Who's Who in Scotland

2nd Edition 1988-89

Carrick Publishing

Published by Carrick Publishing
28 Miller Road, Ayr KA7 2AY
0292 266679

Set by Communitype, Leicester
Printed in Great Britain by Billing & Sons Ltd., Worcester

British Library Cataloguing in Publication Data

Who's Who in Scotland — 2nd ed.
1. Scotland — Bibliographies —
Collections
920'.0411

ISBN 0-946724-19-9

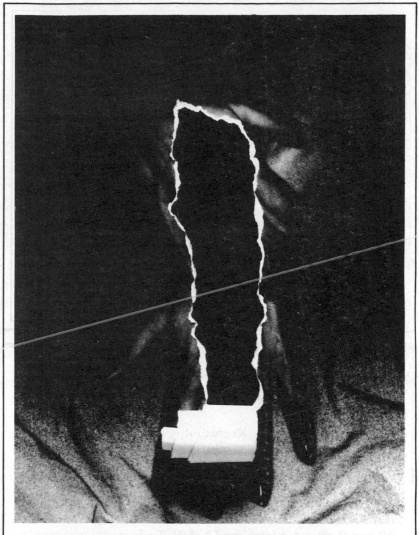

Preface

It is more than two years since the publication of the first edition of Who's Who in Scotland, and the need for a completely revised edition has been obvious for some time.

This second edition contains 4,796 entries compared to 4,539 in the first edition: an increase of 257. However, there are greater changes within the book than this relatively modest overall increase might suggest. From the original edition, about 900 entries have been deleted (mainly through death or retirement) while 3,600 are repeated, suitably amended; and 1,200 entries (25% of the total) appear for the first time in this edition.

All walks of Scottish life are represented: politics and public service, law, religion and education, business and finance, science and medicine, the arts and sport. Prominent Scots living outwith Scotland are not included, except (in a few outstanding cases) where they play a significant and active role in the life of Scotland.

Of the 4,796 entries, biographical details of 4,628 (96%) have been supplied and verified by the entrants themselves. These are signified in the text by the use of a bold type at the start of each entry. In a small number of cases (168), we were unable for one reason or another to have the biographical information verified by the individuals concerned; these entries are signified by the use of italics at the start.

Entries are arranged in alphabetical order, according to surname. A typical entry contains full name, present occupation, date and place of birth, followed by details of family, education and career, publications, recreations and address. The following abbreviations are commonly used: b. (born); m. (married); s. (son); d. (daughter).

Great care has been taken to ensure that information given is accurate and up to date, but during the period in which the book has been in preparation, it is inevitable that some circumstances will have changed. The publishers cannot accept liability for any errors.

Having published our first edition in 1986, and our second in 1988, we intend to publish a third in 1990.

A

Abbott, Mollie Pearson, CBE (1984), OPE, MEd. Member, Convocation, Heriot-Watt University; b. 4.2.28, Peebles. Educ. Edinburgh Ladies' College; Dunfermline College of Physical Education. Assistant Teacher of Physical Education, Norton Park Junior Secondary School, Edinburgh; Visiting Teacher, Blackhall Primary School, Edinburgh; Sole Teacher, Broughton Senior Secondary School, Edinburgh; Temporary Lecturer, Moray House College of Education, Edinburgh, 1952-56; Sole Lecturer, then Senior Lecturer, Ripon Training College, 1956-62; Principal Lecturer, Aberdeen College of Education, 1962-63; HM Inspector of Schools, 1964-70; Principal, Dunfermline College of Physical Education, 1970-83. Past Chairman: Association of Higher Academic Staff in Colleges of Education in Scotland, Scottish Central Committee on Physical Education, Scottish Joint Consultative Committee on Physical Education; former Member: General Teaching Council for Scotland, National Committee for the In-Service Training of Teachers, Scottish Arts Council, Scottish Council of Physical Education, Scottish Sports Council. Recreations: golf; reading; skiing; swimming; walking; wind-surfing, listening to music. Address: (h.) Janefield House, Kirkcudbright, DG6 4UR; T.-0557 30119.

Abbott, Walter Hugh Alexander, MA, MIPM. Chief Careers Adviser, Stirling University, since 1969; b. 2.3.28, Darjeeling, India; m., Anne Judith Scott; 1 s.; 1 d. Educ. Trinity Academy, Edinburgh; Edinburgh University. Diploma, Social Studies. Personnel Trainee, Metropolitan-Vickers Electrical Co. Ltd., 1951-52; MV Electrical Co. Ltd. (latterly named GEC/AEI Power Engineering Co. Ltd.): Recruitment Assistant, Education Department, 1952-56, Senior Assistant, Overseas Recruitment, 1956-58, Senior Assistant, Recruitment and Selection, 1958-61, Head of Recruitment and Non-Engineering Training, 1961-69. Member and former Secretary, Central Scotland Marriage Guidance Council; Selector, Voluntary Service Overseas; serves on various committees of St. Mary's Episcopal Church, Dunblane. Recreations: music (member of three choirs); gardening; reading; theatre; sport. Address: (h.) 51 Argyle Way, Dunblane, FK15 9DX; T.-0786 822937.

Abel, Beverley John, MB, ChB, FRCS(Glas), FRCS(Lond), FRCS(Edin). Consultant Urological Surgeon, Victoria Infirmary, Glasgow, since 1978; Honorary Lecturer in Urology, Glasgow University; b. 7.1.43, Nottingham; m., Wendy Thomas; 1 s.; 2 d. Educ. Carlton Grammar School, Nottingham; Liverpool University. General surgical and urological surgical training, Liverpool, 1967-72; Surgical Research Fellow, Liverpool, 1972-74; Senior Registrar in Urology, Victoria Infirmary, Glasgow, 1975-78. Recreations: fly fishing for salmon; hill-walking. Address: (b.) Victoria Infirmary, Glasgow; T.-041-649 4545.

Aberdeen and Temair, Marchioness of (Beatrice Mary June Gordon), MBE (1971), DL, FRCM, FRSE, DStJ, Hon. LLD (Aberdeen). Musical Director and Conductor, Haddo House Choral Society, since 1945; Chairman, Scottish Children's League, since 1969; Chairman, local Advisory Committee, Aberdeen International Festival of Music and the Performing Arts, since 1980; Governor, Gordonstoun School, since 1971. Address: (h.) Haddo House, Aberdeen, AB4 OER.

Abernethy, Barclay Chivas, MB, ChB, FRCS, FRCSEdin. Consultant Surgeon, Fife Area Health Board, since 1966; Honorary Senior Lecturer, St. Andrews, Edinburgh and Manchester Universities; b. 18.1.28, Aberdeen; m., Isobel Ellen; 1 s.; 2 d. Educ. Robert Gordon's College, Aberdeen; Aberdeen University; Middlesex Hospital, London. Initial medical appointments: Aberdeen Royal Infirmary, Woodend Hospital, Aberdeen, and Northampton General Hospital; Surgical Registrar, Middlesex Hospital, London, 1957-60; Senior Surgical Registrar, East Fife Hospitals, Fife Area Health Board; Examiner, Royal College of Surgeons, Edinburgh. Past President, Kirkcaldy Rotary Club. Recreations: curling (Past President, Markinch Curling Club), gardening; fishing. Address. (h.) The Brackens, 10 Abbots Walk, Kirkcaldy, KY2 5NL; T.-0592 261085.

Abramovich, David Reuben, MB, BS, DGO, PhD, FRCOG. Reader in Obstetrics and Gynaecology, Aberdeen University, since 1984; Honorary Consultant, Grampian Health Board, since 1972; b. 25.10.36, Sydney, Australia; m., Flora; 1 s.; 1 d. Educ. Canterbury Boys' High School; Sydney University. Royal Prince Alfred Hospital, Sydney: House Officer, 1960-61, Registrar in Obstetrics and Gynaecology, 1962-64; Liverpool University: Lecturer in Obstetrics and Gynaecology, 1965, Research Fellow, 1966-70; Senior Lecturer in Obstetrics and Gynaecology, Aberdeen University, 1972-84. Recreation: tennis. Address: (h.) 1 Beaconhill View, Milltimber, Aberdeen; T.-0224 868571.

Adair, Robert, OBE, JP, LCG, TEng, MIMI, TQ. Honorary Sheriff, Shetland, since 1982; Chairman, Shetland Committee for Employment of Disabled, since 1986; part-time Assistant Training Co-ordinator, S.I. Council YTS Schemes, since 1987; b. 8.7.22, Yorkshire; m., Thomasina Jane Yates; 3 d. Educ. Darlington College of Further Education; Jordanhill College of Education. Territorial Army, 1939-46 - RASC, UK and Europe, war service; Member, Executive Committee, NHS General Practitioners, 1955-74; Town and County Councillor, 1963-66; Town Councillor, 1969-74; Chairman, Working Party on NHS Reorganisation, Shetland, 1971-74; Shetland Health Board: Chairman Designate, 1973, Chairman, 1974-85; Member, Scottish Planning Council, NHS, 1974-75; first Chairman, Children's Panel Advisory Committee; Shetland College of Further Education: Lecturer in Engineering, 1966, Senior Lecturer, 1978-87; Chairman, Shetland Scouts County Association; Member, County Valuation Court. Recreations: swimming; golf; computers; reading; horses; fishing; radio. Address: (h.) 41 Gilbertson Road, Lerwick, Shetland, ZE1 OHN; T.-0595 3576.

Adams, Allen. MP (Labour), Paisley North, since 1983 (Paisley, 1979-83); Scottish Chief Whip, since 1986 (Irish Whip, since 1987); Member, Executive Committee, Scottish Council, Labour Party; Member, Executive Committee, Parliamentary Labour Party; b. 16.2.46, Glasgow; m., Katherine Patricia Love; 1 s.; 2 d. Educ. Camphill High School, Paisley; Reid Kerr College, Paisley; Paisley Technical College. Chairman, Paisley Young Socialists, 1963; Paisley Town Councillor, 1968; Strathclyde Regional Councillor, 1971; Vice-Chairman, Strathclyde Social Work Committee, 1974-79; Justice of the Peace. President, Paisley Boys' Brigade. Recreation: boating. Address: (h.) 26 Hunterhill Road, Paisley; T.-041-887 3064.

Adams, David Anstey, MA. Principal, Northern College of Education, formerly Aberdeen College of Education, since 1983; b. 2.3.42, Wakefield, Yorkshire; m., Margaret Ishbel; 1 s.; 1 d. Educ. Harris Academy, Dundee; St. Andrews University. Teacher of English and History, High School of Dundee; Principal Teacher of English, Arbroath Academy; Assistant Director of Education: Angus County Council, Tayside Regional Council. Member: General Teaching Council for Scotland, Scottish Committee for Staff Development in Education, Scottish Examination Board, Committee of Principals of Colleges of Education in Scotland; Chairman: Standing Committee on In-Service Education and Training. Recreations: fishing; shooting. Address: (b.) Northern College of Education, (Aberdeen Campus), Hilton Place, Aberdeen, AB9 1FA; T.-0224 482341.

Adams, Frederick George, MB, ChB, FRCR. Consultant Radiologist, Western Infirmary, Glasgow, since 1971; b. 24.9.38, Aberdeen; m., Allison; 1 s.; 2 d. Educ. Aberdeen Grammar School; Aberdeen University. Chairman, Medical Practitioners' Union (Glasgow), since 1984. Publications: numerous papers on radiology and nuclear medicine. Recreations: contract bridge; swimming. Address: (h.) 54 Terregles Avenue, Glasgow, G41 4LX; T.-041-423 2447.

Adams, Gordon Cassie, MBE. Member, Aberdeen District Council, since 1974; b. 4.2.24, Aberdeen; m., Jean Murray; 2 d. Commissioned Officer, Reconnaisance Corps, 1942-47. Technical Advisor: Government of Pakistan, 1962-68, University of Minas Gerais, Brazil, 1968-70. JP, 1974-84; Parliamentary candidate, Aberdeen North, 1979; former Secretary, Scotland in Europe Movement, 1979; Leader, Conservative Group, Aberdeen City Council, 1976-84; Member, Aberdeen Local Health Council, 1975-79. Recreations: Indian/African history; music; writing; reading. Address: (h.) 11c Kings Gate, Aberdeen; T.-Aberdeen 645834.

Adams, James Gordon Leitch, MA, PhD. Director of Development, Scottish Tourist Board, since 1983; b. 17.10.40, Glasgow; m., Rowan Hopwood; 1 s.; 1 d. Educ. Dundee High School; St Andrews University; Queen's University, Canada; McGill University. Economist: Canadian Federal Government, 1966-70, Highlands and Islands Development Board, 1970-75; Lecturer, Glasgow University, 1975-82; British Council Visiting Lecturer in India, 1981. Recreations: mountaineering; golf. Address: (h.) 5 Corrennie Drive, Edinburgh; T.-031-447 8073.

Adams, Professor James Hume, MB, ChB, PhD, FRSE, FRCPath, FRCP(Glas). Professor of Neuropathology, Glasgow University, since 1971; b. 31.12.29, Glasgow; m., Eileen Rachel Lawson; 3 s. Educ. Paisley Grammar School; Glasgow University. Specialist Pathologist, RAMC, 1955-57; MRC Research Fellow, Institute of Psychiatry, London, 1957-59; Lecturer/Senior Lecturer/ Reader in Neuropathology, Glasgow University, 1959-71. President, British Neuropathological Society, 1968-76; Secretary-General, International Society of Neuropathology, 1978-86. Publications: three books and more than 100 papers in scientific journals. Recreations: golf; bridge. Address: (h.) 31 Burnhead Road, Newlands, Glasgow, G43 2SU; T.-041-637 1481.

Adams, Robert William, OBE, FCMA, FCCA, JDipMA. Director, John Cairney & Co. Ltd., since 1983; Chairman, Burns Musical Co. Ltd., since 1987; Member, Committee of Management, Hanover Housing Association, since 1982; b. 27.9.22, Glasgow; m., Mary Ann Ritchie; 2 s.; 1 d. Educ. Shawlands Academy, Glasgow. H.C. Stewart & Co., CA, Glasgow; Lieutenant, Parachute Regiment; South of Scotland Electricity Board; James Colledge (Cocoa) Ltd., West Africa; Highland Home Industries Ltd.; Managing Director, A.H. McIntosh & Co. Ltd., until 1982. Member, Glenrothes Development Corporation, 1976-84; former Member: Scottish Sports Council; Council, Institute of Cost and Management Accountants; Scottish Sports Council; former Convenor, Scottish Athletic Coaching Committee. Recreations: tennis; golf. Address: (h.) Achray, Shore Road, Aberdour, Fife; T.-0383 860269.

Adams, William Ralph McClymont, Esq., OStJ, FSA (Scot). Vice President Heraldry Society of Scotland, since 1988 (Secretary, 1983-87); b. 6.3.15, Banton, by Kilsyth; m., Joan Graham Barry; 1 s.; 2 d. Educ. Dollar Academy; Hillhead High School, Glasgow; Perth Academy; Heriot Watt College, Edinburgh; Edinburgh College of Art. Architectural training, Perth and Edinburgh; Civil Servant, 1939-80; specialised in conservation of carved stone, decorated plaster, painted ornament and heraldic blazons; Senior Conservation Officer for Scotland, from 1953; Officer, Most Venerable Order of St John of Jerusalem, since 1982. Recreations: horticulture; photography; research and lecturing on heraldry, history, historic buildings and gardens. Address: (h.) Limegrove, High Street, Gifford, Haddington, East Lothian EH41 4QU; T.- 062 081 617.

Adamson, Donald MacFarlane Reid, MB, ChB. Surgeon; Senior Medical Officer, Dunoon and District General Hospital, since 1984; Police Surgeon, Strathclyde, since 1972; Member, Area Ambulance Committee; Representative, Hospital Division, Area Medical Committee; b. 22.10.27, Ayr; 1 s.; 1 d. Educ. Ayr Academy; Glasgow University. House Officer, Ballochmyle Hospital; Senior House Officer, Stockton and

Thornaby Hospital; Registrar, then Associate Specialist, Dunoon and District General Hospital. Recreations: golf; walking. Address: (h.) Linden Lea, Royal Crescent, Dunoon; T.-Dunoon 4053.

Adamson, Iain Thomas Arthur Carpenter, BSc, MSc, AM, PhD. Senior Lecturer in Mathematical Sciences, Dundee University, since 1965; b. 17.6.28, Dundee; m., Robin Andison; 1 d. Educ. Morgan Academy, Dundee; St. Andrews University; Princeton University. Assistant in Instruction, Princeton University, 1950-52; Lecturer: Queen's University of Belfast, 1952-59, Queen's College, Dundee (St. Andrews University), 1960-65; visiting appointments, University of Western Australia, 1965-66, 1972-73, 1978. President, Edinburgh Mathematical Society, 1983-84; Session Clerk: Dundee Meadowside Church, 1975-81, Meadowside St. Paul's Church, 1982-84; ordained as Auxiliary Minister, Church of Scotland, 1986. Books: Introduction to Field Theory; Rings, Modules and Algebras; Elementary Rings and Modules; Elementary Mathematical Analysis. Recreation: reading. Address: (h.) 3 Chalmers Street, Dundee; T.-0382 42280.

Adamson, Norman Joseph, CB, QC. Legal Secretary to the Lord Advocate and First Parliamentary Draftsman for Scotland, since 1979; b. 29.9.30; m., Patricia Mary Guthrie; 4 d. Educ. Hillhead High School, Glasgow; Glasgow University. Faculty of Advocates, Scotland, 1957; called to English Bar, Gray's Inn, 1959; Army Legal Aid (Civil) (UK), 1956-57; practice at Scottish Bar, 1957-65; Standing Junior Counsel, Bible Board, 1962; Standing Junior Counsel, MoD (Army), 1963-65; Honorary Sheriff Substitute, 1963-65; Parliamentary Draftsman and Legal Secretary, Lord Advocate's Department, London, since 1965. Elder, Church of Scotland. Recreations: music; theatre.

Adamson, Rev. Sidney, MA, BD. Minister, Church of Scotland; b. 3.8.11, Arbroath; m., Margaret T. Sharpe, JP; 1 s. Educ. Dumbarton Academy; Glasgow University and Trinity College; Royal Scottish Academy of Music and Drama. Ministries: St Ninian's, Sanquhar, 1937-47 (including war service), Trinity Church, Renfrew, 1947-54, High Kirk of Rothesay, 1954-59, St Michael's Inveresk, Musselburgh, 1959-85. Moderator of Presbytery: Dumfries, 1939, Dunoon, 1958, Dalkeith, 1964 and 1965; former Moderator, Synod of Lothian and Tweeddale; Army Chaplain, India, 1944-47; Territorial Army Chaplain, 1952-66; Chaplain, Royal British Legion (Scotland), Paisley, Renfrew, Rothesay, Musselburgh, and Honorary Vice President, Edinburgh & Lothian Area Council, 1973; Industrial Chaplain, Babcock & Wilcox Ltd., Renfrew, 1948-54; Chaplain, British Sailors' Society, 1955-85; Editor, Homeward Bound (Forces magazine, India), 1946-47. Publications: Two Centuries of Service (history of Sanquhar congregation), 1939; St Michael's Kirk at Inveresk (four editions between 1963 and 1984). Recreations: (at suitable periods) ballroom dancing; shooting; swimming; (always) reading; theatre; freelance journalism; ex-service welfare. Address: 48 Hailes Gardens, Colinton, Edinburgh, EH13 0JH; T.-031-441 2471.

Adler-Bell, Marianne. Dress Designer, since 1939; Member, Board of Directors, Citizens' Theatre, Glasgow, since 1973; b. 17.1.15, Berlin, Germany; m., John Bell (deceased); 1 s. Educ. Staatliche Augusta Schule, Berlin; Art School, Berlin. Former Vice-Chairman, Citizens' Theatre Society; Committee Member, Glasgow Art Gallery. Awarded Bundesverdienstkreuz (similar in Germany to OBE) for work in furthering Scottish-German relations. Recreations: opera; gardening. Address (h.) 348 Knightswood Road, Glasgow, G13 2BT; T.-041-959 1696.

Affrossman, Stanley, BSc, PhD. Senior Lecturer in Chemistry, Strathclyde University, since 1974; b. 22.9.36, Glasgow; m., Patricia Maclean; 2 d. Educ. Whitehill Senior Secondary School; Glasgow University. Fellow, National Research Council of Canada, Ottawa, 1961-63; Assistant Lecturer, Royal College of Science and Technology, Glasgow, 1963-65; Lecturer, Strathclyde University, 1965-74. Recreations: caravanning; hill-walking. Address: (h.) 46 Stirling Drive, Bearsden, Glasgow; T.-041-942 0287.

Agnew of Lochnaw, Sir Crispin Hamlyn. 11th Baronet (created 1629); Chief of the Agnews; Advocate, since 1982; Unicorn Pursuivant of Arms, 1981-86, Rothesay Herald of Arms, since 1986; b. 13.5.44, Edinburgh; m., Susan Rachel Strang Steel; 2 d. Educ. Uppingham School; Royal Military Academy, Sandhurst. Commissioned Royal Highland Fusiliers, 1964, as 2nd Lieutenant; Major, 1977; Retired, 1981. Member: Royal Navy Expedition to East Greenland, 1966; Joint Services Expedition to Elephant Island, Antarctica, 1970-71; Army Nuptse Himal Expedition, 1975; Army Everest Expedition, 1976; Leader: Army East Greenland Expedition, 1968; Joint Services Expedition to Chilean Patagonia, 1972-73; Army Api Himal Expedition, 1980. Publications: articles in various newspapers and journals. Recreations: mountaineering; offshore sailing. Address: 6 Palmerston Road, Edinburgh, EH9 1TN; T.-031-667 4970.

Agnew, Ian, MA (Hons) (Cantab). Rector, Perth High School, since 1975; b. 10.5.32, Newcastle-upon-Tyne; m., Gladys Agnes Heatherill; 1 d. Educ. King's College School, London; Pembroke College, Cambridge. Assistant Teacher of Modern Languages, Melville College, Edinburgh, 1958-63; Assistant Teacher of Modern Languages, then Principal Teacher of Russian, George Heriot's School, Edinburgh, 1964-70; Housemaster, Craigmount Secondary School, Edinburgh, 1970-73; Deputy, Liberton High School, Edinburgh, 1973-75. Chairman, Tayside Regional Working Party on Religious Education, since 1977; Minute Secretary, Headteachers Association of Scotland, 1979-81; Committee Member, SCCORE; President: Perthshire Musical Festival, 1978-88, Perth Chamber Music Society, since 1982; Senior Vice President, Rotary Club of Perth St. John's; Past Chairman: Barnton and Cramond Conservative Association and West Edinburgh Conservative and Unionist Association; Elder, St. Andrew's Parish Church, Perth; Serving Officer (OStJ), Priory of Scotland of the Most Venenerable Order of St. John. Recreations: music (opera); reading; tennis; gardening. Address: (h.) Northwood, Heughfield Road, Bridge of Earn, Perthshire, PH2 9BH; T.-0738 81 2273.

Agnew, Peter Frank, CA. Chief Executive, Lanarkshire Industrial Field Executive, since 1983; Director, BSC (Industry) Ltd.; Chairman, Association of Steel Closure Enterprise Agencies; b. 31.5.43, Glasgow; m., Patricia Morton; 1 s.; 1 d. Educ. Eastwood School; Glasgow University. IBM; Gilbert-Ash (Scotland) Ltd.; British Steel Corporation; BSC (Industry) Ltd. Recreation: golf. Address: (b.) 116 Cadzow Street, Hamilton, ML3 6HP; T.-Hamilton 891515.

Ailsa, The Marquess of (Archibald David Kennedy), OBE; b. 3.12.25, Witham, Essex; m., Mary Burn; 2 s.; 1 d. Educ. Nautical College, Pangbourne. Commissioned Scots Guards, 1944; served with Royal Northumberland Fusiliers in Korea; commissioned 4/5th Bn., Royal Scots Fusiliers TA (commanded, 1966-68); commanded 3rd Bn., Royal Highland Fusiliers T&AVR; Honorary Colonel, Ayr and Renfrew Bn., Army Cadet Force. Recreation: sailing. Address: (h.) Cassillis, Maybole, Ayrshire, KA19 7JN.

Airlie, 13th Earl of (David George Coke Patrick Ogilvy), KT, GCVO, PC, DL. Lord Chamberlain of Her Majesty's Household; Ensign, Queen's Body-Guard for Scotland (Royal Company of Archers), since 1975; Chairman, General Accident Fire & Life Assurance Corporation plc, since 1987 (Deputy Chairman, 1975-87); Director, Royal Bank of Scotland, since 1980; Trustee, Nuffield Hospitals, since 1985; b. 17.5.26, London; m., Virginia Fortune Ryan; 3 s.; 3 d. Educ. Eton College. Lieutenant, Scots Guards, 1944; serving 2nd Bn., Germany, 1945; Captain, ADC to High Commissioner and C-in-C Austria, 1947-48; Malaya, 1948-49; resigned commission, 1950; Chairman, Ashdown Investment Trust Ltd., 1968-82; Director, J. Henry Schroder Wagg & Co. Ltd., 1961-84 (Chairman, 1973-77); Chairman, Schroders plc, 1977-84; Scottish and Newcastle Breweries plc, until 1983. Deputy Lieutenant, Angus. Address: (h.) Cortachy Castle, Kirriemuir, Angus; T.-Cortachy 231.

Aitchison, James Douglas, MA (Hons), MEd (Hons). Head Teacher, Camphill High School, Paisley, since 1984; b. 2.7.47, Glasgow. Educ. High School of Glasgow; Glasgow University; University of Marburg. Teacher, Lycee Faidherbe, Lille; Principal Teacher, Bearsden Academy; Assistant Head Teacher, Gryffe High School, Houston. Recreations: curling; walking; travel. Address: (h.) 4 Langton Place, Newton Mearns, Glasow, G77 6QZ; T.-041-639 7382.

Aitchison, Thomas Milne, MBE, BL, NP, SSC, FIBA, AAABI. Owner, Aitchison & Co., SSC, Whitburn, West Lothian, since 1984; b. 28.5.30, Longridge, West Lothian; m., Flora Jane Stewart Paris; 3 s. Educ. Bathgate Academy; Edinburgh University. 1st Legal Assistant, Lanark County Council, 1962-67; Depute County Clerk (Senior), Ross and Cromarty County Council, 1967-75; Chief Executive, Ross and Cromarty District Council, 1974-78; Partner, P.H. Young & Co., Solicitors, Whitburn, 1979-83. Recreations: sailing; skiing; photography. Address: (h.) 12 Merlin Park, Dollar, Clackmannanshire; T.-Dollar 3156.

Aitken, Adam Jack, MA, DLitt. Editor, A Dictionary of the Older Scottish Tongue, 1956-86; Editorial Consultant and Pronunciation Editor, Concise Scots Dictionary, 1975-85; b. 19.6.21, Edinburgh; m., Norma Ward Manson; 3 s.; 1 d. Educ. Lasswade Secondary School; Edinburgh University. Assistant Lecturer in English Language, Edinburgh University, 1947-48; Research Fellow, Universities of Glasgow, Aberdeen and Edinburgh, 1948-54; Lecturer, Universities of Glasgow and Edinburgh, 1954-64 (Assistant Editor and Editor, Dictionary of the Older Scottish Tongue); Edinburgh University: Honorary Senior Lecturer, 1965-71, Senior Lecturer (part-time) in English Language, 1971-75, Reader (part-time) in English Language, 1975-79; Chairman, Language Committee, Association for Scottish Literary Studies, 1971-76; Chairman, Universities' Forum for Research on the Languages of Scotland, 1978-81; Vice-President, Scottish Text Society, since 1985; Biennial Sir Israel Gollancz Prize of British Academy, 1981; Honorary Professor, Edinburgh University, since 1984. Publications: Edinburgh Studies in English and Scots, 1971; The Computer and Literary Studies, 1973; Lowland Scots, 1973; Bards and Makars, 1977; Languages of Scotland, 1979. Address: (h.) 5 Bellevue Crescent, Edinburgh, EH3 6ND; T.-031-558 1534.

Aitken, Rev. (Eric) Douglas, MA. Religious Media Consultant, since 1987; Assistant Minister (Youth), Mayfield Church, Edinburgh, since 1987; Consultant Director, Inter-Church Project, Glasgow Garden Festival, since 1987; b. 14.11.33, London; m., Fiona Janet Ritchie; 3 s. Educ. Glasgow Academy; Glasgow University and Trinity College. Apprentice marine engineer, 1950-52; National Service (Army) - 2nd Lt., Royal Artillery, 1956-57 (active service, Malta); Assistant, Kings Park Parish Church, Glasgow, 1960-62; Associate, St. Andrews Church, Nairobi, 1962-66; Senior Minister, 1966-69; Depute Clerk, General Assembly, Presbyterian Church of East Africa, 1963-69; Radio Producer, latterly Senior Radio Producer, BBC Scotland Religious Department, 1969-87; Moderator, Presbytery of Dunfermline, 1978-79; Dunfermline District Councillor, 1980-88 (Leader, Alliance Group and Leader of Opposition, 1984-88); Stanley Mair Memorial Lecturer, Glasgow University, 1988; District Commissioner, Scouts, since 1984; Deputy National Chaplain, Scouts, since 1984. Publication: Words for Living, 1984. Recreations: computers; golf; walking; model railway; photography. Address: (h.) 73 Scotland Drive, Dunfermline, KY12 7TP; T.-0383 726590.

Aitken, Rev. Fraser Robert, MA, BD. Minister, Girvan North Parish Church, since 1984; b. 8.1.53, Paisley. Educ. John Neilson Institution, Paisley; Glasgow University. Assistant D'Anglais, CEG Anduze, France, 1972-73; Probationer Assistant, Fairmilehead Parish Church, Edinburgh, 1977-78; Minister, Neilston Parish Church, 1978-84. Chaplain, Ayr Bn., Boys' Brigade, since 1985; Editor, Ayr Way (Presbytery Supplement), since 1985. Recreations: reading; music. Address: (h.) The Manse, 38 The Avenue, Girvan, Ayrshire; T.-0465 3203.

Aitken, George Pattullo Hogg, TD, BL. Assistant Secretary, Scottish Home and Health Department, since 1975; b. 19.2.30, Dundee; m., Agnes Gray; 5 d. Educ. Morgan Academy; Edinburgh University. Senior Examiner, Estate Duty Office,

Edinburgh, 1958-69; Principal: Scottish Home and Health Department, 1969-72, Scottish Courts Administration, 1972-75. Kirk organist. Address: (b.) St. Andrews House, Edinburgh; T.-031-244 2207.

Aitken, James C., BSc (Hons), DipEd. Rector, Auchinleck Academy, since 1985; b. 1.12.44, Glasgow. Educ. Kilmarnock Academy; Glasgow University. Began teaching career, Marr College, Troon, 1968; Principal Teacher of Geography, St. Michael's Academy, 1969; Assistant Rector, Ardrossan Academy, 1975; Depute Rector, Kilwinning Academy, 1977. Recreations: travel; bird-watching; soccer; gardening. Address: (b.) Auchinleck Academy, Sorn Road, Auchinleck, Cumnock; T.-0290 20617.

Aitken, Professor Robert Cairns Brown, MB, ChB, DPM, MD, FRCPEdin, FRCPsych. Professor of Rehabilitation Studies, Edinburgh University, since 1974 (Vice-Dean, Faculty of Medicine, since 1988); Honorary Consultant in Rehabilitation Medicine, Lothian Health Board, since 1974; b. 20.12.33, Dunoon; m., Audrey May Lunn; 1 s.; 1 d. Educ. Dunoon Grammar School; Cargilfield School, Edinburgh; Sedbergh School, Yorkshire; Glasgow University. Institute of Aviation Medicine, RAF, 1959-62; Orpington and Maudsley Hospitals, 1962-66; Senior Lecturer/Consultant Psychiatrist, Royal Infirmary and Royal Edinburgh Hospital, 1967-74. President, International College of Psychosomatic Medicine, 1985-87; Chairman, Napier College Governors, since 1983; Member, Council for Professions Supplementary to Medicine, since 1983; Editor, Journal of Psychosomatic Research, 1979-85; occasional WHO consultant; Foundation Secretary, then President, Society for Research in Rehabilitation, 1981-83. Publications: papers on measurement of mood; flying phobia; management of disability. Recreations: people, places and pleasures of Edinburgh, Scotland and beyond. Address: (h.) 11 Succoth Place, Edinburgh, EH12 6BJ; T.-031-337 1550.

Aitken, Robin Elliot Guild, TD, MB, ChB, MSc, MFCM. Senior Medical Officer, Scottish Home and Health Department; b. 7.11.39, Edinburgh; m., Gillian Ann Odell (deceased); 1 s.; 1 d. Educ. Robert Gordon's College, Aberdeen; Aberdeen University. Medical Officer, 23 Parachute Field Ambulance, 1965-68; Regimental Medical Officer, 1st Bn., Black Watch, 1968-69; Army Health Specialist, 1969-72; retired as Major, 1972; Community Medicine Specialist, Grampian Health Board, 1972-79. Commanding Officer, 252 Field Ambulance (TA) as Lieutenant Colonel, 1977-79; Regimental Medical Officer (Lieutenant Colonel), 2nd 52nd Lowland Volunteers (TA), 1980-83; Elder, Colinton Parish Church. Recreations: running; mountaineering; skiing; cycling; fishing; shooting. Address: (h.) Carnferg, 31 Dreghorn Loan, Colinton, Edinburgh, EH13 ODF; T.-031-441 6116.

Aitken, William Duff, MM (FG). Director, William Aitken Highland Exports Ltd., since 1973; Member, Board of Directors, Eden Court Theatre, since 1984; Member, Inverness District Council; b. 12.3.27, Newton Mearns; m., Eva Alexandra Kjellsson; 2 d. Educ. Merchant Taylors'; Liverpool Nautical College. Seafaring, 1943-53; tanning industry, 1953-72. Member, SSAT. Recreations: philately; swimming; RNXS; TNAUK. Address: (h) Thistles, 19 Swanston Avenue, Inverness, IV3 6QW; T.-0463 230068.

Aitken, William Russell, MA, PhD, FLA. Bibliographer; b. 7.2.13, Calderbank, Lanarkshire; m., Betsy Mary Murison; 1 d. Educ. Dunfermline High School; Edinburgh University. Assistant Librarian, Scottish Central Library, 1936-40; war service, RAF, 1941-46; County Librarian: Clackmannanshire, 1946-49, Perth and Kinross, 1949-58, Ayr, 1958-62; Lecturer, then Senior Lecturer, latterly Reader, Department of Librarianship, University of Strathclyde, 1962-78. President, Scottish Library Association, 1965; Editor, Library Review, 1964-76. Books: A History of the Public Library Movement in Scotland, 1971; William Soutar's Poems in Scots and English (Editor), 1961, 1975; The Complete Poems of Hugh MacDiarmid (Editor, with Michael Grieve), 1978, 1985; Scottish Literature in English and Scots (a bibliographical guide), 1982; Poems of William Soutar: a new selection (Editor), 1988. Address: (h.) 6 Tannahill Terrace, Dunblane, FK15 0AX; T.-Dunblane 823650.

Aitkenhead, John M., MA (Hons), MEd, JP. Headmaster and Founder, Kilquhanity House International School for Boys and Girls, since 1940; b. 21.5.10, Glasgow; m., Morag MacKinnon; 2 s.; 2 d. Educ. Ardrossan Academy; Glasgow University. Worked in Scottish education system until 1940; conscientious objector during World War II; established school inspired by work and writing of A.S. Neill; ardent Scottish nationalist. Recreations: singing; poetry; Scottish country dancing; Gaelic; gardening. Address: Kilquhanity, Castle Douglas, Kirkcudbrightshire; T.-055 665 242.

Akhtar, Anwar Jamil, BSc, MB, ChB, FRCPEdin. Consultant Physician, Royal Victoria Hospital, Edinburgh, since 1972; Senior Lecturer, Edinburgh University, since 1972; b. 25.7.36, Lahore, Pakistan; m., Valerie Joan Penman; 1 s.; 2 d. Educ. Edinburgh University. MRC Research Fellow, Respiratory Diseases Unit, City Hospital, Edinburgh; Senior Registrar, Professorial Unit, Stobhill Hospital, Glasgow. Recreations: music; dogs; restoring pianolas. Address: (b.) Royal Victoria Hospital, Edinburgh; T.-031-332 2566.

Alcock, Professor Leslie, MA, FSA, FRHistS. Professor of Archaeology, Glasgow University, since 1973; b. 24.4.25, Manchester; m., Elizabeth A. Blair; 1 s.; 1 d. Educ. Manchester Grammar School; Brasenose College, Oxford. 7th Gurkha Rifles, 1943-47; Archaeological Survey of Pakistan, 1950-52; Lecturer, Reader, Professor of Archaeology, University College, Cardiff, 1953-73; Member, Board of Trustees, National Museum of Antiquities of Scotland, 1973-85; Member, Ancient Monuments Board, Scotland, since 1974; Commissioner: Royal Commission on Ancient Monuments of Scotland, since 1977, RCAM Wales, since 1986; President, Cambrian

Archaeological Association, 1982-83; President, Society of Antiquaries of Scotland, 1984-87. Publications: Arthur's Britain, 1971; Economy, Society and Warfare, 1987. Recreations: mountain and coastal scenery; music. Address: (b.) Glasgow University, Glasgow, G12 8QQ; T.-041-330 4422.

Alcock, Stephen Robert, MB, ChB, PhD. Senior Lecturer in Bacteriology, Glasgow University, since 1981; Honorary Consultant in Bacteriology, Greater Glasgow Health Board, since 1981; b. 24.6.45, Sutton Coldfield; m., Jean Margaret Diack; 1 s.; 1 d. Educ. Aberdeen Academy; Bearsden Academy; Aberdeen University. House Officer appointments, Aberdeen Royal Infirmary, 1970; Lecturer, Aberdeen University, 1970-81; consultancy work with diving industry, 1974-81, and Sultanate of Oman, since 1984. Recreations: angling; books. Address (h.) 2 Midlothian Drive, Shawlands, Glasgow; T.-041-645 1521.

Alexander of Ballochmyle, Sir Claud Haggart-, 3rd Bt, JP, BA, MInstMC. Vice Lord-Lieutenant, Ayr and Arran, since 1983; b. 6.1.27; m.; 2 s.; 2 d. Educ. Sherborne; Corpus Christi College, Cambridge. Address: (h.) Kingencleugh House, Mauchline, Ayrshire, KA5 5JL.

Alexander, David Alan, MA (Hons), PhD, ABPS. Senior Lecturer, Medical School, Aberdeen University, since 1980 (Director of Course for the Diploma in Psychotherapy, since 1983); b. 28.8.43, Ellon, Aberdeenshire; m., Anita Alexander. Educ. George Watson's College, Edinburgh; Morgan Academy, Dundee; St. Andrews University; Dundee University. Holder of MRC scholarship; Lecturer in Mental Health, Aberdeen University; Senior Lecturer in Mental Health, Aberdeen University and External Examiner, University of West Indies. Consultant to Police Federation. Publications: co-author of two books and regular contributor to professional journals. Recreations: badminton; squash; climbing; riding. Address: (b.) Department of Mental Health, Medical School, Foresterhill, Aberdeen; T.-Aberdeen 681818.

Alexander, David Crichton, CB. Commandant, Scottish Police College, 1979-87; b. 28.11.26, Aberdour; m., Diana Joyce (Jane) Fisher; 1 s.; 1 step-s.; 2 d. Educ. Edinburgh Academy; Staff College, Camberley; Royal College of Defence Studies. Royal Marines, 1944-77 (2nd Lieutenant to Major-General, including Equerry and Acting Treasurer to Duke of Edinburgh); Director-General, English Speaking Union, 1977-79. Governor, Corps of Commissionaires; Member, Civil Service Final Selection Board; Chairman, Edinburgh Academy; Freeman, City of London; Liveryman, Painter Stainers' Company. Recreations: fishing; golf; gardening. Address: (h.) Carnbee House, by Anstruther, KY10 2RU; T.-033-38-238.

Alexander, David Richard Watson, CBE (1972), MA; b. 12.8.18, Montrose; m., Mrs M.A.E. James; 1 s., 1 d. by pr. m.; 3 step-s. Educ. Montrose Academy; Edinburgh University. Served World War II in Hong Kong, India, Ceylon and Malaya (2nd Royal Scots, 12th Frontier Force Regt. and Force 136 (S.O.E.)); final rank, Lieutenant Colonel; awarded MBE (Mil.) for gallant and distinguished service with S.O.E. behind Japanese lines in Malaya. Colonial Administrative Service: appointed Assistant District Officer, Nigeria, 1946; resigned, 1947; re-appointed, 1948, Administrative Officer, Somaliland - on secondment to Cyrenaica (Libya) for service with War Office, then Foreign Office Administration of African Territories, finally Government of Cyrenaica (latterly as Chief Secretary, Ministry of Interior); transferred to Hong Kong, 1953; appointments: Commissioner Essential Services Corps and Chief Staff Officer Civil Aid Services, Director of Social Welfare, Commissioner of Labour, Director of Urban Services and Chairman, Urban Council, Chairman, Housing Authority; Honourable Member, Legislative Council; retired, 1975. Elected Member, Lothian Regional Council, 1982-86 (Chairman, Planning and Development Committee). Address: (h.) 2 Crarae Avenue, Edinburgh, EH4 3JD.

Alexander, Rev. Douglas Niven, MA, BD. Minister, Erskine Parish Church, Bishopton, since 1970; Convener, Church of Scotland Board of Communication, since 1987; b. 8.4.35, Eaglesham; m., Dr. Joyce O. Garven; 1 s.; 2 d. Educ. Hutchesons' Boys' Grammar School, Glasgow; Glasgow University (President, SRC, 1958); Union Theological Seminary, New York. Assistant Minister, St. Ninian's Church, Greenock, 1961-62; Warden, Iona Community House, Glasgow, 1963-70. Secretary, Scottish Union of Students, 1958; Assessor to Lord Rector, Glasgow University, 1969-71; Chaplain to Erskine Hospital, since 1970; Moderator, Paisley Presbytery, 1984; Mair Memorial Lecturer, Glasgow University, 1987; Chairman, British Churches Committee for Channel 4 TV, 1986-88; Member: Scottish Committee, IBA, National Religious Advisory Committee, IBA, Central Religious Advisory Committee, since 1988. Recreation: researching ways of salmon poachers! Address: The Manse, Newton Road, Bishopton, Renfrewshire, PA7 5JP; T.-0505 862161.

Alexander, Rev. Eric J., MA, BD. Minister, St. George's-Tron Parish Church, Glasgow, since 1977; b. 9.5.32, Glasgow; m., Margaret D. Connell; 1 s.; 1 d. Educ. Allan Glen's School, Glasgow; Glasgow University. Publication: The Search for God, 1962. Address: (h.) 12 Dargarvel Avenue, Glasgow, G41.

Alexander, John Huston, BLitt, MA, DPhil Oxon. Senior Lecturer in English, Aberdeen University, since 1984; Editor, Scottish Literary Journal Supplements, since 1984 (Assistant Editor, Scottish Literary Journal, 1980-83); Editor, The Year's Work in Scottish Literary and Linguistic Studies, since 1987; b. 5.4.41, Coleraine, Northern Ireland; m., Flora Ross; 2 s.; 2 d. Educ. Campbell College, Belfast; St. Edmund Hall, Oxford. Sessional Lecturer in English, University of Saskatchewan, Canada, 1966-67; Lecturer in English, Aberdeen University, 1968-84. Editor, The Scott Newsletter, since 1982. Publications: Two Studies in Romantic Reviewing, 1976; The Lay of the Last Minstrel: Three Essays, 1978; The Reception of Scott's Poetry By His Correspondents: 1796-1817, 1979; Marmion: Studies in Interpretation and Composition, 1981; Scott and his Influence (Editor, with David Hewitt), 1983;

Reading Wordsworth, 1987. Recreation: music. Address: (h.) 45A Queen's Road, Aberdeen, AB1 6YN; T.-0224 317424.

Alexander, Sir Kenneth John Wilson, BSc (Econ), LLD, DUniv, FRSE, CBIM, Hon. Fellow, RIAS. Principal and Vice-Chancellor, Stirling University, 1981-86; b. 14.3.22, Edinburgh; m., Angela-May; 1 s.; 4 d. Educ. George Heriot's School, Edinburgh; School of Economics, Dundee. Taught at Universities of Leeds, Sheffield and Aberdeen; Professor of Economics, Strathclyde University, 1963-80; Chancellor, Aberdeen University, since 1986; Member, Advisory Committee on University of the Air, 1965; Chairman: Committee on Adult Education in Scotland, 1970-73, Social Science Research Council, 1975-76; President, Section F, British Association, 1974; Chairman, Highlands and Islands Development Board, 1976-80; Economic Consultant to the Secretary of State for Scotland, since 1968; Member, Scottish Development Agency, 1975-85; Chairman, Council for Applied Science in Scotland, 1980-85; Governor, Technical Change Centre, 1981-87; Director, Scottish Television Ltd., since 1981; Member, Council for Tertiary Education in Scotland, 1981-82; Deputy Chairman, Scottish Council (Development and Industry), since 1982; Honorary President: The Highland Fund, since 1983; Scottish National Dictionary Association Ltd., since 1983; President, Town and Country Planning (Scottish Section), since 1982; Chairman, Michael Kelly Associates, since 1986; Director, Stakis plc, since 1987; Chairman, Edinburgh Book Festival, since 1987. Publications: The Economist in Business, 1967; Fairfields, a study of industrial change (with C.L. Jenkins), 1971; The Political Economy of Change (Editor), 1976. Recreation: Scottish antiquarianism. Address: (h.) 9 West Shore, Pittenweem, Fife, KY10 2NV; T.-0333 310593.

Alexander, Robert George, OBE, FCBSI. Honorary Sheriff, Paisley, since 1974; b. 9.11.14, Portsmouth; m., Mary Matilda Faith Taylor; 1 s.; 1 d. Educ. Kinross Elementary School; Dollar Academy; Edinburgh University. Qualified as Solicitor, 1937; War Service (Territorial) with Argyll and Sutherland Highlanders (Colour Sergeant), 1939-42; commissioned 10/7 Rajput Regiment, 1942; appointed Deputy Assistant Judge Advocate General, HQ Central Command, India, (Major), 1944; Legal Assistant, 1946; Branch Manager/Divisional Manager, Dunfermline Building Society, 1948; Assistant Secretary/Manager and Secretary/General Manager and Director, Paisley Building Society, 1958-78; retired, 1978. General Commissioner of Income Tax, 1972-75; Member, Renfrewshire Valuation Appeal Committee, 1972-75; Member of Council, Building Societies Association, 1970-75; President: Scottish Building Societies Association, 1973-74, Paisley Chamber of Commerce, 1970-71; Scottish Chairman, National House-Building Council, 1975-81 (Honorary Vice-President, since 1982); Member of Council, National Trust for Scotland, 1971-76; Elder, Church of Scotland, since 1955; Treasurer, Durisdeer Church, since 1980. Recreations: golf; gardening. Address: (h.) Hope Cottage, Durisdeer, Thornhill, Dumfriesshire, DG3 5BJ; T.-084 85 285.

Alexander, Samuel, BL. Honorary Sheriff, Dumbarton, since 1983; b. Glasgow; m., Isabella Kerr Ligertwood; 2 s. Educ. Govan High School; Glasgow University. Senior Partner, Keyden Strang & Co., Solicitors, Glasgow. Recreations: golf; reading. Address: (h.) 1 Hillneuk Avenue, Bearsden, Glasgow, G61; T.-041-942 4674.

Ali, Nasir, MB, BS, DPM, MRCPsych. Consultant Psychiatrist, since 1973; Honorary Senior Lecturer, Aberdeen University, since 1982; b. 21.8.39, Lucknow, India; m., D. Rosemary; 1 s.; 1 d. Address: (h.) Balmachree House, Dalcross, Inverness, IV1 2JQ; T.-Inverness 790602.

Alison, Graham, BSc, MEd. General Secretary, Scottish Further and Higher Education Association, since 1982; b. 15.6.31, Clydebank; m., Norma McA. Perry; 2 d. Educ. Dumbarton Academy; Glasgow University. Education Officer, RAF; Educational Psychologist, Lecturer in Psychology and (until it closed) Vice-Principal, Hamilton College of Education. Recreations: theatre; golf; bowling. Address: (b.) 90 Mitchell Street, Glasgow, G1 3NQ; T.-041-221 0118.

Allan, Andrew D.C., MA (Hons). Head Teacher, Mainholm Academy, Ayr, since 1974; b. 16.4.31, Irvine; m., Margaret M.N. Lamont; 2 d. Educ. Irvine Royal Academy; Glasgow University; Jordanhill College of Education. National Service, RAEC, 1954-56; Mathematics Teacher, Kilmarnock Academy, 1956-58; Principal Teacher of Mathematics: Dalry High School, 1958-62, John Neilson Institution, 1962-65, Kilmarnock Academy, 1965-71; Assistant Head Teacher, Kilmarnock Academy, 1970-72; Depute Head Teacher, Ardrossan Academy, 1972-74. Elder, Church of Scotland, since 1956; President, Alloway Rotary Club, 1986-87; Governor, Craigie College of Education, 1979-87; Member, Education Committee, Church of Scotland. Recreations: golf; walking; travelling. Address: (h.) 46 Taybank Drive, Ayr; T.-Alloway 41067.

Allan, David Smith, BSc (Hons), DipEd. Headmaster, Preston Lodge High School, Prestonpans, since 1970; b. 17.1.35, Prestonpans; m., Alexandra; 2 s.; 1 d. Educ. Preston Lodge School, Prestonpans; Edinburgh University. Teacher, George Heriot's School, Edinburgh, 1958-63; Principal Teacher of Science, Preston Lodge High School, Prestonpans, 1963-70. Hon. President, Preston Lodge FP Club; Past President: Lothian Headteachers Association; Lothian Schools Rugby Union; Member, SRU Youth Marketing Committee. Recreations: rugby committee work; golf. Address: (b.) Preston Lodge High School, Prestonpans, East Lothian; T.-Prestonpans 811170.

Allan, Gary James Graham, LLB. Partner, Hughes Dowdall, Solicitors, Glasgow, since 1986; b. 21.1.58, Aberdeen; m., Margaret Muriel Glass. Educ. Aberdeen Grammar School; Aberdeen University. Apprenticeship, McGrigor Donald and Company, Solicitors, Glasgow and Edinburgh; joined Hughes Dowdall, 1982. Executive Member, Glasgow Bar Association, since 1983; Parliamentary Liaison Officer, Law Society of Scotland, until 1988. Recreations: sport; reading; music; the company of good friends. Address: (b.) 216 Bath Street, Glasgow, G2 4HS; T.-041-332 5321.

Allan, George Alexander, MA (Hons). Headmaster, Robert Gordon's College, Aberdeen, since 1978; b. 3.2.36, Edinburgh; m., Anne Violet Veevers; 2 s. Educ. Daniel Stewart's College, Edinburgh; Edinburgh University. Teacher of Classics, Glasgow Academy, 1958-60; Daniel Stewart's College: Teacher of Classics, 1960-63, Head of Classics, 1963-73 (appointed Housemaster, 1967); Schoolmaster Fellow Commoner, Corpus Christi College, Cambridge, 1972; Deputy Headmaster, Robert Gordon's College, 1973-77. Chairman and former Secretary, Headmasters' Conference (Scottish Division) (Member, National Committee, 1982 and 1983); Governor, Welbeck College, since 1980; Council Member, Scottish Council of Independent Schools, since 1988. Recreations: gardening; golf; music. Address: 24 Woodend Road, Aberdeen, AB2 6YH; T.-0224 321733.

Allan, John Balfour, MA, LLB. Divisional Solicitor, Office of Solicitor to Secretary of State for Scotland, since 1982; b. 11.10.33, Linlithgow Bridge. Educ. George Watson's College, Edinburgh; Edinburgh University. Legal Assistant, Auld & Macdonald, WS, 1958-60; Office of Solicitor to Secretary of State for Scotland: Legal Assistant, 1961-66, Senior Legal Assistant, 1967-71, Divisional Solicitor, 1971-72; Secretary, Scottish Law Commission, 1972-79; Deputy Solicitor to Secretary of State for Scotland, 1979-82. Recreation: men's hockey. Address: (h.) 10 Craigleith Hill Gardens, Edinburgh, EH4 2JJ; T.-031-332 6420.

Allan, John Douglas, BL, DMS, FBIM. Procurator Fiscal for Edinburgh and Regional Procurator Fiscal for Lothians and Borders, since 1983; b. 2.10.41, Edinburgh; m., Helen E.J. Aiton; 1 s.; 1 d. Educ. George Watson's College, Edinburgh; Edinburgh University. Solicitor in private practice, Edinburgh, 1963-67; Procurator Fiscal Depute, Edinburgh, 1967-71; Solicitor, Crown Office, Edinburgh, 1971-76; Assistant Procurator Fiscal, then Senior Assistant Procurator Fiscal, Glasgow, 1976-79; Solicitor, Crown Office, Edinburgh, 1979-83. Part-time Lecturer in Law, Napier College, Edinburgh, 1963-66; Holder, Scout "Medal of Merit"; Session Clerk, Greenbank Parish Church of Scotland. Recreations: Scouts; youth leadership; walking; Church. Address: (b.) 3 Queensferry Street, Edinburgh, EH2 4RB; T.-031-226 4962.

Allan, Norman James Wilson, MA, FSA Scot, FRCS(C), FRCOG. Member, Grampian Regional Council, since 1986; Grampian Representative, COSLA, since 1986; b. 23.4.22, Dufftown; 1 s.; 1 d. Educ. Hutchesons' Grammar School, Glasgow; Aberdeen University; Glasgow University. Merchant Navy; SHO, Hammersmith Hospital, London; Registrar, Edinburgh; Senior Registrar, Northampton; Associate Professor, University of Ottawa; Consultant Obstetrician and Gynaecologist, Ottawa General Hospital; Consultant in Maternal Welfare, Government of Ontario. Publication: Scotland, The Broken Image, 1983. Address: (h.) Glenbrae, 2 Campbell Street, Banff, AB4 1JR; T.-02612 5291.

Allan, Norman Colvin, MB, ChB, FRCP, FRCPath. Consultant Haematologist, Western General Hospital, Edinburgh, since 1967, and part-time Senior Lecturer in Medicine, Edinburgh University; b. 30.6.29, N. Nigeria; m., Margaret Eurwen; 2 s.; 3 d. Educ. Daniel Stewart's College, Edinburgh; Edinburgh University. RAMC, 1953-55; Registrar, 1956-60; Senior Registrar, Haematology, Ibadan, 1960-62; Senior Lecturer, Haematology, Ibadan, 1962-67. Recreation: photography. Address: (h.) 11 Crarae Avenue, Edinburgh, EH4 3JD; T.-031-332 4748.

Allan, Robert. Chief Executive, Scottish Fishermen's Federation, since 1982; b. 14.11.33, Peterhead; m., Moira W. Morrison; 2 d. Educ. Aberdeen Grammar School. Audit Assistant, R.C. Kelman & Shirreffs, CA, Aberdeen, 1949-62; Assistant Secretary, latterly Secretary, Aberdeen Fishing Vessel Owners' Association Ltd. and Scottish Trawlers' Federation, 1962-71; Chief Executive, Aberdeen Fishing Vessel Owners' Association Ltd. and Aberdeen Fish Producers' Organisation Ltd., 1971-82. Recreation: keen follower of the fortunes of Aberdeen FC. Address: (h.) 40 Parkhill Circle, Dyce, Aberdeen, AB2 OFN; T.-0224 724366.

Allanbridge, Lord (William Ian Stewart), QC. Senator of the College of Justice in Scotland, since 1977; b. 8.11.25; m.; 1 s.; 1 d. Educ. Loretto; Glasgow University; Edinburgh University. Sub-Lt., RNVR, 1944-46; called to the Bar, 1951; Advocate-Depute, 1959-64; Home Advocate-Depute, 1970-72; Solicitor-General for Scotland, 1972-74; Temporary Sheriff Principal, Dumfries and Galloway, 1974.

Allardyce, John Grahame, MA; b. 4.10.17, Dublin; m., Euphemia Mary Wilson; 2 s.; 2 d. Educ. Cheltenham College; Royal Military Academy, Woolwich; Christ's College, Cambridge. Commissioned Royal Engineers, 1937; War Service in France, North Africa, Sicily, Italy; mentioned in Despatches (twice); US Bronze Star Medal; later in 52 (Lowland) Division/District, Gibraltar and Malaya and with NATO; retired from Army, 1966, as Lt. Col.; Technical Director, International Standards Organization, Geneva, 1967-79. Fellow, Institute of Linguists; Secretary, Nairn Amenities Protection Society and Civic Trust. Address: (h.) Caskieben, Moss-side, Nairn.

Allcock, Ronald, FIWES, LRSC. Director, Tay River Purification Board, since 1987; b. 9.1.40, Mancot; 1 s.; 1 d. Educ. Holywell Grammar School; Doncaster College of Technology. Research Chemist, Coalite Chemicals, 1962; District Inspector, Trent River Authority, 1966; Divisional Pollution Officer: Yorkshire Water, 1972, Clyde River Purification Board, 1978. Recreations: golf; reading; amateur football. Address: (b.) 1 South Street, Perth, PH2 8NJ; T.-Perth 27989.

Allen, Professor John Anthony, PhD, DSc, FIBiol, FRSE. Director, University Marine Biological Station, Millport, since 1976; Professor of Marine Biology, London University, since 1976; b. West Bridgford; m., Margaret Porteous Aitken; 1 s.; 1 d.; 1 step s. (adopted). Assistant Lecturer, Glasgow University; Reader in Marine Biology, Newcastle upon Tyne University. Member, Natural Environmental Research Council,

1977-83 (Chairman, University Affairs Committee, 1978-83); Member, Nature Conservancy Council, since 1982 (Chairman, Advisory Committee on Science, since 1984); President, Malacological Society of London, 1982-84. Recreations: appreciating gardens; pub lunching; wildlife. Address: (h.) Bellevue, Isle of Cumbrae; T.-0475 530260.

Allen, Professor John Walter, MA, FSAS, FRSE. Professor of Solid State Physics, St. Andrews University, since 1980; b. 7.3.28, Birmingham. Educ. King Edward's High School, Birmingham; Sidney Sussex College, Cambridge. RAF, 1949-51; Staff Scientist, Ericsson Telephones Ltd., 1951-56; Services Electronics Research Laboratory, 1956-68; Visiting Associate Professor, Stanford University, 1964-66; joined Department of Physics, St. Andrews University, 1968. Recreations: archaeology; country dancing. Address: (b.) Department of Physics and Astronomy, St. Andrews University, North Haugh, St. Andrews, Fife, KY16 9SS; T.-0334 76161.

Allen, Professor Kevin John, BA. Professor and Director, European Policies Research Centre, Strathclyde University; b. 25.11.41, Warrington; m., Kirsten Margaret Paton; 1 s.; 1 d. Educ. Boteler Grammar School, Warrington; Nottingham University; Newcastle University. Lecturer in Applied Economics, Glasgow University, 1964-75; Research Fellow, International Institute of Management, Berlin, 1975-77; Co-Director, then Director, Centre for the Study of Public Policy, Strathclyde, 1977-87. Recreations: fly fishing; photography. Address: (b.) Livingstone Tower, 26 Richmond Street, Glasgow; T.-041-552 4400.

Allison, Professor Arthur Compton, BSc, DipNumMath, PhD, MBCS. Professor of Computing Science, Glasgow University, since 1986 (Director, Board of Studies in Information Technology); b. 24.3.41, Belfast; m., Dr. A.J. Allison; 3 d. Educ. Queen's University, Belfast; Glasgow University. Glasgow University, 1962-67; Smithsonian Institution, Boston, 1967-73; Glasgow University, 1973-83; Northeastern University, Boston, 1983-84; Glasgow University, since 1984. Elder, Church of Scotland. Recreations: running; squash; hill-walking. Address: (b.) Department of Computing Science, Glasgow University, Glasgow, G12 8QQ; T.-041-339 8855, Ext. 4453.

Allison, John Andrew, MA, LLB. Solicitor, since 1963; Honorary Sheriff, Cupar, since 1986; b. 10.5.36, Glasgow; m., Elizabeth; 2 s.; 1 d. Educ. Paisley Grammar School; Glasgow University. Legal apprenticeship, McGrigor Donald & Co., Glasgow; Legal Assistant, Glenrothes Development Corporation; Partner, Pagan Osborne & Grace, WS, Fife; Dean, Society of Solicitors for Eastern District of Fife; Member, Council, Law Society of Scotland. Recreations: hill-walking; sailing. Address: (h.) Craigrothie House, by Cupar, Fife; (b.) 12 St. Catherine Street, Cupar, Fife; T.-0334 53777.

Allison, Joseph Philip Sloan, MA (Cantab), CertEd. Headmaster, St. Mary's Music School, Edinburgh, since 1979; b. 6.2.44, Leeds; m., Caroline Margaret Paton; 3 s.; 1 d. Educ. Rugby; Churchill College, Cambridge; Moray House College of Education. Jardine Matheson & Co. Ltd., Hong Kong, 1967-70; Assistant Master, then Assistant Head, Belhaven Hill, Dunbar, 1970-77; Deputy Head, St. Mary's Music School, 1977-79. Recreations: sailing; bird-watching; hill-walking. Address: (h.) 4 Raeburn Street, Edinburgh, EH4 1HY; T.-031-332 9768.

Allison, Marjorie Elisabeth Marion, BSc, MD, FRCP. Senior Lecturer in Medicine, Glasgow University, since 1977; Honorary Consultant Nephrologist, Glasgow Royal Infirmary, since 1977; b. 7.9.40, Glasgow. Educ. Hamilton Academy; Glasgow University. Clinical training in nephrology, Glasgow Royal Infirmary, 1966-69; Research Fellow in Kidney Pathophysiology, University of North Carolina, 1969-72, 1979-81. Publications: contributed chapters on acute kidney failure to textbooks. Recreations: gardening; cooking; medical antiquities. Address: (b.) Renal Unit, Glasgow Royal Infirmary, Glasgow; T.-041-552 3535, Ext. 5292.

Allison, Robert H., MB, ChB, FFARCSI. Consultant Anaesthetist, Dundee Teaching Hospitals, since 1980; b. 10.2.48, Perth; m., Lizbeth Bain, 1 s.; 2 d. Educ. Perth Academy; St. Andrews University. House Surgeon, Maryfield Hospital, Dundee, 1972; House Physician, Bridge of Earn Hospital, Perth, 1973; Registrar in Anaesthesia, Dundee Teaching Hospitals, 1973-77; Senior Registrar in Anaesthesia, Western Infirmary, Glasgow, 1977-80. Recreation: golf (St Andrews University blue, 1969). Address: (h.) 4 Ericht Road, Wormit, Newport-on-Tay, Fife; T.-0382 541415.

Allsop, Douglas Thomson. Executive Director, Scottish Council on Alcohol, since 1979; b. 5.11.32, Arbroath; m., Elizabeth Blair Marshall; 1 s. Educ. Arbroath High School. Clydesdale Bank Ltd., 1949-72 (latterly as Investment Manager); Regional Director, Slater, Walker Ltd., Merchant Bankers, 1973-77. Recreations: gardening; walking. Address: (b.) 137/145 Sauchiehall Street, Glasgow, G2 3EW; T.-041-333 9677.

Allsop, Rev. Thomas Douglas, MA, BD. Minister, Beechgrove Church, Aberdeen, since 1977; b. 2.3.34, Kilmaurs; m., Marion Morrison Urie; 2 s.; 1 d. Educ. Kilmarnock Academy; Glasgow University and Trinity College. Assistant Minister, St. Marnock's, Kilmarnock; Minister: Kirriemuir South (after a union called Kirriemuir St. Andrew's), 1959-65; Minister, Knightswood St. Margaret's, Glasgow, 1965-77. Founder Chairman, Kirriemuir Round Table; Moderator, Dumbarton Presbytery, 1975; Burgess, City of Aberdeen. Recreations: photography; golf; musical appreciation. Address: 156 Hamilton Place, Aberdeen, AB2 4BB; T.-0224 642615.

Alroomi, Dr. Layla, MD, DCH, DTM&H, FRCP. Consultant Paediatrician, Glasgow Royal Maternity Hospital and Sick Children's Hospital, Glasgow, since 1984; b. Baghdad. Educ. Baghdad High School for Girls; Warsaw University. Preregistration posts, Warsaw; entered NHS, UK, 1970. Address: (h.) 68 Dumgoyne Drive, Bearsden, Glasgow, G61 3AW.

Alty, Professor James Lenton, BSc, PhD, FBCS. Professor of Computer Science, Strathclyde University, since 1982; Executive Director, Turing

Institute, Glasgow, since 1984; Chairman, Scottish Human Computer Interaction Centre, since 1982; b. 21.8.39, Haslingden; m., Mary Eleanor; 2 s.; 2 d. Educ. King Edward VII School, Lytham; Liverpool University. Liverpool University: Oliver Lodge Fellow (Nuclear Physics), 1964, Leverhulme Fellow (Metallurgy), 1966; Systems Engineer, Senior Systems Engineer, Account Executive, IBM (UK) Ltd., 1968-72; Director, Computer Laboratory, Liverpool University, 1972-82. Publications: Computing Skills and the User Interface (with M.J. Coombs); Expert Systems - Concepts and Examples (with M.J. Coombs). Recreations: musical composition; mountain climbing; skiing. Address: (b.) The Turing Institute, George House, 36 North Hanover Street, Glasgow, G1 2AD; T.-041-552 6400.

Ambler, Professor Richard Penry, MA, PhD. Professor of Protein Chemistry and Head, Department of Molecular Biology, Edinburgh University; b. 26.5.33, Bexley Heath; m.; 2 d. Educ. Haileybury and ISC; Pembroke College, Cambridge. Research Fellow, Pembroke College, Cambridge, 1959-62; scientific staff, MRC Laboratory of Molecular Biology, Cambridge, 1960-65; joined Department of Molecular Biology, Edinburgh University, 1965. Address: (b.) Department of Molecular Biology, Edinburgh University, Mayfield Road, Edinburgh, EH9 3JR; T.-031-667 1081.

Amin, Sayed-Hassan, LLB, LLM, PhD. Reader in Law, Glasgow College, since 1983; Member, Chartered Institute of Arbitrators, since 1984; international lawyer and Middle East specialist; b. 25.11.48, Persia; m., Elspeth Digby-Grant; 1 s.; 1 d. Educ. University of Tehran; Glasgow University. Lecturer, researcher, administrator and practitioner, Iranian and Islamic law, 1969-79; practitioner of international and Middle East law, since 1979; Senior Lecturer in Law, Glasgow College, 1981-83; Middle East Editor, Oil and Gas Law and Taxation Review, since 1985. Publications: 18 books on international, Middle Eastern and Islamic law. Recreations: walking; book collecting. Address: (h.) Royston, Crown Road North, Glasgow, G12 9DH.

Ancram, Michael Andrew Foster Jude, MA, LLB. Company Director and Writer; b. London; m., Lady Jane Fitzalan-Howard; 2 d. Educ. Ampleforth; Christ Church, Oxford; Edinburgh University. Advocate, Scottish Bar, 1970; MP, Berwickshire and East Lothian, February to September, 1974; Chairman, Conservative Party in Scotland, 1980-83; MP, Edinburgh South, 1979-87; Minister for Home Affairs and Environment, Scottish Office, 1983-87. Director: Northern Corporate Communications, North British Newsprint. Recreations: skiing; folk singing; photography. Address: (h.) 6 Ainslie Place, Edinburgh; T.-031-226 3147.

Anderson, Rev. Andrew Fraser, MA, BD. Minister, Greenside Parish Church, since 1981; b. 2.9.44, Aberdeen; m., Hazel Neary; 2 s. Educ. Harrow School; Magdalen College, Oxford; Edinburgh University. Industrial management, Dickinson Robinson Group Ltd., 1967-77. Recreations: music; gardening. Address: (h.) 80 Pilrig Street, Edinburgh, EH6 5AS; T.-031-554 3277.

Anderson, Charles Mitchell, MA, DPA. Chief Executive, Ettrick and Lauderdale District Council, since 1985; b. 3.9.45, Kirkcaldy; m., Margaret; 2 s. Educ. Kirkcaldy High School; Edinburgh University; Strathclyde University (part-time). Administrative Officer, Irvine Development Corporation; Principal Administrative Officer, Highland Regional Council; Assistant Director of Administration and Legal Services, Central Regional Council; Assistant Secretary, Convention of Scottish Local Authorities. Address: (b.) PO Box 4, Council Chambers, Paton Street, Galashiels, TD1 3AS; T.-0896 4751.

Anderson, David, MBE, JP. Member, Grampian Regional Council, since 1974 (Depute Convener, since 1986; Leader, Liberal Group, since 1982); b. 17.1.16, St. Andrews; m., Jessie Watt Taylor; 2 s.; 1 d. Educ. Madras College, St. Andrews. Employed in forestry, various estates in Fife, until 1939; Sergeant, Royal Corps of Signals, 1939-46; various posts in Forestry Commission, 1946-81, latterly as Chief Forester in charge, Huntly Forest; Member, Aberdeen County Council, 1961-74; Chairman, Education Committee, 1973-74. Chairman, Rhynie Branch, Royal British Legion. Recreation: bowling. Address: (h.) Burmah, 6 Watson Avenue, Huntly, Aberdeenshire, AB5 5BF; T.-Huntly 2878.

Anderson, David Colville, VRD, QC, BA Oxon, LLB; b. 8.9.16, Cupar; m., Juliet Hill Watson; 2 s.; 1 d. Educ. Glenalmond College; Pembroke College, Oxford; Edinburgh University. RNVR, 1935-61; served World War II in destroyers; mentioned in Despatches, 1942; special operation, Norway, 1945; King Haakon VII Freedom Medal; Admiralty's Egerton Prize, 1943; Lieutenant Commander, 1947. Advocate, 1946; Lecturer in Scots Law, Edinburgh University, 1947-60; Standing Junior Counsel, Ministry of Works, 1954-55, and War Office, 1955-57; QC, 1957; Solicitor-General for Scotland, 1960-64; MP (Conservative) for Dumfries, 1963-64; Honorary Sheriff, 1965-72; Chairman, Industrial Appeal Tribunals, 1970-72; Chief Reporter for Public Inquiries and Under-Secretary, Scottish Office, 1972-74; Commissioner, Northern Lighthouses, 1960-64. Subject of play, The Case of David Anderson QC, by John Hale (Lyric, Hammersmith, 1981, etc.). Recreations: travel; hill-walking; golf. Address: (h.) 8 Arboretum Road, Edinburgh, EH3 5PD; T.-031-552 3003.

Anderson, David Rae, MA (Hons), LLB, LLM, WS, NP. Solicitor, since 1961 (Senior Partner in private practice); part-time Legal Chairman, Industrial Tribunals, since 1971; Honorary Sheriff, since 1981; b. 27.1.36, Stonehaven; m., Jean Strachan. Educ. Mackie Academy, Stonehaven; Aberdeen University; Edinburgh University; Australian National University, Canberra. Barrister and Solicitor of Supreme Court of Victoria, Australia, 1962; Legal Officer, Attorney-General's Department, Canberra, 1962-65; part-time research student, Law Faculty, Australian National University, Canberra, and part-time Lecturer in Legal History, 1962-65; returned to Scotland, 1965, in private legal practice, Edinburgh, 1965-67, Alloa and Central Scotland, since 1967; Interim Town Clerk, Burgh of Alva, 1973; former part-time Reporter to Secretary of State for Scotland for public enquiries; former Dean, Society of Solicitors of Clackmannanshire; Member, Council, Law Society of Scotland, and Convener, International Relations Committee; Member, UK Delegation, Council of the Bars and Law Societies of the European Community; Elder, Church of Scotland; Parliamentary candidate, 1970 and 1971; formerly served, RNVR. Recreations: climbing and hill-walking; reading, especially historical biography and English literature; music; interested in current affairs, architecture, stately homes and travel. Address: (h.) 3 Smithfield Loan, Alloa, FK10 1NJ; T.-0259 213096; (b.) 8 Shillinghill, Alloa, FK10 1JT; T.-0259 723201.

Anderson, David William, CBE (1976), OBE (1972), ADC (1981). Chief Executive, Cumbernauld Development Corporation, since 1985; b. 4.1.29, Wooler; m., Eileen Dorothy; 1 s.; 2 d. Educ. St. Cuthbert's Grammar School; Royal Military Academy, Sandhurst; Staff College, Camberley. Army service: private soldier to Brigadier, 1946-82; Chief Executive, North East Fife District Council, 1982-85. Recreations: gardening; walking dogs. Address: (b.) Cumbernauld Development Corporation, Cumbernauld House, Cumbernauld.

Anderson, Don S.H., IPFA, FRVA. Director of Finance and Management Services, Clydesdale District Council, since 1983; b. 9.1.43, Forfar; m., Irene R.; 3 d. Educ. Mackie Academy, Stonehaven. Trainee Accountant, Clackmannan County Council, 1961-66; Accountancy Assistant, Airdrie Town Council, 1966-69; Accountant, Kilmarnock Town Council, 1969-75; Finance Manager, Clydesdale District Council, 1975-83. Recreations: golf; swimming. Address: (b.) District Offices, South Vennel, Lanark, ML11 7JT; T.-0555 61331, Ext. 131.

Anderson, Dorothy Elizabeth, BSc (Hons), MB, ChB, MRCP(UK), DMRD, FRCR. Consultant Radiologist, Glasgow Royal Infirmary, since 1981; Honorary Clinical Lecturer, Glasgow University, since 1982; b. 26.9.50, Glasgow; m., David Anderson; 1 s.; 1 d. Educ. Glasgow University. Pre-registration posts, Stobhill Hospital and Glasgow Royal Infirmary; Respiratory Unit, Knightswood Hospital; trained in radiology, Western Infirmary, Glasgow (Registrar, then Senior Registrar). Recreation: choral singing. Address: (b.) Department of Radiology, Glasgow Royal Infirmary, Alexandra Parade, Glasgow, G31 2ER; T.-041-552 3535, Ext. 5521.

Anderson, Douglas Kinloch, OBE, MA. Chairman, Kinloch Anderson Ltd., Edinburgh, since 1975; Board Member, Scottish Tourist Board, since 1986; President, Edinburgh Chamber of Commerce, since 1988; b. 19.2.39, Edinburgh; m., Deirdre Anne; 2 s.; 1 d. Educ. George Watson's Boys College; St. Andrews University. Joined Kinloch Anderson Ltd., 1962 (fifth generation in family business); Assistant on Master's Court, Edinburgh Merchant Company, 1976-79; elected Honorary Member, St. Andrew's Society of Washington DC, 1985; Member, Edinburgh Festival Council. Recreations: golf; fishing; skiing; watching schoolboy rugby; travel (non-business). Address: (b.) 2/4 Restalrig Drive, Edinburgh, EH7 6JZ; T.-031-661 7241.

Anderson, Douglas M.W., DSc, PhD, CChem, FRSC, FRSE. Reader in Chemistry, Edinburgh University, since 1954; b. 10.11.25, Edinburgh; m., Margaret Joan Laing; 1 s.; 3 d. Educ. Montrose Academy; Edinburgh University. War Service, RAF, 1943-46 (Radar duties). Secretary and General Scientific Adviser, International Natural Gums Association for Research Ltd.; adviser and consultant to industry; Editor, two series of monographs on aspects of analytical chemistry. Recreations: music; angling; philately; all kinds of DIY. Address: (b.) Chemistry Department, The University, Edinburgh, EH9 3JJ; T.-031-667 1081, Ext. 3446.

Anderson, Eric George, MB, ChB, MSc (Med Eng), FRCSEdin, FRCSGlas. Consultant Orthopaedic Surgeon, Western Infirmary and Gartnavel General Hospital, Glasgow, since 1978; Honorary Clinical Lecturer, Glasgow University, since 1978; Clinical Associate, Strathclyde University, since 1979; Lecturer in Surgery, Glasgow School of Chiropody; b. 7.6.40, Alyth; m., Elizabeth C. Cracknell; 1 s.; 2 d. Educ. St. Andrews University; Salford University. Resident Physician, Nottingham City Hospital, 1964-65; Resident and Registrar in Casualty, Orthopaedic Surgery, Plastic Surgery and Surgical Neurology, Dundee Royal Infirmary and Bridge of Earn, 1965-70; Registrar in General Surgery, Brighton Hospitals, 1970-71; Research Registrar in Orthopaedic Surgery, Salford Hospitals, 1971-73; Senior Registrar, Robert Jones and Agnes Hunt Orthopaedic Hospital, Oswestry, and Birmingham Accident Hospital, 1973-78. Member, Editorial Board, Injury; Member, Joint Advisory Panel, Orthotic and Prosthetic Training and Education Council (England and Wales); Hon. Treasurer, British Orthopaedic Foot Surgery Society. Recreations: music; model buses; tramways. Address: (h.) 102 Prestonfield, Milngavie, Glasgow, G62 7PZ; T.-041-956 3594.

Anderson, Gordon Alexander, CA, FCMA. Chairman, Arthur Young, Chartered Accountants, since 1987; b. 9.8.31, Glasgow; m., Eirene Cochrane Howie Douglas; 2 s.; 1 d. Educ. High School of Glasgow. Apprentice CA, Moores Carson & Watson, Glasgow, 1949-54; qualified CA, 1955; National Service, Royal Navy, 1955-57 (Sub Lieutenant); Partner, Moores Carson & Watson, 1958 (firm name changed to McClelland Moores, 1958, Arthur Young McClelland Moores, 1968, Arthur Young, 1985). Director: Bitmac Ltd., since 1984; High School of Glasgow Ltd., 1975-81; Member, Scottish Milk Marketing Board, 1979-85; Institute of Chartered Accountants of Scotland: Member, Council, 1980-84, Vice President, 1984-86, President, 1986-87. Recreations: golf; gardening; rugby football (as spectator). Address: (h.) Ardwell, 41 Manse Road, Bearsden, Glasgow, G61 3PN; T.-041-942 2803.

Anderson, Rev. Professor Hugh, MA, BD, PhD, DD. Professor of New Testament Language, Literature and Theology, Edinburgh University, 1966-85; b. 18.5.20, Galston, Ayrshire; m., Jean Goldie Torbit; 1 s.; 1 s. (deceased); 1 d. Educ. Kilmarnock Academy; Glasgow University. Chaplaincy work, Egypt and Palestine, 1945-46; Lecturer in Old Testament, Glasgow University, 1946-51; Minister, Trinity Church, Pollokshields,

Glasgow, 1951-57; Professor of Biblical Criticism, Duke University, North Carolina, 1957-66; special appointments including A.B. Bruce Lecturer in New Testament, Glasgow University, 1954-57; Katharine McBride Visiting Professor, Bryn Mawr College, Pennsylvania, 1972-73; Kenan Distinguished Visiting Professor, Meredith College, North Carolina, 1982-83; Pendergrass Visiting Professor, Florida Southern College, 1985-86, 1987-88. Awarded Schweitzer Medal from North Carolina History and Science Foundation. Publications: Psalms 1-45; Historians of Israel; The New Testament in Historical and Contemporary Perspective (Editor with W. Barclay); Jesus and Christian Origins; Jesus; The Gospel of Mark: Commentary; 3 and 4 Maccabees (Commentary). Recreations: golf; gardening; music. Address: (h.) 5 Comiston Springs Avenue, Edinburgh, EH10 6NT.

Anderson, Iain Howe, BSc, PhD, CChem, FRSC. Depute Director, Scottish Vocational Education Council, since 1986; b. 8.2.37, Glasgow; m., Anne I. Morrison; 1 s.; 1 d. Educ. Gordon Schools, Huntly; Aberdeen University. Lecturer in Chemistry: Heriot-Watt College, 1961-66, Heriot-Watt University, 1966-71; Assistant Secretary, Scottish Association for National Certificates and Diplomas, 1971-73; Education Officer, then Senior Education Officer, Scottish Technical Education Council, 1973-86. Publications: Chemistry for the Applied Sciences (Co-author); research papers. Recreations: sailing; angling. Address: (h.) 5 Duchess Park, Helensburgh, G84 9PY; T.-0436 3263.

Anderson, Ian, MA, PhD. Senior Lecturer in Mathematics, Glasgow University, since 1985; Editor, Glasgow Mathematical Journal; b. 27.11.42, Haddington; m., Margaret Greig; 2 s. Educ. St. Andrews University; Nottingham University. Assistant Lecturer, then Lecturer, Glasgow University, 1967-85. Publications: A First Course in Combinatorial Mathematics, 1974; Combinatorics of Finite Sets, 1987; more than 20 research papers. Recreations: music; hill-walking; Crusaders. Address: (b.) Department of Mathematics, Glasgow University, Glasgow, G12 8QW; T.-041-339 8855, Ext. 4751.

Anderson, James Alexander, BL, NP. Solicitor, since 1948; Member, Glasgow and North Argyll Legal Aid Committee, 1960-86; Honorary Sheriff at Oban, since 1980; b. 17.5.21, Glasgow; m., Jean Jeffrey Brown; 2 s.; 1 d. Educ. Elgin Academy; Edinburgh University. Army, 1942-46 (Staff Captain, RA); joined Anderson Banks & Co., Solicitors, Oban, 1950 (Senior Partner, until 1986); Local Representative, Legal Aid Committee, 1960-79; Dean of Faculty, Oban Procurators, 1975-78. Treasurer, Lorn & Mull Presbytery; Treasurer, Oban and District Christian Aid Committee. Recreations: writing; gardening; golf; pool. Address: (b.) 4/6 Stevenson Street, Oban, Argyll; T.-0631 63158.

Anderson, James Frazer Gillan, CBE, JP, DL. Member, Scottish Development Agency, since 1986; Convener, Central Regional Council, 1974-86; b. 25.3.29, Maddiston, by Falkirk; m., May Harley; 1 s.; 1 d. Educ. Maddiston School; Graeme High School, Falkirk. Convener, Stirling County Council, 1971-75; Member: Health and Safety Commission, 1974-80; Montgomery Committee, 1982-84; Scottish Economic Council, 1983-87. Treasurer, Maddiston Old Folks Association. Recreations: gardening; walking; reading. Address: (b.) Viewforth, Stirling; T.-Stirling 73111.

Anderson, James Killoch, OBE, MB, ChB, FFCM, FCR, JP. Unit Medical Officer, Glasgow Royal Infirmary and Royal Maternity Hospital, Glasgow; b. 3.2.23, Johnstone; m., Irene Webster Wilson; 1 s.; 2 d. Educ. High School of Glasgow; Glasgow University. Deputy Medical Superintendent, Glasgow Royal Infirmary and Associated Hospitals, 1954; appointed Medical Superintendent, 1957; District Medical Officer, Eastern District, Greater Glasgow Health Board, 1974; Unit Medical Officer, Unit East 1, Greater Glasgow Health Board, 1984. Corps Commandant and Council Member, St. Andrew's Ambulance Association, 1957-82; Member of Committee, Scottish Ambulance Service, 1957-74; Director, North Parish, Washing Green Society, Glasgow, since 1957; Member, Scottish Technical Education Council, since 1974; Member, Science Development Team, 16-18s Action Plan, Scottish Education Department. Recreations: gardening; golf. Address: (h.) 15 Kenilworth Avenue, Helensburgh, G84 7JR; T.-0436 3739.

Anderson, James Masson, OBE, DL, JP. Farmer, since 1934; Honorary Sheriff, 1977-86; b. 21.3.17, Elgin; m., Phyllis Adam Taylor; 1 s.; 1 d. Educ. Elgin Academy; North of Scotland College of Agriculture. Military Service, 1939-46; Seaforth Highlanders and Dogra Regiment (Indian Army). Member, Moray County Council and Joint County Council for Moray and Nairn, 1961-74; Chairman, Moray District Council, 1974-84. Recreations: reading; walking; gardening; bridge. Address: (h.) Miltonhill, Forres, Moray, IV36 OUA; T.-0343 85 242.

Anderson, John, MA (Hons). Rector, High School of Stirling, since 1982; Chairman, General Teaching Council of Scotland, 1985-87; b. 20.11.37, Oyne, Aberdeenshire; m., Christina M. Murray; 2 d. Educ. Banchory Academy; Aberdeen University. Assistant Teacher, Robert Gordon's College, Aberdeen, 1961-65; Principal Teacher of Geography, Buckie High School, 1965-70; Rector, Speyside High School, 1970-82. Council Member, SCOTVEC; Governor, Scottish Council for Education Technology. Recreations: golf; fishing. Address: (b.) High School of Stirling, Ogilvie Road, Torbrex, Stirling; T.-Stirling 72451.

Anderson of Pittormie, Captain John Charles Lindsay, VRD (and clasp), OStJ, MA (Oxon), LLB, RNR. Solicitor; Consultant to Messrs J.L. Anderson; Honorary Sheriff, Tayside, Central and Fife, since 1986; Arable and Fruit Farmer; Quarrymaster, Fife Redstone and Brackmont Quarries; b. 8.9.08, Cupar; m., Elsie Margaret Begg; 1 s.; 2 d. Educ. St. Salvators, St. Andrews; Glenalmond College; Pembroke College, Oxford; Edinburgh University. Solicitor, since 1931; Member, St. Andrews Town Council, 1938-51 (Honorary Treasurer, 1945-51); Parliamentary candidate (Conservative), West Stirling, 1945;

joined RNVR as Sub Lt., 1930; served World War II, Northern Patrol, Convoys, Gunnery Specialist; Captain, RNR, 1954; commanded HMS Unicorn, Tay Division RNVR/RNR, 1954-59; RNR ADC to The Queen, 1959-60; Founder Governor, Unicorn Preservation Society, since 1968; Member, Business Committee, Edinburgh University General Council, since 1982; Member, Council, Law Society of Scotland, 1983-86; former Dean of Faculty, Cupar; President, Royal Caledonian Curling Club, 1978-79; Chairman: Kirkcaldy Ice Rink, since 1978, Scottish Ice Rinks Association, since 1986, Fife Housing Co. Ltd., Cupar Corn Exchange Co. Ltd., Fife Redstone Quarry Co. Ltd., Brackmont Quarry Ltd.; Honorary President, St. Andrews Branch, Royal British Legion. Recreations: curling; shooting; golf; tennis. Address: (h.) Pittormie, Dairsie, Fife, KY15 4SW; T.-0334 870233.

Anderson, John MacKenzie, MB, ChB, DPath, FRCPath. Consultant Histopathologist, Dundee Hospitals, since 1975; Honorary Senior Lecturer in Pathology, Dundee University, since 1975; b. 13.8.35, Dundee; m., Mary Ursula Nolan; 2 s.; 2 d. Educ. Dollar Academy; St. Andrews University. Medical Officer, RAMC, 1960-63; Assistant Pathologist, Glasgow Royal Infirmary, 1959-60 and 1963-65; Maudsley Hospital, London, 1965-67; Consultant Pathologist, Greenock Hospitals, 1967-69; Stobhill Hospital, Glasgow, 1969-70; Royal Hospital for Sick Children, Edinburgh, 1970-75. Recreations: golf; gardening; music. Address: (b.) Department of Pathology, Ninewells Hospital, Dundee; T.-Dundee 60111, Ext. 2667.

Anderson, Joseph Aitken, BA (Hons), CSD, MBIM. Managing Director, North of Scotland Milk Marketing Board, since 1982; Director, Company of Scottish Cheesemakers, since 1983; Director, Norlink Ltd., since 1985; Chairman, Local Advisory Committee (Moray Firth Area), IBA, since 1986; b. 1.7.36, Prestonpans; m., Sheila Armstrong; 2 s. Educ. Preston Lodge; Open University. Managing Secretary: Carluke Co-operative Society, 1962-65, East Fife Co-operative Society, 1965-71; Depute Chief Executive, Central and East Fife Co-operative Society, 1971-79; Executive Officer and Secretary, Fife Regional Co-operative Society, 1979-82. Member, United Kingdom Dairy Association Council; Chairman, NE Branch, Society of Dairy Technology. Recreations: golf; fly fishing; photography. Address: (b.) 29 Ardconnel Terrace, Inverness; T.-0463 232611.

Anderson, Kathleen Janette, OBE, BSc, PhD, CBiol, FIBiol, CChem, FRSC. Depute Principal, Napier College, Edinburgh, since 1983; b. 22.5.27, Glasgow; m., Mark Elliot Muir Anderson; 1 s.; 1 d. Educ. Queens Park School, Glasgow; Glasgow University. Lecturer, West of Scotland Agricultural College, Glasgow, 1948-54; Johnson and Florence Stoney Research Fellow, University of Sydney, Australia, 1952-53; Commonwealth Travelling Research Fellow, Australia and New Zealand, 1953; Sir James Knott Research Fellow, Durham University, 1955-57; King's College, Durham University: Lecturer in Biochemistry, 1958-59, Lecturer in Microbiology, 1962-63, Lecturer (part-time) in Landscape Horticulture, 1963-65, Lecturer (part-time), Extra-Mural Department, 1959-65; Lecturer (part-time), Department of Extra-Mural Studies, Edinburgh University, 1965-68; Napier College, Edinburgh: Senior Lecturer, Department of Biological Sciences, 1968-69, Head of Department, Biological Sciences, 1969-83. Crown Trustee, National Library for Scotland, since 1981; Deacon, Church of Scotland, 1974-78, Elder, since 1978; CNAA Environmental Sciences Board, 1978-84; Chairman: Joint Committee for Biology, SCOTEC, since 1979, Biology Board D1, SCOTEC, since 1980; Institute of Biology: Chairman, Scottish Branch, 1977-79, Member of Council, 1977-80, Fellowship Committee, 1980-83, Environment Division, 1982-86; Founder Chairman, Heads of Biology in Tertiary Education, 1975-77; Heads of Biology in Polytechnics, 1974-83; Nurse Education Committee, Royal Edinburgh Hospital, 1974-77; Council Member, SCOTVEC, since 1984 (Chairman, Educational Policy Committee); Chairman, Edinburgh Branch, Glasgow Graduates Association, 1985-86; Member, Scottish National Committee, English Speaking Union, since 1987; Trustee, Royal Observatory (Edinburgh) Trust, since 1987. Publications: Discover Lothian Beaches; Holyrood Park Teachers Handbook; Safety in Biological Laboratories. Recreations: knitting; gardening; foreign travel. Address: (b.) Napier College, 219 Colinton Road, Edinburgh, EH14 1DJ; T.-031-444 2266.

Anderson, Kenneth D., MA. Rector, Grove Academy, Broughty Ferry, since 1981; b. 13.11.31, Glasgow; m., Heather; 1 s. Educ. Glasgow Academy; University College, Oxford. Teacher of Classics, Dunfermline High School, 1955-62; Principal Teacher of Classics: Beath High School, 1962-64, Robert Gordon's College, Aberdeen, 1964-72; Assistant Head Teacher, Portobello High School, Edinburgh, 1972-75; Deputy Rector, Perth Grammar School, 1975-81. Recreations: choral singing; Church work. Address: (b.) Grove Academy, Camperdown Street, Broughty Ferry, Dundee; T.-0382 730284.

Anderson, Leslie William. Parliamentary Correspondent, BBC Scotland, since 1984; b. 3.8.40, Edinburgh; m., Alexandra; 2 d. Educ. Daniel Stewarts College, Edinburgh. Reporter, Lennox Herald, Dumbarton, 1960-63; News Reporter, Scottish Daily Mail, Glasgow, 1963-66; Scottish Daily Express: News Reporter, 1966-67, Deputy Industrial Correspondent, 1967-70, Industrial Correspondent, 1970-78; Industrial Correspondent, BBC Scotland, 1979-84. Recreation: rugby (spectating). Address: (h.) 10 Seggielea Road, Jordanhill, Glasgow; T.-041-954 3369.

Anderson, Professor Malcolm, MA, DPhil (Oxon). Professor of Politics, Edinburgh University, since 1979; b. 13.5.34, Knutsford; 2 s.; 1 d. Educ. Altrincham Grammar School; University College, Oxford. Lecturer in Government, Manchester University, 1960-63; Research Fellow, Institut National des Sciences Politiques, 1964-65 and 1986-87; Senior Lecturer, then Professor, Warwick University, 1965-79; Visiting Fellow, Institute of Higher Studies, Vienna, 1977-78; Associate Professor, Sorbonne-Pantheon, 1987-88. Chairman, University Association for Contemporary European Studies. Publications: Government in France, 1970; Conservative Politics in

France, 1974; Frontier Regions in Western Europe, 1983; Women, Equality and Europe (Co-author), 1988. Recreations: walking; reading; photography. Address: (h.) 13 Northumberland Street, Edinburgh, EH3 6LL; T.-031-556 2113.

Anderson, Moira, OBE. Singer; b. Kirkintilloch; m., Dr. Stuart Macdonald. Educ. Ayr Academy; Royal Scottish Academy of Music, Glasgow. Began with Kirkintilloch Junior Choir, aged six; made first radio broadcast for BBC in Scotland, aged eight; was Teacher of Music in Ayr before becoming professional singer; made first professional broadcast, White Heather Club, 1960; has toured overseas, had her own radio and TV series; has introduced Stars on Sunday, ITV; appeared in summer shows, cabaret, pantomime and numerous other stage shows; several Royal Variety performances.

Anderson, Noel Barber, JP, BSc, MICE, CEng, DipTP. Director of Estates and Buildings, (formerly Buildings Officer), Edinburgh University, since 1971; b. 25.12.25, Edinburgh; m., Vera Gair Sutherland; 1 s.; 3 d. Educ. George Watson's Boys College; Edinburgh University. Engineering Assistant, Partridge Earp and Partners; South of Scotland Electricity Board; Lothian River Purification Board; Cumbernauld Development Corporation; Assistant Buildings Officer, Edinburgh University. Member, Board of Management, Edinvar Housing Association. Recreations: hill-walking; pottering. Address: (b.) University of Edinburgh, Old College, South Bridge, Edinburgh; T.-031-667 1011, Ext. 4345.

Anderson, Peter David, MA, PhD, FSA Scot. Conservation Officer, Scottish Record Office, since 1985; b. 10.3.47, Greenock; m., Jean Johnstone Smith; 1 s.; 1 d. Educ. Hutchesons' Grammar School, Glasgow; St. Andrews University; Edinburgh University. Assistant Teacher of History, Cranhill Secondary School, Glasgow, 1972-73; Research Assistant, Scottish Record Office, 1974-80; Registrar, National Register of Archives (Scotland), 1980-83; Secretary, NRA(S), 1984-85. Honorary Secretary, Scottish Oral History Group, since 1984. Publication: Robert Stewart, Earl of Orkney, Lord of Shetland, 1533-93, 1982. Recreations: drawing and painting; drama. Address: 76 Burghmuir Court, Linlithgow, EH49 7LR; T.-Linlithgow 844663.

Anderson, Robert David, MA, DPhil. Reader in History, Edinburgh University, since 1985; b. 11.7.42, Cardiff. Educ. Taunton School, Somerset; Queen's and St. Antony's Colleges, Oxford. Assistant Lecturer, Glasgow University, 1967-69; Lecturer, then Senior Lecturer, Edinburgh University, 1969-85. Publications: Education in France 1848-1870, 1975; France 1870-1914: Politics and Society, 1977; Education and Opportunity in Victorian Scotland, 1983 (winner, Scottish Arts Council Literary Award, 1984). Address: (b.) Department of History, Edinburgh University, Edinburgh; T.-031-667 1011.

Anderson, Robert Geoffrey William, MA, DPhil, FSA, FSA Scot. Director, National Museums of Scotland, since 1985; b. 2.5.44, London; m., Margaret Elizabeth Callis Anderson; 2 s. Educ. St. John's College, Oxford. Assistant Keeper, Royal Scottish Museum, 1970-75; Assistant Keeper, Deputy Keeper, Keeper, Science Museum, 1975-84; Director, Royal Scottish Museum, 1984-85. Dexter Award, American Chemical Society, 1986; President, International Commission on Scientific Instruments, since 1982; President, British Society for History of Science, since 1988. Publications: books on history of science and museology. Address: (b.) Royal Museum of Scotland, Chambers Street, Edinburgh; T.-031-225 7534.

Anderson, William. Editor, The Sunday Post, since 1967; b. 10.2.34, Motherwell; m., Margaret Cross McClelland; 3 s. Educ. Dalziel High School; Glasgow University. Journalist since first producing school newspapers, with interruptions as cook steward, male nurse, medical student and Army officer. Recreations: fishing; sailing; cooking. Address: (b.) Courier Building, Meadowside, Dundee; T.-0382 23131.

Anderson, William Archibald, MC, TD, JP, MA. Member, Shetland Islands Council, since 1982; b. 22.12.19, Edinburgh; m., Patricia Smith (daughter of late Ex-Provost James A. Smith); 2 s. Educ. Daniel Stewart's College; Aberdeen University. Served with Black Watch (RHR), 1939-46. Woollen manufacturer, 1946-52; schoolmaster, 1952-82. Recreations: gardening; golf. Address: (h.) The Sea Chest, East Voe, Scalloway, Shetland; T.-Scalloway 326.

Anderson, Professor Sir (William) Ferguson, Kt (1974), OBE, KStJ, MD, FRCP(Lond), (Glas), (Edin), (C), (I), FACP. Professor Emeritus, Geriatric Medicine, Glasgow University; Chairman, Scottish Retirement Council; Honorary President, Crossroads (Scotland) Care Attendant Scheme; Honorary Vice-President, Age Concern (Scotland); b. 8.4.14, Glasgow; m., Margaret Gebbie; 1 s.; 2 d. Educ. Glasgow Academy; Glasgow University. Assistant Lecturer, Materia Medica, Glasgow University, 1939-41; Major, RAMC, 1941-46; Senior Lecturer, Materia Medica, Glasgow University, 1946-48; Senior Lecturer, Medicine, Welsh National School of Medicine, 1948-52; Honorary Consultant Physician, Cardiff Royal Infirmary, 1948-52; Consultant Physician in Geriatric Medicine and Advisor in diseases of old age and chronic sickness, Western Regional Board, 1952-65; Professor of Geriatric Medicine, Glasgow University, 1965-79. St. Mungo Prize, City of Glasgow; Ed Henderson Award, American Geriatrics Society; Brookdale Award, Gerontological Society of America. Recreation: golf. Address: (h.) Rodel, Moor Road, Strathblane, Glasgow, G63 9EX; T.-Blanefield 70862.

Anderson, William John, MA, CA. Director of Finance, Nairn District Council, since 1984; b. 14.8.49, Nairn; m., Gilliane; 1 s.; 1 d. Educ. Nairn Academy; Aberdeen University. Chartered Accountant, Peat Marwick Mitchell & Co., Glasgow, 1972-76; Director of Finance, Riddoch of Rothiemay Ltd., 1976-84. Treasurer, Elgin Hospice Trust and several other charitable trusts. Recreations: family; golf; fishing. Address: (h.) 60 Manse Road, Nairn; T.-0667 52796.

Anderson, William Lilburn, JP, BSc, FEIS. Head Teacher, Aith Junior High School, Shetland, since 1966; b. 10.3.31, Glasgow; 4 d. Educ. Hillhead High School; Glasgow University. Regional Secretary (Shetland), EIS. Recreation: building. Address: (h.) Schoolhouse, Aith, Bixter, Shetland, ZE2 9NB; T.-0595 81414.

Andrew, William, MA. Writer; b. 31.8.31, Glasgow. Educ. Shawlands Academy, Glasgow; Glasgow University. Taught English in London and Glasgow; turned to full-time writing, 1979; plays for stage, radio and television, including Project Flora, The Best Baby, Behind the Circle; Script Editor, Take The High Road, STV; short stories. Recreations: local history; music. Address: (h.) 24 Queen's Drive, Glasgow, G42.

Andrews, Rev. James Edward, BA, MA, BD, DipCG. Minister, Ardrishaig linked with South Knapdale, since 1985; Convener, Committee on World Mission and Unity, Presbytery of South Argyll, since 1986; b. 2.5.45, Downpatrick, Northern Ireland; m., Margaret Elizabeth McWhirter; 2 s. Educ. Belfast Royal Academy; Magee University College, Londonderry; Trinity College, Dublin; Edinburgh University. Careers Officer, until 1981; licensed, Presbytery of West Lothian, 1984; Assistant Minister, Jedburgh Old Parish Church. Recreations: fishing; reading; sailing. Address: (h.) The Manse, Ardrishaig, Argyll, PA30 8HE; T.-0546 3269.

Angus, David George, MA (Hons), DipEd. Freelance Writer and Lecturer; b. 20.4.25, Brora; m., Florence Jean Manson. Educ. Inverness Royal Academy; Lanark Grammar School; Edinburgh University. Assistant Teacher of English, Beath High School, 1951-59; freelance Writer, Edinburgh, 1959-61; Special Assistant Teacher of English, Alloa Academy, 1961-71; Extramural Lecturer in Scottish Literature, Stirling University, ten years; has published verse in Scots, English and French; contributed prose in Scots to Lallans magazine and The Scotsman and in English to Scots Magazine and The Scotsman; Historian, Edinburgh Wax Museum; former Council Member and Vice-Chairman, Saltire Society; founder Member and former Secretary, Scots Language Society. Publication: Roses and Thorns - Scottish Teenage Verse (Editor). Recreations: historical, literary and genealogical research. Address: (h.) 122 Henderson Street, Bridge of Allan, Stirling, FK9 4HF; T.-832306.

Angus, Rev. James Alexander Keith, TD, MA. Minister, Braemar and Crathie Parish Churches, since 1979; Domestic Chaplain to The Queen; b. 16.4.29, Aberdeen; m., Alison Jane Daly; 1 s.; 1 d. Educ. High School of Dundee; St. Andrews University. Assistant Minister, Glasgow Cathedral, 1955-56; Minister: Hoddam Parish Church, 1956-67, Gourock Old Parish Church, 1967-79. TA: Captain, Royal Artillery, 1950-56, Chaplain, 1957-77; Convener, Committee of Chaplains to HM Forces, General Assembly, 1981-85. Recreations: hill-walking; fishing; golf. Address: (h.) The Manse of Crathie, Crathie, near Ballater, Aberdeenshire; T.-Crathie 208.

Angus, William Jestyn, FIPM, MIMC. Director-Scotland, Knight Wendling Ltd., since 1982; Director, Glasgow Chamber of Commerce; Director, Merchants House of Glasgow; Vice-President, Glasgow and West of Scotland Outward Bound Association; b. 12.12.30, Northumberland; m., Eleanor Gillian Attwood; 1 s.; 1 d. Educ. Gordonstoun School; Harvard Business School. Eighteen years with George Angus & Co. Ltd., latterly part of Dunlop Holdings Ltd.; from 1953 in marketing, export sales, general management and group personnel management; joined Matthew Hall Group, 1971; Senior Consultant, MSL, 1973-82. Recreations: hill-walking; skiing; tennis; wine. Address: (h.) Braeriach, Helensburgh, G84 9AH; T.-0436 2393.

Angus, Col. William Turnbull Calderhead, CEng, MRAeS, FBIM, FIQA. Honorary Sheriff, North Strathclyde, since 1986; b. 20.7.23, Glasgow; m., Nola Leonie Campbell-Gillies; 2 s.; 2 d. Educ. Govan High School; Glasgow University; Royal Military College of Science. Commissioned Royal Regiment of Artillery, 1944; King's African Rifles and GSO2, DAAG (Major), HQ East Africa Command, 1945-47; Technical Staff Course, Royal Military College of Science, 1949-51; TSO2 (Major), Inspectorate of Armaments, 1951-54; BAOR and Cyprus, 1954-57; GSO2 (Major), G(Tech) HQ BAOR, 1957-60; TSO2 (Major), Ordnance Board, 1960-63; TSO2 (Major), Trials Establishment Guided Weapons, RA, 1963-65; postgraduate Guided Weapons Course, Royal Military College of Science, 1965-66; TSO1 (Lt. Col.), Royal Armament Research and Development Establishment, 1966-69; Assistant Director, Guided Weapons Trials (Col.), MOD Procurement Executive, 1970-73; Member (Col.), Ordnance Board, 1973-74; retired, 1974; self-employed holiday cottages proprietor and Scottish Manager for Blakes Holidays; Past President, Campbeltown Rotary Club. Recreations: wood-turning and manufacture of spinning wheels; creationism studies. Address: Kilchrist Castle, Campbeltown, Argyll, PA28 6PH; T.-0586 53210.

Annan, Hugh Ross, BL. Procurator Fiscal, Linlithgow, since 1976; b. 27.12.34, Perth; m., Sheila McNicol; 2 s. Educ. Bell-Baxter School, Cupar; St. Andrews University. Solicitor, 1959; Procurator Fiscal, Cupar, February-October, 1976. Recreations: reading; astronomy. Address: (h.) 14 Deacons Court, Linlithgow, West Lothian; T.-Linlithgow 844684.

Annand, James King, MA. Writer; b. 2.2.08, Edinburgh; m., Beatrice Violet Lindsay; 4 d. Educ. Broughton Secondary School, Edinburgh; Edinburgh University. Assistant Teacher, James Clark School, Edinburgh, 1932-49 (War Service, Royal Navy, 1941-46); Lecturer in Current Affairs, Regent Road Day Release Centre, 1949-53; Principal Teacher of History, James Clark School, 1953-58; Headmaster, Whithorn Junior Secondary School, 1959-62; Principal Teacher of History, Firrhill Secondary School, Edinburgh, 1962-71. Founder Member and holder of various offices, Scottish Youth Hostels Association, since 1931; Council Member: Saltire Society, 1951-54, Historical Association of Scotland, 1954-58; founder Member, Scots Language Society, 1972 (Honorary Vice-President, since 1983); Councillor, Royal Burgh of Whithorn, 1960-62; Editor: The Rebel Student, 1929, Lines Review, 1958-59, Lallans, 1973-83. Awarded Burns Chronicle Poetry Prize, 1955; Scottish Arts Council Special Award for contribution to Scottish poetry, 1979. Publications: Sing it Aince for Pleisure, 1965; Two Voices, 1968; Twice for Joy, 1973; Poems and Translations, 1975; Songs from Carmina Burana, 1978; Thrice to Show Ye, 1979; Dod and Davie, 1986; Early Lyrics by Hugh MacDiarmid (Editor), 1968; A Scots Handsel (Editor), 1980. Recreations: mountaineering; natural history; photography; book-binding. Address: (h.) 173/314 Comely Bank Road, Edinburgh, EH4 1DJ; T.-031-332 6905.

Annand, Louise Gibson, MBE, MA (Hons), AMA. Artist; Member, Royal Fine Art Commission for Scotland, 1979-86; b. 27.5.15, Uddingston; m., Alistair Matheson (deceased). Educ. Hamilton Academy; Glasgow University. Teacher, primary and secondary schools, Glasgow, 1939-49; Assistant, Schools Museum Service, 1949-70; Museums Education Officer, 1970-80. Past Chairman: Scottish Educational Film Association (Glasgow Production Group); Glasgow Lady Artists Club Trust; National Vice-Chairman, Scottish Educational Media Association, 1979-84; President: Society of Scottish Women Artists, 1963-66 and 1980-85; Glasgow Society of Women Artists, 1977-79; Visiting Lecturer in Scottish Art, Regina University, 1982; Chairman, J.D. Fergusson Foundation, since 1982 (Trustee, since 1983); Member, Business Committee, General Council, University of Glasgow, 1981-85 and since 1988; exhibited widely since 1945; produced numerous 16mm films, including the first on Charles Rennie Mackintosh, 1966. Recreations: mountaineering (Ladies Scottish Climbing Club). Address: (h.) 22 Kingsborough Gardens, Glasgow, G12 9NJ; T.-041-339 8956.

Annandale and Hartfell, Earl of (Patrick Andrew Wentworth Hope Johnstone of Annandale and of That Ilk). Farmer; Chief, Clan Johnstone; Baron of the Barony of the Lands of the Earldom of Annandale and Hartfell, and of the Lordship of Johnstone; Hereditary Steward, Stewartry of Annandale; Hereditary Keeper, Keys of Lochmaben Castle; Deputy Lieutenant, Dumfriesshire, since 1987; Member, Dumfries and Galloway Regional Council, 1975-85; b. 19.4.41, Auldgirth, Dumfriesshire; m., Susan Josephine; 1 s.; 1 d. Educ. Stowe School; Royal Agricultural College, Cirencester. Member: Dumfriesshire County Council, 1970-75, Scottish Valuation Advisory Council, 1982, Solway River Purification Board, 1973-85; Underwriter, Lloyds, London, 1976. Address: (b.) Annandale Estates Office, St. Anns, Lockerbie, Dumfriesshire; T.-Johnstone Bridge 317.

Anstruther, Sir Ralph (Hugo), of that Ilk, 7th Bt. of Balcaskie and 12th of Anstruther, KCVO, MC, DL, BA. Equerry to the Queen Mother, since 1959; b. 13.6.21. Educ. Eton; Magdalene College, Cambridge. Major (ret.), Coldstream Guards. Member, Queen's Bodyguard for Scotland (Royal Company of Archers); DL, Fife, 1960; DL, Caithness-shire, 1965. Address: Balcaskie, Pittenweem, Fife; Watten, Caithness.

Antebi, Raymond Nathan, MD, LAH, DPM, FRCP, RCPS(Glas), FRCPsych. Physician Superintendent, Psychiatric Eastern District, Glasgow, since 1987; Honorary Clinical Lecturer in Psychiatry, Glasgow University, since 1966; Psychiatric Adviser on Mental Health to Strathclyde University Student Health Service, since 1980; b. 4.3.30, Gablonz, Czechoslovakia; m., Anna Van Der Velde; 2 s.; 2 d. Educ. Bologna University. Full-time Consultant Psychiatrist to the Health Service since 1964. Recreations: fishing; reading. Address: (h.) Picketlaw House, Montgomery Street, Eaglesham, Glasgow, G76 0AU; T.-Eaglesham 3520.

Anton, Alexander Elder, CBE, MA, LLB, FRSE, FBA; b. 1922; m., Doris May Lawrence; 1 s. Educ. Aberdeen University. Solicitor, 1949; Lecturer, Aberdeen, 1953-59; Professor of Jurisprudence, Glasgow University, 1959-73; Honorary Visiting Professor, 1982-84, Honorary Professor, 1984, Aberdeen University; Member, Scottish Law Commission, 1966-82; Literary Director, Stair Society, 1960-66; Chairman, Scottish Rights of Way Society, 1988. Publications: Private International Law, 1967; Civil Jurisdiction in Scotland, 1984. Recreation: hill-walking. Address: (h.) 9 Baillieswells Terrace, Bieldside, Aberdeen, AB1 9AR.

Arbuthnott, 16th Viscount of (John Campbell Arbuthnott), CBE, DSC, FRSE, FRSA, KStJ, MA. Lord Lieutenant, Grampian Region (Kincardineshire), since 1977; President, Royal Scottish Geographical Society, 1984-87; Chairman, Scottish Widows' Fund and Life Assurance Society, 1984-87; Lord High Commissioner to the General Assembly of the Church of Scotland, 1986 and 1987; b. 26.10.24; m.; 1 s.; 1 d. Educ. Fettes College; Gonville and Caius College, Cambridge. Member, Countryside Commission for Scotland, 1967-71; Chairman, Red Deer Commission, 1969-75; Member, Aberdeen University Court, 1978-84; President, Scottish Landowners Federation, 1974-79; President, Royal Zoological Society of Scotland, since 1976; President, Scottish Agricultural Organisation Society, 1980-83; President, Federation of Agricultural Cooperatives (UK), 1983-87; Deputy Chairman, Nature Conservancy Council, 1980-85, and Chairman, Scottish Committee, NCC; Chairman, Aberdeen and Northern Marts Ltd., since 1986. Address: (h.) Arbuthnott House, by Laurencekirk, Kincardineshire.

Arbuthnott, The Hon. William David, MBE. Regimental Secretary, The Black Watch, since 1978; b. 5.11.27, Colchester; m., Sonja Mary Thomson; 1 s.; 2 d. Educ. Fettes. Army Officer, The Black Watch, since 1948. Recreations: gardening; reading; civil engineering. Address: (h.) The Old Manse, Trochry, by Dunkeld, PH8 ODY; T.-Trochry 205; (b.) RHQ The Black Watch, Balhousie Castle, Hay Street, Perth, PH1 5HS; T.-Perth 21281.

Argyll, 12th Duke of, (Ian Campbell). Chief of Clan Campbell; Hereditary Master of the Royal Household, Scotland; Hereditary High Sheriff of the County of Argyll; Admiral of the Western Coast and Isles; Keeper of the Great Seal of Scotland and of the Castles of Dunstaffnage, Dunoon, and Carrick and Tarbert; b. 28.8.37; m., Iona Mary Colquhoun; 1 s.; 1 d. Educ. Le Rosey, Switzerland; Glenalmond; McGill University, Montreal. Member, Queen's Bodyguard for Scotland (Royal Company of Archers). Address: Inveraray Castle, Inveraray, Argyll.

Armour, Archibald, MA (Hons), FEIS. Head Teacher, Camphill High School, Paisley, 1975-85; b. 3.6.20, Paisley; m., Margaret B.L. Hebditch; 1 s.; 1 d. Educ. Camphill Senior Secondary School, Paisley; Glasgow University. Teacher, Camphill Senior Secondary School, 1950-54; Principal Teacher of English: Abercorn Junior Secondary School, Paisley, 1954-61, Renfrew High School, 1961-68 (Depute Head, 1965-68); Head Teacher, Mount School (later Cowdenknowes High School), Greenock, 1968-75. President, Educational Institute of Scotland, 1976-77 (Vice-President, 1971-72). Recreations: golf; gardening; bridge; Burns Suppers. Address: (h.) Marvin, 9 Douglas Avenue, Elderslie, Johnstone, PA5 9ND; T.-Johnstone 20884.

Armour, Professor James, PhD, Dr hc Utrecht, MRCVS. Professor of Veterinary Parasitology (Personal Chair), Glasgow University, since 1976; Chairman, Advisory Board, Government Institutes on Animal Health, since 1988; b. 17.9.29, Basra, Iraq; m., Irene Morris; 2 s.; 2 d. Educ. Marr College, Troon; Glasgow University. Colonial veterinary service, Nigeria, 1953-60; Research Scientist, Wellcome Ltd., 1960-63; Glasgow University: Research Fellow, 1963-67, Lecturer/Senior Lecturer, 1967-73, Reader, 1973-76; Dean, Faculty of Veterinary Medicine, 1986-89. Chairman, Government Committee on Animal Medicines; Chairman, Editorial Board, In Practice (veterinary journal). Publications: joint author of textbook on veterinary parasitology; edited two books; 150 scientific articles. Recreation: golf. Address: (h.) 10 Willockston Road, Troon, Ayrshire; T.-0292 314068.

Armour, John Campbell (Ian), TD. Regional Donor Organiser, Glasgow and West of Scotland Blood Transfusion Service, since 1983; b. 29.9.48, Glasgow; m., Margaret Catherine Leitch; 2 d. Educ. Bearsden Academy. Served 52nd Lowland Volunteers (TA), 1968-85. Retail travel industry, 1964-74; sales and marketing appointments in travel industry, 1974-82. Member, Executive Council, Scottish National Blood Transfusion Association. Recreations: railway history; bowling; music. Address: (b.) 80 St. Vincent Street, Glasgow, G2 5UA; T.-041-226 4111.

Armour, Mary Nicol Neill, DA, RSA, RSW, RGI, LLD Glasgow (1980). Artist; b. 27.3.02, Blantyre; m., William Armour. Educ. Hamilton Academy; Glasgow School of Art. Elected ARSA, 1941; RSW, 1956; RSA, 1958; RGI, 1977; Honorary President: Glasgow School of Art, 1982; Royal Glasgow Institute of the Fine Arts, 1983; Vice President, Paisley Art Institute, 1983. Guthrie Award, RSA, 1937; Cargill Prize, RGI, 1972. Recreations: gardening; dress-making. Address: 2 Gateside Place, Kilbarchan, PA10 2LY; T.-Kilbarchan 2873.

Armson, Rev. Canon John Moss, MA, PhD. Principal, Edinburgh Theological College, since 1982; Canon, St. Mary's Cathedral, Edinburgh, since 1982; Pantonian Professor of Theology, since 1982; b. 21.12.39, Coalville, Leicestershire. Educ. Wyggeston Grammar School; Selwyn College, Cambridge; St. Andrews University. Chaplain and Fellow, Downing College, Cambridge, 1969-73; Vice-Principal, Westcott House, Cambridge, 1973-82. Recreation: pottering in the garden. Address: The Theological College, Rosebery Crescent, Edinburgh, EH12 5JT; T.-031-337 3838.

Armstrong, Andrew, MB, ChB, FRCPEdin, FRCPGlas. Consultant Physician, Dumfries and Galloway Royal Infirmary, since 1968 (Postgraduate Tutor, since 1981); Honorary Clinical Lecturer, Aberdeen University, since 1968; b. 3.12.29, Edinburgh; m., Dr. Norah Evelyn Stewart; 2 s.; 1 d. Educ. Edinburgh University. Recreations: mountaineering; skiing; curling. Address: (h.) Deil's Dike, Lochmaben, Dumfriesshire; T.-Lochmaben 810514.

Armstrong, Edward Calvert, MBE, KtT, FSA Scot; b. 20.11.16, Langholm. Educ. Langholm Academy. Joined staff of Stevenson & Johnstone, WS, Langholm, 1935; appointed Depute Town Clerk, Langholm, 1939; undistinguished service, RAF, 1940-46; appointed Town Clerk/Town Chamberlain etc., Langholm, 1946; on reorganisation, became Local Government Officer for Eskdale, 1975-81; Member, Dumfries and Galloway Regional Council, 1982-86. Honorary President, Langholm Operatic Society; founder President, Langholm Rotary and Probus Clubs; Chairman, local committee, Earl Haig Fund; Chairman, Langholm, Ewes and Westerkirk Community Council. Recreations: reading; photography; music. Address: (h.) 2 Charlotte Street, Langholm, DG13 ODZ; T.-0541 80810.

Armstrong, John Frederick Cunningham. Chairman, Mallinson-Denny (Northern) Ltd. and Edward Hughes Ltd.; Executive Director, Hunter Timber Limited; Member, Forth Valley Health Board; b. 29.12.39, Glasgow; m., Evelyn Myra Armstrong McKell; 2 s.; 1 d. Educ. Merchiston Castle School. Engineering career with BL culminating as Managing Director, five East African subsidiaries, 1976-81; appointed Managing Director, Mallinson-Denny Scotland, 1981. Recreations: golf; fishing; skiing; curling. Address: (h.) Glenairthrey, 12 Upper Glen Road, Bridge of Allan, Stirling, FK9 4PX; T.-0786 832862.

Armstrong, Rev. William Sinclair, MA, BD. Minister, Penninghame St. John's, Newton Stewart, since 1971; Moderator, Presbytery of Wigtown and Stranraer, 1987-88; b. 7.3.24, Coventry; m., Jessie Clowes Hazle Kerr; 3 d. Educ. Dalziel High School, Motherwell; Glasgow University; Edinburgh University. Member, British Section, Palestine Police Force, 1943-46; Minister: Parish of Rothes, 1951-55, Trinity Church, Renfrew, 1955-66, St. Marnock's Parish Church, Kilmarnock, 1966-71. Sometime Senior County Chaplain, Renfrew and Bute, Army Cadet Force; former Chaplain, HM Prison, Penninghame and Cornwall Park Old Folks' Home; Chaplain, Newton Stewart Hospital. Publication: Trinity Church, Renfrew, 1862-1962. Recreations: reading; theatre; music; gardening; curling. Address: The Manse, Newton Stewart, Wigtownshire, DG8 6HH; T.-0671 2259.

Arnold, James Edward, BA, CertEd. Manager, New Lanark Conservation Trust, since 1974; b. 16.3.45, Glasgow; m., Rose. Educ. Caludon Castle Comprehensive School; York University; London University. Recreations: New Lanark and life. Address: (b.) Mill Number Three, New Lanark, Lanark; T.-0555 61345.

Arnott, Rev. Andrew David Keltie, MA, BD. Minister, Netherlee Church, Glasgow, since 1977; b. 22.7.45, Dunfermline; m., Rosemary Jane Batchelor; 2 s.; 1 d. Educ. George Watson's College, Edinburgh; St. Andrews University; Edinburgh University. Assistant Minister, St. Ninian's Church, Greenock, 1970-71; Minister, Stobhill Church, Gorebridge, 1971-75, and renamed Gorebridge Church, 1975-77. Recreation: fishing. Address: 532 Clarkston Road, Glasgow, G44 3RT; T.-041-637 2884.

Arnott, James Mackay, TD, BL, WS, SSC. Solicitor; Partner, MacRoberts, Glasgow and Edinburgh, since 1963; b. 22.3.35, Blackford, Perthshire; m., Jean Barbara Allan; 3 s. Educ. Merchiston Castle School, Edinburgh; Edinburgh University. National Service, RAF, 1957-60; TA, 1961-77. Council Member, Law Society of Scotland, 1983-85 (Convenor, Law Reform Committee); Secretary, Scottish Building Contract Committee. Recreation: cricket. Address: (b.) 152 Bath Street, Glasgow, G2 4TB; T.-041-332 9988; 27 Walker Street, Edinburgh, EH3 7HX; T.-031-226 2552.

Arnott, Professor Struther, FRS, BSc, PhD, FRSC, FIBiol. Principal and Vice-Chancellor, St. Andrews University, since 1986; b. 25.9.34; m.; 2 s. Educ. Hamilton Academy; Glasgow University. Scientist, King's College, London, 1960-70; Professor of Molecular Biology, Purdue University, 1970.

Aronson, Sheriff Hazel Josephine, LLB. Sheriff of Lothian and Borders at Edinburgh, since 1983; Member, Parole Board for Scotland; b. 12.1.46, Glasgow; m., John A. Cosgrove; 1 s.; 1 d. Educ. Glasgow High School for Girls; Glasgow University. Advocate at Scottish Bar, 1968-79; Sheriff of Glasgow and Strathkelvin at Glasgow, 1979-83. Recreations: reading; walking; opera; foreign travel. Address: (h.) 14 Gordon Terrace, Edinburgh, EH16 7QR; T.-031-667 8955.

Arthur, Alexander David. Member, Shetland Islands Council, since 1986; b. 16.12.24, Lerwick; m., 1, Elizabeth Sandison (deceased); 1 s.; 2 d.; 2, Georgina Herculson. War Service, REME. Member, Shetland Council of Social Service; Vice Chairman, Shetland Citizens Advice Bureau Advisory Committee; Vice Chairman, Shetland Local Health Council; Member, Shetland Islands Area Licensing Board. Recreations: collector of antiques and coins; licensed radio amateur. Address: (h.) Roadside, Girlsta, Shetland, ZE2 9SQ.

Arthur, David S.C., MA (Hons), DipEd. Principal, Lomond School, Helensburgh, 1977-86; Director of Training, DDTA (Dumbarton); b. 23.2.30, Kenya; m., Mary Frost; 3 d. Educ. Loretto School, Musselburgh; Edinburgh University; Moray House College of Education. Assistant Teacher: Larchfield, 1954-56, Melville College, 1957-62; Senior History Master, Robert Gordon's College, 1962-68; Depute Rector, High School of Stirling, 1968-70; Rector, Greenfaulds High School, 1972-76. Chairman: Samaritans Inc., 1960-68, 1972-76; Secretary, Dumbarton District Business Club; Board, Young Enterprise Dunbartonshire. Publication: Someone To Turn To. Recreations: gardening; hill-walking; photography; tennis. Address: (h.) Inverallan, 26 Argyle Street, Helensburgh, G84 8DB; T.-0436 6494.

Arthur, Lt. General Sir Norman, KCB (1985); b. 6.3.31, London (but brought up in Ayrshire, of Scottish parents); m., Theresa Mary Hopkinson; 1 s.; 1 d. Educ. Eton College; Royal Military Academy, Sandhurst. Commissioned Royal Scots Greys, 1951; commanded Royal Scots Dragoon Guards, 1972-74, 7th Armoured Brigade, 1976-77, 3rd Armoured Division, 1980-82; Director, Personal Services (Army), 1983-85; commanded Army in Scotland, and Governor of Edinburgh Castle, 1985-88; retired, 1988; Honorary Colonel, Royal Scots Dragoon Guards, since 1984; Col. Comdt. Military Provost Staff Corps, 1983-88; mentioned in Despatches, 1974. Officer, Royal Company of Archers; Member, British equestrian team (three-day event), 1960. Recreations: riding; country sports; country life. Address: (h.) Newbarns, Colvend, Kirkcudbrightshire.

Arthur, Peter Drummond, BSc, PhD, CEng, MICE, MIStructE. Senior Lecturer in Civil Engineering, Glasgow University, since 1965; b. 4.7.27, Glasgow; m., Jean Brown Robb; 1 s.; 2 d. Educ. Queen's Park Senior Secondary School; Glasgow University. Babtie Shaw & Morton, civil engineers, 1947-51; Assistant, Glasgow University, 1951-52; Lecturer: St. Andrews University, 1952-58, Glasgow University, 1958-64; Visiting Professor, University of Madras, 1964-66; Senior Lecturer, Glasgow University, 1966-81; Reader, University of Malawi, 1981-83. Past Chairman, The Concrete Society - Scotland. Publication: Ultimate Strength Design for Structural Concrete (Co-author). Address: (b.) Department of Civil Engineering, The University, Glasgow, G12 8QQ; T.-041-339 8855.

Ashcroft, William Alexander, BSc, MSc, PhD, FGS. Senior Lecturer, Department of Geology, Aberdeen University, since 1980; b. 16.6.36, Morayshire; m., Margaret Jean Cotching; 2 s. Educ. Aberlour High School; Aberdeen University; Birmingham University. Seismologist, Seismograph Services Ltd., 1959-62; postgraduate student, 1962-65; Assistant Lecturer, then Lecturer, then Senior Lecturer, Aberdeen University, since 1966. Recreation: skiing. Address: (b.) Department of Geology, Marischal College, Broad Street, Aberdeen; T.-Aberdeen 273057.

Ashmall, Harry Alfred, MA, MLitt, FBIM. Rector, Morrison's Academy, since 1979; presenter of religious programmes on radio and television, since 1976; b. 22.2.39, Stirling; m., Edna Reid; 2 d. Educ. Kilsyth Academy; Glasgow University. Teacher and Careers Master, High School of Glasgow, 1961-66; Principal Teacher of History and Modern Studies, Lochend Secondary School; Principal Teacher of History, High School of Glasgow; Rector, Forfar Academy, 1971-79. Member, Executive and Central Committees, World Council of Churches; various national committees, Church of Scotland; Elder and Lay Reader; Member, Scottish Council for Research in Education; Vice-Chairman, Educational Broadcasting Council for Scotland. Publications: The High School of Glasgow: a history, 1976; Belief yet Betrayal, 1971; Preparing a Staff Manual, 1977; Pupils and their courses, 1981. Recreations: reading; skiing; golf. Address: (b.) Morrison's Academy, Crieff, PH7 3AN; T.-0764 3885.

Ashworth, Bryan, MD, FRCP(Lond), FRCP(Edin). Honorary Librarian, Royal College of Physicians of Edinburgh, since 1982; Consultant Neurologist, Royal Infirmary and Western General Hospital, Edinburgh, and Senior Lecturer in Medical Neurology, Edinburgh University, since 1971; b. 5.5.29, Oundle, Northants. Educ. Laxton School, Oundle; Oundle School; St. Andrews University. National Service, RAMC, Northern Nigeria, 1953-55; junior hospital posts, Manchester and Bristol; Wellcome-Swedish Travelling Research Fellow, Karolinska Hospital, Stockholm, 1965-66; Lecturer in Clinical Neurology, Manchester University, and Honorary Consultant Physician, Manchester Royal Infirmary, 1967-71; Director (non-executive), Robert Bailey and Son, PLC, Stockport, since 1978. Publications: Clinical Neuro-ophthalmology, 2nd edition, 1981; Management of Neurological Disorders, 2nd edition, 1985; The Bramwells of Edinburgh, 1986. Recreations: writing; walking. Address: (h.) 13/5 Eildon Terrace, Edinburgh, EH3 5NL; T.-031-556 0547.

Athanas, Christopher Nicholas, MA, LLB. Partner, Dundas & Wilson, Solicitors, Edinburgh, since 1969; b. 26.8.41, Aden; m., Sheena Anne Stewart; 1 s.; 2 d. Educ. Blairmore Preparatory School, Aberdeenshire; Fettes College, Edinburgh; Aberdeen University. Law Apprentice, then Legal Assistant, Paull & Williamsons, Advocates, Aberdeen, 1964-68; Legal Assistant, Dundas & Wilson, Solicitors, Edinburgh, 1968-69. Member, Society of Writers to the Signet; Invited Member, Edinburgh Registrars Group; former Director, Edinburgh Junior Chamber of Commerce. Recreations: art; angling; golf; philately; walking. Address: (b.) Dundas & Wilson, 25 Charlotte Square, Edinburgh; T.-031-225 1234.

Atholl, The Duke of ((George) Iain Murray), DL (Perthshire), MA. Chairman, Westminster Press Ltd.; Chairman, RNLI, since 1979; Vice-President, National Trust for Scotland, since 1975; Honorary President, Scottish Wildlife Trust, since 1974; President, Scottish Landowners Federation, since 1986; b. 19.6.31, London. Educ. Eton; Christ Church, Oxford. Past Convener, Scottish Landowners Federation; Member, Committee on the Preparation of Legislation; Member, Red Deer Commission, 1969-83. Recreations: golf; bridge; shooting; stalking. Address: (h.) Blair Castle, Blair Atholl, Perthshire; T.-Blair Atholl 212.

Atkinson Brian, MM, MNI. Harbour Master, Aberdeen, since 1970; b. 31.7.32, Kingston-upon-Hull; m., Nancy; 2 s.; 2 d. Educ. Hymers College. Ship management, Merchant Navy officer, 1951-62; port management, since 1963. Honorary Secretary and Launching Authority, Aberdeen Branch, RNLI. Recreations: curling; shooting; gardening; DIY; boat construction. Address: (h.) Granuaille, 24 North Deeside Road, Peterculter, Aberdeen, AB1 OQP; T.-Aberdeen 733134.

Auchinachie, Henry Williamson, ACIS, AIB (Scot). Member, Grampian Regional Council (Finance Chairman, 1978-86); Farmer; retired Bank Manager; b. Keith, Banffshire; m., Edith Russell Taylor; 1 s.; 4 d. Educ. Keith Grammar School; Metropolitan College (Correspondence). Cadet Officer, Mercantile Marine; Bank Official (branches, Inspection and Legal Departments, finally Branch Manager). Former JP; former Member: Banchory Town Council; Kincardine County Council; Aberdeen County Council; Deer District Council; Treasurer, Lonmay Parish Church, 30 years; Secretary/Treasurer, Lonmay Public Hall, 33 years; Life Member: British Show Jumping Association; Fraserburgh Burns Club; Co-Founder, Banchory Festival of Scottish Music; Fraserburgh Harbour Commissioner; Member, North East River Purification Board. Recreations: music; horses. Address: (h.) Mill of Crimond, Fraserburgh, Aberdeenshire, AB4 4XQ; T.-0346 32216.

Auld, Margaret Gibson, SRN, SCM, FRCN, MTD, Hon. DSc, CertNA (Edin), MPhil, CBIM. Chief Nursing Officer, Scottish Home and Health Department, 1977-88; b. 11.7.32, Cardiff. Educ. Glasgow; Cardiff High School for Girls; Edinburgh University. Trained, Radcliffe Infirmary, Oxford, 1950-53; midwifery, St. David's Hospital, Cardiff, 1953-54; Queen's Park Hospital, Blackburn, 1953-54; Staff Midwife, then Sister, Cardiff Maternity Hospital, 1955-56; Sister, Queen Mary Hospital, Dunedin, NZ, 1959-60; Departmental Sister, Cardiff Maternity Hospital, 1962-66; Simpson Memorial Maternity Pavilion: Assistant Matron, 1966-68, Matron, 1968-73; Acting Chief Regional Nursing Officer, South-Eastern Regional Hospital Board, 1973; Chief Area Nursing Officer, Borders Health Board, 1973-76. Member: Briggs Committee on nursing; General Nursing Council for Scotland; Central Midwives Board for Scotland; Common Services Agency. Recreations: reading; music. Address: (h.) Staddlestones, Bellwood Road, Milton Bridge, Penicuik, Midlothian, EH26 ONL; T.-Penicuik 72858.

Austin, Richard Keith, WS. Solicitor; Partner, Steedman Ramage & Co., WS, since 1976; b. 29.1.48, Edinburgh; m., Morag Gillespie Webster; 2 s.; 1 d. Educ. Royal High School, Edinburgh; Edinburgh University; LLB; Diploma, History of Art. Elder, Barclay Church, Edinburgh; Curator, Signet Library, Edinburgh. Recreations: music; looking (at pictures and buildings, mainly). Address: (b.) 6 Alva Street, Edinburgh; T.-031-226 3781.

Austin, Trevor Herbert, RGN, RMN, DipNursing. Chief Area Nursing Officer, Borders Health Board, since 1985; b. 21.2.33, Stockport; m., Joan Margaret Hunt; 2 s.; 1 d. Educ. Stockport Grammar School. Nurse training, 1954-59; theatre and ward charge nurse, then Night Superintendent of Nursing, Stepping Hill Hospital, Stockport, 1960-70; Assistant Matron and Principal Nursing Officer, Peel Hospital, Galashiels, 1970-74; Borders Health Board: Group Principal Nursing Officer, 1974-76, Area Nursing Officer (Personnel, Planning and Development), 1976-85. Member, Borders Region Children's Panel, 1972-82; Member, Borders Region Children's Panel Advisory Committee, since 1984. Recreations: music (choral singing and church organ). Address: (h.) 97 Murrayfield Cottages, Buccleuch Road, Selkirk, TD7 5AT; T.-Selkirk 21579.

Avonside, Rt. Hon. Lord (Ian Hamilton Shearer), PC, QC, MA, LLB. Senator of the College of Justice in Scotland, 1964-84; b. 6.11.14; m.; 1 s.; 1 d.

by pr. m. Educ. Dunfermline High School; Glasgow University; Edinburgh University. Admitted, Faculty of Advocates, 1938; RA, 1939-45 (Major); QC (Scotland), 1952; Sheriff of Renfrew and Argyll, 1960-62; Lord Advocate, 1962-64; Chairman, Lands Valuation Court, 1975-84; Chairman, National Health Service Tribunal, Scotland, 1954-62; Chairman, Scottish Valuation Advisory Council, 1965-68.

Axup, William Bernard Noel, CEng, FIMarE. Steelwork Director, Yarrow Shipbuilders Ltd., since 1985; b. 22.6.31, Bubwith, Yorkshire; m., Isabell. Educ. Vale of Leven Academy; Royal Technical College, Glasgow. Apprentice draughtsman, 1948-53; engineer, Merchant Navy, 1953-58; divisional manager, shipbuilding, 1958-71; Yarrow Shipbuilders Ltd.: General Manager Production, 1971-78, Production Director, 1978-79, Deputy Managing Director (Production), 1979-85. Recreations: golf; fishing. Address: (b.) Yarrow Shipbuilders Ltd., South Street, Scotstoun, Glasgow, G14 OXN; T.-041-959 1207, Ext. 4002.

B

Bade, Rev. Raymond John, DipTh. Minister, United Reformed Churches in Edinburgh and Falkirk, since 1965; Vice Chairman, Scottish Churches Council, since 1986; Chairman, Mid Scotland District, United Reformed Church, since 1987; b. 20.4.31, Ilford; m., Cathreen Birrell Kenny. Educ. Ilford County High School; Overdale Theological College, Birmingham. Entered ministry of Churches of Christ, 1957; first charge, Leeds, until 1961; Falkirk Church of Christ, 1961-65; Dalkeith Road, Edinburgh, since 1965, then Falkirk Church additionally, 1985; became United Reformed Church minister after union, 1981. Chairman, Ark Edinburgh Southside Project. Recreations: caravanning; exercising the dog; listening to records. Address: (h.) 88 Dalkeith Road, Edinburgh, EH16 5AF; T.-031-667 2784.

Bader, Douglas, MA (Hons). Rector, Perth Grammar School, since 1985; b. 22.11.41, Stirling; m., May Heather Thomson; 3 s. Educ. Larbert High School; Glasgow University; Jordanhill College of Education. Teacher of Modern Languages, High School of Glasgow, 1965-69; Principal Assistant, Alloa Academy, 1969-71; Principal Teacher, Modern Languages, Alloa Academy, 1971-75; Assistant Rector, Forfar Academy, 1975-79; Depute Rector, Montrose Academy, 1979-85. Recreations: International grade referee, Scottish Basketball Association; senior instructor, British Canoe Union. Address: (h.) Malvern, County Buildings, Methven, Perth, PH1 3QG.

Badger, Ian. Managing Director, Edinburgh Airport, since 1986; b. 31.12.40, Garrowhill; m., Barbara; 1 d. Educ. Coatbridge High School. Ministry of Aviation, 1962-65; British Airports Authority, 1966-86: Assistant Design Manager, Heathrow Planning Manager, Manager Terminal 4, General Manager Edinburgh Airport. Recreation: shooting. Address: (b.) Edinburgh Airport Ltd., Edinburgh, EH12 9DN; T.-031-344 3151.

Bagnall, John Michael, MA (Cantab), DipLib, MIInfSci. University Librarian, Dundee University, since 1987; b. 22.4.45, South Yorkshire; m., Carol. Educ. Mexborough Grammar School; Sidney Sussex College, Cambridge. Diploma in Librarianship, University College, London; Assistant Librarian and Sub-Librarian, Newcastle upon Tyne University. Recreations: music; birdwatching; languages. Address: University Library, Dundee, DD1 4HN; T.-0382 23181.

Bailey, Colin John, BA (Hons), PhD. Art Historian; Head, Department of Humanities, Edinburgh College of Art, since 1982 (Dean of Art and Design, 1984-87); b. 22.5.46, Hastings. Educ. Hastings Grammar School; Leicester University; Nottingham University. Assistant Keeper of British Art, Walker Art Gallery, Liverpool; Librarian, Barber Institute of Fine Arts, Birmingham University; part-time Lecturer in Art History, Department of Extra-Mural Studies, Birmingham University. British Academy Scholar, 1984. Publications: Edward Lear and Knowsley; German Nineteenth-Century Drawings from the Ashmolean Museum; edition of Johann David Passavant's Tour of a German Artist in England; Catalogue of the Collection of Drawings (Volume V), Ashmolean Museum, Oxford. Recreations: hill-walking; snooker; foreign travel. Address: (h.) Church Cottage, West Byres, Ormiston, East Lothian.

Bailey, Michael, BA (Hons). Curator, Maclaurin Art Gallery, Ayr, since 1976; Curator, Kyle and Carrick District Library and Museum Services, since 1976; b. 11.11.37, Stockport; m., Bernadette Donnelly; 3 s. Educ. Moseley Hall; Open University; Meteorological Office College. Meteorologist, 1956-61; marine biology research, UKAEA, 1961-64; meteorologist, 1964-76. Recreations: music and drama; visual arts; travel. Address: (b.) Rozelle House, Rozelle Park, Ayr, KA7 4NQ; T.-0292 45447.

Baillie, Professor John, MA, CA. Johnstone-Smith Professor of Accountancy, Glasgow University, since 1983; Partner, Peat Marwick McLintock (formerly KMG Thomson McLintock), since 1978; b. 7.10.44; m., Annette Alexander; 1 s.; 1 d. Educ. Whitehill School. Member, various technical and professional affairs committees, Institute of Chartered Accountants of Scotland. Recreations: keeping fit; reading; music; golf. Address: (h.) The Glen, Glencairn Road, Kilmacolm, Renfrewshire; T.-Kilmacolm 3254.

Baillie, Marion, MA (Hons). Vice Chairman, Nurse Training Committee, Greater Glasgow Health Board; Member, Examinations Standing Group (Scotland), Occupational Therapy; Chairman, Carers National Association (Strathclyde); Governor, Morrison's Academy. Educ. Glasgow University. Teacher of English, until 1963; Lecturer in English, until 1965; Headmistress, Morrison's Academy Girls' School, until 1972; Assistant Principal, Jordanhill College of Education, until 1987. Address: (h.) 12 Napier Road, Killearn, Glasgow; T.-Killearn 50580.

Baillie, Robert Martin. Senior Lecturer in History of Fine Art, Glasgow University; b. 4.3.20, Edinburgh; m., Patricia Ireland; 2 s.; 1 d. Educ. Royal High School, Edinburgh; Edinburgh College of Art. Teacher of Drawing, Edinburgh College of Art, 1947-50; Lecturer in Painting, Leeds College of Art, 1950-53; Lecturer in History of Art, Glasgow University, 1954; Art Critic, The Glasgow Herald, 1969-79. Regular exhibitor of paintings, Royal Scottish Academy, Royal Glasgow Institute. Recreations: reading; walking. Address: (h.) 2 North Park Villas, Summerlea Road, Thornliebank, Glasgow, G46 8PB; T.-041-638 3890.

Bain, Robert Garden, JP. Farmer; Director, R.G. Bain Ltd., since 1959; Council Member, National Farmers' Union of Scotland; b. 22.2.34, Aberdeen; m., Elizabeth Ann (Lann); 2 s. Educ. Kirkwall Grammar School; Aberdeen Grammar School; Gordonstoun School. Accountancy until 1959. Elder, Church of Scotland; Chairman, local Community Council. Recreations: coin and stamp collecting. Address: Hall of Tankerness, Orkney; T.-0856 86 275.

Bain, Professor William Herbert, MD, FRCS. Titular Professor in Cardiac Surgery, Glasgow University, since 1981; Consultant Cardio-Thoracic Surgeon, since 1962; b. 20.11.27, Kilmacolm; m., Helen Craigie; 2 s.; 1 d. Educ. Glasgow High School; Glasgow University. Graduated MB, ChB; House Officer posts, Glasgow, 1950-51; McIntyre Research Scholar, 1952-53; Registrar in General Surgery, Glasgow Royal Infirmary, 1954-58; Lecturer in Experimental Surgery, Honorary Senior Registrar, 1958-62; Andrews Fellow, University of Chicago, 1961; Senior Lecturer/Reader in Surgery, Glasgow, 1962-81; Consultant Surgeon, Royal Infirmary, Western Infirmary, Stobhill Hospital. Examiner for Glasgow and Edinburgh Royal Colleges; Member, British Standards Institute; Past President, Scottish Thoracic Society; President-Elect, Society of Cardiothoracic Surgeons of Gt. Britain and Ireland. Publications: Blood Flow Through Tissues and Organs, 1968; Essentials of Cardiovascular Surgery, 1974; Intensive Care, 1980. Recreations: sailing; fishing. Address: (h.) 8 Grange Road, Bearsden, Glasgow, G61 3PL; T.-041-942 3846.

Baird, Alister. Chief Executive, Hamilton District Council; b. 11.12.38, Glasgow; m., Lynne; 2 s. Educ. Eastbank Academy, Glasgow. Student Sanitary Inspector, then Assistant Sanitary Inspector, Airdrie Town Council, 1957-63; Senior Assistant Sanitary Inspector, Fife County Council, 1963-65; Depute Director of Environmental Health, East Kilbride Town Council, 1965-75; Director of Environmental Health, Hamilton District Council, 1975-86. Recreations: golf; music; art. Address: (b.) Municipal Buildings, 102 Cadzow Street, Hamilton ML3 6HH; T.-0698 282323.

Baird, Professor David Tennent, BA (Cantab), MB, ChB, DSc, FRCP Edin, FRCOG. Medical Research Council Professor of Reproductive Endocrinology, Edinburgh University, since 1985; Consultant Obstetrician and Gynaecologist, Simpson Memorial Maternity Pavilion, Edinburgh Royal Infirmary, since 1970; b. 13.3.35, Glasgow; m., Frances Lightveld; 2 s. Educ. Aberdeen Grammar School; Aberdeen University; Trinity College, Cambridge; Edinburgh University. After clinical training in endocrinology as well as obstetrics, spent three years (1965-68) as an MRC travelling Research Fellow at Worcester Foundation for Experimental Biology, Shrewsbury, Mass., USA, conducting research on reproductive endocrinology; Deputy Director, MRC Unit of Reproductive Biology, Edinburgh, 1972-77; Professor of Obstetrics and Gynaecology, Edinburgh University, 1977-85; served on a number of national and international committees. Publications: four books on reproduction. Recreations: ski mountaineering; music; sport. Address: (b.) Department of Obstetrics and Gynaecology, Edinburgh University, Centre for Reproductive Biology, 37 Chalmers Street, Edinburgh, EH3 9EW; T.-031-229 2575.

Baird, Isabel Duncan. General Secretary, United Free Church of Scotland, since 1981; b. 15.9.34, Aberdeen; m., Ronald C.F. Baird; 1 s. Educ. Rosemount Secondary School; Central School (commercial course). Shorthand typist, 1950; private secretary, 1953; private secretary to General Secretary, United Free Church of Scotland, 1971-81. Boys' Brigade officer, 1968-77. Recreations: reading; knitting; Boys' Brigade; local/national Church. Address: (b.) 11 Newton Place, Glasgow, G3 7PR; T.-041-332 3435.

Baird, Joyce Deans, MA, MB, ChB, FRCPEdin. Reader in Medicine, Edinburgh University, and Honorary Consultant Physician, Western General Hospital, Edinburgh; b. 24.6.29, Glasgow; m., John Alexander Penman Splitt; 1 d. Educ. St. Leonards School, St. Andrews; Aberdeen University. Medical staff appointments, Royal Infirmary, Edinburgh, 1954-64; Research Fellow, Department for Endocrine and Metabolic Diseases, Western General Hospital, Edinburgh, 1965-68; Medical Officer, Scottish Home and Health Department, 1968-70; Lecturer in Medicine, Western General Hospital, Edinburgh, 1971-76; Vice-President, European Association for the Study of Diabetes. Recreations: music; painting; hill-walking; skiing; travel; reading. Address: (h.) Manor House, Boswall Road, Edinburgh, EH5 3RR; T.-031-552 2030.

Baird, Lt.-Col. Niall Caldecott, (Rt.), OBE. Managing Director, Lossie Holiday Homes, since 1975; b. 14.10.17, London; m., 1, Susan Davidson (m. dissolved); 4 s.; 2, Mrs Elizabeth Bois. Educ. Stowe School; Royal Military College, Sandhurst. Commissioned, Queen's Own Cameron Highlanders, 1937; served in Burma, World War II; Parachute Regiment, 1947-51; commanded 1st Bn., Queen's Own Cameron Highlanders, 1959-61, and 1st Bn., Queen's Own Highlanders, 1961-62; mentioned in Despatches (twice); entered commerce upon retirement, 1963; set up self-catering company, Elgin, 1975. Member, Queen's Bodyguard in Scotland (Royal Company of Archers). Recreations: golf; gardening. Address: Palmers Cross, Elgin, Moray, IV30 1YF; T.-Elgin 7240.

Baird, Lord Provost Susan. Lord Provost, City of Glasgow District Council, since 1988; b. 26.5.40, Glasgow; m., George; 3 s.; 1 d. Educ. St. Mark's Secondary School, Glasgow. Worked in a city centre office; joined Labour Party, 1969; became Councillor for Parkhead, 1974; elected Bailie of the city, 1980; former Convener, Manpower Committee, latterly Vice-Convener, Parks and Recreation Committee. Address: (b.) City Chambers, George Square, Glasgow, G2 1DU; T.-041-221 9600.

Baird, William Bramwell, LLB (Hons), LLM, ACII. Chief Secretary, The Salvation Army, Scotland, since 1984; b. 20.11.27, Glasgow; m., Rita Gravett; 1 s.; 1 d. Educ. Kilmarnock Academy; London University. Salvation Army: served in corps, business and social work, 1949-66, Finance Officer, Pakistan, 1966-69, Secretary, The Mothers' Hospital, 1970-73, Personnel Officer, Social Services, 1973-74, Legal Officer, International Headquarters, 1974-82, Chief Secretary, Social Services, 1982-84. Recreation: music. Address: (h.) 74 Roffey Park Road, Old Hall, Paisley; T.-041-882 3572.

Baird, Rev. William Gordon Glen, DPA, ACII. Minister, Inverkeithing St. John's and North Queensferry Churches, since 1977; b. 7.1.28, Glasgow; m., Morag Thorburn Crichton; 1 s.; 1 d. Educ. William Hulme's Grammar School, Manchester; Glasgow University; Glasgow and West of Scotland Commercial College; Edinburgh University. Inland Revenue, 1944-46; Royal Navy, 1946-48; Ministry of National Insurance, 1948-66; Senior Executive Officer, HM Treasury (O & M Division), Scottish Branch, 1967-68; Training Officer for Scotland, Department of Health and Social Security, 1969-72; student, University of Edinburgh, 1972-74; Assistant Minister, St. Ninian's Church, Corstorphine, Edinburgh, 1974-75. Recreations: gardening; railways; the solitude of the Western Isles. Address: St. Johns Manse, 34 Hill Street, Inverkeithing, Fife; T.-0383 412422.

Baker, Douglas Arthur, BA (Hons). Principal, Bell College of Technology, Hamilton, since 1982; Member, Scottish Council for Research in Education, since 1985; Member, Scottish Council for Open Learning, since 1984; b. 30.6.31, London; m., Joan Mary; 2 s.; 2 d. Educ. County High School, Braintree; Garnett College and Birkbeck College, London. Office of Customs and Excise, 1953-60; Lecturer, Braintree and Harlow Technical College, 1961-66; Director of Education and Welfare, National Union of Students, 1966-68; Secretary, Educational Research Board, SSRC, 1968-69; Deputy Dean of Students, University of East Anglia, 1969-76; Dean of Students, Chelmer Institute of Higher Education, 1976-79; Vice Principal, Lowestoft College of Further Education, 1979-82. Recreations: music; theatre; National Trust for Scotland. Address: (b.) Almada Street, Hamilton, ML3 OJB; T.-0698 283100.

Baker, Professor Michael John, TD, BA, BSc (Econ), DipM, CertITP (Harvard), DBA (Harvard), FInstM, FCAM, FRSA. Professor of Marketing, Strathclyde University, since 1971 (Deputy Principal, since 1984); Chairman, Institute of Marketing, 1987; b. 5.11.35, Debden; m., Sheila; 1 s.; 2 d. Educ. Worksop College; Bede, Gosforth and Harvey Grammar Schools; Durham University; London University; Harvard University. Royal Artillery, 1957 (2nd Lt.); Richard Thomas & Baldwins (Sales) Ltd., 1958-64; Lecturer: Medway College of Technology, 1964-66, Hull College of Technology, 1966-68; FME Fellow, Harvard Business School, 1968-71; Member, Vice-Chairman and Chairman, SCOTBEC, 1973-85; Member, SSRC Management Committee, 1976-80; Dean, Strathclyde Business School, 1978-84; Chairman, Marketing Education Group, 1974-87; Member, SHERT, since 1983; Member, UGC Business and Management Sub-Committee, 1986; Member, Chief Scientist's Committee, since 1985; Governor, CAM; Director: Stoddard Holdings PLC, Scottish Transport Group; Governor, Lomond School. Publications: Marketing New Industrial Products, 1975; Market Development, 1983; Marketing Strategy and Management, 1985; Marketing, 4th edition, 1985; The Marketing Book (Editor), 1987. Recreations: sailing; gardening; travel; DIY. Address: (b.) Strathclyde University, 173 Cathedral Street, Glasgow, G4 ORQ; T.-041-552 4400.

Baker, Thomas Neville, BMet, PhD, DMet, FIM, FInstP, CEng, CPhys. Reader (Head, Division of Metallurgy and Engineering Materials), Strathclyde University, since 1983; b. 11.1.34, Southport; m., Eileen May Allison. Educ. King George V School, Southport; Sheffield University. Research Metallurgist, Nelson Research Laboratories, English Electric Co., Stafford, 1958-60; Scientist, Project Leader, Tube Investments Research Laboratories, Hinxton Hall, Cambridge, 1961-64; Department of Metallurgy, Strathclyde University: SRC Research Fellow, 1965, Lecturer, 1966, Senior Lecturer, 1976. Recreations: music; literature; gardening. Address: (b.) Division of Metallurgy and Engineering Materials, Strathclyde University, Colville Building, 48 N. Portland Street, Glasgow; T.-041-552 4400.

Baldwick, Allan Thomas, JP. Chairman, Annandale and Eskdale District Sports Council, since 1988; Vice-Chairman, Dumfries and Galloway Educational Trust, since 1988; b. 14.11.48, Dumfries; m., Isabella; 1 d. Educ. Lockbertie Academy. Dumfries and Galloway Regional Councillor, since 1986; Annandale and Eskdale District Councillor, since 1988; Hoddom and Ecclefechan Community Councillor, since 1982. Address: (h.) 2 Burnside Gardens, Ecclefechan, Dumfriesshire, DG11 3DJ; T.-05763 622.

Baldwin, Olaf A.C., BL. Solicitor, since 1950; Notary Public; b. 4.1.27, Edinburgh; m., Sheila MacDonald; 1 s.; 1 d. Educ. Dumfries Academy; Edinburgh University. War Service commission, Indian Army; served with 3rd Gurkha Rifles; demobbed T. Captain; enrolled Solicitor, 1950; Qualified Assistant, Partner, then Senior Partner, Whitelaw, Edgar & Baldwin, Dumfries; appointed Honorary Sheriff, Dumfries, 1976; Dean of Faculty of Procurators of Dumfriesshire, 1983-85. Recreations: sailing; skiing. Address: (h.) Castledykes, Glencaple Road, Dumfries; T.-Dumfries 52023.

Balekjian, Wahe Hagop, Dr (Law), Dr (pol sc), PhD. Head of Department and Reader in European Law, Glasgow University, since 1976; Visiting Titular Professor, University of Salzburg, Austria, since 1981; Titular Professor, European Faculty, Land Use Planning, Strasbourg, since 1982; b. 2.10.24, Cairo; m., Eva Birgitta. Educ. College of Arts and Sciences, Cairo; Vienna University;

Manchester University. Diploma, Hague Academy of International Law. Lecturer, Vienna University, 1957-73; Simon Research Fellow, Manchester University, 1963-65; Head of Department, European Studies, National Institute of Higher Education, Limerick, 1973-76. Publications: Legal Aspects of Foreign Investment in the EEC, 1967 (awarded Prize of European Communities, 1967); The Status of Unrecognised States in International Law (published in German, 1971). Recreations: hill-walking; piano playing; languages. Address: (b.) Department of European Law, The University, Glasgow, G12 8QQ; T.-041-339 8855, Ext. 5539.

Balfour of Burleigh, Lord (Robert Bruce), CEng, FIEE. Chairman, Cablevision (Scotland) plc, since 1983; Chairman, The Turing Institute, since 1983; Chairman, Edinburgh Book Festival, since 1981; Director: Bank of Scotland, since 1968 (Deputy Governor, since 1977), Scottish Investment Trust, since 1971, William Lawson Distillers Ltd., since 1984, Tarmac plc, since 1981; b. 6.1.27; m.; 2 d. RN, 1945-48. Chairman, Scottish Arts Council, 1971-80; Forestry Commissioner, 1971-74.

Balfour, 4th Earl of (Gerald Arthur James Balfour), JP; b. 23.12.25; m. Educ. Eton; HMS Conway. Member, East Lothian County Council, 1960-75. Address: (h.) The Tower, Whittingehame, Haddington.

Balfour, Ian Leslie Shaw, MA, LLB, BD, PhD, SSC, NP. Solicitor (Partner, Balfour & Manson), since 1955; b. 16.6.32, Edinburgh; m., Joyce Margaret Ross Pryde; 3 s.; 1 d. Educ. Edinburgh Academy; Edinburgh University. Qualified as Solicitor, 1955; commissioned, RASC, 1955-57; Partner, Balfour & Manson, since 1959; Secretary, Oliver & Son Ltd., since 1959; Fiscal to Law Society of Scotland, since 1981. Baptist Union of Scotland: President, 1976-77, Law Agent, since 1964, Secretary, Charlotte Baptist Chapel, Edinburgh, since 1980, Secretary, Scottish Bapist College, since 1983; Secretary, Elba Housing Society Ltd., since 1969; Director, Edinburgh Medical Missionary Society. Recreations: hill-walking; home computing; lay preaching. Address: (b.) 58 Frederick Street, Edinburgh; T.-031-225 8291.

Balfour, John Charles, OBE, MC, JP, DL, BA. Chairman, Fife Area Health Board, 1983-87; b. 28.7.19; m.; 3 s. Educ. Eton; Trinity College, Cambridge. Royal Artillery, 1939-45 (Major); Member, Queen's Bodyguard for Scotland (Royal Company of Archers), since 1949; Chairman, Fife County Children's Panel, 1970-75, Fife Region Children's Panel, 1975-77; Chairman, Scottish Association of Youth Clubs, 1968-79.

Balfour, Peter Edward Gerald, CBE. Chairman, Charterhouse plc, since 1985; Chairman, Scottish Council (Development and Industry), 1978-85; Director, Royal Bank of Scotland, since 1972; Chairman, Selective Assets Trust and First Charlotte Assets Trust; b. 9.7.21, Woking; m., 1, Grizelda Ogilvy, 2, Diana Wainman; 3 s.; 2 d. Educ. Eton College. Served Scots Guards, 1940-54; joined William McEwan & Co., brewers, 1954; appointed Director, 1958; Director, Scottish Brewers, 1959; Scottish and Newcastle Breweries, 1961 (Chairman and Managing Director, 1970-83); Director and Vice Chairman, RBS Group, 1978; Director, British Assets Trust. Recreations: farming; forestry. Address: (h.) Scadlaw House, Humbie, East Lothian; T.-087 533 252.

Balfour, Robert Melville. Director of Organisation, Scottish Conservative Party, since 1987 (Deputy Director, 1980-87); b. 16.10.34, Hemel Hempstead; m., Margaretta Rose Ferguson; 1 s.; 1 d. Educ. Kingswood School, Bath; Gwydyr Forester Training School, Betwys-y-Coed. National Service, RAF Police, 1952-54; certificated forester, Forestry Commission Research Station, specialising in entomology, 1958-62; sub-postmaster and general store owner, Kilmun, Argyll, 1962-68; Conservative Party agent: Newcastle-upon-Tyne East, 1968-71, West Aberdeenshire, 1971-75, Argyll, 1975-79. Elder, Dean Parish Church, Edinburgh; Past Chairman: Kilmun District Community Council; Kilmun Hall and Recreation Association. Recreations: walking; carpet bowling; philately; wine-making; reading; music; fishing. Address: (h.) 118 East Claremont Street, Edinburgh, EH7 4JZ; T.-031-556 6776.

Balfour, William Harold St. Clair. Solicitor; b. 29.8.34, Edinburgh; m., Patricia Waite (m. dissolved); 1 s.; 2 d. Educ. Hillfield, Ontario; Edinburgh Academy; Edinburgh University. Partner, Balfour & Manson, Solicitors; Clerk to Admission of Notaries Public. Recreations: sailing; walking. Address: (b.) 58 Frederick Street, Edinburgh, EH2 1LS; T.-031-225 8291.

Balharrie, Brigadier John Charles, MBE, MC, KStJ, TD, DL. Deputy Lieutenant, Dunbartonshire; b. 21.12.19, Glasgow; m., Sara Jean Ferguson. Educ. Glasgow Academy. Commissioned, 1938; active service, Middle East and NW Europe, 1939-45, Palestine, Cyprus and Aden, 1945-59; commanded Royal Scots Greys, 1962-64; Chief Staff Officer, 52nd Lowland Division, 1964-67; Commander, Lowland Area, Edinburgh Castle, 1969-73; retired as Brigadier, 1974, and served as Secretary, Lowland TAVR Association, 1974-84. Honorary Colonel, Glasgow and Lanarkshire Bn., Army Cadet Force; President: Glasgow Area HQ Branch, Royal British Legion Scotland, Joint Council, City of Glasgow Naval, Army and Air Force Associations; Member of Chapter, Order of St. John in Scotland; Chairman: Glasgow Branch, Forces Help Society and Lord Roberts Workshops, Glasgow Branch, Royal Scots Dragoon Guards Association; Vice-Convenor, Chaplains Committee, Church of Scotland. Recreations: country pursuits; reading. Address: (h.) Crepigill Lodge, Skeabost Bridge, Isle of Skye, IV51 9PB; T.-047032 244.

Ball, Geoffrey A., FCA. Chairman, CALA plc (Group Managing Director, since 1974); Member, Scottish Arts Council; b. 4.8.43, Bristol; m., Mary Elizabeth; 3 s.; 1 d. Educ. Cotham Grammar School, Bristol. Former Managing Director, Greencoat Properties Ltd.; non-executive Director: Abaco Investments p.l.c.; Scottish Mortgage & Trust p.l.c.; Stenhouse Western Ltd. Member,

Independent Schools Careers Organisation. Recreations: golf; music. Address: (b.) 42 Colinton Road, Edinburgh, EH10 5BT; T.-031-346 0194.

Ball, Professor John Macleod, BA (Cantab), DPhil. Professor of Applied Analysis, Department of Mathematics, Heriot-Watt University, Edinburgh, since 1982; Senior Fellow, Science and Engineering Research Council, 1980-85; b. 19.5.48, Farnham, Surrey. Educ. Mill Hill School; St. John's College, Cambridge. SERC postdoctoral research fellowship, 1972-74, at Department of Mathematics, Heriot-Watt University, and Lefschetz Center for Dynamical Systems, Brown University, Providence, Rhode Island, USA; Heriot-Watt University: Lecturer in Mathematics, 1974-78, Reader in Mathematics, 1978-82. Elected Fellow, Royal Society of Edinburgh, 1980; Whittaker Prize, Edinburgh Mathematical Society, 1981; Junior Whitehead Prize, London Mathematical Society, 1982; Member, editorial boards, Archive for Rational Mechanics and Analysis; Proceedings of Royal Society of Edinburgh (A); Annales de Institut Henri Poincare (Analyse Non Lineaire); Journal of Elasticity; Physica D. Recreations: music; travel. Address: (h.) 11 Gloucester Place, Edinburgh, EH3 6EE.

Ballantyne, Rev. Duncan Alexander, BD, FSA(Scot), CertMin. Minister, Ascog with Craigmore St. Brendan's, Bute, since 1986; b. 30.7.55, Houston, Renfrewshire. Educ. Linwood High School; Trinity College, Glasgow. Former Sales Manager in the jewellery trade; Probationer, Trinity Church, Rothesay, 1985. Voluntary Adult Literacy Teacher. Recreations: hill-walking; badminton. Address: (h.) The Manse, 1 Albany Terrace, Craigmore, Rothesay, Isle of Bute; T.-Rothesay 2506.

Ballinger, Brian Richard, MA, BM, BCh, FRCPEd, FRCPsych, DPM. Consultant Psychiatrist, Dundee Psychiatric Service, since 1971; Honorary Senior Lecturer, Dundee University, since 1971; b. 1.6.37, Newport, Gwent; m., Dr. C. Barbara Ballinger; 2 s. Educ. Manchester Grammar School; University College, Oxford; St. Mary's Hospital Medical School, London. Postgraduate training in London, Oxford, Sheffield and Dundee; special interest in psychiatry of old age; Chairman, Section for Psychiatry of Old Age, Scottish Division, Royal College of Psychiatry. Recreations: painting; music; travel. Address: (b.) Royal Dundee Liff Hospital, Dundee; T.-0382 580441.

Balls, Rev. Ernest George, MA, BD, STM, DD. Clerk to Ardrossan Presbytery, since 1980; b. 25.6.14, London; m., Elspeth Russell Alexander; 2 s.; 1 d. Educ. Perth Academy; St. Andrews University; Union Seminary, New York. Former Convener, Church and Nation Committee, General Assembly; former Representative, Church of Scotland: Central Committee of World Council of Churches, Scottish Religious Advisory Committee to BBC and ITA, Central Religious Advisory Committee to BBC and ITA; Past Chairman, Multilateral Church Conversation. Recreations: gardening; angling. Address: (h.) 67 High Road, Stevenston, KA20 3DZ; T.-Stevenston 63512.

Bamert, Matthias. Principal Guest Conductor, Scottish National Orchestra, since 1985; Director, Musica Nova, since 1985; b. 5.7.42, Ersigen, Switzerland; m., Susan; 1 s.; 1 d. Assistant to George Szell in Cleveland; Assistant to Leopold Stokowski at American Symphony Orchestra; worked under Pierre Boulez, then Lorin Maazel, in Cleveland; Music Director, Swiss Radio Orchestra, 1978-84; made debut with SNO, 1983; recent engagements with Scottish Chamber, Halle, Bournemouth Symphony, CBSO and BBC Scottish Symphony Orchestras. Address: (b.) Scottish National Orchestra, 3 La Belle Place, Glasgow, G3 7LH; T.-041-332 7244.

Bancroft, John Henry Jefferies, MA, MD, FRCP, FRCPsych. Clinical Consultant, MRC Reproductive Biology Unit, since 1976; Honorary Senior Lecturer, Department of Psychiatry, Edinburgh University, since 1976; b. 18.6.36, Peterborough; m., Judy Greenwood; 2 s.; 1 d. Educ. Bedford School; Caius College, Cambridge. Clinical Reader, Department of Psychiatry, Oxford, 1969-76. President, International Academy of Sex Research, 1976-77; Chairman, British Association for Behavioural Psychotherapy, 1983-84; Member, Executive Committee, National Marriage Guidance Council; Member, Scientific Advisory Board, Kinsey Institute for Research in Sex and Gender Reproduction; President, Lothian Marriage Guidance Council, since 1988. Publications: Deviant Sexual Behaviour, 1974; Human Sexuality and its Problems, 1983. Recreations: music; sailing. Address: (h.) 28 Elbe Street, Leith, Edinburgh, EH6 7HW; T.-031-553 7221.

Band, Thomas Mollison. Chief Executive, Scottish Tourist Board, since 1987; Director, Historic Buildings and Monuments, Scottish Development Department, 1984-87; b. 28.3.34, Aberdeen; m., Jean McKenzie Brien; 1 s.; 2 d. Educ. Perth Academy. Principal, Tariff Division, Board of Trade, London, 1969-73; Director (Location of Industry), Department of Industry, Glasgow, 1973-76; Assistant Secretary (Industrial Policy), Scottish Economic Planning Department, 1976-78; Assistant Secretary (Housing), Scottish Development Department, 1978-82; Assistant Secretary (Finance), Scottish Office, 1982-84. Recreations: gardening; skiing; beating. Address: (h.) Heathfield, Pitcairngreen, Perthshire; T.-073 883 403.

Banks, Philip, MA, MEd. HM Inspector of Schools, since 1983; b. 17.1.46, Stockton-on-Tees; m., Inger Haagensen-Banks; 1 s.; 1 d. Educ. St. Chad's College, Wolverhampton; Trinity Hall, Cambridge; Edinburgh University. Teacher, Ipswich Academy and Edinburgh Academy, 1969-73; Principal Teacher of English, Queen Anne High School, Dunfermline, 1973-81; Development Officer, Scottish Education Department, 1981-83. Recreations: reading; squash; walking. Address: (b.) Corunna House, Cadogan Street, Glasgow; T.-041-204 1220.

Bannerman, James Pirie, OBE, JP, FPS, FPSI. Member, Strathclyde Regional Council, since 1982 (Deputy Leader, SLD Group); b. 24.5.35, Glasgow; m., Marjorie Seddon; 1 s.; 1 d. Educ. Glasgow Academy; Strathclyde University. President, Pharmaceutical Society of Great Britain, 1974-76; Member, Medicines Commission, 1978-86; Director, A.G. Bannerman Ltd. Recreations: golf; marathon running; wind-surfing. Address: (h.) 5 Boclair Crescent, Bearsden, Glasgow, G61; T.-041-942 5200.

Barbenel, Professor Joseph Cyril, BDS, BSc, MSc, PhD, LDS RCS(Eng), CBiol, FIBiol, CPhys, FInstP, FRSE. Professor, Bioengineering Unit, Strathclyde University, since 1982 (Head, Tissue Mechanics Division, since 1970); b. 2.1.37, London; m., Lesley Mary Hyde Jowett; 2 s.; 1 d. Educ. Hackney Downs Grammar School, London; London Hospital Medical College; Queen's College, Dundee (St. Andrews University); Strathclyde University. Dental House Surgeon, London Hospital, 1960; National Service, RADC, 1960-61 (Lieutenant, 1960, Captain, 1961); general dental practice, London, 1963; student, 1963-67; Lecturer, Department of Dental Prosthetics, Dental School, Dundee, 1967-69; Senior Lecturer, Strathclyde University, 1970-82. President, Biological Engineering Society; Member of Committee, and Secretary for Standardisation, International Society for Bioengineering and the Skin; Member, Steering Committee, Forum on Clinical Haemorheology; Chairman, Society for Tissue Viability. Recreations: music; theatre. Address: (b.) University of Strathclyde, Bioengineering Unit, 106 Rottenrow, Glasgow, G4 ONW; T.-041-552 4400.

Barber, Professor James Hill, MB, ChB, MD, FRCGP, FRCPSG, DRCOG. Norie Miller Professor of General Practice, Glasgow University, since 1974; Principal, Greater Glasgow Health Board, since 1972; Honorary Consultant, Medicine, Royal and Western Infirmaries, Glasgow, since 1972; b. 28.5.33, Dunfermline; m. (1) Patricia M. Burton (deceased); 1 s.; 3 d.; (2) Helen K. Thain. Educ. Edinburgh Academy; University of Edinburgh. Medical Branch, RAF, 1958-63; General Practitioner: Callander, 1964-66, Livingston, 1966-72; Senior Lecturer, General Practice, Glasgow University, 1972-74. Publications: General Practice Medicine, 1975 and 1985; Towards Team Care, 1980. Recreations: sailing; model fishing-boat construction; photography. Address: (b.) Woodside Health Centre, Barr Street, Glasgow; T.-041-332 9977.

Barber, Rev. Peter Horne, MA, BD. General Secretary, Baptist Union of Scotland, since 1980; b. 25.8.30, Edinburgh; m., Isobel; 1 s.; 2 d. Educ. Boroughmuir Secondary School, Edinburgh; Edinburgh University and New College. Minister: East Kilbride Baptist Church, 1955-73; Upton Vale Baptist Church, Torquay, 1973-80. Centenary President, Baptist Union of Scotland, 1969-70. Recreations: golf; swimming; music. Address: (b.) 14 Aytoun Road, Glasgow, G41 5RT; T.-041-423 6169.

Barclay, Kenneth Forsyth, BL, NP. Secretary, Scottish Law Commission; b. 1.2.38, Glasgow; m., Jean Broom Curwen; 1 s.; 1 d. Educ. Woodside Senior Secondary School, Glasgow; Glasgow University. Solicitor in private practice, 1960-71; Principal Solicitor, Cumbernauld Development Corporation, 1971-73; joined Office of Solicitor to Secretary of State for Scotland, 1973; Legal Secretary, Royal Commission on Legal Services in Scotland, 1976-80, then Divisional Solicitor, Scottish Office. Recreations: golf; walking; tennis; badminton; reading. Address: (b.) 140 Causewayside, Edinburgh, EH19 1PR; T.-031-668 2131.

Barclay, Robert Peter Clarkson, MB, ChB, DCH, FRCPEdin, FRCPGlas. Consultant Paediatrician, Lanarkshire Health Board, since 1975; Honorary Member, Clinical Teaching Staff, Edinburgh University, since 1980; b. 15.4.41, Hawick; m., Alexandra Margaret Whigham; 2 s.; 2 d. Educ. Hawick High School; Edinburgh University. Former Senior Registrar in Paediatrics, Stobhill Hospital, Glasgow. Branch Director, Lanarkshire, Red Cross; Member, Professional Advisory Committee, Scottish Council for Spastics. Address: (h.) 33 Mousebank Road, Lanark, ML11 7PE; T.-0555 4571.

Barker, Pamela Margaret Wentworth, BSc, MB, ChB, DPM, MRCPsych. Consultant Psychiatrist, Highland Health Board, since 1978; Clinical Senior Lecturer in Mental Health, Aberdeen University, since 1981; b. 5.11.29, London. Educ. Ipswich High School; Leeds University. House Physician and House Surgeon, General Infirmary, Leeds; Senior House Officer, Pinderfields General Hospital, Wakefield; Registrar, Stanley Royd Hospial, Wakefield; Assistant Psychiatrist, Yorkshire Regional Health Authority. Recreation: motor vehicle maintenance. Address: (h.) Burnside, Leachkin Road, Inverness, IV3 6NW; T.-0463 234101.

Barker, Thomas Christopher, MA. Secretary to Trustees, Scottish National War Memorial, Edinburgh Castle, since 1987; b. 28.6.28, Brighton; m., Griselda Helen Cormack; 2 s.; 1 d. Educ. Uppingham; New College, Oxford. 2nd Lt., 1st Bn., The Worcestershire Regiment, 1946-48; HM Diplomatic Service: 3rd Secretary, Paris, 1953-55; 2nd Secretary, Baghdad, 1955-58; Foreign Office, 1958-62; 1st Secretary, Head of Chancery and Consul, Mexico City, 1962-67; Counsellor and Head of Chancery, Caracas, 1969-71; Foreign and Commonwealth Office, 1971-75; Under Secretary, Northern Ireland Office, Belfast, 1976. Curator, Scottish National War Memorial, 1978-87; Treasurer, St. Ninian's Cathedral, Perth, 1983-86. Address: (h.) Abdie House, Grange of Lindores, Cupar, KY14 6HX; T.-0337 40286.

Barlow, Professor (Arthur) John, PhD, DIC, BSc, ACGI, MIEE, CEng. Titular Professor, Electronics and Electrical Engineering Department, Glasgow University; b. 17.3.34, Nottinghamshire; m., Alma Marshall; 1 s.; 1 d. Educ. Nottingham High School; Imperial College. Turner and Newall Research Fellow, Imperial College, 1958-61; Glasgow University: Lecturer, 1961-66, Senior Lecturer, 1966-68, Reader, 1968-75. Address: (h.) 5 Auchencruive, Milngavie, Glasgow, G62 6EE.

Barnes, Robin Adam Boyd, MA (Hons), MEd. Director of Education, Shetland Islands Council, since 1975; b. 3.4.27, Glasgow; m., Cecilia; 3 d. Educ. Glasgow Academy; Glasgow University. Royal Navy, 1945-48; Teacher of English, Larkhall Academy, Lanarkshire, 1953-54; Special Assistant Teacher of English, Kelvinside Academy, Glasgow, 1954-64; Assistant Director of Education, Edinburgh, 1964-72; Director of Education, Zetland County Council, 1972-75. Education Officer, RNR Glasgow, 1958-64; Member, East of Scotland Schools/Industry Liaison Working Party with SED, 1966-68; Secretary, Edinburgh Primary Schools Working Party, 1968-72; President, Isleburgh Drama Group, Lerwick, since 1982. Recreations: performing music (piano); walking; gardening. Address: (b.) Education Office, 1 Harbour Street, Lerwick, Shetland, ZE1 OLS; T.-0595 3535, Ext. 254.

Barnet, James Paul, MA, LLB. Partner, Macbeth Currie & Co., Solicitors, since 1965; Council Member, Law Society of Scotland, since 1985 (Convener, Property Marketing Committee, since 1986); b. 20.7.37, Darlington; m., Margaret Smart; 4 s. Educ. Dunfermline High School; Edinburgh University. Admitted as Solicitor, 1961. Local Secretary, Scottish Garden City Housing Society Ltd.; Captain, Scottish Universities Golfing Society, 1980-81; President, Dunfermline Rotary Club, 1985-86. Recreations: golf; reading; quoting Dr. Johnson. Address: (h.) Bonnyton House, Dunfermline, Fife, KY12 9HT; T.-Dunfermline 731011.

Barnetson, Ross St. Clair, MD, FRCP. Consultant Dermatologist, Edinburgh Royal Infirmary, since 1981; part-time Senior Lecturer, Edinburgh University, since 1981; b. 10.10.39, Edinburgh; m., Sheila Ann Corson; 2 d. Educ. Loretto School, Musselburgh; Edinburgh University. House Physician and House Surgeon, Edinburgh Royal Infirmary; service, RAMC, hospitals in Cyprus, West Malaysia and Singapore; Registrar in Dermatology, Edinburgh Royal Infirmary; Clinical Research Physician, MRC Leprosy Project, Addis Ababa, Ethiopia; Lecturer in Dermatology, Edinburgh University. Member, Medical Advisory Board, LEPRA. Recreations: sailing; skiing; tennis; opera. Address: (h.) 32 Queens Crescent, Edinburgh, EH9 2BA; T.-031-667 5173.

Barnett, Robert James Charles, LLB (Hons). Director of Administration and Legal Services and Depute Chief Executive, Western Isles Islands Council, since 1986; Returning Officer, Western Isles Islands Area, since 1986; b. 10.5.53, Birmingham; m., Christine Mary; 1 s.; 1 d. Educ. Homelands Technical High School, Torquay; Bristol Polytechnic; Guildford College of Law. Served articles with Torbay Borough Council, 1975-77; qualified as Solicitor, 1978; Assistant Solicitor, then Senior Assistant, then Principal Assistant Solicitor, Plymouth City Council, 1978-86. Recreations: music; reading; walking; family. Address: (b.) Western Isles Islands Council, Council Offices, Sandwick Road, Stornoway, Isle of Lewis, PA87 2BW; T.-0851 3773.

Barr, Rev. Alexander Craib, MA, BD. Minister, St. Nicholas' Cardonald Parish Church, Glasgow, since 1967; Moderator, Presbytery of Glasgow, 1987-88; b. 10.2.27, Glasgow; m., Agnes Morrison Robertson; 3 d. Educ. Daniel Stewart's College, Edinburgh; Edinburgh University. Ordained Probationer Assistant, Bathgate High Church, 1950-52; Minister: Hawick Burnfoot Parish Church, 1952-58, Methil Parish Church, 1958-67. Moderator, Presbytery of Kirkcaldy, 1964-65. Recreations: gardening; photography. Address: (h.) 104 Lamington Road, Cardonald, Glasgow; T.-041-882 2065.

Barr, Professor Allan David Stephen, BSc, PhD, CEng, FIMechE, FRSE. Jackson Professor of Engineering, Aberdeen University, since 1985; b. 11.9.30, Glasgow; m., Eileen Patricia Redmond. Educ. Daniel Stewart's College, Edinburgh; Edinburgh University. Student apprentice, Bristol Aeroplane Company; Lecturer, Department of Engineering, Edinburgh University; Visiting Associate Professor, Department of Theoretical and Applied Mechanics, Cornell University, USA; Senior Lecturer, then Reader, Department of Mechanical Engineering, Edinburgh University; Professor and Head, Department of Mechanical Engineering, Dundee University. Recreations: fly fishing; oil painting. Address: (b.) Department of Engineering, Kings College, University of Aberdeen, AB9 2UE.

Barr, David, DPE. Director of Physical Education, Dundee University, since 1968; b. 7.3.34, Motherwell; 1 s.; 1 d. Educ. Dalziel High School, Motherwell; Scottish School of Physical Education, Jordanhill College of Education, Glasgow. Physical Fitness Officer, RAF, 1957-60; Games Master, Glyn Grammar School, Ewell, Surrey, 1960-63; Assistant Director of Physical Education, Aberdeen University, 1963-66; Director of Physical Recreation, Bradford University, 1966-68. Played water polo for Scotland, 1955-61, for Great Britain, 1958-61; national water polo coach, Great Britain, 1961-65; director of water polo, Scotland, 1972-75; team manager/coach, water polo, GB at World Student Games, Budapest, 1965, Turin, 1970, Moscow, 1973. Publications: A Guide to Water Polo, 1964; Play Better Water Polo, 1970; Water Polo, 1980. Recreations: golf; gardening. Address: (b.) Department of Physical Education, The University, Dundee, DD1 4HN; T.-Dundee 23181, Ext. 4117.

Barr, Rev. David, MA, BD. Hospital Chaplain, Glasgow Royal Infirmary and Canniesburn Hospital, 1962-84; b. 14.6.14, Airdrie. Educ. Airdrie Academy; Glasgow University and Trinity College. Student Assistant, New Monkland Parish Church, 1935-37; Minister, Kirkintilloch South Church, 1938-42; part-time Hospital Chaplain, Broomhill and Lanfine Hospitals; Minister, St. Mary's, Partick, 1942-62; part-time Hospital Chaplain, Glasgow Western Infirmary, 1960-62. Moderator, Glasgow Presbytery, 1969-70; Chairman, National Association of Whole-Time Hospital Chaplains for England, Scotland and Wales, 1978-82. Recreations: motoring; reading; topography; ecclesiology; medicine. Address: (h.) 17 Victoria Park Gardens South, Broomhill, Glasgow, G11 7BX; T.-041-339 5364.

Barr, David George Dryburgh, MB, ChB, FRCPEd, DCH. Consultant Paediatrician, Lothian Health Board, since 1971; part-time Senior Lecturer, Department of Child Life and Health, Edinburgh University, since 1977; b. 14.2.36, Edinburgh; m., Anna Blair; 2 s.; 1 d. Educ. Daniel Stewart's College, Edinburgh; Edinburgh University. Senior Registrar, Royal Hospital for Sick Children, Edinburgh, 1965-69; Research Fellow, Children's hospital, Zurich, Switzerland, 1969-70; Consultant Paediatrician, Edinburgh Northern and West Fife Hospitals, 1971-77; Consultant Paediatrician, Royal Hospital for Sick Children and Simpson Memorial Maternity Pavilion, since 1977; seconded to Ministry of Health and University of Riyadh, Saudi Arabia, 1980-83. Address: (b.) Royal Hospital for Sick Children, Sciennes Road, Edinburgh; T.-031-667 1991.

Barr, Ian. Chairman, Post Office Scotland (formerly Chairman, Scottish Postal Board), 1984-88; Board Member, Girobank Scotland, since 1984; Chairman, Association for Business Sponsorship of the Arts, Scotland, 1986-88; b. 6.4.27, Edinburgh; m., 1, Gertrud Karla Odefey; 2 d; 2, Margaret Annie McAlpine Barr. Educ. Boroughmuir High School. Post Office: Assistant Postal Controller (North Western Region, England), 1955; Inspector of Postal Services, 1957; Assistant Controller (Planning), 1962 (both in Post Office HQ, London); Principal, 1966, and Member, Civil Service Selection Board, 1966-71; Assistant Secretary, 1971; Regional Director (Eastern Postal Region, England), 1976; Post Office Headquarters Director of Buildings, Mechanisation and Transport, 1978; Director, Post Office Estates Executive, 1981-84; Chairman, Post Office National Arts Committee, 1976-87; President, Conference Europeenne des Postes et des Telecommunications (Batiments), 1982-86; Member, British Materials Handling Board, 1978-81; Member, Scottish Council, CBI, 1984-88; Trustee, St Mary's Music School, since 1986, and Chairman, Management Committee, since 1988; Trustee, Endocrine Research Trust, since 1987; Director, Friedman Camerata of St Andrew, since 1988. Recreations: composing serial music; constructing a metaphysical system. Address: 9 Ravelston Heights, Edinburgh, EH4 3LX.

Barr, Rev. John Gourlay Crichton. Deputy Secretary, Law Society of Scotland, 1978-88; non-stipendiary Priest, Scottish Episcopal Church, since 1985; b. 10.5.23, Berwick-upon-Tweed; m., Mary Wanklyn Branford; 2 s. Educ. Struan School, Berwick; George Watson's College, Edinburgh; Edinburgh University. Royal Navy, 1942-46; mentioned in Despatches, Normandy, 1944; admitted Solicitor, 1947; Partner: Robertson Dempster & Co., Perth, 1956-74, Condie, Mackenzie & Co., Perth, 1974-78. Former Member of Board, Royal Lyceum Theatre and Perth Repertory Theatre (Chairman, 1972-78); Scottish Episcopal Church: Lay Reader, Diocese of St Andrews, 1958-78, Diocesan Registrar, 1974-78; involved in team ministry, St. Mark's Episcopal Church, Portobello, since 1981; Past Chairman: Laity Committee, Scottish Churches Council; Perth Council of Churches; Council Member, Law Society of Scotland, 1968-77; Member, EAST (Ecumenical AIDS Support Team), since 1987 (Secretary, since 1988); Unionist candidate, West Stirlingshire, 1964; Lieutenant, RNVR, 1946. Recreations: theatre; bird-watching; creative writing. Address: (h.) 3 Hamilton Terrace, Edinburgh, EH15 1NB; T.-031-669 3300.

Barr, Sheriff Kenneth Glen, MA, LLB. Sheriff, South Strathclyde, Dumfries and Galloway, at Dumfries, since 1976; b. 20.1.41; m. Educ. Ardrossan Academy; Royal High School; Edinburgh University.

Barratt, Michael, MA (Hons). Headmaster, Rannoch School, since 1982; b. 31.12.40, Edinburgh; m., Valerie Anne Dixon; 1 s.; 1 d. Educ. George Watson's College, Edinburgh; Merchiston Castle School; St. Andrews University; St. Edmund Hall, Oxford. Assistant Master, Epsom College, Surrey, 1964-73; Housemaster, Strathallan School, Perth, 1973-82. Recreations: golf; gardening; mountaineering; theatre. Address: Headmaster's House, Rannoch School, Rannoch, Perth, PH17 2QQ; T.-088 22 332.

Barratt, Oliver William, SDA. Secretary, Cockburn Association (Edinburgh Civic Trust), since 1971; Secretary, Cockburn Conservation Trust, since 1978; b. 7.7.41, Belfast. Educ. Radley College; East of Scotland College of Agriculture. Vice Chairman, Scottish Association for Public Transport; Trustee, Scottish Historic Buildings Trust and Lothian Building Preservation Trust. Recreations: the hills; travel; most of the arts. Address: (h.) 1 London Street, Edinburgh, EH3 6LZ; T.-031-556 5107.

Barrie, Alistair T., BSc (Hons), DipTP, MRTPI. Chief Planning Officer, City of Dundee District Council, since 1974; b. 19.2.38, Dundee; m., Elizabeth; 2 s.; 1 d. Educ. Harris Academy, Dundee; St. Andrews University; Heriot-Watt University. Past Chairman and former Hon. Secretary and Treasurer, Scottish Society of Directors of Planning. Recreation: athletics. Address: (b.) City of Dundee District Council, 21 City Square, Dundee, DD1 3BS; T.-0382 23141, Ext. 4400.

Barron, James Walter. Assistant Secretary, Scottish Home and Health Department (Superannuation and Fire Services), since 1985; b. 22.8.34, Edinburgh; m., Elizabeth Coutts; 2 d. Educ. Broughton Secondary School. Entered Civil Service, 1951, as Clerical Officer, Admiralty (Rosyth); transferred Department of Registers as Assistant Examiner, 1956; Examiner, 1965; Senior Examiner, 1973; seconded Lands Tribunal for Scotland as Clerk, 1970-73; transferred Scottish Office, 1976, as Principal, SDD; transferred Superannuation Division, 1980. Assistant Secretary, Edinburgh University Extra Mural Association; Session Clerk, Portobello St. James Parish Church; Secretary, Portobello Gramophone Society. Recreations: music; reading; rugby; informal further education. Address: (b.) St. Margaret's House, London Road, Edinburgh; T.-031-661 3211.

Barron, Professor Laurence David, DPhil, BSc, MInstP. Professor of Chemistry, Glasgow University, since 1984; b. 12.2.44, Southampton; m., Sharon Aviva Wolf; 1 s.; 1 d. Educ. King Edward VI Grammar School, Southampton; Northern Polytechnic, London; Lincoln College, Oxford. Post-doctoral research, Cambridge University, 1969-75; Ramsay Memorial Fellow, 1974-75; Glasgow University: Lecturer in Chemistry, 1975-80, Reader, 1980-84. Corday-Morgan Medal, Chemical Society, 1977; G.M.J. Schmidt Memorial Lecturer, Weizmann Institute of Science, 1984; F.L. Conover Memorial Lecturer, Vanderbilt University, 1987. Publication: Molecular Light Scattering and Optical Activity, 1982. Recreations: walking; music; radio-controlled model aircraft. Address: (b.) Chemistry Department, The University, Glasgow, G12 8QQ; T.-041-339 8855.

Barrow, Professor Geoffrey Wallis Steuart, MA (Hons), BLitt, DLitt, FBA, FRSE, FSA, FSA Scot, FRHistS, Hon. DLitt (Glasgow). Sir William Fraser Professor of Scottish History and Palaeography, Edinburgh University, since 1979;

b. 28.11.24, Headingley, Leeds; m., Heather Elizabeth Agnes Lownie; 1 s.; 1 d. Educ. St. Edward's School, Oxford; Inverness Royal Academy; St. Andrews University; Pembroke College, Oxford. Royal Navy and RNVR (Sub-Lieutenant), 1943-46; Lecturer in History, University College, London, 1950-61; Professor of Medieval History, Newcastle-upon-Tyne University, 1961-74; Professor of Scottish History, St. Andrews University, 1974-79. Member, Royal Commission on Historical Manuscripts, since 1984; Royal Historical Society: Council Member, 1963-74, Joint Literary Director, 1964-74, Vice President, 1982-86; Past Chairman of Council, Scottish History Society (President, 1973-77); President, Saltire Society, 1987. Publications: Feudal Britain, 1956; Acts of Malcolm IV, 1960; Robert Bruce, 1965 and 1982; Acts of William I, 1971; The Kingdom of the Scots, 1973; The Scottish Tradition (Editor), 1974; The Anglo-Norman Era in Scottish History, 1980; Kingship and Unity: Scotland 1000-1306, 1981. Recreations: hill-walking; visiting graveyards; travel. Address: (h.) 12A Lauder Road, Edinburgh, EH9 2EL; T.-031-668 2173.

Barry, Rt. Rev. Mgr. John Charles McDonald, MA (Cantab), DCL. Parish Priest, St. Mark's RC Church, Edinburgh, since 1977; b. 26.9.17, Edinburgh. Educ. Abbey School, Fort Augustus; Trinity College, Cambridge; University of Fribourg, Switzerland; Oscott College, Birmingham; Gregorian University, Rome. Ordained priest, 1944; appointed Curate, St. Patrick's, Kilsyth; sent to Rome to study canon law, 1946; appointed to St. Cuthbert's, Edinburgh, 1949; transferred to St. Anthony's, Polmont, 1950; St. Andrew's College, Drygrange: Lecturer, 1953, Rector, 1960. Editor, Canon Law Abstracts, Canon Law Society of Great Britain, 1959-84; Consultor to the Pontifical Commission for the Revision of Canon Law, 1966-78. Recreations: golf; walking. Address: St. Mark's, Oxgangs Avenue, Edinburgh, EH13 9HX; T.-031-441 3915.

Bartlett, Professor Christopher John, BA, PhD, FRHistS. Professor of International History, Dundee University, since 1978 (Head of Modern History Department, 1983-88); Member, Scottish Examination Board, 1984-88; b. 12.10.31, Bournemouth; m., Shirley Maureen Briggs; 2 s. Educ. Queen Elizabeth's Grammar School, Wimborne; University College, Exeter; London School of Economics. Assistant Lecturer, Edinburgh University, 1957-59; Lecturer, University of the West Indies, Jamaica, 1959-62; Lecturer, Queen's College, Dundee, 1962-68; Reader, Dundee University, 1968-78. Publications: Great Britain and Sea Power 1815-53; Castlereagh; The Long Retreat; The Rise and Fall of the Pax Americana; A History of Postwar Britain 1945-74; The Global Conflict 1880-1970. Address: (b.) Department of History, The University, Dundee.

Bartlett, Keith, MB, BCH, FRCR, DMRT, FRCPE. Consultant Radiotherapist, Aberdeen Royal Infirmary, since 1979; b. 10.6.44, Tredegar, Monmouthshire; m., Lilian M. Davis; 1 s.; 2 d. Educ. Pontllanfraith Grammar School; Welsh National School of Medicine, Cardiff. Four years in Canadian hospitals, latterly (1977-78) as Consultant; returned to UK, 1978; pioneered use of RF hyperthermia in cancer in Scotland, 1983. Recreations: music; renovating old cars; electronics. Address: (h.) 58 Victoria Street, Dyce, Aberdeen, AB2 OEE; T.-0224 722221.

Barty, James Webster, OBE (1981), MA, LLB. Retired Solicitor; Honorary President, Scottish Law Agents Society, since 1984; b. 9.3.12, Dunblane; m., Elisabeth Beryl Roebuck; 1 s.; 2 d. Educ. Hurst Grange School, Stirling; Fettes College, Edinburgh; St. Andrews University; Edinburgh University. Qualified as Solicitor, 1935; Partner, Tho. & J.W. Barty, Dunblane, 1937-84; Scottish Law Agents Society: Secretary, 1940-82, President, 1982-84; Honorary Sheriff, since 1970. Clerk, Dunblane Cathedral Kirk Session, 1949-69; Council Member, Friends of Dunblane Cathedral, 1940-84 (Vice-Chairman, 1974-84). Recreations: life-long interest in sport (rugby, tennis, cricket, badminton) and in all arts, including theatre, opera, ballet, literature and painting. Address: (h.) Easterton, Argaty, Doune, Perthshire; T.-0786 841 372.

Basson, John Vincent, MB, ChB, BSc (Hons), MPhil, MRCPsych. Principal Medical Officer, Scottish Home and Health Department; b. 23.11.45, Manchester. Educ. De La Salle College, Salford; Edinburgh University. Fellowship in Community Psychiatry, 1976-78; Member, Secretary of State's Committee on Difficult Prisoners, 1979-82; Chairman, Edinburgh Cyrenian Trust. Recreations: gardening; keep fit; golf; travel. Address: (b.) St. Andrew's House, Edinburgh; T.-031-244 2805.

Bastable, Arthur Cyprian, OBE, BSc, CEng, FIEE, FBIM. General Manager, Ferranti plc, Dundee, 1958-86; Director, Ferranti Astron Ltd., 1983-86; Director, Ferranti Industrial Electronics Ltd., 1984-86; Deputy Chairman, Dundee Port Authority, since 1981 (Member, since 1967, Convener, Corporate Planning Committee, since 1975); b. 9.5.23, Kobe, Japan; m., Joan Cardwell; 1 s.; 1 d. Educ. St. Georges School, Harpenden; Manchester University. Joined Ferranti, 1950; President, Dundee & Tayside Chamber of Commerce, 1970-71 (Convener, Overseas Trade and Development, since 1973); Member, Tayside Development Authority, 1972-75; Vice-Chairman, Board of Governors, Dundee College of Technology, 1975-77; Member, Scottish Council, CBI, 1980; Member, Dundee Project Steering Committee, since 1983; Director: Edinburgh Instruments Ltd., 1983-85; Taytec Ltd., 1985-88; Dundee Unitech Ltd., since 1985; Dundee and Tayside ITEC Ltd., 1985-88. Recreations: sailing; skiing; ornithology. Address: (h.) Hunters Moon, 14 Lorne Street, Monifieth, Dundee, DD5 4DU.

Baster, Jeremy, BA, MPhil. Director of Economic Development, Orkney Islands Council, since 1985; b. 5.2.47, New York; m., Miriam Landor; 2 s.; 1 d. Educ. Leighton Park School, Reading; St. John's College, Oxford; University College, London. Early career in consultancy; Economist, Scottish Council (Development and Industry), 1975-80; Economist, Orkney Islands Council, 1980-85. Fellow, The Smallpeice Trust; Director, Soulisquoy Printmakers Ltd. Address: (b.) Council Offices, School Place, Kirkwall, KW15 1NY; T.-0856 3535.

Batchelor, Sir Ivor (Ralph Campbell), Kt (1981), CBE, FRCPEdin, FRCPsych, DPM, FRSE. Member, Scottish Hospital Endowments Research Trust, since 1984; Emeritus Professor of Psychiatry, Dundee University; b. 29.11.16; m.; 1 s.; 3 d. Educ. Edinburgh Academy; Edinburgh University. Squadron Leader, RAFVR, 1941-46. Professor of Psychiatry, Dundee University, 1967-82; Chairman, Committee on Staffing Mental Deficiency Hospitals, 1967-70; MRC: Chairman, Clinical Research Board, 1973-74, Neuro-Sciences Board, 1974-75; Member, Royal Commission on the National Health Service, 1976-79.

Bates, Peter James, CertSocAdmin, DipSocWk. Director of Social Work, Tayside Regional Council, since 1987; Chairman, Manpower Committee, Association of Directors of Social Work, since 1986; b. 6.5.45, Birmingham; m., Ann Gordon; 1 s.; 3 d. Educ. Birmingham University. Left school at 15 and completed five year apprenticeship; became active in youth work and community action in Handsworth; attended Birmingham University from the age of 23; moved to Scotland, 1969, as a social worker in Greenock; senior social worker, Edinburgh, later Director of a Community Development Project in the Grassmarket; a Social Work Manager with Lothian Regional Council; Principal Child Care Officer, later Deputy Director of Social Work, Strathclyde Regional Council. Publication: Resource Allocation in Health Care, 1979. Recreations: running; climbing; photography. Address: (b.) Social Work Department, Tayside House, 28 Crichton Street, Dundee, DD1 3RN; T.-Dundee 23281.

Baxby, Keith, BSc, MB, BS, FRCS. Consultant Urological Surgeon, Tayside Health Board, since 1977; Honorary Senior Lecturer, Dundee University, since 1977; b. 17.4.44, Sheffield. Educ. King Edward VII School, Sheffield; Durham University. House Officer, Royal Victoria Infirmary, Newcastle-upon-Tyne, 1968-69; Surgical Registrar, Newcastle University Hospitals, 1969-73; Northern Counties Kidney Fund Research Fellow, 1973-74; Senior Urological Registrar, Newcastle General Hospital, 1974-77; Visiting Professor of Urology, Louisiana State University, 1981; WHO Fellow in Clinical Urodynamics, 1984. Recreation: deer stalking. Address: (b.) Department of Urology, Royal Infirmary, Dundee; T.-0382 23125.

Baxter, Carole Mary, BSc. Co-Presenter, The Beechgrove Garden, BBC Scotland, since 1986 (Head Gardener, The Beechgrove Garden, since 1984); b. 30.6.57, Maidstone; m., Dr. Michael R. Baxter. Educ. Maidstone School for Girls; Sussex University. Undergardener, Kildrummy Castle Gardens Trust, Aberdeenshire, 1979-80; Gardener/Caretaker, Aberdeen University Air Squadron, 1980-83; Assistant Gardener, The Beechgrove Garden, Aberdeen, 1983-84. Publication: The Beechgrove Garden (Co-author). Recreations: skiing; walking; swimming; gardening. Address: (b.) BBC, Beechgrove Terrace, Aberdeen, AB9 2ZT; T.-0224 625233.

Baxter, Mary Ross, MBE, MA, LRAM. Chief Executive Scotland, Book Trust Scotland, since 1960; b. 23.9.27, Glasgow. Educ. Park School, Glasgow; Glasgow University. John Smith & Son, Booksellers, Glasgow, 1952-56; British European Airways, Glasgow Office, 1956-60; National Book League (now known as Book Trust), since 1960; started the Scottish Office in 1961. Honorary Member, Scottish Library Association; Vice President, International PEN Scottish Centre. Recreations: music; books; home-decorating; cooking; gardening. Address: (b.) 15A Lynedoch Street, Glasgow, G3 6EF; T.-041-332 0391.

Baxter, Professor Murdoch Scott, BSc (Hons), PhD, CChem, FRSC. Director, Scottish Universities Research and Reactor Centre, since 1985; Professor (Personal Chair), Glasgow University, since 1985; Executive Editor, International Journal of Environmental Radioactivity, since 1984; b. 12.3.44, Glasgow; m., Janice Baxter; 1 s. Educ. Hutchesons' Boys' Grammar School, Glasgow; Glasgow University. Visiting Research Fellow, State University of NY, 1969-70; Lecturer in Chemistry, Glasgow University, 1970-85; Visiting Research Consultant, International Atomic Energy Agency, Marine Radioactivity Laboratories, Monaco, 1981-82. Publications: scientific research papers on natural and artificial radioactivity in the environment. Recreations: sports; photography. Address: (b.) Scottish Universities Research and Reactor Centre, East Kilbride, Glasgow, G75 0QU; T.-03552 20222, Ext. 2609.

Baxter, (William) Gordon, OBE, DL, LLD, BSc. Chairman, W.A. Baxter & Sons Ltd., since 1971; b. 8.2.16, Fochabers, Moray; m., Ena E. Robertson; 2 s.; 1 d. Educ. Ashville College, Harrogate; Aberdeen University. ICI Explosives Ltd., 1940-45 (Research and Development Manager, various military projects); joined family business, 1946; appointed Managing Director, 1947; Member, British Export Council Committee for Exports to USA, 1964-69. Director, Grampian Regional Board, Bank of Scotland; Member of Council, Royal Warrent Holders Association, London; Member, Scottish Conservative Party's Business Group. Recreations: fishing; tennis. Address: (h.) Speybank House, Fochabers, Moray; T.-0343 820393.

Bayliss, Anthony Paul, MB, ChB, FRCR, DMRD. Consultant Radiologist, Aberdeen Royal Infirmary, since 1975; b. 7.2.44, Oldham; m., Margaret Anne; 3 s. Educ. Oldham Hulme Grammar School; St. Andrews University. Medical Intern., Mount Sinai Hospital, Minneapolis, 1969-70; House Officer, Ballochmyle Hospital, Ayrshire, 1970-71; Trainee Radiologist, Western Infirmary, Glasgow, 1971-75. Recreation: golf. Address: (h.) 1 Marchbank Road, Bieldside, Aberdeen; T.-Aberdeen 861229.

Bealey, Professor Frank William, BSc (Econ) (Hons). Professor of Politics, Aberdeen University, since 1964; b. 31.8.22, Bilston, Staffordshire; m., Sheila Hurst; 1 s.; 2 d. Educ. King Edward VI Grammar School, Stourbridge; London School of Economics. Extra-Mural Lecturer, Manchester University, 1951-52; Lecturer, Keele University, 1952-64; Temporary Lecturer, Birmingham University, 1958-59. Treasurer and founder Member, Society for the Study of Labour History, 1960-63; Convener, Committee for Social Science, Aberdeen University, 1970-74 and since 1986; Fellow, Royal Historical Society, 1971; Editorial Board,

Political Studies, 1975-83; Visiting Fellow, Yale University, 1980. Publications: Labour and Politics 1900-1906 (Co-author); Constituency Politics (Co-author); The Social and Political Thought of the British Labour Party; The Post Office Engineering Union; The Politics of Independence (Co-author); Democracy in the Contemporary State. Recreations: reading poetry; darts; eating and drinking; watching football and cricket. Address: (h.) 355 Clifton Road, Aberdeen, AB2 2DT; T.-Aberdeen 484689.

Beastall, Graham Hedley, BSc, PhD, MRCPath. Top Grade Biochemist (Endocrinology), Glasgow Royal Infirmary, since 1981; Honorary Lecturer, Glasgow University, since 1983; b. 11.12.47, Liverpool; m., Judith; 2 s. Educ. Liverpool Institute High School for Boys; Liverpool University. Lecturer in Biochemistry, Liverpool University, 1971-72; Lecturer in Steroid Biochemistry, Glasgow University, 1972-76; Senior Biochemist (Endocrinology), then Principal Biochemist (Endocrinology), Glasgow Royal Infirmary, 1976-81. Secretary, Caledonian Society for Endocrinology, since 1984; Area Commissioner, Greater Glasgow Scout Council. Recreations: Scouting; gardening; sport. Address: (b.) Department of Clinical Biochemistry, Royal Infirmary, Glasgow, G4 OSF; T.-041-552 3535, Ext. 4444.

Beat, Janet Eveline, BMus, MA. Composer; Lecturer, Royal Scottish Academy of Music and Drama, since 1972; b. 17.12.37, Streetly. Educ. High School for Girls, Sutton Coldfield; Birmingham University. Freelance Orchestral Player, 1960s; Lecturer: Madeley College of Education, 1965-67, Worcester College of Education, 1967-71; founder Member, and former Council Member, Scottish Society of Composers; writes musical criticism for The Scotsman; G.D. Cunningham Award, 1962; her compositions include The Gossamer Web, a dance drama for soprano, piano, percussion and tape, commissioned for Edinburgh Festival Fringe, 1975, Dancing on Moonbeams, an electronic fantasy, 1980 (released on gramophone record), Journey of a Letter, commissioned by the Scottish Postal Board and Scottish Ballet, 1986 and Fireworks in Steel, commissioned by Scottish National Orchestra Society for Musica Nova, 1987; her works have received performances throughout Scotland as well as in Switzerland, Poland, North America, South America, Greece and Japan. Recreations: travel; reading; photography. Address: (h.) 5 Letham Drive, Glasgow, G43 2SL; T.-041-637 1952.

Beaton, John Fyffe, CA, ARVA. Director of Finance, Kyle and Carrick District Council, since 1983; b. 18.10.35, Kirkcaldy; m., Frances Irene; 2 s. Educ. Kirkcaldy High School. Assistant Accountant, Inverness County Council, 1964-67; Junior Depute City Chamberlain, Perth, 1967-70; Depute Chamberlain, Ayr Town Council, 1970-74; Director of Finance, North-East Fife District Council, 1974-83. Address: (h.) 4 Broadwood Park, Alloway, Ayr, KA7 4XE; T.-Alloway 42743.

Beattie, Alastair, MA, LLB. Chief Executive, Caithness District Council, since 1974; b. 11.10.37, Aberdeen; m., Rosaline; 2 s.; 1 d. Educ. Robert Gordon's College, Aberdeen; Aberdeen University. Legal/Principal Legal Assistant, Dumfries County Council, 1961-67; Caithness County Council: Depute County Clerk, 1967-74, Chief Executive, 1974. Recreations: bowls; gardening; bridge. Address: (b.) Council Offices, Market Square, Wick, Caithness; T.-0955 3761.

Beattie, Alistair Duncan, MD (Hons), FRCPGlas, FRCPLond. Consultant Physician, Southern General Hospital, Glasgow, since 1976; Honorary Clinical Lecturer, Glasgow University, since 1977; Honorary Secretary, Royal College of Physicians and Surgeons, Glasgow, since 1983; b. 4.4.42, Laurencekirk; m., Gillian Margaret McCutcheon; 3 s.; 2 d. Educ. Paisley Grammar School; Glasgow University. Junior hospital appointments, Royal Infirmary and Western Infirmary, Glasgow, 1965-69; Department of Materia Medica, Glasgow University: Research Fellow, 1969-73, Lecturer, 1973-74; MRC Research Fellow, Royal Free Hospital, London, 1974-75. Honorary Treasurer, Medical and Dental Defence Union of Scotland. Recreations: golf; music. Address: (h.) 228 Queen Victoria Drive, Glasgow, G13 1TN; T.-041-959 7182.

Beattie, Henry Thomson, OBE (1974). Member, Perth and Kinross District Council, since 1980 (Convenor of Architectural Services, 1982-85, Leader, Conservative Group, 1985-86); b. 14.6.20, Glasgow; m., Harriet Hall Hughes; 2 s. Educ. Hutchesons' Grammar School, Glasgow. Pilot, RAF, 1944-45; joined Rivers Steam Navigation Co., 1946; Controlling Agent, Assam, 1954-64 (Director, Assam Sillimamite Co. Ltd., 1956-64); General Manager, Assam Railways & Trading Co. Ltd., 1965-73; Chairman, Nocte Timber Co. Ltd., 1965-73; Housemaster, Morrison's Academy, Crieff (retired, 1985). Appointed MBE, 1963, for services to British people during Chinese incursion into India; Chairman, Assam branch, UK Citizens Association, 1968-72; Chairman, Crieff Community Council, 1975-78. Recreations: fencing; golf. Address: The Cottage, Rectory Road, Crieff, PH7 3DZ; T.-Crieff 2295.

Beattie, Rev. Walter Gordon, MA, BD. Minister, Arbroath Abbey Church, since 1977; b. 25.4.32, Aberdeen; m., Catherine Fiona Matheson; 1 s.; 2 d. Educ. Robert Gordon's College, Aberdeen; Aberdeen University. Assistant Minister, St. Machar's Cathedral, Aberdeen, 1956-57; Minister: Sorbie Parish, Wigtownshire, 1957-62; Fraserburgh West Church, 1962-77. Hospital and school Chaplain. Recreations: reading; gardening; walking. Address: Abbey Church Manse, 51 Cliffburn Road, Arbroath, Angus, DD11 5BA; T.-Arbroath 72196.

Beaumont, Phillip Barrington, BEcon (Hons), MEcon, PhD. Reader, Department of Social and Economic Research, Glasgow University, since 1986 (Senior Lecturer, 1984-86); b. 13.10.49, Melbourne, Australia; m., Patricia Mary Ann McKinlay. Educ. Camberwell High School, Melbourne; Monash University, Melbourne; Glasgow University. Research Fellow, then Lecturer, Glasgow University, 1976-84; Visiting Professor: Massachusetts Institute of Technology, Boston, 1982, McMaster University, 1986, Case Western Reserve University, 1988. Publications: Bargaining in the Public Sector, 1978; Safety at Work and the Trade Unions, 1981; Job Satisfaction in Public Administration, 1983; The Decline of Trade Union Organization, 1987. Recreations: tennis; badminton; shooting; fishing. Address: (b.) The University, Glasgow, G12 8QQ; T.-041-339 8855.

Bechhofer, Professor Frank, MA. Professor of Social Research, Edinburgh University, since 1987 (Director, Research Centre for Social Sciences, since 1984); b. 10.10.35, Nurnberg, Germany; m., Jean Barbara Conochie; 1 s.; 1 d. Educ. Nottingham High School; Queens' College, Cambridge. Junior Research Officer, Department of Applied Economics, Cambridge University, 1962-65; Edinburgh University: Lecturer in Sociology, 1965-71, Reader in Sociology, 1971-87. Address: (b.) Research Centre for Social Sciences, 56 George Square, Edinburgh, EH8 9JU; T.-031-667 1011, Ext. 6322.

Beck, Professor John Swanson, BSc, MD, FRCPGlas, FRCPEdin, FRCPath, FIBiol, FRSE. Professor of Pathology, Dundee University, since 1971; Honorary Consultant Pathologist, Tayside Health Board, since 1971; b. 22.8.28, Glasgow; m., Marion Tudhope Paterson; 1 s.; 1 d. Educ. Glasgow Academy; Glasgow University. House Officer, Western Infirmary and Royal Hospital for Sick Children, Glasgow, 1953-54; Trainee Pathologist, Western Infirmary and Glasgow University, 1954-63; Clinical Research Fellow, National Institute for Medical Research, London, 1960-61; Senior Lecturer in Pathology, Aberdeen University, 1963-71. Chairman, Biomedical Research Committee, Chief Scientist Organisation, Scottish Home and Health Department, since 1983 (Member, Chief Scientist Committee, since 1983); Chairman, Breast Tumour Panel, Medical Research Council, since 1979; Member, Tayside Health Board, since 1983; Member, Medical Advisory Group, LEPRA, since 1988; Member, National Biological Standards Board, since 1988; former Member, Cell Biology and Disorders Board, Medical Research Council; former Assistant Editor, Journal of Pathology. Recreation: DIY. Address: (b.) Department of Pathology, Ninewells Hospital and Medical School, PO Box 120, Dundee, DD1 9SY; T.-0382 60111, Ext. 2169.

Beckett, Rev. David Mackay, BA, BD. Minister, Greyfriars Tolbooth and Highland Kirk, Edinburgh, since 1983; Secretary, General Assembly Panel on Doctrine; b. 22.3.37, Glasgow; m., Rosalie Frances Neal; 2 s. Educ. Glenalmond; Trinity Hall, Cambridge; St. Andrews University. Assistant Minister, Dundee Parish Church (St. Mary's), 1963-66; Minister, Clark Memorial Church, Largs, 1966-83. Convener, Committee on Public Worship and Aids to Devotion, General Assembly, 1978-82; President, Church Service Society, 1986-88. Publication: The Lord's Supper, 1984. Address: (h.) 12 Tantallon Place, Edinburgh, EH9 1NZ; T.-031-667 8671.

Beck-Slinn, George Arthur. Honorary Sheriff, Dingwall; retired bank manager; b. 30.7.13, Henley on Thames; m., Hilda J. Gordon (see Hilda Jean Beck-Slinn); 1 s.; 1 d. Educ. Robert Gordon's College, Aberdeen. Joined Union Bank of Scotland, Aberdeen, 1931; War service, 1940-46 (Captain, Royal Artillery); rejoined Union Bank of Scotland, 1946; Manager, Gatehouse of Fleet, 1953-55; Manager, Bank of Scotland, Gatehouse of Fleet, 1955-64, Dingwall, 1964-73. Recreations: bridge; travel; photography. Address: (h.) Dromore, Tulloch, Dingwall, Ross-shire; T.-0349 62170.

Beck-Slinn, Hilda Jean. Honorary Sheriff, Dingwall; b. 15.3.15, Aberdeen; m., George A. Beck-Slinn (qv); 1 s.; 1 d. Educ. Aberdeen Central School. Metropolitan police officer, London; Children's Officer, Stewartry of Kirkcudbright; Probation Officer, Ross and Cromarty. Recreations: reading; travel; bridge. Address: (h.) Dromore, Tulloch, Dingwall, Ross-shire; T.-0349 62170.

Bedborough, William F., MA (Hons), DipEdTech. Rector, Forfar Academy, since 1979; b. 6.11.42, Glasgow; m., Sheena J. McLullich; 1 s.; 1 d. Educ. Hutchesons' Boys' Grammar School, Glasgow; Glasgow University. Assistant Teacher (History), Hutchesons' Boys Grammar School, 1965-68; Special Assistant Teacher (History), Hamilton Academy, 1968-69; Principal Teacher (History), Bellshill Academy, 1969-72; Assistant Rector, Arbroath Academy, 1972-75; Depute Rector, Galashiels Academy, 1975-79. Recreations: sailing; golf; squash; Forfar Rotary Club; Strathmore Speakers Club. Address: (b.) Forfar Academy, Taylor Street, Forfar; T.-0307 64545.

Beeston, Michael Harding, ARMCM, GRSM. Viola Player, Edinburgh Quartet, since 1971; b. 11.5.48, Blackpool; m., Janet Bond; 1 s.; 2 d. Educ. Royal Manchester College of Music. Sub-Principal Viola, BBC Scottish Symphony Orchestra; Principal Viola, Scottish Chamber Orchestra; present teaching appointments: Royal Scottish Academy of Music, St. Mary's Music School, Edinburgh; frequent appearances as soloist in concertos/recitals; occasional adjudicator. Address: (h.) 119 Craigleith Road, Edinburgh, EH4 2EH; T.-031-332 8691.

Begg, Hugh MacKemmie, MA, PhD, DipTP, MRTPI, MBIM, MCIT, MInstPet. Director, Department of Town and Regional Planning, Duncan of Jordanstone College of Art, Dundee, since 1981; b. 25.10.41, Glasgow; m., Jane Elizabeth Harrison; 2 d. Educ. High School of Glasgow; St. Andrews University; University of British Columbia. Lecturer in Political Economy, St. Andrews University; Research Fellow, Tayside Study; Lecturer in Economics, Dundee University; Assistant Director of Planning, Tayside Regional Council; Visiting Professor, Technical University of Nova Scotia; Consultant, UN Regional Development Project, Saudi Arabia; Consultant, Industry Department Scotland. Recreations: local history; reading; rugby. Address: (h.) 4 Esplanade, Broughty Ferry, Dundee; T.-0382 79642.

Begg, Norman Roderick Darroch, MA, LLB. Secretary, Aberdeen University; b. 23.12.41, London; m., Fiona Schofield; 2 d. Educ. Aberdeen Grammar School; Aberdeen University. Administrative Assistant, East Anglia University, 1964-66; Aberdeen University, since 1966: Administrative Assistant; Assistant Secretary; Registry

Officer; Clerk to Senatus; Deputy Secretary. Member, Children's Panel, Grampian Region, since 1984; Past Chairman, Aberdeen Studio Theatre Group; Director, Edinburgh Festival Fringe Society, 1980-83. Recreation: amateur drama. Address: (h.) Rae's Cottage, Udny Green, by Ellon, Aberdeenshire; T.-06513 2065.

Begg, Robert William, CBE (1977), MA, CA, FRSA. Member, Museums and Galleries Commission, since 1988; b. 19.2.22; m., Sheena Margaret Boyd; 2 s. Educ. Greenock Academy; Glasgow University. Royal Navy, 1942-46 (Lt., RNVR) (Despatches). Consultant, Moores & Rowland, since 1987 (Partner, Mann Judd Gordon, Glasgow, 1951-86). Honorary Treasurer, Royal Philosophical Society of Glasgow, 1952-62; Honorary Treasurer, Royal Glasgow Institute of Fine Arts, 1975-87, President, since 1987; Member, Board of Governors, Glasgow School of Art, 1955-77 (Chairman, 1970-76); Trustee, National Galleries of Scotland, since 1974 (Chairman, 1980-87); Council Member, National Trust for Scotland, since 1984 (Executive, since 1985); Member of Court, Glasgow University, since 1986. Address: (h.) 3 Colquhoun Drive, Bearsden, Glasgow, G61 4NQ; T.-041-942 2436.

Begg, Thomas N.A., JP, BA. Historian and Lecturer; Member, Council of Management, Scottish Special Housing Association, since 1980; b. 8.1.42, Stirling; m., Mary E.; 1 d. Educ. Balfron High School; Strathclyde University. Publications: The CWD File, 1980; Fifty Special Years, 1987. Recreations: hill-walking; music; reading. Address: Department of Applied Consumer Studies, Queen Margaret College, Edinburgh; T.-031-339 8111.

Behan, Peter Oliver, MD, ChB, FRCP(Lond), FRCP(I), FRCP(Glas), FACP. Consultant Neurologist, Greater Glasgow Health Board, since 1976; Reader in Neurology, Glasgow University, since 1976; b. 8.7.35, Co. Kildare; m., Dr. Wilhelmina Behan; 2 s.; 1 d. Educ. Sir John Cass College, London; Leeds University Medical School. Demonstrator in Pathology, Cambridge University, 1965-66; Research Fellow in Psychiatry, Harvard University, 1966-67; Special Research Fellow, Oxford University, 1968-70; Lecturer in Neurology, then Senior Lecturer, Glasgow University, 1971-76. Patron, Motor Neurone Disease Association of Scotland; awarded Pattison Medal for contributions to neurology; Chief Editor, Journal of Neuroimmunology. Recreations: salmon fishing; Samuel Johnson. Address: (h.) 17 South Erskine Park, Bearsden, Glasgow; T.-041-942 5713.

Belch, Alexander Ross, CBE (1972), LLD Strathclyde (1978), BSc, FRSE, FRINA, CBIM, CEng. Company Director; Chairman, Irvine Development Corporation; b. 13.12.20, London; m., Janette Finnie Murdoch; 4 d. Educ. Morrison's Academy, Crieff; Glasgow University. Lithgows Ltd.: Director and General Manager, 1954, Managing Director, 1964; Managing Director, Scott Lithgow Group, 1969-80; part-time Member, Organising Committee for British Shipbuilders, and Member, Board, British Shipbuilders, 1976-79; Shiprepair Adviser, Gibraltar Government, 1982-83; Deputy Chairman, Jebsens Drilling plc; Chairman: Jebsens Travel Ltd., Gleddoch Hotels Ltd., Capelrig Ltd., Murray Hotels (Crieff) Ltd., Kelvin Travel Ltd., Altnacraig Shipping plc; a Director: Orico Systems Ltd., Jebsens (UK) Ltd., J.H. Carruthers & Co. Ltd.; President, Shipbuilders and Repairers National Association, 1974-76; former Member, Scottish Regional Board, British Railways. Past Chairman, Mining Machinery Economic Development Committee; Chairman, Trustees of the Scottish Maritime Museum; Member, Board of Governors, Morrison's Academy, Crieff. Address: A.R. Belch Associates Ltd., 9 Clairmont Gardens, Glasgow, G3 7LS; T.-041-332 8651.

Bell, Albert Elliot, MA, MB, ChB, MFCM. Honorary Senior Lecturer, Department of Community Medicine, Edinburgh University, since 1987; b. 26.11.24, Edinburgh; m., Dr. Fiona McCully; 3 s. Educ. Glasgow University. Industry, 1939-51 (RAF, 1944-47); Deputy Medical Superintendent, Glasgow Royal Infirmary Group, 1962-63; Assistant Dean, Faculty of Medicine, Glasgow, 1963-70; Scottish Home and Health Department, 1970-85 (Senior Medical Officer); Community Medicine Specialist, Fife Health Board, 1985-87. Recreation: golf. Address: (h.) 6B Juniper Park Road, Edinburgh; T.-031-453 3692.

Bell, Alexander Gilmour, BL. Chief Reporter for Public Inquiries, Scottish Office, since 1979; b. 11.3.33; m.; 4 s. Educ. Hutchesons' Grammar School, Glasgow; Glasgow University. Solicitor, 1954; joined Scottish Office as Legal Officer, 1967; appointed Deputy Chief Reporter, 1973.

Bell, Sheriff Andrew Montgomery, BL. Sheriff of Glasgow and Strathkelvin, at Glasgow, since 1984; b. 21.2.40, Edinburgh; m., Ann Margaret Robinson; 1 s.; 1 d. Educ. Royal High School, Edinburgh; Edinburgh University. Solicitor, 1961-74; called to Bar, 1975; Sheriff of South Strathclyde, Dumfries and Galloway, at Hamilton, 1979-84. Address: (h.) 5 York Road, Edinburgh, EH5 3EJ; T.-031-552 3859.

Bell, Sheriff Archibald Angus, QC (Scot), MA, LLB. Sheriff of Glasgow and Strathkelvin, at Glasgow, since 1973; b. 13.4.23; m.; 2 s. Educ. The Leys School, Cambridge; St. Andrews University; Glasgow University. Royal Navy, 1941-45 (Sub Lt., RNVR); admitted, Faculty of Advocates, 1949; Reporter, Court of Session Cases, 1952-55. President, Scottish Cricket Union, 1975.

Bell, Colin John, MA (Hons). Broadcaster; Journalist; Author; b. 1.4.38, London; m., Caroline Rose Bell; 1 s.; 3 d. Educ. St. Paul's School; King's College, Cambridge. Journalist, The Scotsman, 1960-62 and 1975-78; Journalist/Contributor, London Life, Sunday Times, Sunday Telegraph, Daily Mirror, Sunday Mail, etc.; Lecturer, Morley College, 1965-68; College Supervisor, King's College, Cambridge, 1968-75; Parliamentary candidate (SNP), West Edinburgh, 1979; European Parliamentary candidate (SNP), North East Scotland, 1979; Vice-Chairman, SNP, 1978-84; Campaign Director, Euro Election, 1984. Publications: City Fathers, 1969; Boswell's Johnson, 1971; Scotch Whisky, 1985; Radical Alternative (Contributor), 1978; The Times Reports (Series) (Editor). Recreations: jazz; Scottish history. Address: (h.) Cockburnhill, Balerno, Midlothian.

Bell, Donald Atkinson, BSc, PhD, FIMechE, CEng, MIEE. Director, National Engineering Laboratory, since 1983; b. 28.5.41, Belfast; m., Joyce Louisa Godber; 2 s. Educ. Royal Belfast Academical Institution; Queen's University, Belfast; Southampton University. National Physical Laboratory, Teddington, 1966-77; Electronics Applications Division, Department of Industry, 1978-82. Address: (b.) National Engineering Laboratory, East Kilbride; T.-03552 20222.

Bell, George Armour, JP, BSc, MB, ChB. Member, Lanarkshire Health Board (Chairman, Finance Committee); b. 8.7.20, Bellshill; m., Elizabeth Davidson Porteous; 2 s. Educ. Bellshill Academy; Glasgow University. War Service, 609 Squadron, SMO Prestwick, SMO Brize Norton, RAF. Retired General Practitioner, Bellshill; Founder Chairman, Crime Prevention Panel, Bellshill and District; Red Cross Detachment Medical Officer, Bellshill; Member, Management Committee, Citizens Advice Bureau; Chairman, Lanarkshire Branch, Tenovus Scotland; Founder Chairman, Community Council for Mossend; Honorary Medical Officer, Bellshill Bn., Boys Brigade; President, Bellshill Branch, Arthritis Care; Honorary Member, Rotary. Address: (h.) Chudleigh, 449 Main Street, Bellshill, Lanarkshire, ML4 1DB; T.-749084.

Bell, George Scott, AIB, AIB (Scot). Honorary Sheriff, Tayside, Central and Fife, at Dunfermline, since 1976; General Commissioner of Income Tax, Dunfermline District, since 1976; b. 27.6.14, Johnstone; m., 1, Agnes Ewing Stark (deceased); 2, Violet Woolcock; 1 d. Educ. Madras College, St. Andrews. Began career with British Linen Bank, St. Andrews, 1931; as Member, RAFVR, called up for active service, 1939; mentioned in Despatches, 1946; British Linen Bank: Assistant Trustee Manager, 1952, Manager, Linlithgow, 1957, Manager, Dunfermline, 1963 (merged with Bank of Scotland, 1971); part-time Lecturer in banking subjects, Heriot-Watt College, Edinburgh, three years; Examiner, Institute of Bankers in Scotland, 10 years; retired from Bank, 1974. Elder, Church of Scotland, since 1957; at various times Treasurer, St. Michael's Church, Linlithgow, and St. Margaret's Church, Dunfermline. Recreations: golf; bowls. Address: (h.) Kilrymont, 16 Over Haven, Limekilns, Dunfermline, Fife, KY11 3JH; T.-0383 872484.

Bell, G. Susan, ACIS. Founder Director, Scotland Direct (Holdings) Limited; Gourmet Scotland Limited; Bell Lawrie of Biggar (Developments) Ltd.; Board Member, SCOTVEC; b. 31.8.46; m., Arthur J.A. Bell; 2 s.; 2 d. Educ. College of Commerce, Glasgow. Investment Analyst, Edinburgh, 1970-74; Conservative Parliamentary candidate: Motherwell, 1970, Caithness & Sutherland, February 1974; Chairman, Conservative Candidates Association, 1971-74; Member, Council, CBI Scotland; Founder Chairwoman, Phoenix Group, 1987; Board Member, Scottish Tourist Board, 1983-88; Member, Council, National Trust for Scotland, 1983-88. Recreations: garden; riding; reading. Address: (h.) Culter House, Coulter, Biggar; T.-0899 20064.

Bell, Emeritus Professor Henry B., BSc, PhD, FIM, CEng. Professor of Metallurgy, Strathclyde University; b. 3.7.22, Greenock; m., Barbara M. Smith; 1 d. Educ. Greenock High School; Royal College of Science and Technology. Assistant Metallurgist, Scotts Shipbuilding and Engineering Company; Research Assistant, Lecturer, Reader, Metallurgy Department, Strathclyde University; Visiting Professor, Concepcion University, Witwatersrand University, Toronto University; Distinguished Visiting Scientist, National Research Council, Halifax. Kroll Medallist, Metals Society; Member, Editorial Panel, Ironmaking and Steelmaking. Recreation: gardening. Address: (h.) 89 Finlay Rise, Milngavie, Glasgow G62 6QL; T.-041-956 1473.

Bell, Jeanne Elisabeth, BSc, MD, MRCPath. Senior Lecturer in Pathology, Edinburgh University, since 1984; Honorary Consultant in Neuropathology, Western General Hospital, Edinburgh, since 1984; b. 10.8.42, England; m., Dr. Denis Rutovitz; 1 s. Educ. Newcastle-upon-Tyne University. Lecturer, Department of Anatomy, Newcastle-upon-Tyne, 1967-70; part-time Scientific Officer, MRC Clinical and Population Cytogenetics Unit, Edinburgh, 1975-79; Senior Registrar in Paediatric Pathology, Royal Hospital for Sick Children, Edinburgh, 1979-84. Address: (b.) Neuropathology Laboratory, Western General Hospital, Crewe Road, Edinburgh, EH4 2XU; T.-031-332 2525.

Bell, John Alexander, BEd, JP. Secretary for Scotland, Professional Association of Teachers, since 1983; Member, Kirkcaldy District Council, 1984-88; b. 19.4.46, Glasgow; m., Catherine Roy Rankine. Educ. St. Augustine's School, Glasgow; Glasgow University; Jordanhill College of Education. Principal Teacher of Modern Studies, Glenrothes High School, 1975-83; Member, Scottish Joint Negotiating Committee (School Education), since 1983. Recreations: running; walking; reading; music. Address: (h.) 17 Cardean Way, Balgeddie, Glenrothes, Fife; T.-0592 742550; (b.) 22 Rutland Street, Edinburgh, EH1 2AN; T.-031-229 7868, 031-228 4231.

Bell, Neil, MusB, GRSM, ARMCM, ARCO, CertEd. Director of Music, Broughton High School, Edinburgh, and Director, Lothian Specialist Music Scheme, since 1980; b. 17.10.43, York; m., Gillian Gray; 1 s. Educ. Nunthorpe Grammar School, York; Manchester University; Royal Manchester College of Music. Assistant Music Master, Cheadle Hulme School, 1967; Head of Music, West Bridgford School, Nottingham, 1971; joined teaching staff, South Nottinghamshire School of Music, becoming Vice Principal, then Principal; professional Singer, formerly with BBC Northern Singers, now John Currie Singers; Musical Director: Dundee Choral Union, Maccabee Singers. Recreations: the arts; gardening; hill-walking. Address: (b.) Broughton High School, Carrington Road, Edinburgh, EH4 1EG; T.-031-332 7805.

Bell, Robin, MA, MSc. Writer; b. 4.1.45, Dundee; m., Suzette; 2 d. Educ. Morrison's Academy, Crieff; St. Andrews University; Perugia University, Italy; Union College, New York; Columbia University, New York. Director of Information, City University of New York, Regional Opportunity Program; Assistant Professor, John Jay College of Criminal Justice, City University of New

York; Member, US Office of Education Task Force in Educational Technology; Audio-Visual Editor, Oxford University Press; Editor, Guidebook series to Ancient Monuments of Scotland; Secretary, Poetry Association of Scotland; Journalist and Broadcaster; Scottish Radio and Television Industries Award for Best Radio Feature, 1985; Sony Award, Best British Radio Documentary, 1985. Publications: (poetry): The Invisible Mirror; Culdee, Culdee; Sawing Logs; Strathinver: A Portrait Album 1945-53; Collected Poems of James Graham, Marquis of Montrose (Editor). Recreations: books; walking. Address: (h.) 38 Dovecot Road, Edinburgh, EH12 7LE; T.-031-334 5241.

Bell, Sheriff Principal Stewart Edward, MA (Cantab), LLB (Glas), QC. Sheriff Principal of Grampian, Highland and Islands, since 1983 (retired May, 1988); b. 4.8.19, Glasgow; m., 1, Isla Spencer (deceased); 2, Mavis Kydd; 3 d.; 2 step d. Educ. Kelvinside Academy; Trinity Hall, Cambridge; Glasgow University. Commissioned Loyal Regiment, 1939; served with 2nd Bn. in Singapore and Malaya, 1940-42; PoW in Singapore and Korea, 1942-45; admitted Advocate, 1948; practised in Malacca, Malaya as Advocate and Solicitor, 1949-51; at Scottish Bar, 1951-61; Sheriff of Lanarkshire (later of Glasgow and Strathkelvin) at Glasgow, 1961-82. Honorary Pipe-Major, Royal Scottish Pipers Society, 1975-77; Past President and former Honorary Pipe Major, Glasgow Highland Club; Trustee, Scottish Far East PoW Association. Recreation: Highland bagpipe. Address: (h.) The Little House, Thurlow Road, Nairn IV12 4HJ; T.-0667 52131.

Bell, Thomas Grant Law, LDS, RFPS(Glas). Regional Dental Officer, Scottish Home and Health Department, since 1979; b. 17.2.26, Motherwell; m., Edith Barnett Porter; 1 s.; 1 d. Educ. Bellshill Academy; Anderson College of Medicine; Glasgow Dental Hospital and School. Captain, Royal Army Dental Corps, 1949-51; Assistant in general practice, 1951-54; Senior Dental Officer, Burgh of Motherwell and Wishaw, 1955-65; Principal in general practice, 1965-79; former Secretary and Treasurer and Past Chairman, Lanarkshire Section, BDA; Past Chairman, Local Dental Committee, Lanarkshire, and Lanarkshire Steering Committee, NHS Reorganisation; Lanarkshire Health Board: former Dental Secretary, Area Dental Committee, and former Member, GP Sub-Committee and Dental Service Committee; former Honorary Visiting Dental Surgeon, Edinburgh Dental Hospital. Recreations: fishing; shooting; boating. Address: (h.) Cabrach, 10 Laburnum Crescent, Wishaw, ML2 7EH; T.-0698 384930.

Beloff, Halla, BSc, PhD, FBPS. Senior Lecturer, Department of Psychology, Edinburgh University, since 1963; b. 11.5.30; m., John Beloff; 1 s.; 1 d. Educ. South Hampstead High School; London University; Illinois University; Queen's University, Belfast. Former Editor, British Journal of Social and Clinical Psychology; former Member, Psychology Committee, Social Science Research Council; President, British Psychological Society, 1983-84. Occasional broadcaster, BBC Radio Scotland; Convener, Committee on Arts, Scottish Council on Disability, since 1986. Publications: Psychology Survey 5 (Co-Editor), 1984; Camera Culture, 1985, Getting into Life, 1986; Psychology Survey 6, 1987. Recreations: following the arts and not being shocked by the new; needlework. Address: (h.) 6 Blacket Place, Edinburgh, EH9 1RL; T.-031-667 3200.

Belton, Neville Richard, BSc, PhD, CChem, MRSC. Senior Lecturer, Department of Child Life and Health, Edinburgh University, since 1975; Honorary Biochemist, Lothian Health Board; b. 5.10.37, Nottingham; m., Elisabeth Foster Inglis; 1 s.; 1 d. Educ. Nottingham High School; Birmingham University. Research Associate, Children's Memorial Hospital, Chicago, 1963-67; Lecturer in Pharmacology and Associate in Paediatrics, Northwestern University, Chicago, 1964-67; Lecturer, Department of Child Life and Health, Edinburgh University, 1967-75. Member: DHSS Working Party on the Composition of Infant Foods, 1974-80; Committee, Nutrition Society (Scottish Group). Recreations: travel; sport (squash, tennis, hockey); music. Address: (h.) 6 Bernard's Crescent, Edinburgh, EH4 1NP; T.-031-332 0392.

Beltrami, Joseph, BL, NP. Solicitor (Beltrami & Co.); b. 15.5.32, Rutherglen; m., Brigid D.; 3 s. Educ. St. Aloysius College, Glasgow; Glasgow University. Intelligence Corps, 1954-56 (Sgt.); qualified as Solicitor, 1956; specialised in criminal law; has instructed in more than 500 murder cases; closely associated with two cases of Royal Pardon. Chairman, soccer testimonials: Jim Johnstone and Bobby Lennox, 1976; Danny McGrain, 1980. Publications: The Defender, 1980; Glasgow - A Celebration (Contributor), 1984. Recreations: bowls; soccer; snooker; writing; boxing. Address: (h.) 5 St. Andrew's Avenue, Bothwell, Lanarkshire; T.-Bothwell 852374.

Benington, (Charles) Kenneth, BSc, PhD, CEng, MIMechE. Technical Director, Vickers Marine Engineering Division, since 1981; b. 1.4.31, Belfast; m., Margaret Malcolm; 1 s.; 1 d. Educ. Dalriada Grammar School, Ballymoney; Queen's University, Belfast; Heriot-Watt University. Graduate apprentice and design engineer, Associated Electrical Industries Ltd., 1953-60; Assistant Chief Engineer, Trials, British Ship Research Association, 1960-63; Lecturer, Heriot-Watt University, 1963-72; Senior Engineer, Marine Industries Centre, Newcastle University, 1972-74; Brown Brothers & Co. Ltd.: Systems Manager, 1974-75; Technical Manager, 1975-77; Technical Director, 1977-80; Assistant Managing Director and Technical Director, 1980-81. Member, Executive Committee, Scottish Engineering Employers' Association, since 1984. Address: (b.) Vickers Marine Engineering Division, Rosebank Works, Broughton Road, Edinburgh EH7 4LF.

Bennet, Donald John, BSc, MS, PhD, CEng, MIMechE. Senior Lecturer, Department of Thermodynamics, Strathclyde University, since 1975; Author; b. 6.11.28, London; m., Eileen Anne Lowry; 2 s. Educ. Melville College, Edinburgh; Heriot-Watt College, Edinburgh. RAF, 1952-55; Instructor, Outward Bound Trust, 1955-56; Lecturer: Royal Technical College, Glasgow, 1956-61; University of British Columbia, Canada, 1961-62; Lecturer, Strathclyde University, 1963-75.

Member, Countryside Commission for Scotland, since 1982; Chairman, Scottish branch, Combined Heat and Power Association, 1982-85; Honorary Secretary, Scottish Mountaineering Club, 1967-80; President, Scottish Mountaineering Club, 1986-88. Publications: Elements of Nuclear Power, 1971; The Staunings Alps, 1971; The Southern Highlands, 1971; Scottish Mountain Climbs, 1980; The Western Highlands, 1982; The Munros (Editor), 1985. Recreations: photography; mountaineering; skiing. Address: (h.) 4 Morven Road, Bearsden, Glasgow, G61 3BU; T.-041-941 1387.

Bennet, George Charters, BSc, MB, ChB, FRCS. Consultant Orthopaedic Surgeon, Royal Hospital for Sick Children, Glasgow, since 1982; Honorary Clinical Lecturer, Glasgow University, since 1982; b. Edinburgh; m., Louise Spilsbury; 3 s. Educ. Holy Cross Academy; Edinburgh University Medical School. General surgical training, Edinburgh and London; training in orthopaedic surgery, London, Oxford, Southampton and Toronto. Publications: Paediatric Hip Disorders, 1987; papers on children's orthopaedics in various journals. Recreation: hill-walking. Address: (b.) Department of Orthopaedic Surgery, Royal Hospital for Sick Children, Yorkhill, Glasgow, G3 8SJ; T.-041-942 3676.

Bennett, Bruce, MB, ChB (Hons), MD (Hons), FRCP, MRCPath. Reader in Medicine, Aberdeen University; b. 5.7.38, Gorakphur, India; m., Dr. G. Adey Bennett. Educ. Brechin High School; Aberdeen University. Aberdeen University: Ashley Mackintosh Research Fellow, 1964; MRC Junior Research Fellow, 1965; Lecturer in Medicine, 1967; Eli Lilly Travelling Research Fellow, then Visiting Research Fellow, Case Western Reserve University, Cleveland, Ohio, 1970-72; Wellcome Senior Research Fellow, Aberdeen University, 1973; appointed Senior Lecturer, 1978. Address: (b.) Department of Medicine, Polwarth Building, Foresterhill, Aberdeen; T.-0224 681818, Ext. 53025.

Bennett, David Andrew, MA, LLB, WS, NP. Partner, A.C. Bennett & Robertsons, WS, Edinburgh and Glasgow, since 1964; Chairman, Oswalds of Edinburgh Ltd., since 1964; b. 27.3.38, Edinburgh; m., Marion Miller Park; 2 d. Educ. Melville College, Edinburgh; Fettes College, Edinburgh; Edinburgh University. Chairman and Director, Jordan Group Ltd.; Member, Council, Law Society of Scotland, since 1984. Session Clerk, Liberton Kirk, since 1975; Honorary Secretary, Scottish Hockey Association, 1973-82; Scottish Editor, Palmer's Company Law, since 1970, and Gore-Browne on Companies, since 1975. Recreations: most sports and arts. Address: (b.) 16 Walker Street, Edinburgh, EH3 7NN; T.-031-225 4001.

Bennett, Howard Grimwade. Publisher and Managing Director, The Oban Times Ltd., since 1983; b. 17.6.40, London; m., Joan Peake Hughes; 1 s.; 1 d. Educ. Lady Manners Grammar School, Derbyshire. Reed International, 1959-65; The McCorquodale Group, 1966-75; Holmes McDougall Ltd., 1975-81; Petersburg Press, USA, 1981-83. Recreations: classical music; modern art; dreaming of sailing. Address: (h.) 27 St. Bernards Crescent, Edinburgh, EH4 1NR.

Bennett, John Herbert Buteux, BA, PhD. Senior Lecturer in French, Glasgow University, since 1971; b. 24.3.24, London; m., Constance Celia Bound; 1 s. Educ. Queen Elizabeth Grammar School, Darlington; Queen Mary College, London. Served World War II, 1943-46, WS/Lt., Durham Light Infantry (wounded NW Europe, mentioned in Despatches); Belgian Government research scholarship, 1951-52; Assistant Teacher of French, 1954-60; Senior Modern Languages Master, 1960-67; Lecturer, Glasgow University, 1967-71; Chief Examiner in French ("A Level"), Schools Examinations Department, London University, 1974-79; Head, Department of French Language and Literature, Glasgow University, 1985-87. Recreation: chess. Address: (b.) French Department, Glasgow University, Glasgow, G12 8QL; T.-041-339 8855.

Bennett, Roderick, BSc, PhD, CChem, MRIC, MIBiol, MIHEc. Head, School of Home Economics, Robert Gordon's Institute of Technology, since 1972; b. 14.9.37, Sheffield; m., Morag Hamilton. Educ. Sheffield University. Recreations: sailing; squash. Address: Robert Gordon's Institute of Technology, Schoolhill, Aberdeen, AB9 1FR; T.-Aberdeen 633611.

Bennett, Ronald Alistair, CBE (1986), QC (Scot), MA, LLB. Vice-President for Scotland, Value Added Tax Tribunals, since 1977; Chairman, War Pensions Tribunal, since 1984; Member, Scottish Medical Practices Committee, 1976-88; b. 11.12.22; m., Margret Magnusson; 3 s.; 3 d. Educ. Edinburgh Academy; Edinburgh University; Balliol College, Oxford. Lt., 79th (Scottish Horse) Medium Regiment, RA, 1943-45; Captain, attached RAOC, India and Japan, 1945-46; called to Scottish Bar, 1947; Standing Counsel to Ministry of Labour and National Service, 1957-59; Sheriff-Principal: Roxburgh, Berwick and Selkirk, 1971-74, South Strathclyde, Dumfries and Galloway, 1981-82, North Strathclyde, 1982-83; Chairman, Medical Appeal Tribunals (Scotland), since 1971; Chairman, Agricultural Wages Board for Scotland, since 1973; Chairman, Local Government Boundary Commission for Scotland, since 1974; Chairman, Industrial Tribunals (Scotland), since 1977. Address: (h.) Laxamyri, 46 Cammo Road, Barnton, Edinburgh, EH4 8AP.

Bennie, Ernest Harry, MB, ChB, FRCPsych. Consultant Psychiatrist, Leverndale Hospital, since 1970; Honorary Clinical Lecturer, Glasgow University; b. 12.11.38, Glasgow; m., Norma Bennie; 2 s.; 1 d. Educ. Queens Park Senior Secondary School, Glasgow; Glasgow University. General medical career, three years; began psychiatric specialty, Duke Street Hospital, Glasgow, 1965. Recreations: yachting; sailing. Address: (b.) Leverndale Hospital, 510 Crookston Road, Glasgow, G53 7TU; T.-041-882 6255.

Bennie, Thomas, FIB (Scot). General Manager, Bank of Scotland, since 1984; b. 7.11.32, Falkirk; m., Jean M. Bennie; 2 s.; 2 d. Educ. Falkirk High School. British Linen Bank (later merged with Bank of Scotland): entered, 1949; appointed Assistant Superintendent of Branches, 1969; Assistant General Manager, Bank of Scotland Finance Co. Ltd., 1973; Deputy Chief Executive and Assistant Director, British Linen Bank Ltd. (subsidiary of Bank of Scotland), 1977; appointed Director, British Linen Bank Ltd., 1978; Divisional General Manager, Bank of Scotland International Division, 1980-84. Recreations: fishing; golf; bowls; gardening. Address: (b.) Bank of Scotland, The Mound, Edinburgh, EH1 1YZ; T.-031-243 5561.

Bentham, Professor Richard Walker, BA, LLB, Barrister. Professor of Petroleum and Mineral Law and Director of the Centre for Petroleum and Mineral Law Studies, Dundee University, since 1983; b. 26.6.30, Holywood, Co. Down; m., Stella Winifred Matthews; 1 d. Educ. Campbell College, Belfast; Trinity College, Dublin. Lecturer in Law: Tasmania University, Hobart, 1955-57; Sydney University, New South Wales, 1957-61; Legal Department, British Petroleum Co., 1961-83 (Deputy Legal Adviser to the Company, 1979-83). Council Member: British Branch, International Law Association; International Bar Association (Section on energy and natural resources law); elected FRSA, 1986. Recreations: cricket; military history and military modelling. Address: (h.) West Bryans, 87 Dundee Road, West Ferry, Dundee; T.-0382 77100.

Berry, Professor David Richard, MA, MSc, PhD, DSc, CBiol, FIBiol. Professor, Department of Bioscience and Biotechnology, Strathclyde University; b. 1.3.41, Huddersfield; m., Elisabeth Ann; 1 s.; 1 d. Educ. Holme Valley Grammar School; St. Peter's College, Oxford. Scientific Officer, Glaxo Ltd., Ulverston, 1962-64; graduate student, 1964-70; Lecturer, then Senior Lecturer, then Reader, Strathclyde University. Address: (b.) Department of Bioscience and Biotechnology, Strathclyde University, George Street, Glasgow; T.-041-552 4400.

Berry, John, CBE (1968), DL (Fife) (1969), BA (Cantab), MA (Cantab), PhD (St. Andrews) Hon. LLD Dundee (1970), FRSE (1936). Adviser and Consultant on environmental and wildlife conservation; b. 5.8.07, Edinburgh; m., Hon. Bride Fremantle; 2 s.; 1 d. Educ. Ardvreck School, Crieff; Eton College; Trinity College, Cambridge. Salmon Research Officer, Fishery Board for Scotland, 1930-31; Biological Research Station, University College, Southampton: Research Officer, 1932-36; Director, 1936-39; Chief Press Censor for Scotland, 1940-44; Biologist and Information Officer, North of Scotland Hydro-Electric Board, 1944-49; Director of Nature Conservation in Scotland, 1949-67; consultancy work since 1968. Honorary Life Member, Swiss League for Protection of Nature, 1946; founder Member (1948), International Union for Conservation of Natural Resources and first President, International Union Commission on Ecology; Member, Executive Board, International Waterfowl Research Bureau, 1963-72; Honorary Corresponding Member, Danish Natural History Society, since 1957; Vice-President and Honorary Life Fellow, Royal Zoological Society of Scotland, since 1959; Honorary Life Fellow: Wildfowl Trust, 1983; Glasgow Natural History Society, 1951; Member, Dundee University Court, 1970-78. Recreations: natural history (especially water birds and fish); music. Address: (h.) Tayfield, Newport-on-Tay, Fife, DD6 8HA; T.-0382 543118.

Berry, William, MA, LLB, WS, NP. Partner, Murray Beith & Murray, WS, Edinburgh, since 1967; Director: Scottish Life Assurance Co.; Scottish American Investment Co. Plc; Fleming Universal Investment Trust Plc; and other companies; b. 26.9.39, Newport-on-Tay; m., Elizabeth Margery; 2 s. Educ. Ardvreck, Crieff; Eton College; St. Andrews University; Edinburgh University. Interests in farming, forestry, etc. Member, Council/Board: Edinburgh Festival Society (Deputy Chairman, since 1985); New Town Concerts Society Ltd.; Thistle Foundation; New Club, Edinburgh; performer in three records of Scottish country dance music. Recreations: music; shooting; forestry. Address: (b.) 39 Castle Street, Edinburgh, EH2 3BH; T.-031-225 1200.

Besson, John Alexander Owen, BSc, MB, ChB, DPM, MRCPsych. Senior Lecturer in Mental Health, Aberdeen University, since 1985 (Wellcome Senior Lecturer, 1981-85); Honorary Consultant Psychiatrist, since 1981; b. 29.6.44, New Amsterdam, Guyana; m., Margaret Jean Adair. Educ. Edinburgh University. Consultant Psychiatrist, Lothian Health Board, 1977-80. Address: (b.) Department of Mental Health, University Medical Buildings, Foresterhill, Aberdeen; T.-Aberdeen 681818.

Best, Professor Jonathan James Kerle, MB, ChB, MSc, FRCPEdin, FRCR. Professor and Head, Department of Medical Radiology, Edinburgh University, since 1979; Honorary Consultant Radiologist, Lothian Health Board, since 1979; b. 29.11.42, Bristol; m., Elizabeth Margaret Frances McLean; 2 s.; 1 d. Educ. Kelly College; Edinburgh University; London University. Senior Registrar, Radiology, Hammersmith Hospital; Tutor in Radiology, Royal Post-Graduate Medical School; Senior Lecturer, Diagnostic Radiology, Manchester University; Honorary Consultant Radiologist, South Manchester District (Teaching). Address: (h.) 5 Merchiston Avenue, Edinburgh, EH10 4PJ; T.-031-229 6791.

Bevan-Baker, John Stewart, FRCO. Composer and freelance Musician; b. 3.5.26, Staines, Middlesex; m., June Mary Findlay; 1 s.; 4 d. Educ. Blundells School, Tiverton; Royal College of Music, London. Bevin boy, 1944-46; City Carillonneur, Aberdeen, 1958-63; Music Teacher in London, Aberdeen, Highlands of Scotland, and Glasgow. Recreations: gardening; reading; conservation. Address: (h.) 12 Academy Street, Fortrose, Ross-shire, IV10 8TW; T.-0381 20936.

Beveridge, George William, MB, ChB, FRCPE. Consultant Dermatologist, Edinburgh Royal Infirmary, since 1965; Honorary Senior Lecturer, Edinburgh University, since 1965; b. 23.2.32, Edinburgh; m., Janette Millar; 2 s.; 2 d. Educ. Dollar Academy; Edinburgh University. President, Scottish Dermatological Society, 1982-85; Elder, Church of Scotland. Recreations: golf; gardening. Address: (h.) 8 Barnton Park View, Edinburgh, EH4 6HJ.

Beveridge, John Lawrence, BSc, DipAgric(Cantab), MS (Iowa), MA. Deputy Principal, East of Scotland College of Agriculture, since 1986; b. 23.7.33, Glasgow; m., Margaret Ann; 1 s.; 2 d. Educ. Hillhead High School; Glasgow University;

Cambridge University; Iowa State University. Research Assistant, University College of North Wales, 1958-59; University Demonstrator, Cambridge University, 1959-65; Lecturer: West of Scotland Agricultural College, 1965-69, Edinburgh University, 1969-81; Assistant to Principal, East of Scotland College of Agriculture, 1981-86. Recreations: music; gardening; golf. Address: (h.) St Andrews, Duns Road, Gifford, Haddington, East Lothian, EH41 4QW; T.-062-081 694.

Bewick, James Thomas, MA. Rector, Morgan Academy, Dundee, 1970-87; b. 2.5.25, Glasgow; m., Jane C.B. Brash; 1 s.; 1 d. Educ. Albert Road Academy, Glasgow; Glasgow University. War Service, Royal Navy, 1943-46; Teacher of English, Wishaw High School, 1950-54; Principal Teacher of English, Gordon Schools, Huntly, 1954-61; Aberdeen Academy: Principal Teacher of English, 1961-68; Depute Rector, 1968-70. Member: Central Committee on English, 1966-71; Scottish Examination Board, 1981-84; 16 plus Action Plan Development Team, Inter-Disciplinary Studies, 1983-85; Board of Governors, Dundee College of Education, 1983-87; College Council, Dundee College of Commerce, 1981-86. Recreations: reading; pursuing an interest in the arts; gardening; travelling, particularly in France. Address: (h.) 6 Bingham Terrace, Dundee, DD4 7HH; T.-Dundee 455509.

Bewsher, Peter Dixon, MB, ChB, MD, FRCPE. Reader in Therapeutics, Aberdeen University, since 1977; Honorary Consultant Physician, Grampian Health Board, since 1969; b. 6.4.34, Cockermouth; m., Marlyn Crichton; 2 s.; 1 d. Educ. Cockermouth Grammar School; St. Andrews University. Medical Registrar, Aberdeen Hospitals; Research Associate, Indiana University; Lecturer, then Senior Lecturer in Therapeutics, Aberdeen University. Recreations: music; golf; hill-walking. Address: (h.) 83 Abbotshall Drive, Cults, Aberdeen, AB1 9JJ; T.-Aberdeen 868078.

Biddulph, Lord (Robert Micueal Christian); b. 6.1.31; m., Lady Mary Maitland; 2 s.; 1 d. Educ. Canford; RMA, Sandhurst; RAC, Circencester. 16th/5th Lancers; Lloyds of London; Roxburgh County Councillor; Sporting Manager and Partner. Recreations: shooting; fishing. Address: (h.) Makerstoun, Kelso, TD5 7PA; T.-05736 234.

Biggart, Samuel Douglas, BSc, ARCST. Managing Director, Strathclyde Chemical Co. Ltd., since 1962; Director, Paisley and Renfrew Enterprise Trust; Director, Renfrew Development Co.; b. 23.1.33, Glasgow; m., Aileen Guthrie Wilson; 2 s.; 1 d. Educ. Fettes College, Edinburgh; Royal College of Science and Technology. National Service, 1955-57; Trainee Manager, G. J. Weir, 1957-59; Management Consultant, Inbucon Ltd., 1959-62. Director, Glasgow Chamber of Commerce, 1986-87. Recreations: sailing; shooting; golf. Address: (h.) Glenshian, Newton of Beltrees, Lochwinnoch, Renfrewshire; T.-0505 842823.

Biggart, Thomas Norman, CBE (1984), WS. Partner, Biggart Baillie & Gifford, WS, Solicitors, Glasgow and Edinburgh, since 1959; b. 24.1.30; m., Eileen Jean Anne Gemmell; 1 s.; 1 d. Educ. Morrison's Academy, Crieff; Glasgow University. Royal Navy, 1954-56 (Sub-Lt., RNVR). Law Society of Scotland: Council Member, 1977-86; Vice-President, 1981-82; President, 1982-83; President, Business Archives Council, Scotland, 1977-86; Member, Executive, Scottish Council (Development and Industry), since 1984; Member, Scottish Tertiary Education Advisory Council, 1984-87; Member, Scottish Records Advisory Council, since 1985; Director: Clydesdale Bank, since 1985; New Scotland Insurance Group, since 1986; Honorary Member, American Bar Association, 1982; OStJ, 1968. Recreations: golf; hill-walking. Address: (h.) Gailes, Kilmacolm, Renfrewshire, PA13 4LZ; T.-Kilmacolm 2645.

Binns, John Kenneth, MB, ChB, FRCPEdin, FRCPsych. Physician Superintendent, Leverndale Hospital, Glasgow, since 1969 (Consultant Psychiatrist, since 1964); Honorary Clinical Lecturer, Glasgow University, since 1964; b. 25.6.28, Halifax; m., Sylvia Sharp; 1 s.; 1 d. Educ. Rishworth School, West Yorkshire; Edinburgh University. Fulbright Scholar and Rotating Intern., Erie, Pa., 1951-52; Medical Officer, RAMC, 11th Hussars, 1952-54; psychiatric training, Royal Edinburgh Hospital, 1956-64. Member of numerous professional committees at various times. Publication: Psychiatry in Medical Practice (Contributor). Recreations: gardening; photography. Address: (h.) 1 Balvie Avenue, Giffnock, Glasgow, G46 6NE.

Birnie, Rev. Charles John, MA. Minister of Aberdour linked with Tyrie, since 1982; b. 19.7.25, Kininmonth, Lonmay; m., Isabel Moir; 2 s.; 1 d. Educ. Peterhead Academy; Kings College, Aberdeen; Christs College, Aberdeen. Higher Diploma in Religious Education. Teacher of English, Bowmore, Islay, 1950-53; Head Teacher: Watten Primary School, Caithness, 1953-59; Melness Junior Secondary School, Sutherland, 1959-61; English-teaching posts in Banffshire, 1961-67; Minister, Annbank, Ayrshire, 1969-82. Publication: Makar's Quair anthology (Editor), 1968. Recreations: composition of original bothy ballads; collecting Scottish anecdotes; writing scripts featuring vocabulary and rural life of Buchan; country concerts. Address: The Manse, Tyrie, Fraserburgh, AB4 4DN; T.-Memsie 325.

Birnie, George David, BSc, PhD. Senior Scientist, Beatson Institute for Cancer Research, since 1969; Honorary Lecturer in Biochemistry, Glasgow University, since 1982; b. 8.8.34, Gourock; m., Jean Gray McCaig; 2 s.; 1 d. Educ. Gourock High School; Greenock High School; Glasgow University. Assistant Lecturer in Biochemistry, Glasgow University, 1959-60; Postdoctoral Fellow, McArdle Memorial Laboratory, University of Wisconsin, 1960-62; Scientist, Imperial Cancer Research Fund Laboratories, London, 1962-69. Kitchener Scholarship, 1952-56; Fulbright Travel Scholarship, 1960-62; US Public Health Service Fellowship, 1960-62; Member, Editorial Boards, British Journal of Cancer and Experimental Cell Biology; editor of five books, author of more than 100 papers. Deacon, Giffnock Congregational Church. Recreation: gardening. Address: (b.) Beatson Institute for Cancer Research, Garscube Estate, Switchback Road, Bearsden, Glasgow, G61 1BD; T.-041-942 9361.

Birss, Rev. Alan David, MA (Hons), BD (Hons). Minister, Paisley Abbey, since 1988; b. 5.6.53, Ellon; m., Carol Margaret Pearson. Educ. Glenrothes High School; St. Andrews University; Edinburgh University. Assistant Minister, Dundee Parish Church (St. Mary's), 1978-80; Minister, Inverkeithing Parish Church of St. Peter, 1982-88. Secretary, Scottish Church Society; Member, Council, Church Service Society. Address: The Manse of Paisley Abbey, 15 Main Road, Castlehead, Paisley, PA2 6AJ; T.-041-889 3587.

Bishop, Alan Henry, MA (Hons). Principal Establishment Officer, Scottish Office, since 1984; b. 12.9.29, Edinburgh; m., Marjorie Anne Conlan; 1 s.; 1 d. Educ. George Heriot's School, Edinburgh; Edinburgh University. Private Secretary to Parliamentary Under Secretaries of State for Scotland, 1958-59; Principal, Department of Agriculture and Fisheries for Scotland, 1959; First Secretary, Food and Agriculture, Copenhagen and The Hague, 1963-66; Assistant Secretary: Commission on the Constitution, 1969-73, Devolution Division, Scottish Office, 1973-76, Health Building and Liaison Divisions, SHHD, 1976-80; Assistant Under-Secretary of State, Scottish Office, London, 1980-84. President, Scottish Bridge Union, 1979-80. Recreation: contract bridge. Address: (b.) Scottish Office Personnel Divisions, 16 Waterloo Place, Edinburgh, EH1 3DN; T.-031-244 3938.

Bishop, Gordon, MA (Hons), DipEd. Head Teacher, Tarbert Academy, since 1984; Vice-Convener, EIS Central Advisory Committee for English, since 1981; b. 17.12.35, Glasgow; m., Jean Bonner; 2 s. Educ. Possil Senior Secondary School, Glasgow; Glasgow University. Taught in further education and schools, since 1966; Principal Teacher of English: Woodside Secondary School, Glasgow, 1972-75, Elgin Academy, 1975-77; Head Teacher, Tobermory High School, 1977-84. Recreations: golf; badminton; music; theatre. Address: (b.) Tarbert Academy, School Road, Tarbert, Argyll, PA29 6TE; T.-08802 269.

Bisset, Lt. Col. Alexander Galletly, FCIT. Secretary, Multiple Sclerosis Society in Scotland, since 1981; b. 5.10.30, Edinburgh; m., Elizabeth Margaret Bertram; 2 d. Educ. George Watson's College; Royal Military Academy, Sandhurst. Commissioned Royal Army Service Corps, 1951; transferred to Royal Corps of Transport, 1965; attached to Ministry of National Defence, Ottawa, 1971-73; commanded 151 (Greater London) Regiment RCT(V), 1974-77; staff, HQ Eastern District, 1977-80. Member, Committee on Mobility, Scottish Council on Disability; Elder, Cramond Kirk. Address: (b.) 27 Castle Street, Edinburgh, EH2 3DN; T.-031-225 3600.

Bisset, Rev. Peter Thomas, MA, BD. Evangelist, Church of Scotland, since 1974; Warden, St. Ninian's Training Centre, Crieff, since 1974; b. 16.6.27, Motherwell; m., Margaret Russell; 1 s.; 2 d. Educ. Rutherglen Academy; Glasgow University. Minister: Livingstone Church, Stevenston, 1953-60, Rutherford Church, Glasgow, 1960-68, High Church, Bathgate, 1968-74. Publications: Ten Growing Churches (Contributor); Prospects for Scotland (Contributor); The Kirk and Her Scotland. Recreations: music; walking. Address: St. Ninian's, Comrie Road, Crieff, Perthshire, PH7 4BG; T.-0764 3766/7.

Bissett, Norman, MA (Aberdeen), MPhil (Yale), MA (Lancaster). Representative, The British Council, Scotland, since 1984; b. 19.7.38, Burntisland, Fife; m., Faith Lillian Svajian; 3 s. Educ. Aberdeen Academy; Aberdeen University; Aberdeen College of Education; Yale; Lancaster University. British Council Lecturer, Beirut, 1965-66; Head of English Department, Faculty of Political Science, Ankara University, 1969-71; Director, Anglo-Uruguayan Cultural Institute, Montevideo, 1971-75; Director of Studies, British Institute, Barcelona, 1975-79; English Language Officer, The British Council, Egypt, 1980-84. Recreations: books; art; music; hill-walking. Address: (b.) The British Council, 3-4 Bruntsfield Crescent, Edinburgh, EH10 4HD; T.-031-447 4716.

Black, Antony, MA (Cantab), PhD (Cantab). Senior Lecturer in Political Science, Dundee University, since 1980; author; b. 23.6.36, Leeds; m., Sarah Kieme; 3 s.; 1 d. Educ. Shrewsbury School; King's College, Cambridge. Assistant Lecturer, Department of Political Science, Queen's College, Dundee, 1963-66; Lecturer, Department of Political Science, Dundee University, 1967-80; Visiting Associate Professor, School of Government and Public Administration, The American University, Washington, DC, 1975-76. Publications: Monarchy and Community: political ideas in the later conciliar movement (1430-50); Council and Commune: the Council of Basle and the 15th-century heritage; Guilds and civil society in European political thought from the 12th century to the present; State, Community and Human Desire. Recreation: hill-walking. Address: (b.) Department of Political Science, Dundee University, Dundee; T.-Dundee 23181, Ext. 4592.

Black, Hugh Blair, MA (Hons). Head Teacher, Greenock High School, 1968-85; Minister, Struthers Memorial Church, Greenock, since 1956; b. 22.7.22, Kilmacolm; m., Isobel B.M. Wright; 3 d. Educ. Greenock High School; Glasgow University; Jordanhill College of Education. History Teacher, latterly Principal Teacher of History, Port Glasgow High School, 1951-64; Head Teacher, Mount School, Greenock, 1964-68. Chairman, Central Committee on Social Subjects, seven years; Chairman, Social Subjects Centre, Jordanhill, seven years. Address: (h.) 27 Denholm Street, Greenock; T.-Greenock 87432.

Black, Professor Robert, QC, LLB (Hons), LLM. Professor of Scots Law, Edinburgh University, since 1981; Joint General Editor, The Laws of Scotland: Stair Memorial Encyclopaedia, since 1987; Temporary Sheriff, since 1981; b. 12.6.47, Lockerbie. Educ. Lockerbie Academy; Dumfries Academy; Edinburgh University; McGill University, Montreal. Advocate, 1972; Lecturer in Scots Law, Edinburgh University, 1972-75; Senior Legal Officer, Scottish Law Commission, 1975-78; practised at Scottish bar, 1978-81; QC, 1987. Publications: An Introduction to Written Pleading, 1982; Civil Jurisdiction: The New Rules, 1983. Recreations: beer and books, not necessarily in that order. Address: (h.) 6/4 Glenogle Road, Edinburgh, EH3 5HW; T.-031-557 3571.

Black, Robert William, MA (Hons, Econ), MSc (Town Planning), MSc (Public Policy). Chief Executive, Stirling District Council, since 1985; b. 6.11.46, Banff; m., Doreen Mary Riach; 3 s.; 1 d. Educ. Robert Gordon's College, Aberdeen; Aberdeen University; Heriot-Watt University; Strathclyde University. Nottinghamshire County Council, 1971-73; City of Glasgow Corporation, 1973-75; Strathclyde Regional Council, 1975-85. Fellow, Royal Statistical Society. Recreations: hill-walking; cycling; golf; swimming; music and art. Address: (b.) Municipal Chambers, Stirling, FK8 2HU; T.-Stirling 79000.

Blackie, John Walter Graham, BA (Cantab), LLB. Lecturer in Scots Law, Edinburgh University, since 1975; Director, Blackie & Son Ltd., publishers, since 1970; Advocate, since 1974; b. 2.10.46, Glasgow; m., Jane Ashman. Educ. Uppingham School; Peterhouse, Cambridge; Harvard; Merton College, Oxford; Edinburgh University. Open Exhibitioner, Peterhouse, Cambridge, 1965-68; St. Andrews Society of New York Scholar, Harvard, 1968-69; practised at Scottish bar, 1974-75. Recreation: music. Address: (h.) The Old Coach House, 23A Russell Place, Edinburgh, EH5 3HW; T.-031-552 3103.

Blacklaws, Allan Farquharson, OBE, CBIM, CIPM. Human Resource Consultant, since 1983 (Dunedin Management Services); b. 24.7.24, Glasgow; m., Sylvia Noble; 3 d. Educ. Whitehill School, Glasgow; University College, Swansea. Personnel Director, Scottish & Newcastle Breweries p.l.c., 1962-83; original Member, National Industrial Relations Court; Member: Employment Appeal Tribunal; ACAS Panel of Arbitrators. Recreation: bowls. Address: (h.) Craigmore House, 25 Craigmillar Park, Edinburgh, EH16 5PE; T.-031-667 3765.

Blacklock, Lt. Col. Michael David. Director of Marketing Services, National Trust for Scotland, since 1984; b. 30.4.28, London; m., Patricia Mary Ann Johnston; 1 s.; 1 d. Educ. Charterhouse; Royal Military Academy, Sandhurst. Regular Army Officer, Royal Scots Greys, 1948-72 (Instructor, Staff College, Camberley, 1967-68, Commanding Officer, Royal Scots Greys, 1969-71, Defence Fellowship, Edinburgh University, 1972); Development Secretary, National Trust for Scotland, 1973. Recreations: shooting; fishing. Address: (h.) Stable House, Maxton, St. Boswells, Roxburghshire; T.-0835 23024.

Blackwood, Robert Whyte. Honorary Sheriff-Substitute, North Strathclyde, since 1961; b. 14.5.07, Kilmarnock; m., Mary Hately Dinwoodie (deceased); 2 d. Educ. Kilmarnock Academy; Merchiston Castle School, Edinburgh; Leeds University. RAF, 1941-46; Member, Kilmarnock Town Council, 1947-51; Additional Commissioner for Income Tax, Cunninghame Sub-Division, Ayrshire, 1950-57; General Commissioner for Income Tax, Ayrshire Sub-Area of Strathclyde, 1957-82 (Chairman of Commissioners, 1974-82); Member, Advisory Committee, Kilmarnock, Trustee Savings Bank of Glasgow, 1950-75 (Chairman, 1961-65); Member, Valuation Appeals Committee, Ayrshire Sub-Area of Strathclyde, 1965-80; Director, Ayrshire Mission to the Deaf, 1966-81 (Chairman, 1974-80). Recreations: golf; fishing. Address: (h.) 3 Howard Street, Kilmarnock, KA1 2BP; T.-Kilmarnock 42834.

Blair, Alastair William, MB, ChB, FRCPE, DCH. Consultant Paediatrician, Fife Area Health Board, since 1970; Honorary Senior Lecturer: Department of Biochemistry and Microbiology, St. Andrews University, since 1975; Department of Child Life and Health, Edinburgh University, since 1979; Secretary, Scottish Paediatric Society, since 1987; b. 11.8.36, Preston; m., Irene Elizabeth McFee; 2 s. Educ. Harris Academy, Dundee; St. Andrews University. House Officer/Senior House Officer: Arbroath Infirmary; Maryfield Hospital, Dundee; Kings Cross Hospital, Dundee; Hospital for Sick Children, Great Ormond Street, London; Lecturer in Child Health, St. Andrews University; Registrar in Medical Paediatrics, Hospital for Sick Children, Great Ormond Street, London; Lecturer in Child Health, Aberdeen University; Wellcome-Swedish Research Fellow, Karolinska Children's Hospital, Stockholm; Senior Registrar in Paediatrics, Southmead Hospital, Bristol. Publication: Prenatal Paediatrics: a handbook for obstetricians and paediatricians (Co-author and Editor), 1971. Recreations: private aviation; camping; restoring old property; sailing; jazz. Address: (h.) Bellcraig Farm, by Leslie, Fife, KY6 3JE; T.-0592 741754.

Blair, James Eric, BL. Solicitor, since 1948; Honorary Sheriff, since 1980; b. 18.3.23, Airdrie. Educ. Glasgow Academy; Glasgow University. Member, Executive Committee, Abbeyfield Airdrie Society; Past Captain, Airdrie Golf Club. Recreation: golf. Address: (h.) Dunedin, Forrest Street, Airdrie.

Blair, John Samuel Greene, OBE (Mil), TD, OStJ, BA, ChM, FRCSEdin, FICS, D(Obst)RCOG. Consultant Surgeon, Perth Royal Infirmary, since 1966; Honorary Senior Lecturer in Surgery, Dundee University, since 1967; Vice President, Scottish Society of the History of Medicine, since 1987; b. 31.12.28, Wormit, Fife; m., Ailsa Jean Bowes; 2 s.; 1 d. Educ. Dundee High School; St. Andrews University. National Service, RAMC, 1952-55; Tutor, Department of Anatomy, St. Salvator's College, St. Andrews, 1955; surgical and research training, Manchester, Dundee, Cambridge, London, 1957-65; Member, Court of Examiners, Royal College of Surgeons of Edinburgh, 1965; postgraduate Clinical Tutor, Perth, 1966-74; first North American Travelling Fellow, St. Andrews/Dundee Universities, 1971; TA Advisor to various Army Medical Ministry of Defence Departments, 1973-79; Secretary, Tayside Area Medical Advisory Committee, 1974-83; Member, Education Advisory Committee, Association of Surgeons, 1984-88; Secretary, Perth and Kinross Division, British Medical Association, 1982; Member, Scottish Council and Chairman's Sub-Committee, BMA, 1985-88; Honorary Colonel (TA), RAMC; Elder, Church of Scotland. Publications: books on medical history and anatomy. Recreations: golf; history; travel; bridge. Address: (h.) 143 Glasgow Road, Perth; T.-Perth 23739.

Blair, John Woodman, BA (Oxon), LLB, WS. Solicitor; b. 25.1.37, Edinburgh; m., Claire Lucy Ford; 1 s.; 2 d. Educ. Radley College; BNC, Oxford; Edinburgh University. National Service, Scots Guards; Partner, Strathern & Blair, WS; Senior Partner; Director, British Investment Trust. Recreations: gardening; pigeon racing. Address: (h.) Clint, Dunbar, East Lothian.

Blair, Robin Leitch, MB, ChB, FRCSEdin, FRCS(C), FACS. Head, Department of Otolaryngology, Dundee University, since 1984; Consultant Otolaryngologist, Tayside Health Board, since 1984; b. 28.11.45, Gourock; m., Elizabeth Anne White; 2 d. Educ. Greenock Academy; Edinburgh University; University of Toronto. House Surgeon, Royal Infirmary, Edinburgh; Lecturer, Department of Anatomy, Glasgow University; Assistant Professor, Department of Otolaryngology, University of Toronto. Address: (b.) Department of Otolaryngology, Ninewells Hospital and Medical School, Dundee, DD1 9SY; T.-0382 60111, Ext. 2726.

Blair, Robin Orr, MA, LLB, WS. Executive Partner, Dundas & Wilson, CS, since 1988. Educ. Rugby School; St. Andrews University; Edinburgh University. Partner, Dundas & Wilson, since 1967; Honorary Secretary, Association of Edinburgh Royal Tradesmen. Address: (b.) 25 Charlotte Square, Edinburgh, EH2 4EZ; T.-031-225 1234.

Blair, Rev. Thomas James Loudon, MA, BD. Minister, Galston Parish Church, since 1980; Clerk, Irvine and Kilmarnock Presbytery, since 1985; b. 24.7.40, Glasgow; m., Patricia Anne Bell; 1 s.; 2 d. Educ. Hutchesons' Grammar School, Glasgow; Glasgow University. Minister: Campsie Trinity and Milton of Campsie, 1965-71; Wallacetown Parish Church, Dundee, 1971-80; Mid Craigie Parish Church, Dundee (temporarily linked with Wallacetown), 1975-80. Recreations: golf; reading. Address: The Manse, Galston, Ayrshire; T.-Galston 820246.

Blair-Cunynghame, Sir James (Ogilvy), Kt (1976), OBE, FBIM, CIPM, FIB, MA; b. 28.2.13. Educ. Sedbergh School; King's College, Cambridge. Served World War II, RA and Intelligence, Mediterranean and Europe; Lt.-Col., 1944. Chairman, Royal Bank of Scotland Group plc, 1968-78; Chairman, Royal Bank of Scotland plc, 1971-76; Chairman, Williams & Glyn's Bank plc, 1976-78; Deputy Chairman, Provincial Insurance plc, since 1979; Member, Queen's Bodyguard for Scotland (Royal Company of Archers); Hon. LLD, St. Andrews, 1965; Hon. DSc (SocSci), Edinburgh, 1969; Hon. FRCSEd, 1978.

Blair-Kerr, Sir Alastair, KB (1973), MA, LLB. President of the Court of Appeal for Bermuda, since 1979; President of the Court of Appeal for the Bahamas, 1978-81; Member, Gilbraltar Court of Appeal, 1981-86; b. 1.12.11, Killin, Perthshire; m., Esther Margaret Fowler Wright; 1 s.; 1 d. Educ. McLaren High School, Callander; Edinburgh University. Solicitor, 1939; Advocate, Scots bar, 1951; Advocate and Solicitor, Singapore, 1939-41; Straits Settlements Volunteer Force, 1941-42; escaped from Singapore, 1942; Indian Army: Staff Capt., "A" Bombay District HQ, 1942-43; DAAG 107 Line of Communication area HQ, Poona, 1943-44; British Army: GS02, War Office, 1944-45; SO1 Judicial, BMA Malaya, 1945-46; Colonial Legal Service (HM Overseas Service), Hong Kong: Magistrate, 1946-48; Crown Counsel, 1949; President, Tenancy Tribunal, 1950; Crown Counsel, 1951-53; Senior Crown Counsel, 1953-59; District Judge, 1959-61; Puisne Judge, Supreme Court, 1961-71; Senior Puisne Judge, Supreme Court, 1971-73; Acting Chief Justice of Hong Kong; President, various commissions of inquiry. Recreations: music; walking. Address: Gairn, Kinbuck, Dunblane, Perthshire, FK15 ONQ; T.-0786 823377.

Blake, Professor Christopher, FRSE, MA, PhD. Bonar Professor of Applied Economics, Dundee University, 1974-88; Chairman, Glenrothes Development Corporation, since 1987; b. 28.4.26; m.; 2 s.; 2 d. Educ. Dollar Academy; St. Andrews University. Royal Navy, 1944-47; teaching posts, 1951-53; Assistant, Edinburgh University, 1953-55; Stewarts & Lloyds Ltd., 1955-60; Lecturer, then Senior Lecturer, St. Andrews University, 1960-67; Senior Lecturer, then Professor of Economics, Dundee University, 1967-74; Director, Alliance Trust plc, since 1974; Director, William Low & Co. plc, since 1980 (Chairman, since 1985). Recreation: golf. Address: (h.) Westlea, Wardlaw Gardens, St. Andrews, Fife, KY16 9DW.

Blakey, Rev. Ronald Stanton, MA, BD, MTh. Deputy Secretary, Department of Education, Church of Scotland, since 1981; Secretary, Assembly Council, from 1 Aug., 1988; b. 3.7.38, Glasgow; m., Kathleen Dunbar; 1 s. Educ. Hutchesons' Boys' Grammar School, Glasgow; Glasgow University. Minister: St. Mark's, Kirkconnel, 1963-67; Bellshill West, 1967-72; Jedburgh Old Parish with Edgerston and Ancrum, 1972-81. Member, Roxburgh District Council, 1974-80 (Chairman of Council, 1977-80); Religious Adviser, Border Television, 1973-81; Member, Borders Region Children's Panel, 1974-80; JP, 1974-80. Publication: The Man in the Manse, 1978. Recreation: collecting antiquarian books on Scotland. Address: (h.) Flat 3, 21 Stuart Crescent, Edinburgh, EH12 8XR.

Blanche, John Jamieson, CA. Director, Allied Lyons PLC; Chairman: William Teacher & Sons Ltd., since 1985, Allied Distillers Limited; Director, Hiram Walker/Allied Vintners Limited; b. 10.7.29, Paisley; m., Fiona; 1 s.; 1 d. Educ. Glasgow Academy; Strathallan School. Hardie Caldwell, CA, Glasgow, 1954-56; Sales Manager, J.J. Blanche & Co. Ltd., 1956-60; Divisional Manager, Victoria Wine Co. Ltd., 1960-69; Financial Director, William Grant & Sons (Standfast) Ltd., 1967-85; Chairman and Managing Director, Stewart & Son of Dundee, 1969-79; Managing Director, William Teacher & Sons Ltd., 1979-85. Governor, Strathallan School; Council Member, Scotch Whisky Association; Scottish Council Member, CBI; President, Junior Chamber Scotland, 1967. Recreations: golf; camping; hill-walking; gardening. Address: (b.) 14 St. Enoch Square, Glasgow, G1 4BZ; T.-041-204 2633.

Blaxter, Professor John Harry Savage, MA (Oxon), DSc (Oxon), FRSE. Deputy Chief Scientific Officer, Scottish Marine Biological Association, Oban, since 1985; Reader, then Hon. Professor, Stirling University, since 1969; b. 6.1.29, London;

m., Valerie Ann McElligott; 1 s.; 1 d. Educ. Berkhamsted School; Brasenose College, Oxford. SO, then SSO, Marine Laboratory, Aberdeen, 1952-64; Lecturer, Zoology Department, Aberdeen University, 1964-69; PSO, 1969, SPSO, 1974, Scottish Marine Biological Association, Oban. Recreations: sailing; gardening. Address: (h.) Letterwalton House, Ledaig, Oban, PA37 1RY; T.-0631 72206.

Blight, David Philip, BSc, MSc, PhD, CEng, FIMechE, FIAgrE, FSA Scot, FRSA. Managing Director, CH-Farms Ltd.; Director, Scottish Institute of Agricultural Engineering, 1977-87; b. 25.3.30, Truro; m., Catherine Montgomery; 2 d. Educ. St. Austell County Grammar School; Reading University; Durham University; King's College, Newcastle-upon-Tyne. Research Assistant, King's College, Newcastle-upon-Tyne, 1953-55; Scottish station, National Institute of Agricultural Engineering: Scientific Officer/Senior Scientific Officer, 1955-66; Head of Cultivations and Farm Transport section, 1966-71; Head of Agricultural Department, Scottish Institute of Agricultural Engineering, 1971-77. Recreations: genealogy; history of technology; photography. Address: (h.) 4 Midmar Gardens, Edinburgh, EH10 6DZ; T.-031-447 4540; (b.) CH-Farms Ltd., 18 Woodside Crescent, Glasgow, G3 7UU; T.-041-332 9755.

Blyth, Professor Thomas Scott, BSc, DSc (St. Andrews), D-es-Sc (Paris), FRSE, FIMA. Professor of Pure Mathematics, St. Andrews University, since 1977; b. 3.7.38, Newburgh, Fife; m., Jane Ellen Christine Pairman; 1 d. Educ. Bell-Baxter High School, Cupar; St. Andrews University. NATO Research Scholar, Sorbonne, 1960-63; St. Andrews University: Lecturer in Mathematics, 1963-72, Senior Lecturer, 1972-73, Reader, 1973-76; Visiting Lecturer, University of Western Australia, 1966; Visiting Professor, University of Western Ontario, 1968-69. Past President, Edinburgh Mathematical Society; former Executive Editor, Proceedings A, Royal Society of Edinburgh; Corresponding Member, Royal Society of Sciences of Liege. Publications: Residuation Theory (Co-author), 1972; Set Theory and Abstract Algebra, 1975; Module Theory, 1977; Algebra Through Practice, Books 1 to 6 (Co-author), 1984-85; Categories, 1986; Essential Student Algebra, Volumes 1 to 5 (Co-author), 1986. Address: (h.) Wheaton Cottage, 4 Main Street, Strathkinness, Fife, KY16 9RU; T.-0334 85661.

Blyth, William, MA, LLB, BCom, SSC, NP. Director of Administration, City of Edinburgh District Council, since 1980; b. 3.8.37, Kirkcaldy; m., Anna Cecilia; 2 s.; 1 d. Educ. George Heriot's School, Edinburgh; Edinburgh University. Edinburgh Corporation: Head of Conveyancing and Contracts, 1971; Senior Depute Director of Administration, 1974. Recreation: gardening. Address: City Chambers, High Street, Edinburgh; T.-031-225 2424.

Boag, Archibald, BSc. Rector, Lossiemouth High School, since 1973; b. 1.7.31, Ardnadam, Dunoon; m., Fiona Wilson Mackenzie; 2 s. Educ. Dunoon Grammar School; Glasgow University; Jordanhill College of Education. National Service, 2nd Lt., Royal Artillery, 1955-57; Teacher of Mathematics and Science, Dunoon Grammar School, 1957-61; Principal Teacher of Mathematics, Bankhead Academy, Bucksburn, 1961-73. Publication: Mathematics for General Education (Chairman of Joint Authors). Recreations: bridge; bowling; sailing. Address: (h.) Torfness, James Street, Lossiemouth, Moray, IV31 6QZ; T.-034 381 2544.

Boag, Hugh Alexander, MA, DipEd, MLitt. Senior Lecturer in German, Strathclyde University, since 1972; b. 10.12.30, Glasgow; m., 1, Alexandrina Milligan (deceased); 1 s.; 1 d.; 2, Patricia Smith. Educ. Woodside School; Glasgow University; Jordanhill College of Education. Flt. Lt., RAF, 1955-58 (Air Ministry Examiner for Scotland and Northern Ireland); school teacher, Glasgow Corporation, 1958-62; Lecturer in Modern Languages, Scottish College of Commerce, 1962-64; Lecturer in German, Strathclyde University, 1964-72. Past Chairman, Hyndland Residents' Association; Chairman, St. Andrew Society of Glasgow, since 1980. Recreations: swimming; hill-walking. Address: (h.) 16 Kirklee Road, Glasgow, G12 0ST.

Boddy, Francis Andrew, MB, ChB, FRCPEdin, FFCM, DPH. Director, Social Paediatric and Obstetric Research Unit, Glasgow University, since 1978; b. 1.3.35, York; m., Adele Wirszubska; 2 d. Educ. Prince Henry's Grammar School, Otley; Edinburgh University. Research Associate, New York City Department of Health; Senior Lecturer, Department of Community Medicine, Glasgow University. Honorary Secretary, Society for Social Medicine, 1982-87. Publication: General Practice Medicine (Co-Editor), 1975. Recreations: fishing; photography. Address: (b.) 1 Lilybank Gardens, Glasgow, G12; T.-041-339 3118.

Boe, Norman W., LLB (Hons). Deputy Solicitor to Secretary of State for Scotland, since 1987; b. 30.8.43, Glasgow; m., Margaret; 1 s.; 1 d. Educ. George Heriot's School, Edinburgh; Edinburgh University. Legal apprenticeship, Lindsays WS, 1965-67; Legal Assistant, Menzies & White, WS, 1967-70; Office of Solicitor, Scottish Office: Legal Assistant, 1970, Senior Legal Assistant, Divisional Solicitor. Recreations: golf; dog-walking; holidaying. Address: (b.) New St. Andrew's House, Edinburgh; T.-031-244 4884.

Bogle, Rev. Thomas Cranston, BD, CPS, HDipREd. Minister, Parishes of Lochside and Terregles, Dumfries, since 1986; b. 7.7.39, Hawick; m.; 1 s.; 3 d. Educ. Hawick High School; St. Andrews University; Edinburgh University; Moray House College of Education. Teacher, Donaldson's School, 1964-65; Youth Leader, Govan Old, 1965-66; Moray House, 1970-71; Teacher, Westwood, Easterhouse, 1971-77; Headmaster/Missionary, Out Skerries, 1977-83; Minister, Selkirk Heatherlie with Caddonfoot, 1983-86. Recreations: shouting at referees; learning languages. Address: (h.) 27 St. Anne's Road, Dumfries; T.-Dumfries 52912.

Bold, Alan. Writer; b. 20.4.43, Edinburgh; m., Alice Howell; 1 d. Educ. Broughton Secondary School; Edinburgh University. Full-time writer and visual artist since 1966; has published numerous books of poetry including: To Find the New;

The State of the Nation; a selection in Penguin Modern Poets 15; In This Corner: Selected Poems 1963-83; collaborated on A Celtic Quintet, Haven and Homage to MacDiarmid; Editor, numerous anthologies, including: The Penguin Book of Socialist Verse; The Martial Muse; Cambridge Book of English Verse 1939-75; Making Love; The Bawdy Beautiful; Mounts of Venus; Drink To Me Only; The Poetry of Motion; books of criticism including: Thom Gunn & Ted Hughes; George Mackay Brown; The Ballad; Modern Scottish Literature; MacDiarmid: The Terrible Crystal; Muriel Spark; MacDiarmid: A Critical Biography; Editor: The Thistle Rises: a MacDiarmid Miscellany; The Letters of Hugh MacDiarmid; has exhibited Illuminated Poems in a variety of venues; regular contributor to Glasgow Herald, and occasionally to The Scotsman, New Statesman, Times Literary Supplement, and Tribune. Recreations: walking; playing alto saxophone; watching films; gardening. Address: (h.) Balbirnie Burns East Cottage, near Markinch, Glenrothes, Fife, KY7 6NE; T.-0592 757216.

Bolton, Lyndon, Managing Director: Alliance Trust PLC, Dundee, Second Alliance Trust PLC; b. 24.1.37, London; m., Rosemary Jane Toler Mordaunt; 2 s. Educ. Wellington College; Royal Military Academy, Sandhurst. National Service, Royal Artillery, 1955-57; Deloitte Plender Griffiths & Co., London, 1957-63; Alliance Trust, Dundee, since 1964; Trustee, Trustee Savings Bank, 1963-83; Board Member, TSB Group, 1979-83; Director, TSB Group and TSB Scotland, since 1983; Director, General Accident Fire and Life Assurance Corporation PLC, since 1982. Governor, Dundee College of Education, 1980-85; Member of Court, Dundee University, since 1985. Recreations: sailing; golf; fishing; painting. Address: (h.) Arrat's Mill, Brechin, Angus, DD9 7PR; T.-Bridge of Dun 220.

Bonallack, Michael Francis, OBE. Secretary, Royal and Ancient Golf Club of St. Andrews, since 1983; b. 31.12.34; m., Angela Ward; 1 s.; 3 d. British Amateur Champion, 1961-65-68-69-70; Captain, Walker Cup Team, 1971; Chairman, Golf Foundation, 1977-83; President, English Golf Union, 1982.

Bond, Professor Michael R., MD, PhD, FRCSEdin, FRCPsych, FRCPSGlas, DPM. Professor of Psychological Medicine, Glasgow University, since 1973; b. 15.4.36, Balderton, Nottinghamshire; m., Jane; 1 s.; 1 d. Educ. Magnus Grammar School, Newark; Sheffield University. Vice-Principal, Glasgow University; sub-committees, University Grants Committee; Councillor, International Association for the Study of Pain. Recreations: reading; music; painting. Address: (b.) 6 Whittinghame Gardens, Great Western Road, Glasgow; T.-041-334 9826.

Bone, Ian, MB, ChB, FRCP. Consultant Neurologist, Institute of Neurological Sciences, Glasgow, since 1978; Honorary Clinical Lecturer, Glasgow University, since 1978; b. 10.12.45, Reading; m., Isabel Drummond; 1 s.; 2 d. Educ. Bradfield College; St. Andrews University. Lecturer in Neurology, Leeds University, 1976-78. Publications: Neurology and Neurosurgery Illustrated (Co-author); papers on infective, vascular and degenerative diseases of the nervous system. Recreations: opera; cinema; detective novels; watching sport. Address: (h.) 11 Herries Road, Glasgow, G41 4DE; T.-041-423 6992.

Bone, Thomas R., CBE, MA, MEd, PhD, FCCEA. Principal, Jordanhill College of Education, since 1972; Chairman, Council for National Academic Awards Committee for Teacher Education, since 1987; Vice-Chairman, General Teaching Council for Scotland, since 1986; b. 2.1.35, Port Glasgow; m., Elizabeth Stewart; 1 s.; 1 d. Educ. Port Glasgow High School; Greenock High School; Glasgow University; Jordanhill College. Teacher of English, Paisley Grammar School, 1957-62; Lecturer in Education, Jordanhill College, 1962-63; Lecturer in Education, Glasgow University, 1963-67; Head of Education Department, Jordanhill College, 1967-71. Member, Dunning Committee, 1975-77; Chairman, Educational Advisory Council, IBA, 1985-88; Vice-Chairman: Scottish Examination Board, 1977-84; Scottish Tertiary Education Advisory Council, 1984-87; Chairman: Scottish Council for Educational Technology, 1981-87; Standing Conference on Studies in Education, 1982-84; Council for National Academic Awards Board for Organisation and Management, 1983-87. Publication: School Inspection in Scotland, 1968. Recreation: golf. Address: (b.) Jordanhill College of Education, Southbrae Drive, Glasgow, G13 1PP; T.-041-959 1232.

Boney, Professor Arthur Donald, BSc, PhD, DSc, CBiol, FIBiol, FRSE, FLS. Emeritus Professor of Botany, Glasgow University, since 1984; b. 31.5.25, Plymouth; m., Rosemary Mavis Hocking; 2 s. Educ. Plympton Grammar School, Devon; Plymouth College of Technology; University College, Exeter. Assistant Master, Tamar Secondary School, Plymouth, 1948-50; Lecturer, Plymouth College of Technology, 1950-63; Lecturer, then Senior Lecturer, Department of Botany, University College of Wales, Aberystwyth, 1963-69; Senior Lecturer, then Reader, then Professor, Department of Botany, Glasgow University, 1969-84. British Phycological Society: Council Member at various times; Honorary Secretary, 1971-75, Vice-President, 1976-78, President, 1978-80; Member, Committee of Management, University Marine Biological Station, Millport, 1970-75; Council Member, Scottish Marine Biological Association, 1980-82, 1983-85. Recreations: walking; reading. Address: (h.) 15 Falkland Street, Glasgow, G12 9PY; T.-041-339 3333.

Bonnar, Anne Elizabeth, MA. General Manager, Traverse Theatre, since 1986; b. 9.10.55, St. Andrews; m., Fernley Thompson; 1 s.; 1 d. Educ. Dumbarton Academy; Glasgow University; City University, London; Jordanhill College of Education. Theatre Manager, Young Vic Theatre, London, 1980; Director, Circuit, 1982, 1983; Press and Publicity, Mayfest, 1984, 1985; Publicity Officer, Citizens' Theatre, Glasgow, 1981-85; Arts Public Relations Consultant, 1985-86. Address: (b.) Traverse Theatre, 112 West Bow, Grassmarket, Edinburgh; T.-031-226 2633.

Bonnar, George Coutts, BSc (Hons), MSc, TEng, MIProdE. Depute Principal, West Lothian College of Further Education, since 1980; b. 22.2.36,

Motherwell; m., Cecilia W.; 1 s.; 1 d. Educ. Wishaw High School; Strathclyde University; Birmingham University. Apprentice draughtsman/design engineer, then Assistant to Services Engineer, Colvilles Ltd., Motherwell, 1953-62; Assistant Teacher, Coatbridge Technical College, 1962-65; Senior Assistant Teacher, then Head of Engineering Department, Bathgate Technical College, 1965-73; Depute Principal, Galashiels College of FE, 1973-80. Recreations: Sunday School superintendent; Rugby Club supporter. Address: (h.) Beechwood, 12 Muir Road, Bathgate, West Lothian; T.-0506 55125.

Bonner, Geoff, BSc, MRTPI. Assistant Chief Executive, Highland Regional Council, since 1986; b. 13.1.54, Luton; m., Sandy; 1 s.; 1 d. Educ. Luton Grammar School; Luton VI Form College; University of Aston in Birmingham; City of Birmingham Polytechnic. Planning Assistant, Luton Borough Council, 1975-79; Principal Planning Assistant, West Midlands County Council, 1979-85; Assistant Executive, West Midlands County Council, 1985-86. Secretary, Scottish Sub-Committee of the European Bureau for Lesser-Used Languages; Member, Steering Committee, Local Government Chronicle Management Game. Recreation: dabbling. Address: (b.) Regional Buildings, Glenurquhart Road, Inverness; T.-0463 234121.

Bonney, Norman Leonard, BSc (Econ), MA, PhD. Member, Aberdeen City Council, since 1974 (Convenor, Town Planning Committee, 1981-85); Lecturer, Aberdeen University, since 1971; m., 4.3.44, Great Yarmouth; 1 s.; 2 d. Educ. Great Yarmouth Grammar School; London School of Economics; Chicago University. Research Scientist, Institute of Juvenile Research, Chicago, 1968-71. Member: Executive Committee, Scottish Council (Development and Industry), 1974-84; Planning Committee, COSLA, 1981-85; Management Committee, Planning Exchange, 1981-85. Recreations: walking; swimming; tennis. Address: (b.) Department of Sociology, Edward Wright Building, Aberdeen University, Aberdeen; T.-0224 272760.

Bonomy, John, MA, LLB. Chief Executive and Director of Administration, Motherwell District Council, since 1983; b. 25.4.38, Motherwell; m., Isabella Margaret; 3 s. Educ. Dalziel High School, Motherwell; Glasgow University. Depute Town Clerk: Arbroath, 1966; Motherwell and Wishaw, 1966-74; Director of Administration, Motherwell, 1974-83. Recreations: golf; reading. Address: (b.) Civic Centre, Motherwell; T.-Motherwell 66166.

Borley, Lester. Director, National Trust for Scotland, since 1983; b. 7.4.31; m.; 3 d. Educ. Dover Grammar School; London University. Chief Executive, Scottish Tourist Board, 1970-75; Chief Executive, English Tourist Board, 1975-83.

Borthwick, Professor Edward Kerr, MA (Aberdeen), MA, PhD (Cantab). Professor of Greek, Edinburgh University, since 1980; b. 9.6.25, Aberdeen; m., Betty Jean Orton; 2 s.; 1 d. Educ. Aberdeen Grammar School; Aberdeen University; Christ's College, Cambridge. Croom Robertson Fellow, Aberdeen University, 1948-51; Lecturer in Classics, Leeds University, 1951-55; Edinburgh University: Lecturer in Greek, 1955-67, Senior Lecturer, 1967-70, Reader, 1970-80. Recreations: music; tennis; golf. Address: (h.) 9 Corrennie Drive, Edinburgh, EH10 6EQ; T.-031-447 2369.

Borthwick of that Ilk, Lord (John Henry Stuart Borthwick), TD (1943), GCLJ, DL, JP. 23rd Lord Borthwick; Baron of Heriotmuir, Borthwick and Locherwart; Chairman: Heriotmuir Properties Ltd., since 1965; Heriotmuir Exporters Ltd., since 1972; Director, Ronald Morrison & Co. Ltd., since 1972; b. 13.9.05, Borthwick; m., Margaret Frances Cormack (deceased); 2 s. Educ. Fettes College, Edinburgh; King's College, Newcastle-upon-Tyne. Diploma in Agriculture. Formerly RATA, re-employed 1939; served NW Europe, Allied Military Government Staff (Junior Staff College, SO 2), 1944; CCG (CO 1, Lt.-Col.), 1946; Department of Agriculture for Scotland, 1948-50; farming own farms, 1950-71; National Farmers Union of Scotland: Midlothian Branch Committee, 1963; Mid and West Lothian Area Committee, 1967-73 (President, 1970-72); Council Member, 1968-72; Member: Lothians Area Committee, NFU Mutual Insurance Society, 1969-85; Chairman, Monitoring Committee, Scottish Tartans, 1976; Scottish Southern Regional Committee, Wool Marketing Board, 1966-85; Chairman, Area Committee, South of Scotland Electricity Board Consultative Council, 1972-76; Member, Midlothian County Council, 1937-50; Member: Local Appeal Tribunal (Edinburgh and the Lothians), 1963-75; Midlothian Valuation Appeal Committee, 1966; Member: Standing Council of Scottish Chiefs; The Committee of the Baronage of Scotland; Member Corresponding, Istituto Italiano di Genealogie e Araldica, Rome and Madrid, 1964; Honorary Member: Council of Scottish Clans Association, USA, 1975; Royal Military Institute of Canada, 1976; Kt of Justice and Honour, GCLJ (Grand Croix, 1975); CL (Commander of the Rose of Lippe), 1971; NN, 1982. Recreations: shooting; travel; history. Address: Crookston, Heriot, Midlothian, EH38 5YS; T.-Heriot 232.

Bosomworth, Marjorie Douglas, MA (Hons). Head Mistress, St. Margaret's School, Aberdeen, since 1970; b. 4.10.28, Glasgow. Educ. Glasgow High School for Girls; Glasgow University. Albert Senior Secondary School, 1951-53; Jordanhill College School, 1953-57; Hamilton Academy, 1957-65; Golspie High School/Girls' Hostel, 1965-70. Member, Aberdeen Committee, Save the Children Fund; Burgess, Guild of Aberdeen. Recreations: music; gardening. Address: (b.) St. Margaret's School for Girls, 17 Albyn Place, Aberdeen, AB9 1RH; T.-0224 584466.

Bouchier, Professor Ian Arthur Dennis, MB, ChB, MD, FRCP, FRCPEdin, FRSE. Professor of Medicine, Edinburgh University, since 1986; b. 7.9.32, Cape Town, South Africa; m., Patricia Norma Henshilwood; 2 s. Educ. Rondebosch Boys High School; Cape Town University. Instructor in Medicine, School of Medicine, Boston University, 1964; London University: Senior Lecturer in Medicine, 1965; Reader in Medicine, 1970; Professor of Medicine, Dundee University, 1973-86. Member: Court, Dundee University; Chief Scientist Committee, Scotland; Council,

Royal Society, Edinburgh; Medical Research Council; Secretary General, World Organization of Gastroenterology; former Dean, Faculty of Medicine and Dentistry, Dundee University; Chairman, Education Committee, British Society of Gastroenterology. Publications: Clinical Skills (2nd edition), 1982; Gastroenterology (3rd edition), 1982; Textbook of Gastroenterology, 1984; Inflammatory Bowel Disease, 1986. Recreations: music; history of whaling; cooking. Address: (b.) Department of Medicine, Royal Infirmary, Edinburgh, EH3 9YW; T.-031-229 2477, Ext. 2055.

Boulton, Frank Ernest, BSc, MB, BS, MD, FRCPath. Deputy Director, Edinburgh Regional Blood Transfusion Service, since 1981; b. 25.5.41, Ashford, Middlesex; m., Elizabeth Ruth Westcott (deceased); 4 s. Educ. Godalming County Grammar School; St. Thomas's Hospital Medical School, London University. Pre-registration House Officer, London and Portmouth, 1966-67; Casualty Officer, Birmingham Accident Hospital, 1967; Trainee Pathologist (Lecturer), St. Thomas's Hospital, 1967-70; Senior Lecturer (Haematology), London Hospital Medical College, 1971-75; Senior Lecturer and Consultant Haematologist, Liverpool University and Hospitals, 1975-80. Chairman, Edinburgh Branch, and former Member, UK National Executive, Medical Campaign Against Nuclear Weapons; Member, Executive Group, Centre for Human Ecology, Edinburgh University. Recreation: music (player of trombone and clarinet). Address: (h.) 83 West Castle Road, Edinburgh, EH10 5AU.

Bovey, Keith S., BL. Solicitor, since 1951; President, Scottish CND; b. 31.7.27, Renfrew; m., Helen Cameron; 1 s.; 1 d. Educ. Paisley Grammar School; Glasgow University. Army, 1944-48. Publication: Misuse of Drugs, A Handbook for Lawyers. Address: (b.) 313 Byres Road, Glasgow, G12 8UH; T.-041-339 8474.

Bowen, Sheriff Edward Farquharson, TD, LLB. Sheriff of Tayside, Central and Fife, at Dundee, since 1983; b. 1.5.45, Edinburgh; m., Patricia Margaret Brown; 2 s.; 2 d. Educ. Melville College, Edinburgh; Edinburgh University. Admitted Solicitor, 1968; Advocate, 1970; Standing Junior Counsel, Scottish Education Department, 1976; Advocate Depute, 1979-83. Served RAOC TA/TAVR, 1964-80. Recreation: golf. Address: (h.) Westgate, 12 Glamis Drive, Dundee.

Bowen, Stanley, CBE (1972). Honorary Sheriff, Lothian and Borders, since 1975; b. 4.8.10, Carnoustie; m., Mary Shepherd Greig; 2 s.; 1 d. Educ. Barry School, Angus; Grove Academy, Dundee; University College, Dundee. Qualified as Solicitor in Scotland, 1932; entered Procurator Fiscal service, 1933; Depute Procurator Fiscal, Hamilton, 1937; Interim Procurator Fiscal, Airdrie, 1938; Crown Office: Legal Assistant, 1941, Principal Assistant, 1945, Crown Agent for Scotland, 1967-74; since 1974, has served on a number of bodies connected with criminal procedure, police administration, forensic pathology services, the law of human transplants and the care and resettlement of offenders; Chairman, Corstorphine Trust. Recreations: golf; gardening. Address: (h.) Achray, 20 Dovecot Road, Corstorphine, Edinburgh, EH12 7LE; T.-031-334 4096.

Bowey, Professor Angela Marilyn, BA (Econ), PhD, FIPM, FIMS. Director, Pay Advice and Research Centre, since 1976; Commissioner, Equal Opportunities Commission, 1980-86; Member, Police Advisory Board for Scotland, since 1983; Governor, Scottish Police College, since 1984; b. 20.10.40, Blackpool; 3 s.; 2 d. Educ. Withington Girls' School, Manchester; Manchester University. Worked as Mathematician on design of refuelling cycles for nuclear power stations; Assistant Lecturer in Sociology, Elizabeth Gaskell College of Education, Manchester, 1967-68; Research Associate, then Lecturer, Manchester Business School, 1968-76; Professor of Business Administration, Strathclyde University, 1976-86. Member, Scottish Economic Council, 1980-83; Editor, Management Decision, 1979-82; author of eight books and numerous articles on pay, productivity, manpower planning and organisation theory. Address: (h.) Craigard, Arrochar, G83 7AA; T.-03012 277.

Bowie, Graham Maitland, MA, LLB. Chief Executive, Lothian Regional Council, since 1986 (Director of Planning, 1975-86); b. 11.11.31, Alloa; m., Jennifer; 1 s.; 2 d. Educ. Alloa Academy; St. Andrews University; Glasgow University. Glasgow Chamber of Commerce, 1957-59; Ford Motor Co., 1959-64; Edinburgh Corporation Education Department, 1964-69; Inner London Education Authority, 1969-75. Recreations: music; golf; walking. Address: (b.) Lothian Regional Council, Regional Headquarters, George IV Bridge, Edinburgh, EH1 1UQ; T.-031-229 9292.

Bowling, Dudley James Francis, DSc, BSc, PhD, CBiol, MIBiol. Reader in Plant Science, Aberdeen University, since 1981; b. 20.5.37, Kingston upon Hull; m., Sheila Mary Daun. Educ. Hull Grammar School; Nottingham University; Aberdeen University. Aberdeen University: Assistant in Botany, 1961; Lecturer in Botany, 1963; Senior Lecturer in Botany, 1974; Visiting Scientist, DSIR, Palmerston North, New Zealand, 1976-77. Publication: Uptake of Ions by Plant Roots, 1976. Recreations: gardening; model railways. Address: (b.) Department of Plant Science, St. Machar Drive, Old Aberdeen, AB9 2UD; T.-Aberdeen 272693.

Bowman, Allan John, MA, CQSW, DMS. Director of Social Work, Fife, since 1986; b. 3.1.50, Perth; m., Marilyn Norah Cosgrove; 1 s.; 3 d. Educ. Perth Academy; Edinburgh University; Robert Gordon's Institute of Technology; Anglian Regional Management Centre. Social Worker and Senior Social Worker, Dundee Corporation, then Tayside Region, 1972-78; Senior Social Worker, Depute Area Social Work Organiser and Area Social Work Organiser, Essex County Council, 1978-84; Depute Director and Director of Social Work, Fife Regional Council, 1985-86. Member, Tayside Education/ Industry Liaison Committee, 1977-78; Chair, Essex BASW, 1982-84. Recreations: horse racing; guitar; theatre; swimming; cricket; golf. Address: (b.) Social Work Department, Flemington Road, Glenrothes, KY7 5QG; T.-0592 754411, Ext. 3755.

Bowman, Bernard Neil, LLB, NP. Senior Partner, Gray Robertson & Wilkie, Solicitors, Dundee, Forfar and Blairgowrie, since 1984; Secretary:

Dundee Institute of Architects, since 1970, Dundee Building Trades' (Employers) Association, since 1970, Tayside Construction Safety Association, since 1975, Dundee Construction Industry Group Training Association, since 1970; Joint Secretary, Local Joint Council for Building Industry, since 1970, and Local Joint Apprenticeship Committee for the Building Industry, since 1970; Director, High School of Dundee, since 1980; Assessor to Lord Dean of Guild, Guildry Incorporation of Dundee, since 1974 (Lord Dean of Guild, since 1987); b. 11.11.43, Dundee; m., Pamela Margaret Munro Wright; 2 d. Educ. High School of Dundee; Edinburgh University; St. Andrews University. Apprenticeship, Sturrock Morrison & Gilruth, Solicitors, Dundee, 1967; Admitted Solicitor, 1969; Partner, Gray Robertson & Wilkie, 1971. President, Scottish Counties Cricket Board, 1981; Committee Member and National Selector, Scottish Cricket Union, 1974-83, now Vice-President; Honorary Secretary, Tenovus Tayside. Recreations: cricketophile; Highland cattle. Address: (b.) 27 Bank Street, Dundee; T.-0382 222667.

Bowman, Professor William Cameron, BPharm, PhD, DSc, FIBiol, FPS, FRSE, HonFFARCS. Deputy Principal/Vice Principal Elect, Strathclyde University (Head, Department of Physiology and Pharmacology, 1966-87); b. 26.4.30, Carlisle; m., Anne Wylie Stafford; 1 s.; 1 d. Educ. Carlisle Grammar School; London University. RAF (commissioned officer), 1955-57; Lecturer, then Reader in Pharmacology, London University, 1952-66. Dean, School of Pharmaceutical Sciences, Strathclyde University, 1974-77; Member: Nomenclature Committee, BP Commission, 1964-67; Biology Committee, MOD, 1966-75; TCT and SEAR Sub-Committees, CSM, 1972-83; Biomedical Research Committee, SHHD, 1980-85; Chairman, Committee, British Pharmacological Society, 1981-84. Publications: Textbook of Pharmacology, 1968, 1980; Pharmacology of Neuromuscular Function, 1980; Dictionary of Pharmacology, 1986. Address: Department of Physiology and Pharmacology, Strathclyde University, Glasgow, G1 1XW; T.-041-552 4400.

Bown, Professor Lalage Jean, OBE, MA (Oxon), DrUniv (Open University), FRSA. Professor and Director, Department of Adult and Continuing Education, Glasgow University, since 1981; b. 1.4.27, Croydon. Educ. Wycombe Abbey School, Buckinghamshire; Cheltenham Ladies' College; Somerville College, Oxford. Resident Tutor: University College of the Gold Coast, 1949-55; Makerere University College, Uganda, 1955-59; successively Tutorial Advisor, Assistant Director, Deputy Director, Extra-Mural Department, Ibadan University, 1960-66 (Associate Professor, 1962-66); Director of Extra-Mural Studies and Professor Ad Personam, University of Zambia, 1966-70; Professor of Adult Education, Ahmadu Bello University, Nigeria, 1971-76; successively Professor of Adult Education and Dean of Education, Lagos University, 1977-80. Former Member, Scottish Community Education Council; Member: Board of Trustees, National Museums of Scotland; Research and Publications Committee, Scottish Institute of Adult and Continuing Education; Board of Governors, Newbattle Abbey College; Council, INSITE Trust; Board of Governors, Bell College, Hamilton; Board, The British Council; Governing Body, Institute of Development Studies; Past President, British Comparative and International Education Society; Past President, Development Studies Association; Honorary Vice-President, National Union of Townswomen's Guilds; Honorary Vice-President, WEA. Publications: eight academic books. Recreation: travel. Address: (b.) Department of Adult and Continuing Education, Glasgow University, 57-61 Oakfield Avenue, Glasgow, G12 8LW; T.-041-339 8855, Ext. 4392.

Bowser of Argaty and the King's Lundies, David Stewart, JP, BA (Agric). Trustee, Scottish Forestry Trust (Chairman, 1987); Member, Queen's Bodyguard for Scotland (Royal Company of Archers); b. 11.3.26; m.; 1 s.; 4 d. Educ. Harrow; Trinity College, Cambridge. Captain, Scots Guards, 1944-47; Forestry Commissioner, 1974-82; President, Highland Cattle Society, 1970-72; Member, Perth County Council, 1954-61. Address: Auchlyne, Killin, Perthshire.

Boyd, Alan Robb, LLB, BA, NP. Legal Adviser, Irvine Development Corporation, since 1984; b. 30.7.53, Glasgow; m., Frances Helen Donaldson; 2 d. Educ. Irvine Royal Academy; Dundee University. Admitted Solicitor, 1976; Principal Legal Assistant, Shetland Islands Council, 1979-81; Principal Solicitor, Glenrothes Development Corporation, 1981-84. Council Member, Law Society of Scotland, since 1985 (Chairman, Public Service and Commerce Group, since 1986). Recreations: golf; music; gardening. Address: (b.) Perceton House, Irvine, Ayrshire, KA11 2AL; T.-0294 214100.

Boyd, Brian, MA, MEd. Head Teacher, Hunter High School, East Kilbride, since 1986; b. 25.4.48, Glasgow; m., Margo Nicol; 1 s. Educ. Glasgow University. Teacher of English, St. Stephen's High School, Port Glasgow, 1970-72; Principal Teacher of English: St. Aelred's High School, Paisley, 1972-73, St. Cuthbert's High School, Johnstone, 1974-79; Assistant Head Teacher, Barrhead High School, 1979-83; Head Teacher, Barrhead High School, 1983-86. Member: Scottish Central on English, 1977-80; SED Task Group on Guidance, since 1983. Recreations: soccer; reading; addressing meetings on whole school policies. Address: (b.) Hunter High School, Crawford Drive, East Kilbride; T.-East Kilbride 3224363.

Boyd, Colin David, BA (Econ), LLB. Advocate, since 1983; b. 7.6.53, Falkirk; m., Fiona Margaret MacLeod; 1 d. Educ. Wick High School; George Watson's College, Edinburgh; Manchester University; Edinburgh University. Solicitor, 1978-82. Member, National Executive Committee, Campaign for a Scottish Assembly, 1980-82, 1985-88. Recreations: reading; photography; hill-walking. Address: (h.) 11B Grange Road, Edinburgh; T.-031-667 5771.

Boyd, Edward. Playwright; b. 11.5.16, Stevenston, Ayrshire. Worked with Unity Theatre, Glasgow, 1945-49, as Stage Manager, occasional Actor and finally Producer (Heartbreak House and An Inspector Calls); has written extensively for television, including The Odd Man series (Screen Writer's Guild Award), The Lower Largo Sequence, The View from Daniel Pike; author of the book The Dark Number, 1973; film script, Robbery, 1967.

Boyd, Gavin, CBE (1977), MA (Hons), LLB. Consultant, Boyds, Solicitors, since 1978; Chairman, Scottish Opera Theatre Royal, since 1973; Chairman, J.W. Galloway, since 1983; b. 4.8.28; m., Kathleen Elizabeth Skinner; 1 s. Educ. Glasgow Academy; Glasgow University. Partner, Boyds, Solicitors, 1955-77; Director, Stenhouse Holdings Ltd., 1970-79 (Chairman, 1971-78); Director, Scottish Opera, since 1970; Director, North Sea Assets plc, since 1972; Director, Paterson Jenks plc, 1972-81; Director, Scottish Television plc, since 1973; Director, Ferranti plc, since 1975; Director, British Carpets plc, 1977-81; Director, Merchant House of Glasgow, since 1982. Chairman, Court, Strathclyde University, since 1983; Hon. LLD, Strathclyde, 1982. Recreations: music and the performing arts; yacht racing; cruising. Address: (h.) 4A Prince Albert Road, Glasgow, G12 9JX.

Boyd, Ian Mair, MSc, CA. Group Finance Director, The Weir Group PLC, since 1981; b. 4.9.44, Ayr; m., Theodora; 2 s.; 1 d. Educ. Ayr Academy; London Business School. The Weir Group PLC: Financial Controller International Division, 1975-78, Group Chief Accountant, 1978-81. Council Member, Institute of Chartered Accountants of Scotland. Recreations: golf; hill-walking; fishing. Address: (b.) The Weir Group PLC, Cathcart, Glasgow, G44 4EX; T.-041-637 7111.

Boyd, James Ferguson, MD, FRCPEdin, FRCPath, FRCPSGlas. Senior Lecturer in Pathology of Infectious Diseases, Glasgow University, since 1961; Honorary Consultant Pathologist, Greater Glasgow Health Board, since 1961; b. 6.5.25, Kilbirnie, Ayrshire; m., Christina M. MacLeod; 2 s.; 2 d. Educ. Hillhead High School, Glasgow; Carrick Academy, Maybole; Glasgow University. Resident, Hairmyres Hospital, East Kilbride, and Royal Alexandra Infirmary, Paisley, 1948-49; Royal Army Medical Corps, 1949-51; Resident, Western Infirmary, Glasgow, 1951-52; trainee posts in pathology, Western Infirmary, Glasgow, and Area Laboratory, Stirling Royal Infirmary, 1952-57; Lecturer in Pathology, Glasgow University, 1957-61, with secondment to Royal Maternity Hospital and Royal Hospital for Sick Children, Glasgow; Senior Lecturer, Ruchill Hospital, Western Infirmary and Gartnavel General Hospital, Glasgow, since 1961. Recreations: golf; walking. Address: (h.) 44 Woodend Drive, Jordanhill, Glasgow, G13 1TQ; T.-041-959 2708.

Boyd, John Morton, CBE, PhD, DSc, FRSE, FIBiol, FRSA, HonFRSGS, HonFRZSS. Consultant to the Forestry Commission, since 1985; Consultant to North of Scotland Hydro-Electric Board, since 1985; Consultant to National Trust for Scotland, since 1985; b. 31.1.25, Darvel; m., Winifred Isobel Rome; 4 s. Educ. Darvel School; Kilmarnock Academy; Glasgow University. War service, 1943-47 (Flt. Lt., RAF). Nature Conservancy Council: Regional Officer, 1957-68, Assistant Director, 1969-70, Director (Scotland), 1971-85; Nuffield Travel Fellow, Mid-East and East Africa, 1964-65; Leader, British Jordan Expedition, 1966; Member, Royal Society Aldabra Expedition, 1967; Member, Council, Royal Zoological Society of Scotland, 1963-69, since 1980; Member, BBC Scotland Agricultural Advisory Committee, 1973-76; Member, Council, National Trust for Scotland, 1971-85; Member, Council, Royal Society of Edinburgh, 1978-81; Member, Seals Advisory Committee, NERC, 1973-79; Member, Consultative Panel on Conservation of Phoenix and Line Islands (Central Pacific), since 1981; Co-Chairman, Area VI Anglo-Soviet Environmental Protection Agreement, 1977-85; Member, Council, Scottish Wildlife Trust, since 1985; Vice-President, Scottish Conservation Projects Trust, since 1985; Member, Commission on Ecology, IUCN, since 1976; General Editor (Island Biology), Edinburgh University Press, since 1985; Neill Prize, Royal Society of Edinburgh, 1985. Publications: St. Kilda Summer (Co-author), 1960; Mosaic of Islands, 1963; Highlands and Islands (Co-author), 1964; Travels in the Middle-East and East Africa, 1966; Island Survivors (Co-author), 1974; The Natural Environment of the Hebrides (Co-author), 1979 and 1983; Fraser Darling's Islands, 1986. Recreations: hill-walking; travel; painting; photography. Address: (h.) 57 Hailes Gardens, Edinburgh, EH13 OJH; T.-031-441 3220; Balephuil, Tiree, Argyll; T.-Scarinish 521.

Boyd, Michael, MA (Hons). Artistic Director, Tron Theatre, Glasgow, since 1984; b. 6.7.55, Belfast; m., Marcella Evaristi. Educ. Latymer Upper School, London; Daniel Stewart's College, Edinburgh; Edinburgh University. Trainee Director, Malaya Bronnaya Theatre, Moscow; Staff Director, Belgrade Theatre, Coventry; Associate Director, Crucible Theatre, Sheffield; freelance work, Lyric Hammersmith, Haymarket Leicester, Royal Court, Traverse Edinburgh, Cambridge Theatre Co. Recreations: reading; music; TV. Address: (b.) Tron Theatre, Trongate, Glasgow; T.-041-552 3748.

Boyd, William Dalziel, MB, ChB, FRCPEdin, FRCPsych, DPM. Commissioner, Mental Welfare Commission for Scotland, since 1984; Consultant Psychiatrist, Lothian Health Board, since 1967; Honorary Senior Lecturer, Edinburgh University, since 1967; b. 9.11.30, Cupar, Fife; m., Betty Ledingham Gordon; 3 s.; 1 d. Educ. Trinity College, Glenalmond; Edinburgh University. National Service, Royal Army Medical Corps; training posts at Rosslynlee Hospital, Midlothian; Edinburgh Royal Infirmary; Royal Edinburgh Hospital; Consultant Psychiatrist: Herdmanflat Hospital, Haddington; Royal Edinburgh Hospital; Physician Superintendent, Royal Edinburgh Hospital. Chairman: Scottish Division, Royal College of Psychiatrists; Edinburgh and Leith Old People's Welfare Council. Recreation: improving old houses and old gardens. Address: (h.) Kirkbrae House, 10 Randolph Cliff, Edinburgh, EH3 7UA; T.-031-225 3289.

Boyd, William John, MBE (1985), BL. Solicitor; Partner, Bishop & Co., now Bishop and Robertson Chalmers, since 1983 (Sole Partner, Murray Macgregor & Co., Glasgow, 1958-83); b. 16.2.25, Darvel; m., Celia Barbara Ford; 1 d. Educ. Darvel H.G. School; Strathallan School; Glasgow University. War Service, 1943-47; Secretary,

National Federation of Property Owners and Factors of Scotland and Property Owners and Factors Association, Glasgow, Ltd., 1958-83; Member, General Council, British Property Federation. Recreations: golf and other sports. Address: (h.) 42 Braidholm Road, Giffnock, Glasgow, G46 6HS; T.-041-637 5972.

Boyes, John, MA (Hons). HM Inspector of Schools, since 1974; b. 20.5.43, Greenock; m., Margaret Anne Peat; 1 s.; 1 d. Educ. Greenock High School; Glasgow University. Taught French and German, Alloa Academy and Denny High School, 1967-74. Recreation: crossing i's and dotting t's. Address: (b.) Scottish Education Department, Corunna House, 29 Cadogan Street, Glasgow; T.-041-204 1220.

Boyle, Rt. Rev. Mgr. Hugh Noonan, PhL, STL. Administrator, Metropolitan Cathedral Church of St. Andrew, Glasgow, since 1983 (Canon, Chapter of Metropolitan Cathedral Church, since 1984); Prelate of Honour, since 1987; Archivist, Archdiocese of Glasgow, since 1973; b. 14.1.35, Glasgow. Educ. St. Aloysius' College, Glasgow; Glasgow University; Pontifical Scots College and Pontifical Gregorian University, Rome, 1956-63. National Service, RAF, 1954-56; ordained priest, Rome, 1962; Assistant Priest: St. Philomena's, Glasgow, 1963-66, St. Eunan's, Clydebank, 1966-76; Archdiocese of Glasgow: Assistant Archivist, 1967-73; Chancellor, 1976-83. Editor, Catholic Directory for Scotland and Western Catholic Calendar, since issues of 1975; Member: Scottish Catholic Communications Commission, 1979-87; Scottish Catholic Heritage Commission, since 1981; Patron, Hutcheson's Hospital, since 1983. Recreations: music (listening); walking. Address: St. Andrew's Cathedral House, 90 Dunlop Street, Glasgow, G1 4ER; T.-041-221 3096.

Boyle, Iain Thomson, BSc (Hons), MB, ChB, FRCP, FRCP (London and Glasgow). Reader in Medicine, Glasgow University and Glasgow Royal Infirmary, since 1984; Depute Medical Advisor, Strathclyde University, since 1980; b. 7.10.35, Glasgow; m., Elizabeth Johnston Carmichael; 1 s.; 2 d. Educ. Paisley Grammar School; Glasgow University. Lecturer in Medicine, Glasgow University and Glasgow Royal Infirmary, 1964-70; Hartenstein Research Fellow, Wisconsin University, 1970-72; Senior Lecturer in Medicine, Glasgow University and Glasgow Royal Infirmary, 1973-84. Editor, Scottish Medical Journal, 1978-83; Co-Editor, Bone, since 1983; Council Member, Royal College of Physicians and Surgeons, since 1984; Secretary: Scottish Society for Experimental Medicine, since 1984; Scottish Society of Physicians, since 1984; President, Caledonian Philatelic Society, 1983-84. Fletcher Prize, Royal College of Physicians and Surgeons of Glasgow, 1973. Recreations: philately; Scottish social history; angling; gardening; golf. Address: (h.) 7 Lochbrae Drive, High Burnside, Rutherglen, Glasgow, G73 5QL.

Boyle, Sheriff John Sebastian, BL. Sheriff of South Strathclyde, Dumfries and Galloway, at Airdrie, since 1983. Educ. St. Aloysius College, Glasgow; Glasgow University. Solicitor, Glasgow, 1955-83; President, Glasgow Bar Association, 1962-63; Member, Scottish Arts Council, 1966-72; Council Member, Law Society of Scotland, 1968-75; Member, Criminal Injuries Compensation Board, 1975-83.

Boyle, John Stirling. MA, DPA. Director of Public Affairs (Scotland), British Railways Board, since 1983; b. 17.9.39, Paisley; m., Helen Dickson Wallace; 2 s.; 1 d. Educ. Camphill School, Paisley; Glasgow University. Schoolteacher, William Quarrier School, 1960-61; Journalist, Sunday Post, 1961-63; Technical Writer, Harland Engineering Company, 1963-64; Health Education Officer, Stirling County Council, 1964-66; Public Relations Officer, Heriot-Watt University, 1966-73 (also PR Consultant to National Housebuilders Registration Council, 1969-73); Director of External Relations, Scottish Council (Development and Industry), 1973-83. Council Member, National Youth Orchestra of Scotland, 1983-86; Member, Greater Glasgow Tourist Board. Address: (h.) The Smiddy, Inverallan Road, Bridge of Allan; (b.) ScotRail House, 58 Port Dundas Road, Glasgow, G4 OHG; T.-041-332 9811.

Boyle, Sir Lawrence, KB, JP, DL, BCom, PhD, IPFA, CBIM. Financial and Management Consultant; Director: Scottish Mutual Assurance Society; Pension Fund Property Unit Trust, 1979-88; Short Loan & Mortgage Co. Ltd., 1980-87; Visiting Professor, Strathclyde Business School, 1980-85; b. 31.1.20, Balerno, Midlothian; m., Mary McWilliam; 1 s.; 3 d. Educ. Holy Cross Academy, Leith; Edinburgh University. Depute County Treasurer, Midlothian County Council, 1951-62; Glasgow Corporation: Depute City Chamberlain, 1962-70, City Chamberlain, 1970-74; Chief Executive, Strathclyde Regional Council, 1974-80. Member of Court, Strathclyde University, 1980-85 (Chairman, Finance Committee); Chairman, Scottish National Orchestra, 1980-84; Member, Committee of Inquiry into the Functions and Powers of the Islands Councils of Scotland, 1982-84; Member, Committee of Inquiry into the Conduct of Local Authority Business, 1985-86. Recreation: music. Address: (h.) 24 Broomburn Drive, Newton Mearns, Glasgow, G77 5JF; T.-041-639 3776.

Boys, John, ARSA, DA, FRIBA, FRIAS. Partner, John Boys Architects; Commissioner, Royal Fine Arts Commission for Scotland; b. 23.8.28, Kirriemuir, Angus; m., Bridget Jensen; 2 s.; 1 d. Educ. Glasgow School of Art; Dundee School of Art. Royal Army Education Corps, Egypt and Kenya, 1946-48. Founder Member, New Glasgow Society; case worker, The Architectural Heritage Society; former Council Member, RIAS; former Assessor: RIAS; RIBA; New Saltire Society Planning Award. Recreations: painting; rough gardening; curling; sailing. Address: (b.) 19 Woodside Place, Glasgow, G3 7QL; T.-041-332 2228.

Bradley, Professor Anthony Wilfred, MA, LLB (Cantab). Professor of Constitutional Law, Edinburgh University, since 1968; Editor, Public Law, since 1986; Solicitor of the Supreme Court (England and Wales), since 1960; b. 6.2.34, Dover; m., Kathleen Bryce; 1 s.; 3 d. Educ. Dover Grammar School; Emmanuel College, Cambridge. Fellow, Trinity Hall, Cambridge, 1960-68; Visiting Reader in Law, University College of Dar es Salaam, 1966-67; Dean, Faculty of Law, Edinburgh University, 1979-82. Chairman, Social Security Appeal Tribunal, Edinburgh and Lothians; Chairman, Edinburgh Council for the Single Homeless; Member, Social Studies Sub-Committee, University Grants Committee. Recreations: walking; music. Address: (b.) Old College, South Bridge, Edinburgh, EH8 9YL; T.-031-667 1011.

Bradley, Professor Paul Frank, MB, BS, BDS, FDSRCS(Eng), FDSRCS(Edin), MRCS. Professor of Oral and Maxillofacial Surgery, Edinburgh University, since 1983; b. 9.8.35, Birmingham; m., Ceinwen Susan; 1 s.; 1 d. Educ. King Edward School, Birmingham; London University; Birmingham University. Assistant Professor of Oral Surgery, University of Washington, USA, 1971; Senior Lecturer in Oral and Maxillofacial Surgery, Liverpool University, 1972-77; Consultant in Oral and Maxillofacial Surgery, Clwyd AHA, 1977-83. Former Council Member, British Association of Oral and Maxillofacial Surgeons; Hunterian Professor, Royal College of Surgeons, England, 1983. Publication: Cryosurgery of the Maxillofacial Region, 1986. Recreations: amateur theatre; painting; fishing. Address: 53 Nile Grove, Edinburgh EH10 4RE; T.-031-447 2166.

Brady, Paul A., BSc (Hons), PhD. Assistant Secretary, Scottish Office; b. 28.7.49, Glasgow; 2 s.; 1 d. Educ. St. Mungo's Academy, Glasgow. Joined Scottish Office, 1974; posts in Industry, Police, Education and Energy areas, 1974-88; currently heading team advising on electricity privatisation; Private Secretary to Parliamentary Under Secretary of State, Scottish Office, 1977-79. Recreations: walking; music; reading; golf. Address: (b.) Industry Department for Scotland, New St. Andrew's House, Edinburgh; T.-031-244 4671.

Braid, James, JP. Member: North East Fife District Council, since 1980; Fife Regional Council, since 1981; b. 1.4.12, St. Monans, Fife; m., Alison Cruickshank; 1 s.; 2 d. Educ. Waid Academy, Anstruther. RAF (flying), 1940-52; Provost of St. Monans and Member, Fife County Council, 1952-75; Member, North East Fife District Council and Fife Regional Council, 1975-78; Member: Executive Committee, St. Andrews and North East Fife Area Tourist Board, since 1983; Forth River Purification Board, since 1980; Trustee and Committee Member, Scottish Fisheries Museum, since 1982. Freeman of St. Monans. Recreations: bowling; football. Address: (h.) 16 West Shore, St. Monans, Fife, KY10 2BT; T.-St. Monans 262.

Brain, Rev. Isobel Jarvie, MA. Minister, Ballantrae Parish Church, since 1987; b. 4.7.30, Glasgow; m., Rev. E.J. Brain; 1 d. Educ. Hillhead High School; Glasgow University; Jordanhill College. Teacher in Glasgow, 1952-62; Head, English Department, then Deputy and Head Teacher in Liverpool secondary schools, 1963-85; Attached Assistant Minister, Jordanhill Parish Church, 1985-86. Recreations: music; theatre; reading biographies. Address: (h.) The Manse, Ballantrae, Girvan, KA26 0NH; T.-046583 252.

Braithwaite, Robert Barclay, BSc, CEng, FICE, MASCE. Assistant General Manager and Harbour Engineer, Aberdeen Harbour Board, since 1986; b. 17.2.48, Glasgow; m., Christine Isobel Ross; 2 s. Educ. Hutchesons' Boys' Grammar School; Strathclyde University. Graduate/Assistant Engineer, Rendel Palmer & Tritton, Consulting Civil Engineers, London, 1969-74; Deputy Harbour Engineer, 1974-75, Harbour Engineer, 1976-86, Aberdeen Harbour Board. Member, Maritime Engineering Group Board, Institution of Civil Engineers; Chairman, Aberdeen Maritime Museum Appeal. Recreatios: hill-walking; badminton; other sports; reading. Address: (b.) Harbour Office, 16 Regent Quay, Aberdeen, AB9 1SS; T.-0224 592571.

Brand, Professor Charles Peter, MA, PhD. Professor of Italian, Edinburgh University, since 1966 (Vice-Principal, since 1984); b. 7.2.23, Cambridge; m., Gunvor Hellgren; 1 s.; 3 d. Educ. Cambridgeshire High School; Trinity Hall, Cambridge. Lecturer in Italian, Cambridge University, 1952-66; Fellow and Tutor, Trinity Hall, Cambridge, 1958-66. Editor, Modern Language Review, 1970-76. Publications: Italy and the English Romantics, 1957; T. Tasso, 1965; L. Ariosto, 1974; Writers of Italy (Editor). Recreations: sport; gardening. Address: (h.) 21 Succoth Park, Edinburgh, EH12 6BX; T.-031-337 1980.

Brand, Hon. Lord (David William Robert Brand), QC (Scot). Senator of the College of Justice in Scotland, since 1972; b. 21.10.23; m., 1, Rose Josephine Devlin (deceased); 4 d.; 2, Bridget Veronica Lynch. Educ. Stonyhurst College; Edinburgh University. Commissioned Argyll and Sutherland Highlanders, 1942; Captain, 1945; admitted Faculty of Advocates, 1948; Advocate-Depute, 1957-59; Senior Advocate-Depute, 1964; Sheriff of Dumfries and Galloway, 1968; Sheriff of Roxburgh, Berwick and Selkirk, 1970; Solicitor-General for Scotland, 1970-72.

Brand, Janet Mary Valentine, BA (Hons), DipTP, MRTPI. Senior Lecturer, Strathclyde University, since 1973; b. 19.4.44, Bath; m., Robert E. Lamb; 1 d. Educ. County High School for Girls, Brentwood; Exeter University; Mid Essex Technical College. Local authority appointments in Departments of Planning, Essex County Council, London Borough of Barking and City of London, 1965-70; Senior Lecturer, Department of Planning, South Bank Polytechnic, 1970-73. Convener, Education Committee, Scottish Branch, RTPI; Moderator and Reviser, SCOTVEC, since 1978. Recreations: skiing; gardening; family pursuits; travelling. Address: (b.) Centre for Planning, Strathclyde University, Livingstone Tower, Richmond Street, Glasgow; T.-041-552 4400, Ext. 3905/6.

Brand, John Arthur. Senior Lecturer in Politics, Strathclyde University; b. 4.8.34, Aberdeen; 1 d. Educ. Aberdeen Grammar School; Aberdeen University; London School of Economics. Assistant in Politics, Glasgow University, 1959-61; Lecturer in Politics, Reading University, 1961-63; Lecturer in the Politics of Education, London University, 1963-64; joined Strathclyde University as Lecturer in Politics, 1964. Chairman: Campaign for a Scottish Assembly, 1979-83; Glasgow Community Relations Committee, 1968-71. Recreations: skiing; tennis; music. Address: (h.) 17 Kew Terrace, Glasgow, G12 OTE; T.-041-339 1675.

Branscombe, Professor Peter John, MA (Oxon), PhD. Professor of Austrian Studies, St. Andrews University, since 1979; b. 7.12.29, Sittingbourne, Kent; m., Marina Riley; 2 s.; 1 d. Educ. Dulwich College; Worcester College, Oxford; Bedford College, London. Joined St. Andrews University, 1959, as Lecturer, then Senior Lecturer, in German. Governor, Royal Scottish Academy of Music and Drama, 1967-73; served on Awarding Panel for Schlegel-Tieck Prize, 1971-79 (Convener, 1974-77); Member: Music Committee, Scottish Arts Council, 1973-80; Scottish Arts Council, 1976-79; Chairman, SAC Working Party investigating the record industry in Scotland, 1976-77; Chairman, Conference of University Teachers of German in Scotland, 1983-85. Publications: Heine: Selected Verse, 1967 (2nd edition, 1986); Austrian Life and Literature 1780-1938; Eight Essays (Editor), 1978; Schubert Studies (Editor), 1982. Recreations: natural history; walking; music; theatre. Address: (b.) Department of German, The University, St. Andrews, Fife, KY16 9PH; T.-St. Andrews 76161, Ext. 331.

Brant, Douglas, CIPFA, FRVA, MBIM. Director of Finance, Strathkelvin District Council, since 1974; b. 27.6.42, Motherwell; m., Valerie Margaret; 1 s.; 1 d. Educ. Dalziel High School, Motherwell; Scottish College of Commerce. Trainee and Accountancy Assistant, Burgh of Motherwell and Wishaw, 1959-64; Burgh of Bishopbriggs: Assistant and Depute Town Chamberlain, 1964-68, Town Chamberlain, 1968-75. Past Chairman, Scottish Branch, CIPFA. Recreations: golf; curling. Address: (b.) PO Box 4, Tom Johnston House, Civic Way, Kirkintilloch, G66 4TJ.

Bratton, Kenneth, BSc (Econ), FREconS. Secretary, Commissioner for Local Administration in Scotland, since 1976; b. 8.1.31, Billingham-on-Tees; m., Lesley Moira Lendrum; 1 s.; 1 d. Educ. Grammar School, West Hartlepool; London University. Ministry of Health, London, 1947-51; Sales Officer, Dorman Long Ltd., 1951-60; student teacher, 1961-62; lecturing appointments, Ipswich and Darlington, 1962-70; Senior Lecturer, Head of Management and Business Studies, Falkirk College of Technology, 1970-75; part-time Course tutor in Public Administration, Open University, 1976-80. Recreations: walking; travel; good food. Address: (b.) 5 Shandwick Place, Edinburgh, EH2 4RG; T.-031-229 4472.

Bray, Jeremy William, PhD. MP (Labour), Motherwell South, since 1983; Opposition Spokesman on Science and Technology, since 1983; b. 29.6.30, Hong Kong; m., Elizabeth Trowell; 4 d. Educ. Aberystwyth Grammar School; Kingswood School, Bath; Jesus College, Cambridge; Harvard University. Technical Officer, Wilton works, ICI, 1956-62; MP, Middlesbrough West, 1962-70; Member, Select Committee on Nationalised Industries, 1962-64; Chairman, Labour Science and Technology Group, 1964-66; Member, Economic Affairs Estimates Sub-Committee, 1964-66; Parliamentary Secretary, Ministry of Power, 1966-67; Joint Parliamentary Secretary, Ministry of Technology, 1967-69; Director, Mullard Ltd., 1970-73; Chairman, Fabian Society, 1971-72; Co-Director, Programme of Research into Econometric Methods, Imperial College, 1971-74; Consultant, Battelle Research Centre, Geneva, 1973; Senior Research Fellow, Strathclyde University, 1974, and Visiting Professor, 1974-79; Deputy Chairman, Christian Aid, 1972-83; MP, Motherwell and Wishaw, 1979-83; Member, Treasury and Civil Service Select Committee, 1979-83; Chairman, Sub-Committee, Treasury and Civil Service Select Committee, 1981-82. Publications: Decision in Government, 1970; Production Purpose and Structure, 1982. Recreation: sailing. Address: (b.) House of Commons, London, SW1A OAA.

Breaks, Michael Lenox, BA, DipLib, MIInfSc. Librarian, Heriot-Watt University, since 1985; b. 12.1.45, Plymouth; m., Barbara; 1 s.; 1 d. Educ. St. George's College, Weybridge; Leeds University. Assistant Librarian: University College, Swansea, York University; Social Services Librarian, University College, Cardiff, 1977-81; Deputy Librarian, University College, Dublin, 1981-85. Honorary Secretary, Institute of Information Scientists (Scottish Branch). Recreations: gardening. Address: (h.) 15 Corrennie Gardens, Edinburgh, EH10 6DG; T.-031-447 7193.

Brechin, Robert Hood. Managing Director, Brechin Brothers Ltd., since 1966; President, Royal Caledonian Curling Club, 1987-88; b. 16.8.30, Glasgow; m., Avril Anne Anderson; 3 s. Educ. Glasgow Academy; Strathallan. Commissioned HLI, 1949; Argyll and Sutherland Highlanders, 1949-50; joined family business, 1950. Renfrewshire County Councillor, 1967-70; elected to Council, Royal Caledonian Curling Club, 1981. Recreations: golf; sailing; curling. Address: (h.) 5 Newtonlea Avenue, Newton Mearns, Glasgow; T.-041-639 1861.

Bremner, David Neill, MB, ChB, FRCSEdin. Consultant General Surgeon, Borders Health Board, at Borders General Hospital, Melrose, since 1976; b. 4.2.42, Forfar; m., Janette Marlyn; 3 s.; 1 d. Educ. Forfar Academy; Queen's College, St. Andrews University. House Surgeon, Inverness Hospitals, 1966-68; Assistant Surgeon, Hadera, Israel, 1968-69; Registrar Surgeon: Ayr hospitals, 1969-71, Edinburgh hospitals, 1971-74; Senior Registrar, Professorial Department of Surgery, Edinburgh, 1974-76. South Medical Advisor, Scottish Rugby Union; Honorary Vice President, Gala Rugby Club; Regional Advisor, Royal College of Surgeons of Edinburgh. Recreations: gardening; rugby. Address: (h.) 26 Abbotsford Road, Galashiels, TD1 3DS; T.-0896 2558.

Bremner, James W., FCCA, ARVA, MBIM. Director of Finance, Highland Regional Council, since 1975; b. 29.5.33, Forfar; m., Ethel; 1 s.; 1 d. Educ. Forfar Academy. RAF, 1951-54; Accountant, Angus County Council, 1955-65; Ross and Cromarty County Council: Depute County Treasurer, 1965-70; County Treasurer, 1970-75. Elected Member, Chartered Association of Certified Accountants, since 1982. Recreation: golf. Address: (b.) Highland Regional Council, Glenurquhart Road, Inverness; T.-0463 234121.

Brewis, (Henry) John, MA (Oxon). Lord Lieutenant, Wigtown, since 1982; Member, Agriculture Industry Advisory Council, since 1985; b. 8.4.20,

Scarborough; m., Faith MacTaggart Stewart; 3 s.; 1 d. Educ. Eton College; New College, Oxford. Royal Artillery (Major), 1940-46; Barrister-at-law, Middle Temple, 1946-51; Wigtown County Council, 1955-59 (Chairman, Finance Committee); MP (Conservative), Galloway, 1959-74; PPS to Lord Advocate, 1960-61; Chairman, Select Committee on Scottish Affairs, 1971-72; Member, European Parliament, 1973-75. Regional Chairman, Scottish Landowners Federation, 1978-80; Chairman, Scottish Timber Growers, 1980-83; Director, Border Television p.l.c., since 1977. Recreations: forestry; gardening. Address: (h.) Ardwell House, Stranraer, Wigtownshire.

Brian, Paul Vaughan, BSc. Rector, Biggar High School, since 1985 (Rector, Hutchesons' Grammar School, Glasgow, 1984-85); b. 14.6.42, Wokingham; m., Helen Margaret Balneaves; 1 s.; 1 d. Educ. Perth Academy; Edinburgh University; Heriot-Watt College. Assistant Headmaster, Garnock Academy, Kilbirnie, 1974; Depute Rector, Marr College, Troon, 1977; Headteacher, Gryffe High School, Bridge of Weir, 1979. Scientific Officer, Scottish Hindu Kush Expedition, 1968. Recreations: mountaineering; golf; gardening. Address: (b.) Biggar High School, Biggar, Lanarkshire.

Bridges, Professor Roy Charles, BA, PhD, FRGS, FRHistS. Professor of History, Aberdeen University, since 1988 (Chairman, African Studies Group, since 1983); b. 26.9.32, Aylesbury; m., Jill Margaret Bridges; 2 s.; 2 d. Educ. Harrow Weald County Grammar School; Keele University; London University. Lecturer in History, Makerere University, Uganda, 1960-64; joined Aberdeen University as Lecturer, 1964; Senior Lecturer, 1971-88; Head, History Department, 1977-82 and 1985-88; Secretary, African Studies Group, 1966-83. Member, History Panel, Scottish Examination Board, since 1983; Visiting Professor, Indiana University; President, Aberdeen Branch, Historical Association; Treasurer, Scottish Institute of Missionary Studies. Publications: Nations and Empires (Co-author), 1969; J.A. Grant in Africa, 1982. Recreations: cricket; geology; walking. Address: (b.) Department of History, King's College, Aberdeen, AB9 2UB; T.-Aberdeen 272452.

Broadie, Alexander, MA, BLitt, PhD. Reader in Philosophy, Glasgow University. Educ. Edinburgh University; Balliol College, Oxford. Publications: A Samaritan Philosophy, 1981; George Lokert: Late-Scholastic Logician, 1983; The Circle of John Mair, 1985; Introduction to Medieval Logic, 1987. Address: (b.) Philosophy Department, The University, Glasgow, G12 8QQ; T.-041-339 8855.

Brock, Professor David John Henry, BA (Oxon), PhD, MRCPath, FRSE. Professor of Human Genetics, Edinburgh University, since 1985; Director, Human Genetics Unit, Edinburgh University, since 1983; b. 5.6.36, London; m., Sheila Abercromby; 4 s. Educ. Diocesan College, Cape Town; Cape Town University; Oxford University. Postdoctoral Fellow: Massachussets Institute of Technology, 1962-63; Harvard University, 1963-66; Oxford University, 1966-67; Senior Scientific Officer, ARC Animal Breeding Research Organisation, 1967-68; joined Edinburgh University as Lecturer in Human Genetics, 1968; appointed Reader, 1978. Address: (b.) Human Genetics Unit, Western General Hospital, Edinburgh; T.-031-332 7917.

Brockie, Rev. Colin Glynn Frederick, BSc(Eng), BD. Minister, Grange Church, Kilmarnock, since 1978; b. 17.7.42, Westcliff-on-Sea, Essex; m., Barbara Katherine Gordon; 2 s.; 1 d. Educ. Musselburgh Grammar School; Aberdeen Grammar School; Aberdeen University. Probationer Assistant, Mastrick Church, Aberdeen, 1967-68; Minister, St. Martin's Church, Edinburgh, 1968-78. Chaplain, Ayrshire Mission to the Deaf, since 1982; Honorary Secretary and Treasurer, Scottish Church History Society. Recreations: billiards; photography; computing. Address: Grange Manse, 51 Portland Road, Kilmarnock; T.-Kilmarnock 25311.

Brockington, John Leonard, MA, DPhil. Senior Lecturer in Sanskrit, Edinburgh University, since 1982 (Head of Department, since 1975); b. 5.12.40, Oxford; m., Mary Fairweather; 1 s.; 1 d. Educ. Mill Hill School; Corpus Christi College, Oxford. Lecturer in Sanskrit, Edinburgh University, 1965-82. Publications: The Sacred Thread, 1981; Righteous Rama, 1984. Address: (h.) 99 Cluny Gardens, Edinburgh, EH10 6BW; T.-031-447 7580.

Brocklebank, Ted. Head of Documentaries, Grampian Television, since 1985 (Head of News and Current Affairs, 1977-85); b. 24.9.42, St. Andrews; 2 s. Educ. Madras College, St. Andrews. D.C. Thomson, Dundee, 1960-63; Freelance Journalist, 1963-65; Scottish TV, 1965-70; Reporter, Grampian TV, 1970-76. Won BAFTA Award for What Price Oil?; Radio Industries Club of Scotland Special Award (Documentary) for Tale of Two Cities; eight-part series on world oil business networked on Channel Four and throughout USA on PBS. Recreations: rugby; music; reading; living in Scotland. Address: (b.) Grampian TV, Queen's Cross, Aberdeen, AB9 2XJ.

Brocklesby, Professor David William, Dr.Vet.Med. (Zurich), FRCPath, FRCVS. Professor of Tropical Animal Health and Director, Centre for Tropical Veterinary Medicine, Edinburgh University, since 1978; b. 12.2.29, Grimsby; m., Jennifer Mary Hubble; 1 s.; 3 d. Educ. Sedbergh School, Yorkshire; Royal Veterinary College, London; London School of Hygiene and Tropical Medicine. Veterinary Research Officer, East African Veterinary Research Organisation, Muguga, Kenya (Head, Division of Protozoal Diseases), 1955-66; Head, Department of Animal Health, Fisons Pest Control Ltd., Saffron Walden, 1966-67; Head, Department of Parasitology, ARC Institute for Research on Animal Diseases, Compton, Berkshire, 1967-78. Member, Editorial Board: Research in Veterinary Science; British Veterinary Journal; Tropical Animal Health and Production; Member, Council, Royal College of Veterinary Surgeons. Recreations: worrying; reading The Times; watching TV. Address: (b.) Centre for Tropical Veterinary Medicine, Easter Bush, Roslin, Midlothian; T.-031-445 2001.

Brodie, David M., BSc. Chairman, Scottish Parent Teacher Council, since 1982; Personnel Manager, British Steel Corporation, Scottish Steel and

Tube Works, since 1984; b. 5.1.44, Bothwell, Lanarkshire; m., Phyllis; 1 s.; 1 d. Educ. Coatbridge High School; Glasgow University. Education and Training Officer, Colvilles Ltd., 1965-69; Personnel Manager, Marinite Ltd., Cape Group, 1969-71; British Steel Corporation: Graduate Recruitment Co-ordinator, General Steels Division, 1971-74; Senior Industrial Relations Officer, Head Office (London), 1974-77; Industrial Relations Manager, Scottish Division (Heavy Works), 1977-80; Personnel Manager, BSC Plates (Scotland), 1980-84. Scottish Parent Teacher Council: Member, since 1980; Vice-Chairman, 1981-82; Member: Consultative Committee on Curriculum, 1983-87; General Teaching Council for Scotland, since 1987. Recreations: play a little golf (badly) and occasionally watch Airdrieonians play soccer (equally badly!). Address: (b.) British Steel Corporation, Clydesdale Works, Bellshill, Lanarkshire, ML4 2RR; T.-0698 749233.

Brodie, Martin Jeffrey, MD, FRCP(G). Consultant Physician and Clinical Pharmacologist, since 1981; Honorary Clinical Lecturer, Glasgow University, since 1981; b. 14.1.46, Glasgow; m., Sheila Marilyn; 1 s.; 1 d. Educ. Hutchesons' Boys Grammar School; Glasgow University. Lecturer in Materia Medica, Glasgow University, 1974-77; Lecturer in Clinical Pharmacology, Royal Postgraduate Medical School, London, 1977-81. Vice-Chairman, Committee of Management, Prescribers' Journal, DHSS, London, 1987; Chairman, West of Scotland Epilepsy Research Group. Publications: Practical Prescribing; 180 medical reviews and papers. Recreations: chess; reading; sleeping. Address: (b.) Clinical Pharmacology Unit, University Department of Medicine, Western Infirmary, Glasgow; T.-041-339 8822, Ext. 4572.

Brodie, Very Rev. Peter Philip, MA, BD, LLB, DD. Minister, St. Mungo's, Alloa, 1947-86; b. 22.10.16, Airdrie; m., Constance Lindsay Hope; 3 s.; 1 d. Educ. Airdrie Academy; Glasgow University; Trinity College, Glasgow. Minister, St. Mary's, Kirkintilloch, 1942-47; Moderator, General Assembly of the Church of Scotland, 1978-79; Convener, General Administration Committee, 1976-80; Business Convener, 1976-80; Vice Convener, General Trustees, 1973-85; Chairman, General Trustees; Chairman, Judicial Commission, 1983-87; former Chairman, Joint Report, Methodist/Church of Scotland Conversation; Moderator, Synod of Forth, 1976. Recreations: gardening; fishing. Address: 13 Victoria Square, Stirling, FK8; T.-0786 64763.

Brodie, Robert, MA, LLB. Solicitor to Secretary of State for Scotland, since 1987 (Deputy Solicitor, 1984-87); b. 9.4.38, Dundee; m., Jean Margaret McDonald; 2 s.; 2 d. Educ. Morgan Academy, Dundee; St. Andrews University; Queen's College, Dundee. Scottish Office: Legal Assistant, 1965; Senior Legal Assistant, 1970; Deputy Director, Scottish Courts Administration, 1975; Assistant Solicitor, Scottish Office, 1982. Recreations: music; hill-walking. Address: (h.) 45 Stirling Road, Edinburgh; T.-031-552 2028.

Brodie, William, BSc, CBiol, MIBiol. Rector, Wallace High School, Stirling, since 1984; b. 16.9.37, Hamilton; m., Helen Bland; 1 s.; 1 d. Educ. Hamilton Academy; Glasgow University; Paisley College of Technology. Teacher, Wishaw High School, 1965-67; Principal Teacher of Biology, Hutchesons' Grammar School, Glasgow, 1967-74; Assistant Rector, Graeme High School, Falkirk, 1974-79; Depute Rector, Kirkintilloch High School, 1979-81; Rector, Balfron High School, 1981-84. Governor, Moray House College of Education; Chairman, Central Region Secondary Headteachers' Association. Recreations: golf; tennis; gardening. Address: (b.) Wallace High School, Dumyat Road, Stirling; T.-0786 62166.

Brodie of Brodie, (Montagu) Ninian Alexander, DL, JP; b. 12.6.12, Forres; m., Helena Penelope Budgen (deceased); 1 s.; 1 d. Educ. Eton. Trained Webber-Douglas School of Dramatic Art, 1933-35; professional Actor and Director, occasional broadcasts, 1935-40; served with Royal Artillery, including North Africa and Italy, 1940-45; returned to stage, with occasional films and broadcasts, 1945-50; managed estate, market garden, etc., Brodie Castle, from 1950; gave Brodie Castle and part of estate to National Trust for Scotland, 1979; voluntary work as guide etc., since 1980. Life Member, National Trust for Scotland. Recreations: shooting; hill-walking; collecting paintings. Address: (h.) Brodie Castle, Forres, Moray, IV36 0TE.

Brodley, John Inglis, DA, RIBA, ARIAS. Director of Architectural and Technical Services, Kirkcaldy District Council, since 1980; b. 11.2.24, Dunfermline; m., Isabel. Educ. Dunfermline High School; Edinburgh College of Art. Royal Engineers, 1942-47; Assistant Architect, City of Glasgow, 1951-55; Chief Assistant Architect, Burgh of Hamilton, 1955-61; Depute Burgh Architect, Burgh of Kirkcaldy, 1961-75; Depute Director of Architectural and Technical Services, Kirkcaldy District Council, 1975-80. Recreations: golf; gardening. Address: (b.) Forth House, Abbotshall Road, Kirkcaldy, KY1 1RU; T.-0592 261144.

Brooker, William Dixon, BSc. Director, Department of Adult Education and Extra-Mural Studies, Aberdeen University, since 1981; b. 13.12.31, Calcutta; m., Margaret Laura Parkinson; 1 s.; 1 d. Educ. Aberdeen Grammar School; Aberdeen University. Principal Teacher of Geography: Aberlour High School; Keith Grammar School; King Richard School, Dhekelia, Cyprus; Keith Grammar School; Tutor Organiser in Extra-Mural Studies, Aberdeen University, 1966. President, Scottish Mountaineering Club, 1972-74 (Honorary Editor, SMC Journal, 1975-86); Vice-Chairman: Mountaineering Council of Scotland, 1979-81; Scottish Mountain Leader Training Board, 1978-80. Recreations: mountaineering; skiing; travel; photography. Address: (h.) 25 Deeview Road South, Cults, Aberdeen; T.-0224 861055.

Brookes, Brian Sydney, MBE, BSc, MSc, MIBiol. Freelance Naturalist and Ecologist, and Consultant in environmental education and conservation, since 1985; b. 4.5.36, Beckenham, Kent; m., Margaret Mary; 3 s.; 1 d. Educ. Beckenham and Penge Grammar School; King's College, London; Dundee University. Teaching in London schools, seven years; Assistant Warden, field centre in Devon, two years; Warden, Kindrogan Field Centre, Perthshire, 18 years. Sometime Council Member, Botanical Society of the British Isles; various committees, Scottish Wildlife Trust. Recreations: bee-keeping; photography. Address: (h.) Borelick, Trochry, Dunkeld, Perthshire, PH8 0BX; T.-035 03 222.

Brookes, Douglas Whittaker, TD. Secretary, Inverness and District Chamber of Commerce, since 1980; b. 3.1.19, Sheffield; m., May; 1 s.; 1 d. War Service, 1939-46 (Captain, RE); AI Welders Ltd., Inverness, 1946-80: Sales Manager; Sales Director; Managing Director and Chief Executive. Served with local regiment, TA, Lovat Scouts, 1950-66 (latterly Major, Second-in-Command). Recreations: golf; hill-walking; reading. Address: (h.) 13A Island Bank Road, Inverness, IV2 4QN; T.-0463 233570.

Brooks, Professor Charles Joseph William, PhD, DSc, DIC, ARCS, CChem, FRSC, FRSE. Titular Professor of Chemistry, Glasgow University, since 1976; b. 28.9.27, London; m., Gillian M.W. Staniforth; 1 s.; 1 d. Educ. Surbiton County Grammar School; Royal College of Science, London University. Assistant Lecturer, Department of Chemistry and Biochemistry, St. Thomas's Hospital, London, 1954-56; Member, MRC scientific staff, research units, Glasgow, 1956-63; Chemistry Department, Glasgow University: Lecturer, 1963; Senior Lecturer, 1966; Reader, 1973; Visiting Professor: Baylor College of Medicine, Houston, Texas, 1963 and 1965; Japan Society for Promotion of Science, 1977; Walker-Ames Professor, University of Washington, Seattle, May 1987. Editor, Gas Chromatography - Mass Spectrometry Abstracts, 1974-85; Member, Editorial Advisory Board: Biomedical & Environmental Mass Spectrometry; Journal of Chromatography Biomedical Applications; Journal of High Resolution Chromatography and Chromatography Communications; Rapid Communications in Mass Spectrometry; Editorial Advisor, Biochemical Journal. Recreations: travel; music. Address: (b.) Chemistry Department, Glasgow University, Glasgow, G12 8QQ; T.-041-339 8855.

Brooks, Professor David Neil, BA, MSc, PhD. Titular Professor, Department of Psychological Medicine, Glasgow University, since 1984; b. 6.3.44, Huddersfield; m., Christine; 2 s.; 1 d. Educ. William Hulme's Grammar School, Manchester; University of Wales; Leeds University; Glasgow University. Senior Lecturer in Clinical Psychology, Glasgow University, 1972-84. Head of Postgraduate Training Course in Clinical Psychology, Glasgow University; Member, EEC Working Group on Head Injury; Member, Neuroscience Grants Committee, Medical Research Council, 1979-85; Secretary, MRC Co-ordinating Group on Rehabilitation After Acute Brain Damage. Recreations: shooting; working. Address: (h.) 16 Dougalston Gardens North, Milngavie, Glasgow, G62 6HN.

Brooks, James, BTech (Hons), MPhil, PhD, FRSC, CChem, FGS, FInstPet, AssocBIT. Senior Partner, Brooks Associates Glasgow, since 1986; Visiting Lecturer, Glasgow University, since 1978; Chairman/Director, Petroleum Geology '86 Limited, since 1985; b. 11.10.38, Co. Durham; m., Jan Slack; 1 s.; 1 d. Educ. Bradford University. Research Scientist, British Petroleum, 1969-75; Senior Research Fellow, Bradford University, 1975-77; Research Associate/Section Head/Senior Scientist, British National Oil Corporation/Britoil PLC, 1977-86. Geological Society: Vice President, 1984-87, Secretary, since 1987; Founder and Chairman, The Petroleum Group; Member, House of Delegates, AAPG. Publications: 13 books; 70 research papers. Recreations: travel; reading; writing; sport (English soccer!); Christian work. Address: (h.) 10 Langside Drive, Newlands, Glasgow, G43 2EE; T.-041-632 3068.

Brooks, Patrick William, BSc, MB, ChB, DPM, MRCPsych. Senior Medical Officer, Scottish Home and Health Department, since 1981; b. 17.5.38, Hereford. Educ. Hereford High School; Bishop Vesey's Grammar School, Sutton Coldfield; Edinburgh University. Royal Edinburgh and associated hospitals, including State Hospital, Carstairs, and Western General Hospital, Edinburgh: Senior House Officer, 1964-66; Registrar, 1966-69; Senior Registrar, 1969-74; Medical Officer, Scottish Home and Health Department, 1974-81. A founder Member, Edinburgh Festival Fringe Society, 1959 (Vice-Chairman, 1964-71); Chairman, Edinburgh Playhouse Society, 1975-81; Secretary, Lothian Playhouse Trust, 1981-83; Chairman, Scottish Arts Lobby (SALVO); Secretary and Treasurer, Edinburgh Friends of Scottish Ballet. Recreations: opera; ballet; music; theatre; cinema; modern Scottish art; travel. Address: (h.) 11 Thirlestane Road, Edinburgh, EH9 1AL.

Broom, Andrew Munro, MA, LLB. Deputy Keeper, Scottish Record Office, since 1985; b. 18.3.33, Glasgow; m., Katherine Mary Scott; 1 s.; 1 d. Educ. Hutchesons' Boys' Grammar School, Glasgow; Glasgow University; Edinburgh University. National Service, RASC, 1955-57; PA to Deputy Director, Army Legal Services, War Office, 1956-57; joined Scottish Record Office as Assistant Keeper, Grade II, 1957; Grade I, 1963; Secretary, National Register of Archives (Scotland), 1963-71; seconded to Registrar-General for Scotland as Departmental Record Officer, 1974-77; Secretary, Committee on Conservation and Restoration, International Council on Archives, 1981-88. Chairman, Society of Archivists (Scottish Region). Recreations: swimming; photography; assisting Edinburgh Hospitals Broadcasting Service. Address: (b.) Scottish Record Office, HM General Register House, Edinburgh, EH1 3YY; T.-031-556 6585.

Broster, Rev. David, BA. Minister, Kilbirnie: St. Columba's, since 1983; b. 14.3.44, Liverpool; m., Margaret Ann; 2 d. Educ. Liverpool Institute High School; United Theological College, University of Wales; Open University. Dip., Theology; Cert., Pastoral Studies. Ordained by Presbyterian Church of Wales, 1969; Minister: Park Place, Tredegar, Gwent, 1969-78, Clubmoor Presbyterian Church of Wales, Liverpool, 1978-83; Clerk, Association in East, Presbyterian Church of Wales, 1981-83. Recreations: computers; gardening; advanced driving. Address: St. Columba's Manse, Kilbirnie, Ayrshire, KA25 7JU; T.-0505 683342.

Brough, Colin, MB, ChB, DPH, DIH, FFCM, FRCPE. Chief Administrative Medical Officer, Lothian Health Board, since 1980; b. 4.1.32, Edinburgh; m., Maureen Jennings; 4 s.; 1 d. Educ. Bell Baxter School, Cupar; Edinburgh University. House Officer, Leicester General Hospital and Royal Infirmary, Edinburgh, 1956-57; Surgeon-Lt., Royal Navy, 1957-60; GP, Leith and Fife, 1960-64; Deputy Medical Superintendent, Royal Infirmary, Edinburgh, 1965-67; ASMO, PASMO, Deputy SAMO, South-Eastern Regional Hospital Board, Scotland, 1967-74; Community Medicine Specialist, Lothian Health Board, 1974-80. Recreations: golf; shooting; fishing; first aid. Address: (h.) The Saughs, Gullane, East Lothian, EH31 2AL; T.-Gullane 842179.

Broun, Rev. Canon Claud Michael, BA (Oxon). Rector, Greyfriars, Kirkcudbright, and St. Mary's, Gatehouse of Fleet, since 1988; b. 9.2.30, Edinburgh; m., Janice Ann Watson; 2 s.; 1 d. Educ. Edinburgh Academy; Brasenose College, Oxford. Rector: St. Cuthbert's, Cambuslang, 1962-75, St. Mary's, Hamilton, 1975-88; Canon, St. Mary's Cathedral, Glasgow, since 1983. Editor, Truth and Unity newsletter. Recreations: cricket; hill-walking; crosswords. Address: Greyfriars Rectory, 54 High Street, Kirkcudbright, DG6 4JX; T.-0557 30580.

Brown, Alan Cameron, BSc (Hons), PhD, CBiol, MIBiol. Principal, Lauder Technical College, Dunfermline, since 1987; b. 18.1.43, Rothesay; m., Noel Robertson Lyle. Educ. Rothesay Academy; Glasgow University. Assistant Teacher of Science, Ayr Academy, 1969-70; Principal Teacher of Biology, Loudon Academy, 1970-71; Principal Teacher of Biology, Ravenspark Academy, 1971-72; Depute Director of Education, Berwick County Council, 1972-75; Assistant Director of Education, Borders Regional Council, 1975-80; Depute Principal, Galashiels College of FE, 1980-84; Depute Principal, Borders College of FE, 1984-87. Recreations: cycling; swimming. Address: (b.) Lauder Technical College, Halbeath, Dunfermline, Fife; T.-Dunfermline 726201.

Brown, Professor Alan Geoffrey, BSc, MB, ChB, PhD, FRSE, FIBiol. Professor of Veterinary Physiology, Edinburgh University, since 1984; b. 20.4.40, Nottingham; m., Judith Allen; 1 s.; 1 d. Educ. Mundella School, Nottingham; Edinburgh University. Assistant Lecturer, then Lecturer in Veterinary Physiology, Edinburgh University, 1964-68; Beit Memorial Fellow for Medical Research, 1968-71; Research Fellow supported by MRC, 1971-74; Lecturer, then Reader in Veterinary Physiology, Edinburgh University, 1974-84; holder, MRC Research Fellowship for academic staff, 1980-85. Member, Editorial Boards, several scientific journals. Recreations: music; gardening; walking; reading. Address: (b.) Department of Preclinical Veterinary Sciences, Edinburgh University, Edinburgh, EH9 1QH; T.-031-667 1011.

Brown, Catherine, FSA Scot. Freelance Food Writer, since 1973; b. Glasgow; m., Iain Brown; 2 d. Educ. Hutchesons Grammar School; Queens College, Glasgow. Lecturer, catering subjects; professional cook in hotels and restaurants; senior researcher, Scottish Hotel School, for book, British Cookery, published 1976; freelance consultant and food writer; Partner, Tourism Advisory Services. Publications: Scottish Regional Recipes, 1981; Scottish Cookery, 1985; A Flavour of Edinburgh, 1986. Recreations: cooking and eating; fishing. Address: (h.) 13 Kirklee Terrace, Glasgow, G12 0TH; T.-041-339 7095.

Brown, Charles, JP. Member, Glasgow District Council, since 1980; full-time official, National Union of Tailor and Garment Workers, since 1956; b. 4.11.21, Stirling; m., Margaret; 2 d. Educ. Pirn Street Advanced School, Glasgow. Governor, Baillies Institution; former Member, Glasgow Northern Hospital Board; Past Chairman, Glasgow Trades Council. Recreations: bowling; swimming; golf. Address: (h.) 340 Golfhill Drive, Glasgow, G31 2NY.

Brown, Professor Charles Malcolm, BSc, PhD, DSc, FRSA, FIBiol, FRSE. Professor of Microbiology, Heriot-Watt University, since 1979 (Head, Department of Brewing and Biological Sciences); Director, Riccarton Laboratory, Fermentech Ltd., since 1984; b. 21.9.41, Gisland; m., Diane Mary Bryant; 3 d. Educ. Houghton-le-Spring Grammar School; Birmingham University. Lecturer in Microbiology, Newcastle-upon-Tyne University, 1966-73; Senior Lecturer, Dundee University, 1973-79. Editor-in-Chief, Microbiological Sciences; Council Member: Scottish Marine Biological Association; Society for General Microbiology; Director, Bioscot Ltd. Recreations: music; walking. Address: (b.) Heriot-Watt University, Chambers Street, Edinburgh, EH1 1HX; T.-031-225 8432.

Brown, Professor Charles Victor, BA, PhD, FRSA. Professor of Economics, Stirling University, since 1970; b. 11.5.35, New Haven, Connecticut; m., Sara Ann Cook; 2 s. Educ. Haverford College; Massachusetts Institute of Technology; London University. Lecturer in Economics, Ibadan University, 1959-64; Lecturer in Economics, then Senior Lecturer, Glasgow University, 1964-70. Publications: Government and Banking in Western Nigeria, 1964; Nigerian Banking System, 1966; Economic Principles Applied (Editor), 1970; Public Sector Economics (Co-author), 3rd edition, 1986; Taxation and Labour Supply (Editor), 1981; Taxation and the Incentive to Work, 2nd edition, 1983; Unemployment and Inflation, 1984. Recreations: archaeology; sailing. Address: (b.) Department of Economics, Stirling University, Stirling; T.-0786 73171, Ext. 2618.

Brown, Colin Murray, CA. Chairman, Scottish Unit, The Stock Exchange, since 1987; b. 31.3.41, Glasgow; m., Patricia Mary Gillies; 2 s.; 1 d. Educ. Glenalmond. Qualified CA, 1967; joined Maclay Nairn and Ward, 1968; appointed Partner, 1973; Partner/Director, Campbell Neill & Co., Stockbrokers, since 1981. Recreation: golf. Address: (h.) Ardlui, Gryffe Road, Kilmacolm, Renfrewshire.

Brown, Daniel Martin, MA (Hons). Principal, Barmulloch College, since 1977; b. 4.12.28, Clydebank; m., Isabella Montgomery; 1 s.; 1 d. Educ. Clydebank High School; Dumbarton Academy; Glasgow University; Jordanhill College. Education Officer, RAF, 1952-54 (final rank, flying officer); Teacher of English and History: Vale of Leven Academy, 1954-56; Gordon Schools, Huntly, 1956-62; Teacher of English, Dunfermline High School, 1962-64; Senior Lecturer in English, Langside College of Further Education, Glasgow, 1964-70; Cardonald College, Glasgow: Head, Department of Communication Arts, 1970-75; Depute Principal, 1975-77. Chairman, Moderating Committee, SCOTBEC, 1975-78; Further Education Representative, Strathclyde Regional Council, 1980-83; Member, Officer Group on Post-Compulsory Education; Further Education Representative, Strathclyde Regional Council Joint Planning Group for Training in Community Work; College Organiser, College Public Speaking Annual Competition, Glasgow Junior Chamber of Commerce, 1978-86. Recreations: reading (especially 20th-century novelists); theatre; films; angling; bowling. Address: (h.) 45 Lanton Road, Newlands, Glasgow, G43 2SR; T.-041-637 8169.

Brown, David Blair, MA, LLB. Rector, Dunfermline High School, since 1983; b. 6.5.38, Glasgow; m., Marjory Kathleen Muir; 2 s.; 1 d. Educ. Hutchesons' Boys Grammar School, Glasgow; Glasgow University; Jordanhill College of Education. Teacher, Hutchesons' Boys Grammar School; Principal Teacher of History, Renfrew High School, 1970-74; Assistant Rector, Stonelaw High School, 1974-78; Depute Rector and Acting Head, Dalbeattie High School, 1978-81; Assistant Rector, Musselburgh Grammar School, 1981-83. Member, children's panel, since 1976; Church activities. Recreations: walking; cycling; gardening; motoring; ski-ing; theatre; music. Address: (h.) Damar, 130 Terregles Avenue, Maxwell Park, Glasgow, G41; T.-041-423 0604.

Brown, David Henry. Principal, Scottish Home and Health Department, since 1983; b. 13.5.40, Edinburgh; m., Catherine Agnes Moffat; 1 s.; 3 d. Educ. Broughton Senior Secondary School, Edinburgh. Scottish Tourist Board, 1969-72; Scottish Council (Development and Industry), 1973-77; Scottish Education Department, 1978-83 (Secretary, Scottish Council for Community Education, 1979-82). Recreations: hill-walking; road-running. Address: (h.) 23 Pentland Grove, Edinburgh, EH10 6NR; T.-031-445 1724.

Brown, Denis, MSc, FCCA. Director of Finance, Edinburgh University, since 1984; b. 27.8.42, Manchester; 4 s.; 1 d. Educ. Manchester Central Grammar School; Bradford University. Audit practice; Accountant, Shell UK; Systems Analyst, British Leyland; Corporate Finance Executive Assistant, Commercial Union, London, 1972-75; Financial Controller, Procon UK, 1975-77; Director of Finance, Open University, 1977-84. Address: (b.) Old College, South Bridge, Edinburgh, EH18 9YL; T.-031-667 1011, Ext. 4246.

Brown, Professor Donald Houston, JP, BSc, PhD, DSc. Professor in Inorganic Chemistry, Strathclyde University, since 1983; b. 26.2.30, Kilmarnock; widower; 2 s.; 1 d. Educ. Kilmarnock Academy; Glasgow University. Recreations: golf; bridge. Address: (h.) 4 Howard Street, Kilmarnock; T.-Kilmarnock 21632.

Brown, Ewan, MA, LLB, CA. Director: Noble Grossart Ltd., since 1971; Scottish Transport Group; Scottish Development Finance; John Wood Group Plc; Pict Petroleum Plc; b. 23.3.42, Perth; m., Christine; 1 s.; 1 d. Educ. Perth Academy; St. Andrews University. Session Clerk, Mayfield Parish Church, Edinburgh; Governor, Edinburgh College of Art. Recreations: family; golf; skiing; Scottish watercolours. Address: (b.) 48 Queen Street, Edinburgh; T.-031-226 7011.

Brown, George, BL. Chief Executive Officer, Dunfermline District Council, since 1974; b. 2.1.33, Falkirk; m., Sarah; 2 s.; 1 d. Educ. Falkirk High School; Edinburgh University. Solicitor. Assistant Solicitor: Allan Dawson Simpson & Hampton, WS, 1954-55; Falkirk Burgh, 1955-59; Dunfermline Burgh, 1959-62; Town Clerk and Chamberlain, Linlithgow Burgh, 1962-70; Town Clerk and Chief Executive, Bathgate Burgh, 1970-74. Vice-Chairman, Scottish Branch, SOLACE. Recreations: gardening; philosophy. Address: (b.) City Chambers, Dunfermline, Fife; T.-Dunfermline 722711.

Brown, George Mackay, OBE, MA, Hon. MA (Open University), Hon. LLD (Dundee), Hon DLitt (Glasgow), FRSL. Poet and story-teller; b. 17.10.21, Stromness, Orkney. Educ. Stromness Academy; Newbattle Abbey College; Edinburgh University. Author of: (short stories) A Calendar of Love, A Time to Keep, Hawkfall, The Sun's Net, Andrina; (poetry) Selected Poems, Winterfold, Voyages; (novels) Greenvoe, Magnus, Time in a Red Coat, The Golden Bird; various plays for stage and television; three books for children; Editor, Selected Prose of Edwin Muir; two books on Orkney. Winner, 1988 James Tait Black prize for The Golden Bird. Address: (h.) 3 Mayburn Court, Stromness, Orkney, KW16 3DH.

Brown, Gordon. MP (Labour), Dunfermline East, since 1983; b. 20.2.51. Educ. Kirkcaldy High School. Second Student Rector, Edinburgh University; Past Chairman, Scottish Labour Party; former Journalist, Scotish Television.

Brown, Gordon Lamont. Scottish Rugby International and British Lion; Author and After-Dinner Speaker; b. 1.11.47, Troon; m., Linda; 1 s.; 1 d. Educ. Marr College, Troon. Bank Clerk, British Linen Bank, 1965-71; Building Society Manager: Leicester Building Society, 1971-76, Bristol & West Building Society, since 1976. Played for Scotland, 30 times; toured with British Isles Rugby Team ("Lions"), New Zealand 1971, South Africa 1974, New Zealand 1977; holds world record for number of tries scored by a forward on a tour (eight); Vice-Chairman, Stars Organisation for Spastics (Scotland); Finance Committee Member, National Playing Fields Association. Publications: Broon from Troon (autobiography); Rugby is a Funny Game (rugby anecdotes). Recreation: golf. Address: (h.) 65 Bentinck Drive, Troon, Ayrshire; T.-0292 314070.

Brown, Hamish Macmillan. Author, Lecturer, Photographer and Mountaineer; b. 13.8.34, Colombo, Sri Lanka. Educ. several schools abroad; Dollar Academy. National Service, RAF, Middle East/East Africa; Assistant, Martyrs' Memorial Church, Paisley; first-ever full-time appointment in outdoor education (Braehead School, Fife); served many years on Scottish Mountain Leadership Board; has led expeditions world-wide for mountaineering, skiing, trekking, canoeing, etc. Publications: Hamish's Mountain Walk, 1979 (SAC award); Hamish's Groats End Walk, 1981 (Smith's Travel Prize shortlist); Time Gentlemen, Some Collected Poems, 1983; Eye to the Hills, 1982; Five Bird Stories, 1984; Poems of the Scottish Hills (Editor), 1982; Speak to the Hills (Co-Editor), 1985; Travels, 1986; The Great Walking Adventure, 1986; Hamish Brown's Scotland, 1988; Climbing the Corbetts, 1988. Recreations: gardening; "bird" philately; books; music. Address: 21 Carlin Craig, Kinghorn, Fife, KY3 9RX; T.-0592 890422.

Brown, Hugh Dunbar; b. 18.5.19; m., Mary Glen Carmichael; 1 d. Educ. Allan Glen's School; Whitehill Secondary School, Glasgow. Former Civil Servant, Ministry of Pensions and National Insurance; Member, Glasgow Corporation, 1954; Magistrate, Glasgow, 1961; MP (Lab), Glasgow Provan, 1964-87; Parliamentary Under Secretary of State, Scottish Office, 1974-79. Recreation: golf. Address: (h.) 29 Blackwood Road, Milngavie, Glasgow, G62 7LB.

Brown, Ian Forbes, FIB (Scot). Director and Chief Executive, British Linen Bank, since 1979; Director: Motherwell Bridge Holdings Ltd., since 1983; Wilson Distributors (Scotland) Ltd., since 1986; Chairman, IFA Inc., Chicago, since 1987; Chairman, Gillies Melville Associates Limited, since 1986; Director, Anglo Scottish Properties PLC, since 1988; b. 5.3.29, Glasgow; m., Margaret Catherine; 1 s.; 1 d. Educ. Glasgow High School. Has spent entire career with Bank of Scotland, apart from five years spent in Canada; executive responsibilities in Bank of Scotland International Division. Recreations: golf; travelling; reading. Address: (h.) 22 Cammo Gardens, Edinburgh, EH4 8EQ; T.-031-339 1640.

Brown, Ian Johnston Hilton, MA (Hons). Rector, Lanark Grammar School, since 1986 (Rector, Strathaven Academy, 1976-86); b. 5.10.37, Aberdeen. Educ. Royal High School, Edinburgh; Edinburgh University; Moray House College of Education. Teacher, Kirkcaldy High School, 1961-66; Principal Teacher, Bishopbriggs High School, 1966-71; Assistant Head Teacher, Cathkin High School, 1971-74; Depute Rector, Hunter High School, 1974-76. Recreations: hill-walking; badminton. Address: (b.) Lanark Grammar School, Lanark, ML11 9AQ; T.-Lanark 2471.

Brown, James Armour, RD, BL, FSA (Scot). Partner, Kerr, Barrie & Duncan (formerly Kerr, Barrie & Goss), Solicitors, Glasgow, since 1957; b. 20.7.30, Rutherglen; m., Alexina Mary Robertson McArthur; 1 s. Educ. Rutherglen Academy; Glasgow University. National Service, Royal Navy, 1951-53; commissioned RNVR, 1952; served with Clyde Division, RNVR/RNR, 1953-72; Captain, 1972; Senior Reserve Supply Officer on staff of Admiral Commanding Reserves, 1973-76; Naval ADC to The Queen, 1975-76; Member, Suite of Lord High Commissioner to General Assembly of Church of Scotland, 1961-63; Session Clerk, Stonelaw Parish Church, Rutherglen, 1964-81; Member, Church of Scotland Committee on Chaplains to HM Forces, 1975-82 (Vice-Convener, 1979-82); Clerk, Incorporation of Bakers of Glasgow, since 1964; Deacon, Society of Deacons and Free Preseses of Glasgow, 1978-80; Member, Glasgow Committee, Order of St. John of Jerusalem, since 1961 (Chairman, since 1982); Member, Chapter of the Priory of Scotland of the Order of St. John, since 1970; KStJ, 1975; Preceptor of Torphichen, Priory of Scotland, since 1984; Hon. Chairman, Orders and Medals Research Society (Scottish Branch), since 1987. Recreations: music; historical research. Address: (h.) 25 Calderwood Road, Rutherglen, Glasgow, G73 3HD; T.-041-647 2051.

Brown, Jenny, MA (Hons). Director, Edinburgh Book Festival, since 1983; b. 13.5.58, Manchester; m., Adam Zyw; 2 s. Educ. George Watson's College; Aberdeen University. Assistant Administrator, Edinburgh Festival Fringe Society, 1980-82. Address: (b.) 25A SW Thistle Street Lane, Edinburgh, EH2 1EW; T.-031-225 1915.

Brown, Professor John Campbell, BSc, PhD, DSc, FRAS, FRSE. Professor of Astrophysics, Glasgow University, since 1984; b. 4.2.47, Dumbarton; m., Dr. Margaret I. Brown; 1 s.; 1 d. Educ. Dumbarton Academy; Glasgow University. Glasgow University Astronomy Department: Research Assistant, 1968-70, Lecturer, 1970-78, Senior Lecturer, 1978-80, Reader, 1980-84; Nuffield Fellow, 1983-84; Kelvin Medallist, 1983-86; DAAD Fellow, Tubingen University, 1971-72; ESRO/GROC Fellow, Space Research Laboratory, Utrecht, 1973-74; Visitor: Australian National University, 1975, High Altitude Observatory, Colorado, 1977; NASA Associate Professor, Maryland University, 1980; NSF Fellow, University of California at San Diego, 1984; Brittingham Professor, University of Wisconsin, 1987. SERC Solar System Committee, 1980-83; Council, Royal Astronomical Society, 1984-87 (Vice-President, 1986-87); Member, International Astronomical Union, since 1976. Recreations: cycling; walking; painting; lapidary; conjuring; photography; woodwork. Address: (b.) Department of Physics and Astronomy, Glasgow University, Glasgow, G12 8QW; T.-041-330 5182.

Brown, John Clouston, AIB (Scot). Member, Orkney Islands Council, since 1978; b. 4.10.14, Stromness, Orkney; m., Maria Sinclair Flett; 2 s.; 1 d. Educ. Stromness Academy. Joined Union Bank of Scotland Ltd., Stromness, Orkney, 1931; RAF, Burma and India, 1941-45; Manager, Stromness Branch, Union Bank of Scotland (subsequently Bank of Scotland), 1954-74. Past Chairman, Stromness Golf Club; former Secretary: Stromness Chamber of Commerce, Kirkwall Arts Club; former Treasurer, Orkney Agricultural Society. Recreations: golf; fishing; drama. Address: (h.) Breck, Birsay, Orkney, KW17 2LY; T.-Birsay 349.

Brown, Rev. Joseph, MA. Minister, Yetholm, Linton, Morebattle and Hownam, since 1967; b. 2.10.27, Edinburgh; m., Dolina MacDonald; 1 s.; 1 d. Educ. George Heriot's School; Edinburgh University; New College, Edinburgh. Royal Army Chaplain's Department, 1954-57 (attached, Cameron Highlanders); Minister: Kilbrandon and Kilchattan, Argyll, 1957-63, St. Ninian's Musselburgh, 1963-67. Recreations: working glebe; gardening; music. Address: The Manse, Kirk Yetholm, Kelso, Roxburghshire; T.-Yetholm 308.

Brown, Kenneth Clarke, CIPFA. Director of Finance, Nithsdale District Council, since 1984; b. 28.5.44, Dumfries; m., Olivia; 1 s.; 1 d. Educ. Dumfries Academy. Commenced career as Audit Examiner with District Audit in Chelmsford, 1966; moved to Carlisle; appointed Chief Internal Auditor, Skelmersdale and Holland UDC, 1971; moved to similar post, Chorley Borough Council, 1974; Depute Director of Finance, Nithsdale District Council, 1976-84. Honorary Treasurer, Ellisland Trust. Recreations: golf; football; keep-fit; DIY. Address: (h.) Kilmory, 51 Rotchell Park, Dumfries, DG2 7RL; T.-0387 54889.

Brown, Madeline, MB, ChB, MRCPsy, DPsy. Consultant Child Psychiatrist, Royal Aberdeen Children's Hospital, since 1982; b. 30.10.37, Aberdeen; m., Ian R. Brown; 2 s. Educ. Aberdeen Academy; Aberdeen University. Recreations: hill-walking; badminton; drama. Address: (h.) 37 Argyll Place, Aberdeen; T.-0224 633996.

Brown, Neil Dallas, DA, ARSA. Painter; Lecturer, Department of Fine Art Studies (Painting Studios), Glasgow School of Art, since 1979; b. 10.8.38, Elgin; m., Georgina Ballantyne; 2 d. Educ. Bell Baxter High School, Cupar; Duncan of Jordanstone College of Art, Dundee; Royal Academy Schools, London. Visiting Lecturer, School of Design, Duncan of Jordanstone College of Art, since 1968; Visiting Lecturer in Painting, Glasgow School of Art, since 1976; since completing training, 28 one-man exhibitions, in Dundee, Manchester, Edinburgh, London (eight), Glasgow, York, Basle, Paris, Stirling, Belfast, Aberdeen and Kirkcaldy; won 10 awards for painting; has been Guest Artist, Dollar Summer School for the Arts, Croydon College of Art, Strathclyde University, Ulster Polytechnic, Grays School of Art (Aberdeen), Maryland Institute College of Art (Baltimore), Newport College of Art (Wales). Recreations: fishing; running. Address: (h.) Tayside, 55 Cupar Road, Newport-on-Tay, Fife, DD6 8DF; T.-542130.

Brown, Ormond John. Honorary Sheriff of Tayside, Central and Fife, at Stirling, since 1982; b. 30.1.22, Gourock; m., Margaret Eileen Beard; 2 d. Educ. Gourock High School; Greenock High School. Entered Sheriff Clerk service, Scotland, 1939; served Second World War, 1941-45, Outer Hebrides, North Africa, Italy, Greece, Austria; Training Organiser, Scottish Court Service, 1957; Sheriff Clerk of Perthshire, 1970; Principal Clerk of Justiciary, 1971-75; Principal Clerk of Session and Justiciary, 1975-82. Past Chairman, Royal British Legion, Dunblane; Past Captain, Dunblane New Golf Club. Recreations: listening to music; playing indifferent but enthusiastic golf; gardening; remembering the great days of the Clyde steamers; hoping for the revival of Greenock Morton. Address: (h.) Ormar, 29 Atholl Place, Dunblane, Perthshire; T.-0786 822186.

Brown, Professor Peter Evans, PhD, FRSE. Professor of Geology, Aberdeen University, since 1973; b. 5.4.30, Kendal; m., Thelma Smith; 2 s. Educ. Kendal School; Manchester University. Mineralogist/Geologist, Geological Survey of Tanganyika; Lecturer/Senior Lecturer in Geology, Sheffield University. Fellow, Geological Society. Recreations: mountaineering; exploration. Address: (b.) Department of Geology and Mineralogy, Aberdeen University, Marischal College, Aberdeen, AB9 1AS; T.-0224 40241, Ext. 273.

Brown, Professor Peter Melville, MA (Oxon), DPhil. Professor Emeritus, Glasgow University, since 1986 (Stevenson Professor of Italian, 1975-86); b. 7.7.26, Todmorden; m., Aileen Taylor Tough; 2 s.; 1 d. Educ. Todmorden Grammar School; Magdalen College, Oxford; Scuola Normale Superiore, Pisa. Aberdeen University: Assistant Lecturer in Italian, 1955-57, Lecturer in Italian, 1957-66, Senior Lecturer in Italian, 1966-72; Professor of Italian, Hull University, 1972-75. Publication: Lionardo Salviati: A Critical Biography, 1975. Recreation: travel. Address: (h.) 23 Osborne Place, Aberdeen, AB2 4BX; T.-0224 640473.

Brown, Peter Robert, MB, BCh, DTM&H, DA, FFARCS. Consultant Anaesthetist, Perth Royal Infirmary, since 1975; b. 19.11.31, Manchester; m., Ann Kathleen; 1 s.; 1 d. Educ. Oswestry, Bradford and Altrincham Grammar Schools; Queen's University, Belfast. Short service commission, RAMC, 1960-64; Consultant, Huddersfield Royal Infirmary, 1967-75. Faculty Tutor, Faculty of Anaesthetists, Royal College of Surgeons, England, 1983-85; Chairman, Division of Anaesthesia, Perth Royal Infirmary, 1985-88. Recreations: golf; photography; music; World War I aviation literature; gardening; decorating. Address: (h.) Craig House, by Pitcairngreen, Perth; T.-073 884 268.

Brown, Ralph Alexander Stark, MA, LLB. Procurator Fiscal, Cupar, since 1977; b. 16.6.27, Glasgow; m., Mary Bell; 1 s. Educ. Glasgow Academy; Glasgow University. Solicitor: private practice, 1956-71, local government, 1971-74; Procurator Fiscal service, since 1974. Recreations: music; gardening; travel; photography. Address: (b.) County Buildings, Cupar, Fife, KY15 4LS; T.-Cupar 54991.

Brown, Robert Edward, LLB (Hons), NP. Solicitor; Member, Glasgow District Council, and Leader, Liberal Group, since 1977; b. 25.12.47, Newcastle-upon-Tyne; m., Gwen Morris; 1 s.; 1 d. Educ. Gordon Schools, Huntly; Aberdeen University. Legal apprenticeship, Aberdeen, 1969-71; Procurator Fiscal Depute, Dumbarton, 1972-74; Assistant, then Partner, Ross Harper & Murphy, Rutherglen and Glasgow, since 1974. Parliamentary candidate (Liberal), Rutherglen, October 1974, 1979, 1983, 1987; first Liberal, Glasgow District Council; former Secretary, North Aberdeen Liberals; former Member, Scottish Liberal Party Executive and Local Government Organiser; Debates Convenor, Strathclyde Junior Chamber, 1973; Chairman, Rutherglen Citizens' Advice Bureau, 1980-83; Honorary President, Rutherglen Bowling Club, since 1977. Recreations: politics; reading; history; science fiction. Address: (h.) 3 Douglas Avenue, Rutherglen, Glasgow; T.-041-634 2353.

Brown, Robert Thomson. Member (SNP), Kilmarnock and Loudoun District Council, 1984-88; b. 26.12.26, Kilmarnock; m., Isobel Sandford Paton; 2 s.; 1 d. Educ. Dreghorn School. Royal

Artillery, 1945-47 (Gunner); Massey-Ferguson, 1949-80; Member (SNP), Kilmarnock and Loudoun District Council, 1977-80; Member, Electricity Consultative Council, 1977-81; Chairman, Crosshouse Community Council, 1980-83; Steward (Curator), Irvine Burns Club. Recreation: study of life and works of Robert Burns. Address: (h.) Wellwood, 28A Eglinton Street, Irvine, KA12 8AS; T.-Irvine 74511.

Brown, Rev. Robin Graeme, BA, BD. Principal, St. Colm's Education Centre and College, since 1984; b. 27.11.32, Alverstoke, Hampshire; m., Sibyl Enid Clark; 1 s.; 2 d. Educ. Fettes College, Edinburgh; Cambridge University; Edinburgh University; Heidelberg University. Principal, St. Columba's College, Alice, South Africa, 1971-73; Leader, Iona Community, 1974-81. Address: (h.) 24 Inverleith Terrace, Edinburgh, EH3 5NU; T.-031-332 1156.

Brown, Ronald. MP (Labour), Edinburgh Leith, since 1979; b. June, 1940. Educ. Ainslie Park High School, Edinburgh. Member, Lothian Regional Council, 1974-79.

Brown, Sally, BSc, MA, PhD. Director, Scottish Council for Research in Education, since 1986; b. 15.12.35, London; m., Professor Charles Brown; 2 s. Educ. Bromley High School GPDST; University College, London; Smith College, Massachusetts; Stirling University. Lecturer in College of Education, London, and College of Technology, Nigeria; University Lecturer, Nigeria; School Science Teacher, Helensburgh; University Researcher, Stirling; Research Adviser to Scottish Education Department. Publications: 50 (articles, monographs, books) on educational research and education generally. Recreations: squash; sailing. Address: (b.) 15 St John Street, Edinburgh, EH8 8JR; T.-031-557 2944.

Brown, William, CBE (1971). Managing Director, Scottish Television, since 1966 (Deputy Chairman, since 1974); b. 24.6.29, Ayr; m., Nancy Jennifer Hunter; 1 s.; 3 d. Educ. Ayr Academy; Edinburgh University. STV: London Sales Manager, 1958-61, Sales Director, 1961-63, Deputy Managing Director, 1963-66. Lord Willis Award for services to TV, 1982; Royal Television Society Gold Medal for outstanding services to TV, 1984; Chairman, Council, ITCA, 1968-69, 1978-80; Director, ITN, 1972-77; Director, ITP, since 1968; Director, Channel 4, 1980-84; Director, Scottish Amicable Life Assurance Society, since 1981. Recreation: golf. Address: (b.) STV, Cowcaddens, Glasgow, G2 3PR.

Brown, William, BL, SSC, NP. Solicitor; Senior Partner, Ranken & Reid, SSC; b. 18.3.32, Dunfermline; m., Anne Sword; 2 d. Educ. Dunfermline High School; Edinburgh University. National Service commission, RAOC, 1952; joined Ranken & Reid, 1960. Member, Society of High Constables of Edinburgh. Recreations: golf; music; shooting. Address: (h.) Glenavon, 45 Barnton Avenue, Edinburgh, EH4 6JJ; T.-031-336 4227.

Browne, Ronald Grant, DA. Folk Entertainer ("The Corries"), since 1961; Portrait Painter, since 1979; b. 20.8.37, Edinburgh; m., Patricia Isabella Elliot; 2 s.; 1 d. Educ. Boroughmuir School, Edinburgh; Edinburgh College of Art. Teacher of Art and Painting, 1959-63; folk entertaining, 1963-79; folk entertaining and portrait painting, since 1979.

Browning, Professor George Kenneth Spencer, BSc, PhD, MBCS. Titular Professor of Text Manipulation and Related Studies, Computer Publishing Unit, Glasgow University, since 1987 (Director of Computing Services, 1970-87); Managing Director, Computing Services (University of Glasgow) Ltd., since 1982; b. 3.12.38, Dumfries; m., Dr. Janet Paton Finlayson; 2 d. Educ. Glasgow Academy; Glasgow University. Assistant Lecturer, then Lecturer, Department of Natural Philosophy, Glasgow University, 1963-70. Member: Programme Committee, National Development Programme in Computer Assisted Learning, 1973-77, Standing Committee, Inter-University Committee on Computing, 1978-81; Editor, IUCC Bulletin (now University Computing), 1980-82; Honorary Treasurer, Kilmardinny Music Circle, Bearsden. Recreation: listening to music. Address: (h.) Arnprior, 48 Mitre Road, Jordanhill, Glasgow, G14 9LE; T.-041-959 5753.

Browning, J. Robin, BA (Hons), FIB (Scot). Joint General Manager, Bank of Scotland, since 1986 (Divisional General Manager, 1983-86); b. 29.7.39, Kirkcaldy; m., Christine Campbell; 1 s.; 1 d. Educ. Morgan Academy, Dundee; Strathclyde University. Bank of Scotland: Assistant Management Accountant, 1971-74, Assistant Manager (Corporate Planning), 1974-77; British Linen Bank Ltd.: Manager, 1977-79, Assistant Director, 1979-81, Director, 1981-82; Assistant General Manager, Bank of Scotland, 1982-83. Chairman, Tax and Accountancy Committee, Equipment Leasing Association, 1980-82. Recreations: curling; gardening; DIY enthusiast. Address: (b.) Management Services Division, Bank of Scotland, 2 Bankhead, Crossway North, Sighthill, Edinburgh, EH11; T.-031-443 4111.

Browning, Margaret Callan Kirk, BSc. Clinical Biochemist; Principal Biochemist, Department of Biochemical Medicine, Ninewells Hospital, Dundee, since 1979; Honorary Lecturer, Dundee University, since 1978; b. 14.6.39, Edinburgh. Educ. James Gillespie's High School for Girls; Edinburgh University. Research Assistant, Department of Pharmacology and Therapeutics, Queen's College, Dundee, 1961-63; Assistant Lecturer, 1963-64; Basic Grade Biochemist, Department of Steroid Biochemistry, Royal Infirmary, Glasgow, 1964-66; Senior Biochemist, Department of Clinical Chemistry, Maryfield Hospital, and latterly Department of Biochemical Medicine, Ninewells Hospital, Dundee, 1966-79. Recreations: gardening; reading; handicrafts; travel; cooking. Address: (h.) Norwood, 4 Wellpark Terrace, Newport-on-Tay, Fife, DD6 8HT; T.-0382 54 2140.

Brownlie, Alistair Rutherford, OBE, MA, LLB, SSC. Solicitor; Secretary, Society of Solicitors in the Supreme Courts of Scotland, since 1970; b. 5.4.24, Edinburgh; m., Martha Barron Mounsey. Educ. George Watson's Boys College, Edinburgh; Edinburgh University. Served World War II as radio operator, 658 Air OP Squadron, RAF, in Europe and India; apprenticed to J. & R.A.

Robertson, WS; thereafter Solicitor in private practice, Edinburgh; former Member, Council, Law Society of Scotland; Legal Aid Central Committee; founder Member and Past President, Forensic Science Society; Member, Government Technical Panel 9 on instrumental breath analysis; Member, Scottish Legal Aid Board; Elder, Church of Scotland and Congregational Union of Scotland. Recreations: the pen, the spade and the saw. Address: (h.) 8 Braid Mount, Edinburgh; T.-031-447 4255.

Brownlie, Rev. Gavin Dunipace, MA. Minister, Ladyloan St. Columba's Church, Arbroath, since 1961; b. 9.6.27, Glasgow; m., Frances Duff; 2 s.; 1 d. Educ. Hillhead School; Glasgow High School; Hamilton Academy; Glasgow University. Assistant Minister, St. Bride's, Edinburgh, 1953-55; Minister, Redding and Westquarter Parish Church, 1955-61. Founder Chairman, Arbroath Children's Panel Advisory Committee, 1970-74; Member, Tayside CPAC, 1974-78; Member, Tayside Education Committee, 1982. Recreations: golf; bowling; curling; bridge; swimming. Address: Ladyloan Manse, Dishlandtown Street, Arbroath, DD11 1QU; T.-0241 72356.

Brownlie, William Steel, MC, TD, MA; b. 12.10.23, Cambusnethan; m., 1, Margaret Mitchell (deceased); 2, Netta Russell (deceased); 1 s.; 1 d. Educ. Greenock Academy; Glasgow University. Royal Armoured Corps, 1942-47; 2nd Fife and Forfar Yeomanry, 1944-47; Captain, NW Europe; Ayrshire (ECO) Yeomanry, 1950-68; Lt.-Col. Commanding, 1966-68; Teacher, John Neilson High School, Paisley, 1951-84 (Principal Teacher, Modern Languages); Contributor, Lingo Column, Times Educational Supplement; Editor, The Scottish Schoolmaster; Editor, The Yeoman (Ayrshire Yeomanry). Publications: The Proud Trooper (History of the Ayrshire Yeomanry), 1964; Thirteen Letters from a Scottish Solider (Editor), 1988. Recreations: military history; philately; photography; philology; whisky. Address: (h.) Orchard Cottage, Law Brae, West Kilbride, KA23 9DD; T.-0294 822216.

Bruce, David, MA. Director, Scottish Film Council, since 1986; b. 10.6.39, Dundee; m., Barbara; 1 s.; 1 d. Educ. Dundee High School; Aberdeen Grammar School; Edinburgh University. Freelance (film), 1963; Assistant Director, Films of Scotland, 1964-66; Director, Edinburgh International Film Festival, 1965-66; Promotions Manager, Mermaid Theatre, London, 1966-67; Executive Officer, British Universities Film Council, 1967-69; joined Scottish Film Council as Assistant Director, 1969; Depute Director, SFC and Scottish Council for Educational Technology, 1977-86. Chairman, Mental Health Film Council, 1982-84; Chairman, Scottish Society for History of Photography, 1983-86. Recreations: movies; music; photo-history. Address: (b.) Dowanhill, 74 Victoria Crescent Road, Glasgow, G12 9JN; T.-041-334 9314.

Bruce, George, OBE (1984), MA, LittD. Writer/ Lecturer; b. 10.3.09, Fraserburgh; m., Elizabeth Duncan; 1 s.; 1 d. Educ. Fraserburgh Academy; Aberdeen University. Teacher, English Department, Dundee High School, 1935-46; BBC Producer, Aberdeen, 1946-56; BBC Talks (Documentary) Producer, Edinburgh, with special responsibility for arts programmes, 1956-70; first Fellow in Creative Writing, Glasgow University, 1971-73; Visiting Professor, Union Theological Seminary, Richmond, Virginia, and Writer in Residence, Prescott College, Arizona, 1974; Visiting Professor of English, College of Wooster, Ohio, 1976-77; Scottish-Australian Writing Fellow, 1982; E. Hervey Evans Distinguished Fellow, St. Andrews Presbyterian College, North Carolina, 1985; Vice-Chairman, Council, Saltire Society; Council Member, Advisory Council of the Arts in Scotland; Extra-Mural Lecturer, Glasgow, St. Andrews and Edinburgh Universities; Executive Editor, The Scottish Review, 1975-76. Publications: verse: Sea Talk, 1944; Selected Poems, 1947; Landscapes and Figures, 1967; Collected Poems, 1970; The Red Sky, 1985; Perspectives: poems 1970-86, 1987; prose: Scottish Sculpture Today (Co-author), 1947; Anne Redpath, 1974; The City of Edinburgh, 1974; Festival in the North, 1975; Some Practical Good, 1975; as Editor: The Scottish Literary Revival, 1962; Scottish Poetry Anthologies 1-6 (Co-Editor), 1966-72. Recreation: visiting friends. Address: 25 Warriston Crescent, Edinburgh, EH3 5LB; T.-031-556 3848.

Bruce, John Wilkinson, AHWC, CChem, MRSC, BSc, BA. Member: Dumfries and Galloway Regional Council, since 1986; Annandale and Eskdale District Council, 1984-88; b. 10.2.25, Leith; 2 d. Educ. Broughton Secondary School, Edinburgh; Heriot-Watt College, Edinburgh. Industrial Chemist: Stewart and Lloyds, Corby, 1945-47, SCWS Junction Mills, Leith, 1947-52; Teacher: Earlston, Berwickshire, 1954-58, Duns, 1958-63; Principal Teacher of Science, Langholm, 1963-83 (also Deputy Rector, 1965-83). Educational Institute of Scotland: President, Berwickshire Branch, 1962-63, President, Dumfriesshire Branch, 1968-69; President, Langholm Congregational Church, 1966-70; Member, Langholm Town Council, 1966-72, and 1973-75; President, Honours Graduate Teachers' Association, 1980-84. Recreations: bridge; bowls; amateur operatics; philosophy. Address: (h.) 14 John Street, Langholm, Dumfriesshire, DG13 OAD.

Bruce, Malcolm Gray, MA, MSc. MP (Liberal), Gordon, since 1983; Liberal Parliamentary Spokesman on Scottish Affairs, 1983-85, on Energy, since 1985, on Trade and Industry, since 1987; Alliance Employment Spokesman, 1987; Vice-Chairman, Political, Scottish Liberal Party, 1975-84; Rector, Dundee University; b. 17.11.44, Birkenhead; m., Jane Wilson; 1 s.; 1 d. Educ. Wrekin College; Strathclyde University; St. Andrews University. Trainee Journalist, Liverpool Daily Post & Echo, 1966-67; Section Buyer, Boots the Chemist, 1968-69; Fashion Retailing Executive, A. Goldberg & Sons, 1969-70; Research and Information Officer, NESDA, 1971-75; Marketing Director, Noroil Publishing, 1975-81; Director, Aberdeen Petroleum Publishing; Editor/Publisher, Aberdeen Petroleum Report, 1981-83; Co-Editor, Scottish Petroleum Annual, 1st and 2nd editions. Recreations: reading; music; theatre; hill-walking; cycling; travel. Address: (h.) East View, Woodside Road, Torphins, Aberdeenshire, AB3 4JR; T.-033982 386.

Bruford, Alan James, BA, PhD. Archivist, School of Scottish Studies, Edinburgh University, since 1965; Editor, Tocher, since 1971; b. 10.5.37, Edinburgh; m., Morag B. Wood; 1 d. Educ. Edinburgh Academy; Winchester College; St. John's College, Cambridge; Edinburgh University. Junior Research Fellow, 1965; Assistant Lecturer, 1965; Lecturer, 1968; Senior Lecturer, 1984; fieldwork throughout Scotland, especially Orkney and Shetland, collecting folktales and other traditions, songs, fiddle music and oral history; Treasurer, Scottish Association of Magazine Publishers, 1974-79; Chairman, Scottish Oral History Group, since 1987; Organising Secretary, 7th Congress, International Society for Folk-Narrative Research, 1979. Publications: Gaelic Folk-Tales and Mediaeval Romances, 1969; The Green Man of Knowledge and Other Scots Traditional Tales, 1982. Recreations: music (traditional, baroque, composition); travel in Scotland; quizzes. Address: (h.) South Mains, West Linton, Peeblesshire, EH46 7AY; T.-0968 60562.

Brumfitt, Professor John Henry, MA, DPhil (Oxon). Emeritus Professor, St. Andrews University, since 1986 (Professor of French, 1969-86); b. 5.4.21, Shipley; m., 1, Patricia Renee Grand; 2, Margaret Anne Ford; 1 s.; 2 d. Educ. Bradford Grammar School; Queen's College, Oxford. Laming Travelling Fellow, Queen's College, Oxford, 1947-48; Lecturer in French, University College, Oxford, 1948-51; St. Andrews University: Lecturer in French, 1951-59, Senior Lecturer, 1959-69; Member, Editorial Boards, French Studies and Forum for Modern Language Studies. Publications: The French Enlightenment; Voltaire Historian. Address: (h.) 22 Buchanan Gardens, St. Andrews, Fife; T.-0334 73079.

Brunt, Peter William, MD, FRCP(Lond), FRCP(Edin). Consultant Physician, Aberdeen Royal Infirmary, since 1970; Clinical Senior Lecturer in Medicine, Aberdeen University, since 1970; Physician to The Queen in Scotland, since 1984; b. 18.1.36, Prestatyn; m., Marina Evelyn Anne Lewis; 3 d. Educ. Manchester Grammar School; King George V School; Liverpool University. Recreations: mountaineering; music. Address: (h.) 17 Kingshill Road, Aberdeen, AB2 4JY; T.-Aberdeen 314204.

Bryant, Anthony B., FRICS. Regional Representative, Highlands, National Trust for Scotland, since 1986; b. 25.1.38; m., Jane E.A.; 1 s.; 1 d. Educ. Bryanston School. Trained as land agent, Chatsworth Estate, 1956-60, returning there 1964-69 after working for the Duchy of Cornwall; joined National Trust for Scotland as Depute Factor, 1969; Factor, 1976; Head Factor, 1984. Recreations: music; painting. Address: (b.) Abertarff House, Church Street, Inverness; T.-Inverness 232034.

Bryden, Bill. Director/Writer; Associate Director, National Theatre, since 1974; Head of Drama, BBC Scotland, since 1985; b. 12.4.42, Greenock; m., Hon. Deborah Morris; 1 s.; 1 d. Educ. Greenock High School. Researcher, STV, 1964; Assistant Director, Royal Court Theatre, 1966; Associate Director, Royal Lyceum Theatre, Edinburgh, 1969; Member, Board of Directors, Scottish Television, 1982-85; Director (National Theatre): The Mysteries, Glengarry Glen Ross; author of plays: Willie Rough, Benny Lynch; film scripts: Long Riders, Ill Fares The Land, The Holy City. Recreation: music. Address: (b.) BBC, Queen Margaret Drive, Glasgow; T.-041-339 8844.

Bryden, John Stephens, MB, ChB, MSC, FFCM, DipSocMed, MBCS. Community Medicine Specialist, Greater Glasgow Health Board, since 1984; Health Information Consultant; b. 20.11.32, Glasgow; m., Dr. Grace Macfarlane; 1 s.; 2 d. Educ. Rothesay Academy; Glasgow University; Strathclyde University. National Service; accident and emergency medicine; general practice, Glasgow; Medical Superintendent, Royal Alexandra Infirmary, Paisley; Chief Administrative Medical Officer, Argyll and Clyde Health Board; Senior Epidemiologist, Scottish Head Injury Management Study; Director, PIMMS (medical manpower database). Recreation: railways. Address: (b.) 225 Bath Street, Glasgow, G2 4JT; T.-041-204 2755.

Bryson, Archibald Gordon Stuart, CA. Chartered Accountant, since 1935; a Director, Scottish Society for the Prevention of Cruelty to Animals, 1953-87; a Director, Royal Blind Asylum, 1950-87; b. Edinburgh; m., Eleanor; 1 d. Educ. Edinburgh Academy. CA, India, 1935-46; RINVR, 1941-46; CA, Edinburgh, 1946-87. Honorary Treasurer, British Ornithologists Union, 1956-76. Address: (h.) 48 Frogston Road West, Edinburgh, EH10 7AJ; T.-031-445 1082.

Bryson, William McNicol, FIMI. Director, Scottish Motor Trade Association, since 1985; b. 6.3.28, Lanark; m., Marion Rankin Cowper; 1 s.; 1 d. Educ. Lanark Grammar School. Trained as aircraft mechanic, RAF Technical School, Cosford; Rossleigh Ltd.: joined as salesman/buyer, 1949; General Manager, Glasgow, 1961-71; Marketing Director, Edinburgh, 1971-73; Managing Director and General Manager, 1973-77; Regional Director and Managing Director, Heron Rossleigh, 1977-82; Deputy Chairman and Managing Director, Taggart Motor Group, 1982-85. Lord Cornet, Royal Burgh of Lanark, 1959. Recreations: shooting; horse-riding; classic cars. Address: (h.) Marclann, 3 Friarsfield Road, Lanark; T.-0555 2817.

Buccleuch, 9th Duke of, and Queensberry, 11th Duke of (Walter Francis John Montagu Douglas Scott), KT (1978), VRD, JP. Lt.Comdr., RNR; Captain, Queen's Bodyguard for Scotland (Royal Company of Archers); Lord Lieutenant of Roxburgh, since 1974, and of Ettrick and Lauderdale, since 1975; b. 23.9.23, London; m., Jane McNeill, daughter of John McNeill, QC, Appin, Argyll; 3 s.; 1 d. Educ. Eton; Christ Church, Oxford. Served World War II, RNVR; MP (Conservative), Edinburgh North, 1960-73; PPS to the Scottish Office, 1961-64; Chairman, Conservative Party Forestry Committee, 1967-73; Chairman, Royal Association for Disability and Rehabilitation, since 1978; President: Royal Highland and Agricultural Society of Scotland, 1969, St. Andrew's Ambulance Association, Royal Scottish Agricultural Benevolent Institution, Scottish National Institution for War Blinded, Royal Blind Asylum and School, Galloway Cattle Society,

East of Scotland Agricultural Society, 1976, Commonwealth Forestry Association; President (Scotland), Malcolm Sargent Cancer Fund for Scotland; Vice-President: Royal Scottish Society for Prevention of Cruelty to Children, Disablement Income Group Scotland, Disabled Drivers Motor Club, Spinal Injuries Association; Honorary President: Animal Diseases Research Association, Scottish Agricultural Organisation Society; DL: Selkirk, 1955, Midlothian, 1960, Roxburgh, 1962, Dumfries, 1974. Address: Bowhill, Selkirk; T.-Selkirk 20732; and Drumlanrig Castle, Thornhill; T.-Thornhill 30248.

Buchan, Alexander Stewart, MB, ChB, FFARCS. Consultant Anaesthetist, since 1975; b. 7.9.42, Aberdeen; m., Henrietta Young Dalrymple; 1 s. Educ. Loretto School; Edinburgh University. Anaesthetic training in Edinburgh, apart from work in Holland, 1972; appointed Consultant in NHS, 1975; Royal Infirmary, Edinburgh, Royal Hospital for Sick Children, and Princess Margaret Rose Orthopaedic Hospital; in private anaesthetic practice, since 1975; Treasurer, Edinburgh and East of Scotland Society of Anaesthetists. Recreations: sailing; fishing; golf. Address: (h.) 21 Chalmers Crescent, Edinburgh, EH9 1TS; T.-031-667 1127.

Buchan, Andrew Strachan, FIB (Scot). Local Director, Scotland, Barclays Bank PLC, since 1985; b. 12.1.31, Peterhead; m., Jean Eleanor Gilmore; 2 s. Educ. Peterhead Academy; Manchester Business School; Administrative Staff College, Henley. Various managerial posts, Royal Bank of Scotland plc, Edinburgh, Glasgow and London, 1963-77; General Manager (Central Region), Royal Bank of Scotland plc, 1977-85. Council Member, Institute of Bankers in Scotland, 1981-85 (Examiner in Practical Banking, 1968-72); Treasurer for Scotland, Scottish Appeals Committee, Police Dependants' Trust, 1978-85. Recreation: golf. Address: (b.) Barclays Bank PLC, 35 St. Andrew Square, Edinburgh, EH2 2AD; T.-031-557 2733.

Buchan, Gilbert, CBE, RD, MBE. Honorary President, Scottish Fishermen's Federation, since 1982; Honorary President, Scottish Pelagic Fishermen's Association, since 1982; b. 25.5.12, Inverallochy; m., Jessie; 3 d. Educ. Inverallochy School (left aged 14). Fishing since 1927; skipper, since 1933, owner, since 1942; Royal Navy, RNR, 1938 (Lt.Cmdr., RNR, ret., 1962); Director, then Vice-Chairman, Scottish Herring Producers; Scottish Fishermen's Federation: Director, 1974, Vice-President, 1977, President, 1978-82; Member, Herring Industry Board Consultative Group, 1965-80; founder Director, Scottish Fishermen's Producer Organisation, 1974-80; Member, Sea Fish Industry Authority, 1980-82. Recreation: golf. Address: (h.) 7 Mid Street, Inverallochy, Aberdeenshire; T.-034 65 2278.

Buchan, Janey. Member, European Parliament, for Glasgow, since 1979; b. 30.4.26; m., Norman Buchan (qv); 1 s. Past Chairman, Scottish Gas Consumers' Council; former Vice-Chairman, Education Committee, Strathclyde Regional Council.

Buchan, Norman, MA. MP (Labour), Paisley South, since 1983; Opposition Spokesman for the Arts; b. 27.10.22, Helmsdale; m., Janey Kent (see Janey Buchan); 1 s. Educ. Kirkwall Grammar School; Hyndland Secondary School; Glasgow University. Royal Tank Regiment (North Africa, Sicily and Italy), 1942-45; Teacher of English and History; MP, Renfrewshire West, 1964-83; Parliamentary Under Secretary, Scottish Office, 1967-70; Opposition Spokesman on Agriculture, Fisheries and Food, 1970-74; Minister of State, MAFF, March 1974 (resigned, October 1974); Opposition Spokesman on: Social Security, 1980-81, Food, Agriculture and Fisheries, 1981. Publications: 101 Scottish Songs (Editor); The Scottish Folksinger (Editor), 1973; The MacDunciad, 1977. Address: (h.) 72 Peel Street, Glasgow, G11 5LR; T.-041-339 2583.

Buchan, Tom, MA (Hons). Writer; b. 19.6.31, Glasgow; 2 s.; 1 d. Educ. Aberdeen Grammar School; Balfron High School; Jordanhill College School; Glasgow University. Professor of English, Madras University; Director, Community House, Glasgow; Senior Lecturer in English, Clydebank College of Further Education; Artistic Director, Craigmillar Festival; Director, Kalachaitanya Madras Theatre Company; Director, Offshore Theatre Company, Edinburgh; Director, Dumbarton Festival. Publications: Happy Landings; Dolphins at Cochin; Poems 1969-72; Exorcism; Forwords; (plays) Tell Charlie Thanks for the Truss; The Great Northern Welly Boot Show (with Billy Connolly); Knox and Mary; Over The Top; Bunker; God. Address: (h.) 5 Sydenham Road, Glasgow G12 9NT; T.-041-339 3558.

Buchan of Auchmacoy, Captain David William Sinclair, JP. Chief of the Name of Buchan; b. 18.9.29; m.; 4 s.; 1 d. Educ. Eton; Royal Military Academy, Sandhurst. Commissioned Gordon Highlanders, 1949; ADC to GOC, Singapore, 1951-53; Member, London Stock Exchange; Member, Queen's Bodyguard for Scotland (Royal Company of Archers). Address: (h.) Auchmacoy House, Ellon, Aberdeenshire.

Buchanan, Derek Watson King, MB, ChB, MRCGP. Scottish Secretary, British Medical Association, 1981-85; b. 6.9.24, Dundee; m., Sandra; 2 d. Educ. Morgan Academy; Dundee High School; St. Andrews University. House Surgeon, Dundee Royal Infirmary, 1946-47; Captain, RAMC, 1947-49; general practice, 1949-73; Assistant Scottish Secretary, BMA, 1974-81. Secretary, Dundee Local Medical Committee, 1960-73; Member: Dundee Executive Council, NHS, Ninewells Hospital Board of Management; County Director, Dundee Branch, British Red Cross Society; Honorary Surgeon, St. Andrews Ambulance Association. Recreation: golf. Address: c/o Alexander Moffat & Co., WS, 13A Alva Street, Edinburgh, EH2 4PH.

Buchanan, Jane Helen Park, JP. Member, Fife Health Board, 1979-87; Travel Consultant, since 1982; b. Perth; m., James Buchanan; 1 s.; 1 d. Educ. Morrison's Academy, Crieff; Ross's Commercial College. Member, North East Fife District Council, 1976-80 (Chairman, Recreation and Tourism Committee, 1977-80); Vice Chairman,

North East Fife Conservative Association, since 1977; Director: Scottish Agritours, since 1982, Scottish Farmhouse Holidays, since 1983. Nuffield Farming Scholarship, 1981. Recreations: bridge; golf; curling. Address: Drumtenant, Ladybank, Fife, KY7 7UG; T.-0337 30451.

Buchanan, Professor John Grant, MA, PhD, ScD, CChem, FRSC, FRSE. Professor of Organic Chemistry, Heriot-Watt University, Edinburgh, since 1969; b. 26.9.26, Dumbarton; m., Sheila Elena Lugg; 3 s. Educ. Dumbarton Academy; Glasgow Academy; Christ's College, Cambridge. Research Fellow, University of California, Berkeley, 1951-52; Research Assistant, Lister Institute of Preventive Medicine, London, 1952-54; Newcastle-upon-Tyne University: Lecturer in Organic Chemistry, 1955, Senior Lecturer, 1962, Reader, 1965. Council Member, Royal Society of Edinburgh, 1980-83; Member, Editorial Board: Carbohydrate Research, since 1965, Nucleosides and Nucleotides, since 1982; Council Member, Royal Society of Chemistry, 1980-81 and 1982-85. Recreations: golf; listening to music. Address: (h.) Evergreen, 61 South Barnton Avenue, Edinburgh, EH4 6AN; T.-031-312 6296.

Buchanan, Percival William, MA (Hons), LLB. Director of Administration and Legal Services, Central Regional Council, since 1974; b. 17.9.25, Airdrie; m., Anna Dunlop Barron; 1 s.; 1 d. Educ. Peterhead Academy; Aberdeen University. Legal Assistant, Butchart & Rennet, Advocates, Aberdeen, 1954-56; Senior Legal Assistant, Corporation of the City of Aberdeen, 1957-62; Burgh of Alloa: Depute Town Clerk, 1962-63, Town Clerk, 1963-74. Member, Scottish Arts Council and its Music Committee, 1972-75; Chairman, Society of Directors of Administration in Scotland, 1983-84; Chairman, Board of Examiners in the Law and Practice of Registration in Scotland, 1978-87; Chairman, British Institute of Management (Central Scotland Branch), 1986-87. Recreations: music; hill-walking; sailing. Address: (b.) Viewforth, Stirling, FK8 2ET; T.-0786 73111.

Buchanan, William Menzies, DA. Head of Fine Art Studies, Glasgow School of Art, since 1977; b. 7.10.32, Caroni Estate, Trinidad, West Indies. Educ. Glasgow School of Art. Art Teacher, Glasgow, 1956-61; Exhibitions Officer, then Art Director, Scottish Arts Council, 1961-77. Chairman, Stills Gallery, Edinburgh, 1987. Publications: Scottish Art Review, 1965, 1967, 1973; Seven Scottish Painters catalogue, IBM New York, 1965; The Glasgow Boys catalogue, 1968; Joan Eardley, 1976; Mr Henry and Mr Hornel Visit Japan catalogue, 1978; Japonisme in Art (Contributor), 1980; A Companion to Scottish Culture (Contributor), 1981; The Stormy Blast catalogue, Stirling University, 1981; The Golden Age of British Photography (Contributor), 1984; The Photographic Collector (Contributor), 1985; Willie Rodger: A Retrospective (Contributor to catalogue), 1986. Recreations: gardening; cooking. Address: (b.) Glasgow School of Art, 167 Renfrew Street, Glasgow, G3 6RQ; T.-041-332 9797.

Buchanan-Jardine, Andrew Rupert John, MC. Landowner; Deputy Lieutenant; b. 2.2.23, London; 1 s.; 1 d. Educ. Harrow; Royal Agricultural College. Joined Royal Horse Guards, 1941; served NW Europe; retired as Major, 1949. Joint Master, Dumfriesshire Foxhounds, 1950; JP. Recreation: country pursuits. Address: (h.) Dixons, Lockerbie, Dumfriesshire; T.-Lockerbie 2508.

Buchanan-Smith, Alick. MP (Conservative), Kincardine and Deeside; b. 8.4.32, Currie, Midlothian; m., Janet Lawrie; 1 s.; 3 d. Educ. Edinburgh Academy; Glenalmond; Cambridge University; Edinburgh University. Parliamentary Under Secretary, Scottish Office, 1970-74; Minister of State, MAFF, 1979-83; Minister of State, Department of Energy, 1983-87. Address: (b.) House of Commons, London, SW1A 0AA.

Buchanan-Smith, Robin D., BA, ThM. Member, Board of Directors, Scottish Television, since 1982; Chancellor's Assessor, St. Andrews University, 1981-85; b. 1.2.36, Currie, Midlothian; m., Sheena Mary Edwards; 2 s. Educ. Edinburgh Academy; Glenalmond; Cambridge University; Edinburgh University; Princeton Theological Seminary. Minister, Christ's Church, Dunollie, Oban, 1962-66; Chaplain, St. Andrews University, 1966-73. Chaplain: 8th Argylls, 1962-66, Highland Volunteer, 1967-69; British Council of Churches Preacher to USA, 1968; Commodore, Royal Highland Yacht Club, 1977-81. Recreations: sailing; Scotland. Address: Isle of Eriska, Ledaig, Argyll, PA37 1SD; T.-0631 72 371.

Bullough, Professor Donald Auberon, MA, FSA, FRHistS. Professor of Mediaeval History, St. Andrews University, since 1973 (Dean, Faculty of Arts, since 1984); b. 13.6.28, Stoke; m., Belinda Jane Turland; 2 d. Educ. Newcastle-under-Lyme High School; St. John's College, Oxford. National Service, RA, 1946-48; studied abroad, 1950-52; Fereday Fellow, St. John's College, Oxford, 1952-55; Lecturer, Edinburgh University, 1955-66 (Reader Elect, 1966); Warden, Holland House, Edinburgh University, 1960-63; Visiting Professor, Southern Methodist University, 1965-66; Professor of Mediaeval History, Nottingham University, 1966-73; Director, Paul Elek Ltd., 1968-79; Acting Director, British School at Rome, 1984 (Chairman, Faculty of History, Archaeology and Letters, 1975-79); Ford's Lecturer in English History, Oxford University, 1979-80; Andrew Mellon Lecturer, Catholic University, Washington, 1980; Raleigh Lecturer, British Academy, 1985. Recreations: talk; looking at buildings; postal history. Address: (h.) 23 South Street, St. Andrews, Fife, KY16 9QS; T.-0334 72932.

Bundy, Alan Richard, BSc, PhD. Professorial Fellow, Department of Artificial Intelligence, Edinburgh University, since 1987; b. 18.5.47, Isleworth; m., D. Josephine A. Maule; 1 d. Educ. Heston Secondary Modern School; Springgrove Grammar School; Leicester University. Tutorial Assistant, Department of Mathematics, Leicester University, 1970-71; Edinburgh University: Research Fellow, Metamathematics Unit, 1971-74, Lecturer, Department of Artificial Intelligence, 1974-84, Reader, 1984-87; AISB: Editor, Newsletter, 1973-76, Treasurer, 1977-80; Editorial Board: Artificial Intelligence Journal, Journal of Automated Reasoning. Publications: Artificial Intelligence: An Introductory Course, 1978; The Computer Modelling of Mathematical Reasoning,

1983; The Catalogue of Artificial Intelligence Tools, 1984; Symbolic Computation (Series Editor). Recreations: wine and beer making; walking. Address: (b.) Department of Artificial Intelligence, Edinburgh University, 80 South Bridge, Edinburgh, EH1 1HN; T.-031-225 7774.

Bunney, Herrick, LVO, BMus, FRCO, ARCM, FRSAMD. Organist and Master of the Music, St. Giles' Cathedral, Edinburgh, since 1946; b. London; m., Mary Howarth Cutting; 1 s.; 1 d. Educ. University College School; Royal College of Music. Organist to Edinburgh University, until 1981; former Conductor: Edinburgh Royal Choral Union, Edinburgh University Singers, The Elizabethan Singers (London), St. Cecilia Singers; Council Member, Edinburgh International Festival, National Youth Orchestra of Scotland. Recreations: hill-walking; bird-watching. Address: (h.) 3 Upper Coltbridge Terrace, Edinburgh, EH12 6AD; T.-031-337 6494.

Burdon, Professor Roy Hunter, BSc, PhD, FRSA, FRSE. Professor of Molecular Biology and Chairman, Department of Bioscience and Biotechnology, Strathclyde University, since 1985; m., Margery Grace Kellock; b. 27.4.38, Glasgow; 2 s. Educ. Glasgow Academy; St. Andrews University. Assistant Lecturer, Glasgow University, 1959; Research Fellow, New York University, 1963; Glasgow University: Lecturer in Biochemistry, 1964, Senior Lecturer, 1967, Reader, 1974, Professor (Titular), 1977; Guest Professor of Microbiology, Polytechnical University of Denmark, 1977-78; Governor, West of Scotland College of Agriculture; Biochemical Society (UK): Honorary Meeting Secretary, 1981-85, Honorary General Secretary, 1985. Recreations: music; painting; golf. Address: (h.) 144 Mugdock Road, Milngavie, Glasgow, G62 8NP; T.-041-956 1689.

Burgess, John Moncrieff, BSc, MIEDO. Director of Research and Development, Shetland Islands Council, since 1975; b. 8.9.36, Scousburgh; m., Patricia Margaret; 2 s. Educ. Anderson Educational Institute; Aberdeen University. Lecturer, North of Scotland College of Agriculture, 1961-64; Assistant Lands Officer, then Lands Officer, Department of Agriculture and Fisheries for Scotland, 1964-75. Recreations: boating; fishing. Address: (b.) 93 St. Olaf Street, Lerwick, Shetland; T.-0595 3535.

Burgess, Moira, MA, FLA. Novelist and Short Story Writer; b. 19.3.36, Campbeltown; m., Archie Stirling (deceased); 1 s.; 1 d. Educ. Campbeltown Grammar School; Strathclyde University. Librarian, 1953-73; author of: The Day Before Tomorrow (novel), 1971; A Rumour of Strangers (novel), 1987; Editor, short story anthologies: Streets of Stone (with Hamish Whyte), 1985, and The Other Voice, 1987; compiler, The Glasgow Novel, 2nd edition, 1985 (bibliography). Recreations: reading; embroidery; theatre.

Burley, Lindsay Elizabeth, MB, ChB, FRCPE, MRCGP. Unit General Manager, East Unit, Lothian Health Board, and Consultant Physician in Geriatric Medicine, Edenhall Hospital, Musselburgh; b. 2.10.50, Blackpool; m., Robin Burley. Educ. Queen Mary School, Lytham; Edinburgh University. Address: (b.) Edenhall Hospital, Musselburgh, East Lothian, EH21 7TZ; T.-031-665 2546.

Burnett, Charles John, CStJ, DA, AMA, FSAScot. Dingwall Pursuivant of Arms; Curator of Fine Art, Scottish United Services Museum, Edinburgh Castle, since 1985; Vice-President, Heraldry Society of Scotland, since 1986; Vice-Patron, Genealogical Society of Queensland, since 1986; b. 6.11.40, Sandhaven, by Fraserburgh; m., Aileen E. McIntyre; 2 s.; 1 d. Educ. Fraserburgh Academy; Gray's School of Art, Aberdeen; Aberdeen College of Education. Advertising Department, House of Fraser, Aberdeen, 1963-64; Exhibitions Division, Central Office of Information, 1964-68 (on team which planned British pavilion for World Fair, Montreal, 1967); Assistant Curator, Letchworth Museum and Art Gallery, 1968-71; Head, Design Department, National Museum of Antiquities of Scotland, 1971-85. Heraldic Adviser, Girl Guide Association in Scotland, since 1978; Librarian, Priory of the Order of St. John in Scotland, since 1987; Council Member, Society of Antiquaries of Scotland, since 1986. Recreations: reading; visiting places of historic interest. Address: (h.) 3 Hermitage Terrace, Morningside, Edinburgh; T.-031-447 5472.

Burnett, Michael Rodger, BSc. Farmer, since 1960; Director, Scottish Agricultural Colleges; Development Officer, Scottish Agricultural Organisation Society; b. 26.7.35, Edinburgh; 1 s.; 2 d. Educ. Morrison's Academy, Crieff; Edinburgh University. Chairman, Highland Region Education Committee, 1973-77; President, National Farmers Union of Scotland, 1977-79; Chairman, BBC Agricultural Advisory Committee for Scotland, since 1980; Parliamentary Liberal candidate: Caithness and Sutherland, 1974, Moray, 1984. Reader, Church of Scotland. Recreations: bridge; golf. Address: (h.) Pulrossie Farm, Dornoch, Sutherland; T.-086 288 206.

Burnett, Robert Gemmill, LLB, SSC, NP. Solicitor, since 1972; b. 18.1.49, Kilmarnock; m., Patricia Margaret Masson; 1 d. Educ. George Heriot's School, Edinburgh; Edinburgh University. Apprentice, then Assistant, then Partner, Drummond & Co. Vice President, Society of Procurators of Midlothian; Secretary, Lothian Allelon Society; Solicitor to General Teaching Council. Recreations: cricket; golf; gardening. Address: (b.) 31/32 Moray Place, Edinburgh; T.-031-226 5151.

Burnett, Rodney Alister, MB, ChB, FRCPath. Consultant Pathologist responsible for diagnostic services, University Department of Pathology, Western Infirmary, Glasgow, since 1985; b. 6.6.47, Congleton; m., Maureen Elizabeth Dunn; 2 d. Educ. Sandbach School; St. Andrews University. Lecturer in Pathology, Glasgow University, 1974-79; Consultant in administrative charge, Department of Pathology, Stobhill Hospital, Glasgow, 1979-85. Secretary, Association of Clinical Pathologists, Caledonian Branch. Address: (h.) 134 Brownside Road, Cambuslang, Glasgow, G72; T.-041-641 3036.

Burns, James, JP. Member, Strathclyde Regional Council, since 1974; b. 8.2.31, Shotts; m., Jean Ward; 2 s. Educ. St. Patrick's School, Shotts; Coatbridge Technical College. Engineer, NCB, 1948-71; Member: Lanark County Council, 1967-

75, Lanarkshire Health Board, 1973-77; Strathclyde Regional Council: Chairman, General Purposes Committee, 1975-82; Vice-Convener, 1978-82; Convener, 1982-86. Recreations: fishing; golf. Address: (h.) 57 Springhill Road, Shotts, ML7 5JA; T.-Shotts 20187.

Burnside, Andrew MacLaren, MA (Hons). Chief Statistician, Scottish Office, since 1984; b. 18.6.44, Glasgow; m., Anna; 3 s.; 1 d. Educ. Hyndland Secondary School, Glasgow; Glasgow University. Various posts in statistics and administration, Scottish Office, since 1966. Recreations: music; gardening; bee-keeping; canal restoring. Address: (h.) Arbuthnot House, Dorrator Road, Falkirk; T.-0324 34785.

Burstall, Professor Rodney M., MA, MSc, PhD. Professor of Computer Science, Edinburgh University, since 1979; b. 11.11.34, Liverpool; m., Seija-Leena; 3 d. Educ. George V Grammar School, Southport; King's College, Cambridge; Birmingham University. Operational Research Consultant, Brussels, 1959; Operational Research and Programming, Reed Paper Group, Kent, 1960; Research Fellow, Birmingham University, 1962; Research Fellow, Lecturer, Reader, Professor, Department of Artificial Intelligence, Edinburgh University, 1964-79. Emissary to UK for Venerable Chogyam Trungpa Rinpoche, Buddhist Meditation Master, 1982. Address: (b.) Department of Computer Science, Edinburgh University, King's Buildings, Mayfield Road, Edinburgh, EH9 3JZ; T.-031-667 1081.

Burton, Anthony Winston, OBE, BA (Hons). Director, The Planning Exchange, since 1975; b. 14.10.40, Leicester; 2 s.; 1 d. Educ. Wyggeston; Keele University. Member, National Consumer Council; Member, Council, The Consumers' Association; Director, Elise, Brussels. Address: (h.) 9 Marchmont Terrace, Glasgow, G12; T.-041-334 7697.

Burton, Lord (Michael Evan Victor Baillie). Landowner and Farmer; Member, Inverness District Council, since 1984; Executive Member, Scottish Landowners Federation, since 1963; b. 27.6.24, Burton-on-Trent; m., 1, Elizabeth Ursula Foster Wise (m. diss.); 2, Coralie Denise Cliffe; 2 s.; 4 d. Educ. Eton; Army. Scots Guards, 1942 (Lt., 1944); Lovat Scouts, 1948; Member, Inverness County Council, 1948-75; JP, 1961-75; Deputy Lieutenant, Inverness, 1963-65; has served on numerous committees. Recreations: shooting, fishing and hunting (not much time); looking after the estate. Address: Dochfour, Inverness; T.-046 386 252.

Bushe, Frederick, RSA (1987), DA, DAE. Sculptor, since 1956; Director, Scottish Sculpture Workshop, since 1979; b. 1.3.31, Coatbridge; m., Fiona M.S. Marr; 1 d.; 3 s., 1 d. by pr. m. Educ. Our Lady's High School, Motherwell; Glasgow School of Art. Lecturer in Sculpture: Liverpool College of Education, 1962-69, Aberdeen College of Education, 1969-79; full-time Artist since 1979; established Scottish Sculpture Workshop and Scottish Sculpture Open Exhibition; exhibited in numerous one man and group exhibitions, since 1962. Recreation: listening to music. Address: (h.) Rose Cottage, Lumsden, Huntly, Aberdeenshire; T.-046 46 723.

Busuttil, Professor Anthony, MD, FRCPath, DMJ(Path). Regius Professor of Forensic Medicine, Edinburgh University, since 1987; Honorary Consultant Pathologist, Lothian Health Board, since 1976; Police Surgeon, Lothian and Borders Police, since 1980; b. 30.12.45, Rabat, Malta; m., Angela; 3 s. Educ. St. Aloysius' College, Malta; Royal University of Malta. Junior posts, Western Infirmary, Glasgow; Lecturer in Pathology, Glasgow University. Address: (h.) 78 Hillpark Avenue, Edinburgh, EH4 7AL; T.-031-336 3241.

Bute, 6th Marquess of (John Crichton-Stuart), JP. Hereditary Sheriff of Bute; Hereditary Keeper of Rothesay Castle; b. 27.2.33; m., 1, Nicola Weld-Forester (m. diss.); 2 s.; 1 d.; 1 d. (deceased); 2, Jennifer Percy. Educ. Ampleforth College; Trinity College, Cambridge. Chairman, Scottish Standing Committee for Voluntary International Aid, 1964-68; Chairman, Council and Executive Committee, National Trust for Scotland, 1969-84 (Vice-President, since 1984); Chairman: National Museums of Scotland, since 1985; Scottish Committee, National Fund for Research into Crippling Diseases, since 1966; Historic Buildings Council for Scotland, since 1983; Scottish Advisory Committee of the British Council, since 1987; Chairman, Museums Advisory Board (Scotland), 1984-85; Trustee, National Galleries of Scotland, 1980-86; Member, Countryside Commission for Scotland, 1970-78; Honorary Sheriff-Substitute, Bute, 1976; Convener, Buteshire County Council, 1967-70; DL Bute, 1961; Lord Lieutenant, 1967-75; Hon. LLD, Glasgow, 1970; Hon. FRIAS, 1985. Address: (h.) Mount Stuart, Rothesay, Isle of Bute.

Buthlay, Kenneth, MA, DipAppLin. Senior Lecturer in Scottish Literature, Glasgow University, since 1966; b. 19.7.25, London; m., Sheila McLeod (deceased); 1 s.; 1 d. Educ. Aberdeen Grammar School; Aberdeen University; Cornell University; Edinburgh University. BBC Producer, 1953-55; Professor of English Literature, University of Sao Paulo, Brazil, 1956-64. Editor, Scottish Literary Journal, since 1985. Publications: Hugh MacDiarmid, 1964, 1982; many articles in critical journals. Address: (b.) 6 University Gardens, Glasgow, G12 8QH; T.-041-339 8855.

Butler, Anthony Robert, BSc, PhD, DSc, AKC. Reader in Chemistry, St. Andrews University, since 1965; b. 28.11.36, Croydon, Surrey; m., Janet Anderson. Educ. Selhurst; King's College, London; Cornell University. Consulting Editor, Longman-Cartermill Publishing, 1980; Lecturer, Fleming Centenary Celebration, Darvel, 1981. Recreations: hill-walking; road-running; music; writing Chinese characters. Address: (h.) Red Gable, Denhead, St. Andrews; T.-033485 521.

Butler, Rev. John Michael Francis, DipTh, DipMS, MBIM, MIPM. Minister of Religion (Congregational), since 1953; b. 12.3.28, Petersfield; m., Charlotte Matilda; 2 s.; 1 d. Educ. Churchers College, Petersfield; New College, London. Minister: Laira and Plympton Congregational Churches, 1953-59; Helensburgh Congregational Church, 1959-64. Recreations: Christian activity; reading and book reviewing; sailing; bad photography. Address: (h.) 2 Southview, Dalmuir, Clydebank, G81 3LA; T.-041-952 1338.

Butler, Vincent Frederick, RSA. Sculptor. Address: (h.) 17 Deanpark Crescent, Edinburgh, EH4 1PH; T.-031-332 5884.

Butlin, Ron, MA, DipAECD. Poet and Novelist; b. 17.11.49, Edinburgh. Educ. Dumfries Academy; Edinburgh University. Writer in Residence, Lothian Region Education Authority, 1979, Edinburgh University, 1981, 1984-85; Scottish/Canadian Writing Exchange Fellow, University of New Brunswick, 1983-84. Publications: poetry: Stretto, 1976; Creatures Tamed by Cruelty, 1979; The Exquisite Instrument, 1982 (Scottish Arts Council Book Award); Ragtime in Unfamiliar Bars, 1985 (SAC Book Award, Poetry Book Society recommendation); prose: The Tilting Room (short stories), 1983 (SAC Book Award); The Sound of My Voice (novel), 1987. Recreations: music; travel. Address: (h.) 9 Moncrieff Terrace, Edinburgh, EH9 1NB; T.-031-667 0394.

Butter, David Henry, MC. Lord Lieutenant, Perth and Kinross, since 1975; Landowner and Company Director; b. 18.3.20, London; m., Myra Alice Wernher; 1 s.; 4 d. Educ. Eton College; Oxford University. Served in World War II, 2nd Lt., Scots Guards, 1940; served in Western Desert, North Africa, Sicily and Italy (ADC to GOC 8th Army, 1944); Temporary Major, 1946; retired, 1948; Brigadier, Queen's Bodyguard for Scotland (Royal Company of Archers); President, Highland TAVR, 1979-84; Member, Perth County Council, 1955-74; Deputy Lieutenant, Perthshire, 1956; Vice Lieutenant, Perthshire, 1960-71; Lord Lieutenant of County of Perth, 1971-75, of Kinross, 1974-75; Governor, Gordonstoun School, 1954-86; Governor, Butterstone House School; Honorary President, Perthshire Battalion, Boys Brigade. Recreations: golf; skiing; travel; shooting. Address: Cluniemore, Pitlochry, Perthshire; T.-0796 2006.

Butter, Professor Peter Herbert. Regius Professor of English Language and Literature, Glasgow University, 1965-86; b. 7.4.21, Coldstream; m., Bridget Younger; 1 s.; 2 d. Educ. Charterhouse; Balliol College, Oxford. Royal Artillery, 1941-46; Lecturer in English, Edinburgh University, 1948-58; Professor of English, Queen's University, Belfast, 1958-65. Secretary/Treasurer, International Association of University Professors of English, 1965-71. Publications: Shelley's Idols of the Cave, 1954; Francis Thompson, 1961; Edwin Muir, 1962; Edwin Muir: Man and Poet, 1966; Shelley's Alastor, Prometheus Unbound and Other Poems (Editor), 1971; Selected Letters of Edwin Muir (Editor), 1974; William Blake: Selected Poems (Editor), 1982; The Truth of Imagination: Uncollected Prose of Edwin Muir (Editor), 1988. Recreations: gardening; hill-walking. Address: (h.) Ashfield, Prieston Road, Bridge of Weir, Renfrewshire, PA11 3AW; T.-Bridge of Weir 613139.

Butterfield, Alan W., MA, DipEd, JP. Rector, Hamilton Grammar School, since 1971; b. 1.5.33, Dundee; m., Rosemary; 1 s.; 1 d. Educ. Dundee High School; St. Andrews University. Teacher of English and History, Harris Academy, Dundee; Special Assistant of English and History, Dunfermline High School; Principal Teacher of English: Broxburn Academy, Trinity Academy, Edinburgh; Depute Rector, Falkirk High School. President, Headteachers' Association of Scotland, 1984-85. Recreation: Rotary. Address: (h.) 23 Langside Road, Bothwell, Lanarkshire; T.-853505.

Butters, Benjamin. Chairman and Managing Director, Butters Engineering Services Ltd., since 1980; Member, Lands Valuation Appeal Tribunal; Chairman, Glasgow College of Nautical Studies; Director, Glasgow Chamber of Commerce; b. 28.3.27, Glasgow; m., Norah Lindsay Hill; 1 s.; 2 d. Educ. Loretto; Glasgow Technical College. Sales Director, Butters Bros & Co. Ltd., 1954-63; Managing Director, Butters Cranes Ltd., 1963-78; Director, Abbot Engineering Ltd., 1960-78; Past President, Scottish Engineering Employers Association; Chairman, Fyfe Chambers, since 1986. Recreation: golf (Royal Troon). Address: (h.) Flat 8, 4 Barcapel Avenue, Newton Mearns, Glasgow, G77 6QJ; T.-041-639 3128.

Butterworth, Professor George Esmond, BSc, MSc, DPhil, FBPsS. Professor and Head, Department of Psychology, Stirling University, since 1985; b. 8.11.46, Hanover, West Germany; 1 s.; 1 d. Educ. Southern Grammar School, Portsmouth; North East London Polytechnic; Birmingham University; Oxford University. Lecturer and Senior Lecturer in Psychology, Southampton University, 1974-85. Secretary, International Society for Study of Behavioural Development, 1981-85; Member, National Panel of Assessors, Scottish Home and Health Department, since 1987; Chairman, Developmental Psychology Section, British Psychological Society, 1986-88; Editor, British Journal of Developmental Psychology, since 1988. Recreation: antique shops. Address: (b.) Department of Psychology, Stirling University, Stirling, FK9 4LA; T.-0786 73171.

Butterworth, Neil, MA, HonFLCM. Head, Music Department, Napier College, Edinburgh, 1968-87; Music Critic, Times Educational Supplement, since 1983; Broadcaster; b. 4.9.34, Streatham, London; m., Anna Mary Barnes; 3 d. Educ. Rutlish School, Surrey; Nottingham University; London University; Guildhall School of Music, London. Lecturer, Kingston College of Technology, 1960-68; Conductor: Sutton Symphony Orchestra, 1960-64, Glasgow Orchestral Society, 1975-83; Chairman, Incorporated Society of Musicians, Edinburgh Centre, since 1981; Churchill Fellowship, 1975. Publications: Haydn, 1976; Dvorak, 1980; Dictionary of American Composers, 1983; Aaron Copland, 1984; Samuel Barber, 1988. Recreations: autographs; collecting books and records; giant jigsaw puzzles. Address: (h.) The White House, Inveresk, Musselburgh, Midlothian; T.-031-665 3497.

Buxton, Paul Kenneth, MA (Cantab), MB, BChir, FRCP(C), FRCPEdin. Consultant Physician in Dermatology, Fife Health Board and Royal Infirmary, Edinburgh, since 1981; Member, Clinical Teaching Staff, Edinburgh University, since 1981; b. 28.2.36, Harrar, Ethiopia; m., Heather; 1 s.; 1 d. Educ. Trinity College, Cambridge; St. Thomas's Hospital, London. Dermatologist, Royal Jubilee Hospital, Victoria, BC, Canada, 1971-81. President, Fife Branch, BMA, 1986-87; Fellow, Royal Society of Medicine; Member, Ethical Committee, Fife Health Board;

Member, Editorial Board, Ethics and Medicine. Publication: ABC of Dermatology. Recreations: seafaring; books; art; country pursuits. Address: (h.) Old Inzievar House, Dunfermline, KY12 8HA; T.-0383 880297.

Buyers, Thomas Bartlett, OBE, CEng, MIMechE. HM Chief Inspector of Prisons for Scotland, since 1985; b. 21.3.26, Chelmsford; m., Agnes Lodge; 3 d. Educ. Glasgow Academy; Glasgow University. Technical and management posts, BP Chemicals Ltd., Grangemouth and Baglan, S. Wales, 1951-73; Director of Engineering, Offshore Supplies Office (Department of Energy), Glasgow, 1973-75; BP Representative/Commissioning Manager, Sullom Voe, Shetland, 1975-80; Special Projects Manager, BP Chemicals, London, 1980-84. Address: (b.) St. Andrew's House, Edinburgh; T.-031-244 2332.

Byers, Rev. Alan James. Minister, Gamrie linked with King Edward, since 1988; b. 7.4.26, Girvan; m., Mairi Catriona Laing; 3 s.; 1 d. Educ. Girvan Secondary School; Edinburgh University; New College. RAF, 1944-48; Chaplain to hydro-electric workers' camps, 1955-56; Assistant Minister, Ardchattan, 1959; Minister: Presbyterian Church of Ghana (Northern Ghana), 1960-71; Boddam Parish Church, Peterhead, 1971-88. Recreations: photography; DIY. Address: The Manse, King Edward, Banff, AB4 3NB; T.-02616 258.

Byron, Stuart, FCA. Executive Director, Ross Hall Hospital, Glasgow, since 1981; b. 2.7.43, Fareham; m., Linda Dorey; 1 s.; 2 d. Educ. Lysses School, Fareham; Barton-Peveril Grammar School. Recreations: sailing; golf; reading. Address: (b.) 221 Crookston Road, Glasgow, G52 3NQ; T.-041-810 3151.

C

Caddie, James Murdoch, MBIM. Chief Executive Officer, Epilepsy Association of Scotland, since 1977; b. 2.11.27, Glasgow; m., Grace Betty (deceased); 2 d. Educ. Whitehill Senior Secondary School, Glasgow. Administrator: South of Scotland Electricity Board, 1948-71, National Health Service, 1971-77. Member: local Health Council, 1978-83; Glasgow Council for Welfare of the Disabled; Chairman, Joint Epilepsy Associations Committee, 1980-88. Recreations: gardening; travel. Address: (b.) 48 Govan Road, Glasgow, G51 1JL; T.-041-427 4911.

Caddy, Brian, BSc, PhD, CChem, MRIC. Senior Lecturer in Forensic Science and Director, Forensic Science Unit, Strathclyde University, since 1978; b. 26.3.37, Burslem, Stoke-on-Trent; m., Beryl Ashworth; 1 s.; 1 d. Educ. Middleport Secondary Modern School; Longton High School; Sheffield University. Strathclyde University: MRC Research Fellow, 1963, Lecturer in Forensic Science, 1966. Council Member, Forensic Science Society. Recreations: music; reading; gardening; walking the dog; relaxing. Address: (b.) Forensic Science Unit, Strathclyde University, Glasgow; T.-041-552 4400.

Cadell, Colin Simson, CBE, DL, MA, AMIEE; b. 7.8.05, Colinton; m., Rosemary Elizabeth Pooley; 2 s.; 1 d. Educ. Merchiston; Edinburgh University; Ecole Superieure d'Electricite. Commissioned RAF, 1926; Director of Signals, RAF, 1944; ADC, 66 Group, 1946; Managing Director, International Aeradio, 1947; Chairman, Edinburgh Airport Consultative Committee, 1972-83. Member, Royal Company of Archers (Queen's Bodyguard for Scotland); Legion of Merit (US). Address: (h.) 2 Upper Coltbridge Terrace, Edinburgh, EH12; T.-031-337 2666.

Cadell, Patrick Moubray, BA, FSA (Scot). Keeper of Manuscripts, National Library of Scotland, since 1983; b. 17.3.41, Linlithgow; m., Sarah King; 2 s.; 1 d. Educ. Merchiston Castle School, Edinburgh; Cambridge University; Toulouse University. Information Officer, British Museum; Assistant Keeper, Department of MSS, British Library, then National Library of Scotland. Clerk, Abbey Court of Holyrood; Recorder of the Council of Lord High Commissioners; Past President, West Lothian History and Amenity Society. Recreations: walking; music. Address: (b.) National Library of Scotland, George IV Bridge, Edinburgh, EH1 1EW; T.-031-226 4531.

Caird, Professor Francis Irvine, MA, DM, FRCP, FRCPSGlas. David Cargill Professor of Geriatric Medicine, Glasgow University, since 1979; b. 24.8.28, Glastonbury; m., Angela Margaret Alsop (deceased); 1 s.; 2 d. Educ. Winchester College; New College, Oxford. Medical Registrar, General Hospital, Birmingham, and RPGMS, Hammersmith; Senior Registrar and Medical Tutor, Radcliffe Infirmary, Oxford; Senior Lecturer and Reader in Geriatric Medicine, Glasgow University. Recreation: travel. Address: (h.) 4 Colquhoun Drive, Bearsden, Glasgow, G61 4NQ; T.-041-942 7785.

Caird, James Bowman, MA (Hons), DipEd. Council Member (former Vice-President), Association for Scottish Literary Studies; retired HM Inspector of Schools; b. 6.7.13, West Linton; m., Janet H. Kirkwood; 2 d. Educ. Boroughmuir School, Edinburgh; Edinburgh University; The Sorbonne, Paris; Moray House College of Education. Assistant Teacher of English: Wick High School, 1938, Trinity Academy, Edinburgh, 1938-40; Army Service (Royal Artillery, Army Education Corps), 1940-46; Principal Teacher of English, Peebles High School, 1946-47; HM Inspector of Schools in Dumfries, Glasgow, Stirlingshire and the Highlands, 1947-74. Past President, Inverness Field Club; Member, Culloden Committee, National Trust for Scotland. Recreations: reading; continental travel; TV viewing. Address: 1 Drummond Crescent, Inverness; T.-0463 232858.

Caird, Professor James Brown, MA (Edin), D de l'Univ (Rennes). Professor of Geography, Dundee University, since 1975; b. 3.4.28, Perth; m.,

Isa Macaskill; 1 s.; 3 d. Educ. Perth Academy; Edinburgh University; Rennes University. RAF, Education Branch, 1952-55; Assistant, Lecturer, Senior Lecturer, Glasgow University, 1955-64, 1966-74; Reader and Acting Head of Department, Ife University, Nigeria, 1964-66; Dean, Faculty of Environmental Studies, Dundee University, 1975-78. Member, Dundee University Court, 1979-87; Elder, Church of Scotland, since 1960; President, Abertay Historical Society, 1985-87. Recreations: angling; gardening. Address: (h.) 3 Hyndford Street, Dundee, DD2 1HQ; T.-0382 67748.

Cairncross, Robert George, MB, ChB, FRCP (Ed), MRCGP. Deputy Secretary, Scottish Council for Postgraduate Medical Education, since 1984; Honorary Lecturer, Centre for Medical Education, Dundee University, since 1984; b. 6.7.44, Dundee. Educ. Robert Gordon's College, Aberdeen; Aberdeen University. Registrar, Lothian Health Board, 1972-75; trainee General Practitioner, Edinburgh University, 1975-76; Lecturer in Medical Education, Dundee University, 1976-81; Educational Adviser, College of Medicine, ABHA, Saudi Arabia, 1981-83; Project Director, Dundee University, 1983-84. Address: (b.) Scottish Council for Postgraduate Medical Education, 8 Queen Street, Edinburgh, EH2 1JE; T.-031-225 4365.

Cairney, John, BA. Writer, Actor and Director; Director, Shanter Productions and Theatre Consultants (Scotland), since 1968; Director, John Cairney & Company Ltd., since 1984; b. 16.2.30, Baillieston, Glasgow; m., 1, Sheila Cowan (m. diss.); 2, Alannah O'Sullivan; 1 s. by pr. m.; 4 d. by pr. m. Educ. St. Mungo's Academy; Royal Scottish Academy of Music and Drama (Diploma in Drama). Stage actor: Glasgow Citizens' Theatre, 1953-54, Bristol Old Vic, 1954-56; film actor: Rank Organisation, 1956-65, ABPC, Columbia Pictures, 1956-65; TV actor, BBC, London, 1965-68; Founder Director, Burns Festival, Ayr, 1975-79; numerous stage appearances include Hamlet, Cyrano de Bergerac and The Entertainer, and one-man show as Robert Burns; also A Burns Experience, 1984; Burns - The Musical, 1986; wrote and directed, 1970-85: A Mackintosh Experience, The William McGonagall Story, The Private Life of R.L.S., The Ivor Novello Story, The Scotland Story, The Robert Service Story, Oscar Wilde, Blackout, and Dorothy Parker, for Shanter Productions; played leading role in TV serials and series: This Man Craig, 1965-67, Burns, 1968, Scotch on the Rocks, 1971, Taggart, 1986. Jubilee Medal, 1977. Publication: The Man Who Played Robert Burns (Autobiography). Recreations: theatre biographies; city street walking. Address: 44 St. Vincent Crescent, Glasgow, G3 8NG; T.-041-221 2785.

Cairns, Gordon McLean, MA, LLB, NP. Solicitor; Honorary Sheriff, Stranraer, since 1981; b. 31.7.38, Calcutta; m., Elizabeth; 1 s.; 1 d. Educ. Edinburgh Academy; Edinburgh University. Solicitor in private practice, since 1961. Address: (h.) Birchgrove, Whitehouse Road, Stranraer; T.-0776 2984.

Cairns, Rev. John Ballantyne, LTh, LLB. Parish Minister, Riverside Church, Dumbarton, since 1985; Convener, Church of Scotland Committee on Maintenance of the Ministry, since 1984; Joint Convener, Church of Scotland Board of Ministry and Mission, since 1984; b. 15.3.42, London; m., Dr. Elizabeth Emma Bradley; 3 s. Educ. Sutton Valence School, Kent; Bristol University; Edinburgh University. Messrs Richards, Butler & Co., Solicitors, City of London, 1964-68; Administrative Assistant, East Lothian County Council, 1968-69; Assistant Minister, St. Giles, Elgin, 1973-75; Minister, Langholm, Ewes and Westerkirk Parish Churches, 1975-85, also linked with Canonbie, 1981-85; Clerk, Presbytery of Annandale and Eskdale, 1980-82; Divisional Chaplain, Strathclyde Police. Recreations: golf; curling. Address: (b.) High Street, Dumbarton, G82 1NB; (h.) 5 Kirkton Road, Dumbarton, G82 4AS.

Cairns, Robert, MA, DipEd. Member, City of Edinburgh District Council, since 1974 (Chairman, Planning and Development Committee, since 1986); b. 16.7.47, Dundee; m., Pauline Reidy; 2 s. Educ. Morgan Academy; Edinburgh University; Moray House College of Education. Assistant Editor, Scottish National Dictionary, 1969-74; Parliamentary candidate (Labour), North Edinburgh, 1973, February 1974; Teacher, James Gillespie's High School, since 1975; Vice Chairman, Edinburgh Old Town Committee; Board Member: Edinvar Housing Association, Old Town Trust, Old Town Community Development Project. Recreations: gardening; theatre. Address: (h.) 223 Ferry Road, Edinburgh; T.-031-552 3027.

Cairns, Robert Alan, BSc, PhD, MInstP. Reader in Applied Mathematics, St. Andrews University, since 1985; b. 12.3.45, Glasgow; m., Ann E. Mackay. Educ. Allan Glen's School, Glasgow; Glasgow University. Lecturer in Applied Mathematics, St. Andrews University, 1970-83; Senior Lecturer, 1983-85; Consultant, UKAEA Culham Laboratory, since 1984. Committee Member, Plasma Physics Group, Institute of Physics, 1981-84; Member, Editorial Board, Plasma Physics, 1983-85. Publication: Plasma Physics, 1985. Recreations: music (listening to and playing recorder and baroque flute); golf; hill-walking. Address: (b.) Department of Applied Mathematics, St. Andrews University, North Haugh, St. Andrews, Fife, KY16 9SS; T.-0334 76161, Ext. 8150.

Calder, Professor Andrew Alexander, MD, FRCP(Glas), FRCOG. Professor of Obstetrics and Gynaecology, Edinburgh University, since 1987; Consultant Gynaecologist, Edinburgh Royal Infirmary and Consultant Obstetrician, Simpson Memorial Maternity Pavilion, Edinburgh, since 1987; b. 17.1.45, Aberdeen; m., Valerie Anne Dugard; 1 s.; 2 d. Educ. Glasgow Academy; Glasgow University. Clinical training posts in obstetrics and gynaecology, 1969-72: Queen Mother's Hospital, Western Infirmary, Royal Maternity Hospital and Royal Infirmary, (all Glasgow); Research Fellow, Nuffield Department of Obstetrics and Gynaecology, Oxford University, 1972-75; Lecturer in Obstetrics and Gynaecology, Glasgow University, 1975-78, Senior Lecturer, 1978-86. Secretary, Munro Kerr Society for the Study of Reproductive Biology, 1980-86; Blair Bell Memorial Lecturer, RCOG, 1977; WHO Travelling Fellow, 1985. Recreations: music; golf; curling. Address: (h.) 21 Braid Avenue, Edinburgh, EH10 4SR; T.-031-447 0490.

Calder, Angus Lindsay, MA, DPhil. Staff Tutor in Arts, Open University in Scotland, since 1979; Co-Editor, Journal of Commonwealth Literature, 1980-87; Convener, Scottish Poetry Library, 1983-88; b. 5.2.42, Sutton, Surrey; m., 1, Jennifer Daiches; 1 s.; 2 d.; 2, Catherine Kyle. Educ. Wallington County Grammar School; Kings College, Cambridge. Lecturer in Literature, Nairobi University, 1968-71; Visiting Lecturer, Chancellor College, Malawi University, 1978. Member, Board of Directors: Fruitmarket Gallery, Royal Lyceum Theatre Company; Editorial Committee, Cencrastus; Eric Gregory Award for Poetry, 1967. Publications: The People's War: Britain 1939-1945, 1969 (John Llewellyn Rhys Memorial Prize); Revolutionary Empire, 1981 (Scottish Arts Council Book Award). Recreations: curling; cricket. Address: (b.) 60 Melville Street, Edinburgh, EH3 7HF; T.-031-226 3851.

Calder, Jenni, BA, MPhil. Freelance Writer; Publications Editor, National Museums of Scotland, Edinburgh, since 1987; b. 3.12.41, Chicago, Illinois; 1 s.; 2 d. Educ. Perse School for Girls, Cambridge; Cambridge University; London University. Freelance writer, 1966-78; taught and lectured in Scotland, England, Kenya and USA; Lecturer in English, Nairobi University, 1968-69; Education Officer, Royal Scottish Museum, 1978-87. Chairperson, Scottish Branch, Royal Anthropological Institute; Member, Scottish Writers Against the Bomb. Publications: Chronicles of Conscience: a study of George Orwell and Arthur Koestler, 1968; Scott (with Angus Calder), 1969; There Must be a Lone Ranger: the Myth and Reality of the American West, 1974; Women and Marriage in Victorian Fiction, 1976; Brave New World and Nineteen Eighty Four, 1976; Heroes: from Byron to Guevara, 1977; The Victorian Home, 1977; The Victorian Home from Old Photographs, 1979; RLS, A Life Study, 1980; The Robert Louis Stevenson Companion (Editor), 1980; Robert Louis Stevenson and Victorian Scotland (Editor), 1981; The Strange Case of Dr Jekyll and Mr Hyde (Editor), 1979; Kidnapped (Editor), 1981; Catriona (Editor), 1981; The Enterprising Scot (Editor), 1986; Island Landfalls (Editor), 1987; Bonny Fighters: The Story of the Scottish Soldier, 1987; Open Guide to Animal Farm and Nineteen Eighty Four, 1987. Recreations: music; films; walking the dog. Address: (h.) 18 Springfield Road, South Queensferry, West Lothian; T.-031-331 2765.

Calder, John, Honorary Sheriff, Lothians; Vice Lieutenant, West Lothian; b. 11.7.14, Dundee; m., Vida Carmichael; 1 s.; 1 d. Educ. Morgan Academy, Dundee; University College, Dundee; Edinburgh University. Solicitor; Depute Town Clerk, Kirkcaldy; County Clerk, West Lothian; retired. District Governor, Rotary International District 102, 1962; Verdienstkreuz Am Bande (FDR) awarded by Bundesprasident, 1983. Address: (h.) Woodlands, 8 Dundas Street, Bo'ness, West Lothian; T.-0506 822311.

Calder, Robert Russell, MA. Critic, Philosophical Writer, Historian of Ideas, Poet, Freelance Journalist, Book Reviewer; b. 22.4.50, Burnbank. Educ. Hamilton Academy; Glasgow University; Edinburgh University. Editor: Chapman, 1974-76, Lines Review, 1976-77; Theatre Critic and Feature Writer, Scot, 1983-86; various writings on Edwin Muir; poetry: Il Re Giovane, 1976, Ettrick & Annan, 1981; Serapion, 1988. Recreations: music - opera singing; jazz piano. Address: (h.) 23 Glenlee Street, Burnbank, Hamilton, ML3 9JB; T.-0698 824244.

Calderwood, Robert, LLB (Hons). Chief Executive, Strathclyde Regional Council, since 1980; b. 1.3.32; m., Meryl Anne; 3 s.; 1 d. Educ. William Hulme's School, Manchester; Manchester University. Town Clerk: Salford, 1966-69, Bolton, 1969-73, Manchester, 1973-79. Address: Strathclyde Regional Council, Regional HQ, 20 India Street, Glasgow, G2 4PF.

Caldwell, David Cleland, SHNC, MA, BPhil. Secretary, Robert Gordon's Institute of Technology, since 1984; b. 25.2.44, Glasgow; m., Ann Scott Macrae; 1 s.; 1 d. Educ. George Watson's College, Edinburgh; St. Andrews University; Glasgow University. Warwick University: Lecturer in Politics, 1969-76, Administrative Assistant, 1976-77, Assistant Registrar, 1977-80; Registry Officer, Aberdeen University, 1980-84. Member: Warwick District Council, 1979-80, Grampian Regional Council, 1983-84; Parliamentary candidate (Labour), North East Fife, 1983; Member, Aberdeen Grammar School Council, since 1983 (Chairman, since 1985); Member, St. Andrews University Court, since 1986. Address: (b.) Robert Gordon's Institute of Technology, Schoolhill, Aberdeen, AB9 1FR; T.-0224 633611.

Caldwell, David Hepburn, MA, PhD, FSAScot. Curator in Charge of the Scottish Medieval Collections, Royal Museum of Scotland; b. 15.12.51, Kilwinning, Ayrshire; m., Margaret Anne McGovern; 2 d. Educ. Ardrossan Academy; Edinburgh University. Joined staff, National Museum of Antiquities, 1973. Publications: The Scottish Armoury, 1979; Scottish Weapons and Fortifications, 1981. Recreation: travelling. Address: (h.) 3 James Park, Burntisland, Fife, KY3 9EW; T.-872175.

Caldwell, Rev. James, MA. Minister of Religion (retired); former Member, Tayside Health Board; b. 12.5.16, Larkhall, Lanarkshire; m., Marjory Bruce Harvie; 2 s.; 1 d. Educ. Hamilton Academy; St. Andrews University; St. Mary's College, St. Andrews. Ordained by Glasgow Presbytery; Assistant Minister, Govan Old Parish Church, 1943; inducted Rossland Church, Bishopton, 1945; inducted Kirriemuir, 1952; Moderator, Forfar Presbytery, 1955-56; translated to Shawlands Old Parish Church, 1958; became Minister, united charge with Langside Avenue Church, 1963; Chaplain, Victoria Infirmary, Glasgow, 1962-78; translated to Abernethy and Dron Parish Church, Perthshire, 1978; linked with Arngask, Glenfarg, 1979; Member, Advisory Board of Church of Scotland, 1980-81; Moderator, Perth Presbytery, 1983-84; first Chairman, Glasgow (SE) Health Council, 1975-78; Tayside Health Board: Convener, General Medical Practitioners' Committee and Special Leave Committee, 1984-85; Vice Chairman, Arbroath Probus Club, 1988-89. Recreations: walking; gardening; travel; choral singing; writing and journalism. Address: (h.) 26 Dalhousie Place, Arbroath, DD11 2BT; T.-Arbroath 70670.

Caldwell, Sheila Marion, BA (Hons). Head, St. Columba's School, Kilmacolm, 1976-87; b. England; m., Major Robert Caldwell, TD. Educ. Tunbridge Wells Grammar School; University College, London. Founder/Principal, Yejide Girls' Grammar School, Ibadan, Nigeria; first Principal, Girls' Secondary (Government) School, Lilongwe, Malawi; Depute Head, Mills Grammar School, Framlingham, Suffolk. Treasurer, Secondary Heads' Association, Scotland, 1984-87. Recreations: exploring new places and new ideas; reading; walking; music/opera; interior design (theory and practice). Address: (h.) 27 Oxford Road, Renfrew, PA4 0SJ; T.-041-886 2296.

Callaghan, Thomas Stanley, MB, BCh, BAO (Hons), MD, MRCP (UK). Consultant Physician, Stracathro Hospital, since 1982; Honorary Senior Lecturer, Ninewells Hospital and Dundee University Medical School, since 1982; Visiting Physician, Sunnyside Royal Hospital, since 1985; b. 11.2.48, Limavady, Co. Londonderry; m., Irene Helen Bowie; 1 s.; 1 d. Educ. Limavady Grammar School; Queen's University, Belfast. Part-time Lecturer, Dundee College of Technology; Elder, Church of Scotland. Recreations: reading; shooting; walking. Address: (h.) The Mary Acre, Argyll Street, Brechin, DD9 6JL; T.-03562 4725.

Callen, Rev. John Robertson, MA, BD. Minister, Lochgilphead Parish Church, since 1962; Member, Committee to Elect the Moderator of the General Assembly; b. 12.12.35, Glengarnock; m., Isobel Annie Morrison; 2 s. Educ. Spier's School; Glasgow University and Trinity College. Moderator: Inveraray Presbytery, 1966, South Argyll Presbytery, 1983; Chaplain, Lochgilphead Hospitals; Local Office-Bearer, National Bible Society of Scotland, since 1963; Lochgilphead Secretary, Christian Aid, since 1966; first Chairperson, Lochgilphead Community Council, 1977-79; Leader, Holy Land tour, 1983; Lyon Court grant of arms, 1968. Publication: Social Directory of Lochgilphead, 1972. Recreations: hill-walking; cycling. Address: Parish Manse, Manse Brae, Lochgilphead, Argyll, PA31 8QZ; T.-0546 2238.

Calman, Professor Kenneth Charles, MD, PhD, FRCP, FRCS, FRSE. Dean of Postgraduate Medicine, Glasgow University, since 1984; b. 25.12.41, Glasgow; m., Ann; 1 s.; 2 d. Educ. Allan Glen's School, Glasgow; Glasgow University. Lecturer in Surgery, Western Infirmary, Glasgow, 1968-72; MRC Clinical Research Fellow, London, 1972-73; Professor of Oncology, Glasgow University, 1974-84. Recreations: golf; jogging; gardening. Address: (h.) 585 Anniesland Road, Glasgow; T.-041-954 9423.

Cameron, Alan Iain, BSc. Rector, Ellon Academy, since 1981; b. 21.9.41, Southend, Argyll; m., Elizabeth Margaret; 2 s.; 1 d. Educ. Campbeltown Grammar School; Glasgow University; Jordanhill College of Education. Science Teacher, Campbeltown Grammar School, 1964-67; Head of Science, Invergordon Academy, 1967-73; Head of Chemistry, Mackie Academy, 1973-77; Depute Rector, Selkirk High School, 1977-81. Elder, Church of Scotland. Recreations: music; drama; art; most sports. Address: (h.) The Neuk, Station Road, Ellon, Aberdeenshire; T.-20130.

Cameron, Allan John, MBE, VL, JP. Member, Ross and Cromarty District Council, since 1975; Farmer and Landowner, since 1947; b. 25.3.17, Edinburgh; m., Elizabeth Vaughan-Lee; 2 s.; 2 d. Educ. Harrow; Royal Military College. Regular officer, Queen's Own Cameron Highlanders, 1936-47 (ret. Major); Member, Ross and Cromarty County Council, 1955-75 (Chairman, Education Committee, 1962-75); former Commissioner: Red Deer Commission, Countryside Commission for Scotland; former Member, BBC Council for Scotland; President, Royal Caledonian Curling Club, 1963; President, International Curling Federation, 1965-69. Recreations: curling; golf; shooting; fishing; gardening. Address: (h.) Allangrange, Munlochy, Ross and Cromarty; T.-046381 249.

Cameron, Rev. Charles Millar, BA, BD, PhD. Minister, St. Ninian's Parish Church, Dunfermline, since 1980; b. 31.5.51, Glasgow; m., Sharon Elizabeth Tweed; 1 s. Educ. Woodside Secondary School, Glasgow; Stirling University; Glasgow University. World Alliance of Reformed Churches Scholar, Western Theological Seminary, Michigan, 1978-79. Publications: The Bible, 1987; The Problem of Polarization: An Approach Based on the Writings of G.C. Berkouwer, in press. Address: 51 St. John's Drive, Dunfermline, KY12 7TL; T.-0383 722256.

Cameron of Lochiel, Colonel Sir Donald (Hamish), KT (1973), CVO, TD, JP. 26th Chief of the Clan Cameron; Lord Lieutenant, County of Inverness, 1971-86; Chartered Accountant; b. 12.9.10; m.; 2 s.; 2 d. Educ. Harrow; Balliol College, Oxford. Lt.-Col. commanding: Lovat Scouts, 1944-45; 4/5th Bn. (TA), Queen's Own Cameron Highlanders, 1955-57; Colonel, 1957 (TARO); Vice-Chairman, Royal Bank of Scotland, 1969-80; Chairman, Culter Guard Bridge Holdings Ltd., 1970-76; Chairman, Scottish Widows Life Assurance Society, 1964-67; President, Scottish Landowners Federation, 1979-84; President, Royal Highland and Agricultural Society of Scotland, 1971, 1979, 1987; Member, Scottish Railways Board (Chairman, 1959-64). Address: (h.) Achnacarry, Spean Bridge, Inverness-shire.

Cameron, Dugald, DA, FCSD. Head of Design, Glasgow School of Art, since 1982; Director, Squadron Prints, since 1977; Industrial Design Consultant, since 1965; b. 4.10.39, Glasgow; m., Nancy Inglis. Educ. Glasgow High School; Glasgow School of Art. Industrial Designer, Hard Aluminium Surfaces Ltd., 1962-65; Visiting Lecturer, Glasgow School of Art, 1963-70; Head of Product Design, Glasgow School of Art, 1970-82. Member: Engineering Advisory Committee, Scottish Committee, Council of Industrial Design, since 1966, Industrial Design (Engineering) Panel and 3D Design Board, CNAA, since 1978, Scottish Committee of Higher Education, Design Council, since 1984. Recreations: railways; flying (lapsed private pilot). Address: (h.) Achnacraig, Skelmorlie, Ayrshire.

Cameron, Duncan Inglis, JP, BL, CA. Director of Administration and Secretary, Heriot-Watt University, since 1965; b. 26.8.27, Glasgow; m., Elizabeth Pearl Heron; 2 s.; 1 d. Educ. Glasgow High School; Glasgow University. RAF, 1945-48; CA apprentice, Alfred Tongue & Co., 1948-51; Qualified Assistant, Cooper Brothers & Co., 1951-52; Assistant Accountant, Edinburgh University, 1952-65; Commonwealth Universities Administrative Fellow, 1972. President, Edinburgh Junior Chamber of Commerce, 1962-63; Governor, Keil School, Dumbarton, 1967-85; Chairman of Council, Royal Scottish Geographical Society, 1983-88 (Trustee, since 1973); Chairman, Bioscot Ltd., 1983-84; Chairman, Edinburgh Conference Centre Ltd., since 1987; Director, Heriot-Watt Computer Application Services Ltd., since 1987; Member, Universities Central Council on Admissions, since 1967; Chairman, Edinburgh Society of Glasgow University Graduates, 1984-85; Session Clerk, St. Ninian's Church, Corstorphine, since 1969. Officer of the Royal Norwegian Order of St. Olav, 1979. Recreations: travel; photography. Address: (b.) Heriot-Watt University, Riccarton, Edinburgh, EH14 4AS; T.-031-449 5111.

Cameron, Ewen Cameron, OBE, JP. Sheep and Highland Cattle Breeder; Managing Director: Lochearnhead Hotel, since 1947, Lochearnhead Development Company, since 1955; Member, Perth and Kinross District Council, since 1980 (Convenor, Leisure and Recreation Committee); Member, Tayside Health Board; Member, Scottish Sports Council; Member, Electricity Consultative Council for the North of Scotland; b. 23.12.26, Lochearnhead; m., Davina Anne Frew; 1 s.; 1 d. Educ. Glenalmond College (Victor Ludorum). Royal Navy (South East Asia Command), 1944-47; played rugby for Perthshire Acas, 1946-50; Member: Perth County Council, 1964-75, Stirling District Council, 1974-77 (Environmental Health Convener); Vice-Chairman, Cumbernauld Development Corporation, 1973-77 (Member, 1963-73); former Member, Consultative Council, Scottish Tourist Board; Chairman, British Water Ski Federation, 1965-70; President, Balquhidder, Lochearnhead and Strathyre Highland Games; Chairman, Visiting Committee, Perth Prison, 1980-84; Vice-President, Royal Highland Agricultural Society, 1981. Highland Games Champion of Scotland (Heavy Events), 1953. Recreations: curling; shooting; golf; dominos. Address: (h.) Ben Ouhr, Lochearnhead, Perthshire; T.-05673 231.

Cameron, Professor George Gordon, BSc, PhD, DSc, FRSE. Professor of Physical Chemistry, Aberdeen University, since 1984; b. 1.12.32, Stirling; m., Aileen Elizabeth Sinclair; 1 s.; 2 d. Educ. Stirling High School; Glasgow University. Lecturer in Chemistry, St. Andrews University, 1961; Lecturer in Physical Chemistry, then Senior Lecturer, then Reader, Aberdeen University, 1966-84. Recreations: outdoor activities (walking, skiing); music. Address: (b.) Department of Chemistry, Aberdeen University, Aberdeen, AB9 2UE; T.-0224 272903.

Cameron, Gordon Stewart, RSA, DA. Artist; b. 27.4.16, Aberdeen; m., Ellen Malcolm, RSA. Educ. Robert Gordon's College, Aberdeen; Gray's School of Art, Aberdeen. Part-time Lecturer, Gray's School of Art, 1946-51; Lecturer, Dundee College of Art, 1952; Senior Lecturer, Duncan of Jordanstone College of Art, 1967-81; elected, ARSA, 1958, Academician, 1971; work in public galleries in Scotland and in private collections in various parts of the world. Address: (h.) 7 Auburn Terrace, Invergowrie, Dundee; T.-Dundee 562318.

Cameron, Hector MacDonald, OBE, MD, FRCPath. Senior Lecturer in Pathology, Edinburgh University, since 1974; Honorary Consultant, Lothian Health Board, since 1974; Honorary Consultant, Borders Health Board, since 1982; b. 20.12.22, Aberdeen; m., Frances Maude Majury; 2 s.; 2 d. Educ. Methodist College, Belfast; Queen's University, Belfast. Consultant Pathologist: Stobhill Hospital, Glasgow, 1956-64, University Department of Pathology, Glasgow Royal Infirmary, 1964-70; Honorary Lecturer, Glasgow University, 1964-70; Professor of Pathology, Nairobi University, 1967-74. Publication: Liver Cell Cancer (Co-Editor), 1976. Recreations: music; hill-walking. Address: (h.) 25 Gallowhill, Peebles, EH45 9BG; T.-0721 21172.

Cameron, Rev. Professor James Kerr, MA, BD, PhD, FRHistS. Professor of Ecclesiastical History, St. Andrews University, since 1970; b. 5.3.24, Methven; m., Emma Leslie Birse; 1 s. Educ. Oban High School; St. Andrews University; Hartford Theological Seminary, Hartford, Connecticut. Ordained as Assistant Minister, Church of the Holy Rude, Stirling, 1952; appointed Lecturer in Church History, Aberdeen University, 1955; Lecturer, then Senior Lecturer in Ecclesiastical History, St. Andrews University; Dean, Faculty of Divinity, 1978-83. President: Ecclesiastical History Society, 1976-77, British Sub-Commission, Commission Internationale d'Histoire Ecclesiastique Comparee, since 1979; Vice-President, International Association for Neo-Latin Studies, 1979-81. Publications: Letters of John Johnstone and Robert Howie, 1963; First Book of Discipline, 1972; contributions to: Acta Conventus Neo-Latini Amstelodamensis, 1973; Advocates of Reform, 1953; The Scottish Tradition, 1974; Renaissance and Renewal in Christian History, 1977; Reform and Reformation: England and the Continent, 1979; Origins and Nature of the Scottish Enlightenment, 1982; A Companion to Scottish Culture. Recreation: gardening. Address: (h.) Priorscroft, 71 Hepburn Gardens, St. Andrews, KY16 9LS; T.-0334 73996.

Cameron, Hon. Lord (John Cameron), KT (1978), Kt (1954), DSC, LLD (Aberdeen and Edinburgh), DLitt (Heriot-Watt), HRSA, FRSGS. Senator of the College of Justice in Scotland and Lord of Session, 1955-85; b. 1900; m., 1, Eileen Dorothea Burrell (deceased); 1 s.; 2 d.; 2, Iris Shepherd. Educ. Edinburgh Academy; Edinburgh University. Served First World War with RNVR; Advocate, 1924; Advocate-Depute, 1929-36; QC (Scot), 1936; RNVR, 1939-44 (Despatches); Sheriff of Inverness, Elgin and Nairn, 1945; Sheriff of Inverness, Moray, Nairn and Ross and Cromarty, 1946-48; Dean, Faculty of Advocates, 1948-55; DL Edinburgh, 1953-84; Hon. FRSE, 1983; Hon. FBA, 1983; DUniv, Edinburgh, 1983.

Cameron, John Alastair, QC, MA (Oxon). Vice-Dean, Faculty of Advocates, since 1983; President, Pensions Appeal Tribunal for Scotland, since 1985; b. 1.2.38, Newcastle-upon-Tyne; m., Espeth Mary Dunlop Miller; 3 s. Educ. Trinity College, Glenalmond; Pembroke College, Oxford. Called to the Bar, Inner Temple, 1963; admitted Member, Faculty of Advocates, 1966; Advocate-Depute, 1972-75; Standing Junior Counsel to Department of Energy, 1976-79, Scottish Development Department, 1978-79; Legal Chairman, Pensions Appeal Tribunals for Scotland, since 1979. Publication: Medical Negligence: an Introduction, 1983. Recreations: travel; sport; Africana. Address: (h.) 4 Garscube Terrace, Edinburgh, EH12 6BQ; T.-031-337 3460.

Cameron, Professor John Robinson, MA, BPhil. Regius Professor of Logic, Aberdeen University, since 1979; b. 24.6.36, Glasgow; m., 1, Mary Elizabeth Ranson (deceased); 2, Barbara Elizabeth Blair; 1 s.; 2 d. Educ. Dundee High School; St. Andrews University. Harkness Fellow, USA, 1959-61; Lecturer in Philosophy, Queen's College, Dundee, 1962 (Dundee University from 1967); appointed Senior Lecturer in Philosophy, 1973. Recreation: bricolage. Address: (b.) Department of Philosophy, Aberdeen University, King's College, Aberdeen, AB9 2UB; T.-Aberdeen 272365.

Cameron, (John Roderick) Hector, LLB, NP. Partner, Bishop and Robertson Chalmers, Solicitors, since 1973; b. 11.6.47, Glasgow; m., Rosemary Brownlee; 1 s.; 1 d. Educ. High School of Glasgow; Friends School, Wigton; St. Andrews University. Admitted Solicitor, 1971; Partner, Bishop, Milne Boyd & Co., 1973; Chairman, Glasgow Junior Chamber of Commerce, 1981; Managing Partner, Bishop & Co., 1985; Director, Merchants House of Glasgow, 1986; Director, Glasgow Chamber of Commerce, 1987. Chairman, Strathclyde Appeal Committee, Help the Aged. Recreations: reading; gardening; sailing; golf. Address: (b.) 129 St. Vincent Street, Glasgow, G2 5JF; T.-041-248 4672.

Cameron, Rev. Dr. John Urquhart, BA, BSc, PhD, BD, ThD. Minister, Parish of Broughty Ferry, since 1974; b. 10.6.43, Dundee; m., Jill Sjoberg; 1 s.; 1 d. Educ. Falkirk High School; St. Andrews University; Edinburgh University; University of Southern California. Marketing Executive, Beechams, London, 1969-73; Assistant Minister, Wellington Church, Glasgow, 1973-74; Chaplain, Royal Naval Reserve, 1976-81; Marketing Consultant, Pergamon Press, Oxford, 1977-81; Religious Education Department, Dundee High School, since 1980; winter sports Journalist, since 1981; Chaplain, Royal Caledonian Curling Club. National and international honours in both summer and winter sports, 1960-83; sports scholarship, University of Southern California, 1962-64. Recreations: golf; skiing; curling. Address: St. Stephen's Manse, 33 Camperdown Street, Broughty Ferry; T.-0382 77403.

Cameron, Joseph Gordon Stuart, MA, LLB, WS. Solicitor; Partner, Stuart & Stuart, WS; b. 4.2.27, Uddingston; m., Celia Margaret; 3 s.; 1 d. Educ. George Watson's Boys' College; Edinburgh University. National Service, 1948-49; qualified, 1952; Lecturer in Conveyancing, Edinburgh University, 1955-66. Honorary Secretary and Treasurer, Royal Celtic Society; Honorary Treasurer, Edinburgh Angus Club. Publication: The Law of Landlord and Tenant in Scotland (Co-author), 1967. Recreations: gardening; hill-walking. Address: (b.) 23 Rutland Street, Edinburgh, EH1 2RN; T.-031-228 6449.

Cameron, Provost Kenneth, JP. Provost of Nithsdale District Council, since 1984 (Chairman, Policy and Resources Committee, since 1984); b. 26.2.33, Glasgow; m., Mary McGeorge Coupland; 1 s.; 2 d. Educ. Dumfries High School. Fire brigade employee (retired); Past Chairman: Dumfries District Council, Dumfries Area Education Committee, Locharbriggs Community Council; Member, Nithsdale District Council, since 1975; Member, Electricity Consultative Council for South of Scotland District; Depute Traffic Commissioner; Member, COSLA. Recreation: former SFA referee. Address: (h.) 59 Wallamhill Road, Locharbriggs, Dumfries; T.-0387 710367.

Cameron of Lochbroom, Lord (Kenneth John Cameron), Life Baron (1984), PC (1984), MA (Oxon), LLB, QC. Lord Advocate, since 1984; b. 11.6.31, Edinburgh; m., Jean Pamela Murray; 2 d. Educ. Edinburgh Academy; Corpus Christi College, Oxford; Edinburgh University. Advocate, 1958; Queen's Counsel, 1972; President, Pensions Appeal Tribunal for Scotland, 1976; Chairman, Committee of Investigation Under Agricultural Marketing Act 1958, 1980; Advocate Depute, 1981; Hon. Bencher, Lincoln's Inn. Recreations: fishing; sailing. Address: (h.) 10 Belford Terrace, Edinburgh.

Cameron, Monica Joan, BA (Oxon), MA, PGCE. Headmistress, St. Margaret's School, Edinburgh, since 1984; b. 27.2.31, Alloa; m., Rev. D.E.N. Cameron; 2 s.; 2 d. Educ. Cheltenham Ladies' College; St. Hugh's College, Oxford; Durham University. Deputy Head, Northallerton Grammar School, 1974-82; Assistant Head, Firrhill High School, Edinburgh, 1983-84. Recreations: Christian activities; walking; reading. Address: (h.) 6 Redford Terrace, Colinton, Edinburgh; T.-031-447 3870.

Cameron, Rev. Dr. Nigel Malcolm de Segur, MA (Cantab), BD, PhD. Warden, Rutherford House, Edinburgh, since 1982; b. 5.8.52, Folkestone; m., Shenach Jean McKerracher Stringer; 1 s.; 3 d. Educ. Bradford Grammar School; Emmanuel College, Cambridge; New College, Edinburgh. Assistant Minister, Dunblane Cathedral, 1977-78; Associate Minister, Holyrood Abbey Church, Edinburgh, 1982-85; General Editor, Evangel, A Quarterly Review of Biblical, Practical and Contemporary Theology, 1981-87; Editor: Scottish Bulletin of Evangelical Theology, since 1983, Ethics and Medicine, since 1984; Member, Board of Social Responsibility, Church of Scotland, since 1986; Theological Consultant to CARE Trust, since 1987. Publications: Evolution and the Authority of the Bible, 1983; Pulpit and People (Co-Editor), 1986; Abortion: the Crisis in Morals and Medicine (Co-author), 1986; The Challenge of Evangelical Theology (Editor), 1987; Embryos and Ethics, The Warnock Report in Debate (Editor), 1987; Biblical Higher Criticism and the Defense of Infallibilism in Nineteenth Century Britain, 1987; Medicine in Crisis, a Christian Response (Co-Editor), 1988. Recreation: writing, especially to The Times. Address: (h.) 7 Durham Road, Edinburgh; T.-031-554 1206.

Cameron, Rev. Peter Scott, LLB, BD, PhD, LRAM. Lecturer, New Testament Department, Edinburgh University, since 1987; Minister, Church of Scotland, since 1983; b. 2.8.45, Edinburgh; m., Elizabeth Watson; 2 s.; 1 d. Educ. Fettes College; Royal Academy of Music; Edinburgh University; Cambridge University; Tubingen University. Solicitor, Edinburgh, 1970-73; Procurator Fiscal Service, Dundee, 1979-83; Minister, St. Philip's Church, Joppa, Edinburgh, 1984-87. German Academic Exchange Service Scholarship, 1977-78. Publication: Violence and the Kingdom, 1984. Recreation: music. Address: (b.) New College, Mound Place, Edinburgh.

Cameron, Richard William Grant, DA, RIBA, DipTP, MRTPI, ARIAS. Director of Planning, Highland Regional Council, since 1981; b. 2.5.37, Edinburgh; m., Mary Elizabeth Cheyne; 2 d. Educ. Royal High School, Edinburgh; Edinburgh College of Art; Heriot-Watt University. Assistant Architect, Richard E. Moira and B.L.C. Moira Architects, 1959-63; Assistant Planning Officer: Livingston Development Corporation, 1963-66, Central Mortgage and Housing Corporation, Canada, 1966-69; Planning Consultant, Department of National Defence, Canada, 1969-70; Depute Planning Officer: Inverness County Council, 1970-75, Highland Regional Council, 1975-81. External Examiner, Civic Design, Heriot Watt University; Member: Culloden Sub-Committee, National Trust for Scotland; Highland Area Farming, Forestry and Wildlife Advisory Group; Scottish Committee, Nature Conservancy Council. Recreations: bagpipe playing; golf; sailing. Address: (b.) Regional Buildings, Glenurquhart Road, Inverness; T.-0463 234121.

Cameron, Rev. William John, MA, BD. Principal Emeritus, Free Church of Scotland College, since 1977; b. 29.11.07, Brora; m., 1, Lilias Rownsfell Brown (deceased); 2, Murdina Macaulay Smith; 1 s.; 2 d. Educ. Nicolson Public Higher Grade School, Stornoway; Edinburgh University; Free Church College, Edinburgh. Minister, Free Church of Scotland: Burghead, Morayshire, 1932-50, Buccleuch-Greyfriars, Edinburgh, 1950-53; Professor of New Testament Language and Theology, Free Church College, 1953-77 (Principal, 1973-77); Principal Clerk, Free Church of Scotland General Assembly, 1963-76 (Moderator, 1977). Publications: contributions to: New Bible Commentary, 1953; Baker's Dictionary of Theology, 1960; The New Testament from 26 Translations, 1967; Zondervan Pictorial Bible Encyclopedia, 1975; Illustrated Bible Dictionary, 1980. Recreation: walking. Address: (h.) 19 Kilmaurs Road, Edinburgh, EH16 5DA; T.-031-667 6121.

Campbell, Ailsa Morag, BSc, PhD, FRSE. Reader in Biochemistry, Glasgow University; b. 16.3.43, Aberdeen: m., Thomas Campbell (m. diss.); 1 s.; 1 d. Educ. Laurel Bank School, Glasgow; Edinburgh University; Glasgow University. Appointed Lecturer in Biochemistry, Glasgow University, 1969; Visiting Professor, Vanderbilt University, Tennessee, 1978. Recreations: gardening; music. Address: (b.) Department of Biochemistry, Glasgow University, G12 8QQ; T.-041-339 8855, Ext. 4627.

Campbell, Alan Grant, LLB. Director of Law and Administration, Grampian Regional Council, since 1984; b. 4.12.46, Aberdeen; m., Susan Black; 1 s.; 2 d. Educ. Aberdeen Grammar School; Aberdeen University. Aberdeen County Council: Law apprentice/Solicitor, 1968-72, Senior Legal Assistant, 1972-75; Grampian Regional Council: Assistant Director of Law and Administration, 1975-79, Depute Director, 1979-84. Seminar Leader, Diploma in Legal Practice, Aberdeen University. Recreation: cycling. Address: Woodhill House, Westburn Road, Aberdeen, AB9 2LU; T.-0224 682222, Ext. 2111.

Campbell, Professor Alexander George Macpherson, MB, ChB, FRCPEdin, DCH. Professor of Child Health, Aberdeen University, since 1973; Honorary Consultant Paediatrician, Grampian Health Board, since 1973; b. 3.2.31, Glasgow; m., Sheila Mary Macdonald; 1 s.; 2 d. Educ. Dollar Academy; Glasgow University. Paediatric Registrar, Royal Hospital for Sick Children, Edinburgh, 1959-61; Senior House Officer, Hospital for Sick Children, London, 1961-62; Assistant Chief Resident, Children's Hospital of Philadelphia, 1962-63; Fellow in Paediatric Cardiology, Hospital for Sick Children, Toronto, 1963-64; Fellow in Fetal and Neonatal Physiology, Nuffield Institute for Medical Research, Oxford, 1964-66; Lecturer in Child Health, St. Andrews University, 1966-67; Assistant, then Associate Professor of Paediatrics, Yale University School of Medicine, 1967-73. Member, Grampian Health Board; Editorial Committee, Archives of Disease in Childhood. Recreation: golf. Address: (b.) Department of Child Health, Aberdeen University, Aberdeen; T.-0224 681818, Ext. 52471.

Campbell, Alistair Bromley, OBE. Member, Scottish Land Court, since 1981; Chairman, Scottish Conservation Projects Trust, since 1984; b. 23.6.27, Charing, Kent; m., Rosemary Pullar; 1 s.; 2 d. Educ. Tonbridge School. Training in agriculture, 1944-47; self-employed Farmer, 1948-81; Agricultural Consultant, Adviser, Arbiter, Valuer, 1968-81; Agricultural Adviser and Valuer, South of Scotland Electricity Board, 1972-81; Vice-Chairman, Countryside Commission for Scotland, 1972-81; Member, Secretary of State's Panel of Agricultural Arbiters, 1968-81; Member, Council of Management, Strathcarron Hospice, Denny; former Council Member, British Trust for Conservation Volunteers (Chairman, Scottish Regional Committee, 1975-84); Church Warden, St. Mary's Episcopal Church, Dunblane, since 1960; Honorary Vice-President and a Director, Doune and Dunblane Agricultural Society; former Convener, Legal Committee, NFU of Scotland; General Commissioner of Income Tax, since 1971; Chairman, Scottish Executive Committee, Association of Agriculture, 1980-86. Recreations: work; shooting; enjoying countryside; farming. Address: (h.) Grainston Farm, Kilbryde, Dunblane, Perthshire, FK15 9NF; T.-0786 823304.

Campbell, Alistair John. Secretary, Industrial Tribunals (Scotland), since 1979; b. 12.10.29, Inverness; m., Helen MacKay Murray; 1 s.; 1 d. Educ. Royal Academy, Inverness. Ministry of Labour, 1946-47; Royal Artillery, 1948-49; Ministry of Labour, from 1950; Employment Exchange Manager, Isle of Skye, 1960-69, Outer Hebrides, Stornoway, 1970-79. Captain, TA (Queen's Own Cameron Highlanders and 51st Highland Volunteers), 1964-73. Recreations: deer stalking; shooting; fishing; outdoor activities. Address: (h.) Greshornish, 7 Northbank Road, Kirkintilloch, Glasgow, G66 1EZ; T.-041-776 3371.

Campbell, Rev. Andrew Blair, BD. Parish Minister, St. Columba's: Argyll Square Church, Oban, since 1979, and Kilmore and Oban, since 1984; b. 25.6.53, Edinburgh; m., Fiona Margaret Hay McRobbie. Educ. North Berwick High School; New College, Edinburgh. Assistant Minister, St. Michael's Church, Linlithgow, 1978-79. Moderator, Presbytery of Lorn and Mull, 1982-83; Moderator, Synod of Argyll, 1983-84; Area Officer, Argyll and Bute Trust, since 1985; Director, National Bible Society of Scotland, since 1980; Broadcaster and Chairman, Oban Hospital Radio, 1981-85. Recreations: hill-walking; skiing; reading. Address: (h.) Strathearn, Breadalbane Street, Oban, Argyll; T.-0631 62322.

Campbell, Arthur McLure. Principal Clerk of Session and Justiciary, Scotland, since 1982; b. 15.8.32, Glasgow. Educ. Queen's Park School, Glasgow. Admiralty Supplies Directorate, 1953-54; entered Scottish Court Service (Sheriff Clerk Branch), 1954; Departmental Legal Qualification, 1956; Sheriff Clerk Depute, Kilmarnock, 1957-60; Sheriff Clerk of Orkney, 1961-65; seconded HM Treasury (O. & M.), 1965-69 (Secretary, Lord Chancellor's Committee on Re-sealing of Probates and Confirmations, 1967-68, and Secretary, Scottish Office Committee on Money Transfer Services, 1968-69); Sheriff Clerk, Airdrie, 1969-72; Principal, Scottish Court Service Staff Training Centre, 1973-74; Assistant Sheriff Clerk of Glasgow, 1974-81. Chairman, Sheriff Clerks' Association, 1971-72; Member, Secretary of State for Scotland's Review Body on Use of Judicial Time in the Superior Courts, 1985-86. Address: (b.) Parliament House, Edinburgh, EH1 1RQ; T.-031-225 2595.

Campbell, Catherine, JP, BSc, BA (Hons), MSc. Educational Psychologist; Member, Scottish Milk Marketing Board, since 1981; Chairman, Cumbernauld "I" Tech, since 1984; b. 10.1.40, Glasgow; m., John Campbell; 2 s.; 1 d. Educ. Notre Dame High School; Glasgow University; Open University; Strathclyde University. Teacher of Mathematics, 1962-68; Member, Cumbernauld and Kilsyth District Council, 1969-78; Member, Cumbernauld Development Corporation, 1975-84. Jubilee Medal, 1977. Recreations: horse riding; homecrafts. Address: (h.) 10 Westray Road, Cumbernauld, G67 1NN; T.-023 67 24834.

Campbell, Rev. Colin, MA, BD, DipTh. Minister, Williamwood Parish Church, Glasgow, since 1949; b. 30.8.16, Greenock; m., Margaret Thomson Paton; 2 s. Educ. Greenock Academy; Hutchesons' Boys Grammar School, Glasgow; Glasgow University; Trinity College. Minister: Erskine Church, Kilwinning, 1940-44, East Church, Johnstone, 1944-49. Recreations: golf; swimming; classical music; reading. Address: Birnam, 4 Golf Road, Clarkston, Glasgow, G76 7LZ; T.-041-638 1215.

Campbell, Colin MacIver, MA (Hons). Head Teacher, Westwood Secondary School, Easterhouse, Glasgow, since 1977; b. 31.8.38, Ralston, Paisley; m., Evelyn J.M.; 3 s. Educ. Paisley Grammar School; Glasgow University; Jordanhill College of Education. Teacher: Hillhead High School, 1961-63, Paisley Grammar School, 1963-67; Principal Teacher, Greenock Academy, 1967-73; Depute Head Teacher, Merksworth High School, Paisley, 1973-77. Elder, Church of Scotland; Chairman, Renfrew West/Inverclyde SNP; Past Chairman, Kilbarchan Civic Society; former Chairman, Kilbarchan Community Council; SNP candidate, 1987. Recreations: jogging; military history; DIY; politics. Address: (h.) Braeside, Shuttle Street, Kilbarchan, Renfrewshire; T.-Kilbarchan 2713.

Campbell, Sir Colin Moffat, Bt, MC. Chairman, James Finlay plc, since 1975; b. 4.8.25; m., Mary Anne Chichester Bain; 2 s.; 1 d. (deceased). Educ. Stowe. Scots Guards, 1943-47 (Captain); joined James Finlay & Co. Ltd., 1947. President, Federation of Kenya Employers, 1962-70; Chairman, Tea Board of Kenya, 1961-71; Chairman, East African Tea Trade Association, 1960-61, 1962-63, 1966-67; Member, Scottish Council, CBI, 1979-85; Member, Council, CBI, since 1981; Deputy Chairman, Commonwealth Development Corporation, since 1983. Recreations: gardening; racing; cards. Address: (h.) Kilbryde Castle, Dunblane, Perthshire.

Campbell, David A., MA. Assistant Secretary, Scottish Office, since 1978; b. 5.11.34, Concepcion, Chile; m., Philippa Louise Bunting; 1 s.; 3 d. Educ. Oundle; King's College, Cambridge. King's Own Scottish Borderers, 1956-58; travel in the Antipodes and Africa, 1958-60, as tram conductor, docker, schoolmaster and Private Secretary to the Commissioner of the Cameroons; HM Diplomatic Service, 1960-78. Trustee, Rudolf Steiner School of Edinburgh. Recreations: books; the arts; horses. Address: (h.) Old Costerton, Midlothian; T.-Humbie 682.

Campbell, David Ross, FISD, MInstM. Chairman and Chief Executive, West Independent Newspapers Ltd.; Chairman: Guthrie Newspaper Group; Glasgow Guardian Group; Alloa Printing and Publishing Co.; Director, Clyde Cablevision Ltd.; Director, Strathclyde News Holdings Ltd.; b. 27.9.43, Glasgow; m., Moira. Educ. Whitehill School, Glasgow; James Watt Memorial College, Greenock. Previously worked for: international marine radio company; Union Castle SS Company; Sperry Rand; Scottish and Universal Group of companies. President, Glasgow Chamber of Commerce (Director, since 1981); Director, Ardrossan, Saltcoats and Stevenston Enterprise Trust, since 1985; Hon. Vice President, The Prince and Princess of Wales Hospice; Member, Commonwealth Press Union; Liveryman of the City of London. Recreations: golf; walking; swimming. Address: (b.) Herald Street, Ardrossan, KA22 8BX; T.-0294 64321.

Campbell, Donald, MA, FEIS. Rector, Castle Douglas High School, since 1967; b. 21.9.27, Tarbert, Harris; m., Doreen Watson Fergusson; 2 s.; 1 d. Educ. Sir E. Scott School, Tarbert; Portree Secondary School; Edinburgh University. Teacher of Mathematics: Peterhead Academy, Castle Douglas High School; Principal Teacher of Mathematics: Dalbeattie High School, Castle Douglas High School; Deputy Rector, Castle Douglas High School. Chairman, Castle Douglas Cancer Relief Committee; Session Clerk, St. Ringan's Church, Castle Douglas. Recreations: gardening; peat cutting. Address: (h.) Rockville, Ernespie Road, Castle Douglas; T.-0556 2127.

Campbell, Professor Donald, CBE, MB, ChB, FFARCS, FRCP(Glas), FRCS(Eng). Professor of Anaesthesia and Dean of Medicine, Glasgow University; Chairman, Scottish Council for Postgraduate Medical Education; b. 8.3.30, Rutherglen; m., Catherine Conway Bradburn; 1 s.; 3 d. Educ. Pitlochry High School; Hutchesons Grammar School, Glasgow; Glasgow University. Honorary Consultant Anaesthetist, Greater Glasgow Health Board; former Dean, Faculty of Anaesthetists, Royal College of Surgeons of England; former Vice-President, Royal College of Surgeons of England; Past President, Scottish Society of Anaesthetists; former Vice-President and Member of Council, Association of Anaesthetists of Great Britain and Ireland; Member, Medical Advisory Committee, British Council. Recreations: curling; angling. Address: (b.) 27 Tannoch Drive, Milngavie, Glasgow, G62 8AR; T.-041-956 1736.

Campbell, Doris Margaret, MD, MRCOG. Senior Lecturer in Obstetrics and Gynaecology and Reproductive Physiology, Aberdeen University, since 1984; b. 24.1.42, Aberdeen; m., Alasdair James Campbell; 1 s.; 1 d. Educ. Aberdeen High School for Girls; Aberdeen University. Resident house officer posts, Aberdeen, 1967-69; Research Fellow, Aberdeen University, 1969-73; Registrar in Obstetrics and Gynaecology, Aberdeen Hospitals, 1973-74; Lecturer in Obstetrics and Gynaecology and Physiology, Aberdeen University, 1974-84. Former Member, Scottish Women's Hockey Council. Recreations: bridge; badminton; guiding. Address: (h.) 77 Blenheim Place, Aberdeen; T.-Aberdeen 639984.

Campbell, Duncan, BSc, DipLD, MICF, ALI. Director, Countryside Commission for Scotland, since 1988; b. 23.9.35, Rangoon; m., Morny; 2 s. Educ. Merchiston Castle School, Edinburgh; Edinburgh University; Newcastle upon Tyne University. National Service, Royal Horse Artillery, 1954-56; Forestry Commission: Forest Manager, 1960-73, Landscape Architect, 1973-80, Head, Environment Branch, 1980-88. Recreations: landscape appreciation; fishing. Address: (b.) Battleby, Redgorton, Perth, PH1 3EW; T.-0738 27921.

Campbell, Rev. Effie Crawford, BD. Minister, Crichton West Church, Cumnock, since 1981; Moderator, Synod of Ayr, since 1987; b. 7.3.22, Glasgow; m., George Campbell; 1 d. Educ. Battlefield Secondary School, Glasgow; Glasgow University. Before marriage, office worker, SCWS; housewife for 25 years, before full-time study; first ordained woman minister in Ayr Presbytery; first woman to be Moderator, Synod of Ayr. Recreations: reading; knitting; motoring; speaking. Address: The Manse, 46 Ayr Road, Cumnock, KA18 1DW; T.-0290 20119.

Campbell, Wing Commander George, MBE, EsqStJ, DL, MBIM. County Director, British Red Cross Society (Dunbartonshire), since 1983; b. 24.11.22, Renton; m., Marion T.H. Halliday; 1 s.; 1 d. Educ. Vale of Leven Academy. Joined RAF, 1941; served in UK, India, Burma, Malaya, Singapore; demobilised, 1946, and continued in Royal Air Force Voluntary Reserve (Training Branch), serving with Air Training Corps; formed 2319 (Vale of Leven) Squadron, 1956; appointed to Wing Staff, Glasgow, and Western Wing, 1973; promoted to Wing Commander, 1978; retired, 1983; attended Bisley Shooting as competitor, coach, and team captain for 42 years; Chairman, County Scout Committee; Vice Chairman, Duke of Edinburgh Award (County Co-ordinating Committee); Elder, Church of Scotland; County Representative, Royal Air Forces Benevolent Fund; Past President, Dumbarton Rotary Club; Past Chairman, RNLI, Dumbarton Branch. Address: (h.) Valeview, Comley Bank, Oxhill, Dumbarton; T.-Dumbarton 63700.

Campbell, Rev. George Houstoun. Minister, John Knox Church, Stewarton, since 1971; b. 29.4.27, Glasgow; m., Elspeth Gibb Campbell Adams; 1 s.; 3 d. Educ. Whitehill Senior Secondary School, Glasgow; Glasgow University; Trinity College. Post Office and Civil Service, 1941-52; Missionary of Church of Scotland to Church of Central Africa Presbyterian, Malawi, 1957-71. Moderator, Presbytery of Irvine and Kilmarnock, 1980-81; President, Scottish Feed the Minds. Publications: Lonely Warrior; Tikuwababitiziraci Wana? Recreations: reading; gardening; visiting new places. Address: John Knox Manse, 27 Avenue Street, Stewarton, Kilmarnock, KA3 5AP; T.-0560 82418.

Campbell of Croy, Baron (Gordon Thomas Calthrop Campbell), PC (1970), MC (and Bar). Consultant, oil industry, since 1975; Director, Alliance and Leicester Building Society and Chairman of its Scottish Board; Chairman, Stoic Insurance Services, since 1979; b. 8.6.21; m.; 2 s.; 1 d. Educ. Wellington. Commissioned, Regular Army, 1939; RA, 1942 (Major); wounded, 1945; entered HM Foreign Service, 1946 and served in the Foreign Office, at the UN, in the Cabinet Office and in the Embassy in Vienna; MP (Conservative), Moray and Nairn, 1959-74; Secretary of State for Scotland, 1970-74; Chairman, Scottish Committee, International Year of Disabled, 1981; Trustee, Thomson Foundation, since 1980; Chairman, Advisory Committee on Pollution of the Sea, since 1987. Address: (h.) Holme Rose, Cawdor, Nairnshire.

Campbell, Hugh Hall, QC, BA (Hons), MA (Oxon), LLB (Hons), FCIArb. Queen's Counsel, since 1983; b. 18.2.44, Glasgow; m., Eleanor Jane Hare; 3 s. Educ. Glasgow Academy; Trinity College, Glenalmond; Exeter College, Oxford; Edinburgh University. Called to Scottish Bar, 1969; Standing Junior Counsel to Admiralty, 1976. Recreations: music; hill-walking; golf. Address: (h.) 12 Ainslie Place, Edinburgh, EH3 6AS; T.-031-225 2067.

Campbell, Ian, MA, PhD. Reader in English Literature, Edinburgh University; b. 25.8.42, Lausanne, Switzerland. Educ. schools in Lausanne, Rothiemay, Findochty, Buckie and Stonehaven; Aberdeen University; Edinburgh University. Joined Edinburgh University as Assistant Lecturer, then Lecturer in English Literature; visiting appointments in France, Switzerland, Germany, Canada and USA. President, Carlyle Society; Associate Editor, Carlyle Letters; Past President, Scottish Association for the Speaking of Verse. Recreations: music; sport; travel; history. Address: (b.) Department of English, Edinburgh University, George Square, Edinburgh, EH8 9JX; T.-031-667 1011.

Campbell, Ian Gordon, ARIAS, RIBA. Director of Architectural Services, East Lothian District Council, since 1975; b. 5.9.30, Paisley; m., Caryl; 2 s. Educ. Paisley Grammar School; Glasgow School of Architecture. Royal Engineers, 1955-57; Paisley Corporation: Architectural Assistant, 1952-55, Assistant Architect, 1957-61; Chief Architect, Royal Burgh of Rutherglen, 1961-65; Group Architect, Crudens, 1965-71; Burgh Architect, Royal Burgh of Irvine, 1971-75. Secretary, Association of Chief Architects of Scottish Local Authorities, 1978-80 (President, 1980-82); Council Member, RIAS, 1982-85; Area Commissioner, East Lothian Scout Council, 1981-87. Recreations: hill-walking; fishing; painting. Address: (b.) Council Buildings, Court Street, Haddington EH41 3HA.

Campbell, Sir Ian, CBE, OStJ, VRD, JP. Finance Director, Scottish Conservative Party, since 1977; Director, Collins Halden (Scotland), since 1987; Director, Travel System Ltd., since 1987; b. 3.2.23, Edinburgh; m., Marion Kirkhope Shiel; 1 d. Educ. Daniel Stewart's College, Edinburgh. Royal Navy, 1942-46; Royal Naval Reserve, 1946-64 (retired with rank of Commander); John Line & Sons, 1948-61 (Area Manager, West of England); Managing Director, MacGregor Wallcoverings Ltd., 1965-77. Councillor, City of Edinburgh, 1984-88; Member, Transport Users Consultative Committee for Scotland, 1981-87. Recreations: golf; vintage cars; water colour painting. Address: (h.) Merleton, 10 Boswall Road, Edinburgh, EH5 2PR; T.-031-552 4825.

Campbell, Ian William, BSc, MB, ChB, MRCP (UK), FRCPEdin. Consultant Physician, Victoria Hospital, Kirkcaldy, since 1978; Honorary Senior Lecturer, Department of Medicine, Edinburgh University, since 1978; Honorary Senior Lecturer, Department of Biochemistry, St. Andrews University, since 1978; b. 23.11.45, East Wemyss, Fife; m., Catherine McEwan Burgess; 1 s.; 2 d. Educ. Buckhaven High School; Edinburgh University. Senior Medical Registrar, Medical Registrar and Registrar, Diabetes and Metabolism, Edinburgh Royal Infirmary; SHO, Eastern General Hospital, Edinburgh. Member, Medical Advisory Council, British Diabetic Association; Council Member, International Study Group of Insulin Treatment with Implantable Devices, Vienna and Minneapolis. Publication: Diagnosis and Management of Endocrine Diseases (Co-author), 1981. Recreations: tennis; squash; golf. Address: (h.) Strathearn, 19 Victoria Road, Lundin Links, Fife, KY8 6AZ; T.-0333 320533.

Campbell, Sir Ilay Mark, MA (Oxon). Chairman, Christie's Scotland, since 1978; Director, High Craigton Farming Co.; b. 29.5.27, Edinburgh; m., Margaret Minette Rohais Anderson; 2 d. Educ. Eton; Christ Church, Oxford. Christie's: Scottish Agent, 1968, Joint Scottish Agent, 1973; President, Association for the Protection of Rural Scotland; Honorary Vice-President, Scotland's Garden Scheme; Trustee, Crarae Gardens Charitable Trust, since 1978; former Member, Council, Executive Committee and Gardens Committee, National Trust for Scotland; former Scottish Representative, National Arts Collection Fund. Recreations: heraldry; genealogy; collecting heraldic bookplates. Address: (h.) Crarae Lodge, Inveraray, Argyll, PA32 8YA; (b.) Cumlodden Estate Office, Inveraray, Argyll, PA32 8YA; T.-0546 86633.

Campbell, James, BL. Town Clerk Depute, Glasgow District Council, since 1974; b. 20.3.37, Glasgow; m., Leslie Jane Mickel Campbell; 1 s.; 1 d. Educ. Glasgow High School; Glasgow University. Glasgow Corporation: Legal Assistant, Planning Committee, 1959, Chief Solicitor, Housing Committee, 1973. Recreations: golf; bridge. Address: (b.) Town Clerk's Office, City Chambers, Glasgow, G2 1DU; T.-041-227 4515.

Campbell, John Craig. Governor, Robert Gordon's Institute of Technology; Director, Langstane Press Ltd., Aberdeen, since 1946; b. 28.3.15, Aberdeen; m., Anna Wilson Harrison; 1 s. Educ. Morgan Academy, Dundee. Past President, Aberdeen Master Printers; Past Chairman, South Aberdeen Conservative Association; former Member: Manpower Services Commission (Scotland), Scottish Master Printers Education Committee, Paper Publishing Industry Training Board, Grampian Regional Council, Grampian/Tayside Area Manpower Board, Convention of Scottish Local Authorities, Scottish Joint Negotiating Committee (Education). Recreation: golf. Address: (h.) 110 Mastrick Drive, Aberdeen; T.-0224 691122.

Campbell, Rev. Keith, BSc, BD. Minister, Broughty Ferry: St. Aidan's, Dundee, since 1968; Member, Tayside Health Board; Chairman, St Aidan's Project; b. 19.12.32, Gourock; m., Christine Mary Beaton MacFarlane; 1 s. (deceased); 2 d. Educ. Strathallan School; Glasgow University. Minister, Edinkillie, Morayshire, 1963-68. Past Chairman, Dundee Local Health Council; former Depute Chairman, Dundee College of Education. Recreations: swimming; sailing; gardening; photography. Address: St. Aidan's Manse, 63 Collingwood Street, Barnhill, Dundee; T.-0382 79253.

Campbell, Kenneth Murray, MA, LLB, WS. Solicitor; Secretary, Royal Scottish Agricultural Benevolent Institution, since 1966; Secretary, Scottish Agricultural Arbiters' Association, since 1966; b. 20.10.30, Dumfries; m., Madeleine Jean Gillie; 1 s.; 1 d. Educ. Dumfries Academy; Edinburgh University. Education Officer, RAF, 1954-56; Solicitor in private practice, Edinburgh, since 1956. Publication: Connell on the Agricultural Holdings (Scotland) Acts (Joint Editor, 6th edition). Recreations: gardening; reading. Address: (b.) 10 Dublin Street, Edinburgh; T.-031-556 2993.

Campbell, Malcolm, MA (Hons), PhD. Reader in Greek, St. Andrews University, since 1984 (Chairman, since 1987); b. 10.11.43, Shrewsbury; m., Dorothy Helen Fear; 2 s. Educ. Boroughmuir School, Edinburgh; Edinburgh University; Balliol College, Oxford. Lecturer, St. Andrews University, since 1968. Publications: A Commentary on Quintus Smyrnaeus, Posthomerica XII, 1981; Echoes and Imitations of Early Epic in Apollonius Rhodius, 1981; Index verborum in Apollonium Rhodium, 1983; Studies in the Third Book of Apollonius Rhodius' Argonautica, 1983; A Lexicon to Triphiodorus, 1985; Index verborum in Moschum et Bionem, 1987. Recreations: music; philately. Address: (b.) Department of Greek, The University, St. Andrews, Fife.

Campbell, Robert Craig, BSc, MInstM. Policy Research Director, Scottish Council (Development and Industry), since 1986 (Director, Overseas Projects Unit, 1984-86); b. 29.4.47, Glasgow; m., Elizabeth Helen C.; 2 d. Educ. Glasgow Academy; St. Andrews University. Scottish Council: Research Executive, 1970-77, Research Director, 1977-84. Recreation: angling. Address: (b.) Scottish Council (Development and Industry), 23 Chester Street, Edinburgh; T.-031-225 7911.

Campbell, Robert Kenneth, BSc (Hons), DipEd, CPhys, MInstP. Rector, Greenock Academy, since 1967; President, Headteachers' Association of Scotland, 1987-88; b. 10.2.27, Paisley; m., Patricia Stephenson; 2 d. Educ. George Heriot's School, Edinburgh; Edinburgh University; Moray House College of Education; Heriot-Watt College. Research Physicist, Unilever Ltd., Port Sunlight, 1948-50; teacher training, 1950-51; Teacher of Mathematics and Science, Daniel Stewart's College, 1951-56; Senior Teacher of Science, Government High School, Nassau, 1956-59; Teacher of Mathematics and Science, Daniel Stewart's College, 1959-60; Principal Teacher of Science, Websters Seminary, Kirriemuir, 1960-62; Principal Teacher of Physics, Paisley Grammar School, 1962-67. Past President, Greenock Rotary Club; Elder, Ashton Church of Scotland; Chairman, Fort Matilda Playing Fields Union. Recreations: golf; bridge. Address: (h.) 98 Newark Street, Greenock, PA16 7TG; T.-0475 22727.

Campbell, Rev. Roderick D.M., BD, FSA Scot. Minister, Mearns Parish Church, since 1979; b. 1.8.43, Glasgow; m., Susan Norman; 2 d. Educ. Daniel Stewart's College, Edinburgh; Arbroath High School; Jordanhill College of Education; New College, Edinburgh University. Teacher, Technical Subjects, Glasgow, Tanzania and London, 1967-70; Associate Minister, St. Andrew's, Nairobi, 1975-78; Chieftain, Caledonian Society of Kenya, 1978; founder Member, Undugu Society of Kenya, 1975; Chairman, Institute of Advanced Motorists (Kenya), 1977-78. Convener, Lodging House Mission, Glasgow Presbytery, 1981-86; Convener, National Church Extension Committee, Church of Scotland, since 1987; Chaplain, 1/52 Lowland Volunteers, TA; Chairman, Glasgow Churches Council for Overseas Students, since 1987; Vice Chairman, Eastwood Conservative Association, since 1988. Recreations: swimming; sailing. Address: The Manse of Mearns, Newton Mearns, Glasgow, G77 5BU; T.-041-639 1410.

Campbell, Thomas. Member, Perth and Kinross District Council, since 1983; Chairman, George Campbell & Son Ltd., Edinburgh and Perth, since 1983; Chairman, Perthshire Tourist Board; b. 13.8.25, Edinburgh; m., Sheila Margaret; 3 s. Educ. Melville College, Edinburgh; Manchester University. Royal Engineers, 1943-47; worked in family business, 1948-54; Unilever: Ghana and Nigeria, 1954-69, UK, 1969-73. Recreation: golf. Address: Balnabeggan, Bridge of Cally, Perthshire.

Campbell, Professor Thomas Douglas, BA (Oxon), MA, PhD. Professor of Jurisprudence, Glasgow University, since 1979; Mental Welfare Commissioner for Scotland, since 1984; b. 3.3.38, Lenzie; 1 s.; 1 d. Educ. Loretto School; Glasgow University; Oxford University. National Service, 1956-58 (2nd Lt., 1st Regt., Royal Horse Artillery); Glasgow University: Lecturer in Politics, 1964-69, Lecturer in Moral Philosophy, 1969-73; Professor of Philosophy, Stirling University, 1973-79. Publications: Adam Smith's Science and Morals, 1970; Seven Theories of Human Society, 1981; The Left and Rights, 1983. Recreations: golf; dog walking. Address: (h.) 228 Nithsdale Road, Glasgow, G41; T.-041-427 4493.

Campbell, Walter Menzies, CBE, QC, MA, LLB. MP (Liberal), North East Fife, since 1987; Advocate, since 1968; Queen's Counsel, since 1982; part-time Chairman, VAT Tribunal, 1984-87; Member: Legal Aid Central Committee, 1983-86, Scottish Legal Aid Board, 1986-87; Chairman: Medical Appeal Tribunals, 1985-87, Royal Lyceum Theatre, Edinburgh, 1984-87; Member, Broadcasting Council for Scotland, 1984-87; b. 22.5.41, Glasgow; m., Elspeth Mary Urquhart. Educ. Hillhead High School, Glasgow; Glasgow University; Stanford University, California. President, Glasgow University Union, 1964-65; took part in Olympic Games, Tokyo, 1964; AAA 220-yards champion, 1964, 1967; Captain, UK athletics team, 1965; 1966 Commonwealth Games, Jamaica; UK 100-metres record holder, 1967-74. Advocate Depute, 1977-80; Standing Junior Counsel to the Army in Scotland, 1980-82. Parliamentary candidate (Liberal): Greenock and Port Glasgow, February, 1974, and October, 1974, East Fife, 1979, North East Fife, 1983; Chairman, Scottish Liberal Party, 1975-77; Member: UK Sports Council, 1965-68; Scottish Sports Council, 1971-81. Recreations: all sports; music; theatre. Address: (b.) House of Commons, London, SW1A 0AA; T.-01-219 4446.

Campbell, Rev. William John, MA. Minister, Free Church of Scotland, Portree, since 1983; b. 18.11.33, Garrabost, Lewis; m., Margaret Mary Morrison; 1 s.; 2 d. Educ. Nicolson Institute; Aberdeen University; Free Church College, Edinburgh. National Service, RAMC, 1955-57; Actuarial Clerk, Scottish Mutual Assurance Society, Glasgow; Minister: Detroit, Michigan, 1968-72, Park, Lewis, 1972-83. Address: Free Church Manse, Portree, Isle of Skye; T.-0478 2678.

Campbell, William Kilpatrick, MA (Hons). Director, Mainstream Publishing, since 1978; b. 1.3.51, Glasgow; m., Marie-France Callie; 2 d. Educ. Kilmarnock Academy; Edinburgh University. Postgraduate research, Universities of Edinburgh and California; world travel, 1975; Publications Manager, Edinburgh University Student Publications, 1976-78. Publications: Alternative Edinburgh (Co-Editor), 1972; Another Edinburgh, 1976. Recreations: soccer; tennis; swimming; wine; books; people. Address: (b.) 7 Albany Street, Edinburgh, EH1 3UG; T.-031-557 2959.

Campbell-Gibson, Lt.Comdr. R.N. (Ret.) Hugh Desmond. Member, Council, Association for Protection of Rural Scotland; Member, Executive Committee, and County Organiser, Argyll, Scotland's Gardens Scheme; b. 18.8.24; m., Deirdre Wilson; 2 s.; 1 d. Educ. Royal Naval College, Dartmouth. Naval cadet, 1937-41; served Royal Navy, 1941-60; war service convoy duties, Atlantic and Mediterranean; farmed Glenlussa, by Campbeltown, 1960-68; farmed and ran hotel, Dunmor, Seil, Argyll, 1969-83. Chairman, Kilmelford and Kilninver Community Council. Recreations: gardening; skiing. Address: (h.) Tighnamara, Melfort, Kilmelford, Argyll; T.-Kilmelford 224.

Campbell-Preston, Robert Modan Thorne, OBE, MC, TD. Vice-Lieutenant of Argyll and Bute; b. 7.1.09; m., The Hon. Angela Murray (deceased); 1 d. Educ. Eton; Christ Church, Oxford. Lt., Scottish Horse, 1930; Lt.-Col., 1945; Hon. Col., Fife & Forfar Yeomanry/Scottish Horse, 1962-67; retired Member, Royal Company of Archers (Queen's Bodyguard for Scotland); Joint Managing Director, Alginate Industries Ltd., 1949-74; DL, 1951; JP, 1950; Silver Star, USA, 1945; Chairman, Argyll and Bute Trust. Recreations: shooting; fishing; gardening. Address: Ardchattan Priory, by Oban, Argyll; T.-Bonawe 274.

Campsie, Alistair Keith, SDA. Author, Journalist and Piper; b. 27.1.29, Inverness; m., Robbie Anderson; 2 s.; 1 d. Educ. West Sussex High School; Lanark Grammar School; West of Scotland College of Agriculture. Inspector of Agriculture, Sudan Government Service, 1949; Cocoa Survey Officer, Nigeria, 1951; experimental staff, National Institute of Agricultural Engineering (Scotland), 1953; Country Editor, Weekly Scotsman, 1954; Sub-Editor, Verse Writer, Scottish Daily Mail, 1955; Founder Editor, East African Farmer and Planter, 1956; Chief Sub-Editor, Weekly Scotsman, 1957; designed and appointed first Editor, Geneva Weekly Tribune, 1958; Chief Feature Writer, Scottish Daily Mail, 1959; Columnist, Science Correspondent and Senior Writer, Scottish Daily Express, 1962-73. Publications: Poems and a Pibroch (with Hugh MacDiarmid), 1972; By Law Protected, 1976; The MacCrimmon Legend or The Madness of Angus Mackay, 1980; We Bought a Country Pub (under pen-name Alan Mackinnon), 1984; Perfect Poison, 1985; Pibroch: the Tangled Web (radio series), 1985; Dundas or How They Murdered Robert Burns (play), 1987; The Clarinda Conspiracy (in press). Recreations: bagpipes (playing and composing); good whisky; self-important people. Address: Piper's Restaurant and Private Hotel, Union Place, Montrose; T.-0674 72298.

Canavan, Dennis, BSc (Hons), DipEd. MP (Labour), Falkirk West, since 1983; b. 8.8.42, Cowdenbeath. Educ. St. Bride's and St. Columba's School, Cowdenbeath; Edinburgh University. Principal Teacher of Mathematics, St. Modan's High School, Stirling, 1970-74; Assistant Head, Holyrood High School, Edinburgh, 1974; Leader, Labour Group, Stirling District Council, 1974; MP, West Stirlingshire, 1974-83; Chairman, Scottish Parliamentary Labour Group, 1980-81; Vice-Chair, PLP Northern Ireland Committee, since 1983; Member, Foreign Affairs Select Committee, since 1982; Parliamentary Spokesman for Scottish Committee on Mobility for Disabled, since 1976, and Scottish Spina Bifida Association, since 1976; Honorary President, Milton Amateurs Football Club. Recreations: marathon running; hill-climbing; fishing; swimming; football (former Scottish Universities football internationalist). Address: (h.) 15 Margaret Road, Bannockburn, Stirling, FK7 OJG; T.-0786 812581.

Candlish, Kenneth Henry, BL, JP, DL. Retired Solicitor; Deputy Lieutenant, Berwickshire; Clerk, Berwickshire Lieutenancy; b. 22.8.24, Edinburgh; m., Isobel Robertson-Brown; 2 d. Educ. George Watson's; Edinburgh University. Depute County Clerk, West Lothian, 1951-64; County Clerk, Berwickshire, 1964-75. Recreations: photography; wine-making; music. Address: (h.) The Elms, Duns, Berwickshire; T.-Duns 83298.

Cannon, Professor Thomas, BSc (Hons), FRSA, FIntFxp, FIPDm. Professor of Business Studies, Stirling University; Founder Director, Scottish Enterprise Foundation; Council Member, SCOTVEC; Member, Executive, Scottish Business in the Community; b. 20.11.46, Liverpool; m., Frances Constable; 1 s.; 1 d. Educ. St. Francis Xaviers School, Liverpool; Borough Polytechnic. Research Assistant, Aske Research; Research Associate, Warwick University; Lecturer, Enfield College of Technology; Brand Manager, Imperial Group; Lecturer, Durham University. Publications: Basic Marketing; Advertising: The Economic Implications. Recreations: soccer fan, especially Everton FC; walking; squash; being with family. Address: (h.) 2 Westerton Drive, Bridge of Allan, Stirling; T.-Stirling 73171.

Cant, Harry Wallace, MA, LLB, WS, NP. Solicitor, since 1954; Clerk and Treasurer, Iona Cathedral Trust, 1965-85; b. 5.7.18, Edinburgh; m., Mary Fleming Hamilton; 3 s.; 1 d. Educ. George Watson's College, Edinburgh; Edinburgh University. War Service, 1939-46 (Capt., Royal Artillery, 51st Highland Division, Western Desert, Sicily, France and Germany); wounded France, 1944; Partner: Menzies & Thomson, WS, 1954, J. & F. Anderson, WS, 1966; Consultant, J. & F. Anderson, WS, since 1984. Secretary, Edinburgh Musical Festival Association, 1958-67; Secretary, Scottish Society of Women Artists, 1960-68; Treasurer, Scottish Action on Dementia, 1987. Recreations: golf; reading. Address: (h.) 77 Craiglockhart Road, Edinburgh, EH14 1EL; T.-031-441 3512.

Caplan, Sheriff Principal Philip Isaac, MA, LLB, QC. Sheriff Principal of North Strathclyde, since 1983; b. 24.2.29, Glasgow; m., Joyce Stone (2nd m.); 2 s.; 2 d. Educ. Eastwood School; Glasgow University. Solicitor, 1952-56; called to Bar, 1957; Standing Junior Counsel to Accountant of Court,

1964-70; Chairman, Plant Varieties and Seeds Tribunal, Scotland, 1977-79; Sheriff of Lothian and Borders, at Edinburgh, 1979-83; Member, Sheriff Courts Rules Council, 1984; Commissioner, Northern Lighthouse Board, since 1983; Chairman, Scottish Association for the Study of Delinquency, since 1985; Member, Advisory Council on Messengers at Arms and Sheriff Officers, 1987. ERPS (1988), AFIAP (1985). Recreations: photography; sailing; bridge; music; reading. Address: (h.) Auchenlea, Torwood Hill Road, Rhu, Dunbartonshire; T.-0436 820359.

Capperauld, Ian, MB, ChB, DObst, RCOG, FRCSEdin, FRCSGlas. Executive Director, Research and Development, Ethicon Ltd., since 1969; Consultant Surgeon, since 1962; Medical Director, Huntly Nursing Home, since 1981; Member, Lothian Health Board, since 1981; b. 23.10.33, New Cumnock; m., Wilma Hyslop Young; 2 s. Educ. Cumnock Academy; Glasgow University; Edinburgh University. Served as Major, RAMC, 1959-69 (Consultant Surgeon). Recreations: fishing; shooting. Address: (b.) Ethicon Ltd., PO Box 408, Bankhead Avenue, Edinburgh; T.-031-453 5555.

Carbery, Professor Thomas Francis, OBE, MSc, PhD, DPA. Professor of Business Information, Strathclyde University, since 1985; Member: Scottish Legal Aid Board, since 1986, Data Protection Tribunal, since 1985, Press Council, since 1987; b. 18.1.25, Glasgow; m., Ellen Donnelly; 1 s.; 2 d. Educ. St. Aloysius' College, Glasgow; Glasgow University; Scottish College of Commerce. Cadet navigator/meteorologist, RAF, 1943-47; civil servant, 1947-61; Lecturer, then Senior Lecturer, Scottish College of Commerce, 1961-64; Strathclyde University: Senior Lecturer in Government-Business Relations, 1964-75, Head, Department of Office Organisation, 1975-79, Professor of Office Organisation, 1979-85. Member: Independent Broadcasting Authority, 1970-79, Broadcasting Complaints Commission, 1981-86, Royal Commission on Gambling, 1975-77, Transport Users Consultative Committee (Chairman, Scottish TUCC), 1975-81, Scottish Consumer Council (latterly Vice-Chairman), 1976-84; Chairman, Scottish Transport Research Group, 1983-87; Vice-Chairman, Glasgow Fabian Society; Member, Church of Scotland Committee on Higher Education, 1986-87; Chairman, Scottish Branch, Public and Co-operative Enterprise; Chairman, Strathclyde University Inter-denominational Chaplaincy Committee, 1981-87; Joint Editor, Bulletin of Society for Co-operative Studies; Chairman, Scottish Catholic Communications Commission; Member, Scottish Catholic Education Commission. Recreations: conversation; watching television; spectating at association football; very bad golf. Address: (h.) 32 Crompton Avenue, Glasgow, G44 5TH; T.-041-637 0514.

Cargill, Kenneth George, MA, LLB. Editor, News and Current Affairs, Television, BBC Scotland, since 1988; b. 17.2.47, Arbroath. Educ. Arbroath High School; Edinburgh University. BBC TV Scotland: Researcher, Current Affairs, 1972; Reporter, Current Account, 1973; Film Director, Public Account, 1978; Producer, Current Account, 1979, Agenda, 1981, People and Power (London), 1983; Editor of the day, Reporting Scotland, 1983; Editor, Scotland 2000, 1986-87; Deputy Editor, News and Current Affairs, Television, 1984-88. Address: (b.) BBC, Broadcasting House, Queen Margaret Drive, Glasgow, G12 8DG; T.-041-330 2450.

Carlton, George, OBE, BCom (Hons), BL, FCIS, RD. Member, Local Government Boundary Commission for Scotland, since 1980; Deputy Chairman, Local Government Boundary Commission, since 1985; Local Commissioner of Income Tax (Lanarkshire), since 1982; Senior Tutor (part-time), Glasgow University, 1980-86; b. 25.6.23, Coatbridge; m., Helen Clark Love; 3 s. Educ. Coatbridge High School; Glasgow University; London University. Lanarkshire County Council: Solicitor, 1954-57, Deputy County Clerk, 1957-74, County Clerk, 1974-75; Director of Administration, Strathclyde Regional Council, 1975-80; Senior Tutor (part-time), Strathclyde University, 1980-84. Founder Chairman, Society of Directors of Administration in Scotland, 1975-77; Past President: Uddingston Cricket Club; Uddingston Cricket and Sports Club; Past Captain, Bothwell Castle Golf Club; Elder, Church of Scotland. Recreations: golf; curling; reading; watching cricket. Address: (h.) Kingarth, Fairyknowe Gardens, Bothwell, Glasgow, G71 8RW; T.-Bothwell 853181.

Carlyle, Walter, JP. Member, Dumfries and Galloway Regional Council, since 1975 (Chairman, Roads and Transportation Committee, since 1978); Traffic Commissioner, since 1982; Business Executive; b. 29.4.16, Wamphray, Dumfriesshire; m., Mary Jardine. Educ. Lockerbie Academy. Served 79th armoured division, France and Germany, 1942-45; elected Member, Lockerbie Burgh Council, 1950 (Bailie, 1958); Provost of Lockerbie, 1962-75; Member, Dumfries County Council, 1962-75; Deputy Traffic Commissioner, 1975; Chairman, local Rating Appeals Panel, since 1983. Recreations: golf; curling; Rotary and Church activities. Address: (h.) Pinehurst, 1 Glenannan Avenue, Lockerbie, Dumfriesshire, DG11 2EG; T.-Lockerbie 3050.

Carlyle, Walter, BSc, ARIC. General Manager, BP Oil Grangemouth Refinery Limited, since 1987; b. 5.4.37, Bo'ness; m., Beatrice S. Henderson; 2 s.; 1 d. Educ. Bo'ness Academy; Heriot-Watt University. BP: Development Chemist, Aden Refinery, 1961-67, Branch Manager, Design, Refineries Department, 1967-75, Manager, Investment Branch, London, 1980-82, Manager, Development Division, Manufacturing, London, 1982, Assistant Works Manager, BP Oil Grangemouth Refinery Ltd., 1982, Works Manager, Grangemouth, 1983-87. Council Member, CBI Scotland. Recreations: golf; walking; the performing arts. Address: (b.) BP Oil Grangemouth Refinery Limited, Bo'ness Road, Grangemouth, FK3 9XQ; T.-Grangemouth 483422.

Carmichael, George Laurin Murray, MB, ChB, FFARCS, DA. Consultant Neuroanaesthetist, Western General Hospital, Edinburgh, since 1979; b. 24.8.41, Edinburgh; m., Rosalind Eileen Virtue; 1 s.; 1 d. Educ. Edinburgh Academy; Edinburgh University. House Physician, Northern General Hospital, Edinburgh; House Surgeon, Edinburgh Royal Infirmary; Medical

Officer, RAF (appointments in Singapore, Lincoln, Bahrain); Registrar, Department of Anaesthetics, Edinburgh Royal Infirmary; Anaesthetist, Newfoundland; Anaesthetist, British Red Cross Teams, Cambodia and Angola; Senior Registrar, Edinburgh Royal Infirmary. Training Officer, Edinburgh Branch, British Red Cross Society; Council Member, North British Pain Association; Executive Member, BMA Hospital Specialists and Consultants Committee; Council Member, Scottish Society of Anaesthetists; Medical Advisor to film, Killing Fields. Recreations: yachting; gardening. Address: (h.) 38 Liberton Brae, Edinburgh; T.-031-664 5265.

Carmichael, Hugh Alisdair, MB, ChB, MRCP. Consultant Physician, Vale of Leven Hospital, Alexandria, since 1979; b. 21.11.45, Dingwall; m., Rosamund Mary Brannan; 1 s.; 3 d. Educ. Ardrossan Academy; Glasgow University. Glasgow Royal Infirmary: Resident House Surgeon, 1970-71, Resident House Physician, 1971, Senior House Officer in Haematology, 1971-72, Senior House Officer in Medicine, 1972-74, Registrar in Medicine and Gastroenterology, 1974-77; Senior Registrar in Medicine, Western Infirmary, Glasgow, and Gartnavel Hospital, 1977-79. Address: (b.) Vale of Leven Hospital, Alexandria, Dunbartonshire; T.-Alexandria 54121.

Carmichael, Ian Henry Buist, MA, LLB. Advocate; b. 17.5.25, Dundee; m., Jean Cowie Davidson; 2 d. Educ. High School of Dundee; Edinburgh University. Solicitor, 1951-57; Advocate, 1958-62; Procurator Fiscal Service, 1964-85; in practice as Advocate, since 1985. Founder Chairman, Area 39, Round Table; Chairman, Glasgow District Council, Congregational Union of Scotland, 1981-83. Publication: Sudden Deaths and Fatal Accident Inquiries, 1986. Recreations: photography; music; woodworking; model railways. Address: (h.) 4 Fleurs Avenue, Glasgow; T.-041-427 6367.

Carmichael, Sir John, KBE (1955). Chairman, St. Andrews Links Trust, since 1984; b. 22.4.10; m.; 1 s.; 3 d. Educ. Madras College, St. Andrews; St. Andrews University; University of Michigan. Financial and Economic Adviser to Sudan Government, 1955-59; Member, UK Delegation, General Assembly, United Nations, 1959; Member, Scottish Industrial Development Advisory Board, 1972-79; Deputy Chairman, Independent Television Authority, 1960-64; Chairman, Herring Industry Board, 1962-65; Director, Fisons Ltd., 1961-80; Director, Grampian Television, 1965-72; Director, Jute Industries Ltd. (later Sidlaw Industries Ltd.), 1966-80; Director, Royal Bank of Scotland, 1966-80; Member, Social and Economic Committee, EEC, 1973-74.

Carmichael, Margaret Mary, BMus, ARCM. Principal, Oxenfoord Castle School, Pathhead, since 1979; b. 1.2.40, Alyth, Perthshire. Educ. Bedford High School; Guildhall School of Music and Drama, London. Head of Music, City of London School for Girls, 1970-74; Lecturer in Music, Goldsmiths' College, London University, 1975-78. Chairman, Music at Oxenfoord, Scottish Independent Schools' Orchestra. Recreations: theatre; travel. Address: (b.) Oxenfoord Castle School, Pathhead, Midlothian, EH37 5UD; T.-0875 320241.

Carmichael of Kelvingrove, Baron (Neil George Carmichael). Life Peer; b. 1921; m., Catherine McIntosh Rankin; 1 d. Educ. Royal College of Science and Technology, Glasgow. Former Member, Glasgow Corporation; MP (Labour), Woodside, 1962-74, Kelvingrove, 1974-83; Joint Parliamentary Secretary, Ministry of Transport, 1967-69; Parliamentary Secretary, Ministry of Technology, 1969-70; Parliamentary Under-Secretary of State, DoE, 1974-75, DoI, 1975-76.

Carmichael, Peter, CBE, DSc. Group Director, East, Scottish Development Agency, since 1982; b. 26.3.33, Dunblane; m., June; 2 s.; 4 d. by pr. m. Educ. McLaren High School, Callander; Glasgow University. Design engineer, Ferranti Ltd., Edinburgh, 1958-65; Hewlett-Packard, South Queensferry: Project Leader, 1965-67, Production Engineering Manager, 1968-73, Engineering Manager, 1973-75, Manufacturing Manager, 1975-76, Division General Manager, 1976-82, Joint Managing Director, 1980-82. Chairman, Wigtown Rural Development Company; Non-Executive Director, Studio Ink, Aberdour. Recreations: fishing; antique clock restoration. Address: (h.) 86 Craiglea Drive, Edinburgh; T.-031-447 6334.

Carmichael of Carmichael (Richard John). 26th Baron of Carmichael, since 1980; 30th Chief of Name and Arms of Carmichael, since 1981; Chartered Accountant; Farmer; b. 1.12.48, Stamford; m., Patricia Margaret Branson; 1 s.; 2 d. Educ. Hyton Hill Preparatory School; Kimbolton School; Coventry College of Technology. Audit Senior, Coopers and Lybrand, Tanzania, 1972; Audit Manager, Granger Craig Tunnicliffe, Tauranga, New Zealand, 1974; ACA, 1971; FCA, 1976; Factor/Owner, Carmichael Estate, 1980; claims family titles: Earldom of Hyndford, Viscountcies of Inglisberry and Nemphlar, and Lordship Carmichael of Carmichael. Member, Supreme Council of Scottish Chiefs; Secretary Carmichael Anstruther District Charitable Association; New Zealand Orienteering Champion, 1977; Grade One Controller, British Orienteering Federation. Recreations: orienteering; skiing; Clan Carmichael Association. Address: Carmichael House, Carmichael, by Biggar, Lanarkshire, ML12 6PG; T.-08993 336.

Carmichael, William Fleming, PhD, CEng, MICE, DipAd, FRSA. Depute Head, Department of Architecture, Edinburgh College of Art and Heriot-Watt University, since 1984; Dean of Environmental Studies, Heriot-Watt University; b. 24.2.23, Brechin; m., D.H. Martin; 3 d. Educ. Brechin High School; Heriot-Watt University. Local government engineering posts, Brechin, Kirkcaldy, Dundee, Fife; Army Service, Royal Engineers (Lt.); Lecturer, School of Architecture, Dundee; Consulting Engineer/Partner, R. Cowan & Associates. RIBA Research Fellow, 1957. Recreations: golf; hill-walking; music. Address: (h.) 97 Gardiner Road, Edinburgh; T.-031-332 2818.

Carmichael, William George, BL. Procurator Fiscal, Hamilton, since 1987 (Procurator Fiscal, Airdrie, 1981-87); b. 26.2.33, Glasgow; m., Elizabeth Gemmell; 1 s.; 2 d. Educ. Eastwood School; Glasgow University. Legal Assistant: Hamilton Town

Council, 1958-60, Argyll County Council, 1960-62, Ayr Town Council, 1962-64; joined Procurator Fiscal service, 1965. Recreations: golf; squash; music. Address: (b.) 28 Clydesdale Street, Hamilton.

Carnall, Geoffrey Douglas, MA, BLitt. Reader in English Literature, Edinburgh University, since 1969; b. 1.2.27, Croydon, Surrey; m., Elisabeth Seale Murray; 1 s.; 2 d. Educ. Perse School, Cambridge; Magdalen College, Oxford. Lecturer in English, Queen's University, Belfast, 1952-60; Lecturer, then Senior Lecturer in English Literature, Edinburgh University, 1960-69. Chairman, Edinburgh Council for Nuclear Disarmament, 1963-70; Elder, South-East Scotland Monthly Meeting, Society of Friends (Quakers), 1970-87; Chairman, Edinburgh Christian Campaign for Nuclear Disarmament, 1982-85; Vice-Chair, Scottish Christian CND, since 1987. Publications: Robert Southey and His Age, 1960; Robert Southey, 1964; The Mid-Eighteenth Century (Volume 8, Oxford History of English Literature) (Co-author), 1979. Recreation: demonstrating against nuclear weapons. Address: (b.) Department of English Literature, David Hume Tower, George Square, Edinburgh, EH8; T.-031-667 1011.

Carnegie, Leslie Thompson, CBE (1980), BL, JP, Solicitor. Chief Executive, Dumfries and Galloway Regional Council, 1974-85; Honorary Sheriff, since 1960; b. 16.8.20, Aberdeen; m., Isobel Jane McCombie, JP. Educ. Aberdeen Grammar School; Aberdeen University. Legal Department, Aberdeen Corporation, 1939-48; Depute County Clerk, East Lothian, 1948-54; County Clerk, Dumfries County Council, 1954-75. Past President, Society of County Clerks in Scotland; Clerk, Dumfries Lieutenancy, 1954-85. Recreations: gardening; music appreciation; sporting activities. Address: (h.) Marchhill Park, Dumfries.

Carnegy of Lour, Baroness (Elizabeth Patricia), DL. Life Peer, since 1982; Member, House of Lords Select Committee on European Communities, since 1984; President for Scotland, Girl Guides Association, since 1979; Member of Council and of Finance Committee, Open University, since 1984; Member, Scottish Economic Council, since 1980; Trustee, National Museums of Scotland, since 1987; Member, Administrative Council, Royal Jubilee Trusts, since 1984; Partner, Lour Farms; b. 28.4.25. Educ. Downham School. Cavendish Laboratory, Cambridge, 1943-46; Girl Guides Association: Training Adviser for Scotland, 1958-62 and for Commonwealth HQ, 1963-65; co-opted Angus County Council Education Committee, 1967-75; Councillor, Tayside Regional Council, 1974-82; Chairman, Education Committee, 1976-82; Chairman, Working Party on Professional Training in Community Education Scotland, 1975-77; Commissioner, Manpower Services Commission, 1979-82, and Chairman, Committee for Scotland, 1980-83; Member, Scottish Council for Tertiary Education, 1979-84; Chairman, Scottish Council for Community Education, 1980-88; Honorary Sheriff, 1969-84; Deputy Lieutenant, District of Angus, 1988; Fellow, Royal Society of Arts, 1987. Address: (h.) Lour, Forfar, Angus, DD8 2LR; T.-0307 82 237.

Carnie, Colin Greig, DIC, CEng, MICE. Partner, Crouch and Hogg, since 1966; b. 12.11.34, Glasgow; m., Elizabeth Haddo Neill; 3 s.; 2 d. Educ. Loretto; Imperial College, London. Engineer, Crouch and Hogg, 1962-66. Director, Scottish Industrial Estates Corporation, 1972-78; Member, Glasgow Action, since 1986; Member, Broadcasting Council for Scotland, 1973-78; Director, Glasgow Chamber of Commerce; Vice Chairman, The Salmon Conservancy; Honorary Consul in Scotland for Costa Rica. Recreations: fishing; sailing; shooting. Address: (b.) 18 Woodside Crescent, Glasgow, G3 7UU; T.-041-332 9755.

Carr, John Roger, JP, FRICS. Director, Moray Estates Development Co., since 1954; Chairman, Countryside Commission for Scotland, since 1986; Member, Macaulay Land Use Research Institute, since 1987; b. 18.1.27, Ackworth, Yorkshire; m., Cathrine Elise Dickson-Smith; 2 s. Educ. Ackworth & Ayton (Quaker) School. Factor, Walker Scottish Estates Co., Ballater; Factor, subsequently Director and General Manager, Moray Estates Development Co., Forres; former Convenor, Scottish Recreational Land Association; former Council Member, Scottish Landowners Association; former District Councillor, Moray. Recreations: walking; gardening; shooting. Address: (b.) Estates Office, Forres, Moray; T.-03097 2213.

Carr, Rev. Walter Stanley, MA. Minister, St. Columba's Parish Church, Largs, since 1966; b. 3.3.24, Edinburgh; m., Margaret Linton Spittal; 2 d. Educ. George Heriot's School, Edinburgh; Edinburgh University; New College, Edinburgh. Minister: St. Paul's Parish Church, Dunfermline, 1951-64, Avon Street and Brandon Parish Church, Hamilton, 1964-66; former Moderator: Dunfermline and Kinross Presbytery, Ardrossan Presbytery; Chairman, Paton Trust; Chaplain, Royal British Legion, Largs. Recreations: gardening; swimming; artist. Address: (h.) 17 Beachway, Largs, KA30 8QH; T.-Largs 673107.

Carrol, Charles Gordon, MA, DipEd. Director, Commonwealth Institute, Scotland, since 1971; b. 21.3.35, Edinburgh; 3 s. Educ. Melville College, Edinburgh; Edinburgh University; Moray House College of Education. Education Officer: Government of Nigeria, 1959-65, Commonwealth Institute, Scotland, 1965-71. Lay Member, Press Council, 1978-83. Recreations: walking; angling; reading; cooking. Address: (h.) 11 Dukehaugh, Peebles; T.-0721 21296.

Carroll, Robert Peter, MA, PhD. Reader, Department of Biblical Studies, Glasgow University, since 1986; b. 18.1.41, Dublin; m., Mary Anne Alice Stevens; 2 s.; 1 d. Educ. High School, Dublin; Trinity College, Dublin University; Edinburgh University. After postgraduate degree, worked as swimming pool attendant, barman, brickie's mate, secondary school teacher; Glasgow University: Assistant Lecturer in Semitic Languages, 1968, Lecturer in Old Testament Language and Literature, 1969, Senior Lecturer in Biblical Studies, 1981. Publications: When Prophecy Failed, 1979; From Chaos to Covenant, 1981; Jeremiah: A Commentary, 1986. Recreations: cinema; cricket; beer-drinking; day-dreaming; writing imaginary books in my head. Address: (h.) 5 Marchmont Terrace, Glasgow, G12 9LT; T.-041-339 0440.

Carse, George, MA, BL; b. 30.10.19, Edinburgh; m., Ann Elisabeth C. Rankine; 1 d. Educ. Edinburgh Academy; Edinburgh University. Assistant, St. Cuthbert's Parish Church, Edinbugh, 1943-44; Chaplain, Royal Navy, 1944-47; Minister: Lethendy and Kinloch Parish Church, 1947-49, Liberton Northfield Parish Church, 1949-59; admitted Faculty of Advocates, 1965. President, Edinburgh Natural History Society, 1967-70; President, Lothians Branch, Scottish Wildlife Trust, since 1978; Chairman, Liberton Association, 1967-73. Recreations: walking; ornithology; natural history. Address: (h.) 121 Liberton Brae, Edinburgh, EH16 6LD; T.-031-664 2070.

Carson, Thomas Richard, BSc (Hons), PhD, FRAS. Reader in Astrophysics, St. Andrews University; b. Enniskillen, Northern Ireland; m., Ursula Margaret Mary Davies; 1 s. Educ. Portora Royal School; Queen's University, Belfast. Assistant Lecturer, Department of Natural Philosophy, Glasgow University; Senior Scientific Officer, UK Atomic Weapons Research Establishment, Aldermaston; Senior Lecturer, Department of Astronomy, St. Andrews University; Visiting Professor, Colorado University; Senior Research Associate, NASA Institute for Space Studies, New York; Visiting Staff Member, Los Alamos National Laboratory, University of California. Publication: Atoms and Molecules in Astrophysics (Editor, with M.J. Roberts), 1972. Recreations: squash; tennis; swimming; skiing. Address: (h.) 7 Cairnsden Gardens, St. Andrews, Fife, KY16 8SQ; T.-0334 73813.

Carter, Christopher John, BA (Hons), PhD, MRTPI, FBIM, FRSA. Vice Principal, Duncan of Jordanstone College of Art, since 1981; b. 5.2.41, Capel, Surrey; m., Ann Fisher Prince; 1 s.; 1 d. Educ. Ottershaw School, Chertsey, Surrey; Birmingham University; Glasgow University. Town Planning Assistant, Cumbernauld Development Corporation, 1963-64 and 1967-68; Visiting Lecturer in Geography, Brock University, St. Catharines, Ontario, 1968-69; Lecturer/Senior Lecturer in Planning, Glasgow School of Art, 1969-76; Principal Lecturer in Planning, Coventry (Lanchester) Polytechnic, 1976-78; Senior Lecturer/ Head, Department of Town and Regional Planning, Duncan of Jordanstone College of Art, 1978-81. Winner, RTPI Prize, 1970. Publications: Innovations in Planning Thought and Practice at Cumbernauld New Town 1956-62; The Designation of Cumbernauld New Town (case study) (Coauthor). Recreations: skiing; running; photography; music. Address: (h.) 39 Haston Crescent, Kinnoull, Perth; T.-0738 36802.

Carter, Professor David Craig, MB, ChB, MD, FRCSEdin, FRCSGlas. Regius Professor of Surgery, Edinburgh University, since 1988; Honorary Consultant, Edinburgh Royal Infirmary, since 1988; b. 1.9.40, Penrith; m., Ilske; 2 s. Educ. St. Andrews University. Lecturer in Clinical Surgery, Edinburgh University, 1969-74; 12-month secondment as Lecturer in Surgery, Makerere University, Kampala, Uganda, 1972; Senior Lecturer in Surgery, Edinburgh University, 1974-79; St. Mungo Professor of Surgery, Glasgow University, 1979-88; Honorary Consultant, Glasgow Royal Infirmary, 1979-88; 12-month secondment as Associate Professor of Surgery, University of California, 1976. Council Member, Royal College of Surgeons of Edinburgh, 1980. Moynihan Prize, 1973; James IV Association of Surgeons Travelling Fellow, 1975. Recreations: golf; music. Address: (b.) University Department of Surgery, Royal Infirmary, Glasgow, G31 2ER; T.-041-552 3535.

Carter, George Robert, MIPM, MBIM. Personnel Services Controller, Christian Salvesen PLC, since 1974; Director, Christian Salvesen (Food Services) Ltd., since 1977; Member, CBI (Scotland) Council, since 1980 (Chairman, Employment Committee, 1980-87); Member, Manpower Services Committee (Scotland), 1980-87; b. 26.2.31, Youghal, Ireland; m., Margaret Elizabeth Andrew; 2 s.; 1 d. Educ. Christian Brothers Primary and Secondary School. Merchant Navy, 1949-54; trade union official, 1954-63; various personnel management roles, Chrysler (UK) Ltd., 1963-68; Consultant, Department of Employment, 1968-70; Personnel Director, Beaverbrook Newspaper Group, 1970-74. Member: Administration Committee, Scottish Business Education Council, 1977-79, CBI Industrial Relations Committee (Scotland), 1977-80. Recreations: music; reading; photography. Address: (h.) 12A Ravelston Park, Edinburgh, EH4 3DX; T.-031-332 7914.

Carter, Tom, OBE, ACIS, ACMA, CIPFA. Chairman, Castlehill Housing Association; Chairman, Partnership Housing Ltd.; Director of Finance, Grampian Regional Council, 1975-87; b. 27.12.23, Carlisle; m., Gill (m. diss.); 2 s. Educ. Birkenhead Park High School. 7th Bn., Royal Tank Rgt., 1942-44; various clerical posts, mainly with former LMS Railway, 1939-47; Birkenhead: Clerk, Parks and Cemeteries Department, 1947-48, Accountancy Assistant, 1948-55; Technical Assistant, rising to Assistant Secretary, former IMTA, 1955-61; Deputy County Treasurer, Holland (Lincolnshire), 1961-68; County Treasurer, Moray and Nairn, 1968-75. Past Chairman, Directors of Finance (Scotland) Section, CPFA; Member, Local Government Finance Working Party; former Commissioner, Public Works Loan Board. Recreations: walking; bridge; gardening; winemaking; reading. Address: (h.) 24 Gordon Road, Mannofield, Aberdeen, AB1 7RL.

Cartwright, Rev. Alan Charles David, BSc, BD. Minister, Parishes of Fogo and Swinton with Leitholm, since 1976, with Ladykirk with Whitsome, since 1978; b. 14.7.47, Glasgow; m., Mary Elizabeth Lawson Bissett; 1 s.; 2 d. Educ. Hutchesons Boys Grammar School; Strathclyde University; Glasgow University. Project Leader, Wiggins Teape Ltd., 1968-72; Assistant Minister, Cameron with Largoward with St. Leonard's, 1975-76. Moderator, Synod of the Borders, 1982-83; Moderator, Duns Presbytery, 1984-85. Recreations: athletics; studying local history; drinking coffee. Address: The Manse, Swinton, Duns, Berwickshire, TD11 3JJ; T.-Swinton 228.

Carty, Matthew John, MB, ChB, FRCSEdin, FRCPSGlas, FRCOG. Consultant Obstetrician and Gynaecologist, Southern General Hospital, Glasgow, since 1977; b. 8.3.42, Hamilton; m., Caroline Martin; 2 s.; 2 d. Educ. St. Aloysius College, Glasgow; Glasgow University. Lecturer in Midwifery, Nairobi University, Kenya, 1970-71; Lecturer in Midwifery, Glasgow University, 1972-77. Recreations: squash; golf; tennis; jogging. Address: (h.) 31 Monreith Road, Newlands, Glasgow; T.-041-632 1033.

Cash, John David, BSc, MB, ChB, PhD, FRCPath, FRCPE. National Medical Director, Scottish National Blood Transfusion Service, since 1979; Honorary Professor, Department of Clinical Pharmacology, Edinburgh University, since 1987; b. 3.4.36, Reading; m., Angela Mary Thomson; 1 s.; 1 d. Educ. Ashville College, Harrogate; Edinburgh University. Edinburgh and South East Scotland Blood Transfusion Service: Deputy Director, 1969, Regional Director, 1974. Adviser in Blood Transfusion, WHO. Recreations: fishing; gardening. Address: (b.) Scottish National Blood Transfusion Service, Headquarters Unit, Ellen's Glen Road, Edinburgh, EH17 7QT; T.-031-664 2317.

Caskie, Rev. Donald Murdoch, MA, HCF; b. 27.2.08, Glasgow; m., Jane (Sheana) Mathieson; 3 s.; 1 d. Educ. Buchanan Institute and John Street Secondary; Glasgow University and Trinity College. Minister: Cumbrae, 1932-37, Coatbridge: Coats, 1937-47; Army Chaplain, 1941-45; Minister, Monkton and Prestwick, 1947-81; Moderator, Presbytery of Ayr, 1960-61. Past President, Prestwick Rotary Club; Life Member and Past President, Prestwick Burns Club. Address: (h.) 5 Tramore Crescent, Prestwick KA9 1LT; T.-Prestwick 78534.

Caskie, Rev. J. Colin, BA, BD. Parish Minister, Carnoustie, since 1983; Member, Assembly Board of Stewardship and Finance, since 1984; b. 17.8.47, Glasgow; m., Alison McDougall; 2 s.; 1 d. Educ. Knightswood Secondary School; Strathclyde University; Glasgow University. Parish Minister, Penilee, Glasgow, 1977-83. Recreations: railways; gardening. Address: 44 Terrace Road, Carnoustie, Angus, DD7 7AR; T.-0241 52289.

Catley, Brian John, MA, PhD. Senior Lecturer in Biochemistry, Department of Brewing and Biological Sciences, Heriot-Watt University, since 1978; b. 15.11.36, Salisbury, Wiltshire; m., Elizabeth Ferguson Eyres; 1 s.; 1 d. Educ. Bradford Grammar School; St. Catherine's College, Oxford. Research Chemist, Ilford Ltd., 1961-64; Assistant Lecturer, London University, 1965-67; Guest Investigator, Rockefeller University, New York, 1967-68; Assistant Professor, Miami University, 1968-72; Lecturer, Heriot-Watt University, 1972-78. Convenor, Reserve Management Committee, Balerno, Scottish Wildlife Trust. Recreations: photography; travel. Address: (b.) Department of Brewing and Biological Sciences, Heriot-Watt University, Chambers Street, Edinburgh; T.-031-225 8432, Ext. 170.

Cattanach, John Harkness, VM, JP. Member, Highland Regional Council, 1982-86; Member, Nairn District Council, since 1974; b. 19.1.19, Torbermory; m., Williamina Fraser; 1 s. Educ. Kingussie Secondary School; Skerry's College, Glasgow. Army Officer, 1938-46 (Captain); ran own business, 1946-50; accountant, 1950-55; own business, 1956-74. Awarded Order of the Silver Cross of Virtuti Militari by the Polish Government in exile; Hon. Lt. Col., Polish Armed Forces (Govt. in exile). Address: (h.) Lorne House, Geddes, by Nairn, IV12 5SB; T.-06677 279 and 397.

Catto, Graeme R.D., MB, ChB (Hons), MD (Hons), FRCP, FRCPGlas. Reader in Medicine, Aberdeen University, since 1985; Honorary Consultant Physician/Nephrologist, since 1977; b. 24.4.45, Aberdeen; m., Joan Sievewright; 1 s.; 1 d. Educ. Robert Gordon's College; Aberdeen University. Research Fellow/Lecturer/Senior Lecturer in Medicine, Aberdeen University, 1970-85; Harkness Fellow of Commonwealth Fund of New York, 1975-77 (Fellow in Medicine, Harvard Medical School and Peter Bent Brigham Hospital, Boston). Recreations: curling; fresh air; France. Address: (b.) Department of Medicine, Aberdeen University, Foresterhill, Aberdeen, AB9 2ZB; T.-0224 681818.

Cawdor, 6th Earl (Hugh John Vaughan Campbell), FSA, FRICS; b. 6.9.32; m., 1, Cathryn Hinde (m. diss.); 2 s.; 3 d.; 2, Countess Angelika Ilona Lazansky von Bukowa. Educ. Eton; Magdalen College, Oxford; Royal Agricultural College, Cirencester. Address: (h.) Cawdor Castle, Nairn.

Cay, David Robert Bellamy, MA, LLB, FSA Scot. Advocate, since 1954; Reporter to Scottish Legal Aid Board, since 1986; b. 7.11.29, Aberdeen; m., Elizabeth Lorna Jamieson (see Elizabeth Lorna Cay); 1 s.; 1 d. Educ. Aberdeen Grammar School; Aberdeen University. Standing Counsel, Ministry of Labour (subsequently Department of Employment and Productivity); Standing Counsel, Department of Transport; defended last man to be hanged in Scotland. Recreations: golf; reading; travel. Address: (h.) 12 India Street, Edinburgh, EH3 6EZ; T.-031-225 3640.

Cay, Elizabeth Lorna, MD, FRCPsych, MRCPEdin, DPM. Consultant in Rehabilitation Medicine, since 1975; Honorary Senior Lecturer, Edinburgh University, since 1976; b. 11.1.31, Cawdor, Nairn; m., David Robert Bellamy Cay (qv); 1 s.; 1 d. Educ. Elgin Academy; Peebles Burgh and County High School; Edinburgh University. Temporary Advisor, WHO; Chairman, Edinburgh Committee for Coordination of Services for the Disabled. Recreations: convertibles; breeding dogs; travel. Address: (h.) 12 India Street, Edinburgh, EH3 6EZ; T.-031-225 3640.

Chadwick, Professor Charles, MA, DU (Paris). Professor of French, Aberdeen University, since 1968; b. 23.11.24, Widnes; m., Nora O'Brien. Educ. Grammar School, Widnes; Liverpool University; Paris University. Lecturer, Liverpool University, 1951-65; Reader, Manchester University, 1965-68; Dean, Faculty of Arts, Aberdeen, 1982-85. Publications: Etudes Sur Rimbaud, 1959; Mallarme, 1961; Symbolism, 1971; Verlaine, 1973; Rimbaud, 1979. Recreation: gardening. Address: (h.) The Beeches, William Street, Torphins, Aberdeenshire, AB3 4JR; T.-033982 489.

Chadwick, Vivian Anthony, MBIM, MATM. Deputy General Manager, Scotrail, since 1986; Consultant, Organisation and Management Development, since 1984; b. 11.7.35, Greenwich; m., Jeanette Philipson; 1 s.; 1 d. Educ. Stratford upon Avon Grammar School; Germany; Canada; New Zealand. Joined BR, 1956, after National Service; held various management posts in Operations, Marketing and Training, including Passenger Operations Manager, BRB, and Regional Operations Manager Scotland. Publication: Changing Trains (Co-author). Recreations: walking; travel; history. Address: (h.) 19 Rockville Grove, Linlithgow, EH49 6BZ; T.-0506 843326.

Chalmers, Evelyn Margot. Secretary, Scottish Committee, Council on Tribunals, since 1984; b. 7.10.29, Edinburgh; m., Tom Chalmers; 1 s.; 1 d. Educ. James Gillespie's High School for Girls. Various posts, Scottish Office, including Assignment Officer in Organisation and Methods; policy work for Scotland in the European Community. Recreations: journalism; gardening. Address: (b.) 20 Walker Street, Edinburgh; T.-031-220 1236.

Chalmers, Patrick Edward Bruce, NDA, BScA. Controller, BBC Scotland, since 1983; b. 26.10.39, Chapel of Garioch, Aberdeenshire; m., Ailza Catherine Reid McGibbon; 3 d. Educ. Fettes College, Edinburgh; North of Scotland College of Agriculture; Durham University. Joined BBC as Radio Talks Producer, Scotland, 1963; TV Producer, 1965; Senior Producer, Aberdeen, 1970; Head of Television, Scotland, 1979-82; General Manager, Co-Productions, TV, London, 1982. Member, Grampian Region Children's Panel, 1974-79. Recreations: skiing; gardening. Address: (b.) BBC, Queen Margaret Drive, Glasgow.

Chalmers, Robert John, BSc, MSc, PhD, CBiol, MIBiol. Vice Principal, The Queen's College, Glasgow, since 1984; b. 25.3.47, Glasgow; m., Cynthia Mackay; 3 s. Educ. Hyndland Senior Secondary School; Aberdeen University; Glasgow University. Research Assistant, Glasgow University, 1971-73 and 1975-77; Scientific Officer, DAFS, 1973-75; Lecturer, then Senior Lecturer, Queen's College, Glasgow, 1978-84. Elder, Church of Scotland. Recreations: angling; gardening. Address: (h.) Law House, Sandford, Strathaven, Lanarkshire; T.-0357 21162.

Chalmers-Watson, Keith, SDA. Farmer, since 1964; Chairman and Managing Director, D.C. Watson & Sons (Fenton Barns) Ltd.; b. 20.7.45, Edinburgh; m., Kirsteen Henderson; 3 d. Educ. Loretto; East of Scotland Agricultural College. Chairman, Ardtaraig Salmon Ltd.; Director: Fenton Barns (Scotland) Ltd., David Morin (Builders) Ltd., Fenton Barns (Mushrooms) Ltd. Council Member: World Pheasant Association, British Turkey Federation. Recreations: rare game-bird conservation and aviculture. Address: Fenton Barns, North Berwick, East Lothian; T.-062 085 225.

Chapman, Charles Duncan, OBE, MA, LLB. Honorary Sheriff, since 1960; b. 11.2.13, Denny, Stirlingshire; m., Margaret Martin Henry (deceased); 1 s.; 1 d. Educ. Morrison's Academy, Crieff; Edinburgh University. Legal apprentice; Royal Artillery, 1939-45 (Major, 1943); Kirkcaldy Town Council, 1945-75: Legal Assistant, Depute Town Clerk, Town Clerk; Chief Executive, Kirkcaldy District Council, 1975-78. Past Chairman, Law Committee, Convention of Burghs; former Member, Central Probation Council; served on a number of Government committees and working parties; former Council Member, Law Society of Scotland; Director, Link Housing Association; Chairman, Kirkcaldy Citizens' Advice Bureau. Publication: The Licensing Scotland Act 1976. Recreation: bowling. Address: (h.) 15 Stanley Park, Kirkcaldy; T.-0592 201270.

Chapman, Francis Ian, FRSA, CBIM. Chairman and Chief Executive, William Collins PLC, since 1981; Chairman, Radio Clyde Ltd., since 1972; Chairman, Council, Strathclyde University Advisory Board, since 1985; b. 26.10.25, St. Fergus, Aberdeenshire; m., Marjory Stewart Swinton; 1 s.; 1 d. Educ. Shawlands Academy, Glasgow; Ommer School of Music; Royal Scottish Academy of Music. War Service: RAF air crew cadet, 1943-44; National Service coal mines, 1945-47. William Collins: trainee, 1947, Sales Representative, New York Branch, 1950, General Sales Manager, London, 1955, appointed to main operating Board as Group Sales Director, 1959; appointed to Board, William Collins (Holdings) Ltd. as Joint Managing Director, 1967; Deputy Chairman, William Collins (Holdings) Ltd., 1976; Chairman, William Collins Publishers Ltd., 1979; Chairman, Hatchards Ltd., since 1976; Board Member, Pan Books Ltd., 1962-84; Chairman, Harvill Press Ltd., since 1976; Board Member, Book Tokens Ltd., since 1981; Member, Governing Council, SCOTBIC, since 1983; Board Member, IRN Ltd., 1983-85; President, Publishers Association, 1979; Trustee, Book Trade Benevolent Society, since 1982; Board Member, Scottish Opera Theatre Royal Ltd., 1974-79; Director, Stanley Botes Ltd., since 1985; Non-Executive Director, Guinness PLC, since December 1986; Joint Chairman and Chief Executive, Harper and Row, New York, since 1987. Scottish Free Enterprise Award, 1985. Recreations: golf; swimming; skiing; music. Address: (b.) Westerhills Road, Bishopbriggs, Glasgow, G64 2QT.

Chapman, Professor John N., MA, PhD, FInstP. Titular Professor, Physics and Astronomy, Glasgow University, since 1988; b. 21.11.47, Sheffield; m., Judith M.; 1 s.; 1 d. Educ. King Edward VII School, Sheffield; St. John's College and Fitzwilliam College, Cambridge. Research Fellow, Fitzwilliam College, Cambridge; Lecturer, Glasgow University. Former officer: British Joint Committee for Electron Microscopy and Institute of Physics. Publication: Quantitative Electron Microscopy (Co-Editor). Recreations: photography; walking; squash. Address: (b.) Department of Physics and Astronomy, Glasgow University, Glasgow, G12 8QQ; T.-041-339 8855, Ext. 4462.

Chapman, Robert Sutherland, MB, ChB (Hons), FRCP(Glas), FRCP(Edin), FRCP(Lond). Consultant Dermatologist, Greater Glasgow Health Board and Forth Valley Health Board, since 1971; Clinical Lecturer, Glasgow University, since 1973; b. 4.6.38, Cults, Aberdeenshire; m., Dr. Rosalind S. Slater; 2 s.; 1 d. Educ. Turriff Academy; Aberdeen University. House Officer, Aberdeen Royal Infirmary; Research Fellow, Department of Materia Medica and Therapeutics, Aberdeen University; Registrar and Senior Registrar in Dermatology, Aberdeen Hospitals; Senior Registrar in Dermatology, Middlesex Hospital and St. John's Hospital for Diseases of the Skin, London. Recreations: gardening; hill-walking. Address: (h.) 4 Seafield Avenue, Bearsden, Glasgow, G62 3LB; T.-041-942 8993.

Charlton, Professor Graham, BDS, MDS, FDSRCS. Professor of Conservative Dentistry and Head of Department, Edinburgh University, since 1978; b. 15.10.28, Newbiggin-By-Sea, Northumberland; m., Stella Dobson; 2 s.; 1 d. Educ. Bedlington Grammar School; St. John's, York; Durham University. Teaching Certificate. Teacher in Northumberland, 1948-52 (including period of National Service); Dental School, 1952-58; general dental practice, 1958-64; Lecturer, then Senior Lecturer/Honorary Consultant, Bristol University, 1964-78 (Clinical Dean, Dental School, Bristol, 1975-78). Dean of Dental Studies, Edinburgh University, 1978-83. Address: (b.) Dental School, Chambers Street, Edinburgh, EH1 1JA; T.-031-225 9511.

Cherry, Rev. Alastair Jack, BD. Minister, Stamperland Parish Church, Glasgow, since 1987 (Scoonie Kirk, Leven, 1982-87); b. 13.3.44, Glasgow; m., Fiona Mairi Murchison; 2 s. Educ. Bellahouston Academy, Glasgow; Glasgow University. Staff, Clydesdale Bank Ltd., 1964-76; studied for ministry, 1976-82. Recreations: music; dramatic art; walking; a little golf. Address: Manse of Stamperland, 109 Ormonde Avenue, Glasgow, G44 3SN; T.-041-637 4976.

Chester, Richard Waugh, GRSM, ARCM. Administrator, National Youth Orchestra of Scotland, since 1987; b. 19.4.43, Hutton Rudby; m., Sarah Chapman-Mortimer; 1 s.; 2 d. Educ. The Friends' School, Great Ayton; Royal Academy of Music. Flautist: BBC Northern Ireland, 1965, Scottish National Orchestra, 1967; Conductor; Teacher; Examiner. Director, Glasgow Festival Strings. Recreations: squash; swimming; cricket; food and drink. Address: (h.) Milton of Cardross, Port of Menteith, Stirling, FK8 3JY; T.-08775 634.

Chesworth, Air Vice-Marshal George Arthur, CB (1982), OBE (1972), DFC (1954). Chief Executive, Glasgow Garden Festival (1988) Ltd., since 1985; b. 4.6.30, Beckenham; m., Betty Joan Hopkins; 1 s. (deceased); 2 d. Educ. Carshalton and Wimbledon. Joined RAF, 1948; commissioned, 1950; 205 Flying Boat Sqdn., FEAF, 1951-53; RAF Germany, RAF Kinloss, RAF St Mawgan, 1956-61; RN Staff Coll., 1963; MoD, 1964-67; OC 201 Nimrod Sqdn., 1968-71; OC RAF Kinloss, 1972-75; Air Officer in Charge, Central Tactics and Trial Orgn., 1975-77; Director, RAF Quartering, 1977-80; C. of S. to Air Comdr. CTF 317, during Falkland campaign, 1982; C. of S., HQ 18 Gp., RAF, 1980-84. Address: (h.) Pindlers Croft, Lower Califer, Forres, Moray, IV36 0RN; T.-Forres 74136.

Cheyne, Rev. Professor Alexander Campbell, MA (Hons), BLitt, BD, HonDLitt (Memorial University, Newfoundland). Professor of Ecclesiastical History, Edinburgh University, 1964-86; Principal, New College, Edinburgh, 1984-86; Moderator, Edinburgh Presbytery, Church of Scotland, 1987-88; b. 1.6.24, Errol, Perthshire. Educ. Kirkcaldy High School; Edinburgh University; Oriel College, Oxford; Basel University, Switzerland. National Service, Black Watch and RAEC (Instructor, Army School of Education), 1946-48; Glasgow University: Assistant Lecturer, 1950-51, Lecturer in History, 1951-53; New College and Basel University, 1953-57; Lecturer in Ecclesiastical History, Edinburgh University, 1958-64. Carnegie Scholar, 1948-50; Aitken Fellow, 1956-57; Visiting Professor, Wooster College, Ohio, 1973; Chalmers Lecturer (Trinity College, Glasgow, and Christ's College, Aberdeen), 1976-80; Visiting Fellow, Wolfson College, Cambridge, 1979; Burns Lecturer, Knox College, Dunedin, New Zealand, 1980. Publications: The Transforming of the Kirk: Victorian Scotland's Religious Revolution, 1983; The Practical and the Pious: Essays on Thomas Chalmers 1780-1847 (Editor), 1985; contributions to: Reformation and Revolution: Essays presented to Hugh Watt, 1967, The Westminster Confession in the Church Today, 1982; introduction to Movements of Religious Thought in Britain during the Nineteenth Century, 1971. Recreations: classical music; walking; foreign travel. Address: (h.) 12 Crossland Crescent, Peebles, EH45 8LF; T.-0721 22288.

Cheyne, Alexander Ian, MB, ChB, DPM, FRCPsych, MRCP(Glas). Consultant Psychiatrist, Gartnavel Royal Hospital, Glasgow, since 1972; Consultant Psychiatrist, Leverndale Hospital, Glasgow, since 1970; Senior Registrar, Gartnavel Royal Hospital, Glasgow, since 1968; b. 29.9.30, Rangoon, Burma; m., Jean MacDonald Edmonds; 3 d. Educ. Aberdeen Grammar School; Aberdeen University. House Officer: Aberdeen Royal Infirmary, 1954-55, Glasgow Royal Infirmary, 1955; Medical Officer, RAMC, 1955-57; Trainee, general practice, Banchory, 1957-58; Principal, general practice, Cambridgeshire, 1958-64; Registrar, Crichton Royal, Dumfries, 1965-67; Psychiatrist, Hillcrest Hospital, Adelaide, 1967-68. Recreations: farming; golf; walking. Address: (h.) 34 Thorn Road, Bearsden, Glasgow; T.-041-942 2439.

Chick, Jonathan Dale, MA (Cantab), MB, ChB, MPhil, MRCP, FRCPsych. Consultant Psychiatrist, Royal Edinburgh Hospital, since 1979; part-time Senior Lecturer, Edinburgh University, since 1979; b. 23.4.45, Wallasey; m., Josephine Anna; 2 s. Educ. Queen Elizabeth Grammar School, Darlington; Corpus Christi College, Cambridge; Edinburgh University. Posts in Edinburgh teaching hospitals, 1971-76; scientific staff, MRC Unit for Epidemiological Studies in Psychiatry, 1976-79. Adviser, WHO; awarded Royal College of Psychiatrists Research Medal and Prize. Publication: Drinking Problems (Co-author), 1984. Recreations: music; literature; visual arts. Address: (h.) 8 Abbotsford Park, Edinburgh; T.-031-447 6027.

Chisholm, Rev. Archibald Freeland, MA. Minister, Braes of Rannoch with Foss and Rannoch, since 1984; b. 27.10.32, Glasgow; m., Margaret Downer Rice; 4 d. Educ. Perth Academy; St. Andrews University; New College, Edinburgh.

Minister, Bantu Presbyterian Church of South Africa, Gordon Memorial, Natal, 1958-67; Tutor, Federal Theological Seminary of Southern Africa, 1964-65; Minister: Stamperland Parish Church, Glasgow, 1968-76, St. Andrew's Parish Church, Leven, 1976-84. Address: The Manse, Kinloch Rannoch, Pitlochry, PH16 5QA; T.-08822 381.

Chisholm, Duncan Douglas, MB, ChB, MRCPsych, DPM. Consultant Child and Adolescent Psychiatrist, Department of Child and Family Psychiatry, Royal Aberdeen Children's Hospital, since 1975; Clinical Senior Lecturer, Department of Mental Health, Aberdeen University, since 1975; b. 8.10.41, Grantown-on-Spey; m., Rosemary Galloway Doyle; 2 d. Educ. Grantown Grammar School; Aberdeen University. Pre-registration House Officer, Aberdeen, 1965-66; post-registration Senior House Officer/ Registrar, Royal Cornhill Hospital and Ross Clinic, Aberdeen, 1966-70; Senior Registrar in Child and Adolescent Psychiatry, 1970-75 (including one-year sabbatical, Clarke Institute of Psychiatry, Toronto, 1973-74). Chairman, Grampian Family Conciliation Service; Committee Member, Association for Family Therapy, Grampian Branch. Recreations: reading; chess; crosswords; literature, history and culture of Scotland and Scottish Highlands. Address: (h.) Figurettes, 51 Fountainhall Road, Aberdeen, AB2 4EU; T.-0224 640074.

Chisholm, Duncan Fraser. Managing Director, Duncan Chisholm & Sons Ltd., Inverness, since 1979; Member, Inverness District Council, since 1984; Member, Board of Governors, Eden Court Theatre, Inverness, since 1984; President, Clan Chisholm Society, since 1978; b. 14.4.41, Inverness; m., Mary Rebecca MacRae; 1 s.; 1 d. Educ. Inverness High School. Council Member, Inverness, Loch Ness and Nairn Tourist Board, since 1979; President, Inverness and Highland Chamber of Commerce, 1983-84 (Vice-President, 1982-83); Elder, Church of Scotland; Past President, Inverness Wine Appreciation Society; Assistant Area Scout Commissioner, 1975-78. Recreations: swimming; badminton. Address: (b.) 47-53 Castle Street, Inverness; T.-0463 234599.

Chisholm, Professor Geoffrey Duncan, ChM, FRCS, FRCSEdin. President, Royal College of Surgeons of Edinburgh, since 1988; Professor of Surgery, Edinburgh University, since 1977; Director, Nuffield Transplant Unit, Edinburgh, since 1977; Honorary Senior Lecturer, Institute of Urology, London University, since 1972; b. 30.9.31, Hawera, New Zealand; m., Angela Jane; 2 s. Educ. Malvern College; St. Andrews University. Research Fellow, John Hopkins Hospital, Baltimore, 1961-62; Consultant Urological Surgeon, Hammersmith Hospital, London, 1967-77; Honorary Senior Lecturer, Royal Postgraduate Medical School, 1967-77. Chairman, British Prostate Group, 1975-80; Vice President, British Association of Surgical Oncologists, 1980-81; President, British Association of Urological Surgeons, 1985-87; Chairman, European Society of Urological Oncology and Endocrinology, since 1985; Council Member, Royal College of Surgeons of Edinburgh, since 1984; Managing Editor, Urological Research, 1977-81; Editor, British Journal of Urology, since 1977. Publications: Scientific Foundation of Urology (Joint Editor); Clinical Practice in Urology (Series Editor). Recreations: gardening; wine tasting; squash racquets. Address: (h.) 8 Ettrick Road, Edinburgh, EH10 5BJ; T.-031-229 7173.

Chiswick, Derek, MB, ChB, MPhil, MRCPsych. Honorary Senior Lecturer in Forensic Psychiatry, Edinburgh University, since 1988; Consultant Forensic Psychiatrist, Lothian Health Board, since 1988; b. 7.1.45, Hampton, Middlesex; m., Ann Williams; 3 d. Educ. Preston Manor County School, Wembley; Liverpool University. Parole Board for Scotland: Member, 1983-88, Vice-Chairman, 1984-88; Chairman, Working Group on Suicide Precautions, Glenochil Young Offenders' Institution and Detention Centre, 1984-85. Recreation: relaxing with family. Address: (h.) 6 St. Catherine's Place, Edinburgh, EH9 1NU; T.-031-667 2444.

Christian, Professor Reginald Frank, MA (Hons) (Oxon). Professor of Russian and Head of Department, St. Andrews University, since 1966; b. 9.8.24, Liverpool; m., Rosalind Iris Napier; 1 s.; 1 d. Educ. Liverpool Institute High School; Queen's College, Oxford. RAF, 1943-46 (aircrew), flying on 231 Sqdn. and 6 Atlantic Ferry Unit (Pilot Officer, 1944); Foreign Office (British Embassy, Moscow), 1949-50; Lecturer and Head of Russian Department, Liverpool University, 1950-55; Senior Lecturer, then Professor of Russian and Head of Department, Birmingham University, 1955-66; Visiting Professor: McGill University, Montreal, 1961-62, Institute of Foreign Languages, Moscow, 1964-65; Dean, Faculty of Arts, St. Andrews University, 1975-78; Member, University Court, 1971-73, 1981-85. President, British Universities Association of Slavists, 1967-70; Member, International Committee of Slavists, 1970-75; Honorary Vice-President, Association of Teachers of Russian; Member, UGC Arts Sub-Committee on Russian Studies. Publications: Russian Syntax (with F.M. Borras), 1959 and 1971; Korolenko's Siberia, 1954; Tolstoy's War and Peace: A Study, 1962; Russian Prose Composition (with F.M. Borras), 1964 and 1974; Tolstoy: A Critical Introduction, 1969; Tolstoy's Letters, edited, translated and annotated, 1978; Tolstoy's Diaries, edited, translated and annotated, 1985. Recreations: violin; fell-walking; Russian philately; formerly association football. Address: (h.) The Roundel, St. Andrews, Fife; T.-St. Andrews 73322.

Christie, Alexander Duncan, PhD, BSc, CEng, MIEE, AFRAeS. Head, Department of Diagnostic Ultrasound, Ninewells Medical School, Dundee, since 1971; b. 14.6.30, Detroit; m., Beatrice R. Phemister; 2 d. Educ. Robert Gordon's College, Aberdeen; Aberdeen University. Pilot, RAF, 1953-63; Lecturer, Bristol College of Technology, 1963-67; Lecturer, Aberdeen University, 1967-70; Principal Physicist, Tayside Health Board, and Honorary Senior Lecturer, Dundee University, from 1971; Hon. Professor, WHO Collaborating Centre, University of Zagreb, 1986; Visiting Professor, University of Hong Kong, 1988-89. Publication: Ultrasound and Infertility, 1981. Address: (b.) Department of Obstetrics and Gynaecology, Dundee University, Dundee; T.-0382 60111.

Christie, Rev. Andrew Cormack, LTh. Minister, Ferryhill North Church, Aberdeen, since 1984; b. 25.5.35, Stonehaven; m., Norma Rosemary Scott Watson; 2 s.; 1 d. Educ. Mackie Academy, Stonehaven; Banchory Academy; Aberdeen College of Commerce; Christ's College, Aberdeen; King's College, Aberdeen. Grocer, Northern Co-operative Society Ltd., 18 years; Assistant Minister, St. George's, Tillydrone; Minister, Clatt linked with Rhynie, 1975-84. Former Community Councillor, Rhynie. Recreations: supporting Aberdeen FC; golf. Address: 50 Sycamore Place, Aberdeen, AB1 2SZ; T.-0224 580865.

Christie, Campbell. General Secretary, Scottish Trades Union Congress, since 1986; b. 23.8.37, Carsluith, Kirkcudbrightshire; m., Elizabeth Brown Cameron; 2 s. Educ. Albert Senior Secondary School, Glasgow; Woolwich Polytechnic, London. Civil Servant, Department of Health and Social Security, 1954-72; National Officer, then Deputy General Secretary, Society of Civil and Public Servants, 1972-86. Member, EEC Economic and Social Committee; Member, MSC Committee for Scotland; Member, Scottish Economic Council; Director, Wildcat Theatre Company, Scottish National Orchestra, Theatre Royal Opera Company. Address: (h.) 31 Dumyat Drive, Falkirk; T.-0324 24555; (b.) 16 Woodlands Terrace, Glasgow, G5; T.-041-332 4946.

Christie, Very Rev. James, SJ, MA, MSc, CQSW, MInstGA. Director, The Garnethill Centre, Glasgow, since 1980; Superior, The Jesuit Community, Craighead Retreat House, since 1983; b. 3.7.40, Bellshill, Lanarkshire. Educ. Our Lady's High School, Motherwell; St. Aloysius College, Glasgow; Campion Hall, Oxford; Columbia University; Southampton University; London School of Economics. Ordained Priest, Society of Jesus, 1970; parish work and training in Paris, 1970-71; on staff of Fons Vitae Institute, Johannesburg, 1971-72; School Counsellor, Wimbledon College, 1973-75; Depute Director, The Dympna Centre, London, 1977-80. Recreation: hill-walking. Address: Craighead Retreat House, Bothwell, Glasgow, G71 8AU; T.-Hamilton 285300.

Christie, John Belford Wilson, CBE, BA (Cantab), LLB, HonLLD (Dundee, 1977). Advocate; b. 4.5.14, Allanton, Lanarkshire; m., Christine Isobel Syme Arnott; 4 d. Educ. Merchiston Castle School; Cambridge University; Edinburgh University. Admitted to Faculty of Advocates, 1939; on active service, RNVR, 1939-46; Sheriff-Substitute, Western Division, Dumfries and Galloway, 1948-55; Sheriff of Tayside, Central and Fife, at Dundee, 1955-83. Member, Parole Board for Scotland, 1967-73; Member: Queen's College Council, St. Andrews University, 1960-67, University Court, Dundee University, 1967-75; Honorary Lecturer, Department of Private Law, Dundee University; Knight of the Holy Sepulchre of Jerusalem, 1988. Recreation: golf. Address: (h.) Annsmuir Farm, Ladybank, Fife; T.-0337 30480.

Christie, John Fulton, MB, ChB, FRCP, FRCS. President, Scottish Association for the Deaf, since 1982; President, West of Scotland Region, National Deaf Children's Society; b. 18.12.02, Glasgow; m., Clare Lyle Lang; 2 d. Educ. Glasgow Academy; Glasgow University. Consultant Otolaryngologist, Western Infirmary, Glasgow; Lecturer in Diseases of the Ear, Nose and Throat, Glasgow University; Consultant Otolaryngologist, West of Scotland Neurosurgical Unit; Otolaryngologist, Dunbartonshire School Medical Service and Ascertainment Team. Address: (h.) 15 Helensburgh Drive, Glasgow, G13 1RR; T.-041-959 2411.

Christie, Robert Alexander, LLB. Chief Executive and Director of Administration, Berwickshire District Council, since 1977; b. 24.1.45, Preston. Educ. Balshaw's Grammar School, Leyland, Lancashire; St. Andrews University. Dumfries County Council: Principal Legal Assistant, 1969-71, Depute County Clerk, 1971-73; Depute County Clerk, Argyll County Council, 1973-75; Depute Director of Administration, Argyll and Bute District Council, 1975-76; Chief Executive, Lochaber District Council, 1976-77. Recreations: cooking; reading; listening to music. Address: (b.) District Council Offices, 8 Newtown Street, Duns, Berwickshire, TD11 3DT; T.-0361 82600.

Christie, Terry, BSc (Hons). Head Teacher, Musselburgh Grammar School, since 1987 (Ainslie Park High School, 1982-87); Manager, Meadowbank Thistle FC, since 1980 (Director, since 1983); b. 16.12.42, Edinburgh; 2 s.; 1 d. Educ. Holy Cross Academy, Edinburgh; Edinburgh University. Depute Rector, Trinity Academy, 1978-82. Played football for Dundee, Raith Rovers and Stirling Albion, 1960-74; Coach, Meadowbank Thistle, 1978-80. Recreations: golf; bridge; snooker; reading. Address: (h.) 76 Meadowfield Terrace, Edinburgh, EH8 7NU; T.-031-661 1486.

Christie, Sheriff William James, LLB. Sheriff of Tayside, Central and Fife, at Kirkcaldy, since 1979; b. 1.11.32; m.; 3 s. Educ. Holy Cross Academy, Edinburgh; Edinburgh University. Private practice, 1956-79; Member, Council, Law Society of Scotland, 1975-79.

Christie, William W., DSc, PhD. Assistant Director (Science), Hannah Research Institute, Ayr; b. 18.8.39, Kirkcaldy; m., Norma; 2 s. Educ. Buckhaven High School; St. Andrews University. Joined Hannah Research Institute, 1967. Publications: Lipid Analysis; Lipid Metabolism in Ruminant Animals. Recreation: gardening. Address: (b.) Hannah Research Institute, Ayr; T.-0292 76013.

Christman, Rev. William James, BA, BD. Minister, Ayr St. Columba, since 1981; b. 6.9.38, Joplin, Missouri; m., Georgina Boyle; 2 d. Educ. Joplin High School, Missouri; Grinnell College, Iowa; Edinburgh University; Harvard University. Assistant Lecturer in Ecclesiastical History, Edinburgh University, 1963-65; Minister: Richmond Craigmillar Parish Church, Edinburgh, 1965-69, Lochwood Parish Church, Easterhouse, Glasgow, 1970-76, Lansdowne Parish Church, Glasgow, 1977-81. Honorary President, Scottish Churches' Football Association, 1980-85. Publication: The Christman File, 1978. Recreation: music. Address: 2 Hazelwood Road, Ayr, KA7 2PY; T.-Ayr 283125.

Clapperton, Chalmers Moyes, MA (Hons), PhD. Reader in Geography, Aberdeen University, since 1987; b. 9.8.38, Hawick; m., Elizabeth

Morag Thomson; 2 s. Educ. Hawick High School; Edinburgh University. Aberdeen University: Assistant in Geography, 1962, Lecturer, 1963, Senior Lecturer, 1972. Expedition Leader to Antarctica, 1967, Spitsbergen, 1972, Iceland, 1974, South America-Andes, 1970, 1975, 1976, 1983, 1985, 1986; Member of Council, Royal Scottish Geographical Society. Publication: Scotland: A New Geography (Editor), 1983. Recreations: rugby coaching; golf; tennis; squash; skiing; hill-walking; gardening. Address: (b.) Department of Geography, Aberdeen University, Aberdeen, AB9 2UF; T.-Aberdeen 272346.

Clark, Alastair Trevor, CBE (1976), LVO (1974), MA (Oxon). Barrister; Member, Scottish Museums Council, since 1980 (Chairman, 1981-84 and since 1987); Member, Lothian Health Board, since 1981; Member, City of Edinburgh District Council, 1980-88; Member, Race Relations Assessors Panel, Scottish Sheriff Courts, since 1983; Member, Edinburgh Academical Club Council, 1978-84 and since 1986; a Governor, Edinburgh Filmhouse, 1980-84 and since 1987; Member, National Museums of Scotland Charitable Trust, since 1987; b. 10.6.23, Glasgow; m., Hilary Agnes Mackenzie Anderson. Educ. Giffnock Academy; Glasgow Academy; Edinburgh Academy; Magdalen College, Oxford; Inns of Court (Middle Temple); Ashridge Management College. War service, Queen's Own Cameron Highlanders and Royal West African Frontier Force, Nigeria, India and Burma, 1942-46; Administrative Branch, HM Colonial Service (later HMOCS): Nigeria, 1949-59 (Secretary to Cabinet, Northern Region; Senior District Officer), Hong Kong, 1960-72 (Director of Social Welfare; Deputy and Acting Director of Urban Services; Acting Chairman Urban Council; Clerk of Councils; Principal Assistant Colonial Secretary, etc.), Western Pacific, 1972-77 (Chief Secretary Western Pacific High Commission; Deputy and Acting Governor, Solomon Islands); retired, 1977; Vice-President, Hong Kong Scout Association, 1965-72; Joint Founder, HK Outward Bound School; Honorary Secretary, St. John's Cathedral Council, 1963-72; Country Leader Fellowship to USA, 1972; Selector, Voluntary Service Overseas, 1978-80; Leverhulme Trust Grant, 1979-81; Vice-Chairman, Committee of Area Museum Councils, 1983-84; Member: Secretary of State's Museums Advisory Board, 1983-85, Museums Association Council, 1983-86; Trustee, National Museums of Scotland, 1985-87; Member, Edinburgh International Festival Council, 1980-86; a Director, Royal Lyceum Theatre Company, 1982-84; Member, Court of Directors, Edinburgh Academy, 1979-84. Recreations: music; books; theatre; netsuke; cartophily. Address: (h.) 11 Ramsay Garden, Edinburgh, EH1 2NA; T.-031-225 8070.

Clark, Alex. Member, Board of Directors: Mayfest (Founder and Vice-Chairman), Scottish Opera, Scottish Ballet, Glasgow Jazz Festival, Glasgow Film Theatre, Scottish Early Music Consort; Member, Executive Committee, Advisory Council for the Arts in Scotland; Member, Executive Committee, Scottish Arts Lobby Voice (S.A.L.V.O.); Trustee, James Milne Memorial Trust; Trustee, Hugh MacDiarmid Memorial Trust; b. 2.1.22, Larkhall; m., Jessie Beveridge McCulloch; 1 s.; 1 d. Educ. Larkhall Academy. Grain miller, 1936-39; coal miner, 1939-53; political organiser, 1953-69; Scottish and Northern Ireland Secretary, British Actors Equity Association, 1969-84; created the post of STUC Arts Officer, 1985-87; founder Member, Boards, Scottish Youth Theatre, Scottish Theatre Company, Royal Lyceum Theatre Company; also served on Boards of Pitlochry Festival Theatre and Cumbernauld Theatre Company; Member, Scottish Arts Council's Review Committee on Scottish Theatre Company, 1987; Member, Working Party on a National Theatre for Scotland, 1987; Lord Provost's Award for services to the city of Glasgow, 1987; Member, STUC Entertainment and Arts Committee, since foundation. Recreations: reading; music; theatre; walking. Address: (h.) 77 Albert Road, Glasgow, G42 8DP; T.-041-423 4846.

Clark, Alistair Campbell, MA, LLB. Partner, Blackadder, Reid, Johnston (formerly Reid, Johnston, Bell & Henderson), Solicitors, Dundee, since 1961; Honorary Sheriff, Tayside Central and Fife, since 1986; Council Member, Law Society of Scotland, since 1982 (Vice President, 1988); b. 4.3.33, Dundee; m., Evelyn M. Clark; 3 s. Educ. Grove Academy, Broughty Ferry; St. Andrews University. Dean, Faculty of Procurators and Solicitors in Dundee, 1979-81; Secretary, Royal Dundee Blind Craft Products; Past Chairman, Broughty Ferry Round Table; Past President, Claverhouse Rotary Club, Dundee. Recreations: family; travel; erratic golf. Address: (b.) 34 Reform Street, Dundee; T.-0382 29222.

Clark, David Findlay, MA, PhD, CPsychol, FBPsS. Director, Area Clinical Psychology Services, Grampian Health Board, since 1966; Clinical Senior Lecturer, Department of Mental Health, Aberdeen University, since 1966; b. 30.5.30, Aberdeen; m., Janet Ann Stephen; 2 d. Educ. Banff Academy; Aberdeen University. Flying Officer, RAF, 1951-53; Psychologist, Leicester Industrial Rehabilitation Unit, 1953-56; Senior, then Principal Clinical Psychologist, Leicester Area Clinical Psychology Service, and part-time Lecturer, Leicester University and Technical College, 1956-66; WHO short-term Consultant, Sri Lanka, 1977; various lecturing commitments in Canada and USA, since 1968. Honorary Sheriff, Grampian and Highlands; former Governor, Aberdeen College of Education; Member, Grampian Children's Panel, 1970-85; Safeguarder (in terms of Social Work Scotland Act), since 1985; Past Chairman, Clinical Division, British Psychological Society. Publication: Help, Hospitals and the Handicapped, 1984. Recreations: photography; squash; sailing; chess; guitar playing; painting and drawing. Address: (h.) Glendeveron, 8 Deveron Terrace, Banff, AB4 1BB; T.-026 12 2624.

Clark, Guy Wyndham Nial Hamilton. Director, Greig, Middleton & Co. Ltd. (Stockbrokers), since 1976; b. 28.3.44, Wiltshire; m., Brighid Lovell; 2 s.; 1 d. Educ. Sunningdale School; Eton College. Commissioned Coldstream Guards, 1962-66; Stock Broker (John Stein & Co.), South Africa, 1966-72; Fund Manager, Murray Johnstone & Co., 1972-76; joined R.C. Greig, subsequently Greig Middleton & Co. Ltd., as Stockbroker and Director of company. JP, 1983;

DL, Renfrewshire, 1988; Honorary Secretary, Royal Caledonian Hunt, 1984. Recreations: shooting; fishing; racing (Steward, Ayr Racecourse). Address: (h.) Braeton House, Inverkip, Renfrewshire; T.-0475 520619.

Clark, Rev. John, FPhS. Minister, St. Blane's, Dunblane, 1980-88; b. 28.6.23, Kilmarnock; m., Mary Cameron Graham; 2 d. Educ. Kilmarnock Academy; Glasgow University; Trinity College, Glasgow. RAC, 1942-46; Assistant Minister, Riccarton Parish Church, Kilmarnock, 1948-49; Minister, St. Serf's Church, Dysart, 1949-55; first Minister, Drumry: St. Mary's Parish Church, Drumchapel, Glasgow, 1955-60; Minister, Kennoway Parish Church, 1960-80; Moderator, Kirkcaldy Presbytery, 1966-67; Moderator, Stirling Presbytery, 1984-85. Publication: New Ways to Worship (Contributor), 1980. Recreations: driving; swimming; painting; crosswords; listening to music. Address: (h.) 25 Buchan Drive, Dunblane, FK15 9HW.

Clark, Kenneth James, CBE, MA, LLB, JP. Chief Executive, Borders Regional Council, since 1974; b. 30.4.33, Perth; m., Marion; 3 s. Educ. Dundee High School; St. Andrews University. National Service, Queen's Own Cameron Highlanders, 1955-57; Legal and Administrative Assistant, Roxburgh County Council, 1962-63; Banff County Council: Legal and Administrative Assistant, 1963-64, Assistant County Clerk, 1964-65, Deputy County Clerk, 1965-66; Deputy County Clerk, Berwick County Council, 1966-71; County Clerk, Ross and Cromarty County Council, 1971-74. Member, Working Group for Scotland on Handling of Complaints against the Police, 1974; Member, Committee of Inquiry into Local Government in Scotland (The Stodart Committee), 1981. Address: (b.) Regional Headquarters, Newtown St. Boswells, Melrose, TD6 OSA; T.-0835 23301.

Clark, Leslie, MA, BSc, MEd. HM Chief Inspector of Schools, since 1980; b. 24.6.29, Newcastle-upon-Tyne; m., Anne; 2 d. Educ. Rutherford College for Boys, Newcastle; Kings College, Durham University. Teacher, Bo'ness Academy, 1951-55; Principal Teacher, Kelso High School, 1955-61; Lecturer, Jordanhill College of Education, 1961-65; HM Inspector of Schools, 1965-80. Recreations: walking; swimming; Spanish language. Address: (b.) Corunna House, 29 Cadogan Street, Glasgow, G2 7LP.

Clark, Robert John Whitten. Head, Fisheries Regimes Fishstock Management, Marketing and Trade Division, Department of Agriculture and Fisheries for Scotland, 1985-87; b. 29.9.32, Edinburgh; m., Christine Margaret Reid; 1 s.; 1 d. Educ. George Heriot's School, Edinburgh. Scottish Education Department: various appointments, 1949-69, including Private Secretary to Secretary of Department, 1960-61, Head, Teacher Training Branch, 1967-69, Head, Schools Branch, 1969-73, Head, Children's Hearings Branch, Social Work Services Group, 1973-75, Head, Children's Division, Social Work Services Group, 1975-76, Head, List D (Approved) Schools Division, Social Work Services Group, 1976-79; Head, Home Defence and Emergency Services Co-ordination Division, Scottish Home and Health Department, 1979-85. Former Captain and Past President, Edinburgh and District Civil Service Golfing Society; Captain, Scottish Education Department Golf Club, 1984-85; former Vice-Captain, Scottish Civil Service Golfing Society. Recreations: travel; golf; reading; gardening. Address: (h.) 39 Gordon Road, Edinburgh, EH12 6LZ; T.-031-334 4312.

Clark, Robert Phillip, SSC, NP. Solicitor; Senior Partner, Hendry and Fenton, since 1976; b. 20.4.20, Dundee; m., Helen Joan Forman; 3 s. Educ. Logie Secondary School, Dundee; University College, Dundee. Commenced legal training, 1937; War service, 1940-45: Royal Armoured Corps; Royal Military College, Sandhurst; commissioned 2nd Fife & Forfar Yeomanry; Regimental Signals Officer; wounded 1944; resumed legal training, 1947-50; qualified Solicitor, 1950; Court procurator, 1952-56; Honorary Sheriff of Tayside Central and Fife at Dundee, since 1977; former Dean, Faculty of Procurators and Solicitors in Dundee; former Vice-President, Scottish Law Agents Society; Clerk, Hammerman Incorporation of Dundee. Recreations: tennis and golf; hill-walking; photography. Address: (h.) Old Bank House, Alyth, Perthshire; (b.) 21 South Tay Street, Dundee; T.-Dundee 22785.

Clark, Robert William, MA (Cantab). Chief Executive, Nobel's Explosives Company Ltd., since 1986; Member, CBI Scottish Council, since 1986; b. 27.6.37, Middlesbrough; m., Moira Elizabeth; 1 s.; 1 d. Educ. Acklam Hall Secondary Grammar School, Middlesbrough; Trinity College, Cambridge University. Heavy Organic Chemicals Division (engineering and production management), ICI Ltd., 1960-71; London Business School, 1971-72; ICI Ltd.: senior management positions, Petrochemicals Division, 1972-78, appointed Director, Petrochemicals Division, 1978, Director, Petrochemicals and Plastics Division, 1981, Director, Nobel's Explosives Company Ltd., 1984. Board Member, Tees and Hartlepool Port Authority, 1981-84; Member, Advisory Committee on Major Hazards, 1981-84; Sloan Fellow, London Business School. Recreations: gardening; walking; travel. Address: (b.) Nobel House, Stevenston, KA20 3LN; T.-0294 87600.

Clark, Roland Arthur, MB, ChB, BSc (Hons), MRCP(UK), FRCP. Consultant Physician, Kings Cross/Ninewells Hospitals, Dundee, since 1977; Honorary Senior Lecturer in Medicine, Dundee University, since 1977 (Head, Department of Respiratory Diseases, since 1985); b. 8.9.40, Bexleyheath; m., Ann Havard; 2 s.; 4 d. Educ. Dartford Grammar School; Edinburgh University; Zagreb University; Ibadan University. House Officer, Senior House Officer, Research Fellow and Registrar, Departments of Respiratory Diseases, Cardiology, Neurology, Gastroenterology and General Medicine, Edinburgh University; Senior Registrar, Departments of Medicine/Respiratory Diseases, Sheffield University; Consultant Physician and Honorary Lecturer, Lodge Moor/Northern General Hospitals, Sheffield, and Department of Medicine, Sheffield University. Recreations: golf; fishing; gardening; photography; archaeology. Address: (h.) 4 Lawhead Road East, St. Andrews, Fife; T.-0334 77025.

Clark, Terence Gilbert, CEng, MIProdE, MMS, LHSM. Chief Administrator and Secretary, Tayside Health Board, since 1986; b. 19.3.39, Bristol; m., Jennifer Mary; 1 s.; 1 d. Educ. Katharine Lady Berkeley's Grammar School; Bristol College of Science and Technology. Design engineer, 1955-64; work study officer, East Anglian Regional Health Board, 1964-70; Chief Work Study Officer, then General Administrator, Tayside Health Board, 1970-86. Recreations: squash; vintage cars and motorcycles. Address: (b.) Vernonholme, Riverside Drive, Dundee; T.-Dundee 645151.

Clark, William, MA (Hons). Rector, Galashiels Academy, since 1985; b. 21.2.47, Kirkcaldy; m., Anne Kay Whitworth. Educ. Kirkcaldy High School; Buckhaven High School; Edinburgh University. HM Inspector of Taxes, 1971-73; Teacher, Craigmount High School, Edinburgh, 1973-77; Principal Teacher of Modern Studies, Tynecastle High School, Edinburgh, 1977-80; Assistant Headteacher, Boroughmuir High School, Edinburgh, 1980-83; Depute Principal, Wester Hailes Education Centre, Edinburgh, 1983-85. Publications: The Contemporary World: Conflict or Cooperation, 1979; The Great Powers, 1983. Recreations: rugby; soccer; photography; travel; folk music. Address: (b.) Galashiels Academy, Elm Row, Galashiels; T.-0896 4788.

Clark, William. Scottish Political Correspondent, Glasgow Herald, since 1981; b. 18.8.39, Motherwell; m., Anne F. Henry, AIMLT; 1 s.; 2 d. Educ. Dalziel High School. Indentured Motherwell Times, 1956-61; Deputy Night News Editor, Scottish Daily Mail, Glasgow, 1961-68; Scottish Industrial Correspondent, Glasgow Herald, 1976-81. Address: (b.) 195 Albion Street, Glasgow.

Clarke, Peter, CBE, BSc, PhD, LLD, CChem, FRSC. Chairman, Scottish Vocational Education Council, since 1985; Chairman, Aberdeen Enterprise Trust, since 1984; Chairman, Council for National Academic Awards Committee for Scotland, 1982-87; Member, Council for Professions Supplementary to Medicine, 1977-85; Director, Aberdeen Shipbuilders Ltd., since 1986, and Hall Russell Ltd., since 1986; Director, Creative Capital Nominees Ltd., since 1983; b. 18.3.22, Mansfield; m., Ethel; 2 s. Educ. Queen Elizabeth's Grammar School, Mansfield; University College, Nottingham. Principal, Robert Gordon's Institute of Technology, Aberdeen, 1970-85. President, Association of Principals of Colleges, 1980-81; Member, Science and Engineering Research Council, 1978-82; President, Aberdeen Welsh Society, 1979-80; President, Aberdeen Business and Professional Club, 1976-77. Recreations: gardening; swimming. Address: (h.) Dunaber, 12 Woodburn Place, Aberdeen, AB1 8JR; T.-0224 311132.

Clarke, Peter James, MA (Cantab). Secretary to the Forestry Commissioners, since 1976; b. 16.1.34, London; m., Roberta Anne Browne; 1 s.; 1 d. Educ. Enfield Grammar School; St. John's College, Cambridge. Executive Officer, War Office, 1952-62; Higher Executive Officer, 1962; Senior Executive Officer, Forestry Commission, 1967; Principal, 1972; Principal, Department of Energy, 1975. Recreations: gardening; hill-walking; sailing. Address: (h.) 5 Murrayfield Gardens, Edinburgh, EH12 6DG; T.-031-337 3145.

Clarke, Thomas, CBE, JP. MP (Labour), Monklands West, since 1983; Shadow Minister for UK Social Services; b. 10.1.41, Coatbridge. Educ. Columba High School, Coatbridge. Former Assistant Director, Scottish Council for Educational Technology; Provost of Monklands, 1975-82; Past President, Convention of Scottish Local Authorities; MP, Coatbridge and Airdrie, 1982-83; author, Disabled Persons (Services Consultation and Representation) Act, 1986. Recreations: films; walking; reading. Address: (h.) 27 Wood Street, Coatbridge, ML5 1LY.

Clayson, Christopher William, CBE (1974), OBE (1966), MB, ChB, DPH, MD, FRCPEdin, FRCPLond, Hon.FACP, Hon.FRACP, Hon.FRCP(Glas), Hon.FRCGP. Physician (retired); b. 11.9.03, Ilford. Educ. George Heriot's School, Edinburgh; Edinburgh University. Assistant Physician: Southfield Sanatorium, Edinburgh, 1931-44, City Hospital, Edinburgh, 1939-44; Lecturer, Edinburgh University, 1939-44; Medical Superintendent, Lochmaben Sanatorium, 1944-48; Consultant Physician, Dumfries and Galloway Hospitals, 1948-68; President, RCPEdin, 1966-70; Chairman, Departmental Committee on Scottish Licensing Law, 1971-73; Chairman, Scottish Council on Postgraduate Medical Education, 1970-74; William Cullen Prizeman, RCPEdin, 1978. Address: (h.) Cockiesknowe, Lochmaben, Lockerbie, DG11 1RL; T.-0387 810231.

Cleall, Charles, MA, BMus, ADCM, FRCO(CHM), GTCL, LRAM, HonTSC. Editor, Journal, Ernest George White Society, since 1983; Registered Teacher, The School of Sinus Tone, since 1985; Author; b. 1.6.27, Heston, Middlesex; m., Mary Turner; 2 d. Educ. Hampton School, Middlesex; Trinity College, London; University College of North Wales. Command Music Adviser, RN, Plymouth, 1946-48; Professor of Solo Singing and Voice Production, Trinity College of Music, London, 1949-52; Conductor, Glasgow Choral Union, 1952-54; BBC Music Assistant, Midland Region, 1954-55; Music Master, Glyn City School, Ewell, 1955-66; Conductor, Aldeburgh Festival Choir, 1957-60; Organist and Choirmaster, St. Paul's, Portman Square, W1, 1957-61; Guildford PC, 1961-65; Lecturer in Music, Froebel Institute, 1967-68; Adviser in Music, London Borough of Harrow, 1968-72; Warden, Education Section, ISM, 1972-72; Northern Divisional music specialist, HM Inspectorate of Schools in Scotland, 1972-87. Recreations: watching sea-birds; writing; reading; walking; local history. Address: (h.) 10 Carronhall, Stonehaven, Kincardineshire, AB3 2HF.

Cleland, John, BSc (Hons). Depute Principal, Kilmarnock College, since 1984; b. 3.11.35, Darvel; m., Janet G. Ross; 1 s.; 1 d. Educ. Darvel Junior Secondary School; Kilmarnock Academy; Glasgow University. Assistant Teacher of Mathematics, then Assistant Teacher of Science, Kilmarnock Academy; Assistant Teacher of Chemistry, then Senior Assistant Teacher, then Head of Department, Kilmarnock Technical College; Head, Department of Mathematics and Science, Kilmarnock College. FE Representative, SCEEB Chemistry Syllabus Panel, 1974-77; Joint Setter, SCE "H" Grade Chemistry, 1984; Member, Ayr Friends of the Hospice Committee. Recreations: bridge; golf. Address: (b.) Holehouse Road, Kilmarnock, KA3 7AT; T.-0563 23501.

Clements, Professor John Barklie, BSc, PhD, FRSE. Titular Professor in Virology, Glasgow University, since 1987 (Reader, 1984-87); b. 14.3.46, Belfast. Educ. Belfast Royal Academy; Queen's University, Belfast. Research Fellow, California Institute of Technology, 1971-73; joined Institute of Virology, Glasgow University, 1973; Cancer Research Campaign Travelling Fellow, Department of Biochemistry and Molecular Biology, Harvard University, 1983; Council Member, Society for General Microbiology, 1984. Recreations: walking; golf; music. Address: (b.) Department of Virology, Institute of Virology, Glasgow University, Glasgow; T.-041-330 4027.

Clemson, Gareth, BMus (Auckland), BMus (Edinburgh). Teacher of violin and viola, since 1975; Composer, since 1956; b. 1.10.33, Thames, New Zealand; m., Thora Clyne; 2 s.; 1 d. Educ. St. Peter's School, New Zealand; King's College, New Zealand; Auckland University. Music teaching, New Zealand, Edinburgh and West Lothian, 1960-65; String Teacher, West Lothian, 1975-85, Fife Region, since 1985; lessons in composition from Thomas Wilson, 1963-65; chamber works including Nexus I and II, Waters of Separation, The Singing Cat, Invocation; broadcasts, New Zealand and Scotland; Founder, Chameleon Ensemble; recent compositions, Imago for violin and viola, Cronos for strings, Stray Birds for voice and ensemble and Five What-Nots for guitar. Recreations: drawing and painting; photography; philately; cats. Address: (h.) Tillywhally Cottage, Milnathort, Kinross-shire, KY13 7RN; T.-Kinross 64297.

Clerk of Penicuik, Sir John Dutton, 10th Bt, CBE (1966), VRD, FRSE, JP. Lord Lieutenant of Midlothian, since 1972; b. 30.1.17; m.; 2 s.; 2 d. Educ. Stowe. Brigadier, Queen's Bodyguard for Scotland (Royal Company of Archers). Address: (h.) Penicuik House, Penicuik, Midlothian, EH26 9LA.

Clifford, Timothy Peter Plint, BA, AMA. Director, National Galleries of Scotland, since 1984; b. 26.1.46, England; m., Jane Olivia Paterson; 1 d. Educ. Sherborne; Perugia University; Courtauld Institute, London University. Manchester City Art Galleries: Assistant Keeper, Department of Paintings, 1968-72, Acting Keeper, 1972; Assistant Keeper (First Class): Department of Ceramics, Victoria and Albert Museum, London, 1972-76, Department of Prints and Drawings, British Museum, London, 1976-78; Director, Manchester City Art Galleries, 1978-84. Chairman, International Committee for Museums of Fine Art, 1980-83; Member, Museums and Galleries Commission, since 1983; Member, Executive Committee, Scottish Museums Council; Vice President, Turner Society, 1984; FRSA. Recreations: shooting; bird-watching; collecting butterflies and moths. Address: (b.) National Galleries of Scotland, The Mound, Edinburgh, EH2 2EL.

Clive, Eric McCredie, MA, LLB, LLM, SJD. Full-time Member, Scottish Law Commission, since 1981; b. 24.7.38, Stranraer; m., Kay McLeman; 1 s.; 3 d. Educ. Stranraer Academy; Stranraer High School; Edinburgh University. Department of Scots Law, Edinburgh University: Lecturer, 1962-69, Senior Lecturer, 1969-75, Reader, 1975-77, Professor, 1977-81. Publications: The Law of Husband and Wife in Scotland, 2nd edition, 1982; Scots Law for Journalists (Co-author), 5th edition, 1988. Recreations: gardening; bee-keeping; hill-walking; skiing; chess. Address: (h.) 14 York Road, Edinburgh, EH5 3EH; T.-031-552 2875.

Clunie, Henry, DipTech, JP. Honorary Sheriff, since 1967; b. 30.6.07, Leith; m., Harriot Shearer Wilson; 1 s.; 1 d. Educ. Trinity Academy, Leith; Moray House College of Education. Deputy Rector, Dornoch Academy, 1968-72; Town Councillor, Royal Burgh of Dornoch, 1958-74 (Provost, 1965-74); created Freeman of the Burgh, 1973; appointed Commissioner of Income Tax; Member, Sutherland District Council, 1974-78. Recreations: music; amateur drama. Address: (h.) 29 Macdonald Road, Dornoch, Sutherland; T.-0862 810201.

Clunies-Ross, Professor Anthony Ian, BA (Melbourne), MA (Cantab). Professor in Economics, Strathclyde University, since 1978; b. 9.3.32, Sydney, New South Wales; m., Morag McVey; 2 s.; 2 d. Educ. Knox Grammar School, Sydney; Scotch College, Melbourne; Melbourne University; Pembroke College, Cambridge. Tutor in History, Melbourne University, 1958-59; Lecturer, then Senior Lecturer in Economics, Monash University, 1961-67; Senior Lecturer, then Professor in Economics, University of Papua New Guinea, 1967-74; Temporary Lecturer, then Senior Lecturer in Economics, Strathclyde University, 1975-78. Chairman, Australian Student Christian Movement, 1963-66; Member, St. Andrews Diocesan Synod, Scottish Episcopal Church, 1984-86. Publications: One Per Cent: The Case for Greater Australian Foreign Aid, 1963 (Co-author); Australia and Nuclear Weapons (Co-author), 1966; Alternative Strategies for Papua New Guinea, (Co-author), 1973; The Taxation of Mineral Rent (Co-author), 1983; Migrants from Fifty Villages, 1984. Recreations: swimming; gardening. Address: (h.) Railway Cottage, Kinbuck, Dunblane, Perthshire, FK15 ONL; T.-Dunblane 822684.

Clyde, Hon. Lord (James John Clyde), QC (Scot), BA (Oxon), LLB. Senator of the College of Justice, since 1985; b. 29.1.32, Edinburgh; m., Ann Clunie Hoblyn; 2 s. Educ. Edinburgh Academy; Corpus Christi College, Oxford; Edinburgh University. Called to Scottish Bar, 1959; QC, 1971; Advocate Depute, 1973-74; Chancellor to Bishop of Argyll and the Isles, 1972-85; a Judge of the Courts of Appeal of Jersey and Guernsey, 1979-85; Chairman, Medical Appeal Tribunal, 1974-85; Chairman, Committee of Investigation for Scotland on Agricultural Marketing, 1984-85; Chairman, Scottish Valuation Advisory Council, since 1987 (Member, since 1972); Member, UK Delegation to CCBE, 1978-84 (Leader, 1981-84). Director, Edinburgh Academy, since 1979; Trustee and Manager, St. Mary's Music School, since 1976; Trustee, National Library of Scotland, since 1978. Recreations: music; gardening. Address: (h.) 9 Heriot Row, Edinburgh, EH3 6HU; T.-031-556 7114.

Clydesmuir, Baron (Ronald John Bilsland Colville), KT (1972), CB (1965), MBE (1944), TD. Lord Lieutenant, Lanarkshire, since 1963; Captain, Queen's Bodyguard for Scotland (Royal Company of Archers); b. 21.5.17; m.; 2 s.; 2 d. Educ. Charterhouse; Trinity College, Cambridge. Served in The Cameronians (Scottish Rifles), 1939-45; commanded 6/7th Bn., The Cameronians, TA, 1953-56; Director, Colvilles Ltd., 1958-70; Governor, British Linen Bank, 1966-71; Governor, Bank of Scotland, 1972-81; Director, Scottish Provident Institution, 1954-88; Director, Barclays Bank, 1972-82; Chairman, North Sea Assets Ltd., 1972-88; Scottish Council (Development and Industry): Chairman, Executive Committee, 1966-78, President, 1978-87; President, Scottish Council of Physical Recreation, 1964-72; Hon. LLD, Strathclyde, 1968; Hon. DSc, Heriot-Watt, 1971. Address: (h.) Langlees House, Biggar, Lanarkshire.

Clyne, Rev. Douglas Roy, BD. Minister, Old Parish Church, Fraserburgh, since 1973; b. 9.11.41, Inverness; m., Annette Taylor; 1 s. Educ. Inverness High School; Aberdeen University. Accountancy (Inverness County Council and Highland Printers Ltd.), 1956-68; studied for the ministry, 1968-72; Assistant Minister, Mastrick Parish Church, Aberdeen, 1972-73. Address: Old Parish Church Manse, 97 Saltoun Place, Fraserburgh, AB4 5RY; T.-0346 28536.

Coates, Leon, MA (Cantab), LRAM, ARCO. Lecturer in Music, Edinburgh University, since 1965; b. 15.6.37, Wolverhampton; m., Heather Patricia Johnston. Educ. Derby School; St. John's College, Cambridge. Composer, pianist, organist, St. Andrew's and St. George's Church, Edinburgh, since 1981; Conductor: Edinburgh Chamber Orchestra, 1965-75, Edinburgh Symphony Orchestra, 1973-85; Conductor, Edinburgh Studio Orchestra, since 1986; Harpsichordist, Scottish Baroque Ensemble, 1970-77; broadcasts as pianist and harpsichordist; compositions broadcast on Radio 3, Radio 4 Scotland and Radio Eireann. Recreation: hill-walking. Address: (h.) 31 Scotland Street, Edinburgh, EH3; T.-031-556 2240.

Coats, Sir William David, Kt, DL, HonLLD (Strathclyde), 1977. Chairman, Coats Patons PLC, 1981-86; Deputy Chairman, Clydesdale Bank PLC, since 1985; b. 25.7.24, Glasgow; m., The Hon. Elizabeth L.G. MacAndrew; 2 s.; 1 d. Educ. Eton College. Joined J. & P. Coats Ltd., 1948, as management trainee; held various appointments and became a Director, 1957; appointed Director, Coats Patons PLC, on its formation, 1960; Deputy Chairman, 1979. Chairman, Glasgow Coordinating Committee, Cancer Research Campaign. Recreations: golf; shooting. Address: (h.) The Cottage, Symington, Ayrshire, KA1 5QG.

Cobbe, Professor Stuart Malcolm, MA, MD, FRCP. Professor of Medical Cardiology, Glasgow University, since 1985; b. 2.5.48, Watford; m., Patricia Frances; 3 d. Educ. Royal Grammar School, Guildford; Cambridge University. Training in medicine, Cambridge and St. Thomas Hospital, London; qualified, 1972; specialist training in cardiology, National Heart Hospital, London, and John Radcliffe Hospital, Oxford; research work, University of Heidelberg, 1981; Consultant Cardiologist and Senior Lecturer, Oxford, 1982-85. Recreation: walking. Address: (b.) Department of Medical Cardiology, Queen Elizabeth Building, Royal Infirmary, Glasgow, G3; T.-041-552 3535, Ext. 5388.

Cochran, Hugh Douglas, BA (Oxon), LLB. Advocate in Aberdeen, since 1958; b. 26.4.32, Aberdeen; m., Sarah Beverly Sissons; 4 s.; 2 d. Educ. Loretto; Trinity College, Oxford; Edinburgh University. Partner: Cochran & Macpherson, 1958-80, Adam, Cochran & Co., since 1980. Secretary: Blairmore School Educational Trust Ltd., since 1959, Aberdeen Association for the Prevention of Cruelty to Animals, since 1972; Member, Grampian Health Board, since 1983; Registrar, Diocese of Aberdeen and Orkney, since 1984. Recreations: sailing; collecting stamps. Address: 6 Bon Accord Square, Aberdeen, AB9 1XU; T.-Aberdeen 588913.

Cochran, Matt. Director (Scotland), Advisory, Conciliation and Arbitration Service, since 1981; b. 8.3.29, Glasgow; m., Mary Kathleen; 2 s. Department of Employment, Glasgow, Edinburgh, London; Foreign and Commonwealth Office, USA, Mexico, Central America; Manpower Services Commission, Edinburgh; ACAS, Glasgow. Address: (b.) Advisory, Conciliation and Arbitration Service, 123/157 Bothwell Street, Glasgow; T.-041-204 2677.

Cochran, William, MB, ChB, FRCSEdin, FRCSGlas. Consultant Paediatric and Neonatal Surgeon and Consultant in charge Accident and Emergency Department, Royal Hospital for Sick Children, Glasgow, since 1977; Honorary Clinical Lecturer, Glasgow University, since 1978; b. 4.5.27, Sandhead, Wigtownshire; m., Pamela White; 2 s.; 1 d. Educ. Allan Glen's School, Glasgow; Fraserburgh Academy; Aberdeen University. Demonstrator, Department of Anatomy, Aberdeen University; Paediatric Surgical Registrar, Edinburgh Northern Group Hospitals; Senior Paediatric Surgical Registrar, Royal Hospital for Sick Children, Belfast; Consultant Paediatric Surgeon, Belfast Hospitals and Honorary Clinical Lecturer, Queen's University, Belfast. Member, Special Advisory Committee (A/E) to Committee for Higher Surgical Training. Address: (h.) 4 Greenwood Drive, Bearsden, Dunbartonshire, G61 2HA; T.-041-943 0579.

Cochran, Professor William, BSc, PhD, MA, FRS, FRSE. Professor of Natural Philosophy, Edinburgh University, 1975-87; b. 30.7.22, Newton Mearns; m., Ingegerd Wall; 1 s.; 2 d. Educ. Boroughmuir School, Edinburgh; Edinburgh University; Cambridge University. Demonstrator/Lecturer/Reader, Cambridge University, 1948-64; Fellow, Trinity Hall, Cambridge, 1953-64; Professor of Physics, Edinburgh University, 1964-75; Dean, Faculty of Science, 1978-81; University Vice Principal, 1984-87; Honorary Fellow, Trinity Hall, Cambridge, since 1983; awards from Institute of Physics, 1966, Royal Society, 1978,

Franklin Institute, 1985. Recreations: family history; Scots verse. Address: (h.) 71 Clermiston Road, Edinburgh; T.-031-334 6612.

Cochrane, Alexander Kitchener, DL. Retired Company Chairman; b. 6.6.16, Edinburgh; m., Ethel Scott Seatter; 3 s. Educ. Morrison's Academy. Commissioned TA RE, 1937; served 1939-45; attached Indian Army, 1940-45, and on deputation to Government of India; joined family business and retired as Chairman of group, Cochrane Vehicle Holdings Ltd. Recreations: fishing; shooting; gardening. Address: Mount Chasse, Broomieknowe, Lasswade, EH18 1LN; T.-031 663 7906.

Cochrane, Derek John, BSc (Hons), MEng (Dist), MICE, MIWEM. Area Manager, Scotland, British British Waterways Board, since 1979; b. 5.1.51, Edinburgh; m., Elspeth Tait; 2 d. Educ. Portobello Secondary School; Heriot-Watt University; Glasgow University. British Gas, 1969-72; James Williamson & Partners, Consulting Engineers, 1972-73; Trent River Authority, later Severn Trent Water Authority, 1973-79. Honorary Press Officer, West of Scotland Association, Institution of Civil Engineers. Recreations: golf; walking. Address: (h.) 8 Crossburn Avenue, Milngavie, Glasgow; T.-041-956 1482.

Cockburn, Professor Forrester, MD, FRCPGlas, FRCPEdin, DCH. Samson Gemmell Professor of Child Health, Glasgow University, since 1977; b. 13.10.34, Edinburgh; m., Alison Fisher Grieve; 2 s. Educ. Leith Academy; Edinburgh University. Early medical training, Edinburgh Royal Infirmary, Royal Hospital for Sick Children, Edinburgh, and Simpson Memorial Maternity Pavilion, Edinburgh; Research Fellow in Paediatric Metabolic Disease, Boston University; Visiting Professor, San Juan University, Puerto Rico; Nuffield Fellow, Institute for Medical Research, Oxford University; Wellcome Senior Research Fellow, then Senior Lecturer, Department of Child Life and Health, Edinburgh University. Publications: a number of textbooks on paediatric medicine, neonatal medicine, nutrition and metabolic diseases. Recreation: sailing. Address: (b.) University Department of Child Health, Royal Hospital for Sick Children, Yorkhill, Glasgow, G3 8SJ; T.-041-339 8888.

Cockburn, James Masson Thomson, BSc (Hons), CEng, FICE, FIWEM, FBIM. Director of Water Services, Grampian Regional Council, since 1988; b. 22.1.47, Aberdeen; m., Avril; 2 s. Educ. Robert Gordon's College; Dundee University. Assistant Engineer, East of Scotland Water Board, 1969-75; Assistant Divisional Manager (Dundee), Department of Water Services, Tayside Regional Council, 1975-76; Assistant Director, Department of Water and Sewerage, Dumfries and Galloway Regional Council, 1976-79; Depute Director, Department of Water Services, Grampian Regional Council, 1979-88. Past President, Scottish Section, Institution of Water Engineers and Scientists; Member of Council, Institution of Water and Environmental Management, 1987-88. Recreations: hill-walking; sailing; skiing; curling; Rotary. Address: (b.) Grampian Regional Council, Woodhill House, Westburn Road, Aberdeen, AB9 2LU; T.-0224 682222, Ext. 2351.

Cockburn, John Shearer, MB, ChB, ChM, FRCSEdin. Consultant Cardiothoracic Surgeon, Aberdeen Royal Infirmary, since 1978; Clinical Senior Lecturer in Cardiothoracic Surgery, Aberdeen University, since 1978; b. 25.8.42, Turriff; m., Ethel Mary Mitchell Duncan; 1 s.; 1 d. Educ. Gordon Schools, Huntly; Keith Grammar School; Aberdeen University. Pre-registration Resident Medical Officer, then Senior House Officer in Thoracic Surgery, Aberdeen Royal Infirmary, 1966-68; Senior House Officer in General Surgery, Llandough Hospital, Cardiff, 1968-69; Registrar in Surgery, Aberdeen Royal Infirmary, 1969-73, and Research Fellow, Uppsala, Sweden, 1971-72; Registrar in Cardiac Surgery, Glasgow Royal Infirmary, 1973-74; Senior Registrar in Cardiothoracic Surgery, London and Southampton, 1974-77. Recreations: music (clarinet playing); squash; snooker; soccer; rugby. Address: (h.) Castleton House, 15 The Chanonry, Old Aberdeen, AB2 1RP; T.-Aberdeen 493957.

Cocker, Douglas, DA, ARSA. Sculptor, since 1968; Lecturer in Sculpture, Grays School of Art, Aberdeen, since 1982; b. 23.3.45, Alyth, Perthshire; m., Elizabeth Filshie; 2 s.; 1 d. Educ. Blairgowrie High School; Duncan of Jordanstone College of Art, Dundee. SED Travelling Scholar, Italy and Greece, 1966; RSA Andrew Carnegie Travelling Scholar, 1967; RSA Benno Schotz Award, 1967; Greenshields Foundation (Montreal) Fellowship, 1968-69 (studies in New York and Greece); RSA Latimer Award, 1970; Arts Council of GB Award, 1977; East Midlands Arts Award, 1979; Visiting Artist: Newcastle Polytechnic, Duncan of Jordanstone College of Art, Edinburgh College of Art and Tyler University, Philadelphia. Fourteen one-man exhibitions, 1969-84; numerous group and mixed exhibitions, 1970-85; various commissions. Recreations: reading; travel; sport. Address: (h.) Craigveigh, Gordon Crescent, Aboyne, Aberdeenshire; T.-Aboyne 2011.

Coggins, Professor John Richard, MA, PhD, FRSE. Professor of Biochemistry, Glasgow University, since 1986; b. 15.1.44, Bristol; m., Dr. Lesley F. Watson; 1 s.; 1 d. Educ. Bristol Grammar School; Queen's College, Oxford; Ottawa University. Post-doctoral Fellow: Biology Department, Brookhaven National Laboratory, New York, 1970-72, Biochemistry Department, Cambridge University, 1972-74; Lecturer, Biochemistry Department, Glasgow University, 1974-78, Senior Lecturer, 1978-86. Chairman, Molecular Enzymology Group, Biochemical Society, 1982-85; Chairman, Biophysics and Biochemistry Committee, SERC, 1985-88. Recreations: sailing; travelling. Address: (b.) Department of Biochemistry, Glasgow University, Glasgow, G12 8QQ; T.-041-339 8855, Ext. 5267.

Cohen, Cyril, OBE (1986), FRCPEdin, FRCPGlas. Consultant Physician in Geriatric Medicine, since 1962; Honorary Senior Lecturer, Dundee University, since 1962; Member, Chief Scientist's Committee for Research on Equipment for the Disabled and the Health Service Research Committee; former Director, Scottish Hospital Advisory Service; b. 2.11.25, Manchester; m., Sarah E. Nixon; 2 s. Educ. Manchester Central

High School; Victoria University, Manchester. Embarked on career in geriatric medicine, 1952. Past Member/Chairman, Angus District and Tayside Area Medical Committees; Secretary/Chairman, Tayside Area Hospital Medical Services Committee; Member, Scottish and UK Central Committee, Hospital Medical Services, and Chairman, Geriatric Medicine Sub-committee; Past Chairman, Scottish Branch, British Geriatric Society (former Council Member); Member, Panel on Nutrition of the Elderly, COMA; Chairman, Advisory Committee on the Elderly, Scottish Health Education Group. Honorary Vice-President, Dundee and District Branch, British Diabetic Association; Life Member, Manchester Medical Society; Past President, Montrose Burns Club; Member, Forfar School Council; Chairman, Radio North Angus (Hospital Radio); Secretary, Aberlemno Community Council. Recreations: photography; short walks; being at home. Address: (h.) Mansefield, Aberlemno, Forfar, DD8 3PD; T.-030-783 259.

Cohen, George Cormack, MA, LLB. Advocate; b. 16.12.09, Glasgow; m., Elizabeth Wallace; 1 s.; 1 d. Educ. Kelvinside Academy, Glasgow; Glasgow University. Admitted to Faculty of Advocates, 1935; Sheriff of Caithness at Wick, 1944-51; Sheriff of Ayrshire at Kilmarnock, 1951-55; Sheriff of Lothians and Peebles at Edinburgh, 1955-66. Recreations: gardening; travel. Address: (h.) 37B Lauder Road, Edinburgh, EH9 1UE; T.-031-668 1689.

Cohen, Professor Philip, BSc, PhD, FRS, FRSE. Royal Society Research Professor, Dundee University, since 1984; b. 22.7.45, London; m., Patricia Townsend Wade; 1 s.; 1 d. Educ. Hendon County Grammar School; University College, London. Science Research Council/NATO postdoctoral Fellow, Department of Biochemistry, University of Washington, 1969-71; Dundee University: Lecturer in Biochemistry, 1971-78, Reader in Biochemistry, 1978-81, Professor of Enzymology, 1981-84. Federation of European Biochemical Societies Anniversary Prize, 1977; Colworth Medal, British Biochemical Society, 1978. Publication: Control of Enzyme Activity, 1976. Recreations: chess; golf; natural history. Address: (h.) Inverbay, Invergowrie, Dundee, DD2 5DG; T.-0382 562328.

Coke, Professor Simon, MA (Oxon). Professor of International Business, Edinburgh University, since 1972; b. 27.6.32, Bicester, Oxfordshire; m., Diana Margaret Evison; 1 s.; 2 d. Educ. Ridley College, Ontario; Pembroke College, Oxford. Marketing Executive, Beecham Overseas, 1958-64; General Manager, Japan, etc., Johnson & Johnson, 1964-68; Head, Department of Business Studies, Edinburgh University, 1984; Dean, Scottish Business School, 1981-83; Director: Japan Asset Trust, Jigtal Ltd., Lastolite Ltd. Address: (b.) Department of Business Studies, Edinburgh University, 50 George Square, Edinburgh, EH8 9JY; T.-031-667 1011.

Cole, Professor Alfred John, BSc, MSc, PhD, FBCS. Professor of Computational Science, St. Andrews University, since 1969; b. 11.4.25, London; m., Christina Brotherson Carnie; 1 s. Educ. Preston Manor County School; University College, London. Lecturer: Heriot-Watt College, Edinburgh, 1952-55, Queen's College, Dundee, 1955-61; Senior Lecturer and Director, Computing Laboratory, Leicester University, 1961-65; Reader and Director, Computing Laboratory, St. Andrews University, 1965-69 (Head, Department of Computational Science). Publication: Macroprocessors, 1976. Recreations: beer and winemaking; concertina playing; East Fife FC supporter. Address: (h.) Inisheer, Barnyards, Kilconquhar, Fife; T.-033 334 378.

Cole-Hamilton, Arthur Richard, BA, CA, FIB(Scot). Chief Executive, Clydesdale Bank PLC, since 1987; b. 8.5.35, Kilwinning; m., Prudence Ann; 1 s.; 2 d. Educ. Ardrossan Academy; Loretto School; Cambridge University. Partner, Brechin Cole-Hamilton & Co., CA, 1962-67; various appointments, Clydesdale Bank, 1967-82; appointed Chief General Manager, 1982, Director, 1984. Former Council Member, Institute of Chartered Accountants of Scotland (Chairman, Finance and General Purposes Committee, 1984); Chairman, Committee of Scottish Clearing Bankers, since 1985; Director, Glasgow Chamber of Commerce, since 1985; Trustee, National Galleries of Scotland, since 1986. Recreation: golf. Address: (b.) 30 St. Vincent Place, Glasgow; T.-041-248 7070.

Cole-Hamilton, Professor David John, BSc, PhD, FRSC, FRSE. Irvine Professor of Chemistry, St. Andrews University, since 1985; b. 22.5.48, Bovey Tracey; m., Elizabeth Ann Brown; 2 s.; 2 d. Educ. Haileybury and ISC; Hertford; Edinburgh University. Research Assistant, Temporary Lecturer, Imperial College, 1974-78; Lecturer, Senior Lecturer, Liverpool University, 1978-85. Sir Edward Frankland Fellow, Royal Society of Chemistry, 1984-85; Corday Morgan Medallist, 1983. Address: (b.) Department of Chemistry, The Purdie Building, St. Andrews, Fife, KY16 9ST; T.-0334 76161.

Coleman, Eric Norman, MD, FRCPEdin, FRCPGlas. Consultant Physician and Physician-in-Charge, Department of Cardiology, Royal Hospital for Sick Children, Glasgow, since 1961; Honorary Clinical Lecturer in Child Health, Glasgow University, since 1964; b. 22.6.25, Ayr. Educ. Bearsden Academy; Glasgow University. Captain, RAMC, 1949-51; Senior Registrar, Royal Hospital for Sick Children, Glasgow, 1957-58; Lecturer in Child Health, Glasgow University, 1958-61. Honorary Secretary, Scottish Paediatric Society, 1964-80; President, Society of Cardiological Technicians, 1975-78; Regional Postgraduate Adviser in paediatrics; Chairman of Examiners for the Diploma in Child Health, Glasgow; Medical Adviser, Society of Cardiological Technicians. Recreations: music; theology. Address: (b.) Royal Hospital for Sick Children, Glasgow, G3 8SJ; T.-041-339 8888, Ext. 591.

Colin, Professor Andrew John Theodore, MA, FIEE, FBCS, CEng. Professor of Computer Science, Strathclyde University, since 1970; b. 22.6.36, London; m., Veronica Parsons; 2 s.; 2 d. Educ. Gordonstoun; Christ Church, Oxford; Birkbeck College, London. Assistant Lecturer in Computer Science, Birkbeck College, 1958-60; Lecturer, Institute of Computer Science, London

University, 1960-65; Lecturer and Reader in Computer Systems, Lancaster University, 1965-70. Recreations: hill-walking; choral singing. Address: (h.) 21 Queensborough Gardens, Glasgow, G12 9PP; T.-041-339 8297.

Collee, Professor John Gerald, MD, FRCPath, FRCPEdin. Professor and Head, Department of Bacteriology, Edinburgh University, since 1979; Chief Bacteriologist, Edinburgh Royal Infirmary, since 1979; b. 10.5.29, Bo'ness; m., Isobel McNay Galbraith; 2 s.; 1 d. Educ. Bo'ness Academy; Edinburgh Academy; Edinburgh University. House Physician, 1951-52; Army medical service, 1952-54 (Captain, RAMC); General Practitioner, 1954-55; Lecturer in Bacteriology, Edinburgh, 1955-63; WHO Visiting Professor of Bacteriology, Baroda, India, 1963-64; Edinburgh University: Senior Lecturer and Honorary Consultant Bacteriologist, 1964-70, Reader in Bacteriology, 1970-74, Personal Professor of Bacteriology, 1974-79; Editor and Past Chairman, Journal of Medical Microbiology. Recreations: woodwork; mechanics; fishing; music; painting. Address: (b.) Department of Bacteriology, University Medical School, Teviot Place, Edinburgh, EH8 9AG; T.-031-667 1011, Ext. 2207.

Collie, George Francis, CBE (Civil), MBE (Military), JP, BL. Honorary Sheriff, Grampian Region, at Aberdeen, since 1974; retired Advocate in Aberdeen and Notary Public; b. 1.4.09, Aberdeen; m., Margery Constance Fullarton Wishart; 2 s. Educ. Aberdeen Grammar School; Aberdeen University. Partner, then Senior Partner, James & George Collie, Advocates in Aberdeen; Deputy Chairman, then Chairman, Board of Management for Aberdeen Special Hospitals, 1952-68. Honorary Colonel, 51st Highland Division, RASC (TA) and later Honorary Colonel, 153 Highland Regiment, RCT (V), 1964-72. Address: (h.) Morkeu, Cults, Aberdeen, AB1 9PT; T.-0224 867636.

Collie, Ian, MA, MEd, MBIM, FSA Scot. Director of Education, Central Regional Council, since 1975; b. 20.7.33, Grantown-on-Spey; m., Helen; 1 s.; 1 d. Educ. Kingussie Secondary School; Aberdeen University; Glasgow University. Army, 1956-58; teacher, Renfrewshire, 1958-64; lecturer, Glasgow, 1964-66; Junior Assistant Director of Education, then Senior Assistant Director, Stirlingshire, 1966-69; Depute Director, Dunbartonshire, 1969-73; Sole Depute, Stirlingshire, 1973-75. Chairman, Scottish Committee on Open Learning. Publication: Selections from Modern Writings (Editor). Recreations: hill-walking; squash. Address: (b.) Viewforth, Stirling; T.-Stirling 73111, Ext. 503.

Collins, Kenneth Darlingston, BSc (Hons), MSc. Member (Labour), European Parliament, since 1979; b. 12.8.39, Hamilton; m., Georgina Frances Pollard; 1 s.; 1 d. Educ. St. John's Grammar School; Hamilton Academy; Glasgow University; Strathclyde University. Steelworks apprentice, 1956-59; University, 1960-65; Planning Officer, 1965-66; WEA Tutor, 1966-67; Lecturer: Glasgow College of Building, 1967-69, Paisley College of Technology, 1969-79; Member: East Kilbride Town and District Council, 1973-79, Lanark County Council, 1973-75, East Kilbride Development Corporation, 1976-79; Chairman, NE Glasgow Children's Panel, 1974-76; European Parliament: Deputy Leader, Labour Group, 1979-84, Chairman, Environment Committee, 1979-84 (Vice-Chairman, 1984-87), Socialist Spokesman on Environment, Public Health and Consumer Protection, since 1987. Honorary Vice-President: International Federation on Environmental Health, Institute of Trading Standards Administration, Royal Environmental Health Institute of Scotland; Honorary Associate, British Veterinary Association. Recreations: music; boxer dogs; cycling. Address: (b.) 11 Stuarton Park, East Kilbride, G74 4LA; T.-03552 37282.

Collins, Kenneth E., PhD, MRCGP. Vice-Chairman, Glasgow Jewish Board of Education, since 1985; Honorary Secretary, Glasgow Jewish Representative Council, since 1984; b. 23.12.47, Glasgow; m., Irene Taylor; 1 s.; 3 d. Educ. High School of Glasgow; Glasgow University. General medical practitioner in Glasgow, since 1976; Medical Officer, Newark Lodge, Glasgow, since 1978; Research Associate, Wellcome Unit for the History of Medicine, Glasgow University. Publications: Aspects of Scottish Jewry, 1987; Go and Learn: International Story of the Jews and Medicine in Scotland, 1988. Address: (b.) c/o Glasgow Jewish Board of Education, Calderwood Road, Glasgow, G43.

Collins, William John Neilson, BDS, MSc, FDSRCPS, FETC. Dental Surgeon; Director, School of Dental Hygiene, Glasgow Dental Hospital, since 1979; Honorary Lecturer, Glasgow University, since 1980; specialist dental practice (periodontics), since 1983; b. 25.3.40, Cowdenbeath; m., Vanda; 1 s.; 2 d. Educ. St. Columba's High School, Cowdenbeath; St. Andrews University; London University; Glasgow College of Physicians and Surgeons. Army Officer, RADC, 1963-79 (retired with rank of Lt. Col.). Member, Council, National Examining Board for Dental Surgery Assistants, since 1980 (Chairman, 1983-87); TA Officer (Lt. Col.), since 1979; Chairman, Children's Panel Advisory Committee, West Lothian, since 1986; Secretary, Soldiers, Sailors, Airmen Families Association (West Lothian), since 1985. Publications: Self Assessment Book for Dental Hygienists; Guide to Periodontics (Co-author); Handbook for Dental Hygienists, 2nd edition (Co-author). Recreations: Rotary Club; Catenian Association; golf. Address: (h.) Brucefield, Marjoribanks Street, Bathgate, West Lothian, EH48 1AH; T.-0506 632658.

Colquhoun of Luss, Captain Sir Ivar (Iain), 8th Bt, JP, DL. Honorary Sheriff; Chief of the Clan; b. 4.1.16; m.; 1 s.; 1 d.; 1 s. (deceased). Educ. Eton. Address: (h.) Camstraddan, Luss, Dunbartonshire.

Colraine, James, MA (Hons), FSA Scot. Rector, Dumbarton Academy, since 1970; b. 4.12.30, Clydebank; m., Olive McLean; 1 d. Educ. Dumbarton Academy; Glasgow University; Jordanhill College of Education. Army (National Service), 1954-56; Assistant in Classics, Jordanhill College School, 1957-61; Principal Teacher of Classics: Broxburn Academy, 1961-64, Cumbernauld High School, 1964-68; Depute Rector, Clydebank High School, 1968-70. Elder, New Kilpatrick Parish

Church, Bearsden. Recreations: golf; bowls; walking; music; reading; snooker. Address: (b.) Dumbarton Academy, Dumbarton, G82; T.-Dumbarton 63373.

Colvin, David. Chief Social Work Adviser, Scottish Office, since 1980; b. 31.1.31, Glasgow; m., Elma Findlay; 2 s.; 3 d. Educ. Whitehill School, Glasgow; Glasgow University; Edinburgh University. Probation Officer, Glasgow, 1955-60; Psychiatric Social Worker, Scottish Prison and Borstal Service, Scottish Home and Health Department, 1960-61; Senior Psychiatric Social Worker, Crichton Royal Hospital, Child Psychiatric Unit, 1961-65; Director, Family Casework Unit, Paisley, 1965-66; Welfare Officer, SHHD, 1966-68; joined SED as Social Work Adviser, 1968. Senior Associate Research Fellow, Brunel University, 1978; Honorary Adviser, British Red Cross, since 1982. Recreations: collector; swimming; climbing; golf; gardens; social affairs. Address: (h.) 13 Eton Terrace, Edinburgh, EH4 1QD; T.-031-343 3870.

Compton, John Cole, BSc (Agric) (Hons). Member, Advisory Committee for Scotland, Nature Conservancy Council, since 1981; Council Member, Scottish Wildlife Trust, since 1982; Member, Executive Committee, National Trust for Scotland, since 1987; Member, Scottish Agricultural Research and Development Advisory Council, since 1987; Member, Tay River Purification Board, since 1964; b. 1.1.23, Chippenham; m., Elizabeth Beatrice Cox; 2 d. Educ. Blundell's; Edinburgh University. Commissioned Royal Engineers, War service, 1941-45; mixed farming in Angus since 1949; former NFU Branch Chairman; non-party Angus County Councillor, 1968-75; Past Chairman, Scottish Polo Association. Recreations: riding; sailing; wildlife and countryside matters at home and overseas; foreign travel. Address: (h.) Ward of Turin House, Forfar, DD8 2TF; T.-030 783 253.

Condliffe, John, BA (Oxon), MPhil. Director, Finance and Information, Scottish Development Agency, since 1987 (Director, North East, 1984-87); b. 17.9.46, Portsmouth. Educ. Portsmouth Grammar School; Magdalen College, Oxford; University College, London. Corporate planning, Greater London Council; Industrial Development Executive, London Docklands Development Team; Senior Lecturer in Economics, Polytechnic of Central London; Head of Area Programmes, Scottish Development Agency. Recreations: music; visual arts. Address: (b.) Scottish Development Agency, 120 Bothwell Street, Glasgow; T.-041-248 2700.

Conn, Stewart. Poet and Playwright; Head, Radio Drama Department, BBC Scotland; b. 1936. Author of numerous stage plays, including Breakdown, Glasgow Citizens', 1961; I Didn't Always Live Here, Citizens', 1967; The Burning, Royal Lyceum, Edinburgh, 1971; Thistlewood, Traverse, Edinburgh, 1975; Count Your Blessings, Pitlochry Festival Theatre, 1975; poetry including An Ear to the Ground (Poetry Book Society Choice) and Under the Ice (SAC Book Award); Literary Advisor, Royal Lyceum Theatre, 1973-75; former Member, Drama Panel, Scottish Arts Council.

Connarty, Michael, BA, DipEd, DCE, JP. Member, Stirling District Council, since 1977 (Council Leader, since 1980); Teacher of learning impaired children, since 1975; b. 3.9.47, Coatbridge; m., Margaret Doran; 1 s.; 1 d. Educ. St. Patrick's High School, Coatbridge; Stirling University; Jordanhill College of Education; Glasgow University. Member, Scottish Executive, Labour Party; Chair, Labour Party Scottish Local Government Committee; Member, Convention of Scottish Local Authorities; Vice-Chair, Socialist Educational Association, 1983-85; Council Member, Educational Institute of Scotland, 1984-85; Founding Secretary, Labour Coordinating Committee (Scotland). Address: (h.) 25 Princes Street, Stirling, FK8 1HQ.

Connelly, David, MA (Oxon), FSAScot. Director, Historic Buildings and Monuments, Scottish Office, since 1987; b. 23.2.30, Halifax; m., Audrey Grace Salter; 1 s.; 1 d. Educ. Heath Grammar School, Halifax; Queen's College, Oxford. Colonial Administrative Service, Tanganyika, 1954-62; Assistant Secretary, St. Andrews University, 1962-63; Principal, Commonwealth Relations Office, 1963-64; First Secretary, British High Commission, New Delhi, 1964-66; Principal, Scottish Office, 1966-73; Assistant Secretary, 1973-87. Recreations: opera; literature; history; architecture; walking the hills; squash; country life. Address: (b.) 20 Brandon Street, Edinburgh, EH3 5RA; T.-031-244 3068.

Conner, Alan N., MB, ChB, FRCSEdin, FRCSGlas. Consultant Orthopaedic Surgeon, Royal Hospital for Sick Children, Glasgow, since 1971; Honorary Clinical Lecturer, Glasgow University, since 1973; b. 28.9.36, Bellshill; m., Jane T. Lang; 2 s. Educ. Glasgow Academy; Glasgow University. Previously Registrar and Senior Registrar, University Department of Orthopaedics, Western Infirmary, Glasgow, and Senior Registrar, Kenyatta National Hospital, Nairobi. Past Preses, Wellington Church, Glasgow; Past Chairman, Glasgow Area Council for Accident and Orthopaedic Surgery; Trustee, British Scoliosis Society; Governor, Glasgow Academicals' War Memorial Trust. Publications: various papers, mainly on spinal deformity and other orthopaedic problems in childhood. Recreations: sailing; golf; computers; drawing/painting; escaping to Fife. Address: (h.) 14 Ballater Drive, Bearsden, Glasgow, G61 1BY; T.-041-942 5576; 5 Muttoes Court, St. Andrews, KY16 9AE.

Connon, Iain Urquhart, MRTPI. Director of Planning, Dunfermline District Council, since 1986; b. 14.8.39, Perth; m., Eileen Margaret; 2 d. Educ. Perth Academy; Dundee College of Art. Rowand, Anderson, Kinninmouth & Paul, Architects, Edinburgh, 1962-67; Robert Matthew, Johnson Marshall & Partners, Architects, Edinburgh, 1967-70; Planning Department, Royal Burgh of Dunfermline, 1970-75; Dunfermline District Council, since 1975. Recreation: outdoor pursuits. Address: (b.) 3 New Row, Dunfermline, KY12 7NN; T.-0383 736321.

Connor, Professor James Michael, MD, BSc (Hons), MB, ChB (Hons), MRCP. Professor of Medical Genetics and Director, West of Scotland Regional Genetic Service, since 1987 (Wellcome

Trust Senior Lecturer and Honorary Consultant in Medical Genetics, Glasgow University, 1984-87); b. 18.6.51, Grappenhall, England; m., Dr. Rachel A.C. Educ. Lymm Grammar School, Cheshire; Liverpool University. House Officer, Liverpool Royal Infirmary; Resident in Internal Medicine, Johns Hopkins Hospital, USA; University Research Fellow, Liverpool University; Instructor in Internal Medicine, Johns Hopkins Hospital, USA; Consultant in Medical Genetics, Duncan Guthrie Institute of Medical Genetics, Yorkhill, Glasgow. Publications: Soft Tissue Ossification, 1983; Essential Medical Genetics (Co-author), 1984 (2nd edition, 1987); Self-Assessment in Medical Genetics (Co-author), 1985. Recreations: fly fishing; sailing; skiing. Address: (h.) Westbank Cottage, 84 Montgomery Street, Eaglesham; T.-Eaglesham 2626.

Conti, Rt. Rev. Mario Joseph, STL, PhL. Bishop of Aberdeen, since 1977; Member, Secretariat for the Promotion of Christian Unity, Rome, since 1984; Member, International Commission for English in the Liturgy, 1978-87; b. 20.3.34, Elgin. Educ. St. Marie's Convent; Springfield School, Elgin; Blairs College, Aberdeen; Scots College, Pontifical Gregorian University, Rome. Ordained priest, Rome, 1958; Curate, St. Mary's Cathedral, Aberdeen, 1959-62; Parish Priest, St. Joachim's, Wick and St. Anne's, Thurso, 1962. Member, Order of Merit, Italian Republic; President-Treasurer, SCIAF, 1977-85; President, National Liturgy Commission, 1978-86; Chairman, Scottish Catholic Heritage Commission; President, Commission for Christian Doctrine and Unity, since 1986. Recreations: music; art. Address: Bishop's House, 156 King's Gate, Aberdeen; T.-0224 319154.

Cook, Fraser Murray, OBE, BSc, MIMechE, CEng, FInstPet. Chairman, Highlands and Islands Development Consultative Council, 1986-88; Vice Chairman, Forth Ports Authority, since 1985; Member, Court, Stirling University, since 1986; b. 29.12.17, Conon Bridge, Ross-shire; m., Eve Smith Reid. Educ. Inverness Royal Academy; Morgan Academy, Dundee; St. Andrews University. Engineering graduate apprentice, Pumpherston Oil Co. Ltd., 1939-41; REME, South East Asia Command, 1941-46; Assistant to Manager, Pumpherston Oil Co. Ltd., 1946-48; Production Engineer, latterly Oil Construction Engineer, Southern Africa, 1948-53; Engineer, BP Oil Grangemouth Refinery Ltd., 1953-56; Manager, Pumpherston Oil Co. Ltd., 1956-62; Works Manager: BP Oil Grangemouth Refinery Ltd., 1962-66, BP Oil Llandarcy Refinery Ltd., 1966-69; General Manager, then Managing Director and General Manager, BP Oil Grangemouth Refinery Ltd., 1969-77. Chairman, Cumbernauld Development Corporation, 1983-86. Recreations: some golf; photography. Address: Littleton Cottage, Cultoquhey, by Crieff, Perthshire, PH7 3NF; T.-Crieff 3537.

Cook, Rev. James Stanley Stephen Ronald Tweedie, BD, DipPSS. Minister, Hamilton West Parish Church, since 1974; b. 18.8.35, Tullibody; m., Jean Douglas McLachlan; 2 s.; 1 d. Educ. Whitehill Senior Secondary School, Glasgow; St. Andrews University. Apprentice quantity surveyor, Glasgow, 1953-54; regular soldier, REME, 1954-57; Assistant Preventive Officer, Waterguard Department, HM Customs and Excise, 1957-61; Officer, HM Customs and Excise, 1961-69; studied for the ministry, 1969-74. Chairman, Cruse (Lanarkshire); Member, National Training Group, Cruse, since 1987; Chairman, Hamilton Crime Prevention Panel, 1986-87; Member, Action Research for Crippled Child Committee, since 1977; Provincial Grand Master, Lanarkshire (Middle Ward), 1983-88. Recreations: music; photography. Address: West Manse, 43 Bothwell Road, Hamilton, ML3 OBB; T.-Hamilton 458770.

Cook, Rev. John Weir, MA, BD. Minister, St. Philip's, Joppa, since 1988 (Henderson Church, Kilmarnock, 1970-88); b. 10.2.37, Greenock; m., Elizabeth Anne Gifford; 1 s.; 2 d. Educ. Greenock Academy; High School of Glasgow; Glasgow University. Peter Marshall Scholar, Princeton, 1962; Minister, St. Andrews Church, Calcutta, 1963-70; Chairman, Clinical Theology Association, since 1984; accredited by British Association for Counselling, 1984. Recreations: reading; sport; after-dinner speaking. Address: 6 St. Mary's Place, Edinburgh, EH15 2DF; T.-031-669 2410.

Cook, Michael David, CA, IPFA. General Manager, Dumfries and Galloway Health Board, since 1985; b. 30.1.45, Glasgow; m., Deirdre; 1 s.; 1 d. Educ. Wishaw High School; Glasgow University. Treasurer, Orkney Health Board, 1973-74; Area Management Accountant, then District Finance Officer, Ayrshire and Arran Health Board, 1974-82; Treasurer, Dumfries and Galloway Health Board, 1982-85. Recreations: sailing; reading; hill-walking. Address: (b.) Nithbank, Dumfries; T.-0387 53181.

Cook, Robin. MP (Labour), Livingston, since 1983 (Edinburgh Central, 1974-83); b. 28.2.46. Educ. Aberdeen Grammar School; Royal High School, Edinburgh; Edinburgh University. Former Tutor and Organiser in Adult Education; contested Edinburgh North, 1970; former Vice-Chairman, PLP Defence Group; Past Chairman, Housing Sub-Committee, Scottish Labour Group; Opposition Spokesman on Trade, since 1986.

Cooke, David John, BSc, MSc, PhD, FBPsS. Top Grade Clinical Psychologist, Douglas Inch Centre, Glasgow, since 1984; Honorary Lecturer, Glasgow University, since 1984; b. 13.7.52, Glasgow; m., Janet Ruth Salter. Educ. Larbert High School; St. Andrews University; Newcastle-upon-Tyne University; Glasgow University. Clinical Psychologist, Gartnavel Royal Hospital, 1976-83; Cropwood Fellow, Institute of Criminology, Cambridge University, 1986. Recreations: sailing; opera; cooking. Address: (b.) Douglas Inch Centre, 2 Woodside Terrace, Glasgow, G3 7UY; T.-041-332 3844.

Cooke, Joseph Henry, BSc (Hons), MA, DipEd. Head Teacher, Kyle Academy, Ayr, since 1985; b. 30.12.32, Kingston, St. Vincent, West Indies; m., Mary A. Marshall; 3 s. Educ. Methodist College, Belfast; Queen's University, Belfast. Teacher, Down High School, Downpatrick, 1956-67; Head, Geography Department: Strathearn

School, Belfast, 1967-74, Ravenspark Academy, Irvine, 1975-79; Assistant Head Teacher, then Depute Head Teacher, Garnock Academy, Kilbirnie, 1979-85. Elder, Alloway Parish Church. Recreations: travel; bowls; photography; gardening; DIY. Address: (h.) 3 Corsehill Park, Ayr, KA7 2UG; T.-0292 284745.

Cooke, Nicholas Huxley, MA (Oxon). Director, The Scottish Conservation Projects Trust, since 1984; b. 6.5.44, Godalming, Surrey; m., Anne Landon; 2 s.; 3 d. Educ. Charterhouse School; Worcester College, Oxford. Retail management, London, 1967; chartered accountancy training, London, 1968-71; British International Paper, London, 1972-78; Director (Scotland), British Trust for Conservation Volunteers, 1978-84. Council Member, Trust for Urban Ecology; Member, Council, National Trust for Scotland. Recreations: fishing; walking; photography; outdoor conservation work. Address: (b.) Balallan House, 24 Allen Park, Stirling, FK8 2QG; T.-0786 79697.

Cooper, Professor Neil Louis, BA, MA, BPhil, FRSE. Professor in Moral Philosophy, Dundee University, since 1981 (Head, Department of Philosophy, since 1980); b. 25.4.30, Ilford; m., Beryl Barwell Turner; 1 s.; 1 d. Educ. Westminster City School; City of London School; Balliol College, Oxford (Domus Exhibitioner); Senior Scholar, New College, Oxford, 1953-55; John Locke Scholar, 1954. RAF, 1948-49; Lecturer in Philosophy, Queen's College, St. Andrews University, 1956-67; Dundee University: Senior Lecturer in Philosophy, 1967-69, Reader in Philosophy, 1969-81, Dean of Students, Faculty of Social Sciences and Letters, 1972-74, Member of Senate, since 1978, and of Court, since 1986; Editorial Chairman, The Philosophical Quarterly, since 1985; FRSE, 1987. Publications: The Definition of Morality (Contributor), 1970; Weakness of Will (Contributor), 1971; The Diversity of Moral Thinking, 1981; Philosophers on Education (Contributor), 1986. Recreations: conversation; reading; listening to music; playing with ideas. Address: (h.) 2 Minto Place, Dundee, DD2 1BR; T.-Dundee 66518.

Cooper, Patricia, BA, DMS, CertEd. Lecturer in Consumer Studies, Robert Gordon's Institute of Technology, Aberdeen, since 1983; Council Member, Scottish Consumer Council, since 1987; Member, Food Policy Committee, National Consumer Council, since 1988; b. 24.11.42, South Elmsall; m., John M. Cooper; 2 s. Teacher/Lecturer in Home Economics, since 1963. Member, British Telecom Consumer Liaison Panel, 1986; Secretary, Aberdeen Consumer Group, 1985. Recreations: entertaining; reading diverting novels. Address: (b.) R.G.I.T., Kepplestone Premises, Queens Road, Aberdeen, AB9 2PG; T.-0224 633611.

Cooper, Ronald, CEng, FICE, FIAS. Director of Technical Services, Edinburgh District Council, since 1983; b. 12.11.36, Aberdeen; m., Diane; 3 s.; 1 d. Educ. Aberdeen Academy. Apprentice civil engineer, Aberdeen Harbour Board; National Service, Royal Engineers; Engineer, Aberdeen Corporation; Depute Master of Works, Edinburgh Corporation; Director of Building Control, Edinburgh District Council, 1974-83. Recreations: golf; work. Address: (b.) City Chambers, High Street, Edinburgh; T.-031-225 2424, Ext. 5300.

Cooper, Sheena M.M., MA. Rector, Aboyne Academy and Deeside Community Centre; Chairman, Religious Advisory Council for Scotland, since 1987; b. 7.3.39, Bellshill. Educ. Dalziel High School, Motherwell; Glasgow University. Teacher of History, Dalziel High School, Motherwell, 1962-68; Lecturer in History, Elizabeth Gaskell College of Education, Manchester, 1968-70; Woman Adviser, then Assistant Rector, Montrose Academy, 1970-76; Rector, John Neilson High School, Paisley, 1976-83. Member: Council for Tertiary Education in Scotland, 1979-83, Scottish Examination Board, since 1984, Scottish Vocational Education Council, since 1985, Religious Advisory Council, BBC, since 1980; President, Education Section, British Association for Advancement of Science, 1978-79. Recreations: golf; singing; walking. Address: (b.) Aboyne Academy and Deeside Community Centre, Aboyne; T.-0339 2222, Ext. 24.

Copeman, George E., MBE. Honorary Sheriff, Banff and Buchan; b. 11.12.03, Hornsey, Middlesex; m., Dorothy Mary Busby; 1 d. Former Director and Manager, Crosse & Blackwell Ltd., Peterhead; war-time Canning Adviser, Ministry of Food, for North of Scotland; former Treasurer, Magistrate and Chairman, Peterhead Public Health and Water Committee; former Member: Aberdeen County Council, North-East Counties Police Board, Herring Industry Advisory Council, Scottish Council (Development and Industry) Manpower Committee, Peterhead Scottish Week Committee. Address: (h.) 2 Lochside Road, Denmore Park, Bridge of Don, Aberdeen, AB2 8AE; T.-0224 704481.

Coppock, Professor John Terence, CBE, MA, PhD, FBA, FRSE. Emeritus Professor of Geography, Edinburgh University; Secretary and Treasurer, Carnegie Trust for the Universities of Scotland, since 1986; Member, Scottish Sports Council, 1976-88; b. 2.6.21, Cardiff; m., Sheila Mary Burnett; 1 s.; 1 d. Educ. Penarth County School; Queens' College, Cambridge. Civil Servant, 1938-47 (Lord Chancellor's Department, Ministry of Works, Customs and Excise); War Service, Army, 1939-46 (Commissioned, 1941); Departmental Demonstrator, Department of Geography, Cambridge University, 1949-50; University College, London: Assistant Lecturer, 1950-52, Lecturer, 1952-64, Reader, 1964-65; Ogilvie Professor of Geography, Edinburgh University, 1965-86. Institute of British Geographers: Vice-President, 1971-73, President, 1973-74; Vice-President, Royal Scottish Geographical Society, since 1975; Vice-President, British Academy, 1985-87. Recreations: walking; natural history; listening to music. Address: (b.) Carnegie Trust for the Universities of Scotland, 22 Hanover Street, Edinburgh, EH2 2EN; T.-031-220 1217.

Corbet, Professor Philip Steven, BSc, PhD, DSc, ScD, FIBiol, FESC, FRSE. Professor of Zoology, Dundee University, since 1980 (part-time, since

1987) (Head, Department of Biological Sciences, 1983-86); b. 21.5.29, Kuala Lumpur, Malaysia; m., Mary Elizabeth Canvin; 1 d. by pr. m. Educ. Dauntsey's School, Wiltshire; Reading University; Gonville and Caius College, Cambridge. Zoologist, East African Fisheries Research Organisation, Jinja, Uganda, 1954-57; Entomologist: East African Virus Research Organisation, Entebbe, Uganda, 1957-62; Entomology Research Institute, Canada Department of Agriculture, Ottawa, 1962-67; Director, Research Institute, Canada Department of Agriculture, Belleville, Ontario, 1967-71; Professor and Chairman, Department of Biology, Waterloo University, Ontario, 1971-74; Professor and Director, Joint Centre for Environmental Sciences, Canterbury University and Lincoln College, New Zealand, 1974-78; Professor, Department of Zoology, Canterbury University, New Zealand, 1978-80. Entomological Society of Canada: President, 1971, Gold Medal, 1974, Fellow, 1976; Commonwealth Visiting Professor, Cambridge University, 1979-80; Member, Committee for Scotland, Nature Conservancy Council, 1986; Societas Internationalis Odonatologica, Member of Honour, 1985; President, British Dragonfly Society, since 1983. Publications: A Biology of Dragonflies, 1962; research papers on medical entomology. Address: (h.) The Old Manse, 45 Lanark Road, Edinburgh, EH14 1TL; T.-031-443 4685.

Corbett, Donald, RMN, JP. Member, Highland Regional Council, since 1974; Member, Inverness District Council, since 1971; b. 7.2.25, Inverness; m., Isobel; 5 s.; 2 d. Educ. Inverness High School. Chairman: Highland Region Heart Fund, Inverness Building Authority; Vice-Chairman, Highland Region General Purposes Committee; Member, Inverness Justices Advisory Council. Recreations: reading; gardening. Address: (h.) 51 Kessock Road, Inverness; T.-0463 232831.

Corfield, Harry, CEng, FIMinE, FIQ. HM Principal District Inspector of Mines and Quarries, Scotland and North East England District, since 1985; b. 29.6.31, Wigan; m., Margaret; 1 s. Educ. Hindley and Abram Grammar School; Wigan Mining and Technical College. Colliery management, NCB, Lancashire, 1960-74; HM Inspectorate of Mines and Quarries, since 1974. Recreation: reading. Address: (b.) Belford House, Belford Road, Edinburgh; T.-031-225 3686.

Cormack, Professor Richard Melville, MA, BSc, DipMathStat, PhD, FRSE. Professor of Statistics, St. Andrews University, since 1972; Member, Natural Environment Research Council, since 1983; Member, Scottish Universities Council on Entrance, since 1982; Member, Council, Freshwater Biological Association, since 1987; b. 12.3.35, Glasgow; m., Edith Whittaker. Educ. Glasgow Academy; Cambridge University; London University (External); Aberdeen University. Lecturer in Statistics, Aberdeen University, 1956-66; Assistant Professor, University of Washington, 1964-65; Senior Lecturer, Edinburgh University, 1966-72. Honorary Secretary, Biometric Society (British Region), 1970-77; President (International), Biometric Society, 1980-81. Publications: The Statistical Argument; Sampling Biological Populations (Editor), Spatial and Temporal Analysis in Ecology (Editor). Recreations: photography; music; hill-walking. Address: (h.) 58 Buchanan Gardens, St. Andrews, Fife; T.-0334 76970.

Cormie, James E.D., BL. Chief Executive and Director of Administration and Legal Services, Perth and Kinross Council, since 1981; b. 30.7.30, Edinburgh; m., Stella Anne Moir; 1 s.; 1 d. Educ. Robert Gordon's College, Aberdeen; Aberdeen University. Solicitor, private practice, 1953-55; Solicitor, Aberdeen Town Council, 1955-66; Depute Town Clerk, Perth, 1966-75; Director of Administration and Legal Services, Perth and Kinross District, 1975-81. Clerk to Lieutenancy, Perth and Kinross; Company Secretary: Perth and Kinross Recreational Facilities Ltd., Perth Festival of the Arts Ltd., Bowerswell Memorial Homes (Perth) Ltd.; Member, Society of High Constables of the City of Perth; Member, Secretary of State's Advisory Committee on Scotland's Travelling People. Recreations: cine photography; golf; hill-walking. Address: (b.) Council Building, 2 High Street, Perth, PH1 5PH; T.-0738 39911.

Cornish, Melvyn David, BSc, PGCE. Senior Assistant Secretary (Planning), Edinburgh University, since 1987; b. 29.6.48, Leighton Buzzard; m., Eileen Joyce Easterbrook; 1 s.; 1 d. Educ. Cedars Grammar School, Leighton Buzzard; Leicester University. Chemistry Teacher, Jamaica and Cumbria, 1970-73; Administrator, Leicester Polytechnic, 1973-78; Senior Administrative Officer, then Assistant Secretary, Edinburgh University, 1978-87. Recreations: walking; cinema; travel; family. Address: (b.) Old College, South Bridge, Edinburgh; T.-031-667 1011.

Cornwell, Professor John Francis, PhD, BSc, DIC, ARCS, FRSE. Professor of Theoretical Physics, St. Andrews University, since 1979 (Chairman, Physics Department, 1984-85); b. 28.1.37, London; m., Elizabeth Margaret Burfitt; 2 d. Educ. Ealing Grammar School; Imperial College, London. Lecturer in Applied Mathematics, Leeds University, 1961-67; St. Andrews University: Lecturer in Theoretical Physics, 1967-73, Reader, 1973-79. Publications: Group Theory in Physics, two volumes, 1984; Group Theory and Electronic Energy Bands in Solids, 1969. Recreations: sailing; hill-walking; tennis; badminton; golf. Address: (b.) Department of Physics and Astronomy, St. Andrews University, North Haugh, St. Andrews, Fife, KY16 9SS; T.-0334 76161.

Cornwell, Keith, BSc, PhD, CEng, FIMechE. Reader in Mechanical Engineering, Heriot-Watt University, since 1987; b. 4.4.42, Abingdon; m., Sheila Joan Mott; 1 s.; 1 d. Educ. City University, London. Research Fellow, then Lecturer, Middlesex Polytechnic; Lecturer, Heriot-Watt University. Publication: The Flow of Heat. Recreations: walking; old cars. Address: (h.) 33 Park Avenue, Duddingston, Edinburgh, EH15 1JS.

Corrie, John Alexander. Farmer; MP (Conservative), North Cunninghame, 1983-87 (Bute and North Ayrshire, 1974-83); b. 1935; m.; 1 s.; 2 d. Educ. Kirkcudbright Academy; George Watson's College, Edinburgh; Lincoln Agricultural College, New Zealand. Commissioned from the ranks, New Zealand Army, 1957; National Chairman, Scottish Young Conservatives, 1964; Council Member, National Farmers Union of Scotland, 1965; Chairman, Kirkcudbright Conservative Association, 1966; Lecturer, British Wool Marketing Board, 1967-74, and Agricultural Training Board, 1969-74; appointed Scottish Conservative spokesman on education, 1974; Member, European Parliament, 1975 and 1977-79; Vice President, EEC/Turkey Committee; appointed Opposition Whip, 1975 (resigned, 1976); elected to Council, Belted Galloway Cattle Society, 1978; PPS to Secretary of State for Scotland, 1979-81; elected to Council, National Cattle Breeders Association, 1979; introduced private member's Bill on abortion law reform, 1979; Chairman, Scottish Conservative Backbench Committee, 1981; elected Leader, Conservative Group on Scottish Affairs, 1982; Member, Council of Europe, 1983-87; Member, Western European Union (Defence Committee), 1983-87; private member's Bill on diseases of fish, 1982-83; farms family farm in Kirkcudbright. Address: (h.) Park of Tongland, Kirkcudbright, DG6 4NE.

Corsar, Charles Herbert Kenneth, OBE, TD, JP, DL, MA. Farmer, since 1953; Secretary for Scotland, Duke of Edinburgh's Award, 1966-87; b. 13.5.26, Edinburgh; m., Mary Drummond Buchanan-Smith (see Mary Drummond Corsar); 2 s.; 2 d. Educ. Merchiston Castle; King's College, Cambridge. Commissioned, The Royal Scots TA, 1948; commanded 8/9 Bn.,The Royal Scots TA, 1964-67; Edinburgh and Heriot-Watt Universities OTC, 1967-72; TA Colonel, 1972-75; Hon. ADC to The Queen, 1977-81; Honorary Colonel, 1/52 Lowland Volunteers, 1975-87; Chairman, Lowland TA and VR Association, since 1984; Zone Commissioner, Home Defence, East of Scotland; County Councillor, Midlothian, 1958-67; Deputy Lieutenant, Midlothian; Vice President, The Boys Brigade, 1970, and President, Edinburgh Bn., Boys Brigade, 1969-87 (Hon. President, Edinburgh Bn., since 1987); Chairman, Scottish Standing Conference of Voluntary Youth Organisations, 1973-78; Governor: Merchiston Castle School, Clifton Hall School; Chairman, Wellington List D School, 1978-84; Chairman, Earl Haig Fund Scotland, since 1984; Secretary, Royal Jubilee and Princes' Trusts (Lothian and Borders); Member, Scottish Sports Council, 1972-75; Elder, Church of Scotland, since 1956. Recreations: gardening; bee-keeping; shooting. Address: (h.) Burg, Torloisk, Ulva Ferry, Isle of Mull; T.-Ulva Ferry 289; 11 Ainslie Place, Edinburgh, EH3 6AS; T.-031-225 6318.

Corsar, The Hon. Mrs Mary Drummond, MA. Chairman Scotland, Women's Royal Voluntary Service, since 1981; Vice Chairman, Women's Royal Voluntary Service, since 1984; Member, Parole Board for Scotland, since 1982; b. 8.7.27, Edinburgh; m., Colonel Charles H.K. Corsar (qv); 2 s.; 2 d. Educ. Westbourne, Glasgow; St. Denis, Edinburgh; Edinburgh University. Midlothian Girl Guides: Secretary, 1951-66, County Commissioner, 1966-72; Deputy Chief Commissioner, Girl Guides Scotland, 1972-77; Member, Executive Committee, Trefoil Centre, since 1975; Member, Visiting Committee, Glenochil Detention Centre, since 1976; Member, Management Committee, Church of Scotland Youth Centre, Carberry, 1976-82; Honorary President, Scottish Women's Athletic Association; Governor, Fettes College; Member of Convocation, Heriot Watt University. Recreation: hill-walking. Address: 19 Grosvenor Crescent, Edinburgh; T.-031-337 2261.

Cottrell, Professor Glen Alfred, BSc, PhD, DSc. Professor of Neuropharmacology, St. Andrews University; b. 19.8.38, London; m., Ann Rainbow; 2 s.; 1 d. Educ. Shene Grammar School; Southampton University. Research Fellow, Harvard; Lecturer, Senior Lecturer, Reader, St. Andrews University. Recreations: sailing; running. Address: (h.) 34 Grange Road, St. Andrews, KY16 8LF; T.-0334 74985.

Coull, Professor Alexander, BSc, PhD, CEng, FRSE, FICE, FIStructE, DSc. Regius Professor of Civil Engineering, Glasgow University, since 1977; b. 20.6.31, Peterhead; m., Frances Bruce Moir; 1 s.; 2 d. Educ. Peterhead Academy; Aberdeen University. Research Assistant, MIT, USA, 1955; Structural Engineer, English Electric Co. Ltd., 1955-57; Lecturer in Engineering, Aberdeen University, 1957-62; Lecturer in Civil Engineering, Southampton University, 1962-66; Professor of Structural Engineering, Strathclyde University, 1967-76. Chairman, Clyde Estuary Amenity Council, 1981-86; awarded Telford Premium, 1973, and Trevithick Premium, 1974, Institution of Civil Engineers. Publications: Tall Buildings, 1967; Fundamentals of Structural Theory, 1972. Recreations: golf; hill-walking. Address: (h.) 11 Blackwood Road, Milngavie, Glasgow, G62 7LB; T.-041-956 1655.

Coull, James West. Honorary Sheriff, Dundee, since 1971; b. 30.5.14, Dundee; m., Jean Fairley; 1 s.; 1 d. Educ. Morgan Academy, Dundee; St. Andrews University. Solicitor (retired) and Notary Public; Burgh Prosecutor, Carnoustie, 1963-75. Recreations: gardening; watercolour painting. Address: (h.) 22 Dalhousie Street, Carnoustie, Angus.

Coull, Rev. Morris Cowper, BD. Minister, Hillington Park Parish Church, Glasgow, since 1983; b. 12.4.41, Largs; m., Ann Duthie; 1 s.; 1 d. Educ. Allan Glen's School; Newbattle Abbey College; Glasgow University; Trinity College. Assistant Minister, Bearsden South Parish Church, 1972-74; Minister, New Cumnock (Old) Parish Church, 1974-83. Address: 61 Ralston Avenue, Glasgow, G52; T.-041-882 7000.

Coull, Samuel. Member, Grampian Regional Council, since 1978 (Chairman, Water Services Committee); Member, Banff and Buchan District Council, 1977-88; b. 21.6.40, Peterhead; m., Ann F.S. Barclay; 1 d. Educ. Peterhead Academy. Member, Peterhead Harbour Trust. Recreations: gardening; reading. Address: (h.) 16 Lendrum Terrace, Stirlinghill, Boddam, Aberdeenshire; T.-Peterhead 76323.

Coulsfield, Hon. Lord (John Cameron Taylor), QC, BA, LLB. Senator of the College of Justice, since 1987; b. 24.4.34, Dundee; m., Bridget Deirdre Sloan. Educ. Fettes College; Corpus Christi College, Oxford; Edinburgh University. Admitted to Faculty of Advocates, 1960; Queen's

Counsel, 1973; Lecturer in Public Law, Edinburgh University, 1960-64; Advocate Depute, 1977-80; Keeper of the Advocates Library, 1977-87; Chairman, Medical Appeal Tribunals, 1985-87; Judge of the Appeal Courts of Jersey and Guernsey, 1986-87. Address: (h.) 17 Moray Place, Edinburgh.

Couper, Robert Jackson, FIH, FBIM, MIIM, MRSH, MSAAT, MHTTA. Director of Housing, Argyll and Bute District Council, since 1974; b. 20.4.27, Paisley; m., Ann Templeton; 2 s.; 1 d. Educ. Camphill Secondary School, Paisley; Glasgow School of Architecture; Royal College of Technology, Glasgow; Glasgow College of Commerce; Glasgow College of Building. Apprentice architect, Abercrombie & Maitland, 1945-53; Royal Navy, 1945-48; Burgh of Milngavie: Architectural Assistant, 1953-68, Interim Burgh Surveyor, 1968, Assistant Burgh Surveyor (Housing), 1968-70; Housing Manager, Burgh of Port Glasgow, 1970-74; part-time Lecturer, Glasgow College of Building, 1970-74. Session Clerk, St. Lukes Church of Scotland, 1964-72; Vice Chairman, Scottish Local Authorities Special Housing Group, 1976-86; Chairman, Strathclyde Chief Housing Officers Group, 1980-83; Chairman, Association of Chief Housing Officers (Northern Area), 1984; Secretary, Chief Officers Group, Scottish Branch, Institute of Housing, since 1984. Recreations: sailing; art; heraldry. Address: (b.) Kilmory, Lochgilphead, Argyll, PA31 6RT; T.-0546 2127.

Courtney, James McNiven, BSc, PhD, Dr sc nat, ARCST, CChem, FRSC, FPRI. Reader, Bioengineering Unit, Strathclyde University, since 1986; (Senior Lecturer, 1981-86); Visiting Professor, Wilhelm Pieck University, Rostock, GDR, since 1978; b. 25.3.40, Glasgow; m., Ellen Miller Courtney; 2 s.; 1 d. Educ. Whitehill Senior Secondary School; Royal College of Science and Technology; Strathclyde University. Rubber technologist: MacLellan Rubber Ltd., Glasgow, 1962-65, Uniroyal Ltd., Dumfries, 1965-66; Lecturer, Bioengineering Unit, Strathclyde University, 1969-81. Recreation: football supporter (Glasgow Rangers). Address: (b.) Strathclyde University, Bioengineering Unit, 106 Rottenrow, Glasgow; T.-041-552 4400.

Coutts, Findlay Macrury, MA, LLB. Director of Administration, Dunfermline District Council, since 1975; b. 16.3.43, Aberdeen; m., Christine; 1 s.; 1 d. Educ. Aberdeen Grammar School; Aberdeen University. Law apprentice/Legal Assistant, Hamilton Town Council, 1966-69; Town Clerk, Cupar, 1969-75. Recreations: good food; golf; town twinning. Address: (b.) City Chambers, Dunfermline; T.-Dunfermline 722711.

Coutts, Brigadier Francis Henderson, CBE, DL. Trustee, The Seagull Trust; b. 8.7.18, Glasgow; m., Morag Russell Fullerton; 2 d. Educ. Glasgow Academy; Army Staff College, Camberley. Metropolitan Police, 1937-40; in the ranks, London Scottish, 1940-41; commissioned King's Own Scottish Borderers, 1941-73; Colonel, 1970-80. General Secretary, Royal British Legion Scotland and Earl Haig Fund Scotland, 1973-83; President, Scottish Rugby Union, 1977-78; Elder, Colinton Parish Church; Joint President, Friends of St. Andrew's, Jerusalem; Member, Management Committee, Royal British Legion Housing Association. Recreations: gardening; golf; Grouse; piping. Address: (h.) 5 Gillsland Road, Edinburgh, EH10 5BW; T.-031-337 4920.

Coutts, Rev. Fred, MA, BD. Minister, Mastrick Parish Church, Aberdeen, since 1984; b. 13.1.47, Forfar; m., Mary Lawson Fraser Gill; 2 s.; 1 d. Educ. Brechin High School; Dollar Academy; St. Andrews University; Edinburgh University. Assistant Minister, Linwood Parish Church, 1972-74; Minister, Buckie North, 1974-84. Chairman: Buckie Community Council, 1981-83, Moray Firth Community Radio Association, 1982-83. Recreations: music; photography; home computing. Address: 13 Beechgrove Avenue, Aberdeen, AB2 4EZ; T.-Aberdeen 638011.

Coutts, Herbert, SBStJ, FMA, FSAScot. City Curator, Edinburgh City Museums and Art Galleries, since 1973; b. 9.3.44, Dundee; m., Angela E.M. Smith; 1 s.; 3 d. Educ. Morgan Academy, Dundee. Assistant Keeper of Antiquities and Bygones, Dundee City Museums, 1965-68; Keeper, 1968-71; Superintendent, Edinburgh City Museums, 1971-73; Vice-President, Museum Assistants Group, 1969-70; Member: Government Committee on future of Scotland's National Museums and Galleries, 1979-80; Council, Museums Association, 1977-78, and since 1987; Council, Society of Antiquaries of Scotland, 1981-82; Board, Scottish Museums Council, since 1985; Museums Adviser, COSLA, since 1985. Contested Angus South (Lab), 1970. Publications: Ancient Monuments of Tayside; Tayside Before History; Edinburgh: An Illustrated History; guide books and exhibition catalogues. Recreations: family; gardening; opera; writing; reading; walking. Address: (h.) Kirkhill House, Queen's road, Dunbar, EH42 1LN; T.-0368 63113.

Coutts, John R.T., BSc, PhD. Reader in Obstetrics and Gynaecology/Reproductive Medicine, Glasgow University, since 1987; b. 10.7.41, Dundee; m., Marjory R.B.; 1 s.; 2 d. Educ. Morgan Academy, Dundee; St. Andrews University. Dundee University: Research Fellow in Obstetrics and Gynaecology, 1966-69, Honorary Lecturer in Obstetrics and Gynaecology, 1969-70; Lecturer, then Senior Lecturer, Glasgow University, 1970-87. Publication: The Functional Morphology of the Human Ovary (Editor). Recreations: squash; bowling. Address: (b.) Department of Obstetrics and Gynaecology, Glasgow Royal Infirmary, 10 Alexandra Parade, Glasgow; T.-041-552 3535.

Coutts, Norman Alexander, BSc, MB, ChB, FRCP(Glas), FRCP(Edin), FRCP(Lond). Consultant Paediatrician, Argyll and Clyde Health Board and Royal Hospital for Sick Children, Glasgow, since 1969; Honorary Clinical Lecturer, Paediatrics, Glasgow University, since 1980; b. 20.1.33, Glasgow; m., Margaret Sargeant; 2 s.; 1 d. Educ. Woodside School, Glasgow; Glasgow University. House Officer posts, Glasgow, 1958-59; Captain, RAMC, 1959-61; Registrar posts, Lincoln, Leeds, York and Glasgow, 1961-69. Member of Council, British Paediatric Association, 1985-88. Recreations: walking; philately. Address: (h.) 1 Elm Gardens, Bearsden, Glasgow, G61 3BH; T.-041-942 7194.

Coutts, T(homas) Gordon, MA, LLB, QC. Queen's Counsel, since 1973; b. 5.7.33, Aberdeen; m., Winifred K. Scott; 1 s.; 1 d. Educ. Aberdeen Grammar School; Aberdeen University. Advocate, 1959; Chairman, Industrial Tribunals, 1972; Chairman, Medical Appeal Tribunals, 1984. Recreations: golf; stamp collecting. Address: (h.) 6 Heriot Row, Edinburgh.

Cowan, Brigadier Colin Hunter, CBE, DL, MA, FRSA, CEng, MICE. Chief Executive, Cumbernauld Development Corporation, 1970-85; b. 16.10.20, Edinburgh; m., Elizabeth Williamson (deceased); 2 s.; 1 d. Educ. Wellington College; Trinity College, Cambridge. Commissioned, Royal Engineers, 1940; service in India and Burma, Royal Bombay Sappers and Miners, 1942-46; staff and regimental appointments, UK and Malta, 1951-60; commanded Field Engineer Regiment, Germany, 1960-63; Defence Adviser, UK Mission to UNO, New York, 1964-66; Chief Staff Officer to Engineer-in-Chief (Army), Ministry of Defence, 1966-68; Brigadier, Engineer Plans (Army), Ministry of Defence, 1968-70. Chairman, Services Resettlement Committee, Scotland. Recreations: hill-walking; photography; music. Address: (h.) Hillcroft, Dullatur, by Glasgow, G68 OAW; T.-023-67 23242.

Cowan, David Lockhart, MB, ChB, FRCSEdin. Consultant Otolaryngologist, City Hospital, Royal Hospital for Sick Children and Western General Hospital, Edinburgh, since 1974; Honorary Senior Lecturer, Edinburgh University; b. 30.6.41, Edinburgh; m., Eileen M. Masterton; 3 s.; 1 d. Educ. George Watson's College, Edinburgh; Trinity College, Glenalmond; Edinburgh University. Scottish Representative, Council, British Association of Otolaryngologists. Publications: Logan Turner's Diseases of the Ear, Nose and Throat (Co-author); Paediatric Otolaryngology (Co-author). Recreations: golf; all sport. Address: (h.) 28 Braid Hills Road, Edinburgh, EH10 6HY; T.-031-447 3424.

Cowan, Professor Ian Borthwick, MA, PhD, FRHistS. Professor in Scottish History, Glasgow University, since 1983; b. 16.4.32, Dumfries; m., Anna Little Telford; 3 d. Educ. Dumfries Academy; Edinburgh University. Education Officer, RAF, 1954-56; Assistant Lecturer in Scottish History, Edinburgh University, 1956-59; Lecturer in History, Newbattle Abbey College, 1959-62; Glasgow University: Lecturer in Scottish History, 1962-70, Senior Lecturer, 1970-77, Reader, 1977-83. Treasurer: Scottish History Society, Scottish Historical Trust; Past President, Scottish Church History Society; Vice President, The Historical Association; Member, Irish Manuscripts Advisory Committee on Papal Records. Publications: The Parishes of Medieval Scotland, 1967; Scottish Supplications to Rome 1428-32 (with A.I. Dunlop), 1970; The Enigma of Mary Stewart, 1971; The Scottish Covenanters 1660-1689, 1976; Medieval Religious Houses: Scotland (with D.E. Easson), 1976; Renaissance and Reformation in Scotland (with D. Shaw), 1982; The Scottish Reformation, 1982; Knights of St. John of Jerusalem in Scotland (with P.H.R. Mackay and A. Macquarrie), 1983; Ayrshire Abbeys: Crossraguel and Kilwinning, 1986; Mary Queen of Scots, 1987. Recreation: travel. Address: (h.) 119 Balshagray Avenue, Glasgow, G11 7EG; T.-041-954 8494.

Cowan, John, BSc (Hons), MSc, PhD, FIStructE, FICE. Director, Open University in Scotland, since 1987 (Professor of Engineering Education, Heriot Watt University, 1982-87); b. 19.3.32, Glasgow; m., Audrey Walker Cowan; 3 s.; 1 d. Educ. High School of Glasgow; Edinburgh University; Heriot-Watt University. Design engineer, Blyth & Blyth, Edinburgh, 1952-64; joined Heriot-Watt College as Lecturer, 1964; awards, Institution of Structural Engineers and Czech Ministry of Higher Education, for work in engineering education research. Vice Chairman, Scottish Schoolboys' Club. Recreations: reading; music; photography. Address: (b.) 60 Melville Street, Edinburgh, EH3 7HF; T.-031-226 3851.

Cowan, Robert, LLD, MA. Chairman, Highlands and Islands Development Board, since 1982; Board Member, Scottish Development Agency; Member, Broadcasting Council for Scotland, since 1984; b. 27.7.32, Edinburgh; m., Margaret Morton Dewar; 2 d. Educ. Edinburgh Academy; Edinburgh University. Fisons Ltd., 1958-62; Wolsey Ltd., 1962-65; PA Management Consultants Ltd., 1965-82. Hon. LLD, Aberdeen University, 1987. Recreations: gardening; sailing. Address: (h.) The Old Manse, Farr, Inverness-shire; T.-08083 209.

Cowan, Robert L., MA, LLB. Regional Secretary, Lothian Regional Council, since 1982; b. 27.9.36, Edinburgh; m.; 3 children. Educ. Leith Academy, Edinburgh; Edinburgh University. Legal Assistant: Edinburgh Corporation, 1959-62, Perth County Council, 1962-64; Assistant Town Clerk, Burgh of Hawick, 1964-65; Edinburgh Corporation: Principal Legal Assistant, 1965-71, Depute Town Clerk, 1971-75; Deputy Director of Administration, Lothian Regional Council, 1975-82. Address: (b.) Regional Headquarters, George IV Bridge, Edinburgh; T.-031-229 9292.

Cowe, Alan Wilson, MA, LLB. Secretary and Clerk, Church of Scotland General Trustees, since 1964; b. 9.8.38, Kelso; m., Agnes Cunningham Dick. Educ. Dunfermline High School; Edinburgh University. Law apprentice, Simpson Kinmont & Maxwell, WS, Edinburgh; Assistant to Secretary, Church of Scotland General Trustees, 1963-64. Recreations: long-distance running; hill-walking. Address: (b.) 121 George Street, Edinburgh; T.-031-225 5722.

Cowie, Rev. Gordon Strachan, MA, LLB, Advocate. Minister, Birnie and Pluscarden, since 1986; b. 10.6.33, Aberdeen; 3 s.; 1 d. Educ. Aberdeen Grammar School; Aberdeen University. 2nd Lt., RPC, 1958-60; Lecturer, International and Comparative Law, St. Andrews University, 1960-67; Glasgow University: Senior Lecturer in Public Law, 1967-73, Professor of Public Law, 1973-86, Dean, Faculty of Law, 1977-79; Member, Joint Standing Committee on Legal Education in Scotland, 1977-82; Convener, Diploma in Legal Practice Central Liaison Committee, 1979-82; ordained as Minister, Church of Scotland, 1986; Member, Scottish Working Group for Justice/All

Souls Review of Administrative Law in UK; former Consultant, Scottish Branch, Institute of Trading Standards Administration; Governor, Anderson's Institution, Elgin. Recreations: golf; gardening; antiquities. Address: The Manse of Birnie, Elgin, Moray, IV30 3SU; T.-0343 2621.

Cowie, Professor John McKenzie Grant, BSc, PhD, DSc, CChem, FRSC, FRSE. Professor of Chemistry of Materials, Heriot-Watt University, since 1988 (Professor of Chemistry, Stirling University, 1973-88); b. 31.5.33, Edinburgh; m., Agnes Neilson Campbell; 1 s.; 1 d. Educ. Royal High School, Edinburgh; Edinburgh University. Assistant Lecturer, Edinburgh University, 1956-58; Research Officer, National Research Council of Canada, Ottawa, 1958-67; Lecturer, Essex University, 1967-69; Senior Lecturer, Stirling University, 1969-73. Vice Chairman, Scottish Spinal Cord Injury Association; Hon. President, Council of Social Services (Stirling District). Recreations: reading; painting; listening to music. Address: (h.) Traquair, 50 Back Road, Dollar, Clackmannanshire; T.-Dollar 2031.

Cowie, Hon. Lord (William Lorn Kerr Cowie), MA (Cantab), LLB (Glas). Senator of the College of Justice in Scotland, since 1977; b. 1.6.26, Glasgow; m., Camilla Henrietta Grizel Hoyle; 2 s.; 2 d. Educ. Fettes College, Edinburgh; Clare College, Cambridge; Glasgow University. RNVR, 1944-47 (Sub. Lt.); Member, Faculty of Advocates, 1952; QC, 1967. Member, Parole Board for Scotland; Honorary President, Family Conciliation Service (Lothian). Recreation: fishing. Address: (h.) 20 Blacket Place, Edinburgh; T.-031-667 8238.

Cowley, Professor Roger A., MA, PhD, FRS, FRSE, FInstP. Professor of Physics, Edinburgh University, since 1970; b. 24.2.39, Woodford Green; m., Sheila Joyce Wells; 1 s.; 1 d. Educ. Brentwood School, Essex; Cambridge University. Research Fellow, Trinity Hall, Cambridge, 1962-64; Research Officer, Atomic Energy of Canada, 1964-70. Address: (b.) Department of Physics, Edinburgh University, Mayfield Road, Edinburgh; T.-031-667 1081.

Cowley of Innerwick, Victor Charles Vereker, TD, JP, DL. Land Owner and Baron of Innerwick, since 1960; Farmer; b. 4.4.18, Glasgow; m., Moyra McClure; 1 s.; 2 d. Educ. St. Mary's, Melrose; Merchiston Castle School. Young master printer, 1937; commissioned, RATA, 1939; served France, North Africa, Sicily, Italy, Burma, Indo China; Col. Depute CRA 51st Highland Division; Chairman, Brownlie Scandrett and Graham Ltd. (retired 1960); Vice Convener, East Lothian County Council, 1973; Regional Councillor, Lothian, 1975; Commissioner of Income Tax, East Lothian, 1965-87. Recreations: shooting; golf. Address: Crowhill, Innerwick, Dunbar, EH42 1QT; T.-036 84 279.

Cowpe, Jonathan George, BDS (Hons), FDSRCS Ed, PhD. Senior Lecturer in Dental Surgery, Dundee University, since 1985; Honorary Consultant in Oral Surgery, since 1985; b. 23.4.52, Manchester; m., Marianne. Educ. Cheltenham College; Manchester University. Resident House Officer in Oral Surgery, Manchester Dental Hospital, 1975-76; Resident Senior House Officer in Oral Surgery, Bolton General Hospital, 1976-78; Dundee Dental Hospital: Registrar in Oral Surgery, 1978-80, Lecturer and Honorary Senior Registrar in Oral Surgery, 1980-84. Toller Research Prize, 1981; Howard Elder Research Prize, 1983; President, Dundee Dental Club, 1985-86. Recreations: golf; squash; hill-walking. Address: (h.) Kinbank, 9 Bay Road, Wormit, Fife; T.-Newport 541767.

Coyle, Very Rev. Mgr. Francis Coyle, JCL. Parish Priest, St. Philomena's, Glasgow; b. 2.8.24, Glasgow. Educ. St. Aloysius College, Glasgow; St. Peter's College, Bearsden; Gregorian University, Rome. Assistant Priest, St. Andrew's Cathedral, 1949-52; Secretary, Archdiocese of Glasgow, 1952-68; Personal Secretary, Archbishop Scanlan, 1968-72; Assistant Priest, St. Charles, 1952-71; Chancellor, Archdiocese of Glasgow, 1971-74; Catholic Representative, Strathclyde Region Education Committee, 1974-83; Vice President, Catholic Education Commission, 1974-83. Chaplain of Honour to the Pope, 1972; JP, Glasgow, 1980. Recreations: golf; photography. Address: St. Philomena's, 1255 Royston Road, Glasgow, G33; T.-041-770 4237.

Cracknell, (William) Martin. Chief Executive, Glenrothes Development Corporation, since 1976; b. 24.6.29, Leicester; m., Gillian Goatcher; 2 s.; 2 d. Educ. St. Edwards School, Oxford; Royal Military Academy, Sandhurst. Army, Royal Green Jackets, 1947-69; British Printing Industries Federation, 1969-76. Board Member: Glenrothes Enterprise Trust; New Enterprise Development; Member, Executive, Scottish Council (Development and Industry); Chairman, Glenrothes University Industry Dining Club; Chairman, Committee for Scotland, German Chamber of Industry and Commerce in the UK. Address: (b.) Balbirnie House, Glenrothes, Fife; T.-0592 754343.

Cradock, John Whitby, CA. Chairman, Richard Irvin & Sons Ltd., since 1980; Chairman, Aberdeen Harbour Board, since 1984; Director, Trustee Savings Bank Scotland, since 1986; b. 28.6.29, Beckenham, Kent; m., Vina McInnes; 3 s. Educ. Aberdeen Grammar School. Recreations: golf; curling. Address: (h.) 100 Kings Gate, Aberdeen; T.-0224 313901.

Craig, Alex. R., BSc. Headmaster, Hillhead High School, Glasgow, since 1976; b. 27.10.28, Cleland; m., Nessie; 2 s.; 1 d. Educ. Wishaw High School; Glasgow University. Secretary, Wishaw Bowling Club. Recreations: bowling; photography; DIY. Address: (b.) Hillhead High School, Oakfield Avenue, Glasgow; T.-041-339 8200.

Craig, Emeritus Professor Gordon Younger, BSc, PhD, FIGeol, FRSE. Emeritus Professor of Geology, Edinburgh University, since 1984; President, International Commission on the History of the Geological Sciences, since 1984; b. 17.1.25, Milngavie; m., Elizabeth Mary; 2 s. Educ. Hillhead High School; Bearsden Academy; Glasgow University; Edinburgh University. Joined Edinburgh University as Lecturer, 1947; James Hutton Professor of Geology, 1967-84. Publications: Geology of Scotland (Editor), 1983; James Hutton: The Lost Drawings (Co-author), 1977; A Geological

Miscellany (Co-author), 1982. Recreations: golf; gardening. Address: (h.) 14 Kevock Road, Lasswade, Edinburgh, EH18 1HT; T.-031-663 8275.

Craig, James, OBE, MA, LLB, WS, NP. Retired Solicitor; b. 15.9.14, Ardrossan; m., Alice Norris Leith; 1 s.; 1 d. Educ. Aberdeen Grammar School; Aberdeen University. Qualified as Solicitor, 1938; Royal Navy and Fleet Air Arm (Lt. Cmdr., RNVR); former Assistant Registrar of Friendly Societies for Scotland; former Assistant Certification Officer for Trade Unions and Employers Associations; former Treasurer, HM Commissioners Trust Funds for Queen Victoria School, Dunblane; former Secretary and Treasurer, Scottish Naval, Military and Air Force Veterans Residences. Recreation: now only golf. Address: (h.) 12 Royal Circus, Edinburgh; T.-031-226 6432.

Craig, James Leith Johnstone, MA, LLB, WS. Solicitor; Assistant Registrar of Friendly Societies for Scotland, since 1981; Assistant Certification Officer for Trade Unions and Employers Associations for Scotland, since 1980; b. 23.5.44, Aberdeen; m., Susan Mary McDowell; 1 s.; 1 d. Educ. George Watson's College; Edinburgh University. Apprentice, W. & J. Burness, WS, Edinburgh, 1966-68; Assistant, A. & J.L. Innes, Solicitors, Kirkcaldy, 1968-71; Partner, R. Addison Smith & Co., WS, Edinburgh, 1972-82; Partner, Balfour & Manson, Solicitors, Edinburgh, since 1982. Recreations: golf; skiing. Address: (b.) 58 Frederick Street, Edinburgh; T.-031-225 8291.

Craig, John Alexander, BSc, DipTP, MICE, MIHT, MRTPI, FRSA. Head, Department of Town and Country Planning, Edinburgh College of Art/Heriot-Watt University, since 1978; Dean, Faculty of Environmental Studies, Heriot-Watt University, 1983-86; b. 18.5.32, Warrington, Lancashire; m., Jessie Crawford Inglis; 1 s.; 2 d. Educ. Invergordon Academy; Glasgow University; Edinburgh College of Art. National Service, RAF, 1955-57; Structural Engineer, P. & W. McLellan Ltd., Glasgow, 1957-59; Assistant Civil Engineer: Cumbernauld Development Corporation, 1959-63, Livingston Development Corporation, 1963-66; Lecturer, Department of Town and Country Planning, Edinburgh College of Art, 1966-78; private practice as Consultant Civil Engineer, 1968-77; part-time Lecturer, Coatbridge Technical College, 1957-63; Examiner, Glasgow and West of Scotland Committee for Technical Education, 1961-63; Member, Executive Committee, Scottish Branch, RTPI, 1979-83. Recreations: gardening; DIY house and car maintenance. Address: (h.) 1 Newland Avenue, Bathgate, West Lothian, EH48 1EE; T.-0506 53824.

Craig, John Warrender, LDS, FDS, RCSE, DPD. Chief Administrative Dental Officer, Lothian Health Board, since 1974; Specialist in Community Dental Health; Honorary Senior Lecturer, Department of Preventive Dentistry, Edinburgh University, since 1974; b. 21.3.28, South Africa; m., Hazel Campbell Henry; 2 s. Educ. George Heriot's School, Edinburgh; Edinburgh University; St. Andrews University. Chief Dental Officer, Inverness County Council, 1958; Senior Hospital Dental Officer, Eastern Regional Hospital Board, and Clinical Lecturer in Operative Dental Surgery, Department of Orthodontics and Children's Dentistry, St. Andrews University, 1961; Chief Dental Officer, City of Edinburgh, 1965. British Dental Association: former Secretary, Highland and Dundee Sections, President, East of Scotland Branch, 1976-77; British Paedodontic Society: Chairman, East of Scotland Branch, 1970-73, National President, 1972-73; National President, British Association for the Study of Community Dentistry, 1978-79. Publications: The Management of Traumatized Incisor Teeth of Children (Co-author), 1970. Recreations: squash; music; gardening. Address: (h.) 1 Liberton Gardens, Edinburgh, EH16 6JX; T.-031-664 3195.

Craig, Rev. John Wilson, MA, BD. Minister, St. Stephen's Comely Bank Parish Church, since 1963; b. 5.2.25, Paisley; m., Helen McArthur; 3 s. Educ. Camphill Secondary School, Paisley; Glasgow University. Student Assistant: Sherwood Church, Paisley, 1948-50, Cardonald Church, Glasgow, 1950-51; Minister, Radnor Park Church, Clydebank, 1951-63. Industrial Chaplain, Ferranti (Edinburgh). Recreations: stamp collecting; walking; touring. Address: 8 Blinkbonny Crescent, Edinburgh, EH4 3NB; T.-031-332 3364.

Craig, Rev. Maxwell Davidson, MA, BD, ThM. Minister, Wellington Church, Glasgow, since 1973; Chaplain to the Queen in Scotland, since 1986; Convener, Church and Nation Committee, Church of Scotland, 1984-88; b. 25.12.31; m., Janet Margaret Macgregor; 1 s.; 3 d. Educ. Bradford Grammar School; Harrow School; Oriel College, Oxford; Edinburgh University. National Service, 1st Bn., Argyll and Sutherland Highlanders (2nd Lt.), 1954-56. Assistant Principal, Ministry of Labour, 1957-61; Private Secretary to Parliamentary Secretary, 1959-61; left London and civil service to train for ministry of Church of Scotland, 1961; ThM, Princeton, 1965; Minister, Grahamston Parish Church, Falkirk, 1966-73; Chairman: Falkirk Children's Panel, 1970-72, Hillhead Housing Association Ltd., since 1975; Member, Strathclyde Children's Panel, since 1973. Recreations: hill-walking; dinghy sailing; squash. Address: 27 Kingsborough Gardens, Glasgow, G12 9NH; T.-041-339 3627.

Craig, Rev. Neil Douglas, MA, BD. Minister, Craignair linked with Urr, 1980-87; b. 7.8.22, Waterbeck; m., Florence Grimmond Sproul; 1 s.; 1 d. Educ. Royal High School, Edinburgh; Edinburgh University. Minister: St. Andrews Church, Hawick, 1947-53, Carstairs and Carstairs Junction, 1953-61, Craignair Church, Dalbeattie, 1961-80; former Convener, Youth Committee, Lanark Presbytery; Convener, Maintenance of the Ministry Committee, Dumfries Presbytery; Convener, General Assembly Committee on Probationers and Transference of Ministers. Chairman: Dalbeattie Nursing Association, Lindsay Trust (Dalbeattie). Recreations: cricket; golf; gardening. Address: (h.) Langdale, Lochanhead, Dumfries; T.-0387 73 222.

Craig, Very Rev. Professor Robert, CBE (1981), MA, BD, STM, PhD, DLitt, LLD, DD, Hon. FZweIE, Hon. CF. Moderator, General Assembly of the Church of Scotland, 1986-87; b. 22.3.17, Markinch, Fife; m., Olga Wanda Strzelec; 1 s.; 1 d. Educ. Coaltown of Balgonie and Falkland Public Schools; Bell-Baxter, Cupar; St. Andrews University; Union Theological Seminary, New York. Assistant Minister, St. John's Kirk, Perth, 1941-42; ordained, 1942; served as Army Chaplain, 1942-47, in Europe and Middle East; mentioned in Despatches, Normandy, 1944; STM Union Theological Seminary, 1948; Deputy Leader, Iona Community, 1948-50; Professor of Divinity, Natal University, 1950-57; Professor of Religion, Smith College, Northampton, Mass., USA, 1957-63; Professor of Theology, 1963-80, Principal and Vice-Chancellor, 1969-80, University of Zimbabwe (formerly Rhodesia); Minister, St. Andrew's Scots Memorial Church, Jerusalem, 1980-85; Hon. CF, 1947; Hon. LLD, Witwatersrand, 1979, Birmingham, 1980, Natal, 1981; Hon. DLitt, Zimbabwe, 1981; Honorary Fellow, Zimbabwe Institution of Engineers, 1976; Golden Jubilee Medal, Witwatersrand University, 1977; City of Jerusalem Medal, 1985. Address: (h.) West Port, Falkland, Fife, KY7 7BL; T.-033757 238.

Craig, Robert Harvey, RD, CA. Chartered Accountant in professional practice, since 1955; Honorary Sheriff, North Strathclyde at Campbeltown, since 1986; b. 18.12.29, Campbeltown; m., Marion Caldwell; 1 s.; 1 d. Educ. Campbeltown Grammar School; Glasgow University. Admitted to Institute of Chartered Accountants of Scotland, 1953; Fleet Air Arm, 1953-55; later commanded a Naval Reserve minesweeper; Director of various companies, including Chairman, West Coast Motor Service Co. Recreations: sailing; skiing. Address: (h.) Ferndean, Campbeltown, Argyll, PA28 6EN; T.-0586 52495.

Craig, Robert James, MB, ChB, MRCPsych, MPhil. Consultant Psychiatrist; Consultant, Rosslynlee Hospital; b. 13.5.47, Newcastle; m., Elaine Catherine May; 1 s. Educ. Daniel Stewart's College; Edinburgh University. House Officer: Head Injuries and Neurosurgery, Edinburgh Royal Infirmary and Western General Hospital, Edinburgh, General Medicine, Eastern General Hospital, Edinburgh; Senior House Officer, General Medicine, Edenhall Hospital, Musselburgh; Registrar, Psychiatry, Rosslynlee Hospital, Roslin; Senior Registrar, Psychiatry, Royal Edinburgh Hospital. Address: (b.) Rosslynlee Hospital, Roslin, Midlothian, EH25 9QE; T.-031-440 2313.

Craik, Professor Alexander Duncan Davidson, BSc, PhD, FRSE. Professor of Applied Mathematics, St. Andrews University, since 1988 (Reader, 1974-87); b. 25.8.38, Brechin; m., Elizabeth Mary Farmer; 1 s.; 1 d. Educ. Brechin High School; St. Andrews University; Cambridge University. St. Andrews University: Lecturer in Applied Mathematics, 1963-70, Senior Lecturer, 1970-74. Publication: Wave Interactions and Fluid Flows, 1985. Address: (h.) 92 Hepburn Gardens, St. Andrews, KY16 9LN; T.-0334 72992.

Craik, Sheriff Roger George, QC (Scot), MA, LLB. Sheriff of Lothian and Borders, at Edinburgh, since 1984; b. 22.11.40; m.; 1 s.; 1 d. Educ. Lockerbie Academy; Breadalbane Academy, Aberfeldy; George Watson's Boys' College; Edinburgh University. Solicitor, 1962; Orr Dignam & Co., Pakistan, 1963-65; called to Scottish Bar, 1966; Advocate Depute, 1980-83.

Craik, Wendy Ann, BA, PhD. Senior Lecturer in English, Aberdeen University, since 1972; b. 7.2.34, London; 1 s. Educ. Tiffin School, Kingston-on-Thames; Leicester University. Part-time Tutor, WEA and University Extension Courses, Vaughan College, Leicester, 1959-63; Principal English Teacher, Oadby Beauchamp Grammar School, Leicester, 1963-65; Lecturer in English, Aberdeen University, 1965-72. Publications: Jane Austen: the Six Novels; Jane Austen in her Time; Elizabeth Gaskell and the 19th Century Novel; The Bronte Novels. Address: (b.) Department of English, Kings College, Aberdeen; T.-0224 272632.

Cramb, Rev. Erik McLeish, LTh. Parish Minister, Yoker, Glasgow, since 1984; Chaplain to Yarrows Shipbuilders Ltd., since 1984; b. 26.12.39, Glasgow; m., Elizabeth McLean; 2 s.; 3 d. Educ. Woodside Secondary School, Glasgow; Glasgow University and Trinity College. Minister: St. Thomas' Gallowgate, Glasgow, 1973-81, St. Paul's United Church, Kingston, Jamaica, 1981-84. Socialist; Member, Iona Community; Member, Disablement Income Group. Recreation: supports Partick Thistle. Address: (h.) 15 Coldingham Avenue, Glasgow, G14 0PX; T.-041-952 1738.

Cramond, Kenneth William, BL. Chief Executive, Roxburgh District Council, since 1986; b. Arbroath; m., Georgina B. Silver; 3 s. Educ. St. Andrews University. Legal Assistant, Clydebank Town Council; Senior Legal Assistant, Inverness County Council; Town Clerk Depute, Hawick Town Council; Director of Administrative and Legal Services, Roxburgh District Council. Address: (b.) District Council Offices, High Street, Hawick, TD9 9EF; T.-0450 75991.

Cramond, Ronald Duncan, CBE (1987), MA, FBIM, FSA Scot. Commissioner, Countryside Commission for Scotland, since 1988; Deputy Chairman, Highlands and Islands Development Board, 1983-88; Trustee, National Museums of Scotland, since 1985; Member, Scottish Tourist Board, 1985-88; b. 22.3.27, Leith; m., Constance MacGregor (deceased); 1 s.; 1 d. Educ. George Heriot's School; Edinburgh University. Commissioned Royal Scots, 1950; entered War Office, 1951; Private Secretary to Parliamentary Under Secretary of State, Scottish Office, 1956; Principal, Department of Health for Scotland, 1957; Mactaggart Fellow, Glasgow University, 1962; Haldane Medallist in Public Administration, 1964; Assistant Secretary, Scottish Development Department, 1966; Under Secretary, 1973; Under Secretary, Department of Agriculture and Fisheries for Scotland, 1977. Publication: Housing Policy in Scotland, 1966. Recreations: golf; hill-walking; testing a plastic hip. Address: (b.) c/o Countryside Commission for Scotland, Battleby, Redgorton, Perth.

Crampin, Stuart, BSc, PhD, ScD, FRSE, FRAS. Deputy Chief Scientific Officer (Individual Merit), British Geological Survey, since 1987; Honorary Professor, Geophysics Department,

Edinburgh University, since 1988; Chairman, IASPEI Commission on Wave Propagation in Real Media, since 1983; b. 22.10.35, Tiptree, Essex; m., Roma Eluned Williams; 2 d. Educ. Maldon Grammar School; King's College, London; Pembroke College, Cambridge. Research Fellow, Uppsala University, 1963-65; Gassiot Fellow in Seismology, NERC, 1966-69; Principal Scientific Officer, Institute of Geological Sciences, 1969-76; Senior Principal Scientific Officer (Individual Merit), British Geological Survey, 1976-87; Conrad Schlumberger Award, EAEG, 1986. Recreations: hill-walking; travelling. Address: (b.) British Geological Survey, Murchison House, West Mains Road, Edinburgh, EH9 3LA; T.-031-667 1000.

Crampsey, Robert A. McN., MA (Hons), ARCM. Freelance Broadcaster and Writer; b. 8.7.30, Glasgow; m., Dr. Veronica R. Carson; 4 d. Educ. Holyrood School, Glasgow; Glasgow University; London University (External). RAF, 1952-55 (demobilised in rank of Flt. Lt.); Head of History Department, St. Aloysius College, Glasgow, 1967-71; Assistant Head Teacher, Holyrood Secondary School, 1971-74; Rector, St. Ambrose High School, Coatbridge, 1974-86. Winner, Brain of Britain, BBC, 1965; Churchill Fellow, 1970; semi-finalist, Mastermind, 1972-73; BBC Sports Commentator. Publications: History of Queen's Park FC; Puerto Rico; The Manager; The Scottish Footballer; The Edinburgh Pirate (Arts Council Award); The Run Out; Mr Stein (a biography); The Young Civilian; The Glasgow Golf Club 1787-1987; The Empire Exhibition; The Somerset Cricket Quiz Book; The Surrey Cricket Quiz Book. Recreations: travel; things Hispanic; listening to and playing music; cricket. Address: (h.) 15 Myrtle Park, Glasgow, G42; T.-041-423 2735.

Crawford, Henry Paton Fowler, MBE. Member, Scottish Agricultural Development Council; Member, Scottish Agricultural Consultative Panel; b. 14.1.21, Harthill; m., Robina Cessford; 2 s.; 1 d. Educ. Harthill School. Left school aged 14 and worked on farm for 17 years; took up post as District Organiser, Scottish Farm Servants Union (subsequently known as the Scottish Agriculture, Horticulture and Forestry Section, TGWU); appoined Sectional Secretary for Scotland; now retired. Address: (h.) 9 Woodside Park, Kelso, Roxburghshire; T.-Kelso 24328.

Crawford, Iain Padruig. Author, Journalist, Playwright and Broadcaster; b. 21.1.22, Inverness; 3 s.; 1 d. Educ. Inverness Academy; Jordanhill College School, Glasgow. Cadet in Merchant Navy, Officer in Royal Navy, 1939-46; Journalist, 1947-51; BBC, 1951-55; freelance Writer, 1955-59; Journalist in Scotland and London, 1959-64; worked as Film Critic and Travel Editor, Sunday Express; TV programmes and plays for ATV, Harlech, BBC; Publicity Director: Edinburgh International Festival, 1973-80, Scottish Opera, 1980-81; author of plays, Broomstick over Badenoch and Under The Light, and books including The Burning Sea, The Sinclair Exclusive, Scare The Gentle Citizen, The Cafe Royal, The Profumo Affair, London Man, The Havana Cigar, What About Wine, Gateway to Wine, Wine on a Budget, Make Me a Wine Connoisseur, Open Guide to Royal St. George's and Sandwich, Open Guide to Royal Troon and Kyle, Open Guide to the Old Course and St. Andrews; Open Guide to Turnberry and Carrick; Open Guide to Royal Lytham & St. Annes; Held in Trust (book of TV series); The Sea Dominies; eight-part film series, Held in Trust, STV. Recreations: music; golf; wine; watching rugby; other people's archaeology; French; Italian. Address: (h.) 42 Braid Crescent, Edinburgh, EH10 6AU; T.-031-447 1497.

Crawford, Earl of, and Balcarres, Earl of (Robert Alexander Lindsay), PC, DL. Premier Earl of Scotland; Head of House of Lindsay; b. 5.3.27; m., Ruth Beatrice; 2 s.; 2 d. Educ. Eton; Trinity College, Cambridge. Grenadier Guards, 1945-49; MP (Conservative), Hertford, 1955-74, Welwyn and Hatfield, February to September, 1974; Minister of State for Defence, 1970-72; Minister of State for Foreign and Commonwealth Affairs, 1972-74; Chairman, Lombard North Central Bank, 1976-80; Director, National Westminster Bank, since 1975; Director, Scottish American Investment Co., since 1978; Vice-Chairman, Sun Alliance & London Insurance Group, since 1975; Chairman, Royal Commission on Ancient and Historical Monuments of Scotland, since 1985; First Crown Estate Commissioner, 1980-85; Deputy Lieutenant, Fife. Address: (h.) Balcarres, Colinsburgh, Fife, KY9 1HL.

Crawford, Robert Caldwell. Composer; b. 18.4.25, Edinburgh; m., Alison Braedine Orr; 1 s.; 1 d. Educ. Melville College, Edinburgh; Keswick Grammar School; Guildhall School of Music, London. Freelance Composer and Critic until 1970; BBC Music Producer, 1970-85; Chairman, Music Advisory Committee for Sir James Caird's Travelling Scholarships Trust, since 1978. Recreations: carpentry; hill-walking; gardening; beekeeping. Address: (h.) 12 Inverleith Terrace, Edinburgh, EH3 5NS; T.-031-556 3600.

Crawford, Professor Robert MacGregor Martyn, BSc, DocSciNat (Liege), FRSE, FInstBiol. Professor of Plant Ecology, St. Andrews University, since 1977; b. 30.5.34, Glasgow; m., Barbara Elizabeth Hall; 1 s. Educ. Glasgow Academy; Glasgow University; Liege University; Munich University; Moscow University. Lecturer, then Reader in Botany, St. Andrews University; Past President, Edinburgh Botanical Society; Editor, Flora. Recreations: European languages; music; photography. Address: (b.) The University, St. Andrews, KY16 9AJ; T.-0334 76161.

Crean, Gerard Patrick, PhD, FRCPEdin, FRCPGlas. Consultant Physician-in-charge, Gastro-Intestinal Centre, Southern General Hospital, Glasgow, since 1967; Director, Diagnostic Methodology Research Unit, Southern General Hospital, Glasgow, since 1970; Honorary Lecturer, Glasgow University, since 1970; b. 1.5.27, Courtown Harbour, County Wexford; m., Janice Dodds Mathieson; 1 s.; 2 d. Educ. Rockwell College, Cashel, County Tipperary; University College, Dublin. House appointments, Mater Misericordiae Hospital, Dublin, Western General Hospital, Edinburgh and Edinburgh Royal Infirmary; Registrar, then Senior Registrar, Western General Hospital, Edinburgh; Member, scientific staff, Medical Research Council Clinical Endocrinology Unit, Edinburgh; Honorary Lecturer,

Department of Therapeutics, Edinburgh University; Visiting Professor in Physiology, Pennsylvania University. Clarke Prize, Edinburgh Pathological Club; contributed to several textbooks. Past President, British Society of Gastroenterology; Honorary Secretary, Scottish Fiddle Orchestra. Recreations: fiddle playing; traditional music; history of Antarctic exploration; golf. Address: (h.) St. Ronan's, Duchal Road, Kilmacolm, PA13 4AY; T.-Kilmacolm 2504.

Cresser, Malcolm Stewart, PhD, DIC, BSc, ARCS, FRSC, CChem. Reader, Department of Soil Science, Aberdeen University, since 1986; b. 17.4.46, London; m., Louise Elizabeth Blackburn; 1 s.; 2 d. Educ. St. Ignatius College, Tottenham; Imperial College, London. Lecturer, then Senior Lecturer, Department of Soil Science, Aberdeen University, 1970-86; awarded 11th SAC Silver Medal, 1984. Publications: Solvent Extraction in Flame Spectroscopic Analysis; Environmental Chemical Analysis (Co-author); Acidification of Freshwaters (Co-author). Recreations: painting; drawing; gardening. Address: (b.) Department of Soil Science, Meston Walk, Old Aberdeen, AB9 2UE; T.-0224 272259.

Cresswell, Lyell Richard, BMus (Hons), MusM, PhD. Composer; b. 13.10.44, Wellington, New Zealand; m., Catherine Mawson. Educ. Victoria University of Wellington; Toronto University; Aberdeen University. Music Organiser, Chapter Arts Centre, Cardiff; Forman Fellow in Composition, Edinburgh University; Canadian Commonwealth scholarship, 1969-70; Dutch Government bursary, 1974-75; Ian Whyte Award, 1978; APRA Silver Scroll, 1979; Cramb Fellow, Glasgow University, 1982-85. Address: (h.) 4 Leslie Place, Edinburgh, EH4 1NQ; T.-031-332 9181.

Crichton, Charles Maitland Makgill, of That Ilk. Owner, Monzie and Largo Estates, since 1968; Managing Director, Monzie Joinery Ltd., since 1970; b. 25.7.42, Crieff; m., Isla Susan Gloag; 1 s. Educ. Winchester. Economics Intelligence Department, Bank of England, 1963-68. President, Crieff Branch, NFU; Chairman, Kinross and West Perthshire Conservative Association; Conservative candidate, Greenock and Port Glasgow, 1983, Northumbria (European Election), 1984. Recreation: cross-country skiing. Address: Monzie Castle, Crieff, Perthshire; T.-0764 3110.

Crichton, Rev. James, MA, BD, MTh. Minister, Crosshill linked with Dalrymple, since 1981; b. 1.10.44, Glasgow; m.; 2 s.; 1 d. Educ. Eastbank Academy; Glasgow University. Minister, Crosshill, 1969-81; Chaplain, Ayr County Hospital, 1982-84; Member, South Ayrshire Health Council, since 1984; Moderator, Ayr Presbytery, 1984-85; Chairman, Scottish Reformation Society, since 1982. Publications: The Story of the Crosshill Churches; The Carrick Covenanters; Ayr Presbytery 1581-1981 (Co-author). Recreation: worrying about Rangers. Address: 30 Garden Street, Dalrymple, Ayrshire; T.-Dalrymple 263.

Crichton, John. Member, Western Isles Islands Council, since 1974 (Chairman, Manpower Committee, since 1978; Vice-Chairman, Policy and Resources Committee, since 1984); Chairman, Stornoway Trust, since 1983; Chairman, Crofters Union, since 1985; Liaison Officer and Assessor, Crofters Commission, since 1979; b. 27.3.23, Stornoway; m., Joan Finlayson; 2 s.; 1 d. Educ. Knock Public School. Address: (h.) 21 Swordale, Point, Isle of Lewis, PA86 0BP.

Crichton, Maurice, CA. Director, Woolwich Equitable Building Society and Chairman, Scottish and Northern Ireland Local Board, since 1977; Board Member and Vice Chairman, East Kilbride Development Corporation, since 1975; Director, Macphie of Glenbervie Ltd., since 1986; b. 4.6.28, Glasgow; m., Diana Russell Lang; 3 s.; 1 d. Educ. Kelvinside Academy; Cargilfield School; Sedbergh School. Partner, Touche Ross & Co., Chartered Accountants, 1955-86. Collector, Trades House of Glasgow, 1986-87; Member, Board, Bield Housing Association; Elder, Paisley Abbey. Recreations: golf; music; trout fishing; shooting. Address: (h.) Hall of Caldwell, Uplawmoor, Glasgow; T.-050 585 248.

Crichton, Robert, MC, DL, JP, SDA. Farmer; b. 17.11.22, Linlithgow; m., Joan Patricia Watts, BSc; 3 s.; 2 d. Educ. Edinburgh Academy; Edinburgh and East of Scotland College of Agriculture. Army, 1942-46, 2nd Lothians and Border Horse; agricultural student, 1947-49; farming, since 1949. Commandant, Edinburgh, Lothians and Peebles Army Cadet Force, until 1963; JP, since 1958; Deputy Lieutenant, County of West Lothian, since 1961. Recreation: gardening. Address: Niddry Mains, Winchburgh, Broxburn, West Lothian, EH52 6QR; T.-0506 890213.

Crichton, Thomas Kennedy, MBIM. Director of Industrial Liaison, Heriot-Watt University, Edinburgh, since 1982; b. 4.8.25, Edinburgh; m., Davida Anne Whiteford; 1 s.; 3 d. Educ. Daniel Stewart's College, Edinburgh; Heriot-Watt College, Edinburgh. Entered Royal Navy, 1943; commissioned, 1944; active service in light coastal forces in Channel, North Sea and Atlantic; Parts and Service Manager, James Ross & Sons (Motors) Ltd., Edinburgh, 1947-62; Divisional Manager, SAAB (Gt. Britain) Ltd., 1962-78; joined Heriot-Watt University, 1979. Director: Edinburgh Petroleum Development Services Ltd., Loch Ness Wellington Association Ltd.; Elder, Cramond Kirk. Recreations: walking and gardening; rugby and motor sport spectating. Address: (b.) Unilink, Heriot-Watt University, Riccarton, Edinburgh, EH14 4AS; T.-031-449 5111.

Critchley, Frank. Honorary Sheriff, Grampian, Highland and Islands, since 1984; b. 7.10.14, Inverness; m., Joyce; 1 s.; 1 d. Educ. Inverness Royal Academy; George Watson's College, Edinburgh; Edinburgh University. Solicitor, 1938-84; Royal Corps of Signals, 1939-46 (Major); President, Inverness Rotary Club, 1954-55; Member, Craig Dunain Hospitals Board of Management, 1952-58 (Chairman of Finance); Registrar, Diocese of Moray Ross and Caithness, 1971-86; Member, Council, Law Society of Scotland, 1971-77; Dean, Faculty of Solicitors of Inverness-shire, 1979-82. Recreations: reading; walking; gardening; golf; theatre. Address: (h.) Malwa, 9 Mayfield Road, Inverness; T.-Inverness 233516.

Critchlow, Howard Arthur, BDS, FDSRCS(Eng), FDSRCPS(Glas). Consultant Oral Surgeon (Honorary Clinical Lecturer), Glasgow Dental Hospital, Stobhill General Hospital and Royal Hospital for Sick Children, Glasgow, since 1976; b. 22.4.43, Littleborough; m., Avril; 1 s.; 1 d. Educ. Nottingham High School for Boys; Sheffield University. General dental practice, Sheffield; oral surgery training posts. Chairman, Greater Glasgow Health Board Area Dental Committee and Dental Ethical Committee; Chairman, Glasgow Northern Hospitals Ethical Committee. Recreations: gardening; hill-walking; riding; running. Address: (b.) Glasgow Dental Hospital and School, 378 Sauchiehall Street, Glasgow, G2 3JZ; T.-041-332 7020.

Croan, Sheriff Thomas Malcolm, MA, LLB. Sheriff of North Strathclyde at Kilmarnock, since 1983; b. 7.8.32, Edinburgh; m., Joan Kilpatrick Law; 1 s.; 3 d. Educ. St. Joseph's College, Dumfries; Edinburgh University. Admitted to Faculty of Advocates, 1956; Standing Junior Counsel, Scottish Development Department, 1964-65 and (for highways work), 1967-69; Advocate Depute, 1965-66; Sheriff of Grampian, Highland and Islands at Banff and Peterhead, 1969-83. Recreation: sailing. Address: (h.) Overdale, 113 Bentinck Drive, Troon.

Crofton, Sir John Wenman, KB, MD, FRCP, FRCPE. Vice-Chairman, Scottish Committee, Chest, Heart and Stroke Association, since 1976; Chairman, Tobacco and Health Committee, International Union Against Tuberculosis and Lung Disease, since 1984; b. 27.3.12, Dublin; m., Eileen Chris Mercer, MBE; 2 s.; 3 d. Educ. Tonbridge; Sidney Sussex College, Cambridge. Professor of Respiratory Diseases, Edinburgh University, 1952-77; Dean, Faculty of Medicine, 1963-66; Vice-Principal, 1969-70; President, Royal College of Physicians of Edinburgh, 1973-76; Chairman, Scottish Health Education Co-ordinating Committee, SHHD, 1981-86. Recreations: history; music; mountains. Address: (h.) 13 Spylaw Bank Road, Edinburgh, EH13 0JW; T.-031-441 3730.

Crofts, Roger Stanley, BA, MLitt, CertEd. Assistant Secretary, Highlands and Tourism Division, Industry Department for Scotland, since 1984; b. 17.1.44, Leicester. Educ. Hinckley Grammar School; Liverpool University; Leicester University. Research Assistant in Geography: Aberdeen University, 1966-72, University College, London, 1972-74; entered Scottish Office, 1974; Senior Research Officer, 1974-78; Principal Research Officer, 1978-84. Recreations: gardening; choral singing; hill-walking. Address: (h.) 19 Manor Place, Edinburgh, EH3 7DX; T.-031-225 1177.

Cromar, Robert Lindsay, FIB (Scot), AMP (Harvard). General Manager, Bank of Scotland, since 1982; a Director, Glasgow Chamber of Commerce, since 1982; a Director, Queen's Park Football Club, since 1965; Trustee, Hutchesons Education Trust, since 1986; b. 8.10.31, Glasgow; m., Anne Henderson; 2 s.; 1 d. Educ. Hutchesons Grammar School. Bank of Scotland: Clerk, 1948-52, Inspector, 1952-68, Manager, 1968-73, Senior Manager, 1973-78, Assistant General Manager, 1978-82. Recreation: golf. Address: (b.) 110 St. Vincent Street, Glasgow, G2 5EJ; T.-041-221 7071.

Cromartie, Earl of (Roderick Grant Francis Mackenzie), MC, TD, JP, DL. Chief of the Clan Mackenzie; b. 24.10.04; m., 1, Dorothy Downing Porter (m. diss.); 2 d.; 2, Olga Mendoza (m. diss.); 1 s.; 3, Lilias Richard MacLeod. Educ. Charterhouse; Sandhurst. Major, Seaforth Highlanders (retired); Convener: Ross and Cromarty County Council, 1971-75, Ross and Cromarty District Council, 1975-77; Honorary Sheriff; Freeman of Ross and Cromarty, 1977. Address: (h.) Castle Leod, Strathpeffer, Ross and Cromarty, IV14 9AA.

Crombie, John Somerville Brand, BL, WS, NP. Partner, Alex. Morison & Co., WS, Edinburgh, since 1956; Director, Financial Marketing Consulting Group PLC; Director, Alna Press Ltd., since 1955; Director, Key Housing Association Ltd.; Director, Scotcap Ltd.; b. 10.8.29, Coatbridge; m., Isabella Rankin Cursiter; 3 d. Educ. Royal High School, Edinburgh; Edinburgh University. Formerly Secretary, Edinburgh Branch, Scottish Society for the Mentally Handicapped and Chairman, SSMH and Key Housing Association; Elder, Church of Scotland. Recreations: gardening; golf; curling; music. Address: (b.) 33 Queen Street, Edinburgh, EH2 1LE; T.-031-226 6541.

Crompton, Professor David William Thomasson, MA, PhD, ScD, FIBiol. John Graham Kerr Professor of Zoology, Glasgow University, since 1985; b. 5.12.37, Bolton; m., Effie Mary Marshall; 1 s.; 2 d. Educ. Bolton School; Sidney Sussex College, Cambridge. National Service, commission, King's Own Royal Regiment, 1957; Assistant in Research, Cambridge University, 1963-68; Fellow, Sidney Sussex College, 1964-85; Vice-Master, 1981-83; Lecturer in Parasitology, Cambridge University, 1968-85; Joint Editor, Parasitology, 1972-82; Adjunct Professor, Division of Nutritional Sciences, Cornell University, New York, since 1981; Aquatic Life Sciences Committee, Natural Environment Research Council, 1981-84; Director, Company of Biologists Ltd., since 1985; Member, WHO Expert Committee on Parasitic Diseases, since 1985; Scientific Medal, Zoological Society of London, 1977. Recreations: mountain walking; fishing; books; bull terriers. Address: (b.) Department of Zoology, Glasgow University, Glasgow, G12 8QQ; T.-041-330 5395; (h.) 7 Kirklee Terrace, Glasgow, G12 0TQ; T.-041-357 2631.

Crompton, Graham Kenneth, MB, ChB, FRCPE. Consultant Physician, Lothian Health Board, since 1969; Senior Lecturer (part-time) in Medicine and Respiratory Medicine, Edinburgh University, since 1969; b. 14.2.35, Salford; 2 s. Educ. Salford Grammar School; Edinburgh University. Appointed Consultant Physician, 1969; Director of Studies, Faculty of Medicine, 1977; Member, Medical Advisory Committee, Asthma Society, 1981. Publications: Diagnosis and Management of Respiratory Diseases; chapters in five medical text books; numerous papers. Recreation: watching sport. Address: (h.) 1B/3 Fairacre Court, Abbotsford Crescent, Edinburgh, EH10 5DY; T.-031-447 1022.

Crosbie, Ian Martin, FCII. Member, Lothian Regional Council, 1982-88; b. 26.5.22, Edinburgh; m., Lily; 1 s. Educ. Daniel Stewart's College, Edinburgh. Joined Scottish Life Assurance Company, 1939; RAF, 1941-46; management, Scottish Life Assurance Company, 1970-84; Council Member, Insurance Society of Edinburgh, 1973-83 (Honorary Treasurer, 1978-83). Vice-Moderator, Society of High Constables of Edinburgh. Recreations: golf; tennis; travel; music; gardening; photography. Address: (h.) 4 Braehead Avenue, Edinburgh, EH4 6BA; T.-031-339 6233.

Crosby, William Scott, CBE (1982), BL. Lawyer; b. 31.7.18, Hawick; m., Margaret Elizabeth Bell; 3 s. Educ. Hawick High School; Edinburgh University. Army Service, 1939-46; Croix de Guerre, 1945; acted as Brigade Major 152 Brigade, 1945; Partner, Storie, Cruden & Simpson, Advocates, Aberdeen, since 1949; Chairman, Grampian Health Board, 1973-82; President, Society of Advocates in Aberdeen, 1984-85. Recreations: golf; swimming; walking; music; language study; gardening. Address: (h.) 82 Beaconsfield Place, Aberdeen; T.-Aberdeen 643067.

Crosfield, Very Rev. George Philip Chorley, MA (Cantab). Provost, St. Mary's Cathedral, Edinburgh, since 1970; b. 9.9.24, London; m., Susan Mary Jullion; 1 s.; 2 d. Educ. George Watson's College, Edinburgh; Selwyn College, Cambridge. Royal Artillery, 1942-46 (Captain); Priest, 1952; Assistant Curate: St. David's, Pilton, Edinburgh, 1951-53, St. Andrew's, St. Andrews, 1953-55; Rector, St. Cuthbert's, Hawick, 1955-60; Chaplain, Gordonstoun School, 1960-68; Canon and Vice-Provost, St. Mary's Cathedral, Edinburgh, 1968-70. Recreations: walking; reading; carpentry. Address: (h.) 8 Lansdowne Crescent, Edinburgh, EH12 5EQ; T.-031-225 2978.

Crossling, Frank Turner, MB, ChB, FRCSG, FRCSEng. Consultant General Surgeon, Stobhill General Hospital, Glasgow, since 1962; b. 16.8.27, Aberdeen; m., Margaret Elizabeth Abdy; 1 s. Educ. Robert Gordon's College, Aberdeen; Aberdeen University. Series of surgical posts in Aberdeen, London and Glasgow; seconded to University of East Africa, Nairobi, 1967, to help set up a medical school. Recreations: photography; classical music; gardening; dry fly fishing. Address: (h.) 28 North Grange Road, Bearsden, Glasgow, G61 3AF; T.-041-943 0409.

Crowe, Professor Malcolm Kenneth, DPhil, CEng, MIEE, FBCS. Professor of Computing Science, Paisley College of Technology, since 1985; b. 13.1.48, Dublin; m., Margaret Elaine Erskine. Educ. Sandford Park School, Dublin; Trinity College, Dublin; St. Catherine's College, Oxford. Postgraduate work, Oxford; joined staff of Paisley College of Technology as Lecturer in Mathematics, 1972; promoted Senior Lecturer, 1981; Head of Department, 1985; Dean, School of Information, Social and Management Sciences, 1988. Chairman, Scottish Homosexual Rights Group, 1978-80. Address: (h.) 21 Torridon Avenue, Glasgow, G41 5AT; T.-041-427 3767.

Cruickshank, Alistair Booth, MA. Secretary, Royal Scottish Geographical Society, since 1986; Member, Forth Valley Health Board, since 1977; b. 3.8.31, Dumfries; m., Sheena Carlin Brown; 2 s.; 1 d. Educ. High School of Stirling; Glasgow University; Georgia University. Flying Officer, Education Branch, RAF, 1956-58; Glasgow University, 1958-61; Nottingham University, 1961-65; Glasgow University, 1965-86. Member, Clackmannan District Council, 1974-77; Area Chairman, Scout Association, Clackmannanshire, since 1986. Recreations: fishing; travel. Address: (b.) 10 Randolph Crescent, Edinburgh, EH3 7TU; T.-031-225 3330.

Cruickshank, Robert James, SSC. Honorary Sheriff at Ayr; b. 1.8.15, Irvine; m., Isabella Jackson McDougall; 1 d. Educ. Cumnock Academy; Edinburgh University. Depute Procurator Fiscal: Aberdeen, 1943-47, Ayr, 1947-51; Senior Depute Procurator Fiscal, Edinburgh, 1951-54; Procurator Fiscal: Falkirk, 1954-58, Ayr, 1959-76. Address: (h.) Corncairn, 5 Abbot's Way, Doonfoot, Ayr, KA7 4EZ; T.-Ayr 41533.

Cruttenden, Timothy Peter, BEd, DipPE, FILAM. Director of Recreation and Leisure Services, East Kilbride District Council, since 1980; b. 6.9.45, Portsmouth; m., Hazel; 2 s. Educ. Warblington School, Havant; Bristol University; St. Paul's, Cheltenham. Taught in Hampshire and Gloucestershire, 1967-72; sports centre management, 1973-77; recreation administration, since 1977. Winner, Sports Council Management Award, Scotland, 1977; served on various national bodies and working parties, including Countryside Commission for Scotland and Scottish Sports Council. Recreations: squash; hockey; golf; sailing. Address: (b.) Civic Centre, East Kilbride, G74 1AB; T.-03552 28777.

Cull, Roger Ewart, BSc (Hons), PhD, MB, ChB, FRCPE. Consultant Neurologist, Royal Infirmary, Edinburgh, since 1981; Senior Lecturer in Medical Neurology, Department of Clinical Neurosciences, Edinburgh University, since 1981; b. 24.10.47, Leigh, Lancs; m., Dr. Ann M. Cull; 2 d. Educ. Rydal School, Colwyn Bay; Edinburgh University. House Physician, Western General Hospital, Edinburgh, 1971-72; House Surgeon, Longmore Hospital, Edinburgh, 1972; MRC Research Fellow, Department of Physiology, Edinburgh University, 1972-75; Lecturer in Medical Neurology, Edinburgh University, 1976-79; Clinical Lecturer in Neurology, National Hospital for Nervous Diseases, London, 1979-81. Recreations: jazz guitar and piano (Member, Edinburgh Medical Jazz Quartet). Address: (b.) Department of Medical Neurology, Royal Infirmary, Lauriston Place, Edinburgh; T.-031-229 2477.

Cullen, Hon. Lord (William Douglas Cullen), QC, MA, LLB. Senator of the College of Justice, since 1986; b. 18.11.35; m.; 2 s.; 2 d. Educ. Dundee High School; St. Andrews University. Called to Scottish Bar, 1960; Standing Junior Counsel to HM Customs and Excise, 1970-73; Advocate-Depute, 1978-81; Chairman, Medical Appeal Tribunal, 1977-86.

Culshaw, Professor Brian, BSc, PhD, CEng, MIEE. Professor of Electronics, Strathclyde University, since 1983; b. 24.9.45, Ormskirk; m., Patricia Brigid Cargan; 2 d. Educ. Ormskirk Grammar School; University College, London. Research Fellow, Cornell University, 1970; Technical Staff Member, Bell Northern Research,

Ottawa, 1970-73; University College, London: Research Fellow, 1974-75, Lecturer, 1975-82; Senior Research Fellow, Stanford University, 1982; Reader, University College, London, 1983. Recreations: walking; photography; music and opera; theatre. Address: (h.) Cromdale, Gryffe Road, Kilmacolm, Renfrewshire, PA13 4BD; T.-050587 2460.

Cuming, Henry George, CBE, MA, PhD, DIC, CEng, FIMA, MRAeS. Principal, Dundee College of Technology, since 1969; b. 11.12.27, London; m., Valerie Margaret Bennett; 1 s.; 1 d. Educ. Owen's School, London; St. Catharine's College, Cambridge; London University. Scientific Officer, Royal Aircraft Establishment, Farnborough, 1951-55; Lecturer in Mathematics, Birmingham College of Advanced Technology, 1955-58; Senior Lecturer in Mathematics, 1958-60; Head, Department of Aeronautical Engineering, Lanchester College of Technology, Coventry, 1960-66; Depute Principal, Napier College of Science and Technology, Edinburgh, 1966-69. Address: (b.) Bell Street, Dundee, DD1 1HG; T.-0382 27225.

Cumming, James. Sheriff Clerk, Hamilton, since 1985; b. 3.10.43, Glasgow; m., Katrina M. Anderson; 1 s.; 1 d. Educ. Whitehill Senior Secondary School, Glasgow. Sheriff Clerk Depute, Glasgow, Peterhead, Dumbarton, Glasgow; Sheriff Clerk, Haddington; Depute Clerk of Justiciary, Parliament House. Recreations: reading; swimming. Address: (b.) Sheriff Clerk's Office, Almada Street, Hamilton; T.-Hamilton 282957.

Cumming, James William Hunter, RSA, RSW, DA, PPSSA. Painter; b. 24.12.22, Dunfermline; m., Betty Elston; 1 s.; 1 d. Educ. Dunfermline High School; Edinburgh College of Art; Edinburgh University. RAF Volunteer Reserve, 1941-46 (flew SEAAF); Lecturer, Drawing, Painting, History of Art, Edinburgh, 1950-60; Senior Lecturer, Mural Department and School of Drawing and Painting, Edinburgh, 1960-82; President, Society of Scottish Artists, 1958-61; contributor to BBC radio and television arts programmes, 1958-68; elected ARSA and RSW, 1962; wrote outline and script for film, Three Scottish Painters; Member, Broadcasting Council for Scotland, 1969-75; elected Royal Scottish Academician, 1970; Treasurer, RSA, 1973-78; Council Member, National Academic Awards of Great Britain, 1974-79 (Fine Art Board Assessor and Member, Committee for Research Degree Awards); Secretary, RSA, 1978-80; Royal Scottish Academy Award, 1951; awarded scholarship in the Humanities, International Seminar, Harvard University, 1964; awarded Prize by Royal Scottish Society of Painters in Watercolour, 1977; Lothian Region Award, RSW Centenary Exhibition, Edinburgh, 1980. Recreation: watching the world go by. Address: Studio, Swallow Cottage, Lennel, near Coldstream, Berwickshire; T.-0890 2064.

Cumming, Robert Currie, BL, FIBS, ACIB, FRCSEdin (Hon.). Chairman, English Speaking Union - Scotland, since 1984; Non-Executive Director, Adam & Co. PLC, since 1983; b. 21.5.21, Strathaven; m., Mary Jean McDonald Crombie. Educ. Hutchesons' Grammar School, Glasgow; Glasgow University. Former Executive Director, Royal Bank of Scotland Group PLC and Royal Bank of Scotland PLC. Trustee and Finance Convener, Royal Scottish Geographical Society; Member, Finance Committee, Royal Blind Asylum; Member, Investment Committee and Finance Committee, Royal College of Surgeons, Edinburgh; Representative to University Conference, Stirling University. Recreations: fishing; golf; walking. Address: (h.) 3 Succoth Park, Edinburgh, EH12 6BX; T.-031-337 1910.

Cumming, Ronald Patrick, MB, ChB, FRCSEdin. Consultant Surgeon, Shetland Hospitals, 1957-85; Honorary Senior Lecturer in Surgery, Aberdeen University, 1980-85; b. 15.8.23, Golspie; m., Norma Gladys Kitson; 2 s. Educ. Golspie Secondary School; Aberdeen University. General practice assistant, Huntly and Rhynie, Aberdeenshire; Assistant Lecturer in Anatomy, Aberdeen University; junior surgical posts in Worcester, Burnley, and Aberdeen; Fellow: British Medical Association, Association of Surgeons of Great Britain and Ireland. JP; Honorary Sheriff; Chairman, Shetland Committee for Employment of Disabled People, until 1985; former Member, Lerwick Town Council and Shetland County Council; Junior Bailie, Lerwick Town Council, 1972-75; President, Shetland Fiddlers, 1973-85. Publication: Aspects of Health and Safety in Oil Development (Co-Editor). Recreations: golf; badminton; gardening; reading; music. Address: (h.) 62 Hammerfield Avenue, Aberdeen; T.-0224 313192.

Cummins, John George, MA, PhD. Reader in Spanish, Aberdeen University, since 1980 (Head, Department of Spanish, since 1979); b. 26.9.37, Hull; m., Elaine S. Rockett; 2 s.; 1 d. Educ. Malet Lambert School, Hull; Manchester University. Assistant in Spanish, St. Andrews University, 1961-63; Lecturer in Spanish, Birmingham University, 1963-64; Aberdeen University: Lecturer in Spanish, 1964-72, Senior Lecturer in Spanish, 1972-80. Recreations: shooting; fishing. Address: (b.) Department of Spanish, King's College, Aberdeen University, Old Aberdeen; T.-Aberdeen 27254.

Cunningham, Rev. Iain Dickson, MA, BD (Hons). Minister, Kirkton Parish Church, Carluke, since 1987; b. 12.4.54, Port Glasgow; m., Dawn Gibson; 1 s.; 2 d. Educ. Hamilton Academy; Glasgow University. Assistant Minister, Castlehill Church, Ayr, 1978-80; Minister, Duntocher Trinity Parish Church, 1980-87. Recreations: painting; song-writing; music-making; sports; reading; gardening. Address: (h.) Kirkton Manse, Station Road, Carluke, ML8 5AD; T.-0555 71262.

Cunningham, Professor Ian M.M., CBE, FRSE, FIBiol, FRAgS, Hon. Assoc. RCVS, Bsc, PhD. Member of Council: Agriculture and Food Research Council; National Trust for Scotland; Royal Society of Edinburgh; Countryside Commission; Farm Animal Welfare Council; Member, Hill Farming Advisory Committee, Scotland; Professor of Agriculture, Glasgow University, and Principal, West of Scotland Agricultural College, 1980-87; b. 30.9.25, Kirknewton; m., Agnes Whitelaw Frew. Educ. Lanark Grammar School; Edinburgh University. Assistant Economist,

West of Scotland Agricultural College, 1946-47; Lecturer in Agriculture, Durham School of Agriculture, 1947-50; Lecturer, then Senior Lecturer, Edinburgh University, 1950-68; Director, Hill Farming Research Organisation, 1968-80. Member: Farm Animal Welfare Council, Hill Farming Advisory Committee, Scotland; George Hedley Memorial Award for services to the sheep industry; Massey Ferguson Award for services to British agriculture; Hon. Assoc., RCVS. Address: (h.) Glenburnie, Boghall, Biggar Road, Edinburgh.

Cunningham, James M., JP, BSc. Director, D.C. Watson & Sons, since 1974; Director, Fenton Barns (Mushrooms) Ltd., since 1988; b. 25.11.43, Falkirk; m., Marion Cunningham; 3 s. Educ. George Heriot's, Edinburgh; Edinburgh Univesity. Cadzow Sheep Co., 1967-69; Abbotsford Premixing Co., Vancouver, 1970-72; Consultant, J. Bibby (Agriculture). Vice-Convener, Poultry, NFU of Scotland; Elder, Gullane Parish Church. Recreations: badminton; boardsailing. Address: (h.) Carlops, Marine Terrace, Gullane, East Lothian; T.-062 084 2280.

Cunningham, Rev. John, JCD. Roman Catholic Priest; President, Roman Catholic Scottish National Tribunal, since 1986; b. 22.2.38, Paisley. Educ. St. Mary's College, Blairs, Aberdeen; St. Peter's College, Cardross; Scots College and Gregorian University, Rome. Assistant Priest, Our Lady of Lourdes, Bishopton, 1964-69; Professor of Canon Law, St. Peter's College, Cardross and Newlands (Glasgow), 1967-81; Advocate of the Roman Catholic Scottish National Tribunal, 1970-82; Assistant Priest, St. Columba's, Renfrew, 1974-86; Vice-President, RC Scottish National Tribunal, 1982-86. Address: 22 Woodrow Road, Glasgow, G41 5PN; T.-041-427 3036.

Cunningham, John Wylie Rodger. Director General and Secretary, St. Andrew's Ambulance Association, since 1983; b. 4.4.45, Kilmarnock; m., Agnes Margaret Elizabeth (Margot). Educ. Irvine Royal Academy. Entered journalism with George Outram group, including several years with the Glasgow Herald; moved into administration, 1968, and spent eight years on secretariat of National Farmers Union of Scotland; joined Charles Barker Scotland as senior Public Relations Executive. Recreations: cinema and theatre; sport, especially cricket and rugby; eating out; military history; writing; walking; hard work. Address: (h.) Birnam Lodge, Stevenston Road, Kilwinning, Ayrshire; T.-0294 52338.

Curle, Professor Samuel Newby, BSc, MSc, PhD, FRSE. Gregory Professor of Applied Mathematics, St. Andrews University, since 1967 (Dean, Faculty of Science, 1982-85); b. 18.6.30, Sunderland; m., Shirley Kingsford Campion; 3 s.; 1 d. Educ. Bede School, Sunderland; Manchester University. Assistant Lecturer, Mathematics Department, Manchester University, 1953-54; Scientific Officer, Aerodynamics Division, National Physical Laboratory, 1954-61; Southampton University: Reader, Department of Aeronautics/Astronautics, 1961-64, Reader, Department of Mathematics, 1964-67. Orville Wright Prize, Royal Aeronautical Society, 1963; Secretary, Methodist International House, Southampton, 1964-67. Recreations: music; cricket; soccer. Address: (b.) Mathematical Institute, North Haugh, St. Andrews, KY16 9SS; T.-0334 76161.

Curran, Professor Sir Samuel Crowe, Kt, DL, MA, BSc, PhD, DSc, FInstP, FInstE, FRSE, FRS, CEng, DEng, FEng. Visiting Professor of Energy Studies, Glasgow University; Scientific Adviser to various organisations; b. 23.5.12, Ballymena, Northern Ireland; m.; 3 s.; 1 d. Educ. Wishaw High School; Glasgow University; Cambridge University; California University. Research, Glasgow University, Cambridge University; war research, MAP and Ministry of Supply in radar and atom bomb (Manhattan project); staff, Physics Department, Glasgow University; Chief Scientist, UKAEA at AWRE (also on board, UKAEA, Harwell); Principal, Royal College of Science and Technology, Glasgow; Principal and Vice-Chancellor, Strathclyde University. Publications: books on nuclear radiation and energy topics. Recreations: golf; horology. Address: (h.) 93 Kelvin Court, Glasgow, G12 OAH; T.-041-334 8329.

Currie, Professor Sir Alastair Robert, Kt, MB, ChB, Hon DSc, Hon LLD, FRCP, FRCPEdin, FRCPGlas, FRCSE, FRCPath, FRSE. Chairman, Board of Governors, Beatson Institute for Cancer Research; Honorary Treasurer, Cancer Research Campaign; Member, UK Coordinating Committee on Cancer Research; Member, Board of Directors, Inveresk Research International Ltd.; Emeritus Professor of Pathology, Edinburgh University; b. 8.10.21, Isle of Islay; m., Jeanne Marion Clarke, MB, ChB; 3 s.; 2 d. Educ. High School of Glasgow; Glasgow University. Lecturer and Senior Lecturer in Pathology, Glasgow University and Glasgow Royal Infirmary, 1945-59; Head, Division of Pathology, Imperial Cancer Research Fund, London, 1959-62; Regius Professor of Pathology, Aberdeen University, 1962-72; Professor of Pathology, Edinburgh University, 1972-86. Recreation: reading. Address: (h.) 42 Murrayfield Avenue, Edinburgh, EH12 6AY; T.-031-337 3100.

Currie, Alexander Monteith, OBE, BA, BLitt. Secretary, Edinburgh University, since 1978; b. 2.5.26, Stevenston; m., Pamela Mary Breeze; 2 s. Educ. Stevenston Higher Grade School; Portmadoc Grammar School; Bangor University; St. Catherine's College, Oxford. Administrative Officer, Manchester University, 1952-61; Academic Secretary, Liverpool University, 1962-65; Registrar and Secretary, Sheffield University, 1965-78. Address: (h.) 13 Moray Place, Edinburgh, EH3 6DT; T.-031-225 7775.

Currie, Rev. David Edward Paxton, BSc, BD. Minister, West Kirk, East Kilbride, since 1983; b. 27.6.50, Glasgow; m., Gwen; 2 s.; 2 d. Educ. Hunter High School, East Kilbride; Duncanrig Senior Secondary School, East Kilbride; Strathclyde University; Glasgow University. Apprentice metallurgist, Rolls Royce, Hillington, 1967-70; studied, Strathclyde University, 1970-74; Rolls Royce: Production Engineer, Hillington, 1974-77, Development Engineer, East Kilbride, 1977-79; studied for the ministry, 1979-82; probationery year, Rutherglen Stonelaw, 1982-83. Recreations:

reading; music; hill-walking; skiing. Address: 1 Barr Terrace, West Mains, East Kilbride, G74 1AP; T.-East Kilbride 20753.

Currie, James W., BSc (Hons), DRTC, FIEE, CEng. Chief Engineer, Generation Design and Construction, South of Scotland Electricity Board; b. 25.7.24, Ayr; m., Mary E. Procter; 1 s.; 1 d. Educ. Irvine Royal Academy; Glasgow University; Royal Technical College. Army Service, 1944-47; Kennedy & Donkin, Consulting Engineers, 1947-52; Montreal Engineering Company, Canada and Venezuela, 1952-55; Associated Industrial Consultants, 1955-56; Kennedy & Donkin, Consulting Engineers, 1956-62; joined SSEB, 1962. Past President: Scottish Ski Club, Scottish National Ski Council; former Vice President, British National Ski Federation. Recreations: skiing; golf; sailing. Address: (b.) SSEB, Cathcart House, Spean Street, Glasgow, G44 4BE; T.-041-637 7177.

Currie, John (Ian) C., CChem, MRSC, FIWEM. Director and River Inspector, Tweed River Purification Board, since 1964; b. 19.10.33, Glasgow; m., Margaret A.; 3 s.; 1 d. Educ. Shawlands Academy, Glasgow; Paisley Technical College. Assistant Inspector and Chemist, Tweed River Purification Board, 1955-61; Assistant Inspector, Clyde River Purification Board, 1961-64; Pollution Prevention Officer, Usk River Authority, 1964. Recreation: golf. Address: (b.) Burnbrae, Mossilee Road, Galashiels; T.-0896 2425.

Currie, Rev. Robert, MA. Community Minister, Partick, Glasgow, since 1984; Chaplain, Queen Mother's Hospital, Glasgow, since 1978; Assistant Chaplain, Royal Hospital for Sick Children, Glasgow, since 1984; b. 9.12.24, Aberdeen; m., Sheila Thomson; 1 s.; 2 d. Educ. Robert Gordon's College; Central School, Aberdeen; Aberdeen University; Christ's College, Aberdeen. Minister: Boquhanran, Clydebank, 1955-69, Dowanhill, Glasgow, 1969-84; Member, Publications Committee, Convener, Reviewing Committee, Iona Community, 1972-87; Convener, Mainland Committee, Iona Community, 1986-88; Honorary Secretary, Scottish Pastoral Association (now defunct); Chaplain, West of Scotland Wing Air Training Corps, 1959-69. Recreation: listening to choral, organ and orchestral music. Address: 61 Dowanside Road, Glasgow, G12 9DL; T.-041-334 5111.

Currie, Professor Ronald Ian, CBE (1977), FIBiol, FRSE, BSc (Hons). Senior Research Fellow, Grant Institute of Geology, Edinburgh University, since 1988; Director and Secretary, Scottish Marine Biological Association, 1966-87; b. 10.10.28; m., Cecilia de Garis; 1 s.; 1 d. Educ. Glasgow University; Copenhagen University. Joined Royal Naval Scientific Service, 1949; seconded to National Institute of Oceanography; William Scoresby Expedition, South Africa, 1950; Discovery Expedition, Antarctica, 1951; Chairman, Biological Planning Committee, International Indian Ocean Expedition, 1960; Indian Ocean Expedition, 1963 and 1964; Secretary: International Association for Biological Oceanography, 1964-66 (President, 1966-70), Scientific Committee on Oceanic Research, International Council of Scientific Unions, 1972-78; Honorary Secretary, Challenger Society, 1956-88; Honorary Professor, Heriot-Watt University, 1979. Recreations: cooking; hill-walking; shooting; local history. Address: (h.) Kilmore House, Kilmore, by Oban, Argyll; T.-Kilmore 248.

Curtis, Professor Adam Sebastian Genevieve, MA, PhD. Professor of Cell Biology, Glasgow University, since 1967; b. 3.1.34, London; m., Ann Park; 2 d. Educ. Aldenham School; Kings College, Cambridge. University College, London: Honorary Research Assistant, 1957-62, Lecturer in Zoology, 1962-67. Director, Company of Biologists Ltd., since 1961; Governor, Westbourne School, since 1985; Council Member, Royal Society of Edinburgh, 1983-86, Society of Experimental Biology, since 1985; Assessor, Glasgow University Court, since 1987; Editor, Scottish Diver magazine, since 1978; President, Scottish Sub-Aqua Club, 1972-76. Recreations: sports diving; gardening. Address: (h.) 2 Kirklee Circus, Glasgow, G12 0TW; T.-041-339 2152.

Curtis, G. Ronald, BSc, CEng, FICE, FSA Scot. Reservoir Safety Engineer, North of Scotland Hydro-Electric Board, 1971-87; Member, British National Committee on Large Dams; Chairman, Historic Roads and Bridges Committee, Association for the Protection of Rural Scotland, since 1983; b. 24.4.25, Edinburgh; m.; 4 s. Educ. George Watson's College, Edinburgh; Edinburgh University. Design of sewage works, J.D. & D.M. Watson, Consulting Civil Engineers, London, 1947-49; design and construction of sewerage and water supply schemes, Babtie Shaw and Morton, Consulting Civil Engineers, Glasgow, 1949-58; joined North of Scotland Hydro-Electric Board, 1958. Elder, Church of Scotland, 1962-87; Leader, Scout Movement, 1943-75. Recreations: Scotland; archaeology; historic Highland roads and bridges; megalithic astronomy. Address: (h.) 4 Braid Mount Rise, Edinburgh, EH10 6JW.

Cusine, Douglas James, LLB. Senior Lecturer in Conveyancing and Professional Practice of Law, Aberdeen University, since 1982; b. 2.9.46, Glasgow; m., Marilyn Calvert Ramsay; 1 s.; 1 d. Educ. Hutchesons' Boys' Grammar School; Glasgow University. Solicitor, 1971; Lecturer in Private Law: Glasgow University, 1974-76, Aberdeen University, 1977-82. Publication: Marine Pollution: Law and Practice (Co-Editor), 1980; Cases and Materials in Commercial Law (Co-Editor), 1987; A Scots Conveyancing Miscellany (Editor), 1987; various articles on medico-legal issues and conveyancing. Recreations: swimming; walking; bird-watching. Address: (h.) New Mearns, Downies, Portlethen, Aberdeen; T.-0224 780334.

Cuthbert, James R., MA, MSc, DPhil. Chief Statistician, Scottish Education Department, since 1982; b. 20.7.46, Irvine. Educ. Glasgow University; Sussex University. Lecturer in Statistics, Glasgow University, 1970-74; civil servant (Scottish Office and HM Treasury), since 1974. Address: (b.) Scottish Education Department, 43 Jeffrey Street, Edinburgh.

Cuthbert, William Moncrieff, DL, FRSA. Chairman, Clyde Shipping Company (Director, since 1971); Chairman of Council and Executive Committee, National Trust for Scotland, since 1984; b.22.6.36; m., Caroline Jean Balfour Mitchell; 2 s.; 1 d. Educ. Shrewsbury School. Chairman, Scottish Amicable Life Assurance Society (Director, since 1976); Director, the Murray Johnstone managed Investment Trusts, since 1982; Member, Executive Board, Lloyd's Register of Shipping, since 1982. Member, Council, Royal Glasgow Institute of Fine Arts, since 1981; Member, Royal Company of Archers (Queen's Bodyguard for Scotland), since 1968; Governor, Glasgow School of Art. Address: (b.) 78 Carlton Place, Glasgow, G5 9TG; T.-041-429 2181.

Cuthbertson, Sir David Paton, CBE, MD, DSc, LLD (Glasgow and Aberdeen), FRSE, FRCPE, Hon. DSc (Rutgers, USA), Dr hon causa (Zagreb), Hon. FRCSE, Hon. FRCPath, Hon. FRIFST, Hon. FRCPE. Honorary Research Fellow, Glasgow University; Honorary President, International Union of Nutritional Sciences; b. 9.5.00, Kilmarnock; m., Jean Prentice Telfer (deceased); 2 s.; 1 d. Educ. Kilmarnock Academy; Glasgow University; University of Leipzig. Clinical Biochemist and Lecturer in Pathological Biochemistry, Glasgow University, 1926-34; Grieve Lecturer in Physiological Chemistry, Glasgow University, 1934-45; seconded to Medical Research Council, 1943-45; Medical Adviser, Glasgow Home Guard and Garrison Lt. Col.; Director, Rowett Research Institute, 1945-65; former Honorary President, British Nutrition Foundation; Honorary Member: American Institute of Nutrition, Finnish Biochemical and Microbiological Society, European Society of Parenteral and Enteral Nutrition. Recreations: golf; gardening; water colour painting. Address: (h.) Glenavon, 11 Willockston Road, Troon, KA10 6LD; T.-Troon 312028.

Cuthbertson, Iain. Actor; b. 4.1.30. Acted, Citizens', Glasgow, 1958-60; made London debut with the Citizens' in Gay Landscape, 1958; played title role in The Wallace, Edinburgh Festival, Edinburgh Festival, 1960; Member, Pitlochry Festival company, 1961; General Manager and Director of Productions, Citizens', 1962-65; there created the role of Armstrong in Armstrong's Last Goodnight; Associate Director, Royal Court Theatre, London, 1965; there played Musgrave in Sergeant Musgrave's Dance; Director, Perth Theatre, 1967-68; played the leading role in Sutherland's Law (TV series).

Cuthbertson, Ian Jardine, LLB, NP. Managing Partner, Dorman, Jeffrey & Co., Solicitors, Glasgow and Edinburgh, since 1979; b. 8.5.51, Glasgow; m., Sally Jane; 1 s.; 2 d. Educ. Jordanhill College School, Glasgow; Glasgow University. Apprenticeship, Messrs Boyds; admitted as Solicitor, 1974; Partner, Messrs Boyds, 1978; jointly founded firm of Dorman Jeffrey & Co., 1979. Honorary Legal Adviser, St. Mungo Group, Riding for the Disabled Association. Recreations: rugby; swimming; reading; computers. Address: (b.) Madeleine Smith House, 6/7 Blythswood Square, Glasgow; T.-041-221 9880; 20 Ainslie Place, Edinburgh; T.-031-225 9999.

Cuthbertson, Rev. Malcolm, BA, BD (Hons). Minister, Easterhouse: St. George's and St. Peter's, since 1984; b. 3.4.56, Gorbals; m., Deborah Diane Beaubrun. Educ. Grangemouth High School; Stirling University; Aberdeen University. Assistant, Crown Court Church, London, 1983-84. Vice-Chairman, Trustees, Easterhouse Youth Project. Recreations: table tennis; squash. Address: (h.) 2/1, 2 Lochdochart Road, Easterhouse, Glasgow, G34 0PZ; T.-041-773 2667.

Cuthell, Rev. Thomas Cuthbertson, MA, BD. Senior Minister, St. Cuthbert's Parish Church, Edinburgh, since 1976; b. 18.2.41, Falkirk. Educ. Bo'ness Academy; Edinburgh University. Assistant Minister, St. Giles Cathedral, Edinburgh, 1964-66; Minister, North Kirk, Uphall, 1966-76. Recreations: yacht racing; music; squash. Address: (h.) 22 Learmonth Terrace, Edinburgh, EH4 1PG; T.-031-332 6138.

Cuthill, Robert M. Managing Editor, Glasgow Herald, since 1981; b. 8.6.29, Glasgow; 1 s.; 1 d. Educ. Niagara Falls Collegiate Vocational Institute, Ontario. The Scotsman, 1946-50 (including National Service, Royal Navy); Reporter, Reynolds News, 1950-51; Reporter, Greenock Telegraph, 1951-60; Greenock District Reporter, Glasgow Herald and Evening Times, 1960-67; news desk, Glasgow Herald, 1967-69; News Editor, Glasgow Herald, 1969-81. Recreations: golf; gardening; Scrabble. Address: (b.) 195 Albion Street, Glasgow, G1 1QP; T.-041-552 6255.

Cutler, James R., BSc (Hons). Deputy Director, DAFS Agricultural Scientific Services, Edinburgh, since 1987 (Head, Pesticides and Pest Control Division, since 1982); b. 27.9.31, Ranchi, India; m., Elizabeth Johnston; 1 s.; 1 d. Educ. St. Paul's School, Darjeeling; Banff Academy; Aberdeen University. Stored Products Entomologist: West African Stored Products Research Unit, Nigeria, 1955-59, DAFS, Agricultural Scientific Services, 1959-74; Head, Pesticides Usage Survey Unit, DAFS, 1974-82. Recreations: gardening; angling; woodworking. Address: (b.) DAFS, East Craigs, Edinburgh, EH12 8NJ; T.-031-339 2355.

Czerkawska, Catherine Lucy, MA (Hons); MA (postgraduate). Freelance Writer and Dramatist; b. 3.12.50, Leeds; m., Alan Lees; 1 s. Educ. Queen Margaret's Academy, Ayr; St. Michael's Academy, Kilwinning; Edinburgh University; Leeds University. Began by writing and reading poetry; on leaving university, wrote and published two books of poetry (White Boats and A Book of Men); taught EFL in Finland and Poland for three years; returned to Scotland to work as Community Writer in Fife; thereafter, full-time freelance Writer working on radio and television drama, original plays and adaptations, short stories, features, etc.; author, Fisherfolk of Carrick; Pye Radio Award, Best Play of 1980, for Oh Flower of Scotland; Scottish Radio Industries Club Award, 1983, for Bonnie Blue Hen. Recreations: karate; swimming; travel; local history; cookery; films. Address: c/o A.D. Peters and Co. Ltd., 10 Buckingham Street, London, WC2N 6BU; T.-01-839 2556.

D

Dagg, John Hunter, MD (Hons), FRCPGlas, FRCPEdin. Consultant Physician, Western Infirmary, Glasgow, since 1972; Honorary Lecturer in Medicine, Glasgow University, since 1962; b. 23.3.33, Rutherglen. Educ. High School of Glasgow; Glasgow University. Junior hospital posts, Glasgow and Paisley, 1958-65; Senior US Public Health Service Fellow, University of Washington Medical School, 1965-67; Senior Wellcome Fellow in Clinical Science, University Department of Medicine, Western Infirmary, Glasgow, 1968-72. Honorary Curator, Art Collection, and other activities, Royal College of Physicians and Surgeons, Glasgow; Member, Medical Advisory Committee, Greater Glasgow Health Board. Recreations: classical music, especially as pianist; hill-walking; gardening. Address: (h.) 26 Westbourne Gardens, Glasgow, G12; T.-041-334 2981.

Daiches, David, MA (Edin), DPhil (Oxon), Hon. DLitt (Edinburgh, Glasgow, Sussex, Brown), Docteur de l'Universite (Sorbonne), DUniv (Stirling). Writer; b. 2.9.12, Sunderland; m., Isobel J. Mackay (deceased); 1 s.; 2 d. Educ. George Watson's College, Edinburgh; Edinburgh University; Balliol College, Oxford. Professor of English, Cornell University, 1946-51; University Lecturer in English and Fellow of Jesus College, Cambridge, 1951-61; Professor of English, Sussex University, 1961-77; Director, Institute for Advanced Studies in the Humanities, Edinburgh University, 1980-86. President, Saltire Society, 1981-87; Past President, Association for Scottish Literary Studies. Publications: numerous works of criticism and biography. Recreations: music; talking. Address: (h.) 12 Rothesay Place, Edinburgh, EH3 7SQ.

Daiches, Lionel Henry, MA, LLB. Queen's Counsel, since 1956; Fellow, International Academy of Trial Lawyers, since 1976; b. 8.3.11, Sunderland; 2 s. Educ. George Watson's College, Edinburgh; Edinburgh University. Solicitor, Scotland, 1936-39; Army service, 1940-46, including Judge Advocate-General's Branch, Central Mediterranean Forces, North Africa and Italy (including Anzio Beachhead); Advocate, Scots Bar, 1946; QC Scotland, 1956; broadcaster on television and radio. Publication: Russians at Law, 1960. Recreations: walking and talking. Address: (h.) 10 Heriot Row, Edinburgh, EH3 6HU; T.-031-556 4144.

Dalby, Martin, BMus, ARCM. Head of Music, BBC Scotland, since 1972; b. 25.4.42, Aberdeen; m., Hilary. Educ. Aberdeen Grammar School; Royal College of Music. Music Producer, BBC Radio 3, 1965-71; Cramb Research Fellow in Composition, Glasgow University, 1971-72; freelance Composer. Recreations: flying; railways; bird-watching; hill-walking. Address: (h.) 23 Muirpark Way, Drymen, near Glasgow, G63 ODX; T.-0360 60427.

Dale, Alan, RIBA, ARIAS, ACIArb. Group Director West, Scottish Development Agency, since 1977; b. 19.7.33, Huddersfield; m., Alison Mary; 2 d. Educ. Royal Technical College, Salford; Manchester Art School. Harry S. Fairhurst & Son, Architects, Manchester; Derek Lovejoy & Partner, Architects, Manchester; Chief Architect, Fairclough; Scottish Development Agency. Recreation: fishing. Address: (b.) 120 Bothwell Street, Glasgow; T.-041-248 2700.

Dale, Brian Graeme, LLB, WS, NP. Partner, Brooke & Brown, WS, Dunbar, since 1974; Convener, Board of Administration, General Synod, Scottish Episcopal Church, since 1980; b. 20.11.46, London; m., Judith Gail de Beaufort Franklin; 4 s.; 2 d. Educ. Bristol Grammar School; Aberdeen University. Legal apprentice, Shepherd & Wedderburn, WS, Edinburgh, 1968-70; Assistant, then Partner, Stuart & Stuart Cairns & Co., WS, Edinburgh, 1970-85; Treasurer, 1971, Secretary, 1974, Registrar, 1974, Diocese of Edinburgh, Scottish Episcopal Church; Secretary, St. Mary's Music School Trust Ltd.; Honorary Secretary, Abbeyfield Society (Dunbar) Ltd. Recreations: music; sport in general; singing; family life. Address: (h.) 2 Newhouse Terrace, Dunbar, East Lothian; T.-Dunbar 62059.

Dale, Colin, BSc, MBIM. Manager, Scotland and Northern Ireland, British Technology Group, since 1979; b. 2.3.39, Edinburgh; m., Norma Mary Reilly; 1 s.; 2 d. Educ. Royal High School, Edinburgh; Heriot-Watt University. Research Chemist in industry, 1962-69; Executive, Scottish Council (Development and Industry), 1969-77; Manager, Scottish Development Agency, 1977-79. Member, Council, Stow College, Glasgow; Member, Council, West Scotland Technology Centre, Glasgow; Member, Committee, Harmeny Athletic Club, Edinburgh. Recreations: outdoors; gardening; athletics; reading history. Address: (b.) 23 Chester Street, Edinburgh, EH3 7ET; T.-031-220 2860.

Dale, Jack, MA, BD, STM. Further and Higher Education Secretary, Educational Institute of Scotland, since 1985; b. 15.5.38, Glasgow; m., Dr. Maureen G. Dale; 1 s.; 2 d. Educ. North Kelvinside Secondary School, Glasgow; Glasgow University; Union Theological Seminary, New York. Minister, Glengarry Parish, Church of Scotland, 1964-67; Senior Lecturer in Philosophy, Paisley College of Technology, 1967-85. Address: (h.) Westbrae, Gartmore, Stirling, FK8 3RJ; T.-Aberfoyle 360.

Dale, Professor John Egerton, BSc, PhD, FRSE. Professor of Plant Physiology, Edinburgh University, since 1985 (Head, Department of Botany, since 1987); b. 13.2.32, London; m., Jacqueline Joyce Benstock; 1 s.; 2 d. Educ. City of London School; Kings College, London. Plant Physiologist, Empire Cotton Growing Corporation, Uganda, 1956-61; Lecturer in Botany, then Reader, Edinburgh University, 1961-85. Secretary, Society for Experimental Biology, 1974-79; Secretary General, Federation of European Societies of Plant Physiology, 1978-84. Publications: 90 papers on growth of leaves and related topics. Recreations: travel; gardening. Address: (h.) The Old Bothy, Drem, North Berwick, EH39 5AP; T.-062 085 394.

Dale, Professor Richard Steele, BSc (Econ), PhD. Professor of International Banking and Financial Studies, since 1985; Barrister-at-Law; b. 20.4.43, Oxford; m., Mary Valentine; 1 s.; 1 d. Educ. Marlborough College; London School of Economics. Executive, N.M. Rothschild & Sons Ltd., 1973-77; SSRC Research Fellow, University of Kent, 1977-79; Lecturer in International Finance, Bath University, 1979-84; leave of absence, 1982-83, to take up Rockefeller Foundation International Relations Fellowship, based at Brookings Institution, Washington DC. Publications: Anti-Dumping Law in a Liberal Trade Order, 1979; Managing World Debt, 1983; The Regulation of International Banking, 1984. Recreation: walking. Address: (b.) 9 Blackford Hill View, Edinburgh, EH9 3HD; T.-031-667 6227.

Dalgety, Ramsay Robertson, QC, LLB (Hons). Advocate, 1972, Queen's Counsel, 1986, Temporary Sheriff, 1987; b. 2.7.45, Edinburgh; m., Mary Margaret Bernard; 1 s.; 1 d. Educ. High School of Dundee; St. Andrews University. Member, City of Edinburgh District Council, 1974-80; Director, Scottish Opera Ltd., since 1980; Chairman/Director, Venture Shipping Ltd., since 1983; Trustee, Opera Singers Pension Fund (London), since 1983; Director, Scottish Opera Theatre Trust Ltd., since 1987. Address: 196 Craigleith Road, Edinburgh, EH4 2EE; T.-031-332 1417.

Dalgleish, Robert Goodfellow Dakers, MBE, JP. Member, Edinburgh District Council, 1974-77, 1980-88 (first Convener, Information Processing); Chairman, Edinburgh District Licensing Board, 1984-88; b. 8.3.30, Edinburgh; m., Margaret Catherine Heron; 3 s.; 1 d. Educ. George Heriot's School; Heriot-Watt College. Apprentice industrial chemist, laboratory technician, draughtsman, spares engineer and engineering designer, Ferranti; worked briefly at Tugela Ferry Mission Hospital, South Africa, 1957; Member, Lothian Health Board, 1976-80; Chairman, Edinburgh Health Council, 1981-84. Sunday School teacher, 15 years; youth club leader, 17 years; trade union steward, 15 years; Member, Church of Scotland Society, Religion, Technology Project, 14 years; Congregational lay preacher, 14 years; Past Chairman, Leith Labour Party. Recreations: being at home; studying light aircraft design; genealogy; swimming; photography. Address: (h.) 1 Granton Park Avenue, Edinburgh.

Dalhousie, Earl of (Simon Ramsay), KT, GCVO, GBE, MC, LLD. Lord Lieutenant, County of Angus, since 1967; Lord Chamberlain to Queen Elizabeth, the Queen Mother, since 1965; Chancellor, Dundee University, since 1977; b. 17.10.14, London; m., Margaret Elizabeth Mary Stirling; 3 s.; 2 d. Educ. Eton; Christ Church, Oxford. Major, 4/5 Black Watch TA; served overseas, 1939-45 (prisoner); MP, Forfar, 1945-50; Conservative Whip, 1946-48; Governor-General, Federation of Rhodesia and Nyasaland, 1957-63. President: Save the Children Fund, Scotland, Victoria League in Scotland. Address: (h.) Brechin Castle, Brechin, Angus; T.-035-62 2176.

Dall, John Lamont Cameron, OBE (1987), OStJ, MD, FRCP(Glas), DU (Ottawa). Consultant Physician in Geriatric Medicine, Victoria Infirmary, Glasgow, since 1967; Honorary Clinical Lecturer (Geriatrics), Glasgow University, since 1967; Visiting Professor (Geriatric Medicine), University of Ottawa, since 1982; b. 15.10.29, Glasgow; m., Dr. Lilian Margaret Gibson; 2 d. Educ. Shawlands Academy, Glasgow; Hutcheson's Boys' Grammar School, Glasgow. National Service, RAMC, 1954-56; junior hospital appointments in medical specialties, 1956-63. Publications: papers on heart disease/hyptertension; textbook chapters on heart disease of the elderly. Recreation: golf. Address: (b.) Victoria Geriatric Unit, Mansionhouse Road, Glasgow, G42.

Dalrymple, Major The Hon. Colin James, DL, JP, BA. Farmer and Landowner, since 1956; b. 19.2.20, Ford, Midlothian; m., Fiona Jane Edwards; 1 s.; 3 d. Educ. Eton College; Trinity College, Cambridge. Served with Scots Guards, 1939-56; Member, Midlothian County Council, 1967-75; active supporter, Scottish Landowners Federation and National Farmers Union of Scotland. Recreations: shooting; fishing. Address: Oxenfoord Mains, Dalkeith.

Dalrymple, Sir Hew (Fleetwood) Hamilton-, 10th Bt (created 1697), KCVO, 1985 (CVO, 1974). Lord Lieutenant, East Lothian, since 1987; Vice-Chairman, Scottish & Newcastle Breweries, 1983-86 (Director, 1967-86); Chairman, Scottish American Investment, since 1985 (Director, since 1967); b. 9.4.26; m., Lady Anne-Louise Mary Keppel; 4 s. Educ. Ampleforth; HDD Staff College, Camberley, 1957. Commissioned Grenadier Guards, 1944; DAAG HQ 3rd Division, 1958-60; Regimental Adjt., Grenadier Guards, 1960-62; retired, 1962; Lieutenant, Queen's Bodyguard for Scotland (Royal Company of Archers), Adjutant, 1964-85; President: East Lothian Scout Council, East Lothian Council for Voluntary Services; DL, East Lothian, 1964; JP, 1987. Address: Leuchie, North Berwick, East Lothian; T.-North Berwick 2903.

Dalrymple, John Francis, BA, PhD, MInstP, CPhys, FSS. Lecturer in Management Science, Stirling University, since 1979; Chairman, Scottish Association of Children's Panels, since 1983; b. 18.9.49, Rosyth; 1 d. Educ. St. Andrew's High School, Kirkcaldy; Stirling University; Strathclyde University. Research Fellow, then Lecturer, Department of Applied Physics, Strathclyde University, 1974-79. Member, Strathclyde Region Children's Panel, since 1977. Recreations: skiing; walking; reading; swimming. Address: (b.) Department of Business and Management, Stirling University, Stirling, FK9 4LA; T.-0786 73171, Ext. 2606.

Dalrymple-Hamilton of Bargany, Captain North Edward Frederick, DL, JP, CVO (1961), MBE (1953), DSC (1943). Ensign, Queen's Bodyguard for Scotland (Royal Company of Archers); b. 17.2.22; m., 1, Hon. Mary Colville (deceased); 2 s.; 2, Antoinette Beech. Educ. Eton. Royal Navy: Director of Naval Signals, 1965, Director, Weapons Equipment Surface, 1967, retired, 1970. Address: (h.) Lovestone House, Bargany, Girvan, Ayrshire.

Dalton, Dorothy, BL. Executive Director, Scottish Community Education Council, since 1985; b. 4.7.35, Kilbarchan; m., Rodger Guy Dalton; 1 d. Educ. Paisley Grammar School; Glasgow University. Solicitor in private practice; Reporter to Children's Panel, West Lothian; Assistant Director of Planning, Lothian Region. Chairman, Brook Advisory Centre, Edinburgh. Recreations:

golf; photography; bee-keeping. Address: (b.) Atholl House, 2 Canning Street, Edinburgh, EH3 8EG; T.-031-229 2433.

Daly, Rev. Robert, MA, JP. Parish Minister, linked charges of Inchture and Kinnaird, since 1954, Longforgan, since 1963, Abernyte, since 1982; Prison Chaplain, Castle Huntly, since 1963; b. 9.12.20, Glasford; m., Winifred Muriel Emslie; 1 s.; 4 d. Educ. High School of Glasgow (Captain of School, 1937-38); Aberdeen University and Christ's College. War service, Royal Corps of Signals, 1941-45 (Captain); Justice of the Peace, Perth and Dundee; Chaplain, Royal Caledonian Curling Club; Moderator, Dundee Presbytery; Chairman, Carse of Gowrie School Council. Recreations: curling; golf. Address: (h.) The Manse, Longforgan, Dundee, DD2 5HB.

Dalyell, Tam. MP (Labour), Linlithgow (formerly West Lothian), since 1962; Weekly Columnist, New Scientist, since 1967; b. 9.8.32, Edinburgh; m., Kathleen Wheatley; 1 s.; 1 d. Educ. Edinburgh Academy; Harecroft; Eton; King's College, Cambridge; Moray House, Edinburgh. National Service, Scots Greys; Teacher, Bo'ness Academy, 1957-61; Deputy Director of Studies, Ship-School Dunera, 1961-62; Member, Public Accounts Committee, 1962-66; PPS to R.H.S. Crossman, 1964-70; Vice-Chairman, Parliamentary Labour Party, 1974-76; Member, European Parliament, 1975-78; Member, National Executive Committee, Labour Party, 1986-87. Publications: Case for Ship Schools, 1959; Ship-School Dunera, 1961; Devolution: the end of Britain?, 1978; A Science Policy for Britain, 1983; One Man's Falklands, 1983; Misrule, 1987. Address: (h.) The Binns, Linlithgow, EH49 7NA; T.-0506-83 4255.

Dalzel-Job, Patrick. Deputy Lieutenant, Lochalsh, since 1979; b. 1.6.13, London; m., Bjorg Bangsund (deceased); 1 s. Educ. Berkhamsted; in Switzerland. Owner/Master, topsail schooner Mary Fortune, mainly Norwegian and Arctic waters, until start of Second World War; as a junior Sub Lt., organised landing of Allied Expeditionary Force, North Norway, 1940, and evacauation of civilians from Narvik before German bombing; thanked by King of Norway; Special Service Operations, Norway, France, Germany; Canadian Navy, post-war; retired to West Highlands, 1960. Publication: The Settlers, 1957. Recreations: skiing; sailing; woodland garden. Address: (h.) Nead-An-Eoin, by Plockton, Ross-shire; T.-0599 84244.

Dalziel, Colonel William Alexander, CBE (1980), OStJ, TD, JP, DL, KLJ. Chairman, Transport Users Consultative Committee for Scotland; Chairman, Gas Consumers Council for Scotland; Chairman, Magistrates Committee, Edinburgh; Deputy Lord Lieutenant, Edinburgh, since 1977; b. 6.5.21, Dumbarton; m., Elizabeth Alexander Melville; 1 d. Army Service (Colonel); Deputy Chief Signals Officer, Scottish Command; worked in retail clothing trade, transport industry, fishing industry. Recreations: golf; gardening. Address: (h.) Gowanfield, 6 Orchard Road South, Edinburgh, EH4 3HF.

Dangerfield, Nancy. Chair, Scottish Campaign for Nuclear Disarmament, since 1986; Speech Therapist, NHS; b. Glasgow; 1 s.; 1 d. Educ. Riverside Senior Secondary School, Glasgow; Jordanhill College of Education; Glasgow University. Shorthand typist, 1951-59; houseworker, 1959-67; mature student, 1967-71. Joined Scottish Campaign for Nuclear Disarmament Committee, 1978. Recreations: badminton; swimming; theatre; cinema. Address: (h.) 2 Merkland Drive, Kirkintilloch, Glasgow; T.-041-776 6651.

Daniels, Peter William, MA (Hons). Chief Executive, Clydesdale District Council, since 1983; b. 8.6.49, Wishaw; m., Anne; 2 s.; 1 d. Educ. Brandon High School, Motherwell; Dalziel High School, Motherwell; Glasgow University; Jordanhill College of Education. Lecturer (A) in Public Administration, Bell College of Technology, Hamilton, 1972-75; Personal Assistant to Chief Executive, Renfrew District Council, 1975-81; Assistant Chief Executive, Leicester City Council, 1981-83. Member, Scottish Symphony Orchestra Trust; former elected Member, East Kilbride District Council; former Vice-Chairman, Manpower Committee, COSLA. Recreations: classical music; chess; cycling; running. Address: (b.) Clydesdale District Council, District Offices, South Vennel, Lanark, ML11 7JT; T.-Lanark 61331.

Darling, Alistair Maclean. MP (Labour), Edinburgh Central, since 1987; Advocate; b. 28.11.53; m. Educ. Aberdeen University. Admitted Faculty of Advocates, 1984; Member, Lothian Regional Council, 1982-87.

Darwent, Rt. Rev. Frederick Charles, LTh (Hon). Bishop of Aberdeen and Orkney, since 1978; b. 20.4.27, Liverpool; m., 1, Edna Lilian Waugh (deceased); 2 d.; 2, Roma Evelyn Fraser. Educ. Warbreck School, Liverpool; Ormskirk Grammar School; Wells Theological College, Somerset. Followed a banking career, 1943-61; War Service, Far East, 1945-48; ordained Deacon, 1963, Priest, 1964, Diocese of Liverpool; Curate, Pemberton, Wigan, 1963-65; Rector: Strichen, 1965-71, New Pitsligo, 1965-78, Fraserburgh, 1971-78; Canon, St. Andrew's Cathedral, Aberdeen, 1971; Dean of Aberdeen and Orkney, 1973-78. Recreations: amateur stage (acting and production); calligraphy; music. Address: (b.) Diocesan Office, 16 Crown Terrace, Aberdeen, AB1 2HD; T.-Aberdeen 580172.

Das, Sachinandan, MB, BS, FRCR, DMRT. Consultant in administrative charge, Ninewells Hospital, Dundee, and Head, University Department, Dundee University, since 1987; Chairman, Area Oncology Committee, since 1987; Council Member, Scottish Radiological Society, since 1987; Regional Postgraduate Education Advisor in Radiotherapy and Oncology, since 1987; b. 1.8.44, Cuttack, India; m., Dr. Subhalaxmi; 1 s.; 1 d. Educ. Ravenshaw Collegiate School; SCB Medical College, Cuttack, India; Utkal University. Senior House Officer in Radiotherapy, Plymouth General Hospital, 1969-70; Registrar in Radiotherapy and Oncology, then Senior Registrar, Mersey Regional Centre for Radiotherapy, Liverpool, 1970-77; Member: Standing Scottish Committee, National Medical Consultative Committee, Scottish Paediatric Oncology Group, Joint Radiological Safety Committee, Radiation Hazards Sub-Committee, Area Oncology Committee.

Recreations: hill-walking; table tennis; reading. Address: (h.) Grapevine, 42 Menzieshill Road, Dundee, DD2 1PU; T.-Dundee 642915.

Datta, Dipankar, MB, BS, FRCPGlas. Consultant Physician (with special interest in gastroenterology), since 1975; b. 30.1.33, Chittagong, India; m., Dr. J.B. Datta (qv); 1 s.; 1 d. Educ. Calcutta University. Former Member, Central Executive Committee, Scottish Council, United Nations Association; Vice Chairman, UN Association Glasgow; Chairman, Overseas Doctors' Association, Scottish Division; former Member, Lanarkshire Health Board; Member, Executive Committee, Scottish Council, Royal Commonwealth Society for the Blind. Recreations: reading - history, economics and international politics. Address: (h.) 9 Kirkvale Crescent, Newton Mearns, Glasgow, G77 5HB; T.-041-639 1515.

Datta, Jean Bronwen, MB, ChB, MRCP(Glas), DObstRCOG, DCH. Associate Specialist in Infectious Diseases, Belvidere Hospital and Ruchill Hospital, Glasgow, since 1970; Honorary Clinical Lecturer, Glasgow University, since 1985; b. 2.2.32, Glasgow; m., Dr. Dipankar Datta (qv); 1 s.; 1 d. Educ. Rutherglen Academy; Glasgow University. Various hospital appointments, including Registrar in Paediatrics, Sheffield Children's Hospital and Royal Maternity Hospital, Glasgow. Publication: Infections in Current Medical Practice (Contributor), 1986. Recreations: walking; skiing; gardening; music. Address: (h.) 9 Kirkvale Crescent, Newton Mearns, Glasgow, G77 5HB; T.-041-639 1515.

Davey, Christopher John, BA (Hons), FSA Scot. Senior Lecturer in History, Dundee University, since 1979 (Member, University Court, since 1981); b. 25.10.38, Epsom; m., Nancy Taylor; 1 s.; 1 d. Educ. Steyning Grammar School; London School of Economics. Temporary Assistant Lecturer, Sheffield University; Assistant Lecturer, then Lecturer, Queen's College, St. Andrews University; Lecturer, Dundee University, 1967-79; (first) Students' Assessor on Senate, 1968-71; Dean of Students, Faculty of Arts and Social Sciences, 1975-79; elected Member of Senate, 1971-81; Chairman, University External Liaison Committee, since 1979. Chairman, Dundee Area Scout Council; Secretary, Dundee Historical Association (President, 1978-81); Council Member, Abertay Historical Society (President, 1977-79); President, Dundee Association of University Teachers, 1971-73. Recreations: watching birds; writing poetry; collecting goss china. Address: (b.) Department of Modern History, University of Dundee, Dundee; T.-0382 23181.

Davidson, Alan Ingram, ChM, FRCSEdin, DObstRCOG. Consultant Surgeon, Aberdeen Royal Infirmary, since 1974; Honorary Senior Lecturer in Surgery, Aberdeen University, since 1974; b. 25.3.35, Aberdeen; m., Margaret Elizabeth Mackay; 1 s.; 1 d. Educ. Robert Gordon's College, Aberdeen; Aberdeen University. House Officer, Aberdeen Royal Infirmary, 1959-60; National Service, Royal Army Medical Corps, 1960-62; Lecturer, Department of Pathology, Aberdeen, 1963-64; Registrar and Senior Registrar, Aberdeen Royal Infirmary, 1964-74. Recreations: gardening; watching TV; music. Address: (h.) 20 Hillview Road, Cults, Aberdeen; T.-Aberdeen 867347.

Davidson, Anthony Beverley, MA, CA, FCMA, FIB (Scot). Senior Executive Director, TSB Scotland plc, since 1983; b. 25.12.47, Dundee; m., Avril Rose; 2 s.; 2 d. Educ. Morgan Academy, Dundee; St. Andrews University. Deloitte Haskins & Sells, 1970-75; Lothian Regional Council, 1976-77; TSB, Tayside and Central Scotland, 1977-78; TSB Group Central Executive, 1979-82; TSB Scotland, since 1983. Council Member: Institute of Bankers in Scotland, 1984, Association of Accounting Technicians, 1987. Recreations: golf; photography; skiing. Address: (h.) Ingleton, Whim Road, Gullane, East Lothian, EH31 2BD; T.-0620 842146.

Davidson, Arthur Ian Greenwood, MB, ChB, PhD, ChM, FRCS(Edin). Consultant Surgeon, Tayside Health Board, and Honorary Senior Lecturer, Dundee University, since 1972; b. 29.1.37, Aberdeen; m., Doreen Ross; 1 s.; 2 d. Educ. Aberdeen Grammar School; Aberdeen University. House Officer, Professorial Surgical and Medical Units, Aberdeen Royal Infirmary, 1960-61; Lecturer in Anatomy, Aberdeen University, 1961-62; Research Fellow, Department of Cardiovascular Surgery, Western Reserve University, Cleveland, Ohio, 1963-64; Registrar and Lecturer in Surgery, Aberdeen Royal Infirmary, 1964-67; Senior Registrar in Surgery, Aberdeen Royal Infirmary, 1967-71. Keith Gold Medal in Surgery, 1960. Recreations: reading; golf; theatre. Address: (h.) 3 Kincarrathie Crescent, Perth, PH2 7HH; T.-Perth 25727.

Davidson, Hon. Lord (Charles Kemp Davidson), MA, LLB, FRSE. Chairman, Scottish Law Commission, since 1988; Senator of the College of Justice, since 1983; Deputy Chairman, Boundaries Commission for Scotland, since 1985; b. 13.4.29, Edinburgh; m., Mary Mactaggart; 1 s.; 2 d. Educ. Fettes College, Edinburgh; Oxford University; Edinburgh University. Advocate, 1956; QC (Scot), 1969; Keeper, The Advocates Library, 1972-77; Vice Dean, Faculty of Advocates, 1977-79; Dean, 1979-83; Procurator to the General Assembly of the Church of Scotland, 1972-83; Chairman, National Health Service Tribunal for Scotland, 1970-83. Address: (h.) 22 Dublin Street, Edinburgh, EH1 3PP; T.-031-556 2168.

Davidson, Professor Colin William, BSc, DipER, PhD, CEng, FIEE, FRSA. Professor of Electrical and Electronic Engineering, Heriot-Watt University, since 1985; b. 18.9.34, Edinburgh; m., Ranee M.N. Cleland; 2 d. Educ. George Heriot's School; Edinburgh University. Lecturer, Edinburgh University, 1956-61; Electronics Engineer, Nuclear Enterprises (GB) Ltd., 1961-64; Lecturer, Heriot-Watt College/University, 1964-67; Associate Professor, Chulalongkorn University, Bangkok, 1967-68; Senior Lecturer, Heriot-Watt University, 1968-85; Dean of Engineering, 1976-79 and 1984-87, Head of Department, 1979-87. Member of Council, Institution of Electrical Engineers. Recreation: sailing (Royal Highland Yacht Club). Address: (h.) 20 East Barnton Avenue, Edinburgh, EH4 6AQ; T.-031-336 5806.

Davidson, Douglas, DCR, SRR. Area Adviser in Radiography, Aberdeen Royal Infirmary, since 1982; Member, Grampian Health Board, since 1978; Council Member, College and Society of Radiographers, 1982-85; b. 8.2.32, Aberdeen; m., Margaret Farquhar; 1 s.; 1 d. Educ. Robert Gordon's College, Aberdeen; Grampian School of Radiography. National Service, RAMC, 1950-52; Radiographer: Chalmers Hospital, Banff, 1954-55, Aberdeen Royal Infirmary, since 1955. Harry West Memorial Award, 1986. Recreations: golf; swimming; watching sport of all kinds. Address: (h.) 23 Ronaldsay Road, Aberdeen, AB2 6ND; T.-0224 310486.

Davidson, Duncan Lewis Watt, BSc (Hons), MB, ChB, FRCPEdin. Consultant Neurologist, Tayside Health Board, since 1976; Honorary Senior Lecturer in Medicine, Dundee University, since 1976; b. 16.5.40, Kingston, Jamaica; m., Dr. Anne V.M. Maiden; 4 s.; 1 d. Educ. Knox College, Jamaica; Edinburgh University. House Officer, Senior House Officer, Registrar and Senior Registrar posts in medicine and neurology, Edinburgh, 1966-75; Peel Travelling Fellowship, Montreal, 1973-74; MRC clinical scientific staff, MRC Brain Metabolism Unit, Edinburgh, 1975-76. Recreations: gardening; golf. Address: (h.) Brooksby, Queens Terrace, St. Andrews, Fife; T.-0334 76108.

Davidson, Eric Dalgleish, DA (Edin), RIBA, FRIAS. Director, Scottish Health Service, Common Services Agency, Building Division, since 1985; b. 7.9.28, Musselburgh; m., June Mary Ryman; 2 s.; 2 d. Educ. Musselburgh Grammar School; Heriot-Watt University; Edinburgh College of Art. Assistant Regional Architect, South Eastern Regional Hospital Board, 1961-74; Lecturer in Advanced Practice and Management, Department of Architecture, Edinburgh University, 1966-74; Assistant Director and Chief Architect, Scottish Health Service, Common Services Agency, Building Division, 1974-85. Council Member, RIAS; Member, Scottish Building Contract Committee; Member, Scottish Building Standards Committee (Research Sub-Committee). Address: (h.) 27 Belgrave Road, Edinburgh, EH12 6NG; T.-031-334 5231.

Davidson, James Duncan Gordon, MVO (1947). Chief Executive, Royal Highland and Agricultural Society of Scotland, since 1970; b. 10.1.27. Educ. RN College, Dartmouth; Downing College, Cambridge. Royal Navy, 1944-55; MP, West Aberdeenshire, 1966-70.

Davidson, Rev. Ian Murray Pollock, MA, BD. Minister, Allan Park South Church and Church of the Holy Rude, Stirling, since 1985; Convener, Fabric Committee of General Trustees, Church of Scotland, since 1985; b. 14.3.28, Kirriemuir; m., Isla; 2 s. Educ. Montrose Academy; St. Andrews University. National Service, 1949-51; Minister: Crieff North and West Church (St. Andrew's), 1955-61, Grange Church, Kilmarnock, 1961-67, Cambuslang Old Church, 1967-85; Convener, Maintenance of the Ministry Committee and Board, Church and Ministry Department, 1981-84; General Trustee, since 1975. Publication: At the Sign of the Fish (history of Cambuslang Old Parish Church), 1975. Recreations: travel; photography; reading; writing. Address: (h.) 21 Drummond Place, Stirling, FK8 2JE; T.-0786 74154.

Davidson, John, MA. Director, CBI Scotland, since 1979; b. 26.7.30, Bearsden, Dunbartonshire; m., Marilyn Menzies Anderson; 2 d. Educ. Glasgow Academy; Trinity College, Glenalmond; St. John's College, Cambridge; Royal College of Science and Technology, Glasgow. North British Locomotive Co. Ltd., Glasgow, 1954-56; Singer Manufacturing Co. Ltd., Clydebank, 1958-65; Scottish Conservative Central Office, 1965-75; Director, Scottish Federation of Housing Associations, 1975-79; Member: Manpower Services Committee for Scotland, since 1979, Duke of Edinburgh Award Scheme, Scottish Committee; Trustee: Bield Retirement Housing Trust, Scottish Housing Association Charitable Trust, Scottish Disability Foundation; Member, Salvation Army Housing Association (Scotland). Recreations: photography; cattle raising; sailing. Address: (h.) Rinnans, Balfron, Stirlingshire; T.-041-332 8661.

Davidson, John F., MB, ChB, FRCPEdin, FRCPath. Consultant Haematologist, Glasgow Royal Infirmary, since 1969; b. 11.1.34, Lumphanan; m., Laura G. Middleton; 1 s.; 1 d. Educ. Robert Gordon's College, Aberdeen; Aberdeen University. Surgeon Lt., RN; Registrar in Medicine, Aberdeen Royal Infirmary; Research Registrar in Medicine, then Senior Registrar in Haematology, Glasgow Royal Infirmary. Secretary, British Society for Haematalogy, 1983-86; Editor, Progress in Fibrinolysis, Volumes I to VII; Chairman, International Committee on Fibrinolysis, 1976-84; Co-Editor in Chief, Fibrinolysis. Recreation: gardening. Address: (b.) Department of Haematology, Glasgow Royal Infirmary, Glasgow; T.-041-552 3535, Ext. 5125.

Davidson, John Knight, MD, FRCPEdin, FRCPGlas, FRCR, FRACR (Hon). Consultant Radiologist in administrative charge, Western Infirmary/Gartnavel General Hospital, Glasgow, since 1967; Consultant Radiologist, Ross Hall Hospital, since 1984; b. 17.8.25, Edinburgh; m., Edith E. McKelvie; 2 s.; 1 d. Educ. George Watson's Boys College, Edinburgh; Edinburgh University. Royal Army Medical Corps, 1949-51; Senior Registrar, St. Bartholomews Hospital, London, 1956-60; Council Member: Medical and Dental Defence Union for Scotland, since 1971, Royal College of Radiologists, since 1984; Chairman, Standing Scottish Committee, Royal College of Radiologists, since 1985; Member, Bone Necrosis Group, Decompression Sickness Panel, MRC, since 1965; Consultant Adviser, US Navy, on diving medicine, 1974-78; Rohan Williams Travelling Professor, Australasia, 1977; Diwand Chand Aggarwal Lecturer, India, 1988. Chairman, Examining Board, FRCR, 1976-79; Member, Scottish Sub-Committee on Distinction and Meritorious Service Awards, 1982-84; Council

Member, Royal Glasgow Institute for the Fine Arts; Editor, Aseptic Necrosis of Bone. Recreations: golf (Member, R. & A.); bridge; the arts; opera; meeting people. Address: (h.) 31 Newlands Road, Glasgow, G43 2JG; T.-041-632 3113; (b.) Consulting Rooms, 901 Sauchiehall Street, Glasgow, and Ross Hall Hospital, Glasgow.

Davidson, John Marr, MA, LLB, WS. Partner, W. & J. Burness, WS, 1954-86; b. 22.6.23, Lanark; m., Sylvia Russell; 1 s.; 1 d. Educ. Edinburgh Academy; Edinbrgh University. Service in Italy, Middle East, Europe, with Cameronians (Scottish Rifles), attaining rank of Captain, 1942-46; Law Apprentice, then Partner, Auld and Macdonald, WS, 1946-54. High Constable, Holyrood; Director, various limited companies. Recreations: shooting; fishing; travel. Address: (h.) 66 Barnton Park Crescent, Edinburgh, EH4 6EN; T.-031-339 5387.

Davidson, Julie Wilson. Television Critic, Glasgow Herald, since 1981; Freelance Contributor, BBC, Granada TV, The Times, The Observer, etc., since 1981; b. Motherwell; m., Harry Reid (qv); 1 d. Educ. Aberdeen High School for Girls. Trainee Journalist, D.C. Thomson Ltd., Dundee, 1961-64; Feature Writer and Sub-Editor, Aberdeen Press & Journal, 1964-67; The Scotsman: Feature Writer, 1967-77, Columnist, 1977-81. Columnist/Critic of the Year, Scottish Press Awards, 1985; Critic of the Year, Scottish Press Awards, 1988. Recreations: reading; walking; travelling; lunching. Address: (h.) 15 Albion Buildings, Ingram Street, Glasgow; T.-041-552 8403.

Davidson, Neil Forbes, BA, LLB, MSc, LLM. Advocate; b. 13.9.50, St. Andrews; m., Regina Sprissler. Educ. Stirling University; Bradford University; Edinburgh University. Analyst, Scrimgeour Vickers, London, 1972-73; Executive, Noble Grossart Ltd., Edinburgh, 1974; Speechwriter, London, 1975; legal training, 1977-79; practice at Scottish Bar, since 1979. Publications: Scrimgeour's North Sea Oil and Gas Review, 1973; Judicial Review in Scotland. Recreation: taekwondo. Address: (h.) 2 Moray Place, Edinburgh, EH3 6DS; T.-031-225 6177.

Davidson, Neil McDonald, MA, DM, FRCP, FRCPEdin. Consultant Physician, Eastern General Hospital, Edinburgh, since 1978; Senior Lecturer in Medicine, Edinburgh University, since 1978; Assistant Director of Studies (Medicine), Edinburgh Postgraduate Board for Medicine, since 1985; b. 15.5.40, Leamington Spa; m., Jill Ann; 3 s.; 1 d. Educ. Epsom College; Merton College, Oxford; St. Thomas's Hospital, London. House Officer, St. Thomas's Hospital and Hammersmith Hospital, London; Medical Registrar, St. Thomas's Hospital, London; Senior Medical Registrar, Lecturer and Senior Lecturer in Medicine, Ahmadu Bello University, Zaria, Nigeria; Lecturer in Medicine, Edinburgh University. Recreation: collecting antique maps. Address: (h.) 43 Blackford Road, Grange, Edinburgh, EH9 2DT; T.-031-667 3960.

Davidson, Professor Robert, MA, BD, DD. Professor of Old Testament Language and Literature, Glasgow University, since 1972; Principal, Trinity College, Glasgow, since 1981; b. 30.3.27, Markinch, Fife; m., Elizabeth May Robertson; 5 s.; 4 d. Educ. Bell-Baxter School, Cupar; St. Andrews University. Lecturer in Biblical Studies, Aberdeen University, 1953-60; Lecturer in Hebrew and Old Testament Studies, St. Andrews University, 1960-66; Lecturer/Senior Lecturer in Old Testament, Edinburgh University, 1966-72. Publications: The Bible Speaks, 1959; The Old Testament, 1964; Geneses 1 - 11, 1973; Genesis 12 - 50, 1979; The Bible in Religious Education, 1979; The Courage to Doubt, 1983; Jeremiah Volume 1, 1983; Jeremiah Volume 2, Lamentations, 1985; Ecclesiastes, Song of Songs, 1986. Recreations: music; gardening. Address: (h.) 357 Albert Drive, Glasgow, G41 5PH; T.-041-427 5793.

Davidson, Ronald J.L., MD, FRCPEdin, FRCPath. Senior Lecturer in Haematology, Aberdeen University, since 1972; b. 14.1.30, Inverkeilor, Arbroath; m., Winifred Nicol Scott; 1 s.; 2 d. Educ. Arbroath High School; St. Andrews University. House Officer posts, Dundee Royal Infirmary; RAMC, Malaya; Assistant Lecturer, Department of Pathology, Dundee University; Registrar in Medicine, Dundee Royal Infirmary; Senior Registrar in Haematology, Western Infirmary, Glasgow; Consultant in Haematology, City Hospital, Aberdeen, 1964-72. Past Chairman: Caledonian Branch, Association of Clinical Pathologists, Grampian Area Committee for Hospital Medical Services. Recreations: golf (Royal Aberdeen GC); gardening. Address: (h.) Whittycroft, 24 Primrosehill Avenue, Cults, Aberdeen, AB1 9NL; T.-Aberdeen 867206.

Davidson, William Keith, CBE, JP, FRCGP, DPA. Chairman, Scottish Health Service Planning Council; Vice President (and Fellow), British Medical Association; Member, General Medical Council; Member, Scottish Health Service Policy Board, since 1985; General Medical Practitioner, since 1952; b. 20.11.26, Glasgow; m., Dr. Mary W.A. Davidson; 1 s.; 1 d. Educ. Coatbridge Secondary School; Glasgow University. Honorary President, Glagow Eastern Medical Society, 1984-85. Recreation: gardening. Address: (h.) Dunvegan, Hornshill Farm Road, Stepps, Glasgow, G33 6DE; T.-041-779 2103.

Davidson, William Powell, MREHIS, MInstWM, MILAM. Director of Environmental Health, Stewartry District Council, since 1982; Secretary, Scottish Food and Drugs Co-ordinating Committee, since 1983; b. 28.8.48, Paisley; m., Elizabeth Ann Davidson; 1 s. Educ. Camphill Senior Secondary School, Paisley; Langside College, Glasgow; Bell College, Hamilton. Trainee, then Assistant Sanitary Inspector, Renfrew County Council, 1966-71; Sanitary Inspector, Paisley Burgh Council, 1971-72; Assistant District Sanitary Inspector, Perth and Kinross Joint County Council, 1972-75; Area Environmental Health Officer, Argyll and Bute District Council, 1975-76; Regional Manager, Ciba Geigy Public Hygiene Project, Saudi Arabia, 1976-77; Senior Environmental Health Officer, Perth and Kinross District Council, 1977-79; Depute Director of Environmental Health, Stewartry District Council, 1979-82. Recreations: golf; gardening; travel; jogging; football. Address: (b.) Environmental Health Department, Dunmuir Road, Castle Douglas; T.-0557 30291.

Davie, Elspeth, DA. Writer; b. Kilmarnock; m., George Elder Davie; 1 d. Educ. George Watson's College; Edinburgh University; Edinburgh Art College. Taught Art for several years in the Borders, Aberdeen and Northern Ireland; author of three novels: Providings, Creating A Scene, Climbers on a Stair; four collections of short stories: The Spark, The High Tide Talker, The Night of the Funny Hats, A Traveller's Room; two Arts Council Awards; received Katherine Mansfield Prize, 1978. Recreations: reading; walking; films. Address: (h.) 155/17 Orchard Brae Gardens, Edinburgh, EH4; T.-031-332 8297.

Davie, Ivor Turnbull, MB, ChB, FFARCS. Consultant Anaesthetist, Western General Hospital, Edinburgh, since 1971; Honorary Senior Lecturer, Edinburgh University, since 1979; Lecturer, Central Midwives Board (Scotland), since 1974; b. 23.2.35, Edinburgh; m., Jane Elizabeth Fleischmann; 1 s.; 1 d. Educ. Royal High School, Edinburgh; Edinburgh University. Member, Board of Examiners, Faculty of Anaesthetists, Royal College of Surgeons of England (Primary FFARCS, 1978-84, Part II FFARCS, 1985-86, Part III FFARCS, since 1987); Tutor, Faculty of Anaesthetists, since 1979; Member, Editorial Board, British Journal of Obstetrics and Gynaecology, 1980-84; Visiting Medical Officer, Westmead Centre, Sydney, NSW, 1983. Address: (b.) Department of Anaesthesia, Western General Hospital, Edinburgh, EH4 2XU; T.-031-332 2525.

Davie, Robert Alastair, MA, BCom. Secretary/Director, Sea Fish Industry Authority, since 1981; b. 28.10.38, Edinburgh; m., Carol Haig; 2 s. Educ. George Watson's College; Edinburgh University. Recreation: golf. Address: (h.) 4 Riselaw Place, Edinburgh, EH10 6HP; T.-031-447 5168.

Davies, Alan, MA, PhD, DipEd, DipGenLing. Reader in Applied Linguistics, Edinburgh University, since 1984; b. 17.2.31, Neath; m., Anne Margaret; 1 s.; 3 d. Educ. Alderman Newton's School, Leicester; Corpus Christi College, Oxford. Assistant Teacher, 1955-62: Royal Grammar School, High Wycombe, Queen Elizabeth's School, Barnet and Kamusinga Secondary School, Kenya; Senior Research Associate, Birmingham University, 1962-65; Lecturer, then Senior Lecturer, Edinburgh University, 1965-84; Professor and Head of Department of English, Tribhuvan University, Kathmandu, Nepal, 1969-71 (on secondment). Chairman, British Association of Applied Linguistics, 1976-79; Secretary General, International Association of Applied Linguistics, 1978-81; President, TESOL (Scotland), 1983-86; Member, British Council English Teaching Advisory Committee, 1979-85; Editor, Applied Linguistics, since 1984. Publications (as Editor): Language Testing Symposium, 1968; Problems of Language and Learning, 1975; Language and Learning in Early Childhood, 1977; Testing and Experimental Methods, 1977; Language and Learning in Home and School, 1979; Interlanguage, 1984. Recreations: Quakerism; cycling. Address: (b.) Edinburgh University, Department of Applied Linguistics, 14 Buccleuch Place, Edinburgh, EH8 9LN; T.-031-667 1011.

Davies, Christopher Henry, BA (Hons), DipEd, FBIM. Managing Director, Nairn Floors Ltd., Kirkcaldy, since 1983; b. 6.11.39, Wolverhampton; m., Elisabeth; 2 s. Educ. Wolverhampton Grammar School; University College, Durham; Queens' College, Cambridge. General Manager: Commercial Plastics GMBH, Austria, Nairn Australia; International Operations Director, Nairn International Ltd., Newcastle; Sales/Marketing Director, Nairn Floors Ltd., Kirkcaldy; Managing Director, Forbo Nairn Ltd., Kirkcaldy. Recreations: music; walking; board-sailing; golf. Address: (h.) 7 West Carnethy Avenue, Colinton, Edinburgh; T.-0592 261111.

Davies, David Lloyd, MD, FRCP. Senior Lecturer in Medicine, Glasgow University, since 1973; Honorary Consultant Physician; b. 1.3.38, Swansea; m., Catherine G. Drummond; 1 d. Educ. Llandovery College; St. Mary's Hospital, London. Various hospital appointments: St. Mary's Hospital, London, Colonial Hospital, Gibraltar, Postgraduate Medical School, Hammersmith, Chelmsford and Essex Hospital, Western Infirmary, Glasgow. Recreations: marquetry; music; gardening; sport. Address: (h.) 9 Matilda Road, Pollokshields, Glasgow, G41; T.-041-423 0052.

Davies, David Somerville, FTCL, ARCM. Artistic Director, Paragon Ensemble, since 1980; b. 13.6.54, Dunfermline. Educ. Dunfermline High School; Royal Scottish Academy of Music; Edinburgh University; Marseille Conservatoire. Assistant Principal Flute, Scottish National Orchestra; Principal Flute, Scottish Opera; Freelance Recitalist and Conductor; Assistant Conductor, Marseille Opera; awarded Tovey Memorial Prize; Clutterbuck Scholarship; Sir James Caird Scholarship; Scottish Arts Council Music Award; Scottish International Education Trust Award; Performing Rights Society/Scottish Society of Composers Award for services to contemporary Scottish music. Recreations: reading; photography. Address: (b.) c/o Paragon Ensemble, 148 Queens Drive, Glasgow, G42 8QN; T.-041-423 1718.

Davies, Ivor, MA, DipEd, PhD. Director of Facilities Planning, Scottish Sports Council, since 1975 (Executive Member of Council, since 1987); b. Scotland. Educ. Edinburgh University. Founded and developed Department of Geography, Lakehead University, Thunder Bay, Ontario, and became first Chairman of Department. Recreations: sport; music. Address: (b.) 1 St. Colme Street, Edinburgh, EH3 6AA; T.-031-225 8411.

Davies, Terry, BSc (Hons), MSc, MInstP, FIPC. Depute Principal, Telford College of Further Education, Edinburgh, since 1985; b. 14.12.40, Llanelli. Educ. Llanelli Boys' Grammar School; University College of Swansea; Nottingham University. Lecturer (Physics), Middlesex Polytechnic, then Preston Polytechnic, 1964-73; Depute Head, Department of Engineering, Science and Construction, Lewes Technical College, 1973-79; Head, Department of Science, Mathematics and Computing, Telford College of Further Education, Edinburgh, 1979-85. Recreations: rugby; cricket; squash; tennis. Address: (b.) Crewe Toll, Edinburgh, EH4 2NZ; T.-031-332 2491.

Davis, Christine A.M., MA, DipEd. Chairman, Electricity Consultative Council for the North of Scotland, since 1980 (Member, since 1974); Member, North of Scotland Hydro-Electric Board, since 1980; Member, Scottish Legal Aid Board, since 1986; Member, Scottish Economic Council, since 1987; Member, General Convocation, Strathclyde University, since 1987; b. 5.3.44, Salisbury, Wiltshire; m., Robin John Davis; 2 d. Educ. Perth Academy; Ayr Academy; St. Andrews University; Aberdeen University; Aberdeen College of Education. Teacher of History and Modern Studies, Cumbernauld High School and High School of Stirling, 1967-69; joined Dunblane Town Council and Perth and Kinross Joint County Council, 1972; undertook research in Canada on Ontario Hydro and small claims in Ontario courts, 1977-78. Active Member, Religious Society of Friends (Quakers). Recreations: embroidery; bird-watching; walking. Address: (h.) 24 Newton Crescent, Dunblane, Perthshire, FK15 ODZ; T.-Dunblane 823226.

Davis, Margaret Thomson. Novelist; b. Bathgate; 2 s. Educ. Albert Secondary School. Worked as children's nurse; Red Cross nurse; short story writer; novelist; author of autobiography, The Making of a Novelist; novels include The Breadmakers, A Baby Might Be Crying, A Sort of Peace, The Prisoner, The Prince and the Tobacco Lords, Roots of Bondage, Scorpion in the Fire, The Dark Side of Pleasure, A Very Civilised Man, Light and Dark, Rag Woman Rich Woman, Daughters and Mothers; Committee Member: International PEN (Scottish Branch); Society of Authors; Lecturer in Creative Writing; Honorary President, Strathkelvin Writers Club; Committee Member, Swanwick Writers' School. Recreations: reading; travelling; being with friends. Address: c/o London Management, 235/241 Regent Street, London W1A 2JT.

Davis, Robert Gunn. Member, Mental Welfare Commission for Scotland, since 1984; Social Work Adviser (Mental Health), Strathclyde Region, since 1977; b. 11.5.38, Edinburgh; m., Mildred Bennett; 1 s.; 1 d. Educ. Daniel Stewart's College, Edinburgh. Certificate of Qualification in Probation Work, Jordanhill College, 1968. Probation Officer, City of Glasgow, before 1969; Senior Social Worker, then Social Work Training Officer, Lanark County Council, 1970-75; Recruitment and Training Officer, Strathclyde Region Social Work Department, 1975-77. Founder Member, British Association of Social Workers. Recreations: vintage/classic motorcycle and vehicle rallies. Address: (h.) 5 Braid Green, Livingston, West Lothian, EH54 8PN; T.-Livingston 39148.

Davison, Edward Cowper, MA, DipEd. Assistant Secretary, Scottish Education Department, since 1984; b. 31.10.40, Darlington; m., Anna Fay Henderson; 2 d. Educ. Dame Allan's School, Newcastle-upon-Tyne; Glasgow University; London University Institute of Education. Assistant Master, Tottenham County School, 1964-68; administrative staff, Glasgow University, 1969-75; Principal: Scottish Education Department, 1975-79, Department of Agriculture and Fisheries for Scotland, 1979-82, Scottish Office Central Services, 1982-84. Address: (h.) 14 Plewlands Terrace, Edinburgh, EH10 5JZ; T.-031-447 3289.

Davison, Peter Sinclair, BSc, PhD, ARIC, MIInfS. Director of Research, Scientific Documentation Centre Ltd., since 1962; Member, Fife Regional Council, since 1975; b. 21.1.30, Edinburgh; m., Joan Plummer; 1 s.; 1 d. Educ. George Watson's Boys' College, Edinburgh; Edinburgh University. RAF, 1956-58 (Flt. Lt.); Technical Officer (Research), ICI Ltd., Billingham, 1958-59; established Scientific Documentation Centre, 1958; Editor for European Commission: Euroabstracts, 1977-83, European Environmental Science Synopses, 1983; Parliamentary candidate (Conservative): Hamilton, 1979, Dunfermline West, 1983; initiated Rescue Rossend and other campaigns to preserve Scottish heritage. Recreations: travel; admiring man's cultural heritage; DIY. Address: (h.) Halbeath House, Dunfermline, Fife, KY12 OTZ; T.-0383 723535.

Dawson, Professor John Alan, BSc, MPhil, PhD, MIPDM. Fraser of Allander Professor of Distributive Studies, Stirling University, since 1983; b. 19.8.44, Hyde; m., Jocelyn Barker; 1 s.; 1 d. Educ. Lady Manners School, Bakewell; University College, London; Nottingham University. Lecturer, Nottingham University; Lecturer, Senior Lecturer, Reader, St. David's University College, Wales; Visiting Lecturer, University of Western Australia; Visiting Research Fellow, Australian National University; Visiting Professor, Florida State University. Former Member, Distributive Trades Committee, NEDC; former Honorary Secretary, Institute of British Geographers. Publications: Evaluating the Human Environment, 1973; Man and His World, 1975; Computing for Geographers, 1976; Small-Scale Retailing in the UK, 1979; Marketing Environment, 1979; Retail Geography, 1980; Commercial Distribution in Europe, 1982; Teach Yourself Geography, 1983; Shopping Centre Development, 1983; Computer Methods for Geographers, 1985. Recreations: sport; writing. Address: (b.) Stirling University, Stirling; T.-0786 73171.

Dawson, Mary, PhD, FPS. Reader in Pharmacy, Strathclyde University; b. West Maryston. Educ. Airdrie Academy; Royal Technical College, Glasgow. Career spent almost entirely in Department of Pharmacy, Strathclyde University. Awarded Felix Wankel International Prize for research and Pharmaceutical Society's Charter Silver Medal; member of numerous committees concerned with pharmacy, the health service and animal welfare. Recreations: motor sport; photography. Address: (b.) Department of Pharmacy, Strathclyde University, Glasgow, G1 1XW; T.-041-552 4400.

Dawson, Thomas Cameron, SBStJ. Vice Chairman, Rangers Football Club, since 1984; Managing Director, Dawson Motors, Helensburgh, since 1963; Vice Chairman, Glasgow International Sports; b. 12.1.29, Rhu; m., Margaret McFadzean; 1 s. Educ. Hermitage Academy. Army Service, Royal Military Police, three years. Recreation: flying (private pilot's licence). Address: (h.) Sunnyside House, 34 West King Street, Helensburgh, G84 8EB; T.-0436 3860.

Dean, Alan, ChM, FRCSEdin. Vice-President, Royal College of Surgeons of Edinburgh, since 1986; Honorary Consultant Surgeon, Royal Infirmary, Edinburgh, since 1965; b. 12.1.32, Reigate; m., Fidelity Montagu-Pollock; 1 s.; 2 d. Educ. Inverurie Academy; Aberdeen University. Honorary Secretary, Royal College of Surgeons of Edinburgh, 1977-82; Member, Council, Association of Surgeons of Great Britain and Ireland. Address: (b.) Royal College of Surgeons of Edinburgh, Nicolson Street, Edinburgh, EH8 9DW.

Deane, Robert Fletcher, MB, ChB, MSc, FRCSEdin, FRCSGlas. Consultant Urological Surgeon, since 1971; b. 25.3.38, Glasgow; m., Sylvia Allison Yuill; 3 s. Educ. Hillhead High School, Glasgow; Glasgow University. Consultant Urologist, Western Infirmary, Glasgow, since 1971; Senior Consultant Surgeon to Family Planning Association, Glasgow; Member, Specialist Advisory Committee (Urology); Founder, Board of Intercollegiate Specialty Board in Urology. Publication: Urology Illustrated. Recreations: golf; music. Address: (h.) 27 Bellshaugh Lane, Glasgow, G12 0PE; T.-041-334 8102.

Deans, Rev. Graham Douglas Sutherland, MA, BD (Hons). Minister, St. Mary's Parish Church, Dumfries, since 1987; b. 15.8.53, Aberdeen; m., Marina Punler. Educ. Mackie Academy, Stonehaven; Aberdeen University. Assistant Minister, Craigsbank Parish Church, Corstorphine, 1977-78; Minister, Denbeath and Methilhill Parish Churches, 1978-87; Depute Clerk and Treasurer, Kirkcaldy Presbytery, 1981-87. Publication: A History of Denbeath Church, 1980. Recreation: music. Address: 47 Moffat Road, Dumfries, DG1 1NN; T.-0387 54873.

Deans, Rodger William, CB. Regional Chairman, Social Security Appeal Tribunal and Medical Appeal Tribunals for Scotland, since 1983; b. 21.12.17, Perth; m., Joan Radley; 1 s.; 1 d. Educ. Perth Academy; Edinburgh University. Served World War II, RA and REME, Major; Military Prosecutor, Palestine, 1945-46; Solicitor to Secretary of State for Scotland and to HM Treasury, 1971-80 (Assistant Solicitor, 1962-71, Senior Legal Assistant, Scottish Office, 1951-62, Legal Assistant, 1947-50); Consultant Editor, Green & Son, Edinburgh, 1981-82; Senior Chairman, Supplementary Benefit Appeal Tribunals, 1982-84. Recreations: hill-walking; gardening. Address: (h.) 25 Grange Road, Edinburgh, EH9 1UQ; T.-031-667 1893.

de Bono, David Paul, MA, MD (Cantab), FRCPEdin. Consultant Physician, Cardiac Department, Edinburgh Royal Infirmary, since 1979; part-time Senior Lecturer, Department of Medicine, Edinburgh University, since 1980; b. 19.1.47, Sliema, Malta; m., Anne Fingleton; 2 s. Educ. St. Edward's College, Malta; Downside School; Trinity Hall, Cambridge; St. George's Hospital, London. Fellow and Director of Medical Studies, Trinity Hall, Cambridge; Lecturer in Cardiovascular Medicine, Oxford University. Recreations: model aeroplanes; sailing. Address: (h.) 8 Lygon Road, Edinburgh, EH16 5QE; T.-031-667 5526.

Demarco, Richard, OBE, RSW, SSA. Artist; Director, Richard Demarco Gallery, since 1966; External Assessor, Stourbridge College of Art, since 1988; b. 9.7.30, Edinburgh; m., Anne Muckle. Educ. Holy Cross Academy, Edinburgh; Edinburgh College of Art. National Service, KOSB, 1954-56; Art Master, Duns Scotus Academy, Edinburgh, 1957-67; Vice-Chairman, Board, Traverse Theatre Club, 1963-67; Director, Sean Connery's Scottish International Education Trust, 1972-73; Member, Board of Governors, Carlisle School of Art, 1970-74; Member, Edinburgh Festival Society, since 1971; Contributing Editor, Studio International, 1982-84. Gold Order of Merit, Polish People's Republic; Order of Cavaliere Della Republica Italiana; Scottish Arts Council Award for services to Scotland's visual arts, 1975; Honorary Member, Scottish Arts Club and Chelsea Arts Club. Publications: The Road to Meikle Seggie; The Artist as Explorer. Recreation: walking "The Road to Meikle Seggie". Address: (h.) 23(a) Lennox Street, Edinburgh; T.-031-343 2124.

Denholm, James Allan, CA. Director, William Grant & Sons Ltd., since 1975; Chairman, East Kilbride Development Corporation, since 1983 (Member, since 1979); Director, Scottish Mutual Life Assurance Society, since 1987; Director, Scottish Cremation Society Limited, since 1980; b. 27.9.36, Glasgow; m., Elizabeth Avril McLachlan, CA; 1 s.; 1 d. Educ. Hutchesons Boys Grammar School, Glasgow; Institute of Chartered Accountants of Scotland. Apprenticed, McFarlane Hutton & Patrick, CA, Glasgow (Sir William McLintock prizeman); Chief Accountant, A. & W. Smith & Co. Ltd., Glasgow, 1960-66; Secretary, William Grant & Sons Ltd., since 1966; Council Member, Institute of Chartered Accountants of Scotland, 1978-83. Director and Treasurer, Glasgow YMCA, 1966-79; Chairman, Glasgow Junior Chamber of Commerce, 1972-73; Member, CBI Scottish Legal Panel, since 1987; Elder, New Kilpatrick Parish Church, since 1971; Visitor of the Incorporation of Maltmen in Glasgow, 1980-81; President, 49 Wine and Spirit Club of Scotland, 1983-84; Trustee: Scottish Chartered Accountants Trust for Education, The Queen's College, Glasgow Educational Trust, Scottish Cot Death Trust; Fellow, Society of Antiquaries of Scotland, since 1987. Recreations: shooting; golf; curling. Address: (h.) Greencroft, 19 Colquhoun Drive, Bearsden, Glasgow; T.-041-942 1773.

Dennis, Richard Benson, PhD, BSc. Managing Director, Edinburgh Instruments Ltd.; Senior Lecturer, Heriot-Watt University; Founder, Mutek Gmbh, West Germany; b. 15.7.45, Weymouth; m., Beate Stamm; 2 d. Educ. Weymouth Grammar School; Reading University. SRC Postdoctoral Fellow, Reading; Guest Fellow, Freiburg University, 1968-70; Lecturer/Senior Lecturer, Heriot-Watt University, since 1970; Alexander von Humboldt Fellow, Munich University, 1976-78; Founder Committee Member, UK Laser and Electro-Optic Trade Association; Joint Winner, Department of Industry EPIC Award (Education in Partnership with Industry and Commerce), 1982. Recreations: bridge; sport. Address: (b.) Edinburgh Instruments Ltd., Riccarton, Currie, Edinburgh; T.-031-449 5844.

Denny, Margaret Bertha Alice, OBE, DL, BA (Hons), PhD. Member, Council and Executive Committee, National Trust for Scotland, since

1974 (Vice President, since 1981); b. 30.9.07, Chatham; m., Edward Leslie Denny. Educ. Dover County School; Bedford College for Women, London University. Entered Civil Service as Principal, Ministry of Shipping, 1940; Assistant Secretary, 1946; Under Secretary, 1957; Governor, Bedford College; Member, Scottish Advisory Council for Civil Aviation, 1958-67; Member, Western Regional Hospital Board, 1960-74; Member, Scottish Committee, Council of Industrial Design, 1961-71; Member, General Advisory Council, BBC, 1962-66; Member, General Nursing Council, Scotland, 1963-78; Member, Board of Management, State Hospital, Carstairs, 1966-76; Vice-Chairman, Argyll and Clyde Health Board, 1974-77; County Commissioner, Girl Guides, Dunbartonshire, 1958-68; DL, Dunbartonshire, since 1973; Officer, Order of Orange Nassau, 1947. Recreations: gardening; needlework; music. Address: (h.) Gartochraggan Cottage, Gartocharn, by Alexandra, Dunbartonshire; T.-038 983 272.

Deregowski, Professor Jan Bronislaw, BSc, BA, PhD, DSc, FBPsS. Professor of Psychology, Aberdeen University, since 1986 (Reader, 1981-86); b. 1.3.33, Pinsk, Poland; m., Eva Loft Nielsen; 2 s.; 1 d. Educ. London University. Lecturer, then Senior Lecturer, Aberdeen University, 1969-81. Publications: Illusions, Patterns and Pictures: a cross-cultural perspective; Distortion in Art. Address: (b.) Department of Psychology, King's College, Old Aberdeen, AB9 2UB; T.-Aberdeen 272247.

Dervaird, Hon. Lord (John Murray), MA (Oxon), LLB (Edin). Senator of the College of Justice, since 1988; b. 8.7.35, Stranraer; m., Bridget Jane Godfrey; 3 s. Educ. Stranraer schools; Edinburgh Academy; Corpus Christi College, Oxford; Edinburgh University. Advocate, 1962; QC, 1974; Law Commissioner (part-time), 1979-88; Chairman, Committee on International Arbitration, since 1986. Vice-President, Agricultural Law Association (of UK), since 1985 (Chairman, 1979-85). Publications: Stair Encyclopaedia of Scots Law (Contributor); articles on legal and ornithological subjects. Recreations: farming; gardening; bird-watching; music. Address: (b.) Court of Session, Edinburgh.

Derwent, Lavinia, MBE. Writer; b. Jedburgh, Roxburghshire. Educ. Jedburgh Grammar School. Creator of Tammy Troot; author of numerous books for children including the Macpherson books and Sula series; author of autobiographical books, including A Breath of Border Air, Lady of the Manse and Beyond the Borders; TV broadcaster; Past President, Scottish PEN. Address: (h.) 1 Great Western Terrace, Glasgow, G12 OUP; T.-041-334 9172.

Desselberger, Ulrich, MD, MRCPath, MRCP(Glas). Senior Lecturer in Virology, Glasgow University, and Honorary Consultant Virologist, Greater Glasgow Health Board, since 1979; b. 22.7.37, Darmstadt, Germany; m., Elisabeth Wieczorek; 2 s.; 2 d. Educ. Ludwig Georgs-Gymnasium, Darmstadt; Universities of: Frankfurt/Main, Marburg/Lahn, Berlin/West, Paris. Research Assistant, Institutes of Pathology, RVK and Klinikum Westend, Berlin, 1968-69; Research Assistant then Consultant, Institute of Virology, Hannover Medical School, Hannover, 1970-76; Fulbright Research Fellow, Department of Microbiology, Mount Sinai School of Medicine, New York, 1977-79. Editorial Board, Journal of Medical Virology; Journal of General Virology; Archives of Virology. Address: (b.) Institute of Virology, Glasgow University, Church Street, Glasgow, G11; T.-041-339 8822.

Devereux, Alan Robert, CBE, DL, CEng, FIProdE, CBIM. Chairman, Scottish Tourist Board, since 1980; Director, Scottish Mutual Assurance Society, since 1976; Director, Walter Alexander PLC, since 1980; Scottish Adviser, Hambros Bank Ltd., since 1984; Director, Hambro Scotland Ltd., since 1984; Member, British Tourist Authority, since 1980; Director, Solsgirth Investment Trust Ltd., since 1981; b. 18.4.33, Frinton-on-Sea; m., 1, Gloria Alma Hair (deceased); 1 s.; 2, Elizabeth Tormey Docherty. Educ. Colchester School; Clacton County High School; Mid Essex Technical College. Marconi's Wireless Telegraph Company: apprentice, 1950-55, Standards Engineer, 1955-56; Technical Production Manager, Halex Division, British Xylonite Company, 1956-58; Technical Sales Manager, SPA Division, Sanitas Trust, 1958-65; General Manager, Dobar Engineering, 1965-67; various managerial posts, Norcros Ltd., 1967-69; Group Managing Director, Scotcros Ltd., 1969-78; Deputy Chairman, Scotcros Ltd., 1978-80. CBI: Chairman, Scotland, 1977-79 (Deputy Chairman, 1975-77), Council Member, 1972-84, Member, President's Advisory Committee, 1979; UK Regional Chairman, 1979; Chairman, Small Industries Council for Rural Areas of Scotland, 1975-77; Member, Scottish Development Agency, 1977-83; Chairman, Scottish Appeals Committee, Police Dependants' Trust; Member: David Livingstone Memorial Trust; Malcolm Sargent Cancer Fund for Children; Scottish Free Enterprise Award, 1978; Deputy Lieutenant, Renfrewshire, since 1985. Recreations: work; amateur radio; reading. Address: (h.) 293 Fenwick Road, Giffnock, Glasgow, G46 6UH; T.-041-638 2586.

Devine, Rt. Rev. Joseph. Bishop of Motherwell, since 1983; b. 7.8.37. Educ. Blairs College, Aberdeen; St. Peter's College, Dumbarton; Scots College, Rome. Ordained Priest in Glasgow, 1960; Assistant Priest, Glasgow, 1965-67; Lecturer in Philosophy, St. Peter's College, Dumbarton, 1967-74; a Chaplain to Catholic students, Glasgow University, 1974-77; Titular Bishop of Voli and Auxiliary to Archbishop of Glasgow, 1977-83.

Devine, Professor Thomas Martin, BA, PhD, FRHistS. Professor in History, Strathclyde University, since 1988; Chairman, Economic and Social History Society of Scotland, 1984-88; b. 30.10.46, Motherwell; m., Catherine Mary Lynas; 2 s.; 3 d. Educ. Our Lady's RC High School, Motherwell; Strathclyde University. Lecturer, then Senior Lecturer and Reader, Department of History, Strathclyde University, 1969-88; Visiting Professor, University of Guelph, Canada, 1983 and 1988; Joint Founding Editor, Scottish Economic and Social History, 1980-84. Publications: The Tobacco Lords, 1975; Lairds and Improvement in Enlightenment Scotland, 1979; Ireland and Scotland 1600-1850 (Co-Editor), 1983; Farm

Servants and Labour in Lowland Scotland 1770-1914, 1984; A Scottish Firm in Virginia 1767-77, 1984; People and Society in Scotland 1760-1830 (Co-Editor), 1988; The Great Highland Famine, 1988. Recreations: walking and travelling in the Hebrides; watching Celtic FC. Address: (b.) Department of History, McCance Building, 16 Richmond Street, Glasgow, G1 1XQ; T.-041-552 4400, Ext. 2235.

de Vink, Peter Henry John, BComm. Managing Director, Edinburgh Financial and General Holdings Ltd., since 1978; b. 9.10.40, Amsterdam; m., Jenipher Jean Murray-Lyon; 1 s.; 1 d. Educ. Edinburgh University. National Service, Dutch Army, 1961-63; Edinburgh University, 1963-66; Ivory and Sime Investment Managers, 1966-78, latterly as Director. Address: (b.) 7 Howe Street, Edinburgh, EH3 6TE; T.-031-225 6661; (h.) Cotswold, 46 Barnton Avenue, Edinburgh.

Dewar, Donald Campbell, MA, LLB. MP (Labour), Glasgow Garscadden, since 1978; Opposition Spokesman on Scottish Affairs, since 1983; b. 21.8.37, Glasgow; 1 s.; 1 d. Educ. Glasgow Academy; Glasgow University. Practised as Solicitor in Glasgow; MP, Aberdeen South, 1966-70; PPS to Tony Crosland, 1967; Chairman, Select Committee on Scottish Affairs, 1980-81; Member, Scottish front bench team, since 1981; elected to Shadow Cabinet, 1984. Address: (h.) 23 Cleveden Road, Glasgow, G12; T.-041-334 2374.

Dewar, Hugh, ACIS. Chief Executive and Secretary, Royal Scottish Automobile Club, since 1980; b. 14.11.36, Newmilns; m., Irene Anne; 1 s.; 1 d. Educ. Edinburgh Academy. Farming and accountancy in Zimbabwe, 1959-73; Lithgows (Holdings) Ltd., 1974-80; Member, RAC British Motor Sport Council, since 1981; Joint Secretary, Standing Joint Committee, RAC, AA and RSAC, since 1981. Steward, RAC. Recreations: golf; curling; rugby (watching). Address: (h.) 9 Craignethan Road, Whitecraigs, Glasgow, G46 6SQ; T.-041-639 8597.

Dewar, Ian Kennedy, SDA, NDA, FRAgS. Regional Training Adviser Scotland, Agricultural Training Board, since 1967; b. 16.1.31, Keltneyburn; m., Jane Dickson Mackenzie; 3 s.; 1 d. Educ. Breadalbane Academy, Aberfeldy; East of Scotland College of Agriculture. HM Forces, 1954-56 (Sergeant Instructor); Teacher, Fife, 1956-59; Organiser of Agricultural Education, Berwickshire, 1959-67. Recreations: gardening; reading; drystone dyking. Address: (h.) School House, Redgorton, Perth, PH1 3EL; T.-Stanley 828882.

Dewar, Lawrence, MIGD. Chief Executive, Scottish Grocers' Federation, since 1980; b. 12.1.36, Blackford; m., Nancy Kelly; 2 s.; 2 d. Educ. Dunfermline High School. Grocer of the Year, 1967; President, Scottish Grocers' Federation, 1975; Member, Board, SCOTBEC, 1981-85; Member, Sector "O" Board, SCOTVEC, since 1986; Secretary, Institute of Grocery Distribution (Scottish Branch), 1984. Recreations: golf; reading; TV. Address: (b.) 3 Loaning Road, Edinburgh, EH7 6JE; T.-031-652 2482.

Dewar, Richard Houston, DA, FRIBA, FRIAS. Chairman, Board of Governors, Duncan of Jordanstone College of Art, since 1977; Senior Partner, W.M. Wilson and Partners, Architects, Dundee, 1971-88 (Consultant, since 1988); b. 13.1.21, Ardler, by Meigle; 1 s.; 1 d. Educ. Forfar Academy; Dundee Institute of Art and Technology. Military Service, 1940-46. President, Dundee Institute of Architects, 1975-77; Governor, Dundee Institute of Art and Technology, 1968-72. Address: (b.) W.M. Wilson & Partners, 26 Castle Street, Dundee; T.-0382 22099.

Dick, David, OBE, DIC, CEng, FIEE, FIERE, FRSA. Principal, Stevenson College of Further Education, 1969-87; Chairman, Fire Services Examination Board (Scotland), 1968-86; Member, Construction Industry Training Board, 1976-85; Member, Electrical Engineering Services Committee, CITB, since 1976-88; b. 20.3.29, Edinburgh; m., Muriel Elsie Margaret Buchanan; 5 d. Educ. Boroughmuir School, Edinburgh; Heriot-Watt College, Edinburgh; Imperial College, London. Head, Department of Electrical Engineering, Coatbridge Technical College, 1960-64; Depute Principal, Napier College of Science and Technology, Edinburgh, 1964-69. MSC: Chairman, Lothian District Manpower Committee, 1981-82, Member, Lothian and Borders Area Manpower Board, 1982-85; Member and Chairman, various committees, Scottish Technical Education Council and Scottish Business Education Council; Past Chairman, Scottish Committee, Institution of Electronic and Radio Engineers; Honorary President, Edinburgh and District Spastics Association. Recreations: music (flute); gardening. Address: (h.) 34 Hillside Crescent, Edinburgh.

Dick, Professor David Andrew Thomas, MB, ChB, MA, DPhil, DSc. Cox Professor of Anatomy, Dundee University, since 1968; b. 11.6.27, Glasgow; m., Elizabeth Graham Reid; 3 s. Educ. Hillhead High School, Glasgow; Glasgow University; Balliol College, Oxford. Demonstrator of Anatomy: Glasgow University, 1953-55, Oxford University, 1955-58; Carlsberg-Wellcome Research Fellow, Copenhagen, 1958-59; University Lecturer in Anatomy, Oxford, 1959-67; US Public Health Service Research Fellow, Duke University, Durham, North Carolina, 1966-67. Publication: Cell Water, 1966. Recreation: hill-walking. Address: (b.) Department of Anatomy, Dundee University, Dundee, DD1 4HN; T.-Dundee 23181.

Dick, Professor Heather M., MD, FRCPGlas, FRCPath, FIBiol, FRSE. Professor of Medical Microbiology, Dundee University, since 1984; Visiting Professor (Immunology), Strathclyde University, since 1981; b. 14.11.32, London; m., Alex. L. Dick; 1 d. Educ. Harris Academy, Dundee; Queen's College, Dundee (St. Andrews University). Resident House Officer, Dundee Royal Infirmary and Ruchill Hospital, Glasgow, 1957-59; Assistant, Department of Bacteriology, St. Andrews University, 1959-61; Lecturer, Department of Bacteriology, Glasgow University, 1964-71; Consultant in Clinical Immunology, Glasgow Royal Infirmary, 1971-84. Publication: Topley and Wilson's Principles of Bacteriology and Immunity, 7th edition (Joint Editor, Volume 1). Recreation: music. Address: (b.) Department of Medical Microbiology, Ninewells Hospital, Dundee, DD1 9SY; T.-0382 60111, Ext. 2166.

Dick, James, BA, DMS. Director of Social Work, Highland Regional Council, since 1986; b. 19.5.39, Kirkcaldy; m., Isabella Hazell Grieve; 1 d. Educ. Open University; Robert Gordon's Institute of Technology; Jordanhill College of Education. Probation Officer, Edinburgh Combined Probation Area, 1967-69; Child Care Officer/ Social Worker, Moray and Nairn County Councils, 1969-71; Senior Social Worker, Perth and Kinross County Councils, 1971-73; Principal Social Worker/Divisional Officer, Borders Region, 1973-78; Divisional Officer, Banff/ Buchan, Grampian Region, 1978-85; Senior Depute Director, Highland Region, 1985-86. Recreations: golf; gardening; bowls. Address: (h.) Heatherlie, 31 Sunnyside, Culloden Moor, by Inverness; T.-Inverness 790727.

Dick, Sheriff John Alexander, MC (1944), QC (Scot), MA, LLB. Sheriff Principal of Glasgow and Strathkelvin, 1980-86; b. 1.1.20; m. Educ. Waid Academy, Anstruther; Edinburgh University. London Scottish, 1940; commissioned Royal Scots, 1942; called to Scottish Bar, 1949; Lecturer in Public Law, Edinburgh University, 1953-60; Sheriff of Lothians and Borders, at Edinburgh, 1969-78; Sheriff Principal of North Strathclyde, 1978-82.

Dick, Rev. John Hunter Addison, MA (Hons), MSc, BD (Hons). Minister, Ferryhill South, Aberdeen, since 1982; b. 27.12.45, Dunfermline; m., Gillian Averil Ogle-Skan; 3 s. Educ. Dunfermline High School; Edinburgh University. Research Assistant, Air Pollution Survey, Edinburgh University, 1967-70; Senior Tutor in Geography, Queensland University, Australia, 1970-78; student of divinity, 1978-81; Assistant Minister, Fairmilehead Parish Church, Edinburgh, 1981-82. Recreations: music; philately. Address: The Manse, 54 Polmuir Road, Aberdeen, AB1 2RT; T.-0224 586933.

Dick, Rev. Thomas, MA. Minister of Dunkeld, since 1974; b. 23.8.26, Rutherglen; m., Annie Margaret Muir McBride; 2 s. Educ. Rutherglen Academy; Glasgow University. Irvine (Relief) Church, 1951-61; Scotstoun East Church, 1961-74. Past President, Kelvin Rotary Club; former Moderator, Dunkeld and Meigle Presbytery. Recreations: gardening; hill-walking; music. Address: Cathedral Manse, Dunkeld, Perthshire, PH8 OAW; T.-03502 249.

Dickie, Rev. Michael Mure, BSc (Agric). Minister, Ayr: Castlehill, since 1967; b. 7.7.28, Glasgow; m., Marjory Jack Smith; 1 s.; 2 d. Educ. Dundee High School; Melville College, Edinburgh; Edinburgh University. 2nd Bn., Royal Scots; Minister: Rothiemay Parish, 1955-61, St. David's Church, Bathgate, 1961-67; Member, West Lothian Education Committee, 1963-67; first Chairman, Ayr Burgh Children's Panel; Secretary, Steering Committee for Community Councils in Ayr; Member, Forehill and Holmston Community Council, three years; Chaplain, "R" Division, Strathclyde Police. Recreations: hill-walking; drawing. Address: Castlehill Manse, 3 Hillfoot Road, Ayr, KA7 3LF; T.-Ayr 267332.

Dickie, Thomas, JP. Chairman, Garnock Valley Development Executive, since 1984; Member, Cunninghame District Council, since 1975 (Convener, 1980-84); Chairman, Cunninghame District Licensing Board, since 1980; Treasurer, Cunninghame North Constituency Labour Party; b. 5.12.30, Beith; m., Janette Coulter Brown. Educ. Beith Academy; Speirs' Secondary School; Glasgow and West of Scotland Commercial College. Office boy to Personnel Manager, Redpath Engineering Ltd., 1946-80; Member, Board, Irvine Development Corporation, 1981-84; Chairman, Kilbirnie Labour Party, since 1967; Treasurer, Cunninghame North Constituency Labour Party. Recreations: caravanning; walking; music. Address: (h.) 45 Loadingbank Court, Kilbirnie, Ayrshire, KA25 6JX; T.-0505 682205.

Dickinson, Professor Harry Thomas, BA, DipEd, MA, PhD, DLitt, FRHistS. Professor of British History, Edinburgh University, since 1980; Professor of British History, Nanjing University, since 1987; b. 9.3.39, Gateshead; m., Jennifer Elizabeth Galtry; 1 s.; 1 d. Educ. Gateshead Grammar School; Durham University; Newcastle University. Teacher of History, Washington Grammar School, 1961-64; Earl Grey Fellow, Newcastle University, 1964-66; History Department, Edinburgh University: Assistant Lecturer, 1966-68, Lecturer, 1968-73, Reader, 1973-80; Visiting Professor, Nanjing University, China, 1980 and 1983. Fulbright Scholar, 1973; Huntington Library Fellowship, 1973; Folger Shakespeare Library Fellowship, 1973; Winston Churchill Fellow, 1980; Leverhulme Award, 1986-87; Ahmanson Fellowship, UCLA, 1987. Publications: Bolingbroke; Walpole and the Whig Supremacy; Liberty and Property; British Radicals and the French Revolution; The Correspondence of Sir James Clavering; Politics and Literature in the 18th Century; The Political Works of Thomas Spence; Caricatures and the Constitution 1760-1832. Recreations: reading; swimming. Address: (h.) 44 Viewforth Terrace, Edinburgh, EH10 4LJ; T.-031-229 1379.

Dickinson, Professor John Philip, MA, MSc, PhD, AASA CPA, ACIS, FRSA, FBIM. Professor of Accountancy, Glasgow University, since 1985; b. 29.4.45, Morecambe; m., Christine Houghton; 1 s.; 2 d. Educ. Morecambe Grammar School; Cambridge University; Leeds University. Lecturer, Department of Management Studies and Associate Lecturer in Operational Research, Leeds University, 1968-71; Lecturer, Department of Accounting and Finance, Lancaster University, 1971-75; Senior Lecturer, Department of Accounting and Finance, University of Western Australia, 1975-80; Senior Lecturer, Department of Accountancy, Dundee University, 1980-81; Professor of Accountancy, Stirling University, 1981-85. Publications: Portfolio Theory, 1974; Risk and Uncertainty in Accounting and Finance, 1974; Statistics for Business Finance and Accounting, 1976; Portfolio Analysis and Capital Markets, 1977. Recreations: photography; wine and beer-making; travel. Address: (b.) Department of Accounting and Finance, Glasgow Business School, 65-69 Southpark Avenue, Glasgow, G12 8LE; T.-041-330 5428.

Dick-Smith, William Leslie, OBE, BL, FCIS. Chief Executive and Director of Administration, Stewartry District Council, since 1974; Clerk to the Lieutenancy; Clerk of the Peace; Clerk to

Stewartry Educational Trust; Clerk to Creetown Flood Relief Trust; Clerk to Stewartry Licensing Board; b. 12.1.27, Stirling; m., Mary Dalrymple; 1 d. Educ. Stirling High School; Falkirk High School; Bathgate Academy; Edinburgh University. Legal apprentice/Assistant, Cowan & Dalmahoy, WS, Edinburgh, 1946-49; Legal Assistant: Falkirk Town Council, 1949-51, Stewartry of Kirkcudbright County Council, 1951-62; Depute County Clerk, Dumfries County Council, 1962-68; Senior Depute County Clerk, Stewartry of Kirkcudbright County Council, 1968-72; County Clerk, 1972-75. Member, Executive Committees, Society and Association of Local Authority Chief Executives (Scottish Branches), since 1975; Queen's Silver Jubilee Medal; Session Clerk, St. George's Church, Dumfries; Member, Dumfries and Kirkcudbright Presbytery, Church of Scotland. Recreations: DIY pursuits; gardening; walking. Address: (b.) Council Offices, Kirkcudbright; T.-0557 30291.

Dickson, Captain Alexander Forrest, OBE, RD, FRIN. Commissioner of Northern Lighthouses, since 1979; b. 23.6.20, Edinburgh; m., Norma Houston; 3 s.; 2 d. Educ. George Watson's; Leith Nautical College. Apprentice, P. Henderson and Co., 1936-39; Royal Navy service in destroyers, 1939-45; Lecturer, Leith Nautical College, 1945-49; Shell International Marine Co. Ltd., 1949-79 (Director Operations, 1968-79). Recreations: fishing; gardening; golf. Address: (h.) Birchburn, Kenmore, Perthshire; T.-08873 283.

Dickson, Campbell S., MA, DipEd. Rector, Nairn Academy, since 1987; b. 25.11.44, Edinburgh; m., Sylvia Isabel Mary; 2 s. Educ. Boroughmuir High School, Edinburgh; Edinburgh University. Teacher of Modern Languages, Dunfermline High School, 1968-71; Principal Teacher of Modern Languages, Golspie High School, 1971-79; Assistant Rector, Banff Academy, 1979-82; Depute Rector, Lochaber High School, 1982-87. Member, Scottish Central Committee on Modern Languages, 1977-80. Recreations: sport (squash, skiing); walking; wood-turning; reading. Address: (b.) Nairn Academy, Duncan Drive, Nairn, IV12 4RD; T.-0667 53700.

Dickson, Ian Archibald. Secretary to Northern Lighthouse Board, since 1987; b. 3.5.42, Edinburgh; m., Moira Evelyn McLean; 1 s. Educ. George Heriot's, Edinburgh. Northern Lighthouse Board: Executive Officer, 1960-73, Personnel Officer, 1973-77, Deputy Secretary, 1977-86. Elder, Church of Scotland. Address: (b.) 84 George Street, Edinburgh; T.-031-226 7051.

Dickson, James Holms, BSc, MA, PhD, FLS. Senior Lecturer in Botany, Glasgow University, since 1979; b. 29.4.37, Glasgow; m., Camilla Ada Lambert; 1 s.; 1 d. Educ. Bellahouston Academy; Glasgow University; Cambridge University. Assistant, then Senior Assistant in Research, Botany School, Cambridge University, 1961-70; Member, Royal Society Expedition to Tristan da Cunha, 1962; Research Fellow and Official Fellow, Clare College, Cambridge, 1963-70; Lecturer in Botany, Glasgow University, 1970-79. President, Glasgow Natural History Society, 1976-79 and since 1987; Leader, Trades House of Glasgow Expedition to Papua New Guinea, 1987; Scientific Adviser to Britoil's exhibition, Glasgow Garden Festival, 1988. Recreation: gardening. Address: (h.) 113 Clober Road, Milngavie, Glasgow, G62 7LS; T.-041-956 4103.

Dickson, Leonard Elliot, CBE, MC, TD, DL, BA (Cantab), LLB. Retired Solicitor; b. 17.3.15, Edinburgh; m., Mary Elisabeth Cuthbertson; 1 s.; 1 d. Educ. Uppingham; Magdalene College, Cambridge; Glasgow University. 1st Bn., Glasgow Highlanders HLI, 1939-46; former Senior Partner, Dickson, Haddow & Co., Solicitors, Glasgow (retired, 1985); Clerk, Clyde Lighthouses Trust, 1953-65; Secretary, Glasgow Society of Sons of Clergy, 1953-83; serving Officer, TA, 1939-55 (Lt. Col. commanding 1st Bn., Glasgow Highlanders, 1952-55); Chairman, Lowland TAVR, 1968-70; Member, Glasgow Executive Council, NHS, 1956-74 (Vice Chairman, 1970-74). Recreations: travel; gardening. Address: (h.) Bridge End, Gartmore, Stirling, FK8 3RR; T.-087 72 220.

Dillon, J. Shaun H., DRSAM (Comp), FSA Scot. Professional Musician; Composer, Oboist and Teacher of Woodwind; b. 30.12.44, Sutton Coldfield. Educ. Berwickshire High School; Fettes College; Royal Scottish Academy of Music; Guildhall School of Music. Studied composition with Frank Spedding and Edmund Rubbra; awarded prize for composition for Leicestershire Schools Orchestra, 1965; commissions from various bodies, including Scottish Amateur Music Association; Instructor of Woodwind: Edinburgh Corporation, 1967-72, Aberdeen Corporation (latterly Grampian Region), 1972-81; Freelance Musician, since 1981; sometime Director of Music, St. Mary's Cathedral, Aberdeen; two Suites of Airs and Graces for strings published; Secretary, Association of Instrumental and Vocal Specialists, 1975-78. Recreations: reading, especially history, literature; crosswords; playing flute (badly) in ceilidh bands. Address: (b.) 34 Richmond Street, Aberdeen, AB2 4TR; T.-Aberdeen 630954.

Dilworth, Rev. Gerard Mark, OSB, MA, PhD, FRHistS, FSA Scot. Keeper, Scottish Catholic Archives, Edinburgh, since 1979; b. 18.4.24. Educ. St. Andrew's School, Edinburgh; Fort Augustus Abbey School, Invernessshire; Oxford University; Edinburgh University. Fort Augustus Abbey School: Senior Modern Languages Master, 1956-59, Headmaster, 1959-72; Parish Priest, Fort Augustus, 1974-79; Editor, The Innes Review, 1979-84. Publications: The Scots in Franconia; George Douglas: priest and martyr. Address: (b.) Columba House, 16 Drummond Place, Edinburgh, EH3 6PL; T.-031-556 3661.

Dixon, Charles, BSc, PhD, FIMA, FRMetS, MBCS. Senior Lecturer in Mathematics, Dundee University, since 1976 (Adviser of Studies, Faculty of Science and Engineering, since 1975); b. 27.2.35, Dundee. Educ. Morgan Academy, Dundee; St. Andrews University. Assistant Lecturer in Mathematics, Queen's College, Dundee, and St. Andrews University, 1957-60; Research Assistant, Department of Meteorology, Imperial College, London, 1960-62; Lecturer in Mathematics, Queen's College, Dundee, then Dundee University, 1962-76; Visiting Senior Lecturer, University of Western Australia, 1969 and 1974;

Visiting Professor, New Mexico State University, 1980. President, Dundee YMCA; Vice-President, Dundee Bn., Boys Brigade. Publications: Applied Mathematics of Science and Engineering, 1971; Numerical Analysis, 1974; Advanced Calculus, 1981. Recreations: squash; curling; playing bagpipes. Address: (b.) Department of Mathematics and Computer Science, Dundee University, Dundee, DD1 4HN; T.-0382 23181, Ext. 4495.

Dixon, Professor Geoffrey Richard, BSc, PhD, FIHort. Professor of Horticulture, Strathclyde University, since 1987; Head, Department of Horticulture, West of Scotland College, Ayr, since 1987 (Chairman, Plant and Environmental Sciences Division); b. 13.6.42, London; m., Kathleen Hilda Dixon; 1 s.; 1 d. Educ. Pewley County School, Guildford; Wye College, London University. Plant Pathologist, National Institute of Agricultural Botany, Cambridge, 1968-78; Head, Horticulture Division and Chairman, Crop Production and Protection Group, Aberdeen School of Agriculture, 1978-87. Recreations: gardening; photography; travel; hill-walking. Address: (b.) Horticulture Department, West of Scotland Agricultural College, Auchincruive, Ayr, KA6 5HW; T.-0292 520331.

Dixon-Carter, Clare. Vice-Chairman, Scottish Branch Council, British Red Cross Society, since 1986; b. 18.9.38, London. Educ. Moira House School, Eastbourne. Technical staff, EMI; hotel management, 1959-65; Assistant Regional Organiser for Scotland, World Wildlife Fund, 1969-77; joined Inverness-shire Branch, British Red Cross Society, 1965; Branch Director, 1979-86; awarded British Red Cross Society Voluntary Medical Service Medal, 1983; BRCS Badge of Honour for Distinguished Service and Life Membership of Society, 1986. Recreations: photography; travel; music. Address: (h.) Easter Balnabaan, Drumnadrochit, Inverness-shire, IV3 6UX; T.-04562 310.

Dobash, Rebecca Emerson, BA, MSc, PhD. Reader, Sociology and Social Policy, Stirling University, since 1972; b. Indiana; m., Russell Dobash. Educ. University of Washington. International Victimology Society Award for Outstanding Publications. Publications: Violence Against Wives; Violence Against Wives in Scotland; The Imprisonment of Women; Young People and the Criminal Justice System; The Financial Aspects of Divorce. Recreations: travel; food; gardening; walking. Address: (h.) Glenesk, Perth Road, Dunblane, Perthshire.

Dobie, Margaret G.C., MA, DipSocStud. Member, Broadcasting Council for Scotland, since 1987; Chair, Children's Panel Advisory Group, since 1985; Chair, Dumfries and Galloway Children's Panel Advisory Committee, since 1982; b. Galloway; m., James T.J. Dobie; 3 s. Educ. Benedictine Convent, Dumfries; Dumfries Academy; Edinburgh University. Medical Social Worker; Chair, Dumfries and Galloway Regional Children's Panel; Social Worker, Child Guidance Service, Dumfries; National Secretary, Scottish Association for the Study of Delinquency; Chair, Dumfries & Galloway Valuation Panel. Recreations: travel; tennis; reading cookery books and detective novels. Address: (h.) Mansepark, Kirkgunzeon, Dumfries, DG2 8LA; T.-038 776 661.

Dobson, Ronald Matthew, MA, PhD. Senior Lecturer in Agricultural Zoology, Glasgow University, since 1974; b. 18.12.25, Blackburn, Lancashire; m., Ruth Hilda Nash; 2 s.; 3 d. Educ. Queen Elizabeth's Grammar School, Blackburn; Cambridge University; London University. Insect Infestation Inspector, Ministry of Food, then Department of Agriculture for Scotland, 1945-49; Research Assistant, Wye College, London University, 1950-53; Scientific Officer, then Senior Scientific Officer, Rothamsted Experimental Station, 1953-59; Lecturer, Glasgow University, 1959-74. Fellow, Royal Entomological Society of London; Honorary Editor, Glasgow Naturalist. Publications: Insects and Other Invertebrates in Colour (adaptation); numerous scientific and natural history articles. Recreations: music; house renovation; boating. Address: (h.) 664 Clarkston Road, Glasgow, G44 3YS; T.-041-637 3476.

Dodd, Raymond Henry, MA, BMus, ARAM. Cellist and Composer; Head, Department of Music, Aberdeen University; b. 31.3.29; m., Doreen Joyce; 1 s.; 1 d. Educ. Bryanston School; Royal Academy of Music; Worcester College, Oxford. Music Master, Sedbergh School, 1951-55; Aberdeen University: Lecturer in Music, 1956, Senior Lecturer in Music, 1971; Visiting Professor of Music, Wilson College, USA, 1972-73. Various orchestral and chamber music compositions; a Governor, Royal Scottish Academy of Music and Drama; a Director: North East of Scotland Music School, Scottish Music Information Centre; awarded Szymanowski Medal, Polish Ministry of Art and Culture, 1982. Recreation: Indian music. Address: (h.) 14 The Chanonry, Old Aberdeen, Aberdeen, AB2 1RP; T.-0224 485752.

Doig, Andrew, MB, ChB, FRCPEdin, FRCP. Consultant Physician, Edinburgh Royal Infirmary, since 1963; Senior Lecturer in Medicine, Edinburgh University, since 1963; b. 18.12.24, Edinburgh; m., Anne Bisset Duthie; 1 s.; 1 d. Educ. Boroughmuir School, Edinburgh; Edinburgh University; Illinois University. Junior medical posts, Edinburgh Royal Infirmary and Victoria Hospital, Burnley; Assistant Lecturer in Medicine, Edinburgh University; postdoctoral Research Fellow, United States Public Health Service; Past President, Scottish Society of Physicians. Recreations: hill-walking; photography. Address: (h.) 13 Nile Grove, Edinburgh, EH10 4RE; T.-031-447 4160.

Doig, Very Rev. Andrew Beveridge, MA, BD, DD. Moderator, General Assembly of the Church of Scotland, 1981-82; b. 18.9.14, Carluke; m., 1, Nan Carruthers (deceased); 1 d.; 2, Barbara Young; 1 s.; 1 d. Educ. Hyndland Secondary School, Glasgow; Glasgow University; Trinity College, Glasgow; Union Theological Seminary, New York. Missionary, Church of Scotland, to Nyasaland, 1939; Senior Chaplain to the Forces, East Africa Command, 1940-45; Secretary, Blantyre Mission Council, 1946-53; Member: Government Advisory Committee on African Education, 1948-53, Nyasaland Legislative Council, 1946-53; seconded from missionary service to be Nominated Member for African Interests, Central Africa Federal Assembly, 1953-58; General Secretary, Blantyre Synod, Church of Central Africa, Presbyterian, 1958-62; Minister, St. John's and King's Park, Dalkeith, 1962-72; Clerk, Dalkeith Presbytery, 1965-72; Member, Overseas Council, Church of Scotland, and Convener, Christian Aid, 1967-70; General Secretary, National Bible Society of Scotland, 1972-82; Member, Executive Committee for Europe in worldwide United Bible Societies, 1974-82. Recreation: golf. Address: (h.) The Eildons, Moulin Square, Pitlochry, PH16 5EW; T.-0796 2892.

Doig, James Alexander, MB, ChB, FRCSEdin, FRCSGlas. Consultant Surgeon in Otolaryngology, Glasgow Royal Infirmary, since 1960, and in administrative charge, since 1978; Consultant in Neuro-otology, Institute of Neurological Sciences, since 1970; Honorary Clinical Lecturer, Glasgow University, since 1960; Consultant Otolaryngologist, Strathclyde University, since 1980; b. 1926, Dundee; m., Pamela Alison Mais; 1 d. Educ. Dundee High School; St. Andrews University. House Surgeon, Aberdeen Royal Infirmary; House Physician, Dundee Royal Infirmary; House Surgeon (Otolaryngology), Dundee Royal Infirmary; Temporary Major, RAMC; Registrar (Otolaryngology), Aberdeen Royal Infirmary; Registrar (General Surgery), Bangour General Hospital; Senior Registrar (Otolaryngology), Aberdeen Royal Infirmary; Consultant Surgeon (Otolaryngology), Law Hospital. President, Scottish Otolaryngological Society, 1985. Publications: papers in various medical journals and Contributor to Scientific Foundations of Neurology. Recreations: gardening; fishing; music. Address: (b.) 901 Sauchiehall Street, Glasgow, G3 7TD; T.-041-339 5550.

Doig, John Scott. Regional Sheriff Clerk, Grampian Highland and Islands; b. 24.11.38, Dundee; m., Margaret; 1 s.; 1 d. Educ. Harris Academy, Dundee. Sheriff Clerk Service since 1956 in Glasgow, Perth, Campbeltown, Linlithgow, Glasgow, Dumbarton; Secretary, Sheriff Court Rules Council, 1973-79. Recreations: bowls; snooker. Address: (b.) The Castle, Inverness; T.-0463 230782.

Dolan, Philip John, DASS. Area Manager, Social Work, Strathclyde, since 1976; Executive Member, Scottish Council on Disability, since 1982; b. 26.4.36, Glasgow; m., Sheila Reid; 1 s. Educ. St. Mungo's Academy, Glasgow; Glasgow University; Hull University. Printing industry, 1951-64; entered social work service, 1968. Member, Hamilton/East Kilbride Health Council, 1975-82 (Chairman, 1978-80); Member, Prison Local Review Committee, since 1976; Executive Member, Haemophilia Society (Scottish Group), since 1976. Recreations: music; reading; travel. Address: (h.) 160 Camphill Avenue, Langside, Glasgow, G41 3DT; T.-041-649 0050.

Donachy, John Archibald, OBE, MA, FBIM. Director, The Polecon Co. Ltd., since 1970; Governor, British Film Institute, since 1974; Chairman, Scottish Film Council, since 1984; b. Edinburgh; m., Jilly Pollard; 1 s.; 1 d. Educ. George Heriot's School; High School of Glasgow; Glasgow University. Recreations: gardening; golf; cooking; films; music. Address: (b.) 22A Rutland Square, Edinburgh, EH1 2BB; T.-031-228 6391.

Donald, George Malcolm, ARSA, RSW, DA, ATC, MEd. Lecturer, Edinburgh College of Art; Printmaker; b. 12.9.43, Ootacamund, South India; 1 s.; 1 d. Educ. Robert Gordon's College; Aberdeen Academy; Edinburgh College of Art; Hornsey College of Art; Edinburgh University. Joined Edinburgh College of Art as Lecturer, 1969; Visiting Lecturer, five Faculties of Art in India, 1979; Visiting Professor of Art, 1981, and Visiting Professor, Drawing and Anatomy, 1985, University of Central Florida; Visiting Professor, Strasbourg, 1986, Belgrade, 1987; Latimer Award, RSA, 1970; Guthrie Award, RSA, 1973; Scottish Arts Council Bursary, 1973; RSA Gillies Bequest Travel Award to India, 1978; SAC Travel and Study Award, Indiana, 1981; RSA Gillies Prize, 1982; RSW Mary Marshall Brown Award, 1983; RGI Cargill Award, 1987; former Council Member: SSA, Printmakers Workshop (Edinburgh); former Member, Scottish Arts Council Awards Committee; one man shows, Florida, 1985, Helsinki, 1985, Edinburgh Festival, 1985, Belgrade, 1987, Florida, 1987. Address: (b.) Edinburgh College of Art, Lauriston Place, Edinburgh; T.-031-229 9311.

Donald, James Forrest. Director, His Majesty's Theatre, Aberdeen, since 1971; b. 14.3.34, Aberdeen; m., Anne Gerrie; 1 s.; 1 d. Educ. Gordonstoun School. Recreation: golf. Address: (b.) His Majesty's Theatre, Aberdeen; T.-Aberdeen 637788.

Donald, James Turner, BSc (Eng). General Manager, Common Services Agency, Scottish Health Service, since 1986; Member, Management Committee, Common Services Agency, since 1986; b. 12.9.36, Paisley; m., Muriel Elizabeth Donald; 1 s.; 1 d. Educ. Gordonstoun; Glasgow University. Inveresk Group Ltd.: joined, 1962; General Manager, Woodhall, 1970-72, Caldwells, 1972-74, Carrongrove, 1974-76, Westfield, 1981-85; Director, 1976-81, Divisional Chairman, 1974-80. Chairman, Scottish Division, British Paper and Board Federation, 1976-79; Regional Councillor, CBI Scotland, 1976-82. Recreations: horses; photography; sailing. Address: (b.) Trinity Park House, South Trinity Road, Edinburgh, EH5 3SE; T.-031-552 6255.

Donaldson, David Abercrombie, RSA, RP, RGI, LLD, DLitt. Painter; Painter and Limner to The Queen in Scotland, since 1977; b. 29.6.16, Chryston; m., Maria Krystyna Mora-Szorc; 1 s.; 2 d. Educ. Coatbridge Secondary School; Glasgow School of Art. Head of Painting School, Glasgow School of Art, 1967-81; Hon. LLD, Strathclyde, 1971. Recreations: music; cooking. Address: (h.) 5 Cleveden Drive, Glasgow, G12 0SB; T.-041-334 1029.

Donaldson, Rev. David, MA, BD (Hons). Minister, Whitfield Parish Church, Dundee, since 1983; b. 6.7.43, Glasgow; m., Jean Martha Lacey; 1 s.; 3 d. Educ. Glasgow Academy; Glasgow University.

Assistant Minister, Cardonald Parish Church, Glasgow; Church of Scotland Missionary in Taiwan; Minister, St. David's Parish Church, Bathgate. Recreations: squash; tennis; badminton. Address: 55 Chirnside Place, Dundee, DD4 0TE; T.-Dundee 739757.

Donaldson, Professor Gordon, CBE, DLitt, FBA, FRSE. HM Historiographer in Scotland, since 1979; Professor Emeritus, since 1979; b. 13.4.13, Edinburgh. Educ. Royal High School, Edinburgh; Edinburgh University; London University. Assistant, Scottish Record Office, 1938-47; Lecturer in Scottish History, Edinburgh University, 1947; Reader, 1955; Professor of Scottish History and Palaeography, 1963; Member, Royal Commission on the Ancient and Historical Monuments of Scotland, 1964-82; Member, Scottish Records Advisory Council, 1964-87; President: Scottish Ecclesiological Society, 1963-65, Scottish Church History Society, 1964-67, Scottish History Society, 1968-72, Scottish Record Society, since 1981, Stair Society, since 1987. Publications: The Making of the Scottish Prayer Book, 1954; Register of the Privy Seal of Scotland, V-VIII, 1957-82; Life in Shetland under Earl Patrick, 1958; Scotland: Church and Nation, 1960, 1972; Scottish Reformation, 1960, 1972; Scotland: James V to James VII, 1965; The Scots Overseas, 1966; Northwards by Sea, 1966, 1978; Scottish Kings, 1967, 1977; First Trial of Mary Queen of Scots, 1969; Mary Queen of Scots, 1974; Scotland: The Shaping of a Nation, 1974, 1980; The Queen's Men, 1983; Isles of Home, 1983; Scottish Church History, 1985. Address: (h.) 6 Pan Ha', Dysart, Fife, KY1 2TL; T.-0592 52685.

Donaldson, Professor Gordon Bryce, MA, PhD, FInstP. Professor, Department of Physics and Applied Physics, Strathclyde University, since 1985; b. 10.8.41, Edinburgh; m., Christina Martin; 1 s.; 1 d. Educ. Glasgow Academy; Christ's College, Cambridge. Cavendish Laboratory, Cambridge, 1962-65; Lecturer in Physics, Lancaster University, 1966-75; Strathclyde University: Lecturer, 1976, Senior Lecturer, 1978; Visiting Scientist and Fulbright Scholar, University of California, 1975; Visiting Professor, University of Virginia, 1981. Governor, Glasgow Academicals War Memorial Trust. Address: (b.) Department of Applied Physics, Strathclyde University, Glasgow, G4 ONG; T.-041-552 4400.

Donaldson, Professor Iain Malcolm Lane, BSc, MB, ChB, MA, FRCPE, MRCP. Professor of Neurophysiology, Edinburgh University, since 1987; b. 22.10.37; m.; 1 s. Educ. Edinburgh University. House Physician and Surgeon, Research Fellow, Honorary Lecturer, Honorary Senior Registrar, Departments of Medicine and Surgical Neurology, Edinburgh University, 1962-69; Anglo-French Research Scholarship, University of Paris, 1969-70; Research Officer, University Laboratory of Physiology, Oxford, 1970-79; Fellow and Tutor in Medicine, St. Edmund Hall, Oxford, 1973-79; Professor of Zoology, Hull University, 1979-87; Emeritus Fellow, St. Edmund Hall, Oxford, since 1979. Recreation: studying the past. Address: (b.) Department of Pharmacology, Edinburgh University, 1 George Square, Edinburgh.

Donaldson, James Andrew, BDS, BA. Principal in general dental practice; Dental Adviser in General Dental Practice to British Antarctic Survey; Member, Grampian Regional Council, since 1986 (Chairman, Finance and General Purposes Committee, 1986-87); Member, Scottish Valuation Advisory Council; b. 28.2.57, Glasgow; m., Dr. Patricia H. Winter; 1 d. Educ. Coatbridge High School; Dundee University; Open University. Member, Aberdeen District Council, 1984-86. Recreations: skiing; squash; scuba diving. Address: (h.) The Manse, Bridge Street, Cruden Bay, Aberdeenshire; T.-0779 813313.

Donaldson, James Roy, MB, ChB, FRCPath, DipRCPath, DipBact, NDD, CDD. Consultant Bacteriologist, Greater Glasgow Health Board, since 1981; b. 24.12.27, Glasgow; m., Flora Macdonald; 1 s.; 1 d. Educ. Bearsden Academy; Glasgow University; London University; West of Scotland Agricultural College. Dairy technologist, 1948-50; general medical practitioner, 1958-65; Regular Army, Aden, BAOR, UK, Malaysia, 1965-81, to rank of Lt. Col. and Consultant Medical Microbiologist. Recreations: trout fishing; gardening; golf. Address: (h.) Hopedale, South Broomage Avenue, Larbert, FK5 3LF; T.-0324 551739.

Donaldson, James T., BA (Hons), MEd. HM Inspector of Schools, since 1982; b. 4.3.45, Ecclefechan; m., Maureen; 1 s.; 2 d. Educ. Wallace Hall Academy; Strathclyde University; Edinburgh University. Lecturer, Edinburgh College of Commerce, 1968-73; Lecturer/Senior Lecturer, Queen Margaret College, Edinburgh, 1973-79; Head, Department of Business Studies, Telford College of Further Education, Edinburgh, 1979-82. Recreations: golf; running. Address: (b.) Room 4/31, New St. Andrew's House, Scottish Education Department, St. James Centre, Edinburgh, EH1; T.-031-556 8400.

Donaldson, Robert, MA, PhD. Keeper, Division 2, Department of Printed Books, National Library of Scotland, since 1975; b. 13.12.26, Edinburgh; m., Elizabeth Macpherson; 1 s.; 1 d. Educ. George Heriot's School, Edinburgh; Edinburgh University. Assistant Librarian, Edinburgh University Library, 1949-59; Sub-Librarian (Keeper of Special Collections), Glasgow University Library, 1959-62; National Library of Scotland: Assistant Keeper, Department of Printed Books, 1962-72, Deputy Keeper, Department of Printed Books, 1972-74. Editor, The Bibliotheck, 1959-69; President, Edinburgh Bibliographical Society, 1977-80; Chairman, Scottish Group, University, College and Research Section, Library Association, 1980-82; Chairman, Rare Books Group, 1983-86. Recreation: listening to music. Address: (b.) National Library of Scotland, George IV Bridge, Edinburgh, EH1 1EW; T.-031-226 4531.

Donaldson, (William) Blair (MacGregor), MB, ChB, FRCS, DO. Consultant Ophthalmic Surgeon, since 1979; Senior Lecturer in Ophthalmology, Aberdeen University, since 1979; b. 24.12.40, Edinburgh; m., Marjorie Stuart; 1 d. Educ. Edinburgh Academy; Edinburgh University. Junior hospital appointments in Tasmania and Scotland. Recreations: skiing; tennis; golf. Address: (h.) 45 Carlton Place, Aberdeen, AB2 4BR; T.-0224 641166.

Donnelly, Dougie. Radio and Television Broadcaster, since 1976; b. 7.6.53, Glasgow; m., Linda; 2 d. Educ. Hamilton Academy; Strathclyde University. Studied law at University; joined Radio Clyde to present music programmes, 1976, and BBC TV Scotland as Sports Presenter and Commentator, 1978; Presenter, Friday Night With Dougie Donnelly, BBC TV Scotland (two series); Presenter, Dougie Donnelly Mid Morning Show, Radio Clyde (ninth year). Scottish Radio Personality of Year, 1979, 1982 and 1985; Scottish TV Personality of Year, 1982; Member: Stars Organisation for Spastics, Lords Taverners. Recreations: golf; reading; socialising; work. Address: (b.) c/o David John Associates, 10 Queen's Gate Lane, Glasgow, G12 9DF; T.-041-357 0532.

Donnison, Professor David. Professor of Town and Regional Planning, Glasgow University, since 1980; b. 19.1.26. Lecturer: Manchester University, 1950-53, Toronto University, 1953-55; London School of Economics and Political Science: Reader, 1956-61, Professor, 1961-69; Director, Centre for Environmental Studies, London, 1969-75; Supplementary Benefits Commission, 1975-80. Address: (b.) Glasgow University, Glasgow, G12 8RT.

Donovan, Professor Robert John, BSc, PhD, CChem, FRSC, FRSE. Professor of Chemistry, Edinburgh University, since 1979; b. 13.7.41, Nantwich; m., Marion Colclough; 1 d. Educ. Sandbach School; University College of Wales, Aberystwyth; Cambridge University. Research Fellow, Gonville and Caius College, 1966-70; Edinburgh University: Lecturer in Physical Chemistry, 1970-74, Reader in Chemistry, 1974-79. Member, Physical Chemistry Panel, Science & Engineering Research Council, 1977-80; Member, Management Committee, SERC Synchrotron Radiation Source, Daresbury, 1977-80; Member, SERC Synchroton Radiation Facility Committee, 1979-84, Laser Facility Committee, since 1987; awarded Corday-Morgan Medal and Prize, Royal Society of Chemistry, 1975; Member, Faraday Council, Royal Society of Chemistry, 1981-83. Recreations: hill-walking; skiing; sail-boarding; cross-country riding. Address: (b.) Department of Chemistry, Edinburgh University, West Mains Road, Edinburgh, EH9 3JJ; T.-031-667 1081 (Ext. 3408).

Doran, Frank, LLB. MP (Labour), Aberdeen South, since 1987; b. 13.4.49, Edinburgh; m., Pat; 2 s. Educ. Dundee University. Solicitor with own business in Dundee; Member, General Management Committee, Dundee City Labour Party; Party Solicitor in Dundee; Lecturer and Writer on child care and mental health law; Founder Member, Scottish Legal Action Group and "Scottish Child"; Past Chairman, Dundee Association for Mental Health. Recreations: football; cinema. Address: (h.) 12 Laurelbank, Dundee; T.-0382 27086.

Dorman, Arthur Brian, LLB, FBIM. Solicitor; Founding and Senior Partner, Dorman, Jeffrey & Co., Glasgow and Edinburgh; b. 21.6.45, Glasgow; m., Christine Angela; 1 s.; 1 d. Educ. Hillhead High School; Glasgow University. Recreation: occasional golf. Address: (b.) Madeleine Smith House, 6/7 Blythswood Square, Glasgow, G2 4AD; T.-041-221 9880.

Dorward, Adam Paterson, FCFI. Member, Borders Health Board (Convener, Finance Committee), since 1978; a Governor, Scottish College of Textiles; b. 11.6.22, Galashiels; m., Jean MacPherson Ovens; 2 s. Educ. Sedbergh School; St. John's College, Cambridge; Dundee School of Economics; Tailor & Cutter Academy; Stevenson College. RAF, 1942-46 (Flt. Lt. Pilot, Flying Instructor); J. & J. Dorward Ltd., Gala Forest: joined, 1946, appointed Designer/Production Manager, 1948, appointed Director, 1952, Managing Director, 1972, Chairman, 1978; negotiated amalgamation with Dawson International, remaining Managing Director for 18 months; administration, Youth Opportunities Programme and Youth Training Scheme, Borders Regional Council, 1982-84; Business Consultant, 1984; Production Co-ordinator, clothing manufacturer, 1985-87. Town and County Councillor, 1955-60; Member, Board, Galashiels Further Education College, 1955-60; Deacon, Galashiels Manufacturers' Corporation, 1960; a Governor, St. Mary's Preparatory School, Melrose, 1960; Council Member, Clothing Manufacturers' Federation of GB, 1973-81; Chairman, Scottish Clothing Manufacturers' Association, 1975-79; Past Chairman, Border Counties TSB; former Trustee, TSB of South of Scotland; Member, Eildon Housing Association, since 1978; Trustee, R.S. Hayward Trust. Recreations: sports; gardening. Address: (h.) Caddon Lynns, Clovenfords, Galashiels, TD1 3LF; T.-0896 85 259.

Dorward, David Campbell, MA, GRSM, LRAM. Composer, since 1944; Music Producer, BBC, since 1962; b. 7.8.33, Dundee; m., Janet Offord; 1 s.; 2 d. Educ. Morgan Academy, Dundee; St. Andrews University; Royal Academy of Music. Teaching, 1960-61; Freelance, 1961-62. Arts Adviser, Lamp of Lothian Collegiate Trust, since 1967; Member, Scottish Arts Council, 1972-78; Consultant Director, Performing Right Society, since 1985; Patron's Fund Award, 1958; Royal Philharmonic Prizewinner, 1958; compositions include four string quartets, symphony, four concertos, Tonight Mrs Morrison (one-act opera), A Christmas Carol (musical), and incidental music for TV, radio, film and stage. Recreations: photography; computers; walking in the country. Address: (h.) 10 Dean Park Crescent, Edinburgh, EH4 1PH; T.-031-332 3002.

Douglas, Rev. Andrew Morrison, MA. Minister, High Church, Hilton, Aberdeen; Minutes Clerk, Aberdeen Presbytery; Moderator, Aberdeen Presbytery, 1987-88; b. 23.2.30, Orange, Australia; m., Margaret Rennie; 2 s.; 2 d. Educ. Robert Gordon's College; Aberdeen University. Minister: Lochcraig Church, Fife, 1957-63, Bonaccord St. Paul's, Aberdeen, 1963-72, Southesk, Brechin, 1972-77. Chaplain, Aberdeen Maternity and Sick Children's Hospitals, 1968-71. Recreations: gardening; games. Address: 25 Argyll Place, Aberdeen, AB2 4HU; T.-Aberdeen 636672.

Douglas, Rev. Colin Rutherford, MA, BD, STM. Minister, Livingston Ecumenical Parish, since 1987 (Airdrie St. Columba's, 1973-87); b. 10.4.42, Leven. Educ. George Watson's College; Dundee

High School; Loretto School; St. Andrews University; Edinburgh University. Scottish half-mile Schools Champion, 1960. Address: 202 Norman Rise, Livingston, West Lothian, EH54 6NW; T.-0506 410668.

Douglas, Rev. Iain Mackechnie, MA, BD, MPhil, DipEd. Minister, St. Andrew's Parish Church, Montrose, since 1980; b. 25.6.35, Eccles, Berwickshire; m., E.W. Shirley Harris; 2 s. Educ. Eccles Public School; George Watson's Boys' College, Edinburgh; Edinburgh University. Missionary, Church of Scotland, 1960-68; ordained, Madras Diocese, Church of South India, 1960; Lecturer, Tamilnad Theological College, 1963-68; Teacher of Religious Education, Hawick High School, 1969-74; Principal Teacher of Religious Education, Morgan Academy, Dundee, 1974-80. Publications: Famulus Christi (Contributor), 1976; Sacris Erudiri (Contributor), 1974-75. Address: 49 Northesk Road, Montrose, DD10 8TQ; T.-Montrose 72060.

Douglas, Rev. Ian Percy, LTh. Minister, Craigiebuckler Parish Church, Aberdeen, since 1982; b. 2.5.38, Inverurie; m., Celia Gerrard; 2 s. Educ. Inverurie Academy; Aberdeen University. Junior Salesman, Isaac Benzie Ltd., Aberdeen, 1954-56; 1st Bn., Seaforth Highlanders, 1956-59; Departmental Manager, Isaac Benzie Ltd., 1960-65; Training and Personnel Officer, House of Fraser, 1965-67; studied for the ministry, 1967-73; Minister, Viewforth Parish Church, Edinburgh, 1974-82. TA Chaplain, 205 General Hospital Unit, 1979-81; Patron, Aberdeen Trinity Hall; Burgess of Guild of Burgh of Aberdeen. Recreations: music; bowls. Address: Craigiebuckler Manse, Springfield Road, Aberdeen, AB1 8AA.

Douglas, James Hall, MA, LLB. Honorary Sheriff, since 1983; b. 16.9.21, Glasgow; m., Louisa Hemsworth. Educ. Whitehill Senior Secondary School, Glasgow; Glasgow University. RAF, 1940-46; Procurator Fiscal service, 1951-82, at Ayr, Glasgow, Stranraer and Dunfermline; Procurator Fiscal, Dunfermline, 1967-82. Recreations: reading; gardening; music; philately. Address: (h.) 1 Canmore Grove, Dunfermline, KY12 OJT; T.-Dunfermline 725486.

Douglas, James Turner, Honorary Sheriff, since 1971; retired Solicitor; b. 12.9.16, Perth; m., Isobel Barrie Campbell; 1 s.; 1 d. Educ. Perth Academy; Edinburgh University. Qualified as Solicitor, 1939; Army, 1939-45 (POW, Germany, 1940-45); Solicitor in Perth, 1945-83 (Senior Partner, Macnab, Gordon & Douglas, 1962-83). President, Scottish Golf Union, 1972-74; Past Captain, Craigie Hill and Blairgowrie Golf Clubs; Past Captain and President, Perthshire Rugby Club; Past President: Perth Rotary Club, Society of Solicitors of City and County of Perth. Recreations: golf; in younger days, rugby. Address: (h.) 1 Springbank, Isla Road, Perth, PH2 7HB; T.-Perth 21576.

Douglas, John Aitken, DPE, DMS, MBIM, FILAM. Director of Recreation Services, Inverclyde District Council, since 1974; b. 8.4.41, Duns; m., Anne; 1 s.; 1 d. Educ. Berwickshire High School, Duns; Scottish School of Physical Education, Jordanhill College of Education; Glasgow College of Technology. Teacher of Physical Education, Dollar Academy, 1963-65; Assistant Lecturer in Physical Education, Glasgow University, 1965-66; Lecturer in Physical Education, Strathclyde University, 1966-67; Manager, Bellahouston Sports Centre, Glasgow, 1967-71; Recreation Officer, Bishopbriggs Burgh Council, 1971-74. Churchill Fellow, 1970; Past Chairman: British and Irish Basketball Federation, 1972-73, Association of Recreation Managers, 1973-74 and 1979-80; former Member, National Executive, Institute of Leisure and Amenity Management, and Past Chairman, Scottish Region; Member, Executive, Association of Directors of Recreation, Leisure and Tourism; Officer Adviser, COSLA. Recreations: hockey; squash; caravanning; skiing; sailboarding. Address: (b.) Municipal Buildings, Greenock; T.-0475 24400.

Douglas, Marshall Neil, AFA, ABIM. Member, Borders Regional Council, since 1988; President, Roxburgh and Berwickshire SNP, since 1988; Chairman, Borders Association of SNP Councillors, since 1988; b. 7.1.57, Birmingham; m., Lynda Howlett; 1 s.; 1 d. Educ. Fairfax High School, Sutton Coldfield; Scottish College of Textiles. Treasurer, Roxburgh, Selkirk and Peebles Constituency Association, 1979; SNP Election Agent, Tweeddale, Ettrick and Lauderdale, 1983; SNP Parliamentary candidate, Roxburgh and Berwickshire, 1987. Recreations: walking and photography; reading; languages. Address: (h.) 48 Plora Terrace, Innerleithen, Peeblesshire, EH44 6LT; T.-0896 830720.

Douglas, Neil James, MD, FRCP. Senior Lecturer in Respiratory Medicine, Edinburgh University, since 1983; Consultant Physician, since 1983; Secretary, British Thoracic Society, 1988-90; b. 28.5.49, Edinburgh; m., Dr. Sue Galloway; 1 s.; 1 d. Educ. Dundee High School; Trinity College, Glenalmond; St. Andrews University; Edinburgh University. Lecturer in Medicine, Edinburgh University, 1974-83; MRC Travelling Fellow, University of Colorado, 1980-81. Recreations: fishing; gardening; eating. Address: (b.) Department of Respiratory Medicine, City Hospital, Greenbank Drive, Edinburgh; T.-031-447 1001.

Douglas, Patricia. Director, Charles Rennie Mackintosh Society; m., Thomas H. Douglas; 2 s. Consulting Civil Engineer. Scottish Committee Member, Royal Society of Arts; until recently Chairman/Secretary, DIA Scotland. Recreations: tennis; bridge. Address: (b.) Queen's Cross, 870 Garscube Road, Glasgow, G20 7EL; T.-041-946 6600.

Douglas, Richard. MP (Labour), Dunfermline West, since 1983 (Dunfermline, 1979-83); b. 4.1.32. Educ. Govan High School; Co-operative College; Strathclyde University. MP, Stirlingshire East and Clackmannan, 1970-74; Member, Public Accounts Committee, 1979-83.

Douglas, Sadie Naomi. Administrative Director, Scottish Civic Trust, since 1983; b. Huddersfield; m., Alexander Douglas (deceased); 1 s. Educ. Longley Hall, Huddersfield; Huddersfield Technical College. Worked with Oxfam, 1966-70; Organising Secretary, Facelift Glasgow, 1970-73; Trust Secretary, Scottish Civic Trust, 1973-83. Member, Countrywide Holiday Association

(President, Glasgow CHA Club); Member, Scottish Countryside Activities Council. Recreation: hill-walking. Address: (h.) Hillhouse, Ardneil Avenue, West Kilbride, Ayrshire, KA23; T.-0294 822465; (b.) 24 George Square, Glasgow, G2 1EF; T.-041-221 1466.

Douglas-Hamilton, Lord James Alexander, MA, LLB. MP (Conservative), Edinburgh West, since 1974; Parliamentary Under Secretary of State, Scottish Office, for Home Affairs and the Environment, since 1987; b. 31.7.42, Strathaven; m., Susan Buchan; 4 s. Educ. Eton; Balliol College, Oxford; Edinburgh University. Advocate at Scots Bar, 1968; Member, Edinburgh Town Council, 1972; Scottish Conservative Whip, 1977; a Lord Comr, HM Treasury, and Government Whip for Scottish Conservative Members, 1979-81; PPS to Malcolm Rifkind MP, at Foreign Office, later Scottish Office; Captain, Cameronian Coy., 2nd Bn., Lowland Volunteers (RARO), 1972; Honorary President, Scottish Amateur Boxing Association, since 1975; President, Royal Commonwealth Society in Scotland, since 1979; President, Scottish Council, United Nations Association, since 1981. Oxford Boxing Blue, 1961; President, Oxford Union Society, 1964. Publications: Motive For A Mission: The Story Behind Hess's Flight to Britain, 1971; The Air Battle for Malta: The Diaries of a Fighter Pilot, 1981; Roof of the World, 1983. Recreations: golf; forestry. Address: (h.) 12 Quality Street Lane, Davidsons Mains, Edinburgh; T.-031-336 4213.

Douglas-Home, Hon. (Lavinia) Caroline, FSA Scot. Estate Factor, Douglas and Angus Estates, since 1959; Trustee, National Museum of Antiquities of Scotland, 1982-85; Deputy Lieutenant, Berwickshire, since 1983; b. 11.10.37 (daughter of Baron Home of the Hirsel, KT, PC). Educ. privately. Woman of the Bedchamber (Temporary) to Queen Elizabeth the Queen Mother, 1963-65; Lady-In-Waiting (Temporary) to HRH Duchess of Kent, 1966-67. Recreations: hunting; fishing; reading; antiquities. Address: (h.) Dove Cottage, The Hirsel, Coldstream, Berwickshire; T.-0890 2834.

Dourish, James Anthony, MA (Hons). Rector, Trinity High School, Renfrew, since 1979; b. 7.2.37, Glasgow; m., Honor Burns; 3 s.; 1 d. Educ. St. Aloysius' College, Glasgow; Glasgow University. Teacher of Classics, St. Aloysius' College, Glasgow, 1960-67; Principal Teacher of Classics: St. Gregory's, Glasgow, 1967-71, Holyrood, Glasgow, 1972-73; Assistant Head Teacher, St. Margaret Mary's, Glasgow, 1974-77; Depute Head Teacher, Cardinal Newman High School, Bellshill, 1977-79. Choirmaster/Organist, St. Andrew's Cathedral, Glasgow, 1975-82; Past President, Rutherglen Lawn Tennis Club. Recreations: tennis; hill-walking; music. Address: (h.) 46 Viewpark Drive, Burnside, near Glasgow; T.-041-647 1021.

Douse, Cuthbert, MBE, ALCM. Chairman, Scottish Standing Conference of Voluntary Youth Organisations; Chairman, Strathclyde Regional Conference of Voluntary Youth Organisations; Member, Management Committee, Scottish Environmental and Outdoor Centres Association Ltd.; b. 21.4.22, Clydebank; m., Agnes M.F.; 1 s. Educ. Clydebank High School. Warden, Hamiltonhill Community Centre, Glasgow; Further Education Assistant, Dunbarton County Council; Organiser of Youth and Community Service, Dunbarton County Council; Principal Community Education Officer (retired), Dunbarton Division, Strathclyde Regional Council. Recreation: bowling. Address: (h.) 25 Hillfoot Avenue, Dumbarton, G82 3JX; T.-0389 62081.

Dow, Alexander Arthur, MA. Director of Administration and Legal Services, Glenrothes Development Corporation, since 1981; b. 18.12.35, Alyth; m., Elizabeth Lindsay Macmillan; 2 s.; 1 d. Educ. Blairgowrie High School; St. Andrews University; Cambridge University. District Officer, HMOCS, Northern Rhodesia/Zambia, 1958-69; Solicitor, Glenrothes Development Corporation, 1972-81. Recreations: gardening; reading; walking; golf. Address: (b.) Balbirnie House, Glenrothes, Fife, KY7 6NR; T.-0592 754343.

Dow, Lt. Col. Leslie Phillips Graham, OBE. Producer, Edinburgh Military Tattoo, since 1975; b. 13.1.26, Glasgow; m., Joan Robinson; 2 d. Educ. Belhaven Hill, Dunbar; Marlborough College. Commissioned, The Cameronians (Scottish Rifles), 1946; 1st Bn., Gibraltar, Trieste, Hong Kong and Malaya, 1947-51; C-in-C's Staff, Singapore, 1952-54; Adjt., 1st Bn., 1955; Staff College, 1956; Staff (Brigade Major), 1957-59; Company Commander, 1st Bn., Kenya and BAOR, 1959-61; Company Commander, RMA, Sandhurst, 1962-64; MA to GOC Kenya, 1965; with 1st Bn., 1966-68; commanded in Aden until standdown, Douglas, Lanarkshire, May, 1968; voluntary retirement, 1969. Member, The Monks of St. Giles. Recreations: shooting; gardening; French wine; classical music; composing indifferent light verse. Address: (h.) 22A Northumberland Street, Edinburgh, EH3 6LS; T.-031-557 0467.

Dowdalls, Edward Joseph, JP, BSc. Principal, Coatbridge College; b. 6.3.26, Coatbridge. Educ. Our Lady's High School, Motherwell; Glasgow University. Member, Coatbridge Burgh Council, 1958-74 (Provost, 1967-70); Member, Lanarkshire Health Board, 1973-81 (Chairman, 1977-81). Recreations: reading; watching sport. Address: (h.) 72 Drumpellier Avenue, Coatbridge; T.-Coatbridge 23889.

Downie, Rev. Alexander George. Minister, Saline linked with Blairingone, since 1958; b. 15.6.23, Tarland; m., Jean; 1 s.; 2 d. Educ. Morpeth Grammar School; St. Andrews University. Army, 1942-47; commissioned, 1945, attached to 1st Mahratta Light Infantry; with British Occupation Forces, Japan, 1947; promoted Captain, 1947. Assistant Minister, St. Ninian's Parish Church, Stirling, 1951-53; Minister, Saline Parish Church, 1953-58. Moderator, Dunfermline and Kinross Presbytery, 1964-65. Address: The Manse, Saline, Fife; T.-New Oakley 852240.

Downie, James Hubert. FRSA. Deputy Lieutenant; Vice-Chairman, Western Isles Health Board; Barrister; b. 13.5.23, Northwood, Middlesex; m., Joyce Wyllie Milne; 3 d. Educ. Merchant Taylor's School, Northwood. Royal Navy, 1941-58 (retired as Lt.-Comdr); Shell-Mex & BP Ltd.: joined, 1959, Manager, Industrial Relations and Manpower Division, 1966-67, Manager, Trade Relations Division, 1967-75. Recreations: angling; gardening; bird-watching. Address: (h.) Dumarin Strond, Isle of Harris, Western Isles; T.-0859 82 247.

Downie, Professor Robert S., MA, BPhil, FRSE. Professor of Moral Philosophy, Glasgow University, since 1969 (Stevenson Lecturer in Medical Ethics, 1984-88); b. 19.4.33, Glasgow; m., Eileen Dorothea Flynn; 3 d. Educ. High School of Glasgow; Glasgow University; Queen's College, Oxford. Tutor, Worcester College, Oxford, 1958-59; Glasgow University: Lecturer in Moral Philosophy, 1959-68, Senior Lecturer, 1968-69; Visiting Professor: Syracuse University, New York, 1963-64, Dalhousie University, Nova Scotia, 1976. Publications: Government Action and Morality, 1964; Respect for Persons, 1969; Roles and Values, 1971; Education and Personal Relationships, 1974; Caring and Curing, 1980; Healthy Respect, 1987. Recreation: music. Address: (b.) Department of Philosophy, Glasgow University, G12 8QQ; T.-041-339 8855.

Downs, Ian, DipArch, DipTP, RIBA, MRTPI, FRIAS, FRSA. Chief Architect/Planner and Director of Technical Services, Irvine Development Corporation; b. 21.2.37, Withensea, East Yorkshire; 1 s.; 1 d. Educ. Withensea High School; Hull School of Architecture; Manchester University. Architect, Cumbernauld Development Corporation, 1960-63; Architect/Planner: United States (private practice, working on New Towns), 1964-65, Wilson & Womersely, 1965-66; Group Architect, Livingston Development Corporation, 1966-69; Assistant Chief Architect: Redditch Development Corporation, 1969-76, West Midlands Metropolitan County Council, 1976-79. Recreation: sailing. Address: (b.) Irvine Development Corporation, Perceton House, Irvine; T.-Irvine 214100.

Dowson, Henry Richard, BSc, PhD, FRSE. Reader in Mathematics, Glasgow University, since 1975; Editor-in-Chief, Glasgow Mathematical Journal, since 1975; b. 2.3.39, Newcastle-upon-Tyne. Educ. Royal Grammar School, Newcastle-upon-Tyne; King's College, Newcastle-upon-Tyne; St. John's College, Cambridge. Assistant Lecturer, Department of Pure Mathematics, University College of Swansea, 1963-65; Lecturer, Department of Mathematics, Newcastle-upon-Tyne University, 1965-66; Assistant Professor, Illinois University, 1966-68; Department of Mathematics, Glasgow University: Lecturer, 1968-73, Senior Lecturer, 1973-75. Publication: Spectral Theory of Linear Operators, 1978. Recreation: bridge; numismatics. Address: (b.) Department of Mathematics, University Gardens, Glasgow, G12 8QW; T.-041-339 8855, Ext. 5179.

Doyle, Rev. David Wallace, MA (Hons), BD (Hons). Minister, St. Mary's Parish Church, Motherwell, since 1987 (Tulliallan and Kincardine Parish Church, 1977-87); b. 12.4.48, Glasgow; m., Alison Wightman Britton; 1 s.; 1 d. Educ. High School of Glasgow; Glasgow University; Corpus Christi College, Cambridge. Assistant Minister, East Kilbride Old Parish Church, 1973-74; Black Fellowship, awarded by Glasgow University for postgraduate study at Cambridge, 1974-77. Recreations: music; reading. Address: Manse of St. Mary's, 19 Orchard Street, Motherwell, ML1 3JE.

Doyle, Rev. Ian Bruce, MA, BD, PhD. Joint Secretary, Department of Ministry and Mission, Church of Scotland, since 1984; b. 11.9.21, Methil, Fife; m., Anne Watt Wallace; 2 s. Educ. Buckhaven High School; St. Andrews University; New College, Edinburgh. Served with Church of Scotland Huts, Germany, 1945-46; Assistant to Rev. D.P. Thomson, Evangelist, 1946; Minister: St. Mary's, Motherwell, 1946-60, Eastwood, Glasgow, 1960-77; Convener: Home Mission Committee, 1970-74, Home Board, 1974-77; Secretary, Department of Home Mission, 1977-84; Secretary, Prison Chaplaincies Board, since 1977; Religious Advisor to Scottish Television, since 1975. Publications: This Jesus; Covenanting Theology; DP, a memoir of Dr. D.P. Thomson. Recreation: reading. Address: (h.) 21 Lygon Road, Edinburgh; T.-031-667 2697.

Draper, Ivan Thomas, MB, ChB, FRCPEdin, FRCPGlas. Consultant Neurologist, Institute of Neurological Sciences, Glasgow, since 1965; b. 11.9.32, Derby; m., Muriel May Munro. Educ. Bemrose School; Aberdeen University. Fellow, Department of Medicine, Johns Hopkins Hospital, Baltimore, 1962-63. Past President, Scottish Ornithologists Club. Publication: Lecture Notes on Neurology, 6th Edition. Recreations: birds; books; fish. Address: (b.) Institute of Neurological Sciences, Southern General Hospital, Govan Road, Glasgow.

Draper, Professor Paul Richard, BA, MA, PhD. Professor of Finance, Strathclyde University, since 1986 (Esmee Fairbairn Senior Lecturer in Finance, 1978-86); b. 28.12.46, Hayes; m., Janet Margaret; 1 s.; 1 d. Educ. Exeter University; Reading University; Stirling University. Lecturer: St. Andrews University, Edinburgh University. Publication: Scottish Financial Sector (Co-author), 1988. Recreations: renovating country cottages; home computing. Address: (b.) 19 Upper Gray Street, Newington, Edinburgh; T.-031-667 4087.

Draper, Professor Ronald Philip, BA, PhD. Regius Chalmers Professor of English, Aberdeen University (Professor, since 1973, Head of Department, since 1984); b. 3.10.28, Nottingham; m., Irene Margaret Aldridge; 3 d. Educ. Nottingham High School; Nottingham University. Tutorial Assistant, Nottingham University, 1951-53; Education Officer, RAF, 1953-55; Lecturer in English, Adelaide University, 1955-56; Leicester University: Assistant Lecturer in English, 1957-58, Lecturer, 1958-68, Senior Lecturer, 1968-73. Publications: D.H. Lawrence, 1964; D.H. Lawrence (Profiles in Literature), 1969; D.H. Lawrence, The Critical Heritage (Editor), 1970; Hardy, The Tragic Novels (Editor), 1975; George Eliot, The Mill on the Floss and Silas Marner (Editor), 1978; Tragedy, Developments in Criticism (Editor), 1980; Shakespeare, A Midsummer Night's Dream, 1980; Shakespeare, Cymbeline, 1980; Lyric Tragedy, 1985; Shakespeare, The Winter's Tale, 1985; D.H. Lawrence, Sons and Lovers, 1986; Hardy, Three Pastoral Novels (Editor), 1987; Shakespeare, Twelfth Night, 1988; The

Literature of Region and Nation (Editor), 1988. Recreations: reading; listening to music; walking. Address: (b.) English Department, Taylor Building, King's College, Old Aberdeen, AB9 2UB; T.-0224 272623.

Drever, Harry Sinclair, MBE, JP, AIB (Scot). Consultant, Gerald Eve & Co., Chartered Surveyors, London, since 1974; Chairman, Hjaltland Housing Association Ltd., 1982-87; Honorary Sheriff, Grampian, Highlands and Islands at Shetland, since 1961; b. 28.10.05, St. Margaret's, Hope, Orkney. Educ. St. Margaret's Hope Secondary School. Union Bank of Scotland Ltd. and Bank of Scotland, 1921-70 (Manager, Lerwick and Scalloway Branches, 1950-70); Shetland County Councillor, 1958-70 (sometime Chairman, Finance Committee); Member, Board of Management, Shetland Hospitals, 1959-70 (latterly Chairman, Finance Committee); Chairman, Zetland Territorial and Air Forces Association, until 1968; former Honorary Secretary, Shetland Branch, National Savings Committee; former Honorary Treasurer: Shetland Branch, British Red Cross Society, Shetland Tourist Association, Shetland Dog Trials Association, Shetland Swimming Pool Association. Recreations: golf; billiards; restoring antique furniture. Address: (h.) Vogalee, 78 St. Olaf Street, Lerwick; T.-0595 3783.

Drummond, Alastair Wilson, MB, ChB, MRCPsych. Director, Scottish Hospital Advisory Service, since 1988; b. 7.5.32, Cumbria; m., Jean; 2 s. Educ. Ulverston Grammar School; Manchester University. Consultant Psychiatrist, West Cumberland Hospital, Whitehaven, 1963-82, Rosslynlee Hospital, Roslin, 1982-87. Recreations: fishing; bee-keeping; skiing; music. Address: (h.) 10 Crichton Cottages, Pathhead, Midlothian, EH37 5UY; T.-Ford 320445.

Drummond, George Gordon, BSc, CEng, MInstEnergy, MAIME, CBIM. Board Member, Highlands and Islands Development Board, 1977-87; Vice Chairman, Cromarty Firth Port Authority, since 1983; Chairman, Scottish Board, British Institute of Management, 1983-88; Director, Gordon Drummond Consultancy Ltd.; b. 9.9.26, Dundee; m., Jennie Cook Lowe; 1 s.; 1 d. Educ. High School of Dundee; St. Andrews University; Liverpool College of Technology; Administrative Staff College, Henley. Trainee, Scottish Gas Board; Project Engineer, North Western Gas Board; Senior Project Engineer, British Aluminium Co. Ltd.; BACO: Manager, Kinlochleven, Production Manager, London, Manager, Warrington Factories, Manager, Invergordon; Managing Director, BA Primary Aluminium Ltd., Inverness. Publication: The Invergordon Smelter: A Case Study in Management, 1977. Recreations: mountaineering; music; reading; current affairs. Address: (h.) 8 Fairways, Altonburn Road, Nairn, IV12 5NB.

Drummond, Humphrey, MC. Writer and Farmer; b. 18.9.22, Old Buckenham, Norfolk; m., Cherry Drummond, 16th Baroness Strange; 3 s.; 3 d. Educ. Eton; Trinity College, Cambridge. Captain, 1st Mountain Regiment; former General Secretary, Council for Preservation of Rural Wales; Welsh Representative, National Trust; Chairman, Society of Authors (Scotland), 1976-82. Publications: Our Man in Scotland; The Queen's Man; The King's Enemy; Falconry For You; Falconry. Recreations: mechanical musical instruments; pre-Raphaelitism. Address: Megginch Castle, Errol, Perthshire; T.-Errol 222.

Drummond, Rev. John Whiteford, MA, BD. Minister, Rutherglen West Parish Church, since 1986; b. 27.6.46, Glasgow; m., Barbara S. Grant; 1 s.; 3 d. Educ. Bearsden Academy; Glasgow University. Probationer Assistant, St. Francis-in-the-East Church, Bridgeton, Glasgow, 1970-71; ordained Assistant, King's Park Parish Church, Glasgow, 1971-73; Minister, Linwood Parish Church, 1973-86. Chairman, Johnstone and District Christian Aid Committee, 1981-86. Recreations: family; reading. Address: (h.) 12 Albert Drive, Rutherglen, Glasgow, G73 3RT; T.-041-643 0234.

Drummond, Rev. Norman Walker, MA, BD. Headmaster, Loretto School, since 1984; b. 1.4.52, Greenock; m., Lady Elizabeth Kennedy; 2 s.; 2 d. Educ. Crawfordton House, Dumfriesshire; Merchiston Castle School; Fitzwilliam College, Cambridge; New College, Edinburgh. Chaplain to the Forces, 1976-82; Depot, The Parachute Regiment and Airborne Forces, 1977-78; 1st Bn., The Black Watch (Royal Highland Regiment), 1978-82; Chaplain, Fettes College, 1982-84. Member of Court, Heriot-Watt University; Member, Scottish Committee, Duke of Edinburgh's Award Scheme; Chairman, Musselburgh and District Council of Social Services. Publication: The First Twenty Five Years (the official history of the Black Watch Kirk Session). Recreations: rugby football; cricket; golf; curling; traditional jazz; Isle of Skye. Address: Pinkie House, Loretto School, Musselburgh, East Lothian; T.-031-665 2567.

Drummond, Rev. Robert Hugh. Minister, Pitsligo Parish Church, since 1981, linked with Sandhaven Parish Church, 1985; b. 18.11.25, Ajmer, India; m., May Cummings; 4 s. Educ. George Watson's College; St. Andrews University; Edinburgh University. Student Assistant Minister, Liberton Northfield; Assistant Minister: St. Giles' and St. Columba's, Elgin, North Church, Aberdeen; Army Chaplain; Minister: Eskdalemuir Parish Church, Kilmuir-Easter Parish Church, Thornton Parish Church. Recreations: cycling; swimming; tennis; golf; hill-walking; violin. Address: Pitsligo Manse, 49 Pitsligo Street, Rosehearty, Fraserburgh, AB4 4JL; T.-03467 237.

Drummond, Thomas Anthony Kevin, LLB, QC. Advocate Depute, Crown Office, since 1985; b. 3.11.43, Howwood, Renfrewshire; m., Margaret Broadley; 1 d. Educ. Blairs College, Aberdeen; St. Mirin's Academy, Paisley; Edinburgh University. Civil Service, 1962-66; Solicitor, 1970-74; Bar, since 1974; QC, 1987. Cartoonist (Tak), Scots Law Times, since 1981. Recreations: shooting; hill-walking. Address: (h.) Pomathorn House, Howgate, Midlothian; T.-Penicuik 74046.

Dryden, Professor Myles Muir, BSc (Econ), MBA, PhD. Professor of Management Studies, Glasgow University, since 1972; b. 21.9.31, Dundee; m., Margaret Mary Cargill; 1 s.; 1 d. Educ. Kirkcaldy High School; London School of Economics; Cornell University. National Service, 1st Bn., Black Watch, BAOR, 1950-52; Assistant Professor of Finance, Sloan School of Industrial Management, Massachusetts Institute of Technology, 1960; Lecturer, then Reader in Economics, Edinburgh University, 1963-72; appointed to first Chair of Management Studies, Glasgow University, 1972 (Head of Department, until 1980); Member, Scottish Business School Council, 1975-79; has published in a number of professional journals; research on capital budgeting, share price behaviour and portfolio management. Recreations: pottering about either in boats, in the garden, or with microcomputers. Address: (b.) Department of Management Studies, 55 Southpark Avenue, Glasgow, G12 8LF; T.-041-330 4664.

Drysdale, Thomas Henry, LLB, WS. Solicitor; Partner, Shepherd & Wedderburn, WS, Edinburgh, since 1967 (Managing Partner, since 1988); b. 23.11.42, Buchlyvie; m., Caroline Shaw; 1 s.; 2 d. Educ. Cargilfield; Glenalmond; Edinburgh University. Chairman, Lothian Ski Racing Association, since 1987. Recreations: skiing; walking. Address: (b.) 16 Charlotte Square, Edinburgh, EH2 4YS; T.-031-225 8585.

Dudley Edwards, Owen, BA, FRHistS. Reader in Commonwealth and American History, Edinburgh University, since 1979; b. 27.3.38, Dublin; m., Barbara Balbirnie Lee; 1 s.; 2 d. Educ. Belvedere College, Dublin; University College, Dublin; Johns Hopkins University, Baltimore. Visiting Lecturer in History, University of Oragon, 1963-65; Assistant Lecturer in History, Aberdeen University, 1966-68; Lecturer in History, Edinburgh University, 1968-79; Visiting Lecturer, California State University of San Francisco, 1972-73; Visiting Associate Professor, University of South Carolina, 1973; Journalist and Broadcaster, notably for Irish Times, since 1959, and BBC, since 1969; contributor to various journals, especially The Scotsman. Life Member: American Historical Association, Organisation of American Historians; External Examiner: Queen's University, Belfast, Bradford University, Manchester University. Publications: Celtic Nationalism (with Gwynfor Evans, Ioan Rhys and Hugh MacDiarmid), 1968; The Sins of Our Fathers - Roots of Conflict in Northern Ireland, 1970; The Mind of an Activist - James Connolly, 1971; P.G. Wodehouse - a Critical and Historical Essay, 1977; Burke and Hare, 1980; The Quest for Sherlock Holmes: a Biographical Study of Arthur Conan Doyle, 1982; Eamon de Valera, 1987; as Editor/Contributor: 1916 - The Easter Rising (with Fergus Pyle), 1968; Conor Cruise O'Brien Introduces Ireland, 1969; James Connolly: Selected Political Writings (with Bernard C. Ransom), 1973; Scotland, Europe and the American Revolution (with George Shepperson), 1976; Christmas Observed (with Graham Richardson), 1981; Edinburgh (with Graham Richardson), 1983. Recreations: Scottish Nationalism; playing chess badly. Address: (b.) Department of History, Edinburgh University, George Square, Edinburgh; T.-031-664 3526.

Duff, John Hume, MA (Cantab), MA (Edin), DipEd (Oxon). Rector, Kelvinside Academy, since 1980; b. 24.4.40, Edinburgh. Educ. St. Mary's School, Melrose; Edinburgh Academy; Corpus Christi College, Cambridge; Edinburgh University; Brasenose College, Oxford. Housemaster and Head of History Department, Kelly College, Tavistock, Devon, 1967-80. Major, TA. Recreations: squash rackets; skiing; hill-walking; foreign travel. Address: (b.) Kelvinside Academy, 33 Kirklee Road, Glasgow, G12 OSW; T.-041-357 3376.

Duff, Robert Beauchamp (Robin), MBE (1987), MA (Cantab). President, The Scottish Ballet, since 1984; Chairman, Air Transport Users Committee, since 1984; b. 27.2.15, London. Educ. Winchester; Trinity College, Cambridge. BBC Announcer and War Correspondent; Bureau Chief, Paris, then New Delhi, for Daily Express; Personal Assistant to HH Maharaja of Bundi; Chairman, Health and Welfare Committee, Aberdeen County Council, 1957-64; Past Chairman, Transport Users Committee; former Member: Scottish Housing Advisory Committee, Scottish Hygiene Advisory Committee, Meat and Livestock Commission; Chairman, The Scottish Ballet, 1974-84; Hotelier; Broadcaster; Laird of Meldrum and Byth. Recreations: gardening; travel. Address: (h.) Meldrum House, Aberdeenshire, AB5 OAE; T.-065-12 2294.

Duffield, Brian Snowden. Director, Scottish Centre for Physical Education, Movement and Leisure Studies, Moray House College, Edinburgh, since 1987; b. 27.8.43, Doncaster; m., Irene Mary Scott; 3 s.; 1 d. Educ. Doncaster Grammar School; Hull University. Tourism and Recreation Research Unit, Department of Geography, Edinburgh University, 1967-83 (Senior Research Fellow and Deputy Director, 1976-81, Director, 1981-83); Vice Principal, 1983-86, Acting Director, 1987, Dunfermline College of Physical Education; Tourism and Research Fellowship, Bergen University, 1981; Corresponding Editor, Leisure Sciences, since 1984; Publications: Recreation in the Countryside: a spatial analysis (Co-author), 1975; The Leisure Planning Process (Co-author), 1979; Rationale for Public Sector Investment in Leisure (Co-author), 1986; Leisure Focus: the Role of Local Authorities in Leisure, Recreation and Tourism, 1986; The Countryside We Want (Contributing author), 1987. Recreations: politics; conversation; art and literature; squash; work. Address: (h.) 26 Elbe Street, Leith, Edinburgh, EH6 7HW; T.-031-553 7896.

Duffty, Paul, MB, ChB, MRCP, LMCC. Consultant Paediatrician, since 1982; Senior Lecturer in Child Health, Aberdeen University, since 1982; b. 1.9.46, Leeds; m., Lesley Marjory Macdonald; 2 d. Educ. Leeds Central High School; Aberdeen University. Lecturer in Child Health, Aberdeen University, 1972-75; Trainee in General Practice, Aberdeen, 1975-76; Lecturer in Child Health, Aberdeen University, 1976-78; Fellow in Neonatology, Toronto University, 1978-80; Staff Paediatrician, Hospital for Sick Children, Toronto, and Assistant Professor, Toronto University, 1980-82. Recreations: hill-walking; cross-country skiing; philately. Address: (h.) 13 Louisville Avenue, Aberdeen; T.-0224 317072.

Duffus, John Henderson, BSc, PhD, DSc, CBiol, MIBiol, CChem, FRSC. Senior Lecturer in Environmental Toxicology, Heriot-Watt University, since 1980. Educ. Arbroath High School; Edinburgh University; Heriot-Watt University. Research Fellow: Warwick University, 1965-67, Edinburgh University, 1967-70; Lecturer, Heriot-Watt University, 1970-80; WHO Consultant, Toxicology and Chemical Safety, since 1981. Publications: Environmental Toxicology, 1980; Carbohydrate Metabolism in Plants (Co-author), 1984; Environmental Toxicology and Ecotoxicology, 1986; Magnesium in Mitosis and the Cell Cycle (Co-author), 1987; Yeast: A Practical Approach (Co-Editor), 1988. Address: (b.) Heriot-Watt University, Chambers Street, Edinburgh, EH1 1HX; T.-031-225 8432.

Duffy, Mgr. Francis Provost, VG. Vicar General to RC Bishop of Galloway, since 1975; Parish Priest, Troon, since 1982; b. 15.10.14, Edinburgh. Educ. Holy Cross Academy, Edinburgh; Blairs College, Aberdeen; Pontifical Scots College, Rome; Gregorian University, Rome. Ordained Priest (Rome), 1938; Curate, Ayr, 1939-41; Professor, Blairs College, Aberdeen, 1941-55; parish work in various towns, since 1955; Monsignor, since 1972. RC Religious Adviser, Scottish Television, 1958-78; Member, Dumfries Education Committee, 1963-72; Composer of congregational Church music and hymns. Address: 4 Cessnock Road, Troon, KA8 6NJ; T.-Troon 313541.

Duffy, John Alastair, BSc, PhD, DSc, CChem, FRSC. Senior Lecturer in Chemistry, Aberdeen University, since 1977; Consultant to British Steel Corporation, since 1987; Chairman, Molten Salts Discussion Group, Royal Society of Chemistry, since 1986; b. 24.9.32, Birmingham; m., Muriel F.L. Ramsay; 1 s.; 1 d. Educ. Solihull School, Warwickshire; Sheffield University. Research Chemist, Albright & Wilson, Oldbury, 1958-59; Lecturer in Inorganic Chemistry, Wolverhampton Polytechnic, 1959-61; Senior Lecturer in Inorganic Chemistry, NE Wales Institute, 1961-65; Lecturer in Chemistry, Aberdeen University, 1966-77; Assessor in Inorganic Chemistry for Ordinary and Higher National Certificates and Diplomas in Scotland, 1971-82; Consultant to Schott Glaswerke, Mainz, West Germany, since 1984; Past Chairman, NE Scotland Section, Royal Society of Chemistry. Publication: General Inorganic Chemistry, 1966. Recreations: 20th-century opera; music. Address: (h.) 35 Beechgrove Terrace, Aberdeen, AB2 4DR; T.-0224 641752.

Duffy, Sheila Sinclair, MA. Women's Editor, Radio Clyde, since 1973; Freelance Journalist, since 1967; b. 6.8.46, Silloth, Cumberland; m., Paul Young; 2 d. Educ. Boroughmuir School, Edinburgh; Edinburgh University. Auxiliary nurse, Edinburgh Royal Infirmary, 1965-66; croupier, Edinburgh night club, 1966-67; graduate trainee, Scottish Television, 1967-68; Reporter, Scottish Television, 1968-73; Presenter, Dateline Early/Edinburgh Film Festival programmes/Moneywise. Recreations: children; husband; genealogy; cooking; reading; cake decorating; walking; sampler embroidery. Address: (b.) Young Casting Agency, 7 Beaumont Gate, Glasgow; T.-041-339 5180.

Dukes, Professor Paul, BA (Cantab), MA, PhD. Professor of History, Aberdeen University, since 1988; b. 5.4.34, Wallington; m., Rosemary Mackay; 1 s.; 1 d. Educ. Wallington County Grammar School; Cambridge University. Advisory Editor, History Today. Publications: several books on aspects of Russian, American and European history. Recreations: hill-walking; travel. Address: (b.) History Department, Aberdeen University, Aberdeen; T.-0224 272000.

Dulverton, 2nd Baron (Frederick Anthony Hamilton Wills), CBE, TD, MA, DL; b. 19.12.15, London; m., Ruth Violet Mary; 2 s.; 1 d. Educ. Eton; Magdalen College, Oxford. Commissioned Lovat Scouts, 1935 (Major, 1943); President: Bath and West Agricultural Society, 1973, Three Counties Agricultural Society, 1975, Timber Growers United Kingdom, 1983; Chairman, Dulverton Trust; Council Member, WWF (UK) and Wildfowl Trust; awarded Gold Medal, Royal Forestry Society. Recreations: field sports; nature photography. Address: (h.) Fassfern, Kinlocheil, Fort William, Inverness-shire; T.-039783 232.

Dunbar, John Greenwell, MA, FSA, FSA Scot, HonFRIAS. Secretary, Royal Commission on the Ancient and Historical Monuments of Scotland, since 1978; b. 1.3.30, London; m., Elizabeth Mill Blyth. Educ. University College School, London; Balliol College, Oxford. joined staff, Royal Commission on the Ancient and Historical Monuments of Scotland, 1953; Member, Ancient Monuments Board for Scotland, since 1978. Publications: The Historic Architecture of Scotland, 1966; Accounts of the Masters of Works, Volume 2 (1616-1649), (Joint Editor), 1982. Address: (h.) Paties Mill, Carlops, by Penicuik, Midlothian, EH26 9NF; T.-West Linton 60250.

Dunbar-Nasmith, Rear Admiral David Arthur, CB, DSC, DL. Chairman, Moray and Nairn Newspaper Company, since 1982; Member, British Waterways Board, 1980-87; Director, Cairngorm Chairlift Company, since 1973; b. 21.2.21, Glen of Rothes, Rothes; m., Elizabeth Bowlby; 2 s.; 2 d. Educ. Lockers Park; Royal Naval College, Dartmouth. To sea, 1939; War service, Atlantic and Mediterranean; Commanding Officer, HM Ships Haydon, 1943-44, Peacock, 1945-46, Moon, 1946, Rowena, 1946-48, Enard Bay, 1951, Alert, 1954-56, Berwick and 5th Frigate Squadron, 1961-63, Commodore Amphibious Forces, 1966-67; Naval Secretary, 1967-70; Flag Officer Scotland and Northern Ireland, 1970-72; Member, Highlands and Islands Development Board, 1972-83 (Chairman, 1981-82, Deputy Chairman, 1972-81); Member: Countryside Commission for Scotland, 1972-76, North of Scotland Hydro Electric Board, 1982-85; Gentleman Usher of the Green Rod to the Order of the Thistle; Vice Lieutenant, County of Moray; Member, Queen's Bodyguard for Scotland (Royal Company of Archers). Recreations: sailing; shooting; skiing. Address: (h.) Glen of Rothes, Rothes, Moray; T.-03403 216.

Dunbar-Nasmith, Professor James Duncan, CBE, BA, DA, RIBA, PPRIAS, FRSA, FRSE. Professor and Head, Department of Architecture, Heriot-Watt University and Edinburgh College of Art, 1978-88; Partner, The Law and Dunbar-Nasmith Partnership, Architects, Edinburgh and Forres, since 1957; b. 15.3.27, Dartmouth. Educ. Lockers Park; Winchester College; Trinity College, Cambridge; Edinburgh College of Art. Lt., Scots

Guards, 1945-48; ARIBA, 1954; President: Edinburgh Architectural Association, 1967-69, Royal Incorporation of Architects in Scotland, 1971-73; Member, RIBA Council, 1967-73 (Vice-President and Chairman, Board of Architectural Education, 1972-73); Council, ARCUK, 1976-84, Board of Education, 1976-88 (Vice Chairman, 1977); Member: Royal Commission on Ancient and Historical Monuments of Scotland, since 1972, Ancient Monuments Board for Scotland, 1969-82 (interim Chairman, 1972-73), Historic Buildings Council for Scotland, since 1966; Trustee: Scottish Civic Trust, Architectural Heritage Fund, Theatres Trust; Member: Edinburgh New Town Conservation Committee, Executive Committee of Europa Nostra; Deputy Chairman, Edinburgh Festival Society, 1981-85. Recreations: music; theatre; skiing; sailing. Address: (b.) 16 Dublin Street, Edinburgh, EH1 3RE; T.-031-556 8631.

Duncan, Andrew Raymond, CA. Partner, Frame Kennedy & Forrest, since 1973; Member, Council, Institute of Chartered Accountants of Scotland, since 1987; Secretary, Highland Craftpoint, since 1980: b. 19.11.47, Glasgow; m., Carol Ann; 1 s.; 1 d. Educ. Hutchesons' Boys Grammar School. Trained with Cooper Brothers, Glasgow; former Highland Area Secretary, Institute of Chartered Accountants of Scotland. Recreations: fishing; golf; walking. Address: (h.) Enrick House, Balnain, Glenurquhart, Inverness-shire.

Duncan, Angus, OBE, FRICS. Deputy Chief Quantity Surveyor, Scottish Development Department, since 1974; Assistant Director, SDD Building Directorate, since 1978; b. 4.12.28, Sorbie. Educ. Bell-Baxter School, Cupar; Newbattle Abbey College; Heriot-Watt College. Joined Department of Health for Scotland, 1957, dealing with prison buildings, later advising various Scottish Office Departments on housing, education, and health building matters. Chairman, Quantity Surveyors Committee, Scottish Branch, RICS, 1982-83. Recreations: travel; walking; photography; reading; watching TV documentaries. Address: (h.) 4/9 Dun-Ard Garden, Oswald Road, Edinburgh, EH9 2HZ; T.-031-667 1596.

Duncan, Professor Archibald Alexander McBeth, MA, FBA, FRSE, FRHistS. Professor of Scottish History, Glasgow University, since 1962; b. 17.10.26, Pitlochry; m., Ann Hayes Sawyer; 2 s.; 1 d. Educ. George Heriot's School, Edinburgh; Edinburgh University; Balliol College, Oxford. Lecturer: Balliol College, 1950-51, Queen's University, Belfast, 1951-53, Edinburgh University, 1953-61; Leverhulme Fellow, 1961-62; Clerk of Senate, Glasgow University, 1978-83. Publications: Scotland, The Making of the Kingdom; revised 3rd edition of W.C. Dickinson's Scotland from Earliest Times to 1603; Regesta Regum Scottorum, v., 1988; The Acts of Robert I 1306-29, 1988. Recreation: swimming. Address: (h.) 17 Campbell Drive, Bearsden, Glasgow, G61 4NF: T.-041-942 5023.

Duncan, David Graham Bruce, DipArch, DipTP, RIBA, MRTPI, RIAS. Director of Planning, City of Edinburgh District Council, since 1988; b. 23.8.36, Derby; m., Helen Teresa; 2 s. Educ. George Heriot's School, Edinburgh; Edinburgh College of Art. Architect/Planner, R.E. & B.L.C. Moira, Architects and Planning Consultants, Edinburgh, 1960-63; Architect/Planner, Government of State of Singapore, 1963-67; Assistant Planner, then Depute County Planning Officer, East Lothian County Council, 1967-75; Director of Planning, East Lothian District Council, 1975-88. Planning Advisor, COSLA. Address: 1 Cockburn Street, Edinburgh; T.-031-225 2424.

Duncan, Donald Maclachlan, BL, NP, FInstD. Solicitor, since 1948; Honorary Sheriff, Grampian Highland and Islands, at Inverness; b. 18.7.11, Cardross; m., Sarah Faulds Wynne; 1 s.; 1 d. Educ. Alexandria Academy; Royal Technical College, Glasgow; Glasgow University. Former Procurator Fiscal Depute and JP Fiscal, Inverness; Clerk to Commissioners of Income Tax; Clerk to Lord Lieutenant, Ross and Cromarty. Honorary President, Scottish Cross Country Union; Life Vice-President, Scottish Amateur Athletic Association; former Member, British Athletic Board. Recreations: fishing; shooting. Address: (h.) Wyndon, Culcabock Road, Inverness.

Duncan, Eric Gosman, BSc (Hons), PhD. Senior Lecturer in Botany, Department of Biology and Preclinical Medicine, St. Andrews University, since 1975; b. 1.6.31, Broughty Ferry; m., Irene Paul Macleod; 1 d. Educ. Madras College, St. Andrews; St. Andrews University. Berry Scholar, St. Andrews University; Lecturer in Botany: Bedford College, London University, 1956-61, St. Andrews University, 1962-75. Recreations: radio and electronics; photography; golf. Address: (h.) 8 Greenside Place, St. Andrews, KY16 9TH; T.-0334 74043.

Duncan, Geoffrey Cheyne Calderhead, BL, NP. Partner, Kerr, Barrie & Duncan, since 1970; b. 6.10.29, Whitecraigs, Glasgow; m., Lorna Dowling; 1 s.; 1 d. Educ. Belmont House School; Glasgow Academy; Glasgow University. Partner, Aitken, Hamilton & Duncan, 1951-70; Chairman, Glasgow Junior Chamber of Commerce, 1963-64; Director, The Girls' School Company Ltd., 1964-87 (Chairman, 1977-87); Chairman, St. Columba's School, 1972-83; Director, The West of Scotland School Company Ltd., since 1972; Director, Glasgow School of Art, since 1987; Member, Board of Management, Glasgow South Western Hospitals, 1964-69; Member, Clyde River Purification Board, 1969-75; Director, Glasgow Chamber of Commerce, 1972-87; Chairman, Glasgow Post Office Advisory Committee, 1974-84; Member, Post Office Users' National Council, 1974-87; Chairman, Post Office Users' Council for Scotland, 1984-87; Chairman, Advisory Committee on Telecommunications for Scotland, 1984-87; Secretary, Clyde Cruising Club, 1964-69; Secretary, International Clyde Regetta, 1967; Council Member, Clyde Yacht Clubs' Association, 1967-73; Member, Scottish Council, Royal Yachting Association, 1967-73; Director, The Merchants' House of Glasgow, since 1982; Member, Glasgow Committee, Royal National Lifeboat Institution, since 1980; Council Member, Royal Faculty of Procurators in Glasgow, 1981-84; Trustee, George Craig Trust Fund, since 1980; Trustee, Ferguson Bequest Fund, since 1987; Member, Executive Committee, Abbeyfield Quarrier's Society, since 1981 (Chairman, 1988); Member,

Council of Management, Quarrier's Homes, since 1985; Director, The Scottish Cremation Society Ltd., since 1982. Recreations: sailing; golf; curling; photography. Address: (h.) Westwood, Bridge of Weir, Renfrewshire; T.-Bridge of Weir 612566.

Duncan, Graham John, MA, CA. Chairman and Chief Executive, Leisure Business Projects Ltd., since 1988; Chairman, Cable Television Association, since 1987; b. 8.2.51, Edinburgh; m., Margaret; 2 d. Educ. Robert Gordon's College, Aberdeen; Aberdeen University. Trained and qualified as CA with Thomson McLintock & Co., Aberdeen; appointed Audit Manager, 1976; transferred to Glasgow, 1978; Senior Group Manager, 1979; joined Arthur Andersen & Co., Glasgow, 1981; headed new office in Aberdeen, 1982; joined Aberdeen Cable TV as Finance Director, 1984; Managing Director, 1986-88. Member, Management Board, AID (International Alliance for Distribution by Cable). Publication: Going into Business (Co-author). Recreations: swimming; trying to relax with a young family. Address: (h.) 87 Newburgh Road, Bridge of Don, Aberdeen; T.-0224 822238.

Duncan, Ian Douglas, MB, ChB, FRCOG. Senior Lecturer in Obstetrics and Gynaecology, Dundee University, since 1978; Honorary Consultant in Obstetrics and Gynaecology, Tayside Health Board, since 1978; Secretary, International Federation for Cervical Pathology and Colposcopy, since 1987; b. 7.11.43, Edinburgh; m., Jennifer Ross Conacher; 2 s.; 1 d. Educ. Harris Academy, Dundee; St. Andrews University. House Officer, Surgery and Medicine, Maryfield Hospital, Dundee, 1967-68; Senior House Officer, Urology, Ballochmyle Hospital, Mauchline, 1968-69; Registrar in Obstetrics and Gynaecology, Dundee Royal Infirmary, 1969-72; Faculty Fellow in Gynaecologic Oncology, Duke University Medical Center, 1972-74; Senior Registrar/Lecturer in Obstetrics and Gynaecology, Ninewells Hospital, Dundee, 1974-78. John Kynoch Scholarship, 1967; Senior Fulbright Scholarship, 1972; British Society for Colposcopy and Cervical Pathology: Treasurer, 1979-82, Secretary, 1982-85, President, 1985-88; Treasurer, British Gynaecological Cancer Society, 1985-88, President, since 1988; Deacon, Bonnetmaker Craft of Dundee, since 1987. Recreations: golf; gardening. Address: (h.) Invertay, 299 Strathmartine Road, Dundee, DD3 8NS; T.-Dundee 826628.

Duncan, Rev. James, BTh, DipTh, MPhS, FSA Scot. Minister, Blair Atholl and Struan, since 1980; b. 28.1.26, Glasgow; m., Christine Margaret Fisher; 2 s. Educ. Eastbank Academy, Glasgow; Glasgow University. War Service, 1943-46; seconded to Colonial Office, London, 1944; seconded to Australian Army in British North Borneo; ADC Chief Civil Affairs Staff Officer, British Borneo; Harrisons and Crosfield, British Borneo, 1946-47; various Sales Representative jobs, until 1956; joined Unilever (Batchelors Catering Supplies) as Special Accounts Manager. Recreations: music; watching TV; wine-making; good food and wine. Address: The Manse, Blair Atholl, Pitlochry, PH18 5SX; T.-079681 213.

Duncan, Professor James Lindsay, BVMS, PhD, MRCVS. Professor in Veterinary Parasitology, Glasgow University, since 1987; b. 26.2.41, Law, Carluke; m., Helen M.; 1 s.; 1 d. Educ. Wishaw High School; Glasgow University. Veterinary Practice, UK, and clinical teaching posts, Kenya, 1964-70; Glasgow University: Research Fellow, Department of Veterinary Parasitology, 1970-76, Lecturer, 1976-79, Senior Lecturer, 1979-82, Reader, 1982-87; Consultant, joint FAO/IAEA Animal Health Division, International Atomic Energy Agency, Vienna; Co-author of several textbooks. Recreations: tennis; squash; golf; music. Address: (h.) Woodside Farm, Crossford, Carluke, Lanark, ML8 5QN; T.-0555 86254.

Duncan, James Wann, MBE, JP, MIMFT. Vice-Chairman, Tayside Health Board (Convener, General Purposes Committee); Convener, Personnel and Accommodation Sub-Committee, Management Committee, Common Services Agency; b. 14.7.25, Dundee; m., Hilda Mackenzie Gray; 3 d. Educ. Stobswell Secondary School; Dundee College of Technology. Former Convener, Property Equipment Supplies Committee, General Board of Management, Dundee General Hospitals; former Vice-Convener, General Purposes Committee, General Board of Management, Dundee Northern Hospitals; former Member, Dundee Town Council (Senior Magistrate); former Convener: Dundee Art Galleries and Museums Committee, Further Education Committee, Dundee Police Committee; former Member, Board of Governors, Scottish Police College; Member, Dundee District Council, 1974-77 (Convener, Planning and Development Committee); Chairman, Dundee City Labour Party, 1960-62; former Member, Scottish Council, SDP; Scottish Representative, National Committee for Dental Technicians, USDAW; former Member: STUC Health and Social Services Committee, Dundee University Court. Recreations: golf; gardening; DIY. Address: (h.) 13 Clive Road, Downfield, Dundee, DD3 8LP; T.-0382 825488.

Duncan, John Lindsay, BSc, PhD, DSc, FRSE. Reader in Chemistry, Aberdeen University, since 1982; Convener, Science Panel, Scottish Universities Council on Entrance, since 1983; b. 3.2.37, Edinburgh; m., Anne Shearer; 2 d. Educ. Melville College, Edinburgh; Edinburgh University. ICI Research Fellow, Reading University, 1961-64; Aberdeen University: Lecturer, 1964-74, Senior Lecturer, 1974-82; Chairman, SEB/CCC Joint Working Party to revise Certificate of Sixth Year Studies, Chemistry Syllabus, 1978-80. Publication: High Resolution Vibration-Rotation Spectroscopy, 1983. Recreations: music; art; gardening. Address: (b.) Department of Chemistry, Aberdeen University, Meston Walk, Old Aberdeen, AB9 2UE; T.-0224 272911.

Duncan, Malcolm, MA, LLB. Chief Executive and Secretary, East Lothian District Council, since 1987; b. 14.7.45, Cupar; m., Stephanie; 1 s.; 1 d. Educ. Royal High School, Edinburgh; Edinburgh University. Legal apprentice, Midlothian County Clerk, 1969-72; East Lothian District Council: Legal Assistant, 1972-75, Director of Administration, 1974-87. Address: (b.) Council Buildings, Haddington, East Lothian, EH41 3HA; T.-062 082 4161.

Duncan, Thomas, NP. Solicitor, since 1940; Honorary Sheriff, since 1981; b. 17.6.17, Glasgow; m., Jean Gardner Skeoch; 2 d. Educ. Glasgow University. Qualified as Solicitor, 1940; Army, 1940-46 (Major, RA, Rhine Army); enrolled as Solicitor, 1946. President, Montrose Branch, Royal British Legion, Scotland; Past President, Montrose Chamber of Commerce; Past Captain, Royal Albert Golf Club. Recreation: golf. Address: 192 High Street, Montrose, Angus; T.-0674 72533.

Duncan, William Neil Murdoch, BSc, PhD. Shellfish Farmer, since 1982; b. 7.10.47, Perth; m., Ileene Mackie-Campbell. Educ. Rannoch School; Aberdeen University; Durham University. Research Biologist (Animal Ecology), Durham University, 1972-82. Member, Committee, Scottish Shellfish Growers Association and various other industry committees; Convenor, Fish Farming Committee, NFU of Scotland; author of more than 40 published papers in ecology, animal behaviour and natural history. Recreations: travel; writing; shooting; fishing; riding; gardening; natural history; art; reading. Address: (h.) Baravalla, Tarbert, Argyll; T.-088 02 583.

Duncan Millar, Ian Alastair, CBE, MC, MA, MICE, CEng, DL, JP. Chairman, Consultative Committee on Freshwater Fisheries, 1981-86; Vice President, Scottish Landowners Federation, since 1986; Member, Queen's Bodyguard for Scotland (Royal Company of Archers); b. 22.11.14, Alloa; m., Louise Reid McCosh; 2 s.; 2 d. Educ. Greshams School, Holt; Trinity College, Cambridge. Civil Engineer, Sir Alexander Gibb & Partners, 1937-51 (except War years); War Service, Corps of Royal Engineers, Western Desert, Europe (with Highland Division); wounded; twice mentioned in Despatches; retired as Major; Resident Engineer i/c Pitlochry Dam and Power Station, 1946-51; Member: Perth and Kinross County Council, 1946-74 (Convener, 1970-74), Tayside Regional Council, 1974-78 (Convener, 1974-78), North of Scotland Hydro Electric Board, 1956-70 (Depute Chairman, 1970-72); Director: Macdonald Fraser & Co., Perth, 1961-84, United Auctions (Scotland) Ltd., 1963-74 (Chairman, 1967-74); fought Parliamentary elections as Liberal, Banff, 1945, Kinross and West Perth, 1949 and 1963. Director, Hill Farming Research Organisation, 1966-78; Chairman, Scottish Branch, Institute of Fisheries Management, 1980-83; Vice President, Royal Highland and Agricultural Society of Scotland, 1972. Recreations: fishing; shooting; knowing about salmon. Address: (h.) Reynock, Remony, Aberfeldy, Perthshire; T.-Kenmore 400.

Dundas, Charles Robert, TD, MB, ChB, FFARCS, FRCP, RCPSGlas. Senior Lecturer in Anaesthesia, Aberdeen University, since 1976; b. 20.6.34, Glasgow; m., Dr. Valerie Flook. Educ. Grangemouth High School; Edinburgh University. House Surgeon and House Physician, Falkirk and District Royal Infirmary, 1959-60; Aberdeen Royal Infirmary: Senior House Officer in Anaesthesia, 1960-62, Research Fellow, then Senior Registrar in Anaesthesia, 1962-69; Consultant Anaesthetist, Grampian Health Board, 1970-76. Major, RAMC (V), 372 MFST. Recreations: fishing; gardening; sailing. Address: (b.) Department of Surgery, Aberdeen University, Aberdeen.

Dundee, Earl of (Alexander Henry Scrymgeour). Hereditary Royal Standard-Bearer for Scotland; A Lord in Waiting (Government Whip), since 1986; b. 5.6.49; m., Siobhan Mary Llewellyn; 1 s.; 3 d. Educ. Eton; St. Andrews University.

Dundonald, 15th Earl of (Iain Alexander Douglas Blair); b. 17.2.61; m., Marie Beatrice Louise Russo. Educ. Wellington College; Royal Agricultural College, Cirencester. Company Director. Address: Lochnell Castle, Ledaig, Argyll.

Dunlop, Alastair Barr, FRICS. Member, Lothian Health Board, since 1983; Chairman, Central and South, Scottish Conservative and Unionist Association, 1985-88; b. 27.12.33, Calcutta; m., Catriona C.L.H. MacLaurin; 1 s.; 1 d. Educ. Radley. National Service, 1952-54 (active service, Malaya: 2nd Lt., 1st Bn., RWK); commerce, City of London, 1954-58; agricultural student, 1959-61; Land Agent, Inverness, 1962-71 (Partner, Bingham Hughes & Macpherson); Joint Founding Director, Martin Paterson Associates Ltd., 1971. Chairman, Edinburgh and Borders Branch, RICS, 1977; Life Member, Institute of Directors; Chairman, Edinburgh Branch, World Wildlife Fund; President, Edinburgh South Conservative Association; small farm/woodland interest in Galloway. Recreations: golf; skiing; fine arts. Address: 46 Dick Place, Edinburgh, EH9 2JB; T.-031-667 5343.

Dunlop, Alexander Scott, MA (Hons). Rector, Blairgowrie High School, since 1978; b. 24.2.34, Stevenston; m., Elspeth Jean Mitchell; 4 s. Educ. Stevenston Higher Grade School; Ardrossan Academy; Glasgow University; Jordanhill College. Teacher: Irvine Royal Academy, 1957, Ardrossan Academy, 1959; Special Assistant, Ardrossan Academy, 1965; Principal Teacher of English, Stevenston High School, 1968; Assistant Rector, Auchenharvie Academy, 1971; Depute Rector, Garnock Academy, Kilbirnie, 1974. Organist and Choirmaster: St. John's Church of Scotland, Ardrossan, 1958-68, St. Cuthbert South Beach Church, Saltcoats, 1968-78, St. Andrew's, Blairgowrie, since 1984; Member, Royal College of Organists; Fellow, National Chrysanthemum Society; Member, National Rose Society. Recreations: music; growing and exhibiting chrysanths, sweet peas, roses; golf. Address: (b.) The High School, Blairgowrie, Perthshire, PH10 6PW; T.-Blairgowrie 3445/6.

Dunlop, Rev. Alistair John, MA, FSA Scot. Minister, Saddell and Carradale, since 1979; Presbytery Clerk, South Argyll, since 1986; b. 18.3.39, Glasgow; m., Elaine Marion Seton Smith; 4 s. Educ. Hutchesons' Boys' Grammar School; Glasgow University; Trinity College, Glasgow. Assistant Minister, Dunblane Cathedral, 1964-65; Minister: Kirriemuir St. Ninian's, 1965-70, Beith: High, 1970-79; Moderator: Ardrossan Presbytery, 1974-75, South Argyll Presbytery, 1982. Scout Leader, 28th Argyll Scout Troop. Recreations: gardening; TV watching; thinking about working. Address: The Manse, Carradale, Campbeltown, Argyll, PA28 6QG; T.-058 33 253.

Dunlop, Eileen. Children's Writer; Headmistress, Dollar Academy Preparatory School, since 1980; b. 13.10.38, Alloa; m., Antony Kamm (qv). Educ.

Alloa Academy; Moray House College. Publications: Robinsheugh, 1975; A Flute in Mayferry Street, 1976; Fox Farm, 1978; The Maze Stone, 1982 (SAC Book Award); Clementina, 1985 (SAC Book Award); The House on the Hill, 1987; (with Antony Kamm) Scottish Verse to 1800, 1985; A Book of Old Edinburgh, 1983. Recreations: reading; gardening; theatre. Address: (h.) 46 Tarmangie Drive, Dollar, FK14 7BP; T.-Dollar 2007.

Dunlop, Frank, CBE (1977), BA (Hons). Director, Edinburgh International Festival, since 1983; b. 15.2.27. Educ. Kibworth Beauchamp Grammar School; University College, London. Administrator and Associate Director, National Theatre of Gt. Britain, 1967-71; Founder, 1969, Director, 1969-78 and 1980-83, The Young Vic. Address: (b.) Edinburgh International Festival, 21 Market Street, Edinburgh.

Dunn, Bill, BA. Chief Executive, Ayr Locality Enterprise Resource Trust (ALERT), since 1988 (Managing Director, Garnock Valley Development Executive, 1984-88); b. 26.2.48, Ayr; m., Sheila; 2 s.; 2 d. Educ. Ayr Academy; Strathclyde University. Transport Manager, National Freight Corporation/British (later Scottish) Road Services, 1970-73; Administrator, Ayrshire Joint Police Committee, 1973; Internal Audit Department, British Steel Corporation, Glasgow, 1973-81; Garnock Valley Task Force: Project Co-ordinator, 1981-83, Business Development Consultant, 1983-84. Recreations: family; golf; football; music; DIY; model railways. Address: (b.) 88 Green Street, Ayr, KA8 8BG; T.-0292 264181.

Dunn, Douglas Eaglesham, BA, FRSL, Hon.LLD (Dundee, 1987). Writer, since 1971; b. 23.10.42, Inchinnan. Educ. Renfrew High School; Camphill Senior Secondary School, Paisley; Hull University. Books of poems: Terry Street, 1969, The Happier Life, 1972, Love or Nothing, 1974, Barbarians, 1979, St. Kilda's Parliament, 1981, Elegies, 1985, Selected Poems, 1986, Northlight, 1988; Secret Villages (short stories), 1985; books edited: A Choice of Lord Byron's Verse, 1974, The Poetry of Scotland, 1979, A Rumoured City: New Poets from Hull, 1982; Two Decades of Irish Writing: a Critical Survey, 1975; author of radio and TV plays, and TV films using commentaries in verse. Gregory Award, 1968; Somerset Maugham Award, 1972; Geoffrey Faber Memorial Prize, 1975; Hawthornden Prize, 1982; Whitbread Award for Poetry and Whitbread Book of the Year Award, 1985. Honorary Visiting Professor, Dundee University, 1987; Honorary Fellow, Humberside College, 1987. Address (b.) c/o Faber & Faber Ltd., 3 Queen Square, London, WC1N 3AV.

Dunn, Rev. William Stuart, LTh. Minister, Crosshill Parish Church, Motherwell, since 1982; b. 17.4.41, Portlethen, Kincardineshire; m., Elspeth Mairi MacPhail; 1 s.; 3 d. Educ. Mackie Academy, Stonehaven; Christs College and Aberdeen University. Apprentice Chartered Accountant, 1959; began divinity course, Christs College, Aberdeen, 1964; licensed by Aberdeen Presbytery, 1969; Assistant, North and East Church of St. Nicholas, Aberdeen, 1969-70; Minister, Dreghorn and Pearston Old Parish Church, 1970-82. Recreations: music; sport; gardening; motoring; boating. Address: Crosshill Manse, 15 Orchard Street, Motherwell, ML1 3JE; T.-0698 63410.

Dunnachie, James Francis, JP. MP (Labour), Glasgow Pollok, since 1987; b. 17.11.30; m. Councillor, Glasgow Corporation, 1972-74, Glasgow District Council, 1974-77, Strathclyde Regional Council, 1978-87.

Dunne, John Joseph, MA (Hons), MPhil, PHL, AFBPsS. Principal Clinical Psychologist, Community Clinical Psychology Service, Forth Valley Health Board, since 1985; Honorary Lecturer in Psychology, Stirling University, since 1986 (Director, Macmillan Nursing Research Project, since 1987); Director, Church of Scotland Clergy Stress Research Project, since 1988; b. 31.8.42, Kirkcaldy; m., Marie Anne Cecile. Educ. Blairs College, Aberdeen; Gregorian University, Rome; St. Andrews University; Edinburgh University. Clinical Psychologist, Royal Edinburgh Hospital, 1977-81; Senior Clinical Psychologist (Primary Care), Dedridge and Craigshill Health Centres, Livingston, 1981-85; Honorary Fellow, Edinburgh University, since 1984. Address: (b.) Community Clinical Psychology Service, Department of Psychology, Stirling University, Stirling; T.-0786 73171, Ext. 2082.

Dunnet, Professor George Mackenzie, OBE, BSc, PhD, DSc, FRSE, FIBiol, FRSA. Regius Professor of Natural History, Aberdeen University, since 1974 (Dean, Faculty of Science, 1984-87); Chairman, Salmon Advisory Committee; Chairman, Shetland Oil Terminal Environmental Advisory Group, since 1977; b. 19.4.28, Dunnet, Caithness; m., Margaret Henderson Thomson; 1 s.; 2 d. Educ. Peterhead Academy; Aberdeen University. Research Fellow, Oxford University, 1952; Research Officer, CSIRO, Australia, 1953-58; Lecturer/Senior Lecturer in Zoology, Aberdeen University, 1958-71; Professor of Zoology, Aberdeen University, 1971-74; Senior Research Fellow, DSIR, New Zealand, 1968-69. Member, Committees: The Nature Conservancy, Nature Conservancy Council, Natural Environment Research Council, British Council; Chairman, Advisory Committees for Protection of Birds (Scotland, and England and Wales); Council Member, Scottish Marine Biological Association; President, British Ecological Society, 1979-81. Recreations: walking; croquet. Address: (h.) Whinhill, Inverebrie, Ellon, Aberdeen, AB4 9PT; T.-03587 215.

Dunnett, Alastair MacTavish, HonLLD (Strathclyde). Director, Thomson Scottish Petroleum Ltd., 1979-87; b. 26.12.08, Kilmacolm; m., Dorothy Halliday (see Dorothy Dunnett); 2 s. Educ. Overnewton School; Hillhead High School, Glasgow. Entered Commercial Bank of Scotland Ltd., 1925; Co-Founder, The Claymore Press, 1933-34; Glasgow Weekly Herald, 1935-36; The Bulletin, 1936-37; Daily Record, 1937-40; Chief Press Officer, Secretary of State for Scotland, 1940-46; Editor: Daily Record, 1946-55, The Scotsman, 1956-72; Managing Director, Scotsman Publications Ltd., 1962-70 (Chairman, 1970-74);

Chairman, Thomson Scottish Petroleum Ltd., Edinburgh, 1971-79; Member, Executive Board, Thomson Organisation Ltd., 1973-78; Director, Scottish Television, 1975-79; a Governor, Pitlochry Festival Theatre, 1958-84; Member: Press Council, 1959-62, Scottish Tourist Board, 1962-70, Council, National Trust for Scotland, 1962-70, Scottish International Education Trust, Scottish Theatre Ballet Committee, Scottish Opera Committee. Publications: Treasure at Sonnach, 1935; Heard Tell, 1946; Quest by Canoe, 1950; Highlands and Islands of Scotland, 1951; The Donaldson Line, 1952; The Land of Scotch, 1953; The Duke's Day, No Thanks to the Duke, 1978; Among Friends (autobiography), 1984; author of plays: The Original John Mackay, 1956; Fit to Print, 1962. Recreations: sailing; riding; walking. Address: (h.) 87 Colinton Road, Edinburgh, EH10 5DF; T.-031-337 2107.

Dunnett, Dorothy. Writer, since 1960; Portrait Painter, since 1950; b. 25.8.23, Dunfermline; m., Alastair M. Dunnett (qv); 2 s. Civil Service: Assistant Press Officer, Scottish Government Departments, Edinburgh, 1940-46, Executive Officer, Board of Trade, Glasgow, 1946-55; Trustee for the Secretary of State for Scotland, Scottish National War Memorial, since 1962; Director, Scottish Television p.l.c., since 1979; Member, Scottish Executive Committee, Book Trust, since 1984; Fellow, Royal Society of Arts, since 1986; Trustee, National Library of Scotland, since 1986; Council Member, Insite Trust, since 1986. Publications (novels): Game of Kings, 1961; Queens' Play, 1964; The Disorderly Knights, 1966; Dolly and the Singing Bird, 1968; Pawn in Frankincense, 1969; Dolly and the Cookie Bird, 1970; The Ringed Castle, 1971; Dolly and the Doctor Bird, 1971; Dolly and the Starry Bird, 1973; Checkmate, 1975; Dolly and the Nanny Bird, 1976; King Hereafter, 1982; Dolly and the Bird of Paradise, 1983; Niccolo Rising, 1986; The Spring of the Ram, 1987. Contributor to Scottish Short Stories, anthology, 1973. Recreations: travel; medieval history; opera; orchestral music; ballet. Address (h.) 87 Colinton Road, Edinburgh, EH10 5DF; T.-031-337 2107.

Dunning, Norman Moore, BA (Oxon), CQSW. Divisional Manager (East and North Scotland), RSSPCC, since 1987; Chairman, British Association for the Study and Prevention of Child Abuse and Neglect, since 1986; Honorary Lecturer, Department of Child and Adolescent Psychiatry, Glasgow University, since 1984; b. 15.4.50, Crewe; m., Diana Mary; 2 s. Educ. Sandbach School; Jesus College, Oxford; Manchester University. Probation Officer, City of Manchester and Salford, 1973-75; Social Worker, NSPCC, 1975-77; Leader, RSSPCC Overnewton Centre, Glasgow, 1978-87. Joint Director, Family Research Project and Child Abuse Interventions Research Project, Glasgow University; Member, Council and Professional Advisory Group, Childline. Recreations: running; cycling; swimming. Address: (h.) 7 The Ness, Dollar, Clackmannshire; T.-0836 700790.

Dunpark, Hon. Lord (Alastair McPherson Johnston), TD, BA, LLB. Senator of the College of Justice and Lord of Session, since 1971; b. 15.12.15; m., 1, Katharine Margaret Mitchell (deceased); 3 s.; 2, Kathleen Elizabeth Macfie. Educ. Stirling High School; Merchiston Castle School; Jesus College, Cambridge; Edinburgh University. RA (TA), 1939-46 (mentioned in Despatches); Major, 1943; admitted, Faculty of Advocates, 1946; various appointments as Standing Junior Counsel to Government Departments, 1948-58; Assistant, Department of Roman Law, 1946-50, and Tutor in Scots Law, 1947-68, Edinburgh University; QC, 1958; Sheriff Principal of Dumfries and Galloway, 1966-68; Member, Scottish Law Commission, 1968-71; Chairman, RA Association, Scotland, 1960-75; Chairman, Cockburn Association (Edinburgh Civic Trust), 1969-74; Chairman, Edinburgh Legal Dispensary, since 1961; Chairman, St. George's School for Girls, Edinburgh, since 1973; President, Lothian Marriage Guidance Council, 1972-86. Publications: Walton's Law of Husband and Wife (Joint Editor, 3rd edition), 1951; Gloag and Henderson's Introduction to the Law of Scotland (Joint Editor, 7th edition), 1968. Recreations: walking; occasional golf and fishing. Address: (h.) 17 Heriot Row, Edinburgh, EH3 6HP; T.-031-556 1896.

Dunsire, Thomas, MA, LLB, WS. Partner, J. & J. Milligan, WS, Edinburgh (now Morton, Fraser & Milligan, WS), since 1951; b. 16.11.26, Rangoon, Burma; m., Jean Mary. Educ. Morrison's Academy, Crieff; Edinburgh University. Royal Navy; Solicitor and WS, 1950. Chairman, Governors, Morrison's Academy, since 1984. Recreations: formerly rugby, football, golf and cricket. Address: (h.) 40 Liberton Brae, Edinburgh.

Durie, Alastair, MA, PhD, FRHistS. Senior Lecturer, Economic History, Aberdeen University, since 1982 (Director, Overseas Office, since 1986); b. 4.8.46, Edinburgh; m., Catherine Elizabeth; 1 s.; 1 d. Educ. Edinburgh Academy; Edinburgh University. Lecturer and Writer on Scottish economic and social history; Member, Scottish History Council, 1976-80; Visiting Professor of History, University of Guelph, Canada, 1983; Council Member, British Universities Transatlantic Committee, since 1984; Adviser to Overseas Students, 1976-86. Publications: The Scottish Linen Industry in the Eighteenth Century, 1978; The Ogilvies of Auchiries, A Banffshire Family in South Carolina, 1981; George Washington Wilson and Edinburgh, 1987. Recreations: squash; shooting; snooker. Address: (b.) Overseas Office, Aberdeen University, Aberdeen; T.-0224 272023.

Durnin, Professor John V.G.A., MA, MB, ChB, DSc, FRCP, FRSE, FIBiol. Professor of Physiology, Glasgow University, since 1977; b. 23.4.23, Stirling; m., Joan Grimshaw; 4 s.; 2 d. Educ. Robert Gordon's College, Aberdeen; Aberdeen University; Glasgow University. Resident Hospital Officer in Medicine, Surgery and Clinical Pathology, four years; Lecturer/Reader, Institute of Physiology, Glasgow University; WHO and FAO Consultant in Nurtrition in several developing countries, including Burma, Ghana, Ethiopia, Mexico, Peru and Chile; Honorary Civilian Consultant to the Army in Physiology and Nutrition.

Member, Board of Directors, Scottish Ballet. Recreations: golf; skiing; hill-walking; ballet. Address: (h.) Buchanan Castle, Drymen, Glasgow; T.-Drymen 60677.

Durward, William Farquharson, MB, ChB, FRCP(Edin), FRCP(Glas). Consultant Neurologist, Greater Glasgow and Lanarkshire Health Boards, since 1977; Honorary Clinical Lecturer in Neurology, Glasgow University, since 1978; Director, Cloburn Quarry Co. Ltd.; b. 16.9.44, Kilmarnock; m., Ann Roy Paterson; 1 s.; 1 d. Educ. Glasgow University; Boston University. Employed by NHS, since 1968; specialist training grades, 1969-77. Recreations: walking; reading; railway conservation. Address: (h.) Overdale, 20 South Erskine Park, Bearsden, Glasgow, G61 4NA; T.-041-942 3143.

Dutch, Henry D.M., FIPR, FSA (Scot). Head of Public Relations, Strathclyde Regional Council, since 1975. Educ. Montrose Academy. Journalist, Glasgow Herald, 1954-67; Public Relations Officer: Scottish Special Housing Association, 1967-72, Corporation of City of Glasgow, 1972-75. Auxiliary Minister, Church of Scotland. Recreations: golf; walking; hill-climbing. Address: (b.) Strathclyde House, 20 India Street, Glasgow, G2 4PF; T.-041-227 3425.

Duthie, Professor John Hume, MA, PhD, DipEd. Professor of Education, Stirling University, since 1973; b. 25.10.33, Galashiels; m., Doreen Plummer; 1 s.; 1 d. Educ. Galashiels Academy; Langholm Academy; Dumfries Academy; Hawick High School; Edinburgh University; Durham University. School Teacher; Lecturer, Moray House College of Education; Research Director, Scottish Primary School Survey, SED; Lecturer, then Senior Lecturer, Stirling University. Publications: The Primary School Survey: A Study of the Teacher's Day; Auxiliaries in the Classroom. Recreations: music (jazz); cooking; gardening; photography. Address: (h.) Cairnhill, Doune Road, Dunblane, Perthshire; T.-Dunblane 822213.

Duthie, Norman, LDS, MDS. Senior Principal Dental Surgeon, Norman Duthie and Associates, since 1953; Honorary Senior Lecturer, Dundee University, since 1981, and Hospital Practitioner, Dundee Dental School, since 1978; Regional Adviser in General Dental Practice, North Eastern Regional Postgraduate Medical Education Committee, since 1983; b. 7.11.26, Aberdeen; m., Ethel Audrey Connon; 2 s. Educ. Robert Gordon's College, Aberdeen; St. Andrews University; Dundee University. Army (REME), 1944-48; Assistant Dental Surgeon, General Practice, 1953-54; part-time Assistant Dental Surgeon, Department of Dental Prosthetics, Dundee Dental Hospital, 1968-78; Honorary Lecturer, Dundee University, 1968-81. Served on: Aberdeen Local Dental Committee, Aberdeen NHS Executive Council, General Dental Services Committee, General Dental Services Committee (Scottish Sub-Committee), British Dental Association (Scottish Committee), Board of Management, British Dental Guild, Scottish Standing Dental Advisory Committee. Address: (h.) 1 Gladstone Place, Queen's Cross, Aberdeen; T.-0224 322959.

Duthie, Sir Robert Grieve, CBE (1978), CA, LLD, CBIM, FRSA. Chairman: Scottish Development Agency, since 1979, Britoil PLC, since 1988, Insight International Tours Ltd., Capital House Investment Management PLC, since 1988; Director: Insight Group PLC, Carclo Engineering Group PLC, since 1986, Investors Capital PLC, since 1986, Sea Catch PLC, since 1987, Royal Bank of Scotland plc, since 1978, British Assets Trust plc, since 1977; b. 2.10.28, Greenock; m., Violetta Noel Maclean; 2 s.; 1 d. Educ. Greenock Academy. Apprentice Chartered Accountant, Thomson Jackson Gourlay and Taylor, CA, 1946-51; joined Blacks of Greenock, 1952; appointed Managing Director, 1962; Chairman, Black & Edgington, 1972-83. Chairman, Inverkip Society, 1966; Director, Greenock Chamber of Commerce, 1966; Member, Clyde Port Authority, 1971-83 (Chairman, 1977-80); Director, Greenock Provident Bank, 1969-75 (Chairman, 1975); Member, Scottish Telecommunications Board, 1972-77; Council Member, Institute of Chartered Accountants of Scotland, 1973-78; Member: East Kilbride Development Corporation, 1976-78, Strathclyde Region Local Valuation Appeal Panel, 1976-83; CBI Tax Liaison Officer for Scotland, 1976-79; Chairman, Made Up Textile Association of Great Britain, 1972; Member: British Institute of Management Scottish Committee, 1976, Glasgow and West of Scotland Committee, Scottish Council (Development and Industry), 1975-79; Captain: Greenock Club, 1972, Greenock Cricket Club, 1960-61; Commissioner, Queen Victoria School, Dunblane, since 1972; Commissioner, Scottish Congregational Ministers Pension Fund, since 1973; Member, Scottish Economic Council, since 1980; Member of Council, Royal Caledonian Curling Club, since 1984; Treasurer, Nelson Street EU Congregational Church, Greenock, since 1970. Awarded Honorary Degree of Doctor of Laws, Strathclyde University, 1984. Recreations: curling; golf. Address: (h.) Fairhaven, 181 Finnart Street, Greenock, PA16 8JA; T.-Greenock 22642.

Duxbury, Professor Geoffrey, BSc, PhD. Professor of Physics and Applied Physics and Chairman of Department, Strathclyde University; b. 6.11.42, Blackburn; m., Mary R.; 1 s.; 1 d. Educ. Cheadle Hulme School; Sheffield University. Junior Research Fellow, National Physical Laboratory, 1967-69; Research Assistant, Research Associate, Lecturer in Chemical Physics, Bristol University, 1970-80; Senior Lecturer/Reader, Strathclyde University, 1981-86. Marlow Medal, Faraday Division, Royal Society of Chemistry, 1975. Address: (b.) Department of Physics and Applied Physics, Strathclyde University, Glasgow, G4 0NG; T.-041-552 4400.

Dyer, Iain James Anthony, MBE, JP, MA, LLB, DL. Member, Board, The Housing Corporation, since 1983; Lecturer in Private Law, Glasgow University, since 1980; b. 21.4.38, Tanzania; m., Elizabeth Anne Barry; 2 s. Educ. Dumfries Academy; Glasgow University. Parliamentary candidate (Conservative), Hamilton, 1964, 1967; Member, City of Glasgow Council, 1974-88; Lord

Provost's Assessor, Court of Glasgow University, 1977-80; Leader of the Opposition and Bailie, 1984-88; Deputy Lieutenant, City of Glasgow, since 1987; Vice Chairman, Scottish Housing Training Board, 1985-88. Recreation: music. Address: (h.) Orleans, 2 Dalziel Drive, Glasgow, G41 4PT; T.-041-423 5949.

Dyer, James A.T., MB, ChB (Hons), MRCPsych. Consultant Psychiatrist, Royal Edinburgh Hospital, since 1981; Honorary Senior Lecturer in Psychiatry, Edinburgh University, since 1981; b. 31.12.46, Arbroath; m., Lorna M.S.; 2 s.; 1 d. Educ. Bo'ness Academy; Robert Gordon's College, Aberdeen; Aberdeen University. House jobs in Aberdeen hospitals, 1970-71; Trainee General Practitioner, Skene, Aberdeenshire, 1971-72; junior clinical appointments, then Senior Registrar in Psychiatry, Royal Edinburgh Hospital, 1972-77; Scientific Officer, MRC Unit for Epidemiological Studies in Psychiatry, Edinburgh, 1977-80. Member, Medical Campaign Against Nuclear Weapons (Chairman, Scottish Working Party on Psychosocial Issues and War). Recreations: holidays; eating out; home and family. Address: (h.) 86 Morningside Drive, Edinburgh, EH10 5NT; T.-031-447 8148.

Dyke, Michael Christopher, CIPFA. Director of Finance, Glenrothes Development Corporation, since 1988; b. 25.12.46, Blackpool. Educ. St. Joseph's College, Blackpool; Manchester College of Commerce. Deputy Director of Finance, Alnwick DC, 1973-78, North East Derbyshire DC, 1978-80; Assistant Director of Finance, then Director of Finance/Depute Chief Executive, North East Fife District Council, 1980-87. Professional Advisor, CIPFA, to St. Andrews University; Co-ordinator, CIPFA Scottish Branch Weekend School, 1987-88; Member, Scottish Branch Executive Committee, CIPFA. Recreations: swimming; reading; walking; music; travel in Scotland. Address: (b.) Unicorn House, Glenrothes, Fife.

E

Eadie, Alexander. MP (Labour), Midlothian, since 1966; b. 23.6.20. Educ. Buckhaven Senior Secondary School. Former Miners' Agent; contested Ayr, 1959 and 1964; Under Secretary of State for Energy, 1974-79.

Eadie, John, BSc (Hons), FRAgS. Director, Scottish Forestry Trust (Director, Hill Farming Research Organisation, 1980-87); b. 6.11.30, Polton, Midlothian; m., Jean Young Dunlevie; 1 s.; 2 d. Educ. Linlithgow Academy; Edinburgh University. National Agricultural Advisory Service, MAFF, 1954-61; Hill Farming Research Organisation: joined, 1961, Head of Animal Production and Nutrition, 1974-80. Research Medal, Royal Agricultural Society of England, 1978. Address: (b.) Scottish Forestry Trust, c/o TG (UK), 5 Dublin Street Lane, Edinburgh, EH1; T.-031-557 0944.

Earnshaw, Rev. Phillip, BA, BSc, BD. Minister, Parish of Stromness and Graemsay, Orkney, since 1986; b. 27.12.38, Holmfirth, near Huddersfield; m., Anne R.P. MacAndrew; 2 s.; 1 d. Educ. Penistone Grammar School; Open University; Stirling University; Glasgow University. Recreations: music; gardening; walking; astronomy. Address: (h.) The Manse, Stromness, Orkney, KW16 3AP; T.-0856 850 203.

Eason, Professor George, MSc, PhD, FIMA, FRSE. Professor of Mathematics for Applied Scientists, Strathclyde University, since 1970; b. 19.3.30, Chesterfield; m., 1, Olive Holdstock (deceased); 2, Esme Beryl Burgess; 2 d. Educ. Clay Cross Tupton Hall Grammar School; Birmingham University; Keele University. Scientific Officer, RARDE, Ministry of Defence, 1954-56; Lecturer in Applied Mathematics, Newcastle-upon-Tyne University, 1957-61; Senior Lecturer, then Reader, Strathclyde University, 1961-70; Visiting Professor, Wisconsin University, 1968-69. IMA: Chairman, Scottish Branch, 1974-76, Council Member, 1976-79. Publication: Mathematics and Statistics for the Biosciences (Co-author). Recreations: hill-walking; jogging; music. Address: (h.) 1 Greenfield Court, Balfron, Glasgow, G63 OQG; T.-0360 40546.

Eastmond, Clifford John, BSc, MD, FRCP. Consultant Rheumatologist, Grampian Health Board, since 1979; Clinical Senior Lecturer, Aberdeen University, since 1979; b. 19.1.45, Ashton-under-Lyne; m., Margaret Wadsworth; 2 s.; 1 d. Educ. Audenshaw Grammar School; Edinburgh University. House Officer posts, Edinburgh, one year; moved to Liverpool for further training, subsequently to Rheumatism Unit, Leeds. Elder, Church of Scotland. Recreations: golf; skiing; hill-walking; swimming; music. Address: (h.) Whinmoor, 34 Leslie Crescent, Westhill, Skene, Aberdeenshire; T.-0224 741009.

Easton, Rev. David John Courtney, MA, BD. Minister, Burnside Parish Church, Glasgow, since 1977; b. 7.10.40, Bogota, Colombia; m., Edith Stevenson; 2 s.; 1 d. Educ. Arbroath High School; Aberdeen University. Minister, Hamilton-Bardrainney Parish Church, Port Glasgow, 1967-77. Past Chairman, Scottish Tear Fund Advisory Committee; Member, Rutherford House Council. Recreation: music. Address: 59 Blairbeth Road, Burnside, Rutherglen, Glasgow, G73 4JD; T.-041-634 1233.

Easton, Robert William Simpson, CBE (1980), CEng, FIMechE, FIMarE, FRINA. Chairman and Managing Director, Yarrow Shipbuilders Ltd., since 1979; Chairman, Clyde Port Authority, since 1983; Director, Supermarine Consortium Ltd., since 1986; b. 30.10.22, Glasgow; m., Jean Fraser; 1 s.; 1 d. Educ. Govan High School,

Glasgow; Royal Technical College, Glasgow. Apprentice, Marine Engineer, 1939-51; Manager, Yarrow & Co. Ltd., 1951-65; Yarrow Shipbuilders Ltd.: Director, 1965-70, Deputy Managing Director, 1970-77, Managing Director, 1977-79; Main Board Director, Yarrow & Co. Ltd., 1971-77. Vice-President, Clyde Shipbuilders Association, 1972-79; Member, Worshipful Company of Shipwrights, 1982; Freeman, City of London, 1982; Council Member, RINA, 1983; Trustee, Seagull Trust, 1984. Recreations: sailing; golf; walking; family. Address: (h.) Springfield, Stuckenduff Road, Shandon, Dunbartonshire, G84 8NW; T.-0436 820 677.

Easton, Robin Gardner, MA, DipEd. Rector, High School of Glasgow, since 1983; b. 6.10.43, Glasgow; m., Eleanor Mary McIlroy; 1 s.; 1 d. Educ. Kelvinside Academy; Sedbergh School; Christ's College, Cambridge; Wadham College, Oxford. Teacher of French and German, Melville College, Edinburgh, 1966-72; Housemaster and Deputy Head, French Department, Daniel Stewart's and Melville College, 1972-78; Head, Modern Languages, George Watson's College, 1979-83. Elder, Church of Scotland; former Council Member, Scripture Union. Recreations: rugby; tennis; hill-walking; visiting ancient monuments. Address: (h.) 21 Stirling Drive, Bearsden, Glasgow, G61 4NU; T.-041-943 0368.

Eastwood, Martin Anthony, MB, MSc, FRCPE. Consultant Gastroenterologist, Western General Hospital, since 1968; Reader in Medicine, Edinburgh University, since 1987; b. 7.8.35, Hull; m., Jenny; 3 s.; 1 d. Educ. Minster Grammar School, Southwell; Edinburgh University. Lecturer in Therapeutics, Royal Infirmary, Edinburgh, 1964-68; Consultant Physician, in charge of Wolfson Gastrointestinal Laboratory, since 1968; Chairman, Medical Staff Committee, Western General Hospital, 1985-88. Publications: papers on physiology of the colon; Human Nutrition and Dietetics (Co-Editor), 1986. Address: (b.) Wolfson Laboratory, Gastrointestinal Unit, Western General Hospital, Edinburgh, EH4 2XU; T.-031-332 2525.

Ebsworth, Professor Evelyn A.V., BA, PhD, MA, ScD, FRSE. Crum Brown Professor of Chemistry, Edinburgh University, since 1967; b. 14.2.33, Richmond, Yorkshire; m., Mary Salter (deceased); 1 s.; 3 d. Educ. Marlborough School; King's College, Cambridge. Fellow, King's College, Cambridge, 1957-59; Research Associate, Princeton University, 1958-59; Christ's College, Cambridge: Fellow; Demonstrator, 1959-64; Lecturer, 1964-67; Tutor, 1964-67. President, Dalton Division, Chemical Society (Vice-President, Society, 1976-79); Fellow, Royal Institute of Chemistry; Chemical Society Award for Main Group Element Chemistry, 1979; Kipping Award, American Chemical Society, 1980; Corresponding Member, Gottingen Academy of Sciences, 1983. Recreation: opera. Address: (b.) Chemistry Department, Edinburgh University, Kings Buildings, West Mains Road, Edinburgh, EH9 3JJ; T.-031-667 1081, Ext. 3417.

Eccles, Alexander Charles William Anderson, RD*, BA, LLB, WS. Temporary Sheriff, since 1984; part-time Chairman, Social Security Appeals Tribunals, since 1985, and Rent Assessment Committee, since 1975; b. 8.1.33, Newcastle upon Tyne; m., Judith Margaret Hardy; 2 s.; 2 d. Educ. Loretto; Gonville and Caius College, Cambridge; Edinburgh University. National Service, 1951-53 (commissioned HLI); TA, Royal Scots, 1953-59; qualified Solicitor and WS, 1960; Assistant with various firms and local authorities, 1960-68; Partner, J.L. Anderson & Co., Solicitors, Cupar, Kinross, Glenrothes and Cowdenbeath, 1968-84. Lt. Cdr., RNR, 1966-85; Rugby Blue, Edinburgh University (played for Scottish Universities and Durham County). Recreations: rugby; squash; reading military history. Address: (h.) 19A Queens Gardens, St. Andrews, Fife, KY16 9TA; T.-St. Andrews 72505.

Eddison, James Andrew, MA, FICE, FRSE. Deputy Chairman, Scottish Life Assurance Company; Director, Merchiston Developments (Edinburgh) Ltd.; Chairman, Burrell Contracts plc; Deputy Chairman, Edinburgh Old Town Trust; b. 9.5.21, Aberdeen; m., Mary J. Rayner; 1 s.; 1 d. Educ. Rugby; Trinity College, Cambridge. Recreations: fishing; gardening; grandchildren. Address: (h.) Lennox Lea, Currie, Midlothian, EH14 6AR; T.-031-449 3289.

Ede, Donald Albert, BSc, MS, PhD, FRSE, FRSA, FIB. Reader in Zoology, Glasgow University, since 1971; b. 4.5.26, Brighton; m., Eleanor Lambert; 2 s. Educ. Varndean School, Brighton; London University; Northwestern University, USA; Edinburgh University. Assistant Lecturer, Edinburgh University, 1953-56; Lecturer, Wye College, London University, 1957-62; Principal Scientific Officer, Poultry Research Centre, Edinburgh, 1962-70; Visiting Lecturer: Iowa University, Massachusetts University, McGill University, Poona University. Recreation: painting. Address: (h.) 5 Learmonth Terrace, Edinburgh, EH4 1PG.

Eden, Tim Osborn Bryan, MB, BS, D(Obst)RCOG, MRCP, FRCPEdin. Consultant Paediatric Haematologist/Oncologist, Royal Hospital for Sick Children, Edinburgh, since 1982; part-time Senior Lecturer, Edinburgh University, since 1982; b. 2.4.47, Birmingham; m., Randi Forsgren; 1 s.; 1 d. Educ. Grimsby Wintringham Grammar School; University College and Hospital, London. House Physician, University College Hospital, London; Senior House Physician (Obstetrics), Isle of Wight; Registrar, Paediatrics, Royal Hospital for Sick Children, Edinburgh; Registrar, Haematology, Edinburgh Hospitals; Postdoctoral Fellow, Stanford University, California; Lecturer in Child Life and Health, Edinburgh University; Consultant Clinical Haematologist, Bristol Children's Hospital. Chairman, Scottish Paediatric Oncology Group; Coordinator, MRC Eighth Childhood Leukaemia Trial; Member, Scottish Committee, Malcolm Sargent Fund. Recreations: family; politics. Address: (b.) Royal Hospital for Sick Children, Edinburgh; T.-031-667 1991.

Edge, David Owen, BA, MA, PhD, FRAS, FRSA. Director, Science Studies Unit, Edinburgh University, since 1966 (Reader in Science Studies, since 1979); b. 4.9.32, High Wycombe; m., Barbara Corsie; 2 s.; 1 d. Educ. Aberdeen Grammar School; Leys School, Cambridge; Gonville and Caius College, Cambridge. Assistant Physics Master, Perse School, Cambridge; Producer, Science Unit, Talks Department, BBC Radio, London, 1959-66; Senior Fellow, Society for the Humanities, and Senior Research Associate, Science, Technology and Society Program, Cornell University, 1973; Member, Edinburgh University Court, 1983-86; Scottish HQ Adviser for Students, Scout Association, 1966-85; President (Past Chairman), Scout & Guide Graduate Association; Circuit Steward, Methodist Church, Edinburgh and Forth Circuit, 1983-86; Editor, Social Studies of Science, since 1971; Member, various CNAA panels and committees, since 1972; President, Society for Social Studies of Science (4S), 1985-87. Publications: Astronomy Transformed (Co-author), 1976; Science in Context (Co-Editor), 1982. Recreations: hill-walking; music; watching sport - especially soccer and baseball. Address: (h.) 25 Gilmour Road, Edinburgh, EH16 5NS; T.-031-667 3497.

Edmonds, Richard John, MIFireE. Firemaster, Lothian and Borders Fire Brigade, since 1985; b. 13.4.40, Norwich; m., Ann; 1 s.; 1 d. Educ. King Edward VI Grammar School, Norwich. Norfolk Fire Service, 1959; Kent Fire Brigade, 1962; London Fire Brigade, 1965; Worcester City and County Fire Brigade, 1966; Cambridgeshire Fire Brigade, 1976; Kent Fire Brigade, 1977. Recreations: Rotary; bridge. Address: (b.) Fire Brigade HQ, Lauriston Place, Edinburgh, EH3 9DE; T.-031-228 2401.

Edward, Professor David Alexander Ogilvy, CMG, QC, MA, LLB. Salvesen Professor of European Institutions, Edinburgh University, since 1985; Advocate, since 1962; Trustee, National Library of Scotland, since 1966; Member, Law Advisory Committee, British Council; Chairman, Continental Assets Trust plc; Director, Adam & Company plc; Director, Harris Tweed Association Ltd.; Member, Panel of Arbitrators, International Centre for Settlement of Investment Disputes; Specialist Adviser to House of Lords Select Committee on the European Communities; Chairman, Hopetoun House Preservation Trust; b. 14.11.34, Perth; m., Elizabeth Young McSherry; 2 s.; 2 d. Educ. Sedbergh School; University College, Oxford; Edinburgh University. National Service, RNVR, 1956-57 (Sub-Lt.); admitted Advocate, 1962; Clerk, Faculty of Advocates, 1967-70, Treasurer, 1970-77; President, Consultative Committee, Bars and Law Societies of the European Community, 1978-80. Address: (h.) 32 Heriot Row, Edinburgh, EH3 6ES; T.-031-225 7153; (b.) Centre of European Governmental Studies, University of Edinburgh, EH8 9YL; T.-031-667 1011, Ext. 4215.

Edwards, Professor Arthur David, BSc, DIC, PhD, FICE, CEng, FRSA. Professor of Civil Engineering, Head of Department and Dean, Faculty of Engineering, Herot-Watt University; 11.11.25, Eastbourne; m., Jean Margaret; 1 s.; 1 d. Educ. Eastbourne Grammar School; Northampton Engineering College; Imperial College of Science and Technology, London. Various appointments in civil engineering industry, 1950-56; Imperial College of Science and Technology, London: Lecturer in Civil Engineering, 1957-66, Senior Lecturer, 1966-80. Telford Premium, ICE, 1970, 1973, 1983. Recreations: music; sailing; snooker. Address: (b.) Department of Civil Engineering, Heriot-Watt University, Riccarton, Edinburgh, EH14 4AS; T.-031-449 5111.

Edwards, Professor Christopher Richard Watkin, MA, MB, BChir, MD, FRCP, FRCPEdin. Professor of Clinical Medicine, Edinburgh University, since 1980; Honorary Consultant Physician, Lothian Health Board, since 1980; Chairman, Department of Medicine, Western General Hospital, since 1981; b. 12.2.42, Irvinestown, Northern Ireland; m., Dr. Sally Edwards; 2 s.; 1 d. Educ. Marlborough; Cambridge University. Junior House Officer posts, St. Bartholomew's Hospital; Senior House Officer posts, Brompton and Hammersmith Hospitals; Lecturer, St. Bartholomew's Hospital Medical College, 1968-72; Visiting Fellow, Bethesda, USA, 1972-73; Senior Lecturer and Honorary Consultant Physician, St. Bartholomew's Hospital, 1975-80. Recreations: drawing; painting; golf. Address: (b.) Department of Medicine, Western General Hospital, Edinburgh; T.-031-332 2525.

Edwards, Elizabeth Alice, BSc, SRN, SCM. Chief Area Nursing Officer, Tayside Health Board, since 1988 (Dumfries and Galloway Health Board, 1980-88); b. Coleraine. Educ. Coleraine High School; Edinburgh University. Ward Sister, Royal Victoria Hospital, Belfast, 1960-65; nursing in North America, 1966-67; Department Sister and Assistant Matron, Royal Victoria Hospital, Belfast, 1967-69; full-time student at University, 1969-72; Principal Nursing Officer, Edinburgh Northern Hospitals Group, 1972-74; District Nursing Officer, North Lothian District, Lothian Health Board, 1974-80. Member, National Board for Nursing, Midwifery and Health Visiting for Scotland, 1983; Member, United Kingdom Central Council for Nursing, Midwifery and Health Visiting, 1984. Address: (b.) Tayside Health Board, Vernonholme, Riverside Drive, Dundee.

Edwards, Frederick Edward, RD (and Clasp), BA, FBIM, FISW. Director of Social Work, Strathclyde Regional Council, since 1976; b. 9.4.31; m.; 2 s.; 1 d. Educ. St. Edward's College, Liverpool; Glasgow University. Director of Social Work: Moray and Nairn, 1969-74, Grampian, 1974-76.

Edwards, George Lowden, CEng, MIMechE, MIProdE, FBIM, FInstPet. Head of Public Affairs, Clydesdale Bank PLC; Trustee, Scottish Civic Trust; Member, Scottish National Committee, English-Speaking Union; b. 6.2.39, Kirriemuir; m., Sylvia Izatt; 1 d. Educ. Webster's Seminary, Kirriemuir; Dundee Institute of Technology. Production Engineer, Burroughs Machines Ltd., Cumbernauld, 1961-64; Development Division, Scottish Council (Development and Industry), Edinburgh, 1964-67; General Manager, GR Designs Ltd., Perth, 1967-68; London Director, Scottish Council (Development and Industry), 1968-78; Manager, Public Affairs Scotland, Conoco (UK) Ltd., Aberdeen, 1978-83; Manager, Public Affairs, Conoco (UK) Ltd., 1983-85. Council Member, Institute of Petroleum. Recreations: music; travel; food and wine. Address: (h.) 1 Back Dean, Ravelston Terrace, Edinburgh, EH4 3UA.

Edwards, Ian Douglas, BSc, PhD. Education Officer, Royal Botanic Garden, Edinburgh, since 1983; Secretary, Botanical Society of Edinburgh, since 1985; Deputy Chief Scientist, Operation Raleigh, since 1987; b. 31.1.56, Grays; m., Teresa Margaret Darwin; 1 s.; 1 d. Educ. Aveley High School; Lancaster University; Aberdeen University. Institute of Terrestrial Ecology, Banchory, 1977-80; Forestry Research Institute, Malawi, 1980-82. Recreations: travel; mountaineering; natural history. Address: (b.) Royal Botanic Garden, Inverleith Row, Edinburgh, EH3 5LR; T.-031-552 7171.

Edwards, Paul Geoffrey, MA (Cantab), BA. Reader in English Literature, Edinburgh University; b. 31.7.26, Birmingham; m., Maj Ingbritt Nilsson; 2 d. Educ. St. Philip's School, Birmingham; Hatfield College, Durham; Emmanuel College, Cambridge. Taught English, St. Augustine's College, Cape Coast, Ghana, 1954-57; Lecturer in English, Sierra Leone University, 1957-63; joined Edinburgh University, 1963; Visiting Professor, at various times: University of California, New York State University, Bangkok University, Singapore University. Publications: West African Narrative, 1963; Through African Eyes, 1966; Equiano's Travels, 1967; Legendary Fiction in Medieval Iceland (Co-author), 1970; Black Personalities in the Era of the Slave Trade (Co-author), 1983; Icelandic Sagas (Co-translator). Recreations: teaching; translating sagas. Address: (h.) 82 Kirk Brae, Edinburgh, EH16 6JA.

Edwards, Rev. Canon Peter John Smallman, BD, MTh, FSJ. Rector, St. Ninian's Church, Invergordon, since 1981; Synod Clerk, Diocese of Moray, Ross and Caithness, since 1985; Principal, Moray Ordination Course, 1981-88; b. 22.4.48, Hereford. Educ. Haverfordwest Grammar School; University College of North Wales, Bangor; Lincoln Theological College. Curate, Llanelli, 1973-76; Precentor, Inverness Cathedral, 1976-77; Rector, Walton West with Talbenny and Haroldston West, South Wales, 1977-81; Canon, Inverness Cathedral, since 1981; Examining Chaplain to Bishops of Moray, since 1981, and St. David's, since 1982. Address: St. Ninian's Rectory, 132 High Street, Invergordon; T.-Invergordon 852392.

Egginton, Gay, BSc (Hons), PGCE. Headmistress, Laurel Bank School, Glasgow, since 1984; b. 28.2.44, Woking. Educ. St. George's School, Edinburgh; Harrogate College, Yorkshire; London University. Teacher of Chemistry, Priory Comprehensive School, Lewes, 1965-70; Head of Chemistry, Priory County Grammar School, Shrewsbury, 1970-75; Head of Chemistry and Upper School, St. Margaret's School, Edinburgh, 1975-84. Executive Member, Girls' School Association (Scottish Chairman). Recreations: travel; theatre. Address: (b.) Laurel Bank School, 4 Lilybank Terrace, Glasgow, G12.

Eilbeck, Professor John Christopher, BA, PhD, FIMA, FRSE. Head, Department of Mathematics, Heriot-Watt University, since 1984 (Professor, since 1986); b. 8.4.45, Whitehaven; m., Lesley; 3 s. Educ. Whitehaven Grammar School; Queen's College, Oxford; Lancaster University. Royal Society European Fellow, ICTP, Trieste, 1969-70; Research Assistant, Department of Mathematics, UMIST, Manchester, 1970-73; Heriot-Watt University: Lecturer, Department of Mathematics, 1973-80, Senior Lecturer, 1980-85, Reader, 1985-86; Long-term Visiting Fellow, Center for Nonlinear Studies, Los Alamos National Laboratory, New Mexico, 1983-84. Publications: Rock Climbing in the Lake District (Co-author), 1975; Solitons and Nonlinear Wave Equations (Co-author), 1982. Recreation: mountaineering. Address: (b.) Department of Mathematics, Heriot-Watt University, Riccarton, Edinburgh, EH14 4AS; T.-031-449 5111.

Elders, Rev. (Iain) Alasdair, MA, BD. Minister, Broughton McDonald Parish Church, Edinburgh, since 1973; b. 17.4.39, Sunderland; m., Hazel Stewart Steven; 1 s.; 1 d. Educ. Daniel Stewart's College, Edinburgh; Edinburgh University. Assistant Minister: Edinburgh: St. Andrew's, 1961-63, Edinburgh: High (St. Giles Cathedral), 1963-65; Minister, Cumbernauld: Abronhill (church extension charge), 1965-73. Secretary, Cumbernauld Council of Churches, 1967-72; Chairman, Council of East End Churches of Edinburgh, 1978-82; Chairman, New Town Community Council, since 1986; Scout Commissioner, since 1966 (Assistant Area Commissioner, since 1983). Address: Broughton McDonald Manse, 103 East Claremont Street, Edinburgh, EH7 4JA; T.-031-556 7313.

Elgin, 11th Earl of, and Kincardine, 15th Earl of, (Andrew Douglas Alexander Thomas Bruce), KT (1981), DL, JP; 37th Chief of the Name of Bruce; Lord Lieutenant, Fife Region, since 1987; Brigadier, Queen's Bodyguard for Scotland (Royal Company of Archers); Member, Nationwide Anglia Building Society (Scottish Board); Chairman, Scottish Money Management Association; President, Royal Scottish Automobile Club; b. 17.2.24; m., Victoria Usher; 3 s.; 2 d. Educ. Eton; Balliol College, Oxford. President, Scottish Amicable Life Assurance Society, since 1975; Chairman, National Savings Committee for Scotland, 1972-78; Member, Scottish Postal Board, since 1980; Lord High Commissioner, General Assembly, Church of Scotland, 1980-81; Grand Master Mason of Scotland, 1961-65; President, Royal Caledonian Curling Club, 1968-69; Hon. LLD, Dundee, 1977, Glasgow, 1983. Address: (h.) Broomhall, Dunfermline, KY11 3DU.

Eliott of Stobs, Sir Arthur Francis Augustus Boswell, 11th Bt. Chief of the Clan Elliot; b. 2.1.15; m., Frances Aileen McClean; 1 d. Educ. Harrow; King's College, Cambridge. 2nd Lt., King's Own Scottish Borderers TA, 1939; Major, 1944; King's African Rifles, 1941-45; Member, Queen's Bodyguard for Scotland. Publication: The Elliots - The Story of a Border Clan, 1986. Address: Redheugh, Newcastleton, Roxburghshire.

Elliot, Sir Gerald Henry. Chairman, Christian Salvesen PLC, since 1981; Chairman, Scottish Provident Institution, since 1983; Chairman, Scottish Opera, since 1987; b. 24.12.23, Edinburgh; m., Margaret Ruth Whale; 2 s.; 1 d. Educ. Marlborough College; New College, Oxford. Managing Director, Christian Salvesen PLC, 1973-81. Chairman, Scottish Arts Council, 1980-86; Vice Chairman, Scottish Business in the Community, since 1987; Chairman, Prince's Scottish Youth Business Trust, since 1987; Chairman, BioTal Limited, since 1987; Trustee, National Museums of Scotland, since 1987; Member of Court, Edinburgh University, since 1984; Chairman, Scottish Unit Managers Ltd., since 1984; Chairman of Trustees, David Hume Institute, since 1985; Fellow, Royal Society of Edinburgh, since 1977; Honorary Consul for Finland in Edinburgh and Leith, since 1957. Address: (b.) 50 East Fettes Avenue, Edinburgh, EH4 1EQ; T.-031-552 7101.

Elliot, John. Farmer; Director, Rowett Research Institute; Regional Member, British Wool Marketing Board, for Southern Scotland; b. 29.5.47, Duns, Berwickshire; m., Joan Kathleen Wight; 1 s.; 1 d. Educ. St. Mary School, Melrose; Edinburgh Academy. Nuffield Scholar, US and Canada, 1982; Session Clerk, Kirk of Lammermuir. Recreations: spectator sports; reading; writing; agriculture. Address: Rawburn, Duns, Berwickshire, TD11 3PG; T.-036 17 221.

Elliot, Thomas, JP. Farmer; a Director, Royal Highland and Agricultural Society of Scotland; a Director, Animal Diseases Research Association; Member, Hill Farming Research Advisory Committee for Scotland; b. 6.4.26, Galashiels; m., Patrena Jennifer Mundell; 1 s.; 2 d. Educ. St. Mary's School; Loretto. President, Border Area, NFU of Scotland, 1974-76; Chairman, Selkirk Branch, 1968; President, South Country Cheviot Society, 1971-73; Member, Southern Regional Committee, British Wool Board. Played rugby, Gala RFC, 1945-58; 14 caps for Scotland, 1955-58; Barbarians, 1956; British Lions, South African tour, 1955. "Border Man of the Year", Tweeddale Press, 1979; Elder and Session Clerk, Caddonfoot Church. Recreations: watching rugby; reading books; farming. Address: Newhall, Clovenfords, Galashiels; T.-Clovenfords 260.

Elliot of Harwood, Baroness (Katharine Elliot), DBE (1958), JP. Life Peer; b. 15.1.03; m., Rt. Hon. Walter Elliot, PC, CH (deceased). Educ. Abbot's Hill, Hemel Hempstead; Paris. Chairman: National Union of Conservative and Unionist Associations, 1956-67, Carnegie UK Trust, 1940-86, Consumer Council, 1963-68; UK Delegate to General Assembly, United Nations, 1954-56-57; Member, Roxburgh County Council, 1946-75 (Vice-Convener, 1974); Member, King George's Jubilee Trust, 1936-68; Hon. LLD, Glasgow, 1959. Address: (h.) Harwood, Bonchester Bridge, Hawick, Roxburghshire.

Elliott, Robert F., BA (Oxon), MA. Senior Lecturer in Political Economy, Aberdeen University, since 1982; b. 15.6.47, Thurlow, Suffolk; m., Susan Elliott Gutteridge; 1 s. Educ. Haverhill Secondary Modern School, Suffolk; Ruskin College and Balliol College, Oxford. Joined Aberdeen University, 1973, as Research Fellow, then Lecturer; acted as Consultant to numerous public and private sector organisations, including McGaw Committee of Inquiry into Civil Service Pay, the EEC Commission and Highlands and Islands Development Board, on issues of pay and employment. Publications: books on Pay in the Public Sector, 1981; Incomes Policies, Inflation and Relative Pay, 1981; Incomes Policy, 1981. Recreations: music; reading; golf. Address: (h.) 11 Richmondhill Place, Aberdeen, AB2 4EN, T.-0224 314901.

Elliott, Hon. Lord (Walter Archibald Elliott), QC, MC, BL. President, Lands Tribunal for Scotland, since 1971; Chairman, Scottish Land Court, since 1978; Brigadier, Queen's Bodyguard for Scotland (Royal Company of Archers), since 1983; b. 6.9.22, London; m., Susan Isobel MacKenzie Ross; 2 s. Educ. Eton College; Edinburgh University. 2nd Bn., Scots Guards, 1943-45 (Staff Captain, 1947); Advocate and at the Inner Temple, Barrister-at-Law, 1950; QC (Scotland), 1963. Publication: Us and Them: a study of group consciousness, 1986. Recreations: gardening; skiing; shooting. Address: (h.) Morton House, 19 Winton Loan, Edinburgh, EH10 7AW; T.-031-445 2548.

Ellis, Charles William, BA (Hons), LLD. Chairman, Grampian Health Board, since 1982; Member, Whitley Council for Professions Allied to Medicine, since 1987; b. 15.11.21, Horsham, Sussex; m., Maureen Patricia Radley; 1 s.; 3 d. Educ. Oxted County School; University College London. Indian Army and Royal Artillery, 1941-64; completed degree in modern history, 1964-66 (begun in 1940-41); Junior Lecturer to Head, School of Social Studies, Robert Gordon's Institute of Technology, Aberdeen, 1966-85. Councillor, City of Aberdeen, 1971-75 (Convener, Education Committee, 1974-75); Councillor, Grampian Regional Council, 1974-78 (Leader, Labour Group). Recreations: International affairs; family; genealogy. Address: (h.) 50 Hammerfield Avenue, Aberdeen, AB1 6LJ; T.-Aberdeen 310098.

Ellis, Jean B.M., OBE, BSc, MB, ChB, JP. Member, Mental Welfare Commission for Scotland, 1984-88; Member, Scottish Hospital Endowment Research Trust, since 1978; President, Aberdeen and NE Association for Mental Health; b. 13.9.20, Poona, India; m., Richard T. Ellis (qv); 2 s.; 2 d. Educ. Malvern Girls College; Aberdeen University. Past Chairman: Aberdeen Marriage Guidance Council, Royal Cornhill and Associated Hospitals Board of Management; former Member: NE Regional Hospital Board, Nurses and Midwives Whitley Council (Management Side), Grampian Health Board. Address: (h.) 18 Rubislaw Den North, Aberdeen, AB2 4AN; T.-0224 316680.

Ellis, John Russell, BA (Oxon). General Manager, ScotRail; Council Member, CBI Scotland; Member, Governing Council, ScotBic; b. 21.5.38, Chipping Campden; m., Jean Eileen; 2 d. Educ. Rendcomb College, Cirencester; Pembroke College, Oxford. Joined British Rail as graduate management trainee, 1962; held various management appointments, latterly as Assistant General Manager, Eastern Region, then Deputy General Manager, Southern Region. Recreations: hockey; cricket; walking. Address: (b.) ScotRail House, 58 Port Dundas Road, Glasgow; T.-041-332 9811.

Ellis, Laurence Edward, MA, AFIMA. Rector, The Edinburgh Academy, since 1977; b. 21.4.32, Great Yarmouth; m., Elizabeth Ogilvie; 2 s.; 1 d.

Educ. Winchester College; Trinity College, Cambridge. National Service, Rifle Brigade, 1950-52 (2nd Lt.); Assistant Master and Housemaster, Marlborough College, 1955-77. Reader, Church of England; Co-author, SMP Mathematics texts; article in Dictionary of National Biography on A.L.F. Smith. Recreations: music; reading; crosswords; woodwork. Address: (h.) 50 Inverleith Place, Edinburgh, 3.

Ellis, Richard Tunstall, OBE, DL, MA, LLB. Director and Chairman, TSB Scotland plc, since 1986; Director, TSB Group plc, since 1986; Chairman and Trustee, Trustee Savings Bank Scotland, 1983-86; Chairman, TSB Group Pension Trust Ltd., since 1976; b. 6.9.18, Liverpool; m., Jean Bruce Maitland Porter (see Jean B.M. Ellis); 2 s.; 2 d. Educ. Merchant Taylors School, Crosby; Silcoates School, Wakefield; Aberdeen University. Captain, Royal Signals, 1939-45 (POW, Germany); Chairman of Governors, Dunfermline College of Physical Education, 1964-67; Governor, Aberdeen College of Education, 1969-75; Member: Scottish Board, Norwich Union Insurance Society, 1973-80, Aberdeen Board, Bank of Scotland, 1972-82, Aberdeen University Court, since 1984, Council, National Trust for Scotland, since 1984; Chairman, Aberdeen Branch, Institute of Directors, 1983-87. Recreations: golf; hill-walking; skiing. Address: (h.) 18 Rubislaw Den North, Aberdeen, AB2 4AN; T.-0224 316680; (b.) 0224 640471.

Elvidge, John William, BA (Oxon). Assistant Secretary, Scottish Office Housing Division; b. 9.2.51, Edmonton, Middlesex. Educ. Sir George Monoux School, Walthamstow; St. Catherine's College, Oxford. Recreations: appreciating other people's creativity; observing other people's politics. Address: (b.) Room 417, St. Andrews House, Edinburgh, EH1; T.-031-244 2231.

Emmanuel, Professor Clive Robert, BSc (Econ), MA, PhD, ACIS. Arthur Young Professor of Accounting, Glasgow University; b. 23.5.47; m.; 1 s.; 2 d. Educ. UWIST; Lancaster University; UCW, Aberystwyth. Steel Company of Wales, Port Talbot, 1964-68; Lecturer, Lancaster University, 1974-78; Senior Lecturer, then Reader, UCW, Aberystwyth, 1978-87; Associate Professor, University of Kansas, 1980-82. Address: (b.) Department of Accounting and Finance, Glasgow University, Glasgow.

Emond, William John, BSc, FIMA, FSS. Vice Principal, Dundee College of Technology, since 1985; b. 23.8.42, Bellshill; m., Helen Catherine Elliott; 1 s.; 2 d. Educ. Allan Glen's School; Strathclyde University. Lecturer, then Senior Lecturer, polytechnics in England; former Head, Department of Mathematics and Computer Studies, Dundee College of Technology; Member, General Teaching Council; Member, SCOTVEC; Member, SCRE. Past Chairman: Alyth Musical Society, Perthshire Youth Brass Association. Recreations: golf; curling; choral singing. Address: (h.) Kinbrae, Alyth, Perth, PH11 8ES; T.-08283 2446.

Emslie, Rt. Hon. Lord (George Carlyle), MBE, PC, LLD, FRSE. Lord Justice General of Scotland, since 1972; Lord President of the Court of Session, since 1972; b. 6.12.19, Glasgow; m., Lilias Ann Mailer Hannington; 3 s. Educ. High School of Glasgow; Glasgow University. Commissioned A. & S.H., 1940; served War of 1939-45 (Despatches), North Africa, Italy, Greece, Austria, 1942-46; p.s.c. Haifa, 1944; Brigade Major (Infantry), 1944-46; Advocate, 1948; Advocate-Depute (Sheriff Courts), 1955; QC (Scotland), 1957; Sheriff of Perth and Angus, 1963-66; Dean, Faculty of Advcoates, 1965-70; Senator of the College of Justice, 1970-72; Chairman, Scottish Agricultural Wages Board, 1969-73; Member, Council on Tribunals (Scottish Committee), 1962-70; Hon. Bencher, Inner Temple, 1974, and Inn of Court of N. Ireland, 1981; PC, 1972; Baron (Life Peer), created 1980. Recreation: golf. Address: (h.) 47 Heriot Row, Edinburgh, EH3 6EX; T.-031-225 3657.

Emslie, John Frederick. Member, Kincardine and Deeside District Council, since 1980 (Chairman, Planning Committee, since 1984); Chairman, Kincardine and Deeside Tourist Board, since 1985; Electrical Contractor, since 1952; b. 27.6.29, Stonehaven; m., Alice Moira Christie; 2 s.; 2 d. Educ. Mackie Academy, Stonehaven. Served apprenticeship, 1945-50; National Service, 1950-52; began own business, 1952. Chairman, Kincardine and Deeside Recreation Grounds Trustees, since 1981; Deputy Provincial Grand Master, Masonic Order. Recreations: golf; swimming; cycling; walking. Address: 11-13 Ann Street, Stonehaven; T.-Stonehaven 62417.

Emslie-Smith, Donald, MD (Hons), ChB, FRCP, FRCPEdin. Reader in Medicine, Dundee University, since 1971 (Head, Department of Medicine, 1986-87); Honorary Consultant Physician (Cardiologist), Tayside Health Board, since 1961; b. 12.4.22, Aberdeen; m., Ann Elizabeth Milne; 1 s.; 1 d. Educ. Trinity College, Glenalmond; Aberdeen University. House Physician, Aberdeen Royal Infirmary; RAFVR (Medical Branch), UK and Middle East; Registrar in Cardiology, Dundee Royal Infirmary; Edward Wilson Memorial Research Fellow, Baker Institute, Melbourne; Tutor and Senior Registrar in Medicine, Royal Postgraduate Medical School and Hammersmith Hospital, London; Senior Lecturer in Medicine, St. Andrews University. Council Member, Association of Physicians of Great Britain and Ireland, 1977-80; Chairman, British Cardiac Society, 1987; President, Harveian Society of Edinburgh, 1986-87, Harveian Orator, 1987. Publications: Textbook of Physiology (Co-author and Editor) (11th edition, 1988); Accidental Hypothermia, 1977. Recreations: fly-fishing; dinghy-sailing; music. Address: (b.) University Department of Medicine, Ninewells Hospital and Medical School, Dundee, DD1 9SY; T.-0382 60111.

English, Peter Roderick, BSc (Hons), NDA (Hons), PhD. Senior Lecturer in Animal Husbandry, Aberdeen University; b. 9.3.37, Glen Urquhart, Inverness-shire; m., Anne Dunlop Mackay; 2 s.; 1 d. Educ. Balnain Public School; Arnisdale School; Glen Urquhart Senior Secondary School; Inverness Royal Academy; Aberdeen University. Farm Manager; Aberdeen University: Assistant Lecturer, Research Fellow, Lecturer. Won David Black Award, 1984, for major contribution to British pig industry. Publications: The

Sow - Improving Her Efficiency; Glen Urquhart. Recreations: athletics; shinty (first Editor, Shinty Yearbook); writing; travel; hard labour. Address: (h.) Arnisdale, 13 Fintray Road, Aberdeen, AB1 8HL; T.-Aberdeen 319306.

Entwistle, Professor Noel James, BSc, PGCE, PhD, FBPsS. Bell Professor of Education, Edinburgh University, since 1978; Director, Godfrey Thomson Unit for Educational Research, since 1978; b. 26.12.36, Bolton; m., Dorothy Bocking; 1 d. Educ. King's School, Ely; Sheffield University; Aberdeen University. Teacher, Rossall School, Fleetwood, 1961-64; Research Fellow, Aberdeen University, 1964-68; Department of Educational Research, Lancaster University: Lecturer, 1968, Senior Lecturer, 1971, Professor, 1972. Editor, British Journal of Educational Psychology, 1975-79; Governor, St. Margaret's School, Edinburgh; Chairman, Innovation, Research and Development Committee, Microelectronics in Education Committee. Recreations: reading; walking; golf. Address: (b.) 10 Buccleuch Place, Edinburgh, EH8 9JT; T.-031-667 1011.

Erickson, Professor John, MA, FRSE, FBA. Director of Defence Studies, Edinburgh University, since 1967; b. 17.4.29, South Shields; m., Ljubica; 1 s.; 1 d. Educ. South Shields High School; St. John's College, Cambridge. Research Fellow, St. Antony's College, Oxford; Lecturer, Department of History, St. Andrews University; Lecturer/Reader, Department of Government, Manchester University; Reader/Professor, Defence Studies, Edinburgh University. President, Association of Civil Defence and Emergency Planning Officers, until 1984; Visiting Professor, Yale University, 1987. Publications: The Soviet High Command, 1962; The Road to Stalingrad, 1975; The Road to Berlin, 1984; Soviet Ground Forces, An Operational Assessment, 1986. Recreation: model-making. Address: (b.) 31 Buccleuch Place, Edinburgh; T.-031-667 1011.

Erskine, Donald Seymour, DL, FRICS. Factor and Director of Estates, National Trust for Scotland, since 1961; b. 28.5.25, London; m., Catharine Annandale McLelland; 1 s.; 4 d. Educ. Wellington College. RA (Airborne), 1943-47 (Captain); Pupil, Drumlanrig Estate, 1947-49; Factor, Country Gentlemen's Association, Edinburgh, 1950-55; Factor to Mr A.L.P.F. Wallace, 1955-61. Member, Queen's Bodyguard for Scotland (Royal Company of Archers); Deputy Lieutenant, Perth and Kinross; Elder, Church of Scotland. Recreations: shooting; singing. Address: (h.) Cleish House, Cleish, Kinross-shire; T.-057 75 232.

Erskine, Sir (Thomas) David, 5th Bt, JP. Vice Lord-Lieutenant, Fife Region, since 1981; b. 31.7.12; m.; 2 s.; 1 d. (deceased). Educ. Eton; Magdalene College, Cambridge. Retired Major, Indian Corps of Engineers; Convener, Fife County Council, 1970-73; DL, Fife, 1955-81.

Erskine-Hill, Sir Robert, 2nd Bt. Chairman, Life Association of Scotland, 1960-86; b. 6.2.17; m.; 2 s.; 2 d. Educ. Eton; Trinity College, Cambridge. RNVR, 1939-45; Partner, Chiene & Tait, CA, 1946-80; Member, Queen's Bodyguard for Scotland (Royal Company of Archers).

Espley, Arthur James, MB, ChB, DObstRCOG, FRCSEdin. Consultant Orthopaedic Surgeon, Bridge of Earn Hospital, since 1981; Honorary Senior Lecturer, Department of Orthopaedic and Traumatic Surgery, Dundee University, since 1981; b. 19.2.44, Southend; m., Erica Strang, 1 s.; 1 d. Educ. Belfast Royal Academy; Edinburgh University (Rugby Blue, 1968). Member, Scottish and British Universities Rugby XV, 1968; Surgeon Lt. Commander, RNR, 1978. Chairman, Medical Staff Society, Perth Royal Infirmary. Recreations: golf; gardening; curling. Address: (h.) Couttie Bridge Cottage, Coupar Angus, PH13 9HF; T.-0828 27301.

Essery, David James. Under Secretary, Department of Agriculture and Fisheries for Scotland, since 1985; b. 10.5.38, Greenock; m., Nora Loughlin Sim; 2 s.; 1 d. Educ. Royal High School, Edinburgh. Entered Department of Health for Scotland, 1956; Private Secretary to Minister of State, Scottish Office, 1968-69; Principal, Scottish Development Department, 1969-76; Assistant Secretary, Scottish Economic Planning Department, 1976-81, Scottish Development Department, 1981-85. Recreations: reading; music; cricket; squash. Address: (b.) Chesser House, 500 Gorgie Road, Edinburgh; T.-031-443 4020.

Eunson, Edwin Russell, OBE (1986), KFO, JP. Convener, Orkney Islands Council, since 1978 (Chairman, Policy and Resources Committee, since 1978); b. 25.12.17, Kirkwall; m., Margaret Ross Nicolson. Educ. Kirkwall Grammar School. Member, Kirkwall Town Council, 1947-68 (Dean of Guild, 1955, Treasurer, 1955-57, Bailie, 1957-68); Member, Orkney County Council, 1947-55; Member, Orkney Islands Council, since 1974 (Chairman: Development, Planning and Control Committee, 1974-77, Social Work and Environmental Health Committee, 1977-78); Member: Highlands and Islands Development Consultative Council; Scottish Council (Development and Industry) Executive Committee, 1974-87; Chairman, Orkney Committee for Employment of Disabled Persons; Member, Policy Committee, COSLA; Session Clerk, Kirkwall East Church, 1955-87; Chairman: Orkney Liberal Association, 1962-78, Orkney Council of Social Service, 1968-74, Kirkwall Chamber of Commerce, 1970-72; Commander, Royal Norwegian Order of Merit. Recreations: reading; walking dogs. Address: (h.) Newhallea, Glaitness Road, Kirkwall, Orkney; T.-0856 3367.

Evans, Charles, CEng, MIMechE, MIRTE. Chief Executive and Managing Director, Lothian Regional Transport plc, since 1986 (Director of Public Transport, Lothian Regional Council, 1978-86); Chairman, Bus and Coach Council - Scotland; b. 30.8.37, Chadderton, Lancashire; m., Cherie; 3 s.; 1 d. Educ. North Chadderton Secondary Modern School; Oldham Technical College. Apprentice Engineer/Engineer, Oldham Corporation Passenger Transport, 1952-63; Assistant Engineer, Manchester Corporation, 1963-65; Edinburgh Corporation: Assistant Chief Engineer, 1965-71, Chief Engineer, 1971-75; Depute Director, Lothian Regional Council, 1975-78. President, Bus and Coach Council, 1986-87. Recreations: golf; caravanning. Address: (b.) 14 Queen Street, Edinburgh, EH2 1JL; T.-031-554 4494.

Evans, Sheriff George James, MA, LLB. Sheriff of Glasgow and Strathkelvin, at Glasgow, since 1983; b. 16.7.44; m.; 2 d. Educ. Ardrossan Academy; Glasgow University; Edinburgh University. Advocate, 1973.

Evans, James, RD, JP, DL, BSc, CEng, FRINA, MIMechE. Managing Director, Eyemouth Boat Building Co. Ltd., since 1968; Chairman, Berwickshire District Council, since 1980; Chairman, Fishing Boat Builders Association, since 1979; b. 9.5.33, South Shields; m., Patricia Alexena Kerr; 1 s.; 2 d. Educ. Merchiston Castle School; Kings College, Durham. Apprenticeship, 1950-56; Royal Navy, 1956-58; YARD, 1958-63; UKAEA, 1963-68; RNR, 1956-80 (retired as Captain (E) RNR); Member, Eyemouth Burgh Council, 1972-75; Berwickshire County Council; Vice-Chairman and Finance Chairman, Berwickshire District Council, 1974-80; Member, Fishing Industry Safety Group; awarded Silver Medal, Nuclear Engineering Society, 1962; Hon ADC, The Queen, 1979-80; Deputy Lieutenant, Berwickshire, since 1978; Chairman, Berwick Freemen's Guild, since 1975. Address: (h.) Makore, Northburn View, Eyemouth, Berwickshire; T.-Eyemouth 50231.

Evans, Peter Geoffrey, BMus, ARCM. Freelance Pianist, Teacher and Conductor, since 1974; Member, Scottish Arts Council, since 1984; b. 13.1.50, Redhill, Surrey. Educ. Trinity School, Croydon; Edinburgh University; Hochschule fur Musik, Vienna. Solo piano recitals and performances in various duos and ensembles throughout Britain, as well as in West Germany, Austria, Japan, USA and USSR; frequent broadcasts, BBC Radio 3 and Radio Scotland and recordings for BBC TV, Scottish TV, French Radio, Swedish Radio, Hyperion Records; concerto appearances as soloist with all major professional orchestras in Scotland and National Youth Orchestra of Scotland; Principal Conductor and Co-Founder, Meadows Chamber Orchestra, Edinburgh; close association with the chamber music and masterclasses of Sandor Vegh's International Musicians' Seminar, Cornwall; Member, SAC Music Committee, since 1982. Recreations: theatre; films; tennis; golf. Address: (h.) 114 Comiston Road, Edinburgh, EH10 5QL; T.-031-447 6414.

Evans, Robin Anthony, BSc, MChemA, CChem, FRSC, AIFST. Public Analyst, Tayside Regional Council, since 1975; b. 23.8.39, Penarth, South Glamorganshire; m., Jennifer; 2 s.; 1 d. Educ. Penarth Grammar School; University College of South Wales and Monmouthshire, Cardiff. Assistant Analyst, Glamorgan County Council, 1961-70; Principal Assistant Analyst, Bristol Corporation, 1970-73; Public Analyst and Agricultural Analyst, Dundee Corporation, 1973-75. Recreations: golf and sport in general; hospital radio; media action; gardening. Address: (b.) 24 Mains Loan, Dundee, DD4 7AA; T.-0382 455909.

Evaristi, Marcella Silvia, MA (Hons). Writer/Actor; b. 19.7.53, Glasgow; m., Michael Boyd (qv). Educ. Notre Dame High School for Girls; Glasgow University. Playwright in residence, St. Andrews University, 1979-80; Fellowship in Creative Writing, Sheffield University, 1982-84; Writer in Residence, Glasgow and Strathclyde Universities, 1984-85; plays: Scotia's Darlings, Hard to Get, Wedding Belles and Green Grasses, Eve Set the Balls of Corruption Rolling, Commedia, Checking Out the Works, Terrestrial Extras, The Hat; revues: Sugar and Spite, Mouthpieces; Pye Award, best playwright new to television, 1982; Evening Standard Nomination, best new play (for Commedia), 1984-85. Recreation: cooking. Address: (h.) 14 Woodlands Drive, Glasgow, G4 9EH; T.-041-334 8237.

Eveling, Stanley, BA, BPhil. Playwright; retired University Teacher of Philosophy; University Fellow, Edinburgh University, since 1984; Television Critic, The Scotsman, since 1970; b. 4.8.25, Newcastle-upon-Tyne; m., Kate Howell; 2 s.; 2 d. Educ. Rutherford College, Newcastle-upon-Tyne; King's College, Newcastle; Lincoln College, Oxford. Usual drab academic life; writer of 26 plays for radio, TV and stage, some much travelled and still travelling, many produced for Edinburgh Festival and Traverse Theatre. Recreations: golf; tennis; computer studies. Address: (h.) 30 Comely Bank, Edinburgh, EH4 1AJ; T.-031-332 1905.

Everett, Robert Anthony, BA, BSc, CPhys, MInstP, AFIMA, ASTA. Headteacher, Fort Augustus Secondary School, since 1971; b. 5.6.31, Battle, Sussex; m., Christina Laird Hastings Brown; 3 s.; 2 d. Educ. St. Mary's Academy, Bathgate; Edinburgh University; Moray House College of Education; Open University. National Service, Royal Signals; Teacher of Science, Bathgate Academy; Principal Teacher of Science, Dornoch Academy; Principal Teacher of Physics: Camphill Senior Secondary School, Paisley, Galashiels Academy; Headteacher, Leverhulme Memorial Secondary School, Leverburgh, Isle of Harris. Sometime Secretary, Fort Augustus Village Council; Secretary, Fort Augustus/Glenmoriston Community Council; Past Chairman, Fort Augustus Royal British Legion (Scotland); Elder, Fort Augustus Church of Scotland. Recreation: swimming. Address: (h.) The Schoolhouse, Fort Augustus, Inverness-shire, PH32 4DR; T.-0320 6235.

Ewan, Edmund Alan, MA, DipEd, DPhil. Vice-Principal, Moray House College of Education, Edinburgh, since 1984; b. 30.10.31, Bridge of Earn; m., Elizabeth Miller Calder; 2 s. Educ. Perth Academy; St. Andrews University; Oxford University. Assistant Director of Education, Fife County Council, 1961-66; Head, Department of Educational Management and Administration, Moray House College of Education, 1967-84. Honorary Secretary, Scottish Association for Educational Management and Administration, 1972-81 (Vice-Chairman, since 1986); Honorary Secretary, British Educational Management and Administration Society, 1974-83. Recreation: hill-walking. Address: (b.) Moray House College of Education, Holyrood Road, Edinburgh, EH8 8AQ; T.-031-556 8455.

Ewen, Robert, OBE, TD, MA. Secretary of the University Court, Glasgow University, since 1985; b. 3.3.39, Clydebank; m., Eleanor Irene Grayson; 1 s.; 1 d. Educ. Inverness Royal Academy; Aberdeen University. Aberdeen University: Clerk, Faculty of Arts, 1964-73, Clerk, Senatus Academicus, 1973-79, Deputy Secretary, 1976-85.

Lt. Col., Royal Engineers (TA). Recreations: golf; squash; shooting; hill-walking. Address: (b.) University of Glasgow, Glasgow, G12 8QQ; T.-041-339 8855.

Ewing, David John, MA, MD, FRCPEdin. Wellcome Trust Senior Lecturer in Medicine, Edinburgh University, since 1980; Honorary Consultant Physician, Lothian Health Board; b. 27.8.40, London; m., E. Anne Bellamy; 2 d. Educ. Dulwich College; Jesus College, Cambridge; Guy's Hospital, London. Former Lecturer in Medicine, Edinburgh University. Recreations: reading; walking; cathedral and church architecture. Address: (b.) Department of Medicine, Royal Infirmary, Edinburgh, EH3 9YW.

Ewing, Harry. MP (Labour), Falkirk East, since 1983 (Stirling and Falkirk, 1971-74, Stirling, Falkirk and Grangemouth, 1974-83); b. 20.1.31; m.; 1 s.; 1 d. Educ. Beath High School, Cowdenbeath. Under Secretary of State, Scottish Office, 1974-79.

Ewing, Margaret Anne, MA, BA (Hons). MP (Moray), since 1987; Parliamentary Leader and Vice President, SNP, since 1987; b. 1.9.45, Lanark; m., Fergus Stewart Ewing. Educ. Biggar High School; Glasgow University; Strathclyde University; Jordanhill College. Schoolteacher, 1968-74 (Principal Teacher of Remedial Education, St. Modan's, Stirling, 1972-74); SNP MP (East Dunbartonshire), 1974-79; Freelance Journalist, 1979-81; Co-ordinator, West of Scotland CSS Scheme, 1981-87. Recreations: grdening; reading; arts in general. Address: (h.) 22 Kinneddar Street, Lossiemouth, Moray; T.-034381 2287.

Ewing, Winifred Margaret, MA, LLB, NP. Member (SNP), European Parliament, since 1975; President, Scottish National Party; b. 10.7.29, Glasgow; m., Stewart Martin Ewing; 2 s.; 1 d. Educ. Queen's Park School; Glasgow University. Solicitor, since 1952; former Secretary and President, Glasgow Bar Association; President, Soroptimist Club (Glasgow), 1966; MP (SNP), Hamilton, 1967-70, Moray and Nairn, 1974-79; first Vice President of Group (European Democratic Alliance) in European Parliament. Recreations: walking; reading; painting; swimming. Address: (h.) Goodwill, Lossiemouth, Morayshire.

F

Fagan, Ken. President, COSLA, 1986-88; Leader, City of Dundee District Council, 1982-86; Deputy Chairman, British Sections, IULA/CEMR; b. 5.5.44, Perth; m., Joan; 2 s.; 2 d. Educ. Perth Academy; Dundee College of Technology (Diploma, Management Studies). Dundee District Council: elected, 1977, City Treasurer, 1980-82. Executive Member, Scottish Labour Party, 1982-84; Member, Labour Party NEC Local Government Sub-Committee. Address: (b.) City Chambers, Dundee; T.-Dundee 23141.

Fair, James Stuart, MA, LLB, WS, NP. Solicitor; Senior Partner, Thornton Oliver, WS, Dundee; Honorary Sheriff; Lecturer in Taxation, Dundee University; Clerk, Commissioners of Inland Revenue (Dundee District); Director of private investment trust companies; b. 30.9.30, Perth; m., Anne Lesley Cameron; 2 s.; 1 d. Educ. Perth Academy; St. Andrews University; Edinburgh University. Member: Dundee Port Authority, Dundee University Court, Tayside Health Board; Past President, Dundee and Tayside Chamber of Commerce & Industry; Chairman, Review Committee, Perth Prison; Member, Scottish Solicitors' Discipline Tribunal, 1978-88; former Council Member, Society of Writers to Her Majesty's Signet. President, Dundee Choral Union. Address: (h.) Beechgrove House, 474 Perth Road, Dundee, DD2 1LL.

Fairbairn of Fordell, Sir Nicholas Hardwick, QC, KLJ, KOSJ, KPR, FSA(Scot), MA, LLB. MP (Conservative), Perth and Kinross, since 1983; Queen's Counsel, since 1972; b. 24.12.33, Edinburgh; m., Suzanne Mary Wheeler; 3 d. Educ. Loretto; Edinburgh University. Called to the Scots Bar, 1957; MP, Kinross and West Perthshire, 1974-83; Solicitor General, 1979-82; Commissioner of Northern Lighthouses, 1979-82. Honorary President and Founder: Society for Preservation of Duddingston, Edinburgh Brook Advisory Centre; Honorary President, Dysart and Dundonald Pipe Band; Trustee, Royal Museums of Scotland; Vice President, Society of Scottish Women Artists. Publications: Alastair MacLean's Scotland (Contributor); A Life is Too Short. Recreations: painting; broadcasting. Address: (h.) Fordell Castle, by Dunfermline, Fife.

Fairgrieve, Brian David, OBE, DL, MB, ChB, FRCSEd. General Surgeon, Falkirk Royal Infirmary, 1960-87; Deputy Lieutenant, Falkirk and Stirling Districts; b. 21.2.27, Glasgow. Educ. Glasgow Academy; Glasgow University. RMO, 2/6th Gurkha Rifles, 1952-54; initial medical training, Western Infirmary, Glasgow, Stobhill General Hospital, Killearn Hospital; Area Scout Commissioner, 21 years; Senior Vice President, Falkirk Rotary Club; Lecturer and Examiner, Scottish Police College; Member, Council, St. Andrew's Ambulance Association; Director, Incorporated Glasgow Stirlingshire & Sons of the Rock Society; Hon. Vice President, Grangemouth Rugby Club; awarded Silver Wolf, 1983, and OBE, 1986, for services to Scouting. Recreations: photography; travel. Address: (h.) 19 Lyall Crescent, Polmont, Falkirk, FK2 0PL; T.-0324 715449.

Fairgrieve, James Hanratty, DA, ARSA, RSW. Painter; Lecturer in Drawing and Painting, Edinburgh College of Art, since 1968; b. 17.6.44, Prestonpans; m., Margaret D. Ross; 2 s.; 1 d. Educ. Preston Lodge Senior Secondary School; Edinburgh College of Art. Postgraduate study, 1966-67; Travelling Scholarship, Italy, 1968; President, SSA, 1978-82; exhibited in Britain and Europe, since 1966. Recreation: angling. Address: (h.) Burnbrae, Gordon, Berwickshire; T.-Gordon 357.

Fairgrieve, Sir (Thomas) Russell, CBE, TD, JP. Chairman, Crawford Halls Partnership, Edinburgh; Director, William Baird & Co., PLC, since 1975; Director, Bain Dawes (Scotland) Ltd., Edinburgh, since 1984; b. 3.5.24, Galashiels; m., Millie Mitchell; 1 s.; 3 d. Educ. St. Mary's School, Melrose; Sedbergh School, Yorkshire. Commissioned, 8th Gurkha Rifles (Indian Army), 1943; Company Commander, 1/8th Gurkha Rifles, 1944-46 (Burma, Malaya and Java); TA, 4th KOSB, 1947-63 (Major). Director, Laidlaw & Fairgrieve Ltd., 1953-68 (Managing Director, 1958-68); Director, Dawson International PLC, 1961-73 (Group Yarn Sales Director, 1965-68); Chairman, Scottish Young Conservatives, 1950-51; President, Scottish Conservative Association, 1965-66; MP, Aberdeenshire West, 1974-83; Chairman, Scottish Conservative Group for Europe, 1974-78; Scottish Conservative Whip, 1975; Chairman, Scottish Conservative Party, 1975-80; Under-Secretary of State for Scotland, 1979-81; Member, Consultative Assembly, Council of Europe and WEU, 1982-83. Address: (h.) Pankalan, Bolside, Galashiels; T.-0896 2278.

Fairlie of Myres, David Ogilvy, MBE. Landowner; Chairman, East Fife Branch, Arthritis and Rheumatism Council; b. 1.10.23, Edinburgh. Educ. Ampleforth College, York; Oriel College, Oxford. Officer, Royal Signals, Europe, Ceylon, Singapore, Java, Malaya, Korea, SHAPE Paris; retired, 1959; former Cupar District Commissioner and Fife Area Commissioner for Scouts; awarded Silver Acorn and Silver Wolf; DL, Fife; JP; Member, Queen's Bodyguard for Scotland; Knight of the Holy Sepulchre of Jerusalem. Publication: Fairlie of that Ilk. Recreations: genealogy; photography; walking; shooting; gardening; beekeeping. Address: Myres Castle, Auchtermuchty, Cupar, Fife, KY14 7EW.

Fairrie, Lt. Col. Adam Angus. Regimental Secretary, Queen's Own Highlanders, since 1978; b. 9.12.34, Bromborough; m., Elizabeth Rachel Pryor; 1 s.; 1 d. Educ. Stowe; Royal Military Academy, Sandhurst. Commissioned, Queen's Own Cameron Highlanders, 1955; to Queen's Own Highlanders, 1961; Staff College, Camberley, 1966; National Defence College, Latimer, 1973-74; Commanding Officer 1st Bn. Queen's Own Highlanders, 1974-77. Publication: Cuidich 'n Righ (a history of the Queen's Own Highlanders). Address: (b.) RHQ, Queen's Own Highlanders, Cameron Barracks, Inverness; T.-Inverness 224380.

Fairweather, Andrew Burton, TD, BA, MBIM. Director of Office Management, Scottish Office, since 1982; b. 26.2.31, Edinburgh; m., Elizabeth Brown; 3 s. Educ. Royal High School, Edinburgh; Edinburgh University; Open University. Clerical Officer, HM Customs and Excise, 1949; Executive Officer: Accountant of Court for Scotland, 1949, Department of Health for Scotland, 1951 (Secretary, Scottish Medical Practices Committee, 1954-58); Higher Executive Officer, Department of Health for Scotland and Scottish Development Department, 1958; Senior Executive Officer, Scottish Development Department, 1965 (Secretary, Rent Assessment Panel for Scotland, 1965-67); Principal: Chief Administrative Officer, Civil Service College, Edinburgh, 1970, Scottish Economic Planning Department, 1972, Scottish Development Department, 1974 (Secretary, Local Government Staff and Property Commissions, 1974-77), Scottish Office Central Services, 1981; Senior Principal, Scottish Office Central Services, 1982. Rifle Brigade, RAEC; Royal Scots (TA) and Royal Corps of Transport (TA); Commanding Officer, 495 Liaison Unit (BAOR), Royal Corps of Transport (TA), 1977-81; Colonel, Regular Army Reserve of Officers, 1982. Address: (h.) 127 Silverknowes Gardens, Edinburgh.

Falconer, Allan Leslie. Chairman and Managing Director, Tyock Development Co. Ltd., since 1962; Honorary Sheriff, since 1974; b. 1.6.10, Elgin; m., Margaret Mackenzie Fraser; 3 d. Educ. Elgin Academy; Edinburgh University. Major, Seaforth Highlanders; Recreations: golf; curling; bowling. Address: (h.) 10 Pond Park Place, New Elgin, Elgin; T.-Elgin 84262.

Falconer, Ian McLeod, BSc, CEng, MICE. Buildings Officer, Dundee University, since 1979; b. 21.7.31, Aberdeen; m., Brenda; 2 s.; 1 d. Educ. Aberdeen Academy; Aberdeen University. Worked in hydro-electric, building and civil engineering contracting throughout Scotland until 1979; commissioned in Royal Engineers during National Service, 1956; appointed Specialist Adviser, House of Commons Committee on Scottish Affairs, 1982, for inquiry into dampness in housing. Recreations: swimming; golf; Rotary; reading. Address: (b.) The University, Dundee; T.-0382 23181.

Fallon, Ronald John, BSc, MD, FRCPath, FRCPGlas. Consultant in Laboratory Medicine, Ruchill Hospital, Glasgow, since 1961; Honorary Lecturer in Bacteriology, Immunology and Infectious Diseases, Glasgow University, since 1961; b. 1.2.28, Wallasey; m., Valerie Frances Kirkham; 4 d. Educ. Wallasey Grammar School; Liverpool University. Temporary Assistant Lecturer in Bacteriology, Liverpool University, 1953-55; Junior Bacteriologist, Royal Naval Hospital, Plymouth, 1955-57; Lecturer in Bacteriology, Glasgow University, 1957-61. Member: Advisory Committee on Dangerous Pathogens, Microbiological Advisory Committee DHSS; Member, Microbiology Sub-Committee, Scientific Services Advisory Group, Scottish Health Services Council; Past Chairman, Scottish Branch, British Society for the Study of Infection; Past Chairman, Central Sterilising Club. Recreations: singing; country dancing; gardening. Address: (b.) Department of Laboratory Medicine, Ruchill Hospital, Glasgow; T.-041-946 7120.

Fargus, Brian Alfred, OBE, DL; b. 3.1.18, Ollerton; m., Shiona Margaret Lay MacKichan; 1 s.; 1 d. Educ. Cargilfield; Rugby; Royal Military College, Sandhurst; Staff College, Camberley. Commissioned The Royal Scots, 1938; served Hong Kong, 1938-41, and North West Europe - Adjutant, 8th Bn., The Royal Scots, 1944-45; C.O. Depot The Royal Scots, 1957-59; Senior Intelligence Officer, Middle East Command, 1966-67; Colonel General Staff, HQ Scotland, 1968-70; Military Attache, British Embassy, Pretoria, 1971-72; Assistant Regimental Secretary, then Regimental Secretary, The Royal Scots, 1973-83.

Recreations: golf; gardening; fishing. Address: St. Arvans, Nisbet Road, Gullane, East Lothian, EH31 2BU; T.-0620 84 2440.

Farquhar, Charles Don Petrie, JP, DL. Area Manager, Community Industry, since 1972; Member, Dundee District Council, since 1974; b. 4.5.37, Dundee; m., Mary Martin Gardiner; 2 d. Educ. Stobswell Secondary School; Dundee Trades College; NCLC. Time-served engineer; elected Dundee Corporation, 1965; former Magistrate and Chairman of various Committees; served Royal Engineers (TRG NCO); Supervisory Staff, Plant Engineering Division, NCR; elected Dundee District Council, 1974; Lord Provost and Lord Lieutenant, City of Dundee District, 1975-77; Chairman, District Licensing Board and District Licensing Committee; Chairman, Tayside Committee for Employment of Disabled People. Recreations: fresh-water angling; numismatics; DIY; pool; golf. Address: (h.) 15 Sutherland Crescent, Dundee, DD2 2HP.

Farquhar, William John, MA, DSA, FHSM. Secretary, Scottish Health Service Planning Council, since 1985; Director, Planning Unit, Scottish Home and Health Department, since 1987; b. 29.5.35, Maud, Aberdeenshire; m., Isabel Henderson Rusk; 4 s. Educ. Peterhead Academy; Aberdeen University; Manchester University. National Administrative Trainee, Scottish Health Service; Hospital Secretary, Whitehaven Hospital, Cumberland; Deputy Secretary and Treasurer, West Cumberland Hospital Management Committee; Regional Staff Officer, South-Eastern Regional Hospital Board; Deputy Secretary, Eastern Regional Hospital Board; Lothian Health Board: District Administrator, South Lothian District, then Administrator, Operational Services. Council of Europe Medical Fellowship, 1988. Recreations: gardening; walking. Address: (h.) Craigengar, 7 Harelaw Road, Colinton, Edinburgh, EH13 0DR; T.-031-441 2169.

Farquharson, Captain Colin Andrew, JP, DL, FRICS. Lord Lieutenant of Aberdeenshire, since 1987; Chartered Surveyor and Land Agent, since 1953; Member, Grampian Health Board, since 1981; Director, MacRobert Farms (Douneside), 1971-87; b. 9.8.23; m., 1, Jean Sybil Mary Hamilton (deceased); 2 d.; 1 d. deceased; 2, Clodagh, JP, DL, widow of Major Ian Houldsworth of Dallas, Morayshire. Educ. Rugby. Grenadier Guards, 1942-48; ADC to Field Marshal Sir Harald Alexander (Earl Alexander of Tunis), 1942-48; Member, Board of Management, Royal Cornhill Hospitals, 1962-74; Chairman, Gordon Local Health Council, 1975-78; DL, Aberdeenshire, 1966; Vice Lord Lieutenant, Aberdeenshire, 1983-87; Member, Queen's Bodyguard for Scotland (Royal Company of Archers), since 1964. Recreations: shooting; fishing; farming. Address: Whitehouse, Alford, Aberdeenshire.

Farquharson, Gordon Alexander, MA, DipEd. Head Teacher, Tobermory High School, since 1984; b. 7.2.42, Dumfries; m., Elizabeth M. Naismith; 1 s. Educ. Dumfries Academy; Edinburgh University; Moray House College of Education. Teacher of English, Dumfries Academy, 1966-70; Assistant Principal Teacher of English, Queen Anne High School, Dunfermline, 1970-72; Principal Teacher of English, Dunoon Grammar School, 1972-84. Elder, Church of Scotland; Director, Mull Little Theatre. Recreations: drama; choral singing. Address: (h.) Avoch, Western Road, Tobermory, Isle of Mull; T.-0688 2405.

Farrell, Sheriff James Aloysius, MA, LLB. Sheriff of Lothian and Borders, at Edinburgh, since 1986 (Glasgow and Strathkelvin, 1984-86); b. 14.5.43; m.; 2 d. Educ. St. Aloysius College; Glasgow University; Dundee University. Admitted, Faculty of Advocates, 1974; Advocate-Depute, 1979-83.

Farrow, Robert Henry, FIHT. Member, Highland Regional Council; b. 19.2.23, London; 2 d. Educ. Battersea Polytechnic. War Service, Royal Navy; local politics, Somerset (sometime Chairman, Somerset County Council SE Area Planning Committee); Mayor of Chard, 1973-74 and 1974-75; Member: CBI Northern Committee, Highlands and Islands Fire Board; Chairman, Nairn Divisional Planning Committee; Liveryman, City of London, Worshipful Company of Paviors; Council Member, North of Scotland Branch, Institution of Highways and Transportation. Recreations: golf; dramatics; local government service; Rotarian. Address: (h.) 5 Rowan Place, Nairn, 1V12 4TL; T.-Nairn 52809.

Farry, James. Secretary, The Scottish Football League, since 1979; b. 1.7.54, Glasgow; m., Elaine Margaret; 1 s.; 1 d. Educ. Queens Park Secondary School; Hunter High School; Claremont High School. Recreations: occasional fishing; regular spectating football matches. Address: (b.) 188 West Regent Street, Glasgow, G2 4RY; T.-041-248 3844.

Fasken, Robert Alexander, CBE. Governor, Eden Court Theatre, Inverness; Honorary Vice-President, Scottish Youth Hostels Association; b. 5.11.22, Edinburgh; m., Nancy Blanch; 1 s. Educ. George Watson's College. Department of Agriculture and Fisheries for Scotland, 1939-65; Secretary, Advisory Panel on Highlands and Islands, 1961-65; Secretary, Highlands and Islands Development Board, 1965-75; Member, HIDB, 1975-84; Chairman, Highlands and Islands Tourism Council, 1976-84; Member, Scottish Tourist Board, 1975-84. Recreations: reading; chess; gardening. Address: (h.) 79 Stratherrick Road, Inverness, IV2 4LL; T.-0463 233378.

Faulkner, Professor Douglas, WhSch, PhD, RCNC, FEng, FRINA, FIStructE, FRSA. Professor and Head, Department of Naval Architecture and Ocean Engineering, Glasgow University; b. 29.12.29, Gibraltar; m., Isobel Parker Campbell; 3 d. Educ. Sutton High School, Plymouth; HM Dockyard Technical College, Devonport; Royal Naval College, Greenwich. Aircraft carrier design, 1955-57; production engineering, 1957-59; structural research, NCRE Dunfermline, 1959-63; Assistant Professor of Naval Construction, RNC, Greenwich, 1963-66; Structural Adviser to Ship Department, Bath, 1966-68; Naval Construction Officer attached to British Embassy, Washington DC, 1968-70; Member, Ship Research Committee, National Academy of Sciences, 1968-71; Research Associate and Defence Fellow, MIT, 1970-71; Structural Adviser, Ship Department, Bath, and Merrison Box Girder Bridge

Committee, 1971-73; UK Representative, Standing Committee, International Ship Structures Congress, 1973-85; Member, Marine Technology Board, Defence Scientific Advisory Council; Head, Department of Naval Architecture and Ocean Engineering, Glasgow University, since 1973. Recreations: hill-walking; music; chess; GO. Address: (h.) 57 Bellshaugh Place, Glasgow, G12 OPF; T.-041-330 4303.

Fawkes, Rev. George Miller Allan, BA, BSc. Minister, Lonmay linked with Rathen West, since 1979; b. 20.3.35, Glasgow; m., Beatrice B.A. Forbes; 1 s.; 1 d. Educ. Irvine Royal Academy; Glasgow University; Open University; Aberdeen University. FSS, 1961-71; MInstP, 1976-80. Statistician, Pilkington Bros., St. Helens, 1957-58; Education Officer, RAF, 1958-61; Statistician, Stewarts and Lloyds, Clydesdale Works, 1961-64; Lecturer, Inverness Technical College, 1964-77. Buchan Presbytery: Moderator, 1986-88, Convener, Maintenance of the Ministry Committee, 1984-88; Chaplain, Buchan Division, Girls' Brigade, 1985-86. Recreations: reading; family history; relationship between religion and science. Address: The Manse, Lonmay, Fraserburgh, AB4 4UJ; T.-0346 32227.

Fenton, Alexander, CBE, MA, BA, DLitt, FRSE, FSA, FSA Scot. Director, National Museum of Antiquities of Scotland, since 1978; Research Director, National Museums of Scotland, since 1985; b. 26.6.29, Shotts; m., Evelyn Elizabeth Hunter; 2 d. Educ. Turriff Academy; Aberdeen University; Cambridge University. Senior Assistant Editor, Scottish National Dictionary, 1955-59; part-time Lecturer, English as a Foreign Language, Edinburgh University, 1958-60; National Museum of Antiquities of Scotland: Assistant Keeper, 1959-75, Deputy Keeper, 1975-78; part-time Lecturer, Department of Scottish History, Edinburgh University, since 1974; Honorary Fellow, School of Scottish Studies, since 1969; Foreign Member: Royal Gustav Adolf Academy, Sweden, since 1978, Royal Danish Academy of Sciences and Letters, since 1979; Honorary Member: Volkskundliche Kommission fur Westfalen, since 1980, Hungarian Ethnographical Society, since 1983; Jury Member, Europa Prize for Folk Art, since 1975; President, Permanent International Committee, International Secretariat for Research on the History of Agricultural Implements; Secretary, Permanently Standing Organising Board, European Ethnological Atlas; President, Scottish Vernacular Buildings Working Group; Secretary, Scottish Country Life Museums Trust; Secretary and Trustee, Friends of the Dictionary of the Older Scottish Tongue; Secretary, Scotland Inheritance Fund; Co-Editor: Tools and Tillage, since 1968, The Review of Scottish Culture, since 1984. Publications: The Various Names of Shetland, 1973, 1977; Scottish Country Life, 1976 (Scottish Arts Council Book Award); The Diary of a Parish Clerk (translation from Danish), 1976; The Island Blackhouse, A Guide to the Blackhouse at 42 Arnol, Lewis, 1978; A Farming Township, A Guide to Auchindrain, the Museum of Argyll Farming Life, 1978; The Northern Isles, Orkney and Shetland, 1978 (Dag Stromback Award); The Rural Architecture of Scotland (Co-author), 1981; The Shape of the Past 1, 1985; If All The World Were a Blackbird (translation from Hungarian), 1985; The Shape of the Past II, 1986; 'Wirds an' Wark 'e Seasons Roon on an Aberdeenshire Farm, 1987; Country Life in Scotland, Our Rural Past, 1987. Recreation: languages. Address: (b.) National Museums of Scotland, Queen Street, Edinburgh, EH2 1JD; T.-031-225 7534.

Fenton, Professor George Wallace, MB, FRCPEdin, FRCPsych, MRCP, DPM. Professor of Psychiatry, Dundee University, since 1983; Honorary Consultant Psychiatrist, Tayside Health Board, since 1983; b. 30.7.31, Londonderry; m.; 1 s. Educ. Ballymena Academy; Queen's University, Belfast. Lecturer, Academic Department of Psychiatry, Middlesex Hospital, 1964-66; Maudsley Hospital, London: Consultant Psychiatrist, 1967-75, Consultant in Charge, Epilepsy Unit, 1969-75, Consultant Neurophysiologist, 1968-75; Senior Lecturer, Institute of Psychiatry, London University, 1967-75; Professor of Mental Health, Queen's University, Belfast, 1976-83. Publications: Event Related Potentials in Personality and Psychopathology (Co-author), 1982; numerous papers on clinical neurophysiology and neuropsychiatry. Recreations: sailing; history; literature. Address: (b.) University Department of Psychiatry, Ninewells Hospital, Dundee, DD1 9SY; T.-Dundee 60111, Ext. 2121.

Fenwick, Hubert Walter Wandesford. Architectural Historian and Lecturer; b. 17.7.16, Glasgow. Educ. Huntley School, New Zealand; Royal Grammar School, Newcastle-upon-Tyne. Architectural student; qualified, 1950; office of Ian G. Lindsay, then Lorimer & Matthew, Edinburgh; gave up architectural career, 1958; RIBA Examiner for Scotland in History of Architecture, until post abolished; Assistant Secretary and PRO, Scottish Georgian Society, 1960-65; Council Member, Cockburn Association, 1966; Scottish Editor, Church Illustrated, 1959-64; Editor and Manager, Edinburgh Tatler and Glasgow Illustrated, 1966-67; regular contributor to Scots Magazine, 25 years, and other journals. Publications: Architect Royal; Auld Alliance; Scotland's Historic Buildings; Scotland's Castles; Chateaux of France; Scotland's Abbeys and Cathedrals; View of the Lowlands; Scottish Baronial Houses. Recreations: foreign travel; architectural history; sketching and photography (for own books and articles); gardening. Address: 15 Randolph Crescent, Edinburgh, 3; T.-031-225 7982.

Fenwick, Kenneth George, FIH. Director of Housing, Angus District Council, since 1987; Treasurer and Director, Forfar Athletic Football Club Ltd.; b. 28.7.38, Forfar; m., Marion Elizabeth Anderson; 3 s.; 1 step d. Educ. Forfar Academy; Dundee Technical College. Town Planning Assistant, Angus County Council, 1956-57 and 1960-62 (National Service, RAF, 1958-60); Housing Assistant, Glenrothes Development Corporation, 1962-65; Housing Manager, Selkirk Town Council, 1965-66; District Housing Officer, Glenrothes Development Corporation, 1966-67; Assistant Town Factor, then Town Factor, Forfar Town Council, 1967-75; Depute Director/Area Housing Manager, Angus District Council, 1975-76; Director of Housing, Glenrothes Development Corporation, 1976-82; Director of Housing, Kirkcaldy District Council, 1982-87. Recreations:

football; swimming; hill-walking; reading. Address: (b.) County Buildings, Forfar, Angus; T.-Forfar 65101.

Ferguson, Ian Alexander, ARIBA, ARIAS, FRTPI, AMBIM. City Architect, City of Aberdeen District Council, since 1975; b. 9.8.31, New Deer, Aberdeenshire; m., Grace; 2 d. Educ. Peterhead Academy; School of Architecture, Aberdeen; Edinburgh College of Art. City Architect's Department, Aberdeen, 1956-57, Perth, 1957-62; Depute Burgh Architect and Town Planning Officer, then Burgh Architect and Town Planning Officer, Falkirk, 1962-74; Director of Architectural Serices, Central Region, 1974-75. Recreations: bowling; gardening; caravanning. Address: St. Nicholas House, Broad Street, Aberdeen, AB9 1AX; T.-0224 642121.

Ferguson, James, ARCST, BSc, PhD, DSc, FRSC, CChem. Reader, Department of Chemistry and Head, Fibre and Textile Research Unit, Strathclyde University, since 1981; b. 30.3.35, Paisley; m., Jean Leslie; 2 s.; 2 d. Educ. Camphill Secondary School, Paisley; Glasgow University; Royal College of Science and Technology. Research Chemist, Shell Research, 1960-63; Lecturer in Textile Chemistry, Strathclyde University, 1963-76; Senior Lecturer, 1976-81; Consultant to UNIDO, 1985 and 1987. Deacon, Incorporation of Weavers of Glasgow, 1984-88; President, British Society of Rheology, 1988-90; Visiting Professor, Ohio University, 1988. Recreations: golf; travel. Address: 29 Limetree Crescent, Newton Mearns, Glasgow, G77 5BJ; T.-041-639 3405.

Ferguson, James Brown Provan, MB, ChB, DipSocMed, FFCM. Senior Medical Officer, Scottish Home and Health Department, since 1984; b. 23.10.35, Armadale; m., Sheila Capstick; 3 d. Educ. Bathgate Academy; Edinburgh University. Group Medical Superintendent, Edinburgh Northern Hospitals; District Medical Officer, North Lothian District, Lothian Health Board. Elder, Inverleith Church, Edinburgh. Recreations: art; reading; walking. Address: Scottish Home and Health Department, St. Andrews House, Edinburgh, EH1 3DE.

Ferguson, James Murray, BSc (Econ), MPhil, DipEd, FCIS, FBIM, FRSA, FSA Scot. Principal, Aberdeen College of Commerce, since 1982; b. 21.4.28, Almondbank, Perthshire; m., Moira McDougall; 2 d. Educ. Perth Academy; London University; Edinburgh University; Dundee University; Moray House College of Education. Military Service, 1946-79: full-time, Army Emergency Reserve, Territorials, T&AVR, Regular Army Reserve of Officers (final rank of Major); variety of business appointments, mainly in insurance, investment and finance, 1952-64; lectureships in range of management subjects, various higher educational establishments, 1965-76; Principal, Elmwood College, Fife, 1976-82. Governor: Further Education Staff College, Coombe Lodge, Bristol, 1982-87, Aberdeen College of Education, 1983-87. Recreations: sporting: badminton, tennis, hill-walking; non-sporting: reading, writing, public speaking, local history studies. Address: (h.) 45 Desswood Place, Aberdeen, AB2 4EE; T.-Aberdeen 631480.

Ferguson, John Gordon, MA, BSc. Rector, Linlithgow Academy, since 1972; b. 5.2.27, Edinburgh; m., Rose; 2 d. Educ. George Heriot's School, Edinburgh; Edinburgh University; Heriot-Watt University. Royal Navy, 1946-49; Assistant Teacher of Mathematics: Lasswade Senior Secondary School, 1950-55, Royal High School, Edinburgh, 1955-58; Linlithgow Academy: Principal Teacher of Mathematics, 1959-71, Depute Rector, 1971-72. Member, Modular Mathematics Organisation, since 1972; President, Linlithgow and Bo'ness Rotary Club, 1985-86. Recreation: bowling. Address: (h.) Willowdene, St. Ninian's Road, Linlithgow; T.-0506 844270.

Ferguson, Keith, MA, LLB, DPA. Secretary, Accounts Commission, since 1985; b. 18.8.28, Dundee; m., Jean S. Anderson; 2 s.; 1 d. Educ. Robert Gordon's College, Aberdeen; Aberdeen University. Depute Town Clerk, then Town Clerk, Buckhaven and Methil, 1953-62; Director of Administration and Legal Services, Glenrothes Development Corporation, 1962-81. Publications: A History of Glenrothes; An Introduction to Local Government in Scotland; Stair Memorial Encyclopaedia (Contributor). Recreations: writing; swimming; golf. Address: (b.) 18 George Street, Edinburgh; T.-031-226 7346.

Ferguson, Kenneth Gordon, FRICS, JP. Senior Partner, Ferguson and Partners, Chartered Quantity Surveyors, since 1979; Member, City of Edinburgh District Council, since 1977; b. 17.2.44, Edinburgh; m., Jennifer Day Love; 2 d. Educ. Leith Academy; Heriot-Watt University; Napier College. Vice-President, Scottish Conservative and Unionist Association, 1985-87; Chairman, Planning Committee, Edinburgh District Council, 1983-84. Recreations: gardening; writing; travel. Address: (h.) Glebeside, 2 Pentland Avenue, Edinburgh, EH13 0HZ; T.-031-441 3046.

Ferguson, Leonard, MBE (1968), FIH, FRSH. Director of Housing Management, Scottish Special Housing Association, since 1969; b. 30.1.26, Glasgow; m., Valerie A.; 3 s.; 1 d. Educ. Gourock High School. Clerk, British Rail, 1941-43; Ft. Sergeant, RAF, 1943-48; Clerk, Marine Department, British Rail, 1948-50; Clerk, Housing Department, Greenock Corporation, 1950-51; Assistant Housing Manager, Scottish Special Housing Association, 1951-56; Housing Manager, UK Atomic Weapons Establishment, Aldermaston, 1956-57; Housing Manager: Aberdeen County Council, 1957-63, East Kilbride Development Corporation, 1963-69. Member, Management Committee, Ark Housing Association; Past Chairman, Chief Officers Group, Institute of Housing, Scotland. Recreations: gardening; sailing; hill-walking. Address: (b.) 15/21 Palmerston Place, Edinburgh, EH12 5AJ; T.-031-225 1281.

Ferguson, Patricia Ann Hatrick, BSc, AMICE, JP. Director, Hatrick Bruce Group, since 1977; Chairman, Fife Health Board, since 1987 (Vice Chairman, 1985-87); Member, General Practice Finance Corporation, since 1984; Member, Glenrothes Development Corporation, since 1985; b. Dundee; m., Euan Bruce Ferguson. Educ. St. Margaret's, Aberdeen; St. Andrews University; Royal Military College of Science. Resident Engineer, Redpath Dorman Long (North Sea), 1973-

77. Recreations: dressage; music. Address: (h.) Lydiard House, Milton of Balgonie, Glenrothes, Fife, KY7 6QD; T.-0592 758305.

Ferguson, Robert Greig, MREHIS, MIWM. Director of Environmental Health, Caithness District Council, since 1974; b. 30.7.42, Saltcoats, Ayrshire; m., Ruth; 1 s.; 2 d. Educ. Ardrossan Academy; School of Building, Cambuslang; David Dale College, Glasgow; Coatbridge Technical College; Dundee University. Student Sanitary Inspector, Ayr County Council, 1961-65; Assistant Sanitary Inspector: Ayr County Council, 1965-66, Clackmannan County Council, 1966-67; District Sanitary Inspector, Angus County Council, 1967-70; Caithness County Council: Depute County Sanitary Inspector, 1970-71, County Sanitary Inspector, 1971-74. Recreations: golf; snooker; cartophily; bowls. Address: (b.) Council Offices, 77 High Street, Wick; T.-Wick 3761, Ext. 236.

Ferguson, Rev. Ronald, MA, BD, ThM. Leader, Iona Community, since 1981; b. 27.10.39, Dunfermline; m., Cristine Jane Walker; 2 s.; 1 d. Educ. Beath High School, Cowdenbeath; St. Andrews University; Edinburgh University; Duke University. Journalist, Fife and Edinburgh, 1956-63; University, 1963-71; ordained Minister, Church of Scotland, 1972; Minister, Easterhouse, Glasgow, 1971-79; exchange year with United Church of Canada, 1979-80; Deputy Warden, Iona Abbey, 1980-81. Publications: Geoff: A Life of Geoffrey M. Shaw, 1979; Grace and Dysentery, 1979; Chasing the Wild Goose, 1988; The Whole Earth Shall Cry Glory (Co-Editor), 1985. Recreation: supporting Cowdenbeath Football Club. Address: (h.) 54 Ibrox Terrace, Glasgow, G51 2TB; T.-041-427 5609.

Ferguson, William, BSc, CEng, FICE, FIWEM. Assistant Chief Engineer, Scottish Development Department, since 1977; b. Ayr; m., Helen Moir Manson; 1 s.; 1 d. Educ. Ayr Academy; London University; Delft Technological University. Commissioned Royal Engineers, 1946-48. Various appointments in civil and public health engineering, including Chief Assistant Engineer, Midlothian County Council, and Engineering Inspector, Scottish Development Department. Chairman, Scottish Centre, Institution of Public Health Engineers, 1969-70. Recreations: family; DIY; skiing. Address: (h.) 13 Barnton Park Drive, Edinburgh, EH4 6HF; T.-031-336 4602.

Ferguson, William James. Farmer, since 1954; Vice Chairman, Aberdeen and District Milk Marketing Board; Vice Chairman, North of Scotland College of Agriculture, since 1984; b. 3.4.33, Aberdeen; m., Carroll Isobella Milne; 1 s.; 3 d. Educ. Turriff Academy; North of Scotland College of Agriculture. National Service, 1st Bn., Gordon Highlanders, 1952-54, serving in Malaya during the emergency. Member, Scottish Country Life Museums Trust Ltd.; Member, Technical Committee, Crichton Royal Dairy Farm, Dumfries; Member, Council of Scottish Agricultural Colleges; Member, BBC Scottish Rural and Agricultural Affairs Advisory Committee. Recreations: golf; field sports. Address: Rothiebrisbane, Fyvie, Turriff, Aberdeenshire, AB5 8LE; T.-06516 213.

Fergusson of Kilkerran, Sir Charles, 9th Bt; b. 10.5.31; m., Hon. Amanda Mary Noel-Paton; 2 s. Educ. Eton; Edinburgh and East of Scotland College of Agriculture.

Fergusson, James A., MB, ChB, MRCGP. Regional Medical Officer, Scottish Home and Health Department, since 1973; b. 17.7.24, Glasgow; m., Christine Irvine; 2 s.; 1 d. Educ. Hillhead High School; Glasgow University. Medical Assistant: Gynaecology Department, Western Infirmary, Glasgow, 1948, Obstetric Department, Stobhill Hospital, Glasgow, 1948-49, Medical Department, Victoria Infirmary, Glasgow, 1949; General Medical Practitioner, Glasgow, 1949-73; Physician, Cowglen Hospital, 1964-73. Session Clerk, Giffnock South Parish Church. Publication: Potassium Studies in Elderly, 1971. Recreations: golf; fishing; bowls. Address: (h.) 10 Dorian Drive, Glasgow, G76 7NP; T.-041-638 9847.

Fergusson, Thomas Edgar Syme, MB, ChB, MRCGP, DRCOG. Regional Medical Officer, Scottish Home and Health Department, since 1974; b. 24.10.29, Glasgow; m., Charis Wilson Boyle; 1 s.; 2 d. Educ. Hillhead High School; Glasgow University. General Practitioner, 1954-74; part-time Medical Officer, Duntocher Hospital, 1961-74. Recreations: golf; gardening; music. Address: (h.) 1 Edgehill Road, Bearsden, Glasgow, G61 3AD; T.-041-942 0380.

Fernie, Professor Eric Campbell, BA, FSA, FSA Scot. Watson Gordon Professor of Fine Art, Edinburgh University, since 1984; b. 9.6.39, Edinburgh; m., Margaret Lorraine; 1 s.; 2 d. Educ. Marist Brothers College, Johannesburg; Witwatersrand University; London University. Lecturer, Witwatersrand University, 1964-67; East Anglia University: Lecturer, 1967-74, Senior Lecturer, 1974-84, Dean, School of Fine Art and Music, 1977-81. Publications: The Architecture of the Anglo-Saxons; The Communar and Pitancer Rolls of Norwich Cathedral Priory (Co-author). Address: (b.) 19 George Square, Edinburgh, EH8 9LD; T.-031-667 1011.

Ferrier, Alan Gray, TD, DL. Manager, Norwich Union Insurance Group, Wick, since 1973; b. 23.5.39, Glasgow; m., Jean; 1 s.; 1 d. Educ. Hillhead High School; Strathclyde University. Joined Norwich Union, 1962; commissioned TA, 1964; appointed Company Commander, Infantry, 1976; Deputy Lieutenant, Caithness, since 1984; appointed Squadron Commander, Royal Engineers, 1986; Chairman, Earl Haig Fund, Wick; Past President, Wick Rotary Club; Member, Northern Area and Highland TAVRA; Squadron Commander, 236 Field Squadron (ADR) (V), Royal Engineers; Company Commander, 3/51 Highland Volunteers, Wick. Recreation: fishing. Address: (h.) 81 Willow Bank, Wick, Caithness, KW1 4PE; T.-0955 3178.

Ferrier, Professor Robert Patton, MA (Cantab), BSc, PhD, FInstP, FRSE. Professor of Natural Philosophy, Glasgow University, since 1973; b. 4.1.34, Dundee; m., Valerie Jane Duncan; 2 s.; 1 d. Educ. Morgan Academy, Dundee; Queen's College, Dundee, St. Andrews University. Scientific Officer, AERE Harwell, 1959-61; Research

Associate, Massachusetts Institute of Technology, 1961-62; Senior Research Assistant, Cavendish Laboratory, Cambridge, 1962-65; Fellow, Fitzwilliam College, Cambridge, 1964-73; Assistant Director of Research, Cavendish Laboratory, Cambridge, 1965-71; Lecturer in Physics, Cambridge University, 1971-73; Guest Scientist, IBM Research Division, California, 1972-73. Member, Physics Committee, SERC, 1979-82 (Chairman, Semiconductor and Surface Physics Sub-Committee, 1979-82). Recreations: tennis; reading crime novels; garden and house maintenance. Address: Department of Physics and Astronomy, The University, Glasgow, G12 8QQ; T.-041-330 5388.

Ferrier, Rev. Walter McGill, MA (Hons), BD. Minister, St. Andrew's Church, North Berwick, since 1952; b. 20.4.18, Buckhaven, Fife; m., Gillian Mary George; 2 s. Educ. Bathgate Academy; Edinburgh University. Assistant Minister, St. Michael's Church, Dumfries; Minister, High Church, Airdrie, 1946-52. Member, North Berwick Community Council, 1975-79; President, North Berwick Rotary Club, 1973. Publications: The North Berwick Story, 1980; The Last Hundred Years (history of Church), 1983. Recreations: repairing and maintaining talking books for the blind; local history; wine-making. Address: Manse of St. Andrew, 50 St. Baldred's Road, North Berwick, EH39 4PU; T.-0620 2803.

Fewson, Professor Charles Arthur, BSc, PhD, FRSE, FIBiol. Titular Professor, Department of Biochemistry, Glasgow University, since 1982; b. 8.9.37, Selby, Yorkshire; m., Margaret C.R. Moir; 2 d. Educ. Hymers College, Hull; Nottingham University; Bristol University. Research Fellow, Cornell University, New York, 1961-63; Department of Biochemistry, Glasgow University: Assistant Lecturer, 1963-64, Lecturer, 1964-68, Senior Lecturer, 1968-79, Reader, 1979-82. Recreation: watching cricket. Address: (h.) 39 Falkland Street, Glasgow, G12 9QZ; T.-041-339 1304.

Fiddes, Sheriff James Raffan, QC (Scot). Sheriff of South Strathclyde, Dumfries and Galloway, at Hamilton, since 1977; b. 1.2.19. Educ. Aberdeen Grammar School; Glasgow University; Balliol College, Oxford. Advocate, 1948.

Fielding, Mary. Chairman, Sutherland Tourist Board, since 1985; Member, Sutherland District Council, since 1984; b. 21.2.30, Cleethorpes; m., Ronald Fielding; 1 s.; 2 d. Secretary, Sutherland Federation, SWRI, 1979-85 (Chairman, 1985); President, Red Cross, Brora, since 1984. Recreation: Producer, Youth Drama Group, annual pantomimes, etc. Address: (h.) Montrose Cottage, 1 High Street, Brora.

Fife, 3rd Duke of (James George Alexander Bannerman Carnegie). Master of Southesk; b. 23.9.29; m., Hon. Caroline Cicely-Dewar (m. diss.); 1 s.; 1 d. Educ. Gordonstoun. National Service, Scots Guards, 1948-50; Royal Agricultural College; Clothworkers' Company and Freeman, City of London; President, ABA, 1959-73, Vice-Patron, 1973; a Vice-Patron, Braemar Royal Highland Society; a Vice-President, British Olympic Association. Address: Elsick House, Stonehaven, Kincardineshire, AB3 2NT.

Finch, Professor Ronald George, BA (Hons), MA, PhD. Professor of German Language and Literature, Glasgow University, since 1974; b. 19.10.25, Barmouth, Wales; m., Esther Marian Martin; 1 s.; 1 d. Educ. Ardwyn School, Aberystwyth; University College of Wales, Aberystwyth. University College of Wales, Aberystwyth: Assistant, Department of German, 1948, Assistant Lecturer in German, 1949, Lecturer, 1951; Queen's University, Belfast: Grade A Lecturer in German, 1954, Senior Lecturer, 1962, Reader, 1968, Professor, 1970. Recreations: walking; foreign travel. Address: (b.) Department of German Language and Literature, Modern Languages Building, Glasgow University, Glasgow, G12 8QQ; T.-041-339 8855.

Findlay, Alexander, MBE. Mental Welfare Commissioner, since 1986; b. 9.5.26, Dundee; m., Margaret Milne; 2 s. Educ. Harris Academy, Dundee. Joined GPO Telephones as apprentice, 1942; worked in various divisions until retiring from Executive Grouping, 1984. Chief Scout's Award for services to Scouting, 1978; Penicuik Town Councillor, 1971-74; Member, Lothian Health Board, 1974-84, Chairman, 1984-86; Member, Royal Edinburgh Hospital Group, 1971-74. Address: (h.) 54 Rullion Road, Penicuik, Midlothian; T.-0968 73443.

Findlay, Charles Graham, JP, BDS. Honorary Sheriff, since 1980; Dental Surgeon, since 1953; b. 18.1.31, Rutherglen; m., Margaret Elizabeth; 2 s.; 2 d. Educ. Allan Glen's School, Glasgow; Glasgow University. Dental Surgeon, RAF, then General Dental Practitioner, Stranraer; Member, Licensing Appeals Court; Member, Wigtownshire Justices Committee; Past Chairman, Local Dental Council; Representative, Local Dental Council, on Dumfries and Galloway Health Board; Past Chairman, Stranraer and District Round Table; Past President, South of Scotland Golfers Association. Recreations: golf (former Champion, South of Scotland and Wigtownshire). Address: (h.) Broadstone House, Stranraer, DG9 0EX; T.-0776 3833.

Findlay, Donald Russell, QC, LLB (Hons). Advocate, since 1975; Member, Lothian Health Board; Vice Chairman, Leith Conservative and Unionist Association; b. 17.3.51, Cowdenbeath; m., Jennifer E. Borrowman. Educ. Harris Academy, Dundee; Dundee University. Sometime Lecturer in Commercial Law, Heriot-Watt University. Recreations: Glasgow Rangers FC; Egyptology; archaeology; wine. Address: (b.) Advocates Library, Parliament House, Parliament Square, Edinburgh, EH1 1RF; T.-031-226 2881.

Findlay, James Gordon, OBE (1979), QJM, JP. Member, Tayside Regional Council, since 1975; Chairman, Angus Justices Committee, 1968-87; Farmer, since 1945; Director, Animal Diseases Research Organisation; Member, Hill Farming Advisory Committee, since 1962; b. 31.8.16, Angus; m., Annie Lamond; 1 s.; 3 d. Educ. Morgan Academy. Shepherd, 1931-39; soldier, 1939-45; Farm Manager, 1945; Governor, East of Scotland College of Agriculture, 1954-70; County Councillor, 1951-75; Vice-Convener, County of Angus, 1971-75 (Chairman, Planning Committee, 1968-75); Chairman, District Courts Association of Scotland, 1983-84; President, Blackface Sheep Breeders Association, 1974-76; Life Member, Royal Highland and Agricultural Society. Publication: Sel La V. Recreations: dog handling; historical study; dialect preservation. Address: (h.) Linrie Herdhill, Kirriemuir, Angus; T.-Kirriemuir 73427.

Findlay, Richard, DDA. Managing Director, Radio Forth, since 1977; m., Elspeth; 2 s.; 1 d. Educ. Royal Scottish Academy of Music and Drama. Chairman, Association of Independent Radio Contractors, 1984-86; former Hon. President, Heriot Watt University Students Association and Member, University Court; Director: Scottish and Irish Radio Sales Ltd., Cablevision (Scotland) PLC, Chalford Communications Ltd. Address: (b.) Radio Forth Ltd., Forth House, Forth Street, Edinburgh.

Findlay, Richard Martin, LLB, NP. Partner, Ranken & Reid, SSC, Edinburgh, since 1979; b. 18.12.51, Aberdeen. Educ. Gordon Schools, Huntly; Aberdeen University. Trained, Wilsone & Duffus, Advocates, Aberdeen; Legal Assistant, Commercial Department, Maclay Murray & Spens, Glasgow and Edinburgh. Company Secretary: Edinburgh Capital Group Limited, Edinburgh Arts and Entertainment Limited, Edinburgh Music Theatre Co. Limited, Activity Travel Limited and Edinburgh International Jazz Festival. Recreations: music; theatre; opera; cinema. Address: 7 Albyn Place, Edinburgh, EH2 4NN; T.-031-226 6576.

Fine, Anne, BA (Hons). Writer; b. 7.12.47, Leicester; m., Kit; 2 d. Educ. Northampton High School for Girls; Warwick University. Published books: for children: The Summer-house Loon, 1978, The Other, Darker Ned, 1979, The Stone Menagerie, 1980, Round Behind the Ice-house, 1981, The Granny Project, 1983, Scaredy Cat, 1985, Anneli the Art Hater, 1986, Madame Doubtfire, 1987, Crummy Mummy & Me, 1988, A Pack of Liars, 1988, Bill's New Frock, 1989, Goggle-Eyes, 1989; for adults: The Killjoy, 1987. Recreations: reading; walking. Address: (b.) c/o Murray Pollinger, 4 Garrick Street, London, WC2E 9BH.

Fink, Professor George, MB, BS, MD, MA, DPhil. Director, MRC Brain Metabolism Unit, since 1980; Honorary Professor, Edinburgh University, since 1984; b. 13.11.36, Vienna; m., Ann Elizabeth; 1 s.; 1 d. Educ. Melbourne High School; Melbourne University; Hertford College, Oxford. House Officer appointments, Royal Melbourne and Alfred Hospitals, 1961-62; Demonstrator and Lecturer, Department of Anatomy, Monash University, 1963-64; Nuffield Dominions Demonstrator, Oxford, 1965-67; Senior Lecturer, Monash University, 1968-71; University Lecturer, Oxford, 1971-80; Official Fellow and Tutor in Physiology and Medicine, Brasenose College, Oxford, 1974-80. Member of Council, European Neuroscience Association, 1980-82. Publications: Neuropeptides: Basic and Clinical Aspects (Co-Editor), 1982; Neuroendocrine Molecular Biology (Co-Editor), 1986; numerous papers on neuroendocrinology and psychoneuroendocrinology. Recreations: skiing and squash. Address: (b.) MRC Brain Metabolism Unit, Department of Pharmacology, Edinburgh University, 1 George Square, Edinburgh, EH8 9JZ; T.-031-667 1011, Ext. 2509.

Finlay, Ian, CBE, MA, HRSA, FRSA. Professor of Antiquities, Royal Scottish Academy; Writer and Art Historian; b. 2.12.06, Auckland, New Zealand; m., Mary Scott Pringle; 2 s.; 1 d. Educ. Edinburgh Academy; Edinburgh University. Joined Royal Scottish Museum, 1932; Deputy Regional Information Officer Scotland (Ministry of Information), 1942-45; Secretary, Royal Fine Art Commission for Scotland, 1953-61; Royal Scottish Museum: Keeper, Department of Art and Ethnography, 1955-61, Director, 1961-71. Former Member: International Council of Museums, Counseil de Direction Gazette des Beaux Arts; former Vice-Chairman, Scottish Arts Council; Freeman, City of London; Member, Livery Worshipful Company of Goldsmiths; Guest, State Department, US, 1960. Publications: Scotland, 1945; Scottish Art, 1945; Art in Scotland, 1948; Scottish Crafts, 1948; A History of Scottish Gold and Silver Work, 1956; Scotland (enlarged edition), 1957; The Lothians, 1960; The Highlands, 1963; The Lowlands, 1967; Celtic Art: An Introduction, 1973; Priceless Heritage: The Future of Museums, 1977; Columba, 1979 (Scottish Arts Council Award); A History of Scottish Gold and Silver Work (new edition), 1988. Address: (h.) Currie Riggs, Balerno, Midlothian, EH14 5AG; T.-031-449 4249.

Finlayson, Alan Fergus, OBE, MA, LLB, NP. Regional Reporter, Lothian Regional Council, since 1975; b. 19.12.34, Dumfries; m., Dorothy Christine Ebbs; 2 s. Educ. Dumfries Academy; George Watson's College, Edinburgh; Edinburgh University. Partner, Ranken & Reid, SSC, Edinburgh, 1965-70; Reporter to Children's Panel, City of Edinburgh, 1970-75. Address: (b.) 1-3 Howden Street, Edinburgh, EH3 9HH; T.-031-667 9431.

Finlayson, Geoffrey Beauchamp Alistair Moubray, MA, BLitt, FRHistS. Reader in Modern History, Glasgow University, since 1982; b. 17.7.34, Campsie; m., Elizabeth Frew Dempster; 2 d. Educ. Melville College, Edinburgh; Glasgow Academy; Glasgow University; Balliol College, Oxford. Joined Glasgow University, 1959, as Assistant Lecturer, then Lecturer, then Senior Lecturer (Head, Department of Modern History, 1979-82); Visiting Professor, Queens College of City University of New York, 1972-73. Session Clerk, Newlands (South) Church, Glasgow, 1977-82; Member, History Panel, Scottish Universities Council on Entrance; Observer, History Panel, Scottish Examination Board; Observer, Joint Working Party on Revision of Higher and Post-Higher History; Life Member, Fife, Kinross and Clackmannan Society; Member of Committee, Hutchesons' Grammar School Association, 1987-89. Publications: The Seventh Earl of Shaftesbury, 1981 (Scottish Arts Council Book Award); England in the Eighteen Thirties, Decade of Reform, 1969; Philanthropy, Self-Help and the State in Britain 1830-1979, in press. Recreations: music: cricket. Address: (h.) 11 Burnhead Road, Glasgow, G43 2SU; T.-041-637 2418.

Finlayson, Niall Diarmid Campbell, MB, ChB, PhD, FRCP, FRCPEdin. Consultant Physician, Edinburgh Royal Infirmary, since 1973; Honorary Senior Lecturer, Department of Medicine, Edinburgh University, since 1973; b. 21.4.39, Georgetown, Guyana; m., Dale Kristin Anderson; 1 s.; 1 d. Educ. Loretto School, Musselburgh; Edinburgh University. Lecturer in Therapeutics, Edinburgh University, 1965-69; Assistant Professor of Medicine, New York Hospital-Cornell Medical College, New York, 1970-72. Address: (h.) 10 Queens Crescent, Edinburgh, EH9 2AZ; T.-031-667 9369.

Finn, Cecil Thomas. Fisherman (Skipper/Owner), since 1950; Chairman, Clyde Fishermen's Association, since 1985; Vice-President, Scottish Fishermen's Federation, since 1984; b. 15.4.36, Campbeltown; m., Shirley Graham; 1 s.; 1 d. Educ. Campbeltown Grammar School. Lifetime of fishing; Executive of Clyde Fishermen's Association for 25 years. Recreations: indoor and outdoor bowling; snooker. Address: (h.) Gleaner Lea, Stronvaar Road, Campbeltown, Argyll; T.-0586 52823.

Finn, Kathleen, DCE. Schoolteacher; Immediate Past President, Educational Institute of Scotland; Vice Convenor, Strathclyde EIS; Teacher Representative, Strathclyde Education Committee; Member, National Salaries Committee; Convenor, National Women's Advisory Committee; Member, STUC Women's Committee and Education and Training Committee; b. 22.2.43, Glasgow. Educ. Possil Secondary School; Jordanhill College. Union activist since start of teaching career. Member, Board of Directors, Wildcat; Member, Trade Union Committee, Mayfest. Recreations: swimming; reading; political theatre; cat lover. Address: (h.) 18 Marywood Square, Glasgow, G41 2BJ; T.-041-423 1796.

Finnie, James Ross, CA. Member, Inverclyde District Council, since 1977; Assistant Director, Singer & Friedlander Ltd.; b. 11.2.47, Greenock; m., Phyllis Sinclair; 1 s.; 1 d. Educ. Greenock Academy. Member, Executive Committee, Scottish Council (Development and Industry), 1976-87; Convener, Planning and Development Committee, Inverclyde District Council, 1977-80; Chairman, Scottish Liberal Party, 1982-86. Address: (h.) 91 Octavia Terrace, Greenock, PA16 7PY; T.-0475 31495.

Finniston, Sir Harold Montague, Kt, FEng, FRS, FRSE, PhD, Hon. GGIA. Business Industrial Consultant and Chairman/Director of a number of companies; b. 15.8.12, Glasgow; m., Miriam Singer; 1 s.; 1 d. Educ. Allan Glen's School, Glasgow; Royal College of Science and Technology. Began scientific career as Lecturer, Royal College of Science and Technology, 1933; Stewart & Lloyds Steel Company; Chief Officer, Scottish Coke Research Committee; Royal Naval Scientific Service during Second World War; Chief Metallurgist, UKAEA, Harwell, 1948-58; joined C.A. Parsons Company, 1959, as Managing Director of its subsidiary, IRD; Chairman, IRD, 1968-77; Deputy Chairman, later additionally Chief Executive, British Steel Corporation, 1967-73; Chairman, BSC, 1973-76; Director, Sears Holdings Ltd. and Chairman, Sears Engineering Ltd., 1976-79. Chairman: Council, Scottish Business School; Prison Reform Trust; Scottish Enterprise Foundation; Young Enterprise Scotland; Chancellor, Stirling University, since 1979; Honorary Doctorates include DSc, Strathclyde; LLD, Glasgow; DUniv, Stirling; Chairman, Government Committee of Inquiry into the Engineering Profession, 1977-79. Recreations: spectator sport; swimming; walking.

Firth, Professor William James, BSc, PhD, CPhys. Professor of Physics, Strathclyde University, since 1985; b. 23.2.45, Holm, Orkney; m., Mary MacDonald Anderson; 2 s. Educ. Perth Academy; Edinburgh University; Heriot-Watt University. Lecturer to Reader, Physics, Heriot-Watt University, 1967-85. Recreation: sports (Edinburgh University Hockey Blue, 1967-68). Address: (b.) John Anderson Building, 107 Rottenrow, Glasgow, G4 0NG.

Fisher, Rev. Ian Riddock, MA. Minister, Fernhill and Cathkin Parish Church, Rutherglen, since 1972; Convener, St. Andrew Press Executive Committee, since 1985; Vice-Chairman, National Bible Society of Scotland, since 1987; b. 12.2.33, Glasgow; m., Mairi Matheson; 2 d. Educ. Kelvinside Academy, Glasgow; Glasgow University; Edinburgh University. Scottish Travelling Secretary, Inter-Varsity Fellowship, 1960-64; Minister, Maybole West Parish Church, 1964-72. Recreations: walking; reading. Address: 82 Blairbeth Road, Rutherglen, Glasgow, G73 4JA; T.-041-634 1508.

Fisher, Idris, MITD. Regional Manager for Scotland and North East England, Skills Training Agency, Manpower Services Commission, since 1986; b. 5.5.34, Markham, Gwent; m., Marian Wynne Fisher; 1 s.; 1 d. Educ. Dartford Technical College. Apprentice engineer, Vickers Armstrong Ltd.; research, Atomic Weapons Research Establishment; Instructor, Ministry of Labour and National Service; Tutor-Instructor, Training College, Department of Employment; Skill Centre Manager, Training Service Agency, MSC. Recreation: amateur cinematography. Address: (b.) Skills Training Agency, Training Commission, 5 Kirk Loan, Corstorphine, Edinburgh, EH12 7HD; T.-031-334 9821.

Fisher, Kenneth Holmes, BA, ACIS, AInstM, DipABCC. Depute Principal, Barmulloch College, Glasgow, since 1987; b. 19.3.41, Glasgow. Educ. Hillhead High School, Glasgow. Administrative appointments, Colvilles Ltd., 1957-67; Lecturer and Senior Lecturer, Anniesland College, Glasgow, 1967-75; Head, Department of Business Studies, Cumbernauld College, 1975-80; Head, Department of Commerce, Anniesland College, Glasgow, 1980-86. Address: (b.) Barmulloch College, 186 Rye Road, Glasgow, G21 3JY; T.-041-558 9071.

Fitzgerald, William Knight, CBE, LLD, JP, DL. Convener, Tayside Regional Council, 1978-86; Chairman, Tay Road Bridge Joint Board, 1975-86 (and 1970-73); b. 19.3.09, Potchestroom, South Africa; m., 1, Elizabeth Grant (deceased); 2, Margaret Wilkie; 3 s. Educ. Robertson Grammar School, South Africa. Member, Dundee University Court, 1970-86; former Lord Provost of Dundee and City Treasurer; Past President, Convention of Scottish Local Authorities; former Member, Board of Directors, Dundee High School; former Vice Chairman, Dundee College of Art and Technology; President, Dundee Battalion, Boys' Brigade; Honorary President: Dundee Business Club, Dundee and District Retirement Council; Chairman, Dundee Prisoners' Aid Society; President, Tayside Community Relations Council; Chairman, Dundee Community Relations Council, 1978-86. Recreations: gardening; reading. Address: (h.) 1 Roxburgh Terrace, Dundee; T.-Dundee 68475.

Fleming, Archibald Macdonald, MA, BCom, PhD. Director of Continuing Education, Strathclyde University, since 1987 (Director, Management Development Programmes, Strathclyde Business School, 1984-87); Lecturer, Department of Information Science, Strathclyde University, since 1968; Consultant on Management Training and Development, since 1970; b. 19.6.36, Glasgow; m., Joan Moore; 1 s.; 1 d. Educ. Langholm Academy; Dumfries Academy; Edinburgh University. W. & T. Avery, 1961-63; IBM (UK) Ltd., 1963-64; Sumlock Comptometer Ltd., 1964-68; Consultancies: Scottish Co-operative Wholesale Society, 1969, Hotel and Catering Industry Training Board, 1971, Scottish Engineering Employers Association, 1973. Member, Strathclyde Children's Panel; Member, Committee on Food Processing Opportunities in Scotland, Scottish Council (Development and Industry). Publication: Scottish Business Dictionary (with B. McKenna). Recreation: reading, observing and talking on Scotland and the Scots. Address: (b.) 16 Richmond Street, Glasgow, G1 1XQ.

Fleming, Professor George, BSc, PhD, FEng, FICE, FRSA, MIWEM. Professor of Civil Engineering, Strathclyde University, since 1985; Member of Council, Institution of Civil Engineers, since 1986; Member, Environment Committee, SERC, since 1986; b. 16.8.44, Glasgow; m., Irene Fleming; 2 s.; 1 d. Educ. Knightswood Secondary School, Glasgow; Strathclyde University; Stanford University, California. Research Assistant, Strathclyde University, 1966-69, Stanford University, 1967; Senior Research Hydrologist, Hydrocomp International, California, 1969-70; Research Associate, Stanford University, 1969-70; Director and Vice President, Hydrocomp International, Palo Alto and Glasgow, 1970-79; Lecturer, then Senior Lecturer, then Reader in Civil Engineering, Strathclyde University, 1971-85; Visiting Professor, University of Padova, Italy, since 1980; Vice Dean, Engineering Faculty, Strathclyde University, 1984-87. Publications: Computer Simulation in Hydrology, 1975; The Sediment Problem, 1977; Deterministic Models in Hydrology, 1979. Recreations: farming; fishing; food; film-making. Address: (b.) John Anderson Building, 107 Rottenrow, Glasgow, G4 0NG; T.-041-552 4400, Ext. 3168.

Fleming, Ian, RSA, RSW, RWA, DA, LLD (Aberdeen University, 1984). Painter; b. 19.11.06, Glasgow; m., Catherine Margaret Weetch; 1 s.; 2 d. Educ. Hyndland School, Glasgow; Glasgow School of Art; Jordanhill College of Education. Lecturer, Glasgow School of Art, 1931-40; War Service, 1940-43: Glasgow Police (Maryhill F Division), direct commission into Army, 1943-46, service in Normandy, Belgium, Germany; Lecturer, Glasgow School of Art, 1946-48; Warden, Patrick Allen-Fraser Art College, Hospitalfield, 1948-54; Head, Grays School of Art, Robert Gordon's Institute of Technology, 1954-72. Recreations: none, except art. Address: (h.) 15 Fonthill Road, Aberdeen, AB1 2UN; T.-0224 580680.

Fleming, Maurice. Editor, The Scots Magazine, since 1974; b. Blairgowrie; m., Nanette Dalgleish; 2 s.; 1 d. Educ. Blairgowrie High School. Trained in hotel management before entering journalism; worked on various magazines; has had four full-length plays performed professionally, as well as one-act plays by amateurs; founder Member: Traditional Music and Song Association of Scotland, Scottish Poetry Library; Chairman, Blairgowrie, Rattray and District Civic Trust; Past Chairman, Blair in Bloom. Recreations: theatre; reading; bird-watching; enjoying the countryside; folksong and folklore. Address: (h.) Craigard, Perth Road, Blairgowrie; T.-Blairgowrie 3633.

Fleming, Thomas Bryan, CA. Director, MM Finishes Ltd., Ardrossan; Council Member, Institute of Chartered Accountants of Scotland; b. 31.7.32, Glasgow; m., Mary Christine St. Clair Reid (deceased); 1 s.; 1 d. Educ. Allan Glen's School. Apprentice Chartered Accountant, 1949-55; RAF, 1956-57; Audit Clerk, Fraser, Lawson & Laing, CAs, 1958-61; Accountant, Blackwood, Morton & Sons Ltd., 1961-70; Financial Director, then Managing Director, Metallic Manufacturing Co. Ltd., 1970-86. Recreations: music; mountaineering. Address: (h.) Cottage No. 1, The Stables, Swindridge Muir, Dalry, Ayrshire; T.-029 483 2020.

Fleming, Tom. Actor and Director; b. 29.6.27, Edinburgh. Co-Founder, Edinburgh Gateway Company, 1953; directed and acted in numerous productions there; joined Royal Shakespeare Company at Stratford upon Avon, 1962, and played several classical roles, including Brutus in Julius Caesar, the Earl of Kent in King Lear, and the title role in Cymberline; toured with RSC in USSR, USA and Europe, 1964; appointed Director, new Royal Lyceum Theatre Company, 1965; there played title role in Galileo; appeared on television in title role of Jesus of Nazareth; Television Commentator on ceremonial occasions; played Divine Correction, The Thrie Estates, Edinburgh Festival, 1959 and 1973; author of play, Miracle at Midnight; former Artistic Director, Scottish Theatre Company.

Fletcher, Colonel Archibald Ian, OBE. Justice of the Peace for Argyll and Bute, since 1971; Deputy Lieutenant, since 1975; President, Cowal Area, NFU of Scotland, since 1987; b. 9.4.24, London; m., Helen Clare De Salis; 1 s.; 2 d. Educ. Ampleforth College. Recruit, Guards Depot, 1942; Troop Leader, 3rd Tank Bn., Scots Guards, NW Europe, 1944-45; served Palestine, N. Africa, Malaya, Kenya; commanded 1st Bn., Scots Guards, 1963-66, Malaya and Borneo, and Regiment, 1967-70; retired to farm in Argyll; County Councillor, 1972-74; Member, NFU of Scotland Council, 1972-85, Honorary President, 1985-86; Council Member, Timber Growers UK, since

1986; Chairman, Colintraive and Glendaruel Community Council, since 1977. Recreation: country pursuits. Address: (h.) Dunans, Glendaruel, Colintraive, Argyll; T.-Glendaruel 235.

Fletcher, Professor Roger, MA, PhD, FIMA, FRSE. Professor of Optimization, Department of Mathematics and Computer Science, Dundee University, since 1984; b. 29.1.39, Huddersfield; m., Mary Marjorie Taylor; 2 d. Educ. Huddersfield College; Cambridge University; Leeds University. Lecturer, Leeds University, 1963-69; Principal Research Fellow, then Principal Scientific Officer, AERE Harwell, 1969-73; Senior Research Fellow, then Senior Lecturer, then Reader, Dundee University, 1973-84. Member of Council and Associate Editor, Math. Programming Society; Visiting Professor, Universities of Kentucky, Calabria, New South Wales. Publications: Practical Methods of Optimization, 2nd edition, 1987. numerous others. Recreations: hill-walking; music; bridge. Address: (h.) 43 Errol Road, Invergowrie, Dundee, DD2 5BX; T.-0382 562452.

Fletcher, Stewart, BSc, MIBiol, MB, ChB, FRCPath, FRCS(Ed). Senior Lecturer in Pathology, Edinburgh University; Honorary Consultant, Lothian Health Board; b. 8.4.32, Glasgow; m., Lorna Campbell Dryburgh; 3 d. Educ. Hillhead High School, Glasgow; Glasgow University. Bacteriologist, Western Infirmary, Glasgow, 1959-61; Pathologist, Glasgow University (Western Infirmary and Royal Hospital for Sick Children), 1961-66. Recreations: reading, thinking and working in the sciences and engineering. Address: (h.) 56 Polwarth Terrace, Edinburgh, EH11 1NJ; T.-031-337 5504.

Flett, Ian Stark, CBE (1984), MA, MEd, ABPS. Chairman, Scottish Centre for Tuition of the Disabled, since 1980; Chairman, National Association for Gifted Children Scotland, since 1985; b. 26.1.20, Aberdeen; m., Moyra. Educ. Aberdeen Grammar School; Aberdeen University; Aberdeen College of Education. RAF, Signals and Intelligence Branch, 1940-46; Teacher, Aberdeen, 1947-49; Adviser, Durham, 1949-54; Assistant Education Officer, Lancashire, 1954-59; Deputy, 1959-63; Deputy Education Officer, City of Hull, 1963-66; Member, Dalegacy Institute of Education, Hull University, 1963-66; Director of Education, Fife, 1966-85; General Secretary, Association of Directors of Education in Scotland, 1975-85; President, 1979-80; Adviser to Association of County Councils, 1970-74; Principal Adviser, Convention of Scottish Local Authorities, 1975-84; Member, Consultative Committee on the Curriculum, 1977-87; Member, General Teaching Council, 1976-84; Governor, Craiglockhart College of Education, 1977-83; Chairman, Scottish Association of Educational Management and Administration, 1981-84. Recreations: music; gardening. Address: (h.) 5 Townsend Place, Kirkcaldy, Fife, KY1 1HB; T.-0592 260279.

Flett, James. JP. Honorary Sheriff, Lothians and Borders; Past Chairman, City of Edinburgh Valuation Appeal Committee; b. 26.1.17, Findochty; m., Jean Walker Ross; 1 s. Educ. Findochty Public School; Heriot-Watt University; Royal Military College, Sandhurst. Commissioned Seaforth Highlanders; Chief Official, Royal Burgh of Linlithgow (retired). Governor, West Lothian Educational Trust; former Member, JP Advisory Committee; former Member, Scottish Home Department Interviewing Committee at Edinburgh Prisons; former Member, West Lothian Licensing Board. Address: (h.) Craigenroan, Linlithgow, West Lothian; T.-Linlithgow 842344.

Flint, Professor David, TD, MA, BL, CA, FRSA. Professor of Accountancy, Glasgow University, 1964-85 (Vice-Principal, 1981-85); b. 24.2.19, Glasgow; m., Dorothy Mary Maclachlan Jardine; 2 s.; 1 d. Educ. High School of Glasgow; Glasgow University. Royal Signals, 1939-46 (Major; mentioned in Despatches); Partner, Mann Judd Gordon & Company, Chartered Accountants, Glasgow, 1951-71; Lecturer (part-time), Glasgow University, 1950-60; Dean, Faculty of Law, 1971-73; Council Member, Scottish Business School, 1971-77; Institute of Chartered Accountants of Scotland: President, 1975-76, Vice-President, 1973-75, Convener, Research Advisory Committee, 1974-75 and 1977-84, Convener, Working Party on Future Policy, 1976-79, Convener, Public Sector Committee, since 1987, Convener, Taxation Review and Research Sub-Committee, 1960-64; Trustee, Scottish Chartered Accountants Trust for Education, 1981-87; Member, Management Training and Development Committee, Central Training Council, 1966-70; Member, Management and Industrial Relations Committee, Social Science Research Council, 1970-72 and 1978-80; Member, Social Sciences Panel, Scottish Universities Council on Entrance, 1968-72; Chairman, Association of University Teachers of Accounting, 1969; Member, Company Law Committee, Law Society of Scotland, 1976-85; Scottish Economic Society: Treasurer, 1954-62, Vice-President, 1977-88, Hon. Vice-President, since 1988; Member, Commission for Local Authority Accounts in Scotland, 1978-80; President, European Accounting Association, 1983-84. Recreation: golf. Address: (h.) 16 Grampian Avenue, Auchterarder, Perthshire, PH3 1NY; T.-0764 63978.

Flockhart, (David) Ross, BA, BD. Director, Scottish Council for Voluntary Organisations, since 1972; b. 20.3.27, Newcastle, NSW, Australia; m., Pamela Ellison Macartney; 3 s.; 1 d.; 1 d. (deceased). Educ. Knox Grammar School, Sydney; Sydney University; Edinburgh University. Royal Australian Engineers, 1945-46; Chaplain to Overseas Students, Edinburgh, 1955-58; Parish Minister (Church of Scotland), Northfield, Aberdeen, 1958-63; Warden, Carberry Tower, Musselburgh, 1963-66; Lecturer and Senior Lecturer, School of Community Studies, Moray House College of Education, 1966-72; Member, Scottish Arts Council, 1976-82; Trustee, Community Projects Foundation. Recreations: bee-keeping; sailing; bread-baking. Address: (h.) Longwood, Humbie, East Lothian; T.-Humbie 208.

Florence, Professor Alexander Taylor, BSc, PhD, DSc, CChem, FRSC, FRSE, FPS. James P. Todd Professor of Pharmacy, Strathclyde University, since 1976; b. 9.9.40, London; m., Elizabeth Catherine McRae; 2 s.; 1 d. Educ. Queen's Park School, Glasgow; Glasgow University; Royal College of Science and Technology, Glasgow. Strathclyde University: Medical Research Council Junior Fellow, 1965-66; Lecturer, then Senior Lecturer, in Pharmaceutical Chemistry, 1966-76; Member, Committee on Safety of Medicines, CSM, since 1981; Vice Chairman, Chemistry, Pharmacy and Standards Sub-Committee, CSM (Member, since 1972); Member, Greater Glasgow Health Board, since 1987; Member, Nuffield Inquiry into Pharmacy, 1984-85. British Pharmaceutical Conference Science Award, 1974; Harrison Memorial Medal, Pharmaceutical Society of Gt. Britain, 1986. Recreations: organ music; painting; writing. Address: (b.) Strathclyde University, Department of Pharmacy, Royal College, Glasgow, G1 1XW; T.-041-552 4400, Ext. 2135.

Florey, Professor Charles Du Ve, MD, MPH, FFCM. Professor of Community Medicine, Dundee University, since 1983. Instructor, Assistant Professor, Yale University, 1963-69; Member, Scientific Staff, MRC, 1969-71; Senior Lecturer, then Reader, then Professor, St. Thomas's Hospital Medical School, 1971-83; Member, Committee on Data Protection, 1976-78. Publications: Introduction to Community Medicine; Methods for Cohort Studies of Chronic Airflow Limitation. Address: (b.) Department of Community Medicine, Ninewells Hospital and Medical School, Dundee, DD1 9SY; T.-0382 60111.

Fluendy, Malcolm A.D., MA, DPhil, DSc, CChem, FRSC, MInstP, FRSE. Reader in Chemistry, Edinburgh University; b. 28.3.35, London; m., Annette Pidgeon; 2 s. Educ. Westminster City School; Balliol College, Oxford. National Service, 1953-55 (Lt., Royal Signals); Royal Naval Scientific Service, 1955-56; Balliol College, Oxford, 1956-62; Research Fellow: University of California, Berkeley, 1962-63, Harvard University, 1963-64; joined Edinburgh University as Lecturer, 1964. Chairman, Molecular Beam Group, Chemical Society, 1974-79. Publication: Molecular Beams. Recreations: sailing; cruising (yachtmaster). Address: (b.) Department of Chemistry, West Mains Road, Edinburgh, EH9 3JJ; T.-031-667 1081.

Forbes, Professor Charles Douglas, DSc, MD, MB, ChB, FRCP, FRCPGlas, FRCPEdin. Professor of Medicine, Dundee University, and Honorary Consultant Physician, Tayside Health Board, since 1987; b. 9.10.38, Glasgow; m., Janette MacDonald Robertson; 2 s. Educ. High School of Glasgow; Glasgow University. Assistant Lecturer in Materia Medica, Glasgow University; Lecturer in Medicine, Makerere, Uganda; Registrar in Medicine, Glasgow Royal Infirmary; Reader in Medicine, Glasgow University; Fellow, American Heart Association; Fullbright Fellow; Director, Regional Haemophilia Centre, Glasgow. Recreation: gardening. Address: (h.) East Chattan, 108 Hepburn Gardens, St. Andrews, KY16 9LT; T.-0334 72428.

Forbes, Very Rev. Graham J.T., MA, BD. Provost, St. Ninian's Cathedral, Perth, since 1982; b. 10.6.51, Edinburgh; m., Jane Miller; 3 s. Educ. George Heriot's School, Edinburgh; Aberdeen University; Edinburgh University. Curate, Old St. Paul's, Edinburgh, 1976-82; Chairman, Canongate Youth Project, 1977-83; Chairman, Lothian Association of Youth Clubs, 1981-88; Member, Scottish Community Education Council, 1982-88; Chairman, Scottish Intermediate Treatment Resource Centre, since 1982; Member, Edinburgh Area Board, Manpower Services Commission, 1980-83; Chairman, Youth Affairs Group, Scottish Community Education Council, 1982- 88; Non-Executive Director, Radio Tay, since 1987. Address: St. Ninian's House, 40 Hay Street, Perth, PH1 5HS.

Forbes, Sheriff John Stuart, MA, LLB. Sheriff of Tayside, Central and Fife, at Dunfermline, since 1980; b. 31.1.36; m.; 1 s.; 2 d. Educ. Glasgow High School; Glasgow University. Solicitor, 1959-61; Advocate, 1962-76; Sheriff of Lothian and Borders, 1976-80.

Forbes, 22nd Lord (Nigel Ivan Forbes), KBE (1960), JP, DL. Premier Lord of Scotland; Director, Grampian Television Ltd., 1960-88; Director, Blenheim Travel Ltd., 1981-88; Chairman, Rolawn Ltd., since 1975; President, Scottish Scout Association, since 1970; b. 19.2.18; m., Hon. Rosemary Katharine Hamilton-Russell; 2 s.; 1 d. Educ. Harrow; Sandhurst. Retired Major, Grenadier Guards; Representative Peer of Scotland, 1955-63; Minister of State, Scottish Office, 1958-59; Member, Scottish Committee, Nature Conservancy, 1961-67; Member, Aberdeen and District Milk Marketing Board, 1962-72; Chairman, River Don District Board, 1962-73; President, Royal Highland and Agricultural Society of Scotland, 1958-59; Member, Sports Council for Scotland, 1966-71; Chairman, Scottish Branch, National Playing Fields Association, 1965-80; Deputy Chairman, Tennant Caledonian Breweries Ltd., 1964-74. Address: (h.) Balforbes, Alford, Aberdeenshire, AB3 8DR; T.-0336 2516.

Forbes, Captain William Frederick Eustace. Vice Lord-Lieutenant of Stirling and Falkirk, since 1984; b. 6.7.31; m.; 2 d. Educ. Eton. Coldstream Guards, 1950-59; Chairman, Scottish Woodland Owners' Association, 1974-77; Chairman, Scottish Branch, National Playing Fields Association, since 1980. Address: (h.) Dinning House, Gargunnock, Stirling, FK8 3BQ.

Ford, Harold Frank, BA, LLB; b. 17.5.15, Dirleton, East Lothian; m., Lucy Mary Burnet; 1 s.; 3 d. Educ. University College, Oxford; Edinburgh University. War Service, 1940-45, Lothians and Borders Yeomanry; PoW, Germany; Scottish Bar, 1945; Legal Adviser to UNRRA and IRO in British Zone of Germany, 1947; Sheriff Substitute of Forfar and Arbroath, 1951-71; Sheriff at Perth, 1971-80. Governor, Patrick Allan Fraser of Hospitalfield Trust, Arbroath; Chairman, Perth Prison Visitors' Centre. Recreations: gardening; golf. Address: Millhill, Meikleour, Perth, PH2 6EF; T.-Caputh 311.

Ford, James Allan, CB, MC. Author; Trustee, National Library of Scotland, since 1981; b. 10.6.20, Auchtermuchty; m., Isobel Dunnett; 1 s.; 1 d. Educ. Royal High School, Edinburgh; Edinburgh University. Employment Clerk, Ministry of Labour, 1938-39; Executive Officer, Inland Revenue, 1939-40; Captain, The Royal Scots, 1940-46 (POW, Far East, 1941-45); Executive Officer, Inland Revenue, 1946-47; Department of Agriculture for Scotland, 1947-66 (Assistant Secretary,

1958); Registrar General for Scotland, 1966-69; Under Secretary, Scottish Office, 1969-79. Publications (novels): The Brave White Flag, 1961; Season of Escape, 1963; A Statue for a Public Place, 1965; A Judge of Men, 1968; The Mouth of Truth, 1972. Recreations: trout fishing; gardening. Address: (h.) 29 Lady Road, Edinburgh, EH16 5PA; T.-031-667 4489.

Ford, James Angus, MB, ChB, FRCPEdin, FRCPGlas, DCH. Consultant Paediatrician, since 1975; Chairman, Scottish Council, British Medical Association; Chairman, Scottish Committee of Hospital Medical Services, 1983-86; b. 5.11.43, Arbroath; m., Dr. Veronica T. Reid. Educ. Kelvinside Academy; Glasgow University. House appointments: Glasgow Royal, Southern General, Stobhill, Belvidere; Registrar/Senior Registrar, Stobhill; Consultant appointments: Rutherglen Maternity Hospital, Royal Hospital for Sick Children, Glasgow; Territorial Army: six years, 6/7th Bn., Cameronians (Scottish Rifles), Captain; BMA: Chairman, Hospital Junior Staff Committee (Scotland), Deputy Chairman, HJSC (UK), Member of Council (Scottish and UK), Member, Joint Consultants Committee (Scottish and UK). Recreation: gardening. Address: (h.) 20 Ralston Road, Bearsden, Glasgow; T.-041-942 4273.

Fordyce, James Alexander Oswald, JP. Seed Potato Merchant and Farmer; Member, Tayside Regional Council; b. 25.10.26, Auchterarder; m., May Mitchell Stark; 3 d. Educ. Auchterarder High School; Morrison's Academy, Crieff. Member, Auchterarder Town Council, 1957-74 (Provost, seven years); Tayside Regional Council: Vice-Convener, 1981-86, Convener of Education, 1980-82, Convener, Road & Transport Committee, 1982-86, Vice-Chairman, Conservative Group, 1986; President: Auchterarder Curling Club, 1985; Auchterarder Golf Club, 1983; Auchterarder Horticultural Society, 1980; President, Potato Trade Association, 1965-75; Member, Board of Governors, Morrison's Academy, Crieff. Recreations: curling; bowling; golf. Address: (h.) Merrion, Western Road, Auchterarder; T.-Auchterarder 2215.

Fordyce, William Cairns, BSc, MEd. Director of Education, Dumfries and Galloway Region, since 1987; b. 27.8.39, Peterculter; m., Olive Jeannie; 1 s.; 4 d. Educ. Borden Grammar School, Sittingbourne; Aberdeen University; Aberdeen College of Education. Teaching, 1964-68; Assistant Director of Education: County of Dumfries, 1968-69, County of Aberdeen, 1969-72; Depute Director of Education: County of Aberdeen, 1972-75, Grampian Region, 1975-87. Address: (b.) 30 Edinburgh Road, Dumfries; T.-Dumfries 61234.

Forrest, Professor Sir (Andrew) Patrick (McEwen), Kt (1986), BSc, MD, ChM, FRCS, FRCSEdin, FRCSGlas, DSc (Hon), LLD, FACS (Hon), FRACS (Hon), FRCR (Hon), FRSE. Regius Professor of Clinical Surgery, Edinburgh University, since 1970; b. 25.3.23, Mount Vernon, Lanarkshire; m., Margaret Anne Steward; 1 s.; 2 d. Educ. Dundee High School; St. Andrews University. House Surgeon, Dundee Royal Infirmary; Surgeon Lieutenant, RNVR; Mayo Foundation Fellow; Lecturer and Senior Lecturer, Glasgow University; Professor of Surgery, Welsh National School of Medicine. Member: Medical Sub-Committee of University Grants Committee, Medical Research Council, Scientific Advisory Committee of Cancer Research Campaign; Chief Scientist (part-time), Scottish Home and Health Department, 1981-87; Council Member, Royal College of Surgeons of Edinburgh; Advisory Board for Research Councils; Civilian Consultant (Surgery), Royal Navy; Chairman, Working Group, Breast Cancer Screening. Secretary and President, Surgical Research Society; President, Association of Surgeons of Great Britain and Ireland; Secretary, Scottish Society of Experimental Medicine; Member, Kirk Session, St. Giles Cathedral. Publications: Prognostic Factors in Breast Cancer (Co-author), 1968; Principles and Practice of Surgery (Co-author), 1985. Recreation: sailing. Address: (b.) Edinburgh University, Department of Surgery, Royal Infirmary, Edinburgh, EH3 9YW; T.-031-228 1783.

Forrest, Robert Grant. Chairman, Grant Forrest and Partners Ltd., since 1972; b. 20.5.47, Glasgow. Educ. Glasgow Academy. Trainee Account Executive, Peter A. Menzies Advertising, 1965-68; Account Executive, Rex Publicity, 1968-71; Scottish Manager, Riley Advertising, 1971-72. Secretary, Foxhounds Association. Recreations: water skiing; foxhunting. Address: Pegasus House, 375 West George Street, Glasgow, G2 4LW; T.-041-226 3711.

Forrest, Walter Hill, MA, DipEd. Headmaster, Stronsay Secondary School, since 1956; b. 4.3.23, Lanark; m., Paula Buchanan; 1 s.; 2 d. Educ. Larkhall Academy; Glasgow University. Commissioned service, Royal Navy; Headmaster, Flotta Primary School, Orkney, 1951-56. Reader, Church of Scotland. Recreation: gardening. Address: (b.) Stronsay Secondary School, Orkney; T.-Stronsay 246.

Forrester, Professor Alexander Robert, BSc, PhD, DSc, FRSC, FRSE. Professor of Chemistry, Aberdeen University, since 1985 (Head of Department, since 1987); b. 14.11.35, Kelty, Fife; m., Myrna Ross; 1 s.; 3 d. Educ. Alloa Academy; Stirling High School; Heriot-Watt University; Aberdeen University. Lecturer, Paisley Technical College, 1959-60; PhD, Aberdeen, 1960-63; Aberdeen University: Assistant Lecturer, 1963-65, Lecturer, 1965-77, Senior Lecturer, 1977-82, Reader, 1982-85. Recreation: golf. Address: (b.) Chemistry Department, Aberdeen University, Aberdeen; T.-Aberdeen 272944.

Forrester, Professor Duncan Baillie, MA (Hons), BD, DPhil. Principal, New College, Edinburgh, since 1986, and Professor of of Christian Ethics and Practical Theology, since 1978; Chairman, Edinburgh Council of Social Service, 1983-86; Church of Scotland Minister; b. 10.11.33, Edinburgh; m., Rev. Margaret McDonald; 1 s.; 1 d. Educ. Madras College, St. Andrews; St. Andrews University; Chicago University; Edinburgh University. Part-time Assistant in Politics, Edinburgh University, 1957-58; Assistant Minister, Hillside Church, Edinburgh, and Leader of St. James Mission, 1960-61; as Church of Scotland Missionary, Lecturer and then Professor of Politics, Madras Christian College, Tambaram, South India, 1962-

70; ordained Presbyter, Church of South India, 1962; part-time Lecturer in Politics, Edinburgh University, 1966-67; Chaplain and Lecturer in Politics, Sussex University. Publications: Caste & Christianity, 1980; Encounter with God (Co-author), 1983; Studies in the History of Worship in Scotland (Co-Editor), 1984; Christianity and the Future of Welfare, 1985; Theology and Politics, 1988; Just Sharing (Co-author), 1988. Recreations: hill-walking; reading; listening to music. Address: (h.) 25 Kingsburgh Road, Edinburgh, EH12 6DZ; T.-031-337 5646.

Forrester, Frederick Lindsay, MA (Hons), DipEd, MBIM, FEIS. Organising Secretary, Educational Institute of Scotland, since 1975; b. 10.2.35, Glasgow; m., Ann V. Garrity; 1 s.; 1 d. Educ. Victoria Drive Senior Secondary School, Glasgow; Glasgow University; Jordanhill College of Education. Teacher of English, Glasgow secondary schools, 1962-64; Teacher of English and General Studies, Coatbridge Technical College, 1964-67; Assistant Secretary, Educational Institute of Scotland, 1967-75. Contributor to Times Educational Supplement Scotland. Recreations: walking; cycling; swimming; foreign travel. Address: (h.) 28 Liberton Drive, Edinburgh, EH16 6NN; T.-031-664 4797.

Forrester, John McColl, MA, BM, BCh, DObstRCOG, MRCGP. Senior Medical Officer, Scottish Home and Health Department, since 1985; b. 15.9.23, Roslin; m., Hilary Margaret; 1 s.; 2 d. Educ. Edinburgh Academy; St. Andrews University; Oxford University. Formerly Senior Lecturer in Physiology, Edinburgh University. Publication: Companion to Medical Studies (Editor). Recreations: travel; photography. Address: (h.) 120 Morningside Drive, Edinburgh, EH10 5NS.

Forrester, Professor John Vincent, MD, FRCSEdin. Cockburn Professor of Ophthalmology, Aberdeen University, since 1984; Honorary Consultant Ophthalmologist; b. 11.9.46, Glasgow; m., Anne Gray; 2 s.; 2 d. Educ. St. Aloysius College, Glasgow; Glasgow University. Ophthalmologist in training, Glasgow hospitals, 1972-79; MRC Travelling Fellow, Columbia University, New York, 1976-77; Consultant Ophthalmologist, Southern General Hospital, Glasgow, and Honorary Clinical Lecturer, Glasgow University, 1979-84. Recreation: family life. Address: (h.) 12 Urie Crescent, Stonehaven; T.-0569 62303.

Forsyth of That Ilk, Alistair Charles William, JP, FSCA, FSA Scot, FInstPet, CStJ. Baron of Ethie; Chief of the Name and Clan of Forsyth; b. 7.12.29; m., Ann Hughes; 4 s. Educ. St. Paul's School; Queen Mary College, London. Company Director; Priory Chapter, Most Venerable Order of St. John of Jerusalem, since 1978; Member, Angus District Council, since 1988 (Chairman, Industrial Committee). Recreations: Scottish antiquities; hill-walking. Address: (h.) Ethie Castle, by Arbroath, Angus, DD11 5SP.

Forsyth, Constance Catherine, MB, ChB, MD, FRCPLond, FRCPEdin. Reader, Department of Child Health, Dundee University, since 1975; b. 25.7.23, Edinburgh. Educ. George Watson's Ladies' College, Edinburgh; Edinburgh University. Carnegie Research Scholar, Edinburgh University; Research Fellow, Toronto University; Registrar, then Research Fellow, Hospital for Sick Children, Great Ormond Street, London; Dundee University: Lecturer, Department of Child Health, 1955-62, Senior Lecturer, 1962-75. Recreations: hill-walking; golf; swimming; bridge; music; travelling; caravanning. Address: (h.) 5A Glamis Drive, Dundee, DD2 1QG; T.-Dundee 66412.

Forsyth, Professor David J.C., MA (Hons). Professor, Department of Economics, Strathclyde University, since 1985; b. 4.6.40, Elgin; m., Gillian A. Dunmore (deceased); 4 s. Educ. Elgin Academy; Aberdeen University. Economics Lecturer: Strathclyde, 1963-64, Aberdeen, 1964; Visiting Professor, Ghana University, 1971-72; Senior Lecturer, Strathclyde University, 1973-80; UNDP Special Advisor on Technology Policy, Fiji, 1982-83; Reader in Economics, Strathclyde University, 1980-85. Publications: books on American investment in Scotland and technology policy. Recreations: cricket; golf; squash; antiquarianism. Address: (b.) Department of Economics, Strathclyde University, Cathedral Street, Glasgow; T.-041-552 4400, Ext. 3840.

Forsyth, James, MA. Head, Department of Russian, Aberdeen University, since 1964; b. 8.12.28, Edinburgh; m., 1, Mary A. Brown; 2, Tanya Maseeva; 3, Josephine Newcombe; 1 d. Educ. George Heriot's School; Edinburgh University. Edinburgh Public Library, 1946-58; Russian Department, Keele University, 1958-61; Russian Department, Glasgow University, 1961-64. Publications: Russian through Reading (Co-author), 1962; Practical Guide to Russian Stress, 1963; A Grammar of Aspect, 1970; Chuckle with Chekhov (Co-author), 1975; Listening to the Wind, 1977. Recreations: walking; swimming; art; listening to music. Address: (h.) 9 Kirkbrae Avenue, Cults, Aberdeen; T.-Aberdeen 861727.

Forsyth, Michael Bruce, MA. Parliamentary Under Secretary of State, Scottish Office, since 1987; MP (Conservative), Stirling, since 1983; 1983; b. 16.10.54, Montrose; m., Susan Jane; 1 s.; 2 d. Educ. Arbroath High School; St. Andrews University. National Chairman, Federation of Conservative Students, 1976; Member, Westminster City Council, 1978-83; Member, Select Committee on Scottish Affairs; Honorary President, Scottish Federation of Conservative Students; Parliamentary Private Secretary to the Foreign Secretary, 1986-87. Publications: Reservicing Britain; Reservicing Health; The Myths of Privatisation; Down with the Rates; Politics on the Rates; The Case for a Poll Tax. Recreations: mountaineering; astronomy. Address: House of Commons, London, SW1.

Forteviot, 3rd Baron (Henry Evelyn Alexander Dewar), MBE (1943), DL; b. 23.2.06; 2 s.; 2 d. Educ. Eton; St. John's College, Oxford. Black Watch (RHR), 1939-45; Deputy Lieutenant, Perth, 1961; Chairman, John Dewar & Sons Ltd., 1954-76. Address: (h.) Dupplin Castle, Perth.

Fortune, David Ramsay, CA. Vice President, Citibank NA, Edinburgh, since 1988; b. 14.5.47, Edinburgh; m., Phyllis Margaret N. Ewing; 3 d.

Educ. Fettes College; Institute of Chartered Accountants of Scotland. Senior Accountant, Whinney Murray, London, 1973-76; appointed Assistant Manager, Chemical Bank, London and Edinburgh, 1977-80; joined Citibank, 1980, and appointed Resident Vice President, Edinburgh Branch, 1982; Director, Stanecastle Assets Ltd., 1986-87. Recreations: shooting; yachting; gardening. Address: (h.) 15 Kingsburgh Road, Edinburgh, EH12 6DZ; T.-031-337 1556.

Forty, Professor Arthur John, BSc, PhD, DSc, FRSE. Principal and Vice-Chancellor, Stirling University, since 1986; b. 4.11.28, Shrivenham; m., Alicia Blanche Hart; 1 s. Educ. Headlands School, Swindon; Bristol University. RAF, 1953-56; Senior Scientist, Tube Investments Ltd., 1956-58; Lecturer, Bristol University, 1958-64; founding Professor of Physics, Warwick University, 1964-86; Pro-Vice-Chancellor, Warwick Univ., 1970-86; Member, UGC, 1982-86 (Vice-Chairman, 1985-86); Member, Computer Board, Universities and Research Councils, 1982-85 (Chairman, since 1988); Member, British Library Board, since 1987; author of "Forty Report" on future facilities for advanced research computing. Recreations: dinghy sailing; gardening. Address: (h.) Principal's House, Stirling University, Stirling, FK9 4LA.

Forwell, Harold Christie. Senior Partner, Carlton Bakeries, Kirkcaldy, since 1955; Member, Fife Health Board; Member, Industrial Tribunals (Scotland); Director, Kirkcaldy District Chamber of Commerce; b. 16.8.25, Kirkcaldy; m., Isobel Russell Stuart; 1 s.; 1 d. Educ. George Watson's College, Edinburgh; Queen's University, Belfast. Past Chairman, National Joint Committee for Scottish Baking Industry; former Member, Retail Wages Council (BFCS Scotland); Past President: Scottish Association of Master Bakers, Kirkcaldy Rotary Club. Queen's Jubilee Medal, 1977. Recreations: sailing; travel. Address: (h.) 4 West Fergus Place, Kirkcaldy, Fife; T.-0592 260474.

Foster, John, CBE, FRICS, FRTPI, RIBA, ARIAS, FRSA. Director, Countryside Commission for Scotland, 1968-85; b. 13.8.20, Glasgow; m., Daphne Househam. Educ. Whitehill School, Glasgow; Royal Technical College, Glasgow. Surveyor with private firm in Glasgow, 1937; Air Ministry during War; Assistant Planning Officer: Kirkcudbright County Council, 1945-47, Holland Joint Planning Committee, Lincolnshire, 1947-48; Deputy County Planning Officer, Holland County Council, 1948-52; Deputy Planning Officer, Peak Park Planning Board, 1952-54; Director, Peak District National Park Board, 1954-68. Honorary Vice-President, Countrywide Holidays Association; Honorary Fellow, Royal Scottish Geographical Society; Member, Planning and Development Divisional Council, RICS (Penfold Silver Medallist); Life Member, National Trust for Scotland. Recreations: walking; swimming; photography; philately; reading; travel. Address: (h.) Birchover, Ferntower Road, Crieff, PH7 3DH; T.-0764 2336.

Foster, Professor John Odell, MA, PhD. Professor of Applied Social Studies, Paisley College, since 1981; b. 21.10.40, Hertford; m., Renee Prendergast. Educ. Guildford Grammar School; St. Catherine's College, Cambridge. Postdoctoral Research Fellow, St. Catherine's College, Cambridge, 1965-68; Lecturer in Politics, Strathclyde University, 1966-81. Publications: Class Struggle and the Industrial Revolution, 1974; Politics of the UCS Work-In, 1986. Recreation: hill-walking. Address: (h.) 9 Taransay Street, Glasgow, G51; T.-041-440 0437.

Foster, Professor Roy, MA, DPhil, DSc, FRSC, FRSE. Emeritus Professor; Professor of Physical-Organic Chemistry, Dundee University, 1969-86; b. 29.7.28, Leicester; m., Delwen Eluned Rodd; 1 s.; 2 d. Educ. Wyggeston School, Leicester; Wadham College, Oxford. Research Fellow, Department of Pharmacology, Oxford University, 1953-56; Queen's College, Dundee (St. Andrews University): Senior Edward A. Deeds Fellow, 1956-59, Lecturer in Organic Chemistry, 1959-63, Senior Lecturer, 1963-66, Reader, 1966-67 (thence Dundee University, 1967-69). British Association for the Advancement of Science: Member of Council, Member, General Committee, Chairman, Tayside and Fife Branch, 1977-84; Dundee University: sometime Member of Court, Dean, Faculty of Science, Head, Department of Chemistry. Recreation: gardening. Address: (b.) Chemistry Department, Dundee University, Dundee, DD1 4HN; T.-0382 23181.

Fotheringham, John, OBE, FRAgS. Chairman: Scottish Seed Potato Development Council, since 1981, North of Scotland Innovation Services Ltd., since 1986, Grampian Employers Network, since 1987, Deeside Salmon Fisheries Board, since 1985, Aberdeen University Research and Industrial Services Ltd., since 1985; Director: Stewart Milne Group Ltd., since 1986, ESK Foods Holdings Ltd., since 1987; Chairman, Grampian Regional Transport Ltd., since 1987; b. 5.6.23, Kincardine, Fife; m., Isobel Mary Ballantyne; 1 s.; 2 d. Educ. Dunfermline High School. Royal Navy, 1941-47 (Lt., RNVR); National Bank of Scotland Ltd., 1947-49; District Manager, J. Bibby and Sons Ltd., 1949-53; Assistant Manager, Barclay, Ross & Hutchison Ltd., Aberdeen, 1953-55; Managing Director, Northern Agricultural Lime Co., Aberdeen, 1955-64; Unilever Ltd., 1964-72 (latterly Managing Director, United Agricultural Merchants Ltd.); Managing Director, North Eastern Farmers Ltd., 1971-86; Chairman, Grampian Tractors Ltd., 1976-87; Director, National Pig Development Co. (Scotland) Ltd., 1973-87. Member, Scottish Agricultural Organisation Society Ltd., 1972-86; President, United Kingdom Agricultural Supply Trade Association, 1977-78; Member: Aberdeen Harbour Board, since 1978, Co-operative Development Agency, since 1984; Convener, Scottish Rotary Youth Leadership Award Scheme, since 1984; Council Member, Aberdeen Chamber of Commerce, since 1984; Member, Aberdeen University Court, since 1984; Grampian Industrialist of the Year, 1983. Recreations: golf; swimming. Address: (h.) St. Helens, Earlsferry, Fife, KY9 1AF; T.-0333 330 600.

Foulds, Professor Wallace Stewart, MD, ChM, FRCS, FRCSGlas, DO. Tennent Professor of Ophthalmology, Glasgow University, since 1964; Honorary Consultant Ophthalmologist, Greater Glasgow Health Board, since 1964; b. 26.4.24,

London; m., Margaret Holmes Walls; 1 s.; 2 d. Educ. George Watson's Boys College, Edinburgh; Paisley Grammar School; Glasgow University. RAF Medical Branch, 1946-49; training posts, Moorfields Eye Hospital, London, 1952-54; Research Fellow, Institute of Ophthalmology, London University, and Senior Registrar, University College Hospital, London, 1954-58; Consultant Ophthalmologist, Addenbrookes Hospital, Cambridge, 1958-64; Honorary Lecturer, Cambridge University and Research Fellow, London University, 1958-64; Past President: Ophthalmological Society of UK, Faculty of Ophthalmologists; Past Chairman, Association for Eye Research. Recreations: sailing; diving. Address: (b.) Tennent Institute of Ophthalmology, Glasgow University, Western Infirmary, Glasgow, G11 6NT; T.-041-339 8822, Ext. 4640.

Foulis, Alan Keith, BSc, MD, MRCPath. Consultant Pathologist, Royal Infirmary, Glasgow, since 1983; b. 25.5.50, Glasgow; m., Anne Don Foulis; 1 s.; 1 d. Educ. Glasgow Academy; Glasgow University. Trained in pathology, Western Infirmary, Glasgow, following brief flirtation with surgery at Aberdeen Royal Infirmary; C.L. Oakley Lecturer, Pathological Society, Oxford, 1987; Bellahouston Medal, Glasgow University, 1987. Publications: research papers on diseases of the pancreas. Recreations: choral and Leider singing; walking; cycling; arctophilia; natural history. Address: (h.) 32 Tannoch Drive, Milngavie, Glasgow; T.-041-956 3092.

Foulkes, George, JP, BSc. MP (Labour and Co-operative), Carrick, Cumnock and Doon Valley, since 1979; Opposition Spokesman on Foreign Affairs, since 1984; b. 21.1.42, Oswestry; m., Elizabeth Anna; 2 s.; 1 d. Educ. Keith Grammar School; Haberdashers' Aske's School; Edinburgh University. President, Scottish Union of Students, 1964-66; Director: European League for Economic Co-operation, 1967-68, Enterprise Youth, 1968-73, Age Concern Scotland, 1973-79; Chairman: Lothian Region Education Committee, 1974-79, Education Committee, COSLA, 1975-79; Rector's Assessor, Edinburgh University, 1968-71. Recreation: boating; watching football (Heart of Midlothian and Ayr United). Address: (h.) 8 Southpark Road, Ayr, KA7 2TL; T.-Ayr 265776.

Fowlie, Hector Chalmers, MB, ChB, FRCPEdin, FRCPsych, DPM. Vice-Chairman, Mental Welfare Commission for Scotland, since 1984; Consultant Psychiatrist, since 1963; b. 21.6.29, Dundee; m., Christina N.M. Walker; 2 s.; 1 d. Educ. Harris Academy, Dundee; St. Andrews University. House Officer, Maryfield Hospital, Dundee, and Perth Royal Infirmary; Registrar, Dundee Royal Mental Hospital; Lecturer, Department of Psychiatry, Medical School, Dundee University; Consultant Psychiatrist and Deputy Physician Superintendent, Gartnavel Royal Hospital, Glasgow; Physician Superintendent, Royal Dundee Liff and Strathmartine Hospitals; Consultant Psychiatrist, Tayside Health Board. Sometime Vice-Chairman, Parole Board for Scotland; Member, Tayside Health Board; Council of Europe Scholar; Consultant, WHO. Recreations: reading; walking. Address: (h.) 21 Clepington Road, Dundee; T.-0382 41926.

Fox, George Frew, CA. Chairman, Dundee United Football Club; b. 18.11.13, Carnoustie; m., Violet J. Low; 2 d. Educ. Grove Academy, Dundee. Commenced practice as CA, 1938; War Service, 1940-46; resumed practice, 1946; retired, 1978; former Treasurer, Scottish Football Association (Life Member); Life Member: Carnoustie Golf Club, Broughty Golf Club, Forfarshire Football Association, Tayside Athletic Club; Honorary President, Carnoustie Panmure FC; Honorary Vice President, Broughty Operatic Society. Recreation: golf. Address: (h.) 17 Lochty Street, Carnoustie, Angus.

Fox, John Edward, BDSEdin, FDS, RCSEdin. Consultant Oral Surgeon, Tayside Health Board, since 1972; Honorary Senior Lecturer, Dundee University, since 1972; b. 30.6.31, Birmingham; m., Valerie May Anderson; 2 s.; 2 d. Educ. Haverfordwest Grammar School; Edinburgh University. Left school at 16 and followed a business career; entered Edinburgh University to study dentistry, 1957; Lecturer in Periodontology, Edinburgh Dental School; Registrar in Oral Surgery, Edinburgh Royal Infirmary; Senior Registrar in Oral Surgery, St. James Hospital, Leeds. Chairman, Scottish Committee for Hospital Dental Services. Recreations: sailing; hill-walking. Address: (h.) 16 Corsie Avenue, Perth, PH2 7BS; T.-Perth 29145.

Foxall, Professor Gordon Robert, BSc, MSc, PhD. Professor of Marketing, Strathclyde, since 1987; b. 16.7.49; m.; 1 d. Educ. Salford Univ.; Birmingham Univ. Lecturer, Newcastle-upon-Tyne University, 1972-79; Lecturer, Birmingham University, 1980-83; Senior Lecturer, then Reader, Cranfield Institute of Technology, 1983-86. Recreations: reading; walking. Address: (b.) Strathclyde University, Glasgow.

Fraile, Professor Medardo, PhD. Writer; Emeritus Professor in Spanish, Strathclyde University, since 1985; b. 21.3.25, Madrid; m., Janet H. Gallagher; 1 d. Educ. Madrid University. Teacher of Spanish language and literature, Ramiro de Maeztu Secondary School, Madrid, 1956-64; Assistant in Spanish, Southampton University, 1964-67; Strathclyde University: Assistant Lecturer in Spanish, 1967-68, Lecturer, 1968-79, Reader, 1979-83, Personal Professor, 1983-85. Travelling Scholarship for authors, 1954; Premio Sesamo for short story writing, 1956; literary grant, Juan March Foundation, 1960; Book of the Year award, 1965; La Estafeta Literaria Prize for short stories, 1970; Hucha de Oro Prize for short stories, 1971; research grant, Carnegie Trust, 1975. Publications: several collections of short stories, a novel and books of literary criticism. Recreations: swimming; walking. Address: (h.) 24 Etive Crescent, Bishopbriggs, Glasgow, G64 1ES; T.-041-772 4421.

Frain, Ian Millar, MA, JP. Rector, Mearns Academy, since 1968; b. 29.9.27, Auckland, New Zealand; m., Lorna; 3 d. Educ. Robert Gordon's College, Aberdeen; Aberdeen University. Provost of Laurencekirk, 1978; Kincardine and Deeside District Council: Chairman, 1975-84, Vice-Convener, since 1984; Chairman, Kincardine and Deeside Area Tourist Board, 1982-84. Convener, Laurencekirk Meals on Wheels Service. Recreations: rugby (Gordonian rugby "cap"); tennis; golf. Address: (h.) The Firs, Laurencekirk; T.-Laurencekirk 458.

Frame, Roger Campbell Crosbie, CA. Secretary, Royal Scottish Society of Painters in Water Colours, since 1986; Secretary, Glasgow Eastern Merchants and Tradesmen's Society, since 1983; Treasurer, Glasgow Group of Artists, since 1983; b. 7.6.49, Glasgow; m., Angela M. Everisti; 2 s.; 1 d. Educ. Glasgow Academy. Qualified CA, 1973; formed Frame & Co., CA, 1976. Deacon, Incorporation of Coopers of Glasgow, 1985-86. Recreations: clay pigeon shooting; art. Address: (b.) 29 Waterloo Street, Glasgow, G2 6BZ; T.-041-226 3838.

France, Professor Peter, MA, PhD. Professor of French, Edinburgh University, since 1980; b. 19.10.35, Londonderry; m., Sian Reynolds; 3 d. Educ. Bradford Grammar School; Magdalen College, Oxford. Fellow, Magdalen College, Oxford, 1960-63; Lecturer, then Reader in French, Sussex University, 1963-80; French Editor, Modern Language Review, 1979-85. Publications: Racine's Rhetoric, 1965; Rhetoric and Truth in France, 1972; Poets of Modern Russia, 1982; Diderot, 1982; Rousseau: Confessions, 1987. Address: (b.) 4 Buccleuch Place, Edinburgh, EH8 9LW; T.-031-667 1011.

Francey, David Maxwell, FRSA, MInstAM, MInstVT. Public Relations and Promotions Director, The Child and Family Trust; Management and Public Relations Consultant; Freelance Broadcaster; b. 22.2.24, Glasgow; m., Sheila Cameron; 1 s. Educ. Hyndland School, Glasgow; Learmonth College, Edinburgh; Stow College. RAF VR (wartime); Ministry of Civil Aviation; Ministry of Transport; Scottish Gas Board; South of Scotland Electricity Board; Freelance Sports Reporter and Commentator, BBC, 1952-87; has broadcast major football events from more than 20 countries. Publication: And It's All Over (autobiography). Recreations: public speaking; singing; conversation; football at all levels. Address: (h.) 57 Arisdale Crescent, Newton Mearns, Glasgow, G77 6HB; T.-041-639 4638.

Francis, John Michael, BSc, ARCS, PhD, DIC. Director Scotland, Nature Conservancy Council, since 1984; b. 1.5.39, London; m., Eileen; 2 d. Educ. Gowerton Grammar School, near Swansea; Imperial College of Science and Technology, London University. CEGB Berkeley Nuclear Laboratories, 1963-70; Director, Society, Religion and Technology Project, Church of Scotland, 1970-74; Senior Research Fellow, Heriot-Watt University, 1974-76; Principal, Scottish Development Department, 1976-81; Assistant Secretary, Scottish Office, 1981-84. Consultant, World Council of Churches, 1970-83; Chairman, SRT Project, Church of Scotland; Member, Oil Development Council for Scotland, 1973-76; Member, Advisory Committee for Scotland, Nature Conservancy Council, 1973-76; Council Member, National Trust for Scotland, since 1984; Chairman, Edinburgh Forum, since 1986. Publications: Scotland in Turmoil, 1972; Changing Directions, 1973; Facing Up to Nuclear Power, 1976. Recreations: theatre; hill-walking; ecumenical travels. Address: (h.) 49 Gilmour Road, Newington, Edinburgh, EH16 5NU; T.-031-667 3996; (b.) Scottish Headquarters, Nature Conservancy Council, 12 Hope Terrace, Edinburgh, EH9 2AS; T.-031-447 4784.

Franklin, Mark Newman, MA (Oxon), PhD. Reader in Political Science, Strathclyde University; Social Research Consultant; b. 29.1.42; m., Carole Elizabeth Madelaine; 1 s.; 1 d. Educ. Dauntsey's School; Balliol College, Oxford; Cornell University. Visiting Fellow, St. Anne's College, Oxford, 1968; joined Strathclyde University as Lecturer in Politics, 1969; Visiting Professor, Chicago University, 1974-75, and Senior Study Director, National Opinion Research Center; Senior Visiting Fellow, Edinburgh University, 1977-78; Scientific Study Director, European Science Foundation, 1984-85; Visiting Professor, University of Iowa, 1984-85; Visiting Fellow, All Souls College, Oxford, 1987-88; sometime Consultant, Equal Opportunities Commission, and other public bodies. Publications: A User's Guide to the SCSS Conversational Statistical System, 1980; The Decline of Class Voting in Britain, 1985; The Community of Science in Europe, 1988. Recreations: sailing (yachtmaster); swimming; music; theatre. Address: (b.) Department of Politics, Strathclyde University, Glasgow, G1 1XQ; T.-041-552 4400.

Franks, Graham, RGN, RMN, RNMH, DipN, AHSM. Chief Area Nursing Officer, Fife Health Board, since 1987; b. 30.10.43, Leicester; m., V.J. Franks. Educ. Guthlaxton Grammar School, Leicester. Manager, Patient Care Services, East Cumbria Health Authority; Director of Nursing Services, Carlisle Acute Hospitals; Area Nurse Planning/Personnel, Cumbria Area Health Authority; Regional Nursing Officer, Newcastle Regional Hospital Board. Address: (b.) Glenrothes House, Fife; T.-Glenrothes 754355.

Fraser, Brian Mitchell, BA (Hons), PhD, DGA. Director of Personnel, Glasgow University, since 1982; b. 31.7.43, Paisley; m., Hannah Orr Weir Burt; 3 s. Educ. Camphill High School, Paisley; London University; Strathclyde University. Civil Servant, 1962-70; Senior Administrator, Paisley College of Technology, 1970-78; Lecturer in History, Glasgow College of Technology, since 1977; Boys' Brigade historian and leader. Publications: Sure and Stedfast - A History of the Boys' Brigade (Co-author), 1983; A Legacy of Scots (Co-author), 1988. Recreations: youth work; golf; family. Address: (h.) Dunedin, Holehouse Road, Eaglesham; T.-Eaglesham 2416.

Fraser, Callum George, BSc, PhD, FAACB, FACB. Top Grade Biochemist, Ninewells Hospital and Medical School, since 1983; Honorary Senior Lecturer, Dundee University, since 1983; b. 3.1.45, Dundee; m., Stella Sim; 2 d. Educ. Dunfermline High School; Perth Academy; Aberdeen University. Postdoctoral Fellow, National Research Council of Canada, 1969-70; Lecturer in Chemical Pathology, Aberdeen University, and Honorary Biochemist, Grampian Health Board, 1970-75; Chief Clinical Biochemist, Flinders Medical Centre, South Australia, 1975-83; Honorary Senior Lecturer, then Honorary Associate Professor, Flinders University of South Australia, 1975-83. Member, Education Committee, International Federation of Clinical Chemistry; Member, Commission on Teaching of Clinical Chemistry, International Union of Pure and Applied Chemistry; Member, Editorial Boards, Advances in Clinical Chemistry and Clinical Physiology and Biochemistry. Recreations: gardening; reading; travel. Address: (b.) Department of Biochemical Medicine, Ninewells Hospital, Dundee, DD1 9SY; T.-0382 60111.

Fraser, Sir Campbell, BCom, LLD (Strathclyde), DUniv (Stirling), CBIM, FRSE. Chairman, Scottish Television plc, since 1975; Director, British Petroleum Co. plc, since 1978; Director, BAT Industries plc, since 1980; b. 2.5.23, Dunblane; m., Maria Harvey McLaren; 2 d. Educ. McLaren High School, Callander; Glasgow University; Dundee School of Economics. Many positions in Dunlop company (Sole Managing Director, 1972-78, Chairman, 1978-83); Board Member: Bridgewater Paper, Tandem Computers, Green Park Health Care (Chairman), Alexander Proudfoot plc; President, Confederation of British Industry, 1982-84 (Deputy President, 1981-82); Vice President, Scottish Opera; Trustee, The Economist; Visiting Professor, Stirling University; Member of Court, St. Andrews University; President, Society of Business Economists, 1973-85; Past Chairman, Strathclyde University Business School. Recreations: reading; walking; supporting Dundee Football Club. Address: (b.) Scottish Television plc, 7 Adelaide Street, London, WC2N 4LZ; T.-01-836 1500.

Fraser, Charles Annand, CVO, WS, DL. Partner, W. & J. Burness, WS, since 1956; Purse Bearer to Lord High Commissioner to General Assembly of Church of Scotland, since 1969; Chairman, Japan Assets Trust PLC; Director: Adam and Company PLC, Walter Alexander PLC, Anglo Scottish Investment Trust PLC, British Assets Trust PLC, W. & J. Burness Trustees Ltd., Edinburgh American Assets Trust PLC, Edinburgh Old Town Trust, Edinburgh Venture Enterprise Trust, Grosvenor Developments, Scottish Widows' Fund and Life Assurance Society, Scottish Television PLC, Scottish Business in the Community, Signetics (UK) Ltd., Solsgirth Investment Trust Co. Ltd.; Vice Chairman, United Biscuits (Holdings) PLC; b. 16.10.28, Humbie, East Lothian; m., Ann Scott-Kerr; 4 s. Educ. Hamilton Academy; Edinburgh University. Served on Court, Heriot-Watt University; Council Member, Law Society of Scotland, 1966-72; Trustee, Scottish Civic Trust. Recreations: gardening; skiing; squash; piping. Address: (h.) Shepherd House, Inveresk, Midlothian; T.-031-665 2570.

Fraser, David McKee, BSc, MB, ChB, FRCPEdin. Consultant Physician, Milesmark Hospital, Dunfermline, since 1979; Postgraduate Clinical Tutor, West Fife, since 1981; Honorary Senior Lecturer, Department of Medicine, Edinburgh University, since 1979; b. 11.4.47, Dunfermline; m., M. Joan Park; 1 s.; 1 d. Educ. Dunfermline High School; Edinburgh University. Junior hospital posts, South-East Regional Hospital Board, then Lothian Health Board, 1971-79. Address: (h.) Gowan Brae, 120 Garvock Hill, Dunfermline.

Fraser, Douglas Jamieson. Poet; b. 12.1.10, Edinburgh; m., Eva Nisbet Greenshields; 2 s.; 1 d. Educ. George Heriot's School. Spent 44 years with Standard Life Assurance Company, Edinburgh; awarded Queen's Silver Jubilee Medal. Publications: Landscape of Delight; Rhymes o' Auld Reekie; Where the Dark Branches Part; Treasure for Eyes to Hold. Recreation: painting. Address: (h.) 2 Keith Terrace, Edinburgh, EH4 3NJ; T.-031-332 5176.

Fraser, Elwena D.A. Honorary Sheriff, Tayside, Central and Fife, since 1982; Member, Rateable Valuation Appeal Committee, 1975-85; Governor, Dundee College of Technology, since 1969; b. 5.9.31, Lowestoft; m., Dr. Ian Tuke Fraser; 2 s.; 1 d. Educ. Craigholm School, Glasgow; Calder Girls' School, Seascale. Journalist, Scottish Daily Express, 1950-54; Member, Perth Town Council, 1969-72; Member, Education Committee, Perth County Council, 1969-72; Member, Dundee University Adult Education Committee, 1969-72; Member, Executive Committee, Perth Tourist Association, 1969-72; Member, Executive Committee, Perth Festival of the Arts, 1971-81; Board Member, Perth College of Further Education, 1972-78 (Chairman, 1975-78); Honorary Manager, Trustee Savings Bank (Perthshire), 1973-75; Member, Gas Consumers Council for Scotland, since 1973; Member, BBC Broadcasting Council for Scotland, 1977-80. Recreation: gardening. Address: (h.) 15 Spoutwells Avenue, Scone, Perthshire, PH2 6RP; T.-0738 51310.

Fraser, Hugh Donald George, QPM, DipSM, OStJ, FBIM, MIPM, MIIRSM. Senior Assistant Secretary, Heriot-Watt University, since 1971; Member, Lothian Regional Council, since 1982; Honorary Secretary, Scottish Chamber of Safety, since 1979; b. Edinburgh; m., Margaret Jane Stothard; 1 s.; 2 d. War Service, RAF Aircrew, 1939-45 (Pilot); Edinburgh City Police, 1941-71; Chief Superintendent, Research and Planning Branch, Home Office, London, 1966-68; Deputy Commandant, Scottish Police College, 1968-71. Honorary Secretary, Edinburgh and District Spastic Association, 14 years; Member: Edinburgh Accident Prevention Council, Lothian Retirement Committee. Recreations: Burns' enthusiast; work with senior citizens; jogging; the theatre. Address: (h.) 181 Braid Road, Edinburgh, EH10 6JA; T.-031-447 1270.

Fraser, Ian Ross, MA (Hons), MEd. Rector, Inverness Royal Academy, since 1971; b. 16.4.30, Carmyle, Lanarkshire; m., Trudy C. Marshall; 3 s.; 1 d. Educ. Aberdeen Grammar School; Aberdeen University; Aberdeen College of Education. Principal Teacher of Geography, Elgin Academy, 1960-66; Rector, Waid Academy, Anstruther, 1966-71; Member, Ruthven Committee on Ancillary Staff in Secondary Schools, 1973-76; Honorary Secretary, 1975-77, and President, 1978-79, Headteachers' Association of Scotland; Chairman, Highland Region Curriculum Coordinating Group, 1980-84; Chairman, Scottish Central Committee on Social Subjects, 1981-83; Chairman, Steering Committee, S1/2 Social Subjects Development Programme, 1983-87; Member, Scottish Consultative Council on the Curriculum, SCCC Board of Management, SCCC Secondary Committee (Convener). Recreations: tennis; badminton; fishing; hill-walking. Address: (h.) Yendor, Dores Road, Inverness, IV2 4XE; T.-0463 232862.

Fraser, Ian Scott, BSc (Econ), LLB, DEc, DPA, FBIM. Barrister-at-Law; Advocate; b. 21.7.18, Dundee; m., Kathleen Mary Fraser; 1 s.; 1 d. Educ. Fort William High School; London University. Civil Service: Admiralty, 1936-46, Ministry of Pensions and National Insurance, 1946-55 and 1961-63, Treasury, 1955-57 (seconded to NATO (Shape) Paris 1956-57); United Nations official, 1957-61 and 1963-76, serving in Ethiopia and other African countries, New York, Middle East, and South America; travel and further education, 1976-81; practising Advocate, 1981-86; Chairman, Board of Directors, Scottish Rights of Way Society Ltd., 1983-86; Life Member, National Trust for Scotland and Royal Scottish Geographical Society. Recreations: travel; photography; motor caravanning; walking. Address: (h.) 1 Mayfield Gardens, Edinburgh, EH9 2AX; T.-031-667 3681.

Fraser, Professor Sir James David, 2nd Bt, FRCSEdin, FRCS, ChM, BA, MB, ChB. Postgraduate Dean, Faculty of Medicine, Edinburgh University, since 1981; b. 19.7.24; m.; 2 s. Educ. Edinburgh Academy; Magdalen College, Oxford. President, Royal College of Surgeons of Edinburgh, 1982-85.

Fraser, James Edward, MA (Aberdeen), BA (Cantab). Under Secretary, Scottish Home and Health Department, since 1981; b. 16.12.31, Aberdeen; m., Patricia Louise Stewart; 2 s. Educ. Aberdeen Grammar School; Aberdeen University; Christ's College, Cambridge. Royal Artillery, 1953-55 (Staff Captain, "Q", Tel-El-Kebir, 1954-55); Assistant Principal, Scottish Home Department, 1957-60; Private Secretary to Permanent Under-Secretary of State, Scottish Office, 1960-62; Private Secretary to Parliamentary Under-Secretary of State, Scottish Office, 1962; Principal, 1962-69: SHHD, 1962-64, Cabinet Office, 1964-66, HM Treasury, 1966-68, SHHD, 1968-69; Assistant Secretary: SHHD, 1970-76, Scottish Office Finance Division, 1976; Under Secretary, Local Government Finance Group, Scottish Office, 1976-81. President, Scottish Hellenic Society, Edinburgh and South East Scotland. Recreations: reading; music; walking; Greece, ancient and modern. Address: (b.) St. Andrew's House, Edinburgh, EH1 3DE.

Fraser, John, MA. Rector, Mackie Academy, Stonehaven, since 1975; b. 8.8.36, Inverness; m., Judith Helen Procter; 2 d. Educ. Inverness Royal Academy; Aberdeen University; Aberdeen College of Education. Teacher, Harris Academy, 1960-66; Principal Teacher of History, Buckie High School, 1966-72; Assistant Head Teacher and Depute Rector, Peterhead Academy, 1972-75; Governor, Aberdeen College of Education, since 1984; Member: GTC, 1979-83, Grampian Region Education Committee, 1975-78; Regional Convener, SSTA, since 1975. Conductor: Buckie Choral Union, 1968-72, Peterhead Choral Society, 1972-75; Organist in various churches; President, Stonehaven Rotary Club, 1988-89. Recreations: music; DIY. Address: (b.) Slug Road, Stonehaven; T.-Stonehaven 62071/2.

Fraser, John A.W., MA, FEIS, JP, DL. Headmaster, Scalloway Junior High School, 1966-88; Deputy Lieutenant for Shetland, since 1985; b. 9.11.28, Lerwick; m., Jane Ann Jamieson; 2 s. Educ. Anderson Educational Institute; Edinburgh University; Moray House College of Education. Education Officer, RAF, 1950-52; Teacher, Baltasound Junior Secondary School, 1952-54; Head Teacher: Haroldswick Primary School, 1954-59, Aith Junior High School, 1959-66. Former Member, National Council, EIS; Member, Hjaltland Housing Association. Recreation: committees! Address: (h.) Broadwinds, Castle Street, Scalloway, Shetland; T.-Scalloway 644.

Fraser, Rev. John Gillies. Chairman, Lord's Day Observance Society, Scottish Council, since 1985; Chairman, Church of Scotland Total Abstainers Society, since 1980; Vice-Chairman, National Church Association, since 1986; Minister, Elderpark Macgregor Parish Church, Glasgow, 1970-86; b. 5.7.14, Glasgow; m., Jessie MacKenzie Mayer; 1 s.; 3 d. Educ. Shawlands Academy; Glasgow University and Trinity College. Public Assistance Department (later Social Service Department), Glasgow Corporation, 1931-48; Ministry of National Insurance, 1948; divinity student, 1948-50; Minister/Missionary, Church of Scotland, Northern Rhodesia, 1950-60; Minister, Macgregor Memorial Church, 1960-70. Scottish Assistant Secretary, Crusaders' Union, 1935-47; Secretary, South West Glasgow Sunday School Union, 1942-47. Recreation: gardening. Address: (h.) 17 Beaufort Gardens, Bishopbriggs, Glasgow, G64 2DJ; T.-041-772 2987.

Fraser, Keith James, FILAM, DipLD. Director of Parks and Recreation, City of Glasgow District Council, since 1981; b. 11.9.32, Blackpool; m., Margaret; 1 s.; 1 d. Educ. Blackpool Grammar School. Youth gardener/gardener Class II, Blackpool Parks Department, 1949-50 and 1953-56; probationer, Royal Botanic Gardens, Edinburgh, 1956-59; junior technical assistant, Stoke-on-Trent Parks Department, 1959-62; horticultural assistant, City of Glasgow Parks and Botanic Gardens Department, 1962-65; Deputy Director of Parks and Cemeteries, City of Belfast, 1965-69; Depute Director of Parks and Botanic Gardens, City of Glasgow, 1969-74; Director of Parks, City of Glasgow District Council, 1974-81. Recreations: cricket; swimming; reading; gardening. Address: (b.) 20 Trongate, Glasgow, G1 5ES; T.-041-227 5058.

Fraser, Kenneth Nicholson. Director of Environmental Health, Dunfermline District Council, since 1975; b. 11.7.32, Dunfermline; m., Christine Robertson; 1 s.; 2 d. Educ. Dunfermline High School; Heriot-Watt College, Edinburgh. Apprentice, then Assistant Sanitary Inspector, 1949-63; Dunfermline Town Council, 1964-75, latterly as Chief Sanitary Inspector and Inspector of Cleansing. Chairman, Scottish Centre, Institute of Wastes Management, 1986-88. Recreations: golf; rugby; gardening. Address: (h.) 1 Perdieus Mount, Dunfermline, KY12 7XE; T.-0383 722341.

Fraser, Peter, QC. Solicitor-General for Scotland, since 1982; MP, Angus East, 1983-87 (Angus South, 1979-83); b. 29.5.45. Educ. Loretto

School; Gonville and Caius College, Cambridge; Edinburgh University. Advocate; Lecturer in Constitutional Law, Heriot-Watt University, 1971-75; Chairman, Scottish Conservative Lawyers Law Reform Group, 1976.

Fraser, Raymond Morris, LLB (Hons). Advocate, since 1971; b. 16.2.47, Edinburgh. Educ. George Heriot's School, Edinburgh; Edinburgh University. Conservative Parliamentary candidate, Orkney and Shetland, October, 1974; instigator of visit to Angola, 1976, to defend British mercenaries at war crimes trial. Address: (h.) Bonaly Tower, Edinburgh; T.-031-441 3804.

Fraser, Robert W., BSc (Hons), CEng, FICE, FIWEM. Director, Water and Drainage Services, Borders Regional Council, since 1981; b. 13.5.39, Kirkcaldy; m., Elizabeth; 1 s.; 1 d. Educ. Kirkcaldy High School; Edinburgh University. Address: (b.) West Grove, Waverley Road, Melrose, TD6 9SJ; T.-Melrose 2056.

Fraser, Simon William Hetherington, LLB, NP. Partner, Flowers & Co., Solicitors, Glasgow, since 1976; Temporary Sheriff, since 1987; b. 2.4.51, Carlisle; m., Sheena Janet; 1 d. Educ. Glasgow Academy; Glasgow University. Glasgow Bar Association: Secretary, 1977-79, President, 1981-82. Recreations: cricket; snooker. Address: (b.) 134 Holland Street, Glasgow; T.-041-221 5344.

Fraser, Rt. Hon. Thomas, PC (1964); b. 18.2.11, Lesmahagow; m., Janet M. Scanlon (deceased); 1 s.; 1 d. Educ. Lesmahagow Higher Grade School. Worked in coal mines (underground), 1925-43; branch official, Miners' Union, 1938-43; MP (Lab), Hamilton, 1943-67; Parliamentary Under Secretary of State for Scotland, 1945-51; Member, Shadow Cabinet, 1956-64; Minister of Transport, 1964-65, and Member of Cabinet; Member, Royal Commission on Local Government in Scotland, 1966-69; Chairman, North of Scotland Hydro-Electric Board, 1967-73; Member, South of Scotland Electricity Board, 1967-73; Member, Highlands and Islands Development Board, 1967-70; Chairman, Scottish Local Authorities Staff Commission, 1973-78; Chairman, Commission for Local Authority Accounts in Scotland, 1974-79; Chairman, SLA Property Commission, 1976-78; Freeman of Hamilton, 1964. Recreation: gardening. Address: (h.) 15 Broompark Drive, Lesmahagow, Lanark; T.-0555 893223.

Fraser, Professor William Douglas, BSc, MSc, PhD, FRICS. Professor and Head, Department of Land Economics, Paisley College, since 1986; b. 3.1.40, Edinburgh. Educ. Edinburgh Academy; London University; Strathclyde University. Partner, Bingham, Hughes and Macpherson, Chartered Surveyors, Inverness, 1970-72; Lecturer, Department of Land Economics, Paisley College, 1972-83; Lecturer, Centre for Property Valuation and Management, City University, London, 1983-86. Publication: Principles of Property Investment and Pricing, 1984. Recreations: climbing; squash. Address: (b.) Department of Land Economics, Paisley College, High Street, Paisley, PA1 2BE; T.-041-887 1241.

Fraser, William Hamish, MA, DPhil. Senior Lecturer in History, Strathclyde University, since 1977 (Dean, Faculty of Arts and Social Studies, since 1987); b. 30.6.41, Keith; m., Helen Tuach; 1 d. Educ. Keith Grammar School; Aberdeen University; Sussex University. Lecturer in History, Strathclyde University, 1976-77; Co-Editor, Scottish Economic and Social History. Publications: Trade Unions and Society 1850-1880, 1973; Workers and Employers, 1981; The Coming of the Mass Market, 1982; Conflict and Class: Scottish Workers 1700-1838, 1988. Recreations: hill-walking; skiing; cleaning canals. Address: (h.) 112 High Station Road, Falkirk, FK1 5LN; T.-0324 22868.

Fraser, William Irvine, MD, FRCPsych, DPM. Consultant Psychiatrist, since 1969; part-time Senior Lecturer, Edinburgh University, since 1975; Editor, Journal of Mental Deficiency Research, since 1983; b. 3.2.40, Greenock; m., Joyce Gilchrist; 2 s. Educ. Greenock Academy; Glasgow University. Physician Superintendent, Lynebank Hospital, Fife, 1974-78; Council Member, International Association for Scientific Study of Mental Handicap, since 1982. Publications: Care and Training of the Mentally Handicapped; Communication with Normal and Retarded Children. Recreation: sailing. Address: (h.) 10 Merchiston Avenue, Edinburgh; T.-031-229 7017.

Fraser, Sir William Kerr, GCB (1984), LLD, FRSE. Principal and Vice Chancellor, Glasgow University, from October 1988; Permanent Under Secretary of State, Scottish Office, 1978-88; b. 18.3.29; m., Marion Anne Forbes; 3 s.; 1 d. Educ. Eastwood Secondary School; Glasgow University. RAF, 1952-55; various posts in Scottish Office, 1955-78, including Principal Private Secretary to Secretary of State for Scotland, 1966-67. Address: (b.) Glasgow University, Glasgow, G12 8QQ; T.-041-339 8855.

Fraser of Tullybelton, Lord, Walter Ian Reid, Hon. LLD; b. 3.2.11, Glasgow; m., Lady Mary Ursula Cynthia Gwendolen Macdonell; 1 s. Educ. Repton; Balliol College, Oxford; Glasgow University. Admitted Faculty of Advocates, 1936; Lecturer in Constitutional Law, Glasgow University, 1936; Army - Royal Artillery and Staff - UK and Burma, 1939-45; Lecturer in Constitutional Law, Edinburgh University, 1945; QC, 1953; Senator of the College of Justice, 1964; Lord of Appeal in Ordinary, 1975; retired, 1985; Life Peer and Privy Counsellor; Hon. Fellow, Balliol College, Oxford. Vice-President, The Stair Society, 1987. Publication: Outline of Constitutional Law, 1938, 2nd edition 1948. Recreation: walking. Address: Tullybelton House, Bankfoot, Perthshire; T.-Bankfoot 87312.

Freeman, Christopher Paul, BSc, MB, ChB, MPhil, MRCPsych. Consultant Psychiatrist, Royal Edinburgh Hospital, Edinburgh, since 1980; Senior Lecturer, Department of Psychiatry, Edinburgh University, since 1980; Psychiatric Tutor, Royal Edinburgh Hospital, since 1983; b. 21.4.47, York; m., Heather; 2 s. Educ. Nunthorpe School, York; Edinburgh University. Royal College of Psychiatrists Gaskell Gold Medal. Recreations: tennis; squash; growing bonsaii trees. Address: (h.) 59 Braid Avenue, Edinburgh, EH10; T.-031-447 5211.

Freeman, Peter A., MA (Cantab), MB, BChir, FRCS, FRCS(Glas). Consultant Orthopaedic Surgeon, Victoria Infirmary and Associated Hospitals, Glasgow, since 1961; Surgeon in Charge, West of Scotland Spinal Injuries Unit, Philipshill Hospital, Busby, since 1980; b. 24.1.25, Birmingham; m., Daphne Nicholson Crockett; 1 s.; 2 d. Educ. Christ's College, Cambridge; St. Bartholomew's Hospital, London. House Surgeon appointments, London, 1949-54; SHO and Registrar, Robert Jones and Agnes Hunt Orthopaedic Hospital, Oswestry, 1954-57; Senior Registrar, Western Infirmary, Glasgow, 1957-61; Orthopaedic Assistant, Massachusetts General Hospital, Boston, 1959-61. Recreations: fishing; military history. Address: (h.) Flat 1, 36 Mansion House Road, Glasgow, G41 3DW.

Freer, Professor John Henry, BSc, MSc, PhD. Titular Professor in Microbiology, Glasgow University, since 1986 (Reader, 1982-86; Head, Department of Microbiology, since 1984); b. 17.11.36, Kasauli, India; m., Jocelyn Avril Williams; 4 d. Educ. Durham University; Nottingham University; Birmingham University. Lecturer in Microbiology, New South Wales University, Australia, 1962-65; New York University Medical Centre: Associate Research Scientist, then Assistant Professor, Microbiology, 1965-68; Senior Lecturer, Microbiology Department, Glasgow University, 1968-82; Senior Editor, Journal of General Microbiology. Publication: Bacterial Protein Toxins (Joint Editor), 1984; 90 scientific articles. Recreations: sailing; painting. Address: (b.) Department of Microbiology, Glasgow University, 56 Dumbarton Road, Glasgow, G11 6NU; T.-041-339 8855, Ext. 4002/4642.

Freshney, Robert Ian, BSc, PhD. Senior Lecturer, Department of Medical Oncology, Glasgow University, since 1984; b. 16.2.38, Paisley; m., Mary Struthers; 1 s.; 1 d. Educ. Ayr Academy; Glasgow University. Research Fellow, Biochemistry Department, Glasgow University, 1963-64; Postdoctoral Research Fellow, Department of Zoology, Wisconsin University, 1964-65; Research Fellow, Biochemistry Department, Glasgow University, 1965-66; Member, Research Staff, Beatson Institute for Cancer Research, Glasgow, 1966-81; Lecturer, Department of Medical Oncology, Glasgow University, 1981-84. Member, Editorial Board, Anticancer Research and Cytotechnology. Publications: Culture of Animal Cells; Animal Cell Culture: A Practical Approach. Recreations: photography; DIY activities; painting. Address: (h.) 24 Greenwood Drive, Bearsden, Glasgow, G61 2HA; T.-041-942 4782.

Frew, Rev. Michael William, BSc, BD. Church of Scotland Regional Organiser for Evangelism, since 1987; b. 16.5.51, Edinburgh; m., Margaret Smith; 3 s.; 1 d. Educ. Broughton Senior Secondary School, Edinburgh; Edinburgh University. Minister, Alloa West, 1978-87. Recreations: family life; hill-walking. Address: (h.) and (b.) 52 Rose Crescent, Perth, PH1 1NT; T.-0738 27722.

Friedman, Leonard Matthew. Artistic Director, Scottish Ensemble, since 1969; Artistic Director, Friedman Ensemble (and Players), since 1973; Duo Recitalist with Allan Schiller, since 1982; b. 11.12.30, London; 2 s.; 3 d. Educ. Coopers Company School; Guildhall School of Music and Drama. Founder/Co-Founder/Leader/or Director of: Hadyn Orchestra, Kalmar Chamber Orchestra, Tilford Bach, London Bach, Bremen Bach, Northern Sinfonia, Cremona Quartet, International Mozart Ensemble, Friedman Ensemble, Scottish Baroque, Aleph Ensemble, Scottish Ensemble; Guest Leader/Deputy Leader of: Royal Philharmonic, Bremen Philharmonic, Westphalia Symphony, English Opera Group, Glyndebourne, Scottish Opera, Scottish Ballet, Italian Opera Company, Festival Ballet, English Chamber, Scottish Chamber, Royal Ballet, etc.; numerous broadcasts, summer schools, festivals, lectures, records; Gold Medal, Guildhall School of Music and Drama; Citizen of the Year, Edinburgh, 1980, for aiding the development of SBE, SCO and Queen's Hall; Leader, Scottish Philharmonic, Edinburgh Festival, 1987. Recreations: relative religion; philosophy; cricket; politics (global). Address: (h.) 17a Dublin Street, Edinburgh, EH1 3PG; T.-031-556 2398.

Friel, Edward J. Chief Executive, Greater Glasgow Tourist Board and Convention Bureau; b. 20.9.41, Londonderry; m., Eleanor Watt. Educ. Londonderry. Manager - North America, Northern Ireland Tourist Board, New York; Director Marketing and Public Relations, Scottish Opera; Regional Manager London, Swan National Car Rental; Regional Manager SE England, Hertz International Car Rental. Member, Boards: Scottish Opera, Mayfest, Glasgow International Jazz Festival, Glasgow International Dance Festival, Glasgow International Choral Festival, Theatre Royal; Chairman, Glasgow Branch, UNICEF; West of Scotland Committee, Institute of Directors. Recreations: the arts; golf; reading. Address: (h.) Culmore, Kirkhouse Road, Killearn, Glasgow, G63 9NB; T.-0360 50016.

Friend, James, MA, MB, ChB, FRCPEdin. Consultant in Thoracic Medicine, Grampian Health Board, since 1973; Clinical Senior Lecturer in Medicine, Aberdeen University, since 1973; b. 2.6.38, Edinburgh; m., Elizabeth; 1 s.; 2 d. Educ. Edinburgh Academy; Gonville and Caius College, Cambridge; Edinburgh University. Hospital posts in Edinburgh and Oxford; Dorothy Temple Cross Fellowship, Seattle, 1971-72; British Thoracic Society: Secretary, Research Committee, 1980-84, Council Member, since 1983, Treasurer, since 1986. Recreation: the Scottish hills. Address: (b.) City Hospital, Aberdeen, AB2 1NJ; T.-0224 681818, Ext. 58303.

Frizzell, Rev. Robert Stewart, BD, LTh. Minister, Balshagray Parish Church, Glasgow, since 1975; Senior Chaplain, Barlinnie Prison, Glasgow, since 1982; b. 24.6.34, Motherwell; m., Elizabeth; 2 d. Educ. Bellshill Academy; Glasgow University and Trinity College; Baptist Theological College of Scotland. Baptist ministry, 1961-71; entered Church of Scotland ministry, 1971. Address: 20 St. Kilda Drive, Glasgow, G14 9JN; T.-041-954 9780.

Froude, Rev. J. Kenneth, MA, BD (Hons). Minister, St. Brycedale Church, Kirkcaldy, since 1979; b. 8.12.50, Glasgow. Educ. Hillhead High School; Aberdeen University. Trained in personnel management; Assistant Minister, Northfield, Aberdeen, 1978-79; Education Convener, Kirkcaldy Presbytery; Member, local Careers Service Committee. Recreations: running; singing; squash; mountaineering. Address: 6 East Fergus Place, Kirkcaldy; T.-0592 264480.

Fry, Derek John, MA, DPhil, BM, BCh. Senior Lecturer in Anatomy, Dundee University, since 1978; b. 19.8.43, London; m., Carol; 2 d. Educ. Dulwich College; Oxford University; St. Bartholomew's Hospital Medical School. House Physician, Medical Professorial Unit, St. Bartholomew's Hospital, London, 1970; House Surgeon, Royal Sussex County Hospital, Brighton, 1970-71; Dundee University: Demonstrator in Anatomy, 1971-72, Lecturer in Anatomy, 1972-78. Treasurer, Scottish Churches Action for World Development; World Development and Lay Social Responsibility Secretary, Scottish District, Methodist Church. Recreations: hill-walking; early music; squash; gardening; amusing children. Address: (h.) 28 Westfield Road, Broughty Ferry, Dundee, DD5 1ED; T.-Dundee 79430.

Fullarton, John Hamilton, ARIBA, ARIAS, DipTP. Director of Technical Services, Scottish Special Housing Association, since 1979; b. 21.2.31, Dalry, Ayrshire; m., Elvera Peebles; 1 s. Educ. Dalry High School; Glasgow School of Art; Royal Technical College, Glasgow; Edinburgh College of Art. Architect with local authorities before joining Scottish Office, 1964; Superintending Architect, Scottish Development Department, 1970-78; Head of New Towns, Construction Industry Division, Scottish Economic Planning Department, 1978-79. Research Fellowship, Urban Planning, Edinburgh College of Art, 1966-67. Publications: Scottish Housing Handbooks: Space Standards, 1969; Housing for the Elderly, 1970; Waverley Park Conservation Study, 1977. Address: (h.) 7 Queens Crescent, Edinburgh, EH9 2AZ; T.-031-667 5809.

Fullarton, Morag Elizabeth, BA, DipDSD. Artistic Director, Borderline Theatre Company, Ayr, since 1979; b. Ipswich. Has directed theatre productions in most of the major theatres in Scotland; most recent productions include Hogg, a biographical account of the life of James Hogg, for the Edinburgh Festival, and Dario Fo's Trumpets and Raspberries on national tour. Address: (h.) 13 Belmont Crescent, Glasgow, G12 8EU.

Fulton, Rikki. Actor; b. 15.4.24, Glasgow; m., Kate Matheson. Educ. Whitehill Secondary School. Invalided out of RNVR as Sub-Lt., 1945; began professional career broadcasting with BBC in Glasgow; Presenter, BBC Showband, London, 1951-55; appeared in numerous pantomimes and revues with Howard & Wyndham from 1955, including Five Past Eight shows; television work including Scotch & Wry (creator, Rev. I.M. Jolly) and starring roles in The Miser, A Winter's Tale and an episode of Bergerac; films including The Dollar Bottom, Gorky Park, Local Hero, Comfort and Joy and The Girl in the Picture; played leading role in stage production of Let Wives Tak Tent, 1981. Scottish TV Personality of the Year, 1963 and 1979; Best Light Entertainment Performance of the Year, 1969 and 1983; President's Award, Television and Radio Industries Club, 1988. Recreations: bridge; chess; reading; music (listening and piano); writing; painting. Address: (b.) Richard Stone Management, London, WC2N; T.-01-839 6421.

Fulton, William Francis Monteith, BSc, MD (Hons), MB, ChB, FRCP, FRCPGlas, FRCPEdin. Reader, Department of Materia Medica, Glasgow University, 1977-84; Consultant Physician, Stobhill General Hospital, Glasgow, 1958-84; b. 12.12.19, Aberdeen; m., Dr. Frances I. Melrose; 1 s.; 1 d. Educ. Bryanston School, Dorset; Glasgow University. Resident Physician and Surgeon, Western Infirmary, Glasgow, 1945-46; National Service, Merchant Navy, 1946-48 (Ship's Surgeon); joined National Health Service, 1950; Research Assistant, Cardiology, Edinburgh University, 1952-53; Senior Lecturer, Department of Materia Medica, Glasgow University, 1958-77; Senior Fellow, Cardiology, Johns Hopkins Hospital, Baltimore, 1963-64; Foundation Professor of Medicine, Nairobi University, 1967-72. Publications: The Coronary Arteries, 1965; Modern Trends in Pharmacology and Therapeutics, 1967. Address: (h.) Woodhill, Braemar, AB3 5XX; T.-033 83 239.

Fulton, Sheriff William John, BL. Sheriff of Grampian, Highlands and Islands at Inverness, since 1976; b. 17.12.40, Glasgow; m., Marion Thomson Freeland; 1 s.; 1 d. Educ. Glasgow Boys' High School; Glasgow University. Wright & Crawford, Solicitors, Paisley: Assistant, 1963, Partner, 1968-76. Founder Member, Black Isle Theatre Club. Recreations: amateur drama; golf; military history. Address: (b.) The Castle, Inverness; T.-Inverness 230782.

Furnell, James R.G., MA (Hons), DCP, PhD, ABPsS. Consultant Clinical Psychologist (Child Health), Forth Valley Health Board, since 1980; b. 20.2.46, London; m., Lesley Anne Ross; 1 s.; 1 d. Educ. Leighton Park Society of Friends School, Reading; Aberdeen University; Glasgow University; Stirling University. Clinical Psychologist, Royal Hospital for Sick Children, Glasgow, 1970-72; Senior Clinical Psychologist, Forth Valley Health Board, 1972-80. Member, National Consultative Committee of Scientists in Professions Allied to Medicine, 1984-87 (Secretary, Clinical Psychology Sub-Committee); Member, Forth Valley Health Board, 1984-87; Chairman, Division of Clinical Psychology, British Psychological Society, 1988. Recreations: flying; cross-country skiing. Address: (h.) Glensherup House, Glendevon, by Dollar, Perthshire, FK14 7JY; T.-Glendevon 234.

Furness, Professor Nicholas Arthur, BA, Drphil. Professor of German, Edinburgh University, since 1969; b. 9.12.23, Newcastle-upon-Tyne; m., Sylvia Bone; 1 s.; 3 d. Educ. Royal Grammar School, Newcastle-upon-Tyne; King's College, Newcastle; Innsbruck University. Temporary Lecturer in German, King's College, Newcastle, 1952-53; Assistant Lecturer in German, Manchester University, 1953-54; Lecturer, then Senior Lecturer in German, Edinburgh University, 1954-69. Recreations: travel; theatre; gardening; painting and paperhanging; music. Address: (b.)

Department of German, David Hume Tower, George Square, Edinburgh, EH8 9JX; T.-031-667 1011.

Furness, Professor Raymond Stephen, BA, MA, PhD. Professor of German, St. Andrews University, since 1984; b. 25.10.33, Builth Wells; m., Janice Fairey; 1 s.; 2 d. Educ. Welwyn Garden City Grammar School; University College, Swansea. Modern Languages Department, University of Manchester Institute of Science and Technology; Department of German, Manchester University. Publications: Expressionism; Literary History of Germany 1890-1945; Wagner and Literature. Recreation: old horror films. Address: (h.) The Dirdale, Boarhills, St. Andrews, KY16 8PP; T.-033 488 469.

Furness, Lt. Col. Simon John, DL. Landowner; b. 18.3.36, Ayton. Educ. Charterhouse; RMA, Sandhurst. Commissioned Durham Light Infantry, 1956, 2nd Lt.; served Far East, UK, Germany; active service, Borneo, Northern Ireland; retired, 1978. Member, Council and Executive, National Trust for Scotland (Chairman, Gardens Committee); Chairman, Eyemouth Museum Trust. Recreations: field sports; gardening. Address: Netherbyres, Eyemouth, Berwickshire, TD14 5SE; T.-08907 50337.

Furniss, James Cyril, MPhil, DTSc, ARTCS, CTex, FTI, MInstM, FRSA. Principal, Scottish College of Textiles, since 1976; b. 17.7.31, Sale, Cheshire; m., Jennifer Mary; 1 s. Educ. Sale County Grammar School; Leeds University; Royal Technical College, Salford. Textile Producer, Joshua Hoyle & Sons Ltd., Manchester; Research Technologist, British Rayon Research Association, Manchester; Assistant Lecturer, Lecturer, Senior Lecturer in Textiles, latterly Head of Department of Textiles, Carpet Technology and Associated Subjects, Kidderminster College; Vice-Principal, East Warwickshire College, Rugby. Member and former Secretary, Committee of Principals of Central Institutions, Scotland; former Member, Board of Management, Highland Craftpoint Ltd., Inverness; Director, Scottish Textile & Technical Centre Ltd., Galashiels; Past Chairman, Central Institutions Committee for Educational Technology; Member: Design Council, Scottish Design Council, Council of CNAA. Recreations: hill-walking; gardening; travel; music; theatre. Address: (b.) Scottish College of Textiles, Galashiels; T.-Galashiels 3351.

Fyall, Andrew. Director, Public Relations and Tourism, City of Edinburgh, since 1976; b. 13.11.32, Port Gordon; m., Elizabeth; 1 s.; 2 d. Educ. Kirkcaldy High School. Foreign Correspondent/Feature Writer, Daily Express, 1955-76. Recreation: golf. Address: (b.) 3 Princes Street, Waverley Market, Edinburgh; T.-031-557 2727.

Fyfe, James Eckford, MBE, BL. Solicitor; b. 1.6.20, Glasgow; m., Isobel M. Buchanan; 3 s. Educ. High School of Glasgow; Glasgow University. Chairman, Glasgow Social Security Appeal Tribunal, since 1985; Vice-Chairman, Argyll and Clyde Health Board, 1983-85; Past Preses, The Grand Antiquity Society of Glasgow. Recreations: golf; bridge. Address: (b.) 190 St. Vincent Street, Glasgow; T.-041-204 2833.

Fyfe, Maria, BA (Hons). MP, Glasgow Maryhill, since 1987; Vice-Chair, Parliamentary Labour Party Employment Committee, since 1987; b. 25.11.38, Glasgow; 2 s. Educ. Notre Dame High School, Glasgow; Strathclyde University. Glasgow District Councillor, 1980-87; Senior Lecturer, Central College of Commerce, 1977-87; Member, Scottish Executive Committee, Labour Party, 1981-87. Address: (b.) House of Commons, London, SW1A 0AA; T.-01-219 4430.

Fyfe, Thomas, MD, FRCP. Consultant Physician, Southern General Hospital, Glasgow, since 1978; Honorary Clinical Lecturer, Glasgow University, since 1976; Member, Inverclyde District Council, 1984-88; b. 7.1.39, Gourock; m., Katherine Copland; 2 s.; 1 d. Educ. Greenock Academy; Glasgow University. Recreations: golf; bridge. Address: (h.) Drummochy, Kilmacolm; T.-Kilmacolm 2367.

Fyfe, William Morton, MD, FRCP, FRCPGlas, FRCPEdin, DCH. Consultant Paediatrician, Stobhill Hospital and Royal Hospital for Sick Children, Glasgow; b. 27.4.23, Glasgow; m., Elizabeth L. Millar; 2 s.; 2 d. Educ. High School of Glasgow; Glasgow University. House Physician, Stobhill Hospital, Glasgow, 1945; National Service, RAMC, 1946-48; Paediatric Registrar, Stobhill Hospital and Royal Hospital for Sick Children, Glasgow; Consultant Paediatrician, Renfrewshire. Recreations: golf; skiing; gardening. Address: (h.) 77 Drymen Road, Bearsden, Glasgow; T.-041-942 2166.

Fyfe, William Stevenson, OBE (1987). Chairman, Ayrshire and Arran Health Board, since 1981; Member, UK Nursing and Midwifery Staffs Negotiating Council, since 1985; Chairman, Coastal Crafts and Printing Ltd., since 1982; Fellow, Institution of Industrial Managers, since 1985; b. 10.6.35, Glasgow; m., Margaret H.H. Auld; 1 s.; 1 d. Educ. Dollar Academy; Scottish College of Commerce. Town Councillor, Prestwick, 1967-73 (Magistrate, 1970-73, Acting Treasurer, 1971-73); Ayr County Councillor, 1970-73; apppointed to Ayrshire and Arran Health Board, 1973 (Financial Convener, 1973-81); Member, Scottish Health Service Planning Council; Chairman, Scottish Chairmen's Gradings Committee; Member, Management Side, Re-organisation Sub-Committee (Scotland), General Whitley Council. Recreation: golf. Address: (h.) Ford House, Pennyglen, Culzean, KA19 8JW.

Fyfe, William Stuart Fraser, BSc (Agric). Depute Principal, Elmwood Agricultural and Technical College, Cupar, since 1960; b. 26.5.29, Dundee; 2 s.; 1 d. Educ. Morgan Academy, Dundee; Aberdeen University. Teacher of Science Subjects, Webster Seminary, Kirriemuir, 1955; Lecturer of Agricultural Subjects, Elmwood Agricultural Centre, Cupar, 1956. Head of Centre (Non-Vocational Evening Classes), Elmwood, 1980; Member, Careers Literature Working Party, Agricultural Training Board. Recreations: hill-walking; skiing; international holidays; family. Address: (h.) Royston, Carslogie Road, Cupar, Fife; T.-0334 55090.

G

Galbraith, James Donald, MA, MLitt, DipMedStud. Curator of Historical Records, Scottish Record Office, since 1984; b. 26.4.43, Aberdeen; m., Dr. Frances Jennifer Shaw. Educ. Robert Gordon's College, Aberdeen; Aberdeen University. Executive Officer, Ministry of Aviation, 1962; Scottish Record Office: Research Assistant, 1970, Senior Research Assistant, 1974, Assistant Keeper, 1976. Captain, 3/51st Highland Volunteers, 1982. Publications: Calendar of Documents relating to Scotland 1108-1516; St. Machar's Cathedral: The Celtic Antecedents (Co-Editor). Recreations: hill-walking; skiing; manuscript illumination; early music. Address: (h.) 118 Mayfield Road, Edinburgh; T.-031-667 5723.

Galbraith, Russell. Controller of Features & Sport, Scottish Television, since 1985 (Assistant Controller of Programmes, 1983-85); b. 8.2.35, Glasgow; m., Harriet; 1 s.; 3 d. Educ. Govan High School, Glasgow. Staff Reporter, Glasgow Evening News, 1955-57; Sunday Mail, 1957-58; The Scotsman, 1958-62; STV, since 1962: Reporter, Here and Now, 1962-64, Programme Editor, News and Current Affairs, 1964-66, Producer/Director, 1966-72, Head of News, Current Affairs and Sport, 1972-79, Programme Administration Controller, 1979-83. Won Radio Industries Club of Scotland Award, Best Programme, 1970, for Debate, 1971 for Patterns of Folk; Executive Producer, I Can Hear You Smile, RTS Best Regional Programme Award, 1984; Sir William in Search of Xanadu, Gold medal winner, documentary section, New York Film & TV Festival, 1984; Television and Radio Industries Club Scotland, Best Documentary, for Gone for a Soldier, 1985. Recreations: cycling; curling; chess. Address: (b.) STV, Cowcaddens, Glasgow, G2 3PR.

Galbraith, Samuel Laird, BSc, MB, ChB, MD, FRCSGlas. MP (Labour), Strathkelvin and Bearsden, since 1987; Neurosurgeon, Institute of Neurological Sciences, Glasgow; b. 18.10.45. Educ. Glasgow University. Consultant in Neurosurgery, Greater Glasgow Health Board, 1978-87.

Gall, James, LDS, RFPS. Deputy Chief Dental Officer, Scottish Home and Health Department, 1976-87; Honorary Visiting Dental Surgeon, Glasgow Dental School and Hospital, since 1964; Senior Dental Adviser, Prisons Division, Scottish Office, and Senior Dental Adviser, Supplies Division and Building Division, Common Services Agency, NHS, 1977-87; b. 21.4.24, Wishaw; m., Margaret Law Cran; 1 s.; 2 d. Educ. Bellshill Academy; Glasgow University. General Dental Practitioner, 1948-74; joined SHHD as Dental Officer, 1974; elected to local Dental Committee, Lanarkshire, 1958-74 (Member, Executive Council); Member, Area Dental Committee, Lanarkshire Health Board, 1974-85; Dental Member, Scottish Dental Estimates Board, 1971-74; Chairman, Scottish Branch, British Society of Medical and Dental Hypnosis Society, 1970 (National Chairman, 1977-80, President, 1980-82); International Fellow, American Society of Clinical Hypnosis; Life Founder Fellow, Federation Dentaire International; Provincial Fellow, Royal Society of Medicine; Life Fellow, Royal Zoological Society of Scotland. President, Clyde Toastmasters Club, 1962; served in Boys Brigade as Officer, 1st Bellshill. Publication: Modern Trends in Hypnosis (Contributor), 1983. Recreations: gardening; golf; boating; music; reading; bridge; football. Address: (h.) The Bungalow, Douglas Gardens, Uddingston, Glasgow; T.-Uddingston 812878.

Gallacher, Tom. Writer; b. 16.2.34, Alexandria. Stage plays: Our Kindness to 5 Persons, 1969; Mr Joyce is Leaving Paris, 1971; Revival, 1972; Three to Play, 1972; Schellenbrack, 1973; Bright Scene Fading, 1973; The Only Street, 1973; Personal Effects, 1974; A Laughing Matter, 1975; Hallowe'en, 1975; The Sea Change, 1976; A Presbyterian Wooing (adapted from Pitcairne's The Assembly), 1976; The Evidence of Tiny Tim, 1977; Wha's Like Us - Fortunately!, 1978; Stage Door Canteen, 1978; Deacon Brodie (adapted from Stevenson and Henley), 1978; Jenny, 1979; Natural Causes, 1980; The Parole of Don Juan, 1981; The Treasure Ship (adapted from Brandane), 1982. Publications: (fiction): Hunting Shadows, 1981; Apprentice, 1983; Journeyman, 1984; Survivor, 1985; The Jewel Maker, 1986; The Wind on the Heath, 1987. Address: (b.) Michael Imison Playwrights Ltd., 28 Almeida Street, London, N1 1TD.

Gallagher, Rt. Rev. Monsignor Hugh Canon. Parish Priest, St. Mary's, Greenock, since 1972; Diocesan Treasurer, since 1964; Canon of Cathedral Chapter, since 1975; b. 30.4.20, Clydebank. Educ. St. Patrick's High School, Dumbarton; St. Peter's College, Bearsden. Assistant Priest, Gourock, 1945-56; Vice Rector, Royal Scots College, Valladolid, Spain, 1956-63; Chaplain, Little Sisters of the Poor, Greenock, 1964-69; Parish Priest, St. Columba's, Renfrew, 1969-72; Prelate of Honour by Pope John Paul II, 1987. President, Inverclyde Voluntary Association for Mental Health. Recreations: golf; music. Address: St. Mary's Rectory, 14 Patrick Street, Greenock, PA16 8NA; T.-Greenock 21084.

Gallagher, James Moore, MA, LLB, NP. Director of Administration and Legal Services, East Kilbride District Council, since 1975; b. 2.5.27, Bellshill; m., Margaret Ann; 3 s.; 1 d. Educ. Our Lady's High School, Motherwell; Glasgow University. Successively with East Kilbride Development Corporation, Burgh of East Kilbride and East Kilbride District Council, since 1953. Recreation: bowling. Address: (b.) Civic Centre, East Kilbride; T.-East Kilbride 28777.

Gallagher, Sister Maire T., OBE, MA (Hons), DCE. Superior, Convent of Notre Dame, Dumbarton; Sister of Notre Dame Religious Congregation, since 1959; Chairman, Consultative Committee on the Curriculum, since 1987 (Chairman, Committee on Secondary Education, 1983-87); Member, Main Committee, 1986; b. 27.5.33, Glasgow. Educ. Notre Dame High School, Glasgow; Glasgow University; Notre Dame College of Education. Principal Teacher of History, Notre Dame High School, Glasgow; Lecturer in Secondary Education, Notre Dame College of Education; Headteacher, Notre Dame High School, Dumbarton, 1974-87. Member, Consultative

Committee on the Curriculum, since 1976; Member, Executive, Secondary Heads Association (Scottish Branch), 1976-83; Coordinator, Christian Life Movement Groups, West of Scotland. Recreations: reading; dress-making; bird-watching. Address: (h.) Convent of Notre Dame, Cardross Road, Dumbarton, G82 4JH; T.-Dumbarton 62361

Gallois, Ramues William, BSc, DIC, PhD, CEng, FIMM. Head, Geological Survey of Scotland, since 1986; b. 8.11.37, Coventry; m., Barbara Mary Wilkins; 3 s. Educ. King Henry VIII School, Coventry; Birmingham University; Imperial College. Geologist, British Geological Survey, 1960-82; Regional Geologist for South West England, 1982-86. Recreations: natural history; badminton; painting. Address: (b.) Murchison House, West Mains Road, Edinburgh, EH9 3LA; T.-031-667 1000.

Galloway, George. MP (Glasgow Hillhead), since 1987; Vice-Chair, Parliamentary Foreign Affairs Committee; b. 16.8.54, Dundee; m., Elaine Fyffe; 1 d. Educ. Harris Academy, Dundee. Production Worker, Michelin Tyres, 1974; Dundee Labour Party Organiser, 1977; General Secretary, War on Want, 1983. Chairman, Scottish Labour Party, 1981-82; Member, Scottish Labour Party Executive Committee, 1974-84; Founder and first General Secretary, Trade Union Friends of Palestine, 1979. Recreations: football; music; films. Address: (b.) House of Commons, Westminster, London; T.-01-219 6922.

Galpern, Baron (Myer Galpern), Kt (1960), DL, JP. Life Peer; b. 1903. Educ. Glasgow University. Lord Provost of Glasgow, 1958-60; MP (Labour), Glasgow Shettleston, 1959-79; Hon. LLD, Glasgow, 1961.

Galt, Rose Ann, MA (Hons), FEIS. Chairperson, General Teaching Council for Scotland, since 1987; Member, National Executive, EIS, since 1976; Vice-Chairman, Scottish Council for the Validation of Courses for Teachers, since 1987; Member, Scottish Examination Board, since 1982; Vice-Chairperson, Scottish Committee for Staff Development in Education; b. 19.3.37, Glasgow; m., William Galt; 1 d. Educ. Possil Secondary School, Glasgow; Glasgow University; Jordanhill College. Started teaching, Albert Secondary, Glasgow, 1960; appointed Principal Teacher (Guidance), 1970; after career break, resumed teaching, Our Lady's High School, Cumbernauld, 1971, and became Principal Teacher of English, Greenfaulds High School, 1975; EIS: Chairman, Glasgow Local Association, 1970-71, President, Dumbarton Local Association, 1976-77; National Vice-President, 1978-79, National President, 1979-80; Convener, Education Committee, General Teaching Council, 1982-86, and Vice-Chairperson, 1985-87; Member, European Trade Union Committee on Equal Opportunities, since 1986; Member, Strathclyde Regional Council Equality Working Party, 1986-87. Recreations: reading; cooking; fiendishly difficult crosswords. Address: (h.) 38 Meadow View, Cumbernauld, Glasgow; T.-0236 722028.

Garden, Neville Abbot. Presenter, BBC Radio Scotland (Good Morning Scotland, since 1978, and The Musical Garden, since 1979); Writer and Lecturer on musical and media matters; b. 13.2.36, Edinburgh; m., Jane Fowler; 1 s., 1 d.; 3 d. by pr. m. Educ. George Watson's College, Edinburgh. Reporter, Sub-Editor, Feature Writer, Evening Dispatch, 1953-63; Daily Columnist and Music Critic, Edinburgh Evening News, 1963-64; Senior Feature Writer, Scottish Daily Express, 1964-78; Music Critic and Columnist, Sunday Standard, 1981-83; regular Contributor to magazine programmes and Presenter, Arts in Scotland, Prospect, Twelve Noon, BBC Radio, 1952-78. Child Actor, Children's Hour, etc., 1948-52; Founder Member, Edinburgh Symphony Orchestra, 1965; Conductor: Edinburgh Grand Opera, seven years; Edinburgh Ballet Theatre, nine years, Edinburgh Chamber Orchestra; Musical Director, Southern Light Opera Company, since 1979. Address: (b.) BBC, 5 Queen Street, Edinburgh.

Gardiner, Austen James Sutherland, MB, ChB, MD, MRCP, FRCPGlas, FRCPEdin. Consultant Physician and Postgraduate Tutor, Monklands Hospital, Lanarkshire, since 1976; b. 27.1.34, Aberdeen; m., Ruth Duncan; 2 s.; 1 d. Educ. Aberdeen Grammar School; Aberdeen University. Research in junior teaching post, University Department of Surgery and Medicine, Aberdeen; Registrar and Senior Registrar (Internal) Medicine, Aberdeen Teaching Hospital; Honorary Elective of Medicine, Department of Medicine; Research Fellow, Department of Medicine, Magill University, Montreal, 1968-70; Senior Registrar, Aberdeen Group of Teaching Hospitals, 1970-76. Recreations: golf; shooting; fishing. Address: (h.) Farringford, St. Margaret's Drive, Dunblane; T.-0786 822124.

Gardner, Agnes Jardine, MBE, JP. Vice-Chairman, North East Fife District Council, since 1984 (Vice-Chairman, Housing Committee, since 1976); Vice-Chairman, Scottish National Housing and Town Planning Council, since 1980; m., Thomas Gardner; 1 d. Educ. Blairgowrie High School. Apprenticeship in legal firms; Diploma, Scottish Local Government Law and Finance; Town Clerk, St. Monans, 1972-75; Member, Anstruther Town Council, 1958-75; Honorary Secretary, East Neuk of Fife Branch, Cancer Relief. Recreations: reading; gardening. Address: (h.) Westerlea, Anstruther, Fife; T.-0333 310759.

Gardner, David Alistair. Chairman: Moray Firth Radio Limited, since 1980, Hi-Line, Dingwall, since 1985; b. 10.10.30, Glasgow; m., Sheila Maree Stewart; 1 d. Educ. Fettes College, Edinburgh; Ross Hall, Scottish Hotel School, Glasgow. National service, RAF, 1949-50; involved in hotel/licensed trade as Manager/Owner/Director, since 1950; Past President, Inverness and Highland Region Licensed Trade Association; freelance, BBC Radio, 1958-80; own programme, Moray Firth Radio, since 1982; former Senior Bailie, Dornoch Town Council; former Member, Sutherland County Council; Past Chairman, North of Scotland Water Board. Co-Founder, Inverness Hospitals Broadcasting Service. Recreations: broadcasting; travel; golf. Address: (h.) Altyre, 10 Abertarff Road, Inverness, IV2 3NW; T.-0463 230684.

Gardner, Raymond Alexander. Features Editor, Glasgow Herald, since 1978 (also "Trencherman", Restaurant and Hotel Critic, since 1982, and weekly wine column); b. 6.11.44, Glasgow. Educ. High School of Glasgow. Various editorial positions, Fleet Street and Scotland; Columnist, Travel Writer and Author; Contributor to A la Carte, Harpers, Quick Magazine (Munich), Options, The Scotland Book, Motor Boat and Yachting, Radio Clyde, Radio Scotland, RTE. Publications: Land of Time Enough - A Journey Through the Waterways of Ireland; Glasgow - A Celebration (Contributor). Recreation: doing nothing on boats in Ireland. Address: (b.) Glasgow Herald, 195 Albion Street, Glasgow, G1; T.-041-552 6255.

Garner-Smith, Brigadier Kenneth James, OBE, DL, MA. Deputy Lieutenant, Inverness-shire, since 1964; Honorary Sheriff, Inverness-shire, since 1967; Member, Queen's Bodyguard for Scotland (Royal Company of Archers), since 1953; b. 30.3.04; m., Mary Macdonald of Aird and Vallay; 1 s.; 2 d. Educ. Charterhouse; Trinity College, Oxford. Commissioned Seaforth Highlanders, 1925; campaigns: Palestine (Despatches, 1936), North Africa, 1942-43; Staff College (various staff appointments); Military Attache: HM Embassy, Oslo, 1945-48, HM Embassy, Ankara, 1954-57; Member, Inverness County Council, 1961-75; Chairman, Inverness CC Education Committee, 1967-75. Address: (h.) Cottage of Aird, Aird House, Inverness, IV1 2AA; T.-0463 231212.

Garraway, Professor William Michael, MD, MSc, MRCP, FRCGP, FFCM, DObstRCOG, DCH. Professor of Community Medicine, Edinburgh University, since 1983; b. 26.1.42, Dumfries; m., Alison Mary Haggart; 1 s.; 1 d. Educ. Carlisle Grammar School; Edinburgh University; London University; Mayo Graduate School of Medicine. Lecturer, Department of Community Medicine, Edinburgh University, 1972-77 (Senior Lecturer, 1978-81); Consultant Epidemiologist, Mayo Clinic, Rochester, USA, 1981-83. Recreations: hill-walking; cross-country skiing. Address: (b.) Medical School, Teviot Place, Edinburgh, EH8 9AG.

Garrett, James Allan, MB, ChB, FRCSEdin, FRCSGlas. Consultant Surgeon, Stobhill Hospital, Glasgow, since 1967; b. 8.3.28, Glasgow; m., Margaret Keddie; 1 s.; 1 d. Educ. Hutchesons' Grammar School, Glasgow; Glasgow University. Captain, RAMC, 1952-54; House Officer, Registrar and Senior Registrar, Glasgow Royal Infirmary, 1954-67. Address: (h.) 12 Richmond Drive, Cambuslang, Glasgow, G72 8BH; T.-041-641 3333.

Garrity, Rev. Thomas Alan Whiteway, BSc, BD. Minister, The Auld Kirk of Ayr (St. John The Baptist), since 1982; b. 13.7.43, Glasgow; m., Elizabeth Caroline Whiteford; 2 d. Educ. Allan Glen's School; Glasgow University; Edinburgh University. Assistant Minister, Dundee Parish Church (St. Mary's); Minister, Fraserburgh South. Recreations: photography; golf. Address: The Manse, 58 Monument Road, Ayr; T.-Ayr 262580.

Gartside, Peter, BEd (Hons). Freelance education and training consultant; Research Officer, Scottish Council for Research in Education, 1987-88; Advisor, Scottish Council for Educational Technology, 1980-86; Secretary, Scottish Committee on Open Learning, 1983-86; b. 31.10.32, Oldham; m., Kathleen; 1 s. Educ. East Oldham High School; Chester Diocesan Training College; Charlotte Mason College of Education. National Service, Royal Scots Greys, 1951-53; Teacher, Hollinwood County Secondary School, Oldham, 1955-57; Housemaster, The Blue Coat School, Oldham, 1957-68; Head of House, Hattersley County Comprehensive School, 1968-70; Warden, Workington Teachers' Centre, Cumbria, 1970-76; Education Department, Independent Broadcasting Authority, 1977-78; Warden, West Cumbria Teachers' Centre, 1978-79. Former Honorary Secretary, National Committee of Teachers' Audio/Visual Aids Groups; former Member, BBC Radio Carlisle Education Education Advisory Panel. Recreations: walking; travel; music. Address (h.) 73 Argyle Way, Dunblane, FK15 9DY.

Garvie, Alexander Femister, MA. Reader, Department of Greek, Glasgow University, since 1987 (Senior Lecturer, 1972-87); b. 29.1.34, Edinburgh; m., Jane Wallace Johnstone; 1 s.; 1 d. Educ. George Watson's College, Edinburgh; Edinburgh University; Cambridge University. Assistant, then Lecturer, Department of Greek, Glasgow University, 1960-72; Visiting Gillespie Professor, College of Wooster, Ohio, 1967-68; Visiting Assistant Professor, Ohio State University, 1968; Visiting Professor, University of Guelph, 1986. Publications: Aeschylus' Supplices: Play and Trilogy, 1969; Aeschylus Choephori: Introduction and Commentary, 1986. Recreations: music; hill-walking. Address: (h.) 93 Stirling Drive, Bishopbriggs, Glasgow; T.-041-772 4140.

Garvie, Ian Graham Donaldson, MA (Hons), BLitt, DipEd. Rector, Auchmuty High School, Glenrothes, since 1976; b. 7.6.29, Perth; m., Margaret M.C. McIntosh. Educ. Perth Academy; Edinburgh University; Moray House College; Exeter College, Oxford. RAF Education Branch; Assistant Teacher, Classics, Special Assistant Teacher, High School of Stirling; Principal Teacher, Bellshill Academy; Principal Teacher, Assistant Rector, Dunfermline High School. Assistant Secretary, Headteachers' Association of Scotland; Chairman, Mid-Fife Newstape (talking newspaper for the blind); Committee Member, Fife Society for the Blind. Recreation: hill-walking. Address: (h.) 23 Lakeside Road, Kirkcaldy, KY2 5QJ; T.-0592 756554.

Gaskin, Professor Maxwell, DFC (and bar), MA. Jaffrey Professor of Political Economy, Aberdeen University, 1965-85; b. 18.11.21, Liverpool; m., Brenda Stewart; 1 s.; 3 d. Educ. Quarry Bank School, Liverpool; Liverpool University. War Service, RAF, 1941-46; Lecturer and Senior Lecturer in Economics, Glasgow University, 1951-65; Head, Department of Political Economy, Aberdeen University, 1965-81; Economic Consultant to Secretary of State for Scotland, 1965-87; Member, Scottish Agricultural Wages Board, since 1972; Chairman, Foresterhill and Associated Hospitals Board, 1972-74; Chairman, Flax and Hemp and Retail Bespoke Tailoring Wages Councils, since 1978; Member, Civil Engineering EDC, 1978-84; Chairman, Section F, British Association, 1978-79; President, Scottish Economic Society, 1981-84; Fellow, Royal Economic Society. Publications: The Scottish Banks: A Modern Survey, 1965; North East Scotland: A Survey of its Development Potential (Co-author), 1969; Economic Impact of North Sea Oil on Scotland (Co-author), 1978; Employment in Insurance, Banking and Finance in Scotland, 1980; The Political Economy of Tolerable Survival (Editor), 1981. Recreations: music; gardening. Address: (h.) Westfield, Ancrum, Roxburghshire, TD8 6XA; T.-08353 237.

Gaston, Rev. Arthur Raymond, MA, BD. Minister, Dollar with Muckhart with Glendevon, since 1975; Director, National Bible Society of Scotland, since 1980; b. 25.5.36, Atherstone; m., Evelyn Wilson Mather; 1 s.; 2 d. Educ. Gordon Schools, Huntly; Aberdeen University; Scottish Congregational College. Teacher of Mathematics, King's Park School, Glasgow; preparatory study for service with London Missionary Society; Principal, Theological College, Fianarantsoa, Madagascar, 1962-67 (also District Missionary and Head of senior school); entry to Church of Scotland following return to Britain, 1967; Minister, Sauchie Parish Church, 1969-75. Member, Board of Governors, Dollar Academy. Recreations: walking; lepidoptery; water-colour painting. Address: Dollar Manse, 2 Manse Road, Dollar, FK14 7AJ; T.-Dollar 2601.

Gavin, Kevin George, MA (Hons), DipEd. HM Inspector of Schools, since 1985; b. 4.7.48, Aberdeen; 1 d. Educ. Aberdeen Academy; Aberdeen University; Aberdeen College of Education. Assistant Head Teacher, Silverwood Primary School, Kilmarnock, 1974-77; Head Teacher, Monkton Primary School, 1977-80; Adviser in Primary Education: Grampian, 1980-83, Strathclyde, 1983-85. Recreations: walking; gardening; art; motor-cycling. Address: (b.) HM Inspector of Schools Office, 29 Cadogan Street, Glasgow; T.-041-204 1220.

Gayre of Gayre and Nigg, Lt. Col. Robert, MA, DPhil, DFSc, DSc; Grand Commander, Order of St. Lazarus; b. 6.8.07; m., Mary Nina Terry (deceased); 1 s. Educ. Edinburgh University; Exeter College, Oxford. Commissioned Officer, Supplementary Reserve Royal Artillery, 1931; War Service, 1939; transferred to Regular Army Reserve, 1941; Staff Officer for Education, HQ Airborne Forces, 1941; Major HQ, Oxford District, 1941; Lt. Col., Educational Adviser, Allied Military Government for Italy, 1943; Professor of Anthropology, University of Saugor, India, 1954. Member, Royal Society of Naples. Recreation: sailing. Address: Minard Castle, Argyll.

Geary, Martin Charles, RD, MA, LLB. Advocate, since 1980; b. 25.8.50, Taplow, Berkshire; m., Irene Maud Bailey; 2 d. Educ. Abingdon School; Edinburgh University. Qualified as Solicitor, 1979; commenced pupillage at Bar, 1979; called to Bar, 1980. Member, Royal Naval Reserve, since 1969 (Lt. Commander). Recreations: walking; skiing; sailing. Address: (b.) Advocates Library, Parliament House, Edinburgh, EH1 1RF; T.-031-226 5071.

Geddes, Rev. Alexander John, MA, BD. Minister, The Langstane Kirk, Aberdeen, since 1979; b. 27.7.36, Aberdeen; m., Elizabeth M.S. Henderson; 1 s.; 2 d. Educ. Robert Gordon's College, Aberdeen; High School of Stirling; Glasgow University. Assistant Minister, St. Machar's Cathedral, Aberdeen, 1960-61; Minister: St. Andrew's, Peebles, 1961-66, St. John's, Paisley, 1966-79. Convener, Church of Scotland In-Service Training Committee and Vice-Convener, Education for the Ministry Committee, 1983-86; Selection School Assessor, since 1987. Recreations: photography; golf; tennis; reading; watching sport. Address: (h.) 14 Norfolk Road, Aberdeen, AB1 6JR; T.-0224 319747.

Gellatly, Ian Robert George, CA. Past President, Scottish Football League; Past Chairman, International Committee, Scottish Football Association; Director, Dundee Football Club PLC, since 1969 (Chairman, 1972-86); b. 5.11.38, Dundee; m., Anne May Horsburgh; 1 s.; 1 d. Educ. Dundee High School; Lathallan Preparatory School; Merchiston Castle School. Partner, Miller McIntyre Gellatly, CA, Dundee, since 1964. Recreations: golf; curling. Address: (h.) Mains of Fowlis, Invergowrie, by Dundee; T.-Longforgan 229.

Gemmell, Curtis Glen, BSc, PhD, MIBiol, MRCPath. Senior Lecturer, Department of Bacteriology, Glasgow University, since 1976; Honorary Bacteriologist, Greater Glasgow Health Board, since 1976; b. 26.8.41, Beith, Ayrshire; m., Anne Margaret; 2 d. Educ. Spier's School, Beith; Glasgow University. Glasgow University: Assistant Lecturer, 1966-68, Lecturer, 1968-69; Paisley College of Technology: Lecturer, 1969-71, Senior Lecturer, 1971-76; Visiting Assistant Professor, University of Minnesota, Minneapolis, 1979-80. Recreations: gardening; golf. Address: (h.) Sunninghill, 19 Lawmarnock Crescent, Bridge of Weir, PA11 3AS; T.-Bridge of Weir 613350.

Gennard, Professor John, BA (Econ), MA (Econ), FIPM. Professor of Industrial Relations, Strathclyde University, since 1981; Dean, Strathclyde Business School, since 1987; b. 26.4.44, Manchester; m., Florence Anne Russell; 1 s.; 1 d. Educ. Hulme Grammar School for Boys; Sheffield University; Manchester University. Research Officer, Industrial Relations Department, then Lecturer in Industrial Relations, London School of Economics, 1968-81. Publications: The Reluctant Militants (Co-author), 1972; Financing Strikers, 1978; Industrial Relations and Job Security, 1979; The Closed Shop in British Industry, 1984. Recreations: football; swimming; politics; trade unions; food and drink. Address: (h.) 4 South Avenue, Carluke, Lanarkshire; T.-0555 51361.

George, Albert Harold. Member, Shetland Health Board, since 1983; Fire Officer, Sullom Voe Terminal, since 1978; b. 23.3.40, London; m., Valerie Constance; 3 s. Educ. St. Mary's School, Hornsey. Flour Confectioner, 1956-61; Fireman, Middlesex Fire Brigade, 1961-65; Leading Fireman, then Sub Officer, Gloucestershire Fire Service, 1967-78. Area Scout Commissioner, Shetland, since 1981; presented with Scout Association Award (Silver Acorn), 1988. Recreations: gardening; walking. Address: (h.) 7 Vista Vird, Brae, Shetland, ZE2 9SL; T.-Brae 487.

George, John Charles, FSA(Scot), FHS. Kintyre Pursuivant of Arms, since 1986; b. 15.12.30, London; m., Margaret Mary Maria Mercedes Weld. Educ. Ampleforth. Lt., Hertfordshire Yeomanry, 1951-54; films and television advertising, 1952-62; College of Arms, 1962-72; Earl Marshal's Liaison Officer with the Churchill family, 1965; Green Staff Officer, Prince of Wales's Investiture, 1969; Garioch Pursuivant, 1976. Chairman, Philbeach Light Opera Society, 1961-63; Vice President, BBC "Mastermind" Club, 1979-81. Publications: The Puffin Book of Flags, 1975; The French Heralds (paper), 1985; numerous historical articles. Recreations: English light opera and musical comedies; hagiographies; sports. Address: (h.) 115 Henderson Row, Edinburgh, EH3 5BB; T.-031-557 1605.

George, Professor William David, MB, BS, FRCS, MS. Professor of Surgery, Glasgow University, since 1981; b. 22.3.43, Reading; m., Helen Marie Moran; 1 s.; 3 d. Educ. Henley Grammar School; London University. Lecturer in Surgery, Manchester University, 1973-77; Senior Lecturer in Surgery, Liverpool University, 1977-81. Member, National Committees, British Association of Surgical Oncology and Surgical Research Society. Recreations: veteran rowing; golf. Address: (b.) University Department of Surgery, Western Infirmary, Glasgow, G11 6NT; T.-041-339 8822.

Gerrard, John Henry Atkinson, RIBA, ARIAS, DA (Edin), MA (Cantab), FRSA. Technical Director, Scottish Civic Trust, since 1984; b. 15.9.34, Leicester; m., Dr. Margaret Mackay. Educ. Abbotsholme; Corpus Christi College, Cambridge; Edinburgh College of Art. Assistant Architect: Sheffield Corporation, 1961-63, Planning Department, Oxford City Council, 1965-68; Assistant Director, Scottish Civic Trust, 1968-84. Recreation: travelling hopefully. Address: (b.) Scottish Civic Trust, 24 George Square, Glasgow; T.-041-221 1466.

Gerrard, Michael Anthony, MA, AIL. Chief Executive, Shetland Islands Council, since 1983; b. 17.8.35, London; m., Heather Margaret; 1 s.; 3 d. Educ. Finchley Grammar School; Lincoln College, Oxford. John Dale Ltd., London, 1959-63; Coates Bros. & Co. Ltd., London, 1963-74; Secretary, Haringey Community Health Council, 1974-77; Secretary, Association of Community Health Councils for England and Wales, 1977-83. Address: (b.) Town Hall, Lerwick; T.-0595 3535.

Gerrie, John Hutchison. Chief Executive, Clyde Publishing Ltd., since 1987; Chief Executive, Greenock Telegraph, Glasgow Post Series, Paisley and Renfrewshire Gazettes, Helensburgh Advertiser Series; b. 27.12.44, Glasgow; 1 s.; 2 d. Educ. Kelvinside Academy, Glasgow; Strathclyde University; Central College of Commerce, Glasgow. Journalist, Hamilton Advertiser; PR Consultant, Glasgow, Belfast and Dublin; Editor, Kirkintilloch Herald; Editor and Managing Director, Project Scotland; Development Director, Morton Newspaper Group; Managing Director, Paton-Cook Ltd.; Chairman, DSB Photographic Services Ltd.; Chairman, Strathclyde News Holdings. Captain, 32 (Scottish) Royal Signals (V). Recreations: farming; breeding dogs and small domestic animals; TA. Address: (b.) 18/20 Gordon Street, Paisley, PA1 1XB; T.-041-889 8873.

Gerson, Jack Barton. Dramatist and Novelist; b. 31.7.28, Glasgow; 1 d. Educ. Hillhead High School, Glasgow. RAF, two years; worked in advertising and cinema distribution, 1949-59; writing full-time since 1959; won BBC Television Play Competition, 1959, for Three Ring Circus; has written more than 100 hours of television drama; created two series, The Regiment and The Omega Factor; 14 radio plays; novels include Whitehall Sanction, Assassination Run, Treachery Game, The Back of the Tiger, and Deaths Head Berlin. Recreations: cinema; reading; swimming; Caribbean Islands; sleeping in front of television set. Address: (b.) c/o Harvey Unna & Stephen Durbridge, 24 Pottery Lane, Holland Park, London, W11 4LZ; T.-01-727 1346.

Gerstenberg, Frank Eric, MA (Cantab), PGCE. Principal, George Watson's College, Edinburgh, since 1985; b. 23.2.41, Balfron; 1 s.; 2 d. Educ. Trinity College, Glenalmond; Clare College, Cambridge; London University. Assistant Master, Kelly College, Tavistock, 1963-67; Housemaster and Head of History, Millfield School, 1967-74; Headmaster, Oswestry School, 1974-85. Governor, Beaconhurst School, Bridge of Allan. Recreations: skiing; sailing; travelling; music. Address: (h.) 27 Merchiston Gardens, Edinburgh, EH10 5DD; T.-031-337 6880.

Gerver, Elisabeth, BA (Hons), MA, PhD. Director, Scottish Institute of Adult and Continuing Education, since 1983; b. 15.4.41, Winnipeg; m., Dr. David Gerver (deceased); 1 s.; 1 d. Educ. Wolfville High School, Nova Scotia; Dalhousie University, Canada; Toronto University; King's College, London. Lecturer in Communications, Newcastle upon Tyne Polytechnic, 1968-69; part-time staff, Open University, 1971-84; Lecturer in Communication, Queen Margaret College, Edinburgh, 1974-83; Director, Scottish Community Education Microelectronics Project, Glasgow, 1981-82. Council Member, Scottish Community Education Council, 1979-83; Member, BBC Continuing Education Advisory Council, 1983-86; Executive Member, Scottish Institute of Adult Education, 1979-83 (Chairman, 1980-83); Vice-President, European Bureau of Adult Education, 1986-88; Member, Board of Directors, Network Scotland Ltd., 1984-88; Governor, Queen Margaret College, 1985-88; Chair, Editorial Board, Computers in Adult Education and Training, since 1986; Member, IBA Educational Advisory Council, since 1988. Publications: Computers and Adult Learning, 1984; Humanising Technology, 1985. Recreations: spare time spent with children, at the performing arts, in the garden and on the hills. Address: (b.) 30 Rutland Square, Edinburgh, EH1 2BW; T.-031-229 0331.

Gibbons, John Ernest, PhD, DipArch, DipTP, ARIBA, ARIAS, FSA(Scot), FRSA. Director of Building and Chief Architect, Scottish Office, since 1984; b. 20.4.40, Halesowen; m., Patricia Mitchell; 1 s.; 2 d. Educ. Oldbury Grammar

School; Birmingham School of Architecture, Aston University; Edinburgh University. Lecturer, Birmingham School of Architecture and Aston University, 1962-65; Research Fellow, Architecture Research Unit, then Lecturer in Architecture, Edinburgh University, 1966-72; Principal, Architect's Division, Scottish Development Department, 1972-78; Visiting Research Scientist, CSIRO, Melbourne, 1975; Assistant Director, Building Directorate, SDD, 1978; Deputy Director, Scottish Office Building Directorate, 1982-84. Member of Council, EAA and RIAS, 1977-80; Member, Council, ARCUK, since 1984; Assessor, Design Council, 1984-88. Address: (h.) Crichton House, Pathhead, Midlothian, EH37 5UX; T.-0875 320085.

Gibbs, Ronald Percy, OBE. Chairman, PHAB Scotland, since 1984; Concert Organiser, Edinburgh Bach Society, since 1981; Convener, History Section, The Cramond Association, since 1983; b. 1.6.21, London; m., Margaret Eleanor Dean; 3 s.; 1 d. Educ. Owen's School, Islington. Ministry (later Department) of Transport, 1938-81; set up the Ports Office for Scotland in Edinburgh, 1973, and remained Head of that Office until retiral in 1981. Board Member, PHAB Ltd. and Vice-Chairman, Handicabs (Lothian) Ltd.; Member, Council, Old Edinburgh Club. Recreations: transport and communications; music; local and industrial history; photography. Address: (h.) 13 Inveralmond Drive, Edinburgh, EH4 6JX; T.-031-312 6034.

Gibson, Rev. Alexander Cameron, MRCVS. Minister, Eskdalemuir, Hutton, Corrie and Tundergarth, since 1980; b. 21.7.26, New Cumnock; m., Janet Mary Wyllie, MA; 4 s. Educ. Carrick Academy; Glasgow Veterinary College; Glasgow University and Trinity College. Veterinary Surgeon, Maybole and Ilfracombe, 1950-60; Minister: Fenwick, 1962-68, Nairn Old, 1968-80. Founder Member, Lochgoin and Fenwick Covenanters' Trust; twice Presbytery Moderator; Past Chairman, Nairn Health Council; Counsellor, Churches' Selection Schools. Publications: Vet in Vestry and Poultry in Pulpit (under pen name Alexander Cameron). Recreations: gardening; golf; music; former football player. Address: Hutton Manse, Boreland, by Lockerbie, Dumfriesshire; T.-Boreland 213.

Gibson, Sir Alexander (Drummond), KB (1977), CBE (1967), Hon. RAM, Hon. FRCM, Hon. FRSAM, Hon. RSA, OStJ, FRSE, FRSA, Hon. LLD (Aberdeen), Hon. DMus (Glasgow), DUniv (Stirling), Hon. Doctor (Open University), LRAM, ARCM, ARCO. Conductor Laureate, Scottish Opera, since 1987 (Artistic Director, 1962-85, Music Director, 1985-87); Honorary President, Scottish National Orchestra, since 1985 (Principal Conductor and Musical Director, 1959-84); b. 11.2.26, Motherwell; m., Anne Veronica Waggett; 3 s.; 1 d. Educ. Dalziel High School, Motherwell; Glasgow University; Royal College of Music; Mozarteum, Salzburg, Austria; Accademia Chigiano, Siena, Italy. Royal Signals, 1944-48; Repetiteur and Assistant Conductor, Sadler's Wells Opera, 1951-52; Assistant Conductor, BBC Scottish Orchestra, Glasgow, 1952-54; Sadler's Wells Opera: Staff Conductor, 1954-57, Musical Director, 1957-59; Principal Guest Conductor, Houston Symphony Orchestra, 1981-82 and 1982-83. Freeman, Burgh of Motherwell and Wishaw, 1964; St. Mungo Prize, 1970; Arnold Bax Memorial Medal for Conducting, 1959; ISM Musician of the Year Award, 1976; Sibelius Medal, 1978; Musician of the Year, British Music Year Book, 1980.

Gibson, Archibald Turner, FIB (Scot). General Manager, Bank of Scotland, since 1988 (Joint General Manager, 1983-88); b. 6.6.32, Paisley; m., Ellen Campbell McNiven; 1 s.; 2 d. Educ. Paisley Grammar School; Harvard Business School. Bank of Scotland: Assistant General Manager, International Division, 1974-80, Divisional General Manager, Marketing and Development, 1980-83. Recreations: tennis; gardening; theatre; art. Address: (b.) Bank of Scotland, Head Office, The Mound, Edinburgh; T.-031-243 5554.

Gibson, Edgar Matheson, MBE, TD, DL, DA. Assistant Rector, Kirkwall Grammar School, since 1988; Chairman, St. Magnus Cathedral Fair, since 1982; Chairman, Northern Area, Highland TA&VR Association, since 1987; Deputy Lieutenant, Orkney, since 1976; b. 1.11.34, Kirkwall; m., Jean McCarrick; 2 s.; 2 d. Educ. Kirkwall Grammar School; Gray's College of Art, Aberdeen. National Service, 1958-60; TA and TAVR service to 1985 with Lovat Scouts, reaching Lt. Col.; Battalion Second in Command, 2/51 Highland Volunteers, 1973-76; Joint Services Liaison Officer for Orkney, 1980-85; Cadet Commandant, Orkney Lovat Scouts ACF, 1979-86, Honorary Colonel, since 1986. Recreations: painting; sculpture; whisky tasting. Address: (h.) Transcona, New Scapa Road, Kirkwall, Orkney; T.-0856 2849.

Gibson, Eric Robert, IPFA. Director of Finance, North East Fife District Council, since 1988 (Director of Finance, Roxburgh District Council, 1986-88); b. 14.7.49, Duns; m., Angelina; 1 d. Educ. Berwickshire High School. Trainee Accountant, then Accountant, Berwick County Council, 1966-75; Section Accountant, then Chief Accountant, Grampian Regional Council, 1975-86. Recreations: golf; garden; reading; family. Address: (b.) County Buildings, Cupar, Fife.

Gibson, Rev. Henry Montgomerie, MA, BD. Minister, The High Kirk, Dundee, since 1979; b. 11.6.36, Wishaw; m., Dr. Anne Margaret Thomson; 1 s. Educ. Wishaw Academy; Hamilton Academy; Glasgow University. Assistant Minister, Glasgow Cathedral, 1960; Minister: Carmunnock Parish Church, Glasgow, 1961-71, Aberfeldy, 1971-79; Convener, Church of Scotland Working Party on Alcohol and Drugs, 1975-81. Recreations: reading; table tennis (occasionally). Address: High Kirk Manse, 6 Adelaide Place, Dundee, DD3 6LF; T.-Dundee 22955.

Gibson, Rev. Ivor, MA (Hons), FSA (Scot). Minister, Abercorn and Dalmeny, since 1980; b. Kirkcaldy; m., Margaret T.B. Gillespie; 1 s.; 1 d. Educ. Kirkcaldy High School; Aberdeen University and Christ College. Ordained Assistant, Cardonald Church, Glasgow; Minister, Kelty North Parish Church; Tutor Organiser of Adult Education; Teacher of Religious Education. Recreations: reading; walking; local history; listening to music. Address: The Manse, Dalmeny, South Queensferry; T.-031-331 1869.

Gibson, John Alan, MD, FLS, FSA. Director, Scottish Natural History Library, since 1974; Chairman, Clyde Area Branch, Scottish Wildlife Trust, since 1969; Honorary Secretary, British Medical Association, since 1957; b. 15.5.26, Kilbarchan; m., Dr. Mary M. Baxter; 1 d. Educ. Lindisfarne School; Paisley Grammar School; Glasgow University. Family Doctor, village of Kilbarchan; Editor, The Scottish Naturalist (founded 1871); Scottish Representative, Society for the Bibliography of Natural History; Scientific Meetings Secretary, Society for the History of Natural History; Chairman, Scottish Natural History Trust; Honorary Secretary, Scottish Society for the Protection of Birds; Chairman, Friends of Glasgow University Library; Honorary Secretary, Clyde Birds Club; Gold Medal, Scottish Society for the Protection of Birds, 1967. Publications: over 300 scientific papers and books on Scottish natural history. Recreations: natural history; golf (Royal Troon). Address: (h.) Foremount House, Kilbarchan, PA10 2EZ; T.-Kilbarchan 2410.

Gibson, Rev. Professor John Clark Love, MA, BD, DPhil. Head, Department of Hebrew and Old Testament Studies, Edinburgh University, since 1983; b. 28.5.30, Coatbridge; m., Agnes Gilmour Russell, MA ; 4 s.; 1 d. Educ. Coatbridge High School; Glasgow University; Magdalen College, Oxford. Licensed as Probationer, Church of Scotland, 1956; Assistant Minister, Bellshill West, 1956; Minister, Newmachar, 1959-62; Edinburgh University: Lecturer in Hebrew and Semitic Languages, 1962-73, Reader, 1973-87, Professor, since 1987. Publications: Textbook of Hebrew Inscriptions, 1971; Textbook of Aramaic Inscriptions, 1975; Canaanite Myths and Legends, 1978; Textbook of Phoenician Inscriptions, 1982; Daily Study Bible (Old Testament) (General Editor and author of volumes on Genesis and Job), 1981-86; Reader's Digest Family Guide to the Bible (Features Editor), 1984; The Bible in Scottish Life and Literature (Contributor), 1988. Recreations: Burns; golf. Address: 10 South Morton Street, Edinburgh; T.-031-669 3635.

Gibson, Peter Robert, MA (Hons). Director, Scottish Consumer Council, since 1977; b. 11.9.47, Dunlop, Ayrshire; m., Amanda Kate Britain. Educ. Glasgow Academy; Elk Grove Senior High School, California; St. Andrews University; University of California, Davis. Teaching Assistant, University of California, Davis, 1969-70; Marketing Trainee, Unilever, 1970-71; Regional Organiser, Shelter, Surrey and Hampshire, 1971-73; National Groups Organiser, War on Want, 1973-74; Director, Shelter Scotland, 1974-77. Member, Scottish Housing Advisory Committee, 1977-79; Founder Member, Scottish Homeless Group, 1977; Member, Council for Freedom of Information. Recreations: home improvement (involuntary); Italy; eating out; trashy TV and cinema; cats. Address: (h.) Dunluce House, Prospect Road, Dullatur, G68 OAN; T.-02367 24247.

Gifford, Professor the Rev. Douglas John, TD, BLitt, MA (Oxon), FSA. Professor of Spanish, St. Andrews University, since 1975; Non-Stipendiary Episcopalian Chaplain to St. Andrews University, since 1981; Director, The Renaissance Group, since 1955; b. 21.7.24, Buenos Aires; m., Hazel Mary Collingwood; 4 s.; 1 d. Educ. Wycliffe and Queen's College, Oxford. British Army Intelligence Corps, 1943-47; served in Normandy and Holland with 51st Highland Division; Lecturer, then Senior Lecturer, St. Andrews University, 1950-75; Commanding Officer, University OTC, 1960-67 (retired with rank of Lt. Col.); ordained in Episcopal Church of Scotland, 1981. Publications: Textos linguisticos del medioevo espanol (Co-author), 1959; Carnival & Coca-Leaf (Co-author); Gods, Spirits and Warriors, Mythology of Central and South America; The Fool and the Trickster (Co-author); Spain, A Companion to Spanish Studies (Co-author). Recreations: squash; golf; music. Address: 3 Balfour Place, St. Andrews, KY16 9RQ; T.-0334 72742.

Gilbert, Colin, BA (Hons). Head of Comedy, BBC Scotland, since 1986; b. 3.4.52, Glasgow; m., Joanna; 1 s.; 1 d. Educ. St. Paul's School; York University. Script Editor, Not The 9 O'Clock News, 1980-82; Producer: A Kick Up the Eighties, 1983, Naked Radio, 1984, Naked Video and City Lights, 1986 and 1987. Address: (b.) BBC Scotland, Queen Margaret Drive, Glasgow, G12 8DG.

Gilchrist, Sir Andrew Graham, KCMG (1964), BA (Oxon). Fruitgrower and Author, formerly Diplomat; b. 19.4.10, Lesmahagow; m., Freda Grace Slack (deceased); 2 s.; 1 d. Educ. Edinburgh Academy; Exeter College, Oxford. Foreign Service, 1933-70, including appointments as Ambassador at Reykjavik, Djakarta, Dublin, with time out for two years Army service (Major, Force 136) in South-East Asia; on retirement, made Chairman, Highlands and Islands Development Board, 1970-76. Publications: Bangkok Top Secret; Cod Wars and How to Lose Them; five novels (latest, Death of an Admiral, 1988). Recreations: music; fishing; curling (oldest member, Lesmahagow Curling Club). Address: (h.) Arthur's Crag, Hazelbank, by Lanark; T.-055586 263.

Gilchrist, Bernard, MBE, MA (Hons) (Oxon). Chief Executive, Scottish Wildlife Trust, 1965-85; b. 20.5.19, Manchester; m., Jean W. Gregory; 2 s.; 1 d. Educ. Manchester Grammar School; Queen's College, Oxford. Tanganyika: Forest Officer, HM Colonial/Overseas Civil Service, 1942-62 (Conservator of Forests, 1960), Conservator of Forests, Tanganyika/Tanzania Government Service, 1962-65. Recreations: countryside; natural history; hill-walking; photography. Address: (h.) 9 Murrayfield Gardens, Edinburgh, EH12 6DG; T.-031-337 3869.

Gilchrist, James. Vice Chairman, Conservative Group, Lothian Regional Council; Member, Manpower Services Commission, since 1985; b. 1.7.42, Edinburgh; m., June Gilchrist; 1 s.; 2 d. Educ. George Heriot's School, Edinburgh. Elected to Lothian Regional Council, 1975; Chairman, Education Committee, 1982-84, Finance Committee, 1984-86; Vice Chairman, Napier College, 1982-85; Member, Edinburgh University Court, 1982-86. Address: (b.) 19 St. Andrew Square, Edinburgh, EH1 2YE; T.-031-225 2211.

Gilchrist, Thomas, BSc, PhD, CChem, FRSC. Managing Director, Ross Fraser Ltd. and Giltech Ltd., since 1984; b. 18.6.36, Ayr; m., Fiona Christina Brown; 2 d. Educ. Ayr Academy; Glasgow University. Assistant Lecturer in Chemistry, Glasgow University, 1961-62; Research Chemist: Canadian Industries Ltd., Quebec, 1962-64, ICI Ltd., Stevenston, Ayrshire, 1964-69; Strathclyde University: Lecturer in Bioengineering, 1969, Head, Division of Artificial Organs, Bioengineering Unit, 1972, Senior Lecturer in Bioengineering, 1975-84. Section Editor, International Journal of Artificial Organs. Recreations: golf; curling. Address: (h.) The Lodge, 67 Midton Road, Ayr, KA7 2TW; T.-Ayr 266088.

Giles, Sir Alexander Falconer, KBE (1965), CMG (1960), MBE (Mil.); b. 16.9.15, Dumfries; m., Margaret Elinor Watson Burnett; 2 step s.; 1 step d. Educ. Edinburgh Academy; Edinburgh University; Balliol College, Oxford. 2nd Lt., Royal Scots, 1940; Att. RWAFF, 1941, 81 Div.; Lt. Col. Comd. 5th Bn., Gold Coast Regiment, 1945; Cadet, Colonial Service, Tanganyika, 1947; Administrator, St. Vincent, BWI, 1955-62; Resident Commissioner, Basutoland, 1962-65 (British Government Representative there, 1965-66). President, Oxford Union Society, 1939; Chairman, Victoria League in Scotland, 1968-70; Member, General Council, Royal Overseas League, 1972-75. Recreation: the printed word. Address: (h.) 4 Royal Crescent, Edinburgh, EH3; T.-031-556 7416.

Giles, Cecilia Elspeth, CBE, MA. Assistant Secretary, Edinburgh University, 1972-87; Committee of Vice-Chancellors and Principals' Administrative Training Officer (seconded part-time), 1983-85; b. Dumfries. Educ. Queen Margaret's School, Yorkshire; Edinburgh University. Administrative staff, Khartoum University, 1956-57; joined Administrative staff, Edinburgh University, 1957; Member, Church of Scotland Board of Stewardship and Finance, since 1986; Vice-President, Edinburgh University Graduates' Association, since 1987; Chairman, Conservative Political Centre Committee in Scotland. Publication: Tourism in Scotland (Co-author). Recreations: entertaining friends, family and godchildren; theatre. Address: (b.) Old College, South Bridge, Edinburgh, EH8 9YL.

Gilles, Professor Dennis Cyril, BSc, PhD, FRSE, FRSA, FIMA, FBCS. Professor of Computing Science, Glasgow University, since 1966; b. 7.4.25, London; m., Valerie Mary Gardiner; 2 s.; 2 d. Educ. Chislehurst and Sidcup Grammar School; Imperial College, London. Mathematician, Scientific Computing Service Ltd., London, 1949-55; Research Fellow, Computing Machine Laboratory, Manchester University, 1955-57; Director, Computing Laboratory, Glasgow University, 1957-66. Address: (h.) 21 Bruce Road, Glasgow, G41 5EE; T.-041-429 7733.

Gillespie, Adam, BSc (Hons), CPhys, MInstP. Head Teacher, Greenfaulds High School, Cumbernauld, since 1986; b. 22.3.44, Glasgow; m., Agnes C. Ferrie; 2 s. Educ. Glasgow University. Teacher of Physics, Dumbarton Academy, 1966-68; Principal Teacher of Physics, Jordanhill College School, 1968-78; Assistant Head Teacher, then Depute Head Teacher, Vale of Leven Academy, 1978-86. Former Member, Scottish Branch Committee, Institute of Physics. Recreations: music; gardening; walking. Address: (h.) 9(B) West Montrose Street, Helensburgh, G84 9NF; T.-0436 6157.

Gillespie, Archibald, CA, ACMA, IPFA. Director of Finance, Strathclyde Regional Council, since 1986; b. 4.9.35, Greenock; m., Alice Finlayson; 2 s.; 2 d. Educ. Greenock High School. Chief Internal Auditor, Greenock Corporation, 1964-67; County Treasurer, Bute County Council, 1967-75; Senior Depute Director of Finance, Strathclyde Regional Council, 1975-86. Member, Public Sector Committee, Institute of Chartered Accountants of Scotland; Member, Executive Committee, CIPFA, Scottish Branch. Recreations: golf; badminton. Address: (h.) 64 South Street, Greenock; T.-0475 81904.

Gillespie, Professor John Spence, MB, ChB, PhD, FIBiol, FRCPGlas, FRSE. Professor and Head of Department of Pharmacology, Glasgow University, since 1968; b. 5.9.26, Dumbarton; m., Jemima Simpson Ross; 4 s.; 1 d. Educ. Dumbarton Academy; Glasgow University. National Service as RMO, 1950-52; McCunn Research Scholar in Physiology, Glasgow University, 1953-55; Faulds Fellow, then Sharpey Scholar, Physiology Department, University College, London, 1955-57; Lecturer in Physiology, Glasgow University, 1957-59; Sophie Fricke Research Fellow, Royal Society, Rockefeller Institute, 1959-60; Glasgow University: Senior Lecturer in Physiology, 1961-63, Henry Head Research Fellow, Royal Society, 1963-68; Vice-Principal, Glasgow University, since 1983; Honorary Secretary, Physiological Society, 1966-72; Council Member, Research Defence Society, 1974-77; Committee Member, British Pharmacological Society, 1973-76. Recreations: gardening; painting. Address: (b.) Department of Pharmacology, Glasgow University, Glasgow, G12 8QQ; T.-041-339 8855, Ext. 481.

Gillies, Anne Bethea, MA, LLB. Advocate; Honorary Sheriff of South Strathclyde, Dumfries and Galloway, at Lanark, since 1960; Member, Valuation Appeal Panel, Strathclyde, since 1974; b. 12.4.22, Lochgilphead, Argyll; m., Sheriff Principal M.G. Gillies, T.D., Q.C. (qv). Educ. Sherborne School for Girls, Dorset; Edinburgh University. Served in WAAF, until 1946; called to Scottish Bar, 1951; married, 1954. Recreations: gardening; cats. Address: (h.) Redwalls, Biggar, Lanarkshire, ML12 6HA; T.-Biggar 20281.

Gillies, Col. Hugh Stewart, MC, BA, DL, JP; b. 9.12.15, New Abbey; m., Christina Susan Maud; 2 s.; 2 d. Educ. Loretto School; Jesus College, Cambridge. 2nd Lt., KOSB, 1936, UK; Lt., KOSB, 1939, UK, France, Belgium; Captain, KOSB, 1940, France, Belgium, UK; Major, KOSB, Para, and Staff, 1940, UK, France, Belgium, Holland, Germany, Palestine, Egypt, Singapore, Malaya; Lt. Col., SAS Regiment, 1958, UK; Colonel, SAS Regiment, 1961, UK; retired from Army, 1964; Civil Servant under MOD, 1964-81. Nithsdale District Councillor, 1975-81. Recreation: gardening. Address: Kindar House, New Abbey, Dumfries; T.-New Abbey 202.

Gillies (Maurice) Gordon, TD (and Bar), QC (Scot). Sheriff Principal of South Strathclyde, Dumfries and Galloway, since 1982; b. 17.10.16;

m., Anne Bethea McCall-Smith (see Anne Bethea Gillies). Educ. Aberdeen Grammar School; Merchiston Castle; Edinburgh University. Advocate, 1946; Advocate Depute, 1953-58; Sheriff of Lanarkshire (later South Strathclyde, Dumfries and Galloway), 1958-82.

Gillies, Professor William, MA (Edin), MA (Oxon). Professor of Celtic, Edinburgh University, since 1979; b. 15.9.42, Stirling; m., Valerie; 1 s.; 2 d. Educ. Oban High School; Edinburgh University; Corpus Christi College, Oxford; Dublin University. Dublin Institute for Advanced Studies, 1969-70; Lecturer, Edinburgh University, 1970-79. Director, Acair Ltd., Comunn na Gaidhlig. Recreations: walking; gardening; music. Address: (h.) 67 Braid Avenue, Edinburgh, EH10 6ED.

Gillis, Charles Raphael, MD, MRCP(Glas), FFCM. Director, West of Scotland Cancer Surveillance Unit, since 1973; Head, World Health Organisation Collaborating Centre for Community Cancer Care, since 1987; Honorary Clinical Lecturer, Glasgow University, since 1973; b. 23.10.37, Glasgow; m., Judith Ann Naftalin; 1 s.; 1 d. Educ. High School of Glasgow; Glasgow University. Lecturer in Epidemiology and Preventive Medicine, then Senior Lecturer and Honorary Consultant Epidemiologist, Glasgow University, 1965-73. Chairman, Cancer Education Co-ordinating Group of the UK and Republic of Ireland, since 1985; Chairman, West of Scotland Oncological Association, since 1985. Address: (b.) West of Scotland Cancer Surveillance Unit, Ruchill Hospital, Bilsland Drive, Ruchill, Glasgow, G20 9NB; T.-041-946 7120.

Gillon, Rev. Charles Blair, BD. Parish Minister, Ibrox, Glasgow, since 1980; b. 19.8.38, Montrose; m., Linda Smith; 3 s.; 2 d. Educ. Morgan Academy, Dundee; George Heriot's, Edinburgh; Trinity College, Glasgow University. Library Assistant, Edinburgh Corporation Libraries, 1954-59; Senior Library Assistant, Edinburgh University Library, 1959-63; Librarian, Animal Breeding Library, Commonwealth Agricultural Bureau, Edinburgh, 1963-69; student, 1970-75; Parish Minister, Kilbarchan East, 1975-80. Member, Incorporation of Skinners, Trades House, Glasgow. Address: 3 Dargarvel Avenue, Glasgow, G41 5LD; T.-041-427 1282.

Gillon, Hamish William, FFA, FPMI. Assistant General Manager, Scottish Provident Institution, since 1980; b. 22.1.40, Edinburgh; m., Sandra; 1 s.; 1 d. Educ. Royal High School, Edinburgh. Various appointments, Scottish Provident Institution, since 1965. Chairman, Development Working Group, The Scout Association. Address: (b.) 6 St. Andrew Square, Edinburgh, EH2 2YA; T.-031-556 9181.

Gilmore, Stan, BA (Hons), MEd (Hons), DipEd, DipRSAMD. Lecturer in Continuing Education, Stirling University, since 1972; Vice-Chairman, Buildings and Property Committee, Strathclyde Regional Council, since 1982; b. 11.1.29, New York City; m., Anne J.J.; 1 s.; 1 d. Educ. North Kelvinside School, Glasgow; Jordanhill College of Education; University College, London. Various teaching appointments in primary and secondary schools, 1956-62; Lecturer: Central College of Commerce, Glasgow, 1962-66, Hamilton College of Education, 1966-72. Director, Prince and Princess of Wales Hospice. Recreations: theatre-going; travel; reading. Address: (h.) 11 Poplar Drive, Lenzie, Glasgow, G66 4DN; T.-041-776 1409.

Gilmour, Colonel Allan Macdonald, OBE, MC (and Bar), DSC (USA). Lord Lieutenant of Sutherland, since 1972; Member, Highland Regional Council, since 1976; Member, Sutherland District Council, 1974-88 (Chairman, 1974-78); b. 23.11.16, Edinburgh; m., Jean Wood; 3 s.; 1 d. Educ. Cargilfield, Edinburgh; Winchester College; Trinity College, Oxford. Commissioned Seaforth Highlanders, 1939; served War in Middle East, Sicily and NW Europe; Regimental and Staff appointments, 1945-69, including Instructor, Staff College, Quetta, and Chief of Staff, Ghana Armed Forces; Member, Sutherland County Council, 1970; Member, Highland Health Board, 1974 (Chairman, 1982-84); DL, Sutherland, 1969; Member: Highland River Purification Board, since 1978, Highlands and Islands Development Consultative Council, 1980-88; Chairman, East Sutherland Council of Social Service, 1972-76; Board Member, Scottish National Orchestra Society, 1976-86. Recreation: fishing. Address: (h.) Invernauld, Rosehall, Lairg, Sutherland; T.-054 984 204.

Gilmour, Andrew Parr, BSc (Hons). Rector, Rothesay Academy, since 1983; b. 26.4.46, Glasgow; m., Elizabeth Morrison MacPherson; 1 s.; 2 d. Educ. Allan Glen's School, Glasgow; Glasgow University. Teacher of Chemistry, Allan Glen's School, 1969; Dunoon Grammar School: Principal Teacher of Chemistry, 1972, Assistant Rector, 1975; Depute Head Teacher, Mearns Castle High School, 1981. Recreations: sailing; badminton; rugby (spectating nowadays); swimming. Address: (h.) Millford, 34 Mount Stuart Road, Rothesay, Isle of Bute; T.-Rothesay 3336.

Gilmour, Douglas Graham, BSc (Hons), MB, ChB, MD, FRCS. Consultant Vascular Surgeon, Glasgow Royal Infirmary, since 1983; b. 15.4.47, Glasgow; m., Evelyn Jean; 2 s.; 2 d. Educ. Kelvinside Academy, Glasgow; Glasgow University. House Surgeon/Physician, then Senior House Officer/Registrar in Surgery, Western Infirmary, Glasgow, 1971-77; Glasgow Royal Infirmary: Senior Registrar in Surgery, 1977-80, Senior Lecturer (Honorary Consultant) in Surgery, 1980-83. Recreations: family; golf; skiing. Address: (b.) Vascular Surgery Department, Royal Infirmary, Glasgow; T.-041-552 3535, Ext. 5503.

Gilmour, Hugh Montgomery, MB, ChB, FRCPath. Senior Lecturer in Pathology, Edinburgh University, since 1979; Honorary Consultant, Lothian Health Board, since 1979; b. 17.5.43, Edinburgh; m., Alison Mary Little; 2 s. Educ. George Heriot's School; Edinburgh University. House Officer appointments in medicine and surgery, Bangour General Hospital, 1967-68; Lecturer, Department of Pathology, Edinburgh University, 1968-79. Recreations: golf; gardening. Address: (b.) University Medical School, Teviot Place, Edinburgh, EH8 9AG; T.-031-667 1011.

Gilmour, Sir John Edward, 3rd Bt, DSO, TD, JP, BA. Lord Lieutenant of Fife, 1980-87; b. 24.10.12, Edinburgh; m., Ursula Mabyn Wills; 2 s. Educ. Eton College; Trinity Hall, Cambridge; Dundee School of Economics. Served with Fife and Forfar Yeomanry, 1939-45; served on Fife County Council, 1951-61; MP (Conservative), East Fife, 1961-79; Chairman, Conservative Party in Scotland, 1965-67; Lord High Commissioner, General Assembly, Church of Scotland, 1982, 1983. Recreation: gardening. Address: (h.) Montrave, Leven, Fife, KY8 5NY; T.-Leven 26159.

Gilmour, William McIntosh, OStJ, BL. Honorary Sheriff, Dumbarton; Lawyer; b. 9.3.23, Newcastle-upon-Tyne; m., Elinor Adams. Educ. Hillhead High School; Cally House, Gatehouse of Fleet; Glasgow University. Early experience with legal firms in Glasgow; became Partner, latterly Senior Partner, in firm in Dunbartonshire; now in practice in Glasgow; former Dean, Faculty of Solicitors in Dunbartonshire; founder Member and Past President, Clydebank Rotary Club; Past Deacon, Society of Deacons and Free Presces; Chairman for Dunbartonshire, Order of St. John; Member, Incorporation of Gardeners (Glasgow Trades House). Recreations: dog-walking (formerly, motor sport). Address: (h.) 65 Killermont Road, Bearsden, Glasgow; T.-041-942 0498.

Gilmour, Rev. William Mayne, MA, BD. Minister, Lecropt Kirk, Bridge of Allan, since 1983; b. 18.10.42, Glasgow; m., Helen Grant Dewar; 1 s.; 1 d. Educ. Albert Secondary School, Glasgow; Aberdeen University. Minister: Townhead Church, Coatbridge, 1969-79, Chalmers linked with Lecropt Church, Bridge of Allan, 1979-83. Recreation: reading. Address: Lecropt Kirk Manse, 5 Henderson Street, Bridge of Allan, FK9 4NA; T.-0786 832382.

Gilray, George, MB, ChB, DPH, FFCM. Principal Medical Officer, Scottish Home and Health Department; b. 6.11.29, Edinburgh; m., Anne Bertram Pringle; 2 s.; 2 d. Educ. George Heriot's School, Edinburgh; Edinburgh University. After pre-registration hospital appointments, served in RAF Medical Branch, 1955-76. Recreations: reading; sailing. Address: (h.) 10 Barntongate Avenue, Edinburgh, EH4 8BB; T.-031-339 1431.

Gimingham, Professor Charles Henry, BA, PhD, ScD, FRSE, FIBiol. Regius Professor of Botany, Aberdeen University, 1981-88; b. 28.4.23, Leamington; m., Elizabeth Caroline Baird; 3 d. Educ. Gresham's School, Holt, Norfolk; Emmanuel College, Cambridge. Research Assistant, Imperial College, London, 1944-45; Department of Botany, Aberdeen University: Assistant, 1946-48, Lecturer, 1948-61, Senior Lecturer, 1961-64, Reader, 1964-69, Professor, since 1969, Head of Department, 1981-88; Member: Scottish Committee of Nature Conservancy, 1966-69, Scottish Advisory Committee, Nature Conservancy Council, 1970-80, Countryside Commission for Scotland, since 1980; President, Botanical Society of Edinburgh, 1982-84; Member, Board of Management, Hill Farming Research Organisation, 1981-87; Member, Governing Body, Aberdeen College of Education, 1981-87; Member, Council of Management, Macaulay Institute for Soil Research, 1983-87; Member, Board of Management, Macaulay Land Use Research Institute, since 1987; British Ecological Society: Joint Secretary, 1956-61, Vice-President, 1962-64, Joint Editor, Journal of Ecology, 1975-78, President, 1986-87. Publications: Ecology of Heathlands, 1972; Introduction to Heathland Ecology, 1975. Recreations: hill-walking; photography; history and culture of Japan. Address: (h.) 2 Carden Terrace, Aberdeen.

Gimson, George Stanley, QC (Scot). Chairman, Pensions Appeals Tribunals, Scotland, since 1975; Chairman, Medical Appeal Tribunals, since 1985; b. 1915. Educ. High School of Glasgow; Glasgow University. Advocate, 1949; Sheriff Principal of Aberdeen, Kincardine and Banff, 1972-74; Sheriff Principal of Grampian, Highland and Islands, 1975-82; Member, Edinburgh Central Hospitals Board, 1960-70 (Chairman, 1964-70); Director, SNO Society Ltd., 1962-80; Trustee, National Library of Scotland, 1963-76; Chairman, RSSPCC, Edinburgh, 1972-76; Hon. LLD, Aberdeen, 1981. Address: (h.) 11 Royal Circus, Edinburgh, EH3 6TL.

Ginsborg, Professor Bernard Lionel, PhD, DSc, FRSE. Professor of Pharmacology, Edinburgh University, since 1976; b. 22.1.25, London; m., Andrina Taffler; 2 d. Educ. Owen's School, London; Reading University; University College, London. Medical Research Council Scholar, then Stothert Research Fellow of the Royal Society, University College, London, 1951-56; Lecturer in Biophysics, University College, London, 1956-57; Scientific staff, Medical Research Council, 1957-62; Lecturer, then Reader, Department of Pharmacology, Edinburgh University, 1962-76 (Head of Department, 1980-85). Address: (b.) Department of Pharmacology, University Medical School, 1 George Square, Edinburgh, EH8 9JZ; T.-031-667 1011.

Girdwood, John Millar, DSAA, MITSA. Director of Consumer Protection, Grampian Regional Council, since 1985; b. 4.6.31, Glasgow; m., Mabel Sarah Ferrol; 1 s.; 1 d. Educ. John Street School, Glasgow. Glasgow Corporation Weights and Measures Department, 1954-66; Inspector of Weights and Measures, Fife County Council, 1966-67; returned to Glasgow, 1967; Divisional Inspector, 1968; Assistant Director of Consumer Protection, Strathclyde Regional Council, 1975. Recreations: jogging; water colour painting; sketching. Address: (b.) 77/79 King Street, Aberdeen; T.-0224 649966.

Girdwood, Richard Stuart Haxton, LLB, WS, NP. Barrister and Solicitor in the Supreme Court of Victoria, Australia; Director, Legal Practice Unit, Edinburgh University, since 1979; b. 3.5.47, Edinburgh; m., Roberta Anne Egan; 3 s. Educ. George Watson's College; Edinburgh University. Legal practice in Edinburgh firm; Corporate Solicitor, Melbourne, Australia; Lecturer, Department of Scots Law, Edinburgh University. Recreations: horse riding; antiquarian books. Address: (b.) Faculty of Law, Edinburgh University, Old College, South Bridge, Edinburgh; T.-031-667 1011.

Girdwood, Professor Ronald Haxton, CBE, MB, ChB (Hons), MD, PhD, FRCPEd, FRCP, FRCPI, FRCPath, Hon. FACP, Hon. FRACP, FRSE. President, Royal College of Physicians of Edinburgh, 1982-85; Chairman, Scottish National Blood Transfusion Association, since 1981; b. 19.3.17, Arbroath; m., Mary Elizabeth Williams; 1 s.; 1 d. Educ. Daniel Stewart's College, Edinburgh; Edinburgh University; Michigan University. Army service, RAMC, UK and India, 1942-46, successively as Lt., Captain, Major and Lt.-Col. (when posted to Burma); Lecturer, then Senior Lecturer, Reader in Medicine, Edinburgh University, 1946-62; Research Fellow, Michigan University, 1948-49; Consultant Physician, Edinburgh Royal Infirmary, 1950-82; Professor of Therapeutics and Clinical Pharmacology, Edinburgh University, 1962-82 (Dean, Faculty of Medicine, 1975-79); Chairman, Scottish Group, Nutrition Society, 1961-62; President, British Society for Haematology, 1963-64; Chairman, Executive Committee, Edinburgh and SE Scotland Blood Transfusion Association, since 1970; Member, UK Committee on Safety of Medicines, 1972-83; Chairman, Medico-Pharmaceutical Forum, 1985-87; Member, Board of Governors, St. Columba's Hospice, since 1985; Suniti Panja Gold Medal, Calcutta School of Tropical Medicine, 1980; given the Freedom of Sirajgunj, Bangladesh, 1984. Publications: editor of four medical books and more than 300 medical papers. Recreations: writing; photography. Address: (h.) 2 Hermitage Drive, Edinburgh, EH10 6DD; T.-031-447 5137.

Glasgow, 10th Earl of (Patrick Robin Archibald Boyle). Television Director/Producer; b. 30.7.39; m., Isabel Mary James; 1 s.; 1 d. Educ. Eton; Paris University. Sub.-Lt., RNR, 1959-60; Producer/Director, Yorkshire TV, 1968-70; freelance Film Producer, since 1971; formed Kelburn Country Centre, 1977. Address (b.) South Offices, Kelburn Estate, Fairlie, Ayrshire.

Glashan, John Irvine, CA. Director of Finance, Ross and Cromarty District Council, since 1975; b. 23.8.38, Nairn; m., Elizabeth; 2 s.; 1 d. Educ. Aberdeen Grammar School; Forres Academy; Ballater Junior Secondary School. Accountant, City of Aberdeen, 1964-67; Depute County Treasurer, Moray and Nairn Joint County Council, 1968-75. Area Treasurer, Ross and Sutherland Scout Association. Recreation: bowling. Address: (b.) Council Offices, Dingwall; T.-Dingwall 63381.

Glass, Alexander, MA, DipEd. Rector, Dingwall Academy, since 1977; b. 1.6.32, Dunbar; m., Edith Margaret Duncan Baxter; 3 d. Educ. Dunbar Grammar School; Edinburgh University; Heidelberg University; University of Aix-en-Provence. Teacher of Modern Languages, Montrose Academy, 1958-60; Special Assistant Teacher of Modern Languages, Oban High School, 1960-62; Principal Teacher of Modern Languages, Nairn Academy, 1962-65; Principal Teacher of French and Assistant Rector, Perth Academy, 1965-72; Rector, Milne's High School, Fochabers, 1972-77. Chairman, COSPEN; former President, Highland Secondary Headteachers' Association; former Chairman, Highland Region Working Party for Modern Languages; Regional Chairman, Highland Region Children's Panel; Reader, Church of Scotland; Chairman, Highland Division, Scottish Community Drama Association and Inverness District, SCDA; Secretary, Scottish Secondary Schools' Travel Trust; Chairman, Highland Branch, Scottish Association for the Study of Delinquency. Recreations: amateur drama; foreign travel; Rotary. Address: (h.) Craigton, Tulloch Avenue, Dingwall, IV15 9LH; T.-0349 63258.

Glasser, Professor Fredrik Paul, BA, BSc, PhD, DSc, FInstCeram, FIM, FRSE. Professor of Chemistry, Aberdeen University, since 1983; b. 2.5.29; m., Dr. Lesley Scott Dent; 1 s.; 2 d. Educ. Aberdeen University. Research Fellow, Pennsylvania State University, 1957-59; Aberdeen University: Research Fellow, 1959-61, Lecturer, Senior Lecturer, Reader. Chairman, Grampian Region Children's Panel Advisory Committee, 1988-89. Address: (b.) Department of Chemistry, Aberdeen University, Meston Walk, Old Aberdeen, AB9 2UE; T.-0224 272906.

Glen, Alastair Campbell Agnew, MD, BSc, FRCP(Glas). Consultant Clinical Biochemist, Victoria Infirmary, Glasgow, since 1970; Honorary Clinical Lecturer, Glasgow University, since 1982; b. 3.8.36, Glasgow; m., Lesley Gordon; 2 s.; 1 d. Educ. Glasgow Academy; Glasgow University. Research Associate, Massachusetts Institute of Technology, 1966. Recreations: almost anything from skiing and angling to Scottish politics. Address: (h.) 276A Nithsdale Road, Glasgow, G41 5LP; T.-041-427 2131.

Glen, Eric Stanger, MB, ChB, FRCSGlas, FRCSEdin. Consultant Urological Surgeon, Walton Urological Teaching and Research Centre, Southern General Hospital, Glasgow; Honorary Clinical Lecturer, Glasgow University; Member, Surgical Examination Panel, Royal College of Physicians and Surgeons of Glasgow; b. 20.10.34, Glasgow; m., Dr. Patricia. Educ. Glasgow University. Pre-Consultant posts, Western and Victoria Infirmaries, Glasgow; Ship Surgeon, Royal Fleet Auxiliary. Member, Steering Group on Incontinence, King's Fund, London; Founder and former Secretary, International Continence Society; Founder, Urological Computing Society. Recreations: travel; writing; computer applications. Address: (h.) 9 St. John's Road, Pollokshields, Glasgow, G41 5RJ; T.-041-423 0759.

Glen, James Robert, CA. Managing Director, The Scottish Investment Trust PLC, since 1981 (Manager, since 1969); Chairman, The Scottish Life Assurance Co., since 1987 (Director, since 1971); b. 27.5.30, Perth; m., Alison Helen Margaret Brown; 3 s. Educ. Merchiston Castle School. 2nd Lt., RA, 1954-56; Secretary, C.W. Carr, 1956-58; Baillie, Gifford & Co., 1958-62; joined Scottish Investment Trust, 1962. Address: (b.) 6 Albyn Place, Edinburgh; T.-031-225 7781.

Glen, Norman MacLeod, CBE, TD, MA, JP. Leader, Conservative Group, Dumbarton District Council, since 1974; b. 22.12.11, Glasgow; m., Dr. Janet M.S. Glen (deceased); 2 s.; 2 d. Educ. Glasgow Academy; Glasgow University. Retail trade as Buyer, Director and Managing Director, John Glen & Co. Ltd., Glasgow, 1932-74; War Service, six years; TA (mostly 474 HAA

Regt RA), 1938-56 (Lt. Colonel, 1954-56); Parliamentary candidate (Liberal), 1945, (Conservative), 1951, 1955, 1959, 1964, 1966 and By-Election, Woodside, 1962; elected, Helensburgh Town Council, 1966 (last Provost of Helensburgh, 1970-75); Elder, West Kirk of Helensburgh. Recreation: walking. Address: (h.) Flat 11, Queen's Court, Helensburgh, G84 7AH; T.-0436 3497.

Glenarthur, 4th Baron (Simon Mark Arthur), Bt. Minister of State, Foreign and Commonwealth Office, since 1987; b. 7.10.44; m.; 1 s.; 1 d. Educ. Eton. Retired Major, 10th Royal Hussars (PWO); Helicopter Captain, British Airways, 1976-82; a Lord in Waiting, 1982-83; Parliamentary Under Secretary of State: Department of Health and Social Security, 1983-85, Home Office, 1985-86; Minister of State, Scottish Office, 1986-87; Member, Queen's Bodyguard for Scotland (Royal Company of Archers). Address: (b.) House of Lords, London, SW1A 0PW.

Glencross, Rev. William McCallum, LTh. Minister, Macdonald Memorial Church, Bellshill, since 1973; b. 29.7.34, Sanquhar; m., Agnes Jane Crate; 3 d. Educ. Sanquhar Academy; Dumfries Academy; Glasgow University. Mining Surveyor, NCB, 1950-63; Parish Minister, Whalsay and Skerries (Shetland Islands), 1968-73. Address: Macdonald Memorial Manse, 346 Main Street, Bellshill, Lanarkshire; T.-Bellshill 842177.

Glennie, Charles Milne, MA, PhD. Registrar General for Scotland, since 1982; b. 29.10.34, Edinburgh; m., Eileen Margaret Mason; 1 d. Educ. Fettes College; Edinburgh University; Cambridge University; Yale University. Address: (b.) New Register House, Edinburgh, EH1 3YT; T.-031-556 3952.

Gloag, Matthew Irving. Director, Matthew Gloag & Son Ltd., since 1971; b. 1.12.47, Perth; m., Dilly Moon; 2 d. Chairman, Scottish Licensed Trade Association, 1984-85. Address: (b.) 33 Kinnoull Street, Perth, PH1 5EU; T.-0738 21101.

Glover, John Hardie, OBE, RSA, FRIBA, FRIAS. Consultant Architect (retired), Sir Basil Spence Glover & Ferguson, since 1980; b. 21.2.13, North Berwick; m., Laura Milicent James; 1 s.; 1 d. Educ. North Berwick High School; Edinburgh College of Art, School of Architecture. When qualified, joined firm of Leslie Graham Thomson, Architect, 1936; served RE, 1940-46, Britain and India; joined Council of Industrial Design as Exhibition Officer; joined Basil Spence, 1947 (Partner, 1948-80). Recreations: fishing; gardening; furniture-making. Address: (h.) The Coach House, Belford Place, Edinburgh; T.-031-332 6107.

Glover, Sue, MA. Writer; b. 1.3.43, Edinburgh; m., John Glover; 2 s. Educ. St. George's School, Edinburgh; Montpellier University; Edinburgh University. Original drama and other scriptwriting for radio, television and theatre; theatre productions include The Seal Wife, Edinburgh Festival, 1980, An Island in Largo, Byre Theatre, 1981, The Bubble Boy, Glasgow Tron, 1981, The Straw Chair, Traverse Theatre, 1988; televised version of The Bubble Boy won a silver medal, New York Film and Television Festival, and a merit, Chicago International Film Festival, 1983. Recreations: house and garden. Address: Castlefield Cottage, Castlebank Road, Cupar, Fife; T.-Cupar 53664.

Goddard, Kenneth George, BA, IPFA. Director of Finance, Skye and Lochalsh District Council, since 1981; b. 14.1.47, Pembroke Dock; m., Jennifer; 2 s. Educ. Pembroke Grammar School; St. Davids University, Lampeter. Inland Revenue, 1970-72; Pembroke Borough Council, 1972-74; South Pembrokeshire District Council, 1974-78; joined Skye and Lochalsh District Council, 1978. Address: (b.) Park Road, Portree, Isle of Skye, IV51 9EP; T.-0478 2341.

Godden, Anthony John, BSc (Hons), MRSH, AIHE. Principal, West Lothian College of Further Education, since 1987; b. 26.3.46, Swansea; m., Kelly; 1 s.; 1 d. Educ. Dynevor Grammar School; North East London Polytechnic; Open University. Lecturer, Bridgnorth College of Further Education, 1970-73; Social Tutor, Airedale and Wharfedale College of Further Education, 1973-75; Warden, Mildmay Hall, and Head, Section of General Studies and Information Sciences, Essex Institute of Higher Education, 1975-78; Assistant Inspector, Kent County Council Education Department, 1978-82; Principal, Gainsborough College of Further Education, 1982-86. Member, Board of Management, Community Opportunities West Lothian Ltd. Recreations: armchair sport; theatre; guitar; travel. Address: (b.) West Lothian College, Marjoribanks Street, Bathgate, EH48 1QJ; T.-0506 634300.

Godden, Tony Richard Hillier, CB, BSc (Econ). Secretary, Friends of the Royal Scottish Academy, since 1987; Secretary, Scottish Development Department, 1980-87; b. 13.11.27, Barnstaple; m., Marjorie Florence Snell; 1 s.; 2 d. Educ. Barnstaple Grammar School; London School of Economics. Commissioned, RAF Education Branch, 1950; entered Civil Service, 1951; first appointed to Colonial Office; Private Secretary to Parliamentary Under Secretary of State, 1954-55; seconded to Cabinet Office, 1957-59; joined Scottish Home Department, 1961; Assistant Secretary, Scottish Development Department, 1964; Under Secretary, 1969; Secretary, Scottish Economic Planning Development, 1973-80. Address: c/o New Club, Edinburgh, EH2 2BB.

Godfray, Martin Francis, BSc, CChem, FRSC, MChemA. Public Analyst, Official Agricultural Analyst and Scientific Adviser, Lothian, Borders and Highland Regional Councils and Orkney and Shetland Islands Councils, since 1980; b. 10.5.45, Barry, Glamorgan; m., Heather Jean; 1 s.; 2 d. Educ. Barry Boys Grammar Technical School; Birmingham University. Deputy Public Analyst and Deputy Agricultural Analyst, London Boroughs of Southwark, Greenwich, Islington and Tower Hamlets, 1973-80. Address: (b.) Regional Laboratory, 4 Marine Esplanade, Edinburgh, EH6 7LU; T.-031-553 1171.

Godman, Norman. MP (Labour), Greenock and Port Glasgow, since 1983; b. 1937. Educ. Hull University. Teacher and former Shipwright.

Gold, Alexander (Lex) Muncie. Director for Scotland, Training Commission, since 1987; b. 14.12.40, Rigside; m., Eleanor; 1 s.; 1 d. Educ. Lanark Grammar School. Sub-Editor, Daily Record; professional footballer; joined Civil Service, Glasgow, 1960; Inland Revenue, two years; Civil Service Department, four years; Home Office, 21 years. Recreations: theatre; opera; reading; football; golf; running. Address: (b.) 9 St. Andrew Square, Edinburgh; T.-031-225 8500.

Goldberg, Professor Sir Abraham, KB, MD, DSc, FRCP, FRCPEdin, FRCPGlas, FRSE. Regius Professor of the Practice of Medicine, Glasgow University, since 1978; Chairman, Committee on Safety of Medicines, 1980-86; b. 7.12.23, Edinburgh; m., Clarice Cussin; 2 s.; 1 d. Educ. Sciennes School, Edinburgh; George Heriot's School, Edinburgh; Edinburgh University. House Physician, Royal Hospital for Sick Children, Edinburgh, 1946-47; RAMC, 1947-49 (granted rank of honorary Major on discharge); Nuffield Research Fellow, UCH Medical School, London, 1952-54; Eli Lilly Travelling Fellow in Medicine (MRC), Department of Medicine, Utah University, 1956; Glasgow University: Lecturer in Medicine, 1956-57, Titular Professor of Medicine, 1967-70, Regius Professor of Materia Medica, 1970-78. Chairman, Grants Committee 1, Clinical Research Board, MRC, 1973-77; Member, Chief Scientist's Committee, SHHD, 1977-83; Chairman, Biomedical Research Committee, SHHD, 1977-83; Editor, Scottish Medical Journal, 1962-63. Publications: Disorders of Porphyrin Metabolism (Co-author), 1987; Recent Advances in Haematology (Joint Editor), 1971; Clinics in Haematology "The Porphyrias" (Co-author), 1980. Recreations: medical history; literature; writing; walking; swimming. Address: (b.) Glasgow University, Department of Medicine, Gardiner Institute, Western Infirmary, Glasgow, G11 6NT; T.-041-339 2800.

Goldie, David. Farmer; Member, Scottish Training Committee, Agricultural Training Board, 1982-86; Member, Scottish Agricultural Development Council, 1983-86; Director, Royal Highland and Agricultural Society, since 1976 (Chairman of Directors, 1987-88); b. 30.7.37, Dumfries; m., Ann Irving; 3 s. Educ. Wallace Hall Academy, Closeburn, Thornhill. Chairman, Annandale Young Farmers Club, 1958-59; Elder and Treasurer, Ruthwell Church, since 1968; founder Chairman, local Community Council, 1978-81; Chairman, Dumfries Agricultural Society, 1977-79. Address: (h.) Longbridgemuir, Clarencefield, Dumfries; T.-038 787 210.

Goodall, Alexander, MA (Hons). Principal, Wester Hailes Education Centre, since 1982; b. 25.8.38, Dolphinton, Peebles-shire; 1 s.; 1 d. Educ. Portobello High School; Edinburgh University; Moray House College of Education. Teacher of History, Niddrie Marischal Secondary School, 1961-64; Education Officer, Teso College, Uganda, 1964-69; Preston Lodge High School: Principal Teacher of History, 1969-74, Assistant Head Teacher, 1974-78; Depute Principal, Wester Hailes Education Centre, 1978-82. Editor, Scottish History Teaching Review. Publication: Economics and Development (Co-author). Recreations: trout angling; rubber bridge. Address: (b.) 5 Murrayburn Drive, Edinburgh; T.-031-442 2201.

Goodall, Henry Bushman, MB, ChB, MD, FRCPath. Retired; President, Association of Clinical Pathologists, 1986-87; Reader in Haematology, Dundee University, 1981-86; b. 18.6.21, Dundee; m., Janet McIntosh; 1 s.; 1 d. Educ. Errol Public School; Perth Academy; St. Andrews University. Junior House Officer, 1944-45; Trainee Pathologist, 1944-46; RAMC, 1946-48; Lecturer in Pathology, St. Andrews University, 1948-58; Senior Lecturer, Universities of St. Andrews and Dundee, 1958-81. Former Member, Scientific Services Advisory Group, SHHD (Chairman, Haematology Committee); Past Chairman, Dundee Round Table. Recreations: gardening; golf; photography. Address: (h.) 16 Hazel Avenue, Dundee, DD2 1QD; T.-0382 65247.

Gooday, Professor Graham W., BSc, PhD. Professor of Microbiology, Aberdeen University, since 1984; b. 19.2.42, Colchester; m., Margaret A. Mealing; 1 s.; 2 d. Educ. Hove Grammar School for Boys; Bristol University. VSO, Sierra Leone, 1964; Research Fellowships: Leeds University, 1967, Glasgow and Oxford Universities, 1969; Lecturer, Senior Lecturer, Reader, Aberdeen University, 1972-84; Member, Aquatic Life Sciences Committee, NERC, 1984-87; Council Member, British Mycological Society, 1974-77; Council Member, Society for General Microbiology, 1976-80; awarded first Fleming Lectureship, Society for General Microbiology, 1976. Recreation: open countryside. Address: (b.) Department of Genetics and Microbiology, Marischal College, University, Aberdeen, AB9 1AS; T.-0224 273147.

Goodman, Anthony Eric, MA (Oxon), BLitt (Oxon), FRHistS. Reader in History, Edinburgh University, since 1983; b. 21.7.36, London; m., Jacqueline; 1 d. Educ. Selhurst Grammar School, Croydon; Magdalen College, Oxford. Joined staff, Edinburgh University, 1961. Secretary, Edinburgh Branch, Historical Association, since 1975. Publications: The Loyal Conspiracy, 1971; A History of England from Edward II to James I, 1977; The Wars of the Roses, 1981; A Traveller's Guide to Medieval Britain (Co-author), 1986; The New Monarchy, 1471-1534, 1988. Recreation: getting to know the Borders. Address: (h.) 23 Kirkhill Gardens, Edinburgh, EH16 5DF; T.-031-667 5988.

Goodwin, Matthew Dean, CBE, CA. Chairman, Hewden Stuart PLC; Director, Murray Ventures PLC; Director, Murray Technology PLC; Director, F/S Assurance; Member, Irvine Development Corporation; Honorary Treasurer, Scottish Conservative Party; b. 12.6.29, Dalserf; m., Margaret Eileen Colvil; 2 d. Educ. Glasgow Academy. Recreations: shooting; bridge; farming. Address: (b.) 135 Buchanan Street, Glasgow; T.-041-221 7331.

Goold, Lord (James Duncan), Life Peer (1987), Kt (1983), CA, FRSA, FCIOB, FFB, DL. Chairman, Scottish Conservative Party, since 1983; Director: Mactaggart & Mickel Ltd., since 1965, American Trust PLC, since 1984, Gibson & Goold Ltd., since 1978, Edinburgh Oil & Gas PLC, since 1987; b. 28.5.34, Glasgow; m., Sheena Paton; 2 s.; 1 d. Educ. Glasgow Academy. President: Scottish Building Contractors' Association,

1971, Scottish National Federation of Building Trades Employers, 1977-78; Honorary Treasurer, Scottish Building Employers' Federation, 1979-81; Chairman, Conservative Board of Finance Scotland, 1980-83; Honorary Treasurer, Scottish Conservative and Unionist Association, 1980-83; Honorary President, Eastwood Conservative Association, since 1978; Chairman, East Renfrewshire Conservative Association, 1974-77; Chairman, CBI Scotland, 1981-83; Member, Scottish Hospital Endowments Research Trust; Governor, Glasgow Academy; Elder, Mearns Parish Church; Trustee, Ferguson Bequest; Vice President, Tenovus-Scotland. Recreations: golf; tennis; walking. Address: (b.) 107 West Regent Street, Glasgow, G2 2BH; T.-041-332 0001.

Gordon, (Alexander) Esme, RSA, FRIBA, FRIAS; b. 12.9.10, Edinburgh; m., Betsy McCurry; 2 s.; 1 d. Educ. Edinburgh Academy; School of Architecture, Edinburgh College of Art; RIBA. Owen Jones Scholar, 1934; worked for three years in London office of Sir John Burnet; Tait & Lorne, FFRIBA; set up own practice as Architect in Edinburgh, 1936; War Service, RE, Europe; President, Edinburgh Architectural Association, 1955-57; Member, Scottish Committee, Arts Council of GB, 1959-67; Honorary Secretary, RSA, 1972-77. Publications: A Short History of St. Giles Cathedral, 1954; The Principles of Church Building, Furnishing, Equipment and Decoration, 1963; The Royal Scottish Academy 1826-1976, 1976; The Making of the Royal Scottish Academy, 1988. Recreations: drawing; travel; gardening. Address: (h.) 10a Greenhill Park, Edinburgh, EH10 4DW; T.-031-447 7530.

Gordon, Allan Jan, MA (Cantab), BSc, MB, ChB, MRCOG. Consultant Obstetrician and Gynaecologist, Elsie Inglis Maternity and Bruntsfield Hospitals, Edinburgh, since 1981; b. 23.6.46, Glasgow; m., Elizabeth Margaret Elliott; 1 s.; 1 d. Educ. Hillhead High School, Glasgow; Glasgow University. House Officer, Glasgow Royal Infirmary; Senior House Officer posts in Obstetrics, Gynaecology and Pathology, Western Infirmary, Royal Infirmary, Royal Maternity and Queen Mother's Hospital, Glasgow; Registrar in Obstetrics and Gynaecology, Royal Infirmary and Royal Maternity Hospital, Glasgow; Clinical Lecturer, Cambridge University, 1978-81. Member, Iona Community. Recreations: music; reading; jogging; hill-walking. Address: (b.) Elsie Inglis Maternity Hospital, Edinburgh.

Gordon, Boyd. Fisheries Consultant; Fisheries Secretary, Department of Agriculture and Fisheries for Scotland, 1982-86; b. 18.9.26, Musselburgh; m., Elizabeth Mabel Smith; 2 d. Educ. Musselburgh Grammar School. Military Service, Royal Scots; joined Civil Service, initially with Ministry of Labour, then Inland Revenue; joined Department of Agriculture and Fisheries for Scotland, 1953; Principal dealing with Salmon and Freshwater Fisheries Administration and Fisheries Research and Development, 1962-73; Assistant Secretary, Agriculture Economic Policy, EEC Co-ordination and Agriculture Marketing, 1973-82. Recreations: golf; gardening; local Church matters. Address: (h.) 87 Duddingston Road, Edinburgh; T.-031-669 4380.

Gordon, George, MA (Hons), PhD. Dean, Faculty of Arts and Social Studies, Strathclyde University, 1984-87; Senior Lecturer in Geography, since 1980, Director of Academic Practice, since 1987; Governor, Jordanhill College of Education, since 1982 (Chairman, since 1987); b. 14.11.39, Edinburgh; m., Jane Taylor Collins; 2 d. Educ. George Heriot's School; Edinburgh University. Edinburgh University: Vans Dunlop Scholar, 1962-64, Demonstrator, 1964-65; Strathclyde University: Assistant Lecturer, 1965-66, Lecturer, 1966-80; served on SUCE and SCE Geography Panels; Member: SCOVACT; General Teaching Council for Scotland; Council, Royal Scottish Geographical Society; Recorder, Section E, British Association for the Advancement of Science; former Member, General Assembly of Open University; Member, Senate and Court, Strathclyde University. Publications: Regional Cities of the UK 1890-1980 (Editor), 1986; Perspectives of the Scottish City (Editor), 1985; Scottish Urban History, 1983; The Making of Scottish Geography (Co-author), 1984; Settlement Geography, 1983; Urban Geography, 1981. Recreations: theatre-going; watching sport. Address: (b.) Department of Geography, Strathclyde University, Richmond Street, Glasgow; T.-041-552 4400, Ext. 3606.

Gordon, George, MB, ChB, FRCSE, FRCOG. Consultant Obstetrician and Gynaecologist, Dumfries and Galloway, since 1969; b. 4.9.36, Markinch, Fife; m., Rosemary Gould Hutchison; 1 s.; 1 d. Educ. Bell Baxter School; Edinburgh University. Senior Registrar, Western General Hospital, Edinburgh, 1966-69; Chairman, Scottish Confidential Enquiry into Maternal Mortality; Member, Central Midwives Board for Scotland, 1978-84; External Examiner, Edinburgh University, 1978-82; Examiner, FRCS Edinburgh and DRCOG London; Secretary, RCOG Scottish Executive; Administrative Consultant, Alexandra Hospice Unit; Honorary Secretary, Dumfries and Stewartry Division, BMA, 1975-87. Recreations: music; Scottish literature; golf; gardening. Address: (b.) Dumfries and Galloway Royal Infirmary, Bankend Road, Dumfries, DG1 4AP.

Gordon, George Park Douglas, BSc (Hons). HM Chief Inspector of Schools, Education (Basic and Special), since 1986; b. 23.10.37, Peterhead; m., Karein L.M.; 1 s.; 1 d. Educ. Peterhead Academy; Aberdeen University; Aberdeen College of Education. Teacher of Science, Peterhead Academy, 1961-64; Principal Teacher of Science, Dornoch Academy, 1964-67; Assistant Adviser in Science, Glasgow, 1967-69; HM Inspector of Schools, 1969-75, Higher Grade, 1975-86. Elder, St. Paul's Church, Milngavie. Recreations: golf; squash; gardening; reading; walking; spending winter Saturdays watching football and supporting Aberdeen FC. Address: (h.) Suilven, 8 Ewing Walk, Fairways, Milngavie, G62 6EG; T.-041-956 5131.

Gordon, Sheriff Gerald Henry, QC, MA, LLB, PhD, LLD. Sheriff of Glasgow and Strathkelvin, since 1978; b. 17.6.29, Glasgow; m., Marjorie Joseph; 1 s.; 2 d. Educ. Queen's Park Senior Secondary School; Glasgow University. Advocate, 1953; Procurator Fiscal Depute, Edinburgh, 1960-65; Edinburgh University: Head, Department of

Criminal Law and Criminology, 1965-72, Personal Professor of Criminal Law, 1969-72, Dean, Faculty of Law, 1970-73, Professor of Scots Law, 1972-76; Sheriff of South Strathclyde, Dumfries and Galloway, at Hamilton, 1976-77; Member, Interdepartmental Committee on Scottish Criminal Procedure, 1970-77. Publications: Criminal Law of Scotland, 1967, 1978; Renton & Brown's Criminal Procedure (Editor), 1972, 1983. Recreations: Jewish studies; coffee conversation; swimming. Address: (h.) 52 Eastwoodmains Road, Giffnock, Glasgow; T.-041-638 8614.

Gordon, Rev. Canon Hugh. Chaplain, St. Joseph's House, Edinburgh; b. 18.11.10, Inverness. Educ. Stonyhurst College, Lancashire; Heriot-Watt College, Edinburgh; Oscott College, Birmingham. Ordained, 1937; Curate, Inverness, 1937; Army Chaplain, 1940 (Egypt and El Alamain, 51st Highland Division); Osnabruck, 1946, developing civilian parish church and first Catholic school in Germany after the fall of Hitler; Priest: Selkirk, St. Andrews, Edinburgh St. Margaret's and St. John the Evangelist, Linlithgow St. Michael's; founded Linlithgow Scripture Centre for Christian Unity; former Executive Member, Scottish Catholic Lay Apostolate Council; Member: Commission for Christian Doctrine and Unity; Order of Christian Unity; Fellowship of St. Andrew. Recreations: anything to help restoration of Christian unity; stopped tennis, golf, fishing. Address: 47 Gilmore Place, Edinburgh, EH3 9NG; T.-031-229 1929.

Gordon, James Stuart, CBE, MA (Hons). Managing Director, Radio Clyde, since 1973; Chairman, Scottish Exhibition Centre, since 1983; Member, Scottish Development Agency, since 1981; Member, Glasgow University Court, since 1984; b. 17.5.36, Glasgow; m., Anne Stevenson; 2 s.; 1 d. Educ. St. Aloysius College, Glasgow; Glasgow University. Political Editor, STV, 1965-73. Winner, Observer Mace Debating Tournament, 1957; Sony Special Award for Services to Radio, 1984; Member, Committee of Inquiry into Pay and Conditions of Teachers in Scotland, 1986. Recreations: his children; genealogy; golf. Address: (b.) Radio Clyde, Clydebank Business Park, Clydebank; T.-041-941 1111.

Gordon, Canon Kenneth Davidson, MA. Rector, St. Devenick's Episcopal Church, Bieldside, Aberdeen, since 1971; Examining Chaplain to Bishop of Aberdeen and Orkney, 1978-86; Warden of Lay Readers, Diocese of Aberdeen and Orkney, since 1978; b. 27.12.35, Edinburgh; m., Edith Jessica Newing; 2 s. Educ. George Heriot's School, Edinburgh; Edinburgh University; Tyndale Hall, Bristol. Curate, St. Helens Parish Church, Lancashire, 1960-66 (with charge of St. Andrew's Mission Church, 1962-66); Vicar, St. George the Martyr's Parish Church, Bolton, 1966-71; Canon, St. Andrew's Cathedral, Aberdeen, since 1981. Member, Faith and Order Board, and Liturgy Committee, General Synod, Scottish Episcopal Church. Recreations: bird-watching; golf; photography; model railways. Address: The Rectory, Bieldside, Aberdeen, AB1 9AP; T.-0224 861552.

Gordon, Rev. Peter Mitchell, MA, BD. Minister, Airdrie West Parish Church, since 1985; b. 1.7.30, Aberdeen; m., Fiona Selby McDonald; 2 s. Educ. Aberdeen Grammar School; Aberdeen University. Minister: Camperdown, Dundee, 1959-65, Brechin Cathedral, 1965-85. Recreations: gardening; local and family history. Address: West Parish Manse, Arthur Avenue, Airdrie; T.-023 64 63022.

Gordon, Professor William Morrison, MA, LLB, PhD. Douglas Professor of Civil Law, Glasgow University, since 1969; Solicitor (non-practising), since 1956; b. 3.3.33, Inverurie; m., Isabella Evelyn Melitta Robertson; 2 s.; 2 d. Educ. Inverurie Academy; Robert Gordon's College, Aberdeen; Aberdeen University. National Service, Royal Navy, 1955-57; Assistant in Jurisprudence, Aberdeen University, 1957-60; Glasgow University: Lecturer in Civil Law, 1960-65, Senior Lecturer in Law, 1965-69 (and Sub-Dean of Faculty); Dean of Faculty, 1974-76. Elder, Jordanhill Parish Church; Literary Director, The Stair Society. Publications: Studies in Transfer of Property by Tradition, 1970; articles. Recreation: golf. Address: (b.) Department of Legal History, Stair Building, University, Glasgow, G12 8QQ; T.-041-339 8855, Ext. 5387.

Gordon-Duff, Col. Thomas Robert, MC, JP. Lord Lieutenant of Banffshire, 1964-87; b. 1911; m., Jean Moir (deceased); 1 s. Educ. Eton; Sandhurst. 2nd Lt., Rifle Brigade, 1932; served World War II; retired, 1947; Lt.-Col., 5/6 Bn., Gordon Highlanders (TA), 1947; Convener, Banff County Council, 1962-70. Address: (h.) Drummuir, Keith, Banffshire.

Goring, Rev. Iain McCormick, BSc, BD. Minister, Callander Kirk, since 1985; b. 22.7.50, Edinburgh; m., Janet Page; 2 s.; 1 d. Educ. Dunfermline High School; Edinburgh University. Civil Service (DHSS, London), 1971-72; after BD, Assistantship, St. Luke's, Milngavie, 1975-77; Minister, Lochwood Church, Glasgow, 1977-85. Address: The Manse, Aveland Park Road, Callander, Perthshire, FK17 8EN; T.-0877 30097.

Gorman, Brian, MA. Director, English-Speaking Union in Scotland, since 1984; b. 31.10.51, Wishaw. Educ. Our Lady's High School, Motherwell; Glasgow University; Jordanhill College of Education. Teacher of Modern Studies, Columba High School, Coatbridge, 1974-76; Principal Teacher of Modern Studies, St. John's High School, Dundee, 1976-78; Group Travel and Transport Manager, Cotters Travel and Leisure Group, 1978-84. Recreations: theatre; debating. Address: (b.) 23 Atholl Crescent, Edinburgh; T.-031-229 1528.

Gorrie, Donald Cameron Easterbrook, OBE, MA, JP. Leader, Social and Liberal Democrat Group: Lothian Regional Council, since 1974, City of Edinburgh District Council, since 1980; b. 2.4.33, India; m., Astrid Salvesen; 2 s. Educ. Hurst Grange, Stirling; Oundle School; Corpus Christi College, Oxford. Schoolmaster: Gordonstoun School, 1957-60, Marlborough College, 1960-66; Scottish Liberal Party: Director of Research, 1969-71, Director of Administration,

1971-75; Edinburgh Town Councillor, 1971-75. Former Scottish native record holder, 880 yards. Address: (h.) 54 Garscube Terrace, Edinburgh, EH12 6BN; T.-031-337 2077.

Gosden, Roger Gordon, BSc, PhD, FZS, FIBiol. Senior Lecturer in Physiology, Medical School, Edinburgh University, since 1976; b. 23.9.48, Ryde, Isle of Wight; m., Carole Ann Walsh; 2 s. Educ. Chislehurst and Sidcup Grammar School; Bristol University; Cambridge University. MRC Research Fellow, Cambridge University, 1973-74 and 1975-76; Population Council Research Fellow, Duke University, USA, 1974-75; Visiting Scientist, University of Southern California, 1979 and 1982. Executive Member, Church and Nation Committee, Church of Scotland. Publication: Biology of Menopause, 1985. Recreations: natural history; painting. Address: (b.) Department of Physiology, University Medical School, Edinburgh, EH8 9AG; T.-031-667 1011.

Goskirk, Rev. John Leslie, LTh. Minister, Lairg Parish Church, since 1968, and Rogart Parish Church, since 1970; b. 16.3.38, Glasgow; m., Myra Hendry Fisher; 2 s.; 2 d. Educ. High School of Glasgow; Glasgow University and Trinity College. Clerk, Sutherland Presbytery; Past Chairman, former Golspie, Rogart and Lairg District Council; Past Chairman, Lairg Community Council. Address: The Manse, Lairg, Sutherland.

Gosling, Allan Gladstone, RIBA, RIAS, DipArch. Director, Scottish Services, Property Services Agency, since 1983; b. 4.7.33, Preston; m., Janet Pamela; 1 s.; 1 d. Educ. Kirkham Grammar School; Birmingham School of Architecture. Private practice, Birmingham, 1957-59; National Service, Royal Artillery, 1959-61 (2nd Lt.); Works Organisation Architect, War Office, 1961-63; Architect, Ministry of Housing, 1963-72; PSA: Regional Works Officer, North West Region, 1972-76, Director, Midland Region, 1976-83. Recreations: DIY; gardening; walking. Address: (h.) 8 Winton Terrace, Firemilehead, Edinburgh.

Goss, Rev. Alister John, BD. Industrial Organiser, Inverclyde, Scottish Churches Industrial Mission, since 1987; b. 4.10.44, Edinburgh; m., Dorothy May; 1 s.; 1 d. Educ. James Clark School, Edinburgh; Glasgow University; Edinburgh University. Minister, Carnock Parish Church, 1975; Hertfordshire and Bedfordshire Industrial Mission, 1980; Tutor, St. Albans Ministerial Training, 1984-85. Address: 79 Weymouth Crescent, Gourock, PA19 1HR; T.-0475 38944.

Gossip, Michael A.J., JP, BL, NP, FBIM. Chief Executive, Argyll and Bute District Council, since 1974; b. 27.4.33, Edinburgh; m., Margaret; 1 s.; 2 d. Educ. George Watson's Boys' College, Edinburgh; Edinburgh University. Legal Assistant, Midlothian County Council, 1955-57; Dumfries County Council: Senior Legal Assistant, 1957-60, Depute County Clerk, 1960-71; Argyll County Council: Depute County Clerk, 1971-72, County Clerk, 1972-75. Recreations: bowls; gardening. Address: (b.) Kilmory Castle, Lochgilphead, Argyll; T.-0546 2127.

Gotts, Iain McEwan, DipLE, DipTP, ARICS, MRTPI. Director, PEIDA Ltd., Planning, Economic and Development Consultants, since 1976; b. 26.2.47, Glasgow; m., Pamela; 1 s.; 2 d. Educ. Jordanhill College School, Glasgow; Paisley College of Technology; Heriot-Watt University/Edinburgh College of Art. Trainee Surveyor, British Rail Property Department, Glasgow, 1965-68; further education, 1968-72, Surveyor/Land Economist, Wright & Partners, Edinburgh, 1972-76. Recreations: music; golf; rugby refereeing. Address: (b.) 10 Chester Street, Edinburgh, EH3 7RA; T.-031-225 5737.

Goudie, Professor Robert Barclay, MD, FRCPGlas, FRCPath, FRSE. St. Mungo (Notman) Professor of Pathology (Emeritus), Glasgow University; b. 13.11.28, Glasgow; m., Lilian Duke Munro; 3 s.; 1 d. Educ. Hutchesons' Grammar School; Glasgow University. Squadron Leader, RAF Medical Branch, Institute of Pathology and Tropical Medicine, Halton, 1954-56; Lecturer, Senior Lecturer, Reader, University Department of Pathology, Western Infirmary, Glasgow, 1956-70; Nuffield Fellow in Medicine, Cambridge University, 1959-60. Recreation: golf. Address: (b.) University Department of Pathology, Royal Infirmary, Glasgow, G4 OSF; T.-041-552 3535, Ext. 5327.

Gough, Robert Kerr Livingstone, JP. Convener, Fife Regional Council, since 1978; Member, Forth Ports Authority, since 1970; Vice Chairman, Glenrothes Development Corporation, since 1978; b. 1.8.24, Buckhaven; m., Margaret; 2 s. Educ. Buckhaven High School. Member, Buckhaven and Methil Town Council and Fife County Council, 1956; Vice Convener, Fife Regional Council, 1975; Member: Forth Road Bridge Joint Board, 1979, Tay Road Bridge Joint Board, 1979, Forth River Purification Board, 1979. Recreations: gardening; welfare of the young and old and physically handicapped. Address: (h.) 46 Stark Street, Buckhaven, Fife; T.-Buckhaven 713308.

Gow, Sheriff Neil, QC (Scot), MA, LLB, FSA Scot. Sheriff of South Strathclyde, at Ayr, since 1976; b. 24.4.32; m.; 1 s. Educ. Merchiston Castle School; Glasgow University; Edinburgh University. Captain, Intelligence Corps (BAOR); Advocate, 1957-76.

Gowenlock, Professor Brian Glover, CBE, PhD, DSc, CChem, FRSC, FRSE. Professor of Chemistry, Heriot-Watt University, since 1966 (Dean, Faculty of Science, 1969-72, and since 1987); Member, University Grants Committee, 1976-85; Assessor Member, Scottish Tertiary Education Advisory Council, 1984-87; b. 9.2.26, Oldham; m., Margaret Davies; 1 s.; 2 d. Educ. Hulme Grammar School; Manchester University. Assistant Lecturer, then Lecturer in Chemistry, University College of Swansea, 1948-55; Lecturer, then Senior Lecturer in Chemistry, Birmingham University, 1955-66; Visiting Scientist, National Research Council of Canada, Ottawa, 1963; Erskine Memorial Fellow, Canterbury University, Christchurch, 1976. Recreations: genealogy; foreign travel. Address: (h.) 49 Lygon Road, Edinburgh, EH16 5QA; T.-031-667 8506.

Gowland, David Alexander, BA, PhD, PGCE. Senior Lecturer in Modern History, Dundee University, since 1982 (Convener, Committee for

Contemporary European Studies, since 1979); b. 1.4.42, Reading; m., Helen Janet Mackinlay; 3 d. Educ. Culford; Manchester University; London University. Dundee University: Assistant Lecturer in Modern History, 1967-69, Lecturer in Modern History, 1970-81, Dean of Students, Faculty of Arts and Social Sciences, 1979-83; Honorary Lecturer, Civil Service College, 1970-76. Publications: Common Market or Community?, 1973; Methodist Secessions, 1979; Scottish Methodism in the Early Victorian Period, 1981; European Community, Past Present and Future, 1987. Recreation: golf. Address: (b.) Department of Modern History, Dundee University, Dundee; T.-Dundee 23181.

Grace, John, BSc, PhD. Reader in Plant Ecology, Edinburgh University, since 1986; b. 19.9.45, Northampton; m., Elizabeth Ashworth; 2 s.; 1 d. Educ. Bletchley Grammar School; Sheffield University. Lecturer, Edinburgh University, 1970-86. Co-Editor, Functional Ecology, since 1986; Technical Editor, International Society for Biometeorology, since 1983; Member, Terrestrial Life Sciences Committee, Natural Environment Research Council, since 1986; Council Member, British Ecological Society, since 1983. Publications: Plant Response to Wind, 1977; Plants and their Atmospheric Environment (Co-Editor), 1981; Plant-atmosphere Relationships, 1983. Recreations: hill-walking; cycling; fishing; bridge. Address: (h.) 25 Craiglea Drive, Edinburgh, EH10 5PB; T.-031-447 3030.

Grace, Very Rev. Canon Thomas Augustine. Parish Priest, St. Aidan's, Johnstone, since 1987 (St. Peter's, Glenburn, Paisley, 1974-87); Member, Cathedral Chapter, Diocese of Paisley, since 1979; b. 6.11.19, Glasgow. Educ. St. Mungo's Academy, Glasgow; St. Peter's Theological College, Bearsden. Ordained to priesthood, St. Andrew's Cathedral, Glasgow, 1944; Curate: St. Joseph's, Stepps, 1944-47, St. John's, Barrhead, 1947-68, St. Ninian's, Gourock, 1968-70; Parish Priest, St. Mungo's, Greenock, 1970-74. Recreations: reading; music; gardening. Address: St. Aidan's, Tower Road, Johnstone, PA5 0AD; T.-Johnstone 20900.

Gracie, Alistair. Head of News and Current Affairs, Grampian Television, since 1986; b. 25.2.48, Aberdeen; m., Wendy; 1 s.; 2 d. Educ. Aberdeen Grammar School. Joined Aberdeen Journals as Trainee Journalist, 1966; worked on Press and Journal as Reporter and Evening Express as Sub-Editor; moved into television as Researcher/Reporter, 1972; Grampian Television: News Editor, 1974, Programme Editor, 1978. Recreations: mountaineering; squash; running; photography; reading; painting. Address: (b.) Grampian TV, Queen's Cross, Aberdeen, AB9 2XJ.

Graeme, Malcolm Laurie, SBStJ, VRD, MA, MB, BChir, MFCM, DPH, MRCS, LRCP; b. 16.9.19, Guernsey; m., Dr. Patricia Doreen Shurly, MB, BS, MRCP; 1 d. Educ. Stowe; Jesus College, Cambridge; St. George's Hospital Medical School (Devitt-Pendlebury Scholarship). Surgeon, Lt.-Surgeon, Lt. Cdr., RNVR/RNR, 1944-64; Public Health Service, London County Council, London Borough of Barnet and London Borough of Enfield, 1957-70; Medical Branch, Civil Service, Departments of Education and Science and Health and Social Security, 1970-79; Ordained Elder, Church of Scotland, 1970; Clerk to Congregational Board and Member, Kirk Session, Ceres Parish Church, since 1987; Life Governor, Royal Scottish Corporation of London; District Councillor (Conservative), NE Fife, 1980-84; Member, Fife Health Board, 1983-87; Hon. Vice-President, NE Fife Conservative Association, 1987; Chairman, Fife and Kinross Committee, King George's Fund for Sailors and Member, Scottish Council, 1987; Life Member, St. John Association of Scotland and Member, Fife Committee. Recreation: gardening. Address: (h.) Little Baltilly, Ceres, by Cupar, Fife, KY15 5QG; T.-Ceres 238.

Graesser, Neil Walter, MIFM. Chairman, Highland River Purification Board, since 1976; Chairman of the Council, Association of Scottish District Salmon Fishery Boards, since 1969; Member, Management Committee, Atlantic Salmon Trust, since 1969; Freshwater Fisheries Consultant, since 1950; Landowner, since 1967; b. 22.10.28, Froncysyllte, North Wales; m., Audrey Jennifer Christianna Tapp; 1 s.; 1 d. Educ. Oundle; Llysfasi Farm Institute. Brief period in RAF; studied farming; managed a farm, 1950-67; made life's study of salmon and salmon fishing; author of books on salmon and salmon fishing. Recreations: shooting; fishing. Address: Rosehall, Lairg, Sutherland, IV27 4BD; T.-Rosehall 202.

Graham, Rev. A. David M., BA, BD. Minister, Rutherford Parish Church (Rutherford Celebration Centre, Rutherford Bible Village), Aberdeen, since 1983; b. 17.7.40, Tralee; m., Mary A. Taylor; 2 s.; 1 d. Educ. Wesley College, Dublin; Methodist College, Belfast; Queen's University, Belfast; Glasgow University. Assistant, South Leith Parish; Secretary for Christian Education, Scottish National Council of YMCAs; Minister, Anderston Parish, Glasgow; Warden, Iona Abbey. Recreations: jogging; climbing. Address: 22 Osborne Place, Aberdeen, AB2 4DA; T.-0224 648041.

Graham, Dennis C., DSc, PhD, CChem, FRSC, FInstBiol, FRSA, FRSE. Director, Agricultural Scientific Services, Department of Agriculture and Fisheries for Scotland, since 1981; b. 2.12.29, Carlisle. Educ. Carlisle Grammar School; Durham University; Edinburgh University. Recreation: cultivation of alpine plants. Address: 447 Lanark Road, Edinburgh, EH14 5BA; T.-031-453 3459.

Graham, James, MB, ChB, FRCSGlas, FRCSEdin. Consultant Orthopaedic Surgeon, Western Infirmary and Gartnavel General Hospital, Glasgow, since 1976; Honorary Clinical Lecturer, Glasgow University, since 1976; b. 2.3.36, Stonehouse; m., Wilma Edith Melville; 1 s.; 1 d. Educ. Hamilton Academy; Glasgow University. House Officer posts, Western Infirmary and Southern General Hospital, Glasgow; basic surgical training, Vale of Leven Hospital, Alexandria, and Western Infirmary, Glasgow; orthopaedic training in Western Infirmary, Royal Hospital for Sick Children and Southern General Hospital, Glasgow and Massachusetts General Hospital;

appointed Senior Lecturer in Orthopaedics and Honorary Consultant Orthopaedic Surgeon, Western Infirmary and Gartnavel General Hospital, 1972; research, teaching and clinical fellowship to Harvard University and Massachusetts General Hospital, Boston, 1968-69; British Orthopaedic Association ABC Travelling Fellowship to North America, 1974. Recreations: rugby (watching); golf (participating); DIY. Address: (b.) Department of Orthopaedics, Western Infirmary, Glasgow, G11 6NT; T.-041-339 8822.

Graham, Marquis of (James Graham). Brigadier, Queen's Bodyguard for Scotland (Royal Company of Archers), since 1986 (Member, since 1965); b. 6.4.35; m., Catherine Elizabeth MacDonell; 2 s.; 1 d. Educ. Loretto. Order of St. John, 1978. Council Member, National Farmers' Union of Scotland, 1982-84, and since 1987. Address: (h.) Auchmar, Drymen, Glasgow.

Graham, James Walker, BComm, DipComm, FHCIMA. Senior Lecturer, Scottish Hotel School, Strathclyde University, since 1965; b. 30.6.27, Wishaw; m., Jennie Stirrat; 2 d. Educ. Wishaw High School; London University; Scottish College of Commerce. Lecturer in Management Studies, Scottish College of Commerce, 1955-60; Senior Lecturer, Scottish Hotel School, 1960-64. Secretary, Scottish Management Development Committee, Hotel and Catering Institute, 1962-65; Chairman, Curriculum Development Committee, hotel and catering courses, SCOTEC, 1972-75; Member, curriculum development and course assessment panels, HCIMA, 1967-75; Vice-Dean, School of Business and Administration, Strathclyde University, 1975-77; Dean, 1977-78; Member, National Council for Educational Awards (Hotel and Catering Studies), Dublin, 1978-81; Member, Scottish Advisory Committee, Hotel and Catering Training Board, 1978-83; National Councillor and Member, Executive, HCIMA, 1979-86; Member, Consumer and Leisure Studies Panel, CNAA, since 1987; Chairman, Opera Catering Services Ltd., Scottish Opera, 1975-87; Member, Scottish Opera Advisory Council; Elder, St. Nicholas, Lanark. Recreations: walking; golf; music; gardening. Address: (h.) 4 Nemphlat Hill, Lanark, ML11 7PN; T.-0555 2797.

Graham, John James, OBE, MA, FEIS. Member, Shetland Islands Council (Vice-Chairman, Education Committee), since 1982; Chairman, Shetland Movement, since 1982; Joint Editor, The New Shetlander, since 1956; b. 12.7.21, Lerwick; m., Beryl Smith; 3 s.; 2 d. Educ. Lerwick Central Secondary School; Edinburgh University. RAF Training Command, 1941-44, Bomber Command, 1944-46; Principal Teacher of English, Anderson Educational Institute, Lerwick, 1950-66; Headmaster: Lerwick Central Secondary School, 1966-70, Anderson High School, Lerwick, 1970-82; Member: Consultative Committee on the Curriculum, 1976-80, Broadcasting Council for Scotland, 1981-84; President, Shetland Folk Society. Publications: A Grammar and Usage of the Shetland Dialect (Co-author); Northern Lights (Joint Editor); The Shetland Dictionary; Shadowed Valley (novel). Recreations: local history; golf. Address: (h.) 26 King Harald Street, Lerwick, Shetland; T.-Lerwick 3425.

Graham, John Michael Denning, LLB (Hons), NP. Solicitor and Notary Public, since 1970; Chairman, Kilmacolm Developments Ltd.; Director: John Smith & Son (Glasgow) Ltd.; Scot-Care Group Ltd.; Chairman, Rent Assessment Committee, Glasgow, since 1983; b. 7.9.44, Kirkintilloch; m., Christina Jeanne Sinclair; 2 s. Educ. Royal Belfast Academical Institution; Queen's University, Belfast. Joint Senior Partner, Paterson Robertson & Graham, Solicitors, since 1971. Recreations: tennis; golf; hang-gliding. Address: (h.) St. Michael's, Garngaber Avenue, Lenzie, G66; T.-041-221 7691.

Graham, Professor Neil Bonnette, BSc, PhD, CChem, FRSC, FPRI. Professor in Chemical Technology, Strathclyde University, since 1973; Director, Polysystems Limited, since 1980; b. 23.5.33, Liverpool; 1 s.; 3 d. Educ. Alsop High School, Liverpool; Liverpool University. Research Chemist, Research Scientist, Canadian Industries Ltd., MacMasterville PQ, Canada, 1956-67; Assistant Group Head, then Group Head, Polymer Chemistry, ICI, Runcorn, Cheshire. Member: Advisory Committee on Dental and Surgical Materials, 1980-86, and sometime member of various committees, Society of Chemical Industry, Royal Society of Chemistry and Plastics and Rubber Institute; Chairman, Glasgow Membrane Group, since 1986; Member, International Editorial Boards, Biomaterials, Biomedical Polymers and Journal of Controlled Release; Governor and Trustee, Keil School; Trustee, James Clerk Maxwell Trust. Recreations: music; walking. Address: (b.) Strathclyde University, Department of Pure and Applied Chemistry, Thomas Graham Building, 295 Cathedral Street, Glasgow, G1 1XL; T.-041-552 4400, Ext. 2133.

Graham, Nigel John O. Member, Highland Regional Council, since 1983; b. 28.7.27, Worcestershire; m., Margaret; 2 s.; 2 d. Educ. Marlborough College. Highland Light Infantry, 1945-53; TA, Queen's Own Cameron Highlanders, 1953-61; farmer, 1953-83; Member, Nairn County Council, 1966-72. Chairman: Highlands and Islands Conservative Council, Inverness Nairn and Lochaber Conservative Association. Recreation: bird-watching. Address: (h.) Househill, Nairn; T.-Nairn 53241.

Graham, Sir Norman William, Kt (1971), CB (1961), MA, DLitt (Heriot-Watt), DUniv (Stirling), FRSE; b. 11.10.13, Dundee; m., Catherine Mary Strathie; 2 s.; 1 d. Educ. High School of Glasgow; Glasgow University. Assistant Principal, Department of Health for Scotland, 1936; Principal, Ministry of Aircraft Production, 1941; Principal Private Secretary to Minister, 1944; Assistant Secretary, Department of Health for Scotland, 1945; Under Secretary, 1956; Secretary, Scottish Education Department, 1964-73. Recreations: golf; gardening. Address: (h.) 6 Chesterhall Steading, Longniddry, East Lothian; T.-0875 52130.

Graham, Ronald Cairns, MB, ChB, DipSocMed, FRCP, FFCM. General Manager, Tayside Health Board, since 1985; Honorary Senior Lecturer, Dundee University, since 1969; b. 8.10.31, Airdrie; m., Christine Fraser Osborne; 2 s.; 1 d. Educ. Airdrie Academy; Glasgow University.

Deputy Medical Superintendent, Edinburgh Royal Infirmary; Assistant Senior Administrative Medical Officer, South-Eastern Regional Hospital Board; Eastern Regional Hospital Board: Deputy Senior Administrative Medical Officer, Senior Administrative Medical Officer; Chief Administrative Medical Officer, Tayside Health Board, 1973-85. Recreation: fishing. Address: (h.) 34 Dalgleish Road, Dundee; T.-Dundee 43146.

Graham, Thomas. MP (Labour), Renfrew West and Inverclyde, since 1987; b. 1944; m.; 2 s. Member, Strathclyde Regional Council, since 1978.

Graham, William, MA. Freelance Writer; b. 27.2.13, Carluke; m., Jean C. Simpson; 1 s.; 1 d. Educ. Wishaw High School; Glasgow University; Jordanhill College of Education. Organist; Teacher; Nurseryman; Airman; Author. Former Secretary and President, Ayr Burns Club; Past Preses, Scots Language Society. Publications: That Ye Inherit; Twa-Three Sangs and Stories; The Talking Scots Quiz Book; The Scots Word Book; October Sunset; The Handy Guide to Scots. Recreations: music; gardening. Address: (h.) 48 Mount Charles Crescent, Alloway, Ayrshire; T.-Ayr 43701.

Grainger, David Shepherd, JP. Provost and Chairman, Clydebank District Council, since 1985; Member, Countryside Commission for Scotland, since 1986; b. 3.8.43, Edinburgh; m., Sarah; 1 d. Educ. Clydebank High School; Lennox Technical College. Recreations: music; reading. Address: (h.) 4 Napier Court, Old Kilpatrick, Glasgow; T.-Duntocher 78867.

Grainger, John McGregor Leighton, FTS. Director of Tourism, Perthshire Tourist Board, since 1982; b. 3.9.43, Aberdeen; m., Kathleen; 1 s.; 2 d. Assistant Tourist Officer, Aberdeen Town Council, 1959-67; Tourism Manager, Dunbar Town Council, 1967-69; Tourism Manager, Perth Tourist Association, 1969-74; Senior Tourist Officer, Tayside Regional Council, 1974-82. Recreations: fishing; hill-walking. Address: (b.) P.O. Box 33, George Inn Lane, Perth; T.-0738 27958.

Grains, Florence Barbara, JP. Chairman, Shetland Health Board, since 1985; Member, Shetland Islands Council, since 1986; b. 2.11.32, Shetland; m., Alistair M. Grains; 4 s. Educ. Whiteness School, Shetland; Lerwick FE Centre. Retired Sub-postmaster, Whiteness, Shetland. Executive Member, Shetland Council of Social Service; Chairman, Alting Debating Society; Trustee, Shetland Amenity Trust; Chairman, Shetland Branch, Post Office Users Council for Scotland; Supervisor, Whiteness and Weisdale Playgroup; Cub Scout Leader; Executive Member, SWRI. Address: (h.) Hoove, Whiteness, Shetland; T.-0595 84 243.

Grant, Angus Watt. Member, Central Regional Council, 1982-86; b. 15.7.19, Ballater; m., Margaret Grant Park, MA. Educ. Aldenham School, Hertfordshire; Manchester Business School. Management Trainee, 1936-39; commissioned, Royal Marines, 1939-46; Personnel Officer/Manager, Dunlop Rubber Co., Birmingham and Durban (South Africa), 1946-52; Regional Director, National Development and Management Foundation, South Africa, 1953-54; Manager, Employment and Training, Stanvac Refining Co., Durban, 1954-56; Chairman, Executive Committee, Executive Director, Management Services and PA to Chairman, United Tobacco Co. Ltd., Johannesburg, 1956-74; Manager, Senior Management Studies, BAT Industries Ltd., 1974-80. Past Chairman: Programme Committee, Institute of Directors (South Africa Branch), Industrial Council for the Tobacco Industry, South Africa; former Member, Executive Committee, Computer Society of South Africa, and National Development and Management Foundation, South Africa. Recreations: rifle and pistol shooting; photography; cooking. Address: (h.) 11 Mid Shore, Pittenweem, Fife, KY10 2NL.

Grant, Colin Drummond, BSc, PhD, CEng, FIChemE. Reader in Chemical and Process Engineering, Strathclyde University, since 1983; b. 3.6.46, Glasgow; m., Maida Elizabeth; 2 s. Educ. Fettes College, Edinburgh; Strathclyde University. Student Apprentice, Babcock and Wilcox Ltd., 1963-67; Strathclyde University: Research Student, 1967-70, Lecturer, 1970-82, Senior Lecturer, 1982-83. Secretary, Scottish Branch, Institution of Chemical Engineers, 1975-83. Recreations: mountaineering; tennis; squash. Address: (h.) 28 Essex Drive, Jordanhill, Glasgow, G14; T.-041-959 7148.

Grant, Donald, GIFireE. Firemaster, Highland Regional Council, since 1985; b. 11.1.41, West Linton; 1 s. Educ. Inverness High School. Fireman, 1961; Instructor, Scottish Fire Service Training School, 1965; Sub Officer, 1967; Station Officer, 1968; Assistant Divisional Officer, 1974; Divisional Officer, 1974; Deputy Firemaster, 1976. Chairman, British Fire Service Sports and Athletics Association; Chairman, Scottish Fire Service Sports and Athletics Association. Recreations: SFA referee; various sports. Address: The Limit, Lentran, Inverness; T.-0463 83616.

Grant, Donald Blane, TD, CA. Chairman, Scottish Legal Aid Board, since 1986; Partner, Thomson, McLintock & Co., 1950-86; Chairman, Tayside Health Board, since 1984; Chairman, Dundee and London Investment Trust PLC; b. 8.10.21, Dundee; m., Lavinia Margaret Ruth Ritchie; 3 d. Educ. Dundee High School. Royal Artillery, 1939-46 (retired as Major). Chairman: Mathew Trust, Caird Travelling Scholarships Trust. Recreations: golf; fishing; shooting; gardening. Address: (h.) 24 Albany Road, Broughty Ferry, Dundee, DD5 1NT.

Grant, Ian David, CBE, FRAgS. Farmer; President, National Farmers Union of Scotland, since 1984; b. 28.7.43, Dundee; m., Eileen May Louisa Yule; 3 d. Educ. Strathallan School; East of Scotland College of Agriculture. Farms at Thorn, Alyth. Chairman, EEC Cereals Working Party, 1982-88 and International Federation of Agricultural Producers, Grains Committee, since 1984; Vice Chairman, East of Scotland Farmers Ltd.; Council Member, SAOS Ltd., 1980-87; Council Member, Royal Smithfield Club. Recreations: shooting; swimming; music. Address: (h.) Thorn, Alyth, Blairgowrie, PH11 8NP; T.-082-83 2253.

Grant, Ian Faulconer Heathcoat, JP, DL. Director: Croftinloan (Holdings) Ltd., since 1983, First Charlotte Assets Trust PLC, since 1982, Glenmoriston Estates Limited, since 1964, Glenmoriston Gold & Silversmiths Limited, since 1978, Highland Forest Products PLC, since 1983, Highland Mobiles Limited, since 1978, Japan Assets Trust PLC, since 1981, MacDougalls Advertising PLC, since 1985, McKinroy Limited, since 1981, Pacific Assets Trust PLC, since 1985, Royal Bank of Scotland PLC, since 1982, Royal Bank of Scotland Group plc, since 1985, SWOAC Holdings Ltd., since 1986, Worldwide Value Fund Inc. (USA), since 1986, Thomas Tait & Sons Limited, since 1984; b. 3.6.39, Singapore; m., Sally; 1 s.; 3 d. Educ. Cargilfield; Sedbergh; Liverpool College of Commerce. ICI Ltd., 1957-62; various positions, Jardine Matheson & Co. Ltd., Hong Kong, 1962-73, culminating in directorship on Main Board of parent company, as well as directorships in a number of associate companies. Address: (b.) Glenmoriston Estates Ltd., Glenmoriston, near Inverness; T.-0320 51202.

Grant, Rev. James Gordon, MA, BD. Minister, Dean Church, Edinburgh, since 1987 (Portland Church, Troon, 1965-87); Vice-Convener, Board of World Mission and Unity, Church of Scotland, 1984-87; b. 5.7.32, Glasgow; m., Susan Ann Hewitt; 2 s.; 1 d. Educ. High School of Stirling; St. Andrews University. Ordained, 1957; Probationer Assistant, St. Mungo's Parish Church, Alloa, 1957-59; Minister, Dyce Parish Church, Aberdeen, 1959-65; Convener, Inter-Church Relations Committee, 1983-84. Recreations: golf; climbing; ornithology. Address: (h.) 1 Ravelston Terrace, Edinburgh, EH4 3EF; T.-031-332 5736.

Grant, Major James MacAlpine Gregor, TD, NDA, MRAC. Landowner and Farmer, since 1961; b. 18.2.38, Nakuru, Kenya; m., Sara Marjory; 3 d. Educ. Eton; Royal Agricultural College, Cirencester. National Service, Queen's Own Cameron Highlanders, 1957-58; TA with 4/5th Queen's Own Cameron Highlanders; Volunteers with 51st Highland Volunteers. Address: Roskill House, Munlochy, Ross-shire, IV8 8PA; T.-Munlochy 207.

Grant, James Shaw, CBE, LLD, FRSE, FRAgS, MA. Author; b. 22.5.10, Stornoway; m., Catherine Mary Stewart. Educ. Nicolson Institute, Stornoway; Glasgow University. Editor, Stornoway Gazette, 1932-63; Governor, Pitlochry Festival Theatre, 1954-84 (Chairman, 1971-83); Member, Crofters Commission, 1955-78 (Chairman, 1963-78); Director, Grampian TV, 1969-80; Member: Highlands and Islands Development Board, 1970-82, Scottish Advisory Committee, British Council, since 1972; Chairman, Harris Tweed Association Ltd., 1972-84; Member, Council, National Trust for Scotland, 1979-84; Governor, Eden Court Theatre, since 1980 (Vice Chairman, since 1987); author of plays: Tarravore, The Magic Rowan, Legend is Born, Comrade the King. Publications: Highland Villages, 1977; Their Children Will See, 1979; The Hub of My Universe, 1982; Surprise Island, 1983; The Gaelic Vikings, 1984; Stornoway and the Lews, 1985; Discovering Lewis and Harris, 1987. Address: (h.) Ardgrianach, Inshes, Inverness; T.-Inverness 231476.

Grant, Professor John Paxton, LLB, LLM. Professor and Head, Department of Public and European International Law, Glasgow University, since 1988 (Dean, Faculty of Law and Financial Studies, since 1985); b. 22.2.44, Edinburgh; m., Elaine E. Sutherland. Educ. George Heriot's School, Edinburgh; Edinburgh University; Pennsylvania University. Lecturer, Faculty of Law: Aberdeen University, 1967-71, Dundee University, 1971-74; Senior Lecturer, Department of Public International Law, Glasgow University, 1974-88; Visiting Professor: Saint Louis University School of Law, 1981, Northwestern School of Law, Lewis and Clark College, 1984 and 1986; Member, Children's Panel: Aberdeenshire and Kincardine, 1970-71, Dundee, 1971-74, Strathclyde, 1974-81. Publications: Independence and Devolution (Editor), 1976; The Impact of Marine Pollution: Law and Practice (Joint Editor), 1980; The Encyclopaedic Dictionary of International Law (Joint General Editor), 1985. Recreations: walking; travelling. Address: (h.) 87 Warrender Park Road, Edinburgh, EH9 1EW; T.-031-229 7705.

Grant, John Peters, FCCA. Honorary Sheriff, Inverness, since 1963; b. 24.12.98, Leith; m., Agnes M.R. Beaumont; 1 d. Educ. Broughton School, Edinburgh. Inland Revenue (Inspector of Taxes), 39 years; Councillor, Nairn Town Council and Moray and Nairn County Council, five years; Vice Chairman, Moray and Nairn Valuation Committee, and General Commissioner of Income Tax, until the age of 75. Freelance sports journalist. Recreations: golf; bowling. Address: (h.) 16 Seabank Road, Nairn, IV12 4EU; T.-Nairn 53376.

Grant, Kenneth Alexander, MB, ChB, FRCOG. Consultant Obstetrician Gynaecologist, Forth Valley Health Board, since 1977; Honorary Clinical Lecturer, Aberdeen University, since 1984; b. 1.4.43, Invergarry, Inverness-shire; m., Grace Muir Allen Pettigrew; 2 s.; 1 d. Educ. Lochaber High School; Edinburgh University. Training posts in teaching hospitals and district hospitals in Central Scotland, 1967-77; Honorary Clinical Lecturer, Glasgow University, 1977; Fellowship, Royal College of Obstetrics and Gynaecology, 1986. Recreations: photography; archery; hill-walking. Address: (h.) Compthall, Sunnyside Road, Brightons, by Falkirk; T.-0324 715794.

Grant, Very Rev. Malcolm Etheridge, BSc (Hons), BD (Hons). Provost and Rector, Cathedral Church of S. Mary the Virgin, Glasgow, since 1981; b. 6.8.44, Maidstone; m., Katrina Russell Nuttall; 1 d. Educ. Dunfermline High School; Edinburgh University; Edinburgh Theological College. Assistant Curate: S. Mary's Cathedral, Glasgow, 1969-72, Grantham Parish Church, in charge of Church of the Epiphany, Earlesfield, 1972; Team Vicar, Earlesfield, Grantham Team Ministry, 1972-78; Priest-in-Charge, S. Ninian's, Invergordon, 1978-81; Examining Chaplain to Bishop of Moray, Ross and Caithness, 1979-81; Member, Highland Region Education Committee, 1979-81. Address: S. Mary's Cathedral Rectory, 45 Rowallan Gardens, Glasgow, G11 7LH; T.-041-339 4956.

Grant, Maurice Alexander, MA. Principal, Industry Department for Scotland, since 1983; b. 1.1.41, Portree; m., Isabel Alison MacDonald; 1 d. Educ. Dunoon Grammar School; Glasgow

University. Executive Officer: Department of Health for Scotland, 1961-62, Scottish Development Department, 1962-66; Higher Executive Officer, then Senior Executive Officer, Scottish Development Department, 1966-81; Principal, Scottish Economic Planning Department, 1981-83. Recreation: collecting antiquarian books. Address: (h.) 8 Nantwich Drive, Edinburgh, EH7 6QS; T.-031-669 7347.

Grant, Murdo Macdonald, MA (Hons), DipEd. Rector, Kingussie High School, since 1968; b. 20.3.32, Drumnadrochit; m., Cora Laing Gerrard; 2 s.; 1 d. Educ. Glen Urquhart Secondary School; Aberdeen University. Commissioned Service, RAF, 1955-57; Teacher, Nairn Academy; Principal Teacher of English, Golspie High School, 1964-68. Chairman, Badenoch & Strathspey Music Festival; Elder, Church of Scotland; Board Member, Cairngorm Recreation Trust. Recreation: West Coast cruising. Address: (h.) Tor Na Sith, West Terrace, Kingussie, Inverness-shire; T.-05402 498.

Grant, Professor Nigel Duncan Cameron, MA, Med, PhD. Professor of Education, Glasgow University, since 1978; b. 8.6.32, Glasgow; m., Valerie Keeling Evans; 1 s.; 1 d. Educ. Inverness Royal Academy; Glasgow University. Teacher of English, Glasgow secondary schools, 1957-60; Lecturer in Education, Jordanhill College of Education, 1960-65; Lecturer in Educational Studies, then Reader, Edinburgh University, 1965-78. Past Chairman and President, British Comparative and International Education Society; former Executive Member, Comparative Education Society in Europe; Past Chairman, Scottish Educational Research Association; Chairman, Scottish Universities Council for Studies in Education; Educational Consultant, Comann Sgoiltean Da-Chananach Ghlaschu; Member, Executive Committee, Advisory Council for the Arts in Scotland; Member, Editorial Board, Comparative Education. Publications: Soviet Education, 1964; Society, Schools and Progress in Eastern Europe, 1969; Education and Nation-Building in the Third World (Editor and Co-author), 1971; A Mythology of British Education (Co-author), 1974; Scottish Universities: The Case for Devolution (Co-author), 1976; Patterns of Education in the British Isles (Co-author), 1977; The Crisis of Scottish Education, 1982. Recreations: theatre; music; poetry; natural history; languages; art; travel; calligraphy. Address: (b.) Department of Education, Glasgow University, Glasgow, G12 8QQ; T.-041-339 8855.

Grant, Professor Peter Mitchell, BSc, PhD, CEng, MIEE. Professor of Electronic Signal Processing, Edinburgh University, since 1987; Director, EUMOS, Edinburgh, since 1985; b. 20.6.44, St. Andrews; m., Marjory Renz; 2 d. Educ. Strathallan School; Heriot-Watt University; Edinburgh University. Member, Communications Sub-Committee, Science and Engineering Council; Member, Electronics Divisional Board, IEE; Honorary Editor, Proceedings IEE (Part F). Publication: Adaptive Filters (Co-Editor), 1985. Address: (b.) Department of Electrical Engineering, Edinburgh University, Edinburgh, EH9 3JL; T.-031-667 1081.

Grant of Dalvey, Sir Patrick Alexander Benedict, 14th Bt, FSA Scot, LLB. Chieftain of Clan Donnachy; Company Director; b. 5.2.53; m., Dr. Carolyn Elizabeth Highet; 2 s. Educ. St. Conleth's College, Dublin; The Abbey School, Fort Augustus; Glasgow University.

Grant of Rothiemurchus, John Peter, DL. Landowner; Director: Scot Trout Limited, Cairngorm Recreation Trust; b. 22.10.46, Rothiemurchus; m., Philippa; 1 s.; 2 d. Educ. Gordonstoun. Past Chairman: Scottish Recreational Land Association; British Deer Producers Society; Highland Region Forestry, Farming and Wildlife Advisory Group; former Member, Forestry Commission Regional Advisory Committee; Patron, Highland Hospice. Recreations: skiing; shooting. Address: (b.) Rothiemurchus Estate Office, Aviemore; T.-0479 810647.

Grant-Wood, John, MA (Hons). Headmaster, Firrhill High School, Edinburgh, since 1975; b. 8.6.31, Ashton-under-Lyne; m., Pamela Irene; 1 s. Educ. Audenshaw Grammar School; Edinburgh University. Bank of Scotland; RAF; Headmaster, Livister Primary School, Shetland; Senior Housemaster, United World College of the Atlantic, South Wales; Depute Headmaster, Firrhill High School; twice elected to Court, Heriot-Watt University; Council Member, Headteachers Association of Scotland; Past President, Scottish Area, Secondary Heads Association; President, Lothian Heads Association. Publication: Educating for Tomorrow (Contributor). Recreations: travel; railways; canals; music. Address: (h.) Rossarden, 20 Greenhill Gardens, Edinburgh; T.-031-447 3882.

Granville, 5th Earl (Granville James Leveson Gower), MC. Lord Lieutenant, Western Isles, since 1983 (Vice Lord-Lieutenant, 1976-83); b. 6.12.18; m.; 2 s.; 1 d. Educ. Eton. Served Second World War, Tunisia and Italy; mentioned in Despatches.

Grassie, Professor Norman, BSc, PhD, DSc, CChem, FRSC, FRSE. Emeritus Professor of Chemistry, Glasgow University, since 1984; b. 28.5.24, Aberdeen; m., Catherine Beaton; 1 s.; 2 d. Educ. Nicolson Institute, Stornoway; Aberdeen University. DSIR Senior Research Fellow, Birmingham University, 1948-50; ICI Research Fellow, Glasgow University, 1950-55; Glasgow University: Lecturer, 1955, Senior Lecturer, 1963, Reader, 1967, Titular Professor, 1971; Visiting Professor, Universities of: Mainz, 1967, Delaware, 1969, Malaysia, 1975-77, Merida (Venezuela), 1979. Publications: numerous books, mainly on topics related to polymer stability and degradation. Recreations: bridge; hill-walking; ballroom dancing; grandchildren; Church activities. Address: (h.) 15 Lovat Avenue, Bearsden, Glasgow, G61 3LQ; T.-041-942 8768.

Gratwick, Adrian Stuart, MA (Cantab), DPhil (Oxon). Reader in Humanity, St. Andrews University, since 1983; b. 31.3.43, Stanmore, Middlesex; m., Jennifer Rosemary Clark; 2 s. Educ. St. Aloysius' College, Glasgow; St. Brendan's College, Bristol; St. John's College, Cambridge; Balliol College, Oxford. St. Andrews University: Assistant Lecturer in Humanity, 1966, Lecturer,

1969. Recreations: walking; gardening; woodwork. Address: (b.) Department of Humanity, St. Salvator's College, St. Andrews, Fife; T.-0334 76161, Ext. 492.

Gravestock, Martin John. Crown Estate Receiver for Scotland, since 1985; b. 31.8.52, Carshalton, Surrey; m., Olwyn Claire; 3 s. Educ. Sutton County Grammar School. Crown Estate Office, since 1969: Legal, Foreshore and Seabed, General, and London Branches; Head, Personnel Branch, 1984; Head, Foreshore and Seabed Branch, 1984-85. Recreations: cars; gardening. Address: (b.) 10 Charlotte Square, Edinburgh; T.-031-226 7241.

Gray, Adam, NDA, NDD. Farmer; Director, Royal Highland Agricultural Society, since 1976; Director, Scottish Milk Marketing Board, since 1981; Governor, West of Scotland Agricultural College, since 1976; b. 6.8.29, Borgue, Kirkcudbright; m., Elaine West Russell; 3 s. Educ. George Watson's Boys College; West of Scotland Agricultural College. Nuffield Scholar, 1955; Past President, Stewartry NFU; Member, NFU Council; former Council Member, British Simmental Cattle Society; Vice Chairman, Scottish Agricultural Arbiters Association; Vice-Chairman, Scottish Dairy Council; Past Chairman, SW Scotland Grassland Society; former Chairman, Kirkcudbright District Council; Honorary President, Stewartry Agricultural Society; Chairman, Scottish Agricultural Arbiters Association; Council Member, Hannah Research Institute; Secretary, Kirkcudbright Burns Club; Past President, Kirkcudbright Rotary Club. Recreations: rugby; local history. Address: (h.) Ingleston, Borgue, Kirkcudbright; T.-05577 208.

Gray, Alasdair. Artist and Writer; b. 28.12.34, Glasgow; m., nobody, now; 1 s. Educ. Whitehill Senior Secondary School; Glasgow Art School. Part-time Art Teacher, 1958-62; Scene Painter, 1963-64; has since lived by drawing, painting, writing; Glasgow People's Palace has a collection of his portraits and cityscapes; has a mural in Palacerigg nature reserve, Cumbernauld. Publications: novels: Lanark; 1982 Janine; The Fall of Kelvin Walker; anthologies: Unlikely Stories, Mostly; Lean Tales (this last also containing work by Jim Kelman and Agnes Owens). Scottish National Library has a collection of his unpublished plays and other material. Recreations: reading; talking to friends; drinking; walking. Address: (h.) 39 Kersland Street, Glasgow, G12.

Gray, Rev. Alastair H., MA, BD. Minister, Haddington West linked with Garvard and Morham, since 1985; b. 7.4.53, Glasgow; m., Anne Buck; 1 s.; 2 d. Educ. Coatbridge High School; St. Andrews University. Minister, Methil Parish Church, 1978-85. Publications: Local Church Evangelism, 1987; Pray Today, 1987. Recreations: photography; golf; philately; music. Address: 15 West Road, Haddington; T.-062 082 2213.

Gray, Alexander, MA, LLB. Honorary Sheriff, Dumbarton; b. 6.5.12, Glasgow; m., Margaret; 2 s. Educ. Hillhead High School; Glasgow University; Edinburgh University. Recreation: Gaelic. Address: (h.) Borraichill, 116 Frederick Crescent, Port Ellen, Isle of Islay, PA42 7BQ.

Gray, Charles Ireland, JP. Leader, Strathclyde Regional Council, since 1986 (Depute Leader, 1978-86); b. 25.1.29, Gartcosh; m., Catherine; 3 s.; 2 d. Educ. Coatbridge High School. Local government, since 1958; Director, Scottish Exhibition and Conference Centre; former Vice-Chairman, East Kilbride Development Corporation; former Member: Scottish Development Agency, Clyde Port Authority; former Vice-Chairman, Planning Exchange. Recreations: music; reading; local government. Address: (b.) Strathclyde House, 20 India Street, Glasgow, G2 4PF.

Gray, Ethel Marian, CBE, JP, MA, LLD, FEIS. Convener, Adult Access to Education, Scottish Institute of Adult and Continuing Education, since 1988 (President of Institute, 1984-87); Vice-Chairman, Board of Governors, The Queen's College, Glasgow, since 1980; Chairman, Education Project for Older People, Age Concern Scotland, 1982-85; b. 19.4.23, Glasgow; m., George Deans Gray (qv). Educ. Hutchesons' Girls Grammar School; Paisley Grammar School; Glasgow University. Teacher of English, 1946-52; Lecturer in English and Drama, Jordanhill College, 1952-63; Founding Principal, Craigie College of Education, Ayr, 1963-75; Director, Scottish Adult Literacy Agency, 1976-79; Chairman, National Book League Scotland, 1977-81; Member of Court, Chairman of Staffing Committee and Joint Faculty Staff Review Board, Heriot-Watt University, 1979-84; Adviser in Adult Education, IBA, since 1983; Member, Scottish Tertiary Education Advisory Council, 1984-87; Member, Steering Committee, Open College in Lothian, since 1987; Member, Executive Committee, Scottish Centre for the Tuition of the Disabled, since 1987; Member, STV Education Advisory Committee, since 1981; Member, Scottish Community Education Council, 1979-85 (Chairman, Communications and Technology Group and Chairman, Management Committee, Micro-Electronics Project); Member, Crawford Commission on Radio and Television Coverage, 1973-75; Member, Committee of Enquiry on the Police, 1977-79; Member, Consultative Committee on the Curriculum, 1965-71. Recreations: reading; travelling; theatre. Address: (h.) 7 Greenbank Crescent, Edinburgh, EH10 5TE; T.-031-447 5403.

Gray, George Bovill Rennie, DL, CDA, FBIM. Farmer; Chairman, G.B.R. Gray Ltd., since 1952; Member, Board of Management, and Chairman, Development Committee, Hanover (Scotland) Housing Association Ltd.; Vice-President, Animal Diseases Research Association, Moredun, since 1974; Director, Moredun Animal Health Ltd.; b. 5.3.20, Edinburgh; m., Anne Constance Dale; 4 s.; 2 d. Educ. Clayesmore School, Dorset; Edinburgh and East of Scotland College of Agriculture. Past Chairman, East Lothian Area Committee, National Farmers Union of Scotland; former Convenor, Cereals Committee, NFU of Scotland; former Member, Seed Production Committee, National Institute of Agricultural Botany, Cambridge; a Director, West Cumberland Farmers Ltd., 1955-85; Director, Scottish Society for Research in Plant Breeding, since 1957 (Trustee, since 1977); Member, Pig Industry Development Authority, 1958-68; Chairman, Oxford Farming Conference, 1972; a Director, E. Lothian and

Border Area Growers Ltd., Eyemouth, 1972-84; Member, Agricultural and Veterinary Sub-Committee, UGC, 1972-82; Member, Lothian Regional Council, 1974-82; Member, Scottish Advisory Board, British Institute of Management, since 1978; Member, Scientific Research Panel, Home Grown Cereals Authority, 1973-80; Chairman, East Lothian Conservative and Unionist Association, 1985-87; Elder, Church of Scotland; former Assistant County Scout Commissioner; Director, Cruden Foundation. Recreations: gardening; arboriculture. Address: Smeaton, East Linton, EH40 3DT; T.-0620 860275.

Gray, George Deans, CBE, MA. Member, Board of Education, Church of Scotland, 1980-87; b. 23.5.08, Edinburgh; m., Ethel Marian Rennie (see Ethel Marian Gray). Educ. Royal High School, Edinburgh; Edinburgh University. Teacher of Classics: Musselburgh Grammar School, 1931-37, George Watson's College, Edinburgh, 1937-45; Principal Teacher, Royal High School, Edinburgh, 1946-59; Secretary, Scottish Council for the Training of Teachers, 1959-66; Registrar (first), General Teaching Council for Scotland, 1966-72; Honorary General Secretary, Scottish Secondary Teachers Association, 1945-59; Chairman: Classical Association (Edinburgh and SE Centre), 1968-73, Scottish Dyslexia Association, 1980-82. Recreations: choral singing; classical music; piano; gardening. Address: (h.) 7 Greenbank Crescent, Edinburgh, EH10 5TE; T.-031-447 5403.

Gray, His Eminence Cardinal Gordon Joseph, MA, DD, FEIS. Archbishop of St. Andrews and Edinburgh, 1951-85; b. 10.8.10. Educ. Holy Cross Academy, Edinburgh; St. Joseph's, Sussex; St. John's, Surrey. Ordained Priest, 1935; Assistant Priest: St. Andrew's, Fife, 1935-41; Parish Priest, SS Mary and David, Hawick, 1941-47; Rector, St. Mary's College, Blairs, 1947-51; named Cardinal, 1969 (first resident Scottish Cardinal). Address: (h.) The Hermitage, Gillis College, Whitehouse Loan, Edinburgh, EH9 1BB.

Gray, Hugh Spence, FCCA, FRVA. Director of Finance, Hamilton District Council, since 1975; b. 7.1.29; m., Mabel; 1 d. Educ. Wishaw Senior Secondary School; Glasgow College of Commerce. Lanark County Council, 1952-59; Hamilton Town Council, 1959-75. Recreations: walking; reading; gardening. Address: (b.) 102 Cadzow Street, Hamilton, ML3 6HN; T.-Hamilton 282323, Ext. 122.

Gray, Iain George Fowler. Finance Officer, Department of Agriculture and Fisheries for Scotland and Scottish Education Department, since 1984; b. 3.5.39, Glasgow. Educ. Albert Road Academy, Glasgow; Roseburn, Edinburgh; Royal High School, Edinburgh. Joined War Office as Executive Officer, 1960; PS/DUS (B), 1964-65; joined Scottish Office as Assistant Principal, 1965, Principal, 1969; SED to 1971; Private Secretary to Minister of State, 1971-72; SDD, 1973; SEPD, 1973-77; DAFS (Assistant Secretary), 1978-84. Recreations: golf; badminton. Address: (b.) New St. Andrews House, Edinburgh; T.-031-244 5124.

Gray, James Allan, MB, ChB, FRCPEdin. Consultant in Communicable Diseases, City Hospital, Edinburgh, since 1969; part-time Senior Lecturer, Department of Medicine, Edinburgh University, since 1969; Assistant Principal Medical Officer, Scottish Widows' Fund, Edinburgh, since 1979; Vice-President, British Society for the Study of Infection, since 1987; b. 24.3.35, Bristol; m., Jennifer Margaret Newton Hunter; 1 s.; 2 d. Educ. St. Paul's School, London; Edinburgh University. House Surgeon and Physician posts, Edinburgh and Middlesbrough; Short Service Commission, RAF Medical Branch, 1960-63; Senior House Officer, Research Fellow and Registrar posts, Edinburgh, 1965-67; Registrar, Bristol Royal Infirmary, 1967-68; Senior Registrar, Royal Free Hospital (Department of Infectious Diseases), London, 1968-69; Assistant Director of Studies (Medicine), Edinburgh Post-Graduate Board, 1976-84; Fellow, Royal Medical Society (Senior President, 1958-59); Founder Editor, Res Medica, 1957-58; Assistant Editor, Journal of Infection, 1979-86. Publications: Antibacterial Drugs Today (Co-author), 1983; Infectious Diseases (Co-author), 1984. Recreations: hill-walking; pottery collecting; photography. Address: (h.) St. Andrews Cottage, 15 Lauder Road, Edinburgh, EH9 2EN; T.-031-667 4124.

Gray, Professor James Robertson, BSc, DipActMaths, FFA, FIMA, FSS. Professor and Head, Department of Actuarial Mathematics and Statistics, Heriot-Watt University, since 1971; b. 21.2.26, Dundee; m., Catherine McAulay Towner. Educ. High School of Dundee; Edinburgh University. Actuarial Trainee, Scottish Life Assurance Company, 1947-49; St. Andrews University: Lecturer in Mathematics, 1949-50, Lecturer in Statistics, 1950-62, Senior Lecturer in Statistics (also Head of Department), 1962-71; Heriot-Watt University: established first Department of Actuarial Science in UK; Dean, Faculty of Science, 1978-81; Council Member, Faculty of Actuaries, 1969-87 (Vice President, 1983-87); Vice-Chairman, Scottish Examination Board, since 1984 (Convener of Examinations Committee, since 1982); former Vice-Chairman, Scottish Universities Council on Entrance; Past Chairman: Scottish Branch, Institute of Mathematics and Its Applications, Edinburgh Branch, Royal Statistical Society. Recreations: golf; hill-walking; bridge; music; Rotary. Address: (h.) Green Gables, 9 Cammo Gardens, Edinburgh, EH4 8EJ; T.-031-339 3330.

Gray, John Alexander. Broadcasting Consultant, since 1978; b. 5.7.18, London. GPO Film Unit, 1937-39; BBC, 1940-78, mainly in News and Monitoring, and in programme departments in Scotland. Director, Scottish Ballet. Recreation: hill-walking. Address: (h.) 13 Comely Bank Row, Edinburgh, EH4 1EA; T.-031-332 8270.

Gray, John William Reid, MA, LLB, Advocate; b. 24.12.26, Aberdeen. Educ. Aberdeen Grammar School; Aberdeen University. Resident Magistrate, Uganda, 1954-62; Temporary Procurator-Fiscal Depute, Glasgow, 1962-63; Lecturer in Private Law, Queen's College, Dundee, then Dundee University, 1964-84; Warden, Airlie Hall, 1966-75; Member of Senate, 1971-75. Fellow, Saltzburg Seminar, 1964. Publications: articles in legal journals. Address: (h.) 24 Park Road, Dundee, DD3 8LA; T.-0382 815866.

Gray, Muriel, BA (Hons). Broadcaster; Rector, Edinburgh University; b. Glasgow. Educ. Glasgow School of Art. Worked as an illustrator; then as a designer with National Museum of Antiquities; was member of rock band, The Family Von Trapp; had own show with Radio Forth; was frequent presenter on Radio 1; co-presented The Tube, Channel 4; had own arts programme, The Works, Tyne Tees; own music programme, Studio 1, Border TV; presented Casebook Scotland, BBC Scotland; Frocks on the Box, Thames TV; Acropolis Now, ITV; now presents The Media Show; first woman Rector, Edinburgh University. Recreation: being in the Scottish Highlands - gets grumpy and miserable if can't be up a mountain every few weeks. Address: (b.) Schoolhouse Management, 63 Frederick Street, Edinburgh, EH2 1LH.

Gray, Peter Michael David, MA, DPhil, MBCS. Senior Lecturer, Department of Computing Science, Aberdeen University, since 1985; b. 11.2.40, Abingdon; m., Doreen F. Ross; 1 s.; 1 d. Educ. Abingdon School; Queens' College, Cambridge; Jesus College, Oxford. Systems Analyst, Plessey Co., Poole, 1966-68; Research Fellow, Computer Research Group, Aberdeen University, 1968-72; Lecturer in Computing Science, Aberdeen University, 1972-84. Reader, Church of Scotland. Publication: Logic, Algebra and Databases. Recreation: croquet. Address: (b.) Department of Computing Science, King's College, Aberdeen, AB9 2UB; T.-0224 272292.

Gray, Robert, OStJ, JP, LLD. Lord Provost of Glasgow, 1984-88; Lord Lieutenant of Glasgow, 1984-88; Chairman, Greater Glasgow Tourist Board, since 1984; b. 3.3.28, Glasgow; m., Mary McCartney; 1 d. Educ. St. Mungo's Academy; Glasgow College of Building. Joiner; Clerk of Works; Lecturer and Senior Lecturer in Building Subjects; elected Member, Glasgow District Council, 1974; Chairman, Licensing Committee, 1975-77; Vice Chairman, JP Committee, 1976-77; City Treasurer, 1980-84; Member, Scottish Confederation of Tourism; President, Prince and Princess of Wales Hospice; Honorary President, Save the Children Fund; Trustee, University of Glasgow Trust; Patron, Glasgow Branch, British Red Cross Society. Recreations: walking; spectator sports; reading; opera; music. Address: (b.) City Chambers, Glasgow, G2 1DU; T.-041-227 4002.

Gray, Professor Sidney John, BEc, PhD, FCCA, AASA CPA, ACIS, MBIM. Professor of Accountancy, Glasgow University, since 1978 (Head, Department of Accountancy, 1980-87, and Director, Glasgow Business School, since 1986); b. 3.10.42, Woodford; m., Hilary Fenella Jones; 1 s.; 1 d. Educ. Bedford Modern School; Sydney University; Lancaster University. Peirce Leslie and Co. Ltd., UK and India, 1961-67; Burns Philp Pty Ltd., Australia, 1967-68; Tutor in Accounting, Sydney University, 1972; Lecturer in Accounting and Finance, Lancaster University, 1974-78; Secretary General, European Accounting Association, 1982-83; Member, Accounting Standards Committee for UK and Ireland, 1984-87; Chairman, British Accounting Association, 1987. Publications: International Financial Reporting, 1984; Information Disclosure and the Multinational Corporation, 1984; International Accounting and Transnational Decisions, 1983. Recreations: golf; tennis; travel. Address: (h.) 21 Lampson Road, Killearn, Stirlingshire, G63 9PD; T.-0360 50707.

Gray, Sir William Stevenson, Kt (1974), JP, DL. Solicitor and Notary Public; Chairman: Glasgow Independent Hospital Ltd. (Ross Hall Hospital), since 1982; b. 3.5.28; m.; 1 s.; 1 d. Educ. Hillhead High School; Glasgow University. Chairman, Scottish Special Housing Association, 1966-72; Chairman, Irvine New Town Development Corporation, 1974-76; Chairman, Scotland West Industrial Promotion Group, 1972-75; Chairman, Scottish Development Agency, 1975-79; Lord Provost, City of Glasgow, and Lord Lieutenant, County of the City of Glasgow, 1972-75; Hon. LLD: Strathclyde, 1974, Glasgow, 1980.

Gray of Contin, Baron (James (Hamish) Hector Northey Gray), PC (1982). Life Peer; b. 28.6.27; m.; 2 s.; 1 d. Educ. Inverness Royal Academy. Queen's Own Cameron Highlanders, 1945-48; Member, Inverness Town Council, 1965-70; MP (Conservative), Ross and Cromarty, 1970-83; Minister of State, Department of Energy, 1979-83; Minister of State, Scottish Office, 1983-86.

Green, Lawrence Love. Senior Secretary (Region 4), National Union of Seamen, Scotland and North East England; Joint Chairman, Scottish District Maritime Board; b. 17.9.23, Glasgow; m., Eileen Egan; 3 s. Educ. Lambhill Street Secondary School. Seafaring from 1940; entered trade union movement in 1955 as full-time officer, National Union of Seamen. Vice-Chairman, Port Welfare Committee; Member, Management Committee, Veteran Seafarers Association. Recreations: spectator sports (soccer, boxing, rugby). Address: (h.) 1425 Paisley Road West, Glasgow; T.-041-882 6954.

Green, Malcolm Robert, MA, DPhil. Chairman, Education Committee, Strathclyde Regional Council, since 1982; Chairman, Education Committee, Convention of Scottish Local Authorities, since 1978; Lecturer in Roman History, Glasgow University, since 1967; b. 4.1.43, Leicester; m., Mary Margaret Pratley; 1 s.; 2 d. Educ. Wyggeston Grammar School, Leicester; Magdalen College, Oxford. Address: (b.) Strathclyde House, 20 India Street, Glasgow, G2 4PF; T.-041-227 3453.

Greene, John Gerald, MA, PhD. Head of Psychological Services, Western District, Greater Glasgow Health Board; Clinical Lecturer, Glasgow University; b. 10.3.38, Glasgow; m., Dr. Elisabeth Rose Hamil; 2 s.; 2 d. Educ. St. Aloysius College, Glasgow; Glasgow University. Trainee Clinical Psychologist, Crichton Royal Hospital, Dumfries, 1962-64; Senior Psychologist, 1965-70; Principal Psychologist, Gartnavel Royal Hospital, Glasgow, 1970-82; Top Grade Psychologist, Greater Glasgow Health Board, since 1982; Chairman, National (Scotland) Scientific Consultative Committee on Clinical Psychological Services, 1985; Secretary (1975-77) and Chairman (1977-79), Consultative Committee on Psychological Services, Greater Glasgow Health Board; Secretary and Treasurer, Scottish Branch Committee, Division of Clinical Psychology, 1977-81. Publications: The Social and Psychological Origins of the Climacteric Syndrome, 1984; Clinical Psychology in the Scottish Health Service (Co-author), 1984. Recreations: music; tennis. Address: (b.) Psychology Department, Gartnavel Royal Hospital, Glasgow, G12 OXH.

Greene, John Henderson, MA, LLB. Partner, MacRoberts, Solicitors, Glasgow, Edinburgh and London; b. 2.6.32, Kilmarnock; m., Catriona McGillivray Scott; 1 s. Educ. Merchiston Castle School, Edinburgh; Edinburgh University. Assistant, Joseph Kirkland & Son, Solicitors, Saltcoats, 1958-60; Assistant, MacRobert Son & Hutchison, Solicitors, 1960 (appointed Partner, 1961); Law Society of Scotland: Vice-Convener, Company Law Committee, former Member, Bankruptcy and Liquidation Committee; former Council Member, Royal Faculty of Procurators, Glasgow; founder Chairman, Troon Round Table, 1964; Vice-Captain, Royal Troon Golf Club, 1987; Elder, Portland Church, Troon; President, Glasgow Ayrshire Society, 1985-86. Publication: Law and Practice of Receivership in Scotland (Co-author). Recreations: golf; gardening. Address: (h.) Silvertrees, 7 Lady Margaret Drive, Troon, KA10 7AL; T.-Troon 312482.

Greenhalgh, Professor James Francis Derek, MA, MS, PhD. Professor of Animal Production and Health, Aberdeen University, since 1978; b. 4.10.32, Frodsham, Cheshire; m., Isoline Gee; 3 s. Educ. King's School, Chester; Cambridge University; Illinois University; Aberdeen University. Lecturer in Agricultural Chemistry, Edinburgh School of Agriculture, 1959-63; Senior (then Principal) Scientific Officer, Rowett Research Institute, Aberdeen, 1963-78; Editor, Animal Feed Science and Technology. Publication: Animal Nutrition (Co-author). Recreations: hockey; hillwalking. Address: (b.) School of Agriculture, 581 King Street, Aberdeen, AB9 1UD; T.-Aberdeen 480291.

Greenock, William, MA. Principal, Clydebank College, since 1984; b. 3.2.37, Glasgow; 2 d. Educ. Allan Glen's School; Glasgow University. Teacher, secondary schools, 1959-65; David Dale College, 1965-68; Langside College, 1968-70; Reid Kerr College, 1970-75; Anniesland College, 1975-82; Ayr College, 1982-84. Session Clerk, Langside Parish Church, Glasgow. Recreation: golf. Address: (b.) Clydebank College, Kilbowie Road, Clydebank, G81 2AA; T.-041-952 7771.

Greenwood, David, MA. Director, Centre for Defence Studies, Aberdeen University, since 1976; b. 6.2.37, Rochdale, Lancashire; m., 1, Helen Ramshaw (m. diss.); 2 s.; 2, Margaret McRobb. Educ. Manchester Grammar School; Liverpool University. Education Branch, RAF, 1959-66; Economic Adviser, Ministry of Defence, 1966-67; Aberdeen University: Lecturer in Higher Defence Studies, 1967-70, Senior Lecturer, 1970-74, Reader, since 1974; Member, Honeywell Advisory Council, 1982-85; Director, BDMI Ltd., since 1984; Consultant to several organisations in Europe and North America; Member, Foreign and Commonwealth Office Advisory Panel on Arms Control and Disarmament; Member, Editorial Advisory Board, Strategic Studies. Publications: Budgeting for Defence, 1972; numerous monographs, reports, etc. Address: (h.) Lindores, Kinmuck, Inverurie, AB5 0LY; T.-0467 20561.

Greer, Rev. Arthur David Courtenay, MA, LLB, DMin. Minister, Dunscore with Glencairn and Moniaive, since 1985; b. 20.2.30, Glasgow; m., Kathleen Slessor; 1 s.; 3 d. Educ. Prestwick Public and High Schools; Ayr Academy; Glasgow University (Trinity College); NYTS. Assistant Minister, St. Quivox, Ayr, 1954-55; Minister: Presbyterian Church of Jamaica and Grand Cayman, 1956-63, Kelvingrove Church, Glasgow, 1964-78; Department of Education Staff Tutor, St. Colm's College, Edinburgh, 1978-81; Associate Minister, Whitfield, Dundee, 1981-85. Recreation: youth hostelling. Address: The Manse, Wallaceton, Auldgirth, Dumfries; T.-Dunscore 245.

Gregson, William Derek Hadfield, CBE, DL, DFH, CEng, FIEE, CBIM, FRSA. Commissioner of Northern Lighthouses; Director: Anderson Strathclyde, Brammer plc, East of Scotland Industrial Investments PLC; Consultant, ICI; b. 27.1.20; m., Rosalind Helen Reeves; 3 s.; 1 d. Educ. UK and Switzerland. Director, Ferranti Holdings, 1983-85; Deputy Chairman, British Airports Authority, 1975-85; Director, British Telecom (Scotland), 1977-85. Recreations: woodwork; books; automation in the home. Address: (h.) 15 Barnton Avenue, Edinburgh, EH4 6AJ; T.-031-336 3896.

Grier, Arnold Macfarlane, MB, ChB, FRCSEdin. Consultant Ear, Nose and Throat Surgeon, Highland Health Board, since 1962; Chairman, Scottish Association for the Deaf; b. 5.9.21, Musselburgh; m., Elisabeth J. Kluten; 2 s.; 1 d. Educ. Musselburgh Grammar School; Edinburgh University. Recreations: gardening; aviculture. Address: (h.) Elmbank, 68 Culduthel Road, Inverness; T.-Inverness 234682.

Grier, Scott, MA, CA. Managing Director, Loganair Limited, since 1983; b. 7.3.41, Kilmacolm; m., Frieda Gardiner; 2 s. Educ. Greenock High School; Glasgow University. Apprenticed, Grahams Rintoul & Co., 1962-66; Accountant, Ardrossan Harbour Company, 1967-76; Loganair: Financial/Commercial Manager and Secretary, 1976, Financial Director, 1977. Recreations: golf; philately. Address: (h.) Lagavulin, 15 Corsehill Drive, West Kilbride, KA23 9HU; T.-0294 823138.

Grieve, Professor Andrew Robert, DDS, BDS, FDS RCSEd. Professor of Conservative Dentistry, Dundee University, since 1980 (Senior Adviser of Studies in Dentistry, since 1982); Consultant in Restorative Dentistry, Tayside Health Board, since 1980; b. 23.5.39, Stirling; m., Frances M. Ritchie; 2 d. Educ. Perth Academy; St. Andrews University. Junior hospital appointments and general dental practice; Lecturer in Operative Dental Surgery and Dental Therapeutics, St. Andrews University, 1963-65; Lecturer in Conservative Dentistry, Birmingham University, 1965; appointed Senior Lecturer and Consultant in Restorative Dentistry, Birmingham Area Health Authority (Teaching), 1975. Member, Dental Council, Royal College of Surgeons of Edinburgh; President, British Society for Restorative Dentistry, 1986-87; Council Member, Royal Odonto-Chirurgical Society of Scotland; Chairman, Tayside Area Dental Advisory Committee. Recreation: hill-walking. Address: (b.) Department of Conservative Dentistry, Dental School, The University, Dundee, DD1 4HN; T.-0382 26041.

Grieve, Rev. David Shepherd Allan, MA, BD. Minister, linked Parishes of Carmyllie, Colliston and Arbirlot, since 1983 (Colliston and Arbirlot, since 1982); b. 8.12.25, Forfar; m., Marjory Elizabeth Ross Bell; 2 s.; 2 d. Educ. Forfar Academy; Glasgow University; Edinburgh University; Jordanhill College of Education. RNVR, 1944-47; staff, Brechin High School; Cairns Parish Church, Cowdenbeath; St. Andrew's Parish Church, Peterhead; Principal Teacher of Religious Education, Kirkcaldy High School; Adviser in Religious Education, Strathclyde Regional Council. Recreations: landscape gardening; travel; music. Address: Manse of Arbirlot, by Arbroath, DD11 2NX.

Grieve, John. Actor; b. Glasgow. Trained, Royal Scottish Academy of Music and Drama (James Bridie Gold Medallist), followed by five full seasons, Citizens' Theatre, Glasgow; also appeared in Guthrie's production of The Anatomist, Citizens', 1968; numerous other performances on the Scottish stage, including leading roles in The Bevellers, The Flouers o' Edinburgh, The Good Soldier Schweik, Twelfth Night; television work includes The Vital Spark, Oh Brother, Doctor at Sea, New Year shows; numerous appearances in pantomime; appeared with Scottish Theatre Company in Waiting for Godot, 1985. Address: (b.) c/o David White Associates, 2 Ormond Road, London, Surrey, TW10 6TH.

Grieve, Kathleen Zia, MBE, BSc. Organiser, Network Scotland Ltd., 1975-85; b. 25.9.20, Aberdeen; m., Rev. G.M. Denny Grieve; 2 s.; 1 d. Educ. St. Margaret's School for Girls, Aberdeen; Aberdeen University. Technical Assistant, BBC, 1941-44; service in Church of Scotland from 1944, including National Vice-Convener, Home Board, four years, National President, Woman's Guild, 1966-69; represented Church of Scotland, World Alliance of Reformed Churches meeting, Nairobi, 1970; Member, Church of Scotland Committee of Forty (Honorary Secretary, 1972-78); appointed Organiser, Scottish Telephone Referral Service for Adult Literacy (which became Network Scotland Ltd.), 1975; founder Member, then Honorary Secretary, Dyslexia Scotwest; founder Member, Trustee and Administrator, Pet Fostering Service Scotland, 1985-87. Recreations: walking dog; reading; sewing; catering; upholstery; chess; motoring; gardening. Address: (h.) 13 Montgomerie Terrace, Ayr, KA7 1JL; T.-0292 261768.

Grieve, Professor Sir Robert, Kt (1969), MA, FRSE, FRTPI, MICE. Honorary Professor, Heriot-Watt University, since 1986; Professor Emeritus, Glasgow University; b. 11.12.10; m.; 2 s.; 2 d. Educ. North Kelvinside School, Glasgow; Royal College of Science and Technology, Glasgow. Local government, 1927-44; Civil Service, 1946-54; Chief Planner, Scottish Office, 1960-64; Professor of Town and Regional Planning, Glasgow University, 1964-74; Chairman, Highlands and Islands Development Board, 1965-70. Gold Medal, RTPI, 1974; Hon. DLitt, Heriot-Watt; Hon. LLD, Strahclyde; Hon. FRIAS.

Grieve, Hon. Lord (William Robertson Grieve), VRD (1958), QC (Scot), MA, LLB. Senator of the College of Justice in Scotland, since 1972; Chairman, Board of Governors, St. Columba's Hospice, since 1983; b. 21.10.17, Glasgow; m., Lorna St. John Benn; 1 s.; 1 d. Educ. Glasgow Academy; Sedbergh School; Glasgow University. Served with Royal Navy as an RNVR officer, 1939-45; Advocate, Scots Bar, 1947; QC, 1957; Sheriff Principal, Renfrew and Argyll, 1964-72; Judge of Appeal, Jersey and Guernsey, 1971-72; Chairman, Governors, Fettes Trust, 1978-86. President, Glasgow University Union, 1938. Recreations: golf; painting. Address: (h.) 20 Belgrave Crescent, Edinburgh, EH4 3AJ; T.-031-332 7500.

Griffiths, Nigel, JP. MP (Labour), Edinburgh South, since 1987; b. 20.5.55; m., Sally McLaughlin. Educ. Hawick High School; Edinburgh University; Moray House College of Education. Secretary, Lothian Devolution Campaign, 1978; Rights Adviser, Mental Handicap Pressure Group, 1979-87; City of Edinburgh District Councillor, 1980-87 (Chairperson, Housing Committee); Member, Edinburgh Festival Council, 1984-87; Member, Edinburgh Health Council, 1982-87; Executive Member, Edinburgh Council of Social Service, 1984-87; Member, Wester Hailes School Council, 1981. Recreations: travel; live entertainment; badminton; hill-walking; rock-climbing; architecture; reading; politics. Address: (h.) 39 Thirlestane Road, Edinburgh, EH9 1AP; T.-031-447 1947.

Griffiths, Professor Peter Denham, BSc, MD, LRCP, MRCS, FRCPath, MBCS, FBIM. Professor of Biochemical Medicine, Dundee University, since 1968 (Vice-Principal, 1979-85, Dean of Medicine and Dentistry, since 1985); Consultant, Tayside Health Board, since 1966; b. 16.6.27, Southampton; m., Joy Burgess; 3 s.; 1 d. Educ. King Edward VI School, Southampton; Guy's Hospital, London University. House appointments, Guy's Hospital, 1956-57; Junior Lecturer in Physiology, Guy's Hospital, 1957-58; Registrar and Senior Registrar, Guy's and Lewisham Hospitals, 1958-64; Consultant Pathologist, Harlow Hospitals Group, 1964-66; Senior Lecturer in Clinical Chemistry/Honorary Consultant, St. Andrews University, then Dundee University, 1966-68. Member, General Medical Council, since 1986; President, 1987-89, and sometime Chairman of Council, Association of Clinical Biochemists; Director, Drug Development Scotland; Director, Dundee Repertory Theatre. Recreations: music; theatre; domestic activities. Address: (b.) Department of Biochemical Medicine, Ninewells Hospital and Medical School, Dundee, DD1 9SY; T.-0382 60111, Ext. 2164.

Grigor, Kenneth McNeill, BSc, MB, ChB, MD, MRCPath. Senior Lecturer in Pathology, Edinburgh University, since 1980; Honorary Consultant in Pathology, Edinburgh Royal Infirmary, since 1980; b. 15.5.44, Glasgow; m., Jacqueline Hardie; 3 d. Educ. Kelvinside Academy, Glasgow; Glasgow University. Hospital attachments and pathology training in Glasgow, 1969-71; cancer research and pathology, London, 1971-78; pathology, Edinburgh, since 1979. Recreations: gardening; rugby refereeing. Address: (h.) 6 Barnton Gardens, Edinburgh, EH4 6AF; T.-031-336 2824.

Grimes, Alistair Bernard, MA (St. Andrews), MA (Durham), PhD (Edinburgh). Assistant Director, Scottish Council for Voluntary Organisations, since 1984; b. 30.5.51, London. Educ. King Edward VI Grammar School, Nuneaton; St. Andrews University; Durham University; Edinburgh University. Age Concern Scotland, 1978-79; Social Policy Officer, Scottish Council of Social Service, 1979-82; Senior Research Officer (Social Work), Lothian Regional Council, 1982-84. Founder Member, Past Chairman, Scottish Education and Action for Development. Publications: Cold as Charity, 1980; The Form of Ideology (Contributor), 1981; Scotland: The Real Divide, 1983. Recreations: good films; bad television; reading about France; thinking about France; eating in France; telling other people about France. Address: (h.) 108 Newhaven Road, Edinburgh, EH6 4BR; T.-031-553 1965.

Grimmond, Iain William, BAcc (Hons), CA. Treasurer, Erskine Hospital for Disabled Ex-Servicemen, since 1981; b. 8.8.55, Girvan; m., Marjory Anne Gordon Chisholm; 1 s.; 1 d. Educ. Hutchesons' Boys Grammar School; Glasgow University. Trainee CA, Ernst & Whinney, Glasgow, 1976-79; Assistant Treasurer, Erskine Hospital, 1979-81. Elder, Giffnock South Parish Church; Honorary Auditor, Paisley Art Institute. Recreations: golf; badminton; reading. Address: (h.) 9 Wemyss Avenue, Crookfur, Newton Mearns, Glasgow, G77 6AR; T.-041-639 4894.

Grimond, Baron (Joseph Grimond), TD, PC. Life Peer; Leader, Parliamentary Liberal Party, 1956-67; Chancellor, University of Kent at Canterbury, since 1970; b. 29.7.13; m., Hon. Laura Miranda (see Lady Laura Miranda Grimond); 2 s.; 1 d.; 1 s. deceased. Educ. Eton; Balliol College, Oxford. Called to the Bar, Middle Temple, 1937; Fife and Forfar Yeomanry and Staff 53 Division (Major), Second World War; Director of Personnel, European Office, UNRRA, 1945-47; Secretary, National Trust for Scotland, 1947-49; MP (Liberal), Orkney and Shetland, 1950-83; Rector: Edinburgh University, 1960-63, Aberdeen University, 1969-72; Hon. LLD: Edinburgh, 1960, Aberdeen, 1972, Birmingham, 1974, Buckingham, 1983; Hon. DCL, Kent, 1970; DUniv, Stirling, 1984.

Grimond, Lady Laura Miranda. President, Women's Liberal Federation, 1984-86; Honorary Sheriff, Kirkwall, since 1977; Member, Board of Trustees, National Museum of Antiquities of Scotland, 1972-85; Member, Ancient Monuments Board of Scotland, since 1980; b. 13.10.18, London; m., Rt. Hon Lord Grimond of Firth (qv); 2 s.; 1 s. (deceased); 1 d. Educ. privately; Schwarzwald Gymnasium, Vienna; College Sevigne, Paris. Magistrate, Richmond, Surrey, 1955-59; fought West Aberdeenshire as Liberal, 1970; Member, Orkney Islands Council, 1974-81 (Chairman: Housing Committee, 1974-76, Services Committee, 1978-80); first Chairman, Orkney Heritage Society. Address: (h.) The Old Manse of Firth, Kirkwall, Orkney.

Grinyer, Professor John Raymond, MSc, FCA. Professor of Accountancy and Business Finance, Dundee University, since 1976 (Head, Department of Accountancy and Business Finance, since 1976, Dean, Faculty of Law, 1984-85); b. 3.3.35, London; m., Shirley Florence Marshall; 1 s.; 2 d. Educ. Central Park Secondary Modern School, London; London School of Economics. London Electricity Board, 1950-53; National Service, RAMC, 1953-55; Halifax Building Society, 1955-56; Martin Redhead & Co., Accountants, 1956-60; Hope Agar & Co., Chartered Accountants, 1960-62; Kemp Chatteris & Co., Chartered Accountants, 1962-63; Lecturer, Harlow Technical College, 1963-66; City of London Polytechnic, 1966-71; Cranfield School of Management, 1971-76; Chairman, British Accounting Association, 1980-81, and Scottish Representative, since 1984. Recreations: golf; dinghy sailing; Member, Royal Tay Yacht Club. Address: (b.) The University, Dundee, DD1 4HN; T.-Dundee 23181, Ext. 4192.

Grinyer, Professor Peter Hugh, MA (Oxon), PhD. Esmee Fairbairn Professor and Chairman, Department of Management, St. Andrews University, since 1979 (Vice-Principal of the University, 1985-87, Acting Principal, 1986); b. 3.3.35, London; m., Sylvia Joyce Boraston; 2 s. Educ. Balliol College, Oxford; London School of Economics. Senior Managerial Trainee, Unilever Ltd., 1957-59; Personal Assistant to Managing Director, E.R. Holloway Ltd., 1959-61; Lecturer and Senior Lecturer, Hendon College of Technology, 1961-64; Lecturer, The City University, London, 1965-69; The City University Business School: Senior Lecturer and Co-ordinator of Research, 1969-72, Reader, 1972-74, Professor of Business Strategy, 1974-79. Member, Sub-Committee on Management and Business Studies, University Grants Committee, 1979-85; Director, Glenrothes Enterprise Trust, 1983-86; Consultant to NEDO on Sharpbenders Project, 1984-86; Non-Executive Director: John Brown plc, 1984-86, Don Bros. Buist plc (now Don and Low (Holdings) Ltd.) since 1985, Ellis and Goldstein plc, since 1987. Recreations: mountain walking; golf; listening to music. Address: (b.) Department of Management, St. Andrews University, St. Salvator's College, St. Andrews, Fife, KY16 9AL; T.-0334 76161, Ext. 8102.

Groat, John Malcolm Freswick, MBE, JP, DL. Company Director: J.M.F. Groat & Sons Ltd., Orkney Seaport Supplies Ltd.; Member, Orkney Health Board, since 1979; Member, Orkney Islands Council Pilotage Committee; Postmaster, Longhope, Orkney, since 1964; Secretary, Longhope Lifeboat, since 1962; b. 9.9.23, Longhope, Orkney; m., Edna Mary Yule. War service: joined RAFVR as Air Crew Cadet, 1943; operational service with No. 576 and No. 150 Lancaster Squadrons No. 5 Group, Bomber Command, RAF, until 1945, then in India and as Officer i/c transport, Air Command South East Asia, Changi, Singapore, until 1947; Clerk, Hoy and Walls District Council, 1953-74; Clerk, School Management Committee, Walls and Flotta, 1953-74; Registrar of Births etc., Hoy and Walls, 1953-74; Provincial Grand Master, Orkney and Zetland, 1979-84; Trustee, Longhope Lifeboat Disaster Fund, since 1969; Agent, Shipwrecked Mariners Society; Secretary, Longhope British Legion, 1948-53; Secretary, Longhope Sailing Club, 1950-60; Director, Orkney Islands Shipping Co., 1974-87; Member, Coastguard Lifesaving Company, Longhope, 1947-61; Founder Member, Orkney Flying Club, 1949; Secretary/Treasurer, Walls and Hoy Agricultural Society, 1950-60; R.W. Master, Lodge St. Colm No. 1022, 1964-69. Address: (h.) Moasound, Longhope, Orkney; T.-241.

Groom, Rev. Colin John, MA. Member, Fife Regional Council, since 1982; Secretary, West Fife Local Health Council, since 1986; b. 29.1.34, Harrow; m., Eileen; 1 s.; 1 d. Educ. Harrow County Grammar School; Wesley House, Cambridge University; New College, Edinburgh University. Methodist Minister, Shropshire, 1960-67; Methodist Minister and Industrial Chaplain, Leeds, 1967-70; Minister, Cardenden Parish Church, 1972-82; Chairman, Civil Defence Nuclear Free Zone Sub-Committee and Vice-Chairman, Voluntary Services Sub-Committee, Fife Regional Council; Co-Chairman, Railway Development Society (Scotland), 1983-84; Member, Scottish Committee, Christian Socialist Movement. Recreations: hill-walking; cross country skiing. Address: (h.) 28 Woodend Road, Cardenden, Fife, KY5 ONE; T.-0592 720432.

Grossart, Angus McFarlane McLeod, LLD, MA, CA. Advocate; Merchant Banker; Chairman of the Trustees, National Galleries of Scotland, since 1988; Director: Hewden Stuart plc, since 1988, Alexander and Alexander, New York, since 1984, American Trust PLC, since 1973, Edinburgh Fund Managers PLC, since 1983 (Chairman), Noble Grossart Limited, since 1969, The Royal Bank of Scotland plc, since 1982, The Scottish Investment Trust PLC, since 1973 (Chairman); b. 6.4.37, Glasgow; m., Gay Kerr Dodd; 1 d. Educ. Glasgow Academy; Glasgow University. CA apprentice, Thomson McLintock, 1958-62; Advocate, Scottish Bar, 1962-69; Managing Director, Noble Grossart Ltd., since 1969. Former Editor, British Tax Encyclopaedia and British Tax Review. Recreations: golf; restoring castle in Fife. Address: (b.) 48 Queen Street, Edinburgh, EH2 3NR; T.-031-226 7011.

Grosset, Alan George, MA, LLB, WS, NP. Partner, Alex. Morison & Co., WS; b. 18.1.42, Edinburgh; m., Gloria; 1 s.; 1 d. Educ. Royal High School, Edinburgh; Edinburgh University. Law Society of Scotland "Troubleshooter" from inception of scheme, until 1987; President, Scottish Lawn Tennis Association, 1983-84; Council Member, Lawn Tennis Association, since 1980; first Chairman, Scottish Sports Association, since 1984; Member, Scottish Sports Council, since 1984. Recreations: golf; tennis; squash; computers and the law. Address: (b.) 33 Queen Street, Edinburgh; T.-031-226 6541.

Groves, C. Arthur, JP. Member, Borders Regional Council, since 1986; Chairman, Justices Committee, Ettrick and Lauderdale, since 1984; Chairman, General Inland Revenue Commissioners, since 1983; b. 28.11.24, London. Educ. Raine's Foundation, London. Selkirk Town Council, 1961-75 (Hon. Treasurer); former Selkirk County Councillor (Chairman, Finance Committee). Recreation: equestrian activities. Address: (h.) 24 Hillview Crescent, Selkirk, TD7 4AZ; T.-0750 21126.

Grove-White, Ion Greer, MA (Cantab), MB, BChir, FFA RCS(Eng). Consultant Anaesthetist, Angus Hospitals and Dundee Teaching Hospitals, since 1973; b. 5.7.39, London; m., Patricia Sheila Forbes Annand; 3 s.; 1 d. Educ. Rugby School; St. John's College, Cambridge; London Hospital Medical College. House Officer, The London Hospital, also Aberdeen City Hospitals; Registrar and Senior Registrar, Aberdeen Hospitals. Chairman, Montrose District Scout Association; Member, Scottish American Community Relations Committee; Member, Scottish Council, BMA; Past Chairman, Angus Division, BMA; Past President, North East of Scotland Society of Anaesthetists. Recreation: hill-walking. Address: (h.) White House, Hillside, Montrose, Angus, DD10 9HZ; T.-067483 466.

Guild, Ivor Reginald, CBE, MA, LLB, WS. Partner, Shepherd & Wedderburn, WS, since 1950; Procurator Fiscal to the Lyon Court; b. 2.4.24, Dundee. Educ. Cargilfield; Rugby; New College, Oxford; Edinburgh University. Chairman: First Scottish American Trust PLC, Northern American Trust PLC, Edinburgh Investment Trust PLC; Director: Fleming Universal Trust PLC, Fulcrum Investment Trust. Editor, Scottish Genealogist; Bailie, Abbey Court of Holyroodhouse; Trustee, Edinburgh University; Secretary and Treasurer, Stair Society. Recreations: golf; genealogy. Address: (b.) 16 Charlotte Square, Edinburgh, EH2 4YS; T.-031-225 8585.

Guild, Stuart Alexander, TD, BL, NP. Writer to the Signet, since 1950; Senior Partner, Guild and Guild WS; b. 25.1.24, Edinburgh; m., Fiona Catherine MacCulloch; 1 s.; 2 d. Educ. Edinburgh Academy; George Watson's College, Edinburgh; Queen's University, Belfast; Edinburgh University. Royal Artillery, 1942-47; Territorial Army (RA), 1947-65; County Cadet Commandant, Lothian Bn., ACF, 1967-69; Honorary Treasurer and Shooting Convener, Army Cadet Force Association (Scotland); Council Member, Army Cadet Force Association; Member, Lowland TA & VR Association; Member, Royal Artillery Council of Scotland; Chairman, Scottish Smallbore Rifle Association; President, Lothian & Peebles Home Guard Rifle Association; Vice-Chairman, Lothian Smallbore Shooting Association; Governor, Melville College Trust; Chairman, Sandilands Memorial Trust; Assistant, The Company of Merchants of the City of Edinburgh, 1972-75. Recreations: golf; target shooting; photography. Address: (b.) 5 Rutland Square, Edinburgh; T.-031-229 5394.

Gunn, Alexander Anton, MB, ChB, CHM, FRCSEdin. Consultant Surgeon, Bangour General Hospital, since 1964; b. 25.2.28, Edinburgh; m., Dorothy Robinson; 1 s.; 3 d. Educ. Edinburgh Academy; Edinburgh University. Council Member: Royal College of Surgeons, Edinburgh, Scottish Council for Postgraduate Medical Education,

British Journal of Surgery; Member, Health Service Research Committee (Scotland); National Panel, NHS Scotland; Examiner: Royal College of Surgeons, Edinburgh, Edinburgh University. Recreations: golf; fishing; sketching; gardening. Address: (h.) 4 Corrennie Drive, Edinburgh, EH10 6EQ; T.-031-447 1339.

Gunn, Bunty Moffat, OBE (1981), JP, DSCHE. Chairman, Lanarkshire Health Board, since 1981; b., 4.9.23, Perth; m., Hugh McVane Houston Gunn; 3 s.; 1 d. Educ. Grange School for Girls; Grangemouth High School. Member: Lanark County Council, 1970-73, Strathclyde Regional Council, 1973-82; Chairman, Scottish Council for Health Education, 1974-80; Member, Lanarkshire Health Board, since 1973; Vice-President, Royal British Legion, CS and W Branch, 1978; Member, CSA Management Committee, since 1985. Recreations: golf; theatre; light classical music; reading. Address: (h.) 198 Dukes Road, Burnside, Rutherglen, G73 5AA.

Gunn, James Forsyth Grimmond, BSc, CEng, FICE, FIStructE, ACIArb, MConsE. Chairman, Blyth & Blyth Group, since 1987; Director, Blyth & Blyth Associates, since 1976; b. 5.8.36, Edinburgh; m., Brenda; 1 s.; 1 d. Educ. George Watson's Boys' College; Edinburgh University. Construction Engineer, Bovis, London and Manchester, 1960-61; joined Blyth & Blyth, 1962; Manager, Belfast Office, 1964-70; Associate, Edinburgh Office, 1970; Partner/Director, Edinburgh, 1976. Member, Scottish Council, CBI. Recreations: golf; fishing; hill-walking; music. Address: (h.) 8A Glencairn Crescent, Edinburgh, EH12 5BS; T.-031-226 6975.

Gunn, Professor Lewis Arthur, MA. Professor of Administration, Strathclyde Business School, Strathclyde University, since 1972; b. 10.4.35, Aberdeen; m., May Florence Findlay; 2 d. Educ. Robert Gordon's College, Aberdeen; Aberdeen University. English-Speaking Union Teaching Assistant, Cornell University, 1957-59; Lecturer in Government, Manchester University, 1959-66; Senior Lecturer in Politics, Glasgow University, 1966-72; Civil Service Professor of Administration, Civil Service College, 1974-79. Publications: Policy Analysis for the Real World (Co-author), 1985. Address: (b.) Strathclyde Business School, Strathclyde University, Glasgow, G4 0GE; T.-041-552 4400.

Gunn, Marion Ballantyne, MA (Hons), BA. Head of Roads and Transport, Division I, Scottish Development Department, since 1987; b. 31.10.47, Glasgow; m., Donald Hugh Gunn. Educ. Jordanhill College School; Dumfries Academy; Edinburgh University; Open University. Management Trainee, Lewis's, Bristol, 1969-70; various posts, SED and SDD, since 1970; Research Fellow, Glasgow University, 1983-84. Recreations: Scottish country dancing; gardening; squash. Address: (h.) 32 Warriston Avenue, Edinburgh, EH3 5NB; T.-031-552 4476.

Gunstone, Professor Frank Denby, BSc, PhD, DSc, FRSC, FRSE, CChem. Professor of Chemistry, St. Andrews University, since 1971; b. 27.10.23, Chadderton; m., Eleanor Eineen Hill; 2 s.; 1 d. Educ. Oldham Hulme Grammar School; Holt High School, Liverpool; Liverpool University. Lecturer, Glasgow University, 1946-54; St. Andrews University: Lecturer, 1954-59, Senior Lecturer, 1959-65, Reader, 1965-71. Lipid Award, American Oil Chemists' Society, 1973; Hildith Lecturer, 1975; Kaufmann Lecturer, 1976. Address: (h.) Rumgally House, Cupar, Fife, KY15 5SY; T.-0334 53613.

Guthrie, James King, BSc, CEng, MICE. Director, Scotland Tarmac Construction Ltd.; b. 22.12.29, Glasgow; m., Katherine; 1 s.; 4 d. Educ. Jordanhill College School; Glasgow University. National Service, Royal Engineers, 1955-57 (2nd Lt.); Senior Engineer, G. Wimpey Ltd., 1957-64; Project Manager, A.M. Carmichael Ltd., 1964-70; Area Manager/Director, Tarmac Construction Ltd., 1970-80; Director, Aberdeen Construction Group PLC, 1981-86. Recreations: golf; sailing; music. Address (h.) Forest Lodge, Dollar, FK14 7LT; T.-02594 2600.

H

Haddow, Rev. Angus Halley, BSc. Minister, Garthdee Parish Church, Aberdeen, since 1981; Clerk, Aberdeen Presbytery, since 1981; b. 27.11.32, Wishaw; m., Marjory Walsh; 1 s.; 2 d. Educ. Wishaw High School; Glasgow University and Trinity College. Science Teacher, Greenfield Secondary School, 1957-60; Assistant Minister, Newarthill, 1962-63; Minister: Largo St. David's Parish Church, 1963-71, Trinity Parish Church, Aberdeen, 1971-81. Recreations: reading; parapsychology; hill-walking; music. Address: 27 Ramsay Gardens, Aberdeen, AB1 7AE; T.-Aberdeen 317452.

Hadley, Geoffrey, BSc (Hons), PhD. Convener, Grampian Regional Council, since 1986; Honorary Senior Lecturer, Aberdeen University, since 1985; Consultant Microbiologist, since 1985; b. 7.2.32, Stoke-on-Trent; m., Barbara Jean Ross; 3 d. by pr. m. Educ. Longton High School; Birmingham University. Research Fellow, Nottingham University, 1956-58; Lecturer, Glasgow University, 1958-60; Lecturer, then Senior Lecturer, Aberdeen University, 1960-85; seconded to University of Malaya, 1967-68; Member, Aberdeen County Council, 1973-75, Grampian Regional Council, since 1974; Vice-President, British Mycological Society, 1987. Recreations: classical music; home brewing and wine-making; cricket; cycling; DIY. Address: (b.) Woodhill House, Westburn Road, Aberdeen, AB9 2LU; (h.) 74 Don Street, Aberdeen, AB2 1UU; T.-0224 682222.

Haggart, Rt. Rev. Alastair Iain Macdonald, MA, LLD. Retired Bishop; b. 10.10.15, Glasgow; m., Mary Scholes; 2 d. Educ. Edinburgh Theological College; Durham University. Curate, St. Mary's Cathedral, Glasgow; Curate, St. Mary's, Hendon,

London; Precentor, St. Ninian's Cathedral, Perth; Rector, St. Oswald's, King's Park, Glasgow; Synod Clerk, Diocese of Glasgow; Provost, St. Paul's Cathedral, Dundee; Principal, Theological College; Bishop of Edinburgh; Primus, Scottish Episcopal Church. Recreations: walking; reading; music; asking people questions. Address: (h.) 19 Eglinton Crescent, Edinburgh, EH12 5BY; T.-031-337 8948.

Haggart, David Ballantine, JP, MA. Head of Careers Service, Aberdeen University, since 1963; b. 15.3.34, Dundee; m., Gwendolen Hall; 3 s. Educ. Aberdeen Grammar School; Aberdeen University. National Service, Band of Royal Corps of Signals, 1956-58; Teacher, Perth and Kinross County Council, 1958-59; Youth Employment Officer, City of Aberdeen, 1959-63; Member, Justices' Committee, Aberdeen, since 1976; Chairman, Ferryhill Community Council, 1976-82; Housing Management Convener, Castlehill Housing Association, since 1984; Chairman, Aberdeen and NE Scotland Music Festival, 1982-84; Writer and Producer, educational television programmes, including The Interview (Royal Television Society award); regular radio broadcasts, mainly on religious programmes; Presenter, Sunday Best, Northsound Radio, since 1981. Recreations: songwriting; motoring; local history. Address: (h.) 24 Polmuir Road, Aberdeen, AB1 2SY; T.-0224 584176.

Haggart, Mary Elizabeth, OBE. Chairman, Scottish Board of Nursing Midwifery and Health Visiting, 1980-83; b. 8.4.24, Leicester; m., Rt. Rev. A.I.M. Haggart (qv). Educ. Wyggeston Grammar School for Girls, Leicester; Leicester Royal Infirmary and Children's Hospital. Leicester Royal Infirmary: Staff Nurse, 1947-48, Night Sister, 1948-50, Ward Sister, 1950-56, Night Superintendent, 1956-58, Assistant Matron, 1958-61; Assistant Matron, Brook General Hospital, London, 1962-64; Matron, Dundee Royal Infirmary and Matron Designate, Ninewells Hospital, Dundee, 1964-68; Chief Nursing Officer, Board of Managements, Dundee General Hospitals and Ninewells Hospital, 1968-73; Chief Area Nursing Officer, Tayside Health Board, 1974-82; President, Scottish Association of Nurse Administrators, 1972-77; Member, Scottish Board, Royal College of Nursing, 1965-70; Member, General Nursing Council for Scotland, 1965-70 and 1978-82; Member, Standing Nursing and Midwifery Committee, 1971-74 (Vice Chairman, 1973-74); Member, Action on Smoking and Health Scotland, 1978-82 (Chairman, Working Party, Smoking and Nurses); Governor, Dundee College of Technology, 1978-82; Honorary Lecturer, Department of Community Medicine, Dundee University and Medical School, 1980-82; Member, Management Committee, Carstairs State Hospital, 1982; Member, United Kingdom Central Council for Nursing Midwifery and Health Visiting, 1980-82; Member, Scottish Hospital Endowments Research Trust, since 1986. Recreations: walking; music; travel. Address: (h.) 19 Eglinton Crescent, Edinburgh, EH12 5RY; T.-031-337 8948.

Haggarty, Rev. William Gordon, DipEd, LTh, CPS. Minister, North Church of St. Andrew, Aberdeen, since 1976; b. 27.4.41, Glasgow; m., Wendy H. Nicoll; 1 d. Educ. High School of Glasgow; Glasgow University; Edinburgh University; New College, Edinburgh. Constable, City of Glasgow Police (Gorbals Division and Road Patrol), 1962-65; divinity course, New College, 1966-69; Assistant, Dunblane Cathedral, 1970-71; Minister, Glasgow Chryston, 1971-76. Honorary Vice-President, Aberdeen Bn., Boys Brigade; Chaplain: Aberdeen Lifeboat; Aberdeen, Strathspey and Reel Society; Grampian Fire Brigade; HM Theatre, Aberdeen; Grampian Police. Recreations: badminton; walking; family. Address: The Manse, 51 Osborne Place, Aberdeen, AB2 4BX; T.-0224 646429.

Haggarty, William McLaughlan, TD, BL. Solicitor, since 1950; Senior Partner, Mathie Morton Black & Buchanan, Ayr; Honorary Sheriff, South Strathclyde, Dumfries and Galloway; b. 22.2.26, Glasgow; m., Olive Dorothy Mary Speirs; 1 s.; 1 d. Educ. High School of Glasgow; Glasgow University. War Service, Merchant Navy, 1943-47; Chairman, National Insurance Tribunal, North and South Ayrshire, since 1963; Lt. Col. Commanding 264 (Scottish) Regiment, Royal Corps of Transport (TA), 1966; Dean, Ayr Faculty of Solicitors, 1982; Governor, Craigie College of Education, Ayr, 1983; Director, Ayrshire Labels Ltd. Recreations: golf; travel; gardening. Address: (b.) 4 Alloway Place, Ayr; T.-0292 263549.

Hagman, Eric Martin, CA. Managing Partner, Arthur Andersen & Co., Scotland, since 1980; Chairman, Royal Scottish Automobile Club; Chairman, ICAS Audit Practice Committee; Member, ICAS Audit Accountancy Working Party; Member, Council, CBI Scotland; Member, Council, Royal Glasgow Institute of the Fine Arts; Treasurer, Strathclyde Police Dependants Trust; b. 9.7.46, Glasgow; m., Valerie; 4 s.; 1 d. Educ. Kelvinside Academy. Recreations: sailing; skiing; tennis; squash; wine. Address: (h.) Eriska, 49 Sutherland Avenue, Pollokshields, Glasgow; T.-041-427 0471.

Hague, Clifford Bertram, MA, DipTP, MRTPI. Senior Lecturer, Heriot-Watt University/Edinburgh College of Art, since 1973; Course Tutor, Open University, since 1974; b. 22.8.44, Manchester; m., Irene; 1 s.; 3 d. Educ. North Manchester Grammar School; Magdalene College, Cambridge; Manchester University. Planning Assistant, Glasgow Corporation Planning Department, 1968-69; Lecturer, Department of Town and Country Planning, Heriot-Watt University/Edinburgh College of Art, 1969-73; Council Member, Royal Town Planning Institute (Past Chairman, Scottish Branch). Publication: The Development of Planning Thought: A Critical Perspective, 1984. Recreation: cricket. Address: (b.) Department of Town and Country Planning, Edinburgh College of Art, Edinburgh, EH3 9DF; T.-031-229 9311.

Haig of Bemersyde, The Earl (George Alexander Eugene Douglas), OBE, DL, MA, ARSA, KStJ. Painter; b. 15.3.18, London; 1 s.; 2 d. Educ. Cargilfield; Stowe School; Christ Church, Oxford. 2nd Lt., Royal Scots Greys, 1938; retired on account of disability, 1951 (rank of Captain); attended Camberwell School of Arts and Crafts; paintings in many public and private collections; served Second World War; taken prisoner, 1942;

Member, Royal Fine Art Commission for Scotland, 1958-61; Chairman, SE South East Scotland Disablement Advisory Committee, 1960-73; Trustee, Scottish National War Memorial, since 1961 (present Chairman); Trustee, National Galleries of Scotland, 1962-72; Member, Scottish Arts Council, 1968-74; Past Chairman, Royal British Legion Scotland; President, Earl Haig Fund Scotland/Royal British Legion Scotland, 1980-86; President, Scottish Branch, Officers Association; President, Scottish Craft Centre, 1952-73; Vice President, Scottish National Institution for War Blinded and of Royal Blind Asylum, since 1960. Recreations: fishing; shooting. Address: (h.) Bemersyde, Melrose, TD6 9DP; T.-08352 2762.

Haksar, Vinit, BA, MA, DPhil. Reader in Philosophy, Edinburgh University, since 1980; b. 4.9.37, Vienna; 2 s.; 1 d. Educ. Doon School; Oxford University. St. Andrews University: Assistant in Philosophy, 1962-64, Lecturer, 1964-69; Lecturer in Philosophy, Edinburgh University, 1969-80. Publications: Equality, Liberty and Perfectionism, 1979; Civil Disobedience, Threats and Offers, 1986. Recreation: tennis. Address: (h.) 63 Findhorn Place, Edinburgh; T.-031-667 3474.

Haldane, Johnston Douglas, MB, FRCPEdin, FRCPsych, DPM. Psychotherapist and Consultant; b. 13.3.26, Annan; m., Kathleen McKirdy; 3 s. Educ. Lockerbie Academy; Dumbarton Academy; Dumfries Academy; Edinburgh University. Consultant Psychiatrist, Department of Child and Family Psychiatry, Stratheden Hospital, Cupar; Senior Lecturer, Department of Mental Health, Aberdeen University. Recreations: gardening; the arts. Address: (h.) Tarlogie, 54 Hepburn Gardens, St. Andrews, Fife, KY16 9DG.

Halford-MacLeod, Lt.-Col. Aubrey Philip Lydiat, MA (Hons). Army Officer, Black Watch (RHR), since 1962; Chief of Staff, Scottish Division, The Castle, Edinburgh, since 1988; b. 28.4.42, Bagdad; m., Alison Fiona Brown; 2 s.; 1 d. Educ. Winchester College; Magdalen College, Oxford. Entry into Sandhurst, 1961; commissioned into Black Watch as 2nd Lt., 1962; Lt., 1964; Captain, 1968; Adjutant, then Training Major, 1/51 Highland, Perth, 1970-74; Major, 1975; Lt.-Col., 1985; appointed Commanding Officer, Glasgow and Strathclyde Universities OTC. Recreations: walking the dogs; shooting; fishing; opera; model soldiers; curling. Address: (h.) 291 Colinton Road, Edinburgh, EH13 0PR; T.-031-441 5809.

Halford-MacLeod, Aubrey Seymour, CMG, CVO, MA (Oxon); b. 15.12.14, Birmingham; m., Giovanna M. Durst; 3 s.; 1 d. Educ. King Edward School, Birmingham, and abroad; Magdalen College, Oxford. HM Diplomatic Service, Third Secretary, Foreign Office, 1937; Bagdad, 1939; Office of Minister of State, Algiers, 1943; reopened Embassy, Rome, 1944; Secretary, Advisory Council Italy, and Political Adviser to Allied Control Commission, 1943-46; PPS to Permanent Under Secretary, Foreign Office, 1946-49; Deputy Secretary-General, Council of Europe, 1949-52; Tokyo, 1953-55; Libya, 1955-57; Kuwait, 1957-59; Munich, 1959-65; Ambassador to Iceland, 1965-70. Director, Scottish Opera, 1972-77; President, Scottish Society for Northern Studies, 1972-75; Vice-President, Clan MacLeod Society of Scotland; Adviser, Scottish Council (Development and Industry), 1970-77. Recreations: fishing; ornithology. Address: (h.) Mulag House, North Harris, Western Isles, PA85 3AB; T.-Harris 2054.

Halford-MacLeod, Ruairidh, FSA Scot, FSTS. President, travel tour company, since 1986; b. 7.2.44, Alexandria, Egypt; m., Anne S. McDougall; 1 s.; 1 d. Educ. Winchester College; St. Andrews University. Short-service commission, Queen's Own Highlanders (Seaforth and Camerons), 1969-72; Secretary, Harris Craft Guild, 1972-76; Secretary, Harris Council of Social Service, 1973-76; Community Worker, Scottish Council of Voluntary Organisations, 1976-86; Secretary, Rural Forum, 1984-86; Editor, Clan MacLeod Magazine, 1974-82; Vice President, Clan MacLeod Society of Scotland, since 1984; Vice-Chairman, Scottish Tartans Society, since 1987; Associate Professor of Scottish History, North Idaho College, Idaho, since 1980. Recreations: curling; writing. Address: (h.) 49 Upper Greens, Auchtermuchty, Fife, KY14 7BX; T.-0337 28631.

Hall, Professor Denis R., BSc, MPhil, PhD, FInstP, FIEE, CEng. Professor of Optoelectronics, Heriot-Watt University, since 1986; b. 1.8.42; m.; 1 s.; 1 d. Educ. Manchester University; London University; Case Western Reserve University. NRC Postdoctoral Fellow, NASA Goddard Space Flight Center, 1971-72; Senior Research Scientist, AVCO Everett Research Laboratory, Boston, 1972-74; Principal Scientific Officer, Royal Signal and Radar Establishment, 1974-79; Senior Lecturer/Reader, Department of Applied Physics, Hull University, 1979-86. Address: (b.) Heriot-Watt University, Chambers Street, Edinburgh.

Hall, Samuel James, BL, NP, WS. Solicitor, since 1951; Partner, Robson, McLean, Paterson, WS, since 1957; Legal Assessor, Professional Conduct Committee, United Kingdom Central Council for Nursing, Midwifery and Health Visiting; Solicitor to the Ministry of Defence (Navy Department) in Scotland; b. 29.5.30, Edinburgh; m., Olive Douglas Kerr; 2 s.; 1 d. Educ. Daniel Stewart's College, Edinburgh; Edinburgh University. Officer, Royal Army Service Corps, until 1953. Recreations: golf; good food. Address: (h.) 2 Wardie Road, Edinburgh; T.-031-552 1836.

Hall, Simon Robert Dawson, MA. Warden, Glenalmond College, since 1987; b. 24.4.38, London; m., Jennifer Harverson; 2 s. Educ. Tonbridge School; University College, Oxford. 2nd Lt., 7th Royal Tank Regiment, 1956-58; Assistant Master, Gordonstoun School, 1961-65; Joint Headmaster, Dunrobin School, 1965-68; Haileybury: Assistant Master, 1969-79, Senior Modern Languages Master, 1970-76, Housemaster, Lawrence, 1972-79, Second Master, 1976-79; Headmaster, Milton Abbey School, 1979-87. 21st SAS Regt. (TA), 1958-61; Intelligence Corps (V), 1968-71; FRSA, 1983. Recreations: reading; music; motoring; sailing; hill-walking. Address: (h.) The Warden's House, Glenalmond College, Glenalmond, Perth, PH1 3RY; T.-Glenalmond 205.

Hall, William, DFC, FRICS. Member, Lands Tribunal for Scotland, since 1971; Member, Lands Tribunal for England and Wales, since 1979; Honorary Sheriff, Paisley, since 1974; b. 25.7.19, Paisley; m., Margaret Semple Gibson; 1 s.; 3 d. Educ. Paisley Grammar School. Pilot, RAF, 1939-45 (Despatches); Senior Partner, R. & W. Hall, Chartered Surveyors, Paisley, 1949-79; Chairman, Royal Institution of Chartered Surveyors in Scotland, 1971; Member, Valuation Advisory Council, 1970-80; Executive Member, Erskine Hospital, since 1976. Recreation: golf. Address: (h.) Windyridge, Brediland Road, Paisley, PA2 9HF; T.-Brediland 3614.

Hall, William Andrew McDonald, MA (Hons). Head Teacher, Dalry Secondary School, Kirkcudbrightshire, since 1973; b. 12.2.37, Airdrie; m., Catherine R.; 1 s.; 2 d. Educ. Airdrie Academy; Glasgow University. Teacher of History, Hamilton Academy, 1962-66; Principal Teacher of History, Mackie Academy, Stonehaven, 1966-73. Recreations: reading; golf; Airdrieonians Football Club; cinema. Address: (b.) Dalry Secondary School, St. John's Town of Dalry, Kirkcudbrightshire, DG7 3UU; T.-064 43 259.

Hall, (William) Douglas, OBE (1985), BA, FMA. Keeper, Scottish National Gallery of Modern Art, 1961-86; b. 9.10.26, London; m., 1, Helen Elizabeth Ellis (m. diss.); 1 s.; 1 d.; 2, Matilda Mary Mitchell. Educ. University College School, Hampstead; University College and Courtauld Institute of Art, London University, 1948-52. Intelligence Corps, 1945-48 (Middle East); Manchester City Art Galleries: Keeper, Rutherston Collection, 1953-58, Keeper, City Art Gallery, 1958-59, Deputy Director, 1959-61; Member, Edinburgh International Festival Council (Executive Committee); Governor, Glasgow School of Art. Recreations: music; travel; gardening; wall-building. Address: (h.) 4 Northumberland Place, Edinburgh, EH3 6LQ; T.-031-557 3393; Laidlaws, Spottiswood, Gordon, Berwickshire, TD3 6NQ; T.-05784 277.

Halliburton, Ian Scott. Director, James Finlay Financial Services Ltd., since 1981; b. 30.1.43, Huddersfield; m., Anne Whitaker; 1 s.; 1 d. Educ. Royal High School, Edinburgh; Royal Scottish Academy of Music and Drama (Diploma). General banking training, Royal Bank of Scotland, 1961-63; RSAMD, 1963-66; Jordanhill College of Education (teaching of speech and drama), 1966-67; professional actor, 1967-70; Sales Consultant, Imperial Life Assurance Co. of Canada, 1970-71; insurance broking, Towry Law & Co. (Scotland) Ltd., 1971-78, James Finlay Financial Services Ltd., since 1978. Vice-Chairman, Third Eye Centre (Glasgow) Ltd.; Chairman, Platform Music Societies Ltd.; Member, Scottish Arts Council. Recreations: hill-walking; listening to music; supporting the arts. Address: 259 Garrioch Road, Glasgow, G20 8QZ; T.-041-946 5426.

Halliday, Clive Benson, MIFireE. Firemaster, Strathclyde Regional Council, since 1984; b. 27.1.35, Prestatyn, North Wales; m., Margaret Morwena; 1 s.; 1 d. Fireman to Divisional Officer, Manchester Fire Brigade, 1960-74; Senior Divisional Officer, Greater Manchester Fire Service, 1974-78; Assistant/Deputy Chief Fire Officer, Staffordshire Fire Brigade, 1978-82; Chief Fire Officer, Northern Ireland Fire Brigade, 1982-84. Recreations: choral singing; fishing. Address: (b.) Fire Brigade Headquarters, Bothwell Road, Hamilton; T.-0698 284200.

Halliday, James, MA, MLitt, JP. Chairman, Scots Independent Newspapers; Member, National Council, Scottish National Party; Principal Lecturer in History, Dundee College of Education, 1979-87; b. 27.2.27, Wemyss Bay; m., Olive Campbell; 2 s. Educ. Greenock High School; Glasgow University. Teacher: Ardeer FE Centre, 1953, Kildonan Secondary School, Coatbridge, 1954-56, Uddingston Grammar School, 1956-58, Dunfermline High School, 1958-67; Lecturer in History, Dundee College of Education, 1967-79. Chairman, Scottish National Party, 1956-60; Parliamentary candidate: Stirling and Falkirk Burghs, 1955 and 1959, West Fife, 1970. Publications: World in Transformation - America; Scotland The Separate; Story of Scotland (Co-author). Recreations: reading; folk music; football spectating. Address: (h.) 15 Castleroy Crescent, Broughty Ferry, Dundee, DD5 2LU; T.-Dundee 77179.

Halls, Michael, FREHIS, FRSH. Director of Environmental Services, Ettrick and Lauderdale District Council, since 1975; b. 6.12.39, Galashiels; m., Sheila; 1 s.; 1 d. Educ. Galashiels Academy; Heriot-Watt. Trainee Burgh Surveyor, Galashiels Town Council, 1959-63; Additional Public Health Inspector, Thame Urban District Council, 1963-64; Galashiels Town Council: Assistant Burgh Surveyor and Sanitary Inspector, 1964-68, Depute Burgh Surveyor, 1968-71, Burgh Surveyor, 1971-75. Last Honorary Secretary, Scottish Institute of Environmental Health, 1978-83; first Senior Vice-President, Royal Environmental Health Institute of Scotland. Recreation: golf; philately; wine-making/drinking; music; eating. Address: (b.) PO Box 4, Paton Street, Galashiels, TD1 3AS; T.-0896 4751.

Hamblen, Professor David Lawrence, MB, BS, PhD, FRCS, FRCSEdin, FRCSGlas. Professor of Orthopaedic Surgery, Glasgow University, since 1972; Honorary Consultant in Orthopaedic Surgery, Greater Glasgow Health Board, since 1972; Visiting Professor to National Centre for Training and Education in Prosthetics and Orthotics, Strathclyde University, since 1981; Hon. Consultant Orthopaedic Surgeon to Army in Scotland; b. 31.8.34, London; m., Gillian; 1 s.; 2 d. Educ. Roan School, Greenwich; London University. The London Hospital, 1963-66; Teaching Fellow in Orthopaedics, Harvard Medical School/Massachusetts General Hospital, 1966-67; Lecturer in Orthopaedics, Nuffield Orthopaedic Centre, Oxford, 1967-68; Senior Lecturer in Orthopaedics/Honorary Consultant, Edinburgh University/South East Regional Hospital Board, 1968-72; Member, Chief Scientist Committee, SHHD, since 1983; Member, Editorial Board, Journal of Bone and Joint Surgery, 1978-82 and since 1985; Member, Physiological Systems Board, Medical Research Council, 1983-88; Chairman, British

Orthopaedic Association Education Sub-Committee, since 1986. Recreation: golf. Address: (b.) University Department of Orthopaedic Surgery, Western Infirmary, Glasgow, G11 6NT; T.-041-339 8822.

Hamer-Hodges, David William, MS, FRCS, FRCSE. Consultant Surgeon, Western General Hospital, Edinburgh, since 1979; Honorary Senior Lecturer, Edinburgh University, since 1979; b. 17.10.43, Portsmouth; m., Gillian Landale Kelman; 3 s.; 1 d. Educ. Portsmouth Grammar School; University College London. Senior Registrar, Aberdeen Teaching Hospitals; Research Fellow, Harvard Medical School; Resident Surgical Officer, St. Mark's Hospital, London. Address: (b.) 14 Moray Place, Edinburgh; T.-031-225 4843.

Hamill, Sir Patrick, Kt (1984), QPM, OStJ. Chief Constable of Strathclyde, 1977-85; Member, General Convocation, Strathclyde University; b. 29.4.30, Clydebank; m., Nellie Gillespie; 4 s.; 1 d. Educ. St. Patrick's High School, Dumbarton. Joined Dunbartonshire Constabulary, 1950, and rose through the ranks until promoted Chief Superintendent, 1970; transferred to City of Glasgow Police, 1972; appointed Assistant Chief Constable, 1974; joined Strathclyde Police, 1975, and attended the Royal College of Defence Studies, 1976; President, Association of Chief Police Officers (Scotland), 1982-83, Honorary Secretary and Treasurer, 1983-85; Member, Board of Governors: St. Aloysius College, Glasgow, St. Andrew's College of Education, Bearsden. Recreations: walking; gardening; golf.

Hamilton, Alexander Macdonald, CBE (1979), MA, LLB. Senior Partner, McGrigor Donald, Solicitors, Glasgow, 1977-88, Joint Senior Partner, since 1988; Director, Royal Bank of Scotland, since 1978; Chairman, Scottish Committee, Scottish Council of the Scout Association, since 1986; b. 11.5.25; m., Catherine Gray; 2 s.; 1 d. Educ. Hamilton Academy; Glasgow University. RNVR, 1943-46; Law Society of Scotland: Member, Council, 1970-82, Vice-president, 1975-76, President, 1977-78; President, Glasgow Juridical Society, 1955-56; Session Clerk, Cambuslang Old Parish Church, since 1968; Vice-Chairman, Cambuslang Community Council, since 1978. Recreations: golf; sailing; swimming. Address: (h.) 30 Wellshot Drive, Cambuslang, Glasgow, G72 8BT; T.-041-641 1445.

Hamilton, 15th Duke of, and Brandon, 12th Duke of (Angus Alan Douglas Douglas-Hamilton). Premier Peer of Scotland; Hereditary Keeper of Palace of Holyroodhouse; b. 13.9.38; m., 1, Sarah Scott; 2 s.; 2 d.; 2, Jillian Robertson. Educ. Eton; Balliol College, Oxford. Flt.-Lt., RAF (retired, 1967); flying instructor, 1965; Instrument Rating Examiner, 1966; Test Pilot, Scottish Aviation, 1971-72; Chairman, Hamilton & Kinneil Estates Ltd.,1973; Member, Queen's Bodyguard for Scotland (Royal Company of Archers), since 1975; KStJ, 1975, Prior for Scotland, 1975-82; Honorary Member, Royal Scottish Pipers, 1977; Council Member, Cancer Research Campaign, 1978; Honorary Air Commodore, Maritime Headquarters Unit 2, R.Aux.AF, 1982. Address: (h.) Lennoxlove, Haddington, East Lothian.

Hamilton, Christine Jean (Gordon), JP, BSc (Agr), NDD, CDD. A Director, Royal Highland Agricultural Society of Scotland (Glasgow Region), since 1977; a Director, Royal Scottish Agricultural Benevolent Institution (Lanarkshire); b. 24.6.19, Huntly, Aberdeenshire; m., Matthew Hamilton (deceased); 2 s.; 2 d. Educ. Gordon Schools, Huntly; Aberdeen University; North of Scotland College of Agriculture; West of Scotland College of Agriculture. Address: Woolfords, Cobbinshaw, West Calder, EH55 8LJ; T.-Auchengray 224.

Hamilton, Rev. David Gentles, MA (Hons), BD (Hons). Curriculum Officer, Church of Scotland Department of Education; b. 31.10.40, Glasgow; m., Elsa Catherine Nicolson; 2 s. Educ. Woodside Senior Secondary School, Glasgow; Glasgow University. Electrical engineering design work, 1956-63; Assistant to Church of Scotland congregations of Barlanark, Merrylea, High Carntyne, 1963-71; ordained, 1971; Minister, Troon St. Meddans, 1971-78; Hastie Memorial Lectureship, Glasgow University, 1975-77; Theologian in Residence, Arkansas College and First Presbyterian Church, USA, 1976; Convener, Division on Children, Church of Scotland Department of Education, 1977-80; Convener, Youth Committee, Church of Scotland, 1978; Minister, Bearsden South Church, 1978-80; Chairman, British Council of Churches Consultative Group on Ministry among Children, 1982-86; Chairman, European Conference on Christian Education, 1986-89; Director, Church Advisorate on Special Educational Needs, since 1988; author and editor of Christian education publications, videos. Publications: Children - The Challenge to the Church; Children at the Table. Recreations: hill-walking; jazz trumpet; Mozart; gardening; spy thrillers. Address: (h.) 79 Finlay Rise, Milngavie, Glasgow.

Hamilton, Douglas P., BSc (Hons), DipEd, JP. Member, North East Fife District Council, since 1974; a Director, Byre Theatre, St. Andrews; b. 8.9.26, St. Andrews; m., Pamela J. McKane; 1 s. Educ. St. Andrews University. Management Trainee/Production Manager, Unilever, 1948-51; Teacher, 1952-58; Assistant Training Manager, UKAEA, 1958-60; Lecturer, then Head, Department of Science Mathematics, Kingsway Technical College, Dundee, 1960-84. Depute Traffic Commissioner; Member, St. Andrews Links Management Committee; Member, Endowment Committee, Madras College; Vice-Chairman, Planning Committee, North East Fife District Council. Recreations: golf; music (Church organ); gardening. Address: (h.) Craigston, 38 Craig Road, Tayport, Fife, DD6 9LE.

Hamilton, Frank D. Director (Scotland), Royal Society for the Protection of Birds, since 1972; b. 13.11.32, Edinburgh; m., Kathleen; 1 s.; 1 d. Educ. George Watson's College, Edinburgh. Various posts in industry; joined RSPB, 1958, based first in London, then at HQ, Bedfordshire; developed UK film shows, education, sales and membership; established office in Northern Ireland; returned to Scotland, 1970. Vice President, Scottish Ornithologists Club; Member, Secretary of State for Scotland's Forum on the Environment and previous Advisory Committee on Protection of Birds; Scottish Representative, International

Council for the Protection of Birds (British Section); has sat on Council of Irish Wildbird Conservancy. Recreations: bird-watching and bird surveys; walking; wine-making; tropical fish; model railways. Address: (h.) 23 Campbell Road, Longniddry, East Lothian, EH32 ONP.

Hamilton, Ian Robertson, QC (Scot), BL; b. 13.9.25, Paisley; m., Jeannette Patricia Mari Stewart; 1 s.; 1 s., 2 d. by pr. m. Educ. John Neilson School, Paisley; Allan Glen's School, Glasgow; Glasgow University; Edinburgh University. RAFVR, 1944-48; called to Scottish Bar, 1954, and to Albertan Bar, 1982; Founder, Castle Wynd Printers, Edinburgh, 1955; Advocate Depute, 1962; Director of Civil Litigation, Republic of Zambia, 1964-66; Hon. Sheriff of Lanarkshire, 1967; retired from practice to work for National Trust for Scotland and later to farm in Argyll, 1969; returned to practice, 1974; Sheriff of Glasgow and Strathkelvin, May-December, 1984; returned to practice; Founder and Chairman, Whichway Trust for young offenders; Chief Pilot, Scottish Parachute Club, 1979-80. Publications: No Stone Unturned, 1952; The Tinkers of the World, 1957 (Foyle award-winning play). Recreation: sailing. Address: (b.) Advocates' Library, Parliament House, Edinburgh, EH1 1RF.

Hamilton, Rev. Ian William Finlay, BD, LTH, ALCM, AVCM. Minister, Nairn Old Parish Church, since 1986; b. 29.11.46, Glasgow; m., Margaret McLaren Moss; 1 s.; 2 d. Educ. Victoria Drive Senior Secondary School, Glasgow; Glasgow University and Trinity College. Initially employed in banking, then in music publishing; ordained, Alloa North Parish Church, 1978. Publication: A Century of Christian Witness; several children's talks published in the Expository Times. Recreation: music (organ and piano). Address: Nairn Old Parish Church Manse, 3 Manse Road, Nairn, IV12 4RN; T.-0667 52203.

Hamilton, Loudon Pearson, CB (1987), MA (Hons). Secretary, Department of Agriculture and Fisheries for Scotland, since 1984; b. 12.1.32, Glasgow; m., Anna Mackinnon Young; 2 s. Educ. Hutchesons Grammar School, Glasgow; Glasgow University. National Service, RA, 1953-55 (2nd Lt.); Inspector of Taxes, Inland Revenue, 1956-60; Assistant Principal, Department of Agriculture and Fisheries for Scotland, 1960; Private Secretary to Parliamentary Under Secetary of State for Scotland, 1963-64; First Secretary, Agriculture, British Embassy, Copenhagen and The Hague, 1966-70; Assistant Secretary, Department of Agriculture and Fisheries for Scotland, 1973-79; Principal Establishment Officer, Scottish Office, 1979-84. Address: (b.) DAFS, Chesser House, 500 Gorgie Road, Edinburgh, EH11 3AN; T.-031-443 4020.

Hamilton, Steven Fraser, JP, BL, DPA, DMS. Town Clerk and Chief Executive, City of Glasgow District Council, since 1979; b. 10.10.31, Glasgow; m., Dorothy; 1 s.; 1 d. Educ. Victoria Drive Senior Secondary School, Glasgow; Glasgow University; Glasgow College of Technology. Began as Law Apprentice in Town Clerk's Office, Glasgow, 1948; graduated and qualified as Solicitor; appointed Legal Assistant, 2A, 1953; promoted to IA, 1957; Senior Legal Assistant, 1959; Principal Legal Assistant, 1962; Town Clerk Depute, Glasgow, 1973; Director of Administration and Legal Services, 1974. Recreations: golf; bridge; listening to music; opera; ballet. Address: (b.) City Chambers, Glasgow, G2 1DU; T.-041-227 4501.

Hamilton, William, MB, ChB, MD, FRCPGlas, FRCPEdin, DPH, DCH. Paediatrician and Paediatric Endocrinologist, Department of Child Health, Royal Hospital for Sick Children, Glasgow, since 1961; University Senior Lecturer, since 1962; b. 22.12.22, Holytown, Lanarkshire; m., Elizabeth Janet Beveridge; 2 s. Educ. Holytown Public School; Dalziel High School, Motherwell; Glasgow University. House Physician/House Surgeon posts, Glasgow, 1952-54; general practice, 1954-56; Registrar medical post, Inverness, 1957-61; Senior Registrar in Paediatrics, 1961-62. Advisor on Postgraduate and Undergraduate Education and Training, Fatah Medical School, Tripoli, Libya. Publications: Clinical Paediatric Endocrinology, 1972; Surgical Treatment of Endocrine Disease. Recreations: gardening; vintage car enthusiast. Address: (h.) 81 Woodend Drive, Glasgow, G13 1QF; T.-041-954 9961.

Hamilton, Professor (William) Allan, BSc, PhD, FIBiol, FRSE. Professor of Microbiology, Aberdeen University (Head, Department of Genetics and Microbiology); Director, Aberdeen University Research and Industrial Services (AURIS) Ltd.; Chairman, National Collections of Industrial and Marine Bacteria Ltd.; b. 4.4.36, Glasgow. Educ. Hutchesons' Boys Grammar School; Glasgow University. Postdoctoral Research Fellow: Illinois University, 1961-62, Rio de Janeiro University, 1962-63; Scientist, Unilever Research, Bedford, 1963-67; Lecturer/Senior Lecturer, Department of Biochemistry, Aberdeen University, 1967-75; Senior Lecturer/Reader, Department of Microbiology, Aberdeen University, 1975-80. Council, Society of General Microbiology, 1972-76, 1985-89. Recreations: sailing; wine; skiing; fishing. Address: (h.) 175 Queen's Road, Aberdeen, AB1 8BS; T.-0224 313434.

Hamilton-Grierson, Philip John, MA. Deputy Chairman, Highlands and Islands Development Board, since 1988; b. 10.10.32, Inveresk; m., Pleasaunce Jill Cardew; 1 s.; 2 d. Educ. Rugby School; Corpus Christi College, Oxford. Contracts Manager, Bristol Aircraft Ltd.; Economic Adviser, Joseph Lucas Industries Ltd.; Secretary to Liberal Parliamentary Party; Assistant to Managing Director, John Wallace & Sons Ltd.; Director, Gallaher Ltd. Fellow, Royal Society of Arts. Recreations: hill-walking; tennis; music. Address: (b.) 27 Bank Street, Inverness, IV1 1QR; T.-Drumchardine 387.

Hamlin, Professor Michael John, BSc, FEng, FICE, FIWEM, MASCE. Principal and Vice-Chancellor, Dundee University, since 1987; b. 11.5.30; m., Augusta; 3 s. Educ. St. John's College, Johannesburg; Bristol University; Imperial Coll., London. Consultant on water resources problems; Birmingham University: Professor, Water Engineering, 1971, Head of Department,

1980, Pro-Vice-Chancellor, 1985, Vice-Principal, 1986. Address: (b.) Dundee University, Dundee, DD1 4HN.

Hammerton, Desmond, BSc, CBiol, FIBiol, FIWEM, FBIM, FRSE. Director, Clyde River Purification Board, since 1975; Consultant, World Health Organisation, since 1977; b. 17.11.29, Wakefield, Yorkshire; m., Jean Taylor; 2 s.; 2 d. Educ. Harrow Weald County School; Birkbeck College, London University. Assistant Biologist, Metropolitan Water Board, 1953-55; Research Biologist, Bristol Waterworks, 1955-58; Principal Assistant, Lothians River Purification Board, 1958-62; Director, Hydrobiological Research Unit, Khartoum University, 1962-71; Deputy Director, Clyde River Purification Board, 1971-74. Member, Aquatic Life Sciences Grants Committee, Natural Environment Research Council, 1975-79; Member, Marine Pollution Monitoring Management Group and its Steering Committee, since 1974; Member, Steering Committee for the Development of Environmental Quality Objectives and Standards, Department of Environment, 1981; Member, Scottish Council, Institute of Biology, 1973-76; elected to Committee of Environment Division, Institute of Biology, 1977 (Chairman, Environment Division, 1980-82); Member, Terrestrial and Freshwater Sciences Committee, Natural Environment Research Council, since 1976; Representative, Institution of Water Engineers and Scientists, Acid Rain Working Group, Watt Committee on Energy, 1983-84. Recreations: chess; tennis; hill-walking. Address: (h.) 7 Fairfield Place, Bothwell, Glasgow, G7 8RP; T.-Bothwell 852261.

Hammond, John, BSc, BDS, FDS, HDD, DipEd. Senior Lecturer in Prosthodontics, Glasgow University, since 1973; Consultant Dental Surgeon, Greater Glasgow Health Board, since 1973; b. 6.7.28, Airdrie; m., Mary M. Stewart; 1 s.; 1 d. Educ. Airdrie Academy; Glasgow University. Education Officer, RAF, 1951-55; Lecturer in Prosthodontics, Glasgow University, 1961-73; Secretary, Dental Council, Royal College of Physicians and Surgeons (Glasgow), 1976-83; Chairman, Lanarkshire Area Dental Committee, 1977-80. President, Glasgow Dental Students Society, 1958-59; President, Lanarkshire Golf Association, 1967-68. Recreations: golf; photography. Address: (b.) Glasgow Dental Hospital and School, 378 Sauchiehall Street, Glasgow; T.-041-332 7020.

Hampson, Stephen F., MA, BPhil. Assistant Secretary, Industry Department for Scotland, since 1984; b. 27.10.45, Grimsby; m., Gunilla Brunk; 1 s.; 1 d. Educ. The Leys School, Cambridge; University College, Oxford. Lecturer, Department of Political Economy, Aberdeen University, 1969-71; Economist, National Economic Development Office, 1971-75; Economic Adviser, Scottish Office, 1975-78 and 1982-84; First Secretary, British High Commission, New Delhi, 1978-81. Recreation: modern Indian literature. Address: (h.) Glenelg, Park Road, Kilmacolm, Renfrewshire; T.-Kilmacolm 2615.

Haney, Rev. Hugh Baird. Minister, John Ross Memorial Church for the Deaf, Glasgow, since 1982; b. 3.7.29, Irvine; m., Catherine Murray Campbell; 1 s.; 1 d. Educ. Kilmarnock Academy. Missionary to the Deaf, 1960-66; Minister to the Deaf in Falkirk, 1966-75, in Renfrewshire, 1975-82. Recreations: reading; travel; gardening; DIY. Address: Dungoyne, 132 Sandy Road, Renfrew, PA4 OBX; T.-041-886 3115.

Hanley, Clifford. Writer and Performer; Emeritus Professor, York University, Toronto; b. 28.10.22, Glasgow; m., Anna Clark; 1 s.; 2 d. Educ. Eastbank Academy, Glasgow. Journalist, since 1940; Novelist, since 1957; Songwriter; Broadcaster; Member, Scottish Arts Council, 1965-72; Member, Inland Waterways Advisory Council, 1970-73; Professor of Literature, York University, Toronto, 1979-80. Publications: Dancing in the Streets; Love from Everybody; The Taste of Too Much; Nothing but the Best; The System; The Redhaired Bitch; It's Different Abroad; The Italian Gadget; The Chosen Instrument; The Scots; Another Street, Another Dance. Recreations: music; talk; golf. Address: (h.) 36 Munro Road, Glasgow, G13 1SF.

Hanley, Very Rev. Hugh Hanley, SCJ, STL. Superior, Smithstone House, Kilwinning, since 1983; b. 8.8.51, Port Glasgow. Educ. Woodcote Hall, Newport, Shropshire; St. Joseph's, Malpas, Cheshire. Member, Sacred Heart Fathers, 1970; ordained Priest, St. John's, Port Glasgow, 1976; Smithstone House, Kilwinning, 1976-77; Holy Rood Church, Market Rasen, 1977-78; St. John Ogilvie's, Bourtreehill, Irvine, 1978-80; Gregorian University, Rome, 1980-82; Dehon House, Little Sutton, South Wirral, 1982-83. Recreations: various sports; reading. Address: Smithstone House, Kilwinning, Ayrshire, KA13 6PL; T.-0294 52515.

Hanlon, Rt. Rev. John Breslin, STB. Parish Priest, St. Mary's, Lochee, Dundee, since 1981; b. 27.8.30, Dundee. Educ. Lawside Academy, Dundee; Seminaire St. Sulpice, Paris; Catholic University, Paris, 1952-57 (BTheol). National Service, Army, 1948-50; Assistant Priest: St. Andrew's Cathedral, 1957, St. Leonard's, Dundee, 1957-60, Alloa, 1960-64, St. Mary's, Lochee, 1964-66; Parish Priest: Carnoustie/Monifieth, 1966-72, St. Teresa's, Dundee, 1972-76; Administrator, St. Andrew's Cathedral, 1976-81. RC Representative, Education Committee, Tayside Regional Council, 1973-81; Dunkeld Representative, John Ogilvie Committee, 1964-76; Prelate of Honour to Pope Paul VI, 1976; Vicar-General, Diocese of Dunkeld, 1975-81. Recreations: Scottish history; coins/medals/stamps; bowls. Address: St. Mary's, 41 High Street, Lochee, Dundee, DD2 3AP; T.-0382 611282.

Hannabuss, Susan Spencer, MA (Oxon), ACIS. Secretary and Treasurer, North of Scotland College of Agriculture, since 1982; b. 25.8.46, London. Educ. Paddington and Maida Vale High School for Girls; Lady Margaret Hall, Oxford. Teacher of English, Beckenham, Kent; Research Assistant, Inspectorate of Ancient Monuments and Historic Buildings, London and Edinburgh; Open University Tutor in Scotland; Departmental Secretary, Robert Gordon's Institute of Technology; Assistant Secretary, North of Scotland College of Agriculture. Publication: Biographical Dictionary of Painters in Scotland 1300-1700 (Co-

Editor). Recreations: theatre; reading; riding; swimming; calligraphy; embroidery; cookery. Address: (b.) North of Scotland College of Agriculture, School of Agriculture, 581 King Street, Aberdeen, AB9 1UD; T.-0224 480291.

Hannay of Kirkdale and That Ilk, Ramsay William Rainsford. Landowner, Farmer, Caravan Park Operator, since 1964; Barrister-at-Law, Inner Temple; b. 15.6.11, India; m., Margaret Wiseman; 1 s.; 1 d. Educ. Winchester College; Trinity College, Cambridge (Hons. degree in Law). Called to the Bar and practised in the Bankruptcy Court; called up for service in the Forces, 1939; commissioned, HLI; served throughout the War in Europe, with a short spell in USA and Canada; demobilised with rank of Major; Legal Assistant, then Assistant Solicitor, Board of Trade, 1946-64; Honorary Sheriff, Stewartry of Kirkcudbright; Member, Queen's Bodyguard for Scotland (Royal Company of Archers); President, Dumfries and Galloway Boy Scouts Association; Chief of the Clan Hannay. Recreations: sailing; shooting; fishing. Address: (h.) Cardoness, Gatehouse-of-Fleet, Kirkcudbrightshire; T.-Mossyard 207.

Harbison, Rev. David John Hislop, MA, BD. Minister, Beith High Church, since 1979; b. 26.8.33, Greenock; m., Winifred Grace Harley Wright; 1 s.; 2 d. Educ. Greenock Academy; Glasgow University. Minister: Whalsay & Skerries (Shetland), 1958-67, Hillhouse, Hamilton, 1967-79. Recreations: fishing; golf. Address: 2 Glebe Court, Beith, KA15 1ET; T.-Beith 2686.

Hardie, Douglas Fleming, CBE, JP, FRSA. Chairman and Managing Director, Edward Parker & Co. Ltd., since 1960; Deputy Chairman, Scottish Development Agency, since 1978; Chairman, A.G. Scott Textiles Ltd., since 1985; b. 26.5.23, Dundee; m., Dorothy Alice Warner; 2 s.; 1 d. Educ. Trinity College, Glenalmond. Trooper, 58 Training Regt., RAC, 1941; commissioned RMA Sandhurst, 1942, 1 Fifc & Forfar Yeomanry Flamethrowing Tank Regt., NW Europe, 1942-46 (Despatches), Major. Director: Dayco Rubber (UK) Ltd., since 1956, Clydesdale Bank plc, since 1981, The Alliance Trust plc, since 1982, The Second Alliance Trust plc, since 1982, Alliance Trust (Finance) Ltd., since 1982, SECDEE Leasing, since 1982, Alliance Trust (Nominees) Ltd., since 1982, Grampian Television plc, since 1984; Member: CBI Grand Council, London, 1976-85, Scottish Economic Council, since 1977; Councillor, Winston Churchill Memorial Trust, since 1985; Director, Prince's Scottish Youth Business Trust, 1987; Past President, Dundee Rotary Club; Vice-President, Fife & Forfar Yeomanry Regimental Association; Trustee, St. Andrews Links Trust; Deacon Convener, Nine Incorporated Trades of Dundee, 1951-54; Elder, Dundee Parish Church (St. Mary's). Recreations: golf; fishing. Address: (h.) 6 Norwood Terrace, West Park, Dundee, DD2 1PB.

Hare, Rev. Malcolm McNeill Walker, BA, BD. Minister, St. Kentigern's, Kilmarnock, since 1979; b. 21.11.28, Bangor, N. Ireland; m., Dr. Margaret Kathleen Buick Knox; 1 s.; 1 d. Educ. Sullivan Upper School, Holywood, Co. Down; Trinity College, Dublin; New College, Edinburgh. Minister: Charing Cross, Grangemouth, 1956-63, Langside Hill, Glasgow, 1963-79. Chairman, Scottish Council of the Leprosy Mission, 1982-85. Recreations: golf; music; gardening. Address: (h.) 21 Raith Road, Fenwick, Ayrshire; T.-Fenwick 388.

Hare, Professor Paul Gregory, BA, BPhil, DPhil. Professor of Economics and Head of Department, Heriot-Watt University, since 1985; b. 19.3.46, Hull; m., Susan Jennifer Robertson; 1 s.; 2 d. Educ. Malet Lambert High School, Hull; St. John's College, Cambridge; Nuffield College, Oxford. Technical Officer, ICI, 1967-68; Lecturer, Birmingham University, 1971-72; Lecturer, Senior Lecturer, Reader, Stirling University, 1972-85. Member, Lothian Region Children's Panel. Recreations: hill-walking; reading; listening to choral music. Address: (h.) 34 Saughtonhall Drive, Edinburgh, EH12 5TN; T.-031-337 7329.

Hare Duke, Rt. Rev. Michael Geoffrey, BA, MA. Bishop of St. Andrews, Dunkeld and Dunblane, since 1969; b. 28.11.25; m.; 1 s.; 3 d. Educ. Bradfield College; Trinity College, Oxford. Sub-Lt., RNVR, 1944-46; Deacon, 1952; Priest, 1953. Address: Bishop's House, Fairmount Road, Perth, PH2 7AP; T.-0738 21580.

Hargreave, Timothy Bruce, MB, MS, FRCSEdin, FRCS. Senior Lecturer, Department of Surgery, Edinburgh University, since 1978; Honorary Consultant Urological and Transplant Surgeon, Western General Hospital, Edinburgh, since 1978; b. 23.3.44, Lytham; m., Molly; 2 d. Educ. Harrow; University College Hospital, London University. Senior Registrar: Western Infirmary, Glasgow, University College Hospital, London; Medical Officer, Paray Mission Hospital, Lesotho. President, British Andrology Society. Publications: Diagnosis and Management of Renal and Urinary Disease; Male Infertility (Editor). Recreation: skiing. Address: (h.) 39 Murrayfield Gardens, Edinburgh; T.-031-337 3879.

Harkness, William, LLB, CA. Director and Secretary, The Weir Group PLC, since 1982; b. 1.4.43, Glasgow; m., Maura Brogan; 1 s. Educ. Greenock Academy; Glasgow University. Qualified as Chartered Accountant, 1967; admitted as Solicitor, 1970; joined The Weir Group as Legal Assistant, 1971, Group Secretary, 1977. Recreations: golf; bridge. Address: (h.) 51 Esplanade, Greenock; T.-0475 23000.

Harle, John Tate, BSc (Hons), MS, FRAgS. Managing Director, Cluny Home Farms Ltd., since 1966; Chairman, Scottish Agriculture Research and Development Advisory Council; Member, Advisory Committee, Animal and Grassland Research Stations; Member, Governing Body: Grassland Research Institute, 1981-85, Rowett Research Institute, since 1983; Member, Aberdeen and District Milk Marketing Board, since 1983; b. 3.9.41, Washington, England; m., Margaret Muriel; 2 s. Educ. Bede Grammar School, Sunderland; Durham University; Iowa State University. Part-time Lecturer, Agricultural

Economics, Aberdeen University. Recreations: hill-walking; skiing; squash; classical guitar. Address: Little Ley Farmhouse, Tillyfourie, Inverurie, Aberdeenshire, AB3 7SA; T.-033 03 355.

Harley, Roy Macgregor, LLB, NP, SSC. Solicitor; b. 29.10.48, Glasgow; m., Yvonne Mazodier; 1 d. Educ. Hermitage Academy, Helensburgh; Aberdeen University. Solicitor in private practice, Edinburgh, since 1972; Council Member, SSC, 1983; Tutor in Criminal Law, Edinburgh University, 1984. Address: (h.) 14 Dean Park Crescent, Edinburgh, EH4 1PH.

Harper, Professor Alexander Murray, MB, ChB, MD (Hons). Professor of Surgical Physiology, Glasgow University, since 1981; Honorary Consultant Clinical Physiologist, Greater Glasgow Health Board, since 1970; b. 31.5.33, Glasgow; m., Charlotte Maria Fossleitner; 2 s.; 1 d. Educ. Hutchesons' Grammar School; Glasgow University. House Physician and Surgeon, Southern General Hospital and Glasgow Royal Infirmary, 1957-58; McIntyre Research Scholar in Clinical Surgery, Glasgow Royal Infirmary, 1958-60; Scientific Assistant, Medical Research Council, 1960-63; Wellcome Senior Research Fellow in Clinical Science and Honorary Lecturer in Surgery, Glasgow University, 1963-68; Glasgow University: Senior Lecturer in Surgery and Surgical Physiology, 1968-69, Reader, 1969-81. Editor in Chief, Journal of Cerebral Blood Flow and Metabolism, since 1981; David Patey Prize, Surgical Research Society, 1966; H.G. Wolff Award, American Association for Study of Headache, 1968; Gold Medal, British Migraine Association, 1976; Honorary Fellow, American Heart Association (Stroke Council), 1980. Recreations: fishing; contract bridge; gardening. Address: (b.) Wellcome Surgical Institute, Glasgow University, Garscube Estate, Bearsden Road, Glasgow, G61 1QH; T.-041-942 2248.

Harper, Rev. Anne J. McInroy, BD, STM, MTh. Minister, Linthouse St. Kenneth's Parish Church, since 1984; Vice-Convener, Education Committee, and Adult Section Convener, Parish Education Committee, Presbytery of Glasgow; b. 31.10.49, Glasgow. Educ. Camphill Senior Secondary School, Paisley; Glasgow University; Union Theological Seminary, New York. Graduate Fellow, Union Theological Seminary, and Assistant Minister, 2nd Presbyterian Church, New York City, 1974-75; research, Church history and liturgics, Glasgow University, 1975-78; Assistant Minister, Abronhill Church, Cumbernauld, 1978-79; Christian Education Field Officer, Church of Scotland Department of Education, 1979-84. Holder (first woman), The Scots Fellowship awarded by Union Theological Seminary, New York, 1974. Address: 51 Morriston Crescent, Deanpark, Renfrew, PA4 0XW; T.-041-885 1557.

Harper, Professor Anthony John, BA, MA, PhD, CertEd. Professor of German Studies, Strathclyde University, since 1979; b. 26.5.38, Bristol; m., Sandra; 1 s.; 2 d. Educ. Clifton College, Bristol; Bristol University; Exeter University. Lecturer, Department of German, Edinburgh University, 1962-79. Publications: German Today (Co-author), 1967; David Schirmer - A Poet of the German Baroque, 1977; Time and Change, Essays on German and European Literature, 1982; Schriften zur Lyrik Leipzigs 1620-1670, 1985; The Song-Books of Gottfried Finckelthaus, 1988 Address: (b.) Department of Modern Languages, Strathclyde University, 26 Richmond Street, Glasgow, G1 1XQ; T.-041-552 4400.

Harper, Rev. David Little, BSc, BD (Hons). Minister, St. Meddan's Church, Troon, since 1979; b. 31.10.47, Moffat; m., Janis Mary Clark; 2 s. Educ. Morton Academy, Thornhill; Dumfries Academy; Edinburgh University. Assistant Minister, Cumbernauld St. Mungo's, 1971-72; first Minister, New Erskine Parish Church, 1972-79. Member, Scottish Advisory Committee, Independent Broadcasting Authority, 1974-79; Scottish Member, Religious Advisory Panel, IBA, 1978-79. Recreations: squash; golf; hill-walking. Address: St. Meddan's Manse, 27 Bentinck Drive, Troon, Ayrshire; T.-0292 311784.

Harper, Douglas Ross, BSc, MD, FRCSEdin, FRCSEng, FRCSGlas. Consultant Surgeon, Forth Valley Health Board, since 1976; Examiner, Royal College of Surgeons of Edinburgh, since 1979; Examiner, Royal College of Surgeons of Glasgow, since 1987; Honorary Senior Lecturer, Department of Clinical Surgery, Edinburgh University, since 1976; b. 16.2.40, Aberdeen; m., Dorothy Constance Wisely; 1 s.; 3 d. Educ. Aberdeen Grammar School; Aberdeen University. House Officer, Registrar and Fellow in Vascular Surgery, Aberdeen Royal Infirmary, 1967-73; Senior Registrar, Edinburgh Royal Infirmary, 1973-76. Elder, Bridge of Allan Chalmers Church of Scotland. Recreations: hill-walking; geology; woodwork. Address: (h.) Glenallan, 16 Upper Glen Road, Bridge of Allan, Stirlingshire, FK9 4PX; T.-0786 832242.

Harper, Edward James, MA, BMus, ARCM, LRAM. Composer, since 1957; Lecturer in Music, Edinburgh University, since 1964; Director, New Music Group of Scotland, since 1973; b. 17.3.41, Taunton; m., Dorothy Caroline Shanks. Educ. King Edward VI School, Guildford; Royal College of Music, London; Christ Church, Oxford. Main works as a Composer: Piano Concerto, 1971, Bartok Games, 1972, Ricercari in Memoriam Luigi Dallapiccola, 1975, Fanny Robin (chamber opera), Chester Mass, 1979, Clarinet Concerto, 1981, Hedda Gabler (opera, commissioned for Scottish Opera), 1985; Fantasia V (for chamber orchestra), 1985; The Mellstock Quire (chamber opera), 1987. Address: (h.) 7 Morningside Park, Edinburgh, EH10 5HD; T.-031-447 5366.

Harper, John Ross, MA, LLB. Senior Partner, Ross Harper & Murphy, Solicitors, since 1962; b. 20.3.35, Glasgow; m., Ursula; 2 s.; 1 d. Educ. Hutchesons' Boys Grammar School; Glasgow University. Temporary Sheriff; Parliamentary Commissioner; Professor of Law, Strathclyde University; Past President, Glasgow Bar Association; President, Law Society of Scotland; Executive Member, International Bar Association; former Chairman, Scottish Society of Conservative Lawyers; former Parliamentary candidate (Conservative), Hamilton and West Renfrewshire; Honorary Secretary, Scottish Conservative & Unionist Association. Publications: Glasgow

Rape Case; My Client My Lord; A Practitioner's Guide to the Criminal Courts; Fingertip Criminal Law; Rates Revaluation; Devolution. Recreations: angling; bridge; shooting. Address: (b.) 163 Ingram Street, Glasgow; T.-041-552 6343.

Harris, Gordon Scott, BSc, PhD, FRSC, CChem. Senior Lecturer, Chemistry Department, St. Andrews University, since 1965; b. 28.9.31, Alexandria; m., Eleanor Mackay; 2 s. Educ. Vale of Leven Academy; Glasgow University; Sidney Sussex College, Cambridge University. Ramsay Memorial Fellowship, Cambridge University, 1956-58; ICI Research Fellowship, Glasgow University, 1958-59; Lecturer in Chemistry, Glasgow University, 1959-65; Member: Dalton Council, Royal Society of Chemistry, 1977-80, Science Panel, Scottish Universities Council on Entrance, 1977-84, Scottish Examination Board, 1979-82. Recreations: gardening; golf; walking. Address: (b.) Chemistry Department, St. Andrews University, St. Andrews, Fife; T.-St. Andrews 76161.

Harrison, Anthony Frederick, CEng, FIEE, FIERE, FBIM. Director of Telecommunications, Scottish Office, since 1974; b. 20.2.29, Northampton; m., Doreen Caughlin; 1 s. Educ. Tollington Grammar School, London; Hendon Technical College. Began career in GPO, London and Dollis Hill Research Station; helped introduce first error-correcting radiotelegraph system; joined MEL Equipment Ltd. as Project Manager, 1962; designed first GPO Data Test Set; joined Marconi Space and Defence as Project Group Manager, 1968; Leader, European Consortium, providing all electronics, communications and guidance for European Space Tug; Head of Telecommunications, Greater London Council, 1972-74. Address: (b.) St. Andrews House, Regent Road, Edinburgh, EH1 3DE; T.-031-244 2645.

Harrison, Bryan Desmond, BSc, PhD, FRS, FRSE. Head, Virology Division, Scottish Crop Research Institute, since 1984; b. 16.6.31, Purley, Surrey; m., Elizabeth Ann Latham-Warde; 2 s.; 1 d. Educ. Whitgift School, Croydon; Reading University. Agricultural Research Council Postgraduate Research Student, 1952-54; Scientific Officer, Scottish Horticultural Research Institute, 1954-57; Senior and Principal Scientific Officer, Rothamsted Experimental Station, 1957-66; Scottish Horticultural Research Institute/Scottish Crop Research Institute: Principal Scientific Officer, 1966, Senior Principal Scientific Officer (Individual Merit), 1969, Deputy Chief Scientific Officer (Individual Merit), 1981; Honorary Professor, Department of Biochemistry and Microbiology, St. Andrews University, 1987; Honorary Visiting Professor, Dundee University, 1988; Past President, Association of Applied Biologists. Recreation: gardening. Address: (b.) Scottish Crop Research Institute, Invergowrie, Dundee, DD2 5DA; T.-0382 562731.

Harrison, Cameron, BSc (Hons), MEd. Rector, The Gordon Schools, Huntly, since 1982; b. 27.8.45, Mauchline, Ayrshire; m., Pearl; 1 s.; 1 d. Educ. Cumnock Academy; Strathclyde University; Glasgow University; Stirling University. Teacher, Greenock Academy, 1968-71; Principal Teacher of Physics, Graeme High School, Falkirk, 1971-79; Depute Rector, Kirkcudbright Academy, 1979-82; various involvements with SCEEB (now SEB) as setter etc. and with CCC Sub-Committees (Member, JWP on Higher Physics, 1976-79); Member, several research advisory committees; Chairman, Scottish Central Committee for Physical Education. Recreations: lay preacher; used to play rugby (still pretends to!); music; will admit, under pressure, to singing rather badly. Address: (h.) Kirkside, Cairney, Huntly, AB5 4TR; T.-0466 87207.

Harrison, Derek John, BSc, FICFor. Forestry Consultant and Valuer; Member, Red Deer Commission, since 1965; b. 11.6.26, Stoke Poges; m., 1, Janet Leslie Mennie Kennedy; 2 s.; 1 d.; 2, Shirley Ann Hurlston Jones. Educ. Eastbourne College; Aberdeen University; Queens College, Cambridge. War Service, Fleet Air Arm; Assistant Superintendent, Somaliland Police; Woodlands Manager, Moray Estates Development Company, 1960-77; Fellow, Institute of Chartered Foresters. Recreations: sailing; shooting; stalking; fishing; prodding bureaucrats. Address: Cornhill, Ardgay, Sutherland, IV24 3BP; T.-08632 319.

Harrison, Lloyd, BA (Oxon). Rector, Dollar Academy, since 1984; b. 4.8.34, Bradford; m., Moira Middlemas; 2 s.; 1 d. Educ. Bradford Grammar School; Queen's College, Oxford. Head of Classics: Trinity College, Glenalmond, 1960-68, Leeds Grammar School, 1968-70; Deputy Head, Colne Valley High School, 1970-75; Head: Steyning Grammar School, West Sussex, 1975-78, Northallerton Grammar School, 1979-84. Recreations: books; gardens; walking and running in lonely places. Address: (h.) 2 Academy Place, Dollar, Clackmannanshire; T.-025 94 2160.

Harrison, Professor Robert Graham, BSc (Hons), PhD, FRSE. Professor of Physics, Heriot-Watt University, since 1987; b. 26.2.44 Oxford; m., Rowena Indrania; 1 s.; 1 d. Educ. Wanstead High School; London University. Postgraduate and postdoctoral research, Royal Holloway College, London, and Culham Laboratories, UKAEA, 1966-72; Lecturer, Bath University; joined Physics Department, Heriot-Watt University. Publications: 130 scientific publications, including editorship of two books. Address: (b.) Physics Department, Heriot-Watt University, Riccarton, Currie, Edinburgh, EH14 4AS; T.-031-449 5111.

Harrison, Sydney, OBE. Proprietor, Paisley and Renfrewshire Gazette Group, 1963-87; Chairman, James Paton Ltd., Printers, 1970-87; Editor, Scot, 1981-87; b. 13.4.13, Glasgow; m., Joan Morris. Educ. Whitehill School, Glasgow. Journalist, various newspapers, 1927-37; Sub-Editor, Glasgow Herald, 1938-39; Army, 1939-46 (Lt.-Col., 1944); Editor, Scottish Field, 1946-63; Director, Scottish Counties Newspapers, 1950-63; Councillor, 4th District, Renfrewshire, 1956-67; Member, Council of Industrial Design, Board of Trade, 1955-65; Honorary Member, Scottish PEN; President, Paisley Burns Club, 1984-85; Past President, Rotary Club of Paisley. Recreations: curling; motoring; caravanning; travel. Address: (h.) Aviemore, Brookfield, Renfrewshire, PA5 8UG; T.-Johnstone 20634.

Hart, Maidie (Jenny Marianne), MA (Hons). Founder President, Scottish Convention of Women, since 1981; b. 15.12.16, Brookfield, Renfrewshire; m., William Douglas Hart; 2 d. Educ. St. Columba's School for Girls, Kilmacolm; St. Andrews University. Church of Scotland: Vice Convener, Home Board, 1967-70, National Vice-President, Woman's Guild, 1967-70, National President, Woman's Guild, 1972-75, Elder, since 1974; Executive Member, Women's National Commission, 1974-76; Member, Coordinating Committee, UK International Woman's Year, 1974-76 (Chairwoman, Scottish Steering Committee); first Chairwoman, Scottish Convention of Women, 1977; Vice President, British Council of Churches, 1978-81; Church of Scotland Delegate to World Council of Churches, 5th Assembly, 1975, WCC European Conference, 1978, WCC Human Rights and Mission Women's Conference, 1980, WCC Sheffield International Conference, 1981. Recreations: travel; walking; family; reading; garden; cooking. Address: (h.) Westerlea, Chapelhill, Dirleton, East Lothian, EH39 5HG; T.-062-085 278.

Hart, Professor Ralph Thomas, BCom, MA, FSS, FBIM, FInstD. Professor and Head, Business School, Robert Gordon's Institute of Technology, since 1970; Director: Wall Colmonoy Ltd., Pontardawe, South Wales, since 1964, John Fleming & Co. (Holdings) Ltd., since 1986, Aberdeen and District Milk Marketing Board, since 1979; b. 20.4.30, Newcastle-upon-Tyne; m., Hazel Margaret Norton; 2 s.; 1 d. Educ. Dame Allan's Boys' School; King's College, Durham; Strathclyde University. Industrial appointments, 1950-59, with Electricity Authority, Metal Box Co. Ltd. and National Coal Board; Lecturer, Municipal College of Commerce and Rutherford College of Technology, Newcastle, 1959-62; Senior Lecturer, Scottish Woollen Technical College, 1962-65; Head, Management Studies, Scottish College of Textiles, 1965-70; Dean, Faculty of Arts, Robert Gordon's Institute of Technology, 1974-79; Member: Board for Diploma in Commerce, since 1969; Scottish Business Education Council, 1973-85 (Chairman, Professional Studies Sector Committee); Member, various committees and boards, Council for National Academic Awards, 1973-83; Chairman, Appeals Committee, Aberdeen, Scottish Health Service, 1974; Member, MSC Training of Trainers Advisory Group, 1981-84; Member, Domestic Coal Users Consumers Council, since 1985. Recreations: fly fishing; tennis; Continental touring. Address: (h.) Grefsen House, Findon Village, Aberdeen; T.-Aberdeen 780330.

Hart, Bishop William. Roman Catholic Bishop of Dunkeld, 1955-81; b. 9.9.04, Dumbarton. Educ. St. Mungo's Academy, Glasgow; St. Mary's College, Blairs; Le Grand Seminaire, Coutances. Ordained Priest, 1929; Assistant: St. Mary's, Hamilton, 1929-33, St. John's, Glasgow, 1933-39; Army Chaplain, 1939-45; Assistant, St. Michael's, Parkhead, Glasgow, 1945-48; Assistant Rector, Royal Scots College, Valladolid, 1948-49; Parish Priest, St. Saviour's, Glasgow, 1951-55; Scottish Episcopal Conference: President, Ecumenical Commission, 1969-77, President, National Lay Apostolate Council, 1969-70. Address: (h.) Wellburn House, Liff Road, Lochee, Dundee, DD2 2QT.

Harte, Ben, BA, MA, PhD (Cantab), FRSE, FGS. Reader in Geology, Edinburgh University, since 1981; b. 30.5.41, Blackpool; m., Angela Elizabeth Kelly; 1 s.; 2 d. Educ. Salford Grammar School; Trinity College, Cambridge. Geology Department, Edinburgh University: Assistant Lecturer, 1965-67, Lecturer, 1967-81; Guest Investigator, Carnegie Institution of Washington, 1974-75; Visiting Associate Professor, Yale University, 1982. Vice-President, Edinburgh Geological Society, 1981-83; Chairman, Metamorphic Studies Group, Geological Society of London and Mineralogical Society of Great Britain and N. Ireland, 1983-85; Editor, Journal of Petrology, 1978-85. Recreations: sport (squash, tennis); joinery. Address: (b.) Grant Institute of Geology, West Mains Road, Edinburgh, EH9 3JW; T.-031-667 1081.

Hartnoll, Mary C., BA (Hons). Director of Social Work, Grampian Regional Council, since 1978; b. 31.5.39, Bristol. Educ. Colston's Girls School, Bristol; Bedford College, London University; Liverpool University. Child Care Officer, Dorset County Council, 1961-63; various posts, Reading County Borough, 1963-74; Berkshire County Council: Assistant Director, 1974-75, Divisional Director, 1975-77. Member, Board of Directors: National Institute of Social Work, Northsound Radio. Recreations: natural history; walking. Address: (b.) Woodhill House, Westburn Road, Aberdeen, AB9 2LU; T.-0224 682222, Ext. 2570.

Hartshorn, Christina, BA, MSc, DipCG. Enterprise Officer, Women in Scotland, since 1986; b. 18.12.46, Birmingham; 1 d. Educ. Bartley Green Girls' Grammar School, Birmingham; Essex University; Stirling University. Careers Officer, Senior Careers Officer, Fife Regional Council; Lecturer, Napier College, Edinburgh; Tutor, Extra Mural Development, Edinburgh University; Freelance Careers Advisor and Counsellor. Equal Opportunities Fellowship, German Marshall Fund of the United States, 1987. Recreations: friends; hill-walking; clarinet. Address: (b.) Scottish Enterprise Foundation, Stirling University, Stirling; T.-0786 73171.

Harvey, Professor Alan L., BSc, PhD. Personal Professor in Physiology and Pharmacology, Strathclyde University, since 1986; b. 23.6.50, Glasgow. Educ. Hutchesons', Glasgow; Strathclyde University. Lecturer in Physiology and Pharmacology, Strathclyde University, 1974-83; Senior Lecturer, 1983-86. British Pharmacological Society Sandoz Prize, 1983; British Pharmaceutical Conference Science Award, 1983. Publication: The Pharmacology of Nerve and Muscle in Tissue Culture, 1984. Address: (b.) Department of Physiology and Pharmacology, Strathclyde University, Glasgow, G1 1XW; T.-041-552 4400.

Harvey, Jake, DA, ARSA. Sculptor; b. 3.6.48, Kelso; 1 s.; 2 d. Educ. Kelso High Secondary School; Edinburgh College of Art. Travelling Scholarship to Greece, Agean Islands, Crete, 1971; ARSA, 1977; commissioned to make Hugh MacDiarmid Memorial Sculpture, 1982; Charles Mackintosh Memorial, 1985; Newcraighall Mining Memorial, 1987-88; Lecturer in Sculpture.

Recreation: fishing. Address: (h.) Maxton Cross, Maxton, St. Boswells, Roxburghshire; T.-0835 22650.

Harvie, John, MA (Hons). Headteacher, Claremont High School, since 1980; b. 17.8.33, Dalry, Ayrshire; m., Jean D.T. Wallace; 1 s.; 1 d. Educ. Dalry Senior Secondary School; Glasgow University. Teacher: Kilbirnie Junior Secondary School, 1959-61, Duncanrig Secondary School, East Kilbride, 1961-70; Claremont High School: Principal Teacher of Modern Languages, 1970-73, Head of Upper School, 1973-75; Headteacher, Rosehall High School, Coatbridge, 1975-80. Chairman, East Kilbride Headteachers Association; Senior Vice President, East Kilbride Rotary Club. Recreations: golf; watching football. Address: (h.) Murrayfield, 3 Clamps Grove, East Kilbride, Glasgow, G74 2EZ; T.-East Kilbride 21352.

Harwood, Raymond Jeffrey, BSc, PhD, CChem, FRSC. Vice Principal and Head, Department of Technology, Scottish College of Textiles; b. 14.11.40, Birmingham; m., Cynthia Mary; 3 s. Educ. Central Grammar School; Manchester University. Continuous career in education, since 1966; Joint Secretary, Salaries Committee, Central Institutions Academic Staff, 1976-78; Member, Academic Board, Napier College, since 1979; Director, Scottish Textile and Technical Centre, since 1984. Training Officer, Mountain Rescue Committee of Scotland, 1976-81. Recreations: mountaineering/mountain rescue. Address: (b.) Scottish College of Textiles, Galashiels, Selkirkshire, TD1 3HF; T.-0896 3351.

Hastie, Robert Malcolm, FRICS. Director of Technical Services, North East Fife District Council; b. 7.1.46, Glasgow; m., Kirsteen D.; 1 s.; 1 d. Educ. Jordanhill College School, Glasgow; Glasgow College of Building. James Barr & Sons, Glasgow; George Wimpey, Perth; Arbroath Town Council; Tayside Regional Council. Recreations: sailing; golf. Address: (h.) 2 Letham Place, St. Andrews, Fife; T.-0334 76931.

Hatwell, Anthony, DipFA (Lond). Sculptor; Head, School of Sculpture, Edinburgh College of Art, since 1969; b. 21.6.31, London; m., Elizabeth; 2 d. Educ. Dartford Grammar School; Slade School of Fine Art; Borough Polytechnic; Bromley College of Art. Exhibited recently: Scottish Arts Council Edinburgh Festival Exhibition, 1978; British Sculpture in the 20th Century, Whitechapel Gallery, 1981; Built in Scotland exhibition in Edinburgh, Glasgow, and London, 1983; Slade Postgraduate Scholarship, 1956; Boise Travelling Scholarship, 1957; Assistant to Henry Moore, 1958; Member, London Group, 1959-69 (Vice-President, 1961-63); works in collections of Scottish National Gallery of Modern Art, Arts Council of GB, Scottish Arts Council and private collections. Address: (b.) Edinburgh College of Art, Lauriston Place, Edinburgh.

Havergal, Giles. Director, Citizens' Theatre, Glasgow, since 1969; b. 9.6.38. Artistic Director, Palace Theatre, Watford, 1966-68.

Hawkins, Anthony Donald, BSc, PhD, FSA Scot, FRSE. Director of Fisheries Research for Scotland, since 1987 (Deputy Director, 1983-87); Honorary Professor, Aberdeen University; b. 25.3.42, Dorset; m., Susan Mary; 1 s. Educ. Poole Grammar School; Bristol University. Entered Scottish Office as Scientific Officer, Marine Laboratory, Aberdeen, 1965; Senior Scientific Officer, 1969, Principal Scientific Officer, 1972, Senior Principal Scientific Officer, 1978, Deputy Chief Scientific Officer, 1983; conducts research into behaviour and physiology of fish; awarded A.B. Wood Medal, Institute of Acoustics, 1978; Honorary Lecturer in Marine Biology, St. Andrews University. Publications: books on fish physiology and aquarium systems. Recreations: reading; angling; soccer; breeding whippets. Address: (b.) Marine Laboratory, PO Box 101, Victoria Road, Torry, Aberdeen; T.-0224 876544.

Haworth, John Roger, BA (Hons), RTPI, MCIT. Head, Economic Development Unit, Ross and Cromarty District Council; b. 4.2.46, Worsley, Manchester; m., Margaret; 2 s.; 2 d. Educ. Bolton School; Manchester University. Planning Assistant, Stirling County Council, 1968-71; Ross and Cromarty County Council: Assistant Planning Officer, 1971-73, Assistant Planning Officer (Western Isles), 1973-74; Director of Planning and Development, Western Isles Islands Council, 1974-87. Recreations: reading; music; films; history; travel. Address: (b.) Council Offices, Dingwall, Ross & Cromarty, IV15 9QN; T.-0349 63737.

Hay, Alan, BA, FSA Scot. Genealogist and Record Agent; Council Member, Royal Celtic Society, since 1984; Council Member, Scottish Tartans Society, since 1984 (Honorary Secretary, 1985-86) and Trustee, Scottish Tartans Museum; b. 26.9.62, Ellon, Aberdeenshire. Freelance Genealogist, 1982; Consultant, Burke's Peerage, 1984; Niadh Nask, 1984; Genealogist and Archivist, Clan Hay, 1983. Recreations: climbing; shooting; squash; heraldry. Address: (h.) 2 Kirkhill Gardens, Potterton, Aberdeen; T.-Balmedie 43424.

Hay, Ann Catherine, OBE. Secretary, Scottish Conservative and Unionist Association, since 1981; b. Forres. Educ. Forres Academy. Agent, Edinburgh Pentlands Conservative Association, 1963-65; National Organiser, Scottish Young Conservatives, 1965-68; Secretary, Federation of Conservative Students, 1969-72; Agent, High Peak (Derbyshire) Conservative Association, 1973-76; Deputy Director, Scottish Conservative Party, 1976-81. Recreations: reading; music; sewing; DIY. Address: (b.) 3 Chester Street, Edinburgh, EH3 7RF; T.-031-226 4426.

Hay, Francis Walker Christie, OBE, DL, MA (Hons). Deputy Lieutenant, Banffshire, since 1988; Convener, National Welfare Committee, Royal British Legion Scotland, since 1969; Area Chairman, Royal British Legion Scotland, Aberdeen, Banff and Kincardine, since 1981; b. 20.3.23, Aberdeen; m., Margaret Anne Castel; 2 s.; 1 d. Educ. Robert Gordon's College, Aberdeen; Aberdeen University. Commissioned into Reconnaissance Corps, 1943; gazetted Captain, 1947; Teacher of History, 1950-58; Special Assistant, Turriff Academy, 1958-63; Principal Teacher of History, Breadalbane Academy, Banff Academy, 1963-74; Assistant Rector, Banff Academy,

1974-88; Member, Banffshire Education Committee, 1961-75. Recreations: furniture making; amateur dramatics. Address: (h.) 11 Fife Street, Banff, AB4 1JB; T.-02612 2285.

Hay, James Taylor Cantlay, BSc (Hons), FInstPet, AAPG. Regional Manager, North Africa/Mid East/SE Asia, Britoil plc, since 1987; Chairman of Governors, Robert Gordon's Institute of Technology, Aberdeen, since 1985; Member, Aberdeen Beyond 2000, since 1986; b. 13.6.35, Huntly; m., Mary Gordon Davidson; 1 s.; 2 d. Educ. Banchory Academy; Aberdeen University. Geologist, Iraq Petroleum Co. Ltd., Iraq, 1958-66; Head of Geology, Abu Dhabi Petroleum Co. Ltd., Abu Dhabi, 1967-71; Lecturer in Geology, Aberdeen University, 1971-74; Senior Production Geologist, Burmah Oil, London, 1974-76; various management roles, BNOC, Aberdeen and Glasgow, 1977-80; General Manager, BNOC/Britoil, Aberdeen, 1980-87. Recreations: golf; birdwatching. Address: (h.) 67 Fountain Hall Road, Aberdeen; T.-0224 645955.

Hay, John McWhirter. Sheriff Clerk and Auditor of Court, Dunfermline, since 1980; b. 27.4.43, Glasgow; m., Mary Wilkie Munro; 3 d. Educ. Clydebank High School. Clerical Officer: Glasgow Sheriff Court, 1960-63, Dumbarton Sheriff Court, 1963-65; Second Class Depute, Glasgow Sheriff Court, 1965-71; First Class Depute, Ayr Sheriff Court, 1971-80. Captain, Troon St. Meddans Golf Club, 1975; Match Secretary, Dunfermline Golf Club, 1981-83. Recreations: versatile sportsman, first love golf (single figure handicap, since 1972). Address: (b.) Sheriff Clerk's Office, 1/6 Carnegie Drive, Dunfermline, Fife; T.-Dunfermline 724666.

Hay, Kenneth McLennan, BEM, ISM, KCLJ, KMLJ, FSA(Scot). Commissioner to Lord Erroll Clan Hay Society, since 1978; Secretary-General, The Monarchist League; Chairman, Royal Celtic Society; b. 20.2.18, Edinburgh; m., 1, Irene Mary Roberts; 2, Fiona Dubois MacDonald; 1 s. (deceased). Educ. Flora Stevenson School, Edinburgh. War service, 1939-46: Royal Signals, Scotland, War Office, Burma; retired Executive, GPO; Member, National Committee, Post Office and Civil Service Sanatorium Society; a Governor, Benenden Chest Hospital; Honorary Vice-President, Edinburgh Gaelic Choir; Publicity Convenor, St. Andrew Society; former Secretary-General, Grand Commandery Lochore, Military and Hospitaller Order of St. Lazarus of Jerusalem. Publication: Story of the Hays. Recreations: hill-walking; singing; dancing; literature; history; theatre; arts. Address: (h.) 12 St. Peter's Place, Edinburgh, EH3 9PH; T.-031-228 1376.

Hay, Patricia Mary. President, Scottish Ladies' Golfing Association, since 1985; b. 17.3.13, Inverness; m., Lt. Col. G.H. Hay, DSO (deceased); 2 s.; 2 d. Educ. Lansdowne House, Edinburgh. Address: (h.) 106 Polwarth Terrace, Edinburgh.

Hay, Professor Robert Walker, BSc, PhD, CChem, FRSC, FRSE. Professor of Chemistry, St. Andrews University, since 1988; b. 17.9.34, Stirling; m., Alison Laird; 1 s.; 3 d. Educ. Stirling High School; Glasgow University. Assistant Lecturer, Glasgow University, 1959; subsequently worked at Esso Research; Lecturer, Senior Lecturer and Reader, Victoria University, Wellington, New Zealand, 1961; Reader, Stirling University, 1971; Professor, Stirling University, 1984. Publications: Bioinorganic Chemistry, 1984; numerous scientific papers. Recreations: walking; travel; caravanning; reading. Address: (b.) Chemistry Department, St. Andrews, KY16 9AJ; T.-0334 76161.

Hay, William Flett, CBE (1986). President, Scottish Fishermen's Federation, since 1982; Member, Sea Fish Industry Authority, since 1983; b. 7.10.29, Findochty; m., Sheila Reid; 1 s.; 1 d. Educ. Portsoy School. Took up sea going career in the fishing industry at the age of 14; took command of own vessel, 1954; retired from active sea going career, 1984; Chairman, Scottish White Fish Producers' Association, 1976-82. Recreation: bowling. Address: (h.) Mara Vista, Marine Terrace, Portsoy, Banffshire; T.-0261 42454.

Hayes, Sir John Osler Chattock, KCB, OBE. Lord Lieutenant of Ross and Cromarty, Skye and Lochalsh, 1977-88; Deputy Chairman, Gordonstoun School, 1977-86; b. 9.5.13; m., Hon. Rosalind Mary Finlay; 2 s.; 1 d. Educ. Royal Naval College, Dartmouth. War service, 1939-45, Atlantic/HMS Repulse/Singapore/Russian Convoys/Malta; Real Admiral, Naval Secretary to First Lord of Admiralty, 1962-64; Vice Admiral/Rear Admiral, Flag Officer 2nd in command Western Fleet, 1964-66; Vice Admiral, Flag Officer Scotland and Northern Ireland, 1966-68; Member, Queen's Bodyguard for Scotland (Royal Company of Archers), since 1969; President, King George's Fund for Sailors, Scotland, 1968-79; Vice Patron, Royal National Mission for Deep Sea Fishermen, since 1968. Recreations: music; writing; walking. Address: (h.) Arabella House, by Tain, Ross and Cromarty, IV19 1QJ; T.-Nigg Station 293.

Heading, Robert Campbell, BSc, MD, FRCP. Consultant Physician, Edinburgh Royal Infirmary, since 1975; Senior Lecturer in Medicine, Edinburgh University, since 1975; b. 3.7.41, Stepps, Lanarkshire; m., Patricia Mary Goldie; 2 s.; 1 d. Educ. Birkenhead School; King Edward's School, Birmingham; Edinburgh University. Chairman, Medical Staff Committee, Edinburgh Royal Infirmary, since 1987. Address: (h.) 20 Frogston Road West, Edinburgh, EH10 7AJ; T.-031-445 1552.

Healy, Raymond Michael, BSc. Headmaster, Lourdes Secondary School, Glasgow, since 1987 (Rector, Our Lady's High School, Cumbernauld, 1976-86); b. 8.7.40, Glasgow; m., Margaret Bradburn; 2 s. Educ. St. Aloysius College, Glasgow; Glasgow University; Jordanhill College of Education. Research Department: Babcock & Wilcox Ltd., Renfrew, 1961-62, Sandeman Bros., Glasow, 1962-63; Teacher: St. Margaret Mary's Secondary School, Glasgow, 1964-65, St. Aloysius College, Glasgow, 1965-69; Principal Teacher of Chemistry, St. Aloysius College, Glasgow, 1969-72; Assistant Headteacher, St. Andrew's High

School, Clydebank, 1972-74; Depute Headteacher, St. Patrick's High School, Dumbarton, 1974-76. Member, Scottish Central Committee on Science, 1978-81. Recreation: golf. Address: (b.) Lourdes Secondary School, 47 Kirriemuir Avenue, Glasgow, G52 3DF.

Heaney, Henry Joseph, MA, FLA. University Librarian and Keeper of the Hunterian Books and MSS, Glasgow University, since 1978; b. 2.1.35, Newry, Northern Ireland; m., Mary Elizabeth Moloney. Educ. Abbey Grammar School, Newry; Queen's University, Belfast. Assistant Librarian, Queen's University, Belfast, 1959-62; Librarian, Magee University College, Londonderry, 1962-67; Deputy Librarian, New University of Ulster, 1967-69; Assistant Secretary, Standing Conference of National and University Libraries, 1969-72; Librarian: Queen's University, Belfast, 1972-74, University College, Dublin, 1975-78. Member, Advisory Committee on Public Library Service, Northern Ireland, 1965; Chairman, NI Branch, Library Association, 1966, 1973; Trustee, National Library of Scotland, since 1980; Chairman, British Library Ad Hoc Working Party on Union Catalogues, 1982; Member: British Library Reference Division Advisory Committee, since 1982, British Library Lending Division Advisory Committee, 1983-86, British Eighteenth Century Short Title Catalogue Committee, since 1983, Standing Committee, University Libraries Section, IFLA, since 1986. Address: (b.) Glasgow University Library, Hillhead Street, Glasgow, G12 8QE; T.-041-330 5633.

Hearne, John Michael, BMus, MMus. Secretary and Past Chairman, Scottish Society of Composers; Freelance Composer and Professional Singer; Chairman, Scottish Music Advisory Committee, BBC; Member, Central Music Advisory Committee, BBC; Lecturer, Aberdeen College of Education, 1970-87; b. 19.9.37, Reading; m., Margaret Gillespie Jarvie. Educ. Torquay Grammar School; St. Luke's College, Exeter; University College of Wales, Aberystwyth. Teaching, Rugeley, Staffordshire, 1959-60; Warehouseman/Driver, Torquay, 1961-64; Teaching: Tonlistarskoli Borgarfjardar, Iceland, 1968-69, UCW Aberystwyth, 1969-70; Composer, vocal, instrumental and incidental music; Member, John Currie Singers; McEwen Commission, Glasgow University, 1979; President, Garioch Lions Club, 1984-85; Chorus Manager, Aberdeen International Youth Festival, since 1978; won Radio Forth Trophy, 1985, for most outstanding work on Edinburgh Festival Fringe. Recreations: motoring and travel (1954 Daimler Roadster). Address: (h.) Smidskot, Fawells, Keith-Hall, Inverurie, AB5 OLN; T.-065 182 274.

Heasman, Michael Anthony, FRCPEdin, FFCM, DPH. Director, Information Services Division, Scottish Health Service, Common Services Agency, 1974-86; Expert in Health Statistics, World Health Organisation, 1965-88; Honorary Senior Lecturer, Department of Community Medicine, Edinburgh University, 1976-86; b. 9.9.26, Colchester; m., Barbara Nelly Stevens; 1 s.; 1 d. Educ. Felsted School; St. Mary's Hospital, London University. RAF Medical Branch, 1948-53; Research Fellowships, London School of Hygiene, 1954-56; Medical Statistician, General Register Office, London, 1956-61; Senior Medical Officer, Ministry of Health, 1961-65; Principal Medical Officer, Scottish Home and Health Department, 1965-74. Recreations: hill-walking; literature. Address: (h.) 1 Monkrigg Steading, Haddington, East Lothian, EH41 4LB.

Heatly, Peter, CBE, DL, BSc, CEng, FICE. Chairman, Peter Heatly & Co. Ltd., since 1958; Chairman, Scottish Sports Council, 1975-87; Chairman, Commonwealth Games Federation, since 1982; b. 9.6.24, Edinburgh; m., Mae Calder Cochrane. Educ. Leith Academy; Edinburgh University. Structural Designer, Redpath Brown & Co. Ltd., 1946; Lecturer in Civil Engineering, Edinburgh University, 1948. Chairman, International Diving Committee. Recreations: swimming; gardening; travel. Address: (h.) Lanrig, Balerno, Edinburgh, EH14 7AJ; T.-031-449 3998.

Hector, Gordon Matthews, CMG (1966), CBE (1961), MA (Oxon). Chairman, Scottish Council, Victoria League; Vice President, The St. Andrew Society; Secretary to Assembly Council, General Assembly of Church of Scotland, 1980-85; b. 9.6.18, Aberdeen; m., Dr. Mary Forrest Gray; 1 s.; 2 d. Educ. St. Mary's School, Melrose; Edinburgh Academy; Lincoln College, Oxford. HM Colonial Administrative Service and Overseas Civil Service, 1946-66: District Commissioner, Kenya, Secretary, Kenya Road Authority, Secretary to Government of Seychelles, 1952-55, Acting Governor, 1953, Deputy Resident Commissioner and Government Secretary, Basutoland (now Lesotho), 1956-64, Deputy British Government Representative, Lesotho, 1965-66; Aberdeen University: Clerk to University Court, 1967, Deputy Secretary, 1976-80. OBE, 1955. Fellow, Commonwealth Fund, 1939; Burgess of Guild, Aberdeen; Chairman, West End Community Council, Edinburgh; Court of Directors, Edinburgh Academy, 1967-75; Member, Board of Managers, Oakbank List D School. Recreations: town and country walking; railways ancient and modern; grandchildren. Address: (h.) 18 Magdala Crescent, Edinburgh, EH12 5BD; T.-031-346 2317.

Hedley, Professor Anthony Johnson, MB, ChB, MD, DipSocMed, MRCP, MFCM, FRCPEdin, FRCPGlas, FRCPLond, FFCM, HonMD (Khon Kaen, Thailand). Henry Mechan Professor of Public Health, Glasgow University, since 1983; b. 8.4.41, Greenmount, Lancashire; m., Elizabeth-Anne Walsh. Educ. Rydal; Aberdeen University; Edinburgh University. Research Fellow in Materia Medica, Aberdeen University, 1966-69; Honorary Assistant and Registrar in Therapeutics and Pharmacology, Dundee University, 1969-72; Fellow in Community Medicine, Scottish Health Service, 1972-74; Lecturer in Community Medicine, Aberdeen University, 1974-76; Senior Lecturer in Community Health, Nottingham University, 1976-83; Medical Adviser, Faculties of Medicine and Public Health, University of Khon Kaen, Thailand. Recreations: running; target shooting; photography. Address: (b.) Department of Community Medicine, Glasgow University, Glasgow, G12 8QQ; T.-041-330 5013.

Hedley, James, BA (Hons), DipEd, Hon.MCGLI, FRSA. Principal, Inverness College of Further and Higher Education, since 1979; b. 1.11.34,

Newcastle upon Tyne; m., Barbara Wilson; 2 d. Educ. Heaton Grammar School; King's College, Durham. Lecturer, Stockton-Billingham Technical College, 1959-67; Head of Department, Inverness Technical College, 1968-72; Vice-Principal, SE Northumberland Technical College/North Tyneside College of Further Education, 1973-79. Member, Highlands and Islands Area Manpower Board, 1982-85; Honorary Member, City and Guilds of London Institute, since 1983; Member, Manpower Services Committee, Scotland, 1985-88; Member, Scottish Examination Board, since 1986; Member, Forestry Training Council, Education Scotland, since 1987. Recreations: theatre; music; swimming; cricket; Newcastle United FC. Address: (b.) 3 Longman Road, Inverness, IV1 1SA; T.-Inverness 236681.

Heggie, Douglas Cameron, MA, PhD, FRAS. Reader in Mathematics, Edinburgh University, since 1985; b. 7.2.47, Edinburgh; m., Linda Jane Tennent; 2 d. Educ. George Heriot's School, Edinburgh; Trinity College, Cambridge. Research Fellow, Trinity College, Cambridge, 1972-76; Lecturer in Mathematics, Edinburgh University, 1975-85. Council Member, Royal Astronomical Society, 1982-85; President, Commission 37, International Astronomical Union, 1985-88. Publications: Megalithic Science; scientific papers on dynamical astronomy. Recreations: family life; walking; music. Address: (b.) Edinburgh University, Department of Mathematics, King's Buildings, Edinburgh, EH9 3JZ; T.-031-667 1081, Ext. 2936.

Heller, Martin Fuller Vernon. Actor, since 1947; b. 20.2.27, Manchester; m., Joyce Allan; 2 s.; 4 d. Educ. Rondebosch Boys High School, Cape Town; Central School of Speech Training and Dramatic Art, London. Compass Players, 1948-52; repertory seasons and/or individual productions at following Scottish theatres: St. Andrews Byre, Edinburgh Gateway, Glasgow Citizens' (eight seasons), Edinburgh Royal Lyceum, Edinburgh Traverse, Dundee Repertory, Perth Repertory, Pitlochry Festival; Founder Member, Prime Productions, 1986; appeared in England at Morecambe, Preston, Carlisle, Birmingham, Coventry, Leicester and Hammersmith; extensive television and radio work; Equity: Member, Scottish Committee, National Council, three times; Member, Scottish Arts Council, 1975-82 (latterly Chairman, Drama Committee); Board Member, Scottish Youth Theatre; Observer, Board, Royal Lyceum Theatre; Board Member, Pitlochry Festival Theatre; Governor, Royal Scottish Academy of Music and Drama, since 1982. Recreations: politics; history; listening to music. Address: (h.) 54 Hermiston, Currie, Midlothian, EH14 4AQ; T.-031-449 4055.

Hemingway, Dennis, BSc, FSS, AFIMA. Secretary, Scottish Nursery Nurses' Board, since 1974; Consultant, Education Training and Administrative Services, since 1988; b. 28.6.35, Wakefield; m., Rosalie; 1 s.; 3 d. Educ. Normanton Grammar School; Leeds University. Technical Engineer, Bristol Aeroplane Company, 1955-60; Assistant Lecturer, Lecturer and Senior Lecturer, Bristol Technical College, 1960-65; Deputy Secretary, then Secretary, Union of Lancashire and Cheshire Institutes, 1965-74; Chief Officer, Scottish Technical Education Council, 1974-85; Depute Director, Scottish Vocational Education Council, 1985-87. Chairman, Ayrshire Branch, Leukaemia Research Fund. Recreations: bridge; sailing; swimming. Address: (h.) 6 Kilnford Crescent, Dundonald, Kilmarnock, KA2 9DW; T.-0563 850057.

Hemingway, Professor R. Gordon, MSc, PhD, FIBiol. Professor of Veterinary Animal Husbandry, Glasgow University Veterinary School, since 1969; b. 6.4.25, Sheffield; m., Dorothy E. Adam; 2 d. Educ. King Edward VII School, Sheffield; Leeds University. Ministry of Agriculture and Fisheries, 1946-48; Royal Agricultural College, Cirencester, 1948-53; joined Glasgow University, 1953. Past Chairman: Agriculture Group, Society of Chemical Industry, Scottish Group, Nutrition Society. Recreations: golf; gardening; grandchildren. Address: (h.) Eaglesfield, Milndavie Road, Strathblane, Glasgow, G63 9EL; T.-0360 70044.

Hemming, Sarah Catherine, MA (Hons). Arts Journalist; Co-Editor, The List, since 1985; b. 6.2.59, Stoneleigh, Surrey. Educ. Chesterfield High School, Liverpool; Edinburgh University; Freiburg University. Has written for various publications, including The Independent, The Times, Glasgow Herald, Drama, Edinburgh Review, Plays and Players; has reviewed for BBC Radio; co-founded The List (arts magazine), 1985; Scottish Critic, arts page, The Independent, since 1987; edited Festival Times, 1983. Recreations: not much time!; sporadically go walking/running/swimming; reading. Address: (h.) 27 Rutland Street, Edinburgh; T.-031-228 1266.

Hemmings, Douglas Thorley, OBE, DPA, FBIM. Chief Executive Officer, Cumnock and Doon Valley District Council, since 1975; b. 29.12.26, Leeds; m., Aloisia; 1 s.; 1 d. Educ. Ayr Academy. Ayr County Council, 1952-75. Member, Board of Management, Cumnock and Doon Enterprise Trust; President, Burns Memorial Homes, Mauchline. Address: (h.) 2 Broadwood Park, Ayr; T.-Alloway 42742.

Henderson, Andrew Kerr, MB, ChB, FRCP. Consultant Physician, County Hospital, Oban, since 1977; Postgraduate Tutor in Medicine, since 1980; Honorary Clinical Lecturer, Glasgow University, since 1981; b. 1.3.46, Hawick; m., Doreen Innes Wilkinson; 1 s.; 2 d. Educ. Glasgow Academy; Glasgow University. Medical Registrar, Western Infirmary, Glasgow; Medical Registrar/Senior Registrar, Glasgow Royal Infirmary. Chairman, Counties Branch, Scottish Schoolboys' Club. Recreations: gardening; hill-walking. Address: (h.) Birkmoss, North Connel, Argyll; T.-Connel 379.

Henderson, Douglas Mackay, CBE, BSc, FLS, FRSE, VMH. Administrator, Inverewe Garden, National Trust for Scotland, since 1987; Queen's Botanist in Scotland, since 1987; b. 30.8.27, Blairgowrie; m., Julia Margaret Brown; 1 s.; 2 d. Educ. Blairgowrie High School; Edinburgh University. Scientific Officer, Department of Agriculture, Scotland, 1948-50; Research Botanist, Royal Botanic Garden, Edinburgh, 1950-70; Curator, Royal Society of Edinburgh, 1978-87; Secretary, International Association of Botanical Gardens,

1969-81; Regius Keeper, Royal Botanic Garden, Edinburgh, 1970-87; Honorary Professor, Edinburgh University, since 1982. Recreations: natural history; painting; sailing; cooking. Address: (h.) Inverewe House, Poolewe, Wester Ross, IV22 2LQ; T.-044 586 200.

Henderson, Elizabeth Kidd, MA (Hons), MEd (Hons). Headmistress, Westbourne School, since 1970; b. 25.5.28, Dunfermline. Educ. Dunfermline High School; Edinburgh University; St. Andrews University. Mathematics Teacher, Morrison's Academy, Crieff; Second Master, Mathematics, Dundee High School; Principal Teacher of Mathematics, Aberdeen High School; former Secretary, Mathematics Panel, Scottish Examination Board; President, Scottish Area, Secondary Heads Association; President, Glasgow Mathematical Association. Chairman, Community Council. Publication: Modern Mathematics for Schools (Co-author). Recreations: walking; golf. Address: (b.) Westbourne School, 1 Winton Drive, Glasgow, G12 OPY; T.-041-339 6006.

Henderson, Rt. Rev. George Kennedy Buchanan, MBE, BA, JP. Bishop of Argyll and the Isles, since 1977; b. 5.12.21, Oban; m., Isobel Fergusson Bowman. Educ. Oban High School; Durham University. Assistant Curate, Christ Church, Glasgow, 1943-48; Chaplain, Bishop of Argyll and the Isles, 1948-50; Rector, St. Andrew's, Fort William, 1950-77; Canon, St. John's Cathedral, Oban, 1962; Dean of Argyll, 1974. Honorary Burgess of Fort William, 1973; Honorary Sheriff, 1974. Address: Bishop's House, 7 Achnalea, Onich, by Fort William, PH33 6SA; T.-Onich 240.

Henderson, Rev. Grahame McLaren, BD. Minister, Castle Street Church, Dingwall, since 1987 (Glengarry linked with Kilmonivaig, 1974-87); b. 10.6.43, Aberdeen; m., Kathleen Munro Moir; 1 s.; 1 d. Educ. Robert Gordon's College, Aberdeen; Aberdeen University; Edinburgh University. David Henderson (Jewellers) Ltd., Aberdeen, 1959-66; Probationer Assistant, Kirknewton and East Calder, 1973-74. Chairman, Lochaber High School Schools' Council, 1979-82; Moderator, Lochaber Presbytery, 1979-80; Moderator, Synod of Southern Highlands, 1980-82. Recreations: ship cruising; railways; caravanning. Address: 16 Achany Road, Dingwall, Ross-shire, IV15 9JB; T.-0349 63167.

Henderson, Iain, BA, LLB, NP. Procurator Fiscal, Oban; b. 20.12.39, Lochaber; m., Margaret Lydia. Address: (b.) Sheriff Court, Albany Street, Oban; T.-0631 64088.

Henderson, (James Stewart) Barry, MBCS. MP (Conservative), North East Fife, 1983-87 (East Fife, 1979-83, East Dunbartonshire, February to October, 1974); Manager, Special Projects, DRG Transcript, Glenrothes, since 1987; Management Consultant, 1976-79; b. 29.4.36, Kirkcaldy; m., Janet; 2 s. Educ. Lathallan and Stowe Schools. National Service, Scots Guards, 1954-56; employed in electronics and computer industry, 1957-66 and 1970-75; Information Officer, Scottish Conservative Party, 1966-70; Member, Select Committee on Scottish Affairs, 1980-87; Vice-Chairman, Parliamentary Information Technology Committee, 1987; Chairman, Scottish Conservative Members Committee, 1983-84; Parliamentary Private Secretary to Treasury Minister, 1984-87. Address: (h.) Old Gillingshill, by Anstruther, Fife.

Henderson, John, RIBA, ARIAS. Director of Property Services, Dumfries and Galloway Regional Council, since 1979; b. 22.12.31. Educ. School of Architecture, Dundee. Architect's Department, Bank of Scotland, 1956-61; Dumfries County Council: Principal Assistant, 1961-70, Depute County Architect, 1971-73; Assistant to Chief Executive, Dumfries and Galloway Regional Council, 1974-79. Address: (b.) Park House, 2 Annan Road, Dumfries; T.-0387 61234.

Henderson, John Harley, JP. Member, City of Dundee District Council, since 1974 (Convener of Housing, since 1984); Teacher of Mathematics, St. John's High School, Dundee, since 1976; b. 17.8.41, Dundee; m., Peggy Henderson; 1 s.; 1 d. Educ. Lawside Academy, Dundee; Dundee College of Technology. Former Divisional Council Secretary, AUEW-TASS; Dundee District Council: former Secretary and Leader, Administration Group, former Convener of Cleansing, former Convener of Planning and Development; Member, Housing Committee, COSLA; Member, Board of Governors, Dundee College of Technology. Address (h.) 24 Burrelton Gardens, Dundee; T.-0382 811982.

Henderson, John Thomson, BSc, DipRTC, CEng, FIEE. Chief Executive, Scottish Engineering Training Scheme, since 1987; b. 10.10.25, Glasgow; m., Robina Michael Macdonald Henderson; 1 s.; 2 d. Educ. Rutherglen Academy; Royal Technical College, Glasgow; Glasgow University. Lt., REME, 1946-48; Graduate Apprentice and Engineer, Metropolitan Vickers, 1949-53; Electrical Engineer, John Dalglish, 1953-56; Senior Technical Officer, then Technical Manager, then Director and Chief Engineer, Scottish Cables, 1956-77; Marketing Manager (Far East and Pacific), BICC Supertension Cables, 1978-86. IEE: Chairman, SW Scotland Sub-Centre, Chairman, Power Section, Scotland, Chairman, Scottish Centre. Recreations: golf; garden. Address: (h.) 25 Crawfurd Road, Burnside, Glasgow, G73 4JZ; T.-041-634 4936.

Henderson, Admiral Sir Nigel Stuart, GBE (1968), KCB (1962), DL. Deputy Lieutenant, Stewartry of Kirkcudbright, since 1973; b. 1.8.09; m.; 1 s.; 2 d. Educ. Cheltenham College. Director-General of Training, Admiralty, 1960-62; C-in-C Plymouth, 1962-65; Admiral, 1963; Head, British Defence Staffs, Washington, and UK Representative, Military Committee, NATO, 1965-68; Chairman, Military Committee, NATO, 1968-71.

Henderson, Thomas Wilson. Director, John Turnbull & Sons Ltd., Hawick, since 1983; Member, Ettrick and Lauderdale District Council, since 1974; Provost of Selkirk, since 1978; b. 28.9.41, Selkirk; m., Catherine Helen Herbert; 2 s. Educ. Selkirk Public School; Selkirk High School; Scottish College of Textiles; Paisley College of Technology. Served apprenticeship as dyer with George Roberts & Co. Ltd., Selkirk, 1957-61; Dyer, 1961-78; Assistant Manager, John Turnbull

& Sons Ltd., Hawick, 1978-83; involved in management buy-out, 1983; Member, Selkirk Town Council, 1973-75; Corporate Member, Society of Dyers and Colourists; holder of various offices, Transport and General Workers Union, since 1970; Organiser, Scottish National Party, Ayr Constituency, 1967-70. Recreations: hill-walking; horse-riding; reading; folk music; jazz; football; cricket. Address: (h.) Raehurst, 1 Raeburn Meadow, Selkirk; T.-0750 20821.

Henderson, Sheriff William Crichton, MA, LLB. Sheriff of Tayside, Central and Fife, at Stirling, since 1972; b. 10.6.31; m.; 2 d. Educ. George Watson's Boys' College; Edinburgh University. Solicitor, 1954; called to Scottish Bar, 1957; practised as Advocate, 1957-68; Sheriff of Renfrew and Argyll, at Paisley, 1968-72; Chairman, Supreme Court Legal Aid Committee, 1967-68.

Henderson, William Leonard Edgar, BSc (Hons). Principal, Falkirk College of Technology, since 1984; b. 9.5.39, Kilmarnock; m., Janette Anne; 2 d. Educ. Camphill School, Paisley; London University. Lecturer, Engineering and Associated Subjects, Anniesland College, 1966-68; Lecturer, Engineering Subjects, Stow College/Glasgow College of Technology, 1968-70; Senior Lecturer in Engineering, Anniesland College, 1970-74; Head, Department of Science and Mathematics, Cardonald College, 1974-77; Depute Principal, Kingsway Technical College, Dundee, 1977-84; Member, Council for Tertiary Education in Scotland, 1979-83; Member/Convener, Mathematics Panel, SCEEB, 1975-81; Member, CCC, 1987, MEC, 1987; Member, SCOTVEC NC Committee, 1987. Recreations: walking; microelectronics. Address: (b.) Falkirk College of Technology, Grangemouth Road, Falkirk, FK2 9AD; T.-0324 24981.

Hendrie, Eric. Deputy Leader, Labour Group, Grampian Regional Council, since 1978 (Education Spokesperson, Labour Group, since 1978); b. 11.9.25, Glasgow; m., Isabel; 1 s.; 1 d. Educ. Lambhill School, Glasgow; Royal Technical College, Glasgow. Councillor: Aberdeen Corporation, 1970-75, Grampian Regional Council, since 1975. Address: (h.) 37 New Park Road, Aberdeen, AB2 6UT; T.-0224 691723.

Hendry, Professor Alan, BSc (Hons), PhD, CEng, FICeram, MIM, MInstP. Personal Professor in Metallurgy, Strathclyde University, since 1988 (Reader in Ceramics, 1985-88); b. 29.1.47, Ochiltree; m., Jean Carey Kerr; 1 s.; 1 d. Educ. Cumnock Academy; Strathclyde University. Postdoctoral Research Associate, Newcastle University, 1971-75; Research Officer, Midlands Region, CEGB, 1975-76; Lecturer in Metallurgy and Assistant Director, Wolfson Research Group for High Strength Materials, Newcastle University, 1975-85. Council Member, Scottish Branch, Institute of Physics and Vice-President, SAM. Address: (h.) Ardleven, 23 Campbell Drive, Bearsden, Glasgow, G61 4NF; T.-041-942 3169.

Hendry, Professor Arnold William, BSc, PhD, DSc, FICE, FIStructE, FRSE. Professor of Civil Engineering, Edinburgh University, since 1964; b. 10.9.21, Buckie; m., Elizabeth Lois Alice Inglis; 1 s.; 1 d. Educ. Buckie High School; Aberdeen University. Assistant Civil Engineer, Sir William Arrol & Co. Ltd., Glasgow, 1941-43; Lecturer in Civil Engineering, Aberdeen University, 1943-49; Reader in Civil Engineering, King's College, London, 1949-51; Professor of Civil Engineering and Dean, Faculty of Engineering, Khartoum University, 1951-57; Professor of Building Science, Liverpool University, 1957-63. Recreations: walking; DIY; bird-watching. Address: (h.) 2 Castlelaw Road, Edinburgh, EH13 ODN; T.-031-441 4141.

Hendry, Joy McLaggan, MA (Hons), DipEd. Editor, Chapman Magazine, since 1972; Writer; b. 3.2.53, Perth; m., Ian Montgomery. Educ. Perth Academy; Edinburgh University. Former teacher; Co-Editor, Chapman, 1972-76, Sole Editor, since 1976; Deputy Convener, Scottish Poetry Library Association, 1983-88; Convener, Committee for the Advancement of Scottish Literature in Schools; Member AdCas; Scottish National Theatre Steering Committee; Campaign for a Scottish Assembly; writes poetry; gives lectures and talks and performances of poetry and song; radio critic, The Scotsman; theatre reviewer. Publications: Scots: The Way Forward; Poems and Pictures by Wendy Wood (Editor); The Land for the People (Co-Editor); Critical Essays on Sorley MacLean (Co-Editor). Recreations: going to theatre; cinema; reading. Address: 15 Nelson Street, Edinburgh; T.-031-557 2207.

Hendry, Leo Brough, MSc, MEd, PhD, FBPS. Head, Education Department, Aberdeen University, since 1988; b. 12.11.35, Glasgow; m., Philomena Walsh; 2 d. Educ. Hermitage Academy, Helensburgh; Jordanhill College of Education, Glasgow; Bradford University; Leicester University; Aberdeen University. School Teacher in Scottish and English schools, including two posts as Head of Department, 1957-64; Lecturer in Education and Physical Education, College of St. Mark and St. John's, Chelsea, London University Institute, 1964-66; Head of Human Movement Studies, Trinity and All Saints' Colleges, Leeds University Institute, 1966-71; Lecturer in Education, then Senior Lecturer, Aberdeen University, 1971-88. Member, Scottish Council for Research in Education, 1983-86. Publications: School, Sport, Leisure: three dimensions of adolescence, 1978; Adolescents and Leisure, 1981; Growing Up and Going Out, 1983; Personality and Performance in Physical Education and Sport (Co-author), 1974; Physical Education in England (Co-author), 1976; Towards Community Education (Co-author), 1980; The Nature of Adolescence (Co-author), 1988. Recreations: golf; writing; broadcasting; presenting papers at international conferences. Address: (b.) Department of Education, Aberdeen University, Aberdeen, AB9 2UB; T.-0224 40241, Ext. 6588.

Henriksen, Henry Neil, BSc, MEd. Rector, The James Young High School, since 1982; b. 2.9.33, Edinburgh; m., Edith Robb; 2 s. Educ. Royal High School, Edinburgh; Edinburgh University; Strathclyde University. Taught at Portobello, Falkirk High, Forrester; Depute Head, Penicuik High School. Recreations: television; climbing Allermuir. Address: (h.) 16 Redford Loan, Edinburgh, EH13 OAX; T.-031-441 2282.

Henry, Alastair William. Farmer, since 1952; Member, Grampian Regional Council, since 1982; Member, Countryside Commission for Scotland, since 1988; b. 14.5.29, Laurencekirk; m., Olive Margaret Chaplin; 1 d. Educ. Montrose Academy. British Red Cross: Director, Kincardine and Deeside Branch, 1973-82, Council Member, Scotland, since 1974; North Angus & Mearns Conservative Association: Chairman, 1974-77, President, 1977-80; Chairman, NE Scotland Conservative Euro Constituency, 1978-81; Vice President, Scottish Conservative & Unionist Association, 1981-83; Chairman, Kincardine and Deeside Members Centre, National Trust for Scotland, 1980-82; Governor, Royal Aberdeen Workshops for the Blind, since 1982; Director, Haven Products Ltd. (Sheltered Workshops), since 1979; Elder, Church of Scotland, since 1960. Recreations: politics; gardening. Address: Hatton, Laurencekirk, Kincardineshire; T.-067 484 202.

Henry, Gordon Edward, DA, MCSD. Director of Development and Tourism, Aberdeen City Council, since 1977; b. 23.9.37, Elgin; m., Elizabeth Browne; 2 s. Educ. Elgin Academy; Grays School of Art; Aberdeen College of Education. Art Teacher, Lecturer and Freelance Designer, 1960-63; Aberdeen University Press: Staff Designer, 1963-69, Design Manager, 1969-71, Company Director, 1971-75; City of Aberdeen: Depute Director PR, 1975-77, Director of Information and Tourism, 1977. Director, Aberdeen Tourist Board and Gordon District Tourist Board. Recreations: painting; golf; swimming; reading. Address: (b.) St. Nicholas House, Aberdeen, AB9 1DE; T.-0224 642121.

Henry, Professor Peter (formerly H.P. Zuntz), MA (Oxon), DipEd (Leeds). Professor of Slavonic Languages and Literatures, Glasgow University, since 1975; b. 21.4.26, Marburg, Germany; m., Brenda Grace Lewis (m. diss.); 1 s.; 3 d. Educ. St. Knud's Skole, Copenhagen; Mellemskole, Birkerod, Denmark; St. Edward's School, Oxford; St. John's College, Oxford. Left Germany, 1936; Denmark, 1936-39, then Britain; Royal Tank Regiment, 1943-47; Senior Master, St. John's College Choir School, Cambridge, 1952; Russian Instructor, Joint Services School for Linguists, Coulsdon, 1952-54; Senior German Master, Haverfordwest Grammar School, 1954-57; Lecturer in Russian, Liverpool University, 1957-63; Senior Lecturer in Charge, Department of Russian Studies, Hull University, 1963-74. Editor, Scottish Slavonic Review, since 1983; Honorary Vice-President, Association of Teachers of Russian. Publications: Russian prose composition, three volumes, 1964-65; edited texts (Pushkin, Chekhov, Bunin, Paustovsky); two-volume anthology of Soviet satire; Gazeta: Clippings from the Soviet Press (with K. Young); A Hamlet of His Time: Vsevolod Garshin; translations: V. Garshin: From the Reminiscences of Private Ivanov and Other Stories (with L. Tudge); also Sholokhov, Paustovsky, Tendryakov, etc. Recreations: travel; music; theatre. Address: (b.) Department of Slavonic Languages and Literatures, Hetherington Building, Glasgow University, Glasgow, G12 8QQ; T.-041-339 8855, Ext. 5587.

Henshelwood, James, JP, FISMM, MInstM, MBIM, AMNI. Director, Glasgow Chamber of Commerce, since 1976; Director, Bridgegate Trust, since 1982; Director, Mayfest Ltd., since 1983; b. 18.2.22, Glasgow; m., Mavis Irene Watson (deceased); 3 s.; 2 d. Educ. Allan Glen's School; Whitehill Senior Secondary School; Royal Technical College, Glasgow. Joined Merchant Navy as cadet, 1938, and "swallowed the anchor" in 1953 as Master Mariner; Independent Councillor, Johnstone, 1966-69 (Burgh Treasurer); represents Institute of Marketing on board of Glasgow Chamber of Commerce; Chairman, Nautical Institute, West of Scotland. Recreations: golf; sailing; walking. Address: (h.) 72 Globe Court, Calderwood, East Kilbride, Glasgow, G74 3QZ; T.-03552 38851.

Hepburn, Professor Ronald William, MA, PhD. Professor of Moral Philosophy, Edinburgh University, since 1975; b. 16.3.27, Aberdeen; m., Agnes Forbes Anderson; 2 s.; 1 d. Educ. Aberdeen Grammar School; Aberdeen University. Assistant, then Lecturer, Department of Moral Philosophy, Aberdeen University, 1952-60; Visiting Associate Professor, New York University, 1959-60; Professor of Philosophy and Head of Department, Nottingham University, 1960-64; Professor of Philosophy, Edinburgh University, 1964-75; Stanton Lecturer, Cambridge University, 1965-68; Heslington Lecture, York University, 1970; Margaret Harris Lectures on Religion, Dundee University, 1974. Publications: Christianity and Paradox, 1958; Wonder and Other Essays, 1984. Recreation: hill-walking. Address: (b.) Department of Philosophy, David Hume Tower, George Square, Edinburgh, EH8 9JX; T.-031-667 1011.

Hepworth, James Michael, BA. Senior Lecturer in Sociology, Aberdeen University, since 1981; b. 21.12.38, Wakefield; m., Marian Bywell; 1 s.; 2 d. Educ. Ossett Grammar School; Kibworth Beauchamp Grammar School; Hull University. Assistant Careers Advisory Officer, Sutton Coldfield, 1961-65; Assistant Lecturer in Social Studies, Monkwearmouth College of Further Education, Sunderland, 1965-66; Lecturer in Sociology, Teesside Polytechnic, Middlesbrough, 1967-71; Senior Lecturer in Sociology, Lanchester Polytechnic, Coventry, 1971; Lecturer in Sociology, Aberdeen University, 1972-81. Company Secretary, Theory, Culture and Process; Founder Member, Centre for the Study of Adult Life; Member, Crime Writers Association. Publications: Blackmail, 1975; Confession: Studies in Deviance and Religion (Co-author), 1982; Surviving Middle Age, 1982. Recreations: gardening; literature and art; walking. Address: (h.) Rose Cottage, Whiterashes, Aberdeen, AB5 OQP; T.-Whiterashes 319.

Herbert, Rodney Andrew, BSc, PhD, CBiol, MIBiol. Senior Lecturer in Microbiology, Dundee University, since 1982; b. 27.6.44, York; m., Helen Joyce Macpherson Millard; 2 s. Educ. Archbishop Holgate's Grammar School, York; Bradford University; Aberdeen University. Research Fellow, Edinburgh University, 1970-71; Lecturer in Microbiology, Dundee University, 1971-82. Convener, Scottish Branch, Society of General Microbiology; Senior Visiting Scientist: British Antarctic Survey, 1976-77, Ross Sea, Antarctica, 1982-83. Recreations: music; walking; gardening. Address: (b.) Department of Biological Sciences, Dundee University, Dundee, DD1 4HN; T.-Dundee 23181, Ext. 608.

Herbison, Rt. Hon. Margaret McCrorie, PC (1964), MA, LLD (Hon.); b. 11.3.07, Shotts. Educ. Bellshill Academy; Glasgow University. Teacher, 1930-45; MP for Lanarkshire North, 1945-70; Joint Under-Secretary of State, Scottish Office, 1950-51; Minister of Pensions and National Insurance, 1964-66; Minister of Social Security, 1966-67; Chairman, Select Committee on Overseas Aid, 1968-70; Lord High Commissioner to General Assembly of Church of Scotland, 1970; Hon. LLD, Glasgow University, 1970; Scotswoman of the Year, 1970; Member, Royal Commission on Standards of Conduct in Public Life, 1975-76; Lay Observer, 1975-76; Chairman, Labour Party, 1956-57. Recreations: reading; gardening. Address: (h.) 8 Mornay Way, Shotts, ML7 4EG; T.-Shotts 21944.

Herd, James Peter, MBE, WS, NP. Partner, Beveridge, Herd & Sandilands, WS, Kirkcaldy, since 1951; Honorary Sheriff, Kirkcaldy, since 1987; b. 18.5.20, Kirkcaldy; m., Marjory Phimister Mitchell; 3 s.; 2 d. Educ. Edinburgh Academy; St. Andrews University; Edinburgh University. Army Service as Major, Black Watch, UK and South East Asia, 1939-46; Local Director, Royal Insurance Group, since 1951; Trustee, Kirkcaldy and District Trustee Savings Bank, 1952-83; Director, Kirkcaldy Ice Rink Limited, since 1982; Director, Kirkcaldy Abbeyfield Society. Recreations: curling; gardening. Address: (b.) 1 East Fergus Place, Kirkcaldy, Fife, KY1 1XT; T.-0592 261616.

Herdman, John Macmillan, MA (Hons), PhD (Cantab), DipTh. Writer, since 1963; b. 20.7.41, Edinburgh; m., Dolina Maclennan. Educ. Merchiston Castle School, Edinburgh; Magdalene College, Cambridge. Creative Writing Fellow, Edinburgh University, 1977-79; Scottish Arts Council bursaries, 1976 and 1982; Scottish Arts Council Book Award, 1978. Publications: Descent, 1968; A Truth Lover, 1973; Memoirs of My Aunt Minnie/Clapperton, 1974; Pagan's Pilgrimage, 1978; Stories Short and Tall, 1979; Voice Without Restraint: Bob Dylan's Lyrics and Their Background, 1982; Three Novellas, 1987. Recreations: reading; walking; listening to music. Address: (h.) Woodlands, St. Andrew's Crescent, Bridge of Tilt, Blair Atholl, Perthshire, PH18 5SX; T.-Blair Atholl 403.

Heriot, Rev. Charles Rattray, BA. Minister, Brightons Parish Church, since 1967; Clerk, Falkirk Presbytery, Church of Scotland, since 1980; b. 9.4.31, Glasgow; m., Audrey J.L. Scott; 1 s.; 1 d. Educ. Hyndland Senior Secondary School; Glasgow University and Trinity College. Minister, Kenmure Parish Church, 1962-67. Member, Brightons Community Council. Recreations: reading; walking. Address: The Manse, Brightons, Falkirk, FK2 OJP; T.-Polmont 712062.

Herries, Sir Michael, OBE, MC, DL, LLD, DLitt. Chairman, The Royal Bank of Scotland Group plc; Chairman, The Royal Bank of Scotland plc; b. 28.2.23, Castle Douglas; m.; 2 s.; 1 d. Educ. Eton; Trinity College, Cambridge. KOSB, 1942-47, NW Europe and Middle East, Captain (Acting/Major); Jardine, Matheson & Co. Ltd., Hong Kong, Japan, Singapore, latterly as Chairman and Managing Director; Chairman, Matheson & Co. Ltd., 1970-75; appointed a Director, The Royal Bank of Scotland plc, 1972; Chairman, Scottish Mortgage and Investment Trust PLC; Director, Scottish Widows' Fund and Life Assurance Society (Chairman, 1981-84); Chairman, Enterprise Trust for Nithsdale, Annandale, Eskdale and the Stewartry of Kirkcudbright, since 1984; Member, Royal Company of Archers, since 1973; knighted, 1975; DLitt, Heriot-Watt, 1984; Deputy Lieutenant, Stewarty of Kirkcudbright. Recreation: shooting; walking in the Galloway Hills. Address: (b.) 42 St. Andrew Square, Edinburgh, EH2 2YE; T.-031-556 8555.

Herron, Very. Rev. Andrew, ATCL, MA, BD, LLB, DD, LLD. Moderator, General Assembly of Church of Scotland, 1971; b. 29.9.09, Glasgow; m., Joanna Fraser Neill; 4 d. Educ. Strathbungo H.G. School; Albert Road Academy; Glasgow University and Trinity College. Minister: Linwood, 1936-40, Houston and Killellan, 1940-59; Clerk, Glasgow Presbytery, 1959-81. Baird Lecturer, 1985. Publications: Record Apart, 1972; Guide to the General Assembly, 1976; Guide to Congregational Affairs, 1979; Guide to the Presbytery, 1982; Kirk by Divine Right, 1985; Guide to the Ministry, 1987; Guide to Ministerial Income, 1987; contributed article on Houston to Third Statistical Account. Address: (h.) 36 Darnley Road, Glasgow, G41 4NE; T.-041-423 6422.

Herschell, David John, FSA Scot. Trustee and Council Member, Scottish Tartans Society; b. 26.10.44, London; m., Hazel Joyce Giddins; 1 s.; 1 d. Editor, Tartans (Journal, Scottish Tartans Society); Convener, Junior Section, Scottish Tartans Society. Publication: Rev. Francis Edward Robinson (1833-1910) - His Background and Early Life. Recreations: Scottish history and culture; campanology. Address: (h.) Braidon, Ancaster Lane, Comrie, Perthshire, PH6 2DT; T.-0764 70666.

Hesketh, Nigel George Francis. Member, Stewartry District Council, since 1984; Founder, Galloway Lodge Preserves, 1970; b. 10.5.45, Simla, India; m., Fiona Mary Wylie; 1 s. Educ. Stowe School; Royal Military Academy, Sandhurst. Served with 4th/7th Royal Dragoon Guards; Member, Inner Temple. Community Councillor, Gatehouse-of-Fleet; Chairman, Gatehouse-of-Fleet Burns Club. Publication: Commercial English for Foreign Correspondents. Recreation: classical modern studies. Address: (h.) Bleachfield, Gatehouse-of-Fleet, Stewartry of Kirkcudbright; T.-Gatehouse 357.

Hetherington, Professor (Hector) Alastair, MA. Emeritus Professor in Media Studies, Stirling University, since 1987; b. 31.10.19, Llanishen, Glamorgan; m., Sheila Cameron; 2 s.; 2 d.; 1 step s.; 2 step d. Educ. Corpus Christi College, Oxford. Army, 1940-46; Glasgow Herald, 1946-50; The Guardian, 1950-75 (Foreign Editor, 1953-56, Editor, 1956-75); BBC Scotland, 1976-79; Director, Scotquest (film company), since 1982; Chairman, The Scott Trust (owners, The Guardian and Manchester Evening News), since 1984; various films for Channel Four. Publications: Guardian Years, 1981; News, Newspapers and Television, 1985. Recreation: hill-walking. Address: (h.) 38 Chalton Road, Bridge of Allan, Stirling, FK9 4EF; T.-0786 832168.

Hetherington, Rev. Robert MacArthur, MA, BD. Minister, Barrhead South and Levern Parish Church, since 1977; b. 29.9.37, Kilmarnock; m., Inge Olderdissen; 3 s. Educ. Kilmarnock Academy; Worcester College for Blind; Edinburgh University; Marburg University. Lecturer in Philosophy, Madras Christian College, 1965-69; Scottish Braille Press, 1969-71; Inverbrothock Parish Church, Arbroath, 1971-77. Member, Cleric's Group, Royal National Institute for the Blind, since 1982; Member, Board of Directors, Glasgow and West of Scotland Society for the Blind, since 1978. Recreations: music; hill-walking. Address: 3 Colinbar Circle, Barrhead, Glasgow, G78 2BE; T.-041-880 6654.

Hewitt, David S., MA, PhD. Senior Lecturer in English, Aberdeen University, since 1982; b. 22.4.42, Hawick; m., Angela Catherine Williams; 1 s.; 1 d. Educ. Melrose Grammar School; George Watson's College, Edinburgh; Edinburgh University; Aberdeen University. Aberdeen University: Assistant Lecturer in English, 1964, Lecturer, 1968; Treasurer, Association for Scottish Literary Studies, since 1973; Editor-in-Chief, Edinburgh Edition of the Waverley Novels, 1984; President, Edinburgh Sir Walter Scott Club, 1988-89; Elder, Cathedral Church of St. Machar, Old Aberdeen; Managing Editor, New Writing Scotland, 1983-86. Publications: Scott on Himself (Editor), 1982; Literature of the North, 1983; Scott and His Influence, 1984; Longer Scottish Poems, Vol. 2 1650-1830, 1987. Address: (b.) Department of English, Aberdeen University, Aberdeen, AB9 2UB; T.-0224 272634.

Heywood, Barry Keith, MA, LLB. Procurator Fiscal, Inverness, since 1986; b. 24.7.46, Oldham; m., Mary A.; 1 s.; 1 d. Educ. Kirkcaldy High School; Edinburgh University. Procurator Fiscal Depute, Ayr, 1971-77, Glasgow, 1977-78; Procurator Fiscal, Wick, 1978-83; Assistant Procurator Fiscal, Glasgow, 1983-86. Recreations: walking; Roman and Byzanine history; "railway buff". Address: (b.) 2 Baron Taylor's Street, Inverness, IV1 1QL; T.-0463 224858.

Hider, Calvin Fraser, MB, ChB, FFARCS. Consultant Anaesthetist, Edinburgh Royal Infirmary, since 1964; Honorary Senior Lecturer, Faculty of Medicine, Edinburgh University; b. 29.5.30, Glasgow; m., Jean M.D. Dott; 3 d. Educ. George Watson's Boys College, Edinburgh; Edinburgh University. Medical training, Dumfries and Galloway Royal Infirmary and Edinburgh Royal Infirmary; RNVR, Surgeon (Lt.-Cdr.), 1955-64. Recreations: sailing; sheep-breeding (Jacob). Address: (h.) Marchwell Cottage, Penicuik, Midlothian, EH26 OPX; T.-0968 72680.

Higgs, Professor Peter Ware, BSc, MSc, PhD, FRS, FRSE. Professor of Theoretical Physics, Edinburgh University, since 1980; b. 29.5.29, Newcastle-upon-Tyne; m., Jo Ann Williamson; 2 s. Educ. Cotham Grammar School, Bristol; King's College, London. Postdoctoral Fellow, Edinburgh University, 1954-56, and London University, 1956-58; Lecturer in Mathematics, University College, London, 1958-60; Lecturer in Mathematical Physics, then Reader, Edinburgh University, 1960-80. Hughes Medal, Royal Society, 1981; Rutherford Medal, Institute of Physics, 1984. Recreations: music; walking; swimming. Address: (h.) 2 Darnaway Street, Edinburgh, EH3 6BG; T.-031-225 7060.

Higham, Rev. Robert David, BD. Minister, Parish of Gordon with Greenlaw with Legerwood with Westruther, since 1985; b. 13.3.37, Bolton; m., Diana Mai Cochrane; 3 d. Educ. Bolton School; National Leathersellers College, London; Christ's College, Aberdeen. Technical management, tanneries in Bolton, Galashiels and Edenbridge, 1960-69; Technical Editor, then Editor, Leather (journal), 1969-80; undergraduate, Faculty of Divinity, Aberdeen Univesity, 1980-84; Assistant Minister, North Church of St. Andrew, Aberdeen, 1984-85. Secretary, India Ministries Fellowship; Secretary, Scottish Evangelical Theology Society; Governor, Northumbria Bible College. Recreations: hill-walking; music (choral). Address: The Manse, Greenlaw, Duns, Berwickshire, TD10 6XF; T.-03616 218.

Highgate, James Brown, CBE (1981), MA, LLB, JP. Consultant, Miller Thompson Brownlie Watson, Solicitors; former Senior Partner, Brownlie Watson & Beckett, Solicitors; b. 18.6.20, Glasgow. Educ. High School of Glasgow; Glasgow University. Served, Royal Artillery and Royal Indian Artillery, 1941-46 (demobilised as Major); appointed General Commissioner of Income Tax, 1969 (appointed Chairman, Glasgow North Division, 1981); Member, Strathclyde Advisory Board, Salvation Army, since 1970; Joint Honorary Secretary, Scottish Conservative and Unionist Association, 1973-86 (appointed President, 1987); Honorary President, Hamilton and Motherwell North Conservative Constituencies; Elder, Park Church of Scotland, Uddingston; Governor, High School of Glasgow. Recreations: golf; travel. Address: (h.) Broomlands, 121 Kylepark Drive, Uddingston, Glasgow; T.-Uddingston 813377.

Hill, Richard Inglis, BSc (Hons), FICE, FIHT. Director of Roads and Transportation, Borders Regional Council, since 1974; b. 8.5.33, Callander; m., Margaret; 2 s. Educ. McLaren High School, Callander; Royal College of Science and Technology, Glasgow. Perth and Kinross Joint County Council: student assistant, 1951-53, graduate assistant, 1954-56, Assistant Engineer, 1958-59, Senior Engineer, 1959-61, Senior Supervisory Engineer, 1961-65, Assistant County Surveyor, 1965-72; County Surveyor and Engineer, Selkirk County Council, 1972-75. Past Chairman, Scottish Branch, County Surveyors' Society. Recreations: golf; music. Address: (b.) Regional HQ, Newtown St. Boswells, Melrose, TD6 OSA; T.-St. Boswells 23301.

Hill, Professor William George, BSc, MS, PhD, DSc, FRSE, FRS. Professor of Animal Genetics, Edinburgh University, since 1983; b. 7.8.40, Hemel Hempstead; m., C. Rosemary Austin; 1 s.; 2 d. Educ. St. Albans School; London University; University of California; Iowa State University;

Edinburgh University. Edinburgh University: Assistant Lecturer, 1965-67, Lecturer, 1967-74, Reader, 1974-83; Visiting Research Associate, Iowa State University, 1967-68-69-72; Visiting Professor: University of Minnesota, 1966, Iowa State University, 1978, North Carolina State University, 1979; Consultant Geneticist: Cotswold Pig Development Co., since 1965, British Friesian Cattle Society, since 1978; Member, AFRC Animals Research Grant Board, since 1986. Recreations: farming; bridge. Address: (h.) 4 Gordon Terrace, Edinburgh, EH16 5QH; T.-031-667 3680.

Hillhouse, Muriel Muir Harvey, MA. Solicitor, since 1932; Honorary Sheriff, South Strathclyde, Dumfries and Galloway, at Ayr, since 1983; b. 14.11.07, Ayr. Educ. Ayr Academy; Glasgow University. Address: 16 Carrick Park, Ayr, KA7 2SL; T.-Ayr 263472.

Hillhouse, (Robert) Russell, MA. Permanent Under-Secretary of State, Scottish Office, since 1988; b. 23.4.38, Glasgow; m., Alison Fraser; 2 d. Educ. Hutchesons' Grammar School, Glasgow; Glasgow University. Entered Home Civil Service as Assistant Principal, Scottish Education Department, 1962; Principal, 1966; HM Treasury, 1971; Assistant Secretary, Scottish Office, 1974; Scottish Home and Health Department, 1977; Principal Finance Officer, Scottish Office, 1980; Under-Secretary, Scottish Education Department, 1985; Secretary, 1987. Recreation: making music. Address: (b.) St. Andrew's House, Regent Road, Edinburgh, EH1 3DG; T.-031-556 8400.

Hillis, William Stewart, MB, ChB, MRCP, FRCPGlas. Senior Lecturer in Clinical Pharmacology, Glasgow University, since 1979; Honorary Consultant Cardiologist, Glasgow Area Health Board, since 1979; b. 28.9.43, Elderslie, Renfrewshire; m., Anne Marshall Craigie; 3 s.; 1 d. Educ. Clydebank High School; Glasgow University. House Officer in Surgery, Western Infirmary, Glasgow, 1967; House Officer in Medicine, Southern General Hospital, 1968-70; Registrar/Senior Registrar in Cardiology, Glasgow Royal Infirmary, 1970-77 (Research Fellow in Cardiology, Vanderbilt University Hospital, Nashville, Tennessee, 1973-74); Consultant Physician, Stobhill Hospital, 1977-79; Honorary Physician, Scottish Football Association, since 1980. Publication: Treatment of Cardiovascular Disease (Co-author). Recreation: football. Address: (h.) 20 Airthrey Avenue, Jordanhill, Glasgow; T.-041-959 1699.

Hillman, John Richard, BSc, PhD, CBiol, FIBiol, FLS, FBIM, FRSE. Director, Scottish Crop Research Institute, since 1986; Visiting Professor, Dundee University and Strathclyde University, since 1986; b. 21.7.44, Farnborough, Kent; m., Sandra Kathleen Palmer; 2 s. Educ. Chislehurst and Sidcup Grammar School; University of Wales. Assistant Lecturer, 1968, and Lecturer, 1969, Physiology and Environmental Studies, Nottingham University; Lecturer, 1971, Senior Lecturer, 1977, Reader, 1980, Professor of Botany, 1982, Glasgow University. Recreations: landscaping; building renovations; horology; reading. Address: (b.) Scottish Crop Research Institute, Invergowrie, Dundee, DD2 5DA; T.-0382 562731.

Hills, Graham John, PhD, DSc, CChem, FRSC, FRSE, Hon DSc (Lodz and Southampton), Hon LLD (Glasgow). Principal and Vice-Chancellor, Strathclyde University, since 1980; b. 9.4.26, Leigh-on-Sea; m., Mary Jane McNaughton; 1 s.; 3 d. Educ. Westcliff High School for Boys; Birkbeck College and Imperial College, London University. Lecturer in Physical Chemistry, Imperial College, 1949-62; Professor of Physical Chemistry, Southampton University, 1962-80; Visiting Professor, University of Western Ontario, 1968; Visiting Professor and National Science Foundation Fellow, Case-Western Reserve University, Ohio, 1968-69; Visiting Professor, Buenos Aires University, 1976; Member, Pay Review Board for Nurses, Midwives and Professions Allied to Medicine, since 1983; Member, Advisory Council on Science and Technology, since 1987; (Non-Executive) Member: Scottish Post Office Board, since 1986, Britoil Board, since 1988; President, International Society of Electrochemistry, 1982-84; Director, Glasgow Chamber of Commerce, since 1981; Member, Glasgow Action, since 1985; President, Friends of Glasgow Cathedral, since 1987; Commander Insignia, Order of Merit of Polish People's Republic; Commander Insignia, Royal Norwegian Order of Merit. Publications: Reference Electrodes, 1961; Polarography, 1964. Recreations: music; hill-walking; European politics. Address: (b.) Principal's Office, McCance Building, 16 Richmond Street, Glasgow, G1 1XQ; T.-041-552 4400, Ext. 2000.

Himsworth, Professor Richard Lawrence, MD, FRCPLond, FRCPEdin. Regius Professor of Medicine, Aberdeen University, since 1985; Honorary Consultant Physician, Aberdeen Royal Infirmary, since 1985; b. 14.6.37, London; m., Sara Margaret Tattersall; 2 s.; 1 d. Educ. Westminster School; Trinity College, Cambridge; University College Hospital, London. Lecturer in Medicine, University College Hospital Medical School, 1967-71; MRC Travelling Fellowship, Columbia University, New York, 1969-70; MRC scientific staff, Clinical Research Centre, 1971-85 (Assistant Director, 1978-82). Member, NW Thames Regional Health Authority, 1982-85. Recreation: painting. Address: (h.) Mains of Kebbaty, Midmar, Aberdeenshire, AB3 7QL; T.-Sauchen 430.

Hind, Archie. Novelist and Playwright; b. 1928. Author of The Dear Green Place, 1966; former Writer in Residence to the community in Aberdeen.

Hine, Professor Harry Morrison, MA, DPhil (Oxon). Scotstarvit Professor of Humanity, St. Andrews University, since 1985; b. 19.6.48, Portsmouth; m., Rosalind Mary Ford; 1 s.; 1 d. Educ. King Edward's School, Birmingham; Corpus Christi College, Oxford. P.S. Allen Junior Research Fellow, Corpus Christi College, 1972-75; Lecturer in Humanity, Edinburgh University, 1975-85. Editor (Joint), The Classical Review, since 1987. Publication: An Edition with Commentary of Seneca, Natural Questions, Book Two, 1981. Recreations: walking; reading. Address: (h.) 33 Drumcarrow Road, St. Andrews, Fife, KY16 8SE; T.-0334 74459.

Hingston, David Robert, LLB, NP. Procurator Fiscal, Caithness, since 1983; 29.7.48, Assam, India; m., Sylvia Isobel Reid; 2 s.; 1 d. Educ. Morrison's Academy, Crieff; Edinburgh University. Private practice, Edinburgh; joined Procurator Fiscal service, 1975 (Kirkcaldy, Dunfermline, Edinburgh); seconded to Scottish Law Commission; then Edinburgh Office; Tutor in Criminal Law, Demonstrator Criminal Procedure. Group Scout Leader; Vice Chairman, Schools Council; Trustee, Children's Centre Trust Fund; Secretary, Faculty of Procurators of Caithness. Publication: Stair Memorial Encyclopaedia. Recreations: fitting 36 hours into 24; fishing. Address: (b.) Procurator Fiscal's Office, Sheriff Court House, Wick, Caithness; T.-Wick 2197/8.

Hirst, Michael William, LLB, CA. Vice Chairman, Scottish Conservative Party, since 1987; MP (Conservative), Strathkelvin and Bearsden, 1983-87; Member, Select Committee on Scottish Affairs, 1983-87; Parliamentary Private Secretary, Department of Energy, 1985-87; b. 2.1.46, Glasgow; m., Naomi Ferguson Wilson; 1 s.; 2 d. Educ. Glasgow Academy; Glasgow University. Partner, Peat Marwick Mitchell & Co., Chartered Accountants, until 1983; Company Director, Consultant to various companies; Partner, Garrigue Hirst & Associates; contested: Central Dunbartonshire, February and October, 1974, East Dunbartonshire, 1979; Chairman, Scottish Conservative Candidates Association, 1978-81; Preses, Weavers Society of Anderston; Member, Executive Committee, Princess Louise Scottish Hospital, Erskine; Elder, Kelvinside Hillhead Parish Church. Recreations: golf; hill-walking. Address: (h.) Enderley, Baldernock Road, Milngavie, Glasgow, G62 8DU; T.-041-956 1213.

Hitchman, Professor Michael L., BSc, DPhil, CChem, FRSC. Young Professor of Chemistry, Strathclyde University, since 1984 (Chairman, Department of Pure and Applied Chemistry, since 1986); b. 17.8.41, Woburn, Bedfordshire; m., Pauline J. Thompson; 1 s.; 2 d. Educ. Stratton Grammar School, Biggleswade; Queen Mary College and King's College, London University; University College, Oxford. Assistant Lecturer in Chemistry, Leicester Regional College of Technology, 1963-65; Junior Research Fellow, Wolfson College, Oxford, 1968-70; ICI Postdoctoral Research Fellow, Physical Chemistry Laboratory, Oxford University, 1968-70; Chief Scientist, Orbisphere Corporation, Geneva, 1970-73; Staff Scientist, Laboratories RCA Ltd., Zurich, 1973-79; Lecturer, then Senior Lecturer, Salford University, 1979-84. Royal Society of Chemistry: Chairman, Electroanalytical Group, Treasurer, Electrochemistry Group; Science and Engineering Research Council: Member, Chemistry and Non Metallic Materials Committees. Publications: Ring-disk Electrodes (Co-author), 1971; Measurement of Dissolved Oxygen, 1978. Recreations: family; keep fit; walking; sailing; skiing; DIY; theatre-going. Address: (b.) Department of Pure and Applied Chemistry, Strathclyde University, 295 Cathedral Street, Glasgow, G1 1XL; T.-041-552 4400.

Hoare, Peter, DM, MA, BM, BCH, MRCPsych. Consultant Psychiatrist, Royal Hospital for Sick Children, Edinburgh, since 1980; part-time Senior Lecturer, Edinburgh University, since 1980; b. 30.10.45, Liverpool; m., Barbara Jane; 1 s.; 2 d. Educ. St. Mary's College, Crosby, Liverpool; Oxford University. Former Lecturer, Department of Psychiatry, Oxford University. Recreations: squash; opera. Address: (b.) Department of Child and Family Psychiatry, Royal Hospital for Sick Children, 3 Rillbank Terrace, Edinburgh; T.-031-668 2251.

Hobsbaum, Professsor Philip Dennis, MA, PhD, LRAM, LGSM. Titular Professor of English Literature, Glasgow University, since 1984 (Reader in English Literature, 1979-84); b. 29.6.32, London; m., Rosemary Phillips. Educ. Belle Vue Grammar School, Bradford; Downing College, Cambridge; Sheffield University. Lecturer in English, Queen's University, Belfast, 1962-66; Lecturer, then Senior Lecturer in English Literature, Glasgow University, 1966-79. Publications: The Place's Fault, 1964; In Retreat, 1966; Coming Out Fighting, 1969; A Theory of Communication, 1970; A Reader's Guide to Charles Dickens, 1972; Women and Animals, 1972; Tradition and Experiment, 1979; A Reader's Guide to D.H. Lawrence, 1981; Essentials of Literary Criticism, 1983; A Reader's Guide to Robert Lowell, 1988. Recreation: walking the dog. Address: (b.) Department of English Literature, Glasgow University, Glasgow; T.-041-339 8855.

Hodges, Desmond W.H., OBE, FRIAS. Director, Edinburgh New Town Conservation Committee, since 1972; b. 25.9.28, Dublin; m., Margaret Elisabeth Anderson; 2 d. Educ. St. Columba's College, Rathfarnham, Co. Dublin. Architect practising in Dublin and Belfast, 1957-72; Visiting Lecturer, Queen's University, Belfast, 1967-78; Consultant Architect, Methodist Church in Ireland, 1964-87. Founder Member, Ulster Architectural Heritage Society; Member, Council, Cockburn Association and Architectural Heritage Society of Scotland. Address: (h.) 14 Shandon Street, Edinburgh; T.-031-337 4929.

Hoey, James Francis, BL, LMRTPI. Chief Executive, City of Dundee District Council, since 1981. Address: (b.) City Chambers, Dundee, DD1 3BY; T.-Dundee 23141.

Hollands, Clive Thomas Patrick. Director, Scottish Society for the Prevention of Vivisection, since 1970; Secretary, St. Andrew Animal Fund, since 1970; Secretary, Committee for the Reform of Animal Experimentation, since 1979; b. 26.4.29, London; m., Euphemia Garrett; 1 s.; 1 d. Educ. St. Clement Danes School, London; St. Mary's College, Liverpool. Royal Navy, 1946-53; Marine Personnel Officer, Caltex Ltd. for Overseas (Tankship) UK Ltd., 1953-66; joined Scottish Society for the Prevention of Vivisection, 1966; Advisory Director, World Society for the Protection of Animals; Patron, Zoo Check; Member, Scottish Churches Council Community, Justice and Peace Committee; Member, International Network for Religion and Animals Advisory Board, Washington DC; Member, Home Secretary's Animal Procedures Committee. Publication: Compassion is the Bugler - the Struggle for Animal Rights, 1980. Recreations: Scouting; walking; gardening. Address: (h.) Katrina, 6 Orchardhead Road, Edinburgh, EH16 6HL; T.-031-664 5206.

Hollis, Peter Desmond, MA (Hons), DipEd. Headmaster, Forrester High School, Edinburgh, since 1969; b. 23.4.25, Portsmouth; m., Morag McDonald; 2 s.; 1 d. Educ. Portsmouth Grammar School; Edinburgh University; Cambridge University. War service, Royal Artillery, 1943-47; university, 1947-51; Administrative Officer, HM Overseas Civil Service, 1951-57; teacher training, Moray House, Edinburgh, 1957-58; Teacher, then Principal Teacher of English, Edinburgh, 1958-68; Headmaster, Carrickvale Secondary School, 1968-69. Recreation: foreign travel. Address: (h.) Druim, 63 Bonaly Road, Edinburgh, EH13 0PB; T.-031-441 3660.

Holloway, Rt. Rev. Richard Frederick. Bishop of Edinburgh, since 1986; b. 26.11.33; m.; 1 s.; 2 d. Educ. Kelham College; Edinburgh Theological College; Union Theological Seminary, New York. Curate, St. Ninian's, Glasgow, 1959-63; Priest-in-Charge, St. Margaret and St. Mungo's, Glasgow, 1963-68; Rector, Old St. Paul's, Edinburgh, 1968-80. Address: (b.) The Diocesan Centre, Walpole Hall, Chester Street, Edinburgh, EH3 7EN; T.-031-226 3359.

Holmes, George Dennis, CB (1979), DSc, FRSE, FICfor. Forestry Consultant, since 1987; b. 9.11.26, Conwy; m., Sheila Rosemary; 3 d. Educ. John Bright's School, Llandudno; University of Wales, Bangor. Forestry Commission, 1948-86 (Director General, 1976-86). Chairman, Scottish Council for Spastics, since 1986. Recreations: fishing; sailing; golf. Address: (h.) 7 Cammo Road, Barnton, Edinburgh, EH4 8EF; T.-031-339 7474.

Holmes, Professor John Cameron, BSc, MS, PhD. Professor of Crop Production, Edinburgh University, since 1984; Head, Crop Division, Edinburgh School of Agriculture, since 1984; b. 3.4.25, Kilmadock Parish; m., Ellen Miller Hamilton; 1 s.; 2 d. Educ. Stirling High School; Edinburgh University; Iowa State University. Royal Navy, 1943-46; Lecturer and Senior Lecturer in Agriculture, Edinburgh University, 1949-74; Head of Crop Advisory and Development, East of Scotland College of Agriculture, 1974-84. Consultant with FAO, Africa and near East, since 1978; President, European Association for Potato Research, 1987-1990. Recreations: golf; skiing; reading. Address: (b.) Edinburgh School of Agriculture, West Mains Road, Edinburgh, EH9 3JG; T.-031-667 1041.

Holmes, Professor Peter Henry, BVMS, PhD, MRCVS. Head, Department of Veterinary Physiology, Glasgow University, since 1978; b. 6.6.42, Beverley; m., Ruth Helen Holmes; 2 d. Educ. Beverley Grammar School; Glasgow University. Lecturer, Senior Lecturer, Reader, Titular Professor in Veterinary Physiology, Glasgow University, since 1969; various overseas projects in East Africa, particularly in Ethiopia. Recreations: sailing; hill-walking. Address: (b.) Department of Veterinary Physiology, Glasgow University Veterinary School, Bearsden Road, Glasgow; T.-041-339 8855, Ext. 5793.

Holroyd, Rev. Gordon, BTh, FPhS, FSA (Scot). Parish Minister, St. Clements, Dingwall, since 1979; b. 13.7.29, Glasgow; m., Linda Jean Munro; 1 s.; 2 d. Educ. Jordanhill College School, Glasgow; Trinity College, Glasgow. National service, RAMC; salesman, building trade; Minister: Walls, Shetland, 1959-64, Tongue, 1964-67, Isle of Mull, 1972-79. Assistant Secretary, Social Service, Edinburgh, 1967-72. Recreations: woodturning; Member, Guild of Master Craftsmen. Address: St. Clements Manse, Dingwall, Ross-shire; T.-Dingwall 63379.

Home of the Hirsel, Rt. Hon. Lord (Alexander Frederick Douglas-Home), KT; Life Peer; b. 2.7.03, London; m., Elizabeth Alington; 1 s.; 3 d. Educ. Eton College; Christ Church, Oxford. Minister of State, Scottish Office, 1951-55; Secretary of State: Commonwealth Office, 1955-60, Foreign Office, 1960-63; Prime Minister, 1963-64; Secretary of State, Foreign and Commonwealth Office, 1970-74. Publications: The Way The Wind Blows (autobiography), 1976; Border Reflections, 1979; Letters to a Grandson, 1984. Recreations: fishing; shooting; gardening. Address: (h.) The Hirsel, Coldstream, Berwickshire; T.-0890 2345.

Home Robertson, John David. MP (Labour), East Lothian, since 1983 (Berwick & East Lothian, 1978-83); b. 5.12.48, Edinburgh; m., Catherine Brewster; 2 s. Educ. Ampleforth College; West of Scotland Agricultural College. Farmer; Member: Berwickshire District Council, 1974-78, Borders Health Board, 1975-78; Chairman, Eastern Borders Citizens' Advice Bureau, 1976-78; Member, Select Committee on Scottish Affairs, 1979-83; Chairman, Scottish Group of Labour MPs, 1983; Scottish Labour Whip, 1983-84; Opposition Front Bench Spokesman on Agriculture, 1984-87, on Scotland, since 1987. Address: (b.) House of Commons, Westminster, London, SW1A OAA; T.-01-219 4135.

Homfray, John L., TD, DL, FCA. Chairman, Iona Cathedral Trust Management Board, since 1982; b. 5.8.16, Darjeeling, India; m., Elizabeth M. Shand; 2 s.; 1 d. Educ. Sherborne. Captain, RA 80 Field Regiment, 1940-45 (mentioned in Despatches); Director, Clyde Shipping Co. Ltd., Glasgow, 1948-81; Deputy Lieutenant, Dunbartonshire, since 1975. Lt. Col., City of Glasgow Artillery, RATA, 1953-57; Vice Chairman, Glasgow Aged Seamen Relief Fund; Director, Sailors Orphan Society of Scotland. Recreations: shooting; travelling; curling. Address: (h.) Ardballachan, Bracklinn Road, Callander, Perthshire; T.-0877 30256.

Hood, Daniel, MA (Hons), LLB (Hons). Member (SNP), Tayside Regional Council, since 1986; COSLA Representative, since 1987; SCOTVEC Assessor, since 1984; b. 5.12.26, Glasgow; m., Avril Ballantyne; 3 s. Educ. Whitehill Senior Secondary School, Glasgow; Glasgow University. Royal Navy, 1945-47; Marketing Officer, Nigerian Government Service, 1955-57; Barister-at-Law (Gray's Inn); Head, Department of Business Studies, Falkirk College of Technology, 1962-69; Depute Principal, Dundee College of Commerce, 1969-82. Past President, Scottish Further and Higher Education Association; elected Member, National Council, SNP. Recreations: hill-walking; foreign travel; caravanning; reading. Address: (h.) 12 Braehead Drive, Carnoustie, Angus; T.-0241 52422.

Hood, Rev. (Elizabeth) Lorna, MA, BD. Minister, Renfrew North, since 1979; Member, Scottish Churches Council, since 1982; b. 21.4.53, Irvine; m., Peter Finlay Hood; 1 d. Educ. Kilmarnock Academy; Glasgow University. Delegate, World Alliance of Reformed Churches, Ottawa, 1982. Recreation: reading. Address: (h.) 1 Alexandra Drive, Renfrew; T.-041-886 2074.

Hood, James. MP (Labour), Clydesdale, since 1987; b. 16.5.48; m. 2 c. Educ. Motherwell Technical College. Former NUM official.

Hood, Professor Neil, FRSE, MA, MLitt. Director, Locate in Scotland, Scottish Development Agency, since 1987; Professor of Business Policy, Department of Marketing, Strathclyde University, since 1979; Associate Dean, Strathclyde Business School, 1982-85, Dean, 1985-87; Co-Director, Strathclyde International Business Unit, 1983-87; b. 10.8.43, Wishaw; m., Anna Watson Clark; 1 s.; 1 d. Educ. Wishaw High School; Glasgow University. Research Fellow, Scottish College of Textiles, 1966-68; Lecturer/Senior Lecturer, Paisley College of Technology, 1968-78; Economic Adviser, Scottish Economic Planning Department, 1979; Visiting Professor of International Business, University of Texas, Dallas, 1981; Visiting Professor, Institute of International Business, Stockholm School of Economics, since 1982; Director, Euroscot Meat Exports Ltd., 1981-85; Economic Consultant to Secretary of State for Scotland, since 1980; Director, Scottish Development Finance Ltd., since 1984; Investment Adviser, Castleforth Fund Managers, since 1984; Director, LIFE Ltd., 1984-86; Board Member, Irvine Development Corporation, 1985-87; Director, Prestwick Holdings PLC, 1986-87; President, European International Business Association, 1985-86. Publications: Industrial Marketing - A Study of Textiles (Co-author), 1970; Chrysler UK: A Corporation in Transition (Co-author), 1977; The Economics of Multinational Enterprise (Co-author), 1979; European Development Strategies of US Multinationals Located in Scotland (Co-author), 1980; Multinationals in Retreat: The Scottish Experience (Co-author), 1982; Multinational Investment Strategies in the British Isles (Co-author), 1983; Industry, Policy and the Scottish Economy (Co-Editor), 1984; Transnational Corporations in the Textile Industry (Co-author), 1984; Foreign Multinationals and the British Economy (Co-author), 1987; Strategies in Global Competition (Co-Editor), 1987; Scottish Financial Sector (Co-author), 1988. Recreations: swimming; reading; gardening. Address: (h.) Teviot, 12 Carlisle Road, Hamilton, ML3 7DB; T.-0698 424870.

Hook, Professor Andrew Dunnet, MA, PhD. Bradley Professor of English Literature, Glasgow University, since 1979 (Head, Department of English Literature, since 1982); b. 21.12.32, Wick; m., Judith Ann (deceased); 2 s.; 1 d. Educ. Wick High School; Daniel Stewart's College, Edinburgh; Edinburgh University; Manchester University; Princeton University. Edinburgh University: Assistant Lecturer in English Literature, 1961-63, Lecturer in American Literature, 1963-70; Senior Lecturer in English, Aberdeen University, 1970-79; CNAA: Chairman, Committee for Humanities, Member Committee for Academic Affairs; Chairman, Scottish Universities Council on Entrance English Panel; Member, Scottish Examination Board, since 1984. Publications: Scotland and America 1750-1835, 1975; American Literature in Context 1865-1900, 1983; Scott's Waverley (Editor), 1971; Charlotte Bronte's Shirley (Editor, with Judith Hook), 1974; Dos Passos: A Collection of Critical Essays (Editor), 1974; The History of Scottish Literature II, 1660-1800 (Editor), 1987. Recreations: theatre; opera; catching up on reading. Address: (b.) Department of English Literature, Glasgow University, Glasgow, G12 8QQ; T.-041-339 8855, Ext. 4226.

Hope, Colin John Filshill, SBStJ, BA, FCII, FCIS, FCIT, FBIM, MInstM, DipM. Member, Council, Insurance Ombudsman Bureau, since 1981; Deputy Chairman, Transport Users Consultative Committee for Scotland, since 1979; Director, Merchants House of Glasgow, since 1988 (and 1981-87); Member, Air Transport Committee, Association of British Chambers of Commerce, since 1986; Governor, Keil School, since 1986; Governor, Glasgow Educational and Marshall Trust, since 1986; Member, General Convocation, Strathclyde University, since 1980; b. 24.6.24, Dullatur; m., Jean Calder Douglas; 1 s.; 2 d. Educ. Glasgow High School; Glasgow Academy; Open University. RAF, 1942-47; joined Stenhouse & Partners, 1947; appointed Director, 1949; served in many capacities, including Managing Director, Stenhouse International; joined Norman Frizzell Scotland Ltd. as Managing Director, 1974; additionally Director, Norman Frizzell UK Ltd., 1976-81; Director, G.T. Senior, 1981-83 (Consultant, 1983-85); a Director, Glasgow Chamber of Commerce, 1979-88. Member: Scottish Consumer Council, 1979-85, Electricity Consultative Council for Scotland, 1979-87, Glasgow Airport Consultative Committee, since 1984. Address: (h.) Omaha, 4 Munro Drive East, Helensburgh, G84 9BS; T.-0436 3091.

Hope, James Arthur David, QC, BA, LLB. Dean, Faculty of Advocates, since 1986; QC, since 1978; b. 27.6.38, Edinburgh; m., Katharine Mary Kerr; 2 (twin) s.; 1 d. Educ. Edinburgh Academy; Rugby School; St. John's College, Cambridge; Edinburgh University. National Service, Seaforth Highlanders, 1957-59; admitted Faculty of Advocates, 1965; Standing Junior Counsel to Inland Revenue, 1974-78; Advocate Depute, 1978-82; Chairman, Medical Appeal Tribunal, 1985-86; Legal Chairman, Pensions Appeal Tribunal, 1985-86. Publications: Gloag and Henderson's Introduction to Scots Law (Joint Editor, 7th edition, Assistant Editor, 8th and 9th editions); Armour on Valuation for Rating (Joint Editor, 4th and 5th editions); (Contributor) Stair Memorial Encyclopaedia of Scots Law. Address: (h.) 34 India Street, Edinburgh, EH3 6HB; T.-031-225 8245.

Hope, William, MA. Rector, Elgin High School, since 1978; b. 26.9.43, Scotland; m., Patricia Miller. Educ. Dalbeattie High School; Kirkcudbright Academy; Edinburgh University; Jordanhill College of Education. Alloa Academy: Assistant

Teacher, Principal Teacher of Guidance; Assistant Rector, Lochaber High School. Chairman, Moray Branch, UNICEF; Vice Chairman, Elgin and District Branch, Cancer Relief; Chairman, Edinburgh University Club of Moray. Recreations: umpiring hockey and cricket; fishing. Address: (b.) Elgin High School, High School Drive, Elgin, Moray; T.-0343 45181/2.

Hopwood, Sylvia Elaine, MB, ChB, DPM. Psychiatrist, Tayside Region, and Honorary Lecturer, Dundee University, since 1962; b. 25.2.38, Salford; 2 d. Educ. Leeds University. Medical and neurological training, Leeds, 1960-62; psychiatric training, Dundee, 1962. Treasurer, Gowrie Housing Association; Member, National Schizophrenia Fellowship and Manic Depressive Fellowship. Publications: many articles on alcoholism, depression and schizophrenia. Recreations: lace-making; embroidery; gardening. Address: (h.) 6 Strips of Craigie Road, Dundee, DD4 7PZ; T.-0382 41065.

Horden, Professor John Robert Backhouse, MA, MLitt, DHL, FSA, FSA(Scot), FRSL. Professor Emeritus and Honorary Professor of Bibliographical Studies, Stirling University; b. Warwickshire; m., Aileen Mary Douglas (deceased); 1 s. Educ. Oxford University; Cambridge University; Heidelberg University; Sorbonne; Lincoln's Inn. Former Director, Centre for Bibliographical Studies, Stirling University; former Director, Institute of Bibliography and Textual Criticism, Leeds University; former Tutor and Lecturer in English Literature, Christ Church, Oxford; Visiting Professorial appointments, Universities of Pennsylvania State, Saskatchewan, Erlangen-Nurnberg, Texas at Austin, Munster; Editor, Dictionary of Scottish Biography, since 1982; Cecil Oldman Memorial Lecturer, 1971; Marc Fitch Prize for Bibliography, 1979; founded Stirling University Press, 1985. Publications: Francis Quarles: A Bibliography of his Work to 1800, 1953; Francis Quarles' Hosanna and Threnodes (Editor), 1960; Annual Bibliography of English Language and Literature (Editor), 1967-75; English and Continental Emblem Books (22 vols.) (Editor), 1968-74; Dictionary of Concealed Authorship, Vol. 1 (Editor), 1980; initiator and first editor, Index of English Literary Manuscripts, four volumes, 1980-87; Everyday Life in Seventeenth-Century England, 1974; John Freeth: Political Ballad Writer and Inn Keeper, 1985. Recreations: golf (representative honours); music; painting. Address: (b.) Department of English Studies, Stirling University, Stirling, KF9 4LA.

Horlick, Sir John (James Macdonald), 5th Bt. Director, Highland Fish Farmers, since 1978; b. 9.4.22; m.; 1 s.; 2 d. Educ. Eton; Babson Institute of Business Administration, USA. Captain, Coldstream Guards, Second World War; former Depute Chairman, Horlicks Ltd. Address: (h.) Tournaig, Poolewe, Achnasheen, Ross-shire.

Horn, David Bowes, BSc, PhD, CChem, FRSC, FRCPath, FRSE. Head, Department of Clinical Chemistry, Western General Hospital, Edinburgh, 1966-87; Honorary Senior Lecturer in Clinical Chemistry, Edinburgh University, 1966-87; b. 18.8.28, Edinburgh; m., Shirley Kay Riddell; 2 d. Educ. Daniel Stewart's College, Edinburgh; Heriot-Watt University, Edinburgh; Edinburgh University. Senior Grade Biochemist: Vale of Leven Hospital, Alexandria, 1956, Queen Elizabeth Hospital, Birmingham, 1959; Biochemist, Royal Victoria Infirmary, Newcastle-upon-Tyne, and Honorary Lecturer, Department of Clinical Biochemistry, Newcastle-upon-Tyne University, 1959. Past Chairman, Scottish Region, Association of Clinical Biochemists (former Member, ACB National Council); Past Chairman, Scientific Services Advisory Group Clinical Chemistry Sub-Committee; Royal Society of Chemistry Representative, Mastership in Clinical Biochemistry Examination Board. Recreations: gardening; walking. Address: (h.) 2 Barnton Park, Edinburgh, EH4 6JF; T.-031-336 3444.

Hornby, John Murgatroyd, FCCA, ATII, FRVA. Director of Finance, Bearsden and Milngavie District Council, since 1975; b. 6.3.32, London; m., Helen Anne; 2 d. Educ. George Watson's Boys' College, Edinburgh. William Bishop & Co., CA, Edinburgh, 1948-56; Wylie & Hutton, CA, Edinburgh, 1956-57; N.C. Campbell & Co., CA, Haddington, 1957-64; Town Chamberlain, Royal Burgh of Haddington, 1964-67; Burgh Chamberlain, Burgh of Milngavie, 1967-75. Address: (b.) Boclair, Bearsden, Glasgow, G61 2TQ; T.-041-942 2262.

Horne, Allan Maxwell, BL. Consultant to Grigor & Young, Solicitors, Elgin, since 1984; Honorary Sheriff, Elgin, since 1981; b. 24.2.17, Brora; m., Margaret Ross; 1 d. Educ. Elgin Academy; Edinburgh University. Royal Artillery, 1940-46: commissioned 128th Field Regiment, 51st (4) Division, served as Air Observation Pilot, 1945-46, demobilised with rank of Captain; Legal Assistant, Inverness, 1946-49; Partner, Grigor & Young, Solicitors, Elgin, 1949-83, retiring as Senior Partner; Burgh Prosecutor, Elgin, 1950-75. Recreation: golf. Address: (h.) Melford, 11 Fleurs Place, Elgin; T.-Elgin 2833.

Horne, Rev. Archibald Sinclair. Minister, Reformed Presbyterian Church of Scotland, since 1955; Secretary/Lecturer, Scottish Reformation Society, since 1964; b. 9.3.27, Cockenzie, East Lothian; 2 s.; 1 d. Educ. Preston Lodge Secondary School; New College, Edinburgh. Fisherman, 1941-46; Army (Royal Signals), 1946-48; retail fish trade, 1949-54; Student Minister, then Minister, Reformed Presbyterian Church, Loanhead, 1954-63. Editor, Bulwark, magazine of Scottish Reformation Society, since 1981. Publications: Torchbearers of the Truth, Sketches of the Covenanters, 1968; In The Steps of the Covenanters, 1974. Recreations: weight training; golf; photographing and recording locations of historical events. Address: (b.) 17 George IV Bridge, Edinburgh, EH1 1EE; T.-031-220 1450.

Horne, Norman John, MA (Hons). Headmaster, Harlaw Academy, Aberdeen, since 1985; b. 10.12.37, Turriff, Aberdeenshire; m., Ann Gavin; 1 s.; 2 d. Educ. Aberdeen Grammar School; Aberdeen University. Teacher of Classics, Hamilton Academy, 1961-66; Principal Classics Teacher: Nicolson Institute, Stornoway, 1966-71, Inverness Royal Academy, 1971-72; Assistant Rector, Inverness High School, 1972-77; Rector,

Milne's High School, Fochabers, 1977-85. Recreations: sport (golf, table tennis); music (jazz). Address: (h.) 11 Beechwood Gardens, Westhill, Skene, Aberdeen; T.-Aberdeen 743831.

Horne, Norman Wemyss, MB, ChB, FRCPE. President, Europe Region, International Union Against Tuberculosis; Chairman (Scotland), Chest, Heart and Stroke Association; b. 6.4.18, Aberdeen; m., Barbara Munro Ross; 4 s. Educ. George Watson's College, Edinburgh; Edinburgh University. Squadron Leader, RAFVR, 1941-46; Consultant Physician, City Hospital, Edinburgh (retired); Senior Lecturer in Respiratory Medicine, Edinburgh University, 1953-83. President, British Thoracic Society, 1980-81. Recreations: gardening; music. Address: (h.) 10 Corrennie Gardens, Edinburgh; T.-031-447 3384.

Horner, Rev. Alan Philip, BA, BD. Chairman, Methodist Synod in Scotland, since 1982; Methodist Minister, since 1958; b. 8.3.34, Northallerton; m., Margaret Adams; 2 d. Educ. Stockton-on-Tees Grammar School; King James I Grammar School, Bishop Auckland; Durham University; Manchester University. Ministry: Kendal, 1958-62, Harlow, 1962-68, Warrington, 1968-77, Chester, 1977-82. Recreations: walking; photography; gardening; swimming; music; poetry. Address: 7 Rowanlea Drive, Giffnock, Glasgow, G46 6BS; T.-041-633 1434.

Horner, Professor Robert Malcolm Wigglesworth, CEng, BSc, PhD, MICE, MBIM. Professor of Engineering Management, since 1986, and Head, Department of Civil Engineering, since 1985, Dundee University; b. 27.7.42, Bury; m., Beverley Anne Wesley; 1 s.; 1 d. Educ. The Bolton School; University College, London. Civil Engineer, Taylor Woodrow Construction Ltd., 1966-77; Lecturer, Department of Civil Engineering, Dundee University, 1977-83, Senior Lecturer, 1983-86. Founder Chairman, Dundee Branch, Opening Windows on Engineering; Winner, CIOB Ian Murray Leslie Award, 1980 and 1984. Recreations: squash; gardening. Address: (h.) Westfield Cottage, 11 Westfield Place, Dundee, DD1 4JU; T.-0382 25933.

Hornibrook, John Nevill, VRD, BSc, CEng, FIChemE, FInstD. Works Director, Roche Products Ltd., Dalry, Ayrshire, since 1981; Member, CBI Scottish Regional Council; Member, Executive Committee, Scottish Council (Development and Industry); Visiting Professor of Chemical and Process Engineering, Strathclyde University; Director, Garnock Valley Development Executive; b. 25.10.28, Gerrards Cross, Buckinghamshire; m., Dr. (Norma) Gillian Newbury; 2 d. Educ. Wellington College; Birmingham University. National Service, Royal Navy, 1949-51 (Sub-Lt., (E) RNVR, later promoted to Lt.-Cdr., RNR); Assistant Production Superintendent, Trinidad Leaseholds, BWI, 1951-55; Senior Chemical Engineer, Power Gas Corporation, 1955-58; Monsanto Chemicals Ltd., 1958-72: Senior Chemical Engineer, London, Technical Manager, Alta Labs, Bombay, Production Superintendent, Ruabon, North Wales; joined Roche Products Ltd., Dalry, 1972 (Works Manager, 1973-81). Vice-President, Institution of Chemical Engineers, 1983-85; Director, Ayrshire Chamber of Industries, since 1975; Member, Scottish Regional Committee, Chemical Industries Association. Recreations: sailing; gardening. Address: (b.) Roche Products Ltd., Dalry, Ayrshire, KA24 5JJ; T.-029 483 2345.

Horobin, John Charles, BSc, PhD. Assistant Director, Centre for External Services, St. Andrews University, since 1974; b. 13.2.45, Long Eaton; m., Jean Margaret; 1 s.; 1 d. Educ. Long Eaton Grammar School; King's College, London University; Durham University. Tutor-Organiser, WEA, Plymouth and West Devon, 1971-74. Honorary International Secretary, Scottish Institute of Adult and Continuing Education; Honorary Secretary, Universities Council for Adult and Continuing Education (Scotland). Address: (b.) Centre for External Services, St. Andrews University, 66 North Street, St. Andrews, KY16 9AH; T.-0334 73429.

Horsburgh, Charles Paton, JP, BL. Senior Town Clerk Depute, City of Glasgow District Council, since 1974; Clerk, City of Glasgow Licensing Board, since 1980; b. 19.12.27, Edinburgh; m., Patricia Morris; 2 d. Educ. Queen's Park Secondary School, Glasgow; Glasgow University. Thirty years with Glasgow Corporation, rising from Apprentice Solicitor to Principal Solicitor, specialising in court work. Honorary Treasurer, Sherwood Church of Scotland, Paisley. Recreations: music; photography; motoring. Address: (b.) Town Clerk's Office, City Chambers, Glasgow, G2 1DU; T.-041-227 4504.

Horsman, Graham Joseph Vivian, OBE (1977), JP, MA. Chairman, Forth Valley Health Board, 1977-85; Member, Scottish Health Service Planning Council, 1977-85; Extra-Parliamentary Commissioner Under Private Legislation Procedure (Scotland) Act, 1976-86; b. 10.11.19, London; m., Ruth Guest; 2 s.; 2 d. Educ. Whitgift School; Trinity College, Oxford. Councillor, County Borough of Reading, 1946-47; Member, Stirling and Clackmannan Hospitals Board of Management, 1966-69; Chairman, Stirling, Falkirk and Alloa Hospitals Board of Management, 1970-74; Member, Forth Valley Health Board, 1973-77; Member, Committee to Review Assessment in the Third and Fourth Years of Secondary Education in Scotland (Dunning Committee), 1975-77. Chairman, Dollar Civic Trust, 1970-78; Vice-Chairman, Scottish Association of Citizens' Advice Bureaux, 1976-78 (Council Member, 1973-78). Recreations: music; reading; walking. Address: (h.) 9 Tarmangie Drive, Dollar, Clackmannanshire; T.-Dollar 2575.

Horspool, William McKie, BSc, PhD, DSc, CChem, FRSC, FRSE. Reader in Organic Chemistry, Dundee University, since 1972; b. 12.8.36, Kilmarnock; m., Una Macfarlane Hamill; 1 s.; 1 d. Educ. Kilmarnock Academy; Strathclyde University; Glasgow University. Postdoctoral Associate, Columbia University, New York, 1964-65; Lecturer in Organic Chemistry, Queen's College, St. Andrews, 1965-72; Visiting Professor, Wisconsin University, 1974; Visiting Professor, Complutense University, Madrid, 1985. Publication: Aspects of Organic Photochemistry, 1976; Synthetic Organic Photochemistry (Editor), 1984; numerous papers in scientific journals. Recreations:

gardening; DIY construction; choral singing (Treasurer, Dundee Choral Union); local church affairs (Session Clerk, Fowlis and Liff). Address: (h.) Waulkmill, Liff, by Dundee, DD2 5LR.

Hossack, Roma Leonora, JP. Member, Grampian Regional Council; Vice Chairman, Housing, Moray District Council; b. 25.9.37, Elgin. Member: Elgin Town Council, 1972-74, Moray District Council, since 1974, Grampian Regional Council, since 1977; Secretary, Elgin Welfare Committee; Member, Visiting Committee, Porterfield Prison, Inverness. Address: (h.) 46 Gordon Street, New Elgin, Moray; T.-Elgin 7776.

Houldsworth, David Henry, LLB, WS. Solicitor, since 1975; b. 19.2.53, Forres; m., Sarah Jane Hogg. Educ. Eton College; Edinburgh University. Member, Queen's Bodyguard for Scotland (Royal Company of Archers), since 1984. Recreations: skiing; fishing; golf; shooting. Address: (h.) 2 Primrose Bank Road, Edinburgh; Dallas Lodge, Forres, Moray.

House, Jack. Journalist and Author; b. 16.5.06, Glasgow. Left school at 15; trained as a CA; became a newspaperman, 1928; worked on all three Glasgow evening newspapers; during the War, served as a Corporal in the Gordon Highlanders, subsequently as Captain (Scenario Editor), Army Kinematograph Service; numerous appearances on TV and radio (former Member, Scottish Round Britain Quiz team); appeared professionally with Charles Macdona Players and Scottish National Players, 1929-32; Editor, Scottish Stage magazine, c. 1930; Critic and Adjudicator, amateur stage; author of numerous books, including Down the Clyde, Scotland for Fun, Square Mile of Murder, The Heart of Glasgow, Pavement in the Sun, Portrait of the Clyde, Glasgow Old and New.

Houslay, Professor Miles Douglas, BSc, PhD, FRSE, FRSA, FIBiol, CBiol. Gardiner Professor of Biochemistry, Glasgow University, since 1984; b. 25.6.50, Wolverhampton; m., Rhian Mair; 2 s.; 1 d. Educ. Grammar School, Brewood, Stafford; University College, Cardiff; King's College, Cambridge; Cambridge University. ICI Research Fellow and Fellow, Queens' College, Cambridge, 1974-76; Lecturer, then Reader in Biochemistry, UMIST, 1976-82; Selby Fellow, Australian Academy of Science, 1984; Colworth Medal, Biochemical Society of Great Britain, 1984; Honorary Research Fellow, California Metabolic Research Foundation, since 1981; Editor in Chief, Cellular Signalling; Deputy Chairman, Biochemical Journal; Editorial Board, Biochimica Biophysica Acta; Committee Member, Biochemical Society, 1982-85. Publication: Dynamics of Biological Membranes. Address: (b.) Department of Biochemistry, Glasgow University, Glasgow, G12 8QQ; T.-041-339 8855, Ext. 624.

Housley, Edward, MB, ChB, FRCPEdin, FRCP. Consultant Physician, Edinburgh Royal Infirmary, since 1970; part-time Senior Lecturer, Department of Medicine, Edinburgh University, since 1970; b. 10.1.34, Chester, USA; m., Alma Mary; 1 d. Educ. Mundella Grammar School, Nottingham; Birmingham University. Postgraduate training, Department of Medicine, Birmingham University and McGill University, Montreal. Recreation: crossword puzzles. Address: (h.) 48/1 Coltbridge Avenue, Edinburgh, EH12 6AH.

Housley, Richard Sutton, TEng, MCIT, AMIRTE. Head of Internal Transport, Strathclyde Regional Council, since 1975; b. 9.4.26, Airdrie; m., Grace; 2 s. Educ. Airdrie Academy. Depute Transport Manager, Lanark County Council, 1968; Transport Manager, Lanark County Council, 1973. Recreations: bowls; golf; curling. Address: (b.) Strathclyde House, 20 India Street, Glasgow, G2 4PF; T.-041-204 2900.

Houston, Professor George Frederick Barclay, MA, BLitt. Professor, Department of Political Economy, Glasgow University, since 1970; b. 26.10.20, Edinburgh; m., 1, Lilias Adam (deceased); 2, Jean Blackley; 1 s.; 3 d. Educ. George Heriot's School; Edinburgh University; Balliol College, Oxford. Lecturer, 1951, Senior Lecturer, 1966, in Agricultural Economics, Glasgow University; Consultant: FAO, OECD, SOEC, HIDB; Member, British Wool Marketing Board. Publications: Third Statistical Account of Dumfriesshire (Editor); Agrarian Change in the Scottish Highlands (Co-author). Recreations: golf; swimming. Address: (b.) Department of Political Economy, Glasgow University, Glasgow; T.-041-339 8855.

Houston, Rev. Graham Richard, BSc (Hons), BD (Hons), MTh. Minister, Letham St. Mark's Church, Perth, since 1982; b. 3.5.50, Glasgow; m., Irene Elizabeth Robertson; 1 s.; 2 d. Educ. Hutchesons' Boys' Grammar School, Glasgow; Strathclyde University; Aberdeen University. Assistant, Architectural Research Project, Govan, 1972-73; Assistant Minister, Palmerston Place Church, Edinburgh, 1976-77; Minister, Kildonan and Loth Church, Sutherland, 1978-82. Convener, Home Mission Committee, Presbytery of Perth, since 1987. Recreations: squash; jogging. Address: (h.) 35 Rose Crescent, Perth; T.-0738 24167.

Houston, Stewart Robertson, LLB. Procurator Fiscal, Lanark, since 1981; b. 6.1.48, Hamilton; 3 d. Educ. Lanark Grammar School; Edinburgh University. Law Apprentice, then Solicitor, J. & A. Hastie, SSC, Edinburgh, 1970-73; Depute City Prosecutor, Edinburgh, 1973-75; Depute Procurator Fiscal, Edinburgh, 1975-76; Legal Assistant, Crown Office, 1976-77; Depute Procurator Fiscal, Edinburgh, 1977-78; Depute Procurator Fiscal, Dumbarton, 1979-81. Recreations: badminton; swimming; walking; modern languages. Address: (h.) Kirkfield, 21 Rowhead Terrace, Biggar, Lanarkshire; T.-0899 20418.

Houstoun, Andrew Beatty, OBE, MC, DL, JP. Vice President, Scottish Landowners Federation, since 1984; Scottish Member, European Landowners Organisation, 1976-86; b. 15.10.22, Cranleigh; m., Mary Elizabeth Spencer-Nairn; 4 s. Educ. Harrow. Regular Army, 1941-56; retired as Major, 1st The Royal Dragoons; farming, Angus and Perthshire, since 1956; commanded Fife and Forfar Yeomanry/Scottish Horse (TA), 1962-65; Angus County Councillor, 1966-75 (Vice Chairman, Education Committee); Convener, Scottish Landowners Federation, 1979-82; Chancellor's Assessor, Dundee University Court, since 1981; Vice Lord Lieutenant, Angus, since 1986. Address: Lintrathen Lodge, Kirriemuir, Angus, DD8 5JJ; T.-057 56 228.

Howard, Deborah Janet, MA (Cantab), MA (Lond), PhD, FSA. Member, Royal Fine Art Commission for Scotland, since 1987; Lecturer in Architectural History, Department of Architecture, Edinburgh University, since 1982; b. 26.2.46, Westminster; m., Professor Malcolm Sim Longair (qv); 1 s.; 1 d. Educ. Loughton High School; Newnham College, Cambridge; Courtauld Institute of Art. Fellow, Clare Hall, Cambridge, 1972-73; Lecturer in History of Art, University College, London, 1973-76; Visiting Lecturer, Yale University, 1977, 1980. Editor, Journal of the Architectural Heritage Society of Scotland. Publications: Jacopo Sansovino: Architecture and Patronage in Renaissance Venice, 1975, 1987; The Architectural History of Venice, 1980, 1987. Recreations: music; hill-walking; skiing; gardening. Address: (b.) Department of Architecture, Edinburgh University, 20 Chambers Street, Edinburgh, EH1 1JZ; T.-031-667 1011.

Howard, Very Rev. Donald, BD, AKC. Provost, St. Andrew's Cathedral, Aberdeen, since 1978; Honorary Canon, Christ Church Cathedral, Hartford, Connecticut, since 1979; b. 21.1.27, Hull. Educ. London Unviversity. Design Engineer, English Electric Co.; Assistant Priest, Saltburn, North Yorkshire; Rector: Warrenton and Hartswater, N. Cape, South Africa, St. John's, East London, South Africa, Holy Trinity, Haddington. Address: (h.) 15 Morningfield Road, Aberdeen, AB2 4AP; T.-Aberdeen 314765.

Howard, Ian, MA (Hons), ARSA. Head of Painting, Duncan of Jordanstone College of Art, Dundee, since 1986; b. 5.11.52, Aberdeen; m., Ruth D'Arcy; 2 d. Educ. Aberdeen Grammar School; Edinburgh College of Art; Edinburgh University. Travelling scholarship to Italy, 1976; part-time Lecturer in Painting, Gray's School of Art, Aberdeen, 1977 (appointed full-time, 1980); Scottish Arts Council Award, 1979, Bursary, 1985-86; numerous one-man and group exhibitions. Recreations: reading; eating. Address: (h.) 66 Camphill Road, Broughty Ferry, Dundee; T.-Dundee 79395.

Howard-Luck, Clive Andrew, DMA, DCA, FITSA, ACIS. Director of Consumer and Trading Standards, Strathclyde Regional Council, since 1977; b. 27.2.31, Folkestone; m., Babs; 1 s.; 2 d. Educ. Harvey Grammar School, Folkestone. Technical Assistant, Weights and Measures, Folkestone, 1948-55; Provincial Inspector of Weights and Measures, Kenya, 1955-64; Chief Inspector, Weights and Measures, Royal Tunbridge Wells Borough, 1964-74; Chief Trading Standards Officer, City of Westminster Consortium, 1974-77. International and Standards Officer, ITSA, since 1974; Chairman, Factory Enforcement Working Party, LACOTS, 1983-84. Recreations: hill-walking; history of military organisations. Address: (b.) Strathclyde House, 20 India Street, Glasgow, G2 4PF; T.-041-227 3105.

Howat, Robert C.L., MB, ChB, FRCOG. Consultant Obstetrician and Gynaecologist, Royal Maternity Hospital and Royal Infirmary, Glasgow, since 1974; b. 10.7.38, Kilmarnock; m., Janet; 2 s.; 1 d. Educ. Irvine Royal Academy; Glasgow University. House Officer: Glasgow Royal Infirmary, Ayrshire Central Maternity Hospital; General Practitioner: Inverbervie, Glenrothes; Senior House Officer: Ayrshire Central, Stracathro Hospital, Brechin, Kilmarnock Infirmary; Registrar: Falkirk Infirmary, Victoria Infirmary and Royal Maternity Hospital, Glasgow; Senior Registrar, Dundee Teaching Hospitals. Honorary Medical Adviser, Scottish Amateur Swimming Association. Recreations: swimming; golf; gardening. Address: (h.) 1 Coxdale Avenue, Kirkintilloch; T.-041-776 6828.

Howe, Rev. Andrew Youngson, BTh. Minister, Alness, Ross-shire; b. 4.3.28, Dundee; m., Dorothy Alison Thomson; 1 s.; 2 d. Educ. Dundee High School; Queen's College, Dundee; London University. Staff Sergeant, Royal Army Ordinance Corps; Trainee Buyer, then Assistant Buyer, Swan & Edgar, London; Minister, Church of Scotland; commission, RAF VR (T); Assessor, Church of Scotland Schools for Selection of Candidates for the Ministry. Chairman, Alness Academy School Council; Chairman, Easter Ross Save the Children Fund; Honorary Member, Dingwall Rotary Club. Recreations: gardening; model railways. Address: Rosskeen Manse, 15 Perrins Road, Alness, Ross-shire; T.-0349 882265.

Howe, Professor James Alexander Macgregor, MA, PhD. Head, Department of Artificial Intelligence, Edinburgh University, since 1978 (Professor of Artificial Intelligence, since 1985); b. 7.7.37, Glasgow; m., Nan Harvie Bell; 1 s.; 2 d. Educ. Kelvinside Academy, Glasgow; St. Andrews University; Cambridge University. Senior Assistant in Research, Laboratory of Experimental Psychology, Cambridge University, 1964-66; Research Fellow, Lecturer, Senior Lecturer, Reader, Department of Artificial Intelligence, Edinburgh University, 1967-85; Chairman, IKBS Advisory Group, Alvey Directorate; Founder and Chairman, Artificial Intelligence Applications Institute, Edinburgh University; Member, Ordnance Survey's Science and Technology Advisory Committee. Recreations: skiing; curling; gardening. Address: (h.) 26 Essex Road, Edinburgh, EH4 6LJ; T.-031-339 5390.

Howgego, Joseph, MA (Hons) (Cantab). HM Chief Inspector of Schools, since 1982; b. 4.4.33, Crewe; m., Anne Barbara; 4 s. Educ. Manchester Grammar School; Queens' College, Cambridge. Teaching posts: Birkenhead School, 1955-61, King's School, Chester, 1961-64, King George V School, Southport, 1964-67; HM Inspector of Schools, 1968-82. Chairman, Gullane, Aberlady and Drem Community Council, 1975-77. Recreations: golf; walking; music (choral singing). Address: (h.) Bank House, Main Street, Gullane, East Lothian, EH31 2HD; T.-0620 842348.

Howie, Andrew Law, CBE, FRAgrS. Chairman, Robert Howie & Sons, since 1982; Chairman, Scottish Milk Marketing Board, since 1982; b. 14.4.24, Dunlop; m., Joan Duncan; 2 s.; 2 d. Educ. Glasgow Academy. Joined Robert Howie & Sons, 1941; War Service, RN; became Director, 1965; President, Scottish Compound Feed Manufacturers, 1968-70 and 1983-85; President, Compound Animal Feed Manufacturers National Association, 1971-72; Director, Scottish Corn

Trade, 1976-78; Vice-President/Feed, UK Agricultural Supply Trade Association, 1980-81; Chairman, Scottish Council, UKASTA, 1985-87; Director, Scottish Milk Marketing Board, since 1980. Recreations: golf; gardening. Address: (h.) Newmill House, Dunlop, Kilmarnock, KA3 4BQ; T.-0560 84936.

Howie, Sir James William, Kt (1969), LLD, MD, FRCP, FRCPath, FIMLS, Hon. ARCVS; b. 31.12.07, Oldmeldrum, Aberdeenshire; m., Isabella Winifred Mitchell; 2 s.; 1 d. Educ. Robert Gordon's College, Aberdeen; Aberdeen University. Specialised in bacteriology as applied to infectious diseases and agriculture; RAMC, 1939-45, Nigeria and War Office; Professor of Bacteriology, Glasgow University, 1951-63; Medical Director, Public Health Laboratory Service, 1963-73; Honorary Physician to the Queen, 1965-68; Past President: BMA, Royal College of Pathologists, Association of Clinical Pathologists, Institute of Sterile Services Management. Recreations: golf; music. Address: (h.) 34 Redford Avenue, Edinburgh, EH13 0BU; T.-031-441 3910.

Howie, John Cameron, IPFA, ARVA. Chief Executive, Stewartry District Council, since 1988; b. 22.9.41, Perth; m., Kathleen N.; 1 d. Educ. Perth Academy. Chief Accountant, Perth and Kinross Joint County Council, 1967; Depute County Treasurer, Ross and Cromarty County Council, 1970; County Treasurer, Kirkcudbright County Council, 1972; Director of Finance and Housing, Stewartry District Council, 1975-88. Recreations: golf; swimming; all sports; reading. Address: (h.) Kinclaven, Hardgate, Castle Douglas, DG7 3LD.

Howie, Professor John Garvie Robertson, MD, PhD, MRCPE, FRCGP. Professor of General Practice, Edinburgh University, since 1980; b. 23.1.37, Glasgow; m., Elizabeth Margaret Donald; 2 s.; 1 d. Educ. High School of Glasgow; Glasgow University. Registrar, Laboratory Medicine, Western Infirmary, Glasgow, 1962-66; General Practitioner, Glasgow, 1966-70; Lecturer/Senior Lecturer in General Practice, Aberdeen University, 1970-80; Member: Biomedical Research Committee, SHHD, 1977-81, Health Services Research Committee, SHHD, 1982-86, Chief Scientist Committeee, SHHD, since 1987, Committee on the Review of Medicines, since 1986; Chairman, Heads of Departments of General Practice Group. Publication: Research in General Practice. Recreations: golf; gardening; music. Address: (h.) 4 Ravelrig Park, Balerno, Midlothian, EH14 7DL; T.-031-449 6305.

Howie, Professor John Mackintosh, MA, DPhil, DSc, FRSE. Regius Professor of Mathematics, St. Andrews University, since 1970; b. 23.5.36, Chryston, Lanarkshire; m., Dorothy Joyce Miller; 2 d. Educ. Robert Gordon's College, Aberdeen; Aberdeen University. Assistant in Mathematics, Aberdeen University, 1958-59; Assistant, then Lecturer in Mathematics, Glasgow University, 1961-67; Senior Lecturer in Mathematics, Stirling University, 1967-70; visiting appointments: Tulane University, 1964-65, State University of New York at Buffalo, 1969-70, University of Western Australia, 1968, Monash University, 1979; Dean of Science, St. Andrews University, 1976-79. President, Edinburgh Mathematical Society, 1972-73; Vice-President, London Mathematical Society, 1984-86; Convener, SCEEB Mathematics Panel, 1970-73; Chairman, Scottish Central Committee on Mathematics, 1975-81; Member, Committee to Review Examinations (Dunning Committee), 1975-77; Chairman, Governors, Dundee College of Education, 1983-87; Keith Prize, Royal Society of Edinburgh, 1979-81. Publications: An Introduction to Semigroup Theory, 1976; papers in mathematical journals. Recreations: music; gardening. Address: (b.) Mathematical Institute, St. Andrews University, North Haugh, St. Andrews, KY16 9SS; T.-0334 76161.

Howie, Professor Peter William, MD, FRCOG. Professor of Obstetrics and Gynaecology, Dundee University, since 1981; b. 21.11.39, Aberdeen; m., Anne Jardine Quigg; 1 s.; 1 d. Educ. High School of Glasgow; Glasgow University. Astor Foundation Research Fellow, Royal College of Pathologists, 1970-71; Lecturer, then Senior Lecturer, Department of Obstetrics and Gynaecology, Glasgow University, 1971-78; Clinical Consultant, Medical Research Council Reproductive Biology Unit, Edinburgh, 1978-81. Recreations: golf; watching sport. Address: (h.) 8 Travebank Gardens, Monifieth, Dundee, DD5 4ET; T.-0382 534802.

Howie, William Forbes, DL, JP, BSc, CEng, MIEE, BA. Chairman, Supplementary Benefit Appeal Tribunal, Stirling and Falkirk, since 1973; Justice of the Peace, since 1974; Deputy Lieutenant, Stirling and Falkirk District, since 1981; General Commissioner of Income Tax, since 1983; b. 13.8.20, Falkirk; m., Janet M. Campbell; 2 s.; 1 d. Educ. Falkirk High School; Glasgow University; Open University. RAF, during Second World War (demobbed as Flight Lieutenant); Managing Director, Thomas Laurie & Co. Ltd., 1956-81; appointed Chairman, Children's Panel Advisory Committee, Falkirk, 1970; Chairman, Forth Valley Scouts, since 1978; Session Clerk, St. Andrews Church, Falkirk, since 1979; set up Stirling and District Amateur Football Association, 1951 (its first Secretary); set up Falkirk Section, Scottish Wildlife Trust, 1984. Recreations: golf; bowls; colour photography; gardening; wildlife. Address: 12 Gartcows Crescent, Falkirk, FK1 5QH; T.-Falkirk 24128.

Howitt, Lewis Finnigan, MB, ChB, DPH, FFCM, FRCP. Community Medicine Specialist, Lothian Health Board, since 1986; b. 27.5.28, Aberdeen; m., Sheila Helen Elizabeth Burns; 1 s.; 1 d. Educ. Aberdeen Central School; Aberdeen University. Medical Officer, RAF; Medical Officer, Counties of Roxburgh and Selkirk Public Health Department; Medical Officer, then Senior Medical Officer, City of Edinburgh Public Health Department; Deputy Medical Officer of Health, Counties of Midlothian and Peebles Public Health Department; Senior Medical Officer, Scottish Home and Health Department. Recreations: gardening; golf. Address: (h.) 27 Cluny Drive, Edinburgh, EH10 6DT; T.-031-447 5849.

Howson, Alexander, ALA. Director of Libraries and Museums, Falkirk District Council, since 1975; b. 22.3.38, Motherwell; m., Nancy. Educ. Dalziel High School; Scottish School of Librarianship. Various posts, Lanark County Library, 1956-66; Students' and Reference Librarian, Stafford County Library, 1966-67; Depute County Librarian, Aberdeenshire, 1967-69; Burgh Librarian, Falkirk, 1969-75. President, Scottish Library Association, 1981; Member, British Library Advisory Committee on Lending Services, 1979-82. Recreation: golf. Address: (b.) Public Library, Hope Street, Falkirk, FK1 5AU; T.-Falkirk 24911, Ext. 2204.

Hoyle, Robert Stansfield, BSc, FBIM. Director, Direct Labour, Edinburgh District Council, since 1986; b. 23.3.35, Darlington; m., Wenna. Various positions, UK, USA, Germany, Libya, Univac Division, Sperry Rand, 1963-68; Marketing Manager, IBM, Libya, Lebanon, Kuwait, 1968-73; OECD Consultant, Turkey, visiting Assistant Professor, Middle East Technical University, 1973-76; Management Services Superintendent, CDM, Namibia, 1976-77; Deputy Programme Control Manager, Parsons Corporation, Saudi Arabia, 1979-80; Director, Corporate Services, Building Works Department, Glasgow District Council, 1982-86. Address: (b.) 33 Murrayburn Road, Edinburgh, EH14 2TF.

Hubbuck, Professor John Reginald, MA (Cantab), MA, DPhil (Oxon), FRSE. Professor of Mathematics, Aberdeen University, since 1978 (Head, Department of Mathematics, 1980-85); President, Edinburgh Mathematical Society, 1985-86; b. 3.5.41, Girvan; m., Anne Neilson; 1 s.; 1 d. Educ. Manchester Grammar School; Queens' College, Cambridge; Pembroke College, Oxford. Fellow: Gonville and Caius College, Cambridge, 1970-72, Magdalen College, Oxford, 1972-78. Recreation: hill-walking. Address: (h.) 8 Fonthill Terrace, Aberdeen, AB1 2UR; T.-0224 588738.

Huckle, Derek Arthur, CA, FBIM, FIIM, FCCA. Principal, Kirkcaldy College of Technology, since 1984; b. 25.1.30, Newtown St. Boswells; m., Janette; 2 d. Educ. Galashiels Academy. National Service, 1954-56; paper making, 1956-70; further education, since 1970. Member, Committees, Institute of Chartered Accountants of Scotland, British Institute of Management, Institution of Industrial Managers, SCOTVEC. Address: (b.) Kirkcaldy College of Technology, St. Brycedale Avenue, Kirkcaldy, KY1 1EX; T.-0592 268591.

Hudson, Christopher Sydney, DSO (and Bar), FBIM, CPIM. Board Member, Scottish Council for Voluntary Organisations; b. 1.8.16, Tunbridge Wells; m., Ruth Julia Risse; 1 d. Educ. privately, in Switzerland. Army Service, Royal Fusiliers and SOE, 1940-45 (Lt.-Col.); Control Commission for Germany (British and US Sectors), 1946-53; Personnel Manager in overseas companies, Shell International Petroleum Co., Israel, Trinidad, Zaire, Algeria; seconded to International Labour Organisation, Geneva, 1966; Executive in charge of Personnel, Training and Industrial Relations, Bank of Scotland, 1968-80. Croix de Guerre with Palme. Recreations: golf; swimming. Address: (h.) Invereil House, North Berwick, East Lothian, EH39 5DH; T.-0620 3646.

Hudson, Rev. Eric Vallance, LTh. Religious Programmes Officer, Scottish Television, since 1978; Minister, Church of Scotland, since 1971; b. 22.2.42, Glasgow; m., Lorna Mary Miller; 1 s.; 1 d. Educ. Paisley Grammar School; Wollongong High School, NSW; Christ's College, Aberdeen and Aberdeen University. Sub-Editor, D.C. Thomson & Co. Ltd., Dundee, 1961-66; Senior Assistant Minister, New Kilpatrick Parish Church, Bearsden, 1971-73; Minister, Kintore Parish Church, 1973-78. Address: (b.) Cowcaddens, Glasgow, G2 3PR; T.-041-332 9999.

Huggins, Astrid Ilfra, JP, MA, DipSocAdmin. Member, Lothian Regional Council, since 1978 (Conservative Spokeswoman on Education); b. 19.4.36, Edinburgh; m., Martin Huggins (m. diss.); 2 d. Educ. Harrogate College; Edinburgh University. Former Editor, Focus on Social Work and Service in Scotland; former Member, Broadcasting Council for Scotland; Member, Mental Welfare Commission for Scotland; Member, Scottish Community Education Council; former Member, General Teaching Council and Scottish Examination Board. Recreations: skiing; travel; art. Address: (h.) 11 Ann Street, Edinburgh, EH4 1PL; T.-031-332 1455.

Hughes, Professor Ian Simpson, BSc, PhD, FInstP, FRSE. Professor and Head, Department of Physics and Astronomy, Glasgow University, since 1971; b. 1.11.30, Liverpool; m., Isobel Mary; 1 s.; 1 d. Educ. High School of Glasgow; Glasgow University. Research Fellow, Nuclear and Particle Physics, Glasgow University, 1955-57; Research Associate, Particle Physics, Duke University and Lawrence Radiation Laboratory, Berkeley, USA, 1957-58; Lecturer, Senior Lecturer, Reader, Department of Natural Philosophy, Glasgow University, 1958-71; Member, Nuclear Physics Board, Science and Engineering Research Council, 1969-73 and 1980-83 and of numerous SERC Committees. Recreations: literature - poetry, fiction, travel, history; mountaineering; music. Address: (b.) Department of Physics and Astronomy, Glasgow University, Glasgow, G12 8QQ; T.-041-339 8855.

Hughes, Professor John, BSc, CEng, FIMechE. Professor and Director, National Centre for Prosthetics and Orthotics, Strathclyde University, since 1972; b. 20.4.34, Renfrew; m., Margaret Scoular Crichton; 2 d. Educ. Camphill School; Strathclyde University. Worked in shipbuilding and engineering, 1950-63; Strathclyde University: Lecturer in Mechanical Engineering Design, 1963-67, Senior Lecturer, Bioengineering Unit, 1967-72; President, International Society for Prosthetics and Orthotics. Recreations: golf; gardening. Address: (b.) Strathclyde University, Curran Building, 131 St. James' Road, Glasgow, G4 OLS; T.-041-552 4049.

Hughes, Robert. MP (Labour), Aberdeen North, since 1970; b. 3.1.32; m.; 2 s.; 3 d. Educ. Powis Secondary School, Aberdeen; Robert Gordon's College, Aberdeen; Benoni High School, Transvaal; Pietermaritzburg Technical College, Natal. Engineering apprenticeship, South African Rubber Company, Natal, 1949-54; draughtsman, C.F. Wilson & Co., Aberdeen, 1954-70; Member, Aberdeen City Council, 1962-71; Chairman,

Aberdeen City Labour Party, 1961-69; Member, Select Committee on Scottish Affairs, 1971; Opposition Junior Spokesman on Scottish Affairs, 1972-74; Parliamentary Under Secretary of State, Scottish Office, 1974-75; Chairman, Select Committee on Scottish Affairs, 1981; Opposition Junior Spokesman on Transport, 1981-83; Opposition Principal Spokesman on Agriculture, 1984-85, on Transport, since 1985; Member, General Medical Council, 1976-79; Chairman, Anti Apartheid Movement, since 1976. Address: (b.) House of Commons, London SW1A 0AA.

Hughes, Professor Sean Patrick Francis, MS, FRCSEdin, FRCSEdin Orth, FRCS, FRCSI. George Harrison Law Professor of Orthopaedic Surgery, Edinburgh University, since 1979; Honorary Consultant Orthopaedic Surgeon, Edinburgh Royal Infirmary and Princess Margaret Rose Orthopaedic Hospital, Edinburgh; b. 2.12.41, Farnham; m., Felicity Mary Anderson; 1 s.; 2 d. Educ. Downside School; London University. Senior Registrar, Orthopaedics, Middlesex Hospital and Royal National Orthopaedic Hospital; Research Fellow, Mayo Clinic, USA; Director of Orthopaedic Unit, Royal Postgraduate Medical School, London; Council Member, Royal College of Surgeons of Edinburgh. Publications: Musculoskeletal Infections (Co-Editor), 1986; The Principles and Practice of Musculoskeletal Surgery (Co-Editor), 1987. Recreations: golf; sailing; lying in the sun. Address: (h.) 9 Corrennie Gardens, Edinburgh; T.-031-447 1443.

Hughes, Rt. Hon. Lord (William Hughes), PC (1970), CBE (1956), DL, LLD. Company Director; b. 22.1.11, Dundee; m., Christian Clancher Gordon; 2 d. Educ. Balfour Street School; Dundee Technical College. ARP Controller, Dundee, 1939-43; Armed Forces, 1943-46 (commissioned 1944, demobilised as Captain, 1946, served India, Labuan and Burma); Member, Dundee Town Council, 1933-36 and 1937-61; City Treasurer, 1946-47; Lord Provost, 1954-60; Chairman, Eastern Regional Hospital Board, 1948-60; Member, Court, St. Andrews University, 1954-63; Member, Council, Queen's College, Dundee, 1954-63; Member, Committee on Civil Juries, 1958-59; Member, Committee to Inquire into Registration of Title to Land, 1960-62; Member, North of Scotland Hydro Electric Board, 1957-64; Member, Scottish Transport Council, 1960-64; Chairman, Glenrothes Development Corporation, 1960-64; Chairman, East Kilbride Development Corporation, 1975-82; Chairman, Royal Commission on Legal Services in Scotland, 1976-80; Joint Parliamentary Under Secretary of State for Scotland, 1964-69; Minister of State for Scotland, 1969-70 and 1974-75; President, Scottish Federation of Housing Associations, since 1975; Member, Council of Europe and Western European Union, 1976-87; Hon. Member, Council of Europe, since 1987. Recreation: gardening. Address: (h.) The Stables, Ross, Comrie, Perthshire; T.-0764 70557.

Hughes, William Young, CBE. Chairman and Chief Executive, Grampian Holdings plc, since 1985 (Chief Executive, 1976-85); b. 12.4.40, Milnrow, Lancaster; m., Anne Macdonald Richardson; 2 s.; 1 d. Educ. Firth Park Grammar School, Sheffield; Glasgow University; Strathclyde University; Heriot-Watt University. Partner, R. Gordon Drummond, 1966-70; Managing Director, MSJ Securities Ltd., 1970-76. Chairman, CBI Scotland, 1987-89; Member, Governing Council, Scottish Business in the Community. Recreations: Member, Glenbervie and Gleneagles Golf Clubs. Address: (b.) Stag House, Castlebank Street, Glasgow, G11 6DY; T.-041-357 2000.

Hughes Hallett, David John, FRICS. Director, Scottish Landowners' Federation, since 1982; Secretary, Scottish Recreational Land Association, since 1982; b. 19.6.47, Dunfermline; m., Anne Wright; 2 s.; 1 d. Educ. Fettes College. Trained in estate management, Kerse Estates, and with Strutt and Parker, Edinburgh and Ipswich; miscellaneous work in Australia; Past Chairman, Royal Institution of Chartered Surveyors in Scotland (Past Chairman, RICS Land Agency and Agriculture Committee, Scotland, and of RICS Edinburgh Area). Recreations: sailing; shooting. Address: (b.) 18 Abercromby Place, Edinburgh; T.-031-556 4466.

Hume, Sir Alan (Blyth), Kt, CB, MA. Chairman, Edinburgh New Town Conservation Committee, since 1975; b. 5.1.13, Broxburn; m., Marion Morton Garrett; 1 s.; 1 d. Educ. George Heriot's School, Edinburgh; Edinburgh University. Scottish Office: entered, 1936, Under Secretary, Scottish Home Department, 1957-59, Assistant Under Secretary of State, 1959-62, Under Secretary, Ministry of Public Building and Works, 1963-64, Secretary, Scottish Development Department, 1965-73; Chairman, Ancient Monuments Board for Scotland, 1973-81. Recreations: golf; fishing. Address: (h.) 12 Oswald Road, Edinburgh, EH9 2HJ; T.-031-667 2440.

Hume, James Douglas Howden, CBE, BSc, CEng, FIMechE, Hon. LLD (Strathclyde). Chairman and Managing Director, Drimard Limited, since 1988; Non-Executive Director, Macfarlane Thirsk Limited, since 1987; b. 4.5.28, Melbourne, Australia; m., June Katharine Spriggs; 1 s.; 2 d. Educ. Loretto; Strathclyde University; Glasgow University. Royal Artillery, 1944-46 (2nd Lt.); engineering training: James Howden & Company Limited, 1948-54, Production Engineering Limited, 1954-55; James Howden & Company Limited: Production Manager, 1955-56, appointed Director, 1957, Joint Managing Director, 1960, Managing Director, 1963; Howden Group PLC: Managing Director, 1968, Deputy Chairman and Managing Director, 1973, appointed Chairman, 1987 (removed from Chairmanship, November 1987). Address: (b.) Drimard Limited, 22 East Lennox Drive, Helensburgh, Dunbartonshire, G84 9JD; T.-0436 5132.

Hume, John Robert, BSc, ARCST, FSA Scot. Senior Lecturer in Economic History, Strathclyde University (on assignment to Historic Buildings and Monuments as Inspector of Ancient Monuments, since 1984); Member, Inland Waterways Amenity Advisory Council, since 1974; Member, Industrial Archaeology Sub-Committee, English Heritage, since 1985; Chairman, Seagull Trust, since 1978; Trustee, Scottish Maritime Museum, since 1983; b. 26.2.39, Glasgow; m., Catherine Hope Macnab; 4 s. Educ. Hutchesons' Boys' Grammar School; Glasgow University; Royal College of Science and Technology. Assistant

Lecturer, Lecturer, Senior Lecturer in Economic History, Strathclyde University, since 1964. Member, Ancient Monuments Board for Scotland, 1981-84; Director, Scottish Industrial Archaeology Survey, 1978-84. Publications: The Industrial Archaeology of Glasgow; The Industrial Archaeology of Scotland; as Co-author: Workshop of the British Empire: Engineering and Shipbuilding in the West of Scotland; Beardmore: the History of a Scottish Industrial Giant; The Making of Scotch Whisky; A Bed of Nails: a History of P. MacCallum & Sons Ltd.; Shipbuilders to the World: a History of Harland and Wolff; Steam Entertainment; Historic Industrial Scenes: Scotland; Industrial History in Pictures: Scotland; Glasgow's Railway Stations. Recreations: photography; reading. Address: (h.) 28 Partickhill Road, Glasgow, G11 5BP.

Humphrey, James Malcolm Marcus, OStJ, MA, FRICS. Grand Master Mason of Scotland, since 1983; Member, Grampian Regional Council; b. 1.5.38, Montreal, Canada; m., Sabrina Margaret Pooley; 2 s.; 2 d. Educ. Eton College; Oxford University. Conservative Parliamentary candidate, North Aberdeen, 1966; Council Member, National Farmers Union of Scotland, 1968-73; Member, Aberdeen County Council, 1970-75 (Chairman of Finance, 1973-75); Chairman of Finance, Grampian Regional Council, 1974-78 (Leader, Conservative Group, 1974-78); Chairman, Clinterty Agricultural College Council; Member, Queen's Bodyguard for Scotland (Royal Company of Archers); Chairman, North of Scotland Board, Eagle Star Group. Recreations: shooting; fishing; photography. Address: (h.) Dinnet, Aboyne, Aberdeenshire.

Hunt, Tony, MA, BLitt, FSA. Reader in French, St. Andrews University, since 1979; b. 21.3.44, Bebington. Educ. Birkenhead School; Worcester College, Oxford. Lecturer in French, St. Andrews University, 1968-79; Visiting Professor, Westfield College, London, 1986-88; British Academy Research Reader, 1986-88; Honorary Treasurer, Anglo-Norman Text Society; Chief Bibliographer, British Branch, International Courtly Literature Society; Member, Editorial Board: Rhetorica (University of California), Cambridge Studies in Mediaeval Literature, Westfield Publications in Medieval Studies; Advisory Editor, Arthurian Literature. Recreation: playing the double-bass. Address: (b.) Department of French, St. Andrews University, St. Andrews, Fife; T.-0334 76161, Ext. 352.

Hunt, Rev. Trevor George, BD (Hons), CPS. Minister, linked parishes of Evie, Rendall and Firth, since 1986; b. 28.3.42, Deal, Kent; m., Pauline Hazel Keen; 1 s.; 2 d. Educ. Aberdeen University and Christ College. Scientific Assistant, National Institute for Research in Nuclear Science; Senior Electronics Techician, Imperial College of Science and Technology, then Robert Gordon's Institute of Technology. Hon. Treasurer, Reformation Translation Fellowship; Hon. Secretary, Christian Reformed Tapes; Hon. Chairman, Orkney Care Core. Address: Finstown Manse, Orkney, KW17 2EG; T.-0856 76 328.

Hunter, A. Colin J., BA. Head Teacher, Tiree High School, since 1985; b. 26.9.47, Falkirk; 2 s.; 1 d. Educ. Falkirk High School; Stirling University. Entered teaching, 1972; Teacher, Falkirk High School and Forres Academy; Principal Teacher of Biology, Whitfield High School, Dundee; Depute Head Teacher, Auchtercairn Secondary School, Gairloch. Honorary Treasurer, Stirling University Graduates Association. Recreations: gardening; golf; walking. Address: (h.) Cornaigmore Schoolhouse, Isle of Tiree, Argyll, PA77 6XA; T.-087 92 556.

Hunter, Sheriff Adam Kenneth Fisher, MA (Hons), LLB. Sheriff of North Strathclyde (formerly Renfrew and Argyll), at Paisley, since 1953; b. 1920; m.; 1 s.; 2 d. Educ. Dunfermline High School; St. Andrews University; Edinburgh University. Called to Bar, 1946; Chairman, Supreme Court Legal Aid Committee, 1949-53.

Hunter, Rev. Archibald MacBride, MA, BD, PhD, DPhil, DD. Professor of New Testament, Aberdeen University, 1945-71 and Master of Christ's College, Aberdeen, 1957-71; Author of books on the New Testament; b. 16.1.06, Kilwinning; m., Margaret Wylie Swanson; 1 s.; 1 d. Educ. Hutchesons' Grammar School, Glasgow; Glasgow University; Oxford University; Marburg University. Church of Scotland Minister, Comrie, Perthshire, 1934-37; Yates Professor of New Testament, Mansfield College, Oxford, 1937-42; Minister, Kinnoull, Perth, 1942-45; Hastie Lecturer, 1938; Lee Lecturer, 1950; Sprunt Lecturer, Richmond, Virginia, 1954; author of 30 books. Recreations: walking; fishing. Address: (h.) Dunira, 32 Gartconnell Road, Bearsden, Glasgow; T.-041-942 3406.

Hunter, Edward Anthony, BSc, MPhil. Principal Scientific Officer, Scottish Agricultural Statistics Service, Edinburgh University, since 1967; b. 12.2.43, Newcastle-upon-Tyne; m., Janet M. Bruce; 1 s.; 1 d. Educ. Lasswade Secondary School; Edinburgh University. Recreations: playing bridge; reading. Address: (b.) Scottish Agricultural Statistics Service, Edinburgh University, King's Buildings, Edinburgh; T.-031-667 1081, Ext. 2605.

Hunter, George Alexander, OBE (1980), SBStJ. Secretary, Commonwealth Games Council for Scotland, since 1978; Founder Governor, Scottish Sports Aid Foundation, since 1980; b. 24.2.26, Edinburgh; m., Eileen Elizabeth. Educ. George Watson's College, Edinburgh. Served with Cameronians, seconded to 17th Dogara Regiment, Indian Army, 1944-47 (Captain); Lawson Donaldson Seeds Ltd., 1942-82 (Director, 15 years); Secretary, Scottish Amateur Rowing Association, 1948-78 (President, 1978-84); Adviser, Sports Aid Foundation, since 1979; Treasurer, Commonwealth Games Council for Scotland, 1962-78; Member, Scottish Sports Council, 1976-84 (Chairman, Games and Sports Committee, 1976-84); Chairman, Scottish Standing Conference for Sport, 1977-84. Address: (h.) 139 Old Dalkeith Road, Edinburgh; T.-031-664 1070.

Hunter, Ian, BL. Solicitor; Honorary Sheriff, Dumfries, since 1986; b. 12.8.27, Kanpur, India; m., Christina Scott Victoria Crombie; 3 s.; 3 d. Educ. Greenock Academy; Glasgow University. Served apprenticeship, Greenock; worked as Court Procurator in Glasgow and thereafter in general legal business in Dunoon and Lockerbie; Chairman, Social Security Appeal Tribunal (Dumfries); Dean, Faculty of Procurators of Dumfriesshire. Recreations: chess; gardening. Address: (h.) Linwood, Douglas Terrace, Lockerbie, DG11 2DZ; T.-05762 2549.

Hunter, Jack. District Head Postmaster, Aberdeen, since 1986; b. 17.9.34, Kirkcaldy; m., Mary Helen; 2 s.; 2 d. Educ. Leven Junior Secondary School. Telegram messenger, then postman, Leven, 1950-56; clerical and executive grade appointments, 1956-79; Assistant Head Postmaster, Greenock, 1980; Head Postmaster, Oban, 1981, Kilmarnock, 1985. Recreations: gardening; angling; reading; music. Address: (b.) Letter District Office, Crown Street, Aberdeen, AB9 1AA; T.-Aberdeen 576141, Ext. 201.

Hunter, James, MA (Hons), PhD. Director, Scottish Crofters Union; b. 22.5.48, Duror, Argyll; m., Evelyn; 1 s.; 1 d. Educ. Oban High School; Aberdeen University; Edinburgh University. Previously writer, journalist and broadcaster specialising in rural and Highland issues. Publications: The Making of the Crofting Community, 1976; Skye The Island, 1986. Recreations: anything that has nothing to do with crofting. Address: (b.) Old Mill, Broadford, Isle of Skye, IV49 9AQ; T.-047 12 529.

Hunter, James Albert, TD, LRCPE, LRCSE, LRFP&SG. Chairman, Social Work Committee, Shetland Islands Council; b. 2.5.14, Eshaness, Shetland; m., Helena Fraser (deceased); 4 s.; 2 d. Educ. Anderson Educational Institute, Lerwick; School of Medicine, Royal Colleges, Edinburgh. Captain, Royal Army Medical Corps, 1940-46; Medical Officer: Bangour Hospital, Midlothian, 1946, Bridge of Earn Hospital, Perthshire, 1946-47; Junior Assistant Tuberculosis Officer, Edinburgh, 1947; General Practitioner, Bixter and Voe, Shetland, 1947-78. Recreations: photography; fishing. Address: (h.) Kohima, Gott, Shetland, ZE2 9SG; T.-Gott 367.

Hunter, Hon. Lord (John Oswald Mair Hunter), VRD. Senator of the College of Justice in Scotland, 1961-86; b. 21.2.13; m.; 1 s.; 1 d. Educ. Edinburgh Academy; Rugby; New College, Oxford; Edinburgh University. Served Second World War (mentioned in Despatches); Lt.-Comdr., RNVR (retired, 1949); called to Bar, Inner Temple, 1937; admitted, Faculty of Advocates, 1937; QC (Scot), 1951; Advocate Depute (Home), 1954-57; Sheriff of Ayr and Bute, 1957-61; Chairman, Scottish Law Commission, 1971-81; Chairman, Scottish Council on Crime, 1972-75; Deputy Chairman, Boundary Commission for Scotland, 1971-76; Honorary President, Scottish Association for Study of Delinquency, since 1971.

Hunter, John Andrew Adam, BSc, MB, ChB, FRCPE. Consultant Physician in Rehabilitation Medicine, Lothian Health Board, since 1976; part-time Senior Lecturer in Rehabilitation Studies, Edinburgh University, since 1977 (Head, Rehabilitation Studies Unit, since 1988); b. 20.10.43, Perth; m., Hazel Watson; 1 s.; 1 d. Educ. Bell Baxter High School, Cupar; St. Andrews University. House Officer in Medicine and Orthopaedic Surgery, 1968-69; Lecturer in Biochemistry, Rheumatism Research Centre, Manchester University, 1969-72; Senior House Officer in Medicine, University Hospitals of South Manchester, 1972-74; Lecturer in Rheumatology, Manchester Royal Infirmary and Manchester University, 1974-76; Treasurer, Society for Research in Rehabilitation; Temporary Advisor to WHO on Rehabilitation. Recreations: singing; deep sea fishing. Address: (h.) 37 Gilmour Road, Edinburgh, EH16 5NS; T.-031-667 5333.

Hunter, Professor John Angus Alexander, BA, MD, FRCPEdin. Grant Professor of Dermatology, Edinburgh University, since 1981; b. 16.6.39, Edinburgh; m., Ruth Mary Farrow; 1 s.; 2 d. Educ. Loretto School; Pembroke College, Cambridge; Edinburgh University. Research Fellow, Institute of Dermatology, London, 1967; Registrar, Department of Dermatology, Edinburgh Royal Infirmary, 1968-70; Exchange Research Fellow, Department of Dermatology, Minnesota University, 1968; Lecturer, Department of Dermatology, Edinburgh University, 1970-74; Consultant Dermatologist, Lothian Health Board, 1974-80; Member: Executive Committee of Investigative Group, British Association of Dermatologists, 1974-76; Executive Committee, British Association of Dermatologists, 1977-79; SEC, Scottish Dermatological Society, 1980-82; Specialist Advisory Committee, (Dermatology), Joint Committee on Higher Medical Training, 1980-87 (Chairman, 1986-88); Medical Appeal Tribunal, since 1982; Scottish Committee for Hospital Medical Services, 1983-85. Publication: Common Diseases of the Skin (Co-Editor). Recreations: music; gardening; tropical fish; golf. Address: (h.) Leewood, Rosslyn Castle, Roslin, Midlothian, EH25 9PZ; T.-031-440 2181.

Hunter, Mollie. Writer; Chairman, Society of Authors in Scotland; b. 30.6.22, Longniddry; m., Thomas McIlwraith; 2 s. Educ. Preston Lodge School. Freelance Journalist, until 1960; Writer of various types of fiction (fantasy, historical novels, "realism") for children of varying age groups; 25 titles published, including Talent Is Not Enough, on the craft of writing for children; travelled extensively (Australia, New Zealand, Canada, USA); Lecturer on writing for children; Writer-in-Residence, Dalhousie University, Halifax, Canada, on several occasions; awarded Arbuthnot Lectureship, 1975, and Carnegie Medal, 1975. Recreations: reading; gardening; music. Address: The Shieling, Milton, by Drumnadrochit, Inverness-shire; T.-04562 267.

Hunter, Robert Dalglish, MBE (1960). Senior Partner, R.D. Hunter and Company, Solicitors and Notaries, Cumnock, 1941-76 (Consultant, 1976-87); Honorary Burgess, Burgh of Cumnock and Holmhead, since 1974; Honorary Sheriff of Ayr, since 1974; b. 4.8.13, Cumnock; m., Mary Reid Park; 2 s.; 2 d. Educ. Cumnock Academy; Glasgow University. Town Clerk, Cumnock, 1941-75 (Depute Town Clerk, 1936-41); JP Procurator Fiscal, 1941-75; District Prosecutor, 1975-76; Clerk, Cumnock Burgh Police Court, 1941-75; Manager, then Joint Manager, Cumnock and New Cumnock Branches, Commercial Bank of Scotland, later National Commercial Bank, ultimately Royal Bank of Scotland, 1941-76; Company Secretary: Cumnock Knitwear Ltd., 1964-65, Holyrood Knitwear Ltd., 1964-66, Falmer Manufacturing Company (Cumnock) Ltd., 1964-66; Chairman: Kyle Knitwear Ltd., 1966-76, West Sound Radio Ltd., 1980-83 (Honorary President, since 1986); Member, Scottish Board of Directors, Century Insurance Company Ltd., 1947-76; served Boy Scout movement, 35 years, latterly as Member, Ayrshire Scout Council; Medal of Merit from Chief Scout, 1955 (Bar, 1965); served Soldiers', Sailors' and Airmens' Families Association, 50 years, since 1980 as President, SSAFA in Ayrshire; Member: Committee of Management, Scottish Orchestra, 1941-46, Ayrshire Army Cadet Force League, 1950-77, Scottish Advisory Council, BBC, 1950-52, Scottish Music Advisory Committee, BBC, 1952-55; Chairman: Kilmarnock Theatre Trust, 1958-59, Ayrshire Music Festival, 1959-61 (President, 1962-64); Member, ITA (Scottish Committee), 1959-65; Convention of Royal Burghs of Scotland: Chairman, Committee on Music, the Arts and Broadcasting, 1964-66, Vice-Chairman, Committee on Industry and Transport, 1968-70; Member, Committee of Enquiry on Library Services in Scotland, 1965-66; Scottish Arts Council: Member, 1966-73, Chairman, Working Party on Touring Arrangements, 1970-71, Chairman, Working Party on Ballet and Dance in Scotland, 1972-73, Member, Regional Development Committee, 1975-77; Chairman, South Ayrshire Constituency Conservative Party, 1967-70; Member, Broadcasting Council for Scotland, 1968-74; Chairman, Scottish Civic Entertainment Association, 1970-80 (Life President, since 1980); Member: MacRobert Advisory Council, Stirling University, since 1970, Scottish Information Service for the Disabled, 1973-78; President, Ayr Chamber of Commerce, 1977-79. Recreations: listening to and promoting good music (founded Cumnock Music, 1948); swimming (won annual Loch Linnhe Swim from Trislaig to Fort William, 1938, in record-breaking time - record stood for 36 years); motoring; well-known Burnsian. Address: (h.) The Homestead, Cumnock, Ayrshire, KA18 1AP.

Hunter, Robert Leslie Cockburn, MA, LLB, WS, FCI (Arb). Chairman, Industrial Tribunals (Scotland), 1976-85; Chairman, Social Security Appeal Tribunals, since 1983; Lecturer in Law, Aberdeen University, since 1971; b. 31.12.34, Polmont, Stirlingshire; m., Joan Gwendolen Mappin (m. diss.); 2 s. Educ. Loretto School; St. Andrews University; Edinburgh University. National Service, Royal Signals, 1953-55; Law Apprentice, Gillespie and Paterson, WS, Patrick and James, WS, 1960-63; Assistant Solicitor, Patrick and James, WS, 1963-64; Legal Assistant, Inverness County Council, 1964-66; Lecturer in Jurisprudence, Dundee University, 1966-71; occasional Lecturer, Petroleum Training Institute, Stavanger, Norway, 1982-84; Honorary Secretary, Aberdeen Association of University Teachers, 1974-75; Governor, Robert Gordon's Institute of Technology, since 1982 (Chairman, 1982-85); Elder, Queen's Cross Church of Scotland, Aberdeen, since 1982. Publication: The Law of Arbitration in Scotland, 1987. Recreations: choral singing; reading (in literature, history and philosophy); cycling. Address: (h.) Primrose Cottage, Place of Tilliefoure, by Monymusk, Inverurie, Aberdeenshire, AB3 7JB; T.-Monymusk 357.

Hunter, Russell. Actor; b. 18.2.25, Glasgow. Former shipyard worker; began acting as an amateur; made professional debut with Glasgow Unity Theatre, 1947; appeared in repertory with Edinburgh Gateway, Edinburgh Traverse and Glasgow Citizens'; acted with the RSC, Bristol Old Vic and at the Old Vic, London; played title role in The Servant o' Twa Maisters, 1965, opening production of Edinburgh Civic Theatre Company; played The Pope in Galileo, also at Royal Lyceum; played The Gravedigger in Hamlet, Assembly Hall, Edinburgh Festival; took title role in Cocky, one-man play, 1969; played Jock, solo play, 1972.

Hunter, William, MA. Columnist, Glasgow Herald; b. 16.8.31, Paisley; m., Mo; 1 s.; 1 d. Educ. Paisley Grammar School; Glasgow University. Publications: The Saints; Bell the Cage! Recreation: weeding. Address: (h.) 233 Fenwick Road, Glasgow; T.-041-638 1323.

Hunter, William Hill, CBE, CA, JP, DL. Partner, McLay, McAlister & McGibbon, CA, since 1946; Director, J. & G. Grant, Glenfarclas Distillery, since 1966; b. 5.11.16, Cumnock; m., Kathleen Cole; 2 s. Educ. Cumnock Academy. Enlisted as private, RASC, 1940; commissioned Royal Artillery, 1941; Staff Captain, Middle East, 1944-46; Director: Abbey National Building Society (Scottish Advisory Board), 1966-86, City of Glasgow Friendly Society, 1966-88 (President, 1980-88); Member, CBI Scottish Council, 1978-84. President, Renfrew West and Inverclyde Conservative and Unionist Association, since 1972; President, Scottish Unionist Association, 1964-65; contested (Unionist), South Ayrshire, 1959 and 1964; Hon. Treasurer, Quarrier's Homes, since 1972; Hon. Financial Advisor, Erskine Hospital, since 1980; Chairman, Salvation Army Advisory Board in Strathclyde, since 1982; Chairman, Salvation Army Housing Association Scotland Ltd., since 1986; admitted to Distinguished Order of Auxiliary Service of Salvation Army, 1981; Deacon Convener, Trades House of Glasgow, 1986-87. Recreations: gardening; golf; swimming; music. Address: (h.) Armitage, Kilmacolm, PA13 4PH; T.-050587 2444.

Hunter Blair, Francis, JP. Chairman, Galloway Cattle Society of Great Britain and Ireland, since 1986; b. 29.10.30, Lincoln; m., Joyce Adeline Mary Graham; 4 s.; 1 d. Educ. Royal Naval College, Dartmouth; West of Scotland Agricultural College. President, Stewartry Branch, National Farmers' Union of Scotland, 1968-69; Council Member, NFU of Scotland, 1969-70; Vice President, Royal Highland and Agricultural Society of Scotland, 1987; several periods of office as Secretary and President, local agricultural shows; Past Chairman, now Secretary, Carsphairn Community Council; Elder, Carsphairn Kirk. Recreations: country pursuits; reading. Address: Marbrack, Carsphairn, Castle Douglas, Stewartry of Kirkcudbright; T.-Carsphairn 207.

Hunter Blair, James, DL. Landowner and Forester; SW Scotland Representative, Christies, Auctioneers, since 1984; b. 18.3.26, Ayr. Educ. Eton; Oxford. Scots Guards, 1944-48; University, 1948-50; merchant bank, London, 1951-53; managed family estate, since 1953. Past President, Royal Scottish Forestry Society; former Vice-President,

Royal Highland Society; Chairman, Opera West. Recreations: shooting; fishing; going to the opera. Address: Blairquhan, Maybole, Ayrshire; T.-Straiton 239.

Hurford, Professor James Raymond, BA, PhD. Professor of General Linguistics, Edinburgh University, since 1979; b. 16.7.41, Reading; m., Sue Ann Davis; 2 d. Educ. Exeter School; St. John's College, Cambridge; University College, London. Research Fellow, System Development Corporation, Santa Monica, California, 1967-68; Assistant Professor, University of California, 1968-71; Lecturer, Senior Lecturer, Lancaster University, 1972-79. Publications: The Linguistic Theory of Numerals, 1975; Semantics: A Coursebook (Co-author), 1983; Language and Number, 1987. Recreations: gardening; recorder playing. Address: (h.) 14 East Brighton Crescent, Portobello, Edinburgh.

Hutcheon, Andrew William, MB, ChB, MD, MRCP, FRCP. Consultant Physician to Aberdeen Hospitals, since 1978; Consultant Medical Oncologist, since 1978; Senior Lecturer in Medicine, Aberdeen University, since 1978; b. 21.5.43, Aberdeen; m., Christine Gray Cusiter; 1 s.; 2 d. Educ. Robert Gordon's College, Aberdeen; Aberdeen University. House Physician, Aberdeen Royal Infirmary, 1968; House Surgeon, Balfour Hospital, Orkney, 1969; Western Infirmary, Glasgow: Senior House Physician, 1970, Registrar in General Medicine, 1971; University Department of Medicine, Glasgow: Research Fellow, 1973, Senior Registrar, 1975; Senior Registrar, Royal Marsden Hospital, London, 1977. Recreations: skiing; curling; long distance running. Address: (h.) Moreseat, 159 Midstocket Road, Aberdeen, AB2 4LU; T.-0224 637204.

Hutcheon, Laura Louise, BSc (Hons), MSc. Chairman, Social Work Committee, Grampian Regional Council, since 1986; b. 30.12.59, Great Bookham. Educ. Wimbledon High School for Girls GPDST; Royal Holloway College, London University; Aberdeen University. Research Assistant, then Lecturer, Department of Bio-Medical Physics, Aberdeen University, 1981-85; Financial Consultant, Legal and General Assurance Society, 1985-87; Grampian Regional Councillor (Social and Liberal Democrats), since 1984. Recreations: reading; cooking; swimming. Address: (h.) 9 Princess Drive, Dyce, Aberdeen, AB2 0JX; T.-0224 723057.

Hutcheson, Rev. Norman McKenzie, MA, BD. Minister, Dalbeattie with Haugh of Urr, since 1988 (Saint Andrew's Parish Church, Kirkcaldy, 1973-88); b. 11.10.48, Leven, Fife; m., Elizabeth Gilchrist Anderson; 2 d. Educ. Hillhead High School, Glasgow; Glasgow University; Edinburgh University. Member, General Assembly Committees, since 1975: Finance, Practice and Procedure, Social Responsibility, Education for the Ministry; Moderator: Kirkcaldy Presbytery, 1984, Synod of Fife, 1985. Recreations: walking; photography; Rotary. Address: The Manse, Dalbeattie, Kirkcudbrightshire.

Hutchinson, Peter, BSc, PhD, CBiol, MIBiol, MIFM. Assistant Secretary, North Atlantic Salmon Conservation Organization, since 1986; b. 26.5.56, Glasgow; m., Jane MacKellaig; 1 s.; 1 d. Educ. Queen Elizabeth's Grammar School, Blackburn; Edinburgh University. Project Coordinator, Surface Water Acidification; Research Biologist: Institute of Terrestrial Ecology, Edinburgh University. Recreations: golf; squash; rugby union; angling. Address: (h.) 57 Craiglea Drive, Morningside, Edinburgh.

Hutchison, Rev. Alexander Scott, MA, BD, DD. Hospital Chaplain, The City and Associated Hospitals, Aberdeen, since 1986 (Minister, Rubislaw Parish Church, Aberdeen, 1968-86); b. 22.7.26, Uddingston, Glasgow; m., Gillian Alice Curry; 2 s.; 4 d. Educ. Bell-Baxter School, Cupar; St. Andrews University and St. Mary's College. Church of Scotland Chaplain to Overseas Students, 1954-59; Minister, Ceres, Fife, 1959-68; Chairman, International Year of Disabled People (Aberdeen), 1981; former Member, Post Office Users Council (Scotland); Disabled Scot of the Year, 1982; Honorary DD, St. Andrews; Burgess (Aberdeen). Recreation: bread and broth making. Address: Linsue, Drumoak, Aberdeenshire, AB3 3AA; T.-033 08 705.

Hutchison, David, MA, MLitt. Senior Lecturer in Communication Studies, Glasgow College of Technology, since 1975; b. 24.9.44, West Kilbride; m., Pauleen Frew; 2 d. Educ. Ardrossan Academy; Glasgow University. Tutor/Organiser, WEA (West of Scotland), 1966-69; Teacher, Reid Kerr College, Paisley, 1969-71; Lecturer in Communication Studies, Glasgow College of Technology, 1971-75; Member, West Kilbride District Council, 1970-75 (Chairman, 1972-75); Member, Scottish Film Council, since 1987; Member, General Advisory Council, BBC, since 1988; author of play, Deadline, Pitlochry Festival Theatre, 1980. Publications: The Modern Scottish Theatre, 1977; Headlines: the Media in Scotland (Editor), 1978. Recreations: walking; swimming; the arts. Address: (b.) Department of Humanities, Glasgow College of Technology, Cowcaddens Road, Glasgow, G4 OBA; T.-041-332 7090.

Hutchison, Lt.-Comdr. Sir (George) Ian Clark, Kt (1954). Member, Queen's Bodyguard for Scotland (Royal Company of Archers); b. 4.1.03; m., Sheena Campbell (deceased); 1 d. Educ. Edinburgh Academy; RN Colleges. Joined Navy, 1916; Member, Edinburgh Town Council, 1935-41; rejoined Navy, 1939; MP (Unionist), Edinburgh West, 1941-59; Deputy Lieutenant, County of City of Edinburgh, 1958-84.

Hutchison, Rev. Henry, BD, BEd, MA, MLitt, PhD, DipRE, LLCM. Minister, Carmunnock Parish Church, Glasgow, since 1977; b. 4.5.23, Alloa; m., Ann Sheila Maree Ross; 1 s. Educ. Alloa Academy; Dollar Academy; Edinburgh University; Glasgow University; Jordanhill College of Education; Toronto University. War service, RAF; Minister: Erksine Church, Saltcoats, 1948-53, Crosshill-Victoria Church, Glasgow, 1953-57, St. Paul's Presbyterian Church, Peterborough, Ontario, 1957-60; Principal, Stanstead College, Quebec, 1960-63; Assistant Professor of Education, Brandon University, Manitoba, 1965-67; Lecturer in Education, Glasgow University, 1967-77; Moderator, Peterborough Presbytery, Ontario, 1959. Publications: The Church and

Spiritual Healing, 1955; A Faith to Live By, 1959; The Beatitudes and Modern Life, 1960; Scottish Public Educational Documents, 1973; Kirk Life in Old Carmunnock, 1978; Carmunnock Church 1854-1947, 1979; God Believes in You!, 1980; Well I'm Blessed!, 1981, Have a Word with God, 1981; Healing through Worship, 1981; A Faith that Conquers, 1982. Recreations: music; bowls; walking. Address: 161 Waterside Road, Carmunnock, Glasgow, G76 9AJ; T.-041-644 1578.

Hutchison, Ian Somerville, OBE, JP. Chairman, Eastwood District Licensing Board; Member, Eastwood District Council (Chairman of Planning); Vice Chairman, Scottish National Housing & Town Planning Council; Member, Scottish Valuation Advisory Council, 1982-86; Member, Historic Buildings Council for Scotland, since 1983; Managing Director, Timbertection Ltd., since 1973; b. 10.4.28, Glasgow; m., Aileen Wallace; 2 s.; 2 d. Educ. Hutchesons' Boys' Grammar School. Elected to First (Eastwood) District Council, 1967, Renfrew County Council, 1970, Eastwood District Council, 1974; Provost, Eastwood, 1974-80; Delegate, COSLA, since 1975 (Vice President, COSLA, 1979-82); Member, Management Committee, Planning Exchange; Member, Renfrewshire Valuation Appeals Committee; Governor, The Queen's College, Glasgow, since 1973 (Chairman of Governors, since 1980). Recreations: gardening; fishing. Address: (h.) 39 Hazelwood Avenue, Newton Mearns, Glasgow, G77 5QT; T.-041-639 2186.

Hutchison, James Kenneth, CA. Vice-Chairman and Chief Executive, Scottish Sports Council, since 1972; b. 3.7.34, Edinburgh. Educ. George Heriot's School; Edinburgh University. CA apprentice and Audit Assistant, 1952-59; RAF Officer, Secretarial Branch, 1959-63; Scottish Council of Physical Recreation: Depute Secretary, 1964-68, General Secretary, 1968-72; Trustee and Honorary Secretary, Scottish Disability Foundation; Trustee, Scottish Physical Recreation Fund; Past Chairman, Edinburgh Sports Club Ltd.; Past President, George Heriot's School (FP) Rugby Club. Recreations: golf; swimming; theatre; good food and wine. Address: (b.) 1 St. Colme Street, Edinburgh, EH3 6AA; T.-031-225 8411.

Hutchison, Sir Peter Craft, Bt, BA. Chairman, Hutchison & Craft Ltd., Insurance Brokers, and associated/subsidiary companies; Director, Stakis plc, since 1979; Board Member, Scottish Tourist Board, 1981-87; Member, British Waterways Board, since 1987; Chairman, Board of Trustees, Royal Botanic Garden, Edinburgh; b. 5.6.35, London; m., Virginia Colville; 1 s. Educ. Eton; Magdalene College, Cambridge. National Service, Royal Scots Greys (2nd Lt.); Northern Assurance Co. (London); Director of various companies involved in banking, engineering, etc.; Past Chairman, Ailsa Shipbuilding Co. Ltd.; Deacon, Incorporation of Hammermen of Glasgow, 1984-85. Recreations: plant hunting; gardening; calligraphy. Address: (h.) Milton House, Milton, by Dumbarton, G82 2TU; T.-Dumbarton 61609.

Hutchison, Professor William McPhee, BSc, PhD, DSc, FIBiol, CBiol, FLS, FRSE. Research Professor, Strathclyde University, since 1987 (Personal Professor in Parasitology, 1971-87); b. 2.7.24, Glasgow; m., Isabella Duncan McLaughland; 2 s. Educ. Eastwood High School; Glasgow University; Strathclyde University. Glasgow University Athletic Club Blue, 1949; University Fencing Champion, 1949; Scottish Open Fencing Champion, 1949. Robert Koch Prize, 1970; Robert Koch Medal. Recreations: reading; music; gardening; DIY. Address: (h.) 597 Kilmarnock Road, Glasgow, G43 2TH.

Hutton, Alasdair Henry, MBE, TD, MEP. Member, European Parliament, since 1979; b. 19.5.40, London; m., Deirdre Mary Cassels (see Deirdre Mary Hutton); 2 s. Educ. Dollar Academy; Brisbane State High School. Trainee technician, Radio 4BH Brisbane, 1956; Clemenger Advertising, Melbourne, 1957-59; Newspaper Reporter, The Age, Melbourne, 1959-61, Aberdeen Journals, 1962-64; Broadcaser, BBC, 1964-79. Trustee, Community Service Volunteers; Patron, Volonteurop; Life Member, John Buchan Society; Honorary Chairman, Hawick Conservative Club. Recreation: Territorial Army, Parachute Regiment. Address: (b.) 34 Woodmarket, Kelso, TD5 7AX; T.-0573 24369.

Hutton, Deirdre Mary. Council Member, Scottish Consumer Council, since 1986; Member, Music Committee, Scottish Arts Council, since 1986; Member, Scottish Consultative Committee on the Curriculum, since 1987; b. 15.3.49, Haddington; m., Alasdair Hutton (qv); 2 s. Educ. Sherborne School for Girls; secretarial college. Research Assistant, Glasgow Chamber of Commerce, 1976-81; seconded to Scotland is British Campaign and Scotland Says No Campaign during devolution referendum, 1979. Recreations: music; reading. Address: (h.) Rosebank, Shedden Park Road, Kelso, TD5 7PX; T.-0573 24368.

Hutton, James Thomas, ARCM. Composer; Visiting Teacher of Music, since 1960; b. 12.5.23, Glasgow; m., Anne Jamieson Bowes; 1 s. Educ. Provanside Secondary School; Glasgow University; Royal Scottish Academy of Music. Worked for Renfrewshire Education Authority, 1960-64, Lanarkshire Education Authority, since 1964; entirely self-taught Composer of orchestral music; works include two symphonies, two concert-overtures, piano concerto, chamber music, and works for brass band, solo piano and organ; has also composed and arranged music for jazz orchestras and groups. Recreation: playing jazz piano. Address: (h.) 88 Warwick, East Kilbride; T.-East Kilbride 25895.

Hyslop, Kenneth Alexander, BSc. Rector, Leith Academy, since 1983; b. 7.12.39, Edinburgh; m., Sheena Isabel Hyslop; 1 s.; 1 d. Educ. Boroughmuir Secondary School; Heriot-Watt University. Science Teacher, Currie High School, 1964-69; Newbattle High School: Principal Teacher of Science, 1969-72, Assistant Headteacher, 1972-73; Deputy Headteacher, Broughton High School, 1973-77; Headteacher, Castlebrae High School, 1977-83. Address: (b.) Leith Academy, Duke Street, Edinburgh; T.-031-554 0606.

I

Idiens, Dale, BA, DipEd. Keeper, Department of History and Applied Art, National Museums of Scotland; b. 13.5.42, Prestatyn. Educ. Wycombe High School, High Wycombe; Leicester University. Royal Scottish Museum, Department of Art and Archaeology: Assistant Keeper in Charge of Ethnography, 1964, Deputy Keeper, 1979, Keeper, 1983. Address: (b.) Royal Museum of Scotland, Chambers Street, Edinburgh; T.-031-225 7534.

Illingworth, Sir Charles Frederick William, Kt (1961), CBE (1946). Regius Professor of Surgery, Glasgow University, 1939-64; Honorary Surgeon to The Queen, in Scotland, 1961-65; Extra Surgeon, since 1965; b. 8.5.99; m., Eleanor Mary Bennett (deceased); 4 s. Educ. Heath Grammar School, Halifax; Edinburgh University.

Illingworth, Richard Penry, TD, FRICS. Chief Land Agent, Forestry Commission, since 1985; b. 18.1.33, London; m., Elspeth Hutcheson; 2 s. Educ. Bedales School. Address: (b.) 231 Corstorphine Road, Edinburgh, EH12 7AT; T.-031-334 0303.

Illsley, William Allen, BA, MA, DipEd, PhD, FRSA. Principal, Dundee College of Education, 1979-86; b. 24.9.21, Startforth, near Barnard Castle; m., Doris Gorrey; 2 s. Educ. Barnard Castle School; St. Chad's College, Durham University; St. Andrews University. War service, Grenadier Guards, Reconnaissance Corps and 2nd Royal Lancers (Indian Army); teaching; Senior Education Officer, Northern Nigeria; Dundee College of Education: Lecturer, Senior Lecturer, Assistant Principal. Publications: text books on the teaching of Shakespeare and English; County of Angus volume, Third Statistical Account of Scotland (Editor). Recreations: angling; gardening; walking. Address: (h.) Dromore, Strathern Road, West Ferry, Dundee; T.-0382 79301.

Imrie, Ian. Industrial Editor, Glasgow Herald, since 1966 (Air Correspondent, since 1963); b. 26.4.26, Dundee. Educ. Kirkcaldy High School. Recreation: golf. Address: (h.) 34 Rankin Drive, Largs, Ayrshire; T.-0475 672509.

Inglis, Rev. Donald Bain Carrick, MA, MEd, BD. Minister, St. Andrew's Parish Church, Turriff, since 1983; b. 17.12.41, Aberdeen; m., Yvonne M.S. Cook; 1 s.; 2 d. Educ. Aberdeen Grammar School; Aberdeen University; Aberdeen College of Education; Glasgow University. Teacher of English and History at Aberdeen and Ellon Academy, 1964-68; Educational Psychologist, then Senior Educational Psychologist, Lanarkshire, 1968-72; Assistant Minister, Bathgate High Church, 1975-77; Educational Psychologist, then Senior Educational Psychologist, Fife, 1977-83. Former Member, Executive Committee, Psychologists' Section, Educational Institute of Scotland; Convener, Education Committee, Buchan Presbytery, 1984-88. Recreations: violin playing; swimming; hill-walking; cycling. Address: St. Andrew's Manse, Balmellie Road, Turriff, Aberdeenshire, AB5 7DP; T.-Turriff 63240.

Inglis, Professor James Alistair Macfarlane, CBE (1984), MA, LLB. Professor of Conveyancing, Glasgow University, since 1979; Professor of Professional Legal Practice, since 1984 (first holder of Chair); Partner, McClure, Naismith, Anderson & Gardiner, Solicitors, Glasgow, since 1956; b. 24.12.28, Kilmarnock; m., Mary Elizabeth Howie; 2 s.; 3 d. Educ. Kilmarnock Academy; Fettes College; St. Andrews University; Glasgow University. Qualified as Solicitor, 1952; Member: Board of Management, Victoria and Leverndale Hospitals, 1964-74, Greater Glasgow Health Board, 1975-83; President, Rent Assessment Panel for Scotland, 1976-87; Chairman, Glasgow Hospitals Auxiliary Association, since 1985; Convener, Ad Hoc Committee, Church of Scotland, into Legal Services of Church, 1978-79; Session Clerk, Caldwell Parish Church, since 1963. Address: (h.) Crioch, Uplawmoor, Glasgow; T.-Uplawmoor 315.

Inglis, John, RSW, FSA(Scot), DA. Painter and Lecturer; b. 27.7.53, Glasgow; m., Heather; 2 s.; 1 d. Educ. Hillhead High School; Gray's School of Art. Travelling scholarships to Italy, 1976; Member, Dundee Group, 1979-84; one-man exhibitions: Aberdeen, 1976 and 1977; Glasgow, 1980, Skipton, 1981; Scottish Arts Council Award, 1981; RSA Keith Prize, 1975; SAC Bursary, 1982; RSA Meyer Oppenheim Prize, 1982; RSW EIS Award, 1987. Address: (h.) 21 Hillview Road, Larbert, Stirlingshire; T.-0324 558891.

Inglis, William Caldwell, MA (Hons). Rector, Largs Academy, since 1973; b. 22.12.36, Ayr; m., Helga Goldschmidt; 2 s.; 3 d. Educ. Ayr Academy; Glasgow University. Teacher of History, Irvine Royal Academy, 1959-64; Principal Teacher of History, Geography and Modern Studies, Dalmellington High School, 1964-66; Principal Teacher of History and Modern Studies, Cumnock Academy, 1966-70; Depute Rector, Auchinleck Academy, 1970-72. Founder President, Irvine Royal Academicals Rugby Football Club. Recreation: gardening; swimming. Address: (b.) Largs Academy, Flatt Road, Largs; T.-0475 675421.

Ingram, Adam Paterson, JP. MP (Labour), East Kilbride, since 1987; b. 1.2.47; m. Educ. Cranhill Secondary School. Member, East Kilbride District Council, 1980-87 (Leader, 1984-87); Member, Policy Committee, COSLA, 1984-87.

Ingram, Hugh Albert Pugh, BA (Cantab), PhD (Dunelm). Lecturer in Botany (Ecology), Dundee University, since 1966; Trustee, National Museums of Scotland, since 1987; Vice-Chairman (Conservation and Science), Scottish Wildlife Trust, 1982-87; b. 29.4.37, Rugby; m., Dr. Ruth Hunter; 1 s.; 1 d. Educ. Lawrence Sheriff School, Rugby; Rugby School; Emmanuel College, Cambridge; Hatfield College, Durham. Demonstrator in Botany, University College of North Wales, Bangor, 1963-64; Staff Tutor in Natural Science, Department of Extra-Mural Studies, Bristol University, 1964-65; Member, UK Committee, International Peat Society; Member, Museums and Galleries Commission Working Party on the non-national museums of Scotland, 1984-86. Recreations: music (clarinet, piano); literature; rural history; hill-walking. Address: Johnstonfield, Dunbog, Cupar, Fife, KY14 6JG.

Ingram-Brown, Leslie, FInstSMM, MBIM, MRIN. Editor, Nautical Magazine, since 1980; Joint Managing Director, Brown, Son & Ferguson Ltd., since 1980; b. 24.5.47, Glasgow; m., Susanna. Educ. Shawlands Academy; Hutchesons' Boys' Grammar School; Glasgow College of Commerce. Brown, Son & Ferguson Ltd.: Assistant Company Secretary, 1968-72, Company Secretary/Director, 1972-80. Recreations: curling; cricket; golf; reading. Address: (b.) 4/10 Darnley Street, Glasgow, G41 2SD.

Inkson, Robert Henry Ewen, BSc, FSS, FIS. President, General Assembly of Unitarian and Free Christian Churches, 1988-89; Head, Department of Statistics, Macaulay Institute for Soil Research, 1968-87; b. 1.10.24, Aberdeen; m., Jean Davidson McArthur. Educ. Aberdeen Central School; Aberdeen University. Macaulay Institute for Soil Research: Scientific Officer, 1951-54, Senior Scientific Officer, 1954-63, Principal Scientific Officer, since 1963. Chairman, Aberdeen Unitarian Church. Recreations: music; gardening. Address: (h.) 39 Woodend Place, Aberdeen, AB2 6AP; T.-0224 315304.

Innes, James, BSc, CEng, MICE, FIHT. Assistant Chief Road Engineer, Scottish Development Department, since 1985; b. 7.8.44, Helmsdale; m., June Pearson; 1 s.; 1 d. Educ. Woodside Secondary School, Glasgow; Strathclyde University. Lanark County Council, 1966-67; Inverness County Council, 1967-73; Scottish Development Department, 1973-84; Department of Transport (Superintending Engineer), 1984-85. Recreation: golf. Address: (b.) Room 3/70, New St. Andrews House, Edinburgh, EH1 3SZ; T.-031-244 4337.

Innes, Norman Lindsay, BSc, PhD, DSc, FIBiol, FIHort. Head, Plant Breeding Division, Scottish Crop Research Institute, since 1984 (Deputy Director, since 1986); b. 3.5.34, Kirriemuir; m., Marjory Niven Farquhar; 1 s.; 1 d. Educ. Websters High School, Kirriemuir; Aberdeen University; Cambridge University. Senior Cotton Breeder: Sudan, 1958-66, Uganda, 1966-71; Head, Cotton Research Unit, Uganda, 1972; National Vegetable Research Station, Wellesbourne: Head, Plant Breeding Section, 1973-84, Deputy Director, 1977-84; Honorary Lecturer, then Honorary Professor, Birmingham University, 1973-84; Governing Board Member, International Crops Research Institute for Semi-Arid Tropics, India, 1982-88; Honorary Professor: St. Andrews University, since 1985, Dundee University, since 1988; Governing Board Member, International Potato Centre, Peru, since 1988; Chairman, British Association of Plant Breeders, 1982-84; Member, Oxfam Council of Trustees, 1982-85. Recreations: golf; photography; travel. Address: (b.) Scottish Crop Research Institute, Invergowrie, Dundee, DD2 5DA; T.-0382 562731.

Innes, Richard Threlfall, BA, LLB. Honorary Sheriff, Fife; retired Solicitor; b. 5.9.00, Kirkcaldy; m., Jean Davidson; 2 s.; 3 d. Educ. Cargilfield; Fettes; Oxford University; Edinburgh University. Former Secretary, Kirkcaldy Chamber of Commerce; former Clerk, Commissioners of Income Tax. Recreations: gardening; golf. Address: (h.) 14 Boglily Road, Kirkcaldy, Fife; T.-0592 263287.

Innes of Edingight, Malcolm Rognvald, CVO, MA, LLB, WS, FSA Scot, KStJ. Lord Lyon King of Arms, since 1981; Secretary to Order of the Thistle, since 1981; b. 25.5.38, Edinburgh; m., Joan Hay; 3 s. Educ. Edinburgh Academy; Edinburgh University. Carrick Pursuivant, 1958; Marchmont Herald, 1971; Lyon Clerk and Keeper of the Record, 1966; Member, Queen's Bodyguard for Scotland (Royal Company of Archers); President, Scottish Heraldry Society. Recreations: archery; shooting; fishing. Address: (b.) Court of the Lord Lyon, HM New Register House, Edinburgh; T.-031-556 7255.

Ireland, James Cecil Hardin. Trustee, Scottish Rugby Union, since 1951 (President, 1950-51); b. 10.12.03, Glasgow; m., Margaret Stewart McLean. Educ. High School of Glasgow. Singer Manufacturing Co. Ltd.; William Younger & Co. Ltd.; War service, RNVR and Royal Marines, 1940-46; Dundee Manager, William Younger & Co. Ltd.; London Manager, Scottish & Newcastle Breweries (retired, 1968); rugby international, 1925-26-27; Scottish Rugby Union Committee, 1936; international Referee, 1938-39; Chairman, four Home Unions Tours Committee, 1946-51; Honorary Vice President, South Africa Rugby Board, 1964; President, Glasgow High School Club, 1964-65; Elder, St. Columba's Church of Scotland, London, 1960-68. Recreations: spectating at all sports; renewing friendships. Address: (h.) 10 Abbots View, Polmont, FK2 0QL; T.-Polmont 713400.

Ireland, Dr. Kenneth, OBE, DUniv, FRSA, FTS, BL. Freelance Arts Marketing Consultant, since 1984; Consultant, Hanover Fine Arts (Edinburgh); b. 17.6.20, Edinburgh; m., Moira Lamb; 2 s. Educ. Edinburgh Academy; Edinburgh University. Law Apprentice, Steedman Ramage & Co., WS, Edinburgh, 1938-41; War service: Royal Artillery, Gnr/L Bdr., 1941-42, Intelligence Corps, Sgt./S. Sgt./WO II, 1942-46; Lt. (TA), 1948-52; General Manager: Park Theatre, Glasgow, 1946-49, Pitlochry Festival Theatre, 1951-52; Pitlochry Festival Society Ltd.: General Manager and Secretary, 1953-57, Festival Director and Secretary, 1957-83 (retired, 1984); Board Member, Scottish Tourist Board, 1966-69; Chairman, Tourist Association of Scotland, 1967-69; Deputy Chairman, Scottish Tourist Consultative Council, 1977-83; Directorships: Federation of Scottish Theatre, Scottish Opera Theatre Royal, Scottish International Gathering Trust; Vice-Chairman, Campaign for an International Opera Theatre of Scotland; Member: Scottish Corps of Retired Executives (SCORE/EVENT), Advisory Council for the Arts in Scotland, Scottish Opera Advisory Council, Queen Margaret College (Edinburgh) Drama Advisory Board; Trustee: J.D. Fergusson Art Foundation, International Opera Theatre of Scotland; ESU Scotland Thyne Scholarship, 1970; Bill Heron Trophy, 1981 (first recipient for services to tourism). Recreations: foreign travel; theatre-going; galleries; reading. Address: (h.) 10 Ravelston Rise, Edinburgh, EH4 3LH; T.-031-346 2292.

Ireland, Sheriff Ronald David, QC. Sheriff Principal, Grampian, Highland and Islands, since 1988; b. 13.3.25, Edinburgh. Educ. George Watson's College, Edinburgh; Balliol College, Oxford

(Scholar); Edinburgh University. Advocate, 1952; Clerk, Faculty of Advocates, 1957-58; Professor of Scots Law, Aberdeen University, 1958-71; QC, 1964; Dean, Faculty of Law, Aberdeen University, 1964-67; Chairman, Board of Management, Aberdeen General Hospitals, 1964-71; Sheriff, Lothian and Borders at Edinburgh, 1972-88; Director, Scottish Courts Administration, 1975-78. Address: (h.) 6a Greenhill Gardens, Edinburgh, EH10 4BW.

Irons, Norman MacFarlane, CEng, MIMechE, MCIBSE, JP, DL. Partner, Building Services Consulting Engineers, since 1983; Member, City of Edinburgh District Council, since 1976; b. 4.1.41, Glasgow; m., Anne Buckley; 1 s.; 1 d. Held various posts as Consulting Engineer; founded own practice, 1983; SNP Group Leader, Edinburgh District Council. Recreation: stalwart of Lismore Rugby Club, since 1959. Address: (h.) 141 Saughtonhall Drive, Edinburgh, EH12 5TS; T.-031-337 6154.

Ironside, Leonard. Member, Grampian Regional Council, since 1982; Patron, Grampian Special Olympics for Handicapped; Commonwealth Professional Wrestling Champion, since 1981; b. 16.2.50, Aberdeen. Educ. Hilton Academy, Aberdeen. Section Manager, Department of Health and Social Security, since 1976. Won Commonwealth Professional Wrestling Championship at Middleweight, 1979; lost Championship, 1981; regained title, 1981; gained European Lightweight title, 1985. Recreations: yoga teacher; also plays tennis, squash, badminton; cycling. Address: (h.) 42 Hillside Terrace, Portlethen, Kincardineshire; T.-Aberdeen 780929.

Irvine, Andrew Robertson, MBE (1979). Rugby Player; b. 16.9.51, Edinburgh; m., Audrey; 2 d. Educ. George Heriot's School, Edinburgh; Edinburgh University. Captained George Heriot's School, Scottish Schools, Heriots FP, Edinburgh, Scotland; holds records for: most international points scored (273 for Scotland, 28 for British Lions in three tours (nine tests)) and most tries scored by a full back (10); made international debut against All Blacks, 1972; 51 caps for Scotland; works as a Chartered Surveyor.

Irvine, Ian James, CA. Managing Director, George Outram & Company, since 1986; b. 30.5.36, Blantyre, Malawi; m., Margaret; 1 s.; 1 d. Educ. Robert Gordons College, Aberdeen. Trained as Chartered Accountant with F.A. Ritson & Co., Aberdeen, and Wilson, Stirling & Co., Glasgow; qualified as CA, 1959; National Service, RAPC, 1959-61; Chief Accountant, George Outram & Company Ltd., 1965, and additionally Assistant Company Secretary, 1971; appointed a Director and Company Secretary, 1975, and Financial Director, later that year. Director, Glasgow Opportunities Enterprise Trust; Member, Glasgow Action; Director, Glasgow Chamber of Commerce; Director, Scottish Business in the Community. Address: (b.) 195 Albion Street, Glasgow, G1 1QP; T.-041-552 6255.

Irvine, James Williamson, MBE, JP, MA, FEIS. Honorary Sheriff, Lerwick, since 1977; b. 10.3.17, Virkie, Shetland; m., Isabella E. White; 1 s.; 1 d. Educ. Virkie Public School; Anderson Educational Institute; Edinburgh Unversity; Moray House College of Education. Army, 1940-46; Further Education Officer, Shetland, 1946-50; Teacher in Shetland, 1950-77; Headmaster, Lerwick Central School, 1966-77. First Chairman, Shetland Movement. Publications: Footprints, 1980; Up-Helly-Aa, 1982; Lerwick, 1985; Dunrossness, 1987. Recreation: reading. Address: (h.) Brekkheim, 4 Midgarth Crescent, Lerwick, Shetland Isles.

Irvine, John Rutherford, JP. Chairman, Roxburgh District Council, since 1980; Honorary Provost of Hawick, since 1982; b. 14.6.40, Hawick; m., Eileen Millar; 1 s. Educ. Hawick High School; Henderson Technical College, Hawick. Joined Roxburgh District Council, 1975; Vice-Convener, Housing Committee, 1977-80. Address: (h.) Airenlea, 3 Teviot Crescent, Hawick, Roxburghshire; T.-0450 75959.

Irvine-Fortescue, James William, MA (Hons), CA, JP, DL, KLJ, FSA Scot. Commissioner of Income Tax, County of Kincardine, since 1957; Chairman, Grampian Region Valuation Appeal Committee, since 1975; b. 7.6.17, Wilmslow; m., Margaret Guise Yates; 3 s.; 1 d. Educ. Aberdeen Grammar School; Edinburgh Academy; Aberdeen University. War Service: Royal Army Pay Corps, 1940-46, service in India and Ceylon, 1942-46 (Major and Staff Paymaster); JP and Magistrate, Kincardineshire, 1957; Member, Kincardine County Council, 1952-73; Chairman, Lower Deeside District Council, 1964-73. President, Deeside Field Club, 1981-86; a Vice President, Royal Society for Asian Affairs, 1983-88; Past President, Auchinleck Boswell Society; Past Chairman, Aberdeen Music Festival. Recreations: family history research; foreign travel. Address: (h.) Kingcausie, Maryculter, Aberdeen, AB1 0AR; T.-0224 732224.

Irvine Robertson, Alexander, TD, DL, MA, LLB. Solicitor, since 1936; Honorary Sheriff, Tayside, Central and Fife; b. 12.11.12, Stirling; m., Jean Margaret Fraser; 3 s.; 1 d. Educ. Fettes College, Edinburgh; Edinburgh University. Territorial Army, 1931-53 (retired, Bt. Colonel); Councillor, Royal Burgh of Stirling, 1946-50; Chairman, Stirlingshire T & AF Association, 1965-68; Secretary, Stirlingshire and Clackmannanshire (later Central Region) Valuation Appeal Committee, 1956-85; Chairman, Visiting Committee, Cornton Vale Borstal Institution, 1960-70; Session Clerk, Church of the Holy Rude, Stirling, 1958-85. Publication: Peacetime (History of 7th Bn., Argyll and Sutherland Highlanders, 1908-58). Recreations: reading; golf. Address: (h.) 6 Abercromby Place, Stirling; T.-Stirling 74526.

Irving, Rev. Douglas Robert, LLB, BD, WS. Minister, Kilbirnie: Auld Kirk, since 1984; b. 24.5.51, Stranraer; m., Hilary Frances Bell. Educ. Stranraer High School; Dundee University; Edinburgh University. Solicitor, 1974-80. Chairman, Kilbirnie and Glengarnock Community Council. Recreations: bee-keeping; music; reading. Address: Manse of the Auld Kirk, 49 Holmhead, Kilbirnie, KA25 6BS; T.-0505 682348.

Irving, Gordon, MA (Hons). Writer, Journalist and Broadcaster; b. 4.12.18, Annan; m., Elizabeth Dickie; 1 s. Educ. Dumfries Academy; Edinburgh University. Staff Journalist, Daily Record, Edinburgh and Glasgow; Reuters' News Agency, London; TV Guide, Scotland; The Viewer, Scotland; Freelance Writer/Journalist, since 1964; Scotland Correspondent, Variety, New York. Publications: Great Scot! (biography of Sir Harry Lauder); The Good Auld Days; The Solway Smugglers; The Wit of the Scots; The Wit of Robert Burns; The Devil on Wheels; Brush Up Your Scotland; Annie Laurie; Take No Notice and Take No More Notice! (World's Funniest Signs); The First 200 Years (Story of Dumfries and Galloway Royal Infirmary). Recreations: video; motoring to Spain; collecting trivia; fighting bumbling bureaucrats. Address: (h.) 36 Whittingehame Court, Glasgow, G12 OBG; T.-041-357 2265.

Irving, James Wyllie, TD, SSC. Solicitor, since 1937; Partner, Primrose & Gordon, Dumfries; Honorary Sheriff, South Strathclyde, Dumfries and Galloway, at Dumfries, since 1963; Notary Public; b. 21.4.14, Dumfries; m., Henrietta Mary Purcell. Educ. Fettes College; Glasgow University. Cheshire Regiment, 1939-45 (Major); Territorial Army, KOSB, 1948-59 (Major); Civil Defence Depute Group Controller, SW Scotland, 1960-68; Secretary, County of Dumfries Valuation Appeal Committee, 1956-72; Chairman, South West Scotland Local Employment Committee, 1960-74; Member, Board of Management, Dumfries and Galloway Hospitals, 1965-71 (Chairman, 1968-71); Chairman, Board of Management, Dumfries and Galloway and Crichton Royal Hospitals, 1972-74; Chairman, Dumfries and Galloway Health Board, 1973-80; Secretary, Dumfries and Kirkcudbrightshire Ploughing Association, 1955-72; Chairman, Local Board of Directors, Scottish Union and National Insurance Company. Recreation: gardening. Address: (h.) Kirkbrae (the Old Manse), Lochrutton, near Dumfries; T.-Lochfoot 301.

Irving, John Black, BSc, MB, ChB, FRCPE. Consultant Physician, Bangour General Hospital, since 1980; Honorary Senior Lecturer, Edinburgh University, since 1985; Consultant Cardiologist, Edinburgh Royal Infirmary, since 1980; b. 25.11.43, Lanark; m., Elspeth Mary; 2 s.; 1 d. Educ. Selkirk High School; Edinburgh University. British Heart Foundation Research Fellow, University Department of Medicine, Edinburgh, 1970-72; Registrar, Cardiac Department, Western General Hospital, Edinburgh, 1972-74; Registrar, Edinburgh Royal Infirmary, 1974-75; Research Fellow, Department of Cardiology, University of Washington, Seattle, 1975-76; Senior Registrar in Cardiology, Edinburgh Hospitals, 1976-79. Recreations: curling; hill-walking. Address: (b.) Bangour General Hospital, Broxburn, West Lothian, EH52 6LR; T.-0506 81334.

Irving, John Bruce, BSc, MSc, PhD. Director of Information Technology, Dumfries and Galloway Regional Council, since 1986; b. 19.6.42, Lenzie; m., Margaret Anne McWilliam, MB, ChB; 2 s.; 1 d. Educ. Lenzie Academy; Glasgow University. Owner, Bonshaw Tower, the seat of the Irving Clan since 1022; research, National Engineering Laboratory, East Kilbride, 1969-78; Project Coordinator, then Information Systems Manager, Chloride Technical Ltd., Manchester, 1978-85. Past President: Ayrshire Philatelic Society, Dumfries Philatelic Society; awards received at national stamp exhibitions. Recreations: outdoor pursuits; family history; philately. Address: (h.) Bonshaw Tower, Kirtlebridge, Lockerbie, DG11 3LY; T.-O46 15 256.

Irving, Ronald Eckford Mill, MA, DPhil (Oxon). Reader in Politics, Edinburgh University, since 1981; b. 14.7.39, Glasgow; m., Christine Mary Gaudin; 4 d. Educ. Merchiston Castle School; St. Edmund Hall, Oxford. Schoolmaster, 1961-65; Lecturer in Politics: Bristol University, 1968-69, Edinburgh University, 1969-81. Publications: Christian Democracy in France, 1973; The First Indochina War: French and American Policy in Vietnam 1945-54, 1975; The Christian Democratic Parties of Western Europe, 1979. Recreations: golf; piping. Address: (h.) 76 Murrayfield Gardens, Edinburgh, EH12 6DQ; T.-031-337 3663.

Irwin, Professor David George, MA, PhD, FSA, FRSA. Professor of History of Art and Head of Department, Aberdeen University, since 1970; b. 24.6.33, London; m., Francina Sorabji; 1 s.; 1 d. Educ. Holgate Grammar School, Barnsley; Queen's College, Oxford (Exhibitioner); Courtauld Institute of Art, London University. Lecturer in History of Fine Art, Glasgow University, 1959-70; Past President, British Society for 18th Century Studies; former Council Member, Walpole Society; former Member, Art Panel, Scottish Arts Council; Committee Member, Aberdeen Art Gallery; Committee Member, Scottish Georgian Society; elected Member, International Association of Art Critics; won Laurence Binyon Prize, Oxford, 1956. Publications: English Neoclassical Art; Paul Klee; Visual Arts, Taste and Criticism; Winckelmann, Writings on Art; John Flaxman, Sculptor, Illustrator, Designer; Scottish Painters, At Home and Abroad, 1700 to 1900 (with Francina Irwin). Recreations: swimming; walking; travel. Address: (b.) Department of History of Art, King's College, Old Aberdeen, Aberdeen, AB9 2UB; T.-0224 40241.

Irwin, Ian Sutherland, CBE (1982), BL, CA, IPFA, FCIT, CBIM, FInstD. Chairman and Chief Executive, Scottish Transport Group, since 1987; Chairman, Scottish Bus Group Ltd. and Caledonian MacBrayne Ltd., since 1975; Chairman, Scottish Transport Investments Ltd., since 1975; Chairman, SBG Engineering Ltd., since 1987; a Director: British Transport Advertising Ltd., since 1985, Scottish Mortgage & Trust plc, since 1986; Vice-President, International Union of Public Transport, since 1981; b. 20.2.33; m.; 2 s. Educ. Whitehill Senior Secondary School, Glasgow; Glasgow University. President, Bus and Coach Council, 1979-80.

Isaac, David Gilmour Davies, MA (Hons) (Oxon), PhD. Rector, Hutchesons' Grammar School, Glasgow, 1978-84; b. 13.7.24, Fochriw, Glamorgan; m., Sheena Reith Steele; 1 s.; 1 d. Educ. Sir Edward Lewis's School, Pengam, Glamorgan; Jesus College, Oxford (Oxford v. Cambridge association football, 1942); Edinburgh University. House Tutor and Scholarship Historian, Edinburgh Academy, 1945-62 (House Master, 1959-62); Headmaster, King Henry VIII School, Abergavenny, 1962-68; Rector, Marr College, Troon, 1968-78; Member, Headmasters' Conference,

1978-84; Council Member and Editor, Welsh Headmasters' Review; Secretary, Edinburgh Academical Football Club, 1959-62; Governor, Wellington School, Ayr; Elder, Portland Church, Troon; President, Troon Arts Guild, 1987. Recreations: golf; music; wine-making. Address: (h.) 1 Polo Gardens, Troon, Ayrshire; T.-0292 313804.

Ivory, Brian Gammell, MA (Cantab), CA. Director, The Highland Distilleries Company plc, since 1978; Director, Matthew Gloag & Son Ltd., since 1987; Managing Director, The Highland Distilleries Company PLC, since 1988; Member, Scottish Arts Council, since 1983 (Chairman, Combined Arts Committee; Vice Chairman of the Council, since 1988); Member, Arts Council of Great Britain, since 1988; b. 10.4.49, Edinburgh; m., Oona Mairi MacPhie Bell-MacDonald (see Oona Mairi MacPhie Ivory); 1 s. Educ. Eton College; Magdalene College, Cambridge. Recreations: the arts; farming; hill-walking. Address: (h.) Brewlands, Glenisla, by Blairgowrie, Perthshire, PH11 8PL; 12 Ann Street, Edinburgh, EH4 1PJ.

Ivory, Oona Mairi MacPhie, MA (Cantab), ARCM. Professional Musician; Director, The Scottish Ballet; b. 21.7.54, Ayr; m., Brian Gammell Ivory (qv); 1 s. Educ. King's College, Cambridge; Royal Scottish Academy of Music and Drama; Royal Academy of Music. Recreations: visual arts; sailing. Address: (h.) Brewlands, Glenisla, by Blairgowrie, Perthshire, PH11 8PL; 12 Ann Street, Edinburgh, EH4 1PJ.

Izod, (Kenneth) John, BA (Hons), PhD. Senior Lecturer, Department of Film and Media Studies, Stirling University, since 1978; b. 4.3.40, Shepperton; m., Irene Chew Geok Keng; 1 s.; 1 d. Educ. Prince Edward School, Harare City, Zimbabwe; Leeds University. Clerk articled to Chartered Accountant, 1958-63; Projectionist, mobile cinema unit, 1963; Lecturer in English, New University of Ulster, 1969-78; Member, Scottish Film Council, since 1978 (and of its Executive, since 1984); Chairman, Stirling Film Theatre, since 1982. Publication: Reading the Screen, 1984; Hollywood and the Box Office 1895-1986, 1988. Address: (b.) Film and Media Studies, University, Stirling, FK9 4LA; T.-0786 73171.

J

Jack, Professor Robert Barr, MA, LLB. Joint Senior Partner, McGrigor Donald, Solicitors, Glasgow and Edinburgh; Professor of Mercantile Law, Glasgow University, since 1978; b. 18.3.28; m., Anna Thorburn Thomson; 2 s. Educ. Kilsyth Academy; High School of Glasgow; Glasgow University. Admitted a Solicitor in Scotland, 1951; Member: Company Law Committee, Law Society of Scotland, 1971 (Convener, 1978-85); Scottish Law Commission, 1974-77; Scottish Observer, Department of Trade's Insolvency Law Review Committee, 1977-82; Member, DOT Advisory Panel on Company Law, 1980-83; Member, Council for the Securities Industry, 1983-85; Lay Member, Council of the Stock Exchange, 1984-86; Independent Member, Board, Securities Association Ltd., since 1986; Chairman, Review Committee on Banking Services Law, since 1987; Chairman: Brownlee plc, Timber Merchants, Glasgow, 1984-86 (Director, 1974-86); Joseph Dunn (Bottlers) Ltd., Soft Drink Manufacturers, Glasgow, since 1983; Director: Bank of Scotland, since 1985; Scottish Metropolitan Property plc, since 1980; Scottish Mutual Assurance Society, since 1987; Clyde Football Club Ltd., since 1980; Chairman, Scottish National Council of YMCAs, 1966-73; President, Scottish National Union of YMCAs, since 1983; Governor, Hutchesons' Educational Trust, Glasgow, 1978-87 (Chairman, 1980-87); Chairman, The Turnberry Trust, since 1983. Publications: lectures and articles on various aspects of company law and the statutory regulation and self-regulation of the City. Recreations: golf; hopeful supporter of one of Glasgow's less fashionable football teams; a dedicated lover of Isle of Arran which serves, regrettably less frequently, as a retreat and restorative. Address: (h.) 39 Mansewood Road, Glasgow, G43 1TN; T.-041-632 1659; (b.) Pacific House, 70 Wellington Street, Glasgow, G2 6SB; T.-041-248 6677.

Jack, Professor Ronald Dyce Sadler, MA, PhD. Professor of Scottish and Medieval Literature, Edinburgh University, since 1987; Member, Consultative Committee on the Curriculum, since 1987; b. 3.4.41, Ayr; m., Christabel Margaret Nicolson; 2 d. Educ. Ayr Academy; Glasgow University; Edinburgh University. Department of English Literature: Assistant Lecturer, 1965, Lecturer, 1968, Reader, 1978, Associate Dean, Faculty of Arts, 1971-73; Visiting Professor, Virginia University, 1973-74; Member, Universities Central Council on Admissions, 1973-76; Pierpont Morgan Scholar, British Academy, 1976; Advising Editor, Scotia, since 1980; Member, Scottish Universities Council on Entrance, since 1981; Governor, Newbattle Abbey College, since 1984. Publications: Robert MacLellan's Jamie the Saxt (Co-Editor), 1970; Scottish Prose 1550-1700, 1972; The Italian Influence on Scottish Literature, 1972; A Choice of Scottish Verse 1560-1660, 1978; The Art of Robert Burns (Co-author), 1982; Sir Thomas Urquhart, The Jewel (Co-author), 1984; Alexander Montgomerie, 1985; Scottish Literature's Debt to Italy, 1986; The History of Scottish Literature, Volume 1, 1988. Recreations: golf; zoology; theatre. Address: (b.) Department of English Literature, Edinburgh University, David Hume Tower, George Square, Edinburgh, EH8 9JX.

Jackson, Anthony Arthur, MA, MSc, FICDDip. Member, Fife Regional Council, 1978-86; Lecturer in Economics, St. Andrews University, since 1973; Member, General Council, Institute of Civil Defence, since 1981; founding partner, Economic Services (economic consultants), 1986; b. 18.6.46, London; m., Alicia; 3 d. Educ. Westminster City School; Gonville and Caius College, Cambridge; Reading University. Agricultural Economist, Malawi Government, 1968-71; St. Andrews University: Stanley Smith Senior Fellow, 1971-73, Assistant Dean of Students, Faculty of Arts, 1983-86; FAO/FFHC Food and Nutrition Consultant, Malawi Government, 1973-76; Warning Officer, 1975-81, and Sector Scientific Adviser, UKWMO, since 1981; Editor, Journal of Institute of Civil Defence, since 1982; Group Leader, Conservative Group, Fife Regional Council, 1982-86; Director, Byre Theatre; Diploma, Institute of Civil Defence and Gerald Drewitt Medal, 1980. Recreations: theatre; cricket; philately. Address: (h.) Creinch, Peat Inn, by Cupar, Fife, KY15 5LH; T.-033-484 275.

Jackson, David Edward Pritchett, MA, PhD (Cantab). Senior Lecturer in Arabic Studies, St. Andrews University, since 1984 (Chairman, Department of Arabic Studies, 1979-86); b. 9.12.41, Calcutta, India; m., Margaret Letitia Brown. Educ. Tynemouth School; Rossall School; Pembroke College, Cambridge. Research Fellow, Pembroke College, Cambridge, 1967-70; St. Andrews University: Assistant Lecturer, Arabic Language and Literature, 1967-68, Lecturer in Arabic Studies, 1968-84. Publication: Saladin (Co-author). Recreations: the river; music; food; golf. Address: (h.) 5 River Terrace, Guardbridge, by St. Andrews, Fife, KY16 OXA; T.-Leuchars 561.

Jackson, Eileen. Author; b. 18.4.26, Bristol; m., John Tunnard Jackson; 3 d. Short story/article writer, 1935-74; novels, since 1974; first novel, published USA, 1976, UK, 1978; 12 novels in over 45 editions and 10 languages; pseudonyms: Helen May, Linda Comer, Elizabeth Warne; also publishes as Eileen Jackson; Membership Secretary, Society of Authors in Scotland, since 1987; President, Strathclyde Writers, since 1985; Lecturer. Recreations: reading; book collecting; swimming; golf; travel. Address: (h.) 3 Ashgrove Lane, Maybole, Ayrshire, KA19 8BQ; T.-0655 82675.

Jackson, Jack, BSc (Hons), PhD, MIBiol, CIBiol. HM Inspector of Schools, since 1983; b. 31.5.44, Ayr; m., Sheilah Margaret Fulton; 1 s.; 3 d. Educ. Ayr Academy; Glasgow University; Jordanhill College of Education. Demonstrator, Zoology Department, Glasgow University, 1966-69; Lecturer in Zoology, West of Scotland Agricultural College, 1969-72; Assistant Teacher of Biology, Cathkin High School, 1972-73; Principal Teacher of Biology, Ayr Academy, 1973-83. Senior Examiner and Setter, Scottish Examination Board, 1978-83; Director, Board, Scottish Youth Theatre, 1979-82; Member, Scottish Council, Institute of Biology, 1980-83. Recreations: family life; gardening; hill-walking; conservation. Address: (b.) HM Inspector of Schools' Office, 231 Corstorphine Road, Edinburgh; T.-031-316 4639.

Jackson, Jim, BA (Hons). Assistant Director, Scottish Council for Voluntary Organisations, since 1984; b. 10.2.47, Bradford; m., Jennie Deacon; 1 s.; 1 d. Educ. Stand Grammar School, Whitefield; West Ham College of Technology; Open University. Adventure playground leader, Stevenage, 1970-72; Community Development Officer, Stevenage, 1972-75; Senior Community Development Officer, Stockport, 1975-77; Principal Assistant, Community Services & Development, Wirral Borough Council, 1977-81; Consultant, Voluntary Services Unit, Home Office, 1981-84. Recreations: folk music; jazz; hill-walking; reading. Address: (h.) 1 Ventnor Place, Edinburgh, EH9 2BP; T.-031-667 3121.

Jackson, Joseph Michael, BA, PhD. Senior Lecturer in Economics, Dundee University, since 1967; b. 23.2.25, Newport, Gwent; m., Miriam Cecily Andrews; 3 s.; 2 d. Educ. Newport High School; University College of Wales, Aberystwyth; Manchester University. Temporary Clerk, Ministry of War Transport, 1941-43; RAF, 1943-46; Research Assistant, University College of Wales, Aberystwyth, 1949-52; Assistant Lecturer in Economics, Bedford College, London University, 1952-55; Lecturer in Economics, Queen's College, Dundee, 1958-67. Member: Board of Management, Dundee Northern Hospital Group, 1970-74, Scottish Catholic Education Commission, 1972-87, Secretariat for the Laity, since 1986. Publications: The Control of Monopoly in the United Kingdom (Co-author), 1960; Family Income, 1963; Human Values and the Economic System, 1966; Wages and Labour Economics, 1970; Little's Economics for Students (revised), 1971; Dundee Volume, Third Statistical Account of Scotland, 1977. Recreations: swimming; music; photography. Address: (b.) Department of Economics, The University, Dundee, DD1 4HN; T.-Dundee 23181, Ext. 4378.

Jackson, Richard Dodds, MA, DipEd. Assistant Secretary (Primary Health Care), Scottish Home and Health Department, since 1986; b. 13.9.37, Galashiels; m., Brenda Routledge Jackson; 1 s.; 1 d. Educ. St. Mary's School, Melrose; Royal High School, Edinburgh; St. Andrews University; Moray House College of Education. Teacher of English, Broughton Secondary School, Edinburgh, and Daniel Stewart's College, Edinburgh, 1961-70; HM Inspector of Schools and FE Colleges, 1970-75; Scottish Education Department: Temporary Principal, Arts Branch, 1975-78, Assistant Secretary, Social Work Services Group, 1978-82; Deputy Director (Personnel and Supplies), Scottish Prison Service, 1982-86. Recreation: theatre and opera work. Address: (b.) St. Andrew's House, Regent Road, Edinburgh; T.-031-244 2455.

Jackson, Robert Penman, MIBM. Director of Public Works, City of Dundee District Council, since 1984; b. 2.4.47, Dunfermline; m., Helen Paxton; 1 s.; 1 d. Educ. Beath Senior High School, Cowdenbeath; Napier College of Science and Technology, Edinburgh. RSAS Diploma. Burgh Surveyor and Sanitary Inspector, Lochgelly Town Council, 1971-75; Assistant Director of Technical Services, Dunfermline District Council, 1975-84. Honorary Secretary, Lochgelly Old Folks' Reunion Committee. Recreations: golf; squash. Address: (b.) 353 Clepington Road, Dundee; T.-Dundee 23141, Ext. 4729.

Jacobs, Raymond Alexander. Golf Correspondent, Glasgow Herald, since 1963; b. 13.1.31, Accrington. Educ. Loretto School. Recreation: batching up. Address: (b.) 195 Albion Street, Glasgow, G1 1QP; T.-041-552 6255.

Jahoda, Professor Gustav, MSc, PhD, FBPS. Emeritus Professor of Psychology, Strathclyde University; b. 11.10.20, Vienna; m., Jean Catherine Buchanan; 3 s.; 1 d. Educ. London University. Oxford Extra-Mural Delegacy; Manchester University; University of Ghana; Glasgow University. Past President (now Fellow), International Association for Cross-Cultural Psychology. Recreations: fishing; gardening. Address: (b.) Department of Psychology, Strathclyde University, 155 George Street, Glasgow, G1 1RD; T.-041-552 4400.

James, C. Peter, PPIWPC (Dip), FIWEM. Director, Solway River Purification Board, 1954-87; b. 30.4.27, Manchester; m., Grace Irene; 1 s.; 1 d. Educ. Sale Grammar School; Manchester College of Technology. Trainee Inspector, Lancashire Rivers Board, 1943-51; District Inspector, Yorkshire Ouse River Board, 1951-54. President, Institute of Water Pollution Control, 1980-81 (Honorary Treasurer, 1981-87); WHO Consultant on Water Pollution Control Management; holder Arthur Sidney Bedell Award, American Water Pollution Control Federation; President, Dumfries Rotary Club, 1984-85; awarded Queen's Silver Jubilee Medal, 1977. Recreations: haaf-net fishing; photography; gardening; wine making. Address: (h.) Gullsway, Glencaple, Dumfries, DG1 4RF; T.-Glencaple 285.

James, David Sheard, MB, ChB, DipEd, DCH, DPM, FRCPsych. Consultant Child Psychiatrist, Royal Hospital for Sick Children, Glasgow, since 1971; Visiting Psychiatrist, Thorntoun Residential School, near Kilmarnock, since 1971; b. 19.2.39, Harrogate; m., Hilary; 1 s.; 2 d. Educ. Warwick School; Sheffield University. Paediatrics, Sheffield Children's Hospital; Registrar in Psychiatry, Mapperley Hospital, Nottingham; Research Registrar, United Sheffield Hospitals; Senior Registrar, Child Psychiatry, Birmingham Children's Hospital and Charles Burns Clinic. Publication: Families Without Hope (Co-author), 1975. Recreations: motor vehicles; model railway. Address: (h.) Waterside, Lochlibo Road, Uplawmoor, Glasgow, G78 4AA; T.-Uplawmoor 269.

James, Keith, BSc, PhD, DSc, FIBiol, FRCPath, FRSE. Reader in Immunology, Edinburgh University, since 1977; b. 15.3.38, Cumbria; m., Valerie Spencer Jubb; 3 s. Educ. Whitehaven Grammar School; Birmingham University. Research Fellow, Birmingham University, 1962-64; Research Assistant, University of California, 1964-65; Senior Lecturer, Edinburgh University, 1965-77; Consultant in Immunology and Biotechnology for Scottish National Blood Transfusion Service, since 1987. Past Chairman, Treasurer and Education Secretary, British Society for Immunology. Publications: Introducing Immunology (Co-author); numerous scientific papers. Recreations: hill-walking; photography. Address: (h.) 23 Crosswood Crescent, Balerno, Edinburgh, EH14 7LX; T.-031-449 5583.

James, Professor (William) Philip (Trehearne), MA, MD, DSc, FRCP, FRCPEdin, FRSE. Director, Rowett Research Institute, Aberdeen, since 1982; Research Professor, Aberdeen University, since 1983; b. 27.6.38, Liverpool; m., Jean Hamilton Moorhouse; 1 s.; 1 d. Educ. Bala School, North Wales; Ackworth School, Yorkshire; University College, London. Senior House Physician, Whittington Hospital, London, 1963-65; Clinical Research Scientist, Medical Research Council Tropical Metabolism Research Unit, Kingston, Jamaica, 1965-68; Harvard Research Fellow, Massachusetts General Hospital, 1968-69; Wellcome Trust Research Fellow, MRC Gastroenterology Unit, London, 1969-70; Senior Lecturer, Department of Human Nutrition, London School of Hygiene and Tropical Medicine, and Honorary Consultant, UCH, 1970-74; Assistant Director, MRC Dunn Nutrition Unit, and Honorary Consultant Physician, Addenbrooke's Hospital, Cambridge, 1974-82. Sir David Cuthbertson Lecturer; Van den Berghs & Jurgens Reporting Award; Amos Memorial Lecturer; Sir Thomas Middleton Memorial Lecturer; Sir Stanley Davidson Memorial Lecturer; Member, Panel on Diet and Heart Disease, Department of Health; Member, Committees on Toxicity and on Irradiated and Novel Foods; Food Advisory Committee, Ministry of Agriculture; Chairman, Nutrition Sub-Committee, Coronary Prevention Group; Chairman, WHO Committee on Nutrition Policy, 1989; Chairman, FAO Commission on National Energy Needs, 1987-88; author, WHO report on Nutrition and European Health. Address: (b.) Rowett Research Institute, Greenburn Road, Bucksburn, Aberdeen, AB2 9SB; T.-0224 712751.

Jameson, John Valentine McCulloch, JP, BSc, FRICS. Convener, Dumfries and Galloway Regional Council, since 1983; Partner, G.M. Thomson & Co., Chartered Surveyors, since 1970; b. 5.10.33, Twynholm, Stewartry of Kirkcudbright; m., Mary Irene Butters; 1 s.; 2 d. Educ. Rugby School; College of Estate Management (External). Commissioned 4/7 Royal Dragoon Guards, 1952-54; Shell Petroleum Co., London, 1954-57; Richard Costain (Canada) Ltd., Toronto, 1958-64. Member and Bailie, Gatehouse-of-Fleet Town Council, 1970-75; Chairman, Finance Committee, Dumfries and Galloway Regional Council, 1975-83; Chairman, Dumfries and Galloway Tourist Association, 1978-82; Chairman, Scottish Branch, Royal Institution of Chartered Surveyors, 1981-82; Council Member, National Trust for Scotland, 1980-84; Treasurer, Anwoth and Girthon Kirk Session. Recreations: gardening; shooting; squash; hill-walking. Address: (h.) Hillfoot, Gatehouse-of-Fleet; T.-05574 389.

Jamie, David Mitchell, FRICS, MRTPI. Director of Planning, Lothian Regional Council, since 1986; b. 11.8.41, Edinburgh; m., Eileen; 1 s.; 1 d. Educ. North Berwick High School; Heriot-Watt University; Edinburgh College of Art. Chartered Surveyor in private practice, Edinburgh and Glasgow, 1959-67; Town Planner in local government, since 1967. Chairman, Planning and Development Division, RICS in Scotland, 1986-88. Recreations: sailing; skiing; theatre. Address: (b.) 12 St. Giles Street, Edinburgh, EH1 1PT; T.-031-229 9292.

Jamieson, David. Honorary Sheriff, South Strathclyde, Dumfries and Galloway, since 1976; Past Chairman, Rent Tribunals, Lanarkshire; a Chairman, National Insurance and Supplementary Benefit Tribunals, Lanarkshire; b. 10.8.17, Glasgow; m., Pauline Bainbridge; 1 d. Educ. Albert Road Academy, Glasgow; Glasgow University. Six years in HM Forces during Second World War; practising Solicitor in Hamilton; Honorary

Secretary, Uddingston Ratepayers and Electors Committee, since 1946. Publications: Uddingston, The Village (parts one to five), 1974-84; Uddingston in Picture Postcards, 1984. Recreation: horticulture. Address: (b.) 22 Clydesdale Street, Hamilton; T.-Hamilton 281767.

Jamieson, Morley. Writer; b. 29.5.17, Newlandrig, Midlothian; m., Flora Macdonald; 1 s.; 1 d. Educ. (left school at early age due to serious illness); Newbattle Abbey College, Dalkeith; Coleg Harlech, Gwynedd. Quarryman, 1932-39; Bookseller, 1942-81; won Scottish Arts Council Award, 1980. Publications: The Old Wife (short stories), 1972; Nine Poems, 1976; Ten Poems, 1978; Notes on the Short Story, 1980. Recreation: conversation. Address: (h.) Viewbank Cottage, Lasswade, Midlothian, EH18 1AL; T.-031-663 8734.

Japp, William Wilson, FCCA, JP. Chief Executive, Nithsdale District Council, since 1984; b. 5.9.29, Dundee; m., Helen; 2 s.; 2 d. Educ. Harris Academy, Dundee. Dundee Corporation: Clerical Assistant, 1947-56, Accountancy Assistant, 1956-61; Assistant Town Chamberlain, Arbroath Town Council, 1961-64; Depute Town Chamberlain, Dumfries Town Council, 1964-75; Director of Finance, Nithsdale District Council, 1975-84. Address: (b.) Municipal Chambers, Buccleuch Street, Dumfries; T.-0387 53166.

Jardine, Sir (Andrew) Rupert (John) Buchanan-, 4th Bt, MC, DL. Landowner; b. 2.2.23; m., Jane Fiona Edmonstone (m. diss.); 1 s.; 1 d. Educ. Harrow; Royal Agricultural College. Retired Major, Royal Horse Guards; Joint Master, Dumfriesshire Foxhounds, 1950; Deputy Lieutenant, Dumfriesshire, 1978. Address: (h.) Dixons, Lockerbie, Dumfriesshire.

Jardine, Sheriff James Christopher Macnaughton, BL. Sheriff, of Glasgow and Strathkelvin at Glasgow, since 1979 (previousy of North Strathclyde at Dumbarton, and of Stirling, Dunbarton and Clackmannan at Dumbarton); b. 18.1.30, Glasgow; m., Vena Kight; 1 d. Educ. Glasgow Academy; Gresham House; Glasgow University. Lt., RASC, 1950-52; admitted as Solicitor in Scotland, 1953; in practice as principal (Nelson & Mackay), from 1955; Partner, McClure Naismith Brodie & Co., Glasgow, 1956-69; Secretary, Glasgow University Graduates Association, 1956-66; Member, Business Committee, Glasgow University General Council, 1964-67; a Vice-President, Sheriffs Association, 1976-79; Member, Joint Probation Consultative Committee for Strathclyde Region, since 1981. Recreations: enjoyment of theatre, opera and music; swimming. Address: (b.) Sheriffs' Chambers, Sheriff Court of Glasgow and Strathkelvin, 1 Carlton Place, Glasgow, G5; T.-041-429 8888.

Jardine, Leslie Thomas, LLB. Director of Economic Development, Dumfries and Galloway Regional Council, since 1986; b. 4.6.49, Dumfries; m., Angela; 1 s. Educ. Dumfries Academy; Glasgow University. Law apprentice, then Legal Assistant, Dumfries County Council, 1972-75; Policy Planning Assistant, then Regional Public Relations Officer, Dumfries and Galloway Regional Council, 1975-86. Solicitor. Recreation: riding (Chairman, Dumfries and Galloway Branch, British Horse Society). Address: (b.) 118 English Street, Dumfries; T.-0387 53141.

Jardine, Robert, MA. Rector, Queen Margaret Academy, Ayr, since 1977; b. 15.6.30, Renton, Dunbartonshire; m., Norah Tiernan; 1 s.; 1 d. Educ. St. Patrick's High School, Dumbarton; Glasgow University. Teacher: St. Augustine's Secondary School, Glasgow, 1956-61, St. Aloysius College, Glasgow, 1961-67; Principal Teacher of Modern Languages, then Assistant Head Teacher, Holyrood Secondary School, Glasgow, 1967-77. Recreations: music; tennis; golf. Address: (h.) 18 Auchendoon Crescent, Ayr, KA7 4AS; T.-0292 265223.

Jardine, Stewart, BSc (Hons). Head Teacher, Carrick Academy, Maybole, since 1982; b. 8.1.42, Crosshill, Ayrshire; m., Kathleen E.A. Passant; 2 s. Educ. Carrick Academy, Maybole; Glasgow University; Jordanhill College of Education. Girvan Academy: Teacher of Science, 1964-68, Principal Teacher of Physics, 1968-74, Assistant Head Teacher, 1974-76, Depute Head Teacher, 1976-82; Member, CNAA Committee on Teacher Education. Past Chairman, Girvan and District Round Table; Captain, Turnberry Golf Club. Recreations: golf; reading; computing. Address: (h.) 8 Connor Court, Girvan; T.-0465 3508.

Jardine, William Graham, BSc, MSc, PhD, ScD, FGS. Reader, Department of Geology, Glasgow University, since 1978; b. 13.3.27, Glasgow; m., Elizabeth Ann Garven; 3 s.; 1 d. Educ. Allan Glen's High School, Glasgow, 1939-44; Glasgow University; McGill University, Canada; Emmanuel College, Cambridge. National Service, 1950-52 (2nd Lt., Royal Signals, GHQ Signals Regiment, Suez Canal Zone); Soil Survey, Scotland: Scientific Officer, 1955-58, Senior Scientific Officer, 1958-59; Glasgow University: Lecturer, Department of Geology, 1959-66, Senior Lecturer, 1966-78. Council Member, Geological Society of Glasgow, 1961-64; Quaternary Research Association (of Britain): Secretary, 1970-74, Vice-President, 1974-76; Secretary-General, Tenth Congress, International Union for Quaternary Research (INQUA), Birmingham, 1977; President, INQUA Sub-Commission on Shorelines of NW Europe, 1977-82; INQUA Sub-Committee, British National Committee for Geology, 1966-82; President, Glasgow Archaeological Society, 1981-84; Editorial Advisory Board, Quaternary Science Reviews, 1984-87; E.J. Garwood Fund, Geological Society of London, 1963; Member, Congregational Board, 1961-81, and Kirk Session, since 1978, Westerton (Bearsden) Church of Scotland. Recreation: Westerton Male Voice Choir. Address: (b.) Department of Geology, Glasgow University, Glasgow, G12 8QQ; T.-041-339 8855, Ext. 5443.

Jarvie, Norman Dobson, MB, ChB, FRCGP, DObstRCOG. General Practitioner, Crieff; Chairman, Scottish Council, Royal College of General Practitioners, since 1987; Provost, East Scotland Faculty, RCGP, since 1987; Chairman, National Medical Consultative Committee (GP Sub-Committee), since 1988; b. 31.3.36, Glasgow; m., Dr. Anne Jarvie; 2 s.; 1 d. Educ. Rutherglen Academy; Glasgow University. Medical Officer to Crieff Cottage Hospital, Ardvreck School and Morrison's Academy, since 1964; Chairman, Local Medical Committee, Perth and Kinross Division, 1978-80; President, Perth and

Kinross Division, BMA, 1980; Chairman, Scottish Association of General Practitioner Hospitals, 1981-85; General Practitioner Tutor, Dundee University. Recreations: sailing; golf. Address: (b.) Health Centre, Crieff, PH7 3SA; T.-0764 2456.

Jarvis, Geoffrey, FRIBA, FRIAS. Architect in private practice; Consultant, William Nimmo & Partners, Architects, since 1987; b. 9.1.28, London; m., Rosalind Bailey; 2 s.; 2 d. Educ. Kelvinside Academy; Glasgow Academy; Glasgow School of Architecture. Worked for two years in Philadelphia and New York (Marcel Breuer); returned to Glasgow, setting up in private practice; Consultant to National Trust for Scotland, 1972-87; principal works include Culzean Country Park Centre; Clan Donald Centre, Skye; Chatelherault, Hamilton; Edinburgh Castle Visitor Reception Feasibility Study; Past Chairman, Glasgow Tree Lovers' Society; former Honorary Secretary and Chairman, New Glasgow Society; Co-Founder and Vice-Chairman, Clyde Fair International, 1972-73; three Europa Nostra Diplomas of Merit; one Civic Trust Award of Exceptional Merit. Recreations: travel and sight-seeing; local and Scottish history; Glasgow; family. Address: (b.) 7 Fitzroy Place, Glasgow, G3 7RH; T.-041-226 4981.

Jarvis, Professor Paul Gordon, PhD, Fil dr, FRSE. Professor of Forestry and Natural Resources, Edinburgh University, since 1975; b. 23.5.35, Tunbridge Wells; m., Margaret Susan Gostelow; 1 s.; 2 d. Educ. Sir Anthony Brown's School, Brentwood; Oriel College, Oxford. PhD study, Sheffield University, 1957-60; Postdoctoral Fellow, NATO, Institute of Plant Physiology, Uppsala University, 1960-62; Fil dr, Uppsala University, 1963; Senior Lecturer in Plant Physiology, Royal College of Agriculture, Uppsala; Aberdeen University: Lecturer in Botany, 1966-72, Senior Lecturer, 1972-75. Council Member, Society for Experimental Biology, 1977-80; Commissioner, Countryside Commission for Scotland, 1976-78; Member, Governing Body, Scottish Crops Research Institute, 1977-86; Co-Founder and Sectional Editor, Plant, Cell and Environment; Co-Founder and Editor, Current Advances in Ecological Sciences; serves on various other editorial or review boards. Address: (h.) Belmont, 47 Eskbank Road, Dalkeith, Midlothian, EH22 3BH; T.-031-663 8676.

Jarvis, Roland John, CBIM. Managing Director and Group Chief Executive, Low and Bonar PLC, since 1984; b. 23.6.32, London; m., Pamela; 2 s.; 2 d. Educ. Royal Liberty School. Ford Motor (Planning and Analysis), 1965; Group Comptroller, AEI/GEC, 1967; Financial Controller, Chrysler, 1970; Financial Director, Crane Fruehauf, 1972; TI Raleigh Industries: Financial Director, 1976-80, Managing Director, 1980-84. Recreations: tennis; golf; music. Address: (b.) Bonar House, Faraday Street, Dundee, DD1 9JA.

Jarvis, William. Solicitor; Honorary Sheriff, since 1962; Clerk to Lieutenancy; b. 19.4.11, Dunfermline; m., Helen Dalrymple; 2 s. Educ. Dunfermline High School; Edinburgh University. Partner, Wilson & Jarvis, Solicitors, Alloa, 1937-86; Member, National Health Executive Council, 1963-73; Member, Forth Valley Health Board, 1973-78; Honorary Secretary, Clackmannanshire Boy Scouts Association, 15 years; Honorary Treasurer, Alloa YMCA, 25 years; Elder, West Church, Alloa, since 1947; Founder Member and Past Chairman, Abbeyfield (Alloa and District) Society; President, Alloa Rotary Club, 1961. Recreation: bowling. Address: (h.) Greycraigs, 142 Claremont, Alloa; T.-Alloa 212466.

Jasinski, Alfons B., DA, RSW. Artist; Teacher of Art; b. 14.9.45, Falkirk; m., Ann E.M. Conlan; 1 s.; 2 d. Educ. St. Modan's High School, Stirling; Edinburgh College of Art. Travelling Scholarship to Italy, 1969; began teaching, Balwearie High School, Kirkcaldy, 1969 (now Assistant Principal Teacher of Art); Latimer Award, RSA, 1975; one-man exhibitions: Loomshop, 1971-72-74-76-80-82, Kirkcaldy Art Gallery, 1974, The Scottish Gallery, 1976, Cornerstone, Dunblane, 1976, Gallery 22, Cupar, 1984; works in various public and private collections. Address: (h.) 15 Normand Road, Dysart, Fife, KY1 2XN; T.-0592 52505.

Jauncey, Hon. Lord (Charles Eliot Jauncey), QC (Scot), BA, LLB. Senator of the College of Justice in Scotland, since 1979; b. 8.5.25; m., 1, Jean Cunninghame Graham (m. diss.); 2 s.; 1 d.; 2, Elizabeth Ballingal (m. diss.); 3, Camilla Cathcart; 1 d. Educ. Radley; Christ Church, Oxford; Glasgow University. Served Second World War (Sub-Lt., RNVR); Advocate, 1949; QC (Scot), 1963; Sheriff Principal of Fife and Kinross, 1971-74; Honorary Sheriff Substitute of Perthshire, 1962; Member, Queen's Bodyguard for Scotland (Royal Company of Archers), 1951; Member, Historic Buildings Council for Scotland, since 1971.

Jeeves, Professor Malcolm Alexander, MA, PhD (Cantab), FBPsS, FRSE. Professor of Psychology, St. Andrews University, since 1969, and Director, Medical Research Council Cognitive Neuroscience Research Group; Vice-Principal, St. Andrews University, 1981-85; b. 16.11.26, Stamford, England; m., Ruth Elisabeth Hartridge; 2 d. Educ. Stamford School; St. John's College, Cambridge University. Lt., 1st Bn., Sherwood Foresters, BAOR, 1945-48; Exhibitioner, St. John's College, Cambridge, 1948-52; research and teaching, Cambridge and Harvard Universities, 1952-56; Lecturer, Leeds University, 1956-59; Professor and Head, Department of Psychology, Adelaide University, 1959-69 (Dean, Faculty of Arts, 1963-64); Member: Council, SERC, since 1985, Neuroscience and Mental Health Board, MRC, since 1985, Council, Royal Society of Edinburgh, since 1985; Chairman, Executive Committee, International Neuropsychological Symposium; Editor, Neuropsychologia; Cairns Memorial Lecturer, Australia, 1986; New College Lecturer, University of NSW, 1987. Publications: Analysis of Structural Learning (Co-author); Psychology Survey No. 3 (Editor); Experimental Psychology: An introduction for biologists; The Effects of Structural Relations upon Transfer (Co-author); Thinking in Structures (Co-author); Behavioural Science and Christianity (Editor); Free to be Different (Co-author); Psychology and Christianity: The View Both Ways; The Scientific Enterprise and Christian Faith; Psychology: Through the eyes of faith (Co-author). Recreations: walking; music; fishing.

Address: (b.) Department of Psychology, St. Andrews University, St. Andrews, KY16 9JU; T.-0334 76161.

Jeffares, Professor Alexander Norman, MA, PhD, DPhil, Dde'lU, FAHA, FRSE, FRSL, FRSA. Professor of English Studies, Stirling University, 1974-86; Honorary Professor, since 1987; Managing Director, Academic Advisory Services Ltd.; Director, Colin Smythe Ltd.; b. 11.8.20, Dublin; m., Jeanne Agnes Calembert; 1 d. Educ. The High School, Dublin; Trinity College, Dublin; Oriel College, Oxford. Lecturer in Classics, Trinity College, Dublin, 1943-45; Lector in English, Groningen University, 1946-48; Lecturer in English Literature, Edinburgh University, 1949-51; Professor of English Language and Literature, Adelaide, 1951-56; Professor of English Literature, Leeds, 1957-74. Secretary, Australian Humanities Research Council, 1954-57; Honorary Fellow, Australian Academy of Humanities; Founding Chairman, Association for Commonwealth Literary and Language Studies, 1966-68 (Honorary Life Fellow); Founding Chairman, International Association for Study of Anglo-Irish Literature, 1968-70 (Honorary Life President, since 1973); Member, Scottish Arts Council (Chairman, Literature Committee, 1977-83, Vice Chairman, 1980-84); Member, Arts Council of GB, 1980-84; Chairman, National Book League Scotland, 1985-87, Book Trust Scotland, since 1987; Board Member, Book Trust, since 1987; President, International PEN, Scottish Centre, since 1986; Vice-President, Royal Society of Edinburgh, since 1988; Vice-Chairman, Muckhart Community Council, since 1979. Publications: Yeats: Man and Poet; Seven Centuries of Poetry; The Scientific Background (Co-author); A Commentary on the Poems of Yeats; A Commentary on the Plays of Yeats (Co-author); History of Anglo-Irish Literature; Restoration Drama; New Commentary on Poems of Yeats; Brought up in Dublin (poems); Brought up to Leave (poems); An Irish Childhood (Co-Editor); A Jewish Childhood (Co-Editor). Recreations: drawing; painting; restoring old houses. Address: (h.) Craighead Cottage, Fife Ness, Crail, Fife; T.-0333 50898.

Jefferson, Gordon Cort, BSc, MSc, PhD, MPS. Secretary, Scottish Department, Royal Pharmaceutical Society of Gt. Britain, since 1988 (Head, Department of Pharmacy, Heriot-Watt University, 1983-88); Member, National Pharmaceutical Consultative Committee; b. 12.9.35, Edenfield, Lancs; m., Jean Margaret Perkin; 2 s. Educ. Bacup and Rawtenstall Grammar School; Lancaster Royal Grammar School; Manchester University. Benger Research Fellow, then Teaching Assistant, Department of Pharmacology, Manchester University, 1960-62; Lecturer in Pharmacology, then Senior Lecturer, Department of Pharmacy, Heriot-Watt College/University, 1962-83. Recreations: golf; railway history; amateur interest in architecture. Address: (h.) 5 Cherry Tree Crescent, Balerno, Edinburgh, EH14 5AY; T.-031-449 3549.

Jeffery, Professor Jonathan, MA, BSc, DPhil, CChem, FRSC, CBiol, FIBiol, FRSA, FRSE. Professor of Biochemistry, Aberdeen University, since 1983; b. 29.7.35, Liverpool; m., Christa Torriano-Williams; 2 d. Educ. Liverpool Institute High School; Jesus College, Oxford University. Research Biochemist, ICI, 1962-66; Aberdeen University: Lecturer in Chemical Pathology, 1966-72, Lecturer in Biochemistry, 1972-74, Senior Lecturer in Biochemistry, 1974-83. Recreations: country walks; some interest in theatre, visual arts and music. Address: (b.) Department of Biochemistry, Aberdeen University, Marischal College, Aberdeen, AB9 1AS; T.-0224 272000.

Jeffrey, Rev. Eric William Sinclair, MA, JP. Minister, Bristo Memorial Church, Craigmillar, Edinburgh, since 1978; b. 12.2.29, Coatbridge; m., Carol Elizabeth Dover Wilson; 4 s.; 2 d. Educ. High School of Glasgow; Glasgow University and Trinity College. Missionary in Malawi, 1954-69; Minister, Dalmeny and Abercorn, 1969-78. Recreations: playing double bass; cricket umpire; golf. Address: 3 Spence Street, Edinburgh, EH16 5AG; T.-031-668 2722.

Jeffrey, Ian William McDonald, PhD, FDS, LDS, RCSEdin. Senior Lecturer in Conservative Dentistry, Dundee University, since 1978; b. 11.1.31, Edinburgh; m., Jean McKenzie; 2 s.; 1 d. Educ. George Heriot's, Edinburgh; John Bright Grammar School, Llandudno; Edinburgh University. National Service, Egypt, 1953-55; Colonial Service, Uganda, 1955-58; Registrar, Eastern Regional Hospital Board, 1959-60; Lecturing Staff, Dundee University, since 1960; Examiner, Royal College of Surgeons, Edinburgh; Visiting Lecturer, Nairobi University. Recreations: mountaineering; travel; house and car maintenance; photography. Address: (h.) Norwood, McKenzie Street, Carnoustie, Angus; T.-Carnoustie 52405.

Jeffrey, John J., BSc (Hons), BA (Ed), DipEd, CEng, MRINA. Depute Principal, Inverness College of Further and Higher Education, since 1970; Liaison Officer (Inverness), Open University, since 1972; b. 29.7.35, Greenock; m., Norma May McGregor; 1 s.; 2 d. Educ. Greenock High School; Strathclyde University; Open University; Aberdeen University; Paisley College of Technology. Began career as apprentice/design draughtsman, Scott Lithgow (Shipbuilders), 1950-61; Nuclear Power Station Engineer, English Electric, Leicester, 1961-63; Lecturer in Naval Architecture/Engineering, then Senior Lecturer, Kirkcaldy College of Technology, 1963-67; Second Depute Principal, Aberdeen Technical College, 1967-70. Recreations: golf; tennis; computing. Address: (b.) Inverness College of Further and Higher Education, 3 Longman Road, Longman South, Inverness; T.-0463 236681.

Jeffrey, Rev. Stewart Duncan, BSc, BD. Minister, St. George's-Tillydrone Parish Church, Aberdeen, since 1978; b. 14.8.32, Kirkintilloch; m., Margaret Scott Bane; 3 d. Educ. Lenzie Academy; Glasgow University. National Service, Royal Artillery; management trainee; Minister: Berriedale and Dunbeath Ross Church, Caithness, St. Kentigern's Parish Church, Kilmarnock. Recreation: badminton. Address: (h.) 1 Gordon's Mills Road, Aberdeen, AB2 2YU; T.-Aberdeen 491000.

Jeffreys-Jones, Rhodri, BA (Wales), PhD (Cantab). Senior Lecturer in History, Edinburgh University, since 1983; b. 28.7.42, Carmarthen; m.,

Janetta Carolina Minkiewicz; 2 d. Educ. Ysgol Ardudwy; University of Wales; Cambridge University; Michigan University; Harvard University. Tutor: Harvard, 1965-66, Fitzwilliam College, Cambridge, 1966-67; Assistant Lecturer, then Lecturer, Edinburgh University, 1967-83; Fellow, Charles Warren Center for the Study of American History, Harvard, 1971-72. Publications: Violence and Reform in American History; American Espionage: From Secret Service to CIA; Eagle Against Empire: American Opposition to European Imperialism 1914-82 (Editor); The Growth of Federal Power in American History (Joint Editor); The CIA and American Democracy. Recreations: squash; snooker; vegetable gardening. Address: (b.) Department of History, Edinburgh University, William Robertson Building, George Square, Edinburgh, EH8 9JY; T.-031-667 1011.

Jenkins, David, BMus, PhD. Academic Registrar, Moray House College of Education, since 1984; b. 30.5.44, Dundee; m., Dr. Janet Jenkins; 2 s.; 1 d. Educ. Perth Academy; Edinburgh University. Assistant Teacher, Tynecastle Secondary School, Edinburgh, 1968-70; Lecturer, then Vice-Principal, Callendar Park College of Education, Falkirk, 1970-82; Lecturer and Clerk to Board of Studies, Moray House College of Education, 1982-84. Recreations: music; gardening. Address: (h.) 18 Blacket Place, Edinburgh, EH9 1RL; T.-031-667 2885.

Jenkins, Robin, MA. Novelist; b. 11.9.12; m.; 1 s.; 2 d. Educ. Hamilton Academy; Glasgow University. Author of: Happy for the Child, The Thistle and the Grail, The Cone-Gatherers, Guests of War, The Missionaries, The Changeling, Some Kind of Grace, Dust on the Paw, The Tiger of Gold, A Love of Innocence, The Sardana Dancers, A Very Scotch Affair, The Holy Tree, The Expatriates, A Toast to the Lord, A Far Cry from Bowmore, A Figure of Fun, A Would-be Saint, Fergus Lamont.

Jenner, Rev. Albert. Minister, Kingussie, since 1973; Clerk, Abernethy Presbytery, since 1981; b. 7.4.24, Glasgow; m., Isabel MacKenzie MacDonald. Educ. Hillhead High School; Alva Academy; Edinburgh University. War Service, Royal Armoured Corps, 1942-47; Student Assistant, Prestonfield Church, Edinburgh, 1949-50; Minister: Kinnettles, 1951-56, Kelvinside Old, Glasgow, 1956-66, St. Andrew's-Trinity, Johnstone, 1966-73; Moderator: Abernethy Presbytery, 1975-76, Synod of Southern Highlands, 1977-78; Chairman, Kingussie High School Council, since 1975; Chaplain and Past President, Kingussie Branch, Royal British Legion Scotland; Programme Convener, Badenoch and Strathspey Music Festival. Recreations: music; reading; golf. Address: The Manse, West Terrace, Kingussie, Inverness-shire, PH21 1HA; T.-Kingussie 311.

Jennett, Professor Bryan, MD, FRCS. Professor of Neurosurgery, Glasgow University, since 1968 (Dean, Faculty of Medicine, 1981-86); Director, MRC Head Injury Programme, since 1979; b. 1.3.26, Twickenham, Middlesex; m., Professor Sheila Jennett (qv); 3 s.; 1 d. Educ. King's College, Wimbledon; King George V School, Southport; Liverpool University. Lecturer in Neurosurgery, Manchester University; Rockefeller Travelling Fellow, University of California; Hunterian Professor, Royal College of Surgeons of England. Member, Medical Research Council; Member, Chief Scientist Committee, Scotland; Rock Carling Fellow. Publications: Epilepsy After Non-Missile Head Injuries; Introduction to Neurosurgery; High Technology Medicine - Benefits and Burdens. Recreations: writing; cruising under sail. Address: (h.) 83 Hughenden Lane, Glasgow, G12 9XN.

Jennett, Professor Sheila, MD, PhD, FRCPGlas. Titular Professor in Physiology, Glasgow University, since 1985; b. 28.1.26, Liverpool; m., Professor Bryan Jennett (qv); 3 s.; 1 d. Educ. Aigburth Vale High School, Liverpool; Liverpool University. Junior hospital appointments in surgery, spinal injuries, geriatrics and respiratory medicine, 1949-62; Lecturer, then Senior Lecturer, then Reader in Physiology, Glasgow University, 1963-85. Committee Member, Physiological Society, 1981-85. Recreations: sailing; music; walking. Address: (h.) 83 Hughenden Lane, Glasgow, G12 9XN.

Jennings, James, JP. Convener, Strathclyde Regional Council, since 1986; b. 18.2.25; m., 1, Margaret Cook Barclay (deceased); 3 s.; 2 d.; 2, Margaret Mary Hughes, JP; 2 d. Educ. St. Palladius School, Dalry; St. Michael's College, Irvine. Steel industry, 1946-79. Member: Ayr County Council, 1958, Strathclyde Regional Council, 1974 (Vice-Convener, 1982-86); Chairman: Ayr CC Police and Law Committee, 1964-70, Ayrshire Joint Police Committee, 1970-75, North Ayrshire Crime Prevention Panel, 1970-82, Police and Fire Committee, Strathclyde Regional Council, 1978-82; contested Perth and East Perthshire, 1966; Vice-President, St. Andrew's Ambulance Association; Patron, Association of Youth Clubs in Strathclyde; Honorary President: Scottish Retirement Council, Princess Louise Scottish Hospital (Erskine Hospital); Honorary Vice-President: SNO Chorus, Royal British Legion Scotland (Dalry and District Branch); JP, Cunninghame, 1969 (Chairman, Cunninghame Justices Committee, since 1974); Chairman, Official Side, Police Negotiating Board, since 1986. Recreation: local community involvement. Address: (h.) 4 Place View, Kilbirnie, KA25 6BG; T.-Kilbirnie 3339.

Jennings, Kevin, MB, FRCP. Consultant Cardiologist, Aberdeen Royal Infirmary, since 1983; b. 9.3.47, Charleville, Eire; m., Heather; 2 s. Educ. Downside; St. Bartholomew's Hospital, London. Registrar: King's College Hospital, London, London Chest Hospital; Senior Registrar, Freeman Hospital, Newcastle-upon-Tyne. Recreations: theatre; ballet; golf; windsurfing. Address: 58 Rubislaw Den South, Aberdeen, AB2 6AX; T.-Aberdeen 311466.

Jillings, Lewis George, MA (Hons), PhD. Senior Lecturer in German, Stirling University, since 1982 (Member, University Court, 1978-85); b. 7.1.42, Auckland; m., Margaret Nicholas; 2 d. Educ. Auckland Grammar School; Auckland University; Basel University; London University. Lecturer in German, Stirling University, 1968-82; Giessen University, West Germany, 1987-88. Vice-Chairman, Stirling Burgh Liberals, 1983-87; Assistant Secretary, British Branch, International

Arthurian Society, 1980-85. Publications: Martin Luther Selections, 1977; Diu Crone of Heinrich von dem Turlein, 1980; Notes on Steppenwolf by Hermann Hesse, 1981. Recreations: reading; politicking. Address: (h.) 2 Royal Gardens, Stirling; T.-Stirling 62225.

Jimack, Professor Peter David, BA, PhD. Professor of French, Stirling University, since 1972; b. 29.9.30, London; m., Christine Mary; 1 s.; 3 d. by pr. m. Educ. Tottenham Grammar School; Southampton University. Assistant Master: Churcher's College, Petersfield, 1954-57, Cotham Grammar School, Bristol, 1957-58; Birmingham University: Assistant Lecturer, 1959-61, Lecturer, 1961-66, Senior Lecturer, 1966-72. Recreations: gardening; swimming; watching films. Address: (h.) 6 Banavie Road, Glasgow, G11 5AN; T.-041-334 5926.

Johnson, David (Charles), MA, BA, PhD. Composer; Musical Historian; Cellist, McGibbon Ensemble, since 1979; 27.10.42, Edinburgh; 1 s. Educ. Aberdeen University; St. John's College, Cambridge. Part-time teaching jobs, since 1970: Rudolf Steiner School of Edinburgh, Napier College, Edinburgh, Open University; Member, Scottish Music Information Centre Advisory Committee, since 1983; Postdoctoral Fellowship, Music Faculty, Edinburgh University, 1979-80; awarded Scottish Arts Council Writer's Bursary, 1979; Musical Correspondent, Glasgow Herald and Musical Times; compositions include four operas, an orchestral suite, chamber music, songs, etc. Publications: Music and Society in Lowland Scotland, 1972; Scottish Fiddle Music in the 18th Century, 1984; contributions to the New Grove Dictionary of Music, 1981. Address: (h.) 1 Hill Square, Edinburgh, EH8 9DR; T.-031-667 7054.

Johnson, Sir Ronald (Ernest Charles), Kt (1970), CB (1963), MA (Cantab). Chairman, Fire Service Research and Training Trust, since 1976; retired Civil Servant; b. 3.5.13, Portsmouth; m., Elizabeth Gladys Nuttall; 2 s.; 1 s. deceased. Educ. Portsmouth Grammar School; St. John's College, Cambridge. RNVR, Intelligence Eastern Fleet, 1944-45; entered Scottish Office, 1935; Secretary, Scottish Home and Health Department, 1963-72; Secretary of Commissions for Scotland, 1972-78. Chairman, Civil Service Savings Committee for Scotland, 1963-78; Member, Scottish Records Advisory Council, 1975-81; Member, Committee on Administration of Sheriffdoms, 1981-82; President, Edinburgh Bach Society, 1973-86; President, Edinburgh Society of Organists, 1980-82; JP, Edinburgh, since 1971. Recreation: church organ. Address: (h.) 14 Eglinton Crescent, Edinburgh, EH12 5DD; T.-031-337 7733.

Johnson, Roy Arthur, CA. Partner, Coopers & Lybrand, Glasgow, since 1966, and Cork Gully, Glasgow, since 1981; Council Member, Institute of Chartered Accountants of Scotland, since 1984; b. 3.3.37, Wanstead, Essex; m., Heather Campbell; 2 s. Educ. Lancing College. Deacon, Incorporation of Cordiners, Glasgow, 1976-77; Director, Glasgow Chamber of Commerce, since 1988; Collector, Trades House of Glasgow, since 1988. Recreations: golf; gardening; photography. Address: (b.) Kintyre House, 209 West George Street, Glasgow; T.-041-248 2644.

Johnson-Marshall, Professor Emeritus Percy Edwin Alan, CMG, DipArch, MA, RIBA, FRTPI, RIBA, DistTP. Director, Patrick Geddes Centre for Planning Studies; Professor of Urban Design and Regional Planning, Edinburgh University, 1964-85; Partner, Percy Johnson-Marshall and Partners, since 1960; b. 20.1.15, Ajmer, India; m., April Bridger; 3 s.; 4 d. Educ. Queen Elizabeth School, Kirkby Lonsdale; School of Architecture, Liverpool University. Various posts, local government, 1936-38; Senior Planning Architect, Coventry City Council, 1938-41; War Service, Royal Engineers, India and Burma, 1941-46; Advisor to Government of Burma for National Outline Plan, 1945-46; Regional Planning Officer, Ministry of Town and Country Planning, 1946-48; Planner in charge, London's Comprehensive Development Areas, LCC, 1949-59; Senior Lecturer, then Reader, Edinburgh University, 1959-64. Member: RIBA Council, 1951-75, RTPI Council, 1950-75, RIAS Council, 1964-74; former Vice-President, International Society for City and Regional Planners; Consultant on Human Settlements, UN Stockholm Conference on Environment; Member, Commonwealth Human Ecology Council, since 1973; Vice President, 1st International Congress on Planning of Major Cities, Mexico City, 1981. Recreations: reading; writing; travel. Address: (h.) Bella Vista, 64 The Causeway, Duddingston, Edinburgh, EH15 3PZ; T.-031-661 2019.

Johnston, Alan Charles Macpherson, BA (Hons) (Cantab), LLB. Queen's Counsel (1980); b. 13.1.42, Stirling; m., Anthea Jean Blackburn; 3 s. Educ. Edinburgh Academy; Loretto School; Jesus College, Cambridge; Edinburgh University. Advocate, 1967; Standing Junior Counsel, Scottish Home and Health Department, 1972; Treasurer, Faculty of Advocates, since 1977; Advocate Depute, 1978-82; Chairman: Industrial Tribunal, since 1982, Medical Appeal Tribunal, 1985. Publication: Introduction to Law of Scotland 7th Edition (Joint Editor). Address: (h.) 3 Circus Gardens, Edinburgh; T.-031-225 1862.

Johnston, Alastair J.C., BSc, CEng, FIProdE, FBIM. Managing Director, Gates Rubber Co. Ltd.; Chairman, Holden and Fisher Ltd.; Director, Duncan Honeyman Ltd.; Member, CBI Scottish Council; Deputy Chairman, Enterprise Trust, Dumfries; b. 16.9.28, Dundee; m., Morag Campbell; 2 s. Educ. Harris Academy, Dundee; St. Andrews University. Apprenticeship, Caledon Shipyard, Dundee; Industrial Engineering Manager, North British Rubber Co., Edinburgh; Plant Manager, Armstrong Cork Co., Gateshead; Director and General Manager, William Briggs Ltd., Dundee; Managing Director: Permanite Ltd., Waltham Abbey, Trident Equipment Ltd., Ware. Address: (h.) 8 Ravelston Park, Edinburgh, EH4 3DX; T.-031-332 8409.

Johnston, Sheriff Alexander Graham, LLB, BA. Sheriff of Glasgow and Strathkelvin, at Glasgow, since 1985 (Grampian, Highland and Islands, 1982-85); b. 16.7.44; m.; 2 step d.; 2 s. by pr. m. Educ. Edinburgh Academy; Strathallan School; Edinburgh University; University College, Oxford. Solicitor and WS, 1971; Partner, private practice, 1972-82.

Johnston, Brian Bernard, BMSc, MB, ChB, DPM, MRCPsych. Consultant Psychiatrist, Royal Dundee Liff Hospital, since 1984, with special interest in drug and alcohol dependence; Honorary Senior Lecturer, Department of Psychiatry, Dundee University, since 1984; b. 16.5.38, Dundee; m., Mary Delaney; 2 s.; 1 d. Educ. Lawside Academy, Dundee; Queen's College, St. Andrews; Dundee University. Telecommunications engineer, Post Office Engineering Department, 1954-65; National Service, RAF, Singapore, Malaya, 1956-58; medical student, 1965-72; House Officer, Orthopaedic Surgery/General Medicine, Dundee Royal Infirmary, 1972-73; Senior House Officer, Registrar, Senior Registrar in Psychiatry, Royal Dundee Liff Hospital, 1973-79; Consultant Psychiatrist, Stratheden Hospital, Cupar, 1979-84. Recreations: jogging; golf; skating; swimming; hill-walking. Address: (h.) Ad Astra, 127 Kinghorne Road, Lawside, Dundee, DD3 6PW; T.-Dundee 28146.

Johnston, David Scott, BA. Director and General Secretary, National Farmers' Union of Scotland, since 1978; b. 18.12.32, Dundee; m., Sheila Kirkby; 3 s. Educ. Harris Academy, Dundee; Rutherford Grammar School, Newcastle; Hatfield College, Durham University. Economics Researcher, Tube Investments, Birmingham, until 1957; joined NFU of Scotland as Assistant Secretary, 1957 (Deputy General Secretary, 1972-78); UK Representative, General Experts Committee, COPA, three years; Member of Praesidium, COPA. Recreation: mountaineering. Address: (b.) 17 Grosvenor Crescent, Edinburgh, EH12 5EN; T.-031-337 4333.

Johnston, Frederick Patrick Mair, MA. Chairman, Johnston Press PLC (formerly F. Johnston & Co. Ltd.), since 1973; Chairman, The Dunn & Wilson Group Ltd., since 1976; b. 15.9.35, Edinburgh; m., Elizabeth Ann Jones; 2 s. Educ. Morrison's Academy, Crieff; Lancing College, Sussex; New College, Oxford. Editorial Department, Liverpool Daily Post and Echo, 1959; Assistant Secretary, The Times Publishing Co. Ltd., 1960; Company Secretary, F. Johnston & Co. Ltd., 1969. Chairman, Central Scotland Manpower Committee, 1976-83; Member, Press Council, since 1974; President, Scottish Newspaper Proprietors' Association, 1976-78; Treasurer, Society of Master Printers of Scotland, 1981-86; Senior Vice-President, The Newspaper Society, since 1988. Recreations: reading; travelling. Address: (b.) 53 Manor Place, Edinburgh, EH3 7EG; T.-031-225 3361.

Johnston, Gary Hugh. Member, Highland Regional Council, since 1982; Past President, Inverness and Highland Chamber of Commerce; Member, Board of Governors, Eden Court Theatre, since 1982; Building Consultant, since 1978; b. 5.5.57, Inverness; m., Terry S. Educ. Millburn Academy, Inverness; Inverness College. Address: (b.) G.H. Johnston, Building Consultants, 51 Castle Street, Inverness; T.-0463 237229.

Johnston, Grenville Shaw, OBE, TD, KCSG, DL, CA. Chartered Accountant, since 1968; Territorial Army Officer (Lt. Col.), since 1964; b. 28.1.45, Nairn; m., Marylyn Jean Picken; 2 d. Educ. Blairmore School; Fettes College. Qualified in Edinburgh with Scott Moncrieff Thomson & Sheills; Thomson McLintock & Co., Glasgow, 1968-70; joined family firm, W.D. Johnston & Carmichael, Elgin, 1970; Senior Partner, 1975. Commanding Officer, 2nd 51st Highland Volunteers, 1983-86; Deputy Lieutenant of Moray, since 1980; Knight Commander, Order of St. Gregory, 1982, for work for Pluscarden Abbey; OBE for services to Territorial Army; Chairman, Grampian Committee, Royal Jubilee Trusts; Governor, Gordonstoun School; Chairman, Moray Venture Capital Fund Ltd.; Director, Moray Enterprise Trust; Secretary, Moray Local Health Council; Member, Education Committee and Members Services Committee, Institute of Chartered Accountants of Scotland. Recreations: shooting; fishing; hockey; running; golf. Address: (h.) Pendennis, Forteath Avenue, Elgin, IV30 1PB; T.-Elgin 2578; (b.) 7/9 Commerce Street, Elgin; T.-0343 7492.

Johnston, Professor Ian Alistair, BSc, PhD, FRSE. Professor of Comparative Physiology (Personal Chair), Director, Gatty Marine Laboratory, St. Andrews University, since 1985 (Chairman, Department of Biology and Preclinical Medicine); b. 13.4.49, Barking, Essex; m., Dr. Rhona S. Johnston. Educ. Addey and Stanhope Grammar School, London; Hull University. NERC Postdoctoral Research Fellow, Bristol University, 1973-75; Lecturer in Physiology, St. Andrews University, 1976-84; Reader, 1984-85; Visiting Senior Lecturer, Department of Veterinary Physiology, Nairobi University, 1981; Visiting Scientist, British Antarctic Survey base, Signy Island, South Orkneys, 1983-84; awarded Scientific Medal, Zoological Society of London. Recreations: photography; walking; reading. Address: (b.) Department of Biology and Preclinical Medicine, St. Andrews University, St. Andrews, KY16 8LB; T.-0334 76161, Ext. 7104.

Johnston, Jacqueline, BA (Hons), DEduc. Senior Education Officer and Secretary, Educational Broadcasting Council, Scotland, since 1983; b. 3.8.48, Falkirk. Educ. Kilsyth Academy; Strathclyde University. Teacher (Geography), Larbert High School; Assistant Principal Teacher of Geography, then Principal Teacher, Bathgate Academy; Education Officer, BBC, West of Scotland. Recreations: hill-walking; interior design; gardening. Address: (h.) 26 Castle Terrace, Edinburgh; (b.) 5 Queen Street, Edinburgh; T.-031-225 3131.

Johnston, James George, BSc (Hons). Headteacher, Leverhulme Memorial School, Leverburgh, Harris, since 1984; b. 1.5.54, Glasgow; m., Marilyn. Educ. Cumbernauld High School; Glasgow University. Recreations: cooking; fishing; reading. Address: The Schoolhouse, Leverburgh, Harris, Western Isles; T.-0859 82208.

Johnston, James Kenneth Buchanan, TD, BL. Senior Partner, Brown Mair Mackintosh & Co., Solicitors, Glasgow, since 1982 (Partner, since 1950); Chairman, Royal Yachting Association Scotland, since 1986; b. 4.9.15, Stirling; 1 d. Educ. Stirling High School; Glasgow University. Organist and Choirmaster, 1930-39; Service in Territorial Army, 1936-39; War Service in Middle East and Far East, 1939-44 (rank of Lt.-Col.); graduated a Solicitor, 1945. Commodore, Royal Scottish Motor Yacht Club, 1968-71, Hon. Commodore, since 1987; Legal Adviser, Royal Yachting Association Scotland; awarded RYA Award, 1983, for services to yachting. Address: (h.) 47 Poplar Avenue, Newton Mearns, Glasgow; T.-041-639 7238.

Johnston, John Robert, BSc, PhD, FIBiol. Reader, Department of Bioscience and Biotechnology, Strathclyde University, since 1983; b. 6.10.34, Leven, Fife; m., Janet Bonthrone Reekie; 3 s. Educ. Buckhaven High School; St. Andrews University. Teaching Associate, University of California, Berkeley; Research Scientist, Brewing Research Foundation, Nutfield, Surrey; Royal Society Latin America Exchange Fellow, 1970-71, Mexico City; Lecturer, then Senior Lecturer, Strathclyde University, 1964-83. Vice-President, Royal Philosophical Society of Glasgow. Recreations: outdoor activities; theatre and music; community affairs. Address: (b.) Department of Bioscience and Biotechnology, Strathclyde University, Glasgow, G1 1XW; T.-041-552 4400.

Johnston, Robert, BL. Solicitor, since 1951; Notary Public, since 1951; Honorary Sheriff, Dumfries, since 1971; b. 26.3.26, Burnmouth, Berwickshire; m., Mary Ross Wilson. Educ. Kirk High School, Cleveland, Ohio; Eyemouth High School; St. Andrews University; Edinburgh University. Solicitor, Balfour & Manson, SSC, Edinburgh, 1951-55; Partner, Austins, Solicitors, Dalbeattie, since 1955; Town Clerk, Dalbeattie, 1961-71; JP Procurator Fiscal, Kirkcudbrightshire, 1956-71; former Council Member, Law Society of Scotland; Member, Scottish Solicitors Discipline Tribunal, since 1982. Recreations: sailing; angling. Address: (h.) Aldouran, Southwick Road, Dalbeattie, Kirkcudbrightshire; T.-0556 610449.

Johnston, Robert Neilson, MD, FRCP, FRCPEdin. Consultant Physician in Respiratory Medicine; Honorary Senior Lecturer, Dundee University, since 1955; b. 13.12.21, Buluwayo, Southern Rhodesia; m., 1, Muriel Bryan; 2, Elizabeth Semple; 1 s.; 2 d. Educ. Aberdeen Grammar School; Aberdeen University. War Service, RAMC, Gold Coast, West Africa; Medical Registrar, Brompton Hospital, London; Fulbright Scholar and Visiting Fellow, Columbia University Bellevue Hospital, New York; Assistant Physician, Department of Respiratory Medicine, Hammersmith Hospital, London. Member, Research Committee, BTA; Past President, Scottish Thoracic Society; Council Member, Scottish Branch, Chest, Heart and Stroke Association. Recreation: gardening. Address: (h.) 50 Albany Road, West Ferry, Dundee, DD5 1NW; T.-Dundee 78538.

Johnston, Rev. Robert W.M., MA, BD, STM. Minister, Temple-Anniesland Parish Church, Glasgow, since 1984; b. 5.6.34, Cupar; m., Fiona M. McNab; 1 s.; 1 d. Educ. Ayr Academy; Glasgow University; Union Theological Seminary, New York. Teacher, Sharman's Cross High School, Solihull, 1960-64; Minister: Hamilton Memorial Parish Church, Clydebank, 1964-72, Anniesland Cross Parish Church, Glasgow, 1972-84. Moderator, Presbytery of Glasgow, 1986-87. Recreations: golf; music. Address: 76 Victoria Park Drive North, Glasgow, G14 9PJ; T.-041-959 5835.

Johnston, Sir Russell, KB (1985), MA (Hons). MP (Liberal), Inverness, Nairn and Lochaber (formerly Inverness), since 1964; Member, UK Delegation, Council of Europe, since 1984; b. 28.7.32, Edinburgh; m., Joan Graham Menzies; 3 s. Educ. Carbost Public School; Portree High School; Edinburgh University; Moray House College of Education. National Service: commissioned into Intelligence Corps and 2nd i/c British Intelligence Unit, Berlin, 1958-59; History Teacher, Liberton Secondary School, Edinburgh, 1961-63; Research Assistant, Scottish Liberal Party, 1963-64; Joint Parliamentary Adviser, Educational Institute of Scotland, 1964-70; Member, Royal Commission on Local Government in Scotland, 1966-69; Parliamentary Spokesman for Scottish National Federation for the Welfare of the Blind, since 1967; Parliamentary Representative, Royal National Institute for the Blind, since 1977; Member, Select Committee on Scottish Affairs, 1969; Parliamentary Adviser, Scottish Police Federation, 1971-75; Scottish Liberal Party: elected to Executive, 1961, and Organisation Committee, 1962, Vice Chairman, 1965, Chairman, 1970-74, Leader, 1974-88; Liberal Party Spokesman on Education, 1964-66, on Foreign Affairs, 1970-75 and 1979-85, on Scotland, 1970-73, 1975-83, 1985-88, on Devolution, 1975, on Defence, 1983-88; Member, European Parliament, 1973-75 and 1976-79; Vice President, European Liberal Group and Group Spokesman on Regional Policy, 1973-75; Vice President of the Parliament's Political Committee, 1976-79; Member, Western European Union Assembly and Representative to Council of Europe, 1984-85, and since 1987; Interim Leader, Scottish Social and Liberal Democrats, 1988. Recreations: reading; photography; shinty (Vice Chief, Camanachd Association, since 1987). Address: (h.) House of Commons, London, SW1A OAA; T.-01-219 5180.

Johnston, Thomas Lothian, MA, PhD, DL, FRSA, FRSE, CBIM. Principal and Vice-Chancellor, Heriot-Watt University, since 1981; b. 9.3.27, Whitburn; m., Joan Fahmy; 2 s.; 3 d. Educ. Hawick High School; Edinburgh University; Stockholm University. Lecturer in Political Economy, Edinburgh University, 1953-65; Professor of Economics, Heriot-Watt University, 1966-76; Chairman, Manpower Services Committee for Scotland, 1977-80; academic appointments in other countries: Illinois University, 1957, 1962-63, Queen's University, Canada, 1965, Western Australian Institute of Technology, 1979, Visiting Professor, International Institute for Labour Studies, Geneva, 1973; Arbitrator, Chairman of Wages Councils, since 1964. Publications: Collective Bargaining in Sweden, 1962; Economic Expansion and Structural Change, 1963; The Structure and Growth of the Scottish Economy (Co-author), 1971; Introduction to Industrial Relations, 1981. Recreations: gardening; walking. Address: (h.) 14 Mansionhouse Road, Edinburgh, EH9 1TZ; T.-031-667 1439.

Johnston, Very Rev. William Bryce, MA, BD, DD. Minister, Colinton Parish Church, since 1964; Chaplain to The Queen in Scotland, since 1981; b. 16.9.21, Edinburgh; m., Ruth Margaret Cowley; 1 s.; 2 d. Educ. George Watson's College, Edinburgh; Edinburgh University. Chaplain to the Forces, 1945-49; Minister: St. Andrew's Church, Bo'ness, 1949-55, St. George's Church, Greenock, 1955-64; Chaplain, HM Prison, Greenock, 1959-64; Convener, General Assembly Committees: Adult Christian Education, 1970-72, Church and Nation, 1972-76, Inter-Church Relations, 1979-81; Moderator of the General Assembly, 1980; Cunningham Lecturer, New College, 1968-71; Visiting Lecturer in Social Ethics, Heriot-Watt University, since 1966; Member, Broadcasting Council for Scotland, 1983-87. Publications: translations of Karl Barth and John Calvin. Recreations: organ-playing; bowls. Address: (h.) The Manse of Colinton, Edinburgh, EH13 0JR; T.-031-441 2315.

Johnston, William Greer, MBA, CA. Managing Director, Sutherland Transport and Trading Co. Ltd., since 1969; Member, Highland Health Board, since 1983; b. 10.12.40, Old Kilpatrick; m., Moira Alice Haldane Smith; 3 s.; 1 d. Educ. Clydebank High School; Glasgow University. Qualified Chartered Accountant, 1962; various posts in accounting firms, then in engineering and car retail distribution, 1962-69; Member, Highland Regional Council, 1974-78 (Chairman, Education Committee); District Councillor, 1974-80 (Chairman, Environmental Health and Leisure and Recreation). Chairman, Scripture Union Scotland, 1979-84; Treasurer, Scripture Union International, since 1985. Recreations: photography; stamp collecting; family. Address: (h.) Beannach, Lairg, Sutherland; T.-0549 2113.

Johnston, William John, BSc (Hons), DipEd(Tech). Rector, Aberdeen Grammar School, since 1987; b. 17.8.47, Kilmarnock; m., Katie Mary Maclean; 3 d. Educ. Spier's School, Beith; Glasgow University. Marketing Assistant, ICI Silicones, 1969-70; Teacher: Cranhill Secondary, 1971-73, Perth High School, 1973-75; Assistant Principal Teacher, Glenrothes High School, 1975-78; Principal Teacher, Millburn Academy, 1978-81; Assistant Rector, Kingussie High School, 1981-84; Depute Rector, Culloden Academy, 1984-87. Address: (b.) Aberdeen Grammar School, Skene Street, Aberdeen; T.-0224 642299.

Johnstone, Alexander Henry, BSc, PhD, DipREd, CChem, FRSC. Reader in Chemical Education, Glasgow University, since 1984 (Head, Science Education Research Group, since 1972); Chairman, Education Research Group, Royal Society of Chemistry, since 1987; b. 17.10.30, Edinburgh; m., Martha Y. Cuthbertson; 2 s. Educ. Leith Academy; Edinburgh University; Glasgow University; Moray House College of Education. Commissioned, Royal Corps of Signals; Assistant Teacher of Chemistry, George Watson's College, Edinburgh; Head, Chemistry Department, High School of Stirling; Lecturer, then Senior Lecturer in Chemistry, Glasgow University. Vice-President, Royal Society of Chemistry (President, Education Division); Consultant to Consultative Committee on the Curriculum. Recreations: hill-walking; photography; archaeology; lay preaching. Address: (b.) Department of Chemistry, The University, Glasgow, G12 8QQ; T.-041-339 8855, Ext. 5172.

Johnstone, David C.M., MA. Rector, Plockton High School, since 1976; b. 17.3.33, Dumfries; m., Jeanette Lamont; 1 s. Educ. Dumfries Academy; Edinburgh University. Teacher of Russian, High School of Stirling, 1960-70; Careers Adviser, Edinburgh University, 1971-72; Gracemount High School, Edinburgh: Assistant Headteacher, 1972-74, Deputy Headteacher, 1974-76. Recreation: music (Church organist). Address: (b.) Plockton High School, Plockton, Ross-shire, IV52 8TU; T.-059 984 372.

Johnstone, Frank D., MD, FRCOG. Consultant Obstetrician and Gynaecologist, Lothian Health Board, since 1978; Senior Lecturer in Obstetrics and Gynaecology, Edinburgh University, since 1978; b. Ayr; 3 s. Educ. Aberdeen Grammar School; Aberdeen University. Resident Surgical Officer, Hammersmith Hospital, London, Queen Charlotte's Hospital, London, and Chelsea Hospital for Women, London, 1970-73; Registrar and Lecturer, Aberdeen Maternity Hospital, 1973-77; Senior Lecturer, University of Nairobi, 1977-78; Visiting Professor, University of Kuwait, 1984-85. Recreations: mountain climbing; squash. Address: (b.) Department of Obstetrics and Gynaecology, 37 Chalmers Street, Edinburgh; T.-031-229 2575.

Johnstone, Ian Temple, MA (Cantab), LLB (Edin), WS, NP. Partner, Biggart Baillie & Gifford, WS, formerly Baillie & Gifford WS and Biggart Lumsden & Co.; b. 25.2.23, Edinburgh; m., Frances Ferenbach; 3 d. Educ. Edinburgh Academy; Corpus Christi College, Cambridge; Edinburgh University. Royal Artillery, 1942-46 (final rank of Staff Captain after transfer to Q Movements Burma Command); qualified, 1949; Director, Friends Provident Life Office, since 1964; Director, Inch Kenneth Kajang Rubber PLC, since 1970; Chairman, Baillie Gifford Shin Nippon PLC, since 1985; General Commissioner of Income Tax; Past President, Scottish Lawn Tennis Association; Council Member, Lawn Tennis Association, 1969-79; Chairman, St. Margaret's School, Edinburgh Limited. Recreations: following sport - football, tennis, cricket, rugby; listening to music; photography; gentle hill-walking. Address: 45 Moray Place, Edinburgh, EH3; T.-031-225 2021.

Johnstone, John Raymond, BA, CA. Chairman: Murray Johnstone Ltd., since 1984 (Managing Director, 1968-88); Honorary President, Scottish Opera; Director, Scottish Amicable Life Assurance Society (Chairman, 1983-85); b. 27.10.29, London; m., Susan Sara; 5 step s.; 2 step d. Educ. Eton; Trinity College, Cambridge. Investment Analyst, Robert Fleming & Co. Ltd., London, 1955-60; Partner (CA), Brown, Fleming & Murray (later Whinney Murray & Co.), 1960-68; Chairman: Dominion Insurance Co. Ltd., Dominion Insurance Holdings Ltd., Kemper-Murray Johnstone International Inc., Landel Insurance Holdings Ltd., Murray Electronics PLC, Murray Technology Investments PLC; various other Directorships; Member: Scottish Economic

Council; Scottish Committee, Nature Conservancy Council. Recreations: fishing; shooting; opera; farming. Address: (h.) Wards, Gartocharn, Dunbartonshire.

Johnstone, Professor William, MA (Hons), BD. Professor of Hebrew and Semitic Languages, Aberdeen University, since 1980; Minister, Church of Scotland, since 1963; b. 6.5.36, Glasgow; m., Elizabeth M. Ward; 1 s.; 1 d. Educ. Hamilton Academy; Glasgow University; Marburg University. Aberdeen University: Lecturer in Hebrew and Semitic Languages, Aberdeen University, 1962-72, Senior Lecturer, 1972-80, Dean, Faculty of Divinity, 1983-87. Recreation: alternative work. Address: (h.) 37 Rubislaw Den South, Aberdeen, AB2 6BD; T.-Aberdeen 316022.

Jolly, Douglas, BSc (Hons). Rector, Viewforth High School, since 1981; b. 30.6.38, Dundee; m., Elizabeth Smith; 2 d. Educ. Grove Academy, Broughty Ferry; St. Andrews University. Principal Teacher of Physics, Lawside Academy, 1964-72; Assistant Rector, Craigie High School, 1972-75; Depute Rector, Arbroath High School, 1975-81; Member, Central Committee for Science Teaching in Scotland, 1972-75. Committee Member, Balbirnie Park Golf Club; Elder, Markinch Parish Church. Recreations: golf; gardening; travel. Address: (h.) 16 Orchard Drive, Glenrothes, Fife; T.-Glenrothes 757039.

Jones, Professor Arthur Stanley, BSc, PhD, CBiol, FIBiol, FBIM. Strathcona-Fordyce Professor of Agriculture, Aberdeen University, Principal, North of Scotland College of Agriculture and Head, Department of Agriculture, Aberdeen University, since 1986 (Deputy Director, Rowett Research Institute, 1983-86, Head, Department of Applied Nutrition and Chairman, Division of Applied Sciences 1973-86); b. 17.5.32, Belfast; m., Mary Margaret Smith; 3 s.; 1 d. Educ. Gosforth Grammar School; Durham University; Aberdeen University. Farmed, 1960-84; Kirkley Hall Farm Institute and Durham University, 1951-55; Military Service, 1955-57; Agricultural Research Council Scholarship, 1957-58; joined Rowett Research Institute, 1959. Recreations: sailing; gardening; flying. Address: (b.) School of Agriculture, 581 King Street, Aberdeen, AB9 1UD; T.-0224 480291.

Jones, Colin Irving, FCA, ATII. Chartered Accountant; Lecturer in Accounting and Taxation, since 1973; Member, Ettrick and Lauderdale District Council, since 1983 (Vice-Convener, Environmental Health); b. 10.3.33, Gateshead; m., Mary June Henrietta Hine; 1 s. Educ. Gateshead Grammar School. National Service, RAF; worked in industry, 1960-73. Parliamentary candidate, 1983; Elder, Lilliesleaf Kirk; Secretary, Rotary District 102. Recreation: music. Address: (h.) Rigfoot, Midlem, Selkirk, TD7 4QF, T.-Lilliesleaf 306.

Jones, David Adams, MA, MSc, DipStat, FSS. Director, Information and Statistics Division, Scottish Health Service, since 1986; b. 23.4.33, Fochriw; m., Fiona Janet Hill; 2 s.; 1 d. Educ. The Lewis School, Pengam, Glamorgan; Jesus College, Oxford. Lt., Royal Navy; Industrial Statistician, British Nylon Spinners; Lecturer in Statistics, UWIST; Statistician and Chief Statistician, Welsh Office; Director of Statistics, Scottish Health Service. Recreations: squash; hill-walking. Address: (b.) Trinity Park House, Edinburgh; T.-031-552 6255.

Jones, Professor Douglas Samuel, MBE, MA, DSc, HonDSc, FIMA, FRSE, FRS. Ivory Professor of Mathematics, Dundee University, since 1964; President, Institute of Mathematics and its Applications; b. 10.1.22, Corby, Northamptonshire; m., Ivy Styles; 1 s.; 1 d. Educ. Wolverhampton Grammar School; Corpus Christi College, Oxford. Flt.-Lt., RAF; Commonwealth Fellow, Massachusetts Institute of Technology; Lecturer, Manchester University; Professor, Keele University; Visiting Professor, New York University; Member, University Grants Committee; Chairman, Mathematics Committee; Computer Board; Member, Open University Visiting Committee; won Van der Pol Gold Medal; Keith Prize, RSE; Naylor Prize, LMS. Recreation: not answering questionnaires. Address: (b.) Department of Mathematics and Computer Science, The University, Dundee, DD1 4HN; T.-Dundee 23181.

Jones, Rev. Edward Gwynfai, BA (Hons). Minister, St. Rollox Church of Scotland, Glasgow, since 1967; Convener, Unions and Readjustments Committee, Glasgow Presbytery, 1981-86; b. 20.5.37, Aberystwyth, Wales; m., Elspeth Mary Margretta; 2 d. Educ. Pontardawe Grammar School, Wales; Durham University; Westminster Theological College, Cambridge. Minister, Tow Law Presbyterian Church, Co. Durham, 1964-67. Address: 42 Melville Gardens, Bishopbriggs, Glasgow, G64 3DE; T.-041-772 2848.

Jones, Keith Greig, LLB. Director of Legal Services and Depute Chief Executive, Kincardine and Deeside District Council, since 1985; b. 10.9.48, Edinburgh; m., Margaret. Educ. Aberdeen Grammar School; Aberdeen University. Various appointments in private legal practice, 1969-75; joined Law and Administration Department, Kincardine and Deeside District Council, 1975. Address: (b.) Viewmount, Stonehaven, AB3 2DQ; T.-0569 62001.

Jones, Professor Peter (Howard), MA. Professor of Philosophy, Edinburgh University, since 1984; Director, Institute for Advanced Studies in the Humanities, since 1986; b. 18.12.35, London; m., Elizabeth Jean Roberton; 2 d. Educ. Highgate School; Queens' College, Cambridge. Regional Officer, The British Council, London, 1960-61; Research Scholar, Cambridge University, 1961-63; Assistant Lecturer in Philosophy, Nottingham University, 1963-64; Edinburgh University: Lecturer in Philosophy, 1964-77, Reader, 1977-84; Visiting Professor of Philosophy: Rochester University, New York, 1969-70, Dartmouth College, New Hampshire, 1973, 1983, Carleton College, Minnesota, 1974, Oklahoma University, 1978, Baylor University, 1978; Distinguished Foreign Scholar, Mid-America State Universities, 1978; Visiting Fellow, Humanities Research Centre, Australian National University, 1984; Trustee, National Museums of Scotland, since 1987; Member, Edinburgh University Court, since 1987; Governor, Morrison's Academy, Crieff, since

1984; Member, Scottish Council, ISCO; Founder Member, The Hume Society, 1974. Publications: Philosophy and the Novel, 1975; Hume's Sentiments, 1982; A Hotbed of Genius, 1986; Philosophy and Science in the Scottish Englightenment, 1988. Recreations: opera; chamber music; the arts, including architecture; travel; photography. Address: (b.) Institute for Advanced Studies in the Humanities, Hope Park Square, Edinburgh, 8; T.-031-662 4174.

Jones, Rev. Robert Alexander, CA, LTh. Minister, Marnoch, Aberchirder, since 1985; b. 14.7.31, Montreal; m., Margaret Johnston; 1 s.; 2 d. Educ. Robert Gordon's College, Aberdeen; Aberdeen University; Glasgow University. National service (commission, Royal Army Pay Corps), 1954-56; Chartered Accountant, Price Waterhouse, 1956-58; Assistant Chief Accountant, Sunbeam Electric Ltd., 1958-60; Financial Director, Callander's Garages Ltd., Glasgow, 1960-62; Minister, Allan Church, Bannockburn, 1966-85. Recreation: golf. Address: Manse of Marnoch, Aberchirder, Banffshire, AB5 5TS; T.-046-65 276.

Jones, Rodney, BSc (Hons). Head, Fish Team, Marine Laboratory, Aberdeen, since 1985; b. 21.12.27, Cheltenham; m., Sheila Clouston; 1 s.; 2 d. Educ. Cheltenham Grammar School; Liverpool University. Marine Laboratory, Aberdeen: Scientific Officer, 1948-54, Senior Scientific Officer, 1954-63, Principal Scientific Officer, 1963-78, Senior Principal Scientific Officer, since 1978. Address: (b.) Marine Laboratory, Aberdeen; T.-Aberdeen 876544.

Jones, William. Sheriff Clerk, Dumfries, and Joint Auditor, Sheriff Court, Dumfries, since 1983; b. 20.12.42, Dingwall; m., Norma Anne McElnay; 1 s.; 1 d. Educ. Hamilton Academy. Clerk, Sheriff Clerks' Branch, Scottish Court Service, 1961-65; Sheriff Clerk Depute: Perth, 1966-69, Edinburgh, 1969-74; Training Officer, Scottish Court Service Staff Training Centre, Glasgow, 1974-77; Sheriff Clerk Depute, Dunfermline, 1977-79; seconded Scottish Courts Administration, Edinburgh, 1979-83. Recreations: gardening; reading; music. Address: (h.) 8 Craigvale Court, Dumfries, DG1 4QH; T.-0387 65013.

Jones, Rev. William Gerald, MA, BD, ThM, FSA(Scot). Minister, Kirkmichael with Straiton St. Cuthbert's, since 1985; b. 2.11.56, Irvine. Educ. Dalry High School; Garnock Academy, Kilbirnie; Glasgow University; St. Andrews University; Princeton Theological Seminary, Princeton, New Jersey. Student, The Chapel of the University of Glasgow, 1976-78; student attachments: Hope Park Church, St. Andrews, 1978-79, Ryehill Church, Dundee, 1979-80, High Church, Paisley, 1980-82; seconded to First Presbyterian Church, Philadelphia, and Swarthmore Presbyterian Church, Pennsylvania, 1983; Assistant Minister, Glasgow Cathedral, 1983-85. Freeman Citizen of Glasgow, 1984; Member, Incorporation of Gardeners of Glasgow, 1984; Convener, Administration Committee, Presbytery of Ayr, since 1988; Member, General Assembly Panel on Worship and of Liturgical Committee responsible for revision of 1979 "Book of Common Order", since 1987; Member, Council, Church Service Society; Founder Member, Scottish Society for Reformation History; Member, Maybole Schools Council, since 1986. Recreations: music (especially organ, classical, opera); reading; writing; research. Address: The Manse, Kirkmichael, Maybole, Ayrshire, KA19 7PJ; T.-Kirkmichael 286.

Jordan, Gerard Michael, CEng, BEng, CEng, MIMechE. Director, Dounreay Nuclear Power Development Establishment, UKAEA, since 1987; b. 25.9.29; m., Vera Peers; 1 s.; 1 d. Educ. Grange School, Birkenhead; Liverpool University. Marine Engineering Officer, 1950-55; Group Engineer, Thomas Hedley Ltd., 1956-59; UKAEA: Principal Professional and Technical Officer, 1959-73, Band Grade Officer, 1973-80, Assistant Director (Safety and Reliability Directorate), 1980, Assistant Director (Engineering and Safety, Dounreay), 1980-84, Deputy Director (Engineering, Northern Division), 1984-85, Director of Engineering (Northern Division), 1985-87. Recreations: hobby electronics; DIY; fishing. Address: (b.) Dounreay Nuclear Power Development Establishment, Thurso, Caithness, KW14 7TZ.

Jordan, Col. Howard Alfred John, MBE, FCIT. Director, Scottish Engineering Employers' Association, since 1980; b. 26.3.36, Edinburgh; m., Patricia Ann Tomlin; 1 s.; 1 d. Army, 1954-80; Lt. Col., Royal Corps of Transport; service in UK (including Northern Ireland), Singapore, BAOR; commanded 154 (Lowland) Transport Regiment RCT(V). Chairman, Carmunnock Community Council, since 1980; Chairman, Strathclyde Group, National Council for Conservation of Plants and Gardens, since 1983; Honorary President, Carmunnock British Legion, since 1980; Member, Lowland TA Council, since 1981; Member, CBI Scotland Employment Committee, since 1981; County Comdt., Glasgow and Lanarkshire ACF, since 1988. Address: (b.) 105 West George Street, Glasgow, G2 1QL; T.-041-221 3181.

Joughin, Michael, CBE, JP, CBIM, FRAgS. Chairman, North of Scotland Hydro-Electric Board, since 1983; Member, South of Scotland Electricity Board; Farmer, since 1952; b. 26.4.26, Devonport; m., 1, Lesley Roy Petrie; 2, Anne S.H. Hutchison; 1 s.; 1 d. Educ. Kelly College, Tavistock, Devon. Royal Marines, 1944-52 (Lt.); seconded, Fleet Air Arm, 1946-49 (ditched off Malta, 1949, invalided, 1952). Chairman, North of Scotland Milk Marketing Board, 1974-83; Past Chairman, Grassland and Forage Committee, JCC; Chairman, Scottish Agricultural Development Council, 1971-80; Chairman, Governors, North of Scotland College of Agriculture, 1969-72; President, National Farmers Union of Scotland, 1964-66; Deputy Lieutenant, County of Moray, 1974-80; Governor: Rowett Research Institute, Aberdeen, 1968-74, Scottish Plant Breeding Station, 1969-74, Animal Diseases Research Association, Edinburgh, 1969-74; Chairman, Governors, Blairmore Preparatory School, near Huntly, 1966-72; Member: Scottish Constitutional Committee (Douglas-Home Committee), 1969-70, Intervention Board for Agricultural Produce, 1972-76, National Economic Development Council for Agriculture, 1967-70; Past Chairman, NEDC Working Party on Livestock; Member: Agricultural Marketing Development Executive Committee, 1965-68, British Farm Produce Council, 1965-66; former Member: Selection Committee, Nuffield Farming Scholarships, Awards Committee, Massey-Ferguson National Award for Services to UK Agriculture; Chairman: North of Scotland Grassland Society, 1970-71, Elgin Market Green Auction Co., 1969-70; Founder Presenter, Country Focus (farming programme), Grampian Television, 1961-64 and 1967-69; Captain, 11th Bn., Seaforth Highlanders (TA), 1952-53. Recreation: sailing. Address: (h.) Elderslie, Findhorn, Moray; T.-03093 0277.

Jung, Roland Tadeusz, BA, MA, MB, BChir, MD, MRCS, LRCP, MRCP, FRCPEdin. Consultant Physician (Specialist in Endocrinology and Diabetes), since 1982; Honorary Senior Lecturer, Dundee University, since 1982; b. 8.2.48, Glasgow; m., Felicity King; 1 d. Educ. St. Anselm's College, Wirral; Pembroke College, Cambridge; St. Thomas Hospital and Medical School, London. MRC Clinical Scientific Officer, Dunn Nutrition Unit, Cambridge, and Honorary Senior Registrar, Addenbrooke's Hospital, Cambridge, 1977-79; Senior Registrar in Endocrinology and Diabetes, Royal Postgraduate Medical School, Hammersmith Hospital, London, 1980-82. Publication: Endocrine Problems in Oncology (Co-Editor), 1984. Recreation: gardening. Address: (b.) Department of Medicine, Ninewells Hospital and Medical School, Dundee; T.-Dundee 60111.

K

Kamm, Antony, MA. Freelance Editor and Writer; b. 2.3.31, London; m., Eileen Dunlop (qv). Educ. Charterhouse; Worcester College, Oxford. Editorial Director, Brockhampton Press, 1960-72; Senior Education Officer, Commonwealth Secretariat, 1972-74; Managing Editor (Children's Books), Oxford University Press, 1977-79; Consultant to UNESCO and other international organisations, 1963-76; Chairman, Children's Book Group, The Publishers Association, 1963-67, and of Children's Book Circle, 1963-64; played cricket for Middlesex, 1952. Publications include: Choosing Books for Younger Children, 1976; Scotland, 1988; (with Eileen Dunlop): Edinburgh, 1982; The Story of Glasgow, 1983; Kings and Queens of Scotland, 1984; and other information books for children on Scottish themes; several anthologies. Recreations: work; watching sport on TV. Address: (h.) 46 Tarmangie Drive, Dollar, FK14 7BP; T.-02594 2007.

Kane, Jack, OBE, JP, DL, Dr hc (Edin). Honorary Vice-President, Age Concern Scotland, since 1986; Honorary President: Workers Educational Association (SE Scotland), Craigmillar Festival Society, Jack Kane Centre; b. 1.4.11, Addiewell, Midlothian; m., Anne Murphy; 1 s.; 2 d. Educ. Bathgate Academy. Librarian, 1937-55; War Service, Royal Artillery, 1940-46; District Secretary, Workers Educational Association (SE Scotland), 1955-76; Chairman, South of Scotland Electricity Consultative Council, 1977-80; Chairman, Board of Trustees, National Galleries of Scotland, 1975-80; Councillor, Edinburgh, 1938-75 (Bailie, 1947-51, Lord Provost, 1972-75). Recreations: reading; walking. Address: (h.) 88 Thirlestane Road, Edinburgh, EH9 1AS; T.-031-447 7757.

Karolyi, Otto Jozsef, BMus, AMusTCL. Senior Lecturer and Head, Department of Music, Stirling University, since 1978; b. 26.3.34, Paris; m., Benedikte Uttenthal; 1 s. Educ. Champagnat French-Hungarian School, Budapest; Werboczy and Berzsenyi Gymnasiums, Budapest; Bela Bartok Conservatoire, Budapest; Akademie fur Musick und danstellende kunst, Wien; Trinity College of Music, London; London University. Freelance writing; WEA Tutor, ILEA and Oxford districts; Tutor, Extra-Mural Department, London University; Director of Music, Hampden House School; Music Therapist, St. John's Hospital, Stone and Napsbury Hospital, St. Albans; Visiting Lecturer, London University, Imperial College of Science and Technology; Tutor and Head, Department of Musicianship, Watford School of Music; part-time Tutor and Counsellor, Open University; Senior Lecturer, City of Leeds College of Music. Publications: Introducing Music; Modern British Music. Recreations: languages; literature; the arts. Address: (b.) Stirling University, Stirling; T.-0786 73171.

Kay, Sir Andrew Watt, Kt (1973). Chairman, Scottish Hospital Endowments Research Trust, since 1983; Regius Professor of Surgery, Glasgow University, 1964-81; b. 14.8.16; m.; 2 s.; 2 d. Educ. Ayr Academy; Glasgow University. Part-time Chief Scientist, Scottish Home and Health Department, 1973-81.

Kay, Michael, BSc, PhD. Principal Scientific Officer, Rowett Research Institute, since 1974; Head, Animal Husbandry Division, North of Scotland College of Agriculture, since 1979; Beef Leader, Scottish Agricultural Colleges, since 1987; b. 10.3.38, York; m., Moira G. Kay; 1 s.; 1 d. Educ. St. Peter's School, York; Leeds University; Aberdeen University. Joined Rowett Research Institute, 1963. Recreations: sport; gardening; DIY. Address: (b.) School of Agriculture, 581 King Street, Aberdeen, AB9 1UD; T.-0224 480291.

Kay, William, MA. Freelance Broadcaster/Writer/Producer; b. 24.9.51, Galston, Ayrshire; m., Maria Joao de Almeida da Cruz Dinis; 2 d. Educ. Galston High School; Kilmarnock Academy; Edinburgh University. After graduation, money earned on oil rig; launched working tour of Thailand, South Korea, Hawaii, Canada, USA, Mexico; worked as researcher; Producer, Odyssey series, Radio Scotland; produced about 40 documentaries on diverse aspects of working-class oral history. Commandeur d'Honneur, Commanderie du Bontemps de Medoc et des Graves. Publications: Odyssey: Voices from Scotland's Recent Past (Editor); Odyssey: The Second Collection (Editor); Knee Deep in Claret: A Celebration of Wine and Scotland (Co-author); Made in Scotland (poetry); Jute (play for radio); Scots - The Mither Tongue; They Fairly Mak Ye Work (for Dundee Repertory Theatre); Lucky's Strike (play for radio). Recreations: the weans; languages; films; Dundee United. Address: (h.) 72 Tay Street, Newport on Tay, Fife, DD6 8AP.

Kean, Eric Maclean, JP, FRICS. Consultant, Kean, Kennedy and Partners, since 1975; Member, Edinburgh District Council, since 1974; b. 17.10.19, Edinburgh; m., June Patricia Makin. Educ. George Heriot's; Heriot-Watt. Senior Partner, Kean, Kennedy and Partners, 1945-75; Edinburgh Town Council: Member, 1965-75, Chairman, Planning Committee, 1968-71, Bailie/Senior Bailie, 1971-74; Edinburgh District Council: Chairman, Licensing Board, 1978-82, Deputy Chairman of Council, 1982-84. Recreation: golf. Address: (h.) 55 St. Alban's Road, Edinburgh; T.-031-667 2233.

Keane, Professor Simon Michael, MA, LLB, PhD, CA. Professor of Accountancy, Glasgow University, since 1983; b. 8.4.33, Glasgow; m., Mary; 1 d. Educ. St. Aloysius College; Glasgow University. Investigating Accountant, Admiralty, 1965-67; Lecturer, Glasgow College of Commerce, 1967-69; Glasgow University: Lecturer, 1969-81, Reader, 1981-83. Publications: Efficient Market Hypothesis, 1980; Stock Market Efficiency, 1983. Recreations: golf; painting. Address: (b.) 67 Southpark Avenue, Glasgow, G12; T.-041-339 8855.

Kearney, Sheriff Brian, MA, LLB. Sheriff of Glasgow and Strathkelvin, since 1977; b. 25.8.35; m.; 3 s.; 1 d. Educ. Greenock Academy; Glasgow University. Solicitor, 1960; Partner, Biggart, Lumsden & Co., 1965; Sheriff of North Strathclyde, at Dumbarton, 1974-77.

Kee, A. Alistair, MA, BD, STM, PhD. Reader, Department of Theology and Religious Studies, Edinburgh University, since 1988 (Head, Department of Religious Studies, Glasgow University, 1976-88); b. 17.4.37, Alexandria; m., Anne Paterson; 1 s.; 1 d. Educ. Clydebank High School; Glasgow University; Union Theological Seminary, New York. Lecturer: University College of Rhodesia, 1964-67, Hull University, 1967-76; Senior Lecturer, then Reader, Glasgow University, since 1976; Visiting Professor, Augusta College, Georgia, 1982-83; Director, SCM Press Ltd.; Governor, Merchiston Castle School, Edinburgh; delivered Jaspers Lectures, Ripon Hall, Oxford, 1975; Ferguson Lectures, Manchester University, 1986. Publications: The Way of Transcendence; A Reader in Political Theology; Constantine Versus Christ; Being and Truth; Domination or Liberation. Address: (b.) Department of Theology and Religious Studies, Edinburgh University, New College, Mound Place, Edinburgh, EH1 2LX; T.-031-225 8400.

Keegan, James Douglas, LLB, SSC, NP, ACI (Arb). Solicitor, since 1975; Senior Partner, Keegan Walker & Co, SSC, since 1987; Notary Public, since 1975; Council Member, Law Society of Scotland, 1982-85; b. 25.9.51, Uddingston; m., Anne Kirkland; 1 d. Educ. Our Lady's High School, Motherwell; Strathclyde University. Apprentice, John James Teague, 1973-75; joined Constable Farquarson & Co. as Assistant, 1975, Partner, 1976; Partner, Drummond & Co., 1978-87; Secretary, Faculty of Procurators of Linlithgowshire, 1981-84; Chairman, Lowlands Building Services (Scotland) Ltd., since 1985. Recreations: nothing abnormal. Address: (b.) Pentland House, Almondvale, Livingston; T.-Livingston 30042.

Keenan, J. Melvin. Aberdeen District Officer, Transport and General Workers Union, since 1977; Member: Sea Fish Industry Authority, since 1981, Offshore Petroleum Industry Training Board, since 1984, Oil Industry Advisory Committee to Health and Safety Commission, since 1984; b. 13.6.49, Falkirk; m., Nancy; 2 s. Educ. St. Modan's High School, Stirling; Stow College, Glasgow; Esk Valley Technical College. Inveresk Paper Co., 1964-70; BP Chemicals International Ltd. and BP Oil Ltd., 1970-76. Member, EEC Joint Committee on Social Problems in Sea Fishing, since 1978; Trustee, Scottish Trawler Fishermen's Pension Scheme, since 1981. Publications: Fishing: The Way Forward (Co-author), 1980; The Future Through the Keyhole, 1988. Recreations: country life; poetry. Address: (b.) 44 King Street, Aberdeen; T.-0224 645271.

Keenan, Peter. Boxer; b. 1929, Glasgow; m., Cissy; 1 s.; 2 d. Won Scottish Flyweight title, 1948, before turning professional; won two Lonsdale belts outright; British Champion, 1951-53, 1954-59; Empire Champion, 1955-59; European Champion, 1951-52, 1953; failed to beat Vic Toweel, 1952, for World title; promoted boxing in Glasgow for a number of years.

Keir, Professor Hamish Macdonald, BSc, PhD, DSc, CBiol, FIBiol, CChem, FRSC, FRSE. Professor of Biochemistry, Aberdeen University, since 1968 (Vice-Principal, 1982-84); Vice-Chairman of Governors, Macaulay Land Use Research Institute, since 1987; Vice-Chairman, Board of Governors, Rowett Research Institute, Aberdeen, since 1972; b. 5.9.31, Moffat; m., Eleanor Louise Campbell; 1 s.; 2 d. Educ. Ayr Academy; Glasgow University; Yale University. Honorary Secretary, The Biochemical Society, 1970-77, Chairman, since 1986; Member, Cell Board, Medical Research Council; Scottish Home and Health Department, BRC; Chairman, IMB, Natural Environment Research Council; Member, Ethical and Research Committees, Grampian Health Board; President of Council, Federation of European Biochemical Societies; Governor, Longridge Towers; Member, Board of Governors, North of Scotland College of Agriculture; serves on Committees, International Union of Biochemistry; Member: Science and Engineering Research Council (Biology); University Grants Committee (Biology); Royal Society - British National Committee on Biochemistry; Chairman, Universities of Scotland Joint Purchasing Consortium; Member, Committee, Grampian Region, Tenovus-Scotland. Recreations: piano; golf; travel. Address: (b.) Department of Biochemistry, Aberdeen University, Marischal College, Aberdeen, AB9 1AS; T.-0224 273121.

Keith of Kinkel, Baron (Henry Shanks Keith), PC (1976). Life Peer, since 1977; Lord of Appeal in Ordinary, since 1977; b. 7.2.22; m.; 4 s.; 1 d. Educ. Edinburgh Academy; Magdalen College, Oxford; Edinburgh University. Served Second World War (mentioned in Despatches); Advocate, 1950; Barrister, Gray's Inn, 1951; QC

(Scot), 1962; Sheriff Principal of Roxburgh, Berwick and Selkirk, 1970-71; Senator of the College of Justice in Scotland, 1971-77; Chairman, Scottish Valuation Advisory Council, 1972-76.

Kelbie, Sheriff David, LLB (Hons); Sheriff of Grampian, Highland and Islands, at Aberdeen and Stonehaven, since 1986 (North Strathclyde, at Dumbarton, 1979-86); b. 28.2.45, Inverurie; m., Helen Mary Smith; 1 s.; 1 d. Educ. Inverurie Academy; Aberdeen University. Passed Advocate, 1968; Associate Lecturer, Heriot-Watt University, 1971-76; Secretary, Scottish Congregational College, 1974-82. Recreations: sailing; hill-walking; reading; learning. Address: (h.) 38 Earlspark Drive, Bieldside, Aberdeen.

Kellas, Professor James Grant, MA, PhD, FRHistS. Professor in Politics, Glasgow University, since 1984; b. 16.5.36, Aberdeen; m., Norma Rennie Craig; 2 s.; 1 d. Educ. Aberdeen Grammar School; Aberdeen University; London University. Tutorial Fellow in History, Bedford College, London University, 1961-62; Assistant in History, Aberdeen University, 1962-64; Glasgow University: Lecturer in Politics, 1964-73; Senior Lecturer, 1973-77, Reader, 1977-84. Member, Study of Parliament Group. Publications: Modern Scotland, 1968, 1980; The Scottish Political System, 1973, 1975, 1984. Recreations: mountaineering; music. Address: (b.) Department of Politics, Glasgow University, Glasgow, G12 8RT; T.-041-339 8855.

Kellett, Roger John, MA, MB, BChir, FRCP, FRCPEdin. Consultant Physician, Eastern General Hospital, Edinburgh, and Roodlands General Hospital, Haddington, since 1975; part-time Senior Lecturer in Medicine, Edinburgh University, since 1975; b. 17.6.40, Bradford; m., Anne Margaret Watson Lewis; 2 d. Educ. Bradford Grammar School; Emmanuel College, Cambridge. House Surgeon and House Physician, The London Hospital, 1964-65; Medical Registrar, Chelmsford Group of Hospitals, 1966-69; Lecturer in Medicine, Western Infirmary, Glasgow, 1969-75; former Member, Lothian Health Board. Address: (h.) 5 Burgess Terrace, Edinburgh, EH9 2BD; T.-031-667 0300.

Kelly, Barbara Mary, DipEd. Chairman, Scottish Consumer Council, since 1985; Member, National Consumer Council, since 1985; Journalist and Broadcaster; Partner in dairy farming enterprise; b. 27.2.40, Dalbeattie; m., Kenneth A. Kelly (qv); 1 s.; 2 d. Educ. Dalbeattie High School; Kirkcudbright Academy; Moray House College. Former Vice-Chairman, SWRI; Duke of Edinburgh's Award: former Chairman, Scottish Advisory Committee and former Member, UK Advisory Panel; Vice-Chairman, Rural Forum, Scotland; Chairman, Dumfries and Galloway Area Manpower Board, Manpower Services Commission; Trustee, Scottish Children's Bursary Fund. Recreations: painting; music. Address: (h.) Barncleugh, Irongray, Dumfries, DG2 9SE; T.-0387 73210.

Kelly, Kenneth Archibald. Dairy Farmer; b. Glasgow; m., Barbara Mary Prentice (see Barbara Mary Kelly); 1 s.; 2 d. Educ. Glasgow Academy; Sedbergh; West of Scotland College of Agriculture. Elected to Stewartry County Council, 1969, Dumfries and Galloway Regional Council, 1974 (Vice-Chairman, Planning; Chairman, Public Protection); Past Chairman, North British Hereford Breeders Association; Past President, Dumfries Rugby Club; Elder, Irongray Kirk. Recreations: shooting; fishing; curling; music; sailing. Address: (h.) Barncleugh, Irongray, Dumfries, DG2 9SE; T.-0387 73210.

Kelly, Michael, CBE (1983), OStJ, JP, BSc(Econ), PhD, LLD, DL. Public Relations Consultant, since 1984; Chairman, Royal Scottish Society for the Prevention of Cruelty to Children, since 1987; President, Strathclyde Branch, Institute of Marketing, since 1986; b. 1.11.40, Glasgow; m., Zita Harkins; 1 s.; 2 d. Educ. St. Joseph's College, Dumfries. Assistant Lecturer in Economics, Aberdeen University, 1965-67; Lecturer in Economics, Strathclyde University, 1967-80; Lord Provost of Glasgow, 1980-84; Rector, Glasgow University, 1984-87; Member, Association of Business Sponsorship of the Arts (Scottish Committee), since 1986; Director: SITE Ltd.; Eglinton Stone Group Ltd.; Clyde Cablevision Ltd.; British Historic Buildings Trust; British Tourist Authority Medal for services to tourism, 1984; Robert Burns Award from University of Old Dominion, Virginia, for services to Scottish culture, 1984; Scot of the Year, 1983; Radio Scotland News Quiz Champion, 1986, 1987; Radio Scotland Christmas Quiz Champion, 1987; Honorary Mayor of Tombstone, Arizona; Kentucky Colonel, 1983. Recreations: supporting Celtic; philately; philumeny. Address: (b.) 95 Bothwell Street, Glasgow, G2 7HY; T.-041-204 2580.

Kelly, Patrick Joseph, BSc, CEng, MICE. Scottish Officer, National Union of Civil and Public Servants, since 1986; Member, STUC General Council, since 1986; b. 26.10.50, Glasgow; m., Rhona Marie; 2 d. Educ. St. Mungo's Academy; Glasgow University. Civil Engineer, 1973-86; National Executive, NALGO, 1979-86. Address: (b.) 7 Royal Terrace, Edinburgh; T.-031-556 0407.

Kelly, Thomas McDowall. Chairman, Water and Sewerage, Dumfries and Galloway Regional Council, since 1986; Vice-Chairman, Central and South West Scotland Electricity Consultative Council, since 1986; COSLA Representative, since 1986; b. 14.2.36, Mochrum Park. Educ. Wigtown High School. National Commercial Chairman, Transport & General Workers Union; Chairman, Manpower Services Area Committee, Dumfries and Galloway. Recreations: golf; skiing; cycling; walking. Address: 27 Anwoth Avenue, Dumfries, DG2 9QJ; T.-0387 62987.

Kelnar, Christopher J.H., MA, MD, FRCP, DCH. Consultant Paediatric Endocrinologist, Royal Hospital for Sick Children, Edinburgh, since 1983; Senior Lecturer, Department of Child Life and Health, Edinburgh University, since 1983; b. 22.12.47, London; m., Alison; 1 s.; 2 d. Educ. Highgate School, London; Trinity College, Cambridge; St. Bartholomew's Hospital, London. Research Fellow, Paediatric Endocrinology, Middlesex Hospital, London, 1979-81; Senior Registrar, Hospital for Sick Children, Great Ormond Street, London, and Tutor, Institute of

Child Health, London, 1981-83. Publications: The Sick Newborn Baby, 1981 (2nd edition, 1986). Recreations: music; gardening. Address: (b.) Royal Hospital for Sick Children, Sciennes Road, Edinburgh, EH9 1LF; T.-031-667 1991.

Kelso, David Elliot, BSc, MEd, FIPM, FBIM. HM Inspector, Scottish Education Department, since 1985; b. 25.3.45, Glasgow; m., Dorothy Louise Christie; 1 s.; 2 d. Educ. St. Joseph's College, Dumfries; Edinburgh University; Glasgow University; Dundee University. Personnel Officer, Singer (UK) Ltd., Clydebank, 1968-69; Personnel Manager, Rank Organisation, Kirkcaldy, 1969-71; Lecturer in Management, Glasgow College, 1971-73; Senior Lecturer, Dundee College of Commerce, 1973-76; Head, Department of Commerce and Business Studies, Falkirk College, 1976-83; Assistant Principal, 1983-85. Convener, Scottish Humanist Council. Recreations: running; esperanto; hill-walking. Address: (h.) Lomond, St. Mary's Drive, Dunblane, Perthshire; T.-0786 822605.

Kelty, William. Chairman, General Purposes Commitee, Grampian Regional Council, since 1978; b. 4.3.16, Keith; m., Margaret Rogers; 1 s.; 1 d. Educ. Keith Grammar School; Newstead School, Perthshire; Royal Technical College, Glasgow. Elected, Keith Town Council, 1946 (Chairman, Water Services; Dean of Guild); Chairman, Keith Football Club; twice Chairman, Keith Rotary Club; Chairman, Keith Swimming Pool Fund. Address: (h.) 43 Moss Street, Keith, AB5 3HH.

Kemball, Professor Emeritus Charles, MA, ScD, HonDSc, CChem, FRSC, MRIA, FRSE, FRS. Emeritus Professor of Chemistry, Edinburgh University, since 1983; b. 27.3.23, Edinburgh; m., Kathleen Purvis Lynd; 1 s.; 2 d. Educ. Edinburgh Academy; Trinity College, Cambridge. Fellow, Trinity College, 1946-54 (Junior Bursar, 1949-51, Assistant Lecturer, 1951-54); Demonstrator in Physical Chemistry, Cambridge University, 1951-54; Professor of Physical Chemistry, Queen's University, Belfast, 1954-66 (Dean, Faculty of Science, 1957-60, Vice-President, 1962-65); Professor of Chemistry, Edinburgh University, 1966-83 (Dean, Faculty of Science, 1975-78). President, Royal Institute of Chemistry, 1974-76; President, Royal Society of Edinburgh, 1988; Meldola Medal, RIC, 1951; Corday-Morgan Medal, 1958; Tilden Lecturer, 1960; Surface and Colloid Chemistry Award, Chemical Society, 1972; Ipatieff Prize, American Chemical Society, 1962; Gunning-Victoria Jubilee Prize, Royal Society of Edinburgh, 1976-80. Recreations: hill-walking; card games; wine-making. Address: (h.) 5 Hermitage Drive, Edinburgh, EH10 6DE; T.-031-447 2315.

Kemp, Professor Alexander George, MA (Hons). Professor of Economics, Aberdeen University, since 1983; b. Blackhall, Drumoak, Aberdeenshire. Educ. Robert Gordon's College, Aberdeen; Aberdeen University. Economist, Shell International Petroleum, London, 1962-64; Lecturer in Economics, Strathclyde University, 1964-65; Lecturer, then Senior Lecturer, then Reader, Aberdeen University, 1966-83. Specialist Adviser to House of Commons Select Committee on Energy; Economic Consultant to Secretary of State for Scotland; Consultant to UN Centre for Transnational Corporations; Consultant to Commonwealth Secretariat. Publications: 70 books and papers on petroleum economics. Address: (b.) Department of Economics, King's College, Aberdeen, AB9 2TY; T.-0224 272168.

Kemp, Arnold, MA. Editor, Glasgow Herald, since 1981; b. 15.2.39; m., Sandra Elizabeth; 2 d. Educ. Edinburgh Academy; Edinburgh University. Sub-Editor: The Scotsman, 1959-62, The Guardian, 1962-65; The Scotsman: Production Editor, 1965-70, London Editor, 1970-72, Deputy Editor, 1972-81. Recreations: music; reading; theatre. Address: (b.) 195 Albion Street, Glasgow, G1; T.-041-552 6255.

Kemp, Professor Martin John, MA, FRSA, HRSA, HFRIAS. Professor of Fine Arts, St. Andrews University, since 1981 (Associate Dean, 1983-87); b. 5.3.42, Windsor; m., Jill Lightfoot; 1 s.; 1 d. Educ. Windsor Grammar School; Cambridge University; London University. Lecturer: Dalhousie University, Nova Scotia, 1965-66, Glasgow University, 1966-81. Trustee: National Galleries of Scotland, 1982-87, Victoria and Albert Museum, London, since 1985; Honorary Professor of History, Royal Scottish Academy, since 1985; Honorary Fellow, Royal Institute of Architects in Scotland; Member, Institute for Advanced Study, Princeton, 1984-85; Slade Professor, Cambridge University, 1988; Benjamin Sonnenberg Visiting Professor, Institute of Fine Arts, New York University, 1988. Publication: Leonardo Da Vinci: The Marvellous Works of Nature and Man (1981 Mitchell Prize for Best First Book in Art History). Recreation: sport (especially hockey). Address: (h.) Orillia, 45 Pittenweem Road, Anstruther, Fife; T.-0333 310842.

Kendell, Professor Robert Evan, MD, FRCP, FRCPsych. Professor of Psychiatry, Edinburgh University, since 1974 (Dean, Faculty of Medicine, since 1986); Member, Medical Research Council, 1984-88; Member, WHO Expert Advisory Panel on Mental Health, since 1979; b. 28.3.35, Rotherham; m., Ann Whitfield; 2 s.; 2 d. Educ. Mill Hill School; Cambridge University; King's College Hospital Medical School. Visiting Professor, University of Vermont College of Medicine, 1969-70; Reader in Psychiatry, Institute of Psychiatry, London University, 1970-74. Gaskell Medal, Royal College of Psychiatrists, 1967; Paul Hoch Medal, American Psychopathological Association, 1988. Publications: The Classification of Depressive Illnesses, 1968; The Role of Diagnosis in Psychiatry, 1975; Companion to Psychiatric Studies (Editor), 1983 and 1988. Recreations: walking up hills; overeating. Address: (h.) 3 West Castle Road, Edinburgh, EH10 5AT.

Kennedy, Angus Johnston, MA, PhD. Reader in French Language and Literature and Head of Department, Glasgow University; b. 9.8.40, Port Charlotte; m., Marjory McCulloch Shearer; 2 d. Educ. Bearsden Academy; Glasgow University. Glasgow University: Assistant Lecturer in

French, 1965, then Lecturer, Senior Lecturer; former Secretary, British Branch, International Arthurian Society. Publications: books on Christine de Pizan. Address: (b.) French Department, Glasgow University, Glasgow; T.-041-339 8855, Ext. 4589.

Kennedy, Professor Arthur Colville, MD, FRCP(Lond), FRCPE, FRCP(Glas), FRCPI, FRSE, FACP(Hon.), FRACP (Hon.). Consultant Physician, Royal Infirmary, Glasgow, since 1959; Muirhead Professor of Medicine, Glasgow University, since 1978; President, Royal College of Physicians and Surgeons of Glasgow, since 1986; b. 22.10.22, Edinburgh; m., Agnes White Taylor; 1 s. (deceased); 2 d. Educ. Whitehill School, Glasgow; Glasgow University. Medical Officer, RAFVR, 1946-48; junior NHS posts, 1948-57; Lecturer in Medicine, Glasgow University, 1957; Senior Lecturer, 1961; Reader, 1966; Titular Professor, 1969; responsible for establishment of Kidney Unit, Glasgow Royal Infirmary, 1959; Chairman, MRC Working Party in Glomerulonephritis, since 1976; Member, Executive Committee, National Kidney Research Fund, 1976-83; Expert Adviser to WHO on Renal Disease; Adviser to EEC on Nephrology in Developing Countries; Chairman, Professional and Linguistic Assessments Board (PLAB), GMC, since 1987; President, Royal Medico-Chirurgical Society of Glasgow, 1971-72; President, European Dialysis and Transplant Association, 1972-75; President, Scottish Society of Physicians, 1983-84; President, Harveian Society of Edinburgh, 1985; Member, Greater Glasgow Health Board, since 1985. Recreations: gardening; walking; reading; photography. Address: (h.) 16 Boclair Crescent, Bearsden, Glasgow, G61 2AG; T.-041-942 5326.

Kennedy, Charles Peter, MA (Hons). MP (SLD, formerly SDP), Ross, Cromarty and Skye, since 1983; b. 25.11.59, Inverness. Educ. Lochaber High School, Fort William; Glasgow University; Indiana University. President, Glasgow University Union, 1980-81; Winner, British Observer Mace for Student Debating, 1982; Journalist, BBC Highland, Inverness, 1982; Fulbright Scholar, Indiana University (Bloomington Campus), 1982-83. Chairman, SDP Council for Scotland, 1986-88; SDP Spokesman on Health and Social Services, and Scotland, 1983-87; Alliance Election Spokesman, Social Security, Jan.-June, 1987; Member, Select Committee on Social Services, 1985-87; SLD Interim Joint Spokesman, Social Security, 1988; Member, Select Committee on House of Commons Televising, 1988; occasional journalist and broadcaster. Recreations: reading; writing. Address: (b.) House of Commons, London, SW1A 0AA; T.-01-219 5090.

Kennedy, Dermot, MB, ChB, FRCP(Glas), DRCOG. Consultant Physician, Department of Infectious Diseases, Ruchill Hospital, Glasgow, since 1978; Honorary Clinical Lecturer, Glasgow University, since 1978; b. 1.1.44, Glasgow; m., Catherine Ann McLaughlin; 1 s. Educ. St. Aloysius College; Holyrood School; Glasgow University. Glasgow University: Lecturer in Infectious Diseases, 1971-75, Epidemiology of Infectious Diseases, 1975-78; Postdoctoral Fellow, Yale University, 1977; Member, Medical Research Council and Scottish Home and Health Department Committees on AIDS and Home Office Committees on Drug Abuse (Advisory Council on Misuse of Drugs). Publications: Contributor to four books on AIDS, atypical pneumonia and legionnaires disease, respiratory infections and extrapulmonary tuberculosis. Recreations: music; history; walking; Scottish affairs; French impressionism. Address: (h.) 81 Randolph Road, Glasgow, G11; T.-041-357 1100.

Kennedy, Frederick John, LLB. Regional Reporter, Strathclyde Regional Council; b. 22.6.40, Grantham; m., Eleanor Mae Watson; 1 s.; 1 d. Educ. High School of Glasgow; Glasgow University. Private, industrial and local government legal practice; former Reporter to the Children's Panel, City of Glasgow; former Director of Administration, Fife Regional Council. Recreations: golf; reading; gardening. Address: (b.) McIver House, 51 Cadogan Street, Glasgow, G2; T.-041-227 6171.

Kennedy, Professor Gavin, BA, MSc, PhD. Professor of Defence Finance, Heriot-Watt University; Managing Director, Negotiate Ltd., Edinburgh; b. 20.2.40, Collingham, Yorkshire; m., Patricia Anne; 1 s.; 2 d. Educ. London Nautical School; Strathclyde University. Lecturer: Danbury Management Centre, NE London Polytechnic, 1969-71, Brunel University, 1971-73. Lecturer, National Defence College, Latimer, 1972-74; Senior Lecturer in Economics, Strathclyde University, 1973-85. Publications: Military in the Third World, 1974; Economics of Defence, 1975; Bligh, 1978 (Yorkshire Post Book of the Year, 1979); Death of Captain Cook, 1978; Burden Sharing in NATO, 1979; Mathematics for Innumerate Economists, 1982; Defence Economics, 1983; Invitation to Statistics, 1983; Everything is Negotiable, 1984; Negotiate Anywhere, 1985; Macro Economics, 1985; Superdeal, 1985; The Economist Pocket Negotiator, 1987; Captain Bligh: the man and his mutinies, 1988. Recreation: reading. Address: (h.) 22 Braid Avenue, Edinburgh; T.-031-447 3000.

Kennedy, James Henry, MB, ChB, MRCOG. Consultant in Obstetrics and Gynaecology, Royal Maternity Hospital and Royal Infirmary, Glasgow, since 1983; b. 23.4.49, Glasgow; m., Hilary Lawson Sim; 1 s.; 1 d. Educ. High School of Glasgow; Glasgow University. Recently Lecturer in Obstetrics and Gynaecology, Glasgow University. Scottish cricket internationalist, 1970-71. Recreations: cricket; curling. Address: (h.) 5 Penrith Avenue, Glasgow, G46.

Kenny, Gavin N.C., BSc (Hons), MD, FFARCS. Senior Lecturer in Anaesthesia, Glasgow University, since 1982; b. 31.1.48, Glasgow; m., Dr. Joan W. Prentice. Educ. Hutchesons' Boys' Grammar School; Glasgow University. Lecturer in Anaesthesia, Glasgow University, 1977-82; Visiting Professor, Duke University, 1981; Visiting Consultant, Groote Schuur Hospital, Capetown, 1983; Guest Visitor, South African Association of Anaesthetists, 1984; has served on variety of committees for anaesthesia and postgraduate medical education in Scotland and England; Editorial Assistant, British Journal of Anaesthesia. Recreations: sailing; skiing; music. Address: (b.) University Department of Anaesthesia, Glasgow Royal Infirmary, Glasgow; T.-041-552 3535, Ext. 5454.

Kent, Rev. Arthur Francis Stoddart. Minister, Monkton and Prestwick North Parish Church, since 1981; b. 30.1.34, Glasgow; m., Isla Glen McLean; 2 d. Educ. Hutcheson's Boys' Grammar School; Glasgow University and Trinity College. Minister: United Church of Jamaica and Grand Cayman, 1965-73, Bellshill West Parish Church, 1973-81. Recreations: gardening; golf. Address: 40 Monkton Road, Prestwick, KA9 1AR; T.-Prestwick 77499.

Keppie, Joseph L., BSc(Agric) (Hons). Senior Principal Scientific Officer, Department of Agriculture and Fisheries for Scotland; b. 11.12.28, Paisley; m., Laura Brand; 1 s.; 1 d. Educ. Cardonald School, Glasgow; Paisley Grammar School; Aberdeen University. Entered Department of Agriculture and Fisheries for Scotland, 1954. Past President, Kinross-shire Agriculture Society; Past Chairman, St. Kilda Club Committee. Recreations: dog walks; photography; mountains and moorlands; Scottish flora. Address: (h.) The Hollies, High Street, Kinross.

Kerevan, George, JP, MA (Hons). Member, City of Edinburgh District Council, since 1984 (Convener, Cultural Sub-Committee and Economic Development Sub-Committee); Senior Lecturer in Economics, Napier College, Edinburgh, since 1982, and Director, Scottish Coal Project, since 1986; b. 28.9.49, Glasgow. Educ. Glasgow University; Edinburgh University. Lecturer in Economics, Napier College, Edinburgh, 1974; Editor: Scottish Socialist, 1976-77, Bulletin of Scottish Politics, 1980-83; Member, Editorial Board, Local Economy, since 1985; Editor, Scottish Energy News, since 1986; broadcasts and writes on Scottish politics and economics; Member: Edinburgh Festival Council, Royal Lyceum Theatre Board, Traverse Theatre Board (former Secretary), 7:84 Theatre Board, Assembly Productions Board. Publication: The Case for Scottish Coal (Co-author). Recreations: collecting contemporary Scottish art; cooking; cats. Address: (h.) 14a Dalkeith Street, Edinburgh, EH15; T.-031-669 8234.

Kermack, Sheriff Stuart Ogilvy, BA (Oxon), LLB. Sheriff of Tayside, Central and Fife, at Forfar and Arbroath, since 1971; b. 9.7.34, Edinburgh; m., Barbara Mackenzie; 3 s.; 1 d. Educ. Glasgow Academy; Jesus College, Oxford; Glasgow University. Called to Scottish Bar, 1958; Sheriff, Elgin and Nairn, 1965. Secretary, Scottish Branch, Howard League for Penal Reform. Address: (h.) 7 Littlecauseway, Forfar, Angus; T.-Forfar 64691.

Kernohan, Robert Deans, MA. Editor, Life and Work, The Record of the Church of Scotland, since 1972; Journalist, Writer and occasional Broadcaster; b. 9.1.31, Mount Vernon, Lanarkshire; m., Margaret Buchanan Bannerman; 4 s. Educ. Whitehill School, Glasgow; Glasgow University; Balliol College, Oxford. RAF, 1955-57; Editorial Staff, Glasgow Herald, 1957-67 (Assistant Editor, 1965-66, London Editor, 1966-67); Director-General, Scottish Conservative Central Office, 1967-71; Freelance Journalist and Broadcaster, 1972. Chairman, Federation of Conservative Students, 1954-55; Conservative Parliamentary candidate, 1955, 1959, 1964; Elder, Cramond Kirk, Edinburgh. Publications: Scotland's Life and Work, 1979; William Barclay, The Plain Uncommon Man, 1980; Thoughts through the Year, 1985; Our Church, 1985. Recreations: rugby-watching; travel; pontification. Address: (b.) 121 George Street, Edinburgh, EH2 4YN; T.-031-225 5722.

Kerr, Alastair Ian Grant, MB, ChB, FRCSGlas, FRCSEdin. Consultant Otolaryngologist, Edinburgh Royal Infirmary, since 1979; Honorary Senior Lecturer, Edinburgh University, since 1979; b. 28.4.45, Elderslie; m., Elizabeth Wilson Carswell; 1 s.; 2 d. Educ. John Neilson Institution, Paisley; Glasgow University. Trainee in Surgery, Western Infirmary, Glasgow, 1969; specialised in otolaryngology, from 1973; Senior Registrar, Edinburgh Royal Infirmary, 1975 (Consultant, 1977). Publications: Clinical Otolaryngology (Contributor); Logan Turners Diseases of Throat, Nose and Ear (Contributor); The New Medicine Otolaryngology (Contributor); Paediatric Otolaryngology. Recreations: golf; squash; tennis. Address: (b.) ENT Department, Edinburgh Royal Infirmary, Edinburgh; T.-031-229 2477.

Kerr, Allan MacDonald, LLB. Solicitor; Director of Law and Administration, Nairn District Council, since 1984; b. 10.6.53, Glasgow; m., Mairi; 2 s. Educ. Bishopbriggs High School; Glasgow University. Law apprentice, later qualified Assistant, McGettigan & Co., Solicitors, Glasgow, 1976-78; Principal Legal Assistant, later Solicitor, Western Isles Islands Council, 1978-82; Clerk of Court, Motherwell District, 1982-84. Recreations: family; motoring; reading. Address: (b.) The Court House, High Street, Nairn; T.-0667 55523.

Kerr, David Alexander, MC, TD, JP, DL; b. 30.9.16, Inverkip; m., (Elizabeth) Phoebe Coxwell Cresswel; 1 s.; 1 d. Educ. Canford School. Joined Westburn Sugar Refineries Ltd., Greenock, 1936; joined 5/6 Bn., Argyll & Sutherland Highlanders, 1936; mobilised, 1939, serving in France, Belgium, North Africa, Italy, Palestine and Syria; MC, 1945; mentioned in Despatches; returned to Westburn, 1946; Technical Director, 1949; Refinery Director, 1955; Joint Managing Director, 1960; Managing Director, 1967; Chairman, 1972; Director, Tate & Lyle Refineries Ltd., 1976-79; retired, 1979. County Commissioner, County of Renfrew Scout Association, 1964-70, County Chairman, 1971-73; Area President, since 1976; Chief Commissioner for Scotland, 1977-81; Honorary Chief Commissioner, since 1981. Recreations: garden; philately; photography; donkeys. Address: (h.) Whitefarland, 88 Octavia Terrace, Greenock, PA16 7PY; T.-Gourock 31980.

Kerr, Finlay, MB, ChB, DObsRCOG, FRCPEdin, FRCPGlas. Consultant Physician, Raigmore Hospital, Inverness, since 1976; Honorary Senior Lecturer, Aberdeen University, since 1976; Board Director, Highland Hospice, since 1985

(Chairman, Board of Directors, 1985-87); b. 8.8.41, Edinburgh; m., Margaret Ann Carnegie Allan; 1 s.; 2 d. Educ. Keil School; Glasgow University. House Physician and Surgeon, Western Infirmary, Glasgow; House Physician, Ruchill Hospital, Glasgow; House Surgeon, Queen Mother's Hospital, Glasgow; Senior House Officer, Western Infirmary, Glasgow; Fellow, University of Southern California; Lecturer in Medicine, then Senior Registrar in Medicine, Edinburgh Royal Infirmary. Recreations: sailing; skiing; walking. Address: (h.) Glendale, 11 Devlin Crescent, Inverness; T.-0463 234779.

Kerr, Francis Robert Newsam, OBE, MC, DL, JP; b. 12.9.16, Ancrum; m., Anne Frederick Kitson; 2 s.; 1 d. Educ. Ampleforth College. Officer, Royal Scots (Lt-Col.), retired, 1960; Farmer, Berwickshire. Address: (h.) The Lodge, Blanerne, Duns, TD11 3PZ; T.-Chirnside 483.

Kerr, Hugh, BSc. Head Teacher, Greenock High School, since 1985; b. 25.12.42, Airdrie; m., Sylvia; 1 s.; 2 d. Educ. Greenock High School; Glasgow University. Teacher of Chemistry, John Neilson High School, 1966-72; Principal Teacher of Chemistry, Greenock Academy, 1972-76; Depute Head Teacher (Community), Port Glasgow High School, 1976-85. Recreations: canoeing; running; gardening. Address: (h.) Heathfield, Horsewood Road, Bridge of Weir; T.-612687.

Kerr, Isabel Dunlop. Member, Greater Glasgow Health Board, 1983-86; Warden, Guild of Aid, Gorbals, Glasgow, since 1974; b. 24.10.21, Glasgow; m., Charles Ferguson Kerr; 1 s.; 1 d. Educ. Bellahouston Academy; Queen's College (as mature student). Assistant Secretary, City of Glasgow Society of Social Service; Paisley Burgh Social Work Department; Guild of Aid. President, Soroptimist International, Glasgow South, 1980-81; Marriage Guidance Counsellor. Recreations: reading; cooking; flower arranging. Address: (h.) 3 Darnley Place, Maxwell Park, Glasgow, G41 4NA; T.-041-424 3997.

Kerr, John, CA. Director, Scottish Association of Young Farmers' Clubs, since 1985; b. 17.5.46, Tarbolton; m., Mary Paterson; 1 s.; 2 d. Educ. Ayr Academy; Institute of Chartered Accountants of Scotland. Indentured to McClelland Moores & Co., Glasgow, 1963-68; qualified CA, 1968; Audit Senior, McClelland Moores & Co., 1968-70; joined William Grant & Sons Ltd., Paisley, 1970; appointed Chief Accountant, 1973; resigned, 1985. Chairman of Council, Scottish Young Farmers, 1976-77; Chairman, European Committee for Young Farmers, 1980-82. Recreations: family; reading; amateur drama; gardening; home decorating. Address: (b.) Young Farmers' Centre, Ingliston, Edinburgh, EH28 8NE.

Kerr, Robert James, MA (Hons), PhD. Rector, Peebles High School, since 1986; Chairman, Central Support Group for Social and Vocational Skills, Scottish Education Department, since 1986; b. 14.6.47, Jedburgh; m., Isobel Grace Atkinson; 2 s.; 1 d. Educ. Kelso High School; Edinburgh University. Assistant Teacher, Lochaber High School, 1973-75; Assistant Principal Teacher of Geography, Forrester High School, 1976-77; Principal Teacher of Geography, Douglas Ewart High School, 1977-82; Assistant Rector, Elgin High School, 1982-85; Depute Rector, Forres Academy, 1985-86. Recreations: ornithology; skiing; hill-walking; fishing; photography; travel. Address: (h.) Enniskerry, Eshiels, Peebles, EH45 8NA; T.-0721 22298.

Kerr, Robert Reid, MA (Oxon), LLB, TD, OStJ; b. 7.5.14, Greenock; m., Mona; 3 d. Educ. Cargilfield; Trinity College, Glenalmond; Hertford College, Oxford; Glasgow University. War, France, North Africa (1st Army), Italy, Greece; admitted Advocate, 1946; Sheriff, Fort William, Banff, 1952, Falkirk, 1969. Address: (h.) Bagatelle, 14 Rennie Street, Falkirk, FK1 5QW; T.-0324 22046.

Kerr, William John Stanton, BDS, FDS, RCSEdin, MDS, FFD, RCSIrel, DOrthRCS. Reader in Orthodontics, Glasgow Dental Hospital and School, since 1988; Honorary Consultant in Orthodontics, since 1978; b. 12.7.41, Belfast; m., Marie-Francoise; 1 d. Educ. Campbell College, Belfast; Queen's University, Belfast. Address: (b.) Glasgow Dental Hospital and School, 378 Sauchiehall Street, Glasgow, G2 3JZ; T.-041-332 7020.

Kerr, Lt.-Col. (Rtd.) William Walker, MBIM. General Secretary, Scottish Central Council Branch, British Red Cross Society, since 1985; b. 17.4.30, Haddington; m., Jacqueline Mary Sanctuary; 1 s.; 1 d. Educ. Knox Academy, Haddington; Royal Military Academy, Sandhurst. Army, Royal Highland Fusiliers, 1948-80. Recreations: hill-walking; skiing; swimming; bird-watching; stamp-collecting. Address: (b.) Alexandra House, 204 Bath Street, Glasgow, G2 4HL; T.-041-332 9591.

Kerridge, Professor David Frank, BSc, FIS. Professor of Statistics, Aberdeen University, since 1966; b. 27.12.31, Southampton; m., Audrey Heslop (deceased); 2 d. Educ. Barton Peveril School; Southampton University. Statistician, Medical Research Council; Lecturer in Statistics, Sheffield University; Research Fellow, Aberdeen University. Recreations: chess; music. Address: (b.) Edward Wright Building, Dunbar Street, Old Aberdeen, AB9 2TY; T.-0224 272605.

Kerrigan, Professor Herbert Aird, MA, LLB (Hons). Advocate, since 1970; b. 2.8.45, Glasgow; 1 s. Educ. Whitehill School, Glasgow; Aberdeen University; Keele University; Hague Academy. Lecturer in Criminal Law and Criminology, Edinburgh University; Lecturer in Scots Law, Edinburgh University; Visiting Professor, University of Southern California, since 1979; Member, Longford Commission, 1972; Church of Scotland: Elder, 1967 (now at Greyfriars Tolbooth and Highland Kirk), Reader, 1969, elected Member, Assembly Council, 1981. Publications: An Introduction to Criminal Procedure in Scotland, 1970; Ministers for the 1980s (Contributor), 1979; The Law of Contempt (Contributing Editor), 1982. Recreation: travel. Address: (h.) 20 Edinburgh Road, Dalkeith, Midlothian, EH22 1JY; T.-031-660 3007.

Kershaw, Peter Whaley, MD, FRCPsych, FRCPEdin, DPM, DObstRCOG. Physician Superintendent, Gartnavel Royal Hospital, Glasgow, since 1985 (Consultant Psychiatrist, since 1970); Honorary Clinical Lecturer, Department of Psychological Medicine, Glasgow University, since 1970; b. 23.2.35, Bradford, Yorkshire; m., Irene Patricia Gibson; 1 s.; 1 d. Educ. Thornton Grammar School, Bradford; Edinburgh University. House Officer posts, Bradford Royal Infirmary, Edinburgh Royal Infirmary, St. Luke's Hospital, Bradford, and Southern General Hospital, Glasgow; Research Fellow, Department of Therapeutics, Edinburgh University; Lecturer, Department of Psychological Medicine, Glasgow University; Consultant Psychiatrist, Ravenscraig Hospital, Greenock. Publication: Rehabilitation in Psychiatric Practice (Contributor). Recreations: running; hill-walking; orienteering; music; art; painting. Address: (h.) Overdale, 2 Carse View Drive, Bearsden, Glasgow, G61 3NJ; T.-041-942 8525.

Khan, Kabir-Ur-Rahman, BA (Hons), LLB, LLM, PhD. Senior Lecturer, Department of Public International Law, Edinburgh University, since 1982 (Lecturer, 1965-81); b. 2.2.25, Firozpur Jhirka, India; m., Isobel Thomson; 1 d. Educ. Raj Rishi College, Alwar; Government College, Ajmere; Agra University; Sind University; Open University; London University. Barrister-at-Law, Gray's Inn, 1955; Advocate, High Court of Pakistan, Lahore, 1958-61. Member, Lothian Community Relations Council; Member and Co-Chairman, Edinburgh Inter-Faith Association. Publications: The Law and Organisation of International Commodity Agreements, 1982; International Law of Development, in press. Recreations: walking; keep fit; Urdu poetry. Address: (h.) 5 Heriot Row, Edinburgh, EH3 6HU; T.-031-556 2229.

Kidd, Professor Cecil, BSc, PhD, FIBiol. Regius Professor of Physiology, Aberdeen University, since 1984; b. 28.4.33, Shotley Bridge, Co. Durham; m., Margaret Winifred; 3 s. Educ. Queen Elizabeth Grammar School, Darlington; King's College, Newcastle-upon-Tyne; Durham University. Demonstrator in Physiology, King's College, Newcastle-upon-Tyne; Lecturer/Senior Lecturer/Reader in Physiology, Senior Research Associate in Cardiovascular Studies, Leeds University. Recreations: squash; gardening. Address: (b.) Department of Physiology, Marischal College, Aberdeen University, Aberdeen; T.-0224 40241, Ext. 300.

Kidd, David Hamilton, LLB, LLM, WS, NP. Partner, Biggart Baillie & Gifford, WS, since 1978; b. 21.9.49, Edinburgh; m., Geraldine Stephen; 2 s. Educ. Edinburgh Academy; Edinburgh University. Research Assistant, Law Faculty, Queen's University, Belfast, 1976-77. Former Secretary, Scottish Legal Computer Research Trust; Society for Computers and Law: Council Member, 1982-84, Secretary, since 1984; Member, Organisation and Methods Committee, Law Society of Scotland, since 1981. Recreations: cycling; skiing; sailing. Address: (b.) 3 Glenfinlas Street, Edinburgh, EH3 6YY; T.-031-226 5541.

Kidd, Frank Forrest, CA, ACTII. Partner, Coopers & Lybrand, Chartered Accountants, since 1979; b. 4.5.38, Dundee; m., Beryl Ann Gillespie; 2 s.; 2 d. Educ. George Heriot's School; Ballards. CA Apprentice, 1955-60; Partner, Wylie & Hutton, 1962-79; Honorary Professor, Department of Accountancy and Business Law, Stirling University; President, Institute of Chartered Accountants of Scotland. Recreations: squash; golf; walking. Address: (b.) George House, 126 George Street, Edinburgh, EH2 4JZ; T.-031-226 2595.

Kidd, Professor Ian Gray, MA (St. Andrews), MA (Oxon). Professor of Greek, St. Andrews University, 1976-87; b. 6.3.22, Goretty, Chandernagore, India; m., Sheila Elizabeth Dow; 3 s. Educ. Dundee High School; St. Andrews University; Queen's College, Oxford. St. Andrews University: Lecturer in Greek, 1949, Senior Lecturer, 1965; Visiting Professor, University of Texas at Austin, 1965-66; Member, Institute for Advanced Study, Princeton, 1971-72; St. Andrews University: Personal Professor of Ancient Philosophy, 1973-76, Provost of St. Leonard's College, 1978-83; Member, Institute for Advanced Study, Princeton, 1979-80. Publication: Posidonius, The Fragments, 1972. Recreations: music; reading. Address: (h.) Ladebury, Lade Braes Lane, St. Andrews, Fife, KY16 9EP; T.-0334 74367.

Kidd, Jean Buyers, BA, DipMusEd, LRAM, ARCM. Music Director, Junior and Youth Choruses, Scottish National Orchestra, since 1978; b. Macduff, Banffshire; widow. Educ. Buckie High School; Royal Scottish Academy of Music; Open University. Taught in various Glasgow schools and for many years, Principal Teacher of Music, Bellahouston Academy; former Conductor, Bellahouston Music Society; gave instruction in music and drama to women in Duke Street Prison; former Secretary, Scottish Certificate of Education Examination Board. Recreations: reading; playing chamber music; gardening; craft work. Address: (h.) Carolside, Gowanlea Road, Comrie, Perthshire, PH6 2HD; T.-Comrie 70856.

Kidd, Dame Margaret Henderson, DBE, QC, Hon.LLD (Dundee and Edinburgh); b. 14.3.00, Carriden; m., Donald Somerled Macdonald, WS (deceased); 1 d. Educ. Linlithgow Academy; Edinburgh University. Admitted Advocate, Scottish Bar, 1923; practised as Advocate, 1923-60; Editor, Session Case Reports, Scots Law Times, 1942-76; King's Counsel, 1948; Keeper, Advocates' Library, 1956-71; Sheriff-Principal, Dumfries & Galloway, 1960-66, Perth & Angus, 1966-75; Chairman, East and South of Scotland Society for Welfare of the Blind, 1966-72; Council Chairman, Queen's Nursing Institute (Scotland), 1976-81; Honorary Legal Adviser, Scottish Association of Occupational Therapists, 1958-70. Recreation: walking. Address: (h.) 5 India Street, Edinburgh, EH3 6HA; T.-031-225 3867.

Kiely, John, BSc, MSc. HM Inspector of Schools, 1961-85; b. 27.6.25, Tugby, Leicestershire; m., Mary Macdonald; 3 s.; 1 d. Educ. Bicester County School; Bristol University. Instructor-Lt., Royal Navy, 1945-48. Assistant Master, King Edward VII School, Sheffield, 1950-51; Second Mathematics Master, Grimsby Wintringham Grammar

School, 1952-55; Senior Lecturer, Royal Naval College, Dartmouth, 1955-58; Head, Mathematics Department, Blundells School, Tiverton, 1958-61. Recreations: reading; gardening. Address: (h.) Suffolkhill House, 28 Dalbeattie Road, Dumfries, DG2 7PL; T.-Dumfries 63429.

Kiernan, Wolfgang E.S., MB, BCG, FRCPsych, FRCPEdin, FRCPGlas, DipPsych(Ed). Consultant Psychiatrist; Physician Superintendent, Gartnavel Royal Hospital, Glasgow, 1980-85; Honorary Clinical Lecturer, Department of Psychological Medicine, Glasgow University, since 1967; b. 25.1.32, Lisburn, Northern Ireland; m., Diana; 2 d. Educ. St. Malachy's College, Belfast; Queen's University, Belfast. Lecturer in Psychological Medicine, Edinburgh University, 1960-66; Regional Adviser in Mental Health, SE Asia Region, World Health Organisation, 1975-76; Consultant to WHO on Mental Health matters in SE Asia. Honorary Medical Secretary, Mental Health Foundation (Scotland); Member, Expert Advisory Panel on Mental Health, WHO. Recreations: piano; reading; walking; skiing. Address: (h.) 10 Colquhoun Drive, Bearsden, Glasgow, G61 4NQ; T.-041-942 3197.

Kilbrandon, Lord (Charles James Dalrymple), BA, LLB, LLD, DSc (SocSci); Life Peer; Privy Councillor; b. 15.8.06, Coylton, Ayrshire; m., Ruth Caroline Grant; 2 s.; 3 d. Educ. Charterhouse; Balliol College, Oxford; Edinburgh University. Advocate, 1932; War Service, RA, 1939-45; King's Counsel, 1949; Sheriff of Ayr and Bute, 1954-57, of Perth and Angus, 1957; Dean, Faculty of Advocates, 1957; Senator of the College of Justice, 1959; Lord of Appeal in Ordinary, 1971-77; Honorary Fellow of Balliol, 1970; Honorary Bencher of Gray's Inn, 1971; Visitor of Balliol, 1974-86; Chairman of a number of Departmental Committees and Royal Commission on the Constitution. Address: (h.) Kilbrandon House, Balvicar, by Oban, Argyll, PA34 4RA; T.-Balvicar 239.

Kilgour, Alistair Crichton, BSc, PhD, FBCS. Senior Lecturer, Computing Science Department, Glasgow University, since 1984; b. 14.8.40, Glasgow; m., Margaret; 3 s. Educ. Allan Glen's School, Glasgow; Glasgow University. Scientific Programmer, English Electric Computers Ltd., 1963-66; Research Associate, Computer-Aided Design Project, Edinburgh University, 1966-74; Lecturer, Computing Science Department, Glasgow University, 1974-84. Recreations: theatre; films; reading; conservation. Address: (b.) Department of Computing Science, Glasgow University, Glasgow, G12 8QQ; T.-041-339 8855.

Kilgour, Walter B., LLB, DPA, MBIM, NP. Director of Administration, Strathkelvin District Council, since 1985; b. 31.3.53, Glasgow; m., Linda M.; 1 d. Educ. Hutchesons' Boys' Grammar School; Glasgow University. Solicitor, Renfrew District Council, 1975; Senior Solicitor, Motherwell District Council, 1978; Principal Solicitor, Central Regional Council, 1980; Depute District Secretary, Falkirk District Council, 1982. Address: (b.) Tom Johnston House, Kirkintilloch, G66 4TJ; T.-041-776 7171.

Kilmarnock, 7th Baron (Alastair Ivor Gilbert Boyd). Chief of the Clan Boyd; b. 11.5.27; m., 1, Diana Mary Gibson (deceased); 2, Hilary Ann Bardwell; 1 s. Educ. Bradfield; King's College, Cambridge. Lt., Irish Guards, 1946; Chief SDP Whip, House of Lords, 1983-86.

Kimbell, Professor David Rodney Bertram, MA, DPhil, LRAM, FRSA. Professor of Music, Edinburgh University, since 1987 (Professor of Music, St. Andrews University, 1979-87); b. 26.6.39, Gillingham, Kent; m., Ingrid Else Emilie Lubbe; 1 s.; 2 d. Educ. Dartford Grammar School; Kent College, Canterbury; Worcester College, Oxford. Lecturer in Music, Edinburgh University, 1965-78. Publication: Verdi in the Age of Italian Romanticism, 1981. Recreations: walking; miscellaneous sports. Address: (h.) 3 Bellevue Crescent, Edinburgh, EH3 6ND; T.-031-556 5480.

Kincraig, Hon. Lord (Robert Smith Johnston), QC (Scot), BA (Hons), LLB. Senator of the College of Justice in Scotland, 1972-88; Chairman, Parole Review Body for Scotland; b. 10.10.18, Glasgow; m., Margaret Joan Graham; 1 s.; 1 d. Educ. Strathallan; St. John's College, Cambridge; Glasgow University. Member, Faculty of Advocates, 1942; Advocate-Depute, 1953-55; QC (Scot), 1955; Home Advocate Depute, 1959-62; Sheriff of Roxburgh, Berwick and Selkirk, 1964-70; Dean, Faculty of Advocates, 1970-72. Recreations: golf; gardening; curling. Address: (h.) Westwood, Longniddry, East Lothian; T.-Longniddry 52849.

Kinder, Tony, BSc (Hons), MA. Chair, Lothian Enterprise Board; Chair, Lothian Regional Council Employment Committee; b. 19.6.49, Middlesbrough; m., Irene; 1 s.; 1 d. Educ. Cleveland High School; Bradford University. Full-time Union Convener; Tutor in Trade Union Education; Secretary, Edinburgh District Labour Party. Recreation: walking. Address: (h.) 8 Woodhall Terrace, Juniper Green, Edinburgh; T.-031-453 4011.

King, Alexander, DMS, ACMA, FMS. Convener, Policy and Resources Committee, Angus District Council, since 1984; b. 6.10.44, Dunfermline; 1 d. Educ. Arbroath High School; Dundee College of Technology. William R. Stewart & Sons (Hacklemakers) Ltd.: Management Services Manager, 1973-80, Management Accountant, since 1980. Scottish Region Treasurer, Institute of Management Services, 1967-82; Constituency Treasurer, Angus, Scottish National Party, since 1980. Recreations: gliding; theatre; walking.

King, Charles, MA (Hons). Member, Grampian Regional Council, since 1986; Member, Council, Association of Scottish Literary Studies, 1971-88; b. 29.10.19, Edinburgh; m., Vera Gall Thomson; 1 s.; 2 d. Educ. Trinity Academy, Edinburgh; Edinburgh University; Moray House College of Education. Served in Army, Shetland, Orkney, Malta; taught, Scottish schools; appointed Adviser in English, Aberdeen City, then Grampian Region; edited Twelve Modern Scottish Poets, 1971, 1986. Recreations: golf; Scottish country dancing; travel. Recreations: golf; Scottish country dancing; travel. Address: (h.) 36 Hammerfield Avenue, Aberdeen; T.-0224 310403.

King, Emeritus Professor James Lawrence, MA, PhD, FIMA. Professor (Emeritus), Edinburgh University, since 1983; Governor, Strathallan

School, Perthshire; b. 14.2.22, London; m., Pamela Mary Ward Hitchcock; 1 s.; 1 d. Educ. Latymer Upper School; Jesus College, Cambridge. Navy Department, 1942-68 (Admiralty Research Laboratory, 1942-61; Chief Scientist, Naval Construction Research Establishment, Dunfermline, 1961-68); Regius Professor of Engineering, Edinburgh University, 1968-83. Recreation: walking. Address: (h.) 16 Lyne Park, West Linton, Peeblesshire.

Kininmonth, Sir William (Hardie), Kt (1972), PPRSA, FRIBA, FRIAS. Architectural Consultant; b. 8.11.04; 1 d. Educ. George Watson's College, Edinburgh; Edinburgh College of Art. President, Royal Scottish Academy, 1969-73; President, Edinburgh Architectural Association, 1951-53; Member, Royal Fine Arts Commission for Scotland, 1952-65; Council Member, RIBA, 1951-53; former Senior Partner, Sir Rowand Anderson, Kininmonth and Paul, Architects, Edinburgh; Hon. LLD, Dundee, 1975.

Kinloch, John, JP, BSc. Farmer; b. 30.1.41; m., Jeanette Elizabeth MacDonald; 1 s.; 2 d. Educ. Morrison's Academy, Crieff; Edinburgh University. Council Member, National Farmers Union of Scotland, 1974-83 (Convener, Labour and Machinery Committee, 1978-83); Member, Advisory Committee on Birds, 1977-85; former Member: Scottish Agricultural Development Council; Scottish Committee, Scottish Institute of Agricultural Engineering; Elder, Church of Scotland, since 1966. Recreations: walking; hill-walking. Address: Clathybeg, Gask, Crieff, Perthshire, PH7 3PH; T.-0738 73 213.

Kinnaird, Alison, MA, FGE. Glass Engraver and Artist; Clarsach Player; b. 30.4.49, Edinburgh; m., Robin Morton; 1 s.; 1 d. Educ. George Watson's Ladies College; Edinburgh University. Freelance glass artist, since 1971; exhibitions in Edinburgh, 1978, 1981, 1985, in London, 1988; work in many public and private collections; professional musician, since 1970; has produced three LPs as well as film and TV music; served on Council, Scottish Craft Centre, 1974-76; Council, SSWA, 1975-76; Member, BBC Scottish Music Advisory Committee, 1981-84; Member, BBC Broadcasting Council for Scotland, 1984-88; awarded SDA/CCC Craft Fellowship, 1980; Glass-Sellers of London Award, 1987. Recreations: children; cooking; garden. Address: (h.) Shillinghill, Temple, Midlothian, EH23 4SH; T.-Temple 328.

Kinninmont, Tom, MA, PhD. Television Drama Producer, BBC Scotland, since 1982; Chairman, Scottish Youth Theatre, since 1981; Trustee, Scottish Film Training Trust, since 1986; Member, Advisory Committee, Glasgow European City of Culture 1990; Playwright; b. 8.6.50, Irvine; m., Kate; 1 d. Educ. Irvine Royal Academy; Glasgow University; Cornell University, New York. Publishing Research Fellow, National Library of Scotland, 1976-78; Radio Drama Producer, BBC, 1978-82. Vice-Chairman, Scottish Society of Playwrights, 1977-81; author of plays: The Provost, 1977, Britannica, 1978, Second Thoughts, 1982, Identical Twins, 1984. Recreations: family life; reading; writing; cinema; theatre. Address: (b.) BBC, Queen Margaret Drive, Glasgow; T.-041-339 8844.

Kinnis, William Kay Brewster, MA, BL, PhD, DPA. Solicitor and Notary Public; Senior Partner, Miller Jackson, Solicitors, Lenzie, since 1982; Partner, Murdoch Jackson, Solicitors, Glasgow, since 1963 (Senior Partner, since 1987); b. 5.1.33, St. Andrews; m., Agnes Inglis Erskine, MA; 2 d. Educ. Hamilton Academy; Glasgow University; London University (External). Partner: MacArthur Stewart & Orr, Solicitors, Oban and Lochgilphead, 1959-62; Town Clerk and Burgh Chamberlain, Lochgilphead, 1960-62; Council Member, Royal Faculty of Procurators, 1980-83; Governor, Baillie's Institution, since 1983. Choral Scholar, Glasgow University, 1954-58; Choirmaster, Lochgilphead Parish Church, 1959-62; Reader, Church of Scotland, since 1960. Recreations: choral singing; swimming; reading; travel. Address: (b.) 10 Woodside Place, Glasgow, G3 7QJ; T.-041-332 9207.

Kinross, Lord (Christopher Patrick Balfour), LLB, WS. Solicitor, since 1975; b. 1.10.49, Edinburgh; m., Susan Jane Pitman; 2 s. Educ. Eton College; Edinburgh University. Honorary Treasurer: British Digestive Foundation Appeal for Scotland; James IV Association of Surgeons. Recreation: pistol, rifle and shotgun shooting; deer stalking; military vehicle restoration. Address: (b.) 16 Charlotte Square, Edinburgh; T.-031-225 8585.

Kintore, 12th Earl of (James Ian Keith), DL, CEng, AIStructE. Chief of Clan Keith; b. 25.7.08, Edinburgh; m., Delia Virginia Georgina Loyd; 2 s.; 1 d. Educ. Eton College; Royal School of Mines, London. UK Delegate to Council of Europe and Western European Union, 1954-64; Member, Grampian Regional Council, 1974-78; Commissioner for Income Tax; Past Chairman, Scottish-American Community Relations Committee, RAF, Edzell; Member, Queen's Bodyguard for Scotland (Royal Company of Archers), since 1932. Recreations: shooting; fishing; sailing; travel. Address: (h.) Glenton House, Rickarton, Stonehaven, AB3 2TD; T.-0569 63071.

Kirby, Professor Gordon William, MA, PhD, ScD, CChem, FRSC, FRSE. Regius Professor of Chemistry, Glasgow University, since 1972; b. 20.6.34, Wallasey; 2 s. Educ. Liverpool Institute High School; Liverpool Technical College; Gonville and Caius College, Cambridge. Imperial College, London: 1851 Exhibition Senior Studentship, 1958-60, Assistant Lecturer, 1960-61, Lecturer, 1961-67; Professor of Organic Chemistry, Loughborough University of Technology, 1967-72. Corday-Morgan Medal and Prize, Royal Society of Chemistry, 1969; Tilden Lectureship, Royal Society of Chemistry, 1974-75. Recreation: hill-walking. Address: (b.) Department of Chemistry, Glasgow University, Glasgow, G12 8QQ; T.-041-339 8855, Ext. 416/417.

Kirk, David, MA, BM, BCh, DM, FRCS. Consultant Urological Surgeon, Greater Glasgow Health Board, since 1982; Honorary Clinical Lecturer, Glasgow University, since 1984; b. 26.5.43, Bradford; m., Gillian Mary Wroot; 1 s.; 2 d. Educ. King Edwards School, Birmingham; Balliol College, Oxford; Oxford University Clinical Medical School. Resident House Physician and House Surgeon, Radcliffe Infirmary, Oxford; University

Demonstrator, Oxford; clinical surgical posts, Oxford and Bristol; surgical Registrar appointment, Sheffield; academic surgical research, Sheffield University; Senior Registrar in General Surgery, then in Urology, Bristol. Chairman (former Treasurer/Secretary), Scottish Urological Oncology Group; Council Member, Urology Section, Royal Society of Medicine, 1984-87. Recreation: skiing; hill-walking; classical music. Address: (h.) Woodend, Prospect Road, Dullatur, Glasgow, G68 0AN; T.-0236 720778.

Kirk, Gordon, MA, MEd. Principal, Moray House College of Education, since 1981; Chairman, Educational Broadcasting Council, Scotland, since 1985; b. 8.5.38, Dunfermline; m., Jane D. Murdoch; 1 s.; 1 d. Educ. Camphill Secondary School, Paisley; Glasgow University. Lecturer in Education, Aberdeen University, 1965-74; Head, Education Department, Jordanhill College of Education, 1974-81; Member, Munn Committee on the Curriculum of the Secondary School, 1974-77; Member: General Teaching Council for Scotland, since 1984, Consultative Committee on the Curriculum, since 1984, Council for National Academic Awards, since 1979; Chairman, Scottish Council for Research in Education, since 1984; Publications: Scottish Education Looks Ahead (Assistant Editor), 1969; Curriculum and Assessment in the Scottish Secondary School, 1982; Moray House and Professional Education (Editor), 1985; The Core Curriculum, 1986; Teacher Education and Professional Development, 1988. Recreations: walking; golf; bridge. Address: (h.) Craigroyston, Broadgait, Gullane, East Lothian; T.-0620 843299.

Kirk, James Foster, BSc. Rector, Tain Royal Academy, since 1979; b. 31.8.41, Bellshill; m., Margo McFarlane; 1 s.; 1 d. Educ. Hamilton Academy; Glasgow University. Entered teaching, 1963; promoted to Principal Teacher of Science, then Principal Teacher of Guidance, then Assistant Rector; moved from Lanarkshire to Highlands, 1975. Recreations: gardening; wine-making; badminton. Address: (h.) The Barn House, Delny, Invergordon, Ross-shire; T.-Kildary 2564.

Kirkbride, George, CEng, FICE, FIHTE, FIBM. Director of Roads, Grampian Regional Council, since 1983; b. 26.5.33, Willington; 1 s.; 2 d. Educ. Aireborough Grammar School; Bradford Technical College. Pupil, Aireborough Urban District Council, 1949-54; Senior Engineer, Bradford Corporation, 1956-59; Senior Engineer, then Chief Assistant, Crewe Borough, 1959-66; Principal Engineer, then Project Coordinator, Wolverhampton Borough, 1966-72; Depute City Engineer, Dundee City, 1972-75; Regional Roads Engineer, Fife Regional Council, 1975-83. Council Member, FUMPO; Governor, Dundee College of Technology. Recreations: cycling; swimming. Address: (b.) Woodhill House, Ashgrove Road West, Aberdeen; T.-Aberdeen 682222.

Kirkhill, Baron (John Farquharson Smith). Life Peer; b. 7.5.30; m.; 1 step-d. Educ. Robert Gordon's College, Aberdeen. Lord Provost, Aberdeen, 1971-75; Minister of State, Scottish Office, 1975-78; Chairman, North of Scotland Hydro-Electric Board, 1979-82; Hon. LLD, Aberdeen, 1974.

Kirkpatrick, Alastair Elliot, MB, ChB, DMRD, FFR, FRCR, FRCSEdin. Consultant Radiologist in Administrative Charge, Royal Infirmary, Edinburgh, since 1986; Director of Radiology, Lothians Breast Screening Programme, since 1988; Consultant Radiologist, Edinburgh Breast Screening Project, since 1978; b. 7.2.40, West Kirby. Educ. Calday Grange County Grammar School; Edinburgh University. House Officer appointments, Royal Infirmary, Edinburgh, and Northern Hospital, Dunfermline, 1964-65; trained in radiology, Royal Infirmary, Edinburgh, 1966-68; junior staff appointments, Western General Hospital and Royal Infirmary, Edinburgh, 1968-72; Staff Radiologist, Toronto General Hospital, 1972-73; Consultant Radiologist, Royal Infirmary and Longmore Hospitals, Edinburgh, from 1973. Director, Scottish Aircraft Collection Trust. Recreations: gardening; Bonsai; radio-modelling. Address: (b.) Department of Radiology, Royal Infirmary, Edinburgh; T.-031-229 2477.

Kirkpatrick, Ian Denbeigh, MA, LLB, WS, NP. Solicitor; b. 15.12.40, Jedburgh; m., Jean S.; 2 s.; 2 d. Educ. Jedburgh Grammar School; Edinburgh Academy; Edinburgh University. Partner: Turnbull Simson & Sturrock, WS, Jedburgh, P. & J. Stormonth Darling, WS, Kelso, J.D. Clark & Allan, WS, Duns; Reporter, Roxburgh Children's Panel, 1970-75; Member, Council, Law Society of Scotland, 1982-88; Hon. Vice-President and former Captain, Jed-Forest RFC; former Captain, Minto GC. Recreations: reading; golf; watching rugby. Address: (h.) Folly Cottage, Minto, Hawick; T.-0450 87 465.

Kirkwood, Archy, BSc, NP. MP (Social and Liberal Democrat), Roxburgh and Berwickshire, since 1983; b. 22.4.46, Glasgow; m., Rosemary; 1 s.; 1 d. Educ. Cranhill School; Heriot-Watt University. Former Personal Assistant to Rt. Hon. David Steel (qv); Solicitor. Recreation: music. Address: (b.) House of Commons, London, SW1A OAA; T.-01-219 3000.

Kirkwood, Colin Bennie. Publishing Director, John Bartholomew & Son Ltd., since 1986; b. 6.12.51, Glasgow; m., Isabel Mary Johnstone. Educ. Glasgow Academy; Napier College, Edinburgh. Production Editor, NFER Publishing Company, Windsor, 1972-74; General Books Editor, Blackie & Sons Ltd., Glasgow, 1974-77; joined John Bartholomew & Son Ltd., 1977; Chairman, Scottish Young Publishers Society, 1979; Chairman, Scottish Publishers Association, 1984-86; Board Member, Edinburgh Book Festival, since 1984. Recreations: sailing; walking; skiing; tennis. Address: (h.) 16 Broughton Place, Edinburgh, EH1 3RX; T.-031-556 3312.

Kirkwood, Ralph C., BSc, PhD, FRSE. Reader in Biology, Strathclyde University, since 1981; b. 6.7.33, Glasgow; m., Mair Enid; 3 s. Educ. Jordanhill College School, Glasgow; Glasgow University; University of Wales, Aberystwyth. Lecturer, Botany Department, West of Scotland Agricultural College, 1959-64; Strathclyde University: Lecturer, Biology Department, 1964-72, Senior Lecturer, 1972-81; Governor, West of Scotland Agricultural College. Publication: Herbicides and Plant Growth Regulators (Co-author). Recreations: sailing; photography; natural history; walking. Address: (b.) Department of Bioscience and Biotechnology, Biology Division, Todd Centre, Strathclyde University, Glasgow, G1 1XW; T.-041-552 4400.

Kitchen, John Philip, MA, BMus, PhD (Cantab), FRCO, LRAM. Lecturer in Music, Edinburgh University, since 1987 (Lecturer in Music, St. Andrews University, 1976-87); Concert Organist, Harpsichordist, Pianist; b. 27.10.50, Airdrie. Educ. Coatbridge High School; Glasgow University; Cambridge University. Harpsichordist/Organist, Scottish Early Music Consort, Stanesby Recorder Trio, St. Andrews Baroque Trio; BBC and commercial recordings; music reviewer. Recreations: more music; entertaining; doing housework. Address: (b.) Faculty of Music, Alison House, 12 Nicolson Square, Edinburgh, EH8 9DF; T.-031-667 1011.

Klein, Bernat, CBE, FSIAD. Chairman and Managing Director, Bernat Klein Ltd., since 1981; b. 6.11.22, Senta, Yugoslavia; m., Margaret Soper; 1 s.; 2 d. Educ. Senta, Yugoslavia; Bezalel School of Arts and Crafts, Jerusalem; Leeds University. Designer: Tootal, Broadhurst, Lee, 1948-49, Munrospun, Edinburgh, 1949-51; Chairman and Managing Director, Colourcraft, 1952-62; Managing Director, Bernat Klein Ltd., 1962-66; Chairman and Managing Director, Bernat Klein Design Ltd., 1966-81. Member, Design Council, 1962-68; Member, Royal Fine Art Commission for Scotland, 1981-87. Publications: Eye for Colour, 1965; Design Matters, 1975. Recreations: tennis; reading. Address: High Sunderland, Galashiels; T.-0750 20730.

Kleinpoppen, Professor Hans, DipPhys, Dr re nat & habil, FRSE. Professor of Experimental Physics, Stirling University, since 1968; b. 30.9.28, Duisburg, Germany. Educ. Giessen University; Heidelberg University; Tubingen University. Visiting Fellow, Colorado University, 1967; Visiting Associate Professor, Columbia University, New York, 1968; Stirling University: Head, Physics Department, 1970-72, Director, Institute of Atomic Physics, 1975-81. Publication: Physics of Atoms and Molecules (Series Editor). Address: (b.) Atomic and Molecular Physics Department, Stirling University, Stirling.

Klopper, Professor Arnold, MB, ChB, MD, PhD, FRCOG. Professor of Reproductive Endocrinology, Aberdeen University, 1976-87; Consultant Obstetrician and Gynaecologist, since 1960; b. 8.2.22, Ventersburg, South Africa; m., Mary Katherine Turvey. Educ. Brebner College, Bloemfontein, South Africa; Witwatersrand University, Johannesburg. Hospital residency appointments, Johannesburg and London; Clinical Research Fellow, MRC, Guy's Hospital, and Clinical Endocrinology Research Unit, Edinburgh; appointed to permanent senior scientific staff, MRC, Obstetric Medicine Research Unit, Aberdeen, 1958; Aberdeen University: Senior Lecturer, 1966, Reader, 1972. Honorary Fellow, National Obstetrical Societies, USA, Italy, Finland and Singapore. Publications: Fetus and Placenta; Placental Proteins. Recreations: fishing; shooting; training dogs; watching other people work. Address: (b.) Department of Obstetrics and Gynaecology, Royal Infirmary, Aberdeen; T.-0224 681818, Ext. 3323.

Knight, Alanna, FSA Scot. Novelist; b. Co. Durham; m., Alistair Knight; 2 s. Educ. Jesmond High School. Writing career began, 1965; novels: Legend of the Loch, 1969 (RNA First Novel Award), The October Witch, 1971, This Outward Angel, 1971, Castle Clodha, 1972, Lament for Lost Lovers, 1972, The White Rose, 1974, A Stranger Came By, 1974, The Wicked Wynsleys, 1977; historical novels: The Passionate Kindness, 1974, A Drink for the Bridge, 1976, The Black Duchess, 1980, Castle of Foxes, 1981, Colla's Children, 1982, The Clan, 1985; Estella, 1986; Enter Second Murderer, 1988; plays: The Private Life of R.L.S., 1973, Girl on an Empty Swing, 1977; non-fiction: The Robert Louis Stevenson Treasury, 1985; RLS in the South Seas, 1986; radio short stories, plays and documentaries; Lecturer in Creative Writing, WEA, 1971-75; Organiser, Meet The Author, Aberdeen, 1973-75; Committee Member: Society of Authors of Scotland, 1972-84; Scottish PEN, 1972-82; Aberdeen Writers' Workshop (Founder and Chairman). Recreations: walking; reading; creative knitting. Address: (h.) 24 March Hall Crescent, Edinburgh, EH16 5HL; T.-031-667 5230.

Knight, Joan, OBE. Artistic Director, Perth Theatre, since 1968; b. 27.9.24, Walton-Le-Dale, Lancashire. Educ. Lark Hill Convent School. Trained, Bristol Old Vic Theatre School; Director and Administrator, Castle Theatre, Farnham, five years; Director, Ludlow Festival, three years; Director of Productions, Pitlochry Festival Theatre, two years; freelance productions for Bristol Old Vic, Birmingham Repertory, Nottingham Playhouse, Royal Lyceum, Edinburgh, Traverse Theatre, Yvonne Arnaud Theatre, Scottish Theatre Company, etc.; directed The Mousetrap, London; Member, Scottish Arts Council (Chairman, Dance and Mime Committee); Governor, Queen Margaret College, Edinburgh. Recreations: cooking; swimming; walking. Address: (b.) Perth Theatre, High Street, Paisley.

Knill-Jones, Robin Peter, MA, MB, BChir, MSc, DPH, FRCP, MFCM. Senior Lecturer in Clinical Epidemiology, Glasgow University, since 1979; Honorary Community Medicine Specialist, Greater Glasgow Health Board, since 1984; b. 26.4.40, Freshwater; m., Jennifer Gillian Sykes; 3 d. Educ. Malvern College; Cambridge University; St. Bartholomew's Hospital, London. Research Registrar in Medicine, Liver Unit, King's College Hospital, London; Research Fellow, Department of Medicine, Glasgow University; Honorary Senior Registar, Department of Medicine, Western Infirmary, Glasgow, 1973-79; Medical Director, Glasgow People's Marathon; President, European Society for Medical Decision Making. Recreations: unmanaged countryside; microlepidoptera; not smoking; occasional sailing and skiing. Address: (b.) University Department of Community Medicine, 2 Lilybank Gardens, Glasgow, G12 8QQ; T.-041-330 5010.

Knops, Professor Robin John, BSc, PhD, FRSE. Professor of Mathematics, Heriot-Watt University, Edinburgh, since 1971 (Vice Principal, since 1988); b. 30.12.32, London; m., Margaret; 4 s.; 2 d. Educ. Nottingham University. Nottingham University: Assistant Lecturer in Mathematics, 1956-59, Lecturer in Mathematics, 1959-62; Newcastle-upon-Tyne University: Lecturer in Applied Mathematics, 1962-68, Reader in Continuum Mechanics, 1968-71; Head, Department of Mathematics, Heriot-Watt University, 1971-83; Visiting Professor: Cornell University, 1967 and 1968; University of California, Berkeley, 1968; Pisa University, 1974; Ecole Polytechnique Federale Lausanne, Switzerland, 1980; Royal Society of Edinburgh: Council Member, since 1982, Executive Committee Member, 1982-86, Meetings Secretary, 1982-87, Chief Executive Editor, Proceedings A, 1982-87, Curator, since 1987; President, Edinburgh Mathematical Society, 1974-75; Member, Executive Committee, International Society for the Interaction of Mechanics and Mathematics, 1980-84. Publications: Uniqueness Theories in Linear Elasticity (Co-author), 1971; Theory of Elastic Stability (Co-author), 1973. Recreations: walking; reading. Address: (b.) Department of Mathematics, Heriot-Watt University, Edinburgh, EH14 4AS; T.-031-449 5111.

Knowlton, Richard James, CBE (1983), QFSM, FIFireE, FBIM. HM Chief Inspector of Fire Services, Scotland, since 1984; b. 2.1.28, Southampton; m., Pamela V.; 1 s. Educ. Bishop Wordsworth's School, Salisbury. 42 Commando, Royal Marines, 1945; Fireman, Southampton Fire Brigade, 1948; Station Officer, Worcester City and County, 1959; London Fire Brigade: Assistant Divisional Officer, 1963, Divisional Commander, 1967; Firemaster: South Western Scotland, 1971, Strathclyde, 1975; Chairman, London Branch, Institution of Fire Engineers, 1969; awarded Winston Churchill Fellowship, 1969; UK President, Chief and Assistant Chief Fire Officers Association, 1980; UK Chairman, Fire Services National Benevolent Fund, 1980; British Representative, Council, European Association of Professional Fire Officers, 1979-85; President, Scottish District Fire Service Sports and Athletics Association, 1985; awarded Queen's Fire Service Medal, 1977. Address: (b.) St. Andrew's House, Edinburgh, EH1 3DE; T.-031-244 2342.

Knox, Col. Bryce Muir, MC (and Bar), CStJ, TD, BA (Cantab). Lord Lieutenant, Ayr and Arran, since 1974; b. 4.4.16, Edinburgh; m., Patricia Mary Dunsmuir; 1 s.; 1 d. Educ. Stowe; Trinity College, Cambridge. County of Ayr: Deputy Lieutenant, 1953, Vice Lieutenant, 1970-74; Chairman, W. & J. Knox Ltd., Kilbirnie, 1970-78; Vice-Chairman, Lindustries Ltd., 1979 (Director, 1953-79); served with Ayrshire (ECO) Yeomanry, 1939-45, North Africa and Italy (CO, 1953-56, Hon. Col., 1960-71); Honorary Colonel, Ayrshire Yeomanry Squadron, Queen's Own Yeomanry, 1971-77; President, Lowland TA & VR, 1978-83; Member, Queen's Bodyguard for Scotland (Royal Company of Archers). Publications: brief historical notes of the Ayrshire Yeomanry; History of the Eglinton Hunt. Recreation: country sports. Address: (h.) Martnaham Lodge, by Ayr; T.-Dalrymple 204.

Knox, Professor James David Edgar, MD, FRCPEdin, FRCGP. Professor and Head, Department of General Practice, Dundee University, since 1970; NHS Principal, Medical School Teaching Practice, Westgate Health Centre, Dundee, since 1979; b. 12.3.27, Edinburgh; m., Catherine Mary Bell; 1 s.; 1 d. Educ. George Watson's College, Edinburgh; Edinburgh University. Medical Officer, RAF Medical Branch, 1950-55; Registrar posts, Royal Infirmary and Northern General Hospital, Edinburgh, 1955-60; Principal, NHS general practice, West Granton Medical Group, Edinburgh, 1963-70. Member, Professional and Linguistic Assessment Board, GMC. Publication: Presentations in Primary Care, 1985. Recreations: fishing; music. Address: (h.) 369 Blackness Road, Dundee; T.-0382 67635.

Knox, John, RSA, RGI, RSW. Head of Painting Studios, Glasgow School of Art, since 1981; b. 16.12.36; m.; 1 s.; 1 d. Educ. Lenzie Academy; Glasgow School of Art. Staff, Duncan of Jordanstone College of Art, Dundee, 1965-81; work in several permanent collections; Member, Scottish Arts Council, 1974-79; Member, Board of Trustees, National Galleries of Scotland, 1982-87.

Knox, Professor John Henderson, BSc, PhD, DSc, FRSC, CChem, FRSE, FRS. Director, Wolfson Liquid Chromatography Unit, Edinburgh University, since 1972 (Emeritus Professor of Physical Chemistry and Honorary Fellow since 1984); b. 21.10.27, Edinburgh; m., Josephine Anne Wissler; 4 s. Educ. George Watson's Boys College, Edinburgh; Edinburgh University; Cambridge University. Edinburgh University: Lecturer, 1953-66, Reader, 1966-74, Professor, 1974-84. Recreations: skiing; hill-walking; sailing. Address: (h.) 67 Morningside Park, Edinburgh; T.-031-447 5057.

Knox, Robert, MA, LLB, WS. Senior Partner, Boyd, Jameson & Young WS, Edinburgh, since 1983; Solicitor, since 1959, Partner, since 1962; Solicitor to Ministry of Defence (Army) in Scotland, since 1980; Honorary Consul for Belgium in Edinburgh, since 1982; b. 23.5.35, Paisley; m., Jill Mackness; 2 s.; 1 d. Educ. Paisley Grammar School; Glasgow University; Manchester University; Edinburgh University. Member, Lord Maxwell's Committee on Civil Jurisdiction and Enforcement. Recreations: gardening; photography; foreign travel; music. Address: (b.) 89 Constitution Street, Leith, Edinburgh; T.-031-554 3333.

Knox, William. Author and Journalist; b. 20.2.28, Glasgow; m., Myra Ann McKill; 1 s.; 2 d. Educ. Eastwood School. Deputy News Editor, Evening News, Glasgow, 1957; Scottish Editor, Kemsley Newspapers, Glasgow, 1957-60; News Editor, Scottish Television, 1960-62; Freelance Author and Broadcaster, since 1962; author of about 50 books, including novels of crime, sea and adventure; awarded Police Review Award for best novel of British police procedures, 1987 (The Crossfire Killings); Presenter Crime Desk, STV, since 1977; William Knox Collection established Boston University, USA; Past President and Honorary Member, Association of Scottish Motoring Writers; former Member, Scottish Committee, Society of Authors; Past President, Eastwood Rotary Club;

Honorary Editor, Scottish Lifeboat, RNLI. Recreations: motoring; photography; dogs. Address: (h.) 55 Newtonlea Avenue, Newton Mearns, Glasgow, G77 5QF.

Konstam, Peter George, OBE, MD (Frankfurt), FRCSEdin. Honorary Sheriff, Orkney Islands; b. 19.4.08, Frankfurt-on-Main, Germany; m., Dr. Sheila Ritchie; 1 s. Educ. Lessing Gymnasium, Frankfurt; Berlin University; Frankfurt University. Senior Registrar to Professor of Surgery, Aberdeen University; Major, RAMC; Associate Professor of Surgery, Ibadan University; Consultant Surgeon, Orkney Hospitals (retired, 1974). Recreations: piano playing; reading; gardening. Address: (h.) Thule, St. Ola, Orkney Isles; T.-Kirkwall 2821.

Krajewski, Andrew Stephen, BSc, MB, ChB, PhD, MRCPath. Senior Lecturer in Pathology, Edinburgh University, since 1983; Honorary Consultant Pathologist, Lothian Health Board, since 1983; b. 28.11.51, Bishops Stortford; 2 s. Educ. Hertford Grammar School; Edinburgh University. Edinburgh University: Lecturer in Pathology, 1975-82, MRC Research Fellow, 1978-81. Address: (h.) 11 Dundas Street, Edinburgh, EH4.

Kreitman, Norman, FRCPsych, FRCPEdin, MD. Director, MRC Unit for Epidemiological Studies in Psychiatry, since 1971; Honorary Professor, Department of Psychiatry, Edinburgh University, since 1986; b. 5.7.27, London; m., Suzanne; 1 s.; 1 d. Educ. King's College, London; Westminster Hospital. Recreations: literature; angling. Address: (h.) 24 Lauder Road, Edinburgh, EH9 2JF; T.-031-667 4346.

Kuenssberg, Nicholas Christopher D., BA (Hons) (Oxon), FCIS, FBIM. Director, Coats Viyella Plc, since 1986; Chairman, Dynacast International Ltd., since 1978; Non-Executive Director, South of Scotland Electricity Board, since 1984; Member, West of Scotland Board, Bank of Scotland, 1984-88; Director, Standard Life Assurance Company, since 1988; Visiting Fellow, 1985-87, Visiting Professor since 1988, Strathclyde Business School; b. 28.10.42, Edinburgh; m., Sally Robertson; 1 s.; 2 d. Educ. Edinburgh Academy; Wadham College, Oxford. Worked overseas, 1964-78; appointed Director, J. & P. Coats Ltd., 1978. Recreations: squash; languages; opera; travel; printing/publishing. Address: (b.) Coats Viyella Plc, 155 St. Vincent Street, Glasgow, G2 5PA; T.-041-221 8711.

Kyle, James, DSc, MCh, FRCS. Consultant Surgeon, Aberdeen Royal Infirmary, since 1959; Chairman, Representative Body, British Medical Association, since 1984; Chairman, Scottish Joint Consultants Committee, since 1984; b. 26.3.25, Ballymena, Northern Ireland; m., Dorothy Elizabeth Galbraith; 2 d. Educ. Ballymena Academy; Queen's University, Belfast. Scholarship to Mayo Clinic, USA, 1950; Tutor in Surgery, Royal Victoria Hospital, Belfast, 1952; Lecturer in Surgery, Liverpool University, 1957; Senior Lecturer in Surgery, Aberdeen University, 1959-60. Member, Grampian Health Board, 1973-77; Chairman, Scottish Committee for Hospital Medical Services, 1976-79; elected Member, General Medical Council, since 1979. Publications: Peptic Ulcer; Pye's Surgical Handicraft; Crohn's Disease; Scientific Foundations of Surgery. Recreations: Fellow, Royal Philatelic Society, London; licensed radio amateur, GM4 CHX. Address: (h.) Grianan, 74 Rubislaw Den North, Aberdeen, AB2 4AN; T.-Aberdeen 317966.

Kyle, Kenneth Francis, MB, ChB, BAO, MCh (Hons), FRCS, FRCSI. Consultant Urologist, Western Infirmary, Glasgow; b. 19.8.34, Belfast; m., Barbara M. Wilson; 1 s.; 1 d. Educ. Coleraine Academical Institution; Queen's University, Belfast. Previously Urologist, Royal Beatson Memorial Hospital and Stonehouse Hospital; Founder Renal Transplantation Surgeon, Western Infirmary, Glasgow, 1968; first world percutaneous renal transplant pyelolysis, 1984; Honorary Lecturer in Urology, Glasgow University. Publication: Surgery (Contributor). Recreations: golf; hill-walking; travelling; wine-drinking; music; opera. Address: (h.) 13 Campsie View Drive, Blanefield, Glasgow, G63 9JE; T.-Blanefield 70522.

Kyle, Robert, MBE, DL, NP. Honorary Sheriff, Strathclyde, at Airdrie; Deputy Lieutenant, County of Dunbarton; b. 28.3.19, Strathaven; m., Pauline Watson; 3 s.; 1 d. Educ. Strathaven Academy; Hamilton Academy; Glasgow University. War service, six years; Legal Assistant, Kilmarnock Town Council, 1946-48; Depute Town Clerk, Airdrie Town Council, 1948-52; Town Clerk, Kirkintilloch Town Council, 1952-68; Town Clerk and Manager, Cumbernauld Town Council, 1968-74; Chief Executive, Cumbernauld and Kilsyth District Council, 1974-81. Past President, Dumbartonshire Golf Union. Recreations: golf; angling. Address: (h.) 23 Middlemuir Road, Lenzie, Glasgow, G66 4NA; T.-041-776 1861.

Kynoch, Gordon Bryson, CBE, TD, DL, JP. Director, G. & G. Kynoch plc, Keith, since 1922 (former Managing Director and Chairman); Honorary Sheriff, County of Banff, since 1950; b. 8.5.04, Keith; m., Nesta Alicia Janet Thora; 2 s. (inc. 1 deceased); 3 d. Educ. Cargilfield, Edinburgh; Trinity College, Glenalmond. Served Second World War with 14th Army and Gen. HQ India Command; Lt.-Col. (Ret.), Gordon Highlanders (TA); President, Keith and District Branch, Royal British Legion. Address: (h.) Skara Brae, Broomhill Road, Keith, Banffshire; T.-Keith 2507.

L

Lacey, James Binnie, MA (Hons). Rector, Carnoustie High School, since 1973; b. 16.5.36, Kirkliston, West Lothian; m., Margot Elizabeth Munro; 2 d. Educ. Royal High School, Edinburgh; Edinburgh University. Principal Teacher of Geography: St. Mary's Academy, Bathgate, 1963-67, Forrester Secondary School, Edinburgh, 1967-71; Assistant Rector, Perth High School,

1971-72. Captain, Carnoustie Mercantile Golf Club, 1974-76; Member, Board of Directors, Dundee Repertory Theatre, 1974-78; Member, Tayside Education Committee, 1975-79; Governor, Dundee College of Education, 1979-83; Member, SCCTE, 1982-84; Honorary President, Carnoustie HSFP Rugby Club, since 1978. Recreations: rugby; golf; curling; reading. Address: (b.) Carnoustie High School, Shanwell Road, Carnoustie, Angus; T.-0241 52601.

Lacome, Myer, MSCD, MSTD, FRSA, MInstPkg. Principal, College of Art, Dundee, since 1979 (Head of Design School, since 1962); b. 13.11.27, Liverpool; m., Jacci; 1 s.; 2 d. Educ. Liverpool College of Art. National Service, RAF, 1945-47; Design Consultant: New York, 1947-49, London, 1950-59; Senior Lecturer in 3D Design; Consultant Designer to national companies and regional authorities, since 1960; has served on Design Council, SIAD, Crafts Council, Scottish Film Council, CNAA and various national visual arts and education committees; Chairman, Scottish Arts Council Fine Art Committee; Member, 20th Century Consultative Committee, Royal Scottish Museum. Recreation: self-confessed culture vulture. Address: (b.) College of Art, Perth Road, Dundee; T.-0382 23261.

Lacy, Rev. David William, BA, BD. Minister, Knightswood: St Margaret's, since 1977; b. 26.4.52, Inverness; m., Joan Stewart Robertson; 1 s.; 1 d. Educ. Aberdeen Grammar School; High School of Glasgow; Strathclyde University; Glasgow University. Assistant Minister, St. George's West, Edinburgh, 1975-77. Convener, Glasgow Presbytery Committee on Communications, 1979-84. Recreations: music; golf; swimming. Address: 26 Airthrey Avenue, Glasgow, G14 9LJ; T.-041-959 1094.

Laidlaw, Basil Henderson, BSc, MSc, AH-WC, FIMA, MBCS. Vice Principal, Bell College of Technology, Hamilton, since 1986; b. 10.6.40, Edinburgh; m., Catherine Alexandra Currie; 2 d. Educ. Kirkcaldy High School; Edinburgh University; Heriot-Watt University; St. Andrews University. Lecturer, Kirkcaldy Technical College, 1968-72; Senior Lecturer, then Head, Department of Mathematics and Computing, Bell College of Technology, 1972-86. Recreations: chess; rugby (spectator); football; films; theatre. Address: (b.) Almada Street, Hamilton, ML3 0JB; T.-0698 283100.

Laidlaw, Professor James Cameron, MA, PhD. Professor of French, Aberdeen University, since 1975 (Vice-Principal, 1984-86); b. 3.3.37, Ecclefechan; m., Elizabeth Fernie Bosomworth; 1 s.; 2 d. Educ. George Watson's College, Edinburgh; Edinburgh University; Trinity Hall, Cambridge. Research Fellow, Trinity Hall, Cambridge, 1961-63; Lecturer in Medieval French, Queen's University, Belfast, 1963-65; University Assistant Lecturer (from 1969 University Lecturer) in French, and Fellow, Trinity Hall, Cambridge, 1965-74; Visiting Fellow, Gonville and Caius College, Cambridge, 1986-87. Member Arts Sub-Committee, University Grants Committee; Honorary Secretary, Modern Humanities Research Association, 1961-67. Publications: The Future of the Modern Humanities (Editor), 1969; The Poetical Works of Alain Chartier, 1974. Recreations: walking; cycling. Address: (h.) 2 The Chanonry, Old Aberdeen, Aberdeen, AB2 1RP; T.-Aberdeen 482875.

Laing, Rev. David Doig. Secretary, Urban/Industrial Mission, Congregational Union of Scotland, since 1971; Member, Strathclyde Regional Council, since 1978; b. 29.11.36, Edinburgh; m., Ruth; 2 s.; 1 d. Educ. Norton Park Junior Secondary School, Edinburgh; Glasgow University; Scottish Congregational College, Edinburgh. Minister, Govan Congregational Church, 1968-72; Community Minister, Easterhouse, since 1972; Founder Member, Glasgow Industrial Mission Team, 1970; chaired working party on physically handicapped, 1980-82; Chaplain, Glasgow Tigers Speedway Team; Chairman, COSLA Social Work Committee; Chairman, Strathclyde Regional Social Work Committee. Recreations: Citizens' Theatre; Scottish Ballet; science fiction; soccer (season ticket holder, Hibernian); speedway racing. Address: 71 Whirlow Road, Glasow, G69 6QE; T.-041-771 1746.

Laing, Professor Ernest William, MA, PhD, FInstP, FRSE. Titular Professor, Department of Physics and Astronomy, and Dean, Faculty of Science, Glasgow University; b. 12.2.31, Braine-Le-Comte, Belgium; m., Olive Jean Guild Melville; 2 s. Educ. John Neilson School, Paisley; Glasgow University. Senior Scientific Officer, UKAEA Harwell, 1957-60; Glasgow University: Lecturer, 1960-66, Senior Lecturer, 1966-76, Reader, 1976-80, Titular Professor, since 1980. Publication: Plasma Physics, 1979. Recreation: music. Address: (b.) Department of Physics and Astronomy, Glasgow University, Glasgow, G12 8QQ; T.-041-330 4464.

Laing, James Findlay, MA (Hons). Under Secretary, Industry Department for Scotland, since 1979; b. 7.11.33, Nairn; m., Christine Joy Canaway; 1 s. Educ. Nairn Academy; Edinburgh University. Assistant Principal and Principal, Scottish Office, 1957-68; Principal, HM Treasury, 1968-71; Assistant Secretary, Scottish Office, 1972-79. Recreations: squash; chess. Address: (b.) New St. Andrew's House, Edinburgh, EH1 3TA; T.-031-244 4609.

Laing, Marshall George, MA, LLB. Solicitor; Honorary Sheriff; b. 31.1.23, Aberdeen; m. Educ. Robert Gordon's College, Aberdeen; Aberdeen University. Legal Assistant: Guild & Guild, WS, Edinburgh, 1949-50, Davidson & Garden, Aberdeen, 1950-55, Wilkinson & Grist, Hong Kong, 1955-59, J.L. Anderson & Co., Cupar, 1959-62; Partner: Craig and Geddes, Dumfries, 1942-76, Symons & MacDonald, Dumfries, since 1976. Recreations: golf; Loreburn Speakers' Club. Address: (h.) 3 Richmond Avenue, Dumfries; T.-Dumfries 53871.

Laird, Alexander Peddie, BL, SSC, NP. Consultant, Bell & Scott, WS, Edinburgh; b. 14.6.24, Edinburgh; m., Elizabeth Anne Melrose; 2 d. Educ. Daniel Stewart's College, Edinburgh; Edinburgh University. Joined Army, 1943; commissioned, Royal Artillery; served with 51 (Highland) Division, 1944, and with 6th Airborne Division, 1944-46, in Europe and Palestine;

served with Air Observation Post, Royal Artillery, 1946-47, in Palestine; demobilised as Captain, 1947; set up in private practice, 1951. Elder, Cramond Kirk (former Session Clerk). Recreations: golf; walking; gardening. Address: (h.) 2 Barnton Avenue, Edinburgh, EH4 6AP.

Laird, Endell Johnston. Editor-in-Chief, Daily Record and Sunday Mail; b. 6.10.33, Forfar; m., June Stanners Keenan; 1 s.; 2 d. Educ. Forfar Academy. Worked for Dundee Courier, Daily Express, Evening Times, Daily Record. Recreations: golf; bridge. Address: Sunday Mail, Anderston Quay, Glasgow, G3 8DA.

Laird, James Steel, MA, LLB. Solicitor; Partner, McGrigor Donald & Co. (now McGrigor Donald) since 1961; b. 6.9.32, Kilmarnock; 2 d. Educ. Prestwick High School; Ayr Academy; Glasgow University. Served legal apprenticeship, McGrigor Donald & Co., from 1952. Chairman, Pollok School Company (Craigholme School); Member, Giffnock and Thornliebank Community Council. Recreation: golf. Address: (h.) 32 Milverton Road, Whitecraigs, Glasgow.

Lamb, Rev. A. Douglas, MA, FSA Scot. Minister, Dalry: St. Margaret's, since 1973; b. 9.11.36, Glasgow; m., Jean A. Beattie; 3 s.; 1 d. Educ. Hermitage School, Helensburgh; Glasgow University and Trinity College; Princeton Theological Seminary. Assistant Minister: 1st Presbyterian Church, Philadelphia, 1963, Airdrie West, 1963-65; Minister, Unst, Shetland, 1965-73. Sometime Secretary, Unst Council of Social Service; Editor, Unst Guide Book; sometime President, Garnock Valley Rotary Club; sometime Moderator: Shetland Presbytery, Ardrossan Presbytery. Recreations: hill-walking; history. Address: St. Margaret's Manse, Dalry, Ayrshire; T.-029 483 2234.

Lamb, Douglas, MB, ChB, FRCSEdin. Consultant Orthopaedic Surgeon, Princess Margaret Rose Orthopaedic Hospital and Royal Infirmary, Edinburgh, since 1954; b. 21.12.21, Edinburgh; b. Joan; 3 s.; 1 d. Educ. Brentwood School; Edinburgh University. Council Member, Royal College of Surgeons, Edinburgh; Editor, The Practice of Hand Surgery. Recreations: gardening; walking. Address: (h.) 16 Corrennie Gardens, Edinburgh, 10; T.-031-447 5866.

Lamb, Professor John, CBE, BSc, MSc, PhD, DSc, FInstP, FAcoustSocAmerica, HonFInstAcoustics, FIEE, FEng, FRSE. James Watt Professor of Electronics and Electrical Engineering, Glasgow University, since 1961; b. 26.9.22, Accrington; m., Margaret May Livesey; 2 s.; 1 d. Educ. Accrington Grammar School; Manchester University. Ministry of Supply, 1943-46; Lecturer, 1946-56, Reader, 1956-61, in Electrical Engineering, Imperial College, London University; Assistant Director, Department of Electrical Engineering, Imperial College, London University, 1958-61; Vice-Principal, Glasgow University, 1977-80; Member, National Electronics Council, UK, 1963-78; Member, Council for National Academic Awards, 1964-70; Chairman, Scottish Industry/University Liaison Committee in Engineering, 1969-71; President, British Society of Rheology, 1970-72; Council Member, Royal Society of Edinburgh, 1980-83, and since 1986; Member, British National Committee for Radio Science, 1983-87; Scientific Adviser, Industry Department for Scotland, since 1987. Recreations: walking; wine-making; music. Address: (h.) 5 Cleveden Crescent, Glasgow, G12 OPD; T.-041-339 2101.

Lamb, Professor Joseph Fairweather, MB, ChB, BSc, PhD, FRCPEdin, FRSE, FRSA. Chandos Professor of Physiology, St. Andrews University, since 1969; Chairman, Save British Science Society, since 1986; Senior Secretary, Physiological Society, 1982-85; b. 18.7.28, Brechin; 5 s.; 1 d. Educ. Brechin High School; Edinburgh University. National Service, 1947-49; House Surgeon, Dumfries Royal Infirmary, 1955-56; House Physician, Eastern General Hospital, Edinburgh, 1956; Research Scholar, then Lecturer, Edinburgh University, 1957-61; Lecturer, then Senior Lecturer, Glasgow University, 1961-69; Editor, Journal of Physiology, 1968-74; Examiner, College of Surgeons of Edinburgh, Glasgow, London; Examiner, Universities of Aberdeen, Dundee, Edinburgh, Bristol, Leeds, Southampton, Lagos, Malaysia, etc. Publication: Essentials of Physiology, 1980. Recreations: boat-building; sailing; amateur radio. Address: (h.) Kenbrae, Millbank, Cupar, KY15 5DP.

Lamb, Colonel Tom Bell Maxwell, OBE, CStJ, MA, FSA (Scot), DL. Retired Colonel, HM Forces; Deputy Lord Lieutenant, Argyll & Bute, since 1987; b. 23.11.18, Lanark; m., Sheina Barclay Dempster; 2 s.; 1 d. Educ. Lanark Secondary School; Heriot-Watt College. Commercial Bank of Scotland, 1935-38; Chartered Bank of India, 1938-39; Regular Officer, Queen's Own Cameron Highlanders, 1940-70; staff, Stirling University, 1970-75; Controller, The Burn, Edzell, 1975-84. Croix de Guerre, 1945; Meritorious Service Decoration (Singapore), 1964; mentioned in Despatches, 1945; Commander of St. John, 1982. Recreation: golf (Member, R. & A.). Address: (h.) Seafield, Kilchattan Bay, Isle of Bute; T.-Kilchattan Bay 682.

Lambert, John, FMS, FBIM, FIIM. Regional Manager Scotland, Chusid Lander, Human Resource Consultants, Glasgow, since 1986; b. 17.4.34, Blyth, Northumberland; m., Constance; 2 d. Educ. Blyth Grammar School; Rutherford College of Technology, Newcastle. Managerial appointments in general management, personnel and management services; Manager, O. & M. Consultancy Services, Co-operative Wholesale Society, 1969-72; Head, Personnel and Management Services, Burgh of Greenock, 1973-75; Director, Personnel and Management Services, Renfrew District Council, 1975-80; General Manager, RTITB, Livingston Motec, 1980-84; Director, Scotland and Northern Ireland, British Institute of Management, 1984-86. Captain, Largs Golf Club, 1984-85; President, Associated Clubs of Clyde, 1986-87. Recreations: golf; photography; music. Address: (h.) 72 Greenock Road, Largs, Ayrshire; T.-0475 672402.

Lambie, Rev. Andrew Elliot, BD. Minister, linked parishes of Carmichael, Covington, Thankerton and Pettinain, since 1985; b. 10.12.26, Glasgow; m., Elizabeth McCulloch Duncan; 2 s.; 1 d. Educ.

Allan Glen's School, Glasgow; Glasgow University and Trinity College. Minister: Linnvale Church, Clydebank, 1957-64, Lerwick and Bressay, Shetland, 1964-80; Clerk, Shetland Presbytery, 1970-78; Associate Minister, Ellon Parish Church, 1980-85. President, Lerwick Choral Society, 1977-80. Recreations: gardening; walking. Address: The Manse, Thankerton, near Biggar, Lanarkshire; T.-Tinto 333.

Lambie, David, BSc (Hons), DipEd, FEIS. MP (Labour), Cunninghame South, since 1970; b. 13.7.25, Saltcoats; m., Netta Merrie; 1 s.; 4 d. Educ. Ardrossan Academy; Glasgow University; Geneva University. Teacher, Glagow Corporation, 1950-70. Secretary, All Party Committee for Energy Studies, since 1980; chaired Select Committee on Scottish Affairs, 1981-87; UK Member, Council of Europe and Western European Union, since 1987. Recreation: watching junior football. Address: (h.) 11 Ivanhoe Drive, Saltcoats, Ayrshire, KA21 6LS; T.-0294 64843.

Lamond, June Rose. Member, Grampian Regional Council, since 1978; Member, Grampian Health Board, 1975-87; b. 12.6.33, Aberdeen; m., James A. Lamond, MP; 3 d. Educ. Aberdeen Demonstration School; Aberdeen College of Commerce. Member, Aberdeen District Council, 1974-77; Director, Grampian Regional Transport Ltd.; Chairperson, Aberdeen Women's Aid. Recreation: tennis. Address: (h.) 15 Belvidere Street, Aberdeen; T.-Aberdeen 638074.

Lamont, Colin C., MA, PhD. Headmaster, Gracemount High School, Edinburgh, since 1983; b. 6.10.44, Glasgow; m.; 2 s. Educ. Robert Gordon's College, Aberdeen; Aberdeen University; Edinburgh University. Teacher, Merchiston Castle School, Edinburgh; Principal Teacher, Robert Gordon's College, Aberdeen; Adviser in English, Renfrew Division, Strathclyde. Address: (b.) Gracemount High School, Lasswade Road, Edinburgh, EH16 6TZ; T.-031-664 7440.

Lamont, Rev. Stewart Jackson, BSc, BD. Minister, Church of Scotland, since 1972; Freelance Journalist and Broadcaster (Religious Affairs Correspondent, Glasgow Herald), since 1980; b. 8.1.47, Broughty Ferry. Educ. Grove Academy, Broughty Ferry; St. Andrews University. General Council Assessor, St. Andrews University Court, 1970-82; Producer, BBC Religious Department, 1972-80; Freelance Radio and Television Presenter and Producer; part-time Minister, Abernyte, 1980-82. Publications: The Third Angle, 1978; Is Anybody There?, 1980; Religion and the Supernatural (Co-author), 1985; Religion Inc. (Scientology), 1986; Scotland 2000 (BBC TV), 1987. Winner, Scottish Schools Debating Competition, 1965; President of the Union, St. Andrews, 1969. Recreations: cooking; music; foreign travel. Address: 3 Doune Quadrant, Glasgow, G20 6DN; T.-041-946 3629.

Lamont-Brown, Raymond, MA, AMIET, MJS, FSA (Scot). Author and Broadcaster; Lecturer, Department of Adult Education, St. Andrews University, since 1978; Founder, Japan Research Projects, since 1965; b. 20.9.39, Horsforth, Leeds; m., Dr. Elizabeth Moira McGregor. Educ. Wheelwright Grammar School, Dewsbury; Bradford Technical College; SOAS; Nihon Daigaku, Japan. Honorary Secretary/Treasurer, Society of Authors in Scotland; Past President, St. Andrews Rotary Club. Publications: 41 published books, including Discovering Fife; Phantoms of the Sea. Address: (h.) 3 Crawford House, 132 North Street, St. Andrews, Fife, KY16 9AF; T.-0334 74897.

Lamprell-Jarrett, Peter Neville, KCSG, KCHS, PPIAAS, FIAS, FFB, FSA(Scot), FRSA. Partner, Archard & Partners, Architects and Surveyors, since 1954; b. 23.6.19, Margate; m., Kathleen Furner; 1 s.; 1 d. Educ. Vernon House Preparatory School; Cliftonville College. Architectural Assistant, LCC (later GLC) Housing Department, 1947-49; Deputy Controller of Works, Land Settlement Association, 1950-54; President, Incorporated Association of Architects and Surveyors, 1967-68; Kt. Commander, Equestrian Order Holy Sepulchre of Jerusalem, 1974; Kt. Commander, Pontifical Order of St. Gregory the Great, 1975; responsible for design of many Catholic schools and churches; Freeman, City of London; Life Vice President, London Caledonian Catholic Association; Past Chairman, Archdiocese of Westminster Catholic Parents and Electors Association. Recreations: painting; walking; fishing; classical music. Address: (h.) Carrick House, Carrick Castle, by Lochgoil, Argyll, PA24 8AF; T.-Lochgoilhead 394.

Lander, Ronald, BSc. Chairman and Managing Director: Scotlander plc, since 1985, Scetlander Ltd., since 1986; Director, Centre for Entrepreneurial Development, Glasgow University, since 1985; b. 5.8.42, Glasgow; m., Elizabeth Stirling; 2 s. Educ. Allan Glen's School; Glasgow University. Chairman and Managing Director, Lander Grayburn & Co. Limited, 1970-83; Deputy Managing Director, Lander Alarm Company (Scotland) Limited, 1975-79; Managing Director, Lander Alarms Limited and Lander Alarms (Scotland) Limited, 1979-85; Chairman, Lander & Jess Limited, 1983-87. Member, CBI Scottish Council, 1977-83 and since 1984; founding Chairman, CBI Scotland's Smaller Firms' Working Group, 1977-80; Chairman, Scottish Fire Prevention Council, 1979-80; Vice-Chairman, CBI Scotland Education and Training Committee, 1986-87; Member: Kincraig Committee (review of parole system and related matters), since 1987, Manpower Services Committee for Scotland (now Training Commission), since 1987; founder Chairman, Local Employer Network (LENS) Scottish Co-ordinating Committee, 1987; Chairman, CBI Scotland Education and Training Committee, since 1987; Director, SCOTVEC, since 1987; Companion IEE, 1986. Address: (b.) 1 Bowmont Gardens, Glasgow, G12 9LR; T.-041-357 1659.

Lang, Lt.-Gen. Sir Derek, KCB (1967), DSO (1944), MC (1941), DL; b. 7.10.13, Guildford; 1 s.; 1 d. Educ. Wellington College; RMC, Sandhurst. Director of Army Training, 1964-66; GOC-in-C, Scottish Command, and Governor of Edinburgh Castle, 1966-69. President, Army Cadet Force Association (Scotland), 1974-86. Recreations: golf; fishing; shooting; music. Address: (h.) Templeland, Kirknewton, Midlothian, EH27 8DJ; T.0506 883211.

Lang, Ian Bruce, OStJ, BA. MP (Conservative) Galloway and Upper Nithsdale, since 1983 (Galloway, 1979-83); Minister of State, Scottish Office, since 1987 (Parliamentary Under Secretary of State, Scottish Office, 1986-87, and at Department of Employment, 1986); b. 27.6.40, Glasgow; m., Sandra Caroline Montgomerie; 2 d. Educ. Lathallan School; Rugby School; Sidney Sussex College, Cambridge. Member, Select Committee on Scottish Affairs, 1979-81; Honorary President, Scottish Young Conservatives, 1982-84; Trustee, Glasgow Savings Bank and West of Scotland TSB, 1969-82; Lord Commissioner of HM Treasury, 1983-86; Scottish Whip, 1981-83; Vice-Chairman, Scottish Conservative Party, 1983-87; Member, Queen's Bodyguard for Scotland (Royal Company of Archers), since 1974; Insurance Broker and Company Director, 1962-81. Address (b.) House of Commons, Westminster, London, SW1A OAA.

Langan, John. National Officer, Association of Scientific, Technical and Managerial Staffs, 1974-85; Member, Employment Appeal Tribunals; Chairman, Industrial and Social Conditions Committee, Scottish Council (Development and Industry); Member, Scottish Industrial Development Advisory Board; b. 30.12.24, Greenock; m., Margaret; 1 d. Educ. St. Columba's High School; James Watt Technical College. Active in trade union affairs since 1947; full-time Officer with Coppersmiths' Union, 1956; joined ASSET as a full-time Officer, 1965; Member, General Council, Scottish Trades Union Congress, since 1976 (Chairman of Congress, 1983-84); has chaired a number of STUC Committees and Sub-Committees; Member, Council of Tribunals for Scotland, since 1988; Member, Board of Governors, Scottish Police College, 1977-81; Chairman, Glasgow District Manpower Services Committee, 1978-82; Member, Scottish Economic Planning Committee, 1979-82; Member: Scottish Anti-Alcohol Unit, Scottish Labour History Society. Recreations: football and cricket (spectating only); golf and bowls (participating). Address: (h.) 8 Margaret Street, Greenock, PA16 8AS; T.-0475 20547.

Langlands, Robert Craig, BSc, BSc (Eng), MSc, CEng, FIEE. Depute Principal, Clydebank College, since 1974; b. 25.5.26, Glasgow; m., Rita Anna Rappo; 2 s. Educ. Hyndland School, Glasgow; Strathclyde University; Glasgow University; London University. College Apprentice, Metropolitan-Vickers Electrical Co. Ltd., Manchester; Teacher, David Dale College, Glasgow; Senior Lecturer in Electrical Engineering, Coatbridge College; Lecturer in Electrical Engineering, Glasgow University; Head, Department of Electrical Engineering, Stow College, Glasgow; Head, Department of Electrical and Electronic Engineering, Glasgow College of Technology. Recreations: Scout Association; radio; music. Address: (h.) 104 Norse Road, Glasgow, G14 9EO; T.-041-959 6892.

Lansdowne, 8th Marquess of (George John Charles Mercer Nairne Petty-Fitzmaurice), PC (1964); b. 27.11.12; m., 1, Barbara Chase (deceased); 2 s.; 1 d.; 1 d. deceased; 2, Polly Carnegie (m. diss.); 3, Gillian Ann Morgan (deceased). Educ. Eton; Christ Church, Oxford. Served Second World War (Major, 1944); Lord-in-Waiting to The Queen, 1957-58; Minister of State for Colonial Affairs, 1962-64, and for Commonwealth Relations, 1963-64; Member, Queen's Bodyguard for Scotland (Royal Company of Archers); Chairman, Victoria League in Scotland, 1952-56. Address: (h.) Meikleour House, Perthshire.

Lappin, Carolyn Anne, MA (Hons). Administrator, Scottish Youth Theatre, since 1984; b. 12.1.61, Glasgow; m., Stephen McGrath. Educ. Smithycroft Secondary School, Glasgow; Glasgow University. Front of House Assistant, Citizens' Theatre, 1982-84. Treasurer, Scottish National Association of Youth Theatre; Treasurer, West Lothian Youth Theatre. Address: (b.) 48 Albany Street, Edinburgh, EH1 3QR; T.-031-557 2224.

Lapsley, Professor Irvine MacLaren, BCom, PhD, CA. Professor of Accountancy, Stirling University, since 1986; Director, Institute of Public Sector Accounting Research, Stirling University, since 1987; b. 28.4.49, Grangemouth; m., Pamela Anne Wright. Educ. Grangemouth High School; Falkirk High School; Edinburgh University. Lecturer, Department of Accounting and Business Method, Edinburgh University, 1974-85; Research Fellow, Centre for Industrial, Economic and Business Research, Warwick University, 1976-78; Visiting Research Fellow, Centre for Industry, Business and Administration, Warwick University, 1983; Arthur Young Fellow in Public Sector Accounting, Stirling University, 1987-88. Member: Accounting Standards Committee's Public Sector Liaison Group; Public Sector Committee, Institute of Chartered Accountants of Scotland. Recreations: swimming; athletics; soccer; rugby. Address: (b.) Department of Accountancy and Business Law, Stirling University, Stirling, FK9 4LA; T.-0786 73171.

Larg, Ian, FCCA, MBIM. Financial Director, North of Scotland Milk Marketing Board, since 1987; b. 12.8.56, Dundee; m., Fiona Margaret. Educ. Morgan Academy, Dundee; Dundee College of Technology. Audit Senior, then Audit Manager, Scott Oswald & Co., CA, Inverness; Group Chief Accountant, A. Tulloch & Sons (Holdings) Ltd., Inverness; Financial Controller, Elbar Industrial PLC, London. Recreations: music; golf; tennis. Address: (h.) Caberfeidh, Braes of Dunvournie, by Culbokie, Ross-shire; T.-034 987 247.

Larkin, Professor Maurice John Milner, MA, PhD. Professor of Modern European History, Edinburgh University, since 1976; b. 12.8.32, Harrow on the Hill; m., Enid Thelma Lowe; 1 s.; 1 d. Educ. St. Philip's Grammar School, Birmingham; Trinity College, Cambridge. Assistant Lecturer, then Lecturer, Glasgow University, 1958-65; Lecturer, then Senior Lecturer, then Reader, Kent University, 1965-76. Publications: Gathering Pace: Continental Europe 1870-1945, 1969; Church and State after the Dreyfus Affair, 1974; Man and Society in Nineteenth-Century Realism, 1977; France since the Popular Front, 1988.

Recreations: bird-watching; music; films. Address: (b.) History Department, Edinburgh University, Edinburgh, EH8 9JY; T.-031-667 1011.

Larner, Professor John Patrick, MA, FRHistA. Titular Professor of History, Glasgow University, since 1979; b. 24.3.30, London; m., Christina Ross (deceased); 2 s. Educ. Finchley Grammar School; New College, Oxford. Rome Medieval Scholar, British School of Rome, 1954-57; Lecturer, Glasgow University, 1957-79. Publications: Lords of Romagna, 1965; Culture and Society in Italy, 1971; Florentine Society 1382-1494, 1972; Italy in the Age of Dante, 1980. Recreations: hill-walking; photography. Address: (b.) Department of Medieval History, The University, Glasgow, G12 8QQ; T.-041-339 8855.

Last, Professor Frederick Thomas, DSc, ARCS, FRSE. Applied Biologist; Honorary Professor, Forestry and Natural Resources, Edinburgh University, since 1972; Visiting Professor, Soil Science, Newcastle upon Tyne University, since 1986; Consultant (Atmospheric Pollution), Commission of the European Communities, since 1986; b. 5.2.28, Wembley; m., Pauline Mary Cope; 2 s. Educ. Haberdashers' Aske's Hampstead School; Imperial College of Science and Technology, London. Rothamsted Experimental Station, Herts, 1950-61; Chief Plant Pathologist to Government of Sudan, 1956-58; Head, Mycology and Bacteriology, Glasshouse Crops Research Institute, Sussex, 1961-69; Visiting Professor, Pennsylvania State University, 1969-70; Member of Directorate, Institute of Terrestrial Ecology, Midlothian, 1970-86; Commissioner, Red Deer Commission, 1981-86. Publications: Tree Physiology and Yield Improvement (Joint Editor), 1976; Land and its Uses, Actual and Potential: An Environmental Appraisal (Joint Editor), 1986. Recreations: gardening; philately; travelling. Address: (h.) Furuly, Seton Mains, Longniddry, East Lothian, EH32 0PG; T.-0875 52102.

Last, Professor Rex William, BA, MA, PhD, FRSA. Professor of Modern Languages, Dundee University, since 1981; b. 30.6.40, Ipswich; m., Oksana S.; 2 s. Educ. Northgate Grammar School, Ipswich; Hull University. Lecturer, Senior Lecturer, Reader in Modern German Literature, Hull University; Honorary Life Member, Association for Literary and Linguistic Computing; Director, Lochee Publications. Publications: books on Hans Arp, Erich Kastner, E.M. Remarque, German Dadaist literature, computer applications in language teaching, study skills. Recreation: flying. Address: (h.) Oak Villa, New Alyth, PH11 8NN; T.-082 83 2154.

Latham, Professor John Derek, JP, MA, DPhil, DLitt (Oxon), FRAS, FSA Scot. Iraq Professor of Arabic and Islamic Studies and Head, Muir Institute, Edinburgh University, since 1982; b. 5.4.27, Wigan; m., Jean Elisabeth Coulstock; 1 s.; 1 d. Educ. Wigan Grammar School; Pembroke College, Oxford. HM Treasury Research Fellow, Oxford, 1950-53; Associate Professor and Curator, Middle East Collections, Hoover Institution, Stanford University, California, 1957-58; Lecturer, then Reader in Arabic, Manchester University, 1958-82; Visiting Fellow, St. Cross College, Oxford, 1975. Examiner, Civil Service Commission, since 1968; Member: Middle East Libraries Committee, since 1967 (Chairman, 1971-79), British Society for Middle Eastern Studies, since 1973 (President, 1985-87), Medieval Latin Dictionary Committee (British Academy), since 1970, Fontes Historiae Africanae Committee (British Academy), since 1970 (Chairman, 1971-79); Member, Advisory Committee, Journal of Semitic Studies, 1976-82; General Editor (Joint) and Contributor, Cambridge History of Arabic Literature, since 1982; Editor: Islamic Quarterly, 1970-74, Bulletin of British Society for Middle Eastern Studies, since 1974; Contributor, Encyclopaedia of Islam, since 1957; Consultant, Supplement to Oxford English Dictionary, since 1984, and New Oxford English Dictionary, since 1985; Trustee, E.J.W. Gibb Memorial, since 1985 (Chairman of Trustees, since 1988). Publications: several books; numerous papers. Recreations: none (for want of time). Address: (b.) Muir Institute, 7-8 Buccleuch Place, Edinburgh, EH3 9LW; T.-031-667 1011.

Lauderdale, Earl of (Patrick Francis Maitland), BA (Hons) (Oxon). Company Director; b. 17.3.11, Walsall; m., Stanka Lozanitch; 2 s.; 2 d. Educ. Lancing College; Brasenose College, Oxford. Journalist, Fleet Street, 1934-39; War Correspondent, Poland, 1939; Balkans/Danubian Correspondent, The Times, 1939-41; War Correspondent, the Pacific, Greece, Yugoslavia, News Chronicle, 1941-43; Foreign Office, 1943-45; Editor, The Fleet Street Letter Service, 1945-51; MP (Conservative), Lanark, 1951-59; Peer, since 1968; Chairman, Lords Energy Committee, 1974-79; Founder/Deputy Chairman, Parliamentary Group for Energy Studies, since 1983; Guardian, Shrine of Our Lady of Walsingham, since 1963. Recreations: reading; travel; pilgrimages to St. Mary's, Haddington. Address: (h.) 12 St. Vincent Street, Edinburgh; T.-031-556 5692.

Laughland, Andrew William, FRFPSGlas, FRCSEdin, FRCOG. Consultant Obstetrician and Gynaecologist, Glasgow Royal Maternity Hospital and Victoria Infirmary, since 1963; b. 8.2.27, Glasgow; m., Anne Packe Johnstone. Educ. High School of Glasgow; Glasgow University. DADMS 1st Infantry Division, 1952-53; Tutor, Department of Obstetrics and Gynaecology, Liverpool University, 1958-59. Member, Council, Royal College of Obstetricians and Gynaecologists, 1970-76. Recreations: hill-walking; fishing; gardening. Address: (h.) 27 Sutherland Avenue, Glasgow, G41 4HG; T.-041-427 1704.

Laver, Professor John David Michael Henry, MA (Hons), DipPh, PhD. Professor of Phonetics, Department of Linguistics, Edinburgh University, since 1985; Director, Centre for Speech Technology Research, Edinburgh University, since 1984; b. 20.1.38, Nowshera, Pakistan; m., Sandy Hutcheson; 3 s.; 1 d. Educ. Churcher's College, Petersfield; Edinburgh University. Assistant Lecturer, then Lecturer in Phonetics, Ibadan University, 1963-66 (Exchange Lecturer, Edinburgh University, 1964-65); Lecturer, then Senior Lecturer in Phonetics, Edinburgh University, 1966-80; Reader and Head of Subject for Phonetics, 1980-84; Visiting Assistant Professor, Department of Linguistics, University of California, 1971; Visiting Research Fellow, Macquarie University, Sydney, 1982; Information Technology Fellowship, Edinburgh, 1983-84. Publications: Communication in Face to Face Interaction (Joint Editor), 1972; Phonetics in Linguistics (Joint Editor), 1973; Voice Quality, 1979; The Phonetic Description of Voice Quality, 1980; The Cognitive Representation of Speech (Joint Editor), 1981; The Prospect of Future Speech Technology (Co-author), 1987; Proceedings of the European Conference on Speech Technology (Co-Editor), 1987; Aspects of Speech Technology (Co-Editor), 1988. Address: (b.) Centre for Speech Technology Research, Edinburgh University, 80 South Bridge, Edinburgh; T.-031-225 8883.

Laverack, Professor Michael Stuart, BSc, PhD, FIBiol, FRSE. Professor of Marine Biology, St. Andrews University, since 1969; b. 19.3.31, Croydon; m., Maureen Ann; 2 s.; 1 d. Educ. Selhurst Grammar School; Southampton University. Scientific Officer, Nature Conservancy, 1958-60; Lecturer, then Senior Lecturer in Zoology, St. Andrews University, 1960-69. Publications: Lecture Notes in Invertebrate Zoology (Co-author); Physiology of Earthworms. Recreations: photography; walking; gardening; music. Address: (h.) Branxton, Boarhills, St. Andrews, Fife; T.-0334 88241.

Law, Alistair Geekie Robertson, JP, MB, ChB. General Medical Practitioner (retired); Member, Tayside Health Board; Immediate Past Chairman, Scottish Council, British Medical Association; b. 26.12.23, Dundee; m., Dr. Marion M.T. Roy; 1 s.; 2 d. Educ. Morgan Academy, Dundee; St. Andrews University. Hospital appointments; RAF. Fellow, BMA; Member, Bonnetmaker Craft. Recreation: golf. Address: (h.) Ianmhor, 21 Thomson Street, Dundee; T.-Dundee 69259.

Law, Graham Couper, MA (Cantab), ARSA, RIBA, FRIAS. Partner, The Law & Dunbar-Nasmith Partnership, Architects, since 1957; b. 28.9.23, Glasgow; m., Isobel Evelyn Alexander Drysdale; 1 s.; 3 d. Educ. Merchiston Castle School; Kings College, Cambridge. Royal Engineers, 1941-46; ARIBA, 1951; Council Member: Edinburgh Architectural Association, 1964-69, Royal Incorporation of Architects in Scotland, 1965-67; Member: Architects Registration Council, 1967-75, ARCUK Professional Purposes Committee, 1967-73; Chairman, Workshop and Artists Studio Provision (Scotland) Ltd., 1977-81; Member, RIAS Investigation Committee, 1979-85; Associate, Royal Scottish Academy, 1980. Recreations: drawing; skiing; fishing; shooting. Address: (b.) 16 Dublin Street, Edinburgh, EH1 3RE; T.-031-556 8631.

Law, Hamish T., BSc, PhD. Senior Lecturer, Department of Orthopaedic Surgery, Edinburgh University, since 1982; Vice-President, International Society for Hybrid Microelectronics, since 1986; Partner, Teviot Associates, since 1986; b. 7.7.27, Dundee; m., Emma Emmerson. Educ. Elgin Academy; Edinburgh University. Research Laboratory, British Thomson-Houston Co. Ltd., Rugby; Ferranti Ltd., Edinburgh (Chief Engineer, Valve Department); Varian Associates, Palo Alto, California (Senior Scientist); Ferranti Ltd., Edinburgh (Manager, Microelectronics Department); Director, Othopaedic Bio-Engineering Unit, Princess Margaret Rose Hospital, Edinburgh. Publication: Upper Limb Deficiencies in Children - Surgical Prosthetic and Orthotic Management; numerous papers. Recreations: sailing; curling; music. Address: (h.) 8 Learmonth Terrace, Edinburgh, EH4 1PQ; T.-031-332 5795.

Law, James, QC, MA, LLB. Queen's Counsel, since 1971; b. 7.6.26, Irvine; m., Kathleen Margaret Gibson (see Kathleen Margaret Law); 2 s.; 1 d. Educ. Kilmarnock Academy; Girvan High School; Glasgow University. Admitted to Faculty of Advocates, 1951; Advocate Depute, 1957-64; Member, Criminal Injuries Compensation Board, since 1970. Address: 7 Gloucester Place, Edinburgh, EH3 6EE; T.-031-225 2974.

Law, Kathleen Margaret, MA, LLB. Partner, Balfour & Manson, Solicitors, since 1978; Member, VAT Tribunal, Scotland; b. 11.2.26, Dumbarton; m., James Law, QC (qv); 2 s.; 1 d. Educ. Dumbarton Academy; St. Andrews University; Glasgow University. Admitted as Solicitor, 1952; Tutor in Conveyancing, Edinburgh University, 1978-79. Recreations: family; good holidays; good food; music. Address: (b.) 58 Frederick Street, Edinburgh, EH2 1LS; T.-031-225 8291.

Lawrence, James Ronald, BSc (Hons), MB, ChB, MD, FRCPGlas. Consultant Physician, Dumfries and Galloway Royal Infirmary, since 1982; Honorary Senior Lecturer, Aberdeen University, since 1982; b. 16.6.45, Bonnybridge; m., Sheena Jessie Patterson Cordiner. Educ. Denny High School; Glasgow University. SHO, Registrar, then Senior Registrar, Stobhill General Hospital, Glasgow, latterly in University Department of Materia Medica; Clinical Pharmacologist, Hoechst (UK) Ltd. Member, Medical/Scientific Section, British Diabetic Association. Publications: various papers on clinical pharmacology, with particular reference to diabetes and endocrinology. Recreations: hill-walking; reading; gardening. Address: Moncreiffe, Islesteps, Dumfries, DG2 8ES; T.-Dumfries 55507.

Lawrence, John Henry, FCA. Honorary Sheriff, Kilmarnock; b. 4.5.05, Cardiff; m., Kathleen Clare Craig; 3 s. Educ. Cardiff High School. Senior Clerk, Deloitte & Co., CA, London, 1929-37; Assistant Secretary, Richardsons Westgarth & Co., Wallsend, 1938-42; Director and Secretary, Glenfield & Kennedy Ltd., Kilmarnock, 1942-70; former Council Member, Glasgow Management Association; Past Chairman, Glasgow Branch, Institute of Office Management; former Director, Kilmarnock Chamber of Industries; former Member, Taxation Committee, CBI; former Committee Member, Athlone Foundation; former Secretary and President, Kilmarnock Rotary Club; former Director, Ayrshire Branch, British Red Cross Society; former Chairman, Ayrshire Branch, English Speaking Union. Recreations: music; golf; bridge. Address: (h.) 10 Wilson Avenue, Troon, KA10 7AF; T.-0292 312776.

Lawrie, Nigel Gilbert, BSc, PhD. Head Teacher, Port Glasgow High School, since 1985; b. 2.6.47, Edinburgh; m., Janet Clark Warnock; 1 d. Educ. Bearsden Academy; Strathclyde University. Chemistry Teacher, Hermitage Academy, Helensburgh, 1972-75; Principal Teacher of

Chemistry, Dunoon Grammar School, 1975-81; Assistant Head Teacher, Garnock Academy, 1981-84; Depute Head Teacher, Castlehead High School, Paisley, 1984-85. Chief Moderator for Social and Vocational Skills, Scottish Examination Board, 1985-87; President, Scottish Association for Teachers of Social and Vocational Skills, 1984-87. Recreations: reading; gardening; football. Address: (b.) Port Glasgow High School, Marloch Avenue, Port Glasgow; T.-0475 705921.

Lawson, Alexander Adamson Hutt, MD, FRCPEdin. Consultant Physician, Fife Health Board, since 1969; Honorary Senior Lecturer, Edinburgh University, since 1979; Medical Adviser, War Pensions Appeal Tribunal, Scotland, since 1979; b. 30.7.37, Dunfermline; m., Barbara Helen Donnet; 3 s.; 1 d. Educ. Dunfermline High School; Edinburgh University. Consultant Member, Clinical Teaching Staff, Faculty of Medicine, Edinburgh University, since 1971; Postgraduate Tutor in Medicine, West Fife, 1973-81; Medical Assessor, General Medical Council, since 1982; Member, Fife Health Board, since 1981; President, West Fife Medical Society, 1982-83; Life Trustee, Carnegie Dunfermline Trust and Carnegie United Kingdom Hero Fund, since 1980; Life Trustee, Carnegie United Kingdom Trust, since 1983; Member, Committee of Safety, Efficacy and Adverse Reactions of Drugs (Committee, Safety of Medicines, DHSS, London), 1982-84; Member, Specialist Advisory Committee (UK) HCMT - General (Internal) Medicine, 1984-88; UK Representative to European Union of Medical Specialties, Monospecialty Committee for General Medicine, since 1986. Publication: Common Acute Poisonings. Address: (h.) 2 Park Avenue, Dunfermline, Fife, KY12 7HX; T.-Dunfermline 726435.

Lawson, Rev. Alexander Hamilton, THM, THD, FPhS. Minister, Kilbowie Parish Church, Clydebank, since 1955; b. 16.9.21, Toronto, Canada; m., Martha Stevenson Macdonald; 1 s.; 1 d. Educ. Coatbridge Senior Secondary School; Glasgow University and Trinity College; American Bible College, Chicago; Metropolitan College of Law, St. Albans. RAF, 1941-46; Minister, Prestonpans Grange, 1950-55; Moderator, Dumbarton Presbytery, 1970-71; Member, Education Committee, General Assembly, eight years; served 15 years on Dunbartonshire Education Committee (Chairman, General Sub-Committee, 1967-70); Joint Chairman, Religious Education/EIS Group, 1963-74; Governor, Hamilton College of Education, 1967-72; Member, British Atlantic Committee and Representative Speaker, International Conferences, Wolfheze, 1983, and Amsterdam, 1986; Member, SSAS Executive; writer in Press; occasional TV and radio programme participant. Publication: The Moral Challenge of Defence Controversy in Our Nuclear Era. Recreations: table tennis and snooker; reading and gardening. Address: 1 Glebe Park, Mansewood, Dumbarton, G82 3HE.

Lawson, David Hamilton, MD, FRCPEdin, FRCPGlas, FCP. Consultant Physician, Glasgow Royal Infirmary, since 1973; Visiting Professor, Strathclyde University, since 1976; Visiting Scientist, Boston Collaborative Drug Surveillance Program, USA, since 1970; b. 27.5.39, Glasgow; m., Alison Diamond; 3 s. Educ. High School of Glasgow; Glasgow University. Junior doctor positions, Royal Infirmary and Western Infirmary, Glasgow; Senior Scientist, Boston Collaborative Drug Surveillance Program, Boston. Committee on Review of Medicines, DHSS, London: Member, since 1979, Vice Chairman, 1985-86, Chairman, since 1987; Member, Committee on Safety of Medicines, DHSS, London, since 1987; Member, Health Services Research Committee, Office of Chief Scientist, Scottish Home and Health Department, 1984-88. Publication: Clinical Pharmacy and Hospital Drug Management (Co-Editor). Recreations: hill-walking; ornithology; photography. Address: (h.) 43 Drumlin Drive, Milngavie, Glasgow, G62 6NF; T.-041-956 2962.

Lawson, Fettes Grafton. Retired Solicitor (Lawson, Coull & Duncan, Dundee); Honorary Sheriff, Tayside, Central and Fife at Dundee; b. 27.6.18, Dundee; m., Lily Norrie Latto; 1 s.; 2 d. Educ. Alloa Academy. Apprenticeship, 1937 (War Service, 1939-45); qualified, 1946; retired, 1987. Dean, Faculty of Procurators and Solicitors in Dundee, 1973-75. Recreations: reading; walking; gardening. Address: (h.) 33 Fairfield Road, West Ferry, Dundee, DD5 1PL; T.-Dundee 79613.

Lawson, Ian, MA, DipEd. Farmer; Member, Moray District Council; Member, Grampian Regional Council; b. 1.4.28, Rouen, France; m., Margaret; 2 s.; 1 d. Educ. St. George's College, Surrey; St. Andrews University. Member, Perth and Kinross District Council, 1978-80; Governor, Outward Bound, Loch Eil Centre; Committee Member, Moray Branch, British Red Cross; Member, Local Area Health Council; Director, Moray Enterprise Trust. Recreations: hill-walking; skiing. Address: Easter Califer, Forres, Moray, IV36 0RN; T.-0309 72536.

Lawson, John Philip, BSc, FEIS. Chairman, Scottish Youth Hostels Association, since 1980; Headteacher, St. Joseph's School, Linlithgow, since 1974; b. 19.8.37, Bathgate; m., Diana Mary Neal. Educ. St. Mary's Academy, Bathgate; Edinburgh University; Moray House College of Education. Teacher, West Lothian, since 1962; Member, West Lothian Children's Panel, 1972-81; Member, SYHA National Executive, since 1966; Vice-Chairman, SYHA, 1975-80; Member, International Youth Hostel Federation delegation to China, 1984; a Director, Scottish Rights of Way Society, since 1979; a Director, Gatliff Hebridean Hostels Trust, since 1988; President, West Lothian Headteachers Association, 1986-88. Recreations: hill-walking; classical music; reading. Address: (h.) 25 Bolam Drive, Burntisland, Fife, KY3 9HP; T.-0592 872132.

Lawson, Rev. Kenneth Charles, MA. National Adult Adviser, Department of Education, Church of Scotland, since 1984; b. 24.12.34, Agadir, Morocco; m., Mary Elizabeth Anderson; 3 s. Educ. Royal High School, Edinburgh; Preston Lodge School; Stranraer High School; Edinburgh University. Assistant Minister, Brechin Cathedral; Sub-Warden, St. Ninian's Training Centre, Crieff; Minister: Paisley South, Cumbernauld St. Mungo. Trainer, Scottish Association for Counselling. Recreations: walking; reading; painting.

Address: (b.) Group Relations Office, St. Colm's Education Centre and College, 20 Inverleith Terrace, Edinburgh, EH3 5NX; T.-031-332 0343.

Lawson, Norman W.H., FIPA, MCAM, MInstM. Chairman and Chief Executive, Rex Stewart & Associates (Scotland) Ltd.; b. 17.1.37, Kirkintilloch; m., Marion C.M.; 1 s.; 1 d. Educ. Lenzie Academy. Brunning Advertising (Scotland) Ltd.; Director, Struthers Advertising & Marketing Ltd.; Managing Director: Brunning Advertising (Manchester) Ltd.; MCS/Robertson & Scott (Glasgow) Ltd. President, Publicity Club of Glasgow, 1979-80; Chairman, Institute of Practitioners in Advertising (Scotland), 1987-89. Address: (b.) 102 Berkeley Street, Glasgow, G3 7LR.

Lawson, Rev. Ronald George, MA, BD. Parish Minister, St. Andrew's, Dumbarton, since 1976; Moderator, Presbytery of Dumbarton, since 1987; b. 9.9.33, Glasgow; m., Beryl Read; 1 s. Educ. Allan Glen's School; Glasgow University. Student Assistant, St. John's Renfield, Glasgow, 1959-61; Probationer, St. Martin's, Port Glasgow, 1961-63; Parish Minister, Perceton and Dreghorn, 1964-76. Tutor, Counsellor, Group Facilitator, Clinical Theology Association. Recreations: hill-walking; reading; gardening; swimming. Address: 17 Mansewood Drive, Dumbarton, G82 3EU; T.-Dumbarton 62063.

Laybourn, Professor Peter John Robert, MA (Cantab), PhD. Titular Professor in Electronics and Electrical Engineering, Glasgow University, since 1985; b. 30.7.42, London; m., Ann Elizabeth Chandler; 2 d. Educ. William Hulme's Grammar School; Bristol Grammar School; Clare College, Cambridge. Research Assistant, Leeds University, 1963-66; Research Fellow, Southampton University, 1966-71; Lecturer, then Senior Lecturer, then Reader, Glasgow University, 1971-85; Honorary Editor, Part J, IEE Proceedings. Recreations: sailing; boat-building; plant collecting. Address: (h.) Ashgrove, Waterfoot Row, Thorntonhall, Glasgow; T.-041-644 3992.

Laydon, John Patrick, MA, PhD (Cantab). Head of Service Industries, Scottish Development Agency, since 1988; b. 3.6.49, London; 2 s.; 1 d. Educ. St. Edmund's College, Ware; Sidney Sussex College, Cambridge. Scottish Office: Finance Division, 1976, Scottish Education Department, 1977, Housing Division, 1977-78, Private Secretary to Minister of State, 1978-79, Private Secretary to Minister for Industry and Education, 1979-80, Industrial Development Division, 1980-84; European Consultant for West Central Scotland (EEC appointment), 1981-84; Locate in Scotland: Director of Marketing, 1984, Manager, North American Desk, 1985, Manager, International Affairs, 1986, Product Manager Europe, 1987. Address: (h.) 19 Bellevue Place, Edinburgh; T.-031-556 9905.

Lazarowicz, Mark. Member, Scottish Executive, Labour Party, since 1980; Member, Edinburgh District Council, since 1980 (Leader, Labour Group, since 1986). Address: (h.) 15/1 Weir Court, Edinburgh, EH11 4BD; T.-031-442 4761.

Leach, Donald, BSc, FIMA, MInstP, MBCS. Principal, Queen Margaret College, Edinburgh, since 1985; b. 24.6.31, Croydon; m., June Valentine Reid; 2 s.; 1 d. Educ. John Ruskin Grammar School, Croydon; London University (External). Pilot Officer, Navigator, RAF, 1951-53; Physicist, British Jute Trade Research Association, Dundee, 1955-65; Technical Director, A.R. Bolton & Co. Ltd., Edinburgh, 1965-66; Napier College: Lecturer and Senior Lecturer in Mathematics, 1966-68, Head, Department of Mathematics and Computing, 1968-74, Assistant Principal/Dean, Faculty of Science, 1974-85. Member, South-Eastern Regional Hospital Board, 1969-74, and Lothian Health Board, 1977-81; Member: Scottish Health Service Common Services Agency's Advisory Panel on Information Processing, 1979-86, Scottish Health Service Planning Council's Information and Computer Systems Advisory Group, 1981-86, Computer Steering Committee (Chairman), 1981-86; Institute of Mathematics: Council Member, 1978-81, Chairman, Scottish Branch, 1980-83, Member, Joint IMA-Royal Society of London Mathematical Education Committee, 1981-84; Council for National Academic Awards: Member, Combined Studies Science Board, 1975-79, Science Technology and Society Board, 1979-82 (Chairman, 1981-82), Interfaculty Studies Board, 1981-85, Committee for Science and Technology, 1981-84, Committee for Scotland, since 1987; Chairman, Science Technology and Society Association, 1982-85; Chairman, Mathematics and Computing Course Committees, SCOTEC/SCOTBEC, 1981-85; Hon. Secretary, Committee of Principals and Directors of Scottish Central Institutions (COPADOCI), since 1985; Liberal candidate, West Edinburgh, 1959, and East Fife, 1961; Labour candidate, West Perthshire, 1970. Recreations: badminton; walking; skiing; cooking. Address: (h.) 8 Ravelston House Park, Edinburgh, EH4 3LU; T.-031-332 3826.

Leah, Christopher Richard. Provincial Manager (ScotRail), British Railways Board, since 1986; b. 4.12.47, Northampton; m., Prunella Mary Clayton; 3 s. Educ. Towcester Grammar School; London University (Extra Mural). BR: management trainee, Manchester, 1970, Motorail Manager, Kensington Olympia, 1979-81, Personal Assistant to Vice Chairman, BRB, HQ London, 1981-83, Divisional Freight Officer, Birmingham, 1983, Freight Resources Manager, Birmingham, 1983-84, Passenger Marketing Manager (Scotland), 1984-85, Passenger Business Manager (ScotRail), 1985-86. Treasurer, Braco and Greenloaning Community Council. Recreations: travel; industrial archaeology; photography; amateur dramatics. Address: (h.) 6 Greenhaugh Court, Braco, Perthshire; T.-078688 443.

Leake, Professor Bernard Elgey, BSc (Hons), PhD, DSc. Professor of Geology and Keeper of the Geological Collections in the Hunterian Museum, Glasgow University, since 1974; b. 29.7.32, Grimsby; m., Gillian Dorothy Dobinson; 5 s. Educ. Wirral Grammar School; Liverpool University. Leverhulme Postdoctorate Research Fellow, Liverpool University, 1955-57; Lecturer in Geology, then Reader, Bristol University, 1957-74. Lyell Medal, Geological Society, 1977; President, Geological Society, 1986-88; FRSE. Address: (b.) Geology Department, Glasgow University, Glasgow; T.-041-339 8855.

Leathar, Professor Douglas Sutherland, MA, PhD. Professor and Director, Advertising Research Unit, Department of Marketing, Strathclyde University, since 1979; b. 22.5.47, Dumbarton; m., Christine M.; 1 s. Educ. Robert Gordon's College, Aberdeen; Aberdeen University. Senior Account Manager, Research Bureau Limited, London; Senior Research Fellow, Strathclyde University, 1977-79. Recreation: DIY. Address: (b.) 173 Cathedral Street, Glasgow, G4 ORQ; T.-041-552 4400.

LeComber, Peter George, BSc, PhD, DSc, FInstPhys, FIEE, FRSE. Professor of Solid State Physics and Electronics, Dundee University; b. 19.2.41, Ilford, Essex; m., Joy Smith; 1 s.; 1 d. Educ. Leicester University. Research Fellow, Purdue University, USA, 1965-67; SERC Research Fellow, Leicester University, 1967-68; Lecturer, Dundee University, 1968. Awarded Maxwell Premium by IEE, 1983; Duddell Medal, I. of P., 1984; Rank Prize for Opto-Electronics, 1988; Consultant to a number of companies. Recreations: fishing; music; photography. Address: (b.) Department of Applied Physics and Electronic and Manufacturing Engineering, Dundee University, Dundee, DD1 4HN; T.-Dundee 23181.

Ledger, Philip Stevens, CBE, MA, MusB, LLD, FRCM, HonRAM, FRCO. Principal, Royal Scottish Academy of Music and Drama, since 1982; b. 12.12.37, Bexhill-on-Sea; 1 s.; 1 d. Educ. Bexhill Grammar School; King's College, Cambridge. Master of the Music, Chelmsford Cathedral, 1962-65; East Anglia University: Director of Music, 1965-73, Dean, School of Fine Arts and Music, 1968-71; Conductor, Cambridge University Musical Society, 1973-82; Director of Music and Organist, King's College, Cambridge, 1974-82; Editor, Anthems for Choirs 2 and 3; Composer/Editor, Six Carols with Descants. Publication: The Oxford Book of English Madrigals (Editor). Recreations: swimming; theatre. Address: (b.) Royal Scottish Academy of Music and Drama, 100 Renfrew Street, Glasgow, G2 3DB; T.-041-332 4101.

Ledingham, Professor Iain McAllan, MB, ChB, MD (Hons), FRCSEdin, FRCPGlas, FInstBiol, FRSE. Professor of Intensive Care, Glasgow University, since 1980; Honorary Consultant, Western Infirmary, Glasgow, since 1973; Director, Hyperbaric Unit, Western Infirmary, Glasgow, since 1968; b. 26.2.35, Glasgow; m., Eileen Riste; 3 s. Educ. King's Park Senior Secondary School, Glasgow; Central School, Aberdeen; Glasgow University. Western Infirmary, Glasgow: House Officer appointments, 1958-60, Hall Fellow in Surgery, 1960, Senior Research Fellow (MRC), Lecturer/Senior Lecturer/Reader in Surgery; Consultant in Underwater Medicine to Royal Navy; Consultant Adviser to Ministries of Health of Kuwait, Oman and United Arab Emirates; author/editor of several books. Recreations: jogging; swimming; sports; hill-walking; music; woodwork; reading. Address: (h.) 37 Hillside Road, Mansewood, Glasgow, G43 1DB; T.-041-649 8709.

Ledingham, Major James Norman, TD, DL, MA, LLB. Retired Farmer and Solicitor; b. 12.11.11, Perth; m., Helen Matheson Murray; 1 d. Educ. Allan Glen's School, Glasgow; Strathallan School; Glasgow University. Trained and qualified as Solicitor, 1934-39; joined TA, 1938; 1st Bn., Glasgow Highlanders HLI, 1939; Co. Commander, 1941-42; attached Commando Mountain Warfare School, Wales, 1943; posted as Signal Officer to Lovat Scouts, 1944; Italian Campaign, 1944-45; wounded; mentioned in Despatches; Chairman, Sutherland TA Association, since 1964; Sutherland NFU Representative, 1970-76; Vice President, Scottish Mountaineering Club, 1979-81. Recreations: mountaineering; golf. Address: (h.) Kintradwell, Brora, Sutherland, KW9 6LU; T.-040 82 1251.

Lee, Professor Michael Radcliffe, MA, DM, DPhil (Oxon), FRCP, FRCPE. Professor of Clinical Pharmacology, Edinburgh University, since 1984; b. 21.11.34, Manchester; m., Judith Ann Horrocks; 1 s.; 1 d. Educ. Manchester Grammar School; Brasenose College, Oxford. Beit Memorial Fellow for Medical Research; Lecturer in Medicine, Oxford University; Lecturer in Medicine, St. Thomas's Hospital Medical School; Medical Director, then Managing Director, Weddel Pharmaceuticals Ltd.; Senior Lecturer in Clinical Pharmacology, Leeds University. Publications: books on medicine and hypertension. Recreations: gardening; walking; old trains; old books. Address: (b.) Department of Clinical Pharmacology, Royal Infirmary, Edinburgh; T.-031-229 2477, Ext. 2599.

Lees, David Arthur Russell, MB, ChB, DObstRCOG, MRCOG. Consultant Gynaecologist and Obstetrician, Raigmore Hospital, Inverness, and Honorary Clinical Lecturer, Aberdeen University; b. 16.1.48, Elgin; m., Marie Sinclair Bruce; 4 s. Educ. Hamilton Academy; Glasgow University. Registrar in Obstetrics and Gynaecology, Robroyston and Stobhill Hospitals, Glasgow; Senior Registrar in Obstetrics and Gynaecology, Stobhill Hospital and Queen Mother's Hospital, Glasgow. Inverness Area Adviser, Scouting with the Handicapped; holder, Scout Association Medal of Merit. Recreation: Scouting. Address: (h.) Crofthill, Daviot (West), Inverness, IV1 2XQ; T.-0463 85 230.

Lees, Gordon McArthur, MB, ChB, PhD. Reader, Department of Pharmacology, Aberdeen University, since 1981; Secretary, Editorial Board, British Journal of Pharmacology, since 1984; b. 6.9.38, Dundee; m., Doris Irene Manson; 1 s.; 1 d. Educ. Aberdeen Grammar School; Aberdeen University. House Surgeon, Neurosurgical Unit, and House Physician, Professorial Medical Unit, Aberdeen Royal Infirmary, 1961-62; Aberdeen University: Research Fellow, then Lecturer, Department of Physiology, 1962-68, Lecturer, Department of Pharmacology, 1968-72, Senior Lecturer, 1972-81. Research Associate, Loyola University Stritch School of Medicine, Chicago, 1970 (Visiting Professor, 1974); Visiting Research Scholar, Flinders University of South Australia, 1982-83. Recreations: golf; music; astronomy. Address: (b.) Department of Pharmacology and Editorial Office of British Journal of Pharmacology, Aberdeen University, Marischal College, Aberdeen, AB9 1AS; T.-0224 273039 or 273052.

Lees, James George Grahame, MA, LLB, NP. Partner, McLean & Stewart, Solicitors, Dunblane, since 1974; Member, Judicial Commission, and Board of Practice and Procedure, General Assembly of the Church of Scotland; b. 22.6.46, Perth; m., Hazel Margaret Raffan; 1 s.; 2 d. Educ. Dundee High School; St. Andrews University; Edinburgh University. Solicitor, J. & F. Anderson, WS, Edinburgh, 1969-72; Solicitor, McLean & Stewart, Solicitors, Dunblane, since 1972. Elder, Dunblane Cathedral Church of Scotland. Recreations: walking; badminton; tennis; photography; fishing. Address: (h.) Northbank, St. Margaret's Drive, Dunblane, FK15 ODP; T.-Dunblane 822928.

Lefley, John, MA, ACIS. Director, Scottish Association of Master Bakers, since 1983; Member, Employers' Side, Scottish Bakery Joint Industrial Council, since 1982; b. 23.2.39, Kings Lynn; m., Marjorie K.M. Scott; 1 s.; 1 d. Educ. Culford School; Edinburgh University. Assistant Secretary, NFU of Scotland, 1967-82; Director-Designate, Scottish Association of Master Bakers, 1982-83. Various offices, Scottish Liberal Party, from 1956 (none now held). Recreations: inland waterways; playing bridge (badly); politics (desultory); support of anything Scottish. Address: (h.) 3 Riselaw Road, Edinburgh, EH10 6HR; T.-031-447 1535.

Le Gassick, Lt. Col. Cyril Norman, MBE. Regional Representative Grampian, National Trust for Scotland, since 1980; b. 9.4.25, Gillingham; m., Jean; 1 s.; 1 d. Educ. Maidstone School. Regular Army Officer, Royal Corps of Signals, 1946-80; Chief Signal Officer HQ Scotland (Army), 1970-73; Comd. Radio Group, HQ, BAOR, 1973-75. FSA Scot. Recreations: game fishing; shooting; painting. Address: (h.) Pinewood, Pitcaple, Inverurie, Aberdeenshire, AB5 9EE; T.-Pitcaple 634.

Leggate, Peter James Arthur, JP, FRICS. Chartered Surveyor, since 1967; Farmer, since 1972; a Director, Scottish Society for Prevention of Cruelty to Animals; b. 17.10.43; m., Jenifer Susan Gammell; 1 s.; 1 d. Educ. Wrekin College. Qualified as Chartered Surveyor, 1967; Kenneth Ryden & Partners, 1967-70; P.G. Matineau, Jedburgh, 1970-72; Founder, P.J. Leggate & Co., Edinburgh, 1973-79 (Sole Principal, since 1979). Recreations: horses; sailing; skiing. Address: (h.) Birkhill, Earlston, Berwickshire, TD4 6AR.

Legge, Joseph Smith, MD, FRCPEdin. Consultant in Thoracic Medicine, Grampian Health Board, since 1977; Honorary Senior Lecturer, Aberdeen University, since 1977; b. 12.11.43, Portessie, Banffshire; m., Sandra Leisk; 1 s.; 1 d. Educ. Buckie High School; Aberdeen University. Recreations: golf; photography. Address: (h.) 76 Fountainhall Road, Aberdeen; T.-0224 639590.

Leighton, Professor Kenneth, MA, DMus, HonDMus, LRAM, HonFRCM. Reid Professor of Music, Edinburgh University; Composer, Pianist, Conductor; b. 2.10.29, Wakefield; m.; 1 s.; 1 d. Educ. Queen Elizabeth Grammar School, Wakefield; Queen's College, Oxford. Gregory Fellow in Music, Leeds University; Lecturer and Reader in Composition, Edinburgh University; Fellow, Worcester College, Oxford; University Lecturer, Oxford University. More than 100 musical works published, including three symphonies, ten concertos, piano music, chamber music, choral, organ and Church music, two operas. Recreation: walking. Address: (h.) 9 Bright's Crescent, Edinburgh, EH9 2DB; T.-031-667 3113.

Leiper, Joseph, MA, DipEd, ACII. Rector, Oldmachar Academy, since 1983; b. 13.8.41, Aberdeen; m., Moira Taylor; 2 d. Educ. Aberdeen Grammar School; Aberdeen University. Inspector, Commercial Union Assurance, until 1967; Aberdeen University, 1967-72; Aberdeen College of Education, 1971-72; Teacher of English, since 1972. Recreations: hockey; sailing; jogging. Address: (b.) Oldmachar Academy, Jesmond Drive, Bridge of Don, Aberdeen, AB2 8ZJ; T.-0224 820887.

Leishman, Marista Muriel, MA. Representative, Georgian House, and Head of Education, National Trust for Scotland; Director, The Insite Trust for Heritage Interpretation; b. 10.4.32, Beaconsfield; m., Murray Leishman (qv); 1 s.; 3 d. Educ. St. George's School, Ascot; St. Andrews University. Organiser, Ingathering of Funds, National Church Extension; first Co-ordinator, NTS Members' Centres and Youth in Trust; Member, Committees, New Glasgow Society, Cockburn Association, Scottish Museums Council. Recreations: music; painting; writing; hill-walking; gardening. Address: Hunter's House, 508 Lanark Road, Edinburgh, EH14 5DH; T.-031-453 4716.

Leishman, Robert, RSW, DA; b. 30.10.16, Inverkeithing; m., Patricia Stuart Edgar; 3 d. Educ. Dunfermline High School; Edinburgh College of Art. Royal Scots Fusiliers, 1940-46; taught in Germany with Army Educational Corps; painted and taught in Edinburgh, Fife and Dundee; full-time painting, mainly in watercolours, since 1972; elected SSA, 1951; work represented in many public and private collections, UK and abroad; Past President, Dundee Art Society. Recreation: conversational ping-pong. Address: (h.) 15 Charleston Drive, Dundee, DD2 2HF; T.-Dundee 66170.

Leishman, Rev. Robert Murray, MA. Analytical Psychotherapist; Minister, Church of Scotland, since 1957; b. 4.8.31, Edinburgh; m., Marista M. Reith (see Marista Muriel Leishman); 1 s.; 3 d. Educ. George Watson's Boys' College; Edinburgh University; St. Mary's College, St. Andrews. Assistant Minister, St. Ninian's, Larkfield, Greenock; Parish Minister: Moncreiffe Church, Perth, The Barony of Glasgow; Chaplain, Royal Edinburgh Hospital; Lecturer (part-time), Department of Christian Ethics and Practical Theology, Edinburgh University; full-time with Scottish Institute of Human Relations, and private practice, since 1987. Recreations: fishing; golf; gardening; music. Address: Hunter's House, 508 Lanark Road, Edinburgh, EH14 5DH; T.-031-453 4716.

Leitch, Andrew Gordon, BSc, MB, ChB, PhD, FRCPE, FCCP, FSA(Scot). Consultant Physician, Chest Unit, City Hospital, Edinburgh, since 1983; Physician in administrative charge, Royal Victoria Dispensary, since 1983; Honorary Senior Lecturer, Edinburgh University, since 1983; b. 12.12.45, Edinburgh; m., Jean Elizabeth Brawn Miller; 2 s.; 1 d. Educ. Royal High School, Edinburgh; Edinburgh University. Faculty Member, University of Cincinnati School of Medicine, 1978-80; MRC and Wellcome Trust Travelling Fellow, Harvard School of Medicine, Boston, 1981-83. Honeyman Gillespie lecturer, Edinburgh University, 1979; Croom Lecturer, RCPE, 1983. Publication: Respiratory Diseases (Co-author). Recreations: literature; antiquities; golf; squash; fishing. Address: (h.) 16 Wilton Road, Edinburgh, EH16 5NX; T.-031-667 5812.

Leitch, David Alexander. Under Secretary, Social Work Services Group, Scottish Education Department, since 1983; b. 4.4.31, Bournemouth; m., Marie Tain; 2 s.; 1 d. Ministry of Supply, 1948-58; Department of Agriculture and Fisheries for Scotland: Assistant Principal, 1959, Principal, 1963, Assistant Secretary, 1971; Local Government Finance, Central Services: Assistant Secretary, 1976, Under Secretary, 1981. Recreations: climbing; hill-walking. Address: (b.) Scottish Education Department, New St. Andrew's House, Edinburgh.

Leitch, John Stewart, JP. Member, City of Dundee District Council, since 1974; Member, North of Scotland Hydro Electric Board Consultative Committee, since 1979; b. 14.3.27, Musselburgh; m., Evelyn Stephen Donald. Educ. Harris Academy; Brechin High School. Wholesale Merchant, 1942-45; Royal Navy, 1945-47; Wholesale Merchant, 1947-85. Recreation: gardening. Address: (h.) 16 Shaftesbury Park, Dundee, DD2 1LB; T.-Dundee 644182.

Leithead, Walter Douglas Murray, CA, MCIT. Finance Director, Scottish Road Services Ltd., since 1972, and Northern Ireland Carriers Ltd., since 1982; Member, Forth Valley Health Board; b. 29.10.39, Hawick; m., Nancy Ingles; 1 s.; 1 d. Educ. Hawick High School; Glasgow University. Address: (h.) Beechmount, Carronvale Road, Larbert, Stirlingshire; T.-032455 6824.

Leng, Christopher Anthony William, OBE, DL, MA, MRAC. Deputy Lord Lieutenant of Peeblesshire, since 1981; b. 5.4.22, Sheffield; m., Patricia Lillywhite; 2 s.; 2 d. Educ. Downside School; Hertford College, Oxford. Army Captain, 27th Lancers, SOE, five years; TA, 21st SAS, three years; farming, 40 years; Landowner, 40 years; President, Borders Area, NFU of Scotland, 1979; General Commissioner of Inland Revenue. Mentioned in Despatches. Recreations: gardening; fishing; reading. Address: Juniper Bank, Walkerburn, Peeblesshire; T.-089 687 230.

Lenman, Bruce Philip, MA (Aberdeen), MLitt, LittD (Cantab), FRHistSoc. Reader in Modern History, St. Andrews University, since 1983; b. 9.4.38, Aberdeen. Educ. Aberdeen Grammar School; Aberdeen University; St. John's College, Cambridge. Assistant Professor, Victoria University, Canada, 1963; Lecturer in Imperial and Commonwealth History, Queen's College, Dundee (St. Andrews University), 1963-67; Lecturer, Dundee University, 1967-72; United College, St. Andrews: Lecturer, Department of Modern History, 1972-78, Senior Lecturer, 1978-83; British Academy Fellow, Newberry Library, Chicago, 1982; John Carter Brown Library Fellow, Brown University, Providence, RI, 1984. Publications: Esk to Tweed, 1975; An Economic History of Modern Scotland 1660-1976, 1977 (Scottish Arts Council Award); The Jacobite Risings in Britain 1689-1746, 1980 (Scottish Arts Council Award); Scotland 1746-1832, 1981; The Jacobite Clans of the Great Glen 1650-1784, 1984; The Jacobite Cause, 1986. Recreations: golf; squash; badminton; Scottish country dancing; hill-walking. Address: (b.) Department of Modern History, St. Andrews University, St. Andrews, KY16 9AL; T.-0334 76161.

Lenman, John Andrew Reginald, FRSE, MB, ChB, FRCPEdin. Reader in Neurology, Dundee University, since 1960; Honorary Consultant Neurologist, Tayside Health Board, since 1960; b. 28.8.24, Shillong, India; m., Muriel Frances Selby-Brown; 1 s.; 3 d. Educ. Michael Hall; Edinburgh University. House Physician, Edinburgh Royal Infirmary and House Surgeon, Neurosurgical Unit, Bangour Hospital, 1948-49; National Service, RAF, 1949-51 (active service, Singapore); Assistant in Physiology, St. Andrews University, 1952-54; Senior House Officer, Edinburgh Royal Infirmary, 1955-56; Research Fellow and Honorary Registrar, Neurology, Northern General Hospital, Edinburgh, 1956-58; First Assistant in Neurology, Kings College, Newcastle-upon-Tyne and Royal Victoria Infirmary, 1958-59. Publications: Clinical Neurophysiology, 1975; Neurological Therapeutics (Co-author), 1981; Clinical Electromyography, 1983 (Co-author). Recreations: hill-walking; reading; music. Address: (h.) 31 Dundee Road West, Broughty Ferry, Dundee, DD5 1NB; T.-0382 77707.

Lennie, Daniel, JP. Convener and Labour Group Leader, Midlothian District Council, since 1986; Chairman, Midlothian Constituency Labour Party, 1986-88; b. 6.2.47, Edinburgh; m., Thelma Halliday; 2 s.; 1 d. Educ. St. Margaret's School, Loanhead; St. David's School, Dalkeith. Chairman, Midlothian District Licensing Board, 1981-86; AUEW: Shop Steward, 1973-80, Convener, 1977-80, Bertrams Ltd., Edinburgh; Chairman, Bonnyrigg/Lasswade Community Council, 1978-80; Chairman, Bonnyrigg/Lasswade Labour Party, since 1979; President, Dolphin Club for Mentally Handicapped. Recreations: politics; writing bad doggerel. Address: (h.) 10 Sherwood Walk, Bonnyrigg, Midlothian, EH19 3NL; T.-031-660 3492.

Lennox, Iain MacIntyre, MB, ChB, FRCP (Glas), DObstRCOG. Consultant Physician, Geriatric Unit, Victoria Infirmary, since 1980; b. 24.11.48, Glasgow; m., Helen Edith Marshall; 1 s.; 1 d. Educ. Hutchesons' Boys Grammar School, Glasgow; Glasgow University. Secretary, Geriatric Medicine Sub-Committee, Greater Glasgow Area Medical Committee, since 1983; Honorary Medical Adviser, Glasgow Abbeyfield Society. Recreations: golf; badminton. Address: (h.) 29 Langtree Avenue, Whitecraigs, Glasgow, G46; T.-041-638 1480.

Leonard, Robert Charles Frederick, BSc, MD, MB, BS, MRCP, FRCPEdin. Senior Lecturer in Clinical Oncology, Edinburgh University, since 1983; Honorary Consultant Physician, Lothian Health Board, since 1983; b. 11.5.47, Merthyr Tydfil; m., Tania Smith; 3 d. Educ. Merthyr Tydfil

County Grammar School; Charing Cross Hospital Medical School, London. House Officer, Charing Cross, West London and Fulham Hospitals, 1971-73; Senior House Officer, Hammersmith Hospital, 1973; Medical Registrar, Oxford Hospitals, 1974-76; Leukaemia Research Fund Fellow, Oxford University, 1976-79; Senior Registrar and University Lecturer, Royal Victoria and General Hospitals, Newcastle-upon-Tyne, 1979-82; Cancer Research Campaign Travelling Fellow, Dana Farber Cancer Institute and Harvard Medical School, Boston, 1982. Recreations: classical music; reading; soccer. Address: (h.) 19 Craigcrook Road, Edinburgh, EH4 3NQ.

Leonard, Wilfred. Member, Island Policy Committee, Scottish Accident Prevention Council; b. 9.5.12, Humberton, Brafferton, Yorkshire; m., Margaret Ross; 1 s.; 2 d. Educ. Brafferton Church of England School. Staffordshire County Police, 1935-67 (retired in rank of Inspector); Member, Inverness County Council, 1973-74; Past Chairman: Harris District Council, South Harris Agricultural Society, Harris Council of Social Service; former Member: Highlands and Islands Consultative Council; Highlands and Islands Manpower Board, MSC; Member, Western Isles Islands Council, 1974-86 (Chairman, Planning and Development, 1980-86). Recreation: gardening. Address: (h.) Cnoc-Na-Ba, Finsbay, Isle of Harris; T.-Manish 232.

Le Roux, Joan Catherine. Member, Argyll and Clyde Health Board, since 1981; b. 23.4.30, Edinburgh; m., Peter Hugo Le Roux; 3 s. Educ. Mary Erskine College. Member, Argyll and Bute Health Council, 1975-80 (Chairman, 1977-79); Chairman, Argyll Conservative Association, 1976-78 (President, 1978-80); Vice-Chairman, Conservative Women's Scottish Council, 1981-82; Member, Dunoon and Cowal Cancer Research Committee, since 1970 (Chairman, 1982-88). Recreations: reading; sewing; music. Address: (h.) Berryburn, Dunoon, Argyll; T.-0369 2028.

Leslie, Allan Eunson, BSc, FRSH, MREHIS. Director of Environmental Health, Orkney Islands Council, since 1975; b. 15.11.41, Garmouth, Morayshire; m., Vivia Mary Stewart. Educ. Mackie Academy, Stonehaven; Harris Academy, Dundee; Dundee College of Science and Technology; Robert Gordon's College of Further Education; Strathclyde University. Assistant Sanitary Inspector, Dundee Corporation, 1963-64; Assistant Sanitary Inspector, Kincardine County Council, 1964-70; Area Sanitary Inspector, Sutherland County Council, 1970-72. Recreations: gardening; walking; sea fishing; bowls; bridge; reading. Address: (b.) Orkney Islands Council, Environmental Health Department, Council Offices, School Place, Kirkwall, Orkney Isles; T.-0856 3535, Ext. 275.

Leslie, David James, BArch, RIBA, PRIAS. Architect; Partner, Walter Underwood & Partners, since 1987; President, Royal Incorporation of Architects in Scotland, since 1987; b. 15.5.32, Glasgow; m., Olive; 2 s.; 1 d. Educ. Hillhead High School; Glasgow School of Architecture. Qualified, 1957; Registered Architect, 1959; Honorary Secretary, Glasgow Institute of Architects, 1979-82 (Vice President, three times); President, Glasgow Institute of Architects, 1984-86; Governor, Glasgow School of Art; Director, Glasgow Chamber of Commerce; Elder, Netherlee Church, Glasgow; Convener, Festival of Architecture in Scotland, 1984; Convener, Scotstyle Group. Recreations: singing; painting; photography. Address: (b.) 2 La Belle Place, Glasgow, G3 7LH; T.-041-332 7227.

Leslie, Professor Frank Matthews, JP, BSc, PhD, FIMA, FInstP, FRSE. Professor of Mathematics, Strathclyde University, since 1982; b. 8.3.35, Dundee; m., Ellen Leitch Reoch; 1 s.; 1 d. Educ. Harris Academy; Queen's College, Dundee; Manchester University. Assistant Lecturer, Manchester University, 1959-61; Research Associate, MIT, USA, 1961-62; Lecturer, Newcastle University, 1962-68; Visiting Assistant Professor, Johns Hopkins University, USA, 1966-67; Strathclyde University: Senior Lecturer, 1968-71, Reader, 1971-79, Personal Professor, 1979-82; Consultant, RSRE Malvern; Annual Award, British Society of Rheology, 1982. Recreations: golf; hill-walking. Address: (b.) Department of Mathematics, Strathclyde University, Livingstone Tower, 26 Richmond Street, Glasgow, G1 1XH; T.-041-552 4400.

Leslie Melville, Michael Ian, TD, DL, MA, FRICS. Honorary Sheriff, Selkirk Sheriff Court, since 1983; Deputy Lieutenant (West Lothian, 1957, Ettrick and Lauderdale, 1974); Member, Royal Company of Archers (Queen's Bodyguard for Scotland), since 1947; b. 12.8.18; m., Cynthia Hambro (deceased); 1 s.; 2 d. Educ. Eton; Balliol College, Oxford; Open University. TA and War Service, Lovat Scouts (Major, 1945); Chartered Land Agent/Chartered Surveyor (retired); Farmer, Forester, Company Director. Publication: The Story of the Lovat Scouts 1900-1980, 1981. Recreations: riding; field sports; gardening. Address: (h.) Bridgelands Farm, Selkirk, TD7 4PT; T.-0750 20370.

Lessels, Norman, CA. Partner, Chiene & Tait, CA, since 1980; President, Institute of Chartered Accountants of Scotland, 1987-88; Chairman, Standard Life Assurance Company; Chairman, Scottish Eastern Investment Trust PLC; Chairman, New Darien Oil Trust plc; Chairman, Heriot Hotels Ltd; Director, Anderson Strathclyde PLC; Director, The Murrayfield plc; Director, James Lindsay & Son plc; b. 2.9.38, Edinburgh; m., Christine Stevenson; 1 s. Educ. Edinburgh Academy. Partner, Ernst & Whinney, until 1980. Recreations: golf; music; bridge. Address: (b.) 3 Albyn Place, Edinburgh; T.-031-225 7515.

Lessnoff, Michael Harry, MA, BPhil. Reader in Politics, Glasgow University, since 1986; b. 23.1.40, Glasgow. Educ. High School of Glasgow; Glasgow University; Balliol College, Oxford. Assistant Principal, Department of Education and Science, 1965-66; Lecturer, then Senior Lecturer, Department of Politics, Glasgow University, 1966-86; Visiting Associate Professor, College of William and Mary, Williamsburg, USA, 1977-78. Won Snell Exhibition, 1963. Publications: The Structure of Social Science, 1974; Social Contract, 1986. Recreations: literature; art; science; travel. Address: (h.) 58 White Street, Glasgow, G11 5EB; T.-041-334 1799.

Letham, David. President, Scottish Football League, 1981-85; Vice President, Scottish Football Association, 1981-85; b. 7.5.22, Glasgow; m., Nessie Balfour; 1 d. Educ. John Street Secondary School, Glasgow; Scottish School of Physical Education, Jordanhill. RAF, 1942-46; Teacher, John Street Secondary School, 1948-82. Member, Queen's Park FC, since 1939. Address: (h.) 15 Beech Avenue, Newton Mearns, Glasgow, G77 5PP; T.-041-639 1216.

Levein, Charles Peter Alexander, MA, PhD. Senior Principal Research Officer, Scottish Office, since 1977; b. 16.5.40, Devonport; 1 s.; 2 d. Educ. Dunfermline High School; Edinburgh University. Demonstrator, Geography Department, Edinburgh University; Research Officer, Central Planning Research Unit, Scottish Development Department; Senior Research Officer, WC Scotland Planning Team; Principal Research Officer, Scottish Office Urban Deprivation Unit. Recreations: squash; golf; bowls; tennis. Address: (h.) 45 The Wynd, Dalgety Bay, Fife; T.-0383 822952.

Leven and Melville, Earl of (Alexander Robert Melville). Lord Lieutenant, Nairn; Company Director; President, British Ski Federation, 1981-85; Honorary President, Scottish National Ski Council; Chairman, Governors, Gordonstoun School, since 1971; b. 13.5.24, London; m., Susan Steuart-Menzies; 2 s.; 1 d. Educ. Eton. Coldstream Guards, 1942-52 (retired as Captain); ADC to Governor General of New Zealand, 1951-52; Convener, Nairn County Council, 1970-74. Recreations: shooting; fishing; skiing. Address: (h.) Glenferness House, Nairn, IV12 5UP; T.-03095 202.

Lever, Professor William Fred, MA (Oxon), DPhil (Oxon). Titular Professor in Urban Studies, Glasgow University, since 1984; b. 17.4.43, Accrington; m., Marian Frances Hardman; 1 s.; 2 d. Educ. Grammar School, Accrington; St. Peter's College, Oxford University. Tutor in Geography, Oxford University, 1966-67; Lecturer and Senior Lecturer in Urban Studies, then Reader, Glasgow University, 1967-84. Visiting Professor, University of Pittsburgh, University of Texas, University of Seigen; Gutenberg Fellow, University of Mainz. Recreations: travel; theatre; food. Address: (h.) 34 Kirkhouse Road, Blanefield, Glasgow; T.-0360 70536.

Levi, Professor Anthony Herbert Tigar, MA (Oxon), DPhil (Oxon), STL. Emeritus Professor of French Language and Literature, St. Andrews University; b. 30.5.29, London; m., Honor Marjorie Riley; 2 d. Educ. Prior Park College; Oxford University; Munich University. Member, Jesuit Order, 1949-71; Lecturer, Reader, Professor, Warwick University, 1965-71; Lecturer, Christ Church, Oxford, and Tutor, Campion Hall, Oxford, 1965-71. Publications: French Moralists: The Theory of the Passions 1585-1649, 1964; Religion in Practice, 1966; Erasmus, The Praise of Folly (Editor), 1971; Humanism in France, 1970; The Writer and the Artist in France, 1974; Collected Works of Erasmus (Vol. 27 and 28), 1986. Address: (h.) East Castlemount, North Castle Street, St. Andrews, KY16 9BG; T.-St. Andrews 73926.

Levison, Rev. Christopher Leon, MA, BD (Hons). Minister, Paisley High Church, since 1983; b. 7.4.47, Gorebridge, Midlothian; m., Rosemary Anne Milne Logan; 2 d. Educ. George Watson's College; Kirkcaldy High School; St. Andrews University; Edinburgh University. Assistant Minister, South Leith, 1971-73; Minister, Coltness Memorial Church, Newmains, 1973-78 (also Community Councillor); Associate Chaplain, Aberdeen University, 1978-83. Manager and Trustee, Kibble List D School. Recreations: sailing; hill-walking. Address: 178 Glasgow Road, Paisley, PA1 3LT; T.-041-889 3316.

Liddell, Donald John, LLB (Hons). Chief Executive, East Kilbride District Council, since 1988 (Director of Administration and Legal Services, Clydesdale District Council, 1984-88); b. 20.3.50, Hamilton; m., Veronica; 1 s.; 2 d. Educ. Hamilton Academy; Glasgow University. Legal Apprentice/Assistant, Livingston Development Corporation, 1971-75; Legal Assistant/Officer, Clydesdale District Council, 1975-84. Address: (b.) Civic Centre, East Kilbride, G74 1AB; T.-East Kilbride 28777.

Liddell, Helen Lawrie, BA. Director of Personnel and Public Affairs, Scottish Daily Record and Sunday Mail Ltd., since 1988; Scottish Secretary, Labour Party, 1977-88; b. 6.12.50, Coatbridge; m., Dr. Alistair H. Liddell; 1 s.; 1 d. Educ. St. Patrick's High School, Coatbridge; Strathclyde University. Head, Economic Department, STUC, 1971-76; Labour candidate, East Fife, 1974; Economics Correspondent, BBC, 1976-77. Address: (h.) Glenisla, Main Road, Langbank, Renfrewshire; T.-Langbank 344.

Liddell, John Chalmers, MA, LLB. Depute Chief Executive, Grampian Regional Council, since 1979; b. 25.3.46, Dumfries; m., Laura; 2 s.; 1 d. Educ. High School of Glasgow; St. Andrews University. Depute County Clerk, Berwickshire, 1972; Assistant Director of Administration, Borders Region, 1975; Depute Director of Law and Administration, Grampian Region, 1975. Secretary, Aberdeen Ski Club. Recreations: skiing; golf. Address: (b.) Woodhill House, Ashgrove Road West, Aberdeen, AB9 2LU.

Lilwall, Nicholas Brier, BSc, MA, PhD. Head, Agricultural Resource Management Department, Edinburgh School of Agriculture, since 1985; b. 15.8.37, Liverpool; m., Anne; 2 s.; 1 d. Educ. Truro School, Cornwall; Leeds University; Minnesota University. Assistant Lecturer, Leeds University, 1964-66; Research Assistant, Minnesota University, 1967-71; Economist, Edinburgh School of Agriculture, since 1971. Recreation: tennis. Address: (b.) Edinburgh School of Agriculture, 6 South Oswald Road, Edinburgh, EH9 2HH; T.-031-662 4395.

Lincoln, Professor Dennis W., DSc. Director, Medical Research Council Reproductive Biology Unit, Edinburgh, since 1982; b. 21.7.39, Gt. Ellingham; m., Rosemary A. Barrell; 1 s.; 1 d. Educ. Nottingham University; Cambridge University. Research Fellow, Corpus Christi College, Cambridge, 1966-67; Lecturer, Reader, Professor, Faculty of Medicine, Bristol University. Honorary Professor, Faculty of Medicine, Edinburgh University, since 1985. Recreation: ornithology. Address: (b.) Centre for Reproductive Biology, 37 Chalmers Street, Edinburgh, EH3 9EW; T.-031-229 2575.

Lindop, George Black McMeekin, BSc, MB, ChB, MRCPath. Senior Lecturer and Honorary Consultant in Histopathology, Glasgow University, and Honorary Consultant in Histopathology, Western Infirmary, Glasgow, since 1979; b. 28.3.45, Glasgow; m., Sharon Ann Cornell; 2 s.; 1 d. Educ. Hillhead High School; Glasgow University. Senior House Officer/Registrar, then Lecturer/Honorary Senior Registrar, Department of Histopathology, Western Infirmary, Glasgow; Consultant Histopathologist, Ayrshire and Arran Health Board; Consulting Editor, Histology/Histopathology. Recreations: sport; the outdoors; music; cinema. Address: (b.) Department of Pathology, Western Infirmary, Glasgow; T.-041-339 8822.

Lindsay, Alistair, MA, LLB, NP, FSA Scot. Editor, Clan Lindsay Society Publications, since 1947; Consultant, Stewarts, Nicol, D. & J. Hill (Partner, 1948-82); b. 5.2.23, Glasgow; m., Agnes Calder Hamilton Neilson; 1 s.; 1 d. Educ. Pollokshields Secondary School; Larkhall Academy; Glasgow University. Governor, Baillies Institution Free Public Library, six years; Secretary, Old Glasgow Club, 12 years; Secretary, (Glasgow) Ballad Club, 24 years; Life Member, Glasgow Art Gallery and Museums Association; Director: Barloch Proprietors Ltd., Popular Properties Ltd. Publication: The Laird of Barloch 1632-1984, 1985. Recreations: genealogy; local history. Address: (h.) Bruntsfield, 16 Dalziel Drive, Pollokshields, Glasgow, G41; T.-041-423 8440.

Lindsay, James, CBE, BL, CA. Honorary President, Scottish Golf Union, since 1960; Honorary Sheriff, Falkirk; b. 31.10.12, Larbert; m., Margaret Craig Wyllie; 4 s.; 1 d. Educ. Falkirk High School; Glasgow University. Macfarlane Lang & Co. Ltd.: Accountant and Secretary, 1937-57, Director, 1955-73; Director, United Biscuits Ltd., 1957-73; Chairman, The Cake and Biscuit Alliance, 1970-73; President, Scottish Golf Union, 1958-60. Recreations: golf; gardening. Address: (h.) 8 Neilson Street, Falkirk, FK1 5AQ; T.-Falkirk 22248.

Lindsay, Jean Olivia, MA, PhD (Cantab), FRHistS; b. 10.12.10, Bangalore, India; m., H.D.R.P. Lindsay; 1 s.; 2 d. Educ. St. Serfs School, Edinburgh; Brympton School, Gibraltar; three schools in Cologne for children of families serving with BAOR; Queen's College, London; Girton College, Cambridge. Research Fellow, Girton College, 1936-39; War Service, Ministry of Information, 1939-41; Research Department, Foreign Office, 1941-43; SOE, 1943-45; Fellow, Girton College, subsequently Director of Studies in History and University Lecturer, 1947-60; Head Mistress, St. George's School for Girls, Edinburgh, 1960-76; Chairman, Saltire Society, 1983-86. Publications: Trade and Peace with Old Spain; various articles; Editor, Cambridge Modern History, Vol. VII. Recreations: history; drawing; entertaining children. Address: (h.) 3 Ann Street, Edinburgh, EH4 1PL; T.-031-332 3979.

Lindsay, John Maurice, CBE, TD, DLitt, HonFRIAS. Consultant, Scottish Civic Trust (Director, 1967-83); Secretary-General, Europa Nostra, since 1983; b. 21.7.18; m., Aileen Joyce Gordon; 1 s.; 3 d. Educ. Glasgow Academy; Scottish National Academy of Music. Drama Critic, Scottish Daily Mail, 1946-47; Music Critic, The Bulletin, 1946-60; Border Television: Programme Controller, 1961-62, Production Controller, 1962-64, Features Executive and Chief Interviewer, 1964-67. Atlantic-Rockefeller Award, 1946; Editor: Scots Review, 1949-50, The Scottish Review, 1975-85; Member, Historic Buildings Council for Scotland, 1976-87; Council Member, Association of Scottish Literary Studies, since 1983; Trustee, New Lanark Conservation Trust, since 1985; Trustee, National Heritage Memorial Fund, 1980-84; HonDLitt, Glasgow, 1982. Publications: poetry: The Advancing Day, 1940; Perhaps To-morrow, 1941; Predicament, 1942; No Crown for Laughter: Poems, 1943; The Enemies of Love: Poems 1941-45, 1946; Selected Poems, 1947; Hurlygush: Poems in Scots, 1948; At the Wood's Edge, 1950; Ode for St. Andrew's Night and Other Poems, 1951; The Exiled Heart: Poems 1941-56, 1957; Snow Warning and Other Poems, 1962; One Later Day and Other Poems, 1964; This Business of Living, 1969; Comings and Goings: Poems, 1971; Selected Poems 1942-72, 1973; The Run from Life, 1975; Walking Without an Overcoat, Poems 1972-76, 1977; Collected Poems, 1979; A Net to Catch the Winds and Other Poems, 1981; The French Mosquitoes' Woman and other diversions and poems; Requiem for a Sexual Athlete; prose: A Pocket Guide to Scottish Culture; The Scottish Renaissance; The Lowlands of Scotland: Glasgow and the North; Robert Burns: The Man, His Work, The Legend; Dunoon: The Gem of the Clyde Coast; The Lowlands of Scotland: Edinburgh and the South; Clyde Waters: Variations and Diversions on a Theme of Pleasure; The Burns Encyclopedia; Killochan Castle; By Yon Bonnie Banks: A Gallimaufry; Environment: A Basic Human Right; Portrait of Glasgow; Robin Philipson; History of Scottish Literature; Lowland Scottish Villages; Francis George Scott and the Scottish Renaissance; The Buildings of Edinburgh (Co-author); Thank You For Having Me: A Personal Memoir; Unknown Scotland (Co-author); The Scottish Castle: A Constable Guide; Count All Men Mortal: The Story of the Scottish Provident Institution; Victorian and Edwardian Glasgow; Edinburgh: Then and Now (Co-author). Recreations: music; walking. Address: (h.) 7 Milton Hill, Milton, Dumbarton, G82 2TS; T.-Dumbarton 62500.

Lindsay, Nigel Bruce, MA, MLitt. Member, Aberdeen District Council, since 1973 (Convenor, Leisure and Recreation Committee); Chairman, Aberdeen and North Committee, Gas Consumers Council for Scotland, 1984-86; Regional Organiser, Shelter, North of Scotland, since 1975; b. 27.3.48, Scunthorpe. Educ. Aberdeen University. Member, National Executive, Scottish Liberal Party, 1972-76; Member, Aberdeen University Court, 1976-80. Address: (h.) 18 Lochside Terrace, Bridge of Don, Aberdeen; T.-0224 820575.

Lingard, Joan Amelia. Author; Chairperson, Society of Authors in Scotland, 1982-86; Convenor, Scottish Writers Against the Bomb; b. Edinburgh; 3 d. Educ. Bloomfield Collegiate School, Belfast; Moray House College of Education, Edinburgh. First novel published, 1963; has also written plays for TV, including 18-part series, Maggie, adapted from quartet of teenage books; Council Member, Scottish Arts Council, 1980-84 (Member, Literature Committee, 1980-84); novels: Liam's Daughter, 1963; The Prevailing Wind, 1964; The Tide Comes In, 1966; The Headmaster, 1967; A Sort of Freedom, 1968; The Lord on our Side, 1970; The Second Flowering of Emily Mountjoy, 1979; Greenyards, 1981; Sisters By Rite, 1984; Reasonable Doubts, 1986; 17 children's books. Recreations: reading; walking; travelling. Address: (b.) David Higham Associates, 5-8 Lower John Street, Golden Square, London, W1R 4HA.

Lingard, Robin Anthony, MA, FTS. Full-time Member, Highlands and Islands Development Board, since 1988; Member, Scottish Tourist Board, since 1988; b. 19.7.41, Enfield; m., Margaret; 2 d. Educ. Felsted School; Emmanuel College, Cambridge. Joined Ministry of Aviation, 1963; Private Secretary to Joint Parliamentary Secretary, Ministry of Technology, 1966-68; appointments, Department of Industry, DTI, etc., to 1984; Head, Enterprise Unit, Cabinet Office, 1984-85; Head, Small Firms and Tourism Division, Department of Employment, 1985-87. Member, NEDO Sector Group on Tourism and Leisure. Recreations: watching birds; walking; reading; aviation history. Address: (b.) Bridge House, Inverness, IV1 1QR; T.-0463 234171.

Linkie, William Sinclair. Controller, Inland Revenue, Scotland, since 1983; b. 9.3.31, Edinburgh; m., Primrose; 1 s.; 1 d. Educ. George Heriot's, Edinburgh. Entered Civil Service, 1948; served in Edinburgh, Inverness, Cupar, Dundee and East Kilbride; appointments including District Inspector, Edinburgh 6 District, Principal Inspector i/c Centre 1, Principal Inspector i/c Edinburgh 5 District. President, Inland Revenue Sports Association, Scotland; Elder, Church of Scotland. Recreations: golf; choral singing. Address: (b.) 80 Lauriston Place, Edinburgh, EH3 9SL; T.-031-229 9344.

Linklater, Karl Alexander, BVM&S, PhD, FRCVS. Director, Scottish Agricultural Colleges Veterinary Investigation Service, since 1986; President, Association of Veterinary Teachers and Research Workers (Scotland), since 1988; b. 1.9.39, Stromness, Orkney; m., Margaret Carr Gibb; 1 s.; 1 d. Educ. Robert Gordon's College, Aberdeen; Edinburgh University. General veterinary practice, Tarland, Aberdeenshire, 1962-66; North of Scotland College of Agriculture, Aberdeen, 1966-67; Royal (Dick) School of Veterinary Studies, Edinburgh University, 1967-73; East of Scotland College of Agriculture, St. Boswells, 1973-86. President, Sheep Veterinary Society, 1983-85; winner, Alan Baldry Award, 1982. Recreations: sport; gardening; sheep breeding. Address: (h.) Bridge Park, Old Bridge Road, Selkirk; T.-0750 20571.

Linklater, Magnus Duncan. Editor, The Scotsman, since 1988; b. 21.2.42, Harray, Orkney; m., Veronica Lyle; 2 s.; 1 d. Educ. Eton College; Cambridge University. Reporter, Daily Express, Manchester, 1965-66; London Evening Standard: Diary Reporter, 1966-67, Editor, Londoner's Diary, 1967-69; Sunday Times: Editor, Spectrum, 1969-72, Editor, Colour Magazine, 1972-75, News Editor/Features Editor, 1975-83; Managing Editor, The Observer, 1983-86; Editor, London Daily News, 1986-87. Publications: Hoax: the Howard Hughes-Clifford Irving Affair (Co-author); Jeremy Thorpe: A Secret Life (Co-author); The Falklands War (with Sunday Times Insight team); Massacre - the story of Glencoe; The Fourth Reich - Klaus Barbie and the Neo-Fascist Connection (Co-author); Not With Honour - the inside story of the Westland Affair (Co-author). Recreations: tennis; cricket; fishing. Address: (b.) 20 North Bridge, Edinburgh, EH1 1YT; T.-031-225 2468.

Linklater, Marjorie; b. 19.3.09, Edinburgh; m., Eric Linklater (deceased); 2 s.; 2 d. Educ. St. George's School, Edinburgh; Downe House, Newbury, Berkshire; Royal Academy of Dramatic Art, London. Stage career ended, 1930, after appearing in three plays in West End; returned to Scotland and married Eric Linklater, 1933; SSAFA Representative, 1942-45; Member, Ross and Cromarty County Council, 1953-69; served on Inverness Hospital Board; Member, Scottish Arts Council, 1957-63; former Member, Advisory Council, HIDB; Council Member, European Architectural Heritage Year, 1972-75; joined Scottish National Party, 1979, having progressed from Conservative via Liberal; as Chairman of Orkney Heritage Society, 1977-81, led "No Uranium" campaign to prevent uranium mining in Orkney; at present Secretary, Stormy Bank Group opposed to dumping nuclear waste in seabed off Orkney; founder Chairman, Pier Arts Centre Management Committee; helped to initiate Orkney Folk Festival. Recreations: committees; the arts. Address: (h.) 20 Main Street, Kirkwall, Orkney, KW15 1BU; T.-0856 3619.

Lisgo, John, BSc (Econ) (Hons), DipEd (Hons). Principal, Jewel and Esk Valley College, Edinburgh, since 1986 (Lauder Technical College, Dunfermline, 1983-86); b. 8.7.40, Seaham, Durham; m., Norma Ranson Peel; 1 s. Educ. Ryhope School, Sunderland; London School of Economics and Political Science; Durham University. Assistant Teacher of History and Mathematics, Boldon Secondary School, 1962-63; Assistant Lecturer in Economics, then Liaison Officer for Adult Education, Monkwearmouth College of Further Education, 1963-72; Stevenson College of Further Education: Senior Lecturer in Social Studies, 1972-75, Head, Department of Language and Social Studies, 1975-80, Assistant Principal, 1980-83. Convener, Scottish Branch, Association of Principals; Member: City & Guilds Scottish Consultative Committee, MEC, SCOTVEC Sector G Committee. Recreation: swimming. Address: (b.) 24 Milton Road East, Edinburgh, EH15 2PP; T.-031-669 8461.

Lister-Kaye, Sir John, 8th Bt. of Grange. Naturalist; Member, International Committee, World Wilderness Foundation, since 1984; Chairman, Scottish Advisory Committee, RSPB, since 1985; b. 8.5.46; m., Sorrel Deirdre; 1 s.; 2 d. Educ. Allhallows School. Founded field studies centre, Highlands, 1970; founder Director, Aigas Trust, 1979. Publications: The White Island, 1972; Seal Cull, 1979; The Seeing Eye, 1980. Address: (h.) Aigas House, Beauly, Inverness-shire, IV4 7AD.

Liston, William Alexander, BSc, MB, ChB, FRCOG. Consultant in Obstetrics and Gynaecology, Royal Infirmary and Simpson Memorial Maternity Pavilion, Edinburgh, since 1977; Honorary Senior Lecturer, Edinburgh University, since 1977; b. 24.10.41, Edinburgh; m., Kay Elizabeth Adams; 3 s.; 1 d. Educ. Melville College; St. Andrews University; Edinburgh University. Lecturer, Obstetrics and Gynaecology, Aberdeen University, 1972-75; Senior Lecturer, Obstetrics and Gynaecology, Dar Es Salaam University, 1975-77. Recreations: gardening; skiing; hillwalking. Address: (h.) 36A Inverleith Place, Edinburgh; T.-031-552 2994.

Lithgow, Sir William (James), 2nd Bt, DL. Director, Lithgows Ltd.; b. 19.5.34; m., 1, Valerie Helen Scott (deceased); 2, Mary Claire Hill; 2 s.; 1 d. Educ. Winchester College. Chairman, Lithgow Drydocks Ltd., 1967-78; Vice-Chairman, Scott Lithgow Ltd., 1968-78; Chairman, Lithgows Ltd., 1959-84; Chairman, Western Ferries (Argyll) Ltd., 1972-85; Chairman, Campbeltown Shipyard Ltd., since 1970; Director, Bank of Scotland, 1962- 86; Member, Queen's Bodyguard for Scotland (Royal Company of Archers); Past Chairman, Iona Cathedral Trustees Management Board; Hon. LLD, Strathclyde; DL, Renfrewshire, 1970.

Little, Keith, MB, ChB, MD, MRCP, FRCSEdin. Consultant in Accident and Emergency Medicine, Edinburgh Royal Infirmary; b. 26.4.43, Yeadon, Yorkshire; m., Margaret R.; 2 s.; 2 d. Educ. Dalbeattie High School; Dumfries Academy; Edinburgh Medical School. First posts in Edinburgh; moved to Derby as a Registrar in Accident and Emergency Medicine; Consultant, Chester Royal Infirmary, 1974-78. Chairman, Scottish Committee, Medical Commission on Accident Prevention. Publication: Accident and Emergency Resuscitation (Co-author). Recreations: golf; tennis. Address: (b.) Accident and Emergency Department, Royal Infirmary, Edinburgh; T.-031-229 2477.

Littlejohn, William Hunter, DA, RSA, RSW. Head of Fine Art, Gray's School of Art, Aberdeen, 1980-85; b. 16.4.29, Arbroath. Educ. Arbroath High School; Dundee College of Art. Art Teacher: Angus Schools, 1953-56, Arbroath High School, 1956-66; Lecturer, then Head of Painting, Gray's School of Art, 1970-80. Address: (h.) 16 Colvill Place, Arbroath, Angus; T.-Arbroath 74402.

Livingston, David Munro Sheldon, BSc, PhD, FIFST. Dean, Faculty of Science, Robert Gordon's Institute of Technology, since 1982 (Head, School of Nutritional Science, since 1971); b. Montrose; m., Evelyn Irene Soper; 1 s.; 1 d. Educ. Montrose Academy; Aberdeen University. Assistant Lecturer, then Senior Research Fellow, Aberdeen University; Senior Scientific Officer, Rowett Research Institute, Aberdeen; Head of Department, School of Domestic Science, RGIT. Panel Member, SCEEB, 1971-77; Member, Course Committee E4, SCOTEC, since 1972; Member, Dieticians' Board, Education Committee, Liaison Committee, Council for Professions Supplementary to Medicine. Recreations: game and target pistol shooting. Address: (b.) School of Nutritional Science, Robert Gordon's Institute of Technology, Queen's Road, Aberdeen, AB9 2PG; T.-0224 633611.

Livingston, Martin Gerard, MD, MRCPsych. Senior Lecturer in Psychiatry, Glasgow University, since 1983; Honorary Consulant Psychiatrist, Gartnavel Hospitals, since 1983; b. 19.5.53, Glasgow; m., Hilary Monica; 1 s.; 1 d. Educ. Hillhead High School, Glasgow; Glasgow University. Lecturer in Psychiatry, 1979; Honorary Senior Registrar, 1981; Member, Trainees Committee, Royal College of Psychiatrists, 1982; Secretary, Committee on Community Psychiatry and Rehabilitation, Scottish Division, Royal College of Psychiatrists; Vice Chairman, Psychiatric Sub-Committee, Glasgow Area Medical Committee. Recreations: modern writing; photography; cinema. Address: (b.) Department of Psychological Medicine, 6 Whittingehame Gardens, Glasgow, G12 OAA; T.-041-334 9826.

Livingstone, Jeremy Rae Braithwaite, MB, ChB, FRCSEdin, FRCOG. Consultant Obstetrician and Gynaecologist, Simpson Memorial Maternity Pavilion and Royal Infirmary, Edinburgh, since 1968; President, Edinburgh Obstetrical Society, 1986-88; b. 24.9.32, Simla, India; m., Diana Marjorie Cox; 4 d. Educ. Clifton Hall School, Newbridge; Clifton College, Bristol; Edinburgh University. House Officer appointments, Bangour General Hospital and Royal Hospital for Sick Children, Edinburgh; National Service, Royal Navy, 1957-59; training posts, Bangour General Hospital, 1960-62, and Edinburgh, 1962-68; Council Member, Royal College of Obstetricians and Gynaecologists, representing Scottish members, 1972-75; seconded as Chairman, Department of Obstetrics and Gynaecology, King Faisal Specialist Hospital and Research Centre, Riyadh, 1975-77; Civil Consultant in Obstetrics and Gynaecology, Royal Navy in Scotland; Honorary Treasurer and Secretary, Edinburgh Obstetrical Society; Chairman, Lothian Division, Obstetrics and Gynaecology, 1981-84. Publication: Farquharson Textbook of Operative Surgery (Contributor). Recreations: golf; reading; music. Address: (h.) 19 Glencairn Crescent, Edinburgh, EH12 5BT; T.-031-337 4472.

Livingstone, John Stewart, BSc (Hons). Head Teacher, Rosehall High School, Coatbridge, since 1986; b. 12.3.46, Stranraer; m., Catherine Stevenson; 2 d. Educ. Stranraer High School; Glasgow University; Strathclyde University. Teacher of Mathematics, Bellahouston Academy, 1968-74; Principal Teacher of Mathematics, Allan Glen's Secondary School, 1974-81; Assistant Head Teacher, Castlehead High School, 1981-86. Recreations: sport; bridge. Address: (b.) Rosehall High School, Woodhall Avenue, Coatbridge, ML5 5DB; T.-Coatbridge 31166.

Livingstone, Rognvald Maitland, BA, PhD, NDA, NDAgrE, CBiol, MIBiol. Principal Scientific Officer, Rowett Institute, Aberdeen, since 1981; Unit Director, Commercial Scientific Research, since 1985; b. 27.1.35, Aberdeen; m., Rona; 2 s.; 2 d. Educ. Aberdeen Grammar School; North of Scotland College of Agriculture; Essex Institute of Agriculture; Aberdeen University; Open University. Agricultural Engineer, retail trade; military service, Royal Armoured Corps; agricultural research service, since 1958. Member (SLD), Grampian Regional Council; Governor, North of Scotland College of Agriculture. Recreations: skiing; swimming; hill-walking; gardening; reading. Address: (h.) Kirkstane House, Skene, Aberdeenshire, AB3 6XX; T.-0224 743586.

Livingstone of Bachuil, Alastair, MA, LLB, FSA Scot. Baron of Bachuil; b. 1.9.14, Blantyre, Nyasaland; m., Valerie Collins; 2 s.; 3 d. Educ. Loretto School; Edinburgh University; Cambridge University. Sudan political service, 1938-40; 1940-43: commissioned into West Yorkshire Regiment in Khartoum, later Brigade Intelligence Officer, 9th Indian Infantry Brigade, active service in Eritrea and Western Desert; seconded to Palestine Government as Assistant District Commissioner, 1943-47; Executive, Iraq Petroleum Company Ltd., 1948-73. Chairman, Lismore Community Council, 1977-80; Member, Convention of the Baronage of Scotland; Hereditary Keeper of the Pastoral Staff of Saint Moluag; Chairman, 1745 Association; Editor, Muster Roll of Prince Charles Edward Stuart's Army, 1746. Recreations: genealogy; Scottish history; country pursuits. Address: (h.) Bachuil, Isle of Lismore, Argyll; T.-063 176 256.

Llewelyn, John Edward, BA, MA, BLitt. Reader in Philosophy, Edinburgh University, since 1986; b. 1.2.28, Rogerstone, Newport, Gwent; m., Margaret Woolley. Educ. Bassaleg Secondary Grammar School; University College of Wales, Aberystwyth; Edinburgh University; Oxford University. RAF Education Branch; French Air Force College; Liebfrauenschule, Cologne; Department of Philosophy, University of New England, Australia. Publications: Beyond Metaphysics? The Hermeneutic Circle in Contemporary Continental Philosophy, 1985; Derrida on the Threshold of Sense, 1986. Recreation: hill-walking. Address: (b.) Department of Philosophy, David Hume Tower, George Square, Edinburgh, EH8 9JX; T.-031-667 1011.

Lloyd, Charles Heywood, BSc, PhD, MIM. Senior Lecturer, Department of Dental Prosthetics and Gerontology, Dundee University, since 1985; Consultant in Dental Materials, since 1983; b. 15.9.47, Sinoia, Southern Rhodesia; m., Elizabeth Ann Mead; 1 s.; 2 d. Educ. Milton School, Bulawayo; Ellesmere Port Grammar School; Birmingham University. Research Associate, Department of Physical Metallurgy, Birmingham University, 1972-76; Lecturer, Department of Dental Prosthetics, Dundee University, 1976-85. Member, British Standards Committee. Recreations: philately; golf; beer. Address: (b.) Department of Dental Prosthetics and Gerontology, Dundee University, Dundee DD1 4HN; T.-0382 26041.

Lloyd-Jones, Glyn Robin, MA, BA. Author and Novelist; Adviser, Education Department, Dunbartonshire, since 1972; b. 5.10.34, London; m., Sallie Hollocombe; 1 s.; 2 d. Educ. Blundell's School, Tiverton; Selwyn College, Cambridge University; Jordanhill College of Education. Teaching in Scottish secondary schools; Director, Curriculum Development Centre, Clydebank; English-Speaking Union Thyne Travel Scholarship to America, 1974; President, Scottish Association of Writers, since 1981. Publications: children's: Where the Forest and the Garden Meet, 1980; novels: Lord of the Dance (Winner, BBC/Arrow First Novel Competition, 1983); The Dreamhouse, 1985; education books: Assessment: From Principles to Action, 1985; How to Produce Better Worksheets, 1985. Recreations: mountaineering; sea-canoeing; wind-surfing; photography. Address: (h.) 26 East Clyde Street, Helensburgh, G84 7PG; T.-0436 2010.

Loasby, Brian John, BA, MLitt. President, Scottish Economic Society, since 1987; Honorary/ Emeritus Professor of Economics, Stirling University, since 1984; b. 2.8.30, Kettering; m., Judith Ann Robinson; 2 d. Educ. Kettering Grammar School; Emmanuel College, Cambridge. Assistant in Political Economy, Aberdeen University, 1955-58; Bournville Research Fellow, Birmingham University, 1958-61; Tutor in Management Studies, Bristol University, 1961-67; Lecturer in Economics, then Senior Lecturer, then Professor of Management Economics, Stirling University, 1967-84. Member, Council, Royal Economic Society, 1981-86. Publications: The Swindon Project, 1973; Choice, Complexity and Ignorance, 1976; The Mind and Method of the Economist, 1989. Address: (h.) 8 Melfort Drive, Stirling, FK7 0BD; T.-0786 72124.

Lochhead, Liz. Poet and Playwright; b. Motherwell. Educ. Glasgow School of Art. Combined teaching art and writing for eight years; became full-time writer after selection as first holder, Scottish/Canadian Writers' Exchange Fellowship, 1978; former Writer in Residence, Tattenhall Centre, Chester. Publications: Memo for Spring, 1972; Islands, 1978; Grimm Sisters, 1981; Dreaming Frankenstein, 1984; True Confessions, 1985; plays include: Blood and Ice, Dracula, Same Difference, Sweet Nothings, Now and Then, True Confessions.

Lockhart, Sheriff Brian Alexander, BL. Sheriff, Glasgow and Strathkelvin, since 1981; b. 1.10.42, Ayr; m., Christine Ross Clark; 2 s.; 2 d. Educ. Glasgow Academy; Glasgow University. Partner, Robertson Chalmers and Auld, Solicitors, 1967-79; Sheriff, North Strathclyde, at Paisley, 1979-81. Recreations: fishing; golf; squash; family. Address: (h.) 18 Hamilton Avenue, Glasgow, G41; T.-041-427 1921.

Lockhart of the Lee, Angus Hew. Landowner; b. 17.8.46, Dunsyre; m., Susan Elizabeth Normand; 1 s.; 1 d. Educ. Rannoch School, Perthshire; North of Scotland College of Agriculture. Recreations: shooting; water skiing; walking the dog. Address: (b.) Newholm, Dunsyre, Lanark; T.-0968 82254.

Lockley, Stephen Randolph, BSc, CEng, MICE, FICT, MIMunE, MIHT, DipTE. Director General, Strathclyde Passenger Transport Executive, since 1986; b. 19.6.43, Manchester; m., Angela; 2 d. Educ. Morecambe Grammar School; Manchester University. Highway and Planning Engineer, Lancashire County Council, 1964-72; Transportation and Planning Engineer, Lanarkshire County Council, 1972-75; Strathclyde Regional Council: Principal Engineer (Transportation), 1975-77, Depute Director of Policy Planning, 1977-80, Principal Executive Officer, 1980-86. Address: (b.) Consort House, 12 West George Street, Glasgow, G2 1HN; T.-041-332 6811.

Lodge, Adrian Morris, BSc (Hons), MB, ChB, DPM, MRCPsych. Consultant Psychiatrist, Lothian Health Board, since 1978; Honorary Senior Lecturer, Edinburgh University, since 1978; b. 11.5.45, Huddersfield; m., Caroline Lodge; 1 s.; 1 d. Educ. Huddersfield New College; Edinburgh University. Pre-registration year, Western General Hospital, 1969-70; postgraduate training in psychiatry, Royal Edinburgh and Associated Hospitals, 1970-78; now Consultant Psychiatrist (General Psychiatry), Royal Edinburgh Hospital and Hopetoun Unit, Herdmanflat, East Lothian; Chairman, Hopetoun Unit Association. Recreations: squash; caravanning; gardening. Address: (h.) 39 Braid Road, Edinburgh; T.-031-447 4856.

Logan, Andrew, SDA, NDA, FIHort. Farmer; Director, Scotfresh Ltd., since 1984; Governor: National Vegetable Research Station, since 1977, Institute of Horticultural Research, since 1987, Scottish Crop Research Institute, since 1986; Director: Scottish Nuclear Stock Association, since 1983, East of Scotland Growers, since 1987; Member: Horticultural Development Council, since 1986, Scottish Agricultural Research and Development Advisory Council, since 1987, Home Grown Cereals Authority Research and Development Committee, since 1987; Chairman, Dorward Gray Ltd.; b. 24.3.40, Cupar; m., M.L. Fleming; 3 s.; 1 d. Educ. Strathallan School; Edinburgh School of Agriculture. Director: Fifegro, 1973-79, Elba, 1979-84, Central Farmers, 1974-83; Chairman, Soft Fruit and Field Vegetable Committee, Scottish NFU, 1979-83; Member, Scottish Agricultural Development Council, 1983-86; Governor, Strathallan School, since 1986. Recreations: squash; skiing; golf. Address: (h.) Dairsie Mains, Cupar, Fife; T.-Cupar 52808.

Logan, James, CChem, MRIC. Vice-Chairman, Scottish Arts Council, 1984- 88; Member, Arts Council of Great Britain, 1984-88; Director, Scotland the What? comedy revue, since 1970; b. 28.10.27, Haddington; m., Anne Brand; 1 s.; 1 d. Educ. Robert Gordon's Institute. Former Member, Senior Scientific Staff, Macaulay Institute for Soil Research; former Appeal Administrator, Aberdeen Maritime Museum; Founder/Chairman, Friends of Aberdeen Art Gallery and Museums; Committee Member, Aberdeen Art Gallery. Queen's Silver Jubilee Medal. Recreations: theatre; trying to cope with The Guardian's new layout. Address: 53 Fountainhall Road, Aberdeen, AB2 4EU; T.-0224 646914.

Logan, Jimmy. Actor/Manager; Comedian; Chairman, Logan Theatres Ltd., since 1964; Chairman, Rita Theatres Ltd., since 1953; Chairman, Dowanhill Productions Ltd., since 1953; b. 4.4.28, Glasgow; m., Pamela de Wilde Donald; 1 s.; 1 d. Educ. Bellahouston Academy; Gourock High School. One of five children who appeared on stage as The Logan Family; as a youth, toured as an accordionist, juvenile lead and comedian's feed; by the age of 19, was playing star parts at the Metropole, Glasgow; co-starred in the film Floodtide; for many years starred in Five Past Eight (summer revue) and in numerous pantomimes; other stage work includes Rob Roy and A Funny Thing Happened on the Way to the Forum (musicals), The Mating Game and A Bit Between the Teeth (plays); wrote and produced Lauder (one-man show); nine appearances at Royal performances; directed and starred in Jack and the Beanstalk, Eden Court, Inverness, 1984; played Archie Rice in The Entertainer, Byre, St. Andrews, 1984. President, Showbusiness Benevolent Fund; Trustee, Scottish Disability Foundation. Recreations: flying; collecting theatrical memorabilia and old music hall postcards.

Logan, Norman Hunter, MB, ChB, MFCM, DPH, DRCOG, DPA. Community Medicine Specialist, Argyll and Clyde Health Board; Chairman, BMA West of Scotland Committee for Community Medicine; b. 28.8.27, Cleland, Lanarkshire. Educ. High School of Glasgow; Glasgow University. District Medical Officer, Renfrew Health District, 1977-84. President, Clan Maclennan Association; Initiator, Clyde Walkway Project; founder Member and Committee Member, 1975-84, New Lanark Civic Trust; founder Member and Council Member, New Glasgow Society; Honorary President, Cathcart Society; Past President, Glasgow District Council, SNP; Council Member and Heraldic Adviser, the Flag Institute. Publication: A Clyde Walkway, 1973. Recreations: heraldry and vexillology; phonetics; hill-walking; photography. Address: (h.) 12 Kirkwell Road, Glasgow, G44; T.-041-637 2725.

Logan, Robert James, MBE, JP. Vice-Chairman, Lanarkshire Health Board, since 1983; b. 19.4.21, Carnwath; m., Mary Ann Brown Watt. Educ. St. Mary's School, Melrose; Edinburgh Academy. Lanark Branch President and Area Executive Member, National Farmers Union of Scotland; member, Board of Management, Southern Lanark Hospitals, 1962; joined Lanarkshire Health Board, 1974; Member, State Hospital Management Committee, since 1976. Recreations: reading; walking; sport; sea motor boat cruising. Address: (h.) Loganlea, Eastshield, Carnwath, ML11 8LP; T.-Carnwath 840200.

Logan, Rev. Robert James Victor, MA, BD. Minister, Crown Church, Inverness, since 1970; Clerk, Synod of the Southern Highlands, since 1976; Clerk, Inverness Presbytery, since 1980; b. Kilmarnock. Educ. Dundee High School; St. Andrews University; Edinburgh University. Assistant Minister, Auld Kirk of Ayr, 1962-64; Minister, Newton Parish Church, Dalkeith, 1964-70; Member, Church Boundaries' Commission, 1974-75; Clerk, Synod of Moray, 1972-75; Convener, Nomination Committee, General Assembly, 1979-82; Chairman, successful group applying for franchise to operate Moray Firth Radio, 1979-81. Publication: The Lion, The Pit and the Snowy Day. Recreations: classical music; opera; bridge; reading history. Address: (h.) 39 Southside Road, Inverness, IV2 4XA; T.-0463 231140.

Logan, Rt. Rev. Vincent, DipRE. Roman Catholic Bishop of Dunkeld, since 1981; b. 30.6.41, Bathgate. Educ. Blairs College, Aberdeen; St. Andrew's College, Drygrange. Ordained Priest, 1964; Assistant Priest, St. Margaret's, Edinburgh, 1964-66; Corpus Christi College, London, 1966-67; Chaplain, St. Joseph's Hospital, Rosewell, Midlothian, 1966-67; Adviser in Religious Education, Archdiocese of St. Andrews and Edinburgh, 1967; Parish Priest, St. Mary's, Ratho, 1977-81; Vicar Episcopal for Education, Edinburgh, 1978. Address: Bishop's House, 29 Roseangle, Dundee, DD1 4LS; T.-0382 24327.

Logie, John Robert Cunningham, MB, ChB, PhD, FRCS, FRCSEdin. Consultant General Surgeon, Inverness Hospitals, since 1981; b. 9.9.46, Aberdeen; m., Sheila C. Will. Educ. Robert Gordon's College, Aberdeen; Trinity College, Glenalmond; Aberdeen University. House Officer, then Senior House Officer, then Lecturer, Department of Surgery, then Senior Registrar, Aberdeen Royal Infirmary. Recreations: rugby refereeing; garden; railways. Address: (h.) 20 Moray Park Avenue, Culloden, Inverness, IV1 2LS; T.-Inverness 792090.

Long, Hamish Arthur, BSc, PhD. Assistant Director, Scottish Examination Board, since 1986; b. 21.9.41, Edinburgh; m., Elizabeth Anne Stephen; 1 s.; 1 d. Educ. Daniel Stewart's College; Edinburgh University; Moray House College of Education. X-ray crystallographic research, Edinburgh University, 1963-66; Technical Officer, ICI, 1966-67; Science Teacher/Special Assistant, North Berwick High School, 1968-72; Principal Teacher of Science, Dunbar Grammar School, 1972-73; Examination Officer, then Senior Examination Officer, then Statistics and Development Officer, Scottish Examination Board, 1973-86. Recreations: music; gardening; painting. Address: (b.) Ironmills Road, Dalkeith, Midlothian, EH22 1LE; T.-031-663 6601.

Longair, Professor Malcolm Sim, BSc, MA, PhD, LLD (Hons), FRSE. Astronomer Royal for Scotland, since 1980; Regius Professor of Astronomy, Edinburgh University; Director, Royal Observatory, Edinburgh; b. 18.5.41, Dundee; m., Deborah Howard (qv); 1 s.; 1 d. Educ. Morgan Academy, Dundee; Queen's College, Dundee; Trinity College, Cambridge. Fellow, Clare Hall, Cambridge, 1967-80: Research Fellow, 1967-71, Official Fellow, 1971-80, Praelector of Clare Hall, 1971-77; Visiting Assistant Professor of Radio Astronomy, California Institute of Technology, 1972; Visiting Professor of Astronomy, Institute for Advanced Study, Princeton, 1978; Exchange Visitor to USSR Space Research Institute, Moscow, on six occasions, 1975-79; Holder, Research Fellowship, Royal Commission for the Exhibition of 1851, 1966-68; Holder, James Clerk Maxwell Scholarship, Cavendish Laboratory, Cambridge, 1964-66; Holder, James Caird Scholarship, St. Andrews University, 1963-64. Britannica Award for dissemination of knowledge, 1986. Publications: Observational Cosmology (Co-author), 1978; High Energy Astrophysics, 1981; Theoretical Concepts in Physics, 1984. Recreations: music (especially opera); art and architecture (especially Italian). Address: (h.) 41 Cluny Drive, Edinburgh; T.-031-447 9069.

Loraine, John Alexander, DSc, MB, PhD, FRCPEdin, FInstBiol, FRSA, FRSE. Senior Lecturer, Department of Community Medicine, Edinburgh University, since 1979; b. 14.5.24, Edinburgh; m., Alison Blair. Educ. George Watson's Boys' College, Edinburgh; Edinburgh University. Director, MRC Clinical Endocrinology Unit, Edinburgh, 1961-72; Visiting Professor of Endocrinology, Donner Laboratory, University of California, 1964; MRC External Scientific Staff and Honorary Senior Lecturer, Department of Community Medicine, Edinburgh University, 1972-79; Director, Centre for Human Ecology, Edinburgh University, 1978-84; Chairman, Doctors and Overpopulation, since 1972; Vice Chairman, Conservation Society, 1974-87. Publications: Hormone Assays and their Clinical Application (Co-author); Recent Research on Gonadotrophic Hormones (Co-author); Fertility and Contraception in the Human Female (Co-author); Sex and the Population Crisis; The Death of Tomorrow; Reproductive Endocrinology and World Population (Editor); Environmental Medicine (Co-Editor); Understanding Homosexuality (Editor); Syndromes of the Seventies; Here Today...(Co-Editor); Global Signposts to the 21st Century; Energy Policies Around the World. Recreations: reading modern history and political biography; music; bridge. Address: (b.) Department of Community Medicine, Edinburgh University, Medical School, Teviot Place, Edinburgh; T.-031-667 1011.

Lord, Geoffrey, MA, AIB, FRSA. Secretary and Treasurer, Carnegie UK Trust, since 1977; Secretary, The Unemployed Voluntary Action Fund, since 1982; President, Centre for Environmental Interpretation; b. 24.2.28, Rochdale; m., Jean; 1 s.; 1 d. Educ. Rochdale Grammar School; Bradford University. Midland Bank Ltd., 1946-58; Greater Manchester Probation and After-Care Service, 1958-76 (Deputy Chief Probation Officer, 1974-76); Vice-President, Selcare Trust; Trustee, Artlink Edinburgh and The Lothians Ltd.; Honorary Fellow, Manchester Polytechnic, 1987. Publications: The Arts and Disabilities, 1981; Interpretation of the Environment, 1984. Recreations: the arts; philately; walking; enjoying life. Address: (h.) 9 Craigleith View, Edinburgh.

Lorimer, A. Ross, MD, FRCP, FRCPGlas, FRCPEdin. Consultant Cardiologist, Glasgow Royal Infirmary, since 1970; Honorary Lecturer in Medical Cardiology, since 1970; b. 5.5.37, Bellshill; m., Fiona Marshall; 3 s. Educ. Uddingston Grammar School; High School of Glasgow; Glasgow University. Recreations: reading; walking. Address: (b.) Department of Cardiology, Royal Infirmary, Glasgow.

Lorimer, Hew Martin, OBE, HonLLD, RSA. Sculptor in stone; b. 22.5.07, Scotland; m., Mary McLeod Wylie; 2 s.; 1 d. Educ. Loretto School; Edinburgh College of Art. Former PRO, The British Council, Scotland; Royal Scottish Academician (retired), now Senior Academician; Fellow, Royal Society of British Sculptors (retired); Past Chairman, St. Andrews Preservation Trust; Representative in Fife, National Trust for Scotland. Recreations: music; foreign travel. Address: (h.) Kellie Castle, Pittenweem, Fife, KY10 2RF.

Lothian, Sheriff Andrew, MA, LLB. Sheriff of Glasgow and Strathkelvin, since 1979; b. 6.2.42; m.; 2 s.; 2 s. by pr. m. Educ. Trinity College, Glenalmond; St. Andrews University; Edinburgh University. Advocate, 1968; Honorary Lecturer, Glasgow University, since 1984.

Lothian, Professor Niall, BA, CA. Grant Thornton Professor of Accounting and Head, Department of Accountancy and Finance, Heriot-Watt University, since 1987; b. 27.2.48, Edinburgh; m., Carol Miller; 1 s.; 1 d. Educ. Daniel Stewart's College, Edinburgh; Heriot-Watt University. Lecturer, then Senior Lecturer, Department of Accountancy and Finance, Heriot-Watt University, 1973-87; Visiting Professor: IMEDE, Lausanne, 1979-80, INSEAD, Fontainebleau, 1984; Consultant, United Nations Industrial Development Organisation, Vienna, since 1980. Publications: Accounting for Inflation: Issues and Managerial Practices, 1978; Audit Quality and Value for Money, 1983; How Companies Manage R. & D., 1984; Corporate Performance Indicators, 1987. Address: (b.) Department of Accountancy and Finance, Heriot-Watt University, 31-35 Grassmarket, Edinburgh, EH1 2HT; T.-031-225 6465.

Lothian, 12th Marquess of (Peter Francis Walter Kerr), KCVO, DL; b. 8.9.22, Melbourne, near Derby; m., Antonella Newland; 2 s.; 4 d. Educ. Ampleforth College, York; Christ Church, Oxford. Parliamentary Under Secretary, Ministry of Health, 1964; Parliamentary Under Secretary, Foreign and Commonwealth Office, 1970-72; Lord in Waiting, 1972-73; Lord Warden of the Stannaries, 1977-83. Knight of Malta; Ensign, Queen's Bodyguard for Scotland; Chairman of Council, Scottish Branch, British Red Cross, 1973-83. Recreations: music; shooting. Address: Monteviot, Jedburgh, Roxburghshire; T.-08353 288.

Louden, Richard Cameron, MA (Hons), DipEd. Depute Director of Education, Strathclyde Regional Council, since 1982. Educ. Dunfermline High School; Edinburgh University; Moray House College of Education. Depute Director of Education, Dunbarton County Council, 1972-75; Senior Education Officer, Renfrew Division, Strathclyde, 1975-82. Former Member, Consultative Committee on the Curriculum. Address: (b.) Regional Offices, India Street, Glasgow; T.-041-227 2837.

Louden, Rev. Robert Stuart, TD, MA, BD, DD, DLitt. Minister, Church of Scotland, since 1938; b. 11.8.12, Dundee; m., Helen Stewart Wilson; 2 s.; 3 d. Educ. Downfield School; Morgan Academy, Dundee; Edinburgh University; Marburg University; Oxford University. Licensed to preach, 1936; ordained, St. Mary's, Old Aberdeen, 1938; War Service: Chaplain to the Forces, 1939 (Middle East), Prisoner of War, Tobruk, 1942; twice mentioned in Despatches; DACG (TA), Scottish Command, 1958-63; Territorial Decoration (three bars); Minister: Dailly Parish Church, 1945-49, Greyfriars, Edinburgh, 1949-78; Convener, General Assembly Committees: Colonial and Continental, 1957-62, Public Worship, 1965-70; Vice-Convener, Church Hymnary Revision, 1963-73; Vice Chairman and Chairman, Heriot Trust, 1952-75; Vice-President, World Alliance of Reformed Churches, 1964-70; Past President: Scottish Ecclesiological Society, Church Service Society, Scottish Church Society, New College Union, Society for the Relief of the Destitute Sick, Edinburgh Royal Infirmary Samaritan Society; Past Junior and Senior Grand Chaplain, Grand Lodge of Scotland (Masonic); Commandeur de Merite, Order of St. Lazarus of Jerusalem; Order, Cross of St. Mark (second class); President, Edinburgh University Graduates' Association, 1979-80, and Member, University Court, since 1985. Publications: The Church in the World, 1948; The True Face of the Kirk, 1963. Recreations: reading; writing; walking. Address: (h.) 88 Cockburn Crescent, Balerno, Midlothian, EH14 7HU; T.-031-449 4467.

Loudon, John Alexander, LLB, NP, SSC. Solicitor, Messrs J. & A. Hastie, SSC, Edinburgh; Member, Council, Law Society of Scotland; b. 5.12.49, Edinburgh; m., Alison Jane Bruce Laird; 1 s. Educ. Edinburgh Academy; Dundee University. Apprenticeship, Tindal, Oatts and Roger, Solicitors, Glasgow. Secretary, Scottish Division, British Hotels Restaurants & Caterers Association; Secretary, Edinburgh and Lothians Decorators' Association. Recreations: skiing; refurbishing country cottage. Address: (b.) 43 York Place, Edinburgh, EH1 3HT; T.-031-556 7951.

Loudon, John Bruce, MB, ChB, FRCPsych, DPM. Consultant Psychiatrist, Royal Edinburgh Hospital, since 1978 (Deputy Physician Superintendent, since 1980); Honorary Senior Lecturer, Department of Psychiatry, Edinburgh University, since 1978; b. 12.8.43, Edinburgh; m., Susan Mary Lay; 3 s. Educ. Edinburgh Academy; Edinburgh University. Address: (b.) Andrew Duncan Clinic, Morningside, Edinburgh, EH10 5HF; T.-031-447 2011.

Lovat, Sheriff Leonard Scott, BL. Sheriff of South Strathclyde, Dumfries and Galloway, at Hamilton, since 1978; b. 28.7.26, Gourock; m., Elinor Frances McAlister; 1 s.; 1 d. Educ. St. Aloysius College, Glasgow; Glasgow University. Solicitor, 1948; in partnership, 1955-59; also Assistant to Professor of Civil Law, Glasgow University, 1954-63; Procurator Fiscal Depute, Glasgow, 1960; Cropwood Fellow, Institute of Criminology, Cambridge University, 1971; Senior Assistant Procurator Fiscal, Glasgow and Strathkelvin, 1976. Publication: Climbers' Guide to Glencoe and Ardgour (two volumes), 1959 and 1965. Recreations: music; mountaineering; bird-watching. Address: (h.) 38 Kelvin Court, Glasgow, G12 OAE; T.-041-357 0031.

Lovat, 17th Baron (Simon Christopher Joseph Fraser), DSO (1942), MC, TD, JP, DL. 24th Chief of Clan Fraser of Lovat; b. 9.7.11; m., Rosamond Broughton; 4 s.; 2 d. Educ. Ampleforth; Magdalen College, Oxford. Served Second World

War (Captain, Lovat Scouts, 1939, Lt.-Col., 1942, Brig., Commandos, 1943; wounded); Under Secretary of State for Foreign Affairs, 1945. Address: (h.) Balblair, Beauly, Inverness-shire.

Love, Frances Mary. Director, Scottish Marriage Guidance Council, since 1987; Tutor and Lecturer, Scottish Human Relations and Counselling Course, since 1986; Organisational Consultant, SIHR, since 1986; b. 2.7.38, Edinburgh; m., James Love; 1 d. Educ. Broughton Secondary School. Edinburgh Public Library Service; voluntary playleader, Edinburgh Toddlers Playcentres; Pre-School Playgroup Association: playgroup supervisor, fieldworker, Scottish Adviser; General Secretary, Pre-School Playgroups Association; Executive Officer/Company Secretary, Scottish Council for Opportunities in Play Experience (SCOPE). Member, Management Board, Scottish Council of Voluntary Organisations; Member, Executive Committees, Scottish Child & Family Alliance and Scottish Council for Single Parents. Recreations: gardening; reading; theatre; dress-making. Address: (b.) 26 Frederick Street, Edinburgh; T.-031-225 5006.

Love, Professor Philip Noel, CBE (1983), MA, LLB. Professor of Conveyancing and Professional Practice of Law, Aberdeen University, since 1974 (Dean, Faculty of Law, 1979-82; Vice-Principal, since 1986); Member, Scottish Law Commission, since 1986; b. 25.12.39; m., Isabel Leah; 3 s. Educ. Aberdeen Grammar School; Aberdeen University. Admitted Solicitor in Scotland, 1963; Advocate in Aberdeen, since 1963; Partner, Campbell Connon & Co., Solicitors, Aberdeen, 1963-74 (Consultant, since 1974); Law Society of Scotland: Council Member, 1975-86, Vice-President, 1980-81, President, 1981-82; Local Chairman, Rent Assessment Panel for Scotland, since 1972; Member, Joint Standing Committee on Legal Education in Scotland, 1976-85 (Chairman, 1976-80); Chairman, Secretary of State for Scotland's Expert Committee on House Purchase and Sale, 1982-84; Vice-President, Scottish Law Agents Society, 1970; Member, Rules Council, Court of Session, since 1968; Council Member, International Bar Association, 1983-87; Chairman, Aberdeen Home for Widowers' Children, since 1971; President, Aberdeen Grammar School FP Club, 1987-88; Member, Joint Ethical Committee, Grampian Health Board, since 1984 (Chairman, since 1986); Honorary Sheriff, Grampian, Highland and Islands, since 1978. Recreations: rugby (golden oldies version now!); keep fit. Address: (h.) 3A Rubislaw Den North, Aberdeen, AB2 4AL; T.-Aberdeen 313339.

Love, Robert Malcolm, MA (Hons). Controller (formerly Head) of Drama, Scottish Television, since 1979; b. 9.1.37, Paisley. Educ. Paisley Grammar School; Glasgow University; Washington University. Actor and Director, various repertory companies, including Nottingham Playhouse, 1962-65; Producer, Thames TV, 1966-75, including Public Eye, Van Der Valk; freelance Producer, 1976-79, including Thames TV, LWT, Seacastle Film Productions, Scottish TV. Awards including: Commonwealth Festival, New York TV and Film Festival, Chicago Film Festival, Scottish Radio and Television Industries; nominated for International Emmy, New York, 1982. Recreations: reading; music; theatre; travel. Address: (b.) Scottish Television, Cowcaddens, Glasgow.

Loveless, Norman Ernest, MA, PhD. Senior Lecturer in Psychology, Dundee University; b. 9.10.21, London; m., Pamela May Ross; 2 s. Educ. Northern Grammar School, Portsmouth; Edinburgh University. Experimental Assistant, Mine Design Department, Admiralty, 1940-41; Radar Officer, RAF, 1941-47; student, 1947-51; Lecturer in Psychology, St. Andrews University, 1951-52; Lecturer in Industrial Health, Medical School, Newcastle, 1952-59; joined Dundee University as Lecturer, 1959. Recreation: oil painting. Address: (h.) The Limes, Coupar Angus Road, Birkhill, Dundee, DD2 5QE; T.-0382 580425.

Low, Alistair James, BSc, FFA. Director, William M. Mercer Fraser Ltd., Actuaries and Employee Benefit Consultants, since 1986; Non-Executive Director, Scottish Widows Fund, since 1984; Chairman, Championship Committee, Royal and Ancient Golf Club, 1985-88; b. 2.8.42, Dundee; m., Shona Wallace; 2 s.; 1 d. Educ. Dundee High School; St. Andrews University. Partner, Duncan C. Fraser & Co., Consulting Actuaries, 1968-86. Recreations: golf; skiing; bridge. Address: (h.) Thornfield, Erskine Loan, Gullane, East Lothian; T.-0620 843454.

Low, Donald Alexander, MA, BPhil, PhD, FRSE, FSA Scot. Reader in English Studies, Stirling University, since 1981; b. 14.5.39, Greenock; m., Sheona Grant MacCorquodale; 1 s.; 1 d. Educ. Greenock Academy; George Heriot's; Hawick High School; St. Andrews University; Cambridge University. Lecturer in English, St. Andrews University, 1966-72; Lecturer in English, Stirling University, 1972-76. Publications: Robert Burns: The Critical Heritage (Editor), 1974; Critical Essays on Robert Burns (Editor), 1975; That Sunny Dome, 1977; Thieves' Kitchen: The Regency Underworld, 1982; Robert Burns: The Kilmarnock Poems (Editor), 1985; Robert Burns, 1986. Recreations: travel; music. Address: (h.) 17 Chalton Road, Bridge of Allan, Stirlingshire; T.-0786 832661.

Low, Ian Campbell, BSc, CA. Chairman, J.T. Inglis & Sons Ltd., since 1945; b. 15.12.12, Newport, Fife; m., Nora Bolton; 2 d. Educ. Fettes College; St. Andrews University. Deputy Chairman, then Chairman, Low & Bonar PLC, Dundee, 1937-77; Chairman, Dundee and London Investment Trust PLC, 1950-87. Recreations: shooting; fishing; gardening. Address: (h.) Holly Hill, 69 Dundee Road, Broughty Ferry, Dundee, DD5 1NA; T.-0382 79148.

Low, Sir James (Richard) Morrison-, 3rd Bt, DL, DFH, CEng, MIEE. Director, Osborne & Hunter Ltd., Glasgow, since 1956; b. 3.8.25; m., Ann Rawson Gordon; 1 s.; 3 d. Educ. Ardvreck; Harrow; Merchiston; Faraday House, London. Royal Corps of Signals, 1943-47 (Captain). President, Electrical Contractors Association of Scotland, 1982-84; Director, National Inspection Council of Electrical Installation Contractors, 1982-88 (Chairman, Scottish Committee, 1982-88); Chairman, Electrical Industry Liaison Committee, 1986-88; Chairman, Fife Area Scout Council,

1966-84; Chairman, Cupar Branch, East Fife Conservative Association, 1965-78; Trustee, TSB, 1960-80; President, Elecrical Contractors Association of Scotland, 1982-84; DL, Fife, 1978. Address: (h.) Kilmaron Castle, Cupar, Fife.

Lowden, Professor Gordon Stuart, MA, LLB, CA. Chairman, Dundee Port Authority, since 1979; Senior Vice-President, Institute of Chartered Accountants of Scotland, since 1988; Director, Dundee and London Investment Trust PLC, since 1981; b. 22.5.27, Bangkok; m., Kathleen; 2 s.; 1 d. Educ. Dundee High School; Strathallan School; St. John's College, Cambridge; St. Andrews University. Trained with Moody Stuart & Robertson, CA, Dundee; became Partner, 1959; part-time Lecturer/Senior Lecturer, Dundee University, 1955-83; Honorary Professor, Department of Accountancy and Business Finance, Dundee University, since 1987; Member, Board of Governors, Strathallan School. Recreations: golf; watching rugby; bridge. Address: (h.) 169 Hamilton Street, Barnhill, Dundee, DD5 2RE; T.-0382 78360.

Lowe, John Duncan, MA, LLB. Deputy Crown Agent, since 1984; b. 18.5.48, Alloa; m., Jacqueline M.; 2 s. Educ. Hamilton Academy; Glasgow University. Procurator Fiscal Depute, Kilmarnock, 1974-77; Legal Assistant, Crown Office, 1977-79; Senior Procurator Fiscal Depute, Glasgow, 1979-80; Assistant Procurator Fiscal, Glasgow, 1980-83; Assistant Solicitor, Crown Office, 1983-84. Address: (b.) 5/7 Regent Road, Edinburgh; T.-031-557 3800.

Lowe, Martin John Brodie, BSc, PhD. Secretary and Registrar, St. Andrews University, since 1981; b. 10.4.40, Dorking; m., Janet MacNaughtan; 3 s.; 1 d. Educ. Dunfermline High School; St. Andrews University. British Council Officer, with service in Tanzania and South India, 1965-69; Strathclyde University: Administrative Assistant, 1969-71, Assistant Registrar, 1971-73, Secretary to Senate, 1973-81. National Council, Voluntary Service Overseas, 1976-83; Honorary Secretary, then Chairman, Glasgow and West of Scotland VSO Committee, 1973-81. Recreations: piping; hill-walking; family interests. Address: (b.) College Gate, St. Andrews, Fife, KY16 9AJ; T.-St. Andrews 76161.

Lowson, David Murray, CSS, MA. Member, Parole Board for Scotland, since 1981; b. 24.4.20, Carnoustie; m., Catherine Russell Mitchell; 1 s. Educ. Logie School, Dundee; Liverpool University. Toolmaker (after apprenticeship), until 1947; course in youth and community work, 1947-48; course in social science, 1949-51; Probation Officer, 1951-59; Assistant Governor, Prison Service, England, 1959-62; Lecturer, Liverpool University, 1962-80. Member, Parole Board, England and Wales, 1973-76; Warden: University Hall, Liverpool, 1970-80, Liverpool University Settlement, 1963-68; Chairman, Peterlee Community Association, 1955. Recreations: outdoor activities. Address: (h.) 87 High Street, Carnoustie, Angus, DD7 7EA; T.-Carnoustie 52189.

Lucas, Walter Pollock. Company Director; Member, Renfrew District Council, since 1984; b. 17.2.17, Port Glasgow; m., Doreen Ada Bromley; 2 s.; 1 d. Educ. Greenock High School; Herds Commercial College, Greenock; George Commercial College, Greenock. Joined Territorial Army, 1938, as a Gunner, 77th Field Regiment of Artillery; evacuated from Dunkirk, 1940; commissioned, Glasgow Highlanders (9th Bn., HLI), 1941; drafted to India, 1942; seconded to 7/17 DOGRA Regiment, stationed at Fort Salop, North West Frontier; posted to IAOC, 1944, Bombay, as Company Commander, Indian Military Wing; returned to UK, 1945. Vice-Chairman, Paisley Conservative Association, 1980-82; Chairman, Paisley South Conservative Association, 1982; Elder, Paisley Abbey Church, since 1960; Member, Renfrew District Council, 1974-80. Recreations: golf; fresh water fishing. Address: (h.) The Grange, 106 Corsebar Road, Meikleriggs, Paisley, PA2 9PY; T.-041-889 8554.

Ludlam, Christopher A., BSc (Hons), MB, ChB, PhD, FRCP, MRCPath. Consultant Haematologist, Edinburgh Royal Infirmary, since 1980; Director, Edinburgh Haemophilia Reference Centre, since 1980; part-time Senior Lecturer in Medicine, Edinburgh University, since 1980; b. 6.6.46, Edinburgh. Educ. Edinburgh University. MRC Research Fellow, 1972-75; Senior Registrar in Haematalogy, University Hospital of Wales, Cardiff, 1975-78; Lecturer in Haematology, University of Wales, 1979. Address: (b.) Department of Haematology, Royal Infirmary, Edinburgh; T.-031-229 2473.

Lumsden, James Alexander, MBE, TD, BA, LLB, DL. Director, Bank of Scotland, 1958-85; Director, Scottish Provident Institution, 1968-85; b. 24.1.15, Arden, Dunbartonshire; m., Sheila Cross; 3 s. Educ. Cargilfield School, Edinburgh; Rugby School; Corpus Christi College, Cambridge; Glasgow University. Territorial Army, 1937-46; Partner, Maclay Murray & Spens, Solicitors, Glasgow, 1947-82; Director of certain Investment Trust companies managed by Murray Johnstone Ltd., since 1967; Commissioner of Income Tax, County of Dumbarton; Member, Committee on Company Law, 1960-62; Fellow, Law Society of Scotland and Royal Faculty of Procurators, Glasgow. Recreations: shooting; fishing; other country pursuits. Address: (h.) Bannachra, by Helensburgh, Dunbartonshire, G84 9EF; T.-Arden 653.

Lumsden, Professor Keith Grant, MA, PhD. Professor and Director, Esmee Fairbairn Research Centre, Heriot-Watt University, Edinburgh, since 1975; Member, Board of Directors, Hewlett Packard Ltd., since 1982; b. 7.1.35, Bathgate; m., Jean Baillie MacDonald; 1 s. Educ. Bathgate Academy; Edinburgh University; Stanford University, California. Instructor, Department of Economics, then Assistant Professor, Graduate School of Business, Stanford University, 1960-67; Research Associate, Stanford Research Institute, 1965-71; Director, Stanford University Conference: NDTE, 1966, RREE, 1968; Associate Professor, Graduate School of Business, Stanford University, 1968-75; Visiting Professor of Economics, Heriot-Watt University, 1969-70; Director: Economics Education Project, 1969-74, Behavioral Research Laboratories, 1970-72, Capital Preservation Fund Inc., 1971-75, Nielsen Engineering Research Inc., 1972-75; Member,

American Economic Association Committee on Economic Education, 1978-81; Academic Director, Service and Transport Executive Programme (STEP), since 1979; Professor of Economics, Advanced Management College, Stanford University, since 1971; Affiliate Professor of Economics, INSEAD, France; Member, Economics Education 14-16 Project, Manchester University. Publications: The Free Enterprise System, 1963; The Gross National Product, 1964; International Trade, 1965; Microeconomics: A Programmed Book, 1966; Macroeconomics: A Programmed Book, 1966; New Developments in the Teaching of Economics (Editor), 1967; Excess Demand and Excess Supply in World Tramp Shipping Markets, 1968; Recent Research in Economics Education (Editor), 1970; Basic Economics: Theory and Cases, 1973; Efficiency in Universities: The La Paz Papers (Editor), 1974; Economics Education in the United Kingdom, 1980. Recreations: tennis; deep sea sports fishing. Address: (h.) 40 Lauder Road, Edinburgh, EH9 1UE.

Lumsden, William Hepburn Russell, DSc, MD, DTM, DTH, FIBiol, FRCPEdin, FRSE. Scientific and Medical Writer; b. 27.3.14, Forfar; m., Pamela Kathleen Bartram; 2 s.; 1 d. (deceased). Educ. Queen Elizabeth's Grammar School, Darlington; Glasgow University; Liverpool University. MRC Fellow in Tropical Medicine, 1938-41; active service, Malaria Field Laboratories, RAMC, 1941-46; Yellow Fever (subsequently East African Virus) Research Institute, Entebbe, 1947-57; Director, East African Trypanosomiasis Research Organisation, Tororo, 1957-63; Lecturer, Department of Bacteriology, Edinburgh University Medical School, 1963-64; Senior Lecturer, Department of Animal Health, Royal (Dick) School of Veterinary Studies, Edinburgh University, 1964-68; Visiting Professor, Toronto University, 1968; Professor of Medical Protozoology, London School of Hygiene and Tropical Medicine, London University, 1968-79; Senior Editor, Advances in Parasitology, 1978-82; Council Member, Royal Society of Tropical Medicine and Hygiene, 1969-73, 1974-77; Council Member, Royal Zoological Society of Scotland, 1967-68; Member, Expert Advisory Panel on Parasitic Diseases (Trypanosomiasis), WHO, 1962-84; Member, Trypanosomiasis Panel, Ministry of Overseas Development, 1973-79; Member, International Malaria Review Teams, Bangladesh, 1978, Nepal, 1979, Sri Lanka, 1980. Publications: Techniques with Trypanosomes, 1973; Biology of the Kinetoplastida (Editor), 1976 and 1979. Recreations: trout fishing; hill-walking. Address: (h.) 16A Merchiston Crescent, Edinburgh, EH10 5AX; T.-031-229 2702.

Lunan, Charles Burnett, MD, FRCOG, FRCS. Consultant Obstetrician, Royal Maternity Hospital, Glasgow, since 1977; Consultant Gynaecologist, Royal Infirmary, Glasgow, since 1977; b. London; m., Helen Russell Ferrie; 2 s.; 1 d. Educ. High School of Glasgow; Glasgow University. Lecturer, Obstetrics and Gynaecology, Aberdeen University, 1973-75; Senior Lecturer, University of Nairobi, 1975-77; WHO Consultant, Family Planning Programme, Bangladesh, 1984-85. Treasurer, Royal Medico-Chirurgical Society of Glasgow, since 1982; Secretary, Glasgow Obstetrical and Gynaecological Society, 1978-82. Recreations: gardening; photography; hill-walking. Address: (h.) 1 Moncrieff Avenue, Lenzie, Glasgow, G66 4NL; T.-041-776 3227.

Lunan, Duncan Alasdair, MA (Hons), FBIS, DipEd. Author; b. 24.10.45; m., Linda Joyce Donnelly (m. diss.). Educ. Marr College, Troon; Glasgow University. Management Trainee, Christian Salvesen (Managers) Ltd., 1969-70; self-employed (Author), 1970-78; Manager, Astronomy Project, Glasgow Parks Department, 1978-79; SF Critic, Glasgow Herald, 1971-82 and since 1985; regular astronomy column in various papers and magazines; Council Member, Association in Scotland to Research into Astronautics (ASTRA), since 1963 (President, 1966-72 and 1978-85; Secretary, since 1985). Publications: Man and the Stars, 1974; New Worlds for Old, 1979; Man and the Planets, 1983. Recreation: folk music. Address: c/o Campbell, 16 Oakfield Avenue, Hillhead, Glasgow, G12 8JE; T.-041-339 2558.

Lundie, Mary Elizabeth, JP, RGN. Matron, The Princess Louise Scottish Hospital, Erskine, since 1977; b. 11.10.36, Barrhead; m., Peter Lundie; 3 s.; 3 d. Educ. St. Margaret's Convent, Paisley. Trained, Western Infirmary, Glasgow, 1954-58; Staff Nurse, Knightwood Hospital, 1962-65, Southern General Hospital, Glasgow, 1965-66; Sister, Gartloch Hospital, Glasgow, 1966-67; Sister and Nursing Officer, Ruchill Hospital, Glasgow, 1967-75; Nursing Officer, The Princess Louise Scottish Hospital, Erskine, 1975-77. Recreations: reading; walking dogs. Address: (h.) Matron's House, Erskine Hospital, Bishopton, Renfrewshire; T.-041-812 0445.

Lunn, George Michael, BSc, DipHWU. Managing Director, Whyte & Mackay Distillers Ltd., since 1983; Regional Chief Executive - Scotch Whisky, Lonhro PLC, since 1986; Director, Scottish & Universal Investments Ltd., since 1984; Director, Dalmore Distillers Ltd., since 1984; b. 22.7.42, Stirling; m., Jennifer Burgoyne; 3 s.; 1 d. Educ. Kelvinside Academy; Glasgow University; Heriot-Watt University. North of Scotland Distilling Co. Ltd., 1965-68; Distillers Co. (Carbon Dioxide) Ltd., 1968-70; PA Management Consultants, 1970-72; British Carpets Ltd., 1972-78; joined Whyte & Mackay Distillers Ltd., 1978. Council Member, Scotch Whisky Association, since 1986; Governor, Kelvinside Academy, since 1987; Member, Glasgow Action Committee, since 1985. Recreations: golf; tennis. Address: (b.) Whyte & Mackay, Dalmore House, 296-298 St. Vincent Street, Glasgow, G2 5RG; T.-041-248 5771.

Luscombe, Most Rev. Lawrence Edward, OStJ, LLD, DLitt, CA, FSAScot. Primus of the Scottish Episcopal Church, since 1985, and Bishop of Brechin, since 1975; b. 10.11.24; m., Dr. Doris Morgan; 1 d. Educ. Kelham College; King's College, London. Indian Army, 1942-47; Chartered Accountant, 1952; Partner, Galbraith Dunlop & Co. (later Watson and Galbraith), CA, 1953-63; Curate, St. Margaret's, Glasgow, 1963-66; Rector, St. Barnabas', Paisley, 1966-71; Provost, St. Paul's Cathedral, Dundee, 1971-75. Honorary Canon, Trinity Cathedral, Davenport, Iowa, since 1983; Member, Education Committee, Renfrew County Council, 1967-71; Chairman, Governing Body: Glenalmond College, Edinburgh Theological College; Governor, Lathallan School. Address: 7 Shaftesbury Road, Dundee, DD2 1HF; T.-Dundee 644215.

Lyall, Andrew Finlayson Dunnet, LLB, SSC, NP. Solicitor, since 1970; Notary Public, since 1971; Member, Dundee District Council, since 1984; b. 20.10.47, Nairobi; m., Marguerita Fransen Taylor; 1 s.; 1 d. Educ. Prince of Wales School, Nairobi; Morgan Academy, Dundee; St. Andrews University. Enrolled as a Solicitor in Scotland, 1970; Partner, Simpson Boath Lyall & Co., Dundee. Recreation: fishing. Address: (h.) The Dower House, Liff, by Dundee; T.-Dundee 580716.

Lyall, Fiona Jane, DL, MB, ChB, DPH. Family Doctor, Laurencekirk, since 1959; Director, Grampian Television PLC, since 1980; Deputy Lieutenant, Kincardineshire, since 1985; b. 13.4.31, Inverness; m., Dr. Alan Richards Lyall; 1 s.; 1 d. Educ. Inverness Royal Academy; Aberdeen University. Former Member, Laurencekirk Burgh Council; former Kincardine County and Grampian Regional Councillor; Member, Grampian Health Board, 1974, and Kincardine & Deeside Health Council, 1974; Member, Children's Panel Advisory Committee, 1974; Member, Grampian Valuation Appeals Committee; Member, Prince's and Royal Jubilee Trust for Grampian; Treasurer, Action Research for Crippled Child. Recreations: skiing; riding; gardening. Address: Melrose Bank, Laurencekirk, AB3 1AL; T.-05617 258.

Lyall, Ian Alastair, DSC, VRD, DL, FICS; b. 16.3.17, Bangor, Co. Down; m., Eileen Patricia Bennet; 1 d. Educ. Hillhead High School, Glasgow; College of Nautical Studies, Glasgow. Chairman and Managing Director, Roxburgh Henderson & Co. Ltd., 1979-80; Director: British & Burmese Steam Navigation Co. Ltd., 1971-80, Henderson Line Ltd., 1971-80; President, Glasgow Chamber of Commerce, 1978-79; Hon. Consul, Republic of Philippines, since 1965; retired Lt. Commander, RNR, 1963. Recreations: sailing; fishing; shooting. Address: (h.) Rimsdale, 108 East Clyde Street, Helensburgh, Dunbartonshire, G84 7AQ; T.-0436 3976.

Lyall, Michael Hodge, MB, ChB, ChM, FRCSEdin. Consultant Surgeon, Tayside Health Board, since 1975; Honorary Senior Lecturer, Dundee University, since 1975; b. 5.12.41, Methilhill, Fife; m., Catherine B. Jarvie; 3 s. Educ. Buckhaven High School; St. Andrews University. President, Tayside Division, Ileostomy Association of Great Britain; Past President, North Fife Rotary Club. Recreation: computing. Address: (h.) 26 Linden Avenue, Newport on Tay, Fife, DD6 8DU.

Lyddon, William Derek Collier, CB, DLitt, BA, RIBA, DipTP, FRTPI. Chairman, Edinburgh Old Town Committee for Conservation and Renewal; Chairman, Management Committee, Edinburgh School of Environmental Design; Chief Planner, Scottish Development Department, 1967-85; Honorary Professor, Heriot-Watt University; Visiting Professor, Strathclyde University; Vice Chairman, Planning Exchange; b. 17.11.25, Loughton, Essex; m., Marian Louise Kaye Charlesworth; 2 d. Educ. Wrekin College; University College, London. Depute Chief Architect Planner, Cumbernauld Development Corporation; Chief Architect Planner, Skelmersdale Development Corporation. President, International Society of City and Regional Planners, 1981-84. Address: (h.) 38 Dick Place, Edinburgh; T.-031-667 2266.

Lyell, 3rd Baron (Charles Lyell), Bt. Parliamentary Under-Secretary of State, Northern Ireland Office, since 1984; b. 27.3.39. Educ. Eton; Christ Church, Oxford. Scots Guards, 1957-59; CA; Opposition Whip, 1974-79; Government Whip, 1979-84; Member, Queen's Bodyguard for Scotland (Royal Company of Archers). Address: (h.) Kinnordy House, Kirriemuir, Angus.

Lygo, Robert Ernest, BSc. HM Inspector of Schools (Scotland), Higher Grade, since 1972; b. 15.9.29, Warrington; m., Kathleen Mary Newman; 1 s.; 2 d. Educ. Wade Deacon Grammar School; Nottingham University. Station Education Officer, RAF; Teacher of Mathematics, then Head of Department, King Edward VI School, Chelmsford; Deputy Head, Great Baddow Comprehensive School, Chelmsford; HM Inspector of Schools (Scotland). Recreations: walking; gardening. Address: (h.) 25 Charles Crescent, Lenzie, Glasgow, G66 5HH; T.-041-776 4432.

Lyle, Lt.-Col. (Archibald) Michael, DL, JP, MA, BA. Landowner and Farmer; b. 1.5.19; 3 d. Educ. Eton College; Trinity College, Oxford. Hon. Attache, Rome, 1938-39; served 1939-45 with The Black Watch RHR (wounded Normandy, 1944, discharged with wounds, 1946); Lt.-Col., The Scottish Horse RAC (TA), 1953-56; Chairman, T&AFA, 1959-64; Member, Royal Company of Archers, since 1946; Member, Perth and Kinross County Council, 1946-74, Tayside Regional Council, 1974-79; Chairman, Perth College of Further Education, since 1978; JP, Perth, 1950; DL, Perthshire, 1961; Vice Lord Lieutenant, Perth and Kinross, since 1984. Recreations: fishing; shooting; music. Address: Riemore Lodge, Dunkeld, Perthshire; T.-035 04 205.

Lyle, David Angus, MA, LLB, FBIM, FCIS, SSC, NP. Agency Secretary, Scottish Development Agency, and Company Secretary of a number of associated companies, since 1979; b. 7.9.40; m., Dorothy Ann Clark; 1 s.; 3 d. Educ. George Watson's College, Edinburgh; Edinburgh University. Account Executive, advertising agencies, London; indentured, Edinburgh Corporation; Solicitor, Lloyds and Scottish Finance Ltd., Edinburgh; Depute County Clerk, East Lothian County Council; Director of Administration and Law, Dumfries and Galloway Regional Council. Recreations: shooting; golf; bridge. Address: (h.) Ravelston, Glencairn Road, Kilmacolm, Renfrewshire; T.-050587 2321.

Lyons, Sheriff Hamilton, BL. Temporary Sheriff, since 1984; b. 3.8.18, Gourock; m., Jean Cathro Blair; 2 s. Educ. Gourock High School; Greenock High School; Glasgow University. Practised as Solicitor in Greenock, 1940-66; Sheriff, Stornoway and Lochmaddy, 1966-68; Sheriff, North Strathclyde (formerly Renfrew and Argyll), 1968-

84. Council Member, Law Society of Scotland, 1950-66 (Vice-President, 1962-63); Member: Law Reform Committee for Scotland, 1954-64, Committee of Inquiry on Children and Young Persons, 1961-64, Committee of Enquiry on Sheriff Courts, 1963-67, Sheriff Courts Rules Council, 1952-66, Scottish Probation Advisory and Training Council, 1959-69. Recreation: family. Address: (h.) 14 Cloch Road, Gourock, PA19 1AB; T.-0475 32566.

Lyons, Professor Terence John, MA, DPhil. Professor (Colin MacLaurin Chair) of Mathematics, Edinburgh University, since 1985; b. 4.5.53, London; m., Barbara C. Epsom; 1 s.; 1 d. Educ. St. Joseph's College, London; Cambridge University; Oxford University. Junior Research Fellow, Jesus College, Oxford, 1979-81; Hedrick Visiting Assistant Professor, UCLA, 1981-82 (Fulbright Visiting Scholar); Lecturer in Mathematics, Imperial College of Science and Technology, London, 1981-85. Address: (b.) Department of Mathematics, James Clerk Maxwell Building, King's Buildings, Edinburgh, EH9 3JZ; T.-031-667 1081, Ext. 2998.

Lythe, Charlotte Margaret, MA, FSA Scot. Senior Lecturer in Economics, Dundee University, since 1978; b. 15.10.41, Leven, East Yorkshire. Educ. Dundee High School; St. Andrews University. Assistant Lecturer in Political Economy, Aberdeen University; Lecturer in Economics, Queen's College, Dundee, and Dundee University. Director, Tayside Enterprise Board. Recreations: archaeology; local history. Address: (b.) Department of Economics, The University, Dundee, DD1 4HN; T.-0382 23181.

Mc/Mac

McAdam, Robert, MSc, MEd, CEng, MIMechE, MIProdE, AMBIM. Principal, James Watt College, Greenock; b. 7.7.25, Glasgow; m., Elizabeth Campbell Thomson; 3 s.; 1 d. Educ. Gourock High School; Glasgow University; Strathclyde University; Paisley College. Apprentice Engineer, 1941-45; Engineer, Royal Navy, 1945-47; Design Draughtsman, Scott Shipbuilding & Engineering Company, 1947-49; Shipyard Manager, Smith & Houston, 1949-51; Lecturer, Paisley College, 1952-60, Jordanhill, 1960-75. Address: (h.) 67 Caledonia Crescent, Gourock, Renfrewshire; T.-0475 31592.

MacAllan, Harry Bertram Wedderburn, BL. Writer to the Signet, since 1950; Partner, Maclay, Murray & Spens, Solicitors, Glasgow and Edinburgh, since 1967, b. 14.8.20, St. Andrews; m., Grace Edwards (deceased). Educ. Canford School; Edinburgh University. Intelligence Corps, North Africa, Italy, Greece, India and Malaysia, 1939-45; admitted Solicitor in Scotland, 1950, Advocate in Kenya, 1953 (Partner in legal firm in Kenya, until 1964). Publication: Collected Poems, 1940; Contributor of verse to various journals. Recreations: travel; writing; golf. Address: (b.) 151 St. Vincent Street, Glasgow, G2 5NJ; T.-041-248 5011.

McAllion, John, MA (Hons). MP (Lab), Dundee East, since 1987; b. 13.2.48, Glasgow; m., Susan Jean; 2 s. Educ. St. Augustine's Secondary, Glasgow; St. Andrews University. Teacher, History and Modern Studies, St. Saviour's Secondary, Dundee, 1973-78, Social Studies, Balgowan List D School, Dundee, 1978-82; Research Assistant to Bob McTaggart, MP, 1982-86; Regional Councillor, 1984-87; Convener, Tayside Regional Council, 1986-87. Member, Scottish Executive, Labour Party, 1986-88; Senior Vice Chairperson, Dundee Labour Party, 1986, 1987. Recreations: football; reading; music. Address: (h.) 3 Haldane Street, Dundee, DD3 0HP; T.-0382 826678.

McAlpine, Stuart Gemmell, MD, FRCP, FRCPGlas. Consultant Physician, Royal Alexandra Infirmary, Paisley, since 1963; Honorary Clinical Lecturer, Glasgow University, since 1968; President, Scottish Society of Physicians, 1987-88; b. 6.3.27, Glasgow; m., Cynthia Joan McPherson; 2 s.; 1 d. Educ. Glasgow Academy; Glasgow University. Royal Army Medical Corps, 1950-52; medical training, Dumfries and Galloway Royal Infirmary and Glasgow Royal Infirmary; Examiner in Medicine, Glasgow University and Royal College of Physicians and Surgeons of Glasgow; Member, Argyll and Clyde Health Board; President, Royal Medico-Chirurgical Society of Glasgow, 1986-87. Recreations: golf; fishing. Address: (h.) Windyknowe, 168 Southbrae Drive, Glasgow, G13 1TY; T.-041-954 6670.

McAlpine, Thomas, BSc, CEng, MIEE. Director, Glentronic Ltd., Livingston, since 1986; b. 23.9.29, Motherwell; m., Isobel Lindsay; 2 s.; 1 d. Educ. Dalziel High School, Motherwell; Strathclyde University. National Service, REME, 1952-54 (2nd Lt.); Chief Engineer, Belmos Co. Ltd., Bellshill, 1954-58; Chief Development Engineer, Mine Safety Appliances, Glasgow, 1958-62; Managing Director: Rowen Engineering Co. Ltd., Glasgow, 1962-71, Chieftain Industries PLC, Livingston, 1971-85. Executive Vice Chairman Administration, Scottish National Party (former Vice President, SNP); Parliamentary candidate, Clydesdale (Lanark), 1974, 1979, 1983, Dumfries, 1987. Recreations: when young, played rugby, swimming and tennis. Address: (h.) Millrig House, Millrig Road, Wiston, by Biggar, Lanarkshire, ML12 6HT; T.-Lamington 683.

McArdle, Colin S., MD, FRCS, FRCSEdin, FRCSGlas. Consultant Surgeon, University Department of Surgery, Glasgow Royal Infirmary, since 1981; b. 10.10.39, Glasgow; m., June M.C. Merchant; 2 s.; 1 d. Educ. Jordanhill College School; Glasgow University. Senior Registrar in General Surgery, Western Infirmary, Glasgow, 1972-75; Consultant Surgeon: Victoria Infirmary, Glasgow, 1975-78, Glasgow Royal Infirmary, 1978-80. Address: (h.) 4 Collylinn Road, Bearsden, Glasgow.

MacArthur, Rev. Allan Ian, BD, JP. Minister, Lochcarron Parish, since 1973; Member, Crofters Commission, since 1984; District Councillor, since 1984; b. 22.5.28, Marvig, Isle of Lewis; m., Effie Macleod; 1 s.; 6 d. Educ. Nicolson Institute, Stornoway; Glasgow University and Trinity College. Meteorologist, Air Ministry and Falkland Islands Dependencies Survey, Antarctica; teaching; Minister of Religion and Presbytery Clerk. Member, Local Health Council; former Secretary and Vice-Chairman, Community Council. Address: Church of Scotland Manse, Lochcarron, Ross-shire, IV54 8YD; T.-05202 278.

Macarthur, Sheriff Charles Ramsay, QC (Scot). Sheriff of Tayside, Central and Fife, since 1981; m. Educ. Glasgow University. Royal Navy, 1942-46; Solicitor, 1952-59; Scottish Bar, 1960; Sheriff of the Lothians and Borders, 1974-76.

Macarthur, Edith. Actress; b. Ardrossan, Ayrshire. Educ. Ardrossan Academy. Began career, 1948, with Wilson Barrett Company, then Perth Repertory, Gateway Theatre Company, Citizens' Theatre, Glasgow, Bristol Old Vic, Royal Shakespeare Company, Ochtertyre Theatre, Royal Lyceum Theatre Company, West End; television work includes The Borderers, Sunset Song, Weir of Hermiston, Sutherland's Law; the "lady laird" in Take the High Road; recent stage appearances: solo-performance play, Marie of Scotland, Jamie the Saxt and The Thrie Estates for the Scottish Theatre Company at Edinburgh and Warsaw International Festivals, 1986, Judith Bliss in Hay Fever, Royal Lyceum Theatre, 1987, Charley's Aunt, Death of a Salesman, Royal Lyceum, 1988, Daphne Laureola, Pygmalion, Pride and Prejudice, Pitlochry Festival Theatre, 1988. Recreations: music; books. Address: c/o Larry Dalzell Associates Ltd., 126 Kennington Park Road, London, SE11 4DJ.

McArthur, Rev. Farquhar MacDonald, LTh, BD. Minister, Kirk o'Field Pleasance, Edinburgh, since 1974; b. 8.6.39, Glasgow; m., Euphemia MacGilp Lindsay Shaw; 3 d. Educ. St. George's Road Junior Secondary School; Glasgow University; Edinburgh University. Served engineering apprenticeship, Barr & Stroud Ltd., 1955-60; journeyman scientific instrument-maker, 1960-65; relief Teacher of Engineering, 1965-67; Probationer Assistant, then Locum, Renfield. Fieldwork Director, Faculty of Divinity, New College, Edinburgh. Recreations: distance running; swimming; hill-walking; music; reading. Address: (h.) 31 Hatton Place, Edinburgh, EH9 1UA; T.-031-667 7954.

McArthur, John Duncan, BSc (Hons), MB, ChB (Hons), DM, FRCPGlas, MRCP, MRCPEdin. Consultant Physician and Cardiologist, Western Infirmary and Gartnavel General Hospital, Glasgow, since 1978; Honorary Clinical Lecturer, Glasgow University, since 1978; b. 7.1.38, Hamilton; m., Elizabeth A. Bowie; 2 s.; 1 d. Educ. Hamilton Academy; Glasgow University. Junior doctor, Royal Infirmary, Glasgow, and in Ayrshire, 1963-67; St. Colm's College, Edinburgh, 1967-68; Missionary, Church of Scotland, working as Cardiologist at Christian Medical College Hospital, Vellore, India, 1968-73; Senior Registrar, Glasgow Teaching Hospitals, 1974-78. Elder, Killermont Parish Church; Counsellor, Tom Allan Centre; Council Member, Interserve, Scotland. Recreations: DIY; gardening. Address: (h.) 8 Durness Avenue, Bearsden, Glasgow, G61 2AQ; T.-041-942 7330.

Macaskill, Allan Nicolson. Chairman, Lorn, Mid Argyll, Kintyre and Islay Licensing Board, since 1984; Vice Chairman, Tourism, Leisure and Recreation Committee, Argyll and Bute District Council, since 1984; Founder Member, 87 Group; b. 10.2.43, Stirling; m., Elizabeth Dawn; 1 s.; 1 d. Educ. Oban High School; Glasgow High School; Anniesland College of Further Education. Recreations: reading; sport, especially athletics. Address: (h.) Ullinish, Balvicar Farm, by Oban; T.-08523 221.

MacAskill, Norman Alexander, OBE, JP. Vice-Chairman, Crofters Commission, 1966-86; b. 1.11.24, Lochinver; m., Joan Logan Brown; 2 s. Educ. Lochinver Public School; Golspie High School. Customs and Excise Officer; Social Welfare Officer, North West Sutherland; Secretary, North and West Sutherland Council of Social Service; former Chairman: Sutherland Tourist Organisation, Sutherland Valuation Appeals Committee; Member, Highlands and Islands Area Manpower Board, MSC; Member, Scottish Rent Assessment Panel. Recreations: fishing; music; history; archaeology. Address: (h.) 8 Cruamer, Lochinver, Lairg, Sutherland; T.-057 14 291.

Macaulay, Rev. Donald, OBE, JP. Parish Minister, Park, Isle of Lewis, since 1968; Vice Convener, Western Isles Council; Member, HIDB Consultative Council; b. 25.2.26, Great Bernera; m., Catherine Macleod; 3 s.; 3 d. Educ. Great Bernera School; Aberdeen University. Several years a fisherman; Member: Ross and Cromarty County Council, 1969-75, Lewis District Council, 1969-75; Convener, Western Isles Council, 1974-82; Member, COSLA Policy Committee, 1975-82; Member, Comunn na Gaelic. Recreations: fishing; travel; local history; silviculture. Address: Park Manse, Isle of Lewis; T.-0851 88 257.

Macaulay, Donald, MA (Aberdeen), BA (Cantab), DipGenLing. Reader in Celtic, Aberdeen University, since 1980 (Head, Celtic Department, since 1967); b. 21.5.30, Bernera, Isle of Lewis; m., Ella Murray Sangster; 1 s.; 1 d. Educ. Nicolson Institute, Stornoway; Aberdeen University; Cambridge University. Taught: English Language, Edinburgh University, 1958-60; Irish and Gaelic, Trinity College, Dublin, 1960-63; Applied Linguistics, Edinburgh University, 1963-67; Celtic Studies, Aberdeen University, since 1967. Editor, Scottish Gaelic Studies; Secretary, International Committee for the Study of Celtic Cultures, UNESCO; Gaelic poet: Seobhrach as a' Chlaich, 1967; Editor, Nua-bhardachd Ghaidhlig, 1976. Recreations: beagle walking; TV movies. Address: (h.) 106 North Deeside Road, Peterculter, Aberdeenshire, AB1 OQB; T.-0224 732217.

Macaulay, Ewen. Trust Director, Inverclyde Enterprise Trust Ltd., since 1986; b. 12.7.55, Glasgow. Educ. Jordanhill College School, Glasgow. Small Businesses Division, Scottish Development Agency, 1977-84; Director, Motherwell

Enterprise Trust, 1984-86. Recreations: golf; walking. Address: (b.) 64-66 West Blackhall Street, Greenock; T.-0475 892191.

McAvoy, Thomas McLaughlin. MP (Labour), Glasgow Rutherglen, since 1987 (Member, Strathclyde Regional Council, 1982-87); b. 14.12.43, Rutherglen; m., Eleanor Kerr; 4 s. Past Chairman, Rutherglen Community Council, Fernhill Tenants Association and Rutherglen Federation of Tenants Associations. Address: (h.) 70 Kingsburn Grove, Rutherglen, Glasow, G73 2EX; T.-041-643 1954.

MacBain, Gordon Campbell, MB, FRCSGlas, FRCSEdin. Consultant Surgeon, Southern General Hospital, Glasgow, since 1974; b. 29.4.38, Glasgow; m., Margaret Janet Wilson; 1 s.; 1 d. Educ. High School of Glasgow; Glasgow University. Health Service appointments; Leverhulme Research Fellow, Royal College of Surgeons of England; Lecturer in Surgery, Nairobi University; further Health Service posts; Director, Ross Hall Hospital, Glasgow; Trustee, Forum Arts Society. Recreations: golf; squash; skiing; amateur operatics. Address: (h.) 55 Drumlin Drive, Milngavie, Glasgow, G62 6NF; T.-041-956 3388.

Macbeth, Alastair Murdoch, MA, DPhil. Senior Lecturer, Department of Education, Glasgow University, since 1973; b. 26.4.35, Oxford; m., Rosemary; 2 s.; 1 d. Educ. Oundle; Oriel College, Oxford. Pilot, RAF, 1953-55; ICI, 1958-62; Teacher, 1962-67; Headteacher, King George VI Secondary School, Honiara, 1967-72. Educational Adviser: Scottish Parent Teacher Council, European Parents' Association, and various other bodies. Publications: Scottish School Councils, 1980; The Child Between, 1984; Involving Parents, 1988. Recreations: painting; jogging; mountains. Address: (b.) Department of Education, Glasgow University, Glasgow, G12 8QQ.

McCabe, Bernard Thomas. Sheriff Clerk, Arbroath, since 1986; b. 15.11.49, Glasgow; m., Margaret Isabel Gallacher. Educ. St. Mungo's Academy, Glasgow. Joined Civil Service, 1967; Sheriff Court Service, working in various courts; Sheriff Clerk Depute, Lochmaddy, 1974-76; Sheriff Clerk Depute, Paisley, then Glasgow, 1976-86. Recreations: music; reading; gardening. Address: (b.) 88 High Street, Arbroath; T.-0241 76600.

McCabe, Rev. George Elrick, JP, BA. Minister, Dalkeith St. John's and King's Park, 1973-87; b. 3.9.25, Berhampore, India; m., Mollie; 1 s.; 1 d. Educ. Woodstock, Mussoorie, India; Boroughmuir School, Edinburgh; London University; New College, Edinburgh; Open University. Left school to take up farming in the Borders, 1940; Farm and Estate Manager, Dr. Graham's Homes, Kalimpong, India, 1949; ordained Baptist Minister, Port Ellen, Islay, 1958; ordained Church of Scotland Minister, Glendevon linked with Muckhart, 1967; elected Member, Perth and Kinross County Council, 1970; Moderator, Lothian Presbytery, 1977-78; Moderator, Lothian Synod, 1979-80; Director, McCabe Travel, since 1987. Recreations: gardening; travel. Address: (h.) Deolo, 34 Howe Park, Edinburgh, EH10 7HF; T.-031-445 4144.

MacCaig, Norman, OBE, MA, DLitt (Edinburgh), DUniv (Stirling), Lld (Dundee), FRSE, ARSA. Poet; b. 14.11.10, Edinburgh; m., Isabel; 1 s.; 1 d. Educ. Royal High School, Edinburgh; Edinburgh University. Former schoolteacher; former Writer in Residence, Edinburgh University; former Reader in Poetry, Stirling University; publications of poetry: Far Cry, 1943, The Inward Eye, 1946, Riding Lights, 1955, The Sinai Sort, 1957, A Common Grace, 1960, A Round of Applause, 1962, Measures, 1965, Surroundings, 1966, Rings on a Tree, 1968, A Man in my Position, 1969, The White Bird, 1973, The World's Room, 1974, Tree of Strings, 1977, The Equal Skies, 1980, A World of Difference, 1983; Selected Poems, 1971; Penguin Modern Poets 21, 1972; Old Maps and New (selected poems), 1978; Collected Poems, 1985; Voice-over, 1988; Collected Poems (paperback), 1988; Queen's Gold Medal for Poetry, 1986; eight Scottish Arts Council awards, two Society of Authors awards; Heinemann Award, Cholmondely Award. Recreations: literature; music; fishing. Address: 7 Leamington Terrace, Edinburgh, EH10 4JW; T.-031-229 1809.

McCall, James, BSc, MEd, PhD, AFBPsS. Vice-Principal, Jordanhill College of Education, since 1983; b. 14.7.41, Kilmarnock; m., Mary Elizabeth Stuart Maclean; 3 s. Educ. Kilmarnock Academy; Glasgow University; Aberdeen University; Jordanhill College of Education. Teacher of Science, Hillhead High School, Glasgow; Principal Teacher of Physics, Queen's Park Secondary School, Glasgow; Lecturer in Educational Psychology, Aberdeen College of Education; Head, Psychology Department, Jordanhill College of Education; Member, Board of Governors, Glasgow School of Art, since 1986. Publications: Techniques for the Assessment of Practical Skills in Foundation Science, 1983; Techniques for Assessing Process Skills in Practical Science, 1988. Recreations: bridge; golf; skiing. Address: (b.) Jordanhill College of Education, Southbrae Drive, Glasgow, G13 1PP; T.-041-959 1232.

McCall, James Robertson, MA (Hons). Proprietor, James McCall Publishing and Public Relations Consultancy, since 1984; b. 3.1.48, Moffat. Educ. Ayr Academy; Glasgow University. Graduate Trainee, Associated Book Publishers, London, 1970-72; Production Controller, Longman Group, 1972-74; Commissioning Editor, Blackie & Son, Glasgow, 1974, Educational Publishing Director, 1980-84. Joint Founder and first Chairman, Scottish Young Publishers Society, 1977; Member, Board, Educational Publishers Council; Vice Chairman, Scottish Council, Social Democratic Party, 1984-86; contested Dumfries (SDP/Liberal Alliance), 1983 and 1987 General Elections. Recreations: music; gardening; travel; politics. Address: 26 Middlemuir Road, Lenzie, Glasgow, G66 4NA; T.-041-776 4431.

McCallum, Andrew Wilkie, MA (Hons), DipEd. Depute Principal, Ayr College, since 1986; Vice-Chairman, Scottish Youth Theatre, since 1983; b. 20.10.36, Glasgow; m., Wendy; 1 s.; 2 d. Educ. Allan Glen's School, Glasgow; Glasgow University. Training and work as mechanical engineer in Scotland, Zimbabwe and West Africa, 1952-61; Lecturer, Glasgow College of Building, Clydebank College, Glasgow College of Technology,

1966-72; Senior Lecturer, James Watt College, Greenock, 1972-77; Head, Department of General Education, Falkirk College of Technology, 1977-86. Member, Board of Directors, Scottish Youth Theatre, 1978-88; Open University Tutor, 1972-86. Recreations: hill-walking; skiing; swimming; theatre; music; reading. Address: (h.) 94 Talbot Terrace, Scotstounhill, Glasgow, G13 3RX; T.-041-959 8040.

McCallum, Sir Donald Murdo, CBE, DL, BSc, DSc, LLD, DUniv, FEng, FIEE, FRAeS, CBIM, FRSE. Chairman, Scottish Council Development and Industry, since 1985; Director, Ferranti plc, 1970-87; Honorary President: Ferranti Defence Systems Ltd., since 1987, Ferranti Industrial Electronics Ltd., since 1987; Chairman, Scottish Sub-Committee, University Grants Committee, since 1987; b. 6.8.22, Edinburgh; m., 1, Barbara Black (deceased); 1 d.; 2, Margaret Illingworth. Educ. George Watson's Boys' College; Edinburgh University. Admiralty Signal Establishment, 1942-46; Standard Telecommunication Laboratories, 1946; joined Ferranti, 1947; General Manager, Ferranti Scottish Group, 1968-85; Chairman, Scottish Tertiary Education Advisory Council, 1984-87; Trustee, Scottish Civic Trust. Recreations: fishing; photography. Address: (h.) 46 Heriot Row, Edinburgh, 3; T.-031-225 9331.

McCallum, Forbes, MA, DipPM, MIPM. Member, City of Aberdeen District Council, 1977-87 (Convener, Housing (Building and General Purposes) Committee, 1987-88); Lecturer, Business School, Robert Gordon's Institute of Technology, Aberdeen, since 1975; b. 10.6.47, Aberdeen. Educ. Aberdeen Grammar School; Aberdeen University; Robert Gordon's Institute of Technology, Aberdeen. Personnel Officer, Glaxo Laboratories Ltd., 1969-73; Personnel Manager, Richards Ltd., 1973-75. Deputy Chairman, Scottish Liberal Party, 1975-79; Parliamentary candidate (Liberal), North Aberdeen, 1970 and 1974 (February and October). Address: (h.) 43D Jute Street, Aberdeen, AB2 3EX; T.-0224 635661.

MacCallum, Professor James Richard, BSc, PhD, DSc, CChem, FRSC, FRSE. Professor of Polymer Chemistry, St. Andrews University; b. 3.5.36, Kilmartin; m., Eleanor Margaret Thomson; 2 s.; 1 d. Educ. Dumfries Academy; Glasgow University. Technical Officer, ICI Fibres Division, 1961-62; ICI Research Fellow, Aberdeen University, 1962-63; Lecturer, St. Andrews University, 1964. Elder, St. Leonards Church, St. Andrews. Recreation: golf. Address: (h.) 9 Cairnsden Gardens, St. Andrews, Fife; T.-0334 73152.

Maccallum, Norman Ronald Low, BSc, PhD, CEng, FIMechE. Reader in Mechanical Engineering, Glasgow University, since 1982; b. 18.2.31, Walston, Lanarkshire; m., Mary Bentley Alexander; 1 s.; 2 d. Educ. Allan Glen's School, Glasgow; Glasgow University. Assistant in Mechanical Engineering, Glasgow University, 1952-55; National Service, Royal Navy, 1955-57 (final rank: Sub-Lt.); Lecturer in Mechanical Engineering, Glasgow University, 1957-61; Performance Engineer, Rolls-Royce Ltd. (Scottish Group), 1961-62; Lecturer in Mechanical Engineering, then Senior Lecturer, Glasgow University, 1962-72. Joint Session Clerk, Trinity St. Paul's Church, Cambuslang. Recreation: singing. Address: (h.) 43 Stewarton Drive, Cambuslang, Glasgow, G72 8DQ.

McCallum, Tom. Member, Dumfries and Galloway Regional Council, since 1978 (Vice-Chairman, Manpower Committee); Member, Nithsdale District Council, since 1977 (Vice-Chairman, General Purposes Committee); b. 2.10.17, Forth, Lanarkshire; m., Elizabeth Napier Young; 1 s.; 1 d. Educ. Forth School. Entered baking trade in family business; served in Black Watch (RHR), 1939-46 (Sergeant); Master Baker, 1946-72. Treasurer, An Comunn Gaidhealach, Dumfries; Secretary, Age Concern, Dumfries. Recreations: singing; country dancing; meeting people. Address: (h.) 7 Barnton Place, Dumfries, DG1 4HH; T.-0387 62021.

McCalman, Donald, BSc, MEd. HM Inspector of Schools, since 1970; b.26.9.27, Glasgow; m., Mary Jane Elizabeth McMath; 2 s.; 1 d. Educ. Glasgow University. Teacher of Chemistry, Glasgow, 1949-55; Education Officer, Kenya, 1955-57; Surveyor/Base Leader, British Antarctic Survey, 1957-60; Education Officer, Kenya, 1960-63; Lecturer/Senior Lecturer, Dundee College of Education, 1963-70. Polar Medal, 1963. Recreations: sailing; mountaineering. Address: (b.) New St. Andrew's House, St. James Centre, Edinburgh, EH1; T.-031-556 8400.

McCance, Neil Anderson Davis, MBIM, DMS. Secretary, Hannah Research Institute, Ayr, since 1975; b. 19.8.29, Kobe, Japan; m., Anne Rosemary McOwan; 1 s.; 1 d. Educ. Edinburgh Academy; Royal Military Academy, Sandhurst. Commissioned, The Royal Scots (The Royal Regiment), 1949; retired, 1974, with rank of Major after service in UK and abroad. Recreations: mostly countryside pursuits; gardening. Address: (h.) Woodside, Bridgend Mains, Sundrum, by Ayr; T.-0292 570394.

McCann, James Aloysius, MA, LLB. Solicitor and Notary Public; Senior Tutor (Professional Legal Practice), Glasgow University; b. 14.8.39, Glasgow; m., Jane Marion; 3 s.; 1 d. Educ. St. Mungo's Academy, Glasgow; Glasgow University. Former Member, Legal Aid Central Committee; Dean, Faculty of Dunbartonshire Solicitors, 1986-88; Convenor for Law Society PQLE Advocacy Training Course, since 1983; a founding Director, Legal Defence Union in Scotland, 1987; Senior Partner, McCann Fordyce; Member, Law Society of Scotland Legal Aid Committee. Recreations: sailing/windsurfing; chess; music. Address: (b.) 53 High Street, Dumbarton; T.-0389 30340.

McCann, Peter Toland McAree, CBE (1977), OStJ, DL, JP, BL. Solicitor and Notary Public, since 1947; b. 2.8.24, Glasgow; m., Maura Eleanor Ferris; 1 s. Educ. St. Mungo's Academy, Glasgow; Glasgow University. Councillor, Corporation of Glasgow, 1961-75; River Bailie, 1962; Magistrate, 1963-66; Police Judge, 1967-74; JP, since 1967; Lord Lieutenant, 1975-77; Lord Provost, City of Glasgow District, 1975-77; Depute Lieutenant, since 1977; Chairman, St. Thomas More Society for Lawyers, 1960; Chairman, McCann Committee for Provision of Secondary

Education for Physically Disabled Children, 1968; awarded two Golden Swords from HRH Prince Fawaz of Saudi Arabia, 1977-78; awarded Silver and Golden Swords from City of Jeddah, 1975-78; awarded Medal of King Faisal of Saudi Arabia, 1976. Recreations: music; history; model railways; collecting model cars and model soldiers. Address: (h.) Craig En Ross, 31 Queen Mary Avenue, Crosshill, Glasgow, G42 8DS.

McCarrison, Robert, BSc, CBiol, MIBiol. Rector, Marr College, Troon, since 1978; b. 3.11.37, Oxford; m., Janet M. Gibson; 1 s.; 1 d. Educ. Ayr Academy; Glasgow University; Institute of Biology. Assistant Science Teacher, Principal Teacher (Biology), Assistant Rector, Cumnock Academy, 1959-76; Depute Rector, James Hamilton Academy, Kilmarnock, 1976-78. Past President: Ayrshire Science Teachers Association, Ayrshire Biology Panel, Rotary Club of Troon; Treasurer, Kingcase Parish Church, Prestwick. Recreations: golf (Prestwick St. Nicholas); curling (Troon Portland). Address: (b.) Marr College, Dundonald Road, Troon; T.-0292 311082.

McCarthy, James, BSc. Deputy Director (Scotland), Nature Conservancy Council, since 1975; b. 6.5.36, Dundee; m.; 2 s.; 1 d. Educ. Harris Academy, Dundee; Aberdeen University; University of East Africa, Kampala. Military Service, 1954-56 (Royal Marines, commissioned Black Watch, seconded King's African Rifles); Leverhulme Scholar, Makerere College, Kampala, 1959-61; Assistant Conservator of Forests, Tanzania, and Lecturer in Forest Ecology, Forest Training School, 1961-63; Deputy Regional Officer (North England), Nature Conservancy, 1963-69. Churchill Fellow, USA, 1976; Nuffield/Leverhulme Fellow, 1988; Assessor, Scottish Environmental Education Council. Recreation: cross-country skiing. Address: (h.) 6a Ettrick Road, Edinburgh; T.-031-229 1916.

McCartney, Adam Scott, NDD(T). Managing Director, Scottish Pride (Scottish Milk Marketing Board), since 1987; b. 10.3.38, Crieff; m., Kathryn Margaret; 1 s.; 2 d. Educ. Morrison's Academy, Crieff; West of Scotland Agricultural College. Management appointments, Express Dairy Company Ltd., 1961-73; Production Director, then Director of Creameries, Scottish Milk Marketing Board, 1973-87. Recreations: sport; gardening. Address: (h.) 8 Brackendene, Houston, Renfrewshire.

McClellan, John Forrest, MA. Director, Scottish International Education Trust, since 1986; Member, Management Committee, Hanover (Scotland) Housing Association, since 1986; b. 15.8.32, Glasgow; m., Eva Maria Pressel; 3 s.; 1 d. Educ. Aberdeen Grammar School; Aberdeen University. 2nd Lt., Gordon Highlanders and Nigeria Regiment, Royal West African Frontier Force, 1954-56; entered Civil Service, 1956; Assistant Principal, Scottish Education Department, 1956-59; Private Secretary to Permanent Under Secretary of State, Scottish Office, 1959-60; Principal, Scottish Education Department, 1960-68; Civil Service Fellow, Glasgow University, 1968-69; Scottish Education Department: Assistant Secretary, Schools Division, 1969-71, Assistant Secretary, Higher Education Division, 1971-77; Assistant Under Secretary of State, Scottish Office, 1977-80; Under Secretary, Industry Department for Scoland, 1980-85 (retired). Recreations: gardening; walking. Address: (h.) Grangeneuk, West Linton, Peeblesshire; T.-West Linton 60502.

McClelland, David Brian Lorimer, MB, ChB, BSc (Hons), MD, FRCPEdin. Regional Director, Edinburgh and SE Scotland Blood Transfusion Service, since 1979; part-time Senior Lecturer, Department of Clinical Pharmacology, Edinburgh University, since 1979; b. 12.5.44, Dublin; m., Elizabeth Rae; 2 s.; 2 d. Educ. Calday Grange Grammar School, Cheshire; Edinburgh University. Recreations: family; windsurfing. Address: (b.) Regional Transfusion Centre, Royal Infirmary, Edinburgh; T.-031-229 2585.

McClelland, Samuel Edward, BSc, PhD. HM Depute Senior Chief Inspector of Schools, since 1987; b. 8.4.31, Belfast; m., Margaret E. Pike; 3 s. Educ. Methodist College, Belfast; Queen's University, Belfast; Reading University. Research and teaching appointments; HM Inspector of Schools. Recreation: the great outdoors. Address: (b.) Scottish Office, New St. Andrews House, Edinburgh; T.-031-556 8400.

McClelland, Thomas Henry, BAgr, CBiol, MIBiol, ARAgS. Head, Sheep Research and Development, Scottish Agricultural Colleges; b. 10.5.34, Belfast; m., Maureen Mardon; 1 s.; 2 d. Educ. Belfast Royal Academy; Queen's University of Belfast. Lecturer, Government Agricultural College, Northern Ireland, 1959-68; Research Scientist, Animal Breeding Research Organisation, 1968-75; Head, Animal Production Department, West of Scotland Agricultural College, 1975-86. Former Member, Hill Farming Research Organisation governing body; Session Clerk, Ardoch Parish Church, Braco. Recreations: reading; gardening; sport. Address: (b.) East of Scotland College of Agriculture, Bush Estate, Penicuik, Midlothian; T.-031-445 5353.

McClements, Rev. Duncan Elliott, MA, BD, MTh. Minister, Grahamston United Church, since 1976; b. 28.8.40, Glasgow; m., Dorothy Jean Easton; 1 s.; 1 d. Educ. Daniel Stewart's College; Edinburgh University. Minister, Hurlford Reid Memorial Church, 1967-76. Chairman, Kirkcare Housing Association, 1980-84. Recreations: reading; gardening; walking. Address: (h.) 30 Russel Street, Falkirk, FK2 7HS; T.-0324 24461.

McClure, David, RSA, RSW. Painter and Printmaker; b. 20.2.26, Lochwinnoch; m., Joyce D. Flanigan (deceased); 2 s.; 1 d. Educ. Queen's Park School, Glasgow; Glasgow University; Edinburgh University; Edinburgh College of Art. Travelling scholarship, Italy and Spain, 1956-57; staff, Edinburgh College of Art, 1953-55; Fellow of College, 1955-57, travelling and painting in Italy and Sicily; Senior Lecturer, Duncan of Jordanstone College of Art, until 1983 (Head of Painting, 1983-85); one-man exhibitions since 1957 in Edinburgh, Palermo, London, Birmingham, Perth, etc. Publication: John Maxwell (monograph), 1976. Recreations: collecting bric-a-brac; the pianoforte; etymology. Address: (h.) 16 Strawberrybank, Dundee, DD2 1BJ; T.-0382 66959.

McCluskey, Baron (John Herbert McCluskey), QC (Scot), MA, LLB. Senator of the College of Justice in Scotland, since 1984; Life Peer; b. 12.6.29; m.; 2 s.; 1 d. Educ. St. Bede's Grammar School, Manchester; Holy Cross Academy, Edinburgh; Edinburgh University. Admitted Faculty of Advocates, 1955; Advocate-Depute, 1964-71; Sheriff Principal of Dumfries and Galloway, 1973-74; Solicitor General for Scotland, 1974-79; Reith Lecturer, BBC, 1986.

McColl, James Hamilton, NDH, SDH, SHM. Horticulturalist; b. 19.9.35, Kilmarnock; m., Billie; 1 s.; 1 d. Educ. Kilmarnock Academy; West of Scotland Agricultural College. Staff Member, WSAC, Auchincruive, Ayr, 1956-59; Assistant Head Gardener, Reading University Botanic Garden, 1959-61; Horticultural Adviser/Lecturer, Shropshire Education Authority, 1961-67; Horticultural Adviser: MAFF, Leicestershire, Northants and Rutland, 1967-73, North of Scotland College of Agriculture, 1973-78; PRO, Morrison Bowmore Distillers Ltd.; Co-Presenter, The Beechgrove Garden, BBC TV Scotland, since 1978; Trustee, Royal Botanic Gardens, Edinburgh, since 1987. Recreations: golf; curling; music; rugby; fishing. Address: (h.) Ayrshire House, Oldmeldrum, Aberdeenshire; T.-065 12 3955.

MacConnachie, Angus MacLeod, BSc (Hons). Principal Pharmacist, Ninewells Hospital and Medical School, Dundee, since 1974; Honorary Lecturer, Department of Pharmacology and Clinical Pharmacology, Dundee University; Medical Author; b. 3.9.48, Hawick; m., Pamela Joyce Traylen; 2 s.; 1 d. Educ. Boroughmuir School, Edinburgh; Heriot-Watt University, Edinburgh. The London Hospital, 1971-73, latterly as Pharmacist, Grade 1; Senior Pharmacist, Kent and Canterbury Hospital, 1973-74. Publications: Drugs in Nursing Practice (Co-author), 1982 (2nd ed., 1986); various papers. Recreations: rugby union (retired); golf; jogging; cycling; swimming. Address: (b.) Ninewells Hospital and Medical School, Dundee, DD1 9SY; T.-0382 60111, Ext. 2351.

McConnell, Professor Ian F., BVMS, MA, PhD, BVMS, MRCPath, MRCVS, FRSE. Professor of Veterinary Pathology, Edinburgh University, since 1983; b. 6.11.40, Glasgow; m., Anna; 3 s.; 2 d. Educ. St. Aloysius' College, Glasgow; Glasgow University. Wellcome Trust Postdoctoral Research Fellow, Department of Experimental Pathology, ARC Institute of Animal Physiology, Babrahamm, Cambridge, 1970-72; Research Fellow, Clare Hall, Cambridge, 1970-72; Senior Lecturer in Immunology, Royal Postgraduate Medical School, London University, 1972-75; Senior Scientist, MRC Unit on Mechanisms in Tumour Immunity, The Medical School, Cambridge; Member, Governing Body, Animal Virus Research Institute and Houghton Poultry Research Institute. Recreation: hill-walking. Address: (b.) Royal (Dick) School of Veterinary Studies, Summerhall, Edinburgh, EH9 1QH; T.-031-667 1011, Ext. 5322.

McConnell, Jack Wilson, BSc, DipEd. Member, Stirling District Council, since 1984 (Secretary, Labour Group, 1984-88); Teacher, Lornshill Academy, Alloa, since 1983; b. 30.6.60, Irvine. Educ. Arran High School; Stirling University. President, Students Association, Stirling University, 1980-82; Deputy Chairperson, National Union of Students (Scotland), 1982-83; Chairperson, Leisure and Recreation Committee, Stirling District Council, 1986-88; Chairperson, Stirling District Arts Council, 1984-86; Parliamentary candidate, Perth and Kinross, 1987; Member, COSLA Arts and Recreation Committee, 1985-88; Chairperson, Equal Opportunities Committee, Stirling District Council, 1986-88. Address: (h.) 10A Argyll Avenue, Stirling; T.-0786 79470.

McConnell, Walter Scott, PhC, FPS. Community Pharmacist, since 1962; Director, Ayrshire Pharmaceuticals Ltd., since 1964; Past Chairman, Pharmaceutical General Council (Scotland); Member, Local Review Committee, HM Prison, Dungavel; b. 7.4.36, Kilmarnock; m.; 1 s.; 3 d. Educ. Kilmarnock Academy; Royal Technical College, Glasgow. Recreations: curling; golf. Address: (h.) 27 Mauchline Road, Hurlford, Kilmarnock, KA1 5AB; T.-0563 25393.

McCool, Thomas Joseph, BSc (Hons), FRSA. Chief Executive, Scottish Vocational Education Council, since 1986; b. 1.3.39, Bellshill; m., Anne McGurk; 2 d. Educ. Our Lady's High School, Motherwell; Glasgow University; Jordanhill College of Education. Various teaching appointments, 1961-71; Assistant Director of Education, then Depute Director, Renfrewshire, 1971-76; Divisional Education Officer, Renfrew Division, Strathclyde, 1976-86. Member, Munn Committee, 1975-78; Member, Scottish Certificate of Education Examination Board, 1978-86; Chairman, Scottish Central Committee on Guidance, 1981-86. Recreations: golf; swimming; reading. Address: (b.) Hanover House, Douglas Street, Glasgow, G2 7NQ; T.-041-242 2052.

McCormick, David. Vice-Convener, Dumfries and Galloway Regional Council; Trustee Director, Nithsdale, Annan and Eskdale and Stewartry Enterprise Trust, since 1984; b. 5.5.18, Kirkconnel; m., Mary-Ann Edgar Carruthers; 1 s.; 1 d. Educ. Sanquhar Academy. Started in coal-mining, 1934; Underground Deputy, 1954-65; Training Department, NCB, Barony Colliery, 1965-76; elected to Dumfries and Galloway Regional Council, 1978; Vice Chairman, Policy Committee, and Chairman, Training Committee; Chairman, Kirkconnel Co-operative Society; Member, MSC Area Manpower Board; Chairman, Dumfries and Galloway Emergencies and Disaster Fund. Recreations: gardening; photography; motoring. Address: (h.) 21 Libry Street, Kelloholm, Kirkconnel, Dumfriesshire, DG4 6RS; T.-Kirkconnel 401.

MacCormick, Professor (Donald) Neil, MA, LLD, Hon. LLD (Uppsala), FRSE, FBA. Regius Professor of Public Law, Edinburgh University, since 1972; b. 27.5.41, Glasgow; m., Karen (Caroline) Rona Barr; 3 d. Educ. High School of Glasgow; Glasgow University; Balliol College, Oxford. Lecturer in Jurisprudence, Queen's College, Dundee, 1965-67; Fellow, Balliol College, Oxford, 1967-72; Oxford University: CUF Lecturer, 1968-72, Pro-Proctor, 1970-71; Dean, Faculty of Law, Edinburgh University, 1973-76 and 1985-88; Senate Assessor, University Court, 1982-85;

Member, Broadcasting Council for Scotland, since 1985. President, Oxford Union, 1965; Executive Member, Scottish National Party, 1978-81, and Council Member, 1978-84. Address: (h.) Dalhousie Chesters, Bonnyrigg, Midlothian; T.-031-667 1011.

MacCorquodale, Andrew Robb, FRICS. Regional Assessor, Central Regional Council, since 1982; b. 8.5.34, Larbert; m., Helen Walls; 1 s.; 1 d. Educ. Montrose Academy; Larbert High School; Heriot-Watt University. Trainee Valuer, Stirling County Council, 1950; Junior Valuer, Stirling and Clackmannan Joint Valuation Authority, 1956; Depute Assessor, Central Regional Council, 1975. Recreations: sailing; gardening; rugby; art; folk music. Address: (b.) Viewforth, Stirling; T.-Stirling 73111.

McCourt, Peter Aloysius, BSc, AdvDipRE. Rector, St. Mary's Academy, Bathgate, since 1982; b. 14.6.35, Kilwinning; m., Veronica Wilkins; 1 s.; 2 d. Educ. St. Joseph's High School, Kilmarnock; Heriot-Watt University. Royal Corps of Signals, 1954-56; industry, 1956-65; student, 1965-69; St. Augustine's High School: Teacher, 1969, Principal Teacher, Physics, 1970; Depute Head, Holy Rood High School, 1978. Recreations: opera; browsing in bookshops. Address: (h.) 2 Riversdale Road, Edinburgh, EH12 5QN; T.-031-337 4519.

McCracken, William Ian, MA, LLB. Solicitor, since 1950; Honorary Sheriff, since 1986; b. 30.10.24, Troon; m., June Patricia Selvey; 1 s.; 1 d. Educ. Dollar Academy; Edinburgh University. RASC, including two years in West Africa, 1943-47; joined Jenkins and Jardine, Solicitors, Stirling, 1950; became Senior Partner, 1973; Dean, Society of Solicitors and Procurators of Stirling, 1983-85. Former Secretary: Whinwell Children's Home, Stirling; Stirling Chapter of Architects; Stirling Burns Club. Recreations: gardening; walking. Address: (b.) 80 Port Street, Stirling; T.-0786 50366.

McCrae, William Morrice, MB, ChB, FRCPE, FRCP(G). Consultant Physician, Royal Hospital for Sick Children, Edinburgh, since 1965; Senior Lecturer, Department of Child Life and Health, Edinburgh University, since 1965; b. 11.3.32, Hurlford; m., Jennifer Jane Graham. Educ. Kilmarnock Academy; Glasgow University. House Physician/House Surgeon, Royal Infirmary, Glasgow; Captain, RAMC; Hall Fellow in Medicine, Glasgow University; Lecturer, Department of Child Health, Glasgow University. Recreations: gardening; history. Address: (h.) Seabank House, Aberdour, Fife.

McCrone, Iain Alistair, CBE (1987), SDA. Farmer and Company Director; b. 29.3.34, Glasgow; m., Yvonne Findlay; 4 d. Educ. Glasgow Academy; Trinity College, Glenalmond; West of Scotland Agricultural College. Farming on own account, since 1956; Managing Director, McCrone Farmers Ltd., since 1958; began fish farming, 1968; Director, Highland Trout Co. (now McConnell Salmon Ltd.); Director, Otter Ferry Salmon Ltd., since 1974; Member, Fife Regional Council, 1978-82; Parliamentary candidate (Conservative), Central Fife, 1979; Council Member, National Farmers Union of Scotland, 1977-82; Board Member, Glenrothes Development Corporation, since 1980; Member, Fife Health Board, since 1983; Nuffield Farming Scholar, 1966; President, Scottish Conservative and Unionist Association, 1985-87. Recreations: golf; squash; rugby (spectator). Address: (h.) Cardsknolls, Markinch, Fife, KY7 6LP; T.-0337 30267.

McCrone, Robert Gavin Loudon, CB, MA, MSc, PhD, LLD, FRSE. Secretary, Scottish Development Department, since 1987; Chief Economic Adviser, Scottish Office, since 1972; Visiting Professor of Economics, Glasgow University, since 1988; b. 2.2.33, Ayr; m., Alexandra Bruce Waddell; 2 s.; 1 d. Educ. St. Catharine's College, Cambridge; University of Wales; Glasgow University. Fisons Ltd., 1959-60; Lecturer in Economics, Glasgow University, 1960-65; Fellow, Brasenose College, Oxford, 1965-70; Consultant, UNESCO, 1964; Member, NEDC Working Party on Agricultural Policy, 1967-68; Adviser, House of Commons Select Committee on Scottish Affairs, 1969-70; Senior Economic Adviser, Scottish Office, 1970-72; Under Secretary, 1972-80; Secretary, Industry Department for Scotland, 1980-87. Council Member: Royal Economic Society, 1977-82, Scottish Economic Society, since 1982; Visiting Professor, Strathclyde University, 1983-86. Publications: The Economics of Subsidising Agriculture, 1962; Scotland's Economic Progress 1951-60, 1963; Regional Policy in Britain, 1969; Scotland's Future, 1969. Recreation: walking. Address: (b.) St. Andrews House, Regent Road, Edinburgh; T.-031-556 8400.

McCrorie, Ian, BSc. Chorusmaster, Scottish Philharmonic Singers, since 1976; Assistant Rector, Greenock Academy, since 1975; b. 6.5.41, Greenock; m., Olive Simpson Bolton; 2 s. Educ. Greenock Academy; Glasgow University. Founded Toad Choir, Greenock, which appeared in numerous BBC Songs of Praise programmes and won 1975 National Choral Competition, Royal Albert Hall, London; this choir became the nucleus of the Scottish Philharmonic Singers, established in 1976; has prepared the choir to work under several distinguished conductors; Organist and Choirmaster, Mid Kirk of Greenock, since 1964; former Assistant to Arthur Oldham, Edinburgh Festival Chorus; has been Choral Director, International Festival of Youth Orchestras, Aberdeen; has conducted at Festivals in France and Poland, and has taken choir to Israel; Past President and Convener of Cruising, Clyde River Steamer Club; author of numerous booklets and articles on Clyde and West Highland steamers. Recreations: as above! Address: (h.) 72 Newton Street, Greenock; T.-0475 26689.

McCubbin, James Ian, MA, LLB. Solicitor and Legal Adviser to National Health Service in Scotland, since 1984; b. 13.4.26, Edinburgh; m., Thomasina Nicholson Grant; 1 s.; 1 d. Educ. George Heriot's School, Edinburgh; Downing College, Cambridge; Edinburgh University. Legal Assistant, County Councils of Inverness and Renfrew, 1956-59; joined Scottish Hospital Service as Legal Assistant, Central Legal Office, 1959. Address: (b.) Trinity Park House, South Trinity Road, Edinburgh, EH5 3SE; T.-031-552 6255.

McCue, William, OBE (1982), LRAM. Bass Singer; b. 17.8.34, Allanton, Shotts; m., Patricia Carrick; 1 d. Educ. Calderhead High School; Royal Scottish Academy of Music; Royal Academy of Music. Began professional singing career in 1960; his work has included opera, oratorio, recital, concert, cabaret, pantomime and stage musical, radio and TV; has travelled throughout the world, making numerous visits to USA, Canada, USSR, Iceland, Europe and Israel; has made various recordings of Scots songs and Negro spirituals; Director, Scottish Singers Company; former Member, Scottish Arts Council. Recreations: watching all sport; listening to all kinds of music; gardening; escaping to the Scottish countryside. Address: (h.) Sweethope House, Bothwell, Glasgow, G71 8BT; T.-0698 853241.

McCulloch, Henry, BL. Chief Executive and Director of Administration, Badenoch and Strathspey District Council, since 1974; b. 17.12.35, Bieldside, Aberdeen; m., Freda; 1 s.; 2 d. Educ. George Watson's College; Edinburgh University. Legal Assistant: City of Edinburgh, 1960-64, Burgh of Falkirk, 1964-66; Senior Legal and Administrative Assistant, Roxburgh County Council, 1966-68; Depute County Clerk, Dumfries County Council, 1968-74. Recreations: skiing; sailing; golf. Address: (b.) Courthouse, 36 High Street, Kingussie, Inverness-shire, PH21 1JA; T.-054 02 555.

McCulloch, Norman Hamilton. Secretary, Red Deer Commission, since 1978; b. 13.7.30, Longniddry; m., Joyce Ann; 2 s. Educ. Royal High School, Edinburgh. Scottish Education Department, 1947-49; National Service, RAF, 1949-52; rejoined Scottish Education Department, 1952-68; Scottish Economic Planning Department/ Scottish Development Department, 1968-78. Recreations: golf; bridge; conservation; keeping the peace. Address: (b.) Red Deer Commission, Knowsley, 82 Fairfield Road, Inverness, IV3 5LH; T.-0463 231751.

McCunn, Archibald Eddington, BSc (Hons), CEng, MIMechE, FBIM. Board Member, Highlands and Islands Development Board, since 1985; b. 27.5.27, Motherwell; m., Olive Isobel Johnston; 1 s.; 1 d. Educ. Dalziel High School; Strathclyde University. Development Engineer, Colvilles Ltd., Clyde Iron Works, 1952-54; Assistant to General Manager (Construction), Ravenscraig Steelworks, 1954-57; Chief Engineer (Ironworks), Ravenscraig, 1957-63; Senior Consultant, Inbucon/AIC, 1963-67; Divisional Chairman, Stenhouse Industries, 1967-71; Divisional Chairman/Consultant, Grampian Holdings plc, 1971-88; Elder, Church of Scotland, 38 years. Recreations: curling; tennis; painting; music; walking; gardening. Address: (h.) 2 McIntosh Way, Motherwell, ML1 3BB; T.-0698 53500.

McCutcheon, James, MA (Hons). Head Teacher, St. Michael's Academy, Kilwinning, since 1976; b. Kilmarnock; m., Joan Cullinane; 3 s. Educ. St. Joseph's Academy, Kilmarnock; Glasgow University. Principal Teacher of Classics, then Assistant Head Teacher, St. Michael's Academy, Kilwinning; Depute Head Teacher, St. Joseph's Academy, Kilmarnock. President, Kilwinning Rotary Club, 1985-86. Recreations: reading; music; various sports. Address: (h.) 7 Graystones, Kilwinning, Ayrshire.

McDevitt, Professor Denis Gordon, DSc, MD, FRCP, FRCPI, FRCPEd. Professor of Clinical Pharmacology, Dundee University Medical School, since 1984; Honorary Consultant Physician, Tayside Health Board, since 1984; President, Association of Physicians of Great Britain and Ireland, 1987-88; Civil Consultant in Clinical Pharmacology, RAF, since 1987; b. 17.11.37, Belfast; m., Anne McKee; 2 s.; 1 d. Educ. Campbell College, Belfast; Queen's University, Belfast. Assistant Professor of Medicine and Consultant Physician, Christian Medical College, Ludhiana, North India, 1968-71; Senior Lecturer in Clinical Pharmacology and Consultant Physician, Queen's University Medical School, 1971-76; Merck International Fellow in Clinical Pharmacology, Vanderbilt University, Nashville, Tennessee, 1974-75; Reader in Clinical Pharmacology, Queen's University Medical School, 1976-78; Professor of Clinical Pharmacology, Queen's University of Belfast and Consultant Physician, Belfast Teaching Hospitals, 1978-83. Chairman, Clinical Section, British Pharmacological Society, since 1985 (Secretary, 1978-82). Recreations: golf; classical music. Address: (h.) 1 Godfrey Street, Barnhill, Dundee, DD5 2QZ.

McDonald, Alastair. Radio, Television, Stage and Recording Personality; Folk Singer; Programme Presenter and Discussion Guest; Entertainer; b. 28.10.41, Glasgow; m., Anne; 2 s. Educ. Strathbungo Senior Secondary School. Recordings include White Wings, Glencoe and Other Requests, Journey Through Scotland, Heads and Tales, Sing A Song of Scotland, Journey Through Scotland Volume 2. Recreations: inert athlete and hindsight student. Address: (b.) Corban Records, PO Box 2, Glasgow, G44 3LB.

McDonald, Rev. Alexander, BA, CMIWS. Minister, St. Mark's Church, Oldhall, Paisley, since 1974; b. 5.11.37, Bishopbriggs; m., Essdale Helen McLeod; 2 s.; 1 d. Educ. Bishopbriggs Higher Grade School; Whitehill Senior Secondary School, Glasgow; Glasgow University and Trinity College. Management in timber trade, 1952-54; RAF, 1954-56; management in timber trade, 1956-58, motor trade, 1958-62; student, 1962-68; Minister, St. David's, Bathgate, 1968-74. Trustee, Scottish Television Staff Trust; wide range of involvement with Boys' Brigade in Scotland, Scottish Spastics, mentally handicapped children, ACCORD, Christian Aid and many others; regular broadcaster. Recreations: reading; walking; fishing. Address: St. Mark's Church, Glasgow Road, Paisley; T.-041-889 4279.

Macdonald, Alistair, JP. Member, Clydebank District Council, since 1980 (Vice-Chairman, since 1988, Chairman, Environmental Services, since 1984); Member, South of Scotland Electricity Consultative Council, since 1980; b. 29.5.41, Aird, Uig; m., Elizabeth; 2 s. Educ. Dumbarton Academy. Police service, 10 years; staff, British Leyland (Albion Motors), 14 years; Proprietor,

Clydebank Cleaning Service, since 1985; former Vice Chairman, Scottish Area Council, APEX, and Scottish Engineering Advisory Council; founder Member, UB40 (Clydebank Unemployed Workers Centre); Member, Clyde River Purification Board. Recreations: angling; reading; snooker. Address: (h.) 32 Hawthorn Street, Clydebank, Dunbartonshire; T.-Duntocher 79503.

MacDonald, Sheriff Alistair Archibald, MA, LLB, DL. Sheriff of Grampian, Highland and Islands, at Kirkwall and Lerwick, since 1968; b. 8.5.27, Edinburgh; m., Jill Russell; 1 s.; 1 d. Educ. Broughton School; Edinburgh University. Army Service, Intelligence Corps, 1945-48; called to Scottish Bar, 1954; Sheriff Substitute of Caithness, Sutherland, Orkney and Shetland, at Lerwick, 1961-68; Deputy Lieutenant of Shetland, since 1986. Address: (h.) Westhall, Shetland Isles; T.-Lerwick 2711.

Macdonald, Alister Gordon, BSc, PhD. Reader in Physiology, Aberdeen University, since 1984; b. 25.1.40, London; m., Jennifer; 1 s.; 2 d. Educ. Boys' High School, Trowbridge, Wiltshire; Bristol University. University of East Anglia, 1963-69; joined Aberdeen University as Lecturer in Physiology, 1969. Publications: Physiological Aspects of Deep Sea Biology, 1975; Physiological Aspects of Anaesthetics and Inert Gases, 1978. Recreations: hill-walking; badminton; music. Address: (b.) Physiology Department, Marischal College, Aberdeen, AB9 1AS; T.-Aberdeen 273021.

Macdonald, Angus David, MA (Hons) (Cantab), DipEd. Headmaster, Lomond School, Helensburgh, since 1986; b. 9.10.50, Edinburgh; m., Isabelle Marjory Ross; 2 d. Educ. Portsmouth Grammar School; Cambridge University; Edinburgh University. Assistant Teacher, Alloa Academy, 1972-73; Assistant Teacher, Edinburgh Academy, 1973-82 (Exchange Teacher, King's School, Parramatta, NSW, 1978-79); George Watson's College, Edinburgh: Principal Teacher of Geography, 1982, Deputy Principal, 1982-86. Recreations: outdoor recreation; sport; piping; gardening. Address: 8 Millig Street, Helensburgh, Dunbartonshire; T.-0436 2472.

MacDonald, Angus Lamont MacKinnon, DA, RIBA, FRIAS. Chartered Architect; Partner, James Parr & Partners, Architects, since 1973; Past President, Dundee Institute of Architects and former Vice-President, Royal Incorporation of Architects in Scotland; b. 2.9.38, Uig, Isle of Skye; m., Morag A.C. MacLean; 2 s.; 1 d. Educ. Perth Academy; Portree High School; Perth High School; Duncan of Jordanstone College of Art, Dundee. James Parr & Partners, Broughty Ferry: Assistant Architect, 1963, Associate Architect, 1968, Partner, since 1973, Senior Partner responsible for housing etc., 1982; Assessor, Civic Trust Awards, 1983-88; Chairman, Perthshire and Angus Provincial Mod, 1974-88; Chairman, Dundee Highland Society; Director, St. Aiden's Project for Disabled Youngsters, Dundee; President, Broughty Ferry Art Society. Recreations: painting; singing (Gaelic choir and barber shop quartette); canoeing; travel. Address: (h.) Bovain, 2B Arnhall Gardens, Farrington Street, Dundee; T.-0382 65629.

Macdonald, Angus Stewart, CBE, DL, FRAgS. Chairman, Scottish Agricultural Development Council, since 1980; b. 7.4.35, Edinburgh; m., Janet Ann Somerville; 3 s. Educ. Conon Bridge School; Gordonstoun School. Past Chairman and former Vice President, Royal Highland and Agricultural Society; Director: British Wool Marketing Board and associated companies, Reith & Anderson (Tain and Dingwall) Ltd., Gordonstoun School, Aberlour School, Hill Farming Research Organisation, Highlands and Islands Development Board, Panel of Agricultural Arbiters, Grampian Television, Scottish English and Welsh Wool Growers Ltd.; Member, Queen's Bodyguard for Scotland (Royal Company of Archers). Recreation: field sports. Address: Torgorm, Conon Bridge, Dingwall, Ross-shire; T.-0349 61365.

Macdonald, Archibald, MBE, MA, LLB, DL. Senior Partner, R. & R. Urquhart, Solicitor, Forres, since 1965; b. 3.5.24, Hamilton; m., Isobel Jean Ramsay Wright; 2 s.; 1 d. Educ. Fettes College; Edinburgh University. Lt., RNVR, 1942-46: qualified Solicitor, 1950; Partner, R. & R. Urquhart, 1951; Town Clerk, Forres, 1958-75; Honorary Sheriff, 1982; Deputy Lieutenant, Moray, 1983. Recreation: country pursuits. Address: (h.) Chapelton House, Forres, Moray; T.-0309 72786.

MacDonald, Calum Alasdair. MP (Labour), Western Isles, since 1987; b. 7.5.56. Educ. Nicolson Institute; Edinburgh University; University of California at Los Angeles.

MacDonald, Colin Cameron, BA. Chief Research Officer, Scottish Development Department, since 1981; b. 13.7.43, Glasgow; m., Kathryn Campbell; 1 s.; 1 d. Educ. Allan Glen's School; Strathclyde University. Scottish Development Department: Research Officer, Research Services, 1967-70, Senior Research Officer, Research Services, 1970-71, Principal Research Officer, Central Planning Research Unit, 1971-75; Senior Principal Research Officer, Scottish Office Central Research Unit, 1975-81. Recreations: tennis; fishing; music. Address: (b.) Room 5/62, New St. Andrews House, Edinburgh; T.-031-244 4400.

Macdonald, David N., BSc (Hons), DipEd. Head Teacher, Langholm Academy, since 1980; b. 4.11.42, Edinburgh; m., Sandra Crerar-Gilbert; 2 d. Educ. Royal High School, Edinburgh; Heriot-Watt College, Edinburgh. Assistant Teacher of Mathematics: Boroughmuir Secondary School, 1965, Liberton Secondary School, 1966-68; Principal Teacher of Mathematics, Annan Academy, 1968-73; Depute Rector, Annan Academy, 1973-80. Secretary, Langholm Rotary Club. Address: (h.) Sorbie Cottage, Drove Road, Langholm, DG13 0JW; T.-0541 80531.

Macdonald, Donald Alistair, OBE, DipSoc, AAPSW. Mental Welfare Commissioner, Scotland, since 1984; b. 18.2.28, Larbert; m., Grace Catherine; 1 s.; 2 d. Educ. Larbert High School; Edinburgh University. Senior Psychiatric Social Worker, Renfrewshire Mental Hospitals; Senior

Case Work Supervisor, then Training Officer, Staffordshire County Council; Deputy County Welfare Officer, Derbyshire County Council; Director of Social Work, Roxburgh County Council; Director of Social Work, Borders Regional Council (retired). Recreations: gardening; golf; walking. Address: (h.) Northumbria, Darnick, Melrose, Roxburghshire, TD6 9AJ; T.-089682 2250.

MacDonald, Donald Gordon, RD*, BDS, PhD, FRCPath, FDSRCPS(G). Reader in Oral Medicine and Pathology, Glasgow University, since 1982; Consultant Oral Pathologist, Glasgow Dental Hospital, since 1974; b. 5.7.42, Glasgow; m., Emma Lindsay Cordiner; 2 s.; 1 d. Educ. Kelvinside Academy, Glasgow; Glasgow University. Assistant, then Lecturer, Glasgow University, 1964-69; Visiting Associate Professor in Oral Pathology, University of Illinois, 1969-70; Lecturer, Senior Lecturer in Oral Medicine and Pathology, Glasgow University, 1970-82; Editor, Glasgow Dental Journal, 1969-75; Honorary Consultant Forensic Odontologist, Strathclyde Police, since 1976; Honorary Secretary, Association of Head and Neck Oncologists of Great Britain, 1983-87; President Elect, British Society for Oral Pathology, 1987. Recreation: Royal Naval Reserve. Address: (h.) 2 Dougalston Gardens South, Milngavie, Glasgow; T.-041-956 2075.

MacDonald, Donald John, BSc. Rector, Thurso High School, since 1980; b. 25.5.39, Glasgow; 1 s.; 2 d. Educ. Lionel School, Lewis; Govan High School, Glasgow; Glasgow University; Jordanhill College of Education. Teacher of Science, Govan High School; Principal Teacher of Physics: Kirkwall Grammar School, Govan High School; Assistant Head, Linwood High School; Depute Rector, Dingwall Academy; Assistant Divisional Education Officer, Highland Region. Address: (h.) 3 Church Street, Halkirk, Caithness.

MacDonald, Donald Murray, AIB (Scot). Retired Bank Manager; Honorary Sheriff, since 1984; b. 10.6.32, Inverness; m., Irene Foubister Kemp; 2 d. Educ. Inverness Royal Academy. Entered service of Union Bank of Scotland Ltd., 1947; worked in a number of offices throughout Scotland; appointed Accountant, Stornoway Branch, Bank of Scotland, 1971; Assistant Manager, Kirkwall, 1973; Manager, Lochmaddy and Benbecula, 1977; Manager, Portree, 1982 (retired 1986). Treasurer, Celtic Film and Television Association; Treasurer, Church of Scotland, Portree; Treasurer, Portree and District Rotary Club; Chairman, Isle of Skye Piping Society. Recreations: gardening; piping; stalking. Address: (h.) Hillview, Staffin Road, Portree, Isle of Skye, IV51 9HP; T.-0478 2722.

McDonald, Sir Duncan, Kt (1983), CBE (1976), DEng, DSc, BSc, FEng, FH-WC, Hon.FIEE, CBIM, SMIEEE, FRSE, FRSA. Director: General Accident Fire & Life Assurance Corporation plc; Barclays Bank, Scotland; Northern Rock Building Society, Scotland; b. 20.9.21, Inverkeithing; m., Jane Anne Guckian; 3 s.; 1 d. Educ. Inverkeithing Public School; Dunfermline High School; Edinburgh University. Early experience, British Thomson Houston, Rugby (Head, R & D., BTH transformer interests); appointed Chief Transformer Designer, Bruce Peebles, Edinburgh, 1954; became Chief Engineer of company, 1959; Managing Director, 1962; following merger, joined Board, C.A. Parsons, 1969, and Board, Retrolle Parsons Group, 1973; became Chief Executive of Group; first Group Managing Director, Northern Engineering Industries plc, 1977; appointed Chairman and Chief Executive, 1980; Honorary Fellow, Heriot-Watt College, 1962; DSc Heriot-Watt University, 1982; Honorary Fellow, Institution of Electrical Engineers, 1984; awarded first Hon. Doctorate of Engineering by Newcastle upon Tyne University, 1984; Fellow and a Vice-President, Scottish Council (Development and Industry). Recreations: golf; fishing; gardening. Address: (h.) Duncliffe, Kinellan Road, Edinburgh, EH12 6ES; T.-031-337 4814.

Macdonald, Rev. Finlay Angus John, MA, BD, PhD. Minister, Jordanhill Parish Church, Glasgow, since 1977; b. 1.7.45, Watford; m., Elizabeth Mary Stuart; 2 s. Educ. Dundee High School; St. Andrews University. Assistant Minister, Bo'ness Old Kirk, 1970-71; Minister, Menstrie Parish Church, 1971-77; Junior Clerk and Treasurer, Stirling and Dunblane Presbytery, 1973-77; Convener, Church of Scotland Working Group on Children and Communion, 1980-82; Convener, Advance Planning Group, Church of Scotland Youth Education Committee, 1982-84; Co-Editor and Contributor, Children at the Table, 1982; Convener, Legal Questions Committee, Board of Practice and Procedure, 1984-85, 1986-88; Vice-Convener, Business Committee, General Assembly, 1985-88; Chairman, Jordanhill College School PTA Action Committee, 1986-88; first Convener, Board of Managers, Jordanhill School, 1987-88; Member, Board of Governors, Jordanhill College, since 1988. Recreations: music; angling; reading; gardening. Address: (h.) 96 Southbrae Drive, Glasgow, G13 1TZ; T.-041-959 1310.

McDonald, George Alexander, MD, FRCP, FRCPath. Consultant Haematologist, Glasgow Royal Infirmary, since 1964; b. 21.12.24, Cults, Aberdeen; m., Margaret M. Mackie; 2 s.; 1 d. Educ. Milne's High School, Fochabers; Aberdeen University. House Surgeon, then House Physician, Aberdeen Royal Infirmary; Senior Research Fellow, then Lecturer in Medicine, Aberdeen University; Senior Registrar in Haematology, Glasgow Royal Infirmary; Past President, British Society for Haematology; International Counsellor, International Society of Haematology. Publication: Atlas of Haematology (Co-author). Recreations: golf; gardening; fishing. Address: (h.) 21 Blackwood Road, Milngavie, Glasgow, G62 7LB; T.-041-956 3103.

McDonald, Gerard, MA, BA (Hons), DPE. Head Teacher, St. Leonard's Secondary School, Glasgow, since 1983; b. 26.11.39, Motherwell; m., Eileen Mary Gibson; 2 s. Educ. St. Aloysius' College; Glasgow University; Strathclyde University. Teacher, St. Aloysius' College, 1961-71; Principal Teacher, then Assistant Head Teacher, St. Roch's Secondary School, 1971-80; Depute Head Teacher, St. Ninian's High School, Kirkintilloch, 1980-83. Recreations: rugby football; golf. Address: (b.) 62 Lochend Road, Glasgow, G34 ONY; T.-041-771 4986.

Macdonald, Gibson Torbett. Provost, Kyle and Carrick District Council, 1984-88; b. 21.1.33; m., Muirkirk; m., Mary Hastings Logan Lambie; 1 s.; 1 d. Educ. Kilmarnock Academy. National President, Junior Chamber Scotland; Executive Vice President, Junior Chamber International; Chairman, Ayr Branch, Ayr Conservative Association; Chairman, Ayr Conservative Constituency; Town Councillor, Royal Burgh of Ayr; District Councillor, Kyle and Carrick District (held Convenership of Planning, Employment and Policy and Resources Committees); Chairman, Culzean Country Park Joint Committee; Member, COSLA Planning and Town Twinning Committees. Treasurer, Ayrshire Decorative and Fine Arts Society. Recreations: bowling; bridge; computing; philately. Address: (h.) 14 Belmont Avenue, Ayr, KA7 2JN.

Macdonald, 8th Baron, (Godfrey James Macdonald of Macdonald). Chief of the Name and Arms of Macdonald; b. 28.11.47; m., Claire Catlow; 1 s.; 3 d. Address: (h.) Kinloch Lodge, Isle of Skye.

MacDonald, Gus. Director of Programmes, Scottish Television; Television Journalist; b. 20.8.40, Larkhall; m., Teen; 2 d. Educ. Allan Glen's School, Glasgow. Marine engineer, Stephens, Linthouse, 1955-62; Circulation and Publicity Manager, Tribune, 1963-65; Investigative Journalist, The Scotsman, 1965-67; Editor, Financial Scotsman, 1966-67; Investigative Bureau, World in Action, Granada, 1967-69; Editor/Executive Producer, World in Action, 1969-75; successively Head of Current Affairs, Head of Regional Programmes, Head of Features, Granada; Writer/Presenter, Camera: Early Photography, 1979-80, MacDiarmid: Hammer and Thistle; Presenter, variously, World in Action, What the Papers Say, Devil's Advocate, Union World; Election and Party Conference coverage; BAFTA Award, current affairs; National Viewers and Listeners' Association Award, 1985; founder Chairman, Edinburgh International Television Festival, 1976; Visiting Professor, Film and Media Studies, Stirling University, 1985-86. Publications: Grierson: Television and Documentary, 1977; Camera: Victorian Eyewitness, 1979. Recreations: words; pictures; exploring Scotland. Address: (b.) Scottish Television, Cowcaddens, Glasgow, G2 3PR.

Macdonald, Hugh R.M. Advocate, since 1985; b. 24.2.43, Cambridge; m., Margaret Mary Stevenson; 2 s.; 3 d. Educ. Mill Hill School. Scottish Law Commission, 1970-84. Publication: A Guide to the Family Law (Scotland) Act 1985. Recreations: music; rugby; golf. Address: (h.) 13 Danube Street, Edinburgh, EH4 1NN; T.-031-332 5720.

MacDonald, Iain Davies, BMus. Composer; Head of Music, Greenfaulds High School, Cumbernauld, since 1975; Music Director, Cumbernauld Music Centre, since 1982; b. 15.2.51, Greenock; m., Nancy; 1 s.; 1 d. Educ. Allan Glen's School, Glasgow; Glasgow University; Moray House College of Education. Music Teacher, Renfrew High School, 1972-75, Composer (in collaboration with Iain Fraser): Christmas Story (cantata, 1977), American Suite (wind band/choral, 1979, orchestral/choral, 1980), Indecision (musical, 1981); Angel (musical, 1987); Sole Composer and Author, Scottish March (wind band, 1980, wind band and brass band, 1982), Sonatina (wind band, 1982), The Chess Game (musical, 1983), Chances (musical, 1984), Spy (musical, 1988). Recreations: sailing; board sailing. Address: (h.) 8 Main Street, Chryston, Glasgow, G69 9DH; T.-041-779 1595.

Macdonald, Iain Gordon, MA, DipAdEd. Member, Strathclyde Regional Council, since 1982; Membership Development Officer, CWS Scotland, since 1986; b. 20.12.47, Edinburgh; m., Joan Sheila Winter; 1 d. Educ. Melville College, Edinburgh; Edinburgh University. Inner London Education Authority, 1973-79; Member, Scottish Education and Action for Development; Chair, Alternative Employment Study Group; Member: Labour Campaign Group, CND. Recreation: politics. Address. (h.) Station House, Rhu, Dunbartonshire; T.-820719.

Macdonald, Iain Smith, MD, FRCPEdin, FFCM, DPH. Chief Medical Officer, Scottish Home and Health Department, since 1985; b. 14.7.27, Greenock; m., Sheila Foster; 1 s.; 1 d. Educ. Glasgow University. Lecturer in Public Health, Glasgow University, 1955-57; Deputy Medical Officer of Health: County Borough of Bury, 1957-59, County Borough of Bolton, 1959-64; joined Scottish Home and Health Department, 1964. Address: (h.) 36 Dumyat Drive, Falkirk, FK1 5PA; T.-Falkirk 25100.

Macdonald, Ian Hamish, OBE, FIB (Scot), CBIM. Member, South of Scotland Electricity Board, since 1987; Director: Standard Property Investment Plc, Kerarn Ltd., Crescent Japan Investment Trust plc, New Tokyo Investment Trust plc, Macdonald Orr Ltd., TSB Northern Ireland PLC, Morgan Grenfell Scotland Ltd.; Chairman: PR Consultants Scotland Ltd., EFM Dragon Trust PLC, Nationwide Public Relations Ltd., Clan Donald Lands Trust, Scottish Council Foundation; Member, Design Council; b. 30.12.26, Inverness; m., Patricia; 1 d. Educ. Inverness Royal Academy; Inverness Technical College. RAFVR, 1944; Queen's Own Cameron Highlanders, 1945 (Captain, 1948); Mercantile Bank, 1948-59; The Hongkong and Shanghai Banking Corporation: Manager, 1959-72, General Manager, India, 1972-73, General Manager International, 1973-80, Executive Director, 1980-83; Chief General Manager, TSB Scotland, 1983-86, and TSB Scotland PLC, 1986-87; Director, TSB Group PLC, 1986-87. Recreations: fishing; golf; bridge. Address: (h.) First Floor, 24 Moray Place, Edinburgh, EH3 6DA.

McDonald, Professor Janet B.I., MA. Professor of Drama, Glasgow University, since 1979; b. 28.7.41, Netherlee, Renfrewshire; m., Ian James McDonald; 1 d. Educ. Hutchesons' Girls' Grammar School; Glasgow University. Member, Governing Body, Royal Scottish Academy of Music and Drama, since 1979; Chairman, Drama and Theatre Board, Council for National Academic Awards, 1981-85; Chairman, Standing Committee of University Departments of Drama, 1982-85; Chairman, Drama Committee, Scottish Arts

Council, since 1985; Fellow, Royal Society of Arts. Address: (b.) 53 Hillhead Street, Glasgow, G12 8QE; T.-041-339 8855.

McDonald, John, JP, MA (Hons). Rector, Inverness High School, since 1983; b. 29.8.31, Aberdeen; m., Betty M. Christie; 1 s.; 2 d. Educ. Elgin Academy; Aberdeen University; Aberdeen College of Education. Ft. Lt., RAF, Education Branch, 1955-58; Teacher of Geography, Elgin Academy, 1958-60; Principal Teacher of Geography, Nairn Academy, 1960-63; Principal Teacher of Geography, then Depute Rector, Inverness High School, 1963-83. Chairman, Nordic Committee, Scottish National Ski Council. Recreations: skiing; golf; sailing; hill-walking; lapidary; caravanning. Address: (h.) Kirkgate, 3 Seabank Road, Nairn; T.-Nairn 52199.

Macdonald, Rev. John, MA, AEA. Minister, Lochee Old Parish Church, Dundee, 1949-85; Clerk, Synod of Perth and Angus, Church of Scotland, since 1977; b. 31.3.15, Braenish, Uig, Isle of Lewis; m., Eileen Ivy Sheila O'Flynn; 4 s.; 1 d. Educ. Nicolson Institute, Stornoway; Keil School, Dumbarton; Glasgow University; Aberdeen University. War Service, RAF, 1942-46 (Pilot); Chaplain: RAFVR, 1953-56, RAuxAF, 1956-65, ATC, 1965-85. Member: Church and Nation Committee, General Assembly, Dundee and District Retirement Council, Dundee Association of Social Services. Address: (h.) 12 Hyndford Street, Dundee, DD2 1HQ; T.-0382 68655.

Macdonald, Joseph Mackay, FIB (Scot). General Manager, UK Banking, The Royal Bank of Scotland plc, since 1985; b. 16.9.34, Halkirk, Caithness; m., Marlene G. Mackay; 1 s.; 1 d. Educ. Miller Academy, Thurso; Administrative Staff College, Henley. Commercial Bank of Scotland Ltd., 1950-59; National Commercial Bank of Scotland Ltd., 1959-69; Royal Bank of Scotland plc: various appointments, 1969-82, General Manager (Northern Region), 1982-85. Recreations: angling; curling; reading. Address: (b.) 9 Rubislaw Terrace, Aberdeen, AB9 8YQ; T.-0224 646626.

MacDonald, Rev. Kenneth Mackinnon, CertTheo. Free Church Minister, Rosskeen (Invergordon and Alness), since 1984; b. 9.1.35, Skinidin, Skye; m., Reta Cromarty; 2 s.; 2 d. Educ. Portree High School; Free Church College. Army, Seaforth Highlanders, Egypt, Germany, Aden, 1953-55; Uniformed Branch, HM Customs and Excise, Glasgow Docks, London Heathrow, Aberdeen and Stornoway, 1957-80; Free Church College, 1980-84. Member, Western Isles Council, 1973-76; Chairman, Western Isles Branch, Mentally Handicapped Action Committee, 1977-80; Member, Western Isles Children's Panel, 1977-80; capped seven times for Scotland as amateur footballer. Recreations: football; athletics. Address: Rosskeen Free Church Manse, Rosskeen, Invergordon, IV18 OPP; T.-0349 85 2406.

MacDonald, Margo. Broadcaster; b. Hamilton; m., Jim Sillars; 1 step s.; 2 d.; 2 step-d. Educ. Hamilton Academy; Dunfermline College. Teacher, 1963-65; barmaid and mother, 1965-73; Member of Parliament, 1973-74; Broadcaster/Writer, 1974-78; Director, Shelter, Scotland, 1978-81; Radio Forth: Broadcaster, 1981-83, Editor, Topical Programmes, 1983-85.

Macdonald, Rev. Professor Murdo Ewen, MA, BD, DD (St. Andrews), DD (McGill University). Emeritus Professor, Trinity College, Glasgow University; b. 28.8.14, Isle of Harris; 2 s. Educ. Sir Edward Scott School, Harris; Kingussie Secondary School; St. Andrews University. Minister, Portree, Isle of Skye, 1939-40; Chaplain to 4th Camerons, 1940-42; Chaplain to 2nd Paras, 1942; wounded and taken prisoner, North Africa, and spent rest of War in Germany (acted as Chaplain to American Air Force); awarded Bronze Star; Pollock Lecturer in Preaching, Canada; Syme Lecturer in Theology and Preaching, Lutheran Colleges, USA; Ferrie Lecturer in Preaching and Theology, Australia. Publications: Vitality of Faith; Need to Believe; Call to Obey; Crisis of Belief; Call to Communicate; Lost Provinces of Religion. Recreations: mountain climbing (completed Munroes). Address: (h.) 24 Falkland Street, Glasgow, G12; T.-041-334 2087.

Macdonald, Norman Malcolm. Writer; b. 24.7.27, Thunder Bay, Canada; m., Mairi F. Educ. Nicolson Institute; Newbattle Abbey College. New Zealand Air Force, 1949-57; journalism and administration at various periods; Administrator, Fir Chlis (Gaelic theatre company), 1978-80; Secretary, Sabhal Mor Ostaig Gaelic College, 1982-83. Publications: Calum Tod (novel); Fad (poetry); The Shutter Falls, Anna Chaimbeul, The Catechist, The Brahan Seer (plays); Call Na h'Iolaire, Clann-Nighean a Sgadain (historical); The Shutter Falls (television); Storm Witch (screenplay). Recreation: walking. Address: 14 Tong, Isle of Lewis.

Macdonald, Peter Cameron, DL, SDA. Convener, Scottish Landowners Federation, since 1985; Farmer, since 1961; Director, J. Dickson & Son, Gunmakers, since 1968; b. 14.12.37, Edinburgh; m., Barbara Helen Drimmie Ballantyne; 2 step-s. Educ. Loretto; East of Scotland College of Agriculture. Council Member: Scottish Landowners Federation, since 1976, Blackface Sheepbreeders Association, 1970-74; Member, Forth River Purification Board, 1979-87; Director, Royal Highland and Agricultural Society of Scotland, 1985; Deputy Lieutenant, West Lothian, since 1987. Recreations: fishing; shooting; golf. Address: Colzium Farm, Kirknewton, Midlothian, EH27 8DH; T.-0506 880607.

MacDonald, Rev. Peter James, BD, DipMin. National Young Adult Adviser, Church of Scotland, since 1986; b. 22.3.58, Dumbarton; m., Lesley Ann Orr. Educ. Vale of Leven Academy; Trinity College, Glasgow; New College, Edinburgh. Assistant Minister, The Old Kirk of Edinburgh, West Pilton, 1985-86. Convener, Scottish Christian Youth Work Group; Member, British Council of Churches Youth Unit Executive. Recreations: various sports; cinema; theatre; reading; listening to music. Address: (b.) 121 George Street, Edinburgh, EH2 4YN; T.-031-225 5722.

McDonald, Hon. Lord (Robert Howat McDonald), MC (1944), QC (Scot), MA, LLB. Senator of the College of Justice in Scotland, since 1973; b. 15.5.16, Paisley; m., Barbara Mackenzie. Educ. John Neilson Institution, Paisley; Glasgow University. Admitted Solicitor, 1938; KOSB, 1939-46 (mentioned in Despatches); admitted, Faculty of

Advocates, 1946; QC (Scot), 1957; Sheriff of Ayr and Bute, 1966-71; Member, Criminal Injuries Compensation Board, 1964-71; Chairman, Mental Welfare Commission for Scotland, 1964-83; Chairman, General Nursing Council for Scotland, 1970-73. Address: (h.) 5 Doune Terrace, Edinburgh, EH3 6EA; T.-031-225 3586.

Macdonald, Vice-Admiral Sir Roderick Douglas, KBE (1978). Artist; b. 25.2.21; m., 1, Joan Willis (m. diss.); 2 s.; 1 s. deceased; 2, Pamela Bartosik. Educ. Fettes (Captain, Scottish Schoolboys' rugby, 1937-38). Entered Royal Navy, 1939; served at sea throughout War, 1939-45; Cyprus (Despatches, 1957); Commander, Naval Forces Borneo, 1965 (CBE); Captain of the Fleet, 1970; COS to C-in-C, Naval Home Command, 1973-76; ADC to The Queen, 1975; COS to Comdr., Allied Naval Forces Southern Europe, 1976-79. President, Skye Highland Games and Skye Piping Society; Fellow, Nautical Institute (Vice-President, 1976-85); one-man exhibitions, Naples, Edinburgh, London (4). Address: (h.) Ollach, Braes, Skye.

McDonald, Sheena Elizabeth, MA, FRSA. Broadcaster/Journalist, since 1979; b. 25.7.54, Dunfermline. Educ. George Watson's Ladies' College; Edinburgh University; Bristol University. BBC Radio Scotland, 1978-81 (current affairs, arts and features); Presenter/Reporter, Scottish Television, since 1981 (arts, current affairs, politics); Chairman, Traverse Theatre Board of Management; Board Member, Scottish Ballet and Scottish Youth Theatre; Committee Member, Association for Business Sponsorship of the Arts (Scotland); Member, Edinburgh Festival Council. Recreations: cinema/consuming; film/conceiving; swimming. Address: (h.) 29 Northumbrland Street, Edinburgh, EH3 6LR; T.-031-556 1625.

MacDonald, Professor Simon Gavin George, MA, PhD, FInstP, FRSE. Professor of Physics, Dundee University, since 1973 (Head, Department of Physics, 1979-85); Deputy Chairman, Universities General Council on Admissions, since 1983; b. 5.9.23, Beauly, Inverness-shire; m., Eva Leonie Austerlitz; 1 s.; 1 d. Educ. George Heriot's, Edinburgh; Edinburgh University. Junior Scientific Officer, Royal Aircraft Establishment, Farnborough, 1943-46; Lecturer in Physics, St. Andrews University, 1948-57; Senior Lecturer in Physics: University College of the West Indies, 1957-62, St. Andrews University, 1962-67; Dundee University: Senior Lecturer in Physics, 1967-73, Dean of Science, 1970-73, Vice-Principal, 1974-79; Member, Scottish Universities Council on Entrance, 1969-82 (Vice-Convener, 1973-77, Convener, 1977-82); Chairman, Technical Committee, UCCA, 1979-83; Chairman, Board of Directors, Dundee Repertory Theatre, since 1975. Publications: Problems and Solutions in General Physics; Physics for Biology and Premedical Students; Physics for the Life and Health Sciences. Recreations: bridge; golf; fiction writing. Address: (b.) Department of Physics, Dundee University, Dundee, DD1 4HN; T.-0382 23181.

Macdonald, William Alexander, JP, AIB. Honorary Sheriff, since 1972; b. 9.1.21, Banffshire; m., Millicent M. Brodie. Educ. Turriff Academy; Banff Academy. Joined Trustee Savings Bank, 1939; RAF, 1941-46; Manager, Trustee Savings Bank: Stornoway, 1949-52, Peterhead, 1952-84. Chairman: Peterhead Scottish Week, Peterhead Community Centre, Banff Buchan Crime Prevention Panel; Treasurer, Peterhead Aged and Infirm Committee; Treasurer, Frank Jack Court (Housing Association); Session Clerk, Peterhead Old Parish Church, since 1954; Past President, Peterhead Rotary Club. Recreation: gardening. Address: (h.) 6 Kinmundy Road, Peterhead, AB4 6AY; T.-0779 72103.

McDonald, Rev. William James Gilmour, MA, BD, Hon. DD (Edinburgh). Minister, Mayfield Parish Church, Edinburgh, since 1959; b. 3.6.24, Edinburgh; m., Patricia Watson; 1 s.; 2 d. Educ. Daniel Stewart's College; Edinburgh University; Gottingen University. Royal Artillery and Indian Artillery, 1943-46; Parish Minister, Limekilns, 1953-59. Former Convener, Committee on Education for the Ministry; Convener, Assembly Council, 1984-87. Address: 26 Seton Place, Edinburgh, EH9 2JT; T.-031-667 1286.

MacDonell of Glengarry, Air Cdre. Aeneas Ranald Donald, CB, DFC. 22nd Chief of Glengarry; Member, Standing Council of Scottish Chiefs; Trustee, Clan Donald Lands Trust; Trustee, Finlaggan Trust; b. 15.11.13, Baku, Russia; m., 1, Diana Dorothy Keane; 2 s.; 1 d.; 2, Lois Eirene Frances Streatfeild; 1 s.; 1 d. Educ. Hurtspierpoint College; Royal Air Force College, Cranwell. RAF Officer, 1931-64; seconded to Fleet Air Arm, 1935-37; Flying Instructor, 1938-39; Air Ministry; Officer Commanding Spitfire Squadron during Battle of Britain; POW, Germany, 1941-45; Chief Flying Instructor, RAF College, Cranwell; Air Attache, Moscow, 1956-58; Director of Management and Work Study, Ministry of Defence, 1960-64; retired from RAF; Construction Industry Training Board, 1967-72; Head, Commercial Department, Industrial Society, 1972-76; Partner, John Courtis & Partners, Management Selection Consultants; finally retired and moved to Scotland, 1981. Honorary President, Ross and Cromarty Branch, Soliders', Sailors' and Airmen's Families Association. Recreation: bird watching. Address: (h.) Elonbank, 23 Castle Street, Fortrose, Ross-shire, IV10 8TH; T.-0381 20121.

Macdonell, Rev. Alasdair William, MA, BD. Minister, Haddington: St. Mary's, since 1979; b. 28.9.27, Prince Albert, Canada; m., Margaret Stiven; 1 s.; 4 d. Educ. Dundee High School; Fettes College; Pembroke College, Cambridge; New College, Edinburgh. Student Assistant, Kirk of the Canongate, Edinburgh; Assistant Minister, High Kirk of St. Giles; Minister: Uddingston Burnhead, 1955-63, Tarves and Barthol Chapel, Aberdeenshire, 1963-79. Chairman, Whitekirk and Haddington Pilgrimage; Member, Knox Academy Schools Council. Recreations: fiddling (Leader, Haddington Fiddles); hill-walking. Address: St. Mary's Manse, 21 Sidegate, Haddington, EH41 4BZ; T.-062 082 3109.

Macdougall, Alasdair Iain, RD, BSc, MB, ChB, FRCPEdin, FRCPGlas. Consultant Physician, Stobhill General Hospital, Glasgow, since 1968; Honorary Clinical Lecturer, Glasgow University, since 1968; m., Dr. Mary C. Macdougall; 1 s.; 2 d. Educ. Whitehill Secondary School; Glasgow University. Member, Scientific Staff, Medical Research Council, 1953-58; Lecturer in Materia Medica and Therapeutics, Glasgow University, 1964-68. Surgeon Commander, RNR (retired); former Principal Medical Officer, Clyde Division, RNR; Elder, Church of Scotland. Publications: papers on clinical pharmacology, hypertension and renal disease. Recreations: hill-walking; swimming; gardening; opera. Address: (h.) 6 Kelvin Crescent, Bearsden, Glasgow; T.-041-942 2850.

McDougall, A. Neil, MB, ChB, FRCOG. Consultant Obstetrician and Gynaecologist, Rutherglen Maternity Hospital and Royal Samaritan Hospital for Women, Glasgow, since 1981; Honorary Lecturer in Obstetrics and Gynaecology, Glasgow University, since 1986; b. 26.1.45, Bishopbriggs; m., Dr. Marie McDougall; 3 d. Educ. Glasgow Academy; St. Andrews University. Senior House Officer: Stobhill General Hospital, 1971-72, Glasgow Royal Infirmary, 1972, Glasgow Royal Maternity Hospital, 1973; Registrar in Obstetrics and Gynaecology, Royal Maternity Hospital and Royal Samaritan Hospital for Women, Glasgow, 1973-77; Senior Registrar, MRC, Growth and Reproduction Unit, Newcastle upon Tyne, 1977-79; Lecturer in Obstetrics and Gynaecology, Newcastle upon Tyne University, 1979-81. Recreations: yacht racing and cruising. Address: (h.) 37 Brackenrig Crescent, Waterfoot, Eaglesham, by Glasgow, G76 0HF; T.-041-644 4270.

McDougall, Jack Craig, RIBA, FRIAS, FFB, FBIM. Director of Architectural and Related Services, Strathclyde Regional Council, since 1981; b. 10.4.32, Glasgow; m., Elspeth Liddell Nixon; 1 s.; 1 d. Educ. Allan Glen's School, Glasgow; Glasgow School of Art. Depute County Architect: Lanarkshire County Council, 1966, Renfrewshire County Council, 1967; Senior Depute County Architect, Renfrewshire, 1972; Depute Director of Architectural and Related Services, Strathclyde Regional Council, 1974-81. Council Member, RIAS; Senior Vice-President, Glasgow Institute of Architects; Vice President and Secretary, Association of Chief Architects of Scottish Local Authorities; Elder, Church of Scotland, since 1974. Recreations: caravanning; visiting European capital cities; interest in wine. Address: (b.) Department of Architectural and Related Services, Strathclyde House, 20 India Street, Glasgow, G2 4PF; T.-041-227 2100.

Macdougall, Rev. Malcolm McAllister, BD, DChrEd. Minister, St. James' Parish Church, Portobello, Edinburgh, since 1981; b. 20.3.52, Greenock; m., Janet Fiona MacVicar; 1 s. Educ. Greenock Academy; Kelvinside Academy; Edinburgh University. Worked in rope and canvas industry, and in banking, before entering ministry. Recreations: hospital broadcasting; reading; rugby. Address: (h.) 34 Brighton Place, Edinburgh, EH15 1LT; T.-031-669 1767.

MacDougall, Robert Hugh, MB, ChB, DMRT, FRCS, FRCR. Consultant Radiation Oncologist, Lothian Health Board, and Honorary Senior Lecturer in Clinical Oncology, Edinburgh University, since 1986; Honorary Senior Lecturer, St. Andrews University; b. 9.8.49, Dundee; m., Moira Jean Gray; 1 s.; 1 d. Educ. High School of Dundee; St. Andrews University; Edinburgh University. Demonstrator in Anatomy, St. Andrews University; Registrar in Surgery, Aberdeen Royal Infirmary; Lecturer in Clinical Oncology, Edinburgh University; Consultant Radiologist and Oncologist, Tayside Health Board. Recreations: curling; fishing; reading. Address: (b.) Department of Clinical Oncology, Western General Hospital, Edinburgh.

MacDougall of MacDougall, Madam (Coline Helen Elizabeth). 30th Chief of Clan MacDougall; b. 17.8.04; m., Leslie Grahame-Thomson (deceased). Address: (h.) Dunollie Castle, Oban, Argyll.

McDowall, Stuart, CBE, MA. Senior Lecturer in Economics, St. Andrews University, since 1967; Deputy Chairman, Central Arbitration Committee, since 1976; Member, Local Government Boundary Commission for Scotland, since 1982; Member, Monopolies and Mergers Commission, since 1985; b. 19.4.26, Liverpool; m., Margaret B.W. Gyle; 3 s. Educ. Liverpool Institute; St. Andrews University. Master, United College of St. Salvator and St. Leonard, 1976-80. Secretary, Scottish Economic Society, 1970-76; Member, Committee of Inquiry into Powers and Functions of the Islands Councils of Scotland, 1982-84; Arbitrator for ACAS, since 1975. Recreations: golf; hill-walking; gardening; music. Address: (h.) 10 Woodburn Terrace, St. Andrews, Fife, KY16 8BA; T.-0334 73247.

McDowall, William Crocket, MA (Oxon), FRSE. Barrister at Law (Gray's Inn); Member, Board, Irvine Development Corporation, 1981-86; Member, Scottish Joint Negotiating Committee for Teaching Staff in Further Education, 1982-86; b. 16.10.17, Rangoon, Burma; m., Margery Haswell Wilson; 2 s.; 3 d. Educ. Glasgow Academy; Queen's College, Oxford. Sudan Political Service, 1939 (Assistant District Commissioner); Sudan Auxiliary Defence Force, Bimbashi, 1940-42; District Commissioner, 1942-45; Sudan Legal Department, 1946; Judge of the High Court, Sudan, 1951-55; joined ICI Nobel Division, 1955; Chief Executive, Nobel's Explosives Co. Ltd., 1976-79. Honorary Governor, Glasgow Academy; Governor, Glasgow School of Art. Recreations: walking; gardening. Address: (h.) Old Mill, Dunlop, Kilmarnock; T.-Stewarton 84877.

MacDowell, Professor Douglas Maurice, MA. Professor of Greek, Glasgow University, since 1971; b. 8.3.31, London. Educ. Highgate School; Balliol College, Oxford. Schoolmaster, 1954-58; Manchester University: Assistant Lecturer, 1958-61, Lecturer, 1961-68, Senior Lecturer, 1968-70, Reader, 1970-71; Visiting Fellow, Merton College, Oxford, 1969; President, Glasgow Centre, Classical Association of Scotland, 1973-75, 1977-79, 1982-84; Chairman, 1973-76, and Vice President, since 1976, Scottish Hellenic Society; Chairman, Council, Classical Association of Scotland, 1976-82. Publications: Andokides: On the Mysteries, 1962; Athenian Homicide Law, 1963; Aristophanes: Wasps, 1971; The Law in Classical Athens, 1978; Spartan Law, 1986. Address: (b.) Glasgow University, Glasgow, G12 8QQ.

McEwan, David, BSc, CEng, MICE, FCIOB. Principal, Glasgow College of Building and Printing, since 1972; Chairman, Scottish Branch, Association of Principals of Colleges, 1985-87; b. 9.2.27, Beith, Ayrshire; m., Helen Barlow Gebbie; 1 s.; 1 d. Educ. Spiers School, Beith; Glasgow University. Lt., Royal Engineers, during Military Service, 1945-48; Graduate Engineer, Kirkcudbright County Council, 1950-52; Assistant Engineer, Clydebank Town Council, 1952-54; Lecturer and Senior Lecturer, Paisley College, 1954-65; HM Inspector, Scottish Education Department, 1965-67; Principal, Glasgow College of Building, 1967-71. Member, numerous UK and Scottish Committees on education and training and on church buildings. Recreations: travel; photography; wine; food; clan society. Address: (b.) Glasgow College of Building and Printing, 60 North Hanover Street, Glasgow, G1 2BP; T.-041-332 9969.

McEwan, Helen Purdie, MD, FRCOG, FRCSGlas. Consultant Obstetrician and Gynaecologist, Royal Infirmary and Royal Maternity Hospital, Glasgow, since 1972; Honorary Clinical Lecturer, Glasgow University, since 1972; President, Royal Medico Chirurgical Society, Glasgow, 1984-85; b. 8.8.38, Glasgow. Educ. Jordanhill College School; Glasgow University. House Surgeon, Western Infirmary, to Sir Charles Illingworth; Senior House Officer, Gynaecology, Victoria Infirmary and Western Infirmary; Ure Scholar, Western Infirmary; Registrar, Royal Maternity and Royal Samaritan Hospital; Senior Registrar, Glasgow Teaching Hospitals. Member, Advisory Board, Women's Health Concern. Recreations: visiting Western Highlands and Islands; music. Address: (h.) 47 Westland Drive, Glasgow, G14 9PE.

McEwan, Iain, MA (Hons). Rector, Pitlochry High School, since 1986; b. 26.10.39, Perth; m., Nancy Graham; 2 d. Educ. Blairgowrie High School; Aberdeen University. Teacher of History, Lenzie Academy, 1963-67; Principal Teacher of History, Arbroath Academy, 1967-74, Morgan Academy, 1974-81; Depute Rector, Pitlochry High School, 1981-86. Convener, SEB History Panel, 1980-82; Vice President, Scottish Schoolboys' Hockey Association, 1985-87; Vice-Chairman (Administration), Scottish Youth Hockey Board, since 1987. Recreations: photography; hockey; historic aircraft. Address: (h.) 7 Fenton Terrace, Pitlochry, Perthshire; T.-0796 2188; (b.) East Moulin Road, Pitlochry, Perthshire; T.-0796 2900.

McEwan, Louis Vincent, BSc, DipAgrEcon. Head, Fisheries III Division (Structural Policy and Enforcement), Department of Agriculture and Fisheries for Scotland, since 1983; b. 23.7.32, Edinburgh; m., Sheila Brigid Myles Connolly; 4 s.; 1 d. Educ. St. Andrew's Priory; St. Peter's School; Melville College, Edinburgh; Edinburgh University; Reading University; Michigan State University; Glasgow University. Agricultural Economist, DAFS, 1955-72; Kellogg Fellow, Michigan State University, 1961-62; Agricultural Attache, British Embassy, Washington DC, 1972-74; DAFS: Fisheries Economist, 1974-76, Assistant Secretary, 1976; Head, Crops Division, 1976-82, and Capital Grants and Animal Health Division, 1982- 83. Recreations: gardening; golf; music. Address: (b.) Chesser House, Gorgie Road, Edinburgh, EH11 3AW; T.-031-443 4020.

McEwan, Robert Peter, CA. Director: Scottish Consultants International Ltd. (Chairman), Chemflake International Ltd. (Chairman), Kishorn Windows Ltd., Fife Silica Sands Ltd., Bell and Bain Ltd., RDS (Shopfitters) Ltd., Echo Hotels Ltd., Scotia House Ltd., Smith and Telford Ltd., Qualitube Ltd. (Chairman), Bridgegate Trust Ltd.; Director, Scottish Exhibition Centre; b. 21.9.23, Glasgow; m., Mary (Mollie) Howden; 1 s. Educ. High School of Glasgow. Binder Hamlyn, CA, London; Chief Accountant, Sentinel (Shrewsbury) Ltd.; Divisional Director, PA Management Consultants Ltd.; Director of Industry Services, then Director of Finance and of Property Management, Scottish Development Agency. Recreations: golf; gardening. Address: (b.) 120 Bothwell Street, Glasgow; T.-041-248 2700.

McEwan, Sheriff Robin Gilmour, QC, LLB, PhD. Sheriff of Ayr, since 1988 (of Lanark, 1982-88); b. 12.12.43, Glasgow; m., Sheena McIntyre; 2 d. Educ. Paisley Grammar School; Glasgow University. Faulds Fellow in Law, Glasgow University, 1965-68; admitted to Faculty of Advocates, 1967; Standing Junior Counsel, Department of Energy, 1974-76; Advocate Depute, 1976-79; Chairman, Industrial Tribunals, 1981. Publications: Pleading in Court, 1980; A Casebook on Damages (Co-author), 1983; Contributor to Stair Memorial Encyclopaedia of the Laws of Scotland, 1986. Recreations: formerly: football, boxing; now: golf, skating. Address: (b.) Sheriff Court, Ayr, KA7 1DR; T.-Ayr 268474.

MacEwan, Canon Sydney Alfred, MA, DMus. Canon of Argyll and the Isles, since 1956; b. 19.10.08, Glasgow. Educ. St. Aloysius College; Hillhead High School; Glasgow University; Royal Academy of Music, London. International Tenor before becoming Priest (ordained, 1944); Protege of Count John McCormack and Sir Compton Mackenzie; sang in all the great concert halls of the world; recorded for Columbia and Parlophone Companies for 39 years; Member, BBC Advisory Council in Scotland, 1945-50; Member, Education Committee: Argyll, 20 years, Highland Region, until 1976; served in Glasgow, Lochgilphead, Rothesay, Kingussie. Publication: On The High Cs (autobiography), 1974. Recreations: golf; yachting; model Clyde steamers. Address: (h.) Bermuda, 33 Dhailling Road, Dunoon, Argyll.

MacEwen, Charles George, MB, ChB, FRCSEdin, FRCSGlas. Senior Consultant Ophthalmic Surgeon, Glasgow Eye Infirmary, since 1960; Consultant Ophthalmic Surgeon, Nuffield McAlpine Clinic, Glasgow, since 1970; b. 25.3.31, Glasgow; m., Jan J.C. Auld; 3 s.; 1 d. Educ. Whitehill School; Glasgow University. RAMC, 1953-56; Glasgow Eye Infirmary/Western Infirmary, 1956-60. Deacon, Incorporation of Barbers, Trades House of Glasgow, 1970-71; Captain, Glasgow Medical Golf Club, 1971; Examiner, Royal College of Physicians and Surgeons of Glasgow, since 1971; Captain, Cambuslang Golf Club, 1980; Deacon, Incorporation of Tailors, Rutherglen, since 1982; President, Rutherglen Rotary Club, 1982. Recreations: golf; skiing; bridge. Address: (h.) 21 Crawford Gardens, Burnside, Rutherglen, Glasgow; T.-041-634 7233.

McEwen, John, MB, ChB, PhD, MRCP. Medical Director, Drug Development (Scotland) Ltd., since 1983; Honorary Senior Lecturer, Dundee University, since 1983; Honorary Consultant, Tayside Health Board, since 1984; b. 11.4.43, Uddingston; m., Veronica Rosemary Iverson; 1 s.; 1 d. Educ. Ecclesfield Grammar School; St. Andrews University. Resident Physician/Surgeon, Dundee Hospitals, 1966-67; Lecturer in Therapeutics, Dundee University, 1969-75; Visiting Fellow in Clinical Pharmacology, Vanderbilt University, Tennessee, 1972-74; Director of Clinical Pharmacology, Hoechst, UK, 1975-82. Recreations: keyboard instruments; hill-walking; choral singing. Address: (h.) 1 Osborne Place, Dundee, DD2 1BE; T.-Dundee 641060.

MacEwen, Robert Rule (Robin), BL. Solicitor; Honorary Sheriff, Inverness, since 1984; b. 31.1.07, Inverness; m., 1, Elsie Ellis; 2, Marion Pringle or Jack; 1 s. Educ. Inverness Royal Academy; St. Peter's School, York; Edinburgh University. Partner, Stewart, Rule & Co., 1930-67, Rule MacEwen & Co., 1967-77; Consultant, MacLeod & MacCallum, 1977-81; War Service: RAOC, France and Germany, 1944-45 (mentioned in Despatches); Member, Inverness Town Council, 1950-56 (Magistrate and Chairman, Planning Committee); Member, Northern Regional Hospital Board, 1953-56; Dean, Faculty of Solicitors of the Highlands, 1976-79; Chairman, Federation of Scottish Film Societies, 1955; Chairman, Inverness Civic Trust, 1967-72; Chairman, Highlands and Islands Film Guild, 1974-77; Chairman, The Balnbin Trust, 1974-87, Hon. President, since 1987; Member, National Trust Advisory Committee on Culloden; Chairman, Inverness Liberal Association, 1980-81. Address: (h.) 1 Lovat Road, Inverness, IV2 3NT; T.-0463 231197.

McFadden, Jean Alexandra, JP, MA. Vice Lord Lieutenant, City of Glasgow, since 1980; b. 26.11.41; m. Educ. Glasgow University. Glasgow District Council: Leader, Glasgow District Council, 1980-86, Treasurer, since 1986.

McFadyen, Thomas, MB, ChB. Senior Medical Officer, Erskine Hospital, since 1978; b. 30.11.39, Glasgow. Educ. Allan Glen's School; Glasgow University. Appointments, Glasgow Royal Infirmary, Law Hospital, Carluke and Royal Alexandra Infirmary, Paisley. Recreation: golf. Address: (h.) Tigh-Na-Coille, Erskine Hospital, Bishopton, PA7 5PU; T.-041-812 7555.

McFall, John, BSc, MBA, BA. MP (Labour), Dumbarton, since 1987; b. 4.10.44; m.; 3 s.; 1 d. Educ. St. Patrick's School, Dumbarton; Paisley College. Former Schoolteacher.

Macfarlane, Rev. Alwyn James Cecil, BA, MA; b. 14.6.22, Edinburgh; m., Joan Cowell Harris; 1 s.; 1 d. Educ. Cargilfield School, Edinburgh; Rugby School; New College, Oxford; New College, Edinburgh. Captain, 6th Black Watch, North Africa, Italy and Greece, 1940-45; entered Ministry, Church of Scotland, 1951; Minister: Fodderty and Strathpeffer, 1952-59, St. Cuthbert's Church, Edinburgh (Associate), 1959-63, Portobello Old, Edinburgh, 1963-68, Newlands (South), Glasgow, 1968-85; Associate Minister, The Scots' Church, Melbourne, 1985-88. Chaplain to The Queen in Scotland; Member, The Queen's Household in Scotland. Recreations: photography; travel. Address: 4/9 Belhaven Place, Edinburgh.

MacFarlane, Rev. David Cockburn, MA. Minister, Old Parish Church of Peebles, since 1970, with Eddleston Parish Church, since 1977, with Lyne and Manor Parish Church, since 1984; b. 10.6.31, Glasgow; m., Penelope Margaret Broadfoot; 3 s. Educ. High School of Glasgow; Glasgow University and Trinity College. Assistant Minister, Dunblane Cathedral, 1956-58; Minister, Aberlady Parish Church, 1959-70; Moderator: Haddington and Dunbar Presbytery, 1968-69, Melrose and Peebles Presbytery, 1977-78; Warden of Neidpath, 1984; President, Peebles Rotary Club, 1974-75. Publications: Aberlady Parish Church, 1967; The Old Parish Church of Peebles, 1973. Recreations: public speaking; reading; painting. Address: (h.) Old Parish Church Manse, Innerleithen Road, Peebles, EH45 8BD; T.-0721 20568.

McFarlane, Laurence. Sheriff Clerk, Stranraer and Kirkcudbright, since 1984; b. 18.1.54, Kennoway, Fife; m., Angela Berry; 1 s. Educ. Queen Anne High School, Dunfermline. Clerk, Sheriff Clerk's Office, Edinburgh, then Kirkcaldy, 1973-77 ; 2nd Class Depute, Sheriff Clerk's Office, Inverness, then Kirkcaldy, 1977-83; 1st Class Depute, Sheriff Clerk's Office, Greenock, 1983-84. Recreations: reading; music. Address: (h.) Navarre, Main Street, Glenluce, Wigtownshire; T.-05813 285.

MacFarlane, Neil Gerard, FRICS, FRVA, FBIM. Director of Estates, Strathclyde Regional Council, since 1987; b. Glasgow; m., Agnes Beatrix; 2 d. Educ. St. Mungo's Academy, Glasgow; Royal College of Science and Technology. Glasgow Corporation Assessor's Department, then Estates Department; joined Strathclyde Regional Council, 1974 (Head, Estates Department). Executive Member, Scottish Branch, Local Authority Valuers Association; Member, Divisional Committee, General Practice Division, Scottish Branch, RICS. Recreations: bowling; walking; light music. Address: (b.) 20 India Street, Glasgow, G2 4PF; T.-041-204 2900.

Macfarlane, Sir Norman Somerville, Kt (1983). Chairman, Guinness PLC, since 1987; Chairman, United Distillers PLC, since 1987; Chairman and Managing Director, Macfarlane Group (Clansman) PLC, since 1973; b. 5.3.26; m.; 1 s.; 4 d. Educ. High School of Glasgow. Director, Clydesdale Bank, since 1980; Director, General Accident Fire & Life Assurance Corporation plc, since 1984; Chairman, American Trust PLC, since 1984; Member, Board, Scottish Development Agency, since 1979; Chairman, Glasgow Action, since 1985; Vice Chairman, Scottish Ballet, since 1983; President, Royal Glasgow Institute of the Fine Arts, since 1976; Member, Court, Glasgow University, since 1979.

Macfarlane, Peter Wilson, BSc, PhD, FBCS. Reader in Medical Cardiology, Glasgow University, since 1980; b. 8.11.42, Glasgow; m., Irene Grace Muir; 2 s. Educ. Hyndland Senior Secondary School, Glasgow; Glasgow University. Glasgow University: Assistant Lecturer in Medical Cardiology, 1967, Lecturer, 1970, Senior Lecturer, 1974; President, 5th International Congress on Electrocardiology, Glasgow, 1978; Secretary, International Council on Electrocardiology; Author/Editor, ten books. Recreations: playing football; running marathons; playing violin. Address: (h.) 12 Barrcraig Road, Bridge of Weir, PA11 3HG; T.-Bridge of Weir 614443.

Macfarlane, Rev. Thomas Gracie, BSc, PhD, BD. Minister, South Shawlands Parish Church, Glasgow, since 1968; b. 10.6.27, Glasgow; m., Davina Shaw Robertson; 3 s. Educ. Allan Glen's School; Royal Technical College; Glasgow University. Research Metallurgist, 1948-53; ordained, 1956; served under Foreign Mission Committee, Church of Scotland, 1956-61, as Missionary with United Church of Central Africa in Rhodesia; Minister, St. James', Falkirk, 1961-68. Address: 51 Lubnaig Road, Glasgow, G43 2RX; T.-041-637 2331.

MacFarlane, Thomas Wallace, DDS, FRCPath, FDSRCPSGlas. Reader in Oral Medicine and Pathology, Glasgow University, since 1984; Honorary Consultant in Oral Microbiology; b. 12.12.42, Glasgow; m., Nancy McEwan; 1 s. Educ. Hyndland Senior Secondary School; Glasgow University. Assistant Lecturer, Dental Histology and Pathology, 1966-69; trained in Medical Microbiology and Histopathology, Glasgow Royal Infirmary; Lecturer in Oral Medicine and Pathology, 1969-77; organised and ran the diagnostic service in Oral Microbiology, Glasgow Dental Hospital and School; Senior Lecturer in Oral Medicine and Pathology and Consultant in Oral Microbiology, 1977. Recreations: music; reading; painting; walking. Address: (b.) Oral Microbiology Unit, Dental Hospital and School, 378 Sauchiehall Street, Glasgow, G2 3JZ; T.-041-332 7020.

McGarry, Andrew Francis, MA, BA (Hons). Head Teacher, St. Maurice's High School, Cumbernauld, since 1976; b. 21.4.32, Glasgow; m., Mary; 1 s.; 1 d. Educ. St. Mungo's Academy, Glasgow; Blairs College, Aberdeen; Glasgow University; London University (External). RAF, 1954-56; Teacher in Glasgow, Lanarkshire, Stirlingshire, Dunbartonshire, 1963-76. Recreation: golf. Address: (h.) 5 Glamis Gardens, Bishopbriggs, Glasgow, G64 3HP; T.-041-772 2488.

McGarry, James Alexander, MB, FRCOG. Consultant in Obstetrics and Gynaecology; Honorary Clinical Lecturer, Glasgow University; Chairman, Area Sub-Committee in Obstetrics and Gynaecology, Glasgow, since 1982; b. 3.6.30, Mossend, Lanarkshire. Educ. Our Lady's High School, Motherwell; Glasgow University. Surgeon Lt., HMS Bulwark, 1955-56; seconded in charge, Department of Obstetrics and Gynaecology, Kenyatta National Hospital, 1965-67. Address: (h.) 57 Fotheringay Road, Glasgow, G41 4NN; T.-041-423 0938.

McGeough, Professor Joseph Anthony, BSc, PhD, DSc, CEng, FIMechE, FIProdE, MIM. Regius Professor of Engineering and Head, Department of Mechanical Engineering, Edinburgh University, since 1983; Royal Society/SERC Industrial Fellow, 1987-88; b. 29.5.40, Kilwinning; m., Brenda Nicholson; 2 s.; 1 d. Educ. St. Michael's College; Glasgow University; Aberdeen University. Research Demonstrator, Leicester University, 1966; Senior Research Fellow, Queensland University, Australia, 1967; Research Metallurgist, International Research and Development Co. Ltd., Newcastle-upon-Tyne, 1968-69; Senior Research Fellow, Strathclyde University, 1969-72; Lecturer in Engineering, Aberdeen University, 1972-77 (Senior Lecturer, 1977-80, Reader, 1980-83). Chairman, Dyce Academy College Council, 1980-83; Honorary Vice-President, Aberdeen University Athletic Association, since 1981. Publication: Principles of Electrochemical Machining, 1974; Advanced Methods of Machining, 1988. Recreations: gardening; golf; athletics. Address: (h.) 39 Dreghorn Loan, Colinton, Edinburgh, EH13 ODF; T.-031-441 1302.

McGettrick, Professor Andrew David, BSc, PhD, FBCS. Head, Computer Science Department, Strathclyde University, since 1984; b. 15.5.44, Glasgow; m., Sheila Margaret Girot; 5 s.; 1 d. Educ. St. Aloysius College, Glasgow; Glasgow University; Peterhouse, Cambridge. Strathclyde University: Lecturer, 1969-80, Reader in Computer Science, 1980, Professor, 1983. Editor, Addison Wesley's International Computer Science Series, 1980; Chairman, Computing Panel, Scottish Universities Council on Entrance, 1984; Consultancy: SED, EEC, ICL, MOD, NATO. Publications: Algol 68, A First and Second Course; An Introduction to the Definition of Programming Languages; Program Verification Using ADA; Graded Problems in Computer Science. Recreations: squash; running. Address: (b.) Computer Science Department, Strathclyde University, Livingstone Tower, 26 Richmond Street, Glasgow; T.-041-552 4400.

McGettrick, Bartholomew John, BSc (Hons), MEd (Hons). Principal, St. Andrew's College of Education, since 1985; Chairman, Catholic Education Commission for Scotland, 1981-87 (Vice-Chairman, since 1987); Member, Council for Educational Technology, 1982-86; Governor, Scottish Council for Educational Technology, since 1984; Member, Scottish Consultative Council on the Curriculum, since 1988; Member, Council, SCOTVEC, since 1984; Member, General Teaching Council for Scotland, since 1986; Member, Committee for Information and Development Services, CNAA, since 1988; b. 16.8.45, Glasgow; m., Maria McLaughlin; 2 s.; 2 d. Educ. St. Aloysius' College, Glasgow; Glasgow University. Teacher and Head, Department of Geography, St. Aloysius' College, Glasgow, 1968-72; Educational Psychologist, Scottish Centre for Social Subjects, 1972-75; Assistant Principal, then Vice-Principal, Notre Dame College of Education (latterly St. Andrew's College of Education), 1975-85. Member, Council for National Academic Awards, Committee for Education, 1981-85; Chairman, Association of Higher Academic Staff in Colleges of Education in Scotland, 1982-84; Member, Board of Governors, St. Aloysius' College, Glasgow. Recreations: sports (squash, rugby). Address: (h.) 174 Carmunnock Road, Glasgow, G44 5AJ; T.-041-637 8112.

McGhee, John. Director, Scottish Export Office, since 1988; b. 12.9.46, Irvine; m., Linda Christine Whalley; 2 d. Educ. Cumnock Academy; Glasgow University. Board of Trade Investment Grant Office, 1967, Business Statistics Office, 1969; Scottish Development Department, 1971; Scottish Office Management Services Unit, 1974; Department of Agriculture and Fisheries for Scotland - EEC and international fisheries agreements, 1981; Deputy Director, Locate in Scotland, 1986-88. Recreations: reading; music; golf. Address: (b.) Industry Department for Scotland, Alhambra House, 45 Waterloo Street, Glasgow, G2 6AT; T.-041-248 2855.

McGhee, John Francis. Provost, Motherwell District Council, since 1984 (Chairman, Leisure Services Committee, 1977-84); b. 21.10.27, Motherwell; m., Mary T. Hickey; 1 s.; 2 d. Educ. St. Patrick's, Shieldmuir; St. Joseph's, Motherwell. Justice of the Peace. Recreations: reading; golf. Address: (h.) 6 Lammermoor Terrace, Wishaw, ML2; T.-Wishaw 376054.

McGhee, Rev. Robert, DD. Minister, Falkirk St. Andrew's, since 1972; b. 29.7.29, Port Glasgow; m., Mary Stevenson Cunningham; 1 s.; 2 d. Educ. Port Glasgow High School; Greenock High School; Glasgow University and Trinity College. Trained as cashier/bookkeeper, 1945-54; RAF, 1947-49; ordained and inducted to Pulteneytown St. Andrew's, Wick, 1959; Minister, Wick St. Andrew's and Thrumster, 1961-66; Minister, Newbattle, Dalkeith, 1966-72; Convener, Board of Social Responsibility, Church of Scotland, since 1985 (Convener, Community Care, Social Responsibility, 1977-85); Chairman, Lord's Day Observance Society, Scotland, 1970-74; President, Scottish Evangelistic Council, 1982-85; Moderator: Presbytery of Caithness, 1964-65, Presbytery of Falkirk, 1983-84, Synod of Forth, 1985-86. Address: St. Andrew's Manse, 1 Maggie Woods Loan, Falkirk, FK1 5SJ; T.-Falkirk 23308.

McGhie, Fergus Dunsmore Scott, MBE (1985), LCG. Maitre Chef de Cuisine; Principal, Duncraig Castle College, Plockton, 1974-85; b. 25.6.21, Hamilton; m., 1, Margaret E.L. Shanks (deceased); 2 s.; 2, Rosemary G. Tulloch. Educ. Hamilton Academy; Woodside School, Hamilton. War service, Royal Artillery, 1940-46, India, Malaya (PoW, Singapore, Taiwan, Japan). Chef Instructor (and Lecturer), Scottish Hotel School, 1954-60; Head Chef, J.W. Mackie, Edinburgh, 1960-62; Senior Teacher, Catering Subjects, Castlehill School of Baking and Catering, Edinburgh, 1962-67; Head of Section (Professional Cookery), Telford College of Further Education, Edinburgh, 1967-72. Diplome Cordon Culinaire, 1975; Grand Cordon Culinaire; Member, Conseil Culinaire Francaise de Grand Bretagne. Address: (h.) Yasume, 13 Pilmuir Road West, Forres, Moray.

McGhie, James. Honorary Sheriff Substitute of North Strathclyde at Dunoon, since 1982; b. 22.10.15, Alexandria; m., Sarah Malcolm; 2 s. Educ. Vale of Leven Academy. Served in Post Office until 1939; Bloomsbury County Court, 1939-1940; RAF, 1940-46; Newcastle County Court, 1946; Dumbarton Sheriff Court, 1946-50; Oban Sheriff Court, 1950-56; Edinburgh Sheriff Court, 1957; Sheriff Clerk of Orkney, Kirkwall, 1957-61; Sheriff Clerk of Argylll and Bute, Dunoon, 1961-77. Past President, Dunoon Rotary Club and Dunoon Business Club; former Captain, Cowal Golf Club. Jubilee Medal, 1977. Recreations: golf; gardening; philately; DIY. Address: (h.) Ava, West Bay, Dunoon, Argyll.

McGibbon, Alistair, MA, MEd. Rector, Woodlands High School, Falkirk, since 1983; b. 3.10.37, Glasgow; m., Jean Ronald; 2 s.; 1 d. Educ. North Kelvinside School; Glasgow University; Stirling University. Teaching appointments in Glasgow, Guildford, Perth (Western Australia), Papua New Guinea, Central Region. Recreations: golf; Church activities. Address: (b.) Woodlands High School, Rennie Street, Falkirk, FK1 5AL; T.-0324 29615.

McGill, Rt. Rev. Stephen, PSS, STL. Bishop of Paisley, 1968-88; b. 4.1.12, Glasgow. Educ. St. Aloysius College, Glasgow; Blairs College, Aberdeen; Institut Catholique, Paris. Staff, Le Grand Seminaire, Bordeaux, 1939, Le Grand Seminaire, Aix-en-Province, 1940; Spiritual Director, then Rector, Blairs College, Aberdeen, 1940-60; Bishop of Argyll and the Isles, 1960-68. Recreations: caligraphy; golf. Address: 13 Newark Street, Greenock, PA16 7UH.

McGillivray, Rev. (Alexander) Gordon, MA, BD, STM. Clerk, Edinburgh Presbytery, Church of Scotland, since 1973; Depute Clerk, General Assembly, since 1971; b. 22.9.23, Edinburgh; m., Winifred Jean Porter; 2 s.; 2 d. Educ. George Watson's Boys' College, Edinburgh; Edinburgh University; Union Theological Seminary, New York. Royal Artillery, 1942-45; Assistant Minister, St. Cuthbert's Parish Church, Edinburgh; Minister: Waterbeck Church, 1951-58, Nairn High Church, 1958-73. Recreation: golf. Address: 7 Greenfield Crescent, Balerno, Midlothian, EH14 7HD; T.-031-449 4747.

McGillivray, Robert, BSc, CEng, FICE, FIWEM. Chief Engineer, Scottish Development Department, since 1987; b. 11.5.31, Ayr; m., Pauline Davie; 1 s. Educ. Boroughmuir School; Edinburgh University. National Service, 1949-51; training with J. & A. Leslie & Reid, CE, 1955-57; Assistant Engineer, Midlothian County Council, 1957-60; Civil Engineer, Department of Agriculture and Fisheries for Scotland, 1960-72; Principal Civil Engineer, Scottish Development Department, 1972-75; Engineering Inspector, 1975-80; Assistant Chief Engineer, 1980-85; Deputy Chief Engineer, 1985-87. Publication: A History of the Clan MacGillivray (Co-author), 1973. Recreations: music; genealogy; Highland history. Address: (b.) 27 Perth Street, Edinburgh, EH3 5RB; T.-031-244 3036.

McGilvray, Professor James William, MA, MLitt. Professor of Economics, Strathclyde University, since 1975; Director, Fraser of Allander Institute, 1980-86; b. 21.2.38, Glasgow; m., Alison Ann; 1 s.; 1 d. Educ. St. Columba's College, Dublin; Edinburgh University. Recreations: gardening; squash; shooting. Address: (b.) 100 Cathedral Street, Glasgow, G4 0LN; T.-041-552 4400.

McGirr, Professor Edward McCombie, CBE, BSc, MD, FRCP, FRCPEdin, FRCPGlas, FFCM, FACP (Hon.), FRSE. Chairman, Clyde Estuary Amenity Council, since 1986; Chairman, Scottish Council for Postgraduate Medical Education, 1979-85; Emeritus Professor, Glasgow University, since 1981; b. 15.6.16, Hamilton; m., Diane Curzon Woods; 1 s.; 3 d. Educ. Hamilton Academy; Glasgow University. RAMC, 1941-47, including posts as graded physician and specialist in medicine ; appointments in University Department of Medicine, Glasgow Royal Infirmary, 1947-78, latterly Muirhead Chair of Medicine, Glasgow University, and Physician in charge of wards, Glasgow Royal Infirmary; Dean, Faculty of Medicine, Glasgow University, 1974-81; Administrative Dean and Professor of Administrative Medicine, Glasgow University, 1978-81. President, Royal College of Physicians and Surgeons of Glasgow, 1970-72; Chairman, Scottish Health Service Planning Council, 1978-84; Honorary Physician to the Army in Scotland, 1975-81; sometime Member: Greater Glasgow Health Board, National Radiological Protection Board, General Nursing Council for Scotland, National Board for Nursing, Midwifery and Health Visiting; Past President, Royal Medico-Chirurgical Society of Glasgow; Chairman, Scottish Council for Opportunities for Play Experience (SCOPE), 1985-87; Chairman, Working Party on Play in Scotland, 1986-87. Recreations: reading; curling. Address: (h.) Anchorage House, Bothwell, by Glasgow, G71 8NF; T.-0698 852194.

McGlynn, Archie Smith, BA (Hons), MPhil, DipComm, MIIM. HM Chief Inspector of Schools, since 1987; b. Tarbert, Argyll; m., Leah Sutherland Ross; 1 s.; 1 d. Educ. Tarbert Secondary School; Campbeltown Grammar School; Strathclyde University; Glasgow University. Industry and commerce, 1962-64 and 1966-67; Teacher in schools and further/higher education colleges, 1964-69; Depute Principal, Glenrothes and Buckhaven College, 1969-75; HM Inspector of Schools, 1976-87. Recreations: hedgehog preservation; following Fife Flyers. Address: (b.) Room 4/35, New St. Andrew's House, Edinburgh; T.-031-244 4569.

McGlynn, Rt. Rev. Lord Abbot (James Aloysius) Donald, OCSO, STL, SLJ. Monk, Order of Cistercians of Strict Observance, since 1952; Abbot of Nunraw, since 1969; b. 13.8.34, Glasgow. Educ. Holyrood School, Glasgow; St. Bernardine's School, Buckinghamshire; Gregorian University, Rome. President, Scottish Council of Major Religious Superiors, 1974-77; President, British Isles Regional Council of Cistercian Abbeys, 1980-84; Chairman, Union of Monastic Superiors, since 1985; Official Roman Catholic Visitor to the General Assembly, Church of Scotland, 1976 and 1985; Commandeur Ecclesiastique, Military & Hospitaller Order of St. Lazarus of Jerusalem, 1985; Patron, Friends of the Beatitudes, Madras; Patron, Haddington Pilgrimage of St. Mary & the Three Kings. Recreations: iconography; farm work; computer printing. Address: Sancta Maria Abbey, Nunraw, Garvald, Haddington, EH41 4LW; T.-062 083 223.

McGovern, John Gerard, JP, BSc, MRSC. Headteacher, Our Lady's High School, Broxburn, since 1978; b. 16.1.34, Cambuslang; m., Elizabeth Kearney; 2 s.; 3 d. Educ. Our Lady's High School, Motherwell; Glasgow University. National Service, Royal Signals (awarded GSM (Cyprus)); Teacher of Science (Chemistry), Our Lady's High School, Motherwell; Principal Teacher of Science/Chemistry, St. David's High School, Dalkeith; Depute Headteacher: Our Lady's High School, Broxburn, St. David's, Dalkeith. Address: (h.) 85 Ambrose Rise, Dedridge, Livingston, West Lothian; T.-0506 414880.

McGowan, Rev. Andrew T.B., BD, STM. Minister, Trinity Possil and Henry Drummond Church, Glasgow, since 1988; b. 30.1.54, Glasgow; m., June S. Watson; 3 s. Educ. Uddingston Grammar School; Aberdeen University; Union Theological Seminary, New York. Assistant Minister, St. Cuthbert's, Edinburgh, 1978-80; Minister: Mallaig and the Small Isles, 1980-86, Causewayend Church, Aberdeen, 1986-88. Member, Council, Rutherford House, Edinburgh; Moderator, Lochaber Presbytery, 1983-84; Secretary, Scottish Evangelical Theology Society, 1980-85. Recreations: hill-walking; squash; chess; guitar. Address: 35 Springfield Road, Bishopbriggs, Glasgow, G64; T.-041-772 1456.

McGowan, Daniel, MILAM. Director of Recreation and Leisure, Cumbernauld and Kilsyth District Council, since 1978; b. 23.9.41, Coatbridge; m.; 3 s.; 1 d. Educ. St. Patrick's High School, Coatbridge; Coatbridge Technical College. Chairman, Scottish Swimming Coaches Association, since 1980. Recreations: swimming; golf. Address: (b.) Council Offices, Bron Way, Cumbernauld, G67 1DZ; T.-02367 22131.

McGowan, Professor David Alexander, MDS, PhD, FDSRCS, FFDRCSI, FDSRCPSG. Professor of Oral Surgery, Glasgow University, since 1977; Consultant Oral Surgeon, Greater Glasgow Health Board, since 1977; b. 18.6.39, Portadown, Co. Armagh; m., Margaret Vera Macaulay; 1 s.; 2 d. Educ. Portadown College; Queen's University, Belfast. Oral surgery training, Belfast and Aberdeen, 1961-67; Lecturer in Dental Surgery, Queen's University, Belfast, 1968; Lecturer, then Senior Lecturer and Deputy Head, Oral and Maxillofacial Surgery, London Hospital Medical College, 1968-77. Postgraduate Adviser in Dentistry, Glasgow University, since 1977; Chairman, Dental Committee, Scottish Council for Postgraduate Medical Education; Vice-Chairman, Conference of UK Postgraduate Dental Deans/Advisers; Vice-Convener, Dental Council, Royal College of Physicians and Surgeons of Glasgow; former Council Member, British Association of Oral and Maxillofacial Surgeons. Recreations: sailing; music. Address: (b.) Department of Oral Surgery, Glasgow Dental Hospital and School, 378 Sauchiehall Street, Glasgow, G2 3JZ; T.-041-332 7020, Ext. 259.

McGowan, Ian Duncan, BA. Keeper (Catalogues and Automation), National Library of Scotland, since 1978; b. 19.9.45, Liverpool; m., Elizabeth Ann Weir; 2 d. Educ. Liverpool Institute; Exeter College, Oxford. Assistant Keeper, National Library of Scotland, 1971-78. Address: (b.) National Library of Scotland, George IV Bridge, Edinburgh, EH1 1EW; T.-031-226 4531.

McGowan, John, LLB. Solicitor, since 1967; Temporary Sheriff, since 1986; b. 15.1.44, Kilmarnock; m., Elise Smith; 2 s. Educ. St. Joseph's Academy, Kilmarnock; Glasgow University.

Admitted Solicitor, 1967; Council Member, Law Society of Scotland, 1982-85. Recreations: golf; tennis; curling; cricket; listening to music. Address: (h.) 15 Monument Road, Ayr; T.-Ayr 260139.

McGowan, Stuart Watson, MB, ChB, FFARCS, DA. Consultant Anaesthetist, Dundee Teaching Hospitals, since 1964; b. 31.7.29, Uddingston; m., Mabel Wilson; 1 s.; 1 d. Educ. Hutchesons' Boys Grammar School, Glasgow; Glasgow University. President, North-East of Scotland Society of Anaesthetists, 1972; President, Dundee Speakers Club, 1972. Recreations: golf; music; travel. Address: (h.) 41 Whitefauld Road, Dundee, DD2 1RJ; T.-0382 65281.

McGown, Archibald M. Director, Scottish Retirement Council, since 1987; b. 15.11.33, Paisley; m., Janet Robertson; 1 s.; 2 d. Educ. Rutherglen Academy. Managing Director, Elvestead Canned Meat Co. Ltd., 1976-86. Committee Member, Royal Scottish Automobile Club. Recreations: curling; bowling. Address: (b.) 212 Bath Street, Glasgow, G2 4HW; T.-041-332 9427.

McGrain, Daniel Fergus, MBE (1983). Footballer; b. 1.5.50, Glasgow; m., Laraine; 3 c. Former Celtic and Scotland Captain; first club, Maryhill Juniors; signed for Celtic, 1967; first cap against Wales, 1973; played in two World Cups - West Germany, 1974, Spain, 1982; played in seven Scottish Cup Finals; testimonial match, 1980; played more than 600 games for Celtic.

McGrath, John. Artistic Director, 7:84 Theatre Companies, since 1971; Producer/Director, Freeway Films, since 1982; b. 1.6.35, Birkenhead; m., Elizabeth MacLennan; 2 s.; 1 d. Educ. Alun Grammar School, Mold, Clwyd; St. John's College, Oxford. Playwright (more than 35 plays produced professionally in UK and abroad); Writer of film screenplays for feature films and TV plays; Director in theatre and TV; Poet and Songwriter; plays for theatre including Events While Guarding the Bofors Gun and The Cheviot, The Stag and the Black, Black Oil; Visiting Judith E. Wilson Fellow, Cambridge, 1979. Publication: A Good Night Out (lectures). Address: (b.) 7:84 Theatre Co., 31 Albany Street, Edinburgh, EH1 3QN; T.-031-557 2442.

McGrath, Tom. Playwright; b. 23.10.40, Rutherglen. Former Writer in Residence, Traverse Theatre, Edinburgh; plays for the stage include Laurel and Hardy, Traverse, Edinburgh, and Mayfair, London, 1976; The Hardman, Traverse, 1977, UK tour and ICA, London, 1978; Sisters, Theatre Royal, Stratford East, 1978; The Android Circuit, Traverse, 1978.

MacGregor, Alexander Ronald, MB, ChB, MRCGP. Principal in general practice, Kilwinning, since 1980; Medical Officer, Mountain Rescue Committee of Scotland, since 1984; Scottish Representative, Medical Commission, Union Internationale des Association D'Alpinisme; b. 21.2.49, Kilmarnock; m., Margaret Fleming, 3 d. Educ. Annan Academy; Glasgow University. Registrar in Anaesthetics, Glasgow Royal Infirmary, 1975-79; GP trainee, Balfron, Stirling, 1979-80; author of The Nature and Causes of Injuries Sustained in 190 Scottish Mountain Accidents (research report), 1988, and A Review of Scottish Mountain Accidents, conference paper, 1986. Recreations: being on mountains on foot, ski and bicycle; computing; windsurfing. Address: (h.) 8 Ainsdale Court, Kilwinning, KA13 6QD; T.(b.)-0294 54591.

McGregor, Rev. Alistair Gerald Crichton, QC, BA, LLB, WS. Minister, North Leith Parish Church, Edinburgh, since 1987; Temporary Sheriff, 1984-87; b. 15.10.37, Sevenoaks, Kent; m., Margaret Dick Lees or McGregor; 2 s.; 1 d. Educ. Charterhouse; Pembroke College, Oxford; Edinburgh University. Solicitor; Advocate; QC; former Standing Junior Counsel to Queen's and Lord Treasurer's Remembrancer, to Scottish Home and Health Department and to Scottish Development Department; Past Chairman, Discipline Committee, Potato Marketing Board; former Clerk, Rules Council, Court of Session; former Tutor in Scots Law, Edinburgh University; Chairman, Family Care. Publication: Obscenity (Coauthor). Recreations: squash; tennis; swimming; travel; cinema. Address: (h.) 22 Primrose Bank Road, Edinburgh, EH5; T.-031-551 2802.

McGregor, Bobby, MBE (1964). Swimmer; b. 3.4.44, Helensburgh; m., Bernadette. Educ. Falkirk High School; Glasgow College of Architecture. Silver Medal, 4 x 100 m. relay, European Championships, 1962; Gold Medal, 100 m. freestyle, European Championships, 1966; Silver Medal, 110 yards freestyle, Commonwealth Championships, 1962; Silver Medal, 110 yards freestyle, Commonwealth Championships, 1966; Silver Medal, 100 m. freestyle, Olympic Games, 1964; sometime holder, 110 yards world record; now works as an Architect.

McGregor, Rev. Duncan James. Minister, parishes of Channelkirk and Lauder Old, since 1982; b. 17.7.35, Edinburgh; m., Constance Anne Aitchison; 3 s. Educ. Edinburgh Academy; Edinburgh University and New College. Worked in paper trade, then in insurance; Secretary: Scottish Anglers' Association, 1966-82, Anglers' Co-operative Association (Scotland), 1972-78, Scottish Joint Committee for Anglers, 1967-80; called to Ministry, 1982. Life Member, Scottish National Angling Clubs Association and Anglers Co-operative Association (Scotland). Recreations: golf; angling; walking; cycling; reading. Address: The Manse of Lauder, Lauder, Berwickshire; T.-05782 320.

MacGregor of MacGregor, Brigadier Sir Gregor, 6th Bt. 23rd Chief of Clan Gregor; b. 22.12.25; m., Fanny Butler; 2 s. Educ. Eton. Commissioned, Scots Guards, 1944; commanding 1st Bn., Scots Guards, 1966-69; Col. Recruiting, HQ Scotland, 1971; Lt.-Col. commanding Scots Guards, 1971-74; Defence and Military Attache, British Embassy, Athens, 1975-78; Comdr., Lowlands, 1978-80; Member, Queen's Bodyguard for Scotland (Royal Company of Archers). Address: (h.) Bannatyne, Newtyle, Blairgowrie, Perthshire.

McGregor, Ian Alexander, MB, ChB, FRCS, FRPFSG, FRCSGlas, ChM, FRACS, FRCSI, DSc, FACS. Consulting Plastic Surgeon, Glasgow Royal Infirmary; b. 6.6.21, Glasgow; m., Frances

Mary Vint; 3 s. Educ. North Kelvinside Secondary School; Glasgow University. RAMC, 1945-48; Consultant Surgeon, Glasgow Royal Infirmary, 1957; Consultant Plastic Surgeon, Greater Glasgow Health Board, 1959; Visitor, Royal College of Physicians and Surgeons of Glasgow, 1982; Director, West of Scotland Plastic and Oral Surgery Unit, 1980-86; President, Royal College of Physicians and Surgeons of Glasgow, 1984-86. Publications: Fundamental Techniques of Plastic Surgery, 1960; Plastic Surgery for Nurses (Co-author), 1966; Cancer of the Face and Mouth (Co-author). Recreations: music; literature; golf. Address: (h.) 7 Ledcameroch Road, Bearsden, Glasgow, G61 4AB; T.-041-942 3419.

MacGregor, Ian George Stewart, MA, MEd, FBIM. Rector, Bathgate Academy, since 1970; b. 29.12.24, Newcastle-upon-Tyne. Educ. Altrincham Grammar School; Bell-Baxter School, Cupar; St. Andrews University; Edinburgh University; New York University. Assistant Principal, Ministry of Finance, Government of Northern Ireland, 1947-50; Teacher, Buckhaven High School, 1952-53 and 1954-55 (Teaching Fellowship in Psychology, New York University, 1953-54); Principal Administrative Assistant, Edinburgh Corporation Education Department, 1955-59; Assistant Director of Education, Aberdeenshire, 1959-64; Senior Depute Director of Education, West Lothian, 1964-70. Trustee, Edinburgh University General Council Trust; General Council Assessor, Edinburgh University Court; Member, Executive Committee, UCCA; Scottish HQ Commissioner, Scout Association, and Group Scout Leader, 23rd Edinburgh. Recreations: Scouting; photography; travel. Address: (h.) 20 Stewart Avenue, Bo'ness, EH51 9NL; T.-0506 822462.

Macgregor, James Duncan, OBE, MD, FFCM, DPH, DTM&H. Unit Medical Officer, Perth and Kinross, since 1981; Honorary Senior Clinical Lecturer, Department of Community Medicine, Dundee University, since 1982; b. 21.8.27, Invergowrie, Perthshire; m., Rita Moss; 2 s.; 1 d. Educ. Perth Academy; St. Andrews University. House Officer posts, Perth Royal Infirmary and Royal Northern Infirmary, Inverness, 1950-51; joined HM Colonial Medical Service, 1951; posted to Sierra Leone as General Duty MO; transferred to South Pacific Health Service as Senior Medical Officer, 1956; retired from the Overseas Service, 1975, as Director of Medical Services, Solomon Islands; Chief Administrative Medical Officer, Shetland Health Board, 1975; moved to Tayside Health Board as District MO. Red Cross Voluntary Medical Services Medal. Recreations: gardening; hill-walking. Address: (h.) 74 Glasgow Road, Perth, PH2 0PG; T.-Perth 24493.

Macgregor, Janet Elizabeth, OBE, BSc, MB, ChB, MD, FRCPath, FRCOG. Director, Harris Birthright Research Centre, Aberdeen University, since 1988; Specialist, Grampian Health Board, since 1968; Research Fellow, Aberdeen University, since 1960; b. 12.1.20, Glasgow; m., Professor A.G. Macgregor (deceased); 3 s.; 1 d. Educ. Bearsden Academy; Glasgow University. Captain, RAMC, 1943-45; Medical Officer, Maternity and Child Welfare, Glasgow, Sheffield and Edinburgh, 1946-59; Research Fellow, Department of Obstetrics and Gynaecology, Aberdeen University, 1960-66; Medical Assistant, Grampian Health Board, 1966-73; appointed Senior Lecturer, Aberdeen University, 1973. Member, Cytology Sub-Committee, Royal College of Pathologists, 1980-82; Chairman and President, British Society for Clinical Cytology, 1977-83; Member, Medical Advisory Committee, Women's National Cancer Control Campaign, since 1977; Member, IARC (WHO) Study Group on Cervical Cancer, 1978-84; Fellow, International Academy of Cytology, since 1963. Address: (h.) Ardruighe, Clachan, Isle of Seil, Argyll; T.-085-23-427.

McGregor, John Cummack, BSc (Hons), MB, ChB, FRCS, FRCSEdin. Consultant Plastic and Reconstructive Surgeon, Lothian Region, based at Regional Plastic Surgery Unit, Bangour General Hospital, since 1980; Honorary Senior Lecturer in Orthopaedics, Edinburgh University, since 1983; b. 21.4.44, Paisley; m., Moira Imray; 1 s.; 1 d. Educ. Paisley Grammar School; Glasgow University. Initial medical and surgical training, Paisley Royal Alexandra Infirmary, Western Infirmary, Glasgow, Stobhill Hospital, Glasgow, Nottingham City Hospital, Canniesburn Plastic Surgery Unit, Glasgow and Bangour General Hospital. Recreations: tennis; badminton; golf; cacti collecting; budgerigar breeding/showing. Address: (b.) Department of Plastic Surgery, Bangour General Hospital, West Lothian.

McGregor, John Gilmour, MA (Cantab), BSc (Glas), CEng. Honorary Sheriff of South Strathclyde, Dumfries and Galloway, since 1964; b. 19.5.08, Coatbridge; m., Jean Cleland MacLellan; 1 s. Educ. Coatbridge Secondary School; Glasgow University; Cambridge University. Director, Airdrie Savings Bank, 1950-82 (President, 1962-64); former Director, Mid-Scot Training Services Ltd.; former Managing Director and Chairman, Murray & Paterson Ltd. (Engineers), Coatbridge, and Mill Metals Co. Ltd., Coatbridge; former Member, Lanarkshire Scout Area Committee (Chairman, 1969-81). Recreation: golf. Address: (h.) 13 Regent Gate, Bothwell, Glasgow, G71 8QU; T.-0698 815077.

McGrenary, Thomas Joseph, BSc (Hons). Principal, Cumbernauld College, since 1985; b. 12.2.39, Hamilton; m., Marlyn Rodger; 4 s. Educ. Our Lady's High School, Motherwell; Strathclyde University. Lecturing posts, Aberdeen Technical College, 1972-75, and Glasgow College of Food Technology, 1975-80; Further Education Officer, Department of Education, Strathclyde Regional Council, 1980-84; Depute Principal, Ayr College, 1984-85. Recreations: sport; reading. Address: (h.) 42 Buchanan Drive, Rutherglen, G73 3PE; T.-041-647 3974

McGrigor, Captain Sir Charles Edward, 5th Bt. A Vice-President, RNLI, and Convenor, Scottish Lifeboat Council; Member, Queen's Bodyguard for Scotland (Royal Company of Archers); a Deputy Lieutenant, Argyll and Bute; b. 5.10.22; m., Mary Bettine (eldest daughter of the late Sir

Archibald Edmonstone, 6th Bt. of Duntreath); 2 s.; 2 d. Educ. Eton. Joined Army, 1941; Rifle Brigade, North Africa, Italy, Austria (mentioned in Despatches); ADC to Duke of Gloucester, 1945-47. Address: (h.) Upper Sonachan, Dalmally, Argyll.

Macgruer, Michael, RIBA, ARIAS. Director of Architectural Services, Lochaber District Council, since 1986 (District Architect, 1984-86); b. 26.2.51, Inverness; m., Sheena Robertson; 1 s.; 1 d. Educ. Grantown Grammar School; Lochaber High School; Mackintosh School of Architecture, Glasgow. Glasgow District Council: student architect, 1969-77; Project Architect, 1977-83. Address: (b.) Lochaber House, High Street, Fort William; T.-0397 3881.

McGuire, Edward, ARCM, ARAM. Composer; b. 15.2.48, Glasgow. Educ. Royal Academy of Music, London; State Academy of Music, Stockholm. Won National Young Composers Competition, 1969; Rant selected as test piece for 1978 Carl Flesch International Violin Competition; Proms debut, 1982, when Source performed by BBC SSO; String Quartet chosen for 40th Anniversary Concert, SPNM, Barbican, 1983; frequent commissions and broadcasts including Trilogy: Rebirth-Interregnum-Liberation (New Music Group), Euphoria (EIF/Fires of London), Life Songs (John Currie Singers), Songs of New Beginnings (Paragon Ensemble), Quintet II (Lontano); plays flute with Whistlebinkies folk group. Address: c/o Scottish Music Information Centre, 1 Bowmont Gardens, Glasgow, G12; T.-041-334 6393.

McGuire, Ralph Joseph, BSc, MA, MEd. Senior Lecturer in Clinical Psychology, Edinburgh University, since 1971; Honorary Clinical Psychologist, Lothian Health Board, since 1971; b. 2.3.26, Glasgow; m., Beryl Redfern; 1 s.; 4 d. Educ. St. Aloysius' College, Glasgow; Glasgow University. Research Physicist, BICC, 1944-47; Teacher of Mathematics, 1950-54; Lecturer in Mathematics, 1954-57; Clinical Psychologist, Southern General Hospital, Glasgow, 1957-64; Senior Lecturer in Clinical Psychology, Leeds University, 1964-71. Member, Research Committee, Mental Health Foundation. Recreation: listening to music. Address: (b.) Department of Psychiatry, Royal Edinburgh Hospital, Edinburgh, EH10 5HF; T.-031-447 2011.

McHardy, George Jamieson Ross, MA, MSc, BM, FRCPE, FRCP(Lond). Consultant Clinical Respiratory Physiologist, Lothian Health Board, since 1965; Consultant Physician, City Hospital, Edinburgh, since 1966; Senior Lecturer (part-time), Edinburgh University, since 1966; b. 17.11.30, Edinburgh; m., Dr. Valentine Urie Dewar; 2 s.; 1 d. Educ. Wellington College; Brasenose College, Oxford; Middlesex Hospital Medical School. House appointments, Middlesex Hospital, London; National Service (Flt. Lt., RAF Medical branch); Medical Registrar, Middlesex and Hammersmith Hospitals; Tutor in Medicine, Postgraduate Medical School, London, 1964; US Public Health Service Fellow, Department of Environmental Medicine, Johns Hopkins University, Baltimore, 1965. Councillor, Royal College of Physicians of Edinburgh, 1977 and 1981; on Steering Committee, "Fit for Life" Campaign, 1977-82; President, Scottish Thoracic Society, 1986-88. Publications: Davidson's Textbook of Medicine, 15th edition (Contributor); papers on medical subjects. Recreations: music; sailing; skiing. Address: (h.) 6 Ettrick Road, Edinburgh, EH10 5BJ; T.-031-229 9026.

Macharg, John Maitland, MA, FFA. General Manager and Actuary, Scottish Provident Institution, since 1970; b. 22.5.28, Glasgow; m., Madeline Yates; 2 s.; 1 d. Educ. Glasgow High School; Strathallan School; Glasgow University. Joined Scottish Provident, 1955, as Assistant Actuary. President, Faculty of Actuaries, 1985-87. Recreations: golf; skiing; gardening. Address: (b.) 6 St. Andrew Square, Edinburgh, EH2 2YA; T.-031-556 9181.

McIldowie, James Robert, MA, LLB, NP. Solicitor, since 1962; Honorary Sheriff, since 1986; b. 24.9.37, Crieff; m., Isabella Junor (June) Anderson; 2 d. Educ. Morrison's Academy, Crieff; Edinburgh University. Apprentice and Assistant in Edinburgh; joined McLean & Stewart, Dunblane and Callander, 1962; became a Partner, 1963; now Senior Partner. Former Secretary and Treasurer, Highland Pony Society. Recreations: golf; music; theatre; all sports. Address: (b.) 51-53 High Street, Dunblane, Perthshire; T.-0786 823217.

McIlroy, James Roger. Managing Director, Christie's Scotland Ltd., since 1987; Director, Christie Manson and Woods (Australia) Ltd., since 1983; Director, Christie's UK, since 1987; b. 13.2.55, Sydney; m., Lorna Askew; 1 s. Educ. Sydney Church of England Grammar School. James R. Lawson Pty Ltd., Auctioneers, Sydney, 1973-77; Phillips, Auctioneers, London, 1977-78; Specialist in Early Ceramics, Christie's, Auctioneers, London, 1978-87. Publications: A Pictorial History of European Pottery; Techniques of the World's Great Potters (Co-author). Recreations: golf; swimming; surfing; tennis. Address: (b.) 164-166 Bath Street, Glasgow, G2 4TG; T.-041-332 8134.

McIlvanney, William. Novelist; b. 1936, Kilmarnock. Educ. Kilmarnock Academy; Glasgow University. Teacher (Assistant Rector (Curriculum), Greenwood Academy, Irvine, until 1975); Creative Writing Fellow, Strathclyde University, 1972-73; author of Remedy is None, 1966 (joint winner, Geoffrey Faber Memorial Award, 1967), A Gift from Nessus, 1968 (Scottish Arts Council Publication Award, 1969), Docherty, 1975 (Whitbread Award for Fiction, 1975).

McIlwain, Alexander Edward, CBE, MA, LLB, WS, SSC. Senior Partner, Leonards, Solicitors, Hamilton; President, Law Society of Scotland, 1983-84; Honorary Sheriff, South Strathclyde, Dumfries and Galloway, at Hamilton, since 1981; b. 4.7.33, Aberdeen; m., Moira Margaret Kinnaird; 3 d. Educ. Aberdeen Grammar School; Aberdeen University. Commissioned, Royal Corps of Signals, 1957-59; Burgh Prosecutor then District Prosecutor, Hamilton, 1966-76; Dean, Society of Solicitors of Hamilton, 1981-83; Chairman, Legal Aid Central Committee, 1985-87 (Member, 1981-83); Member, Lanarkshire

Health Board, since 1980; Honorary Member, American Bar Association; Member: Central Advisory Committee for Scotland on Justices of the Peace, Council of the Scout Association, Review Committee of Scottish Legal Aid Board; Honorary Vice President, Scottish Lawyers for Nuclear Disarmament; Chairman, Lanarkshire Scout Area, since 1981; Temporary Sheriff, since 1984. Recreations: work; gardening; golf. Address: (h.) 7 Bothwell Road, Uddingston, Glasgow; T.-0698 813368.

MacInnes, Hamish, OBE, BEM. Writer and Designer; b. 7.7.30, Gatehouse of Fleet. Educ. Gatehouse of Fleet. Mountaineer with numerous expeditions to Himalayas, Amazon and other parts of the world; Deputy Leader, 1975 Everest SW Face Expedition; film Producer/Advisor/safety expert, with Zinnemann, Connery, Eastwood, Putnam, etc.; Advisor, BBC TV live outside broadcasts on climbing; author of 18 books on travel and adventure, including two autobiographies and fiction; designed the first all-metal ice axe, Terodactyl ice climbing tools, the MacInnes stretchers; Founder, Search and Rescue Dog Association; Honorary Member, Scottish Mountaineering Club; former President, Alpine Climbing Group; world authority on mountain rescue; Doctor of Laws (Hons), Glasgow University; Hon. DSc, Aberdeen University; President, Guide Dogs Adventure Group; Leader, Glencoe Mountain Rescue Team. Recreations: as above. Address: (h.) Glencoe, Argyll; T.-08552 258.

McInnes, Sheriff John Colin, BA (Hons) (Oxon), LLB. Advocate; Sheriff, Tayside, Central and Fife, at Cupar and Perth, since 1974; b. 21.11.38, Cupar, Fife; m., Elisabeth Mabel Neilson; 1 s.; 1 d. Educ. New Park School, St. Andrews; Cargilfield School, Edinburgh; Merchiston Castle School, Edinburgh; Brasenose College, Oxford; Edinburgh University. 2nd Lt., 8th Royal Tank Regiment, 1956-58; Lt., Fife and Forfar Yeomanry, Scottish Horse, TA, 1958-64; Advocate, 1963; Director, R. Mackness & Co. Ltd., 1964-72; Chairman, Fios Group Ltd., 1970-72; Parliamentary candidate (Conservative), Aberdeen North, 1964; Tutor, Law Faculty, Edinburgh University, 1965-72; in practice, Scottish Bar, 1963-72; Sheriff of Lothian and Peebles, 1972-74. Member, St. Andrews University Court, since 1983. Recreations: fishing; shooting; gardening; photography. Address: (h.) Parkneuk, Blebocraigs, Cupar, Fife; T.-0334 85 366.

McInnes, Marjorie Mary, OBE, AIMSW. Chairman, Scottish Council on Disability, 1980-85; Vice Chairman, Age Concern Scotland, since 1980; b. 21.7.17, Glasgow. Educ. Hutchesons' Girls' Grammar School, Glasgow; Glasgow University; Institute of Medical Social Work. Lady Almoner, Southport General Infirmary, 1942-43; Head Almoner, Hairmyres Hospital, East Kilbride, 1943-48; Head Medical Social Worker: Victoria Infirmary, Glasgow, 1948-55, Western Infirmary, Glasgow, 1955-58; Department of Health for Scotland: Welfare Officer, 1958-62, Chief Welfare Officer, 1962-68; Deputy Chief Social Work Adviser, Social Work Services Group, Scottish Education Department, 1968-78. Chairman, Council of Management, Atholl Baptist Centre, Pitlochry; Member, Council and Executive Committee, Baptist Union of Scotland; Committee Member, Scottish Baptist College; Member, Board of Directors, Glasgow City Mission; Member, Council of Management, Quarriers Homes, Bridge of Weir; Chairman, Barnardo's Fred Martin Project. Recreations: music; reading; out of doors/natural world/walking. Address: (h.) 33 Corrour Road, Glasgow, G43 2DZ; T.-041-632 8959.

McInroy, Charles Colquhoun. Secretary/Treasurer, Queen's Nursing Institute Scotland, since 1983; b. 24.11.21, Edzell; m., Beryl Patricia Moody; 2 s.; 2 d. Educ. Loretto. Army, Queen's Bays, Royal Tank Regiment, and Staff (Captain), 1940-47; Scottish Equitable Life Assurance Society, 1948-81 (Staff Manager). Past Chairman, North Berwick School Council; former Captain, North Berwick Golf Club; former Treasurer, St. Baldred's Episcopal Church, North Berwick. Publication: Scottish Equitable Landmarks 1831-1981, 1981. Recreations: golf; bridge; books. Address: (h.) Arnhall, Fidra Road, North Berwick, EH39 4NE; T.-0260 2762.

McIntosh, Rev. Colin George, MA, BD (Hons). Minister, Dunblane Cathedral, since 1988 (St. John's-Renfield Church, Glasgow, 1976-88); b. 5.4.51, Glasgow; m., Linda Mary Henderson; 2 d. Educ. Govan High School; Glasgow University. Assistant Minister, Corstorphine, Edinburgh, 1975-76. Assessor, Church of Scotland Selection School; Stanley Mair Memorial Lecturer, Glasgow University, 1984. Recreations: gardening; music; reading. Address: (h.) Cathedral Manse, The Cross, Dunblane, FK15 0AQ.

McIntosh, David Bainbridge, MA, MIPM. Director, Scottish Health Service Development Group, since 1987; b. 28.10.42, Oxford; m., Judith Mary Mitchell; 4 d. Educ. Edinburgh Academy; Christ Church, Oxford; London School of Economics. Industrial Relations Adviser, Coats Patons (UK) Ltd., 1972-73; Personnel Manager: J. & P. Coats (UK) Ltd., 1974-79, J. & P. Coats Ltd., 1979-81; Mill Manager: Comphanhia De Linha Coats & Clark LDA Portugal, 1981-84, Hilos Cadena SA Colombia, 1984-87. Former Chief Instructor, Loch Earn Sailing School; Past Chairman, Glasgow and West of Scotland Outward Bound Association. Recreations: golf; sailing; skiing; squash; fishing. Address: (b.) Scottish Health Service Centre, Crewe Road South, Edinburgh, EH4 2LF; T.-031-332 2335.

Macintosh, Farquhar, CBE, MA, DipEd, DLitt, FEIS. Rector, Royal High School, Edinburgh; Chairman, Scottish Examination Board, since 1977; Chairman, School Broadcasting Council for Scotland, 1981-85; Vice-Chairman, School Broadcasting Council for UK, 1984-86; b. 27.10.23, Isle of Skye; m., Margaret M. Inglis; 2 s.; 2 d. Educ. Portree High School; Edinburgh University; Glasgow University; Jordanhill College of Education. Taught, Greenfield Junior Secondary School, Hamilton, Glasgow Academy and Inverness Royal Academy; Headmaster: Portree High School, Oban High School; Member, Highlands and Islands Development Consultative Council and Convener, Education Sub-Committee, 1965-82; Chairman, Jordanhill Board of Governors, 1970-72; Chairman, BBC Secondary

Programme Committee, 1972-80; Member, Court, Edinburgh University; Gaelic Correspondent, Weekly Scotsman, 1953-57. Recreations: hill-walking; sea fishing; Gaelic. Address: (b.) Royal High School, East Barnton Avenue, Edinburgh, EH4 6JP; T.-031-336 2261.

McIntosh, Professor Francis George, BSc, MSc, CEng, MIEE. Professor of Electronic and Electrical Engineering, Robert Gordon's Institute of Technology, since 1984 (Dean, Faculty of Technology, 1984-87, and Head, School of Electronic and Electrical Engineering, since 1982); b. 19.3.42; 1 d. Previously Senior Lecturer, Deputy Head, RGIT. Member, CNAA Electronic Electrical and Control Board, until 1987; Consultant, Board Member, Aberdeen I. Tech Ltd.; Member, Advisory Committee, MEDC; Member, IEE Accreditation Committee; Director, Axon Research Ltd. Address: (b.) RGIT, Schoolhill, Aberdeen, AB9 1FR; T.-0224 633611.

McIntosh, Iain Redford, ARSA, ARBS, MGMC, DA. Sculptor; b. 4.1.45, Peterhead; m., Freida; 2 d. Educ. Peterhead Academy; Gray's School of Art. Recreation: sculpture. Address: (h.) Powmouth, by Montrose; T.-Bridge of Dun 346.

Macintosh, Joan, CBE (1978), MA. Lay Observer for Scotland (Solicitors (Scotland) Act), since 1982; b. 23.11.19; m.; 1 s.; 2 d. Educ. Oxford University. CAB Organiser, Glasgow, 1972-75; Member, Royal Commission on Legal Services in Scotland, 1975-80; Chairman, Scottish Consumer Council, 1975-80; Vice-Chairman, National Consumer Council, 1976-84; Vice President, National Federation of Consumer Groups; Hon. LLD, Dundee, 1982.

McIntosh, Neil William David, ACIS, MIAM, FIPM. Chief Executive, Dumfries and Galloway Regional Council, since 1985; b. 30.1.40, Glasgow; m., Marie Elizabeth Lindsay. Educ. King's Park Senior Secondary School, Glasgow. O. and M. Trainee, Honeywell Controls Ltd., Lanarkshire, 1959-62; O. and M. Assistant, Berkshire, Oxford and Reading Joint Management Services Unit, 1962-64; O. and M. Officer, Stewarts and Lloyds Ltd., Lanarkshire, 1964-66; Senior O. and M. Officer, Lanark County Council, 1966-69; Establishment/O. and M. Officer, Inverness County Council, 1969-75; Personnel Officer, Highland Regional Council, 1975-81; Director of Manpower Services, Highland Regional Council, 1981-85; Clerk, Dumfries Lieutenancy, 1985. Recreations: bowling; hill-walking; antique bottle collecting; local history; youth work. Address: (b.) Regional Council Offices, English Street, Dumfries; T.-0387 53141.

Macintosh, Robert Macfarlan, MA, LLB. Solicitor; Chairman, Rent Assessment Committee, Glasgow, since 1966; Honorary Sheriff Substitute, Dumbarton, since 1975; b. 16.6.17, Dumbarton; m., Ann McLean Kelso; 1 s. Educ. Dumbarton Academy; George Watson's College, Edinburgh; Glasgow University. Qualified as Solicitor, 1949; Local Secretary, Dumbarton Legal Aid Committee, 1950-84; Chairman: Dunbartonshire Rent Tribunal, 1960, Glasgow Rent Tribunal, 1974; Clerk to Commissioners of Income Tax, East and West Dunbartonshire, since 1973; President, Dumbarton Burns Club; Captain, Cardross Golf Club. Recreation: golf. Address: (h.) Ardmoy, Peel Street, Cardross, Dunbartonshire.

McIntyre, Archibald Dewar, MB, ChB, DPH, FFCM, FRCPE, DIH, DTM&H. Principal Medical Officer, Scottish Home and Health Department, since 1977; b. 18.2.28, Dunipace; m., Euphemia Hope Houston; 2 s.; 2 d. Educ. Falkirk High School; Edinburgh University. Senior Medical Officer, Overseas Civil Service, Sierra Leone; Depute Medical Officer of Health, Stirling County Council; Depute Secretary, Scottish Council for Postgraduate Medical Education; Senior Medical Officer, Scottish Home and Health Department. Recreations: gardening; photography. Address: (h.) Birchlea, 43 Falkirk Road, Linlithgow, EH49 7PH; T.-0506 842063.

MacIntyre, David John, MA (Hons). Senior Management Consultant, Arthur Young, since 1987 (Director of Area Operations, Scottish Tourist Board, 1982-87); b. 24.1.45, Fort William; m., Margaret MacKinnon; 1 d. Educ. Lochaber High School; St. Andrews University. Joined British Rail as Planning and Marketing Assistant, 1958; Highlands and Islands Development Board: Statistician, 1970, transferred to Tourism Division, 1971, latterly in charge of all HIDB tourism research and development; also responsible for co-ordinating local network of Area Tourist Boards, before performing that duty on national basis with STB. Recreations: golf; current affairs; gardening. Address: (h.) 8 Stuart Green, Craigmount, Corstorphine, Edinburgh; T.-031-339 6854.

McIntyre, Professor John, CVO, MA, BD, DLitt, DD, DHL, Dr hc, FRSE. Professor of Divinity, Edinburgh University, 1956-86; Honorary Chaplain to The Queen in Scotland, 1974-86 (Extraordinary Chaplain, since 1986); Dean of the Order of the Thistle, since 1974; b. 20.5.16, Glasgow; m., Jessie Brown Buick; 2 s.; 1 d. Educ. Bathgate Academy; Edinburgh University. Ordained, 1941; Locum Tenens, Parish of Glenorchy and Inishail, 1941-43; Minister, Fenwick, Ayrshire, 1943-45; Hunter Baillie Professor of Theology, St. Andrew's College, Sydney University, 1946-56; Principal, St. Andrew's College, 1950-56; Principal Warden, Pollock Halls of Residence, Edinburgh University, 1960-71; Acting Principal and Vice-Chancellor, Edinburgh University, 1973-74, 1979; Principal, New College, and Dean, Faculty of Divinity, 1968-74; Moderator, General Assembly of the Church of Scotland, 1982; Convener, Board of Education, Church of Scotland, 1983-87; former Council Member and Vice President, Royal Society of Edinburgh. Publications: St. Anselm and his Critics, 1954; The Christian Doctrine of History, 1957; On the Love of God, 1962; The Shape of Christology, 1966; Faith, Theology and Imagination, 1987. Recreation: travel. Address: (h.) 22/4 Minto Street, Edinburgh, EH9 1RQ; T.-031-667 1203.

McIntyre, Rev. John, PhL, STL, MA, DipEd. Parish Priest, St. Bride's Church, East Kilbride, since 1986; Secretary, Scottish Catholic Heritage Commission, since 1981; President, Scalan Association, since 1985; b. 12.11.37, Airdrie. Educ. St. Aloysius' College, Glasgow; Gregorian University and Scots College, Rome; Glasgow University. Ordained Priest, 1961; staff member, National Junior Seminary for Scotland, 1968-86; Principal of English, Blairs College, 1975-85; Curator, Blairs College Museum, 1979-85; Rector, Blairs College, 1985-86. Publication: Scotland and the Holy See (Co-Editor), 1982. Recreation: reading. Address: St. Bride's Church, Whitemoss Avenue, East Kilbride, G74 1NN; T.-035 52 20005.

Macintyre, Lorn, BA (Hons), PhD. Freelance Writer; b. 7.9.42, Taynuilt, Argyll; m., Mary. Educ. Stirling University; Glasgow University. Former Head of English, Merchiston Castle School, Edinburgh; Novelist and Short Story Writer; publications include Cruel in the Shadow and The Blind Bend in Chronicles of Invernevis Series. Recreation: work. Address: (h.) Priormuir, by St. Andrews, Fife; T.-0334 76428.

McIntyre, Robert Douglas, MB, ChB, DPH, DUniv, JP, FSC. Honorary Consultant, Stirling Royal Infirmary, since 1974; Chancellor's Assessor, Stirling University; b. 15.12.13, Dalziel; m., Letitia S. MacLeod; 1 s. Educ. Hamilton Academy; Daniel Stewart's College; Edinburgh University; Glasgow University. Consultant Chest Physician, Stirling and Clackmannan Counties, 1951-79; MP, Motherwell and Wishaw, 1945; Chairman, SNP, 1948-56; President, SNP, 1958-80; Honorary Treasurer, Royal Burgh of Stirling, 1958-64; Provost of Stirling, 1967-75; Freeman, Royal Burgh of Stirling. Recreations: sailing; conversation. Address: (h.) 8 Gladstone Place, Stirling; T.-Stirling 73456.

Macintyre, Rev. William John, MA, BD, DD, FSA(Scot). Parish Minister, Crail, Fife, since 1956; b. 15.1.24, Sleat, Skye; m., Christine Thomson Torry; 1 s.; 1 d. Educ. Keil School, Dumbarton; Glasgow University. Captain, A. & S.H., 1943-47, seconded to 2nd K.E.O. Goorka Rifles. Former Moderator, Presbytery of St. Andrews and Synod of Fife. Recreations: line drawing; gardening. Address: The Manse, Crail, Fife, KY10 3UH; T.-Crail 50358.

MacIver, Donald John Morrison, MA (Hons). President, An Comunn Gaidhealach, since 1985; Principal Teacher of Gaelic, Nicolson Institute, since 1973; b. 12.11.42, Stornoway; m., Alice Macleod; 1 s. Educ. Nicolson Institute; Aberdeen University. Teacher of Gaelic, 1968-73. Member, Gaelic Books Council; Director, Acair Publishing Co.; former Editor, Sruth (newspaper of An Comunn Gaidhealach). Publications: Gaelic Oral Composition; Gaelic Language Practice; Gaelic O-Grade Interpretation; Sgriobh Seo; Feuch Seo; Feuch Freagairt; Faic Is Freagair; Camhanaich; Eadar Peann Is Paipear. Recreations: writing (prose and poetry); computing; reading poetry; gardening; Coronation Street. Address: (h.) 32 Goathill Road, Stornoway, Isle of Lewis, PA87 2NL; T.-0851 2582.

MacIver, Duncan Malcolm, CBE (1986). Deputy Director, Scottish Prison Service, 1978-86; b. 7.5.22, Meerut, India; m., Jessie D.T. Neilson; 2 s.; 1 d. Educ. McLaren High School, Callander. Served in Black Watch and Royal Scots, 1939-47, in Ceylon, India and Burma (14th Army), rank of Sgt.; joined Scottish Prison Service as a prison officer, 1948; promoted to Governor grade, 1960; Assistant Governor, Polmont and Barlinnie; Deputy Governor, Polmont and Perth; Governor: Castle Huntly Borstal, 1969-70, Aberdeen Prison, 1970-73; Assistant Inspector of Prisons, 1973-75; Governor (HQ), 1975-76; Governor, Edinburgh Prison, 1976-78; Controller of Operations (Deputy Director), Scottish Prison Service, since 1978. Recreations: golf; gardening. Address: (h.) 3 Caiystane Drive, Edinburgh; T.-031-445 1734.

MacIver, Roy, MA, LLB. Secretary General, Convention of Scottish Local Authorities, since 1986; b. 15.10.42, Stornoway; m., Anne; 3 s. Educ. Nicolson Institute, Stornoway; Edinburgh University; Glasgow University. Legal Assistant, Paisley Corporation; Solicitor/Administrator, Dunfermline Town Council, 1970-72; Assistant County Clerk (Lewis), Ross and Cromarty County Council, 1972-74; Chief Executive, Western Isles Islands Council (Comhairle Nan Eilean), 1974-86. Recreation: jazz. Address: (b.) Rosebery House, 9 Haymarket Terrace, Edinburgh; T.-031-346 1222.

McIvor, Derek Stuart, MA, BA (Cantab). Headteacher, Broxburn Academy, since 1976; Educational Consultant, St. Andrew's Scots School, Buenos Aires, since 1981; b. 24.3.26, Edinburgh; m., Audrey Winifred Gibb; 1 s.; 1 d. Educ. Royal High School; Morrison's Academy, Crieff; Trinity Hall, Cambridge; Moray House College of Education. Teacher, Bo'ness Academy, 1951-54; St. Andrew's Scots School, Buenos Aires: Principal Teacher of History, 1954-61, Depute Headmaster, 1956-61, Acting Headmaster, 1960-61; Teacher of History and Geography, Royal High School, 1961-64; Principal Teacher of History and Modern Studies, Liberton High School, 1964-69; Depute Headteacher, Portobello High School, 1969-76; Member, BBC Council for Scotland, 1970-73, and for the UK, 1973-76. Recreations: golf; snooker; bridge; reading; chess. Address: (h.) 19 Cherry Tree Park, Balerno, EH14 5AQ.

Mackay, Angus Victor Peck, MA, BSc, PhD, MB, ChB, FRCPsych, MRCP. Physician Superintendent, Argyll and Bute Hospital, and MacKintosh Lecturer in Psychological Medicine, Glasgow University, since 1980; Chairman, Research and Clinical Section, Royal College of Psychiatrists (Scotland), since 1981; Psychiatric Representative, Committee on Safety of Medicines, DHSS, since 1983; b. 4.3.43, Edinburgh; m., Elspeth M.W. Norris; 2 s.; 2 d. Educ. George Heriot's School, Edinburgh; Edinburgh University; Churchill and Trinity Colleges, Cambridge. MRC Research Fellow, Cambridge; Member, senior clinical staff, MRC Neurochemical Pharmacology Unit, Cambridge, with appointment as Lector in Pharmacology, Trinity College (latterly, Deputy Director of Unit). Member, Health Service Research Committee of the Chief Scientist for Scotland; Member, Research Committee, Mental Health Foundation; Chairman, Argyll and Clyde Area Psychiatric Sub-Committee; Member, Scottish Executive, Royal College of Psychiatrists. Recreations: rowing; sailing; rhododendrons. Address: (h.) Tigh an Rudha, Ardrishaig, Argyll; T.-0546 3272.

McKay, Sheriff Archibald Charles, MA, LLB. Sheriff of Glasgow and Strathkelvin, since 1979; b. 18.10.29; m.; 1 s.; 3 d. Educ. St. Aloysius' College, Glasgow; Glasgow University. Solicitor, Glasgow, 1957.

Mackay, Charles, CB, BSc, MSc, FIBiol. Chief Agricultural Officer, Department of Agriculture and Fisheries for Scotland, 1975-87; b. 12.1.27, Kinloch, Sutherland; m., Marie A.K. Mitchell; 1 s.; 1 d. Educ. Strathmore School; Lairg Higher Grade Public School; Aberdeen University; Kentucky University. DAFS: Temporary Inspector, 1947-48, Assistant Inspector, 1948-54, Inspector, 1954-64, Senior Inspector, 1964-70, Technical Development Officer, 1970-73, Deputy Chief Agricultural Officer, 1973-75. Recreations: fishing; golf. Address: (h.) 35 Boswall Road, Edinburgh, EH5 3RP; T.-031-552 6063.

MacKay, Colin Hinshelwood, MA (Hons). Political Editor, Scottish Television PLC, since 1973 (Presenter, Ways and Means, 1973-86); Member, Scottish Arts Council, since 1988; b. 27.8.44, Glasgow; m., Olive E.B. Brownlie; 2 s. Educ. Kelvinside Academy, Glasgow; Glasgow University; Jordanhill College of Education. Reporter/Presenter: Border Television Ltd., 1967-70, Grampian Television Ltd., 1970-73; Presenter of political programmes, including all elections and by-elections, STV, since 1973; ITV Commentator: Papal Visit to Scotland, 1982, CBI Conference, Glasgow, 1983. Winner, Observer Mace, 1967 (British Universities Debating Championship); Member, two-man British Universities Canadian Debating Tour, 1967; Commonwealth Relations Trust Bursary to Canada, 1981. Publications: Kelvinside Academy: 1878-1978, 1978; The Scottish Dimension in Central and Eastern Canada, 1981. Recreations: music (especially opera); reading; writing. Address: (b.) Scottish Television PLC, Glasgow; T.-041-332 9999; Press Gallery, House of Commons, London, SW1.

Mackay, David William, CBiol, FIBiol, FIWEM, MIFM, FBIM. Depute Director, Clyde River Purification Board, since 1975; b. 6.4.36, Stirling; m., Maureen. Educ. High School of Stirling; Glasgow University; Strathclyde University. Experimental Officer, Freshwater Fisheries Laboratory, Pitlochry (Department of Agriculture and Fisheries for Scotland), 1959-66; Clyde River Purification Board: Biologist, 1966-68, Marine Survey Officer, 1968-75, Depute Director, 1975-78 and since 1981; Principal Environmental Protection Officer, Government of Hong Kong, 1978-81. Secretary, Scottish Anglers National Association; Consultant, World Health Organization. Recreations: scuba diving; golf; angling. Address: (b.) Rivers House, Murray Road, East Kilbride, Glasgow, G75 OLA; T.-03552 38181.

Mackay, Donald George, MA. Under Secretary, Scottish Development Department, since 1985; b. 25.11.29, Dundee; m., Elizabeth Ailsa Barr; 2 s.; 1 d. Educ. Morgan Academy, Dundee; St. Andrews University. Scottish Home Department, 1953; Assistant Private Secretary to Secretary of State for Scotland, 1959; Assistant Secretary, Royal Commission on the Police, 1962-64; Secretary, Royal Commission on Local Government in Scotland, 1966-69; Scottish Development Department, 1969-79; Department of Agriculture and Fisheries for Scotland, 1979-85. Recreations: hill-walking; photography; music. Address: (h.) 38 Cluny Drive, Edinburgh, EH10 6DX; T.-031-447 1851.

MacKay, Professor Donald Iain, MA. Chairman, PEIDA, since 1976; Professorial Fellow, Heriot-Watt University, since 1982; b. 27.2.37, Kobe, Japan; m., Diana Marjory Raffan; 1 s.; 2 d. Educ. Dollar Academy; Aberdeen University. Professor of Political Economy, Aberdeen University, 1971-76; Professor of Economics, Heriot-Watt University, 1976-82; Director: Adam and Co.; Grampian Holdings; Vice President, Scottish Association of Public Transport; Member, Scottish Economic Council; Economic Consultant to Secretary of State for Scotland; Governor, National Institute of Economic and Social Research. Recreations: tennis; bridge. Address: (h.) Newfield, 14 Gamekeepers Road, Edinburgh; T.-031-336 1936.

Mackay, Donald John, MA, FBIM. Chief Executive, Harris Tweed Association, since 1982; b. 8.6.30, North Uist; m., Rhona MacLeod; 3 d. Educ. Portree High School; Aberdeen University; London University. District Commissioner and Private Secretary/Aide de Camp to Governor, Sierra Leone, 1954-58; Highland Area Officer, Scottish Agricultural Organisation Society, 1958-61; Staff and Management Training Officer, AEA, Dounreay, 1961-63; Personnel and Training Officer, British Aluminium, 1964-65; Director, An Comunn Gaidhealach, 1965-70; Personnel Manager, British Aluminium, Invergordon, 1970-78; External Affairs Manager, Primary Division, British Aluminium, 1978-82. Member, Red Deer Commission, 1966-74; Member, Highland Disablement Advisory Committee, since 1970; Member, Highland Area Group, Scottish Council, since 1971; Member, North of Scotland Electricity Council, 1981-84; Secretary, CBI Highland Area Group, since 1978, Chairman, 1988; Member, HIDB Consultative Council, 1978-81; Member, Nature Conservancy Council Scottish Advisory Committee, 1979-86; MSC Chairman, Highlands & Islands, since 1981; Member, Executive Council, Scottish Council, since 1982; Chairman, CNAG, 1984-86; Chairman, Albyn Housing Society, 1979-83; Director, Fearann Eilean Iarmain, since 1972. Recreations: sailing; shooting; fishing; Gaelic. Address: (h.) Kildonan, Teandalloch, Beauly, by Inverness; T.-0463 231 270.

Mackay, Rev. Canon Douglas Brysson. Rector, Church of the Holy Rood, Carnoustie, since 1972; Synod Clerk, Diocese of Brechin, since 1981; Canon, St. Paul's Cathedral, Dundee, since 1981; b. 20.3.27, Glasgow; m., Catherine Elizabeth; 2 d. Educ. Possil Senior Secondary School; Edinburgh Theological College. Precentor, St. Andrew's Cathedral, Inverness, 1958; Rector, Gordon Chapel, Fochabers, 1961 (also Priest-in-Charge, St. Margaret's Church, Aberlour, 1964); Canon, St. Andrew's Cathedral, Inverness, 1965; Synod Clerk, Diocese of Moray, Ross, Caithness, 1965; Honorary Canon, St. Andrew's Cathedral, Inverness, 1972; Convenor of Youth, Moray Diocese, 1965; Brechin Diocese: Convenor, Social Service Board, 1974, Convenor, Joint Board, 1974, Convenor, Administration Board, 1982; Chairman,

Truth and Unity Movement, 1980-87. President, British Red Cross, Carnoustie, 1974-82; President, British Legion, Carnoustie, 1981; Vice-Chairman, Carnoustie Community Care, 1981; Chairman, Carnoustie Community Council, 1979-81; President, Carnoustie Rotary Club, 1976. Recreations: golf; snooker; reading; music. Address: Holyrood Rectory, Carnoustie, DD7 6AB; T.-Carnoustie 52202.

Mackay, Eileen Alison, MA. Assistant Secretary, Scottish Development Department, since 1987; b. 7.7.43, Helmsdale, Sutherland; m., A. Muir Russell (qv). Educ. Dingwall Academy; Edinburgh University. Research Officer, Department of Employment, 1965-72; Principal: Scottish Office, 1972-78, HM Treasury, 1978-80; Adviser, Central Policy Review Staff, Cabinet Office, 1980-83; Assistant Secretary, Scottish Development Agency and New Towns Division, Industry Department for Scotland, 1983-87; Rural Environment and Nature Conservation Division, Scottish Development Department, since 1987. Address: (b.) New St. Andrews House, Edinburgh.

MacKay, Ian Munro, BComm, CA. Principal, MacKay & Co., Chartered Accountants, Golspie and Dornoch, since 1979; Honorary Sheriff, Dornoch Sheriff Court, since 1985; b. 14.9.47, Brora; m., Maureen; 2 s.; 1 d. Educ. Golspie High School; Edinburgh University. Trained as CA in Edinburgh, qualifying in 1973; has worked in the profession since, spending three years in United Arab Emirates, returning to UK in 1979 to set up own practice. Auditor, Treasurer, Secretary of several local charities and sporting organisations; Secretary/Treasurer, Dornoch Heritage Society, 1981-87. Recreations: curling; local history; garden; following most sports. Address: (h.) 4 Sutherland Road, Dornoch, Sutherland; T.-0862 810333.

Mackay, James Alexander, MA. Author, Journalist and Publisher; Numismatic and Philatelic Correspondent, Financial Times, since 1972; Editor, the Burns Chronicle, since 1978, and The Burnsian, since 1986; b. 21.11.36, Inverness; m., Joyce May Greaves. Educ. Hillhead High School, Glasgow; Glasgow University. Lt., RA Guided Weapons Range, Hebrides, 1959-61; Assistant Keeper, Department of Printed Books, British Museum, in charge of philatelic collections, 1961-71; returned to Scotland as a full-time Writer, 1972; Editor-in-Chief, IPC Stamp Encyclopedia, 1968-72; Columnist on antiques, Financial Times, 1967-72; Trustee, James Currie Memorial Trust, since 1987; Publisher of books on philately and postal history; author of more than 100 books on aspects of the applied and decorative arts, numismatics, philately, postal history; books include Robert Bruce, King of Scots, 1974; Rural Crafts in Scotland, 1976; Scottish Postmarks, 1978; The Burns Federation 1885-1985, 1985; The Complete Works of Robert Burns, 1986; The Complete Letters of Robert Burns, 1987; Burnsiana, 1988. Recreations: travel; languages; music (piano-playing); photographing post offices. Address: (h.) 11 Newall Terrace, Dumfries, DG1 1LN; T.-0387 55250.

Mackay of Clashfern, Lord (James Peter Hymers), Baron (1979), PC (1979), FRSE. Lord High Chancellor of Great Britain, since 1987; b. 2.7.27, Edinburgh; m., Elizabeth Gunn Hymers; 1 s.; 2 d. Educ. George Heriot's School, Edinburgh; Edinburgh University. Lecturer in Mathematics, St. Andrews University, 1948-50; Major Scholar, Trinity College, Cambridge, in Mathematics, 1947, taken up, 1950; Senior Scholar, 1951; BA (Cantab), 1952; LLB Edinburgh (with distinction), 1955; admitted, Faculty of Advocates, 1955; QC (Scot), 1965; Standing Junior Counsel to: Queen's and Lord Treasurer's Remembrancer, Scottish Home and Health Department, Commissioners of Inland Revenue in Scotland; Sheriff Principal, Renfrew and Argyll, 1972-74; Vice-Dean, Faculty of Advocates, 1973-76; Dean, 1976-79; Lord Advocate of Scotland, 1979-84; a Senator of the College of Justice in Scotland, 1984-85. Part-time Member, Scottish Law Commission, 1976-79; Hon. Master of the Bench, Inner Temple, 1979; Fellow, International Academy of Trial Lawyers, 1979; Fellow, Institute of Taxation, 1981; Director, Stenhouse Holdings Ltd., 1976-77; Member, Insurance Brokers' Registration Council, 1977-79; a Commissioner of Northern Lighthouses, 1975-84; Hon. LLD: Edinburgh, 1983, Dundee, 1983, Strathclyde, 1985, Aberdeen, 1987; a Lord of Appeal in Ordinary, 1985-87. Recreation: walking. Address: Lord Chancellor's Residence, House of Lords, London, SW1A 0PW; T.-01-219 3232.

MacKay, John, OBE, MB, ChB, FRCGP. General Medical Practitioner, Govan Health Centre, Glasgow, since 1951; Member, Greater Glasgow Health Board, since 1973; Chairman, Scottish Medical Practices Committee, since 1984; Member, National Board for Nursing, Midwifery and Health Visiting for Scotland; b. 24.7.26, Glasgow; m., Matilda MacLennan Bain; 2 s.; 2 d. Educ. Govan High School; Glasgow University. Junior House Doctor, Victoria Infirmary and Southern General Hospital, Glasgow, 1949; Ship's Surgeon, 1950; Assistant in General Practice, Govan, 1951-52 (Principal, since 1953); Member, Board of Management, Glasgow South West Hospitals, prior to 1973; Tutor, University Department of General Practice, Glasgow; part-time Medical Referee, Scottish Home and Health Department; Honorary Life Manager, Govan Weavers Society; Chairman, Glasgow Local Medical Committee, since 1982; Member, Scottish General Medical Services Committee; Member, Scottish Council for Postgraduate Medical Education. Recreations: angling; golf; gardening. Address: (h.) Moorholm, Barr's Brae, Kilmacolm, Renfrewshire, PA13 4DE; T.-Kilmacolm 3234.

Mackay, John, TD, MA, FInstD. General Manager, Royal Mail Letters, Scotland, N. England and N. Ireland, since 1986; Board Member, Royal Mail Letters, Scottish Post Office Board, since 1985; b. 14.9.36, St. Andrews; m., Barbara Wallace; 1 s.; 2 d. Educ. Madras College; Dunfermline High School; Kirkcaldy High School; Edinburgh University. Army (Lt., East Anglian Regiment), 1959-63; TA, 1964-86, Royal Engineers (Postal and Courier), Colonel; Post Office: Assistant Postal Controller, Wales, N. Ireland, 1963-68, Principal, Post Office HQ, 1968-76, Controller (Personnel and Finance), Eastern Region, 1977-79, Director Philately, Post Office HQ, 1979-84, Controller Royal Mails Scotland, 1985-86. Recreations: ball games, especially cricket;

reading; walking dog; convivial company. Address: (b.) West Port House, Edinburgh, EH3 9HS; T.-031-228 7400.

MacKay, John Angus, MA. Director, Comunn Na Gaidhlig, since 1985; Chairman, Trustees, The Gaelic College, since 1987; b. 24.6.48, Shader, Stornoway; m., Maria F.; 3 s. Educ. Nicolson Institute; Aberdeen University; Jordanhill College. Aberdeen Circulation Rep., D.C. Thomson, 1970-71; Jordanhill College, 1971-72; Teacher, 1972-77; Field Officer, then Development Officer, then Senior Administrative Officer, HIDB, 1977-85. Chairman, Gaelic Youth Radio Trust; Director, Acair (Gaelic publishing company). Recreations: reading; skiing; swimming; running. Address: (h.) 3 Ceann A Tuath, Arnol, Isle of Lewis; T.-0851 71524.

McKay, John Henderson, CBE (1987), BA (Hons), PhD. Lord Provost of Edinburgh, 1984-88; b. 12.5.29, Kirknewton; m., Catherine Watson Taylor; 1 s.; 1 d. Educ. West Calder High School; Open University. Labourer and Clerk, Pumpherston Oil Co. Ltd., 1948-50; National Service, Royal Artillery, 1950-52; Customs and Excise, since 1952. Secretary, Royal Caledonian Horticultural Society. Recreations: gardening; reading; listening to music. Address: (h.) 2 Buckstone Way, Edinburgh, EH10 OPN; T.-031-445 2865.

Mackay, John (Ian) Robb, DipArch, DipTCP. Co-ordinator, Grampian Economic Initiative, since 1987 (Depute Director, NESDA, since 1982); b. 20.6.41, Forfar; m., Elizabeth Victoria; 1 d. Educ. Forfar Academy; Duncan of Jordanstone College of Art, Dundee; Edinburgh College of Art. Qualified as an architect/planner. Recreations: golf; swimming; foreign travel. Address: (h.) 32 West Glebe, Stonehaven, AB3 2HZ; T.-0569 63593.

MacKay, John Jackson, BSc, DipEd. Chief Executive, Scottish Conservative Party, since 1987; b. 15.11.38, Lochgilphead; m., Sheena Wagner; 2 s.; 1 d. Educ. Dunoon Grammar School; Campbeltown Grammar School; Glasgow University; Jordanhill College of Education. Member, Oban Town Council, 1969-74; Member, Argyll Water Board, 1969-74; Principal Teacher of Mathematics, Oban High School, 1969-79; MP for Argyll, 1979-83, for Argyll & Bute, 1983-87; Parliamentary Private Secretary to Secretary of State for Scotland, 1982; Parliamentary Under Secretary of State, Scottish Office, 1982-87; Justice of the Peace for Argyll and Bute. Recreations: fishing; sailing. Address: (b.) 3 Chester Street, Edinburgh, EH3 7RF.

Mackay, John M., MBE. General Manager, Northern Lighthouse Board, since 1977; b. 26.7.28, Chelsea, London; m., Martha; 1 s.; 1 d. Educ. Winchester House, Brackley; RN Colleges, Dartmouth and Greenwich. After training, service in RN General Service ships, 1949-51; service in RN Surveying Service at sea, 1951-67; Commander RN (retd.); Ministry of Defence, 1967-77. Recreations: gardening; Austin Seven. Address: (b.) 84 George Street, Edinburgh, EH2 3DA.

McKay, Rev. Johnston Reid, MA (Glasgow), BA (Cantab). Producer, Religious Programmes, BBC, since 1987; b. 2.5.42, Glasgow. Educ. High School of Glasgow; Glasgow University; Cambridge University. Assistant Minister, St. Giles' Cathedral, 1967-71; Church Correspondent, Glasgow Herald, 1968-70; Minister, Bellahouston Steven Parish Church, 1971-78; frequent Broadcaster; Governor, Paisley College; Minister, Paisley Abbey, 1978-87; Editor, The Bush (newspaper of Glasgow Presbytery), 1975-78; Chairman, Scottish Religious Advisory Committee, BBC, 1981-86. Publications: From Sleep and From Damnation (with James Miller), 1970; Essays in Honour of William Barclay (Joint Editor), 1976; Through Wood and Nails, 1982. Recreations: good music and bad golf. Address: (b.) Religious Broadcasting Department, BBC, Queen Margaret Drive, Glasgow; T.-041-330 2345.

MacKay, Norman, MD, FRCP(Glas), FRCP(Edin). Consultant Physician, Victoria Infirmary, Glasgow, since 1974; Honorary Clinical Lecturer, Glasgow University, since 1974; Chairman, West of Scotland Committee for Postgraduate Education, since 1986; b. 15.9.36, Glasgow; m., Grace Violet McCaffer; 2 s.; 2 d. Educ. Govan High School; Glasgow University. Honorary Secretary: Royal College of Physicians and Surgeons of Glasgow, 1973-83, Standing Joint Committee, Scottish Royal Colleges, 1978-82, Conference of Royal Colleges and Faculties in Scotland, since 1982; Speciality Adviser in Medicine, West of Scotland Committee of Postgraduate Medical Education, since 1982; President, Royal Medico-Chirurgical Society of Glasgow, 1982-83; Member, Area Medical Committee, Greater Glasgow Health Board, since 1987; Vice President, Southern Medical Society, since 1987. Recreations: gardening; walking; golf; association football. Address: (h.) 4 Erksine Avenue, Dumbreck, Glasgow, G41 5AL; T.-041-427 1900.

Mackay, Peter, MA. Under Secretary, Further and Higher Education, Scottish Education Department, since 1987; b. 6.7.40, Arbroath; m., Sarah Holdich; 1 s.; 2 d. Educ. Glasgow High School; St. Andrews University. Teacher, New South Wales, Australia, 1962-63; Assistant Principal, Scottish Development Department, 1963; Private Secretary to Ministers of State, Scottish Office, 1966-68; Principal, Scottish Home and Health Department, 1968-73; Private Secretary to Secretaries of State for Scotland, 1973-75; Assistant Secretary, 1975; Head, Local Government Division, Scottish Development Department, 1979-83; Director for Scotland, Manpower Services Commission, 1983-85; on secondment from Scottish Office to Department of Employment, London (in charge of GB training policy), 1985. Nuffield Travelling Fellowship, 1978-79. Recreations: Scotland; easy mountaineering; dinghy sailing; sea canoeing; tennis. Address: (h.) 6 Henderland Road, Edinburgh, EH12 6BB; T.-031-337 2830.

Mackay, Robert Ostler. Solicitor, since 1930; Notary Public, since 1955; b. 25.12.07, Greenock; m., 1, Dorothy Lilian Johnson (deceased); 2, Irene Isobel Ray Anderson; 1 s.; 2 d. Educ. Greenock Academy; Alyth Public School; Blairgowrie High School; Edinburgh University. Partner: J.C. Richards & Morrice, Solicitors, Fraserburgh, 1939-45, Ferguson & Petrie, Solicitors, Duns, 1945; Honorary Sheriff, Lothian and Borders, at

Duns, since 1981; Council Member, Law Society of Scotland, 1958-79 (Vice-President, 1967-68); Life Member, Cairngorm Club. Recreations: angling; mountaineering. Address: (h.) Nethercraigs, Tighnabruaich, Argyll; T.-0700 811 368.

MacKay, Sheila Stirling. Member, Inverness District Council, since 1980 (Housing Chairman); b. 5.1.39, Inverness; m., Ian Charles MacKay; 2 d. Educ. Inverness Royal Academy. Vice-Chairman, Inverness Housing Committee, since 1984; Member, Board of Governors, Eden Court Theatre, since 1984; Member, Management Committee, Women's Aid; Member, Local Advisory Committee, IBA; Member, Executive Committee, Inverness Nairn and Lochaber Liberal Association. Recreations: reading; gardening. Address: (h.) 92 Culduthel Road, Inverness, IV2 4HH; T.-0463 235448.

Mackay, William Kenneth, BSc, CEng, FICE, FIHT, FRSA, MCIT. Partner, JMP Consultants Ltd. (formerly Jamieson Mackay & Partners), since 1965; Commissioner, Royal Fine Arts Commission for Scotland, since 1981; Board Member, Clyde Port Authority, since 1985; b. 6.6.30, Moyobamba, Peru. Educ. Hillhead High School, Glasgow; Glasgow University. Engineer, NCB, West Fife Area, 1954-57; Senior Engineer, Fife County Council, 1957-59; Group Engineer, Cumbernauld New Town Development Corporation, 1959-65; Consultant, since 1965; Past Chairman, Scottish Branch, Institution of Highways and Transportation; former Member, Planning and Transport Research Advisory Council to UK Government. Recreations: swimming; walking. Address: (b.) JMP (Consultants) Ltd., 20 Royal Terrace, Glasgow, G3 7NY; T.-041-332 3868.

McKean, Charles Alexander, BA, FRSA, FSA Scot. Secretary, Royal Incorporation of Architects in Scotland, since 1979; b. 16.7.46, Glasgow; m., Margaret Yeo; 2 s. Educ. Fettes College; Bristol University. RIBA: Secretary, London Region, 1968-76, Secretary, Eastern Region, 1972-79, Secretary, Community Architecture, 1976-79; Architectural Correspondent, The Times, 1977-83; Director, Wasps; Trustee, Thirlestane Castle; Secretary, RIAS Services Ltd.; author of architectural guides to Edinburgh, Dundee, Stirling, London, Cambridge, Moray; General Editor, RIAS/Landmark Trust Guides to Scotland. Publication: The Scottish Thirties. Recreations: books; glasses; gardens; stately homes. Address: (b.) 15 Rutland Square, Edinburgh; T.-031-229 7205.

McKean, Professor Donald Campbell, MA, DPhil, DSc, FRSE. Professor of Chemistry, Aberdeen University, since 1983 (Head, Department of Chemistry, 1984-87); b. 6.5.28, Sanderstead, Surrey; m., Lucy Marian Homan Thorpe; 4 d. Educ. Tonbridge School; Oxford University. Lecturer, then Senior Lecturer, then Reader, Aberdeen University, 1955-83. Publications: 104 papers in scientific journals. Recreation: hillwalking. Address: (b.) Chemistry Department, Aberdeen University, Aberdeen, AB9 2UE; T.-Aberdeen 272915.

McKean, Rev. Martin James, BD, DipMin. Minister, Cumnock Old Church, since 1984; b. 3.10.57, Edinburgh; m., Audrey Margaret Beat. Educ. John Watson's School, Edinburgh; Edinburgh University. Valuation Assistant, Midlothian County Council and Lothian Regional Council, 1974-75; Cadet Valuer, District Valuer, Lothian, 1975-77; student, 1977-83; Assistant Minister, St. John's Renfield, Glasgow, 1983-84. Part-time Chaplain, Ballochmyle Hospital. Recreations: music; golf; computer programming. Address: The Manse, 33 Barrhill Road, Cumnock, Ayrshire, KA18 1PJ; T.-0290 20769.

McKechnie, George. Editor, Glasgow Evening Times, since 1980; b. 28.7.46, Edinburgh; m., Janequin Claire Seymour Morris; 2 s. Educ. Portobello High School, Edinburgh. Reporter: Paisley & Renfrewshire Gazette, 1964-66, Edinburgh Evening News, 1966, Scottish Daily Mail, 1966-68, Daily Record, 1968-74; Deputy News Editor/ News Editor, Sunday Mail, 1974-76; Assistant Editor, Evening Times, 1976-80. Recreation: reading. Address: (b.) 195 Albion Street, Glasgow, G1 1QP; T.-041-552 6255.

McKeever, Francis Bernard, JP. Member, Falkirk District Council (Housing Chairman, since 1980); Member, Housing Committee, COSLA; b. 8.4.45, Falkirk; m., Elizabeth Liddle; 3 s. Educ. St. Modan's High School, Stirling. Member, Grangemouth Town Council, 1972 (Entertainments Convener, 1973-75, Magistrate, 1974-75); Member: Stirling County Council, 1973-75, Falkirk District Council, since 1974 (Depute Provost, 1980-84). Recreation: fishing. Address: (h.) 57 Thistle Avenue, Grangemouth; T.-Grangemouth 486468.

McKellar, Kenneth, BSc. Singer, Composer, Writer; b. 23.6.27, Paisley; m., Hedy Matisse; 1 s.; 1 d. Educ. John Neilson Grammar School, Paisley; Aberdeen University. Gave first concert in a local hall, aged 13; continued singing while at school, university and during his first two years working in forestry; has made numerous records of classical and popular music; numerous tours, especially in Australia and New Zealand; has appeared a number of times at the London Palladium; made the sound track for the film The Great Waltz; TV work includes Night Music, The Rolf Harris Show, The Good Old Days, At Home with Kenneth McKellar; a Director, Radio Clyde. Recreations: cooking; reading; motor-cycling.

McKelvey, William. MP (Labour), Kilmarnock and Loudoun, since 1979; b. 1934. Educ. Dundee. Former Labour Group Leader, Dundee District Council; former full-time Labour Party and union official.

McKelvie, Campbell John, BSc (Hons), ARCST, FBIM, MICE, MIBM, CEng. Director of Building and Works, Strathclyde Region; b. 1.2.32, Tarbert, Argyll; m., Rhona Paton Smith; 2 s. Educ. Marr College, Troon; Glasgow University; Royal College of Science and Technology. Private sector, 1955-75; Senior Depute Head of Direct Works, Strathclyde Region, 1975-79. Recreations: golf; curling; bridge. Address: (b.) Philip Murray Road, Bellshill, Lanarkshire; T.-Bellshill 749121.

Mackenzie, A(lexander) Graham, MA, ALA. Librarian, St. Andrews University, since 1976; b. 4.12.28, Glasgow; m., E. Astrid MacKinven; 1 s.;

1 d. Educ. Hutchesons' Boys' Grammar School; Glasgow University. Keeper of Science Books, Durham University Library, 1952-60; Sub-Librarian, Nottingham University Library, 1960-61; Deputy Librarian, Brotherton Library, Leeds University, 1961-63; Librarian, Lancaster University, 1963-76, and Director, Library Research Unit, 1970-76. Honorary Treasurer, SCONUL, since 1982. Recreations: golf; Scottish country dancing; baroque music; sailing. Address: (b.) University Library, North Street, St. Andrews, Fife, KY16 9TR; T.-0334 76161.

MacKenzie, Angus Alexander, CA. Chartered Accountant, since 1955; b. 1.3.31, Nairn; m., Catherine; 1 d. Educ. Inverness Royal Academy; Edinburgh University. National Service, RAF, 1955-57; in private practice as CA Assistant in Edinburgh, 1957-59, Inverness, 1959-61; commenced in practice on own account, 1961; Chairman, Highland Group, Riding for the Disabled Association; Director, PLM Helicopters Ltd.; Local Director, Eagle Star Insurance Co. Recreations: shooting; stalking; hill-walking; gardening. Address: (h.) Tigh an Allt, Tomatin, Inverness-shire; T.-Tomatin 270.

Mackenzie, Major Colin Dalzell, MBE, MC, DL. Vice Lieutenant, Inverness-shire, since 1986; b. 23.3.19, Fawley; m., Lady Anne Fitzroy; 1 s.; 3 d. Educ. Eton; RMC, Sandhurst. Page of Honour to King George V, 1932-36; joined Seaforth Highlanders, 1939; ADC to Viceroy of India, 1945-46; Deputy Military Secretary to Viceroy of India, 1946-47; retired, 1949; TA, 1950-56; Inverness County Council, 1949-52; Director, various companies. Recreation: fishing. Address: (h.) Farr House, Inverness, IV1 2XB; T.-Farr 202.

Mackenzie, Colin Scott, DL, BL, NP. Procurator Fiscal, Stornoway, since 1969; Director, Harris Tweed Association Ltd., since 1979; Vice Lord Lieutenant of Islands Area, Western Isles, since 1984; b. 7.7.38, Stornoway; m., Christeen E.D. MacLauchlan. Educ. Nicolson Institute; Fettes College; Edinburgh University. Burgh Prosecutor, Stornoway, 1971-75; JP Fiscal, 1971-75; Deputy Lieutenant and Clerk to Lieutenancy of the Western Isles, 1975; Founder President, Stornoway Flying Club, 1970; Founding Dean, Western Isles Faculty of Solicitors; elected Council Member, Law Society of Scotland, 1985; author of article on Lieutenancy, Stair Memorial Encyclopaedia of Law of Scotland, 1987; President, Stornoway Rotary Club, 1977; Chairman, Lewis Pipe Band, since 1978. Recreation: fishing. Address: (h.) Park House, Matheson Road, Stornoway, Lewis; T.-Stornoway 2008.

Mackenzie, David Chalmers, OBE, BSc (Hons). Headmaster, Falkirk High School, since 1971; b. 1.3.28, Aberdeen; m., E. Finlay; 2 d. Educ. Queen's Park School, Glasgow; Glasgow University. Teacher of Chemistry and Physics, High School of Glasgow, 1952-63; Head of Chemistry and Depute Headmaster, George Heriot's School, Edinburgh, 1963-71; Chairman, Board of Governors, Moray House College of Education, 1977-87; Member: Heriot-Watt University Convocation; Council, Falkirk College of Technology; Trustee and Vice Chairman, Scottish Secondary Schools Travel Trust; Chairman, Central Region Committee, British Heart Foundation; President, Falkirk Burns Club; Past President, Falkirk Rotary Club. Recreations: gardening; bowling; travel. Address: (b.) Falkirk High School, Blinkbonny Road, Falkirk, FK1 5BZ; T.-0324 29511.

Mackenzie, Rev. Gordon Ross, BSc, BD. Minister, Monikie and Newbigging, since 1985; b. 8.1.48, Nairn; m., Sheila Macrae Davis; 1 d. Educ. Nairn Academy; Aberdeen University; Glasgow University. Agricultural Adviser, North of Scotland College of Agriculture (Uist and Barra), 1969-72; divinity student, 1972-75; postgraduate studies, Union Theological Seminary, Virginia, USA, 1975-76; Assistant Minister, Chryston, Glasgow, 1976-77; Minister, Kirkmichael and Tomintoul, 1977-85. Recreations: music; gardening. Address: 59B Broomwell Gardens, Monikie, Dundee, DD5 3QP; T.-Newbigging 200.

MacKenzie, Hugh D., MA (Hons), FEIS, JP. Headteacher, Craigroyston Community High School, since 1972; Director, Craigroyston Curriculum Project, since 1980; b. 29.5.33, Edinburgh; m., Helen Joyce; 1 s.; 1 d. Educ. Royal High School; Edinburgh University; Moray House College of Education, Edinburgh. Education Officer, RAF, 1956-58; Assistant Teacher, Niddrie Marischal Junior Secondary School and Falkirk High School, 1958-62; Principal Teacher: Broxburn Academy, 1962-64, Liberton High School, 1964-70; Deputy Headteacher, Craigmount High School, 1970-72; Scottish Representative, Northern Regional Examination Board, 1973-88; Vice-Chairman, Lothian Regional Consultative Committee, 1984-87; a Director, Royal Lyceum Theatre, Edinburgh, since 1985, Scottish Community Education Council, 1985-88; President, Royal High School Rugby Club; President and Founder Member, Edinburgh Golden Oldies Rugby Club. Recreations: rugby; squash; golf; ornithology; philately; jazz. Address: (h.) 26 Coltbridge Terrace, Edinburgh.

MacKenzie, Ian Kenneth, JP. Chairman, Red Deer Commission, since 1984; Chairman, Highlands and Islands Development Consultative Council, since 1988; Landowner, since 1968; b. 1.3.31, Nairn; m., Margaret Vera Matheson; 2 s.; 2 d. Educ. Inverness Royal Academy. Member, Scottish Agricultural Consultative Panel; Member, Secretary of State's Panel of Arbiters; Director, Royal Highland and Agricultural Society of Scotland, 1980-84. Recreation: field sports. Address: Culblain, 46 Southside Road, Inverness, IV2 4XA; T.-0463 231894.

Mackenzie, Rev. Ian Murdo. Head of Religious Programmes, BBC Scotland, since 1973; b. 3.8.31, Fraserburgh; m., Elizabeth; 1 s.; 1 d. Educ. Fettes College; Edinburgh University. Assistant Organist, St. Giles Cathedral, 1952-60; Editor, Student, Sooth and Breakthrough; Assistant Minister, St. Giles, 1960-62; Assistant General Secretary, Student Christian Movement, 1963-64; Religious Advisor, ABC Television, 1964-67; Executive Producer, Religious Programmes, ABC TV, 1967-68; Executive Producer: From Inner Space, 1966, Don't Just Sit There and Pilgrim's Progress, 1967, The Lion, the Witch, and the Wardrobe, Question 68, and Looking for an Answer, 1968; Executive Producer, Roundhouse, LWT, 1969; Presenter, For Christ's Sake, Grampian TV, 1972; BBC: Series Producer, City of God, Radio Scotland, 1981, Eighth Day and the Yes, No, Don't Know Show, 1975-77, Voyager and Glory Be, 1982-84, Presenter, Angles, 1981, Writer and Presenter, Gates to Space, 1982, Editor, Coast to Coast, 1977. Chairman, Scottish Religious Panel, IBA, 1970-72; Minister, Peterhead Old Parish Church, 1969-73. Publication: Vision and Belief, 1968. Recreations: improvising on the pipe organ and piano; theology; reading newspapers and other fiction; drawing excruciatingly bad cartoons. Address: (h.) 1 Glenan Gardens, Helensburgh, Dunbartonshire.

MacKenzie, James Alexander Mackintosh, FEng, FICE, FIHT. Chief Road Engineer, Scottish Development Department, since 1976; b. 6.5.28, Inverness; m., Pamela D. Nixon; 1 s.; 1 d. Educ. Inverness Royal Academy. Miscellaneous local government appointments, 1950-63; Chief Resident Engineer, Durham County Council, 1963-67; Deputy Director, North Eastern Road Construction Unit, Department of Transport, 1967-71 (Director, 1971-76). Recreations: golf; fishing. Address: (h.) 2 Dean Park, Longniddry, East Lothian, EH32 OQR; T.-Longniddry 52643.

Mackenzie, Rt. Hon. (James) Gregor, PC, JP. MP (Labour), Rutherglen, 1964-87; b. 15.11.27, Glasgow; m., Joan Swan Provan; 1 s.; 1 d. Educ. Queens Park School; Glasgow University; Royal Technical College, Glasgow. Member and Magistrate, Glasgow Corporation, 1952-64; PPS to Rt. Hon. James Callaghan, MP, 1965-70; Shadow Minister for Post and Telecommunications, 1970-74; Under Secretary of State for Industry, 1974-75; Minister of State for Industry, 1975-76; Minister of State for Scotland, 1976-79; Member, Committee of Privileges, House of Commons, 1984-87. Address: 3/2 Nether Craigwell, Edinburgh, EH8 8DR; T.-031-557 5378.

Mackenzie, Keith Roderick Turing, OBE, MC. President, The Golf Foundation; b. 19.1.21, Lucknow, India; m., Barbara Kershaw; 2 s.; 2 d. Educ. Uppingham School; Royal Military College, Sandhurst. 2nd Bn., 6th Gurhka Rifles, 1940-47 (retired Major, 1947); Burmah-Shell Oil Storage and Distributing Co., India, 1947-65; Shell Rhodesia, 1965-66; Secretary, Royal and Ancient Golf Club of St. Andrews, 1967-83. Recreations: golf; gardening. Address: (h.) Easter Edenhill, Kennedy Gardens, St. Andrews; T.-0334 73581.

MacKenzie, Kenneth John, MA, AM. Under Secretary and Principal Finance Officer, Scottish Office, since 1985; b. 1.5.43, Glasgow; m., Irene Mary Hogarth; 1 s.; 1 d. Educ. Birkenhead School; Pembroke College, Oxford; Stanford University, California. Assistant Principal, Scottish Home and Health Department; Principal, Scottish Education Department; Principal Private Secretary to Secretary of State for Scotland; Assistant Secretary, Scottish Economic Planning Department and Scottish Office Finance Division. Session Clerk, St. Cuthbert's Parish Church, Edinburgh; Past President, Edinburgh Civil Service Dramatic Society. Address: (b.) New St. Andrews House, Edinburgh.

MacKenzie, Malcolm Lackie, MA (Hons), MEd. Senior Lecturer in Education, Glasgow University; Vice-Chairman, Scottish Tory Reform Group, since 1988; b. 5.7.38, Clydebank. Educ. Clydebank High School; Glasgow University. Assistant Teacher of English and History, Bearsden Academy, 1961-64; Lecturer in Education, Jordanhill College of Education, 1964-67; joined Department of Education, Glasgow University, 1967; Member, Council of Management, British Educational Administration Society, 1972-76; Member, Working Party set up by CCC on Communication and Implementation of Aims in Secondary Education, 1972-74; Past Chairman, Scottish Association for Educational Management and Administration; Member, Working Party on Educational Policy-making, Administration and Management, Council for Educational Technology for UK, 1974-77; Member, Scottish Central Committee on English, 1978-80; Co-Director, Scottish Schools Councils Research Project, 1976-80; Member, National Advisory Committee on Education, Conservative Party, 1962-82. Address: (h.) 64 Polwarth Street, Hyndland, Glasgow, G12 9TL; T.-041-357 2038.

MacKenzie, Mary, MBE, TD. Member, Grampian Area Health Board, 1981- 85; Member, Industrial Tribunal Panel, 1974-87; Member, National Advisory Council on the Employment of Disabled People, since 1977; Chairman, Grampian Committee for the Employment of Disabled People, since 1981; b. 14.2.18, Rochester, Kent; m., J. Strath MacKenzie; 2 s. Educ. Grammar School for Girls, Rochester; London College of Secretaries. Service in ATS, 1938-46, with rank of Chief Commander (Lt.-Col.); service in WRAC/TA, 1957-63, with rank of Major; Chairman, Aberdeen-Kincardine Disablement Advisory Committee, 1969-81; Member, Royal Cornhill and Associate Hospitals Board of Management, 1964-74; President, SSAFA (Aberdeen); Vice-Chairman, Tenovus (Grampian). Address: (h.) Rynie, Bieldside, Aberdeen, AB1 9AA; T.-0224 867423.

McKenzie, Rev. Morris Glyndwr, BA, LLB. Barrister and Solicitor, Supreme Court of New Zealand; Minister, South Ronaldsay and Burray, since 1978; b. 10.2.28, Invercargill, New Zealand; m., Janette Zena Lewis. Educ. John McGlashan College, Dunedin, New Zealand; Victoria University College, Wellington, New Zealand; University of Otago, Dunedin, New Zealand; St. Mary's College, St. Andrews. New Zealand: Ministry of Social Security, 1947-48, Ministry of Labour, 1948-55, Ministry of Works, 1956-74, District Solicitor, Ministry of Works, Dunedin, 1965-71, District Solicitor, Ministry of Works, Auckland, 1971-74; student, 1974-76; Assistant Minister, St. James, Forfar, 1976-77. Moderator, Orkney Presbytery, 1983-84. Recreations: walking; cycling; travel; reading; music; wine making. Address: Manse of South Ronaldsay and Burray, St. Margaret's Hope, Orkney; T.-St. Margaret's Hope 288.

Mackenzie, Rev. Robert Kenneth, MA, BD, PhD. Minister, Brechin Cathedral, since 1986; b. 13.2.50, Madras; m., Susan R.C. Clinton; 3 d.

Educ. George Watson's College; Edinburgh University. Minister, Creich and Rosehall, Sutherland, 1980-86. Address: (b.) Brechin Cathedral, Brechin, Angus; T.-03562 2783.

McKenzie, Ronald Walker, LLB, NP. Solicitor and Notary Public, since 1974; Temporary Sheriff, since 1987; b. 17.1.49, Dundee; m., Deirdre Mary Fraser; 1 s.; 2 d. Educ. Grove Academy; Dundee High School; Edinburgh University. Elected Member, Council, Law Society of Scotland, 1983; former Convenor, Complaints Committee; present Convenor, Legal Aid Committee; Convenor, Library Committee, Kirkcaldy Law Society. Recreations: rugby football; tennis; restoration of classic and vintage motor cars and cycles. Address: (h.) Old Schoolhouse, Auchtertool, Fife; T.-0592 780391.

Mackenzie, Stuart D., DPE, DYCS, DMS, MBA. Director of Leisure and Recreation, Stirling District Council, since 1982; b. 14.8.46, Glasgow; m., Anita. Educ. Eastbank Academy, Glasgow; Jordanhill College of Education; Glasgow College of Technology; Strathclyde University. Activities Organiser, Scottish Association of Boys Clubs, 1968-70; Area Organiser, Glasgow Education Department, 1970-72; Lecturer, Jordanhill College, 1972-77; Depute Director of Leisure and Recreation, Cunninghame District Council, 1977-82. Executive Committee: Scottish Sports Association for the Disabled, 1975-82, Association of Directors of Leisure, Recreation and Tourism, since 1982. Recreations: squash; video filming; driving. Address: (b.) Beechwood House, St. Ninians Road, Stirling, FK8 2AD; T.-Stirling 79000, Ext. 337.

McKenzie, Rev. William Moncur, DA. Minister, Laurieknowe Troqueer Parish Church, Dumfries, since 1977; b. 30.12.28, Glasgow; m., Margaret Semple Scott; 1 s.; 2 d. Educ. King's Park Secondary School, Glasgow; Glasgow School of Art; Jordanhill Teacher Training College; Trinity College, Glasgow; St. Colm's Missionary College, Edinburgh. Art Teacher in Glasgow, 1951-55; ordained Minister, 1958; Assistant, St. Mary's, Govan; District Missionary, Lubwa, Northern Rhodesia, Livingstonia Mission, Church of Scotland, 1959-65; integrated into United Church of Zambia, 1965; transferred to Kashinda, Mporokoso, 1968, for lay training and Bible translation; left Zambia, 1977. Chaplain, HM Prison, Dumfries, since 1983, ICI Dumfries, since 1978; Secretary/Exegete for Chibemba Bible, Zambia (published, 1983); Committee Member, National Bible Society of Scotland, since 1978. Recreations: walking; camping; gardening. Address: The Manse, Troqueer Road, Dumfries, DG2 7DF; T.-0387 53043.

Mackenzie, William Roderick Simon, ARICS. Member, North East Fife District Council, since 1984; President, Zoological Society of Glasgow and West of Scotland; Chairman, St. Andrews and North East Fife Tourist Board, since 1985; Vice-Chairman, Fife Marriage Counselling Service; b. 2.3.30, Glasgow; m., Margaret Borland Maclachlan; 2 s.; 1 d. Educ. Pollokshields Senior Secondary School, Glasgow; Royal College of Science and Technology, Glasgow. Assistant Quantity Surveyor, Muirhead, Muir & Webster, Glasgow, 1948-64; Quantity Surveyor, Cumbernauld New Town Development Corporation, 1964-69; Senior Quantity Surveyor, Fife County Council, 1969-74; Buildings Office, Dundee University, since 1974. Recreations: writing plays; amateur dramatics; gardening; visiting zoos. Address: (h.) 3 Tarvit Gardens, Cupar, Fife, KY15 5BT; T.-Cupar 52660.

Mackenzie-Robinson, Mhairi Philippa, BA (Hons). Administrator, Edinburgh Festival Fringe, since 1986; b. 10.9.59, Edinburgh. Educ. St. Margaret's School for Girls, Edinburgh; Durham University. Associate Administrator, Edinburgh Festival Fringe, 1982-86. Address: (b.) Fringe Office, 180 High Street, Edinburgh, EH1 1QS; T.-031-226 5257/9.

McKenzie Smith, Ian, RSA, RSW, FRSA, FSS, FMA, FSA (Scot). Director, Aberdeen Art Gallery and Museums, since 1968; b. 3.8.35, Montrose; m., Mary Rodger Fotheringham; 2 s.; 1 d. Educ. Robert Gordon's College, Aberdeen; Grays School of Art, Aberdeen; Hospitalfield College of Art, Arbroath. Teacher of Art, Fife, 1960-63; Education Officer, Council of Industrial Design, Scottish Committee, 1963-68. Member, Scottish Arts Council and Chairman, Art Committee; Executive Committee, Scottish Museums Council; Governor, Edinburgh College of Art; Board Member: Aberdeen Artists Society, Aberdeen Hospitals Art Project, Aberdeen Maritime Museum's Appeal Committee, Aberdeen University Music Committee, Friends of Aberdeen Art Gallery and Museums, Friends of Royal Scottish Academy, National Heritage Scottish Group, Scottish Sculpture Workshop, Scottish Society of Artists, Workshop and Studio Provision, Scotland. Address: (h.) 70 Hamilton Place, Aberdeen, AB2 4BA; T.-0224 644531.

McKeown, Charles. Chairman, Industrial Development Committee, Central Regional Council; Chairman, Board of Directors, Stirling Enterprise Park; b. 27.3.30, Bannockburn; m., Anna Tortolano; 1 s.; 2 d. Educ. St. Modan's High School, Stirling. Engineering apprenticeship, 1945-50 (interrupted by National Service, 1948-50); Henry Ford Co., Detroit, 1955-57. District Councillor, Fallin, Stirling, 1972-73; County Councillor, Bannockburn, 1973-74; Regional Councillor, since 1974. Chairman, Stirlingshire Educational Trust. Recreations: reading; snooker; golf. Address: (h.) 1 Gillespie Place, Whins of Milton, Stirling; T.-0786 812776.

McKichan, Duncan James, BL. Solicitor; Partner, Maclay Murray & Spens, since 1952; Honorary Consul for Canada; Dean, Royal Faculty of Procurators in Glasgow, 1983-86; b. 28.7.24, Wallington, Surrey; m, Leila Campbell Fraser; 2 d. Educ. George Watson's College, Edinburgh; Solihull School; Downing College, Cambridge; Glasgow University. Royal Navy, 1943-46; qualified as Solicitor, 1950. Recreations: gardening; walking; sailing; skiing. Address: (h.) Invermay, Queen Street, Helensburgh; T.-0436 4778.

MacKie, Professor Rona McLeod, MD, FRCP, FRCPGlas, FRCPLond, FRCPath, FRSE. Professor of Dermatology, Glasgow University, since 1973; Honorary Consultant Dermatologist, Greater Glasgow Health Board, since 1978; b. 22.5.40, Dundee; m., Dr. Euan MacKie; 1 s.; 1 d. Educ. Laurelbank School, Glasgow; Glasgow University. Registrar, Department of Dermatology, Western Infirmary, Glasgow, 1970-71; Lecturer in Dermatology, Glasgow University, 1971-72; Consultant Dermatologist, Greater Glasgow Health Board, 1972-78. Recreation: skiing. Address: Department of Dermatology, Glasgow University, Glasgow, G11 6NU; T.-041-339 8855, Ext. 4006.

McKillop, George Armstrong, JP. Provost, East Kilbride District Council, since 1984; Chairman, East Kilbride Sports Council, since 1982; Member, East Kilbride Development Corporation, since 1985; b. 22.3.32, Bellshill; m., Susan; 1 s.; 1 d. Educ. Greenfield Secondary School, Hamilton. Elected to East Kilbride District Council, 1979; Deputy Provost, 1980-84; Chairman, Recreation and Leisure Services Committee, 1980-84. Recreations: reading; local history; bowling. Address: (h.) 30 Laurenstone Terrace, East Kilbride, G74 3BU; T.-East Kilbride 26221.

McKillop, James Hugh, BSc, MB, ChB, PhD, FRCP. Senior Lecturer in Medicine, Glasgow University, since 1982; Honorary Consultant Physician, Glasgow Royal Infirmary, since 1982; b. 20.6.48, Glasgow; m., Caroline A. Oakley; 2 d. Educ. St. Aloysius' College, Glasgow; Glasgow University. House Officer posts, Glasgow Royal Infirmary, Western Infirmary and Royal Hospital for Sick Children, Glasgow, 1972-74; Hall Fellow in Medicine, then Lecturer in Medicine, Glasgow University, 1974-82; Postdoctoral Fellow, Stanford University Medical Center, California, 1979 and 1980. Watson Prize Lectureship, Royal College of Physicians and Surgeons of Glasgow, 1979; Harkness Fellowship, Commonwealth Fund of New York, 1979-80; Robert Reid Newall Award, Stanford University, 1980; Honorary Treasurer, Scottish Society of Experimental Medicine, 1982-87; Honorary Secretary, British Nuclear Cardiology Group, 1982-87; Symposium Editor, Scottish Medical Journal, since 1984; Council Member, British Nuclear Medicine Society, since 1985 (Hon. Secretary, since 1988). Recreations: music (especially opera); history. Address: (h.) 10 Kirklee Circus, Glasgow, G12 OTW; T.-041-339 7000.

McKinlay, Professor David Gemmell, BSc, PhD, ARCST, CEng, FICE, FASCE, FGS, FRSE. Professor Emeritus, Strathclyde University; Geotechnical Consultant; b. 23.8.24, Glasgow; m., Muriel Lees Donaldson; 1 s.; 1 d. Educ. Allan Glen's School, Glasgow; Royal Technical College, Glasgow; Glasgow University. War Service, commissioned RNVR; County Engineer's staff, Dumfries County; civil engineering consultancy; teaching and research, Royal College of Science and Technology, then Strathclyde University. Member, Subsidence Compensation Review Committee, 1984; Council Member, Institution of Civil Engineers, 1979-82, 1983-86; Chairman, Ground Engineering Group Board, 1981-86; Governor, Rotary International District 123, 1987-88. Recreations: estate development; freshwater fishing; travel. Address: (h.) Spylawbank, Burn Road, Darvel, KA17 ODB; T.-0560 22552.

McKinlay, J.T., BSc, CEng, FIMechE. Controller, Computer Aided Engineering, National Engineering Laboratory, since 1984; b. 12.11.39, Glasgow; m., Aileen Watson; 1 s.; 1 d. Educ. Allan Glen's School; Glasgow University. Development Engineer, ICI, Wilton, 1961-63; Design Engineer, British Hydrocarbon Chemicals, Grangemouth, 1963-65; R. & D. in Computer-Aided Design, then Computer Manager, NEL, 1965-75; Computing Industry Sponsorship, then Personal Assistant to Chief Scientist, Department of Industry, London, 1975-78; Chief Executive, Textiles and Other Manufactures Requirements Board, DTI, London, 1978-84. Recreations: gardening; watching rugby; collecting Scotch miniatures. Address: (b.) National Engineering Laboratory, East Kilbride, Glasgow, G75 OQU; T.-035 52 20222.

McKinlay, John William, FIB (Scot). General Manager, Financial Services, Clydesdale Bank PLC, since 1988; b. 1.2.32, Bonhill; m., Betsy Stevenson McNaught; 2 s. Educ. Vale of Leven Academy. Joined Clydesdale Bank, 1948; clerical and junior management posts, 1948-68; Manager, Laurieston, Glasgow, 1968-71, Paisley Road and Scotland Street, 1972; Superintendent of Branches, 1973-75; General Manager's Assistant, 1976-78; Assistant General Manager, 1979-85; General Manager (Administration), 1986; Director, Central Services, 1987; Director, Clydesdale Bank Finance Corporation Ltd., Clydesdale Bank Equity Ltd., Scottish Computer Services Ltd. Member, Council, Institute of Bankers in Scotland; Member of Council, Association for Payment Clearing Services; Director, EFTPOS UK Ltd. Recreation: golf. Address: (b.) 30 St. Vincent Place, Glasgow, G1 2HL; T.-041-248 7070.

McKinney, Alan. National Organiser and Headquarters Director, Scottish National Party, since 1982; b. 16.10.41, Glasgow; m., Elma; 1 s.; 1 d. Educ. Brechin High School. Time-served refrigeration engineer before entering politics full-time as National Organiser, SNP, 1977; former Election Agent, Dundee East; former elected Member, NEC. Played football for Brechin City. Recreation: golf. Address: (b.) Scottish National Party, 6 North Charlotte Street, Edinburgh; T.-031-226 3661.

McKinney, Robert, BSc (Hons), FIIM. Principal, Ayr College, since 1982; b. 17.9.34, Motherwell; m., Elizabeth Jane Newlands; 1 s. Educ. Dalziel High School, Motherwell; Strathclyde University. Head, Department of Science, Thurso Technical College; Head, Department of Science, then Depute Principal, Reid Kerr College. Recreations: curling; bowls; golf. Address: (h.) 34 Greenan Road, Doonfoot, Ayr; T.-0292 45331.

McKinnon, David Douglas, BSc, FFA, FIMA. Director, General Manager and Actuary, Scottish Mutual Assurance Society, since 1982; b. 18.7.26, Larbert; m., Edith June Kyles; 1 s.; 2 d. Educ. High School of Stirling; Glasgow University. Faculty of Actuaries: Fellow, since 1951, President, 1979-81; Chairman, Associated Scottish Life Offices, 1988. Vice Chairman, Church of Scotland

Trust, since 1984. Recreations: golf; gardening. Address: (h.) 4 Carronvale Road, Larbert, Stirlingshire; T.-0324 562373.

Mackinnon, Rev. Duncan. Minister, Plockton and Kyle, since 1973; b. 21.2.24, Tarbert, Haris; m., Marion Macdonald; 1 s.; 1 d. Educ. Tarbert (Harris) Junior Secondary School; Portree High School; Aberdeen University and Christ's College. Merchant Navy, 1942-47 (War Service); Minister: Snizort North Church, Isle of Skye, 1956-65, Ness, Isle of Lewis, 1965-73. Recreations: gardening; fishing; joinery. Address: The Manse, Kyle of Lochalsh, Ross-shire, IV40 8DA; T.-0599 4294.

MacKinnon, Major John Farquhar, MC, DL, JP; b. 27.1.18, Melbourne; m., Sheila Pearce (deceased); 1 s.; 1 d. (deceased); 2, Mrs Anne Swann. Educ. Geelong, Australia; Corpus Christi College, Cambridge (MA). Army, Queen's Own Cameron Highlanders, 1939-46 (Major); twice wounded; Middle East, 1940-41; ADC, Governor General, Union of South Africa, 1942; Staff, UK, 1943-46 (left service due to wounds); Staff, 152 Highland Infantry Brigade (TA), 1949-54; ICI Ltd., Agricultural Division, 1949-73 (Area Manager, London and Cambridge; Regional Manager, Southern England). Secretary, British Field Sports Society, Berwickshire, 1974-80; Elder, Kirk of Lammermuir; Deputy Lieutenant, Berwickshire, since 1987. Recreations: shooting; fishing. Address: (h.) Craigie Lodge, Longformacus, by Duns, Berwickshire; T.-Longformacus 251.

MacKinnon, Lachlan, BL, DPA, FBIM. Chief Executive Officer, Dumbarton District Council, since 1975; b. 9.1.28, Glasgow; m., Rhoda; 2 s.; 2 d. Educ. Stirling High School; Glasgow University. Legal Assistant: Midlothian County Council, 1951-52, Hamilton Town Council, 1952-54; Depute Town Clerk: Rutherglen Town Council, 1954-57, Clydebank Town Council, 1957-67; Town Clerk, Dumbarton Town Council, 1967-75. Honorary Secretary: Dumbarton Senior Citizens Committee, Local Committee of Scottish Veterans' Garden City Association, Dumbarton District Posts and Telecommunications Advisory Committee. Recreations: curling; hill-walking; reading. Address: (b.) Crosslet House, Argyll Avenue, Dumbarton; T.-Dumbarton 65100.

MacKinnon, Niall I., MA (Hons), DipEd. Head Teacher, Braidfield High School, Clydebank, since 1985; b. 6.4.39, Daliburgh, South Uist; m., Eileen; 2 s.; 2 d. Educ. Portree High School; Glasgow University. Teacher, Hillhead High School, 1962-69; Principal Teacher of Classics, Hermitage Academy, 1969-76; Assistant Head Teacher, then Depute Head Teacher, Vale of Leven Academy, 1976-85. Publication: Discovering the Greeks (Co-author), 1977. Recreations: golf; bridge. Address: (b.) Braidfield High School, Queen Mary Avenue, Clydebank, G81 2LR; T.-041-952 3265.

Mackinnon, Roderick. Member, Western Isles Islands Council, since 1986; b. 9.8.28, Castlebay, Isle of Barra; m., Katie-Ann Haggerty-MacKinnon; 1 s.; 1 d. Educ. Castlebay Secondary School; Liverpool College of Technology. Entered Merchant Navy, 1946; qualified as foreign-going Master Mariner, 1961; first command, 1966; became oil marketing executive, 1968; retired, 1983. Honorary Agent: Royal Alfred Seafarers' Society, The Sailors' Children's Society; Deputy Launching Authority, RNLI Castlebay Station. Recreations: fishing; sailing; writing; community work. Address: (h.) 139 Brevig, Castlebay, Isle of Barra, PA80 5UN; T.-Castlebay 242.

MacKinnon, Rev. Roderick MacLean, LTh. Minister, Kilmuir and Logie Easter, since 1981; Clerk, Synod of Ross, Sutherland and Caithness, since 1982; b. 28.3.28, Bunavoneadar, Harris; m., Margaret Smith Robertson; 1 s.; 1 d. Educ. Sir Edward Scott School, Tarbert, Harris; Glasgow University and Trinity College. Lay Missionary, Tiree, 1957-62; Student Assistant, St. Columba, Copland Road, 1962-67; ordained and inducted to Daliburgh, South Uist, 1968; Minister, South Uist, 1978; Member, Committee on Priorities of Mission, General Assembly, 1970-72; Member, Home Board, General Assembly, 1974-81; General Trustee, Church of Scotland, since 1978; Clerk, Uist Presbytery, 1970-81; Chairman, Uist Council of Social Service, 1971-73; Member, Western Isles Islands Council, 1974-81 (Chairman, Social Work Committee, 1978-81); Member, Electricity Consultative Council for North of Scotland, 1977-81, since 1987; Member, Scottish Religious Advisory Committee, BBC, since 1977. Recreation: gardening. Address: The Manse, Delny, Invergordon, Ross-shire; T.-086 284 2280.

Mackintosh, Rev. Aeneas. Information Officer and Communication Adviser, Scottish Episcopal Church (Rector, St. Baldred's, North Berwick, and St. Adrian's, Gullane, 1981-87; Canon, St. Mary's Cathedral, Edinburgh, 1975-87); Senior Tutor, Diocese of Edinburgh, since 1974; b. 1.7.27, Inverness; m., Eileen Mary Barlow; 4 s. Educ. Inverness Royal Academy; Kelham Theological College. Precentor, St. Andrew's Cathedral, Inverness, 1952-55; Curate, St. Augustine's, Wisbech, 1955-57; Rector: St. Matthew, Possilpark, 1957-61, Holy Trinity, Haddington, 1961-65; Town Councillor, Haddington, 1962-65; Diocesan Inspector of Church Schools, 1963; Team Priest, St. John's, Princes Street, Edinburgh, 1965-69, and Rector, St. John's, 1969-81. Address: 31 St. Albans Road, Edinburgh, EH9.

Mackintosh of Mackintosh, Lachlan Ronald Duncan, OBE, JP. 30th Chief of Clan Mackintosh, since 1957; Lord Lieutenant of Inverness, Lochaber, Badenoch and Strathspey, since 1985; Member, Highland Regional Council, since 1974; b. 27.6.28, Camberley; m., Mabel Cecilia Helen ("Celia") Bruce; 1 s.; 2 d.; 1 d. deceased. Educ. R.N. College, Dartmouth. Seaman Officer, Specialist in Communications, Royal Navy, retiring as Lt.-Cdr., 1963; Chairman, Highland Exhibitions Ltd., 1964-85; Vice President, Scottish Conservative and Unionist Association, 1969-71; Member, Inverness County Council, 1970-75; Chairman, Inverness Prison Visiting Committee, 1973-86. Address: Moy Hall, Tomatin, Inverness, IV13 7YQ; T.-Tomatin 211.

Mackintosh, Peter, MIEDO, FInstP. Director of Development, Highland Regional Council, since 1980; b. 7.6.39, Nairn; m., Una; 2 s. Educ. Roses Academic Institute, Nairn. Architectural Assistant: Inverness County Council, 1958-60, Fife

County Council, 1960-62; Ross and Cromarty County Council: Senior Architectural Assistant, 1962-72, Assistant Development Officer, 1972-75; Highland Regional Council: Divisional Development Officer, 1975-78, Assistant Director of Development, 1978-80. Recreations: golf; tennis; photography; walking; gardening; music. Address: (b.) Regional Buildings, Glenurquhart Road, Inverness, IV3 5NX; T.-0463 234121.

Maclachlan, Alistair Andrew Duncan, BA (Hons). Rector, Forres Academy, since 1982; b. 14.3.46, Perth; m., Alison M.S. Love; 2 s. Educ. Perth Academy; Strathclyde University. Teacher in various schools, 1969-71; Principal Teacher of Economics and Business Studies, 1971-74; Assistant Rector, Keith Grammar School, 1974-78; Depute Rector, Elgin High School, 1978-82. Secretary and Treasurer, Keith Agricultural Show, 1972-82; Chairman, Elgin Squash Club, since 1982. Recreations: keeping fit; squash; reading; music. Address: (h.) 82 Duncan Drive, Elgin, Moray, IV30 2NH; T.-Elgin 2193.

Maclagan, Rev. David Willox, MA (Cantab), EdB, ThD, FPRS. Minister, St. John's Parish Church, Largs, since 1972; b. 26.1.31, Port Glasgow; m., Amelia Muirhead; 2 d. Educ. Battersea Grammar School; St. Catharine's College, Cambridge; Glasgow University. Teacher of History, King Edward VI School, Stourbridge; Principal Teacher of History, Shebbear College, North Devon; Minister, Moncreiff Parish Church, East Kilbride. Address: (h.) Flat C, Vanduara, 1 Greenock Road, Largs, Ayrshire; T.-0475 673258.

Maclaren, Allan, MA, PhD. Senior Lecturer in Historical Sociology and Head, Sociology Unit, Strathclyde University; b. 3.11.37, Brechin; m., Marcia Nott; 2 s. Educ. Robert Gordon's College, Aberdeen; Aberdeen University. Worked in printing and publishing industry; former Lecturer, Department of Political Economy, Aberdeen University. Main publications: Religion and Social Class, 1974; Social Class in Scotland (Editor), 1976. Recreations: yachting; photography. Address: (b.) Sociology Unit, Strathclyde University, Glasgow, G1.

McLaren, Bill, MBE (1979). Rugby Union Commentator, BBC; b. 16.10.23; m., Bette; 2 d. Educ. Hawick High School; Woolmanhill College of Physical Education, Aberdeen. Played wing forward for Hawick; had trial for Scotland but forced to withdraw because of illness; became reporter on local newspaper; first live radio broadcast, Glasgow v. Edinburgh, 1953; now main Rugby Union Commentator, BBC; Teacher of Physical Education.

McLaren, Donald Stewart, MD, PhD, DTM&H, FRCP. Reader in Clinical Nutrition, Department of Medicine, Edinburgh University, since 1980; b. 4.2.24, London; m., Olga; 1 s.; 1 d. Educ. Reigate; Edinburgh University. Medical Officer, Moorshead Memorial Hospital, India, 1949-53; Medical Research Officer, East African Institute for Medical Research, Tanzania, 1953-63; Professor of Clinical Nutrition and Director, Nutrition Research Programme, School of Medicine, American University of Beirut, Lebanon, 1962-76; President, Edinburgh Medical Missionary Society. Publications: Nutrition and its Disorders; Nutritional Ophthalmology; Textbook of Paediatric Nutrition; Nutrition in the Community; Colour Atlas of Nutritional Disorders; The Bodytone Maintenance Programme. Recreations: electronic organ; golf; American literature. Address: (b.) Department of Medicine, Royal Infirmary, Edinburgh; T.-031-229 2477, Ext. 2055.

MacLaren, Duncan A.S., BL, NP. Board Secretary, South of Scotland Electricity Board, since 1977; b. 14.5.30, Dunvegan, Isle of Skye; m., Jennifer Jackson; 1 s.; 1 d. Educ. George Watson's Boys' College, Edinburgh; Edinburgh University. Legal and other senior appointments, South of Scotland Electricity Board, 1962-72; Board Secretary, North of Scotland Hydro-Electric Board, 1972-77. Address: (b.) Cathcart House, Spean Street, Glasgow; T.-041-637 7177.

MacLaren, Duncan MacGregor, MA (Hons). Director, Scottish Catholic International Aid Fund (SCIAF), since 1986; b. 22.3.50, Dumbarton. Educ. Clydebank High School; Glasgow University. Assistant Principal, English Section, Institut auf dem Rosenberg, Switzerland, 1973-74; Researcher, Historical Dictionary of Scottish Gaelic, Glasgow University, 1974-75; Researcher, House of Commons, 1975-77; Press Officer, SNP, Edinburgh, 1977-83; Education/Promotion Officer, SCIAF, Glasgow, 1983-86. Member, Third Order of St. Dominic; Member, Roman Catholic Justice and Peace Commission. Publications: Amannan; Dialogue for Development (Editor); Focus on Peace and Justice. Recreation: relaxing in the Highlands. Address: (b.) 43 Greenhill Road, Rutherglen, Glasgow, G73 2SW; T.-041-647 2113.

MacLaren, Iain Ferguson, MB, ChB, FRCSEdin, FRCS. Consultant Surgeon, Royal Infirmary, Edinburgh, since 1974; b. 28.9.27, Edinburgh; m., Dr. Fiona Barbara Heptonstall; 1 s.; 1 d. Educ. Edinburgh Academy; Fettes College; Edinburgh University. Captain, RAMC, Egypt, 1950-52; Surgical Registrar, Royal Hospital for Sick Children, Edinburgh, 1956-58; Senior Surgical Registrar, Royal Infirmary, 1959-63 and 1964-67; Fellow in Surgical Research, Hahnemann Medical College and Hospital, Philadelphia, 1963-64; Consultant Surgeon, Deaconess Hospital, Edinburgh, 1967-85; Vice-President, Royal College of Surgeons of Edinburgh, 1983-86 (Council Member, 1977-83 and since 1987); Fellow, Royal Medical Society (Honorary Treasurer, 1979-85); Chairman, Royal Medical Society Trust, since 1985; Honorary Pipe-Major, Royal Scottish Pipers' Society, 1959-62; Honorary Secretary: Harveian Society of Edinburgh, since 1968, Aesculapian Club, since 1978. Recreations: music; the study of military history; all aspects of Scottish culture. Address: (h.) 3 Minto Street, Edinburgh, EH9 1RG; T.-031-667 3487.

McLaren, John James, MREHIS, MIEHO. Director of Technical Services, Roxburgh District Council, since 1985; b. 2.4.40, Melrose; m., Katharine Parkin; 2 s. Educ. Melrose Grammar School; Galashiels Academy; Heriot-Watt College. City of Aberdeen Council, 1961-63; Reading Borough Council, 1963-67; Goole Rural District Council, 1967-71; Burgh Surveyor, Melrose Town

Council, 1971-75; Roxburgh District Council, since 1975. Junior Vice-President, Royal Environmental Health Institute of Scotland. Recreations: walking; gardening; dry fly fishing. Address: (b.) High Street, Hawick, Roxburghshire, TD9 9EF; T.-0450 75991.

McLatchie, Cameron, OBE, LLB. Chairman and Chief Executive, Scott & Robertson PLC, since 1988; b. 18.2.47, Paisley; m., Helen Leslie Mackie; 2 s.; 1 d. Educ. Boroughmuir School, Edinburgh; Largs High School; Ardrossan Academy; Glasgow University. Whinney Murray & Co., Glasgow, 1968-70; Thomas Boag & Co. Ltd., Greenock, 1970-75; Chairman and Managing Director, Anaplast Ltd., Irvine, 1975-83; this company purchased by Scott & Robertson. Recreations: bridge; golf. Address: (b.) 96 Port Glasgow Road, Greenock; T.-0475 42381.

McLaughlin, Lord Provost Eleanor Thomson, JP. Lord Provost, City of Edinburgh, since 1988; b. Edinburgh; m., Hugh McLaughlin; 1 s.; 2 d. Former Deputy Chairman, Edinburgh District Council, and former Chairman, Housing Committee. Address: (b.) City Chambers, Edinburgh, EH1 1YJ.

MacLaverty, Bernard. Novelist and Short Story Writer; b. Belfast. Former teacher; now writes full-time. Publications: Secrets and other stories; Lamb; A Time to Dance; Cal; The Great Profundo and other stories.

McLay, James Durward, BSc, DipEd. Rector, Douglas-Ewart High School, Newton Stewart, since 1971; b. 8.1.36, Falkirk; m., Catherine May Watson; 1 s. Educ. Denny High School; Glasgow University. Taught in Glasgow, 1958-61; Principal Teacher of Geography, Douglas-Ewart High School, 1960-71. Address: (b.) Douglas-Ewart High School, Newton Stewart, DG8 6JQ; T.-0671 3773.

Maclay, Baron (Joseph Paton Maclay), 3rd Baron; Bt. Chairman and Managing Director, Milton Timber Services Ltd., since 1984; Deputy Lieutenant, Renfrewshire, since 1986; b. 11.4.42; m., Elizabeth Anne Buchanan; 2 s.; 1 d. Educ. Winchester; Sorbonne. Managing Director: Denholm Maclay Co. Ltd., 1970-83, Denholm Maclay (Offshore) Ltd., Triport Ferries (Management) Ltd., 1975-83; Deputy Managing Director, Denholm Ship Management Ltd., 1982-83; Director: Milton Shipping Co. Ltd., 1970-83, Marine Shipping Mutual Insurance Company, 1982-83, Milton Timber Services Ltd., since 1984; President, Hanover Shipping Inc., 1982-83; Director: British Steamship Short Trades Association, 1978-83, North of England Protection and Indemnity Association, 1976-83; Chairman, Scottish Branch, British Sailors Society, 1979-81; Vice-Chairman, Glasgow Shipowners & Shipbrokers Benevolent Association, 1982-83. Address: (h.) Duchal, Kilmacolm, Renfrewshire.

McLean, Allan Campbell. Author; b. 18.11.22, Walney Island; m., Margaret Elizabeth White; 2 s.; 1 d. Educ. Barrow-in-Furness Junior Technical School. Former Chairman, Scottish Council, Labour Party. Won Frederick Niven Award for The Islander (Best Scottish Novel). Recreation: football. Address: (h.) 1 Balmoral Place, Stockbridge, Edinburgh, EH3 5JA.

MacLean, Rev. Andrew Thomas, BA, BD. Chaplain, Strathclyde University, since 1985; b. 1.2.50, Abadan, Iran; m., Alison Douglas Blair; 1 s.; 1 d. Educ. Bearsden Academy; Clydebank Technical College; Stirling University; Edinburgh University. Co-operative Insurance Society, 1967-70; Partner, Janus Enterprises, 1970-72; Probationer, Loanhead, 1979-80; Minister, Aberdeen Stockethill, 1980-85. Vice Convener, Church of Scotland Board of Social Responsibility; Convener, Community Care Sectional Committee. Recreation: sound recording. Address: Chaplaincy Centre, Strathclyde University, John Street, Glasgow; T.-041-552 4400, Ext. 2442.

McLean, Angus, BL, SSC. Solicitor; Honorary Sheriff, Argyll (Dunoon); b. 26.10.12, Kilmartin, Argyll; m., Celia Jane Oliver; 1 s.; 1 d. Educ. Dunoon Grammar School; Glasgow University. Solicitor, Corrigall Ritchie & McLean, Dunoon), 1935; Royal Artillery, 1940-46: 9th/Survey Regiment, 1941-42, commissioned RA, 1942, seconded Indian Army, 1st Indian Survey Regiment, 1943, Staff Captain, Legal & DAJAG, Command HQ, 1944, Major (DAAG), 1945. Member, Council, Law Society of Scotland, 1950-74 (Vice President, 1964); President, Dunoon Business Club; President, Dunoon Rotary Club. Publications: History of Dunoon; Place Names of Cowal. Recreations: travel; gardening. Address: (h.) 21 Ravelston Dykes, Edinburgh, EH4 3JE; T.-031-332 4774.

MacLean, Charles Hector, BL, AE, DL. Consultant Solicitor, Montgomerie & Co., Glasgow, since 1983; Chairman, Association for Relief of Incurables in Glasgow and West of Scotland, since 1964; Deputy Lieutenant, County of Renfrew, since 1987; b. 9.12.13, Glasgow; m., Rachael Malcolm Hutchesson; 2 s.; 2 d. Educ. Canford School; Glasgow University. Pilot Officer, 602 Squadron Auxiliary Air Force, 1936; mobilised, 1939; severely wounded, 1940, as Flt. Commander in Battle of Britain; released in rank of Wing Commander, 1945; Partner, Montgomerie Flemings Fyfe MacLean & Co. (now Montgomerie & Co.), 1947; re-commissioned as wing Commander, RAuxAF to raise and command 3602 Fighter Control Unit. Vice President, Officers Association, Scottish Branch; Member, Committees, Earl Haig Fund Scotland and Erskine Hospital. Address: (h.) 71 Lochwinnoch Road, Kilmacolm, Renfrewshire.

Maclean, Baron (Charles Hector Fitzroy Maclean), Bt, KT (1969), GCVO (1971), KBE (1967), PC (1971), JP. 27th Chief of Clan Maclean; a Permanent Lord in Waiting, since 1984; Lord Lieutenant of Argyll, since 1954; Lieutenant, Queen's Bodyguard for Scotland (Royal Company of Archers); Life Peer; b. 5.5.16; m., Elizabeth Mann; 1 s.; 1 d. Educ. Canford School, Wimborne. Served Second World War (mentioned in Despatches); Chief Commissioner for Scotland, Boy Scouts Association, 1954-59; Chief Scout of the UK and Overseas Branches, 1959-71; Chief Scout of the Commonwealth, 1959-75; Lord Chamberlain of HM Household, 1971-84; Chancellor, Royal Victorian Order, 1971-84; Lord High Commissioner, General Assembly of the Church of Scotland, 1984, 1985; Convenor, Standing Council of Scottish Chiefs; President, Argyll T&AFA. Address: (h.) Duart Castle, Isle of Mull.

MacLean, Colin George, MA. Managing Director, Publishing, Aberdeen University Press, since 1979; b. 3.6.25, Glasgow; m., Moira Smith; 3 s. Educ. Robert Gordon's College, Aberdeen; Aberdeen University. Journalist, Glasgow Bulletin, Daily Telegraph (London), The Times (London); Editor, Times Educational Supplement Scotland, 1965-77; Vice-Chairman, National Youth Orchestra of Scotland, since 1978; President, Scottish Pre-School Playgroup Association, 1980-84; Member, Scottish Arts Council, 1980-84; Member, General Advisory Council, BBC, since 1985. Publication: The Crown & The Thistle (Editor), 1979. Recreation: television. Address: (h.) 3 Cobden Road, Newington, Edinburgh; T.-031-667 5175.

MacLean, Colin MacPhail, BA, BSc, PhD, MIBiol. Principal, Thurso Technical College, since 1983; b. 13.5.35, Glasgow; m., Jean Cameron Armstrong; 2 s. Educ. Victoria Drive School, Glasgow; Glasgow University; Strathclyde University. Member, Post Office Users Council for Scotland; Member, Scottish Advisory Committee to Office of Telecommunications; Member, Management Commitee, Scottish Congregational College; Member, Highlands and Islands Area Manpower Board. Recreations: reading; walking; eating; keeping fit. Address: (b.) Thurso Technical College, Ormlie Road, Thurso; T.-0847 66161.

McLean, David Alexander, FIB. Executive Director: Technology, TSB Scotland PLC, since 1987; b. 6.5.43; m., Linda; 1 s.; 1 d. Educ. Marr College, Troon. Assistant General Manager, then Deputy General Manager, West of Scotland TSB, 1977-83; General Manager, TSB Scotland PLC, 1983-87. Recreations: music; gardening; travel; sport. Address: (b.) Henry Duncan House, 120 George Street, Edinburgh, EH2 4TS; T.-031-225 4555.

Maclean, Sir Donald O.G., FBCO. Deputy Chairman, Scottish Conservative Party, since 1985; President, Scottish Conservative and Unionist Association, 1983-85; Ophthalmic Optician, since 1952; b. Annan; widower; 1 s.; 1 d. Educ. Morrison's Academy, Crieff; Heriot-Watt, Edinburgh. Ophthalmic Optician in Edinburgh, Newcastle, Perth and now Ayr; Chairman, Ayrshire Local Optical Committee, 1986-88; former Member, Transport Users Local Consultative Committee; Chairman, Ayr Constituency Conservative Association, 1971-75; Chairman, West of Scotland Area Council, Scottish Conservative Association, 1977-78-79; Member, National Union Executive Committee, since 1979 (Member, GP Committee, 1983-85); Elder, Church of Scotland; Past President, West Highland Steamer Club; Freeman, City of London. Recreations: photography; reading. Address: (h.) 22 Woodend Road, Alloway, Ayr.

Maclean, Donnie M., DipTechEd. Director, An Comunn Gaidhealach, since 1987; b. 5.9.36, Coll, Isle of Lewis; m., Lynn Kemp; 2 s.; 1 d. Educ. Back Public School; Nicolson Institute, Stornoway; Duncan of Jordanstone College of Art, Dundee; Moray House College of Education, Edinburgh. Fisherman; Civil Servant; Teacher; Producer, BBC Scotland; National Organiser, Scottish Civic Entertainment Association. Councillor representing Coll Division; Playwright. Recreations: drama; photography; the arts; crofting; fishing. Address: (h.) 7A Coll, Back, Isle of Lewis; T.-Back 260.

Maclean of Dunconnel, Sir Fitzroy Hew, 1st Bt, CBE (Mil). 15th Hereditary Keeper and Captain of Dunconnel; b. 11.3.11; m., Hon. Mrs Alan Phipps; 2 s. Educ. Eton; Cambridge. Entered Foreign Office, 1933; served Second World War, Queen's Own Cameron Highlanders and Special Air Service Regiment (Brigadier commanding British Military Mission to Yugoslav partisans, 1943-45); MP (Conservative), Lancaster, 1941-59, Bute and North Ayrshire, 1959-74; Parliamentary Under Secretary of State for War and Financial Secretary, War Office, 1954-57; Member, UK Delegation to North Atlantic Assembly, 1962-74; Member, Council of Europe and WEU, 1972-74; Hon. LLD, Glasgow, 1969, Dundee, 1984; Croix de Guerre, France; Order of Kutuzov, USSR; Partisan Star, 1st Class, Yugoslavia; Order of the Yugoslav Star with Ribbon; Order of Merit, Yugoslavia; President, British Yugoslav Society; Past President, Great Britain-USSR Association; author of works of military history and other books. Address: (h.) Strachur House, Strachur, PA27 8BX.

Maclean, Sheriff Hector Ronald. Sheriff of North Strathclyde, since 1968; b. 1931; m.; 3 d. Advocate, 1959.

MacLean, Ian Teasdale, MA, LLB. Solicitor; Senior Partner, J.D. Mackie & Dewar, since 1982 (Partner, since 1968); Honorary Treasurer, Aberdeen YMCA, since 1970; b. 3.6.40, Stornoway; m., Lavinia May Symonds; 1 s.; 1 d. Educ. Nicolson Institute, Stornoway; Aberdeen University. Qualified as Solicitor, 1964, after three years' indenture with Morice & Wilson, Advocates in Aberdeen; salaried Solicitor, J.D. Mackie & Dewar, Advocates in Aberdeen, 1965-68. Address: (b.) 18 Bon-Accord Square, Aberdeen; T.-0224 596341.

McLean, Jack, DA, MSIAD. Art Teacher, since 1968; Writer and Broadcaster, since 1974; b. Irvine, Ayrshire. Educ. Allan Glen's School, Glasgow; Edinburgh College of Art. Apprentice Welder, 1962-65; various jobs until 1968; Studio Artist, uncertificated Art Teacher, 1968-70; Edinburgh Art College; Jordanhill College of Education; Teacher of Art in Glasgow schools; began writing with Times Educational Supplement with regular column; Columnist, The Scotsman, 1967-81; Columnist, Glasgow Herald, since 1981; Scottish Vice-Chairman and National Executive Member, National Union of Students, 1970-74; Member, Scottish Council, Educational Institute of Scotland, 1981-82; Member, Strathclyde Regional Council Education Committee, since 1986. Commendation, Scottish Press Awards, 1985, 1986; Runner-up, Columnist of the Year, British Press Awards, 1985. Recreations: drinking in public houses (see A. Hind); flashy dressing; not playing tennis. Address: Glasgow Art Club, 185 Bath Street, Glasgow, G2 4HU; T.-041-423 0380, 041-552 6255.

McLean, James, BSc (Hons). Director of Education, Borders Regional Council, since 1974; b. 9.10.31, Glasgow; m., Wendy; 3 s.; 1 d. Educ.

Hyndland Senior Secondary School; Glasgow University. Industrial Assistant, British Petroleum, 1956; Instructor-Lt., Royal Navy, 1957-59; Teacher and Special Assistant Teacher, Dunoon Grammar School, 1960-63; Assistant Director of Education, Dumfriesshire, 1963-66; Depute Director of Education, Stewartry of Kirkcudbright, 1966-72; Director of Education, Peeblesshire, 1972-75. Member, Scottish Sports Council, since 1976; Honorary Treasurer, Association of Directors of Education in Scotland, since 1975. Recreations: Rotary; small-holding; swimming; golf; rugby. Address: (b.) Regional Headquarters, Newtown St. Boswells, Roxburghshire; T.-St. Boswells 23301.

McLean, John David Ruari, CBE, DSC, Croix de Guerre. Typographer and Author; b. 10.6.17, Minnigaff; m., Antonia Maxwell Carlisle; 2 s.; 1 d. Educ. Dragon School, Oxford; Eastbourne College. Royal Navy, 1940-45; Tutor in Typography, Royal College of Art, 1948-51; Typographic Adviser, Hulton Press, 1953-60; The Observer, 1960-62; Art Editor, The Connoisseur, 1962-73; Founder-Partner, Rainbird, McLean Ltd., 1951-58; Founder Editor, Motif, 1958-67; Honorary Typographic Adviser to HM Stationery Office, 1966-80; Senior Partner, Ruari McLean Associates Ltd., 1960-81; Trustee, National Library of Scotland, 1981. Publications: Modern Book Design, 1958; Victorian Book Design and Colour Printing, 1963; Magazine Design, 1969; Jan Tschichold, Typographer, 1975; The Thames & Hudson Manual of Typography, 1980. Recreations: sailing; acquiring books. Address: (h.) Pier Cottage, Carsaig, Isle of Mull; T.-Pennyghael 216.

Maclean, John Robert, DL; b. 24.5.51, Lossiemouth; m., Veronica Mary Lacy Hulbert-Powell; 1 s.; 2 d. Educ. Milton Abbey School. Commissioned into Queen's Own Highlanders, 1971; left Army, 1978, and returned home to farm via Royal Agricultural College, Cirencester; Deputy Lieutenant, County of Moray, since 1987; Member, Royal Company of Archers (Queen's Bodyguard for Scotland), since 1988; Chairman, Elgin Branch, Earl Haig Fund; Member, Committee, Highland Branch, Scottish Landowners Federation. Recreations: shooting; field sports. Address: (h.) Westfield House, near Elgin, Moray.

MacLean, Ranald Norman Munro, BA, LLB, LLM. Queen's Counsel, since 1977; b. 18.12.38, Aberdeen; m., Pamela Ross; 2 s.; 1 d. Educ. Inverness Royal Academy; Fettes College, Edinburgh; Cambridge University; Edinburgh University; Yale University. Advocate, 1964; Advocate Depute, 1972-75; Advocate Depute (Home), 1979-82; Chairman, Scottish Committee, Council on Tribunals, 1985; Member, Council on Tribunals, 1985. Governor, Fettes Trust, since 1977; Trustee, National Library of Scotland, since 1968; Member, Scottish Legal Aid Board, since 1986. Recreations: hill-walking; bird watching. Address: (h.) 12 Chalmers Crescent, Edinburgh, EH9 1TS; T.-031-667 6217.

Maclean, Sir Robert (Alexander), KBE (1973), Kt (1955), LLD. Honorary Life President, A.F. Stoddard & Co. Ltd.; Vice-President, Scottish Council (Development and Industry); Deputy Lieutenant, Renfrewshire; b. 11.4.08, Cambuslang; m., Vivienne Neville Bourke; 2 s.; 2 d. Educ. High School of Glasgow. Partner, later Senior Partner, James Templeton & Co., Glasgow, 1937-45; Chairman, A.F. Stoddard & Co. Ltd., 1946-83. Chairman, Glasgow Junior Chamber of Commerce, 1940; President, Glasgow Chamber of Commerce, 1956-58; Chairman, Scottish Council of Chambers of Commerce, 1960-62; President, Association of British Chambers of Commerce, 1966-68; Regional Controller (Scotland), Board of Trade, 1944-46; Regional Controller, Factory and Storage Control, 1941-44; Chairman, Scottish Industries Exhibitions, 1949, 1954, 1959; Chairman, Scottish Exports Committee, 1966-70; Chairman, Scottish Industrial Estates Corporation, 1955-72; President, British Industrial Exhibition, Moscow, 1966; Member, BNEC, 1966-70; Member, Scottish Aerodromes Board, 1950-61; Member, Export Council for Europe, 1960-64; Vice-Chairman, Scottish Board for Industry, 1952-60. Recreations: golf; fishing. Address: (h.) South Branchal Farm, Bridge of Weir, Renfrewshire, PA11 3SJ; T.-Kilmacolm 2162.

Maclean, William James, DA, ARSA, FSA Scot. Lecturer in Fine Art, Duncan of Jordanstone College of Art, Dundee, since 1982; b. 12.10.41, Inverness; m., Marian Forbes Leven; 2 s.; 1 d. Educ. Inverness Royal Academy; HMS Conway; Grays School of Art, Aberdeen. Postgraduate and Travel Scholarship, Scottish Education Trust Award, Visual Arts Bursary, Scottish Arts Council; Benno Schotz Prize; one-man exhibitions in Rome, Glasgow, Edinburgh and London; group exhibitions in Britain, Europe and North America; represented in private and public collections including Arts Council, British Museum, Scottish National Gallery of Modern Art, Fitzwilliam Museum, Cambridge, and several Scottish galleries. Address: (h.) Bellevue, 18 Dougall Street, Tayport, Fife.

Maclean-Mackintosh, Catherine Margaret Una, MD, PhD, DPH, FFCM. Reader in Community Medicine, Edinburgh University, since 1978; b. 3.7.25, Applecross; m., John P. Mackintosh, MP (deceased); 3 s.; 2 d. Educ. Dingwall Academy; Edinburgh University. Medical posts in Britain after graduation in 1949; clinical work in Aden Colony, 1952-53; research in African cancer epidemiology and African traditional medicine, 1959-63; research in community psychiatry, Scotland, 1964-67 and 1974-75; teacher and researcher, Edinburgh University, since 1967; Member, Medicines Commission, DHSS, since 1986; Member, Health Services Research Committee, SHHD, four years until 1988; writer of many scientific articles and five books; active campaigner for Scottish Assembly; contributor to public debates. Recreations: theatre; the modern novel. Address: (h.) 42 Moray Place, Edinburgh, EH3 6BT; T.-031-226 2181.

MacLeary, Professor Alistair Ronald, MSc, DipTP, FRICS, FRTPI, FRSA. MacRobert Professor of Land Economy, Aberdeen University, since 1976 (Dean, Faculty of Law, 1982-85); President, Planning and Development Division, Royal Institution of Chartered Surveyors, 1984-85; b. 12.1.40, Glasgow; m., Claire Leonard; 1 s.; 1 d. Educ. Inverness Royal Academy; College of Estate Management; Heriot-Watt University;

Strathclyde University. Assistant Surveyor, Gerald Eve & Co., Chartered Surveyors, 1962-65; Assistant to Director, Murrayfield Real Estate Co. Ltd., 1965-67; Assistant Surveyor and Town Planner/Partner, Wright & Partners, 1967-76; seconded to Department of the Environment, London, 1971-73; Member, Committee of Inquiry into the Acquisition and Occupancy of Agricultural Land, 1977-79; Member, Home Grown Timber Advisory Committee, Forestry Commission, 1981-87; Chairman, Board of Education, Commonwealth Association of Surveying and Land Economy; Member, Grampian Region Valuation Panel; Editor, Land Development Studies. Recreations: golf; shooting; skiing; hill-walking. Address: (h.) 164 Forest Avenue, Aberdeen, AB1 6UN; T.-0224 322940.

MacLeay, Very Rev. John Henry James, MA. Dean of Argyll, since 1987; Rector, St. Andrew's, Fort William, since 1978; Canon, St. John's Cathedral, Oban, since 1980; b. 7.12.31, Inverness; m., Jane Speirs Cuthbert; 1 s.; 1 d. Educ. St. Edmund Hall, Oxford. Ordained Deacon, 1957; Priest, 1958; Curate: St. John's, East Dulwich, 1957-60, St. Michael's, Inverness, 1960-62; Rector, St. Michael's, Inverness, 1962-70; Priest-in-Charge, St. Columba's, Grantown-on-Spey and St. John's, Rothiemurchus, 1970-78. Recreations: fishing; reading; visiting old churches and cathedrals. Address: St. Andrew's Rectory, Parade Road, Fort William, PH33 6BA; T.-0397 2979.

MacLehose of Beoch, Baron (Crawford Murray MacLehose), KT (1983), GBE (1976), KCMG (1971), KCVO (1975), DL, Hon. LLD (York, 1983, Strathclyde, 1984). Chairman, School of Oriental and African Studies, since 1985; Chairman, Scottish Trust for the Physically Disabled and Margaret Blackwood Housing Association; Life Peer; 16.10.17; m.; 2 d. Educ. Rugby; Balliol College, Oxford. Served Second World War (Lt., RNVR); joined Foreign Service, 1947; Governor and C-in-C, Hong Kong, 1971-82. Address: (h.) Beoch, Maybole, Ayrshire.

McLeish, Henry Baird, BA (Hons). MP (Labour), Central Fife, since 1987; b. 15.6.48; m.; 1 s.; 1 d. Educ. Heriot-Watt University. Planning Officer, Fife County Council, 1974-75, Dunfermline District Council, 1975-87; Leader, Fife Regional Council, 1982-87.

MacLellan, Sir (George) Robin (Perronet), Kt, CBE, JP. Chairman, Scottish Industrial and Trade Exhibitions Ltd., Edinburgh, since 1981; Director, Nationwide Anglia Building Society (Scotland), since 1969; b. 14.11.15, Liverpool; m., Margaret Robertson; 1 s. Educ. Westbourne School, Glasgow; St. Brides School, Helensburgh; Ardvreck School, Crieff; Clifton College, Bristol; Ecole de Commerce, Lausanne. George MacLellan & Co. Ltd., Flexible Ducting Ltd. (later combined as George MacLellan Holdings) Deputy Chairman, British Airports Authority, 1965-75; President, Glasgow Chamber of Commerce, 1970-71; Director: Investment Trust, Scottish National Trust plc, 1970-85, Govan Shipbuilders Ltd., 1972-74, Nationwide Building Society (main board), 1971-84; Chairman: Scottish Tourist Board, 1974-80, British Tourist Authority, 1974-80, Melville Retirement Homes, General Advisory Board, IBA, 1976-79, British Rail (Scottish Advisory Board), 1977-81; at various times Member, British Export Council for Canada, West Central Scotland Plan Steering Committee, Scottish Industrial Development Board. Past Chairman, Crossroads (Scotland) Care Attendant Scheme; former Deputy Chairman, National Trust for Scotland; Past President, Society of Friends of Glasgow Cathedral; former Member, Court, Strathclyde University; Hon. Fellow, Royal College of Physicians and Surgeons of Glasgow; Fellow, Scottish Council (Development and Industry); Chairman, Strathclyde Tenovus Scotland. Recreations: angling; keeping friendships in good repair; the written and spoken word; useful retirement. Address: (h.) 11 Beechwood Court, Drymen Road, Bearsden, Glasgow; T.-041-942 3876.

McLellan, James Alexander, LLB. Director of Administration, Argyll and Bute District Council, since 1978; b. 23.12.50, Lochgilphead; m., Alexis; 2 s.; 1 d. Educ. Keil School; Glasgow University. Recreations: fishing; rugby; gardening. Address: (b.) Kilmory, Lochgilphead, Argyll, PA31 8RT; T.-0546 2127.

McLelland, John, BVMS, MVSc, PhD, MRCVS. Reader in Veterinary Anatomy, Edinburgh University, since 1981; b. 11.6.37, Kilmarnock; m., Morar; 1 s.; 2 d. Educ. Kilmarnock Academy; Glasgow Academy; Glasgow University; Liverpool University. Pig Industry Development Authority Scholar, Veterinary Hospital, Glasgow University, 1962-63; Egg Marketing Board Scholar, Department of Veterinary Anatomy, Liverpool University, 1964; Assistant Lecturer, then Lecturer, Department of Veterinary Anatomy, Liverpool University, 1964-72; Lecturer, then Senior Lecturer, Department of Veterinary Anatomy, Edinburgh University, 1972-81; Senior Royal Society/Indian National Academy of Sciences Visiting Research Worker, Department of Zoology, Gujarat University, India, 1976; Visiting Lecturer: Vakgroep Funktionele Morfologie, Fakulteit Der Diergeneeskunde, Rijksuniversiteit Te Utrecht, Netherlands, 1980, Department of Veterinary Anatomy, Dar Es Salaam University, 1981, Department of Anatomy and Cellular Biology, Tufts University, Boston, 1984; Chairman, Sub-Committee on Systema Digestorium, International Committee on Avian Anatomical Nomenclature. Publications: Outlines of Avian Anatomy (Co-author), 1975; Form and Function in Birds (Editor), 1979, 1981, 1985; An Introduction to the Functional Anatomy of the Limbs of the Domestic Animals (Co-author), 1984; Birds: Their Structure and Function (Co-author), 1984. Recreations: music; walking; gardening; travel. Address: (h.) 117/10 W. Savile Terrace, Edinburgh; T.-031-662 4588.

MacLennan, Alexander Fraser, BL, SSC, NP, Senior Partner Emeritus, Balfour & Manson, Edinburgh (Partner, 1946-84); b. 17.9.10, Leith; m., F.G. Elwyn Manson; 1 s. Educ. Broughton Secondary School; Scottish Educational Institute, Edinburgh; Edinburgh University. Served with RAF; non-practising Member, Law Society (England); Member, International Bar Association; Honorary Secretary, Edinburgh Legal Dispensary; President, Carrubbers Christian Centre,

Edinburgh; Preaching Evangelist, Edinburgh Presbytery, Church of Scotland. Recreations: walking; golf. Address: (h.) 100 Ravelston Dykes, Edinburgh; T.-031-337 4341.

MacLennan, David Neall, BSc, FIOA. Deputy Director, Marine Laboratory, since 1986; b. 26.9.40, Aberdeen; m., Sheila Cormack; 1 s.; 1 d. Educ. Robert Gordon's College; Aberdeen University. Scientific Officer, AERE Harwell, 1962-67; Marine Laboratory, 1967-73; Head Office, Department of Agriculture and Fisheries for Scotland, 1973-75; returned to Marine Laboratory, 1976. Chairman, ICES Fish Capture Committee. Recreation: bridge. Address: (h.) 2 Stronsay Avenue, Aberdeen; T.-0224 876544.

Maclennan, Professor Duncan, MA, MPhil. Titular Professor in Applied Economics, Glasgow University; Director, Centre for Housing Research, since 1983; Economic Adviser to OECD, Paris, since 1981; Director, Joseph Rowntree Memorial Trust Housing Finance Research Programme, since 1987; b. 12.3.49, Glasgow; m., Ruth Hunter Liddell; 1 s.; 1 d. Educ. Allan Glen's Secondary School; Glasgow University. Lecturer in Applied Economics, Glasgow University, 1974-76; Lecturer in Political Economy, Aberdeen University, 1976-78; Lecturer in Applied Economics, Glasgow University, 1979-82; Chairman, National Steering Group for Care and Repair. Past President, Allan Glen's Rugby Club. Recreations: watching rugby, golf. Address: (b.) Centre for Housing Research, 25 Bute Gardens, Glasgow; T.-041-339 8855.

MacLennan, Finlay, FBIM. Deputy Chief Constable, Northern Constabulary, since 1985; Member, National Broadcasting Council for Scotland; b. 10.4.36, Harris; m., Barbara Patricia; 1 s.; 1 d. Educ. Portree High School; Garnett College, London. National Service, Cameron Highlanders, 1956-58; Metropolitan Police, 1958-85. Member, Board of Management, YMCA, Lambeth, 1979-82. Recreations: squash; shooting; hill-walking; sailing; fishing. Address: (b.) Police Headquarters, Perth Road, Inverness, IV2 3SY; T.-0463 239191.

MacLennan, Graeme Andrew Yule, CA. Investment Director, Ivory & Syme PLC, since 1988; b. 24.8.42, Glasgow; m., Diane; 2 s.; 2 d. Educ. Kelvinside Academy, Glasgow. Edinburgh Fund Managers, 1970-88; Member, External Advisory Council, Centre for Japanese Studies, Stirling University. Recreations: hill-walking; angling. Address: (b.) 1 Charlotte Square, Edinburgh, EH2 4DZ; T.-031-225 1357.

Maclennan, Robert Adam Ross, MA. MP (SLD), Caithness and Sutherland; Joint Interim Leader, Social and Liberal Democrats; Barrister-at-Law; b. 26.6.36, Glasgow; m., Helen Cutter Noyes; 2 s.; 1 d. Educ. Glasgow Academy; Balliol College, Oxford; Trinity College, Cambridge; Columbia University, New York. Parliamentary Private Secretary to Secretary of State for Commonwealth Affairs, 1967; Opposition Spokesman on Scottish Affairs and Defence, 1970; Parliamentary Under-Secretary of State, Department of Prices and Consumer Protection, 1974; Opposition Spokesman on Foreign Affairs, 1979; Founder Member, SDP, 1981, and author of party's constitution; Parliamentary Spokesman on Agriculture, 1981, Home Affairs, 1983, Economic Affairs, 1987; elected Leader, SDP, 1987. Recreations: music; theatre; books. Address: (b.) House of Commons, London, SW1A 0AA; T.-01-219 4133.

MacLennan of MacLennan, Ronald George, Hon-.DLitt (London, 1984). 34th Chief of Clan MacLennan; b. 7.2.25; m., Margaret MacLennan; 1 s.; 2 d. Educ. Boroughmuir Secondary School, Edinburgh; University of Copenhagen. Teacher and Lecturer in Physical Education, 1949-82; Chairman, Kintail Museum Company, since 1983. Grand Cross and Collar, Constantinian Order, St. George, 1985; Count, Holy Roman Empire, 1986. Address: (h.) The Old Mill, Dores, Inverness.

MacLennan, Professor William Jardine, MD, FRCP, FRCPEdin, FRCPGlas. Professor of Geriatric Medicine, Edinburgh University, since 1986; Honorary Consultant Physician in Geriatric Medicine, Lothian Health Board, since 1986; b. 11.2.41, Glasgow; m., Fiona Hannah Campbell; 2 s. Educ. Hutchesons' Boys' Grammar School; Glasgow University. House Physician, Stobhill Hospital, Glasgow, 1964; Hansen Research Scholar, then Assistant Lecturer, then Lecturer, Department of Materia Medica, Glasgow University, 1965-69; Senior Registrar in Geriatric Medicine, Stobhill General Hospital and Glasgow Western Infirmary, 1969-71; Senior Lecturer in Geriatric Medicine, Southampton University, 1971-80; Senior Lecturer, then Reader in Geriatric Medicine, Dundee University, 1980-86. Publications: books on clinical care of the elderly, drugs in the elderly and bone disease in the elderly. Recreations: hill-walking; ship-modelling; playing classical guitar badly. Address: (h.) 26 Caiystane Avenue, Fairmilehead, Edinburgh; T.-031-445 1755.

McLeod, Alistair. Manager, Ayr United Football Club; b. 26.2.31, Glasgow; m., Faye; 2 s.; 1 d. Educ. Queen's Park School. Played football for Queen's Park School, Scottish Schools, Third Lanark, St. Mirren, Blackburn, Hibernian, Ayr United; Manager, Ayr United, Aberdeen, Scotland, Ayr United, Motherwell, Airdrie; led Scotland in World Cup, Argentina.

MacLeod, Angus, CBE (1967), MA, LLB. Honorary Sheriff, Edinburgh, since 1972; b. 2.4.06, Glasgow; m., Jane Winifred Walker (deceased); 3 s. Educ. Hutchesons' Boys' Grammar School, Glasgow; Glasgow University. Qualified Assistant in Legal Practice, Glasgow, 1929-34; Procurator Fiscal Service, 1934-71; Depute Fiscal at Dunfermline, Glasgow, Edinburgh; Senior Depute, Edinburgh, 1934-42; Procurator Fiscal: Dumfries, 1942-52, Aberdeen, 1952-55, Edinburgh, 1955-71; Temporary Sheriff, 1973-77; Chairman, VAT Appeals Tribunal, 1974-77; co-opted Member, Council, Law Society of Scotland, 1967-73; Member, Grant Committee on the Sheriff Court, 1963-67. Recreations: reading; walking. Address: (h.) 7 Oxford Terrace, Edinburgh, EH4 1PX; T.-031-332 5466.

MacLeod, Archibald, OBE, NDA, NDD. Chairman, Crofters Commission, since 1986; b. 23.3.28, Kames, Argyll; m., Sheena Fleming Ferguson; 3 s. Educ. Greenock High School; West of Scotland Agricultural College. Research Assistant, West of Scotland Agricultural College, 1949-53; Officer-in-Charge, Lephinmore Research Farm, Hill Farming Research Organisation, 1953-56; Senior Adviser (North Argyll), West of Scotland Agricultural College, 1956-66; Head of Advisory Services, Argyll Area, 1966-86. Past President: Oban Rotary Club, Oban Speakers Club; founder Chairman, West Cowal YFC; Honorary Vice-President, Lorn Agricultural Society. Recreations: shooting; curling; gardening; reading. Address: (h.) Tarradale, Culloden Road, Westhill, Inverness, IV1 2BJ; T.-Inverness 791598.

MacLeod, Bobby, JP. Musician and Hotelier; b. 8.5.25, Tobermory; m., Jean MacCulloch; 3 s.; 1 d. Educ. Tobermory; Aberdeen. RAF, wartime; Musician and Broadcaster, since 1948; Gold Medal, National Accordeon Organisation, 1957; Honorary Life Member, Glasgow Society of Musicians; Provost of Tobermory, 1963-75; Member, Argyll County Council, 1963-75. Recreations: boating; sailing. Address: (h.) Royal Building, Tobermory; T.-0688 2009.

MacLeod, Calum Alexander, MA, LLB, LLD. Chairman, FS Assurance Ltd., since 1987; Chairman, The Harris Tweed Association Ltd., since 1984; Deputy Chairman, Grampian Television PLC, since 1982; b. 25.7.35, Stornoway; m., Elizabeth M. Davidson; 2 s.; 1 d. Educ. Nicolson Institute; Glenurquhart School; Aberdeen University. Partner, Paull & Williamsons, Advocates, Aberdeen, 1964-80; Member, White Fish Authority, 1973-80; Member, North of Scotland Hydro-Electric Board, 1976-84; Member, Highlands and Islands Development Board, since 1984; Director, Scottish Eastern Investment Trust PLC, since 1981; Aberdeen Board Member, Bank of Scotland, since 1980; Chairman, North of Scotland Investment Company PLC, since 1986. Chancellor's Assessor, Aberdeen University, since 1979; Chairman of Governors, Robert Gordon's College, since 1981; Vice Chairman, Scottish Council of Independent Schools, since 1988; Chairman, SATRO North Scotland, since 1986. Recreations: golf; motoring; hill-walking; reading; music. Address: (h.) 6 Westfield Terrace, Aberdeen, AB2 4RU; T.-0224 641614.

McLeod, Rev. David Campbell, BSc (Hons), MEng, BD (Hons). Minister, Fairmuir Parish Church, Dundee, since 1978; b. 11.1.37, Glasgow; m., Mary Graham Gordon; 2 d. Educ. Dumbarton Academy; Strathclyde University; Glasgow University; Sheffield University. Design and research, YARD, Glasgow, 1960-66; divinity student, then Assistant Minister, St. Columbo Church, Helensburgh, 1966-69; Minister, Martyrs' Church, Paisley, 1969-78. Recreations: tennis; golf; bridge; gardening. Address: 6 Carseview Gardens, Dundee, DD2 1NE; T.-Dundee 641371.

Macleod, Rev. Professor Donald, MA. Professor of Systematic Theology, Free Church College, since 1978; Editor, The Monthly Record, since 1977; Vagrant Preacher, since 1978; b. 24.11.40, Ness, Isle of Lewis; m., Mary Maclean; 3 s. Educ. Nicolson Institute, Stornoway; Glasgow University; Free Church College. Ordained Guy Fawkes Day, 1964; Minister: Kilmallie Free Church, 1964-70, Partick Highland Free Church, Glasgow, 1970-78. Member, Scottish Religious Advisory Committee, BBC. Recreations: dreaming about cricket, fishing and gardening; Gaelic music. Address: (h.) 84 Craiglea Drive, Edinburgh; T.-031-447 6269.

Macleod, Donald Angus David, MB, ChB, FRCS Edin. Consultant General Surgeon, since 1976; Chairman, Lothian Health Board Basic Surgical Training Committee, since 1986; b. 4.3.41, Selkirk; m., Lucile Janette Kirkpatrick; 1 s.; 2 d. Educ. Gordonstoun; Edinburgh University. Assistant Director of Studies (Surgery), Edinburgh Postgraduate Board for Medicine, 1976-86; Chairman, Scottish Committee, Medical Commission for Accident Prevention, 1980-85; Chairman: West Lothian Drug and Therapeutics Committee, since 1978, West Lothian Medical Staff Committee, since 1986; Member: West Lothian Unit Management and New General Hospital Commissioning Team, since 1987; Hon. Medical Adviser, Scottish Rugby Union, since 1969; Member, International Rugby Football Board Medical Advisory Committee, since 1978; Vice-Chairman, Medical Advisory Committee, 13th Commonwealth Games, Scotland, 1984-86; Vice-Chairman, Sports Medicine and Sports Science Consultative Group, Scottish Sports Council, since 1984. Recreation: orienteering. Address: (h.) The Haining, Woodlands Park, Livingston, West Lothian, EH54 8AT.

MacLeod, Donald Ian Kerr, RD*, MA, LLB, WS. Partner, Shepherd & Wedderburn, WS, since 1964; b. 19.4.37, Edinburgh; m., Mary St. Clair Bridge; 1 s.; 2 d. Educ. Aberdeen Grammar School; Aberdeen University; Edinburgh University. Apprentice, MacPherson & Mackay, WS, 1957-60; Assistant, Shepherd & Wedderburn, 1960-64; Solicitor in Scotland to HM Customs and Excise, Department of Employment and Health and Safety Executive, since 1974. Lt.-Cdr. RNR (Retd.); Member, Court of Session Rules Council and Rules of Court Review Group; Past President, East District, Scottish Hockey Association; Church Elder. Recreations: hockey (Class 1 international umpire); golf. Address: (b.) 16 Charlotte Square, Edinburgh, EH2 4YS; T.-031-225 8585.

MacLeod, Donald Roderick, LLB. Advocate, since 1978; b. 24.9.48, Inverness; m., Susan Mary Fulton; 2 d. Educ. High School of Stirling; Glasgow University. Admitted Solicitor, 1973; called to Scottish Bar, 1978; Member, Scottish Executive Council, Labour Party, 1976-77-79; Labour candidate, Kinross and West Perthshire, 1979; Elder, Greenbank Church of Scotland, Edinburgh, since 1987. Recreations: angling; hill-walking; music. Address: (h.) 22 Hermitage Gardens, Edinburgh; T.-031-447 8367.

MacLeod, Duncan James, CBE (1986), CA. Managing Partner, Ernst & Whinney, Glasgow, since 1985; b. 1.11.34, Edinburgh; m., Joanna Bibby; 2 s.; 1 d. Educ. Eton College. Qualified CA, 1958; Partner, Brown Fleming & Murray, 1960; Director: Bank of Scotland, since 1973, Scottish Provident Institution, since 1975, Weir Group Plc, since 1976; Member, Scottish Industrial Development Advisory Board, 1980; Member,

Scottish Tertiary Education Advisory Council, 1984-87. Chief, Glasgow Skye Association. Recreations: golf; shooting. Address: (b.) Savoy Tower, 77 Renfrew Street, Glasgow; T.-041-333 9699.

MacLeod of Fuinary, Baron (Very Rev. George Fielden MacLeod), Bt, MC, BA, DD. Life Peer; Moderator, General Assembly of the Church of Scotland, 1957-58; b. 17.6.95; m., Lorna Helen Janet Macleod (deceased); 2 s.; 1 d. Educ. Winchester; Oriel College, Oxford; Edinburgh University; Union Theological College, New York. Served First World War (Captain, Argyll and Sutherland Highlanders); Collegiate Minister, St. Cuthbert's Parish Church, Edinburgh, 1926-30; Minister, Govan Parish Church, Glasgow, 1930-38; Founder, Iona Community (Leader, 1938-67); Rector, Glasgow University, 1968-71. Address: (h.) 23 Learmonth Terrace, Edinburgh.

MacLeod, Hugh Murdoch, MB, ChB, FRCPE. Consultant Physician, Royal Infirmary, Edinburgh, and Longmore Hospital Geriatric Assessment Unit and Associated Hospitals, since 1964; Principal Medical Officer, Scottish Widows Fund and Life Assurance Society, since 1971; b. 28.6.25, Dornoch; m., Catherine Mackay Shepherd; 1 s.; 1 d.; 1 s. deceased. Educ. Dornoch Academy; Edinburgh University. Registrar posts in Tuberculosis and Chest Medicine, England and Edinburgh; Chest Physician, City Hospital, Edinburgh. Honorary Senior Lecturer in Medicine, Edinburgh University; Registrar, Royal College of Physicians of Edinburgh, 1968-81; Honorary Medical Adviser, Abbeyfield Society. Publications: papers in chest and geriatric medicine. Recreations: art appreciation; gardening; golf. Address: (h.) 3 Forrester Road, Edinburgh, EH12 8AA; T.-031-334 4978.

MacLeod, Professor Iain Alasdair, BSc, PhD, CEng, FICE, FIStructE. Professor of Structural Engineering, Strathclyde University, since 1981; b. 4.5.39, Glasgow; m., Barbara Jean Booth; 1 s.; 1 d. Educ. Lenzie Academy; Glasgow University. Design Engineer, Crouch and Hogg, Glasgow, 1960-62; Assistant Lecturer in Civil Engineering, Glasgow University, 1962-66; Design Engineer, H.A. Simons Ltd., Vancouver, 1966-67; Structural Engineer, Portland Cement Association, Illinois, 1968-69; Lecturer in Civil Engineering, Glasgow University, 1969-73; Professor and Head, Department of Civil Engineering, Paisley College of Technology, 1973-81; Chairman, Scottish Branch, Institution of Structural Engineers, 1985-86. Recreations: climbing; sailing. Address: (b.) Department of Civil Engineering, Strathclyde University, George Street, Glasgow; T.-041-552 4400.

Macleod, Ian Buchanan, BSc, MB, ChB, FRCSEdin. Consultant Surgeon, Royal Infirmary, Edinburgh, since 1969; Honorary Senior Lecturer, Department of Clinical Surgery, Edinburgh University, since 1969; Surgeon to the Queen in Scotland, since 1987; b. 20.5.33, Wigan; m., Kathleen Gillean Large; 1 s.; 1 d. Educ. Wigan Grammar School; Edinburgh University. House Surgeon and House Physician, Royal Infirmary, Edinburgh, 1957-59; National Service, RAMC, Malaya, Singapore, Nepal, 1959-61; appointments, Department of Clinical Surgery, Edinburgh University and Royal Infirmary, Edinburgh, since 1961. Editor, Journal, Royal College of Surgeons of Edinburgh, 1982-87. Publications: Principles and Practice of Surgery (Co-author), 1985; Farquharson's Text Book of Operative Surgery (Contributor), 1986; Companion to Medical Studies (Contributor), 1981, 1985. Recreations: golf; photography. Address: (h.) Derwent House, 32 Cramond Road North, Edinburgh, EH4 6JE; T.-031-336 1541.

MacLeod of MacLeod, John. 29th Chief of Clan MacLeod; b. 10.8.35; m., Melita Kolin; 1 s.; 1 d. Educ. Eton. Address: (h.) Dunvegan Castle, Isle of Skye.

McLeod, John, ARAM, FTCL, LRAM, ARCM, LTCL. Composer, Conductor and Lecturer; Visiting Lecturer, Royal Scottish Academy of Music and Drama; b. 8.3.34, Aberdeen; m., Margaret Murray; 1 s.; 1 d. Educ. Aberdeen Grammar School; Royal Academy of Music, London. Director of Music, Merchiston Castle School, 1974-85; Guest Conductor: Scottish National Orchestra, Scottish Chamber Orchestra, BBC Scottish Symphony Orchestra; Associate Composer, Scottish Chamber Orchestra, 1980-82; Guinness Prize for British Composers, 1979; Radio Forth Award for Composition, 1981; UK Music Education Award, 1982. Recreations: reading; films; theatre; art galleries; walking. Address: (h.) 9 Redford Crescent, Colinton, Edinburgh, EH13 OBS; T.-031-441 3035.

Macleod, Rev. John, MA. Minister, Free Church of Scotland congregation of Duthil-Dores, since 1983; b. 1.1.39, Shawbost, Isle of Lewis; m., Mary Macarthur. Educ. Nicolson Institute, Stornoway; Aberdeen University; Aberdeen College of Education. Torry Academy, Aberdeen: Assistant Teacher of General Subjects, 1961-66, Principal Teacher of Modern Studies, 1966-80. Recreations: gardening; local history. Address: Free Church Manse, Tomatin, Inverness-shire.

MacLeod, Rev. John, MA, DipTh. Minister, Tarbat Free Church of Scotland, Portmahomack, since 1978; b. 14.5.48, Fearn; m., Veda Joy Morrison; 4 s.; 1 d. Educ. Tain Royal Academy; Aberdeen University; Free Church College, Edinburgh. Standard Life Assurance Co., 1969-71; Free Church Missioner to Students, Aberdeen, 1974-75; Free Church Lecturer in Religious Studies, Aberdeen College of Education, 1974-75; Preacher, Highland Church, Vancouver, 1976; Preacher, Free Church of Scotland Western Charge, Prince Edward Island, 1977-78; Convener, Psalmody Committee, Free Church of Scotland, 1982-84; Chairman, Moray Firth Radio Christian Council, since 1983; Publicity Officer, Free Presbytery of Ross, since 1984; Clerk, Training of the Ministry and Admissions Committee, Free Church of Scotland, since 1986. Recreations: squeezing quarts into pint pots and getting blood out of stones. Address: Free Church Manse, Portmahomack, Tain, Ross-shire, IV20 1YL; T.-086287 467.

Macleod, John Alasdair Johnston, DL, MRCGP, DCH, DObsRCOG. General Practitioner, North Uist, since 1973; Secretary, Western Isles Local Medical Committee (GP), since 1977; Deputy

Lieutenant, Western Isles, since 1979; b. 20.1.35, Stornoway; m., Lorna Jean Ferguson; 2 s.; 1 d. Educ. Nicolson Institute; Keil School; Glasgow University. National Service, Royal Navy, 1957-59; hospital posts, Glasgow and London, 1963-73; Non-Executive Director, Olscot Ltd., since 1969; trainer in general practice, since 1975; Visiting Professor, Department of Family Medicine, University of North Carolina, since 1985. Member, Committee of North Uist Highland Gathering; Fellow, Royal Society of Medicine; author of papers and articles, singly and jointly, on aspects of isolated practice. Recreations: boating; horticulture; photography; time-sharing. Address: (h.) Tigh-Na-Hearradh, Lochmaddy, Isle of North Uist, PA82 5AE; T.-08763 333.

MacLeod, John Alexander. Commissioner of Northern Lighthouses, since 1977; b. 31.10.19, Isle of Skye; m., Agnes Campbell Gillespie; 1 s.; 1 d. Educ. Knockbreck Public School; Glasgow Technical College. Merchant Navy career (through the ranks to command), followed by appointment to Marine Superintendent; retired, since 1976. Recreations: gardening; local history. Address: (h.) Halistra, Waternish, Isle of Skye; T.-047 083 206.

Macleod, John Francis Matheson, MA, LLB, NP. Vice-Dean, Faculty of Solicitors of the Highlands; Chairman, Crofters Commission, 1978-86; Member, Council, Law Society of Scotland, since 1988; Solicitor in Inverness, since 1959; b. 24.1.32, Inverness; m., Alexandra Catherine; 1 s. Educ. Inverness Royal Academy; George Watson's College; Edinburgh University. Solicitor, Fife County Council, 1957-59; in private practice, since 1959; Parliamentary candidate (Liberal): Moray and Nairn, 1964, Western Isles, 1966; Chairman, Highland Region, Scottish Liberal Party, until 1978; former Vice-Chairman, Broadcasting Council for Scotland. Address: (b.) 28 Queensgate, Inverness; T.-0463 239393.

MacLeod, John Harvey Aitken, MA (Hons). Rector, Wick High School, since 1977; b. 4.3.36, Vila, New Hebrides; m., Lydia A.W.C. McFarlane; 2 s.; 2 d. Educ. Hamilton Academy; Glasgow University. Taught History and Geography, Kalonga Secondary School, Zambia; Principal Teacher of Geography, Portree High School, Skye; various teaching posts in Fife, latterly as Assistant Rector, Queen Anne High School, Dunfermline; Depute Rector, Oban High School, 1975. Executive Member, Highland Headteachers Association; Lay Preacher. Recreations: photography; music. Address: (h.) Norlands, Ulbster, by Wick, KW2 6AA; T.-Thrumster 265.

MacLeod, Emeritus Professor Malcolm, MD (Hons), FRCPEdin. Professor Emeritus in Renal Medicine, Aberdeen University; b. 9.12.16, Glasgow; m., Elizabeth Shaw Ritchie; 1 s. Educ. Nicolson Institute, Stornoway; Aberdeen University. Military Service, Africa, India, SE Asia, 1940-46 (Medical Specialist, RAMC); Lecturer, Senior Lecturer, Reader in Medicine, 1947-80; Personal Professor in Renal Medicine, Aberdeen University, 1981; Honorary Consultant Physician, Aberdeen Royal Infirmary, 1955-82 and Honorary Consultant in charge, Medical Renal Unit, 1966-82; President, Scottish Society of Physicians, 1980. Recreation: natural history. Address: (h.) 76 Hamilton Place, Aberdeen, AB2 4BA; T.-0224 635537.

MacLeod, Rev. Malcolm, BA, BD. Minister, Arbroath Old Parish Church, since 1984; b. 13.2.53, Stornoway; m., Rev. Ada V. MacLeod; 1 s.; 1 d. Educ. Sir E. Scott Junior Secondary School, Tarbert; Portree High School; Stirling University; Edinburgh University. Assistant, Cadder, 1978-79; Associate, St. Machar's, Aberdeen, 1979-84. Recreations: home computing; reading. Address: (b.) Kirk Square, Arbroath; T.-Arbroath 70253.

Macleod, Rev. Murdo Alexander, MA. Minister, Stornoway Free Church, since 1984; Moderator, Lewis Presbytery, Free Church of Scotland, 1984-85; b. 15.10.35, Stornoway; m., Annie Bella Nicolson; 5 s.; 1 d. Educ. Nicolson Institute, Stornoway; Aberdeen University; Free Church College. Minister: Drumchapel Free Church, Glasgow, 1966-72, Dingwall Free Church, 1972-78, Greyfriars, Inverness, 1978-84. Recreations: walking; talking. Address: Free Church Manse, Stornoway, Lewis; T.-Stornoway 2279.

Macleod, Murdoch, JP. General Manager, Secretary and Treasurer, Stornoway Pier and Harbour Commission, since 1975; Honorary Sheriff; b. 11.8.32, Shawbost, Isle of Lewis; m., Crisybil; 1 s.; 1 d. Educ. Nicolson Institute, Stornoway. Ross and Cromarty Council: Highways Department, 1955-57, Education Department, 1957-65; Stornoway Town Council: Town Clerk's Department, 1965-68, Town Clerk, 1968-75. Member, Transport Users Consultative Committee for Scotland; Past Chairman, District Courts Association; Chairman, Western Isles Justices Committee; Member, Western Isles Health Board; First Deputy Chairman and Chairman, Scottish Small Port Members, British Ports Federation; Chairman: Western Isles Committee for Employment of Disabled Persons, Western Isles Arts Guild, Western Isles District of Scottish Community Drama Association; Vice-Chairman, Lewis Pipe Band; Member, British Airways Consumer Council for Highlands and Islands; Chairman, League of Friends, County Hospital, Stornoway. Recreations: fair weather golf; reading. Address: (h.) 46 Barony Square, Stornoway, Isle of Lewis; T.-0851 3024.

Macleod, Sheriff Norman Donald, QC, MA, LLB. Sheriff Principal of Glasgow and Strathkelvin; b. 6.3.32; m.; 2 s.; 2 d. Educ. Mill Hill School; George Watson's College; Edinburgh University; Hertford College, Oxford. Advocate, 1956; Colonial Administrative Service, Tanganyika, 1957-64; practised, Scots Bar, 1964-67.

MacLeod, Rev. Roderick, MA (Hons), BD, PhD. Minister, Cumlodden and Lochfyneside, Argyll, since 1985; b. 24.6.41, Lochmaddy. Educ. Paible Secondary School; Portree High School; Edinburgh University. Minister, Berneray, North Uist, 1966-85; Member: Western Isles Islands Council, 1974-82, Western Isles Health Board, 1975-79; Clerk, Uist Presbytery, 1981-85; Mackinnon Memorial Lecturer, Cape Breton College, 1979; Visiting Scholar, Harvard Divinity School, 1981; Editor, Gaelic Supplement, Life and Work, since 1980; Founder, Cruisgean (Gaelic newspaper); author of several Gaelic books; writes and broadcasts on Highland affairs in Gaelic and English. Recreations: walking; reading. Address: Furnace, Inverary, Argyll, PA32 8XU.

MacLeod, Rev. William, BSc, ThM. Minister, Partick Free Church, since 1976; b. 2.11.51, Stornoway; m., Marion Johnston; 1 s. Educ. Nicolson Institute; Aberdeen University; Free Church College; Westminster Theological Seminary, USA. Chaplain to Free Church Eventide Home, 1976-79; Free Church Lecturer in Religious Studies, Jordanhill College of Education, 1977-83; Moderator, Glasgow Presbytery, Free Church, 1983-84; Exit Examiner in Theology, Free Church College, 1981-86; Chairman, Lord's Day Observance Society, Glasgow Branch, since 1979; Convener, Church Extension Committee, Free Church, 1984-85. Recreations: reading; gardening; angling. Address: 64 Woodend Drive, Glasgow; T.-041-959 5648.

McLevy, Harry. Regional Officer, Amalgamated Engineering Union, since 1985; Member, General Council, Scottish TUC, since 1986; b. 28.8.36, Dundee; m., Doris Laburn; 3 s.; 1 d. Educ. Logie Junior Secondary. Address: (b.) 145 West Regent Street, Glasgow; T.-041-248 7131.

McLoone, John, BSc, CChem, MRSC. Headteacher, St. Cuthbert's High School, Johnstone, since 1972; b. 14.7.33, Greenock; m., Francisca Albert Rico; 2 s.; 2 d. Educ. St. Columba's High School, Greenock; Glasgow University. Teacher of Science, St. Columba's High School, Greenock, 1957-65; St. Aelred's High School, Paisley: Principal Teacher of Science, 1965-70, Assistant Headteacher, 1970-72. Recreations: bridge; bowls; photography; gardening; reading. Address: (h.) Beechwood, 24 Broomberry Drive, Gourock, Renfrewshire; T.-Gourock 34691.

McLusky, Donald S., BSc, PhD. Senior Lecturer in Biology, Stirling University, since 1977 (Head, Department of Biological Science, 1985); Council Member, Editor of Bulletin, Estuarine and Brackish-Water Sciences Association, since 1983; b. 27.6.45, Harrogate; m., Ruth Alicia Donald; 1 s.; 2 d. Educ. Latymer Upper School, London; Aberdeen University; Stirling University. Stirling University: Assistant Lecturer, 1968-70, Lecturer, 1970-77; Council Member, Scottish Marine Biological Association, 1976-82 and since 1985. Publications: Ecology of Estuaries, 1971; Physiology and Behaviour of Marine Organisms, 1977; The Estuarine Ecosystem, 1981. Recreations: walking; swimming; travel. Address: (h.) 6 Larch Crescent, Doune, Perthshire; T.-0786 841843.

McMahon, Rt. Rev. Mgr. James. Parish Priest, Christ the King, Kings Park, Glasgow, since 1987; Prelate of Honour to Pope John Paul II, since 1980; b. 8.11.21, Paisley. Educ. St. Mirin's Academy, Paisley; Blairs College, Aberdeen; St. Peter's College, Glasgow. Assistant Priest, St. Saviour's, Govan, 1946-57; Spiritual Director, St. Peter's College, 1957-69; Assistant Priest, St. Andrew's Cathedral, Glasgow, 1969-70; Parish Priest, St. John of the Cross, Twechar, Kilsyth, 1970-72; Rector, St. Peter's College, 1972-81; Parish Priest, St. Paul's, Whiteinch, Glasgow, 1981-87; Member, Liturgical Commission, Archdiocese of Glasgow; Vicar Episcopal for Liturgy, Archdiocese of Glasgow, 1979-82. Recreations: golf; swimming; televised sports; reading. Address: Church of Christ the King, 220 Carmunnock Road, Glasgow, G44 5AP; T.-041-637 2882.

McMahon, Hugh Robertson, MA (Hons). Member (Labour), European Parliament, Strathclyde West, since 1984; b. 17.6.38, Saltcoats; m., Helen Paterson Grant; 1 s.; 1 d. Educ. Stevenston High School; Ardrossan Academy; Glasgow University. Schoolteacher in Ayrshire (Largs High, Stevenston High, Irvine Royal Academy, Mainholm Academy); Assistant Head, Ravenspark Academy, 1971-84. Recreation: golf. Address: (b.) Abbeymill Business Centre, Paisley, PA1 1JN; T.-041-889 9990.

McMahon, Rev. Robert James, BD. Minister, Crossford with Kirkfieldbank, since 1976; b. 28.1.27, Glasgow; m., Jessie Millar Steele; 3 s.; 3 d. Educ. Strathbungo School; Glasgow University. Journalist, Glasgow, 1943-56; student, 1953-59; ordained by Glasgow Presbytery, 1959; Missionary, Church of Scotland, Seoni, Central India, 1960-75 (Minister, United Church of Northern India and from 1970 of the Church of North India). Moderator, Lanark Presbytery, 1982. Publication: To God Be The Glory (account of the Evangelical Fellowship of India 1951-1971). Address: The Manse, Crossford, Carluke, ML8 5RE; T.-055-586 415.

McManus, Colin Francis, QFSM, MIFireE. Commandant, Scottish Fire Service Training School, since 1988; b. 15.9.40, Stalybridge; m., Dorothy; 2 d. Educ. Xaverian College, Manchester. Fire service career, 1959-86, starting in Cheshire and ending in Greater Manchester as Deputy Chief Fire Officer, 1981-86; joined Fire Service College as Senior Course Director, then Head of Command Studies. Recreations: golf; gardening. Address: (b.) Scottish Fire Service Training School, Gullane, East Lothian; T.-0620 842236.

McManus, John, BSc, ARCS, PhD, DIC, FRSE, FGS, MIGeol, MIEnvSci. Reader in Geology, St. Andrews University, since 1988; Honorary Director, Tay Estuary Research Centre, since 1979; b. 5.6.38, Harwich; m., J. Barbara Beveridge; 2 s.; 1 d. Educ. Harwich County High School; Imperial College, London University. Assistant, then Lecturer, St. Andrews University, 1964-67; Lecturer, Senior Lecturer, Reader, Dundee University, 1967-88; UNESCO Representative, International Commission on Continental Erosion, 1980-84 and since 1986; Member, Council, Estuarine and Brackish Water Sciences Association; Treasurer, British Sedimentological Research Group; Consultant on Coastal Erosion and Protection to four Regional Councils; Associate Editor, Continental Shelf Research. President: Cupar Choral Association, 1968-78, Cupar Amateur Opera, since 1978. Recreations: music; bird-watching; swimming; stamp collecting. Address: (b.) Department of Geography and Geology, Purdie Building, St. Andrews University, St. Andrews, Fife, KY16 9ST.

McManus, Rev. Matthew Francis. Parish Priest, Kirkcudbright and Gatehouse of Fleet, since 1981; Convenor, Association of Scottish Local

Health Councils, since 1983; b. 22.9.40, Rutherglen. Educ. Sacred Heart High School, Girvan; St. Andrew's College, Drygrange. Ordained, 1965, Assistant Priest, St. Margaret's, Ayr; Parish Priest, New Cumnock, Kirkconnel and Sanquhar, 1976-81; Chairman: Dumfries and Galloway Local Health Council, 1985-87; Chairman, Castle Douglas District CAB, 1984-87; Chairman, Stewartry Council of Voluntary Service, since 1985; Chairman, Stewartry School Council, 1985-87; Member, Scottish Consumer Council, since 1983; Member, Complaints Committee, Law Society of Scotland, since 1985; Secretary, Association of Vocations Directors of Scotland, since 1987. Address: St. Andrew's and St. Cuthbert's, High Street, Kirkcudbright, DG6 4JW; T.-Kirkcudbright 30687.

MacMillan, Professor Andrew, MA, FRIAS, RIBA, ARSA. Principal, Gillespie Kidd & Coia, Architects, since 1966; Professor of Architecture and Head, Mackintosh School of Architecture, Glasgow University, since 1973; b. 11.12.28, Glasgow; m., Angela Lillian McDowell; 1 s.; 3 d. Educ. North Kelvinside Secondary School; Glasgow School of Architecture. Glasgow Corporation, 1945-52; East Kilbride Development Corporation, 1952-54; joined Gillespie Kidd & Coia, 1954 (Partner, 1966); has served as a Member of: CNAA Architecture Board, ARCUK Board of Architectural Education, Scottish Arts Council WASPS Board, GIA Education Committee; Vice President for Education, RIBA; Vice President, Prince and Princess of Wales Hospice, 1981; RIBA Bronze Medal, 1965; RIBA Award for Architecture, four times; RSA Gold Medal, 1975; Concrete Society Award, 1978; Carpenter Award, 1982, 1983; various Saltire Society and Civic Trust awards; Member, Forum, Scottish Churches Architectural Heritage Trust. Recreations: travel; sailing; water colour. Address: (b.) Mackintosh School of Architecture, Glasgow University and Glasgow School of Art, 177 Renfrew Street, Glasgow, G3 6RQ; T.-041-332 9797.

MacMillan, George Gordon, MA (Cantab). Chief of Clan MacMillan; Deputy Lieutenant, Renfrewshire; b. 20.6.30, London; m., (Cecilia) Jane Spurgin; 2 s. Educ. Aysgarth School; Eton; Trinity College, Cambridge. Schoolmaster, Wellington College, 1953-63; Lecturer, Trinity College, Toronto, 1963-64; Lecturer, Bede College, Durham, 1965-74. Owner, small historic house with gardens and woods open to the public. Address: (h.) Finlaystone, Langbank, Renfrewshire, PA14 6TJ; T.-Langbank 285.

MacMillan, Hector. Playwright; b. 1929, Glasgow. Author of: The Rising, Dundee Repertory Theatre, 1973; The Sash, Pool Theatre, Edinburgh, 1973; The Royal Visit, Dundee Repertory, 1974; The Gay Gorbals, Traverse, Edinburgh, 1976; Oh What A Lovely Peace, Scottish Youth Theatre, Edinburgh, 1977; Past Chairman, Scottish Society of Playwrights.

Macmillan, Sheriff Iain Alexander, CBE, LLD, BL. Sheriff of South Strathclyde, Dumfries and Galloway, at Hamilton, since 1981; b. 14.11.23, Oban; m., Edith Janet McAulay; 2 s.; 1 d. Educ. Oban High School; Glasgow University; Scottish Commercial College. RAF (France, Germany, India), 1944-47; Solicitor (Sturrock & Co., Kilmarnock), 1952-81; Council Member, Law Society of Scotland, 1964-79 (President, 1976-77); Chairman, Lanarkshire Branch, Scottish Association for the Study of Delinquency, since 1986. Recreations: golf; hill-walking; photography; music. Address: (h.) 2 Castle Drive, Kilmarnock, Ayrshire; T.-0698 282957.

MacMillan, Rev. James Douglas, MA. Minister, Free Church of Scotland; Professor of Church History and Principles, Free Church College, since 1982; Chairman, Thomas Chalmers Housing Association, since 1984; Chairman, Sub-Committee for Gaelic Religious Broadcasts, BBC, since 1986; b. 30.9.33, Kilchoan; m., Mary Fraser Campbell; 3 s.; 2 d. Educ. Tobermory Junior Secondary School; Aberdeen University; Free Church College. Ordained to St. Columba Free Church, Aberdeen, 1966; translated to St. Vincent Free Church, Glasgow, 1974. Recreations: sea angling; sailing; music; hill-walking. Address: (b.) Free Church College, The Mound, Edinburgh, EH1 2LS; T.-031-226 5286.

McMillan, John Boyd, BSc. Rector, Invergordon Academy, since 1986; b. 16.12.41, Irvine; m., Kathleen Miller; 2 s. Educ. Irvine Royal Academy; Glasgow University; Jordanhill College of Education. Mathematics Teacher: Irvine Royal Academy, 1964-67, Gloucester School, Hohne, BFPO, 1967-72, Invergordon Academy, 1972-74; Principal Teacher of Mathematics, Thurso High School, 1974-82; Assistant Rector, Alness Academy, 1982-86; In-Service Training Co-ordinator, HRC, Inverness, 1986. Football Blue. Recreations: gardening; public speaking. Address: (b.) Invergordon Academy, Academy Road, Invergordon, IV18 0LD; T.-0349 852362.

Macmillan, (John) Duncan, MA, PhD. Reader, Department of Fine Art, Edinburgh University; Curator, Talbot Rice Art Centre, Edinburgh University, since 1979; b. 7.3.39, Beaconsfield; m., Vivien Rosemary Hinkley; 2 d. Educ. Gordonstoun School; St. Andrews University; London University; Edinburgh University. Lecturer, then Senior Lecturer, Department of Fine Art, Edinburgh University; Chairman, Scottish Society for Art History. Recreations: walking; carpentry. Address: (h.) 20 Nelson Street, Edinburgh; T.-031-556 7100.

MacMillan, John MacFarlane Bute, MBE, MC. Chairman, Edinburgh Venture Enterprise Trust (EVENT), since 1982; Chairman, Taste of Scotland Scheme Ltd.; Director, The Murrayfield PLC; b. 12.8.17, Rothesay; m., Rosaline Daphne May Spencer; 1 s.; 1 d. Educ. Allan Glen's School, Glasgow. Regular Army Officer, Royal Artillery, 1939-57; General Manager, then Managing Director, D.S. Crawford Ltd., 1958-62; Director, United Biscuits (Holdings) Ltd., 1962-82; Chairman, D.S. Crawford Ltd., 1979-82; Chairman, UB Restaurants Ltd., 1979-82. Recreations: bird-watching; walking; swimming; tennis. Address: (h.) 24 Cammo Gardens, Edinburgh, EH4 8EQ; T.-031-339 6501.

McMillan, Joyce Margaret, MA (Hons), DipEd. Arts Journalist and Theatre Critic; Radio Critic, Glasgow Herald, since 1983; Scottish Theatre

Critic, The Guardian, since 1984; b. 29.8.52, Paisley. Educ. Paisley Grammar School; St. Andrews University; Edinburgh University. Theatre Reviewer, BBC Radio Scotland and The Scotsman, 1979-81; Theatre Critic, Sunday Standard, 1981-83. Secretary, NUJ Freelance Branch, Edinburgh. Recreations: food; drink; films; music; talking politics; playing with babies. Address: 8 East London Street, Edinburgh, EH7 4BH; T.-031-557 1726.

Macmillan, Marie Alpine, JP. Chairman, Western Isles Health Board, since 1980; b. 26.4.24, Stornoway; m., Ian M. Macmillan, LDS, RFPS; 1 s.; 1 d. Educ. Hyndland School, Glasgow; West of Scotland Commercial College, Glasgow. Chairman: Electricity Consultative Committee, North of Scotland District; Member: Supplementary Benefit Appeals Tribunal, National Insurance Appeals Tribunal; Member, Justices Committee. Recreations: reading; sewing; golf. Address: (h.) 22 Matheson Road, Stornoway, Isle of Lewis; T.-0851 2760.

McMillan, Michael Dale, BSc, LLB, NP. Senior Partner, Sergeants, Solicitors, East Kilbride, since 1978 (Partner, since 1971); Partner, Macdonalds, Solicitors, Glasgow, since 1978; b. 15.2.44, Edinburgh; m., Isobel Ross Mackie; 2 s.; 1 d. Educ. Edinburgh Academy; Edinburgh University. Secretary: East Kilbride Chamber of Commerce, 1971-86 (Treasurer, since 1986), East Kilbride Chamber of Trade, since 1971; Member, East Kilbride Development Corporation, 1979-84; Secretary, Pilgrim Legal Users' Group, since 1985. Captain, East Kilbride Golf Club, 1979. Recreations: golf; sailing; skiing. Address: (h.) Bonnanhill House, Sandford, Strathaven, Lanarkshire; T.-Strathaven 21210.

Macmillan, Rev. William Boyd Robertson, MA, BD. Minister, Dundee Parish Church (St. Mary's), since 1978; Convener, Board of Practice and Procedure, since 1984, and of Business Committee, since 1985, General Assembly, Church of Scotland; b. 3.7.27, Keith; m., Mary Adams Bisset Murray. Educ. Royal High School, Edinburgh; Aberdeen University. Royal Navy, 1946-48; Aberdeen University, 1948-54 (President, SRC, 1953-54); Minister: St. Andrew's Church, Bo'ness, 1955-60, Fyvie Parish Church, 1960-67, Bearsden South Church, 1967-78. President, Church Service Society; Chaplain, City of Dundee District Council. Recreations: golf; reading. Address: Manse of Dundee, 371 Blackness Road, Dundee, DD2 1ST; T.-0382 69406.

McMurray, Donald Brown. Director - Marine and Operations, Clyde Port Authority, since 1987; Director, Ardrossan Harbour Company Ltd., since 1984; Director, Pilotage Authority, since 1983; b. 16.12.32, Glasgow; m., Joan Tulloch; 2 s. Educ. Hyndland Senior Secondary School; Royal College of Technology and Science. Career in Merchant Navy to rank of Master, 1949-68; Clyde Port Authority: Port Control Officer, 1968-71, Depute Harbour Master, 1971-83. Member, Marine Committee, British Ports Association; Member, PSEC Committee, International Ports Association. Recreation: sailing. Address: (b.) Clyde Port Authority, 16 Robertson Street, Glasgow, G2 8DS; T.-041-221 8733.

McMurray, Henry Campbell, BA, MSc (Econ). Director, Scottish Maritime Museum Trust, Irvine, since 1983; b. 27.6.41, Campbeltown; m., Rosemary Jane Elizabeth Law; 1 s.; 2 d. Educ. Campbeltown Grammar School; Dalkeith High School; Leith Nautical College; Leicester University; LSE. Apprentice marine engineer, 1957-62; ships' engineer, 1962-66; Caird Research Fellow, National Maritime Museum, 1970-74; Lecturer in Sociology and Liberal Studies, Southampton College of Higher Education, 1974-75; Research Assistant, then Assistant Keeper, Department of Printed Books and Manuscripts, National Maritime Museum, 1976-83. Member, Industrial Museums Advisory Panel, Scottish Museums Council, since 1984; Oral History Adviser, BBC Radio 4 series, The British Seafarer, 1977-81. Recreations: cinema; sleeping; walking; pottering about the house and garden. Address: (b.) Laird Forge, Gottries Road, Irvine, KA12 8QE; T.-0294 78283.

Macnab of Macnab, Hon. Diana Mary. Chairman, Scotland's Gardens Scheme, since 1983; b. 6.6.36, Edinburgh; m., J.C. Macnab of Macnab (qv); 2 s.; 2 d. Address: (h.) West Kilmany House, Kilmany, Cupar, KY15 4QW.

Macnab of Macnab, James Charles. Executive, Hill Samuel Investment Services Ltd., since 1982; 23rd Chief, Clan Macnab; b. 14.4.26, London; m., Hon. Diana Mary Anstruther-Gray (see Hon. Diana Mary Macnab of Macnab); 2 s.; 2 d. Educ. Radley College; Ashbury College, Ottawa. Served, RAF, Scots Guards, Seaforth Highlanders, 1944-48, gazetted Officer, Royal Federation of Malaya Police Force, 1948-57; managed family estate and farms, 1957-82; former County Councillor, Perth; Member, Central Regional Council, 1978-82; Member, Queen's Bodyguard for Scotland (Royal Company of Archers). Address: (h.) West Kilmany House, Kilmany, Cupar, Fife, KY15 4QW.

Macnab, Joan Catherine Mackenzie, BSc, PhD. Senior Scientist, Medical Research Council Institute of Virology, Glasgow University, since 1980; Honorary Lecturer, Glasgow University, since 1976; b. Netherlee, Glasow; m., Alastair James Macnab; 3 s. Educ. Glasgow High School for Girls; Glasgow University. Early minor appointments in NHS and on grants; Research Assistant to Professor Guido Pontecorvo (Genetics), Glasgow University; Scientist, MRC Institute of Virology. Publications: numerous papers on the role of viruses in oncogenic disease. Recreations: skiing; squash; hill-walking. Address: Medical Research Council, Institute of Virology, Glasgow University, Glasgow, G11 5JR; T.-041-339 8855.

MacNab, Rev. Samuel Gillies, MA, BD, Hon.CF. Minister, St. Luke's and Queen Street Church, Dundee, since 1959; b. 2.10.13, Old Kilpatrick; m., Margaret Miller Maclean; 2 s.; 1 d. Educ. Lossiemouth Higher Grade School; Irvine Royal Academy; St. Andrews University. Assistant Minister, Cupar Old and St. Michael's Church, 1937-38; Minister: Temple Church, Glasgow, 1938-52, Eastbank Church, Glasgow, 1952-56, Irvine Bank and Easton Memorial Church, Darvel, 1956-59. Royal Army Chaplain's Department, 1942-46. Publications: Eastbank Church:

The Story of the Congregation; A Hundred Years: The Story of St. Luke's and Queen Street Church; The Story of the Word: Five Biblical Studies; The Quiet Moment: Daily Prayers and Meditations. Recreations: golf; music. Address: 22 Albert Road, Broughty Ferry, Dundee, DD5 1AZ; T.-Dundee 79212.

McNair, James Burt Oliver, BSc (Hons), DipEd. Headteacher, Waverley Secondary School, since 1976; b. 20.7.33, Bargeddie, Lanarkshire; m., Muriel Eadie; 1 s.; 2 d. Educ. Woodside Secondary School, Glasgow; Glasgow University. Taught, Gambia High School; Principal Teacher of Physics and Assistant Head, North Kelvinside Secondary School; Depute Head, John Street Secondary School; Chairman, SED Joint Working Party on Social and Vocational Skills; Chairman, Drumchapel Citizens' Advice Bureau, 1981-84; Vice Chairman, Scripture Union - Scotland; Director, Drumchapel Community Business. Publication: Basic Knowledge Physics. Address: (b.) 120 Summerhill Road, Glasgow, G15 7LD; T.-041-944 1171.

Macnair, John Bennett, JP. Member, East Lothian District Council, since 1977; b. 28.6.25, Haltwhistle; m., D. Patricia Eldridge; 2 s.; 1 d. Educ. Edinburgh Academy; North Berwick High School; Trinity Academy; Edinburgh and East of Scotland College of Agriculture. Royal Navy, 1942-46. Member, North Berwick Town Council, 1964-75 (Provost, 1971-75); Member, East Lothian County Council, 1967-75 (Vice-Chairman, Education Committee, 1970-75). Vice Chairman, North Berwick Rugby Club; President, North Berwick British Legion; Chairman, North Berwick Boy Scout Executive; Past President, North Berwick Rotary Club. Recreations: shooting; boating; golf; working sheep dogs. Address: (h.) Gilsland, North Berwick, East Lothian.

McNair, Thomas Jaffrey, CBE, MD, FRCSEdin, FRCSEng. President, Royal College of Surgeons of Edinburgh, since 1985; b. 1.3.27, Edinburgh; m., Dr. Sybil M.D. Wood; 1 s.; 1 d. Educ. George Watson's College; Edinburgh University. Consultant Surgeon, Eastern General Hospital, Edinburgh, 1961-64, Chalmers Hospital, Edinburgh, 1964-81, Royal Infirmary, Edinburgh, 1961-87; Surgeon to the Queen in Scotland, 1977-87. Recreation: golf. Address: (h.) 8 Learmonth Terrace, Edinburgh, EH4; T.-031-332 1576.

McNally, Rt. Rev. Anthony Joseph. Rector, Gillis College, Edinburgh, since 1987; Vicar General, Archdiocese of St. Andrews and Edinburgh, since 1985; b. 27.5.32, Edinburgh. Educ. Blairs College, Aberdeen; Seminaire St. Sulpice, Paris. Ordained Priest, 1955; Assistant Priest, Methil, Fife, 1955-63; Missioner, Calabar and Bauchi Province, Nigeria, 1963-67; Assistant Priest, Bonnybridge, 1967-72; Parish Priest, Burntisland, 1972-80, St. Peter's, Morningside, 1980-85; Parish Priest, Musselburgh, and Vicar General, Archdiocese, 1985. Recreations: reading; walking. Address: (b.) 113 Whitehouse Loan, Edinburgh, EH9 1BB; T.-031-447 2807.

McNaught, Peter Cairn, MA, MLitt, FRSA. Principal, Craigie College of Education, Ayr, 1976-87; b. 29.5.25, Glasgow; m., Else Kristine Sandvad; 1 s.; 1 d. Educ. Hutchesons' Boys' Grammar School, Glasgow; Glasgow University. Teacher, Queen's Park and Hutchesons' Boys' Grammar Schools, Glasgow, 1952-58; Lecturer in English, Moray House College of Education, Edinburgh, 1958-60; Principal Lecturer in English, Aberdeen College of Education, 1960-61; Moray House College of Education: Principal Lecturer in Educational Methods and Senior Assistant Principal, 1961-70, Vice-Principal, 1970-75. Vice-Chairman, Scottish Council for the Validation of Courses for Teachers; Member, General Teaching Council for Scotland; Vice-Chairman, West Sound; Member, STV Staff Trust; United Kingdom Award, Council for Educational Technology, 1982; Visiting Professor in English Studies, Strathclyde University, 1988. Recreations: swimming; walking; travel. Address: (b.) Department of Continuing Education, Strathclyde University, Glasgow, G1 1XQ.

Macnaughton, Edwin George, OBE, JP, MA (Hons). Honorary Sheriff; b. 9.5.02, Aberfeldy; m., Annie Meffan (deceased); 2 d. Educ. Breadalbane Academy; Glasgow University. Assistant Teacher: Airdrie Academy, 1923-27, Dalziel High School, 1927-30; Principal Teacher of Classics: Uddingston Grammar School, 1930-32, Airdrie Academy, 1932-44; Headmaster, St. John's Grammar School, Hamilton, 1944-50; Rector, Hamilton Academy, 1950-67. Joint Author: Approach to Latin series, 1938-53, A New Approach to Latin, I, 1973, II, 1974. Address: (h.) 1A Dunchattan Grove, Troon, Ayrshire; T.-0292 316877.

Macnaughton, Rev. Gordon Fraser Hay, MA, BD. Minister, Fenwick Parish Church, since 1985; Member, North Ayrshire Local Health Council, since 1987; b. 27.3.58, Glasgow; m., Isabel Carole Marks. Educ. Glasgow Academy; Glasgow University; Edinburgh University. Assistant Minister, Newlands (South), Glasgow, 1981-85. Secretary, Glasgow Branch, Scottish Schoolboys' Club. Recreations: rugby; wildlife conservation; golf. Address: The Manse, Fenwick, Ayrshire, KA3 6DH; T.-05606 217.

Macnaughton, Edwin George, OBE, JP, MA (Hons). Honorary Sheriff; b. 9.5.02, Aberfeldy; m., Annie Meffan (deceased); 2 d. Educ. Breadalbane Academy; Glasgow University. Assistant Teacher: Airdrie Academy, 1923-27, Dalziel High School, 1927-30; Principal Teacher of Classics: Uddingston Grammar School, 1930-32, Airdrie Academy, 1932-44; Headmaster, St. John's Grammar School, Hamilton, 1944-50; Rector, Hamilton Academy, 1950-67. Joint Author: Approach to Latin series, 1938-53, A New Approach to Latin, I, 1973, II, 1974. Address: (h.) 1A Dunchattan Grove, Troon, Ayrshire; T.-0292 316877.

Macnaughton, James Douglas, BL. Chief Executive, Grampian Regional Council, since 1977; b. 15.12.31, Edinburgh; m., Inger-Marie; 2 s.; 1 d. Educ. Trinity Academy, Edinburgh; Edinburgh University. Colonial Police Service, 1954-62; Aberdeen County Council, 1962-75; Grampian Regional Council, since 1975. Recreations: varied. Address: (b.) Woodhill House, Ashgrove Road West, Aberdeen, AB9 2LU; T.-0224 682222, Ext. 2100.

Macnaughton, Rev. John Anderson, MA, BD. Minister, Hyndland Parish Church, since 1968; b. 30.4.21, London; m., Elizabeth Black Hamilton; 1 s.; 1 d. Educ. High School of Glasgow; Glasgow University. RAF Intelligence, India and Burma, 1941-45; Minister: St. Bride's Parish Church, Glasgow, 1949-57, Park Parish Church, Uddingston, 1957-68. Moderator, Glasgow Presbytery, 1981-82; President, Partick Burns Club, 1985-86. Recreations: golf; hill-walking; theatre-going. Address: Hyndland Manse, 70 Crown Road North, Glasgow, G12 9HW; T.-041-334 1002.

McNaughton, John Ewen, OBE, JP, FRAgS. Chairman, Scotch Quality Beef & Lamb Association, since 1981; Member, British Wool Marketing Board, since 1975; Member, Panel of Agricultural Arbiters, since 1973; Member, Red Deer Commission, since 1975; b. 28.5.33, Edinburgh; m., Jananne Ogilvie Honeyman; 2 s.; 2 d. Educ. Cargilfield; Loretto. Born and bred a hill sheep farmer; after a short spell in America, began farming at Inverlochlarig with father; served on Council, NFU of Scotland; Council Member, Scottish Agricultural Arbiters Association. Elder, Church of Scotland. Recreations: yachting; stalking. Address: Inverlochlarig, Balquhidder, Lochearnhead, Perthshire, FK19 8PH; T.-087 74 232.

Macnaughton, Professor Sir Malcolm Campbell, MD, FRCPGlas, FRCOG, FRSE, FSLCOG (Hon.), FACOG (Hon.), FFARCS (Hon.), FRACOG (Hon.), FIBiol. Professor of Obstetrics and Gynaecology, Glasgow University, since 1970; President, Royal College of Obstetricians and Gynaecologists, London, since 1984; b. 4.4.25, Glasgow; m., Margaret-Ann Galt; 2 s.; 3 d. Educ. Glasgow Academy; Glasgow University. RAMC, 1949-51; Lecturer in Obstetrics and Gynaecology, Aberdeen University, 1957-61; Senior Lecturer, St. Andrews University, 1961-66; Consultant, Eastern Regional, 1966-70. Member, Chief Scientist Committee, SHHD; Member, Biomedical Research Committee and Health Service Research Committee, SHHD; Member, MRC Grant Committee and Cell Systems Board, MRC; Member, Scientific Committee, Hospital Recognition Committee, RCOG; President, RCOG, 1984-87. Chairman, Scottish Perinatal Mortality Advisory Group. Recreations: walking; fishing; curling. Address: (h.) 15 Boclair Road, Bearsden, Glasgow, G61 2AF; T.-041-942 1909.

McNay, W. Gordon, OBE (1978), OStJ, JP, BL. Chief Executive, East Kilbride District Council, since 1975; b. 11.12.25, Wishaw; m., Margaret. Educ. Wishaw High School; Glasgow University. Depute Town Clerk, Burgh of Airdrie, 1952-53; Senior Depute Town Clerk, Burgh of Motherwell and Wishaw, 1953-63; Town Clerk, Burgh of East Kilbride, 1963-75. Recreations: golf; photography; philately. Address: (b.) Civic Centre, East Kilbride, G74 1AB; T.-East Kilbride 28777.

McNee, Sir David Blackstock, Kt, QPM, FBIM, FRSA, CStJ. President, National Bible Society of Scotland; Non-Executive Director and Adviser to a number of public limited companies; b. 23.3.25; m., Isabella Clayton Hopkins; 1 d. Educ. Woodside Senior Secondary School, Glasgow. Joined City of Glasgow Police, 1946; Deputy Chief Constable, Dunbartonshire Constabulary, 1968; Chief Constable: City of Glasgow Police, 1971-75, Strathclyde Police, 1975-77; Commissioner, Metropolitan Police, 1977-82. President, Royal Life Saving Society; Honorary Vice-President, Boys' Brigade, since 1980; Vice-President, London Federation of Boys Clubs, since 1982; Patron, Scottish Motor Neurone Association, since 1982; Freeman, City of London, 1977; President, Glasgow City Committee, Cancer Relief, since 1987. Recreations: fishing; golf; music.

Macneil of Barra, Ian Roderick, BA, LLB, FSA Scot. Wigmore Professor of Law, Northwestern University, Chicago, since 1980; b. 20.6.29, New York City; m., Nancy C. Wilson; 2 s.; 1 d. Educ. Scarborough School; Vermont University; Harvard University. Lt., AUS, 1951-53; Commissioned Officer, USAR, 1950-67; practised law, 1956-59; Member, Cornell Law School Faculty, 1959-72, 1974-80; Visiting Professor, University College, Dar es Salaam, 1965-67, Duke Law School, 1971-72; Professor of Law and Member, Centre for Advanced Studies, Virginia University, 1972-74; Visiting Fellow, Centre for Socio-Legal Studies, Wolfson College, Oxford, 1979, and Edinburgh University Faculty of Law, 1979, 1987; Visiting Professor, Harvard University, 1988-89; Guggenheim Fellow, 1978-79. Member, Standing Council of Scottish Chiefs. Recreations: tennis; reading; historical studies. Address: (h.) Kisimul Castle, Isle of Barra, PA80; T.-Castlebay 300.

McNeil, Neil, MB, ChB, DPH, DPA, FFCM. Director of Community Medicine, Lanarkshire Health Board, since 1976; Honorary Clinical Lecturer, Department of Community Medicine, Glasgow University, since 1973; b. 4.6.31, Glasgow; m., Florence Ward Butterworth; 2 s.; 1 d. Educ. Govan High School; Glasgow University. SHO, Senior Resident, House Physician and House Surgeon, Western Infirmary, Glasgow, 1956-58; Hall Fellow, Glasgow University, 1958-60; Registrar, Western Infirmary, Glasgow, 1960-61; Divisional Medical Officer of Health, City of Glasgow, 1962-65; Principal Lecturer in Health Education and Medical Officer, Jordanhill College, Glasgow, 1965-68; Medical Officer of Health, North-East Hampshire, and Honorary Consultant, Aldershot, 1968-69; Medical Officer, Scottish Home and Health Department, 1969-73; Honorary Lecturer, Departments of Materia Medica and Community Medicine, Glasgow University, 1973-74; Consultant Epidemiologist, Communicable Diseases (Scotland) Unit, Ruchill Hospital, 1973-74; Senior Medical Officer, Scottish Home and Health Department, 1974-76. Dr. MacKinlay Prize in Public Health and Preventive Medicine, Glasgow University, 1962. Publications on community medicine, environmental medicine, public health, immunisation and infectious disease control. Recreations: tennis; photography; natural history; Gaelic language and culture; Scottish history and archaeology. Address: (h.) Claddach, 25 Waterfoot Road, Newton Mearns, Glasgow, G77 5RU; T.-041-639 5165.

McNeill, Billy, MBE. Manager, Celtic Football Club, since 1987; b. 1940, Bellshill; m., Liz; 1 s.; 4 d. Educ. Our Lady's High School, Motherwell. Played for Celtic, retiring in 1975; was first British player to lift European Cup as Captain of Celtic, following defeat of Inter-Milan in Lisbon, 1967; Manager: Clyde, Aberdeen, Celtic, Manchester City; returned to Celtic after eight months as Manager of Aston Villa.

MacNeill, Daniel Anthony, BEM, JP. Provost, Kyle and Carrick District Council, since 1988 (Member, since 1984); b. 25.6.28, Kirkintilloch; m., Agnes Bethia Morgan; 4 s.; 3 d. Educ. Sacred Heart Academy, Girvan. Joined British Rail, 1945; Royal Engineers, 1946-48; Signal Engineering Technician, British Rail, Girvan, 1955; elected local Officer, NUR, 1963 and regional trades Officer, 1969; Member, Ayrshire and Arran Health Board, 1975-79; Vice Chairman, Carrick, Cumnock and Doon Valley Constituency Labour Party. Recreations: reading; walking; music. Address: (h.) 8 Motehill Crescent, Girvan, T.-0465 2455.

McNeill, George Andrew, BSc (Hons), MSc, MRTPI. Director of Physical Planning, West Lothian District Council, since 1978; b. 9.6.47, Edinburgh; m., Thuridur; 2 s. Educ. Musselburgh Grammar School; Edinburgh University. Engineer/Planner, East Lothian District Council, 1972; Depute Director of Planning and Building Control, Midlothian District Council, 1975. Address: (h.) Hiltly, by Linlithgow, West Lothian, EH49 6PJ.

MacNeill, Hector Fletcher, MA. Honorary Sheriff of North Strathclyde at Campbeltown, since 1981; b. 28.9.18, South Knapdale, Argyll; m., Iona Mary Pursell; 1 s.; 2 d. Educ. Keil School; Edinburgh University. RNVR, 1939-46; in action with HMS Hotspur at Battles of Narvik, Matapan and Crete; commanded HM Frigate Keats, 1945-46; Assistant Master, Campbeltown Grammar School, 1947-53, Oban High School, 1953-56; Head Master, Campbeltown primary schools, 1956-83. Member, crew, Campbeltown Lifeboat, 1950-53; President, Campbeltown Horticultural Society, 1963-84; Commodore, Campbeltown Sailing Club, 1968-69; Chairman, Campbeltown Sea Cadets, 1978-83; Member, Presbytery of South Argyll. Recreations: gardening; sailing; woodworking; climbing in Scotland. Address: (h.) Davaar House, Campbeltown, Argyll, PA28 6RE; T.-0586 52349.

McNeill, Ian Cameron, DSc, PhD, BSc. Reader in Chemistry, Glasgow University, since 1977; b. 29.4.32, Glasgow; m., Jessie Robertson Howard; 2 s.; 1 d. Educ. Allan Glen's School, Glasgow; Glasgow University. Assistant in Chemistry, Glasgow University, 1956; ICI Research Fellow, Londonderry Laboratory for Radiochemistry, Durham University, 1958; Lecturer in Chemistry, then Senior Lecturer, Glasgow University, 1961-77. Member, Editorial Board, Polymer Degradation and Stability; Committee Member, Polymer Degradation Discussion Group; Elder, Church of Scotland. Recreations: hill-walking; photography; classical music. Address: (b.) Department of Chemistry, Glasgow University, Glasgow, G12 8QQ; T.-041-339 8855, Ext. 441.

MacNeill, Malcolm Torquil, BL, FSA Scot. Honorary Sheriff, Grampian, Highland and Islands; b. 29.11.19, Bowmore; m., Morag Mackinnon; 2 s.; 1 d. Educ. Dunoon Grammar School; Glasgow University. War Service, The Cameronians (Scottish Rifles), 1939-46 (to Major); Territorial Army, The Cameronians and Parachute Regiment, 1947-52 (to Major); Legal Assistant, Scottish Office, 1950; Procurator Fiscal Depute, 1951; Procurator Fiscal: Moray and Nairn, 1961, Aberdeenshire, 1969; Regional Procurator Fiscal, 1975. Marriage Guidance Counsellor, 1956. Recreations: golf; curling; photography. Address: (h.) 56 Gray Street, Aberdeen; T.-0224 316854.

McNeill, Sheriff Peter Grant Brass, PhD, MA (Hons), LLB. Sheriff of Lothian and Borders at Edinburgh, since 1982; b. 3.3.29, Glasgow; m., Matilda Farquhar Rose; 1 s.; 3 d. Educ. Hillhead High School, Glasgow; Morrison's Academy, Crieff; Glasgow University. Law apprentice, Biggart Lumsden & Co., Glasgow, 1952-55; Carnegie Fellowship, 1955; Faulds Fellowship, 1956-59; Scottish Bar, 1956; Honorary Sheriff Substitute of Lanarkshire, and of Stirling, Clackmannan and Dumbarton, 1962; Standing Junior Counsel to Scottish Development Department (Highways), 1964; Advocate Depute, 1964; Sheriff of Lanarkshire, subsequently of Glasgow and Strathkelvin, at Glasgow, 1965-82; President, Sheriffs' Association, 1982-85. Publications: Balfour's Practicks (Editor), 1962-63; An Historical Atlas of Scotland c. 400 - c. 1600 (Co-Editor), 1975; Adoption of Children in Scotland, 1982. Recreations: legal history; gardening; book-binding. Address: (b.) Sheriffs' Chambers, Sheriff Court House, Lawnmarket, Edinburgh, EH1 2NS; T.-031-226 7181.

MacNeill, Seumas, MA, MInstP. Principal, The College of Piping, since 1945; Editor, The Piping Times, since 1950; b. 12.9.17, Glasgow; m., Janet Boyd; 1 s. Educ. Hyndland School; Glasgow University. Physicist, Royal Technical College, Glasgow, 1940-41; Lecturer, Natural Philosophy Department, Glasgow University, 1941-82. Honorary Secretary, Glasgow District, SYHA, 1943-45. Publications: Tutor for the Bagpipe, Parts 1, 2 and 3 (Co-author); Piobaireachd, the Classical Music for the Bagpipe; Piobaireachd and its Interpretation (Co-author). Recreations: hill-walking; bridge; physics. Address: (h.) 22 Mosshead Road, Bearsden, Glasgow; T.-041-334 3587.

McNeill, William, CEng, MIMechE, MIMarE, MBIM. Principal, Perth College of Further Education, since 1971; b. 30.4.30, Broxburn; m., Jean Shirra Smart; 1 s.; 1 d. Educ. Broxburn High School; Heriot-Watt College. Development Engineer, Scottish Oils Branch, British Petroleum, 1968-71; Engineering Lecturer, Ramsay Technical Institute, 1961-64; Lecturer/Senior Lecturer, Jordanhill College of Education, 1964-67; Head of Engineering, Telford College, 1967-68; Depute Principal, Perth Technical College, 1968-71. Depute Chairman, Friends of Murray Royal Hospital. Recreations: music; golf. Address: (b.) Perth College of Further Education, Crieff Road, Perth, PH1 2NX; T.-Perth 21171.

McNeillie, Isobel Watt, MA (Hons). Headmistress, Craigholme School, Glasgow, since 1975; b. 15.9.30, Johnstone. Educ. Johnstone High School; Paisley Grammar School; Glasgow University. Assistant Teacher, Paisley Grammar School, 1954-60; Exchange Teacher in West Germany, 1958-59; Principal Teacher of German, then Depute Head, Craigholme School, 1960-75. Elder, Church of Scotland, since 1977; Secretary, Secondary Heads Association (Scottish Area), since 1983. Recreations: music; art; bird-watching. Address: (b.) Craigholme School, 72 St. Andrews Drive, Glasgow, G41 4HS; T.-041-427 0375.

McNicol, Professor George Paul, MD, PhD, FRSE, FRCP, FRCPG, FRCPE, FRCPath, FRSA. Principal and Vice-Chancellor, Aberdeen University, since 1981; b. 24.9.29, Glasgow; m., Susan Moira Ritchie; 1 s.; 2 d. Educ. Hillhead High School, Glasgow; Glasgow University. House Surgeon, Western Infirmary, Glasgow, 1952; House Physician, Stobhill General Hospital, Glasgow, 1953; Regimental MO, RAMC, 1953-55; Assistant, Department of Materia Medica and Therapeutics, and Registrar, University Medical Unit, Stobhill General Hospital, 1955-57; University Department of Medicine, Glasgow Royal Infirmary: Registrar, 1957-59, Honorary Senior Registrar, 1961-65; Lecturer in Medicine, 1963-65; Honorary Consultant Physician, 1966-71; Senior Lecturer in Medicine, 1966-70; Reader in Medicine, 1970-71; Professor of Medicine and Honorary Consultant Physician, Leeds General Infirmary, 1971-81; Chairman, Board, Faculty of Medicine, Leeds University, 1978-81; Harkness Fellow, Commonwealth Fund, Department of Internal Medicine, Washington University, 1959-61; Honorary Clinical Lecturer and Honorary Consultant Physician, Makerere UC Medical School Extension, Kenyatta National Hospital, Nairobi, 1965-66. Former Member, Advisory Council on Misuse of Drugs; Chairman, Part I Examining Board, Royal College of Physicians (UK); Member, CICHE; Chairman of the Governors, Rowett Research Institute, Aberdeen. Recreations: skiing; sailing. Address: (h.) Chanonry Lodge, 13 The Chanonry, Aberdeen, AB2 1RP.

Macnicol, Malcolm Fraser, MB, ChB, BSc (Hons), FRCS, MChOrth, FRCSEd (Orth). Consultant Orthopaedic Surgeon, Edinburgh, since 1980; part-time Senior Lecturer, Edinburgh University, since 1980; Honorary Treasurer, Royal College of Surgeons, Edinburgh; Member, Specialist Advisory Committee in Orthopaedic Surgery; b. 18.3.43, Madras, South India; m., Anne Morag; 2 s.; 1 d. Educ. Royal High School, Edinburgh; Edinburgh University. Research Fellow, Harvard University, 1970-71; Senior Lecturer and Orthopaedic Specialist, University of Western Australia, 1978-79. Publications: Basic Care of the Injured Hand; Aids to Orthopaedics; The Problem Knee. Address: (h.) 10 Bright's Crescent, Edinburgh, EH3 2DD; T.-031-667 6609.

McNicoll, Alexander Leonard, MA, LLB. General Secretary, Abbeyfield Scotland, since 1983; b. 15.1.26, Glasgow; m., Catherine Helen Morrison; 1 s.; 1 d. Educ. Pollokshields Secondary School, Glasgow; Glasgow University. Local government solicitor, 1952-82: Dunbarton County Council, 1952-54, Clydebank Town Council, 1954-55, Ayr Town Council, 1955-60, Edinburgh Town Council, 1960-75, Director of Administration, Lothian Regional Council, 1974-82. Address: (h.) 36/4 Glenlockhart Road, Edinburgh, EH14 1BQ; T.-031-444 0627.

McNie, William Malcolm, MA, PhD. Senior Economic Adviser, Economics and Statistics Unit, Industry Department for Scotland, since 1975; b. 18.5.42, Tobermory; m., Mary Philomena; 1 s.; 1 d. Educ. George Watson's College; Caius College, Cambridge University; Columbia University. Economic Assistant, Scottish Office; Economic Adviser, Treasury; Economic Adviser, Customs and Excise. Recreation: golf. Address: (b.) New St. Andrews House, Edinburgh, EH1 3TA; T.-031-556 8400, Ext. 4643.

McOwan, Rennie, FSA Scot. Writer and Broadcaster; b. Stirling; m., Agnes Mooney; 3 s.; 1 d. Educ. Alva Academy. Reporter, Stirling Journal; Sub-Editor, Kemsley Newspapers, Daily Record; Public Relations, Roman Catholic Church; Sub-Editor, Features Writer, Scotsman Publications; Assistant Publicity Secretary, National Trust for Scotland. Correspondent in Scotland for NC News Agency, Washington, and RNS Agency, New York; Scottish Arts Council Lecturer under Writers in Schools scheme; Tutor to writing groups; Contributor to newspapers and magazines in Britain and overseas. Publications: Light on Dumyat; The White Stag Adventure; Walks in the Trossachs and the Rob Roy Country; Discovering the Ochils; contributed to: Walking in Scotland; Poetry of the Scottish Hills; Speak to the Hills; Wild Walks. Recreations: mountaineering; Scottish history and literature. Address: 7 Williamfield Avenue, Stirling, FK7 9AH; T.-0786 61316.

McPartlin, Sheriff Noel, MA, LLB. Sheriff of Grampian, Highland and Islands, at Elgin; b. 25.12.39; m.; 3 s.; 3 d. Educ. Galashiels Academy; Edinburgh University. Solicitor, 1964-76.

MacPhail, Donald John, BSc. Headmaster, Bayble School, Lewis, since 1979; b. 22.10.28, Stornoway; m., Mary Mitchell; 1 s.; 2 d. Educ. Nicolson Institute; Glasgow University. Assistant Teacher of Mathematics and Science, Nicolson Institute, Stornoway, 1959-66; Lecturer in Science, Hamilton College of Education, 1966-71; Headmaster, Leverhulme Memorial School, Harris, 1971-79. Member, Stornoway Trust. Address: (h.) 9 Laxdale, Stornoway, Isle of Lewis; T.-Stornoway 4823.

Macphail, Sheriff Iain Duncan, MA (Hons), LLB. Sheriff of Lothian and Borders at Edinburgh, since 1988; b. 24.1.38; m., Rosslyn Graham Lillias Hewitt; 1 s.; 1 d. Educ. George Watson's College; Edinburgh University; Glasgow University. Admitted Faculty of Advocates, 1963; practice, Scottish Bar, 1963-73; Faulds Fellow in Law, Glasgow University, 1963-65; Lecturer in Evidence and Procedure, Strathclyde University, 1968-69, Edinburgh University, 1969-72; Standing Junior Counsel to Scottish Home and Health Department and Department of Health and Social Security, 1971-73; Extra Advocate-Depute, 1973; Sheriff of Glasgow and Strathkelvin (formerly Lanarkshire), 1973-81; Sheriff of Tayside, Central and Fife at Dunfermline and Alloa, 1981-82; Sheriff of Lothian and Borders at Linlithgow, 1982-88. Chairman, Scottish Association for the Study of Delinquency, 1978-81. Publications: Evidence, 1987; Sheriff Court Practice, 1988. Recreations: music; theatre; reading; writing. Address: (b.) Sheriff Court House, Lawnmarket, Edinburgh, EH1 2NS; T.-031-226 7181.

McPhee, Rev. Duncan Cameron, MA, BD. Joint Secretary-Depute, Department of Ministry and Mission, Church of Scotland, since 1978; b. 26.10.28, Glasgow; m., Elizabeth Anderson MacGregor; 1 s.; 3 d. Educ. Borden Grammar School, Sittingbourne; Glasgow University. Assistant Minister, Barony of Glasgow, 1953-55; Minister: Dalrymple, 1955-61, Airdrie Broomknoll, 1961-78. Assistant Clerk, Hamilton Presbytery, 1964-72; Clerk, 1972-78. Recreations: music; walking. Address: (b.) 121 George Street, Edinburgh, EH2 4YN; T.-031-225 5722.

McPhee, George, BMus, FRCO, DipMusEd, RSAM. Senior Lecturer, Royal Scottish Academy of Music and Drama; Organist and Master of the Choristers, Paisley Abbey, since 1963; b. 10.11.37, Glasgow; m., Margaret Ann Scotland; 1 s.; 2 d. Educ. Woodside Senior Secondary School, Glasgow; Royal Scottish Academy of Music and Drama; Edinburgh University. Studied organ with Herrick Bunney and Fernando Germany; Assistant Organist, St. Giles' Cathedral, 1959-63; joined staff, RSAMD, 1963; Conductor, Scottish Chamber Choir, 1971-75; Conductor, Kilmarnock and District Choral Union, 1975-84; since 1971, has completed 12 recital tours of the United States and Canada; has been both Soloist and Conductor with Scottish National Orchestra; numerous recordings and broadcasts; has taken part in numerous music festivals as Soloist; Adjudicator; Examiner, Associated Board, Royal Schools of Music; Special Commissioner, Royal School of Church Music; Silver Medal, Worshipful Company of Musicians. Recreations: golf; walking. Address: (h.) 17 Main Road, Castlehead, Paisley, PA2 6AJ; T.-041-889 3528.

Macpherson, Sheriff Alexander Calderwood, MA, LLB. Sheriff of South Strathclyde, Dumfries and Galloway, at Hamilton, since 1978; b. 14.6.39; m.; 2 s. Educ. Glasgow Academy; Glasgow University. Solicitor, 1962; private practice, 1962-78.

McPherson, Andrew Francis, BA, DPSA. Co-Director, Centre for Educational Sociology, and Reader in Sociology, Edinburgh University; b. 6.7.42, Louth; 1 s.; 1 d. Educ. Ripon Grammar School; Queen's College, Oxford. Lecturer, Glasgow University, 1965-68; Edinburgh University: Research Fellow, 1968-72, Lecturer, 1972-79, Senior Lecturer, 1979-83, Reader, since 1983. Publications: The Scottish Sixth, 1976; Tell Them from Me, 1980; Reconstructions of Secondary Education, 1983; Governing Education, 1988. Address: (h.) 11 Dalrymple Crescent, Edinburgh.

Macpherson, Archibald Ian Stewart, MB, ChM, FRCSEdin, FRSE. Vice-President, Royal Celtic Society; Vice-President, Clan Macpherson Association; Vice-President, Clan Chattan Association; b. 10.8.13, Newtonmore. Educ. Edinburgh Academy; Fettes College; Edinburgh University. RAMC (Lt. Col.), 1942-47; Rockefeller Scholarship, Presbyterian Hospital, New York, 1948-49; Lecturer, then Senior Lecturer (part-time), Edinburgh University; Consultant Surgeon, Royal Infirmary of Edinburgh, 1954-78, Royal Edinburgh Hospital, 1953-78, Leith Hospital, 1960-67; Vice-President, Royal College of Surgeons, Edinburgh, 1976-79; Editor, Journal, RCSEdin, 1976-81; President, Vascular Surgical Society, 1977; Consultant Surgeon to Army in Scotland; Honeyman Gillespie Lecturer, Edinburgh University, 1952, 1978; Gordon Taylor Medal and Lecturer, 1979; represented Scotland at cricket. Recreations: golf; fishing. Address: (h.) 18 Grange Terrace, Edinburgh, EH9 2LD; T.-031-667 1169.

MacPherson, Archie, BA. Sports Correspondent, BBC Scotland; b. 10.11.34, Glasgow; m.; 2 s. Educ. Coatbridge High School; Jordanhill College. Schoolteacher, 12 years; former Headmaster, Swinton Primary School, Lanarkshire; gave up teaching for broadcasting, 1962; former Rector, Edinburgh University.

MacPherson, Rt. Rev. Colin, STL, LLD. Bishop of Argyll and the Isles, since 1968; b. 5.8.17, Lochboisdale, South Uist. Educ. St. Mary's, Blairs; Propaganda, Rome. Ordained Priest, 1940; Assistant: St. Columba's Cathedral, Oban, 1940-42; Parish Priest: St. Agatha's & St. Anthony's, Knoydart, 1942-51, St. Michael's, Eriskay, 1951-56, St. Mary's, Benbecula, 1956-66, Immaculate Conception, Fort William, 1966-68. Former Member, Inverness County and District Councils; President, Mission Aid Societies Commission, 1972-77; President, Scottish Catholic Lay Apostolate Council, 1970-77; Secretary, Bishops' Conference of Scotland, 1977-82. Address: Bishop's House, Esplanade, Oban, PA34 5AB.

Macpherson, Rev. Colin Campbell Reith, MA, BD. Minister, St. Margaret's Parish Church, Dunfermline, since 1966; b. 8.6.31, Edinburgh. Educ. Aberdeen Grammar School; Merchiston Castle School, Edinburgh; Aberdeen University; Gottingen University; Emmanuel College, Cambridge. Assistant Minister, The Auld Kirk, Ayr, 1958-59; Minister, West Church, Inverurie, 1959-66. Chaplain, Lynebank Hospital, Dunfermline; former Chaplain, 3rd Bn., The Gordon Highlanders (TA). Recreations: books; conversation; walking; visiting stately homes and gardens. Address: (h.) 38 Garvock Hill, Dunfermline, Fife; T.-Dunfermline 723955.

McPherson, Duncan James, MA, SDA. Farmer, since 1959; Vice-Convener, Highland Regional Council; b. 29.10.30, Santos, Brazil; m., Vivian Margaret; 1 s.; 1 d. Educ. Robert Gordon's College, Aberdeen; Aberdeen University. Member, Cromarty Town Council, 1964-75, Ross and Cromarty County Council, 1972-75, Highland Regional Council, since 1974; Highland Area Chairman, Scottish Council (Development and Industry), since 1978; President, Rosemarkie Golf Club; Past President, Black Isle Farmers Society; Chairman, Cromarty Firth Port Authority. Recreations: golf; curling; formerly rugby (Scottish trialist, 1951-56). Address: Cromarty Mains, Cromarty, Ross-shire; T.-038 17 232.

McPherson, Frank Murdoch, MA, PhD, DCP, FBPsS. Director, Tayside Area Clinical Psychology Department, since 1980; b. 2.9.38, Aberdeen; m., Dr. K.M.D. McPherson; 1 s.; 1 d. Educ. Aberdeen Grammar School; Aberdeen University; Edinburgh University. Lecturer in Psychology, Edinburgh University, 1960-66 and 1968-71; Research Fellow, Mental Health Research Fund, 1966-68; Visiting Professor, University of Western Ontario, 1970; Senior Lecturer in Psychology,

Dundee University, 1971-80. Deputy Chairman, National Consultative Committee of Scientists in Professions Allied to Medicine, 1975-78; British Psychological Society: Chairman, Division of Clinical Psychology, 1977-80, Chairman, Joint Standing Committee, BPS and Royal College of Nursing, 1977-80, Chairman, Professional Affairs Board, 1981-84; Member, Scottish Advisory Committee on Top Grade Scientific Posts, since 1984; President, European Federation of Professional Psychologists Associations, since 1982; Temporary Advisor, WHO Regional Office for Europe, since 1982; Member, International Union of Psychological Sciences Committee on Psychology and Health. Recreations: mountaineering; music; supporting Aberdeen FC. Address: (b.) Royal Dundee Liff Hospital, Dundee, DD2 5NF; T.-0382 580441.

Macpherson, Ian, CA. Director and Deputy Chief Executive, British Linen Bank Ltd., since 1979; Director: Low & Bonar PLC, since 1987, Watson & Philip PLC, since 1988, Scottish Unit Managers Ltd., since 1983, Hollingsworth UK Ltd., since 1982; b. 25.3.36; m., Margaret; 1 s.; 1 d. Educ. Morrison's Academy, Crieff. Recreation: golf. Address: (b.) British Linen Bank Ltd., 4 Melville Street, Edinburgh, EH3 7NS; T.-031-243 8304.

Macpherson, Ian Alistair, MBE, CStJ, JP, FIMBM, FCIOB, FFB. Director of Works, East Kilbride Development Corporation; b. 25.1.35, Glasgow; m., Rebecca; 2 d. Educ. Govan High School; Glasgow College of Building and Printing. Freeman Citizen of Glasgow; East Kilbride and Lanarkshire Branch Chairman, Most Venerable Order of St. John; Past President, Institute of Municipal Building Management; Past Chairman, Chartered Institute of Building (Scotland); Vice-President, East Kilbride Chamber of Commerce; Past President, East Kilbride Junior Chamber of Commerce; Member, East Kilbride Committee, British Heart Foundation; Past President, East Kilbride Rotary Club; Past President, Bridgeton Burns Club and East Kilbride Burns Club; Collector, Incorporation of Masons, Trades House of Glasgow. Recreations: golf; curling; raising money for charity; after-dinner speaking. (b.) East Kilbride Development Corporation, Atholl House, East Kilbride, G74 1LU; T.-East Kilbride 35071.

Macpherson, Ian George, BSc, DipEd. Rector, Eastwood High School, since 1977; b. 29.4.37, Perth; m., Gillian Brian; 2 s. Educ. Perth Academy; St. Andrews University; Edinburgh University; Moray House College of Education. Assistant Teacher of Physics, George Heriot's School, Edinburgh, 1959-62; Principal Teacher of Science, Dornoch Academy, Sutherland, 1962-64; Principal Teacher of Physics, Liberton High School, Edinburgh, 1964-69; Adviser in Science, Renfrewshire, 1969-73; Headmaster, Barrhead High School, 1973-77. Member, Strathclyde Executive, Headteachers' Association of Scotland. Recreations: yachting; Ocean Youth Club; Rotary. Address: (h.) 20A Park Road, Paisley, PA2 6JW; T.-041-884 2807.

McPherson, James Alexander Strachan, CBE, MA, BL, LLB, FSA Scot, JP. Lord Lieutenant, Grampian Region (Banffshire), since 1987; Senior Partner, Alexander George & Co., Solicitors, Macduff; Member, Grampian Regional Council, since 1974 (Chairman, Public Protection Committee, 1974-86); Honorary Sheriff, Grampian, Highland and Islands at Banff, since 1972; b. 20.11.27, Wormit, Fife; m., Helen Marjorie Perks; 1 s.; 1 d. Educ. Banff Academy; Aberdeen University. Member, Macduff Town Council and Banff County Council, 1958-75; Provost of Macduff, 1972-75; Convener, Banff County Council, 1970-75; Member, Grampian Health Board, 1974-82; Member, Post Office Users National Council for Scotland, 1976-80; Member, Police Advisory Board for Scotland, 1974-86. Recreations: reading; sailing; swimming. Address: (h.) Dun Alastair, 126 Gellymill Street, Macduff; T.-Macduff 32377.

Macpherson of Drumochter, ((James) Gordon Macpherson), 2nd Baron, JP, FRES, FRSA, FZS. Chairman and Managing Director, Macpherson, Train & Co. Ltd., since 1964; Chairman, A.J. Macpherson & Co. Ltd., since 1973; b. 22.1.24; m., 1, Dorothy Ruth Coulter (deceased); 2 d.; 1 s. deceased; 2, Catherine MacCarthy; 1 s.; 2 d. Educ. Loretto; Wells House, Malvern. RAF, 1939-45. Freeman, City of London. Address: (h.) Kyllachy, Tomatin, Inverness-shire.

McPherson, John, MA, JP. Member, Strathclyde Regional Council; Chairman, Clydebank District Labour Party; b. 27.6.36, Clydebank; m., Roseann Houston; 2 s.; 1 d. Educ. Clydebank High School; Glasgow University. Time-served bricklayer; National Service, 1956-58; elected, Clydebank Town Council, then Clydebank District Council; former Majority Group Leader; last person to be made magistrate, Clydebank Town Council. Recreations: golf; running. Address: (h.) 125 Lennox Drive, Faifley, Clydebank, G81 5DT; T.-Duntocher 73731.

Macpherson, John Hannah Forbes, CBE, OStJ, CA. Chairman, Scottish Mutual Assurance Society, since 1971; Deputy Chairman, TSB Scotland plc, since 1984; Director, TSB Group plc, since 1985; b. 23.5.26, Glasgow; m., Margaret Graham Roxburgh; 1 s. Educ. Glasgow Academy; Merchiston Castle School, Edinburgh. Royal Naval Volunteer Reserve, 1943; Apprentice CA, Wilson Stirling & Co., 1947 (qualified, 1949); Partner, Wilson Stirling & Co. (subsequently Touche Ross & Co.), 1956-86; Chairman: Glasgow Junior Chamber of Commerce, 1965; Scottish Industrial Estates Corporation, 1972, Irvine Development Corporation, 1976; President, Glasgow Chamber of Commerce, 1980; Director: Scottish Metropolitan Property plc, 1986, United Dominions Trust Limited, 1986; Chairman, Glasgow Opportunities Enterprise Trust, 1984; Deputy Chairman, Glasgow Action, 1985; Member, Charity Appeals Committee for Prince and Princess of Wales Hospice, Institute of Neurological Sciences Research; Director, Merchants House and Glasgow Native Benevolent Society; Trustee, Scottish Civic Trust. Recreations: gardening; reading. Address: (h.) 16 Collylinn Road, Bearsden, Glasgow; T.-041-942 0042.

MacPherson, Margaret Hope, MA. Children's Author; b. 29.6.08, Colinton; m., Duncan MacPherson; 7 s. Educ. St. Denis School, Edinburgh;

Edinburgh University. Married, farmed, brought up family; local government, 1945-49; Member, Commission of Inquiry into Crofting, 1951-54 (wrote minority report); Secretary, Skye Labour Party, 1961-84. Publications (children's books): Shinty Boys, 1963; The Rough Road, 1965; Ponies for Hire, 1967; The New Tenants, 1968; Battle of the Braes, 1970; The Boy on the Roof, 1972. Recreations: gardening; watching shinty; football; swimming. Address: (h.) Ardrannach, Torvaig, Portree, Skye; T.-0478 2758.

Macpherson, Peter, FRCP, FRCR, DTCD, FLS. Consultant Neuroradiologist, Institute of Neurological Sciences, since 1970; Honorary Clinical Lecturer, Glasgow University, since 1978; Chairman, Greater Glasgow Area Division of Radiologists, since 1986; b. 10.10.25, Inveraray; m., Agnes Cochrane Davidson; 4 d. Educ. Inveraray Grammar School; Keil School, Dumbarton; Anderson College, Glasgow. House Surgeon, Royal Infirmary, Stirling; Junior Hospital Medical Officer, Robroyston Hospital, Glasgow; Chest Physician, Argyll; Registrar/Senior Registrar, Western Infirmary, Glasgow. Commodore, Oban Sailing Club, 1958-60; President, Glasgow Natural History Society, 1979-81 and 1983-86; Honorary Secretary, Botanical Society of the British Isles, Committee for Scotland, since 1977; Honorary Plant Recorder for Lanarkshire, since 1979. Recreations: natural history; sailing. Address: (h.) Ben Alder, 15 Lubnaig Road, Glasgow; T.-041-632 0723.

Macpherson, Stuart Gowans, MB, ChB, FRCS. Senior Lecturer in Surgery, Glasgow University, since 1977; Honorary Consultant Surgeon, Western Infirmary, Glasgow, since 1977; b. 11.7.45, Glasgow; m., Norma Elizabeth Carslaw; 2 s.; 1 d. Educ. Allan Glen's School, Glasgow; Glasgow University. Surgical training and experience in West of Scotland, with postgraduate training at Harvard Medical School, Boston. Recreations: golf; travelling; reading; family. Address: (b.) Department of Surgery, Western Infirmary, Glasgow, G11 6NT; T.-041-339 8822, Ext. 4710.

Macpherson, Rev. Stewart MacColl, MA. Minister, Dunfermline Abbey, Fife, since 1969; b. 5.11.25, Armadale, West Lothian; m., Janet May Marshall Tennant; 1 s.; 1 d. Educ. Greenock Academy; Edinburgh University and New College. Minister: Swinton Parish Church, near Duns, 1953-58, St. Kentigern's Church, Lanark, 1958-65, Queen's Park West Church, Glasgow, 1965-69; last Moderator, Dunfermline and Kinross Presbytery. Recreations: music; water colour painting; writing; reading. Address: Abbey Manse, 116 Halbeath Road, Dunfermline, Fife, KY11 4LA; T.-Dunfermline 721022.

Macpherson of Cluny (and Blairgowrie), Colonel the Honourable Sir William, KB (1983), TD, MA. 27th Hereditary Chief of the Clan Macpherson (Cluny-Macpherson); b. 1.4.26; m., Sheila McDonald Brodie; 2 s.; 1 d. Educ. Summer Fields, Oxford; Wellington College; Trinity College, Oxford. Scots Guards, 1944-47 (Captain); 21st Special Air Service Regiment (TA), 1951-65 (Lt.-Col. Commanding, 1962-65); Honorary Colonel, 21st SAS, since 1983. Called to the Bar, Inner Temple, 1952; Queen's Counsel, 1971-83; Recorder of the Crown Court, 1972-83; Member, Senate and Bar Council, 1979-83; Bencher, Inner Temple, 1978; Judge of the High Court of Justice (of England and Wales), Queen's Bench Division, 1983; Honorary Member, Northern Circuit, since 1987. Member, Queen's Bodyguard for Scotland (Royal Company of Archers), since 1976; Member, Board of Management, Royal Scottish Corporation. Recreations: golf; fishing; rugby football. Address: (h.) Newton Castle, Blairgowrie, Perthshire; (b.) Royal Courts of Justice, Strand, London, WC2.

Macphie, Charles Stewart. Chairman and Managing Director, Macphie of Glenbervie Ltd., since 1965; President, Bakery and Allied Trades Association, since 1983; Council Member, CBI Scotland; Non-Executive Director, North of Scotland Hydro-Electric Board; Farmer; b. 22.9.29, Baltimore, Maryland; m., Elizabeth Margaret Jill Pearson; 1 s.; 1 d. Educ. Dalhousie Castle School; Rugby. Chairman of Governors, Oxenfoord Castle School; Trustee, Kincardineshire Royal Jubilee Trust. Address: (h.) Knock Hill House, Glenbervie, Kincardineshire; T.-056-94 257.

McQuaid, John, MA (Hons), MEd, PhD. Composer and Psychologist; b. 14.3.09, Lochgelly; m., Mary Darkin. Educ. St. Mungo's Academy, Glasgow; Glasgow University; Edinburgh University. Taught, 1935-40; War Service, 1941-46 (Intelligence Corps), Africa and SE Asia; taught, 1946-51; Psychologist, 1952-77; studied music under Erik Chisholm; numerous broadcasts and public performances of compositions (piano, chamber music, orchestral, etc.). Address: (h.) St. Anne's, 8 Ardrossan Road, Saltcoats, KA21 5BW; T.-0294 63737.

Macquaker, Donald Francis, MA (Oxon), LLB. Chairman, Scottish Health Service Common Services Agency, since 1987; Chairman, Greater Glasgow Health Board, 1983-87; Partner, T.C. Young & Son, Writers, Glasgow, since 1957; Director, Lithgows Limited, since 1987; b. 21.9.32, Stair; m., Susan Elizabeth Finlayson; 1 s.; 1 d. Educ. Winchester College; Trinity College, Oxford; Glasgow University. Former Member, Board of Management, Glasgow Royal Maternity Hospital and Associated Women's Hospital (latterly Vice-Chairman); Chairman, Finance and General Purposes Committee, Greater Glasgow Health Board, 1974-83. Recreations: shooting; fishing; gardening. Address: (h.) Blackbyres, by Ayr; T.-0292 41088.

MacQueen, Professor Jack (John), MA (Glasgow), MA (Cantab), Hon DLitt. Director, School of Scottish Studies, Edinburgh University, since 1969 (Professor of Scottish Literature and Oral Tradition, since 1972); b. 13.2.29, Springboig; m., Winifred W. MacWalter; 3 s. Educ. Hutchesons' Boys Grammar School; Glasgow University; Christ's College, Cambridge. RAF, 1954-56 (Pilot Officer, Flying Officer); Assistant Professor of English, Washington University, St. Louis, Missouri, 1956-59; Edinburgh University: Lecturer in Medieval English and Scottish Literature, 1959-63, Masson Professor of Medieval and Renaissance Literature, 1963-72. Publications: St. Nynia, 1961; Robert Henryson, 1967; Ballattis of Luve, 1970; Allegory, 1970; Progress and Poetry,

1982; Numerology, 1985; Rise of the Historical Novel, 1988; Oxford Book of Scottish Verse (with T. Scott), 1966; A Choice of Scottish Verse 1470-1570 (with W. MacQueen), 1972. Recreations: walking; occasional archaeology; music. Address: (b.) School of Scottish Studies, 27 George Square, Edinburgh, EH8 9LD; T.-031-667 1011, Ext. 6674.

McQueen, James Donaldson Wright, MA, PhD. Deputy Managing Director, Scottish Milk Marketing Board, since 1985; Member: CBI Scottish Council, since 1987, Scottish Dairy Council, since 1983; Director, Taste of Scotland Scheme Ltd., since 1984; b. 14.2.37, Dumfries; m., Jean Evelyn Brown; 2 s.; 1 d. Educ. King's Park School, Glasgow; Glasgow University. Assistant Lecturer, Department of Geography, Glasgow University, 1960-61; Junior Manager, Milk Marketing Board (England and Wales), 1961-62; Scottish Milk Marketing Board: Economist, 1962-70, Marketing Services Manager, 1970-78; Marketing Director, 1978-85. Recreations: golf; gardening; photography. Address: (h.) Ormlie, 53 Kingston Road, Bishopton, Renfrewshire, PA7 5BA; T.-Bishopton 862380.

Macqueen, Julie-Ann, OBE, CQSW, BA, SNNEB. Director, Scottish Council for Single Parents, 1967-88; b. 30.4.28, Jerusalem. Educ. Convent of Notre Dame de Sion, Jerusalem, London, Shropshire; Edinburgh University; Open University. Nursery Nurse in Edinburgh, 1946-54; between 1954 and 1967, held the posts of Personnel Officer, Crawfords Biscuit Factory, Leith, School Welfare Officer, Dundee and Senior Social Worker, Scottish Catholic Child Care Office, Glasgow. Trustee, Buttle Trust for Children; a Vice-President, National Out of School Alliance. Publication: Unmarried Parents and their Children. Recreations: reading; listening to music; cooking; house interiors; antiques; travel; people. Address: (h.) 7 North Park Terrace, Edinburgh, EH4 1DP.

McQuilken, Rev. John Ernest, MA, BD. Minister, Glenaray and Inveraray, since 1983; b. 14.8.27, Port Glasgow; m., Grace Mary Middleton McKenzie; 1 d. Educ. Port Glasgow High School; Greenock High School; Queen's College and St. Mary's College, St. Andrews University. Newspaper Sub-Editor, 1949-62; student, 1962-69; Minister: Drylaw, Edinburgh, 1969-78, Caddonfoot with Heatherlie, Selkirk, 1978-83. Recreations: looking at paintings; poetry; gardening. Address: The Manse, Inveraray, Argyll, PA32 8XT; T.-Inveraray 2060.

Macrae, Rev. Donald Angus, MA, JP. Minister, Tarbert, Harris, since 1956; b. 2.4.18, Miavaig, Isle of Lewis; m., Annie Macleod; 2 s.; 2 d. Educ. Nicolson Institute, Stornoway; Glasgow University. Minister: Sleat, 1942-49, Benbecula, 1949-56. Address: The Manse, Tarbert, Isle of Harris, PA85 3DF; T.-Harris 2231.

MacRae, Duncan Keith, MA, LLB, NP. Partner, Jenkins & Jardine, Solicitors, Stirling, since 1963; b. 24.9.30, Glenshiel, Ross-shire; m., Edith Watson; 2 s. Educ. Plockton; Aberdeen University. Flying Officer, RAF; Partner, McCulloch & MacRae, Solicitors, Grantown-on-Spey, 1956-62; Member, Council, Scottish Law Agents' Society, since 1976 (President, 1988-89); Local Secretary, Macmillan Cancer Relief Society; Director, Stirling Ice Rink Co. Ltd. Recreations: curling; shooting; hill-walking; fishing. Address: (b.) 80 Port Street, Stirling, FK8 2LR; T.-Stirling 50366.

MacRae, John C., BSc, PhD. Head, Physiology Division, Rowett Research Institute, since 1985; b. 10.7.42, Skelmersdale, Lancashire; m., Eileen E.; 2 s. Educ. Ormskirk Grammar School; Newcastle University. Research Scientist, Applied Biochemistry Division, Department of Scientific and Industrial Research, Palmerston North, New Zealand, 1968-71; Research Scientist, Hill Farming Research Organisation, Penicuik, 1972-77; Head, Department of Energy Metabolism, Rowett Research Institute, 1978-85. Member, Editorial Board, British Journal of Nutrition, 1977-83; Committee Member, Scottish Group, Nutrition Society, 1973-75 and 1983-86. Recreations: sport (golf, cricket); family life. Address: (b.) Rowett Research Institute, Greenburn Road, Bucksburn, Aberdeen; T.-Aberdeen 712751.

MacRae, Rev. Malcolm Herbert, MA. Minister, Coalsnaughton Parish Church, since 1986; b. 27.9.45, Lima, Peru. Educ. Inverness High School; Arbroath High School; Free Church College, Edinburgh; Aberdeen University. Minister, West Free, Coatbridge, 1971; Associate Minister, Dunblane Cathedral, 1984; Minister, South Mull, 1985. Leader, Shaftesbury Project Study Group on Theology and Philosophy; Editor, Link. Recreations: sport; sailing; cine-photography; painting. Address: Longriggs Manse, Coalsnaughton, FK13 6LJ; T.-0259 50272.

Macrae, Col. Robert Andrew Alexander Scarth, MBE (1953), JP. Lord Lieutenant of Orkney, since 1972; Farmer; b. 14.4.15; m.; 2 s. Educ. Lancing; Sandhurst. Member, Orkney County Council, 1970-74, Orkney Islands Council, 1974-78; Vice Chairman, Orkney Health Board, 1974-79.

Macrae-Gibson, O. Duncan, MA, DPhil. Reader in English, Aberdeen University, since 1986; b. 30.1.28; m., Frances; 1 s.; 1 d. Educ. Royal Naval College, Dartmouth; St. Catherine's Society, Oxford. Royal Navy, 1949-51; Teacher of maladjusted children, 1955; printing machine assistant, OUP, 1956; Lecturer: Oriel and University Colleges, Oxford, 1957-59, Leicester University, 1959-65; Lecturer, then Senior Lecturer, Aberdeen University, 1965-86. Publications: Learning Old English; (editions) Of Arthour and of Merlin; The Old English Riming Poem. Recreations: hill-walking; skiing; riding; tennis. Address: (b.) Department of English, Aberdeen University, King's College, Old Aberdeen, Aberdeen, AB9 2UB; T.-Aberdeen 272627.

MacRitchie, Professor Farquhar, CBE (1968), MA, LLB, Hon. LLD; Consultant, Burnett & Reid, Advocates, Aberdeen, 1979-85; b. 1.11.02, Isle of Lewis; m., Isobel Ross; 1 s. (deceased). Educ. Aberdeen University. Aberdeen University: Assistant Lecturer in Law, 1940-45, Lecturer in Mercantile Law, 1945-46, Professor of Conveyancing, 1946-74. Honorary Sheriff, Aberdeen; Convener, Legal Education Committee, Law

Society of Scotland, 1955-70; Vice-President, Law Society of Scotland, 1963; Partner, Morice & Wilson, Advocates, Aberdeen, 1939-79; Consultant, Burnett & Reid, Advocates, Aberdeen, 1979-85. Recreation: golf. Address: (h.) 60 Rubislaw Den North, Aberdeen; T.-Aberdeen 315458.

MacRobert, John Carmichael Thomas, MA (Cantab), LLB (Glasgow), NP. Solicitor; Honorary Sheriff; Honorary Secretary and Treasurer, Paisley and District Hospitals Voluntary Service Association, since 1947; b. 26.4.18, Edinburgh; m., Anne Rosemary Millar; 1 s.; 2 d. Educ. Craigflower; Rugby; Queens' College, Cambridge; Glasgow University. Captain, Royal Artillery (Despatches, Burma); Secretary, Local Productivity Committee, 15 years; Member, Council, Law Society of Scotland, 1965-77; Scottish Office Working Parties on Planning Reform and "Planning Exchange"; Hon. Solicitor, subsequently Trustee, Scottish Civic Trust; Council Member, Clyde Estuary Amenity Council; Hon. President (Past Chairman), Paisley South Conservatives. Recreations: sailing; country sports; gardening. Address: (h.) Failte, Colintraive, Argyll; T.-070 084 239.

McSherry, John Craig Cunningham, LLB (Hons), NP. Solicitor, since 1974; b. 21.10.49, Irvine; 2 s. Educ. Ardrossan Academy; Glasgow University. President, University Law Society, 1971-72; Partner, McSherry Halliday, Solicitors; Chairman, Largs and District Citizens' Advice Bureau, 1976-83; Council Member, Law Society of Scotland, 1982-85; Honorary Legal Adviser, Largs CAB and Saltcoats CAB. Recreations: music; skiing; gardening; languages; golf. Address: (b.) 9 Chapelwell Street, Saltcoats, Ayrshire; T.-0294 64366.

McSwan, Malcolm, CA. Managing Director, Racal-MESL Ltd., since 1983; Director, Wolfson Microelectronics Ltd., since 1984; Chairman, West Lothian ITEC Ltd., since 1981; b. 31.8.39, Glasgow; m., Juliet Cowper-Jackson; 2 s. Educ. Royal High School, Edinburgh. Trustee, Central Scotland Countryside Trust. Recreations: renovation; sailing. Address: (b.) Lochend Industrial Estate, Newbridge, Midlothian; T.-031-333 2000.

MacSween, Iain MacLean, BA (Econ), MPhil. Chief Executive, Scottish Fishermen's Organisation, since 1982; b. 20.9.49, Glasgow; m., Jean Gemmill Martin; 3 s.; 1 d. Educ. Knightswood Secondary School; Strathclyde University; Glasgow University. Fisheries Economics Research Unit, 1973-75; Department of Agriculture and Fisheries for Scotland, 1975-77; Scottish Fishermen's Organisation, since 1977; President, European Federation of Fishermen's Organisations. Address: (b.) 601 Queensferry Road, Edinburgh, EH2 6EA; T.-031-339 7972.

MacSween, Malcolm D., MA (Hons), BLitt. Head Teacher, Abronhill High School, Cumbernauld, since 1978; b. 10.10.34, Torridon, Ross and Cromarty. Educ. Golspie High School; Glasgow University. Teacher, Glasgow schools, 1959-71; Assistant Head Teacher, Shawlands Academy, 1971-75; Depute Head Teacher, Stanely Green High School, Paisley, 1975-78. Elder, Church of Scotland; former Member, Scottish Certificate of Examination Board. Recreations: bowls; reading; walking; visiting places of interest in UK. Address: (b.) Abronhill High School, Larch Road, Cumbernauld, Glasgow.

MacSween, Professor Roderick Norman McIver, BSc, MD, FRCPGlas, FRCPEdin, FRCPath, FRSE, FIBiol. Professor of Pathology, Glasgow University, since 1984; Honorary Consultant Pathologist, Western Infirmary, Glasgow, since 1970; b. 2.2.35, Kinloch, Lewis; m., Marjory Pentland Brown; 1 s.; 1 d. Educ. Inverness Royal Academy; Glasgow University. Successively Lecturer, Senior Lecturer, Reader and Titular Professor in Pathology, Glasgow University, 1965-84; Physician/Research and Education Associate, Colorado University Medical Center, Denver, 1968-69; Honorary Fellow, South African Society of Pathologists, 1982; Otago Savings Bank Visiting Professor, Otago University, 1983; Hans Popper Lecturer in Liver Pathology, Columbia University College of Physicians and Surgeons, New York, 1988. President, Royal Medico-Chirurgical Society of Glasgow, 1978-79; Honorary Librarian, Royal College of Physicians and Surgeons, Glasgow; President-Elect, International Academy of Pathology, British Division; Editor, Histopathology (Journal). Publications: Pathology of the Liver, 2nd edition (Co-Editor); Recent Advances in Histopathology, Nos. 11-13; Recent Advances in Hepatology, No. 1. Former Captain, Dunaverty and Machrihanish Golf Clubs. Recreations: golf; gardening; opera; hill-walking; more golf! Address: (b.) University Department of Pathology, Western Infirmary, Glasgow, G11 6NT; T.-041-339 8822, Ext. 4732.

McTaggart, Dick, MBE (1985). Boxer; Coach, Scottish Amateur Boxing Association, since 1983; b. 1935, Dundee. Suffered only 24 defeats in 634 contests; Olympic Gold Medallist, Melbourne, 1956; Olympic Bronze Medallist, Rome, 1960; British Empire Lightweight Champion, 1958; European Lightweight Champion, 1961; British Empire Silver Medallist, 1962; winner of five ABA titles, seven Scottish championships, 32 cups, 57 plaques, 49 medals; Assistant Coach, British Olympic Team, Los Angeles Olympics, 1984; works for Rolls Royce.

McTaggart, Robert. MP (Labour), Glasgow Central, since 1980; b. 2.11.45, Glasgow; m., Elizabeth Jardine; 1 s.; 2 d. Educ. Holyrood Secondary School; Stow College; Glasgow College of Building. Shop Steward, EETPU, Govan Shipbuilders, 1971-77; Member, Glasgow Corporation, 1974-75; Member, Glasgow District Council, 1977-80. Recreations: spectating football, athletics; playing snooker, draughts; reading. Address: (h.) 61 St. Mungo Avenue, Glasgow, G4 OPL; T.-01-219 3450.

MacThomas of Finegand, Andrew, FSA Scot. 19th Chief of Clan MacThomas, since 1970; b. 28.8.42, Edinburgh; m., Anneke Cornelia Susanna Kruyning; 1 s. Educ. in Scotland, then St. Edward's, Oxford. Worked in banking, 1960-66, credit card industry, 1966-82, public affairs, since 1982. Member, Standing Council of Scottish Chiefs; President, Clan MacThomas Society; Vice-President, Clan Chattan Association. Recreations: travel; horse-racing. Address: c/o Clan MacThomas Society, 19 Warriston Avenue, Edinburgh, 3.

MacVicar, Angus, MA, DUniv. Author; b. 28.10.08, Argyll; m., Jean Smith McKerral; 1 s. Educ. Campbeltown Grammar School; Glasgow University. Reporter, Campbeltown Courier, 1931-33; Freelance Author; Army Service, 1940-45 (Captain, RSF); Freelance Author, Journalist, Radio and TV Scriptwriter; published 71 books, including adult novels, children's novels, adult and children's non-fiction, plays; Honorary Sheriff-Substitute, Argyll, 1965; Doctorate, Stirling University, 1985. Recreations: golf; gardening; amateur drama. Address: (h.) Achnamara, Southend, Campbeltown, Argyll, PA28 6RW; T.-0586 83 228.

McVicar, George Christie, DipMusEd, RSAM; Hon.FTSC. Chairman, Scottish Amateur Music Association, since 1982; Examiner, Trinity College of Music, since 1979; Convenor, Saltire Scots Song Competitions, since 1986; b. 17.3.19, Dumbarton. Educ. Dumbarton Academy; Royal Scottish Academy of Music and Drama. Teacher of Music, Dunbartonshire Schools, 1946-54; Lecturer in Music, Moray House College of Education, 1954-56; Adviser in Music to Stirlingshire and subsequently Central Region, 1956-79. Adjudicator Member, British Federation of Music Festivals. Publications: Oxford Scottish Song Book and New Scottish Song Book. Address: (h.) 22 Queen Street, Stirling, FK8 1HN; T.-0786 72074.

McVie, John, BL, WS, NP. Partner, McVies WS; Honorary Sheriff-Substitute, Lothian and Borders; b. 7.12.19, Edinburgh; m., Lindsaye Woodburn Mair; 1 s.; 1 d. Educ. Royal High School; Edinburgh University. Captain, 7/9th Bn., The Royal Scots, 1940-46 (Signal Officer, North West Europe); Solicitor in private practice in Haddington, since 1947; Town Clerk, Royal Burgh of Haddington, 1951-75. Recreations: fishing; golf; motoring. Address: (h.) Ivybank, Haddington, East Lothian; T.-062-082 3727.

McWilliam, Colin Edgar, MA, FRSA, Hon FRIBA. Senior Lecturer, Architectural History and Conservation, Heriot-Watt University and Edinburgh College of Art, since 1978; b. 19.2.28, London; m., Helene Christine Jannink; 1 s.; 2 d. Educ. Charterhouse; Caius College, Cambridge. Formerly: Officer in Charge, Scottish National Buildings Record; Assistant Secretary, National Trust for Scotland; Morgan Professor of Architectural Design, Louisville University. Member, Council, The Victorian Society; Member, Historic Buildings Council for Scotland, 1983-86; Vice President, Architectural Heritage Society of Scotland; Vice President, Edinburgh Antique and Fine Art Society; Hon. Order of Kentucky Colonels. Publications: Scottish Townscape; Buildings of Scotland - Lothian; Edinburgh (Co-author). Recreation: discovering towns and churches. Address: (b.) Edinburgh College of Art, Lauriston Place, Edinburgh, EH3 9DF; T.-031-229 9311.

McWilliam, James, MA (Hons), DipEd. Rector, Lochaber High School, 1970-88; Chairman, Highland Health Board, since 1983; b. 4.10.27, Portsoy, Banffshire; m., Helen C. Brodie; 3 d. Educ. Fordyce Academy, Banffshire; Glasgow University. Teacher of English, Calderhead School, Shotts, 1951; National Service (Royal Army Education Corps), 1951-53; Teacher, Coatbridge High School, 1953; Special Assistant, Beath High School, Cowdenbeath, 1958; Principal Teacher of English, Campbeltown Grammar School, 1961-70. Member, Highland Health Board, since 1978 (Chairman, Practitioners' Committee, 1981); Honorary Sheriff, Grampian, Highlands and Islands, since 1978; Chairman: Lochaber Music Club, League of Friends of Belford Hospital, local committee of British Heart Foundation; Past President: Lochaber Rotary Club, Lochaber EIS, Highland Secondary Headteachers Association. Recreations: music; TV; golf (occasionally). Address: (h.) The Schoolhouse, Camaghael, Fort William; T.-0397 2572.

McWilliam, Robert John, MB, ChB, FRCPG, DO. Consultant Ophthalmic Surgeon; Honorary Lecturer, Glasgow University; Civilian Ophthalmic Specialist for Royal Navy in Scotland; b. Glasgow; m., Louisa R. Denholm; 2 s. Educ. High School of Glasgow; Glasgow University. Recreations: fishing; gardening. Address: (h.) 4 Torridon Avenue, Glasgow, G41; T.-041-427 1204.

McWilliam, Rev. Thomas Mathieson, MA, BD. Minister, Lylesland Parish Church, Paisley, since 1980; b. 12.11.39, Glasgow; m., Patricia Jane Godfrey; 1 s.; 1 d. Educ. Eastwood Secondary School; Glasgow University; New College, Edinburgh. Assistant Minister, Auld Kirk of Ayr, 1964-66; Minister: Dundee St. David's North, 1966-72, East Kilbride Greenhills, 1972-80; Convener, Youth Education Committee, General Assembly, 1980-84; Moderator, Paisley Presbytery, 1985-86. Recreations: sea angling; walking; reading; gardening; bowling. Address: (h.) 28 Southfield Avenue, Paisley, PA2 8BY; T.-041-884 2882.

M

Maan, Bashir Ahmed, JP, DL. Company Director, B.A. Mann & Co. Ltd., since 1981; Honorary Research Fellow, Glasgow University, since 1988; Chairman, Glasgow International Sports Festival Company Ltd., since 1987; b. 22.10.26, Maan, Pakistan; 1 s.; 3 d. Educ. D.B. High School, Quila Didar Singh; Punjab University. Involved in the struggle for creation of Pakistan as a student, 1943-47; organised rehabilitation of refugees from India in Maan and surrounding areas, 1947-48; emigrated to UK and settled in Glasgow, 1953; Founder Secretary, Glasgow Pakistan Social and Cultural Society, 1955-65 (President, 1966-69); Member, Executive Committee, Glasgow City Labour Party, 1969-70; Vice-Chairman, Glasgow Community Relations Council, 1970-75; Member, Glasgow Corporation, 1970-75 (Magistrate, City of Glasgow, 1971-74; Vice-Chairman, then Chairman, Police Committee, 1971-75); Member, National Road Safety Committee, 1971-74 and Scottish Accident Prevention Committee, 1971-75; Member, BBC Immigrant Programmes Advisory Committee, 1972-80; Convenor, Pakistan

Bill Action Committee, 1973; contested East Fife Parliamentary seat, February 1974; President, Standing Conference of Pakistani Organisations in UK and Eire, 1974-77; Police Judge, City of Glasgow, 1974-75; Member, City of Glasgow District Council, 1975-84; Deputy Chairman, Commission for Racial Equality, 1977-80; Member, Scottish Gas Consumers Council, 1978-81; Bailie, City of Glasgow, 1980-84; Member, Greater Glasgow Health Board, since 1981; Deputy Lieutenant, Glasgow, since 1982; Founder Chairman, Scottish Pakistani Association, since 1984; Judge, City of Glasgow District Courts; Chairman, Strathclyde Community Relations Council, since 1986; a Governor, Jordanhill College of Further Education, since 1987; Chairman, Mosque Committee, Islamic Centre, Glasgow, since 1986. Recreations: golf; reading. Address: (h.) 20 Sherbrooke Avenue, Glasgow, G41 4PE; T.-041-427 4057.

Mabon, Rt. Hon. Dr. Dickson, PC (1977), KStL, MB, ChB, DHMSA, MFHom, FRSA, FInstPet, FInstD. Chairman, British Indigenous Technology, since 1984; Chairman, A.H. McIntosh Ltd., since 1985; Chairman, Hall Russell Offshore, since 1986; Chairman, Scottish Social and Liberal Democrats; b. 1.11.25, Glasgow; m., Elizabeth Zinn; 1 s. Educ. North Kelvinside School; Glasgow University. MP, Greenock and Port Glasgow, 1955-83; Joint Parliamentary Under Secretary of State for Scotland, 1964-67; Minister of State for Scotland, 1967-70; Minister of State for Energy, 1976-79. Vice Chancellor, Order of St. Lazarus of Jerusalem; Chairman, SOS Children's Villages. Address: (h.) 2 Sandringham, Largs, KA30 8BT; T.-0475 672293.

Macartney, Rev. William Macleod, MA; b. 11.10.12, Partick; m., Jessie H.I. Low; 1 s.; 2 d. Educ. George Watson's; Edinburgh University; Zurich University. Ordained, 1938; Missionary in Africa, 1938-45; former Minister: Bridge of Weir; Elgin; St. Machar's Cathedral, Old Aberdeen; Hutton and Fishwick; Vienna Community Church; former Member, Health Boards, Elgin and Borders; former Convener, Church of Scotland Publications Committee. Publications: Dr. Aggrey; The Church and the Underdog. Recreations: fishing; writing. Address: (h.) Couttie Cottage, Coupar Angus, PH13 9HF; T.-0282 28152.

Macartney, W.J. Allan, MA, BLitt, PhD. Staff Tutor, Social Sciences, The Open University in Scotland, since 1975; Honorary Fellow, Edinburgh University, since 1981; Member, National Executive Committee, Scottish National Party, since 1984; b. 1941, Accra, Ghana; m., J.D. Anne Forsyth; 2 s.; 1 d. Educ. Elgin Academy; Tuebingen University; Marburg University; Edinburgh University; Glasgow University. Teacher, Eastern Nigeria, 1963-64; Lecturer in Government and Administration, University of Botswana, Lesotho and Swaziland, 1966-74; Research Fellow, Edinburgh University, 1974-75; Honorary Secretary, Unit for the Study of Government in Scotland, 1980-82; Chairman, Scottish Self-Government College, 1982-86; Chairman, Saint Andrew Society, 1978-86; Church of Scotland Elder, since 1979; Parliamentary candidate (SNP), 1970, 1979, 1983, 1987 (International Relations Spokesman, since 1982, Vice-Chairman, since 1985). Publications: Readings in Boleswa Government, 1971; The Referendum Experience: Scotland 1979, 1981; Islands of Europe, 1984; Self-Determination in the Commonwealth, 1987. Recreations: music; languages; walking; vexillogy. Address: (b.) 60 Melville Street, Edinburgh, EH3 7HF; T.-031-226 3851.

Machin, George Ian Thom, MA, DPhil, FRHistS. Reader in Modern History, Dundee University, since 1982; b. 3.7.37, Liverpool; m., Dr. Jane Margaret Pallot; 2 s. Educ. Silcoates School, near Wakefield; Jesus College, Oxford. Research Student and Tutor, Oxford University, 1958-61; Assistant Lecturer, then Lecturer in History, Singapore University, 1961-64; Lecturer in Modern History: St. Andrews University, 1964-67, Dundee University, 1967-75 (Senior Lecturer, 1975-82); Course Tutor, Open University in Scotland, 1971-82. Treasurer, Abertay Historical Society, 1966-73; Treasurer, Dundee Branch, Historical Association, since 1981; Elder, Church of Scotland, since 1981. Publications: The Catholic Question in English Politics 1820 to 1830, 1964; Politics and the Churches in Great Britain 1832 to 1868, 1977; Politics and the Churches in Great Britain 1869 to 1921, 1987. Recreations: culture vulturing; hill-walking; swimming; cooking. Address: (h.) 50 West Road, Newport-on-Tay, Fife, DD6 8HP; T.-0382 543371.

Mack, Donald William, MA. HM Chief Inspector of Schools, since 1984; b. 9.5.32, Dunfermline; m., Catherine; 1 s.; 1 d. Educ. Allan Glen's School, Glasgow; Glasgow University. History Teacher in Glasgow; Lecturer in History, Jordanhill College of Education; Principal Lecturer in Social Studies, Hamilton College of Education; HMI, since 1974. Recreations: photography; rock gardening. Address: (b.) Room 4/108, New St. Andrew's House, St. James Place, Edinburgh; T.-031-556 8400.

Mack, Douglas Stuart, MA, PhD. Lecturer, Stirling University, since 1986; General Editor, Association for Scottish Literary Studies, since 1980; President, The James Hogg Society, since 1982; b. 30.1.43, Bellshill; 2 s. Educ. Uddingston Grammar School; Glasgow University; Stirling University. Research Assistant, National Library of Scotland, 1965-66; Assistant Librarian: St. Andrews University, 1966-70, Stirling University, 1970-86; Editor of various books by James Hogg. Recreations: watching Hamilton Accies; sailing on paddle steamers. Address: (h.) 2 Law Hill Road, Dollar, FK14 7BG; T.-Dollar 2452.

Mack, Jimmy. Broadcaster and Journalist; Presenter, The Jimmy Mack Show, BBC Radio Scotland, since 1979; Presenter, Scotland Today, Scottish Television, since 1985; b. 26.6.34, Greenock; m., Barbara; 1 s.; 1 d. Educ. Lenzie Academy; Bathgate Academy. Insurance Inspector, Guardian Royal Exchange Assurance Co., 1956-70; Producer and Presenter, various programmes, BBC Radio Medway, Kent, 1970-79; since 1979, in addition to daily programme on BBC Radio Scotland also presents Jimmy Mack's Old Gold; Presenter, various programmes, BBC Radios 1, 2 and 4, since 1970; Presenter, various programmes, Grampian TV, since 1980; Television and Radio Industries Club of Scotland Award for best live radio programme, 1986. Publication: Jimmy Mack Show Book, 1984. Recreation: photography. Address: (h.) 38 Douglas Park Crescent, Bearsden, Glasgow, G61 3DN; T.-041-942 0524.

Mackie, Allister Andrew, JP. Member, West Lothian District Council, since 1974 (Labour Group Leader, since 1977 and Leader of Council, since 1984); b. 30.10.30, Toronto, Canada; m., Patricia McGinley; 1 s.; 2 d. Educ. Kilmarnock Academy. Served apprenticeship as compositor, Kilmarnock Herald, 1948-55; RAF, 1952-54; Imperial Father, Scottish Daily Express, Glasgow, 1964-74; Chairman, Scottish Daily News, 1975; Labour candidate, Lothians, European Assembly, 1979. Recreations: reading; politics; bowls; Burns clubs. Address: (h.) 54 Mid Street, Bathgate, West Lothian; T.-Bathgate 53931.

Mackie, Professor Andrew George, MA, PhD, FRSE, FIMA. Professor of Applied Mathematics, Edinburgh University, since 1968; b. 7.3.27, Tain; m., Elizabeth Maud Hebblethwaite; 1 s.; 1 d. Educ. Tain Royal Academy; Edinburgh University; Cambridge University; St. Andrews University. Lecturer, Dundee University, 1948-50; Bateman Research Fellow and Instructor, California Institute of Technology, 1953-55; Lecturer: Strathclyde University, 1955-56, St. Andrews University, 1956-62; Professor of Applied Mathematics, Victoria University of Wellington, New Zealand, 1962-65; Research Professor, Maryland University, 1966-68; Visiting Professor, California Institute of Technology, 1984 and University of New South Wales, Australia, 1985; Vice-Principal, Edinburgh University, 1975-80; Chairman, Scottish Mathematical Council, 1980-84; President, Edinburgh Mathematical Society, 1982-83. Publication: Boundary Value Problems, 1965. Recreation: golf. Address: (h.) 47 Cluny Drive, Edinburgh, EH10 6DU; T.-031-447 2164.

Mackie, Bruce David, JP. Leader, Conservative Group, Tayside Regional Council, since 1986; b. 27.11.32, Dundee; m., Roberta Galloway; 4 s. Educ. Morgan Academy. Former Member, Dundee Corporation; elected to Tayside Regional Council, 1974 (former Planning Convener); Past Chairman, Arts and Recreation Committee, COSLA; former Member, Scottish Sports Council; Governor, Pitlochry Festival Theatre, since 1976; Board Member, Dundee Port Authority, since 1987. Recreations: music; theatre; watching athletics and football. Address: (h.) 60 Elie Avenue, Broughty Ferry, Dundee, DD5 3SJ; T.-0382 78866.

Mackie, (Clarence Roy) Larry, FBIM, LHSM, FIBA, MSc, BSc, DN, RGN, RMN. Executive Director - Nursing, Ministry of Defence and Aviation, Kingdom of Saudi Arabia, since 1987 (Chief Area Nursing Officer, Ayrshire and Arran Health Board, 1984-87); b. 7.6.43, Melita, Manitoba. Educ. Vincent Massey Collegiate Institute, Winnipeg; Sussex University; London University; Aberdeen University; Winnipeg University. Worked in Winnipeg, Toronto, New York, London, Bradford, Divisional Nursing Officer, Lothian Health Board, 1980-83; District Nursing Officer, Greater Glasgow Health Board, 1983-84. Council Member, Scottish Association of Nurse Administrators; elected Member, National Board for Nursing, Midwifery and Health Visiting for Scotland; former Scottish Chairman, RADNO Group; Secretary, Scottish CANOs Group; Member, Information Computer Services Advisory Group for Scotland; Member, Computer Steering Committee Scotland; Member, Standard Systems Committee Scotland; Past Chairman, Lothian Centre, Royal College of Nursing; Past Chairman, Nursing and Midwifery Advisory Committee, Lothian Health Board; former Member, National Nursing and Midwifery Consultative Committee for Scotland. Recreations: reading; walking; skating. Address: (h.) Roseholm, Old Glasgow Road, Stewarton, Ayrshire, KA3 5JW; T.-0560 84617.

Mackie of Benshie, Baron (George Yull Mackie), CBE, DSO, DFC, LLD. Farmer; Liberal Spokesman on Agriculture and Scotland, House of Lords, since 1975; President, Scottish Liberal Party, since 1983; Member, Council of Europe and Western European Union; b. 10.7.19, Aberdeen; m., 1, Lindsay Lyall Sharp; 1 s. (deceased); 3 d.; 2, Mrs Jacqueline Lane. Educ. Aberdeen Grammar School; Aberdeen University. Bomber Command and Air Staff, 1944. Contested South Angus, 1959; Vice-Chairman (Organisation), Scottish Liberal Party, 1959-64; MP (Liberal), Caithness and Sutherland, 1964-66; Chairman, Scottish Liberal Party, 1965-70; contested Caithness and Sutherland, 1970; contested NE Scotland, European Parliamentary Election, 1979; Member, EEC Scrutiny Committee (D), House of Lords; Executive, Inter-Parliamentary Union; Chairman, Industrial Appeal Committee, Pitlochry Festival Theatre, 1979; Chairman, Angus Committee, Salvation Army, 1976-84; Rector, Dundee University, 1980-83. Recreations: golf; shooting; social life. Address: (h.) Ballinshoe, Kirriemuir, Angus; T.-Kirriemuir 73466.

Mackie, Sir Maitland, Kt (1982), CBE (1965), JP. Lord Lieutenant of Aberdeenshire, 1975-87; Farmer; b. 16.2.12; m.; 2 s.; 4 d. Educ. Aberdeen Grammar School; Aberdeen University. Convener, Aberdeen County Council, 1967-75; Chairman, NE Development Authority, 1969-75; Chairman, Aberdeen Milk Marketing Board, 1965-82; Chairman, Oil Policy Committee, Scottish Council (Development and Industry), since 1975; Chairman, Aberdeen Cable Services, since 1983.

Mackie, Maitland, BSc, MA. Farmer; Director, Farmdata, since 1979; b. 21.9.37, Aberdeen; 1 s.; 2 d. Educ. Aberdeen Grammar School; Aberdeen University. Member, Scottish Agricultural Development Council; Chairman, Animals Research Committee, Agricultural and Food Research Council; Council Member, National Farmers Union of Scotland. Recreation: Norway. Address: Westertown, Rothienorman, Aberdeenshire; T.-04675 466.

Macklon, Alan Edward Stephen, BSc, PhD. Head, Plants Division, Macaulay Land Use Research Institute; b. 2.10.36, Dover; m., Bridget Jessamine Carr; 4 s. Educ. Cambridgeshire High School for Boys; Nottingham University; Aberdeen University. Joined Macaulay Institute for Soil Research, 1962; spent a year as Research Associate, Washington State University, 1966-67.

Recreation: gardening. Address: (b.) Macaulay Land Use Research Institute, Craigiebuckler, Aberdeen, AB9 2QJ; T.-Aberdeen 318611.

Maddox, Christopher Edward Ralph, BSc, PhD, CBiol, MIBiol, DipManEd. Principal, Scottish College of Textiles, Galashiels, since 1988 (Vice Principal, Queen Margaret College, Edinburgh, 1983-88); b. 21.11.40; m., Janet; 2 s. Educ. Priory School, Shrewsbury; Birmingham University. MRC Research Fellow, Warwick University, 1965-66; Senior Lecturer, Luton College of Technology, 1966-67; Senior Lecturer, then Principal Lecturer, then Assistant Dean of Studies, Manchester Polytechnic, 1967-77; Head, Department of Molecular and Life Sciences, Dundee College of Technology, 1977-83. Member, SCOTEC Committees for Biology and Medical Laboratory Sciences, 1978-83; Member, Council, Scottish Branch, Institute of Biology, 1979-82; Member, CNAA Combined Studies Board, 1983-87; Member, CNAA Health Studies Committee, since 1987; Member, Health Visiting Joint Committee, UK Central Council for Nursing, Midwifery and Health Visiting. Recreations: reading; watching sports. Address: (b.) Scottish College of Textiles, Galashiels, TD1 3HF; T.-0896 3351.

Magee, James, MBE, OStJ, MCIT, MBIM, MIPM. Member, Employers' Panel, Industrial Tribuals (Scotland), 1981-87; Vice-President, St. Andrews Ambulance Association and Vice-Chairman of Council, 1971-87; Lay Member, Complaints Committee, Law Society of Scotland, 1985-87; b. 8.3.20, Paisley; m., Elizabeth Forbes McKay; 1 s. Educ. Camphill School, Paisley; School of Transport, Derby; British Transport Staff College, Woking. LMS Railway and British Railways, Scotland, 1938-74 (Chief Personnel Officer for Scotland); Chief Staff Officer, British Railways Board, London, 1974-78; Member, CBI Scotland Industrial and Training Committees, 1971-80; Member, Careers Service Advisory Council, Scotland, 1971-74; Member, Central Arbitration Committee, Department of Employment, 1977-80; Council Member, Scottish Action Resource Centre, 1977-82; Trustee, New Templars Halls Trust, Paisley; Chairman, Railway Benevolent Institution (Scottish Committee), since 1980; Member, Paisley Presbytery and Synod of Clydesdale, Church of Scotland, since 1960. Recreations: music (choral); golf; social responsibilities. Address: (h.) 8 Stanely Grove, Paisley; T.-041-884 4370.

Magnusson, Magnus, MA (Oxon), FRSE, FRSA, FSA Scot. Broadcaster; Chairman, Ancient Monuments Board for Scotland, since 1981; b. 12.10.29, Reykjavik, Iceland; m., Mamie; 1 s.; 3 d. Educ. Edinburgh Academy; Jesus College, Oxford. Reporter, Scottish Daily Express; Features Writer, The Scotsman; Co-Presenter, Tonight, BBC TV, 1964-65; Presenter: Chronicle, Cause for Concern, Checkpoint, All Things Considered, Mainly Magnus, BC - The Archaeology of the Bible Lands, Living Legends, Vikings!, Mastermind; Rector, Edinburgh University, 1975-78.

Maher, Michael Alexander Ramsey, JP, ABTI. Convener, Tweeddale District Council; b. 14.5.18, Glasgow; m., Ellaretta Eckford Montgomery; 1 s.; 1 d. Educ. St. Mungo's Academy, Glasgow. Served with 157 Field Ambulance (TA), RAMC, seven years; Training Officer in Civil Defence, Peeblesshire County Council; transferred to Borders Regional Council on re-organisation; held post of Registrar of Births, Deaths and Marriages for Peebles and District; Treasurer, H. Ballantyne Memorial Institute, Walkerburn, 28 years; Chairman: Walkerburn Community Council, Walkerburn OAP Association, St. James Church Parish Council, Innerleithen; Member, COSLA Economic Affairs Committee; President, Probus (Innerleithen, Walkerburn and Traquair); Member: Scottish Borders Tourist Board, Scottish National Housing and Town Planning, Tweeddale District Licensing Board. Recreations: gardening; painting. Address: (h.) 2 Park Avenue, Walkerburn, Peebles-shire; T.-Walkerburn 272.

Maiden, Robert Mitchell, FIB (Scot), FBIM. Managing Director, Royal Bank of Scotland plc, since 1986; Executive Director, Royal Bank of Scotland Group plc, since 1985; b. 15.9.33, Montrose; m., Margaret M. Nicolson. Educ. Montrose Academy. Joined Royal Bank of Scotland, 1950. Recreations: music; golf; hill-walking. Address: (h.) Trinafour, Bonaly Road, Edinburgh; T.-031-441 2858.

Main, Carol B.L.D., BA. Secretary, National Association of Youth Orchestras, since 1979; Administrator, New Music Group of Scotland, since 1982; Scottish Representative, Live Music Now, since 1984; Classical Music Editor, The List, since 1985; b. 21.12.58, Kirkcaldy; m., Colin Heggie. Educ. Kirkcaldy High School; Edinburgh University. Presenter, classical music programmes for BBC, 1988, and Radio Forth, 1983-84; freelance music critic, mainly with Glasgow Herald. Board Director, Edinburgh Festival Fringe Society. Address: (b.) Ainslie House, 11 St. Colme Street, Edinburgh, EH3 6AG; T.-031-225 4606.

Main, James, FRICS. Buildings Officer and Factor, Aberdeen University, since 1979; b. 14.12.30, Aberdeen; m., Norma Scott Miller; 1 s.; 2 d. Educ. Aberdeen Central School; College of Estate Management. Apprentice Assistant, Aberdeen County Architect's Department; Quantity Surveyor, Cumbernauld Development Corporation; Deputy Buildings Officer, Aberdeen University. Address: (h.) 22 Hosefield Avenue, Aberdeen, AB2 4NN; T.-0224 633884.

Main, Kirkland, ARSA, RSW, DA, FEIS. Lecturer in Drawing and Painting, Edinburgh College of Art, since 1969; Dean, Faculty of Art and Design, Heriot-Watt University/Edinburgh College of Art, since 1987; Chairman, Association of Lecturers in Scottish Central Institutions, 1982-86; b. 1.7.42, Edinburgh; m., Geraldine Francis; 1 d. Educ. Daniel Stewart's College; Edinburgh College of Art. Assistant to Vice Principal, Edinburgh College of Art, 1980-83 (Governor, 1979-85); Member, Central Institutions Staffs Salaries Committee, 1977-81; Member, Scottish Joint Negotiating Committee, Further Education, since 1982. Address: (h.) 15 Cramond Village, Edinburgh, EH4 6NU.

Main, Sir Peter (Tester), ERD, MD, LLD (Hon.), FRCPE, CBIM. Director, Scottish Development Agency, since 1986; Director, W.A. Baxter &

Sons Ltd., since 1985; Director, John Fleming & Co. Ltd., since 1985; Chairman, Inveresk Research International, since 1986; b. 21.3.25, Aberdeen; m., 1, Margaret Tweddle (deceased); 2, May Heatherington McMillan; 2 s.; 1 d. Educ. Robert Gordon's College; Aberdeen University. House Surgeon, Aberdeen Royal Infirmary, 1948-49; Captain, RAMC, 1949-51; Medical Officer with Field Ambulance (Suez), 1956; Lt. Col., RAMC (AER), retired 1964; general practice, 1953-57; The Boots Co. PLC: joined Research Department, 1957; Director of Research, 1968; Managing Director, Industrial Division, 1979; Director, 1973-85, Vice Chairman, 1980-81, Chairman, The Boots Co. PLC, 1982-85. Member, National Economic Development Committee, 1984-85; Chairman, Committee of Inquiry into Teachers' Pay and Conditions, Scotland, 1986; Governor, Henley Management College, 1983-86. Recreations: fishing; shooting; Scottish music. Address: Lairig Ghru, Dulnain Bridge, Grantown-on-Spey, PH26 3NT; T.-047985 264.

Mair, Alexander, MBE (1967). Director, Clifton Collier Advertising, Aberdeen, since 1987; Vice President, Aberdeen Chamber of Commerce, since 1987; Chairman, Aberdeen International Football Festival, since 1981; Governor, Robert Gordon's College, Aberdeen, since 1988; b. 5.11.22, Echt; m., Margaret Isobel. Educ. Skene Central School; School of Accountancy, Glasgow. Company Secretary, Grampian TV, 1961-70; appointed Director, 1967; Director and Chief Executive, 1970-87. Chairman, Junior Chamber, Aberdeen, 1960-61. Recreations: golf; skiing; gardening. Address: (h.) Ravenswood, 66 Rubislaw Den South, Aberdeen, AB2 6AX; T.-0224 317619.

Mair, Alistair S.F., MBE, BSc, FBIM. Managing Director, Caithness Glass PLC, since 1977; b. 20.7.35, Drumblade; m., 1, Anne Garrow (deceased); 2, Mary Bolton; 4 s.; 1 d. Educ. Robert Gordon's College, Aberdeen; Aberdeen University. Rolls Royce, Glasgow, 1957-71: graduate apprentice, PA to General Manager, Production Control Manager, Product Centre Manager; RAF, 1960-62 (short-service commission, Technical Branch); Managing Director, Caithness Glass Ltd., 1971-75; Marketing Director, Worcester Royal Porcelain Co., 1975-76. Vice Chairman, Scottish Council, CBI; Member: CBI Council; Manpower Services Committee Scotland; Non-Executive Director, Grampian Television, since 1986. Recreations: gardening; walking; current affairs. Address: (h.) Dungora, Heathcote Road, Crieff, Perthshire, PH7 4AG; T.-0764 2191.

Mair, Douglas, MA, PhD. Senior Lecturer, Department of Economics, Heriot-Watt University, since 1975; b. 3.6.39, Arbroath; m., Ishbel Fraser; 2 s.; 1 d. Educ. Arbroath High School; St. Andrews University. Ford Motor Company, 1960-63; Scottish Council (Development and Industry), 1963-67; joined Heriot-Watt University, 1967; Scottish Development Department (part-time), 1976-77; Secretary, Section F, British Association, 1980-84. Publication: Structure and Growth of Scottish Economy (Co-author), 1971. Recreations: golf; restoration of Victorian property. Address: (h.) Eskdale, 43 Abercorn Terrace, Edinburgh, EH15 2DG; T.-031-669 2511.

Mair, Henry. Poet; b. 4.3.45, Kilmarnock; m., Etta; 1 s.; 1 d. Educ. St. Joseph's High School, Kilmarnock. Originator, 1972, and Secretary, Scottish National Open Poetry Competition; guest, USSR Writers' Union, 1980. Publications: I Rebel, 1970; Alone I Rebel, 1974; Flowers in the Forest, 1978; The Prizewinners, 1987. Address: (h.) 42 Tollerton Drive, Irvine, Ayrshire; T.-Irvine 76381.

Mair, William Wallace, MA. Secretary, Faculty of Actuaries in Scotland, since 1974; Deputy Secretary, Associated Scottish Life Offices, since 1974; b. 19.6.49, Bellshill; m., Sandra Cunningham; 1 s.; 1 d. Educ. Uddingston Grammar School; Glasgow University. Assistant Secretary, Royal Institution of Chartered Surveyors, 1969-72; Secretary, Scottish National Federation of Building Trades Employers, 1972-73. Recreations: badminton; cricket; hill-walking; lay preaching. Address: (b.) 23 St. Andrew Square, Edinburgh, EH2 1AQ; T.-031-557 1575.

Maitland-Titterton, Major David Maitland, TD (1947), MA. Marchmont Herald of Arms to Court of Lord Lyon, since 1982; b. 8.8.04; m.; 2 s. Educ. Queens' College, Cambridge. Commissioned, 1924; Ayrshire Yeomanry, 1926; Assistant District Officer, Political Service, Nigeria, 1927-32; served Second World War (Major, 1942); Liaison Officer with Polish Army, 1944; Staff Officer, 51 Highland Division, 1954-63; Falkland Pursuivant Extraordinary, 1969-71; Ormond Pursuivant, 1971-84; Officer, Order of St. John of Jerusalem. Address: (h.) Moberty, Craigton of Airlie, by Kirriemuir, Angus, DD8 5NW.

Makgill Crichton Maitland, Major John David. Lord Lieutenant of Renfrewshire, since 1980; b. 10.9.25; 1 s.; 1 d. Educ. Eton. Served Second World War, Grenadier Guards, 1944-45; retired, 1957, with rank of Captain; Member, Renfrew County Council, 1961-75; Governor, West of Scotland Agricultural College.

Makin, Professor Brian, BSc, PhD, CEng, FIEE, FInstP. Watson-Watt Professor of Electrical Engineering, Dundee University, since 1974; b. 28.12.35, Sheffield; m., Hazel Phillips; 3 s. Educ. High Storrs Grammar School, Sheffield; Southampton University. Scientific Assistant, Avco-Everett, Massachusetts, 1962-63; Project Engineer, W.G. Pye, Cambridge, UK, 1964-66; Lecturer, then Senior Lecturer, Department of Electrical Engineering, Southampton University, 1966-74. Address: (b.) Electronic Engineering Group, The University, Dundee, DD1 4HN; T.-Dundee 23181, Ext. 4394.

Maksymiuk, Jerzy. Principal Conductor, BBC Scottish Symphony Orchestra, since 1983; b. 9.4.36, Grodno, Poland; m., Irena Kirjacka. Educ. Warsaw Academy of Music. Opera House, Warsaw, 1969, conducting Mozart, Stravinsky and modern works; Director, National Radio Orchestra of Poland, 1972-74; former Music Director, Polish Chamber Orchestra; Composer of music for Polish films. Winner of Polish Cultural Awards for composition and for forming Polish Chamber Orchestra; Polish Cross. Address: (b.) BBC, Queen Margaret Drive, Glasgow, G12 8DG; T.-041-330 2355/3.

Malcolm, David, MA, LLB. Honorary Sheriff, since 1976; b. 20.6.15, Cromarty; m., Helen Liddell Menzies; 2 s. Educ. Cromarty Higher Grade Public School; Fortrose Academy; Glasgow University. 2nd Bn., Glasgow Highlanders and 9th Gurkha Rifles, 1939-46 (attained rank of Major); Partner, J.M. & J. Mailer, Solicitors, Stirling, 1949-81, retiring as Senior Partner; Dean, Stirling Society of Solicitors and Procurators, 1973-75. Honorary Vice-President (and Past Chairman), Stirling and District Choral Union, since 1984; Past President: Stirling Rotary Club, Stirling Bowling Club, Borestone and Stirling Curling Club, Stirling Probus Club, Stirling Burns Club; Elder, St. Columba's Church, Stirling, since 1950. Recreations: bowls; curling; choral singing; music. Address: (h.) 55 Snowdon Place, Stirling, FK8 2JY; T.-0786 73949.

Malcolm, Douglas C., BSc, PhD. Senior Lecturer, since 1978, and Head, Department of Forestry and Natural Resources, since 1987, Edinburgh University; b. 4.12.30, Calcutta; m., M. Jean Wardrop; 4 d. Educ. George Watson's College, Edinburgh; Edinburgh University. District Forest Officer, Forestry Commission, 1954-61; Lecturer, 1961-78. President, Institute of Chartered Foresters. Address: (b.) Department of Forestry and Natural Resources, West Mains Road, Edinburgh, EH9 3JU; T.-031-667 1081.

Malcolm, Robin Neill Lochnell, DL, JP. Farmer, since 1963; Member, Argyll and Bute District Council, since 1976; President, Scottish Agricultural Organisation Society Ltd., 1983-86; b. 11.2.34, Edinburgh; m., Susan Hilary Freeman; 2 s.; 2 d. Educ. Eton; North of Scotland College of Agriculture. National Service, 1st Argyll and Sutherland Highlanders, 1953-54; TA (Captain, 8th Argyll and Sutherland Highlanders), 1955-63; shipping and shipbuilding in London and Glasgow, 1955-63; farming in Argyll, since 1963; Convener, Highlands and Islands Committee, NFU, 1972-74; Chief, Clan Malcolm. Recreations: shooting; swimming. Address: (h.) Duntrune Castle, Kilmartin, Argyll; T.-054 65 283.

Malcolm Smith, Nigel Andrew, RD, MB, ChB, FFARCSEng. Consultant Anaesthetist, Royal Infirmary, Edinburgh, and Princess Margaret Rose Hospital, Edinburgh, since 1978; b. 5.3.36, Edinburgh; m., Elizabeth Ann; 2 s.; 1 d. Educ. Edinburgh Academy; Edinburgh University. House Surgeon, Royal Infirmary, Edinburgh; House Physician, Western General Hospital, Edinburgh; Assistant Surgeon, P. & O. Orient Line; SHO, Registrar, Senior Registrar, Royal Infirmary, Edinburgh; Consultant Anaesthetist, Bangour General Hospital. Medical Branch Training Officer, Royal Naval Reserve. Recreations: Highland bagpipe playing; hill-walking. Address: (h.) 43 Craiglea Drive, Edinburgh, EH10 5PB.

Mallard, Professor John Rowland, BSc, PhD, DSc, FInstP, CEng, FIEE, FRCPath, FRSE. Professor of Medical Physics and Head of Department, Aberdeen University, since 1965; b. 14.1.27; m., Fiona Mackenzie Lawrance; 1 s.; 1 d. Educ. Nottingham University. President, Hospital Physicists Association, 1972-73; Founder President, International Union of Physical Engineering Sciences in Medicine, 1982-85; Founder President, European Society of Nuclear Medicine in Medicine, 1983-85; Member, International Commission of Radiation Units and Measurements, 1985-87; President, Biological Engineering Society, 1978-79; Founder Trustee, Society of Magnetic Resonance in Medicine and Biology, 1982-86; President, International Organisation of Medical Physics, 1979-82. Publications: Nuclear Magnetic Resonance Imaging (Contributor), 1983; NMR Imaging in Liver Disease (Co-author), 1984; Physical Principles and Clinical Applications of NMR (Contributor), 1985; Science and Technology in Europe (Contributor), 1986. Address: (b.) Aberdeen University, Aberdeen, AB9 1FX.

Mallinson, Edward John Harold, MPharm, MPS, FBIM, FRSH. Chief Administrative Pharmaceutical Officer, Lanarkshire Health Board, since 1984; b. 15.3.50, Bingley; m., Diana Gray; 2 d. Educ. Bradford Grammar School; Bradford University. Staff Pharmacist (Ward Pharmacy Services), Bradford Royal Infirmary, 1973-78; District Pharmaceutical Officer, Perth and Kinross District, 1978-83. Royal Pharmaceutical Society of Great Britain: Hon. Secretary, Bradford & District Branch, 1978, Hon. Secretary, Dundee & Eastern Scottish Branch, 1979-83, Hon. Secretary and Treasurer, Lanarkshire Branch, since 1984; Vice Chairman and Secretary, Pharmaceutical Group, Royal Society of Health, since 1986; Chairman, Strathclyde Police/Lanarkshire Health Board Drug Liaison Committee, since 1985; Member, General Synod, Scottish Episcopal Church. Recreations: genealogy; learning Gaelic; walking and cooking. Address: (h.) Malden, North Dean Park Avenue, Bothwell, Glasgow, G71 8HH; T.-0698 852973.

Malone, Desmond Noel Scott, MB, ChB, FRCPEdin. Consultant Physician, Department of Medicine, Milesmark Hospital, Dunfermline, since 1973; Honorary Senior Lecturer, Edinburgh University, since 1981; b. 12.12.34, Edinburgh; m., Kathleen Helena Murray; 2 s.; 2 d. Educ. Mount St. Mary's College, near Sheffield; Edinburgh University Medical School. House Physician, Peel Hospital, Galashiels; Flight Surgeon, Royal Canadian Airforce, Winnipeg; Research Fellow and Registrar, Northern General Hospital, Edinburgh; Medical Registrar, then Senior Medical Registrar, Western General Hospital, Edinburgh. Past Chairman, Fife Area Medical Committee; Past President, West Fife Medical Society. Recreations: fishing; windsurfing. Address: (h.) 2 Dalmeny View, Dalgety Bay, Fife, KY11 5LU; T.-0383 822532.

Malone, Peter Gerald, MA, LLB. Journalist; MP (Conservative), Aberdeen South, 1983-87; b. 21.7.50, Glasgow; m., Dr. Anne Blyth. Educ. St. Aloysius College; Glasgow University. Recreations: opera; music. Address: (h.) 32 Albyn Lane, Aberdeen; T.-Aberdeen 571779.

Manlove, Colin Nicholas, MA, BLitt. Reader in English Literature, Edinburgh University, since 1984; b. 4.5.42, Falkirk; m., Evelyn Mary Schuftan; 2 s. Educ. Dollar Academy; Edinburgh University. Lecturer in English Literature, Edinburgh University, 1967-84. Publications: Modern Fantasy: Five Studies, 1975; Literature and Reality 1600-1800, 1978; The Gap in Shakespeare: The Motif of Division from Richard II to The Tempest, 1981; The Impulse of Fantasy Literature, 1983; Science Fiction: Ten Explorations, 1986; C.S. Lewis: His Literary Achievement, 1987. Address: (b.) Department of English Literature, Edinburgh University, David Hume Tower, George Square, Edinburgh, EH8 9JX; T.-031-667 1011, Ext. 6272.

Mann, Gordon Laurence, DipTP, MRTPI, MInstPet. Director of Physical Planning, Dumfries and Galloway Regional Council, since 1987 (Director of Planning, Shetland Islands Council, 1980-87); b. 28.4.48, Dundee. Address: (b.) English Street, Dumfries, DG1 2DD; T.-0387 53141.

Manners, Professor David John, MA, PhD, ScD, DSc, FRSC, FInstBiol, FRSE. Professor of Biochemistry, Heriot-Watt University, since 1965; b. 31.3.28, Castleford; m., Gweneth Mary Chubbock; 2 s.; 1 d. Educ. Grammar School, Castleford; Fitzwilliam House, Cambridge. Lecturer, then Reader in Chemistry, Edinburgh University, 1952-65; awarded Meldola Medal, Royal Institute of Chemistry, 1957; Alsberg-Schoch Memorial Award, American Association of Cereal Chemists, 1984. Recreations: philately; military history. Address: (h.) 165 Mayfield Road, Edinburgh, EH9 3AY.

Manning, Professor Aubrey William George, BSc, DPhil, FInstBiol, Dr (h c) (Toulouse), FRSE. Professor of Natural History, Department of Zoology, Edinburgh University, since 1973; b. 24.4.30, London; m.; 3 s., inc. 2 by pr. m. Educ. Strode's School, Egham; University College, London; Merton College, Oxford. Research, 1951-54; National Service, Royal Artillery, 1954-56; Lecturer, then Reader in Zoology, Edinburgh University, 1956-73; Member, Scottish Advisory Committee, Nature Conservancy Council, 1982; Member, Advisory Committee on Science, NCC, 1985. Publication: An Introduction to Animal Behaviour, 1979; research papers in biological journals. Recreations: woodland conservation; walking; architecture. Address: (h.) The Old Hall, Ormiston, East Lothian; T.-Pencaitland 340536.

Mansfield and Mansfield, 8th Earl of (William David Mungo James Murray), JP, DL; b. 7.7.30; m., Pamela Joan Foster; 2 s.; 1 d. Educ. Eton; Christ Church, Oxford. National Service, Malayan Campaign; called to Bar, Inner Temple, 1958; Barrister, 1958-71; Member, British Delegation to European Parliament, 1973-75; Minister of State, Scottish Office, 1979-83; Minister of State, Northern Ireland Office, 1983-84; Director: General Accident Fire and Life Assurance Corporation Ltd., 1972-79, and since 1985; The American Trust Ltd., since 1985; Purneys of Scotland Ltd., since 1985; First Crown Estate Commissioner, since 1985. Address: (h.) Scone Palace, Perthshire, PH2 6BE.

Manson, Alexander Reid, SDA. Farmer; Chairman, Buchan Meat Producers Ltd., since 1982; President, Scottish Agricultural Organisation Society Ltd.; Member, Meat and Livestock Commission, since 1986; Trustee, Plunkett Foundation, Oxford, since 1977; Vice-President, Federation of Agricultural Cooperatives, since 1988; b. 2.9.31, Oldmeldrum; m., Ethel Mary Philip; 1 s.; 2 d. Educ. Robert Gordon's College; North of Scotland College of Agriculture. Member, Oldmeldrum Town Council, 1960-65; founder Chairman, Aberdeen Beef and Calf Ltd., 1962. Recreations: golf; bird-watching. Address: (h.) Kilblean, Oldmeldrum, Inverurie, AB5 0DN; T.-Old Meldrum 2226.

Manson, George Inglis, OBE, MB, ChB. Honorary Sheriff, Peterhead, since 1982; b. 8.6.22, Fordoun; m., Helen Johnston; 3 d. Educ. Mackie Academy; Aberdeen University. Assistant in general practice, Peterhead, 1944-48, then Principal, 1948-86; Medical Officer, HM Prison, Peterhead, 1955-87, International Twist Drill Company, Peterhead, 1955-87. Sometime Member and Chairman, former North-East Aberdeenshire Hospitals Board of Management; JP since 1965. Recreations: golf; reading. Address: (h.) Windmill House, 60 Balmoor Terrace, Peterhead, AB4 6ER; T.-0779 73531.

Manson, Thomas Mortimer Yule, MA, DipEd, LLD. Member, Shetland Islands Council, since 1982; b. 9.2.04, Lerwick. Educ. Anderson Educational Institute; Edinburgh University; Moray House College of Education. Trained and qualified as a teacher; entered family printing and newspaper business, 1929; on father's death in 1941, became Proprietor, T. & J. Manson, Lerwick, and Editor, Shetland News (closed, 1963); Reporter, Radio Shetland, 1979-82; Bandmaster, local Boys' Brigade, seven years; Shetland County Scout Commissioner, 14 years (awarded Silver Acorn by Chief Scout); Conductor, Lerwick Brass Band, five years; Secretary, Lerwick Orchestral Society, 41 years; Chairman, Shetland Civic Society, 12 years. Recreation: music. Address: (h.) 93 Gilbertson Road, Lerwick, Shetland; T.-0595 4632.

Mantle, Richard John. Managing Director, Scottish Opera, since 1985; b. 21.1.47, London; m., June Mountain. Educ. Tiffin School, Kingston. Personnel management, Beecham Group, 1969-72; Personnel Manager, J. Walter Thompson Co., 1973-79; Personnel Director, then Deputy Managing Director, English National Opera, 1980-85. Recreations: music; theatre; wine; Church architecture. Address: (b.) 39 Elmbank Crescent, Glasgow, G2; T.-041-248 4567.

Manwaring, Gaye Melodie Anne, MBE, BSc, PhD. Coordinator of Tertiary Education, Northern College of Education, since 1987; Honorary Lecturer in Medical Education, Dundee University, since 1975; Director, Medical Open Learning Service, since 1987; b. 15.10.45, Margate; m., Andrew Henry Wilson. Educ. Exeter University; Edinburgh University. Research Fellow, Glasgow University, 1969-75; Senior Lecturer in Educational Technology, Dundee College of Education, 1975-87. Former Governor, SCET; Member, various Committees of SCET, CET, CNAA; work with MSC, Open Tech, National Extension College, Open College, British Council. Recreations: theatre; gardening; reading; friends; cats. Address: (b.) Northern College of Education (Dundee Campus), Gardyne Road, Dundee, DD5 1NY; T.-0382 453433.

Mappin, Rev. Michael Graeme, BA. Minister, Bower linked with Watten, since 1970; Clerk, Presbytery of Caithness, since 1975; b. 16.3.32, Essex; m., Catherine; 4 s.; 2 d. Educ. Radley College; Pembroke College, Cambridge. Assistant Curate, St. Paul's and St. George's Episcopal Church, Edinburgh, 1960-62; Rector, St. Mungo's Episcopal Church, Balerno, 1962-69; Assistant Minister, Corstorphine Old Parish Church, 1969-70. Recreations: cabinet making; gardening; music. Address: The Manse, Watten, by Wick, Caithness; T.-Watten 220.

Mar, 13th Earl of, and Kellie, 15th Earl of (John Francis Hervey Erskine). Premier Viscount of Scotland; Hereditary Keeper of Stirling Castle; Lord Lieutenant of Clackmannan, since 1966; b. 15.2.21; m., Pansy Constance Thorne; 3 s.; 1 d. Educ. Eton; Trinity College, Cambridge. Major, Scots Guards (retired, 1954); Major, Argyll and Sutherland Highlanders (TA) (retired, 1959); Vice-Convener, Clackmannan County Council, 1961-64; Chairman, Forth Conservancy Board, 1957-68; Chairman, Clackmannanshire T&AFA, 1961-68; Member, Queen's Bodyguard for Scotland (Royal Company of Archers). Address: (h.) Claremont House, Alloa, Clackmannanshire.

Maran, Professor Arnold George Dominic, MB, ChB, MD, FRCS, FACS. Professor of Otolaryngology, Edinburgh University, since 1988; Secretary, Royal College of Surgeons; Consultant Surgeon, Royal Infirmary and City Hospital, Edinburgh, since 1974; b. 16.6.36, Edinburgh; m., Anna; 1 s.; 1 d. Educ. Daniel Stewart's College; Edinburgh University; University of Iowa. Trained in Otolaryngology in Edinburgh and America; former Consultant Otolaryngologist, Tayside Health Board, and Professor of Otolaryngology, West Virginia University. Ten Visiting Professorships to foreign universities. Publications: four books and 80 scientific papers. Recreations: golf; music; travel. Address: (h.) 15 Cluny Drive, Edinburgh, EH10 6DW; T.-031-447 8519.

Marjoribanks, Gerald Brian, BA, LRAM, ALAM. Officer for Scotland, Independent Broadcasting Authority, since 1983; b. 22.7.42, Falkirk; m., Kathleen; 2 s.; 1 d. Educ. Falkirk High School; Edinburgh College of Speech and Drama; Open University. Sports Presenter, Sportsreel, Sportscene, Sportsound, BBC Scotland, 1966-83; Lecturer in Drama, Notre Dame College of Education, 1967-79; Co-ordinator of Learning Resources, Dunfermline College of Physical Education, 1979-80; Head of Public Relations, Cumbernauld Development Corporation, 1980-83. Recreations: drama adjudication; badminton; golf; photography. Address: (h.) Underwood, 33 Maggie Wood's Loan, Falkirk, FK1 5HR.

Marjoribanks, Sir James Alexander Milne, KCMG (1965), MA. Chairman, Scotland in Europe, since 1979; b. 29.5.11, Edinburgh; m., Sonya Patricia Stanley de Brandon (deceased); 1 d. Educ. Edinburgh Academy; Edinburgh University; Strasbourg University. HM Diplomatic Service, 1934-71: served in Peking, Hankow, Marseilles, Jacksonville, New York, Bucharest, Canberra, Luxembourg, Bonn, Brussels, London; Under-Secretary of State, Foreign Office, 1962-65; Ambassador to European Communities, 1965-71. Director, Distillers PLC, 1971-76; Member, Edinburgh University Court, 1976-80; Governing Member, Inveresk Research Foundation; Chairman, Committee for European Community Cultural Co-operation. Recreation: hill-walking. Address: 13 Regent Terrace, Edinburgh; T.-031-556 3872.

Marjoribanks of that Ilk, William Logan, BSc. Member, Standing Council of Scottish Chiefs; b. 26.2.10, Callander; m., Thelma Williamson; 2 s. Educ. Edinburgh Academy; Edinburgh University. Sudan Civil Service, 1932-55; NE of Scotland Representative, National Trust for Scotland, 1955-75. Recreations: gardening; walking; fly-fishing. Address: Kirklands of Forglen, by Turriff, Banffshire, AB5 7JE.

Marker, Commander John (Iain) Hamilton, VRD (and bar), BA, MLitt, FIL, FRMetS, RNR (Rtd.). Depute Principal, Napier College of Commerce and Technology, 1974-87; b. 23.9.24, Greenock; m., Elizabeth Urie Macfarlane. Educ. Ulverston Grammar School; Kings College, Durham University. Assistant Master, Middlesex County Secondary School, 1952-54; Assistant Lecturer in Economics, Kingston College of Advanced Technology, 1954-57; Assistant Lecturer/Lecturer in Economics, Isleworth Polytechnic, 1957-62; Head of Department, West London College, 1962-68; Head of Department, then Depute Principal, Edinburgh College of Commerce, 1968-74. Recreations: golf; reading; gardening. Address: (h.) 2 Cherry Tree Gardens, Balerno, Midlothian, EH14 5SR; T.-031-449 3936.

Marker, William Bennett, MA, MEd. Assistant Principal (In-service Education), Jordanhill College of Education, 1976-86; b. 5.2.28, Greenock; m., Anne Margaret Manthorpe; 1 s.; 1 d. Educ. Ulverston Grammar School; Wadham College, Oxford. Assistant Teacher, Purbrook Park High School, 1954-56; Assistant Housemaster, Woodbridge School, 1956-58; Senior History Master, Queen Elizabeth School, Kirkby Lonsdale, 1958-67; Schoolmaster Fellow, Hull University, 1967; Lecturer/Senior Lecturer in History, Jordanhill College of Education, 1967-72 (Principal Lecturer (In-service), 1972-75). Member, National Committee for the In-service Training of Teachers, 1976-85. Recreations: hill-walking; opera-going. Address: (h.) 2 Huntly Drive, Bearsden, Glasgow, G61 3LD; T.-041-942 6756.

Markland, John A., MA, PhD, ACIS. Chief Executive, Fife Regional Council, since 1986; b. 17.5.48, Bolton; m., Muriel Harris; 4 d. Educ. Bolton School; Dundee University. Demographer, Somerset County Council, 1974-76; Senior Professional Assistant, Tayside Regional Council; Personal Assistant to Chief Executive, then Assistant Chief Executive, Fife Regional Council, 1979-86. Recreations: golf, swimming; cycling. Address: (b.) Fife House, North Street, Glenrothes, Fife; T.-0592 754411.

Marks, Frederick Charles, OBE, MA, LLB, FBIM. General Manager, Scottish Special Housing Association, since 1984; b. 3.12.34, Bellshill; m., Agnes M. Bruce; 3 s.; 1 d. Educ. Wishaw High School; Glasgow University. Depute Town Clerk,

Dunfermline, 1963-68; Town Clerk, Hamilton, 1968-75; Chief Executive, Motherwell, 1974-83. Address: (b.) 9-21 Palmerston Place, Edinburgh, EH12 5AJ; T.-031-225 1281.

Marnoch, Derek George, BSc, ACMA. Chief Executive, Aberdeen Chamber of Commerce, since 1983; b. 30.10.35, Aberdeen; m., Kathleen Howard; 3 s. Educ. Aberdeen Grammar School; Aberdeen University. Recreation: golf. Address: (h.) The Gables, Kirk Road, Stonehaven, AB3 2DX; T.-0569 62709.

Marquis, Mary. Broadcaster; Member, Scottish Arts Council, since 1988. Educ. Dunoon Grammar School; Glasgow University; Royal Scottish Academy of Music and Drama. Presenter, Border TV; joined BBC Scotland as Presenter/Interviewer, Six Ten (nightly news magazine); has presented Today and Nationwide from London; Woman's Hour and Good Morning Scotland from Glasgow; Presenter, Reporting Scotland; has presented own series of profiles (First Person Singular) and classical music programme (Encore) and numerous other arts and current affairs programmes.

Marr, Professor Geoffrey Vickers, BSc, PhD, DSc, CPhys, FInstP, FRSE. Professor of Natural Philosophy, Aberdeen University, since 1981 (Head, Department of Physics); b. 30.1.30, Darlington; m., Jean; 2 s.; 1 d. Educ. Queen Elizabeth Grammar School, Darlington; Manchester University; Reading University. Research Fellow, University of Western Ontario, 1954-57; Lecturer, McGill University, Canada, 1957-59; Physicist, English Electric, Leicester, 1959-61; Lecturer, then Reader, Reading University, 1961-81. Recreations: painting; hill-walking; bee-keeping. Address: (b.) Department of Physics, Aberdeen University, Aberdeen, AB9 2UE; T.-0224 40241.

Marr, Norman G., OStJ, DipArch, ARIBA, FRIAS. Director of Planning and Development, Kincardine and Deeside District Council, since 1975; b. 19.5.37, Aberdeen. Educ. Aberdeen Grammar School; Scott Sutherland School of Architecture, Aberdeen. Architectural Assistant, Aberdeen County Council, 1961-66; Senior Research Assistant, Corporation of the City of Aberdeen, Town Planning Department, 1967-69 (Principal Development Assistant, 1970-75). Organist and Choirmaster, Denburn Parish Church, Aberdeen, since 1956; Secretary, Scottish Federation of Organists. Recreations: organ playing/building; swimming; marathon running; hill-walking. Address: (b.) Viewmount, Arduthie Road, Stonehaven, Kincardineshire; T.-0569 62001.

Marsh, Kenneth James, DPhil (Oxon), ME, BE. Deputy Chief Scientific Officer, National Engineering Laboratory, since 1979; b. 13.2.35, Auckland, New Zealand; m., Margaret Ann Wraight; 1 s.; 1 d. Educ. Auckland Grammar School; Auckland University; St. Catherine's College, Oxford. Spent one year in structural engineering practice; came to UK to undertake research in materials engineering; joined NEL as Senior Scientific Officer, then Principal Scientific Officer; Head, Service Loading Division, 1974. Publications: Metal Fatigue (Co-author), 1974; Full-scale Fatigue Testing of Components and Structures (Editor), 1988. Recreation: hill-walking. Address: (b.) National Engineering Laboratory, East Kilbride, Glasgow; T.-03552 20222.

Marshall, David. MP (Labour), Glasgow Shettleston, since 1979; b. 1941. Member, Glasgow Corporation, 1972-75; Member, Strathclyde Regional Council, 1974-79.

Marshall, Enid Ann, MA, LLB, PhD, Assoc. RICS, ACIArb, FRSA. Solicitor; Reader in Business Law, Stirling University, since 1977; Editor, Scottish Law Gazette, since 1983; Chairman, Social Security Appeal Tribunal, Stirling and Falkirk, since 1984; b. 10.7.32, Boyndie, Banffshire. Educ. Banff Academy; Bell-Baxter School, Cupar; St. Andrews University. Apprentice Solicitor, 1956-59; Lecturer in Law, Dundee College of Technology, 1959-72; Lecturer, then Senior Lecturer, in Business Law, Stirling University, 1972-77. Departmental Editor, Arbitration Section, Journal of Business Law, since 1976. Publications: General Principles of Scots Law; Scottish Cases on Contract; Scottish Cases on Agency; Scottish Cases on Partnerships and Companies; Scots Mercantile Law; Gill on Arbitration; Charlesworth and Cain Company Law (Scottish Editor); Notes on the Law of Property in Scotland (Editor, 3rd edition); M.C. Oliver's Company Law (Reviser, 10th edition). Recreations: veganism; animal welfare. Address: (h.) 24 Easter Cornton Road, Stirling, FK9 5ES; T.-Stirling 78865.

Marshall, Professor Ian Howard, MA, BD, PhD (Aberdeen), BA (Cantab). Professor of New Testament Exegesis, Aberdeen University, since 1979; b. 12.1.34, Carlisle; m., Joyce Elizabeth; 1 s.; 3 d. Educ. Aberdeen Grammar School; Aberdeen University; Cambridge University; Gottingen University. Assistant Tutor, Didsbury College, Bristol; Methodist Minister, Darlington; Lecturer, then Senior Lecturer and Reader in New Testament Exegesis, Aberdeen University. Publications: Kept by the Power of God; Luke: Historian and Theologian; The Origins of New Testament Christology; New Testament Interpretation (Editor); The Gospel of Luke; I Believe in the Historical Jesus; The Epistles of John; Acts; Last Supper and Lord's Supper; Biblical Inspiration; 1 and 2 Thessalonians. Address: (b.) Department of New Testament, King's College, Aberdeen, AB9 2UB; T.-0224 272388.

Marshall, Rev. James Scott, FFA, BA, BD, MDiv. Minister, Lochgoilhead and Kilmorich Church of Scotland, since 1986; b. 1.7.30, Edinburgh. Educ. High School of Glasgow; Bristol University; Edinburgh University. Actuarial Clerk, Scottish Amicable Life Assurance Society, until 1959; Actuary in City of London, until 1964; Assistant Minister, St. Ninian's, Glenrothes, 1971-72, Claremont Church, East Kilbride, 1973-74; Teacher of RE, Earnoch High School, Hamilton, 1975-80; Teacher of Maths and Statistics, Uddingston Grammar School, 1980-83. Recreations: golf; tennis; badminton; walking; swimming; reading. Address: The Manse, Lochgoilhead, Argyll, PA24 8AA; T.-03013 369.

Marshall, Margaret Winton Cowie, RGN, SCM, QN. Member, Moray District Council, 1980-88; Vice President, Speyside and District Council of

Social Service; Member, Highlands and Islands Development Consultative Council; b. 28.11.19, Peterhead; widow; 1 d. Educ. Peterhead Academy. Nursing training, Western General Hospital, Edinburgh, Raigmore Hospital, Inverness, Craigton, St. Andrews, etc.; various nursing posts in Edinburgh, Forfar, Inverness, St. Andrews and Banffshire. WRVS hospital driver and book collector for the forces; Elder, Inveravon Church; founder Member, Glenlivet and Inveravon Community Association (Convener, Welfare Committee). Recreations: music; art; literature; talking with people. Address: (h.) Craighead Cottage, Benrinnes, Aberlour, Banffshire, AB3 9NL; T.-Aberlour 531.

Marshall, Mary Tara, MA, DSA, DASS. Director, Age Concern Scotland, since 1983; b. 13.6.45, Darjeeling, India. Educ. Mary Erskine School for Girls; Edinburgh University; London School of Economics; Liverpool University. Child Care Officer, London Borough of Lambeth, 1967-69; Social Worker, Personal Service Society, Liverpool, 1970-74; Research Organiser, Age Concern, Liverpool, 1974-75; Lecturer in Social Studies, Liverpool University, 1975-83. Publication: Social Work with Old People, 1983. Recreations: photography; bird-watching. Address: (b.) 33 Castle Street, Edinburgh; T.-031-225 5000/1.

Martin, Daniel, MA, BSc, PhD, FRSE, FIMA. Honorary Lecturer in Mathematics, Glasgow University, since 1980; b. 16.4.15, Carluke. Educ. High School of Glasgow; Glasgow University. Lecturer in Mathematics, Royal Technical College, Glasgow, 1938-47; Scientific Officer, Air Navigation Section, Royal Aircraft Establishment, Farnborough, 1941-45; Lecturer in Mathematics, then Senior Lecturer, Glasgow University, 1947-80; Snell Visitor to Balliol College, Oxford, 1975-76. President, Glasgow Mathematical Association, 1958-59; President, Edinburgh Mathematical Society, 1960-61; former Assessor, Church of Scotland's selection schools for candidates for the Ministry. Publications: Solving Problems in Complex Numbers, 1968; An Introduction to Vector Analysis (Reviser), 1970. Recreations: theology; local history; Gaelic. Address: (b.) Department of Mathematics, Glasgow University, Glasgow, G12 8QW; T.-041-339 8855, Ext. 4258.

Martin, David McLeod, DA, RSW, RGI. Painter; b. 30.12.22, Glasgow; m., Isobel Agnes Fowlie Smith; 4 s. Educ. Govan High School; Glasgow School of Art; Jordanhill College of Education. RAF, 1942-46. Principal Teacher, Hamilton Grammar School, 1973-83; retired early to paint full-time; exhibits regularly in Scotland; exhibited RA, 1984; numerous group shows; one man shows, Glasgow, Edinburgh, Perth, Greenock, Newcastle, Stenton; former Vice President, RSW. Address: (h.) The Old Schoolhouse, 53 Gilmour Street, Eaglesham, Glasgow, G76 0LG.

Martin, David Weir, BA (Econ). Member (Labour), European Parliament, for Lothians, since 1984; Leader, British Labour Group, European Parliament, 1987-88, and Vice-President, Socialist Group, since 1987; b. 26.8.54, Edinburgh; m., Margaret Mary Cook; 1 s.; 1 d. Educ. Liberton High School; Heriot-Watt University. Worked as stockbroker's assistant and animal rights campaigner; became Lothian Regional Councillor, 1982; Vice-President, National Playbus Association; Member, Board of Governors, Road Industry Training Board, Livingston MOTEC; Member, Committee, Scottish Society for the Prevention of Vivisection; Director, St. Andrew Animal Fund; Member, West Lothian Develoment Council. Recreations: soccer; reading. Publication: Bringing Common Sense to the Common Market - A Left Agenda for Europe. Address: (h.) 7 Mortonhall Park Gardens, Edinburgh, EH17 8SL; T.-(b.) 031-557 0936.

Martin, Derek Walker, MA, LLB. Chief Executive and Director of Administration, Sutherland District Council, since 1974; b. 4.2.34, Aberdeen; m., Lydia Ann Watson Howard; 1 s.; 1 d. Educ. Robert Gordon's College, Aberdeen; Aberdeen University. Law apprenticeship, Brander and Cruickshank, Advocates in Aberdeen, 1954-57; National Service, 1957-59; Legal and Administrative Assistant, Inverness County Council, 1960-62; Assistant Solicitor, W. & J.S. Gordon, Solicitors, Forfar, 1962-64 (Partner, 1965-67); Assistant County Clerk, then Depute County Clerk, Sutherland County Council, 1967-74; Clerk, Highland River Purification Board (part-time), since 1976. Officer Adviser to Committees of Convention of Scottish Local Authorities; Elder, Church of Scotland. Address: (h.) Glenaveron, Golf Road, Brora, Sutherland; T.-Brora 21455.

Martin, Graham Dunstan, MA, BLitt (Oxon), GradCertEd. Senior Lecturer, French Department, Edinburgh University, since 1982; b. 21.10.32, Leeds; m., 1, Ryllis E. Daniel; 2 s.; 1 d.; 2, Anne M. Crombie; 2 s. Educ. Leeds Grammar School; Oxford University. Teacher: Robert Clack Technical School, Dagenham, 1956, Great Yarmouth Grammar School, 1959; Assistant, Centre Pedagogique Regional, Montpellier, 1962; Teacher, Colchester Royal Grammar School, 1964; Junior Lecturer, then Lecturer, French Department, Edinburgh University, 1965-82. Publications: Paul Valery's Cimetiere Marin, 1971; Language, Truth and Poetry, 1975; The Architecture of Experience, 1981; novels: Giftwish, 1980; Catchfire, 1981; The Soul Master, 1984; Time-Slip, 1986; The Dream Wall, 1987; Half a Glass of Monshine, 1988. Address: (b.) French Department, Edinburgh University, 4 Buccleuch Place, Edinburgh, EH8 9LW; T.-031-667 1011, Ext. 6423.

Martin, Rev. James, MA, BD, DD. Minister, High Carntyne, Glasgow, 1954-87; b. 21.1.21, Motherwell; m., Marion Gordon Greig; 2 d. Educ. Dalziel High School, Motherwell; Glasgow University. Minister, Newmilns West Church, 1946-54; Convener, Publications Committee, General Assembly, 1978-83 and Board of Communications, 1983-87. Publications: Did Jesus Rise from the Dead?; The Reliability of the Gospels; Letters of Caiaphas to Annas; Suffering Man, Loving God; The Road to the Aisle; People in the Jesus Story; A Plain Man in the Holy Land; Listening to the Bible; William Barclay: A Personal Memoir. Recreations: football; operagoing; conversation. Address: 9 Magnolia Street, Wishaw; T.-Cambusnethan 385825.

Martin, James B., BA (Econ). General Secretary, Educational Institute of Scotland, since 1988; b. 6.12.53, Stirling; m., Anne; 1 s.; 1 d. Educ. Larbert High School; Heriot-Watt University; Moray House College of Education. Teacher, Falkirk High School, 1975-79; Field Officer, then Assistant Secretary, EIS, 1979-88. Member, Educational Broadcasting Council for Scotland; Member, Standing Committee on Crime Prevention; Convener, STUC Education and Training Committee. Recreations: football; basketball. Address: (b.) 46 Moray Place, Edinburgh; T.-031-225 6244.

Martin, James Davidson, MA, BD, PhD. Senior Lecturer in Hebrew and Old Testament, St. Andrews University, since 1977 (Chairman, Department of Biblical Criticism and Hebrew, since 1983; Dean, Faculty of Divinity, since 1986); b. 4.5.35, Stirling; m., Frances Margaret Stewart; 1 s.; 2 d. Educ. High School of Stirling; Glasgow University. Minister, Dunscore (Dumfries), 1962-66; Glasgow University: Assistant in Old Testament Language and Literature, 1966-68, Lecturer in Hebrew, 1968-69. Publication: The Book of Judges. Address: (h.) 22 Kilrymont Road, St. Andrews, Fife; T.-0334 77361.

Martin, John S.B., BSc. Assistant Secretary, SDD Housing Division 1, Scottish Office, since 1984; b. 7.7.46, West Kilbride; m., Catriona Meldrum; 1 s.; 1 d. Educ. Bell-Baxter High School, Cupar; St. Andrews University. Assistant Principal, Scottish Education Department, 1968-73; Private Secretary to Parliamentary Under Secretary of State, 1971-73; Principal, Scottish Education Department/Central Services/Scottish Home and Health Department, 1973-79; Rayner Scrutinies, Consultative Committee on the Curriculum/SDD Planning, 1979-80; Assistant Secretary, Highlands and Tourism Division, SEPD/IDS, 1980-84. Recreations: tennis; cricket; philately. Address: (b.) St. Andrews House, Edinburgh; T.-031-244 2014.

Martin, Michael John. MP (Labour), Glasgow Springburn, since 1979; b. 3.7.45. Educ. St. Patrick's Boys' School, Glasgow. Member, Glasgow Corporation, 1973-74, and Glasgow District Council, 1974-79.

Martin, Paul Charles, JP, MA (Hons). Chairman, Conservative Group, Edinburgh City Council; Assistant Director, CBI, Scotland, 1987-88; General Secretary, British Youth Council, Scotland, 1984-87; b. 10.5.58, Edinburgh. Educ. Royal High School, Edinburgh; Edinburgh University. Chairman, Arts and Recreation Committee, Edinburgh, 1983-84; Conservative Parliamentary candidate, East Edinburgh, 1983; Member, Executive Committee, XIII Commonwealth Games, Edinburgh; Member, Edinburgh Festival Council; Director, Lowlands Housing Association Ltd. Address: (h.) 106 Findlay Gardens, Edinburgh, EH7 6HQ; T.-031-554 4878.

Martin, Philip Alexander, BSc (Hons), DRTC, CEng, MIMechE. Principal, Kilmarnock College of Further Education, since 1969; b. 5.10.28, Beith; m., Letitia C. Smith; 3 s.; 2 d. Educ. Spier's School, Beith; Royal Technical College; Glasgow University. Management trainee, Paisley, 1950-52; National Service (commissioned REME), 1952-54; industrial management, 1954-55; Lecturer, then Head, Department of Engineering, then Depute Principal, Kilmarnock College, 1955-69. Past President, Kilmarnock Rotary Club. Recreations: golf; ornithology. Address: (b.) Holehouse Road, Kilmarnock; T.-Kilmarnock 23501.

Martin, Robert, MC, BL. Consultant Solicitor, Wright & Crawford, Paisley, since 1984 (Partner, 1946-84); Honorary Sheriff; b. 5.2.17, Wishaw; m., Dr. Jan J. Martin; 1 s.; 1 d. Educ. Dalziel High School, Motherwell; Glasgow University. War Service, 1940-46: Field Artillery and Parachute Brigade, Singapore, India, Middle East, Italy, Greece, France, Germany (commissioned, 1940). Honorary Vice-President, Paisley Branch, Save the Children Fund; Governor, Imperial Cancer Research Fund. Recreations: golf; swimming. Address: (h.) The Willows, 12 Crosbie Wood, Paisley, PA2 OSG; T.-041-884 2113.

Martyn, Douglas Hamilton, BA. Chief Executive, Strathclyde Business Innovation Centre, since 1986 (Chief Executive, Ardrossan Saltcoats Stevenston Enterprise Trust, 1981-86; Chairman, Ardrossan Saltcoats Stevenston Enterprise Properties Ltd., 1984-86); b. 16.9.44, Lanark; m., Patricia Elizabeth Graham; 1 s.; 1 d. Educ. Strathallan School; Strathclyde University. Assistant Marketing, Satchwell Appliance Controls, East Kilbride; Sales Executive, Rank Xerox, Glasgow; Scottish Regional Manager, Granada Television; Chief Executive, Nationwide TV Services Ltd.; Development Officer, Scottish Development Agency. Recreations: bowling; boating. Address: (h.) 2A Airbles Farm Road, Motherwell, Lanarkshire; T.-Motherwell 68723.

Marwick, Ewan, MA. Secretary and Chief Executive, Glasgow Chamber of Commerce; Secretary, Association of Scottish Chambers of Commerce, since 1982; b. 23.4.52, Edinburgh; m., Helen Daw; 2 s.; 1 d. Educ. Daniel Stewart's College; Edinburgh University. Postgraduate research and consultancy work; Assistant Secretary, Royal Institution of Chartered Surveyors (Scottish Branch); Depute Secretary, Glasgow Chamber of Commerce, 1980-82. A Director, Glasgow Opportunities; Secretary, Glasgow Posts and Telecommunications Advisory Committees. Recreation: field sports. Address: (b.) Glasgow Chamber of Commerce, 30 George Square, Glasgow, G2 1EQ; T.-041-204 2121.

Marwick, George Robert, SDA, DL, JP. Chairman, Swannay Farms Ltd., since 1972; Chairman, Campbeltown Creamery (Holdings) Ltd., since 1974; ; Deputy Lieutenant, County of Orkney, since 1976; Member, Countryside Commission for Scotland, 1978-86; b. 27.2.32, Edinburgh; m., Hanne Jensen; 3 d. Educ. Port Regis; Bryanston; Edinburgh School of Agriculture. Councillor, local government, 1968-78; Vice-Convener, Orkney County Council, 1970-74, Convener, Orkney Islands Council, 1974-78; Chairman, North of Scotland Water Board, 1970-73; Member, Scottish Agricultural Consultative Panel, since 1972 (formerly Winter Keep Panel, 1964-72); Director, North Eastern Farmers Ltd., since 1968; Director, Orkney Islands Shipping Co., 1972-87; Council Member, National Trust for Scotland, 1979-84. Recreations: shooting; tennis; motor sport. Address: (h.) Swannay House, by Evie, Orkney; T.-085-672 365.

Mason, Christopher Michael, MA, PhD. Chairman, Scottish Liberal Party; Member, Strathclyde Regional Council, since 1982; Lecturer in Politics, Glasgow University, since 1966; b. 8.3.41, Hexham; m., Stephanie Maycock; 2 d. Educ. Marlborough College; Magdalene College, Cambridge. Alliance candidate, Glasgow, European Elections, 1984. Publication: Effective Management of Resources: The International Politics of the North Sea, 1979. Recreation: sailing. Address: (h.) 17 Beaumont Gate, Glasgow, G12 9ED; T.-041-339 2840.

Mason, Professor David Kean, CBE, BDS, MD, FRCS, FDS, FRCPath. Professor of Oral Medicine, Glasgow University, since 1967; Dean of Dental Education, since 1980; Honorary Consultant Dental Surgeon, since 1965; b. 5.11.28, Paisley; m., Judith Armstrong; 2 s.; 1 d. Educ. Paisley Grammar School; Glasgow Academy; St. Andrews University; Glasgow University. RAF Dental Branch, 1952-54; Registrar in Oral Surgery, Dundee, 1954-56; Senior Lecturer in Dental Surgery and Pathology, Glasgow University, 1964-67; Honorary Consultant Dental Surgeon, Glasgow, 1964-67; Chairman, National Dental Consultative Committee, 1976-80 and since 1983; Member: Medicines Commission, 1967-80, Dental Committee, MRC, since 1973; Physiological Systems Board, MRC, 1976-80; GDC, since 1976; Dental Committee, UGC, since 1977 (Chairman, since 1983), Joint Committee for Higher Training in Dentistry, since 1977, Dental Strategy Review Group, 1980-81, Scientific Programme Committee, FDI, since 1980, Dental Review Working Party, UGC, 1986-87; Convener, Dental Council, RCPGlas, 1977-80; John Tomes Prize, RCS, 1979. Publications: Salivary Glands in Health and Disease (Co-author); Introduction to Oral Medicine (Co-author); Self Assessment: Manuals I and II (Co-Editor); Oral Manifestations of Systemic Disease. Recreations: golf; tennis; gardening; enjoying the pleasure of the countryside. Address: (h.) Greystones, Houston Road, Kilmacolm, Renfrewshire; T.-Kilmacolm 2001.

Mason, Derek Stevens, CBE (1986), JP, FRICS, FFB. Chairman, Scottish Special Housing Association, since 1981; Partner, John Baxter, Dunn and Gray, Chartered Quantity Surveyors, since 1970; Governor (Vice-chairman, 1987), Hutchesons' Educational Trust, since 1972; b. 21.5.34, Glasgow; m., Jeanette; 2 s.; 1 d. Educ. Allan Glen's School, Glasgow; Royal Technical College (part-time). RICS: Chairman, West of Scotland Junior Sub-Branch, 1965-66, Chairman, Scottish Junior Branch, 1966-67; Councillor, Glasgow Corporation, 1970 and 1972-75, Glasgow District Council, 1974-84 (Deputy Leader, Conservative Group, 1977-80, Bailie, 1977-80); Chairman, Glasgow Sports Promotion Council, 1977-80 (Hon. Vice-President, since 1980); Preceptor, Hutchesons' Hospital, 1978-80; JP, since 1977; Member, Master Court, Incorporation of Masons of Glasgow. Recreations: reading; playing bad golf; watching Clyde FC. Address: (h.) Carinya, 77 Newlands Road, Glasgow, G43 2JP; T.-041-649 2665.

Mason, Douglas C., BSc. Member, Glenrothes Development Corporation, since 1985; Member, Kirkcaldy District Council, since 1974; Parliamentary Research Assistant, since 1979; b. 30.9.41, Dunfermline. Educ. Bradford Grammar School; St. Andrews University. Conservative Party Organising Secretary, 1969-77; Freelance Journalist, since 1977; Member, Fife County Council, 1967-70; Member, Scottish Housing Advisory Committee, 1978-80; contested Central Fife, General Election, 1983; Vice-Convener, General Council Business Committee, St. Andrews University. Domestic Policy Adviser, Adam Smith Institute, since 1984. Publications: Allocation and Transfer of Council Houses (Co-author), 1980; The Qualgo Complex, 1984; Revising the Rating System, 1985; Room for Improvement, 1985; University Challenge, 1986; Time to Call Time, 1986; Ex Libris, 1986; Expounding the Arts, 1987. Recreations: books; music. Address: (h.) 84 Barnton Place, Glenrothes, Fife; T.-0592 758766.

Mason, Gavin John Finlay, MA, LLB. Solicitor; Secretary and Legal Adviser, Strathclyde Passenger Transport Executive, since 1984; b. 15.5.31, Bargeddie, Lanarkshire; m., Patricia Hunter Anderson; 1 s.; 1 d. Educ. Hamilton Academy; Glasgow University. Solicitor in private practice, until 1979, then local government service. Address: (h.) 3 Newark Drive, Glasgow, G41 4QJ; T.-041-423 7496.

Mason, Professor Emeritus John Kenyon French, CBE, MD, LLD, FRCPath, DMJ. Regius Professor of Forensic Medicine, Edinburgh University, 1973-85; b. 19.12.19, Lahore; m., Elizabeth Latham (deceased); 2 s. Educ. Downside School; Cambridge University; St. Bartholomew's Hospital. Regular Officer, Medical Branch, RAF, following War Service; Consultant in charge, RAF Department of Aviation and Forensic Pathology, 1957-73. President, British Association in Forensic Medicine, 1981-83; Swiney Prize in Jurisprudence, 1978. Publication: Forensic Medicine for Lawyers, 2nd Edition; Law and Medical Ethics, 2nd Edition (Co-author); Butterworth's Medico-Legal Encyclopaedia (Co-author). Address: (h.) 66 Craiglea Drive, Edinburgh, EH10 5PF; T.-031-447 2301.

Mason, John Muir, MBE, BL, NP. Solicitor; Partner, Waddell & Mackintosh, Troon; Conductor, Strings of Scotland and Scottish Fiddle Orchestra; b. 21.1.40, Kirkwall; m., Jessica Hilary Miller Groat; 3 s. Educ. Kirkwall Grammar School; Douglas Ewart High School, Newton Stewart; Edinburgh University. Chairman, Rev. James Currie Memorial Trust; Member, Niel Gow Memorial Trust; Honorary Member, Irvine Burns Club; Life Governor, Imperial Cancer Research Fund. Recreation: music, composition and arrangement. Address: (h.) 27 Victoria Drive, Troon, Ayrshire; T.-Troon 312796.

Mason, Peter James, MSc, CEng, FICE, FIHT, MCIT, DipTE. Director of Highways, Lothian Regional Council, since 1981; b. 20.7.33, Newton Abbott; m., Janet Mary Terrill; 1 d. Educ. Watford Boys' Grammar School. Joint Deputy (Planning and Transportation), South Yorkshire County Council, 1973-81. Recreations: gardening; walking. Address: (b.) 19 Market Street, Edinburgh, EH1 1RL; T.-031-229 9292.

Mason, Timothy Ian Godson, MA. Director, Scottish Arts Council, since 1980; b. 11.3.45, Little Chalfont, Buckinghamshire; m., Marilyn Williams; 1 s.; 1 d. Educ. Bradfield College, Berkshire; Christ Church, Oxford. Assistant Manager, Oxford Playhouse, 1966-67; Assistant to Peter Daubeny, World Theatre Season, London, 1967-69; Administrator: Ballet Rambert, 1970-75, Royal Exchange Theatre, Manchester, 1975-77; Director, Western Australian Arts Council, 1977-80. Recreations: arts; family. Address: (b.) 19 Charlotte Square, Edinburgh, EH2 4DF; T.-031-226 6051.

Massie, Allan Johnstone, BA, FRSL. Author and Journalist; b. 16.10.38, Singapore; m., Alison Langlands; 2 s.; 1 d. Educ. Drumtochty Castle; Trinity College, Glenalmond; Trinity College, Cambridge. Schoolmaster, Drumtochty Castle, 1960-71; taught EFL, 1972-75; Creative Writing Fellow, Edinburgh University, 1982-84, Glasgow and Strathclyde Universities, 1985-86; Editor, New Edinburgh Review, 1982-84; Fiction Reviewer, The Scotsman, since 1975; Television Critic, Sunday Standard, 1981-83 (Fraser of Allander Award, Critic of the Year, 1982); Sports Columnist, Glasgow Herald, 1985-88; Columnist, Sunday Times, since 1987. Publications: (novels): Change and Decay in all around I see; The Last Peacock; The Death of Men (Scottish Arts Council Book Award); One Night in Winter; Augustus; (non-fiction): Muriel Spark; Ill Met by Gaslight; The Caesars; Portrait of Scottish Rugby; Colette; 101 Great Scots; Byron's Travels; (as Editor): Edinburgh and the Borders in Verse; (radio play): Quintet in October. Recreations: reading; watching rugby, cricket, racing; walking the dogs. Address: (h.) Thirladean House, Selkirk, TD7 5LU; T.-Selkirk 20393.

Massie, Leslie Alexander, MA, LLB, CM, PJK (Malaysia). Advocate, since 1953; b. 20.5.10, Aberdeen; m., Margot N. Hesketh; 1 d. Educ. Robert Gordon's College, Aberdeen; Aberdeen University. General legal practice as Solicitor in Scotland, 1936-37; Examining Officer's Commission, HM Coal Commission and HM Sasine Office, Scotland, 1938-39; enlisted as private, Royal Scots, 1939; commissioned 2nd Lt., Royal Scots Fusiliers, 1940-42; Captain and Adjutant, 15th (Scottish) Division Infantry Training Battle School, 1943-44; passed SC Military Staff College, Camberley, 1945; Staff Officer (Major), General Headquarters South East Asia Command, XIV Army, 1945; promoted Lt.-Col., Royal Scots Fusiliers, 1945; President, Superior Court (Military) and State Legal Advsier, Malay States of Kedah and Perlis, 1945-46; Assistant Judge-Advocate General GHQ South East Asia Command, 1946-47; President, War Crimes Court, South East Asia, 1947-48; demobilised Army, 1948; passed entry to HM Colonial Legal Service and gazetted as Federal Counsel to Government of Malaya, 1948; later, Senior Federal Counsel; Member, State Executive Council and State Legislative Council in several Malay States and British Settlements; called to Scottish Bar, 1953; took part in deliberations in respect of British Settlement of Malacca, HM Reid Constitutional Commission, 1957; Solicitor-General, Federation of Malaysia, 1959-60; returned to UK, 1961. Recreations: golf; bowling; gardening. Address: (h.) 9 Whitehouse Terrace, Edinburgh, EH9 2EU; T.-031-667 6462.

Masson, Alastair H.B., BA, MB, ChB, FRCSEdin, FFARCS. Consultant Anaesthetist, Edinburgh Royal Infirmary, since 1956; b. 30.1.25, Bathgate; m., Marjorie Nan Paisley-Whyte; 3 s.; 1 d. Educ. Bathgate Academy; Edinburgh University. Visiting Professor of Anesthesiology, South Western Medical School, Dallas, Texas, 1962-63. President, Scottish Society of Anaesthetists, 1978-79; Honorary Archivist, Royal College of Surgeons, Edinburgh; President, Scottish Society of the History of Medicine, 1984-87. Recreations: golf; hill-walking; music; travel. Address: (h.) 13 Osborne Terrace, Edinburgh.

Masterton, Gavin George, FIB (Scot). General Manager, Bank of Scotland, since 1986; b. 19.11.41, Dunfermline; m., Sheila; 3 d. Educ. Dunfermline High School; Harvard University (AMP). Began banking career with British Linen Bank, 1957; branch banking for several years, then to various Head Office functions; appointed Assistant General Manager; initiated bank's move into management buy-out market. Recreations: gardening; walking. Address: (b.) Uberior House, 61 Grassmarket, Edinburgh; T.-031 243 5750.

Mather, Alexander Smith, BSc, PhD. Senior Lecturer, Department of Geography, Aberdeen University, since 1982; Editor, Scottish Geographical Magazine; b. 17.9.43, Aberdeen; m., Grace MacArthur; 1 s. Educ. Maud School; Peterhead Academy; Aberdeen Grammar School; Aberdeen University. Department of Geography, Aberdeen University: Assistant Lecturer, 1967, Lecturer, 1970. Publications: academic papers and monographs; Land Use. Recreation: hill-walking. Address: (b.) Department of Geography, Aberdeen University, Aberdeen, AB9 2UF; T.-0224 272354.

Mather, John, FSCA, FCIS, FCIT. Managing Director, Clyde Port Authority, since 1980; b. 17.12.36, Glasgow. Clyde Navigation Trust (which became Clyde Port Authority): joined, 1953, Director Finance and Marketing, 1974, Deputy Managing Director, 1977; a Director: Ardrossan Harbour Co. Ltd., Qualitube Ltd., Strathclyde Stevedoring Services Ltd.; UK Representative, European Commission's Steering Committee (EHVA); Member, British Ports Federation Management Committee and Council; first Vice-Chairman, National Association of Port Employers; Member, "Negotiating Eight", National Joint Council; Member, Council, Company and Commercial Accountants; Alternate UK Director, International Association of Ports and Harbors (2nd Vice-President, since 1987). Address: (b.) 16 Robertson Street, Glasgow, G2 8DS; T.-041-221 8733.

Matheson, Alexander, JP, MPS. Convener, Western Isles Islands Council, since 1982; Member, Western Isles Health Board, since 1972; Member, Stornoway Trust, since 1967; b. 16.11.41, Stornoway; m., Irene Mary Davidson, BSc, MSc; 2 s.; 2 d. Educ. Nicolson Institute, Stornoway; Robert Gordon's Institute of Technology, Aberdeen. Member: Stornoway Town Council, 1967-75 (Provost, 1971-75), Ross and Cromarty County Council, 1967-75; Chairman, Stornoway Trust, 1971-81; Member, Stornoway Pier and Harbour

Commission, since 1967 (Chairman, 1970-71); Chairman, Development Services, Western Isles Islands Council, 1974-80; Vice-Convener, Western Isles Islands Council, 1980-82; Honorary Sheriff, since 1972; Parliamentary candidate (Labour), 1979; Chairman, Lewis Development Fund (now Western Isles Development Fund), since 1972; President, Islands Commission of the Conference of Peripheral Maritime Regions of Europe, 1987. Address: (h.) 33 Newton Street, Stornoway, Isle of Lewis; T.-0851 2082.

Matheson, Rev. Calum, MA (Hons), DipTh. Minister, Shawbost Free Church, Isle of Lewis, since 1980; b. 27.8.48, Stornoway; m., Betty Broadfoot; 1 s.; 1 d. Educ. Nicolson Institute, Stornoway; Langside College of Further Education, Glasgow; Glasgow University; Free Church College, Edinburgh. Member, Translation Team, Gaelic New Testament, NBSS. Recreations: reading; fishing. Address: The Manse, Shawbost, Isle of Lewis; T.-0851 71 216.

Matheson, Donald, CA, FBIM. Director of Finance, Highlands and Islands Development Board; b. 3.2.36, Inverness; m., Elizabeth; 1 s.; 1 d. Educ. Inverness. Apprentice and Qualified Assistant, Howden and Molleson, Chartered Accountants, Edinburgh, 1958-63; Financial and Management Accountant, Ethicon Ltd., Edinburgh, 1963-67; joined HIDB, 1967. Recreations: Rotary; Church. Address: (b.) Bridge Street, Bank Street, Inverness; T.-0463 234171.

Matheson, Very Rev. James Gunn, MA, BD. Moderator, General Assembly of the Church of Scotland, 1975-76; Minister, Portree, 1973-79; b. 1.3.12; m.; 3 s.; 1 d.; 1 d. (deceased). Educ. Inverness Royal Academy; Edinburgh University. Free Church, Olrig, Caithness, 1936-39; Chaplain to HM Forces, 1939-45 (POW, 1941-43); St. Columba's Church, Edinburgh, 1946-51; Knox Church, Dunedin, New Zealand, 1951-61; Secretary, Stewardship and Budget Committee, Church of Scotland, 1961-73.

Mathewson, Alexander Mackechnie, MB, ChB, MRCGP. General Practitioner, Wishaw, since 1950; Member, Lanarkshire Health Board; b. 13.11.23, Glasgow; m., Dorothy Wightman Reid; 3 s. Educ. Irvine Royal Academy; Glasgow University. Former Captain, RAMC. Past Chairman, Lanarkshire Division, BMA. Recreations: golf; curling. Address: (h.) The Beeches, Wishaw, Lanarkshire, ML2 8LF; T.-0698 384789.

Mathewson, George Ross, CBE, BSc, PHD, MBA, LLD, FRSE, CEng, MIEE, CBIM. Director, Strategic Planning Development, Royal Bank of Scotland Group PLC, since 1987; Director, Royal Bank of Scotland PLC, since 1987; Director: Scottish Investment Trust Ltd., since 1981, EFTPOS UK Ltd., since 1988, Scottish Financial Enterprise, since 1988; Visiting Professor in Marketing, Strathclyde University, since 1984; Chief Executive, Scottish Development Agency, 1981-87; b. 14.5.40, Perth; m., Sheila Alexandra Graham Bennett; 2 s. Educ. Perth Academy; St. Andrews University; Canisius College, Buffalo, New York. Assistant Lecturer, St. Andrews University, 1964-67; Systems Engineer (various positions), Bell Aerospace, Buffalo, New York, 1967-72; ICFC: Executive in Edinburgh Area Office, 1972-74, Area Manager, 1974-79, Director and Assistant General Manager, 1979-81. Recreations: rugby; golf; business. Address: (h.) 29 Saxe Coburg Place, Edinburgh, EH3 5BP.

Mathie, Hugh Alexander, MA, MEd. Rector, McLaren High School, Callander, since 1985; b. 30.7.35, Dundee; m., Margaret Black; 2 s.; 1 d. Educ. Morgan Academy, Dundee; St. Andrews University. Teacher of Classics, Kilsyth Academy and Kirkton High School, Dundee; Principal Teacher of Classics, Kilsyth Academy and Cumbernauld High School; Assistant Rector, Depute Rector, Greenfaulds High School; Rector, Kilsyth Academy. Recreations: hill-walking; golf. Address: (h.) Welwyn, Firpark Terrace, Cambusbarron, Stirling; T.-Stirling 72900.

Mathieson, John George, CBE, TD, DL, BL. Solicitor, Thornton Oliver, WS, Arbroath; b. 15.6.32, Argyll; m., Shirley Bidder; 1 s.; 1 d. Educ. George Watson's College, Edinburgh; Glasgow University. Territorial Army, 1951-76: Commanding Officer The Highland Regiment RA (T), 1967-69, TA Colonel for Highlands, 1972-76, Chairman, Highlands TA Association, 1976-82. Commenced practice as Solicitor in Glasgow, 1955-57; joined practice of Clark Oliver, Arbroath, 1957; now a Senior Partner; Chairman, Scottish Solicitors Discipline Tribunal; Secretary, Angus Housing Association; Chairman, Arbroath Branch, Royal British Legion; Chairman, British Legion Housing Association, Wimberley and Condor Courts, Broughty Ferry and Carnoustie; Deputy Lieutenant, Angus, since 1977; Chairman, Earl Haig Fund, Arbroath; Deputy Chairman, Royal Artillery Council for Scotland; Honorary President, Angus Bn., Boys' Brigade. Recreations: shooting; skiing; golf. Address: (h.) Willanyards, Colliston, Arbroath, Angus; T.-02489 286.

Matthew, Rev. Stewart Graham, MA, BD. National Adult Adviser, Department of Education, Church of Scotland, since 1984; b. 14.11.39, Dundee; m., Irene Nicol Green; 1 s.; 1 d. Educ. High School of Dundee; St. Andrews University. Assistant Minister, St. Columba's, Glenrothes, 1965-66; Teacher of Religious Education, Swinton Comprehensive School, 1966-69; Minister, St. Ninian's Bellfield, Kilmarnock, 1969-79; joined Department of Education as Assistant Secretary (Education), 1979-84; Editor of Frontline materials, Church of Scotland; Scottish Representative on International Committee for the German Kirchentag; regular Columnist, Life and Work magazine. Publication: Leading God's People, 1986. Recreations: guitar; table tennis; motion pictures. Address: (h.) 10 Silverknowes Midway, Davidson Mains, Edinburgh; T.-031-336 5990.

Matthews, Baird, BL. Solicitor in private practice, since 1950; Honorary Sheriff, Kirkcudbright and Stranraer; b. 19.1.25, Newton Stewart; m., Mary Thomson Hope; 2 s.; 1 d. Educ. Douglas Ewart High School; Edinburgh University. Commissioned, Royal Scots Fusiliers, 1944; demobilised as Captain, 1st Bn., 1947; Partner, A. B. & A. Matthews, Solicitors, Newton Stewart, since 1950; Clerk to General Commissioners of Income Tax, Stranraer and Newton Stewart Districts, from 1952; Burgh Prosecutor, Newton Stewart, from 1968; Depute Procurator Fiscal for Wigtownshire, 1970; Chairman, Board of Local Directors, General Accident Fire and Life Assurance Corporation, 1970; Dean of Faculty of Stewartry of Kirkcudbright Solicitors, 1979; Dean of Faculty of Solicitors of the District of Wigtown, 1983; Chairman, Appeals Tribunal, 1984. Recreations: golf; shooting; curling; sailing. Address: (b.) Bank of Scotland Buildings, Newton Stewart, Wigtownshire; T.-0671 3013.

Matthews, Edward. Director, Edinburgh Council of Social Service, since 1974; b. 11.9.37, Brentford, Middlesex; m., Ann Patricia; 1 s.; 1 d. Educ. Finchley Grammar School; St. Edmund's College, Ware. Curate and Borstal Chaplain, 1961-66; Assistant Director, then Deputy Director, Richmond Fellowship, 1966-74; Member, Lothian Health Board, 1983-87; Winston Churchill Fellowship, 1973; Secretary, Edinburgh Lodging House Association; Executive Committee Member: Edinburgh University Settlement, SACRO, Edinburgh Cyrenians, Edinburgh Council for Single Homeless, Grassmarket Area Housing Association. Recreations: woodwork; badminton; gardening. Address: (b.) Edinburgh Council of Social Service, 11 St. Colme Street, Edinburgh, EH3 6AG; T.-031-225 4606.

Matthews, Professor John Burr Lumley, MA, DPhil. Acting Director, Scottish Marine Biological Association; Honorary Professor, Stirling University, since 1984; b. 23.4.35, Isleworth; m., Jane Rosemary; 1 s.; 2 d. Educ. Warwick School; Oxford University. Research Scientist (Zooplankton), Oceanographic Laboratory, Edinburgh, 1961-67; Senior Lecturer, Department of Marine Biology, then Professor of Marine Biology, University of Bergen, 1967-84. Recreations: cross country skiing; gardening; wine-making. Address: (h.) Grianaig, Rockfield Road, Oban, PA34 5DH; T.-0631 62734.

Mattock, Professor John Nicholas, MA, PhD. Professor of Arabic and Islamic Studies, Glasgow University, since 1987; b. 6.1.38, Horsham. Educ. Christ's Hospital; Pembroke College, Cambridge. Research Fellow, Pembroke College, Cambridge, 1963-65; Lecturer in Arabic and Islamic Studies, then Senior Lecturer, Glasgow University, 1965-87. Member, Editorial Board, Journal of Arabic Literature, since 1970; British Representative, European Union of Arabists and Islamists, since 1986. Address: (b.) Department of Arabic and Islamic Studies, Glasgow University, Glasgow, G12 8QQ; T.-041-339 8855, Ext. 5586.

Mauchline, John, PhD, DSc, CBiol, FIBiol, FRSE. Research Biologist, Scottish Marine Biological Association, since 1962; UK Editor, Marine Biology, since 1977; b. 1.7.33, Motherwell; m., Isobel Hopkins Warden; 1 s.; 2 d. Educ. High School of Glasgow; Glasgow University. Research Biologist, UKAEA, 1958-62. Visiting Professor, University of Tokyo, 1976; Visiting Scholar, Memorial University of Newfoundland, 1987. Recreations: fly fishing; painting. Address: (b.) Dunstaffnage, Marine Research Laboratory, P.O. Box 3, Oban, PA34 4AD; T.-Oban 62244.

Maund, Robert Graham, BSc, DipTP, FRTPI. Director of Physical Planning, Strathclyde Regional Council, since 1984; b. 10.11.38, Cheshire; m., Judith L.; 3 s.; 1 d. Educ. Manchester University. City of Manchester: trainee graduate engineer, various planning posts, Assistant City Planning Officer; Greater Manchester Council: Assistant County Planning Officer, Deputy County Planning Officer. Recreations: walking; cross-country running; photography; listening to music; reading; theatre. Address: (b.) Strathclyde House, 20 India Street, Glasgow, G2 4PF; T.-041-227 3626.

Maver, Professor Thomas Watt, BSc (Hons), PhD, FInstE, FRSA. Professor of Computer Aided Design, Department of Architecture and Building Science, Strathclyde University, since 1982 (Head of Department, 1983-85); b. 10.3.38, Glasgow; m., Avril Elizabeth Cuthbertson; 2 d. Educ. Eastwood Secondary School; Glasgow University. Special Research Fellow, Engineering Faculty, Glasgow University, 1961-67; Strathclyde University: Research Fellow, School of Architecture, 1967-70, Director, Architecture and Building Aids Computer Unit, Strathclyde, since 1970; Visiting Professor, Department of Architecture, Technical University, Eindhoven; Past Chairman, Design Research Society. Recreations: family; farming. Address: (h.) 8 Kew Terrace, Glasgow, G12; T.-041-339 7185.

Mavor, Professor John, BSc, PhD, CPhys, FInstP, CEng, FIEE, FIERE. Chair of Electrical Enginering, Edinburgh University, since 1986 (Head, Department of Electrical Engineering, since 1984; Chairman, School of Engineering, since 1987); first holder, Lothian Chair of Microelectronics, 1980-86; b. 18.7.42, Kilwinning; m., Susan Christina; 2 d. Educ. Bromley Technical High School; City University; London University. AEI Research Laboratories, London, 1964-65; Texas Instruments Ltd., Bedford, 1968-70; Emihus Microcomponents Ltd., Glenrothes, 1970-71; joined Edinburgh University, 1971. Chairman, EUMOS Ltd. Recreations: gardening; hill-walking. Address: (b.) Department of Electrical Engineering, Edinburgh University, King's Buildings, Edinburgh, EH9 3JL; T.-031-667 1081, Ext. 3591.

Mavor, Michael Barclay, CVO, MA. Headmaster, Gordonstoun School, since 1979; b. 29.1.47, Kuala Lipis, Malaysia; m., Elizabeth Sucksmith; 1 s.; 1 d. Educ. Loretto; St. John's College, Cambridge. Woodrow Wilson Teaching Fellow, Northwestern University, Evanston, Illinois, 1969-72; Assistant Master, Tonbridge School, 1972-78; Course Tutor (Drama), Open University, 1977-78. Recreations: theatre; writing; fishing; golf. Address: Gordonstoun School, Elgin, Moray, IV30 2RF; T.-0343 830445.

Maxton, John Alston. BA (Oxon), DipEd (Oxon). MP (Labour), Glasgow Cathcart, since 1979; b. 5.5.36, Oxford; m., Christine Elspeth; 3 s. Educ. Lord Williams Grammar School, Thame; University College, Oxford. Lecturer in Social Studies, Hamilton College of Education, before entering Parliament; Chairman, Association of Lecturers in Colleges of Education in Scotland, 1974-78; Member, Scottish Select Committee, 1980-83, Public Accounts Committee, 1983-84; Opposition Treasury and Scottish Whip, 1984-85; Opoosition Scottish Front Bench Spokesperson on Health, Local Government and Transport,

1985-87, on Industry and Local Government Finance, since 1987. Recreations: listenng to jazz (Director, Glasgow International Jazz Festival); running. Address: (h.) 37 Larch Grove, Hamilton, ML3 8NF; T.-0698 43847.

Maxwell, Donald, MA. Professional Singer; b. 12.12.48, Perth. Educ. Perth Academy; Edinburgh University. Former Teacher of Geography; since 1976, professional Singer with British opera companies and orchestras; Principal Baritone, Scottish Opera, 1978-82; Principal Baritone, Welsh National Opera, 1982-85; guest appearances, Royal Opera House, London, as well as France, Belgium, Germany, Canada, Argentina. Recreations: railways; watching cricket. Address: (b.) 12 Victoria Street, Perth; T.-0738 33164.

Maxwell, Ingval, DA, RIBA, ARIAS, FSA Scot. Assistant Director of Works, Historic Buildings and Monuments Directorate, since 1985; b. 28.5.44, Penpont; m., Susan Isabel Maclean; 1 s.; 1 d. Educ. Dumfries Academy; Duncan of Jordanstone College of Art, Dundee. Joined Ministry of Public Buildings and Works as Architect, 1969; Area Architect, then Principal Architect, Ancient Monuments Branch, 1972-85. RIBA Research Award, 1970-71; RIAS Thomas Ross Award, 1988. Recreations: photography; astronomy; aircraft; farm buildings. Address: (h.) 135 Mayfield Road, Edinburgh, EH9 3AN.

Maxwell, John Lyon, MA (Cantab). Member, Stewartry District Council, since 1975; Member, Electricity Consultative Council for South of Scotland District; Farmer; b. 23.9.31, Llanarth, Monmouthshire; m., Lorna Ann Symington; 1 s.; 3 d. Educ. Trinity College, Glenalmond; Emmanuel College, Cambridge. Agricultural Officer, Overseas Agricultural Service, Nyasaland, 1956-64. Recreations: shooting; reading. Address: (h.) Kenmure House, New Galloway, Kirkcudbrightshire; T.-064-42 262.

Maxwell, Hon. Lord (Peter Maxwell), QC, BA, LLB. Senator, College of Justice, since 1973; Chairman, Scottish Law Commission, since 1981; b. 21.5.19, Edinburgh; m., Alison Susan Readman; 1 s.; 2 d. Educ. Wellington College; Balliol College, Oxford; Edinburgh University. Argyll and Sutherland Highlanders and Royal Artillery, 1939-46; called to Scottish Bar, 1951; QC, 1961; Sheriff Principal, Dumfries and Galloway, 1970-73; Member, Royal Commission on Legal Services in Scotland, 1976-80. Address: (h.) 1c Oswald Road, Edinburgh, EH9 2HE; T.-031-667 7444.

Maxwell, Thomas Jefferson, BSc, PhD. Director, Macaulay Land Use Research Institute, since 1987 (Head, Animal Production Department, Hill Farming Research Organisation, 1981-87); Honorary Research Professor, Aberdeen University; b. 7.10.40, Aspatria, Cumbria; m., Christine Patrick Speedie; 1 s.; 1 d. Educ. Silcoates School, Wakefield; Edinburgh University. Specialist Animal Production Adviser, East of Scotland College of Agriculture, 1967-70; Research Scientist, Animal Production Department, Hill Farming Research Organisation, 1970-81. Recreations: reading; squash; hill-walking; choral singing. Address: (b.) Macaulay Land Use Research Institute, Craigiebuckler, Aberdeen.

Maxwell, William Paul, BA (Oxon), DipEd. Rector, Turriff Academy, since 1976; b. 7.1.33, Kirkcaldy; m., Ruth Isobel Alexander; 2 s. Educ. Kirkcaldy High School; Edinburgh Academy; St. Edmund Hall, Oxford. Taught, Daniel Stewart's College, Edinburgh, 1957-67; Principal Teacher of History: Dunfermline High School, 1967-69, Robert Gordon's College, Aberdeen, 1969-72; Assistant Rector, Elgin Academy, 1972-76. Recreations: music; hill-walking; angling. Address: (b.) Turriff Academy, Victoria Terrace, Turriff, AB5 7EE; T.-0888 63216.

Maxwell Davies, Sir Peter, KB (1987), MusB (Hons). Composer; Founder and Artistic Director, St. Magnus Festival, Orkney, 1977-86; Associate Conductor/Composer, Scottish Chamber Orchestra, since 1985; b. 8.9.34, Manchester. Educ. Leigh Grammar School; Royal Manchester College of Music; Manchester University. Director of Music, Cirencester Grammar School, 1959-62; Harkness Fellowship, Princeton University, 1962-64; Professor of Composition, Royal Northern College of Music, Manchester, until 1980; Founder and Artistic Director, Fires of London, 1971-87; Artistic Director, Dartington Summer School of Music, 1979-84; President, Composers Guild of GB, since 1986; Honorary Doctor of Music, Edinburgh University, 1979, Honorary Doctor of Law, Aberdeen University, 1981. Address: (b.) c/o Mrs Judy Arnold, 50 Hogarth Road, London, SW5; T.-01-370 1477.

Maxwell-Irving, Alastair Michael Tivey, BSc, CEng, MIEE, MBIM, AMICE, FSAScot. Antiquarian and Archaeologist; b. 1.10.35, Witham, Essex; m., Esther Mary Hamilton, MA, LLB. Educ. Lancing College; London University. General Electric Company, 1957; English Electric Company, 1960; Assistant Factor, Annandale Estates, 1966; Weir Pumps Ltd., since 1970 (Contracts Manager, Special Projects); founder Member and Secretary, 1975-78, Central Scotland Branch, British Institute of Management. Publications: Genealogy of the Irvings of Dumfries, 1965; The Irvings of Bonshaw, 1968; The Irvings of Dumfries, 1968; Lochwood Castle, 1968; Early Firearms and their Influence on the Military and Domestic Architecture of the Borders, 1974; Cramalt Tower: Historical Survey and Excavations, 1977-79, 1982; Borthwick Castle: Excavations 1979, 1982; Andrew Dunlop (Clockmakers' Company 1701-32), 1984; Hoddom Castle: A Reappraisal of its Architecture and Place in History, 1988. Recreations: architecture and history of the Border towers of Scotland; archaeology; family history and genealogy; Florence and the art and architecture of Tuscany; horology; heraldry; photography; gardening. Address: (h.) Telford House, Blairlogie, Stirling, FK9 5PX.

Maxwell-Scott, Dame Jean (Mary Monica), DCVO (1984). Lady in Waiting to Princess Alice, Duchess of Gloucester, since 1959; b. 8.6.23. VAD Red Cross Nurse, 1941-46. Address: (h.) Abbotsford, Melrose, Roxburghshire, TD6 9BQ.

Maxwell-Scott, Patricia Mary, OBE. Honorary Sheriff of Selkirk, since 1971; b. 11.3.21, Curragh, Dublin; m., Harold Hugh Christian Boulton. Educ. Convent des Oiseaux, Westgate on Sea, Kent. ATP, 1942-45. President, Borders Branch,

Save the Children Fund; President, Spastics Association (Borders); President, Roxburgh Branch, BRCS. Recreations: travelling; reading. Address: (h.) Abbotsford, Melrose, TD6 9BQ; T.-0896 2043.

May, Malcolm Stuart, BA, BD, STM, CQSW. Chief Executive, Dundee Association for Social Service, since 1979; b. 9.9.40, Isle of Shapinsay, Orkney; m., Alison Wood; 1 s.; 1 d. Educ. Kilmarnock Academy; The Gordon Schools, Huntly; Hamilton Academy; Queen's University, Belfast; Glasgow University; Union Theological Seminary, New York. Assistant Minister, The Old Kirk, West Pilton, Edinburgh, 1966-68; staff, Iona Community, Glasgow, 1968-72; social work training, 1972-73; Training Officer, Scottish Council of Social Service, 1973-78. Recreations: reading; choral singing; running; wine-making. Address: (b.) Castlehill House, 1 High Street, Dundee, DD1 1TD; T.-0382 21545.

May, Ranald Stuart, MA, BComm. Senior Lecturer in Economics, St. Andrews University, since 1978; b. 1.5.32, Dundee; m., Jennifer Alison Shewan. Educ. Grove Academy, Dundee; St. Andrews University; Queen's University, Canada. Ft.-Lt., RAF, 1956-59; Finance Officer and Economic Adviser, Shell International Petroleum Company, London and Shell-BP Petroleum Development Company, Nigeria, 1959-63; St. Andrews University: Shell Fellow in Economic Development, 1963-70, Lecturer in Economics, 1970-78. Treasurer, Scottish Economic Society; Arbitrator to ACAS, since 1975. Recreations: golf; gardening. Address: (h.) 1 Albany Place, St. Andrews, Fife; T.-St. Andrews 76161.

Mayfield, Hon. Lord (Ian MacDonald), MC (1945), QC (Scot). Senator of the College of Justice in Scotland, since 1981; b. 26.5.21; m.; 1 s.; 1 d. Educ. Colston's School; Edinburgh University. Served Second World War (Captain, Royal Tank Regiment); called to Bar, 1952; Sheriff Principal of Dumfries and Galloway, 1973; President, Industrial Tribunals for Scotland, 1973-81.

Mearns, James Michie, MA, DL. Rector, Cumbernauld High School, since 1971; Deputy Lieutenant, County of Dunbarton; b. 22.5.30, Inverurie; m., Elizabeth Findlay; 1 s.; 2 d. Educ. Inverurie Academy; Aberdeen University; Aberdeen College of Education. Principal Teacher of Modern Languages, latterly also Depute Head, Currie High School, 1963-71; Assistant Principal Examiner, SCE Examination Board, 1967-70. Recreations: gardening; choral singing; badminton. Address: (h.) 8 Victoria Terrace, Dullatur, Glasgow; T.-02367 27455.

Meek, Brian Alexander, OBE, JP. Columnist, Glasgow Herald; Deputy Chairman, Livingston Development Corporation, since 1986; Director, Capital Publicity Ltd., since 1987; Leader, Conservative Group, Lothian Regional Council, since 1973 (Regional Convener, 1982-86); b. 8.2.39, Edinburgh; m., Frances C. Horsburgh; 1 s.; 1 d. Educ. Royal High School, Edinburgh; Edinburgh Secretarial College. Joined Scotsman Publications as trainee, then Sub-Editor, Features Writer; transferred to Express Newspapers as Feature Writer, Leader Writer and Rugby Correspondent; elected, Edinburgh Corporation, 1969; Leader, Conservative Group, 1970-72; elected as Bailie, 1972; elected, Lothian Regional Council and Edinburgh District Council, 1973; Member, Education Board, Merchant Company. Recreations: golf; theatre. Address: (b.) Lothian Regional Council, Parliament Square, Edinburgh; T.-031-229 9292.

Megson, Raymond James, LLB, NP, SSC. Solicitor; Senior Partner, Megson & Co., SSC, since 1971; b. 4.9.45, Sheffield; m., Kim Frances McCreadie; 3 s.; 1 d. Educ. North Sydney High School; Douglas Ewart School; Edinburgh University. Apprenticeship, Boyd Jameson & Young, WS, Edinburgh; returned to Sydney (where raised); joined Harris & Co., Solicitors; returned to Edinburgh and established own firm, specialising in criminal law; President, Faculty of Procurators of Midlothian (Edinburgh Solicitors Bar Association). Scottish Schools Triple Jump Champion, 1964; Scottish international rugby referee; played rugby for Wigtownshire, Edinburgh University, Musselburgh, Edinburgh Wanderers Co-optimists, Public School Wanderers and Edinburgh District. Recreations: rugby refereeing; golf; badminton; jogging; tennis. Address: (h.) 22 Cluny Drive, Edinburgh; T.-031-447 2343.

Meikle, Elizabeth Aitken, OBE, BPharm, FRPharmS, MCPP. Chief Administrative Pharmaceutical Officer, Greater Glasgow Health Board, since 1978; Assistant Chief Commissioner, Scottish HQ, Scout Association, since 1980; b. 1.8.28, Lenzie, Kirkintilloch. Educ. Frimley and Camberley Secondary School; London University. Chief Pharmacist, Vale of Leven District General Hospital, 1955-73; Area Pharmacist, Glasgow (South) and District Pharmaceutical Officer; served on Grossett and Noel Hall Committees on Hospital Pharmaceutical Service; sometime Chairman, National Pharmaceutical Consultative Committee; Chairman, Scottish Executive, Pharmaceutical Society, 1982-84; Chairman, Working Group on Pharmaceutical Supplies in Residential Homes, 1983. Recreations: gardening; golf; photography; philately; but all restricted by Scouting activities! Address: (h.) Alderbrae, Buchanan Castle Estate, Drymen, G63 OHX; T.-Drymen 60379.

Meikle, Robert Baxter, MA, DipEd. Rector, Alness Academy, since 1975; b. 8.6.33, Kirkliston, West Lothian; m., Adrianne Margaret Stewart; 1 s.; 1 d. Educ. Broxburn High School; Edinburgh University; Moray House College of Education. Sergeant, RAEC, 1956-58; Teacher of Geography and Special Assistant, Bell-Baxter High School, Cupar, 1958-64; Principal Teacher of Geography, then Assistant Rector, Montrose Academy, 1964-75. Chairman, Highland Region Computer Working Party, 1980-84; Chairman, Saltburn Community Council. Publication: Windows on the Geography of Scotland, 1972-73. Recreations: golf; fell-walking; music; photography; art; the works of Robert Burns. Address: (b.) Alness Academy, Alness, Ross and Cromarty; T.-0349 883341.

Mein, William Main, MA (Hons). HM Inspector of Schools, since 1972; b. 1.7.38, Nairn; m., Dorothy Robertson Steele; 2 d. Educ. Nairn Academy; Edinburgh University; Moray House College of Education. Teacher of Mathematics, Robert Gordon's College, Aberdeen, 1961-65; Principal Teacher of Mathematics, Invergordon Academy, 1965-68; Principal Teacher of Mathematics, then Assistant Headteacher, Dingwall Academy, 1968-72. Elder, Crown Church, Inverness. Recreations: angling; photography; gardening. Address: (h.) The Linn, 11 Beaufort Road, Inverness; T.-0463 238617.

Meldrum, James, JP. Member, Strathclyde Regional Council, since 1978 (Chairman, General Purposes Committee, since 1986); b. 17.4.32, Hamilton; 2 s.; 1 d. Educ. St. John's Grammar School, Hamilton. Member, East Kilbride Town Council, 1971-75 (Magistrate, 1972-75, Convener, Parks Committee, 1972-75); Member, East Kilbride District Council, 1974-77; various union branch posts in Boilermakers Society, 1966-73. Recreation: bowls (indoor and outdoor). Address: (h.) 67 Struthers Crescent, Calderwood, East Kilbride; T.-East Kilbride 31156.

Melrose, Rev. James Henderson Loudon, MA (Hons), BD (Hons), MED, FSA(Scot). Lecturer, Jordanhill College of Education, since 1982; Minister of Religion (Moderator, Presbytery of Hamilton, 1987); Lecturer, Extra Mural Department, Glasgow University, since 1972; b. 24.3.30, Glasgow; m., Henrietta Spence Patrick; 3 s. Educ. Forfar Academy; Glasgow University and Trinity College. Ordained Assistant, Barony of Glasgow, 1955-57; Minister, Larbert East, 1958-63; Principal Teacher of Religious Education, 1963-66; Lecturer, Craigie College of Education, 1966-70; Principal Lecturer in Religious Education, Hamilton College of Education, 1970-82. Member, COPE Committee, 1981-85; Member, General Assembly Committee on Education, 1977-81; Vice-Chairman and Chairman, Scottish Covenanters Memorial Association. Recreations: walking; golf; natural history. Address: (b.) Jordanhill College of Education, Southbrae Drive, Glasgow, G13 1PP; T.-01-959 1232.

Melville, Ian Dunlop, MB, ChB, FRCPGlas, FRCPLond. Consultant Neurologist, Institute of Neurological Sciences, Glasgow, since 1965; Honorary Clinical Lecturer, Glasgow University, since 1968; b. 9.11.27, Glasgow; m., Eliza Duffus; 1 s.; 3 d. Educ. Shawlands Academy; Glasgow University. RAF Medical Branch; Medical Registrar, Glasgow Royal Infirmary; Academic Registrar, National Hospital for Nervous Diseases, London; Clinical Research Fellow, Medical Research Council, London; Senior Medical Registrar, Glasgow. Councillor, Royal College of Physicians and Surgeons, Glasgow; Chairman, Research Committee, Epilepsy Association of Scotland. Recreations: golf; photography; chess; motoring. Address: (h.) 9 Mirrlees Drive, Glasgow, G12 OSH; T.-041-339 7085.

Melville, Robert Murray, OBE, MB, ChB, DPH, FFCM. Senior Medical Officer, Scottish Home and Health Department, since 1975; b. 7.1.24, Elgin; m., Elizabeth Mary Munro; 3 s.; 1 d. Educ. Elgin Academy; Edinburgh University. Medical Officer: Colonial Service, Malaya, 1954-57, Colonial Service, Sarawak, 1957-61; Overseas Civil Service, Sarawak: Medical Officer, 1961-65, Senior Medical Officer, 1965-66, Assistant Director of Medical Services (Health), 1967-71; Deputy Medical Superintendent, Bangour General Hospital and Deputy Principal Medical Adviser, Livingston, 1971-74; Medical Officer, Scottish Home and Health Department, 1974-75. Recreations: classical music; history; biography; gardening. Address: (h.) Westfield House, West Calder, West Lothian, EH55 8RB; T.-Livingston 410725.

Melvin, John Middleton, MA, LLB. Solicitor and Estate Agent; Notary Public; Advocate in Aberdeen; b. 2.8.24, Aberdeen; m., Margaret Leslie Robertson; 4 s. Educ. Aberdeen Grammar School; Aberdeen University. Gordon Highlanders, UK, Ireland and Europe, 1944-45, then as Captain, Burma and Far East, until 1948; A.C. Morrison & Richards: joined as Assistant Solicitor, appointed Partner, 1957, Senior Partner, 1978; retired 1987; Consultant, Houghton, Melvin & Co., Solicitors, 1988; former Clerk of the Peace, County of Aberdeen. Recreations: golf; swimming; travel. Address: (h.) 18 Moray Place, Aberdeen, AB2 4AG; T.-Aberdeen 641555.

Mennie, Alastair Douglas, LLB, FSA Scot. Advocate, since 1982; b. 2.10.57, Aberdeen. Educ. Aberdeen Academy; Aberdeen University. Publications: articles in law journals. Address: (h.) 25 Panmure Place, Edinburgh, EH3 9HP; T.-031-229 5604.

Mennie, William Patrick, BL, NP. Partner, Grigor & Young, Solicitors, Elgin and Buckie, since 1964 (Senior Partner, since 1984); b. 11.10.37, Elgin; m., Patricia Leslie Bogie; 2 s.; 1 d. Educ. Elgin Academy; Edinburgh University. Solicitor, 1960; part-time Town Clerk, Dufftown, 1973-75; part-time Depute Procurator Fiscal, Elgin, 1966-74; Member, Property Marketing Committee, Law Society of Scotland, since 1985. Recreation: game shooting. Address: (h.) Innesmill, Urquhart, Elgin; T.-0343 842643.

Menzies, Gordon, MA (Hons), DipEd. Freelance Producer/Director (retired Head of Educational Broadcasting, BBC Scotland); b. 30.7.27, Logierait, Perthshire; m., Charlotte; 2 s.; 1 d. Educ. Breadalbane Academy, Aberfeldy; Edinburgh University. Producer/Director, Who Are the Scots?, 1971, The Chiel Amang Us, 1974, Ballad Folk, 1975, History Is My Witness, 1976, Play Golf with Peter Alliss, 1977, Scotch and Wry, 1978-79, Two Views of Burns, 1979, Barbara Dickson in Concert, 1981-84-86, The World of Golf, 1982, Scotch and Wry Hogmanay, 1980-82-83-84-85-86-87; Editor, The Afternoon Show, 1981-85. Publications: Who Are the Scots?, 1971; The Scottish Nation, 1972; History Is My Witness, 1976; Play Golf, 1977; The World of Golf, 1982; Scotch and Wry, 1986. Recreations: golf; snooker; curling; theatre. Address: (h.) 8 Ingleside, Lenzie, Glasgow, G66 4HN.

Menzies, John Maxwell. Chairman, John Menzies Holdings Ltd., since 1952; b. 13.10.26; m., Patricia Eleanor Dawson; 4 d. Educ. Eton. Lt., Grenadier Guards; Member, Berwickshire County Council, 1954-57; Director: Scottish American Mortgage Co., 1959-63, Standard Life Assurance Co., 1960-63, Vidal Sassoon Inc., 1969-80, Gordon & Gotch plc, 1970-85, Atlantic Assets Trust, since 1973 (Chairman, since 1983), Independent Investment Co. plc, since 1973 (Chairman, since 1983), Fairhaven International Ltd. (formerly Nimslo International), since 1980, Rocky Mountains Oil & Gas, 1980-85, Ivory & Sime plc, 1980-83, Personal Assets PLC, since 1981, Bank of Scotland, since 1984, Guardian Royal Exchange, since 1985. Trustee, Newsvendors' Benevolent Institution, since 1974 (President, 1968-74); Member, Royal Company of Archers, Queen's Bodyguard for Scotland. Recreations: farming; shooting; reading; travel. Address: (h.) Kames, Duns, Berwickshire; T.-Leitholm 202.

Menzies, Neil Graham Finlay, BSc. Scottish Affairs Adviser, ICI, since 1982; b. 14.10.41, Meikleour; m., June Ann Morton; 2 d. Educ. Lower School of John Lyon, Harrow; St. Andrews University. Voluntary Service Overseas, Nigeria, 1964-66; ICI: Teesside, 1966-68, various positions in production, personnel, etc., 1968-82. Member, Executive, Scottish Council; Director, Prince's Scottish Youth Business Trust; Member, Executive, Scottish Business in the Community; Director, ASSET; Director, APL-TO. Address: (b.) ICI, 25 Ravelston Terrace, Edinburgh, EH4 3UB; T.-031-343 3105.

Menzies, Thomas, MB, ChB, FRCSEd, FRCSEng, FRCS, RCPS Glas. Consultant Surgeon, Glasgow Royal Infirmary, 1966-87; b. 28.11.22, Crowborough, Sussex; m., Margaret Ledingham Davidson; 1 s.; 2 d. Educ. Aberdeen Grammar School; Aberdeen University. House Surgeon/House Physician, Aberdeen Royal Infirmary; graded Surgeon, RAMC; Surgical Registrar, Aberdeen Royal Infirmary; Senior Surgical Registrar, Hammersmith Hospital, London, and Tutor in Surgery, Postgraduate Medical School of London. Recreations: gardening; angling; philately. Address: (h.) 62 Manse Road, Bearsden, Glasgow, G61 3PN; T.-041-942 7472.

Mercer, John, MA, DipEd. Headmaster, Belmont House School, since 1972; b. 11.8.40, Glasgow; m., Eileen Margaret; 2 s.; 1 d. Educ. Eastwood Senior Secondary School; Glasgow University; Jordanhill College of Education. Teacher of English/History, Mossvale Secondary School, Paisley, 1962-66; Head Teacher of English, Belmont House School, 1966-72. Elder and former Session Clerk, Mearns Parish Kirk; President, Eastwood Rotary Club, 1986-87. Recreations: golf; skiing; walking; reading; palaeontology. Address: (b.) Belmont House School, Newton Mearns, Glasgow, G77 5DU; T.-041-639 2922.

Mercer, Roger James, MA, FSA, FSA Scot, MIFA. Reader in European Archaeology, Edinburgh University, since 1982; b. 12.9.44, London; m., Susan; 1 s.; 1 d. Educ. Harrow County Grammar School; Edinburgh University. Inspector of Ancient Monuments, AM Division, Department of the Environment, London, 1969-74; Lecturer, Department of Archaeology, Edinburgh University, 1974-82. Treasurer, Society of Antiquaries of Scotland, 1977-87; Chairman, Scottish Group, Institute of Field Archaeologists. Recreations: music; reading; learning. Address: (b.) Department of Archaeology, Edinburgh University, Edinburgh; T.-031-667 1011, Ext. 2548.

Mercer, Ronnie Edward. Director, BSC Ravenscraig, since 1985; b. 3.3.44, Kilwinning; 1 s.; 2 d. Educ. Spiers School, Beith; Paisley College of Technology. Began steel industry career at Glengarnock Works, Ayrshire, as a trainee chemist, 1960; transferred to Ravenscraig Works, 1970, as a member of the production management team; appointed Manager, Continuous Casting Plant, 1977; Works Manager - Iron, 1980. Sydney Gilchrist Thomas Medal, 1982. Recreation: golf. Address: (b.) British Steel Corporation, Ravenscraig Works, Motherwell, ML1 1SW.

Merchant, Bruce Alastair, LLB. Solicitor; Partner, South, Forrest, Mackintosh & Merchant, Inverness, since 1971; Vice-Chairman, Highland Health Board, since 1987 (Member, since 1981); b. 17.5.45, Edinburgh; m., Joan Isobel Sinclair Hamilton; 1 s.; 2 d. Educ. Inverness Royal Academy; Aberdeen University. Council Member, Law Society of Scotland, since 1982; Member: Board of Management for Inverness Hospitals, 1971-74, Inverness Local Health Council, 1975-81. Address: (h.) 3 Crown Circus, Inverness; T.-0463 239980.

Merrylees, Andrew, BArch, DipTP, ARSA, RIBA, FRIAS, FCSD. Architect; Principal, Andrew Merrylees Associates, since 1985; b. 13.10.33, Newmains; m., Maie Crawford; 2 s.; 1 d. Educ. Wishaw High School; Strathclyde University. Sir Basil Spence, Glover and Ferguson: joined, 1957, Associate, 1968, Partner, 1972; awards: RIBA Bronze Medal, Saltire Award, Civic Trust Award, Art in Architecture Award, Royal Scottish Academy Gold Medal. Recreations: oil painting; cooking; tennis; walking. Address: (b.) 4 Heriot Row, Edinburgh, EH3 6HU; T.-031-557 3808.

Meston, Professor Michael Charles, MA, LLB, JD. Professor of Scots Law, Aberdeen University, since 1971; b. 13.12.32, Aberdeen; m., Dorothea Munro; 2 s. Educ. Robert Gordon's College, Aberdeen; Aberdeen University; Chicago University. Lecturer in Private Law, Glasgow University, 1959-64; Aberdeen University: Senior Lecturer in Comparative Law, 1964-68, Professor of Jurisprudence, 1968-71; Honorary Sheriff, Grampian Highland and Islands, since 1972; Vice Principal, Aberdeen University, 1979-82; Trustee, National Museum of Antiquities of Scotland, 1982-85; Governor, Robert Gordon's College, Aberdeen; Member, Grampian Health Board. Publications: The Succession (Scotland) Act 1964; The Matrimonial Homes (Family Protection) (Scotland) Act 1981. Recreations: golf; photography. Address: (h.) 4 Hamilton Place, Aberdeen, AB2 4BH; T.-Aberdeen 641554.

Michie, David Alan Redpath, RSA, RGI, DA. Head, School of Drawing and Painting, Edinburgh College of Art, since 1982; b. 30.11.28, St. Raphael, France; m., Eileen Anderson Michie; 2 d. Educ. Hawick High School; Edinburgh College of Art. Travelling Scholarship, Italy, 1954-55; Lecturer, Grays School of Art, Aberdeen, 1957-61; Lecturer, Edinburgh College of Art, 1961 (Vice Principal, 1974-77). President, Society of Scottish Artists, 1961-63; Member, General Teaching Council for Scotland, 1975-80; Member, Court, Heriot-Watt University, 1979-82; Council

Member, British School at Rome, 1980-85; Guthrie Award, RSA, 1964; David Cargill Prize, RGI, 1977; Lothian Region Award, 1977; Sir William Gillies Award, 1980; one-man exhibitions, Mercury Gallery, London, six times, 1966-83, Lothian Region Chambers, 1977, The Scottish Gallery, 1980, Loomshop Gallery, Lower Largo, 1981, 1987, Mercury Gallery, Edinburgh, 1986. Address: (b.) Edinburgh College of Art, Lauriston Place, Edinburgh; T.-031-229 9311.

Michie, James Alexander Davidson, MA, MEd. Director of Education, Grampian Regional Council, since 1974; b. 1.10.26, Keithhall, Aberdeenshire; m., Lena; 2 s. Educ. Mackie Academy, Stonehaven; Aberdeen University. Assistant Director of Education, Fife County Council, 1959-65; Senior Depute Director of Education: Dundee City Corporation, 1965-67, Aberdeen County Council, 1967-68; Director of Education, Aberdeen County Council, 1968-74. Recreations: golf; curling; gardening; literature; foreign travel. Address: (b.) Woodhill House, Westburn Road, Aberdeen, AB9 2LU; T.-0224 682222, Ext. 2500.

Michie, (Janet) Ray. MP (SLD), Argyll and Bute, since 1987; b. 4.2.34; m.; 3 d. Educ. Aberdeen High School for Girls; Lansdowne House School, Edinburgh; Edinburgh School of Speech Therapy. Former Speech Therapist, Argyll and Clyde Health Board. Address: (b.) House of Commons, SW1A 0AA.

Michie, Robert Cook, BSc, CEng, MICE, ARGTC. Honorary Sheriff, Fort William, since 1972; b. 28.12.17, Aberdeen; m., Margaret Barlow; 3 s. Educ. Robert Gordon's College; Aberdeen University. Agent and Engineer, William Tawse Ltd., Civil Engineering Contractors, 1941-49; Deputy Resident, latterly Resident Engineer, Crouch & Hogg, Consulting Civil Engineers, 1949-52; Managing Director, Highland Lime Co., Quarrymasters, 1952-77; Project Manager for quarry and brickworks, 1977-83. Past President, Lochaber Rotary Club. Recreation: motoring. Address: (h.) Forglen, Banavie, Fort William, PH33 7LX; T.-0397-7-287.

Micklem, Professor Henry Spedding, MA, DPhil (Oxon). Professor of Immunobiology, Edinburgh University, since 1988 (Reader in Zoology, 1973-88); b. 11.10.33, Oxford; m., Lisel Ruth Thomas; 3 s. 1 d. Educ. Rugby School; Oriel College, Oxford. Scientific Staff, Medical Research Council; Research Fellow, Institut Pasteur, Paris; Academic Staff, Department of Zoology, Edinburgh University; Visiting Professor, Department of Genetics, Stanford University. Recreation: music. Address: (b.) Department of Zoology, Edinburgh University, West Mains Road, Edinburgh, EH9 3JT; T.-031-667 1081.

Middleton, Francis, MA, LLB; b. 21.11.13, Rutherglen; m., Edith Muir; 2 s.; 1 d. Educ. Rutherglen Academy; Glasgow University. Solicitor, 1937; Indian Army, 1939 (11 Sikh Regiment); injured, 1942; Judge Advocate General's Branch, 1942-45; 1st Class Interpreter, Urdu, Examiner for India in Punjabi; Advocate, 1946; Sheriff, 1948-78. Serves on boards of various charitable bodies. Recreations: reading; walking; gardening; water divining. Address: (h.) 20 Queens Court, Helensburgh, G84 7AH; T.-0436 78965.

Middleton, Robert, JP. Leader, Labour Group, Grampian Regional Council, since 1979; Chairman, Labour Party in Scotland, 1986-87; b. 28.7.32, Aberdeen; m., Audrey Ewen; 2 s. Educ. Aberdeen Grammar School. Started apprenticeship with Post Office Telephones, 1948; now employed with British Telecom as Band F Engineering Manager; Aberdeen Town Council: elected, 1961, appointed Magistrate, 1963, Chairman of Magistrates, 1965-66, Chairman, Education Committee, 1966-69; contested Banffshire as Labour candidate, 1966; contested Aberdeen South, 1974 (twice) and 1983; elected, Grampian Regional Council, 1975. Publication: North Sea Brose. Recreations: golf; reading; writing not very good poetry; travel. Address: (h.) 9 Stronsay Avenue, Aberdeen, AB2 6HX; T.-0224 313366.

Middleton, Ruth Charlotte, LLB. Secretary/Director, Ark Housing Association Ltd., since 1978; b. 9.9.42, Edinburgh; m., Norman A. Middleton; 1 s.; 1 d. Educ. Berwickshire High School; Edinburgh University. Legal practice, 1965-78. Address: 8 Balcarres Street, Edinburgh, EH10 5JB; T.-031-447 9027.

Midgley, Professor John Morton, BSc, MSc, PhD, CChem, MRCS, FPS. Professor of Pharmacy, Strathclyde University, since 1984 (Chairman and Head of Department, since 1985); b. 14.7.37, York; m., Jean Mary Tillyer; 2 s. Educ. Nunthorpe Grammar School, York; Manchester University; London University. Demonstrator, Manchester University, 1959-61; Assistant Lecturer, School of Pharmacy, London University, 1962-65; Research Associate, Massachusetts Institute of Technology, 1965-66; Lecturer, then Senior Lecturer, School of Pharmacy, London University, 1966-83; Visiting Professor, Florida University; Member: Committee on the Review of Medicines, since 1984, British Pharmacopoeia Committee, since 1985. Recreations: fly fishing; fisheries management; training labradors; gardening; music. Address: (b.) Strathclyde University, Department of Pharmacy, Royal College, 204 George Street, Glasgow, G1 1XW; T.-041-552 4400, Ext. 2125.

Miles, Rex Stafford, MB, ChB, FRCPath. Senior Lecturer, Edinburgh University, since 1976; Honorary Consultant, Lothian Health Board, since 1976; b. 16.11.42, Beeston, Nottinghamshire; m., Janice Isabel Martin; 3 s.; 1 d. Educ. Southwell Minster Grammar School; Edinburgh University. House Physician, Edinburgh Royal Infirmary; House Surgeon, Peel Hospital, Galashiels; Registrar in Bacteriology, Edinburgh University; Lecturer and Honorary Senior Registrar in Bacteriology, Dundee University. Recreations: golf; photography; Border history. Address: (b.) Edinburgh University Medical School, Teviot Place, Edinburgh, EH8 9AG; T.-031-229 2477.

Millan, Rt. Hon. Bruce, PC, CA. MP (Labour), Glasgow Govan, since 1983; b. 5.10.27, Dundee; m., Gwendoline May Fairey; 1 s.; 1 d. Educ. Harris Academy, Dundee. MP, Glasgow Craigton, 1959-83; Parliamentary Secretary for the RAF,

1964-66; Parliamentary Secretary, Scottish Office, 1966-70; Minister of State, Scottish Office, 1974-76; Secretary of State for Scotland, 1976-79; Opposition Spokesman on Scottish Affairs, 1979-83. Address: (h.) 10 Beech Avenue, Glasgow, G41; T.-041-427 6483.

Millan, William Robert, LLB, NP. Director of Administrative and Legal Services, Roxburgh District Council, since 1986; Clerk of the Peace (Roxburgh Commission Area), since 1986; Clerk to the Licensing Board and District Court, since 1986; b. 17.8.52, Glasgow; m., Margaret Hamilton McCulloch; 1 s.; 1 d. Educ. Hillhead High School; Glasgow University. Bannatyne, Kirkwood, France & Co., Writers, Glasgow, 1973-75; Senior Legal Assistant, Cumnock and Doon Valley District Council, 1975-79; Depute Director of Administrative and Legal Services, Roxburgh District Council, 1979-86. Recreations: reading; DIY; gardening; skiing; badminton; golf; vintage cars. Address: (b.) District Council Offices, High Street, Hawick, TD9 9EF; T.-0450 75991.

Millar, Ainslie, TD, FRSAMD, FRVA, JP. Chartered Surveyor, since 1949; Chairman, Board of Governors, Royal Scottish Academy of Music and Drama, 1975-87; b. 9.4.20, Glasgow; m., Morag Bruce; 3 s. Educ. Glasgow Academy; Fettes College; Glasgow University. Commissioned, TA, 1938; War Service, 1939-46; qualified as Surveyor, 1949; served on several RICS Committees, particularly in field of education; Member, Board, Sadlers Wells Trust, latterly English National Opera, 1959-75; Progressive Councillor, Kelvinside Ward, 1964-69; Co-Founder, Scottish Opera, and Board Member, 1960-82; joined Board, RSAMD, 1965; responsible for preparation and submission to Secretary of State for Scotland of petition seeking special facilities for education of greatly gifted children in music and dance, 1970-71; Chairman, Board, Mull Little Theatre, 1980-82; Chairman, Board, Glasgow International Competition for Junior Violinists, 1969-74. Recreations: reading; listening to music; gardening; keyboard strumming; singing. Address: (h.) 18 Gateside Place, Kilbarchan, Renfrewshire.

Millar, Alexander David, MA, LLB, NP. Solicitor, since 1975; Principal, A. David Millar & Co.; Partner, Bird Semple and Crawford Herron (incorporating C. Scott Mackenzie and Company), 1982-86; b. 11.1.50, Selkirk; m., Deborah Stark Goodwin; 2 s. Educ. High School of Stirling; Edinburgh University. Employed by Berwickshire County Council, 1973-75; joined Roxburgh District Council; appointed Solicitor, Western Isles Islands Council, 1975-82. Council Member, Law Society of Scotland, 1981-85; Dean, Western Isles Faculty of Solicitors, 1984-87; Member, Western Isles Health Board, since 1986. Recreations: photography; fishing. Address: (h.) 8 Stewart Drive, Stornoway, Isle of Lewis; T.-0851 4645.

Millar, David A.R., MA. Chaplain, Glasgow University, and Lecturer in Theology and Church History, Faculty of Divinity, since 1964; b. 18.2.25, Glasgow; m., Jean M. Tindal; 1 s.; 1 d. Educ. Glasgow Academy; Glasgow University; St. Andrews University. RAF, India, Germany, 1943-47; Assistant Minister, Wallacetown, Dundee, 1954-56; Minister, Richmond Craigmillar, Edinburgh, 1956-64. Address: (b.) 11 The University, Glasgow, G12 8QG; T.-041-334 8769.

Millar, Geoffrey Thomas, MB, ChB, FRCSEdin, DObstRCOG. Consultant Ophthalmic Surgeon, Royal Infirmary, Edinburgh, since 1968; b. 23.6.35, Edinburgh; m., Vivien Mary Land; 1 s.; 2 d. Educ. Morrison's Academy, Crieff; Melville College, Edinburgh; Edinburgh University. Tutor, Leeds University, 1966. Recreations: golf; sailing; walking. Address: (h.) 22 Dick Place, Edinburgh, EH9 2JJ; T.-031-667 1664.

Millar, Helen Jean, MA. Vice Chairman, Consumers in European Community Group, since 1985; Chairman, Consumer's Committee for Scotland, since 1980; Lecturer in charge, Children's Panel Training, Glasgow University, since 1980; b. 10.10.31, Glasgow; m., William M. Millar (m. diss.); 3 s.; 2 d. Educ. Craigholme School, Glasgow; Glasgow University. Member and Vice-Chairman, Scottish Consumer Council, 1979-87; Chairman, Strathclyde Children's Panel, 1979-81; Vice-Chairman, New Glasgow Society, 1980-87; Founder Member, Board, Tron Theatre Club, Glasgow. Recreations: theatre; arts in general; Glasgow; arguing. Address: (h.) 33 Aytoun Road, Glasgow, G41; T.-041-423 4152.

Millar, Henry Rankin, MB, ChB, BMedBiol (Hons), MRCPsych. Consultant Psychiatrist, Southern General Hospital, Glasgow, since 1980; b. 23.4.47, Aberdeen; m., Frances Morgan; 3 d. Educ. Aberdeen Grammar School; Aberdeen University. House Officer, Aberdeen Royal Infirmary, 1972-73; Junior Fellow in Community Medicine and Honorary Senior House Officer in Medicine, Aberdeen University and Aberdeen Royal Infirmary, 1973-74; Senior House Officer/Registrar in Psychiatry, Royal Edinburgh Hospital, 1975-77; Senior Registrar and Lecturer, Dundee Psychiatric Services and Dundee University, 1977-80. Recreations: golf; walking. Address: (h.) 237 Fenwick Road, Giffnock, Glasgow; T.-041-638 1178.

Millar, Mary Armour, MB, ChB, FRCPGlas, FRCR. Consultant Radiologist, Victoria Infirmary, Glasgow, since 1972; b. 10.8.39, Glasgow. Educ. Queen's Park Senior Secondary School; Glasgow University. Resident House Officer: Stobhill Hospital, Glasgow Royal Infirmary; Victoria Infirmary: Registrar in Medicine, Registrar in Radiology, Senior Registrar. Medical Advisor, Overseas Missionary Fellowship in Scotland; Member, Congregational Board, Sandyford Henderson Memorial Church. Recreations: reading; gardening; hill-walking. Address: (h.) 1 Rosslea Drive, Giffnock, Glasgow, G46 6JW; T.-041-638 3036.

Millar, Peter Carmichael, OBE, MA, LLB, DKS. Deputy Keeper of Her Majesty's Signet, since 1983; Chairman, Church of Scotland General Trustees, 1973-85; Chairman, Mental Welfare Commission for Scotland, since 1983; b. 19.2.27, Glasgow; m., Kirsteen Lindsay Carnegie; 2 s.; 2 d. Educ. Aberdeen Grammar School; Glasgow University; St. Andrews University; Edinburgh University. Royal Navy, 1944-47; Partner, W. & T.P. Manuel, WS, 1954-62; Partner, Aitken Kinnear &

Co., WS, 1963-87; Partner, Aitken, Nairn WS, since 1987; Clerk, Society of Writers to HM Signet, 1964-83. Recreations: golf; hill-walking; music. Address: (h.) 25 Cramond Road North, Edinburgh, EH4 6LY.

Millar, Thomas H., MA, BA (Hons). Head Teacher, James Hamilton Academy, Kilmarnock, since 1976; b. 13.3.24, Glasgow. Educ. Kilmarnock Academy; Glasgow University; London University. Teacher of History, Irvine Royal Academy and Kilmarnock Academy; Principal Teacher of History, Dollar Academy and Auchenharvie Academy; Assistant Head Teacher, Ravenspark Academy; Deputy Head Teacher, Greenwood Academy. Recreations: travelling; reading; sailing. Address: (h.) 18 Charles Drive, Troon, Ayrshire; T.-Troon 312993.

Millar, William McIntosh, OBE, BL. Solicitor; Partner, McClure Naismith Anderson & Gardiner, Solicitors, Glasgow, since 1955; Editor, Journal of the Law Society of Scotland, since 1983; b. 10.9.25, Edinburgh; 3 s.; 2 d. Educ. Glasgow Academy; Fettes College; Glasgow University. Royal Signals, 1943-47 (Captain, 1947); Secretary, Fife Kinross & Clackmannan Charitable Society, 1955-88 (President, 1961-62, and Patron, 1985); Chairman, Strathclyde Housing Society Ltd. and 11 associated housing societies, 1966-75; Member, Scottish Housing Advisory Committee, 1970-75; Founder Member, Scottish Federation of Housing Associations, 1976-78; Trustee, Scottish Housing Associations Charitable Trust, 1980 (Chairman, 1985); Director, Citizens Theatre Ltd. and Chairman, Close Theatre Club, 1969-72; Governor, Royal Scottish Academy of Music and Drama, since 1969; Chairman, Scottish Early Music Association. Recreations: music; writing; avoiding golf and politics. Address: (h.) 34 Cleveden Drive, Glasgow, G12 ORX; T.-041-339 5633.

Miller, Alan Cameron, MA, LLB, FCIT. Advocate; Past Chairman (Scotland), Institute of Transport; b. 10.1.13, Killin, Perthshire; m., Audrey Main; 1 s.; 1 d. Educ. Fettes College; Edinburgh University. Member, Faculty of Advocates, since 1938; Royal Navy, 1940-45; Sheriff, Fort William, 1946-52; Legal Adviser (Scotland) to: British Transport Commission, 1952-62, British Railways Board, 1962-72. Voluntary Tutor, Fettes College. Recreations: golf; music. Address: (h.) 42 Great King Street, Edinburgh; T.-031-556 3800.

Miller, Alastair Robert John Dunlop, BSc, MAg, NDA, FRAgS. Farmer; Chairman, Scotfresh Ltd., since 1973; b. 5.3.37, Tranent; m., Margaret Eileen Lees-Brown; 3 d. Educ. Edinburgh Academy; Rugby; Edinburgh University; Purdue University, USA. Scottish Horticulture Medal. Recreations: golf; travel. Address: (h.) Ferrygate, North Berwick, East Lothian.

Miller, Alexander Ronald, CBE, DUniv (Stirling), FRSA, CBIM. Chairman, Motherwell Bridge Holdings Ltd., since 1958; b. 7.11.15, Bothwell. Educ. Craigflower School; Malvern College; Royal Technical College. Member: Scottish Council, CBI, 1955-82 (Chairman, 1963-65), Design Council, 1965-71 (Chairman, Scottish Committee, 1967), Scottish Economic Planning Council (Chairman, Industrial Committee, 1967-71), British Rail Scottish Board, 1966-70, British Rail Design Panel, 1966-82, General Convocation, Strathclyde University, since 1967, Steering Committee, West Central Scotland Plan, 1970-75, Lanarkshire Health Board, 1973-85 (Chairman, 1973-77), Oil Development Council for Scotland, 1973-78, British Institute of Management Scottish Board, since 1974, College Council, Bell College of Technology, Hamilton, since 1976, Management Committee, Scottish Health Service Common Services Agency (Chairman), 1977-83, Lloyd's Register of Shipping Scottish Committee, since 1977, Lloyd's Register of Shipping General Committee, since 1982, CBI Council, since 1982; Director, Lloyd's Register Quality Assurance Association Ltd., since 1985. President, Lanarkshire Branch, Forces Help Society and Lord Roberts Workshops. Address: (h.) Lairfad Farm, Auldhouse, East Kilbride, G75 9DP; T.-East Kilbride 63275.

Miller, Professor Andrew, MA, BSc, PhD, FRSE, FIBiol. Professor of Biochemistry, Edinburgh University, since 1984; b. 15.2.36, Kelty, Fife; m., Rosemary S.H. Fyvie; 1 s.; 1 d. Educ. Beath High School; Edinburgh University. Assistant Lecturer in Chemistry, Edinburgh University, 1960-62; Postdoctoral Fellow, CSIRO, Melbourne, and Tutor in Chemistry, Ormond College, Melbourne University, 1962-65; Staff Scientist, MRC Laboratory of Molecular Biology, Cambridge, 1965-66; Lecturer in Molecular Biophysics, Oxford University and (from 1967) Fellow, Wolfson College, 1966-83; on secondment as first Director, European Molecular Biology Laboratory, Grenoble Antenne, France, 1975-80. Committee Member: British Biophysical Society, 1972-74, SERC Synchrotron Radiation Facility Committee, 1979-82, Biological Sciences Committee, 1982-85, Neutron Beam Research Committee, 1982-85; Council Member, Institut Laue-Langevin, 1981-85; Member: MRC Joint Dental Committee, 1984-86, UGC Biological Sciences Committee, since 1985; (part-time) Director of Research, European Synchrotson Radiation Facility, Grenoble, since 1986; Member, Advisory Board, AFRC Food Research Institute, since 1985. Address: (b.) Biochemistry Department, Edinburgh University Medical School, Hugh Robson Building, George Square, Edinburgh, EH8 9XD; T.-031-667 1011, Ext. 2336.

Miller, Rev. Charles, MA. Minister, Fowlis Easter and Liff Parish Church, since 1980; Chaplain, Royal Dundee Liff Hospital, since 1980; b. 4.2.26, Kinross; m., Isabella Russell Stewart, MA; 3 s. Educ. St. Mary's School, Dunblane; McLaren High School, Callander; Aberdeen University; St. Andrews University. Assistant Minister, Auld Kirk of Ayr, 1953-54; Minister: Torthorwald, Dumfries, 1953-59, Munro Church, Rutherglen, 1959-65, Cruden, Aberdeenshire, 1965-72, Anstruther Parish Church, 1972-80; former Convener: Overseas Committee, Dumfries Presbytery; Church and Nation and Social Responsibility Committees, Aberdeen Presbytery; Social Responsibility Committee, St. Andrews Presbytery; Member, Scottish Churches Consultative Committee on Road Safety; Member, Governing Council, Institute of Advanced Motorists, since 1964 (President, Scottish Groups Association).

Recreations: caravanning; swimming; landscape painting. Address: 14 Liff Park, Liff, Dundee, Angus; T.-0382 580033.

Miller, Colin Brown, LLB. Solicitor and Notary Public; b. 4.10.46, Paisley; m., Joan Elizabeth Blyth; 3 s. Educ. Paisley Grammar School; Glasgow University. Partner, McFadyen & Semple, since 1971 (Senior Partner, since 1987); Temporary Sheriff, since 1984; Council Member, Law Society of Scotland, since 1983 (Convener, Conveyancing Committee, since 1986); Member, Joint Committee with Keeper of Registers, since 1981. Chairman, Blythswood Housing Association Ltd., since 1981. Recreations: sailing (PS Waverley); photography; work. Address: (b.) 6 Gilmour Street, Paisley; T.-041-889 9291.

Miller, Donald John, BSc, FEng, FIMechE, FIEE. Chairman, South of Scotland Electricity Board, since 1982; b. 9.2.27, London; m., Fay G. Herriot; 1 s.; 2 d. Educ. Banchory Academy; Aberdeen University. Metropolitan-Vickers, 1947-53; British Electricity Authority, 1953-55; Preece Cardew & Rider (Consulting Engineers), 1955-66; Chief Engineer, North of Scotland Hydro-Electric Board, 1966-74; Director of Engineering, SEEB, 1974; appointed Deputy Chairman, 1979. Chairman, Power Division, IEE, 1977. Recreations: gardening; walking; sailing. Address: (h.) Puldohran, Gryffe Road, Kilmacolm, Renfrewshire; T.-Kilmacolm 3652.

Miller, Douglas Hamilton, TD, MREHIS, MIWM. Director of Environmental Health, Banff and Buchan District Council, since 1974; b. 15.3.33, Dunfermline; m., Jean Elizabeth; 2 s.; 3 d. Educ. Dunfermline High School; Heriot-Watt, Edinburgh. Apprentice, then Assistant Burgh Surveyor, Lochgelly, 1950-55; Group Hygienist, RAF, 1956-58; Assistant Sanitary Inspector, Perth, 1958-60; Assistant, then District Sanitary Inspector, then Depute County Sanitary Inspector and Master of Works, then Director of Environmental Health and Master of Works, Banff County Council, 1960-74. Past President, Banff Rotary Club; Administrative Officer in Medical Unit, TA (Major); Elder, Church of Scotland. Recreations: snooker; golf. Address: (h.) Broadcroft, 15 Bellevue Road, Banff, AB4 1BJ; T.-02612 2213.

Miller, Edward, CBE, MA, MEd, MLitt. Director of Education, Strathclyde Regional Council, since 1974; b. 30.3.30, Glasgow; m., Margaret T. McLean; 2 s. Educ. Eastbank Academy; Glasgow University. Junior Depute Director of Education, West Lothian, 1959-63; Senior Assistant Director of Education, Stirlingshire, 1963-66; Depute and Senior Depute Director of Education, Glasgow, 1966-74. Recreations: swimming; sailing; reading. Address: (h.) 58 Heather Avenue, Bearsden, Glasgow, G61 3JG.

Miller, Hugh Craig, BSc, MB, ChB, FRCPEdin. Consultant Cardiologist, Edinburgh Royal Infirmary, since 1975; b. 7.4.42, Edinburgh; m., Isobel Margaret; 1 s.; 1 d. Educ. George Watson's College; Edinburgh University. Registrar, Edinburgh Royal Infirmary, 1969-72; Senior Registrar, Brompton Hospital, London, 1972-75; Research Fellow, Duke University, North Carolina, 1973-74; Fulbright Scholar. Recreations: skiing; sailing. Address: (h.) 12 Dick Place, Edinburgh; T.-031-667 4235.

Miller, Professor Hugh Graham, BSc, PhD, DSc, FICFor, FIBiol, FRSE, FRSA. Professor and Head, Department of Forestry, Aberdeen University, since 1984; b. 22.11.39, Ndola, Zambia; m., Thelma Martin; 1 s.; 1 d. Educ. Kaptagat School, Kenya; Strathallan School; Sutton High School; Aberdeen University. Joined Department of Peat and Forest Soils, Macaulay Institute for Soil Research, 1983. Awarded Institute of Foresters Silvicultural Prize, 1974; selected for International Union of Forest Research Organization's Scientific Achievement Award, 1981. Recreations: curling; sailing; philosophy. Address: (b.) Department of Forestry, Aberdeen University, St. Machar Drive, Aberdeen, AB9 2UU; T.-0224 40241.

Miller, Rev. Ian Hunter, BA, BD. Minister, Bonhill, since 1975; b. 30.5.44, Johnstone; m., Joan Elizabeth Parr; 2 s. Educ. Johnstone High School; Glasgow University; Open University. Travel agent, latterly Branch Manager, A.T. Mays, 1962-69; Assistant Minister, Renfrew Old Kirk, 1974-75. Moderator, Dumbarton Presbytery, 1985-87 (Convener, Planning Committee, since 1985). Recreations: golf; badminton; music; drama. Address: Bonhill Manse, 1 Glebe Gardens, Bonhill, Alexandria, G83 9HR; T.-Alexandria 53039.

Miller, Ian James, MA, LLB. Secretary and Academic Registrar, Napier Polytechnic of Edinburgh, since 1987; b. 21.10.38, Fraserburgh; m., Sheila Mary Hourston; 1 s.; 2 d. Educ. Fraserburgh Academy; Aberdeen University; Edinburgh University. Private legal practice, 1963-68; Senior Legal Assistant, Inverness County Council, 1968-70; Depute County Clerk, then County Clerk, Ross and Cromarty County Council, 1970-75; Chief Executive, Inverness District Council, 1975-77; Director of Law and Administration, Grampian Regional Council, 1977-84; Director, Kildonnan Investments Ltd., Aberdeen, 1984-87. Recreations: golf; curling. Address: (b.) 219 Colinton Road, Edinburgh, EH14 1DJ; T.-031-444 2266.

Miller, James, CBE (1987), MA, FCIOB, FCIArb, CBIM. Chairman and Managing Director, The Miller Group Ltd. (formerly James Miller & Partners) since 1970; Director, Life Association of Scotland Ltd., since 1981; Director, Scottish Exhibition Centre Ltd., since 1983; Director, British Linen Bank Ltd., since 1983; Director, Britoil plc, since 1988; b. 1.9.34, Edinburgh; m., 1, Kathleen Dewar (deceased); 2, Iris Lloyd-Webb; 1 s.; 3 d. Educ. Edinburgh Academy; Harrow School; Balliol College, Oxford. National Service, Royal Engineers. James Miller & Partners Ltd.: joined, 1958, appointed Director, 1960; Scottish Representative, Advisory Committee to the Meteorological Services, since 1980; Chairman, Federation of Civil Engineering Contractors, 1985-86; Deacon Convener, Incorporated Trades of Edinburgh, 1974-77; President,

Edinburgh Chamber of Commerce, 1981-83; Assistant on Court of Merchant Company of Edinburgh, 1982-85. Recreation: shooting. Address: (b.) The Miller Group Ltd., Miller House, 18 South Groathill Avenue, Edinburgh, EH4 2LW; T.-031-332 2585.

Miller, James David Frederick, DUniv (Stirling), MA (Cantab), CBIM, FIPM. Director, Coats Viyella Plc, since 1986; Director, Wolverhampton and Dudley Breweries, since 1984; b. 5.1.35, Wolverhampton; m., Saffrey Blackett Oxley; 3 s.; 1 d. Educ. Edinburgh Academy; Emmanuel College, Cambridge; London School of Economics. National Service, Argyll and Sutherland Highlanders, Cameron Highlanders, commissioned in South Staffords, 1953-55; J. & P. Coats Ltd.: joined, 1958, Training Officer, 1964-66, Personnel Manager, 1969; Personnel Manager, Coats Patons Group, 1970; Director, J. & P. Coats Ltd., 1973; Director, Coats Patons PLC, 1977; Council Member, Outward Bound Ltd.; Governor, Outward Bound Loch Eil Ltd. (Chairman, 1977-84); Member, Court, Stirling University, 1978-84; Director, Scottish National Orchestra, 1984; Director, Edinburgh Academy, 1985; Commissioner, Queen Victoria School, Dunblane, 1987; Member, CBI Employee Involvement Panel. Recreations: gardening; tennis; golf. Address: (b.) Coats Viyella Plc, 155 St. Vincent Street, Glasgow; T.-041-221 8711.

Miller, Professor James Douglas, MD, PhD, FRCSEdin, FRCSGlas, FACS, FRCPEdin. Professor of Surgical Neurology, Edinburgh University, since 1981 (Chairman, Department of Clinical Neurosciences); b. 20.7.37, Glasgow; m., Margaret Scott Rainey; 2 s. Educ. Glasgow Academy; Glasgow University. Surgical Senior House Officer and Registrar, Glasgow, 1962; Neurosurgical Registrar, Institute of Neurological Sciences, Glasgow, 1965; Medical Research Council Fellow, Department of Surgery, Glasgow University, 1967; Senior Registrar in Neurosurgery, Institute of Neurological Sciences, Glasgow, 1969; US Public Health Service Fellow in Neurosurgery, University of Pennsylvania, 1970; Senior Lecturer in Neurosurgery, Glasgow University, 1971; Professor of Neurosurgery, Virginia Commonwealth University, USA, 1975. Recreation: hill-walking. Address: (h.) 36 Cluny Drive, Edinburgh, EH10 6DX; T.-031-447 5828.

Miller, John Dow Booth, MB, ChB, ChM, FRCSEdin, FIBiol. Consultant Surgeon, Dr. Grays Hospital, Elgin, and Honorary Senior Lecturer in Surgery, Aberdeen University; b. 10.7.44, Aberdeen; m., Isobel Stewart Murray; 2 s.; 1 d. Educ. Robert Gordon's College, Aberdeen; Aberdeen University. House Surgeon to Academic Unit, Aberdeen Royal Infirmary, then Senior House Officer, Pathology, Maryfield Hospital, Dundee, 1968-69; Senior House Officer, then Registrar in Surgery, Aberdeen, 1970-75; Research Fellow in Surgery, Harvard University, Boston, 1975-76; Senior Registrar and Lecturer in Surgery, Aberdeen University, from 1976. Address: (h.) Findrassie House, Elgin, Moray, IV30 2PS; T.-0343 7292.

Miller, Rev. John Stewart Abercromby Smith, MA, BD, STM. Minister, Morningside United Church, Edinburgh, since 1975; b. 3.5.28, Gibraltar; m., Lorna Vivien Fraser; 1 s.; 1 d. Educ. Lanark Grammar School; Edinburgh University; Union Theological Seminary, New York. Assistant Minister, St. Giles' Cathedral, Edinburgh, 1953-54; Minister: St. Andrew's, Hawick, 1954-59, Sandyhills, Glasgow, 1959-64, Mortlach and Cabrach, Banffshire, 1964-75; Visiting Instructor, Columbia Theological Seminary, Georgia, 1986; Honorary Associate Minister, Peachtree Presbyterian Church, Georgia, 1986. Recreations: reading; listening to music; exploring Britain. Address: (h.) 1 Midmar Avenue, Edinburgh; T.-031-447 8724.

Miller, Richard Tweedie, BL, WS. Consultant, Pairman Miller & Murray, WS; Secretary, Lothian Local Medical Committee (General Practice), 1956-87; Secretary, General Practitioner Sub-Committee, Lothian Area Medical Committee, 1956-87; b. 11.4.15, Edinburgh. Educ. George Watson's Boys' College; Edinburgh University. WS apprenticeship, Bruce & Kerr, WS, Edinburgh; joined 94th HAA Regiment and served in ADGB throughout World War II; commissioned and latterly served as Brigade Intelligence Officer on staff of 55 Brigade; after the War, joined family legal practice. Voluntary Leader, Tweedie Memorial Boys Club, Edinburgh. Recreations: voluntary youth work; gardening; motoring; rugby football. Address: (b.) 13 Heriot Row, Edinburgh, EH3 6HP; T.-031-557 1558.

Miller, Roger Ogilvy Stewart, BSc, CEng, FCIOB, FFB. Director, The Miller Group Ltd. (formerly James Miller & Partners Ltd.), since 1965; Managing Director, Miller Homes Northern Ltd., since 1970; b. 17.4.36, Edinburgh; m., Jean; 2 s.; 2 d. Educ. Edinburgh Academy; Harrow; Edinburgh University. National Service, 1958-60 (commissioned, Royal Engineers); joined James Miller & Partners Ltd., 1960. President, Building Employers Confederation, 1988; President, Scottish Building Employers Federation, 1978-79; Member, Scottish Committee, NHBC, 1968-79; Member, Scottish Committee, CBI, 1982-86; President, Scottish Housebuilders Association, 1972-74; President, Edinburgh and District Master Builders Association, 1976-77. Recreations: sailing; golf; badminton. Address: (b.) 18 South Groathill Avenue, Edinburgh, EH4 2LW; T.-031-332 2585.

Miller, Ronald Andrew Baird, CBE (1985), CA, BSc. Chairman and Chief Executive, Dawson International PLC, since 1982; b. 13.5.37, Edinburgh. Address: (b.) Dawson International PLC, 9 Charlotte Square, Edinburgh, EH2 4DR.

Miller, Ronald Murdoch. Scottish Officer, Equal Opportunities Commission, since 1978; b. 16.3.33, Dundee; m., Phyllis; 1 s. Educ. Morgan Academy. War Service, Korea/Japan, 1951-53; Youth and Community Worker, Gloucestershire; Deputy Youth and Community Officer, Suffolk; Community Development Officer, Holland (Lincolnshire); Education Researcher (Curriculum), Lanarkshire. Recreations: gardening; rugby referee; ballet (as a spectator); after-dinner speaker. Address: (b.) St. Andrew House, 141 West Nile Street, Glasgow, G1 2RN; T.-041-332 8018.

Miller, Stanley Scott, MB, ChB, ChM, FRCS. Consultant General and Paediatric Surgeon, since 1976; Honorary Senior Lecturer in Surgery, Aberdeen University, since 1976; b. 24.12.38, Whitley Bay; 2 s.; 3 d. Educ. Robert Gordon's College; Aberdeen University. Research Fellow, Department of Surgery, Aberdeen University, 1970; Senior Surgical Registrar, Aberdeen Royal Infirmary, 1970-74; Resident Assistant Surgeon, Hospital for Sick Children, Great Ormond Street, London, 1975. Member, Executive, British Association of Paediatric Surgeons, 1983. Recreations: fishing; skiing; golfing. Address: (h.) 8 Forest Road, Aberdeen, AB2 4BT; T.-0224 38795.

Miller, Stewart O. Director, Miller Farms (Balbeggie); Honorary Member, Perth Branch Committee, National Farmers' Union of Scotland (Branch Chairman, 1955); Director, East of Scotland Farmers, since 1960; Member, Tayside Regional Council, 1978-86; Member, Perth and Kinross District Council, 1980-88; b. 2.4.18, Errol; m., Betty L. Penny; 1 s.; 1 d. Educ. Perth Academy. Started work on farm, 1933; took over farm, 1943; elected, Perth and Kinross County Council, 1958 (Chairman, Housing Committee, 1967-75); elected, Perth Branch Committee, National Farmers' Union of Scotland, 1950 (Branch Chairman, 1955); elected, Council, NFU of Scotland; served on various local committees, local Health Board, Perth Presbytery. Address: (h.) Rosefield, Balbeggie, Perth, PH2 6AT; T.-Kinrossie 236.

Miller, Professor William L., MA, PhD. Edward Caird Professor of Politics, Glasgow University, since 1985; b. 12.8.43, Glasgow; m., Fiona Thomson; 2 s.; 1 d. Educ. Aberdeen Grammar School; Royal High School, Edinburgh; Edinburgh University; Newcastle University. Formerly Lecturer, Senior Lecturer and Professor, Strathclyde University; Visiting Professor, Virginia Tech., Blacksburg, Virginia, 1983-84; also taught at Universities of Essex and Cologne; frequent Contributor to Press and TV; Member, Editorial Boards: Electoral Studies, Political Studies. Publications: Electoral Dynamics, 1977; The End of British Politics?, 1981; The Survey Method in the Social and Political Sciences, 1983; Elections and Voters, 1987; The Quality of Local Democracy, 1988. Address: (b.) Department of Politics, Glasgow University, G12 8RT; T.-041-339 8855.

Milligan, Eric. President, Convention of Scottish Local Authorities, since 1988; Chairman, Finance Committee, Lothian Regional Council, since 1986; b. 27.1.51, Edinburgh; m., Janis. Educ. Tynecastle High School; Napier College of Commerce and Technology. Edinburgh District Councillor, 1974-78; Lothian Regional Councillor, since 1978; Member: Electricity Consultative Council; Napier College Council; Edinburgh Prison Visiting Committee; Royal High School Endowment Trust. Recreation: football. Address: (h.) 22 Hailes Grove, Edinburgh, EH13 0NE; T.-031-441 1528.

Milligan, John, BSc. Head Teacher, Smithycroft Secondary School, Glasgow, since 1985; b. 26.4.38, Castle Douglas; m., Sheena; 1 s.; 1 d. Educ. Castle Douglas High School; Kirkcudbright Academy; Glasgow University; Jordanhill College of Education. Address: (b.) 282 Smithycroft Road, Glasgow, G33 2QU; T.-041-770 5595.

Milligan, Rev. Rodney, FRGS. Minister, Culsalmond linked with Rothienorman, since 1958; b. 27.12.22, Arbroath; m., Jeannie Duguid. Educ. Arbroath High School; St. Andrews University; St. Mary's College. RAFVR, 1941-45; student, 1946-49; ordained as Assistant Minister, Dunfermline Abbey, 1949; Minister, Culsamond, 1951; Moderator: Garioch Presbytery, 1958-59, Gordon Presbytery, 1984-85. Recreations: philately; oenology. Address: 18 Dunnydeer Park, Insch, Aberdeenshire, AB5 6GD.

Millington, Philip Francis, BSc, MSc, PhD. Reader in Bioengineering, Strathclyde University, since 1970, and Co-ordinator, Study Skills and Counselling, Academic Practice, since 1988; b. 14.6.30, Birmingham; m., Rosemary Cooke; 1 s.; 2 d. Educ. St. Philip's Grammar School, Birmingham. Research and Senior Research Associate, Birmingham University, 1956-62; Lecturer in Histology and Physiology, Bristol University, 1962-68. Tutor in Counselling; Faculty Co-ordinator, Schools Liaison, 1987-88; Vice-Chairman (Hon.), CRUSE (Glasgow); Counsellor and trainer to CRUSE, CMAC and Glasgow Hospice; spokesman on marriage and marital relationships, Glasgow Archdiocese. Publication: Skin, 1983. Address: (h.) 27 North Erskine Park, Bearsden, Glasgow; T.-041-942 0495.

Mills, Colin Frederick, MSc, PhD, CChem, FRSC, FRSE. Director, Postgraduate Studies, Rowett Research Institute, since 1986 (Head, Biochemistry Division, 1966-86); b. 8.7.26, Swinton, Lancashire; m., D. Beryl; 1 d. Educ. Altrincham Grammar School; Reading University; London University. ARC Unit for Micronutrient Research, Long Ashton Research Station, Bristol University, 1946-47; Assistant Lecturer in Biochemistry, Wye College, London University, 1947-51; joined Rowett Research Institute, 1951. Member, WHO Experts Committee on Trace Elements in Human Nutrition; Chairman, International Committee for Symposia on Trace Elements in Man and Animals; Royal Society for Chemistry John Jeye Gold Medallist (Environmental Studies). Recreations: music; sailing. Address: (b.) Rowett Research Institute, Bucksburn, Aberdeen, AB2 9SB; T.-0224 712751.

Mills, Derek Henry, BSc, MSc, PhD, FIFM. Senior Lecturer, Department of Forestry and Natural Resources, Edinburgh University, since 1965; b. 19.3.28, Bristol; m., Florence Cameron; 1 s.; 1 d. Educ. Clifton House; Harrogate Grammar School; Queen Mary College, London University. RAF, 1947-49; Scientific Officer, Oceanographic Laboratory, Edinburgh, 1954-56; Assistant Scientist, Fisheries Research Board of Canada, 1956-57; Senior Scientific Officer, Freshwater Fisheries Laboratory, Pitlochry, 1957-65. Consultant Biologist to Anglers' Co-operative Association; Editor, Journal of Aquaculture and Fisheries Management; Member, Training Committee, Institute of Fisheries Management; Member, Council, Committee of Management and Scientific Advisory Panel, Atlantic Salmon Trust; Member, Council, L'Association de Defense du

Saumon Atlantique. Publications: Salmon and Trout; Introduction to Freshwater Ecology; Scotland's King of Fish; Salmon Rivers of Scotland (Co-author); Salmon in Iceland (Co-author); The Fishing Here is Great; Ecology and Management of Atlantic Salmon. Recreations: angling; hill-walking; photography. Address: (h.) 37 Granby Road, Edinburgh, EH16 5NP; T.-031-667 4931.

Mills, Harold Hernshaw, BSc, PhD. Under Secretary, Scottish Development Department, since 1984; b. 2.3.38, Greenock; m., Marion Elizabeth Beattie. Educ. Greenock High School; Glasgow University. Cancer Research Scientist, Roswell Park Memorial Institute, Buffalo, New York, 1962-64; Lecturer, Chemistry Department, Glasgow University, 1964-69; Principal, Scottish Home and Health Department, 1970-76; Assistant Secretary: Scottish Office, 1976-81, Privy Council Office, 1981-83, Scottish Development Department, 1983-84. Address: (b.) Scottish Development Department, St. Andrews House, Edinburgh, EH1 3DD; T.-031-556 8400.

Mills, Kenneth Leslie George, MA, BSc, MB, BChir, FRCS, FRCSEdin, FRCSCanada. Consultant Orthopaedic Surgeon, since 1968; b. 16.8.29, Birmingham; 2 d. Educ. High School of Glasgow; Cambridge University; Westminster Hospital, London. Medical Officer, RAF; Senior Lecturer in Orthopaedic Surgery, Dundee University. Publications: Guide to Orthopaedics (Trauma), 1979; Colour Atlas of Accidents and Emergencies, 1984. Address: (h.) 29 Craigiebuckler Avenue, Aberdeen, AB1 7SL; T.-0224 314077.

Milne, Alastair, MA, MEd, ABPsS. HM Inspector of Schools, since 1970; b. 27.10.29, New Pitsligo; m., Margaret M. McHardy (deceased); 1 s. Educ. Banff Academy; Aberdeen University; Aberdeen College of Education. Teacher, Fyvie School, 1955-57; Educational Psychologist, Aberdeen Child Guidance Service, 1957-60; Lecturer, Senior Lecturer, Principal Lecturer, Dundee College of Education, 1960-70. Recreations: reading; hill-walking. Address: (h.) 52 Kelvin Court, Glasgow, G12 OAE; T.-041-357 3684.

Milne, Brian, MB, ChB, FRCOG. Consultant Gynaecologist and Obstetrician, Highland Health Board (based at Raigmore Hospital, Inverness), since 1978; Clinical Senior Lecturer, Aberdeen University, since 1978; b. 9.1.42, Elgin; m., Mary I.B.; 2 s. Educ. Keith Grammar School; Aberdeen University. House Officer and Senior House Officer appointments, Aberdeen Royal Infirmary; Registrar appointments, Raigmore Hospital, Inverness and Southern General Hospital, Glasgow; Senior Registrar, Obstetrics and Gynaecology, Leicester Royal Infirmary, 1974-78. Recreations: golf; curling; Chairman, Inverness Branch, Aberdeen FC Supporters. Address: (h.) Muirfield House, 28 Muirfield Road, Inverness; T.-0463 222134.

Milne, James Ewen, OBE, FIExport. Director (Exports), Industry Department for Scotland, 1972-88; b. 22.12.28, Glasgow; m., Winifred Jeffrey Lochhead; 1 s.; 1 d. Educ. Whitehill School; Manchester Business School. Clerical Officer, then Executive Officer, Board of Trade, 1946-56; Assistant British Trade Commissioner, Johannesburg, 1956-60, Karachi, 1960-63; Senior Executive Officer, Board of Trade, 1964-66; Assistant Director, Regional Development Grants Office, Glasgow, 1966-72; retired, 1988. Recreations: industrial architecture; bird-watching.

Milne, John Alexander, BA, BSc (Hons), PhD. Head, Animals and Grazing Ecology Division, Macaulay Land Use Research Institute (formerly Hill Farming Research Organisation), since 1988; b. 22.11.43, Edinburgh; m., Janet Erskine; 1 s. Educ. Edinburgh Academy; Edinburgh University; London University; Open University. Joined Hill Farming Research Organisation, 1970. Editor, British Journal of Nutrition. Address: (b.) Bush Estate, Penicuik, Midlothian; T.-031-445 3401.

Milne, John Duff. Broadcasting Journalist, since 1972; b. 13.5.42, Dundee; m., Jennifer Frances Brown; 2 s. Educ. Harris Academy, Dundee. Newspaper Journalist: D.C. Thomson, Dundee, Scotsman Publications, Edinburgh; Broadcasting Journalist: Swiss Broadcasting Corporation, Bern, BBC. Recreations: sport; music. Address: (b.) BBC Scotland, Queen Margaret Drive, Glasgow; T.-041-339 8844.

Milne, Robert Hughes, MInstM. Executive Director, Aberdeen Fish Curers and Merchants Association Ltd., since 1987 (Chief Executive/Secretary, 1983-87); b. 4.6.39, Pittenweem; m., Helen Wilma Masson; 1 s. Educ. Waid Academy, Anstruther. Assistant Chief Fisheries Advisor, then Regional Officer, Herring Industry Board, 1962-73; Development Officer/Secretary, then Secretary General, Scottish Federation of Fishermen's Co-operatives Ltd., Fishing Co-operative Trading (Scotland) Ltd. and Fishing Co-operatives (Manufacturing) Ltd., 1973-83. Served, European Community Social Problems Fisheries Committee, European Community Advisory Committee on Fisheries and Association of European Agricultural and Fisheries Co-operatives, 1973-83; Member, Isle of Man Government's Commission of Inquiry, 1982-83; Secretary, Scottish Fish Merchants Federation Ltd., since 1984; Member, Sea Fish Industry Authority Research and Development Committee and Sea Fish Training Council, since 1983. Chairman, Aberdeen Fish Festival Committee; Burgess of Guild, City of Aberdeen; Council Member, Aberdeen Chamber of Commerce. Recreations: gardening; church activities. Address: (b.) South Esplanade West, Aberdeen, AB9 2FJ; T.-0224 897744.

Milne Home, John Gavin, JP, TD, FRICS. Lord Lieutenant, Dumfries and Galloway, since 1988; Chartered Surveyor and Land Agent; b. 20.10.16, Dumfriesshire; m., Rosemary Elwes; 2 s.; 1 d. Educ. Wellington College; Trinity College, Cambridge. Served 4th Bn., King's Own Scottish Borderers, 1938-45; Factor, Buccleuch Estates Ltd., on Eskdale, Liddesdale and Branxholm Estates, 1945-74; Member, Dumfries County Council, 1949-74; self-employed Land Agent, since 1974. Chairman, Dumfries and Galloway Region, British Field Sports Society, 1976-88. Recreations: country sports; nature study. Address: (h.) and (b.) Kirkside of Middlebie, Lockerbie, Dumfriesshire, DG11 3JW; T.-05763 204.

Milner, A.D., MA, DipPsych, PhD. Reader in Neuropsychology, St. Andrews University, since 1985 (Chairman, Department of Psychology, since 1983); b. 16.7.43, Leeds. Educ. Bradford Grammar School; Lincoln College, Oxford. Research Worker, Institute of Psychiatry, London, 1966-70; Lecturer, then Senior Lecturer, St. Andrews University, 1970-85. Address (b.) Psychological Laboratory, St. Andrews University, St. Andrews, KY16 9JU; T.-0334 76161.

Milner, Professor Arthur John Robin Gorell, BA (Cantab). Professor of Computation Theory, Edinburgh University, since 1984; b. 13.1.34, Yealmpton; m., Lucy; 2 s.; 1 d. Educ. Eton; King's College, Cambridge. National Service, 2nd Lt., Royal Engineers, 1952-54; student, 1954-58; Mathematics Teacher, Marylebone Grammar School, 1959-60; Ferranti Ltd., 1960-63; Mathematics Lecturer, The City University, 1963-68; Research Fellow, University College, Swansea, 1968-70; Research Associate, Artificial Intelligence Laboratory, Stanford University, 1971-72; joined Edinburgh University as Lecturer, 1973. Elected Fellow of the Royal Society, 1988. Publications: Edinburgh LCF (Co-author); A Calculus of Communicating Systems. Recreations: music (oboe and piano); carpentry; walking. Address: (h.) 2 Garscube Terrace, Edinburgh, EH12 6BQ; T.-031-337 4823.

Milton, Professor Anthony Stuart, MA, DPhil (Oxon). Professor of Pharmacology and Head of Department, Aberdeen University, since 1973; b. 15.4.34, London; m., Elizabeth Amaret Freeman; 1 s.; 2 d. Educ. Cranleigh School; St. Catherine's College, Oxford. Lecturer, Dartmouth College Medical School, USA, 1959-60; Research Fellow: Stanford University Medical Center, USA, 1960-61, Edinburgh University, 1961-63; Lecturer, then Senior Lecturer, School of Pharmacy, London University, 1966-73. Recreation: breeding and showing Border Terrier dogs. Address: (h.) Stone Cottage, Baillieswells Road, Bieldside, Aberdeen, AB1 9BQ; T.-0224 868651.

Minto, 6th Earl of (Gilbert Edward George Lariston Elliot-Murray-Kynynmound), OBE (1986), JP. Brigadier, Queen's Bodyguard for Scotland (Royal Company of Archers); Chairman, Scottish Council on Alcohol, since 1973; Deputy Lieutenant, Borders Region, Roxburgh, Ettrick and Lauderdale, since 1983; Member, Borders Regional Council, since 1986; b. 19.6.28; m., 1, Lady Caroline Child-Villiers (m. diss.); 1 s.; 1 d.; 2, Mary Elizabeth Ballantine (deceased). Educ. Eton; Sandhurst. Former Captain, Scots Guards. Address: (h.) Minto, Hawick.

Minto, James Rutherford, OBE, MA, MEd, PhD, DL. General Director, Quarrier's Homes, Bridge of Weir, since 1974; b. 9.4.26, St. Boswells; m., Rosemary; 1 s.; 2 d. Educ. Kirkcudbright Academy; St. Andrews University. Assistant Teacher: Waid Academy, Anstruther, 1951-59, Abraham Lincoln High School, Philadelphia, 1956-57; Headmaster, then Principal, Dr. Graham's Homes, Kalimpong, India, 1959-71. Vice-Chairman, Strathclyde Branch, Epilepsy Association Scotland. Publication: Graham of Kalimpong. Recreation: golf. Address: (h.) Braehead, Quarrier's Homes, Bridge of Weir, Renfrewshire; T.-Bridge of Weir 612414.

Miquel, Raymond Clive, CBE (1981). Chairman and Chief Executive, Belhaven plc, since 1986; Chairman, Scottish Sports Council; b. 28.5.31; m.; 1 s.; 2 d. Educ. Allan Glen's School, Glasgow; Glasgow Technical College. Joined Arthur Bell & Sons Ltd., 1956, as works study engineer; Managing Director, 1968-85; Chairman, 1973-85.

Misra, Prem Chandra, BSc, MBBS, DPM (RCP&S, Edin and Glas), FAGS. Deputy Physician Superintendent, Gartloch Hospital, Glasgow, since 1984; Clinical Lecturer, Glasgow University, since 1976; b. 24.7.41, Lucknow, India; m., Sandhya; 1 s.; 2 d. Educ. KK Degree College and King George's Medical College, Lucknow, India; Lucknow University. Rotating Intern, King George's Medical College Hospital, Lucknow, 1967; Demonstrator, Department of Human Physiology, Lucknow University, 1967; Resident Senior House Officer, General Medicine and Geriatrics, Wigan and Leigh Group of Hospitals, 1968-69; Resident House Surgeon, General Surgery, Wigan Royal Infirmary, 1968-69; Resident House Physician, General Medicine, Whelley Hospital, Wigan, 1969-70; Resident Senior House Officer in Psychiatry, then Resident Registrar in Psychiatry, Bolton District General Hospital, 1970-73; Senior Psychiatric Registrar (Midland Area Consultant Training Scheme), Hollymoor Hospital, Birmingham, 1973-76; Consultant Psychiatrist, Solihull Area Health Authority, 1976; appointed Consultant Psychiatrist, Glasgow Royal Infirmary and Duke Street Hospital, 1976; Consultant in Charge, Acorn Street Day Hospital, 1979. President, Indian Association of Strathclyde, since 1981; Member, Executive Committee: Strathclyde Community Relations Council, 1981-85, Scottish Council for Racial Equality, 1982; Member, Social and Welfare Committee, CRC, for Ethnic Groups and Vietnam Refugees, 1982; awarded Ludwika Bierkoskigo Medal by Polish Medical Association for "outstanding contributions in the prevention and treatment of disabilities"; Secretary, Division of Psychiatry, Eastern District of Glasgow, since 1980; Member: Executive Committee, British Society of Research on Sex Education, International Scientific Committee on Sexuality and Handicap, International Advisory Board of Israel Society of Clinical and Experimental Hypnosis; Executive Committee Member, European Society of Hypnosis; Member, International Committee of Sexologists; Justice of the Peace; President, British Society of Medical and Dental Hypnosis (Scottish Branch). Publications: Modern Trends in Hypnosis; research papers. Address: (b.) Gartloch Hospital, Gartcosh, Glasgow, G69 8EJ; T.-041-771 0771.

Mitchell, Rev. Alexander Bell, BD, DipTechEd.. Minister, St. Leonard's Church, Dunfermline, since 1981; Chairman, Executive Committee, Fife Marriage Counselling Service; b. 28.6.49, Baillieston; m., Elizabeth Brodie; 1 s.; 2 d. Educ. Uddingston Grammar School; New College, Edinburgh. Mechanical Engineer, Motherwell Bridge and Engineering, 1965-70; student, 1970-72; Teacher, Uddingston Grammar School, 1972-75; theology degree, 1975-79; Assistant Minister, Dunblane Cathedral, 1979-81. Chaplain, RAF

Pitreavie. Recreations: badminton; hill-walking. Address: 12 Torvean Place, Dunfermline, KY11 4YY; T.-Dunfermline 721054.

Mitchell, Archibald George, MA, LLB. Depute Chief Executive, Tayside Regional Council, since 1982; Solicitor, since 1958; b. 7.6.31, Cupar; m., Isabel M. MacIntyre; 1 s.; 2 d. Educ. St. Andrews University; Edinburgh University. Address: (h.) 12 East Somerville Place, Dundee; T.-Dundee 24720.

Mitchell, Archie Mackenzie, MITSA. Director of Trading Standards, Tayside Regional Council, since 1980; b. 23.3.35, Cupar; m., Kathleen; 2 s.; 1 d. Educ. Bell-Baxter High School, Cupar. Trainee Inspector of Weights and Measures, Fife, 1953-58; Inspector of Weights and Measures, Glasgow, 1959; Ayr County: District Inspector, 1959-69, Depute Chief Inspector, 1969-75; Chief Inspector Consumer Protection (Ayr Sub-Region), Strathclyde, 1975-77; Depute Director, Grampian, 1977-80. Honorary Secretary, Society of Directors of Trading Standards in Scotland, 1982-86; Adviser on Trading Standards to COSLA and LACOTS, since 1986. Recreations: curling; cricket; rugby. Address: (b.) 1 Riverside Drive, Dundee, DD1 4DB; T.-Dundee 23281.

Mitchell, David William, CBE. Director, Mallinson-Denny (Scotland) Ltd., since 1980; Chairman, Cumbernauld New Town, since 1987; b. 4.1.33, Glasgow; m., Lynda Guy; 1 d. Educ. Merchiston Castle School. Member, Western Regional Hospital Board, 1965-73; Member, Glasgow Rating Valuation Appeal Committee, 1970-74; Council Member, CBI Scotland, 1979-85; Executive Member, Scottish Council (Development and Industry), since 1979; President, Scottish Timber Trade Association, 1980-82; Executive Member, Institute of Directors in Scotland, since 1983; President, Scottish Conservative and Unionist Association, 1980-82. Recreations: golf; shooting; fishing. Address: (h.) Dunmullen House, Blanefield, Stirlingshire, G63 9AJ; T.-0324 483294.

Mitchell, Rev. Duncan Ross, BA (Hons), BD (Hons). Minister, St. Andrews Church, West Kilbride, since 1980; b. 5.5.42, Boddam, Aberdeenshire; m., Sandra Brown; 2 s.; 1 d. Educ. Hyndland Senior Secondary School, Glasgow; Strathclyde University; Glasgow University. Worked in insurance industry, four years; Minister, Craigmailen UF Church, Bo'ness, 1972-80; Convener, Assembly Youth Committee, UF Church, 1974-79; Member: Scottish Joint Committee on Religious Education, 1974-79, Multilateral Conversation in Scotland, 1976-79, Board of Social Responsibility, Church of Scotland, 1983-86; Convener, World Mission and Unity, Ardrossan Presbytery, since 1984; Convener, General Assembly Board of World Mission and Unity, Local Involvements Committee, and Executive Member of the Board, since 1987. Address: St. Andrew's Manse, 7 Overton Drive, West Kilbride; T.-0294 823142.

Mitchell, Iain Grant, LLB (Hons), FSA Scot. Advocate, since 1976; b. 16.11.51, Edinburgh. Educ. Perth Academy; Edinburgh University. Called to Scottish Bar, 1976; Partner, Mitchells of Perth (Dyers and Cleaners), since 1973; Advisor in Scots Law to Lawtel (Prestel Legal Database), since 1983; Past President, Diagnostic Society of Edinburgh; former Vice-President, Edinburgh University Conservative Association; Conservative candidate, Falkirk West, General Election, 1983, and Kirkcaldy, General Election, 1987; Chairman, Trust for an International Opera Theatre of Scotland; Vice-Chairman, Scottish Baroque Ensemble Ltd.; former Chairman, Scottish Philharmonic Club; Member, Scottish Committee, Royal Institute of International Affairs; Member, Conservative Group for Europe and the European Movement; Committee Member, Perth Civic Trust. Recreations: music and the arts; photography; history; travel; writing; building opera houses; finding enough hours in the day. Address: (b.) Advocates Library, Parliament House, High Street, Edinburgh; T.-031-226 5071.

Mitchell, James F.O., MD, DLO, FRCSEdin. Senior Consultant Ear, Nose and Throat Surgeon, Tayside Area, since 1984; Consultant Otolaryngologist, Dundee, Angus and Perth NHS, 1951-87; b. 7.9.21, Edinburgh; 3 s. Educ. George Heriot's School, Edinburgh; Edinburgh University. Army Service, RAMC, 1945-48, Egypt and Palestine, latterly as Major. Chairman, Area Medical Committee, 1981-83; Chairman, British Medical Association, Angus, 1964, and Dundee, 1978. Dundee Chairman, British Subaqua Club, 1969. Recreations: swimming; skiing; caravanning; ornithology; golf; fishing. Address: (h.) 19 Rockfield Crescent, Dundee; T.-0382 66092.

Mitchell, Sheriff (James Lachlan) Martin. Sheriff of Lothian and Borders at Edinburgh, since 1978; b. 13.6.29, Inverness. Educ. Cargilfield; Sedbergh; Edinburgh University. National Service (RN), 1954-55; Sub Lt. (S), RNVR, 1954; Permanent Reserve, 1956-74; Commander, RNR, 1966; retired, 1974; Law Apprentice, 1950-53; Member, Faculty of Advocates, 1957; in practice, 1957-74; Standing Junior Counsel in Scotland to the Admiralty Board, 1963-74; Temporary Sheriff, 1971; Sheriff of Lothian and Peebles, 1974, and as a floating Sheriff, 1974-78; Honorary Sheriff at Inverness, 1983. Recreations: fishing; photography; the gramophone. Address: (b.) Sheriffs' Chambers, Sheriff Court, Lawnmarket, Edinburgh, EH1 2NS; T.-031-226 7181.

Mitchell, John, BSc. Head Teacher, Kilsyth Academy, since 1985; b. 4.1.45, Kirkintilloch; m., Irene; 1 s.; 1 d. Educ. Lenzie Academy; Glasgow University. Taught in Glasgow; Principal Teacher of Physics, Balfron High School and Bishopbriggs High School; Assistant Head Teacher, Kilsyth Academy; Deputy Head Teacher, Knightswood Secondary School. Address: (h.) Kilsyth Academy, Balmalloch, Kilsyth, G65 9NF; T.-0236 822244.

Mitchell, (John) Angus (Macbeth), CB, CVO, MC, LLD(Hon). Chairman of Court, Stirling University, since 1984; Member, Commission for Local Authority Accounts in Scotland, since 1985; Chairman, Scottish Action on Dementia, since 1986; b. 25.8.24, Ootacamund, India; m., Ann Williamson; 2 s.; 2 d. Educ. Marlborough College; Brasenose College, Oxford. Royal Armoured Corps (Captain), 1943-46; Scottish

Office, 1949-84; Principal Private Secretary to Secretary of State for Scotland, 1958-59; Under Secretary, Social Work Services Group, 1969-74; Secretary, Scottish Education Department, 1976-84. Order of Orange-Nassau, 1946; Chairman, Scottish Marriage Guidance Council, 1965-69; Vice-Convener, Scottish Council of Voluntary Organisations, since 1986. Publications: Scottish Office Ministers 1885-1985; Procedures for the Reorganisation of Schools in England, 1986. Recreations: old Penguins; gravestones; maps. Address: (h.) 20 Regent Terrace, Edinburgh, EH7 5BS; T.-031-556 7671.

Mitchell, John Gall, QC, MA, LLB. Social Security (formerly National Insurance) Commissioner, since 1979; b. 5.5.31, Edinburgh; m., Anne Bertram Jardine; 3 s.; 1 d. Educ. Royal High School, Edinburgh; Edinburgh University. Advocate, 1957; Standing Junior Counsel, Customs and Excise, Scotland, 1964-70; a Chairman, Industrial Tribunals, Scotland, 1966-80; Honorary Sheriff of Lanarkshire, 1970-74; Chairman, Supreme Court Legal Aid Committee, 1974-79; a Chairman, Pensions Appeal Tribunals, Scotland, 1974-80. Address: (h.) Rosemount, Park Road, Eskbank, Dalkeith, Midlothian; T.-031-663 2557.

Mitchell, John Logan, QC, LLB (Hons). Queen's Counsel, since 1987; Advocate Depute, 1981-85; b. 23.6.47, Dumfries; m., Christine Brownlee Thomson; 1 s.; 1 d. Educ. Royal High School, Edinburgh; Edinburgh University. Called to Bar, 1974; Standing Junior Counsel to Forestry Commission; Standing Junior Counsel, Department of Agriculture and Fisheries. Address: (h.) 17 Braid Farm Road, Edinburgh; T.-031-447 8099.

Mitchell, Joseph R., OBE, JP. Vice-Convener, Banff and Buchan District Council, since 1975 (Vice-Chairman, Housing Committee); Farmer; Vice-Chairman, North East of Scotland Library Committee, since 1984; b. 15.3.14, Old Deer. Educ. Robert Gordon's College, Aberdeen. Director, Fraserburgh Ltd. and C.E. Heath & Co. (Scotland) Ltd.; Chairman, Buchan Meat Producers, 1954-73; Past Chairman, Buchan Poultry Products; Past Chairman, Aberdeen-Kincardine Area, NFU of Scotland; received Royal Northern Agricultural Society Award, 1984; Chairman, East Aberdeenshire Conservative Association, 1976-78. Recreation: bridge. Address: Coburty Mains, Fraserburgh; T.-Rosehearty 206.

Mitchell, Lyn, BSc (SocSci), MMedSci, RGN, SCM, RSCN, RNT. Chief Executive Officer, National Board for Nursing, Midwifery and Health Visiting for Scotland, since 1986; b. 26.4.40, Elgin; m., David Mitchell; 1 step s.; 1 step d. Educ. Elgin Academy; Edinburgh University; Nottingham University. Ward Sister: Sheffield Children's Hospital, Aberdeen Royal Infirmary; Nurse Teacher, Foresterhill College, Aberdeen; Senior Health Education Officer, Grampian Health Board; Lecturer, Department of Nursing Studies, Edinburgh University; Nursing Adviser, Scottish Health Education Group. Honorary Fellow, Department of Nursing Studies, Edinburgh University. Publication: Teaching for Health. Address: (b.) 22 Queen Street, Edinburgh, EH2 1JX; T.-031-226 7371.

Mitchell, Ross, MA, DSA, FHSM, MIPM. Associate Director, Scottish Hospital Advisory Service, since 1987 (Secretary, Lothian Health Board, 1981-87); b. Glasgow; m., Marion; 1 s. Educ. Hillhead High School, Glasgow; Glasgow University; Manchester University. Eastern Regional Hospital Board: National Administrative Trainee, 1956-58, Administrative Assistant, 1958-60, Work Study Officer, 1960-61; Hospital Secretary, Bridge of Earn Hospital, 1961-65; Deputy Secretary and Treasurer, East Fife Board of Management, 1965-69; Secretary and Treasurer, West Lothian Board of Management, 1969-73; Secretary, Fife Health Board, 1973-81. Recreations: squash; golf; tennis. Address: (h.) 43 Braehead Road, Edinburgh; T.-031-339 1279.

Mitchell, Professor Ross Galbraith, MD, FRCPEdin, DCH. Professor of Child Health, Dundee University, 1973-85, now Emeritus; Member, General Medical Council, 1983-85; b. 18.11.20; m., June Phylis Butcher; 1 s.; 3 d. Educ. Kelvinside Academy, Glasgow; Edinburgh University. Surgeon Lt., Royal Naval Volunteer Reserve, 1944-47; junior medical posts, Edinburgh, Liverpool and London, 1947-52; Rockefeller Research Fellow in Physiology, Mayo Clinic, USA, 1952-53; Lecturer in Child Health, St. Andrews University, 1952-55; Consultant Paediatrician, Dundee Teaching Hospitals, 1955-63; Professor of Child Health, Aberdeen University, 1963-72. Chairman, Editorial Board, Mac Keith Press, since 1980; Chairman, Scottish Advisory Council on Child Care, 1966-68; Dean, Faculty of Medicine and Dentistry, Dundee University, 1978-81; Chairman, Aberdeen Association of Social Service, 1971-72; President, Scottish Paediatric Society, 1982-84; President, Harveian Society of Edinburgh, 1982-83. Recreations: fishing; gardening; languages. Address: (h.) Craigard, Abertay Gardens, Barnhill, Dundee, DD5 2SQ; T.-0382 76983.

Mitchell, Ruthven, BSc (Hons), MB, ChB, MD, FRCPath, FRCPGlas. Regional Director, Glasgow and West of Scotland Blood Transfusion Service, since 1978; b. 28.3.36, Cambuslang; m., Eleanor Forbes Burnside; 1 s.; 1 d. Educ. Hamilton Academy; Glasgow University. Glasgow Royal Infirmary: Medical and Surgical House Officer, 1961-62, Senior House Officer in Pathology, 1962-63, Registrar in Pathology, 1963-65, University Lecturer in Pathology, 1965-68; Consultant Pathologist, Ministry of Health, Tanzania, 1965-67; Deputy Medical Director, Glasgow and West of Scotland Blood Transfusion Service, 1968-78. Recreations: gardening; fishing. Address: (h.) 2 Byron Court, Sweethope Farm Steading, Bothwell, Lanarkshire; T.-0698 853255.

Mitchell, Thomas. Lord Provost, City of Dundee, since 1984; b. 4.9.41, Dundee; m., Gertrude Brown; 2 s. Educ. St. John's High School, Dundee. Elected, City of Dundee District Council,

1980. Recreations: football; hill-walking. Address: (b.) City Chambers, Dundee, DD1 3BY; T.-Dundee 23141.

Mitchison, Professor John Murdoch, ScD, FRS, FRSE. Professor of Zoology, Edinburgh University, since 1963; b. 11.6.22; m., Rosalind Mary Wrong; 1 s.; 3 d. Educ. Winchester College; Trinity College, Cambridge. Army Operational Research, 1941-46; Research Scholar, then Fellow, Trinity College, Cambridge, 1946-54; Lecturer, then Reader in Zoology, Edinburgh University, 1953-62; Member, Edinburgh University Court, 1971-74, 1985-88; Dean, Faculty of Science, 1984-85; Member, Scottish Marine Biological Association, 1961-67; Executive Committee Member, International Society for Cell Biology, 1964-72; Member: Biological Committee, SRC, 1972-75, Royal Commission on Environmental Pollution, 1974-79, Science Board, SRC, 1976-79, Working Group on Biological Manpower, DES, 1968-71, Advisory Committee on Safety of Nuclear Installations, Health and Safety Executive, 1981-84; President, British Society for Cell Biology, 1974-77. Publication: The Biology of the Cell Cycle. Address: (h.) Great Yew, Ormiston, East Lothian, EH35 5NJ; T.-Pencaitland 340530.

Mitchison, Naomi, CBE. Writer; b. 1.11.97, Edinburgh; m., Dick Mitchison; 3 s.; 2 d. Educ. Dragon School, Oxford; St. Anne's College, Oxford. Member: Argyll County Council, 1945-65, Highland Panel, 1945-65, Highland and Island Advisory Council, 1965-75; contested Scottish Universities Parliamentary constituency for Labour; author of about 80 books, including: The Corn King and the Spring Queen; Blood of the Martyrs; The Bull Calves; The Big House; Lobsters on the Agenda; Five Men and a Swan; Cleopatra's People; volumes of autobiography; The Cleansing of the Knife; Images of Africa; Memoirs of a Space Woman; Travel Light; Early in Orcadia. Address: (h.) Carradale House, Carradale, Campbeltown, Argyll.

Mitchison, Professor Rosalind Mary, MA. Professor of Social History, Edinburgh University, 1981-86; b. 11.4.19, Manchester; m., J.M. Mitchison (qv); 1 s.; 3 d. Educ. Channing School, Highgate; Lady Margaret Hall, Oxford. Assistant Lecturer, Manchester University, 1943-46; Tutor, Lady Margaret Hall, Oxford, 1946-47; Assistant: Edinburgh University, 1954-57, Glasgow University, 1962-63; Lecturer: Glasgow University, 1966-67, Edinburgh, from 1967. President, Scottish History Society, 1981-84. Publications: A History of Scotland, 1970; British Population Change since 1860, 1977; Life in Scotland, 1978; Lordship to Patronage: Scotland 1603-1745, 1983. Recreations: walking; skiing. Address: (h.) Great Yew, Ormiston, East Lothian, EH35 5NJ; T.-Pencaitland 340530.

Mithen, Dallas Alfred, CB, BSc, FICFor. President, Institute of Chartered Foresters, 1984-86; Chairman, Forestry Training Council, since 1984; b. 5.11.23; m., 1, Peggy Clarke (deceased); 2, Avril Teresa Dodd; 1 s.; 1 d. Educ. Maidstone Grammar School; University College of North Wales, Bangor. Fleet Air Arm, 1942-46; joined Forestry Commission as District Officer, 1950; Deputy Surveyor, New Forest, and Conservator, SE (England), 1968-71; Senior Officer, Scotland, 1971-75; Head, Forest Management Division, Edinburgh, 1975-76; Commissioner for Harvesting and Marketing, Forestry Commission, 1977-83. Trustee, Central Scotland Countryside Trust, since 1985; President, Forestry Section, BAAS, 1985. Recreations: swimming; walking; gardening. Address: (h.) Kings Knot, Bonnington Road, Peebles, EH45 9HF; T.-0721 20738.

Moffat, Alistair Murray, MA (Hons), MPhil. Executive Producer, Religion, Education, Gaelic, Special Projects, Scottish Television, since 1987; Chairman, Assembly Productions, Edinburgh, since 1983; b. 16.6.50, Kelso; m., Lindsay Thomas; 1 s.; 2 d. Educ. Kelso High School; St. Andrews University; Edinburgh University; London University. Ran Edinburgh Festival Fringe, 1976-81; Arts Correspondent, then Producer, Scottish Television. Council Member, Advertising Standards Authority. Publications: The Edinburgh Fringe, 1978; Kelsae - A History of Kelso from Earliest Times. Recreations: sleeping; supporting Kelso RFC. Address: (b.) Scottish Television, Cowcaddens, Glasgow, G2 3PR.

Moffat of that Ilk, Francis, MC, JP, DL, FSA Scot. Chief of the Name and Arms of Moffat; Deputy Lieutenant, County of Dumfries, since 1957; b. 21.3.15, Moffat; m., Margaret Carrington; 2 d. Educ. Shrewsbury School; Trinity College, Cambridge. Farming in Roxburghshire, 1937-40; War Service, 1940-45: Major, King's Own Scottish Borderers, severely wounded in Germany, 1945; Farmer and Landowner, Dumfriesshire, 1946-76; succeeded father as County Councillor for Moffat and Wamphray, 1948; President, Moffat Show Society, 1950-57 (Honorary President, since 1957); Member, Association of County Councils in Scotland, 1961-75; Vice-Convener, Dumfries County Council, 1961-69, Convener, 1969-75; Chairman: SW Scotland Joint Planning Working Party, 1969-72, SW Scotland Industrial Development Authority, 1972-75; Member, Board of Management, Small Industries Council for Rural Areas of Scotland, 1972-75; Member, Committee for European Investment in Scotland, 1972-74; Member, Scottish Consultative Committee, Scottish Council (Development and Industry), 1972-75; Council Member, Galloway Cattle Society, 1961-72; President, Dumfriesshire Conservative Association, 1978-85. Recreations: historical and genealogical research; walking; reading. Address: (h.) Redacres, Moffat, Dumfriesshire, DG10 9JT; T.-0683 20045.

Moffat, John, MB, ChB, FRCPsych, DPM. Physician Superintendent, Ravenscraig Hospital, Greenock, since 1968 (Consultant Psychiatrist, since 1965); b. 20.11.28, Renfrew; m., Jean Forsyth; 1 s.; 1 d. Educ. Camphill Secondary School; Glasgow University. Member, Argyll and Clyde Area Health Board, since 1981. Address: (h.) 41 Denholm Street, Greenock; T.-0475 20975.

Moir, Alexander Thomas Boyd, MB, ChB, BSc, PhD, FRCPEdin, FRCPGlas, FRCPath, MFOM, MFCM, FIBiol, FIFST. Director, Chief Scientist Office, Scottish Home and Health Department; b. 1.8.39, Bolton; m., Isabel May Sheehan; 1 s.; 2 d. Educ. George Heriot's School, Edinburgh; Edinburgh University. Intern appointment, New York City Hospitals; MRC Scientific/Clinical Scientific Staff, Honorary Registrar/Senior Registrar, Honorary Fellow, Edinburgh University; Senior/Principal Medical Officer, Scottish Home and Health Department. Recreations: playing games; listening to music; reading. Address: (b.) Scottish Home and Health Department, St. Andrews House, Edinburgh, EH1 3DE; T.-031-556 8400.

Moir, Donald Dundas, MD, FFARCS, DA, DRCOG. Consultant Anaesthetist, Queen Mother's Hospital and Western Infirmary, Glasgow, since 1963; Honorary Clinical Lecturer, Glasgow University, since 1970; b. 11.6.29, Kendal, Cumbria; m., Heather Joy Harvey; 2 s. Educ. Hillhead High School, Glasgow; Glasgow University. Junior posts in various Glasgow hospitals, 1952-63; Captain, RAMC, 1953-55; Assistant Professor, Western Reserve University, Cleveland, Ohio, 1961-62. President, Obstetric Anaesthetists Association, since 1984; President, Glasgow and West of Scotland Society of Anaesthetists, 1978-79; Member, Scottish Standing Committee, Faculty of Anaesthetists, 1981-84; British Council Lecturer, Sri Lanka and Israel. Publications: Pain Relief in Labour; Obstetric Anaesthesia and Analgesia. Recreations: golf; walking; gardening. Address: (h.) St. David's Cottage, Madderty St. David's, Crieff, PH7 3PJ; T.-Madderty 328.

Moir, Dorothy Carnegie, MB, ChB, MD, MFCM. Chief Administrative Medical Officer, Forth Valley Health Board, since 1988 (Community Medicine Specialist, since 1979; Honorary Senior Clinical Lecturer in Community Medicine, Aberdeen University, 1979-88); b. 27.3.42, Aberdeen; m., Alexander D. Moir; 3 s. Educ. Albyn School for Girls, Aberdeen; Aberdeen University. Research Fellow in Therapeutics and Pharmacology, 1966-69; Lecturer in Community Medicine, 1970-79. Address: (b.) 33 Spittal Street, Stirling.

Moir, Rev. Ian Andrew, MA, BD. Minister, Old Kirk of Edinburgh, since 1983; b. 9.4.35, Aberdeen; m., Elizabeth; 3 s. Educ. Aberdeen Grammar School; Aberdeen University. Sub-Warden, St. Ninian's Training Centre, Crieff, 1959-61; Superintendent, Pholela High School, Natal, 1962-73; Assistant Secretary, Church of Scotland Overseas Council, 1974-83. Recreations: walking; golf. Address: 24 Pennywell Road, Edinburgh, EH4 4HD; T.-031-332 4354.

Mollison, Professor Denis, MA, PhD. Professor of Applied Probability, Heriot-Watt University, since 1986; Chairman, Mountain Bothies Association, since 1978; Treasurer and Trustee, John Muir Trust; b. 28.6.45, Carshalton; m., Jennifer Hutton; 1 s.; 3 d. Educ. Westminster School; Trinity College, Cambridge. Research Fellow, King's College, Cambridge, 1969; Lecturer in Statistics, Heriot-Watt University, 1973. Elected Member of Council, National Trust for Scotland, 1979-84. Address: (h.) The Laigh House, Inveresk, Musselburgh, EH21 7TD; T.-031-665 2055.

Monaghan, Rt. Rev. James. Titular Bishop of Cell Ausaille and Auxiliary Bishop of St. Andrews and Edinburgh, since 1970; b. 11.7.14, Bathgate. Educ. St. Aloysius', Glasgow; St. Mary's, Blairs; Scots College, Valladolid; St. Kieran's, Kilkenny. Ordained Priest, 1940; Assistant: St. Andrew's, Ravelston, Edinburgh, 1940-42, St. Margaret Mary's, Edinburgh, 1942-47; Chaplain, Little Sisters of the Poor, Edinburgh, 1947-59; Parish Priest, Holy Cross, Edinburgh, 1959; President, Scottish Catholic Communications Commission, 1970-77. Address: 252 Ferry Road, Edinburgh, EH5 3AN.

Monaghan, Captain William. Member, Highland Health Board, since 1975; b. 28.4.36, Dundee; m., Margaret Innes; 2 s.; 1 d. Educ. Rockwell Junior Secondary School, Dundee; Jordanhill College of Education, Glasgow. 1st Bn., Seaforth Highlanders, 1954-57; Salvation Army Officer, 1957-64; social work, 1964-74; Highland Region Social Work Department, 1974-84. Chairman, Inverness Council on Alcoholism, 1982; Bandmaster, Inverness Salvation Army Band, 1970-83. Recreations: reading; gardening; letterpress printing. Address: (h.) 4 Huntly Place, Inverness, IV3 6HA; T.-Inverness 234123.

Moncreiff, 5th Baron (Harry Robert Wellwood Moncreiff), Bt; b. 4.2.15; m., Enid Marion Watson Locke (deceased); 1 s. Educ. Fettes College, Edinburgh. Lt.-Col. (Hon.), RASC (retired). Address: (h.) Tulliebole Castle, Fossoway, Kinross-shire.

Moncrieff, Charles William Kemley, BSc, MA. Rector, Annan Academy, since 1984; b. 12.7.42, Edinburgh; m., Helen Grantham; 1 s.; 1 d. Educ. Ross High School; Edinburgh University; Heriot-Watt University; Moray House College of Education. Teacher of Mathematics and Science: Daliburgh Secondary School, South Uist, Knox Academy, Haddington; Principal Teacher of Mathematics: David Kilpatrick Secondary School, Edinburgh, Gracemount High School, Edinburgh; Assistant Rector, Banff Academy; Depute Rector, Dumfries Academy. Address: (b.) Annan Academy, St. John's Road, Annan, DG12 6AP; T.-Annan 2954.

Moncrieff, Peter Duncan, BSc (Hons), DipEd. Rector, Blantyre High School, since 1974; b. 22.5.28, Perth; m., Doreen J.B. Langlands (deceased); 2 s.; 1 d. Educ. Perth Academy; Edinburgh University; Moray House College of Education. First Assistant, Goodlyburn Primary School, Perth, 1958-60; Head Teacher: Aberuthven Primary School, Perthshire, 1960-61, Mallaig Secondary School, 1961-70; Depute Rector, Stonelaw High School, Rutherglen, 1970-74. Children's Panel Member (Past Chairman, Area 10, Glasgow SE); Governor, National Memorial to David Livingstone. Recreations: golf; badminton; swimming; philately. Address: (h.) 184 Wellhall Road, Hamilton, Lanarkshire; T.-Hamilton 425393.

Mone, Rt. Rev. John Aloysius. Bishop of Paisley, formerly Titular Bishop of Abercorn and Auxiliary Bishop of Glasgow; b. 22.6.29, Glasgow. Educ. Holyrood Secondary School; Seminaire St. Sulpice and Institut Catholique, Paris. Ordained Priest, 1952; Assistant: St. Ninian's, Knightswood, Glasgow, 1952-75, Our Lady and St. George, Glasgow, 1975-79; Parish Priest, St. Joseph's, Tollcross, Glasgow, 1979-84. National Chairman, Catholic Marriage Advisory Council,

1981; Chairman, Scottish Catholic International Aid Fund, 1975-77; President, National Justice and Peace Commission, 1987. Address: 89 Muiryfauld Drive, Glasgow, G31 5RU.

Monelle, Raymond, MA, BMus, PhD, ARCM. Composer; Music Critic, The Independent, The Scotsman and Opera Magazine; Lecturer in Music, Edinburgh University; b. 19.8.37, Bristol; 2 d. Educ. Bristol Grammar School; Pembroke College, Oxford. Address: (h.) Salisbury Green, 18 Holyrood Park Road, Edinburgh, EH16 5AZ.

Monro, Sir Hector, AE, DL, JP. MP (Conservative), Dumfries, since 1964; Farmer; Company Director; b. 4.10.22, Edinburgh; m., Lady (Anne) Monro; 2 s. Educ. Canford School; Cambridge University; Dundee School of Economics. RAF, 1941-46; Royal Auxiliary Air Force, 1946-53 (Honorary Air Commodore, since 1981); Member, Dumfries County Council, 1952-67 (Chairman, Planning Committee and Joint Police Committee); Scottish Conservative Whip, 1967-70; Lord Commissioner, HM Treasury, 1970-71; Minister of Health and Education, Scottish Office, 1971-74; Opposition Spokesman on Scottish Affairs, 1974-75, Sport, 1974-79; Minister of Sport, 1979-81; Member, Nature Conservancy Council, since 1982; Member, Area Executive, NFU, since 1964; Member, Council, National Trust for Scotland, 1983-88; Vice-President, Scottish Rugby Union, 1975, President, 1976-77; Member, Queen's Bodyguard for Scotland (Royal Company of Archers); President: NSRA, since 1987, ACU, since 1983. Recreations: rugby; golf; flying; vintage cars; country sports. Address: (h.) Williamwood, Kirtlebridge, Lockerbie, Dumfriesshire; T.-04615 213.

Montagu-Smith, Group Captain Arthur, DL. Deputy Lieutenant, Morayshire, since 1970; b. 17.7.15; m., Elizabeth Hood Alexander; 1 s.; 1 d. Educ. Whitgift School; RAF Staff College. Joined RAF, 1935; Adjutant 99 Squadron, 1938-39; served Second World War, European Theatre, North Africa and Mediterranean; Flt. Cdr., 264 Squadron, 1940, and 221 Squadron, 1941; OC 248 Squadron, 1942-43; Battle of Britain Gold Rosette, 1940; mentioned in Despatches, 1942; Deputy Director, RAF Training, USA (Washington), 1944; OC 104 Wing, France, 1945; Hon. ADC, Governor, N.I., 1948-49; Air Adviser, New Delhi, 1949-50; RAF Representative, Chiefs of Staff Committee, UN, New York, 1951-53; HM Air Attache, Budapest, 1958-60; retired, 1961; Regional Executive, Small Industries Council and Scottish Development Agency, 1962-80; Member, Elgin District Council, 1967-75; Member, Moray TAFA, 1961-68; Director, Elgin and Lossiemouth Harbour Company, since 1966; Hon. County Representative, Moray and Nairn, RAF Benevolent Fund, since 1964; Chairman, Elgin and Lossiemouth Scottish SPCA, 1971-82; Past President, Victoria League, Moray and Nairn; Past Chairman, Moray Association of Youth Clubs. Recreations: outdoor interests; travel. Address: (h.) Woodpark, by Elgin, Moray; T.-034 384 2220.

Monteith, Lt.-Col. Robert Charles Michael, OBE, MC, TD, JP, DL, OStJ. Vice-Lieutenant of Lanarkshire, since 1964; b. 25.5.14, London; m., Mira Elizabeth Fanshawe; 1 s. Educ. Ampleforth College. CA, Edinburgh; served with Lanarkshire Yeomanry, 1939-45; contested Hamilton Division, 1950 and 1951; County Councillor (Lanarkshire), 1949-74; Chairman, Clydesdale District Council, 1974-84; Member, Mental Welfare Commission for Scotland, 1962-84; Member, East Kilbride Development Corporation, 1972-76; Member, Queen's Bodyguard for Scotland (Royal Company of Archers); Member, SMO Knights of Malta, 1956. Recreations: shooting; curling. Address: (h.) Cranley, Cleghorn, Lanark; T.-0555-870 330.

Monteith, Rev. William Graham, MA, BD, BPhil. Minister, Hoy & Walls linked with Flotta and Fara, since 1985; Convener, Business Committee, Presbytery of Orkney, since 1986; b. 14.11.46, Glasgow; m., Angela Mary Faulkner; 1 s. Educ. Ross High School, Tranent; Edinburgh University; York University. Assistant Minister, St. Andrew's, Drumchapel, 1973-74; Minister, Berwick Wallace Green Church, 1974-85. Former Member, Board of Management, Westerlea School for Spastics. Publications: Disability, Faith and Acceptance, 1987; various papers and articles. Recreations: table games; music; philosophy; lazing around beaches. Address: The Manse of the South Isles, Green Hill, Longhope, Stromness, Orkney, KW16 3PG; T.-0856 70 325.

Montgomery, Alan Lauchlan, FCMA. Finance Director, Scottish Television, since 1983; b. 30.5.50, Glasgow; m., Heather; 1 s. Educ. Duncanrig Senior Secondary School, East Kilbride. Finance Controller, Rank Xerox, Scotland, 1973-77; Head of Financial Planning, Scottish & Newcastle Breweries Ltd., 1977-80; Finance Director, Ellerman Travel & Leisure Ltd., 1980-81; Deputy Finance Director, Playtex UK Ltd., 1981-83. Recreations: golf (Buchanan Castle Golf Club); travel; music; theatre/films; current affairs; food and wine; tennis; football; rugby. Address: (b.) Cowcaddens, Glasgow, G2 3PR; T.-041-332 9999.

Montgomery, Sir (Basil Henry) David, 9th Bt, JP, DL. Chairman, Forestry Commission, since 1979; b. 20.3.31; m., Delia Reid; 1 s.; 4 d.; 1 s. (deceased). Educ. Eton. Black Watch, 1949-51; Member, Nature Conservancy Council, 1973-79; Vice-Lieutenant, Kinross-shire, 1966-74; Deputy Lieutenant, Perth and Kinross, since 1975; Hon. LLD, Dundee, 1977.

Montgomery, Daniel David William, BSc. Director, Electrical Contractors' Association of Scotland, since 1975; Director and Secretary, Scottish Joint Industry Board, since 1975; Director, Scottish Electrical Contractors' Insurance Ltd., since 1975; b. 24.9.37, Banton, Stirlingshire; m., Joan Elizabeth Allan; 2 s. Educ. Kilsyth Academy; Glasgow University; Royal College of Science and Technology; Heriot-Watt University. Student apprentice, Fairfield Shipbuilding and Engineering Co. Ltd. and Rolls Royce Ltd.; graduate training, then Organisation and Methods Officer, Joseph Lucas Ltd., Birmingham, and Uniroyal, Edinburgh; joined Electrical Contractors Association of Scotland, 1965, as Assistant to the Chief Executive. Territorial Army Commission, Royal Engineers, 1963-67. Recreations: golf; hill-walking; reading. Address: (b.) 23 Heriot Row, Edinburgh, EH3 6EW; T.-031-225 7221.

Montgomery, Rev. Robert Aitken. Parish Minister, Quarrier's village, since 1986; Chaplain, Quarrier's Homes, since 1978; b. 25.7.27, Ruthwell, Dumfries; m., Elizabeth Hay; 2 s. Educ. Hutchesons' Grammar School; Glasgow University and Trinity College. Parish Minister: Portsoy, 1955, Fordyce, 1972. Moderator: Presbytery of Fordyce, 1965, of Strathbogie and Fordyce, 1972, of Greenock, 1983; Chairman, various Committees, County of Banff and Grampian Region, until 1978; Chairman, Abbeyfield Quarrier's Society. Recreations: fishing; hill-walking. Address: The Manse, Quarrier's village, Bridge of Weir, Renfrewshire; T.-0505 690498.

Moon, Brenda Elizabeth, MA, FLA. Librarian, Edinburgh University, since 1980; b. 11.4.31, Stoke on Trent. Educ. Oxford University. Assistant Librarian, Sheffield University, 1955-62; Sub-Librarian, then Deputy Librarian, Hull University, 1962-79. Recreations: walking; gardening; canal cruising. Address: (b.) Edinburgh University Library, George Square, Edinburgh; T.-031-667 1011.

Moonie, Lewis George, MB, ChB, MSc, MRCPsych, MFCM. MP (Labour), Kirkcaldy, since 1987; b. 25.2.47; m.; 2 c. Educ. Grove Academy, Dundee; St. Andrews University. Former Senior Registrar (Community Medicine) and Community Medicine Specialist, Fife Health Board; former Member, Fife Regional Council.

Moore, Andrew F., BL. Chief Officer, SCOTBEC, 1980-87 (seconded by SCOTVEC to Stirling University, 1987); b. 5.12.39, Leven; m., Anne MacGregor; 2 s.; 1 d. Educ. Buckhaven High School; Edinburgh University. Examiner, Estate Duty Office, Edinburgh, 1958-63; Assistant, then Depute Secretary, Scottish Council for Commercial Education, 1963-73; Depute Chief Officer, Scottish Business Education Council, 1973-80. Governor, Scottish Council for Educational Technology, 1976-84; Director, Filmhouse, Edinburgh, 1980-85; Honorary Treasurer, British Association for Commercial and Industrial Education, 1979-81; President, Pedagogical Committee, International Society for Business Education and Member, ISBE/SIEC Executive; Member/Trustee, Levenmouth Enterprise Trust; Member, Scottish Council for Research in Education, 1984-87; Hon. Secretary, Scottish Students' Song Book Committee Ltd.; Session Clerk, Scoonie Kirk, Leven; President, Leven YMCA. Recreations: golf; youth work. Address: (h.) Annandale, Linksfield Street, Leven, Fife; T.-Leven 26984.

Moore, Kenneth William, BSc, PhD. Head, Housing (Private Sector) Division, Scottish Development Department, since 1987; b. 31.5.41, Glasgow; m., Sheila Blackwood; 2 d. Educ. Allan Glen's School, Glasgow; Glasgow University. Joined Civil Service, 1967; variously responsible for Land Tenure Reform, Health Services, Scottish Development Agency; Finance Officer, Scottish Education Department, 1980-83, and Department of Agriculture and Fisheries for Scotland, 1983-84; Head, Local Government Division, 1984-87. Recreations: hill-walking; mathematics and computing; cycling; language and languages; bird-watching; music. Address: (h.) 22 Morningside Park, Edinburgh; T.-031-447 2051.

Moore, Michael Ritchie, BSc, PhD, DSc. Senior Lecturer in Medicine, Glasgow University, since 1982; b. 24.1.44, Glasgow; m., Alice Briscoe; 1 s.; 2 d. Educ. Falkirk High School; Glasgow University. Glasgow University: Research Assistant, Department of Medicine, 1967, Department of Materia Medica, 1970, Research Fellow, 1973, Lecturer in Materia Medica, 1975, in Medicine, 1978; Chief Professional Officer, Groote Schuur Hospital, Cape Town, 1982; Senior Research Fellow, MRC/UCT Porphyrias Unit, Cape Town University, 1983. Chairman, Kilsyth Community Council, 1985; Secretary and Director, Clock Theatre, Kilsyth, 1984; Committee Member, Tetrapyrrole Discussion Group, 1975. Publication: Disorders of Porphyrin Metabolism, 1987. Recreations: rock climbing and hill-walking; photography; amateur dramatics; gardening. Address: (b.) Porphyrias Unit, University Department of Medicine, Western Infirmary, Glasgow, G11 6NT; T.-041-339 8822.

Moore, Professor Robert Samuel, BA, PhD. Professor of Sociology, Aberdeen University, since 1976 (Head, Department of Sociology, since 1975); b. 3.6.36, Beckenham, Kent; m., Lindy Ruth Parker; 1 s.; 1 d. Educ. Beckenham and Penge County Grammar School for Boys; Hull University. Royal Navy, 1952-61; Research Associate, Birmingham University, 1964-65; Lecturer, Durham University, 1965-70; Senior Lecturer, then Reader, Aberdeen University, 1971-76. Council Member: Institute of Race Relations, 1972-80, British Association for the Advancement of Science, 1969-76 and 1979-84 (President, Sociology Section, 1984-85); Executive Member, British Sociological Association (former Treasurer, Chairman, 1981-82); Chair, Editorial Board, Sociology, 1984-87; Member, CNAA Social Research Sub-Committee, 1983-87, and CNAA Sociological Studies Board, 1984-87. Publications: Race, Community and Conflict (Co-author), 1967; Pitmen Preachers and Politics, 1974; Slamming The Door: The Administration of Immigration Control (Co-author), 1975; Racism and Black Resistance, 1975; The Social Impact of Oil, 1982. Recreations: gardening; photography. Address: (b.) Department of Sociology, Aberdeen University, Aberdeen, AB9 2TY; T.-0224 272760.

Moorhouse, Professor Robert Gordon, MA, PhD, CPhys, FInstP, FRSE. Titular Professor, Department of Physics and Astronomy (formerly Department of Natural Philosophy), Glasgow University, since 1968; b. 14.3.26, Huddersfield; m., Peggy Gee; 1 s. Educ. Huddersfield College; Cambridge University. Research Fellow and Lecturer, Natural Philosophy, Glasgow University, 1950-61; Principal Scientific Officer, Rutherford-Appleton Laboratory (Science and Engineering Research Council), 1961-67; Reader, Glasgow University, 1967-68. Publication: The Pion-Nucleon System (Co-author). Address: (b.) Department of Physics and Astronomy, Glasgow University, Glasgow, G12 8QQ; T.-041-339 8855.

Moray, Earl of (Douglas John Moray Stuart), BA, FRICS. Chairman, Moray Estates Development Co., since 1974; b. 13.2.28, Johannesburg; m., Malvina Dorothea Murray; 1 s.; 1 d. Educ. Hilton College, Natal; Trinity College, Cambridge. Address: (h.) Darnaway Castle, Forres, Moray.

More, Ian Aitken Ross, BSc, MB, ChB, PhD, MD, FRCPath. Senior Lecturer, Department of Pathology, Glasgow University, since 1978; Consultant, Greater Glasgow Health Board, since 1978; b. 8.8.41, Motherwell; m., Eleanor Russell Gibson. Educ. Hamilton Academy; Glasgow University. BEIT Medical Research Fellow, 1968-71; Lecturer, Glasgow University, 1972-78. Recreations: photography; gardening; electronics. Address: (b.) Pathology Department, Western Infirmary, Glasgow; T.-041-339 8822, Ext. 522.

More, Magnus, MA, BSc, DipEd. Director of Education, Fife Regional Council, since 1985; b. 2.2.34, Wick; m., Audrey; 3 s. Educ. Wick High School; St. Andrews University/Dundee College of Education. Teacher, Oban High School, 1959-62; Principal Teacher, Queen Anne High School, Dunfermline, 1962-67; Assistant Director of Education, Aberdeen County Council, 1967-69; Fife County Council: Assistant Director of Education, 1969-71, Senior Assistant Director of Education, 1971-75, Senior Depute Director of Education, 1975-84. First Chairman, Committee on Special Educational Needs, Consultative Committee on the Curriculum; Member: Convocation, Heriot-Watt University; General Teaching Council; Scottish Committee for Staff Development in Education; Board of Governors, Moray House College; President, Association of Directors of Education in Scotland. Recreations: swimming; golf; gardening. Address: (b.) Fife House, North Street, Glenrothes, Fife, KY7 5LT.

Morgan, Edwin (George), OBE, MA, Hon. DLitt (Loughborough). Freelance Writer (Poet, Critic, Translator), since 1980; Emeritus Professor of English, Glasgow University, since 1980; Visiting Professor of English, Strathclyde University, since 1987; b. 27.4.20, Glasgow. Educ. Rutherglen Academy; High School of Glasgow; Glasgow University. War Service, Royal Army Medical Corps, 1940-46; Glasgow University: Assistant Lecturer in English, 1947, Lecturer, 1950, Senior Lecturer, 1965, Reader, 1971, Titular Professor, 1975; received Cholmondeley Award for Poets, 1968; Hungarian PEN Memorial Medal, 1972; Scottish Arts Council Book Awards, 1968, 1973, 1977, 1978, 1983, 1985; Saltire Society and Royal Bank Scottish Literary Award, 1983; Soros Translation Award (New York), 1985. Publications: (poetry): The Vision of Cathkin Braes, 1952, Beowulf, 1952, The Cape of Good Hope, 1955, Poems from Eugenio Montale, 1959, Sovpoems, 1961, Collins Albatross Book of Longer Poems (Editor), 1963, Starryveldt, 1965, Emergent Poems, 1967, Gnomes, 1968, The Second Life, 1968, Proverbfolder, 1969, Twelve Songs, 1970, The Horseman's Word, 1970, Scottish Poetry 1-6 (Co-Editor), 1966-72; Glasgow Sonnets, 1972, Wi the Haill Voice, 1972, The Whittrick, 1973, From Glasgow to Saturn, 1973, Fifty Renascence Love-Poems, 1975, Rites of Passage, 1976, The New Divan, 1977, Colour Poems, 1978, Platen: Selected Poems, 1978, Star Gate, 1979, Scottish Satirical Verse (Editor), 1980, Poems of Thirty Years, 1982, Grafts/Takes, 1983, Sonnets from Scotland, 1984, Selected Poems, 1985, From the Video Box, 1986, Themes on a Variation, 1988; prose: Essays, 1974, East European Poets, 1976, Hugh MacDiarmid, 1976, Twentieth Century Scottish Classics, 1987; plays: The Apple-Tree, 1982, Master Peter Pathelin, 1983. Address: (h.) 19 Whittingehame Court, Glasgow, G12 OBG; T.-041-339 6260.

Morgan, Professor Henry Gemmell, BSc, MB, ChB, FRCPEdin, FRCPGlas, FRCPath, FRSE. Professor of Pathological Biochemistry, Glasgow University, since 1965; Director, Institute of Biochemistry, Glasgow Royal Infirmary, 1967-88; President, Association of Clinical Biochemists, UK, 1985-87; b. 25.12.22, Dundee; m., Margaret Duncan; 1 d. Educ. Merchiston Castle School, Edinburgh; St. Andrews University. Local Defence Volunteers/Home Guard, 1940-44; Lecturer/Senior Lecturer in Pathology, St. Andrews University, 1948-65; Research Fellow, Johns Hopkins Medical School, Baltimore, 1956; Adviser to SHDD, WRHB, GGHB, London University etc.; Chairman, Medical Staff Committee, Glasgow Royal Infirmary, since 1984; former External Examiner, Universities of Dublin, Leeds and Newcastle; Secretary, Forfarshire Medical Association, 1960-65. Recreation: travel abroad. Address: (h.) Firwood House, 8 Eaglesham Road, Newton Mearns, Glasgow, G77 5BG.

Morgan, Robin Milne, MA, BA. Principal, Daniel Stewart's and Melville College, since 1977, and The Mary Erskine School, since 1979; b. 2.10.30, Stonehaven; m., Fiona Bruce MacLeod Douglas; 3 s.; 1 d. Educ. Mackie Academy, Stonehaven; Aberdeen University; London University. 2nd Lt., Gordon Highlanders, 1952-54; Assistant Master: Arden House Preparatory School, 1955-60, George Watson's College, 1960-71; Headmaster, Campbell College, Belfast, 1971-76. Recreations: music; archaeology; fishing; climbing; deer-stalking. Address: (b.) Queensferry Road, Edinburgh, EH4 3EZ.

Morgan, Tom, CBE, DL, OStJ, JP, NDD, CDD; b. 24.2.14, Aberdeenshire; m., Mary Montgomery McLauchlan; 2 s. Educ. Longside School; West of Scotland College of Agriculture. Unigate PLC, 38 years (Regional Director, Scotland); Councillor, City of Edinburgh Council, 1954-71, City of Edinburgh District Council, 1977-84; City Treasurer, 1968-71; Lord Provost and Lord Lieutenant, 1980-84; Chairman, Edinburgh Military Tattoo and Edinburgh International Festival, 1980-84. Recreations: golf; gardening. Address: (h.) 400 Lanark Road, Edinburgh, EH13 0LX; T.-031-441 3245.

Morison, Hon. Lord (Alastair Malcolm Morison), QC, MA, LLB. Senator of the College of Justice, since 1985; b. 12.2.31, Edinburgh; m., Birgitte Hendil; 1 s., 1 d. by pr. m. Educ. Winchester College; Edinburgh University. Advocate, 1956. Recreation: fishing. Address: (h.) 6 Carlton Terrace, Edinburgh, EH7 5DD; T.-031-556 6766.

Morison, Hugh, MA, DipEd. Under Secretary, Industry Department for Scotland, since 1988; b. 22.11.43, Bognor Regis; m., Marion H. Smithers; 2 d. Educ. Chichester High School for Boys; St. Catherine's College, Oxford. Assistant Principal, Scottish Home and Health Department, 1966-69; Private Secretary to Minister of State, Scottish Office, 1969-70; Principal: Scottish Education Department, 1971-73, Scottish Economic Planning Department, 1973-79 (seconded to Offshore Supplies Office, Department of Energy, 1974-75); Assistant Secretary, Scottish Economic Planning Department, 1979-82; Gwilym Gibbon Research Fellow, Nuffield College, Oxford, 1982-83; Assistant Secretary, Scottish Development Department, 1983-84; Under Secretary, Scottish Home and Health Department, 1984-88. Member of Vestry, St. John's Episcopal Church, Edinburgh. Publication: The Regeneration of Local Economies, 1987. Recreations: sailing; cycling; hill-walking; archaeology. Address: (b.) Alhambra House, 45 Waterloo Street, Glasgow, G2 6AT; T.-041-248 2855.

Morley, Kenneth Donald, BMedBiol (Hons), MB, FRCPEdin, FRACP. Consultant General Physician and Rheumatologist, since 1982; b. 16.4.49, Ripon; m., Susan Margaret Bell Tawse; 2 s.; 1 d. Educ. Dame Allan's Boys School, Newcastle; Aberdeen University. Formerly General Medical Registrar, Christchurch Hospitals, New Zealand; Arthritis and Rheumatism Council Copeman Research Fellow and Honorary Senior Registrar, Hammersmith Hospital, London. Recreations: family; DIY; gardening; hill-walking. Address: (h.) 9 Burnside Road, Invergowrie, Dundee; T.-0382 562673.

Morley, William Neil, RD*, MB, ChB, FRCPEdin, FRCPGlas. Consultant Dermatologist; Civil Consultant to Royal Navy, since 1976; Consultant, Western Infirmary and Royal Hospital for Sick Children, Glasgow, since 1963; Member, Medical Appeal Tribunal, DHSS, since 1977; b. 16.2.30, Bradford; m., Dr. Patricia Morley; 3 s.; 1 d. Educ. Merchiston Castle School; Edinburgh University. House Surgeon and Physician, Edinburgh Royal Infirmary; Surgeon Lt., RNVR, HMS Falcon, Malta; Assistant, Department of Medicine, Edinburgh University; Registrar and Senior Registrar, Dermatology Department, Edinburgh Royal Infirmary. Past President and Secretary, Royal Medical Society; President, Scottish Dermatological Society, 1985-88. Publication: Colour Atlas of Paediatric Dermatology. Recreations: golf; gardening. Address: (h.) Parkhall, Balfron, Glasgow, G63; T.-Balfron 40124.

Morrell, David William James, MA, LLB. Registrar and Secretary, Strathclyde University, since 1973; b. 26.7.33, Glasgow; m., Margaret; 2 s.; 1 d. Educ. George Watson's Boys' College, Edinburgh; Edinburgh University. Administrative Assistant, Durham University, 1957-60; Assistant Registrar and Appointments Officer, Exeter University, 1960-64; Senior Assistant Registrar, Essex University, 1964-66; Academic Registrar, Strathclyde University, 1966-73. Commonwealth Travelling Fellow, 1978; Elder, Church of Scotland. Recreations: hill-walking; fishing; swimming; history of environment. Address: (h.) 29 Barclay Drive, Helensburgh, G84 9RA.

Morrice, Rev. Charles Smith, MA, BD, PhD. Minister, Mauchline Parish Church, since 1976; Convener, Church of Scotland Youth Education Committee, 1984-88; Member, Boys' Brigade Scottish Executive Committee, since 1980; b. 1.12.31, Leitholm, Coldstream; m., Margaret Elizabeth Sutherland; 2 s.; 1 d. Educ. Peterhead Academy; Aberdeen University; Pacific School of Religion, Berkeley, California. Minister: Newarthill Church, Motherwell, 1959-71, St. Andrew's Scots Presbyterian Church, Buenos Aires, 1971-76. Member, Church of Scotland Board of Education, 1980-88. Recreations: walking; swimming; gardening; organ playing. Address: The Manse of Mauchline, 97 Loudoun Street, Mauchline, Ayrshire, KA5 5BQ; T.-Mauchline 50386.

Morrice, J. Kenneth W., MD, FRCPsych, DPM. Honorary Consultant Psychiatrist, Grampian Health Board, and Honorary Fellow, Aberdeen University; in private practice; b. 14.7.24, Aberdeen; m., Norah Thompson; 1 s.; 2 d. Educ. Robert Gordon's College, Aberdeen; Aberdeen University. Served RNVR as Surgeon Lt.; trained in psychiatry, Crichton Royal, Dumfries, and Aberdeen Royal Infirmary; appointed Consultant, Dingleton Hospital, 1956; Honorary Lecturer in Forensic Psychiatry, Edinburgh University; Visiting Psychiatrist, Edinburgh Prison; Consultant, Fort Logan Mental Health Centre, Denver, 1966-67; Consultant Psychiatrist and Senior Clinical Lecturer, Ross Clinic and Department of Mental Health, Aberdeen. Publications: Crisis Intervention; volumes of poetry. Recreations: golf; TV; reading and writing; walking. Address: (b.) 21 Albyn Place, Aberdeen, AB9 1RJ; T.-Aberdeen 572879.

Morris, Alexander Watt, BSc (Hons), MInstP. Principal, Edinburgh Tutorial College and American School of Edinburgh, since 1976; b. 24.11.46, Dunfermline; m., Moira Joan Watson; 1 s. Educ. Dunfermline High School; Edinburgh University. Began teaching career, Musselburgh Grammar School, 1972; Head of Physics, George Watson's Ladies College, 1973 (and to George Watson's College on merger of the schools); founded Edinburgh Tutorial College and American School of Edinburgh. Recreations: good food; hifi; cricket; skiing. Address: (b.) 29 Chester Street, Edinburgh, EH3 7EN; T.-031-225 9888.

Morris, Arthur McGregor, MA, MB, BChir (Cantab), FRCS, FRCSEdin. Consultant Plastic Surgeon, Tayside Health Board, since 1975; Honorary Senior Lecturer in Surgery, Dundee University, since 1975; b. 6.5.41, Heswall, Wirral; m., Victoria Margaret Whitaker; 1 s.; 1 d. Educ. Dulwich College; Selwyn College, Cambridge; Guy's Hospital. House Officer, Guy's Hospital, 1965-66; Anatomy Demonstrator, Newcastle University, 1966-67; Senior House Officer in Surgery, Bristol, 1967-69; Research Registrar, then Casualty Registrar, Guy's Hospital, 1969-71; Plastic Surgery Registrar, Canniesburn Hospital, Glasgow, 1972; Plastic Surgery Senior Registrar, Bangour General Hospital, 1972-75. Recreations: golf; curling; photography; bee-keeping. Address: (b.) Tayside Plastic Surgery Unit, Dundee Royal Infirmary, Dundee; T.-Dundee 23125.

Morris, Arthur Stephen, BA, MA, PhD. Senior Lecturer, Department of Geography, Glasgow University; b. 26.12.36, Broadway, Worcestershire; m., Estela C.; 1 s.; 1 d. Educ. Chipping Campden; Exeter College, Oxford University; University of Maryland; University of Wisconsin. Instructor/Assistant Professor, Western Michigan University, 1964-67; joined Glasgow University as Lecturer, 1967. Publications: South America,

1979; Latin America, 1981. Recreations: gardening; sailing. Address: (h.) The Old Manse, Shandon, near Helensburgh; T.-041-339 8855.

Morris, Jean Daveena Ogilvy, MBE, MA, MEd. Chairman, Parole Board for Scotland, since 1980; b. 28.1.29, Kilmarnock; m., Rev. William J. Morris (qv); 1 s. Educ. Kilmarnock Academy; St. Andrews University. Clinical Psychologist: Royal Hospital for Sick Children, Edinburgh, St. David's Hospital, Cardiff, and Church Village, Pontypridd; Member, Bailie and Convener of Housing, Peterhead Town Council; Member, Aberdeen County Council; Columnist, Aberdeen Press and Journal; Chairman, Christian Action Housing Association; Member, Scottish Federation of Housing Associations; Chairman, Government Committee on Links Between Housing and Social Work (Morris Committee); Chairman, Local Review Committee, Barlinnie Prison. Badminton Blue, St. Andrews University. Recreations: swimming; holidays in France. Address: (h.) 94 St. Andrews Drive, Glasgow, G41 4RX; T.-041-427 2757.

Morris, John Howell, BSc, PhD, DSc, CChem, FRSC. Reader in Inorganic Chemistry, Strathclyde University, since 1986; b. 21.3.38, Cardiff; m., Bethia Reynolds; 3 d. Educ. Cardiff High School; Nottingham University. Research Fellow, Harvard University, 1961-62; Senior Research Associate, Newcastle-upon-Tyne University, 1962-65; Lecturer, then Senior Lecturer, Kingston-upon-Thames College of Technology, 1965-68; Lecturer in Inorganic Chemistry, Strathclyde University, 1968-75, Senior Lecturer, 1975-86; Visiting Associate Professor, Wisconsin University, 1976, Visiting Professor, 1986. Recreation: sailing. Address: (b.) Department of Pure and Applied Chemistry, 295 Cathedral Street, Glasgow, G1 1XL; T.-041-552 4400.

Morris, William, BA, FIOP. Principal, Anniesland College, since 1981; b. 15.5.24, Aberdare, Wales; m., Pauline; 1 s.; 2 d. Educ. Aberdare Boys' Secondary School; Cardiff School of Art; Garnet College, London; London School of Printing and Graphic Arts; Open University. Compositor/Typographer; Lecturer in Typography; Head, Department of Typography and Related Subjects; Depute Principal, Glasgow College of Building and Printing; Board Member, Printing and Publishing Industry Training Board; Member, City and Guilds of London Institute; Board Member and Director, Scottish Vocational Education Council; Chairman, Association of Principals of Colleges (Scottish Branch); Secretary of the Vestry, St. Cyprian's Church, Lenzie; Chairman, Foundation Committee, Kelvin Rotary Club. Recreations: golf; gardening. Address: (h.) 26 Laurel Avenue, Lenzie, Kirkintilloch, Glasgow, G66 4RU; T.-041-776 2716.

Morris, Rev. William James, JP, BA, BD, PhD, LLD, DD, Hon. FRCP&SGlas. Minister, Glasgow Cathedral, since 1967; Chaplain in Ordinary to The Queen in Scotland, since 1969; Chairman, Iona Cathedral Trust, since 1979; b. 22.8.25, Cardiff; m., Jean Daveena Ogilvy Howie (see Jean Daveena Ogilvy Morris); 1 s. Educ. Cardiff High School; University of Wales (Cardiff and Aberystwyth); Edinburgh University. Ordained, 1951; Assistant, Canongate Kirk, Edinburgh, 1949-51; Minister, Barry Island and Cadoxton Presbyterian Church of Wales, 1951-53; Minister: St. David's, Buckhaven, 1953-57, Peterhead Old Parish Church, 1957-67; Chaplain, Peterhead Prison, 1963-67; Chaplain to Lord High Commissioner, 1975-76; Moderator, Deer Presbytery, 1965-66; now Chaplain: Strathclyde Police, Glasgow Academy, High School of Glasgow, Glasgow District Council, Trades House of Glasgow, Glasgow YMCA, West of Scotland Engineers Association, Royal Scottish Automobile Club; Member, Independent Broadcasting Authority, 1979-84 (Chairman, Scottish Advisory Committee); Member, Council of Management, Quarrier's Homes; Member, Convocation, Strathclyde University; Governor, Jordanhill College of Education; Member, Scottish Committee, British Sailors Society; Honorary President, Glasgow Society of Social Service. Publication: A Walk Through Glasgow Cathedral, 1986. Recreation: being good, careful, and happy (not always simultaneously). Address: (h.) 94 St. Andrews Drive, Glasgow, G41 4RX; T.-041-427 2757.

Morrison, Rev. Alistair Hogarth, BTh, DipYCS. Minister, Elgin High Church, since 1985; b. 12.9.43, Glasgow; m., Grace; 1 s.; 1 d. Educ. Jordanhill College School; Aberdeen University. City of Glasgow/Strathclyde Police, 1962-81 (Inspector). Strathclyde Medal for Bravery, 1975. Recreation: hill-walking. Address: 29 Moray Street, Elgin, IV30 1JH; T.-0343 2449.

Morrison, Andrew Neil, MIFireE, DipEdTech. Firemaster, Grampian Region, since 1985; b. 8.9.37, Arbroath; m., Kathleen; 1 s. Educ. Arbroath High School; Dundee College of Technology. Armourer, REME, serving in Malaya, Singapore and Berlin (gained GSM and clasp); joined Fire Service, 1962, with Tayside (then Angus) fire Brigade; joined Grampian as Deputy Firemaster, 1980. Secretary, District No. 7 (Scotland), Chief and Assistant Chief Fire Officers Association. Recreations: golf; curling; swimming. Address: (b.) 19 North Anderson Drive, Aberdeen; T.-0224 696666.

Morrison, Rev. Angus Wilson, MA, BD. Minister, Braid Parish Church, Edinburgh, since 1977; b. 14.2.34, Glasgow; m., Isobel M.S. Taylor; 1 s.; 2 d. Educ. Epsom College, Surrey; Trinity College, Oxford; New College, Edinburgh. Minister: Whithorn, 1961-67, Cults West, Aberdeen, 1967-77; various periods of service on General Assembly Committees, including Overseas Council, Inter-Church Relations, Board of Education and Selection Schools; Observer for World Alliance of Reformed Churches, Vatican Council II, 1963. Recreations: travel; family. Address: 2 Cluny Avenue, Edinburgh, EH10 4RN; T.-031-447 1871.

Morrison, David, ALA. Poet; Short Story Writer; Painter; Sculptor; b. 4.8.41, Glasgow; m., Edna; 1 s.; 1 d. Educ. various schools; Strathclyde University. County Librarian (Caithness), 1972-75; Wick Branch Librarian, Highland Regional Council, since 1981; Editor, Scotia Rampant, since 1985; Promoter, Pulteney Press, since 1985; Organiser, poetry/music events in Caithness; Organiser, Wick Festival of Poetry, Folk and Jazz, seven years; Editor, Scotia Review, 10 years; always Scottish patriot. Recreations: working for Scottish literature and Scotland as a nation; painting; sculpture. Address: (h.) 3 Moray Street, Wick, Caithness; T.-Wick 3703.

Morrison, Donald, BA (Hons), DipComm. Principal, Reid Kerr College, Paisley, since 1987; b. 31.3.42, Durness; m., Carole Davidson; 2 d. Educ. Dornoch Academy; Strathclyde University. Senior Lecturer, Clydebank College, 1965-70; Head, Department of Business Studies, then Depute Principal, James Watt College, Greenock, 1970-87. Recreations: fishing; caravanning; clay pigeon shooting. Address: (b.) Renfrew Road, Paisley, PA3 4DR; T.-041-889 4225.

Morrison, James, ARSA, RSW, DA, DUniv (Stirling). Painter in oil and watercolour; b. 11.4.32, Glasgow; m., Dorothy McCormack; 1 s.; 1 d. Educ. Hillhead High School; Glasgow School of Art. Taught part-time, 1955-58; won Torrance Memorial Prize, RGI, 1958; Visiting Artist, Hospitalfield, 1962-63; Council Member, SSA, 1964-67; staff, Duncan of Jordanstone College of Art, 1965-87; won Arts Council Travelling Scholarship to Greece, 1968; painting in various regions of France, 1976-82; numerous one-man exhibitions since 1956, in Scotland, London, Italy, West Germany, Canada; four works in private collection of Duke of Edinburgh and numerous other works in public and private collections; several group exhibitions since 1980 in UK and Europe. Publication: Aff the Squerr. Recreation: playing in a chamber music group. Address: (h.) Craigview House, Usan, Montrose, Angus; T.-Montrose 72639.

Morrison, Peter, MA, LLB. Singer and Solicitor; b. 14.8.40, Greenock; m., Irene; 1 s.; 1 d. Educ. Greenock Academy; Glasgow University. Town Clerk's Department: Paisley, 1965, Clydebank, 1966-68; private legal practice thereafter; established own legal practice, 1977; began professional singing engagements at University; passed BBC audition, 1969, and began solo broadcasts; first television series, Castles in the Air, 1971; numerous radio, television and theatre appearances in UK and abroad. Recreations: golf; tennis; non-participating cricket and rugby supporter. Address: (b.) 65 Bath Street, Glasgow; T.-041-331 1029.

Morrison, Peter Angus. Member, Crofters Commission, since 1984; Director, Lewis Land Services Ltd.; b. 31.12.45, Isle of Lewis; m., Murdina; 2 d. Educ. Shawbost School; Lews Castle College. Mechanical engineering apprenticeship, then draughtsman, William Beardmore & Co., Glasgow; contracts draughtsman, John Brown Engineering, Clydebank; Lecturer in Mechanical Engineering, Springburn College of Engineering; Senior Lecturer, Engineering Department, Lews Castle College. Recreation: travel. Address: (h.) 52 Newmarket, Stornoway, Lewis; T.-0851 5338.

Morrison, Rev. Roderick, MA, BD. Minister, High Church, Stornoway, Lewis, since 1981; b. 3.7.43, Lochmaddy; m., Christina Ann MacDonald; 1 s.; 1 d. Educ. Lochportan Public School; Glasgow University and Trinity College. Assistant Minister, Drumchapel Old Parish Church, Glasgow, 1973-74; Minister, Carinish Parish Church, North Uist, 1974-81. Recreations: sailing; fishing; shooting. Address: High Church Manse, 1 Goathill Road, Stornoway, Isle of Lewis; T.-Stornoway 3106.

Morrison, Professor Ronald, BSc, MSc, PhD. Professor of Software Engineering, St. Andrews University, since 1985; b. 15.4.46, Glasgow; m., Ann Margaret MacDonald; 1 s.; 1 d. Educ. Eastbank Academy, Glasgow; Strathclyde University; Glasgow University; St. Andrews University. Systems Programmer, Glasgow University, 1968-71; Senior Research Fellow, Lecturer, Reader, St. Andrews University, 1971-85. Past President, Scottish Cross Country Union. Recreations: cross country running; golf. Address: (h.) 8 Trinity Place, St. Andrews, KY16 8SG; T.-0334 75649.

Morrison, William Garth, BA, CEng, MIEE, DL. Farmer; Chief Scout, since 1988; Chief Commissioner of Scotland, The Scout Association, 1981-88; b. 8.4.43, Edinburgh; m., Gillian Cheetham; 2 s.; 1 d. Educ. Pangbourne College; Pembroke College, Cambridge. Service, Royal Navy, 1961-73, retiring with rank of Lt.; farming, since 1973; appointed Director, Scotfresh Ltd., formerly Elba Growers Ltd., 1975; Member, Lothian Region Children's Panel, 1976-83 (Chairman, Midlothian/East Lothian Area Panel, 1978-81); Lamp of Lothian Trustee, 1978; Member, Lothian, Borders and Fife Committee, Prince's Trust, 1979, Lothian and Borders Committee, Prince's and Royal Jubilee Trusts, 1983-88; Member, Society of High Constables of Holyroodhouse, 1979; Deputy Lieutenant, East Lothian, 1984. Recreations: golf; sailing; Scouting. Address: West Fenton, North Berwick, East Lothian; T.-0620 842154.

Morrison, Professor William Russell, BSc, PhD, DSc, FIFST, FRSE. Professor of Food Science, Strathclyde University; b. 14.1.32, Glasgow; m., Anne Ker; 2 s.; 1 d. Educ. High School of Glasgow; Royal College of Science and Technology. Address: (b.) Food Science Division, Strathclyde University, 131 Albion Street, Glasgow, G1 1SD; T.-041-552 4400, Ext. 2209.

Morrocco, Alberto, RSA, RSW, RP, RGI, LLD, DUniv. Painter, since 1938; b. 14.12.17, Aberdeen; 2 s.; 1 d. Educ. Sunnybank School, Aberdeen; Gray's School of Art, Aberdeen. Former Member, Grants Committee, Scottish Arts Council; Member, Royal Fine Art Commission for Scotland. Carnegie Award and Guthrie Award, Royal Scottish Academy; San Vito Romano Prize. Address: Binrock, 456 Perth Road, Dundee; T.-0382 69319.

Morsbach, Helmut, MSc, PhD. Reader in Social Psychology, Glasgow University, since 1983; b. 2.8.37, Rondebosch, South Africa; 2 d. Educ. Bonn University; Stellenbosch University; Hamburg University; Cape Town University. Lecturer in Psychology, Rhodes University, Grahamstown, South Africa, 1964-67; Assistant Professor in Psychology, International Christian University, Tokyo, 1967-69; Lecturer, then Senior Lecturer in Social Psychology, Glasgow University, since 1969. Visiting Professor, International Christian University, 1972, 1987; Volkswagen Foundation

Grant for studies on Japan, 1977-80; Snell Visitor, Balliol College, Oxford, 1982. Recreation: gliding. Address: (b.) Department of Psychology, Glasgow University, Glasgow, G12 8RT; T.-041-339 8855, Ext. 5085.

Morton, Rev. Alasdair J., MA, BD, DipEd, DipRE, FEIS. General Secretary, Department of Education, Church of Scotland, since 1977; b. 8.6.34, Inverness; m., Gillian M. Richards; 2 s.; 2 d. Educ. Bell-Baxter School, Cupar; St. Andrews University; Hartford Theological Seminary. District Missionary/Minister, Zambia (Northern Rhodesia), 1960-65; Chaplain and Religious Education Lecturer, Malcolm Moffat Teachers' College, Serenje, Zambia, 1966-67; Principal, David Livingstone Teachers' College, Livingstone, Zambia, 1968-72; Minister, Greyfriars Parish Church, Dumfries, 1973-77. Recreations: choral singing; gardening. Address: (b.) 121 George Street, Edinburgh, EH2 4YN; T.-031-225 5722.

Morton, Hugh Gloag, MB, ChB, DPM, FRCPsych. Consultant Child and Adolescent Psychiatrist, Tayside Health Board, since 1975; Honorary Senior Lecturer in Psychiatry, Dundee University, since 1975; b. 2.6.43, Perth; m., Isobel Patricia Blair Campbell; 2 s.; 1 d. Educ. Strathallan; St. Andrews University. Training appointments, Dundee Psychiatric Services, 1968-71; Lecturer in Psychiatry, Dundee University, 1971-73; Senior Registrar in Child and Adolescent Psychiatry, St. George's Hospital, London, and Queen Mary's Hospital for Children, Carshalton, 1973-75; Member, Child and Adolescent Mental Health Working Group, Scottish Health Service Planning Council, 1978-83. Publication: Psychiatric Problems in Childhood - A Guide for Nurses (Co-author), 1983. Recreations: classical music; fishing; railways; boating; walking. Address: (h.) 7 Viewmount Road, Wormit, Fife, DD6 8NJ; T.-Newport on Tay 541742.

Morton, 22nd Earl of (John Charles Sholto Douglas), DL; b. 19.3.27; m., Sheila Mary Gibbs; 2 s.; 1 d. Deputy Lieutenant, West Lothian, since 1982.

Morton, William F., MA (Hons). Rector, Coltness High School, Wishaw, since 1974; b. 28.3.32, Glasgow; m., Ena Nicol; 1 d. Educ. Bishopbriggs Higher Grade School; Albert Secondary School, Glasgow; Glasgow University. Hamilton Academy: Teacher, 1956, Special Assistant, 1961, Principal Teacher of English, 1968; Assistant Head Teacher, Hamilton Grammar School, 1973-74. Secretary, Lanarkshire County English Committee, 1971-74; Examiner for Higher Grade English, Scottish Examination Board, 1972-75; Honorary Vice-President, Hamilton Golf Club, since 1981 (Captain, 1976-78); President, Lanarkshire Golf Association, 1974. Address: (h.) The Coach House, Woodlands Gate, Wishaw, Lanarkshire; T.-0698 384790.

Mould, David John, FILAM, MInstBCA. Director of Amenity and Recreation, Falkirk District Council, since 1980; b. 27.5.29, Dundee; 1 s.; 1 d. Educ. Grove Academy. Assistant Parks Superintendent, Carlisle CBC, 1955-60; Deputy Parks and Cemeteries Superintendent, Hornchurch UDC, 1960-65; Assistant Parks Superintendent, then Deputy Head of Recreation and Amenities, then Head of Recreation and Amenities, LB of Havering. Recreations: Church treasurer; country lover; theatre-goer. Address: 8b.) Kilns House, Kilns Road, Falkirk, FK1 5SA; T.-Falkirk 24911.

Moule, Brian, MB, BCh, DMRD, FRCR, MRCP(Glas). Consultant Radiologist, Glasgow Royal Infirmary, since 1966; Honorary Clinical Lecturer, Glasgow University, since 1966; b. 19.9.34, Briton Ferry, Wales; m., Isabel Claire Moule; 1 s.; 1 d. Educ. Neath Grammar School; Welsh National School of Medicine, Cardiff. House Officer in Medicine, then Surgery, Cardiff, 1957-58; Captain, RAMC, 1959-60; Registrar, Senior Registrar in Radiology, 1961-66. Recreations: golf; cricket; walking; reading; music. Address: (h.) Larachmhor, Drymen, Glasgow; T.-036 060 313.

Moule, Rev. Gerald Christopher, BA, BD. Minister, Moffat linked with Wamphray, since 1975; b. 31.8.45, Guildford; m., Patricia Rosemary Parker; 1 s.; 2 d. Educ. Edinburgh Academy; Kelvinside Academy, Glasgow; St. Andrews University; Newcastle upon Tyne University; New College, Edinburgh. Chartered Accountancy articles with Chalmers, Impey & Co., London; Assistant Minister, West Church of St. Nicholas, Aberdeen, 1973-75. Moderator, Presbytery of Annandale and Eskdale, 1980-81 and 1988-89; Secretary and Treasurer, Scottish Journal of Theology. Recreations: cricket; swimming; travel; hill-walking; gardening. Address: St. Andrew's Manse, Moffat, Dumfriesshire, DG10 9EJ; T.-Moffat 20128.

Mountain, Peter, LRAM, FRAM, FRSAMD. Violinist and Conductor; Head, Strings Department, Royal Scottish Academy of Music and Drama, since 1975; Chief String Coach, National Youth Orchestra of Scotland, since 1979; Chairman of Council, Scottish Society of Composers; b. 3.10.23, Shipley; m., Angela Dale; 1 s.; 2 d. Educ. Bingley Grammar School; Royal Academy of Music, London. Wartime Service, Royal Marines; Member, Boyd Neel String Orchestra, 1948-51; Member, Philharmonia Orchestra, 1951-55; Leader, Royal Liverpool Philharmonic Orchestra, 1955-66; Section Leader, London Philharmonic Orchestra, 1966-68; Concert Master, Academy of the BBC, 1968-75; Soloist with most British orchestras; Leader of own string quartet; wide experience as Adjudicator and Orchestral Coach. Recreations: photography; the countryside; walking. Address: (h.) 2 Kew Terrace, Glasgow, G12 OTD; T.-041-339 2204.

Mowat, Alastair, MA (Hons), MBIM, FIWM, MBII. Chairman, Scottish Brewers Ltd., since 1983; Chairman, Scottish & Newcastle (Sales) Ltd., since 1984; Marketing Director, Scottish & Newcastle Breweries Plc, since 1982; b. 12.3.39; m., Alison; 1 s.; 1 d. Educ. Edinburgh Academy; Edinburgh University. Unilever, 1961-64; joined S & NB, 1964 (various functions, including production, selling, personnel and retailing). Recreations: music (jazz and classical); rugby. Address:

(b.) Scottish & Newcastle Breweries Plc, 111 Holyrood Road, Abbey Brewery, Edinburgh; T.-031-556 2591.

Mowat, Bill, MA (Hons), FInstPet. Member, Highland Regional Council, since 1978; Trustee, Wick Harbour, since 1978; b. 13.5.43, Thurso. Educ. Wick High School; Edinburgh University. Vice-President, Scottish Union of Students, 1965-66; Editor, Caithness Courier, 1966-68; Reporter, Daily Record, since 1968; Director, John O'Groats Crafts Ltd., since 1974; Honorary Secretary, Highland Branch, NUJ, 1975-78; Vice-President, Inverness Trades Council, 1977-78. Address: (h.) Balquholly, John O'Groats, Caithness; T.-0955 81360.

Mowat, David McIvor, JP, MA. Chief Executive, Edinburgh Chamber of Commerce, since 1968; b. 12.3.39, Bournemouth; m., Anne Birtwistle; 3 d. Educ. Edinburgh Academy; Edinburgh University. Vice-Chairman, Edinburgh Tourist Group, 1982; Director, Edinburgh Financial and General Holdings Ltd., 1980; Chief Executive: Chamber Developments Ltd., Edinburgh's Capital Ltd.; President, British Chambers of Commerce Executives, 1987. Recreations: swimming; walking. Address: (b.) 3 Randolph Crescent, Edinburgh; T.-031-225 5851.

Mowat, Sheriff John Stuart, MA, LLB. Sheriff of Glasgow and Strathkelvin, since 1974; b. 30.1.23, Manchester; m., Anne Cameron Renfrew; 2 s.; 2 d. Educ. High School of Glasgow; Merchiston Castle School; Glasgow University. Served RAF Transport Command, 1942-46 (Flt.-Lt.); Journalist, 1947-52; Advocate, 1952-60; Sheriff of Fife and Kinross, at Dunfermline, 1960-72, at Cupar and Kinross, 1972-74. Office-Bearer, Scottish Liberal Party, 1954-58; Parliamentary candidate, Caithness and Sutherland, 1955; Secretary, Sheriffs Association, 1968-75 (Vice-President, 1984); Trustee: Carnegie Dunfermline Trust, 1967-74, Carnegie United Kingdom Trust, 1970-74. Recreations: golf; curling; watching football. Address: (h.) 31 Westbourne Gardens, Glasgow, G12 9PF; T.-041-334 3743; Afton, Port Wemyss, Isle of Islay.

Mowat, Norman Ashley George, MB, ChB, FRCP. Consultant Physician and Gastroenterologist, Aberdeen Teaching Hospitals, since 1975; Clinical Senior Lecturer in Medicine, Aberdeen University, since 1975; b. 11.4.43, Cullen; m., Kathleen Mary Cowie; 1 s.; 2 d. Educ. Fordyce Academy; Aberdeen University. House Officer, then Senior House Officer, then Registrar, Aberdeen Teaching Hospitals, 1966-72; Lecturer in Medicine, Aberdeen University, 1972-73; Lecturer in Gastroenterology and Research Associate, Medical College of St. Bartholomew's, London, 1973-75. Visiting Physician to Shetland Islands; publications include Integrated Clinical Sciences: Gastroenterology (Co-Editor), 1985. Recreations: sailing; golf; soccer; reading; photography. Address: (h.) Bucholie, 13 Kings Cross Road, Aberdeen, AB2 4BF; T.-0224 319223.

Muckart, Rev. Graeme Watson MacKinnon, MTheol, FSA Scot. Minister, Erskine Church, Falkirk, since 1983; b. 11.12.43, Dunfermline; m., Mary Elspeth Small; 1 s.; 1 d. Educ. Royal Naval School, Malta; Willesden County Grammar School; Portsmouth Southern Grammar School; Highbury Technical College, Portsmouth; Leeds College of Art; St. Andrews University. Barclays Bank Trustee Department, 1962-64; Trainee Architect, Hampshire County Council, 1964-69; architectural appointments, 1969-76; Member, Resident Staff, Iona Abbey, 1976-78; Assistant Minister, Carrick Knowe Parish Church, Edinburgh, 1982-83; Convener, Social and Community Interests Committee, Presbytery of Falkirk, since 1985; Member, Church of Scotland Board of Social Responsibility; Member, Church of Scotland Church and Nation Committee; Chairman, Falkirk Council of Churches; Member, Iona Community, since 1978. Recreations: painting; photography; heraldry; reading; walking the dog. Address: Erskine Manse, Burnbrae Road, Falkirk, FK1 5SD; T.-0324 23701.

Muir, Rev. Frederick Comery, MA, BD, ThM, ARCM. Minister, Stepps Parish Church, since 1983; b. 26.11.32, Glasgow; m., Christine Elizabeth Dickie; 1 s.; 1 d. Educ. Kelvinside Academy; Glasgow University; Princeton Theological Seminary. Assistant Minister, Cathcart South Church, Glasgow, 1957-58; Teaching Fellow, Princeton Theological Seminary, 1959-60; Minister: St. James' Church, Lossiemouth, 1961-72, Whitehill Parish Church, Stepps, 1972-83. Instructor of Music, Gordonstoun School, 1967-71; Conductor, Strathkelvin Choral Society, 1973-78; Chairman, Scottish Committee, Royal School of Church Music, since 1986; President, Glasgow Society of Organists, 1983-84. Recreations: music-making; hill-walking. Address: 20 Alexandra Avenue, Stepps, Glasgow, G33 6BP; T.-041-779 2504.

Muir, Sir John (Harling), 3rd Bt, TD, DL. Director, James Finlay & Co. Ltd., 1946-81; Member, Queen's Bodyguard for Scotland (Royal Company of Archers); b. 7.11.10; m.; 5 s.; 2 d. Educ. Stowe. Served Second World War (demobilised with rank of Major); Deputy Lieutenant, Perthshire, since 1966. Address: (h.) Bankhead, Blair Drummond, by Stirling.

Muir, Kenneth Walter, BSc, PhD. Reader in Chemistry, Glasgow University, since 1985; b. 2.9.41, Edinburgh; m., Ljubica; 1 s.; 1 d. Educ. Hutchesons' Boys' Grammar School; Glasgow University. Lecturer: Sussex University, Glasgow University. Recreations: foreign travel; reading; walking. Address: (b.) Department of Chemistry, Glasgow University, Glasgow; T.-041-339 8855.

Muir, Trevor, BA. Chief Executive, Midlothian District Council, since 1987; b. 10.7.49, Glasgow; m., Christine Ann; 1 s.; 1 d. Educ. High School of Glasgow; Langside College; Strathclyde University. Scottish Special Housing Association, 1973-77; City of Glasgow District Council, 1977-81; Director of Housing, City of Aberdeen District Council, 1981-87. Recreation: family life. Address: (b.) 1 Eskdaill Court, Dalkeith, Midlothian; T.-031-663 2881.

Muirhead, Douglas Campbell, OBE, BSc (Hons), CEng, MIProdE, FIMC. Chairman, Ardrossan, Saltcoats and Stevenston Enterprise Trust (ASSET), since 1981; Director, Ardrossan, Saltcoats and Stevenston Enterprise Properties Ltd.

(APL); Deputy Chairman, Irvine Development Corporation, since 1983; Past President, Ayrshire Chamber of Industries; Chairman, Prestwick Airport Consultative Committee; Past Chairman, PA Management Consultants Ltd. and Director, PA International Management Consultants Ltd.; b. 21.2.21, Glasgow; m., Sheila Grace Fenton; 2 s.; 1 d. Educ. Allan Glen's School, Glasgow; Glasgow University. Recreation: travel. Address: (h.) Camlarg, 64 South Beach, Troon, Ayrshire; T.-0292 314920.

Muirshiel, 1st Viscount (John Scott Maclay), KT (1973), CH (1962), CMG (1944), PC (1952), DL. Lord Lieutenant of Renfrewshire, 1967-80; Secretary of State for Scotland, 1957-62; b. 26.10.05; m., Betty L'Estrange Astley (deceased). Educ. Winchester; Trinity College, Cambridge. MP, Montrose Burghs, 1940-50, Renfrewshire West, 1950-64; Minister of Transport and Civil Aviation, 1951-52; Minister of State for Colonial Affairs, 1956-57; President, Assembly of WEU, 1955-56; Director, Clydesdale Bank, 1970-82; Hon. LLD: Edinburgh, 1963, Strathclyde, 1966, Glasgow, 1970. Address: (h.) Knapps, Kilmacolm, Renfrewshire.

Mullen, Ian M., BSc, MRPharmS. Chairman, Pharmaceutical General Council (Scotland), since 1986; Vice-Chairman, National Pharmaceutical Consultative Committee, since 1987; Member, UK Advisory Committee on Borderline Substances, since 1986; b. 11.5.46, Stirling; m., Veronica Drummond; 2 s.; 1 d. Educ. St. Modan's High School, Stirling; Heriot-Watt University. Registered MPS, 1970; self-employed community pharmacist, since 1971; elected to Pharmaceutical General Council, 1974; Vice-Chairman, 1983; Member, Forth Valley Health Board, since 1987. Recreations: walking; golf; swimming. Address: (h.) Ardenlea, 11 Arnothill, Falkirk, FK1 5RZ; T.-0324 21806.

Mulrine, Stephen, MA (Hons). Poet and Playwright; Senior Lecturer in Historical Studies, Glasgow School of Art, since 1983 (Lecturer, 1969-83); Extra-Mural Lecturer in Creative Writing, Glasgow University, since 1970; b. 13.3.37, Glasgow; m., Elizabeth S.K. Lees; 2 s.; 1 d. Educ. St. Mungo's Academy; Glasgow University; Edinburgh University. Member, Board of Directors, Glasgow Citizens' Theatre, since 1971; Member, Drama Committee, Scottish Arts Council, 1983-88; author of six television plays, including The Silly Season (Play for Today), BBC 1, and The House on Kirov Street, BBC; numerous radio plays including serials Deacon Brodie and Mary, Queen of Scots; theatre and poetry criticism. Recreations: theatre-going; reading. Address: (h.) 132 Kingswood Drive, Glasgow, G44 4RB; T.-041-649 2183.

Mundell, Christeen, RGN, SCM. Director of Hospital Services, Ross Hall Hospital, Glasgow, since 1986; b. 15.7.48, Dunoon. Educ. Dunoon Grammar School; Glasgow Royal Infirmary and Queen Mother's Hospital, Glasgow. Glasgow Royal Infirmary: Staff Nurse, Surgical Unit, 1971, Sister/Night Duty Surgical Area, 1971-72, Senior Sister in charge of University Department of Surgery Wards, 1972-77, Nursing Officer in charge of University Department of Surgery Wards, Acute Receiving Surgical Wards and Urology Wards, 1977-83; Director of Nursing, Ross Hall Hospital, 1983-85, Director of Clinical Services, 1985-86. Address: (h.) Donrhona, Sandbank, Dunoon; T.-0369 6277.

Munn, Sir James, OBE, MA, LLD, DUniv. Chairman for Scotland, Manpower Services Commission/Training Commission, 1987-88; b. 27.7.20, Bridge of Allan; m., Muriel Jean Millar Moles; 1 d. Educ. Stirling High School; Glasgow University. Indian Civil Service, 1941-48; various teaching appointments, Glasgow, 1949-57; Principal Teacher of Modern Languages, Falkirk High School, 1957-66 (Depute Rector, 1962-66); Principal Examiner in Modern Languages, Scottish Examination Board, 1965-66; Rector: Rutherglen Academy, 1966-70, Cathkin High School, 1970-83; Member, University Grants Committee, 1973-82; Member, Consultative Committee on the Curriculum, 1968-80, Chairman, 1980-87; Chairman, Committee to review the Structure of the Curriculum at S3 and S4, 1975-77; Member of Court, Strathclyde University, 1983-87, Deputy Chairman, since 1987. Address: (h.) 4 Kincath Avenue, High Burnside, Glasgow, G73 4RP; T.-041-634 4654.

Munn, Roy William. Chairman of Finance, Grampian Regional Council, since 1987; b. 2.5.29, Glasgow; m., Anne M.N.; 3 s. Educ. King's Park Senior Secondary School; Strathclyde University. Retired Surveyor of Customs and Excise. Recreations: golf; fishing; photography; writing; sailing. Address: (h.) 18 South Guildry Street, Elgin, Moray.

Munn, Professor Walter Douglas, MA, PhD, DSc, FRSE. Thomas Muir Professor of Mathematics, Glasgow University, since 1973; b. 24.4.29, Kilbarchan; m., Margaret Clare Barlow. Educ. Marr College, Troon; Glasgow University; St. John's College, Cambridge. Scientific Officer, Royal Naval Scientific Service; Assistant in Mathematics, then Lecturer in Mathematics, Glasgow University; Visiting Assistant Professor, Tulane University; Senior Lecturer in Computing Science, then Senior Lecturer in Mathematics, Glasgow University; Professor of Mathematics, Stirling University. Recreations: music; gardening; hill-walking. Address: (b.) Department of Mathematics, Glasgow University, Glasgow, G12 8QW; T.-041-339 8855, Ext. 4207.

Munro, Alexander, MB, ChB, ChM, FRCS. Consultant General Surgeon, Raigmore Hospital, Inverness, since 1978; Clinical Senior Lecturer in Surgery, Aberdeen University, since 1978; b. 5.6.43, Ross and Cromarty; m., Maureen E. McCreath; 2 s.; 1 d. Educ. Fortrose Academy; Aberdeen University. Training in General Surgery at Registrar and Senior Registrar level, Aberdeen Hospitals, 1971-78; specialist training, St. Mark's Hospital, 1977. Recreation: gardening. Address: (h.) 23 Eriskay Road, Inverness; T.-Inverness 223804.

Munro, Rev. David Peacock, MA, BD, STM. Minister, Bearsden North Church, since 1967; Clerk, Presbytery of Dumbarton, since 1986; b. 7.9.29, Paisley; m., Jessie Scott McPherson; 3 d. Educ. Paisley Grammar School; Glasgow University; Union Theological Seminary, New York. Minister, Aberluthnott Parish Church, 1953-56, Castlehill Church, Ayr, 1956-67. Chairman, General Assembly Board of Education, 1974-79; Convener, General Assembly Education Committee, 1981-85; Editor, Children of the Way (Sunday School Programme), Year One, 1981. Publication: Preface to Teaching. Recreations: golf; gardening. Address: North Manse, 8 Collylinn Road, Bearsden, Glasgow; T.-041-942 0366.

Munro, Gordon McKie, BSc, DipEd. Rector, Beath High School, Cowdenbeath, since 1987 (Head Teacher, Tynecastle High School, Edinburgh, 1983-87); b. 4.1.44, Glencraig, Fife; m., Nessy; 4 s. Educ. Beath High School; Edinburgh University; Moray House College of Education. Taught Physics, Beath Senior High School, Cowdenbeath, 1967-69; Tynecastle High School: Principal Teacher of Physics, 1970-72, Assistant Head Teacher, 1972-78, Deputy Head Teacher, 1978-83. Secretary, Christian Assembly Meeting, Gospel Hall, Ballingry, Fife. Recreations: preaching; teaching; reading; walking; gardening; building; looking after a donkey. Address: (h.) The Whins, Nether Milton, Crosshill, Fife, KY5 8AN; T.-0592 860 515.

Munro, John Farquhar, JP. Chairman, Skye and Lochalsh District Council; Haulage and Civil Engineering Contractor; b. 26.8.34, Glenshiel; m., Cecilia Moffat Brown Robertson; 1 s.; 1 d. Educ. Plockton High School; Sea Training College. Merchant marine, 11 years; Member, Highland Regional Council, 1978-82; Chairman, Gaelic Committee, Highland Region, 1978-82; Assessor to Crofters Commission, since 1977; Member, Shipping Advisory Committee, Caledonian MacBrayne; elected, Skye and Lochalsh District Council, 1974; Trustee, Gaelic Language Promotion Trust; Member, Council on Alcoholism, Alcoholics Anonymous; Treasurer, Kintail Parish Church. Recreations: shooting; sailing; drama. Address: (h.) Glomach House, Glenshiel, Wester Ross; T.-059 981 222.

Munro, John Forbes, MB, ChB (Hons), FRCPEdin. Consultant Physician, Eastern General and Edenhall Hospitals, since 1968; part-time Senior Lecturer, Edinburgh University, since 1984; b. 26.6.33, Edinburgh; m., Elizabeth Jean Durell Caird; 3 d. Educ. Edinburgh Academy; Chigwell School, Essex; Edinburgh University. Registrar and Senior Registrar, Edinburgh Royal Infirmary, 1962-68. Recreations: gardening; playing mixed hockey. Address: (h.) Backhill, Carberry, near Musselburgh, East Lothian; T.-031-663 4935.

Munro, Rev. John Pringle Lorimer, MA (Cantab), BD, PhD. Minister, St. Vigeans, linked with Knox's, Arbroath, since 1986; b. 11.5.47, Edinburgh; m., Patricia Ann Lawson; 1 s.; 1 d. Educ. Edinburgh Academy; Christ's College, Cambridge; New College, Edinburgh University. Chaplain, Stirling University, 1977-82; Lecturer, St. Paul's United Theological College, Limuru, Kenya, 1983-85. Recreations: the study of Third World theology; piano; angling. Address: St. Vigeans Manse, Arbroath, Angus, DD11 4RD; T.-0241 73206.

Munro of Foulis, Captain Patrick, TD (1958), DL (1949). 30th Chief of Clan Munro; Vice Lieutenant of Ross and Cromarty, 1968-77; b. 30.8.12; m., Eleanor Mary French; 3 s.; 1 d. Educ. Imperial Service College, Windsor; Sandhurst. 2nd Lt., Seaforth Highlanders, 1933; Captain, 1939; served Second World War (POW); Farmer and Landowner; Honorary Sheriff of Ross and Cromarty. Address: (h.) Foulis Castle, Evanton, Ross-shire.

Munro, Robert William. Author and Journalist; b. 3.2.14, Kiltearn, Ross-shire; m., Jean Mary Dunlop. Educ. Edinburgh Academy. War Service, Seaforth Highlanders and Inter-Services Public Relations Directorate (India), 1940-46; Editorial Staff, The Scotsman, 1933-59 and 1963-69; Editor-in-Chief, Highland News Group, 1959-63; Chairman, Edinburgh Press Club, 1955-57 (President, 1969-71); Honorary Editor, Clan Munro Association, 1939-71 (Vice-President, since 1963); former Council Member: Society of Antiquaries of Scotland, Scottish History Society, Scottish Genealogy Society; Trustee, National Museum of Antiquities of Scotland, 1982-85. Publications: Donald Monro's Western Isles of Scotland and Genealogies of the Clans 1549 (Editor), 1961; Tain Through the Centuries (Co-author, with wife), 1966; The Glorious Privilege: The History of The Scotsman (Co-author), 1967; Kinsmen and Clansmen, 1971; The Northern Lighthouses, 1976; Highland Clans and Tartans, 1977; Edinburgh and the Borders, 1977; The Munro Tree 1734, 1978; Scottish Lighthouses, 1979; Taming the Rough Bounds, Knoydart 1745-1784, 1984; Acts of the Lords of the Isles 1336-1493 (Co-author, with wife), 1986. Recreations: historical research and writing; walking; visiting islands. Address: (h.) 15A Mansionhouse Road, Edinburgh, EH9 1TZ; T.-031-667 4601.

Murchison, Lilian Elizabeth, MB, ChB, PhD, FRCPE, FRCP(Lond). Consultant Physician and Honorary Clinical Senior Lecturer in Medicine, Aberdeen University, since 1976; b. 29.4.36, Aultbea. Educ. Invergordon Academy; Edinburgh University; Glasgow University. Member, Scientific Staff, Atheroma Research Unit, Western Infirmary, Glasgow, 1963-68; Senior Tutor/ Senior Registrar, Department of Medicine, Queen's University, Belfast, 1969-71; Lecturer, Department of Therapeutics and Clinical Pharmacology, Aberdeen University, 1971-76. Recreations: overseas travel; hill-walking. Address: (h.) 9 Highgate Gardens, Aberdeen, AB1 2TZ; T.-0224 588532.

Murchison, Maurine, OBE, MA (Hons). Chairman, Children's Panel Advisory Committee, Highland Region, 1980-85; Member, Consultative Committee on the Curriculum, 1980-87; Member, Highlands and Islands Development Consultative Council, 1978-86; Member, Police Advisory Board for Scotland, since 1985; b. 25.11.35, London; m., Dr. Murdoch Murchison (qv); 3 s.; 2 d. Educ. James Allen's Girls School, Dulwich; Edinburgh University. Secondary school teaching, 1958-60; homemaker and mother, since 1960; Member, Inverness County Children's Panel, 1971-75 (Chairman, 1972-75); Chairman, Highland Region Children's Panel, 1975-80; Member, Inverness Prison Visiting Committee, 1984-85; Member, Panel for Appeals Tribunal, set up under Social Work Scotland Act 1968, since 1983; Assessor under Race Relations Act, since 1982; Past Chairman: Lifeline Inverness, YWCA, Inverness; Conciliator, Grampian Family Conciliation Service, 1988. Recreations: embroidery; group Bible study; reading (ethics and theology). Address: (h.) Riverdale, 22 Hillview Road, Cults, Aberdeen, AB1 9HB; T.-0224 868327.

Murchison, Murdoch, MB, ChB, DObstRCOG, DPH, DIH, FFCM. Chief Administrative Medical Officer, Grampian Health Board, since 1984; Honorary Clinical Senior Lecturer, Aberdeen University, since 1984; b. 27.10.33, Aultbea, Ross-shire; m., Maurine Tallach (see Maurine Murchison); 3 s.; 2 d. Educ. Invergordon Academy; Edinburgh University. Medical Officer of Health, Inverness County Council and Inverness Burgh Council; Community Medicine Specialist and District Medical Officer, Highland Health Board; Police Surgeon, Northern Constabulary; Medical Officer, Highland and Islands Fire Brigade. Member, Community Medicine Consultative Committee UK; Past Chairman, Scottish Committee for Community Medicine, BMA; Past President, Scottish Society for Community Medicine. Recreations: hill-walking; gardening. Address: Riverdale, 22 Hillview Road, Cults, Aberdeen, AB1 9HB; T.-Aberdeen 868327.

Murdoch, Brian Oliver, BA, PhD, AMusTCL. Senior Lecturer in German, Stirling University, since 1975 (Head, Department of German, since 1982); b. 26.6.44, London; m., Ursula I. Riffer; 1 s.; 1 d. Educ. Sir George Monoux Grammar School, Walthamstow; Exeter University; Goettingen University; Freiburg University; Jesus College, Cambridge. Lecturer in German, Glasgow University; Assistant/Associate Professor of German, Illinois University; Lecturer in German, Stirling University. Editor, Scottish Papers in Germanic Studies, since 1981. Recreations: jazz; numismatics; books. Address: (b.) German Department, Stirling University, Stirling, FK9 4LA; T.-0786 73171, Ext. 2270.

Murdoch, Eileen, MA. Headmistress, St. Augustine's High School, Edinburgh, since 1977; b. Edinburgh. Educ. Holy Cross Academy; Edinburgh University; Craiglockhart College. Recreation: choral singing. Address: (b.) St. Augustine's High School, Broomhouse Road, Edinburgh; T.-031-334 6801.

Murdoch, John, FCMA, JDipMA, CIPFA. Director of Finance and Management Services, Irvine Development Corporation, since 1972; b. 31.12.34, Glassford; m., Ann McTaggart Jack; 3 s.; 1 d. Educ. Hamilton Academy; School of Accountancy (Correspondence Courses). Bank Clerk, Bank of Scotland, Hamilton, 1951-53 and 1955-58; National Service, Cameronians (Scottish Rifles), 1953-55; Trainee Cost Accountant, Colvilles Steel Industry, Motherwell, 1958-63; Budget Controller, East Kilbride Development Corporation, 1963-68; Financial Controller, Irvine Development Corporation, 1968-72. Recreations: lay preaching; writing; marathon running; bird-watching. Address: (b.) Irvine Development Corporation, Perceton House, Girdle Toll, Irvine, Ayrshire; T.-Irvine 214100.

Mure, Kenneth Nisbet, MA, LLB, FTII. Advocate, since 1975; b. 11.4.47, Glasgow. Educ. High School of Glasgow; Glasgow University. Part-time Lecturer in Revenue Law, Glasgow University, 1971-83. Address: (b.) Advocates' Library, Edinburgh.

Murison, James, RMN, RGN, BA. Member, Grampian Health Board, since 1975; Superintendent, Willowbank Adult Training Centre and Hostel, since 1967; Deputy Principal Nursing Officer, Bilbohall Hospital, Elgin, since 1960; b. 25.5.29, Aberdeenshire; m., Agnes Gray; 1 s.; 2 d. Educ. Udny Green, Aberdeenshire; Open University; Royal College of Nursing. President: Peterhead Chess Club, since 1968, Longside Tennis Club. Recreations: chess; tennis. Address: (b.) Willowbank Adult Training Centre, Peterhead, Aberdeenshire; T.-St. Fergus 301.

Murphy, Herbert Edward Harnett, ACIT. Regional Director, Scotland and Northern Ireland, Automobile Association, since 1974; b. 31.8.32, Dublin; m., Susan Gillion Hall; 2 s. Educ. Repton School, Derbyshire; Trinity College, Dublin. Member, Transport Committee, Glasgow Chamber of Commerce; Member, Transport Action Scotland Committee. Recreations: sailing; golf; hill-walking. Address: (h.) 20 Donaldfield Road, Bridge of Weir, Renfrewshire, PA11 3JG; T.-0505 613118.

Murphy, Sheriff James Patrick, BL. Sheriff of North Strathclyde, since 1976; b. 24.1.32; m.; 2 s.; 1 d. Educ. Notre Dame Convent; St. Aloysius College, Glasgow; Glasgow University. Solicitor, 1953; Founder, Ross Harper & Murphy, 1961; President, Glasgow Juridical Society, 1962-63; President, Glasgow Bar Association, 1966-67; Member, Council, Law Society of Scotland, 1974-76.

Murphy, James Barrie, MB, ChB, DPM, MRCPsych. Consultant Psychiatrist and Honorary Clinical Lecturer, Gartnavel Royal Hospital, Glasgow; b. 27.7.42, Glasgow; m., Jean Wynn Kirkwood; 1 s.; 1 d. Educ. High School of Glasgow; Glasgow University. Consultant Psychiatrist, Dykebar Hospital, Paisley, 1973-80. Address: (b.) Gartnavel Royal Hospital, 1055 Great Western Road, Glasgow, G12 0XH; T.-041-334 6241.

Murphy, Peter Alexander, MA, MEd. Rector, Whitfield High School, Dundee, since 1976; b. 5.10.32, Aberdeen; m., Margaret Christie; 3 s.; 1 d. Educ. Aberdeen Grammar School; Aberdeen University. Assistant Principal Teacher of English, Aberdeen Grammar School, 1963-65; Principal Teacher of English, Summerhill Academy, Aberdeen, 1965-71; Head Teacher, Logie Secondary School, Dundee, 1971-76. Chairman, Carnoustie Branch, Labour Party; Elder, Carnoustie Church. Publication: Life and Times of Logie School (Co-author). Recreations: hill-walking; hockey; bee-keeping; gardening. Address: (h.) Ashlea, 44 Burnside Street, Carnoustie, Angus; T.-Carnoustie 52106.

Murray, Rev. Alexander, MA. Minister, Free Presbyterian Church of Scotland, since 1954; Member, Highland Regional Council, since 1986 (and 1975-78); b. 1.11.25, Invershin, Sutherland; m., Marjory Graham; 3 s.; 4 d. Educ. Bonar Bridge H.G. School; Selwyn College, Cambridge; Glasgow University. RAFVR, 1944-47; Moderator, Synod of FP Church, 1960 and 1978; Clerk, Foreign Missions Committee, since 1977; Member, Education Committee, Ross and Cromarty County Council, 1960-70, Member of the Council, 1970-75; Vice-Chairman, Social Work Committee, Highland Regional Council, since 1987; Secretary, Applecross Committee, 1965-75. Recreations: loch and sea fishing; swimming. Address: FP Manse, Saval Road, Lairg, IV27 4EH.

Murray, Alexander George, KStG, KLJ, BSc, FBSC(Lond). National Director, Crossroads (Scotland) Care Attendant Schemes, since 1981; m., Margaret Elizabeth; 1 d. Educ. Whitehill School, Glasgow; Glasgow University. Scottish Manager, British subsidiary of Chase Manhatten Bank of America; formed several companies in investment/credit field. Led first Scottish delegation to UNESCO, 1955-56; established Scottish Worldfriends Society and became its first National Director; prominent in Highland societies; Scot of the Year, 1986; Founder and Convener, Caledonian Country Dancing Clubs; former Secretary, West of Scotland Refugee Committee; Past President, East Kilbride Sea Cadet Corps; Member, Organising Committee, East Kilbride National Mod, 1974-75. Recreations: bowling; swimming; walking. Address: (h.) Failte, 51 Eaglesham Road, Clarkston, Glasgow, G76 7TR; T.-041-644 1374.

Murray, Alex. T.L., CEng, BSc, FIEE. Chief Engineer, North of Scotland Hydro-Electric Board, since 1974; b. 27.6.25, Edinburgh; m., Mary; 1 s.; 1 d. Educ. George Heriot's; Heriot-Watt University. General Assistant Engineer, Central Electricity Board, 1947-48; Assistant Section Engineer, SE Scotland Division, British Electricity Authority, 1948-51; various posts, North of Scotland Hydro-Electric Board, since 1951. Recreations: early music performance; amateur radio; hill-walking. Address: (b.) 16 Rothesay Terrace, Edinburgh, EH3 7SE.

Murray, Athol Laverick, PhD, MA, LLB, FRHistS, FSA Scot. Keeper of the Records of Scotland, since 1985; b. 8.11.30, Tynemouth; m., Irene Joyce Cairns; 1 s.; 1 d. Educ. Lancaster Royal Grammar School; Jesus College, Cambridge; Edinburgh University. Research Assistant, Foreign Office, 1953; Scottish Record Office: Assistant Keeper, 1953-83, Deputy Keeper, 1983-84. Chairman of Council, Scottish Record Society. Address: (b.) Scottish Record Office, HM General Register House, Edinburgh, EH1 3YY; T.-031-556 6585.

Murray, David Edward. Chairman and Managing Director, Murray International Holdings; b. 14.10.51, Ayr; m., Louise V. Murray; 2 s. Educ. Fettes College; Broughton High School. Young Scottish Business Man of the Year, 1984; Hon. Doctorate, Heriot-Watt University, 1986; Chairman, UK 2000 (Scotland), 1987; Governor, Clifton Hall School, 1987. Recreations: sports sponsorship, e.g. basketball, hockey, volleyball, etc.; snooker; collecting wine. Address: (b.) South Gyle, Edinburgh; T.-031-317 7000.

Murray, Donald, MA. Head Teacher, Sir Edward Scott School, Tarbert, Isle of Harris, since 1981; b. Port of Ness, Isle of Lewis; 2 d. Educ. Nicolson Institute, Stornoway; Glasgow University. Teacher, Calder Street Secondary School, Glasgow; Teacher, Achnamara Residential School, Argyll; Principal Teacher of Guidance, Victoria Drive Secondary School, Glasgow; Assistant Head Teacher (Curriculum), Kingsridge Secondary School, Glasgow. Recreations: angling; gardening; reading. Address: (h.) Balranald, West Tarbert, Isle of Harris; T.-0859 2339.

Murray, Rev. Douglas Millar, MA, BD, PhD. Minister, Polwarth Parish Church, Edinburgh, since 1981; b. 1946, Edinburgh; m., Dr. Freya M. Smith. Educ. George Watson's College, Edinburgh; Edinburgh University; New College, Edinburgh; Fitzwilliam and Westminster Colleges, Cambridge. Minister: St. Bride's Church, Callander, 1976-80, John Ker Memorial Church in deferred union with Candlish Church, Edinburgh, 1980-81 (became Polwarth Church, 1981). Editor, Liturgical Review, 1979-81; Associate Editor, Scottish Journal of Theology, 1981-87; Convener, Panel on Doctrine, General Assembly, Church of Scotland, since 1986. Publication: Studies in the History of Worship in Scotland (Co-Editor). Recreations: golf; Scottish country dancing; hill-walking; sketching. Address: 9 Merchiston Bank Gardens, Edinburgh, EH10 5EB; T.-031-447 2741.

Murray, Gordon, BSc (Hons), PhD. Director, Scottish Courts Administration, since 1986; b. 25.8.35, Aberdeen; m., Janet Yerrington; 2 s.; 1 d. Educ. Kirkcaldy High School; Edinburgh University. Research Fellow, Atomic Energy Authority of Canada, 1960-62, UKAEA, 1962-65; Lecturer in Physics, Manchester University, 1965-69; Principal, Scottish Home and Health Department, 1970-77; Assistant Secretary, Scottish Education Department, 1977-79, Central Services, 1979-86. Recreations: reading; walking. Address: 26 Royal Terrace, Edinburgh, EH7 5AH; T.-031-556 0755.

Murray, Gordon Lindsay Kevan. Partner, W.J. Burness WS, since 1982; Secretary, Scottish National Orchestra Society Ltd., since 1985; b. 23.5.53, Glasgow; m., Susan Patricia; 3 d. Educ. Lenzie Academy; Edinburgh University. President, Scottish Young Lawyers Association, 1977-78. Address: (b.) 16 Hope Street, Charlotte Square, Edinburgh, EH2 4DD; T.-031-226 2561.

Murray, Gordon Stewart, JP, ARGTC. Member, Strathclyde Regional Council, 1974-86; Member, Cumbernauld and Kilsyth District Council, since 1974; b. 15.7.27, Aberdeen; 1 s.; 1 d. Educ. Aberdeen Grammar School; Aberdeen University; Robert Gordon's College of Technology. First and last Provost of Cumbernauld Burgh, 1968-75; first Provost, Cumbernauld and Kilsyth, 1974-80; Senior Engineer, Cumbernauld Development Corporation, 1964-83; former Vice-Chairman and Vice-President, Scottish National Party; Parliamentary candidate, East Dunbartonshire, 1970,

East Kilbride, 1974 and 1979, Cumbernauld and Kilsyth, 1983. Recreation: part-time crofter. Address: (h.) 17 Arran Drive, Cumbernauld, Glasgow.

Murray, Isobel (Mary), MA, PhD. Writer and Book Reviewer; Senior Lecturer in English, Aberdeen University, since 1974; b. 14.2.39, Alloa; m., Bob Tait. Educ. Dollar Academy; Edinburgh University. Assistant Lecturer, then Lecturer, Department of English, Aberdeen University; books include several editions of Oscar Wilde, introductions to new editions of J. MacDougall Hay's Gillespie and Ian MacPherson's Shepherds' Calendar; edited, Beyond This Limit: Selected Shorter Fiction of Naomi Mitchison; Ten Modern Scottish Novels (with Bob Tait), 1984; wide range of book reviews, especially for The Scotsman, since 1962, and new fiction for Financial Times, 1968-81. Address: (b.) Department of English, King's College, Old Aberdeen, Aberdeen, AB9 2UB; T.-Aberdeen 40241, Ext. 6562.

Murray, Professor James Lothian, BSc, MSc, FIMechE, CEng. Professor of Computer Aided Engineering, Heriot-Watt University, since 1985 (Director, CAE Centre, since 1982); b. 11.6.38, Loanhead; m., Anne Walton; 1 d. Educ. Lasswade Senior Secondary School; Heriot-Watt University. Student apprentice, then Design Engineer, Ferranti Ltd., 1956-66; Heriot-Watt University: Lecturer in Engineering Design, 1966-78, Senior Lecturer in Design and Manufacture, 1978-85, Head, Department of Mechanical Engineering, since 1984. Member, Academic Board, Napier College, Art and Design Panel, SUCE; Board Member, Unilink; Associate Director, Anderson Allan Ltd. Recreation: hill-walking. Address: (b.) Department of Mechanical Engineering, Heriot-Watt University, Edinburgh, EH14 4AS; T.-031-449 5111.

Murray, Rev. John James, DipTh. Minister, Free High Church, Oban, since 1978; b. 11.9.34, Dornoch; m., Cynthia MacPhee; 1 s.; 1 d. Educ. Dornoch Academy; Edinburgh University; Free Church College. Worked with insurance company before joining Banner of Truth Trust, 1960, as Assistant Editor; Secretary, Reformation Translation Fellowship, since 1962; Clerk, Argyll and Lochaber Presbytery, since 1983; Editor, The Bulwark, 1977-80. Address: Free Church Manse, Rockfield Road, Oban, Argyll, PA34 5DQ; T.-0631 62154.

Murray, Jonathan Aidan Muir, BSc, MB, ChB, FRCS, FRACS, MD. Consultant Ear Nose and Throat Surgeon, Edinburgh, since 1983; part-time Senior Lecturer in Otolaryngology, since 1984; b. 16.8.51, Edinburgh; m., Shiona Aitken; 2 s.; 2 d. Educ. Daniel Stewart's College, Edinburgh; Edinburgh University. Address: (h.) The Old Rectory, Lasswade, Midlothian, EH18 1LR; T.-031-660 2694.

Murray, Professor Kenneth, BSc, PhD, FRS. Professor of Molecular Biology, Edinburgh University, since 1976; b. 30.12.30, East Ardsley; m., Noreen E. Parker (see Noreen Elizabeth Murray). Educ. Henry Mellish Grammar School; Birmingham University. Postdoctoral work, Stanford University, California, 1959-64; MRC Scientific Staff, Cambridge, 1964-67; joined Edinburgh University, 1967; leave of absence at European Molecular Biology Laboratory, Heidelberg, 1979-82. Recreations: musical appreciation; reading. Address: (b.) Department of Molecular Biology, Edinburgh University, Mayfield Road, Edinburgh, EH9 3JR; T.-031-667 1081.

Murray, Leonard G., JP, BL. Senior Partner, Levy & McRae, Solicitors, since 1981; Tutor, Glasgow University and Strathclyde University; b. 16.8.33, Glasgow; m., Elizabeth Wilson; 3 s. Educ. St. Mungo's Academy, Glasgow; Glasgow University. Appointed Member, Legal Aid Central Committee, 1978 (Vice Chairman, 1986). After-dinner speaker; founder Director, Speakeasy (Scotland) Ltd., 1987. Recreation: golf. Address: (b.) 13 Bath Street, Glasgow, G2 1HZ; T.-041-331 2311.

Murray, Professor Maxwell, BVMS, DVM, FRCPath, FRSE, PhD. Professor of Veterinary Medicine, Glasgow University, since 1985; b. 3.5.39, Glasgow; m., Christine Madelaine; 1 s.; 2 d. Educ. Shawlands Senior Secondary School; Glasgow University. Animal Health Trust Research Scholarship, 1962-63; Lecturer in Veterinary Pathology, University of Nairobi, 1963-65; Lecturer in Veterinary Pathology, then Senior Lecturer, Glasgow University, 1965-75; Senior Scientist, International Laboratory for Research on Animal Diseases, Nairobi, 1975-85. Recreations: family; football; philosophy. Address: (b.) Department of Veterinary Medicine, Glasgow University Veterinary School, Bearsden Road, Bearsden, Glasgow, G61 1QH; T.-041-339 8855, Ext. 5734.

Murray, Noreen Elizabeth, FRS, PhD. Reader, Department of Molecular Biology, Edinburgh University, since 1982; b. 26.2.35, Burnley; m., Kenneth Murray (qv). Educ. Lancaster Girls' Grammar School; King's College, London; Birmingham University. Research Associate, Department of Biological Sciences, Stanford University, 1960-64; Research Fellow, Botany School, Cambridge, 1964-67; Edinburgh University: Member, MRC Molecular Genetics Unit, Department of Molecular Biology, 1968-74, Lecturer, then Senior Lecturer, Department of Molecular Biology, 1974-80; Group Leader, European Molecular Biology Laboratory, Heidelberg, 1980-82. Recreation: gardening. Address: (b.) Department of Molecular Biology, Edinburgh University, Mayfield Road, Edinburgh, EH9 3JR; T.-031-667 1081.

Murray, Patrick, VRD, WS. Landowner; b. 13.5.11, Edinburgh; m., Doris Herbert Green; 2 d. Educ. Ardvreck, Crieff; Marlborough College. Royal Naval Volunteer Reserve, 1935-55 (Commander); Partner, Murray, Beith & Murray, WS, Edinburgh, 1937-77. Recreations: gardening; forestry; hunting; carriage driving. Address: (h.) Townhead of Cavers, Hawick, Roxburghshire, TD9 8LJ; T.-0450 73604.

Murray, Rt. Hon. Lord (Ronald King Murray), PC (1974). Senator of the College of Justice in Scotland, since 1979; b. 15.6.22; m.; 1 s.; 1 d. Educ. George Watson's College; Edinburgh University; Jesus College, Oxford. Served HM Forces, 1941-46; called to Scottish Bar, 1953; QC (Scot), 1967; Advocate Depute, 1964-67; Senior Advocate-Depute, 1967-70; MP (Labour), Leith, 1970-79; Lord Advocate, 1974-79.

Murray, Rt. Rev. Mgr. Thomas Canon, STL. Parish Priest, Dumbarton, since 1975; b. Wishaw. Educ. Our Lady's High School, Motherwell; Blair's College; Scots College, Rome. Assistant: St. Luke's, Glasgow, Carfin; on staff, Scots College; Parish Priest, Balornock, 1957-75. Address: St. Patrick's, Strathleven Place, Dumbarton, G82 1BA.

Murray, Thomas Stuart, MB, PhD, FRCPGlas, FRCGP, DRCOG. West of Scotland Adviser in General Practice, since 1985; Senior Lecturer in General Practice, Glasgow University, since 1977; b. 22.7.43, Muirkirk; m., Anne Smith; 1 s.; 2 d. Educ. Cumnock Academy; Glasgow University. Early postgraduate work, medicine and cardiology, Glasgow Royal Infirmary; Principal in general practice, Alexandria; Research Fellow in General Practice, then Senior Lecturer in General Practice, Glasgow University. Recreations: travel; sport; reading. Address: (b.) Glasgow University, Glasgow, G12 8QQ; T.-041-339 8855, Ext. 5276.

Murray, Walter Watson, FRICS. Director of Estates, Grampian Regional Council, since 1975. Educ. Royal College of Science and Technology, Glasgow. NE Counties Valuation Committee, Aberdeen: Senior Valuer, 1957-61, Depute Assessor, 1961-67, Assessor, 1967-75. Chairman, Association of Local Authority Valuers, Scottish Branch. Recreation: hill-walking. Address: (b.) Woodhill House, Westburn, Aberdeen, AB9 2LU; T.-0224 682222, Ext. 2440.

Murray, William, JP. Farmer; Chairman, W. Murray (Farming) Ltd., since 1960; Chairman, Border Sheepskins Ltd., since 1966; b. 16.2.17, Gorebridge; m., Fiona Stevenson; 3 s.; 2 d. Educ. Dalhousie Castle School; Merchiston Castle School. Began farming with father, 1934; went to Southern Rhodesia, 1938, to tobacco farm, becoming Manager; served King's African Rifles Defence Force, 1939-42; joined Rhodesian Royal Airforce (invalided out, 1942); returned to UK and became Farm Manager, Redden, Kelso, 1943 (subsequently Tenant and Farmer); acquired Watherston Farm, 1972, and Mid Housebyres Farm, 1983; Committee Member, NFU of Scotland, and Convener, Local Area, 1957-58; Director, Royal Highland and Agricultural Society of Scotland, 1968-84; Treasurer, Sprouston Church, 1950-85; Director, Scottish Agricultural Organisation Society, 1965-70; Convener, Border Union Agricultural Society, 1959-60. Recreations: shooting; foxhunting. Address: Redden, Kelso, Roxburghshire, TD5 8HS; T.-089 083 276.

Murray, William Hutchison, OBE. Author and Mountaineer; b. 18.3.13, Liverpool; m., Anne Burnet Clark. Educ. Glasgow Academy. Union Bank of Scotland, until 1939; Captain, HLI, Western Desert (Prisoner of War, 1942-45); Leader, Scottish Himalayan Expedition, 1950; Deputy Leader, Everest Expedition, 1951; Leader, NW Nepal Expedition, 1953; Commissioner, Countryside Commission for Scotland, 1968-80; Mungo Park Medal, RSGS, 1950; Literary Award, USA Education Board, 1954; Honorary Doctorate, Stirling University, 1975. Publications: Mountaineering in Scotland, 1947; Rock Climbs, Glencoe and Ardgour, 1949; Undiscovered Scotland, 1951; Scottish Himalayan Expedition, 1951; Story of Everest, 1953; Five Frontiers, 1959; The Spurs of Troodos, 1960; Maelstrom, 1962; Highland Landscape, 1962; Dark Rose the Phoenix, 1965; The Hebrides, 1966; Companion Guide to West Highlands, 1968; The Real MacKay, 1969; The Islands of Western Scotland, 1973; The Scottish Highlands, 1976; The Curling Companion, 1981; Rob Roy MacGregor, 1982; Scotland's Mountains, 1987. Recreations: mountaineering; sailing. Address: Lochwood, Loch Goil, Argyll.

Murray-Smith, Professor David James, MSc, PhD, CEng, FIEE, MInstMC. Titular Professor in Electronics and Electrical Engineering, Glasgow University; b. 20.10.41, Aberdeen; m., Effie Smith; 2 s. Educ. Aberdeen Grammar School; Aberdeen University; Glasgow University. Engineer, Inertial Systems Department, Ferranti Ltd., Edinburgh, 1964-65; Glasgow University: Assistant, Department of Electrical Engineering, 1965-67, Lecturer, 1967-77, Senior Lecturer, 1977-83, Reader, 1983-85. Past Chairman, United Kingdom Simulation Council; Member, various committees, Institution of Electrical Engineers; Advisory Director, Scottish Engineering Training Scheme Ltd. Recreations: hill-walking; photography; strong interest in railways. Address: (b.) Department of Electronics and Electrical Engineering, Glasgow University, Glasgow, G12 8QQ; T.-041-339 8855.

Murrie, Sir William Stuart, GCB (1964), KBE (1952), Hon. LLD (Dundee); b. 19.12.03, Dundee; m., Eleanore Boswell (deceased). Educ. Harris Academy, Dundee; Edinburgh University; Balliol College, Oxford. Scottish Office, 1927-35; Department of Health for Scotland, 1935-44; Under Secretary, Offices of War Cabinet, 1944; Deputy Secretary (Civil), Cabinet Office, 1947; Deputy Under Secretary of State, Home Office, 1948-52; Secretary: Scottish Education Department, 1952-57, Scottish Home Department, 1957-59; Permanent Under Secretary of State for Scotland, 1959-64; Chairman, Board of Trustees, National Galleries of Scotland, 1972-75; Member, Council on Tribunals, 1965-77; General Council Assessor, Edinburgh University Court, 1967-75. Address: (h.) 7 Cumin Place, Edinburgh, EH9 2JX; T.-031-667 2612.

Musson, John Nicholas Whitaker, MA (Oxon). Scottish Secretary, Independent Schools Careers Organisation, since 1987 (Warden, Glenalmond College, 1972-87); b. 2.10.27; m., Ann Priest; 1 s.; 3 d. Educ. Clifton College; Brasenose College, Oxford. Served as Guardsman and Lt., Lancashire Fusiliers, 1945-48; HM Overseas Civil Service, 1951-59 (District Officer, N. Nigeria and Lecturer, Institute of Administration, Nigeria); British Petroleum Co., London, 1959-61; Assistant Master and Housemaster, Canford School, Dorset, 1961-72. Scottish Division Chairman, Headmasters' Conference, 1981-83. Recreations: hill-walking; history; fine arts. Address: (h.) 47 Spylaw Road, Edinburgh, EH10 5BP; T.-031-337 0089.

Mutch, Alexander Fyvie, CBE, JP. Member, Grampian Regional Council, since 1974 (first Convener, 1974-82); b. 23.3.24, Aberdeen; m., Freda Mutch; 1 d. Educ. Aberdeen Central School. Convener, Aberdeen Corporation Cleansing Committee, 1963; Vice-Chairman, North-East Water Board, 1968-70; Magistrate, Aberdeen, 1967; Senior Magistrate, 1968; Chairman, Aberdeen Licensing Court, 1968; Member, Aberdeen University Court, 1974-82; Chairman, South Aberdeen Conservative Association, 1964-68 (President, 1968-72); Senior Vice-President, Conservative Party in Scotland, 1972-73 (President, 1973-74); Leader, Conservative Group, Aberdeen Town Council, 1974-75; Governor, Robert Gordon's College, Aberdeen, 1968-70 and since 1974; Honorary President, Grampian-Houston Association; Honorary Citizen, Houston, Texas. Address: (h.) 28 Salisbury Terrace, Aberdeen; T.-Aberdeen 591520.

Mutch, Robert Alexander, BSc, MSc, CEng, MCIBSE. Senior Lecturer, Department of Building, Heriot-Watt University; b. 14.3.33, Edinburgh; m., Maureen Isabel; 1 s.; 1 d. Educ. Broughton Senior Secondary School; Edinburgh University. Teacher: Niddrie Mill Primary School, 1957-60, Edinburgh School of Building and Crafts, 1961-64; Lecturer/Senior Lecturer in Building Science, Department of Building, Heriot-Watt College/University, since 1964. Recreations: reading; badminton. Address: (h.) 22 Duddingston Park, Edinburgh, EH15 1JX; T.-031-669 6735.

Mutch, William Edward Scott, OBE, BSc, PhD, FRSE, FICFor. Senior Lecturer in Forestry and Natural Resources, Edinburgh University, since 1963; b. 14.8.25, Salford; m., Margaret Isobel McKay; 1 d. Educ. Royal High School, Edinburgh; Edinburgh University. HM Colonial Service (Forest Department, Nigeria, as Assistant Conservator of Forests and Silviculturist), 1946; Research Assistant, Oxford University, 1952; Lecturer in Forestry, Edinburgh University, 1953. Head, Department of Forestry and Natural Resources, Edinburgh University, 1981-87; President, Institute of Chartered Foresters, 1982-84 (Institute Medal, 1986); Member: Countryside Commission for Scotland, 1988-92, National Forestry Research Advisory Committee. Publication: Farm Woodland Management. Recreations: cabinet making; hill-walking. Address: (h.) 19 Barnton Grove, Edinburgh, EH4 6EQ; T.-031-339 1400.

Myatt, Mary Elizabeth, BSc (Hons). Headmistress, The Park School, Glasgow, since 1986; b. 4.1.41, Belfast; m., Thomas Myatt. Educ. Omagh Academy; Queen's University, Belfast. Head, Mathematics Department: Dungannon High School for Girls, 1963-66, International School of Hamburg, 1966-68, Ashleigh House School, Belfast, 1968-70, Maida Vale High School, London, 1970-71; Wellington School, Ayr: Head, Mathematics Department, 1971-86, Director of Studies, 1984-86. Area Chairman, National Association of Ladies' Circles, 1978-79. Recreations: bridge; golf. Address: (b.) 25 Lynedoch Street, Glasgow, G3 6EX; T.-041-332 0426.

Myles, David Fairlie. Hill Farmer; Member, North of Scotland Hydro-Electric Board, since 1985; Member, Angus District Council, since 1984; Member, Angus Tourist Board, since 1984; Chairman, Dairy Produce Quota Tribunal for Scotland, since 1984; Member, Potato Marketing Board, since 1988; b. 30.5.25, Cortachy, Kirriemuir; m., Janet I. Gall; 2 s.; 2 d. Educ. Brechin High School. Auctioneer's clerk, 1941-43; Royal Marines, 1943-46; Tenant Hill Farmer, since 1946; Director of auction company, 1963-81; Member, Transport Users Consultative Committee for Scotland, 1973-79; Council Member, NFU of Scotland, 1970-79 (Convener, Organisation and Publicity Committee, 1976-79); Member, Meat Promotion Executive, MLC, 1975-79; Chairman, North Angus and Mearns Constituency Conservative Party, 1971-74; MP (Conservative), Banff, 1979-83; Joint Secretary, Backbench Conservative Agriculture Committee, 1979-83; Secretary, Backbench Conservative European Committee, 1980-83; Member, Select Committee on Agriculture and Select Committee on European Legislation, 1979-83. Recreations: curling; traditional Scottish fiddle music; works of Robert Burns. Address: (h.) The Gorse, Dunlappie Road, Edzell, Brechin, DD9 7UB; T.-035 64 207.

Myles, Thomas Hope Fenton, NP. Solicitor, since 1938; Honorary Sheriff of Tayside Central and Fife, at Perth, since 1982; b. 4.11.16, Kilspindie; m., Marion Merle Elizabeth Leppard; 1 s.; 2 d. Educ. Perth Academy; Edinburgh University. Legal Assistant, 1938-39; RAF, 1939-45; Partner, Campbell, Brooke & Myles, Solicitors, Perth, 1945-82. Recreation: Shetland pony breeding. Address: (h.) Newfargie House, Gateside, Strathmiglo, Fife; T.-05773 339.

N

Nandy, Kashinath, BSc, MSc (Calcutta), MSc (Edinburgh), PhD, FRAS, FRSE. Deputy Chief Scientific Officer, Royal Observatory, Edinburgh, 1977-86; Visiting Professor, Rome University, 1987; b. 1.12.27, Santipur, West Bengal, India; m., Smritilekha; 1 d. Educ. Calcutta University; Edinburgh University. Observatory Assistant, Presidency College Observatory, Calcutta, 1952-59; received International Astronomical Union Grant for Studies Abroad, 1959-60; held Robert Cormack Bequest Fellowship (Royal Society of Edinburgh), 1960-63; Royal Observatory, Edinburgh: Research Fellow, 1963-68, Principal Scientific Officer, 1968-72, Senior Principal Scientific Officer, 1972-77. Fellow, Royal Astronomical Society; Member, International Astronomical Union; Honorary Fellow, Edinburgh University, 1973-87; Honorary Research Fellow, University College, London, 1979-86; elected Fellow, Royal Society of Edinburgh, 1973; Fellow, Royal Society of Liege, 1980. Recreations: reading; travel; photography; surfing. Address: (h.) 36 West Mains Road, Edinburgh, EH9 3BG; T.-031-667 6131.

Naumann, Laurie M. Director, Scottish Council for Single Homeless, since 1978; b. 1943, Saffron Walden; m., Barbara; 2 s.; 3 d. Educ. Edinburgh, Gloucester and Nuremberg Rudolf Steiner; Leicester University. Furniture maker, Gloucestershire; Probation and After Care Officer, Leeds; Social Worker, Edinburgh. Council of Europe Social Fellowship to Finland to study services for the drunken offender, 1976; jointly won Rosemary Delbridge Memorial Trophy for influencing Parliament to legislate, 1983. Recreations: travel; reading; walking; woodwork. Address: (h.) St. Ann's, Alexander III Street, Kinghorn, Fife, KY3 9SD.

Naylor, Arthur, MA, MEd, PhD. Assistant Principal, St. Andrew's College of Education, Bearsden, since 1986; b. 27.2.49, Glasgow; m., Valerie Jean Fox; 2 s.; 1 d. Educ. Holyrood Secondary School, Glasgow; Glasgow University; Jordanhill College of Education. Teacher and Assistant Principal Teacher, 1972-75; Principal Teacher: St. Margaret's High, Paisley, 1975-76 (until amalgamation), Turnbull High, Bishopbriggs, 1976-81; St. Andrew's College of Education: Lecturer in Educational Science, 1981-84, Head of Department, 1984-86. Secretary/Development Officer, Scottish Central Committee on Guidance, 1981-85; Director of national and regional in-service guidance courses for teachers, 1981-84; Member of wide-ranging advisory committees on guidance, 1981-84, and on undergraduate and postgraduate teacher education, since 1984. Recreations: local history; swimming; walking; reading. Address: (b.) St. Andrew's College of Education, Bearsden, G61 4QA; T.-041-943 1424.

Naylor, Graham John, MB, ChB, BSc, DPM, MD, FRCPsych. Reader in Psychiatry, Dundee University, since 1980; Honorary Consultant, Royal Dundee Liff Hospital, since 1970; b. 13.2.40, Sheffield; m., Pamela Hilda Moody. Educ. Firth Park Grammar School, Sheffield; Sheffield University. Consultant Psychiatrist, Royal Dundee Liff Hospital, 1970-72; Senior Lecturer, Department of Psychiatry, Dundee University, 1972-80. Address: (b.) Department of Psychiatry, Ninewells Hospital and Medical School, Dundee; T.-Dundee 60111.

Needham, Ted, PhD, BSc, ARCS, DIC, MIBiol. Fish Farmer; Director: Sea Catch PLC, Pairc Salmon (Lewis) Ltd., Salmon Farms Ltd., North Uist Fisheries Ltd., Atlantic Freshwater PLC, Sea Growers PLC, Sea Salmon PLC, Sea Fish PLC, Silver Salmon PLC, Scallop Kings PLC; Consultant to: Hayes McCubbin MacFarlane, Aberdeen, Highlands and Islands Development Board, Orkney and Shetland Fish Farmers, Landcatch Ltd., Roberts Morris Bray Insurance Brokers; b. 7.7.43, Skipton, Yorkshire; m., Jane; 1 s.; 2 d. Educ. Tonbridge School, Kent; Edinburgh University; Imperial College, London. Kincardine County Councillor, 1973-75; Kincardine and Deeside District Councillor, 1974-77 and since 1979 (Chairman, Environmental Health, Leisure and Recreation Committee); Member, Grampian Region Agriculture and Fisheries Committee; Chairman, Scottish Fish Farmers Association, 1976-77; Convener, Fish Farming Committee, National Farmers Union of Scotland, 1977-79; Consultant to Hayes McCubbin Macfarlane, Aberdeen, Highlands and Islands Development Board, Orkney Islands; Columnist, Fish Farmer Magazine; part-time Lecturer, Stirling University, Inverness Technical College. Recreations: skiing; beef cattle; talking. Address: Home Farm, Maryculter, Aberdeen, AB1 OBA; T.-0224 732310.

Neil, Alex., MA (Hons). Director, Development Options Ltd.; Director, Cumnock and Doon Enterprise Trust, 1984-87; b. 22.8.51, Irvine; m., Isabella Kerr; 1 s. Educ. Dalmellington High School; Ayr Academy; Dundee University. Scottish Research Officer, Labour Party, 1974-76; General Secretary, Scottish Labour Party, 1976-78; Business Manager, Digital Equipment Corporation, 1978-83; Marketing Manager, Future Technology Systems, 1983-84. Recreations: golf; gardening; reading. Address: (h.) Rowallan, Hillside, Patna, Ayrshire; T.-0292 531480.

Neill, David Lindsay. Master Mariner; Ship's Captain, since 1973; Captain, P.S. Waverley, since 1975; b. 21.5.44, Glasgow; m., Jean Shaw Thompson McLachlan; 1 s.; 2 d. Educ. various schools; Glasgow School of Nautical Studies. Deck Apprentice, 1960-64; Ship's Navigating Officer, 1964-70; Ferry Manager (Isle of Skye), 1970-71; Ship's Navigating Officer, 1971-73. Life Member, Paddle Steamer Preservation Society. Recreations: out of door. Address: (b.) Waverley Excursions Ltd., Anderston Quay, Glasgow, G3 8HA; T.-041-221 8152.

Neill, Gordon Webster McCash, DSO, SSC, NP, FInstD. Solicitor and Notary Public; Honorary Sheriff; b. Arbroath; m., Margaret Mary Lamb; 1 s.; 1 d. Educ. Edinburgh Academy. Legal apprenticeship, 1937-39; Pilot, RAF, 1939-46 (DSO, French Croix de Guerres with silver gilt star and silver star); Partner, Neill & Gibb, SSC, 1947; Chairman, Dundee Area Board, British Law Insurance Co. Ltd., 1954; Principal, Neill & Mackintosh, SSC, 1967; Past Chairman, Scottish Gliding Association and Angus Gliding Club Ltd.; Past President, Chamber of Commerce, Arbroath Rotary Club and Society of Solicitors and Procurators in Angus. Recreations: gliding; powered flying; shooting; fishing. Address: (b.) 93 High Street, Arbroath, Angus, DD11 1DS; T.-0241 73314.

Neill, William Wilson, MA (Hons). Poet; b. 22.2.22, Prestwick; m., Doris Marie; 2 d. (by pr. m.). Educ. Ayr Academy; Edinburgh University. Served, RAF; won Sloane Verse Prize and Grierson Verse Prize while at Edinburgh University; Teacher; crowned Bard, Aviemore Mod, 1969; former Editor, Catalyst; former Editor, Lallans (Scots Language magazine); SAC Book Award, 1985; broadcasts, essays in Scotland's three tongues. Publications: Scotland's Castle, 1969; Poems, 1970; Four Points of a Saltire (Co-author), 1970; Despatches Home, 1972; Buile Shuibhne, 1974; Galloway Landscape: Poems, 1981; Cnu a Mogaill: Poems, 1983; Wild Places: Poems, 1985; Blossom, Berry, Fall: Poems 1986; Making Tracks: Poems, 1988. Address: (h.) Burnside, Crossmichael, Castle Douglas, DG7 3AP; T.-055-667 265.

Neilson, James McElfrish, MB, ChB, FRCPLond, FRCPGlas, FRCPEdin, DPH. Consultant Physician, Stobhill General Hospital, Glasgow, since

1964; Consultant Physician in charge, Diabetic Clinics, Glasgow Northern Hospitals, since 1964; Visiting Physician, Kilsyth and Woodside Health Centres, since 1972; b. 5.4.24, Airdrie; m., Joan Morag Orkney; 2 s. Educ. Airdrie Academy; Glasgow University; Edinburgh University. Formerly: Squadron Leader, RAFVR, Honorary Senior Lecturer, Makerere University Medical School (Nairobi), Member, Faculty and Senate, Glasgow University. Honorary Clinical Lecturer, Glasgow University; Examiner in Medicine and Therapeutics, Scottish Triple Qualification; Member, Panel of Examiners, Royal College of Physicians and Surgeons of Glasgow; Examiner in Medicine, Panel of Examiners for the Professional and Linguistic Assessment Board; Visitor, Joint Committee on Higher Medical Training. Recreations: golf; oil painting. Address: (h.) 7 Thorn Drive, Bearsden, Glasgow, G61 4NG; T.-041-942 4585.

Neilson, William, MA, LLB. Senior Principal Legal Officer, Scottish Office, since 1986; b. 10.2.42, Airdrie; m., Celia Ward; 1 s.; 1 d. Educ. Airdrie Academy; Glasgow University. Qualified as Solicitor, 1967; Procurator Fiscal Depute, 1969-73; admitted to Faculty of Advocates, 1974. Recreations: photography; model shipbuilding; cycling. Address: (h.) 1 East Clapperfield, Edinburgh, EH16; T.-031-664 0595.

Nelson, Rev. James Robert, BD, DPTheol. Church of Scotland Minister, Parishes of Calderbank and Chapelhall, since 1986; b. 27.2.45, Bellshill; m., Georgina Roden. Educ. Uddingston Grammar School; St. Andrews University. Recreations: music; hill-walking; penal reform. Address: The Manse, Chapelhall, Airdrie, ML6 8SG; T.-Airdrie 63439.

Nelson, John, TD, JP, DL. Convener, Stewartry District Council, since 1976; Chairman, Solway River Purification Board, since 1986; b. 26.12.18, Irongray, Dumfries; m., Margaret M.C. Shedden; 4 s. Educ. Castle Douglas High School. Farming, 1934-84, except for War years spent with Royal Artillery and Indian Mountain Artillery in Burma; NFU Committee Member, 40 years (Chairman, Stewartry Area, 1960-61); County Councillor, 1971-74; appointed Deputy Lieutenant, 1983. Recreation: horse riding. Address: (h.) Greentop, 4 Castle View, Castle Douglas; T.-Castle Douglas 3143.

Ness, James Stein, FCA. Chief Executive, Monklands District Council, since 1974 (Director of Finance, since 1984); b. 28.3.28, Dunfermline; m., Betty Alice Belsey; 1 s.; 1 d. Educ. Dunfermline High School; Heriot-Watt College, Edinburgh. City and Royal Burgh of Dunfermline, 1943-58; Burgh of Coatbridge: Depute Chamberlain, 1958-67, Chamberlain, 1967-73, General Manager and Town Clerk, 1974-75. Trustee, Summerlee Industrial Heritage Park; Secretary and Director, Monklands Bookshop Ltd.; President, Monklands Rotary Club. Recreations: golf, walking; fishing. Address: Annfield House, 17 Laird Street, Coatbridge, ML5 3LJ; T.-Coatbridge 21379.

Neumann, Jan, CBE, BSc, FEng, FIMechE, FIMarE, MIES, MASME. Director, YARD Ltd., since 1969 (Managing Director, 1978-87); Board Member, SSEB, since 1986; b. 26.6.24, Prague; m., Barbara Joyce Gove; 2 s. Educ. Friends' School, Great Ayton; London University. Flight Engineer, RAF; Design Engineer, English Electric Co., Rugby; various engineering design and management positions in Yarrow Admiralty Research Department; received Denny Gold Medal, IMarE, and Thomas Lowe Gray Prize, IMechE. Recreations: swimming; bowls. Address: (b.) YARD Ltd., Charing Cross Tower, Glasgow, G2 4PP; T.-041-204 2737.

Newall, Stephen Park, DL, Hon. LLD (Strathclyde). Chairman, Court, University of Strathclyde, since 1988; Chairman: Kanthal Limited, since 1980, Bulten Limited, since 1980, NSC Cartons Limited since 1982, Shuna Shipping Ltd., since 1986; Deputy Lieutenant, Dunbartonshire, since 1985; b. 12.4.31, Bearsden, Dunbartonshire; m., Gay Sommerville Craig; 4 s.; 1 d. Educ. Loretto. Commissioned and served with Parachute Regiment, National Service, 1949-51; Sales Manager, A.P. Newall & Co., 1951-57; Managing Director, Bulten-Kanthal Stephen Newall Co. Ltd., 1957-80. Chairman, Epilepsy Association of Scotland, 1982-86; Chairman, Finance Committee, University of Strathclyde, since 1985; Council Member, Quarrier's Homes, since 1983; Council Member, Scottish Business School, since 1983; Secretary of State for Scotland's Nominee on Court of Cranfield, since 1985; Deacon Convener, Trades of Glasgow, 1983-84. Recreations: farming; hill-walking; sailing; music. Address: (h.) Rowaleyn, Rhu, Dunbartonshire; T.-0436 820 521.

Newbould, Peter, BSc, BAgr, DPhil. Assistant Director, Macaulay Land Use Research Institute; b. 24.9.31, Lincoln; m., Doreen Wilson; 1 s.; 1 d. Educ. Priory School, Shrewsbury; Queen's University, Belfast; Lincoln College, Oxford. Research Assistant, Department of Agriculture, Oxford University; ARC Radiobiological Laboratory (subsequently Letcombe Laboratory): Scientific Officer, Senior Scientific Officer, Principal Scientific Officer, Head of Field Studies Section; Senior Principal Scientific Officer, Plants and Soils Department, Hill Farming Research Organisation; General Secretary, Association of Applied Biologists; Member, Editorial Board, Journal of the Science of Food and Agriculture. Recreations: squash; tennis; gardening; photography; reading; amateur dramatics. Address: (b.) Craigiebuckler, Aberdeen, AB9 2QJ; T.-0224 318611.

Newell, Professor Alan F., BSc, PhD, MIEE, CEng. NCR Professor of Electronics and Microcomputer Systems, Dundee University, since 1980 (Director, Dundee University Microcomputer Centre, since 1980); b. 1.3.41, Birmingham; m., Margaret; 1 s.; 2 d. Educ. St. Philip's Grammar School; Birmingham University. Research Engineer, Standard Telecommunication Laboratories; Lecturer, Department of Electronics, Southampton University. Recreations: family life; horse riding. Address: (b.) Microcomputer Centre, Department of Mathematics and Computer Science, The University, Dundee, DD1 4HN; T.-Dundee 23181.

Newis, Kenneth, CB, CVO, MA. Chairman, Queen's Hall (Edinburgh) Ltd.; Member, Historic Buildings Council for Scotland; Member, Edinburgh Old Town Committee for Conservation and Renewal; Vice Chairman of Council, Cockburn Association; Director, Scottish Baroque Ensemble Ltd.; Governor, Royal Scottish Academy of Music and Drama; b. 9.11.16, Crewe; m., Kathleen Barrow; 2 d. Educ. Manchester Grammar School; St. John's College, Cambridge. HM Office of Works, London, 1938-70; Under Secretary, Scottish Development Department, 1970-73; Secretary, 1973-76. Recreation: music. Address: (h.) 11 Abbotsford Park, Edinburgh, EH10 5DZ; T.-031-447 4138.

Newlands, Rev. George McLeod, MA, BD, PhD. Professor of Divinity, Glasgow University, since 1986 (Dean, Faculty of Divinity, since 1988); b. 12.7.41, Perth; m., Mary Elizabeth Wallace; 3 s. Educ. Perth Academy; Edinburgh University; Heidelberg University; Churchill College, Cambridge. Assistant Minister, Muirhouse, Edinburgh, 1969; Lecturer in Divinity, Glasgow University, 1969; University Lecturer in Divinity, Cambridge, 1973; Dean, Trinity Hall, Cambridge, 1982. Publications: Hilary of Poitiers, 1978; Theology of the Love of God, 1980; The Church of God, 1984; Making Christian Decisions, 1985. Recreations: walking; sailing; golf. Address: (h.) 82 Highburgh Road, Glasgow, G12 9EN; T.-041-334 4712.

Newlands, William Jeffrey, MB, ChB, FRCSEdin. Consultant Ear, Nose and Throat Surgeon, Grampian Health Board and Orkney and Shetland Health Boards, since 1981; Clinical Senior Lecturer in Otolaryngology, Aberdeen University, since 1981; b. 9.9.29, Edinburgh; m., Patricia Kathleen St. Quintin Gee; 2 s.; 2 d. Educ. Daniel Stewart's College, Edinburgh; Edinburgh University. House Physician and House Surgeon, Western General Hospital, Edinburgh, 1952-53; Captain, RAMC, 1953-55; specialist training, 1958-65, Royal Infirmary, Edinburgh, Western Infirmary, Glasgow, Royal National Throat, Nose and Ear Hospital, London; Otolaryngologist, Brown Clinic, Calgary, 1966; Consultant ENT Surgeon: Grampian Health Board, 1967-77, County Hospital, Uddevalla, Sweden, 1977-78, Lothian Health Board, 1978-79; Professor of Otolaryngology, King Faisal University College of Medicine, Saudi Arabia, 1979-81. Examiner in Otolaryngology, Part 2 Examination, FRCSEdin. Recreations: travel; music. Address: (h.) 4 Camperdown Road, Aberdeen, AB2 4NU; T.-0224 633784.

Newsam, John Ernest, MB, ChB, FRCSE. Consultant Urological Surgeon, since 1966; Honorary Senior Lecturer, Edinburgh University, since 1968; Chairman, Lothians Division of Surgery, since 1987; b. 24.9.26, Liverpool; m., Avril McCowan; 3 s.; 2 d. Educ. Liverpool Institute; Edinburgh University. Royal Army Medical Corps, 1951-53; House Surgeon, Registrar, Royal Infirmary, Edinburgh, 1953-55; Senior Registrar, Western General Hospital, Edinburgh, 1958-66; Examiner, Royal College of Surgeons of Edinburgh, since 1967; Assistant Editor, British Journal of Urology, since 1978; Member, Council, Royal College of Surgeons of Edinburgh, since 1985. Recreations: golf; reading. Address: (h.) 14 Comely Bank, Edinburgh, EH4 1AN; T.-031-332 6307.

Newton, Ray William, MB, ChB, FRCPEdin. Consultant Physician in charge of diabetes, Ninewells Hospital, since 1977; Senior Lecturer in Medicine, Ninewells Hospital Medical School, since 1983; Senior Lecturer in Clinical Pharmacology, Dundee University, since 1978; b. 8.12.44, Cockermouth; m., Sylvia Spreng; 3 s. Educ. Cockermouth Grammar School; Edinburgh University. Medical Registrar, Royal Infirmary, Edinburgh, 1970-74; Senior Registrar, Ninewells Hospital, Dundee, 1974-77; Chairman, National Youth Diabetes Project, since 1983; Tayside Regional Adviser, Royal College of Physicians of Edinburgh, since 1986; Specialty Adviser in Medicine, Tayside Region, since 1987; Vice-Chairman, Scottish Committee, British Diabetic Association; Secretary, Scottish Society of Physicians, 1978-83. Publication: Endocrinology - The New Medicine (Editor), 1983. Recreations: President, Forthill Sports Club; Member, Royal and Ancient Golf Club. Address: (h.) 70 Seafield Road, Broughty Ferry, Dundee, DD1 3AQ; T.-0382 76239.

Nicholson, (Charles) Gordon (Brown), QC, MA, LLB. Commissioner, Scottish Law Commission, since 1982; b. 11.9.35, Edinburgh; m., Hazel Mary Nixon; 2 s. Educ. George Watson's College, Edinburgh; Edinburgh University. Admitted to Faculty of Advocates, 1961; Advocate Depute, 1968-70; Sheriff of Dumfries and Galloway, at Dumfries, 1970-76; Sheriff of Lothian and Borders, at Edinburgh, 1976-82. Honorary Vice President, Scottish Association for the Study of Delinquency; Chairman, Scottish Association of Victim Support Schemes. Publication: The Law and Practice of Sentencing in Scotland, 1981. Recreation: music. Address: (h.) 1A Abbotsford Park, Edinburgh, EH10 5DX; T.-031-447 4300.

Nicholson, Peter Alexander, LLB (Hons). Legal Editor, W. Green & Son Ltd., since 1981; General Editor, Scots Law Times and Scottish Current Law, since 1985; General Editor, Green's Weekly Digest, since 1986; b. 22.5.58, Stirling; m., Morag Ann Fraser. Educ. High School, Dalkeith; Edinburgh University. Admitted as Solicitor, 1981. Parish Cuncillor, St. Cuthbert's RC Church, Slateford, Edinburgh; Lay Minister of the Eucharist and Chairman of Four Churches (Ecumenical) Council, Slateford. Recreations: choral singing; running; keeping fit. Address: (h.) 1 Buckstone Row, Edinburgh, EH10 6TW; T.-031-445 4311.

Nickson, Sir David Wigley, KBE (1987), CBE (1981), DL, CBIM, FRSE. Chairman, Scottish Development Agency, from 1 Jan., 1989 (Board Member, since 1988); Chairman, Scottish and Newcastle Breweries plc, since 1983; President, Confederation of British Industry, 1986-88 (Chairman, CBI in Scotland, 1979-81); Chairman, Countryside Commission for Scotland, 1983-86; Director, General Accident Fire and Life Assurance Corporation plc; Director, Clydesdale Bank; Director, Edinburgh Investment Trust; b. 27.11.29, Eton; m., Helen Louise Cockcraft; 3 d. Educ. Eton College; Royal Military Academy, Sandhurst. Commissioned, Coldstream Guards,

1949-54; William Collins: joined, 1954, Director, 1961-85, Joint Managing Director, 1967, Vice-Chairman, 1976-83, Group Managing Director, 1979-82; Director: Scottish United Investors plc, 1970-83, Radio Clyde Ltd., 1982-85; Chairman, Pan Books, 1982-83. Member: Scottish Industrial Development Advisory Board, 1975-80, Scottish Economic Council, since 1980, Scottish Committee, Design Council, 1978-81; Vice Chairman, Management Committee, Atlantic Salmon Trust, since 1982; Member, Queen's Bodyguard for Scotland (Royal Company of Archers); Deputy Lieutenant, Stirling and Falkirk, since 1982. Recreations: fishing; bird-watching; the countryside. Address: (h.) Renagour, Aberfoyle, Stirling, FK8 3TF; T.-Aberfoyle 275.

Nicol, Alan, BA, LRAM. National Administrator: Scottish Community Drama Association, since 1985, Scottish Association of Speech and Drama Adjudicators, since 1987; b. 3.6.31, Lewis; m., Jane. Educ. Stretford Grammar School; RADA; Open University. Professional theatre, 1948-59; Highland Adviser, SCDA, 1959-66; Children's Theatre, Aberdeen, 1966-69; Aberdeen College of Education, 1969-85; Visiting Professor, University of Newfoundland, 1980 and 1981; Adjudicator of drama festivals in Dundalk, Gibraltar, New York; conducted workshops in Japan and throughout Europe and America. Address: (b.) 5 York Place, Edinburgh, EH1 3EB; T.-031-557 5552.

Nicol, Rev. Douglas Alexander Oag, MA, BD (Hons). Minister, St. Columba Church, Kilmacolm, since 1982; b. 5.4.48, Dunfermline; m., Anne Wilson Gillespie; 1 s.; 1 d. Educ. Kirkcaldy High School; Edinburgh University; Glasgow University. Assistant Warden, St. Ninian's Centre, Crieff, 1972-76; Minister, Lochside, Dumfries, 1976-82. Chairman, Board of Directors, National Bible Society of Scotland, 1984-87; Convener, Evangelism Committee, Church of Scotland, 1983-88; Joint Convener, Department of Mission and Ministry, since 1988. Recreations: hill-walking; marathon running. Address: 6 Churchill Road, Kilmacolm, Renfrewshire; T.-Kilmacolm 3271.

Nicol, Rev. John Chalmers, MA, BD, AHSM. Minister, Holy Trinity Church, Bridge of Allan, since 1985; b. 6.4.39, Greenock; m., Anne Morrison Macdonald; 1 s.; 1 d. Educ. Greenock Academy; Glasgow University; Princeton Theological Seminary. Assistant Minister, Westwood Parish Church, East Kilbride, 1964-65; Minister: St. Andrews Scots Church, Temperley, Buenos Aires, 1965-69, Bonnyrigg Parish Church, 1970-75; Secretary, Edinburgh Local Health Council, 1975-78; Principal Administrative Assistant, Argyll and Clyde Health Board, 1978-85. Recreations: fishing; wine-making. Address: 29 Keir Street, Bridge of Allan, Stirling, FK9 4QJ; T.-0786 832093.

Nicol, Rev. Thomas James Trail, LVO, MBE, MC, MA, DD. Minister, Church of Scotland; Extra Chaplain to The Queen, since 1979; b. 24.1.17, Skelmorlie, Ayrshire; m., Mary Barnfather Taylor; 2 d. Educ. Edinburgh Academy; Dundee High School; Glasgow Academy; Aberdeen Grammar School; Aberdeen University. OCTU and Commission, Black Watch, 1939-42; ordained as Chaplain to the Forces, 1942; RAChD, 1942-46, attached 51 (H) Division; Minister, St. Luke's, Broughty Ferry, 1946-49; regular commission, RAChD, 1949-72; Assistant Chaplain-General, HQ Scotland, 1967-72; Minister, Crathie, 1972-77; Domestic Chaplain in Scotland to the Queen, 1972-79. Recreations: hill-walking; fishing; golf. Address: (h.) Beech Cottage, Dalginross, Comrie, Perthshire, PH6 2HB; T.-0764 70430.

Nicol, William, CBE, BSc, FCIOB, FInstR. Chairman, Scottish Committee, and Member of Council, CNAA; former Chairman and Managing Director Director, Craig-Nicol Limited; b. 9.9.24, Glasgow; m., Margaret Jean McNeill; 2 s.; 1 d. Educ. High School of Glasgow; Gresham House; Glasgow University. President, Glasgow Master Wrights and Builders' Association, 1953-54; Chairman, Glasgow Local Joint Apprenticeship Committee, 1952-61; Chairman, Scottish Building Apprenticeship Council, 1959-67; Member, Board of Governors, Jordanhill College of Education, 1959-67; Deacon, Incorporation of Wrights in Glasgow, 1963-64; Director, Glasgow Chamber of Commerce, 1965-70 (Chairman, Education Committee); Founder Chairman, Scottish Branch, Chartered Institute of Building, 1963-65 (National President, 1970-71, Honorary Treasurer, 1972-76); Member, Construction Industry Training Board, 1964-85 (Chairman, Building Committee, 1967-72); President, Scottish National Federation of Building Trades' Employers, 1969-70 and 1972-73; Governor, Glasgow College of Building and Printing, 1966-75 (first Chairman, Board of Governors) and Vice-Chairman, then Chairman, new College Council, 1976-82; Vice-Chairman, Scottish Technical Education Council, 1973-78, Chairman, 1978-85; Chairman, British Refrigeration Association, 1975-77, President, 1986; Chairman, Commercial Section, CECOMAF, 1974-77 (President, CECOMAF, 1979-83); Committee Member, Scottish Branch, Institute of Refrigeration, 1977-81 (elected Vice-Chairman, 1979); Member, Heating, Ventilating, Air Conditioning and Refrigeration Equipment - Economic Development Committee, NEDO, 1984-87. Recreations: gardening; walking; reading; golf. Address: (h.) 27 Burnhead Road, Glasgow, G43 2SU; T.-041-637 4097.

Nicoll, Douglas Alexander Smith, JP. Honorary Sheriff, Forfar; b. 24.6.18, Forfar; m., Ella Mary Grant; 1 s.; 2 d. Educ. Forfar Academy. Partner, joinery manufacturing firm, Forfar, from 1936; Managing Director and Chairman upon retirement, 1972; Member, Forfar Town Council, seven years; served on Magistrates' Bench, three years; served on Steering Committee for Community Councils in Angus; Elder, Church of Scotland. Recreations: music; bowling. Address: (h.) Dunvegan, 11 Turfbeg Avenue, Forfar, DD8 3LJ; T.-0307 63232.

Nicoll, Eric Hamilton, CBE, FSA Scot, BSc (Hons), FICE, FIWEM (Dip). Deputy Chief Engineer, Scottish Development Department, 1976-85; b. 15.5.25, Edinburgh; m., Helen Elizabeth Barnes; 1 s.; 1 d. Educ. George Heriot's School, Edinburgh; Edinburgh University. Engineering Assistant: Midlothian County Council

Roads Department, 1945-46, Edinburgh Corporation Water Department, 1946-51; Chief Assistant County Engineer, Midlothian County Council, 1951-62; Scottish Development Department: Engineering Inspector, 1962-68, Senior Engineering Inspector, 1968-72, Assistant Chief Engineer, 1972-75. US Water Pollution Control Federation Arthur Sidney Bedell Award, 1985. Publication: Small Water Pollution Works: Design and Practice, 1988. Recreations: wood sculpture; music; antiquities. Address: (h.) 35 Wardie Road, Edinburgh, EH5 3LJ.

Nicolson, Alasdair George, MA (Hons). Assistant Principal, Jordanhill College of Education, since 1976; b. 6.12.26, Stepps, Lanarkshire; m., Sylvia Hall; 1 d. Educ. Coatbridge High School; Glasgow University. Teacher/Principal, Modern Studies and History, Airdrie High School, 1951-61; Lecturer in Modern Studies, then Head, Modern Studies Department, Jordanhill College of Education, 1961-76; Principal Examiner, Modern Studies, SCEEB, 1965-74; Member, BBC Schools Broadcasting Council Advisory Committee, 1968-74; Member, STV Education Advisory Committee, since 1981; Member, Scottish Central Committee Social Subjects, 1974-81; Chairman, Scottish Council, United Nations Association, since 1982; Chairman, Saltire Education Committee, 1970-76; Chairman, Association of Lecturers in Colleges of Education in Scotland, 1969-72; Chairman, Association for Liberal Education, 1969-72; Executive Member, Council for Education in the Commonwealth, since 1979; Founder Member, Scottish Environmental Education Council; Chairman, West of Scotland District, WEA, since 1982. Publications: The Cold War, 1972; World Today (Co-author); Europe Today (Co-author). Recreations: swimming; travel. Address: (h.) 12 Somerford Road, Bearsden, Glasgow, G61 1AS; T.-041-942 4933.

Nicolson, David M., CA. Office Managing Partner, Peat Marwick McLintock, Edinburgh, since 1988; b. 22.4.42, Edinburgh; m., Elizabeth Finlay Smith; 1 s.; 1 d. Educ. Royal High School, Edinburgh. Qualified as CA with Robertson & Maxtone Graham, Edinburgh, 1964; Peat Marwick Mitchell & Co., London, 1964-67; returned to Robertson & Maxtone Graham, 1967 (now Peat Marwick McLintock). President, Edinburgh Junior Chamber of Commerce, 1975-76. Recreations: golf; tennis; skiing; gardening. Address: (b.) 33/34 Charlotte Square, Edinburgh, EH2 4HF; T.-031-225 1516.

Nicolson, Elisabeth, MA, RGN, SCM. Member for Unst, Shetland Islands Council, since 1986; Community Councillor, South Unst, since 1982; b. 14.3.43, St. Helens; m., James Barron Smith Nicolson. Educ. North Berwick High School; Edinburgh University. Staff nurse, Edinburgh; relief district nurse, Shetland, Orkney and West Lothian; agency nursing, Edinburgh, Paris, Glasgow and London; teaching, English and French, Dunbar Grammar School; midwifery, Rossendale. Recreations: music; singing; dancing; local and family history; conversation. Address: (h.) 16 Nikkavord Lea, Baltasound, Unst, Shetland, ZE2 9XL; T.-095 781 503.

Nimmo, Ian Alister. Editor, Evening News, Edinburgh, since 1976; b. 14.10.34, Lahore, Pakistan; m., Grace; 2 s.; 1 d. Educ. Royal School of Dunkeld; Breadalbane Academy. Commissioned, Royal Scots Fusiliers; Reporter, Sub-Editor, D.C. Thomson, Dundee, 1957; Editor, Weekly Scotsman, Edinburgh, 1961; Features Editor, Press and Journal, Aberdeen, 1966; Editor, Evening Gazette, Middlesbrough, 1970. Vice-President, Newspaper Press Fund. Publications: Robert Burns; Portrait of Edinburgh; The Brave Adventure. Recreations: climbing; fly fishing; gardening; painting. Address: (b.) 20 North Bridge, Edinburgh, EH1 1YT; T.-031-225 2468.

Nisbet, Hugh Haddow, MA (Hons), DipEd. Headteacher, Stanely Green High School, Paisley, since 1977; b. 20.4.40, Barrhead; m., Lilian; 1 s.; 1 d. Educ. Paisley Grammar School; Glasgow University. Teacher, Crookston Castle Secondary School, Glasgow, 1963-69; Principal Teacher of History, Glenwood Secondary School, Glasgow, 1969-71; Assistant Head Teacher: Riverside Secondary School, Glasgow, 1971-75, Crookston Castle Secondary School, 1975-77. Recreations: reading; tropical fish-keeping; junior football; golf. Address: (b.) Stanely Green High School, Foxbar Road, Paisley, PA2 0RT; T.-Brediland 3217.

Nisbet, Professor John Donald, OBE, MA, BEd, PHD, FEIS. Professor of Education, Aberdeen University, 1963-88; b. 17.10.22, Rosyth; 1 s.; 1 d. Educ. Dunfermline High School; Edinburgh University; Aberdeen University. RAF, 1943-46; Teacher, 1946-48; Lecturer, 1949-63; Visiting Professor, San Jose, 1961, 1964, Monash, Australia, 1974, Walkato, New Zealand, 1978. Chairman: Educational Research Board, 1972-75, Scottish Committee on Primary Education, 1974-80, Scottish Council for Research in Education, 1975-78; President, British Educational Research Association, 1975; Editor, British Journal of Educational Psychology, 1967-74; Editor, Studies in Higher Education, 1979-84; Editor, World Yearbook of Education, 1985. Recreations: golf; orienteering. Address: (h.) 7 Lawson Avenue, Banchory, AB3 3TW; T.-03302 3145.

Niven, Catharine, BSc, AMA, FSA(Scot). Curator, Inverness Museum and Art Gallery, since 1984; b. 23.9.52, Denbigh; m., Roger Niven. Educ. Loughton High School; Leicester University. Freelance archaeologist, working in Britain and Scandinavia; Keeper of Antiquities, Rotherham Museum, 1979-81; Assistant Curator (Archaeology), Inverness Museum and Art Gallery, 1981-84. Recreation: music. Address: (b.) Castle Wynd, Inverness, IV2 3ED; T.-0463 237114.

Niven, David, MBE, JP. Leader, Conservative Group, North East Fife District Council, since 1984; b. 28.10.14, St. Andrews; m., Jessie Isabella Miller; 1 s.; 1 d. Educ. Madras College, St. Andrews. Elected to St. Andrews Town Council, 1951; Magistrate, 1959; Provost, 1970; elected to North East Fife District Council, 1974; Chairman, 1980; President, Saint Andrews Society of St. Andrews. Recreations: golf; photography. Address: (h.) 7 John Street, St. Andrews, Fife, KY16 9DB; T.-St. Andrews 74387.

Niven, Peter Stuart Buchanan, LLB. Secretary - Legal Education, Law Society of Scotland; b. 18.8.57, Edinburgh; m., Lynne Temporal. Educ. George Watson's College, Edinburgh; Edinburgh University. Apprenticed to Robson, McLean & Paterson, WS, 1978-80; Qualified Assistant: Fyfe Ireland & Co., WS, 1980-82, Shepherd & Wedderburn, WS, 1982-84. Member, Vestry, Old St. Paul's Scottish Episcopal Church, since 1983. Recreations: tennis; badminton; choral singing; listening to good music; eating out. Address: (h.) 14 Wolseley Crescent, Edinburgh; T.-031-659 6229.

Niven, Stuart Matthew, BSc, DipEd. Director, School of Further Education, Jordanhill College of Education, since 1983; b. 1.3.36, Clydebank; m., Jean K. McPhee; 1 s.; 1 d. Educ. Clydebank High School; Glasgow University. Teacher of Mathematics and Physics: Clydebank High School, 1959, Stow College of Engineering, 1961; Head, Department of Mathematics and Physics, Kilmarnock College, 1964; Jordanhill College of Education: Lecturer in Mathematics, 1967, Senior Lecturer in Further Education, 1968, Principal Lecturer, 1970. Member, CNAA Further Education Board, 1978-84; Chairman, Editorial Board, Journal for Further and Higher Education in Scotland, 1976-83; Chairman, National Liaison Committee on Training of Teachers of Nursing, Midwifery and Health Visiting, since 1983. Publications: Vocational Further Education in Scotland, 1982; Professional Development of Further Education Lecturers in Scotland: Towards Comprehensive Provision, 1987. Recreation: golf. Address: Jordanhill College of Education, 76 Southbrae Drive, Glasgow, G13 1PP; T.-041-959 0044.

Nixon, Christopher William, NDA, CertEd. Principal, Oatridge Agricultural College, since 1985; b. 7.11.45, Grappenhall; m., Susan Doreen Presley; 1 s.; 2 d. Educ. Normain College, Chester; Harper Adams Agricultural College. Lecturer in Agriculture/Extra Mural Lecturer, Newton Rigg, Penrith; Lecturer in Sheep Production/Senior Lecturer, Extra Mural, Bishop Burton; Depute Principal, Oatridge Agricultural College. SCOTVEC Assessor, since 1985. Address: (h.) 1 Avonmill Road, Linlithgow, West Lothian; T.-0506 843559.

Nixon, Mary MacKenzie, OBE, MA (Hons), DipEd. Archivist, Scottish Girl Guides Association, since 1979; b. Port Arthur, Canada. Educ. High School of Stirling; St. Andrews University. Assistant English Teacher, Riverside School, Stirling; Responsible Assistant, History, High School of Stirling, Falkirk High School; Responsible Assistant, English, Falkirk High School; Head, English Department, Grangemouth High School. Girl Guides Association: County Camp Adviser and Chairman, Training Committee, Stirlingshire; Scotland: Ranger Adviser, Training Adviser, Deputy Scottish Chief Commissioner; Co-ordinator, Silver Jubilee Scheme for Unemployed; Chairman, Netherurd Committee, Scottish Girl Guides Association Training Centre, 1981-85. Recreations: genealogy; archaeology; poetry. Address: (h.) Gartlea, 19 Station Road, Bannockburn, FK7 8LE.

Noble, Alastair MacIver, BSc, PhD. HM Inspector of Schools, since 1985; b. 12.4.45, Glasgow; m., Ruth; 1 s.; 1 d. Educ. High School of Glasgow; Glasgow University. Science Teacher, Paisley Grammar School; Principal Teacher of Chemistry, Graeme High School, Falkirk; Curriculum Development Officer, Scottish Curriculum Development Service; BBC Education Officer, West of Scotland. Address: (h.) 1 Craighorn Drive, Falkirk, FK1 5NX; T.-0324 21162.

Noble, Sheriff David, MA, LLB, WS, JP. Sheriff at Oban, Campbeltown and Fort William, since 1983; b. 11.2.23, Inverness; m., Marjorie Scott Smith; 2 s.; 1 d. Educ. Inverness Royal Academy; Edinburgh University. RAF Bomber Command, 1942-46; Miller Thomson & Robertson, WS, Edinburgh, 1950-83. Recreation: sailing. Address: (h.) Woodhouselee, North Connel, Argyll; T.-Connel 678.

Noble, David Hillhouse, LLB. Chief Executive, Skye and Lochalsh District Council, since 1974; b. 27.4.48, Paisley; m., Hilary; 1 s.; 2 d. Educ. Greenock Academy; Glasgow University. Legal and Administrative Assistant, Argyll County Council, 1972-73; Senior Legal and Administrative Assistant, Inverness County Council, 1973-74. Recreations: board sailing; music. Address: (b.) Council Offices, Park Road, Portree, IV51 9EP; T.-0478 2341.

Noble, Rev. George Strachan, DipTh. Minister, Newarthill linked with Carfin, since 1972; b. 29.9.31, Inverallochy, near Fraserburgh; m., Mary Kinsman Addison; 1 s.; 1 d. Educ. Inverallochy Public School; Fraserburgh Academy; Glasgow University; Aberdeen University. Apprentice Auctioneer, fish trade, Fraserburgh, 1948-50; Royal Artillery, 1950-52; Auctioneer, 1952-59; Manager and Director, fishing boat management/fish-selling firm, Fraserburgh, 1959-66; divinity student, 1966-71; Probationer Assistant Minister, Fraserburgh Old Parish Church, 1971-72. Member, Church and Nation Committee, Church of Scotland. Recreation: sport. Address: The Manse, Church Street, Newarthill, Motherwell, ML1 5HS; T.-0698 860316.

Noble (or Nobail), Sir Iain, Bt. of Ardkinglas and Eilean Iarmain. Chairman, Noble and Company Ltd.; b. 8.9.35, Berlin. Educ. in China, Argentina and England; University College, Oxford. Scottish Council (Development and Industry), 1964-69; Noble Grossart Ltd., Edinburgh, 1969-72. Chairman, Seaforth Maritime Ltd., 1972-77; Director, Adam and Company plc, since 1983; Darnaway Venture Capital plc, since 1984; New Scotland Insurance Group PLC, since 1986; Proprietor, Fearann Eilean Iarmain; Member, Edinburgh University Court, 1970-73; Governor, College of Sabhal Mor Ostaig, 1974-84. Editor, Sources of Finance, 1967-69. Recreations: deoc bad, comhradh, orain is ceol le deagh chompanaich. Address: An Lamraig, Eilean Iarmain, An t-Eilean, Sgitheanach, IV43 8QR; T.-047 13-266.

Noble, Professor Iain William, MA, LLB, WS. Professor of Conveyancing, Edinburgh University, since 1973; Partner, Dundas & Wilson CS, Solicitors, Edinburgh, since 1953; b. 6.12.25, Inverness; m., Dr. Mary Evelyn Cameron Bird; 1

s.; 2 d. Educ. Inverness Royal Academy; Edinburgh University. Member, several Committees, Law Society of Scotland. Recreations: fishing; sailing. Address: (b.) 25 Charlotte Square, Edinburgh, EH2 4EZ; T.-031-225 1234.

Noble, Sir (Thomas Alexander) Fraser, Kt (1971), MBE (1947), MA, LLD, FRSE; b. 29.4.18, Cromdale; m., Barbara A.M. Sinclair; 1 s.; 1 d. Educ. Nairn Academy; Aberdeen University. Indian Civil Service, 1940-47; Lecturer in Political Economy, Aberdeen University, 1948-57; Secretary, Carnegie Trust for Scottish Universities, 1957-62; Vice-Chancellor, Leicester University, 1972-76; Principal, Aberdeen University, 1976-81; Past Chairman of numerous public service committees, including Scottish Standing Conference of Youth Service Organisations, Home Office Advisory Committee for Probation and After Care, Television Research Committee; Chairman, UK Committee of Vice Chancellors, 1970-72; former Executive Member of Council, Association of Commonwealth Universities. Recreations: golf; listening to music. Address: (h.) Hedgerley, Victoria Street, Nairn; T.-Nairn 53151.

Noble, Timothy Peter, MA, MBA. Director: Noble & Company Ltd., Waverley Mining Finance plc, Indepent Insurance Co. Ltd.; Chairman, Business Archives Council of Scotland; b. 21.12.43; m., Elizabeth Mary Aitken; 2 s.; 1 d. Educ. University College, Oxford; Gray's Inn, London; INSEAD, Fontainebleau. Recreations: wine; astronomy; spectrology; skiing; tennis; bridge. Address: (h.) Ardnahane, Barnton Avenue, Edinburgh; T.-031-336 3565.

Nodes, Brian Henry. Administrator, Blair Castle, since 1981; Chairman, Grand Tour of Scotland Consortium, since 1986; b. 28.5.32, Hampstead; m., Marlene Leslie; 2 s.; 2 d. Educ. Queen Elizabeth Grammar School for Boys, Carmarthen. Articled pupil, firm of chartered surveyors; served with Intelligence Corps in Far East during National Service; Estate Surveyor, Cawdor Estates, Wales; Administrator, Cawdor Castle, Nairn. Member, The Atholl Highlanders, since 1982. Recreations: rugby; sailing; choral singing; gardening; caravanning; model making. Address: (h.) Golden Grove, Old Blair, Blair Atholl, Pitlochry, PH18 5TX; T.-079 681 320.

Noel-Paton, Frederick Ranald, BA. Group Managing Director, John Menzies plc, since 1986; b. 7.11.38, Bombay; m., Patricia Anne Stirling; 4 d. Educ. Rugby School; McGill University. Investment Analyst, Greenshields Inc., 1962-63; Management Trainee, United Biscuits, 1964; various posts, British United Airways Ltd., 1965-70; various senior executive posts, British Caledonian Airways, 1970-86 (General Manager, West Africa, 1975-79, General Manager, Far East, 1980-86, Director, Caledonian Far East Airways, 1984-86); Director: Pacific Assets Investment Trust plc, since 1986, General Accident Fire and Life Assurance Corporation plc, since 1987, Royal Bank of Scotland plc, since 1988. Recreations: fishing; walking; bird-watching; the arts. Address: (b.) 108 Princes Street, Edinburgh, EH2 3AA; T.-031-225 8555.

Norris, Derrick S., BSc (Hons), FBCS. Director of Computer Services, City of Glasgow, since 1979; b. 17.3.40, Liverpool; m., Pamela Anne; 1 s.; 1 d. Educ. Liverpool Institute; Liverpool University. Statistician/Programmer, Associated Octel, 1963-67; Senior Computer Assistant, Cheshire County Council, 1967-69; Senior Systems Analyst, Lancashire County Council, 1969-74; Deputy Computer Manager, Devon County Council, 1974-78; Assistant County Treasurer (Computer Services), Northamptonshire County Council, 1978-79. Recreations: swimming; walking; shooting; DIY. Address: (b.) 112 Ingram Street, Glasgow, G1 1ET; T.-041-227 4067.

North, Michael James, MA, PhD. Senior Lecturer in Biological Science, Stirling University, since 1985; b. 20.1.48, London. Educ. East Barnet Grammar School; Hertford College, Oxford; Newcastle upon Tyne University. SRC Postdoctoral Fellow, Leicester University and Essex University, 1973-75; Lecturer in Biochemistry, Stirling University, 1975-85. Recreations: gardening; music; supporting Tottenham Hotspur FC. Address: (b.) Department of Biological Science, Stirling University, Stirling, FK9 4LA; T.-0786 73171.

Norton-Smith, Professor John, BA, MA, BLitt, DLitt (Hon.), FRSA. Professor of English, Dundee University, since 1977 (Head, Department of English, since 1977); b. 26.6.31, Philadelphia; m., Marianne Cecil; 1 d. Educ. William Penn Charter School; Magdalen College, Oxford. Lecturer: St. Andrews University, 1960, Hull University, 1961-68; Reader, Reading University, 1968-77. Member, University Council for Scottish Dictionaries, since 1979; Member, Scottish University Examination Committee, since 1985; General Editor, Medieval and Renaissance Authors Series, since 1969. Publications: John Lydgate: Poems, 1966; James I of Scotland: The Kingis Quair, 1971; Geoffrey Chaucer, 1974; The Quare of Jelusy, 1976; M.S. Fairfax 16, 1979; William Langland, 1983; Christopher Marlowe: Doctor Faustus, 1988. Recreations: music; art history. Address: (h.) Glencairn, Tayview Terrace, Newport-on-Tay, Fife; T.-0382 543102.

Norwell, Peter Smith, OBE, TD, JP. Honorary Sheriff, Perth; b. 14.4.12, Perth; m., Elisabeth May Edwards; 3 d. Educ. Dollar Academy. Lt.-Col., RASC, 1944; Secretary, Perthshire Territorial Army Association, 1960-62; Assistant Secretary, Angus, Perthshire and Fife Territorial Army Association, 1962-67; Managing Director, Norwells Perth Footwear Ltd., 1935-60; Town Councillor, Perth, 1946-52; Chairman, Perth Theatre Company, 1968-72. Address: (h.) Greenknowe, Corsiehill, Perth, PH2 7BN; T.-Perth 25681.

Nowell, Professor Ian William, BSc (Hons), PhD, CChem, FRSC. Head, School of Chemistry, Robert Gordon's Institute of Technology, Aberdeen, since 1986; b. 26.4.44, London; 2 d. Educ. Bourne Grammar School; Leicester University. Woodrow Wilson Fellow, Kent State University, 1969-70; Postdoctoral Fellow, University of British

Columbia, 1970-71; Junior Fellow in Inorganic Chemistry, Bristol University, 1971-72; Lecturer in Chemistry, Mid-Cheshire College of FE, 1973-74; Lecturer, Senior Lecturer, Principal Lecturer, Sheffield City Polytechnic, 1974-85. Recreations: hill-walking; golf; skiing; swimming. Address: (b.) Robert Gordon's Institute of Technology, St. Andrew Street, Aberdeen, AB1 1HG; T.-0224 633611.

O

Oakes, David Alexander, BA (Hons), DipEd, CertEd. Head Teacher, Arran High School, since 1972; b. 21.1.34, Leeds; m., Maureen Ridyard; 2 s. Educ. Rothwell Grammar School; Liverpool University; Sheffield University. Commissioned Officer, Aircrew, RAF, 1955-57 (Pilot); Assistant Geography Teacher, Wirral Grammar School for Boys, 1958-63; Head, Geography Department, Rothwell Grammar School, near Wakefield, 1963-67; Principal Teacher of Geography, Arran High School, 1967-72. Secretary/Treasurer, Arran Mountain Rescue Team; Church Elder; Trustee, Arran Heritage Museum; Treasurer, Arran Music Society. Recreations: hill-walking; travel; crosswords; amateur operatics; reading; golf. Address: (h.) Island Bank, Lamlash, Isle of Arran, KA27 8LG; T.-077 06 279.

Oakley, Charles A., CBE, JP, LLD. Honorary President, Glasgow College of Technology, since 1985; Chairman, Central College of Commerce, Glasgow, since 1966; Honorary President, Scottish Film Council, since 1939; Hon. President, Citizens Theatre, Glasgow; b. 30.9.00, Portsmouth; m., Dr. Agnes Stewart (deceased); 2 d. Educ. Devonport High School; Glasgow University. Apprentice, John Brown's Shipyard, 1919-24; qualified naval architect; Lecturer in Industrial Psychology, Glasgow University, 1930-72 (seconded to Civil Service, 1939-53); Scottish Area Officer, Air Ministry; Scottish Controller, Ministry of Aircraft Production, 1940-45; also Controller, North of Ireland, 1944-45; Scottish Controller, Board of Trade, 1945-53; President, Glasgow Chamber of Commerce, 1963-65; President, Association of Scottish Chambers of Commerce, 1966-68. Publications: Men at Work, 1946; The Second City, 1946. Recreation: leading a social life. Address: (h.) 10 Kirklee Circus, Glasgow, G12; T.-041-339 7000.

O Baoill, Colm J.M., MA, PhD. Senior Lecturer in Celtic, Aberdeen University, since 1980; b. 22.9.38, Armagh; m., Frances G.R. O Boyle; 3 d. Educ. St. Patrick's College, Armagh; Queen's University, Belfast. Assistant Lecturer in Celtic, Queen's University, Belfast, 1962-65; Lecturer in Celtic, Aberdeen University, 1966-80. Publications: Bardachd Shilis Na Ceapaich, 1972; Eachann Bacach and Other Maclean Poets, 1979. Address: (h.) 19 King's Crescent, Old Aberdeen, Aberdeen; T.-Aberdeen 637064.

O'Brien, Francis Aloysius, BL, NP. Honorary Sheriff, Dumfries, since 1971; b. 30.8.07, Dumfries; m., Ellen Drysdale Johnstone; 2 d. Educ. St. Joseph's College, Dumfries; Edinburgh University. Depute Procurator Fiscal, 1941-62; Burgh Prosecutor, 1941-44. Dumfries Guild of Players, since 1924: Secretary, 17 years, Treasurer, 3 years, Master, 1973-78, Honorary Life Member, since 1957; Secretary/Treasurer, Dumfries Property Owners, 1941-57; Governor, St. Joseph's College, Dumfries, 1960-82; Dean of Faculty (Dumfriesshire), 1975-77. Recreations: golf; drama. Address: (h.) Belmont, Whinnyhill, Dumfries, DG2 8HE; T.-New Abbey 354.

O'Brien, Sir Frederick William Fitzgerald, KB, QC, MA, LLB. Sheriff Principal, Lothian and Borders, since 1978; Commissioner, Northern Lighthouse Board, since 1965; Convener of Sheriffs Principal, since 1972; b. 19.7.17, Edinburgh; m., Audrey Muriel Owen; 2 s.; 1 d. Educ. Royal High School, Edinburgh; Edinburgh University. Called to Scottish Bar, 1947; QC, 1960; Commissioner, Mental Welfare Commission, 1962-65; Senior Advocate Depute, Crown Office, 1964-65; Sheriff Principal, Caithness, Sutherland, Orkney and Shetland, 1965-75; Interim Sheriff Principal, Aberdeen, Kincardine and Banff, 1969-71; Sheriff Principal, North Strathclyde, 1975-78; Interim Sheriff Principal, South Strathclyde, 1981; Member, Scottish Medical Practices Committee, 1973-76; Member, Scottish Records Advisory Council, 1974-83; Chairman, Sheriff Court Rules Council, 1975-81; Convener, General Council Business Committee, Edinburgh University, 1980-84; Past President, Royal High School FP Club (Honorary President, since 1980). Recreations: music; golf. Address: (h.) 22 Arboretum Road, Edinburgh, EH3 5PN; T.-031-552 1923.

O'Brien, Most Rev. Keith Michael Patrick, BSc, DipEd. Archbishop of St. Andrews and Edinburgh, since 1985; b. 17.3.38, Ballycastle, Northern Ireland. Educ. Saint Patrick's, Dumbarton; Holy Cross Academy, Edinburgh; Edinburgh University; St. Andrew's College, Drygrange; Moray House College of Education. Teacher, St. Columba's High School, Fife; Assistant Priest, Kilsyth, then Bathgate; Spiritual Director, St. Andrew's College, Drygrange; Rector, Blairs College, Aberdeen; ordained Archbishop by Cardinal Gray, 1985. Recreations: music; walking. Address: Saint Bennet's, 42 Greenhill Gardens, Edinburgh, EH10 4BJ.

O'Donnell, Mgr. John. Catholic Priest; b. 18.7.18, Dumbarton. Educ. St. Patrick's High School, Dumbarton; St. Peter's College, Bearsden. Ordained, 1944; Motherwell Diocese: Diocesan Secretary, 1948-56, Diocesan Chancellor and Treasurer, 1956-84; appointed Privy Chamberlain, 1956, Domestic Prelate, 1960. Address: 8 The Clachan, Wishaw, Lanarkshire, ML2 7LR; T.-0698 376866.

O'Farrell, Professor Patrick Neil, BA, PhD, MIPI. Professor of Town and Country Planning, Heriot-Watt University, since 1986; b. 18.4.41; m.; 3 d. Educ. Trinity College, Dublin. Assistant in Geography, Trinity College, Dublin, 1963-65; Assistant Lecturer and Lecturer in Geography, Queen's University, Belfast, 1965-70; Lecturer in

Geography, New University of Ulster, 1971-73; Lecturer, Senior Lecturer and Reader in Planning, UWIST, 1973-86. Recreations: golf; talking; music. Address: (b.) Heriot-Watt University, Chambers Street, Edinburgh, EH1.

Ogden, Professor Raymond William, MA, PhD, FRSE. George Sinclair Professor of Mathematics, Glasgow University, since 1984 (Head of Department, since 1986); b. 19.9.43, Lytham; m., Susanne; 2 s.; 2 d. Educ. Leamington College; Gonville and Caius College, Cambridge. Science Research Council Research Fellow, East Anglia University, 1970-72; Lecturer, then Reader in Mathematics, Bath University, 1972-80; Professor of Mathematics, Brunel University, 1981-84. Publication: Non-linear Elastic Deformations, 1984. Recreations: playing squash; walking; music; gardening. Address: (b.) Department of Mathematics, Glasgow University, Glasgow, G12 8QW; T.-041-339 8855.

Ogilvie-Laing, Gerald, ARSBS. Sculptor; b. 11.2.36, Newcastle upon Tyne. Educ. Berkhamsted School; RMA, Sandhurst. Commissioned Fifth Fusiliers, 1955-60; resigned commission and attended St. Martin's School of Art; lived in New York, 1964-69; Artist in Residence, Aspen Institute for Humanistic Studies, Colorado, 1966; moved to north of Scotland, 1969, and restored ruins of Kinkell Castle; Civic Trust Award, 1971; established a tapestry workshop in north of Scotland; Visiting Professor, University of New Mexico, 1976-77; set up bronze foundry, Kinkell Castle, to produce own work; Member, Art Committee, Scottish Arts Council, 1978-80; worked mainly in New York, 1984-85; Professor of Sculpture, Columbia University, New York, 1986-87; appointed Commissioner, Royal Fine Art Commission for Scotland, 1987; divides time between north of Scotland and New York. Address: (h.) Kinkell Castle, Ross and Cromarty, IV7 8AT; T.-0349 61485.

Ogilvy, Sir David (John Wilfrid), 13th Bt, DL. Farmer and Landowner; Deputy Lieutenant, East Lothian, since 1971; b. 3.2.14; m., Penelope Mary Ursula Hills; 1 s. Educ. Eton; Trinity College, Oxford. RNVR, 1939-45. Address: (h.) Winton Cottage, Pencaitland, East Lothian, EH34 5AT.

Ogle, Ian Henry, CA. Senior Audit Partner (Glasgow), Arthur Young, since 1986; Director: CBI Scottish Council, Glasgow Chamber of Commerce, Scottish Chamber Orchestra, Greater Easterhouse Partnership; Member, Governing Council, SCOTBIC; b. 26.4.34, London; 2 s.; 2 d. Educ. Glasgow Academy. Arthur Young: Executive Partner, 1975-78, Managing Partner, 1978-85, Regional Managing Partner, 1985-86. Recreations: golf; swimming; opera; orchestral music. Address: (b.) George House, 50 George Square, Glasgow, G2 1RR; T.-041-552 4994.

O'Grady, Richard John Peard, MA (Hons). Director/Secretary, Zoological Society of Glasgow and West of Scotland, since 1972; b. 6.7.49, Cambridge; m., Maria Ann; 1 s. Educ. King's School, Bruton; Dundee University. Weekly pets feature, Daily Record, since 1976; D. of E. Inspector of Zoos, since 1982; Member, West of Scotland Committee for the Employment of Disabled People. Recreations: family; son's hobbies; visiting zoos, parks, reserves. Address: (b.) Glasgow Zoo, Calderpark, Uddingston, Glasgow, G71 7RZ; T.-041-771 1185.

Ogston, Rev. David Dinnes, MA, BD. Minister, St. John's Kirk of Perth, since 1980; b. 25.3.45, Ellon, Aberdeenshire; m., Margaret Macleod; 2 d. Educ. Inverurie Academy; King's College and Christ's College, Aberdeen. Assistant Minister, St. Giles' Cathedral, Edinburgh, 1969-73; Minister, Balerno, 1973-80. Publication: White Stone Country. Recreations: late-night films on TV; listening to the blues; Greek and Russian Ikons. Address: 15 Comely Bank Perth; T.-Perth 21755.

Ogston, Professor Derek, MA, MD, PhD, DSc, FRCPEdin, FRCP, FIBiol, FRSE. Professor of Medicine, Aberdeen University, since 1983 (Dean, Faculty of Medicine, 1984-87; Vice-Principal, since 1987); b. 31.5.32, Aberdeen; m., Cecilia Marie; 1 s.; 2 d. Educ. King's College School, Wimbledon; Aberdeen University. Aberdeen University: Lecturer in Medicine, 1962-69, Senior Lecturer in Medicine, 1969-75, MRC Travelling Fellow, 1967-68, Reader in Medicine, 1975-76, Regius Professor of Physiology, 1977-83. Publications: Haemostasis: Biochemistry, Physiology and Pathology (Joint Editor), 1977; The Physiology of Hemostasis, 1983; Antifibrinolytic Drugs: Chemistry, Pharmacology and Clinical Usage, 1984; Venous Thrombosis: Causation and Prediction, 1987. Recreations: gardening; running. Address: (h.) 64 Rubislaw Den South, Aberdeen, AB2 6AX; T.-Aberdeen 316587.

O'Halloran, Sir Charles Ernest, KB. Chairman, Irvine Development Corporation, 1983-85; b. 26.5.24, Liverpool; m., Annie Rowan; 1 s.; 2 d. Educ. Conway Central School, Birkenhead. Member, Ayr Town Council, 1953-74 (Provost, 1964-67); Member, Strathclyde Regional Council, 1974-82 (Convener, 1978-82); Freeman, Ayr Burgh, 1975. Recreations: golf and walking (can be the same). Address: (h.) 40 Savoy Park, Ayr, KA7 2XA; T.-0292 266234.

Oliver, Ian Thomas, QPM, LLB, MPhil, PhD. Chief Constable, Central Scotland Police, since 1979; b. 24.1.40, London; m., Elsie; 2 s.; 1 d. Educ. Grammar School, Hampton, Middlesex; Nottingham University; Strathclyde University. RAF, 1959-61; Constable to Superintendent, Metropolitan Police, 1961-77; Northumbria Police: Chief Superintendent, 1977, Assistant Chief Constable (Management Services), 1978. Clerk/Treasurer, Sir James Duncan Medal Trust; Churchill Fellow, 1986. Publication: Police, Government and Accountability, 1987. Address: (b.) Randolphfield, Stirling, FK8 2HD; T.-0786 73161.

Oliver, Brigadier James Alexander, CB, CBE, DSO (and Bar), TD, DL, LLD. Solicitor; Honorary Sheriff, County of Angus; b. 19.3.06, Arbroath; m., Margaret W. Scott. Educ. Trinity College, Glenalmond. 2nd Lt., Black Watch (TA), 1926; commanded: 7th Black Watch, 1942, 152 Infantry Brigade (Highland Division), 1943, 154 Infantry Brigade (Highland Division), 1944; served World War II in North Africa, Sicily and NW Europe (mentioned in Despatches); ADC to

The Queen, 1953-63; Honorary Colonel, 6/7th Black Watch, 1960-67; Honorary Colonel, 51st Highland Volunteers, 1967-70, Member, Angus and Dundee T&AFA, 1938-59 (Chairman, 1945-59); Past Chairman, Vice President, The Earl Haig Fund Scotland; Vice-Lieutenant, County of Angus, 1967-81. Address: (h.) West Newton, Arbroath, Angus; T.-Arbroath 72579.

Oliver, James Kenneth Murray. Farmer; Director, Royal Highland and Agricultural Society of Scotland, since 1962; b. 1.2.14, Hawick; m., Rhona Mary Purdom Wilkinson; 1 s.; 1 d. Educ. Merchiston Castle, Edinburgh. Army, 1939-46; Director, Andrew Oliver & Son Ltd.; as racehorse trainer, trained almost 1,000 winners under National Hunt Rules; rode winner, Scottish Grand National, 1950; trained five winners, Scottish Grand National; four times runner-up, Grand National; trained winners for the Queen Mother; Financial Director, Doncaster Bloodstock Sales Ltd.; Secretary, Teviotdale Farmers Club. Recreations: hunting; racing; golf; tennis; squash. Address: (h.) Hassendean Bank, Hawick; T.-0450 87 216.

Oliver, Professor Michael Francis, CBE, MD, MDhc (Bologna and Stockholm), FRCP, PRCPEdin, FFCM, FACC, FRSE. Duke of Edinburgh Professor of Cardiology, Edinburgh University, since 1979; Senior Cardiologist and Physician, Edinburgh Royal Infirmary, since 1978; b. 3.7.25, Borth; m., 1, Margaret Y. Abbey; 2 s.; 1 s. (deceased); 1 d.; 2, Helen L. Daniel. Educ. Marlborough College, Wiltshire; Edinburgh University. Consultant Physician, Royal Infirmary, and Senior Lecturer in Medicine, Edinburgh University, 1961; Reader in Medicine, 1973; Personal Professor of Cardiology, 1977; Member, Scientific Board, International Society of Cardiology, 1968-78 (Chairman and Council on Atherosclerosis); Chairman, British Atherosclerosis Group, 1970-75; Member, Cardiovascular Panel, Government Committee on Medical Aspects of Food Policy, 1971-74 and 1982-84; UK Representative, Advisory Panel for Cardiovascular Diseases, World Health Organisation, since 1972; Chairman, BBC-Medical Advisory Group in Scotland, 1975-81; Council Member, British Heart Foundation, 1976-84; Convener, Cardiology Committee, Scottish Royal Colleges, 1978-81; President, British Cardiac Society, 1981-85; President, Royal College of Physicians of Edinburgh, since 1985; Chairman, Honorary Advisory Panel, Cardiovascular Conditions for Fitness to Drive, since 1985; Purkinje Medal, 1981; Polish Cardiac Society Medal, 1984; FRACP, 1988; FRCPI, 1988. Publications: 300 medical and scientific papers and five books. Recreations: questioning; all things Italian. Address: (h.) Barley Mill House, Pencaitland, East Lothian, EH34 5EP.

Oliver, Michael Roger, DipTP, MRTPI. Director of Physical Planning, Argyll and Bute District Council, since 1974; b. 16.11.38, Manchester; m., Janet; 1 s.; 2 d. Educ. Burnage Grammar School; Manchester University. Planning Assistant, Lancashire County Council, 1962-64; Deputy Chief Planning Assistant, Bootle County Borough Council, 1964-69; Senior Planning Assistant, Southport County Borough Council, 1969-70; Principal Planning Officer, Manchester City Council, 1970-73; Depute County Planning Officer, Argyll County Council, 1973-75. Recreations: music; railways; local history. Address: (b.) Kilmory Castle, Lochgilphead, Argyll; T.-0546 2127.

Olver, Professor Richard Edmund, BSc, MB, FRCP, FRCPE. James Mackenzie Professor of Child Health, Dundee; b. 26.10.41; m.; 2 s.; 2 d. Educ. London University. House Officer and Senior House Officer posts, St. Thomas's, Addenbrookes and Brompton Hospitals, 1966-69; Lecturer, Senior Lecturer, Reader, Department of Paediatrics, University College, London, 1969-85; Consultant Paediatrician, University College Hospital, London, 1975-85. Address: (b.) Dundee University, Dundee.

O'Malley, Thomas John, BSc (Hons), DipEd. Headmaster, St. David's High School, Dalkeith, since 1975; Chairman, Lothian Regional Consultative Committee on Secondary Education, 1983-87; Chairman, Catholic Headteachers' Association of Scotland, 1984-86; Member, Scottish Consultative Council on the Curriculum, since 1986; b. 7.4.37, Edinburgh; m., Maureen; 1 s.; 2 d. Educ. Holy Cross Academy, Edinburgh; Edinburgh University; Moray House College of Education. Assistant Teacher, Holy Cross Academy, 1960-63; Principal Teacher of Chemistry, St. Mary's Academy, Bathgate, 1963-67; Principal Teacher of Physical Sciences, Lawrence Park Collegiate Institute, Toronto, 1967-69; Principal Teacher of Chemistry, St. Anthony's Secondary School, Edinburgh, 1969-72; Assistant Head Teacher, Holyrood High School, Edinburgh, 1972-75. Member: Munn Committee, 1975-77, Archbishop O'Brien's Advisory Committee on Education. Recreations: shareholder, Hibernian FC; golf; hill-walking. Address: (b.) Abbey Road, Dalkeith, EH22 3AD; T.-031-663 1961.

O'Neill, Martin (John), BA (Econ). MP (Labour), Clackmannan, since 1983 (East Stirlingshire and Clackmannan, 1979-83); b. 6.1.45; m., Elaine Samuel; 2 s. Educ. Trinity Academy, Edinburgh; Heriot-Watt University. Insurance Clerk, Scottish Widows Fund, 1963-67; Assistant Examiner, Estate Duty Office of Scotland, 1971-73; Teacher of Modern Studies, Boroughmuir High School, Edinburgh, 1974-77, Craigmount High School, Edinburgh, 1977-79; Social Science Tutor, Open University, 1976-79. Member, Select Committee on Scottish Affairs; Opposition Spokesman on Defence. Recreations: watching football; playing squash; reading; listening to jazz; cinema. Address: (h.) 9 Laverock Bank Terrace, Edinburgh.

Orr, Ian, MPS. Pharmacist; Honorary Sheriff, South Strathclyde, Dumfries and Galloway, since 1980; Lord Cornet (Standard Bearer), Lanark, since 1961; b. 14.3.26, Lanark; m., Dora Hickey; 1 s. Educ. Lanark Grammar School; Strathclyde University. National Service, RAMC, Egypt, 1947-49. Past President, Lanark Rotary Club; President, Dante Alighieri Society (Diploma Di Benemerenza and Silver Medal). Recreations: fox-hunting; golf; foreign travel. Address: (h.) Gezira, St. Patrick's Road, Lanark; T.-0555 2810.

Orr, Sir John Henry, Kt (1979), OBE (1972), QPM (1977). Chief Constable, Lothian and Borders Police, 1975-83; b. 13.6.18; m.; 1 s.; 1 d.

Educ. George Heriot's School, Edinburgh. Chief Constable, Dundee, 1960; Chief Constable, Lothians and Peebles, 1968; Past President, Scottish Rugby Union.

Orr, Rev. Norman Bennie, BSc (Hons), ARCST, DipRTC. Industrial Organiser, Scottish Industrial Mission (Glasgow Area), since 1981; b. 26.3.25, Glasgow; m., Catherine Margaret Howie; 2 s.; 1 d. Educ. High School of Glasgow; Morrison's Academy, Crieff; Glasgow University; Royal College of Science and Technology. Design Development Mechanical Engineer, 1948-54; Parish Minister: Hamilton-Bardrainney Parish, Port Glasgow, 1958-66; Chaplain, Dundee University, 1966-73; Worker Priest, James Howden & Co. Ltd., 1974-80. Director, St. Rollox Industrial Development Enterprise Ltd.; Co-ordinator, Scottish Nuclear Freeze Campaign. Recreations: reading; swimming; walking; golf. Address: (h.) 7 Sherbrooke Drive, Glasgow, G41 5AA; T.-041-427 6342.

Orr Ewing, Major Sir Ronald Archibald, 5th Bt; b. 14.5.12; m., Marion Hester; 2 s.; 2 d. Educ. Eton; Sandhurst. Scots Guards, 1932-53 (Major); DL, Perthshire, 1963; JP, Perthshire; Grand Master Mason of Scotland, 1965-69. Address: (h.) Cardross, Port of Menteith, Stirling.

Osborne, Eric Alexander, MB, ChB, FRCSEdin, FRCSGlas, D(Obst)RCOG. Consultant Ear, Nose and Throat Surgeon, Victoria Infirmary, Glasgow; b. 9.4.36, Glasgow; m., Sheilagh Sophie Wilson; 3 d. Educ. Merchiston Castle School, Edinburgh; Glasgow University. Director, Neilston Agricultural Society. Recreations: shooting; fishing; stalking. Address: (h.) Thorterburn Farm, Neilston, near Glasgow, G78 3AX; T.-050585 222.

Osler, Douglas Alexander, MA (Hons), FSA Scot, DipRE. HM Chief Inspector of Schools, Scottish Education Department; b. 11.10.42, Edinburgh; m., Wendy I. Cochrane; 1 s.; 1 d. Educ. Royal High School, Edinburgh; Edinburgh University; Moray House College of Education. Assistant Teacher of History/Careers Master, Liberton Secondary School, Edinburgh, 1965-68; Principal Teacher of History, Dunfermline High School, 1968-74. English Speaking Union Fellowship to USA, 1966. Publications: Queen Margaret of Scotland; Sources for Modern Studies, Volumes 1 and 2. Recreations: bowling; bridge; gardening; reading. Address: (b.) Room 4/103 New St. Andrew's House, Edinburgh.

Oswald, John McLay, MBE, BSc, ARCST. Secretary, Paisley College of Technology, since 1969; b. 11.4.28, Glasgow; m., Isabel Mair; 2 s.; 1 d. Educ. Shawlands Academy; Glasgow University; Royal College of Science and Technology. HM Forces, 1949-51; Clyde Alloy Steel Co. Ltd., Motherwell, 1951-53; Rolls Royce Ltd., Hillington, Glasgow, 1953-55; Pressed Steel Co. Ltd., Linwood, 1956-63; joined Paisley College of Technology, 1963. Vice-Chairman, Scottish Council for Spastics; Past Chairman, National Bureau for Handicapped Students (Scottish Branch). Recreations: gardening; choral music. Address: (h.) 40 Church Road, Giffnock, Glasgow; T.-041-638 2784.

Owen, Professor David Gareth, MA, BD (Hons), PhD, FICE, CEng. Professor of Offshore Engineering, Heriot-Watt University, since 1986 (Head, Department of Offshore Engineering, since 1982); b. 6.11.40, Brecon, Wales; m., Ann Valerie Wright; 2 d. Educ. Christ College, Brecon; Downing College, Cambridge. Graduate Engineer, John Laing & Son, London; Aerospace Engineer, Marconi Space and Defence Systems, Portsmouth; Lecturer in Civil Engineering, Heriot-Watt University; Visiting Professor, University of New Hampshire; Senior Lecturer, Department of Offshore Engineering, Heriot-Watt University. Recreations: music; travelling; skiing. Address: (h.) 7 Oak Lane, Edinburgh, EH12 6XH; T.-031-339 1740.

Owen, Professor Douglas David Roy, MA, PhD. Professor of French, St. Andrews, since 1972; b. 17.11.22, Norton, Suffolk; m., Berit Mariann; 2 s. Educ. Cambridge and County High School; Nottingham High Pavement School; Nottingham University; St. Catharine's College, Cambridge. St. Andrews University: Lecturer, 1951-64, Senior Lecturer, 1964-71, Reader, 1971-72; General Editor, Forum for Modern Language Studies. Publications: Fabliaux (Joint Editor), 1957; The Evolution of the Grail Legend, 1968; The Vision of Hell, 1970; Arthurian Romance: Seven Essays (Editor), 1970; Two Old French Gauvain Romances (Joint Editor), 1972; The Song of Roland (Translator), 1972; The Legend of Roland, 1973; Noble Lovers, 1975; Chretien de Troyes, Arthurian Romances (Translator), 1987. Recreation: golf. Address: (h.) 7 West Acres, St. Andrews, KY16 9UD; T.-St. Andrews 73329.

Owens, Agens. Author; b. 24.5.26, Milngavie; m., Patrick Owens; 2 s.; 4 d. Educ. Bearsden Academy. Worked in shops, factories and offices; came to writing by accident; author of Gentlemen of the West (Autumn Book Award, 1984) and Like Birds in the Wilderness; short stories in Lean Tales. Recreations: walking; reading. Address: (h.) 21 Roy Young Avenue, Balloch, Dunbartonshire; T.-Alexandria 50921.

Owens, Professor David Howard, BSc, ARCS, PhD, FIMA, CEng, MIEE. Professor of Mathematics, Strathclyde University, since 1985; b. 23.4.48, Belper; m., Rosemary; 1 s.; 1 d. Educ. Dronfield Henry Fanshawe Grammar School; Imperial College, London University. Atomic Energy Establishment, Winfrith, Dorchester, 1969-73; Reader in Control Engineering, Sheffield University, 1973-85. Recreations: cycling; small-bore rifle shooting. Address: (b.) Department of Mathematics, Strathclyde University, Livingstone Tower, 26 Richmond Street, Glasgow, G1 1XH; T.-041-552 4400, Ext. 3804.

P

Pacey, Archibald Charles, MA, FEIS. Head Teacher, Greenhall High School, since 1982; Principal Examiner, Scottish Examination Board,

1970-86; b. 29.6.31, Kirkcaldy; m., Joan Marion Margaret Henry; 3 s.; 1 d. Educ. Knox Academy, Haddington; Edinburgh University; Moray House College. Captain, RAEC, in BAOR, 1954-57; Principal Teacher of French, Moray House Demonstration School, 1958-61; Teacher of Modern Languages, Dalkeith High School, 1961-64; Principal Teacher of Modern Languages, then Depute Head Teacher, Lasswade High School, 1964-82. Founder Secretary/Treasurer, Lothian Regional Executive, Educational Institute of Scotland; Honorary Secretary, Haddington Rugby Football Club, 1979-84. Recreations: gardening; DIY; wine-making; Midlothian-Heinsberg Twinning. Address: (h.) Carlowrie Cottage, Barleyknowe Road, Gorebridge, Midlothian; T.-0875 20235.

Pack, Professor Donald Cecil, CBE, MA, DSc, FIMA, FEIS, FRSE. Emeritus Professor, Strathclyde University, since 1986; b. 14.4.20, Higham Ferrers; m., Constance Mary Gillam; 2 s.; 1 d. Educ. Wellingborough School; New College, Oxford. Ordnance Board, Cambridge, 1941-43; Armament Research Department, Ministry of Supply, Fort Halstead, 1943-46; Lecturer in Mathematics, St. Andrews University, 1947-52; Visiting Research Associate, Maryland University, 1951-52; Lecturer in Mathematics, Manchester University, 1952-53; Professor of Mathematics, Strathclyde University, 1953-82 (Vice-Principal, 1968-72); Honorary Professor, 1982-86. Chairman, Scottish Certificate of Education Examination Board, 1969-77; Chairman, Committee of Inquiry into Truancy and Indiscipline in Scottish Schools, 1974-77 ("Pack Report" published by HMSO, 1977); Chairman, National Youth Orchestra of Scotland, since foundation, 1978; Member, Scottish Arts Council, 1980-85; Member: General Teaching Council for Scotland, 1966-73, Dunbartonshire Education Committee, 1960-66; Governor, Hamilton College of Education, 1976-81; Council Member, Royal Society of Edinburgh, 1960-63; Honorary Treasurer and Council Member, Institute of Mathematics and its Applications, 1964-72; Member, International Advisory Committee on Rarefied Gas Dynamics Symposia, 1976-88; Member, British National Committee for Theoretical Mechanics, 1973-78; Council Member, Gesellschaft fuer angewandte Mathematik und Mechanik, 1977-83; Past President: Edinburgh Mathematical Society, Glasgow Mathematical Association; President, Milngavie Music Club, since 1983. Recreations: music; gardening; golf. Address: (h.) 18 Buchanan Drive, Bearsden, Glasgow, G61 2EW; T.-041-942 5764.

Packer, John Aidan, OBE, BA, ATI. Managing Director, John A. Packer (Private Collections) Ltd., Langholm, since 1987; Chairman, The Woolly Mill Co. Ltd., Langholm, since 1987; Trustee, National Galleries of Scotland; b. 19.7.35, Wakefield; m., Carol Lesley Burdin; 1 s.; 2 d. Educ. Queen Elizabeth Grammar School, Wakefield; Munich University; Leeds University. National Service, 1957-59 (commissioned, 1st Bn., KOYLI); joined Reid & Taylor, Langholm, 1959; appointed Director, 1965, Managing Director, 1967-87; Director, Allied Textile Companies, 1973-87; Director, Allied Textile Companies Fine Worsted Division, 1981; first President, The Scottish Woollen Industry, 1983; Director, Scottish Textile and Technical Centre, 1984; Governor, Cumbria College of Art and Design, Carlisle; former Member, Board of Management, British Colour Council; Member, Scottish Committee, Design Council, 1974-79; Member, Design Council, 1976-79; Member, Industrial Design Advisory Committee, 1977-79; Member, Steering Committee on Training of Designers, Confederation of British Wool Textiles; Council Member, National Wool Textile Export Corporation; winner, Scottish Free Enterprise Award, 1979; Patron, Register of Apparel and Textile Designers; Fellow, Society of Antiquaries of Scotland; winner of award by Clothing and Footwear Institute, 1982. Recreations: squash; swimming; collecting antiques. Address: (b.) Ford Mill, Langholm, Dumfriesshire, DG13 0BL; T.-0541 81088.

Page, Christopher Nigel, BSc, PhD, FLS. Principal Scientific Officer, Royal Botanic Garden, Edinburgh, since 1971; Honorary Lecturer, Department of Botany, Edinburgh University, since 1983; b. 11.11.42, Gloucester; m., Pauline Ann; 1 s.; 2 d. Educ. Cheltenham Grammar School; Kings College, Durham; Newcastle-upon-Tyne University. NATO Overseas Research Fellow, Queensland University, 1968-70; Department of Rural Economy, Oxford University, 1970-71. Nuffield/Leverhulme Overseas Travel Fellow, 1976-77; Tutor, Scottish Field Studies Council, since 1973; Editor, British Fern Gazette, 1974-84; Specialist Adviser, International Union for the Conservation of Nature, since 1986. Publications: The Ferns of Britain and Ireland, 1982; Biology of Pteridophytes, 1984; Ferns (New Naturalist), 1988. Recreations: photography; walking; writing. Address: (h.) 17 Silverknowes Crescent, Edinburgh, EH4 5JE; T.-031-336 1142.

Page, John Graham, ChM, FRCS, MB, ChB. Consultant Accident and Emergency Surgeon, Grampian Health Board, since 1981; Honorary Senior Lecturer in Surgery, Aberdeen University, since 1981; b. 16.2.43, Liverpool; m., Sandra; 1 s.; 2 d. Educ. Robert Gordon's College; Aberdeen University. Lecturer in Pathology, Aberdeen University, 1969; Surgical Registrar, Grampian Health Board, 1972; Research Fellow, Harvard University, Boston, 1974; Registrar, Accident and Emergency, Grampian Health Board, 1979. Publications: A Colour Atlas of Accidents and Emergencies, 1984; A Colour Atlas of Plaster Techniques, 1985; A Colour Atlas of Resuscitation Techniques, 1985. Recreations: skiing; sailing. Address: (h.) 16 Kingswood Avenue, Kingswells, Aberdeen, AB1 8AE; T.-Aberdeen 742945.

Palmer, Godfrey Henry Oliver, MIBiol, BSc, PhD, DSc, FIBrew. University Teacher, Department of Brewing and Biological Sciences, Heriot-Watt University, since 1977; Research Consultant; b. 9.4.40, St. Elizabeth, Jamaica; m., Margaret Ann Wood; 1 s.; 2 d. Educ. Shelbourne Secondary Modern School; Highbury County School; Leicester University; Edinburgh University; Heriot-Watt University. Technician, 1958-61; Brewing Research Foundation, 1968-77. Recreations: reading; watching cereal fields; education of deprived children; friends; ball games; music. Address: (b.) Heriot-Watt University, Department of Brewing and Biological Sciences, Edinburgh; T.-031-225 8432.

Palmer, John Carrington, BSc, PhD. Chief Executive Officer, Citizens Advice Scotland, since 1986; b. 24.11.50, Nakuru, Kenya; m., Nicoline; 2 s. Educ. Marlborough College; LSE. Anthropological research, Kenya, 1973-75; Course Co-ordinator, Open University, 1978-80; Voluntary Service Overseas (Field Director, Kenya), 1980-83; VSO Programme Management Officer, London, 1983-86. Recreations: cycling; walking; mini-rugby; skiing; woodcraft folk; cinema. Address: (b.) Atlantic House, 38 Gardner's Crescent, Edinburgh; T.-031-667 0156.

Palmer, Robert Allen, BA (Hons). Director, European City of Culture 1990 and Festivals Director, Glasgow District Council, since 1987 (Drama and Dance Director, Scottish Arts Council, 1980-87); Theatre Director, since 1971; b. 3.6.47, Toronto; m., Lynn Susan Winston; 1 s.; 1 d. Educ. Forrest Hill Collegiate; York University; Central London Polytechnic. Teacher of English and Drama, Inner London Education Authority and Surrey County Council, 1970-72; Director, Theatre Centre for Young People, 1971-73; Director, Theatremakers, MacRobert Arts Centre, Stirling, 1973-75; Director, Theatre Workshop, Edinburgh, 1975-80; Member, Advisory Panels for Drama and Dance, British Council, since 1980. Recreations: cooking; walking; music. Address: (h.) 46A Blacket Place, Edinburgh.

Panton, John, MBE. Professional Golfer; b. 9.10.16, Pitlochry. Won PGA Match-Play Championship, 1956 (Runner-up, 1968); PGA British Seniors', 1967-69; World Seniors', 1967 (defeated Sam Snead for title); Silver King, 1950; Daks, 1951; North British-Harrogate, 1952; Goodwin Foursomes, 1952; Yorkshire Evening News, 1954; Gleneagles-Saxone Am.-Pro. Foursomes, 1956; Woodlawn Invitation Open (West Germany), 1958-59-60; leading British player, Open Championship, 1956; Leader, PGA Order of Merit (Vardon Trophy), 1951; won Scottish Professional Championship, seven times (and joint Champion, once); Ryder Cup player, 1951-53-61; awarded Golf Writers' Trophy, 1967.

Parbrook, Geoffrey Donald, MD, FFARCS. Senior Lecturer in Anaesthesia, Glasgow University, since 1967; Consultant Anaesthetist, Glasgow Royal Infirmary, since 1967; b. Ferryhill, Co. Durham; m., Evelyn; 3 s. Educ. Birmingham University. Eastman Dental Hospital, London, 1959; Newcastle Regional Chest Surgery Centre, 1960-62; Aberdeen Royal Infirmary, 1962-67. Publication: Basic Physics and Measurement in Anaesthesia, 1985. Address: (b.) University Department of Anaesthesia, Royal Infirmary, 8-16 Alexandra Parade, Glasgow, G31 2ER; T.-041-552 3535.

Park, Andy. Drama and Arts Television Producer, BBC Scotland, since 1986; b. 14.8.36, Ayr; m., Nan; 2 s.; 1 d. Educ. Dalmellington High School; Ayr Academy; Glasgow School of Art; Jordanhill College of Education. Producer, BBC Radio 2, 1971-73; Head of Entertainment, Radio Clyde, 1973-78; Controller of Programmes, Radio Forth, 1978; Head of Programmes, Radio Clyde, 1978-81; Commissioning Editor for Music, Channel 4, 1981-85; Head of Light Entertainment Television, BBC Scotland, 1985-86; Composer of jazz, chamber, rock and pop music for television, radio, theatre and cinema in UK and USA; won Billboard Trendsetter Award, New York, 1976; Scotstar Award, 1979; Board Member, Masterconcerts Ltd., 1980-82; Council Member, Scottish Society of Composers, 1980-84; Chairman, BAFTA (Scotland), 1987-89; BAFTA Award: Best TV Drama Series, 1987. Recreations: listening to, writing and playing music; watching football; dreaming of the days when he could play it. Address: (h.) 25A Mansionhouse Road, Glasgow, G41.

Park, Ian Michael Scott, CBE, MA, LLB. Partner, Paull & Williamsons, Advocates, Aberdeen, since 1961; Member, Criminal Injuries Compensation Board, since 1983; Council Member, Law Society of Scotland, 1974-85; b. 7.4.38, Aberdeen; m., Elizabeth M.L. Struthers; 2 s. Educ. Aberdeen Grammar School; Aberdeen University. Assistant to, subsequently Partner in, Paull & Williamsons; Member, Society of Advocates in Aberdeen, since 1962; sometime part-time Assistant, Department of Public Law, Aberdeen University; President, Law Society of Scotland, 1980-81; Chairman, Aberdeen Citizens Advice Bureau; Secretary, Aberdeen Granite Association, 1962-84; frequent broadcaster on legal topics. Recreations: golf; gardening. Address: (h.) 46 Rubislaw Den South, Aberdeen.

Parker, Cameron Holdsworth, BSc. Managing Director, Lithgows Limited, since 1984; b. 14.4.32, Dundee; m., Marylyne Honeyman; 3 s. Educ. Morrison's Academy, Crieff; Glasgow University. Managing Director, latterly also Chairman, John G. Kincaid & Co. Ltd., Greenock, 1967-80; Chairman and Chief Executive, Scott Lithgow Ltd., Port Glasgow, 1980-83; Board Member, British Shipbuilders, 1977-80, 1981-83; Chief Executive, Prosper Enginering Ltd., Irvine, 1983-84. Liveryman, Worshipful Company of Shipwrights; Member, Council, CBI Scotland. Recreation: golf. Address: (b.) Netherton, Langbank, Renfrewshire, PA14 6YG; T.-047554 692.

Parnell, Brian K., BSc, ACGI, DipTP, FRTPI. Head, Department of Planning, Glasgow School of Art, 1976-87; Planning Consultant; b. 18.12.22, Brighton; 2 s.; 1 d. Educ. Varndean School, Brighton; London University; Edinburgh College of Art. Captain, EME, 1943-47; Department of Planning, Midlothian County Council, 1949-57; Depute Planning Officer, Stirling County Council, 1957-64; joined Glasow School of Art, 1964; Commissioner, Countryside Commission for Scotland, 1968-80; part-time Planning Inquiry Reporter, Scottish Office, since 1982. Chairman, Association of Scientific Workers (Scottish Area), 1949-69; Member, Board of Governors, Heriot-Watt College, 1954-56; Chairman, Scottish Branch, Royal Town Planning Institute, 1972-73; Executive Committee Member, National Trust for Scotland, 1973-83; Trustee, Scottish Civic Trust, since 1985. Recreations: sailing; swimming; hill-walking; travel. Address: (h.) 15 Park Terrace, Stirling, FK8 2JT; T.-0786 73843.

Parr, John Brian, BSc (Econ), MA, PhD. Reader in Applied Economics, Glasgow University, since 1980 (Secretary, Centre for Urban and Regional Research, since 1978); Chairman, British Section,

Regional Science Association, 1981-85; b. 18.3.41, Epsom; m., Pamela Jean Harkins; 2 d. Educ. Henry Thornton School; London University; University of Washington. Instructor, University of Washington, 1966; Assistant Professor/Associate Professor, University of Pennsylvania, 1967-75; joined Glasgow University as Lecturer, 1975. Editor, Papers of the Regional Science Association, 1968-75; Associate Editor, Journal of Regional Science, since 1978; Member, Board of Management, Urban Studies, since 1981. Publications: Christaller Central Place Structures (Co-author); Regional Policy: Past Experience and New Directions (Co-Editor); Analysis of Regional Structure: Essays in Honour of August Losch (Co-Editor); Market Centers and Retail Location (Co-author). Address: (b.) Department of Social and Economic Research, Glasgow University, Glasgow, G12 8RT; T.-041-339 8855, Ext. 4724.

Parratt, Professor James Roy, BPharm, MSc, PhD, DSc, MRCPath, DipRelStudies (Cantab), FPS, FIBiol, FRSE. Professor of Cardiovascular Pharmacology, Strathclyde University, since 1983 (Head, Department of Physiology and Pharmacology, since 1986); b. 19.8.33, London; m., Pamela Joan Lyndon Marels; 2 s.; 1 d. Educ. St. Clement Danes Holborn Estate Grammar School; London University. Spent nine years in Nigeria as Head of Pharmacology, Nigerian School of Pharmacy, then in Physiology, University Medical School, Ibadan; joined Strathclyde University, 1967; appointed Reader, 1970; Personal Professor, Department of Physiology and Pharmacology, 1975-83. Chairman, Cardiac Muscle Research Group, 1980-83; Gold Medal, Szeged University, 1975; Honorary Member, Hungarian Pharmacological Society, 1983; Chairman, Universities and Colleges Christian Fellowship; former Vice-Chairman, Scripture Union; Past Chairman, SUM Fellowship; Lay Preacher, Baptist Unions of Scotland and Great Britain; Honorary President, Baptist Lay Preachers Association of Scotland. Recreation: music. Address: (h.) 16 Russell Drive, Bearsden, Glasgow, G61 3BD; T.-041-942 7164.

Parry, John Wynne Lloyd, TD, MA, DM, BSc, FFARCS. Consultant Anaesthetist, Aberdeen Hospitals, since 1966; Clinical Senior Lecturer, Aberdeen University, since 1970; b. 24.3.29, Llandudno; m., Priscilla Rachel Tate; 1 s.; 1 d. Educ. Barmouth Grammar School; Oxford University; University College Hospital, London. Short-service commission, RAF Medical Branch, 1957-60; principal junior anaesthetic appointments, University College Hospital and Hospital for Sick Children, Great Ormond Street, London, 1960-66; Staff Member, Massachusetts General Hospital and Harvard Medical School, Boston, 1963-64 and 1967-68. Past President, NE Scotland Society of Anaesthetists; Assistant Medical Officer, RNLI, Aberdeen; former Member, Senate and Faculty of Medicine, Aberdeen University. Recreations: sailing; skiing. Address: (h.) 18 Woodburn Avenue, Aberdeen, AB1 8JQ; T.-0224 319350.

Parry, Kenneth Michael, OBE, MB, ChB, FRCPEdin, FFCM, FRCGP, DCH. Secretary, Scottish Council for Postgraduate Medical Education, since 1970; b. 28.5.29, Manchester; m., Maureen Anne Jones; 2 s.; 1 d. Educ. Bristol Grammar School; Bristol University. Senior Administrative Medical Officer, Eastern Regional Hospital Board, 1967-70; Council of Europe Medical Fellow, 1974; William Pickles Lecturer, Royal College of General Practitioners, 1977; Australian Universities Commonwealth Senior Fellow, 1980; Honorary Secretary, Association for Study of Medical Education, since 1984. Recreations: music; painting. Address: (h.) 9 Moray Place, Edinburgh, EH3 6DS; T.-031-226 3054.

Parsons, Professor Ian, BSc, PhD, FRSE. Professor of Geology, Edinburgh University, since 1988; b. 5.9.39, Manchester; m., Brenda Mary Reah; 3 s. Educ. Beckenham and Penge Grammar School; Durham University. DSIR Research Fellow, Manchester University, 1963-64; Aberdeen University: Assistant Lecturer, 1964-65, Lecturer, 1965-77, Senior Lecturer, 1977-83, Professor, 1983-88. Former Member, NERC Geological Sciences Research Grants Committee, since 1984 and Geological Sciences Training Awards Committee, since 1983; Vice-President, Mineralogical Society, 1981; Member, NCC Committee for Scotland, since 1985. Recreations: skiing; hill-walking; music. Address: (b.) Grant Institute of Geology, Edinburgh University, West Mains Road, Edinburgh, EH9 3JW; T.-031-667 1081.

Parsons, Professor John William, BSc, PhD, FIBiol. Professor and Head, Department of Soil Science, Aberdeen University, since 1981; b. 20.7.33, Wallasey; m., Gillian Mary; 3 s. Educ. Oldershaw Grammar School; Reading University. Postdoctoral Fellow, Delaware University, 1958-60; Lecturer and Senior Lecturer, Aberdeen University, 1960-81; Visiting Research Fellow, CSIRO Soils Division, Adelaide, 1972-73. Governor, Strathallan School; Member, Council of Management, Macaulay Land Use Research Institute and Board of Management, Scottish Crop Research Institute. Recreations: hill-walking; reading. Address: (b.) Department of Soil Science, Aberdeen University, Aberdeen, AB9 2UE; T.-0224 272257.

Patel, Arvind Rai, MB, ChB, MD, FRCPGlas. Consultant Physician, Western Infirmary, Glasgow, since 1975 (Consultant in Administrative Charge, Accident and Emergency, 1975-88); Honorary Clinical Lecturer in Medicine, Glasgow University, since 1975; b. 27.2.36, Thika, Kenya. Educ. Christ College, Blackheath; Aberdeen University. Junior posts, Aberdeen Royal Infirmary, 1963-65; Senior House Officer and Registrar, Western Infirmary, 1965-70; Research Fellow, University Department of Medicine, Glasgow, 1971-75. Member, various Committees, Greater Glasgow Health Board. Recreations: keeping fit; painting; hill-walking; cooking. Address: (h.) 23 Braemar Crescent, Bearsden, Glasgow, G61 1DE; T.-041-942 5178.

Paternoster, Rev. Canon Michael Cosgrove, MA. Rector, St. James' Episcopal Church, Stonehaven, since 1975; Honorary Canon, St. Paul's Cathedral, Dundee, since 1981; b. 13.5.35, East Molesey, Surrey; m., Careth Osborne. Educ. Kingston Grammar School; Pembroke College, Cambridge; Cuddesdon Theological College.

Deacon, 1961; Priest, 1962; Curate, St. Andrew's, Surbiton, 1961-63; Chaplain to Anglican students in Dundee, 1964-68; Secretary, Fellowship of St. Alban and St. Sergius, 1968-71; Rector, St. James', Dollar, 1971-75; Secretary, Inter-Church Relations Committee, Scottish Episcopal Church, 1975-82; Member, Doctrine Committee, Scottish Episcopal Church, since 1980. Publications: Thou art There Also, 1967; Stronger Than Death, 1972. Recreations: reading; sketching; bird-watching; listening to music. Address: 35 Gurney Street, Stonehaven, Kincardineshire, AB3 2EB; T.-Stonehaven 62694.

Paterson, Ailie Campbell Clark, MA, LLB. Member, Borders Valuation Appeal Panel, since 1982; Trustee and Past Chairman, Edinburgh Home for Babies and School of Mothercraft; Trustee and Past Borders Chairman, Victoria League; Chairman, Melrose Branch, Cancer Relief; b. 29.6.30, Edinburgh; m., Sheriff James Veitch Paterson (qv); 1 s.; 1 d. Educ. Lansdowne House, Edinburgh; Edinburgh University. Called to the Bar, 1954; remained in practice until 1964. Recreations: theatre; visiting stately homes; tapestry. Address: (h.) Sunnyside, Melrose, Roxburghshire; T.-089 682 2502.

Paterson, Professor Alan Alexander, LLB (Hons), DPhil (Oxon). Professor of Law, Strathclyde University, since 1984; b. 5.6.47, Edinburgh; m., Alison Jane Ross Lowdon; 1 s.; 1 d. Educ. Edinburgh Academy; Edinburgh University; Pembroke College, Oxford. Research Associate, Oxford Centre for Socio-Legal Studies, 1972-73; Lecturer, Law Faculty, Edinburgh University, 1973-84; Visiting Professor, University of New Mexico Law School, 1982, 1986. Chairman, Scottish Legal Action Group; Chairman, Scottish Legal Education Trust; Chairman, Scottish Association of Citizens Advice Bureaux Legal Advisory Group. Publications: The Law Lords, 1982; The Legal System of Scotland (Co-author), 1986. Address: (b.) Strathclyde University Law School, 173 Cathedral Street, Glasgow, G4 ORQ; T.-041-552 4400, Ext. 3341.

Paterson, Alexander Brown, MBE, Hon. MA (St. Andrews). Chairman, Byre Theatre, St. Andrews, since 1970; b. 11.4.07, St. Andrews; m., Millie Manson Bridges (deceased); 1 s.; 1 d. Educ. Burgh School, St. Andrews. Founder, Byre Theatre, St. Andrews, 1933 (Administrator, until 1980); wrote several plays including The Open, Re-Union in St. Andrews, The Last Provost, The Herald's Not for Sale, etc.; wrote several guide books on Fife towns and The History of the Byre Theatre; ran a news agency in St. Andrews for more than 50 years and co-edited East Fife Observer; a Director (Past Chairman), Federation of Scottish Theatre; Trustee, Scottish Fisheries Museum; Trustee, Hamada Trust; served in RAF during World War II; STV award for outstanding service to Scottish theatre, 1971; awarded Jubilee Medal, 1977. Recreations: golf; swimming. Address: (h.) 90 Bridge Street, St. Andrews; T.-0334 74493.

Paterson, Betty. Member, Tayside Regional Council, since 1986 (Convener, Equal Opportunities Committee, since 1987); b. 20.12.51, Dundee; m., Ross Paterson; 3 d. Educ. Lawside Academy, Dundee. Member, Executive, Scottish National Federation for the Welfare of the Blind; Board Member: Carolina House, Cleghorn Housing Association; Member, Dundee Labour Party Executive Committee. Recreations: family pursuits; reading; theatre. Address: (h.) 8 Harefield Avenue, Dundee; T.-Dundee 825616.

Paterson, Colin Ralston, MA, DM, MSc, MRCP, FRCPath. Senior Lecturer in Biochemical Medicine, Dundee University, since 1969; Honorary Consultant, Tayside Area Health Board, since 1971; b. 5.10.36, Manchester; m., Sally Hellier; 1 s.; 2 d. Educ. Shrewsbury School; Brasenose College, Oxford; University College Hospital. House Physician, University College Hospital; House Surgeon, Leeds General Infirmary; Assistant Lecturer, Clinical Investigation Unit, Leeds University; Medical Registrar, York. Van den Berghs and Jurgens Nutrition Award, 1972; Chairman, Brittle Bone Society. Publications: Metabolic Disorders of Bone, 1975; Textbook of Physiology and Biochemistry, 9th edition (Co-author), 1976; Textbook of Physiology, 10th edition (Co-author), 1980; Essentials of Human Biochemistry, 1983; Bone Disease in the Elderly (Co-author), 1984; Textbook of Physiology, 11th edition (Co-author), 1988. Address: (b.) Department of Biochemical Medicine, Ninewells Hospital, Dundee, DD1 9SY; T.-0382 60111, Ext. 2517.

Paterson, George Marshall, FBIM, FITD. Depute Secretary (Manpower), Convention of Scottish Local Authorities, since 1986 (Personnel Director, Central Regional Council, 1974-86); b. 29.4.31, Falkirk; m., Pearl Dow; 1 s.; 1 d. Educ. Falkirk Technical School. Entered local government service, 1945. Honorary President, Larbert Amateur Operatic Society; Scottish Area Representative for Region No. 3, National Operatic and Dramatic Association; Elder, Larbert Old Church. Recreation: involvement in the amateur operatic movement. Address: (h.) 3 Dobbie Avenue, Larbert, Stirlingshire, FK5 3EP; T.-Larbert 562752.

Paterson, Lt. Col. Howard Cecil, TD, FSA Scot, FRSA. International Tourism Consultant; Senior Partner, Tourism Advisory Services; Chairman, Scottish International Gathering Trust; b. 16.3.20, Edinburgh; m., Isabelle Mary; 1 s. Educ. Daniel Stewart's College, Edinburgh; Edinburgh College of Art. Army, 1939-49; combat duties during War; personnel selection afterwards; Territorial Army, 1949-70; serves on East Scotland TAVR Committee; Assistant Personnel Manager, Jute Industries Ltd., Dundee, 1949-51; Organising Secretary, Scottish Country Industries Development Trust, 1951-66; Senior Director, Scottish Tourist Board, 1966-81. Vice-Chairman, Scottish Aircraft Collection Trust; Vice-Chairman, John Buchan Society; Member, Scottish Committee, British Horse Society; Member, Executive Committee, Scottish Trekking and Riding Association. Publications: Tourism in Scotland; Flavour of Edinburgh (with Catherine Brown). Recreations: fishing; shooting; riding; writing; gardening; natural history; history. Address: (h.) Dovewood, West Linton, Peeblesshire, EH46 7DS; T.-0968 60346.

Paterson, (James Edmund) Neil, MA. Author; b. 31.12.15, Greenock; m., Rosabelle MacKenzie; 2 s.; 1 d. Educ. Banff Academy; Edinburgh University. Lt., RNVR minesweepers, 1940-45; variously Member, Chairman of Production, Director, Consultant, Films of Scotland, 1954-79; Governor, British Film Institute, 1958-60; Chairman, Literature Committee, Scottish Arts Council, 1967-76; Member, Planning Committee, National Film School, 1969; Governor, Pitlochry Festival Theatre, 1966-76; Governor, National Film School, 1970-80; Member, Arts Council of GB, 1974-76; Director, Grampian Television, 1960-86; Atlantic Award in Literature, 1946; American Academy Award (Oscar), 1959; author of: The China Run, Behold Thy Daughter, And Delilah, Man on the Tight-Rope, The Kidnappers, A Candle to the Devil; various stories and screenplays. Recreations: golf; fishing; bridge. Address: (h.) St. Ronans, Crieff, Perthshire; T.-0764 2615.

Paterson, Rev. (James) Roy (Herkless), MA. Minister, Cairns Church, Milngavie, since 1964; b. 22.2.28, Brechin; m., Elizabeth Moyra Wright; 3 s. Educ. Merchiston Castle School; Edinburgh University. National Service, Royal Signals, 1945-47; Assistant Minister, West Church of St. Nicholas, Aberdeen, 1953-55; Minister, Craigie Parish Church, Perth, 1955-64. Publications: Meeting the Mormons; A Faith for the 1980s. Recreations: golf; photography. Address: 4 Cairns Drive, Milngavie, Glasgow, G62 8AJ; T.-041-956 1717.

Paterson, Sheriff James Veitch, MA (Oxon), LLB (Edin). Sheriff of Lothian and Borders at Jedburgh, Selkirk and Duns, since 1963; b. 16.4.28; m., Ailie Campbell Clark Hutchison (see Ailie Campbell Clark Paterson); 1 s.; 1 d. Educ. Edinburgh Academy; Lincoln College, Oxford; Edinburgh University. Admitted Faculty of Advocates, 1953. Recreations: fishing; shooting; gardening. Address: (h.) Sunnyside, Melrose, Roxburghshire; T.-Melrose 2502.

Paterson, John Gordon, MB, ChB, DRCOG, DCM, FFCM. Community Medicine Specialist, Grampian Health Board, since 1977; Honorary Senior Lecturer, Aberdeen University, since 1977; Regional Adviser in Community Medicine - Faculty Adviser (Scotland), since 1986; b. 19.11.41, Blackburn. Educ. Queen Elizabeth's School, Blackburn; Edinburgh University. Hospital posts in East Lothian and Edinburgh, followed by General Practitioner appointments in North Berwick and Selkirk; transferred to public health duties, 1973, as Assistant Medical Officer of Health, Roxburgh and Selkirk; Scottish Health Service Fellow in Community Medicine, 1974-77. Deputy President, City of Aberdeen Branch, British Red Cross Society. Address: (h.) Bracken Cottage, Schivas, Ythanbank, near Ellon, Aberdeenshire, AB4 0UE; T.-035 87 284.

Paterson, John Lamb, DA, ARIBA, FRIAS, FRSA. Principal, Edinburgh College of Art, since 1984; Architect/Designer, Paterson Associates, since 1966; b. 17.7.31, Sydney, Australia. Educ. Royal High School, Edinburgh; Edinburgh College of Art. Architect, Robert Matthew & Partners, Edinburgh; Lecturer, School of Architecture, Edinburgh College of Art; began practice, Paterson and Associates, Edinburgh; Director, First Year Studies, then Head, School of Design and Crafts, Edinburgh College of Art. Chairman, Scottish Central Committee of Art, 1982-84; Winner, RSA Gold Medal for Architecture. Publications: Imaginary City; Design Odyssey; The World From A Hill; Iona. Recreations: swimming; photography. Address: (h.) 24 Young Street Lane North, Edinburgh; T.-031-225 3725.

Paterson, Rev. John Love, MA, BD, STM, FSA Scot. Minister, St. Michael's Parish Church, Linlithgow, since 1977; b. 6.5.38, Ayr; m., Lorna Begg. Educ. Ayr Academy; Glasgow University; Edinburgh University; Union Theological Seminary, New York. Minister: Presbyterian Church of East Africa, 1964-72, St. Andrew's, Nairobi, 1968-72; Chaplain, Stirling University, 1973-77. Moderator, West Lothian Presbytery, 1985. Recreation: gardening. Address: St. Michael's Manse, Linlithgow, West Lothian; T.-0506 842195.

Paterson, Very Rev. John Munn Kirk, ACII, MA, BD, DD. Minister, St. Paul's Church, Milngavie, 1970-87; b. 8.10.22, Leeds; m., Geraldine Lilian Parker; 2 s.; 1 d. Educ. Hillhead High School; Edinburgh University. Pilot, RAF, 1940-46; Insurance official, 1946-58; ordained Minister, Church of Scotland, 1964; Minister, St. John's Church, Bathgate, 1964-70. Moderator, General Assembly, Church of Scotland, 1984-85; Life Member, Chartered Insurance Institute; Hon. Doctorate, Aberdeen University, 1986. Recreations: fishing; hill-walking. Address: (h.) 58 Orchard Drive, Edinburgh, EH4 2DZ; T.-031-332 5876.

Paterson, (Thomas) Michael, DA. Assistant Head of Educational Programmes, Scottish Television, since 1981; b. 14.4.38, Kirkcaldy; m., Joan; 1 s.; 2 d. Educ. George Watson's Boys' College; Edinburgh College of Art; Moray House College of Education. Teacher of Art, Waid Academy, Anstruther, 1960-64; Special Assistant, George Heriot's, Edinburgh, 1964-67; Head of Art, Marr College, Troon, 1967-69; Lecturer and Programme Director, College Television Service, Craigie College of Education, 1969-80; ETA: Chairman (Scotland), 1979-80, National Executive, since 1978; RTS Awards Convener, 1981-86, Chairman, Scottish Centre, and Member of Council, since 1986; Member, Publicity Committee, General Assembly, Church of Scotland, 1983-86; Member, Board of Communication and Convener A/V Production Unit, Church of Scotland, since 1986. Publication: A Primary Art Course (Co-author). Recreations: golf; painting; gardening; reading. Address: (h.) 1 Laurelbank Road, Maybole, KA19 8BE.

Paterson, Rev. William, BD. Minister, Craigmillar Park Church, Edinburgh, since 1984; b. 5.6.36, Airdrie; m., Evelyn Jean Davie Marshall; 1 s.; 1 d. Educ. Glasgow Academy; Glasgow University. Director, Robert Paterson and Sons Ltd., Airdrie, 1958-72; divinity student, 1971-76; Minister: St. Machar's Ranfurly Church, Bridge of Weir,

1977-84. Director, Society for the Relief of the Destitute Sick; Convener, Edinburgh Presbytery Property Committee. Recreations: motoring; travel. Address: Craigmillar Park Manse, 14 Hallhead Road, Edinburgh, H16 5QJ; T.-031-667 1623.

Paterson, William, BSc (Eng), CEng, MRAeS. Engineer in Chief, Northern Lighthouse Board, since 1987; b. 24.7.40, Neilston; m., Margaret Quirie Forrest Gerrard; 2 s.; 2 d. Educ. Paisley Grammar School; Strathclyde University. Radio Officer, Merchant Navy; Technician, then Engineer, Civil Aviation Authority; Head, Radio Department, Northern Lighthouse Board. Recreation: fair weather golf. Address: (b.) 84 George Street, Edinburgh, EH2 3DA; T.-031-226 7051.

Paterson, Wilma, DRSAM. Freelance Composer/Writer; b. 23.4.44, Dundee; 1 s.; 1 d. Educ. Harris Academy; Royal Scottish Academy of Music. Composition study with Luigi Dallapiccola in Florence; writes all types of music (chamber, orchestral, incidental); music reviews for Glasgow Herald; broadcasts and writes on food and plants. Publications: A Country Cup; Was Byron Anorexic?; Shoestring Gourmet; Flowers and Herbs of the Bible. Address: 27 Hamilton Drive, Glasgow, G12 8DN; T.-041-339 2711.

Paterson-Brown, June, MB, ChB. Commonwealth Chief Commissioner, Girl Guides Association, since 1985; Vice-Chairman, Princes Trust, since 1982; Non-Executive Director, Border Television plc, since 1980; b. 8.2.32, Edinburgh; m., Peter Neville Paterson-Brown; 3 s.; 1 d. Educ. Esdaile School; Edinburgh University. Medical Officer, Family Planning and Well Woman's Clinics, 1959-85; Past Chairman: County of Roxburghshire Youth Committee, Roxburgh Duke of Edinburgh Award Committee; Scottish Chief Commissioner, Girl Guides Association, 1977-82; Chairman, Borders Region Children's Panel Advisory Committee, 1982-85; Chairman, Scottish Standing Conference of Voluntary Youth Organisations, 1983-85; Trustee, MacRobert Trusts, since 1987. Address: (h.) Norwood, Hawick, Roxburghshire; T.-0450 72352.

Patience, Rev. Donald, MA. Minister, Kilmaurs: St. Maurs-Glencairn, since 1963; b. 28.6.28, Blair Atholl; m., Flora Bell Edgar; 1 s.; 1 d. Educ. Kingussie School; St. Andrews University. Assistant, St. Ninian's, Stirling, 1953-54; Chaplain, RAF, 1954-57; Minister, Burns Church, Kilsyth, 1958-63. Moderator, Irvine and Kilmarnock Presbytery, 1981-82; Moderator, Synod of Ayr, 1982-83. Publication: The Kirk at Kilmaurs. Recreations: history (particularly of the clans and tartans); hillwalking; jogging; participated in Glasgow Marathon 1982. Publication: The Kirk at Kilmaurs. Address: The Manse, 9 Standalane, Kilmaurs, Ayrshire; T.-Kilmarnock 38289.

Patience, Donald MacAngus, BSc (Hons). Director Investment, Scottish Development Agency, since 1982; b. 10.3.37, Fearn, Ross and Cromarty; m., Patricia Anne; 3 d. Educ. Tain Royal Academy; St. Andrews University. Research Scientist, General Electric Co., 1960-64; Production Manager, EMI, Middlesex, 1964-67; Area Manager, Liverpool then London, Investors in Industry PLC, 1967-80; Director and Manager, Finance Corporation for Industry, 1980-82. Recreations: tennis; swimming; reading; Stock Exchange investment. Address: (h.) Fir Tops, 2 Camstradden Drive East, Bearsden, Glasgow, G61 4AH; T.-041-943 1236.

Paton, Alasdair Chalmers, BSc, CEng, MICE, MIWEM. Deputy Chief Engineer, Scottish Development Department, since 1987; b. 28.11.44, Paisley; m., Zona G. Gill; 1 s.; 1 d. Educ. John Neilson Institution, Paisley; Glasgow University. Assistant Engineer, Clyde Port Authority, 1967-71; Assistant Engineer, DAFS, 1971-72; Senior Engineer, SDD, 1972-77; Engineer, Public Works Department, Hong Kong Government, 1977-80; Senior Engineer, then Principal Engineer, SDD, 1980-87. Recreations: Rotary; sailing; golf. Address: (b.) 27 Perth Street, Edinburgh; T.-031-244 3035.

Paton, George, MA, MEd, FEIS, FITD. Director, Scottish Council for Educational Technology, since 1986; b. 5.12.31, Rutherglen; m., Barbara Thomson; 2 s. Educ. Rutherglen Academy; Glasgow University. National Service, RAEC, 1953-55; Schoolteacher, 1955-61; Lecturer in English, Jordanhill College of Education, 1961-63; Principal Lecturer in English, then Assistant Principal, Dundee College of Education, 1963-69; Principal, Hamilton College of Education, 1970-81; Assistant Principal, Jordanhill College of Education, 1981-82; Depute Director, Scottish Council for Educational Technology, 1982-86. Executive Committee Member, International Council for Educational Media, since 1983; Member, Library Information Service Committee (Scotland), since 1984; Executive Committee Member, Commonwealth Institute in Scotland, since 1985; Governor, David Livingstone Memorial Trust, since 1971; former Convener, Education Committee, General Teaching Council for Scotland; Member, Consultative Committee on the Curriculum, 1980-83; Member, SCE Examination Board, 1977-81; Past President, Association of Higher Academic Staff in Colleges of Education in Scotland; Elder, Church of Scotland. Recreations: singing; drama; gardening. Address: (b.) 74 Victoria Crescent Road, Glasgow, G12 9JN; T.-041-334 9314.

Paton, Rev. Iain Ferguson, BD, FCIS. Minister, Newlands (South), Glasgow, since 1985; b. 28.1.41, Edinburgh; m., Marjorie Vickers Macdonald; 1 s.; 1 d. Educ. George Watson's College, Edinburgh; Edinburgh University. Royal Bank of Scotland Ltd., 1957-66; Assistant Secretary, John Menzies (Holdings) Ltd., 1966-68; Senior Registrar, Charlotte Registrars Ltd., 1968-70; Secretary, Scottish Sports Council, 1970-75; Faculty of Divinity, Edinburgh University, 1975-79; Assistant Minister, St. Ninians Church, Corstorphine, 1979-80; Minister, Banchory-Ternan West Parish Church, 1980-85. Address: Newlands (South) Manse, 24 Monreith Road, Glasgow, G43 2NY; T.-041-632 2588.

Paton, James Peter Hill, BL. Chief Executive, Falkirk District Council, since 1974; Clerk of the Peace, Falkirk District, since 1975; b. 29.6.31, Glasgow; m., Evelyn Margaret Grant. Educ. Kelvinside Academy; Glasgow University. Local government legal posts, from 1956; Depute County

Clerk, Clackmannan County Council, 1964; Clerk, Central Region Steering Committee, 1973; Executive Committee Member, Society of Local Authority Chief Executives; Chief Officer Adviser, COSLA. Recreations: curling; golf; art; music. Address: (b.) Municipal Chambers, Falkirk, FK1 5RS; T.-Falkirk 24911.

Paton, William, BSc (Hons). Deputy Director, National Engineering Laboratory; b. 29.11.41, Kilwinning; m., Elizabeth Anne; 2 s. Educ. Douglas Ewart School, Newton Stewart; Glasgow University. Consulting Geophysicist, Seismograph Services Ltd., 1963; Management Trainee, Colvilles Ltd., Ravenscraig, 1964; Research Scientist in Materials, NEL, 1965-76; Offshore Supplies Office, 1976-77; Divisional Manager, Materials Engineering Division, then Controller, Design, Materials and Systems Department, NEL, 1977-87. Recreation: golf. Address: (b.) National Engineering Laboratory, East Kilbride, Glasgow; T.-East Kilbride 20222.

Patrick, James McIntosh, RSA, LLD, ROI, ARE. Artist and Landscape Painter; b. 4.2.07, Dundee; m., Janet Watterston (deceased); 1 s.; 1 d. Educ. Morgan Academy, Dundee; Glasgow School of Art. Guthrie Award, RSA, 1935; paintings in numerous national and municipal collections; Hon. LLD, Dundee, 1973; Fellowship, Duncan of Jordanstone College of Art. Address: (h.) The Shrubbery, Magdalen Yard Road, Dundee.

Patterson, Rev. Andrew Ramsay Murray, MA, BD. Minister, Mochrum, since 1984; b. 8.2.49, Newcastle; m., Elizabeth Anne MacIntyre; 1 s.; 1 d. Educ. Epsom College; St. Andrews University; New College, Edinburgh. Organic horticulture, 1971-76; History Teacher, Annan Academy, 1976-81. Recreations: gardening; fishing; beer; walking. Address: 45 Main Street, Kirkinner, Wigtownshire.

Patterson, Professor Edward McWilliam, BSc, PhD, FRSE, FIMA. Professor of Mathematics, Aberdeen University, since 1965; b. 30.7.26, Whitby; m., 1, Joan Sibald Maddick (deceased); 2, Elizabeth McAllan Hunter; 1 d. Educ. Northallerton Grammar School; Ripon Grammar School; Whitby County School; Lady Lumley's Grammar School, Pickering; Leeds University. Research Demonstrator in Mathematics, Sheffield University, 1949-51; Lecturer in Mathematics: St. Andrews University, 1951-56, Leeds University, 1956-59; Aberdeen University: Senior Lecturer in Mathematics, 1960-64, Dean, Faculty of Science, 1981-84; Royal Society Visiting Professor, Malaya University, 1973; awarded MakDougall-Brisbane Prize, Royal Society of Edinburgh, 1962; Vice-President, IMA, 1973-74; President, Edinburgh Mathematical Society, 1964-65; Council Member, London Mathematical Society, 1976-80. Publications: Topology, 1956; Elementary Abstract Algebra (Co-author), 1965; Solving Problems in Vector Algebra, 1968. Address: (b.) Department of Mathematical Sciences, Edward Wright Building, Dunbar Street, Aberdeen, AB9 2TY; T.-0224 272758.

Patterson, John Stitt, MB, ChB, FRCGP. Senior Medical Officer, Scottish Home and Health Department (retired); b. 23.10.23, Arbroath; m., Margaret Madeline Fraser; 3 s.; 2 d. Educ. Arbroath High School; St. Andrews University; Edinburgh University. Army Service, 1942-46; junior appointments in hospital and general practice, 1951-57; Principal in general practice, Westray (Orkney), 1958, Edinburgh, 1961. Secretary, Scottish Council, Royal College of General Practitioners, 1969-72 and 1973-74. Recreations: photography; music; theatre. Address: (h.) 67 Great King Street, Edinburgh; T.-031-556 7647.

Patterson, Rev. John Wallace, BA, BD. Minister, Martyrs Church, St. Andrews, since 1958; Clerk, Presbytery of St. Andrews, since 1972; b. 7.1.23, Coleraine; m., Catherine Mackay Cape; 4 d. Educ. Coleraine Academical Institution; Trinity College, Dublin; St. Andrews University. Minister, Prestwick North, 1950-58. Address: Martyrs Manse, St. Andrews, Fife, KY16 8LG.

Patterson, Walter Moffat, MSc, BSc. HM Inspector of Schools, since 1986; b. 14.6.45, Airdrie; m., Colleen McCrone; 1 s.; 1 d. Educ. Coatbridge High School; Strathclyde University. Lecturer in Statistics, Paisley College; Development Officer, Glacier Metal Co., Kilmarnock, 1973-74; Lecturer in Statistics, Paisley College, 1974-83; Senior Lecturer in Information Technology, MEDC, Paisley College, 1983-86. Recreations: gardening; golf. Address: (b.) Room 3/29, New St. Andrews House, Edinburgh, EH1 3SY; T.-031-244 4528.

Pattison, David Arnold, BSc, PhD. UK Director, Leisure and Tourism Consulting, Arthur Young; Board Director, Scottish National Orchestra; b. 9.2.41, Kilmarnock; m., Anne Ross Wilson; 2 s.; 1 d. Educ. Kilmarnock Academy; Glasgow University. Planning Assistant, Ayr County Council, 1963-64; PhD studies, Glasgow University, 1964-66; Planning Assistant, Dunbarton County Council, 1966-67; Lecturer, Strathclyde University, 1967-70; Head of Tourism, Highlands and Islands Development Board, 1970-81; Chief Executive, Scottish Tourist Board, 1981-85. External Examiner for postgraduate tourism courses, Strathclyde University, 1981-84. Recreations: reading; watching soccer and rugby; golf; gardening. Address: (b.) Arthur Young International, 17 Abercromby Place, Edinburgh, EH3 6LT; T.-031-556 8641.

Pattison, Rev. Kenneth John, MA, BD, STM. Chaplain, Glasgow Royal Infirmary, since 1984; b. 22.4.41, Glasgow; m., Susan Jennifer Brierley Jenkins; 1 s.; 2 d. Educ. Lenzie Academy; Glasgow University; Union Theological Seminary, New York. Missionary of Church of Scotland/Minister, Church of Central Africa Presbyterian, Malawi, 1967-77; Principal, Kapeni Theological College, Blantyre, Malawi, 1975-77; Minister, Park Parish Church, Ardrossan, 1977-84. Recreations: gardening; hill-walking. Address: (h.) 46 Berridale Avenue, Cathcart, Glasgow, G44 3AE; T.-041-637 2697.

Pattullo, David Bruce, BA. Group Chief Executive and a Deputy Governor, Bank of Scotland, since 1988; Director (Non-Executive): British Linen Bank, since 1977, Melville Street Investments (Edinburgh) PLC, since 1973, Standard Life, since 1985, Bank of Wales PLC, since 1986, North West Securities Ltd., since 1986; b. 2.1.38, Edinburgh; m., Fiona Jane Nicholson; 3 s.; 1 d.

Educ. Belhaven Hill School; Rugby; Hertford College, Oxford. National Service commission, Royal Scots (seconded to West Africa); joined Bank of Scotland, 1961; winner, first prize, Institute of Bankers in Scotland, 1964; Manager, Investment Services Department, 1967-71; Deputy Manager, Bank of Scotland Finance Co. Ltd., 1971-73; Chief Executive, Group Merchant Banking Activities, 1973-78; Deputy Treasurer, Bank of Scotland, 1978; Treasurer and General Manager, 1979; Chairman, Committee of Scottish Clearing Bankers, 1987-89; Honorary Treasurer, Malcolm Sargent Cancer Fund for Children in Scotland; Fellow and Vice-President, Institute of Bankers in Scotland. Recreation: tennis. Address: (b.) Bank of Scotland, Head Office, The Mound, Edinburgh, EH1 1YZ; T.-031-243 5555.

Paul, Rev. Alison, MA, BD, DipTEO. Minister, North Motherwell Parish Church, since 1986; b. 18.11.46, Glasgow. Educ. Dumbarton Academy; Glasgow University; Manchester University; Trinity College, Glasgow. Teacher of English, Buckeburg, West Germany, 1970-82; divinity student, 1982-85; Assistant Minister, Helensburgh West Kirk, 1985-86. Former Girl Guide District Commissioner. Recreations: music; reading; walking. Address: North Church Manse, 3 Kirkland Street, Motherwell, ML1 3JW; T.-0698 66716.

Paul, Rev. Iain, BSc, PhD, BD, PhD. Minister, Craigneuk and Belhaven Church, Wishaw, since 1976; b. 15.6.39, Glasgow; m., Elizabeth Henderson Findlay Russell; 1 s.; 1 d. Educ. Govan High School; Strathclyde University; Bristol University; Edinburgh University. Postdoctoral research, Sheffield University, 1967-69; Lecturer in Chemistry, Queen Elizabeth College, London University, 1969-71; Assistant Minister, St. Conal's linked with St. Mark's, Kirkconnel, 1974-75; Member, Centre of Theological Inquiry, Princeton, USA, 1980-81. Publications: Science, Theology and Einstein, 1982; Science and Theology in Einstein's Perspective, 1985; Knowledge of God, Calvin, Einstein, Polyani, 1987. Recreations: writing books; reading; music. Address: 100 Glen Road, Wishaw, ML2 7NP; T.-Wishaw 372495.

Paul, Professor James, DipArch, DipTP, FRIBA, FRIAS, FRTPI, AILA. Professor of Architecture, Duncan of Jordanstone College of Art/Dundee University, since 1983; b. 7.10.29, Toronto; m., Elizabeth; 4 s. Educ. Banff Academy; School of Architecture, Aberdeen; School of Town Planning, Royal Technical College, Glasgow. Architect/Planner, Corporation of City of London, 1954-56; School of Architecture, Dundee: Lecturer, 1956, Senior Lecturer, 1959, Head of School, since 1965; private practice: James Parr and Partners, 1957-59, Johnston and Baxter, 1959-62 (Partner), Baxter, Clark and Paul Architects, 1962-79 (Partner), James Paul Associates, since 1979. Address: (b.) Department of Architecture, Duncan of Jordanstone College of Art/Dundee University, 13 Perth Road, Dundee; T.-0382 23261, Ext. 41.

Paul, John, MB, ChB, PhD, FRSE, FRCPEdin, FRCPGlas, FRCPath. Honorary Senior Lecturer, Department of Pathology, Glasgow University, since 1966 (Director, Beatson Institute for Cancer Research, 1966-87); b. 25.4.22, Wishaw; m., Eleanor Rae Turnbull; 2 s.; 1 d. Educ. Dalziel High School; Glasgow University. Rockefeller Fellow, College of Physicians and Surgeons, New York, 1953-54; Reader (Biochemistry), Glasgow University, 1961-64; Titular Professor (Biochemistry), Glasgow University, 1964-66. Honorary Professor (Biochemistry), Hull University, 1973-87. Publications: Cell and Tissue Culture, and other books; numerous scientific papers. Address: (h.) 115 Kelvin Drive, Glasgow, G20 8QL.

Paul, Professor John P., BSc, PhD, ARCST, CEng, FIMechE, FISPO, cFBOA, FRSA, FRSE. Professor and Head, Bioengineering Unit, Strathclyde University, since 1978; b. 26.6.27, Sunderland; m., Elizabeth R. Graham; 1 s.; 2 d. Educ. Aberdeen Grammar School; Allan Glen's School, Glasgow; Royal College of Science and Technology, Glasgow; Glasgow University. Successively Research Assistant, Lecturer and Senior Lecturer in Mechanics of Materials, Royal College of Science and Technology, subsequently Strathclyde University, 1949-69; Visiting Professor, West Virginia University, 1969-70; Reader, then Personal Professor, Bioengineering Unit, Strathclyde University, 1970-78. Elected President, International Society of Biomechanics, 1987. Publications: Computing in Medicine (Senior Editor), 1981; Biomaterials in Artificial Organs (Senior Editor), 1984; Disability (Co-Editor), 1979; Total Knee Joint Replacement (Co-Editor), 1988. Recreations: formerly rugby; gardening; home maintenance; light reading. Address: (h.) 25 James Watt Road, Milngavie, Glasgow, G62 7JX; T.-041-956 3221.

Paul, Ronald, MA, DipEd. Headmaster, Currie High School, since 1970; b. 6.8.32, Edinburgh; m., Nancy Crawford Logan; 3 s. Educ. Boroughmuir School, Edinburgh; Edinburgh University; Moray House College of Education. Commissioned, RAF, 1955-58; Teacher of Geography, Edinburgh, 1958-65; Principal Teacher, Boroughmuir, 1965-67; Headmaster, James Clark School, Edinburgh, 1968-70. Church Elder; President, Edinburgh Rotary Club, 1982-83; Past President, Lothian Headteachers and Headteachers Association of Scotland; Member, Scottish Examination Board. Recreations: family; travel; reading; music; oil painting. Address: (b.) Currie High School, Dolphin Avenue, Currie, EH14 5RD; T.-031-449 2165.

Pauson, Professor Peter Ludwig, BSc, PhD, CChem, FRSC, FRSE. Freeland Professor of Chemistry, Strathclyde University, since 1959; b. 30.7.25, Bamberg, Germany; m., Lai-ngau Wong; 1 s.; 1 d. Educ. Glasgow University; Sheffield University. Assistant Professor, Duquesne University, Pittsburgh, 1949-51; postdoctoral fellowships: University of Chicago, 1951-52, Harvard University, 1952-53; Lecturer, then Reader, Sheffield University, 1953-59; Visiting Professor: University of Arizona, 1966-67, La Trobe University, Melbourne and Australian National University, Canberra, 1977. Tilden Lectureship, 1960, and Organometallic Chemistry Award, Chemical Society, 1976. Publication: Organometallic Chemistry, 1967. Recreations: skiing; hillwalking; gardening; badminton; listening to music. Address: (b.) Department of Pure and Applied Chemistry, Strathclyde University, Cathedral Street, Glasgow, G1 1XL; T.-041-552 4400.

Pawley, Professor G. Stuart, MA, PhD, FRSE. Professor of Computational Physics, Edinburgh University, since 1985; b. 22.6.37, Ilford; m., Anthea Jean Miller; 2 s.; 1 d. Educ. Bolton School; Corpus Christi College, Cambridge. Lecturer, Edinburgh University, 1964; Reader, 1970; Personal Chair, 1985; Guest Professor, Aarhus University, Denmark, 1969-70. Recreations: choral singing; mountain walking. Address: (b.) Physics Department, Kings Buildings, Edinburgh University, EH9 3JZ; T.-031-667 1081.

Payne, Professor Peter Lester, BA, PhD, FRHistS. Professor of Economic History, Aberdeen University, since 1969; b. 31.12.29, London; m., Enid Christine Rowntree; 1 s.; 1 d. Educ. Brockley County School, London; Nottingham University. Visiting Lecturer in American Economic History, Johns Hopkins University, 1957-58; Lecturer in Economic and Social History, Nottingham University, 1958-59; Colquhoun Lecturer in Business History, Glasgow University, 1959-69; Senior Lecturer in Economic History, Glasgow University, 1964-69; Sherman Fairchild Distinguished Scholar, California Institute of Technology, Pasadena, 1977-78. Member: Business Archives Council, since 1959; Business Archives Council of Scotland; Council, Economic History Society. Publications include: Rubber and Railways in the Nineteenth Century; British Entrepreneurship in the Nineteenth Century; Colvilles and the Scottish Steel Industry; The Early Scottish Limited Companies; The Hydro. Recreations: philately; woodwork. Address: (h.) 68 Hamilton Place, Aberdeen, AB2 4BA; T.-0224 644874.

Peacock, Professor Sir Alan Turner, Kt (1987), DSC, MA, Hon. DUniv (Stirling), Hon. DEcon (Zurich), Hon. DScEcon (Buckingham), FBA. Research Professor in Public Finance, Esmee Fairbairn Centre, Heriot-Watt University, since 1985; Executive Director, David Hume Institute, Edinburgh, since 1985; Chairman, Scottish Arts Council, since 1986; b. 26.6.22, Ryton-on-Tyne; m., Margaret Martha Astell-Burt; 2 s.; 1 d. Educ. Grove Academy; Dundee High School; St. Andrews University. Royal Navy, 1942-45; Lecturer in Economics, St. Andrews, 1947-48; Lecturer, then Reader in Economics, London School of Economics, 1948-56; Professor of Economic Science, Edinburgh University, 1956-62; Professor of Economics, York University, 1962-78 (Deputy Vice Chancellor, 1963-69); Professor of Economics, University College, Buckingham, 1978-80; Principal, then Vice Chancellor, Buckingham University, 1980-84; Chief Economic Adviser, Department of Trade and Industry (on secondment), 1973-76; Member, Royal Commission on the Constitution, 1970-73; Member, Inquiry into Retirement Provision, 1983-85; SSRC Council, 1972-73; President, International Institute of Public Finance, 1966-69; Chairman, Committee on Financing the BBC, 1985-86. Recreations: attempting to write music; jogging; hillwalking. Address: (h.) 8 Gilmour Road, Edinburgh, EH16 5NF; T.-031-667 0544.

Peacock, Peter James. Member, Highland Regional Council, since 1982 (Chairman, Finance Committee); Training and Organisational Consultant; b. 27.2.52, Edinburgh; 2 s. Educ. Hawick High School; Jordanhill College of Education, Glasgow. Community Worker, Orkney Islands, 1973-75. Co-author, Vice-Chairman, subsequently Chairman of successful applicant group for Independent Local Radio franchise, Moray Firth; Member, Scottish Valuation Advisory Committee; former Area Officer, Highlands, Islands, Grampian, Scottish Association of Citizens Advice Bureaux. Recreations: ornithology; watching rugby union; challenging conventional thought. Address: (h.) 68 Braeside Park, Balloch, Inverness; T.-0463 790371.

Peaker, Professor Malcolm, PhD, FZS, FIBiol, FRSE. Director, Hannah Research Institute, Ayr, since 1981; Hannah Professor of Dairy Science, Glasgow University, since 1981; b. 21.8.43, Stapleford, Nottingham; m., Stephanie Jane Large; 3 s. Educ. Henry Mellish Grammar School, Nottingham; Sheffield University; University of Hong Kong. ARC Institute of Animal Physiology, 1968-78; Head, Department of Physiology, Hannah Research Institute, 1978-81. Member, Editorial Board: Journal of Dairy Science, 1975-78, International Zoo Yearbook, 1978-82, Journal of Endocrinology, 1981; Editor, British Journal of Herpetology, 1977-81. Publications: Salt Glands in Birds and Reptiles, 1975; Avian Physiology (Editor), 1975; Comparative Aspects of Lactation (Editor), 1977; Physiological Strategies in Lactation (Co-Editor), 1984. Recreations: vertebrate zoology; natural history; golf; grumbling about bureaucrats. Address: (h.) 13 Upper Crofts, Alloway, Ayr, KA7 4QX; T.-Alloway 43999.

Pearson, Brigadier Alastair Stevenson, CB (1958), DSO, OBE, MC, KStJ, TD. Lord Lieutenant of Dunbartonshire, since 1979; Keeper of Dumbarton Castle, since 1981; b. 1.6.15; m.; 3 d. Educ. Kelvinside Academy; Sedbergh. Served Second World War (Lt.-Col., 1942); ADC to The Queen, 1956-61; Hon. Colonel, 15th (Scottish) Bn., The Parachute Regiment (TA), 1963-77 and since 1983. Address: (h.) Tullochan, Gartocharn, by Alexandria, Dunbartonshire.

Pearson, Donald William Macintyre, BSc (Hons), MB, ChB, MRCP. Consultant Physician, Aberdeen Teaching Hospitals, since 1984; Clinical Senior Lecturer, Aberdeen University, since 1984; b. 5.9.50, Kilmarnock; m., Margaret J.K. Harris; 2 s.; 1 d. Educ. Cumnock Academy; Glasgow University. Registrar, University Department of Medicine, Glasgow Royal Infirmary; Lecturer in Medicine with Aberdeen University, Raigmore Hospital, Inverness; Senior Registrar in General Medicine, Diabetes and Endocrinology, Grampian Health Board. Past President, New Cumnock Burns Club. Recreations: football; computing; music; Scottish poetry. Address: (b.) Diabetic Clinic, Woolmanhill, Aberdeen Royal Infirmary, Aberdeen; T.-0224 681818, Ext. 55491.

Pearson, Keith Philip, MA (Cantab), CertEd, DipEstHisp. Headmaster, George Heriot's School, since 1983; b. 5.8.41, Preston; 2 d. Educ.

Preston Grammar School; Madrid University; St. Catharine's College, Cambridge. Assistant Teacher, then Head of Modern Languages, Rossall School, 1964-72; Head of Modern Languages, then Deputy Principal, George Watson's College, 1972-83. Member, HMC; twice Member, SCCML; Member, Central Committee on the Curriculum, since 1983. Recreations: sport; hill-walking; music; DIY; foreign travel. Address: (h.) 41 Morningside Park, Edinburgh, EH10 5EZ; T.-031-447 5861.

Pearson, Thomas, DPE. Vice President, Scottish Rugby Union, 1987 (Convenor of Coaching and Youth Development, since 1982); b. 4.10.26, Burnside, Fife; m., Elizabeth Hay McDonald; 2 s.; 1 d. Educ. Bell-Baxter School, Cupar; Scottish School of Physical Education, Glasgow. Principal Teacher of Physical Education, Buckhaven High School; Assistant Rector, Buckhaven High School (now retired). Recreations: curling; golf; gardening; Continental travelling. Address: (h.) Lingmoor, Carberry Park, Leven, Fife; T.-0333 26248.

Peat, Jeremy Alastair, BA, MSc. Senior Economic Adviser, Scottish Office, since 1985; b. 20.3.45, Haywards Heath; m., Philippa Ann; 2 d. Educ. St. Paul's School, London; Bristol University; University College London. Economic Assistant/Economic Adviser, Ministry of Overseas Development, 1969-77; Economic Adviser, Manpower Services Commission, 1978-80; Head, Employment Policy Unit, Ministry of Finance and Development Planning, Government of Botswana, 1980-84; Economic Adviser, HM Treasury, 1984-85. Recreations: golf; walking; reading. Address: (b.) Room 5/27, New St. Andrews House, Edinburgh, EH1 3TA; T.-031-244 5104.

Peat, Rev. Stanley William, BSc, PhD, BD. Minister, St. Serf's Parish Church, Edinburgh, since 1984; b. 5.5.29, Edinburgh; m., Elizabeth Eleanor Smith; 1 s.; 1 d. Educ. George Heriot's School, Edinburgh; Edinburgh University. Lecturer, then Senior Lecturer in Physics, Heriot-Watt College/University, 1957-73; Minister, St. John's Church, Carluke, 1977-84. Recreation: golf. Address: 1 Denham Green Terrace, Edinburgh, EH5 3PG; T.-031-552 4059.

Peat, William Wood Watson, CBE, JP, FRAgS. Farmer; National Governor for Scotland, BBC, and Chairman, Broadcasting Council for Scotland, since 1984; b. 14.12.22, Denny; m., Jean McHarrie; 2 s.; 1 d. Educ. Denny Public School. Lt., Royal Signals, NW Europe and India, 1940-46; Broadcaster; National Chairman, subsequently President, Scottish Association of Young Farmers Clubs; Member, Stirling County Council, 1959-75 (Vice Convener, 1967-70); Council Member, NFU of Scotland, 1959-78 (President, 1966-67); Member, Scotish River Purification Advisory Committee, 1960-79; Board of Management, RSNH, 1960-72; General Commissioner of Income Tax, since 1962; Chairman, Scottish Advisory Committee, Association of Agriculture, 1974-79 (Vice-President, since 1979); Council, Hannah Research Institute, 1963-82; Council Member, Scottish Agricultural Organisation Society Ltd., since 1963 (President, 1974-77); Member, British Agricultural Council, 1974-84; Member, Board of Management, Oatridge Agricultural College, 1967-75; Governor, West of Scotland Agricultural College (Chairman, since 1983); Chairman, Scottish Agricultural Colleges Ltd., since 1987; Director, FMC plc, 1974-83; Member, Central Council for Agricultural and Horticultural Co-operation, 1967-83; Member, Co-operative Development Board, since 1983; Member, Board of Management, British Farm Produce Council, 1964-83, BFP Committee, Food from Britain, 1984-87; Chairman, BBC Scottish Agricultural Advisory Committee, 1971-76. Recreations: amateur radio; flying. Address: (h.) 61 Stirling Road, Larbert, FK5 4SG.

Peddie, Richard L., MA, MEd, ABPsS. Vice-Principal, Craigie College of Education; b. 11.6.28, Grangemouth; m., Nan K. Bell; 1 s.; 2 d. Educ. Grangemouth High School; Glasgow University. Royal Signals Officer, Allied Supreme HQ (SHAPE), 1951-53; Teacher, Stirlingshire, 1953-56; Educational Psychologist, Ayrshire, 1956-59; Lecturer, Jordanhill College, 1959-64; Head, Psychology Department, Assistant Principal, Vice-Principal, Craigie College of Education, since 1964; Member, General Teaching Council for Scotland, 1970-78; External Examiner in Education, London University Institute, 1971-76; External Examiner, Hamilton College of Education, 1977-80; Member, Scottish Examination Board, 1980-84; Member, Education Committee, British Psychological Society, 1964-68; Chairman, Glasgow University Educational Colloquium, 1966-67; Chairman, Association of Lecturers in Colleges of Education in Scotland (ALCES), 1967-69; Captain, 51 (H) Infantry Division Signals Regiment (TA), 1953-60; Vice-Chairman, Ayr Children's Panel, 1970-74; Member, Scottish Council for Research in Education, 1962-78; Member, Executive Committee, Scottish Division of Educational and Child Psychology, since 1979; Chairman, Association of Higher Academic Staff in Colleges of Education, 1984-87; Paul Harris Fellow, Rotary Award, 1986; Church of Scotland Elder. Recreations: reading; Rotary; driving; very occasional golf; tennis. Address: (h.) 14 Glenpark Place, Alloway, Ayr, KA7 4SQ; T.-0292 41996.

Peden, Hugh Andrew Mair, JP, MA, LLB, NP. Retired Senior Partner, Peden and Patrick, Solicitors, Glasgow; b. 7.11.20, Glasgow; m., Grace Joyce Parker; 1 s.; 1 d. Educ. High School of Glasgow; Glasgow University. Served in 11 Group Fighter Command, RAF, 1941-46; qualified as a Solicitor and became a Partner in family law firm, 1951. Liberal Party Parliamentary Agent, seven consecutive General Elections since 1959, Eastwood (formerly East Renfrewshire). Recreations: politics; supporting Queens Park FC (of which a member for more than 20 years); reading. Address: (h.) Milrig, Glebe Road, Newton Mearns, Glasgow.

Peden, Professor James McKenzie, BSc, MEng, PhD, CEng, MIChemE, MAIME. Shell Research Professor of Petroleum Engineering and Head, Petroleum Engineering Department, Heriot-Watt University; Director: Edinburgh Petroleum Development Services Ltd., since 1983, Petroleum International Training and Consultancy Ltd., since 1986, Ecodrill Ltd., since 1987; b.

27.9.47, Edinburgh; m., Jacqueline Watson; 1 s.; 1 d. Educ. Darwen Grammar School; Heriot-Watt University. Process Technologist, Shell UK Oil Ltd., 1970-73; Research Engineer, Henry Balfour Ltd., Leven, 1973-74; Sales Development Officer, Distillers Ltd., 1974-75; postgraduate student, 1975-76; Petroleum Engineer, Shell International Petroleum Co., 1976-78; Lecturer, Heriot-Watt University, since 1978. Chairman, Aberdeen Section, Society of Petroleum Engineers, AIME; Member, SPE and I CHEME; Member, International Editorial Review Committee, SPE Dallas. Recreations: golf; bridge. Address: (h.) Dunella, Station Road, Kinross, KY13 7TU; T.-0577 62708.

Peebles Brown, David Adair, MB, ChB, FRCSEdin, FRCSGlas. Consultant Surgeon, Gartnavel General/Western Infirmary, Glasgow, 1963-88; Honorary Clinical Lecturer, Glasgow University, since 1963; b. 4.1.27, Malton, Yorkshire; m., Mary A.F. Findlay; 3 s.; 1 d. Educ. Shrewsbury School; Glasgow University. Commission, 1st Royal Tank Regiment; medical student, junior surgical trainee, then Consultant Surgeon. Recreations: gardening; ornithology. Address: (h.) 3 Falcon Terrace Lane, Glasgow, G20 OAG; T.-041-945 0920.

Peggie, Robert Galloway Emslie, CBE, FCCA, FBCS. Commissioner (Ombudsman) for Local Administration in Scotland, since 1986; b. 5.1.29, Bo'ness; m., Christine; 1 s.; 1 d. Educ. Lasswade High School. Trainee Accountant, 1946-52; Accountant in industry, 1952-57; Edinburgh Corporation, 1957-72: O. and M. Officer, Assistant City Chamberlain, Deputy City Chamberlain, Reorganisation Steering Committee; Chief Executive, Lothian Regional Council, 1974-86. Recreation: golf. Address: (b.) 5 Shandwick Place, Edinburgh, EH2 4RG; T.-031-229 4472.

Pelham Burn, Angus Maitland, JP. Farmer; Vice Lord Lieutenant, Kincardineshire, since 1978; Member, Grampian Regional Council, since 1974; Member, Queen's Bodyguard for Scotland (Royal Company of Archers), since 1968; Director, Bank of Scotland, since 1977; Company Director; b. 13.12.31; m.; 4 d. Educ. Harrow; North of Scotland College of Agriculture. Vice Convener, Kincardine County Council, 1973-75.

Pelly, Frances Elsie, ARSA, DA. Sculptor; b. 21.7.47, Edinburgh. Educ. Morrison's Academy, Crieff; Duncan of Jordanstone College of Art, Dundee. Secondary and primary school teaching, Dumfriesshire, 1973-74; self-employed as Sculptor and part-time lecturing, Dundee, 1974-79; Lecturer in Sculpture, Grays School of Art, Aberdeen, 1979-83. Recreations: learning dressage riding; gardening. Address: 5 Dolphinstone Cottages, Tranent, East Lothian; T.-Tranent 613961.

Pender, Colonel Dinsdale. Territorial Commander for Scotland, Salvation Army, since 1986; b. 22.3.32, London; m., Winifred Dale; 2 d.; 1 s. Educ. Govan Academy; Colfe's Grammar School, London. RAF, 1950-52; commissioned as Salvation Army Officer, 1953; worked in various parts of England, including Bath, Coventry, Manchester; Divisional Commander on Tyneside; Assistant Field Secretary, National Headquarters, London; Chief Secretary in New Zealand; Territorial Commander in Southern Africa. Address: (b.) Houldsworth Street, Glasgow, G3 8DU; T.-041-221 3378.

Pendreigh, David Mackie, MB, ChB, FRCP, FFCM, DPH. Senior Lecturer, Department of Community Medicine, Edinburgh University, since 1978; Honorary Community Medicine Specialist, Lothian Health Board, since 1978; Chief Investigator, WHO Collaborating Centre, Usher Institute, since 1982; b. 13.1.31, Whitburn, West Lothian; m., Gladys Margaret Pendreigh; 2 s.; 1 d. Educ. Bathgate Academy; Edinburgh University. Variety of clinical posts in hospital and general practice, as well as in public health, and two years as a Surgeon Lieutenant in Royal Navy; various posts, Scottish Home and Health Department, 1966-78, latterly as Principal Medical Officer and Director, Scottish Health Services Planning Unit; serves on various NHS Committees. Recreations: walking; tennis; squash. Address: (h.) 22 Bonaly Avenue, Edinburgh, EH13 OET; T.-031-441 1869.

Penman, Ian Dalgleish, CB (1987), MA. Deputy Secretary, Central Services, Scottish Office, since 1984; b. 1.8.31, Glasgow; m., Elisabeth Stewart Strachan; 3 s. Educ. High School of Glasgow; Glasgow University; Balliol College, Oxford. RAF Education Branch, 1955-57; HM Treasury, 1957-58; joined Scottish Office, 1958; Private Secretary to Parliamentary Under Secretary of State, 1960-62; Principal, Scottish Development Department, 1962-70; Assistant Secretary, Establishment Division, 1970-72, Police Division, 1972-78; Under Secretary, Scottish Development Department, 1978-84. Recreations: swimming; travel; music. Address: (h.) 4 Wardie Avenue, Edinburgh, EH5 2AB; T.-031-552 2180.

Penn, Ian Davis, CBiol, MIBiol, AIMLS. Depute Principal, Dumfries and Galloway College of Technology, since 1983; b. 20.3.40, Bromley; m., Valerie Jane Rolston; 1 s.; 1 d. Educ. Colfe's Grammar School, London; North East Surrey College of Technology. Laboratory technician; Assistant Lecturer in Biology, Chelmsford, Essex; Lecturer B in Biology, Bristol Technical College; Senior Lecturer in Science, then Head, Department of Science, Stevenson College, Edinburgh. Institute of Biology: Chairman, Education Division, 1984-86, Chairman, Scottish Branch, 1985-88. Recreation: gardening. Address: (h.) Nithsdale, Edinburgh Road, Dumfries; T.-0387 62269.

Pennington, Christopher Royston, BSc (Hons), MB, ChB, MRCP, MD, FRCPEdin. Consultant Physician (General Medicine and Gastroenterology), since 1979; Honorary Senior Lecturer in Medicine, Dundee University, since 1979; Examiner, MRCP (UK), since 1986; b. 22.2.46, Chard; m., Marcia Jane Barclay, 1 d. Educ. Shebbear College; Manchester University. House Officer, Manchester Royal Infirmary, 1970-71; Registrar in Medicine, Aberdeen Royal Infirmary, 1971-74; Lecturer in Medicine, Dundee University, 1974-79. External Examiner in Medicine, Aberdeen University, 1983-86. Publication: Therapeutic Nutrition: A Practical Guide, 1988. Address: (h.) Balnagowan, Braehead, Invergowrie, Dundee.

Pentland, Brian, BSc, MB, ChB, FRCPE. Consultant Neurologist in Rehabilitation Medicine, since 1982; Senior Lecturer in Orthopaedic Surgery and Neurosciences, Edinburgh University, since 1983; b. 24.6.49, Glasgow; m., Gillian Mary Duggua; 4 s. Educ. Liberton High School, Edinburgh; Edinburgh University. Junior hospital appointments in Edinburgh, Cumbria and Dundee; formerly Lecturer in Neurology in Edinburgh. Recreation: hill-walking. Address: (b.) Astley Ainslie Hospital, Grange Loan, Edinburgh, EH9 2HL; T.-031-447 6271.

Peoples, Robin (Robert John), MA (Hons). Artistic Director, Scottish Youth Theatre, since 1983; b. 9.9.54, Londonderry; m., Lamorna Hutchison; 1 s.; 1 d. Educ. Foyle College, Derry; St. Andrews University. Youth and community work in Northern Ireland; taught at University of Erlangen-Nuremberg, West Germany; awarded Scottish Arts Council Director's Bursary; directed and designed with various theatre companies throughout Scotland. Member, Mime Advisory Committee; Member, Advisory Theatre Committee, Scottish-USSR Society. Recreations: theatre; painting; reading; canoeing. Address: (b.) Scottish Youth Theatre, 48 Albany Street, Edinburgh, EH1 3QR; T.-031-557 2224.

Peploe, Denis Frederic Neil, RSA, DA. Artist; b. 25.3.14, Edinburgh; m., Elizabeth Marion Barr; 1 s.; 1 d. Educ. Edinburgh Academy; Edinburgh College of Art. Fellowship, Edinburgh College of Art, 1939-40; War Service, 1940-46 (RA, Intelligence Corps, SOE); Lecturer, Edinburgh College of Art, 1954-79; elected ARSA, 1956, RSA, 1966; Governor, Edinburgh College of Art, 1982. Recreations: hill-walking; mycology. Address: (h.) 18 Mayfield Gardens, Edinburgh; T.-031-667 6164.

Percy-Robb, Professor Iain Walter, MB, ChB, PhD, FRCPEdin, FRCPath. Professor in Pathological Biochemistry, Glasgow University, since 1984; b. 8.12.35, Glasgow; m., Margaret E. Cormie; 2 s.; 2 d. Educ. George Watson's College, Edinburgh; Edinburgh University. Various clinical posts, 1959-63; research scholar, 1963-65; Lecturer, then Senior Lecturer, then Reader, Edinburgh University, 1965-84; MRC International Travelling Research Fellow, 1972-73; Visiting Associate Professor of Medicine, Cornell University Medical Center, New York, 1972-73; Australian Postgraduate Federation in Medicine Lecturer, 1981; Distinguished Visiting Professor in Medicine, University of Adelaide, 1984. Recreations: golf; gardening. Address: (h.) Rossendale, 7 Upper Glenburn Road, Bearsden, Glasgow.

Perfect, Hugh Epton, BSc. Assistant Principal, Moray House College of Education; b. 9.4.41, London; m., Susan; 2 d. Educ. Haberdasher's Askes' School, Hampstead; Imperial College, London. Teacher, Windsor Grammar School; Lecturer, Bulmershe College of Education, Reading; Lecturer/Senior Lecturer, Biology Department, Moray House College of Education. Member: Scottish Committee for Staff Development in Education and Convener of its Priorities Committee, Scottish Committee on Open Learning, JCCES Standing Committee on In-Service; Convener, JCCES Advisory Committee on Multicultural Education. Recreations: badminton; gardening; micro-computers. Address: (b.) Moray House College of Education, Holyrood Road, Edinburgh, EH8 8AQ; T.-031-556 8455.

Perkins, Professor Peter Graham, BSc, PhD, DSc, CChem, FRSC, CPhys, FInstP, FRSE. Chemical and Computer Consultant; Visiting Professor of Chemistry, Strathclyde University; b. 27.10.32, Ilkeston; m., Kathryn Ann Levison; 5 s.; 3 d. Educ. Henry Mellish Grammar School, Nottingham; Nottingham University. Research Officer, Shirley Institute, Manchester; Lecturer: Sheffield University, Newcastle upon Tyne University; Professor of Chemistry, Strathclyde University; Gastprofessor, Technische Universitat, Vienne. Publications: 180 papers and one book on various aspects of theoretical chemistry. Recreations: mountaineering; skiing; painting; music. Address: (h.) 7 Menzies Terrace, Fintry, Glasgow, G63 OXJ; T.-036086 351.

Perrie, Walter, MA. Poet and Critic; b. 5.6.49, Quarter. Educ. Hamilton Academy; Edinburgh University. Full-time writer since 1975; five collections of poetry, one of which, A Lamentation for the Children, won a Scottish Arts Council book award; critical writings on aesthetics, philosophy of language, Hugh MacDiarmid, W.H. Auden, Muriel Spark and Lord Byron; held Scottish-Canadian writer's exchange fellowship, 1984-85; has lectured widely in Europe and North America; received a Gregory Award for poetry and bursaries from the Merrill-Ingram Foundation (New York) and Scottish Arts Council; Editor, Margin, a quarterly of arts and ideas. Address: The Square Inch, Lower Granco Street, Dunning, PH2 0SQ.

Perry, Clive Graham, MA (Cantab), Hon. MA (Leicester). Festival Director, Pitlochry Festival Theatre, since 1986; b. 17.3.36, Harrow. Educ. Wolverhampton Grammar School; Harrow County Grammar School; Cambridge University. Awarded Thames TV Scholarship to regional theatre, 1960-61; Assistant Director, Derby Playhouse; Associate Director, Castle Theatre, Farnham; Director of Productions, Phoenix Theatre, Leicester; Director, Royal Lyceum Theatre, Edinburgh, 1966-76 (Director of Theatres in Edinburgh, 1971-76); Director, Birmingham Repertory Theatre, 1976-86. Recreation: theatre. Address: (b.) Pitlochry Festival Theatre, Port-Na-Craig, Pitlochry, PH16 5DR; T.-0796 3054.

Perth, 17th Earl of (John David Drummond), PC (1957); b. 13.5.07; m., Nancy Seymour Fincke; 2 s. Educ. Downside; Cambridge University. Lt., Intelligence Corps, 1940; War Cabinet Offices, 1942-43; Ministry of Production, 1944-45; Minister of State for Colonial Affairs, 1957-62; First Crown Estate Commissioner, 1962-77; Member, Court, St. Andrews University, 1967-86; Trustee, National Library of Scotland, since 1968. Hon. LLD; Hon. FRIBA; Hon. FRIAS. Address: (h.) Stobhall, by Perth.

Peterken, Laurence Edwin, MA. General Manager, Greater Glasgow Health Board, since 1986; b. 2.10.31, London; m., 1, Hanne Birgithe Von Der Recke (deceased); 1 s.; 1 d.; 2, Margaret Raynal Blair; 1 s.; 1 d. Educ. Harrow School (Scholar);

Peterhouse, Cambridge (Scholar). Pilot Officer, RAF Regt., Adjt. No. 20 LAA Sqdn., 1950-52; Service Divisional Manager, Hotpoint Ltd., 1961-63; Commercial Director, then Managing Director, British Domestic Appliances Ltd., 1963-68; Director, British Printing Corporation Ltd., 1969-73; Managing Director, Fashion Multiple Division, Debenhams Ltd., 1974-76; Management Auditor, 1976-77; Controller, Operational Services, GLC, 1977-85; President, GLC Chief Officers' Guild, 1983-85; Acting Director, Royal Festival Hall, 1983-85. Recreations: opera; swimming. Address: (h.) 25 Kingsborough Gardens, Glasgow, G12 9NH; T.-041-339 0480.

Peters, David Alexander, MA, DSA, FHSM. General Manager, Borders Health Board, since 1985; b. 18.10.38, Glasgow; m., Moira Cullen Macpherson; 2 s.; 1 d. Educ. King's Park School, Glasgow; Glasgow University; Manchester University. Hospital Secretary, Greenock Royal Infirmary, Eye Infirmary, ENT Hospital, 1963-66; Eastern Regional Hospital Board, Dundee: Principal Administrative Assistant, 1966-68, Assistant Secretary, 1968-71, Principal Assistant Secretary, 1971-74; District Administrator, Renfrew District, Argyll and Clyde Health Board, 1974-81; Secretary, Borders Health Board, 1981-85. Recreations: curling; tennis; sailing; golf; gardening. Address: (h.) Wildcroft, Gattonside, Melrose, TD6 9NP.

Peters, Kenneth Jamieson, CBE, JP, DL, FSA Scot, FBIM, Assoc. MCIT. Member, British Railways (Scottish) Board, since 1982; Member, Girobank, Scotland Board, since 1984; Member, Peterhead Bay Authority, since 1983; Director, Aberdeen Journals Ltd., since 1960; b. 17.1.23, London; m., Arunda Merle Jane Jones. Educ. Aberdeen Grammar School; Aberdeen University. Served Second World War; commissioned Queen's Own Cameron Highlanders; also King's Own Scottish Borderers; editorial staff, Scottish Daily Record and Evening News Ltd., 1947-51; Assistant Editor, Aberdeen Evening Express, 1951-52; Assistant Editor, Manchester Evening Chronicle, 1952-53; Editor, Aberdeen Evening Express, 1953-56; Editor, Press and Journal, Aberdeen, 1956-60; Managing Director, Aberdeen Journals Ltd., 1960-80, Chairman, 1980-81; Director: Thomson North Sea, 1981-88, Thomson Scottish Petroleum, 1981-86, Thomson Forestry Holdings, 1982-88, Highland Printers Ltd., 1968-83; President, Scottish Daily Newspaper Society, 1964-66 and 1974-76; Member, Press Council, 1974-77; Director, Thomson Regional Newspapers, 1974-81; Director, Aberdeen Association of Social Service, 1973-78; Member, Executive, Scottish Council (Development and Industry), since 1982 (Chairman, Aberdeen and North-East Committee, since 1982); Member, Scottish Advisory Committee, British Council, 1967-84; National Committee Member, Films of Scotland, 1970-82. Publications: The Northern Lights, 1978; Burgess of Guild, 1982; Great North Memories, Vol. 1 and Vol. 2 (Editor). Recreations: walking; cricket; rugby football. Address: 47 Abergeldie Road, Aberdeen, AB1 6ED; T.-0224 587647.

Peterson, George Sholto, NP. Solicitor and Notary Public, since 1956; Honorary Sheriff, since 1982; b. 18.9.27, Lerwick; m., Dorothy Hilda Spence; 2 s.; 4 d. Educ. Lerwick Central Public School; Edinburgh University. Secretary, The Shetland Trust; Factor for the Marquess of Zetland; Senior Partner, Tait & Peterson, Solicitors and Estate Agents, Lerwick; Dean, Faculty of Solicitors in Shetland; Honorary Pastor, Ebenezer Church, Lerwick. Recreations: studying theology; reading; fishing. Address: (b.) Bank of Scotland Buildings, Lerwick, Shetland; T.-0595 3010.

Pethrick, Professor Richard Arthur, BSc, PhD, DSc, FRSC, FRSE. Professor in Chemistry, Strathclyde University, since 1983; b. 26.10.42; m., Joan Knowles; 1 s. Educ. North Gloucestershire College, Cheltenham; London University. Editor: British Polymer Journal, Polymer Yearbook; Member, Polymer Committee, European Science Foundation; Member, Committee, MACRO Group, 1979-84. Address: (h.) 40 Langside Drive, Newlands, Glasgow, G43 2QQ; T.-041-552 4400.

Petrie, Professor James Colquhoun, MB, ChB, FRCPEdin, FRCP. Professor of Clinical Pharmacology, Department of Medicine and Therapeutics, Aberdeen University, since 1985; Honorary Consultant Physician, Aberdeen Teaching Hospitals, since 1971; b. 18.9.41, Aberdeen; m., Dr. M. Xanthe P.; 2 s.; 2 d. Educ. Anieres, Geneva; Robert Gordon's College, Aberdeen; Aberdeen University. Senior Lecturer, 1971-81, Reader, 1981-85, Aberdeen University. Chairman, Lecht Ski Company, since 1976. Recreations: ski; golf; fishing. Address: (b.) Department of Medicine and Therapeutics, Aberdeen Royal Infirmary, Foresterhill, Aberdeen, AB9 2ZB; T.-0224 681818.

Phanjoo, Andre Ludovic, MB, ChB, FRCPsych, DPM. Consultant Psychiatrist, Royal Edinburgh Hospital, since 1972; Honorary Senior Lecturer, Department of Psychiatry, Edinburgh University, since 1982; b. 29.9.37, Port Louis, Mauritius; m., Barbara Elizabeth Darwell; 1 s.; 2 d. Educ. Royal College, Port Louis; Edinburgh University. Postgraduate training in psychiatry, Royal Edinburgh Hospital, 1967-70; appointed Consultant Psychiatrist to Royal Edinburgh Hospital and Rosslynlee Hospital, 1972; Consultant in Geriatric Psychiatry, 1982; Consultant, Catholic Marriage Advisory Council. Recreations: hill-walking; playing the guitar; music/opera; cooking. Address: (h.) 29 Blacket Place, Edinburgh, EH9 1RJ; T.-031-667 9809.

Philip, Alistair Erskine, MA, PhD, FBPsS. Area Co-ordinator, Clinical Psychology Service, Lothian Health Board, since 1980; Member, State Hospital Management Committee, since 1980; Honorary Senior Lecturer, Edinburgh University, since 1980; b. 10.7.38, Aberdeen; m., Betty J. McKay; 1 s.; 2 d. Educ. Aberdeen Grammar School; Aberdeen University; Edinburgh University. Scientific staff, MRC Unit for Epidemiological Studies in Psychiatry, Edinburgh University, 1963-71; Head, Psychology Department, Bangour Village Hospital, 1971-80; Chairman, Clinical Psychology Sub-Committee, National Consultative Committee of Scientists in Professions Allied to Medicine, 1981-85. Publication: Suicidal Behaviour (Co-author), 1972. Recreations: playing hockey; going to auctions. Address: (h.) 37 Meggetland Terrace, Edinburgh, EH14 1AP; T.-031-443 2447.

Philip, Rev. George M., MA. Minister, Sandyford-Henderson Memorial Church, since 1956; b. 11.11.25, Bucksburn, Aberdeenshire; m., Patricia Joy Morrison; 2 s.; 1 d. Educ. Bucksburn School; Central Secondary School, Aberdeen; Aberdeen University. Able seaman, Royal Navy, 1943-47; qualified as Member, Institute of Bankers in Scotland, 1949; licensed by Aberdeen Presbytery, 1953. Moderator, Glasgow Presbytery, 1979-80. Publications: Fundamentals of the Faith; School of Discipleship; Commentary on Book of Job; Commentary on Ecclesiastes; Kingdom against Kingdom; Daily Bible Reading Notes. Recreation: gardening. Address: 66 Woodend Drive, Glasgow, G13 1TG; T.-041-954 9013.

Philip, Michael Stuart, MBE, MA (Oxon), BSc, FICF. Reader in Forestry, Aberdeen University, since 1982; b. 4.11.26, London; m., Audrey Elizabeth Rae; 1 s.; 1 d. Educ. Bancroft's; Kings College, London; Keble College, Oxford. Assistant Conservator of Forests, Uganda, 1947-60; Forest Ecologist, Uganda, 1960-62; Conservator of Forests (Research), Uganda, 1962-64; Lecturer, then Senior Lecturer in Forestry, Aberdeen University, 1964-82; Associate Professor of Forestry, Dar-es-Salaam University, 1977-79. Trustee, Scottish Forestry Trust. Publication: Measuring Trees and Forests. Recreations: gardening; fishing. Address: (h.) 45 Hillview Road, Cults, Aberdeen, AB1 9HA; T.-0224 867132.

Philipson, Sir Robin, PPRSA, RA, Hon. RA. Painter; b. 1916, Broughton-in-Furness. Educ. Dumfries Academy; Edinburgh College of Art. KOSB, India, RIASC, 1940-46; joined staff, Edinburgh College of Art, 1947; RSA Guthrie Award, 1951; ARSA, 1952; RSW, 1955; Head, School of Drawing and Painting, Edinburgh College of Art, 1960; RSA, 1962; Visiting Professor of Painting, Colorado University, 1963; Leverhulme Travel Award, 1965; FRSA, 1965; Member, Royal Fine Art Commission for Scotland, 1965; Cargill Award, 1967; Secretary, RSA, 1969; Council Member, Edinburgh Festival Society, 1969; Member, Scottish Advisory Committee, British Council, 1971; President, RSA, 1973-83; elected Honorary Royal Academician, 1974; knighted for service to arts in Scotland, 1976; Honorary Doctorate, Stirling University, 1976; Member, Board of Trustees, National Museum of Antiquities for Scotland, 1976; FRSE, 1978; LLD, Aberdeen University, 1978; elected Member, Royal Academy, 1981; DUniv, Heriot-Watt University, 1985; retired as Head, School of Drawing and Painting, Edinburgh College of Art, 1982; RSA William J. Macaulay Award, 1983. Address: (h.) 23 Crawfurd Road, Edinburgh; T.-031-667 2373.

Phillips, Professor Calbert Inglis, PhD, MD, DPH, FRCS, FRCSEdin, DO, FBOA (Hon.). Professor of Ophthalmology, Edinburgh University; Honorary Consultant Ophthalmic Surgeon, Edinburgh Royal Infirmary; b. 20.3.25, Glasgow; m., C. Anne Fulton; 1 s. Educ. High School of Glasgow; Robert Gordon's College, Aberdeen; Aberdeen University. House Physician and House Surgeon, Aberdeen Royal Infirmary; Registrar, Moorfields Eye Hospital, London; Senior Registrar, St. Thomas' Hospital, London; Research Assistant, Institute of Ophthalmology, London University; Consultant Surgeon, Bristol Eye Hospital; Professor of Ophthalmology, Manchester University. Publications: Clinical Practice and Economics (Editor), 1977; Basic Clinical Ophthalmology, 1984; Glaucoma Ophthalmic Genetics; original papers on glaucoma, etc. Recreation: ophthalmology. Address: (b.) Eye Pavilion, Chalmers Street, Edinburgh, EH3 9HA; T.-031-229 2477, Ext. 2578.

Phillips, John Brydon Mills, MA. Director, Scottish Association for the Care and Resettlement of Offenders, since 1980; b. 15.6.32, Cheadle Hulme; m., Anna; 1 s.; 3 d. Educ. Mill Hill School; Worcester College, Oxford. Teacher: The Leys School, Cambridge, 1955-60, Campbell College, Belfast, 1960-68, Royal Belfast Academical Institution, 1968-74; Director, Northern Ireland Marriage Guidance Council, 1974-79. Recreations: hill-walking; (motor) caravanning. Address: (h.) 1 Saxe Coburg Street, Edinburgh; T.-031-556 9726.

Phillips, John H., MA, PhD. Reader in Biochemistry, Edinburgh University, since 1986; b. 19.2.41, York; m., Kerstin B. Halling; 2 d. Educ. Leighton Park School, Reading; Christ's College, Cambridge. Lecturer in Biochemistry, Makerere University, Uganda, 1967-69; scientific staff, MRC Laboratory of Molecular Biology, Cambridge, 1969-74; Department of Biochemistry, Edinburgh University, since 1974. Recreations: natural history; Scottish mountains; visits to Sweden. Address: (h.) 46 Granby Road, Edinburgh, EH16 5NW; T.-031-667 5322.

Phillips, Rev. Thomas Miller, MA (Hons), BD. Minister, Church of Scotland; b. 31.8.14, Newmains, Wishaw; m., Catherine C. Grigor; 1 s.; 1 d. Educ. Wishaw High School; Glasgow University and Trinity College. Parish Minister: John Knox Church, Stewarton, 1939-45, Mid Kirk of Greenock, 1945-64, West Linton and Carlops, 1964-84. Past Chairman and Lessons Convener, Scottish Sunday School Union; Member, European Committee, former World Council of Christian Education. Recreation: gardening. Address: (h.) 20 Station Road, Biggar, Lanarkshire, ML12 6JN; T.-0899 20197.

Phillips, William Denstone Powell, MB, BCh, MRCOG. Consultant Obstetrician and Gynaecologist, Perth Royal Infirmary, since 1982; Honorary Senior Lecturer, Dundee University; b. 18.2.47, Cardiff; m., Alicia Elizabeth Gregg. Educ. Felsted School; Welsh National School of Medicine. House Surgeon/Physician; Senior House Officer, Obstetrics and Gynaecology, University Hospital of Wales, Cardiff, and John Radcliffe Hospital, Oxford; Registrar, Obstetrics and Gynaecology, UHW, Cardiff; Clinical Fellow, Fetal Intensive Care Unit, University of British Columbia; Lecturer, Aberdeen University. Recreations: shooting; fishing; cricket; golf; gardening. Address: (h.) Greylag House, Forteviot, Perthshire, PH2 9BT; T.-076484 245.

Pickard, Willis Ritchie, MA (Hons). Editor, Times Educational Supplement Scotland, since 1977; Rector, Aberdeen University, since 1988; b. 21.5.41, Dunfermline; m., Ann; 2 d. Educ. Daniel Stewart's College; St. Andrews University. The Scotsman: Leader Writer, 1967-72, Features Editor, 1972-77. Member, Scottish Arts Council; Chairman, Children's Book Committee for Scotland; Liberal candidate, East Fife, 1970 and February, 1974. Address: (b.) 37 George Street, Edinburgh, EH2 2HN; T.-031-220 1100.

Picken, James, MA, DipEd. HM Inspector of Schools, since 1975, Higher Grade, 1985, District Inspector, Glasgow, 1986; b. 7.11.36, Kilmarnock; m., Helen Craig; 1 s. Educ. Kilmarnock Academy; Glasgow University. Teacher, High School of Glasgow; Principal Teacher, Jordanhill College School, Glasgow; Assistant Principal, George Watson's College, Edinburgh. Publication: Ecce Romani. Recreations: philately; chess; music; beach-combing; dogs. Address: (b.) SED, Corunna House, Cadogan Street, Glasgow; T.-041-204 1220.

Pickett, Professor James, BSc (Econ), MLitt. Professor and Director, David Livingstone Institute, Strathclyde University, since 1973; b. 7.6.29, Greenock; m., Janet C. Hamilton; 1 s.; 2 d. Educ. Greenock Academy; School of Economics, Dundee; Paris University; Glasgow University. Statistician, Dominion Bureau of Statistics, Canada; Lecturer, Strathclyde University; Visiting Professor, Saskatchewan University; Special Economic Adviser, UN Economic Commission for Africa; Senior Lecturer and Professor, Strathclyde University. Member, Council for Social Democracy; regular Consultant to UN, OECD, and EEC. Recreations: photography; walking; listening to music; long-suffering support of Greenock Morton. Address: (b.) Strathclyde University, 16 Richmond Street, Glasgow, G1 1XQ; T.-041-552 4400.

Piggott, Elizabeth Ann, MBIM. Secretary/Treasurer, Macaulay Land Use Research Institute, since 1987; b. Lymington. Educ. St. Leonards School, St. Andrews. Hill Farming Research Organization, 1956-66; Scottish Plant Breeding Station, 1966-72; Secretary/Treasurer, Macaulay Institute for Soil Research, 1972-87. Recreations: gardening; travel; snapshot photography. Address: (b.) Craigiebuckler, Aberdeen, AB9 2QJ; T.-0224 318611.

Pighills, Christopher David, MA (Cantab). Headmaster, Strathallan School, Perth, since 1975; b. 27.11.37, Bradford. Educ. Rydal School, North Wales; Christ's College, Cambridge. Assistant Master/Housemaster, Fettes College, 1960-75. Recreations: shooting; dog training; hill-walking; working. Address: (b.) Strathallan School, Perth, PH2 9EG; T.-0738 812546.

Pilcher, Rosamunde. Author; b. 22.9.24, Lelant, Cornwall. Began publishing short stories in Woman and Home, 1945; since then has published hundreds of short stories and 25 novels, including Sleeping Tiger, Under Gemini, Wild Mountain Thyme, The Carousel, Voices in Summer and The Shell Seekers; play, The Dashing White Sergeant. Address: (h.) Over Pilmore, Invergowrie, by Dundee; T.-Longforgan 239.

Pinkerton, Ian W., TD, MB, ChB, FRCPGlas, FRCPEdin. Consultant Physician, Department of Infectious Diseases, Ruchill Hospital, Glasgow, since 1964; Honorary Lecturer in Infectious Diseases, Glasgow University, since 1964; b. 8.10.28, Glasgow; m., Christina Graham; 2 s.; 3 d. Educ. Allan Glen's School, Glasgow; Glasgow University. Junior hospital appointments, Glasgow and Paisley; National Service, RAMC, Egypt, 1952-54; Lt.-Col., RAMC TA; World Health Organisation Fellow, 1971. President, British Society for the Study of Infection; President, Paisley Philosophical Institution; Past President, Royal Philosophical Society of Glasgow; Chairman of Council, St. Andrews Ambulance Association. Recreations: skiing; golf; photography. Address: (h.) 73 Gartmore Road, Paisley, PA1 3NG; T.-041-889 5632.

Pinkerton, John Macpherson, QC, BA, LLB, FSA Scot. Advocate, since 1966; Queen's Counsel, since 1984; b. 18.4.41, East Kilbride. Educ. Lathallan School; Rugby School; Oxford University; Edinburgh University. Clerk, Faculty of Advocates, 1971-77; Standing Junior Counsel, Countryside Commission for Scotland; Standing Junior Counsel, HM Commissioners of Customs and Excise. Chairman: Cockburn Association, Dunimarle Castle Advisory Committee; Member, Scottish Valuation Advisory Council; Trustee, National Library of Scotland. Recreation: mezzotint collecting. Address: (h.) Arthur Lodge, 60 Dalkeith Road, Edinburgh, EH16 5AD; T.-031-667 5163.

Pirie, Henry Ward, OStJ, MA, LLB. Crossword Compiler, Glasgow Herald, and various publications; b. 13.2.22, Edinburgh; m., Jean Jardine; 4 s. Educ. George Watson's College; Edinburgh University. Royal Scots; Indian Army (Grenadiers), 1944; Advocate, 1947; Standing Junior Counsel to the Admiralty in Scotland, 1951; Sheriff-Substitute of Lanarkshire, at Airdrie, 1954-55; Sheriff-Substitute (later Sheriff) of Lanarkshire, at Glasgow, 1955-74. Past President: Glasgow and West of Scotland Watsonian Club, The Lenzie Club. Recreations: opera; bridge; dog-walking. Address: (h.) 16 Poplar Drive, Lenzie, Glasgow, G66 4DN.

Pirie, Professor Hugh Munro, BVMS, PhD, MRCVS, FRCPath. Professor, Department of Veterinary Pathology, Glasgow University, since 1982; Secretary, European Association of Establishments for Veterinary Education, 1988-91; b. 10.4.36, Glasgow; m., Myrtle Elizabeth Stewart Levack; 1 d. Educ. Coatbridge High School; Glasgow University. Rockefeller Foundation Research Fellow, Kenya, 1965; Scientific Editor, Research in Veterinary Science, 1981-88; British Council Specialist, Argentina, 1982, Ethiopia, 1986-87; President, Association of Veterinary Teachers and Research Workers, 1984. Recreations: travel; gardening; hill-walking; swimming; gastronomy. Address: (h.) North East Corner, Buchanan Castle Estate, Drymen, G63 0HX; T.-0360 60781.

Pirie, Sheriff Iain Gordon, MA, LLB. Sheriff of Glasgow and Strathkelvin, since 1982; b. 15.1.33, Dundee; m., Dr. Sheila B. Pirie; 2 s.; 1 d. Educ. Harris Academy, Dundee; St. Andrews University. Procurator Fiscal, Dumfries, 1971-76, Ayr, 1976-79; Sheriff of South Strathclyde, Dumfries and Galloway, 1979-82. Address: (b.) Sheriff Court, 1 Carlton Place, Glasgow, G5 9DA; T.-041-429 8888.

Pirie, John McDonald Strachan, CA. Board Secretary, Scottish Milk Marketing Board, since 1988 (Finance Director, 1983); b. 17.11.38, Ayr; m., Rosetta; 1 s.; 2 d. Educ. Ayr Academy; Glasgow University. Address: (b.) Underwood Road, Paisley; T.-041-887 1234.

Pitt, Douglas Charles, BA, MA, PhD, MBIM. Reader in Public Administration, Strathclyde University, since 1988; b. 13.7.43, Greenock; m., Jean Hamilton Spowart. Educ. Varndean Grammar School, Brighton; Exeter University; Manchester University. Executive Officer, Civil Service, 1961-64; Lecturer, then Senior Lecturer, Strathclyde University, 1973-88. Current research interest: telecommunications deregulation in Britain and the USA. Publications: The Post Office Telecommunications Function, 1980; Public Administration: An Introduction, 1980; Government Departments: An Organisational Analysis, 1981; The Computer Revolution in Public Administration, 1984. Recreations: German; riding; swimming; fishing; skiing; sailing; traditional jazz; bluegrass; opera. Address: (h.) 19 Waterfoot Road, Newton Mearns, Glasgow, G77 5RU; T.-041-639 5359.

Playfair-Hannay of Kingsmuir, Patrick Armour. Farmer; b. 12.7.29, Banstead; m., Frances Ann Roberton; 1 s.; 1 d. Educ. Oundle. National Service, commissioned into RASC; planting tea and rubber in Ceylon, seven years; took up farming in the Border country, 1956. Chairman, Association for Protection of Rural Scotland. Recreation: shooting. Address: Clifton on Bowmont, Kelso, Roxburghshire; T.-057 382 227.

Plotkin, Professor Gordon David, BSc, PhD. Professor in Computer Science, Edinburgh University; b. 9.9.46, Glasgow; m., Lynda Margaret; 1 s. Educ. Glasgow High School for Boys; Glasgow University; Edinburgh University. Lecturer, then Reader, Edinburgh University; British Petroleum Venture Research Fellow, 1981-88; Editor, Information and Control; Series Editor, Oxford University Press. Recreations: chess; hill-walking. Address: (b.) Department of Computer Science, King's Buildings, Edinburgh University, Edinburgh; T.-031-667 1081, Ext. 2775.

Pollock, Alexander, MA (Oxon), LLB. Advocate, Scottish Bar, since 1973; b. 21.7.44, Glasgow; m., Verena Francesca Gertraud Alice Ursula Critchley; 1 s.; 1 d. Educ. Rutherglen Academy; Glasgow Academy; Brasenose College, Oxford; Edinburgh University; Perugia University. Partner, Bonar Mackenzie & Kermack, WS, 1971-73; called to Scottish Bar, 1973; Conservative candidate: West Lothian, General Election, February 1974, Moray and Nairn, General Election, October 1974; MP, Moray and Nairn, 1979-83, Moray, 1983-87; Parliamentary Private Secretary to Secretary of State for Scotland, 1982-86; PPS to Secretary of State for Defence, 1986-87. Member, Queen's Bodyguard for Scotland (Royal Company of Archers), since 1984. Recreations: walking; music. Address: (h.) Drumdarrach, Forres, Moray.

Pollock, John Denton, BSc, FEIS. General Secretary, The Educational Institute of Scotland, 1975-88; b. 21.4.26, Kilmarnock; m., Joyce Margaret Sharpe; 1 s.; 1 d. Educ. Ayr Academy; Royal Technical College, Glasgow; Glasgow University; Jordanhill College of Education. Commissioned Royal Engineers, 1945-48. Teacher, Mauchline Secondary School, 1951-59; Head Teacher, Kilmaurs Secondary School, 1959-65; Rector, Mainholm Academy, Ayr, 1965-74; General Secretary Designate, EIS, 1974. Forestry Commissioner, since 1978; Chairman, Scottish Labour Party, 1959 and 1971; Chairman, STUC, 1981-82 (Vice-Chairman, 1980-81); Member, General Council, STUC, 1975-87; Member, Annan Committee on Future of Broadcasting, 1974-77; Member, Manpower Services Committee Scotland, since 1977; Member, National Broadcasting Council for Scotland, since 1985; Member, World Executive, since 1986, and Chairman, European Committee, since 1980, World Confederation of Organisations of the Teaching Profession; Honorary Vice-President, South West District, SYHA, since 1985. Address: (h.) 52 Douglas Road, Longniddry, East Lothian.

Polwarth, Lord (Henry Alexander Hepburne-Scott), TD, DL, FRSE, FRSA. Vice-Lord-Lieutenant, Borders Region, since 1975; Member, Queen's Bodyguard for Scotland (Royal Company of Archers); Chartered Accountant; Chairman, Scottish Forestry Trust, since 1987; b. 17.11.16; m., 1, Caroline Margaret Hay (m. diss.); 1 s.; 3 d.; 2, Jean Jauncey; 2 step s.; 1 step d. Educ. Eton College; King's College, Cambridge. Served Second World War as Captain, Lothians and Border Yeomanry; former Partner, Chiene and Tait, CA, Edinburgh; Governor, Bank of Scotland, 1966-72, Director, 1974-87; Chairman, General Accident, Fire & Life Assurance Corporation, 1968-72; Director, ICI Ltd., 1969-72, 1974-81; Director, Halliburton Co., 1974-87; Director, Canadian Pacific Ltd., 1975-86; Director, Sun Life Assurance Co. of Canada, 1975-84; Minister of State, Scottish Office, 1972-74; Chairman, later President, Scottish Council (Development and Industry), 1955-72; Member, Franco-British Council, since 1981; Chairman, Scottish National Orchestra Society, 1975-79; Chancellor, Aberdeen University, 1966-86; Hon. LLD: St. Andrews, Aberdeen; Hon. DLitt, Heriot-Watt; DUniv, Stirling. Address: Harden, Hawick; T.-Hawick 72069.

Poole, Sheriff Isobel Anne, LLB. Sheriff of Lothian and Borders; b. 9.12.41, Oxford. Educ. Oxford High School for Girls; Edinburgh University. Advocate. Recreations: country; arts; gardens; friends. Address: (b.) Sheriffs' Chambers, Sheriff Court, Edinburgh, EH1 2NS.

Portchmouth, Rev. Roland John, NDD, ATD. Minister, Church of Scotland, since 1980; b. 4.9.23, London; m., Susan Mary; 1 s.; 3 d. Educ. Kilburn Grammar School; Harrow and Hornsey Colleges of Art; Edinburgh University. Royal Navy, 1942-46; Art Teacher, 1951-61; Lecturer in Art Education and Senior Lecturer in Art, 1961-68. Artist (paintings exhibited, Royal Academy and other London and provincial galleries). Publications: Creative Crafts for Today, 1969; Secondary School Art, 1971; Poetry, 1972; All Kinds of

Paper Crafts, 1972; Working in Collage, 1973; Making Things from the Beach, 1973; The Creatures of the Carp, 1977. Address: The Manse, Meikleour, Perth, PH2 6DZ; T.-025 083 229.

Porte, Andrew Lawrie, BSc, PhD, CChem, FRSC. Reader in Chemistry, Glasgow University, since 1983; b. 24.5.31, Ayr. Educ. Ayr Academy; Glasgow University; Illinois University. Assistant Lecturer, Glasgow University, 1956-58; Fulbright Scholar, Illinois University, 1958-60; Glasgow University: ICI Research Fellow, 1960-61, Lecturer in Chemistry, 1961-72, Senior Lecturer, 1972-83. Recreations: walking; music; languages. Address: (h.) 36 Weymouth Court, 177 Weymouth Drive, Glasgow, G12 OEP; T.-041-334 5059.

Porter, Felix, HNC (Mech), DipTEd. Head Teacher, St. Roch's Secondary School, since 1978; b. 15.1.27, Glasgow; m., Theresa Gallacher; 3 d. Educ. St. Mungo's Academy; Stow College; Jordanhill College. Member, General Education Committee, Engineering Council, since 1983; Chairman, Catholic Headteachers Association of Scotland, since 1986. Recreations: theatre; reading; golf. Address: (h.) 20 Eastercraigs, Glasgow, G31 3LJ; T.-041-554 8264.

Postlethwaite, Professor Roy, BSc, MD, FRCPath. Professor of Virology, Aberdeen University, since 1980; Honorary Consultant Bacteriologist, Grampian Area Health Board, since 1961; b. 26.4.25, Todmorden; m., Joyce; 2 s.; 1 d. Educ. County Grammar School of King Edward VII, Melton Mowbray; Manchester University. Royal Artillery, 1943-47; junior hospital appointments, Manchester Royal Infirmary, 1954-56; Assistant Lecturer/Lecturer in Bacteriology, Manchester University, 1956-61; Senior Lecturer in Bacteriology, Aberdeen University, 1961-80; Nuffield Foundation Medical Fellow, University of Michigan, 1959-60; Visiting Virologist, National Institute for Medical Research, London, 1971-72. Recreations: walking; reading; travel. Address: (b.) Department of Bacteriology, Medical School, Foresterhill, Aberdeen, AB9 2ZD; T.-Aberdeen 681818.

Povey, Rev. John McLintock, MA, BD. Minister, Kirk of Calder Parish Church, since 1981; b. 6.3.56, Glasgow; m., Linda R. Shiells; 1 s.; 1 d. Educ. Paisley Grammar School; Glasgow University. Assistant Minister, Loanhead Parish Church, 1980-81. Chairman, Mid Calder Community Council, since 1984; Chaplain, Drumshoreland Hospital, since 1983. Recreations: swimming; philately; research into local history. Address: 19 Maryfield Park, Mid Calder, Livingston, West Lothian, EH53 0SB; T.-0506 882495.

Power, James Patrick, MA (Hons), BA (Hons). Rector, St. Columba's High School, Gourock, since 1975; b. 2.2.27, Renfrew; m., E. Patricia Currie; 1 s.; 1 d. Educ. St. Mirin's Academy, Paisley; Glasgow University; London University; Jordanhill College of Education. Teacher: St. Columba's High School, Greenock, 1948-52, St. Joseph's Academy, Kilmarnock, 1952-56; Principal Teacher of Science, Sacred Heart High School, Girvan, 1956-60; Principal Teacher of Mathematics, St. Joseph's Academy, Kilmarnock, 1960-63; Head, Department of Mathematics and Science, Ayr Technical College, 1963-74; Mathematics Tutor, Open University, 1971-75; Adviser in Mathematics, County of Lanark, 1974-75. Chairman, Scottish Central Committee on Mathematics, 1981-86; Member: Scottish Education/Industry Committee, 1984-86, CNAA Committee in Scotland, 1983-87, Catholic Education Commission, 1978-87; Chairman, Central Support Group on Mathematics; Honorary Treasurer and Past President, Headteachers' Association of Scotland; President, Gourock Rotary Club, 1984-85; Past President, Greenock and District Catenian Association; Past President, Ayr Amateur Opera Company. Address: (b.) St. Columba's High School, Burnside Road, Gourock, PA19 1XX; T.-0475 33271.

Powrie, John ("Ian"). Musician; b. 26.5.23, Strathardle, Blairgowrie; m., Lillias Robina Mailer; 1 s.; 1 d. Educ. Blairgowrie High School. Began playing violin, aged four; completed graduate examination for London College of Violinists, 1936; made first solo broadcast on BBC, 1936; volunteered for RAF Aircrew, 1943; trained as pilot in Canada; demobbed, 1945; formed band, 1949, and began broadcasting Scottish dance music for BBC; one of original entertainer members, BBC's White Heather Club; completed numerous tours with Andy Stewart; played for the Queen twice at Balmoral; completed 50 years recording with a celebration record with Jimmy Shand, 1983; bought a building company in Perth, Western Australia, 1966 and emigrated there; sold all interests, 1984, and returned to Scotland to retire; honoured by National Association of Accordion and Fiddle Clubs, 1983, and presented with portrait for work in Scottish music. Recreations: flying; farming; fishing; shooting. Address: (h.) Corrieburn, Duchally, Auchterarder, Perth; T.-Auchterarder 62805.

Prag, Thomas Gregory Andrew, MA, FBIM. Managing Director, Moray Firth Radio; b. 2.1.47, London; m., Angela; 3 s. Educ. Westminster School; Brasenose College, Oxford. Joined BBC, 1968, as Studio Manager; Producer, BBC Radio Oxford; Programme Organiser, BBC Radio Highland; first Chief Executive, Moray Firth Radio, 1981. Recreations: family; growing vegetables; chasing deer off vegetables. Address: (b.) Moray Firth Radio, PO Box 271, Inverness, IV1 1UJ.

Prain, Alexander Moncur, CBE (1964). Advocate; b. 19.2.08, Longforgan, Perthshire; m., Florence Margaret Robertson. Educ. Edinburgh Academy; Edinburgh University. Advocate, 1932; Army (Major, Royal Armoured Corps), 1939-46; Sheriff-Substitute, Perthshire, 1946-71; retired. Recreation: reading. Address: (h.) Castellar, Crieff, Perthshire; T.-0764 2270.

Preece, Paul Edward, MD, FRCSEdin, FRCS. Senior Lecturer in Surgery, Dundee University, since 1978; Honorary Consultant Surgeon, Tayside Health Board, since 1978; b. 21.10.40, Great Malvern; m., Heather Margaret Angell; 2 d. Educ. Worcester Cathedral King's School; Welsh National School of Medicine, Cardiff. Pre-registration House Officer, Cardiff and Newport, 1966-67; Senior House Officer posts, Oxford,

Bristol and Birmingham, 1968-70; Rotational Surgical Registrar, South Wales, 1971-72; Tenovus and Medical Research Council Research Fellow, 1973-74; Lecturer in Surgery, Welsh National School of Medicine, 1975-77. Council of Europe Fellowship, Germany, 1975. Recreations: music; vintage cars. Address: (h.) 11 Marchfield Road, Dundee, DD2 1JG; T.-0382 68126.

Preen, Alan Frederick, IPFA, MBIM, FRVA. Treasurer, Orkney Health Board, since 1974; b. 10.11.26, London; m., Elaine. Army, 1944-48; Metropolitan Borough of Battersea: Accountancy/Technical Assistant, 1948-54, Senior Auditor, 1954-60, Senior Accountant, 1960-65; London Borough of Wandsworth: Deputy Chief Accountant, 1965-68, Chief Accountant, 1968-69; Treasurer, Richmond (Yorkshire) Rural District Council, 1969-74 (and Chief Officer, Richmond Public Authorities Joint Computer Committee); Treasurer, Richmondshire District Council, 1973-74. Recreations: travelling; walking; lazing; reading; driving; astronomy. Address: (h.) Midbigging, Grimbister, Firth, Orkney.

Prentice, Rev. George, BA, BTh, ASTA, AIST(LS). Minister, Martyrs' Church, Paisley, since 1969; b. 21.7.32, Motherwell; m., Janet Dunsmuir; 1 s.; 1 d. Educ. Wishaw High School; Glasgow University and Trinity College. Civil Service, 1949-58; National Service, RAF, 1951-53; student, 1958-63; Minister, Townhead Parish Church, Coatbridge, 1964-69. Publication: Church and Congregation. Recreations: teaching swimming; examining life-saving; following football. Address: 12 Low Road, Castlehead, Paisley; T.-041-889 2182.

Prentis, Rev. David Freeman, BSc, MA. Parish Minister, Drumoak and Durris, since 1988 (Rousay, 1982-88); b. 16.6.40, Ilford; m., Michaela Slamova; 4 s. Educ. Ilford County High School for Boys; London University; Leeds University; Cambridge University; Tubingen University; Prague University. Probationer Minister, Methodist Church, Bradford, 1965-67, and Evangelische Kirche, Rheinland, Bonn and Dusseldorf, 1973-75; Minister, Ekir, Neuss, 1975-82. Board Member, Human Life Council; teacher of natural family planning. Recreations: music (viola, violin, recorders); languages (German, Czech). Address: The Manse, Durris, Banchory, Kincardineshire, AB3 3BU; T.-Crathes 557.

Prescott, Professor Laurie F., MA, MB, BChir, MD, FRCPEdin. Honorary Consultant Physician, Edinburgh Royal Infirmary, since 1969; Professor of Clinical Pharmacology, Edinburgh University, since 1985; b. 13.5.34, London; m.; 1 s.; 3 d. Educ. Hitchin Boys Grammar School; Cambridge University; Middlesex Hospital Medical School, London. Research Fellow, Johns Hopkins Hospital, Baltimore, 1963-65; Lecturer in Therapeutics, Aberdeen University, 1965-69; Senior Lecturer in Clinical Pharmacology, Edinburgh University, 1969-74, Reader, 1974-85. British Pharmacological Society Lilly Prize, 1978. Recreations: music; walking; gardening; sailing. Address: (h.) Redfern, 24 Colinton Road, Edinburgh, EH10 5EQ; T.-031-447 2571.

Preston, Ian Mathieson Hamilton, BSc, PhD, FEng, MInstP, FIEE. Deputy Chairman, South of Scotland Electricity Board, since 1983; b. 18.7.32, Bournemouth; m., Sheila Hope Pringle; 2 s. Educ. Kilmarnock Academy; Glasgow University. University Assistant Lecturer, 1957-59; joined SSEB as Assistant Reactor Physicist, 1959; various appointments until Chief Engineer, Generation Design and Construction Division, 1972; Director General, Central Electricity Generating Board, Generation Development and Construction Division, 1977-83. Chairman, British Hydromechanics Research Association, since 1985. Recreations: angling; gardening. Address: (b.) South of Scotland Electricity Board, Cathcart House, Spean Street, Glasgow, G44 4BE; T.-041-637 7177.

Preston-Thomas, Rev. Canon Colin Barnabas Rashleigh. Priest, Scottish Episcopal Church, since 1954; b. 11.6.28, Exford, Somerset; m., Barbara Anne Davidson. Educ. Bristol Grammar School; King's College, London; Edinburgh Theological College. Curate, St. David's, Pilton, 1953-54; Precentor, Perth Cathedral, 1954-60; Prison Chaplain, Perth, 1955-60; Rector: Rosyth with Inverkeithing, 1960-72, St. John's Forfar, 1972-82, Holy Trinity, Pitlochry, with Kilmaveonaig, Blair Atholl, since 1982; Synod Clerk, St. Andrews Diocese; Canon, Perth Cathedral, since 1968; Diocesan Secretary, since 1980. Recreations: theatre; music. Address: The Parsonage, Perth Road, Pitlochry, PH16 5DJ; T.-Pitlochry 2176.

Prettyman, James Arthur, CEng, MIProdE. Executive Director, Leith Enterprise Trust, since 1984; President, Motherwell Bridge Projects Ltd. (Canada), since 1982; Director and General Manager, Motherwell Bridge Pipe Ltd., since 1970; b. 19.3.31, Hatfield, Hertfordshire; m., Wendy Bell; 2 d. Educ. North Western Polytechnic, London; Hatfield Polytechnic. Student Apprentice/Production Engineer, de Havilland Aircraft; Sub-Lieutenant, Royal Navy (Fleet Air Arm); Management Trainee/Production Superintendent, Brush Electrical Engineering Co. (now Hawker Siddeley); Unit Engineer, Glacier Metal; Manufacturing Manager, Ampep Products; Director, Motherwell Bridge Group. Member, Citizens Advice Management Group; Member, Management Committee, Leith Community Association; Convener (Vocation), Leith Rotary Club. Recreations: fitness; swimming: hill-walking. Address: (b.) 25 Maritime Street, Leith, Edinburgh; T.-031-553 5566.

Price, Rev. Peter Owen, CBE, QHC, BA, FPhS. Minister, Blantyre Old Parish Church, Glasgow, since 1985; b. 18.4.30, Swansea; m., 1, Margaret Winifred Trevan (deceased); 3 d.; 2, Marilyn Campbell Murray. Educ. Wyggeston School, Leicester; Didsbury College, Bristol; Open University. Chaplain, Royal Navy, 1960-84, latterly Principal Chaplain, Church of Scotland and Free Churches (Naval), Ministry of Defence, 1981-84. Recreations: clay pigeon shooting; rugby; warm water sailing. Address: The Manse of Blantyre, High Blantyre, Glasgow, G72 9UA; T.-0698 823130.

Price, Robert J., BSc, PhD, DSc. Reader in Geography, Glasgow University; b. 19.7.36, Cardiff; m., Mary Frater; 1 s.; 1 d. Educ. St. Illtyd's College, Cardiff; University of Wales, Aberystwyth;

Edinburgh University. Assistant Professor: Oklahoma University, 1961-62, Oregon University, 1962-63; joined Glasgow University as Lecturer, 1963. Publications: Glacial and Fluvioglacial Land Forms; Highland Land Forms; Scotland's Environment - The Last 30,000 Years. Recreations: sailing; golf. Address: (b.) Department of Geography, Glasgow University, Glasgow, G12 8QQ; T.-041-339 8855, Ext. 5405.

Priest, Professor Eric Ronald, BSc, MSc, PhD. Professor of Theoretical Solar Physics, St. Andrews University, since 1983; b. 7.11.43, Birmingham; m., Clare Wilson; 3 s.; 1 d. Educ. King Edward VI School, Birmingham; Nottingham University; Leeds University. St. Andrews University: Lecturer in Applied Mathematics, 1968, Reader, 1977. Recreations: bridge; walking; swimming; children. Address: (b.) Applied Mathematics Department, St. Andrews University, St. Andrews, KY16 9SS; T.-0334 76161.

Priestley, Graham C., BSc, PhD, CBiol, MIBiol. Senior Lecturer in Dermatology, Edinburgh University, since 1984; b. 11.4.38, Leeds; m., Marjorie; 2 s. Educ. Leeds Grammar School; Durham University; Leeds University; Harvard University. Research Fellow, Leeds University, 1964-66; Research Fellow in Surgery, Harvard University, 1966-68; Project Manager (Dermatology), Beecham Research Laboratories, 1968-70; Research Fellow, Animal Genetics Unit, Edinburgh, 1970-73; Lecturer in Dermatology, Edinburgh University, 1973-84. High Bailiff of the Water of Leith. Publications: Angling in the Lothians, 1983; numerous papers in scientific journals. Recreations: trout fishing; journalism; cricket. Address: (h.) 22 Cherry Tree Crescent, Balerno, Midlothian, EH14 5AL; T.-031-449 4522.

Primrose, Andrew Hardie, BA (Hons) (Oxon), LLB. Solicitor; Partner, Maclay Murray and Spens, Solicitors, Glasgow and Edinburgh; b. 25.9.39, Glasgow; m., 1, Helen Mary Banks (deceased); 2, Meg Owens; 1 s.; 1 d. Educ. Belmont House School; Glenalmond; University College, Oxford; Glasgow University. Member, Scottish Industrial Estates Corporation, 1973-75; Trustee, West of Scotland Trustee Savings Bank, 1978-84; Governor, Belmont House School, Glasgow, since 1983; Vice-Chairman, Section on General Practice, Division 1, International Bar Association; Chairman, Glasgow Junior Chamber of Commerce, 1971-72; President, West of Scotland Football Club, 1981-83; Deacon, Incorporation of Hammermen of Glasgow, 1985-86; Director, Glasgow Chamber of Commerce, since 1986; Clerk, General Council, Glasgow University, since 1987. Recreations: curling; golf; skiing; squash; hill-walking; jogging; riding. Address: (b.) 151 St. Vincent Street, Glasgow, G2 5NJ; T.-041-248 5011.

Pringle, Derek Hair, CBE, PhD, DSc, CPhys, FInstP, FRSE, Hon. FRCSE. Chairman, SEEL Limited, Livingston, since 1980; Director: Melville Street Investments plc, since 1984, Amersham International PLC, 1978-87; Chairman, Bioscot Limited, Edinburgh, 1983-86; b. 8.1.26, Edinburgh; m., Anne Collier Caw; 3 s.; 1 d. Educ. George Heriot's School, Edinburgh; Edinburgh University. Research Physicist, Ferranti Ltd., Edinburgh, 1948-59; Nuclear Enterprises Ltd., Edinburgh: Technical Director, 1960-76, Managing Director, 1976-78, Chairman, 1978-80. Member, National Radiological Protection Board, 1969-81; Member, Court, Heriot-Watt University, 1968-77; President, Edinburgh Chamber of Commerce, 1979-81; Chairman, Association of Scottish Chambers of Commerce, 1985-87; Vice President, Royal Society of Edinburgh, since 1985; Trustee, National Museums of Scotland, since 1985. Recreations: golf; gardening. Address: (h.) Earlyvale, Eddleston, Peeblesshire EH45 8QX; T.-072-13-231.

Pringle, Robert, MB, ChB, ChM, FRCS(Eng), FRCS(Edin), FRCS(Glas). Consultant Surgeon, Ninewells Hospital, Dundee, since 1974; Honorary Senior Lecturer, Dundee University, since 1967; Member, Council, Medical and Dental Defence Union of Scotland, since 1979; b. 23.8.27, Paisley; m., Margaret Anne Mitchell; 1 s.; 2 d. Educ. Camphill School, Paisley; Glasgow University. RAF, 1951-55 (Squadron Leader); Hall Fellow in Surgery, then Registrar in Surgery, Glasgow Royal Infirmary, 1956-59; Senior Registrar in Surgery, Royal Victoria Infirmary, Newcastle upon Tyne, 1960-63; First Assistant in Surgery, Newcastle upon Tyne University, 1963-64; Senior Lecturer in Surgery, St. Andrews University, 1964-67; Consultant Surgeon, Dundee Royal Infirmary, 1964-74. Chairman, Surgical Section, National Medical Consultative Committee, since 1987. Publications: papers and books on various gastroenterological, surgical and scientific topics. Recreations: flying; piano; golf; cycling. Address: (h.) Taynuilt, Kilspindie, Rait, Perthshire, PH2 7RX; T.-082 17 289.

Prior, William Barrett. Chief Officer, Countryside Commission for Scotland, 1987-88 (Secretary, 1971-87); Honorary Vice-President, Scottish Youth Hostels Association, since 1988; Director, Scottish Rights of Way Society Ltd., since 1988; b. 10.1.31, Edinburgh; m., Mary Bain; 1 s.; 2 d. Educ. George Heriot's School, Edinburgh. Department of Agriculture and Fisheries for Scotland, 1947-49; National Service, RAF, 1949-51; DAFS, 1951-67; Nature Conservancy, 1967-71. Address: (h.) 16 Spoutwells Drive, Scone, Perthshire.

Pritchard, Kenneth William, BL, WS, SSC. Secretary, The Law Society of Scotland, since 1976; Secretary, Scottish Council of Law Reporting, since 1976; Clerk, Registrar of Examiners, since 1976; b. 14.11.33, London; Honorary Sheriff, Dundee; m., Gretta Murray; 2 s.; 1 d. Educ. Dundee High School; Fettes College; St. Andrews University. National Service, Argyll and Sutherland Highlanders, 1955-57; 2nd Lt., 1956; TA, 1957-62 (Captain); joined J. & J. Scrimgeour, Solicitors, Dundee, 1957; Senior Partner, 1970-76; Member: Sheriff Court Rules Council, 1973-76, Lord Dunpark's Committee considering Reparation upon Criminal Conviction, 1973-77; Hon. Visiting Professor, Law School, Strathclyde University; Hon. Member, Law Institute of Victoria, 1985; Hon. Member, Law Society of New Zealand, 1987; Hon. Member, Faculty of Procurators and Solicitors in Dundee; Governor, Moray House College of Education, since 1982; Member, National Trust for Scotland Jubilee Appeal

Committee, 1980-82; President, Dundee High School Old Boys Club, 1975-76. Recreation: golf. Address: (h.) 36 Ravelston Dykes, Edinburgh, EH4 3EB; T.-031-332 8584.

Pritchard, Rev. Stanley, MA, OStJ. Appeals Director, Scotland, Royal National Mission to Deep Sea Fishermen; Author; Broadcaster; Preacher; Charity Consultant; b. 18.7.10, Glasgow. Educ. Bellahouston Academy, Glasgow; Glasgow University. Ordained, 1937; Minister, Martyrs Church of Scotland, Kilmarnock, 1938-41; YMCA Huts and Canteen Service, 1941-42; Minister, Williamwood, 1942-48; Church of Scotland Canteens in Europe, 1945-47; BBC, 1948-76: Appeals Organiser, Radio and Television Producer; Special Award for Children's Drama, 1956; Minister, Stevenson Memorial Church, Glasgow, 1968-79. Chairman, Hospital Sunday Fund; Chairman, Action for Disaster; Trustee, Barbirolli Trust; author of six plays; Writer and Director of several films. Publications: They Happened to Me, 1980; Fish and Ships, 1981; Variations on a Theme, 1982. Recreations: opera; travel; making documentary films; public speaking. Address: (h.) 3 Queen Margaret Road, Glasgow, G20 6DP; T.-041-946 4263.

Procter, Robert Hendy, MA. Secretary, Scottish Council, The Scout Association, since 1982; b. 22.1.31, Alloa; m., Elizabeth Rosemary; 1 s.; 2 d. Educ. Fettes College; Trinity Hall, Cambridge. Commissioned, Royal Corps of Signals (2nd Lt.), 1950; Patons & Baldwins Ltd., 1954-79 (General Manager, from 1969); Director, John Gladstone & Co. Ltd., Galashiels, 1980-82. General Commissioner of Income Tax, Clackmannan Division, 1976-80; Honorary Sheriff, Tayside Central and Fife, at Alloa, 1975. Recreations: hill-walking; golf. Address: (h.) 2 Braid Avenue, Morningside, Edinburgh, EH10 6DR; T.-031-447 1140.

Proctor, George Rennet, BSc, PhD, DSc, CChem, FRSC. Reader in Organic Chemistry, Strathclyde University, since 1979; b. 3.5.28, Ampthill, Bedfordshire; m., Christina Ann Fraser; 2 s.; 1 d. Educ. Robert Gordon's College, Aberdeen; Aberdeen University. 2nd Lt., Royal Engineers, 1946-48; RE (TA), 1948-53; Research Chemist, ICI Pharmaceuticals, 1956-58; Research Fellow, Zurich University, 1960; Royal Society Research Fellow, Yale University, 1963; Visiting Expert, National Cancer Institute, Bethesda, 1975-76; Lecturer and Senior Lecturer, Strathclyde University, 1958-79. Recreations: fishing; gardening. Address: (b.) Department of Pure and Applied Chemistry, Strathclyde University, Glasgow, G1 1XL; T.-041-552 4400, Ext. 2389.

Prophit, Professor Penny, BSN, MSN, DNSc, PhD. Professor of Nursing Studies and Head of Department, Edinburgh University, since 1983; b. 7.2.39, Monroe, Louisiana. Educ. Catholic University of America; St. Louis University. Associate Professor and Chairperson of Psychiatric-Mental Health Nursing Department, University of Southern Mississippi, 1974-75; Associate Professor and Chairperson of Graduate Research, Catholic University of America, Washington DC, 1975-78; Professor, Catholic University of Louvain/Leuven, Belgium, 1978-83; Director, Nursing Research Unit, Edinburgh University, 1983-84. Consultant, World Health Organisation. Recreations: playing piano; golf; jogging; writing poetry and short stories. Address: (h.) 51 Thirlestane Road, Edinburgh, EH9 1AP; T.-031-447 2148.

Prosser, (Leslie) Charles, DFA, DAEd. Secretary, Royal Fine Art Commission for Scotland, since 1976; b. 27.10.39, Harrogate; m., Coral; 1 s.; 2 d. Educ. Bath Academy of Art at Corsham Court; Slade School of Fine Art, London University. Assistant Lecturer in Fine Art, Blackpool School of Art, 1962-64; Fine Art research, Royal Academy, Stockholm, 1964-65; Lecturer in Fine Art, Leeds/Jacob Kramer College of Art, 1965-76; research in Art Education, Leeds University, 1974-75. Member, Awards Committee, Royal Incorporation of Architects in Scotland, since 1979; Leverhulme European Arts Research Award, 1964; exhibited paintings; lectured variously on art and design. Recreations: criticising visual arts: sculpting and drawing; cycling; Scottish dancing and hill-walking; plumbing; being not idle in the sun. Address: (h.) 28 Mayfield Terrace, Edinburgh, EH9 1RZ; T.-031-668 1141.

Prosser, Hon. Lord QC, MA (Oxon), LLB. Senator of the College of Justice in Scotland and Lord of Session, since 1986; b. 23.11.34, Edinburgh; m., Vanessa Lindsay; 2 s.; 2 d. Educ. Edinburgh Academy; Corpus Christi College, Oxford; Edinburgh University. Advocate, 1962; Queen's Counsel, 1974; Vice-Dean, Faculty of Advocates, 1979-83, Dean of Faculty, 1983-86. Address: 7 Randolph Crescent, Edinburgh, EH3 7TH; T.-031-225 2709.

Proudfoot, Thomas A., BSc. Rector, Girvan Academy, since 1982; b. 28.2.33, Irvine; m., V. Audrey Howlett; 1 d. Educ. Carrick Academy, Maybole; Glasgow University; Jordanhill College of Education. National Service, Royal Signals; Mathematics Teacher, Irvine Royal Academy and Ravenspark Academy; Assistant Rector, Kilmarnock Academy; Depute Rector, Carrick Academy, Maybole. Elder, Church of Scotland. Recreations: DIY; gardening; badminton. Address: (h.) 8 Ainslie Road, Girvan, KA26 OAY.

Proudfoot, Professor V. Bruce, BA, PhD, FSA, FRSE, FSA Scot. Professor of Geography, St. Andrews University; b. 24.9.30, Belfast; m., Edwina Valmai Windram Field; 2 s. Educ. Royal Belfast Academical Institution; Queen's University, Belfast. Research Officer, Nuffield Quaternary Research Unit, Queen's University, Belfast, 1954-58; Lecturer in Geography: Queen's University, Belfast, 1958-59, Durham University, 1959-67; Hatfield College, Durham: Tutor, 1960-63, Librarian, 1963-65; Visiting Fellow, University of Auckland and Commonwealth Visiting Fellow, Australia, 1966; Alberta University, Edmonton: Associate Professor, 1967-70, Professor, 1970-74; Co-ordinator, Socio-Economic Opportunity Studies and Staff Consultant, Alberta Human Resources Research Council, 1971-72. Vice President, Royal Society of Edinburgh, 1985-88 (Convener, Earth Science Committee, 1983-85); Chairman, Society for Landscape Studies, 1979-83; Vice-President, Society of Antiquaries of Scotland, 1982-85; Chairman, Rural Geographical Study Group, Institute of British

Geographers, 1980-84; Hon. Editor, Royal Scottish Geographical Society, since 1978; Hon. President, Scottish Association of Geography Teachers, 1982-84; Trustee, National Museum of Antiquities of Scotland, 1982-85. Recreation: gardening. Address: (h.) Westgate, Wardlaw Gardens, St. Andrews, KY16 9DW; T.-0334 73293.

Proudfoot, William, FFA. Chief General Manager and Actuary, Scottish Amicable Life Assurance Society, since 1969; b. 4.4.32, Bellshill; 2 d. Educ. Rutherglen Academy. Joined Scottish Amicable, 1948; appointed Assistant Actuary, 1957, Actuary and Secretary for Australia, 1959, Manager and Actuary for Australia, 1961, Assistant General Manager, 1968, General Manager, 1969 (title altered, 1982), Director, 1977. Director, various subsidiaries, Scottish Amicable; Director, Scottish Opera; Director, Securities and Investments Board, 1986. Recreations: golf; music. Address: (b.) Scottish Amicable Life Assurance Society, 150 St. Vincent Street, Glasgow; T.-041-248 2323.

Provan, James Lyal Clark. Member (Conservative), European Parliament, NE Scotland, since 1979; Farmer; b. 19.12.36, Glenfarg, Perthshire; m., Roweena Adele Lewis; 2 s.; 1 d. Educ. Ardvreck School, Crieff; Oundle School, Northants; Royal Agricultural College, Cirencester. National Farmers Union of Scotland: Area President, Kinross, 1965, Fife and Kinross, 1971; Tayside Regional Councillor, 1978-81; Member, Tay River Purification Board, since 1978; European Democratic (Conservative) Spokesman on Agriculture and Fisheries, 1981-87; Questor of European Parliament, since 1987. Recreations: country pursuits; sailing; flying; politics; agriculture. Address: Wallacetown, Bridge of Earn, Perth, PH2 8QA; T.-0738 812243.

Pullar, Robert Alexander, JP. Chairman, Tay River Purification Board, since 1986; Member, Central Scotland Water Development Board, since 1982; Member, Tayside Regional Council, since 1978 (Chairman, Water Services Committee, 1982-86); b. 9.10.49, Perth; m., Nancy; 1 d. Educ. Perth High School. Chairman, Perth Prison Visiting Committee, 1984-85. Recreations: music; politics; bowling; golf. Address: (h.) Glenfinlas, Church Lane, Methven, Perth, PH1 3PQ; T.-073884 200.

Pullen, Ian Michael, MB, BS, MRCPsych. Consultant Psychiatrist, Royal Edinburgh Hospital, since 1980; Honorary Senior Lecturer, Department of Psychiatry, Edinburgh University, since 1980; b. 19.9.46, Hampstead; m., Prue Matthews; 2 s. Educ. Hemel Hempstead Grammar School; London Hospital Medical College; London University. General Practitioner turned Psychiatrist. Publication: Psychological Aspects of Genetic Counselling (Co-Editor); Rehabilitation in Psychiatry (Co-Editor). Address: (h.) 10 Cluny Avenue, Edinburgh, EH10 4RN; T.-031-447 2169.

Punnett, Robert Malcolm, BA, MA (Econ), PhD. Reader in Politics, Strathclyde University, since 1984; b. 1.5.36, Carlisle; m., Marjory Chalmers; 2 d. Educ. Carlisle Grammar School; Sheffield University. Assistant Lecturer in Politics, Sheffield University, 1963-64; Visiting Professor in Political Science: Carleton University, Ottawa, 1967-68, McGill University, Montreal, 1974, McMaster University, Ontario, 1976-77, Virginia Polytechnic Institute, 1988; Visiting Fellow, Australian National University, 1980; Visiting Fellow, University of Western Australia, 1985; Lecturer, then Senior Lecturer, Strathclyde University, from 1964. Publications: British Government and Politics; The Prime Minister in Canadian Government and Politics; Front-Bench Opposition. Recreation: hill-walking. Address: (b.) Politics Department, Strathclyde University, Glasgow, G1; T.-041-552 4400.

Purser, John Whitley, MA (Hons). Composer and Lecturer; Poet, Playwright and Broadcaster; Manager, Scottish Music Information Centre; b. 10.2.42, Glasgow; 1 s.; 1 d. Educ. Fettes College; Glasgow University; Royal Scottish Academy of Music and Drama. Part-time Lecturer in English Literature, Glasgow University, 1981-85; compositions include two operas, numerous orchestral and chamber works; three books of poetry, The Counting Stick, A Share of the Wind and Amoretti; three radio plays and a radio series, A Change of Tune. Recreations: numerous. Address: (b.) 29 Banavie Road, Glasgow, G11 5AW; T.-041-334 6393.

Purvis, John Robert, MA (Hons). International Business Consultant (Managing Partner, Purvis & Co.), since 1973; Member for Scotland, Independent Broadcasting Authority, since 1985; Vice President, Scottish Conservative and Unionist Association, since 1987; b. 6.7.38, St. Andrews; m., Louise Spears Durham; 1 s.; 2 d. Educ. Glenalmond; St. Andrews University. 2nd Lt., Scots Guards, 1956-58; First National City Bank (Citibank NA), London, New York City, Milan, 1962-69; Treasurer, Noble Grossart Ltd., Edinburgh, 1969-73; Director and Secretary, Brigton Farms Ltd., 1969-86; Managing Director, Founder, Owner, Gilmerton Management Services Ltd., since 1973; Member, European Parliament, Mid Scotland and Fife, 1979-84 (Deputy Chief Whip, Group Spokesman on Monetary Affairs, Energy, Research and Technology) Vice Chairman, European Parliament Delegation to the Gulf States; Chairman, IBA Scottish Advisory Committee, since 1985. Member of Council, St. Leonards School, St. Andrews, since 1981; Chairman, Economic, Employment and Industry Committee, Scottish Conservative and Unionist Association, since 1986. Recreations: Italy and Scotland. Address: Gilmerton House, Dunino, St. Andrews, KY16 8NB; T.-0334 75830.

R

Racey, Professor Paul Adrian, MA, PhD, DSc, FIBiol. Professor of Zoology, Aberdeen University, since 1985 (Head of Department, since 1987); b. 7.5.44, Wisbech, Cambridgeshire; m., Anna Priscilla Notcutt; 3 s. Educ. Ratcliffe College,

Leicester; Downing College, Cambridge. Rothamsted Experimental Station, Harpenden, 1965-66; Zoological Society of London, 1966-70; Unit of Reproductive Biology, Liverpool University, 1970-73; joined Department of Zoology, Aberdeen University, 1973. Recreations: riding; sailing; shooting. Address: (b.) Department of Zoology, Aberdeen University, Tillydrone Avenue, Aberdeen, AB9 2TN; T.-0224 272858.

Radford, Professor Peter F., DPE, MSc, PhD. Professor and Head, Department of Physical Education and Sports Science, Glasgow University (Director, Department of Physical Education and Recreation, 1976-87); Member, Scottish Sports Council, since 1983; Chairman, Scottish Consultative Group on Sports Medicine and Sports Science, since 1984; b. 20.9.39, Walsall; m., Margaret M. Beard; 1 d. Educ. Tettenhall College, Wolverhampton; Cardiff University; Purdue University, Indiana; Glasgow University. Assistant Professor, McMaster University, School of Physical Education and Athletics, Hamilton, Ontario, 1967-75. Chairman, Scottish Universities Physical Education Association, 1980-81; Member, Scottish Executive, British Association of Sport and Medicine, 1982-84; Member, Glasgow Sports Promotion Council, since 1982; Member, Sports Council's Drug Abuse Advisory Group, since 1986; holder of world record, 200 metres and 220 yards, 1960; Bronze Medal, 100 metres and 4 x 100 metres Relay, Olympic Games, Rome, 1960; British 100 metres record, set in Paris, 1958, remained unbroken for 20 years. Address: (b.) Department of Physical Education and Sports Science, Glasgow University, Glasgow, G12 8LT; T.-041-339 8855.

Radin, Leon, MA, LLB. Solicitor, since 1952; Honorary Sheriff; b. 27.4.28, Edinburgh; m., Margaret Morton Wood; 1 s.; 2 d. Educ. Royal High School, Edinburgh; Edinburgh University. Pilot Officer (Admin), RAF, 1951-53; Partner, Middleton Ross & Arnot, Solicitors, Dingwall, since 1957; Clerk of the Peace for Ross and Cromarty, 1969-75. Recreation: music. Address: (h.) Dunbeath, Strathpeffer, Ross-shire; T.-Strathpeffer 21271.

Rado, Emil Richard, BSc (Econ). Senior Lecturer in Development Studies, Glasgow University, since 1965; b. 18.1.31, Budapest; m., Anne Forrest Taylor; 1 s.; 2 d. Educ. Ackworth School; University College, London. Research Fellow and Lecturer in Economics, Ghana University, 1953-60; Visiting Professor, Williams College, USA, 1960-61; Lecturer in Economics, Makerere University College, 1961-65; Senior Research Fellow, Nairobi University (on secondment), 1967-70. Council Member, Development Studies Association and African Studies Association, at various times; has acted as Consultant to World Bank, International Labour Office, OECD and several Governments; Member, Central Committee, Quaker Peace and Service. Recreations: running; hill-walking; photography; herb-growing. Address: (h.) 18 Kersland Drive, Milngavie, Glasgow, G62 8DG; T.-041-956 1953.

Rae, Barbara, DA, ARSA, RSW. Painter; Lecturer in Drawing and Painting, Glasgow School of Art, since 1975; b. 10.12.43, Falkirk; 1 s. Educ. Morrison's Academy, Crieff; Edinburgh College of Art; Moray House College of Education. Travelling Scholarship, France and Spain, 1966; Arts Council Awards, 1968, 1975 and 1981; Guthrie Medal, RSA, 1977; May Marshall Brown Award, RSW, 1979; elected Associate, RSA, 1980; RSA Gillies Award, 1983; Calouste Gulbenkian Printmaking Award, 1983; President, Society of Scottish Artists, 1983-84; exhibited in UK, USA and Australia. Recreation: gardening. Address: Studio 7, 30 Elbe Street, Leith, Edinburgh.

Rae, Hugh Crauford. Novelist; b. 22.11.35, Glasgow; m., Elizabeth Dunn; 1 d. Educ. Knightswood School. Prolific popular novelist; author of more than 50 tiles, under a variety of pseudonyms, including Stuart Stern, James Albany and Jessica Stirling; books include (as Hugh C. Rae) Skinner, The Marksman, The Shooting Gallery, Harkfast and Privileged Strangers and (as Jessica Stirling) The Spoiled Earth, The Hiring Fair, The Dark Pasture, Treasures on Earth. Recreation: golf. Address: (h.) Drumore Farm Cottage, Balfron Station, Stirlingshire.

Rae, Rev. Peter Crighton, BSc, BD. Minister, Cowdenbeath North with Kirk of Beath, since 1969; b. 4.10.39, St. Albans; m., Margaret Helen West; 2 d. Educ. Kings College School, Wimbledon; Edinburgh University; New College, Edinburgh. In enginering; Assistant Minister, St. Giles and St. Columba's, Elgin. Founder Member, Cowdenbeath Community Council; former Moderator, Dunfermline Presbytery; has served on various Committees of the General Assembly. Recreations: family; cycling; walking; hymnody. Address: The Manse, Stuart Place, Cowdenbeath, Fife; T.-Cowdenbeath 511033.

Rae, Rita Emilia Anna, LLB (Hons). Advocate; b. 20.6.50, Glasgow. Educ. St. Patrick's High School, Coatbridge; Edinburgh University. Apprentice, Biggart, Lumsden & Co., Glasgow, 1972-74; Assistant Solicitor: Balfour & Manson, Edinburgh, 1974, Biggart, Baillie & Gifford, Glasgow, 1974-76; Solicitor and Partner, Ross Harper & Murphy, Glasgow, 1976-81; Advocate, 1982. Recreations: theatre-going; driving; cycling; walking; opera; music. Address: (h.) 73 Fotheringay Road, Glasgow; T.-041-423 0781.

Rae, Scott Alexander, LLB (Hons), WS, NP. Partner, Morton Fraser & Milligan WS, Edinburgh, since 1970; b. 17.12.44, Edinburgh; m., Annabel Riach; 3 s. Educ. Daniel Stewarts College, Edinburgh; Edinburgh University. Sometime Tutor and Course Leader, Edinburgh University; Law Society of Scotland Examiner in Taxation and Chairman, Board of Examiners; Member, VAT Tribunal (Scotland); Clerk, Incorporated Trades of Edinburgh; Academician, International Academy of State and Trust Law. Recreations: fishing; gardening. Address: (b.) 15-19 York Place, Edinburgh; T.-031-556 8444.

Rae, Thomas Ian, MA, PhD. Keeper of Manuscripts (Cataloguing), National Library of Scotland, since 1972; b. 9.6.26, Norwich; m., Margaret Tickle (m. diss.); 3 s. Educ. Hawick High School; Balliol College, Oxford; St. Andrews University. Royal Navy, 1944-47; Assistant Lecturer in History, Glasgow University, 1951-52; Assistant Lecturer in Medieval History, St. Andrews University, 1952-55; Assistant Keeper, Manuscripts, National Library of Scotland, 1955-72. Secretary, Scottish History Society, 1969-76 (Publication Secretary, since 1976); Chairman, Company of Scottish History, 1978-84; Chairman, Scottish Records Association, 1981-83. Publications: The Administration of the Scottish Frontier 1513-1603, 1966; The Burgh Court Book of Selkirk 1503-1545 (Co-author), 1960, 1969; Scotland in the Time of Shakespeare, 1965. Recreations: reading; music. Address: (h.) 26 Marchmont Crescent, Edinburgh, EH9 1HG.

Raeburn, James B., FCIS. Director, Society of Master Printers of Scotland, since 1984; Director, Scottish Newspaper Publishers' Association, since 1984; b. 18.3.47, Jedburgh; m., Rosemary Bisset; 2 d. Educ. Hawick High School. Edinburgh Corporation, 1964-69; Roxburgh County Council, 1969-71; Electrical Contractors' Association of Scotland, 1972-84 (Secretary, 1975-83). Recreations: golf; squash. Address: (b.) Edinburgh House, 3-11 North St. Andrew Street, Edinburgh, EH2 1JU; T.-031-557 3600.

Raeburn, John Alexander, TD, MB, ChB, PHD, FRCPEdin. Senior Lecturer, Human Genetics Unit, Department of Medicine, Edinburgh University, since 1972; Honorary Consultant Physician, Lothian Health Board, since 1972; b. 25.6.41, Adlington, Macclesfield; m., Arlene Rose; 1 s.; 2 d.; 2 step s. Educ. Loretto School; Edinburgh University. Worked in clinical medicine; now building up a Medical Genetic Service in SE Scotland, providing genetic counselling; Past Chairman, Scottish Down's Syndrome Association; Chairman, Scottish Council, Cystic Fibrosis Research Trust, since 1986; Honorary Medical Adviser to AID for Down's Babies in Edinburgh, since 1977. Recreations: reading; fishing; sketching; cycling to work. Address: (h.) 22 Inverleith Row, Edinburgh, EH3 5QH.

Raeburn, Emeritus Professor John Ross, CBE, FRSE, FIBiol, BSc, MA, PhD. Consultant; b. 20.11.12, Kirkcaldy; m., Mary Roberts; 1 s.; 3 d. Educ. Manchester Grammar School; Edinburgh University; Cornell University. Professor, Agricultural Economics, Nanking University, 1936-37; Research Officer, Oxford University, 1938-39; Statistician, then Head of Agricultural Plans Branch, Ministry of Food, 1939-46; Senior Research Officer, Oxford University, 1946-49; Reader in Agricultural Economics, London University, 1949-59; Professor and Head, Department of Agriculture, Aberdeen University, 1959-78; Principal, North of Scotland College of Agriculture, 1963-78; Consultant to World Bank, since 1979; Vice-President, International Association of Agricultural Economists, 1964-70; President, Agricultural Economics Society, 1964-65. Publication: Agriculture: Foundations, Principles and Development. Recreations: travel; gardening; photography. Address: (h.) 30 Morningfield Road, Aberdeen, AB2 4AQ; T.-0224 314010.

Raffe, David James, BA, BPhil. Reader in Education, Edinburgh University, since 1985 (Co-Director, Centre for Educational Sociology, since 1987); b. 5.5.51, Felixstowe; m., Shirley Paine; 1 s.; 1 d. Educ. The Leys School; New College, Oxford; Nuffield College, Oxford. Edinburgh University: Research Fellow, Centre for Educational Sociology, 1975-79, Lecturer in Education, 1979-85; Deputy Director, Centre for Educational Sociology, 1979-87. Publications: Reconstructions of Secondary Education, 1983; Fourteen to Eighteen, 1984. Recreations: squash; hill-walking. Address: (b.) 7 Buccleuch Place, Edinburgh, EH8 9LW; T.-031-667 1011, Ext. 6499.

Rafferty, George Campbell, BSc, MRCVS, DL. Veterinary Surgeon in general practice, since 1948; b. 1.3.26, Glasgow; m., Jane Lilian Sarsons; 2 s.; 2 d. Educ. Rutherglen Academy; Royal Dick Veterinary College. Qualified, 1948; in practice: Suffolk, 1948-49, Hampshire, 1949-50, Fife, 1951-52, Strathspey, since 1953; appointed Veterinary Zoo Inspector, 1984; Deputy Lieutenant, Inverness-shire, since 1985; Honorary Vice-President, Strathspey Farmers Club. Recreation: work. Address: Seaforth, Seafield Avenue, Grantown-on-Spey, Morayshire; T.-0479 2252.

Rahman, Mohammad Zalilur, MB, BS, FRCPsych, DTM&H. Consultant Psychiatrist, since 1977; Co-Director, Possil Drug Project, since 1984; Honorary Clinical Lecturer, Glasgow University, since 1986; b. 14.11.30, Bangladesh; m., Dr. Syeda K. Nahar; 1 s. Educ. Dhaga University; Edinburgh University. Graduated in medicine, Dhaga; GP in Bangladesh; emigrated to UK, 1969; Psychiatric Tutor, Royal College of Psychiatrists, since 1981; Convener, Working Party on Manpower and Training, Substance Misuse Section, Royal College of Psychiatrists; Treasurer, Psychosomatic Society, Glasgow; former Vice Chairperson, Strathclyde Community Relations Council; President, Bengali and Arabic School, Glasgow; Member and Past President, Bangladesh Association, Glasgow; Member, Broadcasting Council for Scotland. Recreations: gardening; travelling; reading. Address: (h.) Lynedoch, Larch Avenue, Lenzie, Glasgow, G66 4HT; T.-041-776 6428.

Ralston, Andrew Dunlop, BL, NP. Partner, Macnair Clyde & Ralston, Solicitors, Paisley, since 1949 (Senior Partner, since 1981); Honorary Sheriff of North Strathclyde, at Paisley, since 1976; b. 22.5.23, Glasgow; m., Jane Neilson Burns; 3 s. Educ. Allan Glen's School, Glasgow; Glasgow University. Vice-Dean, Faculty of Procurators in Paisley, 1979-81. Honorary Secretary, Scottish Baptist College, 1966-83; Honorary Treasurer, Dennistoun Baptist Church, Glasgow, 1974-77. Recreation: gardening. Address: (b.) 43 High St, Paisley, PA1 2AJ; T.-041-887 5181.

Ramage, John Bradley, ALA, MBIM. Chief Librarian, City of Dundee, since 1982; b. 14.1.42, Airdrie; m., Dorothy Laing Cowan; 1 d. Educ. Airdrie Academy; Scottish School of Librarianship. School Librarian, Broxburn Academy, 1962-63; Chief Assistant Librarian, Burgh of Clydebank, 1963-67; Depute Chief Librarian, Burgh of Coatbridge, 1967-73; City of Dundee: Senior Assistant Chief Librarian, 1973-78, Depute Chief Librarian, 1978-82. Member, Scottish Advisory

Committee, Independent Broadcasting Authority; Secretary, Dundee Film Theatre Committee; Elder, Church of Scotland. Recreations: golf; gardening; home wine-making; DIY. Address: (b.) Central Library, The Wellgate, Dundee, DD1 1DB; T.-0382 23141, Ext. 4323.

Ramage, Professor Robert, BSc, PhD, DSc, MSc, CChem, FRSC, FRSE. Forbes Professor of Organic Chemistry, Edinburgh University, since 1984; b. 4.10.35, Glasgow; m., Joan Fraser Paterson; 3 d. Educ. Whitehill Senior Secondary School, Glasgow; Glasgow University. Fellow, Harvard College and Fulbright Scholar, Harvard University, 1961-63; Woodward Research Institute, Basle, 1963-64; Lecturer, then Senior Lecturer, Liverpool University, 1964-77; Professor, then Head, Department of Chemistry, UMIST, 1977-84; Tilden Lecturer, Royal Society of Chemistry, 1986. Recreations: sports; gardening. Address: (h.) 26 Craigleith View, Ravelston, Edinburgh, EH4 3JZ; T.-031-337 1952.

Ramsay, Professor Donald MacDonald, BSc, PhD, FGS, FRSE. Professor of Geology, Dundee University, since 1980; b. 17.8.32, Glasgow; m., Elma; 1 s.; 2 d. Educ. Allan Glen's School; Glasgow University. Assistant in Geology, Glasgow University, 1957-59; Dundee University: Lecturer in Geology, 1959, Senior Lecturer, 1966, Reader, 1977. Secretary, then British Correspondent, Project 27 (Caledonide Orogen), International Geological Correlation Programme (UNESCO). Recreation: curling. Address: (b.) Department of Geology, The University, Dundee, DD1 4HN; T.-Dundee 23181, Ext. 4439.

Ramsay, Hamish, MRTPI. Director of Planning, Tayside Regional Council, since 1975; b. 23.3.30, Windygates, Fife; m., Sheila; 2 d. Educ. Buckhaven High School; College of Estate Management. Fife County Council: planning apprentice, 1947-52, Junior Planning Assistant, 1954-56; Corporation of Dundee: Planning Assistant, 1956-65, Depute Town Planning Officer, 1965-69, Chief Planning Officer, 1969-75. Vice-Chairman, Duncan of Jordanstone College of Art, since 1978. Recreations: Rotary; walking. Address: (b.) Tayside House, Crichton Street, Dundee; T.-0382 23281.

Ramsay, John Neville David, FInstFF. Retired Chairman, John G. Borland & Peat Ltd., Glasgow; Board Member, Clyde Port Authority, since 1983; b. 18.5.24, Glasgow; m., Olive Doreen; 1 s. Educ. Hutchesons' Boys Grammar School, Glasgow. Joined Anchor Line Ltd., Glasgow, 1940; War Service, RAF (home, North Africa, Italy), 1942-47; John G. Borland & Peat Ltd., Shipbrokers: joined, 1947, appointed Director, 1959, Managing Director, 1978, Chairman, 1980; President, Glasgow and Clyde Shipping Association, 1983; Director, Glasgow Chamber of Commerce, since 1983. Recreations: angling; painting; gardening; music. Address: (h.) Ash Ford, 17 Brackenrig Crescent, Waterfoot, Eaglesham, G76 0HF; T.-041-644 4234.

Ramsay, Rev. Robert John, LLB (Hons), NP, BD. Minister, Glenisla with Kilry with Lintrathen, since 1986; b. 28.10.51, Alyth; m., Sheila Margaret Ball; 2 d. Educ. Blairgowrie High School; Edinburgh University; St. Mary's College, St. Andrews. Apprentice Solicitor and Tutor in Constitutional Law, Dundee University, 1973-75; Lecturer in Private Law, Dundee University, 1975-79; Head, Department of Legal Studies, Administrative College, Port Moresby, Papua New Guinea, 1979-82; Assistant Minister, Kirriemuir Old Church, 1985-86. Honorary Treasurer, Fellowship of Reconciliation in Scotland. Recreations: music; reading; travel. Address: The Manse, Bridgend of Lintrathen, Kirriemuir, Angus; T.-05756 226.

Ramsey, Professor Peter Herbert, MA, DPhil. Professor of History, Aberdeen University, since 1966; b. 19.11.25, Barnet; m., Priscilla Telford; 3 d. Educ. Mill Hill School; Worcester College, Oxford. Assistant, Glasgow University, 1951-55; Lecturer, Bristol University, 1955-65. Publications: Tudor Economic Problems, 1963; The Price Revolution in Sixteenth Century England, 1971. Recreations: reading; music. Address: (h.) Goose Croft House, Kintore, Aberdeenshire; T.-Kintore 32337.

Randall, Rev. David James, MA, BD, ThM. Minister, Doune Parish Church, Macduff, since 1971; b. 5.6.45, Edinburgh; m., Agnes Wardlaw; 3 s.; 1 d. Educ. George Heriot's School; Edinburgh University; Princeton Theological Seminary. Former Moderator, Turriff Presbytery and Buchan Presbytery. Recreation: jogging. Address: (h.) Doune Manse, Macduff, AB4 3QL.

Randall, John Norman, BA, MPhil. Deputy Registrar General for Scotland, since 1985; b. 1.8.45, Keston, Kent; m., Sandra Jane Philpott; 1 s.; 1 d. Educ. Bromley Grammar School; Bristol University; Glasgow University. Assistant Research Officer, Department of Economic Affairs, 1968-70; Economic Assistant, West Central Scotland Plan, 1970-74; Economic Adviser, Scottish Office, 1974-85. Recreations: reading; hill-walking; natural and local history. Address: (b.) General Register Office (Scotland), New Register House, Edinburgh, EH1 3YT; T.-031-556 3952.

Rankeillour, Rt. Hon. Lord. Peer; Member, House of Lords, since 1968; Rear Commodore, House of Lords Yacht Club; Farmer and Landowner; b. 29.5.35. Educ. Ampleforth College; privately. Recreations: agricultural and horticultural equipment/machinery inventor; shooting, hunting, and landscaping on the grand scale. Address: (h.) The Achaderry Estate, Roy Bridge, Inverness-shire; T.-Spean Bridge 206.

Rankin, Alick Michael, CBE (1986). Chief Executive, Scottish & Newcastle Breweries plc, since 1983 (Deputy Chairman, since 1988); Director: Christian Salvesen PLC, since 1986, Edinburgh's Capital, since 1985, Bank of Scotland, since 1987; Vice-Chairman, The Brewers' Society; b. 23.1.35, London; m., Suzetta Nelson; 1 s.; 3 d. Educ. Eton College; Oxford University. Scots Guards, 1953-55; investment banking, Toronto, 1956-59; Scottish & Newcastle Breweries plc, since 1960. Recreations: fishing; shooting; golf; tennis. Address: (b.) Abbey Brewery, 111 Holyrood Road, Edinburgh, EH8 8YS; T. 031 556 2591.

Rankin, Emeritus Professor Robert Alexander, MA, PhD, ScD, FRSAMD, FRSE. Emeritus Professor of Mathematics, Glasgow University, since

1982; b. 27.10.15, Garlieston, Wigtownshire; m., Mary Ferrier Llewelyn; 1 s.; 3 d. Educ. Whithorn School; Fettes College; Clare College, Cambridge. Fellow, Clare College, 1939-51; War work on rockets, 1940-45; Lecturer, Cambridge University, 1945-51; Assistant Tutor, Clare College, 1947-51; Mason Professor of Pure Mathematics, Birmingham University, 1951-54; Professor of Mathematics, Glasgow University, 1954-82 (Clerk of Senate, 1971-78, Dean of Faculties, 1985-88). Vice-President, Royal Society of Edinburgh, 1960-63; Keith Prize, RSE, 1961-63; Member, Secretary of State's Advisory Council on Education, 1959-61; Honorary President, Gaelic Society of Glasgow, since 1969; Vice-President, London Mathematical Society, 1966-68; President, Edinburgh Mathematical Society, 1957-58 and 1978-79. Recreations: music; hill-walking; Gaelic studies. Address: (h.) 98 Kelvin Court, Glasgow, G12 OAH; T.-041-339 2641.

Rankin, Thomas John, MA, FCollP. Head Teacher, Sgoil Dhalabroig, South Uist, since 1981; b. 29.3.47, Glasgow; m., Jean Helen Adams; 2 d. Educ. Strathbungo Secondary School, Glasgow; Glasgow University. Teacher, Bernard Street Junior Secondary School, Glasgow; Teacher, Chizongwe Secondary School, Chipata, Zambia; Deputy Head, Kabulonga School for Boys, Lusaka, Zambia; Examinations Officer, i/c Cambridge School Certificate and London University External Degree Examinations, Ministry of Education, Lusaka; Acting Headmaster, Libala Secondary School, Lusaka; Teacher: West Derby Comprehensive School, Liverpool, Chryston High School, near Glasgow. Address: (b.) Sgoil Dhalabroig, Dalabrog, Isle of South Uist, PA81 5SS; T.-08784 276.

Ransford, Tessa, MA. Director, Scottish Poetry Library; Poet; b. 8.7.38, Bombay; 1 s.; 3 d. Educ. St. Leonard's School, St. Andrews; Edinburgh University; Craiglockhart College of Education. Publicity Department, Oxford University Press, 1958; in Pakistan as wife of missionary, 1960-68; Assistant to the Director, Scottish Institute of Adult Education, 1982-83; books of poetry: Poetry of Persons, 1975, While It Is Yet Day, 1976, Light of the Mind, 1980, Fools and Angels, 1984; Shadows from the Greater Hill, 1987; first prize, Jubilee poetry competition, Scottish Association for the Speaking of Verse, 1974; Scottish Arts Council Book Award, 1980; Founder and Organiser, School of Poets (open learning workshops for practising poets). Recreation: hill-walking. Address: (b.) Scottish Poetry Library, Tweeddale Court, 14 High Street, Edinburgh, EH1 1TE; T.-031-557 2876.

Rattray, Charles McNab Iverson, BSc, MSc, FIMA, FBCS. Senior Lecturer, Department of Computing Science, Stirling University, since 1978; b. 3.9.38, Burrelton; m., May Rattray; 2 s. Educ. Adelaide Boys' High School; Adelaide University; UMIST, Manchester. Engineer, Ferranti Ltd., Salisbury, South Australia, and Manchester, England, 1959-64; Lecturer, UMIST, 1964-69; Senior Lecturer, MacQuarie University, Sydney, 1969-72; variety of research posts and commercial positions, 1972-78. Whitworth Exhibitioner, 1973-74. Publications: Programming Language Semantics; Algebraic Specification for Practical Software Production. Recreation: working. Address: (b.) Department of Computing Science, Stirling University, Stirling, FK9 4LA; T.-0786 73171.

Raven, Alan Martin, BSc (Hons), PhD, CChem, FRSC, MIBiol. Scientific Adviser, Department of Agriculture and Fisheries for Scotland, since 1982; b. 24.1.30, Lewisham, London; m., Yvonne Valerie Simpson; 2 s.; 1 d. Educ. Cockermouth Grammar School; King's College, Durham University, Newcastle-upon-Tyne. Chemical and Animal Nutrition Research Division, Ministry of Agriculture, Northern Ireland: Scientific Officer, 1955-59, Senior Scientific Officer, 1959-67, Principal Scientific Officer, 1967-72; Assistant Lecturer to Senior Lecturer, Agricultural Chemistry Department, Queen's University, Belfast, 1955-72; West of Scotland Agricultural College: Assistant Director (Development), 1972-75, Deputy Principal, 1975-82. Recreations: reading; travel; theatre; gardening. Address: (b.) Department of Agriculture and Fisheries for Scotland, Chesser House, Gorgie Road, Edinburgh, EH11 3AW; T.-031-443 4020.

Rawcliffe, Rt. Rev. Derek Alec, OBE, BA. Bishop of Glasgow and Galloway, since 1981; b. 8.7.21, Manchester; m., Susan Kathryn Speight (deceased). Educ. Sir Thomas Rich's School, Gloucester; Leeds University; College of the Resurrection, Mirfield. Ordained Deacon, 1944; ordained Priest, Worcester, 1945; Assistant Priest, St. George's, Worcester, 1944-47; Assistant Master, then Headmaster, All Hallows School, Pawa, Solomon Islands, 1947-56; Headmaster, St. Mary's School, Maravovo, Guadalcanar, Solomon Islands, 1956-58; Archdeacon of Southern Melanesia, New Hebrides, 1958-74; Assistant Bishop, Diocese of Melanesia, 1974-75; first Bishop of New Hebrides (now Vanuatu), 1975-80. Recreations: music; numismatics. Address: Bishop's House, 48 Drymen Road, Bearsden, Glasgow, G61 2RH; T.-041-943 0612.

Rayner, Colin Robert, MB, BS, MS, FRCS, FRCSEdin. Consultant Plastic Surgeon, Grampian Health Board and Royal Aberdeen Children's Hospital, since 1978; Senior Lecturer in Surgery, Aberdeen University, since 1978; b. 28.10.38, London; m., Margaret Mary; 1 s.; 2 d. Educ. St. George's College, Weybridge; Middlesex Hospital, London. General surgical training and pre-registration posts, Middlesex Hospital, Birmingham Accident Hospital, Kent and Sussex Hospital, 1964-71; SHO Plastic Surgery, East Grinstead Hospital, 1971; Registrar and Senior Registrar in head and neck surgery, Westminster and Royal Marsden Hospital, London, 1972-75; Senior Registrar, South Manchester Teaching Hospital, 1976-78. Recreations: skiing; opera; Russian literature; the works of P.J. Wodehouse. Address: 6 Moray Place, Aberdeen; T.-0224 314216.

Readman, Hope, VMSM (two bars). Chairman of Council, Scottish Branch, British Red Cross Society, since 1986; b. 18.4.29, Glasgow; m., Lt.-Col. Ian R. Readman, MC (deceased); 2 s.; 1 d. Educ. Southover Manor School. British Red Cross Society: enrolled Perth Branch, 1959, President, Perth and Kinross Branch, 1974-84, Vice

Chairman, Scottish Council, 1984-86; Member, Central and Tayside War Pensions Committee, 1975-80; Member, MSC Employment for Disabled, 1983-85; Member, Scottish Veterans' Garden City Association, since 1981; Elder, Dunblane Cathedral; Jubilee Medal. Recreations: music; reading; cooking; sewing. Address: (h.) Gateside of Glasingall, Dunblane, Perthshire; T.-Dunblane 824248.

Redding, Penelope Jane, MB, BS, MRCS, LRCP, MRCPath. Consultant Bacteriologist, Victoria Infirmary, Glasgow, since 1984; Honorary Clinical Lecturer, Glasgow University, since 1985; b. 21.11.50, London; m., Christopher John Vincent; 2 s. Educ. Lycee Francais de Londres; University College, London/Westminster Hospital Medical School. House Surgeon, Gynaecology, Queen Mary's, Roehampton, 1974; House Physician, Medicine, St. Stephen's, Fulham, 1975; Rotating SHO, Pathology, Westminster Hospital, 1975-76; Assistant Lecturer, Microbiology, St. Thomas's Hospital, 1976-77; Registrar, Bacteriology and Immunology, Western Infirmary, 1977-80 (Senior Registrar, 1980-84). Publication: Handbook of Intensive Care (Contributor), 1983. Recreations: skiing; swimming; dress-making; opera; ballet. Address: (b.) Bacteriology Department, Victoria Infirmary, Glasgow, G42 9TY; T.-041-649 4545.

Redman, Timothy, GRSM, ARMCM. Composer and Arranger; Conductor; Organist; 9.11.43, Newcastle-upon-Tyne. Educ. Rutherford Grammar School, Newcastle-upon-Tyne; Royal Manchester College of Music. Teacher of Music and Deputy Headmaster, Salford, Lancashire; Associate Musical Director, Theatre Royal, Newcastle-upon-Tyne, 1973-74; Organist and Master of the Choristers, St. Mary's Cathedral, Glasgow, 1976-79; Associate Director, BBC Scottish Singers, 1977-80; Member, Music Staff, BBC Scotland, since 1974; Founder Chairman, Glasgow Diocesan Music Association, 1976-79 and 1981-83; Musical Director: Helensburgh Savoy Club, BBC Club Singers; compositions include organ and choral music, chamber and orchestral music, music for brass group and concert band. Recreations: cinema; theatre; reading. Address: (h.) 21 Belhaven Terrace West, Kirklee, Glasgow, G12 0UL; T.-041-339 3975.

Redpath, Jean, MBE, DUniv (Stirling). Singer; b. 28.4.37, Leven. Educ. Leven; Buckhaven; Edinburgh University. Singer of traditional Scottish music with particular interest in Burns; has sung in every state in the USA, where she tours several times a year; lectures at summer school, Stirling University, each year; numerous radio and TV appearances, UK, USA and Australia; Kentucky Colonel. Recreations: singing!; photography. Address: resident in Fife.

Rees, Alan Tait, MA (Cantab), CQSW. Assistant Director, Edinburgh Council of Social Service, since 1976; Chairman, Committee on Mobility for Scotland, Scottish Council on Disability, since 1979; Convener, Scottish Community Transport Group, 1983-85; b. 4.8.31, Shanghai, China; m., Alison Margaret; 2 s.; 2 d. Educ. Kingswood School, Bath; Gonville and Caius College, Cambridge; London School of Economics; University College, Swansea. Community Development Officer, Tanzania; Lecturer in Youth and Community Studies, Moray House College; Organising Secretary, Board for Information in Youth and Community Service, Scotland; Senior Community Development Officer, Council of Social Service for Wales. Chairman, Scotland Yard Adventure Centre, Edinburgh; Treasurer, Scottish Committee, British Association of Social Workers; Trustee, Seagull Trust; Secretary, Handicabs (Lothian); Member, Transport Users Consultative Committee for Scotland. Recreations: gardening; painting; DIY. Address: (h.) 20 Seaforth Drive, Edinburgh, EH4 2BZ; T.-031-332 7317.

Rees, Professor Elmer Gethin, BA (Cantab), PhD (Warwick), MA (Oxon), FRSE. Professor, Department of Mathematics, Edinburgh University, since 1979; b. 19.11.41, Llandybie, Wales; m., Mary Elene; 2 s. Educ. Llandeilo Grammar School; St. Catharine's College, Cambridge; Warwick University. Lecturer, Department of Pure Mathematics, Hull University, 1967-69; Member, Institute for Advanced Study, Princeton, 1969-70; Lecturer, Department of Pure Mathematics, University College of Swansea, 1970-71; Tutorial Fellow, St. Catherine's College, Oxford and Lecturer in Mathematics, Oxford University, 1971-79. Publications: Notes on Geometry; Homotopy Theory. Address: (h.) 23 Blacket Place, Edinburgh, EH9 1RJ; T.-031-667 2747.

Reeves, Philip Thomas Langford, RSA, RSW, RE, RGI, ARCA. Artist; b. 7.7.31, Cheltenham; m., Christine MacLaren; 1 d. Educ. Naunton Park School, Cheltenham; Cheltenham School of Art; Royal College of Art, London. Lecturer in Graphic Design, Glasgow School of Art, 1954-70 (Head of Printmaking, since 1970). Address: (h.) 13 Hamilton Drive, Glasgow, G12 8DN; T.-041-339 0720.

Regent, Peter. Writer and Sculptor; b. 8.12.29, Bury St. Edmunds; m., Karola Hood Zurndorfer; 1 d. Educ. Thetford Grammar School; Keble College, Oxford. Nigerian Government Service, 1954-56; Head of African Section/Research Director, Hansard Society, 1956-59; Staff Tutor in Government, Police Staff College, Bramshill, 1959-65; Head, Department of Liberal and Complementary Studies, Duncan of Jordanstone College of Art, Dundee, 1965-75. Member, North East Fife District Council, since 1984; Parliamentary candidate (Liberal/Alliance), North Tayside, 1987. Publication: Laughing Pig (short stories), 1984. Recreation: walking abroad. Address: (h.) Windhover House, Woodmuir Crescent, Newport-on-Tay, Fife; T.-0382 543192.

Reiach, Alan, OBE, RIBA, RSA, RSW. Architect; b. 2.3.10, London; m., Patricia Anne; 1 s.; 1 d. Educ. Edinburgh Academy; Edinburgh College of Art. Apprenticed to Sir Robert Lorimer; Travelling Scholarship to USA, 1935-36; worked in office of Robert Atkinson, London, 1936-37; Architect Planner, Scottish Office, 1940-46; ran own practice, 1949-65; joined Eric Hall & Partners, 1965; retired, 1975; Consultant, 1975-80. Publication: Building Scotland (Co-author), 1940.

Recreation: painting. Address: (b.) Messrs Reiach & Hall, 6 Darnaway Street, Edinburgh; T.-031-225 8444.

Reid, Rev. Albert Brown, BSc, BD. Minister, Trinity Parish Church, Dundee, since 1981; b. 19.1.40, Monifieth, Angus; m., Mary McDonald Pattie; 1 s.; 2 d. Educ. Grove Academy, Broughty Ferry; St. Andrews University; New College, Edinburgh. Assistant, Wallacetown Parish Church, 1964-66; Minister: Cairns Church, Lanark, 1966-72, Letham Kirk, Perth, 1972-81. Recreations: golf; hill-walking; photography. Address: 75 Clepington Road, Dundee; T.-0382 41930.

Reid, Alexander (Alastair) James, FIB (Scot). Senior General Manager, UK Banking, North, The Royal Bank of Scotland plc, since 1986; b. 26.8.35, Edinburgh; m., Sandra Elizabeth Johnston; 1 s.; 1 d. Educ. Kingussie Secondary School. Royal Bank of Scotland: Inspector of Branches, 1972, Assistant Superintendent of Branches (Glasgow), 1972, Manager, Glasgow, Charing Cross West, 1975, Superintendent of Branches (Edinburgh), 1978, various senior appointments, Head Office, 1979-86; President, Institute of Bankers in Scotland; Council Member, The Office of the Banking Ombudsman; Director, Scottish Agricultural Securities Corporation plc; Elder, Craigsbank Church. Recreations: gardening; sport, particularly golf, angling and curling. Address: (b.) 42 St. Andrew Square, Edinburgh, EH2 2YE; T.-031-556 8555.

Reid, Alexander Donaldson, MA (Edin), MA (Oxon). Principal, Newbattle Abbey College, since 1974; b. 26.10.26, Leith; m., Gudrun Naima Sigbritt Andersson; 1 s.; 1 d. Educ. Niddrie Marischal School; Newbattle Abbey College; Edinburgh University; Oxford University. Laboratory Assistant, Edinburgh University, 1941-42; Sales Assistant, G. & J. Paton, 1942-44; Parachute Regiment, 1944-48; Warehouseman, Thomson & Brown Brothers Ltd., 1948-53; Research Assistant, Department of Sociology, LSE, 1959-60; Staff Tutor (Philosophy and Political Theory), Newbattle Abbey College, 1960-74. Recreations: hill-walking; reading; listening to music; film. Address: (h.) Principal's Residence, Newbattle Abbey College, Dalkeith, Midlothian, EH22 3LL; T.-031-663 5568.

Reid, Daniel, MD, FRCPGlas, FFCM, DPH. Consultant, Communicable Diseases (Scotland) Unit, since 1969; Honorary Lecturer, Department of Infectious Diseases, Glasgow University, since 1969; b. 5.2.35, Glasgow; m., Eileen Simpson; 2 d. Educ. Allan Glen's School, Glasgow; Glasgow University. House Surgeon, Victoria Infirmary, Glasgow; House Physician, Southern General Hospital, Glasgow; House Surgeon, Stobhill Hospital, Glasgow; Lt./Captain, Royal Army Medical Corps (attached Royal Northumberland Fusiliers, Hong Kong); Registrar, University Department of Infectious Diseases, Ruchill Hospital, Glasgow; Senior Registrar, Epidemiological Research Laboratory, London. Forbes Fellow, Fairfield Hospital, Melbourne, 1982; Chairman, Advisory Group on Infection, Scottish Health Services Planning Council; Chairperson, Whooping Cough Vaccine Sub-Committee, Medical Research Council. Address: (b.) Communicable Diseases (Scotland) Unit, Ruchill Hospital, Glasgow, G20; T.-041-946 7120.

Reid, David C., MA, MEd. Rector, Kinross High School, since 1985; b. 4.9.43, Motherwell; m., Alison W. Ewing; 1 s.; 1 d. Educ. Wishaw High School; Glasgow University; Jordanhill College; Edinburgh University. Teacher of English, Kirkcaldy High School, 1966-71; Principal Teacher of English, Currie High School, 1971-80; Assistant Rector, Inverkeithing High School, 1980-85. Member/Chairman, English Panel, Scottish Examination Board, 1976-82; Member, IBA Educational Advisory Council (Schools Panels), 1975-86; Chairman, Joint Working Party (English "S" Grade), 1982-83. Recreations: hill-walking; angling; conversation; reading; Scottish traditional architecture. Address: (b.) Kinross High School, Kinross, Kinross-shire, KY13 7AW; T.-0577 62430.

Reid, David James Glover, BSc. Resident Director, Scotland and North of England, IBM United Kingdom Ltd., since 1985; b. 14.8.36, Edinburgh; m., Norma Scott Elder Chalmers; 2 s. Educ. Royal High School, Edinburgh; Edinburgh University. Joined IBM UK Ltd. at Development Laboratory, Winchester; worked in UK and USA; appointed Laboratory Operations Manager, 1983. Member: Scottish Economic Council, Public Policy Committee of Scottish Council (Development and Industry), Scottish Council for Research in Education; Chairman, Executive, Scottish Enterprise Foundation; Member, Executive, SCOTBIC; Director, Edinburgh Chamber of Commerce; Director, Board, Edinburgh Venture and Enterprise Trust; Member, Scottish Committee, Association of Business Sponsorship of the Arts. Address: (b.) 21 St. Andrew Square, Edinburgh; T.-031-556 9292.

Reid, Gavin Clydesdale, MA, MSc, PhD. Senior Lecturer in Economics, Edinburgh University, since 1984; b. 25.8.46, Glasgow; m., 1, Margaret Morrice (m. diss.); 1 s.; 1 step-s.; 2, Maureen Johnson or Bagnall; 1 d.; 1 step.-s. Educ. Frimley and Camberley Grammar School; Aberdeen University; Southampton University; Edinburgh University. Lecturer in Economics, Edinburgh University, 1971-84; Visiting Associate Professor: Queen's University, Ontario, 1981-82, Denver University, Colorado, 1984; Visiting Scholar, Darwin College, Cambridge, 1987-88. Review Editor, 1981-87, Editorial Board, since 1986, Scottish Journal of Political Economy. Publications: The Kinked Demand Curve Analysis of Oligopoly, 1981; Theories of Industrial Organization, 1987; The Small Entrepreneurial Firm (Co-author), 1988. Recreations: music; reading; running; badminton. Address: (b.) Department of Economics, Edinburgh University, George Square, Edinburgh, EH8 9JY; T.-031-667 1011.

Reid, Very Rev. George Thomson Henderson, MC, MA, BD, DD. Minister, Church of Scotland; b. 31.3.10, Leith; m., Anne Guilland Watt; 3 s.; 1 d. Educ. George Watson's Boys College, Edinburgh; Edinburgh University and New College. Minister: Cockenzie, 1935-38, Juniper Green, Edinburgh, 1938-49; Chaplain to the Forces: 3rd

Bn., Scots Guards, 1940-44, Senior Chaplain, 15 (5) Division, 1944-45; awarded MC, 1945; Minister: Claremont Church, Glasgow, 1949-55, West Church of St. Andrew, Aberdeen, 1955-75; awarded Doctorate of Divinity by Aberdeen University, 1971; Chaplain to the Queen, 1972; Moderator, General Assembly, Church of Scotland, 1973-74. Recreations: golf; water-colour painting. Address: (h.) 33 Westgarth Avenue, Edinburgh, EH13 OBB; T.-031-441 1299.

Reid, Harry William, BA (Hons). Deputy Editor, Glasgow Herald, since 1983; b. 23.9.47, Glasgow; m., Julie Davidson (qv); 1 d. Educ. Aberdeen Grammar School; Fettes College; Oxford University. The Scotsman: Education Correspondent, 1973-77, Features Editor, 1977-81; Sports Editor, Sunday Standard, 1981-82; Executive Editor, Glasgow Herald, 1982-83. Recreations: reading; walking; supporting Aberdeen Football Club. Address: (h.) 15 Albion Buildings, Ingram Street, Glasgow; T.-041-552 8403.

Reid, Jimmy. Journalist and Broadcaster; b. 1932. Former Engineer; prominent in campaign to save Upper Clyde Shipbuilders; former Convener of Shop Stewards, AUEW; former (Communist) Member, Clydebank Town Council; joined Labour Party and contested Dundee East, General Election, 1979; Rector, Glasgow University, 1971-74; Columnist, Daily Record, then The Sun.

Reid, John, BA, PhD. MP (Labour), Motherwell North, since 1987; b. 8.5.47; m.; 2 s. Educ. St. Patrick's Senior Secondary School, Coatbridge; Stirling University. Scottish Research Officer, Labour Party, 1979-83; Political Adviser to Rt. Hon. Neil Kinnock, 1983-85; Scottish Organiser, Trade Unionists for Labour, 1985-87.

Reid, Rev. John Kelman Sutherland, CBE, TD, MA, DD. Member, Editorial Board, Scottish Journal of Theology, since 1948; Member, Church of Scotland Board of World Mission and Unity, since 1961; b. 31.3.10, Leith; m., Margaret Winifrid Brookes. Educ. George Watson's College, Edinburgh; Edinburgh University; Heidelberg University; Basel University; Marburg University; Strasburg University. Professor of Philosophy, Calcutta University, 1935-37; Minister, Craigmillar Park Parish Church, Edinburgh, 1939-52; Chaplain to the Forces with Parachute Regiment, 1942-46; Professor of Theology, Leeds University, 1952-61; Chaplain, Territorial Army, 1948-62; Professor of Systematic Theology, Aberdeen University, 1961-76. Publications: Calvin's Theological Treatises (Editor and Translator), 1954; The Biblical Doctrine of the Ministry, 1955; The Authority of Scripture, 1957; Calvin's Concerning the Eternal Predestination of God (Editor and Translator), 1961; Our Life in Christ, 1963; Presbyterians and Unity, 1966; Christian Apologetics, 1969. Recreation: golf. Address: (h.) 8 Abbotsford Court, 18 Colinton Road, Edinburgh, EH10 5EH; T.-031-447 6855.

Reid, Professor John Low, MA, DM, FRCP. Regius Professor of Materia Medica, Glasgow University, since 1978; Consultant Physician, Stobhill Hospital, since 1978; Visiting Professor, Strathclyde University, since 1983; b. 1.10.43, Glasgow; m., Randa Pharaon; 1 s.; 1 d. Educ. Fettes College; Oxford University. MRC Research Fellow, Royal Post Graduate Medical School, London, 1970-73; Travelling Fellow, US National Institutes of Health, Washington, USA, 1973-75; Senior Wellcome Fellow in Clinical Science and Reader in Clinical Pharmacology, Royal Post Graduate Medical School, London, 1975-78. Publications: Lecture Notes in Clinical Pharmacology (Co-author); Clinical Science, 1982-84 (Editor); Handbook of Hypertension (Editor). Recreation: gardening. Address: (b.) Stobhill Hospital, Glasgow; T.-041-558 0111.

Reid, Rev. Martin Robertson Betsworth Coutts. Minister, Falkirk West, since 1968; b. 7.10.28, Dundee; m., Alison Thomson Gordon; 2 s.; 1 d. Educ. Stobswell Central Junior Secondary School, Dundee; Dundee College of Art; St. Andrews University; London University. Piano technician, 1943-55; Minister, Strathy and Halladale, 1960-68. Serves on various voluntary and charitable bodies. Recreations: reading; music; walking; woodwork; gardening; administration. Address: West Manse, 38 Camelon Road, Falkirk, FK1 5JH; T.-0324 23242.

Reid, Patricia Maureen, BL. Member and Director, Scottish Community Education Council, since 1988; b. 29.8.39, Glasgow; m., Graham Douglas Melville Reid; 1 s.; 1 d. Educ. Laurel Bank School, Glasgow; Glasgow University. Qualified as Solicitor, 1961; employed as an Assistant in private practice (part-time, since 1974). Former Adult Leader Trainer, The Girl Guides Association; County Commissioner, City of Glasgow Girl Guides, 1979-82; Scottish Chief Commissioner, 1982-87. Address: (h.) 64 Crown Road North, Glasgow, G12 9HW; T.-041-357 1351.

Reid, Robert Cameron Birnie, BA, CA. Local Senior Partner, Deloitte Haskins & Sells, Aberdeen, since 1980; Chairman, Aberdeen Fund Managers Ltd., since 1984; b. 23.1.28, Aberdeen; m., Pauline; 2 s.; 3 d. Educ. Loretto School; Clare College, Cambridge. National Service, TA; Captain, Royal Corps of Signals; De Zoete & Gorton, Stock Exchange, 1952-53; Price Waterhouse, Toronto, 1953-54; Partner, Meston & Co., CA, Deloitte Haskins & Sells, since 1955. Member, Queen's Bodyguard for Scotland (Royal Company of Archers); Secretary, Aberdeen Squash Racquets Club. Recreations: tennis; skiing; squash. Address: (b.) 6 Golden Square, Aberdeen, AB9 1JB; T.-0224 636555.

Reid, Thomas Shaw Lindsay, CA. Secretary, Shirlaw Allan & Co. Ltd., since 1970; Member, Lanarkshire Health Board, since 1983; b. 16.11.25, Wishaw; m., Rita Mildred Aldred Acum; 2 s.; 1 d. Educ. Hamilton Academy. Apprentice, Thomson McLintock & Co., CA, 1941-43 and 1947-50; RNVR (Sub-Lt. (A)), 1944-47; Peat Marwick Mitchell & Co., CA, 1951-54; Director, G. Brazil & Co. Ltd., 1954-70. Recreation: Motherwell FC spectator. Address: (h.) 26 Rosefield Gardens, Uddingston, G71 7AW.

Reid, William Kennedy, CB, MA. Secretary, Scottish Home and Health Department, since 1984; Chairman of Governors, Scottish Police College; b. 1931, Aberdeen; m., Ann Campbell; 2 s.; 1 d. Educ. George Watson's College; Edinburgh University; Trinity College, Cambridge. Ministry of Education, 1956; Cabinet Office, 1964; Department of Education and Science, 1967; Scottish Office, 1978. Address: (b.) St. Andrews House, Edinburgh; T.-031-556 8400.

Reid, Sheriff William Macpherson, MA, LLB. Sheriff of Tayside, Central and Fife, since 1983; b. 6.4.38; m.; 3 d. Educ. Elgin Academy; Aberdeen University; Edinburgh University. Admitted Advocate, 1963; Sheriff of Lothian and Borders, 1978; Sheriff of Glasgow and Strathkelvin, 1978-83.

Reilly, James, MA, MEd. Principal, Langside College, since 1985; b. 19.4.28, Bellshill; m., Jean Hanlon; 3 s.; 3 d. Educ. St. Mungo's Academy, Glasgow; Glasgow University. Subaltern Infantry, Egypt and Eritrea, 1946-48; Teacher, primary and secondary schools, Glasgow, 1952-58; Ellis Robins High School, Salisbury, Rhodesia, 1958-63; St. Patrick's High School, Coatbridge, 1964; Lecturer and Senior Lecturer, Barmulloch College, 1964-70; Langside College: Head of Department, 1970-84, Depute Principal, 1984-85. Chairman, National Working Party on Special Educational Needs Provision in Further Education, 1987-88; Vice-Chairman, Joint Management Committee, West of Scotland Scheme, Certificate in Social Service; Member: Central Council for Education and Training in Social Work Interim Planning Group (Scotland), Scottish Nursery Nurse Board, Scottish Retirement Council Executive Committee, Glasgow School of Occupational Therapy Advisory Committee. Recreations: golf; music. Address: (b.) Langside College, 50 Prospecthill Road, Glasgow, G42 9LB; T.-041-649 4991.

Reilly, Patrick, MA (Hons), BLitt. Senior Lecturer, Department of English Literature, Glasgow University, since 1964; b. 6.1.32, Glasgow; m., Rose Fitzpatrick; 3 s.; 3 d. Educ. St. Mungo's Academy, Glasgow; Glasgow University. Civil Servant, 1948-50; National Service, RAEC, 1950-52; storeman, labourer, clerk, lamplighter, salesman, 1952-57; Glasgow University, 1957-61; Luke Fellowship, Pembroke College, Oxford, 1961-63; Assistant Lecturer, then Lecturer, Glasgow University, 1964-81. Member, Catholic Education Commission of Scotland, since 1977 (Chairman, Adult Education Committee, since 1983). Publications: Jonathan Swift: The Brave Desponder, 1982; George Orwell: The Age's Adversary, 1985; The Literature of Guilt: from Gulliver to Golding, 1988; Nineteen Eighty-Four: Orwell's Tocsin, 1988; Scottish Catholicism (Contributor), 1979; Fielding: A Collection of Essays (Contributor), 1985. Recreation: football. Address: (h.) 7 Arundel Drive, Bishopbriggs, Glasgow, G64 3JF; T.-041-772 2320.

Reith, David Stewart, LLB, NP, WS. Partner, Lindsays WS, Solicitors, Edinburgh, since 1976; b. 15.4.51, Edinburgh. Educ. Edinburgh Academy; Fettes College; Aberdeen University. Director, Scottish Historic Buildings Trust, since 1985; Secretary: Lothian Building Preservation Trust, since 1984, Ponton House Association, Edinburgh, since 1982; Honorary Solicitor, Architectural Heritage Society of Scotland. Recreations: curling; swimming; photography; wine. Address: (h.) The Studio, 1 Ravelston Park, Edinburgh, EH4 3DX; T.-031-343 2341.

Reith, Fiona Lennox, LLB, WS. Advocate, since 1983; b. 17.7.55, Ipswich; m., David Stewart Reith (qv). Educ. St. Dorothy's Convent, Malta; Perth Academy; Aberdeen University. Solicitor, 1979-82. Recreations: film and theatre-going; eating out; travel; photography. Address: (h.) 12 Clarendon Crescent, Edinburgh; T.-031-332 6401.

Renfrew, Rt. Rev. Charles McDonald, PhL, STL. Assistant Bishop in Glasgow (Titular See Abula), since 1977; b. 21.6.29, Glasgow. Educ. St. Aloysius College, Glasgow; Scots College, Rome; Gregorian University, Rome. Ordained Priest in Rome, 1953; Assistant Priest, Immaculate Conception, Glasgow, 1953-56; Professor of English and Music, and Bursar, St. Mary's College, Blairs, 1956; first Rector, St. Vincent's College, Langbank, 1961; Chaplain to Sisters of Notre Dame, Glasgow, and Vicar General of Glasgow, 1974; ordained Titular Bishop of Abula, 1977; Head, Commission for Pastoral and Social Care, since 1984; Member, Kidney Research Committee Scotland and Second Chance Committee Scotland. Publications: St. Vincent's Prayer Book; Rambling Through Life; Pageant of Holiness. Recreations: classical music; history of Glasgow. Address: 38 Mansionhouse Road, Glasgow, G41; T.-041-649 2228.

Renfrew, Norman, LDS, BChD, JP. Member, Scottish Tourist Board, since 1986; Member, Council, Scottish Special Housing Association, since 1985; North of Scotland Representative, British Dental Association, since 1987; Chairman, Tayside General Dental Practitioners Committee, since 1986; b. 9.6.37, Greenock; m., Dr. Margaret Hodson; 1 s.; 2 d. Educ. Greenock High School; Leeds University. Councillor, Perth Town Council, Perth and Kinross District Council, 1968-84; Provost, Perth and Kinross District, 1977-80; Chairman, Perthshire Tourist Board, 1983-87. Recreations: car restoration; water skiing. Address: (h.) East Lodge, Barnhill, Perth, PH2 7AT; T.-Perth 21097.

Rennie, Archibald Louden, CB, BSc. Chancellor's Assessor, St. Andrews University, since 1985; Vice-Chairman, Advisory Committee on Distinction Awards, since 1985; Member, Council on Tribunals, and its Scottish Committee, since 1987; b. 4.6.24, Guardbridge, Fife; m., Kathleen Harkess; 4 s. Educ. Madras College, St. Andrews; St. Andrews University. Experimental Officer, Minesweeping Research Division, 1944-47; joined Department of Health for Scotland, 1947; Private Secretary to Secretary of State for Scotland, 1962-63; Assistant Secretary, Scottish Home and Health Department, 1963-69; Registrar General for Scotland, 1969-73; Under Secretary, Scottish Economic Planning Department, 1973-77;

Secretary, Scottish Home and Health Department, 1977-84. Chairman, Blacket Association, 1971-73. Recreations: sailing; sea-fishing; gardening; walking; bird-watching. Address: (h.) Baldinnie, 10 Park Place, Elie, Leven, KY9 1DH; T.-0333 330741.

Rennie, Brenda Louise, LLB, NP. Solicitor; Partner, Balfour & Manson, Edinburgh, since 1976; b. 21.12.47, Aberdeen; m., Donald G. Rennie, WS. Educ. Aberdeen Academy; Aberdeen University. Qualified as Solicitor, 1971; Chairman, Finance Committee, Girl Guides Association (Scotland); Member, UK Finance Committee, Girl Guides Association. Recreations: travel; architecture; history; literature. Address: (h.) 7 Blinkbonny Crescent, Edinburgh, EH4 3NB; T.-031-332 3046; (b.) 58 Frederick Street, Edinburgh, EH2 1LS; T.-031-225 8291.

Rennie, Frank William, BSc (Hons), PhD. President, Scottish Crofters Union, since 1985; Scientific Officer, Nature Conservancy Council, since 1985; part-time Earth Science Tutor, Open University, since 1983; b. 18.4.57, Stirling; m., Agnes Gillies. Educ. Alva Academy; Aberdeen University. Liaison Officer, Crofters Commission, since 1986; Member, Scottish Training Committee, Agricultural Training Board, since 1987; Fellow, Arkleton Trust, since 1986. Publications: several books on birds. Recreations: hill-walking; ornithology; skiing; reading. Address: 25 South Galson, Isle of Lewis; T.-0851 85 429.

Rennie, James Alexander Norris, MD, FRCP. Consultant Physician (Rheumatology), since 1979; b. 28.1.47, Dunfermline; m., Margaret; 2 s.; 1 d. Educ. Dunfermline High School; Aberdeen University. Lecturer, Department of Medicine, Aberdeen University, 1973-76; Senior Registrar, General Medicine/Rheumatology, Glasgow, 1976-79. Recreations: DIY; china painting; football. Address: (h.) 13 Belvidere Street, Aberdeen, AB2 4QS; T.-Aberdeen 632172.

Rennie, Rev. James Benjamin, MA. Minister, Leochel Cushnie and Lynturk linked with Tough, since 1983; b. 27.9.33, Craigellachie, Banffshire; m., Margaret Gordon Pirie; 1 s. Educ. Banff Academy; Aberdeen University and Christ's College. Assistant Minister, St. Andrew's Parish Church, Dundee, 1958-59; Minister: Kinlochleven, 1959-67, Blackford, Perthshire, 1967-83. Address: The Manse, Muir of Fowlis, Alford, Aberdeenshire, AB3 8JU; T.-Muir of Fowlis 239.

Rennie, James Stark, BDS, PhD, FDSRCPS, MRCPath. Consultant Oral Pathologist, since 1983; Senior Lecturer, Glasgow University, since 1984; b. 22.5.49, Glasgow; m., Ann Maris Campbell; 2 s. Educ. Coatbridge High School; Glasgow University. Two years as a House Officer, Glasgow Dental Hospital; awarded three year MRC Research Fellowship; Lecturer, Department of Oral Medicine and Pathology, Glasgow University, 1977; Melbourne University Scholarship, 1980; returned to UK, 1982, as Lecturer, Glasgow University; appointed Consultant in Oral Pathology, Glasgow Dental Hospital; Deacon, Incorporation of Skinners of Glasgow, 1986-87. Recreations: golf; squash; fishing. Address: (h.) Southview, 12 Station Road, Balfron, G63 OSY.

Rennie, Professor Michael John, BSc, MSc, PhD. Professor and Head, Department of Physiology, Dundee University, since 1983; Secretary, SIRCO Ltd., since 1985; b. 28.7.46, Wallsend on Tyne; m., Anne MacGregor Gill; 1 s.; 2 d. Educ. Royal Grammar School, Newcastle-upon-Tyne; Hull University; Manchester University; Glasgow University. Research Assistant, Department of Neurology, Glasgow University, 1970-74; MRC Travelling Fellow and Instructor, Washington University, St. Louis, 1974-76; Muscular Dystrophy Association of America Fellow and Instructor, Washington University, 1976-77; Lecturer in Human Metabolism, School of Medicine, University College, London, 1977-79; Wellcome Senior Lecturer, Department of Medicine, University College, London, 1979-83. Member, Editorial Boards: Clinical Science, Medicine in Science and Sports, European Journal of Applied Physiology, European Journal of Clinical Investigation; Editor, Intensive Therapy and Clinical Monitoring; Director, SIRCO Ltd. Recreations: reading; outdoor pursuits; working with hands; cooking. Address: (b.) Department of Physiology, The University, Dundee, DD1 4HN; T.-0382 23181, Ext. 4572.

Rennie, Robert, LLB, PhD. Partner, Ballantyne & Copland, Solicitors, Motherwell, since 1972; b. 30.6.47, Glasgow; m., Catherine Mary; 1 s.; 3 d. Educ. Lenzie Academy; Glasgow University. Apprentice then Legal Assistant, Bishop Milne Boyd & Co., Solicitors, Glasgow; joined Ballantyne & Copland as Legal Assistant, 1971; Member, Law Society of Scotland Conveyancing Committee; Trustee, Lanarkshire Spastics Association; Member, Glasgow Presbytery. Recreation: classical music. Address: (b.) Torrance House, Knowetop, Motherwell, ML1 2AF; T.-0698 66200.

Renton, Rev. Ian Paterson, OStJ, FSA Scot, JP. Minister, St. Colm's Parish Kirk, Dalry, Edinburgh, since 1966; b. 22.3.26, Kirkcaldy; m., Ann Gordon Mutter Macpherson; 2 s.; 1 d. Educ. Sinclairtown and Viewforth Schools, Kirkcaldy; Newbattle Abbey College; Glasgow University; St. Mary's College, St. Andrews. Shipping Clerk, Robert Wemyss & Co., Kirkcaldy, 1941-44; Sergeant, 3rd Bn., Scots Guards, 1944-47; Ministry of Labour, Kirkcaldy, 1947-48; Newbattle Abbey College, 1948-50; Youth Clubs Organiser, Roxburghshire, 1950-53; divinity studies, 1953-58; Assistant Minister, North Kirk, Aberdeen, 1958-60; Minister, St. Mark's Church, Greenwich, London, 1960-66. Member, Edinburgh City Education Committee, 1970-76; Governor: Moray House College, 1971-79, Donaldson's School, Edinburgh, 1972-75, Newbattle Abbey College, 1973-76; Member, General Assembly Committee on Education, 1973-79; Joint Chairman, Scottish Joint Committee on Religious Education, 1974-79; Member, Lothian Region Education Committee, 1977-78; Member, Edinburgh Children's Panel, 1971-74; Executive Member, Broadcasting Council, Radio Forth, 1976-79; Member, DHSS Social Security Tribunal, 1978-84; Member, Church of Scotland Board of Education, 1983-85; Member, Committee on Medical Ethics, Lothian Health Board, since 1984; regular Contributor, BBC, STV, Radio Forth, since 1973. Recreations: climbing; golfing; gardening; drystane diking;

archaeological excavation, Byzantine site, Shelomi, Israel. Address: 1 Merchiston Gardens, Edinburgh, EH10 5DD; T.-031-337 1107.

Renton, Joan Forrest, DA, RSW. President, Scottish Society of Women Artists, since 1988; Vice President, Scottish Arts Club, since 1988; Member, Council, Scottish Artists Benevolent Fund, since 1986; b. 11.8.35; m., Ronald Renton; 2 s.; 1 d. Educ. Dumfries Academy; Shawlands Academy, Glasgow; Hawick High School; Edinburgh College of Art. Practising artist, painting in watercolours and oils; Teacher of Art, Lothian Region, until 1983. Recreations: painting; gardening. Address: (h.) 9 Lennox Row, Trinity, Edinburgh, EH5 3JP; T.-031-552 1209.

Renton, John B., MBE. General Secretary, Scottish Prison Officers' Association, since 1971; b. 7.6.32, Coldsteam; m., A. Marie; 5 s. Educ. Coldstream and Kelso High School. Police Constable, Edinburgh City Police, 1952-58; Scottish Prison Service: Prison Officer, Saughton, 1959-62, Clerk Officer, Barlinnie, 1962-65, Clerk Officer, Dumfries, 1965-67, Principal Clerk Officer, 1967-71. Address: (b.) 21 Calder Road, Edinburgh; T.-031-443 8105.

Renton, Stuart, MBE, ARSA, DA, FRIBA, ARIAS. Architect; Senior Partner, Reiach and Hall, since 1982; b. 15.9.29, Edinburgh; m., Ethnie; 1 s.; 1 d. Educ. Royal High School, Edinburgh; Edinburgh College of Art. Military Service, RAF and RAFVR; Partner, Alan Reiach and Partners, 1957; Partner, Reiach and Hall, 1965; External Examiner, several universities; Assessor for architectural awards schemes; Governor, Edinburgh College of Art, 1985. Recreations: skiing; game fishing. Address: (b.) 6 Darnaway Street, Edinburgh, EH3 6BG; T.-031-225 8444.

Renwick, Professor John Peter, MA, PhD, DLitt. Professor of French, Edinburgh University, since 1980; b. 25.5.39, Gillingham; m., Claudette Gorse; 1 s.; 1 d. Educ. Gillingham Grammar School; St. Bartholomew's Grammar School, Newbury; St. Catherine's College, Oxford; Sorbonne; British Institute in Paris (Leverhulme Research Scholar). Assistant Lecturer, then Lecturer, Glasgow University, 1964-66; Fellow, Churchill College, Cambridge, 1966-72; Maitre de Conferences Associe, Departement de Francais, Universite de Clermont-Ferrand, 1970-71, 1972-74; Professor of French, New University of Ulster, 1974-80 (Pro-Vice-Chancellor, 1978-80). Publications: La destinee posthume de Jean-Francois Marmontel, 1972; Marmontel, Memoires, 1972; Marmontel, Voltaire and the Belisaire affair, 1974; Marmontel, Correspondence, 1974; Catalogue de la bibliotheque de Jean-Baptiste Massillon, 1977; Voltaire et Morangies, ou les Lumieres l'ont echappe belle, 1982; Chamfort Devant La Posterite, 1986; Catalogue de la Bibliotheque du Comte D'Espinchal, 1987. Address: 4 Buccleuch Place, Edinburgh, EH8 2LW; T.-031-667 1011.

Rettie, James Philip, CBE, TD. Chairman, Sea Fish Industry Authority, 1981-87; Trustee: Scottish Civic Trust, since 1982; Farmer; b. 7.12.26, Dundee; m., 1 Helen Grant; 2, Diana Harvey; 2 s.; 1 d. Educ. Trinity College, Glenalmond. Royal Engineers, 1945-48; William Low & Co. PLC, 1948-85 (Chairman, 1980-85); Honorary Col., 227 (ADR) Field Squadron, RE, TAVR, since 1984. Recreations: shooting; gardening; hill-walking. Address: (h.) Wester Ballindean, Inchture, Perthshire, PH14 9QS; T.-082 886 337.

Reynolds, Adrian, DipRADA. Artistic Director, Byre Theatre, St. Andrews, since 1981; b. 3.5.43, Leeds; m., Marion Anne; 2 d. Educ. King Edward's School, Birmingham; Royal Academy of Dramatic Art. Ten years an Actor, two of which at the Mermaid Theatre, one in Vivat! Vivat Regina!, London; Assistant Director, Civic Theatre, Chelmsford, 1969-70; Associate Director, Salisbury Playhouse, 1974-77; Theatre Director, Manitou-Wabing Theatre, Ontario, 1977-79; Guest Director: Nuffield Theatre, Southampton, 1978-79, Lyceum, Edinburgh, 1980, Scarborough, 1981-82. Recreations: supporting Manchester United; writing; walking four dogs. Address: (h.) 2 Woodpark Cottages, Ceres, Fife, KY15 5QU; T.-0334 82 445.

Rhind, William, MA (Hons), BSc. Honorary Sheriff, Grampian, Highlands and Islands; b. 11.9.07, Inverurie; m., Georgia L. Ollason; 1 d. Educ. Inverurie Academy; Aberdeen University; Aberdeen Teacher Training College. Anderson High School, Lerwick: Principal Teacher of Mathematics, 1931-47, Deputy Headmaster, 1947-52, Headmaster, 1952-70. Recreations: bridge; music; reading; angling. Address: (h.) Kelda, 6 Lovers Loan, Lerwick, Shetland; T.-0595 2238.

Rhodes, Joseph, MA (Hons). Rector, Dunoon Grammar School, since 1981; b. 9.12.45, Irvine; m., Ann T. Robertson; 3 s.; 3 d. Educ. Ayr Academy; Glasgow University; Jordanhill College. Assistant Teacher (History), Kilmarnock Academy, 1969-71; Principal Teacher of History, Auchenharvie Academy, 1971-74; Assistant Rector, Garnock Academy, Kilbirnie, 1974-77; Depute Rector, Oban High School, 1977-81. Address: (h.) Firbank, North Campbell Road, Innellan, Argyll; T.-Innellan 387.

Riach, Rev. Donald, BL. Minister, St. Peter's Church, Thurso, since 1965; b. 25.6.36, London; m., Jean Blyth; 3 s.; 1 d. Educ. Newcastle Royal Grammar School; St. Andrews University; Edinburgh University. National Service, 1955-57; Assistant Minister, Newbattle Parish Church, 1963-65. Vice President, Thurso Bible Society. Recreation: walking. Address: 46 Rose Street, Thurso, Caithness, KW14 7HN; T.-Thurso 62456.

Richards, Professor Bryan Edward, BSc, DIC, PhD, CEng, FRAeS, AFAIAA. Mechan Professor of Engineering and Head, Department of Aeronautics and Fluid Mechanics, Glasgow University, since 1980 (Dean of Engineering, 1984-87); b. 30.6.38, Hornchurch, Essex; m., Margaret Dorothy Owen; 2 s.; 2 d. Educ. Palmer's School, Grays, Essex; Queen Mary College, London University. Aerodynamicist, Aircraft, Bristol Aeroplane Company, 1960-62; Research Assistant, Hypersonic Aerodynamics, Department of Aeronautics, Imperial College, 1962-66; Assistant Professor, Associate Professor, then Professor, Von Karman Institute for Fluid Dynamics, Rhode-St-Genese, Belgium, 1966-79. Recreations: sailing;

walking. Address: (b.) Department of Aeronautics and Fluid Mechanics, James Watt Building, Glasgow University, Glasgow, G12 8QQ; T.-041-339 8855, Ext. 4304.

Richards, Glyn, BA, BD, MA, BLitt. Senior Lecturer in Religious Studies, Stirling University, since 1976 (Head, Department of Religious Studies, since 1977); b. 6.8.23, Rhymney; m., Helga; 2 s.; 2 d. Educ. Rhymney Grammar School; University of Wales; McMaster University; Oxford University. Minister of Religion; Extra Mural Lecturer, University of Wales; Tutor, McMaster University, Canada; Lecturer, Carleton University, Ottawa; Lecturer, Stirling University; Visiting Lecturer, International Christian University, Tokyo; Founder and Editor, Scottish Journal of Religious Studies; General Editor, Themes in Comparative Religion. Publications: The Development of Theological Liberalism, 1957; The Philosophy of Gandhi, 1981; A Sourcebook of Modern Hinduism, 1984; Towards a Theology of Religions, 1988. Recreations: travel; golf; reading. Address: (b.) Department of Religious Studies, Stirling University, Stirling; T.-Stirling 73171.

Richards, John Deacon, CBE, AADip, DUniv, ARSA, RIBA, PPRIAS. Senior Consultant to Robert Matthew, Johnson-Marshall and Partners (Chairman, 1983-86); Chairman, Scottish Committee, Housing Corporation, and Board Member, Housing Corporation, since 1982; b. 7.5.31, Shanghai; m., Margaret Brown; 1 s.; 3 d. Educ. Cranleigh School, Surrey; Architectural Association School of Architecture, London. Works include Stirling University, Royal Commonwealth Pool (Edinburgh), Airport Terminals, Edinburgh and Aberdeen, buildings for IBM, Greenock, own offices, Dean Village, Edinburgh; Member, Royal Fine Art Commission for Scotland, since 1975; Agrement Board, 1980-83; Member, Williams Committee on National Museums and Galleries, 1981; Gold Medallist, RSA, 1972; Past President, Royal Incorporation of Architects in Scotland, 1983-85; Governor, Edinburgh College of Art, 1982-87; Trustee, National Galleries of Scotland, since 1986. Recreation: country life. Address: (h.) Lady's Field, Whitekirk, East Lothian; T.-Whitekirk 206.

Richards, Kenneth, BSc (Eng), CEng, FICE, FIWES, FBIM. Director of Water and Drainage, Lothian Regional Council, since 1979; b. 13.5.25, London; m., Patricia; 1 s.; 1 d. Educ. Alleynes School; London University. Various local government posts, 1946-60; Deputy Borough Engineer, Chesterfield, 1960-65; Borough Engineer, High Wycombe, 1965-73; Technical Services Officer, Wycombe District Council, 1973-79. Recreations: hill-walking; music; travel. Address: (b.) 6 Cockburn Street, Edinburgh; T.-031-229 9292.

Richardson, Geoffrey Alan, MA, PhD, CertEd, DipEd (Man). Principal, The Queen's College, Glasgow, since 1976; b. 27.7.36, Preston; m., Jill S.; 2 d. Educ. Hutton Grammar School, Lancashire; Fitzwilliam College, Cambridge; Glasgow University; Exeter University; Sheffield Polytechnic. School teaching, UK/Australia, 1959-66; Lecturer/Senior Lecturer/Warden, Edge Hill College, Lancashire, 1966-72; The Senior Tutor, Ilkley College, Yorkshire, 1972-76. Recreations: music; swimming; walking. Address: (b.) The Queen's College, Glasgow, 1 Park Drive, Glasgow, G3 6LP; T.-041-334 8141.

Richardson, Professor Jeremy John, BA (Hons), MA (Econ), PhD. Professor of Politics, Strathclyde University, since 1982; b. 15.4.42, Bridgnorth; m., Anne; 1 s.; 1 d. Educ. Wenlock Edge School; Keele University; Manchester University. Assistant Lecturer, Lecturer, Senior Lecturer and Reader in Politics, Keele University, 1966-82; Member: Economic and Social Research Council Training Board, Final Selection Board of Civil Service Commission. Publications: Campaigning for the Environment; The Policy-Making Process; Governing Under Pressure; Pressure Groups in Britain; Policy Styles in Western Europe; Unemployment: Policy Responses of Western Democracies; British Politics and Policy Process. Recreations: hill-walking; tennis; gardening. Address: (h.) 1 Duchess Park, Helensburgh, Dunbartonshire; T.-Helensburgh 5321.

Richardson, Michael John, BSc, MSc. Assistant Director and Head, Potato and Plant Health Division, Agricultural Scientific Services, Department of Agriculture and Fisheries for Scotland, since 1979; b. 10.7.38, St. Albans; m., Barbara Anne Cooper; 2 s. Educ. St. Albans County Grammar School; Nottingham University. School teacher, Ripley, Derbyshire, 1959-60; Research Associate, Trent Polytechnic, Nottingham, 1961-64; Plant Pathologist, DAFS, since 1964. Editor, Transactions of the British Mycological Society; Secretary, Scottish Gliding Union. Recreations: gliding; gardening; mycology. Address: (b.) DAFS, Agricultural Scientific Services, East Craigs, Edinburgh, EH12 8NJ; T.-031-339 2355.

Richman, John Christopher Hugh, MSc, BSc, CEng, FRIAgrE, FBIM. Chief Executive, Sea Fish Industry Authority, since 1983; b. 18.4.29, Goole; m., Joan Potts; 2 s. Educ. Hymer's College, Hull; Friends' School, Lancaster; Leeds University; Newcastle University. Managing Diretor, Ransomes (South Africa) Pty; Director, Ransomes, Sims & Jeffries Ltd.; Group Managing Director, The Gascoigne Group. President, Agricultural Engineers' Association. Recreations: sailing; fishing. Address: (h.) 2A Ainslie Place, Edinburgh, EH3 6AR; T.-031-225 8765.

Richmond, H. Anthony, MA (Oxon), PhL, STL. Headmaster, St. Aloysius' College, Glasgow, since 1977; Member, Society of Jesus (Jesuit), since 1949; Catholic Priest, since 1965; b. 7.6.31, Preston. Educ. Preston Catholic College; Heythrop College; Oxford University. First vows, 1951; Teacher: Beaumont College, Old Windsor, 1960-62 and 1966-67, Stonyhurst College, 1968-77 (Depute Headmaster, 1975-77). Recreations: travel; languages; ornithology; jogging; reading (novels, history, politics, theology); music. Address: (b.) 45 Hill Street, Glasgow, G3 6RJ; T.-041-332 3190.

Rickets, Brigadier Reginald Anthony Scott. Managing Director, Irvine Development Corporation, since 1981; Director, Ayrshire Chamber of Industries (President, 1986); Trustee, Scottish Maritime Museum (Irvine); b. 13.12.29, Weybridge; m., Elizabeth Ann Serjeant; 1 s.; 1 d. Educ. St. George's College, Weybridge; Royal

Military Academy, Sandhurst. 2nd Lt., RE, 1949; served with Airborne, Armoured and field Engineers, UK, Cyrenaica, Egypt, Malaya, Borneo, Hong Kong and BAOR; special employment military forces, Malaya, 1955-59; Staff College, Camberley, 1962; Brigade Major, BAOR, 1963-66; Gurkha Independent Field Squadron, 1966-68; Directing Staff, Army Staff College, 1968-70; Commandant, Gurkha Engineers, 1970-73; Chief of Staff, Berlin, 1973-77; Brigadier Chief Engineer, UK Land Forces, 1978-81. Recreation: sailing (DTI Ocean Skipper, RYA Coach/Examiner, Commodore REYC, 1979). Address: (b.) Irvine Development Corporation, Perceton House, Irvine, KA11 2AL; T.-0294 214100.

Ricketts, Rev. Henry Martin, MA, BD; b. 8.8.11, Dundee; m., Margaret Calthorpe Emslie; 1 s. Educ. Morgan Academy, Dundee; St. Andrews University; University of Goettingen. Member, Walker Trust Excavation Team, Istanbul, 1935-36, excavating Palace of Justinian; Minister, Craigiebuckler Parish Church, Aberdeen, 1939-81; Chairman, Royal Scottish Society for Prevention of Cruelty to Children, 1979-87. Recreations: gardening; fishing. Address: (h.) 306 Queen's Road, Aberdeen, AB1 8DT; T.-0224 315783.

Rickman, Professor Geoffrey Edwin, MA, DPhil (Oxon), FSA. Professor of Roman History, St. Andrews University, since 1981; b. 9.10.32, Cherat, India; m., Ann Rosemary Wilson; 1 s.; 1 d. Educ. Peter Symonds' School, Winchester; Brasenose College, Oxford. Junior Research Fellow, Queen's College, Oxford; St. Andrews University: Lecturer in Ancient History, Senior Lecturer, Professor; Visiting Fellow, Brasenose College, Oxford. Council Member, Society for Promotion of Roman Studies; Member, Faculty of Archaeology, History and Letters, British School at Rome (Chairman, 1984- 87). Publications: Roman Granaries and Storebuildings, 1971; The Corn Supply of Ancient Rome, 1985. Recreations: opera; swimming. Address: (h.) 56 Hepburn Gardens, St. Andrews, Fife; T.-St. Andrews 72063.

Riddell, William Thomas Carmichael, OBE, TD, MA. Member (SLD), Strathclyde Regional Council, since 1986; b. 15.4.27, Greenock; m., Elspeth Hill; 1 s.; 1 d. Educ. Fettes College; Gonville and Caius College, Cambridge. Russian interpreter, Army, 1946-48; John Hastie & Co. Ltd., Greenock: Estimator, 1951-58, Director, 1958-76; Industrial Adviser, Cumbernauld Development Corporation, 1978-84; Consultant, Cumbernauld and Kilsyth Enterprise Trust, since 1984. Vice-Chairman, Scottish Liberal Party, 1960-65; OC, 277 (A&SH) Regt. RA (TA), 1963-65; Provost of Greenock, 1968-71. Address: (h.) Muiredge, Garshangan, by Kilmacolm, PA13 4TJ; T.-0475 22971.

Riddle, Gordon Stewart, MA. Principal and Chief Ranger, Culzean Country Park, since 1976 (Deputy Administrator, Culzean Castle and Country Park, since 1982); b. 2.10.47, Kelso; m., Rosemary; 1 s.; 1 d. Educ. Kelso High School; Edinburgh University; Moray House College of Education. Biology and History Teacher, Lasswade High School, 1970-71; National Ranger Training Course, 1971-72; Ranger and Depute Principal, Culzean Country Park, 1972-75; National Park Service (USA) Training Course, 1978; Winston Churchill Travelling Fellowship, USA, 1981. Recreations: sport; gardening; birds of prey; photography; hill-walking; music; writing. Address: (h.) Swinston, Culzean Country Park, by Maybole, Ayrshire; T.-06556 662.

Riddle, Robert William, OBE. General Secretary, Royal British Legion Scotland/Earl Haig Fund (Scotland)/Officers' Association (Scottish Branch), since 1983; b. 19.1.33, Galashiels; m., Ann Mary Munro Millar; 3 d. Educ. Stonyhurst. 2nd Lt., King's Own Scottish Borderers, 1953; Staff College, 1963; Brigade Major, 157 (L) Brigade TA, Glasgow, 1964; Commanding Officer, 1st Bn., King's Own Scottish Borderers, 1971; Military Secretary, CINC BAOR, 1974; Colonel AO 3rd Armoured Division, 1977; Brigadier Scottish Division, 1980; retired, 1983. Colonel, King's Own Scottish Borderers; Member, Queen's Bodyguard for Scotland (Royal Company of Archers). Recreations: field sports; golf; tennis. Address: (h.) Old Harestanes, Blyth Bridge, West Linton, Peeblesshire, EH46 7AH; T.-07215 2255.

Ridley-Thomas, Roger. Managing Director, The Scotsman Publications Ltd., since 1984. The Scotsman Publications Ltd.: Executive Assistant, 1972-74, Assistant Managing Director, 1974-80; Managing Director, Aberdeen Journals Ltd., 1980-84. Past President, Scottish Daily Newspaper Society. Address: (b.) 20 North Bridge, Edinburgh, EH1 1YT; T.-031-225 2468.

Riemersma, Rudolph Arend, BSc, MSc, PhD. Assistant Director, Cardiovascular Research Unit, Edinburgh University, since 1975 (British Heart Foundation Senior Lecturer in Cardiac Biochemistry, since 1979); b. 9.5.43, Hengelo, Netherlands; m., Eva J. Nieuwenhuis; 1 s.; 1 d. Educ. Charlois Lyceum, Rotterdam; Leyden University; Edinburgh University. Biochemist, Department of Cardiology, Academic Hospital, Utrecht; postgraduate research, Royal Postgraduate Medical School, Hammersmith Hospital, London; Research Fellow, Edinburgh University, 1973. Former Vice-President, European Society of Clinical Investigation. Recreations: athletics; skiing; hill-walking; botany. Address: (b.) Cardiovascular Research Unit, Hugh Robson Building, George Square, Edinburgh; T.-031-667 1011.

Rifkind, Malcolm Leslie, QC, LLB, MSc. Secretary of State for Scotland, since 1986; MP (Conservative), Edinburgh Pentlands, since 1974; Minister of State, Foreign and Commonwealth Office, 1983-86; b. 21.6.46, Edinburgh; m., Edith Amalia Steinberg; 1 s.; 1 d. Educ. George Watson's College, Edinburgh; Edinburgh University. Lecturer, University of Rhodesia, 1967-68; called to Scottish Bar, 1970; Opposition Front-Bench Spokesman on Scottish Affairs, 1975-76; Member, Select Committee on European Secondary Legislation, 1975-76; Chairman, Scottish Conservatives' Devolution Committee, 1976; Joint Secretary, Conservative Parliamentary Foreign and Commonwealth Affairs Committee, 1977-79; Member, Select Committee on Overseas Development, 1978-79; Parliamentary Under-Secretary of State, Scottish Office, 1979-82; Parliamentary Under-Secretary of State, Foreign and Commonwealth Office, 1982-83. Address: (b.) House of Commons, London, SW1.

Ripley, Professor Brian David, MA, PhD, FSS. Professor of Statistics, Strathclyde University, since 1983; b. 29.4.52, Farnborough, Hampshire; m., Ruth Mary Appleton. Educ. Farnborough Grammar School; Churchill College, Cambridge. Lecturer, then Reader in Statistics, Imperial College, London University, 1976-83. Member, International Statistical Institute; Member, International Council for Bird Preservation. Publications: Spatial Statistics; Stochastic Simulation. Recreations: natural history; walking; photography. Address: (b.) Department of Mathematics, Strathclyde University, 26 Richmond Street, Glasgow, G1 1XH; T.-041-552 4400.

Risk, Sheriff Douglas James. Sheriff of Grampian, Highland and Islands, at Aberdeen, since 1979; b. 23.1.41; m.; 3 s.; 1 d. Educ. Glasgow Academy; Gonville and Caius College, Cambridge; Glasgow University. Admitted Advocate, 1966; Sheriff of Lothian and Borders, at Edinburgh, 1977-79.

Risk, Sir Thomas Neilson, BL, LLD (Glasgow), FRSE; b. 13.9.22, Glasgow; m., Suzanne Eiloart; 4 s. Educ. Kelvinside Academy, Glasgow; Glasgow University. Flight Lt., RAF, 1941-46; RAFVR, 1946-53; Partner, Maclay, Murray & Spens, Solicitors, 1950-81; Governor, Bank of Scotland, since 1981; Director, Shell UK Ltd., since 1982; Chairman, Scottish Financial Enterprise, since 1986; Director, MSA (Britain) Ltd., since 1958; Director, Standard Life Assurance Company, 1965-88 (Chairman, 1969-77); Director, Howden Group, 1971-87; Director, Merchants Trust, since 1973; Director, British Linen Bank Limited (Governor, 1977-86); Director, Barclays Bank, 1983-85; Member, Scottish Industrial Development Board, 1972-75; Member, Scottish Economic Planning Council, since 1983. Trustee, Hamilton Bequest. Recreation: golf. Address: (h.) 10 Belford Place, Edinburgh, EH4 3DH.

Ritchie, Alastair Newton Bethune. Member, Stirling District Council, since 1977; b. 30.4.21, London; m., Isobel Sinclair; 1 s.; 1 d. Educ. Harrow School; Corpus Christi College, Cambridge. Scots Guards, 1940-58; campaign North-West Europe, 1944-45; wounded; mentioned in Despatches; active service, Malaya and Far East, 1947-49; Canadian Army Staff College, 1951; Assistant Military Attache, Canada, 1952-53; active service, Canal Zone, Egypt, 1954; retired as Major, 1958; Argyll and Sutherland Highlanders TA, 1966-68; Partner, Drunkie Farms, Callander, 1967-81; Partner, Sheppards and Chase, Stock and Money Brokers and Member, Stock Exchange, 1960-85. Member, Queen's Bodyguard for Scotland (Royal Company of Archers), since 1966; Deputy Lieutenant, Central Region (Stirling and Falkirk), since 1979. Recreations: gardening; fishing. Address: (h.) Avonbeith, Callander, Perthshire, FK17 8BN; T.-0877 30078.

Ritchie, Anthony Elliot, CBE, MA, DSc, MD, FCSP, FRCPEd, FRSE, LLD. Secretary and Treasurer, Carnegie Trust for the Universities of Scotland, 1969-86; b. 30.3.15, Edinburgh; m., Elizabeth Lambie Knox; 1 s.; 3 d. Educ. Edinburgh Academy; Aberdeen University; Edinburgh University. Carnegie Scholar, Lecturer and Senior Lecturer in Physiology, Edinburgh University, 1941-48; Professor of Physiology, St. Andrews University, 1948-69; Honorary Consultant, Eastern Regional Hospital Board, 1950-69; Chairman, Scottish Committee on Science Education, 1970-78; Chairman, Scottish University Entrance Board, 1963-69; Member, British Library Board, 1973-80; Member, Houghton Committee on Teachers' Pay; Trustee, National Library of Scotland, Carnegie Trust; Royal Society of Edinburgh: Fellow, 1951, General Secretary, 1966-76, Bicentenary Gold Medal, 1983; Hon. DSc (St. Andrews); Hon. LLD (Strathclyde). Recreations: reading; hill-walking; mechanics; electronics. Address: (h.) 12 Ravelston Park, Edinburgh, EH4 3DX; T.-031-332 6560.

Ritchie, George Fraser, MA, LLB. Solicitor; b. 26.5.42, Dundee; m., Sheila Stewart Anderson; 1 s.; 1 d. Educ. Dundee High School; St. Andrews University; Edinburgh University. Solicitor, private practice, since 1968; Partner, Hendry & Fenton, Solicitors, Dundee, since 1972; Council Member, Law Society of Scotland, since 1979; Convener, Legal Aid, 1982-83; Convener, Professional Remuneration, 1983-87; Convener, Guarantee Fund Committee, 1987-88; Secretary, High School of Dundee Trust Appeal Fund. Recreations: golf; hill-walking; listening to music. Address: (b.) 21 South Tay Street, Dundee; T.-Dundee 22785.

Ritchie, Ian Charles Stewart, MA (Cantab). General Manager, Scottish Chamber Orchestra, since 1984; b. 19.6.53, London; m., Angela Mary Reid; 2 d. Educ. Stowe School; Royal College of Music; Trinity College, Cambridge; Guildhall School of Music and Drama. Promotion Manager, Universal Edition (Music Publishers), 1976-79; General Manager, City of London Sinfonia, 1979-84; Artistic Director, City of London Festival, 1983-84; Member, Advisory Panel on Music, Arts Council of GB, 1983-86; Council Member, National Youth Orchestra of Scotland; Trustee, Scottish Musicians' Benevolent Fund; Director, St. Mary's Music School, Edinburgh; Director, Association of British Orchestras; Trustee, Edinburgh International Lunchtime Concert Trust. Recreations: watching cricket (MCC member); playing various sports (including golf); crosswords. Address: (h.) 8 Duncan Street, Edinburgh, EH9 1SZ.

Ritchie, Professor James McPherson, MA, DrPhil, DLitt. Professor and Head, Department of German, Aberdeen University, since 1987; b. 10.7.27; m.; 2 s.; 1 d. Educ. Aberdeen University; University of Tubingen. Lecturer, Glasgow University, 1954-61; Associate Professor, University of Newcastle, NSW, Australia, 1961-65; Reader, Hull University, 1965-70; Professor, Sheffield University, 1970-87. Recreation: playing the clarinet. Address: (b.) Department of German, Aberdeen University, Aberdeen.

Ritchie, Rev. Malcolm Alexander. Minister, Kilbrandon and Kilchattan, since 1982; b. 8.6.20, Beckenham, Kent; m., Heather Peebles Brown; 2 s.; 1 d. Educ. Dulwich College; King's College, Wimbledon; Edinburgh University and New College. Commissioned, Royal Regiment of Artillery, 1941; honorary rank of Captain, 1946; licensed to preach, 1950; Children's Evangelist and Staff Worker, Scripture Union, 1950; Minister: Broughty Ferry - St. James's, 1955-69, Strathblane, 1969-82; Chairman, Waldensian Missions Aid Society in Scotland, 1979; preached, centenary service of Scripture Union, Assembly Hall, Edinburgh, 1957; Moderator, Presbytery of Lorn and Mull, 1988-89. Recreations: boats; music. Address: The Manse, Easdale, Oban, Argyll; T.-Balvicar 240.

Ritchie, Murray. Journalist; Assistant Editor, Glasgow Herald, since 1981; b. 5.9.41, Dumfries; m., Andree Margaret Bryce; 1 s.; 2 d. Educ. High School of Glasgow. Scottish Farmer, 1958-60; Dumfries and Galloway Standard, 1960-65; Scottish Daily Record, 1965-67; East African Standard, 1967-71; joined Glasgow Herald, 1971. Journalist of the Year, Fraser Press Awards, 1980. Recreations: golf; folk music. Address: (h.) 64 Falloch Road, Milngavie, Glasgow; T.-041-956 1129.

Ritchie, Rev. Walter Millar, ACIS. Minister, Appin with Lismore, since 1981; Clerk, Presbytery of Lorn and Mull, since 1985; b. 16.1.36, Glasgow; m., Heather Bell Russell McNiven; 1 s.; 2 d. Educ. Jordanhill College School; Glasgow University (non-graduate course). Company Secretary and Chief Accountant; studied for the ministry; Minister, Kirkmichael, Straloch and Glenshee. Chaplain, Black Watch Army Cadet Force, 1972-85. Recreation: gardening. Address: The Manse, Appin, Argyll, PA38 4DD; T.-Appin 206.

Ritchie, Professor William, BSc, PhD, FRSGS, FRSE. Professor of Physical Geography, Aberdeen University, since 1979 (Head, Department of Geography, since 1982); b. 22.3.40, Wishaw; m., Elizabeth Armstrong Bell; 2 s.; 1 d. Educ. Wishaw High School; Glasgow University. Research Assistant, Glasgow University, 1963; Assistant Lecturer, Lecturer, Senior Lecturer, Professor, Aberdeen University, since 1964; Visiting Professor/Research Scientist, Lousiana State University, 1971, 1979, 1985, 1986, 1987. Sometime Member: Nature Conservancy Committee for Scotland, Scottish Examination Board, Council of Royal Society of Edinburgh; Past Chairman, Royal Scottish Geographical Society (Aberdeen). Address: (b.) Department of Geography, Aberdeen University, Old Aberdeen; T.-0224 272328.

Ritchie, William Rennie, CBE, BSc (Hons), DipEd. HM Depute Senior Chief Inspector of Schools, since 1984; b. 14.7.28, Kirkcaldy; m., Jan Murrie; 1 s.; 1 d. Educ. Kirkcaldy High School; Edinburgh University. RAF, 1946-48; Physics Teacher, Kirkcaldy High School, 1953-62; Nuffield Foundation, 1962-63; HM Inspector (Science), 1963-73; HM Chief Inspector (Eastern Division, then 16-18 Development), 1973-84. Nuffield Foundation Scholarship, 1962-63; Commonwealth Fellowship (Australia), 1971. Recreations: music, golf. Address: (b.) Scottish Education Department, Room 4/101 New St. Andrews House, Edinburgh; T.-031-244 4521.

Ritson, Bruce, MD, FRCPsych, FRCP(Ed), DipPsych. Consultant Psychiatrist, Royal Edinburgh Hospital, since 1972; Senior Lecturer in Psychiatry, Edinburgh University, since 1972; Consultant, Royal Edinburgh Hospital, since 1972; b. 20.3.37, Elgin; m., Eileen Carey; 1 s.; 1 d. Educ. Edinburgh Academy; Edinburgh University; Harvard University. Trained in medicine, Edinburgh; postgraduate training in psychiatry, Edinburgh, Harvard and California; Director, Sheffield Region Addiction Unit, 1968-71; at present Consultant with special responsibility for alcohol-related problems; Consultant to World Health Organisation on several occasions. Chairman, Howard League in Scotland; Regional Advisor, Medical Council on Alcoholism; Council Member, Action Against Alcohol Abuse; Member, Advisory Group on Alcohol Problems to Health and Safety Executive, EEC. Recreations: friends; squash; theatre. Address: (b.) Andrew Duncan Clinic, Royal Edinburgh Hospital, Morningside Park, Edinburgh; T.-031-447 2011.

Rizvi, Mohammad Bin Ashiq, MA (Econ), LLB, AInstAM. Member, Lothian Regional Council, since 1986; b. 15.12.36, Amroha, India; m., Yasmin; 2 d. Educ. India; Karachi University; London University. Began as Teacher with ILEA, 1963; joined insurance group, 1964, and remained until 1986; took early retirement to devote full time to politics; held various offices in Scottish Conservative Party; first non-white Regional Councillor in UK; Member, Children's Panel Advisory Board; Chairman, Membership Panel, Lothian Community Relations Council; Secretary and Trustee, Central Mosque and Islamic Centre. Recreations: tennis; cricket; reading; Member, Caledonian Club. Address: (h.) 5 Fox Covert Avenue, Edinburgh, EH12 6UQ; T.-031-334 5389.

Roach, Professor Gary Francis, BSc, MSc, PhD. Professor of Mathematics, Strathclyde University, since 1979 (Dean, Faculty of Science, since 1982); b. 8.10.33, Penpedairheol, South Wales; m., Isabella Grace Willins Nicol. Educ. University College, South Wales and Monmouthshire; London University; Manchester University. RAF (Education Branch), Flying Officer, 1955-58; Research Mathematician, British Petroleum Co. Ltd., 1958-61; Lecturer, Manchester University Institute of Science and Technology, 1961-66; Visiting Professor, University of British Columbia, 1966-67; Strathclyde University: Lecturer, 1967-70, Senior Lecturer, 1970-71, Reader, 1971-79. Fellow, Royal Astronomical Society; Fellow, Institute of Mathematics and its Applications; Fellow, Royal Society of Edinburgh; Past President, Edinburgh Mathematical Society. Recreations: mountaineering; photography; philately; gardening; music. Address: (b.) Department of Mathematics, Strathclyde University, Livingstone Tower, 26 Richmond Street, Glasgow, G1 1XH; T.-041-552 4400, Ext. 3800.

Roads, Elizabeth Ann, FSA (Scot). Lyon Clerk and Keeper of the Records, since 1986; b. 5.7.51, West Germany; m., Christopher George William Roads; 1 s. Educ. Lansdowne House School, Edinburgh; Cambridge College of Technology; Study Centre for Fine Art, London. PA: London University Institute of Education, 1970, Christie's, Art Auctioneers, 1971-74, Strathern and Blair, WS, 1974-75, Court of the Lord Lyon, 1975-86; Linlithgow Pursuivant Extraordinary, 1987. Recreations: history; reading; countryside activities. Address: (h.) 9 Denham Green Place, Edinburgh; T.-(b.) 031-556 7255.

Robb, Alan, DA, MA, RCA. Head, School of Fine Art, Duncan of Jordanstone College of Art, Dundee, since 1983; b. 24.2.46, Glasgow; m., Cynthia J. Neilson; 1 s.; 1 d. Educ. Robert Gordon's College, Aberdeen; Grays School of Art; Royal College of Art. Assistant Art Master, Oundle School, 1972-75; Crawford School of Art: Lecturer in Painting, 1975-78, Head of Painting, 1978-80, Head of Fine Art, 1980-83. Member, Fine Art Panel, CNAA, 1986-87; Specialist Advisor, CNAA, since 1987; Director, Art in Partnership and WASPS; first one-man exhibition, New 57 Gallery; exhibitions, 1973 and 1976; Arts Council touring two-man exhibition, 1978-79; regularly exhibits in Scotland. Publication: Irish Contemporary Art, 1980. Address: (b.) Duncan of Jordanstone College of Art, Perth Road, Dundee, DD1 4HT.

Robb, Colin Denholm, BSc (Econ) (Hons). Member, East Kilbride District Council, since 1979; Board Member, East Kilbride Development Corporation, 1983-86; Lecturer in Economics, Bell College, Hamilton, since 1978; b. 14.10.46, Rutherglen; m., Mariet; b. 1 s.; 1 d. Educ. Rutherglen Academy; Glasgow College of Technology; Strathclyde University (postgraduate degree course). Leader, Labour Group, and Chairman, Policy and Resources Committee, East Kilbride District Council, 1980-83. Recreations: reading; hill-walking; photography. Address: (h.) 22 Loch Torridon, East Kilbride, G74 2ET; T.-East Kilbride 24337.

Robb, Gilbert Morris, DA, RIBA, ARIAS. Director of Architectural Services, Falkirk District Council, since 1986; b. 17.10.38, Dundee; m., Edith Robertson; 2 d. Educ. Arbroath High School; Duncan of Jordanstone College of Art. Falkirk Town Council, 1962-74, latterly as Senior Architect; Depute Director of Architectural Services, Falkirk District Council, 1974-86. Recreations: athletics; rugby; horse-riding; swimming. Address: (h.) Treetops, Kilns Road, Falkirk, FK1 5SA.

Robb, Graham, DRSAM. Freelance Musician and Composer; Lecturer in Music; Musical Director and Arranger; b. 7.8.50, Aberdeen; m., Erica Gunn; 2 s. Educ. Aberdeen Grammar School; Royal Scottish Academy of Music. Double bass player, BBC Scottish Symphony Orchestra, 1971-76; freelance double bass and bass guitar player, since 1976; founder Member, "Head" (jazz rock band), 1969-78; formed various jazz-rock bands; music for BBC TV and radio, theatre and schools; commissioned by Platform Jazz Society, 1975, to write 50-minute song cycle; Lecturer in Rock Music, Perth College of Further Education, 1984 (creator of first full-time course in rock music at that college); actively involved with development of SCOTVEC music modules. Recreations: music; preparation and consumption of food and drink. Address: (h.) Tigh-Na-Beithe, Birnam, Perthshire; T.-Dunkeld 371.

Robbins, Professor Keith Gilbert, MA, DPhil, DLitt. Professor of Modern History, Glasgow University, since 1980; b. 9.4.40, Bristol; m., Janet Carey; 3 s.; 1 d. Educ. Bristol Grammar School; Magdalen and St. Antony's Colleges, Oxford. Lecturer in History, York University, 1963-71; Professor of History, University College of North Wales, 1971-79; Raleigh Lecturer, British Academy, 1984; Ford Lecturer, Oxford, 1987; Editor, History, 1979-86; President, Historical Association, since 1988. Publications: Munich 1938, 1968; Sir Edward Grey, 1971; The Abolition of War, 1976; John Bright, 1979; The Eclipse of a Great Power: Modern Britain, 1983; The First World War, 1984; Nineteenth-Century Britain: Integration and Diversity, 1988; Appeasement, 1988. Recreations: music; walking; gardening. Address: (b.) Department of Modern History, Glasgow University, Glasgow; T.-041-339 8855, Ext. 4522.

Robbins, Oliver Charles Gordon, BA (Hons), MIProdE, MIED. Depute Principal, Cambuslang College of Further Education, since 1984; b. 28.4.36, Edinburgh; m., Andrewena Henderson Briggs; 4 s.; 1 d. Educ. Bellevue Secondary School; Open University; Napier College. Apprentice engineer, 1952-57; draughtsman, 1957-60; design draughtsman, Rolls Royce/Ferranti Ltd., 1960-69; Lecturer, Senior Lecturer, Head of Department, Moray College of FE. Recreations: caravanning; martial arts. Address: (h.) 11 Strathaven Road, Lesmahagow, Lanarkshire; T.-Lesmahagow 894617.

Roberts, Edward Frederick Denis, MA, PhD, FRSE, FLA. Librarian, National Library of Scotland, since 1970; b. 16.6.27, Belfast; m., Irene Richardson; 1 s.; 1 d. Educ. Royal Belfast Academical Institution; Queen's University, Belfast. Research Assistant, Department of History, Queen's University, Belfast, 1951-55; National Library of Scotland: Assistant Keeper, Department of Manuscripts, 1955-66, Secretary of the Library, 1966-67; Librarian, Trinity College, Dublin, 1967-70; Honorary Professor, Edinburgh University, 1975. Address: (h.) 6 Oswald Court, Edinburgh, EH9 2HY; T.-031-667 9473.

Roberts, M. Maureen, BSc, MB, BCh, MD. Director, Edinburgh Breast Screening Clinic, since 1979; Consultant, Lothian Health Board; Lecturer and Senior Lecturer, Department of Clinical Surgery, Edinburgh University, 1971-88; b. 15.3.36, Newport, Gwent; m., Robert Ellis; 1 s.; 1 d. Educ. Newport High School for Girls; Welsh National School of Medicine, Cardiff. House Officer appointments, Cardiff and Newport Hospitals; Lecturer, Surgical Unit, Cardiff Royal Infirmary, 1967-71; Lecturer, Department of Clinical Surgery, Edinburgh University, 1971-77 (Senior Lecturer, from 1977). Former Secretary, British Breast Group. Recreations: countryside (especially Scotland); yoga; reading; theatre. Address: (b.) Edinburgh Breast Screening Clinic, Springwell House, 26 Ardmillan Terrace, Edinburgh, EH11 2JL; T.-031-346 1824.

Roberts, Rev. Maurice Jonathon, BA, BD. Minister, Ayr Free Church of Scotland, since 1974; b. 8.3.38, Timperley, Cheshire; m., Alexandra Macleod; 1 d. Educ. Lymm Grammar School; Durham University; London University; Free Church College. Schoolteacher, 14 years; Minister, 14 years; former Editor, Free Church youth magazine; former Convener, Public Questions Committee, Free Church. Recreation: reading. Address: (b.) Free Church Manse, 8 Inverkar Road, Ayr, KA7 2JT; T.-0292 266043.

Roberts, Ronald John, BVMS, MRCVS, PhD, FRCPath, FIBiol, FRSE. Director, Institute of Aquaculture, Stirling University, since 1971; b. 28.3.41; m., Helen Macgregor; 2 s. Educ. Campbeltown Grammar School; Glasgow University. Lecturer, Glasgow University, 1964-71; Consultant: Department of Agriculture and Fisheries for Scotland, 1967-70, Overseas Development Administration, since 1974, United Nations, since 1976; Council Member, Royal Society of Edinburgh, 1980-83; Buckland Professor of Fisheries, Buckland Foundation, 1985; Director: Tarbert Fyne Foods, Stirling Salmon, Stirling Aquatic Technology; Editor, Journal of Fish Diseases. Publications: Fish Pathology; Handbook of Salmon and Trout Diseases; Recent Advances in Aquaculture; Diseases of Asian Catfishes (Co-author). Recreations: golf at Machrihanish Golf Club; squash. Address: (b.) Institute of Aquaculture, Stirling University, Stirling; T.-Stirling 73171.

Roberts, Stewart Muir, OBE, DL, JP, FEIS, BA, MA. Honorary Sheriff, Ettrick and Lauderdale; Governor, Merchiston Castle School, since 1962; b. 4.2.08, Selkirk; m., Marguerite Hugh Considine; 1 s.; 2 d. Educ. Merchiston Castle School; Clare College, Cambridge; Scottish Woollens' Technical College, Galashiels. Director, George Roberts & Co. Ltd., 1936-62 (Managing Director, 1956-62); Director, Roberts, Thorburn and Noble, 1962-73; Army Service, 1943-46; Standard Bearer, Royal Burgh of Selkirk, 1934; Member, Selkirk Town Council, 1935-75 (Provost, 1955-61); Member, Selkirk County Council, 1937-75 (Chairman, County Education Committee, 1948-75); Member and Chairman, Education Committee, Borders Regional Council, 1974-78; Vice-Convenor, Borders Regional Council, 1974-78; Member, Scottish Council on Alcohol, 1975-88; Member, Dunning Committee, 1976-79. Recreations: golf; fishing; curling; bee-keeping. Address: (h.) Tweedknowe, Selkirk; T.-0750 20224.

Robertson, Alexander, MA, PhD. Senior Lecturer, Department of Social Policy, Edinburgh University, since 1981; Head, Department of Social Policy, since 1986; b. 13.8.39, Aberdeen; m., Elaine Walden; 2 s.; 1 d. Educ. Robert Gordon's College; Aberdeen University; Edinburgh University. Research Assistant, Leicester University, 1962-64; Research Officer, Essex University, 1965-66; Lecturer in Sociology, Ipswich Civic College, 1966-68; Scientific Officer, MRC Unit for Epidemiological Studies in Psychiatry, Edinburgh University, 1968-72; Lecturer, Edinburgh University, 1972-81; Visiting Professor, McMaster University, Ontario, 1977; Visiting Professor, University of Padua, 1985. Publications: Improving Social Intervention (Editor), 1983; Social Policy and the Quality of Life (Editor), 1985; Lifestyle Survey (main author), 1987. Recreations: sport; playing violin; languages; music; reading. Address: (h.) 11 Merchiston Park, Edinburgh, EH10 4PW; T.-031-229 1182.

Robertson, Alistair John, BMedBiol (Hons), MB, ChB, MRCPath. Consultant in Administrative Charge, Perth and Kinross Unit Laboratories, since 1982; Consultant Histopathologist, Tayside Health Board, since 1982; Honorary Senior Lecturer in Pathology, Dundee University, since 1982; b. 29.6.50, Aberdeen; m., Frances Elizabeth Smith. Educ. Aberdeen Grammar School; Aberdeen University. House Physician, Ninewells Hospital, Dundee, 1975; House Surgeon, Aberdeen Royal Infirmary, 1976; Senior House Officer in Pathology, Ninewells Hospital, 1976; Lecturer in Pathology, Ninewells Hospital, 1977. Recreations: golf; curling; caravanning; philately. Address: (b.) The Laboratory, Rose Crescent, Perth Royal Infirmary, Perth; T.-Perth 23311.

Robertson, Alistair Raeburn, RD (and clasp), DPA, DSA, FHSM, FBIM. General Manager, Forth Valley Health Board, since 1986; b. 29.5.33, Glasgow; m., Mary Gilchrist Smith; 2 s.; 1 d. Educ. Hyndland Senior Secondary School; Glasgow University; Manchester University. Corporation of Glasgow Education Department, 1949-56; Royal Navy, 1951-53; miscellaneous appointments, Scottish Health Service, 1956-71; Group Secretary and Treasurer, Board of Management for Angus Hospitals, 1971-74; District Administrator, South Eastern District, Greater Glasgow Health Board, 1974-85; Acting Secretary, Greater Glasgow Health Board, 1985-86. Royal Naval Reserve, 1951-79, Captain (Retd); Council Member, Institute of Health Services Management; Past Chairman, Scottish Division, Institute of Health Services Management. Recreations: curling; sailing; gardening. Address: (b.) 33 Spittal Street, Stirling, FK8 1DX; T.-0786 63031.

Robertson, Andrew Alexander, CIPFA, MBCS. Computing and Services Controller, North of Scotland Hydro-Electric Board, since 1983; b. 3.1.35, Cowdenbeath; m., Louise Wilson; 1 s.; 1 d. Educ. Dunfermline High School; Glasgow College of Commerce. Internal Auditor, then Systems and Programming Manager, SSEB; NSHEB: Computer Manager, Computing and Accounting Services Manager, Deputy Chief Financial Officer. Founder Chairman, NE Scotland Branch, British Computer Society. Recreations: golf; gardening; travel. Address: (b.) 16 Rothesay Terrace, Edinburgh, EH3 7SE; T.-031-225 1361.

Robertson, Andrew Ogilvie, LLB. Partner, T.C. Young & Son, Solicitors and Notaries, since 1968; Secretary, Erskine Hospital, since 1976; Secretary, Clydeside Federation of Community Based Housing Associations, since 1978; Secretary, The Briggait Company Ltd., 1982-88; Director, Glasgow Chamber of Commerce, since 1982; Chairman, Post Office Users Council for Scotland, since 1988; b. 30.6.43, Glasgow; m., Sheila Sturton; 2 s. Educ Glasgow Academy; Sedbergh School; Edinburgh University. Director, Merchants House of Glasgow, 1978-85 and 1988. Recreations: climbing; skiing; sailing; running; fishing; shooting. Address: (b.) 30 George Square, Glasgow, G2 1LH; T.-041-221 5562.

Robertson, Brenda Margaret, JP. Member, Orkney Islands Council, since 1974; Member, Children's Panel Advisory Committee; Member, Highlands and Islands Fire Board; b. 8.9.24, Scarborough; m., John MacDonald Robertson, BL, NP; 1 s.; 1 d. Educ. Scarborough Girls' High School; University College, St. Andrews. Wartime service, WRNS (Naval Intelligence); formerly: District Commissioner for Guides, Stromness and West Mainland; Member, Stromness Town Council; County Councillor; Member, Executive Council, NHS; Governor, Aberdeen College of Education. Recreations: reading; arts generally. Address: (h.) Berridale, Stromness, Orkney.

Robertson, Rev. Charles, MA, JP. Minister, Canongate Kirk, since 1978; b. 22.10.40, Glasgow; m., Alison Margaret Malloch; 1 s.; 2 d. Educ. Camphill School, Paisley; Edinburgh University. Assistant Minister, North Morningside Church, Edinburgh, 1964-65; Minister, Kiltearn, Ross and Cromarty, 1965-78. Secretary, Panel on Worship, General Assembly; Chaplain to: Elsie Inglis Memorial Maternity Hospital, the Clan Donnachaidh Society, New Club; Vice-Chairman, Board, Queensberry House Hospital; Governor, St. Columba's Hospice, Edinburgh; Director: Whitedael Housing Association, Edinburgh and East of Scotland Deaf Association; Lecturer, St. Colm's College; Justice of the Peace, City of Edinburgh. Recreations: books; music. Address: Manse of Canongate, Edinburgh, EH8 8BR; T.-031-556 3515.

Robertson, Rev. Daniel McCallum, MA. Minister, Auchinleck, since 1967; b. 20.4.35, Bathgate; m., Anne Moffat Affleck; 2 s.; 2 d. Educ. Bathgate Academy; Edinburgh University and New College. Student Assistant, Broughton Place, Edinburgh, 1958-59; Probationer Assistant, St. Cuthbert's, Edinburgh, 1959-60; Minister: Camelon Trinity, Falkirk, 1960-67, Auchinleck Barony, 1967-80, linked charge of Auchinleck Barony/Peden, 1980-83, and united charge of Auchinleck, since 1983. Representative, Ayr Presbytery, on Cumnock and District Schools Council. Recreations: crosswords; music; gardening; DIY motor mechanics. Address: 28 Mauchline Road, Auchinleck, Ayrshire, KA18 2BN; T.-Cumnock 21108.

Robertson, Sheriff Daphne Jean Black, WS, MA, LLB. Sheriff of Glasgow and Strathkelvin, since 1979; b. 31.3.37; m., Donald Buchanan Robertson, QC. Educ. Hillhead High School; Greenock Academy; Edinburgh University; Glasgow University. Admitted Solicitor, 1961.

Robertson, David Greig, CBE, MA, MEd. Director of Education, Tayside Regional Council, since 1975; b. 29.12.24, Dundee; m., Margaret J.D. Keay; 3 s. Educ. Morgan Academy, Dundee; St. Andrews University. Teacher, Dundee and Dollar, 1952-58; Assistant Director of Education: Berwickshire, 1958-61, Dundee, 1961-64; Director of Education: Selkirkshire, 1964-72, Dundee, 1972-75. Honorary President, Scottish Amateur Music Association; Council Member, National Youth Orchestra of Scotland; Member, Consultative Committee on the Curriculum. Recreations: reading; caravanning; music. Address: (b.) Tayside House, 28 Crichton Street, Dundee, DD1 3RJ; T.-0382 23281, Ext. 3654.

Robertson, Rev. Fergus Alexander, MA, BD. Minister, Dalneigh and Bona Church, Inverness; b. 25.4.45, Malvern; m., A. Valery Macrae; 3 d. Educ. George Heriot's School, Edinburgh; Edinburgh University; St. Andrews University. Assistant Minister, West Pilton, Edinburgh. Moderator, Inverness Presbytery, 1984-85. Recreations: swimming; skiing. Address: The Manse, 9 St. Mungo Road, Inverness; T.-0463 232339.

Robertson, George F., FRICS, FCIArb. Partner, Robertson and Dawson, Chartered Surveyors, Edinburgh, since 1970; Chairman, Scottish Building Contract Committee, since 1983; President, Rent Assessment Panel for Scotland, since 1984; Board Member, Scottish Development Agency; b. 14.7.32, Edinburgh; m., Anne McGonigle; 3 d. Educ. George Heriot's School, Edinburgh; Heriot-Watt College, Edinburgh. Arbiter; Lecturer (part-time), School of Architecture, Edinburgh College of Art/Heriot-Watt University, 1964-84; Chairman, Joint Standing Committee of Architects, Surveyors and Building Contractors in Scotland, 1976-78; Chairman, Board of Governors, Leith Nautical College, 1976-78; Lay Member, Scottish Solicitors Discipline Tribunal, since 1976; Chairman, Scottish Branch, Royal Institution of Chartered Surveyors, 1984-85. Director, Queensberry House Hospital, Edinburgh, 1983-86. Recreations: working; gardening; hill-walking; Greece; researching Scottish market crosses. Address: (h.) Gladsheil, Campbell Court, Longniddry, East Lothian.

Robertson, George Islay MacNeill, MA. MP (Labour), Hamilton, since 1978; Deputy Opposition Spokesman on Foreign and Commonwealth Affairs, since 1981; b. 12.4.46, Port Ellen, Islay; m., Sandra Wallace; 2 s.; 1 d. Educ. Dunoon Grammar School; Dundee University; St. Andrews University. Tayside Study Economics Group, 1968-69; Scottish Organiser, General, Municipal, Boilermakers Union, 1969-78; Chairman, Scottish Labour Party, 1977-78; Member, Scottish Executive, Labour Party, 1973-79; PPS to Secretary of State for Social Services, 1979; Opposition Spokesman on Scottish Affairs, 1979-80, on Defence, 1980-81, on Foreign and Commonwealth Affairs, since 1981; Principal Spokesman on Europe, since 1985; Member of Board, Scottish Development Agency, 1976-78, Scottish Tourist Board, 1974-76; Board of Governors, Scottish Police College, 1975-78; Vice Chairman, British Council; Council Member, Royal Institute of International Affairs; Council Member, National Trust for Scotland, 1976-80, 1983-85; Member, Great Britain/East Europe Centre; Member, Steering Committee, Konigswinter Conference; Council Member, British Atlantic Committee. Recreations: family; photography. Address: (h.) 3 Argyle Park, Dunblane, Perthshire.

Robertson, George Slessor, MD, FFARCS. Consultant Anaesthetist, since 1969; Honorary Senior Lecturer in Anaesthesia, Aberdeen University; b. 30.12.33, Peterhead; m., Audrey E. McDonald; 1 s.; 2 d. Educ. Peterhead Academy; Aberdeen University. Early medical training, Aberdeen, London and Winnipeg. Publications: papers on the ethical dilemmas of non-treatment decisions in the demented elderly. Recreations: golf; hill-walking; picture-framing. Address: (b.) Department of Anaesthesia, Royal Infirmary, Foresterhill, Aberdeen, AB9 2ZB; T.-0224 681818.

Robertson, Harry, IPFA. Director of Finance and Depute Chief Executive, Perth and Kinross District Council, since 1981; b. 7.9.49, Dunfermline; m., Rosemary Elizabeth; 2 s. Educ. Dunfermline High School; Glasgow College of Commerce. Trainee Accountant, Burgh of Burntisland; Accountancy Assistant, Assistant Town Chamberlain, Depute Town Chamberlain, Burgh of Barrhead; Depute Director of Finance, Perth and Kinross District Council. Secretary/Treasurer, Perth Repertory Theatre Ltd.; Chairman, Scottish Branch, CIPFA, 1987-88; Treasurer, Perthshire Tourist Board. Recreations: golf; theatre; badminton. Address: (b.) 2 High Street, Perth, PH1 5PH; T.-Perth 39911.

Robertson, Iain Samuel, LLB, CA, CBIM. Chief Executive, Scottish Development Agency, since 1987; b. 27.12.45, Glasgow; m., Morag; 2 s.; 2 d. Educ. Jordanhill College; Glasgow University. Industry and professional practice, 1966-72; Civil Servant, 1972-83; Director, Locate in Scotland, 1983-86. Chairman, Scottish Development Finance Ltd., since 1987; Chairman, Glasgow Garden Festival 1988 Ltd., since 1987; Director, Japan Assets Trust plc, since 1987. Recreations: golf; reading. Address: (b.) 120 Bothwell Street, Glasgow, G2 7JP; T.-041-248 2700.

Robertson, Maj.-Gen. Ian Argyll, CB (1968), MBE (1947), MA, DL. Deputy Lieutenant, Highland Region (Nairn); b. 17.7.13, Richmond, Surrey; m., Marjorie Violet Isobel Duncan; 2 d. Educ. Winchester College; Trinity College, Oxford. Commissioned Seaforth Highlanders, 1934; commanded 1st Bn., 1954-57; commanded School of Infantry, 1963-64; commanded 51 Highland Division, 1964-66; retired, 1968. Vice-Chairman and Chairman, Royal British Legion Scotland, 1971-74. Recreations: golf; gardening. Address: (h.) Brackla House, Nairn; T.-Cawdor 220.

Robertson, Ian Barr, MA, LLB. Solicitor; Advocate in Aberdeen; Member, Grampian Regional Council, 1974-86 (Chairman, Transportation and Roads Committee, 1978-86); Honorary Sheriff, Grampian, Highland and Islands, at Stonehaven; b. Aberdeen; m., Vi L. Johnston; 2 s.; 1 d. Educ. Mackie Academy; Fettes College; Aberdeen University. King's Regiment and KAR, 1939-46 (Captain); Partner, Cunningham & Robertson, Solicitors, Stonehaven, since 1951; Joint Town Clerk, then Town Clerk, Stonehaven, 1957-75; President, Society of Town Clerks in Scotland, 1973-75; Member, Aberdeen Harbour Board, 1975-86; Member, Peterhead Bay Authority, 1978-88; Past President, Stonehaven Rotary Club; Elder, Stonehaven South. Recreations: rough shooting; fishing; golf; theatre. Address: (h.) 15 Bath Street, Stonehaven; T.-Stonehaven 62879.

Robertson, Ian Macbeth, CB, LVO, HRSA, Hon. DLitt (Heriot-Watt). Chairman, Board of Governors, Edinburgh College of Art, since 1981; b. 1.2.18, Crookedholm, Ayrshire; m., Anne Stewart Marshall. Educ. Melville College; Edinburgh University. Served, Middle East and Italy, Royal Artillery and London Scottish, 1940-46; entered Scottish Office, 1946; Private Secretary to Minister of State, 1951-52, and to Secretary of State for Scotland, 1952-55; Under Secretary, Scottish Office, Scottish Development Department and Scottish Education Department, 1963-78; Secretary of Commissions for Scotland, 1978-83; JP, Edinburgh, 1978. Member, Williams Committee on National Museums and Galleries in Scotland, 1979-81; Chairman, Scottish United Services Museum Advisory Committee, 1970-85; Director, Royal Lyceum Theatre Company, 1978-85. Address: (h.) 8 Colinton Road, Edinburgh, EH10 5DS; T.-031-447 4636.

Robertson, Hon. Lord (Ian Macdonald Robertson), TD (1946), BA, LLB, QC. Senator of the College of Justice in Scotland, 1966-87; Chairman of Governors, Merchiston Castle School, since 1970; b. 30.10.12, Edinburgh; m., Anna Love Glen; 1 s.; 2 d. Educ. Merchiston Castle School, Edinburgh; Balliol College, Oxford; Edinburgh University. Admitted Faculty of Advocates, 1939; served War of 1939-45, 8th Bn., The Royal Scots (The Royal Regiment) - commissioned 1939; Captain/Staff Officer, 44th Lowland Infantry Brigade (15th Scottish Division); Normandy and North West Europe, 1944-45; mentioned in Despatches; Advocate Depute, 1949-51; QC, 1954; Sheriff Principal of Ayr and Bute, 1961-66; Sheriff Principal of Perth and Angus, 1966; Chairman, Medical Appeals Tribunal, 1957-63; Chairman, Scottish Joint Council for Teachers Salaries, 1965-81; Chairman, Scottish Valuation Advisory Council, 1977-86; UK Representative on Central Council, International Association of Judges, 1974-87; General Council Assessor, Edinburgh University Court, 1967-81; Chairman, Edinburgh Centre of Rural Economy and Edinburgh Centre for Tropical Veterinary Medicine, 1967-86; Governor, Merchiston Castle School, 1954-88; Captain, Honourable Company of Edinburgh Golfers at Muirfield, 1970-72. Recreation: golf. Address: (h.) 13 Moray Place, Edinburgh, EH3 6DT; T.-031-225 6637.

Robertson, Rev. Ian William, MA, BD. Minister, Colvend, Southwick and Kirkbean, since 1974; b. 18.12.25, Glasgow; 5 s. Educ. Hutchesons' Grammar School, Glasgow; Glasgow University; Edinburgh University; Marburg University. Minister: Galston New, 1956-65, Crosshill Queen's Park, Glasgow, 1965-74. Publication: Fides Quaerens Intellectum (Translator), 1960. Address: The Manse, Colvend, by Dalbeattie, DG5 4QN; T.-055 663 255.

Robertson, Sir James (Anderson), Kt (1968), CBE (1963), QPM (1961), OStJ, BL. Honorary President: Securicor (Scotland) Ltd., Boys' Brigade (Glasgow Bn.), Royal Scottish Pipe Band Association; President, Cowal Highland Gathering; Chairman, Glasgow Standing Conference of Voluntary Youth Organisations; Chairman, National Children's Home (Scotland Committee); b. 8.4.06, Glasgow; m., Janet Lorraine Gilfillan McFarlane; 2 s.; 1 d. Educ. Provanside School, Glasgow; Glasgow University. Chief Constable of Glasgow, until 1971. Member, Advisory Board, Salvation Army; Chairman, Glasgow Branch, Mental Health Foundation. Recreations: gardening; golf. Address: (h.) 3 Kirklee Road, Glasgow, G12 0RL; T.-041-339 4400.

Robertson, Rev. James Henry, BSc, BD. Minister, Thornliebank Church, since 1985; b. 24.3.49, Edinburgh; m., Morag Margaret Sinclair; 2 s.; 1 d. Educ. Greenhall High School; Edinburgh University. Assistant Minister, Muirhouse, Edinburgh, 1973-75; Minister: St. Ninian's, Greenock, 1975-85. Recreations: squash; singing; gardening; walking. Address: Thornliebank Manse, 73 Rouken Glen Road, Thornliebank, Glasgow, G46 7JD.

Robertson, James Taylor, BSc, FICE, FIWEM, MBIM. Director of Water and Drainage, Central Regional Council, since 1974; b. 2.4.26, Edinburgh; m., Margaret Ruth; 2 d. Educ. George Watson's Boys' College, Edinburgh; Edinburgh University. Apprentice and Assistant, J. & A. Leslie & Reid, 1948-52; New Works Assistant, Colchester Corporation Waterworks, 1952-54; Assistant Supplies Engineer, then Assistant Distribution Engineer, Bristol Waterworks Company, 1954-61; Depute City Water Engineer, Dundee Corporation, 1961-68; Depute Engineer, then Engineer, Mid Scotland Water Board, 1968-75. Council Member, Water Research Centre. Recreations: golf; walking. Address: (b.) Woodlands, Stirling, FK8 2HB; T.-0786 62811.

Robertson, John Davie Manson, OBE (1978), BL, FSA Scot. Chairman, Robertson Group of Companies, since 1980; Director, Stanley Services Ltd.; Chairman, Orkney Health Board, since 1983 (Member, since 1974); Chairman, SCOTMEG, since 1985; b. 6.11.29, Golspie; m., Elizabeth Amelia Macpherson; 2 s.; 2 d. Educ. Kirkwall Grammar School; Edinburgh University. Member: Highlands and Islands Development Consultative Council, Orkney Valuation Appeal Committee; Honorary Vice Consul for Denmark, 1972; Honorary Consul, Federal Republic of Germany, 1976; Honorary Sheriff, Grampian, Highland and Islands, 1977; Past Chairman, Highlands and Islands Savings Committee; Past Chairman, Children's Panel for Orkney, 1971-76; Past Chairman, Children's Panel, Orkney Advisory Committee, 1977-82; former Member, Board of Management, Orkney Hospitals, 1970-74; Member, Rent Assessment Panel for Scotland, 1973-85. Royal Order of Knight of Dannebrog, 1982; Cavelier's Cross of the Order of Merit, 1986. Publication: Uppies and Doonies, 1967. Recreations: squash; rough shooting. Address: (h.) Shorelands, Kirkwall, Orkney; T.-Kirkwall 2530.

Robertson, John William, MA. Secretary, British Linen Bank Ltd., since 1986; Solicitor, since 1971; b. 12.11.43, Dunfermline; m., Alice Rudland; 1 s.; 3 d. Educ. Dunfermline High School; Edinburgh University. Assistant Law Secretary, Bank of Scotland, 1975; Manager, Law Department, Bank of Scotland, London, 1978; Assistant Secretary, British Linen Bank Ltd., 1983. Address: (h.) 52 Findhorn Place, Edinburgh, EH9 2NS; T.-031-667 4229.

Robertson, Lewis, CBE, FRSE, FRSA. Chairman: F.J.C. Lilley plc, since 1986, Triplex Lloyd plc, since 1987, Girobank Scotland, since 1984, Borthwicks plc, since 1985; b. 28.11.22, Dundee; m., Elspeth Badenoch; 3 s.; 1 d. Educ. Trinity College, Glenalmond. Apprentice Chartered Accountant, 1939-42; RAF, 1942-46; entered family textile business, 1946; appointed Managing Director, Robertson Industrial Textiles, 1954; first Managing Director, Scott & Robertson, 1965 (Chairman, 1968); resigned, 1970; Chief Executive, Grampian Holdings, Glasgow, 1971-76 (also Deputy Chairman, 1972-76); Non-Executive Director, Scottish & Newcastle Breweries, 1975-87; Director, IC Industries (International) SA, Geneva, since 1987; Chairman, Scottish Board (and UK Council Member), British Institute of Management, 1981-83; Chairman, Eastern Regional Hospitals Board, 1960-70; Member, Committee of Enquiry into the Relationship of the Pharmaceutical Industry with the NHS, 1965-67; Member, Monopolies (later Monopolies and Mergers) Commission, 1969-76; Deputy Chairman and first Chief Executive, Scottish Development Agency, 1976-81; Member, Scottish Economic Council, 1977-83; Member, Restrictive Practices Court, since 1983; Member, Scottish Post Office Board, since 1984; Trustee, since 1963, and Member, Executive Committee, since 1964, Carnegie Trust for the Universities of Scotland; Member, Court, Dundee University, 1967-70 (first Finance Chairman); Council Member, Scottish Business School, 1978-83; Chairman, Scottish Arts Council, and Member, Arts Council of GB, 1970-71; Chairman, Scottish Advisory Committee, British Council, 1978-87; Council Member, Scottish History Society, since 1984; first Chairman, Policy Committee, Scottish Episcopal Church, 1974-76; Trustee, Foundation for the Study of Christianity and Society; Member, Advisory Board, Edinburgh Edition of the Waverley Novels, since 1986; Director, Friends of Royal Scottish Academy, since 1986; Honorary Doctorate of Laws, Dundee University, 1971. Recreations: work; foreign travel; computer use; music. Address: 32 Saxe Coburg Place, Edinburgh, EH3 5BP; T.-031-332 5221.

Robertson, Noel Farnie, CBE, MA, BSc, PhD, FRSE, FIBiol. Chairman, Scottish Countryside Museums Trust, since 1987; Chairman, Scottish Crop Research Institute; Member, Board of Trustees, Royal Botanic Garden, Edinburgh; b. 24.12.23, Dundalk; m., Doreen Colina Gardner; 2 s.; 2 d. Educ. Trinity Academy; Edinburgh University; Trinity College, Cambridge. Plant Pathologist, West African Cacao Research Institute, Ghana, 1946-48; Lecturer, Plant Pathology, Cambridge University, 1948-59; Professor of Botany, Hull University, 1959-69; Professor of Agriculture, Edinburgh University, and Principal, East of Scotland College of Agriculture, 1969-83. Recreations: gardening; natural history. Address: (h.) Woodend, Juniper Bank, Walkerburn, Peeblesshire, EH43 6DE; T.-089 687 523.

Robertson, Richard Ross, RSA, FRBS, DA. Sculptor; b. 10.9.14, Aberdeen; m., Kathleen May Matts; 2 d. Educ. Paisley Grammar School; Glasgow School of Art; Aberdeen Art School. Work exhibited in Aberdeen public parks and several public buildings in city and county of Aberdeen; also exhibited in several private collections in Britain, America and Holland; retired Lecturer in Sculpture, Gray's School of Art, Aberdeen. Recreations: carving; gardening; walking. Address: (h.) Creaguir, Woodlands Road, Rosemount, Blairgowrie, Perthshire; T.-0250 4970.

Robertson, Robert, CBE, JP, FEIS. Member, Strathclyde Regional Council, 1974-86; b. 15.8.09, Shapensay, Orkney; m., Jean Murdoch Moffatt; 1 s.; 1 d. Educ. Forres Academy; Royal Technical College, Glasgow. Local government service since 1952; Convener, former Renfrewshire County Council; Chairman, former Renfrewshire Education Committee, 13 years; Chairman, Standing Committee for the Supply and Training of Teachers in Further Education (Robertson Report); Member, Board of Governors, Jordanhill College of Education; Member, various College Councils. Recreations: fishing; painting. Address: (h.) 24 Broadwood Park, Alloway, Ayrshire, T.-0292 43820; Castlehill, near Maybole, Ayrshire; T.-029 250 337.

Robertson, Lord Provost Robert. Lord Provost, City of Aberdeen, since 1988; m., Susan. Joined Aberdeen Corporation, 1965, as Labour Member; Grampian Regional Councillor, 1975-79; joined Aberdeen City Council, 1979; Housing Convener, 1980-84; Policy Convener, 1984-87.

Robertson, Rev. Robert Campbell. Community Minister, Church of Scotland (Glasgow City Centre), since 1977; b. 28.2.35, Glasgow. Educ. Allan Glen's School, Glasgow; Glasgow University and Trinity College. Leader, Calton Youth Club, 1965-68; Deputy Warden, Carberry Tower, 1968-72; Warden, Community House, Glasgow, 1972-77. Executive Member, Strathclyde Association of Youth Clubs. Recreations: films; theatre; playing music. Address: 12B/30 St. Vincent Terrace, Glasgow, G3 8UT; T.-041-204 1541.

Robertson, Roderick. Managing Director, Robertsons of Tain Ltd.; Honorary Sheriff, Tain and Dingwall, 1976; b. 24.8.35, Tain; m., Elizabeth Martin Steele; 1 s. Educ. Tain Royal Academy. Agricultural engineering apprenticeship, 1951-56; Army, 1956-59; began in business (agricultural engineering), 1959; elected, Tain Town Council, 1965 (Chairman of Development, Dean of Guild and Senior Bailie); JP, 1975; appointed Member, Valuation Appeal Committee, Ross and Cromarty, Skye and Lochalsh, 1980; Chairman, Justices of the Peace Committee, Ross and Cromarty, 1980; Chairman, Local Royal British Legion Housing Association, 1984; Member, Tain Community Council. Recreations: flying; shooting; fishing; judo. Address: (h.) Craigton, Provost Ferguson Drive, Tain, Ross-shire; T.-0862 2151.

Robertson, Ronald Foote, CBE, MD, FRCPEdin, FRCP, FRCPGlas. Physician to the Queen in Scotland, 1977-85; Consultant Physician, Edinburgh Royal Infirmary, 1974-86; Principal Medical Officer, Scottish Life Assurance Company, 1968-86; b. 27.12.20, Aberdeen; m., Dorothy Wilkinson; 2 d. Educ. Perth Academy; Edinburgh University. Consultant Physician: Leith Hospital, 1959-74, Deaconess Hospital, 1958-83; President, Royal College of Physicians of Edinburgh, 1976-79; President, British Medical Association, 1983-84; Member, General Medical Council, since 1979; Honorary Fellow, College of Physicians and Surgeons, Pakistan, 1977; Honorary FACP, 1978; Honorary FRCPI, 1978; Honorary FRACP, 1979. Recreations: curling; gardening; fishing. Address: (h.) 15 Wester Coates Terrace, Edinburgh, EH12 5LR; T.-031-337 6377.

Robertson, Sidney Park, MBE, TD, JP, VL, BCom. Director, S. & J.D. Robertson & Co. Ltd. Group of Companies; Honorary Sheriff, Grampian, Highlands and Islands, since 1969; Vice Lord Lieutenant of Orkney; b. 12.3.14, Kirkwall; m., Elsa Miller Croy; 1 s.; 1 d. Educ. Kirkwall Grammar School; Edinburgh University. Commissioned, Royal Artillery, 1940 (Despatches, NW Europe, 1945); Lt.-Col. Commanding Lovat Scouts, 1962-65; Brigadier, CRA 51st Highland Division, 1966-67; Chairman, Orkney Hospitals Board of Management/Orkney Health Board, 1965-79; Honorary Area Vice-President (Orkney), Royal British Legion, since 1975; Honorary Colonel, 102 (Ulster and Scottish) Light Air Defence Regiment, Royal Artillery, 1975-80; Hon. Colonel Commandant, Royal Regiment of Artillery, 1977-80; Vice President, National Artillery Association, since 1977; Chairman, Royal Artillery Council of Scotland, 1980-84; Honorary President, Orkney Bn., Boys' Brigade; Vice-President, RNLI, since 1985. Recreations: travel; hill-walking; angling. Address: (h.) Daisybank, Kirkwall, Orkney; T.-0856 2085.

Robins, John F. Company Secretary, Animal Concern (Scotland), since 1988 (Company Secretary, Scottish Anti-Vivisection Society, 1981-88); Co-ordinator, Scottish Animal Rights Network, since 1983; Managing Director, Ethical Promotions Ltd., since 1988; b. 2.1.57, Glasgow; m., Mary E.; 1 s.; 1 d. Educ. St. Ninian's High School. Co-ordinator, Glasgow Energy Group, 1978-80; Green Party activist and candidate, 1978-81; Delegate, Anti-Nuclear Campaign, 1978-81; Vice-Chair, Friends of the Earth (Scotland) Ltd., 1981-82. Recreations: campaigning against hunting, shooting and fishing; catching up on lost sleep. Address: (b.) 121 West Regent Street, Glasgow, G2 2SD; T.-041-221 2300.

Robinson, Helen Mairi Johnstone, MA. Research Associate, Edinburgh Edition of the Waverley Novels, since 1987; Kerr-Fry Award holder, Edinburgh University, since 1985; b. 21.1.45, Glasgow; 1 s.; 1 d. Educ. George Watson's Ladies' College, Edinburgh; Edinburgh University. Scottish National Dictionary: Junior Assistant Editor, 1966, Assistant Editor, 1967, Senior Assistant Editor, 1972; Editor-in-Chief, Concise Scots Dictionary, 1973-85; Member, Advisory Committee, Private Papers of James Boswell, Yale University, since 1987. Publication: Concise Scots Dictionary, 1985. Recreations: music; theatre; reading; travel. Address: (b.) 17a West Crosscauseway, Edinburgh.

Robinson, Stanley Scott, MBE (Mil), TD, BL, SSC. Sheriff of Grampian, Highland and Islands (retired); Honorary Sheriff of Inverness; Honorary Sheriff of Angus; b. 27.3.13, Edinburgh; m., Helen Annan Hardie; 3 s. Educ. Boroughmuir School, Edinburgh; Edinburgh University. Admitted Solicitor, 1935; TA commission, 1936; War service, Royal Artillery, 1939-45; Major; mentioned in Despatches (2); France and Belgium, 1939-40, France and Germany, 1944-45; admitted SSC, 1962; Vice President, Law Society of Scotland, 1970-72; appointed Sheriff, Fort William/Skye/Inverness/Western Isles, 1972; retired, 1985. Publications: Law of Interdict, 1987; Encyclopedia of Laws of Scotland (Contributor). bowling; caravanning. Address: (h.) Drumalin House, 16 Drummond Road, Inverness, IV2 4NB; T.-0463 233488.

Robson, Professor James Scott, MB, ChB (Hons), MD, FRCPEdin, FRCP. Emeritus Professor; Professor of Medicine, Edinburgh University, 1977-86; Physician in charge, Medical Renal Unit, Edinburgh Royal Infirmary, 1959-86; b. 19.5.21, Hawick; m., Mary Kynoch MacDonald; 2 s. Educ.

Hawick High School; Edinburgh University; New York University. RAMC (Captain), India, Palestine and Egypt, 1945-48; Rockefeller Research Fellow, Harvard University, 1949-50; Edinburgh University: Senior Lecturer in Therapeutics, 1959, Reader in Therapeutics, 1961, in Medicine, 1968; Honorary Associate Professor of Medicine, Harvard, 1962; Merck Sharpe & Dome Visiting Professor to Australia, 1968. President, Renal Association, London, 1977-80; sometime Member, Editorial Board, and Deputy Chairman, Clinical Science and other medical journals; Member, Biomedical Research Committee, SH&HD; Chairman, Sub-Committee in Medicine, National Medical Consultative Committee. Publications: Companion to Medical Studies (Co-Editor); many scientific papers on renal physiology and disease. Recreations: gardening; theatre; reading and writing. Address: (h.) 1 Grant Avenue, Edinburgh, EH13 ODS; T.-031-441 3508.

Robson, Robert, MA (Hons). Director, Cumbernauld Theatre, since 1983; b. 21.12.54, Hamilton; m., Annette Liddle; 2 s. Educ. Hamilton Academy; Glasgow University. Community drama worker with Easterhouse Festival Society, 1978-83. Recreation: following the fortunes of Motherwell FC. Address: (h.) 45 Kirkwall, The Village, Cumbernauld, Glasgow; T.-0236 720979.

Robson, Professor William Wallace, FRSE, MA (Oxon). Masson Professor of English Literature, Edinburgh University, since 1972; b. 20.6.23, Plymouth; m., Anne-Varna Moses; 2 s. Educ. Leeds High School and Modern School; New College, Oxford. Assistant Lecturer, King's College, London, 1944-46; Lecturer, Lincoln and Queen's Colleges, Oxford, 1944-46; Fellow, Lincoln College, Oxford, 1948-70; Professor of English, Sussex University, 1970-72; Visiting Professor: University of Southern California, 1953, Adelaide University, 1956, Delaware University, 1963-64; Elizabeth Drew Professor, Smith College, USA, 1968-69; Visiting Fellow: All Souls College, Oxford, 1981, New College, Oxford, 1985. Publications: Critical Essays, 1966; The Signs Among Us, 1968; Modern English Literature, 1970; The Definition of Literature, 1982; A Prologue to English Literature, 1986. Recreations: non-strenuous games of many kinds. Address: (b.) Department of English Literature, Edinburgh University, David Hume Tower, George Square, Edinburgh, EH8; T.-031-667 1011.

Rochester, Professor Colin Herbert, BSc, PhD, DSc, CChem, FRSC, FRSE. Baxter Professor of Chemistry, Dundee University, since 1980; b. 20.3.37, Coventry; m., Jennifer Mary Orrell; 2 s.; 2 d. Educ. Hymers College, Hull; Royal Liberty School, Romford; King's College, London University. Nottingham University: Assistant Lecturer in Physical Chemistry, 1962-64, Lecturer, 1964-72, Reader, 1972-80. Publication: Acidity Functions, 1970. Recreations: fossil collecting; swimming. Address: (b.) Chemistry Department, The University, Dundee, DD1 4HN; T.-0382 23181.

Rochford, Professor Gerard, BA, BSc. Professor of Social Work Studies, Aberdeen University, since 1978; Analytical Psychotherapist; b. 17.12.32, Dorking; m., Anne Prime; 3 s.; 7 d. Educ. Worcester Royal Grammar School; Hull University; Oxford University. Medical Research Council, 1960-63; Lecturer in Psychology: Aberdeen University, 1963-67, Hong Kong University, 1967-70; Lecturer/Senior Lecturer, Aberdeen University, 1970-78. Member, Scottish Association of Analytical Psychotherapists; Case-Discussion Leader, Marriage Guidance Council. Recreations: family; friends; poetry. Address: (h.) 47 Waverley Place, Aberdeen; T.-Aberdeen 644873.

Rodger, Alan, BSc, MB, ChB, DMRT, FRCSEdin, FRCR. Consultant Radiation Oncologist, Western General Hospital, Edinburgh, since 1981; b. 9.6.46, Kirkcaldy. Educ. Kirkcaldy High School; Edinburgh University. Pre-registration hospital posts, Royal Infirmary, Edinburgh, and Victoria Hospital, Kirkcaldy, 1971-72; junior hospital training course in surgery, Royal Infirmary, Edinburgh, 1972-75; Registrar post in Radiotherapy, Western General Hospital, Edinburgh, 1975-77; University Lecturer in Radiotherapy, Western General Hospital, Edinburgh, and MRC Cyclotron Unit, 1977-80; Project Investigator, M.D. Anderson Hospital and Tumour Institute, Houston, 1980-81. Member, several SHHD committees and working parties, and committees of Royal College of Radiologists. Recreations: preparation and eating of good food; good wines; opera sopranos; history and architecture. Address: (h.) 1 Laverockbank Road, Trinity, Edinburgh; T.-031-552 5699.

Rodger, James McPhail, BSc, MEd. Headmaster, Portree High School, since 1971; b. 15.9.33, Cleland, Lanarkshire; m., Jessie Tyre Crawford; 4 d. Educ. Wishaw High School; Glasgow University; Jordanhill College. Flying Officer, RAF, 1956; Teacher of Mathematics, Hamilton Academy, 1959-64; Principal Teacher of Mathematics and latterly Depute Headmaster, Carluke High School, 1964-71. Member, Consultative Committee on the Curriculum, 1980-83. Professional footballer: Glasgow Rangers, 1952-55, St. Mirren, 1955-62, Heart of Midlothian, 1962-65. Recreations: bridge; golf; hill-walking; gardening; reading. Address: (b.) Portree High School, Portree, Isle of Skye; T.-0478 2030.

Rodger, William J., JP. Chairman, Policy and Resources Committee, Kirkcaldy District Council, since 1984; Chairman, Kirkcaldy Licensing Board, since 1984; Chairman, Kirkcaldy Justices Committee, since 1982; b. 14.10.32, Buckhaven; m., Joan; 3 s. Educ. Buckhaven High School. Member, Buckhaven and Methil Town Council, 1971; Member, Kirkcaldy District Council, since 1974. Recreation: golf when time allows. Address: (h.) 70 Kirkland Walk, Methil, Leven, Fife, KY8 2AB; T.-0333 26673.

Roger, Alan Stuart, MBE (Mil), JP. Vice-President, National Trust for Scotland, since 1984; Council Member, Contemporary Art Society, since 1980; Chairman, Bonsai Kai, since 1965; b. 27.4.09, London. Educ. Loretto School; Trinity College, Oxford. Partner, Norris Oakley Bros. and Director, various public companies, 1933; BRC and St. John Ambulance, France, 1940; Ministry of Supply mission to India, 1940-41; Indian Army, 1941-45 and War Office, 1945-52, serving India, Persia, Iraq, Hong Kong; Director of various public companies in UK and Portugal, 1953-79. Trustee, National Galleries of Scotland, 1967-82; Trustee, Crarae Garden Trust. Recreations: gardening; reading. Address: (h.) Dundonnell, by Garve, Ross & Cromarty; T.-085 483 206.

Rogers, Rev. James Murdoch, BA (Hons), BD. Minister, Roseangle Ryehill Church, Dundee, since 1980; Convener, Board of World Mission and Unity, Church of Scotland, 1984-88; Vice-President, British Council of Churches, since 1987; Member, Central Committee, World Council of Churches, since 1988; b. 22.11.28, Limavady, Northern Ireland; m., Doris Young; 2 s. Educ. Coleraine Academical Institution; Queen's University, Belfast; Presbyterian College, Belfast. Minister, Second Presbyterian Church, Saintfield, 1955-65; Moderator, Down Presbytery; Secretary, Irish Council of Churches, 1963-65; Minister, Ryehill Church, Dundee, 1965-80; Chairman, Hospital Sub-Committee, Home Board; Vice-Convener, Overseas Council, Church of Scotland, 1977-80; Chairman, Departmental Board of Overseas Missions and Inter-Church Relations, 1977-83; Exchange Preacher, British Council of Churches, National Council of Churches, USA; Member, Board of Directors, Royal Dundee Institution for the Blind, since 1966. Recreations: golf; gardening; photography; travel; Rotarian. Address: (h.) 15 West Park Road, Dundee, DD2 1NU; T.-Dundee 67460.

Rogerson, Robert William Kelly Cupples, OBE, BArch, FRIBA, FRIAS, FSA Scot, MRSH. Vice Chairman, Scottish Council on Disability; Chairman, Committee on Access for Scotland, 1980-88; Council Member, National Trust for Scotland, 1980-86; b. 14.5.17, Glasgow; m., Mary Clark MacNeill; 1 s.; 1 d. Educ. High School of Glasgow; Strathclyde University. Architect in private practice, 1955-56 and 1958-82 (Partner, Watson Salmond & Gray, 1956-58); Lecturer, School of Architecture, Glasgow School of Art; Past Chairman, Glasgow Building Guardian Committee; Past Chairman, RIAS Trustees of The Hill House, Helensburgh; Founder and Chairman, Glasgow Summer School; former Member, Committee on Artistic Matters, Church of Scotland. Publications: A Place at Work (Co-author); Jack Coia, His Life & Work. Recreations: gardening; travelling abroad. Address: (h.) 49 Roman Court, Roman Road, Bearsden, Glasgow, G61 2NW; T.-041-942 3997.

Rolfe, Mervyn James. Chair, Tayside Education Committee, since 1986; Member, COSLA Education Committee, since 1986; b. 31.7.47, Wisbech; m., Christine; 1 s. Educ. Buckhaven High School. Civil servant, until 1983; Co-ordinator, Dundee Resources Centre for the Unemployed, 1983-87; Vice-Chair, Dundee Trades Council, 1981-82; Governor, Dundee (now Northern) College of Education, since 1986; Member, Dundee University Court, since 1986; Member, Scottish Community Education Council, 1986-88; Member, General Teaching Council, since 1986; Member, Scottish Committee for Staff Development in Education, since 1987; Member, Scottish Institute of Adult Education, since 1986; Member, Scottish Cooperative Development Committee, since 1984; Member, Dundee Heritage Trust, since 1986. Recreatios: reading; politics. Address: (h.) 17 Mains Terrace, Dundee; T.-0382 450073.

Rorke, Professor John, CBE, PhD, BSc, CEng, FIMechE, FRSE. Professor of Mechanical Engineering, Heriot-Watt University, since 1980 (Vice Principal, since 1984); b. 2.9.23, Dumbarton; m., Jane Craig Buchanan; 2 d. Educ. Dumbarton Academy; Royal Technical College, Glasgow. Lecturer, Strathclyde University, 1946-51; Assistant to Engineering Director, Alexander Stephen & Sons Ltd., 1951-56; Technical Manager, then General Manager and Engineering Director, William Denny & Bros. Ltd., 1956-63; Technical Director, then Sales Director, Managing Director and Chairman, Brown Bros. & Co. Ltd. and Chairman, John Hastie of Greenock Ltd., 1963-78; Managing Director, Vickers Offshore Group, 1978 (Director of Planning, Vickers PLC, 1979-80). President, Institution of Engineers and Shipbuilders in Scotland, 1985-87; Council Member, Institution of Mechanical Engineers and Royal Society of Edinburgh. Recreations: bridge; golf. Address: (h.) 3 Barnton Park Grove, Edinburgh; T.-031-336 3044.

Rose, David, BA, NDA, CertEd. Principal, The Barony College, Dumfries, since 1980; Member, Agricultural Training Board, since 1983; b. 6.7.40, Denton, Manchester; m., Pauline Anne Rose; 1 s.; 1 d. Educ. Seale-Hayne College of Agriculture; Open University. Assistant Farm Manager, Wiltshire, 1962-66; Lecturer in Agriculture, Cumbria College of Agriculture and Forestry, 1967-70; Senior Lecturer in Agriculture, Bishop Burton College of Agriculture, 1970-74; Vice-Principal, Oatridge College of Agriculture, 1974-80. Recreation: hill-walking. Address: (b.) Parkgate, Dumfries; T.-038 786 251.

Rosebery, 7th Earl of (Neil Archibald Primrose), DL; b. 11.2.29; m., Alison Mary Deirdre Reid; 1 s.; 4 d. Educ. Stowe; New College, Oxford. Address: (h.) Dalmeny House, South Queensferry, West Lothian.

Rosie, Professor Aeneas Murdoch, BSc, MSc, PhD, CEng, FIEE, MIEEE. Professor of Telecommunications, Strathclyde University, since 1973; b. 6.6.31, Wick; m., June Foley; 1 s.; 1 d. Educ. Wick High School; Glasgow University; Birmingham University. Electronic Engineer, Pye Radio Company; Research Fellow, Birmingham University; Lecturer, Senior Lecturer and Reader, Queen's University, Belfast. Recreations: sailing; formerly squash. Address: (h.) Mill Bridge, Rhu Road Higher, Helensburgh, Dunbartonshire.

Rosie, George. Freelance Writer and Broadcaster; b. 27.2.41, Edinburgh; m., Elizabeth Ann Burness; 2 s.; 1 d. Educ. Trinity Academy, Edinburgh; Edinburgh School of Architecture. Editor, Interior Design magazine, 1966-68; freelance magazine writer, 1968-76; Scottish Affairs Correspondent, Sunday Times, 1976-86; Reporter, Channel 4 TV series Down the Line, 1986-87, Scottish Eye, 1988. Publications: British in Vietnam, 1970; Cromarty, 1975; The Ludwig Initiative, 1978; Hugh Miller, 1982; The Directory of International Terrorism, 1986; as contributor:

Headlines, the Media in Scotland, 1978; Scottish Government Yearbook, 1982; Scotland, Multinationals and the Third World, 1982; World Offshore Oil and Gas Industry Report, 1987. Recreation: hill-walking. Address: (h.) 70 Comiston Drive, Edinburgh, EH10 5QS; T.-031-447 9660.

Rosie, Spencer John, BSc. Member, Orkney Islands Council, since 1982; Co-Founder, The Orkney Movement, 1980 (Chairman, 1980-84); b. 3.11.55, Kirkwall; m., Erica Anne Hourston; 1 s.; 2 d. Educ. Kirkwall Grammar School; Aberdeen University; Robert Gordon's Institute of Technology. First political candidate to be elected to Orkney Islands Council. Address: (h.) Drumlea, Carness Road, Kirkwall, Orkney; T.-Kirkwall 4553.

Rosin, Leslie, BL. Company Director; Member: Eastwood District Council, since 1984 (Vice Convener); Strathclyde Regional Council, since 1986; b. 31.8.31, London; m., Hilary Langman; 1 s.; 2 d. Educ. Hutchesons' Grammar School; Glasgow University. Chairman, Eastwood Conservative Association; Vice chairman, Giffnock and Newlands Hebrew Congregation. Recreation: harpsichord maker. Address: (h.) 23 Greenhill Avenue, Glasgow, G46 6QQ; T.-041-638 3333.

Ross, Alastair Robertson, OStJ, DA, ARSA, FRBS, FSA Scot, FRSA. Artist; Lecturer in Fine Art, Duncan of Jordanstone College of Art, Dundee, since 1966; Scottish Representative and Council Member, Royal Society of British Sculptors, since 1972; b. 8.8.41, Perth; m., Kathryn Margaret Greig Wilson; 1 d. Educ. St. Mary's Episcopal School, Dunblane; McLaren High School, Callander; Duncan of Jordanstone College of Art, Dundee. SED Postgraduate Scholarship, 1965-66; Royal Scottish Academy Carnegie Travelling Scholarship, 1965; Duncan of Drumfork Scholarship, 1965; award winner, Paris Salon, 1967; Medaille de Bronze, Societe des Artistes Francais, 1968; Medaille D'Argent, 1970; Council Member, Society of Scottish Artists, 1972-75; exhibited work widely in UK and abroad. Recreations: genealogy; heraldry; travel. Address: (h.) Ravenscourt, 28 Albany Terrace, Dundee, DD3 6HS; T.-0382 24235.

Ross, Alexander (Sandy), LLB, CYCW. Controller, Arts and Entertainment, Scottish Television, since 1986; b. 17.4.48, Grangemouth; 1 s.; 1 d. Educ. Grangemouth High School; Edinburgh University; Moray House College. Apprentice lawyer, 1971-73; Lecturer, Paisley College, 1974-75; Producer, Granada TV, 1978-86. Member, Edinburgh Town Council, 1971-74; Member, Edinburgh District Council, 1974-78; President, Moray House Students Union, 1976. Recreations: golf; music; reading; watching football. Address: (h.) 7 Murrayfield Avenue, Edinburgh, EH12 6AU; T.-031-337 3679.

Ross, Rev. Andrew Christian, MA, BD, STM, PhD. Senior Lecturer in Ecclesiastical History, Edinburgh University, since 1966 (Principal of New College and Dean, Faculty of Divinity, 1978-84); b. 10.5.31, Millerhill, Lothian; m., I. Joyce Elder; 4 s.; 1 d. (deceased). Educ. Dalkeith High School; Edinburgh University; Union Theological Seminary, New York. RAF, 1952-54; Minister, Church of Central Africa Presbyterian (Malawi), 1958-65; Chairman, Lands Tribunal of Nyasaland, then Malawi Government, 1963-65; Vice Chairman, National Tenders Board, Nyasaland, then Malawi Government, 1963-65. Member, University Court, 1971-73; Convener, Student Affairs Committee, 1977-83; Kerr Lecturer, Glasgow University, 1984; Lecturer, Assembly's College, Belfast, 1985. Publication: John Philip: Missions, Race and Politics in South Africa. Recreation: coaching and watching football. Address: (h.) 27 Colinton Road, Edinburgh; T.-031-447 5987.

Ross, Rev. David Sinclair, BSc, MSc, PhD, BD. Minister, Old Parish Church, Peterhead, since 1978; Church of Scotland Representative, Grampian Regional Education Committee, since 1981; b. 24.7.45, Aberdeen; 2 s. Educ. Aberdeen Academy; Aberdeen University; Glasgow University. Research Chemist, West Germany, 1971-74. Chairman, Peterhead Disabled Club; President, Peterhead Rugby FC; Chaplain, HM Prison, Peterhead, since 1980. Recreations: choral singing; rugby; trout fishing. Address: 49 King Street, Peterhead, AB4 6TA; T.-0779 72618.

Ross, Rt. Hon. Lord (Donald MacArthur Ross), PC, MA, LLB. Lord Justice Clerk, since 1985; a Senator of the College of Justice, since 1977; b. 29.3.27, Dundee; m., Dorothy Margaret Annand; 2 d. Educ. High School of Dundee; Edinburgh University. Advocate, 1952; QC, 1964; Vice-Dean, Faculty of Advocates, 1967-73; Dean of Faculty, 1973-76; Sheriff Principal of Ayr and Bute, 1972-73; Member, Scottish Committee, Council of Tribunals, 1970-76; Member, Committee on Privacy, 1970; Deputy Chairman, Boundary Commission for Scotland, 1977-85. Member, Court, Heriot-Watt University, since 1978, Chairman, since 1984. Hon. LLD, Edinburgh; Hon. DUniv, Heriot-Watt; FRSE. Recreation: gardening. Address: Parliament House, Edinburgh, EH1 1RQ; T.-031-225 2595.

Ross, Professor Donald Sutherland, BSc, PhD, ARCST, FEng, FIMechE, FIProdE, FRSA. Professor of Production Engineering and Head, Department of Design, Manufacture and Engineering Management, Strathclyde University, since 1966; b. 12.7.23, Glasgow; m., Catherine. Educ. Albert Senior Secondary School, Glasgow; London University; Glasgow University; Strathclyde University. Apprentice and Production Engineer, Rolls Royce Ltd., 1939-45; Production Engineer, Vactric Ltd., Airdrie, 1946-47; Teacher, Marr College, Troon, 1947-50; Lecturer, Royal College, Glasgow, 1951-59; Assistant to Works Director, L. Sterne, Hillington, 1960-61; Lecturer/Senior Lecturer, Strathclyde University, 1961-66. Address: (b.) Strathclyde University, Montrose Street, Glasgow, G1 1XJ; T.-041-552 4400, Ext. 2329.

Ross, Duncan, MBE. Principal, Benmore Centre for Outdoor Education, since 1975; Commissioner, Countryside Commission for Scotland, since 1972; Chairman, Scottish Mountain Leader Training Board, since 1987; b. 29.4.33, Sandbank, Argyll; m., Kathryn Dilworth. Educ. Moray House College of Education, Edinburgh. Pilot, RAF, 1951-57; Instructor, National Mountain

Training Centre, Glenmore Lodge, 1963-71; Deputy Principal, Benmore Centre for Outdoor Education, 1971-75. Recreations: mountaineering; sailing; skiing; nature study and conservation; reading. Address: (b.) Benmore Centre for Outdoor Education, by Dunoon, Argyll; T.-0369 6337.

Ross, Ernest. MP (Labour), Dundee West, since 1979; Chair, PLP Foreign Affairs Backbench Group; Convener, Scottish Group of Labour MPs; b. 27.7.42, Dundee; m., June; 2 s.; 1 d. Educ. St. John's Junior Secondary School. Apprentice Marine Fitter, Caledon Shipyard; Quality Control Inspector/Engineer, Timex. Recreations: football; cricket. Address: (b.) House of Commons, London, SW1A OAA; T.-01-219 3480.

Ross, Fiona Jean. Political Reporter, Scottish Television, since 1983; b. 7.11.48, London. Educ. Ayr Academy; Royal Scottish Academy of Music and Drama; Jordanhill College. Teacher of Drama, 1970-74; Journalist, Radio Clyde, 1974-83. Recreations: theatre; travelling; reading. Address: (b.) Scottish Television, Cowcaddens, Glasgow, G2 3PR; T.-041-332 9999.

Ross, Gavin Thomas Nelson, DA, DipTP, MArch, RIBA, ARIAS, FRSA. Vice Principal, Robert Gordon's Institute of Technology, since 1985; b. 14.6.41, Kincardine-on-Forth. Educ. Dollar Academy; Edinburgh College of Art; University of Pennsylvania. Architect: Livingston Development Corporation, 1966-77, Derek Stephenson & Partners, London, 1968-69, Greater London Council, 1969-73, The Edinburgh Consortium, 1973-77; Lecturer, then Principal, Edinburgh College of Art, 1973-84. Honorary Secretary, COPA-DOCI, 1979-84; Member, NAB/UGC/SED Architecture Working Group, 1984-85, and Town Planning Working Group, 1985-86; Member, CNAA Committee of Art and Design, since 1984. Recreations: art; architecture; travel. Address: (h.) 5 Keith Hall, Inverurie, Aberdeenshire, AB5 0LD; T.-0467 24843.

Ross, Graham Tullis, LVO. Director, Scottish Business in the Community (SCOTBIC), since 1982; b. 5.7.28, Edinburgh; m., Margot; 1 s.; 2 d. Educ. George Watson's College, Edinburgh. Director, Macvitties Guest & Co. Ltd., Edinburgh, 1955-65; Managing Director, Macvitties Guest (Edinburgh), A.F. Reid (Glasgow), 1965-71; Managing Director, A.A. Laing Ltd. and Ross Restaurants Ltd., 1971-76; Managing Director, D.S. Crawford (Catering) Ltd., 1976-82. Chairman, Scottish Hotel and Catering Institute, 1968-72; Chairman, Napier College Advisory Committee, 1970-85; former Scottish rugby internationalist. Recreation: hill-walking. Address: (h.) 81 Craiglockhart Road, Edinburgh; T.-031-556 9761.

Ross, Helen Elizabeth, BA, MA (Oxon), PhD (Cantab). Reader in Psychology, Stirling University, since 1983; b. 2.12.35, London. Educ. South Hampstead High School; Somerville College, Oxford; Newnham College, Cambridge. Assistant Mistress, schools in London and Oxfordshire, 1959-61; Research Assistant and student, Psychological Laboratory, Cambridge University, 1961-65; Lecturer in Psychology: Hull University, 1965-68, Stirling University, 1969-72; Senior Lecturer in Psychology, Stirling University, 1972-83; Research Fellow, DFVLR Institute for Aerospace Medicine, Bonn, 1980-81; Leverhulme Fellowship, 1983-84; Fellow, British Psychological Society, since 1986. Publications: Behaviour and Perception in Strange Environments, 1974; E.H. Weber: The Sense of Touch (Co-translator), 1978. Recreations: skiing; curling; hill-walking; traditional music. Address: (b.) Department of Psychology, Stirling University, Stirling, FK9 4LA; T.-0786 73171.

Ross, Rev. James, MA, BD. Minister, Kilsyth Anderson Parish Church; b. 26.4.33, Port Seton; m., Mary Cameron Somerville; 1 s.; 1 d. Educ. Preston Lodge School, Prestonpans; Aberdeen University. Former Assistant Superintendent, Seamen's Bethel, Glasgow. Recreations: gardening; music. Address: (h.) Anderson Manse, Kilsyth, G65 0HR; T.-Kilsyth 822345.

Ross, Rev. John Durham, BA, DipEd. Industrial Chaplain, Dundee Area; b. 8.6.32, Mansfield, Victoria, Australia; m., Violet Cooper Shearer; 1 s.; 1 d. Educ. Wesley College, Melbourne; Melbourne University and Ormond College. Chaplain, RAN, 1958-60; Assistant Minister, Govan Old, Glasgow, 1960-63; Associate Minister, Double Bay, Sydney, Australia, 1964-66; Leader, World Council of Churches ecumenical teams in Italy, later also Co-ordinator of teams in Greece and Cyprus and liaison for North African teams, 1966-73; Minister, Langside, Glasgow, 1974-84. First Chairman, Battlefield and Langside Community Council; Co-Chairman, Langside and Battlefield Caring Service. Address: (h.) 6 Hill Street, Broughty Ferry, Dundee, DD5 2JL; T.-Dundee 78729.

Ross, John Graham, DSO, MBE, TD, DL. Solicitor; Honorary Sheriff, Dundee, since 1971; Deputy Lieutenant, City of Dundee, since 1975; b. 13.4.21, Dundee; m., Kathleen Mary Pain; 3 s.; 1 d. Educ. Dundee High School. Commissioned, Black Watch (RHR), 1939-41, Parachute Regiment, 1941-46, 15th Bn., Parachute Regiment (TA), 1949-53; former Partner, Ross Strachan & Co., Solicitors, Dundee, 1949. Recreation: gardening. Address: (h.) Nether Ridge, Rockcliffe, by Dalbeattie, DG5 4QF.

Ross, Peter Edward, MSc, PhD. Senior Lecturer, Department of Medicine, Dundee University, since 1983; b. 17.10.45, Perth; m., Joan; 2 d. Educ. County High School, Arnold, Nottinghamshire; Dundee University. Postdoctoral Research Fellow, Department of Medicine, Dundee University, 1974-76; non-clinical Lecturer, Department of Medicine, and Honorary Lecturer, Department of Biochemistry, Dundee, 1976-83; Visiting Lecturer, Basrah University, 1979, University of Shenyang, People's Republic of China, 1987. Recreations: squash; travel; reading; music. Address: (b.) Department of Medicine, Ninewells Hospital and Medical School, Dundee, DD1 9SY; T.-Dundee 60111, Ext. 2456.

Ross, Philip Wesley, TD, MB, ChB, MD, MRCP, MRCPath, MIBiol, FLS. Consultant, Edinburgh Royal Infirmary, and Senior Lecturer in Bacteriology, Edinburgh University, since 1973; b. 6.6.36, Aberdeen; m., Stella Joyce Shand; 2 s.; 1 d. Educ. Turriff Academy; Robert Gordon's College, Aberdeen; Aberdeen University. Senior Warden, Edinburgh University, 1972-83. Lt.-Col., RAMC (TA); Officer Commanding Medical Division and Edinburgh Detachment 205 Scottish General Hospital, 1975-80; Examiner, Royal College of Surgeons, Edinburgh, Royal College of Pathologists; Chairman, Lothian Area Division of Laboratory Medicine, since 1987; Elder, Duddingston Kirk, Edinburgh. Publications: papers in scientific and medical journals on streptococci, diseases of mouth, throat and genital tract, antibiotics and cross infection. Recreations: music; playing church organs (formerly organist in three Aberdeen churches); walking; tennis; Perthshire. Address: (h.) 18 Old Church Lane, Duddingston, Edinburgh, EH15 3PX; T.-031-661 5415.

Ross, Thomas Alexander, KStJ, BL, PhD. Senior Partner, Russel & Aitken, WS, Falkirk, Edinburgh and Denny; Honorary Sheriff, Tayside, Central and Fife; b. 18.7.06, Selkirk; m., Eleanor Tyson; 1 s. Educ. Selkirk School; Edinburgh University. Director of Administration, Far Eastern Bureau of Political Intelligence, Department of the Foreign Office in Delhi and Chungking, 1944; Governor, Christ's Hospital. Recreations: travelling; shooting. Address: (b.) Russel & Aitken, WS, King's Court, Falkirk; T.-Falkirk 22888.

Ross, William, FRICS. Director of Economic Development and Estates, City of Edinburgh District Council, since 1984; b. 2.2.41, Rutherglen; m., Margaret; 2 s.; 1 d. Educ. Rutherglen Academy; Glasgow University. Trainee, London County Council; Negotiator, Hillier Parker May and Rowden; Valuer, Glasgow Corporation; District Surveyor, British Rail Property Board; Group Development Surveyor, Maxwell Property Development Company; self-employed; Principal Surveyor (Development), Grampian Regional Council; Depute Director of Estates, Edinburgh District Council. Recreations: gardening; chess; family. Address: (b.) 375 High Street, Edinburgh; T.-031-225 2424, Ext. 5800.

Ross Stewart, David Andrew, OBE, BA (Cantab). Managing Director, John Bartholomew & Son Ltd., since 1968; b. 30.11.30, Edinburgh; m., Susan Olive Routh; 2 s. Educ. Rugby School; Cambridge University. Assistant General Manager, Alex. Cowan & Sons (NZ) Ltd., 1959-62; General Manager, Alex. Cowan & Sons (Stationery) Ltd., 1962-66; General Manager, Spicers (Stationery) Ltd., 1966-68. Vice Chairman, Scottish Provident Institution; Chairman, St. Andrew Trust plc; Director, East of Scotland Industrial Investments plc; Member, Scottish Advisory Board, Abbey National Building Society; Chairman, Trade Development Committee, Scottish Council (Development and Industry). Recreations: fishing; gardening; golf. Address: (b.) 12 Duncan Street, Edinburgh, EH9 1TA; T.-031-667 9341.

Round, Professor Nicholas Grenville, MA, DPhil. Stevenson Professor of Hispanic Studies, Glasgow University, since 1972; b. 6.6.38, Looe, Cornwall; m., Ann Le Vin; 1 d. Educ. Launceston College; Pembroke College, Oxford. Lecturer, then Reader in Spanish, Queen's University, Belfast, 1962-72; Warden, Alanbrooke Hall, Queen's University, Belfast, 1970-72. Publications: Unamuno: Abel Sanche: A Critical Guide, 1974; The Greatest Man Uncrowned: A Study of the Fall of Alvaro de Luna, 1985. Recreations: reading; drawing; politics; hill-walking; music; all aspects of Cornwall. Address: (h.) 11 Dougalston Avenue, Milngavie, Glasgow; T.-041-956 2507.

Rowan, John O'Donnell, PhD, CPhys, FInstP, CEng, FIEE. Deputy Director, West of Scotland Health Boards Department of Clinical Physics and Bio-Engineering, since 1983; Honorary Lecturer in Clinical Physics, Glasgow University, since 1980; Member, National Panel of Assessors for NHS Top Grade Scientists in Scotland, since 1982; b. 5.4.36, Glasgow; m., Maureen Paterson; 2 d. Educ. Victoria Drive Senior Secondary School, Glasgow; Glasgow University. Research Physicist, Barr and Stroud, Glasgow, 1961-63; Electronics Engineer, Scottish Research Reactor Centre, East Kilbride, 1963-66; West of Scotland Health Boards Department of Clinical Physics and Bio-Engineering: Senior Physicist, 1966-71, Principal Physicist, 1971-81, Top Grade Physicist, 1981-83. Honorary Treasurer, Scottish Branch, Institute of Physics, 1972-77; Honorary Secretary, Hospital Physicists Association, 1976-78, and President, 1982-84; Deputy Editor, Physics in Medicine and Biology, 1980-82. Address: (b.) 11 West Graham Street, Glasgow; T.-041-332 6061.

Rowbotham, Samuel Russell, BSc, RIBA, ARIAS, MIH. Director of Housing, City of Dundee District Council, since 1986; b. 10.12.42, Belfast; m., Dorothy; 1 s.; 2 d. Educ. Methodist College, Belfast; Queen's University, Belfast. Local authority Architect, 1971-75; Housing Development Officer, Dundee District Council, 1975-83; Director of Housing and Development, North Kesteven District Council, 1983-86. Address: (b.) 3 Shore Terrace, Dundee.

Rowe, Michael, BA (Hons). Deputy Director Scotland, Employment Service, since 1987; b. 30.5.37, Stoke-on-Trent; m., Kathleen Marie; 2 s. Educ. High School, Newcastle-under-Lyme; St. Catherine's College, Oxford University. Various posts, Department of Employment, 1961-70; First Secretary, UK Delegation to European Communities in Brussels, 1970-72; various posts, London, 1972-81; Benefit Manager, Scotland, Department of Employment, 1981-87. Recreations: family; involvement in youth club activities; enjoying good food and wine. Address: (b.) Employment Service, Office for Scotland, 9 St. Andrew Square, Edinburgh; T.-031-225 8500.

Roxburgh, Andy, DPE. Scottish Football Association National Coach, since 1986, and Technical Director, since 1975; b. 5.8.43, Glasgow; m., Catherine; 1 s. Educ. Bellahouston Academy; Jordanhill College. Primary school Head Teacher, three years; professional footballer, 10 years; clubs: Partick Thistle, Clydebank, Falkirk; Coach, Clydebank, two years; Coaching Director, SFA, 12 years; Manager, Youth, U-21 and Full International teams, over 12-year period; FIFA Instructor, six years. Recreations: music; reading; golf. Address: (b.) 6 Park Gardens, Glasgow; T.-041-332 6372.

Roxburghe, 10th Duke of (Guy David Innes-Ker), b. 18.11.54; m., Lady Jane Meriel Grosvenor; 2 s.; 1 d. Educ. Eton; Sandhurst; Magdalene College, Cambridge. Address: (h.) Floors Castle, Kelso.

Roy, Rev. Alan John, BSc, BD, MA. Minister, Ogilvie & Stobswell, Dundee, since 1985; b. 27.12.34, Edinburgh; m., Roma Mary Hutchison Finlayson; 2 s.; 1 d. Educ. Daniel Stewart's College, Edinburgh; Edinburgh University; Swedish Theological Institute, Jerusalem. Missionary, Church of Scotland, with the United Church of Zambia, 1961-72, first as District Minister, Serenje, then as Tutor, Ministerial Training College, Mindolo, Kitwe; Minister, Park, Dundee, 1972-76; became Minister, United Congregation of Stobswell, 1976. Vice Chairman, Scottish Support Group, Feed the Minds; Chairman, Dundee Auxiliary, Leprosy Mission; Vice Chairman, Crossroads Care Attendant Scheme (Dundee). Recreations: golf; stamp collecting. Address: (h.) 23 Shamrock Street, Dundee, DD4 7AH; T.-Dundee 459119.

Roy, Rev. James Alexander, MA, BD. Minister, Lochee West, Dundee, since 1973; Chairman, Children's Panel for Tayside, 1983-86; Clerk, Dundee Presbytery, Church of Scotland, since 1985; b. 21.2.40, Comrie; m., Sheila Munro Fitzgerald; 1 s.; 2 d. Educ. Morrison's Academy, Crieff; St. Andrews University. Minister, Dunnottar Parish Church, Stonehaven, 1966-73. Address: Churchmount, 3 Coupar Angus Road, Dundee, DD2 3HG; T.-0382 611415.

Royle, Trevor Bridge, MA. Author and Broadcaster; Editor, Lines Review; Literary Editor, Scotland on Sunday; b. 26.1.45, Mysore, India; m., Dr. Hannah Mary Rathbone; 3 s. Educ. Madras College, St. Andrews; Aberdeen University. Editor, William Blackwood & Sons Ltd.; Literature Director, Scottish Arts Council, 1971-79; Council Member, Scottish National Dictionary Association; Scottish Arts Council Book Award, 1983. Publications: We'll Support You Evermore: The Impertinent Saga of Scottish Fitba' (Co-Editor), 1976; Jock Tamson's Bairns (Editor), 1977; Precipitous City: The Story of Literary Edinburgh, 1980; A Diary of Edinburgh, 1981; Edinburgh, 1982; Death Before Dishonour: The True Story of Fighting Mac, 1982; The Macmillan Companion to Scottish Literature, 1983; James and Jim: The Biography of James Kennaway, 1983; The Kitchener Enigma, 1985; The Best Years of their Lives: The Post-War National Service Experience, 1986; War Report: The War Correspondents' View of Battle from the Crimea to the Falklands, 1987; radio plays: Magnificat, 1984; Old Alliances, 1985; Foreigners, 1987; Huntingtower, 1988; A Man Flourishing, 1988. Recreations: rugby football; hill-walking; music. Address: (h.) 6 James Street, Edinburgh, EH15 2DS; T.-031-669 2116.

Ruckley, Charles Vaughan, MB, ChM, FRCSEdin. Consultant Surgeon, Royal Infirmary, Edinburgh, since 1971; part-time Senior Lecturer, Edinburgh University, since 1971; b. 14.5.34, Wallasey; m., Valerie Anne Brooks; 1 s.; 1 d. Educ. Wallasey Grammar School; Edinburgh University. Research Fellow, University of Colorado, 1967-68. Secretary/Treasurer, Vascular Surgical Society of Great Britain and Ireland; Member, Council, Association of Surgeons of Great Britain and Ireland. Recreations: angling; music; skiing. Address: (b.) Vascular Surgery Unit, Royal Infirmary, Edinburgh; T.-031-229 2477.

Runnalls, Graham Arthur, BA, MA, DipGenLing, DLitt. Reader in French, Edinburgh University; b. 21.11.37, Exmouth; m., Anne K.; 2 d. Educ. Exmouth Grammar School; Exeter University. Assistant Lecturer in French, Exeter University, 1962-63; Lecturer in French, North London Polytechnic, 1963-66; joined Edinburgh University as Lecturer, 1966. Honorary President, International Society for the Study of Medieval Theatre. Recreations: opera; sport, especially tennis and running. Address: (h.) 85A Colinton Road, Edinburgh, EH10 5DF; T.-031-337 1737.

Rusby, Sir Cameron, KCB, LVO. Chief Executive, Scottish Society for the Prevention of Cruelty to Animals, since 1983; b. 20.2.26, Sliema, Malta; m., Marion Elizabeth Bell; 2 d. Educ. Wootton Court School, near Canterbury; Royal Naval College, Dartmouth. Thirty nine years in Royal Navy, reaching rank of Vice Admiral; retired, 1982. Recreations: sailing; skiing; equitation. Address: c/o Bank of Scotland, 70 High Street, Peebles, EH45 8AQ.

Russell, (Alastair) Muir, BSc. Head, Local Government Finance Division 1, Scottish Office; b. 9.1.49, Glasgow; m., Eileen A. Mackay (qv). Educ. High School of Glasgow; Glasgow University. Assistant Principal, Scottish Office, 1970; Principal, Scottish Office, 1974; Secretary, Scottish Development Agency, 1975-76; Assistant Secretary, Scottish Office, 1981; Principal Private Secretary to Secretary of State for Scotland, 1981-83; Head, Energy Division, Industry Department for Scotland, 1983-86. Recreations: music; food and wine. Address: (b.) New St. Andrew's House, Edinburgh, EH1; T.-031-244 5002.

Russell, Sheriff Albert Muir Galloway, QC, BA (Oxon), LLB. Sheriff, Grampian, Highland and Islands, at Aberdeen, since 1971; b. 26.10.25, Edinburgh; m., Margaret Winifred Millar; 2 s.; 2 d. Educ. Edinburgh Academy; Wellington College; Brasenose College, Oxford; Edinburgh University. Lt., Scots Guards, 1944-47; Member, Faculty of Advocates, 1951; Standing Junior Counsel to Board of Trade, Department of Agriculture and Forestry Commission; QC (Scot), 1965; Vice Chairman, Board of Management, Southern Group of Hospitals, Edinburgh, 1966-70; Governor, Moray House College of Education, 1965-70. Recreations: golf; music. Address: (h.) Easter Ord House, Skene, Aberdeenshire, AB3 6SQ; T.-0224 740228.

Russell, Rev. Archibald, MA. Minister, Duror linked with Glencoe, since 1979; Clerk, Lochaber Presbytery, since 1982; Moderator, Synod of the Southern Highlands, 1985-87; b. 17.11.24, Cleland, Lanarkshire; m., Elma Sandeman Watson; 2 s. Educ. Wishaw High School; Glasgow University. Assistant, South Dalziel Parish Church, Motherwell; Minister: Holyrood Abbey, Edinburgh, St. Mark's Lancefield, Glasgow, Anderston Parish Church, Glasgow; first Community Minister of Church of Scotland (based at Drumchapel, Glasgow). Founder Editor, Drumchapel News. Recreations: gardening; local history. Address: Manse of Duror and Glencoe, Brecklet, Ballachulish, Argyll, PA39 4JG; T.-085 52 209.

Russell, David Cairns, FRICS. Deputy Director of Building and Chief Quantity Surveyor, Scottish Development Department, since 1980; b. 21.8.30, Glasgow; m., Moira Young Whitehill; 3 s. Educ. Hutchesons' Boys Grammar School, Glasgow; Royal Technical College, Glasgow. Apprentice Quantity Surveyor, 1947-54 (including National Service); appointments in private practice, 1954-68; joined Scottish Development Department, 1968. Recreations: hill-walking; swimming; bridge. Address: (h.) 14 Learmonth Gardens, Edinburgh, EH4 1HB; T.-031-332 5081.

Russell, David Michael, MSc (Eng), BSc (Eng), AKC, CEng, MIEE. HM Inspector of Schools (Further and Higher Education), since 1976; b. 18.6.34, Runwell, Essex; m., Lena; 1 s.; 1 d. Educ. St. Clement Danes Grammar School; King's College, London University; Birmingham University. RAF, 1953-55; Executive Engineer, Cable and Wireless Ltd., 1960-62; Engineer, Decca Radar Ltd., 1962-64; Assistant Professor, American University of Beirut, 1964-67; Senior Lecturer, Middlesex Polytechnic, 1967-70; Technical Consultant, NEC (Japan), Beirut, 1970-72; Senior/Principal Lecturer, Plymouth Polytechnic, 1972-76. Recreations: Member, Edinburgh Festival Chorus and Edinburgh Grand Opera. Address: (h.) 27 Murrayfield Gardens, Edinburgh, EH12 6DG; T.-031-337 5016.

Russell, George, MB, ChB, FRCP. Consultant Paediatrician, Grampian Health Board, since 1969; Honorary Senior Lecturer in Child Health, Aberdeen University, since 1970; b. 2.7.36, Insch; m., Gillian Douglas Simpson; 2 s.; 2 d. Educ. Robert Gordon's College; Aberdeen University. Junior hospital appointments, Aberdeen teaching hospitals; Research Fellow, University of Colorado; Lecturer in Child Health, Aberdeen University; Professor of Paediatrics, University of Riyad, Saudi Arabia. Recreations: walking; photography; working. Address: (h.) 12 Pinewood Avenue, Aberdeen, AB1 8NB; T.-0224 315448.

Russell, George Stuart, BL, CA, WS, OBE. Member, Queen's Bodyguard for Scotland (Royal Company of Archers); former Senior Partner, Strathern and Blair WS; b. 21.1.14, Edinburgh; m.; 1 s.; 3 d. Educ. Edinburgh Academy; Belhaven Hill; Harrow; Edinburgh University. CA, 1937; served Second World War, 1939-45 (Lt. Col.); then pursued a legal career; Fiscal, WS Society, 1973-79; closely involved in work of National Trust for Scotland, 1951-82, now Councillor Emeritus; Treasurer, Iona Community, 1947-65; President, Edinburgh Abbeyfield Society; Vice President, UK, Abbeyfield Society, 1975-83; Trustee, Edinburgh Old Town Trust and Lothian Building Preservation Trust. Recreations: fishing; walking. Address: (h.) 59 Braid Road, Edinburgh, EH10; T.-031-447 6009.

Russell, Rev. John, MA. Minister, Tillicoultry Parish Church, since 1978; b. 29.5.33, Glasgow; m., Sheila Spence; 2 s. Educ. Cathedral School, Bombay; High School of Glasgow; Glasgow University. Licensed by Glasgow Presbytery, 1957; ordained by United Church of Canada, 1959; Assistant Minister: Trinity United Church, Kitchener, Ontario, 1958-60, South Dalziel Church, Motherwell, 1960-62; Minister: Scots Church, Rotterdam, 1963-72, Southend Parish Church, Kintyre, 1972-78; Member of various General Assembly Committees, since 1972; Convener, General Assembly's Committee on Unions and Readjustments, since 1987. Recreations: travel; reading. Address: The Manse, Dollar Road, Tillicoultry, Clackmannanshire, FK13 6PD; T.-0259 50340.

Russell, Michael William, MA. Chief Executive, Network Scotland Ltd. (Director, 1983, Executive Director, 1984-88); b. 9.8.53; m., Cathleen Macaskill; 1 s. Educ. Marr College, Troon; Edinburgh University. Creative Producer, Church of Scotland, 1974-77; Director, Cinema Sgire, Western Isles, 1977-81; Founder and first Director, Celtic Film and Television Festival, 1980; Secretary General, Association for Film and Television in the Celtic Countries, 1981-83. Parliamentary candidate (SNP), Clydesdale, 1987; Executive Vice Chairman, Publicity, SNP, since 1987; Sub-Deacon, Episcopal Church in Scotland; Chairman, Save a Life in Scotland Campaign, 1986-88; Member, Scottish Advisory Committee, National Aids Trust, since 1987; Member, BBC Scottish Continuing Education Advisory Panel, since 1988. Recreation: cookery. Address: (h.) 3 The Terrace, Tillietudlem, by Lesmahagow, Lanarkshire, ML11 9PN; T.-Crossford 276.

Russell, Robin Irvine, MD, PhD, FRCPEdin, FRCPGlas, FACN. Consultant in Charge, Gastroenterology Unit, Royal Infirmary, Glasgow, since 1970; Consultant Physician, Royal Infirmary, Glasgow, and Glasgow University, since 1970; b. 21.12.36, Wishaw; m., Ann Tindal Wallace; 1 s.; 1 d. Educ. Glasgow University. Lecturer, Department of Clinical Medicine, Glasgow University; Member, medical and scientific staff, Medical Research Council Gastroenterology Unit, London. Chairman, British Digestive Diseases Foundation (Scotland). Publications: Elemental Diets, 1981; Investigative Tests and Techniques in Gastroenterology. Recreations: golf; travel; literature; music. Address: (h.) 28 Ralston Road, Bearsden, Glasgow, G61 3BA; T.-041-942 6613.

Russell, Sheriff Terence Francis, BL. Sheriff, North Strathclyde, at Kilmarnock, since 1983; b. 12.4.31, Glasgow; m., Mary Ann Kennedy; 2 d. Educ. St. Mungo's Academy, Glasgow; Glasgow University. Solicitor: Glasgow, 1955-58, Bombay High Court, 1958-63, Glasgow, 1963-81; Sheriff, North Strathclyde, at Oban and Campbeltown and Grampian, Highland and Islands, at Fort William, 1981-83. Recreations: gardening; painting. Address: (h.) 1 Sutherland Avenue, Glasgow, G41; T.-041-427 1745.

Russell, Professor William C., BSc, PhD. Professor of Biochemistry, St. Andrews University, since 1984; b. 9.8.30, Glasgow; m., 1, Dorothy Ada Brown (deceased); 1 s.; 1 d.; 2, Reta McDougall. Educ. Allan Glen's School, Glasgow; Glasgow University. Locke Research Fellow, Institute of Virology, Glasgow, 1959-63; Eleanor Roosevelt International Cancer Fellow, Toronto University, 1963-64; Member, MRC Scientific Staff, National Institute for Medical Research, London, 1964-84; Head, Division of Virology, 1977-84. Editor, Journal of General Virology, 1972-77; Convener, Virus Group, Society for General Microbiology, since 1984. Address: (b.) Department of Biochemistry and Microbiology, St. Andrews University, Irvine Building, North Street, St. Andrews, KY16 9AL; T.-0334 76161.

Rutherford, Walter Angus, BA, ACP. Vice Convener, Annandale and Eskdale District Council; Chairman, Annan Fishery Board, since 1984; Vice Chairman, Dumfriesshire Education Trust, since 1984; b. 24.9.21, Newcastle-upon-Tyne; m., Phyllis; 1 step s.; 1 d. Educ. Heaton Grammar School; Goldsmiths College, London University; Open University. Royal Navy; elected, Annandale and Eskdale District Council, 1977; Reader, Church of Scotland; Member, Dumfriesshire EIS Executive, 1968-82; Honorary Life Member, EIS. Recreations: gardening; reading; swimming. Address: (h.) Holmlea, Eaglesfield, Lockerbie, Dumfriesshire.

Rutherford, William Hay, MA, LLB. Advocate in Aberdeen, since 1949; Consultant, Raeburn Christie & Co. (Partner, 1978-87); Honorary Sheriff, Grampian, Highland and Islands, since 1974; b. 9.11.16, Forres; m., Dr. Jean Aitken Steel Wilson; 1 s.; 2 d. Educ. Forres Academy; Aberdeen University. Law Apprentice, James & George Collie, Advocate, Aberdeen, 1936-39; 51st Highland Division, Royal Signals, 1939-46 (taken prisoner, St. Valery, France, 1940; held prisoner, Stalag VIIIB, Upper Silesia, 1940-45); Legal Assistant, John Angus, Advocate, Aberdeen, 1946-61; Partner, Christie, Buthlay & Rutherford, Advocates, Aberdeen, 1962-78; President, Society of Advocates, Aberdeen, 1985-86; Session Clerk, Kirk of St. Nicholas (City Kirk of Aberdeen), since 1954; President, Royal Northern Agricultural Society, 1980. Recreations: country walking and wildlife study; organisation of equestrian events. Address: 38 Gladstone Place, Queen's Cross, Aberdeen.

Rutherfurd, Richard Napier, JP, BSc (Eng), MB, ChB, MRCGP. Honorary Sheriff; b. 13.5.02, Glasgow; m., Elinor D. Jackson (deceased); 2 s.; 1 d. Educ. Glasgow Academy; Sedbergh School; Glasgow University. Sir William Arrol, 1921-28; Engineer, Central Argentine Railway, 1928-31; Western Infirmary, Glasgow/Royal Hospital for Sick Children, Yorkhill, 1938-39; general practice: Rothesay, 1939, West Kirkby, Cheshire; Captain, RAMC, UK and Egypt, 1942-45; general practice, Kirkcudbright, 1946-70. Local Secretary and Hon. Medical Adviser, RNLI (Lifeboat); last Provost of Royal Burgh of Kirkcudbright. Recreations: sailing; tennis; climbing. Address: (h.) Wester Oakley, Kirkcudbright, DG6 4AH; T.-0557 30410.

Ruthven, Ian Scott, MB, ChB, FRCPEdin, FRCPGlas, DObstRCOG. Consultant Paediatrician, Ayrshire and Arran Health Board, since 1969; Postgraduate Tutor, South Ayrshire Hospitals, 1981-87; b. 9.3.37, Glasgow; m., Louisa Mary Jolly; 1 s.; 2 d. Educ. High School of Glasgow; Glasgow University. Junior hospital - appointments, various Glasgow hospitals and in New Jersey, USA. Chairman, Ayrshire Paediatric Division and Past Chairman Ayrshire and Arran Committee for Hospital Medical Services; Chairman, Ayrshire and Arran Division, BMA, 1987-88; Member, Paediatric Committee, Royal College of Physicians and Surgeons of Glasgow. Recreations: golf; angling; hill-walking. Address: (h.) Westholme, 10 Victoria Drive, Troon, KA10 6EN; T.-0292 313006.

Ryan, James, PhL, BD. Deputy Secretary, Dundee University, since 1980; b. 2.3.31, Denny; m., Winifred Frances O'Donnell; 2 s.; 2 d. Educ. Blairs College, Aberdeen; Gregorian University, Rome. Commissioned, Argyll and Sutherland Highlanders, 1954; seconded Royal West African Frontier Force (1st Bn., Gold Coast Regiment), 1955; Teacher, 1957; HMOCS (Sierra Leone), 1958-64; Chairman, two Commissions of Enquiry, 1963; Assistant Secretary, St. Andrews University, 1964-67; Assistant Secretary, Senior Assistant Secretary, Deputy Secretary, Dundee University, 1967-85. Secretary, Abertay Rotary Club, 1982-85. Recreations: bowling; swimming; reading. Address: (h.) 6 Fontstane Crescent, Monifieth, Dundee, DD5 4JZ; T.-0382 532711.

Ryan, John D., CBE (1986), BDS. Dental Surgeon; Chairman, Argyll and Clyde Health Board, since 1979; Chairman, Information and Computer Services Advisory Group, Scottish Health Services Planning Council, since 1985; b. 10.1.43, Glasgow; m., Margaret; 1 s.; 1 d. Educ. St. Ninian's High School, Kirkintilloch; Glasgow University. Member, 4th District Council, Renfrewshire, 1968-70; Member, Greenock Corporation, 1973-75; Member, Inverclyde District Council, 1974-77; joined Argyll and Clyde Health Board, 1974 (Vice Chairman, 1977-79). Recreations: golf; sailing. Address: (h.) 35 Esplanade, Greenock; T.-0475 27649.

Ryden, Kenneth, MC, DL, FRICS, FRVA; b. 15.2.17, Blackburn; m., Catherine Kershaw Wilkinson; 2 s. Educ. Queen Elizabeth's Grammar School, Blackburn. Served Second World War, Royal Engineers, attached Royal Bombay Sappers and Miners, in India, Burma and Assam, 1940-46; retired Captain; mentioned in Despatches; Ministry of Works, Scotland, 1946-47; attached UK High Commission, India, 1947-50; Senior Estate Surveyor, Scotland, 1950-59; Founder and Senior Partner, Kenneth Ryden & Partners, Chartered Survyors, 1959-74; Chairman, Lothian Region Valuation Appeal Panel, since 1987; Member, Scottish Solicitors' Discipline Tribunal, since 1985. FRCPE, 1985; Master, Company of Merchants of City of Edinburgh, 1976-78. Recreations: golf; fishing; Scottish art. Address: 19 Belgrave Crescent, Edinburgh, EH4 3AJ; T.-031-332 5893.

S

St. Clair-Ford, Robin Sam. General Organiser, Scotland's Gardens Scheme, since 1982; b. 6.6.41, Fareham; m., Alison Frances; 2 s. Educ.

Nautical College, Pangbourne; Royal Military Academy, Sandhurst. Officer, KOYLI, 1961-71 (last appointment, Adjutant Light Infantry Depot, Shrewsbury); Sales Executive, Ashton Containers Ltd., 1971-76; self-employed retailer, 1976-82. Recreations: travel; golf; running a family. Address: (h.) 21 Claremont Crescent, Edinburgh, EH7 4HX; T.-031-557 3444.

Salmon, Thomas Graham, MA, LLB, Hon. FRIAS, SSC, JP. Factor, Lockerby Trust, since 1959; Chairman, Davidson Clinic, Edinburgh Trust, since 1973; Chairman, Scottish Anti-Common Market Council, since 1976; Chairman of Council, St. Andrew Society, since 1986; b. 21.7.10, Edinburgh; m., Annie (Nancy) Hunter Waters. Educ. George Watson's Boys' College, Edinburgh; Edinburgh University. Solicitor, 1934; private practice until retirement in 1981; was Secretary/Treasurer: Edinburgh Section, Cinematograph Exhibitors' Association, Society of Scottish Artists, Scottish Society of Women Artists, Edinburgh Architectural Association, Treasurer, Scottish Modern Arts Association, and Legal Adviser, Scottish Branch, CEA; twice Chairman, South Edinburgh Branch, Scottish Liberal Party; Session Clerk (Church of Scotland), 40 years; Army, during War; served Council, Law Society of Scotland; former Vice-President, SSC Society. Recreations: Scottish activities; gardening; modest tartan collecting. Address: 9 South Gray Street, Edinburgh, EH9 1TE; T.-031-668 1358.

Salmond, Alexander Elliot Anderson, MA (Hons). Economist; MP (SNP), Banff and Buchan, since 1987; Senior Vice-Chair, Scottish National Party, since 1987; b. 31.12.54, Linlithgow; m., Moira McGlashan. Educ. Linlithgow Academy; St. Andrews University. Vice-President: Federation of Student Nationalists, 1974-77, St. Andrews University SRC, 1977-78; Founder Member, SNP 79 Group, 1979; Assistant Agricultural and Fisheries Economist, DAFS, 1978-80; Economist, Royal Bank of Scotland, 1980-87; Parliamentary Spokesperson on Energy, Fishing, Treasury; Member, SNP National Executive, 1981-82, and since 1983. Recreations: golf; reading. Address: (b.) House of Commons, London; T.-01-219 4578; Constituency Office, 17 Maiden Street, Peterhead; T.-0779 70444.

Salmond, Rev. James Sommerville, BA, BD, MTh, ThD. Minister, Holytown Parish Church, since 1979; b. 13.1.51, Broxburn; m., Catherine F. Wildy; 4 d. Educ. West Calder High School; Whitburn Academy; Leeds University; Edinburgh University; Central School of Religion. Serves on the Committees of Scottish Reformation Society, National Church Association, etc.; regular contributor to radio and TV programmes on evangelical issues. Publication: Evangelicals within the Kirk 1690-1843. Recreations: field sports; riding. Address: The Manse, Holytown, Motherwell; T.-Holytown 832622.

Salter, Bruce Lloyd. Member, Grampian Regional Council, since 1980; Director, Scottish National Orchestra Society, since 1983; Director, Voluntary Service, Aberdeen, since 1983; Member, Aberdeen Harbour Board, 1984-86; b. 11.10.58, Aberdeen; m., Linda Westland. Educ. Robert Gordon's College, Aberdeen. Chairman, Aberdeen North Constituency Labour Party, 1979-81; Secretary, Aberdeen District Labour Party, 1987-88. Recreations: drawing; writing; local history; watching sport. Address: (h.) 34 Bethany Gardens, Aberdeen.

Salter, Professor Stephen Hugh, MA (Cantab). Professor of Engineering Design, Edinburgh University, since 1986; b. 7.12.38, Johannesburg; m., Professor Margaret Donaldson. Educ. Framlingham College; Sidney Sussex College, Cambridge. Apprentice aircraft fitter and tool-maker; Research Assistant, Department of Psychology, Cambridge University; Research Fellow, then Lecturer, Department of Artificial Intelligence, then Reader in Mechanical Engineering, Edinburgh University. Recreations: photography; inventing and designing instruments and tools. Address: (b.) Department of Mechanical Engineering, Mayfield Road, Edinburgh University, Edinburgh, EH9 3JL; T.-031-667 1081, Ext. 3276.

Saltoun, Lady (Flora Marjory Fraser). Chief of Clan Fraser; b. 18.10.30; m., Captain Alexander Ramsay of Mar; 3 d. Address: (h.) Cairnbulg Castle, Fraserburgh, Aberdeenshire, AB4 5TN.

Salzen, Professor Eric Arthur, BSc, PhD. Professor of Psychology, Aberdeen University, since 1973 (Head, Department of Psychology, 1977-88); b. 28.4.30, London; m., Heather Ann Fairlie; 2 d. Educ. Wanstead County High School; Edinburgh University. Assistant in Zoology, Edinburgh University, 1954-55; Scientific Officer, HM Overseas Civil Service, 1955-56; Research Assistant and Lecturer in Psychology, Durham University, 1956-60; Lecturer in Zoology, Liverpool University, 1960-64; Associate Professor and Professor of Psychology, Waterloo University, Ontario, 1964-68; Senior Lecturer and Reader in Psychology, Aberdeen University, 1968-73. Recreation: travel. Address: (b.) Psychology Department, King's College, Aberdeen University, Aberdeen; T.-0224 40241.

Sandeman, Mary (Mary Gove Mackinnon). Singer; b. 10.7.47, Edinburgh; m., Dr. Angus J.A. Mackinnon; 2 s. Educ. St. Denis School, Edinburgh. Began to learn Gaelic and singing at aged 10; gained diploma in domestic science and secretarial training; worked in TV Department, Heriot-Watt University, before marrying and going to live in Isle of Harris; lived in Canada for a period; in 1981, had a "No 1" hit record in nine countries with song called Japanese Boy under the stage name of Aneka. Recreations: singing and yet more singing!; travel; walking; being entertained. Address: (h.) 80 Braemar Avenue, Dunblane, Perthshire; T.-0786 825303.

Sandeman, Robert John, LLB, NP, WS, DL. Solicitor, since 1979; Deputy Lieutenant, Stirling and Falkirk Districts, since 1986; Vice-Chairman, Southern Area Committee, Highland TA&VRA;, since 1987; b. 8.1.29, India; m., Enid; 1 s.; 1 d. Educ. Trinity College, Glenalmond; RMA, Sandhurst, Glasgow University. Infantry Officer, 1948-76; Second-in-Command, 1st Bn., The Royal Scots (The Royal Regiment), 1965-67; staff appointments, 1967-76; retired from Regular Army as Major, 1976; law student, 1976-79; commanded Number One Company, Home Service Force (Black Watch), Territorial Army, 1982-85. Member, Queen's Bodyguard for Scotland (Royal Company of Archers), since 1967; Director, Glasgow, Stirlingshire and Sons of the Rock Society, since 1986. Recreations: archery; hill-walking; shooting. Address: (h.) Khyber House, Upper Glen Road, Bridge of Allan, FK9 4PX; T.-0786 832180.

Sandeman, The Hon. Mrs (Sylvia Margaret). Member, Scottish Council on Disability; b. 29.7.49, Irvine; m., Ronald L. Sandeman; 1 d. Educ. Downe House, Newbury. Former Member, Scottish Sports Council. Recreation: sailing. Address: (h.) Rosgaradh, West Dhuhill Drive, Helensburgh, G84 9AW; T.-0436 5105.

Sanders, Samuel Chandrarajan, MBBS, FRCP, DMJ. Consultant Physician, Geriatric Medicine, Glasgow West, since 1976; Honorary Clinical Lecturer, Geriatric Medicine, Glasgow University, since 1977; b. 1.7.32, Jaffna, Sri Lanka; m., Irene Saravanamuttu; 1 s.; 2 d. Educ. Jaffna College, Sri Lanka; Ceylon University. Resident HO, Ceylon, 1957-58; varied experience in medicine, surgery, neurosurgery, public health and forensic medicine, Sri Lanka, 1958-70; postgraduate training, forensic medicine and clinical therapeutics, Glasgow University, Guy's Hospital, London and Edinburgh Royal Infirmary, 1971-72; Registrar, then Senior Registrar, Glasgow Western District, 1973-76. Recreations: sport; reading; fishing. Address: (h.) 28 Hillfoot Drive, Bearsden, Glasgow, G61 3QF; T.-041-942 9388.

Sanderson, Rev. Alastair William Murdoch, LTh, BA. Minister, Shawlands Cross Church, since 1976; b. 27.4.42, Glasgow; m., Elizabeth T.; 3 s.; 1 d. Educ. Clydebank High School; Glasgow University; Open University. Minister, Ervie-Kirkcolm, 1971-76; former Convener, Parish Education Committee, Wigtown and Stranraer Presbytery; serves on various Committees, Glasgow Presbytery. Recreations: swimming; hill-walking. Address: 29 St. Ronans Drive, Shawlands, Glasgow, G41 3SQ; T.-041-632 9046.

Sanderson, Arthur Norman, MBE, MA, DipEd. Regional Director, The British Council, Glasgow, since 1986; b. 3.9.43, Glasgow; m., Issy Halliday; 1 s.; 1 d. Educ. Glasgow Academy; Fettes College; Corpus Christi College, Oxford; Moray House College of Education. Tutor in Maths and English, Foso Training College, Ghana, 1966-68 (VSO); Economics and Careers Master, Daniel Stewart's College, 1969-73; British Council: Assistant Director, Kano, Nigeria, 1974-76, Regional Director, Recife, Brazil, 1976-80, Far East and Pacific Department, London, 1980-83, Assistant, then Acting Representative, Ghana, 1983-86. Recreations: hill-walking; jogging; travel; languages; the arts; DIY. Address: (b.) 6 Belmont Crescent, Glasgow, G12 8ES; T.-041-332 8651.

Sanderson, Eric Fenton, LLB, CA. Director, The British Linen Bank Ltd., since 1984; Non-Executive Director, Airtours PLC, English and Overseas Properties plc; b. 14.10.51, Dundee; m., Patricia Ann Shaw; 3 d. Educ. Morgan Academy, Dundee; Dundee University. Qualified CA with Touche Ross & Co.; joined British Linen Bank Ltd., 1976. Recreations: gardening; photography. Address: (b.) 4 Melville Street, Edinburgh, EH3 7NS; T.-031-453 1919.

Sanderson, Professor Jeffrey John, BSc, PhD. Professor of Theoretical Plasma Physics, St. Andrews University, since 1985 (Reader in Applied Mathematics, 1975-85); b. 25.4.37, Birmingham; m., Mirjana Adamovic; 1 s.; 1 d. Educ. George Dixon Grammar School, Birmingham; Birmingham University; Manchester University. Research Associate, Maryland University, 1961-64; Theoretical Physicist, English Electric Co., Whetstone, 1964-66; Lecturer, then Senior Lecturer in Applied Mathematics, St. Andrews University, 1966-75; Visiting Professor, Department of Physics, College of William and Mary, USA, 1976-77. Publications: Plasma Dynamics (Co-author), 1969; Laser Plasma Interactions (Joint Editor), 1979. Recreations: chess; Scottish country dancing; five-a-side football; cricket. Address: (b.) North Haugh, St. Andrews, KY16 9SS; T.-0334 76161, Ext. 8135.

Sanderson, Very Rev. Peter Oliver, BA, DipTh. Provost, St. Paul's Episcopal Cathedral, Dundee, since 1984; b. 26.1.29, South Shields; m., Doreen Gibson; 2 s.; 1 d. Educ. South Shields High School; St. Chad's College, Durham University. Assistant Curate, Houghton-Le-Spring, Durham, 1954-59; Rector, St. Thomas-Ye-Vale, Jamaica, 1959-63; Chaplain, RAF, 1963-67; Vicar, Winksley-cum-Grantley and Aldfield with Studley, Ripon, 1967-74; Vicar, St. Aidan's, Leeds, 1974-84. Address: Cathedral Rectory, 4 Richmond Terrace, Dundee, DD2 1BQ; T.-0382 68548.

Sanderson, Stewart Forson, MA. Hon. Harold Orton Fellow, Leeds University, since 1983; Member, Scottish Arts Council, since 1983 (Chairman, Literature Committee); b. 23.11.24, Blantyre, Malawi; m., Alison M. Cameron; 2 s.; 1 d. Educ. George Watson's College; Edinburgh University. RNVR, 1943-46; Secretary-Archivist and Senior Research Fellow, School of Scottish Studies, 1952-60; Director, Institute of Dialect and Folk Life Studies, Leeds University, 1960-83; Royal Gustav Adolfs Academy, since 1968; Visiting Professor of Folklore and Folklife, University of Pennsylvania, 1974; Chairman, School of English, Leeds University, 1980-83; President, Folklore Society, 1970-73; Council, Society for Folk Life Studies, 1974-79; Governor, British Institute of Recorded Sound, 1979-83; Committee, Leeds City Museums, 1979-84; British Library Committee, National Sound Archive, since 1983. Publications: Hemingway, 1961; The Secret Commonwealth, 1976; Linguistic Atlas of England, 1978; Studies in Linguistic Geography, 1985; Word Maps, 1987. Recreations: music; fly-fishing; gardening. Address: (h.) Primside Mill Farmhouse, Kelso, Roxburghshire, TD5 8PR; T.-Yetholm 678.

Sanderson, William. Farmer; Director, Royal Highland and Agricultural Society of Scotland; Director and Past Chairman, Aberdeen Angus Producers (South of Scotland) Ltd.; b. 9.3.38, Lanark; m., Netta; 4 d. Educ. Dalkeith High School. Past Chairman, South Midlothian and Lothians and Peeblesshire Young Farmers Clubs; Past Chairman, Dalkeith Agricultural Society;

President, Royal Caledonian Curling Club, 1984-85; Past President, Oxenfoord and Edinburgh Curling Clubs; Scottish Curling Champion, 1971 and 1978 (2nd, World Championship, 1971). Recreations: curling; exhibiting livestock. Address: (h.) Blackshiels Farm, Blackshiels, Pathhead, Midlothian; T.-Humbie 288.

Sanderson, Very Rev. William Roy, MA, DD. Minister, Church of Scotland; Extra Chaplain to The Queen in Scotland, since 1977 (Chaplain-in-Ordinary, 1965-77); b. 23.9.07, Leith; m., Muriel Easton; 3 s.; 2 d. Educ. Fettes College; Oriel College, Oxford; New College, Edinburgh. Ordained, 1933; Assistant Minister, St. Giles' Cathedral, 1932-34; Minister: St. Andrew's, Lochgelly, 1935-39, The Barony of Glasgow, 1939-63, Stenton with Whittingehame, 1963-73; Moderator, Glasgow Presbytery, 1958 and Haddington and Dunbar Presbytery, 1972-74; Moderator, General Assembly, 1967; Hon. DD (Glasgow), 1959; Chairman, Scottish Religious Advisory Committee, BBC, 1961-71; Member, Central Religious Advisory Committee, BBC and ITA, 1961-71; Governor, Fettes College, 1967-77; Honorary President, Church Service Society; President, New College Union, 1975. Recreations: reading; walking. Address: (h.) 1A York Road, North Berwick, EH39 4LS; T.-0620 2780.

Sanderson of Bowden, Lord (Charles Russell Sanderson), KB. Life Peer; Minister of State, Scottish Office; b. 30.4.33, Melrose; m., Frances Elizabeth Macaulay; 2 s.; 2 d. Educ. St. Mary's School, Melrose; Glenalmond College; Bradford University; Scottish College of Textiles. Commissioned, Royal Signals; Partner, Charles P. Sanderson, 1958-87; former Director, Clydesdale Bank, Illgworth Morris, Johnston of Elgin; former Chairman, Shires Investment PLC and Edinburgh Financial Trust; President, Scottish Conservative and Unionist Association, 1977-79; Chairman, National Union of Conservative and Unionist Associations Executive Committee, 1981-86; Chairman, Eildon Housing Association, 1976-83. Recreations: golf; amateur dramatics. Address: (h.) Becketts Field, Bowden, Melrose, Roxburgh.

Sandham, Andrew, BDS, LDSRCS, FDSRCS, DOrth, PhD. Senior Lecturer in Orthodontics, Edinburgh University, since 1982; Consultant Orthodontist (Head, Clinical Department of Orthodontics), Edinburgh Dental School, since 1982; b. 22.1.43, Mansfield, Nottinghamshire. Educ. King Edward VI School, Stourbridge; Durham University. Dentist, Norwegian Health Service, 1966-67; House Surgeon, Birmingham and London, 1967-68; Registrar, Birmingham Dental Hospital, 1968-71; Lecturer in Children's Dentistry and Orthodontics, Dundee University, 1971-74; Lecturer in Orthodontics, Birmingham University, 1974-76; Consultant Orthodontist: Fife Health Board, 1976-78, Birmingham Area Health Authority, 1978-82. Examiner, Royal College of Surgeons, Edinburgh. Recreations: travel; fine art; aviation. Address: (b.) Edinburgh University Dental School, Chambers Street, Edinburgh, EH1 1JA; T.-031-225 9511.

Sandilands, Robert Ian, MA. Deputy Director and General Secretary, National Farmers' Union of Scotland, since 1978 (Assistant General Secretary, 1972-78); b. 23.9.34, Dumfries; m., Frances Margaret Elliot; 1 s.; 2 d. Educ. Langholm Academy; Dumfries Academy; Edinburgh University. Caterpillar Tractor Company Ltd., Tannochside, 1957-60; Secretary, Lanark Area Executive, NFU of Scotland, 1960-72. Recreations: golf; photography; walking. Address: (b.) 17 Grosvenor Crescent, Edinburgh, EH12 5EN; T.-031-337 4333.

Sanford, Professor Anthony John, BSc, PhD, ABPsS. Professor of Psychology, Glasgow University, since 1982 (Head, Department of Psychology, 1983-86); b. 5.7.44, Birmingham; m., Linda Mae Moxey; 1 d. Educ. Waverley Grammar School; Leeds University; Cambridge University. MRC Research Scholar, Applied Psychology Unit, Cambridge; Postdoctoral Research Fellow, then Lecturer in Psychology, Dundee University; Senior Lecturer, then Reader in Psychology, Glasgow University. Gifford Lecturer in Natural Theology, Glasgow, 1983. Publications: Understanding Written Language (Co-author); Models, Mind and Man; Cognition and Cognitive Psychology. Recreations: hill-walking; industrial archaeology; music; cooking. Address: (b.) Department of Psychology, Glasgow University, Glasgow; T.-041-339 8855.

Sang, Christopher T.M., MB, ChB, FRCSEdin, MRCP. Consultant Cardiothoracic Surgeon, Lothian Health Board, since 1982; b. 14.6.43, Georgetown, Guyana; m., Jean Cowan; 1 s.; 2 d. Educ. George Watson's College, Edinburgh; Edinburgh University. General surgery training, Edinburgh, and general medicine and cardiology training, Edinburgh and Canada, 1966-73; cardiovascular and thoracic surgery training, Toronto, Edinburgh, London (Guy's) and Baltimore (Johns Hopkins), 1973-82. Address: (h.) 29 Blackford Hill Grove, Edinburgh, EH2 3HA; T.-031-667 6046.

Sangster, Rev. Ernest George, MA, BD, ThM. Minister, Blackhall St. Columba's Church, Edinburgh, since 1976; b. 19.6.32, Lumphanan, Aberdeenshire; m., Alison Margaret Runcie; 2 s.; 2 d. Educ. Robert Gordon's College, Aberdeen; Aberdeen University; Union Theological Seminary, Richmond, Virginia; Oriel College, Oxford. Chaplain, St. Andrews Colleges, St. Andrews University, 1961-65; Minister, Beechgrove Church, Aberdeen, 1966-76. Governor, Moray House College of Education, 1978-87. Recreations: reading; music; golf; hill-walking. Address: 5 Blinkbonny Crescent, Edinburgh, EH4 3NB; T.-031-332 3070.

Sargent, Professor John Reid, BSc, PhD, FIBiol, FRSE. Head, Department of Biological Science, Stirling University, since 1985; b. 12.10.36, Buckie; m., Elizabeth Jean; 2 d. Educ. Buckie High School; Robert Gordon's College, Aberdeen; Aberdeen University. Lecturer, Biochemistry Department, Aberdeen University, 1964-69; PSO, then Merit SPSO, then Deputy Director, then Director, Institute of Marine Biochemistry, Aberdeen, 1970-85. Council Member, Scottish Marine Biological Association, 1981-87, Marine

Biological Association of UK, since 1988. Recreations: hill-walking; skiing. Address: (h.) 4 Merlin Park, Dollar, Clackmannshire.

Sarson, William C.T., BSc (Hons), MEd. Rector, Mintlaw Academy, since 1981; b. 23.9.38, Edinburgh; m., Lorna E. Black; 3 s. Educ. Lasswade Senior Secondary School; Edinburgh University. Production Engineer, Honeywell Controls, Newhouse; Physics Master, Edinburgh Academy; Principal Teacher of Physics and Assistant Head Teacher, Liberton High School; Depute Rector, Douglas Ewart High School, Newton Stewart. Recreations: swimming; hill-walking; computing. Address: (b.) Station Road, Mintlaw, Peterhead, AB4 8FN; T.-07712 2994.

Saunders, David Stanley, BSc, PhD. Reader in Zoology, Edinburgh University, since 1974; b. 12.3.35, Pinner; m., Jean Margaret Comrie Doughty; 3 s. Educ. Pinner County Grammar School; King's College, London; London School of Hygiene and Tropical Medicine. Joined academic staff, Zoology Department, Edinburgh, 1958; Visiting Professor: Stanford University, California, 1971-72, North Carolina University, 1983. Publications: Insect Clocks; Introduction to Biological Rhythms. Recreations: cycling; gardening; photography. Address: (b.) Department of Zoology, West Mains Road, Edinburgh, EH9 3JT; T.-031-667 1081.

Saunders, Francis William, MBE, ERD, JP, CEng, MICE, MCIOB. Member, Central Regional Council; b. 2.7.06, Liverpool; m., Mary Winifred Service. Educ. Glasgow Academy; Royal Technical College, Glasgow. Civil Engineer, private and public appointments, 1923-39; commissioned, Royal Engineers Regular Army Reserve, 1936; Army service, BEF (France), MEF (Western Desert, Palestine, Transjordan), CMF (Italy, Greece), 1939-47 (mentioned in Despatches); Regular Army Reserve (rank of Lt.-Col.), 1947-61; Civil Engineer, public service, 1947-49; travelled privately in Antipodes, 1949-50; private practice as Civil Engineer, 1950-85. Former Member, Stirling Town Council; President, Glasgow Branch, Royal Engineers Association. Recreations: travel; domestic life. Address: (h.) 1 Royal Gardens, Stirling, FK8 2RJ; T.-Stirling 73975; 37 Shoregate, Crail, KY10 3SU; T.-Crail 50690.

Savage, Rev. Gordon Matthew Alexander, MA, BD. Minister, Maxwelltown West, Dumfries, since 1984; Clerk, Presbytery of Dumfries and Kirkcudbright, since 1987; b. 25.8.51, Old Kilpatrick; m., Mairi Janet MacKenzie. Educ. Glasgow Academy; Edinburgh University. Assistant Minister: Dyce Parish Church, 1975-76, Dunblane Cathedral, 1976-77; Minister: Almondbank, Tibbermore and Logiealmond, 1977-84. Junior Chaplain to Moderator, General Assembly, 1982; Junior Clerk, Perth Presbytery, 1980-83. Recreations: railways; model railways; music. Address: Maxwelltown West Manse, 11 Laurieknowe, Dumfries, DG2 7AH; T.-0387 52929.

Savidge, Malcolm Kemp, MA. Vice-Chairman, Labour Group, Aberdeen City Council, since 1980 (Convener of Libraries, 1984-87); Teacher of Mathematics, Kincorth Academy, Aberdeen, since 1973; b. 9.5.46, Redhill, Surrey. Educ. Wallington County Grammar School, Surrey; Aberdeen University; Aberdeen College of Education. Computer and Production Control Assistant, Bryans' Electronic Instruments Ltd., Mitcham, 1970-71; Mathematics Teacher: Greenwood Dale School, Nottingham, 1971, Peterhead Academy, 1972-73. Baillie, 1982-84; JP, 1984-86; Governor, Aberdeen College of Education, 1980-87; Director, Scottish National Orchestra, 1985-86; Member, Steering Committee, Nuclear Free Zones (Scotland), since 1985; Member, IBA Local Advisory Committee, since 1986; Governor, Robert Gordon's Institute of Technology, since 1980; Educational Institute of Scotland: Aberdeen President, 1977-79, Grampian Regional Secretary, 1978-81, Grampian President, 1983-84, Member, National Council, since 1980, Member, National Executive, 1982-84; Treasurer, Aberdeen City Labour Party, 1981-84. Recreations: exploring life; spectator sport; crosswords and puzzles; reading; real ale; the arts. Address: (h.) 13F Belmont Road, Aberdeen, AB2 3SR; T.-0224 632369.

Savin, John Andrew, MA, MD (Cantab), FRCP, FRCPEdin, DIH. Consultant Dermatologist, Edinburgh Royal Infirmary, since 1971; Senior Lecturer, Dermatology Department, Edinburgh University, since 1971; President Elect, Section of Dermatology, Royal Society of Medicine; b. 10.1.35, London; m., Patricia Margaret Steel; 2 s.; 2 d. Educ. Epsom College; Trinity Hall, Cambridge; St. Thomas's Hospital, London. Royal Naval Medical Service, 1960-64; Registrar to Skin Department, St. George's Hospital, London; Senior Registrar, St. John's Hospital for Diseases of the Skin, and St. Thomas's Hospital, London; Co-Editor, Recent Advances in Dermatology; Associate Editor, British Journal of Dermatology; former Secretary, Scottish Dermatological Society. Recreations: golf; literature. Address: (h.) 86 Murrayfield Gardens, Edinburgh; T.-031-337 7768.

Scaife, Professor John Graham, PhD. Professor of Molecular Parasitology, Edinburgh University, since 1984; b. 23.9.34, Leeds; 2 d. Educ. Leeds Modern School; University College, London. Scientific staff, MRC Microbial Genetics Unit, 1961-74; Senior Lecturer, then Reader, Edinburgh University, 1974-84. Member, MRC Cell Board, 1981-85 (Chairman, Grants Committee, 1982-85). Recreation: gardening. Address: (b.) Department of Molecular Biology, King's Buildings, Mayfield Road, Edinburgh, EH9 3JR; T.-031-667 1081, Ext. 2889.

Schaffer, Professor Heinz Rudolph, BA, PhD, FBPsS. Professor of Psychology, Strathclyde University, since 1970; b. 21.7.26, Berlin; m., Evelyn Blanche; 1 s.; 1 d. Educ. Ackworth School, Yorkshire; Birkbeck College, London. Research Psychologist, Tavistock Clinic, London, 1951-55; Principal Psychologist, Royal Hospital for Sick Children, Glasgow, 1955-63; Lecturer, then Senior Lecturer and Reader, Strathclyde University, 1964-70; Nuffield Fellowship, North Carolina University, 1971; Van Leer Fellowship, Jerusalem, 1976. Council Member, Social Science Research Council, 1976-78; President, Section J, British Association for the Advancement of Science, 1984-85; Chairman, Association for Child Psychology and Psychiatry, 1986-87. Recreations: walking; travelling. Address: (h.) 89 Roman Court, Bearsden, Glasgow, G61 2NW; T.-041-942 0197.

Schofield, Rev. Melville Frederick, MA. Chaplain to Western General and Associated Hospitals, Edinburgh, since 1988; b. 3.10.35, Glasgow; m., Christina Skirving Crookston. Educ. Irvine Royal Academy; Dalkeith High School; Edinburgh University and New College. Ordained Assistant, Bathgate High, 1960-61; Minister, Canal Street, Paisley, 1961-67; Minister, Laigh Kirk, Kilmarnock, 1967-88. Former Moderator, Presbytery of Irvine and Kilmarnock; former Moderator, Synod of Ayr; radio and TV broadcaster; Past President, No. 0 Kilmarnock Burns Club. Recreations: international Burns engagements; golf; after-dinner speaking. Address: (h.) 25 Rowantree Grove, Currie, Midlothian, EH14 5AT; T.-031-449 4745.

Schuster, Ida. Actress; b. Glasgow; m., Dr. Allan Berkeley; 2 s. Founder Member, Glasgow Jewish Institute Players; appeared in leading role in Glasgow Unity Theatre's first production (Awake and Sing), 1941; played Leah in The Dybbuk, Jewish Arts Festival, 1951; Member, Pitlochry Festival Theatre Company, 1974; directed and acted for Glasgow University Arts Theatre; has worked extensively in Scottish theatre, including the Citizens' Theatre, where she acted under five consecutive directorial regimes; one of the original cast of John Byrne's The Slab Boys; three Edinburgh Festivals; recent appearances at Glasgow Citizens' Theatre and Mayfest (in The Steamie); film work including a leading role in Passing Glory, 1986. Address: (h.) 1 Arran Drive, Giffnock, Glasgow, G46 7NL; T.-041-638 6789.

Schwarz, J.C. Peter, MA, BSc, PhD. Vice-Dean, Faculty of Science, Edinburgh University, since 1972 (Senior Lecturer in Chemistry, since 1970); b. 6.5.27, Bremen; m., Catherine Collocott; 3 d. Educ. St. Andrew's College, Dublin; Trinity College, Dublin. Assistant Lecturer in Chemistry, TCD, 1950-53; ICI Fellow, Edinburgh University, 1953-56; Lecturer in Chemistry: TCD, 1956-57, Edinburgh University, 1957-70. Recreations: music; computing. Address: (b.) Faculty of Science Office, West Mains Road, Edinbrgh, EH9 3JY; T.-031-667 1081.

Scobbie, Andrew, FFA. Director and General Manager, FS Assurance Ltd., since 1981; Deputy Chairman, Associated Scottish Life Offices, since 1988; Chairman, Northern Mortgage Corporation Ltd., since 1984; b. 18.8.31, Glasgow; m., Ethel; 1 s.; 1 d. Educ. Allan Glen's School, Glasgow. Qualified as Fellow, Faculty of Actuaries, 1961; Joint Actuary, Scottish Mutual Assurance Society, 1965-72; Actuary and Secretary, FS Assurance Ltd., 1972-81. Recreations: golf; reading; music. Address: (b.) FS Assurance Ltd., 190 West George Street, Glasgow, G2 2PA; T.-041-332 6462.

Scobbie, Irene, BA, MA. Reader and Head, Department of Scandinavian Studies, Edinburgh University, since 1987; b. 16.4.30, Northumberland. Educ. Gosforth County Grammar School; King's College, Durham; University College, London. English Secretary, Cultural Attache's Office, Swedish Embassy, London, 1954-57; research, UCL, 1957-59; Swedish Lecturer, Cambridge University, 1959-64; Head, Scandinavian Department, Aberdeen University, 1964-87. Recreations: opera; walking; visiting Scandinavia. Address: (b.) Department of Scandinavian Studies, Edinburgh University, 18 Buccleuch Place, Edinburgh, EH8 9LN; T.-031-667 1011, Ext. 6766.

Scobie, William Galbraith, MB, ChB, FRCSEdin, FRCSGlas. Consultant Paediatric Surgeon, Lothian Health Board, since 1971; part-time Senior Lecturer, Department of Clinical Surgery, Edinburgh University, since 1971; Assistant Director, Edinburgh Postgraduate Board for Medicine, since 1986; b. 13.10.36, Maybole; m., Elizabeth Caldwell Steel; 1 s.; 1 d. Educ. Carrick Academy, Maybole; Glasgow University. Registrar, General Surgery, Kilmarnock Infirmary; Senior Registrar, Royal Hospital for Sick Children, Glasgow; Senior Registrar, Hospital for Sick Children, London; Senior Paediatric Surgeon, Abu Dhabi, 1980-81. Recreations: fishing; golf; gardening; music. Address: (h.) 598 Queensferry Road, Edinburgh, EH4 6AT; T.-031-339 2306.

Scothorne, Professor Raymond John, BSc, MD, FRSE, FRCSG. Regius Professor of Anatomy, Glasgow University, since 1973; b. 13.6.20, Nottingham; m., Audrey Gillott; 1 s.; 2 d. Educ. Royal Grammar School, Newcastle-upon-Tyne; Leeds University; Chicago University. Lecturer in Anatomy, Leeds University, 1944-50; Senior Lecturer, Glasgow University, 1950-60; Professor of Anatomy, Newcastle-upon-Tyne University, 1960-73. Anatomical Society of Gt. Britain and Ireland: Honorary Secretary, 1967-71, President, 1971-73; President, British Association of Clinical Anatomists, since 1986; Foundation Editor, Clinical Anatomy, since 1988. Recreations: the countryside; labrador dogs. Address: (b.) Department of Anatomy, Glasgow University, Glasgow; T.-041-339 8855.

Scott, Alan Bridgwood, MA. Deputy Director (Monuments), Scottish Development Department, since 1986 (Assistant Secretary, Department of Agriculture and Fisheries for Scotland, 1978-85); b. 18.8.43, Wishaw; m., Judith; 2 d. Educ. Wishaw High School; Glasgow University. Department of Agriculture and Fisheries for Scotland, 1965-68; Private Secretary to Joint Parliamentary Under Secretary of State, 1968-70; DAFS (Fisheries), 1970-72; Diplomatic Service (Office of the UK Permanent Representative to the European Communities, Brussels), 1972-76; DAFS (Livestock Products), since 1976. Address: (b.) 20 Brandon Street, Edinburgh, EH3 5DX.

Scott, Alexander. Writer; b. 1920, Aberdeen; m.; 2 s. Educ. Aberdeen Academy; Aberdeen University. Royal Artillery, 1941-43 (commissioned, 1943); Gordon Highlanders, 1943 (wounded, Normandy, 1944; MC, 1945). Lecturer, then Senior Lecturer in Scottish Literature, Glasgow University; appointed Head, Department of Scottish Literature, 1971; Co-Editor, Scots Review, 1950-51; Editor, Saltire Review, 1954-57; Secretary, Universities Committee on Scottish Literature, 1968; President, Association for Scottish

Literary Studies, 1976; author of (verse and drama): Prometheus 48, The Latest in Elegies, Selected Poems, Untrue Thomas, Mouth Music, Cantrips, Greek Fire, Double Agent, Selected Poems 1943-74, A Double Scotch with Edwin Morgan; (prose) Still Life: William Soutar, The MacDiarmid Makars, Modern Scottish Literature 1920-1975; (plays) Right Royal, Citizens', Glasgow, 1954, Tam O'Shanter's Tryst, Citizens', Glasgow, 1955, Truth to Tell, Citizens', Glasgow, 1958.

Scott, Bill, RSA. Sculptor; Senior Lecturer, Edinburgh College of Art, since 1976 (Lecturer, since 1962); b. 16.8.35, Moniaive; m., Phyllis Owen Scott; 1 s.; 2 d. Educ. Dumfries Academy; Edinburgh College of Art. One-man exhibitions: Compass Gallery, 1972, Stirling Gallery, 1974, New 57 Gallery, 1979, Lamp of Lothian, 1980, Art Space Gallery, 1980; numerous group exhibitions. Address: (h.) 45 St. Clair Crescent, Roslin, Midlothian, EH25 9NG.

Scott, Christopher John, MB, BS, FRCPE. Consultant Physician in Geriatric Medicine, Aberdeen, since 1976; Clinical Senior Lecturer, Aberdeen University, since 1976; Consultant in Charge, Maidencraig House, Aberdeen, since 1983; b. 13.4.45, Gainsborough; m., Rosemary Anne Hislop; 3 s. Educ. Bishop Auckland Grammar School; Newcastle upon Tyne University. House Officer posts, Hexham and Sedgefield; Medical Registrar, Deaconess Hospital, Edinburgh; Senior Registrar, Longmore Hospital, Edinburgh. Recreations: walking; photography; reading; taxi-ing children about. Address: (h.) 51 Forest Road, Aberdeen, AB2 4BN; T.-0224 645881.

Scott, Donald Bruce, MD, FRCPEdin, FFARCS. Consultant Anaesthetist, Edinburgh Royal Infirmary, 1959-86; Member, Board, Faculty of Anaesthetists, Royal College of Surgeons of England, since 1981; President, European Society of Regional Anaesthesians, since 1982; b. 16.12.25, Sydney; m., Joan Isobel White; 4 s.; 2 d. Educ. Hove Grammar School; Edinburgh University. Colonial Medical Service, Ghana, four years; training in anaesthesia, Edinburgh, six years; Consultant, NHS, Edinburgh Royal Infirmary, since 1959. Past President, Scottish Society of Anaesthetists; Past President, Obstetric Anaesthetists Association. Publication: Handbook of Epidural Anaesthesia (Co-author). Recreations: golf; food and wine. Address: (h.) 1 Zetland Place, Edinburgh, EH5 3HU; T.-031-552 3317.

Scott, Duncan, TD, BSc, MIQ. Managing Director, Lochearnhead Watersports Ltd., since 1980; Member, Central Regional Council, since 1986; b. 8.5.46, Farnworth; m., Penelope Ann; 1 s.; 2 d. Educ. Smithills High School; London University. Major, Royal Engineers (TA), since 1969; Member, North of Scotland Hydro Electric Board Consultative Council. Recreation: TA. Address: (h.) Glen Earn House, Lochearnhead, Perthshire, FK19 8PR; T.-05673 245.

Scott, Eoin Flett. Member, Orkney Islands Council (Chairman, Development, Planning & Control Committee, since 1984); Farmer; b. 12.6.42, Orkney. Educ. Stromness Academy. Commissioner of Inland Revenue; Member, Highland TA Volunteer Reserve Association; Governor, Aberdeen College of Education; Member, BBC General Advisory Council; Session Clerk, Firth Church, since 1978. Recreations: archaeology; geology; numismatics. Address: (h.) Redland, Firth, Orkney, KW17 2EU; T.-0856 76 214.

Scott, George Gordon. Solicitor (retired); Honorary Sheriff, Dumfries, since 1971; b. 29.5.12, Dumfries; m., Constance Elizabeth Offord (deceased); 2 d. Educ. Dumfries Academy; Glasgow University. Solicitor in private practice, 1936-80. Has held various Church offices and secretaryships of employers' trade associations. Recreations: gardening; reading. Address: (h.) 166 Annan Road, Dumfries, DG1 3HA; T.-Dumfries 54961.

Scott, Rev. Gideon George, MA, BD, ThM. Minister, St. David's North, Dundee, since 1973, linked with Albany-Butterburn, since 1986; b. 6.8.35, Alexandria; m., Margaret Anne Allan; 2 s. Educ. Dumbarton Academy; Glasgow University; Princeton Theological Seminary. Assistant: St. Stephen's Blythswood, Glasgow, 1961, West Second-Avenue Presbyterian Church, Columbus, Ohio, 1962; Locum Preacher, Rosneath, St. Modan's, 1962; Teacher of Religious Education, Vale of Leven Academy, 1962; Minister, Wester Coates, Edinburgh, 1963-73; Extra-Mural Lecturer in Religion, Dundee University, 1978-79 - 1982-83. Secretary, Scottish Church Theology Society, 1966-71; Regional Tutor in Divinity and Practical Theology to Candidates for the Auxiliary Ministry of the Church of Scotland, since 1983. Recreations: listening to classical music; reading. Address: The Manse, 38 Albany Terrace, Dundee; T.-0382 21394.

Scott, Gordon Ramsay, BSc, MS, PhD, MRCVS. Reader in Tropical Animal Health, Edinburgh University, since 1978; Consultant Virologist, Food and Agricultural Organisation, since 1963; b. 6.7.23, Arbroath; m., Joan Henderson Walker; 1 s.; 2 d. Educ. Arbroath High School; Royal (Dick) Veterinary College, Edinburgh; Wisconsin University. Private practice, 1946-49; Virologist, Veterinary Laboratory, Kabete, Kenya, 1950-52 (Head, Virus Section, 1952-56); Head, Division of Virus Diseases, East African Veterinary Research Organisation, 1956-62; Acting Director, EAVRO, Kenya, 1959, 1962; Lecturer, then Senior Lecturer, Tropical Veterinary Medicine, Edinburgh University, 1963-78. Recreations: biometry; travel. Address: (h.) 22 Frogston Road West, Edinburgh, EH10 7AR; T.-031-445 1658.

Scott, Rev. Ian Gray, BSc, BD, STM. Minister, Greenbank Parish Church, Edinburgh, since 1983; b. 31.5.41, Kirkcaldy; m., Alexandrina Angus; 1 d. Educ. Kirkcaldy High School; St. Andrews University; Union Theological Seminary, New York. Assistant Minister, St. Mungo's, Alloa, 1965-66; Minister: Holy Trinity Church, Bridge of Allan, 1966-76, Holburn Central, Aberdeen, 1976-83; Convener, Panel on Doctrine, General Assembly, 1978-82; part-time Lecturer, Faculty of Divinity, Aberdeen University, 1977-79; founder Member, Ministry and Psychotherapy Group; Trustee, Harry Guntrip Memorial Trust. Past President, Stirling Bn., Boys' Brigade. Recreations: reading; photography; caravanning; golf (so called). Address: 112 Greenbank Crescent, Edinburgh, EH10 5SZ; T.-031-447 4032.

Scott, James Archibald, CB, LVO, MA (Hons). Secretary, Industry Department for Scotland, since 1987 (Secretary, Scottish Education Department, 1984-87); b. 5.3.32, Jaffa, Palestine; m., Dr. Elizabeth A.J. Buchan-Hepburn; 3 s.; 1 d. Educ. Dollar Academy; St. Andrews University; Queen's University, Ontario. RAF Aircrew, 1954-56; joined Commonwealth Relations Office, 1956; First Secretary, UK High Commission, New Delhi, 1958-62 and UK Mission to UN, New York, 1962-65; transferred to Scottish Office, 1965; Private Secretary to Secretary of State for Scotland, 1969-71; Assistant Secretary, Scottish Development Department, 1971; Under-Secretary, Industry Department for Scotland, 1976-84. Recreations: music; golf. Address: (b.) New St. Andrew's House, Edinburgh, EH1 3SY; T.-031-244 4602.

Scott, Rev. James Finlay. Minister, Dyce Parish Church, since 1966; b. 12.11.31, Strachur, Argyll; m., Isobel Macleod Mackie; 1 s.; 1 d. Educ. Keil School, Dumbarton; Aberdeen University; Christ's College, Aberdeen. Assistant Minister, St. Giles, Elgin, 1957-59; Minister, Rhynie with Clatt, 1959-66. Address: 144 Victoria Street, Dyce, Aberdeen, AB2 OBE; T.-0224 722380.

Scott, Jean Grant, BSc (Hons), PGCE, MIBiol. Headmistress, St. George's School for Girls, since 1986; b. 7.10.40, Helmsdale; m., John Scott (deceased); 2 s. Educ. George Watson's Ladies College, Edinburgh; Wellington School, Ayr; Glasgow University; London University Institute of Education. Research Biologist, Glaxo Laboratories Ltd., 1962-65, ICI, Alderley Edge, 1966-67; Lecturer in Biology (part-time), Newcastle-under-Lyme College of Further Education, 1969-70; Teacher of Biology (part-time), Dr. Challoner's High School for Girls, Little Chalfont, 1970-76; Teacher of Biology, Northgate Grammar School, Ipswich, 1976-77; Teacher of Biology, Head of Biology and Senior Mistress, Ipswich High School GPDST, 1977-86. Member, Committee for Biological Sciences, Cambridge University Local Examinations Syndicate, 1982-87; Teacher Moderator for "A" level Social Biology, Cambridge Board, 1983-86. Recreations: skiing; loch fishing; holidays in France; theatre; concerts. Address: (b.) St. George's School for Girls, Garscube Terrace, Edinburgh, EH12 6BG; T.-031-332 4575.

Scott, John, DL, JP. Member, Orkney Islands Council, since 1962; Director, Orkney Islands Shipping Company, since 1962; b. 3.9.21, Papa Stronsay; m., Margaret Ann Pottinger; 4 d. Educ. Stromness Academy. Home Guard; Auxiliary in Charge, HM Coastguard, Westray (retired); Army Cadet Force (Honorary Captain, retired); President, Local Committee, National Farmers Union; Secretary, Westray Baptist Church, 1943-86. Recreations: flying (PPL); sailing; golf; badminton. Address: (h.) Leckmelm, Annfield Crescent, Kirkwall, Orkney, KW15 1NS; T.-0856 3917.

Scott, Rev. John, LTh. Minister, St. Fillan's Church, Aberdour, since 1975; b. 21.6.31, Edinburgh; m., Catherine McLurg; 2 s.; 1 d. Educ. Royal High School, Edinburgh; Edinburgh University. Printing trade, 1947-63; Assistant Minister, Paisley Abbey, 1968-70; Minister, Viewfield Church, Stirling, 1970-75. Chairman, Aberdour Community Council, 1984-87; Moderator, Synod of Fife, 1985-86; Moderator, Presbytery of Dunfermline, 1986-87. Recreation: reading. Address: The Manse, Aberdour, Fife; T.-Aberdour 860349.

Scott, John Andrew Ross, JP. Member, Borders Regional Council, since 1985 (Vice Chairman, Planning, since 1986); Journalist; b. 6.5.51, Hawick; m., Christine Evans Collie; 2 s. Educ. Hawick High School. Worked on father's farm, 1966-74; Journalist, Hawick News, 1977-78, Tweeddale Press Group, since 1978; first SDP Member, Roxburgh District Council (1980-85) and Borders Regional Council; Chairman, Roxburgh District Licensing Board, 1984-85; first Chairman, Borders Area Party, SDP, 1981-84. Recreations: broadcasting for Radio Tweed; writing; music; travel; tennis. Address: (h.) 8 Union Street, Hawick, Roxburghshire; T.-0450 76324.

Scott, Rev. John Leonard, MA, BD. Minister, West Church, Inverurie, since 1966; b. 14.9.24, Edinburgh; m., Jean Macfarlane (deceased); 1 s.; 3 d. Educ Royal High School, Edinburgh; Edinburgh University. Minister, Graham's Road Church, Falkirk, 1957-66. Address: West Manse, Inverurie, Aberdeenshire; T.-0467 20285.

Scott, Mora Joan, DL, MB, ChB. Deputy Lieutenant, Morayshire, since 1983; President, Moray District, Scottish Children's League, since 1968; retired General Practitioner; b. 9.10.17, Beckenham; 1 s.; 2 d. Educ. Albyn School, Aberdeen; Aberdeen University. Past President, Elgin Soroptimist Club; Chairman, RSSPCC Elgin District, since 1983. Recreations: fishing; gardening. Address: St. Michael's, Northfield Terrace, Elgin, Moray; T.-Elgin 3832.

Scott, Paul Henderson, CMG, MA, MLitt. Convener, Advisory Council for the Arts in Scotland, since 1981; Vice-President, Scottish Centre, PEN International, since 1983; b. 7.11.20, Edinburgh; m., B.C. Sharpe; 1 s.; 1 d. Educ. Royal High School, Edinburgh; Edinburgh University. HM Forces, 1941-47 (Major, RA); HM Diplomatic Service in Foreign Office, Warsaw, La Paz, Havana, Montreal, Vienna, Milan, 1947-80. Publications: 1707, The Union of Scotland and England, 1979; Walter Scott and Scotland, 1981; John Galt, 1985; The Age of MacDiarmid (Co-Editor), 1980; In Bed with an Elephant: The Scottish Experience, 1985; A Scottish Postbag (Co-Editor), 1986. Recreation: skiing. Address: (h.) 33 Drumsheugh Gardens, Edinburgh, EH3 7RN; T.-031-225 1038.

Scott, Sheriff Richard John Dinwoodie, MA, LLB. Sheriff of Lothian and Borders at Edinburgh, since 1986 (of Grampian, Highland and Islands, at Aberdeen and Stonehaven, 1977-86); Honorary Reader, Aberdeen University, 1980-86; b. 28.5.39, Manchester; m., Josephine Moretta Blake; 2 d. Educ. Edinburgh Academy; Edinburgh University. Lektor, Folkuniversitet of Sweden, 1960-61; admitted to Faculty of Advocates, 1965; Standing Junior Counsel, Ministry of Defence (Air), 1969; Parliamentary candidate,

1974. Address: (b.) Sheriffs' Chambers, Sheriff Court House, Edinburgh, EH1 2NS; T.-031-226 7181.

Scott, Robert Ian, MA, BLitt, MLitt, DipEd. Rector, Banff Academy, since 1965; b. 30.9.25, Inverness; m., Catherine Jane Johnstone Ralston; 1 s.; 2 d. Educ. Inverness Royal Academy; Queen's Park Senior Secondary School, Glasgow; Glasgow University. Teacher of English, Glasgow, 1953-57; Principal Teacher of English, Nicolson Institute, Stornoway, 1957-61; Deputy Rector, Aberdeen Academy, 1962-65. Past President, Banff Rotary Club. Publication: Poetry Anthology From Barbour to Burns (Editor), 1960. Recreations: tennis; badminton; reading. Address: (b.) Banff Academy, Banff, AB4 1BY; T.-Banff 2591.

Scott, Roy, JP, MB, ChB, MD, FRCSGlas, FRCSEdin, FSA (Scot). Consultant Urologist, Glasgow Royal Infirmary; Honorary Clinical Lecturer, Glasgow University; b. 17.7.35, Wishaw; m., Janette J.C. Dalgleish; 1 s.; 2 d. Educ. Wishaw High School; Glasgow University. RAMC, Kenya, Aden, UK, 1958-61; Assistant Lecturer, Glasgow University, 1961-62; Stobhill Hospital, Glasgow, 1963-67; Glasgow Royal Infirmary, since 1967; Arkansas Traveller; Council Member, British Association of Urological Surgeons, 1983-86; Hon. President, Greenock Medical Faculty, 1987-88; Member, Justices Association for Scotland; Council Member, St. Andrew's Ambulance Association; Member, West of Scotland Association of St. John; President, Sandyford Burns Club; Member, Master Court, Incorporation of Tailors in Glasgow. Publications: Urology Illustrated (Co-author); Modern Practical Nursing (Urology) (Co-author); History of Glasgow Kilwinning No. 4. Recreations: fishing; book collecting; history of Glasgow; gardening; lecturing; Robert Burns; music. Address: (h.) Garrion, 27 Forest View, Kildrum, Cumbernauld; T.-Cumbernauld 22683.

Scott, Thomas Hardy, BPhil, DPS. Hospice Director, Strathcarron Hospice, Denny, since 1979; Adviser for Scotland, Macmillan Cancer Relief Fund, since 1984; b. 11.5.32, Dundee; m., Dorothy K. Shields; 2 s.; 2 d. Educ. Sedbergh School; Edinburgh University; St. Andrews University. Assistant Minister, St. Giles Cathedral, Edinburgh, 1959-61; Minister, Bonnybridge Parish Church, 1961-66; Chaplain, Heriot-Watt University, 1966-79. Chairman, Edinburgh Council of Social Service, 1974-77; Chairman, Joint Committee on Alcohol Related Problems, Lothian Health Board and Social Work Department, 1978-81. Recreation: fishing. Address: (b.) Strathcarron Hospice, Denny, Stirlingshire; T.-0324 826222.

Scott, Tom, MA, PhD. Writer; b. 6.6.18, Glasgow; m., Margaret Heather Fretwell; 1 s.; 2 d. Educ. Hyndland School, Glasgow; Madras College, St. Andrews; Edinburgh University. Began life in building trade, St. Andrews, 1934; War Service (Nigeria, 1941-43); after few jobs in bookshops in London, freelance Writer until belated University studies via Newbattle Abbey College (under Edwin Muir); first published poem in Poetry London, 1940; first volumes, Seeven Poems O Maister Francis Villon, An Ode Til New Jerusalem, The Ship and Ither Poems; then At the Shrine O The Unkent Sodger, Brand the Builder, The Tree, The Dirty Business; edited Oxford Book of Scottish Verse (with John MacQueen), Some Late Medieval Scottish Poets, the Penguin Book of Scottish Verse; for children, Tales of King Robert the Bruce and Tales of Sir William Wallace; criticism: Dunbar, An Exposition of the Poems. Recreations: game fishing; ornithology; music. Address: (h.) 3 Duddingston Park, Edinburgh.

Scott, Walter, CBE, DA, RIBA, FRIAS. Architect, Scott & McIntosh, Edinburgh, since 1964, and Galashiels, since 1975; Member, Borders Health Board, since 1983; b. 26.1.26, Musselburgh; m., Irene Duncan; 1 s.; 2 d. Educ. Musselburgh Grammar School; Edinburgh College of Art; Heriot-Watt University. Royal Engineers, 1944-47 (Captain); joined Architect's Department, South Eastern Regional Hospital Board, 1957; founded Scott & McIntosh, 1964; Member, RIAS Council, 1957-60; President, Scottish Conservative Association, 1970-71; President, Old Musselburgh Club, 1972. Recreations: rugby football; gardening; curling. Address: (h.) The Dell, Gordon, Berwickshire; T.-057381 335.

Scott, Professor William, BSc (Hons), CEng, FIMechE, MIProdE, MBIM. Course Supervisor, Manufacturing Sciences and Engineering, Strathclyde University, since 1978 (Manager, Engineering Applications Centre, since 1982); b. 6.11.26, Giffnock; m., Carol Claire Lewin; 1 s.; 1 d. Educ. High School of Glasgow; Glasgow University. Metropolitan Vickers Electrical Co. Ltd., 1947-51; Compressor Division, James Howden & Co. Ltd., 1951-61; Associated Industrial Consultants Ltd., 1961-63; Department of Production Engineering, 1963-78. Recreation: work. Address: (b.) Room M111, James Weir Building, Strathclyde University, 75 Montrose Street, Glasgow, G1 1XJ; T.-041-552 4400, Ext. 2047.

Scott, Captain William Patrick, OBE, TD, DL. Honorary Sheriff, Grampian, Highland and Islands; Member, Queen's Bodyguard for Scotland (Royal Company of Archers); b. 1.12.10, Lanark; m., Philippa Greig (deceased); 1 s.; 3 d. Educ. Sedbergh. Former Director, Highland Distilleries Co. Ltd.; former Member, Highland TA & VR Association; former County Commissioner, Orkney Boy Scouts; Past Chairman, Orkney LEC; Past Chairman, Orkney RSPB; served with Lanarkshire Yeomanry and on Staff, 206 Infantry Brigade and 184 Infantry Brigade. Recreations: golf; shooting; fishing; gardening. Address: (h.) Kierfiold House, Sandwick, Stromness, Orkney; T.-Sandwick 503.

Scott Brown, Ronald, MA, LLB. Director, Aberdeen Fund Managers Ltd., since 1983; Director, Abtrust Management Ltd., since 1987; b. 14.2.37, Madras; m., Jean Leslie Booth; 3 s. Educ. Aberdeen Grammar School; Aberdeen University. Qualified Solicitor, 1961; Assistant, then Partner, Brander & Cruickshank, Advocates, 1961-83. Member, Board of Governors, Northern College of Education, since 1983. Address: (b.) 10 Queen's Terrace, Aberdeen, AB9 1QJ; T.-0224 631999.

Scott-Dempster, Ronald, BL, WS. Writer to the Signet (Consultant), since 1974; Honorary Sheriff, Perthshire, since 1958; b. 8.5.98, Perth; m., Ann Reid; 1 s.; 2 d. Educ. Perth Academy; Edinburgh University. Lt., Royal Field Artillery, 1916-19; wounded, 1917; Partner, Robertson Dempster & Co., WS, 1924-74; Chairman, Court of Referees, 1933-38; Registrar, Diocese of St. Andrews, 1928-74; Treasurer, Perthshire Nursing Federation, 1933-58; Treasurer, Perth Royal Infirmary, 1938-49; Secretary, Territorial Army Association, Perthshire, 1939-49; Lt.-Col., Army Welfare, Perthshire, 1943-50; Director, General Accident Assurance Co., 1948-74, Yorkshire General Life Assurance, 1950-62, English Insurance Co., 1962-77, Grampian Properties Ltd., 1967-77; Consultant, Condie Mackenzie & Co., WS, 1974-88; Deer Consultant, 1977-82; Convener, Executive Council, Scottish Episcopal Church, 1959-67 (Trustee, 1960-88); Vice-Chairman, Perth Branch, Royal British Legion since formation; Life Member, Gaelic Society of Perth and Royal Scottish Pipers Society. Recreations: golf; deer stalking; gardening; piping; hill-walking. Address: (h.) Tayhill, Dunkeld, Perthshire; T.-03502 277.

Scrimgeour, John Beocher, MB, ChB, DObst, RCOG, FRCOG, FRCS(Edin). Consultant Obstetrician and Gynaecologist, since 1972; Honorary Senior Lecturer in Obstetrics and Gynaecology, Edinburgh University, since 1972; b. 22.1.39, Elgin; m., Joyce Morrin; 1 s.; 1 d. Educ. Hawick High School; Edinburgh University. General Practitioner, Edinburgh, 1963-65; Senior House Officer: Stirling Royal Infirmary, 1965, and Registrar, Eastern General Hospital, Edinburgh, 1966-69; Senior Registrar, Edinburgh Royal Infirmary, 1970-72; Senior Secretary, Edinburgh Obstetrical Society, 1980-85; Chairman, Area Division of Obstetrics and Gynaecology, since 1984; Member, Council, Royal College of Obstetricians and Gynaecologists, 1976-81. Publication: Towards the Prevention of Fetal Malformation, 1978. Recreations: gardening; golf; tennis. Address: (h.) 4 Kinellan Road, Edinburgh, EH12 6ES; T.-031-337 6027.

Seafield, 13th Earl of (Ian Derek Francis Ogilvie-Grant), b. 20.3.39; m., 1, Mary Dawn Mackenzie Illingworth (m. diss.); 2 s.; 2, Leila Refaat. Educ. Eton. Address: (h.) Old Cullen, Cullen, Banffshire.

Seagrave, David Robert, LLB (Hons), SSC, NP. Solicitor and Notary Public; Council Member, Law Society of Scotland, 1981-87; Partner, Seagrave & Co., Solicitors, Dumfries; b. 29.4.43, Berwick-on-Tweed; m., Fiona Lesley Thomson; 1 s.; 1 d. Educ. Newcastle-upon-Tyne; Glasgow University. Banking, insurance, police; Secretary, Enterprise Trust for Nithsdale, Annandale/Eskdale and the Stewartry. Recreations: choral singing; shooting; fishing; golf. Address: (h.) Amulree, Islesteps, Dumfries; T.-Dumfries 64523.

Sealey, Barry Edward, BA (Hons) (Cantab), CBIM. Managing Director, Christian Salvesen PLC, since 1981, and Deputy Chairman, since 1987; b. 3.2.36, Bristol; m., Helen Martyn; 1 s.; 1 d. Educ. Dursley Grammar School; St. John's College, Cambridge. Joined Christian Salvesen, 1958, as Trainee; joined Board, 1969; Director, Scottish Equitable Life Assurance Society; Director, Scottish American Investment Trust; Director, Scottish Transport Group; Council Member and Executive Committee, The Industrial Society; Member of the High Constabulary, Port of Leith. Address: (b.) 50 East Fettes Avenue, Edinburgh, EH4 1EQ; T.-031-552 7101.

Seaton, Professor Anthony, BA, MD (Cantab), FRCPLond, FRCPEdin, FFOM. Director, Institute of Occupational Medicine, Edinburgh, since 1978; OMS Professor of Environmental and Occupational Medicine, Aberdeen University, since 1988; b. 20.8.38, London; m., Jillian Margaret Duke; 2 s. Educ. Rossall School, Fleetwood; King's College, Cambridge; Liverpool University. Assistant Professor of Medicine, West Virginia University, 1969-71; Consultant Chest Physician, Cardiff, 1971-77. Editor, Thorax, 1977-82. Publications: Occupational Lung Diseases; Respiratory Diseases. Recreations: rowing; squash; painting. Address: (h.) 8 Avon Grove, Barnton, Edinburgh; T.-031-336 5113.

Seaton, Robert, MA, LLB. Secretary of the University, Dundee University, since 1973; b. 2.8.37, Clarkston, Renfrewshire; m., Jennifer Graham Jack; 2 s.; 2 d. Educ. Eastwood Secondary School; Glasgow University; Balliol College, Oxford; Edinburgh University. Administrative Assistant, then Senior Administrative Officer, then Assistant Secretary, Edinburgh University, 1962-73. Director, Dundee Repertory Theatre Ltd., since 1980; Director, TAYTEC Limited, since 1985. Recreations: tennis; squash; golf. Address: (h.) Dunarn, 29 South Street, Newtyle, Angus, PH12 8UQ; T.-Newtyle 330.

Selfridge, Rev. John, BTh, BEd(Rel). Minister, Scourie, since 1986; b. 10.8.21, Craigs, N. Ireland; m., Isabella MacMillan MacKenzie; 1 d. Educ. Ballymena Technical School; Metropolitan College and A.B. College, USA. Minister in congregation for those of mixed race in South Africa, 1948-51; travelling evangelist in nine African countries, 1952-70; Organising Secretary, Inter-Church Evangelism Programme, Malawi, 1970-75; Minister, Church of Central Africa Presbyterian, 1975-86; seconded to multi-racial congregation in South Africa, 1980-84. Address: The Manse, Scourie, Lairg, IV27 4TQ; T.-0971 2431.

Sellar, Allan George, OStJ, JP. Provost of Inverness, since 1980; Chairman, Inverness Harbour Trust, since 1980; Chairman, Governors, Eden Court Theatre, since 1980; Chairman, Culloden Committee, National Trust for Scotland, since 1982; b. 10.10.24, Dufftown; m., Margaret Brenda Fraser; 2 s.; 2 d. Educ. Inverness Royal Academy. RAF, 1943-47; began own business, 1956; Political Organiser, 1962-68; elected, Inverness Town Council, 1972; Member, Highland Regional Council, since 1974; Member, Inverness District Council, since 1974. Recreations: golf; caravanning. Address: (h.) 42 Southside Road, Inverness; T.-Inverness 233623.

Semple, Peter d'Almaine, MD, FRCPGlas, FRCPEdin. Consultant Physician and Chest Specialist, Inverclyde District, since 1979; b.

30.10.45, Glasgow; m., Judith Mairi Abercromby; 2 d. Educ. Belmont House, Glasgow; Loretto School, Musselburgh; Glasgow University. Various training posts, Glasgow and Dundee teaching hospitals; Consultant General Physician, Inverclyde Royal Hospital and district (including Bute), 1979; former Postgraduate Medical Tutor, Inverclyde District, and Honorary Clinical Lecturer, Glasgow University. Past Chairman, West of Scotland Branch, British Deer Society. Recreations: salmon fishing; shooting; deer stalking; ornithology; golf; curling; sailing. Address: (h.) Allandale, 11 Barrhill Road, Gourock, PA19 1JX; T.-0475 32720.

Semple, Walter George, BL, NP, ACI Arb. Solicitor; Partner, Bird Semple Fyfe Ireland, WS, Solicitors; b. 7.5.42, Glasgow; m., Dr. Lena Ohrstrom; 3 d. Educ. Belmont House, Glasgow; Loretto School; Glasgow University. President, Glasgow Juridical Society, 1968; Tutor and Lecturer (part-time), Glasgow University, 1970-79; Council Member, Law Society of Scotland, 1976-80; Chairman, Scottish Lawyers European Group, 1978-81; Member, Commission Consultative des Barreaux Europeens, 1978-80, 1984-87; President, Association Internationale des Jeunes Avocats, 1983-84; Vice Chairman, Scottish Branch, Institute of Arbitrators. Recreations: golf; fishing; skiing; music. Address: (h.) 47 Newark Drive, Glasgow, G41 4QA; T.-041-423 7095.

Semple, William David Crowe, BSc (Hons), DipEd, FBIM. Director of Education, Lothian Regional Council, since 1974; b. 11.6.33, Grangemouth; m., Margaret; 1 s.; 1 d. Educ. Grangemouth High School; Falkirk High School; Glasgow University; Jordanhill College, Glasgow; London University. Education Officer, Northern Rhodesia, 1958-64; Zambia: Deputy Chief Education Officer, 1964-66, Chief Education Officer, 1966-67, Acting Director of Technical Education, 1967-68; Edinburgh Corporation: Assistant Director of Education, 1968-70, Depute Director of Education, 1970-74. Member: University Grants Committee, since 1983, Scottish Council for Tertiary Education, 1979-83, UK National Committee for UNESCO, 1981-86; Chairman, Scottish Television Educational Advisory Committee, 1979-85; General Secretary, Association of Directors of Education. Recreation: gardening. Address: (b.) 40 Torphichen Street, Edinburgh; T.-031-229 9166.

Sessford, Rt. Rev. George Minshull. Bishop of Moray, Ross and Caithness, since 1970; b. 7.11.28; m.; 3 d. Educ. St. Andrews University. Curate, St. Mary's Cathedral, Glasgow, 1953; Chaplain, Glasgow University, 1955; Priest-in-Charge, Cumbernauld New Town, 1958; Rector, Forres, 1966.

Sewell, Major Morley Hodkin, MA, PhD, VetMB, MRCVS. Reader in Veterinary Parasitology, Edinburgh University, since 1980; b. 1.9.32, Sheffield; m., Cynthia Margaret-Rose Hanson; 1 s.; 3 d. Educ. King Edward VII School, Sheffield; Cambridge University. Colonial Office Research Scholar, Cambridge, 1957-59; Veterinary Research Officer, Government of Nigeria, 1959-63; Lecturer, then Senior Lecturer, then Reader, Edinburgh University, since 1963. Local Preacher, Methodist Church, since 1958; Vice Chairman, SUM Fellowship, Scottish Committee; Chairman, Midlothian Liberal Association. Recreations: Church; politics; travel. Address: (h.) 14 Craigiebield Crescent, Penicuik, Midlothian.

Shackleton, Rev. William, MA (Hons). Minister, Wellpark West, Greenock, since 1983; b. 19.10.27, Glasgow; m., Margaret Mackenzie Brown; 1 s.; 2 d. Educ. Preston Grammar School; Edinburgh University. Assistant, then Minister, St. Francis-in-the-East, Glasgow, 1955-83. Chairman, Church House Youth Club, Bridgeton; President, Bridgeton Business Club; Patron, Regnal League of Men's Circles. Recreations: writing; golf. Address: 45 Denholm Street, Greenock; T.-0475 21974.

Shand, Jimmy, MBE. Musician and Scottish Country Dance Band Leader; b. 28.1.08, East Wemyss; m., Anne Anderson; 2 s. Educ. East Wemyss School. Has played the accordion and led Scottish danceband at thousands of concert and theatre performances at home and overseas; numerous recordings; several thousand broadcasts. Recreations: motor bikes; sailing.

Shankland, David, JP. Convenor, Cumnock and Doon Valley District Council, since 1984; b. 3.7.43, Mauchline; m., Ellen Park; 1 s.; 2 d. Educ. Cumnock Academy. Member, Cumnock District Council, 1974-75, and Cumnock and Doon Valley District Council, since 1976; Chairman, General Purposes Committee, 1977-80, and Planning Committee, 1980-84; Member, Ayrshire and Arran Health Board, 1978-86; Member, Cumnock and Doon Valley Licensing Court, 1978-86; Chairman, Mauchline Community Association. Recreations: no time. Address: (h.) 38 Welton Road, Mauchline, Ayrshire; T.-0290 50836.

Shanks, Duncan Faichney, ARSA, RGI, RSW. Artist; b. 30.8.37, Airdrie; m., Una Brown Gordon. Educ. Uddingston Grammar School; Glasgow School of Art. Part-time Lecturer, Glasgow School of Art, until 1979; now full-time painter; one-man shows: Stirling University, Scottish Gallery, Fine Art Society, Talbot Rice Art Gallery, Edinburgh University; taken part in shows of Scottish painting, London, 1986, Toulouse, Rio de Janeiro, 1985, Wales, 1988; Scottish Arts Council Award; Latimer and MacAulay Prizes, RSA; Torrance Award, Cargill Award, MacFarlane Charitable Trust Award, RGI. Recreations: music; gardening. Address: (h.) Davingill House, Crossford, by Carluke, Lanarkshire; T.-Crossford 310.

Shanks, Thomas Henry, MA, LLB. Solicitor and Notary Public, since 1956; Honorary Sheriff, Lanark, since 1982; b. 22.10.30, Lanark; m., Sheila Dales Hunter (deceased); 1 s.; 1 d. Educ. Lanark Grammar School; Glasgow University. Intelligence Corps (National Service), 1954-56; Solicitor in general practice, since 1956; Depute Clerk of Peace, County of Lanark, 1961-74; Chairman, Royal Burgh of Lanark Community Council, 1977-80 and 1983-86; Chairman, Lanark Round Table, 1967; Captain, Lanark Golf Club, 1962; Lord Cornet, 1968; Secretary, Lanark Lanimer Committee; Secretary, Clydesdale Upperward Society; Preses, Cairns Church, Lanark; Elder, Church of Scotland. Recreation: golf. Address: (h.) Clydesholm Braes, Lanark.

Sharp, Alexander McLean, JP. Chairman, Fife Regional Planning and Development Committee, since 1974; Chairman, Scottish National Housing and Town Planning Association, since 1982; Chairman, Planning Committee, COSLA, since 1980; Vice Chairman, National Housing and Planning Council (UK), since 1987; b. 13.10.33, Lochgelly; m., Betty Gray; 2 s.; 1 d. Educ. Lochgelly Junior Secondary School. Former Member, Lochgelly Town Council (Provost of Lochgelly, 1973-75); Member, Dunfermline Advisory Board for Justices of the Peace, since 1973; Chairman: Cowdenbeath School Council, Lochgelly Centre Management Committee, Mossmorran/Braefoot Bay Petrochemical Liaison Committee; Vice Chairman, Forth River Bridge Board; Member, Glenrothes Development Corporation, 1978-84; Deputy Chairman, SDA Consultative Committee; Chairman, Central District, Gas Consumer Council; Citizen of the Year, Lochgelly, 1987. Recreations: golf; fishing; local interests. Address: (h.) 119 Main Street, Lochgelly, Fife; T.-Lochgelly 780508.

Sharp, Professor David William Arthur, MA, PhD, CChem, FRSC, FRSE. Professor of Chemistry, Glasgow University, since 1968; Director, Office for International Programmes, Glasgow University, since 1988; Convener, Scottish Council for the Validation of Courses for Teachers, since 1983; b. 8.10.31, Folkestone; m., Margaret Cooper; 1 s.; 2 d. Educ. Harvey Grammar School, Folkestone; Sidney Sussex College, Cambridge. Lecturer, Imperial College, London, 1957-61; Strathclyde University, latterly as Professor, 1965-68; Chairman, Scottish Council for Educational Technology, 1975-81; Council Member, Scottish Universities Council on Entrance, 1974-83; Chairman, Committee of Heads of University Chemistry Departments, 1979-81; Governor, Jordanhill College, 1971-79; Member, Scottish Examination Board, 1977-84; Council Member, Royal Society of Chemistry, 1974-77; Member, Council, Royal Society of Edinburgh, since 1985. Publications: A New Dictionary of Chemistry (Editor); Penguin Dictionary of Chemistry (Editor); J. Fluorine Chemistry (Editor). Recreation: walking. Address: (b.) Department of Chemistry, Glasgow University, Glasgow, G12 8QQ; T.-041-339 8855, Ext. 4418.

Sharp, Sir George, Kt (1976), OBE, JP, DL, GDC. Chairman, Glenrothes Development Corporation, 1978-86; Member, Economic and Social Committee, EEC, 1982-86; b. 8.4.19; m., Elsie May Rodger; 1 s. Educ. Buckhaven High School. Fife County Council: Member, 1945-75, Chairman, Water and Drainage Committee, 1955-61, Chairman, Finance Committee, 1961-72, Convener, 1972-75; Convener, Fife Regional Council, 1974-78; President: Association of County Councils, 1972-74, COSLA, 1975-78; Chairman: Kirkcaldy District Council, 1958-75, Fife and Kinross Water Board, 1967-75, Forth River Purification Board, 1955-67 and 1975-78, Scottish River Purification Advisory Committee, 1967-75, Scottish Tourist Consultative Council, 1979-82; Vice-Chairman, Forth Road Bridge Committee, 1972-78; Member, Scottish Water Advisory Committee, 1962-69, Committee of Enquiry into Salmon and Trout Fishing, 1963, Scottish Valuation Advisory Committee, 1972, Committee of Enquiry into Local Government Finance, 1974-76, Scottish Development Agency, 1975-80, Royal Commission on Legal Services in Scotland, 1978-80; Director, Grampian Television, since 1975; Member, Scottish Board, National Girobank, since 1982; Managing Trustee, Municipal Mutual Insurance Ltd., since 1979. Recreation: golf. Address: (h.) Strathlea, 56 Station Road, Thornton, Fife; T.-Thornton 347.

Sharp, James King, FLA. Director of Libraries, Museums and Art Galleries, Dunfermline District Council, since 1975; b. 27.5.31, Glasgow; m., Elizabeth; 1 s.; 1 d. Educ. Allan Glen's School, Glasgow; Strathclyde University. Library Assistant, Clydebank Public Libraries, 1948-53; Senior Library Assistant, Coatbridge Public Libraries, 1953-56; District Librarian, Lanark County Council, 1956-60; County Librarian, Bute County Council, 1960-65; Librarian and Curator, Dunfermline Town Council, 1965-75. Recreations: golf; motoring; travel. Address: (b.) Library HQ, Abbot Street, Dunfermline, Fife; T.-Dunfermline 723661.

Sharp, John Clarkson Macgregor, MB, ChB, DPH, FFCM, MRCPGlas. Consultant Epidemiologist, Communicable Diseases (Scotland) Unit, Ruchill Hospital, Glasgow, since 1971; b. 20.6.31, New Stevenston, Lanarkshire; m., Elizabeth Anthony Stevenson; 2 d. Educ. Daniel Stewart's College; Edinburgh University. Hospital appointments, Plymouth, Dartford and Bangour; general practice, Edinburgh and Motherwell; Senior Medical Officer, Public Health Department, Edinburgh; Depute County Medical Officer, West Lothian. Honorary Medical Adviser, Scottish Rugby Union. Recreations: golf; curling. Address: (b.) Communicable Diseases (Scotland) Unit, Ruchill Hospital, Glasgow, G20 9NB; T.-041-946 7120.

Sharp, Nigel Ernest, MA. Assistant Secretary, Scottish Office, since 1970; b. 22.5.31, Edinburgh; m., Margaret Martin Taylor; 2 s.; 2 d. Educ. George Watson's College, Edinburgh; St. James School, Maryland, USA; Edinburgh University. National Service, RAEC, 1953-55; Assistant Principal, Scottish Home Department, 1955-60; Principal, 1960-70: Industry and Transport, Housing, Police Administration, Social Work including Children's Hearings; Assistant Secretary, since 1970: NHS General Practitioner Services, Doctors' and Dentists' Remuneration, Trunk Roads, Ancient Monuments, Historic Buildings and Building Control, Law and General, Legal Aid, Land Use. Vice-President, East District, Scottish Hockey Association, to 1988; Elder, Greenbank Church. Recreations: hockey (1,100 goals for Watsonians); crosswords; jogging; reading; doggerel. Address: (b.) Department of Agriculture and Fisheries for Scotland, Chesser House, Gorgie Road, Edinburgh, H11 3AW; T.-031-443 4020.

Shaw, Rev. Alexander James, MA, BD. Minister, Ardclach with Auldearn and Dalmore, Nairn, since 1984; b. 6.6.42, Perth; m., Elspeth Margaret

Walker; 2 s. Educ. Perth Academy; Edinburgh University. Worked with General Accident Fire and Life Assurance Corporation; Minister, West Parish Church, Cowdenbeath, 1968-84. Member, Board of Social Responsibility, Church of Scotland; Member, Moray Firth Radio Christian Council; Chaplain, (Nairn) Air Training Corps; Member, Presbyterian and Reformed Renewal Ministries, Oklahoma City; Reviewer of religious books. Recreations: reading; running; leading pilgrimages to the Holy Land. Address: The Manse, Auldearn, Nairn, IV12 5SX; T.-Nairn 53180.

Shaw, Rev. Alistair Neil, MA (Hons), BD (Hons). Minister, Relief Parish Church, Bourtreehill, Irvine, since 1982; b. 6.7.53, Kilbarchan; m., Brenda Bruce; 1 d. Educ. Paisley Grammar School; Glasgow University. Recreations: foreign travel; ancient history; swimming. Address: 68 Dundonald Road, Dreghorn, Irvine, KA11 4AP; T.-Irvine 216939.

Shaw, Professor Douglas William David, MA, LLB, BD, WS. Professor of Divinity, St. Andrews University, since 1979 (Dean, Faculty of Divinity, 1983-86, Principal, St. Mary's College, since 1986); Minister, Church of Scotland, since 1960; b. 25.6.28, Edinburgh; m., Edinburgh Academy; Loretto; Ashbury College, Ottawa; St. John's College, Cambridge; Edinburgh University. Practised law as WS (Partner, Davidson and Syme, WS, Edinburgh), 1952-57; Assistant Minister, St. George's West Church, Edinburgh, 1960-63; Official Observer, Second Vatican Council, Rome, 1962; Lecturer in Divinity, Edinburgh University, 1963-79; Principal, New College, and Dean, Faculty of Divinity, Edinburgh, 1973-78; Visiting Fellow, Fitzwilliam College, Cambridge, 1978; Visiting Lecturer, Virginia University, 1979. Publications: Who is God?, 1968; The Dissuaders, 1978. Recreations: squash; golf; hill-walking. Address: (h.) 40 North Street, St. Andrews, Fife, KY16 9AQ; T.-0334 77254.

Shaw, Rev. Duncan, BD (Hons), MTh. Minister, St. John's, Bathgate, since 1978; b. 10.4.47, Blantyre; m., Margaret S. Moore; 2 s.; 1 d. Educ. St. John's Grammar School, Hamilton; Hamilton Academy; Trinity College, Glasgow University. Assistant Minister, Netherlee Parish Church, Glasgow, 1974-77. Clerk, West Lothian Presbytery, since 1982. Address: St. John's Parish Church Manse, Mid Street, Bathgate, EH48 1QD; T.-Bathgate 53146.

Shaw, Professor John Calman, BL, CA, FCMA, MBCS. Executive Director, Scottish Financial Enterprise, since 1986; b. 10.7.32, Perth; m., Shirley Botterill; 3 d. Educ. Strathallan; Edinburgh University. Qualified as Chartered Accountant, 1954; Partner, Graham, Smart & Annan, CA, Edinburgh, latterly Deloitte Haskins & Sells, 1960-1987; President, Institute of Chartered Accountants of Scotland, 1983-84; Johnstone Smith Professor of Accountancy, Glasgow University, 1977-83. Lay Director, Scottish Chamber Orchestra; Trustee, David Hume Institute; author of various texts and publications on accountancy. Recreations: music; walking; travel. Address: 91 George Street, Edinburgh, EH2 3ES; T.-031-225 6990.

Shaw, Mark Robert, BA, MA, DPhil. Keeper of Natural History, National Museums of Scotland, since 1983; b. 11.5.45, Sutton Coldfield; m., Francesca Dennis Wilkinson; 2 d. Educ. Dartington Hall School; Oriel College, Oxford. Research Assistant (Entomology), Zoology Department, Manchester University, 1973-76; University Research Fellow, Reading University, 1977-80; Assistant Keeper, Department of Natural History, Royal Scottish Museum, 1980-83. Recreations: field entomology; family life; slash-and-burn gardening. Address: (h.) 48 St. Albans Road, Edinburgh, EH9 2LU; T.-031-667 0577.

Shaw, Richard Wright, MA. Principal, Paisley College of Technology, since 1987; b. 22.9.41, Preston; m., Susan Angela; 2 s. Educ. Lancaster Royal Grammar School; Sidney Sussex College, Cambridge. Assistant Lecturer in Management, then Lecturer in Economics, Leeds University, 1964-69; Lecturer in Economics, then Senior Lecturer, Stirling University, 1969-84; part-time Lecturer, Glasgow University, 1978-79; Visiting Lecturer, Newcastle University, NSW, 1982; Head, Department of Economics, Stirling University, 1982-84; Professor and Head, Department of Economics and Management, Paisley College of Technology, 1984-86; Vice Principal, 1986. Recreations: walking; listening to music. Address: (b.) Paisley College of Technology, High Street, Paisley, PA1 2BE; T.-041-887 1241.

Shaw, Susan Angela, MA (Cantab). Senior Lecturer, Department of Business and Management, Stirling University, since 1985; General Secretary, Federation Europeenne De La Salmoniculture, since 1986; b. 1.6.43, Bristol; m., Richard Shaw; 2 s. Educ. Kingswood Grammar School, Bristol; Girton College, Cambridge. Marketing Executive, ICI Fibres; Lecturer in Economics, Stirling University. Publications: Salmon Economics and Marketing (Co-author); Marketing the Products of Aquaculture. Recreations: hill-walking; opera. Address: (b.) Department of Business and Management, Stirling University, Stirling, FK9 4LA; T.-0786 73171.

Shaw, Thomas Raymond Dunlap, BSc, MD, FRCP. Consultant Cardiologist, Western General Hospital, Edinburgh, since 1983; b. 27.4.43, Dumfries; m., Dr. Paula de Souza Lima; 2 s. Educ. Douglas Ewart High School, Newton Stewart; Glasgow University. Senior House Officer, Western General Hospital, Edinburgh, Edinburgh Royal Infirmary; Registrar, St. Bartholomew's Hospital, London; Senior Registrar, Edinburgh Teaching Hospitals. Recreations: curling; fishing. Address: (b.) Department of Cardiology, Western General Hospital, Crewe Road, Edinburgh, EH4 2XU; T.-031-332 2525.

Shaw-Stewart, Sir Houston (Mark), 11th Bt, MC (1950), TD. Vice Lord Lieutenant, Strathclyde Region (Eastwood, Renfrew and Inverclyde Districts), since 1980; b. 24.4.31; m., Lucinda Victoria Fletcher; 1 s. Educ. Eton. Coldstream Guards, 1949; 2nd Lt., Royal Ulster Rifles, Korea, 1950;

Ayrshire Yeomanry, 1952; Member, Queen's Bodyguard for Scotland (Royal Company of Archers). Address: (h.) Ardgowan, Inverkip, Renfrewshire.

Shearer, Magnus MacDonald, JP. Lord Lieutenant of Shetland, since 1982; Honorary Consul for Sweden in Shetland and Orkney, since 1958; Honorary Consul for Federal Republic of Germany in Shetland, 1972-87; b. 27.2.24; m., Martha Nicolson Henderson; 1 s. Educ. Anderson Educational Institute, Shetland; George Watson's College, Edinburgh. Royal Navy, Atlantic, Mediterranean and Far East, 1942-46; Royal Artillery TA, commissioned 2nd Lt., 1949; TARO, rank Captain, 1959; Honorary Secretary, Lerwick Branch, RNLI, since 1968; Member, Lerwick Town Council, 1963-69; Deputy Lieutenant of Shetland, 1973. Recreations: reading; bird watching; ships. Address: (h.) Birka, Cruester, Bressay, Shetland, ZE2 9EL; T.-0595 82 363.

Shedden, Alexander Denis, BSc, FFA, FSA. President, Faculty of Actuaries in Scotland, 1983-85; Deputy Chief Executive and Secretary, Standard Life Assurance Company, since 1985; b. 7.8.27, Glasgow; m., Catrionia Garland Kerr; 1 s.; 2 d. Educ. Allan Glen's School; Glasgow University. National Service as Education Officer, RAF, 1948-50; Scottish Mutual Assurance Society, Glasgow, 1950-52; Dominion Life Assurance Company, Ontario, Canada, 1952-63; joined Standard Life Assurance Co., 1963. Recreations: bridge; music. Address: (b.) 3 George Street, Edinburgh, EH2 2XZ; T.-031-225 2552.

Sheehan, Sheriff Albert Vincent, MA, LLB. Sheriff of Tayside, Central and Fife, at Falkirk, since 1983; b. 23.8.36, Edinburgh; m., Edna Georgina Scott Hastings; 2 d. Educ. Bo'ness Academy; Edinburgh University. 2nd Lt., 1st Bn., Royal Scots (The Royal Regiment), 1960; Captain, Directorate of Army Legal Services, 1961; Depute Procurator Fiscal, Hamilton, 1961-71; Senior Depute Procurator Fiscal, Glasgow, 1971-74; Deputy Crown Agent for Scotland, 1974-79; Scottish Law Commission, 1979-81; Sheriff of Lothian and Borders, at Edinburgh, 1981-83. Leverhulme Fellow, 1971. Publication: Criminal Procedure in Scotland and France, 1975. Recreations: naval history; travel; sailing. Address: (b.) Sheriff Court House, Falkirk; T.-Falkirk 20822.

Sheehan, Michael John, BSc (Econ), PhD. Member, Aberdeen City Council, 1984-88; Lecturer in International Relations, Aberdeen University, since 1979; b. 26.6.54, London. Educ. Cardinal Vaughan School, London; University College of Wales, Aberystwyth. Associate, Aberdeen Centre for Defence Studies, since 1984; Member, Liberal Party Defence Policy Panel, 1981-88. Publications: The Arms Race, 1983; Pocket Guide to Defence (Co-author), 1986; Arms Control: Theory and Practice, 1988. Recreations: music; astronomy; Aberdeen and Cardiff City Football Clubs. Address: (b.) Department of Politics, Aberdeen University, Dunbar Street, Aberdeen, AB9 2UB; T.-Aberdeen 272726.

Shelton, Richard Graham John, BSc, PhD. Officer-in-Charge, DAFS Freshwater Fisheries Laboratory, Pitlochry, since 1982; b. 3.7.42, Aylesbury; m., Freda Carstairs; 2 s. Educ. Royal Grammar School, High Wycombe; St. Andrews University. Research work, Burnham-on-Crouch Laboratory, MAFF, 1968-72; Assistant to Controller of Fisheries Research and Development, MAFF Fisheries Laboratory, Lowestoft, 1972-76 and (from 1974) DAFS Marine Laboratory, Aberdeen; worked on the population ecology of Crustacea, 1976-82. Recreations: shooting; fishing; steam model railways. Address: (h.) Dalfraoich, Strathtay, Pitlochry, PH9 OPJ; T.-088 74 217.

Shenkin, Alan, MB, ChB, BSc, PhD, MRCP(G), MRCPath. Consultant Clinical Biochemist, Glasgow Royal Infirmary, since 1978; Honorary Clinical Lecturer, Glasgow University, since 1978; b. 3.9.43, Glasgow; m., Leonna Estelle Delmonte; 1 s.; 2 d. Educ. Hutchesons' Grammar School; Glasgow University. Lecturer in Biochemistry, Glasgow University, 1970-74; Senior Registrar in Clinical Biochemistry, Glasgow Royal Infirmary, 1974-78; Royal Society European Exchange Fellow, Karolinska Institute, Stockholm, 1976-77. Chairman, Scottish Group, Nutrition Society, 1981-82; Chairman, Scientific Committee, European Society of Parenteral and Enteral Nutrition; European Editor, Nutrition. Recreations: golf; table tennis; chess; travel. Address: (h.) 1 Netherton Road, Newton Mearns, Glasgow, G77 6ER; T.-041-639 4505.

Shepherd, Professor James, BSc, MB, ChB, PhD, MRCPath. Professor in Pathological Biochemistry, Glasgow University, since 1987 (Reader, 1984-87); b. 8.4.44, Motherwell; m., Janet Bulloch Kelly; 1 s.; 1 d. Educ. Hamilton Academy; Glasgow University. Lecturer, Glasgow University: Biochemistry, 1968-72, Pathological Biochemistry, 1972-77; Assistant Professor of Medicine, Baylor College of Medicine, Houston, Texas, 1976-77; Senior Lecturer in Pathological Biochemistry, Glasgow University, 1977-84; Visiting Professor of Medicine, Geneva University, 1984. Address: (b.) Department of Biochemistry, Royal Infirmary, Glasgow, G4 OSF; T.-041-552 3535, Ext. 5374.

Shepperson, Professor George Albert, MA, CertEd (Cantab), Hon.DUniv (York). William Robertson Professor of Commonwealth and American History, Edinburgh University, 1963-86; Professor Emeritus, since 1986; b. 7.1.22, Peterborough; m., Joyce Irene Cooper; 1 d. Educ. King's School, Peterborough; St. John's College, Cambridge. Commissioned Northamptonshire Regiment; seconded King's African Rifles; War Service, 1941-46; Lecturer, Senior Lecturer, Reader in History, Edinburgh University, 1948-63; various overseas academic appointments, including Visiting Scholar, Du Bois Institute, Harvard, 1986-87; Dean, Faculty of Arts, Edinburgh, 1974-77; Dean, Scottish Universities Summer School, 1971-76; Chairman, British Association for American Studies, 1971-74; Chairman, Mungo Park Bicentenary Committee, 1971; Chairman, David Livingstone Documentation Project, since 1973; Chairman, Commonwealth Institute, Scotland, since 1973; founder Member and former Convener, Centre of African Studies and Centre of Canadian Studies, Edinburgh University; President, St. Andrew Society of Edinburgh, 1970-73; Joint Editor, Oxford Studies in African Affairs,

1969-85. Publications: David Livingstone and the Rovuma; Independent African. Recreations: collecting African and Afro-American documents; theatre. Address: (h.) 23 Ormidale Terrace, Edinburgh; T.-031-337 4424.

Sherrard, Rev. (Henry) Dane, BD. Minister, Buckhaven Parish Church, since 1976; b. 13.3.46, Watford; m., Rachel Joan Hammerton. Educ. Dundee High School; St. Andrews University. President, SRC, St. Andrews, 1965-66; Vice President, Scottish Union of Students, 1966; Assistant, Abronhill Parish Church, 1970; Church of Scotland Minister, Northern Italy (responsible for Seamen's Mission), 1971-76. Area Board Member, MSC, since 1983; Chairman, Aberhill Youth Project, 1979-82; Chairman, Levenmouth Council of Social Service, 1978-82; in 1983, began employment scheme which now employs 800 people. Recreations: theatre and music; a passion for Gilbert and Sullivan and cricket. Address: St. Michael's House, East Lawrence Street, Buckhaven, KY8 1BQ; T.-0592 715546.

Sherratt, Professor David John, BSc, PhD, FRSE. Professor of Genetics, Glasgow University, since 1980; b. 14.6.45, Nuneaton; 1 s.; 2 d. Educ. Loughborough Grammar School; UMIST; Edinburgh University. Research Fellow, California University, 1969-71; Lecturer in Microbial Genetics, Sussex University, 1971-80. Fleming Lecturer, 1982. Recreation: enjoying fresh air. Address: (b.) Department of Genetics, Glasgow University, Church Street, Glasgow, G11 5TS; T.-041-339 8855, Ext. 7113.

Sherrington, Professor David Colin, BSc, PhD, FRSC, CChem. Professor, Department of Pure and Applied Chemistry, since 1987; b. 5.3.45, Liverpool; m., Valerie. Educ. Waterloo Grammar School; Liverpool University. Lecturer, then Senior Lecturer, Strathclyde University, 1971-84; Polymer Science Area Head, Unilever Research, 1984-87; Reader, Strathclyde University, 1987. Editor, Reactive Polymers. Recreation: angling. Address: (h.) 10 Hawthorne Avenue, Lenzie, Glasgow, G66 4RA; T.-041-776 1747.

Sherwood, Professor John Neil, DSc, PhD, CChem, FRSC, FRSE. Burmah Professor of Physical Chemistry, Strathclyde University, since 1983; b. 8.11.33, Redruth, Cornwall; m., Margaret Enid Shaw; 2 d. Educ. Aireborough Grammar School; Bede College, Durham University. Research Fellow, Hull University, 1958-60; Lecturer and Reader, Strathclyde University, 1960-83. Recreations: hill-walking; photography; gardening. Address: (b.) Department of Pure and Applied Chemistry, Strathclyde University, Glasgow, G1 1XL; T.-041-552 4400.

Shewan, Rev. Frederick David Fitzgerald, MA, BD. Minister, Muirhouse Parish Church, Edinburgh, since 1980 (Northesk Parish Church, Musselburgh, 1970-80); Convener, Church and Nation Sub-Committee on Mass Media, 1981-85; Convener, Social and Community Interests Committee, Edinburgh Presbytery, 1983-87; b. 24.3.42, Whiterashes, Aberdeenshire; m., Iris Patricia Barrack; 2 d. Educ. Inverurie Academy; Kings College and Christ's College, Aberdeen University. Convener, Church and Nation Committee, Lothian Presbytery, 1975; Member, Church and Nation Committee, General Assembly, 1977; President, Scottish Church Theology Society, 1978-81. Publication: The Significance of Modern Israel, 1970. Recreations: reading; hill-walking; classic cars; sport and painting. Address: The Manse, 35 Silverknowes Road, Edinburgh, EH4 5LL; T.-031-336 4546.

Shewan, Henry Alexander, CB (1974), OBE (1946), QC, MA, LLB; b. 7.11.06, Aberdeen; m., Ann Fraser Thomson (deceased); 2 s. Educ. Robert Gordon's College, Aberdeen; Aberdeen University; Emmanuel College, Cambridge. Admitted Scottish Bar, 1933; RAFVR, 1940-45 (Squadron Leader); Standing Junior Counsel to Inland Revenue Scotland, 1947-49; QC, 1949; Referee under Coal Industry Nationalisation Act, 1949-55; Chairman, Medical Appeal Tribunal, 1950-55; National Insurance Commissioner, 1955-80. Chairman, General Nursing Council for Scotland, 1960-62. Address: (h.) St. Raphaels, 6 Blackford Avenue, Edinburgh.

Shiach, Sheriff Gordon Iain Wilson, MA, LLB, BA (Hons). Sheriff of Lothian and Borders, at Edinburgh, since 1984; b. 15.10.35, Elgin; m., Margaret Grant Smith; 2 d. Educ. Lathallan; Gordonstoun; Edinburgh University; Open University. Admitted Advocate, 1960; practised as Advocate, 1960-72; Sheriff of Fife and Kinross, at Dunfermline, 1972-79; Sheriff of Lothian and Borders, at Linlithgow, 1979-84. Recreations: orienteering; swimming; music; the theatre. Address: (b.) Sheriff Court House, Lawnmarket, Edinburgh, EH1; T.-031-226 7181.

Shoat, David Robertson. Scottish Secretary, Transport and General Workers' Union, since 1986; b. 14.12.38, Corby; m., Elizabeth Caird; 1 s.; 1 d. Educ. Riverside Secondary School, Stirling. Galashiels District Secretary, TGWU, 1973-81, Aberdeen District Secretary, 1981-86; Representative on: STUC General Council and Sub-Committees, Scottish Council Development and Industry. Recreations: gardening; walking; reading; music. Address: (b.) 290 Bath Street, Glasgow, G2 4LD; T.-041-332 7321.

Shoolbread, James Wilson, BDS, MGDS, RCPS. Chairman, Scottish Dental Estimates Board, since 1984; Director, Dental Estimates Division, Common Services Agency, since 1984; b. 9.7.43, Edinburgh; m., Kathleen Muckart; 2 s. Educ. Bo'ness Academy; Edinburgh University; Royal College of Physicians and Surgeons, Glasgow. General dental practitioner, 1966-84. Member, Forth Valley Health Board, 1981-84; Secretary, Dunblane Sports Club. Recreations: squash; golf; tennis; music; reading. Address: (b.) Trinity Park House, South Trinity Road, Edinburgh; T.-031-552 6255.

Short, Agnes Jean, BA (Hons), MLitt. Writer; b. Bradford, Yorkshire; m., Anthony Short (qv); 3 s.; 2 d. Educ. Bradford Girls' Grammar School; Exeter University; Aberdeen University. Various secretarial, research and teaching jobs, both in UK and abroad; took up writing, 1966; 13 novels, including several with a Scottish setting; also short stories and radio; Constable Award, 1976. Recreations: dog-walking; whisky-tasting; good food; small hills. Address: (h.) 20 The Chanonry, Aberdeen, AB2 1RQ; T.-0224 482277.

Short, Anthony, BSc (Econ), MA, BLitt. Reader in International Relations, Aberdeen University, since 1977 (Warden, Dunbar Hall, since 1967); b. 26.6.29, Singapore; m., Agnes Russell (see Agnes Jean Short); 3 s.; 2 d. Educ. Hele's School, Exeter; University College, Exeter; London School of Economics; University of Virginia; St. Catherine's, Oxford. National Service, Malaya, 1947-49; Lecturer, Bristol University, 1957-60; Lecturer, University of Malaya 1960-66; Visiting Fellow, Senior Lecturer, Reader, Department of Politics, Aberdeen University. Publication: The Communist Insurrection in Malaya 1948-60. Recreations: malt whisky; wood gathering; temperate hill-walking. Address: (h.) Chaplain's Court, The Chanonry, Old Aberdeen; T.-0224 482277.

Short, Emeritus Professor David Somerset, MD, PhD, FRCP, FRCPEdin. Honorary Consultant Physician, Grampian Health Board, since 1983; Emeritus Professor in Clinical Medicine, Aberdeen University, since 1983; b. 6.8.18, Weston-super-Mare, Avon; m., Joan Anne McLay; 1 s.; 4 d. Educ. Bristol Grammar School; Cambridge University; Bristol University. RAMC, 1944-47; Senior Registrar in Medicine/Cardiology, Bristol, National Heart Hospital, London Hospital and Middlesex Hospital, London, 1948-59; Consultant Physician, Aberdeen Hospitals and Senior Lecturer, Aberdeen University, 1960-83; former Physician to The Queen in Scotland. Recreation: walking. Address: (h.) 48 Victoria Street, Aberdeen, AB9 2PL; T.-0224 645853.

Short, James, FITSA, DCA. Director of Trading Standards, Lothian Regional Council, since 1974; b. Paisley. Educ. John Neilson High School. Trained in Paisley Weights and Measures Department, 1950-53; Inspector of Weights and Measures, Glasgow Corporation, 1953-58; Inspector in Charge, Weights and Measures Department, Burgh of Clydebank, 1958-59; Chief Inspector, Burgh of Paisley, 1959-74. Recreations: golf; DIY. Address: (b.) 1 Parliament Square, Edinburgh, EH1 1RF; T.-031-229 9292.

Sibbald, Alexander, BSc. Headteacher, Hazlehead Academy, since 1984; b. 8.4.38, Edinburgh; m., Christina W.M. Mallinson; 1 s.; 1 d. Educ. George Heriot's School; Edinburgh University. Assistant Teacher of Science, Lindsay High School, Bathgate, 1961-63; Lecturer, Regent Road Institute, Edinburgh, 1963-66; Principal Teacher of Science, Castlebrae High School, Edinburgh, 1966-75; Assistant Head/Depute Head, Whitburn Academy, West Lothian, 1975-80; Head Teacher, Kemnay Academy, 1981-84. Recreations: wide range of sports; car restoration. Address: (b.) Groat's Road, Aberdeen; T.-Aberdeen 310184.

Sibbald, John Arnold. Library Consultant; Librarian, Advocates' Library, 1982-88; b. Glasgow; m., Caroline Mary Paton. Educ. George Watson's College; Society of the Sacred Mission, Newark; Edinburgh University. Assistant Librarian, Homerton College, Cambridge, 1966-68; Deighton, Bell & Co., Cambridge, 1969-77; Assistant Librarian, Advocates' Library, 1978-82. Address: (h.) 50 Blacket Place, Edinburgh, EH9 1RJ; T.-031-668 3474.

Sibbett, Professor Wilson, BSc, PhD. Professor of Physics, St. Andrews University, since 1985 (Chairman, Department of Physics and Astronomy, since 1987); b. 15.3.48, Portglenone, N. Ireland; m., Barbara Anne Brown; 3 d. Educ. Ballymena Technical College; Queen's University, Belfast. Postdoctoral Research Fellow, Blackett Laboratory, Imperial College, London, 1973-76; Lecturer in Physics, then Reader, Imperial College, 1976-85. Member, Physics Committee, Science and Engineering Research Council. Recreation: golf (to low standard). Address: (b.) Department of Physics and Astronomy, St. Andrews University, North Haugh, St. Andrews, KY16 9SS; T.-0334 76161.

Sillars, Evelyn Murdoch, MBE, JP, MA. Member, Cunninghame District Council, since 1974; Member, HIDB Consultative Council, since 1975; b. 24.11.23, Ayr; m., Douglas A. Sillars; 4 d. Educ. Ayr Academy; Glasgow University. Intelligence Section, Foreign Office (War Service); Teacher of English and Religious Education; Honorary Secretary, Scottish Committee, War on Want; County Councillor, holding post of County Convener at time of reorganisation (only woman to hold such appointment in Scotland); District Councillor for Arran; Member, Scottish Transport Users Consultative Committee, since 1981; Member, Clyde Shipping Advisory Committee; Executive Member, Arran Council of Social Service; Executive Member, Arran Tourist Association; Centre Organiser for Red Cross; Church Elder. Recreations: music; bridge; bowling. Address: (h.) Mid Mayish House, Brodick, Isle of Arran; T.-0770 2246.

Sillars, James, FBIM; b. 4.10.37, Ayr; m., Margo MacDonald (qv); 1 s.; 3 d. Educ. Ayr Academy. Member, Ayr Town Council and Ayr County Council Education Committee, 1960s; Member, Western Regional Hospital Board, 1965-70; Head, Organisation Department, Scottish TUC, 1968-70; MP, South Ayrshire, 1970-79. Recreation: reading. Address: (h.) 15 Woodburn Terrace, Edinburgh.

Simmers, Brian Maxwell, CA. Partner, Kidsons Simmers, CA (formerly S. Easton Simmers & Co., CA); Director, Scottish Highland Hotels, since 1963; b. 26.2.40, Glasgow; m., Constance Ann Turner; 3 s. Educ. Glasgow Academy; Larchfield; Loretto. Member, Scottish Sports Council, 1981-84; Deputy Chairman, National Playing Fields Association; Governor, Glasgow Academy; Honorary Secretary, Rugby Internationals' Golfing Society; former Member, Finance Committee, British Red Cross (Glasgow). Played rugby for Scotland (seven caps) and Barbarians. Recreations: rugby; golf; shooting; skiing; windsurfing. Address: (b.) 98 West George Street, Glasgow, G2 1PW; T.-041-332 6538.

Simmers, Graeme Maxwell, OBE, CA. Partner, Kidsons Simmers, CA (formerly S. Easton Simmers & Co., CA); Chairman, Scottish Highland Hotels Group Ltd., since 1972; Chairman, Board of Management, British Hotels, Restaurants and

Caterers Association (Chairman, Scottish Division, 1979-81); Vice-Chairman of Governors, Loretto School; b. 2.5.35, Glasgow; m., Jennifer M.H. Roxburgh; 2 s.; 2 d. Educ. Glasgow Academy; Loretto School. Qualified CA, 1959; commissioned, Royal Marines, 1959-61. Member, Scottish Tourist Board, 1979-86; Chairman, HCBA (Scotland), 1984-86; Elder and Treasurer, Killearn Kirk; Member, Championship Committee, Royal and Ancient Golf Club of St. Andrews. Recreations: rugby; golf; skiing; literary society. Address: (h.) Kincaple, Boquhan, Balfron, near Glasgow, G63 ORW; T.-0360 40375.

Simmons, Dennis, CEng, FIEE, FBIM. Chief Commercial Officer, South of Scotland Electricity Board, since 1982; b. 19.9.31, Grimsby. Grimsby Corporation, 1947; Yorkshire Electricity Board, 1954; Eastern Electricity Board, Bedford, 1956; South East Electricity Board, Guildford, 1961; SSEB: Assistant District Engineer, Edinburgh East, 1964, District Engineer, Borders, 1966, District Manager, Ayr, 1967, District Manager, Glasgow South, 1971, Area Engineer, Glasgow/Clyde, 1974, Area Manager, Edinburgh, Fife and Borders, 1979; Recreations: golf; tennis; badminton. Address: (b.) Cathcart House, Spean Street, Glasgow; T.-041-637 7177.

Simpson, David Francis, BL, WS. Honorary Sheriff, Cupar, since 1976; b. 6.4.19, Dundee; m., Jessie Ogilvy Steel Dickie (deceased); 1 s. Educ. Edinburgh Academy; Fettes; Edinburgh University. War Service with Cameronians (Scottish Rifles), 1939-46 (Major); wounded, Germany, 1945; practised as Solicitor in Edinburgh, 1948-50 and Cupar, 1950-82. Recreations: golf; walking; reading. Address: (h.) 17 Hallowhill, St. Andrews, Fife; T.-St. Andrews 73677.

Simpson, Eric William McIntyre, DipEdTech, ALA. Chairman, Glasgow and West Hospital Broadcasting Service, since 1975; Senior Lecturer, Anniesland College, since 1978; freelance broadcaster; b. 18.2.45, Glasgow. Educ. Victoria Drive School, Glasgow; Strathclyde University. Former Administrative Director, Glasgow and West Hospital Broadcasting Service; SCOTVEC Subject Assessor for National Certificate; Member, National Working Party on Resource Based Learning; Radio Judge, Television and Radio Industries Club of Scotland Radio Awards, 1987, 1988. Recreations: reading; spectator sports; listening to radio. Address: (h.) 11 Victoria Park Drive South, Glasgow, G14.

Simpson, Gordon Russell, DSO and bar, LVO, TD. Stockbroker; b. 2.1.17, Tayport; m., Marion Elizabeth King, deceased; 2 s. Educ. Rugby. Member, Edinburgh Stock Exchange, 1938; Partner, Bell Cowan & Co.; Lothians and Border Horse, 1939-46, commanding 2nd Regiment, 1944-46; Chairman, Edinburgh Stock Exchange, 1961-63; Chairman, Scottish Stock Exchange, 1965-66; President, Council of ASE, 1971-73; Deputy Chairman, The Stock Exchange, 1973-78; Director, General Accident, 1967-87, Chairman, 1979-87. DL, Central Region, Stirling and Falkirk Dstricts; Member of Court, Stirling University, 1980-88; Commissioner, Queen Victoria School; Member, Board, Scottish Chamber Orchestra; Member, Executive Committee, Scottish Veterans Garden City Association; Kirk Elder. Recreations: music; skiing; archery; tennis. Address: Bell Lawrie Ltd., 68/73 Queen Street, Edinburgh, EH2 4AE.

Simpson, Hugh Walter, MB, ChB, MD, PhD, FRCPath, FRCP(Glas). Reader in Pathology, Glasgow University, since 1978; Head of Pathology, Glasgow Royal Infirmary, since 1984; b. 4.4.31, Ceres, Fife; m., Myrtle Emslie (see Myrtle Simpson); 3 s.; 1 d. Educ. Bryanston; Edinburgh University. Leader of numerous expeditions to polar and tropical regions; awarded Polar Medal and Mungo Park Medal. Recreation: skiing. Address: (h.) 7 Cleveden Crescent, Glasgow, G12 0PD; T.-041-357 1091.

Simpson, Rev. Ean Macgregor. Minister, Grangemouth Kerse, since 1973; b. 4.2.32, Glasgow; m., Marjorie Patricia Wooley; 1 s. Educ. Dalziel High School; Edinburgh University and New College. Assistant Ordained Minister, Dunfermline Abbey, 1963; Minister, Kilfinan and Tighnabruaich, 1964-73. Past Chairman, Kyles of Bute Tourist Committee; former Vice-Chairman, Grangemouth Community Council. Recreations: steam railways; fishing. Address: 142 Bo'ness Road, Grangemouth, FK3 9BX.

Simpson, Rev. James Alexander, BSc (Hons), BD, STM. Minister, Dornoch Cathedral, since 1976; b. 9.3.34, Glasgow; m., Helen Gray McCorquodale; 3 s.; 2 d. Educ. Eastwood Secondary School; Glasgow University; Union Seminary, New York. Minister: Grahamston Church, Falkirk, 1960-66, St. John's Renfield, Glasgow, 1966-76. Publications: There is a time to ....; Marriage Questions Today; Doubts are not Enough; Holy Wit; Laughter Lines. Recreations: photography; writing articles on golf and Highland life. Address: Cathedral Manse, Dornoch, IV25 3HN; T. 086 2810296.

Simpson, James White, BSc, MCIT, MRIN. Divisional Manager, Marine Services, Forth Ports Authority, since 1986 (Port Manager, Grangemouth, 1982-86); Director, Forth Estuary Towage Ltd., since 1986; b. 30.8.44, St. Andrews; m., Barbara Hutton; 1 s.; 1 d. Educ. Grangemouth High School; Buckhaven High School; Leith Nautical College; Plymouth Polytechnic. Cadet, Furness Prince Lines, 1961-64; Navigating Officer: Shaw Savill Line, 1965-68, Overseas Containers Ltd., 1969-70; Assistant Harbour Master, then Assistant to Port Superintendent, Grangemouth, 1973-77; Port Superintendent, Leith and Granton, 1978-82. Recreation: sailing. Address: (b.) Forth Ports Authority, Tower Place, Leith, EH6 7DB; T.-031-554 4343.

Simpson, Professor John Alexander, MD Hon. (Glasgow), FRCP, FRCPEdin, FRCPGlas, FRSE. Emeritus Professor of Neurology, Glasgow University, since 1987 (Professor of Neurology, 1965-87); Senior Neurologist, Institute of Neurological Sciences, Southern General Hospital, Glasgow, 1965-87; Consultant Neurologist, Civil Service Commission, 1974-87; b. 30.3.22, Greenock; m., Dr. Elizabeth M.H. Simpson; 2 s.; 1 d. Educ. Greenock Academy; Glasgow University. Surgeon-Lieutenant, RNVR; Registrar in Medicine, Southern General Hospital, Glasgow;

Lecturer in Medicine, Glasgow University; MRC Research Fellow, National Hospital for Nervous Diseases, London; Senior Lecturer in Medicine, Glasgow University; Consultant Physician, Western Infirmary, Glasgow; Reader in Neurology, Edinburgh University. President, Association of British Neurologists, 1985-86; Past Chairman, Scottish Epilepsy Association; former Consultant Neurologist to British Army in Scotland; Editor, Journal of Neurology, Neurosurgery and Psychiatry. Recreations: violinist (Glasgow Chamber Orchestra and Scottish Fiddle Orchestra); sailing. Address: (h.) 87 Glencairn Drive, Glasgow, G41 4LL; T.-041-423 2863.

Simpson, John Donald Carmichael, LLB, FRICS, FRVA. Regional Estates Surveyor, Lothian Regional Council, since 1978; b. 14.1.43, Greenock; m., Elizabeth Hastie Fagnen. Educ. Hutchesons Grammar School, Glasgow; London University (External). City Assessor's Office, Glasgow; British Rail Property Board (Scotland); Thomas Binnie & Hendry, Chartered Surveyors, Glasgow; Estates Department, Glasgow Corporation; Depute Head of Estates, Strathclyde Regional Council. Member, Rent Assessment Panel for Scotland. Recreations: golf; music; private flying. Address: (b.) Estates Department, Lothian Regional Council, 7/9 North St. David Street, Edinburgh, EH2 1AW; T.-031-557 5656.

Simpson, John Gruer, MB, ChB (Hons), PhD, FRCPath. Senior Lecturer in Pathology, Aberdeen University, since 1978; Honorary Consultant Pathologist, Grampian Health Board, since 1978; b. 15.5.41, Toronto, Canada. Educ. Fraserburgh Academy; Aberdeen University. Aberdeen Royal Infirmary: Resident Medical Officer, 1965-66, Garden Research Fellow, 1966-67; Aberdeen University: MRC Junior Research Fellow, 1967-68, Lecturer in Pathology, 1968-75; Visiting Professor and NIH Scholar, Michigan University, 1975-77. Treasurer, European Society for Microcirculation; Assistant Editor, Scottish Medical Journal. Recreations: opera; sailing; travel; cooking; red Burgundy. Address: (h.) 37 Thomson Street, Aberdeen, AB2 4QN; T.-0224 637482.

Simpson, John Moir, FRICS, FCIArb. Senior Partner, John M. Simpson & Co., Chartered Quantity Surveyors; Senior Partner, Wilkie & Simpson, Chartered Surveyors; Member, Cumbernauld Development Corporation, since 1983; b. 29.1.28; m., Elizabeth Russell Faulds; 1 s.; 1 d. Educ. Whitehill Secondary School, Glasgow; Royal Technical College, Glasgow. Chief Quantity Surveyor, Cumbernauld Development Corporation, 1965-69. Chairman, Advisory Panel, Glasgow College of Building and Printing, since 1965; Chairman, Valuation Appeals Committee (North Strathclyde); Chairman, Cumbernauld Information and Technology Board; Vice-Chairman, Cumbernauld CAB, since 1976; Member, Board of Management, Cumbernauld and Kilsyth Enterprise Trust; Member, Cumbernauld International Sports Trust; Past President, Cumbernauld Rotary Club and Cumbernauld Burns Club; Member, Executive Committee, Glasgow Association of Burns Clubs. Recreations: bowling; curling. Address: (h.) 17 Glen View, Cumbernauld, Glasgow, G67 2DA; T.-0236 722933.

Simpson, John Montgomery, MA. Senior Lecturer in Scottish History, Edinburgh University, since 1981; b. 27.10.38, Edinburgh; m., Anne Corstorphine; 1 s.; 2 d. Educ. Daniel Stewart's College; St. Andrews University. Department of History, Sheffield University, 1962-64; Department of Scottish History, Edinburgh University, since 1964. Recreations: music; walking. Address: (b.) Department of Scottish History, Edinburgh University, 17 Buccleuch Place, Edinburgh, EH8 9LN.

Simpson, Myrtle Lillias. Author and Lecturer; Member, Scottish Sports Council; Past Chairman, Scottish National Ski Council; b. 5.7.31, Aldershot; m., Dr. Hugh Simpson (qv); 3 s.; 1 d. Educ. 19 schools (father in Army). Writer/Explorer; author of 12 books, including travel, biography, historical and children's; first woman to ski across Greenland; attempted to ski to North Pole (most northerly point reached by a woman unsupported); numerous journeys in polar regions on ski or canoe; Mungo Park Medal. Recreations: climbing; skiing; canoeing. Address: (h.) 7 Cleveden Crescent, Glasgow, G12 0PD; T.-041-357 1091.

Simpson, Patrick William, CA. Chairman, Cockburn Conservation Trust; Director: The Queen's Hall (Edinburgh), Scottish Opera; Member: Edinburgh New Town Conservation Committee, Lothian Building Preservation Trust, Queen's Nursing Institute Scotland, Scotland's Gardens Scheme; b. 14.3.22, Edinburgh; m., Elizabeth Wilson; 1 s.; 1 d. Educ. Rugby. Royal Artillery and Ayrshire Yeomanry, N. Africa and Italy, 1941-46; Partner, Chiene & Tait, CA, 1952-87. Former Member of Council, Edinburgh Festival Society. Recreations: music; skiing; painting. Address: (h.) 23 Moray Place, Edinburgh, EH3 6DA; T.-031-225 8020.

Simpson, Robert Keith, FCCA, IPFA. Controller of Audit, Commission for Local Authority Accounts in Scotland, since 1985; b. 26.7.43, Barrow-in-Furness; m., Brenda Mary Baines; 2 s. Educ. Barrow-in-Furness Grammar School. Accountant, Barrow-in-Furness County Borough Council, 1959-72; Principal Auditor, Bristol City Council, 1972-74; Chief Auditor, Avon County Council, 1974-77; Assistant Director of Finance, South Yorkshire County Council, 1977-82; Depute Controller of Audit, Commission for Local Authority Accounts in Scotland, 1982-85. Former Editor, Audit Bulletin, CIPFA. Publication: Audit in the Public Sector (Co-author). Recreations: archery; hill-walking. Address: (h.) Cerna, 69 Dirleton Avenue, North Berwick; T.-0620 4288.

Sinclair, Allan MacDonald, PhD, FRSE. Reader in Mathematics, Edinburgh University, since 1977; b. 11.7.41, Johannesburg, South Africa; m., Patricia Margaret Bush; 1 s.; 1 d. Educ. Parktown Boys' High School, Johannesburg; Witwatersrand University; Newcastle-upon-Tyne University. Senior Lecturer, 1968-72, and Professor, 1972-73, in Mathematics, Witwatersrand University; Lecturer in Mathematics, Edinburgh University, 1973-77; Visiting Professor, California University, Los Angeles, 1978-79. Recreations: hill-walking; sculpture; Scottish country dancing. Address: (b.) Department of Mathematics, Edinburgh University, James Clark Building, King's Buildings, Mayfield Road, Edinburgh, EH9 3JZ; T.-031-667 1081, Ext. 2812.

Sinclair, 17th Lord (Charles Murray Kennedy St. Clair), LVO. Lord Lieutenant, Dumfries and Galloway Region (District of Stewartry), since 1982; Extra Equerry to the Queen Mother, since 1953; Member, Queen's Bodyguard for Scotland (Royal Company of Archers); b. 21.6.14; m., Anne Lettice Cotterell; 1 s.; 2 d. Educ. Eton; Magdalene College, Cambridge. Served Second World War (mentioned in Despatches); retired Major, Coldstream Guards. Address: (h.) Knocknalling, St. John's Town of Dalry, Castle Douglas, Kirkcudbrightshire.

Sinclair, Rev. Colin Andrew Macalister, BA (Hons), BD (Hons). General Director, Scripture Union Scotland, since 1988 (Minister, Newton-on-Ayr, Ayr, 1982-88); b. 16.9.53, Glasgow; m., Ruth Mary Murray; 1 s.; 1 d. Educ. Glasgow Academy; Stirling University; Edinburgh University. Schools Training Officer, Scripture Union, Zambia, 1974-77; Assistant Minister, Palmerston Place, Edinburgh, 1980-82. Publication: Ministers for the 1980s (Contributor). Recreations: family; reading. Address: 36 Clincarthill Road, Rutherglen, Glasgow, G73 2LQ.

Sinclair, Derek Urquhart, MA (Hons), MB, ChB, MRCGP, DPM. Senior Medical Officer, Scottish Home and Health Department, since 1988 (Medical Officer, 1987-88); b. 10.10.40, Falkirk; m., Dorothy Aalbregt; 1 s.; 2 d. Educ. Grangemouth High School; Falkirk High School; Glasgow University. House Officer, Falkirk and District Royal and Paisley Royal Alexandra Infirmaries, 1964-65; Norwegian State Stipendiary, University of Oslo, 1965-66; Assistant Lecturer in Physiology, Glasgow University, 1966-68; Senior House Officer and Registrar in Psychiatry, Royal Edinburgh Hospital, 1970-72; Principal in general practice, Falkirk, 1972-86; Deputy Police Surgeon, Central Scotland Police, 1972-86; Clinical Assistant in Psychiatry, Bellsdyke Hospital, 1977-86; Regional Medical Officer, Scottish Home and Health Department, 1986-87. Counsellor to Vasectomy Clinic, Forth Valley Health Board, 1977-80; Voluntary Medical Officer, Strathcarron Hospice, 1983-87. Recreations: gardening; walking; fishing. Address: (b.) St. Andrews House, Edinburgh, EH1 3DE; T.-031-244 2833.

Sinclair, Sir John (Rollo Norman Blair), 9th Bt; b. 4.11.28. Educ. Wellington College. Lt., Intelligence Corps, 1948-49; Trustee, The Human Development Trust and the Lynwood Fellowship; Director, Natural Health Foundation, 1982-88. Publications: The Mystical Ladder, 1968; The Other Universe, 1973; The Alice Bailey Inheritance, 1984. Address: (h.) Barrock House, Wick, KW1 4UD.

Sinclair, John, MB, ChB, FRCSEdin. Consultant Urological Surgeon, Southern General Hospital, Glasgow, since 1975; b. 16.7.41, Kilmarnock; m., Ann Sinclair; 1 s.; 1 d. Educ. Edinburgh Academy; Edinburgh University. Junior hospital appointments, Inverness and Stornoway; Locum, general practice, from Applecross to Auchenshuggle. Recreations: hill-walking; swimming; playing drums; buses and bus operation. Address: (h.) 7 Bridgegait, Milngavie, Glasgow, G62 6NT; T.-041-956 3247.

Sinclair, Martin Fraser, MA, CA. Partner, Chiene & Tait, CA, since 1973; Director, Albyn Trust Ltd., since 1973; Director, NESSCO (Aberdeen) Ltd., since 1982; Vice Chairman, English Speaking Union in Scotland (Treasurer, 1973-81); b. 18.7.45, Greenock; m., Patricia Anne Ogilvy Smith; 1 s.; 2 d. Educ. Edinburgh Academy; Edinburgh University. Apprentice, Chiene & Tait, CA; qualified, 1970; Peat Marwick Mitchell & Co., Vancouver, 1970-73. President, Institute of Chartered Accountants Benevolent Association, 1983-84 (Member, Property Committee, since 1979). Athletics Blue, Edinburgh University; Captain, Scottish Universities Athletics Team, 1969. Recreations: skiing; squash; orienteering. Address: (b.) 3 Albyn Place, Edinburgh, EH2 4NQ; T.-031-225 7515.

Sinclair, William John, MBA, CA. Secretary to the Board of Trustees and Financial Controller, National Galleries of Scotland, since 1986; b. 16.12.37, Hong Kong; m., Muriel Rowe; 3 s. Educ. Eastwood Senior Secondary School; Strathclyde University. Recreations: hill-walking; golf. Address: (b.) 83 Princes Street, Edinburgh, EH2 2ER; T.-031-556 8921.

Sinfield, Professor Robert Adrian, BA, DipSoc Admin. Professor of Social Policy, Edinburgh University, since 1979; b. 3.11.38, Wallington, Surrey; m., Dorothy Anne Palmer; 2 d. Educ. Mercers' School, London; Balliol College, Oxford; London School of Economics. Assistant Lecturer/Lecturer/Senior Lecturer/Reader in Sociology, Essex University, 1965-79; Visiting Lecturer in Social Work, Bryn Mawr College and Columbia University, 1969-70; consultancies, OECD, 1965-68, 1970, 1983 and UN, 1970-71; Scientific Adviser to DHSS Chief Scientist, since 1980; Convener and Co-Founder, Unemployment Unit, since 1981. Publications: The Long-Term Unemployed, 1968; Which Way for Social Work?, 1969; Industrial Welfare, 1971; The Workless State (Co-Editor), 1981; What Unemployment Means, 1981. Address: (h.) 12 Eden Lane, Edinburgh, EH10 4SD; T.-031-447 2182.

Singleton, John Francis Maxwell, MA, DL. Deputy Lieutenant, Kincardineshire; Assistant Master, Lathallan School; b. 26.8.16, Colwall; m., Jean Osborne (deceased); 1 s.; 2 d. Educ. Uppingham; Pembroke College, Cambridge. Commissioned Royal Artillery, 1938; served Second World War, BEF, MEF, CMF, BLA; Instructor, Mons Officer Cadet School, 1949-55; Malayan emergency, 1953-54. Vice Chairman, NE TAVRA; County Commissioner for Scouts, Kincardineshire. Recreations: hockey; cricket; golf; shooting. Address: (h.) Scotston of Kirkside, St. Cyrus, Montrose; T.-St. Cyrus 241.

Sischy, Mark, MA, LLB, SSC, NP. Solicitor in private practice, since 1975; President, Society of Solicitors in the Supreme Courts of Scotland; Member, Court of Session Rules Council; Member, Standing Committees, Law Society of Scotland; b. 14.7.45, Johannesburg; m., Judith Lewis; 2 d. Educ. George Watson's College, Edinburgh; Edinburgh University. Recreation: armchair sportsman. Address: (b.) 3 Coates Crescent, Edinburgh; T.-031-225 2121.

Skene, Hugh Crawford. Composer; b. 24.2.19; m., Barbara Land; 1 d. Educ. Bristol. War Service as Camouflage Officer; graduated, 1949; Director of Orchestra, Buxton College; Founder Member and Musical Director, Buxton Opera Group; Director of Orchestras, City of Norwich School, 1953-73; compositions during this period include Derbyshire Rhapsody, Symphony from East Anglia and the cantata Birthday of Jesus; Musical Director, St. Cecilia Chorus and Orchestra, 13 years; returned to Scotland (Hamilton Grammar School), 1973; Musical Director, Blantyre Choral Society; retired from education service, 1983; later compositions include opera on Dumas' The Black Tulip, A Highland Symphony, Hebridean Poem, Concertino for Double Bass and orchestra, Song of the Psalms, various ensembles and fanfares; Fanfare '88, Edinburgh Festival, 1988. Recreation: exploring and photographing remote Scotland. Address: (h.) Crowhills, by Hamilton, Lanarkshire, ML3 7XP; T.-Chapelton 303.

Skinner, Rev. Alistair, BD. Minister, Priestfield Parish Church, Edinburgh, since 1975; b. 22.9.24, Greenock; m., Frances Craigmile; 2 s.; 1 d. Educ. Highlanders' Academy, Greenock; Greenock High School; Hartley-Victoria College, Manchester; Christ's College, Aberdeen. Minister: Dunbar Methodist Church, 1951-54, Lancaster Methodist Circuit, 1954-60, Liverpool Methodist Mission, 1960-63; Assistant Minister, Mastrick Parish Church, Aberdeen, 1963-64; Minister, Douglas and Angus Parish Church, Dundee, 1964-75. Address: 13 Lady Road, Edinburgh, EH16 5PA; T.-031-668 1620.

Skinner, Professor Andrew, MA, BLitt. Clerk of Senate, Glasgow University, since 1983; Daniel Jack Professor of Political Economy, since 1985; b. 11.1.35, Glasgow; m., Margaret Mary Robertson. Educ. Keil School, Dumbarton; Glasgow University; Cornell University, New York. Governor, Jordanhill College. Address: Glen House, Cardross, G82 5ES; T.-038 9841 603.

Skinner, Basil Chisholm, OBE, MA, FSA. Director of Extra-Mural Studies, Edinburgh University, since 1975; Chairman, Hopetoun House Preservation Trust, since 1979; Chairman, Conservation Committee, Scottish Development Agency, since 1979; b. 1923, Edinburgh; m., Lydia Mary Mackinnon; 2 s. Educ. Edinburgh Academy; Edinburgh University. Army Service, Yorkshire Yeomanry and Intelligence Corps; Librarian, Glasgow School of Art, 1951-54; Assistant Keeper, Scottish National Portrait Gallery, 1954-66; joined Edinburgh University as Lecturer, 1966; Council Member, National Trust for Scotland, 1970-75; Governor, Edinburgh Academy, 1973-75; Vice-President, Society of Antiquaries of Scotland, 1975-78; Member, Board of Trustees, National Museum of Antiquities, 1975-78; Trustee, Sir Patrick Geddes Memorial Trust, since 1981; Member, Scottish Museum of the Year Award Panel, since 1981; recipient, George Waterston Memorial Award, 1982. Publications: Scottish History in Perspective, 1966; Scots in Italy, 1966; Lime Industry in Lothian, 1970. Recreations: gardening; walking; travel. Address: (b.) Department of Extra-Mural Studies, 11 Buccleuch Place, Edinburgh, 8: T.-031-667 1011.

Skinner, David Neave, BArch, MLArch, RIBA, ALI. Consultant Landscape Architect; Head, Department of Landscape Architecture, Heriot-Watt University/Edinburgh College of Art; b. 16.12.28; m., Patricia Mary Coulthwaite; 2 s. Educ. Liverpool University; Pennsylvania University. Private practice in landscape architecture in Edinburgh; Professor of Landscape Architecture, School of Architecture and Planning, New Delhi; Landscape Consultant, Ford Foundation, India; Dean, Faculty of Environmental Studies, Heriot-Watt University. Publications: The Coast of Scotland, 1974; The Planning and Design of Rural Roads, 1976. Address: (h.) 5 Fingal Place, Edinburgh, EH9 1JX; T.-031-667 1503.

Slater, Basil Crandles Smith, OBE, MD, MRCP, FRCGP, MFCM, Hon. MCFP (Canada). Community Medical Specialist, Royal Infirmary, Edinburgh; former Director, Scottish Health Services Planning Unit, Scottish Home and Health Department; b. 26.7.28, Broxburn; m., Jean Wallace Simpson; 2 s.; 1 d. Educ. Armadale Public School; Bathgate Academy; Edinburgh University. House Physician, Edinburgh Royal Infirmary, 1952; House Surgeon, Bangour General Hospital, 1953; Surgeon Lieutenant, RNVR, 1953-55; General Practitioner, Harrow, Middlesex and Dalkeith, Midlothian, 1955-75; joined Scottish Home and Health Department, 1975. Former Honorary Secretary and Vice Chairman of Council, Royal College of General Practitioners; former Regional Adviser in General Practice, North West Metropolitan Region; former Vice-President, Section of General Practice, Royal Society of Medicine; first Civilian Consultant in General Practice to Royal Navy. Recreations: bridge (average); bowling (reasonable); fireside sitting (well). Address: (b.) Royal Infirmary, Lauriston Place, Edinburgh; T.-031-229 2477, Ext. 2021.

Slater, Carolyn Louttit (Buchanan), LLB. Secretary, Royal Institution of Chartered Surveyors in Scotland, since 1987; b. 22.12.47, Glasgow; m., John Cameron Slater. Educ. Hutchesons' Girls' Grammar School, Glasgow; Glasgow University. Apprentice Solicitor and Legal Assistant, Glasgow, 1968-74; Lecturer, Department of Land Economics, Paisley College of Technology, 1974-78; Secretary (Legal Education), Law Society of Scotland, 1978-87. Address: (b.) 9 Manor Place, Edinburgh, EH3 7DN; T.-031-225 7078.

Slater, Peter Anderson, MB, ChB, FRCSEdin. Consultant Orthopaedic Surgeon, Stracathro Hospital and Aberdeen Royal Infirmary, since 1978; b. 6.9.41, Aberdeen; m., Isobel; 1 s.; 2 d. Educ. Prince of Wales School, Nairobi; Aberdeen University. House Officer, Aberdeen Royal Infirmary, 1966-67; Lecturer in Pathology, Aberdeen University, 1967-68; Senior House Officer, General Surgery, Aberdeen Royal Infirmary, 1968-70; Registrar, General Surgery, South Teesside Hospitals, 1970-72; Registrar in Orthopaedics, South Birmingham Hospitals, 1972-75; Senior Registrar in Orthopaedics, Aberdeen Royal Infirmary, 1975-78. Board Member, National Centre for Education and Training in Prosthetics and Orthotics, Strathclyde University. Recreations: DIY; reading science fiction. Address: (h.) 6 Argyll Street, Brechin, Angus, DD9 6JL; T.-035 62 2554.

Slater, Professor Peter James Bramwell, BSc, PhD, DSc. Kennedy Professor of Natural History, St. Andrews University, since 1984; b. 26.12.42, Edinburgh; m., Elisabeth Vernon Smith; 2 s. Educ. Edinburgh Academy; Glenalmond; Edinburgh University. Demonstrator in Zoology, Edinburgh University, 1966-68; Lecturer in Biology, Sussex University, 1968-84. Secretary, Association for the Study of Animal Behaviour, 1973-78, President, since 1986; European Editor, Animal Behaviour, 1979-82; Editor, Advances in the Study of Behavior and of Science Progress. Recreations: walking; ornithology; music; disarmament. Address: (b.) Department of Biology and Preclinical Medicine, St. Andrews, Fife; T.-0334 76161, Ext. 7218.

Slaven, Professor Anthony, MA, BLitt, FRHistS. Professor of Business History, Glasgow University, since 1979 (Head, Department of Economic History, since 1979); Director, Centre for Business History in Scotland, since 1987; b. 5.10.37, Blantyre; m., Isabelle Dunsheath Cameron; 1 s.; 2 d. Educ. Hamilton Academy; Glasgow University. Assistant Lecturer, Glasgow University, 1960-62; Lecturer in Geography, Queensland University, 1962-64; Glasgow University: Lecturer in Economic History, 1965-70, Colquhoun Lecturer in Business History, since 1969, Senior Lecturer in Economic History, 1970-79. Council Member, Economic History Society; Member, Editorial Board, Scottish Economic and Social History. Publications: The Development of the West of Scotland; Shipbuilding - A Review of UK Statistics; Dictionary of Scottish Business Biography (Co-Editor). Recreations: walking; golf; DIY. Address: (b.) Department of Economic History, Adam Smith Building, Glasgow University, Glasgow, G12 8QQ; T.-041-339 8855, Ext. 4669.

Slavin, William J., MA, STL. Co-ordinator, Scottish Drugs Forum, since 1986; b. 17.1.40, Bristol. Educ. Blairs College, Aberdeen; Scots College, Rome; Glasgow University. Assistant Priest, Broomhill, Glasgow, 1965-70; Educational Psychologist, Glasgow Child Guidance Service, 1970-75; Deputy Director, Jessore Training Centre, Bangladesh, 1975-80; Secretary, RC Justice and Peace Commission, 1980-85; Assistant Chaplain, Barlinnie Prison. Recreation: An rud Gaidhealach. Address: (b.) 266 Clyde Street, Glasgow, G1 4JH; T.-041-221 1175.

Slawson, Keith Brian, BSc, MB, ChB, FFARCS. Consultant Anaesthetist, Western General Hospital, Edinburgh, since 1966; Honorary Senior Lecturer, Edinburgh University, since 1975; b. 7.9.33, Birmingham; m., Nan; 1 s.; 1 d. Educ. Bradford Grammar School; Edinburgh University. MRC Scientific Assistant, Department of Therapeutics, Edinburgh Royal Infirmary, 1962-63; Lecturer in Anaesthesia, Edinburgh University, 1963-66. Honorary Medical Officer, Scottish Rugby Union. Recreation: refereeing rugby football. Address: (h.) 27 Craigmount View, Edinburgh; T.-031-339 4786.

Sleeman, Professor Brian David, BSc, PhD, DSc, FIMA, FRSE. Professor of Mathematics, Dundee University, since 1978; b. 4.8.39, London; m., Juliet Mary Shea; 2 s.; 1 d. Educ. Tiffin Boys School; Battersea College of Technology; London University. Department of Mathematics and Computer Science, Dundee University: Assistant Lecturer, 1965-67, Lecturer, 1967-71, Reader, 1971-78. Chairman, Scottish Branch, Institute of Mathematics and its Applications, 1982-84; Member, General Synod, Scottish Episcopal Church. Publications: Multiparameter Spectral Theory in Hilbert Space, 1978; Differential Equations and Mathematical Biology, 1983. Recreations: choral music; hill-walking. Address: (b.) Department of Mathematics and Computer Science, Dundee University, Dundee, DD1 4HN; T.-0382 23181.

Sleeman, Professor Derek Henry, BSc, PhD. Professor of Computing Science, Aberdeen University, since 1986; b. 11.1.41, Penzance; m., Margaret G. Rankine; 1 d. Educ. Penzance Grammar School; King's College, London. Leeds University: Computing Assistant, 1965-67, Lecturer in Computational Science, 1967-82, Associate Director, Computer Based Learning Project, 1969-82; Visiting Scientist: Rutgers University, 1979, Carnegie-Mellow University, 1980-81; Senior Consultant, Teknowledge, Palo Alto, CA, 1983-86; Senior Research Associate/Associate Professor, Stanford University, 1982-86. Secretary, SS AISB, 1979-82. Publications: 50 technical papers, including Intelligent Tutoring Systems (Co-Editor). Recreations: hill and coastal path walking; medieval architecture; photography. Address: (b.) Computing Science Department, King's College, Aberdeen University, Aberdeen, AB9 2FX; T.-0224 272288.

Sleigh, James Douglas, MB, ChB, FRCPath, FRCPGlas. Reader in Bacteriology, Glasgow University, since 1984; Consultant Bacteriologist, Glasgow Royal Infirmary, since 1979; b. 5.7.30, Glasgow; m., Rosemary Margaret Smith; 2 s. Educ. Glasgow Academy; Glasgow University. House appointments, Glasgow Western Infirmary, 1953-54; Pathologist, RAMC, 1954-56; Registrar in Bacteriology, Glasgow Western Infirmary, 1956-58; Lecturer in Bacteriology, Edinburgh University, 1958-65; Consultant Clinical Pathologist, Dunbartonshire Hospitals, 1965-69; Senior Lecturer in Bacteriology, Glasgow University, 1969-84; Consultant Bacteriologist, Glasgow Western Infirmary, 1969-79. Publication: Notes on Medical Bacteriology (Co-author). Recreations: seeking non-existent bargains; spending time on Arran. Address: (h.) Clynder, 5 Sutherland Avenue, Glasgow, G41 4JJ; T.-041-427 1486.

Sloane, Professor Peter James, BA (Econ), PhD. Professor of Political Economy, Aberdeen University, since 1984; b. 6.8.42, Cheadle Hulme; m., Avril Mary Urquhart; 1 s. Educ. Cheadle Hulme School; Sheffield University; Strathclyde University. Assistant Lecturer and Lecturer, Department of Political Economy, Aberdeen University, 1966-69; Lecturer in Industrial Economics, Nottingham University, 1969-75; Economic Adviser, Department of Employment Unit for Manpower Studies (on secondment), 1973-74; Professor of Economics and Management, Paisley College, 1975-84. Member, Economic and Social Research

Council, 1979-85; Council Member, Scottish Economic Society, since 1983. Publications: Sex Discrimination in the Labour Market, 1976; Women and Low Pay, 1980; Sport in the Market?, 1980; Equal Employment Issues, 1981; Tackling Discrimination in the Workplace, 1982; Labour Economics, 1985. Recreation: sport. Address: (b.) Department of Economics, Aberdeen University, Edward Wright Building, Dunbar Street, Old Aberdeen, Aberdeen, AB9 2TY.

Small, Peter James, MA, BM, BCh, FRCP, DCH. Consultant Paediatrician, Grampian Health Board, since 1980; Honorary Senior Lecturer in Child Health, Aberdeen University, since 1980; b. 10.10.43, Harrow; m., Janice Lockhart; 3 s.; 1 d. Educ. Merchant Taylors', Northwood; St. John's College, Oxford; Oxford Clinical Medical School. Paediatric House Officer, Inverness Hospitals, 1970; Medical Registrar, Cornwall Hospital (Treliske), 1972; Lecturer in Child Health, Dundee University, 1975; Fellow in Paediatric Endocrinology, University of Manitoba, Winnipeg, 1979. Member, Health Services Human Growth Hormone Committee, 1982-87; Secretary, Scottish Study Group for the Care of Young Diabetics. Recreations: Member, Aberdeen Bach Choir; Lay Clerk, St. Andrew's Cathedral, Aberdeen. Address: (b.) Royal Aberdeen Children's Hospital, Aberdeen, AB9 2ZG; T.-0224 681818, Ext. 53102.

Small, Christopher. Writer; b. 15.11.19, London. Educ. Dartington; Oxford. Literary Editor and Dramatic Critic, Glasgow Herald, 1955-80; author of Ariel Like A Harpy: Shelley, Mary & Frankenstein; The Road to Miniluv: George Orwell, the State & God; The Printed Word: An Instrument of Popularity.

Small, Professor John Rankin, BSc (Econ), FCCA, FCMA. Professor, Department of Accountancy and Finance, Heriot-Watt University, since 1967; Chairman, Commission for Local Authority Accounts in Scotland, since 1983; b. 28.2.33, Dundee; m., Catherine Wood; 1 s.; 2 d. Educ. Harris Academy; Dundee School of Economics. Industry and commerce; Lecturer, Edinburgh University; Senior Lecturer, Glasgow University. Consultant to various organisations; Council Member, Chartered Association of Certified Accountants (President, 1982-83); Vice-Principal, Heriot-Watt University, 1974-78, and since 1987; Chairman, National Appeal Panel for Entry to Pharmaceutical Lists (Scotland), since 1987. Recreation: golf. Address: (b.) Heriot-Watt University, Grassmarket, Edinburgh; T.-031-225 8432.

Small, Ramsay George, MB, ChB, FFCM, FRCPE, DPH. Chief Administrative Medical Officer, Tayside Health Board, since 1986; Honorary Senior Lecturer in Community Medicine, Dundee University, since 1974; b. 5.2.30, Calcutta; m., Aileen Stiven Masterton; 4 s. Educ. Harris Academy, Dundee; St. Andrews University. Assistant Medical Officer of Health, Ayr County Council, 1958 61; Senior Assistant Medical Officer of Health, then Principal Medical Officer, City of Dundee, 1961-74; Community Medicine Specialist, Tayside Health Board, 1974-85. Faculty Adviser, Scotland, Faculty of Community Medicine, 1980-83, Convener Scottish Affairs Committee, 1983-86; Member, National Medical Consultative Committee and Member, Board, Faculty of Community Medicine; Member, Council, Royal College of Physicians of Edinburgh; President, Baptist Union of Scotland, 1972-73; Chairman, Eastern Regional Postgraduate Medical Education Committee, 1980-83; Secretary, Broughty Ferry Baptist Church, since 1969. Recreations: bird-watching; music. Address: 46 Monifieth Road, Broughty Ferry, Dundee, DD5 2RX; T.-Dundee 78408.

Small, Very Rev. Robert Leonard, CBE, MA, DD. Vice Chairman, Age Concern Scotland; Minister of Religion (retired); b. 12.5.05, North Berwick; m., Jane Hay McGregor; 3 s.; 1 d. Educ. North Berwick High School; Edinburgh University and New College. Minister: St. John's, Bathgate, 1931-35, West High, Kilmarnock, 1935-44, Cramond Kirk, Edinburgh, 1944-56, St. Cuthbert's, Edinburgh, 1956-75; Convener, Church of Scotland Committees: Huts and Canteens, Temperance and Morals, Social and Moral Welfare, Stewardship and Budget; Moderator, General Assembly, 1966; Chaplain to The Queen, since 1967; Member, Scottish Advisory Committee on Treatment of Offenders, 1950-66; Chairman, Parole Board for Scotland, 1967-73. Vice-President, Edinburgh Scout Council; Vice-President, Edinburgh Council of Girl Guides; Honorary Vice-President, Boys' Brigade; Regional Chaplain to Air Training Corps, since 1953; OBE, 1957; Chairman, Age Concern Scotland, 1981-83; Chairman, Edinburgh Parkinson's Disease Society. Address: (h.) 5 Craighill Gardens, Edinburgh, EH10 5PY; T.-031-447 4243.

Smart, George Edward, MB, ChB, FRCOG, FRCSEdin. Consultant Obstetrician and Gynaecologist, Simpson Memorial Maternity Pavilion and Royal Infirmary, Edinburgh, since 1976; Honorary Senior Lecturer, Edinburgh University; b. 19.6.35, Shipley, Yorkshire; m., Margaret; 1 s.; 2 d. Educ. Bradford Grammar School; Edinburgh University Medical School. House Physician and Surgeon appointments: Ashford Hospital, Middlesex, 1960, Edinburgh Royal Infirmary, 1961, Bradford Royal Infirmary, St. Lukes Hospital, Bradford, 1962-63; Registrar and Senior Registrar appointments, Simpson Memorial Maternity Pavilion and Royal Infirmary, Edinburgh; Senior Tumor Fellow, State University of New York, 1970-71; Consultant Senior Lecturer, Bristol University, and Honorary Consultant, United Bristol Hospitals, Bristol Maternity Hospital and Southmead Hospital, Bristol, until 1976; Examiner, Royal College of Surgeons, Edinburgh, and Royal College of Obstetricians and Gynaecologists, London. Recreations: swimming; golf; gardening. Address: (h.) Beechcroft, 24 Cramond Road North, Cramond, Edinburgh; T.-031-312 8499.

Smillie, Ian R.D., BL. Chief Executive Officer and Director of Administration, Kyle and Carrick District Council, since 1983; b. 13.9.39, Kilmarnock; m., Margaret; 2 d. Educ. Kilmarnock Academy; Glasgow University. Private practice,

1958-68; Royal Burgh of Ayr, 1968-74 (latterly as Assistant Town Clerk); Director of Administration, Kyle and Carrick District Council, 1974-83. Address: (b.) Burns House, Burns Statue Square, Ayr, KA7 1UP; T.-0292 281511.

Smith, Professor Adam Neil, MD, FRCSE, FRSE. Wade Professor of Surgical Studies, RCSEd, since 1986; Consultant Surgeon, Gastro-Intestinal Unit, Edinburgh, since 1962; b. 27.6.26, Hamilton; m., Sibyl Mary Veitch Johnstone; 1 s.; 3 d. Educ. Lanark Grammar School; Glasgow University. Academic and Health Service appointments, since 1948; Lecturer in Surgery, Glasgow University; Medical Research Council Fellow; Senior Lecturer, Edinburgh University and Western General Hospital. Former Surgical Traveller, James IV Surgical Association; former Council Member, Royal College of Surgeons of Edinburgh. Recreation: golf. Address: (h.) 105 Trinity Road, Edinburgh; T.-031-552 3836.

Smith, Sheriff Agnes Lawrie Addie, LLB. Sheriff of Glasgow and Strathkelvin, since 1982; b. 17.6.47. Educ. Hamilton Academy; Glasgow University. Solicitor, 1969; called to the Scottish Bar, 1976; Solicitor, private practice, 1969-71; Procurator Fiscal Depute, 1971-75.

Smith, Sir Alan, Kt (1982), CBE (1976), DFC (1941) and Bar (1942), DL, JP. President, Dawson International plc, Kinross, since 1982; Chairman, Quayle Munro PLC, Edinburgh, since 1982; b. 14.3.17, South Shields; m., 1, Margaret Stewart Todd (deceased); 2, Alice Elizabeth Moncur; 3 s.; 2 d. Educ. Bede College, Sunderland. Self-employed, 1931-36; Unilever, 1936-39; RAF, 1939-45; Managing Director, Todd & Duncan Ltd., Kinross, 1946-60; Chairman and Chief Executive, Dawson International, Kinross, 1960-82. Board Member, Scottish Development Agency, 1982-87; Kinross Burgh Councillor, 1952-65; Provost of Kinross, 1959-65; Tayside Regional Councillor, since 1979; Financial Convenor, Tayside Region, 1980-86. Recreations: work; sailing. Address: (h.) Ardgairney House, Cleish, by Kinross; T.-05775 265.

Smith, Alan Gordon Rae, MA, PhD, FRHistS. Reader in Modern History, Glasgow University, since 1985; b. 22.12.36, Glasgow; m., Isabel Robertson; 1 s.; 1 d. Educ. Glasgow High School; Glasgow University; University College, London. Research Fellow, Institute of Historical Research, London University, 1961-62; Assistant in History, 1962-64, then Lecturer, Glasgow University, 1964-75; Senior Lecturer in Modern History, 1975-85; Review Editor, History (Journal of the Historical Association), 1984-87. Publications: The Government of Elizabethan England, 1967; The New Europe, 1969; Science and Society in the Sixteenth and Seventeenth Centuries, 1972; Servant of the Cecils: The Life of Sir Michael Hickes, 1977; The Emergence of a Nation State: The Commonwealth of England 1529-1660, 1984. Recreation: watching sport. Address: (h.) 5 Cargil Avenue, Kilmacolm, Renfrewshire; T.-Kilmacolm 2055.

Smith, Alistair Fairley, MA, MD, FRCPEdin, FRCPath. Senior Lecturer in Clinical Chemistry, Edinburgh University, since 1971; Consultant Clinical Chemist, Edinburgh Royal Infirmary, since 1971; b. 5.10.35, Edinburgh; m., Carol Ann; 1 s.; 1 d. Educ. Bootham School, York; Clare College, Cambridge. House Officer posts, London Hospital, 1960-61; House Officer and Junior Assistant Pathologist posts, Addenbrookes' Hospital, Cambridge; Lecturer in Clinical Chemistry, Edinburgh University, 1965-71. Publications: Lecture Notes on Clinical Chemistry (Co-author); Multiple Choice Questions on Clinical Chemistry (Co-author). Recreations: golf; bridge. Address: (b.) Department of Clinical Chemistry, Royal Infirmary, Edinburgh, EH3 9YW; T.-031-229 2477, Ext. 2365.

Smith, Sheriff Charles, MA, LLB, NP. Sheriff of Tayside, Central and Fife at Perth, since 1986; b. 15.8.30, Methil; m., Janet Elizabeth Hurst; 1 s.; 1 d. Educ. Perth Academy; St. Andrews University. Solicitor, 1956; private practice as Principal, 1962-82; Member, Perth Town Council, 1966-68; Interim Depute Procurator Fiscal, 1974-82; Tutor, Dundee University, 1980-82; Member, Council, Law Society of Scotland (Convener, various Committees), 1977-82; Temporary Sheriff, 1977-82; Honorary Tutor, Dundee University, since 1982; Sheriff of Glasgow and Strathkelvin, 1982-86; Member, Council, Sheriffs' Association, since 1987. Recreations: tennis; golf; bridge. Address: (b.) c/o Sheriff Clerk, Sheriff Court, Perth, PH2 8NL; T.-0738 20546.

Smith, C. Christopher, MB, FRCP. Consultant Physician, General Medicine, Aberdeen Royal Infirmary and Consultant in charge, Regional Infection Unit, City Hospital, Aberdeen, since 1973; Honorary Senior Lecturer, Aberdeen University, since 1973; b. 16.5.39, West Indies; 2 s.; 1 d. Educ. Lodge School, Barbados; Edinburgh University. Registrar, Department of Medicine, Edinburgh Royal Infirmary; Registrar, Thoracic Medicine, then Senior Registrar, Infectious Diseases, City Hospital, Edinburgh; Senior Registrar, Department of Therapeutics, Edinburgh Royal Infirmary; former Member, Part I MRCP Examination Board, RCPS; Examiner, MRCP Part II; author of papers, chapters and leading articles on topics in medicine, infection and antimicrobial chemotherapy. Recreations: watching cricket; golf; live theatre; jazz music. Address: (b.) Wards 25/26, Aberdeen Royal Infirmary, Foresterhill, Aberdeen, AB2; T.-Aberdeen 681818.

Smith, David Bruce Boyter, MA, LLB, NP. Director and Chief Executive, Dunfermline Building Society, since 1987; b. 11.3.42, St. Andrews; m., Christine Anne; 1 s.; 1 d. Educ. High School, Dunfermline; Edinburgh University. Legal training, Balfour & Manson, Edinburgh; admitted Solicitor, 1968; Solicitor, Standard Life Assurance Co., 1969-73; Dunfermline Building Society: Secretary, 1974-81, General Manager (Admin.), 1981-86, Deputy Chief Executive, 1986. Chairman, Scottish Liaison Committee, Building Societies Association; Member, Council, NHBC (Scotland); Vice-Chairman, Care and Repair National Committee, Scotland; Director, South Fife Enterprise Trust; Member, Secretary of State's Expert Committee on Valuations and Surveys. Recreations: golf; sailing; the arts. Address: (b.) 12 East Port, Dunfermline, Fife; T.-0383 721621.

Smith, Sheriff David Buchanan, MA, LLB. Sheriff of North Strathclyde at Kilmarnock, since 1975; b. 31.10.36, Paisley; m., Hazel Mary Sinclair; 1 s.; 1 d. Educ. Paisley Grammar School; Glasgow University; Edinburgh University. Advocate, 1961; Standing Junior Counsel to Scottish Education Department, 1968-75; Tutor, Faculty of Law, Edinburgh University, 1964-72; Trustee, Scottish Curling Museum Trust, since 1980. President, Kilmarnock and District History Group. Publications: Curling: An Illustrated History, 1981; The Roaring Game: Memories of Scottish Curling, 1985; contributions to The Laws of Scotand: Stair Memorial Encyclopedia, Vol. 6. Recreations: Scotland - history and culture; curling; music. Address: (b.) Sheriff Court House, Kilmarnock, KA1 1ED; T.-0563 20211.

Smith, Sir David Cecil, Kt, FRS, MA, DPhil. Principal and Vice-Chancellor, Edinburgh University, since 1987; b. 21.5.30; m., Lesley Margaret Collison Mutch; 2 s.; 1 d. Educ. Colston's School, Bristol; St. Paul's School, London; Queen's College, Oxford. Browne Research Fellow, Queen's College, Oxford, 1956-59; Harkness Fellow, University of California, Berkeley, 1959-60; University Lecturer, Department of Agriculture, Oxford University, 1960-74; Wadham College, Oxford: Royal Society Research Fellow, 1964-71, Tutorial Fellow and Tutor for Admissions, 1971-74; Melville Wills Professor of Botany, 1974-80, and Director of Biological Studies, 1977-79, Bristol University; Sibthorpian Professor of Rural Economy, and Fellow of St. John's College, Oxford University, 1980-87. Address: Old College, Edinburgh University, Edinburgh, EH8 9YL.

Smith, Very Rev. David Macintyre Bell Armour, MA, BD, DUniv, JP. Minister, Logie, since 1965; Moderator, General Assembly of the Church of Scotland, 1985; b. 5.4.23, Fort Augustus; m., Mary Kulvear Cumming; 3 s. Educ. Monckton Combe; Peebles High School; St. Andrews University. Minister, Warrender Church, Edinburgh, 1951-61; Exchange Preacher, USA, 1958 and 1961; Minister, Old Partick, Glasgow, 1961-65; Moderator, Stirling and Dunblane Presbytery, 1972-73; Moderator, Perth and Stirling Synod, 1975-76; Vice Convener, Joint Working Party, Church of Scotland, 1980-82; Convener, Church of Scotland Board of Education, 1979-83; Church of Scotland Representative, Stirlingshire Education Committee, 1969-79; Governor, Moray House College of Education, 1983; Member, Central Regional Education Committee, since 1986; Member, Church of Scotland Board of Practice and Procedure, since 1982; Honorary Brother, Guildry of Stirling, 1986. Recreations: philately; gardening. Address: (h.) 34 Airthrey Road, Stirling, FK9 5JS; T.-Stirling 75085.

Smith, Derek Matthew Hutchison, MA, LLB. Honorary Sheriff, Ayr, since 1971; b. 1.10.10, Glasgow; m., Nora Rawling; 1 s.; 1 d. Educ. Glasgow High School; Glasgow University. Practised as Solicitor in Girvan, 1935-77; appointed Burgh Prosecutor, Maybole, 1969; JP Fiscal, Carrick District, 1970; Tory candidate, South Ayrshire, 1951 and 1955; Council Member, Law Society of Scotland, 1965-76 (first Convener, Society's EEC Committee); Member, Girvan Town Council, 19 years (Provost, 1953-56); Past Chairman, Girvan Invasion Committee; Honorary Treasurer, St. John's Episcopal Church, Girvan. Recreation: walking. Address: (h.) 45 The Loaning, Alloway, Ayr; T.-Alloway 41923.

Smith, Douglas Campbell, MREHIS, MRSH, FInstPet. Director of Environmental Health and Trading Standards, Shetland Islands Council; b. 31.3.28, Lerwick; m., Marguerite May Rosalind; 2 s.; 1 d. Educ. Anderson Educational Institute, Lerwick; Heriot-Watt College, Edinburgh. Zetland County Council, 1949-75 (latterly County Sanitary Inspector/Director of Environmental Health); Director of Environmental Health and Consumer Protection, Shetland Islands Council, 1975-77; Director of Protective Services and Housing, 1977-88. Recreations: brass band; photography. Address: (b.) 3 Commercial Road, Lerwick, ZE1 OLX; T.-0595 3535, Ext. 324.

Smith, Douglas Murray, MA (Hons). Rector, Dumfries Academy, since 1980; b. 2.10.39, Glasgow; m., Patricia Katherine Petrie; 2 d. Educ. Hutchesons' Boys Grammar School; Glasgow University. Co-author of mathematics text books. Recreation: sport. Address: (b.) Dumfries Academy, Dumfries; T.-0387 52846.

Smith, (Edward) Alistair, CBE, MA, PhD. Director, Aberdeen University Development Trust, since 1982; Deputy Chairman, Scottish Conservative Party, 1981-86; b. 16.1.39, Aberdeen. Educ. Aberdeen Grammar School; Aberdeen University. Lecturer in Geography, Aberdeen University, 1963-88; President, Scottish Conservative and Unionist Association, 1979-81; Member, Grampian Health Board, since 1983. Publications: Europe: A Geographical Survey of the Continent (Co-author), 1979; Scotland's Future Development (Contributor), 1983. Recreations: travel; photography; music. Address: (h.) 68A Beaconsfield Place, Aberdeen, AB2 4AJ; T.-0224 642932.

Smith, Edward Gordon, BA, BSc, DipEd. Head Teacher, Castlebrae High School, Edinburgh, since 1983; b. 10.11.39, Fochabers; m., Ann Smith; 1 s.; 1 d. Educ. Elgin Academy; Aberdeen University. Education Officer, Uganda and Kenya; Teacher, Hyndland Secondary School; Principal Teacher of Chemistry, North Kelvinside School; Assistant Head Teacher, Firrhill High School; Deputy Head Teacher, Forrester High School. Recreations: sailing; walking; books. Address: (b.) Castlebrae High School, Greendykes Road, Edinburgh, EH16 4DP; T.-031-661 1282.

Smith, Eric Watson, OBE, MIES. Assistant Managing Director/Industrial Relations Director, Yarrow Shipbuilders Ltd.; b. 7.2.31, Glasgow; m., Irene; 2 s. Educ. Whitehill Senior Secondary School; Perth Academy; Royal Technical College, Glasgow. Apprentice Engineer/Draughtsman, A. Stephen & Sons Ltd.; Supervisor, Caterpillar Tractor Ltd.; Superintendent, Engineering Manager, Rootes Motors (Scotland) Ltd.; Plant Engineering Manager, Chrysler UK Ltd.; Works Manager, Yarrow Engineeers (Glasgow) Ltd.; General Manager, Industrial Relations and Personnel, Yarrow Shipbuilders Ltd. Council Member, Institute of Engineers and Shipbuilders, Scotland; Vice Chairman, Council, Anniesland

College; Chairman, Shipbuilding and Allied Industries National Training Association; Executive Panel Member, Marine Builders Training Trust; Freeman, City of London, 1985. Recreations: golf; gardening. Address: (b.) Yarrow Shipbuilders Ltd., Scotstoun, Glasgow, G14 OXN; T.-041-959 1207.

Smith, Francis William, MD, DMRD, FFRRCS (1). Consultant in Nuclear Medicine, Grampian Health Board, since 1979; Clinical Senior Lecturer in Medicine, Aberdeen University, since 1979; b. 8.1.43, Colchester; m., Pamela Anne Cox; 1 s.; 1 d. Educ. Prince Edward School, Harare; Aberdeen University. Studied nuclear medicine, Hospital for Sick Children, Toronto; in 1980 began first clinical trial of magnetic resonance imaging technique, subsequently applied to medical diagnosis worldwide; Guest Lecturer, Australia and New Zealand Society of Nuclear Medicine, 1983; Jameson Memorial Lecturer, Royal College of Physicians and Surgeons of Canada, 1984; Past President, Society for Magnetic Resonance Imaging; Co-Editor in Chief, Magnetic Resonance Imaging. Recreations: swimming; fishing; reading. Address: (h.) 7 Primrosehill Road, Cults, Aberdeen, AB1 9ND; T.-Aberdeen 868745.

Smith, George Ballantyne Pryde, BSc (Hons). Head Teacher, Boclair Academy, since 1976; b. 24.7.31, Glasgow; m., Anne; 3 s. Educ. Albert Secondary School; Strathclyde University; Glasgow University. Teacher: Possil Secondary, Whitehill Secondary, North Kelvinside Secondary; Principal Teacher of Mathematics, Knightswood Secondary; Head Teacher, Eastbank Academy. Recreations: golf; reading. Address: (b.) Inveroran Drive, Bearsden, Glasgow, G61 2PL; T.-041-943 0717.

Smith, Gordon Matthew, DCA, MITSA. Director of Trading Standards, Dumfries and Galloway Regional Council, since 1982; b. 10.11.44, Ayr; m., Moyra; 1 s.; 1 d. Educ. Ayr Academy. Trainee Trading Standards Officer, Ayr County Council, 1962-66; Trading Standards Officer: Lindsey (Lincolnshire) County Council, 1966-68, Lanark County Council, 1968-72; District Trading Standards Officer, 1972-75; Senior Trading Standards Officer, Strathclyde Regional Council, 1975-79; Assistant Chief Trading Standards Officer, Central Regional Council, 1979-82. Recreations: golf; curling; badminton. Address: (b.) 1 Newall Terrace, Dumfries, DG1 1LN; T.-0387 62217.

Smith, Graham Douglas, LLB (Hons). General Manager Scotland - British Airways, since 1987; b. 22.6.48, Broughty Ferry. Educ. Prince Edward School, Salisbury, Rhodesia; Dundee University. Entire working career with BA, including appointments in personnel, industrial relations, line management, marketing. Recreations: golf; tennis; reading; dining. Address: (b.) 134 Renfrew Street, Fleming House, Glasgow; T.-041-333 5216.

Smith, Grahame Francis, MA, PhD. Senior Lecturer, Department of English Studies, Stirling University, since 1970; b. 3.5.33, London; m., Angela Mary; 2 s.; 1 d. Educ. Woodside Senior Secondary School, Glasgow; Aberdeen University; Cambridge University. Taught at California University, Los Angeles, 1963-65, University College, Swansea, 1965-70; secondment to Malawi University, 1982-83. Publications: Dickens, Money and Society, 1968; The Novel and Society: From Defoe to George Elliot, 1984; The Achievement of Graham Greene, 1985. Recreations: cinema; opera; jazz; walking. Address: (b.) Department of English Studies, Stirling University, Stirling, FK9 4LA; T.-078686 3171.

Smith, Rev. G. Richmond N.R.K., OBE, MA, BD. Minister, Church of Scotland, since 1952; b. 2.3.27, Rendall, Orkney; m., Agnes Margaret Elliott Longden. Educ. Anderson Educational Institute, Lerwick; Edinburgh University. Minister: East Parish, Peterhead, 1952-60, West High Parish, Kilmarnock, 1960-65; Theological Secretary, World Alliance of Reformed Churches, 1965-83; lived in Geneva, then retired to Scotland, 1983. Recreations: ornithology; archaeology. Address: (h.) Aignish, Kippford, by Dalbeattie, DG5 4LL; T.-Kippford 624.

Smith, Hamilton, BSc, PhD, CChem, FRSC, FRCPath. Titular Professor of Forensic Medicine (Toxicology), Glasgow University, since 1987; b. 27.4.34, Stirling; m., Jacqueline Ann Spittal. Educ. Kilsyth Academy; Glasgow University. Glasgow University: MRC Fellow, 1960, Special Research Fellow, 1963, Lecturer in Forensic Medicine Department, 1964, Senior Lecturer, 1973, Reader, 1984. Publication: Glaister's Medical Jurisprudence and Toxicology, 13th edition. Recreations: golf (New Club, St. Andrews, Crail Golfing Society); gardening. Address: (b.) Department of Forensic Medicine and Science, Glasgow University, Glasgow, G12 8QQ; T.-041-339 8855.

Smith, Rev. Hugh M.C., LTh. Minister, Cabrach and Mortlach, since 1982; b. 22.2.44, Aberdeen; m., Lily Ann Beaton; 1 s.; 1 d. Educ. Aberdeen Academy; Aberdeen University and Christ's College. Assistant Minister, Cardonald, Glasgow, 1972-73; Minister, Reay, 1973-82. Chairman, Reay Hall Committee, 1974-80; Chairman, Highlands Clubs Council, 1974-76; Member, Church of Scotland Maintenance of the Ministry Committee, 1976-82; Member, Inter Church Relations Committee, 1978-81; Moderator, Caithness Presbytery, 1980-81; Member, Cabrach and Mortlach Community Association, since 1983; Member, Speyside Council of Social Service, since 1983 (Vice Chairman, since 1987). Address: Mortlach Manse, Dufftown, Banffshire.

Smith, Iain Crichton, OBE, LLD (Dundee), DLitt (Glasgow), DLitt (Aberdeen), MA (Hons). Writer; b. 1.1.28, Glasgow; m., Donalda Gillies Logan; 2 step s. Educ. Nicolson Institute, Stornoway; Aberdeen University. Teacher, Oban High School, 1955-77; full-time Writer, since 1977; Member, Literature Committee, Scottish Arts Council; Fellow, Royal Literary Society, books in English: 10 novels, six volumes of short stories, 13 volumes of poetry; books in Gaelic: two novels, five volumes of short stories, four volumes of poetry; translations from Gaelic into English; numerous radio plays in both languages; Poetry Book Society Choice and two recommendations; eight Arts Council awards; awards for Gaelic plays and short stories; award for Gaelic television play; PEN Award, 1970; Scotsman Short Story Award, 1983; Commonwealth Poetry Prize (European Section), 1986; Travelling Scholarship, Society of Authors, 1987. Recreation: reading detective stories. Address: Tigh Na Fuaran, Taynuilt, Argyll; T.-Taynuilt 463.

Smith, Iain William, BA Hons. Member, Fife Regional Council, since 1982; Leader, Opposition SLD Group, since 1986; Agent, NE Fife Social and Liberal Democrats and Constituency Assistant to Menzies Campbell, MP, since 1987; b. 1.5.60, Gateside, Fife. Educ. Bell Baxter High School, Cupar; Newcastle-upon-Tyne University. Advice Worker, then Centre Manager, Bonnethill Advice Centre, Dundee, 1982-85; Agent Organiser, North East Fife Liberal Association. Recreations: watching football, cricket, etc.; real ale. Address: Waterend Road, Cupar, Fife, KY15 5HP; T.-0334 56361.

Smith, Ian Stanley, MB, ChB, FRCSEdin, FRCSGlas, DObstRCOG. Consultant Surgeon, Victoria Infirmary, Glasgow, since 1975; Honorary Clinical Lecturer in Surgery, Glasgow University, since 1975; b. 13.11.39, Glasgow; m., Carole Ann Newby; 1 s.; 1 d. Educ. Glasgow Academy; Glasgow University. Assistant Lecturer in Anatomy, Glasgow University, 1964-65; various junior surgical appointments to hospitals in Western Regional Hospital Board. Examiner in Anatomy and Surgery, Royal College of Physicians and Surgeons of Glasgow; Examiner in Anatomy, Royal College of Surgeons of Edinburgh. Recreations: golf; mah-jongg; wine-making. Address: (h.) Ashford, 16 Albert Drive, Killermont, Bearsden, Glasgow, G61 2PF; T.-041-942 7452.

Smith, James, OStJ, JP, BSc. Rector, St. Patrick's High School, Coatbridge, since 1972; b. 9.1.24, Glasgow; 2 s.; 3 d. Educ. Holyrood Secondary School, Glasgow; Glasgow University; Strathclyde University. Provost of East Kilbride, 1972-75; Member, East Kilbride Development Corporation, 1972-82; Member, Justice of the Peace Advisory Committee for East Kilbride. Recreations: walking; reading. Address: (h.) 19 Capel Grove, East Kilbride.

Smith, James Aikman, TD, BA, LLB. Advocate; Honorary Sheriff, since 1976; b. 13.6.14, Kilmarnock; m., Katharine Ann Millar; 3 d. Educ. Glasgow Academy; Oxford University; Edinburgh University. Admitted Faculty of Advocates, 1939; served Royal Artillery, 1939-46 (Lt. Col., 1944), North Africa, Italy and Austria; Despatches, Bronze Star US; Sheriff Substitute, Renfrew and Argyll, 1948-52, Roxburgh, Berwick and Selkirk, 1952-57, Aberdeen, Kincardine and Banff, 1957-68; Sheriff of Lothians and Borders, 1968-76; President, Sheriffs' Association, 1969-72; Member, UK Departmental Committee on Probation Service, 1959-62; Member, After Care Council (Scotland), 1962-65; UK Delegate to UN Congress on Crime, Japan, 1970; Chairman, Edinburgh and East of Scotland Branch, English Speaking Union, 1970-74; Vice-President, Cairngorm Club, 1962-65; Chairman, Allelon Society, 1970-76; Elder, Church of Scotland, since 1948; has served on various General Assembly Committees. Recreations: hill-walking; gardening; travel. Address: (h.) 16 Murrayfield Avenue, Edinburgh, EH12 6AX; T.-031-337 8205.

Smith, James David, OBE, MA, LLB. Retired Solicitor; Honorary Sheriff of North Strathclyde at Greenock, since 1976; b. 27.10.19, Dumbarton; m., Margaret McGregor Grant; 2 s. Educ. Dumbarton Academy; Glasgow University. Commissioned Highland Light Infantry, 1940; Town Clerk, Dumbarton, 1951-67; Chief Executive, Corporation of Greenock, 1967-75; Visiting Lecturer in Law, Paisley College of Technology, 1976-87. Address: (h.) 42 Octavia Terrace, Greenock, PA16 7SR; T.-0475 23788.

Smith, Rt. Hon. John, QC, MA, LLB. MP (Labour), Monklands East, since 1983 (North Lanarkshire, 1970-83); b. 13.9.38, Dalmally, Argyll; m., Elizabeth Margaret Bennett; 3 d. Educ. Dunoon Grammar School; Glasgow University. Called to Scottish Bar, 1967; QC (Scot), 1983; Parliamentary Under Secretary of State for Energy, 1974-75; Minister of State for Energy, 1975-76; Minister of State, Privy Council Office, 1976-78; Secretary of State for Trade, 1978-79; Member, Shadow Cabinet, since 1979; Principal Opposition Spokesman on Treasury and Economic Affairs; Vice Chairman, Great Britain-USSR Association; a Governor, Ditchley Foundation; National President, Industrial Common Ownership Movement. Recreations: tennis; hill-walking. Address: (h.) 21 Cluny Drive, Edinburgh, EH10 6DW; T.-031-447 3667.

Smith, Rev. John Murdo. Minister, Lochmaddy and Trumisgarry, Uist, since 1963; b. 29.8.27, Shader, Isle of Lewis; m., Mary Margaret Macpherson; 1 s.; 2 d. Educ. Airidhantuim School, Isle of Lewis; Skerry's College, Glasgow; Glasgow University; Aberdeen University. National Service, RAF, 1945-48; Minister, South Uist Howmore, 1956-63; Moderator, Uist Presbytery, 1957, 1973, 1982 (Presbytery Clerk, 1959-71); updated North Uist part, Statistical Account of Scotland; Member, local School Council; Chaplain, Lochmaddy Hospital, since 1963, Hon. Port Chaplain, British Sailors Society, Lochmaddy, since 1963. Recreations: fishing; hill-walking. Address: (h.) The Manse, Lochmaddy, North Uist.

Smith, Rev. John Raymond, MA, BD. President Elect, Congregational Union of Scotland, 1987-88; Minister, School Wynd Congregational Church, Paisley, since 1986; World Mission Secretary, Congregational Union of Scotland, 1978-86; b. 12.4.47, Dumfries; m., Isabel Jean McKemmie; 3 d. Educ. Dumfries Academy; Edinburgh University; Geneva University. Minister, School Wynd Congregational Church, Paisley, 1973-82. European Regional Executive Member, Council for World Mission. Recreations: photography; freelance writing. Address: (b.) The Wynd Centre, 6 School Wynd, Paisley, PA1 2DB; T.-041-887 4647.

Smith, Joseph Raymond, OBE, BSc (Econ), MSc, MA. College Secretary, Dundee College of Technology, since 1983; b. 21.12.28, High Wycombe; m., Jean Margaret Hughes; 1 s.; 1 d. Educ. Royal Grammar School, High Wycombe; LSE. Chief Education Officer, HQ Land Forces, Hong Kong, 1969-72; Lt. Col., Officer Education Branch, 1972-76; Col., Directorate of Army Education, MoD, 1976-78; Col./Chief Inspector, Army Education, 1978-79; Brigadier/Chief Education Officer HQ UK Land Forces, 1979-82; Brigadier/Chief Education Officer, HQ BAOR, 1982-83. Recreations: reading; walking; bird-watching. Address: (b.) 40 Bell Street, Dundee, DD1 1HG; T.-0382 23291.

Smith, Professor Keith, BA, PhD, FRSE. Professor of Environmental Science, Stirling University, since 1986; b. 9.1.38, Marple; m., Muriel Doris Hyde; 1 s.; 1 d. Educ. Hyde County Grammar School; Hull University. Tutor in Geography, Liverpool University, 1963-65; Lecturer in Geography, Durham University, 1965-70; Strathclyde University: Senior Lecturer, 1971-75, Reader, 1975-82, Personal Professor, 1982-84, Professor and Head of Department, 1984-86. Drapers' Company Visiting Lecturer, Adelaide University, 1978; Visiting Principal Scientist, Illinois State Water Survey, 1988; Visiting Professor of Geography, University of Illinois, 1988. Publications: Water in Britain; Principles of Applied Climatology; Human Adjustment to Flood Hazard. Recreations: hill-walking; badminton. Address: (b.) Department of Environmental Science, Stirling University, Stirling, FK9 4LA; T.-0786 73171.

Smith, Lawrence D., BSc. Reader in Agricultural Economics, Glasgow University, since 1977; b. 1939, Bedfordshire; m., Evelyn Mavis Stead; 1 s.; 2 d. Educ. Bedford Modern School; Wye College, London University; Linacre College, Oxford. Departmental Lecturer, Agricultural Economics, Research Institute, Oxford University, 1963-66; Lecturer, then Senior Lecturer in Agricultural Economics, Department of Political Economy, Glasgow University. Recreation: gardening. Address: (b.) Department of Political Economy, Glasgow University, Glasgow; T.-041-339 8855.

Smith, Martin, CBE, FRICS. President, Glasgow Chamber of Commerce, 1984-86; Senior Partner, Doig & Smith, Chartered Quantity Surveyors, 1977-87; Honorary Secretary, RICS in Scotland, 1979-88; b. 16.7.22, Glasgow; m., Margaret Emma; 2 s. Educ. Coatbridge High School. Qualified ARICS, 1948; Chairman, RICS in Scotland, 1974-75; Chairman, Scottish Building Contract Committee, 1975-81; Elder, Church of Scotland; Deacon, Incorporation of Gardeners, 1964-65. Recreations: gardening; golf. Address: (b.) 6 Lynedoch Place, Glasgow, G3 6AQ; T.-041-332 8907.

Smith, Murdoch Mackenzie, MPS, MCPP. Chief Administrative Pharmaceutical Officer, Highland Health Board and Western Isles Health Board, since 1975; b. 10.1.37, Inverness; m., Marianne Fergus. Educ. Inverness Royal Academy; Robert Gordon's Institute of Technology, Aberdeen. Pharmacist, T.S. Davidson, Inverness, 1959-63; Pharmacist, Inverness Hospitals, 1963-67 (Deputy Chief Pharmacist, 1967-72); Principal Pharmacist/Deputy Regional/Area Pharmacist, Northern Regional Hospital Board, 1973-75. Former Member, National Pharmaceutical Consultative Committee; Past Chairman, Northern Scottish Branch, Pharmaceutical Society of GB; Chairman, Cromal Hill Recreation Committee; Past President, Highland Cricket Club and Inverness and District Badminton League; former Member: Ardersier and Petty Community Council, Inverness District Sports Council; former Captain, Highland Cricket Club. Recreations: history; cricket; collecting books and lead soldiers. Address: (h.) Glencoe, Ardersier, Inverness, IV1 2QD; T.-0667 62059.

Smith, Nigel R. Managing Director, David Auld Valves Ltd., since 1976; Member, Executive, Scottish Engineering Employers Association, since 1985; Member, Broadcasting Council for Scotland, since 1986; b. 9.6.41, Girvan; m., Jody; 2 s.; 2 d. Educ. Dollar Academy. Lt., 4/5 Bn., Royal Scots Fusiliers (TA), 1960-67; staff and management appointments, Bowater Paper, Richard Costain, Rank Hovis McDougall. Member, Camden Council Community Relations Committee, 1966-69. Recreations: hill-walking; offshore sailing; opera and choral; reading, particularly biography. Address: (b.) David Auld Valves, Cowlairs Industrial Estate, Finlas Street, Glasgow, G22 5DQ; T.-041-557 0515.

Smith, Peter Dryburgh. Campaign Director, Scottish Conservative Party, since 1987; b. 15.11.45, Edinburgh. Educ. Lasswade High School. Political Agent, South Edinburgh, 1968-70; National Organiser, Scottish Young Conservatives, 1970-72; Sales Manager, Adam Cramond & Son, 1972-74; Political Agent, East and West Renfrewshire, 1974-82; Euro Agent, Strathclyde West, 1979-82; Deputy Director, Scottish Conservative Party, 1982-85; Deputy Central Office Agent for Yorkshire, 1985-87. Recreations: crosswords; reading. Address: (b.) Scottish Conservative Party, 3 Chester Street, Edinburgh, EH3 7RF; T.-031-226 2246.

Smith, Rev. Ralph Colley Philip, MA, STM. Director of Audio Visual Productions, Church of Scotland, since 1985; Minister, Church of Scotland, since 1960; b. 11.3.31, Edinburgh; m., Florence; 2 s. Educ. Edinburgh Academy; St. Andrews University; Edinburgh University; Union Seminary, New York. Minister, Gallatown Church, Kirkcaldy; Religious Broadcasting Assistant, then Producer, Religion, Television, BBC Scotland; Associate Minister, New Kilpatrick Parish Church, Bearsden. Recreations: cello; bowls; golf. Address: (h.) 2 Blackford Hill View, Edinburgh, EH9 3HD.

Smith, Rev. Richard, BD, AICS. Minister, Denny Old Parish Church, since 1983; b. 25.2.38, Redding, Falkirk; m., Georgina Wotherspoon Swinton; 2 d. Educ. Falkirk Technical School; Heriot-Watt College; Glasgow University. Shipbroker, J.T. Salvesen & Co. Ltd., Grangemouth, 17 years; first Minister, linked charge of Barr and Dailly, 1976-1983. Recreation: motoring. Address: Manse of Denny Old, 31 Duke Street, Denny, Falkirk, FK6 6NR.

Smith, Robert Haldane, CA. Managing Director, Charterhouse Development Capital Ltd., since 1985, and Executive Director, Charterhouse Bank Ltd., since 1985; b. 8.8.44, Glasgow; m., Alison Marjorie Bell; 2 d. Educ. Allan Glen's School, Glasgow; Glasgow University. Articled to Robb Ferguson & Co., CA, Glasgow, 1963-68; qualified CA, 1968; ICFC, 1968-82: Area Manager, Brighton, 1973, Business Development Manager, 1978, Assistant General Manager, 1981, Director of several group companies, Investors in

Industry, 1981; General Manager (Corporate Finance Division), The Royal Bank of Scotland plc, 1983-85; Managing Director, National Commercial & Glyns, 1983-85; current Directorships include: TIP Europe PLC, MFI Furniture Group Ltd., A.T. Mays Group plc; Member, Board of Trustees, National Museums of Scotland; Commissioner, Museums and Galleries Commission. Publication: Managing Your Company's Finances (Co-author). Recreations: amateur drama; public speaking; spectator sports; historic and listed buildings; music. Address: (h.) 4 Lauder Road, Edinburgh; T.-031-667 1400.

Smith, Robert Lupton, OBE, JP, FRICS. Director, Association for the Protection of Rural Scotland, since 1981; Chartered Surveyor in private practice, since 1954; b. 26.4.24, Cheadle Hulme; m.; 3 d. Educ. George Watson's College; College of Estate Management; Heriot-Watt College. Chairman, Scottish Junior Branch, RICS, 1952; Member, Scottish Executive Committee, RICS, 1952-60; elected, Edinburgh Town Council, 1962-74 and Edinburgh District Council, 1974-77; Governor, Edinburgh College of Art, since 1963; fought European Election, 1979, as Liberal; Deputy Traffic Commissioner, 1974-78; Chairman, Good Neighbours Housing Association, 1984-87; Scottish Liberal Party: Chairman, Executive Committee, 1971-74, Chairman, 1974, President, 1976-82; Council Member, Royal Scottish Geographical Society, since 1957; Chairman, Scottish Liberal Club, since 1984; Director, Cockburn Conservation Trust Ltd. Recreations: walking; visiting Perthshire and Orkney; reading; looking at fine art. Address: 14A Napier Road, Edinburgh, EH10 5AY; T.-031-229 1898.

Smith, Roger. Editor, Environment Now, since 1987 (Editor, The Great Outdoors, 1977-86); b. 28.11.38, London; m., Terry; 2 d. Educ. Latymer Upper School, London. Past Chairman, Scottish Wild Land Group; elected Council Member, Scottish Conservation Projects Trust; elected Council Member, National Trust for Scotland. Publications: Penguin Book of Orienteering, 1981; The Winding Trail, 1981; Outdoor Scotland, 1981; Weekend Walking, 1982; Visitor's Guide to Scottish Borders, 1983; Jet Guide to Scotland's Countryside, 1985; The Great Outdoors Book of the Walking Year, 1988; Classic Walks in Scotland (Co-author), 1988. Recreations: hill-walking; running; orienteering; Scottish history. Address: (h.) 21 Inver Court, Bainsford, Falkirk, FK2 7UR; T.-0324 32215.

Smith, Roger Galbraith, MB, ChB, FRCPEdin. Senior Lecturer, Department of Geriatric Medicine, Edinburgh University, since 1976; Honorary Consultant Physician in Geriatric Medicine, Lothian Health Board, since 1976; b. 7.7.42, Edinburgh; m., Margaret Lawson; 1 s.; 1 d. Educ. George Watson's College, Edinburgh; Edinburgh University. Surgeon Lieutenant, Royal Navy, 1967-72; Senior Registrar in Geriatric Medicine, 1973-76. Member, Board of Directors, Queensberry House Hospital, Edinburgh. Recreations: golf; curling. Address: (h.) 56 Alnwickhill Road, Edinburgh; T.-031-664 1745.

Smith, Samuel Gordon, BSc, DipEd. Headteacher, Newbattle High School, since 1978; b. 3.4.43, Bonnyrigg; m., Carol Anne Wallace; 2 s. Educ. Lasswade Secondary School; Edinburgh University. Depute Headteacher, Greenhall High School, 1974-77. Address: (h.) 30 Golf Course Road, Bonnyrigg, Midlothian, EH19 2EZ; T.-031-663 8320.

Smith, Professor Stanley Desmond, BSc, PhD, FRS, FRSE, DSc. Professor of Physics, Heriot-Watt University, since 1970; Chairman, Edinburgh Instruments Ltd., since 1971; b. 3.3.31, Bristol; m., Gillian Anne Parish; 1 s.; 1 d. Educ. Cotham Grammar School; Bristol University; Reading University. SSO, RAE, Farnborough, 1956-58; Research Assistant, Department of Meteorology, Imperial College, London, 1958-59; Lecturer, then Reader, Reading University, 1960-70; Head, Department of Physics, Heriot-Watt University, since 1970. Member: Advisory Council for Applied Research and Development, 1985-87, Advisory Council on Science and Technology, 1987-88, Defence Scientific Advisory Committee, SERC Astronomy and Planetary Science and Engineering Boards, Council of Institute of Physics, 1984-87. Recreations: tennis; skiing; mountaineering; golf. Address: (h.) 29D Gillespie Road, Colinton, Edinburgh, EH13 0NW; T.-031-441 7225.

Smith, Stanley William, MA, PhD (Cantab). Senior Lecturer in English, Dundee University, since 1984; Director, Auden Concordance Research Project, since 1987; b. 12.1.43, Warrington; 2 s.; 1 d. Educ. Boteler Grammar School, Warrington; Jesus College, Cambridge. Assistant Lecturer in English, Aberdeen University, 1967-68; Lecturer in English, Dundee University, 1968-84; Visiting Professor, University of Florence, 1987. Publications: A Sadly Contracted Hero: The Comic Self in Post-War American Fiction, 1981; Inviolable Voice: History and Twentieth Century Poetry, 1982; 20th Century Poetry, 1983; W.H. Auden, 1985; Edward Thomas, 1986; W.B. Yeats, 1989. Recreations: the arts; politics; chess; travel. Address: (b.) English Department, The University, Dundee, DD1 4HN; T.-Dundee 23181, Ext. 4418.

Smith, Professor Emeritus Sir Thomas (Broun), Kt, QC, BA, MA, BCL, DCL, LLD, FRSE, FBA. General Editor, Laws of Scotland: Stair Memorial Encyclopaedia, since 1981; Professor Emeritus of Scots Law, Edinburgh University, since 1980; b. 3.12.15, Glasgow; m., Ann Dorothea Tindall; 1 d.; 1 s., 1 d. deceased. Educ. High School of Glasgow; Sedbergh School; Christ Church, Oxford; Edinburgh University. Called to Bar by Gray's Inn, 1938; served Army, 1939-46 (Lt. Col.); admitted Faculty of Advocates, 1947; Professor of Scots Law, Aberdeen University, 1949-58; Professor of Civil Law, 1958-68; Professor of Scots Law, Edinburgh University, 1968-72; Commissioner (part-time), Scottish Law Commission, 1965-72, (full-time), 1972-81; Visiting Professor, Cape Town, Tulane, LSU and Harvard Law Schools; Tagore Professor, Calcutta, 1977; QC, 1956; Member, Academic Advisory Committee, St. Andrews and Dundee Universities, 1964; Hon. Bencher, Gray's Inn; Hon. Member, Law Society of Scotland; Hon. Foreign Member, American Academy of Arts and Sciences; Hon. LLD, Cape Town, Aberdeen and Glasgow Universities. Publications: Doctrines of Judicial Precedent in Scots Law; Scotland: The Development of Its Laws and Constitution; British Justice: The Scottish Contribution; Studies Critical and Comparative; A Short Commentary on the Law of Scotland; Property Problems in Sale, Basic Rights and their Enforcement; Holy Willie. Recreations: reading, especially history; travel. Address: (h.) 18 Royal Circus, Edinburgh, EH3 6SS; T.-031-225 8306.

Smith, Thomas James, MBE, MA, JP. Honorary Sheriff; b. 17.6.05, King Edward Parish, Aberdeenshire; m., Alice Mary Mann; 1 s.; 1 d. Educ. Banff Academy; Aberdeen University. Headmaster: Towie School, 1931-43, New Pitsligo, 1943-48, Peterhead Central School, 1948-70; Member, Peterhead Town Council, 1958-67 and 1970-75; Provost of Peterhead, 1971-75; Chairman, Peterhead Harbour Board and Fcuars' Managers, 1971-75; Member, Grampian Regional Council, 1974-78; President, Peterhead Rotary Club and Professional and Business Men's Club; Chairman, Peterhead Burns Club, 1955-76. Recreation: bowls. Address: (h.) 53 Anderson Drive, Aberdeen; T.-Aberdeen 317922.

Smith, Thomas Stewart, BSc, MEd. Rector, Arbroath Academy, since 1986; b. 3.7.44, Forfar; m., Adrienne Gemmell; 2 s. Educ. Arbroath High School; St. Andrews University; Edinburgh University; Dundee University. Assistant Teacher, Duncanrig Secondary School, East Kilbride, 1968-73; Principal Teacher (Chemistry), Currie High School, 1973-78; Assistant Rector, then Depute Rector, Morgan Academy, Dundee, 1978-86. Recreations: golf; badminton; soccer. Address: (b.) Arbroath Academy, Glenisla Drive, Arbroath, DD11 5JD; T.-0241 72978.

Smith, W. Cairns S., MD, MPH, MFCM. Epidemiologist and Leader, Scottish Heart Health Study, since 1983; Honorary Senior Lecturer in Community Medicine, since 1984; Honorary Community Medicine Specialist, Tayside Health Board, since 1984; b. 8.2.51, Aberdeen; m., Christine Morrison; 2 s.; 2 d. Educ. Aberdeen Grammar School; Aberdeen University. Junior medical career, Aberdeen and Glasgow; Superintendent, Leprosy Hospital in India for three years; developed Leprosy Control Programme in India; Chairman, Leprosy Mission Council for Scotland. Address: (b.) Cardiovascular Epidemiology Unit, Ninewells Hospital and Medical School, Dundee; T.-0382 641764.

Smith, W. Gordon. Writer; b. 13.12.28, Edinburgh. RAF; Journalist; Radio/TV Producer, BBC, 25 years; author of plays: Vincent; Jock; Knox; Sweeter Than All The Roses; A North British Working Man's Guide to the Arts; Wizard; On the Road to Avizandum; Marie of Scotland; Xanadu.

Smith, William Angus, BEM, JP. Chairman, Education Committee, Shetland Islands Council, since 1975 (Vice Chairman, Housing Committee, 1982-85); Vice-Chairman, Lerwick Harbour Trust; b. 20.8.19, Burra Isle, Shetland; m., Daisy Manson; 4 s. Educ. Anderson Educational Institute. Engineer, British Telecomms, 1937-83; Royal Signals, UK, Middle East, Burma, India, Germany, 1940-46; Member, Lerwick Town Council and Zetland County Council, 1967-75; Member, Lerwick Harbour Trust, since 1967 (except for short break); Provost of Lerwick, 1971-74; Member, Shetland Islands Council, since 1975; Member, Shetland Area Health Board, since 1974; Member, Electricity Consultative Council for North of Scotland District, since 1974; Member, Clickimin Recreational Trust. Recreations: crosswords; reading. Address: (h.) 14 Bruce Crescent, Lerwick, Shetland, ZE1 OPB; T.-0595 2121.

Smith, William Anthony. Director, Scottish Office Training Unit, 1982-86; b. 14.9.28, Edinburgh; m., Maureen Enid Graham; 2 s.; 2 d. Educ. George Heriot's School, Edinburgh. Various executive posts, Department of Health and Social Security; Senior O. & M. Officer, HM Treasury; Head of O. & M. Unit, Scottish Office; UN Consultant in Management, Costa Rica, and in Organisation Development, Iran; Personnel Manager, Scottish Office. Past Chairman, Edinburgh Oxfam Committee. Recreations: part-time antiquarian and second-hand bookseller; winemaking; reading and writing about avocados. Address: (h.) 5 Stirling Road, Edinburgh; T.-031-552 1850.

Smith, William E., CEng, MICE, MIHT. Director of Construction, Shetland Islands Council, since 1975; b. 15.2.31, Lerwick; m., Pamela; 1 s.; 2 d. Educ. Anderson Educational Institute. Zetland County Council: Apprentice Road Surveyor, 1949-53, Assistant Engineer, 1954-55, Depute County Surveyor, 1959-75. Recreations: sailing; golf; music. Address: (b.) Grantfield, Lerwick, Shetland, ZE1 ONT; T.-0595 2024.

Smith, William Leggat, CBE, MC, TD, JP, DL, BA (Oxon), LLB, LLD; b. 30.1.18, Kilmarnock; m., Yvonne Menna Williams; 1 s.; 2 d. Educ. Glasgow Academy; Queen's Collee, Oxford; Glasgow University. Commissioned (TA), Cameronians (Scottish Rifles), 1939; served Second World War in UK, Europe, USA; Solicitor, 1947-86; Chairman, Governors, Glasgow Academy, 1972-80; Deacon Convener, Trades of Glasgow, 1964-65; Dean, Royal Faculty of Procurators in Glasgow, 1976-79; Member, Reviewing Committee on Export of Works of Art, 1980-82; Convener, Retirement Scheme of Church of Scotland, 1976-80; Chairman, Charles Rennie Mackintosh Society, 1985-88; Chairman, Indigent Gentlewomen of Scotland Fund, since 1985; Chairman, Glasgow School of Art, since 1975. Recreations: gardening; salmon fishing. Address: (h.) The Cottage, Campsie Glen, Glasgow; T.-0360 311434.

Smith, William Wilson Campbell, MA (Cantab), LLB (Glas). Partner, Biggart Baillie & Gifford, WS, Solicitors, Glasgow and Edinburgh, since 1974; b. 17.5.46, Glasgow; m., Elizabeth Margaret Richards; 2 d. Educ. Glasgow Academy; St. Catharine's College, Cambridge; Glasgow University. Qualified as a Solicitor, 1972; Assistant Solicitor, Herbert Smith & Co., London, 1972-73. Member, various committees, Law Society of Scotland; Member, Joint Insolvency Examination Board; late Collector, Incorporation of Barbers, Glasgow. Recreations: croquet; golf; barbershop singing. Address: (b.) 105 West George Street, Glasgow, G2 1QP; T.-041-221 7020.

Smout, Professor Thomas Christopher, MA, PhD, FRSE. Professor of Scottish History, St. Andrews University, since 1980; b. 19.12.33, Birmingham; m., Anne-Marie; 1 s.; 1 d. Educ. Leys School, Cambridge; Clare College, Cambridge. Department of Economic History, Edinburgh University, 1959-79. Address: (b.) St. Andrews University, St. Andrews, Fife.

Smylie, Henry Gordon, MB, ChB, MD, FRCPath. Senior Lecturer, Department of Bacteriology, Aberdeen University, and Honorary Consultant, Grampian Health Board, Aberdeen Hospitals, since 1964; b. 31.7.26, Aberdeen; 4 s. Educ. Robert Gordon's College; Aberdeen University. Variously employed in the newspaper, clothing and building industries, farming and forestry; three years' volunteer service, Royal Navy, 1944-47; undergraduate, 1948-54; several months in general practice, then Probationer Lecturer, Bacteriology, Aberdeen University, 1955. Recreations: running; gardening. Address: (h.) Birken Lodge, Bieldside, Aberdeen; T.-Aberdeen 861305.

Smyth, Professor John Fletcher, MA, MB, BChir, MD (Cantab), MSc (Lond), FRCPE, FRCP. Professor of Medical Oncology, Edinburgh University, since 1979 (Head, Department of Clinical Oncology, since 1980); Honorary Director, Imperial Cancer Research Fund Medical Oncology Unit, Edinburgh University, since 1980; b. 26.10.45, Dursley; m., Catherine Ellis; 2 d. Educ. Bryanston School; Trinity College, Cambridge. Trained, St. Bartholomews Hospital, Royal Postgraduate Medical School and Institute of Cancer Research, London; National Cancer Institute, Bethesda; University of Chicago; Honorary Consultant Physician, Royal Marsden Hospital and Senior Lecturer, Institute of Cancer Research, London, 1976-79. Governor, Bryanston School. Recreations: flying; music. Address: (h.) 18 Inverleith Avenue South, Edinburgh, EH3 5QA; T.-031-552 3775.

Smyth, Michael Jessop, MA, PhD, FRAS, FRSE. Senior Lecturer, Department of Astronomy, Edinburgh University, since 1965; b. 12.11.26, Hounslow; m., Mary Florence Isabel Speyer; 2 s. Educ. Hounslow College; Selwyn College, Cambridge. Lecturer in Astronomy, Edinburgh University, 1950-54; Assistant Director and Acting Director, Dunsink Observatory, Dublin, 1954-59; Lecturer in Astronomy, Edinburgh University, 1959-65. Member, British National Committee for Astronomy. Recreations: travel; photography; hill-walking; swimming; gardening; winemaking. Address: (b.) Royal Observatory, Edinburgh, EH9 3HJ; T.-031-667 3321.

Snaith, David William, MSc, PhD, CEng, MIM, CChem, FRSC. Principal, Stow College, Glasgow, since 1983; b. 30.6.40, Birmingham; m., Susan Willoughby Tucker; 1 s.; 2 d. Educ. Kings Norton Grammar School, Birmingham; Aston University. Research Chemist, Birmingham Small Arms Co. Ltd.; Assistant Lecturer in Chemistry, Matthew Boulton Technical College, Birmingham, 1965; Lecturer in Chemistry, Ipswich Civic College, 1969; Deputy Head, Department of Science and Metallurgy, North Lindsey College of Technology, Scunthorpe, 1974; Head, Department of Science, North East Liverpool Technical College, 1980. Royal Society of Chemistry: Assistant Secretary, East Anglian Section Committee, 1972-74, Chairman, Southumbria Section, 1977-78. Recreations: hill-walking; photography; music; rifle shooting. Address: (b.) Stow College, 43 Shamrock Street, Glasgow, G4 9LD; T.-041-332 1786.

Sneader, Walter, BSc, PhD, MRPharmS. President, Glasgow Jewish Representative Council, since 1986; Chairman, West of Scotland Council of Christians and Jews, since 1987; Senior Lecturer in Pharmaceutical Chemistry, Strathclyde University; b. 2.11.39, Glasgow; m., Myrna Joan Levine; 2 s.; 1 d. Educ. Glasgow High School; Glasgow University. After a period with National Research Council of Canada, joined Strathclyde University; appointed to National Pharmaceutical Consultative Committee, 1986; former Executive Member, Glasgow Board of Jewish Education; former Hon. Secretary, Jewish Representative Council. Publications: Drug Discovery: The Evolution of Modern Medicines, 1985; Drug Development: From Laboratory to Clinic, 1986. Address: (b.) Department of Pharmacy, Strathclyde University, Glasgow, G1 1XW; T.-041-552 4400.

Snedden, Charles, OBE, OStJ, JP. Deputy Chairman, Scottish Special Housing Association, since 1982; Convener, Central Regional Council, since 1986; Member, University Court, Stirling; b. 28.3.32, Bo'ness; m., Margaret Kidd; 1 s.; 1 d. Educ. Bo'ness Academy. Joined Bo'ness Town Council and West Lothian County Council, 1959; Provost of Bo'ness, 1964-75; Member, Council of Management, Scottish Special Housing Association, since 1978. Honorary President: Bo'ness United FC, Kinneil Colliery Silver Band, West Lothian Golf Club; Trustee and Director, Bo'ness Heritage Trust. Recreations: gardening; reading. Address: Pennvael, 2 Deanburn Grove, Bo'ness, West Lothian, EH51 0NA; T.-0506 822355.

Sneddon, Ian Naismith, OBE (1969), BSc, DSc, BA, MA, FRS, FRSE, FIMA, FRSA. Honorary Research Fellow and Emeritus Professor of Mathematics, Glasgow University; Honorary Visiting Professor of Mathematics, Strathclyde University; Vice-Chairman, Advisory Council, Scottish Opera; Vice-Chairman, Board of Directors, Citizens' Theatre, Glasgow; b. 8.12.19, Glasgow; m., Mary Campbell Macgregor; 2 s.; 1 d. Educ. Hyndland School, Glasgow; Glasgow University; Trinity College, Cambridge. Junior Scientific Officer, Ministry of Supply, 1942-45; William Bryce Fellow, Glasgow University, 1945-46; Lecturer in Natural Philosophy, Glasgow University, 1946-50; Professor of Mathematics, University College of North Staffordshire, 1950-56; Simson Professor of Mathematics, Glasgow University, 1956-85. Hon DSc: Warsaw University, Heriot-Watt University, Hull University; Kelvin Medal, Glasgow University; Makdougall-Brisbane Prize, Royal Society of Edinburgh, 1959; Eringen Medal, Society of Engineering Science, 1979; Copernicus Medal, Polish Academy of Sciences; Gold Medal for Culture (Poland), 1983; Member, Order of the Long Leaf Pine (North Carolina), 1964; Commander, Order of Polonia Restituta, 1969; Commander, Order of Merit of Poland, 1979.

Recreations: music; painting in oils; photography. Address: (h.) 19 Crown Terrace, Glasgow, G12 9ES; T.-041-339 4114.

Soames, Christopher Kenneth, BSc, BIM, JP. Chairman, Education Committee, Orkney Islands Council, since 1986; b. 15.11.43, Birmingham; m., Mary Joan Wilkinson; 3 s.; 1 d. Educ. St. Philip's Oratory School, Birmingham; Birmingham University. Teacher in England, 1962-69; farming in Orkney, since 1970; Member, Orkney Islands Council, since 1982; represents COSLA (Education Committee), Educational Broadcasting Council for Scotland. Recreations: sailing; photography; walking; music; good food and drink. Address: (h.) Brendale, Rousay, Orkney, KW17 2PR; T.-Rousay 234.

Somerville, Donald Robert, LLB, NP. Director of Legal Services, Inverness District Council, since 1984; b. 19.3.53, Edinburgh; m., Margaret; 3 d. Educ. Scotus Academy, Edinburgh; Edinburgh University. Law Apprentice/Legal Assistant, private practice, 1974-77; Principal Legal Assistant, West Lothian District Council, 1977-84. Recreations: hill-walking; jogging; following the Hearts. Address: (b.) Town House, Inverness; T.-0463 239111.

Sommerville, John Kenneth, CA. Partner, French & Cowan, CA, Glasgow, since 1970; Council Member, Institute of Chartered Accountants of Scotland, since 1984; b. 1.3.42, Glasgow; m., Iris Alexa Hutchison; 3 d. Educ. Kelvinside Academy; Glasgow University (during CA course). CA apprenticeship, French & Cowan. Member, Board of Governors, Kelvinside Academy, since 1976 (Chairman of Board, since 1985). Recreations: golf; skiing; running. Address: (b.) 144 St. Vincent Street, Glasgow, G2 5LT; T.-041-221 2984.

Souness, Graeme James. Manager, Rangers Football Club, since 1986; b. 6.5.53, Edinburgh; m., Danielle; 2 s.; 1 d. Educ. Carrickvale Secondary School, Edinburgh. Professional Footballer: Tottenham Hotspur FC, 1969-72, Middlesbrough FC, 1972-78, Liverpool FC, 1978-84, Sampdoria FC, 1984-86. Publication: No Half Measures (autobiography). Address: (b.) Ibrox Stadium, Glasgow, G51 2XD; T.-041-427 5232.

Souness, James McGill, FFA. Managing Director, Life Association of Scotland, since 1984; Vice President, Faculty of Actuaries; b. 9.11.28, Edinburgh; m., Ena; 2 s.; 1 d. Educ. George Heriot's. Qualified Fellow, Faculty of Actuaries, 1956; joined Life Association of Scotland, 1957, as Assistant Actuary, then Secretary, Assistant General Manager, and General Manager. Past President, Edinburgh Chamber of Commerce; Past Chairman, Associated Scottish Life Offices; Finance Convener, Royal Scottish Society for Prevention of Cruelty to Children; Chairman, Music Committee, Scottish Arts Council; Honorary Consul to the Netherlands (Edinburgh). Recreations: hill-climbing; golf; music; gardening. Address: (b.) 10 George Street, Edinburgh; T.-031-225 8494.

Souter, James Gordon, JP, MRCVS, DVSM. Member, Fife Regional Council, since 1976; b. 22.10.06, Stonehaven; m., Grace Elizabeth Geddes, MA (deceased); 1 s.; 2 d. Educ. Aberdeen Grammar School; Royal (Dick) College of Veterinary Studies, Edinburgh University. Assistant in veterinary practice, Ware, Hertfordshire; postgraduate course, Royal (Dick) College of Veterinary Studies; joined staff, MAFF; Veterinary Officer (Assistant), Aberdeen and Aberdeenshire Regional Scheme (later State Veterinary Service); Divisional Veterinary Officer, London; Field Staff, Fife and Kinross. Member, Newport-on-Tay Town Council, 1963-71 (Provost of Newport-on-Tay, 1968-71); Member, Fife County Council, 1968-76. Recreations: rugby football and cricket (now as a spectator). Address: (h.) Dalbradie, Crawford Avenue, Gauldry, Newport-on-Tay, Fife; T.-Gauldry 788.

Souter, William Alexander, MB, ChB (Hons), FRCSEdin. Consultant Orthopaedic Surgeon, Princess Margaret Rose Orthopaedic Hospital and Edinburgh Royal Infirmary, since 1968; Honorary Senior Lecturer, Department of Orthopaedic Surgery, Edinburgh University; b. 11.5.33, Cupar; m., Kathleen Bruce Georgeson Taylor; 1 s.; 2 d. Educ. George Watson's Boys' College, Edinburgh; Edinburgh University. Various House Officer and Registrar appointments, Edinburgh Royal Infirmary and Princess Margaret Rose Orthopaedic Hospital, 1957-61; Registrar in General Surgery, then in Hand Surgery, Derbyshire Royal Infirmary, 1962-64; Senior Registrar in Orthopaedic Surgery, Edinburgh Royal Infirmary and Princess Margaret Rose, 1965-68; Instructor, Department of Orthopaedic Surgery, Washington University, Seattle, 1967; Visiting Professor, Bioengineering Department, Strathclyde University, 1985-88; Examiner, General and Orthopaedic Fellowships, Royal College of Surgeons of Edinburgh; Member, Editorial Board, Journal of Bone and Joint Surgery, 1981-84; first Honorary Secretary, European Rheumatoid Arthritis Surgical Society, 1979-83; Member, Scientific Co-ordinating Committee, Arthritis and Rheumatism Council, 1977-84; Council Member, British Society for Surgery of the Hand, 1976-78; Council Member, British Orthopaedic Association, 1986-88; Trustee, International Opera Theatre of Scotland Trust Fund; Elder, St. George's West Church, Edinburgh. Recreations: music; photography; gardening; skiing; golf. Address: (h.) Old Mauricewood Mains, Penicuik, Midlothian, EH26 ONJ; T.-Penicuik 72609.

Southcott, Barry John, BSc (Econ), ASIA. Director, British Investment Trust; Managing Director, Marketable Securities, British Coal Pension Fund, now CIN Management Ltd., since 1975; b. 27.3.50, London; m., Lesley Anne Parkinson. Educ. Latymer Upper School; Bradford University. Phillips & Drew, 1971-75; British Coal Pension Fund, since 1975. Recreations: tennis; football; music. Address: (b.) 46 Castle Street, Edinburgh.

Southesk, Earl of (Charles Alexander Carnegie), KCVO, DL; b. 23.9.93, Edinburgh; m., 1, H.H. Princess Maud (deceased); 1 s.; 2, Evelyn Campbell. Educ. Eton; Sandhurst. Scots Guards, 1913; ADC to Viceroy of India, 1917-19. Recreations: shooting; fishing. Address: (h.) Kinnaird Castle, Brechin, Angus; T.-067 481 209.

Spawforth, David Meredith, MA (Oxon). Headmaster, Merchiston Castle School, since 1981; b. 2.1.38, Wakefield; m., Yvonne Mary Gude; 1 s.; 1 d. Educ. Silcoates School; Hertford College, Oxford. Assistant Master, Winchester College, 1961-64; Housemaster, Wellington College, 1964-80; BP Education Fellow, Keble College, Oxford, 1977. Recreations: travel - especially France and Italy; theatre; walking. Address: (b.) Merchiston Castle School, Colinton, Edinburgh.

Spear, Professor Walter Eric, PhD, DSc, FRS, FRSE, FInstP. Professor of Physics, Carnegie Laboratory of Physics, Dundee University, since 1968; b. 20.1.21, Frankfurt/Main, West Germany; m., Hilda Doris King; 2 d. Educ. London University. Lecturer in Physics, Leicester University, 1953; Visiting Professor: Purdue University, 1957-58, N. Carolina University, 1965-66; Reader in Physics, Leicester University, 1967-68. Max Born Prize, 1977; Europhysics Prize, 1977; Makdougal-Brisbane Medal, Royal Society of Edinburgh, 1981. Rank Prize for Optoelectronics, 1988. Recreations: music; languages; literature. Address: (b.) Carnegie Laboratory of Physics, Dundee University, Dundee, DD1 4HN; T.-0382 23181, Ext. 4563.

Speirs, Alexander Logan, OBE, MD, FRCP(Lond), FRCP(Glas), DCH. Consultant Paediatrician, Stirling and Falkirk Royal Infirmaries and Royal Hospital for Sick Children, Glasgow, since 1954; b. 4.4.21, Aberdeen; m., Dr. Inez Mary Brebner; 2 d. Educ. Aberdeen Grammar School; Aberdeen University. House Surgeon/Physician, Aberdeen Royal Infirmary; Surgeon Lt., RNVR, 1944-47; junior hospital appoointments, Aberdeen and Glasgow, 1947-54. Member, BBC Advisory Committee on Appeals, 1964-72; Member, Child Health Programme Planning Group, SHHD, 1977-80; Chairman, Vulnerable Families Sub-Committee, 1979; Council Member, British Paediatric Association, 1982-85; Council Member, Royal College of Physicians and Surgeons of Glasgow, 1984-87; President, Scottish Paediatric Society, 1984-85. Recreations: golf; gardening. Address: (h.) 29 Chalton Road, Bridge of Allan, Stirling, FK9 4EF; T.-0786 833276.

Speirs, John A.A., CA, FRICS. Managing Partner, Speirs Parnie & Adam, since 1983 (Partner, since 1964); b. 16.3.37, Glasgow; m., Dorothea Ross Kelly; 1 s.; 1 d. Educ. Merchiston Castle School, Edinburgh. Chairman, Scottish Junior Branch, Royal Institution of Chartered Surveyors, 1969-70; President, Property Owners & Factors Association, Glasgow, 1979-81; Deputy Chairman, West of Scotland TSB, 1982-83; Board Member, TSB Scotland PLC, since 1986; Member, East Kilbride Development Corporation, since 1987; Deacon, Incorporation of Weavers in Glasgow, 1973-74; Governor, Glasgow School of Art, 1982-88; Deacon Convener, Trades of Glasgow, 1985-86; Member of Court, Glasgow University, since 1987; Trustee, Trades Hall of Glasgow Trust. Recreations: angling; shooting; sailing. Address: (h.) Clifton, Moor Road, Strathblane, by Glasgow, G63 9EX; T.-Blanefield 70424.

Speirs, Norman Thomas, BSc, MB, ChB, DMRD, FACI. Consultant Radiologist, Lothian Health Board, since 1958; b. 31.8.24, London; m., Dorothy Glen; 1 d. Educ. George Watson's Boys' College; Edinburgh University. House Surgeon, Royal Infirmary, Edinburgh; Captain, RAMC; specialist training in Radiology; various Registrar appointments, Edinburgh; Consultant Radiologist, Princess Margaret Rose Orthopaedic Hospital, Edinburgh, and Roodlands Hospital, Haddington; entered part-time private practice (now at Murrayfield Hospital, Edinburgh). Past Chairman, Scottish Association of Amateur Cinematographers; elected to National Council, Institute of Amateur Cinematographers (IAC) and awarded its Fellowship, 1981. Address: (h.) 5 Blackbarony Road, Edinburgh, EH16 5QP; T.-031-667 6662.

Speirs, Robert, ACIS. Director of Finance, Britoil plc, since 1983; b. 23.10.36, Liverpool; m., Patricia; 2 s. Educ. Alleynes Grammar School, Uttoxeter. Coopers & Lybrand, 1965-68; Texaco Ltd., 1968-77; BNOC/Britoil, since 1977. Address: (b.) 301 St. Vincent Street, Glasgow, G2 5DD; T.-041-204 2525.

Speirs, William MacLeod. Deputy General Secretary, Scottish TUC; b. 8.3.52, Dumbarton; m., Lynda; 1 s.; 1 d. Educ. John Neilson High School, Paisley; Strathclyde University. Chairperson, 7:84 Theatre Co. (Scotland); Chairperson, West of Scotland Friends of Palestine; Council of Management, War on Want; Governor, Glasgow College of Technology. Recreations: watching St. Mirren FC; playing football and cricket. Address: (b.) STUC, 16 Woodlands Terrace, Glasgow, G3 6DF; T.-041-332 4946.

Speitel, Hans H., PhD. Reader, Department of Scottish Studies, Edinburgh University, since 1987 (Lecturer, since 1963); b. 22.3.37, Erfurt, Germany; m., Inge Jaskulla; 2 d. Educ. Munster University; Kiel University; Frankfurt University; Edinburgh University. Co-Editor, Linguistic Atlas of Scotland, Volumes 1-3; Member, Editorial Board, Atlas Linguarum Europae. Recreations: topography of Edinburgh, London; general literature. Address: (h.) 14 Thirlestane Road, Edinburgh, 9; T.-031-447 3946.

Spence, Professor John, ARCST, BSc, MEng, PhD, DSc, CEng, FIMechE. Chairman and Head, Department of Mechanical and Process Engineering, Strathclyde University, since 1987 (Trades House of Glasgow Professor of Mechanics of Materials, since 1982); b. 5.11.37, Chapelhall; m., Margaret Gray Hudson; 2 s. Educ. Airdrie Academy; Royal College of Science and Technology; Sheffield University. Engineering apprenticeship, Stewarts & Lloyds (now British Steel Corporation); Senior Engineer, then Head of Stress Analysis, Babcock & Wilcox Research Division; Strathclyde University: Lecturer, 1966, Senior Lecturer, Reader. Serves on several national committees, including Institution of Mechanical Engineers, SERC and British Standards Institution. Address: (b.) Department of Mechanical and Process Engineering, Strathclyde University, 75 Montrose Street, Glasgow, G1 1XJ; T.-041-552 4400, Ext. 2324.

Spencer, Rt. Rev. Alfred Raymond, OSB. Abbot, Pluscarden Abbey, Elgin, since 1966; b. 28.6.15, Scopwick, Lincoln. Educ. Panton College, Lincoln; Franciscan Friary, Crawley. Joined Capuchin Franciscan Order, 1934; Priest, 1941; pastoral work in England and Wales; Assistant Novice Master, Pantasaph, North Wales, five years; transferred to Benedictine Abbey, Prinknash, 1951; Novice Master, 1953; elected Conventual Prior of Pluscarden, 1966 (Priory given status of Abbey, 1974); confirmed as first Abbot. Address: Pluscarden Abbey, Elgin, Moray, IV30 3UA; T.-034 389 257.

Spiers, Rev. John McLaren, LTh. Minister, Orchardhill Church, Giffnock, since 1977; b. 12.12.43, Edinburgh; m., Janet Diane Watson; 2 d. Educ. George Watson's College, Edinburgh; Glasgow University. Trainee, Scottish Union and National Insurance Company, 1961-65; University, 1966-71; Probationer Assistant, Drumchapel Old Parish Church, Glasgow, 1971-72; Minister, South Church, Barrhead, 1972-77. Recreations: music; art; country pursuits; family life; various sports. Address: 23 Huntly Avenue, Giffnock, Glasgow, G46 6LW.

Spilg, Walter Gerson Spence, MB, ChB (Hons), FRCPath, MRCPG. Consultant Pathologist, Victoria Infirmary, Glasgow, since 1972, in Administrative Charge, since 1986; Honorary Clinical Lecturer, Glasgow University, since 1973; b. 27.10.37, Glasgow; m., Vivien Anne Burns; 1 s.; 2 d. Educ. Hutchesons' Boys' Grammar School, Glasgow; Glasgow University. Registrar in Pathology, Glasgow Royal Infirmary, 1965-68; Senior Registrar in Pathology, Victoria Infirmary, Glasgow, 1968-69; Lecturer in Pathology, Glasgow University (Western Infirmary), 1969-72. Chairman, Laboratory Division, Victoria Infirmary; Chairman, Laboratory Medicine Committee, West of Scotland Committee for Postgraduate Medical Education; Member, Forensic Pathology Liaison Committee. Recreations: bridge; golf. Address: (h.) 98 Ayr Road, Newton Mearns, Glasgow, G77 6EJ; T.-041-639 3130.

Spratt, Col. Douglas Norman, CBE, TD, DL. Partner, Cameo of Edinburgh, since 1984; b. 18.9.20, Ramsgate; m., Margaret; 1 d. Educ. Sir Roger Manwood's Grammar School, Sandwich, Kent. President, Edinburgh Branch, Institute of Marketing; Honorary Col., 71 (Scottish) Engineer Regiment (V); Chairman, Friends of the Reserve Forces Association, Scotland; Vice Chairman, Action Research in Scotland (Chairman, Edinburgh Committee); Member, High Constables of Edinburgh; Deputy Lieutenant, City of Edinburgh; Member of the Military Attaches London. Recreations: fishing; sailing. Address: (h.) 6 Fernielaw Avenue, Edinburgh, EH13 OEE; T.-031-441 1962.

Sprent, Professor Peter, BSc, PhD, FRSE. Statistician and Author; Professor of Statistics, Dundee University, 1972-85, Professor Emeritus, since 1985; b. 28.1.23, Hobart, Australia; m., Janet Irene Findlater. Educ. Hutchins School, Hobart, Tasmania; Tasmania University; London University. Lecturer in Mathematics, Tasmania University, 1948-57; Statistician, East Malling Research Station, 1958-67; Senior Lecturer in Statistics, Dundee University, 1967-72. Sometime Member, Editorial Boards, Journal of Royal Statistical Society, Journal of American Statistical Association, Biometrics. Publications: Models in Regression and Related Topics; Statistics in Action; Quick Statistics. Recreations: aviation; golf; hill-walking. Address: (h.) 32 Birkhill Avenue, Wormit, Newport-on-Tay, DD6 8PW; T.-0382 541706.

Sprigge, Professor Timothy Lauro Squire. Professor of Logic and Metaphysics, Edinburgh University, since 1979; b. 14.1.32, London; m., Giglia Gordon; 1 s.; 2 d. Educ. Gonville and Caius College, Cambridge. Lecturer in Philosophy, University College, London, 1961-63; Lecturer, then Reader in Philosophy, Sussex University, 1963-79. Publications: The Correspondence of Jeremy Bentham, Volumes 1 and 2; Facts, Words and Beliefs; Santayana: An Examination of his Philosophy; The Vindication of Absolute Idealism; Theories of Existence; The Rational Foundations of Ethics. Recreation: backgammon. Address: (b.) Philosophy Department, David Hume Tower, Edinburgh University, George Square, Edinburgh; T.-031-667 1011.

Sprot of Haystoun, Lt.-Col. Aidan Mark, MC, JP. Lord Lieutenant, Tweeddale, since 1980; Landowner (Haystoun Estate) and Farmer, since 1965; b. 17.6.19, Lilliesleaf. Educ. Belhaven Hill; Stowe. Commissioned, Royal Scots Greys, 1940; served Palestine, 1941-42, Western Desert, 1942-43, Italy, 1943-44, NW Europe, 1944-45; continued serving with Regiment in Germany until 1952, Libya, Egypt and Jordan, 1952-55, UK, 1955-58, Germany, 1958-62; Adjutant, 1944-45; Commanding Officer, 1959-62; retired, 1962. County Councillor, Peeblesshire, 1963-75; DL (Peeblesshire), 1966-80; Member, Queen's Bodyguard for Scotland (Royal Company of Archers), since 1950; County Director, Peeblesshire Branch, Red Cross, 1966-74, Patron, since 1983; County Commissioner, Peeblesshire Scout Association, 1968-73; Honorary Secretary, Royal Caledonian Hunt, 1964-74; President, Lowlands of Scotland TA&V-RA, since 1986. Recreations: country sports; motor cycle touring. Address: (h.) Crookston, by Peebles, EH45 9JQ; T.-Kirkton Manor 209.

Sprott, Gavin Chappell, MA. Head, Working Life Section, National Museums of Scotland and Curator, Scottish Agricultural Museum, Ingliston; b. 23.7.43, Dundee; m., Maureen Turnbull; 2 s.; 1 d. Educ. Edinburgh University. Research Assistant, Scottish Country Life Section, National Museum of Antiquities of Scotland, 1972-79. Recreations: cycling; walking; restoring and sailing old boats. Address: (b.) National Museums of Scotland, Queen Street, Edinburgh, EH2; T.-031-225 7534.

Sprott, Trevor Ferguson, RIBA, FRTPI. Director of Physical Planning, Grampian Regional Council, since 1975; b. 22.4.33, Belfast; m., Patricia M.I.; 1 step s.; 2 step d. Educ. Bangor Grammar School; University College, London; Edinburgh University. Assistant Planner, P.E.A. Johnson-

Marshall, 1960-61; Group Planner, Cumbernauld Development Corporation, 1961-62; Research Planner, Planning Research Unit, Edinburgh University, 1962-63; Senior Principal Planner, Craigavon Development Commission, Northern Ireland, 1963-72; Regional Planning Adviser, North East of Scotland Joint Planning Advisory Committee, 1972-75. Fellow, Salzburg Seminar in American Studies; Member, Academic Advisory Board, Forestry Department, Aberdeen University; Planning Adviser, COSLA Planning Committee and Economic Affairs Committee; Past Chairman, Scottish Society of Directors of Planning; Chairman, Local Authority and Working Party on Digital Mapping and Geographic Information. Recreations: golf; bridge; photography; walking. Address: (b.) Department of Physical Planning, Grampian Regional Council, Woodhill House, Westburn Road, Aberdeen, AB9 2LU; T.-0224 682222, Ext. 2400.

Squire, Geoffrey, DFA, ARSA, RSW, RGI. Senior Lecturer, Glasgow School of Art, since 1971; b. 21.2.23, Cleckheaton; m., Jean Marie; 1 s.; 1 d. Educ. Heckmondwike Grammar School; Leeds College of Art; Ruskin School, Oxford; Slade, London. Fleet Air Arm, Europe and Far East, 1942-46. Lecturer, Glasgow School of Art, 1948; elected ARSA, 1977, RGI, 1980, RSW, 1983. Recreation: vintage motoring. Address: (h.) The Studio, Links Place, Elie, Fife.

Stair, 13th Earl of (John Aymer Dalrymple), KCVO (1978), MBE (1941). Captain General, Queen's Bodyguard for Scotland (Royal Company of Archers), since 1973; b. 9.10.06; m., Davina Bowes-Lyon; 3 s. Educ. Eton; Sandhurst. Colonel (retired), Scots Guards. Address: (h.) Lochinch Castle, Stranraer, Wigtownshire.

Stanforth, Professor Anthony William, BA, MA, Drphil. Professor and Head, Department of Languages, Heriot-Watt University, since 1981; b. 27.7.38, Ipswich; m., Susan Margaret Vale; 2 s. Educ. Ipswich School; King's College, Newcastle (Durham University); Marburg University. Earl Grey Memorial Fellow, Newcastle-upon-Tyne University, 1962-64; Assistant Lecturer, Manchester University, 1964-65; Lecturer, Senior Lecturer, Newcastle-upon-Tyne University, 1965-81; Visiting Assistant Professor, Wisconsin University, 1970-71. Fellow, Royal Society of Arts. Recreation: opera. Address: (b.) Department of Languages, Heriot-Watt University, Riccarton, Edinburgh, EH14 4AS; T.-031-449 5111.

Stanley, Alexander, MA. General Secretary, Scottish Secondary Teachers' Association, since 1985; b. 1.4.45, Wolverhampton. Educ. Wolverhampton Grammar School; Queen's College, Dundee; St. Andrews University. Principal Teacher of History, Rockwell High School, Dundee, 1972-84. Held various offices within SSTA. Recreations: gardening; reading; horse-racing (viewing). Address: (b.) 15 Dundas Street, Edinburgh, EH3 6QG; T.-031-556 5919/0605.

Stanners, Ian Cram, FRICS. Chartered Quantity Surveyor; Chairman, Royal Institution of Chartered Surveyors in Scotland, 1986-87; b. 30.11.38, Glasgow; m., Louise Robertson; 2 d. Educ. Hutchesons' Boys' Grammar School. Chairman, Quantity Surveyors Divisional Committee, Scottish Branch, RICS, 1980-81; Vice Chairman, Scottish Building Contract Committee. Honorary Vice-President, Clyde Amateur Rowing Club. Recreations: rowing; curling. Address: (b.) 21 Woodlands Terrace, Glasgow, G3 6DF; T.-041-332 6032.

Stark, Robert, OStJ, NP. Honorary Sheriff, Tayside Central and Fife; Retired Solicitor; b. 28.8.15, Kirkcaldy; m., Mary Elizabeth; 1 s.; 1 d. Educ. Kirkcaldy High School; Edinburgh University. Solicitor, since 1940; Lt., RNVR, 1941-46; Partner, Innes Johnson & Co., 1952-84. Chairman, Rent Assessment Committee; Secretary, Fife Centre, SMTA, 1954-85; Chairman, Fife Branch, St. John Association, 1984-86; Past Chairman, Central and West Fife Conservative Association; former Honorary Secretary, Forces Help Society and Lord Roberts Workshop; Hon. Treasurer, Edinburgh and Borders Riding for the Disabled Association. Recreations: golf (former Captain, Balbirnie Park GC); gardening. Address: (h.) Croft House, Markinch, Fife.

Stavert, Donald James, JP. Member, West Lothian District Council, since 1980 (Chairman, Finance and Manpower Committee, since 1984); National Chairman, Association of Direct Labour Organisations, 1985-86; b. 3.3.48, Edinburgh; m., Sandra McKay; 2 s. Educ. Penicuik High School. Branch Chairman, East of Scotland, Scottish Graphical Division, SOGAT, 1979-81; Member Scottish Executive, Graphical Division, SOGAT, 1976-81; Vice-Chairman, Housing Committee, West Lothian District Council, 1980-84; Community Councillor, 1978-80; Chairman, Livingston Constituency Labour Party, 1983-85; Chairman, West Lothian Labour Party Publications, since 1983; Secretary, West Lothian Centre for Unemployed. Recreations: swimming; walking; reading. Address: (h.) 18 Macfarlane Place, Uphall, West Lothian.

Steedman, Robert Russell, RSA, RIBA, FRIAS, ALI, DA, MLA. Partner, Morris and Steedman, Architects and Landscape Architects; b. 3.1.29, Batu Gajah, Malaysia; m., Martha Hamilton; 1 s.; 2 d. Educ. Loretto School; School of Architecture, Edinburgh College of Art; Pennsylvania University. Governor, Edinburgh College of Art, since 1974; Commissioner, Countryside Commission for Scotland, since 1980; ARSA, 1973, Academician, 1979; Council Member, RSA, 1981 (Deputy President, 1982-83, Secretary, since 1983); Commissioner, Royal Fine Art Commission for Scotland, since 1983; former Member, Council, RIAS; nine Civic Trust Awards, 1963-78; British Steel Award, 1971; RIBA Award for Scotland, 1974; European Heritage Medal, 1975; Association for the Protection of Rural Scotland, 1977; Borders Region Award, 1984. Address: (h.) 11B Belford Mews, Edinburgh; T.-031-225 1697.

Steel, Very Rev. David, MA, BD, DD, LLD. Minister Emeritus, St. Michael's, Linlithgow, since 1977; b. 5.10.10, Hamilton; m., Sheila E.W. Martin; 3 s. (eldest son: Rt. Hon. David Steel, PC, MP (qv)); 2 d. Educ. St. John's Grammar School, Hamilton; Peterhead Academy; Robert Gordon's College, Aberdeen; Aberdeen University. Minister: Denbeath, Fife, 1936-41, Bridgend, Dumbarton, 1941-46; Associate Secretary, Foreign Mission Committee, Edinburgh, 1946-49; Minister, St. Andrew's, Nairobi and East Africa, 1949-57; Locum, St. Cuthbert's, Edinburgh, 1957-58; Minister, St. Michael's, Linlithgow, 1959-76; Moderator, General Assembly of the Church of Scotland, 1974-75; Visiting Preacher and Lecturer: in America, 1953-87, Lausanne, 1978, Tanzania, 1980; Vice-President: Boys' Brigade, National Bible Society of Scotland, West Lothian Historical and Amenity Society; Member, National Committee, ESU. Publications: History of St. Michael's; The Belief; Preaching through the Year. Recreations: trout fishing; travel. Address: (h.) 39 Newbattle Terrace, Edinburgh, EH10 4SF; T.-031-447 2180.

Steel, Rt. Hon. David (Martin Scott), PC (1977). MP, Tweeddale, Ettrick and Lauderdale, since 1983 (Roxburgh, Selkirk and Peebles, 1965-83); Leader, Liberal Party, 1976-88; Joint Leader, Social and Liberal Democrats, March-July 1988; b. 31.3.38, Kirkcaldy; m., Judith MacGregor; 3 s.; 1 d. Educ. Prince of Wales School, Nairobi; George Watson's College, Edinburgh; Edinburgh University. Assistant Secretary, Scottish Liberal Party, 1962-64; Interviewer, BBC TV Scotland, 1964-65; Presenter, weekly religious programme, STV, 1966-67, for Granada, 1969, for BBC, 1971-76; Liberal Chief Whip, 1970-75; Sponsor, Private Member's Bill to reform law on abortion, 1966-67; President, Anti-Apartheid Movement of Great Britain, 1966-69; Chairman, Shelter, Scotland, 1969-73; Member, British Council of Churches, 1971-75; Vice-President, Liberal International, since 1978; Rector, Edinburgh University, 1982-85; Chubb Fellow, Yale, 1987. Publications: Boost for the Borders, 1964; Out of Control, 1968; No Entry, 1969; The Liberal Way Forward, 1975; A New Political Agenda, 1976; Militant for the Reasonable Man, 1977; New Majority for a New Parliament, 1978; High Ground of Politics, 1979; A House Divided, 1980; Border Country, 1985; The Time Has Come (with David Owen), 1987; Mary Stuart's Scotland (with Judy Steel), 1987. Recreations: angling; vintage motoring. Address: (b.) House of Commons, London, SW1A 0AA; T.-01-219 3373.

Steel, Major Sir (Fiennes) William Strang, 2nd Bt, DL, JP; b. 24.7.12; m., Joan Henderson (deceased); 2 s.; 1 d. (deceased). Educ. Eton; Sandhurst. Retired Major, 17/21st Lancers; Member, Forestry Commission, 1958-73; Convener, Selkirk County Council, 1967-75. Address: (h.) Philiphaugh, Selkirk.

Steele, Alexander Allison, OBE (1986). Honorary Sheriff, Perth, since 1985; Auditor of Court, since 1971; b. 5.10.25, Oakley, Fife; m., Patricia Joyce Hipkins; 1 s.; 2 d. Educ. Boroughmuir Secondary School. Entered Scottish Home Department, 1942; Royal Navy, 1943-46; Scottish Court Service (Sheriff Clerk's Branch), 1950; Sheriff Clerk: Dingwall, 1969-71, Perth, 1971-81, Dundee, 1981-85; Member, Lord Stewart's Committee on Alternatives to Prosecution, 1977-83; Honorary Life Member, Society of Sheriff Court Auditors. Recreations: gardening; swimming; wine-making. Address: (h.) Lyndhurst, Hillend Road, Perth; T.-0738 26611.

Steele, George Thomas, MA (Hons). Rector, Johnstone High School, since 1975; b. 19.8.39, Newquay; m., Janet Mary Craig; 4 d. Educ. Hutchesons' (Boys) Grammar School; Glasgow University; Jordanhill College of Education. Teacher, Queen's Park Secondary School, 1962-65; Teacher, Hutchesons' (Boys') Grammar School, 1965-67; Principal Teacher of Classics, Whitburn Academy, 1967-71; Assistant Head Teacher, then Depute Head Teacher, Hillpark Secondary School, 1971-75. Member, Advisory Council on Misuse of Drugs to Home Office, 1977-83; Member, GGHB Liaison Committee on Alcohol and Drug Misuse, 1977-85. Recreations: DIY; reading; walking; holidays abroad. Address: (b.) Johnstone High School, Beith Road, Johnstone; T.-Johnstone 22173.

Steele, Hugh, MRSanA, MRSH, JP. Honorary Sheriff, since 1974; b. 12.8.16; m., Grace Wyllie Lawrie; 2 s. Educ. Strathaven Academy; Hamilton Academy; Royal Technical College, Glasgow. Assistant Sanitary Inspector, Lanarkshire County Council, 15 years; Depute Chief Sanitary Inspector, Sutherland County Council, 1949-60; Chief Sanitary Inspector (then Director of Environmental Health and Master of Works), Sutherland, 1960-74. Elder, Dornoch Cathedral, 26 years (latterly as Session Clerk); Member, Sutherland Presbytery; Life Member, Royal British Legion Scotland; Honorary Grand Junior Deacon, Grand Lodge of Scotland, for services to freemasonry; General Commissioner of Income Tax, since 1976; Chairman, Stafford Court Committee, Royal British Legion Housing Association Ltd. Recreations: golf; bowling; gardening; Scottish country dancing (teacher). Address: (h.) Stra'ven, Rosebery Avenue, Dornoch, Sutherland, IV25 3SZ; T.-0862 810 325.

Steele, Rev. Leslie McMillan, MA, BD (Hons). Minister, Galashiels Old Parish & St. Paul's, since 1988 (Gardner Church, Macduff, 1973-88); b. 13.12.47, Edinburgh; m., Lillias Margaret Franks; 4 d. Educ. George Heriot's, Edinburgh; Edinburgh University. Assistant Minister, St. Columba's, Largs, 1972-73; Convener, Overseas Interests Committee, Buchan Presbytery, 1980-84; Moderator, Buchan Presbytery, 1983-84. Recreation: DIY. Address: Old Parish Manse, Barr Road, Galashiels, TD1 3HX; T.-0896 2320.

Steele, Thomas Graham. Group Director of Programmes, Radio Forth, since 1978; Director, Radio Tay, since 1987; b. 11.5.45, Lanark; m., Fiona MacAuslane; 1 s.; 1 d. Educ. Larkhall Academy, Larkhall; Skerry's College, Glasgow. Lobby Correspondent, Scottish Daily Mail; TV and Radio Presenter, BBC Glasgow; Producer, BBC Local Radio; Broadcaster, Radio Clyde; Head of News and Current Affairs, Radio Forth. Member, Programming Committee, Association of Independent Radio Contractors, since 1980; Creator, Festival City Radio. Recreations: sailing; walking; reading; conversation. Address: (b.) Forth House, Forth Street, Edinburgh; T.-031-556 9255.

Steer, Christopher Richard, BSc (Hons), MB, ChB, DCH, FRCPE. Consultant Paediatrician; Clinical Tutor, Department of Child Life and Health, Edinburgh University; Hon. Senior Lecturer, Department of Child Life and Health,

Aberdeen University; Hon. Senior Lecturer, Department of Biochemistry, St. Andrews University; b. 30.5.47, Clearbrook, near Plymouth; m., Patricia Mary Lennox. Educ. St. Olaves and St. Saviours Grammar School, London; Edinburgh University. Publications: Textbook of Paediatrics (Contributor); Treatment of Neurological Disorders (Contributor). Recreation: our garden. Address: (b.) Paediatric Unit, Victoria Hospital, Kirkcaldy, Fife; T.-0592 261155.

Stein, Rev. Jock, MA, BD. Joint Warden, Carberry Tower, since 1986 (Minister, Steeple Church, Dundee, 1976-86); b. 8.11.41, Edinburgh; m., Margaret E. Munro; 3 d. Educ. Sedbergh School; Cambridge University; Edinburgh University. Work Study Officer, United Steel Companies, Sheffield; Assistant Warden, St. Ninian's Lay Training Centre, Crieff; publishing and lay training, Presbyterian Church of East Africa. Publications: Ministers for the '80s (Editor); Our One Baptism; In Christ All Things Hold Together (Co-author). Recreations: music; skiing. Address: Carberry Tower, Musselburgh, EH21 8PY.

Steiner, Mark Rudie, LLB, NP. Lawyer, Landowner and Company Director; Principal, Goodman Steiner & Co., Solicitors and Property Agents, Perthshire and Fife; Director, Falcon Hill Pty Ltd.; Member, Scottish Consumer Council; part-time Chairman, Social Security Appeal Tribunal; m., Dr. Eleanor Steiner, DPH, MFCM, MRCGP; 1 s. Educ. Aberdeen University. Editor, Canadian Broadcasting Corporation, Toronto and Montreal; Editor, Swiss Broadcasting Corporation, Berne; Procurator Fiscal in Scotland; Partner and Director of various firms and companies; Past Chairman, Perth Community Relations Council; Delegate, Scottish Council for Racial Equality; Chairman, Central Scotland Society of Conservative Lawyers. Recreations: sailing; writing; broadcasting. Address: (h.) Falcon Hill Farm, Dunning, Perthshire, PH2 0RA; T.-Dunning 300.

Stenhouse, George Alexander, DA, RIBA, ARIAS, DipTP. Director of Architectural Services, West Lothian District Council, since 1975; b. 19.3.35, Buckhaven; 1 s. Educ. Kirkcaldy High School; Edinburgh College of Art. Private practice, 1960-64; Depute Burgh Architect and Planning Officer, 1964-68, Burgh Architect and Planning Officer, 1968-75, City and Royal Burgh of Dunfermline. RIBA Archibald Dawnay Scholar; Past President, Association of Chief Architects of Scottish Local Authorities; Council Member, RIAS. Recreations: golf; gardening; travel. Address: (h.) Braehead, 29 Cromwell Road, Burntisland, Fife; T.-0592 873402.

Stenlake, Professor John Bedford, CBE, PhD, DSc, FPS, CChem, FRSC, FRSE. Honorary Professor, Strathclyde University, since 1982; Chairman, British Pharmacopoeia Commission, since 1980; Member, Medicines Commission, since 1984; b. 21.10.19, Ealing; m., Anne Beatrice Holder; 5 s.; 1 d. Educ. Ealing Grammar School; School of Pharmacy, London. Pilot, RAF, 1942-45; Demonstrator, Assistant Lecturer, Lecturer in Pharmaceutical Chemistry, School of Pharmacy, London, 1945-52; Senior Lecturer in Pharmaceutical Chemistry, Royal College of Science and Technology, Glasgow, 1952-61; Professor of Pharmacy, Strathclyde University, 1961-82. Member, Committee on Safety of Medicines, 1970-79; author of 100 papers, reviews and articles concerned with original research in medicinal chemistry. Recreations: reading; gardening. Address: (h.) Mark Corner, Twynholm, Kirkcudbright.

Stephen, David Smith, MIWM, AMITA. Director of Cleansing, City of Aberdeen District Council, since 1981; b. 7.10.32, Tannochside, Lanarkshire; m., Dorothy; 2 s. Educ. Wishaw High School; Paisley Technical College. Apprentice, Burgh of Motherwell and Wishaw, 1950-54; District Inspector: Burgh of Airdrie, 1954-55, Burgh of Coatbridge, 1956-57, Burgh of Motherwell and Wishaw, 1958-60; Area Transport and Cleansing Officer, Midlothian County Council, 1961-64; Depute Director of Cleansing, City of Aberdeen, 1964-81. Recreations: fishing; boating; shooting. Address: (b.) 38 Powis Terrace, Kittybrewster, Aberdeen, AB2 3QE; T.-0224 482221.

Stephen, Rev. Donald Murray, TD, MA, BD, ThM. Minister, Marchmont St. Giles' Parish Church, Edinburgh, since 1974; b. 1.6.36, Dundee; m., Hilda Swan Henriksen; 2 s.; 1 d. Educ. Brechin High School; Richmond Grammar School, Yorkshire; Edinburgh University; Princeton Theological Seminary. Assistant Minister, Westover Hills Presbyterian Church, Arkansas, 1962-64; Minister, Kirkoswald, 1964-74; Chaplain, TA, 1965-85 (attached to 4/5 Bn., RSF, 205 Scottish General Hospital, 2nd Bn., 52nd Lowland Volunteers); Convener, Committee on Chaplains to Her Majesty's Forces, General Assembly. Recreations: golf; curling. Address: 19 Hope Terrace, Edinburgh, EH9 2AP; T.-031-447 2834.

Stephen, Eric John. Farmer; Director, Aberdeen and Northern Marts Ltd., since 1986; Director, Aberdeen and Northern Estates Ltd., since 1987; b. 2.1.38, Turriff; 1 s.; 3 d. Educ. Inverurie Academy. Member, Scottish Agricultural Wages Board, Scottish Agricultural Training Board; Convener, Employment and Technology Committee, National Farmers Union of Scotland; Board Member, Clinterty College Council; Elder, Auchterless Parish Church, 27 years; Past President, Aberdeen and Kincardine Executive, NFU of Scotland; Director, Royal Northern Agricultural Society; Committee Member, Turriff Show. Recreation: bowling. Address: Lower Thorneybank, Rothienorman, Inverurie, AB5 8XT; T.-08884 233.

Stephen, Frank H., BA, PhD. Reader, Department of Economics, Strathclyde University, since 1986 (Senior Lecturer, 1979-86); Managing Editor, Journal of Economic Studies, since 1982; b. 20.11.46, Glasgow; m., Christine Leathard; 2 d. Educ. Queen's Park Secondary School, Glasgow; Strathclyde University. Research Officer, then Head, Economics Department, STUC, 1969-71; Lecturer, Department of Economics, Strathclyde University, 1971-79. Publications: The Performance of Labour-Managed Firms (Editor), 1982; Firms Organisation and Labour (Editor), 1984; The Economic Analysis of Producers' Cooperatives, 1984; The Economics of the Law, 1988. Address: (b.) Department of Economics, Strathclyde University, Glasgow; T.-041-552 4400.

Stephen, Professor Kenneth William, BDS, DDSc, HDDRCPS, FDSRCS. Professor of Preventive Dentistry, Glasgow University, since 1984 (Head, Department of Oral Medicine and Pathology, since 1980); Consultant-in-charge, Glasgow School of Dental Hygiene, since 1979; b. 1.10.37, Glasgow; m., Anne Seymour Gardiner; 1 s.; 1 d. Educ. Hillhead High School, Glasgow; Glasgow University. General Dental Practitioner, 1960-64; House Officer, Department of Oral Surgery, Glasgow Dental Hospital, 1964-65; Lecturer, Department of Conservative Dentistry, 1965-68, Lecturer, Department of Oral Medicine and Pathology, Glasgow University, 1968-71; Visiting Lecturer, Department of Oral Physiology, Newcastle-upon-Tyne University, 1969-70; Senior Lecturer, Department of Oral Medicine and Pathology, Glasgow University, 1971-80; Reader, 1980-84. Co-President, European Organisation for Caries Research, 1978-79. Recreations: swimming; hill-walking; skiing; gardening. Address: (b.) Dental School, 378 Sauchiehall Street, Glasgow, G2 3JZ; T.-041-332 7020.

Stephen, Nicol Ross, LLB, DipLP, NP. Solicitor, Milne, Mackinnon & Peterkins, Aberdeen, since 1983; Member, Grampian Regional Council, since 1982; b. 23.3.60, Aberdeen. Educ. Robert Gordon's College, Aberdeen; Aberdeen University; Edinburgh University. Trainee Solicitor, C. & P.H. Chalmers, Aberdeen, 1981-83. Past Chairman, Kincardine and Deeside Liberal Association; Depute Leader, Social and Liberal Democrats Group, and Chairman, Planning, Property and Development Committee, Grampian Regional Council; Member, Standing Commission on the Scottish Economy; Member, SLD Scottish Executive and Scottish Policy Committee; Liberal/SDP Alliance candidate, Kincardine and Deeside, 1987. Recreation: golf. Address: (h.) 565 Great Western Road, Aberdeen; T.-Aberdeen 30635.

Stephen, Pamela Judith, BSc (Hons), MB, ChB, MRCP. Consultant in Geriatric Medicine, Perth Royal Infirmary, since 1984; Honorary Senior Lecturer, Department of Medicine, Dundee University, since 1984; b. 29.1.51, Falkirk. Educ. Mary Erskine School for Girls, Edinburgh; Edinburgh University. Pre-registration House Officer and Senior House Officer, Edinburgh, 1975-77; Medical Registrar, Falkirk, 1977-80; Registrar in Rehabilitation Medicine, Edinburgh, 1980-81; Lecturer, Department of Geriatric Medicine, Edinburgh University, 1982-84. Recreations: classical music; theatre and the arts; gardening; travel. Address: (b.) Geriatric Unit, Perth Royal Infirmary, Perth, PH1 1NX; T.-0738 23311.

Stevenson, Rev. Andrew Lockhart, LLB, MLitt, DPA, FPEA. Parish Minister, Balmerino with Wormit, since 1984; b. 12.12.26, Beith; m., Jane Wilson Begg; 1 s.; 2 d. Educ. Spier's School, Beith; Scottish School of Physical Education, Jordanhill; London University; Aberdeen University. National Service, RAF, 1946-48; Teacher, Ayrshire, London and Glasgow, 1948-57; Principal Physical Education Teacher, Aberdeen Grammar School, 1957-66; Lecturer/Senior Lecturer (PE), Aberdeen College of Education, 1966-81. Governor, Aberdeen College of Education, 1976-81; President, Scottish Physical Education Association; Member, Aberdeen District Council, 1976-84 (Convener, Housing, Building and General Purposes Committee, 1979-80). Address: The Manse, 5 Westwater Place, Wormit, Fife, DD6 8NS; T.-Newport-on-Tay 542626.

Stevenson, David, BA, PhD. Reader in Scottish History, Aberdeen University, since 1984; Director, Centre for Scottish Studies, Aberdeen University, since 1984; b. 30.4.42, Largs; m., Wendy B. McLeod; 2 s. Educ. Gordonstoun; Dublin University; Glasgow University. Aberdeen University: Lecturer in History, 1970-80, Senior Lecturer in History, 1980-84. Honorary Secretary, Scottish History Society, 1976-84; Fellow, Royal Historical Society. Publications: The Scottish Revolution 1637-44, 1973; Revolution and Counter-Revolution in Scotland 1644-51, 1977; Alasdair MacColla and the Highland Problem in the 17th Century, 1980; Scottish Covenanters and Irish Confederates, 1981; The Government of Scotland under the Covenanters 1637-51, 1982; Scottish Texts and Calendars (with Wendy B. Stevenson), 1987; The Origins of Freemasonry, 1988; The First Freemasons: The Early Scottish Lodges and their members, 1988. Address: (b.) Department of History, Aberdeen University, Old Aberdeen, AB9 2UB.

Stevenson, David Deas, CBE, BCom, CA. Managing Director, Edinburgh Woollen Mill, since 1972; b. 28.11.31, Hawick; m., Alix Jamieson; 2 d. Educ. Langholm Academy; Dumfries Academy; Edinburgh University. British Steel Corporation, 1966-67; Langholm Dyeing Co., 1967-72. Recreations: squash; horses; running. Address: (b.) Waverley Mills, Langholm, Dumfriesshire, DG13 OEB; T.-0541 80611.

Stevenson, Gerda, DDA. Actress, Singer, Writer, Book Illustrator, Theatre Director; b. 10.4.56, West Linton; m., Aonghas MacNeacail; 1 s. Educ. Peebles High School; Royal Academy of Dramatic Art, London. Has performed with (among others) 7:84 Theatre Co., Scottish Theatre Company (most notably as Queen Anne in Jamie the Saxt), Royal Lyceum Theatre, Edinburgh; performed one-woman play, Barry, Traverse Theatre, Edinburgh; television work includes Clay, Smeddum and Greenden, Square Mile of Murder, Grey Granite, Around Scotland, The Celts, Horizon, Battered Baby (all BBC), The Old Master and Taggart (STV), The Stamp of Greatness (Channel 4); extensive radio work includes title roles in The Bride of Lammermoor and Catriona; performs regularly as singer and story teller with her sister, Savourna Stevenson; directed Uncle Jesus, Edinburgh Festival Fringe, 1987; Assistant Director, Royal Lyceum, Edinburgh, Autumn 1987. Vanbrugh Award, RADA; wrote and illustrated children's book, The Candlemaker and other stories, 1987. Recreation: walking in the country. Address: (h.) 1 Roseneath Terrace, Marchmont, Edinburgh, EH9 1JS; T.-031-229 5652.

Stevenson, James Edward Mackenzie, MA, LLB, NP. Solicitor; Honorary Sheriff Substitute, South Strathclyde, Dumfries and Galloway, at Dumfries; b. 9.11.19, Lockerbie; m., Maureen Mary; 2 s.; 2 d. Educ. Lockerbie Academy; George Watson's Boys College; Edinburgh University. Captain, 131st Field Regiment, RA, Second World War; Partner, McJerrow & Stevenson, Solicitors, Lockerbie; Town Clerk and Chamberlain: Burgh of Lochmaben, 1949-75, Burgh of Lockerbie, 1957-75. Director, South of Scotland Ice Rink, Lockerbie; Clerk, Annan Fishery Board; Clerk, Lockerbie Branch, Earl Haig Fund. Recreations: golf; curling. Address: (h.) Fairfield, St. Brydes Terrace, Lockerbie, Dumfriesshire.

Stevenson, Rev. John, MA (Hons). Rector, Moffat Academy, since 1976; b. 13.12.39, Stewarton; m., Jane Dawson Alexander; 2 s.; 1 d. Educ. Stewarton Higher Grade School; Glasgow University; Jordanhill College of Education. Teacher: Stewarton High School, Kilmarnock Academy, Onthank Junior Secondary School, Grange Academy (Kilmarnock), Largs Academy. Ordained non-stipendiary Deacon, Scottish Episcopal Church, 1987. Address: (h.) Hoppertitty, Beattock, Moffat, Dumfries, DG10 9PJ; T.-06833 337.

Stevenson, John Meikle, BSc, FInstD, FBIM. Farmer; Vice Chairman, Forth River Purification Board, 1982-85; Vice Chairman, Royal Scottish Agricultural Benevolent Institution, since 1982; b. 20.1.31, Aberlady; m., Eileen A.; 2 s.; 1 d. Educ. Trinity College, Glenalmond; Aberdeen University. Councillor, East Lothian County Council, 1961-66; President, East Lothian, National Farmers' Union, 1968-69; Council Member, NFU, 1966-70; Member, Governing Body, British Society for Research in Agricultural Engineering, since 1968; Committee Member, Scottish Institute of Agricultural Engineering, since 1968 (Chairman, since 1984). Recreations: shooting; fishing; gardening; golf. Address: Luffness Mains, Aberlady, East Lothian, EH32 OPZ; T.-Aberlady 212.

Stevenson, John S.K., MB, ChB, FRCGP, D(Obst)RCOG. Senior Lecturer, Department of General Practice, Edinburgh University, since 1968; b. 28.8.29, West Kilbride; m., Helen L. Howes; 3 s.; 1 d. Educ. Ayr Academy; Glasgow University. Principal, general practice, Stevenston, Ayrshire, 1958-68; Member, NHS Executive Council for Ayrshire, 1963-68; Member, Edinburgh and District Council on Alcoholism, 1969-73; Honorary Treasurer, Association of University Teachers of General Practice, 1972-81; Member, BBC Scotland Medical Advisory Group, 1976-84; BBC Scotland Radio Doctor, 1976-78; Member, Biomedical Research Committee, Chief Scientist Organisation, SHHD, 1983-85; Medical Officer, George Heriot's FP Rugby Football Club. Recreations: reading; writing; theatre; travel; holiday golf. Address: (b.) Department of General Practice, Levinson House, 20 West Richmond Street, Edinburgh, EH8 9DX; T.-031-667 1011.

Stevenson, Leslie Forster, MA, BPhil. Reader in Logic and Metaphysics, St. Andrews University, since 1977; b. 15.12.43, Bridgnorth; m., Zinaida Lewczuk. Educ. Friends' School, Lisburn; Campbell College, Belfast; Corpus Christi College, Oxford. Lecturer in Logic and Metaphysics, St. Andrews University, 1968-77. Publications: Seven Theories of Human Nature, 1974; The Metaphysics of Experience, 1982. Recreations: bassoon-playing; hill-walking. Address: (h.) 6 Abbotsford Place, St. Andrews, Fife, KY16 9HQ; T.-0334 74745.

Stevenson, Paul, BSc (Econ). Managing Director, Northsound Radio, since 1986; b. 8.9.46, Tamworth, Staffs; m., Susan Carol; 2 s. Educ. The Regis School, Tettenhall; University College, Cardiff. Advertising Manager, Aberdeen Journals, 1984-86. Director, Scottish and Irish Radio Sales Ltd. Recreations: walking; shooting. Address: (b.) 45 King's Gate, Aberdeen; T.-Aberdeen 632234.

Stevenson, Peter David, MA (Cantab). Chairman, Stevenson Trust Limited, since 1988; b. 6.3.47, Edinburgh; m., Susan Blades; 1 s.; 1 d. Educ. Edinburgh Academy; Trinity College, Cambridge. Non-Executive Director, William Low PLC. Address: (b.) 25 Alva Street, Edinburgh, EH2 4PS; T.-031-557 0900.

Stevenson, Robert Orr, BA, FCIS. Secretary, Scottish Special Housing Association, since 1983; b. 27.4.33, Glasgow; m., Anne. Educ. Trinity College, Glenalmond; Christ's College, Cambridge. Beaverbrook Newspapers Ltd.: General Manager, Sunday Express; General Manager, Daily Express; Group General Manager, Scotland; Director and General Manager, Felixstowe Dock and Railway Company (Chief Executive, Port of Felixstowe); Managing Director, A.M. Tweedie & Co. Ltd. Recreations: golf; opera. Address: (h.) Muirlea, Gifford, East Lothian; T.-Gifford 586.

Stevenson, Ronald, FRMCM. Composer and Pianist; Broadcaster; Author; b. 6.3.28, Blackburn; m., Marjorie Spedding; 1 s.; 2 d. Educ. Royal Manchester College of Music; Conservatorio Di Santa Cecilia, Rome. Senior Lecturer, Cape Town University, 1963-65; BBC Prom debut in own 2nd Piano Concerto, 1972; Aldeburgh Festival recital with Sir Peter Pears, 1973; Busoni documentary, BBC TV, 1974; BBC Radio Scotland extended series on the bagpipe, clarsach and fiddle music of Scotland, 1980-84; Artist in Residence: Melbourne University, 1980, University of W. Australia, 1982, Conservatory of Shanghai, 1985; published and recorded compositions: Passacaglia for Piano, two Piano Concertos, Violin Concerto (commissioned by Menuhin), Prelude, Fugue and Fantasy for Piano, Prelude and Fugue for Organ. Publication: Western Music. Recreations: hill-walking; reading poetry, biographies and politics. Address: (h.) Townfoot House, West Linton, Peeblesshire; T.-0968 60511.

Stevenson, Ronald Harley, MA, LLB. Chief Executive, Highland Regional Council, since 1981; b. 6.1.34, Dunfermline. Educ. Dunfermline High School; Edinburgh University. County Clerk,

Caithness County Council, 1967-75; Joint Director of Law and Administration, Highland Regional Council, 1975-81. Address: (b.) Regional Buildings, Inverness; T.-Inverness 234121.

Stevenson, Sir Simpson, LLD. Provost, Inverclyde District Council, 1984-88; Chairman, Scottish Health Services Common Services Agency, 1983-87; b. 18.8.21, Greenock; m., Jean Holmes Henry. Educ. Greenock High School. Provost of Greenock, 1962-65; Chairman, Western Regional Hospital Board, 1967-73; Chairman, Greater Glasgow Health Board, 1973-83; knighted, 1976; Hon. LLD, Glasgow University, 1982; Member, Royal Commission on NHS, 1976-79. Address: (h.) The Gables, Reservoir Road, Gourock; T.-0475 31774.

Stevenson, Struan John Stirton, JP. Leader of the Administration, Kyle & Carrick District Council, 1986-88 (Chairman, Policy and Resources Committee, 1986-88); Chairman, Conservative Group, COSLA, since 1986; Chairman, Carrick, Cumnock and Doon Valley Conservative Constituency Association, since 1982; Farmer and Director, J. & R. Stevenson Ltd., Ballantrae; b. 4.4.48, Ballantrae; m., Pat; 2 s. Educ. Strathallan; West of Scotland Agricultural College (Diploma in Agriculture). Elected, Girvan District Council, 1971-75; elected, Kyle and Carrick District Council, 1974; Convener, Leisure and Recreation, 1977-80; Convener, Miscellaneous Services Committee, COSLA, 1977-80; Vice Chairman, South Ayrshire Conservative Constituency Association, 1981-82; Vice Chairman, Ayrshire Justices Committee, since 1984; Member, Kyle and Carrick District Licensing Board, 1984-86; Member, Ayrshire and Burns Country Tourist Board; Curator, MacLaurin Trust; Director, Richard Demarco Gallery Ltd., Edinburgh, 1982-87; Member, BBC Agricultural Advisory Committee (Broadcasting Council), since 1984; Member, Institute of Advanced Motorists, since 1981. Recreations: contemporary art collector; photography. Address: (h.) Balig House, Ballantrae, Girvan, KA26 OJY; T.-046583 214.

Stevenson, William Trevor, CBE, DL, FCIT. Chairman, Alex. Wilkie Ltd., since 1977; b. 21.3.21, Peebles; m., Alison Wilson Roy. Educ. Edinburgh Academy. Apprentice Engineer, 1937-41; Engineer, 1941-45; entered family food manufacturing business, Cottage Rusks, 1945; Managing Director, 1948-54; Chairman, 1954-59; Chief Executive, Cottage Rusks Associates, 1965-69; Regional Director, Ranks Hovis McDougall, 1969-74; Director, various companies in food, engineering, hotel and aviation industries, since 1974; founder Chairman, Gleneagles Hotels, 1981-83; Chairman, Scottish Transport Group, 1981-86; Chairman, Hodgson Martin Ventures Ltd., 1982-87; Master, Company of Merchants of City of Edinburgh, 1978-80; Vice President, Edinburgh Chamber of Commerce, 1983-87. Recreations: flying; sailing; curling. Address: (h.) 45 Pentland View, Edinburgh, EH10 6PY; T.-031-445 1512.

Stewardson, Raymond Richard, BA (Hons). Rector, John Neilson High School, Paisley, since 1983; b. 26.9.37, Huyton, Merseyside; m., Aileen Agnes Mackie; 1 s.; 1 d. Educ. Prescot Grammar School; Sheffield University; London University (External). Assistant Teacher; Principal Teacher of Geography; Assistant Head Teacher; Depute Rector. Recreations: swimming; gardening. Address: (b.) John Neilson High School, Paisley, PA1 2QZ; T.-041-889 9451/2.

Stewart, A.J. (Ada F. Kay). Playwright and Author; b. 5.3.29, Tottington, Lancashire. Educ. Grammar School, Fleetwood. ATS Scottish Command; first produced play, 1951; repertory actress, 1952-54; BBC TV Staff Writer/Editor/Adaptor, Central Script Section, 1956-59; returned to Scotland, 1959, as stage and TV writer; winner, BBC New Radio Play competition, 1956; The Man from Thermopylae, presented in Festival of Contemporary Drama, Rheydt, West Germany, 1959, as part of Edinburgh International Festival, 1965, and at Masquers' Theatre, Hollywood, 1972; first recipient, Wendy Wood Memorial Grant, 1982; Polish Gold Cross for achievements in literary field. Publications: Falcon - The Autobiography of His Grace, James the 4, King of Scots, 1970; Died 1513-Born 1929 - The Autobiography of A.J. Stewart, 1978; The Man from Thermopylae, 1981. Recreation: work. Address: 15 Oxford Street, Edinburgh, 8.

Stewart, Alan Aitken. Solicitor; Sole Partner, Curdie & Smith, since 1963; Senior Partner, Curdie Sturrock & Co., since 1983; Clerk, C.K. Marr Educational Trust, since 1970; Honorary Sheriff, Kilmarnock, since 1979; b. 25.1.34, Prestwick; m., Joy; 2 s.; 1 d. Educ. Prestwick High School; Ayr Academy; Glasgow University. Qualified in Law, 1955; Solicitor, 1956; Junior Partner, Curdie & Smith, 1958; Dean, Kilmarnock Faculty of Solicitors, 1978-80; founder Secretary, Kilmarnock and North Ayrshire Junior Chamber of Commerce (President, 1964); Secretary, Federation of Scottish Junior Chamber of Commerce, 1965 (President, 1966); Vice President, Junior Chamber of Commerce International, 1967; Captain, Kilmarnock (Barassie) Golf Club, 1977. Recreations: golf; swimming; snooker. Address: (b.) 1 Howard Street, Kilmarnock; T.-0563 25118.

Stewart, Alasdair Duncan, CA. Financial Director, North of Scotland Hydro-Electric Board, since 1975; b. 24.2.33, Perth; m., Audrey Jean Lind Stewart; 3 s. Educ. Perth Academy. J. & R. Morison & Co., Perth, 1950-59; Stewarts & Lloyds Ltd., Birmingham and Glasgow, 1959-67; P-E Consulting Group, 1967-72; joined North of Scotland Hydro-Electric Board, 1972. Recreation: sailing. Address: (b.) 16 Rothesay Terrace, Edinburgh, EH3 7SE; T.-031-225 1361.

Stewart, Sheriff Alastair Lindsay, BA (Oxon), LLB(Edin). Sheriff of Grampian, Highland and Islands at Aberdeen and Stonehaven, since 1979; b. 28.11.38, Aberdeen; m., Annabel Claire Stewart; 2 s. Educ. Edinburgh Academy; St. Edmund Hall, Oxford; Edinburgh University. Admitted to Faculty of Advocates, 1963; Tutor, Faculty of Law, Edinburgh University, 1963-73; Standing Junior Counsel to the Registrar of Restrictive Trading Agreements, 1968-70; Advocate Depute, 1970-73; Sheriff of Lanarkshire (later South Strathclyde, Dumfries and Galloway) at Airdrie, 1973-79; Hon. Lecturer, Faculty of Law, Aberdeen University, since 1981. Governor, Robert

Gordon's Institute of Technology, since 1982 (Vice Chairman of Governors, 1985-88); Past Chairman, now Hon. President, Grampian Family Conciliation Service; Chairman, Scottish Association of Family Conciliation Services, since 1986; President, North East Wind, since 1986. Publication: Sheriff Court Practice (Contributor), 1988. Recreations: music; reading. Address: (b.) Sheriff's Chambers, Sheriff Court House, Aberdeen, AB9 1AP; T.-0224 572780.

Stewart, Alexander Donald, BA, LLB, WS. Solicitor in private practice in Glasgow, since 1961; Director, Clyde Cablevision Limited, since 1982; Director, Scottish Amicable Life Assurance Society, since 1985; b. 18.6.33, Edinburgh; m., Virginia Mary Washington; 1 s.; 5 d. Educ. Wellington College, Berkshire; Oxford University; Edinburgh University. Hon. Consul for Thailand in Scotland. Recreations: music; skiing; field sports; curling. Address: (h.) Ardvorlich, Lochearnhead, Perthshire; T.-05673 218.

Stewart, Alexander Reavell Macdonald, FRICS, FRVA, ACIArb. Chartered Surveyor; Chairman, Scottish Branch, Royal Institution of Chartered Surveyors, 1985-86; b. 14.2.29, Bearsden; m., Keris Duguid Keir; 2 s.; 2 d. Educ. Merchiston Castle School. President: Property Owners and Factors Association Glasgow, 1968-69, National Federation of Property Owners Scotland, 1978-80. Recreations: trout fishing; piping. Address: (b.) 145 North Street, Glasgow; T.-041-221 9191.

Stewart, Andy. Entertainer; Song Writer; b. 30.12.33, Glasgow; m., Sheila Newbigging; 1 s.: 5 d. Educ. Craigie School, Perth; Arbroath High School. Numerous theatre seasons and concert tours in UK and USA, Canada, Australia, New Zealand, South Africa; toured with White Heather Club; Hogmanay shows for BBC TV, Scottish Television and Grampian Television; TV specials including Andy Stewart Show and White Heather Club; 13 Sauchie Street series (radio); wrote the song A Scottish Soldier, and other ballads and monologues. Recreations: golf; reading; watching old films.

Stewart, Archibald Ian Balfour, CBE, BL (Dist), FSA (Scot). Retired Solicitor; Honorary Sheriff; b. 19.5.15, Campbeltown; m., Ailsa Rosamund Mary Massey; 3 s. Educ. Cheltenham College; Glasgow University. Solicitor, 1938; Town Clerk, Lochgilphead, 1939-46, Campbeltown, 1947-54; Procurator Fiscal of Argyll at Campbeltown, 1941-74; Temporary Sheriff, 1975-88; Secretary, Clyde Fishermen's Association, 1941-74; Churchill Fellow, 1966; President, Scottish Fishermen's Federation, 1970-75; Former Director, Scottish Fishermen's Organisation and Scottish Board, Phoenix Insurance Co. Ltd.; Past President, Kintyre Antiquarian Society; Past Chairman, Argyll and Bute National Insurance Committee, Kintyre Employment Committee; Adviser, North East Atlantic Fisheries Conference, UN Law of Sea Conference. Recreations: local history; genealogy; wine; gardening; idling. Address: (h.) Askomel End, Campbeltown, Argyll, PA28 6EP; T.-0586 52353.

Stewart, Clement A., MA, MEd. Rector, Portlethen Academy, since 1986; b. 9.1.41, Strichen. Educ. Aberdeen Grammar School; Aberdeen University. Teacher of Mathematics, Aberdeen Grammar School, 1963-70; Dunoon Grammar School: Principal Teacher of Mathematics, 1970-72, Assistant Rector, 1972-74, Depute Rector, 1974-77; Head Teacher, Lochgilphead High School, 1977-86. Address: (h.) Kilmory, 12 Martin Avenue, Stonehaven, Kincardineshire, AB3 2LZ; T.-0569 63852.

Stewart, David Roger, TD, MA, BA (Hons), FEIS. Honorary Sheriff, Selkirk, since 1983; b. 3.2.20, Glasgow; m., Gwyneth Ruth Morris; 2 s.; 1 d. Educ. Hyndland Secondary School; Glasgow High School; Glasgow University; London University. Army, 1939-46; Schoolmaster, 1947-65 (Kelvinside Academy, Galashiels Academy); Rector, Selkirk High School, 1965-81; Member: Selkirk Town Council, 1967-75, Borders Education Committee, 1975-81, Borders Regional Council, 1982-86; TA, 1939-64; Member, Borders Local Health Council; Chairman, Selkirk Committee, Cancer Research Campaign. Recreations: golf; caravanning; gardening. Address: (h.) Cairncoed, Hillside Terrace, Selkirk, TD7 4ND; T.-0750 21755.

Stewart, Rt. Hon. Donald James, PC. MP (Scottish National Party), Western Isles, 1970-87; b. 17.10.20, Stornoway; m., Christina MacAulay. Educ. Nicolson Institute, Stornoway. Town and County Councillor, 1951-70; Provost of Stornoway, 1958-64 and 1968-70; Honorary Sheriff. Recreations: photography; fishing; gardening. Address: (h.) Hillcrest, 41 Goathill Road, Stornoway; T.-0851 2672.

Stewart, Douglas Fleming, MA, LLB, WS, NP, FSA Scot. Solicitor (Scotland), Crown Estate Commissioners, since 1970; Partner, J.F. Anderson, WS, since 1961; Secretary, Stewart Society, 1968-87; b. 22.5.27, Sydney, Australia; m., Catherine Coleman; 2 d. Educ. George Watson's College, Edinburgh; Edinburgh University. RAF, 1945-48; Session Clerk, Braid Church, Edinburgh, since 1979; Treasurer, Friends of the Royal Scottish Museum, since 1972; Council Member, Royal Celtic Society, since 1981. Recreation: swimming. Address: (b.) 48 Castle Street, Edinburgh, EH2 3LX; T.-031-225 3912.

Stewart, Ena Lamont. Playwright; b. 10.2.12, Glasgow; m., Jack Stewart (deceased); 1 s. Educ. Woodside School, Glasgow; Esdaile School, Edinburgh. Assistant, Public Library, Aberdeen, 1930-34; Medical Secretary, Radcliffe, Lancashire, 1934-37; Secretary/Receptionist, Royal Hospital for Sick Children, Glasgow, 1937-41; Baillie's Reference Library, Glasgow: Assistant Librarian, 1953-57, Librarian-in-charge, 1957-66; author of plays: Starched Aprons, Men Should Weep, The Heir to Ardmally, Business in Edinburgh, After Tomorrow (unperformed), Walkies Time, Knocking on the Wall, Towards Evening, High Places. Recreations: reading; listening to music. Address: (h.) 5a Monkton Road, Prestwick, KA9 1AP; T.-0292 76355.

Stewart, Sheriff Ewen, BSc (Agr), MA (Econ), LLB. Sheriff at Wick, since 1962, and at Dornoch and Tain, since 1977; b. 22.4.26; m., 1 d. Educ. Edinburgh University. Practised, Scottish Bar, 1952-62; Lecturer on Agricultural Law, Edinburgh University, 1957-62.

Stewart, Francis John, MA (Oxon), LLB, TD. Writer to the Signet (retired); Director, American Trust plc; Member, Queen's Bodyguard for Scotland (Royal Company of Archers); b. 11.5.17, Edinburgh; m., Olga Margaret Mounsey; 3 s.; 1 d. Educ. Cargilfield School, Edinburgh; Loretto School; Trinity College, Oxford; Edinburgh University. 1st Bn., Lothians and Borders Yeomanry; Senior Partner, Murray Beith & Murray, WS, Edinburgh (retired); Past Chairman of Governors, Loretto School; Honorary Consul for Principality of Monaco, 1964-85; Chevalier of the Order of St. Charles. Recreation: gardening. Address: (b.) 39 Castle Street, Edinburgh; T.-031-225 1200.

Stewart, Sir Frederick Henry, KB, BSc, PhD, FRSA, DSc Hon. (Aberdeen, Leicester, Heriot-Watt, Durham, Glasgow), FRS, FRSE, FGS. Professor Emeritus, Edinburgh University, since 1982; Trustee, British Museum (Natural History), 1983-88; Council Member, Scottish Marine Biological Association, since 1983; b. 16.1.16, Aberdeen; m., Mary Florence Elinor Rainbow. Educ. Fettes College, Edinburgh; Robert Gordon's College, Aberdeen; Aberdeen University; Emmanuel College, Cambridge. Mineralogist, Research Department, Imperial Chemical Industries, 1941-43; Lecturer in Geology, Durham University, 1943-56; Regius Professor of Geology and Mineralogy, Edinburgh University, 1956-82; Member, Council for Scientific Policy, 1967-71 (Assessor, 1971-73); Chairman, Natural Environment Research Council, 1971-73; Chairman, Advisory Board for the Research Councils, 1974-79; Member, Advisory Council for Research and Development, 1976-79; University Grants Committee Earth Sciences Review, 1986-87. Lyell Fund Award, 1951 and Lyell Medal, 1970, Geological Society of London; Mineralogical Society of America Award, 1952; Clough Medal, Edinburgh Geological Society; Sorby Medal, Yorkshire Geological Society. Publications: The British Caledonides, 1963; Marine Evaporites, 1963. Recreations: fishing; collecting fossil fish. Address: (h.) 79 Morningside Park, Edinburgh, EH10 5EZ; T.-031-447 2620; House of Letterawe, Lochawe, Argyll, PA33 1AH; T.-083-82 329.

Stewart, Professor George, BSc, PhD, CEng, MIChemE, MAIME. Professor of Petroleum Engineering, Heriot-Watt University, since 1981; Director, Edinburgh Petroleum Development Services, since 1984; b. 4.5.40, Edinburgh; 2 s. Educ. George Heriot's School, Edinburgh; Edinburgh University. Process Engineer, Esso Refinery, Fawley, 1962-63; Assistant Lecturer in Chemical Engineering, Newcastle University, 1963-67; Lecturer in Chemical Engineering, then Senior Lecturer, Heriot-Watt University, 1967-78; Visiting Professor, Texas University, 1976; Senior Reservoir Engineer, Services Techniques Schlumberger, Paris, 1978-81. Recreations: squash; golf; tennis; sailing. Address: (b.) Department of Petroleum Engineering, Heriot-Watt University, Riccarton, Edinburgh, EH14 4AS; T.-031-449 5111, Ext. 2331.

Stewart, George Girdwood, CB, MC, TD, BSc, FICFor, Hon. FLI. Regional Representative for Central and Tayside, National Trust for Scotland, since 1984; Cairngorm Estate Adviser to Highlands and Islands Development Board, since 1988; Chairman, Scottish Wildlife Trust, 1981-87; Member, Countryside Commission for Scotland, 1981-88; Member, Environment Panel, British Railways Board, since 1980; Member, Cairngorm Recreation Trust, since 1986; b. 12.12.19, Glasgow; m., Shelagh Jean Morven Murray; 1 s.; 1 d. Educ. Kelvinside Academy, Glasgow; Glasgow University; Edinburgh University. Royal Artillery, 1940-46 (mentioned in Despatches); Forestry Commission: District Officer, 1949-60, Assistant Conservator, 1960-67, Conservator (Glasgow), 1967-69, Commissioner, Forest and Estate Management, 1969-79. Commanding Officer, 278 (Lowland) Field Regiment RA (TA), 1956-59; President, Scottish Ski Club, 1971-75; Vice President, National Ski Federation of Great Britain, 1975-78; Fellow, Royal Society of Arts. Recreations: skiing; tennis; studying Scottish painting. Address: (h.) Branklyn House, Dundee Road, Perth, PH2 7BB; T.-0738 25535.

Stewart, George Munro, IPFA, FRVA. Director of Finance, Argyll and Bute District Council, since 1975; b. 9.6.29, Keith; m., Margaret Morag; 1 s.; 1 d. Educ. Dingwall Academy. Senior Finance Assistant, Ross and Cromarty County Council, 1947-60; Assistant County Treasurer, Caithness County Council, 1960-65; Town Chamberlain and Housing Manager, Wick Town Council, 1965-67; Town Chamberlain and Collector, Dunoon Town Council, 1967-75. Recreations: golf; gardening; bridge. Address: (b.) Kilmory, Lochgilphead, Argyll; T.-0546 2127.

Stewart, Ian William. Governor, Dundee College of Technology, since 1985; b. 24.3.23, Edinburgh; m., Jane Alison Cunningham; 2 s. Educ. Merchiston Castle School. Pilot, RAF, 1941-46; William Low & Co., PLC, 1946-88 (Managing Director, 1959-83, Deputy Chairman, 1983-88); President, Dundee and Tayside Chamber of Commerce and Industry, 1984-85; Board Member, SCOTVEC, 1985-88. Recreations: golf; gardening. Address: (h.) Greenbank, Barry, Carnoustie, Angus; T.-0241 53043.

Stewart, James Blythe, MA, LLB. Advocate; Senior Lecturer in Law, Heriot-Watt University, since 1976; b. 22.4.43, Methil. Educ. Buckhaven High School; Edinburgh University. Research Assistant, Faculty of Law, St. Andrews University, 1966-67; Assistant Lecturer in Law, then Lecturer, Heriot-Watt University, 1967-76. Recreations: bowls; golf; football spectating. Address: (h.) 3 Comely Bank Terrace, Edinburgh, EH4 1AT; T.-031-332 8228.

Stewart, Rev. James Charles, MA, BD, STM. Minister, Kirk of St. Nicholas, Aberdeen, since 1980; b. 29.3.33, Glasgow. Educ. Glasgow Academy; St. Andrews University; Union Theological Seminary, New York. Assistant Minister, St. John's Kirk of Perth, 1969-74; Minister: St. Andrew's Church, Drumchapel, 1964-74, East Church of St. Nicholas, Aberdeen, 1974-80; Secretary, General Assembly's Committee on Public Worship and Aids to Devotion, 1976-82; Chairman, Aberdeen Civic Society, 1979-81. Address: (h.) 48 Gray Street, Aberdeen; T.-0224 34056.

Stewart, Very Rev. James Stuart, MA, BD, DD. Minister, Church of Scotland, since 1924; Professor Emeritus, Edinburgh University, since 1966;

b. 21.7.96, Dundee; m., Rosamund Anne Barron; 2 s. Educ. Dundee High School; St. Andrews University; University of Bonn on the Rhine. Minister: St. Andrews Church, Auchterarder, 1924-28, Beechgrove Church, Aberdeen, 1928-35, North Morningside Church, Edinburgh, 1935-46; Professor of New Testament, Edinburgh University (New College), 1946-66. Chaplain to the Queen in Scotland; author of ten books on religious themes. Recreation: walking. Address: (h.) St. Raphael's Home, 6 Blackford Avenue, Edinburgh, EH9 2LB.

Stewart, John Allan. MP (Conservative), Eastwood, since 1983 (East Renfrewshire, 1979-83); b. 1.6.42, St. Andrews; m., Susie Gourlay; 1 s.; 1 d. Educ. Bell Baxter High School, Cupar; St. Andrews University; Harvard University. Lecturer in Political Economy, St. Andrews University, 1965-70; Confederation of British Industry: Head, Regional Development Department, 1971, Deputy Director (Economics), 1973, Scottish Secretary, 1976, Scottish Director, 1978; Under Secretary of State, Scottish Office, 1981-86. Recreations: bridge; reading. Address: (b.) House of Commons, London, SW1A OAA; T.-01-219 5110.

Stewart, John Barry Bingham, OBE, BA, CA. Chairman, Martin Currie Ltd.; b. 21.2.31, Edinburgh; m., Ailsa Margaret Crawford. Educ. The Leys School, Cambridge; Magdalene College, Cambridge. Accountancy training, Edinburgh; worked in London, United States and Canada; joined Martin Currie, 1960; Independent Member, Scottish Agricultural Wages Board; Member, Scottish Tourist Board. Recreations: fishing; shooting; golf; skiing. Address: 18 Hope Terrace, Edinburgh, EH9 2AR; T.-031-447 1626.

Stewart, John Stanley, MA, LLB. Solicitor in private practice, since 1952; b. 10.11.25, Glasgow; m., 1, Dr. Marianne F. Stewart; 3 s.; 1 d.; 2, Edna W. Smith. Educ. Bellahouston Academy, Glasgow; Glasgow University. Partner: John W. Stewart & Son, until 1962, Thorburn & Paterson, 1962-70, Paterson Holms & Co., Glasgow, since 1970; also part-time Assistant Lecturer in Commercial/Business Law, Glasgow University, 1962-78 (thereafter part-time Lecturer). Honorary Secretary, Scottish Mountaineering Club, 1958-66; Touring Convener, Scottish Ski Club, 1978-80. Recreations: mountaineering; skiing; sea canoeing; gardening; choral singing. Address: (b.) 113 West Regent Street, Glasgow, G2 2RX; T.-041-248 5341.

Stewart, Kathleen Margaret, MA, LLB, WS, NP. Partner, McGrigor Donald, Solicitors, Edinburgh and Glasgow, since 1988 (Partner, Balfour & Manson, Solicitors, Edinburgh, 1983-87); b. St. Andrews. Educ. Bell Baxter High School, Cupar; St. Andrews University; Sweet Briar College, USA; Edinburgh University. Assistant Lawyer (Corporate Department) in London firm of commercial lawyers, 1975-79, and Scottish firms of commercial lawyers, 1980-83. Committee Member, Edinburgh Committee, Institute of Directors; Member, Company Law Panel, CBI; Committee Member, Business Committee, St. Andrews University; Member, Edinburgh/Stirling Finance and Investment Seminar; Member, EEC Sub-Committee, Company Law Committee, Law Society of Scotland; Director, Edinburgh Chamber of Commerce. Recreations: horse riding; tennis; squash; bad bridge. Address: (b.) 68 Queen Street, Edinburgh; T.-031-225 9221.

Stewart, Louis K., MBE (1964). Senior Deer Officer, Red Deer Commission, since 1960; b. 26.3.29, Ross-shire; m., Margaret S. McPhee; 2 s.; 2 d. Educ. Dingwall Academy. National Service, Royal Artillery, 1947-48; Stalker: Lochiel Estates, 1948-54, Nature Conservancy, 1954-60. President: Scottish Clay Pigeon Association, 1981-83, Inverness Shinty Club, 1981-83. Recreations: clay pigeon shooting (international); curling; fishing. Address: (h.) 22 Laggan Road, Inverness, IV2 4EH; T.-0463 232478.

Stewart, Rev. Norma Drummond, MA, MEd, DipTh, BD. Minister, Strathbungo Queen's Park Church, Glasgow, since 1979; b. 20.5.36, Glasgow. Educ. Hyndland Secondary School, Glasgow; Glasgow University; Bible Training Institute, Glasgow; Trinity College, Glasgow. Teacher, Garrioch Secondary School, Glasgow, 1958-62; Missionary, Overseas Missionary Fellowship, West Malaysia, 1965-74; ordained to ministry, Church of Scotland, 1977. Selection School Assessor; Convener, Education for the Ministry Committee, Glasgow Presbytery; Member, Church of Scotland Panel on Doctrine; occasional Lecturer in Old Testament, Glasgow University, since 1977. Recreation: research in Old Testament studies. Address: 5 Newark Drive, Glasgow, G41 4QJ; T.-041-423 4818.

Stewart, Norman MacLeod, BL, SSC. President, Law Society of Scotland, 1985-86; Senior Partner, Allan, Black & McCaskie, Solicitors, Elgin, since 1984; b. 2.12.34, Lossiemouth; m., Mary Slater Campbell; 4 d. Educ. Elgin Academy; Edinburgh University. Training and Legal Assistant, Alex. Morison & Co., WS, Edinburgh, 1954-58; Legal Assistant: McLeod, Solicitor, Portsoy, 1958-59, Allan, Black & McCaskie, Solicitors, Elgin, 1959-61 (Partner, 1961); Council Member, Law Society of Scotland, 1976-87 (Convener, Public Relations Committee, 1979-81, and Professional Practice Committee, 1981-84). Past President, Elgin Rotary Club; Past Chairman, Moray Crime Prevention Panel; Member, Committee, Police Dependants' Trust (Grampian). Recreations: walking; golf; music; Spanish culture. Address: (h.) Argyll Lodge, Lossiemouth, Moray; T.-034381 3150.

Stewart, Patrick Loudon Mclain, LLB, WS, DL. Senior Partner, Stewart Balfour & Sutherland, Solicitors, since 1982; Secretary, Clyde Fishermen's Association, since 1970; b. 25.7.45, Campbeltown; m., Mary Anne McLellan; 1 s.; 1 d. Educ. Edinburgh Academy; Edinburgh University. Partner, Stewart Balfour & Sutherland, Campbeltown, 1970; former Executive Member, Scottish Fishermen's Federation, and Director, Scottish Fishermen's Organisation Ltd.; member of many Scottish fishing industry committees. Commanding Officer, Campbeltown Unit, Sea Cadet Corps; Member, Sea Cadet Council; Cadet Forces Medal. Recreations: sailing; shooting; youth work. Address: Craigadam, Campbeltown, Argyll, PA28 6EP; T.-0586 52161.

Stewart, Peter Duns, MD, FRCPath, DL. Deputy Lieutenant, Dunbartonshire, since 1973; b. 11.7.15, Oban; m., Doreen M. King; 2 d. Educ. Oban High School; Edinburgh University. Service in RAMC (Regular) - general duties, then Pathologist, 1937-59; Consultant Pathologist, Vale of Leven District General Hospital, 1959-80; Member, Argyll and Clyde Health Board, 1975-83; Territorial Army, 1960-67; Army Cadet Force, 1968-77; Medical Officer, Dunbartonshire BRCS, 1967-80, County Director, 1980-83. Recreation: fishing. Address: (h.) Burnside House, 38 Campbell Street, Helensburgh; T.-Helensburgh 2612.

Stewart, Richard, CBE (1976), JP, Hon. LLD (Strathclyde). Leader, Strathclyde Regional Council, 1974-86; b. 27.5.20, Harthill; m., Elizabeth Peat; 1 d. Educ. Harthill School. Member, Lanark County Council, 15 years; full-time Secretary/Organiser, Labour Party, until 1983; Agent for Rt. Hon. Margaret Herbison, MP, 20 years; Agent, Rt. Hon. John Smith, 1970-83; Member, Board of Directors, Scottish Transport Group, since 1975; President, COSLA, 1984-86; Past Chairman, Scottish Council of Labour Party; Member, Board of Directors, Scottish Exhibition Centre, 1982-86. Recreations: music; chess. Address: (h.) 28 Hawthorn Drive, Harthill, Shotts, Lanarkshire, ML7 5SG; T.-0501 51303.

Stewart, Robert Armstrong, BA, DipTP, FRTPI. Director of Physical Planning and Development, Moray District Council, since 1979; b. Stirling. Planning Assistant, Lanark County Council, 1968-69; Planner, Glasgow, 1969-70; Senior Assistant, then Group Leader: Development Control, West Lothian County, 1970-75; Depute Director: Planning, East Lothian District, 1975-79. Address: (b.) District Headquarters, High Street, Elgin; T.-Elgin 45121.

Stewart, Rev. Robert James, MA, BD, STM. Minister, Bothwell, since 1977; b. 8.7.32, Aberdeen; m., Janette Grier; 1 s.; 1 d. Educ. George Watson's Boys' College, Edinburgh; Edinburgh University; St. Andrews University; Union Theological Seminary, New York. First Minister, new Parish of St. Mark's, Wishaw, 1960-67; Minister, Comrie and Strowan, 1967-77. Recreations: reading; hill-walking; playing the piano. Address: The Manse, Bothwell, Glasgow, G71 8PQ; T.-0698 853189.

Stewart, Robin Reith Wittet, MA, DSA, FHSM. General Manager, Highland Health Board, since 1985 (Secretary, 1974-84); Member, Hospital Committee, EEC, 1980-88; b. 11.8.35, Cambridge; m., Sara Sutherland; 2 d. Educ. George Watson's College, Edinburgh; Edinburgh University; Cambridge University; Manchester University. Depute Secretary and Treasurer, Glasgow Royal Infirmary, 1963-70; Secretary, Northern Regional Hospital Board, 1970-74. Church of Scotland Elder; former President, Inverness and District Choral Society; Past Chairman, Scottish Division, Institute of Health Service Management; former Treasurer, Inverness District Sports Council. Recreations: choral singing; golf; watching rugby. Address: (h.) 20 Crown Avenue, Inverness, IV2 3NF; T.-0463 236493.

Stewart, Ronald Somerville. Head, Food Standards Branch, Department of Agriculture and Fisheries for Scotland, since 1982; b. 6.1.30, Sydney; m., Gwendolene Rita Newton; 2 s. Educ. Harris Academy; Carlisle Grammar School. Joined Scottish Office, 1950; Head of Branch in following Divisions: Prisons, Housing, Town and Country Planning. Address: (b.) Department of Agriculture and Fisheries for Scotland, Chesser House, Gorgie Road, Edinburgh.

Stewart, Professor William Duncan Paterson, BSc, PhD, DSc, FRSE, FRS, FIBiol. Boyd-Baxter Professor of Biology, Dundee University, since 1968 (Vice-Principal, 1985-87); b. 7.6.35, Glasgow; m., Catherine Macleod; 1 s. Educ. Dunoon Grammar School; Glasgow University. Assistant Lecturer, Nottingham University, 1961-63; Lecturer, Westfield College, London University, 1963-68; Visiting Research Worker, Wisconsin University, 1966 and 1968; Visiting Professor, Kuwait University, 1980 and Otago University, New Zealand, 1984. Chairman: Royal Society Biological Education Committee, 1977-80, Royal Society Study Group on the Nitrogen Cycle, 1979-84, Independent Advisory Group on Gruinard Island, since 1986; Trustee, Estuarine and Brackish Water Sciences Association, since 1978; Chairman, International Committee on Microbial Ecology, 1983-87; Council Member, Royal Society, NERC, AFRC, Scottish Marine Biological Association, Marine Biological Association of UK, Freshwater Biological Association, Lenihan Committee, Royal Society Study Group on Science Education. Address: (h.) 45 Fairfield Road, Broughty Ferry, Dundee; T.-0382 76702.

Stewart, William F., MA, DipEd, BA (Hons). Rector, Belmont Academy, Ayr, since 1975; b. 25.1.33, Dreghorn; m., Marion McMillan; 3 d. Educ. Irvine Royal Academy; Glasgow University. Irvine Royal Academy: Teacher (Maths), Special Assistant Teacher (Maths), Principal Assistant (Maths), Principal Teacher (Maths), Depute Rector. Member, National Council, Headteachers Association of Scotland (Convener, Examinations Committee); Headteacher Representative, Ayr College Council; Executive Member, Kyle and Carrick Sports Council. Recreation: golf. Address: (b.) Belmont Academy, Belmont Road, Ayr; T.-0292 281733.

Stewart, Rev. William Thompson, BD, DPS. Minister, Glasford linked with Strathaven East, since 1980; Chairman, Strathaven and District Council of Churches, since 1985; b. 12.4.53, Glasgow; m., Sheila Ann Alison; 1 s. Educ. Shawlands Academy; Glasgow University. Assistant Minister, Rutherglen Stonehouse Parish Church, 1978-79. Address: Westdene, 68 Townhead Street, Strathaven, Lanarkshire, ML10 6BC; T.-Strathaven 21138.

Stewart-Fitzroy, Captain William Wentworth. Honorary Sheriff, Sutherland; b. 28.9.07, Romford, Essex; m., Patricia Grant (deceased); 3 s.; 1 d. Served, Second World War and in Korea; Captain, Royal Navy (retired); Past President, Stewart Society. Recreations: sailing; hill-walking; collector of rocks and minerals. Address: (h.) Nordhvall, Dornoch, Sutherland, IV25 3QN; T.-Dornoch 810584.

Stewart-Tull, Duncan Eric Stewart, BA, MA, PhD. Senior Lecturer in Microbiology, Glasgow University, since 1976; b. 27.6.37, London; m., Ann Virginia Dumbrell; 1 s.; 1 d. Educ. Tiffin School, Kingston-upon-Thames; Trinity College, Dublin; London Hospital Medical College; Glasgow University. Research Assistant, London Hospital, 1962-63; Assistant Lecturer in Bacteriology, then Lecturer, Glasgow University, 1963-76; Royal Society Visiting Professor, Osaka University Dental School, Japan, 1972-73; Visiting Scientist to Institute Pasteur, Paris, 1981. Vice Chairman, Bishopbriggs and Chryston School Council, 1976-78; Chairman, School Attendance Panel, 1975; Secretary, Strathkelvin Queen's Silver Jubilee Committee, 1977-80; President, Bishopbriggs Ratepayers Association, 1980-82; Convener, Scottish Branch, Society for General Microbiology, 1980-84 (Publications Officer of the Society, since 1985). Recreations: renovating an old house; simply being alive. Address: (b.) Department of Microbiology, Glasgow University, Alexander Stone Building, Garscube Estate, Bearsden, Glasgow; T.-041-339 8855.

Stiff, John Barry, GradIFireE. Firemaster, Dumfries and Galloway Fire Brigade, since 1984; b. 17.5.43, Sunderland; m., Catherine Ann; 2 s.; 1 d. Educ. Sunderland County Borough Boys' Technical School. Joined Sunderland Fire Brigade, 1964; South Western Area Fire Brigade, Scotland, 1972; Dumfries and Galloway, 1975. Recreations: cars; caravanning; fishing; outdoor pursuits. Address: Dumfries and Galloway Fire Brigade Headquarters, Brooms Road, Dumfries, DG1 2DZ; T.-0387 52222.

Still, Ronald McKinnon, MB, ChB, FRCOG. Consultant Obstetrician and Gynaecologist, since 1967; Honorary Clinical Lecturer, Glasgow University, since 1967; b. 20.3.32, Helensburgh; 1 s.; 2 d. Educ. Hermitage School, Helensburgh; Glasgow University. House Surgeon/House Physician, Royal Infirmary, Glasgow, 1956-57; Captain, RAMC, seconded Malaya Military Forces, 1957-60; Registrar, Queen Mother's Hospital/Stobhill General Hospital, Glasgow; Senior Registrar, Glasgow Teaching Hospitals. Recreations: golf; music. Address: (h.) 7/3 Whistlefield Court, 2 Canniesburn Road, Bearsden, Glasgow, G61; T.-041-942 3097.

Still, Rev. William. Minister, Gilcomston South Church, Aberdeen, since 1945; Chairman, Trustees, Rutherford House Study Centre, since 1981; b. 8.5.11, Aberdeen. Educ. Aberdeen University and Christ's College. Fish worker in family business; Teacher of music, pianoforte, singing, choral work; Cadet, Salvation Army College, London; Assistant Minister, Springburnhill Parish Church, Glasgow. President, Inter-Varsity Fellowship, 1975-76; President, local University Christian Union, on several occasions. Recreations: walking; music; gardening; art; architecture. Address: 18 Beaconsfield Place, Aberdeen; T.-Aberdeen 644037.

Stimson, Professor William Howard, BSc, PhD, CBiol, FIBiol, FRSE. Professor of Immunology and Head, Immunology Division, Strathclyde University, since 1981; Research Director/Executive Director, May and Baker Diagnostics Ltd., Glasgow; b. 2.11.43, Liverpool; m., Jean Scott Baird; 1 s.; 1 d. Educ. Prince of Wales School, Nairobi; St. Andrews University. Research Fellow, Department of Obstetrics and Gynaecology, Dundee University, 1970-72; Lecturer, then Senior Lecturer, Biochemistry Department, Strathclyde University, 1973-80. Patron, Scottish Motor Neurone Disease Association; holder, Glasgow Loving Cup, 1982-83; Member, Editorial Boards, four scientific journals. Recreations: mechanical engineering; walking. Address: (b.) Immunology Division, Strathclyde University, 31 Taylor Street, Glasgow, G4 ONR; T.-041-552 4400, Ext. 3729.

Stirling, George Scott, MB, ChB, FRCPGlas, FRCPsych, DPM. Former Medical Administrator, Crichton Royal Hospital, Dumfries; b. 20.4.26, Aberdeen; m., Yvonne; 1 s.; 1 d. Educ. Robert Gordon's College, Aberdeen; Aberdeen University. House Physician, Royal Cornhill Hospital, Aberdeen; Medical Branch, RAF; House Physician, Woodend General Hospital, Aberdeen; Fellow in Psychiatry, Crichton Royal, Dumfries; Independent Visiting Psychiatrist to Board of Management, State Hospital, Carstairs; Past Chairman, Forensic Section, Scottish Division, Royal College of Psychiatrists (Member, Executive Committee, Scottish Division); Fellow on Council, Royal College of Psychiatrists, London. Member, National Panel of Specialists; Member, Scottish Committee of Hospital Specialists; Member, Parole Board for Scotland; Council of Europe Travelling Fellow; former Vice-Chairman, SASD (Dumfries). Recreations: fishing; shooting; curling; gardening. Address: (h.) Phyllis Park, Murraythwaite, Dalton, Lockberie, DG11 1DW.

Stirling of Garden, Lt.-Col. James, CBE, TD, FRICS. Lord Lieutenant of Stirling and Falkirk, since 1983; b. 8.9.30; m.; 2 s.; 2 d. Educ. Rugby; Trinity College, Cambridge. Partner, K. Ryden & Partners, Chartered Surveyors, since 1962.

Stirling, Joe. Editor, Scottish Field, since 1988; b. 19.9.35, Glasgow. Educ. Shawlands Academy. Publisher, 1952-59; Advertising Agent, 1959-70; Fine Arts Consultant, 1970-81; Freelance Journalist, 1981-86; Deputy Editor, Scottish Field, 1987. Past President, Glasgow Press Club. Address: (h.) Dalnair Lodge, Croftamie, by Drymen, G63 0EZ.

Stirling, Kenneth W., MA (Hons). Rector, Dalziel High School, Motherwell, since 1978; b. 19.12.26, Aberdeen. Educ. Robert Gordon's College, Aberdeen; Aberdeen University. RAF, 1945-48. Principal Teacher of Modern Languages: Turriff Academy, 1959-62, Beath High School, Cowdenbeath, 1962-72; Assistant Head Teacher, then Depute Rector, Grove Academy, Dundee, 1972-78. Address: (h.) 1 Lower Joppa, Edinburgh, EH15 2ER; T.-031-669 5806.

Stirling, William Norman, IPFA, DPA, FCIT. Scottish Manager, Cipfa Services Ltd., since 1986; b. 26.2.36, Glasgow; m., Edith; 1 s.; 3 d. Educ. Hamilton Academy; Glasgow College of Commerce; Glasgow University. Lanark County Council, 1953-58; Midlothian County Council, 1958-59; Clydebank Town Council, 1959-61; Motherwell and Wishaw Town Council, 1961-73 (Town Chamberlain and Collector of Rates, Local Taxation Officer and Manager, Municipal Bank, 1970-73); Director, Strathclyde Passenger Transport Executive, 1973-86. Director, National Transport Tokens Ltd.; Past Chairman, Scottish Branch, CIPFA. Recreations: golf; Robert Burns. Address: (h.) and (b.) 10 Crawfurd Gardens, High Burnside, Glasgow, G73 4JP; T.-041-634 2728.

Stirling of Fairburn, Roderick William Kenneth, TD, JP. Lord Lieutenant, Ross and Cromarty and Skye and Lochalsh, since 1988; Landowner and Estate Manager; Vice-Chairman, Red Deer Commission (Member, since 1964); Chairman, Highland Region Valuation Appeal Committee, since 1983; Chairman, Scottish Salmon and White Fish Co. Ltd., since 1980; b. 17.6.32; m., Penelope Jane Wright; 4 d. Educ. Wellesley House; Harrow; Aberdeen University. National Service, Scots Guards, 1950-52 (commissioned, 1951); TA service, Seaforth and Queen's Own Highlanders, 1953-69 (retired with rank of Captain); Member, Regional Advisory Committee to Forestry Commission, 1964-85; Local Director, Eagle Star Insurance Co., 1966-85; Director, Moray Firth Salmon Fishing Co. Ltd.; Member, Highland River Purification Board, since 1975; Ross and Cromarty County Councillor, 1970-74 (Chairman of Highways, 1973-74); Member, Ross and Cromarty District Council, since 1984; Chairman, Highland Committee, NPFA (appointed to Scottish Council, 1971); Member, Highland Committee, Scottish Landowners Federation (Chairman, 1974-79). Recreations: wild life management; gardening; curling. Address: (h.) Arcan, Muir of Ord, Ross-shire; T.-Urray 207.

Stirling-Hamilton, Sir Bruce, 13th Bt; b. 5.8.40; m., Stephanie Campbell; 1 s.; 2 d. Educ. Nautical College, Pangbourne; Sandhurst. Commissioned, Queen's Own Highlanders (Seaforth and Camerons), 1961; Captain, 1967; resigned commission, 1971; Management Consultant. Address: (h.) 16 Bath Place, Ayr, KA7 1DP.

Stiven, Frederic William Binning, ARSA, MCSD, DA. Constructivist, Designer and Teacher; Head of Design, Grays School of Art, Aberdeen, 1982-87; b. 25.4.29, Cowdenbeath; m., Jenny Paton; 2 s.; 2 d. Trained Edinburgh College of Art. Constructivist work in numerous public and private collections; exhibited in Edinburgh, Glasgow, Leeds, London, Bergen, Helsinki, Venice and New York; freelance Designer; Royal Scottish Academy Gillies Award, 1985. Address: (h.) Sheallagan, Golf Course Road, Rosemount, Blairgowrie, Perthshire; T.-0250 4863.

Stobo, James, OBE, DL, FRAgS. Farmer; President, Animal Diseases Research Association, since 1980; Chairman of Governors, Longridge Towers School, since 1982; Chairman, Scottish Seed Potato Development Council, since 1988; b. 9.12.34, Lanark; m., Pamela Elizabeth Mary Herriot; 1 s.; 2 d. Educ. Edinburgh Academy. Farming, since 1951; Past Chairman and President, Scottish Association of Young Farmers Clubs; Member, Home-Grown Cereals Authority, 1971-76; President, National Farmers' Union of Scotland, 1973-74; Director, John Hogarth Ltd., Kelso Mills; Member, Secretary of State for Scotland's Panel of Agricultural Arbiters. Vice-President: Scottish National Fat Stock Club, Royal Smithfield Club; Deputy Lieutenant, County of Berwick, 1987. Recreations: game shooting; photography. Address: Fishwick, Berwick-upon-Tweed, TD15 1XO; T.-0289 86224.

Stockdale, Elizabeth Joan Noel, MB, ChB, DMRD, FRCR. Consultant Radiologist, Royal Aberdeen Children's Hospital and Aberdeen Royal Infirmary, since 1980; Clinical Senior Lecturer, Aberdeen University, since 1980; b. Chippenham; m., Christopher Leo Stockdale; 2 s.; 1 d. Educ. Aberdeen University. House Surgeon, Aberdeen Royal Infirmary; Senior House Surgeon, Professorial Surgical Unit, Hospital for Sick Children, Great Ormond Street; Registrar, St. George's Hospital; Senior Registrar, Royal National Orthopaedic Hospital, Royal Marsden Hospital, Atkinson Morley's Hospital. Recreations: theatre; classical music; travel. Address: (h.) 1 Grant Road, Banchory, Kincardineshire, AB3 3UW; T.-03302 3096.

Stockwell, Professor Robert, BSc, MB, BS, PhD. Professor of Anatomy, Edinburgh University, since 1981; b. 26.6.33, Hertford; m., Jill Fyfield; 2 s.; 1 d. Educ. Christ's Hospital; London University. Military Service, Royal Corps of Signals, 1951-53; House Surgeon, St. Thomas's Hospital, London, 1960-61; Lecturer in Anatomy, St. Thomas's Hospital Medical School, 1961-67; Senior Lecturer and Reader in Anatomy, Edinburgh University, 1967-81; Editor, Journal of Anatomy, 1983-86. Publication: Biology of Cartilage Cells. Recreations: music; history; carpentry. Address: (b.) Department of Anatomy, University Medical School, Teviot Place, Edinburgh, EH8 9AG; T.-031-667 1011.

Stodart of Leaston, Rt. Hon. Lord (James Anthony Stodart), PC (1974); b. 6.6.16, Exeter; m., Hazel Usher. Educ. Wellington. MP (Conservative), Edinburgh West, 1959-74; Joint Under Secretary of State, Scottish Office, 1963-64; Parliamentary Secretary, later Minister of State, Ministry of Agriculture, Fisheries and Food, 1970-74; Chairman: Agricultural Credit Corporation Ltd., 1975-87, Committee of Enquiry into Local Government in Scotland, 1980, Manpower Review of Veterinary Profession in UK, 1984-85. Publication: Land of Abundance: a study of Scottish agriculture in the 20th century. Recreations: music; golf; preserving a sense of humour. Addresses: Lorimers, North Berwick; Leaston, Humbie, East Lothian.

Stone, Professor Frederick Hope, MB, ChB, FRCP, FRCPsych. Professor of Child and Adolescent Psychiatry, Glasgow University, 1977-86; Consultant Psychiatrist, Royal Hospital for Sick Children, Glasgow, since 1954; b. 11.9.21, Glasgow; m., Zelda Elston, MA; 2 s.; 1 d. Educ. Hillhead High School, Glasgow; Glasgow University.

Acting Director, Lasker Mental Hygiene Clinic, Hadassah, Jerusalem, 1952-54; World Health Organisation Visiting Consultant, 1960, 1964; Member, Kilbrandon Committee, 1963-65; Secretary-General, International Association of Child Psychiatry, 1962-66; Member, Houghton Committee on Adoption, 1968-72; Chairman, Scottish Division, Royal College of Psychiatrists, 1981-84; Chairman, Child Guidance Trust, since 1985; Chairman, Children's Panel Advisory Committee, since 1988. Publication: Child Psychiatry for Students (Co-author). Address: (h.) 14A Hamilton Avenue, Pollokshields, Glasgow, G41 4JF; T.-041-427 0115.

Stone, Sheriff Marcus, MA, LLB. Sheriff of Lothian and Borders, at Linlithgow, since 1984; b. 22.3.21, Glasgow; m., Jacqueline Barnoin; 3 s.; 2 d. Educ. High School of Glasgow; Glasgow University. Served Second World War; admitted Solicitor, 1949; admitted Faculty of Advocates, 1965; Sheriff of North Strathclyde, at Dumbarton, 1971-76; Sheriff of Glasgow and Strathkelvin, at Glasgow, 1976-84. Publications: Proof of Fact in Criminal Trials, 1984; Cross-examination in Criminal Trials, 1988. Recreations: swimming; music. Address: (b.) Sheriff Court House, Court Square, Linlithgow, EH49 7EQ; T.-Linlithgow 684 2922.

Storey, Gerald Francis, BSc, CEng, FICE, FIHT. Consulting Engineer; former Assistant Chief Engineer, Scottish Development Department; b. 14.5.27, Edinburgh; m., Marjorie Purves; 1 s.; 1 d. Educ. George Heriot's School; Edinburgh University. Argyll County Council; Air Ministry Works Directorate; Macartney Ltd., Contractors; Department of Agriculture and Fisheries; Ministry (now Department) of Transport; seconded to Scottish Office, since 1962. Past Chairman, Scottish Branch, Institution of Highways and Transport; former Member, Road Engineering Board, Institution of Civil Engineers. Recreations: golf; motoring. Address: (h.) Cruivan, 7 Lodgehill Park, Nairn, IV12 4SA; T.-0667 53120.

Stormonth Darling, Sir Jamie Carlisle, Kt, CBE, MC, TD, WS, LLB, MA, Hon. FRIAS, DUniv (Stirling), Hon. LLD (Aberdeen). Chairman, Edinburgh Old Town Trust, since 1987; President, Scottish Conservation Projects Trust, since 1983; Trustee: Pollok Trust (Glasgow) and Holy Rood Brewery Foundation; b. 18.7.18, Battle, Sussex; m., Mary Finella Gammell, BEM, DL; 1 s.; 2 d. Educ. Winchester College; Christ Church, Oxford; Edinburgh University. 2nd Lt., KSOB (Territorial), 1937: Adjutant, 1941, to Lt.-Col. Commanding 52nd (L) Division; Reconnaissance Regiment, RAC, 1945-46; studied law, Edinburgh University, 1946-49; appointed Chief Executive as Secretary, then Director, National Trust for Scotland, 1949-83, then Vice-President (Emeritus). Concerned with various Scottish charities such as Scottish Churches Architectural Heritage Trust, Scotland's Gardens Scheme. Recreations: gardening; walking; golf. Address: (h.) Chapelhill House, Dirleton, North Berwick, EH39 5HG; T.-062 085 296.

Stormonth Darling, Mary Finella, BEM, DL. Chairman, New Generation Housing Association, since 1987; b. 15.4.24, Farnborough; m., Sir Jamie Carlisle Stormonth Darling, qv; 1 s.; 2 d. Educ. Southover Manor School, Lewes; Architectural Association, London. Designed own house, 1974; Elder, Dirleton Kirk and Convener, Fabric Committee, since 1976; Member, Church and Nation Committee, Church of Scotland, 1978-86; Convener, Sub-Committee on International Interests, 1982-84; Member, British Council of Churches, 1980-83; voluntary and charitable work. Recreations: painting and gardening. Address: Chapelhill House, Dirleton, North Berwick, EH39 5HG; T.-062 085 296.

Storrar, George Alexander, MC, BSc, JP. Farmer; Honorary Sheriff; b. 17.9.18, Collessie, Fife; m., Leila Barrie Orchison; 1 s.; 2 d. Educ. Perth Academy; Edinburgh University. Army, 1939-46: Fife and Forfar Yeomanry and Royal Tank Regiment - Major; France, 1940, NW Europe, 1944-46; mentioned in Despatches (2). Trustee, Cupar Savings Bank; Director, Scottish Plant Breeding Station; Member, Fife Valuation Appeal Court. Address: (h.) Halhill, Leckiebank Road, Auchtermuchty, Fife; T.-Auchtermuchty 603.

Stother, Ian G., MA, MB, BChir, FRCSEdin, FRCSGlas. Consultant Orthopaedic Surgeon, Glasgow Royal Infirmary and Nuffield McAlpin Clinic, Glasgow, since 1978; b. Lytham; m., Jacqueline; 2 d. Educ. King Edward VII School, Lytham; Kings College, Cambridge; St. George's Hospital Medical School, London. Honorary Clinical Lecturer, Glasgow University; Honorary Lecturer, Bioengineering Unit, Strathclyde University; Examiner, Royal College of Physicians and Surgeons of Glasgow; Orthopaedic Adviser, Dance School of Scotland and Scottish Ballet. Recreations: classic cars; golf. Address: (h.) 13 Moncrieff Avenue, Lenzie, Glasgow; T.-041-776 5330.

Stott, Rt. Hon. Lord (George Gordon Stott), PC (1964), QC (Scot), MA, LLD, DipEd; b. 22.12.09; m., Nancy Braggins; 1 s.; 1 d. Educ. Edinburgh Academy; Edinburgh University. Advocate, 1936; QC (Scot), 1950; Advocate Depute, 1947-51; Sheriff of Roxburgh, Berwick and Selkirk, 1961-64; Lord Advocate, 1964-67; Senator of the College of Justice, 1967-85. Editor, Edinburgh Clarion. Recreations: Mozart; reading; keeping a diary. Address: (h.) 12 Midmar Gardens, Edinburgh; T.-031-447 4251.

Stout, George Alexander, MA (Hons). Company Director; b. 9.11.27, Dundee; m., Dorothy Smith; 1 s.; 3 d. Educ. Morgan Academy, Dundee; Edinburgh University. Director: Fleming Claverhouse Investment Trust PLC, since 1977, Advent Technology p.l.c., since 1981, Advent Capital Limited, since 1985; Adviser, Joseph Johnston & Sons Ltd., since 1987; Honorary Lecturer, Dundee University. Recreations: golf; curling; gardening; photography; music; travel. Address: (h.) Uplands, Victoria Street, Monifieth, DD5 4HP.

Stoward, Peter John, MA, MSc, DPhil, FInstBiol, DipRMS, FRSE. Reader in Histology (Head, Department of Anatomy and Physiology), Dundee University; b. 27.1.35, Birmingham; m., Barbara Essex Lewis (deceased); 1 d. Educ. King Edward's School, Birmingham; Oriel College, Oxford. Assistant Lecturer, University of Aston in Birmingham, 1958-61; Research Assistant,

Department of Human Anatomy, Oxford University, 1961-63 and 1965-67; International Research Fellow, National Institutes of Health, Bethesda, Maryland, 1964, 1965; Lecturer, Nuffield Department of Orthopaedic Surgery, Oxford University, 1967-68; Senior Lecturer in Anatomy, Dundee University, 1968-75; Visiting Professor, Pavia University, Italy, since 1980; Editor, Histochemical Journal, since 1967. Diocesan Reader, Scottish Episcopal Church. Publications: Histochemistry: The Widening Horizons (Co-author), 1981; Histochemistry of Secretary Processes (Co-author), 1977. Recreations: sailing; walking; reading. Address: (b.) Department of Anatomy and Physiology, The University, Dundee, DD1 4HN; T.-0382 23181.

Strachan, Daniel, OBE, CStJ, KCT, AMM. A Vice-President, St. Andrew's Ambulance Association, and Honorary Corps Commissioner; b. 12.2.17, Greenock; m., Elizabeth Leighton; 1 s.; 1 d. Educ. Greenock High School; Herd's College. Director General, St. Andrew's Ambulance Association, 1959-83; awarded Certificate and Australian Medal of Merit, 1977, in recognition of service to Association; Member, Joint Revision Committee, First Aid Manual; an Honorary Vice-President, West Lowland Area and Greenock Boys' Brigade Batallions. Address: (h.) Whitehill House, 79 Octavia Terrace, Greenock, PA16 7PX; T.-Gourock 35406.

Strachan, Graham Robert, CBE (1977), DL, FEng, FIMechE, FIMarE. Director, Scott Lithgow Ltd., since 1984; b. 1.11.31; m., Catherine Nicol Liston; 2 s. Educ. Trinity College, Glenalmond; Trinity College, Cambridge. Apprentice Engineer, 1950-55; National Service, RNVR, 1955-57; John Brown & Co. (Clydebank) Ltd., 1957-63; John Brown Engineering Ltd.: Director and General Manager, 1966, Managing Director, 1968, Group Managing Director, 1975, Deputy Chairman, 1983-84; Director: British Smelter Constructions Ltd., 1968-73, CJB Offshore Ltd., 1975-80, John Brown & Co. (Overseas) 1976-84; Chairman: JBE Offshore Ltd., 1976-81, JBE Gas Turbines, 1976-84, Stephens of Linthouse Ltd., 1982-84. Member: CBI Oil Steering Group, 1975-79, Executive Committee, Scottish Engineering Employers' Association, 1966-82; Vice-President, Scottish Council (Development and Industry), since 1983; Member, Council, Institution of Engineers and Shipbuilders in Scotland, since 1985; Director, Glasgow Chamber of Commerce, since 1978; Member, Court, Strathclyde University, 1979-83. Recreations: skiing; golf; early jazz. Address: (h.) The Mill House, Strathblane, Stirlingshire; T.-Blanefield 70220.

Strachan, James Gerrit, BSc, MB, ChB, MPhil, MRCPsych. Consultant Psychiatrist, Royal Edinburgh Hospital, since 1981; Honorary Senior Lecturer, Edinburgh University, since 1981; b. Dublin. Educ. Latymer Upper School, London; Edinburgh University. Registrar and Senior Registrar, Royal Edinburgh and Associated Hospitals; Lecturer, Utrecht University; Forensic Psychatrist, Pieter Baan Centrum, Utrecht. Address: (b.) Royal Edinburgh Hospital, Morningside Place, Edinburgh, EH10 5HF; T.-031-447 2011.

Strachan, John, JP, MA, LLB. Senior Partner, Davidson & Garden, Advocates, Aberdeen, since 1969; Director, William Wilson Holdings Ltd., since 1979; Director, Osprey Communications P.L.C., since 1982; Chairman, Hunter Construction (Aberdeen) Ltd., since 1987; b. 9.8.29, Fraserburgh; m., Margaret Cheyne; 1 s.; 2 d. Educ. Fraserburgh Academy; Aberdeen University. National Service, 1954-56 (Sub Lt., RNVR); Partner, Davidson & Garden, Advocates, 1958. Recreations: shooting; fishing. Address: (h.) 64 Forest Road, Aberdeen, AB2 4BL; T.-0224 313906.

Strang, Gavin Steel, BSc (Hons), DipAgriSci, PhD. MP (Labour), East Edinburgh, since 1970; Labour Spokesperson on Employment; b. 10.7.43, Dundee; m., Bettina Smith; 1 s. Educ. Morrison's Academy, Crieff; Edinburgh University. Parliamentary Under Secretary of State, Department of Energy, February to October, 1974; Parliamentary Secretary, Ministry of Agriculture, 1974-79. Recreations: golf; swimming; the countryside. Address: (h.) 80 Argyle Crescent, Edinburgh, EH15 2QD; T.-031-669 5999.

Strang Steel, Malcolm Graham, BA (Cantab), LLB, WS. Partner, W. & J. Burness, WS, since 1973; Member, Council, Law Society of Scotland, since 1984; b. 24.11.46, Selkirk; m., Margaret Philippa Scott; 1 s.; 1 d. Educ. Eton; Trinity College, Cambridge; Edinburgh University. Sometime Chairman, Albyn Housing Society Ltd. Recreations: shooting; fishing; skiing; tennis; reading. Address: (b.) 16 Hope Street, Edinburgh, EH24 4DD; T.-031-226 2561.

Straton, Timothy Duncan, TD, CA, ATII. Partner, Scott-Moncrieff Thomson & Shiells, CA, since 1969; Treasurer, Scottish Society for the Prevention of Cruelty to Animals, since 1985; b. 1.10.42, Edinburgh; m., Gladys Margaret George; 1 s.; 1 d. Educ. Edinburgh Academy. Commissioned as TA Officer, Royal Signals, 1963; transferred to Royal Army Pay Corps, TA, 1973; Unit Paymaster, 32 (Scottish) Signal Regiment (V). Recreations: driving; photography; golf. Address: (b.) 17 Melville Street, Edinburgh, EH3 7PH; T.-031-226 6281.

Street, Margaret Dobson. Vice-Chairman, Saltire Society, since 1984; b. 18.10.20, Hawick; m., Richard Andrew Rutherford Street (deceased); 2 s. Educ. Hawick High School; Alva Academy. Civil Servant, 1938-48; Ministry of Labour and National Service, 1938-47; Ministry of National Insurance (Inspectorate), 1947-48; voluntary work since 1948, apart from freelance writing on household and conservation topics; Honorary Secretary (Past Chairman), Leith Civic Trust; Convener, Friends of North Carr Lightship; Saltire Society Representative, Council, National Trust for Scotland; Secretary, Mungo Park Conservation Committee; Trustee, Robert Hurd Memorial Fund. Recreations: promotion of Scottish cultural activity; conservation; good cooking. Address: (h.) 115 Trinity Road, Edinburgh; T.-031-552 2409.

Stuart, Iain Macnaughton, MA (Hons), DipEd. Depute Chief Executive, Strathclyde Regional Council, since 1981; b. 18.6.34, Alexandria; m.,

Fiona Elizabeth; 2 s.; 1 d. Educ. Morrison's Academy, Crieff; Glasgow University; McGill University. Teacher in Canada, 1957-58; District Officer, N. Rhodesia, 1958-64; Jordanhill College, 1964-65; Teacher, Glasgow Academy, 1965-67; Depute Director of Education, Glasgow Corporation, 1967-73; Education Planner, World Bank, Jamaica, 1973-75; Policy Planning, Strathclyde Regional Council, 1975-81. Recreations: art; running; hill-walking; skiing; sailing; golf. Address: (b.) Strathclyde House, India Street, Glasgow; T.-041-227 3367.

Stuart, William Forbes, BSc, DIC, PhD, FRAS. Head, Geomagnetism Research Group, British Geological Survey; b. 10.11.36, Glasgow; m., Margaret Edith; 2 s. Educ. Queen's Park School, Glasgow; Glasgow University; Royal School of Mines. Research Assistant, Imperial College; Senior Research Fellow, Meteorological Office; Research Geophysicist, British Geological Survey. Recreations: boating; fishing; golf; gardening; jogging; the company of young people. Address: (h.) Anston, St. Ninians Avenue, Linlithgow, EH49 7BP; T.-050-684 2009.

Stuart-Smith, Deryk Aubrey, BSc, MD, FRCPGlas, FRCPEdin. Senior Lecturer, Department of Medicine, Glasgow University, since 1970; Consultant Physician, Western Infirmary, Glasgow, since 1970 (Director, Bone Metabolism Research Unit, since 1971); b. 12.4.27, Simla, India; m., Anne Bennoch; 1 s.; 3 d. Educ. Bishop Cotton School; Glasgow University. Publication: Diagnostic Procedures in Disorders of Calcium Metabolism. Recreations: gardening; theatre; science fiction; science fact. Address: (h.) 30 Dolphin Road, Maxwell Park, Glasgow, G41 4DZ; T.-041-423 2430.

Sturgeon, David, BL. Registrar and Deputy Secretary, Heriot-Watt University, since 1967; b. 10.12.35, Kilwinning; m., Nancy McDougall; 2 s.; 1 d. Educ. Dalry High School, Ayrshire; Glasgow University. National Service (RASC - War Office), 1957-59; Trainee Actuary, Scottish Widows Fund, 1959-61; Administrative Assistant, Royal College of Science and Technology (later, Strathclyde University), 1961-67. Secretary and Treasurer, Edinburgh Society of Glasgow University Graduates, since 1971. Recreations: golf; music (particularly Scottish country dance music). Address: (h.) 10 Dalhousie Road, Eskbank, Midlothian, EH22 3AS; T.-031-663 1059.

Sturrock, Alexander Muir, MBE, TD, Croix de Guere, WS, NP, BA (Oxon); b. 21.9.13, Edinburgh; m., Mary Percival Walsh; 1 s.; 2 d. Educ. Edinburgh Academy; Exeter College, Oxford; Edinburgh University. Commissioned, 1939, KOSB posted 6 KOSB; served in Europe until 1945; Adjutant, 6 KOSB, DAA and QMG, 44 (Lowland) Brigade, DAAG 15 (Scottish) Division; rejoined 4 KOSB (TA), 1947; Burgh Prosecutor, Royal Burgh of Jedburgh; Clerk, Jedburgh District Council; Clerk, River Tweed Commissioners, 1950-82. Recreations: (used to be!) rugby; tennis; golf; shooting; fishing. Address: (h.) Elm Bank, Jedburgh, TD8 6QF; T.-0835 62400.

Sturrock, George McLeish Thomson, MA (Hons). Depute Rector, Menzieshill High School, Dundee, since 1986; Vice-President, Scottish Secondary Teachers' Association, since 1987; Member, Consultative Committee on the Curriculum, since 1987; b. 18.11.51, Dundee; m., Julia Mary; 1 s.; 1 d. Educ. Morgan Academy, Dundee; Jordanhill College. History Teacher, Menzieshill High, 1974-81; Principal Teacher of History, Morgan Academy, 1981-84; Assistant Rector (Curriculum), Perth Grammar School, 1984-86. Chairman, Morgan School Council, 1983-84, Menzieshill School Council, since 1987. Recreations: family; DIY; sport. Address: 9 Panmure Terrace, Dundee, DD3 6HP; T.-Dundee 25107.

Sturrock, Robert Ralph, MB, ChB, DSc. Reader in Anatomy, Dundee University, since 1981; b. 1.7.43, Dundee; m., Norma Duncan; 1 d. Educ. Dundee High School; St. Andrews University. House Surgeon, Perth Royal Infirmary, 1967-68; House Physician, Stirling Royal Infirmary, 1968; Demonstrator, then Lecturer, Anatomy Department, Dundee University, 1968-77; Visiting Associate Professor of Neuroanatomy, Iowa University, 1976; Senior Lecturer, Dundee, 1977-81. Symington Memorial Prize in Anatomy, 1978. Recreations: reading; running; swimming; hill-walking. Address: (h.) 6 Albany Terrace, Dundee; T.-0382 23578.

Subak-Sharpe, Professor John Herbert, FInstBiol, BSc, PhD, FRSE. Professor of Virology, Glasgow University, since 1968; Honorary Director, MRC Virology Unit, Institute of Virology, Glasgow, since 1968; b. 14.2.24, Vienna; m., Barbara Naomi Morris; 2 s.; 1 d. Educ. Humanistisches Gymnasium, Vienna; Birmingham University. Assistant Lecturer, Glasgow University, 1954-56; Member, ARC scientific staff, AVRI Pirbright, 1956-61; Visiting Fellow, California Institute of Technology, 1961; Member, MRC Experimental Virus Unit scientific staff, Glasgow, 1961-68; Visiting Professor, NIH, Bethesda, 1967-68. Visiting Fellow, Clare Hall, Cambridge, 1986; elected Member (Past Chairman, Course and Workshops Committee), EMBO; Trustee (former Secretary and Vice-President), Genetical Society; Chairman, MRC Training Awards Panel, 1986-89; Member, Governing Body, West of Scotland Oncological Organisation, since 1974, and Governing Body, Animal Virus Research Institute, Pirbright, 1986-88; Member, Scientific Advisory Body, Equine Virology Research Institute, since 1987; Member, Medical Research Council Cell Biology and Disorders Board, 1988-92. Recreation: travel. Address: (h.) 17 Kingsborough Gardens, Hyndland, Glasgow, G12 9NH; T.-041-339 1863.

Suckling, Professor Colin James, BSc, PhD, CChem, FRSC, FRSE. Professor of Chemistry, Strathclyde University, since 1984; b. 24.3.47, Birkenhead; m., Catherine Mary Faulkner; 2 s.; 1 d. Educ. Quarry Bank High School, Liverpool; Liverpool University. Lecturer, Department of Pure and Applied Chemistry, Strathclyde University, 1972; Royal Society Smith and Nephew Senior Research Fellow, 1980. Vice Chairman, National Association for Gifted Children in Scotland. Publications: Chemistry Through Models (Co-author), 1978; Biological Chemistry (Co-author), 1980; Enzyme Chemistry, Impact and Applications (Co-author), 1984 Recreations: music; horn playing. Address: (b.) Department of

Pure and Applied Chemistry, Strathclyde Universtiy, 295 Cathedral Street, Glasgow, G1 1XL; T.-041-552 4400.

Suddaby, John Trevor, MA. Deputy Secretary, Edinburgh University, since 1987; b. 28.3.34, Horbury; m., Margaret Helen Steventon; 1 s.; 1 d. Educ. Bradford Grammar School; Jesus College, Cambridge. National Service (Intelligence Corps), 1955-57; Assistant Research Officer, Ministry of Defence, 1958-62; on administrative staff, Edinburgh University, since 1962. Recreations: music; mountain-walking. Address: (b.) Old College, South Bridge, Edinburgh, EH8 9YL; T.-031-667 1011.

Suess, Nigel M., MA, FCIB, FCCA. Director: The British Linen Bank Ltd., since 1979, The Murrayfield p.l.c., since 1982, Lothian Homes Ltd., since 1986; b. 13.12.45, Chelmsford; m., Maureen Ferguson; 1 d. Educ. Chigwell School; Gonville and Caius College, Cambridge. N.M. Rothschild & Sons Ltd., 1967-77 (Assistant Director, 1974-77); joined The British Linen Bank Ltd., 1978. Recreations: mountaineering; chess; ornithology. Address: (b.) 4 Melville Street, Edinburgh, EH3 7NS; T.-031-453 1919.

Sugden, Professor David Edward, MA, DPhil. Professor, Department of Geography, Edinburgh University, since 1987; b. 5.3.41, Paignton; m., Britta Valborg Stridsberg; 2 s.; 1 d. Educ. Warwick School; Jesus College, Oxford. Scientific Officer, British Antarctic Survey, 1965-66; Lecturer/Reader, Department of Geography, Aberdeen University, 1966-86. Recreations: hill-walking; gardening; squash. Address: (b.) Department of Geography, Edinburgh University, Edinburgh, EH8; T.-031-667 1011.

Susskind, Werner, MB, ChB, FRCPGlas, FRCPEdin. Consultant Dermatologist, Victoria Infirmary, Glasgow, since 1965; Honorary Clinical Lecturer in Dermatology, Glasgow University, since 1966; b. 29.4.33, Hamburg; m., Shirley Banks; 2 s. Educ. Hillhead High School, Glasgow; Glasgow University. Recreations: choral singing; photography; golf. Address: (h.) 55 Beech Avenue, Newton Mearns, by Glasgow, G77 5QR; T.-041-639 3265.

Sutherland, Anne Bryson, MB, ChB, MD, FRCSE. President, European Burn Association, since 1987; Consultant Plastic Surgeon (retired); b. 7.1.22, Broxburn. Educ. Bathgate Academy; St. Hilda's School for Girls, Edinburgh; Edinburgh University. Junior medical and surgical posts, Bridge of Earn and Edinburgh; Assistant Surgeon, US Army Surgical Research Unit, Texas; Senior Registrar, then Consultant, Regional Plastic Surgery Service, Bangour General Hospital, Broxburn, and Royal Hospital for Sick Children, Edinburgh. British Association of Plastic Surgeons: Member of Council, 1981-83, President, 1987; British Burn Association: Member of Executive, 1968-73, Chairman, 1982-86. Recreations: walking; skiing; gardening; photography; music. Address: (h.) 41 Ormidale Terrace, Edinburgh, EH12 6EA; T.-031-337 3921.

Sutherland, David Alexander, DDS, FDS, RCPS(G). Chief Administrative Dental Officer, Ayrshire and Arran Health Board, since 1982; Postgraduate Dental Tutor, Glasgow University and Honorary Clinical Teacher, Glasgow University; b. 29.10.44, Glasgow; m., Gillian F.M. Grieve; 2 d. Educ. Paisley Grammar School; Coatbridge High School; Glasgow University. House Officer, Glasgow Dental Hospital; Lecturer, Department of Oral Medicine and Pathology, Glasgow University; Assistant Chief Administrative Dental Officer, Greater Glasgow Health Board. Organist and Choirmaster, Grange Church, Kilmarnock. Recreations: graphic arts; DIY; avoiding TV soaps! Address: (h.) 1 Lochend Road, Troon, KA10 6EU; T.-Troon 311980.

Sutherland, David George Carr, CBE, MC and bar, TD. Farmer, since 1962; Consultant, Control Risks Ltd., since 1985; b. 2.10.20, London; m., 1, Jean Henderson; 2, Christine Hotchkiss; 1 s.; 2 d. Educ. Eton; Sandhurst. War Service, Black Watch and Special Air Service Regiment, Dunkirk, Western Desert, Aegean, Adriatic; mentioned in Despatches; Greek War Cross; command and staff appointments, 1945-55, including British Military Mission to Greece, instructor at Sandhurst, Gold Staff Officer at The Queen's Coronation; retired from the Army, 1955; Ministry of Defence, 1955-80; commanded 21 SAS Regiment, Artists Rifles, TA, 1956-60; Deputy Lieutenant for Tweeddale, since 1974; Non-Executive Director, Asset Protection International Ltd., 1981-85. Member, Queen's Bodyguard for Scotland; Fellow, Royal Geographical Society. Recreations: fishing; shooting; walking. Address: Ferniehaugh, Dolphinton, West Linton; T.-Dolphinton 82257.

Sutherland, David I.M., MA, MEd. Registrar, The General Teaching Council for Scotland, since 1985; b. 22.1.38, Wick; m., Janet H. Webster; 2 s. Educ. Aberdeen Grammar School; Aberdeen University; University of Zurich. Teacher of Modern Languages, Aberdeen Grammar School, 1962-66; Lecturer in Education, Stranmillis College of Education, Belfast, 1966-69; Lecturer in Educational Psychology, Craigie College of Education, Ayr, 1969-72; Assistant Director of Education, Sutherland County Council, 1972-75; Divisional Education Officer (Inverness), then Depute Director of Education, Highland Regional Council, 1975-85. Chairman: Scottish Association for Educational Management and Administration, Scottish Television Educational Advisory Committee; Member: Scottish Council for Research in Education, CNAA (Committee for Teacher Education). Recreations: golf; walking; theatre; reading. Address: (b.) 5 Royal Terrace, Edinburgh, EH7 5AF; T.-031-556 0072.

Sutherland, Elizabeth (Elizabeth Margaret Marshall). Writer; Curator, Groam House Museum, Rosemarkie, since 1982; b. 24.8.26, Kemback, Cupar; m., Rev. John D. Marshall; 2 s.; 1 d. Educ. St. Leonard's Girls' School, St. Andrews; Edinburgh University. Social Worker for Scottish Episcopal Church, 1974-80; author of: Lent Term (Constable Trophy), 1973, The Seer of Kintail, 1974, Hannah Hereafter (Scottish Arts Council Book Award), 1976, The Eye of God, 1977, The Weeping Tree, 1980, Ravens and Black Rain: The Story of Highland Second Sight, 1985, The Gold Key and The Green Life, 1986. Recreations: Highland history; Gaelic language; gardening;

tennis; walking. Address: (h.) 17 Mackenzie Terrace, Rosemarkie, Ross-shire, IV10 8UH; T.-Fortrose 20924.

Sutherland, Rev. Elizabeth Wylie, BD, DPS, DCE. Minister, Balornock North Church, Glasgow, since 1972, linked charge of Balornock North with Barmulloch, since 1983; b. 30.10.31, Stirling. Educ. High School of Stirling; London University; Edinburgh University. Teacher of Religious Education; Tutor, Missionary College, London; Assistant Minister, Muirhouse Church, Edinburgh; Minister, Balornock North Church, Glasgow. Member, Council of Mission to Military Garrisons. Recreations: hill-walking; photography. Address: (h.) 54 Etive Crescent, Bishopbriggs, Glasgow; T.-041-772 1453.

Sutherland, Countess of (Elizabeth Millicent Sutherland). Chief of Clan Sutherland; b. 30.3.21; m., Charles Noel Janson; 2 s.; 1 s. (deceased); 1 d. Educ. Queen's College, London; abroad. Land Army, 1939-41; Laboratory Technician, Inverness and London, 1941-45. Address: (h.) Dunrobin Castle, Sutherland; House of Tongue, Lairg, Sutherland.

Sutherland, George Graham Mackay, MA, FEIS. Member, Skye and Lochalsh District Council, since 1984; b. 10.4.24, Creich, Sutherland; m., Effie Maynard. Educ. Portree High School; Aberdeen University. Former Schoolmaster, Morrison's Academy, Crieff; former Member, Council and Executive, Educational Institute of Scotland; former Member, General Teaching Council, Scotland; former Member, Crieff Town Council; Past Chairman, Crieff Co-operative Society; Member, British Wind Energy Association; Metal Trader; Reclamation Engineer; Director: Highland Wind Ltd., Gordonite Development Ltd., Island Reclamations Ltd. Recreations: work; management of sporting estates. Address: (h.) Glenbrittle, Isle of Skye; T.-047842 223/267.

Sutherland, George Roberton (Roy), MB, ChB, FRCPEdin, FRCPGlas, FRCR, DMRD. Consultant Radiologist in administrative charge, Glasgow Royal Infirmary, Stobhill General Hospital, and associated hospitals; Honorary Clinical Lecturer, Glasgow University, since 1974; Consultant Radiologist, Nuffield McAlpine Hospital, Glasgow and Bon Secours Nursing Home, Glasgow, since 1981; b. 15.12.31, Glasgow; m., Lorna Hunter Murray; 2 d. Educ. George Heriot's School, Edinburgh; Edinburgh University. Former Honorary Secretary, Dunbartonshire Division, BMA; President, Scottish Radiological Society; Council Member, Scottish Thoracic Society; Chairman, Hospital Medical Committee, Northern District, Glasgow; Member, Area Medical Committee Executive, Glasgow; Deputy Chairman, Senior Medical Staffing Committee, Glasgow; Chairman, Ethical Committee, Glasgow Northern Hospitals; Member, Sub-Committee in Radiology, National Medical Consultative Committee; Member, Faculty Board, Royal College of Radiologists and Chairman, Computer Advisory Committee; Member: Scottish Standing Committee, Royal College of Radiologists; Symposium Committee, Royal College of Physicians, Glasgow; Association of Queen's College, Glasgow; Elder, St. George's Tron, Glasgow. Recreations: electronics; amateur radio, repairing old motor cars, or any other mechanical or electrical device; classical music; photography; gardening; golf. Address: (h.) 22 Montrose Drive, Bearsden, Dunbartonshire; T.-041-942 7802.

Sutherland, Hamish Watson, MB, ChB, FRCOG. Clinical Reader (former Acting Head), Department of Obstetrics and Gynaecology, Aberdeen University; Consultant, Grampian Area Health Board; b. 20.10.33, Kinross; m., Frances Cairns; 2 s. Educ. Dollar Academy; St. Andrews University. Resident appointments, Dundee Royal Infirmary; RAMC, 1959-61; Clinical Officer, British Military Hospital, Munster and Hostert; Senior House Officer/Registrar, Dundee, Falkirk and Glasgow; Lecturer/Honorary Senior Registrar, Department of Obstetrics and Gynaecology, Aberdeen University, 1965 (Senior Lecturer, 1970); Representative, Scottish Medical Schools, Central Midwives Board for Scotland, 1979-83; appointed to UK Central Council for Nursing, Midwifery and Health Visiting, 1983; Member, Scottish Executive Committee, Royal College of Obstetricians and Gynaecologists; Past Chairman, Diabetic Pregnancy Study Group, European Association for the Study of Diabetes. Publication: Carbohydrate Metabolism in Pregnancy and the Newborn (four volumes) (Editor). Recreations: sport; art. Address: (h.) Redstones, 9 Marchbank Road, Aberdeen, AB1 9DJ; T.-Aberdeen 867017.

Sutherland, Professor Hugh Brown, SM, FEng, FICE, FIStructE, FRSE. Director, University of Glasgow Trust, since 1987 (Emeritus Professor of Civil Engineering); b. 22.1.20, Glasgow; m., Sheila Doris Oliphant; 1 s.; 1 d. Educ. Allan Glen's School, Glasgow; Royal Technical College; Harvard University. Articled Civil Engineer, 1936-40; Assistant Civil Engineer, Oscar Faber and Partners, 1940-42; Lecturer, Glasgow University, 1942-46; Research Associate, Harvard University, 1947; Research Officer, National Research Council of Canada, 1948; Lecturer, Senior Lecturer, Reader, Professor, Glasgow University (Dean, Faculty of Engineering, 1975-78); Vice-President, Institution of Civil Engineers, 1982-84; Member, various Government Advisory Committees. Recreations: golf; sports administration; gardening. Address: (b.) Glasgow University, Glasgow, G12 8QQ; T.-041-339 8855.

Sutherland, James, CBE (1974), MA, LLB, LLD. Consultant, McClure Naismith Anderson & Gardiner, Solicitors, Glasgow and Edinburgh (Partner, 1951-87); b. 15.2.20; m., 1, Elizabeth Kelly Barr; 2 s.; 2, Grace Williamson Dawson. Educ. Queens Park Secondary School, Glasgow; Glasgow University. Royal Signals, 1940-46; Examiner in Scots Law, 1951-55, and Mercantile Law and Industrial Law, 1968-69, Glasgow University; Chairman, Glasgow South National Insurance Tribunal, 1964-66; Member, Board of Management, Glasgow Maternity and Women's Hospitals, 1964-74 (Chairman, 1966-74); Council Member, Law Society of Scotland, 1959-77 (Vice-President, 1969-70, President, 1972-74); Council Member, International Bar Association, since 1972 (Chairman, General Practice Section, 1978-80, Secretary General, 1980-84, President, 1984-86); Vice-Chairman, Glasgow Eastern Health

Council, 1975-77; Council Member, General Dental Council, since 1975; Deacon, Incorporation of Barbers, Glasgow, 1962-65; Dean, Royal Faculty of Procurators in Glasgow, 1977-80; Member, Court, Strathclyde University, since 1977. Recreation: golf. Address: (h.) Greenacres, 20/1 Easter Belmont Road, Edinburgh, EH12 6EX; T.-031-337 1888.

Sutherland, John Crawford, AIB (Scot). Secretary, Committee of Scottish Clearing Bankers, since 1974. Address: (b.) 19 Rutland Square, Edinburgh, EH1 2DD; T.-031-229 1326.

Sutherland, Margaret Helen. Head Teacher, Farr Secondary School, Bettyhill; b. 15.11.28. Educ. Wishaw High School; West of Scotland Agricultural College; Jordanhill College of Education. Lecturer, Cumberland/Westmorland Farm School; Assistant Teacher of Science, West Lothian; Depute Head, Beauly Secondary School. Founder President, Soroptimist International of Easter Ross; Past Chairman, Ross and Cromarty Conservative Association. Recreations: golf; gardening; Soroptimists; charity work. Address: (h.) Schoolhouse, Bettyhill, Sutherland; T.-064 12 217.

Sutherland, Hon. Lord (Ranald Iain Sutherland), QC (Scot). Senator of the College of Justice, since 1985; b. 23.1.32; m.; 2 s. Educ. Edinburgh Academy; Edinburgh University. Admitted, Faculty of Advocates, 1956; Advocate Depute, 1962-64, 1971-77; QC (Scot), 1969.

Sutherland, Robert, MA, LLB, WS, NP. Senior Lecturer in Private Law, Glasgow University; an Honorary Sheriff, Central, Tayside and Fife, at Stirling; a Chairman, Social Security Appeal Tribunals, Glasgow; Member, Central Region Valuation Appeal Panel; b. 9.9.26, Edinburgh. Educ. George Watson's College; Edinburgh University. Indian Army (Assam Regiment), 1944-47; Partner, Stuart & Stuart, WS, 1955-72. Episcopal Church: between 1965 and 1974 was variously Edinburgh Diocesan Treasurer; Deputy Registrar of the Edinburgh Diocese; Member, Diocesan Council; Member, Representative Church Council; Member, Provincial Allocation Committee; Member, Central Joint Board for Clergy Stipends and Home Mission; Member, Provincial Action for World Development Committee. Recreations: Nordic skiing; sailing; baroque music. Address: Glasgow University, Glasgow.

Sutherland, Sinclair Stewart, MB, ChB, DPM, FRCPsych. Consultant Psychiatrist, Lanarkshire Health Board, since 1985; Physician Superintendent, Hartwood Hospital, Shotts, since 1985; b. 4.1.30, Carluke; m., Dr. Alice Andries; 4 s. Educ. Wishaw High School; Aberdeen University. General Practitioner, Shetland Isles and Aberdeenshire, 1957-60; Psychiatry trainee posts, North Eastern Regional Hospital Board, 1960-65; Research Fellow in Psychiatry, Harvard University, 1964; Consultant Psychiatrist, Greater Glasgow Health Board, Deputy Physician Superintendent, Woodilee and Stoneyetts Hospitals, Glasgow, and Honorary Clinical Lecturer, Glasgow University, 1966-85. Worked with Scottish and Glasgow Marriage Guidance Councils, since 1972. Recreations: golf; motor cycling; clarinet. Address: (h.) Egmont, 51 Belhaven Terrace, Wishaw; T.-0698 372632.

Sutherland, William George MacKenzie, QPM. Chief Constable, Lothian and Borders Police, since 1983; b. 12.11.33, Inverness; m., Jennie Abbott; 2 d. Educ. Inverness Technical High School. Cheshire Police, 1954-73; Surrey Police, 1973-75; Hertfordshire Police, 1975-79; Chief Constable, Bedfordshire Police, 1979-83. Recreations: squash; hill-walking. Address: (b.) Police Headquarters, Fettes Avenue, Edinburgh, EH4 1RB; T.-031-311 3131.

Sutherland, William James, CIPFA, FCMA. Chief Financial Officer, South of Scotland Electricity Board, since 1983; b. 10.6.35, Glasgow; m., Fiona Mackay Begg; 3 s.; 1 d. Educ. Victoria Drive Senior Secondary School, Glasgow; Strathclyde University. Glasgow Corporation, 1952-61; Depute Town Chamberlain, Burgh of Bearsden, 1961-64; Town Chamberlain: Burgh of Bishopbriggs, 1964-68, Burgh of Cumbernauld, 1968-75; Depute Director of Finance, Strathclyde Regional Council, 1975-82. Recreations: golf; table tennis. Address: (b.) South of Scotland Electricity Board, Spean Street, Glasgow, G44 4BE; T.-041-637 7177.

Suttie, James Michael Peter, MRTPI. Director of Planning and Development, Banff and Buchan District Council, since 1980; b. 24.3.48, Arbroath; m., Sylvia; 1 s.; 2 d. Educ. Dundee High School; Duncan of Jordanstone College of Art, Dundee. Principal Planning Officer (Development Control), Dundee Corporation, 1973-75; Principal Planning Assistant (Information), Tayside Regional Council, 1975; Chief Assistant Planning Officer, Fife Regional Council, 1975-80. Honorary Secretary and Treasurer, Scottish Society of Directors of Planning. Recreations: golf; hill-walking; orienteering; driving. Address: (b.) Town House, Low Street, Banff; T.-02612 2521.

Swaffield, Professor John Arthur, BSc, MPhil, PhD, CEng, MRAS, FIWEM, MCIBSE. Professor of Building Services Engineering, Heriot-Watt University, Edinburgh, since 1985; b. 4.3.43, Aberystwyth; m., Jean Winnan; 2 d. Educ. Ardwyn Grammar School, Aberystwyth; Bristol University. Research Fellow, Mechanical Engineering Department, City University, London, 1966-70; Deputy Head, Systems Laboratory, British Aircraft Corporation, Filton, Bristol, 1970-72; Lecturer and Senior Lecturer, Department of Building Technology, Brunel University, 1972-83; Reader in Mechanical Engineering, Brunel University, 1983-85. Recreations: skiing; cinema; political/military history. Address: (b.) Department of Building, Heriot-Watt University, Riccarton, Edinburgh, EH14 4AS; T.-031-449 5111.

Swan, Rev. Andrew Fortune, MA, BD (Hons), DipMin. Minister, Buittle and Kelton linked with Castle Douglas: St. Andrews, since 1983; Vice Chairman, Stewartry Council of Voluntary Organisations; b. 25.3.54, Edinburgh; 2 d. Educ. Fettes College, Edinburgh; Edinburgh University. Convener, Education Committee, Presbytery of Dumfries and Kirkcudbright. Recreations: painting; railways; walking. Address: The Manse, 10 Queen Elizabeth Drive, Castle Douglas, DG7 1HH; T.-0556 2585.

Swan, James Robert Drummond, MA, CBIM. Director, Bass PLC, since 1983 (Chairman, Scottish Division); Chairman and Managing Director, Tennent Caledonian Breweries Ltd.; Director, Hedges and Butler Ltd., since 1982; Chairman, J.G. Thomson & Co. Ltd., since 1982; Director, Maclay & Co. Ltd., since 1986; b. 30.6.34, Dundee; m., Rachel; 1 s.; 1 d. Educ. Edinburgh University. Beecham Group; Dorland Advertising Ltd.; Bass PLC. Past President, Brewers Association of Scotland; Past Chairman, Scottish Licensed Trade Association; Late Visitor, Incorporation of Maltmen in Glasgow; Trustee and Member, Management Committee, Scottish Civic Trust. Recreations: skiing; walking. Address: (b.) 110 Bath Street, Glasgow; T.-041-552 6552.

Swan, Lt. Col. William Bertram, CBE, TD, JP. Lord Lieutenant, Berwickshire, since 1969; Chairman: Rural Forum, Scotland, since 1982, Scottish Veterans' Garden City Association, since 1983; President, Borders Scout Council, since 1976; President, Borders Association of Youth Clubs, since 1977; President, Berwickshire Naturalists' Club, 1987-88; Farmer; b. 19.9.14, Duns; m., Ann Gilroy Hogarth; 4 s. Educ. St. Mary's, Melrose; Edinburgh Academy. Farmer, Blackhouse, Reston, Berwickshire, since 1933; served, 1939-42, with 4th Bn., KOSB (UK and France), 1942-45 with Indian Army; President, National Farmers Union of Scotland, 1961-62; Chairman, Scottish Agricultural Organisation Society, 1966-68; Development Commissioner, 1964-76; President, Scottish Cricket Union, 1972-73; President, Lowlands TA & VRA, 1983-86. Recreation: sport. Address: Blackhouse, Eyemouth, Berwickshire; T.-Duns 82842.

Swanson, Alexander James Grenville, MB, ChB, FRCS. Consultant Orthopaedic Surgeon, since 1980; Acting Head, Department of Orthopaedic Surgery, Dundee University, since 1986; b. 18.10.41, Ecclefechan; 2 s. Educ. Dingwall Academy; St. Andrews University. Postgraduate training: St. Andrews, 1967-68, Edinburgh, 1968-69, Glasgow, 1969-70, Edinburgh, 1970-74, Dunfermline, 1974-75; Lecturer, then Senior Lecturer and Honorary Consultant, Dundee University, 1975-83. Recreations: downhill skiing; cross-country skiing; travel. Address: (b.) Department of Orthopaedic and Traumatic Surgery, Royal Infirmary, Dundee, DD1 9ND; T.-0382 23125.

Swanson, Kenneth M., BSc, PhD, JP, DL. Assistant Director, Technology, Dounreay Nuclear Power Development Establishment, since 1986; b. 14.2.30, Canisbay, Caithness; m., Elspeth J.W. Paton; 2 s.; 1 d. Educ. Wick High School; St. Andrews University. Flying Officer, Pilot, RAF, 1952; Lecturer in Physics, University of Wales, 1955; joined UKAEA, Dounreay, on Fast Reactors, 1958; appointed JP, 1970; DL, Caithness, 1977. Author of papers and patents on the development of plutonium fuels for electricity production. Recreation: farming. Address: Knockglass, Westfield, Thurso; T.-084 787 201.

Swapp, Garden Hepburn, MB, ChB, DObstRCOG, DCH, FRCOG. Consultant Obstetrician and Gynaecologist, since 1966; Clinical Senior Lecturer, Aberdeen University; b. 21.11.29, Kota Bharu, Kelantan, Malaysia; m., Anne Margaret Gillespie, MA, LTCL; 2 s.; 1 d. Educ. Mackie Academy, Stonehaven; Fordyce Academy; Aberdeen University. Sqdn. Leader, RAF Medical Branch; House Officer, Royal Hospital for Sick Children, Glasgow, Aberdeen Maternity Hospital; Lecturer and Senior Lecturer, Department of Obstetrics, Aberdeen University. Recreations: walking; golf. Address: (h.) 38 Gray Street, Aberdeen, AB1 6JE; T.-0224 318302.

Swapp, George David, OBE, MA (Hons), DipEd. Member, Grampian Regional Council, since 1986; b. 25.5.31, Labuan (of Aberdeen parents); m., Eva Jane MacNab; 2 s.; 2 d. Educ. Mackie Academy, Stonehaven; Aberdeen University. RAF Staff College, graduate and directing staff, 1965-68; Ministry of Defence (Training Policy), 1971-74 and 1978-80; promoted Wing Commander, 1971; Board Chairman, RAF Officer and Aircrew Selection Centre, 1974-78; Head, RAF Officer Training Establishment, Bracknell, 1980-83; retired from RAF, 1983. Member, Council, National Trust for Scotland; Chairman, Stonehaven Harbour Committee; Church Elder. Recreations: hill-walking; sailing; local history; geography; protection and enhancement of amenities and woodlands. Address: (h.) 9 Urie Crescent, Stonehaven, AB3 2DY; T.-Stonehaven 64124.

Sweeney, Sister Dorothea, MA (Hons), BA (Hons), PhD. Vice Principal (formerly Assistant Principal), St. Andrew's College of Education, since 1985; b. Glasgow. Educ. Notre Dame High School, Glasgow; Glasgow University; Notre Dame College of Education; Bedford College and LSE, London University; Strathclyde University. Assistant Teacher of English, Our Lady & St. Francis Secondary School, Glasgow, 1960-63; entered Congregation of Sisters of Notre Dame, Sussex, 1963; Assistant Teacher of English, Notre Dame High School, London, 1966-67; Notre Dame College of Education: Lecturer, Department of Psychology, 1970-76, Senior Lecturer, Department of Educational Science, 1976-80. Member, Board of Governors, St. Andrew's College, since 1980; Member, CNAA Inservice Education Board, 1982-87, and Committee for Teacher Education; Member, National Inservice Committee, until 1981; Member, National Inter-College Committee for Educational Research, since 1982; Member, Catholic Education Commission (Scotland), 1973-75. Recreations: creative writing; dance; music; art; sport; drama; technology. Address: (b.) St. Andrew's College of Education, 6 Duntocher Road, Bearsden, Glasgow, G61 4QA; T.-041-943 1424.

Sweeney, William John, DRSAM. Composer; b. 5.1.50, Glasgow; m., Susannah Conway; 1 s.; 1 d. Educ. Knightswood Secondary School; Royal Scottish Academy of Music and Drama; Royal Academy of Music. Studied clarinet and composition, 1967-72; principal compositions: Heights of Maccu Piccu, 1978, String Quartet, 1981, Maqam, 1983, Nine Days, 1976; Sunset Song, 1985. Vice-Chairman, Scottish District Council, Musicians' Union. Recreation: a quiet pint in the Dowanhill Bar. Address: (h.) 37 Lawrence Street, Glasgow, G11 5HD; T.-041-334 9987.

Sweet, Elizabeth Mary, MB, ChB, FRCPEdin, FRCPGlas, FRCR. Consultant Radiologist, Royal Hospital for Sick Children, Glasgow, since 1963, and Queen Mother's Maternity Hospital, Glasgow, since 1964; b. 30.8.28, Bombay. Educ. St. Bride's, Helensburgh; Edinburgh University. President, 22nd Congress, European Society of Paediatric Radiology, Glasgow, 1985. Address: (b.) Royal Hospital for Sick Children, Glasgow, G3 8SJ; T.-041-339 8888.

Swift, Bernard Christopher, BA, MA, PhD. Senior Lecturer in French, Stirling University, since 1973; b. 5.2.37, St. Helens; m., Christine Ramsden; 2 s.; 1 d. Educ. West Park Grammar School, St. Helens; Manchester University; Paris University; Aberdeen University. Lecturing posts, Geneva University, 1961-63, School of Interpreters, Geneva University, 1962-63, Aberdeen University, 1963-72, Saskatchewan University, 1969-70, McMaster University, Ontario, 1970. Chief Examiner for Certificate of Sixth Year Studies, French, since 1972. Recreations: gardening; fine art; photography; music. Address: (h.) 2 Grant Drive, Dunblane, Perthshire, FK15 9HU; T.-0786 824066.

Swinney, John Ramsay, MA. National Secretary, Scottish National Party, since 1986 (Defence Spokesman, SNP, since 1987); b. 13.4.64, Edinburgh. Educ. Forrester High School, Edinburgh; Edinburgh University. Research Officer, Scottish Coal Project, 1987-88; Research Consultant, Development Options Ltd., since 1988; Secretary, Young Scottish Nationalists, 1982-84; SNP: Assistant National Secretary, 1984-86, Acting National Secretary, 1986, Member, National Executive Committee, since 1983; Joint Editor, "Activist" publications, 1985-86. Publication: Defending a Free Scotland (Co-author), 1986. Recreations: reading; classical music. Address: (h.) 27 Gardner's Crescent, Edinburgh, EH3 8DF; T.-031-229 1209.

Swinton, Major General Sir John, KCVO, OBE, DL. Deputy Lieutenant, Berwickshire, since 1980; Brigadier, Queen's Bodyguard for Scotland (Royal Company of Archers), since 1977; Honorary Colonel, 2nd Bn., 52nd Lowland Volunteers, since 1983; National Chairman, Royal British Legion Scotland, since 1986; Council Member, Commonwealth Ex-Servicemen's League, since 1984; Trustee, Scottish National War Memorial, since 1984; Chairman, Thirlestane Castle Trust, since 1984; Trustee, Army Museums Ogilby Trust, since 1978; Chairman, Berwickshire Civic Society, since 1982; Member, Central Advisory Committee on War Pensions, since 1986; b. 21.4.25, London; m., Judith Balfour Killen; 3 s.; 1 d. Educ. Harrow School. Enlisted Scots Guards, 1943; commissioned, 1944; served NW Europe (twice wounded); Malaya, 1948-51 (Despatches); ADC to Field Marshal Sir William Slim, Governor General of Australia, 1953-54; Regimental Adjutant, Scots Guards, 1960-62; Adjutant, RMA, Sandhurst, 1962-64; comd. 2nd Bn., Scots Guards, 1966-68; Lt.-Col. commanding Scots Guards, 1970-71; Commander, 4th Guards Armoured Brigade, BAOR, 1972-73; Brigadier, Lowlands and Commander, Edinburgh and Glasgow Garrisons, 1975-76; GOC London District and Major General comd. Household Division, 1976-79. Coordinator for Scotland, Duke of Edinburgh's Award 25th Anniversary Appeal, 1980 (Honorary Liaison Officer for the Borders, 1983-85); Chairman, Roxburgh and Berwickshire Conservative Association, 1983-85. Address: (h.) Kimmerghame, Duns, Berwickshire; T.-0361 83277.

Syme, James, MB, ChB, FRCPEdin, FRCPGlas. Consultant Paediatrician, Edinburgh, since 1965; Honorary Senior Lecturer, Edinburgh University, since 1970; Vice President, Royal College of Physicians of Edinburgh, since 1985; b. 25.8.30, Fife; m., Pamela; 1 s.; 1 d. Educ. Edinburgh University. Captain, RAMC, 1955-57; Registrar and Senior Registrar posts, up to Consultant appointment, 1965; former Secretary, Royal College of Physicians of Edinburgh. Recreations: gardening; caravanning; visiting old churches. Address: (h.) 13 Succoth Park, Edinburgh, EH12 6BX; T.-031-337 6069.

Symington, Rev. Alastair Henderson, MA, BD. Minister, New Kilpatrick Parish Church, Bearsden, since 1985; b. 15.4.47, Edinburgh; m., Eileen Margaret Jenkins; 2 d. Educ. Daniel Stewart's College, Edinburgh; Edinburgh University; Tubingen University, West Germany. Assistant Minister, Wellington Church, Glasgow, 1971-72; Chaplain, RAF, 1972-76; Minister, Craiglockhart Parish Church, Edinburgh, 1976-85. Contributor, Scottish Liturgical Review. Publications: Westminster Church Sermons, 1984; Reader's Digest Family Guide to the Bible (Co-author), 1985. Recreations: golf; rugby; music; computing. Address: 51 Manse Road, Bearsden, Glasgow, G61 3PN; T.-041-942 0035.

T

Tait, Eric, MBE, BSc (Eng), MPhil. Secretary, Institute of Chartered Accountants of Scotland, since 1984: b. 10.1.45, Edinburgh; m., Jane; 1 s.; 1 d. Educ. George Heriot's School; London University; Royal Military Academy, Sandhurst; Cambridge University. Commissioned, 2nd Lt., Royal Engineers, 1965; mentioned in Despatches; GSO3 HQ 39 Infantry Brigade, 1976; student, Advanced Staff Course, RAF Staff College, Bracknell, 1977; GSO2 SD HQ1 (BR) Corps, 1980; Officer Commanding 7 Field Squadron, RE, 1980-81; Lt. Col., 1982; Directing Staff, Staff College, Camberley, 1982; retired from active list, 1983. Member, Executive, Scottish Council (Development and Industry). Recreations: swimming; hill-walking; reading. Address: (b.) 27 Queen Street, Edinburgh, EH2 1LA; T.-031-225 5673.

Tait, Eric Alexander, BSc. Member, Grampian Health Board, since 1983; Honorary Sheriff, Kincardine and Deeside, since 1983; Emeritus Professor, Aberdeen University; b. 26.2.22, Edinburgh;

m., Margaret Anna Rowter (deceased); 2 s.; 2 d. Educ. King Alfred's Grammar School, Wantage; Aberdeen University. War Service, 1940-46 (Captain, Royal Artillery); student, 1946-50; Colonial Service, Geological Survey, Nigeria, 1950-61 (Principal Geologist); Department of Geology and Mineralogy, Aberdeen University, 1961-82 (Professor and Head of Department, 1972-82). Member, Stonehaven Town Council, 1965-71; Chairman, Stonehaven Community Council, 1975-78; Chairman, Mackie Academy School Council, 1975-82; Vice-Chairman, Kincardine and Deeside Conservative Association, since 1975; Director, Kincardine and Deeside Branch, British Red Cross Society, since 1981. Recreations: travel; reading. Address: (h.) Hingston, 83B Cameron Street, Stonehaven, AB3 2HF; T.-0569 62872.

Tait, Ivan Ballantyne, TD, KStJ, KLJ, FRCS, FRCSEdin, FRCSGlas. Physician in Administrative Charge, Genito-Urinary Medical Services in the West of Scotland; b. 14.9.28, Stepps, Lanarkshire; m., Jocelyn Mary Connel Leggatt; 1 s.; 1 d. Educ. Glasgow Academy; Daniel Stewart's College; Edinburgh University. Col., L/RAMC (V); Representative Knight of Justice, Scottish Priory of the Order of St. John; Liveryman, Worshipful Company of Apothecaries; Freeman, City of London; Honorary Surgeon (TA) to The Queen. Recreations: TA; charitable societies. Address: (h.) 6 Lennox Row, Edinburgh, EH5 3HN.

Tankel, Henry I., MD, FRCSEdin, FRCSGlas. Surgeon, Southern General Hospital, Glasgow, since 1962; Chairman, Glasgow Board of Jewish Education, since 1985; b. 14.1.26, Glasgow; m., Judith Woolfson; 2 s.; 2 d. Educ. High School of Glasgow; Glasgow University. Fulbright Scholar, 1954-55; President, Glasgow Jewish Representative Council, 1974-77; Chairman, Glasgow Hospital Medical Services Committee, 1974-79; Board of Science and Education, 1978-81; President, United Synagogues of Scotland, 1978-85; Treasurer, Scottish Committee for Hospital Medical Services, since 1978; Member, National Panel of Specialists, 1978-82 and since 1987; invited to address General Assembly of Church of Scotland, 1984. Recreations: walking; making model boats. Address: (h.) 26 Dalziel Drive, Glasgow, G41 4PU; T.-041-423 5830.

Tasker, George Leith, CA. Senior Partner, Bird, Simpson & Co., CA, Dundee; b. 28.9.30, Dundee; m., Norma Croll; 3 d. Educ. Morgan Academy, Dundee; Cambridge University. CA training, 1947-53; National Service, RAF, 1953-55; commissioned into RAF Intelligence as interpreter (Russian); Qualified Assistant, Norman J. Bird & Co., CA, 1955-57 (became Partner, 1957, Senior Partner, 1979); Council Member, Institute of Chartered Accountants of Scotland, 1982. Former Council Member, Dundee Civic Trust; Treasurer, Dundee Chamber Music Club; Elder, Church of Scotland. Recreations: music; theatre; travel abroad; art; fishing. Address: (h.) Hammersrang, Pitroddie, Perthshire, PH2 7RJ; T.-082 17 279.

Taylor, Rev. Alan Hunter Stuart, BA (Hons), MA (Hons), BD. Minister, Brydekirk and Hoddam, since 1987; b. 28.3.26, Wick; m., Margaret Riddell McNay; 2 d. Educ. Morrison's Academy, Crieff; St. Andrews University; London University. Royal Signals and Intelligence Corps, Far East, 1944-48; teaching appointments, John Watson's School, Edinburgh, and Coatbridge High School; Assistant Minister, Auld Kirk of Ayr, 1957-58; Minister: Dryfesdale Parish Church, Lockerbie, 1958-65, Aberlour and Craigellachie, 1965-75, Holm, Orkney, 1975-87. Recreations: music; miscellaneous reading; art; gardening; golf; hill-walking. Address: The Manse of Brydekirk and Hoddam, Ecclefechan, Lockerbie, Dumfriesshire; T.-057 63 357.

Taylor, Rev. Andrew Stark, ThB, FPhS. Minister, Union Church, Greenock, since 1959; b. 3.11.28, Glasgow; m., Mary McEwan; 1 d. Educ. Govan Senior Secondary School; Glasgow University and Trinity College. Staff, Donaldson Brothers and Black Ltd., Shipping Agents, 1944-54; Assistant Minister: Linthouse Church, 1955-57, St. Nicholas Church, Glasgow, 1957-59. Address: 72 Forsyth Street, Greenock; T.-0475 21092.

Taylor, Anthony Edward, BA, IPFA. Director of Finance, Fife Regional Council, since 1987; b. 13.4.43; m., Joan Elizabeth; 3 s. (2 by pr. m.); 1 d. Educ. Cowbridge Grammar School, Glamorgan; University College of Wales, Aberystwyth. Research Officer, Lancashire and Merseyside Industrial Development Association, 1966-68; Economist, Cardiff City Council, 1968-70; Assistant Chief Accountant, then Head of Economics Unit, Brighton County Borough Council, 1970-74; Chief Budget Officer, Brighton Borough Council, 1974-79; Assistant Director of Finance, Sandwell Metropolitan Borough Council, 1979-82; Senior Depute Director of Finance, Tayside Regional Council, 1982-87. Member, CIPFA Rating Review Panel; Member, CIPFA (Scotland) Education and Training Executive. Recreations: history; castles; gardening; horse-riding; philately. Address: (b.) North Street, Glenrothes, Fife; T.-0592 754411.

Taylor, Charles Edwin, CBE, BSc, PhD, FRSE, FIBiol. Director, Scottish Crop Research Institute (formerly Scottish Horticultural Research Institute), 1972-86; Vice-President, Association of Applied Biologists (President, 1989); NATO Senior Research Fellow, Instituto di Nematologia Agraria CNR, Bari, Italy; b. 11.9.23, Oystermouth; m., Dorothy N. Taylor; 1 d. Educ. Cardiff High School; University College, Cardiff. Pilot, RAF, 1943-46; Lecturer in Applied Zoology, Nottingham University School of Agriculture, 1949-56; Senior Entomologist, Federation of Rhodesia and Nyasaland, 1956-59; Head, Zoology Section, Scottish Horticultural Research Institute, 1959-72. President, European Society of Nematologists, 1980-84. Address: (h.) Westcroft, Longforgan, Dundee, DD2 5EX; T.-082 67 731.

Taylor, David John, MB, BS, MD, MCRCOG. Senior Lecturer, Obstetrics and Gynaecology, Dundee University, since 1979; Honorary Consultant Obstetrician and Gynaecologist, Ninewells Hospital, Dundee, since 1979; b. 10.8.47, Gateshead; m., Pamela; 1 s.; 2 d. Educ. St. Aidan's Grammar School, Sunderland; Newcastle upon Tyne University. House Officer, Royal Victoria Infirmary, Newcastle upon Tyne, 1970-71; Newcastle Vocational Rotation in Obstetrics and

Gynaecology, 1971-75; Member, scientific staff, MRC Reproduction and Growth Unit, 1975-77; First Assistant, Department of Obstetrics and Gynaecology, Newcastle upon Tyne, 1977-79; Joint Director, EEC Concerted Action into Maternal Alcohol Consumption and its Effects on Pregnancy Outcome and Child Development, 1985. Recreations: golf; badminton; watching all sports. Address: (b.) Department of Obstetrics and Gynaecology, Ninewells Hospital and Medical School, Dundee, DD1 9SY; T.-0382 60111, Ext. 2500.

Taylor, Rev. Ian, BSc, MA, LTh, DipEd. Minister, Abdie & Dunbog and Newburgh, since 1983; b. 12.10.32, Dundee; m., Joy Coupar, LRAM; 2 s.; 1 d. Educ. Dundee High School; St. Andrews University; Durham University; Sheffield University; Edinburgh University. Teacher, Mathematics Department, Dundee High School; Lecturer in Mathematics, Bretton Hall College of Education; Senior Lecturer in Education, College of Ripon and York St. John; Assistant Minister, St. Giles' Cathedral, Edinburgh. Secretary, History of Education Society, 1968-73; extensive work in adult education (appreciation of music and the arts); Director, Summer Schools in Music, St. Andrews University, 1974-82; numerous courses for Edinburgh and Hull Universities and WEA; has played principal roles in opera and operetta; Producer, Gilbert and Sullivan Society of Edinburgh, 1979-87; compiled Theatre Music Quiz series, Radio Tay; presented own operetta, My Dear Gilbert ...My Dear Sullivan, BBC; Writer of revues and documentary plays with music, including Tragic Queen (Mary Queen of Scots), St. Giles' Cathedral, Edinburgh Festival Fringe, 1982, and John Knox (Church of Scotland Video). Publications: How to Produce Concert Versions of Gilbert Sullivan; The Gilbert and Sullivan Quiz Book; The Opera Lover's Quiz Book. Address: The Manse, Cupar Road, Newburgh, Fife, KY14 6HA; T.-0337 40275.

Taylor, John Henry Bindon, MA (Hons), BD, PGCE, DipEd. Head Teacher, Auchenharvie Academy, Stevenston, since 1980; b. 4.11.26, Swansea; m., Constance Jean Tainsh; 3 s.; 1 d. Educ. Swansea Grammar School; Open Exhibitioner in History, Worcester College, Oxford; Glasgow University. Minister: Lincluden, Dumfries, 1952, St. Mary's Presbyterian, Woolston, Southampton, 1956, Irvine St. Andrews, 1960; Teacher, latterly Assistant Rector, Ravenspark Academy, 1969; Depute Head Teacher, Garnock Academy, Kilbirnie, 1978. Chairman, Joint Working Party, Standard Grade Creative and Aesthetic Studies; Convener, Religious Studies Panel, Scottish Examination Board. Recreations: walking; writing; numismatics; railway history. Address: (b.) Auchenharvie Academy, Stevenston, Ayrshire.

Taylor, John McDowall, IPFA, MBIM. City Chamberlain, City of Aberdeen District Council, since 1988; b. 12.2.40, Kilwinning; m., Maureen Agnes Graham Taylor; 2 d. Educ. City Public Senior Secondary School, Glasgow. Various finance posts, Glasgow Corporation, 1956-66; Chief Assistant, then Deputy Borough Treasurer, Dover Borough Council, 1966-71; Principal Accountant, then Assistant Controller of Financial Services, LB of Harrow, 1971-74; Chief Officer, Finance, LB of Ealing, 1974-77; Depute City Chamberlain, then Senior Depute, City of Aberdeen District Council, 1977-88. Director, Aberdeen International Football Festival; Treasurer, Doug Sanders Junior International Golf Tournament. Recreations: golf; football; travel. Address: (b.) Town House, Broad Street, Aberdeen; T.-0224 642121.

Taylor, Rev. Canon John Mitchell, MA. Canon, St. Mary's Cathedral, Glasgow, since 1979; b. 23.5.32, Aberdeen; m., Edna Elizabeth Maitland; 1 s.; 1 d. Educ. Banff Academy; Aberdeen University; Theological College, Edinburgh. Curate, St. Margaret's, Aberdeen; Rector: Holy Cross, Knightswood, Glasgow, St. Ninian's, Pollokshields, Glasgow, St. John the Evangelist, Dumfries. Recreations: angling; hill-walking; sketching; music. Address: St. John's Rectory, 8 Newall Terrace, Dumfries; T.-Dumfries 54126.

Taylor, Rt. Rev. Maurice, STD. Bishop of Galloway, since 1981; b. 5.5.26, Hamilton. Educ. St. Aloysius College, Glasgow; Our Lady's High School, Motherwell; Pontifical Gregorian University, Rome. Royal Army Medical Corps, UK, India, Egypt, 1944-47; Assistant Priest: St. Bartholomew's, Coatbridge, 1951-52, St. Bernadette's, Motherwell, 1954-55; Lecturer, St. Peter's College, Cardross, 1955-65; Rector, Royal Scots College, Spain, 1965-74; Parish Priest, Our Lady of Lourdes, East Kilbride, 1974-81. Episcopal Secretary, Bishop's Conference of Scotland; Vice President, Catholic Institute for International Relations. Publication: The Scots College in Spain, 1971. Address: 8 Corsehill Road, Ayr, KA7 2ST; T.-Ayr 266750.

Taylor, Michael Alan, BA, MSc, MEd, PhD. Principal, Telford College of Further Education, Edinburgh, since 1985; b. 22.12.45, London; m., Maureen Brown. Educ. Sir George Monoux Grammar School, Walthamstow; Middlesex Polytechnic; Lancaster University; Liverpool University; Keele University. Teacher, London secondary schools, 1968-71; Lecturer, Chorley College of Education, 1971-73; Senior and Principal Lecturer, Ulster Polytechnic, 1973-76; Head, School of Social Sciences and Dean, North East Wales Institute of Higher Education, 1976-82 (Director, Institute of Health Education); Depute Principal, Telford College, 1982-84. Recreations: mountaineering; canoeing; skiing; cycling. Address: (b.) Telford College of Further Education, Crewe Toll, Edinburgh, EH4 2NZ; T.-031-332 2491.

Taylor, Michael George, MA (Hons). Rector, St. Joseph's College, Dumfries, since 1982; b. 22.2.43, Coleraine; m., Eileen Forde; 1 s.; 2 d. Educ. St. Aloysius' College, Glasgow; Glasgow University. Head, History Department, St. Conval's High School, Cumnock, 1970-71; Head, History Department, then Assistant Rector, St. Andrew's Academy, Saltcoats, 1971-81; seconded to Chief Executive's Department, Strathclyde Regional Council, 1981-82. President, Ayrshire History Teachers' Association, 1978-81; Member, Catholic Education Commission, 1984-87; Vice Chairman/Chairman, Dumfries Schools' Council, 1987-88. Recreations: reading; education; historical research. Address: (b.) St. Joseph's College, Craigs Road, Dumfries, DG1 4UU; T.-0387 52893.

Taylor, Michael Thomas, MA, MEd. Rector, Dyce Academy, Aberdeen, since 1980; b. 17.2.47, Newcastle upon Tyne; m., Sheena Robertson; 1 s.; 2 d. Educ. Rutherford Grammar School, Newcastle upon Tyne; Trinity College, Cambridge; Aberdeen University. Teacher of Chemistry, Cannock Grammar School, 1969-75; Ellon Academy: Principal Teacher of Guidance, 1975-76, Assistant Head Teacher, 1977-78, Depute Rector, 1978-80. Secretary, Newmachar Community Council; Elder, Newmacher Parish Church. Recreations: hill-walking; music. Address: (h.) Loch-An-Eilan, Newmachar, Aberdeen; T.-065 17 2234.

Taylor, Peter Bruce, MB, ChB, FFARCS. Consultant Anaesthetist, since 1979; Honorary Senior Lecturer in Anaesthesia, Dundee University, since 1979; b. 30.6.44, Newcastle-upon-Tyne; m.; 1 s.; 1 d. Educ. Aberdeen Grammar School; Aberdeen University. Short Service commission, RAF, 1968-74; Anaesthetic Registrar, Aberdeen Royal Infirmary, 1974-75; Anaesthetic Senior Registrar, Nottingham AHA, 1976-79; Instructor in Anaesthesia, Michigan University Hospital, 1977-78. Linkman (Tayside), Association of Anaesthetists of GB and Ireland; Honorary Secretary, North East of Scotland Society of Anaesthetists. Recreations: duplicate bridge; reading; philately (specialist in Machin definitives). Address: (b.) Anaesthetic Department, Ninewells Hospital, Dundee, DD1 9SY; T.-Dundee 60111, Ext. 2475.

Taylor, Sheriff Robert Richardson, MA, LLB, PhD, QC. Sheriff Principal of Tayside Central and Fife, since 1975; Chairman, Sheriff Courts Rules Council, since 1982; b. 16.9.19, Glasgow; m., Martha Birgitta Bjorkling; 2 s.; 1 d. Educ. Glasgow High School; Glasgow University. Called to Scottish Bar, 1944; called to Bar (Middle Temple), 1948; Lecturer in International Private Law, Edinburgh University, 1947-69; Sheriff Principal, Stirling Dumbarton & Clackmannan, 1971-75; contested (Unionist and National Liberal), Dundee East, 1955, Dundee West, 1959 and 1963; Chairman, Central and Southern Region, Scottish Conservative Association, 1969-71; Chairman, Northern Lighthouse Board, 1985-86. Recreations: lapidary; mineral collecting. Address: (h.) 51 Northumberland Street, Edinburgh, EH3 6JQ; T.-031-556 1722.

Taylor, Ross Jenkins, MD, FRCGP, DCH. Senior Lecturer, Department of General Practice, Aberdeen University, since 1978; General Medical Practitioner, Grampian Health Board, since 1980; b. 16.4.43, Glasgow; m., Armida Mary Craig; 2 s.; 2 d. Educ. Thurso High School; Aberdeen University Medical School. RAF Medical Branch, 1965-73; House Officer, Stracathro Hospital, Brechin, 1966-67; Honorary Registrar in Paediatrics, St. George's Hospital, London, 1970; Lecturer, Department of General Practice, Aberdeen University, 1973-78; Academic Member, NHS Prescription Pricing Authority, 1980-83. Butterworth Gold Medal, RCGP, 1977. Recreation: music. Address: (b.) Department of General Practice, Aberdeen University, Foresterhill Health Centre, Westburn Road, Aberdeen, AB9 2AY; T.-0224 697722, Ext. 270.

Taylor, St. Clair S., MA, PhD, DipAnimGen, CIBiol, FIBiol. Senior Principal Scientific Officer, AFRC Animal Breeding Research Organisation, Edinburgh, since 1973; Honorary Lecturer in Animal Growth and Development, Edinburgh University, since 1978; b. 26.6.28, Banchory; m., Helen Margaret Gladstone Bain (m. diss.); 2 s.; 2 d. Educ. Robert Gordon's College, Aberdeen; George Watson's College, Edinburgh; Edinburgh University. Joined AFRC Animal Breeding Research Organisation, 1953 (Head, Department of Growth and Efficiency, 1973-83); Member, AFRC Joint Consultative Organisation Cattle Committee on R. & D. Priorities, 1973-77; awarded British Society of Animal Production's Hammond Memorial Prize, 1970; elected Honorary Fellow, Faculty of Science, Edinburgh University, 1983; Visiting Fellow for 1987, Australian Association of Animal Breeding and Genetics. Recreations: theatre; books; music; wood-carving; clay-modelling; badminton; occasional yoga, cycling and dancing. Address: (b.) Institute of Animal Physiology and Genetics Research, King's Buildings, West Mains Road, Edinburgh, EH9 3JQ; T.-031-667 6901.

Taylor, Professor Samuel Sorby Brittain, BA, PhD. Professor of French, St. Andrews University, since 1977; b. 20.9.30, Dore and Totley, Derbyshire; m., Agnes McCreadie Ewan; 2 d. Educ. High Storrs Grammar School, Sheffield; Birmingham University; Paris University. Royal Navy, 1956-68 (Sub Lt., RNVR); Personnel Research Officer, Dunlop Rubber Co., 1958-60; Institut et Musee Voltaire, Geneva, 1960-63; St. Andrews University: Lecturer, 1963, Reader, 1972, Personal Chair, 1977; Chairman, National Council for Modern Languages, 1981-85; Member, Executive Committee, Complete Works of Voltaire, since 1970; Project Leader, Inter-University French Language Teaching Research and Development Project, since 1980; Chairman, Scottish Joint Working Party for Standard Grade in Modern Languages, 1982-84. Recreations: athletics timekeeping; photography. Address: (b.) Department of French, St. Andrews University, St. Andrews, Fife; T.-0334 76161, Ext. 485.

Taylor of Gryfe, Lord (Thomas Johnston Taylor), Hon. LLD (Strathclyde); b. 27.4.12, Glasgow; m., Isobel. Educ. Bellahouston Academy. Member, Board, Scottish Television, 1968-83; Director: Whiteaway Laidlaw (Bankers), since 1971, Friends Provident, 1972-83, Scottish Metropolitan Property, 1972-88; Member, International Advisory Board, Morgan Grenfell, 1972-88; Chairman, Forestry Commission, 1967-72; Chairman, Economic Forestry, 1972-82; Chairman, Scottish Railways Board, 1969-80; Chairman, Wolfson Trust (Scotland), since 1975; Trustee, Dulverton Trust, since 1979. Recreation: golf. Address: (h.) The Cottage, Auchenames, Kilbarchan, Renfrewshire; T.-050 57 2648.

Taylor, William Gordon, MA, DipTP, MRTPI, FBIM, FIIM. Director, Economic Development and Planning, Fife Regional Council, since 1985; b. 13.2.43, Edinburgh; m., Margaret Frances Carrick McKinnon; 1 s.; 1 d. Educ. George Watson's College; Edinburgh University; Heriot-Watt University. Planning Assistant, Edinburgh Corporation; Area Planning Officer, Fife County Council; Assistant City Planning Officer, Dundee Corporation; Depute Planning Officer, then Director of Physical Planning, Fife Regional Council. Past Chairman, Scottish Society of Directors of Planning; Advisor, EEC Environment Directorate; Advisor on industry and the environment, WHO. Recreations: golf; walking; music; current affairs. Address: (h.) Langdale, 55 Main Street, Dairsie, Fife, KY15 4SR; T.-0334 870503.

Taylor, William Leonard, CBE, BL, JP, DL, Hon. FRTPI. Solicitor; Chairman, Glasgow Citizens' Theatre Ltd., since 1970; Chairman, Planning Exchange, since 1972; Chairman, Scottish Executive, Town and Country Planning Association, since 1953; b. 21.12.16, Glasgow; m., Gladys Carling, 1 s. Educ. Whitehill Secondary School, Glasgow; Glasgow University. Councillor, Glasgow Corporation, 1952-69; Magistrate, City of Glasgow, 1956-60 (Senior Magistrate, 1960-61); Leader, Labour Group, Glasgow Corporation, 1962-69; Leader of Council, 1962-68; Chairman, Livingston Development Corporation, 1965-72 (Member, from 1962); Member, Scottish Advisory Committee on Civil Aviation, 1965-72; Governor, Centre for Environmental Studies, 1966-79; Trustee, Scottish Civic Trust, since 1967; Chairman, Scottish Water Advisory Committee, 1969-72; Member, Extra-Parliamentary Panel under Private Legislation Procedure (Scotland) Act 1936, since 1971; Chairman, Panel of Assessors, River Clyde Planning Study, 1972-74; Chairman, Scottish Advisory Council on Social Work, 1974-81; Vice-Chairman, Commission for Local Authority Accounts in Scotland, 1974-79; Member, Housing Corporation, 1974-80; Member, Scottish Economic Council, 1975-82; Chairman, Scottish Special Housing Association, 1978-81 (Depute Chairman, 1976-78). DL, Glasgow, 1971; Knight, Order of Polonia Restituta (Poland), 1969. Recreations: theatre; reading. Address: (h.) Cruachan, 18 Bruce Road, Glasgow, G41 5EF; T.-041-429 1776.

Taylor, Rev. William Robert, MA, BD. Minister, Slateford Longstone, Edinburgh, since 1986; b. 5.8.58, Airdrie; m., Alison Anne Wason; 1 s. Educ. High School of Glasgow; Glasgow University; Edinburgh University. Assistant Minister, East Kilbride Old Parish Church, 1982-83; Youth Officer, St. Ninian's Centre, Crieff, 1983-86. Recreation: photography. Address: 50 Kingsknowe Road South, Edinburgh, EH14 2JW; T.-031-443 2960.

Teall of Teallach, Dr. D. Gordon, LCP, MEd (Dist.), PhD, FSTS, FSAScot. Executive President and Chairman of the Council, Scottish Tartans Society; b. 8.8.24; m., Eleanor Joan; 2 s.; 2 d. Educ. Warwick School; Coopers Hill College; Leicester University. Former Principal, Priory College, Stamford Baron, County of Cambridge; Council Member, Independent Schools Association, and Chairman, NE England and Scotland Area Committee; Honorary Member, Clan Grant; Honorary Lt.-Col., Militia of the State of Georgia; Member: Manorial Society of Great Britain, Leet of Feudal Lords, University Centre Cambridge, Manx Sailing and Cruising Club, Lloyds of London, Institute of Directors. Royal Humane Society Award for Gallantry. Publications: A Brief History of the Scottish Tartans Society; The Manx Tartans; The Tradesmen and Corporation of Stamford 1485-1750; The District Tartans of Scotland (Co-author). Recreations: sailing; cross-country skiing; horse riding; windsurfing; mountain walking; swimming. Address: (b.) Scottish Tartans Museum, Comrie, Perthshire; T.-0764 70779.

Teasdale, Professor Graham Michael, MB, BS, MRCP, FRCSEdin, FRCSGlas. Professor and Head, Department of Neurosurgery, Glasgow University, since 1981; Consultant Neurosurgeon, Institute of Neurological Sciences, Glasgow, since 1975; b. 23.9.40, Spennymoor; m.; 3 s. Educ. Johnston Grammar School, Durham; Durham University. Postgraduate clinical training, Newcastle-upon-Tyne, London and Birmingham, 1963-69; Assistant Lecturer in Anatomy, Glasgow University, 1969-71; specialist training in surgery and neurosurgery, Southern General Hospital, Glasgow, 1971-75; Senior Lecturer, then Reader in Neurosurgery, Glasgow University, 1975-81. Editor, Society of British Neurosurgeons. Publication: The Management of Head Injuries. Recreations: hill-walking; inshore fishing. Address: (b.) University Department of Neurosurgery, Institute of Neurological Sciences, Southern General Hospital, Glasgow; T.-041-445 2466.

Tebbutt, Michael Laurence, MBIM. Administrator, Culzean Castle and Country Park, and National Trust Representative in Ayrshire, since 1982; b. 23.7.31, Stamford; m., Hazel Taylor; 4 d. Educ. Stamford School, Lincolnshire. Royal Navy, 1950-57; Outward Bound Trust, 1957-61; Joint Iron Council, 1961-64; Stevenage Youth Trust, 1964-67; National Federation of Young Farmers Clubs, 1967-69; Comptroller, Knebworth House and Country Park, 1970-72; Administrator, Weston Park, 1972-82. Vice-President, Wrekin Decorative and Fine Art Society; Chairman, Ayrshire Decorative and Fine Arts Society; Executive Committee Member, Ayrshire and Burns Country Tourist Board. Recreations: sailing; mountaineering; music; heritage; photography. Address: Culzean Castle, Maybole, Ayrshire; T.-06556 274.

Tedder, Rt. Hon. Lord (John Michael Tedder), MA, ScD, PhD, DSc, FRSE. Purdie Professor of Chemistry, St. Andrews University, since 1969; b. 4.7.26, London; m., Peggy Eileen Growcott; 2 s.; 1 d. Educ. Dauntsey's School, Wiltshire; Magdalene College, Cambridge; Birmingham University. Research Fellow: Birmingham University, 1950-52, Ohio State University, 1952-53, Edinburgh University, 1953-55; Lecturer, then Reader, Sheffield University, 1955-64; Roscoe Professor of Chemistry, Dundee University, 1964-68. Member, Board of Management, Macaulay Institute of Soil Research, 1979-87. Publication: Basic Organic Chemistry, Parts 1-5 (Co-author); Valence Theory (Co-author); The Chemical Bond (Co-author); Radicals (Co-author); numerous papers. Recreation: music. Address: (h.) Little Rathmore, Kennedy Gardens, St. Andrews, Fife; T.-St. Andrews 73546.

Telfer, James William, MBE, BSc. Rector, Hawick High School, since 1984; b. 17.3.40, Pathhead, Midlothian; m., Frances Mary; 1 s.; 1 d. Educ. Galashiels Academy; Heriot-Watt University. Assistant Teacher, Galashiels Academy, 1964; moved to Glasgow, 1971, and Edinburgh, 1973, as Principal Teacher; Depute, Deans Community High School, 1978. Rugby player; represented Scotland 25 times, 10 times as Captain; went on two Lions tours to New Zealand and South Africa; Scotland rugby coach, 1980-84; Coach to British Lions, New Zealand, 1983. Recreations: rugby; gardening; walking. Address: (b.) Croft House, Kilncroft, Selkirk, TD7 5AQ; T.-0750 20925.

Telfer, Jaye. Sheriff Clerk, Perth, since 1981; b. Gorebridge. Educ. Dalkeith High School. Women's Royal Naval Service, four years; Civil Service (Scottish Courts Service): began as typist, appointed to clerical grades by open competition, first woman Sheriff Clerk at Perth. Recreations: Siamese cats; reading; gardening. Address: (h.) 2 Alder Drive, Perth; T.-0738 28709.

Telfer, John, BSc (Hons), NDA, NDD, FRAgS. Principal, Clinterty Agricultural College, Aberdeen, since 1968; b. Langholm; m., Katharine Dent; 1 s.; 2 d. Educ. Lockerbie Academy; Wallace Hall Academy; Durham University; West of Scotland Agricultural College. Farm worker, five years; Lecturer, Cumbria College of Agriculture, five years; Day Release Class Organiser, Aberdeen and Kincardineshire, three years. Young Farmers' and Apprenticeship Committees, SCOTVEC; Member, NCA Examination Board; Director, Royal Northern Agricultural Society; Church Elder. Recreation: gardening. Address: (b.) Clinterty Agricultural College, Kinellar, Aberdeen, AB5 OTN; T.-0224 790393.

Telfer, Walter Little, CA. Deputy Group Chief Executive and Group Finance Director, Low and Bonar PLC; b. 3.3.36, Milngavie; m., Margaret Esther Lilias; 1 s.; 1 d. Educ. Elgin Academy; Glasgow University. Joined Low and Bonar, 1975; appointed to parent Board, 1982. Address: (h.) 27 Cedar Road, Broughty Ferry, Dundee, DD5 3BA; T.-0382 79933.

Templeton, Professor Allan, MD, FRCOG. Professor of Obstetrics and Gynaecology, Aberdeen University, since 1985; b. 28.6.46, Glasgow; m., Gillian Constance Penney; 3 s.; 1 d. Educ. Aberdeen Grammar School; Aberdeen University. Junior hospital posts in obstetrics and gynaecology, Aberdeen, 1969-75; Lecturer and Senior Lecturer in Obstetrics and Gynaecology, Edinburgh University, 1976-85. Recreation: mountaineering. Address: (h.) Aultmore, Maryculter, Aberdeen; T.-0224 733947.

Templeton, James Douglas, MB, ChB, FRCPsych. Consultant Psychotherapist, since 1974; Chairman, Division of Psychotherapy, Greater Glasgow Health Board, since 1985; Chairman, Training Committee, Scottish Institute of Human Relations, since 1985; b. 24.11.26, Glasgow; 2 d. Educ. Hutchesons' Grammar School; Glasgow University. Consultant in Adolescent and Family Psychiatry, London, 1969-73; Deputy Medical Director, Cassel Hospital, 1966-73; Consultant in Adolescent and Family Psychiatry, Glasgow, 1973-74. Honorary Clinical Lecturer, Glasgow University, since 1974; Member of Council, Scottish Institute of Human Relations, since 1978; Chairman, Psychotherapy Specialist Advisory Sub-Committee, Joint Committee on Higher Psychiatric Training, 1984-86. Recreations: swimming; sailing; bridge. Address: (h.) 5 Boathouse Avenue, Largs, Ayrshire, KA30 8PW; T.-0475 673815.

Tennant, George, BSc, PhD, CChem, FRSC, FRSE. Reader in Organic Chemistry, Edinburgh University, since 1977; b. 22.2.36, Glasgow; 1 s.; 1 d. Educ. Whitehill Senior Secondary School, Glasgow; Glasgow University. ICI Research Fellow, Aberdeen University, 1961-63; Lecturer: Queen's College, St. Andrews, 1963-65, Edinburgh University, 1965-76; Senior Lecturer, Edinburgh University, 1976-77. Secretary, Heterocyclic Group, Royal Society of Chemistry, 1976-79; Chairman, Edinburgh and SE Scotland Section, Royal Society of Chemistry, 1981-83. Recreations: sport; music; art. Address: (b.) Department of Chemistry, Edinburgh University, West Mains Road, Edinburgh, EH9 3JJ; T.-031-667 1081.

Tennant, Iain Mark, KT (1986). Chairman, Grampian Television PLC, since 1968 (Vice-Chairman, 1960-68); Director, Caledonian Associated Cinemas PLC; Director, Clydesdale Bank PLC; Director, Abbey National Building Society (Chairman, Scottish Advisory Board); Director, Moray and Nairn Newspaper Company Ltd.; Crown Estate Commissioner; Honorary Director, Seagram Company Ltd., Montreal; Lord Lieutenant of Morayshire; Lord High Commissioner to the General Assembly of the Church of Scotland, 1988; b. 11.3.19, North Berwick; m., Lady Margaret Ogilvy; 2 s.; 1 d. Educ. Eton College; Magdalene College, Cambridge. Learned about film production, Welwyn Garden City Film Studios; served in Egypt with 2nd Bn., Scots Guards, 1940-42; became Intelligence Officer, 201 Guard's Brigade; captured at the surrender of Tobruk; prisoner of war, Italy and Germany, until 1945; Founder Member, Moray Sea School, 1949; Council Member, Outward Bound Trust, 15 years; joined Board, Gordonstoun School, 1951 (Chairman, 1957-72); Member, Moray and Nairn County Council, 1956-64 (latterly Vice-Chairman, Education Committee); Member, The Times Publishing Co. Ltd., 1962-66; Member, Board, Cairngorm Sports Development Ltd., 1964-76; appointed Chairman, local Disablement Advisory Committee, 1964; Chairman, Glenlivet and Glen Grant Distilleries Ltd., 1964-70 (Chairman, Glenlivet Distillers Ltd., from 1970); Trustee, King George's Jubilee Trust, London, 1967-71; FRSA, 1971; Trustee, Churchill Trust, 1973-76; Member, Board, Courage Ltd., 1974-77; Chairman, Seagram Distillers Ltd. (in London), 1977-82; CBIM, 1983. Recreations: shooting; fishing. Address: (b.) Innes House, Elgin, Moray; T.-Lhanbryde 2410.

Thaw, David Samson, MBE (M). Retired Solicitor; Honorary Sheriff, Dunoon, since 1973; Honorary Judge Advocate, USA Navy, since 1973; b. 19.1.08, Lanark; m., Violet Lightbody; 1 s.; 2 d. Educ. Lanark Grammar School; Lanark Higher Grade School; Glasgow University. Qualified as

Solicitor, 1930; private practice, 1930-40; volunteered for RAFVR, 1940; released, 1946, with rank of Squadron Leader; Procurator Fiscal Service, 1947; Fiscal, Dunoon District, 1959-73. Recreation: golf (an addict). Address: (h.) 31 Fountain Quay, Kirn, Dunoon, Argyll.

Thin, David Ainslie, BSc. Joint Managing Director, James Thin Ltd., since 1962; Chairman, Melven's Bookshops Ltd., since 1972; Chairman, Book Tokens Ltd., since 1987; b. 9.7.33, Edinburgh; m., Elspeth J.M. Scott; 1 s.; 2 d. Educ. Edinburgh Academy; Loretto School; Edinburgh University. President, Booksellers Association of GB and Ireland, 1976-78. Recreations: golf; travelling; reading. Address: (h.) 60 Fountainhall Road, Edinburgh, EH9 2LP; T.-031-667 2725.

Thom, Arthur David, JP. Member, Falkirk District Council, since 1980 (Chairman, Planning Committee); Executive Committee Member, Forth Valley Tourist Board, since 1988; Member, Scottish National Housing and Town Planning Council, since 1988; Member, Management Committee, Planning Exchange, since 1988; Member, Forth and Clyde Canal Steering Committee, since 1988; Member, Forth River Purification Board, since 1984; Member, COSLA Planning Committee, since 1984; Trustee, Bo'ness Heritage Trust; b. 6.1.46, Glasgow; m., Catherine Jeffrey; 1 s. Educ. Grangemouth High School. Recreations: golf; photography. Address: (h.) 17 Tweed Street, Grangemouth, FK3 8HA.

Thomas, Professor David Brynmor, MB, BS, BSc, DSc, FRCPEdin, FRCPath, FIBiol, FRSE. Bute Professor and Head, Department of Anatomy and Experimental Pathology, St. Andrews University, since 1973; b. 11.10.30, Cefn Coed y Cymmer, Wales; m., Elizabeth Elma Flanagan; 1 s. Educ. Ysgol-y-Graig and Vaynor & Penderyn Secondary School; University College, London; University College Hospital Medical School. House Surgeon, University College Hospital and Royal Northern Hospital; Registrar, Neath General Hospital; Lecturer: Bristol University, University of Wales, Oxford University; Senior Lecturer, Birmingham University; Consultant, Biology Division, Oak Ridge National Laboratory, Tennessee; Master, United College of St. Salvator and St. Leonard, St. Andrews University; West Memorial Lecturer, University College, Cardiff, 1979; Latta Centennial Lecturer, University of Nebraska Medical College, 1986. Recreations: golf; music; photography; walking. Address: (b.) Bute Medical Buildings, St. Salvator's College, St. Andrews, Fife, KY16 9TS; T.-0334 76161, Ext. 7106.

Thomas, Professor Lyn Carey, MA, DPhil (Oxon), FIMA. Professor of Management Science, Edinburgh University, since 1985 (Head, Department of Business Studies, since 1987); b. 10.8.46, Dowlais; m., Margery Wynn Bright; 2 s.; 1 d. Educ. Lewis School, Pengam; Jesus College, Oxford. Research Fellow, University College, Swansea, 1971-74; Lecturer in Decision Theory, then Senior Lecturer, Manchester University, 1974-85; Senior NRC Fellow, Naval Postgraduate School, Monterey, California, 1982-83. Publications: Games, Theory and Applications, 1984; Operational Research Techniques, 1986. Recreations: reading; rugby; rambling. Address: (b.) Department of Business Studies, William Robertson Building, 50 George Square, Edinburgh; T.-031-667 1011.

Thomas, Professor Michael Frederic, MA, PhD, FGS, FRSE. Professor of Environmental Science, Stirling University, since 1980; b. 15.9.33, London; m., Elizabeth Anne Dadley; 1 s.; 1 d. Educ. Royal Grammar School, Guildford; Reading University. Assistant Lecturer in Geography, Magee University College, Londonderry, 1957-60; Lecturer, Ibadan University, Nigeria, 1960-64; Lecturer, then Senior Lecturer, St. Andrews University, 1964-79; visiting appointments, Universities of Canterbury (New Zealand), New South Wales, Natal, and Sierra Leone. Council Member, Royal Scottish Geographical Society; Past Chairman, British Geomorphological Research Group; Member, Scottish Environmental Education Council Executive. Publication: Tropical Geomorphology, 1974. Recreations: listening to music; hill-walking; travel. Address: (b.) Department of Environmental Science, Stirling University, Stirling, FK9 4LA; T.-0786 73171.

Thomas, Professor Michael James, BSc, MBA, FRSA, FInstM. Professor of Marketing, Strathclyde University, since 1987; b. 15.7.33; m.; 1 s.; 1 d. Educ. University College London; Indiana University. Metal Box Co. Ltd., London, 1957-60; Syracuse University Management School, 1960-71; Lancaster University, 1972-86. Recreation: ornithology. Address: (b.) Strathclyde University, Glasgow, G1 1XQ.

Thomas, Professor Phillip Charles, BSc, PhD, FIBiol, CBiol. Principal, West of Scotland College of Agriculture, Auchincruive, Ayr, and Professor of Agriculture, Glasgow University, since 1987; b. 17.6.42, Pontypool; m., Pamela Mary Hirst; 1 s.; 1 d. Educ. Abersychan Grammar School; University College of North Wales, Bangor. Lecturer, Department of Animal Nutrition and Physiology, Leeds University, 1966-71; Research Scientist, Hannah Research Institute, Ayr, 1971-87. Publications: Nutritional Physiology of Farm Animals, 1983; Silage for Milk Production, 1983. Recreations: watching the garden grow; mini-rugby coaching. Address: (b.) West of Scotland College of Agriculture, Auchincruive, Ayr, KA6 5HW; T.-0292 520331.

Thomason, Edward, ACII. Convener, Shetland Islands Council, since 1986; b. 12.8.22, Lerwick; m., Dinah. Educ. Anderson Educational Institute, Lerwick. Councillor, since 1960; Convener, Zetland County Council, 1970-73; Director and Chairman, Sullom Voe Association Ltd. Recreations: fiddle and accordion music; writing magazine articles. Address: (h.) 14 Mounthooly Place, Lerwick, Shetland; T.-0595 2901.

Thompson, Professor Alan Eric, MA (Hons), PhD. Professor, School of Business and Financial Studies, Heriot-Watt University, since 1987; b. 16.9.24; m., Mary Heather Long; 3 s.; 1 d. Educ. Edinburgh University. Edinburgh University: Assistant in Political Economy, 1952-53, Lecturer in Economics, 1953-59 and 1964-71; Professor of the Economics of Government, Heriot-Watt University, 1972-87; MP (Labour), Dunfermline, 1959-

64; Member, Royal Fine Art Commission for Scotland, 1975-80; Chairman, Northern Offshore Maritime Resources Study, since 1974; Governor, Newbattle Abbey College, since 1975 (Chairman, 1980-83); Member, Local Government Boundaries Commission for Scotland, 1975-80; Member, Scottish Council for Adult Education in HM Forces, since 1973; BBC National Governor for Scotland, 1975-79; Governor, Leith Nautical College, 1981-85; Trustee, Bell's Nautical Trust, since 1981; Parliamentary Adviser, Pharmaceutical General Council (Scotland), since 1984; Chairman, Scottish-Soviet Coordinating Commitee for Trade and Technology, since 1985. Publication: Development of Economic Doctrine (Co-author), 1980. Recreation: writing children's stories and plays. Address: (h.) 11 Upper Gray Street, Edinburgh, EH9 1SN; T.-031-667 2140.

Thompson, Colin, CBE, DUniv, FRSE, MA, FMA. Writer, Lecturer and Broadcaster on art and museums; b. 2.11.19, Berkhamstead; m., Jean A.J. O'Connell; 1 s.; 1 d. Educ. Sedbergh; King's College, Cambridge; Chelsea Polytechnic. War Service, FS Wing (CMP) and GCHQ, 1941-45; Lecturer, Bath Academy of Art, Corsham, 1948-54; joined National Gallery of Scotland as Assistant Keeper, 1954; Director, National Galleries of Scotland, 1977-84. Member, Scottish Arts Council, 1976-83; Member, Edinburgh Festival Society, since 1979; founding Chairman, Edinburgh Festival Exhibitions Forum, 1982-85; Chairman, Scottish Museums Council, 1984-87; Member, Board of Governors, Edinburgh College of Art; Trustee, Buccleuch Heritage Trust. Publications: Pictures for Scotland, 1972; Hugo Van Der Goes and the Trinity Panels in Edinburgh (Co-author), 1974. Address: (h.) Edenkerry, Lasswade, Midlothian, EH18 1LW; T.-031-663 7927.

Thompson, Francis George, FIElecIE, MASEE, TEng, FSA Scot. Author of books on Highland subjects; Senior Lecturer, Lews Castle College, Stornoway; Director, An Lanntair Gallery, Stornoway; Director, Western Isles Development Fund; b. 29.3.31, Stornoway; m., Margaret Elaine Pullar; 1 s.; 3 d. Educ. Nicolson Institute, Stornoway. From 1946: supply maintenance electrician, technical writer, assistant publicity manager, lecturer; has held various offices within An Comann Gaidhealach, including editorship of Sruth, bilingual newspaper, 1967-71; books include: Harris and Lewis, 1968; Harris Tweed, 1969; Highlands and Islands, 1974; Crofting Years, 1985; Shell Guide to Northern Scotland, 1987; The Western Isles, 1988. Recreation: writing! Address: Am Fasgadh, 5 Rathad na Muilne, Stornoway, Lewis; T.-0851 3812.

Thompson, Professor Ian Bentley, BA, MA, PhD. Professor of Geography, Glasgow University, since 1976; b. 2.1.36, Dewsbury; m., Helene Lamerant; 4 d. Educ. Bourne Grammar School, Lincolnshire; Durham University; Indiana University. Instructor in Geography, Indiana University, 1954-55; Tutor in Geography, Durham University, 1955-56; Assistant Lecturer in Geography, Leeds University, 1956-59; Lecturer, Senior Lecturer, Reader in Geography, Southampton University, 1959-76. Chevalier des Palmes Academiques, 1985. Recreation: ornithology. Address: (h.) 132 Dowanhill Street, Glasgow, G12 9DN; T.-041-339 6298.

Thompson, John Robert, LLB, NP. Director of Administration, Inverclyde District Council, since 1981; Clerk, Inverclyde Licensing Board and District Court; Clerk of the Peace; Solicitor; b. 23.5.38, Glasgow; 1 s.; 1 d. Educ. Hutchesons' Grammar School; Glasgow University. Address: (b.) Municipal Buildings, Clyde Square, Greenock, PA15 1LY; T.-0475 24400.

Thompson, William Douglas, MB, ChB, PhD, MRCPath. Senior Lecturer in Pathology, Aberdeen University, since 1981; b. 29.10.46, Glasgow; m., Margaret Lilias McNeil Darroch; 3 s. Educ. High School of Glasgow; Glasgow University. Registrar and Lecturer in Pathology, Glasgow Royal Infirmary, 1971-80; Honorary Consultant, Aberdeen Royal Infirmary, since 1981. Recreations: skiing; fishing. Address: (b.) Department of Pathology, Aberdeen Royal Infirmary, Foresterhill, Aberdeen, AB9 2ZD; T.-0224 681818.

Thomson, Alan James Reid, FIB (Scot), MIPM, MBIM. Divisional General Manager (Personnel), Bank of Scotland, since 1982; b. 28.10.35, Airdrie; m., Eileen Isobel Millar; 1 s.; 1 d. Educ. Robert Gordon's College, Aberdeen. Bank of Scotland, since 1952; Staff Manager, 1974; Assistant General Manager (Staff), 1978. Member, Scotland Advisory Committee, Understanding British Industry; Member, Council, Institute of Bankers in Scotland (Convenor, Education Committee). Recreations: golf; swimming. Address: (b.) Bank of Scotland, Staff Department, PO Box 133, 62 George Street, Edinburgh, EH2 2RA; T.-031-243 5212.

Thomson, Rev. Alexander, BSc, BD, MPhil, PhD. Minister, Rutherglen Old Parish Church, since 1985; b. 25.4.47, Motherwell; m., Ann Fraser Smith; 2 s. Educ. Brandon High School and Dalziel High School, Motherwell; Glasgow University; Edinburgh University; Aberdeen University. Industrial Chemist, Dalziel Steel Works, Motherwell; Assistant Minister, New Kilpatrick Church, Bearsden, 1973-75; Minister: St. Columba's, Kilbirnie, 1975-82, Ardler, Kettins, Meigle, 1982-85. Publication: Tradition and Authority in Science and Theology, 1987. Address: 31 Highburgh Drive, Rutherglen, Glasgow; T.-041-647 6178.

Thomson, Alexander McEwan, SSC, NP. Solicitor; b. 13.11.17, Dublin; m., Marjorie May Wood; 2 s.; 1 d. Educ. Daniel Stewart's College; George Heriot's School; Edinburgh University. Partner, Drummond & Reid, 1960-69 and Drummond & Co., WS, 1969-83 (Senior Partner, 1970-83), retired, 1983; Solicitor to General Teaching Council for Scotland, 1966-83; Solicitor to Edinburgh (subsequently Lothian Regional) Assessor; President, Society of Solicitors in the Supreme

Courts of Scotland, 1979-82. Recreations: gardening; shooting. Address: (h.) The Steading, Leithhead, by Kirknewton, West Lothian; T.-0506 883393.

Thomson, Alistair MacLachlan. Director, Scottish Prison Service, 1982- 88; b. 2.7.30, Glasgow; m., Elizabeth McEwan; 2 s.; 1 d. Educ. Allan Glen's School, Glasgow. Entered Civil Service, 1951, as an Executive Officer, Department of Health for Scotland; served in Health Services and Town and Country Planning; Higher Executive Officer, Town and Country Planning, 1959; Assistant Private Secretary to Secretary of State for Scotland, 1964-66; Principal, 1966; Assistant Secretary, Social Work Services, 1975. Recreations: golf; music.

Thomson, Angus William, BSc (Hons), MSc, PhD, DSc, MRCPath, FIBiol. Reader in Immunopathology, Aberdeen University, since 1987; b. 13.2.48, Inverness; m., Robyn Gai Glover; 1 s.; 1 d. Educ. Inverness Royal Academy; Aberdeen University; Birmingham University. Marr-Walker Research Fellow, Department of Pathology, Aberdeen University, 1974-75; Lecturer in Pathology, Aberdeen University, 1975-82; MRC (UK) Senior Travelling Research Fellow, Kolling Institute of Medical Research, Sydney, Australia, 1981-82; Senior Lecturer in Immunopathology, Aberdeen University, 1982-87; numerous publications in cellular immunology; Committee Member, British Society for Immunology, since 1987, and British Transplantation Society, since 1988. Recreations: badminton; wine appreciation. Address: (h.) 57 Denview Road, Potterton, Aberdeen, AB4 OZL; T.-03584 3279.

Thomson, Bryden. Music Director and Principal Conductor, Scottish National Orchestra, since 1988. Educ. Royal Scottish Academy of Music and Drama. Has conducted SNO regularly since 1960s, including three years as Associate Conductor; former Principal Conductor: BBC Philharmonic, BBC Welsh, Ulster Orchestra, RTE Symphony Orchestra; has been Conductor, Norwegian Opera, Royal Opera (Stockholm), Scottish Opera.

Thomson, Colin, BSc (Hons), PhD, FRSC. Senior Lecturer in Theoretical Chemistry, St. Andrews University, since 1970; Regional Director of Research, National Foundation for Cancer Research, since 1977; Director, Association for International Cancer Research, since 1984; b. 6.7.37, Whitby, Yorkshire; m., Maureen Margaret Green; 2 s.; 2 d. Educ. Whitby Grammar School; Leeds University. Postdoctoral Research Fellow, California University, 1961-63; Postdoctoral (NATO) Research Fellow, Cambridge University, 1963-64; Lecturer in Theoretical Chemistry, St. Andrews University, 1964-70; Committee Member, SERC Computational Chemistry Committee, since 1983; Editor, RSC specialist reports. Recreations: jazz and dance band musician, walking; sailing. Address: (h.) 12 Drumcarrow Road, St. Andrews, KY16 8SE; T.-0334 74820.

Thomson, David Kinnear, CBE, TD, CStJ, JP, DL. President, Perth Festival of the Arts, since 1985; Honorary Sheriff, Perth and Kinross, since 1969; b. 26.3.10, Perth. Educ. Perth Academy; Strathallan School. Member, Committee of Management, Trustee Savings Bank, Perth/Tayside, 1959-83; Lord Provost of Perth, 1966-72; Member: Scottish Economic Planning Council, 1968-74, Scottish Council (Development and Industry), 1968-75; Member, IBA, 1969-75; Director, Scottish Opera, 1967-79; Director, Scottish Transport Group, 1972-78; Chairman, Tayside Health Board, 1973-77; Member, Cancer Research Committee (Perth), 1967-87. Recreations: walking; golf; listening to music. Address: (h.) Fairhill, Oakbank Road, Perth.

Thomson, Professor Derick S., MA (Aberdeen), BA (Cantab), DLitt (Univ. of Wales), FRSE. Professor of Celtic, Glasgow University, since 1963; b. 5.8.21, Stornoway; m., Carol Galbraith; 5 s.; 1 d. Educ. Nicolson Institute, Stornoway; Aberdeen University; Cambridge University; University College of North Wales, Bangor. Taught at Edinburgh, Glasgow and Aberdeen Universities before returning to Glasgow as Professor, 1963; Chairman, Gaelic Books Council, since 1968; President, Scottish Gaelic Texts Society; Chairman, Catherine McCaig's Trust; former Member, Scottish Arts Council; first recipient, Ossian Prize, 1974; author of numerous books and articles, including An Introduction to Gaelic Poetry, The Companion to Gaelic Scotland and collections of Gaelic poetry, including collected poems Creachadh na Clarsaich. Address: (h.) 19 Bemersyde Avenue, Glasgow, G41; T.-041-632 7880.

Thomson, Duncan, MA, PhD. Keeper, Scottish National Portrait Gallery, since 1982; b. 2.10.34, Killearn; m., Julia Jane Macphail; 1 d. Educ. Airdrie Academy; Edinburgh University; Edinburgh College of Art; Moray House College of Education. Teacher of Art; Assistant Keeper, Scottish National Portrait Gallery. Member, Art Committee, and Chairman, Exhibition Panel, Scottish Arts Council. Publication: The Life and Art of George Jamesone, 1974. Recreations: literature; walking; looking. Address: (b.) Scottish National Portrait Gallery, 1 Queen Street, Edinburgh, EH2 1JD; T.-031-556 8921.

Thomson, Sir (Frederick Douglas) David, Bt, BA. Deputy Chairman, The Ben Line Group Limited, since 1984 (Director, since 1964); Chairman, Britannia Steamship Insurance Association Limited, since 1986 (Director, since 1965); Director, Life Association of Scotland Ltd., since 1970; Director, Caledonian Offshore PLC, since 1971; Chairman, Through Transport Marine Mutual Assurance Association (Bermuda) Ltd., since 1984 (Director, since 1973); Director, Danae Investment Trust Ltd., since 1979; Director, Cambrian & General Securities PLC, since 1982; Chairman, Jove Investment Trust PLC, since 1983; Director, Martin Currie Pacific Trust PLC, since 1985; Member, Royal Company of Archers (Queen's Bodyguard for Scotland); b. 14.2.40, Edinburgh; m.; 2 s.; 1 d. Educ. Eton; University College, Oxford. Recreations: shooting; skiing; tennis. Address: (h.) Glenbrook House, Balerno, Midlothian; T.-031-449 4116.

Thomson, Iain Marshall, FIA (Scot). Managing Director, United Auctions (Eastern) Limited (formerly Macdonald, Fraser & Co. Limited), since 1986; Director, Perth City Auctions, since 1983; b. 28.9.38, Stirling; 2 d. Educ. Lanark Grammar School; George Watson's College, Edinburgh. Joined Macdonald, Fraser and Co. Ltd., 1955, appointed Director, 1970, Joint Managing Director, 1976; Council Member, Institute of Auctioneers and Appraisers in Scotland, since 1972, Vice President, 1986-88; Member, Board, Royal Highland and Agricultural Society of Scotland, 1981-85; appointed by Secretary of State for Scotland to Panel of Arbiters, 1983; Past Chairman, Perth and District Junior Agricultural Club. Recreations: golf; fishing. Address: (b.) 17 Caledonian Road, Perth, PH1 5QY; T.-0738 26183.

Thomson, James, BA, FRICS, DipRating, FRVA. Lands Valuation Assessor and Electoral Registration Officer, Fife Regional Council, since 1973, and Community Charge Registration Officer, since 1987; b. 12.2.31, Glasgow. Chartered Valuation Surveyor, Glasgow Corporation, until 1957; Fife County Council: Chartered Valuation Surveyor, 1957-68, Depute County Assessor and ERO, 1968-73, County Assessor and ERO, 1973-75. President, Scottish Assessors' Association, since 1986. Address: (b.) Fife House (03), North Street, Glenrothes, Fife, KY7 5LT; T.-0592 757371.

Thomson, John, QFSM, FIFireE. Firemaster, Fife Regional Council, since 1983; b. 2.4.29, Airdrie; m., Janet; 1 s.; 2 d. Educ. Airdrie Academy. Divisional Officer: Grade III, 1968, Grade II, 1974, Grade I, 1975; Acting Senior Divisional Officer, 1976; Deputy/Assistant Firemaster, 1979. Recreation: golf. Address: (b.) Fire and Rescue Service HQ, Strathore Road, Thornton, Kirkcaldy, KY1 4DF; T.-Glenrothes 774451.

Thomson, John Aidan Francis, MA, DPhil, FRHistS. Reader in Mediaeval History, Glasgow University, since 1983; b. 26.7.34, Edinburgh; m., Katherine J.V. Bell; 1 s.; 1 d. Educ. George Watson's Boys' College, Edinburgh; Edinburgh University; Balliol College, Oxford. Glasgow University: Assistant in Mediaeval History, 1960, Lecturer, 1961, Senior Lecturer, 1974. President, Glasgow Archaeological Society, 1978-81. Publications: The Later Lollards 1414-1520, 1965; Popes and Princes 1417-1517, 1980; The Transformation of Mediaeval England 1370-1529, 1983; Towns and Townspeople in the Fifteenth Century (Editor), 1988. Recreations: hill-walking; gardening. Address: (b.) Department of Medieval History, Glasgow University, Glasgow, G12 8QQ; T.-041-339 8855.

Thomson, John Alexander, MD, PhD, FRCPGlas, FRCPLond. Reader in Medicine, University Department of Medicine, Glasgow University, since 1981; Honorary Consultant Physician, Glasgow Royal Infirmary, since 1968; b. 19.4.33, Airdrie; m., Fiona Jane Reid; 2 s.; 2 d. Educ. Hamilton Academy; Glasgow University. House Physician, then House Surgeon, Glasgow Royal Infirmary, 1956-57; Royal Army Medical Corps, 1957-59 (Regimental Medical Officer, 13/18 Royal Hussars); House Surgeon, Glasgow Royal Maternity and Women's Hospital, 1959-60; McIntyre Clinical Research Scholar in Medicine, University Department of Medicine, 1960-61; Registrar in Medicine, then Senior Registrar, University Medical Unit, Glasgow Royal Infirmary, 1961-68; Senior Lecturer in Medicine and Consultant Endocrinologist, Glasgow Royal Infirmary, 1968-81. Address: (b.) University Department of Medicine, Royal Infirmary, 10 Alexandra Parade, Glasgow, G31 2ER; T.-041-552 3535.

Thomson, Rev. John Bruce, MA, BD. Minister, Scone Old Parish Church, since 1983; also Minister, St. David's, Stormontfield, since 1983; Keeper, Benefice Register, Perth Presbytery, since 1984; b. 14.7.44, Edinburgh; m., Margaret Anne Craigen; 1 s.; 1 d. Educ. James Gillespie's Boys' School; George Heriot's School, Edinburgh; Edinburgh University; New College, Edinburgh. Ordained Assistant, Dundee Parish Church (St. Mary's), 1971-74; Minister, Thurso West Church, 1974-83; Moderator, Caithness Presbytery, 1979-80. Contributor, BBC Radio Orkney, Radio Tay, Reflections (Grampian TV), Scotspraise (BBC TV); Chairman, Tay Churches Radio Council, since 1987. Recreations: swimming; golf; Rotary Club of Perth St. John's. Address: The Manse, Burnside, Scone, Perth, PH2 6LP; T.-0738 52030.

Thomson, John C., DDS, LDS, HDD, FDS. Senior Lecturer, Department of Prosthodontics, Glasgow University, and Consultant, Greater Glasgow Health Board, 1968-87; b. 4.2.22, Airdrie; m., Christine M. Rodger; 1 s.; 1 d. Educ. Airdrie Academy; Glasgow Dental Hospital and School. Dental Officer, RAF, 1943-48; General Dental Practitioner, 1948-50; Lecturer, Glasgow University, and Registrar/Senior Registrar, West Regional Hospital Board, 1950-68. President, Glasgow Odontological Society, 1968; Chairman, Board of Governors, Langside College of Further Education, 1971-74; President, West of Scotland Branch, British Dental Association, 1977. Address: (h.) 10 Mosspark Road, Milngavie, Glasgow, G62 8NJ; T.-041-956 2591.

Thomson, Professor Joseph McGeachy, LLB. Professor of Law, Strathclyde University, since 1984; Deputy General Editor, Stair Memorial Encyclopaedia of the Laws of Scotland, since 1985; b. 6.5.48, Campbeltown. Educ. Keil School, Dumbarton; Edinburgh University. Lecturer in Law, Birmingham University, 1970-74; Lecturer in Laws, King's College, London, 1974-84. Recreations: opera; ballet; food and wine. Address: (h.) 140 Hyndland Road, Glasgow; T.-041-334 6682.

Thomson, Professor Kenneth James, MA, MSc, MS. Professor of Agricultural Economics, Aberdeen University, since 1986; b. 30.9.45, Aberdeen; m., Lydia. Educ. Aberdeen Grammar School; Aberdeen University; London University; Iowa State University. Lecturer and Senior Lecturer, Department of Agricultural Economics, Newcastle upon Tyne University, 1972-86; Economics R. & D. Leader, Scottish Agricultural Colleges, since 1987; Editor, Journal of Agricultural Economics, since 1987. Publication: The Cost of the Common Agricultural Policy, 1982. Recreations: viola-playing; mountaineering. Address: (b.) School of Agriculture, 581 King Street, Aberdeen, AB9 1UD; T.-0224 480291.

Thomson, Margaret Catherine, BL. District Administrator, Renfrew District Council, since 1987; b. 13.4.31, Largs. Educ. Greenock Academy;

Glasgow University. Qualified Assistant in private practice; joined Paisley Corporation as Legal Assistant; appointed Junior Depute Town Clerk of Paisley, 1968; Senior Depute Director of Administration, Renfrew District Council, 1974. Recreations: golf; bowling; reading. Address: (b.) Municipal Buildings, Paisley; T.-041-889 5400.

Thomson, Margaret Wallace, OBE (1986), RGN, RSCN, SCM, RNT. Chief Executive Officer, National Board for Nurses, Midwives and Health Visitors for Scotland, 1981-86; b. 8.6.27, Edinburgh. Educ. Mary Erksine School for Girls; Edinburgh University. Registrar, General Nursing Council for Scotland; Education Officer, General Nursing Council for Scotland; Principal Tutor/Tutor, Belfast, Aberdeen, Nigeria, Edinburgh; Ward Sister/Staff Nurse, Edinburgh. Elder, Church of Scotland. Address: (h.) 28 Blinkbonny Gardens, Edinburgh; T.-031-332 3628.

Thomson, Margery Jean, JP. Non-Executive Member, South of Scotland Electricity Board, since 1980; b. 24.2.27, Bearsden; m., John Alexander Thomson; 2 s.; 2 d. Educ. Beacon School, Bridge of Allan; Glasgow College of Domestic Science. Past Chairman, Dumfriesshire Conservative Association; former Vice-Chairman, South of Scotland Euro Constituency. Recreations: gardening; embroidery. Address: (h.) Summerhill House, Annan, Dumfriesshire.

Thomson, Sheriff Nigel Ernest Drummond, MA, LLB. Sheriff of Lothian and Borders, at Edinburgh, since 1976, and at Peebles, since 1983; b. 19.6.26, Aberdeen; m., Snjolaug Magnusson; 1 s.; 1 d. Educ. George Watson's Boys' College; St. Andrews University; Edinburgh University. Called to Scottish Bar, 1953; appointed Sheriff at Hamilton, 1966; Member, Scottish Arts Council, 1978 (Chairman, Music Committee, 1979-84). Honorary President, Strathaven Arts Guild; Honorary Vice-President, Tenovus-Scotland; Honorary President, Scottish Association for Counselling; Chairman, Edinburgh Youth Orchestra. Recreations: music; woodwork; golf. Address: (h.) 50 Grange Road, Edinburgh; T.-031-667 2166.

Thomson, Peter. Returning Officer, Local Plebiscites, since 1984. Admitted Faculty of Advocates, 1946; Sheriff at Wick, 1955-62, at Hamilton, 1962-77; founded Scottish Plebiscite Society, 1947; Returning Officer, annual local plebiscites: Lanark, 1984, Banff, 1985, Hawick, 1986, St. Andrews, 1987. Address: (h.) Haughhead Farm House, Uddingston, G71 7RR; T.-041-641 2843.

Thomson, Rev. Peter David, MA, BD. Minister, Comrie and Strowan with Dundurn, since 1978; b. 4.11.41, St. Andrews; m., Margaret Celia Murray; 1 s.; 1 d. Educ. Dundee High School; Edinburgh University; Glasgow University; Tubingen University. Minister, Balmaclellan with Kells, 1968-78; Moderator, Kirkcudbright Presbytery, 1974-75; Convener, Nomination Committee, General Assembly, 1982-85. Chairman, New Galloway and Kells Community Council, 1976-78. Recreations: haphazardly pursued interests in photography, wildlife, music, theology, current affairs. Address: The Manse, Comrie, Perthshire, Ph6 2HE; T.-0764 70269.

Thomson, Rev. Peter George, MA, BD (Hons). Minister, Fullarton Parish Church, Irvine, since 1953; b. 18.5.20, Campsie Glen; m., Pamela I.M. Thorne; 3 s.; 1 d. Educ. Dunbar Grammar School; Edinburgh University and New College. Warden, New College Settlement, Pleasance, Edinburgh; Chaplain with YMCA, Germany; ordained and inducted, St. David's Church, Buckhaven, 1947; Moderator, Irvine and Kilmarnock Presbytery, 1966-67; Moderator, Synod of Ayr; Convener, National Church Extension, Church of Scotland, 1983-87. Honorary Chaplain, British Sailors' Society; Honorary Burgess, Royal Burgh of Irvine, 1967. Recreations: gardening; golf. Address: Fullarton Parish Manse, Irvine, Ayrshire; T.-Irvine 79909.

Thomson, Robert Scott, BSc, CChem, MRCS. Rector, Larkhall Academy, since 1974; b. 9.6.33, Newtongrange; m., Helen Mary McIntosh; 1 d. Educ. Newbattle Secondary School; Dalkeith High School; Heriot-Watt University. Scientific Technical Officer, NCB, 1950-59; Chemistry Teacher, George Watson's College, 1963-67; Principal Teacher of Chemistry: Dalkeith High School, 1967-70, George Watson's College, 1970-74. Member, Consultative Committee on the Curriculum; Chairman, Committee on Technology; Chairman, Scottish Education Industry Committee. Recreations: reading; gardening; bowling. Address: (b.) Larkhall Academy, Cherryhill, Larkhall, ML9 1QN; T.-Larkhall 881570.

Thomson, Roy Hendry, CStJ, MA (Hons), JP. Chairman, Kincardine and Deeside Social and Liberal Democrats; Chairman, Friends of Aberdeen University Library; b. 27.8.32, Aberdeen; m., Nancy; 3 d. Educ. Aberdeen Grammar School; Aberdeen University. National Service, Gordon Highlanders, 1955-57; personnel and market research, Rowntree & Co. Ltd., 1957-60; Chairman/Director, family motor business, until 1986; former Director, The Scottish Ballet (Chairman, 1983-87); former Member, City of Aberdeen District Council; Past President: Rotary Club of Aberdeen, Mountain Rescue Association, Aberdeen. Recreations: skiing; hill-walking; bee-keeping. Address: (h.) Baillieswells House, Baillieswells Road, Bieldside, Aberdeen, AB1 9BQ; T.-Aberdeen 867960.

Thomson, Stuart James, HND (Agric). General Secretary, Ayrshire Cattle Society of GB and Ireland, since 1984; b. 29.8.54, Kirkwall; m., Carolynne Henderson; 1 s. Educ. Kirkwall Grammar School; School of Agriculture, Aberdeen. Regional Officer, North of Scotland Milk Marketing Board, 1976-84. Recreations: gardening; golf; fishing. Address: (b.) 1 Racecourse Road, Ayr, KA7 2DE; T.-Ayr 267123.

Thomson, Rev. Thomas, MA. Minister, Wardie Parish Church, Edinburgh, since 1961; b. 16.3.20, Edinburgh; m., Mary Euphemia McTavish; 1 s. Educ. George Heriot's School, Edinburgh; Edinburgh University; New College, Edinburgh. War Service, 1940-46 (Captain, Gordon Highlanders); Assistant Minister, North Morningside Church, Edinburgh, 1952-54; Minister, Christ's Church, Dunollie, Oban, 1954-61. Governor, George Heriot's Trust, since 1979; Convener, Department of Home Mission, 1980-83; Joint Convener, **Depart-**

ment of Ministry and Mission, 1983-84; Moderator, Edinburgh Presbytery, 1982. Recreation: music. Address: Wardie Parish Church Manse, 35 Lomond Road, Edinburgh, EH5 3JN; T.-031-552 3328.

Thomson, Thomas James, CBE (1983), OBE (1978), FRCPGlas, FRCPLond, FRCPEdin, FRCPIre. Chairman, Greater Glasgow Health Board, since 1987; b. 8.4.23, Airdrie; m., Jessie Smith Shotbolt; 2 s.; 1 d. Educ. Airdrie Academy; Glasgow University. Lecturer, Department of Materia Medica, Glasgow University, 1953-61; Postgraduate Adviser to Glasgow Northern Hospitals, 1961-80; Honorary Secretary, RCPSGlas, 1965-73; Secretary, Specialist Advisory Committee for General Internal Medicine for UK, 1970-74; Chairman: Medico-Pharmaceutical Forum, 1978-80 (Chairman, Education Advisory Board, 1979-83); Conference of Royal Colleges and Faculties in Scotland, 1982-85; National Medical Consultative Committee for Scotland, 1982-87; President, RCPSGlas, 1982-84; Hon.FACP, 1983; Hon. LLD, Glasgow University, 1988. Publications: Dilling's Pharmacology (Co-Editor); Gastroenterology - an integrated course. Recreations: swimming; golfing. Address: (h.) 1 Varna Road, Glasgow, G14 9NE; T.-041-959 5930.

Thomson, Walter, MBE. Editor, Selkirk Advertiser, 1932-86; Rugby Writer, Sunday Post, since 1931; b. 20.3.13, Selkirk; m., Gerda; 2 d. Educ. Selkirk High School; Heriot-Watt. Army (Captain), 1940-46. Recreation: photography. Address: (h.) Cruachan, Murrayfield, Selkirk; T.-Selkirk 20261.

Thomson, William Andrew Charles. Director, Ben Line Group, since 1978; Chairman, Forth Ports Authority, since 1984; Chairman, Edinburgh Maritime, since 1987; Chairman, British Ports Federation, since 1988; Member, Trinity House Lighthouse Board, since 1984; Managing Director, Edinburgh Tankers, since 1986; Chairman, River Tweed Commissioners; b. 20.1.48, Edinburgh; m., Cecilia Bernadette Gill; 2 s.; 1 d. Educ. Gordonstoun. Short Service commission, 17/21st Lancers. Recreations: shooting; fishing; golf. Address: (b.) 33 St. Mary's Street, Edinburgh; T.-031-557 2323.

Thomson, Rev. William Halliday. Minister, Liberton Northfield Parish Church, Edinburgh, since 1987; b. 21.1.34, Kilmarnock; m., Margaret; 4 d. Educ. James Hamilton Academy; Kilmarnock Academy; Glasgow University and Trinity College. National Service, 1952-54; in commerce, 1949-59; student assistant, Riccarton Parish Church, Kilmarnock, 1963-64; Minister: Broxburn West, 1964-70, John Knox (Gerrard Street), Aberdeen, 1970-76, St. Columba's, Glenrothes, 1976-87. Recreations: swimming; hill-walking; snooker. Address: 9 Claverhouse Drive, Edinburgh, EH16 6BR; T.-031-658 1754.

Thomson, William P.L., MA. Rector, Kirkwall Grammar School, since 1971; b. 9.5.33, Newmilns. Educ. Dundee High School; St. Andrews University. Principal Teacher of History and Geography, then Deputy Headteacher, Anderson High School, Lerwick. Publications: The Little General and the Rousay Crofters; Kelp-Making in Orkney. Address: (b.) Kirkwall Grammar School, Kirkwall, Orkney; T.-0856 2102.

Thorne, Roderick Hugh Frank, MA, PGCE (Cantab), AdvCertEd (Oxon). Head Teacher, Sanday Junior High School, Orkney, since 1984; b. 7.5.47, Maidenhead; m., Sylvia Driscoll; 3 s. Educ. Leighton Park School; Trinity, Cambridge; Christ Church, Oxford. Head Teacher: Fetlar, Shetland, 1971-74, Fair Isle, 1976-81, Bredhurst, Kent, 1981-84. Publications: Fetlar: Some Facts and Stories; Fair Isle School 1878-1978; Shetland Animal Studies; Fair Isle Birds (Co-author). Recreations: natural history; golf; running. Address: Schoolhouse, Sanday, Orkney, KW17 2AY; T.-08575 404.

Thornton-Kemsley, Nigel Scott, CBE (1987), OStJ, DL. Managing Director, Thornton Farms Ltd., since 1956; Chairman, North of Scotland College of Agriculture, since 1982; Director, Royal Highland and Agricultural Society of Scotland, since 1971; Director, Scottish Agricultural Colleges, since 1987; Governor, Rowett Research Institute, since 1981; b. 14.8.33, Chigwell, Essex; m., Judith Gay Sanders; 1 s.; 2 d. Educ. Fettes College; East of Scotland College of Agriculture. National Service: Royal Signals, 1954-56, TA 51st Highland Signal Regiment, 1957-63, 3rd Bn., Gordon Highlanders, 1963-71, OC TAVR Company; Major on retiral; Deputy Lieutenant, Kincardineshire, 1978; President, Aberdeen-Angus Cattle Society, 1981-82; Member, Scottish American Community Relations Council, 1971-80; Chairman, Council, Scottish Agricultural Colleges, 1982-84; Life Governor, Imperial Cancer Research Council, since 1978; Past President, Royal Northern Agricultural Society; Past President, Fettercairn Farmers' Club. Recreation: shooting. Address: Thornton Castle, Laurencekirk, Kincardineshire; T.-056 17 301.

Thorpe, John Elton, BA, PhD. Senior Principal Scientific Officer, Freshwater Fisheries Laboratory, Pitlochry, since 1981; b. 24.1.35, Wolverhampton; m., Judith Anne Johnson; 2 s. Educ. Kingswood School, Bath; Jesus College, Cambridge. Cambridge Expedition to British Honduras, 1959-60 (Leader); Shell International Chemical Co. Ltd., London, 1960-62; joined DAFS Freshwater Fisheries Laboratory, Pitlochry, 1963. Council Member, Fisheries Society of British Isles, 1974-77, 1978-81, since 1985; Editorial Board, Fisheries Management, 1978-84 and Aquaculture and Fisheries Management, since 1985; Chairman, Killiecrankie and Fincastle Community Council, 1976-78. Publications: four books; 100 scientific papers. Recreations: travelling; Baroque music. Address: (b.) Freshwater Fisheries Laboratory, Pitlochry, Perthshire, PH16 5LW; T.-0796 2060.

Thrower, Rev. Charles George, BSc. Minister, Carnbee linked with Pittenweem, since 1970; b. 22.11.37, Barton Turf, Norfolk; m., Dr. Stephanie A.M. Thrower; 1 s.; 3 d. Educ. King Edward VI School, Norwich; Britannia Royal Naval College, Dartmouth. Electrical branch training, H.M.S. Girdle-Ness (Malta), 1960-61; divinity student, 1961-64; probationer, St. Andrews Church, Dundee, 1964-65; missionary appointment, Hampden with Falmouth, Trelawny, Jamaica, 1966-70. Synod of Fife Youth Adviser, 1971-74; equipped Netherbow studio for stereo recording while serving on Church of Scotland

Publications Committee; Chairman, East Neuk of Fife Committee, RSSPCC, since 1974, and Member, RSSPCC Central Committees, since 1976. Recreations: bee-keeping; water colour painting; photography; sailing; gardening; local church history. Address: The Manse, 2 Milton Place, Pittenweem, Fife, KY10 2LR; T.-0333 311255.

Thrower, James Arthur, MA (Dunelm), BLitt (Oxon), PhD (Aberdeen). Director, Centre for the Study of Religions, Aberdeen University, since 1987 (Senior Lecturer in History of Religions, since 1970, and Head, Department of Religious Studies, 1984-87); b. 5.10.36, Guisborough; m., Judith Elizabeth Gauss; 3 d. Educ. Guisborough Grammar School; Durham University; St. Edmund Hall, Oxford University. Staff Tutor, Eastern District, WEA, 1962-64; Lecturer in Philosophy of Religion, Ghana University, 1964-68; Lecturer in Religious Studies, Bede College, Durham University, 1968-70; Visiting Professor: Helsinki University, 1974, Polish Academy of Sciences, 1976; British Council Exchange Scholar, Leningrad University, 1976 and 1978; Visiting Scholar, Gdansk University, 1981 and 1982; Visiting Professor, Aligarh Muslim University, India, 1988; Warden, Balgownie Lodge, Aberdeen University, 1971-82. Publications: A Short History of Western Atheism, 1971; The Alternative Tradition, 1981; Marxist-Leninist "Scientific Atheism", 1983; Marxism-Leninism as the Civil Religion of Soviet Society, 1988. Recreations: listening to music; photography; travelling; gardening. Address: (h.) 233 Clifton Road, Aberdeen; T.-Aberdeen 485641.

Thurso, Viscount (Robin Macdonald Sinclair), 2nd Viscount, 5th Bt. of Ulbster, JP. Lord Lieutenant of Caithness, since 1973; Baron of Thurso; Chairman, Sinclair Family Trust Ltd; Chairman, Lochdhu Hotels Ltd.; Chairman, Thurso Fisheries Ltd.; Director, Stephens (Plastics) Ltd.; Founder and first Chairman, Caithness Glass Ltd.; b. 24.12.22, Kingston Vale; m., Margaret Beaumont Brokensha; 2 s.; 1 d. Educ. Eton; New College, Oxford; Edinburgh University. RAF, 1941-46; Flt.-Lt., 684 Squadron, 540 Squadron; commanded Edinburgh University Air Squadron, 1946; Member, Caithness County Council, 1949, 1952, 1955, 1958; Member, Thurso Town Council, 1957, 1960 (resigned, 1961), 1965, 1968, 1971; President, North Country Cheviot Sheep Society, 1951-54; Chairman, Caithness and Sutherland Youth Employment Committee, 1957-75; Member, Red Deer Commission, 1965-74; President, Highland Society of London, 1980-82; Council Member, Royal National Mission to Deep Sea Fishermen, 1983-85; President, Boys' Brigade, since 1985; Vice Lieutenant, Caithness, 1964-73. Recreations: fishing; shooting; amateur drama. Address: Thurso East Mains, Thurso, Caithness, KW14 8HW; T.-0847 62600.

Thyne, Malcolm Tod, MA. Headmaster, Fettes College, since 1988; b. 6.11.42, Edinburgh; m., Eleanor Christine Scott; 2 s. Educ. The Leys School, Cambridge; Clare College, Cambridge. Assistant Master, Edinburgh Academy, 1965-69; Assistant Master, Oundle School, 1969-80 (Housemaster, 1972-80); Headmaster, St. Bees School, Cumbria, 1980-88. Publications: Periodicity, Atomic Structure and Bonding (Revised Nuffield Chemistry), 1976; contributions to Revised Nuffield Chemistry Handbook for Pupils and Teachers Guides, 1978. Recreation: mountaineering. Address: (b.) Fettes College, Edinburgh, EH4 1QX; T.-031-332 3642.

Timbury, Professor Morag Crichton, MD, PhD, FRCPath, FRCPGlas, FRSE. Professor of Bacteriology, Glasgow University (Royal Infirmary), since 1978; Honorary Consultant Bacteriologist and Virologist, Greater Glasgow Health Board, and Head, Regional Virus Laboratory, Ruchill Hospital, since 1983; b. 29.9.30, Bearsden; m., Gerald C. Timbury (deceased); 1 d. Educ. St. Bride's School, Helensburgh; Glasgow University. Trained in medical bacteriology and virology; Maurice Bloch Research Fellow in Virology; Lecturer in Bacteriology, Senior Lecturer, then Reader in Virology, Glasgow University, 1966-78. Publications: Notes on Medical Virology; Notes on Medical Bacteriology (Co-author). Recreations: reading; military history; mediaeval fortified houses. Address: (b.) Department of Bacteriology, Glasgow Royal Infirmary, Glasgow, G4 0SF; T.-041-552 3535, Ext. 5270.

Timms, Professor Duncan William Graham, BA, PhD (Cantab). Professor, Stirling University, since 1972; b. 11.10.38, Cheltenham; m., Elizabeth Anne Barnes; 1 s.; 1 d. Educ. Pate's Grammar School, Cheltenham; St. Catharine's College, Cambridge. Lecturer, Senior Lecturer, Queensland University, 1962-67; Professor, Auckland University, 1968-72; Deputy Principal, Stirling University, 1978-80 and 1981-84 (Acting Principal and Vice-Chancellor, 1980-81); Visiting Professor, Stockholm University, 1984-85; Chairman, MacRobert Arts Centre. Recreations: map collecting; philately of the South Pacific. Address: (h.) 7 East Claremont, Edinburgh, EH7.

Tinsley, Emeritus Professor Joseph, BSc, PhD, FRSE, FRSC, CChem. Emeritus Professor of Soil Science, Aberdeen University, since 1981; Chairman, DAFS Residual Manurial Values Committee, since 1976; President, Aberdeen YMCA, since 1984; b. 24.7.16, Wootton Bassett; m., Mary Joan Swain; 4 d. Educ. Reading University. Assistant Agricultural Advisory Chemist, MAFF, SE Counties of England, 1938-43; Lecturer in Agricultural Chemistry, Reading University, 1943-58; Reader in Soil Science and Head of Department, Aberdeen University, 1958-71; first Professor of Soil Science, Aberdeen University, 1971-81. President, British Society of Soil Science, 1970-72. Recreations: exploring landscapes in the UK and overseas; support for Christian organisations and aid to third world countries; photography, mainly to illustrate lectures on scientific and travel topics; family interests. Address: (h.) 52 Victoria Street, Aberdeen, AB1 1XA; T.-0224 646552.

Titterington, Professor (Donald) Michael, BSc, PhD, DipMathStat. Titular Professor of Statistics, Glasgow University, since 1982; b. 20.11.45, Marple, Cheshire; m., Mary Hourie Philp; 1 s. Educ. High School of Stirling; Edinburgh University; Cambridge University. Lecturer, then Senior Lecturer, Department of Statistics, Glasgow University, 1972-82; visiting appointments: Princeton University, 1978, State University of New York,

1980, Wisconsin University, 1982, Australian National University, 1982; Associate Editor, Biometrika, 1979-85, Annals of Statistics, 1983-85, and Journal, American Statistical Association, since 1986; Joint Editor, Journal of the Royal Statistical Society, Series B, since 1986; elected Fellow, Institute of Mathematical Statistics, 1986. Publications: Statistical Analysis of Finite Mixture Distributions (Co-author); many journal articles. Recreations: sailing; hill-walking. Address: (b.) Department of Statistics, Glasgow University, Glasgow, G12 8QQ; T.-041-339 8855.

Tivy, Professor Joy, BA, BSc, PhD, FRSE, FRSGS. Professor (Titular), Department of Geography and Topographic Science, Glasgow University, since 1976; Chairman, Scottish Field Studies Association, since 1984; b. 24.8.24, Glasgow. Educ. Masonic Girls School and Alexandra College, Dublin; Trinity College, Dublin University; Edinburgh University. Assistant Mistress, Leeds Girls High School; Research Assistant, Department of Planning, Wakefield; Assistant Lecturer and Lecturer, Department of Geography, Edinburgh University; Lecturer, Senior Lecturer, Reader, Department of Geography, Glasgow University; Visiting Research Fellow, Universite de Strasbourg, 1956, Syracuse University, 1963-64, Cornell University, 1971, Lund University, Arhus University, and Australian National University, 1981-83; Editor, Scottish Geographical Magazine, 1955-65; Secretary and Editor, Scottish Field Studies Association, 1960-75; Member, Scottish Advisory Committee to the Nature Conservancy (Scotland), 1974-80. Publications: The Organic Resources of Scotland - their Nature and Evaluation, 1973; Human Impact on the Ecosystem, 1981; Biogeography: The Role of Plants in the Ecosphere, 1982. Recreations: painting; gardening; tapestry. Address: (h.) 51 Hyndland Road, Glasgow; T.-041-339 3801.

Tocher, Gordon James MacLaren, BMus (Hons). Composer and Piano Teacher; b. 30.12.57, Inverness. Educ. Inverness Royal Academy; Aberdeen University. Taught at several schools in Inverness, 1981-84; freelance, since 1984; Conductor, The Inverness Singers; Assistant Organist, Inverness Cathedral; compositions include piano, chamber and choral works, also choral arrangements of Scottish and other folk songs. Address: (h.) 54 Glenburn Drive, Inverness, IV2 4NE; T.-0463 232345.

Tod, Stewart, DiplArch, FSA Scot. Senior Partner, Stewart Tod & Partners, Architects, Edinburgh, since 1977; b. 30.4.27, West Wemyss; m., A. Vivienne J. Nixon; 2 s.; 2 d. Educ. Buckhaven High School; Edinburgh College of Art. RAF, 1945-49; Stratton Davis & Yates, 1952-55; Falkirk District Council, 1955-57; Carr and Matthew, 1957-60; David Carr Architects, 1960-77. Committee Member, Association for the Preservation of Rural Scotland; General Trustee, Church of Scotland; Member, Church of Scotland Board of Practice and Procedure. Recreation: bee-keeping. Address: (h.) 12 Greenhill Terrace, Edinburgh; T.-031-447 4625.

Todd, Rev. Andrew Stewart, MA, BD, DD. Minister, St. Machar's Cathedral, Old Aberdeen, since 1967; b. 26.5.26, Alloa; m., Janet Agnes Brown Smith; 2 s.; 2 d. Educ. High School of Stirling; Edinburgh University; Basel University. Assistant Minister, St. Cuthbert's, Edinburgh, 1951-52; Minister: Symington, Lanarkshire, 1952; North Leith, 1960; Member, Church Hymnary Revision Comittee, 1963-73; Convener, General Assembly's Committee on Public Worship and Aids to Devotion, 1974-78; Moderator, Aberdeen Presbytery, 1980-81; Vice-Convener, Panel on Doctrine; Member, Church Hymnary Trust; awarded Honorary Doctorate, Aberdeen University, 1982; translator of three theological books from German into English; Honorary President, Church Service Society; Honorary President, Scottish Church Society. Recreations: music; gardening. Address: 18 The Chanonry, Old Aberdeen, Aberdeen; T.-0224 483688.

Tolley, David Anthony, MB, BS (Lond), FRCS, FRCSEdin. Consultant Urological Surgeon, Edinburgh Royal Infirmary, since 1980; Honorary Senior Lecturer, Department of Surgery/Urology, Edinburgh University, since 1980; Director, Scottish Lithotriptor Centre; b. 29.11.47, Warrington; m., Judith Anne Finn; 3 s.; 1 d. Educ. Manchester Grammar School; Kings College Hospital Medical School, London University. House Surgeon and Physician, Kings College Hospital; Lecturer in Human Morphology, Southampton University; Lecturer in Anatomy and Fulbright Fellow, University of Texas at Houston; Surgical Registrar, Hammersmith and Ealing Hospitals, London; Senior Surgical Registrar (Urology), Kings College Hospital, London; Senior Urological Registrar, Yorkshire Regional Training Scheme. Chairman, Bladder Cancer Sub Group, MRC Working Party on Urological Cancer; Past Chairman, Scottish Urological Oncology Group. Recreations: opera; cross-country skiing; motor racing; sailing. Address: (b.) Murrayfield Hospital, Corstorphine Road, Edinburgh; T.-031-334 0363.

Tollin, Patrick, BSc, PhD, FRSE. Reader in Physics, Dundee University, since 1977; b. 22.4.38, Glasgow; m., Marie Collins; 2 s.; 2 d. Educ. St. Aloysius College, Glasgow; Glasgow University; Fitzwilliam College, Cambridge. Assistant Lecturer, Lecturer, Senior Lecturer, Reader, Dundee University, since 1962; Visiting Associate Professor, University of Purdue, Indiana, 1965; Visiting Scientist, University of Western Ontario, 1977-84. Chairman, Monifieth Schools Council. Recreation: golf. Address: (h.) Speybank, 52A Durham Street, Monifieth, Angus; T.-0382 532396.

Tomkinson, Michael John, MSc, PhD. Senior Lecturer in Mathematics, Glasgow University, since 1983; Honorary Treasurer, Scottish Society for Mentally Handicapped; Editor, Glasgow Mathematical Journal; b. 6.7.43, Crewe; m., Jennifer; 2 s. Educ. County Grammar School, Crewe; Birmingham University; Newcastle upon Tyne University. Assistant, Lecturer, Senior Lecturer in Mathematics, Glasgow University, since 1966. Address: (h.) 16 Dumgoyne Drive, Bearsden, Glasgow, G61 3AP; T.-041-942 7284.

Tomlinson, Professor Geoffrey Railton, MSc, PhD. Professor of Mechanical Engineering, Heriot-Watt University, since 1987; b. 21.7.45; m.; 1

s.; 1 d. Educ. Aston University, Birmingham. Graduate apprentice, High Duty Alloys Ltd., Cumbria, 1962-69; Senior Analysis Engineer, Mirrlees Blackstone, 1969-71; Senior Lecturer, Manchester Polytechnic, 1971-79; Lecturer, then Senior Lecturer, Manchester University, 1979-86. Recreations: ornithology; hill-walking. Address: White Cottage, 33 Old Kirk Road, Corstorphine, Edinburgh, EH12 6JX.

Tongue, Christopher Hugh, MA (Cantab), DipEd. Headmaster, Keil School, since 1984; b. 2.4.43, Uppingham; m., Chelsia Tongue; 2 s. Educ. Kingswood School, Bath; Jesus College, Cambridge. Teacher: Kagumo High School, Kenya, 1966-68, Felsted School, Essex, 1968-74, 1976-84, Diocesan College, Cape Town, 1975-76. Recreations: cricket; rugby; music. Address: (b.) Keil School, Helenslee Road, Dumbarton, G82 4AL; T.-0389 62003.

Topps, John H., BSc, PhD, DSc, FRSC. Head, Department of Chemistry, and Chairman, Chemistry and Microbiology Group, Aberdeen School of Agriculture; b. 11.7.29, Southampton; m., Brenda Mary Poe; 2 s.; 2 d. Educ. Purbrook Park County High School; London University. Senior Lecturer in Agricultural Chemistry, Essex Institute of Agriculture, 1956-59; Lecturer, then Senior Lecturer in Animal Nutrition, University of Rhodesia, 1959-67; Lecturer, then Senior Lecturer in Animal Nutrition, Aberdeen University, 1967-77. Recreations: skiing; squash; tennis; gardening. Address: (b.) School of Agriculture, 581 King Street, Aberdeen, AB9 1UD; T.-0224 480291.

Torbet, Thomas Edgar, MB, ChB, FRCSEdin, FRCOG. Consultant Obstetrician and Gynaecologist, since 1967; Honorary Clinical Lecturer, Glasgow University, since 1967; b. 15.3.30, Bearsden; m., Helen Fiona; 1 s. Educ. Morrison's Academy, Crieff; Glasgow University. JP, East Kilbride. Recreations: sailing; skiing. Address: (h.) 10 Easter Road, Busby, Clarkston, Glasgow; T.-041-644 1099.

Torrance, Rev. Professor James Bruce, MA (Hons), BD. Professor of Systematic Theology, Aberdeen University, since 1977 (Dean, Faculty of Divinity, 1978-81); Minister, Church of Scotland, since 1950; b. 3.2.23, Chengtu, Szechwan, West China; m., Mary Heather Aitken; 1 s.; 2 d. Educ. Royal High School, Edinburgh; Edinburgh University and New College; Marburg University; Basle University; Oxford University. RAF, 1943-45; ordained, Invergowrie, Dundee, 1954; Lecturer in Divinity and Dogmatics in History of Christian Thought, 1961, and Senior Lecturer in Christian Dogmatics, 1972, New College, Edinburgh; Visiting Professor of New Testament, Union Theological Seminary, 1960, of Theology, Columbia Theological Seminary, 1965, and Vancouver School of Theology, 1974-75. Convenor, Panel on Doctrine, General Assembly, 1982-86. Recreations: bee-keeping; fishing; swimming; gardening. Address: (h.) Don House, 46 Don Street, Old Aberdeen, Aberdeen, AB2 1UU; T.-0224 481526.

Torrance, Very Rev. Thomas Forsyth, MBE, MA, BD, DrTheol, DLitt, DD, DrTeol, DTheol, DSc, FBA, FRSE. Emeritus Professor, Edinburgh University, since 1979; b. 30.8.13, Chengdu, Sichuan, China; m., Margaret Edith Spear; 2 s.; 1 d. Educ. Canadian School, Chengdu, China; Bellshill Academy, Lanarkshire; Edinburgh University; Basel University; Oriel College, Oxford. Minister: Alyth Barony Parish Church, 1940-47; served as Church of Scotland Chaplain, 1943-45; Minister, Beechgrove Parish Church, Aberdeen, 1947-50; Edinburgh University: Professor of Church History, 1950-52, Professor of Christian Dogmatics, 1952-79; Moderator, General Assembly of the Church of Scotland, 1976-77. Cross of St. Mark, First Class, 1970; Protopresbyter of Greek Orthodox Church (Hon.), 1973; President, Academie Internationale des Sciences Religieuses, 1972-81. Recreations: formerly golf, squash, fishing; now walking. Address: (h.) 37 Braid Farm Road, Edinburgh, EH10 6LE; T.-031-447 3050.

Torrance, Professor Victor Brownlie, BSc, MSc, PhD, FCIOB, FBIM, FRSA, Hon. ARICS. William Watson Professor and Head, Department of Building, Heriot-Watt University, since 1972; b. 24.2.37, Shotts, Lanarkshire; m., Inez Marjorie Ann Jack; 1 s.; 2 d.; 1 step s.; 1 step d. Educ. Wishaw High School; Heriot-Watt College; Heriot-Watt University; Edinburgh University. Associate Professor and Head, Department of Building and Estate Management, Singapore University, 1966-72; Member, Civil Engineering and Transport Committee and Building Sub-Committee, Science Research Council, 1975-78; Member, Building Board, Council for National Academic Awards, 1976-80; Member, Board of Governors, Edinburgh College of Art, since 1973; Member, Building Standards Advisory Committee, Research Sub-Committee, 1982-85; Member, Panel of Visitors, Building Research Establishment, since 1983; Chairman, RIAS Research Steering Committee, 1982-85; President, Chartered Institute of Building; Member, Technology Research Sub-Committee, Council for National Academic Awards, 1983-86; Chairman, Council of Professors of Building, since 1987; Partner, Building and Design Consultants, Edinburgh, since 1976; Consultant, Buildings Investigation Centre. Recreations: music; building; committees; travel; family. Address: (h.) Kerry, 3 Craiginnan Gardens, Dollar, FK14 7JA; T.-02594 2240.

Toth, Professor Akos George, Dr. Jur., PhD. Professor of Law, Strathclyde University, since 1984; b. 9.2.36, Mezotur, Hungary; m., Sarah Kurucz. Educ. Budapest University; Szeged University; Exeter University. Strathclyde University: Lecturer in Law, 1971-76, Senior Lecturer, 1976-82, Reader, 1982-84. Publication: Legal Protection of Individuals in the European Communities, 1978. Recreations: travel; music; opera; theatre; swimming; walking. Address: (b.) Strathclyde University, Law School, 173 Cathedral Street, Glasgow, G4 0RQ; T.-041-552 4400.

Toulmin, David. Hon. MLitt (Aberdeen). Writer; b. 1.7.13, Rathen, Aberdeenshire; m., Margaret Jane Willox; 3 s. Educ. five public/parish schools. From the age of 14 to 65, earned living by manual labour (farm worker); his first article was published by Farmer and Stock Breeder, 1947; wrote short stories in dialect for local newspapers and the Scots Magazine; five stories broadcast on radio by the BBC; a collection was published as Hard Shining Corn, 1972; has published a further seven books; awarded grant by the Scottish Arts Council, 1983; real name, John Reid. Recreations: writing; reading; popular music; cinema; video; television; antiquarian research. Address: (h.) 7 Pittodrie Place, Aberdeen; T.-Aberdeen 634058.

Trabichoff, Geoffrey Colin, AGSM, LGSM. Leader, BBC Scottish Symphony Orchestra, since 1982; Soloist and Recitalist; b. 15.4.46, London; m., Judith Orbach; 1 step s.; 1 d. Leader, Gulbenkian Orchestra, Lisbon, 1974-76; Leader, Mannheim Chamber Orchestra, 1976-78; Leader, Hannover State Orchestra, 1978-81. Address: (h.) 40 Woodend Drive, Jordanhill, Glasgow, G13; T.-041-959 3496.

Trainer, Professor James, MA, PhD. Professor of German, Stirling University, since 1969 (Deputy Principal, 1973-78, 1982-88, Acting Principal, 1975); b. 2.3.32; m., Barbara Herta Reinhard (deceased); 2 s.; 1 d. Educ. St. Andrews University; Free University of Berlin. Lecturer in German, St. Andrews University, 1958-67; Visiting Professor, Yale University, 1964-65; Vice-Convener, SUCE, 1987; Convener, SUCE Modern Languages Panel, 1979-86; Member, Inter University and Polytechnic Council, since 1983; Member, Scottish Examination Board, 1975-82; Member, SED Postgraduate Awards Committee, since 1978; Member, UK Fulbright Committee, since 1985; Trustee, National Library of Scotland, 1986. Recreations: music; cricket; translating. Address: (b.) Stirling University, Stirling; T.-0786 73171.

Tranter, Nigel, OBE, KCLJ, MA (Hon.). Author and Novelist, since 1935; b. 23.11.09, Glasgow; m., May Jean Campbell Grieve (deceased); 1 s. (deceased); 1 d. Educ. St. James' Episcopal School; George Heriot's, Edinburgh. Professional Writer, since 1946; published more than 100 books, including 70 novels; Vice-Convener, Scottish Covenant Association, 1951-55; President, East Lothian Liberal Association, 1960-70; Chairman, National Forth Road Bridge Committee, 1953-57; Chairman, St. Andrew Society of East Lothian, since 1966; President, Scottish PEN, 1962-66 (now Honorary President); Chairman, Society of Authors, Scotland, 1966-70; Chairman, National Book League, Scotland, 1971-73. Vice-Chancellor, Order of St. Lazarus of Jerusalem, 1982-88; Honorary Freeman of Blackstone, Virginia, USA, 1980. Recreations: walking; climbing; genealogy; castle architecture. Address: (h.) Quarry House, Aberlady, East Lothian; T.-Aberlady 258.

Traynor, William. Member, Lanarkshire Health Board, since 1983; Member, Supplementary Appeals Tribunals, since 1982; Secretary, Motherwell and Wishaw District Trades Council, since 1982; b. 9.7.25, Motherwell; m., Jessie; 2 d. Educ. Motherwell Central School. Former Councillor and Magistrate; former Member, Children's Panel; Past Chairman, Motherwell District Committee, RSSPCC; Member, Motherwell College Council; former Organiser, East Kilbride Unemployed Workers Centre; Co-ordinator, Blantyre Crime Prevention Project. Recreations: community work; music; writing poetry. Address: (h.) 117 Milton Street, Motherwell, Lanarkshire; T.-Motherwell 63347.

Trevarthen, Professor Colwyn Boyd, BSc, MSc, PhD. Professor of Child Psychology and Psychobiology, Edinburgh University, since 1984; b. 2.3.31, Auckland; m., Elizabeth Lee Simmons; 3 s. Educ. Auckland Grammar School; Auckland University. Research Fellow, California Institute of Technology, 1962; USPHS Postdoctoral Fellow (CNRS), Marseille, 1963-66; MRC Research Fellow, Psychological Laboratory, Cambridge University, 1966; Research Fellow in Cognitive Studies, Lecturer in Psychology, Harvard University, 1966-68; Senior Research Fellow, California Institute of Technology, 1969-70; Edinburgh University: Lecturer, 1971-72, Reader, 1973-84, Associate Dean, Social Sciences, 1974-75; Visiting Reader or Professor, La Trobe University, Auckland University, California Institute of Technology, Lagos University, Universite Libre de Bruxelles, Natal University, University of Texas at Austin, University of Utah. Recreations: walking; travelling; reading; playing flute. Address: (b.) Department of Psychology, Edinburgh University, 7 George Square, Edinburgh, EH8 9JZ; T.-031-667 1011, Ext. 4441.

Trotter, Alexander Richard. DL, FRSA. Convenor, Scottish Landowners Federation, 1982-85; Member, Nature Conservancy Council, since 1985 (Chairman, Committee for Scotland, since 1985); b. 20.2.39, London; m., Julia Henrietta Greenwell; 3 s. Educ. Eton College. Royal Scots Greys, 1958-68; Member, Berwickshire County Council, 1968-74 (Chairman, Roads Committee, 1972-74); Member, UK Committee, European Year of the Environment, 1986-88; Chairman, Mortonhall Park Ltd., since 1973; Vice-Chairman, Border Grain Ltd., since 1984. Member, Queen's Bodyguard for Scotland (Royal Company of Archers). Recreations: skiing; tennis; riding; shooting. Address: Charterhall, Duns, Berwickshire, TD11 3RE; T.-089 084 301.

Trotter, William, MA. Headteacher, Craigmount High School, Edinburgh, since 1969; b. 7.5.28, Greenock; m., Sylvia Rosemary Hall; 1 s.; 1 d. Educ. Hamilton Academy; Glasgow University; Jordanhill College of Education. Teacher of Modern Languages: Airdrie Academy, 1955-58, Forest Hill School, London, 1958-61; Head of Languages Department, Sedgehill School, London, 1961-65; Lecturer in Modern Languages, High Wycombe College of Technology, 1965-67; Deputy Head, Joseph Leckie School, Walsall, 1967-69; President, Corstorphine Rotary Club, 1988-89. Recreations: reading; music; swimming; light-hearted bridge. Address: (h.) 26 Ormidale Terrace, Edinburgh, EH12 6EQ; T.-031-337 6492.

Trudgill, David L., BSc, PhD. Head, Zoology Department, Scottish Crop Research Institute, since 1972; b. 2.5.42, Leeds; m., Margaret Jean Luckraft; 3 s. Educ. Leeds Grammar School; Ulverston Grammar School; Leeds University; London University. Nematologist, Rothamsted Experimental Station, 1966-72. Chairman, European Plant Protection Organisation ad hoc committee on potato cyst nematodes. Recreations: table tennis; hill-walking; fishing. Address: (b.) Zoology Department, Scottish Crop Research Institute, Invergowrie, Dundee, DD2 5DA; T.-0382 562731.

Truman, Donald Ernest Samuel, BA, PhD, MIBiol, CIBiol. Senior Lecturer, Department of Genetics, Edinburgh University, since 1978 (Head, Department of Genetics, since 1984, Director of Biology Teaching Unit, since 1985); b. 23.10.36, Leicester; m., Kathleen Ramsay; 1 s.; 1 d. Educ. Wyggeston School, Leicester; Clare College, Cambridge. NATO Research Fellow, Wenner-Grenn Institute, Stockholm, 1962-63; MRC Epigenetics Research Group, Edinburgh, 1963-72; Lecturer, Department of Genetics, Edinburgh University, 1972-78; Aneurin Bevan Memorial Fellow, Government of India, 1978. Publications: The Biochemistry of Cytodifferentiation, 1974; Differentiation in Vitro (Joint Editor), 1982; Stability and Switching in Cellular Differentiation, 1982; Coordinated Regulation of Gene Expression, 1986. Recreation: gardening. Address: (b.) Department of Genetics, West Mains Road, Edinburgh, EH9 3JN; T.-031-667 1081.

Truscott, Professor Terence George, BSc, PhD, DSc, CChem, FRSC, FRSE. Professor of Chemistry, Paisley College, since 1974 (Head, Department of Chemistry, since 1974, Dean, School of Science); b. 8.5.39, Bargoed; m., Marylin; 1 d. Educ. Bargoed Grammar School; University of Wales. Postdoctoral Research Fellow, Minnesota University, 1964-65; Lecturer in Physical Chemistry, Bradford University, 1966-71; Research Group Section Leader, INCO Ltd., Canada, 1971-73. Associate Editor, Photochemistry and Photobiology; President, European Society of Photobiology; Chairman, Glasgow and West of Scotland Section, Royal Society of Chemistry. Recreation: bridge. Address: (b.) Paisley College, Department of Chemistry, High Street, Paisley, PA1 2BE; T.-041-887 1241, Ext. 242.

Tucker, John Barry, BA, MA, PhD. Reader in Zoology, St. Andrews University, since 1979; b. 17.3.41, Arundel; m., Janet Stephen Murray; 1 s. Educ. Queen Elizabeth Grammar School, Atherstone; Peterhouse, Cambridge. Fulbright Travel Scholar and Research Associate, Department of Zoology, Indiana University, 1966-68; SERC Research Fellow, Department of Zoology, Cambridge, 1968-69; Lecturer in Zoology, St. Andrews University, 1969-79 (Chairman, Zoology Department, 1982-84). Member: SERC Advisory Group II, 1977-80, SERC Molecular Biology and Genetics Sub-committee, 1986-89, Editorial Board of Development, 1979-88. Recreations: cycling; hill-walking; tennis; reluctant gardener. Address: (b.) Department of Biology and Preclinical Medicine, Bute Building, St. Andrews University, St. Andrews, Fife, KY16 9TS; T.-0334 76161.

Tullis, John Ivor, LDS. Chief Administrative Dental Officer, Highland Health Board, since 1974; b. 26.8.24, Dundee; m., Margaret May McAlpine; 2 s.; 1 d. Educ. High School of Dundee; University College, Dundee. Dental Officer, RADC, 1946-52; retired with rank of Major; Assistant in general practice, 1953; Principal in partnership in general practice, Dundee, 1953; Lecturer in Restorative Dentistry, Edinburgh University, 1969. Past President, North of Scotland Branch, BDA; Past President, Dundee Dental Club. Recreations: cricket; hockey; golf; angling; music. Address: (h.) 4 Cradlehall Park, Westhill, Inverness; T.-0463 791182.

Tullis, Major Ramsey, BA. Vice Lord-Lieutenant of Clackmannanshire, since 1974; Farmer; b. 16.6.16; m., Daphne Mabon; 3 s. Educ. Trinity College, Glenalmond; Worcester College, Oxford. 2nd Lt., Cameronians, 1936; served Second World War (Major, 1943); County Commissioner for Scouts, Clackmannanshire, 1958-73; Income Tax Commissioner, since 1964. Recreations: golf; gardening. Address: (h.) Woodacre, Pool of Muckhart, by Dollar, Clackmannanshire, FK14 7JW.

Tumelty, Michael, MA (Hons). Music Critic, Glasgow Herald, since 1983; b. 31.5.46, Hexham; m., Frances McGinniss; 2 s.; 1 d. Educ. St. Aloysius College, Glasgow; Aberdeen University. Postgraduate research into the music of Debussy, 1974-75; entered teaching, St. Columba's High School, Clydebank (Principal Teacher, 1980-83); served on a variety of working groups on curriculum development; freelance Music Critic, Jewish Echo, 1979-82, and Daily Telegraph, 1982-83; Contributor, Musical Times. Member, Scottish Central Committee on Music, 1982-83. Recreations: family; avid collector of records; photography. Address: (h.) 31 Burlington Avenue, Glasgow, G12 OLJ; T.-041-334 4430.

Tunnell, John, FRAM. Leader, Scottish Chamber Orchestra, since 1974; Professor, Royal Scottish Academy of Music and Drama, since 1974; b. 12.5.36, Stockton-on-Tees; m., Wendy Packard; 2 s.; 1 d. Educ. Bradford Grammar School; Royal Academy of Music (London); Vienna Academy. Member, London String Quartet, 1958-67; founder Member, English Chamber Orchestra and Principal; Leader, Tunnell Piano Trio and Piano Quartet, Thames Chamber Orchestra, 1969-74, and Vesuvius Ensemble of London; frequent solo appearances, recordings. Recreations: hill-walking; gardening; tennis. Address: (h.) Crawhill Manor, by Bathgate, West Lothian; T.-0506 52991.

Tunstall, David P., BSc (Hons), PhD. Reader in Physics, St. Andrews University, since 1978; b. 15.7.39, Wellington, England; m., Rosemarie; 2 s.; 1 d. Educ. Whitchurch Grammar School; University College of North Wales. Research Fellow: Zurich, 1963-64, Grenoble, 1964-65; Lecturer, St. Andrews, 1966-75; Visiting Professor: Cornell, 1973, UCLA, 1979; Senior Lecturer, St. Andrews, 1975-78. Recreations: skiing; hill-walking. Address: (h.) 4 West Acres, St. Andrews, Fife; T.-St. Andrews 73507.

Tunstall-Pedoe, Professor Hugh David, MA, MD, FRCP, FRCPE, FFCM. Professor and Director, Cardiovascular Epidemiology Unit, and Senior Lecturer in Medicine, Ninewells Hospital and Medical School, Dundee, since 1981; Honorary Consultant Cardiologist, since 1981; Honorary Specialist in Community Medicine, since 1981; b. 30.12.39, Southampton; m., Jacqueline Helen; 2 s.; 1 d. Educ. Haberdashers' Aske's School; Dulwich College; King's College, Cambridge; Guy's Hospital Medical School. Junior hospital posts, Guy's, Brompton, National Queen Square and London Hospitals; MRC Social Medicine Unit, 1969-71; Lecturer in Medicine, The London Hospital, 1971-74; Senior Lecturer in Epidemiology and Honorary Physician, and Honorary Community Physician, St. Mary's Hospital and Medical School, London, 1974-81. Chairman, European Society of Cardiology Working Group on Epidemiology and Prevention, 1983-85. Recreations: hill-walking; bee-keeping; golf. Address: (b.) Cardiovascular Epidemiology Unit, Ninewells Hospital and Medical School, Dundee, DD1 9SY; T.-0382 644255.

Turley, Alfred, JP, DCM, CPM. Member, Dumfries and Galloway Regional Council, 1975-86; b. 30.3.13, Dudley; m., Margaret Linn; 1 s. 7th Hussars, 1932-38; Palestine Police, 1938-48; Malayan Police, 1948-50; Colonial Police Medal for Gallantry; Distinguished Conduct Medal awarded by Sultan of Trengganu, Malaya; Member, Dumfries Town Council, 1964-75. Address: (h.) 109 Annan Road, Dumfries, DG1 3EW; T.-0387 55194.

Turmeau, William Arthur, PhD, CEng, FIMechE. Principal, Napier College, Edinburgh, since 1982; b. 19.9.29, London; m., Margaret Moar Burnett; 1 d. Educ. Stromness Academy, Orkney; Edinburgh University; Moray House College of Education; Heriot-Watt University. Royal Signals, 1947-49; Research Engineer, Northern Electric Co. Ltd., Montreal, 1952-54; Mechanical Engineer, USAF, Goose Bay, Labrador, 1954-56; Contracts Manager, Godfrey Engineering Co. Ltd., Montreal, 1956-61; Lecturer, Bristo Technical Institute, Edinburgh, 1962-64; Napier College: Lecturer and Senior Lecturer, 1964-68, Head, Department of Mechanical Engineering, 1968-75, Assistant Principal and Dean, Faculty of Technology, 1975-82. Member, Council, CNAA, since 1982 (and Scotland Committee, since 1983); Member, Council, IMechE, since 1983; Member, Council, Societe Europeene Pour La Formation Des Ingenieurs, since 1983; Member, British Council CICHE, since 1982. Recreations: modern jazz; Leonardo da Vinci. Address: (h.) 71 Morningside Park, Edinburgh, EH10 5EZ; T.-031-447 4639.

Turner, Allan Roderick, MB, ChBEd, FRCSEdin, FRCS. Consultant Surgeon, Dunfermline and West Fife Hospital, since 1979; Honorary Senior Lecturer, Department of Surgery, Edinburgh University, since 1979; b. 18.11.41, Lochmaddy; m., Jean J.C. Macrae; 3 s.; 3 d. Educ. Portree High School; Edinburgh University. Surgical training, Edinburgh, Aberdeen, Liverpool, London; Surgeon to Christian Mission Hospital, Kurdistan, 1973-75; Associate Professor, Department of Surgery, Shiraz University, Iran, 1976. Recreations: gardening; squash; children's hobbies; Celtic languages. Address: (h.) 34 Couston Street, Dunfermline, Fife; T.-Dunfermline 729689.

Turner, Colin William, BSc, AKC. Rector, Glasgow Academy, since 1983; b. 10.12.33, Torquay; m., Priscilla Mary Trickett; 2 s.; 2 d. Educ. Torquay Grammar School; King's College, London University; Exeter University. Edinburgh Academy: Assistant Master, 1958, CCF Contingent Commander, 1960-74, Housemaster, 1975-82. Recreations: mountaineering; caravanning. Address: (h.) 11 Kirklee Terrace, Glasgow, G12 0TH; T.-041-357 1776.

Turner, John R., MA, MusB, FRCO. Organist and Director of Music, Glasgow Cathedral, since 1965; Lecturer, Royal Scottish Academy of Music, since 1965; Organist, Strathclyde University, since 1965; b. Halifax. Educ. Rugby; Jesus College, Cambridge. Recreations: gardening; travel. Address: (h.) 2 Cathkin Cottage, Burnside Road, Glasgow, G73 5RD; T.-041-634 3083.

Turner, Captain John Russell, OBE (1986), MCIT, MIMH, MNI. General Manager, Aberdeen Harbour Board, since 1978; b. 17.6.30, Cheadle Hulme; m., Jean Catherine Baker; 1 s.; 2 d. Educ. Kings School, Macclesfield; Thames Nautical Training College, HMS Worcester; UMIST; Cranfield Institute of Technology. Cadet, Royal Naval Reserve; Navigating Officer: Clan Line, P. & O., Cunard Line; Port of Manchester: Assistant Chief Superintending Stevedore, Dock Traffic Superintendent, Assistant Docks Manager; Deputy General Manager, Aberdeen Harbour Board, 1973-78. Liveryman, Honourable Company of Master Mariners; Member, Management Committee, and Chairman, Medium Ports Committee, British Ports Federation; Council Member, Association of Pilotage Authorities, 1978-84; Vice Chairman and Co-Founder, Scottish Advisory Committee, Netherlands British Chamber of Commerce; Council Member, Aberdeen Chamber of Commerce; Vice Chairman, North of Scotland Export Club, 1982-84; Member, Aberdeen Committee, Royal National Lifeboat Institution; Chairman, Grampian-Houston Association, 1985-87; received Freedom of the City of London, 1972; awarded John Morris Gold Medal, British Industrial Truck Association, 1965. Recreations: golf; travel; historical research; sailing. Address: (b.) Harbour Office, 16 Regent Quay, Aberdeen, AB9 1SS; T.-0224 592571.

Turner, Malcolm, OBE, JP. Member, Strathclyde Regional Council, since 1974; b. 13.12.21, Clydebank; m., Margaret Balfour; 1 s. Educ. Clydebank High School. Member: Clydebank Town Council, 1957-75 (Provost, 1966-69), Dunbarton County Council, 1957-75; Member, Cumbernauld Development Corporation, 1975-83; former Chairman, Central Water Development Board. Recreations: angling; caravanning; bowling; golf. Address: (h.) 10A Duncombe View, Clydebank, Dunbartonshire; T.-041-952 3992.

Turner, Norman William, MILAM, ALA, FBIM, FSA(Scot). Director of Leisure Services, Motherwell District Council, since 1985; Vice-Chairman, Association of Directors of Leisure, Recreation and Tourism, since 1986; b. 12.4.48, Portsmouth. Educ. Portsmouth Technical High School; Brighton Polytechnic. District Librarian, Motherwell District Council; Depute Director of Libraries and Museums, Falkirk District Council; Deputy District Librarian, City of Southampton District; Deputy Borough Librarian, Andover Borough Council. Former Vice-Chairman, Public Libraries Group; former Hon. Treasurer, Scottish Library

Association. Recreations: season ticket holder, Motherwell FC; sport, especially running (four Marathons completed); theatre; cinema; music; national history. Address: (b.) Motherwell District Council, PO Box 14, Civic Centre, Motherwell, ML1 1TW; T.-0698 66166.

Turner, Susan Morag, MA, DipEd, MBATOD, FISW, FCollP, FRSA. Director, Scottish Centre for the Education of the Deaf, since 1970; Hon. Director, Scottish Association for the Deaf, since 1984; b. 5.4.35, Glasgow. Educ. Rutherglen Academy; Glasgow University; Manchester University. Teacher of hearing-impaired children, Glasgow School for the Deaf; Head Teacher: Paisley School for the Deaf, Dundee School for the Deaf; Lecturer, Special Education Department, Moray House College. Member, National Council of Special Education. Address: (h.) 15 Bonaly Brae, Colinton, Edinburgh, EH13 0QF; T.-031-441 7520.

Turner Thomson, Ann Denise. Interior Designer; Member, Scottish Arts Council; b. 23.5.29, Molesey; m., Gordon Turner Thomson; 1 s.; 3 d. Educ. Sherborne School for Girls, Dorset; St. James's Secretarial College, London. Member, Merchandising Committee, National Trust; Council Member, Saltire Society; Member, Saltire Society Housing Awards Panel. Recreations: theatre; opera; reading; sailing; swimming; tennis. Address: 8 Middleby Street, Edinburgh, EH9 1TD; T.-031-667 3997.

Tweedy, Brigadier Oliver Robert. Commandant, Queen Victoria School, Dunblane, since 1985; b. 4.2.30, Newbury; m., Dawn Berrange; 2 s.; 1 d. Educ. Sedbergh School; RMA, Sandhurst. Commissioned, The Black Watch, 1949; commanded 1st Bn., The Black Watch, Scotland, Northern Ireland and Hong Kong, 1971-73; Commander, British Army Advisory Team, Nigeria, 1980-82; Commander, 51 Highland Brigade, 1982-84; ADC to The Queen, 1983; retired, 1985. Recreations: golf; country pursuits. Address: (h.) Inverbraan, Little Dunkeld, Perthshire, PH8 OAD.

Twidell, John W., MA, DPhil. Head, Energy Studies Unit, Strathclyde University, since 1984; b. 4.4.39, Windsor; m., Mary; 2 s.; 1 d. Educ. Maidenhead Grammar School; Lincoln College, Oxford. Lecturer in Physics, Khartoum University, Sudan, 1964-68; Research Fellow, Essex University, 1968-70; Lecturer and Senior Lecturer, Department of Applied Physics, Strathclyde University, 1970-84. Council Member, British Wind Energy Association. Publications (books): Renewable Energy Resources (first and revised ed.); Dictionary of Energy (Co-author); four-volume Proceedings of Energy for Rural and Island Communities; Guide to Small Wind Energy Conversion System. Address: (h.) 21 Lynn Drive, Milngavie, Glasgow.

Tyrrell, Reginald Charles. Farmer and Company Director, since 1970; b. 15.11.30, Essex; m., Lady Caroline Hay. Educ. Forest School. Former Director of companies in audio-visual, film and management training fields, including: Sound-Services Ltd. (Managing), Merton Park Studios Ltd. (Managing), Film Producers' Guild Ltd., Film Facilities Ltd., Management Training Ltd. Deputy Chairman, National Trust for Scotland (Convener, Curatorial Committee); Vice-Chairman, British Fields Sports Society (Chairman, Scotland). Recreations: field sports; meteorology. Address: (h.) Capplegill, Moffat, Dumfriesshire, DG10 9LQ; T.-0683 20525.

U

Underwood, Rev. Geoffrey Horne, BD, FPhS. Minister, Chalmers Memorial Church, Cockenzie, since 1964; b. 6.11.28, Stockport; m., Florence; 3 s.; 1 d. Educ. Alexandra School, Stockport; Manchester University; Edinburgh University. Employed in industry and commerce, 1942-54 (National Service, 1946-49); Minister, Levenshulme URC Church, Manchester, 1958-63; Assistant, Greenbank Church, Edinburgh, 1963-64. Recreations: sailing; swimming; hill-climbing. Address: Braemar Villa, 2 Links Road, Port Seton, EH32 0HA.

Upton, Professor Anthony Frederick, MA (Oxon), AM, FRHistS. Professor of Nordic History, St. Andrews University, since 1984; b. 13.10.29, Stockton Heath, Cheshire; m., Sirkka R.; 3 s. Educ. County Boys' School, Windsor; Queen's College, Oxford. Assistant Lecturer in Modern History, Leeds University, 1952-56; St. Andrews University: Lecturer in Modern History, 1956, Senior Lecturer, 1966, Reader, 1974. Sundry offices, Labour Party in Fife and in educational bodies, e.g. St. Andrews School Council. Recreations: music; literature; politics. Address: (h.) 5 West Acres, St. Andrews, Fife.

Upton, Professor Brian Geoffrey Johnson, BA, MA, DPhil, FRSE. Professor of Petrology, Edinburgh University, since 1982; Executive Editor, Journal of Petrology, since 1983; b. 2.3.33, London; m., Bodil Aalbaek; 2 s.; 1 d. Educ. Reading School; St. John's College, Oxford. Geological survey of Greenland, 1958-60; Postdoctoral Fellow, California Institute of Technology, 1961-62; Edinburgh University, since 1962 (Lecturer in Geology, 1962-72, Reader, 1972-82). Recreations: painting; gardening. Address: (h.) 59 Belwood Road, Milton Bridge, Midlothian, EH26 OQN; T.-0968 73500.

Urbaniak, Stanislaw Joseph, BSc (Hons), MB, ChB, PhD, FRCPEdin, MRCPath. Regional Director, Aberdeen and NE Scotland Regional Transfusion Centre, since 1982; Clinical Senior Lecturer, Department of Medicine, Aberdeen University, since 1982; Consultant, Grampian Health Board, since 1982; b. 26.1.45, Leslie; m., Ann Howard Murison; 2 d. Educ. Llandeilo Grammar School; Edinburgh University. Various medical appointments to Edinburgh hospitals; MRC Research Fellow, MRC Clinical Endocrinology Unit; Senior Registrar, Edinburgh and SE Scotland Regional Transfusion Centre; Consultant Immuno Haematologist and Deputy Director, Edinburgh RTC; part-time Senior Lecturer, Department of Therapeutics and Clinical Pharmacology, Edinburgh University. Recreations: fishing; reading; travelling. Address: (h.) Caledon, 306 North Deeside Road, Cults, Aberdeen, AB1 9SB; T.-0224 867509.

Ure, William, BL. Solicitor; b. 17.12.17, Bishopbriggs; m., Jessie Shanks King Duff (deceased). Educ. Glasgow Academy; Glasgow University. University and legal training, 1935-39; The Cameronians (Scottish Rifles), 1939-46; legal practice, 1946-88 (retired); Deacon, Incorporation of Gardeners of Glasgow, 1972-73; Chairman, West Stirlingshire Conservative Association, 1980-83. Recreation: golf. Address: (h.) Belmont, Bardowie, Milngavie, Glasgow; T.-Balmore 20310.

U'ren, William Graham, BSc (Hons), DipTP, FRTPI. Director of Planning and Technical Services, Clydesdale District Council, since 1982; b. 28.12.46, Glasgow; m., Wendy; 2 d. Educ. Aberdeen Grammar School; Aberdeen University; Strathclyde University. Planning Assistant: Clackmannan County Council, 1970-72, Lanark County Council, 1972-75; Principal and Chief Planning Officer, Clydesdale District Council, 1975-82. Past Chairman, Scottish Society of Directors of Planning. Recreations: sport; bird watching; philately. Address: (b.) District Offices, South Vennel, Lanark, ML11 7JT; T.-Lanark 61331.

Urquhart, Alistair P., OBE, MA. Chairman, Central Support Group for Music, since 1986; Headmaster, Kincorth Academy, Aberdeen, 1971-85; b. 27.7.21, Paisley; m., May Brown (deceased). Educ. John Neilson Institute, Paisley; Glasgow University. War Service, 1941-46 (Captain, Royal Artillery); Teacher of English, then Principal Teacher, Powis Junior Secondary School, Aberdeen, 1947-61; Deputy Headmaster, Summerhill Secondary School, Aberdeen, 1962-66; Headmaster, Old Aberdeen Secondary School, 1966-71. Chairman, Scottish Central Committee on Music, 1979-86; President, Scottish Badminton Union, 1970-72; Captain, Deeside Golf Club, 1986-88. Recreations: golf; badminton; music. Address: (h.) 15 Kingshill Road, Aberdeen; T.-Aberdeen 36100.

Urquhart, Daniel, FCCA. Director of Finance, Banff and Buchan District Council, since 1974; b. 27.4.32, Banff; m., Molly; 1 s.; 1 d. Educ. Banff Academy. Trainee Accountant, Banff County Council, 1955-59; Aberdeen Corporation: Audit Assistant, 1959-61, Accountancy Assistant, 1961-63, Senior Accountancy Assistant, 1963-67; Town Chamberlain, Fraserburgh Town Council, 1967-74. Recreations: golf; bridge; gardening. Address: (b.) St. Leonard's, Sandyhill Road, Banff; T.-Banff 2521.

Urquhart, James Macconnell, MB, ChB, FFCM, DPH. Chairman, Management Committee, Margaret Blackwood Housing for Adult Handicapped, Dundee; Chairman, Council on Disability, Dundee; Deputy Commissioner, Clan Urquhart Association; b. 1.10.18, Wishaw; m., 1, May Harrison (m. diss.); 2, Nora Hanna; 1 s.; 2 d. Educ. Dumfries Academy; High School of Glasgow; Glasgow University. RAF Medical Branch, 1942-68 (retired with rank of Group Captain); War Service, India, Burma; Safety Office, Atomic Trials, Australia, 1956; OC, RAF Hospitals; Community Medicine, Northern Ireland Hospital Authority, 1968-72; Medical Superintendent, Dundee General Hospitals, 1972-75; District Medical Officer, Dundee District, 1975-83. Member, Executive Committee, St. Aidans Project, Dundee; Vice Chairman, Preparation for Retiral Council, Dundee; Trustee, Scottish Trust for Physically Disabled; Trustee, Dundee Trust for Education of Deaf; Member, Diocesan Synod, Brechin, and Provincial Synod, Scottish Episcopal Church. Recreations: reading; photography. Address: (h.) 35 Albany Terrace, Dundee, DD3 6HS; T.-0382 22928.

Urquhart, John Munro, CBE, MA, MEd, FEIS, FSA Scot. Member, Board of Communications, Church of Scotland; b. 16.9.10, Gairloch; m., Adela Margaret Sutherland; 1 s.; 1 d. Educ. Lochgilphead Secondary School; Oban High School; Glasgow University. Schoolmaster, Hutchesons' Boys' Grammar School; Assistant Director of Education, Banffshire; Depute Director of Education, Glasgow; Director of Education, Selkirkshire; Director, Scottish Certificate of Education Examination Board, 1965-75; Consultant Registrar, Caribbean Examinations Council, 1977-78; President, Association of Directors of Education, 1963-64. Boy Scouts County Commissioner, Selkirkshire; edited Statistical Account of Selkirkshire, 1964; District Governor, Rotary District 102, 1980. Recreations: angling; walking; reading; gardening. Address: (h.) 29 Craiglockhart Drive South, Edinburgh, EH14 1JA; T.-031-443 3085.

Urquhart, Rev. Thomas Chalmers, MA, DA. Minister, Arisaig and Moidart, since 1964; b. 14.4.15, Anstruther; m., Janet Mora Vicar Craig; 1 s. Educ. Greenock Academy; Glasgow University; Glasgow School of Art. Spent some time teaching before entering upon theological course at New College, Edinburgh, 1949-51; ordained, Aberdeen, 1953; Minister, Carlisle, Church of Scotland, 1957-63. Recreations: painting; music; gardening; hill-walking. Address: The Manse, Arisaig, Inverness-shire, PH39; T.-06875 227.

Usher, John Richard, BSc (Hons), MSc, PhD, FIMA. Head, School of Mathematical Sciences and Computer Studies, Robert Gordon's Institute of Technology, since 1983; Member, Scottish Examination Board Steering Committee for the Revision of Higher and Post-Higher, since 1987; Member, Council, Institute of Mathematics and its Applications, since 1987 (Chairman, Scottish Branch, 1985-88); b. 12.5.44, London; m., Sheila Mary; 1 d. Educ. St. Nicholas Grammar School; Hull University; St. Andrews University. Lecturer I, then Lecturer II, Teesside Polytechnic, 1970-74; Senior Lecturer, Glasgow College of Technology, 1974-82. Recreations: squash; bridge; hill-walking; philately. Address: (b.) School of Mathematical Sciences and Computer Studies, Robert Gordon's Institute of Technology, St. Andrew Street, Aberdeen; T.-0224 633611, Ext. 363.

V

Valentine, Ian Balfour, CA. Scottish Managing Partner, Binder Hamlyn, Chartered Accountants, since 1985; Finance Convener, Ayrshire and Arran Health Board, since 1982 (Member, since 1981); b. 17.10.40, Glasgow; m., Elaine; 1 s.; 1 d. Educ. Hutchesons' Boys' Grammar School. Partner, J. Wyllie Guild & Ballantine, 1965 (subsequently Binder Hamlyn). Member, Discipline Committee, Area Training Committee and South West Area Committee, Institute of Chartered Acountants of Scotland; Chairman, Ayrshire Association of Chartered Accountants of Scotland, 1976-78; President, Junior Chamber Ayr, 1972-73; Member, Ayr Schools Council, 1976-78; Director, Federation of Scottish Junior Chambers of Commerce, 1973-74; Honorary Secretary and Treasurer, Ayr Rugby Football Club, 1979-84. Recreations: golf; rugby (as spectator); bridge; curling. Address: (b.) 64 Dalblair Road, Ayr; T.-0292 263277.

Valentine, Keith, MA, LLB. Procurator Fiscal, Stirling, since 1976; b. 10.12.32, Perth; m., Anne Florence Ritchie; 1 s.; 2 d. Educ. Perth Academy; Edinburgh University. RAF Education Branch, 1956-59 (Flt.-Lt.); Procurator Fiscal Service, since 1961, Ayr, Glasgow, Edinburgh and Crown Office; other legal experience in private practice and with General Accident Fire and Life Assurance Corporation Ltd. Founder Chairman and currently Scottish Branch Representative, Executive Committee, British Association for the Study and Prevention of Child Abuse and Neglect. Recreations: golf; gardening; swimming; holidays in the sun. Address: (h.) Muircroft, Chalton Road, Bridge of Allan, FK9 4EF.

Vallance, Ramsay, MB, ChB, FRCSGlas, FRCR, DMRD. Consultant Radiologist, Western Infirmary/Gartnavel General Hospital, Glasgow, since 1977; Honorary Clinical Lecturer in Radiology, Glasgow University, since 1979; b. 9.3.45, Port Glasgow; m., Dr. Norma Bryan Stewart; 3 d. Educ. Eastwood Senior Secondary School; Glasgow University. Registrar in Surgery, Western Infirmary/Killearn Hospital, 1970-73; Registrar in Diagnostic Radiology, Southern General Hospital, Glasgow, 1973-75; Senior Registrar in Radiology, Western Infirmary/Gartnavel General Hospital, 1975-77. Church of Scotland Elder. Recreations: photography; classical music; golf. Address: (h.) 56 Russell Drive, Bearsden, Glasgow, G61 3BB; T.-041-942 2931.

Vallance-Owen, Andrew John, MB, ChB, FRCSEdin. Scottish Secretary, British Medical Association, since 1985; Secretary, Scottish Joint Consultants Committee, since 1985; b. 5.9.51, London; m., Frances Mary Glover; 2 s. Educ. Epsom College; Birmingham University. Surgical training, Newcastle upon Tyne, 1977-83 (Melbourne, 1980-81); Provincial Secretary, North of England, BMA, 1983-85. Surg. Lt. Cdr. RNR, HMS Claverhouse. Recreations: music; sailing; gardening. Address: (h.) 6 Midmar Avenue, Edinburgh, EH10 6BS; T.-031-447 5221.

Vardy, Professor Alan Edward, BSc, PhD, CEng, MICE, MASCE. Professor of Civil Engineering, Dundee University, since 1979 (Deputy Principal, since 1985); Director, Wolfson Bridge Research Unit, since 1980; b. 6.11.45, Sheffield; m., Mary Rosalind; 1 s.; 1 d. Educ. High Storrs Grammar School, Sheffield; Leeds University. Lecturer in Civil Engineering, Leeds University, 1972-75; Royal Society Warren Research Fellow, Cambridge University, 1975-79. Recreations: flying; wind-surfing; skiing; music. Address: (h.) Dunholm, 512 Perth Road, Dundee, DD2 1LW; T.-Dundee 66123.

Varley, William Raymond, BSc, DipTP, FICE, MIHT. Deputy Chief Engineer (Bridges), Scottish Development Department, since 1982; b. 7.7.28, Slaithwaite; m., Margaret Elizabeth Jessop; 2 s.; 1 d. Educ. King James Grammar School, Almondbury; Manchester University. National Service, Royal Engineers, 1951-53; Highway Engineering Department, West Riding County Council, 1954-68; Superintending Engineer (Bridges), NERCU, Department of Transport, 1969-81. Recreation: painting. Address: (b.) Room 3/102 New St. Andrews House, Edinburgh, EH1 1SZ; T.-031-556 8400.

Varty, Professor E. Kenneth C., BA, PhD, DLitt, FSA. Stevenson Professor of French, Glasgow University, since 1967; b. 18.8.27, Calke, Derbyshire; m., Hety Benninghoff; 2 d. Educ. Bemrose Grammar School, Derby; Nottingham University. Assistant Lecturer, then Lecturer, Keele University, 1953-61; Lecturer, then Senior Lecturer, Leicester University, 1961-67. Dean, Faculty of Arts, Glasgow, 1980-82; Visiting Lecturer, Warwick University, 1967; Visiting Professor, Jerusalem University, 1977; Visiting Research Fellow, Merton College, Oxford, 1974, and Clare Hall, Cambridge, 1983; Life Member, Clare Hall, 1985. Address: (b.) French Department, Glasgow University, Glasgow; T.-041-339 8855.

Vaughan, Henry William Campbell, DL, JP, MIPS. Lord Provost of Dundee, 1977-80; Deputy Lieutenant, since 1980; b. 15.3.19, Dundee; m., Margaret Cowie Flett; 1 s.; 1 d. Educ. Dundee Training College; Logie and Stobswell Secondary Schools. Stationer, Burns and Harris Ltd., Dundee, 1934-39; RAF (Volunteer Reserve), 1939-46; Chief Buyer, Valentine & Sons, Art Publishers, 1946-64; elected Councillor, 1958; Group Purchasing Officer, Scott & Robertson (Tay Textiles), 1964-75; Stationery Manager, Burns and Harris Ltd., Dundee, 1975-79; Chairman, Tayside Area Council on Alcoholism, 1980-82; Honorary Vice President, Strathspey and Fiddle Society; Lord Lieutenant, 1977-80; awarded Silver Jubilee Medal, 1977. Recreations: cine photography; politics; water colour painting. Address: (h.) 15 Fraser Street, Dundee, DD3 6RE; T.-Dundee 826175.

Venner, Robert Martin, MB, ChB, FRCSEdin. Orthopaedic Surgeon, Western Infirmary, Glasgow, since 1980; Honorary Clinical Teacher, Glasgow University, since 1980; Orthopaedic Surgeon: Vale of Leven Hospital, Ross Hall Hospital; b. 4.1.45, Sutton Coldfield; m., Morag Glen; 2 s.; 1 d. Educ. Aston Grammar School, Birmingham; Birmingham University Medical School. Ship's

Surgeon, P. & O. Steam Navigation Company; Anatomy Demonstrator, Glasgow University; trained in general surgery and orthopaedics, Western Infirmary, Glasgow. Recreation: Eastwood Amateur Swimming Club. Address: (h.) 288 Glasgow Road, Waterfoot, Eaglesham, Glasgow, G76 0EW; T.-041-644 2991.

Vernon, Kenneth Robert, CBE, BSc, FEng, FIEE, FIMechE. Deputy Chairman and Chief Executive, North of Scotland Hydro-Electric Board, since 1973; b. 15.3.23, Dumfries; m., Pamela Hands; 1 s.; 3 d.; 1 d. deceased. Educ. Dumfries Academy; Glasgow University. BTH Co., Edinburgh Corporation, British Electricity Authority, 1948-55; South of Scotland Electricity Board, 1955-56; North of Scotland Hydro Electric Board: Chief Electrical and Mechanical Engineer, 1964, General Manager, 1966, Board Member, 1970; Director, British Electricity International Ltd., since 1976; Board Member, Northern Ireland Electricity Service, 1979-85. Recreation: fishing. Address: (h.) 10 Keith Crescent, Edinburgh, EH4 3NH; T.-031-332 4610.

Vernon, Richard Geoffrey, BSc, PhD. Head, Department of Biochemistry and Physiology, Hannah Research Institute; Honorary Lecturer, Glasgow University, since 1981; b. 19.2.43, Maidstone; m., Mary Christine Cunliffe; 1 s.; 1 d. Educ. Newcastle High School; Birmingham University. Member, Editorial Board, British Journal of Nutrition; Past President, Birmingham University Mountaineering Club; first ascent of Mount Mazinaw, first British ascent, Mount Nautilus. Publication: Physiological Strategies in Lactation (Joint Editor). Recreations: walking; ornithology; mountaineering; bridge; photography. Address: (h.) 29 Knoll Park, Ayr; T.-0292 42195.

Vettese, J.W., MA (Hons), DipEd. Headteacher, Liberton High School, since 1985; b. 31.5.37, Brechin; m., M.L. McLean; 1 s.; 1 d. Educ. Bathgate Academy; Edinburgh University. Assistant Teacher, Wishaw High School; Housemaster, Stratford Academy, New Jersey; Principal Teacher of Geography: Hunter High School, East Kilbride, Garrion Academy, Wishaw; Assistant Head Teacher, Upper School, Coltness High School, Wishaw; Rector, Calderhead High School, 1979-85. Address: (h.) Marchwood House, Kirk Road, Bathgate, West Lothian; T.-Bathgate 633698.

Vickerman, Professor Keith, BSc, PhD, DSc, FRSE, FRS. Regius Professor of Zoology, Glasgow University, since 1984; Consultant Expert on Parasitic Diseases, World Health Organisation, since 1973; b. 21.3.33, Huddersfield; m., Moira Dutton; 1 d. Educ. King James Grammar School, Almondbury; University College, London (Fellow, 1985). Wellcome Lecturer in Protozoology, University College, London, 1958-63; Tropical Research Fellow, Royal Society, 1963-68; Glasgow University: Reader in Zoology, 1968-74; Professor of Zoology, 1974-84, Head, Department of Zoology, 1979-85. Publications: The Protozoa (Co-author), 1967; many papers in scientific and medical journals. Recreations: drawing and painting; gardening. Address: (h.) 16 Mirrlees Drive, Glasgow, G12 OSH; T.-041-334 2794.

Waddell, Professor David Alan Gilmour, MA, DPhil, FRHistS. Professor of Modern History, Stirling University, since 1968; b. 22.10.27, Edinburgh; m., Barbara Box; 2 s.; 1 d. Educ. Royal High School, Edinburgh; St. Andrews University; Oxford University. Lecturer, University College of the West Indies, Jamaica, 1954-59; Lecturer and Senior Lecturer, Edinburgh University, 1959-68; visiting appointments, Trinidad, Colombia and California. Member, Scottish Examination Board, since 1982; President, Scottish Society of the History of Medicine, since 1987. Address: (b.) Department of History, Stirling University, Stirling, FK9 4LA; T.-0786 73171, Ext. 2154.

Waddell, Ronald Muir, BA, MSc. Director, Scottish Social and Liberal Democrats, since 1988 (Political Director, Scottish Liberal Party, 1985-88); b. 15.5.54, Glasgow. Educ. Bearsden Academy; Strathclyde University; Salford University; Cranfield Institute of Technology. Chair, Scottish Young Liberals, 1981-82; Organisation Vice-Chair, Scottish Liberal Party, 1981-82, 1983-85. Recreations: hill-walking; travel; music. Address: (b.) 4 Clifton Terrace, Edinburgh, EH12 5DR; T.-031-337 2314.

Wade, Nicholas James, BSc, PhD. Reader in Psychology, Dundee University, since 1978; b. 27.3.42, Retford, Nottinghamshire; m., Christine Whetton; 2 d. Educ. Queen Elizabeth's Grammar School, Mansfield; Edinburgh University; Monash University. Postdoctoral Research Fellow, Max-Planck Institute for Behavioural Physiology, Germany, 1969-70; Lecturer in Psychology, Dundee University, 1970-78. Publications: The Art and Science of Visual Illusions, 1982; Brewster and Wheatstone on Vision, 1983. Recreations: golf; cycling. Address: (h.) 36 Norwood, Newport-on-Tay, Fife, DD6 8DW; T.-0382 543136.

Wade, Professor Terence Leslie Brian, BA, PhD, FIL. Professor in Russian Studies, Strathclyde University; b. 19.5.30, Southend-on-Sea; m., Mary Isobel McEwan; 2 d. Educ. Southend-on-Sea High School for Boys; Durham University. National Service, Intelligence Corps, 1953-55; War Office Language Instructor, 1955-63; Lecturer, Scottish College of Commerce, Glasgow, 1963-64; Lecturer, Senior Lecturer, Reader, Professor, Strathclyde University, from 1964. Convener, West of Scotland Association of Teachers of Russian; Editor, Journal of Russian Studies, 1980-86: Chairman, Association of Teachers of Russian, 1986-89. Publications: Russian Exercises for Language Laboratories (Co-author); The Russian Preposition "do" and the Concept of Extent; Prepositions in Modern Russian; Russia Today (Co-Editor). Address: 1 Cleveden Crescent, Glasgow, G12 OPD; T.-041-339 3947.

Waite, James A., MA. Rector, Perth Academy, since 1986; b. 9.10.42, Edinburgh; m., Sandra R. MacKenzie; 1 s.; 2 d. Educ. Royal High School, Edinburgh; Edinburgh University. Teacher of English, George Heriot's School, 1965-70; Principal Teacher of English, Campbeltown Grammar School, 1970-71; Principal Teacher of English, then Assistant Head Teacher, Boroughmuir High School, 1971-83; Depute Head Teacher, James Gillespie's High School, 1983-86. Recreations: theatre; literature; music. Address: (b.) Perth Academy, Murray Place, Perth, PH1 1NJ; T.-0738 23491.

Wakeford, Air Marshal Sir Richard (Gordon), KCB (1976), LVO (1961), OBE (1958), AFC (1952). Director, RAF Benevolent Fund, Scotland, since 1978; Chairman, MacRobert Trustees, since 1982; b. 20.4.22, Torquay; m., Anne Butler; 2 s.; 1 d.; 1 d. (deceased). Educ. Montpelier School, Paignton; Kelly College, Tavistock. Entered RAF, 1941; Coastal Command, 1941-45; Transport Command, 1945-47; Training Command, 1947-52; staff duties, including Director of Ops Staff, Malaya, 1952-58; CO, The Queens' Flight, 1958-61; IDC, 1969; Director, Service Intelligence, 1970-73; Commander, Anzuk Force Singapore, 1974-75; Deputy Chief of Defence Staff (Intelligence), 1975-78; retired Air Marshal, 1978. Commissioner, Queen Victoria School, Dunblane; Director, Thistle Foundation; Director, Cromar Nominess; Commander, Order of St. John, 1986. Recreation: fishing. Address: (h.) Earlston House, Forgandenny, Perth, Ph2 9DE; T.-0738 812392.

Walkden, Gordon Mark, BSc, PhD. Member, Kincardine and Deeside District Council, since 1984 (Vice Convener and Chairman, Policy and Resources, since 1988); Senior Lecturer and Research Scientist, Department of Geology, Aberdeen University, since 1987; Geological Consultant to industry; b. 8.6.44, Edinburgh; m., K. Mary M. Begg; 3 c. Educ. Quintin School, London; Manchester University. Past Chairman, Banchory Community Council; scientific author and local historian. Recreations: building restoration; palaeontology. Address: (h.) Banchory, Kincardineshire.

Walker, (Alexander) Percy, DL, MB, ChB, DObstRCOG, MRCGP. Deputy Lieutenant, Ayr and Arran; b. 2.7.16, Irvine; m., Aileen Gerrard; 1 s.; 3 d. Educ. Shrewsbury School; Glasgow University. Temporary Surgeon Lt., RNVR, 1940-46; General Medical Practitioner, Ayr, 1948-81; Adjudicating Medical Officer, DHSS, 1952-87; Senior Medical Officer, Western Meeting Club, Ayr Racecourse, 1955-87. Recreations: golf; gardening; curling; sailing. Address: (h.) Bentfield, Maryborough Road, Prestwick, KA9 1SW; T.-0292 77876.

Walker, Alexander William, JP. Honorary Sheriff, since 1971; Chairman, Finance and General Purposes Committee, Tweeddale District Council, since 1977 (Member of Council, since 1974); Chairman, Tweeddale Licensing Board, since 1975; Chairman, Tweeddale Local Sports Council; b. 10.5.24, Peebles; m., Dorothy Margaret. Educ. Kingsland School; Scottish Woollen and Worsted Technical College. D.B. Ballantyne Bros., 1939-70; Air Training Corps, 1941-43, RAF, 1943-46 (Sergeant); Director, Sonido International Ltd. (formerly Fidelitone International Ltd.); elected, Peebles Town Council, 1960-75; Provost, 1967-70; Burgh Treasurer, 1971-75; held every office, Peebles Town Council; Member, Peeblesshire County Council, 1960-70 (Vice Chairman, Finance Committee); Vice Chairman, Tweeddale District Council, 1974-77; Warden, Neidpath Castle, 1971; former Dean, Guildry Corporation of Peebles; Honorary Member, Peebles Callants Club. Recreations: football in younger days; now enjoys reading political biographies; and, of course, local government, which unfortunately is no longer local or indeed democratic. Address: (h.) Gadeni, 59 High Street, Peebles; T.-Peebles 21011.

Walker, Sir Allan Grierson, KB, QC, MA, LLB, LLD. Sheriff Principal of Lanarkshire, 1963-74; b. 1.5.07, Dumfries; m., Audrey Margaret Glover; 1 s. Educ. Whitgift School; Edinburgh University. Practised at Scottish Bar, 1931-39; Sheriff Substitute, Selkirk and Peebles, 1942-45; Sheriff Substitute, Dumbarton, 1945-50; Sheriff Substitute, Glasgow, 1950-63; Member, Law Reform Committee for Scotland, 1964-70; Chairman, Sheriff Court Rules Council, 1972-74. Publications: The Law of Evidence in Scotland (Co-author); Purves' Scottish Licensing Laws, 7th and 8th editions. Recreations: gardening; walking. Address: (h.) 24 Moffat Road, Dumfries, DG1 1NJ; T.-0387 53583.

Walker, Professor David Maxwell, CBE, QC, MA, PhD, LLD, Hon. LLD, FBA, FRSE. Regius Professor of Law, Glasgow University, since 1958; b. 9.4.20, Glasgow; m., Margaret Knox. Educ. High School of Glasgow; Glasgow University; Edinburgh University; London University. HLI and Indian Army, 1939-46; Advocate, 1948; in practice, Scottish Bar, 1948-54; Professor of Jurisprudence, Glasgow University, 1954-58; Barrister (Middle Temple), 1957; QC (Scot), 1958; Dean, Faculty of Law, Glasgow University, 1956-59; Convener, School of Law, 1984-88. Chairman, High School of Glasgow Trust (School Governor). Publications: Law of Damages in Scotland; The Scottish Legal System; Law of Delict in Scotland; Law of Civil Remedies in Scotland; Law of Prescription in Scotland; Law of Contracts in Scotland; Oxford Companion to Law; Principles of Scottish Private Law (four volumes); The Scottish Jurists; Stair's Institutions (Editor); Stair Tercentenary Studies (Editor); A Legal History of Scotland, Vol. I. Recreations: book collecting; Scottish history; motoring. Address: (b.) Department of Private Law, Glasgow University, Glasgow, G12 8QQ; T.-041-339 8855, Ext. 4556.

Walker, David Morrison, DA, FSA Scot, HFRIAS, Hon. LLD (Dundee). Principal Inspector of Historic Buildings, Scottish Development Department, since 1978; b. 31.1.33, Dundee; m., Averil Mary Stewart McIlwraith; 1 s. Educ. Morgan Academy, Dundee; Dundee College of Art. Voluntary work for National Buildings Record, Edinburgh, 1952-56; National Service, Royal Engineers, 1956-58; Glasgow Education Authority, 1958-59; Dundee Education Authority, 1959-61; Historic Buildings Branch, Scottish Office: Senior Investigator of Historic Buildings, 1961-76, Principal Investigator of Historic Buildings, 1976-78. Alice David Hitchcock Medallion, 1970. Publications: Architecture of Glasgow (Co-author), 1968 (revised and enlarged edition, 1987); Buildings of Scotland: Edinburgh (Co-author), 1984;

Dundee: An Illustrated Introduction (Co-author), 1984; Dundee Nineteenth Century Mansions. Address: (b.) 20 Brandon Street, Edinburgh, EH3 5DX; T.-031-244 2971.

Walker, Ernest John Munro. Secretary, The Scottish Football Association Ltd., since 1977; b. 20.7.28, Glasgow; m., Anne; 1 s.; 2 d. Educ. Queen's Park Secondary School. Army (Royal Horse Artillery), 1946-48; Assistant Secretary, industrial textile company, 1948-58; Assistant Secretary, Scottish Football Association, 1958-77. Director, Euro-Sportring; Director, Scotball Travel and Leisure Ltd.; Member: FIFA Protocol Committee, FIFA World Cup 1994 Inspection Group, UEFA Organizing Committee of the Club Competitions, UEFA Committee for Stadia. Recreations: golf; fishing; music; travel. Address: (b.) 6 Park Gardens, Glasgow, G3 7YF; T.-041-332 6372.

Walker, Esme, CBE, MA, LLB, WS, NP. Chair, Scottish Association of Citizens Advice Bureaux; Member, Equal Opportunities Commission; Member, Scottish Committee of the Council on Tribunals; Member, Lord Chancellor's Committee on Conveyancing; b. 7.1.32, Edinburgh; m., Ian Macfarlane Walker; 1 s. Educ. St. George's School for Girls, Edinburgh; Edinburgh University. Lawyer; Vice Chairman, National Consumer Council, 1984-87; Chairman, Scottish Consumer Council, 1980-85. Address: (h.) Clinton House, Whitehouse Loan, Edinburgh; T.-031-447 5191.

Walker, Ian. Member, Gordon District Council, since 1984; Head Teacher, Westhill Primary School, since 1973; Chairman, Aberdeen Advisory Committee, IBA; Member: Gordon Sports Council, Gordon District Tourist Board; b. 1.6.40, Inverurie; m., Mildred Agnes Rose; 1 s.; 1 d. Educ. Daviot School; Inverurie Academy; Aberdeen College of Education. Assistant Teacher, Insch School, 1963-67; Head Teacher: Finzean School, 1967-69, Kinellar School, 1969-73; Member, Working Party on Mathematics in the Primary School, Grampian Regional Council; Elder, Church of Scotland. Recreations: curling; golf; cricket (Blue, Aberdeen College of Education); reading; listening to all kinds of music; theatre; films. Address: (h.) 11A Arnhall Drive, Westhill, Skene, Aberdeenshire, AB3 6TZ; T.-0224 741783.

Walker, James, CA. Senior Partner, James Rosie & Co., CA, Galashiels and Peebles, since 1968; Chairman, Board of Governors, Scottish College of Textiles; b. 14.6.27, Airdrie; 1 s.; 1 d. Educ. Airdrie Academy. Recreations: golf; bridge. Address: (h.) Broombank, Gattonside, Melrose, Roxburghshire; T.-0896 82 2362.

Walker, John Hyslop, CBE, MA, MEd, PhD. Director, Scottish Examination Board, since 1975; b. 12.3.29, China; m., Jean Wighton Allan; 2 d. Educ. Girvan High School; Glasgow University. National Service (commission, RAF), 1952-54; taught, Cumnock Academy and Kilmarnock Academy, 1954-59; Department of Education, Glasgow University, 1959-62; Assistant Director of Education, Stirlingshire, 1962-65; Depute Director, Scottish Examination Board, 1965-75. Session Clerk, Borthwick Parish Church. Recreations: music; caravanning; hill-walking. Address: (h.) 4 Private Road, Gorebridge, Midlothian; T.-0875 20788.

Walker, Rev. Kenneth Donald Fraser, MA, BD. Minister, Athelstaneford linked with Whitekirk and Tyninghame, since 1976; b. 4.9.42, Tarbert, Argyll; m., Veronica McClay Fraser; 2 s.; 3 d. Educ. Girvan Academy; Edinburgh University. Entered banking profession, 1961; licensed to the Ministry, 1974; Assistant Minister, Bearsden South, 1974; ordained, 1976; a Chaplain to Moderator, General Assembly, 1981. Recreations: gardening; hill-walking. Address: The Manse, Athelstaneford, North Berwick, EH39 5BE; T.-062088 378.

Walker, Leslie James, BSc, CEng, FICE, MIHT. Director of Technical Services, Dunfermline District Council, since 1974; b. 10.12.31, Ferryhill, Co. Durham; m., Beatrice; 2 s. Educ. Acklam Hall Grammar School, Middlesbrough; Edinburgh University. Assistant Resident Engineer, Partridge Earp & Partners, Edinburgh, 1953-60; Dunfermline Town Council: Assistant Engineer, 1960-63, Principal Engineer, 1963-70, Depute Burgh Engineer, 1970-75. Recreation: rugby football. Address: (b.) 7 Abbot Street, Dunfermline; T.-Dunfermline 731751.

Walker, Margaret, MA. Vice-President, Scottish Conservative & Unionist Association, since 1987; b. 4.5.26, Paisley; m., David Maxwell Walker (qv). Educ. Paisley Grammar School; Glasgow University. Manuscript Department, National Library of Scotland, 1948-54; Chairman, Hillhead Conservative & Unionist Association, 1982-86; West of Scotland Conservative Women's Area Committee: Vice-Chairman, 1980-81, Chairman, 1981-83; West of Scotland Conservative Area Council: Vice-Chairman, 1983-85, Chairman, 1985-87. Recreations: music; ballet; conservation; cookery. Address: (h.) 1 Beaumont Gate, Glasgow, G12 9EE; T.-041-339 2802.

Walker, Margaret Mary, MB, ChB, MRCPsych, DObstRCOG. Consultant Psychiatrist in Adult Psychiatry, Duke Street Hospital, Glasgow, since 1977; Honorary Clinical Lecturer, Glasgow University, since 1978; b. 11.6.42, Hammersmith; m., Norman G. Niblock. Educ. Greenhead High School, Huddersfield; Glasgow University. House Officer appointments; medical rotation, Glasgow Royal Infirmary; began psychiatric training in Glasgow, 1972. President, Psychosomatic Society (Glasgow), 1982-84. Recreations: hill-walking; geology; archaeology; photography; foreign travel. Address: (b.) Duke Street Hospital, Glasgow; T.-041-556 5222.

Walker, Michael Giles Neish, CBE, MA (Cantab). Chairman, Sidlaw Group, since 1988 (Chief Executive, 1976-88); b. 28.8.33, Fife; m., Margaret R. Hills; 2 s.; 1 d. Educ. Shrewsbury School; St. John's College, Cambridge. National Service, Royal Dragoons, 1952-54 (2nd Lt.); TA, Fife and Forfar Yeomanry, 1954-72 (Major); joined Jute Industries Ltd., 1958 (subsequently name changed to Sidlaw Group); Director, Dundee and London Investment Trust plc, since 1982; Member, North of Scotland Hydro-Electric Board, since 1982. Address: (b.) Sidlaw Group plc, Nethergate Centre, Dundee, DD1 4BR; T.-0382 23161.

Walker, Thomas Wallace, CBE, BL, FIB (Scot). Chairman, Standard Property Investment plc, since 1987; Chairman, Macdonald Orr Ltd., since 1982; b. 20.7.13, Paisley. Educ. John Neilson Institution, Paisley; Glasgow University. General Manager, British Linen Bank, 1963-71; Treasurer and General Manager, Bank of Scotland, 1970-74 (Director, 1974-84); Deputy Governor, British Linen Bank, 1975-87; founding Chairman, International Energy Bank Ltd., 1973-78; President, Institute of Bankers in Scotland, 1965-67; Director, Life Association of Scotland Ltd., 1978-84; Trustee, Bield Housing Trust; Past Chairman, Abbeyfield Society for Scotland Ltd.; Committee Member (former Treasurer), Malcolm Sargent Cancer Fund for Children (Scotland). Recreation: reading. Address: (h.) Kinfauns, 6 Frogston Terrace, Edinburgh, EH10 7AD; T.-031-445 1164.

Walker, William Buchanan Cowan, MA, LLB. Solicitor; Secretary, Royal Scottish Forestry Society; Farmer and Landowner; b. 27.6.27, Callander; m., Rita Bate; 2 s.; 1 d. Educ. Dollar Academy; Edinburgh Academy; Edinburgh University. Assistant, Robert Stewart & Scott, SSC, Edinburgh; Partner, Henderson and Jackson, WS, Edinburgh; Consultant, Lindsays, WS, Edinburgh; Director, Jamaica Street Ltd.; Director, Glenbervie Estate Co. Ltd.; Director, Garvald School Ltd. Recreations: repairing old buildings; travelling; people watching. Address: (h.) Stoneyknowe, West Linton, Peeblesshire.

Walker, William Connoll, FIPM, FBIM, FRSA. MP (Conservative), Tayside North, since 1979; Defence Spokesman, Scottish Conservative Party, since 1981; b. Dundee; m., Mavis Evelyn; 3 d. Educ. Logie School. Message boy; RAF (commissioned); Training and Education Officer; Director of Personnel; Managing Director. Recreations: gliding; caravanning. Address: (h.) Candletrees, Golf Course Road, Rosemount, Blairgowrie, Perthshire; T.-0250 2660.

Walker-Naddell, Alexander Walker, KStJ, ERD, JP, DL, FRCS, FRCPS, FSA Scot, FRSA. Consultant Orthopaedic and Neuro Surgeon; Hon. Colonel, 304 General Hospital "City of Glasgow" TAVR; b. 25.12.10, Glasgow; m., Iris Elaine Harris; 1 s.; 2 d. Educ. Bellahouston Academy; Glasgow University and St. Mungo College. Qualified in medicine, 1938; War Service, 1939-45; appointed Surgeon, Glasgow Royal Infirmary, 1946; volunteered service to Army; appointed Surgeon in command, S Division, 4 General Hospital, 1952-62; Deputy Lieutenant, City of Glasgow, since 1963; Director, Humane Society, 20 years; District Court Judge, City of Glasgow, to 1981; Fellow, Royal Society of Medicine. Publications: The Slipped Disc and Aching Back of Man, 1985; Fight Old Age, 1987; papers on the medical aspects of atomic warfare, and migraine. Recreations: golf; water polo. Address: 22 Sandyford Place, Charing Cross, Glasgow, G3 7NG; T.-041-221 7571.

Walkingshaw, Francis, NP. Solicitor; Procurator Fiscal, District of Wigtown, since 1983; b. 9.12.42, Edinburgh; m., Penelope Marion Theodosia Brooks McKissock; 2 s. Educ. George Watson's College, Edinburgh. Private practice; joined Procurator Fiscal service, 1975. Dean, Faculty of Wigtown District Solicitors, 1985-87. Recreations: shooting; fishing; food and wine. Address: (b.) Sheriff Court House, Lewis Street, Stranraer; T.-0776 4321.

Wallace, Professor David Alexander Ross, BSc, PhD, FRSA, FRSE. Professor of Mathematics, Strathclyde University, since 1986 (Professor, Stirling University, 1973-86); b. 24.11.33, Cupar. Educ. Stranraer High School; St. Andrews University; Manchester University. Instructor: Princeton University, 1958-59, Harvard University, 1959-60; Research Fellow, then Lecturer, Glasgow University, 1960-65; Senior Lecturer, Aberdeen University, 1965-73. Recreations: culture; tennis; swimming; skiing; badminton. Address: (b.) Department of Mathematics, Strathclyde University, Livingstone Tower, 26 Richmond Street, Glasgow, G1 1XH; T.-041-552 4400.

Wallace, Professor David James, BSc, PhD, FRSE, FRS. Tait Professor of Mathematical Physics, Edinburgh University, since 1979; Director, Edinburgh Concurrent Supercomputer Project; Chairman, Physics Committee, SERC, since 1987; b. 7.10.45, Hawick; m., Elizabeth Anne Yeats; 1 d. Educ. Hawick High School; Edinburgh University. Harkness Fellow, Princeton University, 1970-72; Lecturer in Physics, 1971-78, Reader, 1978-79, Southampton University; Visiting Scientist, Europe, Israel, North and South America. Maxwell Medal, Institute of Physics, 1980. Recreations: running; eating at La Potiniere. Address: (b.) Physics Department, The University, Mayfield Road, Edinburgh, EH9 3JZ; T.-031-667 1081.

Wallace, Rev. Douglas Woodburn, MA (Hons), BD (Hons). Minister, Kilmodan and Colintraive, since 1982; b. 23.9.55, Greenock; m., Janet Rosalind Lee; 2 s. Educ. Greenock Academy; New College, Edinburgh. Member, Church of Scotland Youth Education Committee; Education Convener, Dunoon Presbytery, since 1983. Recreations: long-distance running; music; reading; board games; worship. Address: Kilmodan Manse, Glendaruel, Colintraive, Argyll, PA22 3AA.

Wallace, George, DPA, MInstAM (Dip), FMS, MIPM. Director of Personnel, Perth and Kinross District Council, since 1975; Personnel Officer, Perth and Kinross Recreational Facilities Ltd., since 1987; Personnel Adviser, Bowerswell Memorial Homes, since 1983; b. 5.7.34, Glasgow; m., Elizabeth Hall Graham; 1 s.; 1 d. Educ. Albert Senior Secondary School; Glasgow University. National Service, RAF, 1952-54; Glasgow Corporation, 1954-64; Renfrew County Council, 1964-65; Western Regional Hospital Board, 1965-68; Lanark County Council, 1968-71; LAMSAC, 1971-73; Perth and Kinross Joint County Council, 1973-75. Panel Chairman, British Standards Institution; Elder, Church of Scotland. Recreation: amateur radio. Address: (b.) 2 High Street, Perth, PH1 5PH; T.-0738 39911.

Wallace of Campsie, Baron (George Wallace), JP, DL. Life President, Wallace, Cameron (Holdings) Ltd., since 1981; Life Peer; b. 13.2.15; m. Educ. Queen's Park Secondary School, Glasgow; Glasgow University. Solicitor, since 1950; Honorary Sheriff, Hamilton, since 1971; Chairman, East

Kilbride and Stonehouse Development Corporation, 1969-75; Member, South of Scotland Electricity Board, 1966-68; founder Member, Board, Scottish Development Agency, 1975-78; President, Glasgow Chamber of Commerce, 1974-76; Honorary President, Scottish Section, Town and Country Planning Association, since 1969; Chairman, Scottish Executive Committee, British Heart Foundation, 1973-76; Vice-Chairman, Scottish Retirement Council, since 1975.

Wallace, James Fleming, QC, MA, LLB. Counsel (Draftsman), Scottish Law Commission, since 1979; b. 19.3.31, Edinburgh; m., Valerie Mary Lawrence (deceased); 2 d. Educ. Edinburgh Academy; Edinburgh University. National Service, 1954-56 (2nd Lt., Royal Artillery), 1954-56; TA (Lt., Royal Artillery), 1956-60; practised at Scottish Bar, 1957-60; Parliamentary Draftsman and Legal Secretary to Lord Advocate, 1960-79. Publications: The Businessman's Lawyer (Scottish Supplement); Stair Memorial Encyclopaedia (Contributor). Recreations: hill-walking; choral singing; golf; badminton. Address: (h.) 24 Corrennie Gardens, Edinburgh, EH10 6DB; T.-031-447 1224.

Wallace, James Robert, MA (Cantab), LLB (Edinburgh). MP (SLD, formerly Liberal), Orkney and Shetland, since 1983; Liberal Parliamentary Spokesman on Energy and Fisheries, 1983-85, on Defence and Fisheries, 1985-88; Chief Whip, Liberal Party, 1987-88; first Chief Whip, Social and Liberal Democrats, since 1988; Advocate, since 1979; b. 25.8.54, Annan; m., Rosemary Janet Fraser; 2 d. Educ. Annan Academy; Downing College, Cambridge; Edinburgh University. Called to Scottish Bar, 1979; contested Dumfries, 1979, and South of Scotland Euro Constituency, 1979; Member, Scottish Liberal Party Executive, 1976-85 (Vice-Chairman, Policy, 1982-85); Honorary President, Scottish Young Liberals, 1984-85. Publication: New Deal for Rural Scotland (Co-Editor), 1983. Recreations: golf; reading; travelling (especially between London and the Northern Isles). Address: (h.) Northwood House, Tankerness, Orkney, KW17 2QS; T.-0856 86 383.

Wallace, John Anderson. Chief Executive, Tayside Regional Council, since 1982; b. 10.7.29, Perth; m., Mary; 1 s.; 1 d. Educ. Perth Academy; Edinburgh University. Solicitor, private practice, 1951-54; Solicitor: Dundee Corporation, 1954-60, Cumbernauld Development Corporation, 1960-66; Depute Town Clerk, Dundee Corporation, 1966-75; Depute Chief Executive, Tayside, 1975-82. Recreations: golf; bowls; wine-making; music. Address: (b.) Tayside House, 28 Crichton Street, Dundee; T.-Dundee 23281.

Wallace, John David, MA, DipEd, FSA Scot. International Arbiter and Commissioner, Federation Internationale des Echecs; President, Scottish Junior Chess Association; Council Member, Scottish Chess Association; b. 21.11.21, Bulford; m., Jenefer M.H. Bell (deceased); 1 s.; 1 d. Educ. Tonbridge School; St. Andrews University. Army Service, 1940-46 (Captain, Royal Artillery); teaching appointments in Orkney and Fife, 1954-73; Assistant Rector, Madras College, St. Andrews, 1971-73; founding Headmaster, Abbotsgrange Middle School, Grangemouth, 1974-84. Recreations: bridge; chess; curling; hill-walking. Address: (h.) Kirkheugh Cottage, The Shorehead, St. Andrews, Fife, KY16 9RG.

Wallace of That Ilk, Lt.-Col. Malcolm Robert. 34th Chief (1970); Member, Queen's Bodyguard for Scotland (Royal Company of Archers); b. 14.12.21, Perth. Educ. Stowe. Commissioned, The Black Watch, 1941; served World War II (mentioned in Despatches); served Korean War, 1950-51 (Argyll and Sutherland Highlanders) and 1952 (Black Watch); Australian Staff College, 1955; commanded Argyll and Sutherland Highlanders, 1964-67; Regimental Secretary, The Black Watch, 1967-78. Recreations: shooting; fishing. Address: (h.) Hilton of Gask, Auchterarder, Perthshire; T.-Gask 278.

Wallace Thomas, BSc. President, Scottish Secondary Teachers' Association, since 1987; b. 12.11.41, Glasgow; m., Kathleen May Macqueen; 1 d. Educ. Allan Glen's School; Glasgow University; Jordanhill College. Teacher, 1966; Principal Teacher (Physics), Riverside Secndary, 1971, Albert Secondary, 1984. Elected Vice-President, SSTA, 1974; Vice-President, 1985; elected to General Teaching Council for Scotland, 1979 (re-elected 1983 and 1987); Convener, GTC Supply Committee, 1987; appointed by Secretary of State to Scottish Committee for Staff Development in Education, 1987. Recreation: bagpipes. Address: (h.) 40 Rowallan Gardens, Glasgow, G11 7LJ; T.-041-334 2436.

Wallace, Rev. William Fitch, BDS, BD. Minister, Wick St. Andrew's and Thrumster Church, since 1974; Executive Member, Church of Scotland Board of Social Responsibility, since 1985; Chairman: Wick Schools Council, since 1986, Caithness Local Health Council, since 1987; Member, Scottish Council, ASH, since 1987; b. 6.10.39, Falkirk; m., Jean Wyness Hill; 1 s.; 3 d. Educ. Allan Glen's School; Glasgow University; Edinburgh University. Ordained Assistant, St. George's Tron, Glasgow, 1968-71; Missionary Dentist, Addis Ababa, Ethiopia, 1971-73. Chairman, Caithness Local Health Council, 1975-83; Member, Church of Scotland Social Responsibility Committee, 1975-83; Organising Secretary, Wick Primary Schools Action Group, 1984-86. Recreations: golf; gardening. Address: St. Andrew's Manse, Coronation Street, Wick, KW1 5LS; T.-Wick 3166.

Wallace, William Villiers, MA, FRHistS. Director, Institute of Soviet and East European Studies, Glasgow University, since 1979; b. 15.12.26, Glasgow; m., Gulli Fyfe; 2 s.; 1 d. Educ. Hutchesons' Boys' Grammar School; Glasgow University; London University. RNVR, 1944-47; appointments in History, Pittsburgh University, London University, Aberdeen University, Durham University, 1953-67; Professor of History, New University of Ulster, 1967-79. Chairman, Scottish Branch, Royal Institute of International Affairs; Chairman, Association of University Teachers (Scotland). Address: (b.) Institute of Soviet and East European Studies, Glasgow University, 29 Bute Gardens, Glasgow, G12 8RS; T.-041-330 4579.

Walley, Raymond Peter, CIC. Chairman, Border Crafts Association; Member, Borders Regional Council; Potter; b. 29.8.47, Stoke-on-Trent; m.,

Kathleen Anne; 2 s. Educ. Blessed William Southerne Secondary School; Stoke-on-Trent College of Art. Art Teacher, 1967-69; Pottery Manufacturer, since 1975. Chairman, Innerleithen Branch, Social and Liberal Democrats. Recreation: DIY. Address: (h.) Orchard Mains Lodge, Traquair, Innerleithen, Peeblesshire; T.-0896 830575.

Walls, Professor Andrew Finlay, OBE, MA, BLitt, FSA Scot. Director, Centre for the Study of Christianity in the Non-Western World, since 1982; b. 21.4.28; m., Doreen Mary Harden; 1 s.; 1 d. Librarian, Tyndale House, Cambridge, 1952-57; Lecturer in Theology, Fourah Bay College, Sierra Leone, 1957-62; Head, Department of Religion, Nigeria University, 1962-65; Aberdeen University: Lecturer in Church History, 1966-69, Senior Lecturer, 1969, first Head, Department of Religious Studies, and Riddoch Lecturer in Comparative Religion, 1970, Reader, 1975, Professor of Religious Studies, 1979-85, Emeritus Professor, 1985; Honorary Professor, Edinburgh University, since 1987; Visiting Professor of World Christianity, Yale University, 1988; Co-opted Member, Aberdeen Education Committee, 1971-74; Aberdeen City Councillor, 1974-80; Convener, Arts and Recreation, COSLA, 1978-80; Chairman, Council for Museums and Galleries in Scotland, 1978-81; Vice-Chairman, Committee of Area Museums Councils, 1980-81; Member, Williams Committee on the future of the national museums, 1979-82; Trustee, National Museum of Antiquities of Scotland, 1982-85; Member, Museums Advisory Board for Scotland, 1984-85; Trustee, National Museums of Scotland, 1985-87; Methodist Preacher; Past Chairman, Disablement Income Group, Scotland; President, British Association for the History of Religions, 1977-80; Secretary, Scottish Institute of Missionary Studies; Editor, Journal of Religion in Africa, 1967-86; Member, Scottish Working Party on Religions of the World. Address: (b.) Centre for the Study of Christianity in the Non-Western World, Edinburgh University, New College, Mound Place, Edinburgh, EH1 2LU; T.-031-225 8400.

Walsh, David. Head of Production, Scottish Opera, since 1988; b. Toronto. Educ. University of Windsor, Canada; University of Toronto. Assistant Director, English National Opera, 1978-80; Assistant Director, Frankfurt Opera, 1980; Assistant Artistic Director, Vancouver Opera, 1984-88. Address: (b.) 39 Elmbank Crescent, Glasgow, G2 4PT.

Walsh, David Brian, MB, ChB, MRCPath. Consultant in Clinical Chemistry, Tayside Health Board, since 1973; Honorary Senior Lecturer in Biochemical Medicine, Dundee University, since 1973; b. 3.7.41, Douglas, Isle of Man; m., Maureen; 2 d. Educ. William Hulme's Grammar School, Manchester; Victoria University of Manchester. House Officer posts, St. Woolos Hospital, Newport; Senior House Officer posts in Clinical Pathology, London Hospital and Llandough Hospital, Cardiff; Lecturer in Pathology, Manchester University; Senior Registrar in Chemical Pathology, United Manchester Hospitals. Editor, BEST Database; Regional Adviser, Royal College of Pathologists. Recreations: photography; family. Address: (b.) Department of Biochemical Medicine, Ninewells Hospital, Dundee, DD2 9SY.

Walsh, Ewart Geoffrey, MA, BSc, BM, BCh (Oxon), MD, FRSE, FRCP, FRCPEdin. Reader, Department of Physiology, Edinburgh University; b. 25.11.22, Cheltenham; m., E.P.Y. Watson; 4 d. Educ. Cheltenham Grammar School; Oxford University; Harvard University. Academic career, Edinburgh University, since 1951; WHO Visiting Professor, Baroda Medical School, India, 1963-64. Recreation: playing the flute. Address: (b.) Physiology Department, Teviot Place, Edinburgh, EH8 9AG; T.-031-667 1011.

Walsh, Professor Patrick Gerard, MA, PhD, FRSE. Professor of Humanity, Glasgow University, since 1972; b. 16.8.23, Accrington; m., Eileen Benson Quin; 4 s.; 1 d. Educ. Preston Catholic College; Liverpool University. Lecturer in Ancient Classics, University College, Dublin, 1952-59; Lecturer, Reader, Professor, Department of Humanity, Edinburgh University, 1959-72. Recreations: tennis; travel. Address: (h.) 17 Broom Road, Glasgow, G43 2TP; T.-041-637 4977.

Walsh, Sadie Delores, MB, ChB, MRCPEdin, FRCPEdin. Consultant Physician, Royal Victoria Hospital and Corstorphine Hospital, Edinburgh, since 1980; b. 14.10.32, Kingston, Jamaica; m., John Nuttall; 2 d. Educ. Edinburgh University. House Physician, Roodland General Hospital; House Surgeon, Dumfries and Galloway Royal Infirmary; House Physician, Royal Hospital for Sick Children, Edinburgh; Registrar posts, Respiratory Unit, City Hospital, Edinburgh; general medicine, Western General Hospital, Edinburgh; Registrar, Haematology, Edinburgh Royal Infirmary; Registrar, Geriatric Medicine, Royal Victoria Hospital, Edinburgh; Consultant Physician, Geriatric Medicine, Fife Health Board, 1975-80. Recreations: hill-walking; skiing; swimming. Address: (h.) 8 S.W. Northumberland Street Lane, Edinburgh, EH3 6JD; T.-031-556 7632.

Walton, Professor Ewart Kendall, BSc, PhD, FRSE. Professor of Geology, St. Andrews University, since 1968; b. 28.11.24, Ashington, Northumberland; m., 1, Margaret; 1 s.; 1 d.; 2, Susan Clare; 2 s.; 1 d. Educ. Bedlington Secondary School, Northumberland; King's College, Durham. Assistant, Glasgow University, 1951-54; Lecturer, then Reader, Edinburgh University, 1954-68; Master, United College, St. Andrews, 1972-76. President, Association of Teachers of Geology, 1978-80; Member, Scottish Advisory Committee, NCC, 1982-85; Member, Geology Panel, Scottish Examination Board, 1982-85. Address: (b.) Department of Geography and Geology, Division of Geology, Purdie Building, St. Andrews, Fife, KY16 9ST; T.-0334 76161.

Walton, Professor Henry John, MD, PhD, FRCPE, FRCPsych, DPM, Hon.MD Uppsala. Physician; Professor of International Medical Education, Edinburgh, since 1986; b. 15.2.24, South Africa; m., Sula Wolff. Educ. University of Cape Town; London University; Columbia University, NY; Edinburgh University. Registrar in Neurology and Psychiatry, University of Cape Town, 1946-54; Head, Department of Psychiatry, 1957-60; Senior Registrar, Maudsley Hospital, London, 1955-57; Senior Lecturer in Psychiatry, then Professor of Psychiatry, Edinburgh University, 1962-85; Editor, Medical Education, since 1976; President, Association for Medical Education in Europe, 1972-86, Hon. Life President, since 1986; President, World Federation for Medical Education, since 1983; frequent Consultant to WHO. Publications: as Editor: Small Group Psychotherapy, 1974; Dictionary of Psychiatry, 1985; as Co-Editor: Newer Developments in Assessing Clinical Competence, 1986; as Co-Author: Alcoholism, 1988. Recreations: literature; visual arts, particularly Western painting and Chinese and Japanese art. Address: Medical School, Edinburgh University, Teviot Place, Edinburgh, EH8 9AG; T.-031-226 3125.

Walton, John Christopher, BSc, PhD, DSc. Reader in Chemistry, St. Andrews University, since 1986; b. 4.12.41, St. Albans; m., Jane Lehman; 1 s.; 1 d. Educ. Watford Grammar School for Boys; Sheffield University. Assistant Lecturer: Queen's College, St. Andrews, 1966-67, Dundee University, 1967-69; Lecturer in Chemistry, United College, St. Andrews, 1969-80; Senior Lecturer, 1980-86. Director, Good Health Association (Scotland) Ltd.; Elder, Seventh-day Adventist Church. Recreations: music; philosophy. Address: (b.) Department of Chemistry, St. Andrews University, St. Andrews, Fife, KY16 9ST; T.-0334 76161.

Walton, Kenneth D., BMus, GMusRNCM, ARCO. Manager, Scottish Music Information Centre; Editor, Stretto magazine; Scottish Music Critic, Daily Telegraph, since 1983; Writer and Critic: Classical Music magazine, Glasgow Herald; Broadcaster; Hon. Secretary/Treasurer, Scottish Musicians Benevolent Fund; b. 20.2.58, Paisley; m., Janis H. Goodfellow; 2 d. Educ. Paisley Grammar School; Glasgow University; Royal Northern College of Music, Manchester. Tutor in Music, Glasgow University, 1982-83; Lecturer in Academic Studies, Royal Scottish Academy of Music and Drama, 1985-86, and since 1988; on music staff, Hutchesons' Grammar School, 1987-88. Member, BBC Music Advisory Committee (Scotland); President, Glasgow Society of Organists, 1985-86; Joint Course Organiser and Tutor, Scottish Association for Church Music; Organist and Choirmaster, Lylesland Parish Church, Paisley, since 1982; Conductor, Bridge of Weir Choral Society, 1981-85. Recreations: gardening; good beer; bad golf. Address: (h.) 38 Lancaster Avenue, Beith, Ayrshire, KA15 1AR; T.-Beith 3511.

Walton, Robert. Controller for Scotland, DHSS, since 1986; b. 30.11.30, South Shields; m., Dorothy; 2 d. Educ. South Shields Grammar School. Temporary Clerk, then Clerical Officer, Ministry of Transport, South Shields, 1946-56; Executive Officer, then HEO, National Assistance Board, Liverpool, 1956-65; Senior Executive Officer, DHSS, Rochdale, Oldham and Manchester, 1966-71; Principal, HQ London, 1971-77, Senior Principal Deputy Controller, London West Region, 1977-81; Assistant Secretary Controller, North Eastern Region, 1981-86. Recreations: gardening; walking; DIY. Address: (b.) DHSS, Argyle House, Lady Lawson Street, Edinburgh, EH3 9SH; T.-031-222 5001.

Wannop, Professor Urlan Alistair, MA, MCD, MRTPI. Professor of Urban and Regional Planning, Strathclyde University, since 1981; b. 16.4.31, Newtown St. Boswells; m., Jean; 1 s.; 1 d. Educ. Aberdeen Grammar School; Edinburgh University; Liverpool University. Appointments in public and private practice, 1956-68; Team Leader, Coventry-Solihull-Warwickshire Sub-Regional Planning Study, 1968-71; Director, West Central Scotland Plan, 1972-74; Senior Deputy Director of Planning, Strathclyde Regional Council, 1975-81; Vice-Chairman, Planning Committee, Social Science Research Council, 1978-82; Member, Parliamentary Boundary Commission for Scotland, since 1983. Address: (h.) 43 Lomond Street, Helensburgh, G84 7ES; T.-0436 4622.

Ward, Brian W., FCCA, IPFA. Director of Finance and Depute Chief Executive, Wigtown District Council, since 1983; b. 29.10.52, Chatham, Kent; m., Margaret E.; 1 s.; 1 d. Member of Council, Chartered Association of Certified Accountants; Member: Local Authority (Scotland) Accounts Advisory Committee, CIPFA Local Authority Accounting Development Group; Member and Past President, CACA Public Sector Society in Scotland; Member and Past President, CACA Scottish Branch. Recreation: amateur drama. Address: (b.) District Offices, Sun Street, Stranraer, DG9 7JJ; T.-0776 2151.

Ward, Professor Charles William Romen, MA, PhD, AMSIA. Professor of Accountancy, Stirling University, since 1985; Deputy Principal, since 1988; b. 4.3.40, Yorkshire; m., Susan; 1 s.; 2 d. Educ. Sedbergh School; Cambridge University; Exeter University; Reading University. J. Lyons & Co. Ltd., 1961-63; Thomas Forman & Sons Ltd., 1963-67; Lewes Technical College, 1967-70; Leicester Polytechnic, 1970-74; City of London Polytechnic, 1974-79; Lancaster University, 1979-85. Publication: British Financial Institutions and Markets (Co-author). Recreation: painting. Address: (b.) Department of Accountancy and Business Law, Stirling University, Stirling, FK9 4LA; T.-0786 73171.

Ward, Christopher C., MA (Hons), PhD. Leader of the Administration, Tayside Regional Council, since 1987; b. 24.3.50, Dundee; m., Mary McGregor Ward; 1 s. Educ. Morgan Academy, Dundee; Dundee University. Administrative Assistant, Dundee Corporation; Civil Servant in London, seven years; College and University studies; taught part-time, Town Planning Department, Duncan of Jordanstone College; Development Officer, Dundee Resources Centre for the Unemployed, 1984-87; Councillor, Tayside Regional Council, since 1986. Recreation: watching Dundee United. Address: (b.) 28 Crichton Street, Dundee; T.-Dundee 23281, Ext. 3375.

Ward, David Romen, MA, CertEd. Rector, Hutchesons' Grammar School, since 1987; b. 21.12.35, Newcastle upon Tyne; m., Stella Barbara Anderson; 1 s.; 2 d. Educ. St. Mary's, Melrose; Sedbergh School; Emmanuel College, Cambridge. Assistant Master: Winchester College,

Wellington College; Senior History Master, City of London School; Deputy Headmaster, Portsmouth Grammar School; Head Master, Hulme Grammar School. Member, Admiralty Interview Board. Publications: Fall of Metternich and the Revolution of 1848; British Foreign Policy 1815-1865; Explorations. Address: (h.) 192 Nithsdale Road, Glasgow, G41 5EU; (b.) Hutchesons' Grammar School, Beaton Road, Glasgow, G41 4NW; T.-041-423 2933.

Ward, Emeritus Professor Dennis, MA (Cantab). Chairman, Scottish Slavonic Review; Emeritus Professor of Russian, Edinburgh University, since 1984; b. 1.2.24, Rotherham; m., Doreen Mary Robinson; 2 s.; 1 d. Educ. Rotherham Grammar School; Christ's College, Cambridge. Military service, 1943-47: Queen's Royal Regiment, commissioned into York and Lancaster, 1944, Captain, 1946, Russian Interpreter, Allied Control Commission, Berlin, Liaison Officer to Soviet C-in-C's military mission to British Zone, 1946-47; Edinburgh University: Lecturer in Russian, 1949, Senior Lecturer, 1959, Reader, 1961, Professor, 1963; Acting Director, Russian Language Research Project, Essex University, 1967; sometime President, British Universities Association of Slavists; Heath Visiting Professor, Grinnell College, Iowa, 1982; founded (with P. Henry) Scottish Slavonic Review, 1983; sometime Member, Commission on Research and Development in Modern Languages; Member, Editorial Board, Russian Linguistics. Recreations: looking at pictures; painting pictures; visiting prehistoric settlements. Address: (h.) 21B Clermiston Road, Edinburgh, EH12 6XG; T.-031-334 1184.

Ward, Rev. Michael John, BSc (Hons), BD (Hons). Parish Minister, Kinfauns with St. Madoes Church, since 1983; b. 23.8.56, Barrow-in-Furness; m., Jean Gallan. Educ. Galashiels Academy; Edinburgh University. Assistant Minister, Auchtertool with Burntisland, 1982-83. Convener, World Mission and Unity Committee, Perth Presbytery; Researcher/Producer, Radio Tay, since 1986 (appointed by Tay Churches' Radio Council); Church Representative, Scottish Churches' Action for World Development. Recreations: contemporary art; theatre and cinema; philately; sports. Address: St. Madoes Manse, Glencarse, Perth, PH2 7NF; T.-0738 86 387.

Wardell, Gareth. Producer-Director, Jam Jar Films, since 1985; Founder, Arts Education Trust; b. 26.10.46, Edinburgh. Educ. Royal Scottish Academy of Music and Drama; Glasgow University; Jordanhill College of Education. Trainee Actor and Director, various repertory companies; Teacher of Speech and Drama, John Street Secondary School, Glasgow; Lecturer in Speech and Drama, Moray House College of Education, Edinburgh; Founder/Artistic Director, Scottish Youth Theatre/Young Playwrights Festival; Head of Youth Programmes, BBC TV and Radio (N.I.). Recreations: friends; landscape gardening. Address: c/o Jam Jar Films, Balerno, Edinburgh, EH14 7DH; T.-031-449 7227.

Wardlaw, Professor Alastair Connell, MSc, PhD, DSc, FRSE. Professor of Microbiology, Glasgow University, since 1970; b. 20.1.30, Port of Spain; m., Jacqueline Shirley Jones; 1 s.; 2 d. Educ. Manchester Grammar School; Manchester University. Research Fellow, Western Reserve University, Cleveland, Ohio, 1953-55; Sir Alexander Fleming Research Fellow, St. Mary's Hospital, London, 1955-58; Research Fellow and Research Member, Connaught Laboratories, Toronto, 1958-66; Professor of Microbiology, Toronto University, 1966-70. Member, Marshall Aid Commemoration Commssion. Publication: Sourcebook of Experiments for the Teaching of Microbiology. Recreations: ceramics; gardening; cycle-camping. Address: (h.) 92 Drymen Road, Bearsden, Glasgow, G61 2SY; T.-041-942 2461.

Wardlaw, Douglas, MB, ChB, ChM, FRCSEdin. Consultant Orthopaedic Surgeon to Aberdeen Hospitals, since 1981; Honorary Senior Lecturer, Aberdeen University, since 1981; Clinical Associate, Strathclyde University, since 1977; b. 18.6.45, Stirling; m., Sheila; 1 s.; 1 d. Educ. Dunfermline High School; Edinburgh University. House Officer, Medical Unit, Milesmark Hospital, Dunfermline; Victoria Hospital, Kirkcaldy: House Officer, Surgical Unit; Senior Surgical House Officer; Surgical Registrar; Aberdeen Hospitals: Rotating Registrar, Career Orthopaedic Registrar, Orthopaedic Senior Registrar. Sponsor, Grampian Back Pain Association. Recreations: golf; squash; DIY. Address: (b.) Ward 36, Department of Orthopaedics, Aberdeen Royal Infirmary, Foresterhill, Aberdeen, AB9 2ZB; T.-0224 681818, Ext. 52221.

Wardlaw, Rev. Elliot G.S., BA, BD, DipMin. Minister, Bathgate: St. David's Parish Church, since 1984; Chairman, Board of Directors, BAIT Ltd.; Chairman, West Lothian Community Trust; Convener, Church and Community Committee, West Lothian Presbytery; b. 12.10.56, Edinburgh. Educ. Edinburgh Academy; Edinburgh University. Address: St. David's Manse, 70 Marjoribanks Street, Bathgate, West Lothian; T.-0506 53177.

Warlow, Professor Charles Picton, BA, MB, BChir, MD, FRCP. Professor of Medical Neurology, Edinburgh, since 1987; Honorary Consultant Neurologist, Lothian Health Board; Secretary, Association of British Neurologists; b. 29.9.43; m.; 2 s.; 1 d. Educ. Cambridge University. Lecturer in Medicine, Aberdeen University, 1971-74; Registrar and Senior Registrar in Neurology, National Hospitals for Nervous Diseases, London, and University College Hospital, London, 1974-76; Clinical Lecturer in Neurology, then Clinical Reader, Oxford University, 1976-86. Recreations: sailing; photography; theatre. Address: 3 Mortonhall Hall, Edinburgh, EH9 2HS.

Warner, Graeme Christopher, LLB, WS, NP. Solicitor, Notary and Estate Agent; Partner, Ross Harper & Murphy, WS, Edinburgh, since 1978; b. 20.10.48, Glasgow; m., Rachel Kidd Gear; 1 s.; 1 d. Educ. Strathallan; Edinburgh University. Law apprentice, J. Raymund McCluskey, Edinburgh, 1969-70; Legal Apprentice, then Assistant, then Partner, Boyd Jameson & Young, WS, Leith, 1970-78. Member, Children's Panel; Past Chairman, Family Conciliation Service (Lothian); Voluntary Worker, Pilton Youth Programme. Recreations: upholding the powerless in the face of the powerful; helping people separate with rationality and decorum. Address: (h.) 6 Cottage Park, Edinburgh, EH4 3QL; T.-031-315 2674.

Warner, Rev. Kenneth, DA (Hons), DipTP, RIBA, MRTPI, ARIAS, BD. Minister, Halkirk and Westerdale, since 1981; b. 10.12.38, Glasgow; m., Ann Harriet Sangster Maule-Brown; 2 s. Educ. George Watson's Boys' College; Edinburgh College of Art; St. Andrews University. Architect in private practice, Henry Wylie and Partners, Edinburgh, 1963-66, Sir William Holford and Partners, Glasgow, 1966-69; Town Planning: Glasgow Corporation, 1969-72, Motherwell Town Council, 1972-75; Area Planning Officer: Hamilton District Council, 1975, Orkney Islands Council, 1975-78. Moderator, Caithness Presbytery, 1984-85. Recreations: painting; gardening. Address: Abbey Manse, Halkirk, Caithness; T.-Halkirk 227.

Warren, Alastair Kennedy, TD, MA. Director, Nithsdale Council of Voluntary Service, since 1986; Director, Solway Community Business, since 1987; Chairman, Loch Arthur Village for Mentally Handicapped Adults, since 1985; Trustee, The Enterprise Trust for Nithsdale, Annandale/Eskdale and the Stewartry, since 1984; Chairman, South West Community Cleaners, since 1987; b. 17.7.22, Glasgow; m., Ann Lindsay Maclean; 2 s. Educ. Laurel Bank School; Glasgow Academy; Loretto School; Glasgow University. Served at home and overseas, HLI, 1940-46 (from private to Major); Management Trainee, Stewarts and Lloyds, 1950-53; Glasgow Herald: joined, 1954, Business Editor, 1961-63, City Editor, 1964-65, Editor, 1965-74; Regional Editor, Scottish and Universal Newspapers Ltd., Southern Region, 1974-76; Editor, Dumfries and Galloway Standard, 1976-86. Served with 5/6th Bn., HLI (TA), 1976-78; first Chairman, Stewartry Mountaineering Club, 1976-78; Provost, Royal Burgh of New Galloway and Kells Parish, 1978-81. Recreations: hill-walking; running; swimming; poetry; conversation. Address: (h.) Rathan, High Street, New Galloway, Castle Douglas, DG7 3RN; T.-New Galloway 257.

Warren, Alex. Stewart, OBE, JP, DL; b. 2.6.03, Glasgow; m., Jessie; 2 d. Educ. Allan Glen's School, Glasgow. Former Councillor, Glasgow Corporation; sometime Leader, Progressive Party; Member and Founder, Scottish Committee, Variety Club of Great Britain; Committee Member, Stars Organisation for Spastics (Scotland); Life President, British Council of Dancing. Address: (h.) 191 Southbrae Drive, Glasgow, G13 1TT; T.-041-959 2457.

Warren, Professor Graham Barry, MA, PhD (Cantab). Professor of Biochemistry, Dundee University, since 1985 (Head, Department of Biochemistry); b. 25.2.48, London; m., Philippa Mary Adeline; 4 d. Educ. Willesden County Grammar School; Pembroke College, Cambridge. MRC Fellow, National Institute for Medical Research, London, 1972-75; Stothert Research Fellow of the Royal Society, Department of Biochemistry, Cambridge, 1975-77; Research Fellow, Gonville and Caius College, Cambridge, 1975-77; Group Leader, then Senior Scientist, European Molecular Biology Laboratory, Heidelberg, 1977-85. Address: (h.) 6 Beechwood Terrace, West Park Road, Dundee, DD2 1NW; T.-0382 67755.

Waterman, Professor Peter George, BPharm (Hons), PhD, FLS. Professor in Phytochemistry, Department of Pharmacy, Strathclyde University, since 1987; b. 28.4.46, Langley, Kent; m., Margaret Humble. Educ. Judd School, Tonbridge; London University. Postgraduate Research Assistant, London University, 1968-69; Lecturer, Senior Lecturer, Reader, Department of Pharmacy, Strathclyde University, 1969-87. Pharmaceutical Society Young Scientist of the Year Award, 1979; Phytochemical Society of Europe Tate & Lyle Award for contribution to Phytochemistry, 1984. Recreations: travel; walking. Address: (b.) Phytochemistry Research Laboratories, Department of Pharmacy, Strathclyde University, Glasgow, G1 1XW; T.-041-552 4400.

Waters, Donald Henry. Chief Executive and Director, Grampian Television PLC, since 1987; b. 17.12.37, Edinburgh; m., June Leslie Hutchison; 1 s.; 2 d. Educ. George Watson's, Edinburgh; Inverness Royal Academy. Director, John M. Henderson and Co. Ltd., 1972-75; Grampian Television PLC: Company Secretary, 1975, Director of Finance, 1979; Director: Independent Television Publications Ltd., 1987, Moray Firth Radio Ltd., 1982, Glenburnie Properties Ltd., 1976, Blenheim Travel Ltd., 1981, Cablevision Scotland PLC, 1987. Recreations: gardening; travel. Address: (h.) Balquhidder, 141 North Deeside Road, Milltimber, Aberdeen, AB1 0JS; T.-Aberdeen 867131.

Waters, Rev. Robert, MA. General Secretary, Congregational Union of Scotland, since 1971; b. 8.7.30, Edinburgh; m., Magdalene Forrest; 1 s.; 1 d. Educ. Boroughmuir School, Edinburgh; Edinburgh University; Scottish Congregational College; Chicago University. Recreation: trout fishing. Address: (b.) 340 Cathedral Street, Glasgow, G1 2BQ; T.-041-332 7667.

Waterton, John Brian. Executive Director, Dawson International plc, since 1978; b. 10.3.34, Bradford; m., Jane; 2 s.; 2 d. Educ. Giggleswick College. National Service (commissioned, Royal Artillery), 1952-54; wool textile industry, West Yorkshire, 1954-70, latterly as Joint Managing Director of company within Coats Patons Group; branded consumer durables industry, 1970-77, latterly as Deputy Managing Director of German subsidiaries, British-owned group. Member, Council, CBI Scotland, 1978-80. Recreation: golf. Address: (h.) 23 Danube Street, Edinburgh, EH4 1NN; T.-031-332 5505.

Watker, Rev. E. Raymond. Secretary, Methodist Synod in Scotland, since 1976; b. 18.3.28, Rotherham; m., Shirley H. Millns; 2 d. Educ. Handsworth College, Birmingham. Entered Methodist ministry, 1954; Minister: Tranent and Cockenzie, 1954-61, Peterhead, 1961-66, Clydebank and Drumchapel, 1966-73; Superintendent, Greenock Circuit, 1973-85, Kilsyth Circuit, 1985. Recreations: walking; music; photography. Address: (h.) Dormarky, Glasgow Road, Kilsyth, Glasgow, G65 9AE; T.-0236 823135.

Watkins, Trevor Francis, BA, PhD, FSA, FSA Scot. Senior Lecturer, Department of Archaeology, Edinburgh University, since 1979; Vice-President, Society of Antiquaries of Scotland; b.

20.2.38, Epsom, Surrey; m., Antoinette Marie; 1 s.; 2 d. Educ. Kingston Grammar School; Birmingham University. Research Fellow, Birmingham University, Lecturer, Edinburgh University. Honorary Secretary, British Institute of Archaeology at Ankara; Council Member, British School of Archaeology in Iraq; Director, Scottish Field School of Archaeology. Recreations: walking; bird-watching; music. Address: (b.) Department of Archaeology, Edinburgh University, 19 George Square, Edinburgh, EH8 9JZ; T.-031-667 1011.

Watkinson, Geoffrey, MD, BS (Lond), FRCP (Lond), FRCPGlas. Consultant Physician and Gastroenterologist, Western Infirmary, Garnavel General Hospital and Southern General Hospital, Glasgow, 1969-86; b. 12.5.21, Bolton; m., Marie Christine; 1 s.; 1 d. Educ. Southgate County School; St. Bartholomew's Hospital, London. House Physician and Senior Registrar, Medical Professorial Unit, St. Bartholomew's Hospital; Medical Branch, RAF (Wing Commander); Leeds University, 1948-60, latterly as Senior Lecturer in Medicine and Honorary Consultant; Physician, Leeds General Infirmary and St. James Hospital, Leeds; Rockefeller Travelling Fellowship in Medicine, 1953-54 (Mayo Clinic, Minnesota); Consultant, York Group of Hospitals, 1961-68, latterly as Senior Physician and Chairman, Medical Division. Council Member, Association of Physicians of Great Britain and Ireland; Member, National Committee of the Review of Medicines, 1979-83; Member, Awards Committee for Scotland, 1982-85; Senior Examiner, Membership Examination, Royal College of Physicians of Glasgow and London; Phillip Bushell Lectureship in Australian Gastroenterology, 1969; Council Member and Past President, British Society of Gastroenterology; Secretary General, President and latterly Honorary President, World Organisation of Gastroenterology. Recreations: music; photography; gardening. Address: (h.) 14 Southview Road, Blanefield, Glasgow, G63 9JG; T.-0360 70689.

Watson, Professor Alan Robert, JP, MA, MB, BS, FRCP, FRCPath, DMJ, DTM&H. Regius Professor of Forensic Medicine, Glasgow University, since 1985; Honorary Consultant in Forensic Medicine, Greater Glasgow Health Board, since 1978; Committee Member, Forensic Medicine (Scotland) Committee, since 1982; b. 20.2.29, Reading; m., Jeannette Anne Pitts; 3 s. Educ. Reading School; St. Mary's Hospital, London; Queens' College, Cambridge. Lecturer in Pathology, Glasgow University, 1964-69; University Senior Assistant Pathologist, Cambridge University, 1969-71; elected Fellow of Queen's College and Assistant Director of Studies, 1970; Consultant in Forensic Medicine, SE Asia Region, Delhi, WHO, 1977. Hon. President, Scottish Band of Hope Union. Recreations: Church activities (Baptist lay preacher). Address: (b.) Department of Forensic Medicine and Science, Glasgow University, Glasgow, G12 8QQ; T.-041-339 8855.

Watson, Antony Charles Harington, MB, ChB, FRCSEdin. Consultant Plastic Surgeon, Lothian Health Board, since 1972; part-time Senior Lecturer, Department of Clinical Surgery, Edinburgh University, since 1972; Editor, British Journal of Plastic Surgery, since 1985; b. 14.10.36, London; m., Anne Henderson Spence; 1 s.; 3 d. Educ. Barnard Castle School; Edinburgh University. Surgical training, Edinburgh and Florida. Council Member, British Association of Plastic Surgeons, since 1984; Member, Scottish Committee, Medical Commission for Accident Prevention; Examiner for Fellowship, Royal College of Surgeons of Edinburgh; Secretary, Scottish Melanoma Group, 1980-84. Recreations: playing and listening to music; painting and sculpture; spending time with the family. Address: (h.) 6 Duncan Street, Edinburgh, EH9 1SZ; T.-031-667 4022.

Watson, Archibald Craig, MA, LLB, NP. Honorary Sheriff of South Strathclyde and Dumfries and Galloway, since 1975; b. 19.3.09, Roche, Cornwall; m., Elizabeth Eudora Ogilvie; 1 s.; 1 d. Educ. George Watson's Boys' College, Edinburgh; Edinburgh University. Partner, Gibson & Montgomery, Solicitors, Kirkcudbright, 1943; Town Clerk, Gatehouse of Fleet, 1945-47, Kirkcudbright, 1947-75; Clerk to Dee (Kirkcudbright) Fishery Board; Clerk, Stewartry of Kirkcudbright Faculty of Procurators, 1947-75. Given freedom, Royal Burgh of Kirkcudbright, 1975. Recreation: gardening. Address: (h.) Rosemount, Kirkcudbright, DG6 4EJ; T.-Kirkcudbright 30264.

Watson, Edward Paul, MBII. President, Scottish Licensed Trade Association, since 1986; Vice Chairman, Forth Wines Ltd., since 1986; b. 10.9.25, Aberdeen; m., Isabella Jean Stewart; 2 s.; 1 d. Educ. Aberdeen Grammar School. United Africa Co. (Unilever), Nigeria and Ghana, 1951-66; Proprietor, Park Hotel, Aberdeen, 1966-71; Proprietor, The Grill, Aberdeen, since 1971. Recreations: golf; photography. Address: (h.) 71 Morningfield Road, Aberdeen, AB2 4AP.

Watson, Rev. Elizabeth R.L., BA, BD (Hons). Minister, Kildonan and Whiting Bay Churches, since 1982; Vice-Chairman, Council of Social Services, Isle of Arran; b. 28.3.56, Whitburn. Educ. Whitburn Academy; Edinburgh University. Recreations: walking; swimming; reading. Address: The Manse, Whiting Bay, Isle of Arran, KA27 8RE; T.-07707 289.

Watson, George Alistair, BSc, MSc, PhD, FIMA. Reader, Department of Mathematics and Computer Science, Dundee University, since 1984; b. 30.9.42, Aberfeldy; m., Hilary Mackay. Educ. Breadalbane Academy; Edinburgh University; Australian National University. Demonstrator, Computer Unit, Edinburgh University, 1964-66; Dundee University: Research Fellow, then Lecturer, Mathematics Department, 1969-82; Senior Lecturer, Mathematical Sciences Department, 1982-84. Recreation: gardening. Address: (h.) 5A Albany Road, West Ferry, Dundee, DD5 1PN; T.-Dundee 79473.

Watson, Hamish, MFH, TD, MD, FRCPEdin, FRCP, FAAC. Consultant Physician and Cardiologist, Tayside Area, 1964-85; Chairman, Section of Cardiology, Department of Medicine, Dundee University, 1964-85; Postgraduate Dean and Director of Postgraduate Medical Education, 1970- 85; b. 26.6.23, Edinburgh; m., Lesley Leigh Dick Wood; 1 s. (deceased); 2 d. Educ. George Watson's College; Edinburgh University. President, Association of European Paediatric Cardiologists, 1963-70; Assistant Editor, British Heart Journal, 1964-68; Member, Scientific Board, International Society of Cardiology and Chairman, Council of Paediatric Cardiology, 1966-72; Convenor, Cardiology Committee, Royal College of Physicians of Edinburgh, 1969-75; Member, Specialist Advisory Committee on Cardiovascular Diseases, 1970-74; Member, Scottish Council for Postgraduate Medical Education, 1970-85; Trustee, Royal College of Physicians of Edinburgh, since 1973; Chairman, Standing Committee, Conference of Postgraduate Deans and Directors of Postgraduate Medical Education of Universities of UK, 1975-79. RMO, The Scottish Horse RAC (TA), 1952-57, and Fife and Forfar Yeomanry/Scottish Horse, 1957-67; Member, Masters of Foxhounds Association, since 1985. Publications: numerous books and scientific papers on heart disease. Recreations: fox-hunting; polo; fishing; horticulture; farming. Address: (h.) Nethermains of Kinnaird, Inchture, Perthshire, PH14 9QX; T.-0828 86303.

Watson, James T., MA. Commercial Director, Ferranti Defence Systems Ltd., since 1985; Council Member: CBI Scotland, Electronic Engineering Association; b. 21.1.28, Edinburgh; m., Isobel C.; 2 s. Educ. George Heriot's School, Edinburgh; Edinburgh University. Ferranti, since 1955. Recreation: music. Address: (h.) 14 Trinity Grove, Edinburgh, EH5 3HD; T.-031-552 1433.

Watson, Captain John J. Chief Executive, Dundee Port Authority, since 1986; Member, Medium Ports Committee, British Ports Federation, since 1986; Master Mariner; b. 19.1.39, Barr, Ayrshire; m., Maureen; 1 s. Educ. Girvan High School; Strathclyde University, Glasgow. Merchant Navy, 1954-66; British Transport Docks Board, 1966-80; Harbourmaster, Dundee Port Authority, 1980-86. Member, United Kingdom Pilots Association; former District Commissioner for Scouting, Boothferry; Past President, Goole and District Junior Chamber. Recreations: shooting; golf; fishing. Address: (h.) Thistledhu, Craighie, near Forfar, DD8 2LU; T.-030 781 579.

Watson, Robert Lamb. Member, Grampian Regional Council, since 1986; Director, Fraserburgh Ltd. (Enterprise Trust), since 1986; b. 16.1.46, Fraserburgh; m., Isobel Mary Lovie; 3 d. Educ. Fraserburgh Academy. Army Apprentice, 1963-66; Royal Electrical and Mechanical Engineers, 1966-73; Kelvin Hughes, Fraserburgh, 1973-75; Technical Officer, British Telecom, Fraserburgh, since 1975. General Service Medal (N.I.); Secretary, Scottish National Party, Banff and Buchan, 1984-86; Elder, Tyrie Kirk. Recreations: traditional Scottish music; fishing; birdwatching; football; reading. Address: (h.) Mossend Cottage, Boyndlie, Fraserburgh, AB4 4DX; T.-03466 316.

Watson, Roderick, MA, PhD. Poet; Literary Critic and Writer; Senior Lecturer in English, Stirling University; b. 12.5.43, Aberdeen; m., Celia Hall Mackle; 1 s.; 1 d. Educ. Aberdeen Grammar School; Aberdeen University; Peterhouse, Cambridge. Lecturer in English, Victoria University, British Columbia, 1965-66; collections of poetry include Trio and True History on the Walls; other books include The Penguin Book of the Bicycle, The Literature of Scotland, and MacDiarmid. Recreation: cycling. Address: (h.) 19 Millar Place, Stirling; T.-Stirling 75971.

Watson, Thomas Anderson, MA, DipEd. Rector, The Waid Academy, since 1982; b. 22.2.35, Pittenweem; m., Joyce Paterson; 1 s.; 1 d. Educ. Waid Academy; Edinburgh University. Bank Clerk, 1951-52; Travelling Teacher, Falkland Islands, 1952-56; Teacher, Oakfield Secondary School, 1956-59; student, 1959-64; Principal Teacher of History, Campbeltown Grammar School, 1964-67; Waid Academy: Principal Teacher, 1967-73, Assistant Rector, 1973-79, Depute Rector, 1979-81. Recreations: tennis; walking; photography; music; local history. Address: (h.) 8 Melville Terrace, Anstruther, Fife; T.-0333 310453.

Watt, Archibald, JP, MA, MEd, FEIS, FSA Scot. Honorary Sheriff, Grampian, Highlands and Islands, since 1979; b. 20.5.14, Aberdeen; m., 1, Anne D.M. Ashton (deceased); 2, Elizabeth P. White; 1 d. Educ. Robert Gordon's College, Aberdeen; Aberdeen University; Aberdeen College of Education. Teacher of English, Elgin Academy, 1938; Flt.-Lt., RAF Administrative and Special Duties Branch and RAF Regiment, 1941-46; Mackie Academy: Principal Teacher of English, 1949, Deputy Rector, 1962, retired, 1977; Organist, HM Prison, Aberdeen, 1930-38; WEA Organiser for Adult Education, Elgin, 1946-49; WEA Tutor in Psychology, 1946-51; Founder and Organising Secretary, Stonehaven Music Club, since 1949; Member, National Council, and Chairman, Regional and District Committees, Scottish Community Drama Association, 1949-67; Member, National Executive and District Chairman, School Library Association in Scotland, 1952-73; Elder, Church of Scotland, since 1954; Chairman and/or Member, Kincardine District Committee, EIS, 1956-77; Member, Joint Consultative Committee, Kincardine County Council, 1965-77; Queen's Jubilee Medal, 1977; Organist and Clerk, Congregational Board, South Church, Stonehaven, since 1976; Director, Kinneff Old Church Preservation Trust Ltd., since 1979; Founder Member and President, Stonehaven Probus Club, 1981-82; Committee Member, National Trust for Scotland (Kincardine and Deeside Centre), since 1984; Member, Aberdeen Choral Society, since 1978, and Aberdeen Proms Chorus, since 1985; Chairman, Stonehaven Heritage Society, since 1988; author of Reading Lists for the Secondary School, 1966; Highways and Byways Round Stonehaven, 1976; Highways and Byways Round Kincardine, 1985. Recreations: concert and theatre-going; travel; antiquities and archaeology; brass bands; research; golf; choral singing; hill-walking. Address: (h.) Rutlands, Arduthie Road, Stonehaven; T.-Stonehaven 62712.

Watt, Archibald Scott, LCH, SRCH. Member, Borders Regional Council, since 1974; Member, Lothian and Borders Police Board, since 1974; Member, Borders Health Board, since 1978; b. 21.8.29, Loanhead, Midlothian; m., Mary Corbett McNairn Brown; 1 d. RAF, 1947-49; Chiropodist, in private practice, since 1957; elected, Peebles Town Council and Peeblesshire County

Council, 1973; TA, 1960-62; Past President, Peebles Rotary Club. Recreation: photography. Address: East Rectory, Tweed Brae, Peebles; T.-Peebles 20803.

Watt, Brian, MD, FRCPath, CBiol, FIBiol. Consultant Bacteriologist, City Hospital, Edinburgh, since 1982; Honorary Senior Lecturer, Department of Bacteriology, Edinburgh University, since 1974; b. 6.12.41, Edinburgh; m., Hilary Watt; 2 d. Educ. Rudolf Steiner School; Edinburgh University. Lecturer, Department of Bacteriology, Edinburgh University, 1968-73; Consultant Microbiologist, Western General Hospital, 1973-82. Recreations: fishing; gardening; golf; tennis; singing. Address: (h.) Silverburn House, by Penicuik, Midlothian; T.-Penicuik 72085.

Watt, David Edwin, BSc, PhD, DSc, CPhys, FInstP, MSRP. Member, British Committee for Radiation Units, since 1983; Member, Sub-Committee, International Committee for Radiation Units, since 1983; Member, Physics and Dosimetry Committee, Medical Research Council, since 1984; b. 16.8.30, Glasgow; m., Dorothea Murphy; 1 s. Educ. Shawlands Academy; Glasgow University. Atomic Weapons Research Establishment, UKAEA, 1956-61; UKAEA Production Group, Chapelcross, 1961-69; Department of Medical Biophysics, Dundee University, 1969-84; Department of Physics and Astronomy, St. Andrews University, since 1984; recipient of Founder's Medal, Society for Radiological Protection. Publication: High Sensitivity Counting Techniques, 1964. Recreations: gardening; travel; squash; tennis. Address: (b.) Department of Physics and Astronomy, St. Andrews University, St. Andrews, KY16 9SS; T.-0334 76161.

Watt, Hamish, JP, Hon. LLD (Aberdeen). Member, Grampian Regional Council, since 1984 (Chairman, Education Committee); Rector, Aberdeen University, since 1985; b. 27.12.25, Keith; m., Mary N. Grant; 1 s.; 2 d. Educ. Keith Grammar School; St. Andrews University. MP, Banffshire, 1974-79. Recreation: travel. Address: (h.) Mill of Buckie, Buckie; T.-Buckie 32591.

Watt, James Affleck Gilroy, MB, ChB, MD, FRCPEdin, FRCPsych, DPM. Consultant Psychiatrist, Gartnavel Royal Hospital, since 1971; b. 14.7.34, near Edinburgh; m., Shirley Camilla Wilson; 2 s.; 1 d. Educ. Lasswade Senior Secondary School; Edinburgh University. House Officer in Neurosurgery, Medicine and Neurology, 1958-60; Junior Medical Specialist, RAMC, 1960-64 (BAOR); Registrar in Psychiatry, Bangour, 1964-66; Research Fellow in Psychiatry, Edinburgh, 1966-69; Lecturer in Psychiatry, Dundee, 1969-71. Recreations: skiing; chess; glass engraving. Address: (b.) Gartnavel Royal Hospital, 1055 Great Western Road, Glasgow, G12; T.-041-334 6241.

Watt, James Fergus, BL, DL, AMNI. Honorary President, Aberdeen YWCA (Great Britain) Housing Society Ltd.; Deputy Lieutenant; b. 27.9.16, Aberdeen; m., Elizabeth Ross Angus; 4 d. Educ. Aberdeen Grammar School; Daniel Stewart's College; Edinburgh University. Legal Assistant, Aberdeen Corporation, 1937-40; Royal Navy, 1940-46; Legal Assistant, then Town Clerk Depute, Aberdeen Corporation, 1946-71; Town Clerk, Aberdeen, 1971-77; Member, Scottish Valuation Advisory Council, 1971-75; Member, Accounts Commission, 1978-82. Recreations: climbing; sailing; golf. Address: (h.) 48 Greenbank Crescent, Edinburgh, EH10 5SQ; T.-031-447 2308.

Watt, Jim, MBE (1980). Boxer; b. 18.7.48, Glasgow; m., Margaret; 2 s.; 1 d. Turned professional, 1968; British Lightweight Champion, 1972-73, 1975-77; European Lightweight Champion, 1977-79; World Lightweight Champion, 1979-81; four successful defences of World title; Freedom of Glasgow, 1981. Recreations: golf; playing blues guitar.

Watt, John Maxwell Dalrymple Smith, DPE. Director of Leisure Services, Ross and Cromarty District Council, since 1975; b. 24.1.35, Dingwall; m., Elma MacPherson; 3 s.; 1 d. Educ. Dingwall Academy; Jordanhill College (Scottish School of Physical Education). Principal Teacher of Physical Education: Invergordon Academy, 1960-73, Dingwall Academy, 1973-75. Chairman, Scottish Association of Local Sports Councils. Recreations: hill-walking; cycling; swimming; reading; film-watching. Address: (b.) Council Offices, Dingwall, IV15 9QN; T.-0349 63381.

Watt, Robert Strachan, MA, FBCS. Chairman, Livingston Development Corporation, since 1982; Chairman, Scotbyte Computers Ltd., since 1979; b. 13.10.32, Aberdeen; m., Lorna Beattie; 1 s.; 2 d. Educ. Robert Gordon's College; Aberdeen University. Member, Glenrothes Development Corporation, 1971-78 (Deputy Chairman, 1978-81); Chairman, Management Committee, Scottish New Towns Computer Service, 1977-81; Member, Whitley Council, 1975-81; Council Member, British Computer Society, 1968-69; Elder, Cramond Kirk; Honorary President, Livingston Voluntary Organisations Council; Trustee, Livingston Youth Trust; Honorary President, Livingston Youth Theatre; Member, Edinburgh Airport Consultative Committee; Member of Court, Heriot-Watt University. Recreations: golf; tennis. Address: (b.) 226 Queensferry Road, Edinburgh, EH4 2DQ; T.-031-343 3900.

Watt, William Percy, JP, NCIA. Dairy Farmer; Chairman, Planning Committee, Moray District Council, since 1984 (Member, since 1978); Scottish Member, United Kingdom Seeds Executive, since 1978; b. 29.4.29, Keith; m., Elizabeth Shand; 4 d. Educ. Keith Grammar School; North of Scotland College of Agriculture. President, National Farmers Union of Scotland, 1976-77; Member, Intervention Board for Agricultural Produce. Address: (h.) Auchoynanie, Keith, Moray; T.-05422 2566.

Watters, Ann Margaret, BSc (Hons), JP. Member, Kirkcaldy District Council, since 1984; Assistant Adviser of Science/Environmental Studies, Fife Regional Council, since 1972; b. Wallington, Surrey; m., A. Norman Watters; 1 s.; 1 d. Educ. St. Leonard's School, St. Andrews; London University; Moray House College of Education. Research Chemist and Lecturer, 1947-53; Science Teacher and Lecturer (FE), 1954-72. Chairman,

Kirkcaldy Civic Society, since 1984; Secretary, Save the Wemyss Ancient Caves Society; Secretary, Levenmouth Environmental Society; Member, Tayside and Fife Committee, British Association for the Advancement of Science; established Wemyss Environmental Education Centre, East Wemyss; author of 17 booklets on Fife coastal walks. Recreations: swimming; walking; local history. Address: (h.) 17 Townsend Crescent, Kirkcaldy, KY1 1DN; T.-0592 266361.

Weatherhead, Alexander Stewart, OBE, TD, MA, LLB. Solicitor; Partner, Tindal Oatts, Solicitors, Glasgow, since 1960; b. 3.8.31, Edinburgh; m., Harriett Foye; 2 d. Educ. Glasgow Academy; Glasgow University. Royal Artillery, 1950-52; TA, 1952; Lt. Col. Commanding 277 (A&SH) Field Regiment, RA (TA), 1965-67, The Lowland Regiment, RA (T), 1967 and Glasgow and Strathclyde Universities OTC, 1970-73; Colonel, 1974; TAVR Colonel, Lowlands (West), 1974-76; ADC (TAVR) to The Queen, 1977-81; Honorary Colonel, Glasgow and Strathclyde Universities OTC, since 1982; Vice Chairman, Lowland TAVRA (Convener, Strathclyde Area), since 1987; Council Member, Law Society of Scotland, 1971-84 (Honorary Vice-President, 1983-84); Member, Royal Commission on Legal Services in Scotland, 1976-80; Council Member, Society for Computers and Law, 1973-86 (Chairman, 1981-84); Temporary Sheriff, since 1985. Recreations: sailing; reading; music. Address: (h.) 52 Partickhill Road, Glasgow, G11 5AB; T.-041-334 6277.

Weatherhead, Rev. James Leslie, MA, LLB. Principal Clerk, General Assembly of the Church of Scotland, since 1985; b. 29.3.31, Dundee; m., Dr. Anne Elizabeth Shepherd; 2 s. Educ. High School of Dundee; Edinburgh University and New College, Edinburgh. Temporary Sub-Lt., RNVR (National Service), 1955-56. Licensed by Presbytery of Dundee, 1960, Presbytery of Ayr, 1960; Assistant Minister, Auld Kirk of Ayr, 1960-62; Minister: Trinity Church, Rothesay, 1962-69, Old Church, Montrose, 1969-85. Member, Broadcasting Council for Scotland, 1978-82. Recreations: music; sailing. Address: (b.) Church of Scotland Offices, 121 George Street, Edinburgh, EH2 4YN; T.-031-225 5722.

Weatherston, William Alastair Paterson, MA (Hons). Fisheries Secretary, Department of Agriculture and Fisheries for Scotland, since 1986; b. 20.11.35, Peebles; m., Margaret Jardine; 2 s.; 1 d. Educ. Peebles High School; Edinburgh University. Assistant Principal, Department of Health for Scotland and Scottish Education Department, 1959-63; Private Secretary to Permanent Under Secretary of State, Scottish Office, 1963-64; Principal, Scottish Education Department, 1964-72; Cabinet Office, 1972-74; Assistant Secretary, Scottish Home and Health Department, 1974-77; Scottish Education Department, 1977-79; Central Services, Scottish Office, 1979-82; Director, Scottish Courts Administration, 1982-86. Recreations: reading; music. Address: (b.) Department of Agriculture and Fisheries for Scotland, Chesser House, Gorgie Road, Edinburgh, EH11 3AW; T.-031-443 4020.

Weatherstone, Robert Bruce, CA, TD. Chairman, Lothian Health Board; Director, Christian Salvesen (Managers) Ltd.; Director, Lothian Region Transport plc; Member, Executive Council, and Chairman, Planning and Resources Committee, Scottish Business in the Community; b. 14.5.26, Bangor; m., Elaine Fisher; 1 s.; 1 d. Educ. Edinburgh Academy; Dollar Academy; Edinburgh University. Director/Secretary, J.T. Salvesen Ltd., Grangemouth, 1954-62; Director and Member, Management Committee, Christian Salvesen Ltd., 1962-83; served in TA, latterly as Colonel, for more than 20 years; Trustee and Chairman, Care Committee, Leonard Cheshire Foundation. Recreations: hill-walking; ornithology. Address: (h.) 27 Ravelston Garden, Edinburgh, EH4 3LE; T.-031-337 4035.

Weaver, John Patrick Acton, MA, BA (Hons), BSc, BM Bch, DM, MCh, FRCSEdin, FRCS. Consultant Urologist, Dundee Royal Infirmary; Honorary Senior Lecturer in Surgery, Dundee University; b. 17.11.27, Oxford; m., Mary Catherine Bainbridge Robinson; 2 s.; 1 d. Educ. Ampleforth; Trinity College, Oxford; Guy's Hospital. Demonstrator in Biochemistry, Oxford University; House Surgeon, Guy's Hospital; Senior Surgical Registrar, Royal Victoria Infirmary, Newcastle-upon-Tyne; Lecturer in Surgery, Newcastle-upon-Tyne University. Recreation: gardening. Address: (b.) 229 Strathmartine Road, Dundee; T.-Dundee 89383.

Webb, Professor Jeffrey R.L., BSc, DPhil, FRSE. Titular Professor in Mathematics, Glasgow University, since 1987 (Reader, 1982-87); b. 19.12.45, Stourport-on-Severn; m., Angela Millard; 1 s.; 1 d. Educ. King Charles I School, Kidderminster; Sussex University. Royal Society European Programme Fellowship, 1970-71; Science Research Council Fellowship, Sussex University, 1971-73; Lecturer in Mathematics, Glasgow University, 1973-78 and 1979-82; Visiting Associate Professor, Indiana University, 1978-79; Visiting Professor, Tulane University, New Orleans, 1982. Member, Editorial Board: Proceedings of the Royal Society of Edinburgh, Glasgow Mathematical Journal. Recreations: chess; squash; listening to music. Address: (b.) Mathematics Department, Glasgow University, Glasgow, G12 8QW; T.-041-339 8855, Ext. 5181.

Webb, John Neville, MA, MD (Cantab), FRCPEdin. Consultant Pathologist, Western General Hospital, Edinburgh, since 1969; Honorary Senior Lecturer, Edinburgh University (Chairman and Head, Department of Pathology, Western General Hospital, since 1979); b. 14.1.35, Carmarthen; m., Pauline Wickham Edmondson; 2 s.; 1 d. Educ. Shrewsbury; Peterhouse, Cambridge; St. Thomas's Hospital Medical School. Recreations: book collecting; opera; bird-watching; fast cars. Address: (h.) 56 St. Albans Road, Edinburgh; T.-031-667 2637.

Webster, David. Producer/Director, This is Scotland (stage and screen promotions); Director, Highland Theatre and Highland Discovery Centre, Oban. Address: (h.) Corriebeg, Oban, Argyll, PA34 5DU; T.-0631 63794.

Webster, David Pirie, DPE, LCSP (Phys). Author; Director of Leisure, Recreation and Tourism, Cunninghame District Council, 1975-87; b. 18.9.28, Aberdeen; 4 s.; 2 d. Educ. Crowlees Boys

School; Aberdeen Training College; Woolmanhill College. Senior Technical Representative, Scottish Council of Physical Recreation, 1954-72; Head of Facilities Planning Division, Scottish Sports Council, 1972-74; Director/Administrator, Magnum Leisure Centre, 1974-75. Director of Weightlifting, Commonwealth Games; Secretary General, World Federation of Heavy Events Athletes. Recreations: writing (more than 30 books); Highland Games; fitness and weight training. Address: (h.) 43 West Road, Irvine, Ayrshire, KA12 8RE; T.-0294 72257.

Webster, Derek Adrian, CBE (1979). Chairman and Editorial Director, Scottish Daily Record and Sunday Mail Ltd., 1974-87; Director, Mirror Group Newspapers, 1974-87; Director, Clyde CableVision Ltd., 1982-86; b. 24.3.27; m., Dorothy Frances Johnson; 2 s.; 1 d. Educ. St. Peter's, Bournemouth. Royal Navy, 1944-48; Reporter, Western Morning News, 1943; Staff Journalist, Daily Mail, 1949-51; joined Mirror Group, 1952; Northern Editor, Daily Mirror, 1964-67; Editor, Daily Record, 1967-72. Vice Chairman, Age Concern Scotland, 1977-83; Member, Press Council, 1981-84 (Joint Vice Chairman, 1982-84); Honorary Vice President, Newspaper Press Fund. Recreations: boating; gardening. Address: (h.) Kessog Bank, Blanefield, by Glasgow; T.-Blanefield 70252.

Webster, Jack (John Barron). Author and Journalist; Columnist, Glasgow Herald; b. 8.7.31, Maud, Aberdeenshire; m., Eden Keith; 3 s. Educ. Maud School; Peterhead Academy; Robert Gordon's College, Aberdeen. Reporter, Turriff Advertiser; Reporter/Sub Editor, Aberdeen Press & Journal/Evening Express; Chief Sub-Editor, Scottish Sunday Express; Feature Writer, Scottish Daily Express; Feature Writer, Sunday Standard. Publications: The Dons, 1978; A Grain of Truth, 1981; Gordon Strachan, 1984; Another Grain of Truth, 1988; television films: The Roup, 1986; As Time Goes By, 1987. Address: (b.) Glasgow Herald, 195 Albion Street, Glasgow, G1; T.-041-552 6255.

Webster, Janice Helen, LLB, CPLF. Deputy Secretary, Law Society of Scotland and Secretary, Scottish Lawyers' European Group; b. 2.4.44, Falkirk; m., Hon. Mr Justice Webster, RD, BA (Cantab); 2 d. Educ. Surbiton Girls High School; Larbert High School; Edinburgh University. Apprenticeship, Cochran Sayers and Cook, Glasgow, 1964-67; admitted Solicitor, 1967; NP, 1972; Legal Assistant, then Senior Solicitor, Falkirk Town Council, 1967-71; Alston Nairn & Hogg, Solicitors, Edinburgh, 1971-74; Deputy Secretary, Law Society of Scotland, 1974-80; State Counsel, then Magistrate, Seychelles, 1980-82; rejoined Law Society of Scotland, 1982. Manager, Palmerston Place Church, Edinburgh; Governor, International School, Seychelles, 1980-82. Publication: Professional Ethics and Practice for Scottish Solicitors (Co-author). Recreations: singing; occasional riding and tennis; frequent dog walking! Address: (h.) 35 Queen's Crescent, Edinburgh, EH9 LBA; T.-031-667 8062.

Wedgwood, Robert Amery. Deputy Lieutenant, Dunbartonshire, since 1964; Honorary Sheriff, since 1955; b. 24.3.04, Dumbarton; m., Jean Hope Henderson; 3 s. Educ. Shrewsbury. Marine Engineer; TA, 9th Bn., Argyll and Sutherland Highlanders, 1928, 54th Light AA Regiment, 1939; served as Major during Second World War. Recreations: tennis; golf. Address: (h.) Dalnair House, Croftamie, by Glasgow, G63; T.-Drymen 60962.

Weeple, Edward John, MA. Assistant Secretary, Scottish Home and Health Department, 1980-85, Department of Agriculture and Fisheries for Scotland, since 1985; b. 15.5.45, Glasgow; 3 s.; 1 d. Educ. St. Aloysius' College, Glasgow; Glasgow University. Entered DHSS, London, 1968; Assistant Principal, 1968-73 (Private Secretary to Minister of Health, 1971-73); Principal, 1973-78; transferred to Scottish Office, 1978; Principal (Industrial Development Division, SEPD), 1978-80. Address: (h.) 19 Lauder Road, Edinburgh; T.-031-668 1150.

Weipers, Professor Sir William (Lee), Kt (1966), FRCVS, BSc, DVSM, DUniv (Stirling), DVMS (Glas), RSE; b. 21.1.04, Kilbirnie; m., Mary Maclean (deceased); 1 d. Educ. Whitehill School; Glasgow Veterinary College. General veterinary practice, 1925; postgraduate study, Royal (Dick) Veterinary School, Edinburgh; Department of Veterinary Surgery, Royal (Dick) Veterinary School; private practice, 1930-49; Glasgow University Veterinary School, 1949-74 (Director of Veterinary Education and Professor of Veterinary Surgery); President, Royal College of Veterinary Surgeons, 1964-65. Address: (h.) Snab Cottage, Hardgate, Clydebank, G81 5QS.

Weir, Alan David, MBA, CA. Finance Officer, Glasgow University, since 1982; b. 25.11.37, Edinburgh; m., Alys Taylor Macdonald; 2 s. Educ. Mill Hill; Strathclyde University. National Service (commissioned), Black Watch (RHR) and 4th QONR; served Articles with Touche Ross, London; commercial and industrial experience at Board level. Recreations: golf; hill-walking. Address: (h.) 3 Dumgoyne Drive, Bearsden, Glasgow, G61 3AP; T.-041-942 7936.

Weir, Hon. Lord (David Bruce Weir), QC (Scot), MA, LLB. Senator of the College of Justice in Scotland, since 1985; b. 19.12.31; m.; 3 s. Educ. Kelvinside Academy; Glasgow Academy; The Leys School, Cambridge; Glasgow University. RNR, 1955-64; admitted, Faculty of Advocates, 1959; Advocate Depute for Sheriff Court, 1964; Advocate Depute, 1979-82; Chairman, Medical Appeal Tribunal, 1972-77; Chairman, Pensions Appeals Tribunal for Scotland, 1978-84; Member, Criminal Injuries Compensation Board, 1974-79.

Weir, Professor David Thomas Henderson, MA (Oxon), DPSA, FBIM, FRSA. Head, Department of Management Studies, Glasgow University, since 1980 (Professor of Organisational Behaviour, since 1974); Chairman, Glasgow Business School; b. 10.4.39, Chalfont St. Peter; 2 s.; 1 d. Educ. Bradford Grammar School; Queen's College, Oxford. University posts, Universities of Aberdeen, Leeds, Hull and Manchester, 1961-70; Manchester Business School, 1970-74; Dean, Scottish Business School, 1977-79; Member, Committee of Inquiry into the Engineering Profession, 1977-80; Arbitrator, Milk Industry (Scotland), 1983-88; Director, Gulliver Foods, 1980-82. Publications: Sociology of Modern Britain; Social Problems of Modern Britain; Men and Work in Modern Britain; Cities in Modern Britain; Computerguide III; Key Variables in Social Research; New Sociology of Modern Britain. Recreations: fell-walking; music; sport; cooking; riding. Address: (b.) Department of Management Studies, Glasgow Business School, Glasgow University, G12 8RJ; T.-041-330 5410.

Weir, Professor Donald Mackay, MB, ChB, FRCPEdin, MD (Hons). Professor of Microbial Immunology, Edinburgh University, since 1983; Honorary Consultant, Lothian Health Board, since 1967; b. 16.9.28, Edinburgh; m., Dr. Cecelia Caroline Blackwell; 3 s. Educ. Edinburgh Academy; Edinburgh University. Research Fellow, Medical Research Council, Rheumatism Research Unit, 1957-61; Edinburgh University: Lecturer, Department of Bacteriology, 1961-67, Senior Lecturer, 1967-78, Reader, 1978-83. Publications: Immunology, An Outline for Students of Medicine and Biology; Handbook of Experimental Immunology (Editor); Principles of Infection and Immunity in Patient Care (Co-author, with wife). Recreation: sailing. Address: (h.) 36 Drummond Place, Edinburgh; T.-031-556 7656.

Weir, Jamie, MB, BS, FRCPEdin, DMRD, FRCR. Consultant Radiologist, Aberdeen Royal Infirmary, since 1976; Senior Lecturer, Aberdeen University, since 1976; b. 22.9.45, Woking. Educ. King's College School, Wimbledon; Middlesex Hospital Medical School. House Physician, then House Surgeon, Middlesex Hospital, 1969; Senior House Officer, Ipswich Hospital, 1970-71; Registrar, then Senior Registrar, Radiology, Middlesex Hospital (latterly also Harefield Hospital), 1971-75. Publications: Atlas of Radiological Anatomy (Co-author); Atlas of Clinical Echocardiography (Co-author). Recreation: golf. Address: (b.) Radiology Department, Aberdeen Royal Infirmary, Foresterhill, Aberdeen; T.-0224 681818.

Weir, John Alexander Campbell. Honorary Sheriff, Cupar, since 1981; Member, Fife Valuation Appeal Committee, since 1981; Member, Scottish Legal Aid Board, since 1987; b. 1.4.21, Glasgow; m., Isabel Mary Sharp; 2 s. Educ. Queen's Park Secondary School, Glasgow. Sheriff Clerk Depute, Argyll, 1949-55; Sheriff Clerk of Galloway, 1955-61; Sheriff Clerk Depute, Aberdeen, 1961-66; Sheriff Clerk of Fife, 1966-74; Sheriff Clerk, Dundee, 1974-81. President, Cupar Rotary Club, 1985. Recreations: bridge; golf; bowls. Address: (h.) 16 Tarvit Avenue, Cupar, Fife; T.-Cupar 53451.

Weir, Michael Eckford Lind, MA, LLB, WS, NP, FBIM, FCIArb. Solicitor, since 1961 (formerly Weir and Company WS, now of Ketchen and Stevens WS, Edinburgh); b. 5.5.38, Edinburgh; m., Hazel Dobson Cunningham; 3 s. Educ. George Watson's College, Edinburgh; Edinburgh University. Part-time Member, Secretary of State for Scotland's Panel for Public Enquiries; former Chairman, Rent Assessment Committees; former General Commissioner of Income Tax; President, Edinburgh General Chamber of Commerce, 1966-67; Treasurer, Edinburgh University Sports Union, 1965-80; Honorary Officer, Scottish Paraplegic Association, 1983-85; Member, General Committee, Amateur Athletics Association, 1961-64; Member, Council, National Playing Fields Association for Scotland, 1968-71; Secretary, Legal/Concessions Committee, 1970 Commonwealth Games in Edinburgh, 1968-70; Founder Secretary, Scottish Branch, Institute of Arbitrators, 1967-70; Secretary, Blackface Sheepbreeders Association, 1966-71; Member, Independent Examinations Board, Institute of Valuers and Auctioneers, 1979-83; Full Livery Member, Worshipful Company of Arbitrators of London and Honorary Scottish Correspondent, Canadian Arbitration Association; Member, Panel of the Arbitrators, American Arbitration Association. Publication: Law and Practice of Arbitration in Scotland. Recreations: occasional golf, squash and walking; Scottish history; photography. Address: (h.) 1 Pentland Avenue, Edinburgh; T.-031-441 1977.

Weir, Ronald John, MD, FRCPGlas. Consultant Physician, Western Infirmary and Gartnavel General Hospital, Glasgow, since 1973; Honorary Clinical Lecturer, Glasgow University, since 1973; b. 6.4.35, Glasgow; m., Janette MacKay Wilson; 3 s.; 1 d. Educ. Jordanhill College School, Glasgow; Glasgow University. Junior medical appointments, Western Infirmary, Royal Hospital for Sick Children and Victoria Infirmary, Glasgow; Vale of Leven Hospital; Toronto General Hospital; Research Fellow, MRC Blood Pressure Unit, Glasgow, 1969-73. Convener, Group Relations Committee and Member, Eldership Working Party, Church of Scotland. Recreations: hill-walking; gardening; reading. Address: (h.) 10 Moorfoot Way, Bearsden, Glasgow, G61 4RL; T.-041-943 1367.

Weir, Tom. Journalist and Photographer; Honorary Vice-President, Scottish Rights of Way Society. Former Ordnance Surveyor; climbed in the Himalayas and began professional photography; author of several books on climbing and Scotland; Presenter, Weir's Way, Scottish Television; Columnist, Glasgow Herald.

Weir, William. Director, Ross & Weir, Dairy and Livestock Farmers; Director, Blackshaw Farm Park Ltd.; Vice-Chairman, Scottish Milk Marketing Board, since 1982; Director, Royal Association of British Dairy Farmers, since 1982; b. 9.8.24, Lugar, Ayrshire; m., Margaret Ross; 1 s.; 2 d. Educ. Patna and Dalmellington Schools. Past President: World Federation of Ayrshire Cattle Societies, Ayrshire Cattle Society of Great Britain and Ireland; Past Chairman, Scottish Dairy Council; former Director, Cattle Services, Ayr Ltd. Recreations: occasional game of curling; watching football and athletics. Address: Wheatrig, Kilmaurs, Kilmarnock, Ayrshire; T.-0563 38231.

Weir, Viscount (William Kenneth James Weir), BA. Chairman, The Weir Group PLC, since 1966; Vice-Chairman, J. Rothschild Holdings PLC, since 1985; Director, BICC plc, since 1977; b. 9.11.33, Glasgow; m., 1, Diana MacDougall (m. diss.); 2, Jacqueline Mary Marr; 1 s.; 1 d. Educ. Eton; Trinity College, Cambridge. Member, London Advisory Committee, Hongkong and Shanghai Banking Corporation, since 1980; Deputy Chairman, Charterhouse J. Rothschild PLC,

1983-85; Member, Court, Bank of England, 1972-84; Co-Chairman, RIT and Northern PLC, 1982-83; Director, 1970, Chairman, 1975-82, Great Northern Investment Trust Ltd.; Member, Scottish Economic Council, 1972-85; Director, British Steel Corporation, 1972-76. Recreations: shooting; golf; fishing. Address: (h.) Rodinghead, Mauchline, Ayrshire; T.-Fiveways 233.

Welsh, Andrew Paton, MA (Hons), DipEd. MP (SNP), Angus East, since 1987; b. 19.4.44, Glasgow; m., Sheena Margaret Cannon (see Sheena Margaret Welsh); 1 d. Educ. Govan High School; Glasgow University. Member, Stirling District Council, 1974; MP (SNP), South Angus, 1974-79; SNP Parliamentary Spokesman on Housing, 1974-78, Self-Employed and Small Businesses, 1975-79, Agriculture, 1975-79; Parliamentary Chief Whip, 1977-79; SNP Executive Vice Chairman for Administration, 1979-83; Member, National Executive Committee, SNP, since 1983; Parliamentary candidate, East Angus, 1983; Member, Church and Nation Committee, Church of Scotland, 1984-85; Member, Dundee University Court, 1984-87; Provost, Angus District Council, 1984-87; Member, Angus District Health Council; Member, SCOTVEC Public Administration and Moderating Committees. Recreations: music; horse riding. Address: (h.) 22 Monymusk Road, Arbroath, Angus; T.-0241 76291.

Welsh, Frederick Wright, JP. Chairman, Public Works and Building Control Committee, Dundee District Council, since 1980; Member, Justices Committee, Dundee District; Member, IBA Local Advisory Committee; Member, Scottish Housing Forum; b. Dundee; m., Margaret; 3 s. Educ. Rockwell Secondary School, Dundee. Member, Dundee Corporation, 1973-75 (Convener, Public Libraries, Museums and Art Galleries, 1973-75); Member, Tayside Regional Council, 1974-77 (Labour Group Chief Whip and Further Education Opposition Spokesman, 1974-77); Member, Dundee District Council, since 1977; Member, Central Committee, Gas Consumers Council for Scotland; Member, Perth Prison Visiting Committee; Member, Management Committee, Dundee Resources Centre for Unemployed; Chairman, ADLO Scottish Region and Member, National Council, ADLO; Member, COSLA Miscellaneous Committee; Member, Management Committee, Heat Development (Dundee) Ltd., since 1986; Member, Fire Services Scotland Examination Board, 1973-75. Recreations: gardening; DIY; watching all sports; walking. Address: (h.) 2 McKinnon Street, Dundee, DD3 6JN; T.-0382 27669.

Welsh, Sheena Margaret, MA (Hons), DipEd. Member, Angus District Council, since 1980 (Vice Convener, Housing, since 1984); Teacher of children with learning difficulties, Arbroath Academy, since 1977; Member, Grampian and Tayside Area Manpower Board, since 1986; b. 22.12.48, Dunoon; m., Andrew Paton Welsh (qv); 1 d. Educ. Dunoon Grammar School; Glasgow University. Teacher: Fallin Primary School, 1972-74, Chapelpark Primary School, Forfar, 1974-77; Treasurer, Aldbar WRI, since 1981; elected Member, National Council, SNP, 1984; Chairman, Arbroath Branch, SNP, 1979-81; Member, Independent Local Radio Advisory Committee, Dundee/Perth, since 1980; Member, Electricity Consumers Consultative Committee, Dundee Area, since 1982; Vice Chairman, Angus Local Association, EIS, 1976-77. Recreations: horse riding; cookery; music. Address: (h.) 22 Monymusk Road, Arbroath, Angus; T.-0241 76291.

Wemyss and March, Earl of (Francis David Charteris), KT (1966), Hon. LLD (St. Andrews), Hon. DUniv (Edinburgh), JP, BA. Lord Lieutenant, East Lothian, 1967-87; b. 19.1.12, London; m., Mavis Gordon Lynette Murray; 1 s.; 1 d.; 1 s. (deceased); 1 d. (deceased). Educ. Eton; Balliol College, Oxford. Commissioned, Lovat Scouts (TA), 1932-44; Basutoland Administrative Service, 1937-44; War Service, African Auxiliary Pioneer Corps, Middle East, 1941-44; Chairman, Council, National Trust for Scotland, 1947-67 (President, since 1967); Chairman, Scottish Churches Council, 1964-71; Chairman, Royal Commission on Ancient and Historical Monuments of Scotland, 1949-84; Vice-Chairman, Marie Curie Memorial Foundation; President, Royal Scottish Geographical Society, 1958-62; President, National Bible Society of Scotland, 1960-83; Lieutenant, Queen's Bodyguard for Scotland (Royal Company of Archers). Recreations: countryside and conservation. Address: (h.) Gosford House, Longniddry, East Lothian; T.-Aberlady 200/389.

West, Professor Thomas Summers, CBE, BSc, PhD, DSc, FRSC, FRSE. Director, Macaulay Institute for Soil Research, Aberdeen, 1975-87; b. 18.11.27, Peterhead; m., Margaret O. Lawson; 1 s.; 2 d. Educ. Tarbat School, Portmahomack; Tain Royal Academy; Aberdeen University; Birmingham University. Lecturer in Chemistry, Birmingham University, 1955-63; Imperial College of Science and Technology, London: Reader in Chemistry, 1963-65, Professor of Chemistry, 1965-75. Meldola Medal, Royal Institute of Chemistry; Gold Medal, Society of Analytical Chemistry; President, Society for Analytical Chemistry, 1969-71; Honorary Secretary, Royal Society of Chemistry, 1972-75; President, Analytical Division, International Union of Pure and Applied Chemistry, 1979-81; Secretary General, IUPAC, since 1983; Honorary Research Professor, Aberdeen University, since 1983. Recreations: gardening; motoring; reading; music; fishing. Address: (h.) 31 Baillieswells Drive, Bieldside, Aberdeen, AB1 9AT; T.-0224 868294.

Westcott, Michael John Herbert, BSc (Hons) (Glasgow), Hon. MA (Edinburgh). University Administrative Fellow, Edinburgh University; b. 16.4.19, Plymouth. Educ. Hillhead High School; Glasgow University. Ministry of Home Grown Timber Production, 1940-43; Army (Royal Signals), 1943-48 (retired as Major); Colonial Service, Sierra Leone (Administrative Officer), 1948-61; Administrative Officer, Edinburgh University, 1962-86. Vice-Chairman, Edinburgh Festival Fringe Society; Honorary President, Edinburgh and SE Scotland VSO Group. Recreation: walking. Address: (h.) 2 Kilgraston Court, Kilgraston Road, Edinburgh, EH9 2ES; T.-031-447 8282.

Westwell, Alan Reynolds, MSc, ACT (Hons), CEng, MIMechE, MIProdE, FCIT. Chairman, Managing Director and Chief Executive, Strathclyde Buses Ltd., since 1986 (Director General, Strathclyde Passenger Transport Executive, 1979-86); Vice President, Bus and Coach Council, since 1986; b. 11.4.40, Liverpool; m., Elizabeth Aileen Birrell; 2 s.; 1 d. Educ. Old Swan Technical College; Liverpool Polytechnic; Salford University. Liverpool City Transport, 1956-67; Chief Engineer: Southport Corporation Transport, 1967-69, Coventry Corporation Transport, 1969-72, Glasgow Corporation Transport Department, 1972-74; Director of Public Transport, Tayside Regional Council, 1974-79. President, Scottish Council, Confederation of British Road Passenger Transport, 1983; Chairman, Institution of Mechanical Engineers, Automobile Division, 1982-83; Chairman, Scottish Section, Chartered Institute of Transport, 1983-84. Recreations: golf; swimming; tennis; music; reading. Address: (h.) 12 Glen Drive, Helensburgh, Dunbartonshire, G84 9BJ; T.-0436 71709.

Westwood, Alan, BSc, MSc, PhD, CChem, MRSC, MRCPath. Top Grade Scientist and Head, Department of Paediatric Biochemistry, Royal Hospital for Sick Children, Edinburgh, since 1979; Honorary Senior Lecturer, Edinburgh University, since 1981; b. 2.3.48, Luton; m., Jennifer Anne; 1 s.; 1 d. Educ. Luton Technical School; Liverpool University; Birmingham University. Clinical Biochemist: Broadgreen Hospital, Liverpool, 1969, Birmingham Children's Hospital, 1970, Liverpool Royal Infirmary, 1976, Edinburgh Royal Hospital for Sick Children, 1979. Chairman, Scottish Region, Association of Clinical Biochemists, 1984-87 (Member of Association Council, 1982-85). Recreations: squash; curling; microcomputing. Address: (h.) Fawnspark, Loanstone, by Penicuik, Midlothian, EH26 8PH; T.-Penicuik 78407.

Whaley, Professor Keith, MB, BS, MD, PhD, FRCP, FRCPath. Professor, Department of Pathology, Glasgow University, since 1984; Honorary Consultant in Clinical Immunology; b. 2.9.42, Redcar; m., Mairearad Campbell Whyte; 2 s. Educ. Middlesbrough High School; Newcastle-upon-Tyne University. SHO/Registrar, Medicine/Rheumatology, Centre for Rheumatic Diseases, Glasgow, 1967-69; MRC Research Fellow, then Lecturer, Immunopathology, Glasgow University, 1969-74; Assistant Professor of Medicine, Medical College, Virginia, 1974-76; Lecturer, then Senior Lecturer, then Reader, Glasgow University, 1976-84. Publications: Methods in Complement for Clinical Immunologists; Complement in Health and Disease. Recreations: sailing; jogging; gardening; reading. Address: (b.) Pathology Department, Western Infirmary, Glasgow; T.-041-339 8822, Ext. 4210.

Whaling, Frank, MA, ThD, AAABI, FIBA, FRAS, FWLA, FABI. Senior Lecturer, Religious Studies, Edinburgh University, since 1984; b. 5.2.34; m., Patricia Hill; 1 s.; 1 d. Educ. Christ's College, Cambridge; Wesley House, Cambridge; Harvard University. Minister: Methodist Church, Birmingham, 1960-62; Methodist Church, India, 1962-66; Methodist Church, Eastbourne, 1966-69; Teaching Fellow, Harvard University, 1972-73; Special Teacher in Religious Studies, Edinburgh University, 1973-84; Director: Edinburgh-Farmington Project, Edinburgh and Oxford, 1977-81; Edinburgh-Cook Project, Edinburgh and Gloucester, 1981-83; Council Member, Shap Working Party, London, since 1973; Chairman/President, Scottish Working Party on Religion in Education, since 1975; Council Member, Christian Education Movement in Scotland, since 1979; Chairman, Scottish Churches China Group, since 1986; Chairman, Edinburgh Inter-Faith Assembly, since 1987; Fulbright Fellow, Harvard University, 1981; British Council awards, 1982 and 1984; British Academy Fellow to China, 1982 and 1987; Commonwealth Foundation Award to India, 1985; Moray Trust Award, 1987. Publications: An Approach to Dialogue: Hinduism and Christianity, 1966; The Rise of the Religious Significance of Rama, 1980; John and Charles Wesley in the Classics of Western Spirituality, 1981; The World's Religious Traditions: Current Perspectives in Religious Studies, 1984; Contemporary Approaches to the Study of Religion: The Humanities, 1984, and The Social Sciences, 1985; Religions of the World, 1985; Christian Theology and World Religions: A Global Approach, 1986. Address: (h.) 29 Ormidale Terrace, Murrayfield, Edinburgh, EH12 6EA.

Wheater, Roger John, FRSE, CBiol, FIBiol. Director, Royal Zoological Society of Scotland, since 1972; b. 24.11.33, Brighton; m., Jean Ord Troup; 1 s.; 1 d. Educ. Brighton, Hove and Sussex Grammar School; Brighton Technical College. Commissioned, Royal Sussex Regiment, 1953; served Gold Coast Regiment, 1953-54; 4/5th Bn., Royal Sussex Regiment (TA), 1954-56; Colonial Police, Uganda, 1956-64; Assistant Warden, Murchison Falls National Park, 1961-70; Director, Uganda National Parks, 1970-72; Member, Co-ordinating Committee, Nuffield Unit of Tropical Animal Ecology; Member, Board of Governors, Mweka College of Wildlife Management, Tanzania; Director, National Park Lodges Ltd.; Member, Ugdana National Research Council; Vice Chairman, Uganda Tourist Association; Council Member, 1980, and Vice President, 1986, International Union of Directors of Zoological Gardens; Council Member, 1974, and Vice Chairman, 1980, The National Federation of Zoological Gardens of Great Britain and Ireland; Chairman, Anthropoid Ape Advisory Panel, 1977; President, Association of British Wild Animal Keepers, 1984; Chairman, Membership and Licensing Committee, 1984; Chairman, Working Party on Zoo Licensing Act, 1981-84; Member of Council, National Trust for Scotland, 1973-78, Executive Committee, 1982-87; Chairman, Cammo Estate Advisory Committee, 1980; ESU William Thyne Scholar, 1975; Assessor, Council, Scottish Wildlife Trust, 1973; Consultant, World Tourist Organisation (United Nations), 1980; Vice Chairman, Edinburgh Branch, English Speaking Union, 1977-81; President, Edinburgh Special Mobile Angling Club, 1982-86. Recreations: country pursuits; painting; gardening. Address: (b.) Scottish National Zoological Park, Edinburgh, EH12 6TS; T. 031-334 9171.

Wheatley, Denys Neville, BSc, PhD, DSc, MRCPath, CBiol, FIBiol. Reader in Cell Pathology, Aberdeen University, since 1981; b. 18.3.40,

Ascot; m., Pamela Snare; 2 d. Educ. Windsor Grammar School; London University. Research Fellow, Aberdeen University, 1964; MRC Travelling Fellow, Wisconsin University, 1968-69; US Public Health Service supported Fellowship, 1969-70; Research Fellow, then Lecturer in Pathology, then Senior Lecturer, Aberdeen University, 1970-81. Recreations: music; hill-walking; rowing. Address: (b.) Department of Pathology, University Medical Buildings, Foresterhill, Aberdeen, AB9 2ZD; T.-0224 681818.

Wheatley, Lord (John Wheatley), PC (1947), MA, LLB, LLD, DUniv, Hon. FEIS, KGCSG; b. 17.1.08; m., Agnes Nichol; 4 s.; 1 d. Educ. St. Aloysius College, Glasgow; Mount St. Mary's College, Sheffield; Glasgow University. Called to Scottish Bar, 1932; took silk, 1947; appointed Solicitor General for Scotland, March, 1947, Lord Advocate, October, 1947; elected MP (Labour), East Edinburgh, October, 1947; Senator of the College of Justice, 1954-85; Lord Justice Clerk, 1972-85; created Life Peer, 1970; Chairman, University Court, Stirling University, 1966-74; Chairman, Royal Commission on Local Government in Scotland, 1966-69. Hon. Chairman, RSSPCC Executive Committee, 1956-79; Hon. President, Age Concern (Scotland); Hon. President (Scotland), International Year of Shelter for Homeless. Publication: One Man's Judgement (autobiography), 1987. Recreation: golf. Address: (h.) 3 Greenhill Gardens, Edinburgh, EH10 4BN; T.-031-229 4783.

Wheatley, Sheriff John Francis, BL. Sheriff, Perthshire and Kinross-shire, at Perth, since 1980; b. 9.5.41, Edinburgh; m., Bronwen Catherine Fraser; 2 s. Educ. Mount St. Mary's College, Derbyshire; Edinburgh University. Called to Scottish Bar, 1966; Standing Counsel to Scottish Development Department, 1968-74; Advocate Depute, 1974-78. Recreations: music; gardening. Address: Braefoot Farmhouse, Fossoway, Kinross-shire; T.-Fossoway 212.

Wheelans, James Dunn, CBE, MBE (Mil), BL. Honorary Sheriff, Selkirk, since 1979; b. 19.1.13, Hawick; m., Catherine Laidlaw Sanderson. Educ. Hawick High School; Edinburgh University. Legal Assessor to Scottish Land Court, 1936; War Service, TA, 1939-45 (active service, Europe, demobilised in rank of Lt. Col.); entered private legal practice, Galashiels, 1946; part-time Secretary, Scottish Woollen Technical College, 1949-70; elected to Council, Law Society of Scotland, 1958: Vice-president, 1971-72, President, 1974-76; retired from active legal practice, 1982. Recreations: fishing; gardening; hill-walking; photography. Address: (h.) Lillieslea, Lilliesleaf, Melrose; T.-083 57 304.

Wheeler, Sir (Harry) Anthony, Kt (1988), OBE, PRSA, Hon. RA, Hon. RGI, Hon. RBS, PPRIAS, FRIBA, BArch, MRTPI, DipTP. Consultant, Wheeler & Sproson, Architects and Town Planners, Edinburgh and Kirkcaldy, since 1986; b. 7.11.19, Stranraer; m., Dorothy Jean Campbell; 1 d. Educ. Stranraer High School; Glasgow School of Architecture; Strathclyde University. War Service, Royal Artillery, 1939-46; John Keppie Scholar and Sir Rowand Anderson Studentship, RIBA Grissell Medallist, Neale Bursar; Assistant to City Architect, Oxford, to Sir Herbert Baker & Scott, London; Senior Architect, Glenrothes Development Corporation; began private practice in Fife; Senior Lecturer, Dundee School of Architecture, 1952-58; Saltire Awards and Commendations (22), Civic Trust Awards and Commendations (12); Trustee, Scottish Civic Trust, 1970-83; Member, Royal Fine Art Commission for Scotland; President, Royal Scottish Academy, since 1983. Recreations: sketching and water colours; fishing; music; drama; gardens. Address: (h.) Hawthornbank House, Dean Village, Edinburgh, EH4 3BH.

Whitby, Professor Lionel Gordon, MA, PhD, MD, BChir, FRCP, FRCPEdin, FRCPath, FRSE, FIBiol. Professor of Clinical Chemistry, Edinburgh University, since 1963; Honorary Consultant in Clinical Chemistry, Lothian Health Board, since 1974; b. 18.7.26, London; m., Joan Hunter Sanderson; 1 s.; 2 d. Educ. Eton College; King's College, Cambridge. MRC Scholar for Training in Research, Biochemistry Department, Cambridge University, 1948-51; Fellow, King's College, Cambridge, 1951-55; junior hospital appointments, Middlesex Hospital, London, etc., 1956-58; Registrar in Chemical Pathology, then Assistant Lecturer, Royal Postgraduate Medical School, London, 1958-60; Rockefeller Travelling Fellowship, National Institutes of Health, Bethesda, 1959-60; University Biochemist, Addenbrooke's Hospital, Cambridge, 1960-63; Fellow, Peterhouse, Cambridge, 1961-62; Dean, Faculty of Medicine, Edinburgh University, 1969-72 and 1983-86. Visiting Professor of Chemical Pathology, Royal Postgraduate Medical School, 1974; Vice-Principal, Edinburgh University, 1979-83. Recreations: gardening; photography. Address: (b.) Department of Clinical Chemistry, Royal Infirmary, Edinburgh, EH3 9YW; T.-031-229 2477.

White, David J., BSc (Hons), PhD, JP. Rector, Garnock Academy, since 1974; b. 13.12.32, New York; m., Cecilia Wilson; 1 s.; 3 d. Educ. Strathclyde University; Glasgow University. Address: (h.) 30 Mulgrew Avenue, Saltcoats, Ayrshire, KA21 6HP; T.-0294 62568.

White, David Nathaniel James, BSc, DPhil. Reader in Physical Chemistry, Glasgow University, since 1984; b. 12.2.46, Edinburgh; m., Valerie Joyce; 3 s.; 1 d. Educ. West Hatch Technical High School, Chigwell; University of Wales Institute of Science and Technology; Sussex University. Lecturer in Physical Chemistry, Glasgow University, 1974-84. Former Treasurer, Molecular Graphics Society; former holder, Royal Society European and Ramsay Memorial Fellowships. Recreations: skiing; reading; home computers. Address: (b.) Chemistry Department, Glasgow University, Glasgow, G12 8QQ; T.-041-339 8855.

White, Duncan Bryce. Sheriff Clerk, Edinburgh, since 1981; Commissary Clerk, Edinburgh, since 1981; Sheriff Clerk of Chancery, since 1981; Regional Sheriff Clerk, Sheriffdom of Lothian and Borders, since 1986; b. 3.2.32, Airdrie; m., Ivie White Neill; 2 d. Educ. Coatbridge High School. HM Treasury, 1953; HM Exchequer, 1954; Sheriff Court, Aberdeen, 1955; Sheriff Court, Glasgow, 1961; Sheriff Court, Dunblane,

1964; Principal Training Officer, Scottish Court Service, 1974. Recreations: golf; hill-walking. Address: (h.) Mylnhurst, Old Doune Road, Dunblane, Perthshire; T.-0786 822582.

White, Glenda Ann, BA, MEd (Hons), DCE. HM Inspector of Schools, since 1985; b. 5.4.45, Wallasey. Educ. Queen Elizabeth's Girls' Grammar School, Barnet; Open University; Glasgow University; Manchester University. Teaching appointments, four primary schools in Liverpool and Glasgow, including Assistant Headteacher, Commonhead Primary School, Easterhouse, 1966-72; Lecturer, Callander Park College of Education, Falkirk, 1972-74; Lecturer/Senior Lecturer, Jordanhill College of Education, Glasgow, 1974-85. Awarded first prize by SCRE for thesis on David Stow and Infant Education. Recreations: long distance hill-walking; theatre; music. Address: (h.) 72 Great George Street, Glasgow, G12 8RU; T.-041-339 0893.

White, James Francis, CEng, FICE, FIHT. Director of Roads and Transport, Tayside Regional Council, since 1986 (Senior Depute Director, 1977-86); b. 14.9.30, St. Andrews; m., Winifred Rose Gourlay Robertson; 3 s. Educ. Madras College, St. Andrews; Dundee Technical College. Apprentice road surveyor, Fife County Council, 1948-53; Engineer and Divisional Surveyor, Perth and Kinross County Council, 1953-63; Divisional Surveyor, Hereford County Council, 1963-66; Depute County Surveyor, then County Surveyor, Ross and Cromarty County Council, 1966-75; Depute Director of Roads, Highland Regional Council, 1975-77. Chairman, North of Scotland Branch, Institution of Highways and Transportation, 1976-77; Vice-Chairman, Dundee Branch, Institution of Civil Engineers, 1987-88. Recreations: gardening; golf. Address: (h.) 138 Strathern Road, Broughty Ferry, Dundee, DD5 1BQ; T.-Dundee 76249.

White, Norman Hugh, CA. Partner, Victor T. Fraser & Co., CA, Wick, since 1966; Honorary Sheriff; b. 19.7.31, Liverpool; m., Fiona Shearer; 2 d. Educ. Hillhead High School. National Service (2nd Lt., Highland Light Infantry), 1957-58; employed in professional capacity, 1959-65. Former Member, Supplementary Benefits Appeals Tribunal. Recreation: golf. Address: (h.) 7 West Park, Wick, Caithness; T.-Wick 3162.

White, Robert I.K., BSc, FRICS. Chief Estates Officer, Scottish Development Department, since 1985; b. 22.2.36, Comrie; m., Constance M. Jackson; 2 s. Educ. Larbert High School; Edinburgh University. Joined Ministry of Public Buildings and Works, 1982, serving in Glasgow and Newcastle; Principal Estate Surveyor, PSA, London, 1970-75; Defence Land Agent, NW Europe, 1975-77; Superintending Estate Surveyor, Scotland, PSA, 1977-85. Governor, Rannoch School. Recreations: golf; curling; badminton. Address: (b.) Room 6/52, New St. Andrews House, Edinburgh, EH1 3SZ; T.-031-244 4404.

White, Stephen Leonard, MA, PhD, DPhil. Reader in Politics, Glasgow University, since 1985; b. 1.7.45, Dublin; m., Ishbel MacPhie; 1 s. Educ. St. Andrew's College, Dublin; Trinity College, Dublin; Glasgow University; Wolfson College, Oxford. Lecturer in Politics, Glasgow University, 1971-85. Examiner, Certificate of Sixth Year Studies (Modern Studies), Scottish Examination Board, since 1985; Joint Editor, Coexistence. Publications: Political Culture and Soviet Politics, 1979; Britain and the Bolshevik Revolution, 1980; Origins of Detente, 1986; The Bolshevik Poster, 1988. Address: (h.) 11 Hamilton Drive, Glasgow, G12 8DN; T.-041-334 9541.

Whitecross, John Andrew, LLB, BSc (Econ), DPA, FBIM, FInstAM (Dip.). Chief Executive and Director of Administration, Annandale and Eskdale District Council, since 1981; b. 13.4.44, Glasgow; m., Janet Lomax MacNicol; 2 s. Educ. Hillhead High School, Glasgow; Glasgow University; London University. Town Clerk's Office, Glasgow, 1967-74; Depute Chief Executive, Annandale and Eskdale District Council, 1974-77; Director of Administration and Deputy Chief Executive, Inverness District Council, 1977-81. Recreations: philately; rugby refereeing; jogging. Address: (b.) District Council Chambers, High Street, Annan; T.-Annan 3311.

Whitelaw, Ian Macleod. Assistant Secretary, Department of Agriculture and Fisheries for Scotland, since 1984; b. 20.9.42, Edinburgh; m., Rhoda Margaret Thomson; 1 s.; 1 d. Educ. Royal High School, Edinburgh. Scottish Education Department, 1961-71; Secretary, Scottish Agricultural Development Council, 1971-74; DAFS, since 1974. Recreations: sport; history (Scottish/military). Address: (b.) Department of Agriculture and Fisheries for Scotland, Chesser House, 500 Gorgie Road, Edinburgh, EH11 3AW; T.-031-443 4020, Ext. 2176.

Whitelaw, James Weir, MB, ChB, FRCPEdin, FRCPath, DPath. Consultant Haematologist, Southern General Hospital, Glasgow, since 1960; Chairman, Scottish Committee for Hospital Medical Services, since 1986; Honorary Clinical Lecturer, Glasgow University; b. 9.7.29, Hull; 1 s.; 1 d. Educ. Paisley Grammar School; Glasgow University. House Physician and House Surgeon, Royal Alexandra Infirmary, Paisley; Captain, RAMC; Senior Registrar, Pathology Department, Western Infirmary, Glasgow; Consultant Haematologist, Southern General Hospital, Glasgow; Honorary Clinical Lecturer, Glasgow University. Recreations: travel; bowling. Address: (b.) Department of Haematology, Southern General Hospital, Glasgow, G51 4TF; T.-041-445 2466, Ext. 4119.

Whitelaw, Robert George, MA, MD, FRCOG, DL. Deputy Lieutenant, Fife, since 1969; Honorary Sheriff, since 1978; b. 29.4.13, Motherwell; m., Cicely Mary Ballard; 1 s. Educ. Wishaw High School; Glasgow University. Consultant Obstetrician and Gynaecologist, West Fife Group of Hospitals, 1956-78; External Examiner, Edinburgh University, 1967-71; Examiner: Central Midwives Board for Scotland, General Nursing Council for Scotland, Royal College of Surgeons of Edinburgh, PLAB. Past President, Fife Branch, BMA; Past President, Dunfermline Rotary Club. Publications: various papers, mainly on obstetrical and gynaecological subjects. Recreations: golf; photography; travel. Address: (h.) 64 Garvock Hill, Dunfermline, Fife, KY12 7UU; T.-0383 721209.

Whiteman, Professor Arthur John, BSc, PhD, FInstPet. Professor of Petroleum Geology, Aberdeen University, since 1974; b. 1.1.28, Ormskirk; m., Barbara Ann Chidzey; 2 s.; 2 d. Educ. University College, London; Stanford University; Columbia University. Geologist, Humble Oil and Refining Co. Research Fellowship, Columbia University, 1949-51; Geologist, HM Geologist Survey, Great Britain, 1951-56; Exploration Geologist, Compagnie Des Petroles D'Algerie, Royal Dutch Shell, 1956-60; Consultant Petroleum Geologist, since 1960; Professor of Geology, Khartoum, Sudan, 1960-68; Professor of Petroleum Geology, Ibadan University, Nigeria, 1968-72; Professor of Petroleum Geology, Bergen University, Norway, 1972-74. Publication: Geology of Sudan Republic, 1971; Nigeria: Its Petroleum Geology, Resources and Potential, 1982. Recreation: gardening. Address: (h.) Heugh Head, Aboyne, AB3 5JE; T.-0339 2155.

Whitfield, Professor Charles Richard, MD, FRCOG, FRCPGlas. Regius Professor of Midwifery, Glasgow University, since 1976; Consultant Obstetrician, Queen Mother's Hospital, Glasgow, and Consultant Gynaecologist, Western Infirmary, Glasgow, since 1976; b. 21.10.27, India; m., Marion Douglas; 1 s.; 2 d. Educ. Campbell College, Belfast; Queen's University, Belfast. Resident appointments, Belfast Teaching Hospitals, 1951-53; RAMC, 1953-64 (Senior Specialist in Obstetrics and Gynaecology, 1959-64); Consultant Obstetrician and Gynaecologist, Belfast Teaching Hospitals, 1968-74; Professor of Obstetrics and Gynaecology, Manchester University, 1974-76. Publication: Dewhurst's Postgraduate Textbook of Obstetrics and Gynaecology (Editor). Recreations: trying to remember what they were. Address: (h.) 23 Thorn Road, Bearsden, Glasgow, G61.

Whiting, Professor Brian, MD, FRCPGlas. Titular Professor (Clinical Pharmacology), Glasgow University, since 1986; Consultant Physician (Clinical Pharmacology), since 1972; Chairman, Glasgow Clinical Pharmacology Group, since 1986; b. 6.1.39, Manchester; 2 d. Educ. Stockport Grammar School; Glasgow University. Research and hospital posts, Stobhill General Hospital, Department of Materia Medica, 1965-77; Visiting Professor of Clinical Pharmacology, University of California, San Francisco, 1978-79; returned to Glasgow, 1979; Director, Clinical Pharmacokinetics Laboratory, Department of Materia Medica, Stobhill General Hospital, Glasgow, since 1980; Treasurer, Clinical Section, British Pharmacological Society. Publication: Lecture Notes on Clinical Pharmacology (Co-author). Recreation: electronic music; mountaineering. Address: (h.) 2 Milner Road, Glasgow, G13 1QL; T.-041-959 2324.

Whitley, Rev. Laurence Arthur Brown, MA, BD. Minister, Montrose Old Parish, since 1985 (Busby East and West, 1975-85); b. 19.9.49, Port Glasgow; m., Catherine MacLean MacFadyen; 1 s. Educ. Edinburgh Academy; Edinburgh University; St. Andrews University. Assistant Minister, St. Andrews, Dundee, 1974-75. Parliamentary candidate (SNP), Dumfriesshire, February and October, 1974. Recreation: piping. Address: 2 Rosehill Road, Montrose, Angus, DD10 8ST; T.-Montrose 72447.

Whitson, Angus Grigor Macbeath, LLB. Immediate Past Chairman, Council, Scottish Tartans Society; Honorary Secretary, Angus Branch, British Red Cross Society, since 1969; Company Director; b. 17.3.42, Dundee; m., Elizabeth Marjorie Greville; 2 s.; 1 d. Educ. Loretto School; Edinburgh University. Solicitor, 1966-77; Clerk to the Justices of the Peace for Angus, 1970-76. Recreations: fishing; shooting; sailing; curling; drinking fine spirits and wines. Address: (h.) The Kirklands, by Montrose, Angus.

Whitson, Harold A., CBE, BA; b. 20.9.16, Esher; m., Rowena Pitt; 1 s.; 2 d. Educ. Rugby School; Trinity College, Cambridge. Royal Engineers, 1940-46; Melville, Dundas and Whitson Ltd., 1946-82; East Kilbride Development Corporation, 1962-79; President, Glasgow Chamber of Commerce, 1967-68; Chairman, Irvine Development Corporation, 1979-82; former Director, Scottish National Orchestra; Fellow, Royal Society of Arts. Recreations: gardening; shooting. Address: (h.) Edmonston House, Biggar, ML12 6QY; T.-0899 20063.

Whittemore, Professor Colin Trengove, BSc, PhD, NDA. Professor of Animal Production, Edinburgh University, since 1984; Head, Animal Division, Edinburgh School of Agriculture, since 1984; b. 16.7.42, Chester; m., Chris; 1 s.; 3 d. Educ. Rydal School; Newcastle-upon-Tyne University. Lecturer in Agriculture, Edinburgh University and Head, Animal Production, Advisory and Development, Edinburgh School of Agriculture; Sir John Hammond Memorial Prize for scientific contribution to an understanding of nutrition and growth; Oxford University Blackman Lecture; Royal Agricultural Society of England Gold Medal for research; Mignini Oscar. Recreations: skiing; riding. Address: (b.) Edinburgh University, School of Agriculture, West Mains Road, Edinburgh, EH9 3JG; T.-031-667 1041.

Whittle, Martin John, MB, ChB, MD, MRCOG. FRCP(Glas). Consultant Obstetrician/Gynaecologist, Queen Mother's Hospital, Glasgow, since 1982; b. 6.7.44, London; m., Lindsay Hall; 1 s. Educ. William Grimshaw Secondary Modern School, London. Laboratory technician, 1962-65; medical student, Manchester, 1967-72. Publications: author of chapters/papers on fetal medicine. Recreations: swimming; music; languages. Address: (h.) 67 Fotheringay Road, Pollokshields, Glasgow.

Whittington, Graeme Walter, BA, PhD. Reader in Geography, St. Andrews University, since 1982 (Chairman, Department of Geography and Geology, since 1987); b. 25.7.31, Cranleigh. Educ. King Edward VI Royal Grammar School, Guildford; Reading University. St. Andrews University: Assistant, 1959, Lecturer, 1962, Senior Lecturer, 1972; Visiting Lecturer, Natal University, 1971; Member, British Association Committee on Ancient Fields, 1958-73. Publications: Environment and Land Use in Africa (Co-Editor); An Historical Geography of Scotland (Co-Editor).

Recreations: gardening; classical music. Address: (h.) 3 Leonard Gardens, St. Andrews, Fife, KY16 8RD; T.-0334 76807.

Whyte, David James, MA. Rector, Golspie High School, since 1983; b. 21.2.40, Cupar; m., Judith; 4 s. Educ. Bell Baxter High School; St. Andrews University; Oxford University. Teacher of English, Strathallan School, 1964-67; Special Assistant, Kirkcaldy High School, 1967-69; Principal Teacher of English, Brechin High School, 1969-74; Assistant Head Teacher, Arbroath Academy, 1974-79; Depute Rector, Peterhead Academy, 1979-83. British athletics international, 1958-60; AAA Long Jump Champion, 1959; Oxford rugby blue, 1963; Scottish rugby international, 1964-67 (13 caps); Chairman, NE Aberdeenshire Members' Centre, National Trust for Scotland. Recreation: bridge. Address: (h.) Tigh Geal, Backies, Golspie, Sutherland; T.-Golspie 3572.

Whyte, Donald, JP, FHG, FSG. Consultant Genealogist, Author and Lecturer; b. 13.3.26, Newtongrange; m., Mary Burton; 3 d. Educ. Crookston School, Musselburgh; Institute of Heraldic and Genealogical Studies, Canterbury. Agricultural and horticultural work, 1940-68; professional genealogist, 1968-76; Member, Kirkliston and Winchburgh District Council, 1964-75 (Chairman, 1970-73); Member, West Lothian County Council, 1970-75; founder Member and Vice-President, Scottish Genealogy Society; President, Association of Scottish Genealogists and Record Agents, since 1981. Publications: Kirkliston: A Short Parish History; Dictionary of Scottish Emigrants to USA; Introducing Scottish Genealogical Research; Dictionary of Scottish Emigrants to Canada before Confederation. Address: (h.) 4 Carmel Road, Kirkliston, EH29 9DD; T.-031-333 3245.

Whyte, George B., CEng, MIMechE. Chairman, Electricity Consultative Council, since 1981; Non-Executive Board Member, South of Scotland Electricity Board, since 1981; b. 18.3.26, Kirkcaldy; m., Joan Walden; 1 s.; 2 d. Educ. Kirkcaldy High School; Heriot-Watt College, Edinburgh. Various appointments, Scottish Agricultural Industries P.L.C., Edinburgh, 1949-84 (latterly Chief Engineer); Member, Electricity Consultative Council, since 1971 (Deputy Chairman, 1979-81). Past President, Fertiliser Society. Recreations: golf; gardening; walking. Address: (b.) 249 West George Street, Glasgow; T.-041-248 5588.

Whyte, Rev. Iain Alexander, BA, BD, STM. Minister, Blairhill Dundyvan Parish Church, Coatbridge, since 1987; Convener, Africa Committee, Board of World Mission and Unity, Church of Scotland, since 1987; b. 3.9.40, Stirling; m., Isabel Helen Martin; 2 s.; 1 d. Educ. Sherborne School, Dorset; St. Peter's College, Oxford; Glasgow University; Union Theological Seminary, NY. Assistant Minister, Kildrum, Cumbernauld, 1967-69; Minister and Youth Worker in Ghana, 1969-71; Chaplain to Overseas Students in Glasgow, 1971-74; Lecturer, Falkirk Technical College, 1974-75; Minister, Merksworth Parish Church, Paisley, 1976-81; Chaplain, St. Andrews University, 1981-87. Scottish Churches Representative, Board, Christian Aid, 1980-86 (Chairman, Christian Aid Middle East Committee, 1982-86); Chairman, Scottish Churches Council Race and Community Relations Group, 1981-83; Scottish Representative, Britain/Zimbabwe Society; former Chair, Glasgow Anti-Apartheid Group. Recreations: travel; squash; watching St. Mirren; numismatics; candle-making. Address: (h.) The Manse, 18 Blairhill Street, Coatbridge, ML5 1PG; T.-0236 32304.

Whyte, Rev. James, BD, DipCE. Parish Minister, Broom, Newton Mearns, since 1987; b. 26.4.46, Glasgow; m., Norma Isabella West; 1 s.; 2 d. Educ. Glasgow; Jordanhill College; Glasgow University. Trained as planning engineer; studied community education (Glasgow and Boston, Mass., USA); Community Organiser with Lamp of Lothian Collegiate Trust, Haddington; Organiser of Community Education, Dumbarton, 1971-73; Assistant Principal Community Education Officer, Renfrew Division, Strathclyde Region, 1973-77; entered ministry, Church of Scotland, 1977; Assistant Minister: Barrhead Arthurlie, 1977-78, St. Marks, Oldhall, Paisley, 1978-80; Minister, Coupar Angus Abbey, 1981-87. Recreations: gardening; caravanning; reading. Address: Manse of Broom, 3 Laigh Road, Newton Mearns, Glasgow, G77; T.-041-639 2916.

Whyte, Rt. Rev. Professor James Aitken, MA, LLD. Moderator, General Assembly of the Church of Scotland, 1988-89; Professor of Practical Theology and Christian Ethics, St. Andrews University, 1958-87; b. 28.1.20, Leith; m., Elisabeth Wilson Mill; 2 s.; 1 d. Educ. Daniel Stewart's College, Edinburgh; Edinburgh University. Ordained and commissioned as Chaplain to the Forces, 1945; Minister: Dunollie Road Church, Oban, 1948-54, Mayfield North Church, Edinburgh, 1954-58; Dean of Divinity, St. Andrews University, 1968-72; Principal, St. Mary's College, 1978-82; Kerr Lecturer, Glasgow University, 1969-72; Croall Lecturer, Edinburgh University, 1972-73; Hon. LLD, Dundee University, 1981; President, Society for the Study of Theology, 1983-84. Address: (h.) 13 Hope Street, St. Andrews, Fife; T.-St. Andrews 72323.

Whyte, John Jarvie, BSc (Hons). Rector, Arbroath High School, since 1983; b. Kirkcaldy; m., Ness Reid; 1 s.; 1 d. Educ. Kirkcaldy High School; Edinburgh University; Strathclyde University; Moray House College of Education. Depute Rector, Craigie High School, Dundee, 1980-81; Rector, Rockwell High School, Dundee, 1981-83. Address: (h.) 42 Nolt Loan Road, Arbroath, Angus.

Whyte, Robert, MB, ChB, FRCPsych, DPM. Consultant Psychotherapist, Duke Street Hospital, Glasgow, since 1979; b. 1.6.41, Edinburgh; m., Susan Frances Milburn; 1 s.; 1 d. Educ. George Heriot's, Edinburgh; St. Andrews University. House Officer in Surgery, Arbroath Infirmary, 1966; House Officer in Medicine, Falkirk and District Royal Infirmary, 1967; Trainee in Psychiatry, Dundee Psychiatric Services, 1967-73; Consultant Psychiatrist, Duke Street Hospital,

Glasgow, 1973. Past Chairman, Scottish Association of Analytical Psychotherapists; Member, Scottish Institute of Human Relations. Recreation: running. Address: (h.) Waverley, 70 East Kilbride Road, Busby, Glasgow, G76 8HU; T.-041-644 1659.

Wiggins, Ian Stewart. Chief Fatstock Officer for Scotland, Meat and Livestock Commission, since 1979; b. 19.5.32, Glasgow; m., Jean Hopkirk; 1 d. Educ. Hutchesons Grammar School, Glasgow. Wholesale Meat Supply Association, 1948; joined Ministry of Food, 1954; Department of Agriculture, 1956; appointed District Fatstock Officer, Edinburgh District, 1966; Regional Fatstock Officer, 1968. President, Scottish Lawn Tennis Association, 1979-80; Member, Lawn Tennis Council, 1977-81; Honorary Vice-President, SLTA. Recreations: tennis; squash. Address: (h.) Hilltop, Cults, Aberdeen, AB1 9RN.

Wight, John James. Farmer; Director, Royal Highland and Agricultural Society of Scotland, since 1981; Council Member, British Charolais Cattle Society, since 1984; b. 3.5.38, Crawford; m., Netta S.S. Struthers; 2 s.; 1 d. Educ. Biggar High School. Member, NFU Committee, Biggar; Member, Biggar Show Committee; former Member, NFU Council; former Council Member, North British Hereford Herd Book Society; Past President, Coulter Curling Club. Recreations: curling; golf. Address: Midlock, Crawford, Biggar, Lanarkshire, ML12 6UA; T.-08642 230.

Wightman, Andrew James Scott. District Head Postmaster, Edinburgh; b. 5.5.29, Edinburgh; m., Joan Campbell; 1 s.; 1 d. Educ. George Heriot's School, Edinburgh. GPO: Executive Officer, 1952-54, Assistant Postal Controller, 1954-69; Post Office: Head Postmaster, Chester, 1969-71, Head Postmaster, Edinburgh, 1971-86; District Head Postmaster, Royal Mail Letters, since 1986. Recreations: golf; curling. Address: (h.) 45 Kingsknowe Road South, Edinburgh, EH14 2JP; T.-031-443 3224.

Wilby, John Michael, FASI, MInstTA. Director, Scottish Ambulance Service, since 1985; Ambulance Service Advisor to Scottish Office, since 1985; b. 30.1.39, Rochford, Essex; 2 d. Educ. Rochford, Essex. Ambulanceman/Control Officer, Hertfordshire Ambulance Service, 1960-65; Station Officer, Leicestershire, 1965-69; Assistant Chief Ambulance Officer, Warwickshire, 1969-70; Chief Ambulance Officer: Plymouth, 1970-72, Berkshire and Reading, 1972-74, Dorset, 1974-80; Deputy Chief Officer, Cape Ambulance and Rescue Service, South Africa, 1980-85. Founder and former National Secretary, Ambulance Service Institute of South Africa; former Senior Vice-President, Association of Chief Ambulance Officers; former Editor, Ambulance Journal. Recreations: music; cricket; hill-walking. Address: (b.) National Ambulance Headquarters, Maitland Street, Glasgow, G4 0HX; T.-041-332 6001.

Wild, John Robin, BDS, DPD, JP. Deputy Chief Dental Officer, Scottish Home and Health Department, since 1987 (Chief Administrative Dental Officer, Borders Health Board, 1974-87; Regional Dental Postgraduate Adviser, SE Regional Committee for Postgraduate Medical Education, 1982-87); b. 12.9.41, Scarborough; m., Eleanor Daphne Kerr; 1 s.; 2 d. Educ. Sedbergh School; Edinburgh University; Dundee University. General Dental Practitioner, Scarborough, 1965-71; School Dental Officer, East Lothian, 1971-74; Honorary Member, clinical teaching staff, Edinburgh Dental School, since 1975; former Fellow, Edinburgh University; Past Chairman, Scottish Council, British Dental Association. Recreations: vintage cars (restoration and driving); music; gardening; photography. Address: (h.) Braehead House, St. Boswells, Roxburghshire; T.-0835 23203.

Wilken, Charles Beaton, MBE, TD. Solicitor; Honorary Sheriff, Grampian, Highland and Islands, Elgin, since 1970; Consultant, Allan Black & McCaskie, Solicitors, Elgin; b. 29.3.14, Elgin; m., Mary Ethel Vipond; 4 s. Educ. Elgin Academy; Edinburgh University. Seaforth Highlanders, 1939-46. Recreation: golf. Address: (h.) Kilmorie, 6 Institution Road, Elgin, Moray; T.-Elgin 2707.

Wilkie, Emeritus Professor John Ritchie, MA. Emeritus Professor of German, Aberdeen University, since 1982; b. 24.5.21, Rathen, Aberdeenshire; m., Sheila Ruth Napier; 1 d. Educ. Banff Academy; Aberdeen University; St. John's College, Cambridge; Zurich University. Assistant in German, Aberdeen University, 1945-50; Lecturer, Senior Lecturer, Professor, German Language and Literature, Leeds University, 1950-77; Professor of German, Aberdeen University, 1978-82. Member of Conference of University Teachers of German in Great Britain and Ireland. Publication: A Short History of the German Language (Co-author), 1970. Recreations: music; history (including local history); language and literature; theology. Address: (h.) 90 Desswood Place, Aberdeen, AB2 4DQ; T.-0224 645991.

Wilkie, Neil Keith, MA (Hons). Headteacher, Gairloch High School, (formerly Achtercairn Secondary School), since 1978; b. 5.4.39, Perth; m., Margaret Rawlinson; 1 s. Educ. Perth Academy; Dundee University; Dundee College of Education; East of Scotland College of Agriculture. Sugar planter, Trinidad, six years; resumed academic studies, 1966; Teacher of History and Modern Studies, then Principal Teacher of History, Golspie High School, 1972-78. Elder, Gairloch and Dundonnell Parish Church; Member, Gairloch Community Council. Recreations: sport; fishing; gardening. Address: (h.) Rohallion, Achtercairn, Gairloch, Ross-shire; T.-0445 2221.

Wilkie, Professor (William) Roy, MA. Professor, Department of Administration, Strathclyde University, since 1974; b. 10.6.30, Rutherglen; m., Jill Henzell; 1 s.; 3 d. Educ. Rutherglen Academy; Aberdeen University. Lecturer and Senior Lecturer, Department of Administration, Strathclyde University, 1963-66; Director, J. & J. Denholm (Management) Ltd., 1966-70; Reader and Head, Department of Administration, Strathclyde University, 1966-73. Publications: The Concept of Organization, 1974; Managing the Police, 1986.

Recreations: swimming; movies; jazz; reading. Address: (b.) Strathclyde Business School, 130 Rottenrow, Glasgow; T.-041-552 4400.

Wilkins, Professor Malcolm Barrett, BSc, PhD, DSc, AKC, FRSE. Regius Professor of Botany, Glasgow University, since 1970 (Dean, Faculty of Science, 1985-87); b. 27.2.33, Cardiff; m., Mary Patricia Maltby; 1 s.; 1 d. (deceased). Educ. Monkton House School, Cardiff; King's College, London University. Lecturer in Botany, King's College, London, 1958-64; Lecturer in Biology, then Professor of Biology, East Anglia University, 1964-67; Professor of Plant Physiology, Nottingham University, 1967-70. Rockefeller Foundation Fellow, Yale University, 1961-62; Corporation Research Fellow, Harvard University, 1962-63; Darwin Lecturer, British Association for the Advancement of Science, 1967; elected Corresponding (Honorary) Member, American Society of Plant Physiologists, 1984; Chairman, Life Science Working Group, European Space Agency. Recreations: sailing; fishing. Address: (b.) Botany Department, Glasgow University, Glasgow, G12 8QQ; T.-041-339 8855.

Wilkinson, Alexander Birrell, MA, LLB. Sheriff of Tayside, Central and Fife at Falkirk, since 1986; b. 2.2.32, Perth; m., Wendy Imogen Barrett; 1 s.; 1 d. Educ. Perth Academy; St. Andrews University; Edinburgh University. Advocate, 1959; practised at Scottish Bar, 1959-69; Lecturer in Scots Law, Edinburgh University, 1965-69; Sheriff of Stirling, Dunbarton and Clackmannan, at Stirling and Alloa, 1969-72; Professor of Private Law, Dundee University, 1972-86 (Dean, Faculty of Law, 1974-76 and 1986); a Chairman, Industrial Tribunals (Scotland), 1972-86; Chancellor, Dioceses of Brechin and of Argyll and the Isles, Scottish Episcopal Church; Chairman, Scottish Marriage Guidance Council, 1974-77; Chairman, Legal Services Group, Scottish Association of CAB, 1979-83. Publications: Gloag and Henderson's Introduction to the Law of Scotland, 8th and 9th editions (Co-Editor); The Scottish Law of Evidence. Recreations: collecting books and pictures; reading; travel. Address: (h.) 267 Perth Road, Dundee, DD2 1JP; T.-0382 68939.

Wilkinson, Professor Chris D.W., MA, PhD, FRSE. Titular Professor, Department of Electronics and Electrical Engineering, Glasgow University, since 1982; b. 1.9.40, Blackburn; m., Judith Anne Hughes; 1 s.; 2 d. Educ. Queen Elizabeth's Grammar School, Blackburn; Balliol College, Oxford; Stanford University, California. Engineer, English Electric Valve Company, Chelmsford, 1967-69; Department of Electronics and Electrical Engineering, Glasgow University: Lecturer, 1969, Senior Lecturer, 1975, Reader, 1978. Member, SERC Committees. Recreation: hill-walking. Address: (b.) Department of Electronics and Electrical Engineering, Glasgow University, Glasgow, G12 8QQ; T.-041-339 8855.

Wilkinson, Professor Paul, MA. Professor of International Relations, Aberdeen University, since 1979; Head, Department of Politics and International Relations, since 1985; Writer on conflict and terrorism; b. 9.5.37, Harrow, Middlesex; m., Susan; 2 s.; 1 d. Educ. John Lyon School; University College, Swansea; University of Wales. RAF, 1959-65; Assistant Lecturer in Politics, University College, Cardiff, 1966-68; University of Wales: Lecturer, 1968-75, Senior Lecturer, 1975-77, Reader in Politics, 1978-79; Editorial Adviser, Contemporary Review; Associate Editor, Terrorism: An International Journal; Member, Editorial Board, Conflict Quarterly; Editor, Key Concepts in International Relations; Scottish Free Enterprise Award, 1982; Honorary Fellow, University College, Swansea, 1986; Chairman, Research Foundation for the Study of Terrorism, 1986; Special Consultant, CBS America and ITN, since 1986; Aviation Security Adviser to IFAPA, 1988. Publications: Social Movement, 1971; Political Terrorism, 1974; Terrorism and the Liberal State, 1986 (revised edition); The New Fascists, 1983; Terrorism: Theory and Practice (Co-author), 1979; British Perspectives on Terrorism (Editor), 1981; Contemporary Research on Terrorism (Joint Editor), 1987. Recreations: modern art; poetry; walking. Address: (b.) Department of Politics and International Relations, Aberdeen University, Aberdeen, AB9 2UB; T.-0224 40241.

Wilkinson, Professor Peter Charles, MD, FRSE. Titular Professor in Bacteriology and Immunology, Glasgow University, since 1982; Honorary Consultant in Bacteriology and Immunology, Western Infirmary, Glasgow, since 1970; b. 10.7.32, London; m., Eileen Mary Baron; 2 s.; 1 d. Educ. London Hospital Medical College; London University. House appointments, London Hospital, 1956-58; Flt.-Lt., RAF (Medical Officer), 1958-60; Lecturer in Bacteriology, London Hospital Medical College, 1960-63; Lecturer and Senior Lecturer in Bacteriology and Immunology, Glasgow University, 1964-77; MRC Travelling Fellow, Swiss Research Institute, 1967-69; Reader, Glasgow University, 1977-82; Visiting Professor, Rockefeller University, New York, 1979. Publications: Chemotaxis and Inflammation; A Dictionary of Immunology (Co-author). Recreations: various interests in the arts. Address: (h.) 26 Randolph Road, Glasgow, G11 7LG.

Wilkinson, Richard Matthew, MInstPS, AHSM. Supplies Officer, Lothian Health Board, since 1987; Member, Strathclyde Regional Council, 1978-88; b. 7.9.47, Kilwinning; m., Anne R.R. Hair; 1 s.; 1 d. Educ. Irvine Royal Academy. Civil Servant, 1965-71; Health Service Work Study Officer, 1971-73; Hospital and Health Board Administrator, 1973-80; Supplies Officer, Common Services Agency, 1980-83; Assistant Director, Supplies Division, Common Services Agency, 1973-87. Member, Largs and District Crime Prevention Panel; Member, Isle of Arran Tourist Board; Chairman, West Kilbride Committee, Action Research for the Crippled Child; Chairman, North Cunninghame Conservative and Unionist Association; Member, Executive Council, Scottish Conservative and Unionist Association. Recreations: family; theatre; gardening; charity fund-raising. Address: (h.) The Fort, Ardrossan Road, Seamill, West Kilbride; T.-0294 822755.

Wilkinson, Rev. William Brian, MA (Hons), BD (Hons). Minister, East Church, Kirkwall, since 1987; b. 14.4.42, Edinburgh; m., Janet Cameron Inglis. Educ. Peterhead Academy; High School of

Stirling; Edinburgh University. Assistant Minister, Gilmerton Parish Church, Edinburgh, 1967-69; Minister: Carnock Parish Church, Fife, 1969-74, Christ's Church, Dunollie, Oban, 1974-83, Kilmore and Oban Parish Church (Senior Colleague), 1984-87. Council Member, Royal National Mission to Deep Sea Fishermen, since 1980. Recreations: Gaelic and English choral singing; book (Highland) collecting; walking. Address: East Manse, Kirkwall, Orkney; T.-0856 5469.

Will, David Houston, BL, NP. President, Scottish Football Association, since 1984; Vice-President, UEFA, since 1986; Chairman, Brechin City FC, sincd 1966; Chairman, Scotball Travel and Leisure Ltd., since 1986; b. 20.11.36, Glasgow; m., Margaret; 2 d. Educ. Brechin High School; Edinburgh University. SFA: appointed to Council, 1970; Chairman, Referee and Disciplinary Committee, 1972-80; Treasurer, 1980-83; Vice-President, 1983-84; Member, UEFA Executive Committee, since 1984. Recreations: golf; curling. Address: (h.) Norandale, 32 Airlie Street, Brechin, Angus; T.-03562 2273.

Will, Ronald Kerr, WS. Retired Solicitor; b. 22.3.18, Edinburgh; m., Margaret Joyce Stevenson; 2 s. Educ. Merchiston Castle School; Edinburgh University. Served King's Own Scottish Borderers, 1940-46 (Major); mentioned in Despatches; WS, 1950; former Senior Partner, Dundas & Wilson, CS, Edinburgh; Deputy Keeper of Her Majesty's Signet, 1975-83; Director, Scottish Equitable Life Assurance Society, 1965-88 (Chairman, 1980-83); Director, Scottish Investment Trust PLC, 1963-88; Member, Council on Tribunals, 1971-76; Chairman, Scottish Committee, Merchiston Castle School, 1953-76. Recreations: gardening; shooting; fishing. Address: (h.) Chapelhill Cottage, Dirleton, North Berwick, East Lothian; T.-062 085 338.

Willett, Professor Frank, CBE, MA, FRSE. Director, Hunterian Museum & Art Gallery, Glasgow, since 1976; b. 18.8.25, Bolton; m., Mary Constance Hewitt; 1 s.; 3 d. Educ. Bolton Municipal Secondary School; University College, Oxford. Keeper of Ethnology and General Archaeology, Manchester Museum, 1950-58; Government Archaeologist, Nigeria, 1958-63; Leverhulme Research Fellow, 1964; Research Fellow, Nuffield College, Oxford, 1964-66; Professor of Art History, African Studies and Interdisciplinary Studies, Northwestern University, Evanston, Illinois, 1966-76; Visiting Fellow, Clare Hall, Cambridge, 1970-71; Hon. Corresponding Member, Manchester Literary and Philosophical Society, since 1958; Vice Chairman, Scottish Museums Council, since 1986; Fellow, Royal Anthropological Institute. Publications: Ife in the History of West African Sculpture, 1967; African Art: An Introduction, 1971; Treasures of Ancient Nigeria, Co-author, 1980. Recreation: walking. Address: (b.) Hunterian Museum, Glasgow University, Glasgow, G12 8QQ; T.-041-339 8855.

Williams, Sir Alwyn, Kt, PhD, FRS, FRSE, MRIA, FGS, Hon. FRCPS, Hon. DSc, Hon. LLD. Honorary Research Fellow, Department of Geology, Glasgow University (Principal and Vice-Chancellor, Glasgow University, 1976-88); Non-Executive Director, Scottish Daily Record and Sunday Mail Ltd., since 1984; b. 8.6.21, Aberdare, Wales; m., Edith Joan Bevan; 1 s.; 1 d. Educ. Aberdare Boys' Grammar School; University College of Wales, Aberystwyth. Commonwealth Fund Fellow, US National Museum, 1948-50; Lecturer in Geology, Glasgow University, 1950-54; Professor of Geology, Queen's University, Belfast, 1954-74; Lapworth Professor of Geology, Birmingham University, 1974-76; Member, Scottish Tertiary Education Advisory Council, since 1984; President, Palaeontological Association, 1968-70; President, Royal Society of Edinburgh, since 1985; Trustee and Chairman, Board of British Museum (Natural History), 1971-79; Chairman, Committee on National Museums and Galleries of Scotland, 1979-81; Honorary Fellow, Geological Society of America, since 1970; Foreign Member, Polish Academies of Science, since 1981; Hon. DSc, Universities of Wales, Queen's (Belfast) and Edinburgh; Hon. DCL, Oxford; Hon. LLD, Strathclyde. Address: (h.) 25 Sutherland Avenue, Pollokshields, Glasgow, G41 4HG; T.-041-427 0589.

Williams, Arthur, MPS. Chief Administrative Pharmaceutical Officer, Grampian, Orkney and Shetland Health Boards, since 1981; b. 5.11.32, Tarleton, near Preston; m., Barbara; 1 s.; 1 d. Educ. Hutton Grammar School, near Preston; School of Pharmacy, Leicester. Senior Pharmacist, United Manchester Hospitals, 1957-59; Chief Pharmacist: Jewish Hospital, 1959-62, Macclesfield Hospital, 1962-66; Group Chief Pharmacist to Area Pharmaceutical Officer, 1966-81. Merck, Sharp and Dohme Award, 1979. Recreations: gardening; fell-walking; natural history. Address: (b.) Department of Pharmacy, Aberdeen Royal Infirmary, Foresterhill, Aberdeen, AB9 2XJ; T.-0224 681818, Ext. 52399.

Williams, Brian Owen, MD, MRCP, FRCPGlas. Consultant Physician in administrative charge, Geriatric Medical Service, Gartnavel General Hospital, Glasgow, since 1982; b. 27.2.47, Glasgow; m., Martha MacDonald Carmichael; 2 d. Educ. Kings Park Senior Secondary School, Glasgow; Glasgow University Medical School. Senior Lecturer, Geriatric Medicine, Glasgow University, 1979-82; Consultant Physician in Geriatric Medicine, Victoria Infirmary, Glasgow, 1976-79; Councillor, Royal College of Physicians and Surgeons of Glasgow, 1976-83. Recreations: swimming; running; gardening. Address: (h.) 15 Thorn Drive, High Burnside, Glasgow, G73 4RH; T.-041-634 4480.

Williams, Professor Morgan Howard, BSc Hons, PhD, FBCS, FRSA. Professor and Head, Department of Computer Science, Heriot-Watt University, since 1980; Treasurer, Conference of Professors of Computer Science, since 1986; b. 15.12.44, Durban; m., Jean Doe; 2 s. Educ. Grey High School, Port Elizabeth; Rhodes University, Grahamstown. Physicist in Antarctic Expedition, 1968-69; Rhodes University: Lecturer in Computer Science, 1970-72, Senior Lecturer, 1972-77, Professor and Head of Department, 1977-80. Address: Computer Science Department, Heriot-Watt University, 79 Grassmarket, Edinburgh, EH1 2HJ; T.-031-225 6465, Ext. 550.

Williamson, Rev. Colin Raymond, LLB, BD. Minister, Aberdalgie and Dupplin with Forteviot, since 1984; Convener, Panel on Worship, General Assembly, 1982-86; b. 20.1.42, Belfast; m., Arlene Elizabeth Geddes; 1 s.; 2 d. Educ. Dumbarton Academy; Glasgow University; New College, Edinburgh. Licensed, 1971; Assistant, Ayr Auld Kirk, 1971-72; ordained, 1972; Minister: Auchencairn with Rerrick, 1972-78, Leith St. Paul's, 1978-84. Secretary, Church Service Society. Recreations: country life; music. Address: Manse of Aberdalgie, Perth, PH2 OQD; T.-0738 25854.

Williamson, David, CBE, BL. Chairman, Scottish Schoolboys' Club, since 1964; Chairman, North Merchiston Club, Edinburgh, since 1982; Trustee, Stanley Nairne Memorial Trust, since 1969; b. 13.1.20, Edinburgh; m., Agnes Margaret. Educ. George Heriot's School, Edinburgh; Edinburgh University. Army Service, 1940-46 (Gunner, Lance Bombadier, Bombadier, Sergeant, Officer Cadet, Second Lieutenant, Lieutenant, Captain); Keeper of the Registers of Scotland, 1973-82 (supervised introduction of Registration of Title to Scotland, 1981); Honorary Member, Law Society of Scotland, since 1982; received Keystone Gold Award for services to Boys' Clubs, 1985. Publications: Registration of Title Practice Book (Co-author); The Story of the Scottish Schoolboys' Club (Editor and Co-author). Recreations: walking; enjoying countryside; reading; appreciating music (including opera); watching rugby. Address: (h.) 10 Homeross House, Mount Grange, Edinburgh, EH9 2QX; T.-031-447 3050.

Williamson, Douglas Guthrie, BSc, PhD. Senior Lecturer in Chemistry, Aberdeen University, since 1980; Member, Transport Users Consultative Committee for Scotland, since 1987; Vice Chairman, Scottish Consumer Council, since 1987; b. 2.6.37, Edinburgh; m., Alison J. Donaldson. Educ. Paisley Grammar School; Glasgow University. Research Fellow (DSIR), Glasgow and Cambridge Universities, 1963-65; Lecturer in Chemistry, Aberdeen University, 1965-80. Secretary, Aberdeen Consumer Group, 1978-83. Recreations: hill-walking; gardens. Address: (h.) 150 Broomhill Road, Aberdeen, AB1 6HY; T.-0224 586847.

Williamson, Professor James, CBE, MB, ChB, FRCPEdin. President, British Geriatrics Society; Chairman, Age Concern Scotland; Member, Lothian Health Board; Professor Emeritus, Geriatric Medicine, Edinburgh University; b. 22.11.20, Wishaw; m., Sheila Mary Blair; 3 s.; 2 d. Educ. Wishaw High School; Glasgow University. General medical training in Glasgow hospitals; general practice; training in respiratory medicine, becoming Consultant in Edinburgh, 1954; converted to geriatric medicine, 1959; Consultant, Edinburgh, until 1973; first occupant, Chair of Geriatric Medicine, Liverpool University; first occupant, Chair of Geriatric Medicine, Edinburgh University, 1976-86; Visiting Professor to several North American medical schools. Recreations: reading; walking. Address: (h.) 14 Ann Street, Edinburgh, EH4 1PJ; T.-031-332 3568.

Williamson, John, MD (Hons), FRCS, DO. Consultant Eye Surgeon, Southern General Hospital, Glasgow, since 1966; b. 15.6.35, Broxburn; m., Myra Miller Hardie; 2 s.; 1 d. Educ. Broxburn High School; Edinburgh University. Honorary Clinical Lecturer, Glasgow University; International Award, Texas, 1985, for continued work on the Lacrimal system; Director, Scottish Division, RNIB, 1987. Publications: The Eye in Connective Tissue Disease; The Eye and Its Disorders in the Elderly (Co-author); Diabetes Today (Co-author). Recreations: tennis; gardening; squash; skiing. Address: (h.) Highfield, 4 Balfleurs Street, Milngavie, Glasgow, G62 8HW; T.-041-956 1777.

Williamson, Rev. Magnus James Cameron. Minister, Fetlar linked with Yell, since 1982; b. 9.9.34, Nesting, Shetland; m., Eunice Winifred Mary Williamson; 3 s.; 1 d. Educ. Lerwick; Aberdeen. Lay Missionary: Eday, Orkney, 1965-73, Yell and Fetlar, 1973-82. Past Chairman, Yell and Fetlar School Council; Member, Yell Community Council and Old Haa Trust. Recreation: gardening. Address: The Manse, Mid Yell, Shetland, ZE2 9BN; T.-0957 2283.

Williamson, Raymond MacLeod, MA, LLB. Solicitor, since 1968 (Partner, MacRoberts, Solicitors, Glasgow and Edinburgh, since 1972); Chairman, Scottish National Orchestra Society Limited; Governor, High School of Glasgow; Member, Council, Law Society of Scotland; b. 24.12.42, Glasgow; m., Brenda; 1 s.; 1 d. Educ. High School of Glasgow; Glasgow University. Recreation: music. Address: (h.) 11 Islay Drive, Ryelands Estate, Newton Mearns, Glasgow, G77 6UD; T.-041-639 4133.

Williamson, Richard John. Editor, Evening Express, Aberdeen, since 1986; b. 14.12.35, Dunphail, Moray; m., Lesley Paterson Mutch; 1 s.; 1 d. Educ. Forres Academy. Elder, St. Columba's Church, Aberdeen. Recreations: reading; walking. Address: (b.) Lang Stracht, Mastrick, Aberdeen; T.-0224 690222.

Williamson, Roy M.B., DA. Musician (The Corries); Commercial Fisherman. Author, Flower of Scotland. Recreation: painting.

Willocks, James, MD, FRCOG, FRCPGlas. Consultant Obstetrician and Gynaecologist, Queen Mother's Hospital and Western Infirmary, Glasgow, since 1966; Lecturer in Midwifery, Glasgow University, since 1964; Examiner to the Universities of Glasgow and London, Royal College of Obstetricians and Gynaecologists and Royal College of Physicians and Surgeons of Glasgow; b. 29.7.28, East Kilbride; m., Elizabeth M. Cant; 3 d. Educ. Hutchesons' Grammar School; Glasgow University. Regimental Medical Officer, 2nd Gurkha Rifles, 1952-54; Hall Tutorial Fellow, Glasgow University, 1957; Registrar and Senior Registrar, Glasgow Royal Maternity Hospital, 1958-64; Royal College of Obstetricians and Gynaecologists' Specialist Adviser for the West of Scotland, 1976-81; Chairman, Postgraduate Committee in Obstetrics and Gynaecology, Glasgow University, since 1981; President, Glasgow Obstetrical and Gynaecological Society, 1982-84; former Member: Central Midwives Board for Scotland, Scottish Council for Postgraduate Medical Education; Regional Assessor, Enquiry into Maternal Deaths in Scotland; Member, Advisory Committee on Medical Establishments, SHHD.

Publication: Essentials of Obstetrics and Gynaecology, 3rd edition, 1986. Recreations: medical history; literature; music; walking. Address: (b.) Queen Mother's Hospital, Glasgow, G3 8SH; T.-041-339 8888.

Wills, (Desiree) Pamela, MB, ChB, DPM, MRCPsych. Consultant in Child Psychiatry, Department of Child and Family Psychiatry, Royal Hospital for Sick Children, Edinburgh, and Bangour Village Hospital, since 1976; Honorary Clinical Tutor, Edinburgh University, since 1976; b. 8.10.40, Georgetown, Guyana; 1 s.; 1 d. Educ. St. Rose's High School, Georgetown; St. Joseph's Convent, Girvan; Glasgow University. Registrar in Psychiatry, Royal Edinburgh Hospital, 1970-73; Senior Registrar in Child Psychiatry, Department of Child and Family Psychiatry, Royal Hospital for Sick Children, Edinburgh, 1973-76. Consultant Child Psychiatrist to Falkland School, Fife, since 1985. Recreations: cookery; theatre; music; reading; aerobics. Address: (h.) 33 Comely Bank, Edinburgh, EH4 1AJ; T.-031-343 2533.

Wills, Jonathan W.G., MA (Hons), PhD. Writer and Broadcaster; Illustrator and Painter; Editor, Shetland Times, since 1987; b. 17.6.47, Oxford; m., Lesley M. Roberts; 3 s.; 1 d. Educ. Warwick School; Anderson Educational Institute, Lerwick; Edinburgh University. Reporter, Shetland Times, 1969; Warden and boatman, Noss National Nature Reserve, 1970; Rector, Edinburgh University (first student Rector), 1971; Scottish and NI Organiser, Third World First (Oxfam), 1972; Boatman, Muckle Flugga Lighthouse, Unst, 1974; Reporter, Shetland Times, 1976; Senior Producer/Presenter, BBC Radio Shetland, 1977; News Editor, Shetland Times, 1981; Scottish Correspondent, The Times, 1982; Producer, BBC Radio Scotland, 1983; Freelance and Research Assistant to Alex. Falconer, MEP, 1984; Tutor, Media Studies, STUC and individual trade unions, 1984; Senior Reporter, Shetland Times, 1985; Fraser Press Award, 1981-82, for work on Shetland Times; Labour candidate, Orkney and Shetland, 1974 (twice). Publications: (children's books) Magnus Pole, 1975; Linda and the Lighthouse, 1976. Recreations: sailing other people's boats; ornithology; painting; gardening. Address: (h.) Sundside, Bressay, Shetland, ZE2 9ER.

Wills, Leslie Charles, MB, ChB, FRCSEdin. Consultant ENT Surgeon, since 1975; Clinical Senior Lecturer in ENT, Aberdeen University, since 1975; b. 21.2.40, Aberdeen; m., Frances Cumming Gove; 3 d. Educ. Robert Gordon's College; Aberdeen University. Aberdeen University: Lecturer in Anatomy, Clinical Lecturer in ENT; Clinical Lecturer/Senior Registrar in ENT, Royal National Throat, Nose and Ear Hospital, London. Vice Chairman, Board, NE Society for the Deaf; Council Member, British Association of Otolaryngologists; Governor, Albyn School. Address: (h.) Bogjoran, Pitfodels, Cults, Aberdeen; T.-Aberdeen 868149.

Wilson, Alan Oliver Arneil, MB, ChB, DPM, FRCPsych. Consultant Psychiatrist, Bangour Hospitals, since 1977; Member, Clinical Teaching Staff, Faculty of Medicine, Edinburgh University, since 1979; President, World Association for Psychosocial Rehabilitation, since 1986; Consultant (in Scotland), Ex-Services Mental Welfare Society; Consultant Psychiatrist, Murrayfield Hospital, Edinburgh; b. 4.1.30, Douglas; m., Dr. Fiona Margaret Davidson; 3 s. Educ. Biggar High School; Edinburgh University. RAMC, 1953-55; psychiatric post, Stobhill General Hospital, Glasgow, and Garlands Hospital, Carlisle, 1955-63; Consultant Psychiatrist and Deputy Physician Superintendent, St. George's Hospital, Morpeth, 1963-77. Joint Honorary Secretary, Northern Counties Psychiatric Association; Chairman, Group for Study of Rehabilitation and Community Care, Scottish Division, RCPsych; Member, Ethics Committee, World Association for Social Psychiatry; Chairman, Psychosocial Rehabilitation Scotland. Recreations: golf; folk singing; guitar; "blethering"; former Hibernian FC footballer. Address: (h.) 14 Cammo Hill, Edinburgh, EH4 8EY; T.-031-339 2244.

Wilson, Alexander McArthur, CA, FACCA, ATII. Honorary Sheriff Substitute, Alloa, since 1975; b. 27.9.08, Charlestown, Fife; m., Helen Comrie Scott; 1 s.; 1 d. Educ. Dunfermline High School. Accountancy practice, Dunfermline, 1926-45 (Partner, 1935-45); carried on accountancy practice, Alloa, 1945-78. Elder, Clackmannan Church, since 1949 (Clerk to Board, 16 years, Treasurer, 14 years); former Treasurer, now Honorary Life Member, Alloa Amateur Operatic Society; Past President, Alloa Rotary Club. Recreations: gardening; bowling; Scottish country dancing; bee-keeping. Address: (h.) 7 The Glebe, Clackmannan; T.-0259 213659.

Wilson, Brian, MA (Hons). MP (Labour), Cunninghame North, since 1987; b. 13.12.48, Dunoon; m., Joni Buchanan. Educ. Dunoon Grammar School; Dundee University; University College, Cardiff. Journalist; Publisher and Founding Editor, West Highland Free Press; Contributor to The Observer, Glasgow Herald, etc. First winner, Nicholas Tomalin Memorial Award for Journalism. Address: (b.) House of Commons, London, SW1A 0AA.

Wilson, Catherine Julia. Freelance Opera Singer; Tutor, Royal Northern College of Music, since 1980; b. Glasgow; m., Leonard Hancock. Educ. The Bar Convent, York; Royal Manchester College of Music. Seasons with Glyndebourne Opera Chorus and Arts Council Opera for All, 1958-60; principal roles, Glyndebourne Opera, 1960; Principal, Sadlers Wells Opera, 1960-68; freelance work with Scottish Opera, English National Opera, Opera North, English Opera Group, Welsh Opera, and abroad, since 1968; has toured Russia and America. Address: (h.) 34 Glasgow Street, Glasgow, G12; T.-041-334 7771.

Wilson, Sir Charles Haynes, Kt (1965), MA. Principal and Vice-Chancellor, Glasgow University, 1971-76; b. 16.5.09; m.; 1 s.; 2 d. Educ. Hillhead High School; Glasgow University; Oxford University. Principal, University College of Leicester, 1952-57; Vice-Chancellor, Leicester University, 1957-61.

Wilson, Conrad. Music Critic, The Scotsman, since 1963 (also Wine and Food Correspondent, since 1981); b. 7.11.32, Edinburgh; 1 s.; 1 d. Educ. Daniel Stewart's College, Edinburgh. Music Critic, Evening Dispatch, Edinburgh, 1954-58; Music Editor, Philips Records, Holland, 1958-61; Cultural Correspondent, The Scotsman, London Office, 1961-63. Programme Editor, Edinburgh Festival, 1966-82; freelance Music Lecturer, since 1964; Chairman, Critics' Committee, European Music Year, Arts Council of GB, 1985. Publications: A Critic's Choice, 1966; Scottish Opera, the First Ten Years, 1972; Collins Encyclopedia of Music (revised), 1976; Good Food Facts (Co-author), 1986; Where to Eat Well in Scotland, 1988; Collins Dictionary of Music (revised), 1988. Address: (h.) 10 Leslie Place, Edinburgh; T.-031-343 2866.

Wilson, David Rowan, OBE. Honorary Sheriff, Wigtown; retired Solicitor; b. 1.11.13, Hamilton; m., Helen Kirkland Benson; 1 s. Educ. Hamilton Academy; Glasgow University. Qualified as Solicitor, 1936; Depute County Clerk, then County Clerk, Wigtownshire, 1948-75; Chief Executive, Wigtown District Council, 1975-78. Justice of the Peace, Wigtown District. Recreations: golf; curling. Address: (h.) Morville, Cairnryan Road, Stranraer; T.-0776 2307.

Wilson, Eric, FCIB, AIB (Scot). Managing Director, TSB Scotland plc, since 1987; b. 8.7.35, Durham; m., Irene; 1 s. Educ. Houghton-Le-Spring Grammar School. Various management appointments, Martins Bank and Barclays Bank, 1965-80; Corporate Finance Director, Large Corporate Division, Barclays Bank, 1980-84; TSB Scotland: General Manager - Banking, 1984-85, Senior General Manager, 1985-87, Chief General Manager, 1987. Director: TSB Group plc, TSB Scotland Asset Finance Ltd., TSB Scotland Nominees Ltd., TSB Scotland (Investment) Nominees Ltd., TSB Scotland Home Loans Ltd., TSB Travellers Cheque Services Ltd., TSB Trustcard Ltd., Slater Hogg & Howison Ltd. (Chairman), Evansville Ltd., Kingstar Leasing Ltd., Glythorne Ltd., Snowglen Securities Ltd., Azedcrest Ltd., Scottish Business in the Community; Member, CBI Scottish Council; Member, Executive, Scottish Council (Development and Industry). Recreations: music; squash; running; reading; travelling. Address: (b.) Henry Duncan House, 120 George Street, Edinburgh, EH2 4TS; T.-031-225 4555.

Wilson, Forrest. Children's Author and Crossword Compiler; b. 6.12.34, Renfrew; m., Jean Anderson; 1 d. Educ. Renfrew High School. British Oil and Cake Mills, 1959-68; Scottish Milk Marketing Board, 1968-77; began writing, 1966, full-time, since 1977; creator of Super Gran and author of Super Gran series of books (12), The Adventures of the ABC Mob, Brain Benders, Farm Crosswords. Recreations: theatre-going; composing music. Address: (b.) c/o A.P. Watt, 20 John Street, London, WC1N 2DL.

Wilson, Gerald, MA. Secretary, Scottish Education Department, since 1988 (Under Secretary, Industry Department for Scotland, 1984-88); b. 7.9.39, Edinburgh; m., Margaret; 1 s.; 1 d. Educ. Holy Cross Academy; Edinburgh University. Assistant Principal, Scottish Home and Health Department, 1961-65; Private Secretary, Minister of State for Scotland, 1965-66; Principal, Scottish Home and Health Department, 1966-72; Private Secretary to Lord Privy Seal, 1972-74, to Minister of State, Civil Service Department, 1974; Assistant Secretary, Scottish Economic Planning Department, 1974-77; Counsellor, Office of the UK Permanent Representative to the Economic Communities, Brussels, 1977-82; Assistant Secretary, Scottish Office, 1982-84. Recreation: music. Address: (b.) New St. Andrew's House, Edinburgh, EH1 3SY; T.-031-244 4409.

Wilson, Gordon, MA (Hons), DipEd. Head Teacher, Shawlands Academy, Glasgow, since 1983; b. 9.6.33, Glasgow; m., Sybil Scott Ewing; 2 d. Educ. Allan Glen's School, Glasgow; Glasgow University; Jordanhill College of Education. Teacher of Geography: Shawlands Academy, 1960-64, Langside College, 1964-66; Hyndland Secondary School: Principal Teacher of Geography, 1966-71, Assistant Head Teacher, 1971-74, Depute Head Teacher, 1974-75; Head Teacher, John Street Secondary School, 1975-83. Past President, Headteachers' Association of Scotland. Recreations: badminton; golf. Address: (b.) Shawlands Academy, 31 Moss-side Road, Glasgow, G41 3TR; T.-041-632 1154.

Wilson, Gordon McAndrew, MA, PhD. Principal, Craigie College of Education, since 1988; b. 4.12.39, Glasgow; m., Alison Rosemary Cook; 2 s.; 1 d. Educ. Eastwood Secondary School; Glasgow University; Jordanhill College of Education. Teacher of History and Modern Studies: Eastwood Secondary School, 1963-65, Eastwood High School, 1965-67; Lecturer in Social Studies, Hamilton College of Education, 1967-73 (Head of Department, 1973-81); Principal Lecturer in Inservice Education, then Assistant Principal, Jordanhill College of Education, 1981-88. Publications: Teaching Local History in Lanarkshire, 1972; Alexander McDonald, Leader of the Miners, 1982; Dictionary of Scottish Business Biography (Contributor), 1986. Recreations: reading; gardening; walking; music. Address: (b.) Craigie College of Education, Beech Grove, Ayr, KA8 0SR; T.-0292 260321/4.

Wilson, Hamish Robert McHattie, MA (Aberdeen), MA, PhD (Cantab), AHSM. Unit General Manager, Grampian Health Board, since 1987 (Secretary, 1983-87); b. 19.1.46, Aberdeen. Educ. Robert Gordon's College, Aberdeen; Aberdeen University; Emmanuel College, Cambridge. Entered Health Service administration, 1972; held posts with Grampian Health Board in planning and primary care. Member, Scottish Society of the History of Medicine; Member, Scottish Divisional Council, Institute of Health Services Management. Recreations: music; reading; theatre; cinema; good food and wine. Address: (b.) 42 Queens Road, Aberdeen; T.-Aberdeen 311566.

Wilson of Langside, Baron (Henry Stephen Wilson), PC, QC, LLB. Advocate, since 1946; House of Lords Spokesman for SDP on Scottish Legal Affairs; b. 21.3.16, Glasgow; m., Jessie Forrester Waters. Educ. High School of Glasgow; Glasgow University. Army, 1939-46 (Regimental Officer, HLI and RAC); called to Scottish Bar, 1946; Labour candidate, Dumfries, 1950, 1955, West Edinburgh, 1951; Sheriff, Greenock, 1955-56, Glasgow, 1956-65; Solicitor-General for Scotland,

1965-69; Lord Advocate, 1968-70; Sheriff, Glasgow, 1971-75, Sheriff Principal, Glasgow and Strathkelvin, 1975-77. Recreations: gardening; hill-walking. Address: (h.) Dunallan, Kippen, Stirlingshire, FK8 3HL; T.-Kippen 210.

Wilson, Professor Herbert Rees, BSc, PhD, FInstP, FRSE. Professor and Head, Physics Department, Stirling University, since 1983; b. 28.1.29, Nefyn, Wales; m., Elizabeth Turner; 1 s.; 2 d. Educ. Pwllheli Grammar School; University College of North Wales, Bangor. Research Scientist, Wheatstone Physics Laboratory, King's College, London, 1952-57; Lecturer in Physics, Queen's College, Dundee, 1957-64; Research Associate, Children's Cancer Research Foundation, Boston, 1962; Senior Lecturer and Reader in Physics, Dundee University, 1964-83. Publication: Diffraction of X-Rays By Proteins, Nucleic Acids and Viruses. Recreations: travel; theatre; art. Address: (h.) Lower Bryanston, St. Margaret's Drive, Dunblane, FK15 ODP; T.-0786 823105.

Wilson, Ian Crawford, OBE, JP, BCom, IPFA. Chief Executive, Inverclyde District Council, since 1974; b. 10.4.36, Glasgow. Educ. Dalziel High School; Edinburgh University. Depute County Treasurer, Berwickshire County Council, 1968-71; Town Chamberlain, Greenock Corporation, 1971-74. Recreations: sailing; hill-walking. Address: (b.) Municipal Buildings, Greenock; T.-0475 24400.

Wilson, Ian Dunn. Farmer; Convenor, Milk Committee, National Farmers Union of Scotland, since 1984; Member, Board, Scottish Milk Marketing Board, since 1988; b. 25.4.46, Edinburgh; m., Agnes Jane; 1 s.; 1 d. Educ. Trinity College, Glenalmond; Royal Agricultural College, Cirencester. Recreations: golf; shooting. Address: Drum, Beeswing, Dumfries, DG2 8PB; T.-0387 76240.

Wilson, Rev. Canon Ian George MacQueen, Hon. LTh. Hon. Canon, St. John's Cathedral, Oban, and Cathedral of the Isles, Millport, since 1987 (Dean, Diocese of Argyll and the Isles, 1979-87); b. 6.3.20, Glasgow; m., Janet Todd Kyle. Educ. Albert Road Academy; Edinburgh Theological College. Diocese of Glasgow and Galloway: Deacon, 1950, ordained Priest, 1951, Curate, St. Margaret's Newlands, 1950-52, Priest in charge, St. Gabriel's Govan, 1952-57, Rector, Christ Church, Dalbeattie, 1957-61, Rector, St. John's Baillieston, 1961-64; Diocese of Argyll and the Isles: Rector, St. Paul's Rothesay, 1964-75, Canon, St. John's Cathedral, Oban, 1973-79, Priest in charge, St. Peter's Stornoway, 1975-78, Synod Clerk, Diocese of Argyll and the Isles, 1977-79, Rector, St. John's Ballachulish and St. Mary's Glencoe, 1978-85. Address: The Parsonage, Ardchattan, Bonawe, Oban, Argyll; T.-Bonawe 228.

Wilson, Ian Matthew, CB, MA. Secretary of Commissions for Scotland, since 1987 (Under Secretary, Scottish Education Department, 1977-86); b. 12.12.26, Edinburgh; m., Anne Chalmers; 3 s. Educ. George Watson's College; Edinburgh University. Assistant Principal, Scottish Home Department, 1950; Private Secretary to Permanent Under Secretary of State, Scottish Office, 1953-55; Principal, Scottish Home Department, 1955; Assistant Secretary: Scottish Education Department, 1963, Scottish Home and Health Department, 1971; Assistant Under Secretary of State, Scottish Office, 1974-77. Address: (h.) 1 Bonaly Drive, Edinburgh, EH13 OEJ; T.-031-441 2541.

Wilson, Brigadier James, CBE. Executive Director, Edinburgh Old Town Trust, since 1987; Chief Executive, Livingston Development Corporation, 1977-87; b. 12.3.22, Irvine; m., Audrie Veronica Haines; 3 d. Educ. Irvine Royal Academy; Edinburgh Academy. Served Royal Artillery, 1941-77. Chairman, Soldiers, Sailors and Airmen's Families Association, West Lothian; Chairman, Royal Artillery Association Scotland; Member, Scottish Executive, Town and Country Planning Association; Member, Royal Artillery Council for Scotland; Member, Lothian Area Committee, Lowland Territorial Auxiliary and Volunteer Reserve Association; Member, Scottish Committee, Institute of Directors. Recreations: golf; bridge; sailing. Address: (h.) 2 The Gardens, Aberlady, East Lothian.

Wilson, James, MB, ChB, FFARCS, DORCOG. Consultant in charge of Obstetric Anaesthetics and Analgesia, Simpson Memorial Maternity Pavilion, Edinburgh Royal Infirmary, since 1972; Honorary Senior Lecturer, Department of Anaesthetics, Edinburgh University, since 1976; b. 11.12.29, Edinburgh; m., Helen C.A. Dawson; 2 s.; 1 d. Educ. Boroughmuir Senior Secondary School, Edinburgh; Edinburgh University. RAMC, 1953-56; Assistant, then Principal, general practice, 1956-65; Senior House Officer, then Registrar in Anaesthetics, 1965-67; Senior Registrar in Anaesthetics, then Lecturer in Anaesthesia, Edinburgh University, 1967-69; Consultant Anaesthetist, Leeds Maternity Hospital and Honorary Clinical Tutor, Leeds University, 1969-72; former President and former Secretary, Edinburgh and East of Scotland Society of Anaesthetists. Recreations: curling; gardening; walking; DIY. Address: (h.) 15 Campbell Road, Edinburgh, EH12 6DT; T.-031-357 6763.

Wilson, Rev. James Patterson, MA. Minister, St. Kentigern's Church, since 1966; Vice-Convener, Maintenance of the Ministry Committee, General Assembly of the Church of Scotland, since 1988; b. 1.8.33, Minnigaff; m., Elizabeth Gardner Orr; 2 s.; 1 d. Educ. Paisley Grammar School; Glasgow University. Assistant Minister, Lylesland Church, Paisley, 1958-59; Minister, St. Mary's Parish Church, Hawick, 1959-66. Former Moderator, Presbytery of Lanark and Synod of Clydesdale; Member, Royal Burgh of Lanark Community Council, since 1986; Contributor to Expository Times. Recreation: travel. Address: St. Kentigern's Manse, Lanark; T.-0555 2331.

Wilson, James W., BSc, MSc. Principal, Angus Technical College, Arbroath, since 1967; b. 12.5.30, Alva; m., Catherine; 1 s.; 2 d. Educ. Dollar Academy; Edinburgh University. Atomic energy industry, 1956-60; operational research, Courtaulds Ltd., 1960-63; Industrial Liaison Officer, Dundee College of Technology, 1963-67. Recreations: gardening; bridge; driving. Address: (b.) Angus Technical College, Keptie Road, Arbroath, Angus; T.-0241 72056.

Wilson, James Wiseman, OBE, SBStJ. Director, Wilforge Foundation, since 1970; Director, Sealed Air Corporation (UK) Ltd., since 1980; Director, Wilson Management Ltd., since 1970; b. 31.5.33, Glasgow; m., Valerie Grant; 1 s.; 3 d. Educ. Trinity College, Glenalmond; Harvard Business School. Marketing Director, Scottish Animal Products, 1959-63; Sales Director, then Managing Director, then Chairman, Robert Wilson & Sons (1849) Ltd., 1964-85. National Trust for Scotland: Member of Council, 1977-82 and since 1984, President, Ayrshire Members' Centre; Chairman, Management Committee, Scottish Civic Trust; Honorary President, Skelmorlie Golf Club and Irvine Pipe Band; won Aims of Industry Free Enterprise Award (Scotland), 1980. Recreations: golf; backgammon; skiing; bridge; travelling. Address: (h.) Skelmorlie Castle, Skelmorlie, Ayrshire, PA17 5EY; T.-0475 521127.

Wilson, John McIntyre, BL. Town Clerk and Chief Executive, City of Aberdeen District Council, 1977-88; b. 26.5.23, Aberdeen; m., Lena; 1 s. Educ. Robert Gordon's College, Aberdeen; Aberdeen University. Solicitor, private practice, Aberdeen, until 1960; Corporation of the City of Aberdeen: Solicitor, 1960-69, Second Town Clerk Depute, 1969-71, Senior Town Clerk Depute, 1972-75; Depute Town Clerk and Chief Executive, City of Aberdeen District Council, 1975-77. Address: (b.) Town House, Aberdeen, AB9 1AQ; T.-0224 642121, Ext. 500.

Wilson, John Melville, RIBA, FRIAS, DipTP, MRTPI, FIH. Director of Housing, City of Edinburgh District Council, since 1983; b. 11.9.31, Uphall; m., Mary H.; 2 d. Educ. Lenzie Academy; Clydebank High School; Glasgow School of Architecture; Strathclyde University. Senior Architect, SSHA, 1968-72; Assistant Director of Housing, Edinburgh Corporation, 1972-75; Depute Director of Housing, City of Edinburgh, 1975-83. Recreations: sport; reading. Address: (b.) 23 Waterloo Place, Edinburgh, EH1 3BH; T.-031-225 2424.

Wilson, Professor Leslie Blakett, BSc, DSc, FBCS. Professor and Head, Computing Science Department, Stirling University, since 1979 (Chairman, Board of Studies for Science, since 1984); b. 1.11.30, Newcastle-upon-Tyne; m., Patricia Kinair; 2 d. Educ. Newcastle Royal Grammar School; Durham University. Scientific Officer/Senior Scientific Officer, Naval Construction Research Establishment, Dunfermline, 1951-64; Lecturer/Senior Lecturer in Computing Science, Newcastle-upon-Tyne University, 1964-79; Visiting Associate Professor, Waterloo University, Canada, 1974. Publications: Information Representation and Manipulation Using Pascal; Computational Combinatorics; Comparative Programming Languages: A Conceptual Approach. Recreations: bridge; cinema; fell-walking; golf. Address: (b.) Computing Science Department, Stirling University, Stirling, FK9 4LA; T.-Stirling 73171, Ext. 2577.

Wilson, Michael Jeffrey, BSc, PhD, DSc, FRSE. Research Soil Scientist; Head, Soils and Soil Microbiology Division, Macaulay Land Use Research Institute, since 1983; b. 22.2.37, Liverpool; m., Ann; 2 d. Educ. Merthyr Tydfil County Grammar School; University College of Swansea, Wales. Research Demonstrator in Geology, University College of Cardiff, 1961-64. Secretary, Clay Minerals Group, Mineralogical Society of Gt. Britain, 1978-84. Recreation: cricket. Address: (b.) Department of Mineral Soils, Macaulay Land Use Research Institute, Aberdeen, AB9 2QJ; T.-0224 38611.

Wilson, Professor Peter Northcote, CBE, BSc, MSc, Dip. Animal Genetics, PhD, CBiol, FBiol, FRSE. Professor of Agriculture and Rural Economy, Edinburgh University, since 1983; Principal, Edinburgh School of Agriculture, since 1983; b. 4.4.28, Beckenham, Kent; m., Maud Ethel Bunn; 2 s.; 1 d. Educ. Whitgift School, Croydon; Wye College, London University; Edinburgh University. Lecturer in Agriculture, Makerere College, East Africa; Senior Lecturer in Agriculture, Imperial College of Tropical Agriculture, Trinidad; Professor of Tropical Agriculture, University of West Indies; Head of Biometrics, Unilever Research Laboratory, Bedford; Agricultural Development Director, SLF Ltd., Liverpool; Chief Agricultural Adviser, BOCM Silcock Ltd., Basingstoke. Past President, British Society of Animal Production; Chairman, Frank Parkinson Agricultural Trust, since 1978. Publications: Agriculture in the Tropics (Co-author); Improved Feeding of Cattle and Sheep (Co-author). Recreations: walking; photography; natural history. Address: (b.) School of Agriculture, Kings Buildings, West Mains Road, Edinburgh, EH9 3JG; T.-031-667 1041.

Wilson, Robert Gordon, BL, LLD. Chairman, Scottish National Party, since 1979; Solicitor; b. 16.4.38, Glasgow; m., Edith M. Hassall; 2 d. Educ. Douglas High School for Boys; Edinburgh University. National Secretary, SNP, 1963-71; Partner, law firm, 1965-74; MP, Dundee East, 1974-87; Rector, Dundee University, 1983-86. Recreation: reading; sailing; walking. Address: (h.) 48 Monifieth Road, Dundee, DD5 2RX.

Wilson, Robert Graham, BSc. HM Inspector of Schools (Further Education), since 1976; b. 6.3.42, Johnstone; m., Alexandra A. Macfadyen; 2 d. Educ. Paisley Grammar School; Glasgow University. Depute Headteacher, Port Glasgow High School, prior to appointment as HMI. Address: (h.) Newton, Strachur, Argyll.

Wilson, Roy. General Manager, Pitlochry Festival Theatre, since 1961; b. St. Andrews. Educ. Burgh School and Madras College, St. Andrews. Proprietor, grocer's business, St. Andrews, 1953-59; Assistant Manager, Pitlochry Festival Theatre, 1959-61. Recreations: plays and theatre in general; most forms of classical music, with particular interest in choral singing; listening to records; reading. Address: (h.) Kilrymont, Bruach Lane, Pitlochry, Perthshire, PH16 5DG; T.-Pitlochry 2897.

Wilson, Sydney Gordon Forbes, MD, FRCPEdin. Consultant Paediatrician, Tayside Health Board, since 1964; b. 6.5.24, Inverkeilor; m., Eileen Margaret Beattie; 3 s.; 1 d. Educ. Arbroath High School; Trinity College, Glenalmond; Edinburgh University. House Physician, Hospital for Sick

Children, Great Ormond Street, London, and Neonatal Department, Hammersmith Hospital, London; Fellow, Paediatric Renal Research, Western Reserve University, Cleveland, Ohio; Paediatric Senior Registrar, Dundee Royal Infirmary; First Assistant, Department of Child Health, Newcastle University; Consultant Paediatrician, Sunderland. Recreations: golf; walking; reading. Address: (h.) 11 Rockfield Crescent, Dundee, DD2 1JE; T.-0382 67411.

Wilson, Thomas Black, BSc (Hons), MBCS. Depute Principal, Cardonald College, Glasgow, since 1986; b. 23.12.43, Airdrie; m., Barbara Smith; 1 s.; 1 d. Educ. Cumnock Academy; Glasgow University; Jordanhill College. Principal Teacher, Prestwick Academy, 1969-74; Head, Computing Department, Ayr College, 1974-84; Depute Principal, Barmulloch College, Glasgow, 1984-86. Member, Scottish Central Committee (Mathematics), 1975-82. Recreations: reading; writing; music. Address: (b.) 690 Mosspark Drive, Glasgow, G52 3AY; T.-041-883 6151.

Wilson, Emeritus Professor Thomas Brendan, MA, BMus, ARCM. Composer; b. 10.10.27, Trinidad, Colorado; m., Margaret Rayner; 3 s. Educ. St. Mary's College, Aberdeen; Glasgow University; Royal College of Music. RAF, 1945-48; Glasgow University: Lecturer in Music, Extra-Mural Studies, 1957, Reader in Music, Extra-Mural Studies, 1972, Professor, 1977; Member, Scottish Arts Council, 1966-72; Chairman, Composers Guild; President, Scottish Society of Composers; Member, Advisory Commitee, Scottish Music Archive; elected Member, Royal Society of Musicians; compositions include orchestral, choral-orchestral, chamber-orchestral, opera (including The Confessions of a Justified Sinner), ballet, brass band, vocal music of different kinds, and works for a wide variety of chamber ensembles and solo instruments; numerous commissions. Recreations: golf; talking shop. Address: (h.) 120 Dowanhill Street, Glasgow, G12 9DN; T.-041-339 1699.

Wilson, William, MB, ChB, DO, FRCSEdin. Senior Consultant Ophthalmologist, Glasgow Royal Infirmary, since 1962; Honorary Clinical Lecturer, Glasgow University, since 1962; b. 29.10.28, Glasgow; m., Isobel Smith Mackie; 1 s.; 1 d. Educ. Eastbank Academy; High School of Glasgow; Glasgow University. Consultant Ophthalmologist, Glasgow Royal Infirmary and Vale of Leven Hospital; Ophthalmic Advisor to School Health Service for the City of Glasgow and Dunbartonshire Schools Health Service; Examiner, Royal College of Surgeons of Glasgow and Edinburgh; Consultant Ophthalmologist, Glasgow School for Partially Sighted. Past President, Scottish Ophthalmological Society. Recreations: gardening; DIY. Address: (h.) 34 Calderwood Road, Glasgow, G43 2RU; T.-041-637 4898.

Wilson, Professor William Adam, MA, LLB. Lord President Reid Professor of Law, Edinburgh University, since 1972; b. 28.7.28, Glasgow. Educ. Hillhead High School, Glasgow; Glasgow University. Solicitor, 1951-60; Lecturer in Scots Law, Edinburgh University, 1960-72. Recreation: walking. Address: (h.) 2 Great Stuart Street, Edinburgh; T.-031-225 4958.

Wilson, William Murray, MB, ChB, MRCGP. General Medical Practitioner, Dalry, Ayrshire, since 1949; Medical Advisor, Roche Products, Dalry, Ayrshire, since 1965; Medical Referee, Cunninghame District Council, since 1972; Member, Ayrshire and Arran Health Board; b. 19.1.25, Glasgow; m., Elizabeth Carbine; 3 s. Educ. Eastwood Secondary School; Glasgow University. Past Chairman, Local Medical Committee/GP Committee, Area Medical Committee, BMA Ayrshire Division; former Member, General Medical Services Committee, London and Edinburgh; Elder, St. Margaret's Church, Dalry; former Member, Education for the Ministry Committee, Church of Scotland; Honorary Lecturer, British Red Cross Society, St. Andrew's Ambulance Association. Recreations: travel; photography. Address: (h.) 22 Courthill Street, Dalry, Ayrshire, KA24 5AN; T.-Dalry 2165.

Wilson, William Ogilvie, MA, AHA, JP. Member, Perth and Kinross District Council, since 1980 (Vice Chairman, since 1988); Area Staff Training and Development Officer, Tayside Health Board, since 1987; b. 22.11.47, Broughty Ferry, Dundee; m., Margaret; 2 s. Educ. Perth High School; Dundee University. Assistant Hospital Secretary, then Sector Administrator, Perth Royal Infirmary, 1972-84; Unit Administrator, Tayside Health Board, 1984-87. Chairman, Management Committee, Oakbank Church and Sunday School; Vice Chairman, Perth City III Schools Council; Committee Member, Perth Royal Infirmary League of Friends; Press Officer, Perth and Kinross Liberal Association. Recreations: running; swimming; gardening. Address: (h.) 3 Fairhill Avenue, Perth, PH1 1RP; T.-Perth 26270.

Wilson, Rev. William Stewart, DA. Minister, Kirkcudbright, since 1980; b. 8.3.34, Stromness; m., Sheila Stevens; 1 s.; 1 d. Educ. Stromness Academy; Gray's School of Art; Aberdeen University. Soldier (Instructor, RAEC), two years; Schoolteacher, five years; islander (Fair Isle), nine years; Schoolteacher, four years. Member, Advisory Committee on Artistic Matters, Church of Scotland. Publication: Shipwrecks of Fair Isle, 1970. Recreations: painting; drama; ornithology. Address: 6 Bourtree Avenue, Kirkcudbright; T.-0557 30489.

Wilson, William Walker, BSc, CEng, MIMechE, FBIM. Management Services Controller, South of Scotland Electricity Board, since 1975; b. 9.9.26, Stirling; m., Anne Livingston Ross; 1 s.; 1 d. Educ. Hyndland School, Glasgow; Glasgow University. National Service (commission, RA), 1947-49; engineering posts, SW Scotland Division, BEA, 1949-55; senior engineering posts, CEGB, 1955-62; SSEB: Manager, Braehead Power Station, 1962-67, Manager, Generation Management Services, 1967-72, Group Manager Generation, 1972-75. Recreations: music; golf. Address: (h.) 2 Crosbie Woods, Paisley, PA2 0SG; T.-041-884 8472.

Wilson, W. Stewart, BSc. Rector, Banchory Academy, since 1978; b. 15.5.37, Aberdeen; m., Elizabeth Gorrod; 1 s.; 1 d. Educ. Aberdeen Grammar School; Aberdeen University. Teacher, Aberdeen Grammar School, 1961-66; Principal Teacher of Mathematics, then Deputy Rector,

Banchory Academy, 1966-78. Elder and Clerk, Congregational Board, Banchory Ternan West Parish Church; Past President: Banchory and District Round Table, Rotary Club of Banchory Ternan; Past Chairman, Kincardine and Deeside National Trust Members' Centre; Scottish Headquarters Scout Commissioner for Adult Leader Training, since 1975. Recreations: philately; Robert Burns - his life and works; antique maps of Kincardineshire. Address: (h.) Ibiscus, Rosehill Crescent, Banchory; T.-033-02 3194.

Wilson Smith, Lt. Col. John Logan, OBE. Regimental Secretary, The Royal Scots, since 1983; b. 4.7.27, Harrow; m., Ann Winifred Lyon Corsar; 3 d. Educ. Wellington College. Commissioned, 1946; Lt. Col., 1972; retired, 1977; Chairman, The Royal Scots Association; Director, The Royal Scots Regimental Shop Ltd.; President, SSAFA and FHS, Edinburgh and Midlothian. Recreations: forestry; shooting; fishing. Address: (h.) Cumledge, Duns, Berwickshire, TD11 3TB.

Wiltshire, James Phillip, OBE (1987), BA, PhD. Chairman, Ayrshire Area Manpower Board, since 1983; Member, Ayrshire and Arran Health Board, since 1982; b. 9.5.24, Sheffield; m., Janet Eleanor; 1 s.; 1 d. Educ. Maltby Grammar School; Queens' College, Cambridge. Joined ICI as Research Chemist, Paints Division, Slough, 1947; seconded to Canadian Industries Ltd., Toronto, 1960-62; Research Manager, Nobel Division, ICI, Stevenston, 1969; Policy Group Member, Corporate Laboratory, ICI, Runcorn, 1971; Research and Personnel Director, Nobel's Explosives Co. Ltd., Stevenston, 1973; a CBI Representative, Manpower Services Committee for Scotland, 1980-82; retired from ICI, 1982; Past Chairman, Ayrshire Marriage Guidance Council; former Treasurer, Ayrshire Council on Alcoholism; former Representative, CBI Scotland, on Community Business Scotland; former Member, Scottish Technical Education Council. Recreations: sailing; hill-walking; a little music and opera. Address: (h.) Burnswood, 20 Greenfield Avenue, Alloway, Ayr, KA7 4NW; T.-0292 41502.

Windsor, Malcolm L., PhD, FRSC. Secretary, North Atlantic Salmon Conservation Organization, since 1984; b. 12.4.38, Bristol; m., Sally; 2 d. Educ. Cotham Grammar School, Bristol; Bristol University. Researcher, University of California, 1965-67; fisheries research, Humber Laboratory, Hull, 1967-75; Fisheries Adviser to Chief Scientist, Ministry of Agriculture and Fisheries, London, 1975-84. Secretary, Society for the Preservation of Duddingston Village. Publication: book on fishery products. Recreations: local conservation work; jazz; walking. Address: (b.) 11 Rutland Square, Edinburgh, EH1 2AS; T.-031-228 2551.

Winney, Robin John, MB, ChB, FRCPEdin. Consultant Renal Physician, Edinburgh Royal Infirmary, since 1978; b. 8.5.44, Dunfermline. Educ. Dunfermline High School; Edinburgh University. Recreations: badminton; curling. Address: (h.) 74 Lanark Road West, Currie, Midlothian, EH14 5JZ.

Winning, Most Rev. Thomas Joseph, STL, DCL, DD, FEIS. Archbishop of Glasgow and Metropolitan, since 1974; President, Bishops' Conference of Scotland, since 1985; b. 3.6.25, Wishaw. Educ. Our Lady's High School, Motherwell; St. Mary's College, Blairs; St. Peter's College; Scots College; Gregorian University, Rome. Ordained Priest, Rome, 1948; Assistant Priest, Chapelhall, 1949-50; Rome (DCL, "Cum Laude"), 1953; Assistant Priest, St. Mary's Hamilton, 1953-57; Cathedral, Motherwell, 1957-58; Chaplain, Franciscans of the Immaculate Conception, Bothwell, 1958-61; Diocesan Secretary, Motherwell, 1956-61; Spiritual Director, Scots College, Rome, 1961-66; Advocate of the Sacred Roman Rota, 1965; Parish Priest, St. Luke's Motherwell, 1966-70; Officialis and Vicar Episcopal, Motherwell Diocese, 1966-70; first President, Scottish Catholic Marriage Tribunal, 1970; nominated Titular Bishop of Louth and Bishop Auxiliary, 1971, and ordained by James Donald Scanlan, Archbishop of Glasgow, November, 1971; Parish Priest, Our Holy Redeemer's Clydebank, 1972-74; translated to Glasgow as Archbishop, 1974; Honorary DD (Glasgow), 1983; awarded Glasgow Loving Cup, 1983. Recreations: watching football; listening to music. Address: (h.) 40 Newlands Road, Glasgow, G43 2JD; T.-041-226 5898.

Winter, Charles M., FIB (Scot). Group Chief Executive, Royal Bank of Scotland Group p.l.c., since 1985; b. 21.7.33, Dundee; m., Audrey Hynd; 1 s.; 1 d. Educ. Harris Academy, Dundee. Joined Royal Bank of Scotland, 1949; Director, 1981; Director, Royal Bank of Scotland Group, 1981; President, Institute of Bankers in Scotland, 1981-83; Director, Lloyds & Scottish PLC, 1983-84; Chairman, Committee of Scottish Clearing Bankers, 1983-85; Member, Board of Governors, Leith Nautical College, 1979-82; Treasurer, Commonwealth Games, Scotland, 1986; Chairman, Steering Committee, Inter-Alpha Group of Banks, 1986; Vice-President, Edinburgh Chamber of Commerce and Manufactures, 1987. Recreations: golf; choral music. Address: (b.) Royal Bank of Scotland Group p.l.c., 42 St. Andrew Square, Edinburgh; T.-031-556 8555.

Winton, Alexander, QFSM, MIFireE. Firemaster, Tayside Fire Brigade, since 1985; b. 13.7.32, Perth; m., Jean; 2 s. Perth and Kinross Fire Brigade, 1958; Instructor, Scottish Fire Service Training School, 1962; Lancashire County Fire Brigade, 1967; East Riding of Yorkshire Fire Brigade, 1970; Angus Area Fire Brigade, 1973; Tayside Fire Brigade, 1975; Deputy Firemaster, Tayside Fire Brigade, 1981. Recreations: golf; curling. Address: (h.) 5 Ferndale Drive, Broughty Ferry, Dundee, DD5 3DB; T.-Dundee 78156.

Wishart, David, BSc, PhD. Assistant Secretary, Scottish Education Department, since 1984; b. 5.7.43, London; m., Doreen Pamela Craig Wishart; 3 s. Educ. Kilburn Grammar School; Truro School; St. Andrews University. Statistician, Civil Service Department, London, 1970-75; Principal, Scottish Office, 1975-77; Chief Statistician, Scottish Office, 1977-81; Director of Statistics, Scottish Office, 1981-84. Fellow: British Computer Society, Royal Statistical Society (Vice President, 1986-88). Recreations: cricket; skiing; opera. Address: (h.) 16 Kingsburgh Road, Edinburgh, 12; T.-031-337 1448.

Wither, Andrew, BL. Procurator Fiscal, Moray, since 1976; b. 25.8.29, Stranraer; m., Barbara Jane Clark; 1 s.; 1 d. Educ. Stranraer Academy; Edinburgh University. Deputy Administrator General, Uganda (Colonial Legal Service), 1956-66; joined Procurator Fiscal Service, 1966. Recreation: game shooting. Address: (b.) Sheriff Courthouse, Elgin, IV30 1BU; T.-0343 3594.

Withers, John Alexander (Jack), FCIL. Librarian and Writer-in-Residence, Scottish-German Centre/Goethe Institut, since 1974; Writer; b. Glasgow; m., Beate (Bea) Haertel. Educ. North Kelvinside School; Jordanhill College of Education (Youth and Community Diploma). Left school at 14; worked in garage, electrical industry, labouring, National Service, unemployment, razor-blade salesman; long periods abroad, wandering, wondering, working: France, FRG, Italy, Scandinavia, Spain, North Africa; youth worker; freelance writer; ski instructor; librarian; Scottish republican and radical; plays for radio, TV, theatre; James Kennoway Screenplay Award (shared); Scottish Arts Council Awards; short stories published in numerous journals in UK, Denmark and West Germany. Address: (h.) 16 Belmont Crescent, Glasgow; T.-041-339 9492.

Witney, Brian David, BSc, MSc, PhD, CEng, FIMechE, FIAgrE. Director, Scottish Centre of Agricultural Engineering, since 1987; b. 8.6.38, Edinburgh; m., Maureen M.I. Donnelly; 1 s.; 2 d. Educ. Daniel Stewart's College, Edinburgh; Edinburgh University; Durham University; Newcastle University. Senior Research Associate, Newcastle upon Tyne University, 1962-66; Research Fellow, US Army Research Office, Duke Univ., 1966-67; Senior Scientific Officer, Military Engineering Experimental Establishment, Christchurch; Head, Agricultural Engineering Department, East of Scotland College of Agriculture, Edinburgh, 1970-86. President, Institution of Agricultural Engineers. Publication: Choosing and Using Farm Machines. Address: (b.) Scottish Centre of Agricultural Engineering, Bush Estate, Penicuik, Midlothian, EH26 0PH; T.-031-445 2147.

Wolfe, William Cuthbertson, CA. Secretary, Scottish Poetry Library, since 1985; b. 22.2.24; m.; 2 s.; 2 d. Educ. Bathgate Academy; George Watson's College, Edinburgh. Army, 1942-47; Honorary President (Rector), Students' Association, Heriot-Watt University, 1966-69; contested West Lothian for SNP, 1962, 1964, 1966, 1970, 1974 (twice), 1979; Chairman, SNP, 1969-79, President, 1980-82.

Wolfe Murray, Stephanie. Managing Director, Canongate Publishing Ltd.; b. 27.4.41, Blandford, Dorset; m., Angus; 4 s. Educ. Overstone, Northamptonshire; Florence; Paris. Odd jobs till marriage, 1961; publisher's reader, early 1970s; Past Chairman, Scottish Publishers Association; Council Member, National Book League, Scotland; Member, Publishers Advisory Committee, British Council; Director, Edinburgh Book Festival. Recreations: walking; reading. Address: (h.) 20 Leonard's Bank, Edinburgh; T.-031-557 5888.

Wolrige Gordon, Captain Robert. Member, Grampian Regional Council, 1978-86 (Deputy Chairman, Planning, 1982-86); b. 20.9.28, Esslemont; m., Rosemary Jane Abel Smith; 1 s.; 1 d. (deceased). Educ. Eton College; Royal Military Academy, Sandhurst. Enlisted Grenadier Guards, 1947; commissioned, 1948; Captain, 1953; retired, 1959; Member, Aberdeenshire County Council, 1961-74 (Chairman, Accident Prevention and Civil Defence Committee); farming at Esslemont, since 1959; Grand Master Mason of Scotland, 1974-79; Member, Representative Church Council, 1959-82; Member, Diocesan and Provincial Synod, Scottish Episcopal Church. Recreations: shooting; fishing; history. Address: (h.) Esslemont, Ellon, Aberdeenshire; T.-Ellon 20234.

Wong, Professor Henry H.Y., BSc, PhD, DIC, CEng, FRAeS. Professor, Department of Aeronautics and Fluid Mechanics, Glasgow University; Adviser to the Guangdong Higher Education Bureau, China, since 1985; Adviser to Glasgow University on Chinese Affairs, since 1986, and Director of Special Training Programmes, since 1987; Senior Research Fellow, since 1987; b. 23.5.22, Hong Kong; m., Joan Anstey; 2 s.; 1 d. Educ. St. Stephen College, Hong Kong; Jiao-Tong University, Shanghai; Imperial College, London; Glasgow University. Assistant Lecturer, Jiao-Tong University, 1947-48; Engineer, Armstrong Siddeley, 1949; Structural Engineer, Hunting Percival Aircraft, 1949-51; Senior Structural Engineer, de Havilland Aircraft, 1952-57; Senior Lecturer, Hatfield Polytechnic, 1957-59; Lecturer, Senior Lecturer, then Reader in Aeronautics and Fluid Mechanics, Glasgow University, from 1960; Economic and Technological Consultant to Shantou Special Economic Zone, China, since 1988. Former Treasurer and Vice-Chairman, Kilmardinny Music Circle; Chairman, Glasgow Summer School, since 1979. Recreations: reading; music; painting; swimming. Address: (h.) 77 Antonine Road, Bearsden, Glasgow; T.-041-942 8346.

Wood, Arthur Murdoch Mactaggart, OBE, MA, LLB. General Secretary, RSSPCC, since 1968; b. 15.12.37, Kilbarchan; 2 s.; 2 d. Educ. George Watson's College, Edinburgh; Edinburgh University. Standard Life Assurance Company, 1960-61; Assistant Secretary, RSSPCC, 1961-68. Address: (b.) RSSPCC, Melville House, 41 Polwarth Terrace, Edinburgh, EH11 1NU; T.-031-337 8539.

Wood, Brian Charles Thallon, BL, NP. Solicitor, since 1955; Partner, Charles Wood & Son, Solicitors, Kirkcaldy, since 1956; Honorary Sheriff; b. 8.8.34, Kirkcaldy; m., Tessa; 1 s.; 1 d. Educ. Fettes; Edinburgh University. Part-time Chairman, Industrial Tribunals, 1972-77; part-time Chairman, Rent Assessment Committee, 1987. Recreations: gardens; skiing; mending anything. Address: (b.) 37 Kirk Wynd, Kirkcaldy, Fife; T.-0592 261621.

Wood, Brian James Barry, PhD, BSc, CChem, FRSC. Reader, Division of Applied Microbiology, Strathclyde University, since 1981; b. 11.7.34, Birmingham. Educ. Kings Norton Grammar School, Birmingham; Birmingham University. Research Biochemist, University of California at Davis, 1959-62; Scientist, Unilever Ltd., Bedford, 1962-68; Strathclyde University: Lecturer, 1968-75, Senior Lecturer, 1975-81; Technical

Director, Bean Products Ltd., 1981-84. Representative, Forth and Clyde Canal Society on Glasgow Urban Wildlife Group. Recreations: gardening; Lenzie Rugby FC; work. Address: (b.) Division of Applied Microbiology, Strathclyde University, Glasgow, G1 1XW; T.-041-552 4400.

Wood, Eric Alexander Masterton, MB, ChB, MRCP, FRCPE, FRCPsych. Consultant Psychotherapist, Royal Edinburgh Hospital, since 1965; Senior Lecturer in Psychiatry, Edinburgh University, since 1965; b. 15.2.23, Grangemouth; 4 s. Educ. George Watson's College, Edinburgh; Edinburgh University. House Surgeon, Edinburgh Royal Infirmary; Major, Royal Army Medical Corps; Principal in general practice; Assistant Physician, Royal Edinburgh Hospital; Senior Lecturer in Psychiatry, Leeds University; Hon. Consultant Physician, Department of Psychiatry, Leeds General Infirmary. Member of Council, Scottish Institute of Human Relations; founder Member, Analytical Psychotherapy Training Committee, SIHR; first Chairman, Scottish Association of Analytical Psychotherapists. Recreation: swimming. Address: (h.) 75 Morningside Park, Edinburgh, EH10 5EZ; T.-031-447 5674.

Wood, George Alexander McDougall, BA. Senior Lecturer in English Studies, Stirling University, since 1975; Executive Editor, Edinburgh Edition of the Waverley Novels, since 1986; b. 9.8.38, Hyde. Educ. William Hulme's Grammar School, Manchester; University College, London. Research Assistant, English Department, University College, London, 1962; Librarian, Osborn Collection, Yale University, 1962-66; Fellow, Silliman College, Yale University, 1965-66; Assistant Professor of English, University of California, Santa Barbara, 1966-68; Lecturer, Stirling University, 1968-75. Recreation: railways. Address: (h.) Burn O'Vat, Haining, Dunblane, Perthshire; T.-Dunblane 4878.

Wood, Professor Hamish Christopher Swan, BSc, PhD, CChem, FRSC, FRSE. Professor of Organic Chemistry, Strathclyde University, since 1969; b. 8.5.26, Hawick; m., Jean Dumbreck Mitchell; 1 s.; 1 d. Educ. Hawick High School; St. Andrews University. Lecturer in Chemistry, St. Andrews University, 1950-51; Research Fellow, Australian National University, 1951-53; Lecturer, Senior Lecturer and Reader, Strathclyde University, 1953-69 (Vice-Principal, 1984-86). Address: (b.) Thomas Graham Building, Strathclyde University, 295 Cathedral Street, Glasgow, G1 1XL; T.-041-552 4400.

Wood, Ian Clark, CBE (1982), LLD, BSc, CBIM. Chairman and Managing Director, John Wood Group PLC, since 1967; Chairman, J.W. Holdings, since 1982; b. 21.7.42, Aberdeen; m., Helen Macrae; 3 s. Educ. Robert Gordon's College, Aberdeen; Aberdeen University. Joined family business, John Wood & Sons, 1964; Board Member, Scottish Development Agency; Member, Scottish Economic Council; Member, Aberdeen Harbour Board; Fellow, Royal Society of Arts; Member, Offshore Energy Technology Board; Member, Scottish Sub-Committee, University Grants Committee; Board Director, Royal Bank of Scotland; Chairman, Aberdeen Beyond 2000; Grampian Industrialist of the Year, 1978; Young Scottish Businessman of the Year, 1979; Hon. LLD, 1984. Recreations: squash; family. Address: (b.) John Wood Group PLC, John Wood House, Greenwell Road, East Tullos, Aberdeen; T.-0224 875464.

Wood, Jack Williamson, FRICS, FRVA. Regional Assessor and Electoral Registration Officer, Strathclyde Regional Council, since 1981, and Community Charge Registration Officer, since 1987; Vice President, Scottish Assessors Association; b. 15.3.33, Rutherglen; m., Wilma; 2 d. Educ. Rutherglen Academy; Royal College of Science and Technology. Assistant Chief Surveyor, Glasgow, 1964-75; Strathclyde Region: Depute Assessor, 1975-79, Senior Depute Assessor, 1979-81. Recreations: sport (golf); music; literature. Address: (b.) Strathclyde House II, 20 India Street, Glasgow; T.-041-227 3822.

Wood, James Tweedie. Farmer; Chairman, Royal Highland and Agricultural Society; b. 7.9.40, South Queensferry; m., Christine Margaret; 1 s.; 1 d. Educ. Daniel Stewart's College; Edinburgh School of Agriculture. Past President, Edinburgh Curling Club; Past Chairman, East Area, Young Farmers' Clubs; former Governor, East of Scotland College of Agriculture. Recreations: curling; golfing. Address: (h.) Easter Dalmeny, South Queensferry, EH30 9TS; T.-031-319 1347.

Wood, Michael, BSc (Hons), DipCarto, FRGS. Senior Lecturer in Geography (Cartography), Aberdeen University, since 1983; b. 25.6.41, Insch; m., Margaret Russell Lochhead Barr; 2 d. Educ. Aberdeen Grammar School; Aberdeen University; Glasgow University. Research Assistant, then Assistant Lecturer, Department of Geography, Glasgow University, 1964-69; Lecturer, Department of Geography, Aberdeen University, 1969-83; External Examiner for National Certificates in Cartography, Surveying and Planning in Britain, 1971-78; Council Member, British Cartographic Society, since 1971 (President, 1982-84). Publications: Surveying and Mapping for Field Scientists (Co-author), 1988; papers on cartography and map reading; numerous maps. Recreations: hill-walking; skiing. Address: (b.) Department of Geography, Elphinstone Road, Aberdeen, AB9 2UF; T.-0224 272332.

Wood, Robert Anderson, BSc, MB, ChB, FRCPEdin. Consultant Physician, Perth Royal Infirmary, since 1972; Senior Lecturer in Pharmacology and Therapeutics, Dundee University, since 1972; b. 26.5.39, Edinburgh. Educ. Edinburgh Academy; Edinburgh University. Address: (h.) Ballomill House, Abernethy, Perthshire; T.-Abernethy 201.

Wood, Robert Anthony Bowness, MB, ChB, MRCP, FRCSEdin, FRCS. Senior Lecturer in Surgery, Dundee University, and Honorary Consultant Surgeon; b. 12.4.43, Leeds; m., Dr. Elizabeth Spiers; 2 s.; 2 d. Educ. St. Peter's School, York; Leeds University. House Physician/House Surgeon, Leeds, Glasgow, York, London, 1966-69; Registrar/Lecturer, Leeds, Birmingham, Norwich, Cardiff, 1969-74; Senior Registrar, Cardiff, 1974-75; Research Associate/Instructor, Chicago University, 1975-76; Lecturer in Surgery, Cardiff, 1976. Recreations: hill-walking; classical music.

Address: (b.) Department of Surgery, Ninewells Hospital and Medical School, Dundee, DD1 9SY; T.-0382 60111.

Wood, Stephen Charles, MA, BA (Hons), FSA(Scot). Keeper, Scottish United Services Museum, Edinburgh Castle, since 1983; b. 29.1.52, Wells, Somerset; 1 s. Educ. The Blue School, Wells; Bishop Wordsworth's School, Salisbury; Birkbeck College, London University. Curator, Department of Uniform, National Army Museum, London, 1971-83. Publication: The Scottish Soldier, 1987. Recreations: travel; gastronomy; country matters. Address: (b.) Edinburgh Castle, Edinburgh; T.-01-225 7534.

Wood, William Ferrie, DipArch, DipTP, RIBA, MRTPI. Vice Principal, Edinburgh College of Art, since 1978; b. 23.9.32, Edinburgh. Educ. Daniel Stewart's College, Edinburgh; Edinburgh College of Art. National Service, business, student, 1949-65; Architect/Planner, Robert Matthew, Johnson-Marshall & Partners, Welwyn Garden City, 1965-69; Lecturer, then Senior Lecturer, Department of Town and Country Planning, Heriot-Watt University/Edinburgh College of Art, 1969-78. Recreations: painting; reading; squash. Address: (h.) 26a Dalrymple Crescent, Edinburgh, EH9 2NX; T.-031-667 4370.

Wood-Gush, Professor David Grainger Marcus, PhD, BSc, DipAnimGen, FRSA, FRSE. Honorary Professor, School of Agriculture, Edinburgh University, since 1978; b. 20.11.22, Dordrecht, South Africa; m., Eola Langham Godden; 1 s.; 1 d. Educ. St. Andrews College, Grahamstown, South Africa; Witwatersrand University, Johannesburg; Edinburgh University. Senior Principal Scientific Officer (Special Merit), AFRC, and Head, Ethology Department, AFRC Poultry Research Centre, Edinburgh, 1952-78. Former Chairman, Association for the Study of Animal Behaviour; former President, Society for Veterinary Ethology. Publications: The Behaviour of the Domestic Fowl; Elements of Ethology. Recreations: reading; swimming; hill-walking; historic building preservation. Address: (h.) 26 Nelson Street, Edinburgh, EH3 6LJ; T.-031-556 6488.

Woodruff, Professor Sir Michael (Francis Addison), Kt (1969), DSc, MD, MS, FRCS, FRCSE, FRACS, Hon. FACS, FRSE, FRS. Professor Emeritus, Surgery, Edinburgh University; b. 3.4.11, London; m., Hazel Gwenyth Ashby; 2 s.; 1 d. Educ. Wesley College, Melbourne; Queens College, Melbourne University. House Physician and House Surgeon, Royal Melbourne Hospital; Captain, Australian Army Medical Corps (PoW, Singapore); Tutor in Surgery, Sheffield University, 1946; Senior Lecturer in Surgery, Aberdeen University, 1948; Professor of Surgery, Otago University, 1953, Edinburgh University, 1957-76; research worker, MRC Clinical and Population Cytogenetics Unit, Edinburgh, 1976-86. President, The Transplantation Society, 1972-74. Publications: Deficiency Diseases in Japanese Prison Camps; Surgery for Dental Students; The Transplantation of Tissues and Organs; On Science and Surgery; The Interaction of Cancer and Host. Recreations: sailing; music; tennis. Address: (h.) The Bield, 506 Lanark Road, Juniper Green, Edinburgh, EH14 5DH; T.-031-453 3653.

Woodward, Professor John Frank, BSc, CEng, FICE, FIStructE, FBIM. Vice Principal, Paisley College of Technology; Visiting Professor, Glasgow Business School, since 1970; b. 23.6.33, London; m., Marjorie Isobel; 4 d. Educ. City of Leicester Boys School; Glasgow University. Engineer, latterly Director, associate company, Taylor Woodrow Group, 1956-67; Reader in Management Science, Stirling University, 1968-81. Council Member, Association of Project Managers. Recreations: field sports; skiing. Address: (b.) Paisley College of Technology, High Street, Paisley, PA1 2BE; T.-041-887 1241.

Wooldridge, Ian, BA (Hons). Artistic Director, Royal Lyceum Theatre Company, Edinburgh, since 1984; b. 11.8.46, Swansea. Educ. King Henry VIII School, Coventry; Cardiff University; Bristol University. Stage Manager and Teacher of Drama, 1968-72; Associate Director, Dark and Light Theatre Company, Brixton, 1972-75; freelance Theatre Director and Drama Consultant, Lothian Region Education Authority, 1975-78; Artistic Director, TAG Theatre Company, Glasgow, 1978-84. Address: (b.) Royal Lyceum Theatre, Grindlay Street, Edinburgh, EH3 9AX; T.-031-229 7404.

Worrall, Ernest Paterson, MB, ChB, FRCPsych, DPM. Consultant Psychiatrist: Southern General Hospital, Glasgow, since 1980, Ross Hall Hospital, Glasgow, since 1984, Bon Secours Hospital, Glasgow; b. 28.10.42, Hamilton; m., Jean Price; 1 s.; 1 d. Educ. Hamilton Academy; Glasgow University. Lecturer in Psychiatry, Dundee University, 1973-75; Senior Lecturer in Psychological Medicine, Glasgow University, 1975-80. Recreation: triathlons (as active participant). Address: (b.) Department of Psychiatry, Southern General Hospital, Glasgow, G51 1TF; T.-041-445 2466.

Worthington, Tony, BA, MEd. MP (Labour), Clydebank and Milngavie, since 1987; b. 11.10.41, Hertfordshire; m., Angela; 1 s.; 1 d. Educ. City School, Lincoln; London School of Economics; York University; Glasgow University. Member, Home Affairs Select Committee; Vice Chairman, Labour Party House of Commons Home Affairs Committee. Recreations: running; fishing; gardening. Address: (h.) 24 Cleddans Crescent, Hardgate, Clydebank; T.-0389 73195.

Wotherspoon, (John Munro) Iain, TD, DL. Senior Partner, Macandrew & Jenkins, WS, since 1954; Deputy Lieutenant, Districts of Lochaber, Inverness, Badenoch and Strathspey, since 1982, and Clerk, since 1985; b. 19.7.24, Inverness; m., Victoria Avril Jean Edwards; 2 s.; 2 d. Educ. Inverness Royal Academy; Loretto School; Trinity College, Oxford; Edinburgh University. Lt., Royal Signals, Europe and Burma, 1945-46; TA, 1948-78; Lt.-Col. commanding 51 (Highland) Division Signals, 1963-70; Col. Dep. Cdr. 13 Signals Gp., 1970-72; Hon. Col. 32 (Scottish) Signal Regiment, 1972-78; ADC to The Queen, 1971-76; WS, 1950; Solicitor and Land Owner. Recreations: shooting; fishing; stalking. Address: (h.) Maryfield, 62 Midmills Road, Inverness, IV2 3QL; T.-0463 233642.

Wray, David, MD, BDS, MB, ChB, FDS, RCPSGlas, FDS RCSEdin. Senior Lecturer, Department of Oral Medicine and Oral Pathology, Edinburgh University, since 1983; Honorary Consultant, Lothian Health Board, since 1983; b. 3.1.51, Carshalton; m., Alison; 2 s. Educ. Uddingston Grammar School; Glasgow University. Temporary Lecturer, Department of Oral Medicine, Glasgow University, 1977-79; Fogarty Visiting Associate, National Institutes of Health, Bethesda, 1979-81; Research Fellow, Royal Dental School, London University, 1982. Honorary Secretary and Treasurer, British Society of Oral Medicine. Recreation: fly fishing. Address: (h.) 6 Randolph Cliff, Edinburgh, EH3 7TZ; T.-031-225 6948.

Wray, James. MP (Labour), Glasgow Provan, since 1987; b. 28.4.38; m.; 3 c. Member, Strathclyde Regional Council, since 1976; President, Scottish Federation of the Blind, 1987.

Wright, David Frederick, MA (Cantab). Senior Lecturer in Ecclesiastical History, Edinburgh University, since 1973; b. 2.10.37, Hayes, Kent; m., Anne-Marie; 1 s.; 1 d. Educ. Christ's College, Cambridge; Lincoln College, Oxford. Edinburgh University: Lecturer, 1964-73, Associate Dean, Faculty of Divinity, 1972-76, Dean, since 1988, Convener, General Assembly of Academic Staff, 1972-74, Member, University Court, 1984-87; External Examiner, Universities of Sussex, Liverpool, Durham, Cambridge, etc.; Member, Council of Management, Keston College; Chairman, Tyndale Fellowship for Biblical and Theological Research; Associate Editor, Tyndale Bulletin; Review Editor, Scottish Bulletin of Evangelical Theology. Publications: Common Places of of Martin Bucer, 1972; Essays in Evangelical Social Ethics (Editor), 1979; Lion Handbook History of Christianity (Consultant Editor), 1977; New Dictionary of Theology (Joint Editor), 1988. Recreations: walking; gardening; DIY. Address: (h.) 5 Lockharton Gardens, Edinburgh, EH14 1AU; T.-031-443 1001.

Wright, David John, MB, BS, FFARCS. Consultant Anaesthetist, Western General Hospital, Edinburgh, since 1979; b. 13.4.44, Oswestry; m., Bronwen; 2 s.; 1 d. Educ. Bristol Grammar School; St. Bartholomew's Hospital Medical College, London. Joint Honorary Secretary, Scottish Society of the History of Medicine. Address: (h.) 20 Lennox Row, Edinburgh, EH5 3JW; T.-031-552 3439.

Wright, Douglas Stewart. Director, Keep Scotland Beautiful, since 1973; Chairman, Beautiful Scotland in Bloom, since 1983; b. 22.7.32, Glasgow; m., May Carswell; 1 s.; 2 d. Educ. Albert Road Academy, Pollokshields. Representative, Scottish Field, 1947-58; National Service, 1st Bn., Cameronians Scottish Rifles (Malaya), 1950-52; General Manager, The Scottish Farmer, 1959-66; Appeals Director, Scottish Council for the Care of Spastics, 1966-73. Committee Member, Stars Organisation for Spastics (Scotland); Past President, Glasgow Haggis Club (No. 33). Recreations: hillwalking; specialist in China Tea Clippers. Address: (b.) County Chambers, Cathedral Square, Dunblane, Perthshire, FK15 OAQ.

Wright, Edward, JP. Member, Clydesdale District Council, since 1980 (Leader, Labour Group, since 1984); b. 15.5.52, Motherwell; m., Rita McCutcheon. Educ. Dalziel High School, Motherwell; Bell College of Technology, Hamilton. Engineer, Anderson Strathclyde, Motherwell, since 1968; Shop Steward and Deputy Convener, AUEW (ES), 1975-83; Chairman, Industrial Development, Clydesdale District Council, 1981-84; Director, Lanarkshire Industrial Field Executive, 1982-84; Member, Youth Advisory Committee, STUC, 1975-78; Chairman, Clydesdale Constituency Labour Party, 1984-86; Officer, then Officer in charge, 4th Carluke Company, Boys' Brigade, since 1978. Recreations: golf; bowls. Address: (h.) 4 Lanark Road, Carluke, ML8 4HD.

Wright, Sir Edward (Maitland), Kt (1977), MA, DPhil, LLD, DSc, FRSE. Research Fellow, Aberdeen University, since 1976; b. 1906; 1 s. Educ. Jesus College and Christ Church, Oxford; University of Gottingen. Aberdeen University: Professor of Mathematics, 1935-62, Vice-Principal, 1961-62, Principal and Vice-Chancellor, 1962-76.

Wright, George Gordon. Publisher; b. 25.6.42, Edinburgh. Educ. Darroch Secondary School; Heriot Watt College. Left printing trade, 1973, to develop own publishing company; founder Member, Scottish General Publishers Association; Past Chairman, Scottish Young Publishers Society. Publications: MacDiarmid: An Illustrated Biography, 1977; A Guide to the Royal Mile, 1979; Orkney From Old Photographs, 1981; A Guide to Holyrood Park and Arthur's Seat, 1987. Recreations: history of Edinburgh; photography; jazz. Address: (h.) 25 Mayfield Road, Edinburgh, EH9 2NQ; T.-031-667 1300.

Wright, (Glydon) Bernard, TC, ADPE, MA, FPEA. Director, Scottish School of Physical Education, since 1974; b. 15.3.28, Cwmbran, Gwent; m., Zena; 2 s. Educ. Abersychan Grammar School; Gwent and Cardiff Colleges of Education; Leeds University. Began teaching career, Beckenham and Cray Valley Technical High Schools; Department Head, Forest Hill Comprehensive School, London, 1958; joined Borough Road College, 1962, as Lecturer (later Senior, Principal Lecturer); Conference Director, VIII Commonwealth and International Conference on Sport, Physical Education, Dance, Recreation and Health; has served on numerous national committees, including CNAA Physical Education and Recreation Sports Studies Board, Scottish Central Committee on Physical Education, Physical Education Association (Treasurer), Scottish Council for Physical Education; Visiting Professor, Canada; Consultant in Portugal and Qatar. Recreations: all sporting activities. Address: (b.) Scottish School of Physical Education, Jordanhill College of Education, Southbrae Drive, Glasgow, G13 1PP; T.-041-959 1232, Ext. 242.

Wright, Rev. Iain Alastair Mackay, BA, BD, RNR. Parish Minister, Falkland and Freuchie, since 1984; b. 15.9.57, Edinburgh; m., Caroline Louise Read; 1 s. Educ. George Watson's College; Edinburgh University. Assistant Minister, St. Columba's, Pont Street, London, 1982-84. Serving Officer, RNR; Freeman Citizen of Glasgow; Member, Royal Scottish Society of Arts. Recreations: reading; philately. Address: The Manse, Falkland, Fife, KY7 7AQ; T.-0337 57252.

Wright, Ian William Weir, BSc, DRCST, CEng, MIChemE, CChem, MRIC. Chief Inspector, HM Industrial Pollution Inspectorate, since 1985; b. 22.4.35, Glasgow; m., Mary Stirling; 1 s.; 1 d. Educ. Allan Glen's School, Glasgow; Strathclyde University. Production Chemist, UKAEA, Windscale Works, 1959-63; Chemical Engineer, Scottish Pulp & Paper Mills, 1963-71 (Deputy Technical Manager); HM Industrial Pollution Inspectorate, since 1971. Recreations: DIY; gardening; reading; motoring. Address: (b.) 27 Perth Street, Edinburgh, EH3 5RW; T.-031-244 3056.

Wright, Rev. Kenyon Edward, MA, BA, BSc, MTh. General Secretary, Scottish Churches Council, since 1981; Director, Scottish Churches House, since 1981; b. 31.8.32, Paisley; m., Betty Robinson; 3 d. Educ. Paisley Grammar School; Glasgow University; Cambridge University. Missionary in India, 1955-70; Director, Ecumenical Social and Industrial Institute, Durgapur, India, 1963-70; Director, Urban Ministry, Coventry Cathedral, 1970-74; Canon Residentiary and Director of International Ministry, Coventry Cathedral, 1974-81. Companion of the Order of the Cross of Nails, Coventry Cathedral; Executive Committee Member, Ecumenical Association of Academies and Laity Centres in Europe; Vice-President, Christian Peace Conference. Recreations: reading; walking; travel; living life to the full. Address: (b.) Scottish Churches House, Kirk Street, Dunblane, FK15 OAJ; T.-0786 823588.

Wright, Michael, LLB, LLM, FBIM, FPIM. Assistant Principal, Napier Polytechnic of Edinburgh, since 1983; b. 24.5.49, Newcastle-upon-Tyne; m., Pamela Stothart; 2 s.; 1 d. Educ. Durham Johnson Grammar School; Bearsden Academy; Birmingham University. Lecturer, Bristol Polytechnic, 1970-79; Head of Department, Glasgow College of Technology, 1980-83; Member of various educational and professional bodies; Elder, Balerno Parish Church. Recreation: sport. Address: (b.) Napier College, Sighthill Court, Edinburgh, EH11 4BN; T.-031-444 2266.

Wright, Professor Norman Gray, BVMS, MRCVS, PhD, DVM, FRCPath, FRSE, FIBiol. Professor of Veterinary Anatomy, Glasgow University, since 1975; b. 19.8.39, Kilmarnock; m., Irene Anne Wright; 2 s. Educ. Kilmarnock Academy; Glasgow University. General veterinary practice, Kilmarnock, 1962-63; Assistant Lecturer/Lecturer/Senior Lecturer, Department of Veterinary Pathology, Glasgow University, 1963-75; awarded G. Norman Hall Gold Medal, Royal College of Veterinary Surgeons, 1975. Recreations: fishing; boating. Address: (h.) 50 Kilmardinny Crescent, Bearsden, Glasgow; T.-041-942 3944.

Wright, Patrick George, MA, PhD, DSc. Reader in Chemistry, Dundee University, since 1977; b. 3.10.32, Henstead, near Beccles, Suffolk; m., Margaret Robson; 2 s.; 1 d. Educ. Lowestoft Grammar School; Cambridge University. Research Fellow, Leeds University, 1956-59; various posts, Queen's College, Dundee (subsequently Dundee University), since 1959. Publications: nearly 100 papers in scientific journals. Address: (h.) 16 Duntrune Terrace, West Ferry, Dundee.

Wright, Very Rev. Ronald (William Vernon) Selby, CVO, ChStJ, TD, MA, DD, FRSE, JP. Chaplain, Edinburgh Castle and to the Governor, since 1959; Chaplain, Queen's Bodyguard for Scotland (Royal Company of Archers), since 1973; Extra Chaplain to the Queen, since 1978 (Chaplain, 1961-78); b., 12.6.08, Glasgow. Educ. Edinburgh Academy; Melville College, Edinburgh; Edinburgh University and New College. Minister, The Canongate, 1937-77; Chaplain, 7/9 Royal Scots, 1938-42, 1946-48; Senior Chaplain, 52 Lowland Division, 1942-43; 1O Indian Division, 1944-45; Honorary Senior Chaplain to the Forces, since 1945; Founder Warden, St. Giles (later Canongate) Boys' Club, 1927-78; Moderator: Edinburgh Presbytery, 1963, General Assembly, 1972-73; Radio Padre, BBC, 1942-47; Extra-ordinary Director, Edinburgh Academy, since 1973. Publications: Asking them Questions; Take Up God's Armour; Another Home. Address: (h.) The Queen's House, 36 Moray Place, Edinburgh, EH3 6BX; T.-031-226 5566.

Wright, Tom, BA (Hons). Writer; b. 8.3.23, Glasgow. Educ. Coatbridge High School; Strathclyde University. Served apprenticeship in embossing and stained glass; Army, 1943-47; served in Europe and Far East, including Japan; began to publish poems and short stories after demobilisation; had first play performed, Edinburgh Festival, 1960; author of There Was A Man; began to write radio and television drama, 1963; former Creative Writing Fellow; former Script Editor, BBC Scotland Drama Department; has also been Script Editor and Story Line Editor, Take The High Road, STV; won Festival Fringe Award, 1984, for Talk of the Devil; Past Chairman, Scottish Committee, Writers' Guild, and Scottish Society of Playwrights. Recreation: listening to music. Address: 318 Churchill Drive, Glasgow, G11.

Wylie, Rt. Hon. Lord (Norman Russell Wylie), PC (1970), VRD (1961), BA (Oxon), LLB (Glas). Senator of the College of Justice in Scotland, since 1974; b. 26.10.23, Elderslie; m., Gillian Mary Verney; 3 s. Educ. Paisley Grammar School; St. Edmund Hall, Oxford (Hon. Fellow, since 1975); Glasgow University; Edinburgh University. Fleet Air Arm, 1942-44 (subsequently RNR, Lt.-Cdr, 1954). Admitted Faculty of Advocates, 1952; Standing Junior Counsel to Air Ministry, 1956; Advocate Depute, 1958; QC, 1964; Solicitor General for Scotland, April to October, 1964; MP (Conservative), Edinburgh Pentlands, 1964-74; Lord Advocate, 1970-74. Chairman, Scottish National Committee, English Speaking Union of Commonwealth, 1978-84; Trustee, Carnegie Trust for Universities of Scotland, since 1975. Recreations: shooting; sailing. Address: (h.) 30 Lauder Road, Edinburgh; t.-031-667 8377.

Wylie, Ronald James, OBE, CA, JDipMA. Executive Director, Young Enterprise & U.I. - Scotland; b. 31.8.30, Edinburgh; m., Brenda Margaret Wright; 2 s. Apprentice, John M. Geoghegan & Co. Ltd., 1947-52; National Service, 1953-55; Tullis Russell & Co. Ltd.: Cost Accountant, 1955-59, Accountant, 1959-62, Secretary, 1962-72, joined

Board, 1971, Joint Managing Director, 1973-81, Chief Executive, 1981-85. Elder, Dysart Kirk; former Council Member, British Paper and Board Industry Federation. Recreation: sailing. Address: 123 Dysart Road, Kirkcaldy, KY1 2BB.

Wylie, Rev. William Andrew, MA. North East Industrial Mission Organiser and Offshore Chaplain to Oil Industry, since 1986; b. 17.5.27, London; 4 d. Educ. Glasgow Academy; Glasgow University and Trinity College. Minister: Stepps, 1953-59, Scots Kirk, Lausanne, 1959-67; General Secretary, Scottish Churches Council, 1967-71; Minister, St. Andrew's and St. George's, Edinburgh, 1972-85; Chaplain, Inverclyde Industrial Mission, 1985-86; elected Member, Institute of Petroleum, 1988. Chairman of Governors, Aiglon College, Switzerland. Recreations: hill-walking; golf; broadcasting; music. Address: (h.) Rosebank, Sauchen, Aberdeenshire, AB3 7PA; T.-03303 320; (b.) Salvesen Tower, Blaikies Quay, Aberdeen, AB1 2PW; T.-0224 573181.

Wyllie, Gordon Malcolm, LLB, FSA Scot, NP, WS. Partner, Biggart Baillie & Gifford; Clerk to the Trades House of Glasgow and to Grand Antiquity Society of Glasgow; Depute Clerk to General Commissioners of Inland Revenue, Glasgow North Division; b. Newton Mearns. Educ. Dunoon Grammar School; Glasgow University. Honorary Treasurer, Edinburgh Summer School in Ancient Greek; Director, Bailford Trustees Ltd.; Chairman, Edinburgh Subscription Ball Committee; wrote Scottish contribution to International Bar Association's International Dictionary of Succession Terms. Recreations: music; history and the arts generally; country walks; foreign travel. Address: (b.) 105 West George Street, Glasgow; T.-041-221 7020.

Wyllie, Rev. Hugh Rutherford, MA. Minister, Hamilton Old Parish Church, since 1981; Convener, The Assembly Council, General Assembly, since 1987; b. 11.10.34, Glasgow; m., Eileen E. Cameron, MA; 2 d. Educ. Hutchesons' Grammar School; Glasgow University. Bank of Scotland, 1951-53 (AIBS); RAF, 1953-55; student, 1956-62; Assistant, Glasgow Cathedral, 1962; Minister: Coatbridge Dunbeth, 1965, Cathcart South, 1972; Convener, Stewardship and Budget Committee, General Assembly, 1978-83; Convener, Board of Stewardship and Finance, General Assembly, 1983-86. Recreations: gardening; DIY. Address: Mansewood, Union Street, Hamilton, ML3 6NA; T.-0698 420002.

Y

Yang, Eric Shih-Jung, BSc, MSc, PhD, CEng, FIEE, FIOA. Reader, Department of Electrieal and Electronic Engineering, Heriot-Watt University, since 1985; m., Fei Jeannette; 1 d. Educ. Hong Kong University; Queen Mary College, London University. Senior Scientific Officer, British Rail, 1970-72; Lecturer, then Senior Lecturer, Heriot-Watt University, 1972-85. Publications: Low-Noise Electrical Motors, 1981; Machinery Noise Measurement (Co-author), 1985; Handbook of Electric Machines (Co-author), 1987. Address: Department of Electrical and Electronic Engineering, 31-35 Grassmarket, Edinburgh, EH1 2HT; T.-031-225 6465.

Yarrow, Sir Eric Grant, MBE, DL, CEng, MRINA, FRSE. Chairman, Clydesdale Bank PLC, since 1985 (Director, since 1962); Director, National Australia Bank Ltd., since 1987; b. 23.4.20, Glasgow; m., 1, Rosemary Ann Young (deceased); 1 s. (deceased); 2, Annette Elizabeth Francoise Steven (m. diss.); 3 s.; 3, Joan Botting; 3 step d. Educ. Marlborough College; Glasgow University. Served engineering apprenticeship, G. & J. Weir, 1938-39; Royal Engineers, 1939-45; served Burma, 1942-45 (Major, RE, 1945); Yarrow & Co. Ltd. (later Yarrow PLC): Assistant Manager, 1946, Director, 1948, Managing Director, 1958-67, Chairman, 1962-85, President, 1985-87; Director, Standard Life Assurance Company; President, Executive Committee, Princess Louise Scottish Hospital, Erskine; Council Member, Royal Institution of Naval Architects, since 1957 (Vice President, 1965, Honorary Vice President, 1972); Member, General Committee, Lloyd's Register of Shipping, 1960-87; Deacon, Incorporation of Hammermen in Glasgow, 1961-62; Chairman, Yarrow (Shipbuilders) Ltd., 1962-79; Officer (Brother), Order of St. John, since 1965; Deputy Lieutenant, County of Renfrewshire, since 1970; Prime Warden, Worshipful Company of Shipwrights, 1970-71; Council Member, Institute of Directors, since 1983; President, Smeatonican Society of Civil Engineers, 1983-84; President, The Marlburian Club, 1984. Recreations: golf; shooting. Address: (h.) Cloak, Kilmacolm, Renfrewshire, PA13 4SD; T.-Kilmacolm 2067.

Yemm, Professor Robert, BDS, BSc, PhD, FDS RCS(Edin). Professor and Head, Department of Dental Prosthetics and Gerontology, Dundee University, since 1984; b. 31.1.39, Bristol; m., Glenys Margaret; 1 s.; 1 d. Educ. Bristol Grammar School; Bristol University. Lecturer in Dental Prosthetics, Bristol University; Associate Professor, Department of Oral Biology, Alberta University; Lecturer in Dental Medicine (Oral Biology), then Dental Prosthetics, Bristol University; Senior Lecturer (Honorary Consultant), Dental Prosthetics, Dundee University. Recreation: sailing. Address: (h.) 10 Birkhill Avenue, Wormit, Newport-on-Tay, Fife, DD6 8PX; T.-0382 541819.

Yeomans, Richard Millet, CEng, FIEE, FIMechE. Chief Engineer Generation Operation, South of Scotland Electricity Board, since 1987; b. 19.7.32. Educ. Durban, South Africa; Cornwall Technical College; Bristol College of Technology; Southampton University. Lt., REME; CEGB power stations; Deputy Manager, Longannet Power Station; Deputy Manager and Manager, Inverkip Power Station; Manager, Hunterston A and B Nuclear Power Station; Generation Engineer (Nuclear), SSEB. Recreations: yachting; golf; gardening. Address: (b.) Cathcart House, Spean Street, Glasgow, G44 4BE; T.-041-637 7177.

Young, Daniel Greer, MB, ChB, FRCSEdin, FRCSGlas, DTM&H. Reader in Paediatric Surgery, Glasgow University, since 1984; Honorary Consultant Paediatric Surgeon, since 1967; b. Skipness, Argyll; m., Agnes Gilchrist Donald; 1 s.; 1 d. Educ. Wishaw High School; Glasgow University. Resident Assistant Surgeon, Hospital for Sick Children, London; Senior Lecturer, Institute of Child Health, London University; Honorary Consultant Surgeon, Hospital for Sick Children, London, and Queen Elizabeth Hospital, Hackney, London; Senior Lecturer and Head, Department of Paediatric Surgery, Glasgow University, Honorary Consultant Surgeon, Royal Hospital for Sick Children and Stobhill General Hospital, Glasgow. Honorary Secretary, Lanarkshire Division, British Medical Association; Past President, Royal Medico-Chirurgical Society of Glasgow; Honorary President, Scottish Spina Bifida Association; Member of Council, Royal College of Physicians and Surgeons; Chairman, Intercollegiate Board in Paediatric Surgery; Honorary Member: Hungarian Paichatree Surgical Association, South African Paediatric Surgical Association, American Surgical Paediatric Association. Recreations: curling; fishing; gardening. Address: (b.) Department of Paediatric Surgery, Royal Hospital for Sick Children, Yorkhill, Glasgow, G3 8SJ; T.-041-339 8888, Ext. 389.

Young, Lt.-Gen. Sir David (Tod), KBE (1980), CB (1977), DFC (1952). Chairman, Cairntech Ltd., Edinburgh, since 1983; b. 17.5.26, Edinburgh; m., 1, Joyce Marian Melville (deceased); 2 s.; 2, Joanna Myrtle Oyler Torin. Educ. George Watson's College, Edinburgh. Commissioned The Royal Scots, 1945; Brevet Lt.-Col., 1964; Mil. Assistant, MoD, 1964-67; commanded 1st Bn., The Royal Scots, 1967-69; Col. GS, Staff College, 1969-70; Commander, 12 Mechanized Brigade, 1970-72; Deputy Military Secretary, MoD, 1972-74; Commander Land Forces, Northern Ireland, 1975-77; Director of Infantry, MoD, 1977-80; GOC Scotland and Governor, Edinburgh Castle, 1980-82; Colonel, The Royal Scots, 1975-80; Colonel Commandant: Scottish Division, 1980-82, Ulster Defence Regiment, since 1986; Honorary Colonel, Northern Ireland Regiment Army Air Corps, 1988. Member, Scottish Committee, Marie Curie Foundation, since 1983 (Chairman, 1986); President, Army Cadet Force Association Scotland, since 1984; HM Commissioner, Queen Victoria School, since 1984; Chairman, St. Mary's Cathedral Workshop, since 1986; Member, Board of Governors, St. Columba's Hospice, since 1986. Recreations: golf; sports; music. Address: c/o Adam & Company plc, 22 Charlotte Square, Edinburgh, EH2 4DF.

Young, Edward, MA (Hons). Rector, The Nicolson Institute, since 1968; b. 30.11.25, Motherwell; m., Sheila Hewison; 2 d. Educ. Dalziel High School; Glasgow University. Teacher of English, Hamilton Academy, 1952-61; Principal Teacher of English: Blairgowrie High School, 1961-64, Bell-Baxter High School, 1964-68. Member, Working Party, Transition from School to University, SED, 1970-72; Chairman, Working Party on Drama, SED, 1973-75; Member, Committee on Secondary Education, CCC, 1976-78; Member, Highlands and Islands Development Consultative Council, 1979-87; Member, Post Office Users Council for Scotland, since 1984. Recreations: fly fishing; fly dressing; rugby refereeing; reading; gardening. Address: (h.) 1 Goathill Crescent, Stornoway, Isle of Lewis; T.-0851 2204.

Young, George Bell, CBE, CStJ, CBIM, FInstM. Managing Director, East Kilbride Development Corporation, since 1968; b. 17.6.24; m., 1, Margaret Wylie Boyd (deceased); 1 s.; 2, Joyce Marguerite McAteer. Educ. Queens Park School, Glasgow. RNVR, 1942-45 (Lt., destroyers and mine-sweepers); Journalist and Feature Writer, Glasgow Herald, 1945-48; North of Scotland Hydro-Electric Board, 1948-52; Chief Executive (London), Scottish Council (Development and Industry), 1952-68; Council Member, National Trust for Scotland, 1974-79; Director, Royal Caledonian Schools, since 1957; Chairman, East Kilbride and District National Savings Committee, 1968-78; Trustee, Strathclyde Scanner Campaign; Scottish Chairman, British Heart Foundation, 1975-79; Chairman, East Kilbride Committee, Order of St. John; Honorary Secretary, Saints and Sinners Club of Scotland, since 1982; Chairman, BIM Scotland, since 1988; Member, British Railways (Scottish) Board, since 1985. Recreations: golf; fishing. Address: (b.) East Kilbride Development Corporation, Atholl House, East Kilbride, G74 1LU; T.-East Kilbride 41111.

Young, Hugh Kenneth, CA, FIB (Scot). Secretary and Member, Management Board, Bank of Scotland, since 1984; b. 6.5.36, Galashiels; m., Marjory Bruce Wilson; 2 s.; 1 d. Educ. Edinburgh Academy. National Service, 1959-61; commissioned as 2nd Lt., Royal Scots, subsequently Captain (1966), 1st Bn., 52nd Lowland Volunteers, TAVR; with ICFC Ltd., 1962-67; with Schroders Ltd. group, 1967-73, latterly as Manager, J. Henry Schroder Wagg & Co. Ltd.; Local Director in Edinburgh, Edward Bates & Sons Ltd., 1973-75; joined Bank of Scotland, 1975; Head of Corporate Finance, Bank of Scotland Finance Company Ltd., 1976; Director, The British Linen Bank Ltd., 1978-84 (Deputy Chief Executive, 1982-84). Director: Edinburgh Sports Club Ltd., 1983-87 (Chairman, 1984-87), Bank of Scotland (Jersey) Ltd., 1986 (Chairman), Bank of Wales (Jersey) Ltd., 1986, Pentland Oil Exploration Ltd., 1980-87. Recreations: squash; tennis; hill-walking. Address: (b.) The Mound, Edinburgh, EH1 1YZ; T.-031-243 5562.

Young, Ian Macrae, BSc, CertEd, CBiol, MIBiol. Educational Adviser, Scottish Health Education Group, since 1983; b. 20.7.46, Glasgow; m., Anne Crawford; 2 s. Educ. Rutherglen Academy; Paisley College of Technology. Teacher of Science, Camphill High School, Paisley, 1969; Principal Teacher of Biology, Renfrew High School, 1972; Adviser in Science, Renfrew and Argyll and Bute Divisions, Strathclyde Region, 1978. Publications: The Science of Life (series of biology texts). Recreations: folk song; photography; running. Address: (b.) Scottish Health Education Group, Woodburn House, Canaan Lane, Edinburgh, EH10 4SG; T.-031-447 8044.

Young, James McMicken, FIB, MIBS, MBIM. Member, Clyde Port Authority; Member, Edinburgh Company of Merchants; Treasurer, Scottish Association of Victim Support Schemes; Joint General Manager, Bank of Scotland, 1973-85; Chairman, British Linen Assets PLC; b. 4.10.25, Stranraer; m., Lillian Frances Judith Maran; 1 s.; 1 d. Educ. Stranraer Academy; Stranraer High School. Bank of Scotland: Assistant Manager, London Chief Office, 1965, Assistant Secretary, 1968, Assistant General Manager, Bank of Scotland, and Manager, Bank of Scotland Finance Co. Ltd. (now British Linen Bank Ltd.), 1972, Director, Bank of Scotland Finance Co. Ltd., 1973; Director: British Linen Bank Ltd., British Linen Leasing Ltd., British Linen Shipping Ltd., Capital Leasing Ltd., Capital Leasing (Edinburgh) Ltd., Capital Leasing (London) Ltd., Melville Street Leasing (Edinburgh) Ltd. Recreations: tennis; chess. Address: (h.) 23 Succoth Park, Edinburgh, EH12 6BX; T.-031-337 5479.

Young, John Henderson, OBE (1980), JP, MBIM, MIEx, DL. Leader of the Opposition, Glasgow District Council, since 1988 (Council Member, since 1974); Deputy Lieutenant, Glasgow, since 1981; b. 21.12.30, Glasgow; m., Doris Paterson; 1 s. Educ. Hillhead High School, Glasgow; Scottish College of Commerce. Councillor, Glasgow Corporation, 1964-73, Glasgow District Council, since 1974; Leader, Glasgow City Council, 1977-79; Parliamentary candidate (Conservative), Rutherglen, 1966; Chairman, Cathcart Conservatives, 1964-65, 1968-71, 1987-88; Chairman, Glasgow Conservative Euro Constituency, since 1987; Vice-Chairman, Glasgow Conservatives, 1969-72; Export Manager, Scotch whisky industry; Vice-Chairman, Scottish Pakistani Association; Kentucky Colonel, 1984; Member, Glasgow Sports Promotion Council; Member, Post Office Advisory Committee. Recreations: tennis; reading; history; animal welfare; meeting people. Address: (h.) 4 Deanwood Avenue, Muirend, Glasgow, G44 3RJ; T.-041-637 9535.

Young, John Maclennan, OBE (1987), JP. Convener, Caithness District Council, since 1974; Member, Highland Regional Council, since 1974 (Chairman, Roads and Transport Committee, since 1978); b. 6.6.33, Thurso. Educ. Thurso Miller Academy. Farmer; Member, Caithness County Council, 1961-75; Member, Caithness Western District Council, 1961-75; Chairman, Housing Committee, 1968-73, and Planning Commitee, 1973-75, Caithness County Council; Conservative candidate, Caithness and Sutherland, 1970. Address: (h.) Sordale, Halkirk, Caithness; T.-Halkirk 228.

Young, Raymond Kennedy, BArch, ARIAS. Director, Scotland, The Housing Corporation, since 1978; b. 23.1.46, Newcastle-upon-Tyne; m., Jean; 3 s. Educ. High School of Glasgow; Strathclyde University. Strathclyde University Research Group, 1971-74; Housing Corporation, Glasgow Office, 1974-78. Chairman, Govan Festival. Recreations: music; theatre; railway modelling; no sports. Address: (b.) Rosebery House, 9 Haymarket Terrace, Edinburgh, EH12 5YA; T.-031-337 0044.

Young, Robert W.J., BSc (Hons), PhD, CEng, MICE. HM Inspector of Schools (Staff Inspector), since 1970; b. 14.3.36, Falkirk; m., Cynthia; 2 d. Educ. Melville College, Edinburgh; Edinburgh University. Civil Engineer, British Rail, 1958-61; Edinburgh University, 1961-70, with period of secondment to Khartoum University, Sudan. Recreations: wind-surfing; sailing; skiing; squash. Address: (b.) Room 3/19, Scottish Education Department, New St. Andrews House, St. James Centre, Edinburgh; T.-031-556 8400, Ext. 4534.

Young, Roger, BSc, MBA. Chief Executive, Electronics and Electrical Division, Low & Bonar p.l.c.; b. 14.1.44, Edinburgh; m., Susan; 1 s.; 2 d. Educ. Gordonstoun School; Edinburgh University. Address: (b.) Low & Bonar p.l.c., Bonar House, Faraday Street, Dundee, DD1 9JA; T.-0382 818171.

Young, Professor Stephen, BCom, MSc. Professor of International Marketing, Strathclyde University, since 1987; b. 20.8.44, Berwick upon Tweed; m., Elizabeth Anne Scott; 1 s.; 1 d. Educ. Berwick Grammar School; Liverpool University; Newcastle upon Tyne University. Lecturer in Economics and Management, Dar-es-Salaam Technical College, 1966-67; Economist, Planning Unit, Ministry of Agriculture and Cooperatives, Dar-es-Salaam, 1967-68; Trainee Economist/ Economist, Marketing Economics Department, and Manager, International Economics Department, Milk Marketing Board, 1969-73; Lecturer/ Senior Lecturer in Economics and Management, Paisley College of Technology, 1973-79 and June to September, 1980; Visiting Professor of International Business, Louisiana State University, 1979-80; Senior Lecturer in International Business and Business Policy, Strathclyde Business School, 1980-87 (Director, Strathclyde International Business Unit, from 1983); Visiting Professor of International Business, University of Texas at Dallas, 1982. Assistant Secretary, International Dairy Committee, 1972-73; UK Representative, OECD Dairy Industry Working Party, 1972; UK Representative, EEC milk processing association, ASSILEC, 1972-73; Member, Board, East Kilbride Business Centre, 1984-87. Recreations: mountaineering; swimming; soccer. Address: (h.) The Croft, 12 Stanley Drive, Brookfield, Renfewshire, PA5 8UG; T.-0505 20113.

Young, Sheriff Sir Stephen Stewart Templeton, 3rd Bt. Sheriff of North Strathclyde, since 1984; b. 24.5.47; m.; 2 s. Educ. Rugby; Trinity College, Oxford; Edinburgh University. Sheriff, Glasgow and Strathkelvin, 1984.

Young, Rev. William Galbraith, MA (Hons), BD, PhD. Retired Bishop, Church of Pakistan; retired Minister, Church of Scotland; b. 10.10.17, Greenock; m., Elizabeth Crawford Wiseman; 1 s.; 2 d. Educ. Greenock Academy; Oban High School; Glasgow University. Private, RAMC, 1940-45 (War service overseas, India, Iraq, Persia, Cyprus); Missionary, Church of Scotland, Punjab, Pakistan, 1947-77; Principal, Murree Language School, 1954-55; Vice-President, West Pakistan Christian Council, 1963-64; Editor, Urdu Textbook Project, Theological Education Fund, 1963-77; Professor of Church History, Gujranwala Theological Seminary, 1966-70; Church of Pakistan: Bishop, 1970-77, Chairman, Liturgical Commission, 1970-77, Deputy Moderator, 1974-77; Minister, Resolis and Urquhart Parish Church, 1977-85; Moderator, Chanonry and Dingwall Presbytery, 1979-80; Moderator, Synod of Ross, Sutherland and Caithness, 1981-82; Chairman, Sialkot Inter-Aid Committee (Flood and Refugee Relief), 1973-77; Vice-Chairman, East Ross and Black Isle Council of Social Service, 1980-82. Publications: Handbook of Source Materials for Students of Church History up to 650 AD, 1969; Patriarch, Shah and Caliph, 1974; Church of Pakistan - Experimental Services, 1974; The Parish of Urquhart and Logie Wester, 1984; various publications in Urdu. Recreations: (when young) tennis; (now) choral singing; walking; reading; listening to music. Address: (h.) 29 Ferry Brae, North Kessock, Inverness, IV1 1YH; T.-046 373 581.

Younger of Leckie, 3rd Viscount (Edward George Younger), OBE (1940); b. 21.11.06; m., Evelyn Margaret McClure (deceased); 3 s.; 1 d. Educ. Winchester; New College, Oxford. Served Second World War; Colonel, Argyll and Sutherland Highlanders (TA); Lord Lieutenant, Stirling and Falkirk, 1964-79. Address: (h.) Leckie, Gargunnock, Stirling.

Younger, Rt. Hon. George (Kenneth Hotson), TD (1964), PC (1979), DL. MP (Conservative), Ayr, since 1964; Secretary of State for Defence, since 1986; b. 22.9.31; m., Diana Rhona Tuck; 3 s.; 1 d. Educ. Cargilfield School; Winchester College; New College, Oxford. Argyll and Sutherland Highlanders, 1950-51; 7th Bn., Argyll and Sutherland Highlanders (TA), 1951-65; Director, Tennant Caledonian Breweries Ltd., since 1977; Parliamentary Under Secretary of State, Scottish Office, 1970-74; Minister of State for Defence, 1974; Secretary of State for Scotland, 1979-86; Chairman, Conservative Party in Scotland, 1974-75; Brigadier, Queen's Bodyguard for Scotland (Royal Company of Archers); DL, Stirlingshire.

Younger, Sheriff Robert Edward Gilmour, MA, LLB. Sheriff of Tayside, Central and Fife, at Stirling and Alloa, since 1987; b. 25.9.40, Stirling; m., Helen Jane Hayes; 1 s.; 1 d. Educ. Winchester; New College, Oxford; Edinburgh University; Glasgow University. Advocate, 1968-79; Sheriff of Glasgow and Strathkelvin, at Glasgow, 1979-82, and of Tayside, Central and Fife, at Stirling and Falkirk, 1982-87. Recreations: out of doors. Address: (h.) Old Leckie, Gargunnock, Stirling; T.-Gargunnock 213.

Youngson, Alexander John, CBE, MA, DLitt, Hon.FRIAS. Chairman, Royal Fine Art Commission for Scotland, since 1983; b. 28.9.18, Pakistan; m., Elizabeth Gisborne Naylor; 1 s.; 1 d. Educ. Aberdeen Grammar School; Aberdeen University. Fleet Air Arm, 1939-45; Lecturer, St. Andrews University, 1948-50; Lecturer, Cambridge University, 1950-58; Fellow, Emmanuel College, Professor, Edinburgh University, 1958-74; Director, Research School, Social Sciences, Australian National University, 1974-80; Professor, University of Hong Kong, 1980-82. Publications: Possibilities of Economic Progress, 1959; The Making of Classical Edinburgh, 1966; After the Forty Five, 1970; The Prince and the Pretender, 1985. Recreation: gardening. Address: (h.) 48 Blacket Place, Edinburgh; T.-031-667 2021.

Youngson, George Gray, MB, ChB, PhD, FRCSEdin. Consultant Surgeon, Royal Aberdeen Children's Hospital and Aberdeen Royal Infirmary, since 1985; Honorary Senior Lecturer in Clinical Surgery, Aberdeen University, since 1985; b. 13.5.49, Glasgow; m., Sandra Jean Lister; 1 s.; 2 d. Educ. Buckhaven High School; Aberdeen University. House Officer to Professor George Smith, 1973; Research Fellow, 1975; Registrar in General Surgery, 1975-77; Senior Resident in Cardiac and Thoracic Surgery, University Hospital, London, Ontario, 1979; Lecturer in Clinical Surgery, Aberdeen University, 1981; Clinical Fellow, Paediatric Surgery, Hospital for Sick Children, Toronto, 1983; Lecturer in Surgical Paediatrics and Transplantation, Aberdeen University, 1984. Recreations: sport (tennis and squash); music (piobaireachd, guitar). Address: (h.) 10 Kennerty Park, Peterculter, Aberdeen.

Yule, William. Honorary Sheriff, Tayside, Central and Fife, since 1976; b. 16.2.08, Kirkcaldy; m., Joan Kininmonth; 1 s. Educ. Kirkcaldy High School; George Watson's Boys' College, Edinburgh. President: Wholesale Grocers Association of Scotland, 1955-56, Kirkcaldy Rotary Club, 1957-58; Chairman, East Fife Hospitals Board of Management, 1963-68; Commissioner of Income Tax, 1964-78. Address: (h.) 16 Victoria Gardens, Kirkcaldy, KY1 1DJ; T.-Kirkcaldy 263356.

Z

Ziervogel, Mark Allan, BSc, MB, ChB, DMRD, FRCR. Consultant Paediatric Radiologist, Royal Hospital for Sick Children, Glasgow, since 1978; Honorary Secretary, Scottish Committee, Royal College of Radiologists; b. 25.12.36, Pietersburg, South Africa; m., Toni Levick; 1 s.; 1 d. Educ. Pretoria Boys' High School; Natal University; Glasgow University. Cattle farming, South Africa; hospital appointments, Glasgow, Stirling and New Plymouth (New Zealand). Honorary Lecturer in Radiodiagnosis, Glasgow University; Regional Postgraduate Advisor in Radiodiagnosis for the West of Scotland. Recreations: cycling; tandem touring with wife; squash; music, food and wine. Address: (h.) Robinsfield, Balmore Road, Bardowie, Milngavie, Glasgow, G62 6ER; T.-0360 22268.